HANDBOOK OF
CLINICAL CHILD PSYCHOLOGY

THIRD EDITION

HANDBOOK OF
CLINICAL CHILD PSYCHOLOGY

THIRD EDITION

Edited by

C. EUGENE WALKER

AND

MICHAEL C. ROBERTS

JOHN WILEY & SONS, INC.
New York • Chichester • Weinheim • Brisbane • Singapore • Toronto

Library of Congress Cataloging-in-Publication Data:

Handbook of clinical child psychology / edited by C. Eugene Walker and
    Michael C. Roberts. — 3rd ed.
        p.   cm.
    Includes bibliographical references and indexes.
    ISBN 0-471-24406-6 (cloth : alk. paper)
    1. Clinical child psychology Handbooks, manuals, etc. I. Walker,
C. Eugene (Clarence Eugene), 1939– . II. Roberts, Michael C.
    [DNLM: 1. Child Psychology. 2. Adolescent Psychology. 3. Mental
Disorders—Adolescence. 4. Mental Disorders—Child.   WS 105 H2355
2000]
RJ503.3.H36   2000
618.92'89—dc21
DNLM/DLC
for Library of Congress   99-40629

Printed in the United States of America.

10 9 8 7 6 5 4 3 2 1

This book is dedicated with
admiration and affection to our parents
Olga Thresa Brioli and Lewis G. Walker (C.E.W.);
Winona Clark and J. Kent Roberts (M.C.R.).

Contributors

Gregory A. Aarons, PhD
Assistant Clinical Professor, Department of
    Psychiatry, University of California, San Diego
Research Scientist, Child and Adolescent Services
    Research Center
San Diego, California

Ana M. Abrantes, BA
San Diego State University/University of
    California, San Diego Joint Doctoral Program in
    Clinical Psychology
San Diego, California

Anne Marie Albano, PhD
Child Study Center
Department of Psychiatry
New York University School of Medicine
New York, New York

Arthur D. Anastopoulos, PhD
Department of Psychology
University of North Carolina—Greensboro
Greensboro, North Carolina

Glen P. Aylward, PhD
Department of Pediatrics—School of Medicine
Southern Illinois University
Springfield, Illinois

Declan Barry, MA
Department of Psychology
University of Toledo
Toledo, Ohio

Karen Bartsch, PhD
Department of Psychology
University of Wyoming
Laramie, Wyoming

Michelle L. Bengtson, PhD
Cook Children's Medical Center
Fort Worth, Texas

Sheila Black, PhD
Department of Psychology
University of Alabama
Tuscaloosa, Alabama

Thomas J. Boll, PhD
University of Alabama
Birmingham, Alabama

Tom Bond, PhD
Sleep Disorders Center
Williamsburg Community Hospital
Williamsburg, Virginia

Barbara L. Bonner, PhD
University of Oklahoma Health Sciences Center
Oklahoma City, Oklahoma

Sandra A. Brown, PhD
Professor of Psychology and Psychiatry
University of California
San Diego, California
Chief, Psychology Service
VA San Diego Healthcare System
San Diego, California

Bryan D. Carter, PhD
Bingham Child Guidance Clinic
Department of Psychiatry
University of Louisville School of Medicine
Louisville, Kentucky

David Causey, PhD
Bingham Child Guidance Clinic
Department of Psychiatry
University of Louisville School of Medicine
Louisville, Kentucky

Judith A. Chafel, PhD
Department of Curriculum and Instruction
School of Education
Indiana University
Bloomington, Indiana

Kelly M. Champion, PhD
Department of Psychology
Gustavus Adolphus College
St. Peter, Minnesota

John M. Chaney, PhD
Department of Psychology
Oklahoma State University
Stillwater, Oklahoma

Edward R. Christophersen, PhD
Developmental and Behavioral Sciences
Children's Mercy Hospital
Kansas City, Missouri

Paola Conte, PhD
Ferkauf Graduate School of Psychology
Yeshiva University, Mazer Hall
Bronx, New York

Geraldine Dawson, PhD
Department of Psychology
Center on Human Development and Disability
University of Washington
Seattle, Washington

Jerel E. Del Dotto, PhD, ABPP/CN
Department of Neuropsychology
Foote Hospital
Jackson, Michigan

David DiLillo, PhD
Department of Psychology
University of Missouri-Columbia
Columbia, Missouri

Stephen J. Dollinger, PhD
Department of Psychology
Southern Illinois University
Carbondale, Illinois

Joseph A. Durlak, PhD
Department of Psychology
Loyola University Chicago
Chicago, Illinois

Nancy S. Ehrenreich, JD, LLM
College of Law
University of Denver
Denver, Colorado

Jean C. Elbert, PhD
Department of Psychology
California State University—Northridge
Northridge, California

Michele J. Eliason, PhD
College of Nursing
University of Iowa
Iowa City, Iowa

Sheila Eyberg, PhD
Department of Clinical and Health Psychology
University of Florida
Gainesville, Florida

Donald K. Freedheim, PhD
Department of Psychology
Case Western Reserve University
Cleveland, Ohio

Paul J. Frick, PhD
Department of Psychology
University of New Orleans
New Orleans, Louisiana

David M. Garner, PhD
River Centre Clinic Eating Disorders Program
Sylvania, Ohio

Brenda O. Gilbert, PhD
Department of Psychology
Southern Illinois University
Carbondale, Illinois

Betty N. Gordon, PhD
Department of Psychology
University of North Carolina—Chapel Hill
Chapel Hill, North Carolina

Leilani Greening, PhD
Department of Psychology
University of Alabama
Tuscaloosa, Alabama

Linda Sayler Gudas, PhD
Department of Psychiatry
Children's Hospital Medical Center
Boston, Massachusetts

Robert Habenstein, PhD
Professor Emeritus
Sociology Department
University of Missouri
Columbia, Missouri

Kathryn Gold Hadley, PhD
Department of Sociology
Indiana University
Bloomington, Indiana

Martin Heesacker, PhD
Department of Psychology
University of Florida
Gainesville, Florida

Russell H. Jackson, PhD
Oregon Institute for Disability and Development
Oregon Health Sciences University
Portland, Oregon

Anne K. Jacobs, MA
Clinical Child Psychology Program
University of Kansas
Lawrence, Kansas

James H. Johnson, PhD
Department of Clinical and Health Psychology
University of Florida
Gainesville, Florida

Mark James Johnson, PsyD
INTEGRIS Mental Health
Spencer, Oklahoma

Russell T. Jones, PhD
Department of Psychology
Virginia Tech University
Blacksburg, Virginia

Randy W. Kamphaus, PhD
Department of Educational Psychology, Research, and Measurement
University of Georgia
Athens, Georgia

Ruth Kanfer, PhD
School of Psychology
Georgia Institute of Technology
Atlanta, Georgia

Alain Katic, MD
Department of Psychiatry
The Cambridge Hospital
Harvard Medical School
Cambridge, Massachusetts

Keith L. Kaufman, PhD
Portland State University
Portland, Oregon

Thomas J. Kenny, PhD
University of Maryland
    Medical Center
Baltimore, Maryland

Christina Kephart, MS
Department of Psychology
Virginia Tech University
Blacksburg, Virginia

H. Elizabeth King, PhD
Peachtree Psychological Associates
Atlanta, Georgia

James H. Kleiger, PsyD
Private Practice
Bethesda, Maryland

Gerald P. Koocher, PhD
Department of Psychiatry
Children's Hospital Medical Center
Boston, Massachusetts

Gloria Krahn, PhD
Departments of Pediatrics, Public Health & Preventive Medicine
Oregon Health Sciences University
Portland, Oregon

Ami F. Kuttler, PhD
Department of Psychology
University of Miami
Coral Gables, Florida

Annette M. La Greca, PhD
Department of Psychology
University of Miami
Coral Gables, Florida

Audra K. Langley, MS
Department of Psychology
Virginia Tech University
Blacksburg, Virginia

J. Michael Leibowitz, PhD
Munroe–Meyer Institute
Nebraska Medical Center
Omaha, Nebraska

Jennifer Leonetti, PhD
NW Regional Education Service District
Hillsboro, Oregon

Sacha E. Lindekens, MEd
Department of Psychology
University of Florida
Gainesville, Florida

Thomas R. Linscheid, PhD
Department of Psychology
Columbus Children's Hospital
Columbus, Ohio

Mary Beth Logue, PhD
Department of Pediatrics
University of Oklahoma Health Sciences Center
Oklahoma City, Oklahoma

Robert D. Lyman, PhD
Department of Psychology
University of Alabama
Tuscaloosa, Alabama

Phillip M. Lyons, Jr., JD, PhD
Criminal Justice Center
Sam Houston State University
Huntsville, Texas

William E. MacLean, Jr., PhD
Department of Psychology
University of Wyoming
Laramie, Wyoming

Janet R. Matthews, PhD
Department of Psychology
Loyola University—New Orleans
New Orleans, Louisiana

Lee H. Matthews, PhD
Department of Psychiatry and Neurology
Tulane Medical School
New Orleans, Louisiana

John W. McCaskill IV, PhD
Department of Clinical and Health Psychology
University of Florida
Gainesville, Florida

Elisabeth McMahon, MA
Los Angeles Unified School District
Los Angeles, California

James McPartland, BA
Department of Psychology
University of Washington
Seattle, Washington

Gary B. Melton, PhD
Institute on Family and Neighborhood Life
Clemson University
Clemson, South Carolina

Michael L. Miller, MS
Department of Psychology
University of Wyoming
Laramie, Wyoming

Leonard S. Milling, PhD
Department of Psychology
University of Connecticut
Storrs, Connecticut

Larry L. Mullins, PhD
Department of Psychology
Oklahoma State University
Stillwater, Oklahoma

Greg J. Neimeyer, PhD
Department of Psychology
University of Florida
Gainesville, Florida

Larissa N. Niec, PhD
Central Michigan University
Mt. Pleasant, Michigan

Roberta A. Olson, PhD
Department of Counseling
Oklahoma City University
Oklahoma City, Oklahoma

William C. Orr, PhD
President and CEO
Lynn Health Science Institute
Oklahoma City, Oklahoma

Julie Osterling, PhD
Center for Human Development and Disability
University of Washington
Seattle, Washington

Mary N. Parker, MS
Department of Psychology
Virginia Tech University
Blacksburg, Virginia

Lizette Peterson, PhD
Psychology Department
University of Missouri
Columbia, Missouri

Beeman N. Phillips, EdD
Professor Emeritus
University of Texas—Austin
Austin, Texas

Scott W. Powers
Division of Psychology
Children's Hospital Medical Center
Cincinnati, Ohio

Patricia C. Purvis, PhD
Developmental and Behavioral Sciences
Children's Mercy Hospital
Kansas City, Missouri

Jane Querido, MS
Department of Clinical and Health Psychology
University of Florida Health Sciences Center
Gainesville, Florida

William A. Rae, PhD
Department of Educational Psychology
Texas A&M University
College Station, Texas

L. Kaye Rasnake, PhD
Department of Psychology
Denison University
Granville, Ohio

George A. Rekers, PhD
Department of Neuropsychiatry and Behavioral
  Science
University of South Carolina School of Medicine
Columbia, South Carolina

Lynn C. Richman, PhD
Department of Pediatrics
University of Iowa
Iowa City, Iowa

Michael C. Roberts, PhD, ABPP
Clinical Child Psychology Program
University of Kansas
Lawrence, Kansas

Susan L. Rosenthal, PhD
Division of Adolescent Medicine
Children's Hospital Medical Center
Cincinnati, Ohio

Byron P. Rourke, PhD
Department of Psychology
University of Windsor
Windsor, Ontario
Canada

Sandra W. Russ, PhD
Department of Psychology
Case Western Reserve University
Cleveland, Ohio

Thomas V. Sayger, PhD
Department of Counseling, Education Psychology,
  and Research
University of Memphis
Memphis, Tennessee

Arlene B. Schaefer, PhD
Private Practice
Oklahoma City, Oklahoma

Carolyn S. Schroeder, PhD
University of Kansas
Lawrence, Kansas

Thomas W. Seale, PhD
Department of Pediatrics
University of Oklahoma Health Sciences Center
Oklahoma City, Oklahoma

Stephanie D. Shaffer, MA
Department of Psychology
University of North Carolina Greensboro
Greensboro, North Carolina

William James Shaw, PsyD
Clinical Psychologist
Oklahoma City, Oklahoma

Uma Shenoy, MS
Department of Psychology
Virginia Tech University
Blacksburg, Virginia

Peter L. Sheras, PhD
Curry Programs in Clinical and School Psychology
University of Virginia
Charlottesville, Virginia

Lawrence J. Siegel, PhD
Ferkauf Graduate School of Psychology
Yeshiva University, Mazer Hall
Bronx, New York

Rune J. Simeonsson, PhD, MSPH
School of Education
University of North Carolina
Chapel Hill, North Carolina

Jean Spruill, PhD
University of Alabama
Tuscaloosa, Alabama

Ronald J. Steingard, MD
Department of Psychiatry
The Cambridge Hospital
Harvard Medical School
Cambridge, Massachusetts

Elton G. Stetson, EdD
Department of Elementary Education
Texas A&M University-Commerce
Commerce, Texas

Ranae Stetson, EdD
School of Education
Texas Christian University
Fort Worth, Texas

Wendy L. Stone, PhD
Department of Pediatrics
Vanderbilt School of Medicine
Nashville, Tennessee

Eric M. Vernberg, PhD
Clinical Child Psychology Program
University of Kansas
Lawrence, Kansas

J. Catesby Ware, PhD
Department of Psychiatry
Eastern Virginia Medical Center
Norfolk, Virginia

Cheri Weeks, MS
Department of Psychology
Virginia Tech University
Blacksburg, Virginia

Branlyn E. Werba, MS
Department of Clinical and Health Psychology
University of Florida
Gainesville, Florida

Jennifer Willoughby, PhD
Division of Behavioral and Developmental
 Pediatrics
University of Maryland Medical Center
Baltimore, Maryland

David R. Wilson, PhD
Gadsden Psychological Services
Gadsden, Alabama

Preface

There have been many new and exciting developments in the field of clinical child psychology in the eighteen years since the publication of the first edition of this *Handbook*. Over the years, the *Handbook* has become a standard reference and guide for students, researchers, and clinicians in the field. Hence, the need became evident for a third edition. The fact that a third edition was needed after eight years rather than ten, as with the second, no doubt indicates the increasingly rapid development of the field.

As was the case with the first edition, the purpose of this present volume is to provide a text and reference work dealing in a comprehensive manner with the range of children's psychological problems that confront clinical child psychologists, pediatric psychologists, educators, child psychiatrists, and other mental health professionals. The chapters in this volume have been prepared with a view toward active professionals charged with the care of children. Thus, intervention and management have been emphasized. However, research in the relevant areas has not been slighted. In the majority of cases, the author(s) of the chapter is both a scholar and a clinician. The general format of each chapter provides the reader with practical suggestions and advice for high quality clinical practice combined with a scholarly review of research in the area, The goal has been to bridge the gap between research and practice.

The order of the sections follows from the logical progression of providing a basic background in child development, through diagnosis and treatment, to consideration of more specific disorders and topics. This book is based on the concept that psychological disorders of childhood are best understood in the context of human development. Thus, the chapters in Section One provide a background for conceptualizing both normal and abnormal development in children and their families.

Section Two provides basic information for the application of a wide range of assessment procedures available to the child psychologist in his or her armamentarium. Sections Three, Four, and Five are organized around the three general developmental stages of early life, childhood, and adolescence, respectively. These sections examine in detail the disorders most commonly confronting the clinical child psychologist working with children of that age. Some of the chapters in these sections contain only information about the age group under discussion (e.g., "Clinical Problems of Birth, the Neonate, and the Infant"). Others (e.g., "Psychosomatic Problems in Children") contain some references to such problems in older and/or younger groups but have been placed in this section because most of the unique information needed by the clinical child psychologist pertains to this age group. However, this unique body of information is placed in context with respect to information for the other age groups. Section Six elaborates intervention strategies generally used in clinical child practice. The coverage of these procedures is broad and reflects a wide variety of practices. Finally, Section Seven, on special topics, is an attempt to reflect the developing areas of clinical child psychology. Chapter topics were chosen to reflect the new and innovative issues of social, ethical, clinical, and practical importance to the child, family, and clinician.

The third edition was written on the level of the advanced graduate student and professional. This *Handbook* can be used as a primary text for courses in child psychopathology/treatment as well as in the clinical child practicum portions of training received by advanced graduate students. Additionally, it is hoped that the third edition will prove useful as a reference for practicing clinical child psychologists as well as for related professionals dealing with children and families in a variety of settings (e.g., medicine, social work, education, nursing, and other areas). The third edition is a compendium of the diversity of the problems and excitement of research and practice in clinical child psychology.

In preparing for this third edition, both editors carefully reviewed the content of the first two volumes. We next read all published reviews of those volumes. Profiting from the feedback of our students and colleagues who have used this volume over the years, we decided to add a chapter on "The Psychological Impact of a Parent's Chronic Illness on the Child" one on "Poverty and the Well-Being of Children and Families," and one on "Methods of Research in Developmental Psychopathology and Treatment Effectiveness" because of their timeliness and the important work going on in those areas. Some chapter topics were modified to reflect

the changes in the field. All chapters in the current edition have been rewritten and reworked. In many cases, the emphasis and organization have been significantly changed to reflect the directions that the field has taken in recent years.

As with the first edition, we are pleased to present this volume to all of those professionals who are responsible for or interested in the mental health of children. It is our sincere hope that this volume will make a significant contribution to the welfare of this and succeeding generations.

C. EUGENE WALKER
MICHAEL C. ROBERTS

Oklahoma City, Oklahoma
Lawrence, Kansas

Contents

SECTION THREE

PROBLEMS OF EARLY LIFE

SECTION FOUR

PROBLEMS OF CHILDHOOD

SECTION FIVE

PROBLEMS OF ADOLESCENCE

SECTION SIX

INTERVENTION STRATEGIES

SECTION SEVEN

SPECIAL TOPICS

CHILD DEVELOPMENT

CHAPTER 1

Families and Children in History

ROBERT HABENSTEIN AND ROBERTA A. OLSON

The American family has experienced profound changes in both structure and function during the past three centuries. Throughout history, the family has changed in response to changes in society and, in turn, has influenced society's perceptions of and demands on the family. The unique role of the family as a social unit results from many factors, and the modern family has evolved from earlier forms developed under previous economic and social conditions. The existing social and economic conditions and the prevailing culture and evolving ideology also influence the family continuously.

American society today has many types of families, differing in geographic location, size, ethnic norms, religious orientation, economic status, vocational skills, social class, and lifestyle (Mindel, Habenstein, & Wright, 1998). Moreover, family structures vary greatly in size, lines of authority, rigidity, degree of inclusion of extended kin, roles of family members, child-rearing techniques, and lifestyle (Queen, Habenstein, & Quadagno, 1985). The traditional family unit provides its members with economic status, religious orientation, educational level, sense of identity, and affectional bonds.

Although American families are quite diverse, it is still possible to examine the concept of the family and explore the distinctive characteristics of American families to gain an understanding of how general patterns of family organization and structures have emerged in Western society and how they have changed since the early days of the American colonies. Before considering colonial families, it is helpful to look briefly to their European roots.

EUROPEAN FAMILIES

The origins of family ideology and institutional practice stretch back to the ancient Greek, Roman, and Judeo-Christian cultures, with their systems of patrilineage, patriarchy, extended kinship, and other forms of affiliative bonds. Father-centered families have dominated Western society for several thousand years. The paterfamilias of the ancient Romans stands as an extreme example of authority vested in the male parent. (For the role of Roman mothers as disciplinarians as well as custodians of Roman culture and traditional morality, see the excellent study by Hallett, 1984). Although the role of the father as absolute head of the family is no longer prevalent in American society, it is still a recognizable cultural model among many ethnic groups. (Mindel et al., 1998)

A pervasive, counterbalancing alternative to the ancient patriarchal, patrilineal family has always existed but has received little historical attention. Trumbach, in his comprehensive and anthropologically sophisticated *Rise of the Egalitarian Family* (1978), has delineated a constant dialectical opposition in

Western society between the *patriarchal* (male-dominated) and *kindred* forms of kinship and family organization. "In Western societies," writes Trumbach,

> the patriarchal household was one of ancient provenance. It was enshrined in the *Odyssey* and in the law codes of Exodus and Deuteronomy. Its basic presumption was that at the head of each household stood a man who in his role as master, father, and husband owned his wife, his children, his slaves, his animals, and his land. The authority of master over his household was the model for all dependent relationships, including that of kin and subjects. (p. 3)

In contrast to the system of patrilineage, particularly but not exclusively, barbarian peoples associated with the Dark Ages organized their relations into systems of cognatic kindred:

> Each individual . . . stood at the center of a unique circle of kinsman connected to him through both mother and father and through his spouse. Inheritances were equally divided among all children; the position of women with regard to property and divorce was relatively high; and friendship was a stronger bond than kinship. (p. 14; for a more recent discussion of patriarchal and kindred forms of family organization, see Casey's *History of the American Family*, 1989; Gottlieb 1993)

Through the later centuries of feudalism, the kindred form of family structure declined and was gradually eclipsed by a growth in the ideal of continuity in family lines and the transfer of property through patrilineal inheritance. Primogeniture (inheritance from the father to the firstborn son) and other special rights accorded to the eldest son, the loss of property rights of women, and the turn to paternal relatives instead of friends relegated kindred to secondary status (Trumbach, 1978).

However, as feudalism gave way to mercantilism, colonization, urbanization, and neoindustrialism, the system of kindred organization with its nonpatriarchal mode of kinship reckoning reemerged in European society and spread to America. Today, for example, the mother's and the father's family lines are bilineally recognized. However, the patronymic (the naming of children through the father's line) remains established for all but the very rich and aristocratic and, since the mid-18th century, family

and kinship organization has been oriented more toward males than females. The alternation between kindred and patrilineal family structures, as Trumbach (1978) notes, remains part of the social dynamics of traditional European society.

Whichever family system was currently dominant, it did not operate to the exclusion of the other. Nor did these opposing forms exist in a social vacuum. The simplicity of a patriarchal, patrilineal, primogeniture system of relations and affiliation, which operated to keep property and bloodlines intact, commended it to property-based and agricultural pursuits because it could easily become a building block in larger forms of kinship organizations such as sibs, clans, and even larger societal divisions.

Whether the dominant family form of the times was patriarchal or kindred, the ideal of the large household prevailed from ancient to relatively recent times. It is hardly necessary to point out that some modern religious and ethnic groups, such as Mormons (Shoumatoff, 1985) and Hispanics (Becerra, 1998), still hold tenaciously to the ideal of a large family. Large households through earlier centuries might contain not only many children but also servants, boarders, children from other primary relatives, and members of elder generations (Gottlieb, 1993). The large household could thus function as an economic and protective unit with a ramified division of labor and the potential for survival in troubled and perilous times. The extended family was thus a microcosm of the larger society (Gottlieb, 1993).

Within the large households (and among them, when they were physically close), kinship bonds extended between and across generations. For example, the mother's sister would be available to take charge of the family during the birth of children or during periods of family crisis such as sickness or separation. The maternal aunt has always been a favorite category of kin in Western society. The father's brother by the same token could assist in matters of authority and discipline. Parental siblings have played various roles in the family throughout history, but their role has always been important. The same is true of grandparents.

Although the ideal of large kindreds and households was often approximated, these larger family units always contained a nucleus of husband, wife, and children. This nucleus, when shorn of other kin to form a distinct family unit, has come to be known as the *nuclear* family. The concept of the nuclear family has caused considerable confusion and argument among those who study the family. Nevertheless, in Western society, this small, tightly knit nucleus of husband, wife, and children has always existed within any larger family unit. The larger unit, with its variety of ascending or cross-generational relatives operating under a set of unifying rules and expectations, has come to be called the *extended* family.

Some family researchers and scholars have failed to recognize the enduring historical character of the nuclear family. Instead, they have argued that the nuclear family is a product and foundation of capitalism and the Protestant ethic. Without elaboration, a strong argument can be made that capitalism and Protestantism, in conjunction with the Industrial Revolution of late 18th- and early 19th-century industrialism, did not "produce" the nuclear family (Berger & Berger, 1983; Goody, 1983). On the other hand, it can also be reasonably argued that these major social institutions (and others) have definitely influenced the size and functions of the European and, later, the American family.

Max Weber (1958), for example, contends that the nuclear family originated in the decline of Catholicism and the influences of the Protestant Reformation. The change from a primary focus on religion and the rewards to be gained in heaven to a focus on the earthly rewards of economic gain in the present world profoundly affected the family. The Protestant ethic stressed the need for stronger personal and societal concentration of thought and energy on economic production and consumption. Action in the service of the Lord would replace contemplation. Initially, this change of focus reduced the power of the Church to dictate the actions of family members in their daily lives. Patriarchal power and the importance of family lineage were reduced by the desire for individual achievement. Also important were the mass emigrations to the New World and the later movement westward (Weber, 1958).

Another argument comes from Shorter (1975), who has suggested that the increased striving for personal gain and emotional satisfaction during the Industrial Revolution eventually led to the active pursuit of individual gain, enhanced intimacy, and romanticism, which reduced the influence of extended kin on the nuclear family.

AMERICAN COLONIAL FAMILIES

NEW ENGLAND (1620–1780)

During the colonial period, the ideal family unit provided the setting for economic, educational, social, recreational, and religious functions (Queen et al., 1985). Most early settlers in the New World were either members of nuclear families or single males. Although most grandparents and older parents did not travel to the New World during its early stages of settlement, the ideal of the extended family was not forgotten. This was true even though the forces for disorder and declension in England, particularly in rural areas in the 17th century, along with the beginnings of an urbanization that would transfer attention away from land ownership and toward the production and marketing of industrial goods, disrupted the traditional patriarchal extended family organization (Greven, 1970; Habenstein, 1998).

Early colonists did not necessarily come from extended families. Even those who did found it difficult to transport such families intact to the New World. If the extended family ideal included cousins, aunts, uncles, affinals, and older generations, such an assemblage would almost never be found living under one roof in colonial New England (Demos, 1970). However, a number of close relatives, including married children, might live very near each other. Usually, a male colonist would acquire a modest holding and, with his wife and children, develop it. The typical New England colonial home was not designed to accommodate a large household with many kin (Demos, 1970). For Middle Atlantic and Southern colonial households, the situation was different, particularly on large plantations (Queen et al., 1985).

Among New England colonists, the husband/father would assume a patriarchal role, but kindred, including close and supportive friends, were not forgotten. Male children grew up with the expectation that they would some day acquire the entire family homestead or would receive part of the original holding on which to settle and start a new homestead. In earlier colonial New England, family structure was not clear-cut; it incorporated, in order of importance, patriarchal authority, utilization of both family lines to aid in surviving the hardships of settling, friendships, indentured servants, other primary and nonprimary relatives, primogeniture, and the settling of grown children on nearby family land. Generally, families were large only to the extent that there were many children born into them who survived. Through generations, the nuclear family thus remained dominant but was both buttressed and intruded on by close kin living nearby.

The utility of the large family to rural agricultural pursuits is obvious. The many tasks required in farming can be accomplished through a division of labor with important roles for all members, regardless of age or sex. But the physical environment adds a limiting factor. Goldschmidt (1976) points out that the New England colonists in their farming developed a Northern tradition

> adapted to the relatively hilly lands of the North; the land was held by the farmer himself who was independent in his operation. . . . Hard work, ingenuity, and independence were critical features of the morality that developed in this area, a pattern we have come to know as the "Protestant Ethnic." (p. 4)

Incorporated into the new ethic was a dour and somewhat anxiety-ridden religious ideology called Puritanism that emphasized hard work, prudence, avoidance of ritual and display, rigorous caste lines, and repression of emotional display. Nevertheless, companionship was emphasized as one of the primary purposes of marriage, the family itself to be considered a "little commonwealth" (Bremer, 1976, pp. 176–180).

The Puritan religion considered the birth of children to be a "divine obligation" (Bell, 1971), but children were also considered to be an economic asset. The typical family of the 1790s had eight children (Kephart, 1977). In both the isolated Southern farms and the small New England colonies, large families were able to function as quasi-independent economic units. Children provided economic services for the family by farming the land, learning the family trade, making and storing the food, and helping to build the family home. The struggle for existence in early colonial days did not allow for an extended childhood at home.

Child Rearing

Play and amusement were considered sinful pursuits; education in the home often began at 3 or 4 years of age (Calhoun, 1960). Children's books usually consisted of Bible stories or verses such as "The

Prodigal Daughter" or "The Disobedient Lady Reclaimed." By 1649, some degree of classroom education was required for boys in every New England colony except for Rhode Island. Schools of this period, in session seven or eight hours a day, were equally strict in discipline and in their reliance on religious psalms and scriptures as major teaching tools. Basic knowledge such as reading and mathematics was supplemented by the teaching of practical skills. Boys were taught farming or were trained in their father's trade. Girls were taught domestic skills (Bremer, 1976).

Religious teaching and worship were home-centered. The early Puritan ideology emphasized the role of the family as guardian of the public as well as the private good (Shorter, 1975). Not only did religion specify the approved relationships among family members and their duties and responsibilities to each other, but it also made it a sacred duty of the patriarch to see that the edicts of the church were carried out in the home and community (Bremer, 1976).

The patriarch was responsible for reading daily scriptures in the home and modeling the ethical and moral standards of the community. He was responsible for setting and enforcing the religious and ethical standards of all family members. The patriarch's role of supreme authority in the home was sanctioned and encouraged by the church (Goodsell, 1934). As the Puritan religion waned in favor of less restrictive religious practices, the church's support of patriarchal dominance lessened.

Nevertheless, obedience to parents, the importance of work, the evils of idleness, and strict adherence to church doctrine were always stressed. The father, as the sole guardian of his family, determined the education, religious training, work apprenticeship, distribution of land, and marriage of his children. Children were viewed as easy prey for the devil. Idleness and play were the "devil's playground." The Puritans viewed children as basically depraved, and this perception made it necessary to seek infantile conversions.

Children were confronted from their earliest years with the terrors of Hell, which they could escape only by following what they were taught and avoiding all pleasures of childhood (Calhoun, 1917). Strict discipline and the use of corporal punishment to "break the child's will" were encouraged (Miller & Swanson, 1958). John Robinson, a Pilgrim teacher, advised parents:

Surely, there is in all children (though not alike) a stubbornness and stoutness of mind arising from natural pride which must in the first place be broken and beaten down that so the foundations of their education being layed in humilitie and tractableness other virtues may in their time be built thereon. (quoted in Earle, 1895, p. 192)

Children had no legal rights, and parents had almost unlimited authority in child rearing and discipline. Children were expected to obey their parents without question. A book of etiquette for children entitled *A Pretty Little Pocket Book* instructed children never to speak unless spoken to, never to sit at the dinner table until grace had been spoken, and never to dispute with parents or other adults (Goodsell, 1934).

In a 122-page *Little Book* published in Boston in 1712, Benjamine Wadsworth Trumbull, A.M., pastor of the New England Church of Christ, sought prescriptively to establish the duties of "The Well-Ordered Family." He elaborated in several previously delivered sermons on the duties of husbands and wives, parents and children, as well as masters and servants. Although most of the book is devoted to the husband-wife relationship, the duties of children to their parents consume 10 pages and are subsumed under seven major admonishments: Children should (1) love their parents, (2) fear them, (3) honor them, (4) give diligent heed to their instructions, (5) patiently bear their deserved corrections, (6) obey them, and (7) relieve and maintain them if need requires (Rothman & Rothman, 1972).

Parents had the legal right to punish children severely. Massachusetts and Connecticut had laws that permitted the killing of an "unrully child." The Piscataqua colony passed a law stating, "If any child or children above 16 years of competent understanding, shall curse or smite their natural father or mother, he or they shall be put to death unless it can be sufficiently testified that the parents have been unchristianly negligent of the education of such child" (quoted in Calhoun, 1960, p. 120). Although no record exists of such punishment actually being carried out, parents did use beatings and denial of food as punishment for acts of disobedience (Bell, 1971).

During the colonial period, marriage was considered by the Puritans to be both a spiritual and contractual union. The patriarch of the family arranged the marriages of his children, although the daughter did have the right to refuse the marital agreement. Consensus for marriage was based primarily on the financial ability of the man to support his wife. Love, attraction, and affection were not considered adequate reasons for the arrangement of a marriage.

During the period from colonization to after the American Revolution, the importance of the extended family network increased. The nuclear family of the early colonial days was to some extent replaced or strongly reinforced by the extended family kin network. The extended family provided a strong patriarchal system that encouraged stability, financial interdependence, and the importance of family lineage (Leslie, 1976; Winch, 1952). The status of the extended family stemmed from its land holdings or family enterprise. Membership in a family traditionally defined each member's place in the community. Family membership also defined how far the child would go in school, what trade he or she would learn, whom the child could marry, and where the child would live.

SOUTHERN PLANTATION (1620–1780)

Before dealing with the movement west, it is necessary to add a few paragraphs on the distinctive character of the colonial family of the South. Again, physical environment was a major factor in the development, during that time, of a family type quite different from that of New England. Goldschmidt (1976) has sketched the parameters of the Southern plantation tradition, but Queen et al. (1985) have described the Southern colonial household in some detail:

> There were many Cavaliers and few Puritans. Many of the earliest settlers were detached males seeking their fortunes instead of families seeking homes. There was marked stratification, which involved social distance between first families, yeomen, a pioneer fringe of poor whites, indentured servants, and Negro slaves. Gradually there was built up a social system reminiscent of feudalism and chivalry, though actually very different from anything ever developed in Europe. (p. 209)

On the large plantations, each household was a relatively self-sufficient group that produced a large part of its own food, clothing, and other necessities, erected buildings, made tools, trained its children, cared for its sick, dispensed homemade justice, and provided amusement. Southern households were often much larger and more isolated than those of New England.

Women, who through chivalry were put on a pedestal, nevertheless usually occupied an inferior social position. Through the years, primogeniture had come to prevail, and females were limited in inheritance of land and property. The eldest son would almost always inherit the manor house and principal lands. Thus, lands were kept in the same male line for many generations. The *Virginia Gazette* in 1737 advised women for the "advancement of matrimonial felicity" never to dispute with their husbands under any circumstances. Generally, it was believed that the husband should guide, defend, and provide for the wife, and she was expected to serve him in subjection, be modest in speech and dress, and be a good housewife. It was held that "while marriage was for man a pleasant duty, it was woman's reason for existence" (Spruill, 1938, p. 318). Women were expected to be chaste before marriage and observe marital fidelity afterward. Males were relatively free to exploit both Black and White females sexually.

As in New England, marital selection involved both romantic and practical considerations. Both men and women married at an early age. Courtship with parental consent preceded marriage, but considerations of economic and social status were more important than romantic love as the chief bases for marriage.

Child Rearing
Children in the Southern colonies grew up under varying circumstances, depending on the social class into which they were born (Morgan, 1952). The children of the well-to-do enjoyed comforts provided by nurses, tutors, and governesses; farmer's children were cared for chiefly by their own mothers, but very early, they began to assume responsibilities and to share the work of house, barn, and field. Finally, children of indentured servants and slaves received haphazard attention and were soon incorporated into the workforce.

Birth and death rates both were consistently high. Formal education for children who survived, with the exception of those in upper classes, was limited. There were far fewer schools in the South than in New England, and it is said that only three White men out of five could spell their own name

(Morgan, 1952). Again, in matters of religion, the New England families were more active than the Southern families. But in both the North and the South, marriages were encouraged or almost demanded of single persons, and the expectation of a large family was universal in all colonies. The affectional functions would be underplayed publicly, whether involving children, juveniles, or adults. Queen et al. (1985) summarize:

In general it is correct to say that the (colonial) family was a much more important institution in colonial times than today. Its functions were much more inclusive, almost everyone was a member of some family group, and there were fewer agencies to threaten the family's hold on its members. (p. 216)

MOVEMENT WEST, 1780 TO 1880

The mass movement of the population westward across the Appalachian Mountains to the Mississippi and later to the Pacific Ocean created a major shift in both the functions and organization of the family. Again, nuclear families and single men moved, and the elderly were left behind. Migration created major structural changes in the family system. Throughout history, patriarchal societies are associated with nonmobile extended family units and usually with large households. As young families broke economic and sentimental ties to their parental families, patriarchal control declined.

Children growing up on the frontier might never experience the direct authority of a grandparent and in turn would not learn to expect great control over their own grandchildren. The father continued to be the final authority in the frontier family, but isolation and the struggle for survival led to the wife's acquiring more responsibility and authority in the family. This relationship led to an increased democratization of the family. Changes were made in the laws of inheritance of land and transmission of the family business. No longer were the family lands held intact for future generations. When young adults left the families on the East Coast, the landholdings to which extended and nuclear patriarchal families traditionally had been tied were often sold. The democratic ideology of the new nation demanded an equal distribution of the land among all children, including the females.

The loss of patriarchal power and the breakup of landholdings also led to basic changes in family structure. Family functions also changed, and family status no longer defined the economic, educational, or social limits of the children. Young adults were less restricted in their choice of education, schooling, trade, landholding, and marriage. Fathers no longer arranged marriages, although parental approval of a fiancé's economic abilities might still be a major factor in a marriage. The patriarchal family embedded in a cluster of extended kin living neolocally changed, and in its place emerged a conjugal family system without strong tradition or economic and sentimental ties to the extended kin. Kin were not abandoned, but they were often left behind.

Although the westward movement of young families created a period of loss of kinship and extended family networks, the following generations of pioneers often settled down in small agricultural communities to create a new, perhaps modified, extended kinship network. The new network of kin functioned primarily as a support system. The tradition of powerful patriarchal dominance did not exist even though the patriarchal role might have had strong appeal to males. Another consequence of the pioneer movement westward was the loss of formal education in schools and a return to education in the family homes. The education of children continued to be in the home or in small schools over which parents retained considerable control. Religious practices also remained in the home or small community church.

CHILD REARING

The movement westward also changed child-rearing practices. There was a decline in the practice of "breaking the child's will" (Miller & Swanson, 1958). Use of corporal punishment began to lessen. Etiquette on the frontier changed; children no longer remained silent during meals; they talked more freely with parents and had more freedom to express their opinions. In general, arbitrary patriarchal or parental authority diminished. Children were expected to be working members of the family. Work and home life were one and the same. Adolescence was not a unique stage of development during this period. Young adults contributed to the family work. When they married, the new couple usually moved onto land of their own or onto a nearby piece of parental land. With the loss of patriarchal authority and the emergence of conjugal, more democratic families, independence and self-reliance were most often stressed as important qualities to instill in frontier children.

INDUSTRIAL REVOLUTION, 19TH CENTURY

One of the most dramatic changes in the American family occurred during the Industrial Revolution. Prior to the 1800s, the largest "immigration" was of 10 to 20 million Black slaves primarily into the Southern states. The ethnic composition of the immigrants changed, as did the character of the country's economy. The great influx of Southern, Eastern, and Central European immigrants, mostly of peasant stock, coincided with the rapid surge of industrial and urban growth in America. No longer needed to build the railroads or settle the virgin land of the western states, the new arrivals—Bohemians, Slovaks, Poles, Russians, Russian-Polish Jews, Czechs, and Italians—were directed to the factories and sweatshops of America's slum-ridden cities (Feldstein & Costello, 1974). This large population influx into the cities of America created one of the most dramatic periods of change in the society as well as the family.

SHIFTING ECONOMY AND CHANGING
FAMILY ORGANIZATION

Prior to the early 1800s, the economy was primarily agricultural, and the farm family was a fairly self-sufficient unit. The development of an industrial society dramatically altered many of the traditional family functions. Production of goods and services, for example, was removed from the home. Children were less likely to participate in the family economy of farming or a family trade. Business and industry became structural units outside the home. There was a continual reduction in homemaking activities, and the home became increasingly separate from the workplace. Movement to the cities created a family within which children, for the first time, became an economic liability instead of an economic function. Poor children working in the factories provided some economic contribution to the family but were often a net liability. An interesting development of this era was that children's work was often separated from the previous family work system. A new extension of the kindred principle appeared for the first time when the children and adolescents had the opportunity to form numerous contacts with other children their age. This was the beginning of age-separate functions for adolescents.

The protective functions of the agricultural family included the promise of economic security from childhood to old age. Movement to the cities again was a movement of the young or the nuclear families; the older generations were usually left behind. The industrialization of the country lessened the responsibility and commitment to care for previous generations.

The religious functions of the family during the period of industrialization also witnessed a shift in emphasis. Religious dicta of the agricultural family stressed the family as a religious unit with the father as the head of the family. The family was primarily responsible for the ethical standards of its members. Family prayers and Bible readings were common customs. The advent of the movement to the cities reduced the family's religious functions as large churches and Sunday schools began to assume primary responsibility for religious training to the children and the setting of ethical standards for the community.

The period of rapid change affected the status-conferring functions of the family. In an agricultural community, the family directly participated in defining each member's role in the community. Boys usually followed in their father's occupational footsteps, and girls were expected to become housewives and mothers. Children grew up and usually married within their social class; often, they stayed in the same town as their parents. Industrialization changed the traditions of the family and the family's ability to define the child's occupation within the community. Industrialization not only brought adults to urban areas but offered them the opportunity to "further or better their parents' place in society" (Mead, 1976). Worth began to be defined in terms of the amount of money a person made.

For the first time, women entered the marketplace in large numbers. The previous roles of mother and housewife were expanded. The added cost of child care and the crowding of families into tenement houses created conditions in which the limiting of the number of children in a family was desirable. Women gained the right to own their own

property and to enter into contracts. Unmarried women were now able to leave home and live independently. As noted previously, Shorter (1975) has suggested that the most dramatic changes in the family had their seeds in the period of industrialization and the emergence of capitalism. Previously, unmarried women stayed in the family home and were able to move out only at the time of marriage. Now, the ability to obtain a job for the first time freed women from the family and allowed them an increased opportunity to choose a marriage partner on the basis of emotional needs instead of financial ability. Shorter further suggests that the shift from economic to emotional needs as a basis for marriage initially led to the decrease in extended kinship control and eventually to the increases in the divorce rate of the 20th century.

The increased wealth of families, accompanied by improved health care, allowed more children to live and allowed mothers to spend more time in child rearing and building emotional attachments to children within the family. The strengthened attachment of mother and child led to an increased sense of nuclear family solidarity and the beginning withdrawal of the family unit from the community.

Education prior to industrialization took place in the home or small school. The advent of large urban areas created two major changes. First, children of lower-income families were forced to work in factories. Previously, these children had learned a trade within the family or worked the family farm; now, children from poor families were separated from family production and interaction with other family members. Second, public education in large cities further diluted parental involvement in the teaching of their children. State and federal government agencies increasingly assumed this function.

CHILD REARING

19th-Century Victorianism

As the younger more adventurous segment of American society pushed westward, the burgeoning populace of those remaining in growing urban centers and in established villages and farms were subject to an ideology that had emerged from middle-class England: Victorianism.

Victorianism in the United States presumed a set of ideas and values suitable for guiding the behavior of Americans in all walks of life. Civility, good manners, respect for convention, rational thought and circumspection in dealing with matters large and small would produce a valued end product: the man or woman of *character*. Further, the social institution par excellence to instill such character could only be the family, within which one first learned the moral, religious, ethical, and social precepts of good citizenship. (Queen et al., 1985, p. 94).

We can only look to this period of changing values and practices for their relevance to child rearing, but it might be pointed out that whatever the changing definition of adult behavior (character and morality based in common religious beliefs), considerable leeway was allowed on the part of husbands.

Childhood, Adolescence, and Victorianism
During the last two-thirds of the nineteenth century, childhood and adolescence began to be viewed as distinctly different periods of development. For the first time, children were no longer considered to be miniature adults. Demos and Demos (1969) identify the early period as the beginning of "child-centered families." After 1825, child-rearing books by American authors began to appear, and many sold thousands of copies. Magazines such as *Mother's Magazine* and *Mother's Assistant* were specifically addressed to child care and child-rearing issues (Demos & Demos, 1969). The popularity of these magazines and books indicated society's increased interest in the child and recognition of the importance of child rearing. Changes in the family structure during the 19th century were met with considerable anxiety about the quality of American family life (Wishy, 1968). Child-rearing books stressed the importance of parental authority, the need for strict discipline in early childhood, and the maintenance of this authority throughout the formative years.

As late as midcentury, Bulkeley (1858) advised parents that even the smallest infant reveals a "willfulness that springs from a depraved nature and is intensely selfish." Parents were warned that, if strict discipline was not instituted and maintained, the child would quickly become uncontrollable and would suffer permanent damage. The author appeared to believe that parents were rapidly losing all control and authority over their children and predicted dire consequences if this trend continued. Parents were strongly advised not to "show off" their children to guests because this would create a conceited and selfish child (Child, 1835).

The concept of adolescence began to emerge during this period. The separation of generations, as seen in the "new custom" of holding parties exclusively for young people, was viewed as an alarming development that would endanger the unity of the family if it were to continue (Child, 1835). By 1900, writings on youth gangs, juvenile delinquency, and vocational guidance indicated that society was beginning to recognize and attempt to deal with adolescence as a special period of child development (Demos & Demos, 1969).

G. Stanley Hall, a leader in the child study movement in the late 19th century, was the first to write about adolescence as a separate stage of child development. Hall (1882) published a paper entitled "The Moral and Religious Training of Children" and later *Adolescence: Its Psychology, and Its Relations to Physiology, Anthropology, Sociology, Sex, Crime, Religion, and Education* (1904). These works were the first to describe the "storm and stress" of adolescence. Hall's theory postulated that each individual "lives through each of the major steps in the evolution of the race as a whole" (1904). Adolescence was viewed as a time of great change and confusion. Hall's writings had a profound effect on psychology (Angell, 1904), education (Betts, 1906), child rearing (McKeever, 1913), child labor laws, vocational guidance (Mangold, 1910), and religious training. Adolescence as a separate stage of development was accepted, and the rudimentary beginnings of a youth culture were beginning to be recognized. After 1925, Hall's theories of adolescence were discarded. Judd (1915), King (1903), Mead (1928), and Thorndike (1908) claimed that Hall's theories were too tied to set stages, overemphasized physiological functions, and ignored cultural determinants. Nevertheless, adolescence continued to be recognized and studied as a stage in child development.

TWENTIETH-CENTURY

Perhaps a milestone in the changing attitude toward child care occurred in 1914, when the federal government first published *Infant Care,* a booklet on child rearing for parents. This booklet has been repeatedly revised over the years and provides an interesting indication of the changes in child rearing from 1914 to the present. From 1914 to 1921, parents were warned of the great potential harm in allowing children to act on their autoerotic impulses. Thumb sucking and masturbation were to be promptly and rigorously stopped; otherwise, it was suggested, these behaviors would "grow" beyond control and permanently damage the child. The child was to be bound both hand and foot to the crib so that he or she would not be able to thumb-suck, masturbate, or rub his or her thighs together.

During the period from 1929 to 1938, there was a shift in emphasis. Autoeroticism was considered less of a problem. Regularity in daily living was most important, and strict, early toilet training was stressed. Children were to be fed, weaned, toilet trained, and put to bed on a strict schedule and with firmness. Parents were warned not to yield to the "baby's resistance." A major danger in child rearing was allowing the child to dominate the parents.

Between 1942 and 1945, the watchword was non-interference. Children were viewed as devoid of sexual impulses. Parents were to be "mild" and not to interfere with children's thumb sucking or masturbation. Weaning and toilet training were started later, and punishment for failure was less severe than suggested in earlier editions.

By 1951, there was still the suggestion of mildness in the role of parents. Yet, concerns that had been expressed in 1929 that the child would dominate the parents were once again expressed. Parents were cautioned not to pick up the baby every time he or she cried because this could eventually lead to the child's becoming a tyrant.

During the 1960s, child-rearing guides stressed leniency, recognition of developmental readiness, and the use of positive reinforcement of appropriate behaviors. During the late 1970s and 1980s, some child-rearing books began to focus on teaching reading, language, and math concepts to preschool children. The "fast track" babies and toddlers were rushed from gymnastics, swimming, and foreign language lessons to flash card reading periods. Many child development specialists began to warn of the danger of pushing young children too fast and potentially creating anxious and unhappy youngsters who would be burned out on learning by grade school.

Starting in the 1960s and continuing through the 1990s, an enormous popular literature on child care came into existence. Parents could pick and choose the philosophy of and prescription for child care that suited their own preconceptions. Books have ranged from how to raise children in a fundamentalist Christian family (i.e., Dobson, 1982), in which the use of spankings and strong parental authority are recommended as the best way to raise children, to the final edition of *Baby and Child Care* (1997), in which Benjamin Spock continued to encourage parents to trust in themselves and to be consistent in their rules of parenting. In the 1980s, Terry Brazelton, a pediatrician, became well-known for his supportive and caring style with parents and children. Brazelton, focusing on the parent-child relationship, encouraged parents to understand their child's behavior in terms of the child's developmental stage. The child's behavior was seen as a means of communication about how he or she experiences the world. Parents were asked to take on the role of helping the child to express feelings and learn to cope with normal experiences of childhood such as anxiety, jealousy, and frustration. David Elkind's writings about the developmental stage of adolescence continued to impact the child/adolescent developmental psychologist's research and writings.

Additionally, many child-rearing books in the 1980s and 1990s began to focus on shared parenting and the importance of the father in the child's and adolescent's life. Vastly discrepant groups have supported the importance of the father in the home. The Promise Keepers, a fundamentalist Christian group, encourages fathers to take their "rightful place" as the head of the household and family caretaker. Psychologists and child development experts have encouraged fathers to become more involved in the daily parenting of the infant and child to avoid problems in adolescence. Research and clinical cases have focused on fathers as playing a pivotal role in preventing problems ranging from anorexia to depression, suicide, pregnancy, violence, and drug use. Fathers are encouraged to become more emotionally expressive with their children and to learn to be an active and involved parent in the traditional nuclear family or in the divorced and in blended family settings.

A survey commissioned by the National Committee for the Prevention of Child Abuse (Lung & Daro, 1996) found less than half of all American parents report that they use spankings as a mode of child management. Yet, at the other end of the spectrum, one million children were victims of substantiated abuse and neglect, and 996 children were killed as a result of abuse and neglect (Lung & Daro, 1996). The Department of Health and Human Services estimates from the Third National Incidence Study on Child Abuse and Neglect (Lung & Daro, 1996) that 2.8 million children were considered at risk for abuse and neglect in 1994. This figure is double the number of children considered to be at risk from the prior survey in 1988. The link between substance abuse and child abuse has strengthened over the years. It is estimated that about 9 to 10 million children under the age of 18 are directly affected by substance-abusing parents (Woodside, 1988). Lung and Daro report that in 15 states, on average 40% of the substantiated child abuse cases involved substance-abusing parents.

BIRTHRATES

The fifth consecutive year of overall decline in the birthrate was marked in 1995, when the birthrate was 11% lower than in 1990. The decline is due to the lower number of births to women in their twenties (Ventura, Martin, Curtin, & Mathews, 1998). Although almost one million teens become pregnant each year, the 1995 birth records indicate an overall 4% decline in the birthrates for teens (Henshaw, 1997; Ventura et al., 1998). Black teens had the largest decline (8%) in births. But, overall, 22% of Black teens get pregnant each year as compared to 9% of White and 18% of all Hispanic teens. Teen pregnancies often result in single-parent, low-income families (Maynard, 1996).

MARRIAGE AND DIVORCE RATES

Couples marrying today have about a 50% chance of getting a divorce over their lifetime. Divorce was at its highest peak in 1979, at which time 53% of people obtained a divorce. Divorce has steadily declined since that time. In 1996, the annual divorce rate was 43% (U.S. National Center for Health Statistics, 1997). The divorce rate in 1996 marks a 20-year low. One important reason for the lower divorce rate is that while marriages have declined over the past decade, there has also been a rise in the number of never-married parents. In 1996, children are just as likely to be living with a single never-married parent as with a single divorced parent. Overall, only 68% of all children under the age of 18 live in the traditional two-parent nuclear family. White children more often live with two parents (75%) than Hispanic (62%) or Black (33%)

children (U.S. National Center for Health Statistics, 1997).

An interesting trend over the past two decades is the delaying of the first marriage. Men are marrying at the average age of 26.7 years and women at 24.5 years (U.S. Bureau of the Census, 1998). Many of these young men and women may be the products of divorced families. The delay in the age of marriage and the number of never-married parents may reflect the concerns of making a lifelong commitment to a spouse or a desire to avoid an early marriage and subsequent divorce.

The role of social scientists in the field of child development, with its child-rearing issues, is assumed to be one of leadership and guidance. Our brief historical review of child-rearing literature suggests that, on the contrary, social scientists have often mirrored or fostered society's current beliefs and perceptions concerning children's roles and functions in the family.

POST–WORLD WAR II FAMILY DISORGANIZATION

In the past 50 years, an efflorescence of writings has addressed the changing character and fortune of the American family. The litany of changes is extensive: reduction in family size, sloughing off of extended kin, increased geographic mobility, increasing urbanity, declining community awareness and participation, individualism of family members replacing familism, weakening of traditional roles, impacting class and status systems, economic insecurity related to business cycles, and the inexorable process of shifting traditional family functions toward corporate structures and rationally designed organizations such as schools, churches, businesses, corporations, government agencies, commercialized entertainment and recreation, transportation systems, communications systems, and the like. Traditional functions—protective, economic, religious, educational, status-giving, recreational, and affectional—all of which bound the family together as a major societal entity, were either losing strength or had lost the battle during this era.

ETHNIC DIVERSITY THROUGH WAVES OF IMMIGRATION

During the first decade of the 20th century, America was receiving 600,000 to 700,000 legal immigrants a year, mostly from eastern and south-eastern Europe. The influx from western and northern Europe continued but at a slower pace. The country's industrial pool was nearly overflowing, especially since great numbers of Black migrants had moved from the rural South to northern industrial centers.

The "yellow peril" of Chinese immigrants had been stopped abruptly by federal law in 1882, and popular attention turned toward a new threat, Bolshevism, which appeared to be spreading from Russia to all Western countries, and, because the lair of "bomb-throwing anarchists" was thought to be found among Jews and eastern European immigrants (Shillony, 1991), popular opinion strongly supported the Immigration Acts of 1921 and 1924. Grounded in notions of Nordic supremacy, these laws effectively cut off immigration from all but northwestern European countries for more than 40 years.

A change in public opinion after World War II led, finally, to a revision of these acts. Mindel, Habenstein, and Wright wrote:

> When the 1921 and 1924 Immigration and Nationality Acts were ultimately amended in 1965, many of the more egregious biases were eliminated, quotas were now distributed evenly across countries, and first preference was given to persons wishing to be reunited with their families (although the preference was not extended to Mexico until 1976). In addition, political exceptions were made for Cuba (over 600,000 between 1960 and 1990), Vietnam and Southeast Asian countries (over 600,000 from 1975 to 1990), and Soviet Jews (approximately 150,000). There have also been 150,000 additional refugees from such other countries as Poland, Romania, Iran, Afghanistan, and Ethiopia from 1981 through 1990.
>
> Since 1960 almost 20 million people have legally emigrated to the United States, and an additional 3 to 5 million (in 1995) are estimated to be in the country illegally. Experts estimate the rate of illegal immigration to be about 250,000 to 300,000 per year. (1998, pp. 2–3)

Estimates for total numbers of legal and illegal immigrants, those outstaying their visas, migratory workers who decide to stay in the United States and others in detention vary widely. Immigration writer Roy Beck (1996) suggests the top figure for the mid-1990s of a million a year. Beck follows the contention of economist George Borjas (1994) that a direct relationship exists between a large inflow of unskilled, poorly educated immigrants and a transfer of wealth to the top realm of America's occupational hierarchy. Bluntly put, at the bottom of the occupational pyramid the poorest get poorer and at the top the rich get richer. (See also Reich, 1991.) For a rejection of the Borjas contention, see the excellent *Strangers among Us* by journalist Roberto Suro (1998).

On the other hand, writers such as Sanford J. Ungar have been less interested in the impact of numbers of immigrants than in the positive value of ethnicity of the newcomers, who, in his words, contribute positively to a "benign multiculturalism" (1995, p. 21). Whatever the consequences, and there seem to be many, the last third of the 20th century has seen America leading the world in accepting, for diverse and most often political reasons, immigrants from nearly all parts of the globe.

In the last third of the 20th century, no set of social problems has loomed so important yet so vexingly beclouded by personal, group, regional, and economic interests as the great inflowing of immigrants across the country's borders. Central to nearly all immigration problems is the consequences of what can be called "the family connection." It is almost impossible to talk about immigrants without taking into account nuclear and extended family involvements and their life courses as immigrants search in America for a better world, however sentimentally attached they remain to the one left behind.

CURRENT MAJOR ETHNIC GROUPS

We will consider four major ethnic groups demographically, and then turn to one, Latinos, for critical aspects of their community life.

Latino

Under the new census category of People of Hispanic Origin, immigrants and descendants (some from many generations back) from the Caribbean, Mexico, and Central America are exhibiting dramatic growth in America. This is particularly true for a number of states: those with the largest Hispanic population in 1990 include California, 7.7 million; Texas, 4.3 million; New York, 2.2 million; Florida, 1.6 million; Illinois, 0.9 million; as well as large numbers in other states, mostly in the West and Southwest (Wright, 1998, p. 274).

The majority are Mexicans, who make up 64.1% of the total Hispanic population. Florida is the magnet state for Central Americans, and New York has an imposing number of Puerto Ricans. All major cities have Hispanic enclaves; those in southern California and Texas are expanding rapidly, as are cities in Arizona and New Mexico. In the decade 1980 to 1990, metropolitan areas including Los Angeles, Miami, Dallas/Fort Worth, and Washington, D.C. have had Hispanic increases of 71 to 137%! (Wright, 1998, p. 271).

Asian and Pacific Islander

Far fewer in numbers, with only 2.9% of the U.S. population made up of Asian and Pacific Islanders, these immigrants represent a wide variety of race and ethnic character and of reasons for their entry by the tens of thousands since the end of the war in Vietnam. Refugees came from that country and Cambodia. Business-oriented Koreans, who no longer enter as refugees, but reversing the "yellow peril" appellation, have been welcomed and will soon approach .5 million in number. Chinese and Japanese usually come with a middle-class education and a strong spirit of enterprise, both business and educational. Asian Indians are usually fluent in English and well prepared in business, educational, and technical enterprises. All in all, the arrival of such great numbers of Asian immigrants, literally millions (not all legal by far) during 1975 to 1990, has caused a notable change in population. It has also increased technical and business competition, in California particularly, and to a lesser degree elsewhere in the United States, especially in major cities.

American Indian, Eskimo, and Aleut

About 1,875,000 American Indians and 86,000 Eskimos and Aleuts were living in America in 1990 (Wright, 1998, p. 274). Their increase over the past two decades has been significant, as only 524,000 Indians and 42,000 Alaskan Natives were counted in 1960. Most American Indians live in the southwestern states, California, Arizona, New Mexico, and Oklahoma, with less than one fifth living mostly on the 314 reservations scattered across these states (and a few in the north central, New England, and south Atlantic regions). Of all current developments among American Natives, gambling casinos are a vigorous new enterprise for people always characterized as being of the land.

Afro-American

As is well-known to every grade schooler, African Americans first came to America in a Dutch ship in 1619 as slaves, considered as chattel, subhuman, and excluded from the (White) world of Christianity. Their intrinsic value was gauged in term of their utility. Nearly 400 years later, slavery is a dim historical recollection, but African ancestry remains as viable a concern as does the "Auld sod" for American Irish whose ancestors came to this country during Ireland's potato famines of a century and half ago.

Today, we have the terms "Blacks" (used by the U.S. Bureau of Census), "persons of color" (used by today's social scientists), and "Afro-Americans," now popular with journalists and a majority of persons whose ancestors came from Africa. The Afro-American population today represents a continuous growth through the centuries and has risen to 33.9 million in 1996, an estimated 12.8% of Americans—by far the nation's largest minority group (Wright, 1998, p. 268).

Blacks will continue to increase faster than Whites, with a younger median age of 29.5, which is more than six years below the White median age of 35.7. The Black concentration in cities and the White flight to the suburbs has left many center-city areas with a dominant Black population. Percentages of Blacks in major cities vary but are impressive: by number, New York has (in 1990) 7,323,000; Los Angeles, 3,485,400; Chicago, 2,783,700; Philadelphia, 1,585,600; and Houston, 1,630,600. These are the top six, with a dozen or more cities with an average of .5 million Blacks within city limits. In percentage of total population, the first six are Detroit (76%); Atlanta (67%); Washington, D.C. (66%); Birmingham, Alabama (63%); New Orleans, (62%); and Baltimore (59%) (Wright, 1998, p. 272).

Although the Afro-American population continues to grow faster than the White, in the next 15 years the largest minority group in the United States will be people of Hispanic ancestry. Hispanics will number 39 million in 2010, according to Census Bureau projections, compared to 38 million Blacks (Wright, 1998, p. 272).

BARRIO SOCIETY AND IMMIGRATION

In the previously mentioned *Strangers among Us* (1998), Roberto Suro finds generalities and significant differences among the Latinos (his term) who have streamed into the United States for generations, sharing different fates as they follow different migration channels and build their own ethnic communities or "barrios." In contrast with immigrants from India, for example, Latinos are unlikely to be proficient in English, and for the most part those who have emigrated to this country in the past two decades are woefully short on work skills (Reich, 1991).

Yet, Latinos are traditionally work-oriented, looking for and accepting jobs even if it is necessary for them to start at the bottom of the occupational ladder. Nor in the barrios, as in Black ghettos, is there a constant grinding down of self-respect. For Latinos, the alternative to an unsuccessful existence is at the worst a return to their homeland. For Afro-Americans, Haitians, and other Caribbean Blacks, this option may not be very realistic. If Afro-Americans find their fates in urban ghettos, Haitians might find theirs in work camps and shanty towns, relieved only by transiency. Obviously, color matters, but most Hispanics in this respect slip under the door.

Within the barrios of major American cities, the large, extended, father-dominated, mother-adored, and kinship-oriented family may still be found. But this type of family, though remaining respected, even revered in worship, is undergoing significant changes. Looking beyond simple growth patterns of Hispanic people in the United States, we should become aware of the surging character of their migratory movements and the startling social and personal consequences of the changing relationships between older and younger generations.

However, as noted, intense immigration in short periods carries with it the incipient danger of separation of newcomers and older, established residents. The hiatus usually runs along generational lines, with the young arrivals and barrio-born youth facing difficulty finding jobs, if only as casual laborers. An alternative to low-paid and part-time work is to join street gangs and, absorbing gang culture, finding a new social reality in the street world. It is unnecessary to point out that this alternative can only lead to family stress and dysfunction.

Suro (1998, pp. 31–55) gives a rather startling account of youth of Mayan descent in the Houston barrio rejecting the industry of their parents, who often hold two jobs at the same time to create successful ongoing families. Dismissing school and industry, the Mayan youth preferred moving away from parents and family life into the highly organized, more exciting street gang culture. Drug selling, particularly of crack, a cheaply made cocaine derivative, however dangerous, becomes the enterprise of choice with indubitable monetary reward. Better to push drugs than peddlers' carts! (See also William Finnegan, *Cold New World*, 1998.)

A final blow to the hard-working Hispanic-grounded culture of the parents is to find their daughters also participating in street gang culture, dismissive of parental rules and expectations, and often bringing adolescence to a quick halt with teenage single motherhood. Discouragement in older generations often leads to a grudging reassessment of barrio life in *el norte*, followed by plans for a return to a less productive but much less disturbing life in their homeland (Suro, 1998, pp. 50–55). The social problems, particularly illegal and dangerous activities, associated with the sudden filling of the barrio with the young and unskilled is not only intensely disturbing to its good citizens but, in the minds of Americans everywhere, a threat to urban society itself, with stricter laws and law enforcement as the solution of choice.

ETHNIC GROUPS AND FAMILIES

Assimilation

Distinguishable by language and/or accent, values, folkways, mores, art and artifact, and by awareness of their particular history, ethnic groups are as common in the world as are people. Assimilation, however, is a hit-or-miss process as ethnicity provides so much of one's identity.

The search in America for one superidentity reached its height in the very early part of the 20th century and was expressed in a nationwide effort toward "Americanization" (Ross, 1914). Now at the turn of the century, a true and all-encompassing American identity has pretty much been replaced by the social science concept of "ethnic diversity" or "multiculturalism," and, often by journalists, of the "salad bowl."

Still, exchanging one's ethnic identity for "American" shows up in about 5% of the answers to the census question on race or nationality, and undoubtedly to most citizens, "American" does have an important identity reference beyond the right to vote. It is in the context of family life that ethnicity becomes a cultural impress or template, with its rules and expectations, and within each family, through the interaction of its members over time, the emergence of a body of informal practices that assure the continuation of this indispensable societal entity.

Ethnic Density and Disassimilation
The flip side of ethnic diversity lies in the anxiety to hold onto old customs rather than to accept and observe the new. Writes Sanford J. Ungar (1995):

> [Immigrants] may choose to remain quietly apart from the crowd, to resist being smothered by the materialism and high tech consumerism they see on television and their children bring home from school. Often this means they continue to speak the language they brought with them and make a special effort to pass it on to their children and grandchildren. (p. 20)

This is more likely to be true today in urban areas where ethnic enclaves have reached critical mass and where, to post a poor pun, English is no longer the lingua franca. For example, in one large Catholic church in Anaheim, California, masses are said on Sundays at three different times in English, Vietnamese, and Spanish.

Quite obviously, it is important when planning educational programs to take language spoken at home into account. In the 1990 Census, about a third of all people of Hispanic heritage admitted to speaking English poorly or not at all. Language skills are obviously as important in achieving social and occupational mobility as are work skills.

Yet, the picture of cultural change is highly complicated. In laying out a course of analysis, sociology professor H. L. H. Kitano (cited in Mindel et al., 1998) uses as an example the course of three generations of Japanese in America. Whereas no first-generation member could or would speak English as immigrants, the third generation today is almost totally absorbed into and makes exceptional contributions to the culture and prospects of America (p. 34). Kitano proposes a number of categories for analyzing ethnic family change: (1) freedom of choice of spouse, along with the concept of romantic love; (2) priority placed on conjugal bonds over filial bonds; (3) greater equality of the sexes; (4) more flexibility in sex roles; and (5) higher emotional intensity, with emphasis on sexual, romantic attraction, and consequently greater instability and verbal communication between spouses (p. 34).

Globalization
As the new century begins, questions are being raised about family kinships and ethnic cultural levels to take into account broad-range social, political, and economic movements currently taking place on a global scale. But, given restrictions on space, we can only call attention to this ever-growing level of social reality. With virtually instant global communications and the dynamics of the production of worldly goods, the rapacious quality of trade agreements, and the cost of labor becoming the central factor in corporate business, it is difficult to locate and assess the residual power of the individual, and his or her ethnic connection, facing this deus ex machina (Greider, 1997).

REFERENCES

Alvin, M., & Cavil, D. (1981). *Family life in America 1620–2000.* New York: Revisionary Press.

Angell J. (1904). *Psychology.* New York: Hoyt.

Appleton, M. (1821). *Early education.* London.

Becerra, R.M. (1998). The Mexican-American family. In C.H. Mindel, R.W. Habenstein, & R. Wright (Eds.), *Ethnic families in America: Patterns and variations* (4th ed., pp. 153–171). Upper Saddle River, NJ: Prentice Hall.

Beck, R. (1996). *The case against immigration: The moral, economic, social, and environmental reasons for reducing U.S. immigration back to traditional level.* New York: Norton.

Bell, R. (1971). *Marriage and family interaction* (3rd ed.). Hammed, IL: Renders.

Berger, B., & Berger, P. (1983). *The war over the family: Capturing the middle ground.* New York: Anchor Press/Doubleday.

Betts, G. (1906). *The mind and its education.* New York: Appleton.

Borjas, G.J. (1994). Tired, poor, on welfare. In N. Mills (Ed.), *Arguing immigraton* (pp. 76–80). New York: Simon & Schuster.

Bremer, F.J. (1976). *The Puritan experiment: New England society from Bradford to Edwards.* New York: St. Martin's Press.

Brimelow, F. (1996). *Alien nation: Common sense about America's immigration disaster.* New York: Harper Perennial.

Bulkeley, H. (1858). *A word to parents.* Philadelphia: Presbyterian Board of Publication.

Calhoun, A. (1917). *A social history of the American family: From colonial times* (Vol. 1). Cleveland, OH: Arthur Clark.

Calhoun, A. (1960). *A social history of the American family: Colonial period.* New York: Barnes & Noble.

Casey, J. (1989). *History of the American family*. Oxford, England: Basil, Blackly Ltd.

Child, L. (1835). *The mothers' book*. Boston: Carter Hendee & Babcock.

Demos, J. (1970). *A little commonwealth*. New York: Oxford University Press.

Demos, J., & Demos, V. (1969). Adolescence in historical perspective. *Journal of Marriage and the Family, 31,* 632–638.

Dobson, J. (1982). *Dare to discipline*. New York: Bantam Books.

Earle, A. (1895). *Colonial dames and goodwives*. New York: Macmillan.

Feldstein, S., & Costello, L. (Eds.). (1974). *The ordeal of assimilation*. New York: Anchor Press/Doubleday.

Finnegan, W. (1998). *Cold new world*. New York: Random House.

Goldschmidt, G. (1976, October). *Cecil Gregory Memorial Lecture*. Columbia: University of Missouri.

Goodsell, W. (1934). *A history of marriage and the family*. New York: Macmillan.

Goody, J. (1983). *The development of the family and marriage in Europe*. Cambridge, England: Cambridge University Press.

Gottlieb, B. (1993). *The family in the Western world from the black death to the industrial age*. New York: Oxford University Press.

Greider, W. (1997). *One world: The manic logic of global capitalism*. New York: Simon & Schuster.

Greven, P. (1970). *Four generations: Population, land and family in colonial Andover*. Ithaca, NY: Cornell University Press.

Habenstein, R. (1998). A then and now overview of the immigrant family in America. In C. Mindel, R. Habenstein, R. Wright (Eds.), *Ethnic families in America*. Upper Saddle River, NJ: Prentice Hall.

Hall, G. (1882, January). The moral and religious training of children. *Princeton Review* (pp. 26–48).

Hall, G. (1904). *Adolescence: Its psychology, and its relations to physiology, anthropology, sociology, sex, crime, religion, and education*. New York: Appleton.

Hallett, J. (1984). *Fathers and daughters in Roman society: Women and the elite family*. Princeton, NJ: Princeton University Press.

Henshaw, S.K. (1997, May/June). Teenage abortion and pregnancy statistics by state, 1992. *Family Planning Perspectives*.

Judd, C. (1915). *The psychology of high school subjects*. Boston: Ginn.

Kephart, W. (1977). *The family, society, and the individual* (4th ed.). Boston: Houghton Mifflin.

King, L. (1903). *The psychology of child development*. Chicago: University of Chicago Press.

Leslie, G. (1976). *The family in social context*. New York: Oxford University Press.

Lung, C.T., & Daro, D. (1996). *Current trends in child abuse reporting and fatalities: The results of the 1995 annual fifty-state survey*. Chicago: National Committee for the Prevention of Child Abuse.

Mangold, G. (1910). *Child problems*. New York: Macmillan.

Maynard, R.A. (Ed.). (1996). *Kids having kids: A Robin Hood Foundation special report on the costs of adolescent childbearing*. New York: Robin Hood Foundation.

McKeever, W. (1913). *Training the boy*. New York: Macmillan.

Mead, M. (1928). *Coming of age in Samoa*. New York: Morrow.

Mead, M. (1976). The development of Western family organization. In G.R. Leslie (Ed.), *The family in social context*. New York: Oxford University Press.

Miller, D., & Swanson, G. (1958). *The changing American parent*. New York: Wiley.

Mindel, C.H., Habenstein, R.W., & Wright, R. (Eds.). (1998). *Ethnic families in America: Pattern and variation* (4th ed.). Upper Saddle River, NJ: Prentice Hall.

Morgan, E. (1952). *Virginians at home: Family life in the eighteenth century*. Williamsburg, VA: Colonial Williamsburg, Inc.

National Committee for the Prevention of Child Abuse. (1995). *The results of the 1995 annual fifty-state survey*. Chicago: National Committee for the Prevention of Child Abuse.

Queen, S., & Habenstein, R. (1974). *The family in various cultures* (4th ed.). Philadelphia: Lippincott.

Queen, S., Habenstein, R., & Quadagno, J. (1985). *The family in various cultures* (5th ed.). New York: Harper & Row.

Reich, R. (1991). *The work of nations*. New York: Knopf.

Ross, E.A. (1914). *The old world and the new*. Upper Saddle River, NJ: Prentice Hall.

Rothman, D., & Rothman, S. (Eds.). (1972). *The colonial American family: Collected essays*. New York: Arno Press.

Ruben, R. (1990). Diversity of families. In D.H. Olson & M.K. Hanson (Eds.), *2001: Preparing families for the future* (pp. 36–37). Minneapolis, MN: National Council on Family Relations.

Shillony, B.A. (1991). *The Jews and the Japanese*. Rutland, VT: Charles T. Tuttle.

Shorter, F. (1975). *The making of the modern family*. New York: Basic Books.

Shoumatoff, A. (1985). *The mountain of names*. New York: Simon & Schuster.

Spock, B. (1997). *Baby and child care*. New York: Simon & Schuster.

Spruill, J. (1938). *Women's life and work in the southern colonies*. Chapel Hill: University of North Carolina Press.

Suro, R. (1998). *Strangers among us: How Latino immigration is transforming America*. New York: Knopf.

Thorndike, E. (1908). Notes on childstudy. *Columbia University Contributions to Philosophy, Psychology, and Education, (4),* 143.

Trumbach, R. (1978). *The rise of the egalitarian family.* New York: Academic Press.

Ungar, S.J. (1995). *Fresh blood: The new American immigrants.* New York: Simon & Schuster.

U.S. Bureau of the Census. (1998). *United States population estimates, by age, sex, race, Hispanic origin 1990–1997* (Release PPL-91). Washington, DC: U.S. Government Printing Office.

U.S. National Center for Health Statistics. (1997, July 17). *The report of the final natality statistic, 1995, Vital statistics for the United States (annual) and monthly vital statistics report, 45* (No 11(S) & No. 12). Washington, DC: U.S. Government Printing Office.

Ventura, S.J., Martin, J.A., Curtin, S.C., & Mathews, T.J. (1998). Report of final natality statistic, 1995. *Monthly Vital Statistics Report, 45,* 11(S).

Weber, M. (1958). *The protestant ethic.* New York: Scribners. (Original work published 1930)

Woodside, M. (1988). Research on children of alcoholics: Past and future. *British Journal of Addiction, 83,* 785–792.

Winch, R. (1952). *The modern family.* New York: Hoyt.

Wishy, B. (1968). *The child and the republic.* Philadelphia: University of Pennsylvania Press.

Wright, J.W. (Ed.). (1998). *The New York Times 1998 Almanac* (pp. 261–313). New York: New York Times Co.

CHAPTER 2

Developmental Theories and Clinical Practice

RUNE J. SIMEONSSON AND SUSAN L. ROSENTHAL

Age is usually not a central issue in the provision of psychological services to adults. However, every facet of clinical work with children is influenced by developmental factors. Presenting problems, the nature of assessment, types of diagnoses, and the implementation of interventions will vary significantly if the client is an infant, a preschooler, a school-age child, or an adolescent. The significance of developmental factors in clinical services is recognized by the fact that mental conditions that have their origin in infancy or childhood are assigned a separate section in *DSM-IV* (American Psychiatric Association [APA], 1994). Although *DSM-IV* yields a diagnostic classification for these conditions, it does not define causal factors or frame of treatment. For a comprehensive approach to the clinical activities of assessment, diagnosis, and intervention, it is essential that appropriate consideration is given to the child's age and stage of development. Such an approach can be enhanced by conceptual models that take into account change and continuity in the development of children.

The purpose of this chapter is to review selected models of child development in terms of their contribution to clinical practice. Conceptual frameworks are clearly important in guiding the clinician's approach to defining the problem and carrying out interventions. The formality and explicitness of conceptual frameworks may differ from one clinician to another, with some adhering to established theoretical models and others taking a more eclectic approach. Yet others may draw on subjective insights and personal experiences to address presenting problems. In the past, the provision of clinical services for children drew heavily on psychodynamic and learning models. Increasingly, there is a growing interest in the potential contribution of other models that can inform clinical interventions by taking developmental factors into account.

The field of developmental psychopathology (Luthar, Burack, Cicchetti, & Weisz, 1997) reflects the move toward comprehensive approaches in which developmental aspects of psychopathology in children and youth are considered. This field integrates cross-sectional and longitudinal findings on child development and draws on theories to guide clinical practice. Various models of development are available that could be of value in providing different perspectives on normal and atypical development. To be of value, such models should encompass variability in the nature and rate of development to account for individual differences in sensory, motor, cognitive, communicative, perceptual, and personal domains. Although the models do not directly lead to classification or to assignment of a diagnosis to the child, understanding of typical and atypical development is clearly important for diagnosis. For example, a 3-year-old who has difficulty separating from a parent on the first few days of nursery school would not meet the criteria of separation anxiety. On the other hand, a 7-year-old who demonstrates pervasive and recurrent difficulty in separating from a parent will likely meet the *DSM-IV* criteria for separation anxiety (309.21). With this diagnosis, a model of development is useful to frame the clinician's understanding of etiology and guide implementation of treatment. Furthermore,developmental factors continue to be important in accounting for individual differences of the child in which interactions over time may result in different outcomes for children with similar etiologies.

The increasing diversity of clinical problems presented by children and the range of settings in which they are seen demonstrate the value of child development theories. Client populations range from premature infants to adolescents with chronic illnesses or disabilities and encompass treatment methods ranging from primary prevention (Durlak & Wells, 1997; Simeonsson, 1994) to parent-child interaction training in the home (LaFreniere & Capuano, 1997), individual psychodynamic therapy (Shapiro, 1989), and crisis intervention for children exposed to shock or trauma (Johnson, 1989). Settings include mental health and psychiatric facilities, schools, private offices, correctional facilities, pediatric wards and clinics, and residential and community programs for children with behavioral, affective, and developmental problems. This diversity of children's clinical needs calls for a matching array of conceptual frameworks in the provision of services to children. To be of value, a framework should contribute to an understanding of child and environmental factors that influence child functioning and adaptation. A framework should also facilitate the derivation of intervention goals and strategies.

The models of child development reviewed in this chapter are well established, have historical significance in understanding the development of children, and were selected for their applicability to clinical practice. To facilitate the review, each model was examined with reference to specific dimensions of relevance to clinical concerns. A dimensional review is consistent with the applied focus of this volume and seeks to synthesize, rather than duplicate, more detailed presentations available elsewhere (Lewis & Miller, 1990; Reisman, 1986). In addition to psychosexual, psychosocial, and qualitative developmental models, the review also encompasses behavioral and family life cycle models. Although each model has unique elements applicable to specific problems or situations, benefits may also accrue from an eclectic approach. Such eclecticism does not negate the potential contribution of a given model but rather recognizes that one or more models may be of relevance to clinical concerns under certain conditions. This is in keeping with an earlier conclusion by Reese and Overton (1970) that "at our present state of knowledge, ... eclectic theories seem to be necessary to account for the whole range of human behaviors throughout the life-span" (p. 123).

A DIMENSIONAL APPROACH TO DEVELOPMENTAL MODELS

The dimensions along which models can be reviewed are numerous and vary from basic assumptions to methodological details. In selecting dimensions for this chapter, consideration was given to dimensions identified in earlier contributions (Miller, 1993; Reese & Overton, 1970). The dimensions selected for this review were designed to extract features of each model of particular relevance for clinical applications with children. To this end, four dimensions were specified for each model: major assumptions, explanations of typical development, explanations of atypical development, and clinical implications for assessment and intervention. A brief explanation of each of these dimensions follows.

Major Assumptions. This dimension addresses how the model represents development and change. What is the role of the environment, and what are the assumptions regarding continuities and discontinuities in development?

Explanation of Typical Development. This dimension focuses on how the model accounts for typical development in most children. What defines the expected rate and sequence of typical development of children?

Explanation of Atypical Development. How does the model account for atypical development? What is the basis for differentiating between typical and atypical development? What key variables are assumed to account for atypical development?

Clinical Implications. What are the implications of the model for assessment and intervention? What variables account for behavior change in the child?

REVIEW OF MODELS OF CHILD DEVELOPMENT

The selection of models reviewed in this chapter was based on their being recognized as major conceptual approaches with significant implications for clinical practice. In reviewing the models on the basis of the preceding dimensions, similarities and differences can be identified in terms of clinical implications. Conceptualizations of typical and atypical development, for example, have often focused on particular domains of development (e.g., psychosocial, cognitive). Furthermore, although models usually reflect a focus on psychological variables, there is increasing recognition of the role of biological and environmental variables defining the complex nature of development, for example, in the attention given to social experience in the development of the brain and mental function (Eisenberg, 1995). The nature of these complexities is represented in the transactional model (Sameroff, 1993), which proposes complementary and regulatory roles of genotype, phenotype, and environtype. The concept of developmental psychopathology frames diagnostic and intervention activities from a life span perspective and incorporates concepts of normative development and the typical variance at any given age or stage (Kazdin, 1997). This perspective requires both cross-sectional and longitudinal frameworks for understanding the nature and rate of development.

PSYCHOSEXUAL MODEL

Although the original formulations of Freud constitute the major framework for the psychosexual model of development, there have been a number of revisions and adaptations, each providing unique perspectives on child development. Two important extensions reviewed in this chapter are the approaches of Klein (1958) and Anna Freud (1963), who is credited with extending psychoanalytic

theory to children and pioneering child psychoanalysis (Solnit, 1997).

Major Assumptions

A central assumption of the psychosexual model is that the child's development reflects a continuous striving to gratify needs from infancy through adolescence. A substantial role is assigned to the structural development of the id, ego, and superego, indicative of innate tendencies toward psychological organization. Paralleling assumptions about structural development are qualitative psychosexual stages defined by age-appropriate changes in the focus and nature of need gratification. Drawing on these principles of psychosexual development, Anna Freud (1963) proposed the concept of developmental lines defined as sequences of graduated steps in the emergence of the child's personality. These developmental lines trace the transition from dependency and irrationality toward an increased mastery role of the ego and consist of eight phases covering the period from infancy to adolescence:

1. Biological mother-infant tie.
2. Part object, anaclitic relationship phase.
3. Object constancy phase.
4. Preoedipal ambivalent phase.
5. Object-centered phallic-oedipal phase.
6. Latency period.
7. Preadolescent prelude to "adolescent revolt."
8. Adolescent struggle and stabilization.

Early experience is given major emphasis by the psychosexual model in that beginning in early infancy, the caregiver, usually the mother, serves as a primary source of stimulation for the infant. However, the need to revise psychoanalytic constructs pertaining to early experience is being raised based on findings from neurobiological, cognitive-developmental, information processing, and other research (Lewis, 1995).

Explanation of Typical Development

Typical development within the psychosexual model is defined largely in terms of age-appropriate need gratification. From Anna Freud's perspective, development reflects approved activities repeated by the infant, whereas lack of maternal interest or approval may result in delayed or atypical development in a corresponding developmental line. Klein's (1958) theory is an extension of Freud's original formulation, and she appears to incorporate the concept of qualitative psychosexual stages as a major feature. The child is active in his or her own development, but primarily on a mental plane. A central feature of Klein's theory is the presence of self-destructive and self-preserving instincts in early infancy and the emergence of defensive expressions of projection, introjection, and splitting to deal with anxieties and conflicts. For normal development to occur, a division between the good object and the bad object, between love and hate, should take place in early infancy. As Klein notes, "When such a division is not too severe and yet sufficient to differentiate between good and bad, it forms in my view one of the basic elements for stability and mental health" (pp. 87–88). The resolution of the two conflicting instincts in normal development is thus achieved in part by splitting or differentiating the roles of the id, the ego, and the superego in dealing with conscious and unconscious material.

Explanation of Atypical Development
A central explanation for atypical psychosexual development resides in the failure to gratify needs in an appropriate manner for a particular stage or age. "An uncommon persistence of behaviors beyond the age at which they are appropriate (fixation) or a resumption of immature behaviors (regression) constitute two major forms of psychopathology" (Reisman, 1986, p. 16). Anna Freud (1963) also appears to rely on the concept of incongruence, or inappropriateness of behavior for age or stage, in defining imbalances of developmental lines.

The developmental level achieved by a given child is seen as a result of the interaction of ego, superego development, and drive in response to environmental influences. For the infant and young child, these environmental influences are tied closely to the mother, whereas for the older child, the range is broader, encompassing the family and the social-cultural setting as well. The notion of incongruence as reflective of atypical development also appears in Klein's theory defined in terms of instincts. From this perspective, abnormal development is seen as the failure of the ego to develop adequately in terms of its conscious and unconscious parts. As Klein (1958) notes, "When, however, there is a very rigid barrier produced by splitting, the implication is that development has not proceeded normally" (p. 88). Inadequate ego development may result in subsequent problems of integration and object synthesis.

Clinical Implications
In the psychosexual model, behavior change is seen to occur as a function of maturation as well as adaptation. The child's biological endowment in terms of the id is assumed to account for maturation, and in terms of the ego to account for organizational tendencies. In work with children, the clinician can trace developmental lines by examining them progressively through observation and longitudinal analysis. The clinical utility of the concept of developmental lines can be illustrated in two examples proposed by Anna Freud (1963). Preoedipal ambivalence (Phase 4), for example, is seen as the basis for clinging behavior in the toddler rather than the result of spoiling by the mother. The latency period, or Phase 6 functioning, is seen as necessary for adequate integration into school. Furthermore, disturbances in development of specific phases have been causally linked to separation anxiety (Phase 1), anaclitic depression (Phase 2), and aggressive-destructive behavior (Phase 4) (Freud, 1963).

The importance attributed to early mother-child interactions for subsequent development and elaboration of the nature of the functions of the ego in the very young child are two aspects of Klein's theory with potential clinical significance. The prototype of the internalization process of objects in the infant's relationship with the mother is the infant's introjection of the mother's breasts. In this context, it would seem that the acquisition of new behavior is tied to the function of the ego's "need and capacity not only to split, but also to integrate itself. The more the ego can integrate its destructive impulses and synthesize the different aspects of its objects, the richer it becomes" (Klein, 1958, p. 89).

Although the focus of the psychoanalytic approach has been on intrapsychic phenomena, Cohen (1997) has suggested that one of the major trends in the past 15 years has been a growing recognition of the role of environmental and developmental factors. In addition, there has been an increase in empirical applications to advance the field.

QUALITATIVE-DEVELOPMENTAL MODEL

Major Assumptions
The qualitative-developmental model encompasses Piaget's theory and extension of his theory to areas of social-emotional development (Cowan, 1978). A basic premise of Piaget's theory is that development is the expression of the child's active, progressive

construction of reality: "To present an adequate notion of learning, one first must explain how the subject manages to construct and invent, not merely how he repeats and copies" (Piaget, 1970, p. 704). This constructivist approach posits that reality is, in fact, the product of the interaction between child and environment. The role of action in development is essential because "there can be no experience without action as its source, whether real or imagined, because its absence would mean that there would be no contact with the external world" (p. 721). Development is seen as a process in which successive adaptations result in qualitatively different stages of the child's construction of reality. Thus, although common adaptive processes are found across development, structural change produces four discontinuous qualitative stages that may vary in rate of emergence but not in sequence.

Theories of social cognition have helped to explain the developmental changes of children and adolescents in their understanding of relationships and social contexts. Areas that have been studied frequently are perspective-taking and referential communication as elements of interpersonal understanding (Selman, 1980) and adolescent egocentrism in terms of the imaginary audience and the personal fable (Elkind, 1982).

Explanation of Typical Development

The child's adaptation to physical and psychological reality is a function of the complementary processes of assimilation and accommodation. In assimilation, environmental stimuli are modified to conform to the child's existing cognitive structures, whereas in accommodation, encounters with the environment result in change of cognitive structure. Hunt (1961) has suggested that these processes correspond respectively to inner organization and outward coping. Piaget (1970) has indicated that the essential forms of these processes correspond to play and imitation. Effective adaptation is a relative balance or equilibration of these processes within successive sequential stages of cognitive development leading to formal operations, the stage of equilibrated, mature cognitive functioning.

Explanation of Atypical Development

Significant imbalances between assimilation and accommodation may result in maladaption. If assimilation (organization) predominates over accommodation (coping), extreme results may take the form of egocentric or autisticlike thought and behavior with the environment incorporated into or conforming to existing mental structures. "If assimilation alone were involved in development, there would be no variation in the child's structures. Therefore, he would not acquire new content and would not develop further" (Piaget, 1970, p. 707). Reciprocally, when environmental demands require coping in excess of organization, accommodation predominates over assimilation, and the result may be the expression of imitative behavior. Piaget and his colleagues (Inhelder, 1966; Schmid-Kitsikis, 1973) have also proposed that aberrations of stage transitions may reflect disorders of development in the form of stage fixation, false equilibrium, and oscillations between stages to explain the development of children with mental retardation and emotional disturbance (Inhelder, 1966). Distortions in stage transitions with particular reference to fixation at the preoperational stage have been identified as significant elements of cognitive psychotherapy (Leahy, 1995).

A variety of studies have examined the development of social cognition in atypical children revealing that their understanding of self-other differentiation is significantly delayed compared with that of their more "typical" peers. Illustrative of this thesis is research evidence by Perner, Frith, Leslie, and Peekam (1989) pointing to significant impairments in the theory of mind of children with autism, that is, limitations in the ability to "conceive of mental states in self and others." These findings have been posited as underlying cognitive structures as well as affective dimensions in atypical development, as might be observed, for example, in childhood depression (Feinstein & Berndt, 1995).

Clinical Implications

The notion of disequilibrium implies imbalances between assimilation and accommodation. Acquisition of new behavior can thus be seen as a temporary disequilibrium in which accommodation predominates, requiring a modification of the child's cognitive framework to fit new experiences. As Piaget maintains, there would be no acquisition of new content without accommodation. In this context, accommodation is a repeated process that results in developmental change within and across qualitative stages.

The implication for clinical practice is to provide structured experiences for children that promote cognitive development. Ivey (1991) advocated the application of cognitive-developmental theory for therapy and counseling in which the goal is to promote transitions to more advanced developmental levels. In a similar frame, Noam, Chandler, and LaLonde (1995) have proposed the application of social cognitive theory to clinical contexts to examine the child's construction of meaning about self and others. The role of the clinician is to assess and intervene with children evidencing structural or functional asynchrony. A good example of such an approach is Selman's (1990) pair therapy. The premise of pair therapy is to use activities for two children to promote change along the developmental progression of intimacy (shared experiences) to autonomy (negotiating conflict).

PSYCHOSOCIAL MODEL

Major Assumptions

The major theory contributing to the exploration of psychosocial development is that of Erikson (1962). Erikson extended Freud's formulations and defined the ego as a personality structure to synthesize and coordinate responses to the environment. The ego is assumed to provide direction and control in adaptation to the environment. The child is further assumed to play an active role in development that is both influencing and being influenced by the family (Maier, 1965).

The environment is seen as the dynamic interchange among family members in a sociocultural context. The totality of environment in physical, social, and cultural aspects contributes, along with innate processes, to development. Although the specific manner in which the environment affects the development of a child may be the result of chance, the family and society provide direction for development. Of particular importance for development are cultural forces, which guide and select experiences for the child (Maier, 1965). Special significance is attached to early experience: "The first two years of life, the formative years, provide the foundation for all later motivation and personal disposition" (Maier, 1965, p. 25). In the early development of the ego, play serves a major function in adaptation to demands through organization of experience. The dynamic and developmental significance of play as a form of ego expression is emphasized by Erikson (1940): "The child uses play to make up for the defeats, sufferings and frustrations, especially those

resulting from a technically and culturally limited use of language" (p. 567).

Each of eight qualitative, differentiated stages of ego development and redevelopment is characterized by a crisis or dilemma that needs to be resolved for normal psychosocial development to occur. These stages encompass the five stages originally proposed by Freud and three additional stages dealing with adult development. Each phase involves both a "vertical crisis culminating in an individual psychosocial solution and a horizontal crisis calling for a personally and socially satisfactory solution to the problem of motivational forces" (Maier, 1965, p. 30). The eight developmental phases, each represented by a specific psychosocial crisis to resolve, are:

1. Trust versus mistrust.
2. Autonomy versus shame and doubt.
3. Initiative versus guilt.
4. Industry versus inferiority.
5. Identity and repudiation versus identity diffusion.
6. Intimacy and solidarity versus isolation.
7. Generativity versus self-absorption.
8. Integrity versus despair.

Explanation of Typical Development

Normal development is tied to the resolution and mastery of successive crises across the eight phases. Psychological well-being and developmental maturity reflect the resolution of needs of the ego in the social context. Recent contributions have addressed the fact that these conceptualizations did not adequately reflect gender differences, advancing the premise that male development progresses differently from female development (Gilligan, 1996). These differences include an emphasis on the "Language of rights that protect separation versus the Language of responsibilities that sustain connection" (Gilligan, 1982, p. 210). Similarly, contrasts have been made between the processes of autonomy and attachment. The importance of understanding these perspectives is evident in an expanding literature that further examines differential risk and resilience associated with gender at different developmental stages (Gilligan, 1996).

Explanation of Atypical Development

Atypical development is characterized by the failure to solve a crisis or conflict at a certain phase of development. As such, it may be due to physical as well as psychological factors: "Retardation or failure in the development will rob the individual of his potential supremacy and endanger his whole hierarchy of development" (Maier, 1965, p. 30). Because normal development involves a balance of three affective processes (id, ego, and superego), disturbances of interpersonal relationships reflect imbalances among these processes. Abnormal or atypical development, however, is not viewed as a fixed outcome or an irreversible condition, but rather as a variation of normal processes (Maier, 1965).

Clinical Implications
Erikson accepts the psychodynamic position that libido is a basic force energizing development. Two opposing drives of this basic force contribute to an ongoing struggle between progressive and reactionary facets of the personality across stages of development (Maier, 1965). The recurrent struggle between these polar opposites forms the basis for change in development. The clinical implications of a psychosocial model of development pertain to the importance of a life span emphasis and acknowledge the significance of societal forces of development. The stages of development provide a useful framework for identifying the tasks a child faces at a particular stage. In addition, the stages suggest an organization for the examination of the child's history and its possible impact on the resolution of current crises, with projections for development in adolescence and adulthood. The value of the stage-based approach in psychosocial theory has been extended to therapeutic interventions with adults focusing on the family (Freeman, 1986).

BEHAVIORAL MODEL

Major Assumptions
The behavioral model is different from the previous models reviewed in this chapter in that the focus is on functional aspects of behavior rather than developmental transitions that reflect qualitative changes in the child's experience of the world. Additionally, the behavioral model assumes that past reinforcement histories are related to current behaviors, but does not assume that they are symptomatic of underlying conflicts or failures to master earlier developmental tasks. Although behavioral theories are not developmental in the usual sense of the word, they do contribute to understanding of the development and adaptation in children and thus warrant inclusion. This review builds on the extensive literature in this area, including the classic contributions of Bijou and Baer (1961) and Eysenck (1967) as representative of the behavioral model.

Behavioral models generally adopt a mechanistic view in which the child's behavior is seen as a response to external forces or stimuli. The behavioral approach builds on the importance of observed behavior, the key role of the social environment, and the involvement of natural agents of change (Prinz, 1992). The passive and reactive role of the child is paralleled by the assumption that experiences are accumulated on the basis of a copying theory of knowledge (Reese & Overton, 1970). The mechanistic emphasis further implies that complex behavior is reducible to simpler elements that can be related functionally to specific stimuli or contingencies.

Although it is assumed that behavior is learned and that reinforcement history can account for behavioral development, the focus is generally placed on current rather than past conditions. Because behavior is assumed to be a function of environmental conditions, analysis is made of those stimuli (antecedent or consequent) that influence current behavior and that can be manipulated for behavior change. The environment consists of the range of stimuli that serve to elicit behavior, as in classical conditioning, or that reinforce behavior, as in operant conditioning. Bijou (1967) maintained, "When the environment is dull, routine, unvaried, and limited in range, interactions are restricted" (p. 266). Inadequate reinforcement histories may thus account for deficient or atypical behavioral repertoires in the child's development.

Explanation of Typical Development
A central assumption is that behavior is learned, whether learning takes place by imitation, association, conditioning, or observation. Given the elementary components of stimulus and response (s-r) in behavior acquisition, a variety of s-r combinations can be identified to account for complex behaviors. Normal development thus represents the acquisition of appropriate response repertoires to environmental demands. Such response repertoires can become increasingly complex through forward

and backward chains and account for forms of behavior from simple motor responses to complex verbal learning skills.

Explanation of Atypical Development
Because learning is central to normal development, atypical development is, by extension, seen as an exaggerated form of learned behavior. Abnormal or atypical development may be characterized by inappropriate or deficient behavior repertoires. In the context of mental (developmental) retardation, Bijou (1967) has proposed that environmental variables can account for atypical development through idiosyncratic reinforcement histories. Unpredictable reinforcement, extinction, and severe punishment may each operate to suppress, distort, or extinguish behavioral development. The role of biological factors in behavioral development has been recognized by Eysenck (1967), who has proposed individual differences in conditionability as an aspect of abnormal development. Differences in conditionability may thus predispose individuals to disorders associated with learning aberrations.

Clinical Implications
The primary role attributed to the environment in learning theories implies that behavioral development is largely a function of managing environmental contingencies. Because behavior is assumed to be under stimulus control, new behaviors can be developed and strengthened through management of contingencies. With the assumption that all behaviors are learned, the acquisition of appropriate behaviors and the reduction of inappropriate behaviors can be achieved through the use of behavioral techniques of shaping, chaining, and extinction. Given this model of contingency management, primary caregivers and parents have often played a central role as change agents in differential reinforcement of child behavior (Eyberg, Boggs, & Algina, 1995).

FAMILY LIFE CYCLE MODEL

Major Assumptions
The family life cycle model differs from the previous models in that it focuses on the developmental path of families and incorporates both male and female development rather than the developmental progression of the child as an individual phenomenon (McGoldrick, Heiman, & Carter, 1993). The model proposes that there is a progression of stages that intact families go through as well as stages that typify atypical family progression (e.g., divorce). The model acknowledges the power of both horizontal stressors (i.e., life cycle transitions and unpredictable events such as untimely deaths, illnesses, accidents) and vertical stressors (i.e., family patterns, myths, secrets, and legacies). A primary assumption is that an individual cannot be understood separate from the context of both the nuclear and extended family or the social, economic, or political context.

McGoldrick and colleagues (1993) describe the following development stages for intact families: leaving home—single young adults; the joining of families through marriage—the new couple; families with young children; families with adolescents; launching children and moving on; families in later life.

Explanation of Typical Development
Typical development is perceived in terms of the current patterns of family life and societal views of normalcy. Normal family development varies as it is related to ethnicity, religious identity, socioeconomic status, and the constitution of the family (e.g., intact, divorced, blended). The focus is on the family's ability to progress developmentally.

Explanation of Atypical Development
The family life cycle model assumes that symptoms or dysfunctions are often the result of stress occurring at transition points in the development sequence. Dysfunction of family development may be an expression of extreme horizontal stressors such as serious accidents or illness. Minimal horizontal stress may also produce dysfunction if it occurs in a context in which a vertical stressor such as a family myth plays a significant role.

The emphasis in this model is not to focus on deviations from the norm or to imply that each generation faces a unique new world. Rather, the emphasis is on understanding intergenerational connectedness as a basis for assessing the adaptation and development of a given family. The composition, size, and ethnicity of the family are viewed as significant factors impacting family life transitions (McGoldrick, Giordano, & Pearce, 1996). There is increasing recognition of the role of gender in family life and development, with particular attention given to the experience of women (McGoldrick, Anderson, & Walsh, 1989).

Clinical Implications
The family life cycle model posits that the goal of treatment is to reestablish the family's developmental momentum on a healthy continuum. It points to the need to broaden the focus from the symptomatic individual to the intergenerational family. Assessment should include the evaluation not only of current stressors but of family patterns, secrets, and myths. An example of this assessment process includes obtaining and reading genograms (McGoldrick & Gerson, 1985; Rohrbaugh, Rogers, & McGoldrick, 1992). The family is given support to define its problems in terms of past causes, current stage, and future development. By addressing

vertical and horizontal stressors, the family can be helped to progress developmentally.

SUMMARY

Having reviewed the various models of child development, it may be useful to consider selected features to provide a basis for identifying clinical implications. Although the interpretations are derived from the authors' review of the materials pertaining to each model, alternative interpretations obviously can be derived. Table 2.1 summarizes the theories according to the dimensions specified in this chapter. An overview of the table reveals that the models are characterized by commonalities as well as differences. A comparative analysis along each of the dimensions may facilitate a consideration of implications for clinical service.

Table 2.1 Comparison of developmental models.

Developmental Model	Major Assumptions	Explanation of Typical Development	Explanation of Atypical Development	Clinical Implications
Psychosexual	Drive to gratify needs; primacy of mother-child relationship; centrality of others in development	Correspondence of resolution of conflicting instincts	Imbalance of developmental lines; inappropriate or inadequate resolution of conflicting instincts	Interpretation of discordance in development; intervention to promote age-appropriate need gratification and resolution of conflicts
Qualitative-Developmental	Construction of reality as a function of adaptive mechanisms of assimilation; progressing to equilibrated thought	Qualitative, ordinal developmental stages reflecting structuring and restructuring of experience	Significant asynchrony of assimilation/accommodation; fixation, regression, stage oscillation	Stage-appropriate intervention to promote growth; facilitation of disequilibration to address asynchrony of structure/function
Psychosocial	Formation of identity as central aspect of ego development	Resolution and mastery of crises at successive stages of identity formation	Imbalance of affective processes and failure to master stage crises	Interpreting atypical development in psychosocial stage; intervention to facilitate crisis resolution
Behavioral	Behavior is functionally related to antecedents or consequences in the environment	Acquisition of appropriate response repertoires	Inadequate, inconsistent, or history of reinforcement	Management of antecedents or consequences to effect change in behavior
Family Life Cycle	Stages of family life across generations, reflecting horizontal and vertical dimensions	Developmental stages of family built on connectedness of family members	Dysfunction of family resulting from stress at transition points in family life cycle	Identification, establishment, or reestablishment of family momentum; focus on intergenerational family life cycles

In terms of primary assumptions, all of the models except for the behavioral assume stages of development with critical transition periods. The models vary in the aspects believed to have primary significance and the context in which developmental changes occur. Although the explanatory mechanism for typical and atypical behavior varies for the psychosexual, psychosocial, and qualitative developmental models, all share a common perspective in which individual development and adaptation are seen as a resolution of conflict or imbalance. The family life cycle model differs in that it shifts the focus from the individual to the impact of intergenerational patterns on the mastery of current family tasks. Normal family development is defined in terms of the continuation of developmental momentum. In behavioral models, adaptation and development can be understood in terms of the adequacy of acquired behavioral repertoires.

Each of the models has contributed a particular perspective on how behavior is changed, with associated implications for the nature of treatment. Although there is thematic variation, the psychosexual, psychosocial, and qualitative developmental models all assume that successful completion of earlier stages of development is necessary for mastery of subsequent stages. For these models, the treatment is typically child-focused. The family life cycle model assumes that an understanding of family patterns is essential to promoting child and family progress. Therefore, the treatment usually involves the nuclear family and often grandparents, aunts, and uncles as well. The behavioral model may encompass the child, with the treatment focusing on the family's role in controlling the antecedents and consequences of behaviors. The applicability of models for clinical practice thus varies as a function of several factors, including the nature of the problem, developmental level of the child, and strategy for therapeutic intervention.

It should be emphasized that the utility of models reviewed in this chapter and models elsewhere should not be evaluated on an overall basis but should be considered in terms of their relevance to specific clinical concerns. To this end, evaluation and adoption of clinical frameworks should take into account the criteria of practicality, inclusiveness, and degree of fit with the clinician's philosophy. Specifically, it may be useful to consider the following five elements in the identification of clinical implications of models of child development:

1. *Pragmatic Base.* An important element in terms of a model's usefulness should be the extent to which it is consistent with commonsense notions about child development. Models with a heavy reliance on abstraction and symbolism may be viewed as having limited applicability to specific clinical problems. To the extent that a model is able to present developmental characteristics with greater parsimony in terms of concepts and abstractions, it is likely to have greater utility.

2. *Empirical Base.* A second major element focuses on the model's amenability to empirical validation. There are two aspects to consider in this regard: (a) Is there a database for the model, and if so, is it prospective or retrospective, anecdotal or systematic, and clinical or empirical? (b) Is the model operationalized so as to permit empirical tests of hypotheses generated from it?

3. *Inclusiveness of Normality-Variance.* The manner and extent to which a model can encompass normal as well as atypical development constitute a third element of importance. The comparative review made earlier suggested that some models primarily address normality, whereas others primarily address pathology. Still others appear to be applicable only to certain kinds of pathology and lack breadth to account for variations in type or severity of atypical development. With the trend toward educational and clinical programs that serve younger and more severely involved children, comprehensiveness constitutes a highly desirable element for models of child development. Inhelder's (1966) explication of the qualitative-developmental model illustrates its inclusiveness by encompassing such diverse developmental problems as mental retardation, emotional disturbance, and dyspraxia within central concepts of the model. The applicability of Inhelder's proposals has been validated in empirical research with various special populations.

4. *Developmental Comprehensiveness.* An element related to the normality-pathology dimension is that of developmental comprehensiveness. In this regard, comprehensiveness involves both vertical and horizontal dimensions. Comprehensiveness in a horizontal sense implies that the model encompasses a broad

rather than a narrow segment of the life span. From this perspective, Erikson's (1959) theory of eight life stages represents horizontal comprehensiveness, whereas the focus on infancy and early childhood in Freud's (1963) psychosexual model and infancy through adolescence in the qualitative-developmental model deal with more limited segments of the life span. Vertical comprehensiveness, on the other hand, refers to the breadth of the model to account for development in a variety of domains. Models with limited vertical comprehensiveness focus on a single developmental process such as affective states with minimal attention to other processes such as language, cognition, and perception. The focus on emotional development in the psychosexual model illustrates limited comprehensiveness in this regard. Theories with greater vertical comprehensiveness address, or have the potential to address, correspondences of development across domains. The qualitative developmental model (Piaget's theory), particularly as elaborated in recent years by Selman (1980) and Elkind (1982), exemplifies an approach with vertical comprehensiveness. Not only were Piaget's own efforts relevant to cognitive, perceptual, and linguistic processes of development, but there continue to be applications of the theory to interpersonal concept development and psychopathology.

5. *Applied Relevance.* A final element to consider pertains to the applicability of a model to practical and clinical realities. Although the clinical problems presented by children are not likely to change, the manner and extent of meeting these needs may change as a function of social, legal, and political realities. Economic, political, and social changes occur frequently, with significant clinical implications for habilitative and educational services. Policies and mandates such as deinstitutionalization, primary prevention, and early intervention and mainstreaming of children with disabilities are requiring reformulations of the logic and methods of providing clinical services. The shift in treatment settings from hospital and institutional care in favor of community-based programs for children with significant developmental or emotional problems and the integration and mainstreaming

of exceptional children with normal peers in school settings have been priorities guiding services for children and youth. To ensure that such efforts result in comprehensive and integrative programs, there is a need for conceptual frameworks based on developmental theory and research. Conceptual frameworks are important in that they can provide direction and sequence for clinical efforts by specifying conditions and characteristics of developmental change. The emphasis placed on primary prevention is an example of such an approach (Durlak & Wells, 1997). By juxtaposing treatment goals within developmental theory, clinical strategies and environments can be conceptualized in terms of their contribution to successive stages of personal independence and developmental maturity.

The preceding evaluative elements are selective and clearly not exhaustive. They may be useful in comparing and contrasting models on an informal basis. A specific model may thus be seen to have strength in terms of a particular element, or on an overall basis, or both. In practical terms, the value of any element may be relative to its contribution to the solution of a clinical problem. This approach is consistent with Goldfried's (1980) position on the status of competing orientations in psychotherapy: "We have all 'taken up sides' and have placed far too much emphasis on who is correct, not what is correct" (p. 991). That position is similar to a consideration of the contribution of developmental models. Seeking convergence and rapprochement of a variety of models and theories is a useful goal in clinical work. Support for such a strategy is evident in recommendations for greater collaboration between research and practice to identify effective and validated therapies (Goldfried & Wolfe, 1998).

The examination of conceptual models in this chapter has been a step toward rapprochement of elements and approaches that may be of direct relevance to clinical practice. A further step that could be taken is the systematic review of other models and theoretical approaches not considered here. An interesting model in this regard is the proposed application of Vygotsky's (1962) work in the form of integrated psychotherapy (Ryle, 1991) and for the remediation of higher cognitive functions (Akhutina, 1997). Another interesting application is that of Loevinger's (1976) model of ego development by

Noam (1992). In this application, Noam builds on Loevinger's levels and stages of ego functioning, with development proceeding toward greater maturity and complexity. Yet another step could involve efforts to synthesize different models or approaches. The similarity of the cognitive theories of Piaget, Bruner, and Ausubel, for example, could readily yield common implications for practice (Lawton, Saunders, & Muhs, 1980). Representative contributions involving other approaches have been the synthesis of psychoanalytic and learning theory (Alexander, 1963; Wachtel, 1977), and cognitive developmental theory with psychoanalytic theory (Greenspan, 1979; Weiner, 1975), with cognitive-behavioral therapy (Kinney, 1991), and with reality therapy (Protheroe, 1992). Although these synthesizing efforts have been restricted to certain theories, they illustrate the value of identifying complementarity of different theories and models.

The continuing trends of increasing diversity and complexity of clinical problems, clients, and settings emphasize the need for corresponding diversity of models from which applications can be derived for appropriate clinical services. Kazdin (1997) proposes that for child and adolescent psychotherapy to advance, there is a need for systematic research on questions, outcomes, and treatment forms. The benefit from such an approach is likely to be the provision of more individualized and more developmentally sensitive clinical services for children.

REFERENCES

Akhutina, T.V. (1997). The remediation of executive functions in children with cognitive disorders: The Vygotsky-Luria neuropsychological approach. *Journal of Intellectual Disability Research, 41*(2), 144–151.

Alexander, F. (1963). The dynamics of psychotherapy in light of learning theory. *American Journal of Psychiatry, 120,* 440–448.

American Psychiatric Association. (1994). *Diagnostic and statistical manual of mental disorders* (4th ed.). Washington DC: Author.

Bijou, S.W. (1967). Theory and research in mental (developmental) retardation. In S.W. Bijou & D.M. Baer (Eds.), *Child development: Readings in experimental analysis* (pp. 256–272). New York: Appleton-Century-Crofts.

Bijou, S.W., & Baer, D.M. (1961). *Child development: A systematic and empirical analysis.* New York: Appleton-Century-Crofts.

Cohen, J. (1997). Child and adolescent psychoanalysis: Research, practice and theory. *International Journal of Psycho-Analysis, 78*(Pt. 3), 499–520.

Cowan, P.S. (1978). *Piaget with feeling.* New York: Holt, Rinehart, and Winston.

Durlak, S.A., & Wells, A.M. (1997). Primary prevention mental health programs for children and adolescents: A meta-analytic review. *American Journal of Community Psychology, 25*(2), 115–152.

Eisenberg, L. (1995). The social construction of the human brain. *American Journal of Psychiatry, 152*(11), 1563–1575.

Elkind, D. (1982). Piagetian psychology and the practice of child psychiatry. *Journal of the American Academy of Child Psychiatry, 21,* 435–445.

Erikson, E. (1940). Studies in the interpretation of play: Clinical observations of play disruption in young children. *Genetic Psychology Monograph, 22,* 557–671.

Erikson, E. (1959). Identity and the life cycle: Selected papers [Monograph]. *Psychological Issues.* New York: International Universities Press.

Erikson, E. (1962). Reality and actuality. *Journal of the American Psychoanalists Association, 10,* 451–473.

Eyberg, S.M., Boggs, S.R., & Algina, J. (1995). Parent-child interaction therapy: A psychosocial model for the treatment of young children with conduct problem behavior and their families. *Psychopharmacology Bulletin, 31*(1), 83–91.

Eysenck, H.J. (1967). *The biological basis of personality.* Springfield, IL: Thomas.

Feinstein, S.C., & Berndt, D.J. (1995). Assimilating Piaget: Cognitive structures and depressive reaction to loss. *Adolescent Psychiatry, 20,* 23–28.

Freeman, A. (1986). Understanding personal, cultural, and family schema in psychotherapy: Depression in the family [Special issue]. *Journal of Psychotherapy and the Family, 2*(3–4), 79–99.

Freud, A. (1963). The concept of developmental lines. *Psychoanalytic Study of the Child, 18,* 245–265.

Gilligan, C. (1982). New maps of development: New visions of maturity. *American Journal of Orthopsychiatry, 52,* 199–212.

Gilligan, C. (1996). The centrality of relationship in human development: A puzzle, some evidence and a theory. In G.G. Noam & K. Fischer (Eds.), *Development and vulnerability in close relationships: The Jean Piaget symposium series* (pp. 237–261). Mahwah, NJ: Erlbaum.

Goldfried, M.R. (1980). Toward the delineation of therapeutic change principles. *American Psychologist, 35,* 991–999.

Goldfried, M.R., & Wolfe, B.E. (1998). Toward a more clinically valid approach to therapy research. *Journal of Consulting and Clinical Psychology, 66*(1), 143–150.

Greenspan, S.I. (1979). Intelligence and adaptation: An integration of psychoanalytic and Piagetian developmental psychology. *Psychological Issues, 12*, 1–108.

Hunt, J.M. (1961). *Intelligence and experience.* New York: Ronald Press.

Inhelder, B. (1966). Cognitive development and its contribution to the diagnosis of some phenomena of mental deficiency. *Merrill-Palmer Quarterly, 12*, 299–321.

Ivey, A.E. (1991). *Developmental strategies for helpers: Individual, family, and network interventions.* Pacific Grove, CA: Brooks/Cole.

Johnson, K. (1989). *Trauma in the lives of children.* Claremont, CA: Hunter House.

Kazdin, A.E. (1997). A model for developing effective treatments: Progression and interplay of theory, research and practice. *Journal of Clinical Child Psychology, 26*(2), 114–129.

Kinney, A. (1991). Cognitive-behavior therapy with children: Developmental reconsiderations. *Journal of Rational-Emotive & Cognitive Behavior Therapy, 9*(1), 51–61.

Klein, M. (1958). On the development of mental functioning. *International Journal of Psychoanalysis, 39*, 84–90.

LaFreniere, P.J., & Capuano, F. (1997). Preventive intervention as a means of clarifying direction of effects in socialization: Anxious-withdrawn preschoolers case. *Development and Psychopathology, 9*(3), 551–564.

Lawton, J.T., Saunders, R.A., & Muhs, P. (1980). Theories of Piaget, Bruner, and Ausubel: Explications and implications. *Journal of Genetic Psychology, 136*, 121–136.

Leahy, R.L. (1995). Cognitive development and cognitive therapy: Psychotherapy integration and cognitive psychotherapy [Special issue]. *Journal of Cognitive Psychotherapy: An International Quarterly, 9*(3), 173–184.

Lewis, M. (1995). Memory and psychoanalysis: A new look at infantile amnesia and transference. *Journal of the American Academy of Child and Adolescent Psychiatry, 34*(4), 405–417.

Lewis, M., & Miller, S.M. (Eds.). (1990). *Handbook of developmental psychopathology.* New York: Plenum Press.

Loevinger, J. (1976). *Ego development: Conceptions and theories.* San Francisco: Jossey-Bass.

Luthar, S., Burack, J.A., Cicchetti, D., & Weisz, J.R. (Eds.). (1997). *Developmental psychopathology: Perspectives on adjustment, risk and disorder.* New York: Cambridge University Press.

Maier, H.W. (1965). *Three theories of child development.* New York: Harper & Row.

McGoldrick, M., Anderson, C.M., & Walsh, F. (Eds.). (1989). *Women in families: A framework for family therapy.* New York: Norton.

McGoldrick, M., & Gerson, R. (1985). *Genograms in family assessment.* New York: Norton.

McGoldrick, M., Giordano, J., & Pearce, J.K. (Eds.). (1996). *Ethnicity and family therapy* (2nd ed.). New York: Guilford Press.

McGoldrick, M., Heiman, M., & Carter, B. (1993). The changing family life cycle: A perspective on normalcy. In F. Walsh (Ed.), *Normal family processes* (2nd ed., pp. 405–443). New York: Guilford Press.

Miller, P. (1993). *Theories of developmental psychology.* New York: Freeman.

Noam, G.G. (1992). Development as the aim of clinical intervention: Developmental approaches to prevention and intervention [Special issue]. *Development and Psychopathology, 4*(4), 679–696.

Noam G.G., Chandler, M., & LaLonde, C. (1995). Clinical-developmental psychology: Constructivism and social cognition in the study of psychological dysfunctions. In D. Cicchetti & D.J. Cohen (Eds.), *Developmental psychopathology: Theory and methods* (Vol. 1, pp. 424–464). New York: Wiley.

Perner, J., Frith, V., Leslie, A.M., & Peekam, S.R. (1989). Explanation of the autistic child's theory of mind: Knowledge, belief and communication. *Child Development, 60*, 689–700.

Piaget, J. (1970). Piaget's theory. In P.H. Mussen (Ed.), *Carmichael's manual of child psychology* (3rd ed.). New York: Wiley.

Prinz, R.J. (1992). Overview of behavioural family interventions with children: Achievements, limitations and challenges. *Behaviour Change, 9*(3), 120–125.

Protheroe, D. (1992). Reality therapy and the concept of cognitive developmental stages. *Journal of Reality Therapy, 12*(1), 37–44.

Reese, H.W., & Overton, W.F. (1970). Models and theories of development. In L.R. Goulet & P.B. Baltes (Eds.), *Life-span developmental psychology: Research and theory* (pp. 115–145). New York: Academic Press.

Reisman, J.M. (1986). Models of child psychopathology. In J.M. Reisman (Ed.), *Behavior disorders in infants, children and adolescents* (pp. 5–31). New York: Random House.

Rohrbaugh, M., Rogers, J.C., & McGoldrick, M. (1992). How do experts read family genograms? *Family Systems Medicine, 10*(1), 79–89.

Ryle, A. (1991). Object relations theory and activity theory: A proposed link by way of the procedural sequence model. *British Journal of Medical Psychology, 4*(4), 307–316.

Sameroff, A.J. (1993). Models of development and developmental risk. In C.H. Zenah Jr. (Ed.), *Handbook of infant mental health* (pp. 3–13). New York: Guilford Press.

Schmid-Kitsikis, E. (1973). Piagetian theory and its approach to psychopathology. *American Journal of Mental Deficiency, 77*, 694–705.

Selman, R.L. (1980). *The growth of interpersonal understanding.* New York Academic Press.

Selman, R.L. (1990). *Making a friend in youth: Developmental theory and pair therapy.* Chicago: University of Chicago Press.

Shapiro, T. (1989). The psychodynamic formulation in child and adolescent psychiatry. *Journal of the American Academy of Child Psychiatry, 28,* 675–680.

Simeonsson, R.J. (1994). *Risk & resilience: Promoting the well-being of all children.* Baltimore: Brookes.

Solnit, A.J. (1997). A legacy: Anna Freud's views on childhood and development. *Child Psychiatry and Human Development, 28*(1), 5–14.

Vygotsky, L.S. (1962). *Thought and language.* Cambridge, MA: MIT Press.

Wachtel, P.L. (1977). *Psychoanalysis and behavior therapy.* New York: Basic Books.

Weiner, M.L. (1975). *Cognitive unconscious: A Piagetian approach to psychotherapy.* Davis, CA: International Psychological Press.

CHAPTER 3

Methods of Research in Developmental Psychopathology and Treatment Effectiveness

ERIC M. VERNBERG AND ANNE K. JACOBS

Clinical child psychology relies on an evidence-based, developmentally oriented, conceptual framework, developmental psychopathology, for understanding the nature of problematic behavior throughout childhood and adolescence. This conceptual framework is also essential in designing and evaluating psychological interventions with children and adolescents (Kazdin, 1997; Russ, 1998; Vernberg, Routh, & Koocher, 1992). Clinical child psychology is evolving increasingly into an evidence-based endeavor (Lonigan, Elbert, & Johnson, 1998), and there is a strong need to integrate knowledge derived from basic research in developmental psychopathology with information gained by attempts to treat or prevent child and adolescent psychological disturbances. This chapter describes core issues in research on developmental psychopathology and treatment outcomes, with the goal of demonstrating the value of a full integration of key concepts in intervention and psychopathology.

APPROACHES TO RESEARCH ON DEVELOPMENTAL PSYCHOPATHOLOGY

DESIGN CONSIDERATIONS

Adopting a developmental perspective toward psychopathology focuses attention on continuity and change over time. Prospective, longitudinal designs are crucial to answering certain questions; yet the time, expense, and effort required for these designs forces psychological researchers to rely on mixed retrospective-prospective, accelerated longitudinal, and cross-sectional designs to build a sufficient knowledge base to warrant long-term longitudinal research. Experiments, whether embedded in longitudinal designs or carried out at a single measurement point, remain important as a means of identifying defining features of psychopathology, testing hypotheses about mechanisms underlying dysfunction, and gauging the impact of treatment and prevention efforts.

Cross-Sectional Designs

Cross-sectional designs gather data at only one time point, yet in many ways set the stage for longitudinal research in developmental psychopathology. These designs offer a means of comparing the presentation of symptoms at different ages, gauging the incidence and prevalence of mental disorders in various populations or for different developmental periods, and examining whether hypothesized patterns of association among variables can be documented. Cross-sectional designs are essential for developing measures, formulating problems, and for exploratory studies.

Initial tests of possible causal factors can also be made, especially when cross-sectional designs take advantage of "natural experiments" in which children vary in their level of exposure to an event or experience presumed to alter adaptation (Rutter, 1994). For example, a cross-sectional study of children's adjustment following a natural disaster found evidence consistent with a dose-response relationship among degree of exposure to life-threatening experiences, ongoing disruptions, and intensity of posttraumatic stress symptoms (Vernberg, La Greca, Silverman, & Prinstein, 1996). Support was also found for hypothesized relationships between additional elements of the conceptual model (e.g., access to social support, coping efforts, demographic characteristics) and the level of symptomatology.

The expense and time commitment of longitudinal research are best justified when there is strong cross-sectional evidence on the plausibility of the conceptual framework for the study, the psychometric integrity for measures, and risk or protective factors influencing the emergence or progression of psychopathology. Rutter (1994) argued, "It is crucial that researchers not rush impetuously into the premature use of longitudinal studies" (p. 928). Some forms of psychopathology appear to have a sufficient research base to warrant a strong reliance on fully prospective, long-term longitudinal designs (e.g., disruptive behavior disorders, ADHD), whereas research on other forms of psychopathology, including most internalizing disorders, has reached a level of sophistication where cross-sectional or brief longitudinal designs remain necessary.

Longitudinal Designs

Longitudinal research designs give the advantage of tracking the natural history of child psychopathology, addressing critical issues such as onset, duration, persistence, escalation, and decay of symptoms (Loeber & Farrington, 1994). Gathering information from the same group of children at various times helps researchers trace sequences and paths of development, gauge the effects of life experiences during sensitive developmental periods, and evaluate the significance of possible risk and resilience factors. Longitudinal designs can be retrospective, prospective, or a combination of the two.

Retrospective Longitudinal Designs. In retrospective longitudinal designs, a group of individuals is identified and information about their early development is gathered through self-recollections of their lives, the recollections of others (e.g., mothers' reports of their child's temperament as an infant), or through other means such as school or medical records. Although retrospective research can link early factors with later outcomes, the accuracy of the early reports is often criticized. Whether respondents can accurately remember and report on events that previously happened or if such reports are colored by time or the knowledge of later developmental events calls into question the validity of conclusions drawn from retrospective studies (Briere, 1992). However, some techniques appear to enhance the accuracy of retrospective recall (Willett, Singer, & Martin, 1998). For instance, administrative records help reconstruct event histories more accurately, either by providing data directly or providing anchors for life history calendars (Friedman, Thornton, Camburn, Alwin, & Young-DeMarco, 1988). Asking questions about the context in which events occurred, in addition to whether or not a key event occurred, also appears to increase the accuracy of retrospective reports (Bradburn, Rips, & Shevell, 1987; Friedman et al., 1988).

Prospective Longitudinal Designs. Prospective longitudinal designs involve tracking a cohort of children forward in time. These designs allow researchers to document the emergence and course of psychopathology, yielding valuable clues about factors affecting developmental trajectories and the significance of potential indicators of future functioning. Key constructs can be measured carefully and consistently over time, and sequences of events can be considered. Greater numbers of data collection points improve the measurement of growth trajectories (Willett et al., 1998). Three waves of data are a minimal number for identifying the shape of individual developmental trajectories; each additional wave collected increases the reliability with which change trajectories can be measured, with sharp increases in reliability as the number of waves increases from three to seven. Willett and colleagues argue that researchers should collect extra waves of data at all costs, even if this means fewer children will be followed.

Although prospective studies avoid questions about the validity of retrospective data, other difficulties are encountered. In the time between the beginning of the study and publication of key results, the conceptual framework, methodology, instrumentation, and policy concerns guiding the initial study may become dated or outmoded (Loeber & Farrington, 1994). Keeping all of the participants in a prospective study is difficult as families move away or lose interest. All too often, it is the families who are experiencing greater difficulties who drop out. Loeber and Farrington advise gathering extensive identifying information on participants and their families during the first contact and obtaining permission to search future records (e.g., legal, financial, educational) to help locate participants later. Financial incentives, respect and consideration toward the participants, and stability within the research team also aid in retention.

Period effects are another concern (Willett et al., 1998). Societal changes in education, health care, occupational options, and technology produce notable differences in the experience of childhood as a function of year of birth. Significant changes in the rate of physical maturation and the acquisition of cognitive and social skills have occurred in the 20th century, calling into question the applicability of longitudinal studies begun in previous eras to children born today.

Mixed Retrospective-Prospective Designs.   Most prospective studies in developmental psychopathology begin data collection well after the prenatal period, often at an age just prior to a notable increase in the incidence and prevalence of a specific disorder or problem behavior (e.g., Gjerde & Westenberg, 1998; Loeber, Farrington, Stouthamer-Loeber, Moffitt, & Caspi, 1998). Retrospective information on earlier developmental periods is gathered and participants are followed prospectively. These designs offer

numerous practical advantages and, when retrospective data are of high quality, provide strong scientific evidence of predictive factors and the life course of psychopathology.

Accelerated Longitudinal Designs.   Accelerated longitudinal designs, also referred to as cohort-sequential designs or mixed longitudinal designs, allow researchers to address developmental questions in a shorter time period than required by fully longitudinal designs (Willett et al., 1998). In these designs, two or more age cohorts are followed simultaneously long enough for the younger cohort to reach the same age as the older cohort at the beginning of the study. These designs allow researchers to address the potentially confounding effects of age, year of birth, and cohort-specific idiosyncrasies. For example, if a sample of 5-year-olds born in 1995 and another of 7-year-olds born in 1993 are assessed initially in the same year and tracked for two years, researchers have data covering years 5 through 9, with the capability to test whether the 1995 birth cohort and 1997 birth cohort were similar at age 7. If so, confidence increases in identified age-related trends in development. If not, period or cohort-specific effects, rather than age effects, are operating.

Willett and colleagues (1998) note that the piecing together of developmental trajectories from different age cohorts cannot produce the same level of evidence as full longitudinal designs. They advise using accelerated longitudinal designs when resources are unavailable for a long-term study and the research questions focus on short-term developmental issues rather than longer developmental trajectories. Further, accelerated designs are more likely to yield reliable results in communities with greater residential stability, because higher levels of in- or out-migration make it more difficult to gather different age cohorts that are similar in demographic characteristics and contextual backgrounds. Farrington and colleagues argue for increased use of accelerated longitudinal designs, citing the cost and time effectiveness of this design approach relative to single-cohort long-term longitudinal studies (Farrington, 1991; Loeber & Farrington, 1994).

Experimental Designs

Experimental designs involve manipulation of a key variable with the intention of producing a predictable result on other variables of interest. In the context of developmental psychopathology, differences in responses to experimenter-controlled stimuli by individuals with specific forms of psychopathology often provide critical tests of basic cognitive, physiological, and behavioral processes thought to contribute to specific forms of psychopathology (e.g., Oosterlaan & Sergeant, 1998). Intervention trials offer another level of experimentation. Here, the independent variable (treatment condition) takes weeks or months to deliver, and follow-up assessments of treatment effects create a longitudinal-experimental design (Loeber & Farrington, 1994).

MEASUREMENT CONSIDERATIONS

Measurement is a core issue for developmental psychopathology. Given questions of continuity and change psychopathology for individuals who are also experiencing remarkable growth in cognitive, physical, and social capabilities, it is often a challenge to select attributes that can be tracked throughout the developmental period of interest. Moreover, many research questions require attention to a broad range of factors, from molecular processes to cultural forces. Multiple sources of information are needed for most research questions, as is careful attention to the measurement of key social contextual variables.

Multiple Informants

The use of multiple informants is widely encouraged in research in developmental psychopathology. Although the child's perspective is of great interest, other reporters are needed to make an informed assessment. Sometimes, children are not able to remember or accurately describe important information regarding their symptoms (Emslie & Mayes, 1999). Particularly at very early ages, researchers rely on the reports of adults in children's environments. Parents and teachers are often in a better position to report on the precursors to certain child behaviors as well as to describe the specific behaviors themselves. In addition, trained observers may be used to gather objective information about the child and the environments in which the behaviors occur. As children develop, their reports become more reliable and they can be asked to report on themselves (Edelbrock, Costello, Dulcan, Kalas, & Calabro-Conover, 1985). Self-report is especially valuable when personal information about

internal states, attitudes, or covert activities, such as drug use, is needed (Edelbrock, Costello, Dulcan, Calabro-Conover, & Kalas, 1986; O'Donnell et al., 1998). Youth checklists and interviews are two common ways to gather information directly from the child. In addition to adult and self-report, children's peers may be asked to provide information about the participants. Various peer-report measures such as the Pupil Evaluation Inventory (Pekarik, Prinz, Liebert, Weintraub, & Neale, 1976) and peer nomination instruments (Crick & Bigbee, 1998; D.G. Perry, Kusel, & Perry, 1988) have been used to gather information about children's behaviors, especially overt and relational aggression.

Reports from child, parents, teachers, observers, and peers often show only low to moderate agreement (Canino, Bird, Rubio-Stipec, & Bravo, 1995; Edelbrock et al., 1985; Huddleston & Rust, 1994). Differences between parents' perceptions and child reports in particular have been shown to vary according to the child's age (Edelbrock et al., 1985), gender (Offord, Boyle, & Racine, 1989; Valla, Bergeron, Breton, Gaudet, & Berthiaume, 1993), and level of acculturation (Rousseau & Drapeau, 1998). Although these low levels of agreement may indicate a lack of reliability of certain reporters (Edelbrock et al., 1985), low correlations among informants do not necessarily reflect a shortcoming of any of the methods of data collection. The differences among informants attests to the different vantage points the reporters have to offer concerning a particular problem. Information on internalizing symptoms differs in level of accessibility to the different informants. Although people in the children's environments can witness some behaviors, children will be more knowledgeable about their feelings or fears. It is not surprising, then, that parent-child agreement on internalizing symptoms is much lower than that for externalizing symptoms (Edelbrock et al., 1986; Herjanic & Reich, 1982). Children's behavior also varies in different settings; thus, discrepancies between teacher and parent reports are likely to reflect these differences in behavior instead of a lack of reliability.

In some cases, the lack of agreement among reporters may indicate biases of the reporters or a desire to give a socially appropriate picture of the situation (Rousseau & Drapeau, 1998). In complex family situations, such as domestic violence, gaining perspectives from everyone involved is encouraged as a way to improve the reliability of reports of behavior (Sternberg, Lamb, & Dawud-Noursi, 1998). Likewise, in cases involving families from different cultures, gathering data from numerous sources can help clarify if the expression of symptoms differs by culture (Weisz, Suwanlert, Chaiyasit, Weiss, & Walter, 1987) or if certain informant reports are influenced by cultural beliefs or values (Chang, Morrissey, & Kaplewicz, 1995). Integrating conflicting data from multiple informants can be burdensome, yet it results in a richer view of children and the factors related to their behaviors.

Comprehensive Measurement Plans

Research in developmental psychopathology requires a tremendous breadth of measurement, ranging from molecular indicators of biological and cognitive processes to cultural and social processes (Achenbach, 1990). To test proposed interplay between molecular, intraindividual processes and social contexts, it is essential to identify and measure carefully key constructs at all levels of interest.

Measuring Social Context. A recent consensus panel defined *social context* operationally as "a set of interpersonal conditions, relevant to a particular behavior or disorder and external to, but shaped and interpreted by, the individual child" (Boyce et al., 1998, p. 143). Working from this definition, this panel offered five propositions to guide research on developmental psychopathology (see Table 3.1). Specific research recommendations based on these propositions are intended to produce more precise elucidation of the actual transactions occurring between children with various

Table 3.1 Propositions and recommendations for measuring social context in research on developmental psychopathology.

Propositions	*Recommendations: What Future Research Should Address*
1. Increase study of the complex interplay among the various contexts in an individual's life.	a. The multidimensionality of influences within and across hierarchical levels of children's environments. b. Clearer differentiation between structural and functional aspects of social context. c. The additive, mediating, and moderating relations among social-psychological factors at different hierarchical levels. d. The embeddedness of each context in a broader social milieu.
2. Social contexts change over time in response to changes within the child, in other settings, and in the larger community environment.	a. Child's age and changing developmental status b. Emergence of behavior problems, other early signs of mental disorders in the child. c. Presence or emergence of psychopathological conditions in other members of the child's social contexts. d. Dynamic changes in the breadth or roles of particular social contexts. e. Secular changes in characteristics of the broader social ecology.
3. Contexts impact children, and children change and interpret their contexts.	a. Measurement of social contextual effects on the child and child effects on the social context. b. Modalities of such effects and the means by which children and contexts are mutually developing. c. Differentiation of genetically driven child effects and the individual child's values, dispositions, and propensities that lie between biology and context.
4. Children's perceptions and interpretations influence the impact of the contexts in their lives.	a. Collection of subjective and objective information about children's social contexts. b. Innovative methods, beyond self-report, for assessing children's actual or likely subjective appraisals of their environments. c. New methodologies that attend to the basic psychological and physical needs addressed by childhood social contexts.
5. Contexts should be selected for assessment in light of specific questions or outcomes.	a. The most important level of the contextual domain. b. The salient dimensions within that domain. c. Subjects' developmental stage. d. Theoretical assumptions underlying the search for contextual effects.

Source. Adapted from Boyce et al., 1998.

personal characteristics and their social contexts. Through this effort, the panel called for stronger evidence on the ways social context influences neurobiological processes and events.

Conceptual Issues

Specifying "Mechanisms" Carrying Risk or Psychopathology

The concept of mechanisms as applied in developmental psychopathology research refers to basic mental and biological processes that drive dysfunctional behavior. These mechanisms are thought to influence behavior directly and pervasively by affecting fundamental cognitive functions involved in information processing (Dodge, 1993). Relatively well-articulated mechanism models have been proposed for several specific disorders, with an emphasis on the linkages between behavioral episodes and the emergence of cognitive and biological architectures that eventually produce characteristic responses to environmental stimuli (Brodsky & Lombroso, 1998; Dodge, 1993; B.D. Perry, Pollard, Blakely, Baker, & Vigilante, 1995).

Social-Cognitive Mechanisms. Formulation of psychopathology from a mechanisms perspective requires integration of information from multiple disciplines and research traditions. Dodge (1993) drew from cognitive science, attachment theory, and clinical developmental research on psychopathology to propose social-cognitive mechanisms for the emergence of conduct disorder and depression. His model links early social experiences with the development of knowledge structures, conceptualized as latent mental structures (e.g., schemas, working models, beliefs) that guide information processing in specific encounters in the social environment. These knowledge structures become important foci for research because they are thought to drive information processing, which in turn directly influences thoughts and behavior in specific situations. For example, low self-esteem and a negative self-schema are viewed as knowledge structures leading to social information qualities characteristic of depression, such as filtering out positive cues, hopeless expectations, and poverty of response accessing (Dodge, 1993). These features of information processing are posited to contribute to depressed mood, heightened sensitivity to cues of failure or rejection, and reduced activity level.

Specification of social-cognitive mechanisms allows greater precision in selecting measures and methods by identifying key constructs that must be assessed carefully to test hypothesized linkages among experiences, underlying cognitive structures, information processing, and behavior. Models specifying mechanisms also help organize seemingly disparate pieces of evidence into a more coherent, integrated organizational system.

Genetic Mechanisms. Interest in possible genetic influences on the emergence of psychopathology has drawn increasing attention as advances in molecular science have enabled new techniques for studying gene-behavior relationships (Goldsmith, Gottesman, & Lemery, 1997). At the highly technical end of behavioral genetics research, genetic probes now allow searches for chromosomal regions associated with specific behavioral patterns. "Knockout genetics" enables animal researchers to inactivate specific genes and then observe the effects of these manipulations.

In their recent review of behavior genetics in the context of developmental psychopathology research, Goldsmith and colleagues (1997) argue that the expression of most forms of psychopathology is influenced to some extent by genetics. For many disorders, individuals with the same diagnostic label likely receive genetic influences from different combinations of genetic material. Although a limited number of developmental disorders are linked to single gene mutations, most psychiatric disorders appear to be influenced by multiple genes, acting in complex interactions with each other and environmental influences (Brodsky & Lombroso, 1998). Identification of distinct developmental trajectories is important for research in behavioral genetics in the possible identification of specific subtypes with more homogeneous genetic contributors.

From this perspective, it is extremely important to gather information on family patterns of psychopathology and genetically influenced aspects of child-rearing environments (e.g., Reiss, 1995) in prospective longitudinal studies. More precise, direct measures of key environmental processes (observational and multiple informant data rather than exclusive reliance on self-report) and behavioral or physiological responses to a variety of stimuli are also essential to gain a clearer picture of the interplay between genetic and environmental influences in the development of psychopathology.

Biological Mechanisms. Whether influenced by genetics, environment, or a combination of genes and environment, there is keen interest in biological mechanisms involved in psychopathology (Quay, 1993). The formation of neural connections is determined in part by experience and environmental stimulation, and models have been proposed linking environmental events, psychobiological functioning, and specific forms of psychopathology. For example, extreme experiences in childhood, such as repeated, severe maltreatment, have been proposed to alter brain chemistry and architecture, leading to long-standing disturbances in affect regulation and arousal characteristic of posttraumatic stress disorder and other trauma-related disturbances (B.D. Perry et al., 1995; van der Kolk, 1997). Measurement advances, such as brain imaging and neurotransmitter technology, show promise in developing more complete models to explain the psychobiology of child psychopathology, in turn offering hope for more effective pharmacological, psychological, and environmental treatments for chronic disorders.

RESEARCH ON TREATMENT EFFECTIVENESS

Psychologists have an ethical responsibility to provide their clients with effective treatments. In addition to ethical considerations, clinicians' interest in empirically supported treatments has been further reinforced by changes in the American health care system. Managed care organizations, and attempts to compete with them, are an external source of pressure for practitioners to prove that their services are effective and worthy of reimbursement. It is becoming increasingly evident that clinicians and researchers must work to bridge the gap between research and practice by reducing loyalty to particular orientations and focusing instead on developing, evaluating, and implementing empirically supported treatments that have the greatest potential for evoking positive change in a client's life (Shirk & Phillips, 1991). A central theme in bridging the gap between research and practice is the idea that both researchers and clinicians should influence each other.

EFFECTIVENESS AND EFFICACY

In discussing empirically supported treatments, it is helpful to distinguish between effectiveness and efficacy as two distinct approaches to evaluating a treatment. Efficacy refers to outcome studies that are conducted under tightly controlled conditions (Hoagwood, Hibbs, Brent, & Jensen, 1995). Efficacy studies generally use random assignment, control or comparison groups, exclusion criteria (e.g., leaving out participants with multiple diagnoses), clearly specified treatments of a standard duration, and a high level of control over the conditions of treatment delivery. However, these studies do not necessarily reflect the conditions faced in many clinical practice settings, bringing the generalizability of such studies into question. Efficacy studies are valuable in that they allow researchers to attribute the reduction of symptoms to the specific elements of a treatment. They often represent early steps in the development and evaluation of useful treatments that can later be applied in clinical settings. Efficacy studies help researchers target elements of interventions that may need to be modified to improve outcomes for clients of varying developmental levels or severity of symptoms.

Effectiveness studies, in contrast, test how a treatment is likely to work in a typical clinical setting fraught with the issues that face clinicians, such as comorbidity and varying intensity and duration of treatments (Kazdin, Bass, Ayers, & Rodgers, 1990). Treatment effectiveness studies address clinicians' concerns that their clients and treatment conditions are never as controlled as in laboratory studies. A treatment that reduces symptoms in the laboratory may not be as feasible or effective in a clinical setting, so it is important to track the outcomes of treatments provided outside of the laboratory. Studies in clinical settings are also valuable in that they address moderating factors, such as parental functioning or household composition, that may affect treatment outcome. Effectiveness studies are useful in targeting aspects of treatment delivery that need to be modified to make a research therapy more palatable to clients and clinicians in clinical settings.

Taken together, efficacy and effectiveness studies illustrate the melding of research and practice, which has long been touted as a central tenet of the scientist-practitioner model. Ideally, efficacy studies provide clinicians with information about what interventions appear promising for particular diagnoses, and effectiveness studies aid those who develop treatments in identifying various difficulties of translating their research therapy into practice. Although gaps remain between science and practice in clinical child psychology, efforts to consolidate and evaluate the vast number of treatment outcome studies offer hope of moving closer toward science-guided practice.

EMPIRICALLY SUPPORTED TREATMENTS

Attempts to evaluate the impact of child treatments have evolved over the years from narrative reviews to extensive meta-analyses that evaluate the effects of hundreds of outcome studies. Early evaluations of treatment outcome studies involving children consisted of narrative reviews focused on the use of psychoanalysis and play therapy (Eysenck, 1952; Levitt, 1957, 1963). The discouraging message from these early reviews was that children involved in therapy generally did not improve significantly compared to children who were receiving no treatment (Eysenck, 1952; Levitt, 1957, 1963). More recent reviews included the use of meta-analytical procedures to integrate and evaluate results of outcome studies. These recent meta-analyses demonstrated that children receiving therapeutic interventions did show significant improvements compared to children not receiving treatment; furthermore, behavioral treatments appeared to be more beneficial than other treatment modalities (Casey & Berman, 1985; Kazdin et al., 1990; Weisz & Weiss, 1993; Weisz, Weiss, Alicke, & Klotz, 1987; Weisz, Weiss, Han, Granger, & Morton, 1995). Despite the more optimistic results of recent meta-analyses, the question remains: How do therapists decide which specific treatments are most likely to benefit a particular client?

Standards for Establishing Treatment Effectiveness
Individual studies to determine if a treatment works to alleviate symptoms vary greatly in the number of participants, what is being compared (e.g., pre- and posttreatment behavior, comparison to an alternative treatment), measurement specificity and sensitivity, and documentation of treatment fidelity. As the number of outcome studies grows, increased attention is being paid to evaluating the quality of evidence for efficacy and

effectiveness. General criteria for categorizing psychosocial interventions as "well established" or "probably efficacious" (Chambless et al., 1996) have been tailored specifically for studies involving children and adolescents (Lonigan et al., 1998). Characteristics such as a substantial body of well-designed studies, an adequate number of participants for the statistical analyses, the use of a treatment manual, and a comparison to a placebo, alternative treatment, or control group help categorize the level of evidence for the effects of various treatments for specific problems (see Table 3.2). For example, both well-established and probably efficacious treatments for children need to include the use of manualized interventions and clear descriptions of the samples used to evaluate the treatments (Lonigan et al., 1998). The distinction between well-established and probably efficacious treatments lies in the rigor of the studies showing the treatment to be effective in comparison to a placebo/control group or other established treatments. The cognitive-behavioral treatment manual for anxious children (Kendall, Kane, Howard, & Siqueland, 1990) is an example of a probably efficacious treatment package that has been evaluated across several years through single-subject designs (Kane & Kendall, 1989), randomized clinical trials (Kendall, 1994; Kendall, Flannery-Schroeder, Panichelli-Mindel, & Southam-Gerow, 1997), including subjects with multiple diagnoses (Kendall et al., 1997), and using long-term follow-up (Kendall & Southam-Gerow, 1996).

Seldom will treatments be supported by a body of literature containing all the relevant characteristics. Pediatric psychology treatment outcome studies, for example, often include only a small number of participants due to the rarity of the pediatric conditions under study (Spirito, 1999). Conducting large group design experiments with control conditions may not be feasible. The research literature for some conditions, such as disease-related pain, consists almost exclusively of case studies (Walco, Sterling, Conte, & Engel, 1999). In response to these complications, the Society of Pediatric Psychology modified the criteria for well-established treatments. Treatment manuals are not required if the treatment protocol is specified; groups smaller than 30 participants are acceptable for research of chronic illness; and two multiple baseline designs by independent investigators are viewed as indicators of well-established treatments (Spirito, 1999).

Table 3.2   Criteria for well-established and probably efficacious psychosocial treatments for children.

Well-Established Treatments	*Probably Efficacious Treatments*

1. At least two well-conducted group design studies, conducted by different investigatory teams, showing the treatment to be either
  a. Superior to pill placebo or alternative treatment, OR
  b. Equivalent to an already established treatment in studies with adequate statistical power.
 	
OR
 	
2. A large series of single-case design studies (i.e., $\underline{n} > 9$) that both
  a. Use good experimental design AND
  b. Compare the intervention to another treatment.
 	
AND
 	
3. Treatment manuals used for the intervention preferred.
 	
AND
 	
4. Sample characteristics clearly specified.
	1. Two studies showing the intervention was more effective than a no-treatment control group.
	
	OR
	
	2. Two group design studies meeting criteria for well-established treatments but conducted by the same investigator.
	
	OR
	
	3. A small series of single-case design experiments (i.e., $n > 3$) that otherwise meet Criterion 2 for well-established treatments.
	
	AND
	
	4. Treatment manuals used for the intervention preferred.
	
	AND
	
	5. Sample characteristics clearly specified.

Source: Adapted from Lonigan et al., 1998, p. 141.

Although it may take years for a treatment to be empirically supported, using such criteria should help clinicians identify if a treatment is promising for their client's situation.

TRANSLATING RESEARCH THERAPIES INTO CLINICAL SETTINGS

Despite the encouraging findings of meta-analyses evaluating child therapy in general and advances in evaluating particular treatments, the generalizability of these findings has been questioned due to the fact that most therapies evaluated in research studies were delivered under tightly controlled conditions (Roberts, Vernberg, & Jackson, 2000). Clinicians often express concern that treatment conditions in outcome studies vary greatly from their own experiences. These concerns appear to be legitimate because the level of measured treatment effects for therapies delivered in clinical settings often does not reach that of research therapies (Weisz, Donenberg, Han, & Weiss, 1995).

The relatively lower level of treatment effects in effectiveness studies as compared to efficacy studies indicates that efforts are still needed to bridge the gap between research and practice. First, such efforts would include increasing evaluations of treatments delivered in clinic settings (Weisz, Donenberg, et al., 1995). Evidence on research therapy has been steadily growing, but less effort has been made to track outcomes in clinic settings (Weisz, Donenberg, et al., 1995). A variety of reasons exists for the paucity of research in clinical settings (e.g. lack of time, lack of resources, need to generate income), yet these outcome studies are necessary in understanding the services that most clients are likely to receive. Second, factors related to the relatively stronger effects of research therapy need to be identified (Weisz, Donenberg, et al., 1995). One apparent factor is the greater complexity of cases and severity of symptoms typically found in clinic therapy compared to research therapy (Clarke, 1995; Hoagwood et al., 1995; Kazdin et al., 1990). Not only do clients in clinic settings often present with multiple concerns or diagnoses, but also intervention in the community may involve a variety of service providers in addition to traditional individual or group therapy. Third, efficacious research treatments need to be integrated into clinical sites (Kendall & Southam-Gerow, 1995; Weisz, Donenberg, et al., 1995). Multiple obstacles hinder the transfer of research interventions into clinic settings. In addition to higher rates of comorbidity and more complex service plans, therapists in clinic settings differ greatly in their level of education and experience, opportunities for supervision, and commitment to particular theoretical backgrounds (Kendall & Southam-Gerow, 1995). Greater understanding and acknowledgment of the barriers to delivering research therapies in clinic settings should lead to stronger treatment results in effectiveness studies.

Examine Treatment Feasibility

A common criticism of treatment researchers is that they are isolated from real-world settings and may focus on techniques that are not relevant or feasible in clinic settings (Kendall & Southam-Gerow, 1995). Greater care needs to be taken to ensure that treatments can realistically be applied in a variety of clinical settings, and to evaluate systematically how these treatments fare when introduced in less-controlled settings. Supervision and training needs and availability, cost considerations, and the acceptability of treatments to both providers and consumers all deserve attention.

Determining if the public as well as the professional sectors view the treatment to be useful and appropriate is crucial. Client satisfaction measures can identify elements of treatments that need to be modified if the treatment is to be widely adopted in clinical settings. It is a positive sign that research on treatment acceptability appears to have increased in recent years (Roberts et al., 2000).

Link Treatment to Mechanisms of Dysfunction

Kazdin (1997) proposed a model for developing effective treatments that includes greater emphasis on the conceptualization of the dysfunction as well as researching the factors related to symptoms. Information such as the timing of the onset of symptoms, the pervasiveness of dysfunction and the later results of certain risk factors is important in understanding the problem targeted for treatment. Treatments should be conceptualized based on theories and current knowledge of the dysfunction (Kazdin, 1997). For example, therapists can choose treatments based on an understanding of how and when a child became engaged in a deviant developmental pathway and which of the larger set of empirically supported factors thought to cause and maintain a specific form of psychopathology is operating for this child (Vernberg, 1998). Creating elements in the treatment to target the most likely causes and maintainers of dysfunction should result in a greater likelihood of successful outcomes.

Expand the Scope of Outcomes Evaluated

Once treatments have been implemented, researchers should track client behavior and identify how the processes of the intervention relate to the outcomes (Eddy, Dishion, & Stoolmiller, 1998; Kazdin, 1997). Although evidence of the reduction of overt behavioral symptoms and self-reported distress remains essential, outcome studies should also assess changes in internal processes such as cognition, mood, and physiological factors (Chorpita, Barlow, Albano, & Daleiden, 1998). Although recent attempts have been made to track changes in mood and cognition as well as behaviors (Kazdin, 1994) and to link behavioral interventions with changes in the physiology related to disorders (Hegel & Martin, 1998), some have argued that the increase in outcome studies has coincided with a decrease in research on the underlying mechanisms of change (Safran & Muran, 1994). Rhodes and Greenberg (1994) asserted that investigations of internal mental operations in outcome studies would help bridge the gap between research and practice. Toward this end, treatment studies should be theory-driven in the sense that researchers begin with a theory of how a change will occur, then evaluate both the outward performance of the client and the hypothesized model of internal processes thought to be related to the change.

In addition to change in internal processes, clinicians are often concerned with enhancing a child's functioning in a variety of domains and settings. Helping the child accomplish developmental tasks and handle new challenges competently are worthy treatment goals, but these outcomes are often not tracked in the short-term follow-up assessments typical of many treatment studies. The child's functioning within the family, with peers, and academically should also be of great importance when evaluating a treatment (Kazdin, 1997).

Cost offset also provides a way to further evaluate the impact of a developed treatment. Determining if the use of psychological treatments reduced the need for more expensive medical treatments (Roberts & Hurley, 1997) or other costs such as incarceration is an important way of viewing outcomes in the individual and in the larger society.

Address Comorbidity and Social Context

Evidence of the influence of comorbid conditions and life circumstances of children and their families on treatment selection and outcome is also a high priority (Clarke, 1995; Kazdin, 1995, 1997).

Many children seen in clinical practice meet criteria for more than one disorder. Moreover, clinicians are all too familiar with the impact on child treatment outcomes of social context factors, such as residential instability, divorce, parental job loss, and parental pathology. Despite the frequency of comorbid conditions and adverse social circumstances, such factors are often overlooked in research therapy outcome studies. Assessing the role of these factors in research therapies, rather than ignoring them or using them as a basis for exclusion from treatment, could provide useful information about why a particular treatment may or may not succeed with a particular client. Attention to these potential moderating factors may also result in the determination that multiple interventions are needed for a successful outcome.

Develop Manualized Treatments

Kazdin (1997) emphasized the need for specification of treatments in efficacy and effectiveness studies, typically by developing a manualized description of treatment principles and techniques. Some critics are reluctant to adopt manuals and lament such tools as signifying the death of the art of therapy and unnecessary restrictions on their clinical judgment. Detailed descriptions of interventions, however, are essential for research that attempts to replicate outcomes for promising treatments (Kazdin, 1997; Lonigan et al., 1998). In applied settings, manuals are useful tools for training new therapists and teaching new techniques. Manuals may also broaden accessibility to effective treatments by allowing a wider range of practitioners to adopt empirically supported principles and techniques. The development and use of treatment manuals help address concerns over treatment fidelity when the interventions are provided by therapists who vary greatly in education and experience.

View Treatment from a Developmental Perspective

Instead of focusing exclusively on "fixing" a problem or simply reducing the frequency or severity of symptoms, developmental treatments strive to place children back on an adaptive pathway of development. The children presumably can then use their newly acquired skills to face and adapt to upcoming challenges. Returning a child to an adaptive developmental pathway rarely offers inoculation against all difficulties that a child may encounter, especially as the child develops new cognitive and physical abilities and faces new developmental tasks. Knowledge of the trajectories or sequences by which treatment gains fade over time or fail to generalize to new situations enhances clinical decision making about treatment options. This makes it possible to anticipate the necessity of booster sessions or renewed treatment before symptoms reappear or escalate to dangerous levels. In some cases, psychopathology may endure, and the focus of treatment then is to help children cope with and manage their symptoms (Kendall, 1989). Teaching skills, such as relaxation and pain management techniques, are examples of ways that psychologists can benefit clients by teaching them how to manage difficult situations when a cure is not available.

CONCLUDING REMARKS

The evidence-based, developmentally oriented conceptual framework of developmental psychopathology provides an organizational paradigm for the field of clinical child psychology. Research on the emergence, escalation, and desistance of psychopathology throughout the life span must guide clinical practice. At the same time, intervention research potentially allows essential tests of evidence garnered from longitudinal, cross-sectional, and basic experimental studies. Moreover, intervention research offers hope that we can be more than passive observers of aberrant developmental processes. One of the great challenges for developmental psychopathology research, and for developmental psychotherapy research, is to integrate information from multiple research literatures, which range in focus from societal influence to molecular processes, in such a way that assumptions and propositions can be evaluated empirically. A second great challenge is to apply this evidence-based conceptual framework to treatment decisions for individual children. Resources for research in these areas are precious and scarce, and can be allocated most judiciously by formulating research questions within this overarching macroparadigm.

REFERENCES

Achenbach, T.M. (1990). Conceptualization of developmental psychopathology. In M. Lewis & S.M. Miller

(Eds.), *Handbook of developmental psychopathology: Perspectives in developmental psychology* (pp. 3–14). New York: Plenum Press.

Boyce, W.T., Frank, E., Jensen, P.S., Kessler, R.C., Nelson, C.A., Steinberg, L., & The MacArthur Foundation Research Network on Psychopathology and Development (1998). Social context in developmental psychopathology: Recommendations for future research from the MacArthur Network on Psychopathology and Development. *Development and Psychopathology, 10,* 143–164.

Bradburn, N.M., Rips, L.J., & Shevell, S.K. (1987). Answering autobiographical questions: The impact of memory and inference on surveys. *Science, 236,* 157–161.

Briere, J. (1992). Methodological issues in the study of sexual abuse effects. *Journal of Consulting and Clinical Psychology, 60,* 196–203.

Brodsky, M., & Lombroso, P.J. (1998). Molecular mechanisms of developmental disorders. *Development and Psychopathology, 10,* 1–20.

Canino, G., Bird, H.R., Rubio-Stipec, M., & Bravo, M. (1995). Child psychiatric epidemiology: What we have learned and what we need to learn. *International Journal of Methods in Psychiatric Research, 5,* 79–92.

Casey, R.J., & Berman, J.S. (1985). The outcome of psychotherapy with children. *Psychological Bulletin, 98,* 388–400.

Chambless, D.L., Sanderson, W.C., Shoham, V., Johnson, S.B., Pope, K.S., Crits-Christoph, P., Baker, M.J., Johnson, B., Woody, S.R., Sue, S., Beutler, L.E., Williams, D.A., & McCurry, S. (1996). An update on empirically validated therapies. *Clinical Psychologist, 49,* 5–18.

Chang, L., Morrissey, R.F., & Kaplewicz, H.S. (1995). Prevalence of psychiatric symptoms and their relation to adjustment among Chinese-American youth. *Journal of the American Academy of Child and Adolescent Psychiatry, 34,* 91–99.

Chorpita, B.F., Barlow, D.H., Albano, A.M., & Daleiden, E.L. (1998). Methodological strategies in child clinical trials: Advancing the efficacy and effectiveness of psychosocial treatments. *Journal of Abnormal Child Psychology, 26,* 7–16.

Clarke, G.N. (1995). Improving the transition from basic efficacy research to effectiveness studies: Methodological issues and procedures. *Journal of Consulting and Clinical Psychology, 63,* 718–725.

Crick, N.R., & Bigbee, M.A. (1998). Relational and overt forms of peer aggression: A multi-informant approach. *Journal of Consulting and Clinical Psychology, 66,* 337–347.

Dodge, K.A. (1993). Social-cognitive mechanisms in the development of conduct disorder and depression. *Annual Review of Psychology, 44,* 559–584.

Edelbrock, C., Costello, A.J., Dulcan, M.K., Kalas, R., & Calabro-Conover, N. (1985). Age differences in the reliability of the psychiatric interview of the child. *Child Development, 56,* 265–275.

Edelbrock, C., Costello, A.J., Dulcan, M.K., Calabro-Conover, N., & Kalas, R. (1986). Parent-child agreement on child psychiatric symptoms reported via structured interview. *Journal of Child Psychology and Psychiatry, 27,* 181–190.

Eddy, J.M., Dishion, T.J., & Stoolmiller, M. (1998). The analysis of intervention change in children and families: Methodological and conceptual issues embedded in intervention studies. *Journal of Abnormal Child Psychology, 26,* 53–69.

Emslie, G.J., & Mayes, T.L. (1999). Depression in children and adolescents. *CNS Drugs, 11,* 181–189.

Eysenck, H.J. (1952). The effects of psychotherapy: An evaluation. *Journal of Consulting Psychology, 16,* 319–324.

Farrington, D.P. (1991). Longitudinal research strategies: Advantages, problems, and prospects. *Journal of the American Academy of Child and Adolescent Psychiatry, 30,* 369–374.

Friedman, D., Thornton, A., Camburn, D., Alwin, D., & Young-DeMarco, L. (1988). The life-history calendar: A technique for collecting retrospective data. *Sociological Methodology, 18,* 37–68.

Gjerde, P.F., & Westenberg, P.M. (1998). Dysphoric adolescents as young adults: A prospective study of the psychological sequelae of depressed mood in adolescence. *Journal of Research on Adolescence, 8,* 377–402.

Goldsmith, H.H., Gottesman, I.I., & Lemery, K.S. (1997). Epigenetic approaches to developmental psychopathology. *Development and Psychopathology, 9,* 365–387.

Hegel, M.T., & Martin, J.B. (1998). Behavioral treatment of pulsatile tinnitus and headache following traumatic head injury. *Behavior Modification, 22,* 563–572.

Herjanic, B., & Reich, W. (1982). Development of a structured psychiatric interview for children: Agreement between child and parent on individual symptoms. *Journal of Abnormal Child Psychology, 10,* 307–324.

Hoagwood, K., Hibbs, E., Brent, D., & Jensen, P. (1995). Introduction to the special section: Efficacy and effectiveness in studies of child and adolescent psychotherapy. *Journal of Consulting and Clinical Psychology, 63,* 683–687.

Huddleston, E.N., & Rust, J.O. (1994). A comparison of child and parent ratings of depression and anxiety in clinically referred children. *Research Communications in Psychology, Psychiatry and Behavior, 19,* 101–112.

Kane, M.T., & Kendall, P.C. (1989). Anxiety disorders in children: A multiple-baseline evaluation of a cognitive-behavioral treatment. *Behavior Therapy, 20,* 499–508.

Kazdin, A.E. (1994). *Behavior modification in applied settings.* Pacific Groves, CA: Brooks/Cole.

Kazdin, A.E. (1995). Scope of child and adolescent psychotherapy research: Limited sampling of dysfunctions, treatments, and client characteristics. *Journal of Clinical Child Psychology, 24,* 125–140.

Kazdin, A.E. (1997). A model for developing effective treatments: Progression and interplay of theory, research, and practice. *Journal of Clinical Child Psychology, 26,* 114–129.

Kazdin, A.E., Bass, D., Ayers, W.A., & Rodgers, A. (1990). Empirical and clinical focus on child and adolescent psychotherapy research. *Journal of Consulting and Clinical Psychology, 60,* 733–747.

Kendall, P.C. (1989). The generalization and maintenance of behavior change: Comments, considerations, and the "no-cure" criticism. *Behavior Therapy, 20,* 357–364.

Kendall, P.C. (1994). Treating anxiety disorders in children: Results of a randomized clinical trial. *Journal of Consulting and Clinical Psychology, 62,* 100–110.

Kendall, P.C., Flannery-Schroeder, E., Panichelli-Mindel, S.M., & Southam-Gerow, M.A. (1997). Therapy for youths with anxiety disorders: A second randomized clinical trial. *Journal of Consulting and Clinical Psychology, 65,* 366–380.

Kendall, P.C., Kane, M.T., Howard, B., & Siqueland, L. (1990). *Cognitive-behavioral treatment of anxious children: Treatment manual.* (Available from Philip C. Kendall, Temple University, Department of Psychology, Philadelphia, PA 19122)

Kendall, P.C., & Southam-Gerow, M.A. (1995). Issues in the transportability of treatment: The case of anxiety disorders in youths. *Journal of Consulting and Clinical Psychology, 63,* 702–708.

Kendall, P.C., & Southam-Gerow, M.A. (1996). Long-term follow-up of a cognitive-behavioral therapy for anxiety-disordered youth. *Journal of Consulting and Clinical Psychology, 64,* 724–730.

Levitt, E.E. (1957). The results of psychotherapy with children: An evaluation. *Journal of Consulting Psychology, 32,* 286–289.

Levitt, E.E. (1963). Psychotherapy with children: A further evaluation. *Behavior Research and Therapy, 60,* 326–329.

Loeber, R., & Farrington, D.P. (1994). Problems and solutions in longitudinal and experimental treatment studies of child psychopathology and delinquency. *Journal of Consulting and Clinical Psychology, 62,* 887–900.

Loeber, R., Farrington, D.P., Stouthamer-Loeber, M., Moffitt, T.E., & Caspi, A. (1998). The development of male offending: Key findings from the first decade of the Pittsburgh Youth Study. *Studies on Crime and Crime Prevention, 7,* 141–171.

Lonigan, C.J., Elbert, J.C., & Johnson, S.B. (1998). Empirically supported psychosocial interventions for children: An overview. *Journal of Clinical Child Psychology, 27,* 138–145.

O'Donnell, D., Biederman, J., Jones, J., Wilens, T.E., Milberger, S., Mick, E., & Faraone, S.V. (1998). Informativeness of child and parent reports on substance use disorders in a sample of ADHD probands, control probands, and their siblings. *Journal of the American Academy of Child and Adolescent Psychiatry, 37,* 752–758.

Offord, D.R., Boyle, M.H., & Racine, Y. (1989). Ontario child health study: Correlates of disorder. *Journal of the American Academy of Child and Adolescent Psychiatry, 28,* 856–860.

Oosterlaan, J., & Sergeant, J.A. (1998). Effects of reward and response cost on response inhibition in AD/HD, disruptive, anxious, and normal children. *Journal of Abnormal Child Psychology, 26,* 161–174.

Pekarik, E.G., Prinz, R.J., Liebert, D.E., Weintraub, S., & Neale, J.M. (1976). The Pupil Evaluation Inventory: A sociometric technique for assessing children's social behavior. *Journal of Abnormal Child Psychology, 4,* 83–97.

Perry, B.D., Pollard, R.A., Blakely, T.L., Baker, W.L., & Vigilante, D. (1995). Childhood trauma, the neurobiology of adaptation, and "use dependent" development of the brain: How "states" become "traits." *Infant Mental Health Journal, 16,* 271–291.

Perry, D.G., Kusel, S.J., & Perry, L.C. (1988). Victims of peer aggression. *Developmental Psychology, 24,* 807–814.

Quay, H.C. (1993). The psychobiology of undersocialized aggressive conduct disorder: A theoretical perspective. *Development and Psychopathology, 5,* 165–180.

Reiss, D. (1995). Genetic influence on family systems: Implications for development. *Journal of Marriage and the Family, 57,* 543–560.

Rhodes, R.H., & Greenberg, L. (1994). Investigating the process of change: Clinical applications of process research. In P.F. Talley, H.H. Strupp, & S.F. Butler (Eds.), *Psychotherapy research and practice: Bridging the gap* (pp. 227–245). New York: Basic Books.

Roberts, M.C., & Hurley, L.K. (1997). *Managing managed care.* New York: Plenum Press.

Roberts, M.C., Vernberg, E.M., & Jackson, Y. (2000). Psychotherapy with children and families. In C.R. Snyder & R.E. Ingram (Eds.), *Handbook of psychological change: Psychotherapy processes and practices for the 21st century* (pp. 500–519). New York: Wiley.

Rousseau, C., & Drapeau, A. (1998). Parent-child agreement on refugee children's psychiatric symptoms: A transcultural perspective. *Journal of the American Academy of Child and Adolescent Psychiatry, 37,* 626–629.

Russ, S. (Ed.). (1998). Special section on developmentally-based integrated psychotherapy with children: Emerging models. *Journal of Clinical Child Psychology, 27,* 2–53.

Rutter, M. (1994). Beyond longitudinal data: Causes, consequences, changes, and continuity. *Journal of Consulting and Clinical Psychology, 62,* 928–940.

Safran, J.D., & Muran, J.C. (1994). Toward a working alliance between research and practice. In P.F. Talley,

H.H. Strupp, & S.F. Butler (Eds.), *Psychotherapy research and practice: Bridging the gap* (pp. 206–226). New York: Basic Books.

Shirk, S.R., & Phillips, J.S. (1991). Child therapy training: Closing gaps with research and practice. *Journal of Consulting and Clinical Psychology, 59,* 766–776.

Spirito, A. (1999). Introduction to special series on empirically supported treatments in pediatric psychology. *Journal of Pediatric Psychology, 24,* 87–90.

Sternberg, K.J., Lamb, M.E., & Dawud-Noursi, S. (1998). Using multiple informants to understand domestic violence and its effects. In G.W. Holden & R. Geffner (Eds.), *Children exposed to marital violence: Theory, research, and applied issues* (pp. 121–156). Washington, DC: American Psychological Association.

Valla, J.P., Bergeron, L., Breton, J.J., Gaudet, N., & Berthiaume, C. (1993). Informants, correlates and child disorders in a clinical population. *Canadian Journal of Psychiatry, 38,* 406–411.

van der Kolk, B.A. (1997). The complexity of adaptation to trauma: Self-regulation, stimulus, discrimination, and characterological development. In B.A. van der Kolk, A.C. McFarlane, & L. Weisaeth (Eds.), *Traumatic stress: The effects of overwhelming experience on mind, body, and society* (pp. 182–213). New York: Guilford Press.

Vernberg, E.M. (1998). Developmentally based psychotherapies: Comments and observations. *Journal of Clinical Child Psychology, 27,* 46–48.

Vernberg, E.M., La Greca, A.M., Silverman, W.K., & Prinstein, M.J. (1996). Prediction of posttraumatic stress symptoms in children after Hurricane Andrew. *Journal of Abnormal Psychology, 105,* 237–248.

Vernberg, E.M., Routh, D., & Koocher, G. (1992). The future of psychotherapy with children. *Psychotherapy, 29,* 72–80.

Walco, G.A., Sterling, C.M., Conte, P.M., & Engel, R.G. (1999). Empirically supported treatments in pediatric psychology: Disease-related pain. *Journal of Pediatric Psychology, 24,* 115–167.

Weisz, J.R., Donenberg, G.R., Han, S.S., & Weiss, B. (1995). Bridging the gap between laboratory and clinic in child and adolescent psychotherapy. *Journal of Consulting and Clinical Psychology, 63,* 688–701.

Weisz, J.R., Suwanlert, S., Chaiyasit, W., Weiss, B., & Walter, B.R. (1987). Over and undercontrolled referral problems among children and adolescents from Thailand and the United States: The wat and wai of cultural differences. *Journal of Consulting and Clinical Psychology, 55,* 719–726.

Weisz. J.R., & Weiss, B. (1993). *Effects of psychotherapy with children and adolescents.* Newbury Park, CA: Sage.

Weisz, J.R., Weiss, B., Alicke, M.D., & Klotz, M.L. (1987). Effectiveness of psychotherapy with children and adolescents: A meta-analysis for clinicians. *Journal of Consulting and Clinical Psychology, 55,* 542–549.

Weisz, J.R., Weiss, B., Han, S.S., Granger, D.A., & Morton, T. (1995). Effects of psychotherapy with children and adolescents revisited: A meta-analysis of treatment outcome studies. *Psychological Bulletin, 117,* 450–468.

Willett, J.B., Singer, J.D., & Martin, N.C. (1998). The design and analysis of longitudinal studies of development and psychopathology in context: Statistical models and methodological recommendations. *Development and Psychopathology, 10,* 395–426.

CHAPTER 4

Poverty and the Well-Being of Children and Families

JUDITH A. CHAFEL AND KATHRYN GOLD HADLEY

Despite its genesis as a nation of equal opportunity for all, the United States has become an economically stratified society. U.S. Census Bureau data indicate that the nation has witnessed a long-term trend toward increased income inequality. A comparison of the years 1976 and 1996 shows an increasing share of aggregate wealth possessed by the highest income quintile and a declining share by the lowest (most recent figures; "Money income," 1996). Inclusion of this chapter in the third edition of the *Handbook of Clinical Child Psychology* acknowledges the economic disparity that exists in our society and the consequences of that disparity for a sizable proportion of our nation's children. Today, millions of American children and their families are living in poverty, and the problem is a serious one for our society.

The discussion opens with a definition of poverty, reports on current trends, and highlights some of the more important factors explaining economic want. After briefly considering the stresses on children and families posed by disadvantage, the next section reviews recent research on the health risks, psychosocial risks, and cognitive risks of poverty for children, and ruminates about the concept of risk as a social construction. The third section of the chapter briefly looks at factors and processes within and outside the child that enable

some children in poverty to be more resilient than others, and considers the implications for clinical practice. The final section briefly describes additional ways that the stress associated with poverty may be reduced. The chapter concludes with a number of directions for future inquiry.

DEFINITIONS, TRENDS, AND CAUSES

Although poverty may be defined in a variety of ways (see, e.g., the *Journal of Poverty: Innovations on Social, Political & Economic Inequalities*), this introductory section draws on the official federal government definition because it constitutes the most widely used criterion. The federal government considers a family poor if its pretax cash income falls below a certain standard of need known as "the poverty line" (*Economic Report of the President*, 1998). The threshold is based on the minimal amount of money needed to maintain a nutritionally adequate diet, varies by family size and composition, and is adjusted annually for inflation (Lamison-White, 1997). To illustrate with two examples, the poverty line in 1996 for a family comprising one adult and two children stood at $12,641; for a family of two adults and two children at $15,911 (most recent figures; Lamison-White, 1997). By comparison, the median income for all U.S. families was $40, 611 in 1995 (most recent figure; U.S. Bureau of the Census, 1997b).

There has been considerable discussion in recent years about how accurately and reliably the official measure of poverty identifies poor people (Blank, 1997; Duncan & Brooks-Gunn, 1997; Scarbrough, 1993). The issue is more than academic because the way poverty is defined determines a family's poverty status, its eligibility for assistance, and consequently, its well-being. A 1995 report by the National Research Council (NRC) recommended a number of revisions to address limitations of the current measure (*Economic Report of the President*, 1998). The report suggested expanding the definition of income to include certain benefits (e.g., food stamps, housing subsidies, the Earned Income Tax Credit) that enhance a family's ability to meet its basic consumption needs, and subtracting certain necessary expenditures (e.g., taxes, child support payments, child care expenses) that diminish it. Adding benefits to the calculation of income would lower the poverty count among those receiving substantial noncash assistance, and subtracting taxes and work-related expenses would raise it among low-income working families (Blank, 1997).

The NRC also recommended other changes to more accurately reflect a family's income requirements: (1) basing the measure of consumption used to derive poverty thresholds on clothing and shelter as well as food; (2) taking account of regional variations in housing costs; (3) adjusting the thresholds for family size in a more consistent way; and (4) updating the thresholds to reflect changes in spending patterns over time (*Economic Report of the President*, 1998). The official measure of poverty is limited in still other ways: it neither distinguishes degrees of poverty nor measures its duration (Scarbrough, 1993).

Over the past several decades, the official poverty rate for children (proportion of those poor) has fluctuated, declining sharply between 1960 and 1969, and trending upward between 1969 and 1993, although it has remained near or slightly above 20% since 1981 (*Economic Report of the President*, 1998; Federal Interagency Forum on Child and Family Statistics, 1997). In 1996, the most recent year for which estimates are available, the federal government counted 20.5% of the nations's children poor: 18.3% of all those 6 to 17 years of age, and 22.7% of

all those under 6 years of age. In 1996, 16.3% of all White children were living in poverty, 39.9% of all Black children, and 40.3% of all Hispanic children (*Economic Report of the President*, 1998). The higher proportions of minority children living in poverty indicate that they are more likely than White children to be counted among the poor, although the total number of poor White children is actually higher because there are more White children in our society (Lamison-White, 1997). Though they comprise only about 25% of the total population, children represent a disproportionate share of the nation's impoverished: 40%, with those under age 6 especially vulnerable (Lamison-White, 1997). According to some estimates, economic vulnerability is a condition confronting about half of all U.S. children at least once during their childhood (Duncan & Rodgers, 1988).

Certain dynamics profoundly affecting life circumstances are not reflected in the official government definition of poverty: the extent to which a family's income falls below (or above) the poverty line, and the length of time lived in poverty. In 1996, when 20.5% of all children were officially classified as poor, 43.2% of all children were living either *in poverty or near poverty*, which is defined by the federal government as family income less than twice the poverty line. In that same year, 9% of all children were living *in extreme poverty*, which is defined as family income less than half the poverty line (*Economic Report of the President*, 1998). The figures just cited indicate that the number of children counted as poor depends on the way poverty is determined; that is, poverty is a social construction. Although most of the nation's total poverty population do not remain poor for very long, a substantial minority are impoverished for extremely long periods of time (Blank, 1997). In 1992 and 1993, children were far less likely than nonelderly adults (18 to 64 years of age) to exit out of poverty: 8.3% of children as compared to 3.2% of nonelderly adults were chronically poor in all 24 months of the two years. Children constituted a large proportion of the chronically poor in these years: 47.6%. Black and Hispanic children are far more likely than White children to be poor for extended periods (Duncan & Brooks-Gunn, 1997). From 1992 through early 1994, the median duration of a poverty spell for children lasted 5.2 months (Eller, 1996).

Dynamics such as these are important to consider because of the effect on child development.

Developmental risks for children have been associated with the *degree* to which a family is economically disadvantaged, the *length* of time the deprivation endures, and the *developmental timing* (Baydar, Brooks-Gunn, & Furstenberg, 1993; Duncan & Brooks-Gunn, 1997; Duncan, Brooks-Gunn, & Klebanov, 1994; McLeod & Shanahan, 1996; Steinberg, Catalano, & Dooley, 1981). Intuition, theory, and research all suggest that an infant born into extreme poverty and remaining impoverished for a decade or more of life and an adolescent living at the poverty margin for a single year are not equally disadvantaged, although economic deprivation may have serious consequences for both. The deepest poverty and its most sustained effects often occur among the long-term poor (Blank, 1997). The problem is particularly worrisome for children because of poverty's potential to thwart development.

Before proceeding to the major focus of the chapter, poverty and its relation to child development, an important question to ponder, even briefly, is: Why are so many children and families in our society today poor? The answer to this question is neither simple nor straightforward because poverty results from many interrelated, complex causes (Bianchi, 1993). Space constraints make it impossible to give this complex issue the attention that it deserves. The brief discussion presented here highlights a few of the more important factors explaining poverty: (1) macroeconomic and labor market conditions, (2) changes in family structure, and (3) the extent of government assistance. Readers are referred elsewhere for a more extensive discussion of these and other related issues (see, e.g., Bianchi, 1993; Blank, 1997; Center on Budget and Policy Priorities, 1998; Chase-Lansdale & Brooks-Gunn, 1995; Devine & Wright, 1993; Fitzgerald, Lester, & Zuckerman, 1995; Haveman & Wolfe, 1994; Weinberg, 1996).

THE ECONOMY

Children are poor because they live in families whose income does not provide adequately for the basic necessities of life (Bianchi, 1993). Macroeconomic and labor market conditions influence family income by determining the quantity and quality of jobs available (*Economic Report of the President*, 1998). Historically, the poverty rate has fluctuated with the overall performance of the nation's economy,

but over the past 15 years or so, a more complicated picture has emerged (Bianchi, 1993; Blank, 1997). Today, the connection between the two is mediated by an increasingly complex set of factors: (1) a decline in earnings of less-skilled, less-educated workers relative to more-skilled, more highly-educated workers; (2) a shift in employment away from goods-producing industries toward professional and business services; (3) a shift in employment toward low-wage jobs; (4) the relocation of production jobs overseas; (5) a globalization of trade; (6) an erosion in the real value of the minimum wage; (7) a decline in labor unions, and other factors (Bianchi, 1993; Blank, 1997; Weinberg, 1996). Although a shrinking economy still elevates the poverty rate, an expanding one no longer brings about its decline, although the reasons why are not completely understood (Bianchi, 1993; Blank, 1997). The trend is expected to continue for the foreseeable future (Blank, 1997). Based on the most recent poverty thresholds, full-time, year-round work at a minimum-wage job (hypothetically, 40 hours a week for 52 weeks a year at $5.15 per hour) does not in itself result in income above the poverty line for a family comprising at least one adult and one child (1996 figure; Lamison-White, 1997). The federal Earned Income Tax Credit (EITC) would raise that family's income above the poverty line. The EITC operates like a negative income tax and provides supplemental income to low-wage workers. During the mid-1990s, 65% of poor families with children in which the parents were not elderly or disabled were employed either full or part time, a figure that belies a commonly held assumption that people are poor because of a lack of work effort (Lazere, 1997).

FAMILY STRUCTURE

Over the past several decades, an increase in single-parent families has significantly affected the well-being of children. Increasing proportions of children live with a never-married mother, one who is divorced, or one who is married but not currently living with a husband. Whereas about 8% of all children lived with only their mother in 1960, the number escalated to 24% in 1996, a threefold increase (*Economic Report of the President*, 1998; Federal Interagency Forum on Child and Family Statistics, 1997). In 1996, the poverty rate of children living in female-headed households (49.3%) was nearly five times greater than the poverty rate of those living in married-couple households (10.1%) (*Economic Report of the President*, 1998). The poverty rate of those under 6 years of age was even higher: 58.8% for those in mother-only families, contrasted with 11.5% for those in married-couple families (Lamison-White, 1997). Children living with a mother only are also more likely to be living in deeper poverty and to be among the long-term poor (Blank, 1997; *Economic Report of the President*, 1998; Eller, 1996). The higher poverty risk of female-headed households stems from the fact that most single mothers are not recipients of child support and must get by on a single source of income, and women typically earn less than men (*Economic Report of the President*, 1998). Never-married mothers are at an even greater disadvantage economically than divorced mothers because unmarried childbearing frequently occurs before the completion of schooling, an important indicator of job skill (Hofferth & Moore, cited by Bianchi, 1993). A substantial proportion, 24.1%, of the nation's householders 25 years old and older lacking a high school diploma live in poverty (1995 figure; U.S. Bureau of the Census, 1997b).

Extent of Government Assistance

The Center on Budget and Policy Priorities (CBPP, 1998), a nonpartisan research organization and policy institute, recently examined the effect of government programs on the child poverty rate over time using data collected by the U.S. Census Bureau. For the analysis, the CBPP used two measures of poverty that differ from the official federal government definition: the poverty rate *before* receipt of government benefits and the poverty rate *after* receipt of government benefits. Employing these definitions, the study found that in 1989, government programs reduced the child poverty rate by 4.8% (from 22.8% to 18%), whereas in 1996 they lowered it by 7.5% (from 23.6% to 16.1%). The report attributed the change to increases in a number of government benefit programs. The poverty rate after receipt of government benefits remained nearly the same between 1995 and 1996, a finding that reversed a decade-long pattern of growth in the safety net in reducing child poverty. The decline reflected the participation of fewer children in cash assistance (Aid to Families with Dependent Children [AFDC]) and food stamp programs, and was offset by an expansion of the EITC (Earned Income Tax Credit). The smaller number of children receiving benefits resulted from state welfare reform initiatives that reduced caseloads. Welfare reform enacted by the federal government in 1996 did not represent a major factor in the decline because few of its provisions (e.g., work requirements, time limits on cash assistance, measures to enforce child support) were in effect. As welfare reform proceeds, a continued decline in the number of children eligible for government benefits should further erode the effectiveness of the safety net in reducing the child poverty rate (Center on Budget and Policy Priorities, 1998). Substantial research supports the conclusion that when AFDC recipients lose cash assistance, their total family income is lower after the loss of benefits than before, even though former recipients may be employed full time (Blank, 1997).

Other data provided by the U.S. Department of Health and Human Services (undated) provide more of a historical perspective on the extent to which government assistance plays a role in reducing the poverty rate among children. One reason the rate of reduction is much larger than the figures just cited is that the report examined the effect of a broader array of programs (namely, the federal system of cash and near-cash transfers). In 1979, these transfers reduced poverty among persons in families with related children under age 18 by 37%, in 1983 by 19.1%, in 1989 by 23.9%, in 1993 by 26.5%, and in 1994 by 32.6%. The point that merits emphasis is that governmental assistance substantially affects the child poverty rate, and the effect has varied significantly over time.

Summary

The federal government carefully counts the poor, but the definition used to compile the data may not accurately and reliably identify the economically disadvantaged. Nevertheless, official reports do show that a large proportion of children in our society are residing in families whose income does not provide adequately for the basic necessities of life. The high child poverty rate in the United States is expected to continue for the foreseeable future. The structure of the economy, single parenthood, and recent policy developments support that conclusion (Garbarino, 1990). Demographic data also indicate that the poverty population is characterized by great diversity. That diversity contradicts stereotypical thinking about the poor, for example, that poverty results from a lack of work effort (Chafel, 1993). As a result of economic hardship, millions of our young are growing up in less than optimal environments with adverse consequences for their development.

POVERTY AND CHILD DEVELOPMENT

In what is now widely regarded as a seminal formulation, Bronfenbrenner (1979) proposed that human development never evolves in isolation, but in interaction with an ecological environment that encompasses several interconnected systems: microsystems (the immediate setting of the developing person), mesosystems (linkages among settings where the person actually participates), exosystems (linkages among settings that a person may never enter, but where events happen that affect the person's immediate environment), and macrosystems (generalized patterns of social institutions characteristic of a particular culture or subculture). Most children's ecologies include, for example, family, friends, and school (microsystems), processes involving home and school (mesosystems), connections between the parental workplace and the home (exosystems), and customs, belief systems, and lifestyles (macrosystems). At the time, Bronfenbrenner's theory of environmental interconnections presented a novel way to analyze the impact of various spheres of activity that affect human growth and development. Today, it is accepted as a given, and serves as a cogent reminder that the child of poverty can be understood only in the context of his or her surroundings. When attempting to understand developmental problems and social pathologies, one must look both to the individual as a biological organism and beyond to the wider ecologies surrounding the child (Garbarino, 1990).

For children and families in poverty, these ecologies can be fraught with stress. Poverty has been characterized as "a pervasive rather than bounded crisis distinguished by a high contagion of stressors that grind away and deplete emotional reserves" (McLoyd & Wilson, 1991, p. 105). Research has sought to identify the stressors that affect the poor. Not surprisingly, a report issued by the federal government found that those with family income below

the poverty line and those receiving AFDC scored very low on many measures of material well-being (Short & Shea, 1995). The poor were significantly worse off than the nonpoor, and those on AFDC more so than the income poor. By comparison with their more advantaged peers, the poor were more likely to live in unsafe neighborhoods and to express dissatisfaction with their communities. In addition, they were less likely to be able to meet their rent or mortgage payments, to seek needed medical attention, and to pay their utility bills. They were more likely to have their telephone disconnected, to go without food, or not have enough money to buy food. Other research by Cook and Fine (1995) documents the stress experienced by a single-parent, or working-poor mother trying to juggle conflicting responsibilities. In the woman's own voice:

> I'm a single parent, I'm working, I'm raising my own kids, now I'm taking on somebody else's kid. . . . My father's dying. And I'm just not going to sit idly by, be in school, work, and raise kids and not visit my father sometimes. . . . And my time is very limited. . . I have to be on my job by 1:30. Then I won't see any of my children anymore, which I don't see any of my children during the day at all, anyway. I took on a night job to make ends meet. Now Social Services is telling me now that I've taken on this gig, I have to give up my night job. . . . In order to be with him [the baby] because he needs the time (p. 128).

Some have suggested that rural families may face even greater challenges than urban families in overcoming the environmental obstacles posed by poverty and economic stress. Urban settings may provide greater access to facilities, health care resources, and other services that may not be available to rural families (Orthner, 1986). The sizable proportion of poor children and families living in rural areas and the lack of resources available to them suggest that this group is particularly needy. In recent years, a focus on the urban poor has shifted attention away from the rural poor and may have resulted in an urban bias (Bianchi, 1993; Tarnowski & Rohrbeck, 1993). Given the points just made, the perspective needs to be corrected. Nevertheless, regardless of geographic locale, poverty is a stressor that taxes the coping resources of children and families (Garbarino, 1990).

Poverty is widely acknowledged to be a risk factor with the potential for bringing about adverse consequences (Huston, McLoyd, & Coll, 1994a;

Routh, 1994a). Broadly defined, the concept of risk refers to those "biological and environmental conditions that increase the likelihood of negative developmental outcomes" (Liaw & Brooks-Gunn, 1994, p. 360). Not only is poverty itself a risk factor, but it is associated with numerous other risk factors, including low birthweight, single parenthood, unemployment, unsafe neighborhoods, maternal depression, low social support, welfare dependence, and stressful life events (Huston et al., 1994a; Routh, 1994a). A number of statements can be made about risk factors generally: (1) those who experience them are more likely than those who do not to be affected by negative outcomes; (2) negative outcomes are more likely to result from more rather than fewer risk factors; (3) negative outcomes may be associated with some risk factors more than others; (4) certain combinations of risk factors may bring about certain outcomes; (5) risk factors interact; and (6) the effects of risk factors are cumulative (Brooks-Gunn, Klebanov, & Liaw, 1995; Liaw & Brooks-Gunn, 1994; Rutter, 1979; Sameroff, Barocas, & Seifer, 1984; Sameroff & Seifer, 1990; Sameroff, Seifer, Baldwin, & Baldwin, 1993; Sameroff, Seifer, & Zax, 1982; Schorr & Schorr, 1988; U.S. Bureau of the Census, 1997a; Werner, Bierman, & French, 1971). Research also suggests that risk is not transmitted in a linear or specific fashion (e.g., maternal depression may be linked not only with depression in offspring [a linear model], but also with other less specific outcomes) (Zeanah, Boris, & Larrieu, 1997). As a risk factor, poverty may be so devastating that its effect may impact a child over and above the presence of multiple other risk factors (Huston, 1991; Liaw & Brooks-Gunn, 1994). Research is beginning to illuminate complex and evolving interrelationships among risk factors (Zeanah et al., 1997), but more information is needed about many aspects of risk.

As Schorr and Schorr (1988) cogently put it, "An understanding of risk factors does not lead to reliable predictions about individuals or single events, but does lead to accurate assessments of probabilities" (p. 4). A single risk factor may not be particularly devastating for a child, but the presence of multiple interacting factors does present that child with substantial threat (Schorr & Schorr, 1988). For example, a constitutionally vulnerable child (e.g., a malnourished preschooler suffering from asthma) interacting with an unsupportive environment (e.g., an abusive family situation) is susceptible to

lasting harm. Knowing about risk factors can be very useful in determining intervention strategies. For example, being aware that poor families are likely to experience multiple risks may help in interventions aimed at reducing the number of risks a family experiences as well as recognizing that multiple risks require multiple interventions (M. Hanson & Carta, 1995; Liaw & Brooks-Gunn, 1994; Schorr & Schorr, 1988).

The next several sections review research findings on the health risks, psychosocial risks, and cognitive risks of poverty for children. The effects of poverty on various developmental outcomes are well-known; not so widely recognized are the pathways through which poverty influences these outcomes. The section on psychosocial risks has been framed to consider the processes by which the effects of poverty come about for two reasons: (1) this is the direction that research seems to be turning, and (2) it has the most direct implications for clinical intervention. By comparison, health and cognition are dealt with only briefly, and so these sections focus solely on the correlates of poverty. The studies cited in all three sections have been largely limited to ones utilizing U.S. children as subjects and published within the past five years. The review does not deal with special populations, such as homeless children, abused and neglected children, or teen pregnancy and parenting, because of space constraints as well as the fact that excellent reviews on these topics are available elsewhere (see, e.g., Belsky, 1993; Coley & Chase-Lansdale, 1998; Jencks, 1994).

THE HEALTH RISKS OF POVERTY FOR CHILDREN

Living in poverty places children of all ages at risk for developing health problems. Beginning at the moment of conception and continuing through childhood, impoverished children face more health risks and experience more health problems than do their more economically advantaged peers. Indeed, the health status of an impoverished child is important to consider as it lays a foundation for problems with physical, cognitive, and psychosocial development across childhood. This section examines the physical health of children living in poverty. Drawing on findings from a wide range of research studies, most published within the past five years, we consider the incidence of poor health arising from both internal (physiological) and external (environmental) influences, describe factors and conditions that may account for children's poor health, and outline the developmental implications that may result.

Some poor children do not even survive their first year of life; in fact, infant mortality rates among poor families are 60% higher than those of nonpoor families (Federman et al., 1996). Poor infants who do survive the first year of life face a host of health risks, especially if they are born prematurely and/or are underweight. Not surprisingly, low-income mothers are more likely to give birth to preterm (gestation less than 37 weeks) and low birthweight (less than 2500g) babies (Federman et al., 1996). The mother's lack of adequate prenatal medical care and nutrition contributes to the incidence of low birthweight and infant mortality in poor families (Klerman, 1991). Almost half of poor single mothers reported that they did not receive medical care during the first trimester (Federman et al., 1996). The nutritional habits of the pregnant mother are also important to the unborn child. Indeed, low-income mothers who received nutritional supplements through the Special Supplemental Food Program for Women, Infants, and Children (WIC) during pregnancy reduced the rate of low birthweight infants by 25% (Avruch & Cackley, 1995). In short, a poor child who is born prematurely and underweight faces "a very poor prognosis of functioning within normal ranges in all domains of development" (Bradley et al., 1994, p. 425). Specifically, low birthweight babies may suffer from neurological deficits (Breslau et al., 1994) and exhibit greater classroom behavior problems in school (Klebanov, Brooks-Gunn, & McCormick, 1994).

Children living in poverty are also at greater risk of acquiring and then suffering from infectious diseases. Although they may not die from polio, diphtheria, or tetanus, these preventable diseases can lead to irreversible brain damage that affects cognitive and sensorimotor development (Oberg, Bryant, & Bach, 1995). Children living in poverty also face a higher incidence of some visual, hearing, and dental health problems. In fact, it is poor children who are most likely to have serious, uncorrected vision problems (Schorr & Schorr, 1988). Hearing loss or difficulties may also plague children living in poverty. During the first few years of life, middle ear infections are common for all children, but the

risk is higher in disadvantaged children (Schorr & Schorr, 1988). Additionally, children from impoverished families experience higher levels of dental disease (Call, 1989).

Lack of or inadequate primary medical care as well as lower immunization rates may explain why both the risk of infectious disease and complications resulting from more common medical problems are more prevalent for economically deprived children. Once children are born into poverty, they are less likely to have access to the usual sources of care, are more likely to use neighborhood and community clinics to receive care, and are more likely to wait longer to receive that care (Newacheck, Hughes, & Stoddard, 1996). Also, poor children are about 50% more likely to go without treatment for common but significant health problems than children not living in poverty (Newacheck et al., 1996), and they receive immunizations at rates 10 percentage points lower than their nonpoor peers (Center for Disease Control and Prevention, 1997). Finally, poor children may fail to receive adequate care as a result of inferior or nonexistent insurance coverage as well. About 20% of children living in poverty are not covered by any health insurance at all compared to about 12% of children not living in poverty. Of those poor children covered, most received Medicaid, as opposed to the vast majority of nonpoor children who received coverage through private insurance (Moffitt & Slade, 1997; Snyder & Shafer, 1996).

When considering the developmental detriments that can result from poor health, one can see what an important role consistent primary medical care has in mitigating negative effects. Relatively minor problems such as an ear infection or mild vision impairment, left untreated, may create lasting and profound problems. School-age children may suffer from developmental delays as a result of early, untreated visual and hearing problems. Impaired sight may diminish the child's ability to process visual stimuli and may hinder participation in classroom activities (Schorr & Schorr, 1988). A hearing impairment may also hinder the child's ability to participate in all aspects of academic life, especially because the impairment may render the child unable to process sounds and result in delayed language development (Schorr & Schorr, 1988). Not surprisingly, impaired sight and loss of hearing may manifest themselves as behavior problems or result in poor school performance.

Poor nutrition is another health problem facing children living in poverty. Although severe malnutrition is often associated with developing countries, milder forms are more common in developed nations such as the United States (Brown & Pollitt, 1996). The effects of poor nutrition are lasting, especially when present in very young children. Proper brain development may be hindered, and cognitive deficits ranging from moderate delays to mental retardation may occur (Shirley, 1991). Iron deficiency anemia is another condition that results from poor nutrition and contributes to problems such as shortened attention span, fatigue, and diminished concentration (Oberg et al., 1995). As a result, children who suffer from inadequate nutrition early in life may have trouble in school later.

Economically disadvantaged children who live in low-income areas are at greater risk of exposure to dangerous environmental hazards in the form of lead poisoning and air pollution. Children in communities with large numbers of young children living in poverty (more than 20%) have lead poisoning rates almost nine times higher than those in communities where child poverty rates fall below 5% (Sargent et al., 1995). In addition, low-income people, including children, are also at greater risk of exposure to environmental hazards such as air pollution and toxic waste (Olden, 1996).

Simply put, economically disadvantaged families lack the resources to move away from dangerous areas and out of run-down housing; therefore, children are exposed to environmental dangers on a daily basis. While researchers still work to identify the consequences of long-term exposure to airborne toxins on the health of low-income families (Olden, 1996), we do know what may result after exposure to and ingestion of lead paint. Lead poisoning can lead to verbal, perceptual, motor, and behavior problems, in addition to problems with maintaining focus and attention. All of these problems could place the impoverished child at a developmental disadvantage and thereby lead to diminished school performance (Schorr & Schorr, 1988).

Limited financial resources also inhibit many impoverished families from escaping crime-ridden areas, leaving children exposed to violence and at risk of falling victim to it (Sheehan, DiCara, LeBailly, & Christoffel, 1997). Despite the greater exposure to physical violence, physical injuries are not reported at higher rates among the poor. Reduced access to medical care may decrease the numbers who seek help and thus report their injuries, and those in poverty with a serious injury may be more likely to die from it as well (Kelly & Miles-Doan, 1997).

SUMMARY

Living in poverty limits children's access to adequate health care, insurance coverage, proper nutrition, and safe living environments. The health problems that arise and persist as a result of these conditions often plague children living in poverty throughout their lives. Not only do they cause suffering at the time of the specific illness or onset of the condition, but these health problems may also continue to play an insidious and detrimental role in children's physical, cognitive, and psychosocial development throughout childhood.

THE PSYCHOSOCIAL RISKS OF POVERTY FOR CHILDREN

Unquestionably, poverty affects mental health. The relationship between the two has been referred to as "one of the most well established in all of psychiatric epidemiology" (Belle, 1990, p. 385). Not so well-known are the mechanisms through which these effects come about, and it is these mediating processes that have the most direct implications for clinical intervention. This section focuses on a small collection of studies that seek to illuminate these pathways. Findings from 16 studies are reviewed: 10 with community-level samples, and 6 with nationally-drawn samples. Most focused on White and African-American subjects, a few on Hispanic, and only one included American Indians. Other minorities are noticeably absent. The studies have looked at outcomes for children of a wide variety of ages (from 4 to 22 years), using longitudinal or cross-sectional designs. They have operationalized poverty in different ways: in terms of household income, per capita income, debts, receipt of free or reduced-price school lunch, socioeconomic status, or by means of subjective measures (perceived adequacy of financial resources). Few have considered poverty over time, and none has considered the degree to which subjects were disadvantaged or the developmental timing of the effects of poverty. Most have examined mediating pathways at the level of Bronfenbrenner's microsystem—that is, family processes operating in the child's immediate home environment—although a couple have researched broader neighborhood effects at the level of the macrosystem. The studies have attempted to link these mediating processes with outcomes that are internalizing or externalizing in nature, that is, internal feeling states or outward behaviors. The rather dense discussion that follows reflects the complicated pattern of relationships that researchers have sought to examine in their inquiries.

Although factors from all levels of the economically disadvantaged child's ecological environment affect psychosocial well-being, it is Bronfenbrenner's microsystem-level factors, specifically parenting practices, that are the most well-documented mediators through which poverty impacts children's internalizing and externalizing outcomes. These parenting practices include emotional involvement, behavioral involvement, and use of punishment. Two studies also attempt to identify macrosystem-level factors, neighborhood-level characteristics that affect the economically disadvantaged child's mental health. In general, most studies reviewed here investigate *proximal* mental health outcomes for children by identifying a *single* parenting practice or neighborhood-level factor through which socioeconomic disadvantage influences children's mental health. In addition, a small group of studies highlights more *distal* mental health outcomes for children by uncovering the *multiple,* interlinking pathways between poverty and a host of family-level factors. These include parenting practices as well as parental affect, children's perceptions of their family relationships, and youth self-regulatory competence. Regardless of whether researchers examine poverty's influence through single or multiple mediating pathways, its negative effects on children's mental health remain.

SINGLE MEDIATORS AND PROXIMAL OUTCOMES

Emotional Involvement

The emotional relationship between parent and child is one family process through which poverty impacts a child's affective states as well as behavioral outcomes. In a study using a sample of families with preadolescent children in Iowa (sixth- and eighth-graders) of unspecified race/ethnicity, economic hardship diminished the child's perception

of the quality of the parent-child relationship, which in turn was linked to lower self-esteem (Ho, Lempers, & Clark-Lempers, 1995). The authors concluded that the parent-adolescent relationship suffers in impoverished circumstances and that this diminished emotional connection contributed to reduced feelings of self-worth in the child.

Poverty's influence on the emotional relationship between parent and child also impacts externalizing outcomes. Sampson and Laub (1994) found that living in poverty as well as troublesome early childhood behavior together contributed to a weakened emotional bond between parent and child that was mutually perceived by both. Independent of child disposition, family poverty continued to exert significant and relatively large effects on parent-child attachment. In other words, economic hardship weakened the parent-child attachment and increased the incidence of delinquency in 10- to 17-year-old White boys from Boston. Despite the fact the researchers found that the child's early behavior affected the parenting practice of interest, poverty still played the stronger albeit indirect role in the behavioral outcomes for these boys through a weakened parent-child bond.

In one study by McLeod and Shanahan (1993), mothers' emotional involvement with their children did not mediate the effect of poverty on children's mental health. In a national sample of 4- to 8-year-old White, African-American, and Hispanic children and their mothers, the presence of current poverty (but not persistent poverty) related to a decrease in the emotional responsiveness of the mothers (as measured by the interviewer's perception of the mother's reactions to her child during the child's assessment interview). This finding did not vary by race/ethnicity. Contrary to the researchers' expectations, however, the decrease in emotional responsiveness did not produce significant effects on the internalizing (e.g., anxiety) and externalizing (e.g., antisocial behavior) mental health outcomes for children. We speculate that the reliance on the interviewer's perception of emotional involvement obtained during a brief observation period as the mode of measurement may have contributed to this contradictory finding. Neither the child nor the parent had input into the measure of mothers' emotional responsiveness as they did in the studies where mothers' emotional involvement was found to mediate the effects of poverty on the child's mental health.

In their study of a national sample of White and non-White high school- and college-age children living in a two-parent family, Harris and Marmer (1996) sought to uncover the relatively unexamined effect of the father's emotional involvement on the child's mental health in five groups of families: never poor, temporarily poor, persistently poor, never received welfare, and received welfare. They examined the emotional relationship between the child and both mother and father as buffers against the negative effects of poverty. They found that fathers' involvement did protect the child from some adverse outcomes. The fathers' close emotional relationship with the child reduced the likelihood of delinquent behavior more so among children in *persistently poor* families than for children in the other four groups examined. Mothers' emotional involvement reduced the delinquency outcomes only in *never poor* families. In contrast, fathers' emotional involvement buffered against depression for children who were *temporarily poor, never poor,* or *never received welfare.* Mothers' emotional involvement did not buffer against the effects of depression in any of the groups.

Behavioral Involvement

Parents' behavioral involvement in their child's life also serves as a pathway through which poverty influences children's development in terms of internalizing and externalizing outcomes. Harris and Marmer (1996) examined behavioral involvement on the part of both parents and found that persistently poor parents and parents who received welfare were less likely to participate in joint activities and engage in active, supportive communication with their children than were parents who experienced temporary poverty, no poverty, or never received welfare. Indeed, only the behavioral involvement of mothers who received welfare mediated the effects of poverty on their high school-through college-age children by reducing depressive symptoms as well as delinquency. The behavioral involvement of fathers in all five types of families had no effect on these outcomes.

A mother's role in another dimension of behavioral involvement, a child's schooling, also mediates the effects of poverty on child outcomes. Economic hardship led to a drop in the mother's involvement in her child's schooling (as assessed by the teacher), which in turn led to a drop in both White and African-American preadolescent (fifth–seventh grade) students' self-esteem in a study by Bolger, Patterson, Thompson, and Kupersmidt (1995). The drop in maternal participation, however, had no effect on children's feelings of shyness or anxiety. In the same study, a mother's decreased school involvement also increased the child's aggressiveness and acting-out behaviors. We can see, then, that a mother's weakened connection to the child's school activities due to economic hardship may lead to negative outcomes for her children.

Finally, Sampson and Laub (1994) found that living in poverty as well as troublesome early childhood behavior (such as violent temper tantrums) reduced effective monitoring. Monitoring was operationalized as mother's supervision of the 10- to 17-year-old White boys' behavior in the home as well as the neighborhood. After controlling for children's early problem behavior, however, the researchers found that poverty's effect on maternal supervision was no longer significant. In explaining this finding, the authors speculated that poverty may nevertheless play a role by increasing the child's early negative behavior, and this in turn may lead to the weakening of maternal supervision. So, they speculate that poverty may play a role in decreased maternal supervision but only as it is manifested through the child's early problem behaviors. The researchers did find that later in the child's life, weakened maternal monitoring increased the incidence of delinquency. Overall, their data confirm that poverty does affect boys' behavior through the mother's weakened monitoring role in the preteen and teenage years.

Punishment

Mothers' use of physical punishment is another family process through which poverty affects a child's mental health. Sampson and Laub (1994) found that living in poverty, as well as troublesome early childhood behavior, contributed to the increased use of erratic/punitive discipline toward 10- to 17-year-old White boys. Even when the child's early behavior was statistically controlled, family poverty still had a significant effect on the increased incidence of erratic and harsh discipline. The researchers also found that harsh punishment was linked with an increased incidence of delinquency. Although the child's early behavior affected parenting practices, poverty still played an indirect role in the behavior of these boys, a role mediated by erratic/harsh punishment.

Dodge, Pettit, and Bates (1994) examined the socialization practices of families with 5- to 9-year-old White and African-American children living in Tennessee and Indiana across five socioeconomic classes. The eight socialization practices were (1) maternal warmth, (2) the child's observation of violence both in and outside the home, (3) endorsement of aggressive values, (4) stressful life events, (5) social isolation and the lack of social support, (6) a stable peer group, (7) cognitive stimulation, and (8) harsh discipline. They found a significant negative correlation between the eight factors and socioeconomic status, and observed that the former variables significantly predicted both teacher-rated and peer-rated aggressive behaviors for children. For both the teacher- and peer-rated outcomes, the entire set of variables accounted for a significant portion of the variance, whereas harsh discipline provided the only unique contribution to these outcomes.

In a national sample of 4- to 8-year-old White, African-American, and Hispanic children and their mothers, currently poor mothers demonstrated more harsh or punitive behaviors than nonpoor mothers (McLeod & Shanahan, 1993). Harsh punishment was associated with higher levels of anxiety and depression in their children as well as more antisocial behavior and peer conflict than in children whose mothers spanked less often. The mediating relationship disappeared, however, when the effects of persistent poverty on mothers' punishing behaviors were considered. Using duration of poverty as a measure, the researchers found that persistently poor mothers actually spanked their children less often than other mothers, regardless of race. This finding held regardless of whether the family was currently poor, so the effects of long-term poverty on children's mental health cannot be explained via the mediator of mothers' harsh punishment in this study. This finding highlights the importance of considering the duration of poverty and its impact on the family processes through which children are affected by poverty.

Although research suggests that a mother's use of harsh discipline mediates the relationship between poverty and the child's mental health, we must also remember to consider two important issues: reciprocal effects and duration of poverty. Basing a study on the assumption that mothers' punishing behaviors result only *in* their child's antisocial behavior rather than result *from* it may mask

findings and thus fail to capture the complex relationship between a mother's use of punishment and child outcomes. In addition, failure to consider the effects of duration of poverty on punishing behavior may also result in a failure to capture the actual relationship among poverty, punishment, and outcomes for impoverished children (McLeod & Shanahan, 1993).

Before moving on to consider mediating processes that occur outside the family unit, it is important to note that not all researchers found that parenting practices mediate the effects of poverty on children's mental health. This is an important point to report and discuss briefly, as this finding contradicts the argument made earlier that parenting practices serve as pathways through which poverty affects children. Using data from a national sample of White and African-American families with children 5 to 18 years of age, Mosley and Thomson (1995) found that parental behaviors, as measured by frequency of shared activities between parents and children both inside and outside the home as well as the level of parental control and supervision maintained over the child, were not significantly affected by poverty. Indeed, parenting behaviors did affect child outcomes (e.g., high levels of parental control led to negative effects on boys' temperament), but these behaviors did not serve as mediators of poverty's effects. The crucial poverty–parenting practice link was not established by the data.

Using the same data set to explore the impact of parenting practices on children's mental health, T.L. Hanson, McLanahan, and Thomson (1997) also found that parenting was not strongly or consistently negatively affected by economic resources. The measure of parenting practices included those used in the study just cited as well as measures of praise and punishment of the child and parental aspirations for the child. Consistent with the findings reported by Mosley and Thomson (1995), the authors found that variations in parenting practices did not relate to poverty status, but parenting practices did significantly affect child outcomes. The failure to establish a link between economic status and parenting practices conflicts with findings from a host of other studies examined in this section (Bolger et al., 1995; Dodge et al., 1994; Harris & Marmer, 1996; Ho et al., 1995; McLeod & Shanahan, 1993; Sampson & Laub, 1994). However, this finding may be explained by the measure of income used as well as the discrepancy between timing of the measures; that is, income was reported for the previous year and parenting practices for the current year (T.L. Hanson et al., 1997).

Neighborhood-Level Factors

Two studies have attempted to identify macrolevel factors mediating the effects of poverty on child outcomes. McLeod and Edwards (1995) looked at how neighborhood characteristics affected a national sample of White, African-American, Hispanic, and American-Indian children over the age of 4. They found that for Hispanic children (but not for African Americans or Whites), being currently poor and living in areas with a high proportion of same-race residents provided a buffering effect such that Hispanic children exhibited lower levels of withdrawal, depression, and anxiety as well as reduced levels of disobedience and acting-out behaviors. However, the presence of other *low-income* same-race peers had a negative effect in that this neighborhood characteristic was linked to more externalizing problems for Hispanic children. In sum, peers of the same race provided support, but if those peers were also poor, they did not. For American-Indian children, the variables contributing to increased levels of internalizing and externalizing symptoms were being currently poor and living in an urban environment.

When the duration of poverty was considered (as opposed to currency of poverty), the change in mental health outcomes emerged only for Hispanic children. The authors found that persistent poverty rather than area of residence was linked to internalizing symptoms. Overall, this study indicates that neighborhood characteristics were linked with the mental health of Hispanic and American-Indian youth. As the authors noted, it is important to consider ethnic groups separately rather than combined into one non-White category because there appear to be some real outcome differences by ethnic group.

Elliot et al. (1996) also considered the impact of neighborhood disadvantage on children's mental health, and examined neighborhood organization as a mediating variable. Subjects were 10- to 16-year-old White, African-American, and Latino youth from Chicago and Denver. Using a multidimensional measure of neighborhood disadvantage (poverty, mobility, family structure, and ethnic diversity), the authors found that greater neighborhood disadvantage was linked with weaker neighborhood organization in two ways, through decreased social integration (e.g., less support received from neighbors) and weaker informal controls (e.g., less general respect for authority). The only aspect of neighborhood organization that served as a common mediating variable on *aggregated* rates of adolescent development was informal control. Higher levels of informal control predicted positive outcomes for youth with respect to prosocial competence (e.g., commitment to conventional activities) and having conventional friends, and they lowered the neighborhood rates of problem behavior (e.g., delinquency and drug use). The researchers also analyzed the effects of neighborhood organization on *individual*-level adolescent development but did not examine these with respect to mediating pathways. Although studies examining the impact of macrolevel factors on children's mental health are not as plentiful as those on family processes, findings cited here certainly suggest that neighborhood-level characteristics affect the impoverished child's mental health and point to the importance of considering these factors further in future research.

MULTIPLE MEDIATORS AND DISTAL OUTCOMES

Parental Affect and Family Processes

Family processes as well as parental affect mediated the impact of economic stress on negative mental health outcomes for a sample of White seventh-graders living in two-parent families in rural Iowa (Conger, Ge, Elder, Lorenz, & Simons, 1994). Parents who experienced more adverse economic conditions experienced greater economic pressure (e.g., feeling unable to make ends meet) compared to parents who did not experience adverse economic conditions. That economic pressure led to increased parental depression, which in turn led to marital conflict, and that in turn led to fathers' hostility toward the child. These processes were associated with a greater risk of internalizing and externalizing symptoms in children. In addition, parents who felt greater economic pressure experienced more conflicts with their children over money, but those disputes did not contribute *directly* to negative outcomes for youth. Instead, these disputes contributed *indirectly* to negative outcomes through their influence on increased parental hostility. In sum, adverse economic conditions had a negative impact on mental health outcomes for children in this study.

Using the same data from the previous study, Conger, Conger, and Elder (1997) found that economic hardship (measured by income-to-needs ratio) was significantly related to feelings of economic pressure in White families from rural Iowa. As economic pressure increased, so did financial conflicts between parents. As predicted, increased financial conflicts threatened the mental health of boys as manifested by a drop in self-confidence, but this was not the case for girls. The authors also considered the link between financial conflict and parenting practices. In contrast to other studies, a significant link was not found between parents' financial conflicts and harsher parenting practices. The authors suggest that their narrowly defined measure of marital conflict (based solely on finances) may explain this finding. A more inclusive measure of marital dispute (i.e., a general measure of hostility and negativism between parents) used in the previously cited study did predict harsher parenting. In sum, parental responses to economic pressure mediated the effects of economic hardship on boys' outcomes but not girls' in this study.

In a study using a national sample of White and African-American mothers and their children over 6 years of age, McLeod, Kruttschnitt, and Dornfeld (1994) examined the relationships among poverty, maternal distress, parenting practices, and mental health outcomes for children. The authors found that poor mothers experienced greater maternal distress (as measured by the mother's alcohol use) than nonpoor mothers, regardless of race. The increase in maternal distress, however, did not explain differences in parenting practices across income levels. In addition, poverty did not have a significant impact on maternal affection or spanking. Poverty played neither a direct nor an indirect role in these two parenting practices. The authors noted that their measurement of maternal distress, which used a behavioral indicator of alcohol use rather than an affective indicator such as depression, may have contributed to the observed lack of connection between maternal distress and parenting practices. It remains unclear, however, why poverty did not have the expected negative effect on family practices in this study even though maternal affection and physical punishment were operationalized in a manner similar to other studies where significance was found.

Maternal Affect, Family Processes, and Children's Perceptions

In their study of 241 single African-American mothers and their seventh- and eighth-grade children in a Midwestern city, McLoyd, Jayaratne, Ceballo, and Borquez (1994) found that one measure of economic hardship, past work interruption, was not associated with depression in mothers, but current unemployment was directly associated. However, the link between current unemployment and depression was not mediated by feelings of financial strain, a finding that conflicts with those of other studies reported in the literature. Increased maternal depression led to more negative perceptions of a mother's role, which in turn mediated increased adolescent punishment. (However, increased maternal depression was not associated with harsher punishment if the negative perceptions did not mediate the relationship.) Also, the presence of instrumental support (tangible assistance in the form of goods and services) had a positive impact in that it directly decreased maternal use of physical punishment and indirectly decreased punishment through diminished negative perceptions of the maternal role.

With respect to outcomes for adolescents in this study, mothers' use of physical punishment increased youths' perception of negative relations with the mother, which in turn led to higher levels of cognitive distress in their children. In addition, mothers' punishment increased adolescents' depression both directly and indirectly through its adverse effect on adolescents' perception of the quality of mother-adolescent relations. Maternal punishment neither increased anxiety nor lowered self-esteem in adolescents, but the adolescents' perception of economic hardship did lead to these negative outcomes.

Parental Affect, Family Processes, and Children's Competence

Family processes also mediated the impact of economic stress on mental health outcomes for a sample of African-American 9- to 12-year-olds living in two-parent families in rural Georgia and North Carolina (Brody et al., 1994). Constrained family resources (measured by family's per capita income) led to parental depression and diminished feelings of optimism. Depression was linked to increased conflict (e.g., arguments over child-rearing practices) between parents and lower levels of cocaregiving support (receiving help from spouse in raising child) as perceived by fathers. As expected, diminished parental optimism also led to both parents reporting decreased cocaregiving support, and it also led to increased conflict for fathers. Finally, increased conflict between parents as well as diminished support led to decreased youth self-regulatory competence (ability to plan ahead and persevere in the face of challenges), which led to more depression and disruptive behavior for the children. In sum, once again we see that family processes suffer as a result of economic hardship, and children's mental health is negatively affected.

One final study also explored the mediated relationship between poverty and children's mental health. Brody and Flor (1997) examined family processes contributing to internalizing and externalizing problems for a sample of 6- to 9-year-old African-American children living with their mothers in rural Georgia. According to their data, lack of adequate financial resources was linked to increased maternal depression and lower self-esteem. Mothers' depression was associated with diminished quality of the mother-daughter relationship, and lower self-esteem led to a more nonsupportive relationship between the mother and child as well as less frequently shared family routines, such as regular family playtime for both boys and girls. When these relationships and routines suffered, so did boys' and girls' self-regulatory competence. Children whose self-regulatory competence suffered did not plan ahead before acting or stick to tasks as well as did children in more affluent families. Finally, the child's decreased self-regulatory competence led to more internalizing (depression) and externalizing (antisocial behaviors) outcomes for boys and girls. In addition to pathways already described, disrupted family routines also led *directly* to more internalizing problems for boys.

SUMMARY

The studies just reviewed explore the mediated link between poverty and children's mental health and illuminate the ways in which family processes play

a key role in shaping outcomes for children. Diminished family resources and increased economic burdens translate into weakened family processes for most of the families in these studies. Parents' emotional as well as behavioral involvement with their children diminishes, and their use of harsh physical punishment increases. Children show greater incidence of depression, anxiety, and lower self-esteem while acting out in a more delinquent and antisocial manner. Some neighborhood-level factors also suffer as a result of poverty, and these factors in turn impact children's mental health. Several studies examine the relationship between poverty and children's mental health by exploring not only parenting practices but also parents' affective states as well as youths' self-regulatory competence as pathways through which poverty affects children's outcomes. Like those studies that simply examine the relationship among poverty, parenting practices, and child outcomes, these studies show that parents' emotions, relationships, and parenting practices suffer under economically disadvantaged circumstances, and so does children's mental health. Whether the mediating factors examined are few or many, poverty still threatens the mental health of children.

THE COGNITIVE RISKS OF POVERTY FOR CHILDREN

Not surprisingly, living in poverty endangers a child's cognitive well-being. Several researchers have explored the direct effects of depth, duration, and timing of poverty as well as the effects of welfare receipt on children's reading and math competence and years of schooling completed. These outcomes are only two of the many that might have been considered in this section, but they were selected because they are often cited in the literature and represent important indicators of a child's future success in life. As discussed earlier in this chapter, poverty often co-occurs with other risk factors such as single parenthood and lower education levels of parents. The studies reviewed here examine the effects of poverty by holding these and other factors constant to determine poverty's impact, net of other effects, on children's cognitive outcomes. Space constraints prevent us from presenting a discussion of each set of controls. However, Aber,

Bennett, Conley, and Li (1997) provide an in-depth discussion of control variables commonly employed in these types of studies. In addition, they discuss the importance of researchers' attempts to disentangle the effects of poverty from other factors to determine poverty's impact on child outcomes.

POVERTY'S EFFECTS ON MATH AND READING COMPETENCE

Simply considering a dichotomous measure of parents' income (poor/not poor) at one point in time revealed that in a community-level sample of urban African-American and Hispanic fourth- to sixth-grade students, those living in poverty demonstrated lower reading and math competence than their nonpoor peers (Schultz, 1993). Whereas a dichotomous measure of poverty revealed negative outcomes, researchers discovered that looking at a nondichotomous measure (depth of poverty) provided a more precise account of poverty's negative impacts on children's math and reading competence. Korenman, Miller, and Sjaastad (1995) analyzed data from a national sample of White, African-American, and Hispanic preschool through elementary school–age children (about 4–11 years old), and Smith, Brooks-Gunn, and Klebanov (1997) examined two national samples of 3- to 8-year-old White, African-American, and Hispanic children. Both sets of researchers found that those children who fell right at or just under the poverty line (50%–100% of poverty) exhibited lower math and reading competence than the reference group of nonpoor peers. Children living in the deepest poverty (<50% of poverty) displayed the lowest competence of all. Clearly, depth of poverty reveals more subtle effects on reading and math skills than the dichotomous measure does.

Duration of poverty is also crucial to consider. In a study by Korenman et al. (1995), long-term poverty had a greater negative impact on math and reading skills than short-term poverty did for a national sample of multiracial 4- to 11-year-old children. Smith et al. (1997) found that for two national samples of multiracial 3- to 8-year-old children, living in transient poverty had a significantly negative effect on children's math and reading skills. Those living in persistent poverty, however, demonstrated even lower competencies compared to transiently poor and never poor children. Whereas these two studies examined poverty's impact on cognitive outcomes by holding the race variable constant, Driscoll and Moore (1998) analyzed the effects of poverty on 9- to 14-year-old White and African-American children separately. In this study, poverty's duration did affect cognitive outcomes, but it did so differently for White and African-American children. The reading competencies of White children were negatively affected by short-term poverty but not long-term poverty, whereas the math competencies of African-American children were negatively affected by both short- and long-term poverty.

Finally, two studies considered the developmental timing of poverty in the child's life and the impact that timing had on reading and math competencies. Smith et al. (1997) found that 3- to 8-year-old White, African-American, and Hispanic children who were exposed to poverty in infancy did not display significantly different math and reading skills compared to children who were exposed to poverty in preschool or never lived in poverty at all. By comparison, Dubow and Ippolito (1994) found that exposure to poverty during the preschool years did have a negative impact on a national sample of 5- to 8-year-old White, African-American, and Hispanic children's math and reading competencies. Exposure to poverty later, in elementary school, did not have the same effect. These discrepancies may possibly be explained by the fact that Smith et al. measured poverty for a shorter period of time (only two years) to mark early and late timing, whereas the other researchers utilized a four-year period. In short, it appears that timing in combination with duration makes a difference in cognitive outcomes when duration is measured for a longer period of time.

WELFARE RECEIPT'S EFFECTS ON MATH AND READING COMPETENCE

Two studies examined the impact welfare receipt had on children's math and reading skills. Indeed, because receipt of welfare presupposes low income, the authors' set of control variables necessarily included income to examine welfare's impact on child cognitive outcomes net of other factors. Driscoll and Moore (1998) investigated the effects of both ever receiving welfare and long-term welfare receipt on the cognitive outcomes of 9- to 14-year-old White and African-American children. In the national sample they analyzed, both White and

African-American children who had *ever received welfare* exhibited lower reading skills than White and African-American children who had never received welfare. In addition, White children who had ever received welfare demonstrated lower math skills compared to children who had never received welfare. This was not the case for African-American children. In the case of *long-term* welfare recipients in the same study, White children exhibited lower math skills. African-American children had lower reading skills compared to their same-race peers who experienced either short-term welfare or had never received welfare (Driscoll & Moore, 1998). Once the researchers included additional controls for factors that may have influenced a mother's decision to go on welfare, the strength of the effects for "ever received" and "long-term welfare" variables diminished. The effect was more pronounced for long-term welfare receipt. The authors suggested that "women who are long-term welfare recipients differ in important ways from those that are not, and that these differences have consequences for the cognitive . . . development of their children" (p. 25).

In another study that explored welfare receipt's effects on children's math and reading skills, Moore, Glei, Driscoll, and Zaslow (1998) did not analyze their data separately by race. Nonetheless, they found that for a national sample of White, African-American, and Hispanic 10- and 11-year-old children, children who were *always* living on welfare (during a four-year period) demonstrated significantly lower math and reading competencies compared to never poor children.

POVERTY'S EFFECTS ON YEARS OF
COMPLETED SCHOOLING

Several studies also examined poverty's impact on children's schooling outcomes. Indeed, children living in poverty were likely to complete fewer years of schooling compared to peers not living in poverty (Duncan, 1994; Peters & Mullis, 1997; Teachman, Paasch, Day, & Carver, 1997). Detailed measures of poverty including *duration* and *timing* revealed different effects on years of schooling completed. Analyzing data from a community-level sample of White families, Axinn, Duncan, and Thornton (1997) found that children who lived in low-income status (income at or below 200% of poverty line)

some of the time during childhood completed significantly fewer years of schooling by age 23 compared to those who were never low-income. *Persistent* low income had an even more detrimental impact on years of schooling completed than did transient low income. Peters and Mullis, however, found that for a national sample of White, African-American, and Hispanic youth, children who lived in persistent poverty were no worse off in terms of completed schooling than those who lived in occasional poverty. The authors speculated that differences in duration did not differently affect schooling outcomes because the length of time measured was short (only three years) and was considered only during adolescence rather than in early childhood, a time period others have found to have a significant impact on cognitive outcomes. For example, Axinn et al. found that the *timing of low income* mattered because being poor early in a child's life (from birth through early childhood) but not later (during the teenage years) was associated with fewer years of completed schooling by age 23.

WELFARE'S EFFECTS ON YEARS OF
COMPLETED SCHOOLING

Results for welfare's impact on years of completed schooling are mixed. Peters and Mullis (1997) examined a national data set composed of White, African-American, and Hispanic youth. They found that for Hispanic children, living in a family that received any welfare support during the child's high school years had a *positive* effect on years of schooling completed by age 24 to 25. The authors conjectured that social supports such as Medicaid and Head Start that accompany welfare benefits may have been beneficial to these Hispanic adolescents' cognitive outcomes. In contrast, Duncan (1994) found that a family's greater dependence on welfare as a portion of income (compared to no dependence on welfare) when the child was between 10 and 16 years old was negatively related to years of schooling completed by mid-20s only for African Americans and not Whites from a national sample of youth. Another set of discrepant findings was presented by Teachman et al. (1997). The researchers found that neither duration of welfare receipt (0–2 years during late adolescence) nor proportion of income from welfare (when the child was 14–18 years old) had a significant impact on schooling outcomes for their national sample of White and African-American youth. The range of findings presented here may possibly be explained by at least three factors: (a) varying measures of welfare receipt (e.g., proportion of income from welfare, duration of welfare receipt), (b) varying ages of the youth at time of welfare receipt, and (c) varying control factors used across the three studies.

POVERTY'S EFFECTS ON HIGH SCHOOL GRADUATION

Several researchers also examined poverty's impact on children's chances for graduating from high school. Haveman, Wolfe, and Wilson (1997) found that for a national sample of White and African-American youth, living in a lower-income family was associated with a reduced probability of graduating from high school compared to youth from higher-income families. They also found that living in *persistent poverty* significantly reduced the probability of graduating from high school. Teachman et al. (1997) also found that for a national sample of White and African-American youth, *spending more time* below the poverty line meant that children were less likely to graduate from high school compared to children living just above the poverty line. Whereas these two studies examined poverty's impact on cognitive outcomes by holding race constant, Duncan (1994) considered poverty's effects on high school graduation *separately* for White and African-American males and females. He found that lower family income was significantly related to a greater risk of dropping out of high school for all children in the sample *except* African-American males. We speculate that other factors influencing African-American males may contribute to the risk of becoming a high school dropout, so the effect of poverty net of other factors may not be that substantial.

Finally, Ensminger, Lamkin, and Jacobson (1996) analyzed data from an African-American sample from Chicago and also found that family income did not affect high school graduation chances for African Americans. In contrast to Duncan (1994), this finding held for both males and females. The geographically restricted sample used by Ensminger et al. may explain why these researchers did not find that family income affected the likelihood of these African-American children graduating from high school.

SUMMARY

Poverty has a negative impact on children's math and reading competence as well as years of schooling completed and high school graduation. Although not all studies considered degree, duration, and timing of poverty, those that did often showed how depth and duration of exposure to poverty as well as exposure earlier in a child's life negatively affect children's cognitive outcomes. For the most part, welfare receipt (considered apart from poverty) led to negative consequences for cognitive outcomes, but researchers found it difficult to disentangle welfare's effects from those of poverty and other factors that may lead to welfare receipt in the first place. Controlling for a host of factors is necessary to tease out the impact of poverty and welfare receipt on children's cognitive outcomes.

THE CONCEPT OF RISK: A SOCIAL CONSTRUCTION

Children in poverty are widely referred to as "children at risk." A number of researchers are critical of the term, saying that it is a pejorative label that stigmatizes (Swadener & Lubbeck, 1995a). By suggesting deficiency, it faults the child rather than society for the problem of disadvantage, and deflects attention from the real causes of poverty. Critics of the term contend that a discussion of risk fails to question the societal conditions that perpetuate it. They see the concept as a cultural construction that strengthens the status quo, one that "keeps us from being broadly, radically, and structurally creative" about realizing societal transformation (Swadener & Lubbeck, 1995b, p. 8). They counter the term with another, "children at promise." They believe that the new metaphor communicates the conception of children with the potential for success rather than failure.

Some of Swadener and Lubbeck's (1995a) assertions are well-taken. Negative connotations associated with the at-risk term do mirror society's condescending view of the poor, and our society has refused to initiate any meaningful change on their behalf. However, the alternative metaphor they suggest does not represent an improvement over what it was meant to replace. The large body of literature cited in this chapter attests to the fact that children in poverty are at risk, and the new term merely downplays this fact. A well-intended euphemism, it obscures the special needs of economically vulnerable children in a society all too willing to forget them. Substituting a more agreeable expression (promise) for a less agreeable one (risk) removes from public consciousness any reminder of the fact that poverty threatens a child's development. Some in our society see the at-risk label as providing an opportunity to blame the victim. Use of the at-promise term may offer yet another opportunity. We are an individualistic society that values "lifting oneself up by one's bootstraps." The danger with the at-promise metaphor is that economically disadvantaged children may be expected to epitomize the adage, when a myriad of factors militate against it. Their special needs make it imperative that we acknowledge their at-risk status, and that we urge society to meet its obligation to take action to improve the life circumstances that engender it.

RESEARCH ON RESILIENCY

Not all children living in poverty succumb to adverse outcomes. For some time, researchers have sought to establish why some children develop adequately despite exposure to multiple risk factors, and others do not, that is, why they are resilient. Thinking about economically disadvantaged children in these terms shifts a discussion of their development from a deficit to a strength perspective. To address the issue, Garmezy, Masten, and Tellegen (1984) have suggested three possible explanations. The *compensatory* model proposes that risk factors and protective factors combine additively in the prediction of outcomes, and that protective ("compensating") factors can offset risk factors. The *challenge* model posits that a stressor may enhance successful adaptation; provided that the stressor is not overly challenging, when surmounted, it may actually strengthen competence. The *conditional* model theorizes that protective factors interact with risk factors in such a way as to decrease the likelihood of a negative outcome. The three models may operate simultaneously or successively to buffer a child against adverse consequences; they are not mutually exclusive (Werner, 1990).

Research has identified specific factors and processes that contribute to adaptive outcomes in

children despite adversity. Werner (1990) has summed up three types of protective factors that are emphasized in the research literature: "(1) dispositional attributes of the child that elicit predominantly positive responses from the environment, such as physical robustness and vigor, an easy temperament, and intelligence; (2) affectional ties and socialization practices within the family that encourage trust, autonomy, and initiative; and (3) external support systems that reinforce competence and provide children with a positive set of values" (p. 111). Good nurturing may be provided by parents, but affectional ties may also be developed with alternative caregivers such as grandparents, older siblings, and babysitters, and external support systems may include friends, neighbors, teachers, and others (Werner, 1990; Werner & Smith, 1992). Figures such as these can serve as important buffers of stress. Socialization practices that promote resiliency appear to differ for boys and girls. For boys, these practices are important: (1) greater parental supervision, rules, and structure; (2) encouragement of emotional expressiveness; and (3) the presence of a male role model with whom they can identify. For girls, these practices are important: (1) reliable emotional support from a primary caregiver; (2) an absence of overprotection; and (3) an emphasis on risk taking and independence (Werner, 1990). Other qualities cited in the literature that characterize resilient children are self-esteem and self-confidence. They also seem to possess a belief in their own self-efficacy and an ability to deal with change and adaptations. And they also have a repertoire of social problem-solving strategies (Rutter, 1985). Research has focused more on protective factors and processes operating at the microsystem level (i.e., the individual and family), while downplaying the role that broader social contexts at the level of the macrosystem may play in fostering resiliency (Zimmerman & Arunkumar, 1994).

The dispositional qualities defining individual resilience appear to transcend racial, class, and cultural boundaries, but resiliency does not seem to represent a fixed attribute, nor does it apply to all life domains (Rutter, 1987; Werner & Smith, 1992; Zimmerman & Arunkumar, 1994). An individual's response to a stressful environment may not always be resilient, as circumstances and the need to adapt change. Similarly, a child may show resilience to one form of risk but not to another. As a process, resiliency may operate differently at different phases of development (Zimmerman & Arunkumar, 1994). More information is needed on how processes that are salient for different populations may influence resiliency (e.g., strong ethnic ties) (Zimmerman & Arunkumar, 1994), and how resiliency functions in children at different developmental stages. (For a more extensive discussion, see Haggerty, Sherrod, Garmezy, & Rutter, 1994; Werner, 1990; Werner & Smith, 1992; Zimmerman & Arunkumar, 1994.)

Clinicians can draw on the knowledge that research on resiliency provides to conceive of therapeutic interventions for children and families in poverty. Whereas risks may multiply to a child's detriment, protective elements may accumulate with the opposite effect (Bradley et al., 1994). Interventions can be designed to reduce the number of risk factors to which a child is exposed and to increase the number of protective factors available (Werner, 1990). Four protective processes identified by Rutter (1987) can be used for intervention purposes, namely: (1) lessen the risk impact on the child; (2) decrease negative chain reactions; (3) develop and preserve self-esteem and self-efficacy; and, (4) open up opportunities. Lessening the risk impact involves modifying the meaning or the danger of a risk variable for a child and changing the child's exposure to or involvement with the risk situation. Decreasing chain reactions entails intervening to attenuate the sequelae that follow risk exposure and sustain risk effects. Self-esteem and self-efficacy can be enhanced through two types of experiences: secure and harmonious love relationships, and the successful accomplishment of tasks important to a child. Opportunities may be opened up in a variety of ways, for example, by assisting families in making a physical move away from a disadvantaged environment, or by facilitating the enrollment of a child in a high-quality educational program that may provide a route out of poverty. (See Rutter, 1987; Werner & Smith, 1992, for a fuller discussion.) In sum, research on resiliency has important implications for clinical intervention.

MORE IMPLICATIONS FOR CLINICAL INTERVENTION

The large body of literature reviewed in this chapter attests to poverty's potential to undermine child and family well-being. Although empirical data are sparse on the unique effects of material hardship, and poverty should not necessarily be considered a proxy for it (Huston, McLoyd, & Coll, 1994b), the low-income status of families falling below the poverty line does suggest that they are confronted with intense economic need. By definition, poverty signifies an insufficiency of financial resources, and the challenge to make do can induce considerable stress. Clinicians are well advised to consider the psychological strain associated with material hardship in conceiving of therapeutic interventions. Improving a family's economic status is a primary way to reduce economic stress and the adverse consequences that emanate from it (Conger et al., 1994). Although it may not always be possible to assist families in acquiring a sustainable income, they can be linked to services. A broad, well-integrated network of supports is essential for families experiencing the multiple risks associated with poverty. Services should address basic life requirements such as food, clothing, shelter, and medical care. Direct services should also address improvement of quality of life, for example, through job training, education and literacy skills training, high-quality child care, and parenting programs. Over the course of the past decade or so, influential task forces, commissions, and others have recommended a number of steps that address the problem of poverty generally, and child poverty more specifically (see, e.g., Blank, 1997; Carnegie Corporation of New York, 1994; National Commission on Children, 1993). The recommendations offered by these sources suggest the need to advocate for change at local, state, and national levels.

Empirical research has identified many of the pathways through which poverty affects negative outcomes for children. Some family processes operating at the microsystem level include: (1) diminished emotional connection between parent and child, (2) reduced behavioral involvement of parent with child, (3) disrupted family routines, (4) decreased effective monitoring of children, (5) use of punishment, (6) parental depression, (7) marital conflict, (8) hostility between parent and child, (9) more negative perceptions of a mother's role, and (10) lower levels of cocaregiving support. These process variables denote areas of family functioning amenable to change. They also suggest the importance of focusing on parents as well as children. To illustrate, helping families to improve their life circumstances or to move out of poverty may alleviate depressive symptoms that negatively affect children (Benasich, Brooks-Gunn, & Clewell, 1992). The availability of social support may also reduce feelings of depression as well as help mothers become less punitive with their children and less negative about their maternal role (McLoyd et al., 1994). Parents can also be helped to learn more emotionally responsive ways of interacting with their children and to monitor their children's activities more closely. By placing an emphasis on family processes, researchers have neglected other, broader, macrolevel factors that affect family functioning. The research findings reviewed earlier should not be construed to suggest that parents are solely responsible for negative child outcomes. Other as yet unexamined contextual factors may also play a critical role (Halpern, 1990).

CONCLUSION

Researchers from a variety of disciplines have directed their attention to the psychological impact of poverty on children and families. A sizable number of children and families in our society are poor, and such inquiry is needed to better understand how economic hardship affects them, as well as how to design interventions on their behalf. Important directions for further inquiry that emerge from reviewing the literature (see, e.g., Brody et al., 1994; Huston et al., 1994b; Routh, 1994b) concern the need to (1) examine the effects that degree, duration, and timing of poverty have on all aspects of a child's development; (2) identify the differential effects that poverty and the interventions designed to alleviate poverty have on groups that vary by race, ethnicity, and gender; (3) analyze the ways that societal factors such as racism and discrimination intensify the stresses of economic hardship for some groups; (4) analyze the pathways through which poverty and interventions designed to alleviate the consequences of poverty affect children and families; (5) investigate contextual factors beyond the immediate level of child and family, including school, neighborhood, and community; (6) analyze how children and families that vary by race, ethnicity, and gender subjectively view their experiences with economic hardship; (7) investigate issues of resiliency and adaptive responses to poverty in different ecologies affecting the child; (8) look at rural as well as urban poverty; (9) draw on multidisciplinary frameworks and utilize a variety of research paradigms and methods; and (10) conceptualize policy-relevant research questions, that is, questions with the potential for yielding information useful for policymakers and that have the potential for positively influencing public attitudes toward the poor. Poverty is a dilemma that threatens the well-being of millions of children and families in our society. Democratic ideals demand that we take steps to address the problem.

REFERENCES

Aber, J.L., Bennett, N.G., Conley, D.C., & Li, J. (1997). The effects of poverty on child health and development. *Annual Review of Public Health, 18,* 463–483.

Avruch, S., & Cackley, A. (1995). Savings achieved by giving WIC benefits to women prenatally. *Public Health Reports, 110,* 27–34.

Axinn, W., Duncan, G.J., & Thornton, A. (1997). The effects of parents' income, wealth, and attitudes on children's completed schooling and self-esteem. In G. Duncan & J. Brooks-Gunn (Eds.), *Consequences of growing up poor* (pp. 518–540). New York: Russell Sage Foundation.

Baydar, N., Brooks-Gunn, J., & Furstenberg, F., Jr. (1993). Early warning signs of functional illiteracy: Predictors in childhood and adolescence. *Child Development, 64,* 815–829.

Belle, D. (1990). Poverty and women's mental health. *American Psychologist, 45,* 385–389.

Belsky, J. (1993). Etiology of child maltreatment: A developmental-ecological analysis. *Psychological Bulletin, 114,* 413–434.

Benasich, A., Brooks-Gunn, J., & Clewell, B. (1992). How do mothers benefit from early intervention programs? *Journal of Applied Developmental Psychology, 13,* 311–362.

Bianchi, S. (1993). Children of poverty: Why are they poor? In J. Chafel (Ed.), *Child poverty and public policy* (pp. 91–125). Washington, DC: Urban Institute Press.

Blank, R. (1997). *It takes a nation: A new agenda for fighting poverty.* New York: Russell Sage Foundation.

Bolger, K.E., Patterson, C.J., Thompson, W.W., & Kupersmidt, J.B. (1995). Psychosocial adjustment among children experiencing persistent and intermittent family economic hardship. *Child Development, 66,* 1107–1129.

Bradley, R.H., Whiteside, L., Mundfrom, D., Casey, P., Kelleher, K., & Pope, S. (1994). Contribution of early intervention and early caregiving experiences to resilience in low-birthweight, premature children living in poverty. *Journal of Clinical Child Psychology, 23,* 425–434.

Breslau, N., DelDotto, J.E., Brown, G.G., Kumar, S., Ezhuthachan, S., Hufnagle, K.G., & Peterson, E.L.

(1994). A gradient relationship between low birth weight and IQ at age 6 years. *Archives of Pediatric and Adolescent Medicine, 148,* 377–383.

Brody, G.H., & Flor, D.L. (1997). Maternal psychological functioning, family processes, and child adjustment in rural, single-parent, African-American families. *Developmental Psychology, 33,* 1000–1011.

Brody, G.H., Stoneman, Z., Flor, D.L., McCrary, C., Hastings, L., & Conyers, O. (1994). Financial resources, parent psychological functioning, parent cocaregiving, and early adolescent competence in rural two-parent African-American families. *Child Development, 65,* 590–605.

Bronfenbrenner, U. (1979). *The ecology of human development.* Cambridge, MA: Harvard University Press.

Brooks-Gunn, J., Klebanov, P., & Liaw, F. (1995). The learning, physical, and emotional environment of the home in the context of poverty: The Infant Health and Development Program. *Children and Youth Services Review, 17,* 251–276.

Brown, J.L., & Pollitt, E. (1996, February). Malnutrition, poverty, and intellectual development. *Scientific American,* 38–43.

Call, R.L. (1989). Effects of poverty on children's dental health. *Pediatrician, 26,* 200–206.

Carnegie Corporation of New York. (1994). *Starting points: Meeting the needs of our youngest children.* New York: Author.

Center on Budget and Policy Priorities. (1998). *Strengths of the safety net.* Washington, DC: Author.

Center for Disease Control and Prevention. (1997). Vaccination coverage by race/ethnicity and poverty level among children aged 19–35 months: United States, 1996. *Journal of the American Medical Association, 278,* 1655–1656.

Chafel, J. (1993). *Child poverty and public policy.* Washington, DC: Urban Institute Press.

Chase-Lansdale, P., & Brooks-Gunn, J. (1995). *Escape from poverty: What makes a difference for children?* New York: Cambridge University Press.

Coley, R., & Chase-Lansdale, P. (1998). Adolescent pregnancy and parenthood: Recent evidence and future directions. *American Psychologist, 53,* 152–166.

Conger, R.D., Conger, K.J., & Elder, G.H., Jr. (1997). Family economic hardship and adolescent adjustment: Mediating and moderating processes. In G. Duncan & J. Brooks-Gunn (Eds.), *Consequences of growing up poor* (pp. 288–310). New York: Russell Sage Foundation.

Conger, R.D., Ge, X., Elder, G.H., Jr., Lorenz, F.O., & Simons, R.L. (1994). Economic stress, coercive family process, and developmental problems of adolescents. *Child Development, 65,* 541–561.

Cook, D., & Fine, M. (1995). "Motherwit": Childrearing lessons from African-American mothers of low income. In B. Swadener & S. Lubbeck (Eds.), *Children and families "at promise": Deconstructing the discourse of risk.* Albany, New York: State University of New York Press.

Devine, J., & Wright, J. (1993). *The greatest of evils: Urban poverty and the American underclass.* New York: Aldine de Gruyter.

Dodge, K.A., Pettit, G.S., & Bates, J.E. (1994). Socialization mediators of the relation between socioeconomic status and child conduct problems. *Child Development, 65,* 649–665.

Driscoll, A.K., & Moore, K.A. (1998). *Deprivation and dependency: The relationship of poverty and welfare to child outcomes.* Washington, DC: Child Trends.

Dubow, E.F., & Ippolito, M.F. (1994). Effects of poverty and quality of the home environment on changes in the academic and behavioral adjustment of elementary school-age children. *Journal of Clinical Child Psychology, 23,* 401–412.

Duncan, G.J. (1994). Families and neighbors as sources of disadvantage in the schooling decisions of White and Black adolescents. *American Journal of Education, 103,* 20–53.

Duncan, G.J., & Brooks-Gunn, J. (Eds.). (1997). *Consequences of growing up poor.* New York: Russell Sage Foundation.

Duncan, G.J., Brooks-Gunn, J., & Klebanov, P. (1994). Economic deprivation and early childhood development. *Child Development, 65,* 296–318.

Duncan, G.J., & Rodgers, W. (1988). Longitudinal aspects of childhood poverty. *Journal of Marriage and the Family, 50,* 1007–1021.

Economic Report of the President. (1998). Washington, DC: U.S. Government Printing Office.

Eller, T. (1996, June). *Dynamics of economic well-being: Poverty, 1992–1993. Who stays poor? Who doesn't?* [Online]. Available: http://www.census.gov/prod /2/pop/p70/p70–55.pdf

Elliot, D.E., Wilson, W.J., Huizinga, D., Sampson, R.J., Elliot, A., & Rankin, B. (1996). The effects of neighborhood disadvantage on adolescent development. *Journal of Research in Crime and Delinquency, 33,* 389–426.

Ensminger, M.E., Lamkin, R.P., & Jacobson, N. (1996). School leaving: A longitudinal perspective including neighborhood effects. *Child Development, 67,* 2400–2416.

Federal Interagency Forum on Child and Family Statistics. (1997). *America's children: Key national indicators of well-being* [Online]. Available: http://www.cdc.gov /nchswww/about/otheract/children/child.htm

Federman, M., Garner, T., Short, K., Cutter, W., Keily, J., Levine, D., McGough, D., & McMillen, M. (1996, May). What does it mean to be poor in America? *Monthly Labor Review,* 3–17.

Fitzgerald, H., Lester, B., & Zuckerman, B. (1995). *Children of poverty: Research, health, and poverty issues.* New York: Garland Press.

Garbarino, J. (1990). The human ecology of early risk. In S. Meisels & J. Shonkoff (Eds.), *Handbook of early childhood intervention* (pp. 78–96). Cambridge, England: Cambridge University Press.

Garmezy, N., Masten, A., & Tellegen, A. (1984). The study of stress and competence in children: A building block for developmental psychopathology. *Child Development, 55*, 97–111.

Haggerty, R., Sherrod, L., Garmezy, N., & Rutter, M. (1994). *Stress, risk, and resilience in children and adolescents: Processes, mechanisms, and interventions.* Cambridge, England: Cambridge University Press.

Halpern, R. (1990). Poverty and early childhood parenting: Toward a framework for intervention. *American Journal of Orthopsychiatry, 60*, 6–18.

Hanson, M., & Carta, J. (1995). Addressing the challenges of families with multiple risks. *Exceptional Children, 62*, 201–212.

Hanson, T.L., McLanahan, S., & Thomson, E. (1997). Economic resources, parental practices, and children's well-being. In G. Duncan & J. Brooks-Gunn (Eds.), *Consequences of growing up poor* (pp. 190–238). New York: Russell Sage Foundation.

Harris, K.M., & Marmer, J.K. (1996). Poverty, paternal involvement, and adolescent well-being. *Journal of Family Issues, 17*, 614–640.

Haveman, R., & Wolfe, B. (1994). *Succeeding generations: On the effects of investments in children.* New York: Russell Sage Foundation.

Haveman, R., Wolfe, B., & Wilson, K. (1997). Childhood poverty and adolescent outcomes: Reduced-form and structural estimates. In G. Duncan & J. Brooks-Gunn (Eds.), *Consequences of growing up poor* (pp. 419–460). New York: Russell Sage Foundation.

Ho, C.S., Lempers, J.D., & Clark-Lempers, D.S. (1995). Effects of economic hardship on adolescent self-esteem: A family mediation model. *Adolescence, 30*, 117–131.

Huston, A. (1991). *Children in poverty: Child development and public policy.* Cambridge, England: Cambridge University Press.

Huston, A., McLoyd, V., & Coll, C. (Eds.). (1994a). Children and poverty [Special issue]. *Child Development, 65*, 275–315.

Huston, A., McLoyd, V., & Coll, C. (Eds.). (1994b). Children and poverty: Issues in contemporary research. *Child Development, 65*, 275–282.

Jencks, C. (1994). *The homeless.* Cambridge, MA: Harvard University Press.

Kelly, S.M., & Miles-Doan, R. (1997). Social inequality and injuries: Do morbidity patterns differ from mortality? *Social Science Medicine, 44*, 63–70.

Klebanov, P.K., Brooks-Gunn, J., & McCormick, M.C. (1994). Classroom behavior of very low birth weight elementary school children. *Pediatrics, 94*, 700–708.

Klerman, L. (1991). The health of poor children: Problems and programs. In A.C. Huston (Ed.), *Children in poverty: Child development and public policy* (pp. 136–157). Cambridge, England: Cambridge University Press.

Korenman, S., Miller, J.E., & Sjaastad, J.E. (1995). Long-term poverty and child development in the United States: Results from the NLSY. *Children and Youth Services Review, 17*, 127–155.

Lamison-White, L. (1997). *Poverty in the United States–1996: U.S. Bureau of the Census, current population reports* (Series P60–198). Washington, DC: U.S. Government Printing Office.

Lazere, E. (1997). *The poverty despite work handbook: Data and guidelines for preparing a report on the working poor in each state.* Washington, DC: Center on Budget and Policy Priorities.

Liaw, F., & Brooks-Gunn, J. (1994). Cumulative familial risks and low-birthweight children's cognitive and behavioral development. *Journal of Clinical Child Psychology, 23*, 360–372.

McLeod, J.D., & Edwards, K. (1995). Contextual determinants of children's responses to poverty. *Social Forces, 73*, 1487–1516.

McLeod, J.D., Kruttschnitt, C., & Dornfeld, M. (1994). Does parenting explain the effects of structural conditions on children's antisocial behavior? A comparison of Blacks and Whites. *Social Forces, 73*, 575–604.

McLeod, J.D., & Shanahan, M.J. (1993). Poverty, parenting, and children's mental health. *American Sociological Review, 58*, 351–366.

McLeod, J.D., & Shanahan, M.J. (1996). Trajectories of poverty and children's mental health. *Journal of Health and Social Behavior, 37*, 207–220.

McLoyd, V., & Wilson, L. (1991). The strain of living poor: Parenting, social support, and child mental health. In A. Huston (Ed.), *Children in poverty: Child development and public policy* (pp. 105–135). Cambridge, England: Cambridge University Press.

McLoyd, V.C., Jayaratne, T.E., Ceballo, R., & Borquez, J. (1994). Unemployment and work interruption among African American single mothers: Effects on parenting and adolescent socioemotional functioning. *Child Development, 65*, 562–589.

Moffitt, R.A., & Slade, E. (1997). Health care coverage for children who are on and off welfare. *The Future of Children, 7*, 87–98.

Money Income in the United States–1996. (1998, June 13). (Separate data on valuation of noncash benefits) (P60–197) [Online]. Available: http://www.census.gov/prod/3/97pubs/P60-197.PDF

Moore, K.A., Glei, D.A., Driscoll, A.K., & Zaslow, M.J. (1998). *Ebbing and flowing, learning and growing: Transitions in family economic resources and children's development.* Washington, DC: Child Trends.

Mosley, J., & Thomson, E. (1995). Fathering behavior and child outcomes. In W. Marsiglio (Ed.), *Fatherhood: Contemporary theory, research, and social policy* (pp. 148–165). Thousand Oaks, CA: Sage.

National Commission on Children. (1993). *Next steps for children and families* [Implementation Guide Series]. Washington, DC: Author.

Newacheck, P.W., Hughes, D., & Stoddard, J. (1996). Children's access to primary care: Differences by race, income and insurance status. *Pediatrics, 97*, 26–32.

Oberg, C.N., Bryant, N., & Bach, M. (1995). A portrait of America's children: The impact of poverty and a call to action. *Journal of Social Distress and the Homeless, 4*, 43–56.

Olden, K. (1996). A bad start for socioeconomically disadvantaged children [Editorial]. *Environmental and Health Perspectives, 104*, 462–463.

Orthner, D. (1986, April). *Children and families in the south: Trends in health care, family services, and the rural economy.* Prepared statement for a hearing before the U.S. House of Representatives Select Committee on children, youth, and families, held in Macon, GA. Washington, DC: U.S. Government Printing Office.

Peters, H.E., & Mullis, N.C. (1997). The role of family income and sources of income in adolescent achievement. In G. Duncan & J. Brooks-Gunn (Eds.), *Consequences of growing up poor* (pp. 340–381). New York: Russell Sage Foundation.

Routh, D. (Ed.). (1994a). Impact of poverty on children, youth, and families [Special issue]. *Journal of Clinical Child Psychology, 23*, 346–459.

Routh, D. (Ed.). (1994b). Impact of poverty on children, youth, and families: Introduction to the special issue. *Journal of Clinical Child Psychology, 23*, 346–348.

Rutter, M. (1979). Protective factors in children's responses to stress and disadvantage. In M.W. Kent & J.E. Rolf (Eds.), *Primary prevention of psychopathology: Social competence in children* (Vol. 3, pp. 49–74). Hanover, NH: University Press of New England.

Rutter, M. (1985). Resilience in the face of adversity: Protective factors and resistance to psychiatric disorder. *British Journal of Psychiatry, 147*, 598–611.

Rutter, M. (1987). Psychosocial resilience and protective mechanisms. *American Journal of Orthopsychiatry, 57*, 316–331.

Sameroff, A., Barocas, R., & Seifer, R. (1984). The early development of children born to mentally ill women. In N. Watt, E. Anthony, L. Wynne, & J. Rolf (Eds.), *Children at risk for schizophrenia: A longitudinal perspective* (pp. 482–514). Cambridge, England: Cambridge University Press.

Sameroff, A., & Seifer, R. (1990). Early contributors to developmental risk. In J. Rolf, A. Masten, D. Cicchetti, K. Neuchterlein, & S. Weintraub (Eds.), *Risk and protective factors in the development of psychopathology* (pp. 52–66). Cambridge, England: Cambridge University Press.

Sameroff, A., Seifer, R., Baldwin, A., & Baldwin, C. (1993). Stability of intelligence from preschool to adolescence: The influence of social and family risk factors. *Child Development, 64*, 80–97.

Sameroff, A., Seifer, R., & Zax, M. (1982). Early development of children at risk for emotional disorder. *Monographs of the Society for Research in Child Development, 47* (7).

Sampson, R.J., & Laub, J.H. (1994). Urban poverty and the family context of delinquency: A new look at structure and process in a classic study. *Child Development, 65*, 523–540.

Sargent, J., Brown, M., Freeman, J., Bailey, A., Goodman, D., & Freeman, D. (1995). Childhood lead poisoning in Massachusetts communities: Its association with sociodemographic and housing characteristics. *American Journal of Public Health, 85*, 528–534.

Scarbrough, W. (1993). Who are the poor? A demographic perspective. In J. Chafel (Ed.), *Child poverty and public policy* (pp. 55–90). Washington, DC: Urban Institute Press.

Schorr, L., & Schorr, D. (1988). *Within our reach: Breaking the cycle of disadvantage.* New York: Doubleday.

Schultz, G.F. (1993). Socioeconomic advantage and achievement motivation: Important mediators of academic performance in minority children in urban schools. *The Urban Review, 25*, 221–232.

Sheehan, K., DiCara, J., LeBailly, S., & Christoffel, K. (1997). Children's exposure to violence in an urban setting. *Archives of Pediatrics and Adolescent Medicine, 151*, 502–504.

Shirley, A. (1991). Education and nutrition. *Journal of Health Care for the Poor and Undeserved, 2*, 87–94.

Short, K., & Shea, M. (1995). *Beyond poverty, extended measures of well-being: 1992* [Online]. Available: http://www.census.gov/prod/1/pop/p70–50rv.pdf

Smith, J.R., Brooks-Gunn, J., & Klebanov, P.K. (1997). Consequences of living in poverty for young children's cognitive and verbal ability and early school achievement. In G. Duncan & J. Brooks-Gunn (Eds.), *Consequences of growing up poor* (pp. 132–189). New York: Russell Sage Foundation.

Snyder, T., & Shafer, L. (1996). *Youth indicators: Trends in the well-being of American youth.* Washington, DC: U.S. Government Printing Office.

Steinberg, L., Catalano, R., & Dooley, D. (1981). Economic antecedents of child abuse and neglect. *Child Development, 52*, 975–985.

Swadener, B., & Lubbeck, S. (1995a). *Children and families "at promise": Deconstructing the discourse of risk.* Albany: State University of New York Press.

Swadener, B., & Lubbeck, S. (1995b). The social construction of children and families "at risk": An introduction.

In B. Swadener & S. Lubbeck (Eds.), *Children and families "at promise": Deconstructing the discourse of risk.* Albany: State University of New York Press.

Tarnowski, K., & Rohrbeck, C. (1993). Disadvantaged children and families. In T. Ollendick & R. Prinz (Eds.), *Advances in clinical child psychology* (Vol. 15, pp. 41–79). New York: Plenum Press.

Teachman, J.D., Paasch, K.M., Day, R.D., & Carver, K.P. (1997). Poverty during adolescence and subsequent educational attainment. In G. Duncan & J. Brooks-Gunn (Eds.), *Consequences of growing up poor* (pp. 382–417). New York: Russell Sage Foundation.

U.S. Bureau of the Census. (1997a). *Census brief: America's children at risk* [Online]. Available: http://www.census.gov/prod/3/97pubs/cb-9702.pdf

U.S. Bureau of the Census. (1997b). *Statistical abstract of the United States: 1997.* Washington, DC: Bernan Press.

U.S. Department of Health and Human Services, Office of the Assistant Secretary for Planning and Evaluation. (n.d.). *Trends in the well being of America's children and youth.* Washington, DC: U.S. Government Printing Office.

Weinberg, D. (1996, June). *A brief look at postwar U.S. income inequality* [Online]. Available: http://www.census.gov/pub/hhes/www/img/p60-191.pdf

Werner, E. (1990). Protective factors and individual resilience. In S. Meisels & J. Shonkoff (Eds.), *Handbook of early childhood intervention.* Cambridge, England: Cambridge University Press.

Werner, E., Bierman, J., & French, F. (1971). *The children of Kauai: A longitudinal study from the prenatal period to age ten.* Honolulu: University of Hawaii Press.

Werner, E., & Smith, R. (1992). *Overcoming the odds: High risk children from birth to adulthood.* Ithaca, NY: Cornell University Press.

Zeanah, C., Boris, N., & Larrieu, J. (1997). Infant development and developmental risk: A review of the past 10 years. *Journal of the American Academy of Child and Adolescent Psychiatry, 36,* 165–178.

Zimmerman, M., & Arunkumar, R. (1994). Resiliency research: Implications for schools and policy. *Social Policy Report (Society for Research in Child Development), 8.*

DIAGNOSTIC ASSESSMENT OF CHILDREN

CHAPTER 5

The Process of the Clinical Child Assessment Interview

JANE QUERIDO, SHEILA EYBERG, RUTH KANFER, AND GLORIA KRAHN

In the diagnosis and planning for treatment of childhood disorders, the child interview can be a source of insight into the child's thoughts, feelings, and behavior. The information gathered from a child interview provides the clinician with an understanding of the child's perceptions of the current problems and the child's willingness to participate in treatment. Several structured interviews have been developed to assist clinicians in using the interview as part of the assessment and diagnostic process (e.g., Child Assessment Schedule [CAS], Hodges, Kline, Fitch, McKnew, & Cytryn, 1981; Hodges, Kline, Stern, Cytryn, & McKnew, 1982; Diagnostic Interview Schedule for Children [DISC], Costello, Edelbrock, Dulcan, Kalas, & Klaric, 1984). In addition, the interview with the child can be useful in determining the most effective intervention for the child's condition with respect to his or her level of motivation for treatment.

Through both the direct observation of the child and the content of the child's responses during the interview, the interviewer has the opportunity to gather several types of information. Direct observation of the child's general demeanor and interaction with the parent and interviewer provides information about the child's general social skills and capacity to relate to others. The information gathered from the interview can be used to evaluate the child's coping strategies and determine any behavioral and cognitive aspects associated with the child's condition (Johnson, 1998). Furthermore, the interviewer can learn about the child's perception of his or her condition, family, and social environment. The child interview also offers the interviewer the opportunity to evaluate the consistency of information provided by the parent versus the child. Any conflicting views may provide relevant information about the dynamics of the family and the child's presenting problem.

The child interview is a flexible procedure that is directed by the trained interviewer. By using the child's verbal responses and nonverbal behavior as guides, the interviewer can slow the pace of conversation or redirect the focus of the interview as needed. In addition, the interviewer has the opportunity to resolve any ambiguous responses and clarify any misunderstandings. Children as young as 6 years of age are capable of providing accurate information about their behavior, environment, and cognitions (Hodges & Cools, 1990; La Greca, Kuttler, & Stone, 1992). Therefore, it is the interviewer's responsibility to gain access to the wealth of information that children are capable of providing.

To conduct an interview with a child, the interviewer must be able to communicate with the child effectively. Although treatment manuals on play therapy with children (e.g., McNeil, Hembree-Kigin, & Eyberg, 1996) have addressed the issue of building and maintaining rapport with children, there is a limited amount of research on the skills that are effective in this process. As a result, the beginning child clinician frequently comes into the clinical setting knowing what information is needed from the child assessment interview, but not knowing how to obtain it. Effective child interviewers typically develop their expertise through supervision and trial-and-error experiences in the interview situation.

Process skills are the techniques that interviewers use to guide and direct the interview sequence, build and maintain rapport, and facilitate the resolution of conflicts that may occur during the interview. Such skills are useful throughout the interview process. For example, interviewers often find it necessary to establish a safe and comfortable atmosphere for the child so that he or she will feel comfortable providing the interviewer with personal information. Display of warmth and acceptance is typically integrated with interviewer behaviors to facilitate the gathering of information from the apprehensive child.

The information in this chapter is tailored for the novice child clinician. It provides a repertoire of specific interview skills and strategies to facilitate communication with the preschool to preadolescent child during the assessment interview. Consistent with a developmental perspective, the discussion focuses on the general process skills that explicitly take into account the child's developmental capabilities and limitations. To simplify discussion of the many types of interviewer behaviors that will be considered, process skills are divided into two categories. General communications skills that can be implemented throughout the interview and that serve to build and maintain rapport are described first. Process skills that guide the interview sequence and facilitate resolution of common interview problems are discussed within a chronological model of the child interview in the final section.

GENERAL COMMUNICATION SKILLS

Two continuous process goals throughout the interview are (1) to establish rapport and (2) to maintain child cooperation. We have identified eight basic communication techniques that are helpful in accomplishing these goals. The use of these skills is not limited to interviewing but is frequently implemented in therapy as well. However, the scope of this chapter will be limited to their use in the assessment interview. No single technique is usually sufficient; rather, they are most successfully used in combination and as the situation demands.

ACKNOWLEDGMENTS

An acknowledgment is a verbal or nonverbal response by the interviewer that indicates attention, expresses empathy, or provides feedback to the child. An acknowledgment does not describe or evaluate the child's thoughts or behaviors. Interviewers use acknowledgments to convey to the child that the interviewer is watching or listening, as in the following examples:

CHILD: I drew a flower.
INTERVIEWER: Hmmm.
CHILD: I like talking to you.
INTERVIEWER: (smiles).
CHILD: He took my stuff.
INTERVIEWER: Oh no.

Interviewers must adjust their methods of acknowledgment according to the developmental level of the child. With preschool children, interviewers need to use slightly exaggerated expressions of affect and distinct behaviors to acknowledge the child's thoughts or behaviors effectively. With adolescents, however, interviewers have more flexibility in their expressions of affect or behavioral gestures, and even very subtle acknowledgments will affect the interactions.

Acknowledgments are useful for conveying understanding of the child's thoughts and feelings without interrupting the child's train of thought. A child is often more willing to verbalize his or her feelings and concerns about a topic once the interviewer has shown empathy with the child's point of view. Interviewers need to be aware of their use of acknowledgments and use clinical judgment when deciding whether to acknowledge a child's thought or behavior. Although not evaluative, acknowledgments typically result in elaboration of the child's current topic of conversation. Therefore, caution in the use of acknowledgments is essential to avoid inadvertently reinforcing redundant or irrelevant discussion.

DESCRIPTIVE STATEMENTS

A descriptive statement is a verbal picture of the ongoing behavior of the child, as in the following examples:

> You're drawing lots of colors in your rainbow.
>
> You look sad when you talk about your grandmother.
>
> You're using your indoor voice today.

Descriptive statements are a simple way to give attention to the child and to focus on those aspects of the situation that are likely to interest him or her. With very young children who are generally egocentric, descriptions of their behavior let them know that you notice what they are doing or that you can share their perspective. Descriptive statements provide an easy way to encourage the child to continue ongoing behavior. Perhaps of most importance to the interviewer who is uncertain where to proceed next, descriptive statements can provide a way to maintain communication while planning the next step. When at a loss for words, novice clinicians are sometimes tempted to make personal comments, such as "I liked cars when I was your age" or "I have a brother with that name too," which rarely promote relevant discussion. Children commonly do not clearly describe their feelings in words, although they sometimes express their emotions very clearly through their actions (e.g., drawing) or facial expressions. When the interviewer describes their expressions, children learn that emotions are topics of interest in the interview without feeling pushed to describe the feelings they may be hesitant or unable to verbalize yet.

In choosing an appropriate descriptive statement, the interviewer must consider the child's developmental level. It is important that the child understands the descriptive statement. Therefore, the interviewer must choose age-appropriate vocabulary and short, concise statements when addressing young children. Even when addressing older children, the interviewer must be aware of their ability to comprehend complex language and abstract content. In addition, adolescents often have terms and phrases in their repertoire that have a specific meaning for their age group. Therefore, the interviewer must be cautious in using descriptive statements that reflect ambiguity. It is possible that descriptive statements spoken with good intent could be perceived as offensive by the preadolescent.

REFLECTIVE STATEMENTS

Reflective statements repeat or paraphrase what the child says. They may be literally the same words or they may provide some elaboration or interpretation of what the child said, but they always retain the essential meaning of the child's expression through reflection of the content or the emotion of the child's expression. The following examples are reflective statements:

CHILD: I want the black crayon.
INTERVIEWER: You want the black crayon. (literal)
INTERVIEWER: You need a dark color for the picture of your house. (elaboration)
CHILD: I hid under the covers.
INTERVIEWER: You were really scared by the thunder. (reflection of emotions)

Interviewers use reflective statements to convey acceptance, interest, and understanding. By reflecting the child's ideas, the interviewer gives the child an opportunity to clarify the interviewer's understanding and elaborate with further details. Reflective statements generally result in increased verbal interchange between the interviewer and the child.

REFRAMING

Reframing is a technique in which the interviewer provides the child with a more appropriate interpretation of his or her situation. The following are examples in which the interviewer reframes information that the child has provided:

CHILD: My mom is always getting mad at me for leaving my shoes everywhere. She always says that my room is messy and that I never make my bed.
INTERVIEWER: It sounds like your mom is noticing that you're growing up and you're able to handle more responsibilities. But you don't seem very happy with the way she reminds you of the things you need to do.
CHILD: I keep on trying to study really hard, but I'm still not making good grades. I'm tired of school.

INTERVIEWER: All the effort you've been putting into your school work shows that you really want to do well in school. Every hour you spend studying will bring you closer to getting better grades. But so far, you've found that certain study habits may not work too well for you. In therapy, we can use that strong desire of yours and think of other techniques that may work better for you.

Children tend to be fixed in how they view their environment. When a child has negative views, it is important for the interviewer to recognize the child's feelings and guide the child toward a more appropriate interpretation of the situation. By your acknowledging the child's views and discussing them in a more positive and encouraging light, the child will be exposed to a new way of understanding his or her situation.

PRAISE STATEMENTS

A statement of "labeled praise" indicates approval and specifies exactly what act or event the interviewer is encouraging:

I like how gently you're playing with the toys.

You're doing a good job of telling me what happened.

It sounds like you did the best you could at getting along with her.

The child frequently anticipates assessment as a negative event; genuine labeled praise helps minimize the child's anxiety, and it is a direct expression of acceptance. It also serves to encourage and guide the child's talk in productive directions. The type of labeled praise that the interviewer uses must change according to the developmental level of the child; it is more subtle and less effusive with the older child.

SUMMARY STATEMENTS

Summary statements are used to review information that the child has presented in the preceding segments of the interview. The interviewer briefly describes the information the child has given, as in the following examples:

You've told me that you fight a lot with your sister and you don't think your family loves you. I'd like to know more about how your family treats you.

As I understand things so far, one big problem is school, and another one is your brother's friends. Is that correct?

We've talked about your brothers and your sisters. What is one of your favorite activities that you enjoy doing with your family?

Summary statements can be useful for focusing on a particular topic when the child has presented several content areas. As shown in the first example above, the interviewer uses the summary statement to guide the interview process and solicit the desired information. Summary statements are also useful for confirming the interviewer's understanding of information that the child has presented, as seen in the second example above. The third example shows how interviewers can use summary statements to introduce a new topic of discussion without breaking the flow of conversation. Summary statements are often used when the interviewer wishes to close one area of discussion and introduce a new topic.

AVOID CRITICAL STATEMENTS

Critical statements are verbal statements that indicate disapproval, such as negative "stop" commands and insults to the child. Critical statements may also imply that what the child says, thinks, or does is in some way wrong or bad, as in these examples:

You should know better than that.

Stop climbing out of your chair.

You don't try very hard to remember.

Critical statements foster negative emotional reactions such as anger, resentment, and frustration, and lead to unproductive defensiveness. These statements are particularly detrimental to rapport and may lead the child to act negatively or resistantly for the remainder of the interview. For example, a child who is told that he or she is not trying hard enough may lose the motivation to respond further. Although it is easy to avoid blatant criticism of the child, the interviewer must be vigilant to avoid subtle criticisms, such as "I know you can do better." As an alternative, the interviewer might choose to acknowledge the child's effort by saying "It's a hard job and I can see that you're still trying."

Often, children's negative, aggressive, or destructive behavior can be avoided by structuring the situation at the start (see "Getting Started" later in this chapter). Occasionally, however, negative behavior will be presented that is too harmful or destructive to be continued. If the rules of the playroom have been previously stated, rule-based correction can be used to avoid direct critical statements. For example, a reiteration such as "One of the rules of the playroom is that things cannot be broken" is preferable to "Don't break the doll." In other instances, a critical statement intended to change a child's inappropriate behavior might be restated as an invitation for an incompatible behavior. The following examples demonstrate critical and invitational statements:

CHILD: (hitting head against wall)
INTERVIEWER: Stop hitting your head. (poor)
INTERVIEWER: Come and play at the table. (better)
CHILD: (throwing blocks at interviewer)
INTERVIEWER: I don't like it when you throw blocks at me. (poor)
INTERVIEWER: Put the blocks in the box. (better)
CHILD: (drawing on table)
INTERVIEWER: Don't draw on the table. (poor)
Interviewer: Draw your picture on this paper so you can save it if you want. (better)

There are also situations when inappropriate behavior can simply be ignored. Rather than criticizing, the clinician can watch for positive behaviors and reinforce them when they occur, as in these examples:

CHILD: (climbs on table)
INTERVIEWER: (ignores climbing)
CHILD: (gets off table)
INTERVIEWER: It's safer when you stand on the floor.
INTERVIEWER: Tell me a story about this picture.
CHILD: I can't think of anything.
INTERVIEWER: (ignores statement) What is this girl doing?
CHILD: She's sitting.

INTERVIEWER: She is sitting. I'm glad you told me about part of this picture.

OPEN-ENDED QUESTIONS

An open-ended question, in contrast to a close-ended question, is one that cannot be answered with a simple yes or no. Open-ended questions are generally preferable:

Do you like dolls? (close-ended)

What toys do you like best? (open-ended)

Can you remember anything else about that? (close-ended)

What else can you remember about that? (open-ended)

Was it bad? (close-ended)

What was it like for you? (open-ended)

Open-ended questions lead to more information per question and minimize the possibility of leading the child to a conclusion that is the interviewer's rather than the child's. Open-ended questions are especially useful for opening up new areas of discussion and can facilitate spontaneous, continued conversation. When using open-ended questions with preschool children, it is important to comment on the child's response or encourage the child to elaborate. Young children may not provide all of the information the interviewer is seeking. If the interviewer is seeking information that has not been revealed in the child's response, the interviewer may use close-ended questions to elicit the necessary details (e.g., "You said that you're getting bad grades in school. Are you having trouble doing your school work?").

Open-ended questions that begin with "why" should be avoided. "Why" questions are typically perceived as threatening and lead to defensiveness. Most children referred to a clinician have already been asked "why" many times with respect to their difficulties. Their responses are likely to be post hoc rationalizations rather than the desired information describing the steps leading to the problem behavior. For example, the question "Why did you skip school?" could be better rephrased as "What things about school don't you like?" or "What things do you do instead of going to school?" It is the interviewer's responsibility to determine motivation, therefore it is unproductive to ask the child to make interpretations in the interview.

AGE-APPROPRIATE COMMUNICATION

There are many areas in which an interviewer may alter his or her style depending on the age of the child. The first and most obvious is the vocabulary and sentence structure that is used in talking with a child. It is often difficult for a novice interviewer to translate sophisticated words or concepts into the simple terminology that a young child can understand. For example, in attempting to determine possible reinforcers for use in a token program with a fourth-grader, the child would have difficulty understanding "What kinds of activities are reinforcing for you?" Instead, the clinician might ask, "What things do you like to do?"

One source of confusion for the child is psychological jargon. Many words and phrases that become basic vocabulary to mental health professionals are not familiar to children. Sentences such as "How do you interact with your dad?" and "It sounds like you wanted some feedback from your teacher" contain typical examples. Children are not likely to point out words they do not understand, but these words often lead to misunderstanding and disrupt rapport. Audiotaping an interview for later scrutiny with a supervisor or colleague is often a useful technique for identifying jargon and honing skills for interviewing children.

Young children can become particularly confused with the use of "feeling words," such as "depressed," "anxious," "disappointed," and "guilty." Typically, young children understand few feeling descriptions other than "mad," "sad," "glad," and "scared." To obtain more information about the affective experience of the child, the clinician would do better to work toward having the child describe specific examples behaviorally. Rather than asking "What is it about your mother that angers you?", the clinician can more profitably ask the child "What things does your mother do that make you mad?" At other times, children may use words or phrases incorrectly to describe their feelings. When a child uses sophisticated words to describe feelings, it is advisable to explore the child's understanding of the words. For example, Boggs and Eyberg (1990) suggest that the interviewer prompt

the child to provide clarification by reflecting the child's phrase.

In addition to using clear and simple vocabulary, the interviewer must limit use of qualifying phrases with children. Although the clinician's intent is to increase accuracy when asking a question such as "Where are you most likely to be when you cry?", that information is more apt to be obtained by asking "Where do you cry?" The interviewer must also limit the amount of information conveyed in each sentence. As a general rule, each statement or question should be short and simple and contain only one idea. For example, the interviewer would not want to say "When is it that you feel bad, and what do you do then?" but instead "When do you feel bad?" and then follow obtained leads with subsequent questions.

The use of silences is another important style issue to consider in the child interview. A silence of more than a few seconds is often aversive to children when the primary mode of interaction is verbal (Boggs & Eyberg, 1990). With the preadolescent in particular, an extended silence following an interviewer's question tends to be nonproductive and contributes to resistance. In some cases, the child may perceive the "pregnant silence" as being a challenge or an indication of disapproval from the interviewer. In contrast to the strictly verbal exchange interview often used with the older child, the silences that occur spontaneously during play interactions with younger children can be used productively to allow nonverbal communications.

Decisions about the use of physical contact when interviewing the child have few explicit guidelines. The reasons an interviewer might touch a child are varied and could include the wish to gain a child's attention, to encourage a child to continue in an activity (often used in conjunction with praise), to calm a child, or to demonstrate affection. In general, physical contact is used judiciously and in accordance with the child's history and reactions. Paralleling general societal norms, the interviewer will provide relatively less physical contact to older children. In the play interview, a touch on the child's hand might be used to redirect the child's attention to the task, and a pat on the shoulder might accompany verbal praise. When children wish to hug the interviewer hello or good-bye, they often accept and enjoy an enthusiastic redirection to a "high five." In rare cases where a child exhibits acute emotional distress (such as crying or showing intense fear), the interviewer may feel it important to provide additional physical comforting. In most cases, however, the role of the interviewer is not to provide nurturance. The interviewer can typically minimize emotional distress by using one of the following strategies: (1) offering verbal reassurance, (2) distracting the child toward a pleasant activity, or (3) redirecting the topic to a more neutral area. With young children, for example, the redirection back to toys immediately following a stressful interchange may reduce emotional distress without need for physical comforting. Older children may benefit from having conversation redirected toward areas in which they have personal strengths.

Another way that clinicians sometimes demonstrate nurturance is by sharing a snack or a drink with the child. Opinions on this as a practice in child therapy vary considerably (e.g., Greenspan & Greenspan, 1981). Some clinicians argue that it is critical to respond concretely to the unmet dependency needs of some children, or that use of such primary reinforcers can enhance the clinician's reinforcement valence. We suggest that this is an unnecessary procedure in the child interview. Family health beliefs about many snack foods have assumed increased salience in recent years, and potential problems can be avoided if food is not offered. Although it may be tempting to do so, it is advisable to avoid assuming a parental role with the child during the initial interview.

A final issue to consider in age-related communication pertains to reference points of interest. Children at different developmental levels relate to different media heroes, games, clothing fads, and hobbies. Conversation about current topics can be very effective in establishing rapport. This means that the clinician needs to be familiar with what is current in the child's world and should not rely on recollection of his or her own childhood to determine the child's interests. For interviewers who have daily contact with children, this may not be difficult. For others, deliberate efforts to learn more about the child's world may be necessary. Browsing in toy stores or in the children's section of bookshops and clothing stores or leafing through toy or clothing catalogues can familiarize the clinician with the trade names of popular toys and current trends in collectibles (e.g., Beanie Babies). Watching the Saturday morning cartoons and the after-school to early evening television programs can serve as an introduction to the media heroes of different age

groups. Knowing the traits of the characters a child identifies with may reveal information about the child's values. Simply talking with friends who are parents can provide a wealth of information about popular interests and activities of children of various ages.

CONDUCTING THE INTERVIEW

For heuristic purposes, we divide the child interview process into five successive stages. In each stage, we describe step-by-step interactions that collectively define the interview. Common problems that may arise to interrupt or interfere with forward progress through the stages are also presented along with ways the interviewer can handle these disruptions.

GETTING STARTED

In most instances, the interviewer will meet the family in the waiting room. Prior to approaching the parent and child, the interviewer can make valuable observations about the child's physical appearance, coordination, mood, activity level, location, and responses to parents and others. The interviewer can also observe parent-child interactions and child or family problems. This may be the most naturalistic observation period available.

The introduction to parents and child can take several forms (e.g., Greenspan & Greenspan, 1981; Reisman & Ribordy, 1993). Opinions vary as to whether the interviewer should address the parents or the child first and the degree of formality that is appropriate in these initial introductions. Although some clinicians prefer to avoid using a formal title, others believe that such a procedure is important to establish the nature of the relationship as a helping relationship and different from a casual friendship (Reisman & Ribordy, 1993). A formal introduction, given with a smile and individual attention, is least likely to offend.

Following the introduction to the parents, the interviewer may wait briefly for the parents to introduce their child or may choose to initiate the introduction to the child immediately. The first approach may be preferable when the child appears shy or frightened, when the interviewer wishes to observe a brief sample of how the parents gain the child's cooperation, or when the interviewer wishes to acknowledge the parents' authority. An immediate introduction to the child may be the preferred approach when the interviewer wishes to communicate with and express respect for the child or when it seems important to avoid appearing allied with the parents. This latter approach seems most advantageous with an older child. Of course, if the parents do not make the introduction, the interviewer would turn to the child and do so.

In the introduction to the child, the interviewer might say "Hello Susie, I'm Dr. Jones." Regardless of the child's age, he or she will likely be suspicious of the interviewer. To allay the child's initial apprehension, the interviewer can make brief comments about the child's appearance, dress, or any personal object the child may have brought. Comments such as "That's a big gator on your shirt!" or "What a pretty doll. What is her name?" let children know that the interviewer is interested in them. These comments should be positive, brief, and enthusiastic in nature.

Next, provide information to the child and family about the plan for the session. If the plan is stated while in the waiting room, it can help to alleviate the natural anxiety a family may have about the visit. The plan should clearly tell the child what he or she will be doing, where he or she will be doing it, and where his or her parents will be. There are a number of ways to sequence the interview. For example, the following statements would be appropriate for the younger child:

"I brought a special picture book that you can look at while I talk to your mom and dad. We will be talking in the room right across the hall for a little while. Then we'll come back, and you and I will get a chance to play and talk. If you need anything, you can ask Mrs. Smith [receptionist] right there." (parent interview first)

"I have some special toys and pictures for us in a room just down the hall. Your mom and dad will be working on some papers right here while we play and talk. I want you to come with me, and I will show you where the toys are." (child interview first)

"The four of us will go to the play room so that we can have a chance to talk, and I have some special toys for you to play with." (family interview first)

A typical procedure is to ask the parents to fill out standardized assessment questionnaires about the child and family (see Boggs & Eyberg, 1990) while waiting for the child. Giving this task to the parents at this time can set the stage for asking the child to come to the interview room while the parents are filling out the forms. If the assessment session will include standardized parent-child observations, it can be explained to the child that after a period of play (talk) with the interviewer, he or she will have an opportunity to play (talk) with his or her parents in the playroom.

The walk to the playroom with the child provides additional time to establish rapport. It is useful to chat with the child about interesting and nonthreatening topics (e.g., "It looks like you have new tennis shoes"; "I have a brand new puppet in my office").

POTENTIAL PROBLEMS IN GETTING STARTED

Because beginning clinicians often find it more comfortable to deal with adults, it may be tempting to ignore the child and to focus on the parent. It is important to give children equal time in the waiting room and in the family interview. Of course, there will be times, with younger children particularly, when they cannot be left in the waiting room and must be present during the "parent interview." It is inefficient to try to include a child in interview topics such as developmental history, for example. In this situation, suitable options may include explaining the need to talk to the parents and providing the child with toys, paper and pencil, or a book and separate space in the room. With the highly disruptive child or when sensitive material must be discussed, it is best to obtain a babysitter for the child in the waiting room, such as a clinic staff, or even an understanding colleague for whom you may have to return the favor.

A second potential problem in getting started arises when parents begin to describe the child's problems too soon. Sometimes, parents begin an account of the child's behavior when they first meet the interviewer in the waiting room. This can interfere with initial attempts to establish rapport with the child. The premature offering of information can often be avoided by the early provision of information about the plan for the session or can be gently curtailed by assuring the parents that there will be an opportunity to talk in detail during the interview.

The clinician encounters another kind of problem if a different set of persons than expected is present for the child's interview. This might be a different parent than was expected, more parents than expected (such as both natural and step), and/or additional children. It might also be that the parents are absent, or even the child may be absent. The interviewer will need to be flexible in dealing with these kinds of unanticipated situations and should do so without communicating inconvenience to the family. Occasionally, the clinician may capitalize on unexpected situations by learning more about the family, their values, or their perceptions of the child. After meeting the individuals who are present, it may be necessary to take some time to revise the plan for the session. This can be done by telling the family that some additional forms, toys, or chairs are needed, and asking them to wait a few minutes.

A fourth potential problem in getting started occurs when the child to be interviewed is screaming and crying in the waiting room. The first option available is to wait a few minutes before entering the waiting area to see if the child's distress is brief. Allowing the parent to calm the child may prevent a circumscribed outburst from setting up a negative initial interaction between interviewer and child. If the child continues to cry or begins crying after entry into the waiting room, one of several strategies can be employed. The interviewer may try initially to ignore the crying and proceed to greet the family and describe the plan for evaluation. If the child continues to cry, it may be possible to distract the child by offering him or her a toy and engaging briefly in play. If this too fails, we suggest beginning with the parent interview with the child present. Parents know their children well and will likely be able to calm the child during this time. Making age-appropriate, appealing toys available during this time is a useful strategy.

A related problem encountered occasionally in the waiting room involves difficulties in separation. As a first consideration, most children under the age of 3 or 3.5 years can be expected to resist separating. Unless seeing the child alone is important, it is wise to avoid unnecessary separation for the very young child. Separation problems with children aged 4 years and older can often be prevented by careful and clear structuring of the situation. The child must be told where the parent or relative will wait and younger children need to be shown the specific area. In implementing the separation, it is not a good idea to ask the child if he or she would like to come. This question may unintentionally imply that the child's preference is being solicited. Instead, it is more effective to say "Come with me to the playroom" while offering a hand to the young child. By providing the directive and taking the initiative as if compliance is expected, the interviewer can minimize potential separation problems. Alternatively, it is sometimes effective to provide the child with two choices, either of which is acceptable. For example, the interviewer could ask the child "Would you like to leave your dolly here with your mother, or would you like to bring her with you?" By your providing the child a choice and some semblance of control in the situation, the child may feel more comfortable. Sometimes, carrying a particularly enticing toy (e.g., a bubble-blowing bear), demonstrating it, and then offering the child a chance to play with it but only in the special playroom allows the interviewer to coax a hesitant child into the interview room.

Similar strategies may also be used when separation problems persist. For example, the interviewer can have the parents accompany the child to the interview room and encourage the child to explore the toys. As the child relaxes, the interviewer can increase the one-to-one involvement with the child while remaining focused on play materials. When the child becomes engaged in play, the interviewer can give the parents explicit verbal permission to leave the room. Parents of children who have separation problems may also be ambivalent about separating, particularly if the child begins to protest. If this is the case, the interviewer can give the parents brief verbal assurance, such as "Things will be fine." If this is not enough to reassure the parents or child or both, it may be best to redirect the parents to stay. At this point, any further attempts at separation are likely to be unproductive and have deleterious effects.

SETTING THE STAGE

The initial few minutes with the child in the interview room can be awkward and anxiety-inducing for the novice interviewer. The child typically looks to the adult for guidance regarding appropriate behavior in this new setting. Providing a structure for the child in the initial stages of the interview will reduce the child's anxiety and set the stage for conduct during the session (Calzada, Aamiry, & Eyberg, 1998).

The purpose of the evaluation may determine the degree of structure the clinician will choose to employ initially with the child. If the first objective is to administer standardized tests, a high degree of initial structure is recommended. On the other hand, if direct contact with the child is limited to the unstructured clinical interview, less structure may be needed or desired.

The presence and placement of objects in the room provide the initial means of structuring. By carefully selecting the play materials, the clinician guides the interview to topics of clinical relevance. If the interviewer wishes to assess the child's perceptions of his or her family, for example, then materials relating to houseplay should be prominent. Additional materials made visible to the child during testing or interviewing are likely to be a distraction.

The degree of structure is also influenced by the explicitness and immediacy with which the child is directed to a seat. If the interviewer wishes to have the child remain seated throughout most of the session, it is advisable to direct the child to a seat shortly after entering the room. The interviewer might say "I have a special chair just for you [pointing to the chair]. Sit right here." If it is necessary for the child to remain seated for an extended period of time or if the child is very active, the placement of the child's chair should be planned in advance. By placing the child's chair in a corner of the room blocked on two sides by a table and the interviewer's chair, the child will attempt to leave less often. Gentle physical constraint, along with explicit directions, may also be necessary and usually is not upsetting to the child. For example, the interviewer can hold the child's hands while setting out objects or extend an arm to the child's shoulder if the child starts to get up. Of course, as described earlier, frequent praise of the child for the positive opposite behavior is likely to maintain the child's attention on the tasks. Initial comments such as "You're staying in your chair so well" as well as comments throughout the interview such as "You're trying really hard on this" (young child) or "You're doing a nice job of telling me what happened" (older child) serve to reinforce the ongoing behavior. Most children enjoy being allowed to select a sticker as a prize for staying seated or working on a task. Allowing children to place earned stickers on a paper they can keep is a simple and powerful technique for structuring with disruptive children.

In a play interview, and particularly with the disruptive child, it is advisable to point out to the child what he or she can and cannot do. For example, "Two important rules of the playroom are that you cannot break anything and that you cannot do anything that will hurt you or me." If the behavioral limits are established at the outset, occurrences of rule breaking provide information about how the child responds to rules as well as a means for avoiding direct criticism if the child breaks a rule. Instead, rule-based corrections are possible.

Particularly for the older child, an important consideration in setting the stage for the interview pertains to letting the child know more about what is going to happen. There are a number of ways to broach this topic. It may be that the child will provide initial cues, such as a look of apprehension or a direct question: "Are you going to give me a shot?" At other times, the interviewer will need to bring up the topic in a statement such as "I wonder whether you know what kind of doctor I am." An explanation can vary according to the age of the child. One introduction is as "a doctor for feelings, someone who talks with boys and girls who sometimes feel bad and helps them feel happier." Another introduction might be as "a psychologist, someone who talks with kids and their families when there are some problems and helps them learn better ways of getting along." The interviewer can also alleviate some of the child's concerns by giving the child an opportunity to ask questions about the interview process.

At any point during the interview, the interviewer must be aware that communication problems may occur due to ethnic, cultural, or socioeconomic differences between the interviewer and the child. Verbal and nonverbal behaviors may be misinterpreted by the interviewer or the child due to differences in communication style. For example, differences in the use of gaze patterns can produce miscues and awkward periods. Interviewers must guard against making hasty interpretations and diagnoses when cultural differences exist. The expression of psychopathology is often related to the child's culture (Whaley, 1997). Therefore, the interviewer must be aware that symptoms have different interpretations depending on the child's group membership. In working with a child of a different ethnic, cultural, or social class group, it is essential for the interviewer to study the culture, language, and traditions of the group prior to the interview to become more familiar with the ongoing context in which the child is raised (e.g., Bernal & Knight, 1993; Harris, Blue, & Griffith, 1995; Owomoyela, 1996). The interviewer will also improve the quality of communication by becoming familiar with words or expressions that have special meaning to the child's group.

A final consideration in setting the stage is confidentiality. Confidentiality in relation to children is both an ethical and legal issue; it has been discussed in detail by Melton and Ehrenreich (1992) and Keith-Spiegel and Koocher (1998; Koocher & Keith-Spiegel, 1990). Legally, children have very limited rights to confidentiality. Ethically, however, the confidentiality of information provided by the child depends on both the age of the child and the purpose of the interview. In general, a discussion of confidentiality is unnecessary during the play interview with a preschool-age child (Boggs & Eyberg, 1990). With the preadolescent, unless the interviewer intends to cover highly sensitive topics, introducing the concept of the limits of confidentiality may serve only to confuse or intimidate the child. For most children, it may be best to address confidentiality in broad terms. For example, the interviewer might say "We will be talking about a lot of things today. Then you and I will talk to your parents about the things that are important. This way we can all work together to make things better." The development of trust is fostered more by the warmth and empathy conveyed by the clinician than by verbal assurances of limited confidentiality.

GATHERING INFORMATION

As soon as the process of establishing rapport with the child has been initiated, the gathering of relevant information can begin. The basic information usually desired from child interviews for effective diagnosis and treatment planning includes assessment of (1) intellectual and academic functioning, (2) developmental level, (3) personality functioning, (4) family functioning, (5) social functioning, and (6) temperament and affect. Not all of this information is sought in the child interview; formal psychometric assessment, structured behavioral observations, parent interviews, teacher interviews, and agency contacts serve as important sources of this material. However, the child interview may be particularly useful for assessing the child's perceptions of his or her environment and self, for gaining knowledge about the child's preferences, likes, dislikes, and expectations, for assessing the child's social and emotional skills, and for obtaining specific and sensitive types of information (Mash & Terdal, 1997).

In light of the large number of topics that could be covered in a child interview, it is important that the interviewer select areas carefully. A thorough review of all background information and presenting problem(s) of the particular child can guide the choice of those areas. The interviewer should also review the professional literature relevant to the child's problem, any associated physical or cognitive deficits, and possible treatments. It is a good idea to prepare in advance a brief checklist of the information to be obtained during the interview. To maintain rapport with the child in the face of unanticipated events, however, it is important to remain flexible and not follow an outline rigidly. Periodic reference to the checklist can provide reassurance and help ensure that important topics are not forgotten.

An organizational format that can be helpful is one that proceeds through the child's perceptions about his or her (1) environment, (2) self, and (3) presenting problem(s). Included in environment are peer relations, school, and family; included in self-perceptions might be wishes, interests, and fears. The presenting problem consists of the specific complaint that led to the referral. It may stem from either the environment or the self. Addressing the presenting problem last allows the interviewer to have the opportunity to establish a degree of rapport and trust before addressing the most difficult issues. It also provides the interviewer with a more comprehensive understanding of the child's perception of the problem.

Often, it is useful to employ "selective reflection" to structure the conversation during the interview. This involves listening to the total content but reflecting only that portion of the verbalization that the interviewer wishes to explore further. For example, a child might say "Sometimes I get really mad at my sister, but Mom always takes her side." This presents at least two choices for direction. If the child's relationship with his or her sister seems most important, the response to the child could be "Your sister does some things that make you mad."

On the other hand, if the child's relationship with the mother is the focus, the response could be "Your mother doesn't always seem to understand how you feel." Another technique useful in providing transitions between topic areas is to use a summary statement of the content areas just covered, placing last in the summary the area to be pursued further. This can be followed with a statement such as "I'd like to talk more about [the last point]." Summary statements can also be used to provide closure to a topic area, and then new topic areas can be introduced simply by asking new questions.

An approach that can be used within each of the content areas is to move from the positive, non-threatening topics to the more threatening topics. The problem topic is generally not addressed until the broader context is understood. Younger children can be made to feel more comfortable by beginning with subjects they know and like. Aspects of the child such as age, nursery school, birthday, pets, favorite games, and TV shows are usually safe topics. Older children, who have had more societal contacts, may be relaxed by discussion focused on friends, school, sports, or social activities.

In exploring self-perceptions, the interviewer may initially ask children about what they like best about themselves or what they are most proud of. Discussion of strengths is usually nonthreatening and eases the transition into more threatening topics. For example, asking children to list three positive things about themselves leads logically to asking them to describe three things they would like to be different about themselves. The pairing of positive and negative in this way minimizes the child's reactivity to discussion of threatening topics.

Another procedure the interviewer can use to shift into more direct discussion of a threatening topic area is to acknowledge the source of information before asking the questions. For example, "Your mother said you hit your teacher. What things make you mad at her?" or "You told me before that you don't like school. What things about school don't you like?" These introductions help to legitimize the shift into a threatening area.

Once a threatening topic area has been opened, a child will frequently display resistance. The child may give cues such as becoming silent, changing the subject, saying "I don't know," changing affect, or changing activity. Often, this resistance is an internally imposed protection against embarrassment or fear of disapproval and can prevent the

interviewer from learning important information. If the interviewer does not handle this situation sensitively, rapport can be damaged. Several strategies can help reduce the child's fear. One is to allow the child to play with a toy (e.g., blocks) while talking. This provides an opportunity to fall back on description of play activities as a means of reducing the child's anxiety without having to enter into a new area of discussion. The interviewer can describe the play briefly and then ease the conversation back to the clinical issue. The advantage of this strategy is that it can be used repeatedly without disrupting the natural flow of conversation. A variant of this approach is the use of puppet play. Some children find it easier to express themselves by talking as or to a puppet rather than directly to the clinician. A second strategy for reducing the child's anxiety when dealing with threatening material is to acknowledge the child's discomfort explicitly. By saying "It's all right if you don't feel like talking about that yet," the interviewer not only gives permission for hesitancy in discussion but also establishes the expectation that the child will be ready to discuss the topic in the future and that the clinician may ask again. A third strategy to employ when encountering resistance is to follow, or immediately direct, the child back to a nonthreatening topic and gradually approach the threatening topic again in a different way.

At times, the interviewer may suspect that the child's resistance to talking is more externally imposed. That is, the child may have been directed not to talk about certain things. This situation is perhaps most frequently encountered with children who have been abused. In these instances, gentle questioning needs to convey support and acceptance. One approach is to say "I know that sometimes kids are told not to talk with me about things that have happened. Were you told not to say anything about this to me?" Here, a close-ended question may provide the child the safety of responding with a simple head nod or shake.

Interviewing children in sensitive areas, such as parental divorce, suicidal ideation, and physical or sexual abuse, requires expertise gained through training and supervision. We advise the clinician untrained or inexperienced in these areas to exercise caution when these areas first become evident during a child interview. The discussion we provide is not a substitute for the expertise required in these situations, but is intended to heighten awareness of the issues and recognition of signs that indicate that direct supervision, consultation, or referral should be sought for the interview.

When it becomes evident during an assessment interview that the child's parents are in the process of divorce, the interviewer must be aware of the possibility that information obtained from the child may be subpoenaed by the courts in a child custody dispute. Parents need to be informed that the interviewer is not a child custody expert and will not be able to provide information relevant to custody issues. They also need to be informed that a specific custody evaluation may be sought if they wish information from the child for the custody determination. Similarly, the interviewer inexperienced in custody evaluation should not record unnecessary information that could be taken out of context in a custody dispute. Children in the situation of an impending divorce often have emotional conflicts and disrupted behavior. Young children often experience sadness and fear, whereas older children more often experience anger or ambivalence toward one or both parents (Ashmore & Brodzinsky, 1986). The interviewer should convey to parents the importance of allowing a distinction in confidentiality between a custody evaluation and the treatment a child might need. Children in individual treatment must be allowed to express painful thoughts without feeling disloyal or fearing retribution.

When suicidal ideation is suggested during an assessment interview, the interviewer must rapidly make a number of difficult decisions. These include whether the child can safely return home under parental supervision or whether immediate hospitalization is needed to assure the safety of the child. An interviewer inexperienced in the assessment of child suicide potential must seek supervision or consultation with a knowledgeable colleague on the spot. Epidemiological evidence indicates that attempted suicide in the United States is rare among children under the age of 12 and is likely to be extremely rare among children under age 5 (Hawton, 1986), but it does happen. Once alerted to statements or behaviors that might signal suicidal thoughts or self-injurious behavior, the interviewer might begin by asking the child a general question, such as "What do you do when you are really mad at yourself?" or "What do you want to do when you feel so bad?" Responses that suggest suicidal ideation from older children might be followed with questions aimed at learning more about the nature

and extent of the child's thinking in this area. With a nondisclosing child, it may be necessary to use a close-ended question, such as "Do you ever feel so bad that you think about hurting yourself?" With this topic, interviewers need to communicate their willingness to hear, to understand, and to help the child through statements that encourage the child to elaborate, such as interpretative reflective statements (e.g., "It sounds like sometimes you feel pretty bad about yourself"). It is usually critical that the child's caregivers be interviewed specifically about the child's situation, moods, and behaviors during the assessment as well. Again, if interview information suggests any cause for concern, the inexperienced interviewer should seek expert advice before the child leaves. A primary responsibility is to make certain that a potentially suicidal child is closely monitored by a responsible adult until the concern has passed.

When the novice interviewer becomes aware of behaviors or statements by the child that suggest possible physical or sexual abuse, there are several initial considerations. For the safety of the child, when child abuse is suspected, the suspicion must be reported to authorities, such as child protection agencies, who are able to investigate. The interviewer's questions must be sufficient to determine whether there is a realistic concern to report. They must be thoughtfully and carefully worded so as to convey empathy and safety to the child. They must also in no way influence the child's response. In this situation, it is not the interviewer's task to determine whether abuse conclusively occurred, but only whether there is reason to suspect that it has. When a suspicion is reported to authorities, there will likely be an investigative interview conducted by highly trained individuals, who will tape-record the interview so as to preserve the child's earliest statements and to prevent the necessity of repeated, stressful questioning of the child. Child abuse investigations may lead to allegations of abuse in legal proceedings, where it is important that the novice interviewer be able to testify that his or her questions did not influence the child's subsequent investigative interview. Carefully documenting not only the child's precise statements but also the exact questions and procedures that were conducted is important.

To obtain sufficient information for reporting suspected abuse from children under age 7, nonverbal, indirect procedures are suggested (Wolfe &

McEachran, 1997). For example, statements related to abuse might be asked in the context of drawing or imaginative play where the child may demonstrate the answer nonverbally. Among school-age children, verbal strategies may be employed. Wolfe suggests that the interviewer begin with a general discussion of activities and events the child enjoys and then proceed to more specific questions about fears, worries, and recent negative events. The questions should be phrased in such a way that an inability to recall or a lack of knowledge is acceptable. It is essential to include a discussion about the child's understanding of aggressive behavior and the child's attitude toward conflict with others. Wolfe cautions that the interviewer should (1) avoid leading questions, (2) closely monitor the child for signs of growing fear, agitation, or anxiety, and (3) provide the child with frequent reassurance that he or she will not be harmed for disclosing any information. If necessary, specific questions can be used to obtain clarification. For example, the interviewer may follow up on inconsistencies in a gentle, nonthreatening manner. If the child has used a term that seems inappropriate for his or her age, the interviewer may ask where he or she learned that word. The interviewer must avoid rewarding the answers of the child to avoid affecting the child's responses.

It is during discussion of these most sensitive topics that the issue of confidentiality with the child may need to be directly addressed. It is important for the interviewer to be honest with the child by communicating that the primary goal is to protect the child from being hurt and that this might mean that others will have to be told what he or she says. Interviewers can explain that they will use their best judgment in deciding whether to tell another person this and express the hope that the child will trust this judgment. Ultimately, most clinicians agree that the child should know that he or she has the right to withhold information and that the interviewer will understand and respect the child's decision and will still do everything possible to help and protect the child.

WRAPPING UP

After the relevant topic areas have been explored, it is important to acknowledge any efforts the child has made during the interview in sharing information. A verbal summary of what the interviewer has learned provides the opportunity to demonstrate to the child that he or she has been heard and understood. It is useful at this point, especially with the older child, to ask for any additional information the child might want to offer or for any suggestions the child might have for solving identified problems. This is also the time for the interviewer to convey a desire to help the child with these problems. A final step in wrapping up is to provide the child with as much information as possible about what the interviewer plans to do with the collected information. To protect the child's rights, the child should be informed about what information will be communicated to the parents or others as well as any plans or recommendations regarding intervention. An example of the concluding comments to an assessment interview with a child, where the referring problem is enuresis, might be:

> You and I have done some important talking today. You worked hard at helping me to understand how you feel. It sounds like you have quite a lot of friends to play with and that school is going very well for you in second grade. But it seems like things haven't been as good for you at home with your mom. I guess she, and you too, have been unhappy because you sometimes wet the bed. There are some ways that I can help you learn how to stay dry at night. What I'd like to do now is to have your parents come in so we can all talk together about some of these ways and see if they would like to help us. How does that sound to you?

These final comments exemplify several of the basic interviewer skills discussed in this chapter: acknowledging and praising the child's efforts in the interview, reflecting and summarizing some of the major content areas addressed, and leading from the discussion of the child's strengths into more threatening problem areas. The problems are stated in a way that does not criticize the child, and an open-ended question is used to elicit the child's responses to the plan. The words used are simple and appropriate to the age of the child interviewed. The use of the process skills described in this chapter will enable the beginning clinician to engage the child in the interview process and to conduct an informative interview.

REFERENCES

Ashmore, R.D., & Brodzinsky, D.M. (1986). *Thinking about the family: Views of parents and children.* Hillsdale, NJ: Erlbaum.

Bernal, M.E., & Knight, G.P. (Eds.). (1993). *Ethnic identity: Formation and transmission among Hispanics and other minorities.* Albany: State University of New York Press.

Boggs, S.R., & Eyberg, S. (1990). Interviewing techniques and establishing rapport. In A.M. La Greca (Ed.), *Through the eyes of the child: Obtaining self-reports from children and adolescents* (pp. 85–108). Boston: Allyn & Bacon.

Calzada, E., Aamiry, A., & Eyberg, S.M. (1998). Principles of psychotherapy with behavior problem children. In G.P. Koocher, J.C. Norcross, & S.S. Hill (Eds.), *Psychologist's desk reference* (pp. 257–261). New York: Oxford University Press.

Costello, A.J., Edelbrock, C.S., Dulcan, M.K., Kalas, R., & Klaric, S.H. (1984). *Report on the NIMH Diagnostic Interview Schedule for Children (DIS-C).* Washington, DC: National Institute of Mental Health.

Greenspan, S.I., & Greenspan, N.T. (1981). *The clinical interview with children.* New York: McGraw-Hill.

Harris, H.W., Blue, H.C., & Griffith, E.E. (Eds.). (1995). *Racial and ethnic identity: Psychological development and creative expression.* New York: Routledge & Kegan Paul.

Hawton, K. (1986). *Suicide and attempted suicide among children and adolescents.* Beverly Hills: Sage.

Hodges, K., & Cools, J.N. (1990). Structured diagnostic interviews. In A.M. La Greca (Ed.), *Through the eyes of the child: Obtaining self-reports from children and adolescents* (pp. 109–149). Boston: Allyn & Bacon.

Hodges, K., Kline, J., Fitch, P., McKnew, D., & Cytryn, L. (1981). The child assessment schedule: A diagnostic interview for research and clinical use. *Catalogue of Selected Documents in Psychology, 11,* 56.

Hodges, K., Kline, J., Stern, L., Cytryn, L., & McKnew, D. (1982). The development of a child assessment interview for research and clinical use. *Journal of Abnormal Child Psychology, 10,* 173–189.

Johnson, S.B. (1998). Juvenile diabetes. In T.H. Ollendick & M. Hersen (Eds.), *Handbook of child psychopathology* (3rd ed., pp. 417–434). New York: Plenum Press.

Keith-Spiegel, P., & Koocher, G.P. (1998). *Ethics in psychology: Professional standards and cases.* New York: Random House.

Koocher, G.P., & Keith-Spiegel, P. (1990). *Children, ethics, and the law: Professional issues and cases.* Lincoln: University of Nebraska Press.

La Greca, A.M., Kuttler, A.F., & Stone, W.L. (1992). Interviews and behavioral observations. In C.E. Walker & M.C. Roberts (Eds.), *Handbook of clinical child psychology* (2nd ed., pp. 63–83). New York: Wiley.

Mash, E.J., & Terdal, L.G. (1997). Assessment of child and family disturbance: A behavioral-systems approach. In E.J. Mash & L.G. Terdal (Eds.), *Assessment of childhood disorders* (3rd ed., pp. 3–68). New York: Guilford Press.

McNeil, C.B., Hembree-Kigin, T., & Eyberg, S.M. (1996). *Short-term play therapy for disruptive children.* King of Prussia, PA: Center for Applied Psychology.

Melton, G.B., & Ehrenreich, N.S. (1992). Ethical and legal issues in mental health services for children. In C.E. Walker & M.C. Roberts (Eds.), *Handbook of clinical child psychology* (2nd ed., pp. 1035–1055). New York: Wiley.

Owomoyela, O. (1996). *The African difference: Discourses on Africanity and the relativity of cultures.* Johannesburg, South Africa: Witwatersrand University Press.

Reisman, J.M., & Ribordy, S. (1993). *Principles of psychotherapy with children.* New York: Lexington Books.

Whaley, A. (1997). Ethnicity/race, paranoia, and psychiatric diagnoses: Clinical bias versus sociocultural differences. *Journal of Psychopathology and Behavioral Assessment, 19,* 1–20.

Wolfe, D.A., & McEachran, A. (1997). Child physical abuse and neglect. In E.J. Mash & L.G. Terdal (Eds.), *Assessment of childhood disorders* (3rd ed., pp. 523–568). New York: Guilford Press.

CHAPTER 6

Assessing Children through Interviews and Behavioral Observations

ANNETTE M. LA GRECA, AMI F. KUTTLER, AND WENDY L. STONE

Assessment represents the initial step in all clinical work with children and families. It is the process by which the professional and clients identify the problems of concern, determine clinical diagnoses, and establish treatment plans and recommendations. Beyond initial problem identification, assessment should be a continuous process that enables the clinician to tailor the treatment to the changing needs of the youngster and family and to evaluate the impact of intervention efforts. Interviews and behavioral observations are two common methods of assessment used with children and their families.

In this chapter, we describe the basic elements of these two assessment methods. The focus is on the uses of interviewing and behavioral observations for the purposes of identifying problems or clinical diagnoses, selecting treatment strategies, and evaluating treatment outcome. Our approach to assessment is largely empirical, although we provide examples of interviews and behavioral observations that promise to be clinically useful in a variety of settings.

Since the publication of the first edition of this *Handbook* in 1983, tremendous changes have occurred in the area of child assessment. At that time, behavioral observations were considered to be synonymous with "child assessment" for many clinicians, whereas the use of structured interviews to assess psychological symptomatology in children and adolescents was limited. In fact, at that time, researchers were just beginning to document children's ability to report psychological symptoms in a reliable and valid manner (Herjanic, Herjanic, Brown, & Wheatt, 1975), leading to the initial development of structured diagnostic interviews for use with children (e.g., Herjanic & Reich, 1982; Hodges, Kline, Stem, Cytryn, & McKnew, 1982). In contrast, at the present time, clinical interviews with children are considered to be essential to the child assessment process (La Greca, 1990; Silverman, 1994), and structured diagnostic interviews have proven extremely useful for this purpose. However, the increased prominence of clinical interview methods, coupled with the growth and development of reliable and well-validated behavioral checklists, have been matched by a decline in the use of behavioral observations to assess childhood problems, given their time-consuming nature. Nevertheless, behavioral observations remain useful in many situations, as in the assessment of conduct problems and

The authors express their appreciation to Wendy Silverman, Ph.D., for her thoughtful comments on an earlier draft of this chapter.

attention-deficit behaviors (e.g., Barkley, 1997), parenting skills (e.g., Eyberg & Robinson, 1983), and pain and distress among children undergoing aversive medical procedures (e.g., Blount et al., 1997).

Another major change that has affected the child assessment process is the shift to providing services in the context of managed care (Roberts, M.C., & Hurley, 1997). Managed care and its associated cost-containment approach to service provision has led to greater emphasis on focused assessments and empirically supported treatments (La Greca & Hughes, 1999; Roberts, M.C., & Hurley, 1997). Thus, clinicians are often in the position of determining a child's clinical diagnosis before services can be provided and evaluating treatment outcome to monitor treatment progress and receive reimbursement for services. Thus, focused assessment methods, such as structured interviews, that can assist with problem identification and diagnosis have been gaining favor and are of considerable interest to today's practitioners.

Before discussing interviews and behavioral observations, we review some general guidelines regarding the child assessment process. These guidelines should set the tone for the child assessment process.

CHARACTERISTICS OF CHILD ASSESSMENT

There are important differences between the assessment process for children and that for adults (La Greca, 1990). Unlike adults, children are rarely self-referred for treatment. More typically, referral is initiated by significant others in the child's life (parents, teachers, pediatricians), and in many cases, the referral may bear little relationship to the child's feelings of distress (Evans & Nelson, 1977). In addition, children and youth undergo behavioral, social, emotional, and cognitive changes at a much more rapid pace than adults; thus, their behaviors, feelings, and actions must always be viewed within a developmental context. These two key differences require a different approach to the assessment of children, youth, and their families as compared to adults.

Specifically, the first basic characteristic of child assessment is that it involves *multiple persons* in the child's life, including the child. This contrasts sharply with the adult assessment process, which often involves only the adult client. Because children and adolescents generally are not self-referred for treatment, their input is needed in addition to input from the significant others in their lives. In addition, a child's behavior is often situation-specific (Mash & Terdal, 1997); for example, a child who is well mannered in school may be difficult to control at home (or vice versa). For this reason, input from a number of persons is necessary. Finally, it is important to assess how significant persons in the child's life interact with the child and how their behavior contributes to the child's problem. Parents, teachers, and others (including peers and siblings) have an important impact on the child and are also affected by the child's behavior. Because intervention efforts typically involve multiple persons in addition to the child, the assessment process must similarly adopt a multiperson perspective (see La Greca & Lemanek, 1996).

The second characteristic of child assessment is that *multiple methods* of assessment are desirable. Although the present chapter covers interviews and behavioral observations, skilled professionals do not limit themselves to one or two assessment tools due to the limitations inherent in each method. Interviews, for instance, may provide valuable information about child and family functioning, yet parents' retrospective accounts have shown little stability over time and tend to distort the child's behavior in the direction of precocity (Hetherington & Martin, 1979). Moreover, parents' psychological states, such as the presence of depression, influence their reports of child behavior (Webster-Stratton & Hammond, 1988). Although behavioral observations provide more objective information, they are time-consuming and may be limited by problems with interrater reliability and reactivity of observers (Foster & Cone, 1986). A further reason for using a multimethod perspective is that it permits cross-validation of information obtained from different sources and methods, so that greater confidence can be placed in the conclusions drawn from the assessment data.

A third aspect of child assessment is that a *developmental perspective* is critical to the identification and understanding of many childhood problems. Children undergo rapid and uneven developmental change (Mash & Terdal, 1997); thus, knowledge of age-appropriate functioning is a prerequisite for identifying many childhood problems. For example, nocturnal bed-wetting may be common among 4-year-olds, yet problematic for 9-year-olds.

Another important characteristic of child assessment is the need for *culturally sensitive and appropriate* assessment measures. Recent U.S. demographics indicate that ethnic minority and immigrant youth constitute the fastest growing segment of the child and adolescent population (U.S. Bureau of the Census, 1996). Despite the increased numbers of youth and families from minority backgrounds, assessment and intervention procedures have not kept pace with the shifting demographics and may not be appropriate for children from diverse cultural backgrounds. Considerable concern has been expressed about the need for developing culturally relevant, sensitive, and appropriate assessment methods and intervention procedures for children, youth, and families (e.g., Kazdin, 1993; Reid et al., 1998). To accomplish these goals, assessment and intervention services need to be strength-based rather than deficit-oriented and take into account the notion of culture as both *content* (i.e., a person's worldview, values, view of self and others) and *context* (i.e., patterns of family interactions, ways of relating, environmental stressors and supports) (Koss-Chioino & Vargas, 1992). The field of clinical child psychology, for the most part, has yet to embrace the notion of multicultural competence in its assessment and intervention approaches. The development of culturally sensitive child and family assessments and interventions will be critical in the future (Forehand & Kotchick, 1996).

Finally, evaluating children's *academic and cognitive skills* is often a critical aspect of the child assessment process, although this is rarely the case for adults. Many children are referred due to concerns about school performance and classroom behavior (e.g., learning and attention problems) (Kazdin, Siegel, & Bass, 1990). Consequently, it is often desirable to obtain information about children's cognitive and academic functioning to understand the contributions of their abilities and skills to school-based problems.

In summary, several characteristics of the child assessment process may guide the professional in selecting appropriate assessment procedures. These include involving the child and significant others in the assessment process, using multiple methods of assessment, evaluating the child's behavior relative to developmental and cultural norms, and, when appropriate, obtaining information regarding the child's academic skills and patterns of cognitive functioning.

INTERVIEWS

Interviews are an integral part of the assessment process. They are especially important for obtaining initial information about the child and the family and for establishing rapport. Clinicians must be concerned about the *process* and *content* of the interview; both are addressed in the ensuing discussion.

INTERVIEWS WITH CHILDREN AND PARENTS

Although far more attention has been devoted to the interview process with adults than with children, there has been substantial interest in developing diagnostic interviews for use with children and adolescents (e.g., Costello, Edelbrock, Dulcan, Kalas, & Klaric, 1984; Herjanic & Reich, 1982; Hodges, Kline, Fitch, McKnew, & Cytryn, 1981). Until the 1980s, the relative paucity of information on child interviews reflected concerns about obtaining reliable and valid information from children, compounded by children's cognitive and verbal limitations vis-à-vis the interview situation (La Greca, 1990). However, many of these concerns have been dispelled by demonstrating that children can provide reliable reports of their behavior and psychological symptomatology (e.g., Herjanic et al., 1975) and by developing interview formats that are structured, developmentally appropriate, and geared to children's cognitive and language abilities. Today, interviews with children are essential for understanding the child's perspective and for establishing a positive therapeutic relationship with the child (H.P. Ginsburg, 1997; Hughes & Baker, 1990). Moreover, structured diagnostic child interviews have become a primary assessment tool for epidemiological studies of child and adolescent disorder (e.g., Cuffe et al., 1998; Prescott et al., 1998), for investigations of risk factors for disorder (e.g., Manassis & Hood, 1998), and for treatment outcome studies (e.g., Birmaher et al., 1998; King et al., 1998).

In the sections below, we first provide an overview of the development and use of structured diagnostic interviews. These interviews are essential for clinical research but are also extremely useful in clinical settings. Specifically, structured interviews have gained increasing importance as a result of managed care's emphasis on the use of focused assessments and empirically supported treatments (e.g., Roberts, M.C., & Hurley, 1997). Other clinical advantages of structured diagnostic interviews are that they frame questions in developmentally appropriate ways so that they can be used with children as young as 6 years of age and they provide clinicians with a comprehensive framework for gathering information from children and parents (see Silverman, 1994).

Following the discussion of structured diagnostic interviews, we briefly focus on information regarding interview content and process. Process considerations are important regardless of whether a structured or unstructured interview format is used.

Structured Diagnostic Interviews

Interviews that use a structured format have been most successful in obtaining reliable and valid information from children. Structured interviews are designed so that questions are presented in a standard manner and response expectations are clear. The purpose of most structured interviews is to evaluate the presence or absence of psychiatric symptoms and to establish clinical diagnoses (Silverman, 1994). Most of the research on the structured interview process with children and parents has focused on the reliability of the responses provided and the accuracy of the clinical diagnoses that are generated.

The semistructured interview format developed by Rutter and Graham (1968) paved the way for more recent work in this area. Interviews such as the Child Assessment Schedule, the Diagnostic Interview for Children and Adolescents, and the Diagnostic Interview Schedule for Children were developed for use in clinical and epidemiological research on childhood disorder; however, they also have considerable clinical utility. In general, they provide comprehensive assessments of youngsters' social, emotional, and behavioral functioning, with the intent of deriving clinical diagnoses based on widely used taxonomy systems, such as the *Diagnostic and Statistical Manual of Mental Disorders,* 4th edition (*DSM-IV;* American Psychiatric Association, 1994) or the *International Classification of Diseases* (*ICD-10;* World Health Organization, 1992). In addition, specialized diagnostic interviews have been developed for assessing affective disorders in children and for evaluating anxiety disorders.

Most structured interviews can be used with children as young as 6 years of age. Generally, the interviews require minimal verbal responses and thus do not overtax the child's verbal expressive skills. The interview questions tend to be geared toward children's language capabilities so that the questions are understandable to most children. Also, their standard format and scoring procedures permit the use of these interviews in treatment evaluation and clinical research.

All the interviews described below can be used to derive *DSM-III-R* or *DSM-IV* diagnoses (American Psychiatric Association, 1987, 1994). Parent versions have been developed for the interviews described.

Diagnostic Interview for Children and Adolescents–Revised (DICA-R). The DICA was the first interview schedule developed for use with children (Herjanic et al., 1975) and it is highly structured. (See Hodges & Cools, 1990, and Rogers, 1995 for detailed reviews.) The latest revision, the DICA-R, has three versions: one for *children* age 6 to 12 (DICA-R-C), one for *adolescents* age 13 to 17 (DICA-R-A), and a *parent* version that covers the 6- to 17-year-old age span (DICA-R-P). The interview takes approximately 60 minutes to administer and generally requires a simple yes or no response from the child/adolescent/parent. In the DICA-R, some of the wording was modified to make the interview more conversational, and structured probes were added to increase flexibility. The DICA-R is organized into 15 major sections. The first two sections obtain general and sociodemographic information. Eleven sections cover various mental disorders and symptomatology, including attention deficits, conduct disorders, substance abuse, and mood disorders, as well as dysthymic, anxiety, obsessive-compulsive, posttraumatic stress, eating, elimination, gender identity, somatization, and psychotic disorders. Other interview sections include clinical observations, psychosocial stressors, and menstruation.

Recent studies conducted on the DICA-R support the reliability of this interview. Adequate test-retest reliabilities have been reported for adolescent diagnoses using the DICA-R-A (Boyle et al., 1996), as well as for the DICA-R-P (Boyle et al., 1997). However, some studies have found parent assessments to be more reliable than children's or adolescents' reports, especially for internalizing disorders (Boyle et al., 1993).

Work that has concentrated on diagnostic concordance has found mixed support for the validity of DICA-R. One study that used the DICA-R with children age 6 to 16 years found high rates of concordance between the diagnostic classifications made by child psychiatrists and trained lay interviewers, but low rates of agreement between parents and children/adolescents (Boyle et al., 1993). When responses to specific items were evaluated, parent-child agreement appeared to be highest for concrete, observable, or severe symptoms, and poorest for items relating to youngsters' internal, affective, and cognitive states (e.g., feelings of anxiety and depression) (Boyle et al., 1993).

Other studies have addressed validity by examining the concordance between clinician ratings and child or parent reports (e.g., Carlson, Kashani, Thomas, Vaidya, & Daniel, 1987; Ezpeleta et al., 1997). In one study of 137 child and adolescent outpatients and their parents, agreement between the DICA-R-C/DICA-R-A and the best-estimate clinical diagnoses was low to moderate for most diagnostic categories (Ezpeleta et al., 1997). Only conduct disorder showed a high level of agreement among children, adolescents, and clinicians. Parent-clinician agreement was moderate to good for attention-deficit hyperactivity disorder, conduct disorder, posttraumatic stress disorder, and encopresis for reports of both children and adolescents; however, poor concordance was found for obsessive-compulsive disorder, dysthymic disorder, and bulimia (Ezpeleta et al., 1997).

In summary, the DICA-R has promising empirical support for its reliability, although studies of its validity have revealed mixed results. Further research is necessary to address the interview's psychometric properties, with attention devoted to evaluating its concordance with other well-validated structured interviews and rating scales. Nevertheless, one advantage of the DICA-R is the availability of an adolescent version and its emphasis on child and adolescent confidentiality.

Diagnostic Interview Schedule for Children (DISC). The DISC (Costello et al., 1984) was developed primarily as a research tool for clinical and epidemiological studies and was modeled on the adult-oriented Diagnostic Interview Schedule. The DISC was designed to be administered by laypersons with minimal training in interview techniques. It is a highly structured interview for youngsters 6 to 17 years of age and takes approximately one hour to administer; there is also a parent version. The DISC was recently revised (DISC-R) to be compatible with *DSM-III-R* criteria (Piacentini et al., 1993; Shaffer et al., 1993), although subsequent studies have led to further changes. The current DISC is

Version 2.3 (Shaffer et al., 1996). The DISC-2 uses *DSM-III-R* criteria to identify 31 childhood diagnoses and is organized into 19 diagnostic sections with related diagnoses grouped into 6 diagnostic modules (i.e., anxiety, mood, disruptive, substance abuse, psychotic, and miscellaneous disorders). Questions regarding age, context of onset, impairment, and treatment history are included as part of the interview. Responses to questions in the DISC-2 are mostly limited to yes, no, sometimes, or somewhat. Parallel child and parent versions are available and generally cover the same behaviors and symptoms. A shortened version is also available to use with teachers. Computer algorithms based on *DSM-III-R* criteria yield diagnoses based on child, parent, or combined child and parent interviews.

Recent studies have found excellent reliability for both the DISC-R (Schwab-Stone et al., 1993; Shaffer et al., 1993) and the DISC-2 (Jensen et al., 1995; Shaffer et al., 1996). Using parent reports, test-retest reliabilities of the DISC-2 have been good to excellent for attention-deficit hyperactivity disorder, conduct disorder, dysthymia and major depressive disorder, oppositional defiant disorder, and simple phobias, but poor for all other anxiety disorders (Shaffer et al., 1996). For the child-report DISC-2, the highest test-retest reliabilities were obtained for social phobia, oppositional defiant disorder, conduct disorder, separation anxiety disorder, and depression/dysthymia (Shaffer et al., 1996). Higher test-retest reliabilities for the DISC-2 have been found when combined parent and child reports arc used (versus single informant) and in clinical versus community samples (Jensen et al., 1995).

Few validity studies have been conducted on the DISC-R and DISC-2, although existing results are encouraging. In 1993, Piacentini and colleagues examined concurrent criterion validity by comparing results of the DISC-R and clinician-generated diagnoses. Diagnostic agreement for the DISC-R was good for disruptive behavior disorders but not for major depressive disorder; child-clinician agreement was lower for all disorders. More recent studies have found the DISC-2 to have good to excellent sensitivity for certain "rare" disorders, including eating disorders, major depression, obsessive-compulsive disorder, psychosis, tic disorders, and substance use disorders (Fisher et al., 1993).

In summary, the DISC-2 is a comprehensive structured interview that is widely used, particularly with older children and adolescents. It is useful for assessing risk factors for psychiatric dysfunction, patterns of psychopathology, and overall levels of clinical impairment. In fact, the DISC-2 has been widely used in studies of child and adolescent disorder and in the field trials for *DSM-IV* (e.g., Lahey, Applegate, McBurnett, et al., 1994; Lahey, Applegate, Barkley, et al., 1994). Although the DISC (and its revisions) has been established as a reliable instrument, its diagnostic effectiveness with inpatient populations need to be examined. (See Rogers, 1995, for more details.)

The Child Assessment Schedule (CAS). The CAS was developed specifically to address concerns regarding the difficulty of establishing rapport with children when using structured interviews (Hodges et al., 1981, 1982). This semistructured interview uses a conversational format to enhance rapport; it is low in structure and high in flexibility, but requires highly trained interviewers for its administration. The CAS is used primarily with children between 7 and 12 years, although the most recent version has been used with adolescents (Miller-Johnson, Lochman, Coie, Terry, & Hyman, 1998). The CAS takes about 60 minutes to administer. The initial section consists of 75 items that cover 11 content areas: friends, school, family, activities, fears, worries, self-image, mood, somatic concerns, expression of anger, and thought disorder symptomatology. Most item responses are coded yes or no. The second part contains questions about the onset and duration of symptoms, and the final section consists of 53 items that are scored by the examiner after the interview has been completed (e.g., grooming, activity level, etc.).

There is considerable psychometric support for the CAS. Internal consistency has been demonstrated for all symptom scales (Hodges, Saunders, Kashani, Hamlett, & Thompson, 1990) and for nine content scales (Hodges & Saunders, 1989). Furthermore, moderate to high interrater reliability has been obtained for the total CAS, the individual content areas, and the symptom complex scales (Hodges, Gordon, & Lennon, 1990; Verhulst, Althaus, & Berden, 1987). Moreover, test-retest reliability appears to be satisfactory for the total CAS score, the content scales, and the following diagnostic categories: conduct disorder, major depressive episode, oppositional disorder, dysthymia, and separation anxiety (Hodges, Cools, & McKnew, 1986, 1989).

With respect to validity, the CAS can discriminate among psychiatric, pediatric, and healthy populations (e.g., Hodges, Kline, Barbero, & Flanery, 1985;

Verhulst et al., 1987). Discriminant validity also was supported in a study examining a nonreferred and hospitalized sample of adolescents (Barrera & Garrison-Jones, 1988). Hodges et al. (1982) examined the concurrent validity of the CAS and found that the total CAS score correlated with mothers' reports of the number and severity of child problems on the Child Behavior Checklist (Achenbach, 1991). However, parent-child agreement has been found to be low for internalizing problems but moderate for externalizing problems. (See Hodges & Cools, 1990; Rogers, 1995, for further discussion.)

In summary, data on the reliability and validity of the CAS are promising. The CAS possesses qualities that are conducive to using this structured interview in clinical and research settings. Additional investigation of the psychometric properties of this scale would enhance the utility of this diagnostic interview. To our knowledge, a *DSM-IV* version of the interview has not been developed as yet.

Schedule for Affective Disorders and Schizophrenia in School-Age Children (K-SADS). The K-SADS (Orvaschel, Puig-Antich, Chambers, Tabrizi, & Johnson, 1982; Puig-Antich & Chambers, 1978) is a semistructured interview, modeled after the Schedule for Affective Disorders and Schizophrenia (Endicott & Spitzer, 1978), to assess psychiatric disturbance in youth age 6 to 18 years. It is the most widely used interview for the study of clinical depression in children and adolescents (e.g., Williamson et al., 1998); however, it also assesses conduct disorder, separation anxiety, phobias, attention-deficit disorder, and obsessive-compulsive disorder. The K-SADS was designed to be administered only by highly trained professionals with extensive training in diagnostic assessment. The same administration procedure is used for parents and children, with the parents interviewed first. It is recommended that the interviewer use information obtained from the parent interview to guide the child interview. Each interview takes approximately 60 minutes to administer. Any discrepancies between parent and child reports are resolved using clinical judgment (Ambrosini, 1988).

There are two versions of the K-SADS, one that assesses current episodes of disorder (the Present Episode version, K-SADS-P) and one that assesses lifetime symptomatology (the Epidemiological version, K-SADS-E). In the Epidemiological version (Orvaschel et al., 1982), the questions are asked twice to determine whether a symptom was present in the past and whether a symptom is currently present. In the Present version, questions are also asked twice, with the first to determine the severity of the symptom at its worst during the present episode and the second to determine the severity of the symptom within the past week.

Limited data are available on the psychometric properties of the most recent versions of the K-SADS. However, in a sample of disturbed children and their parents, test-retest reliability over a 2- to 3-day period revealed an average interclass correlation of .55 for individual items and .68 for the 12 summary scales (Chambers et al., 1985). Diagnostic agreement also was established for nonmajor depressive disorders, conduct disorder, and major depressive disorder, but not for anxiety disorders (Chambers et al., 1985). Similarly, concordance between parent and adolescent inpatients has been found to be good for depressed mood and thoughts and conduct disorder, but poor for anxiety disorder (Apter, Orvaschel, Laseg, Moses, & Tyano, 1989). Higher concordance has been found with adolescents and in populations with greater levels of impairment (Weissman, Warner, & Fendrich, 1990).

Validity has been established comparing groups of children and adolescents using the Children's Depression Inventory (CDI) and the K-SADS. McCauley, Mitchell, Burke, and Moss (1988) found a modest correlation between the CDI and K-SADS in groups of psychiatric patients with a major depressive disorder, with major depression within the past year, and with diagnoses other than depression. In addition, the K-SADS appears to be sensitive to treatment effects in preadolescent children with affective disorders (Puig-Antich et al., 1979). However, discriminant validity has not yet been established for the K-SADS.

In summary, the K-SADS is a widely used interview to assess child and adolescent depression. Advantages of using the K-SADS are that it allows for the assessment of present and lifetime symptomatology and that it includes ratings of symptom severity. Although reliability has been established for symptoms of depression and conduct disorder, questions still remain about the reliability of the K-SADS for anxiety disorders.

Anxiety Disorder Interview Schedule for Children (ADIS-C). The ADIS-C (Silverman & Nelles, 1988), a downward extension of the Anxiety Disorder Interview Schedule (DiNardo, O'Brian, Barlow,

Waddell, & Blanchard, 1983), was developed to address the absence of a psychometrically sound interview for diagnosing anxiety disorders in children. It is developmentally sensitive, using visual prompts (e.g., "thermometers" to obtain fear ratings; "calendars" to indicate time periods for symptoms) and simple wording of questions so that it can be easily understood by children (see Silverman, 1991, 1994). The most recent version, the ADIS-IV-C (Silverman & Albano, 1996), uses *DSM-IV* diagnostic criteria. This semistructured interview can diagnose anxiety disorders, mood disorders, externalizing disorders, and related behavioral disturbances in youth 6 to 17 years of age. It provides quantifiable data regarding anxiety symptomatology, as well as the etiology, course, and functional analysis of anxiety disorders. The ADIS-IV-C has two separate interviews, one for the parent and one for the child. The administration time for each interview is approximately 60 minutes, and information from both sources is combined to form an overall composite diagnosis (Silverman, 1991, 1994).

Although reliability studies have not yet been conducted on the ADIS-IV-C, high test-retest and interrater reliabilities have been found using the *DSM-III* and *DSM-III-R* versions (Silverman & Rabian, 1995). Silverman and Eisen (1992) examined the test-retest reliability of the ADIS-C in a sample of 50 outpatients and their parents, finding that kappas ranged from .64 for overanxious disorder to .84 for specific phobia. In addition, moderate to high interrater reliability was demonstrated in a sample of 51 outpatients using paired clinician ratings (Silverman & Nelles, 1988). The clinical utility of the ADIS-C has been demonstrated in several studies (e.g., Ollendick, Hagopian, & Huntzinger, 1991).

Overall, the ADIS-C is the only diagnostic interview specifically developed to assess children with anxious or phobic disorders and it is widely used for this purpose (e.g., DiBartolo, Albano, Barlow, & Heimberg, 1998; G.S. Ginsburg, La Greca, & Silverman, 1998). The coverage of anxious and phobic disorders is more extensive and complete than in other structured interviews.

Use of Structured Interviews with Parents
All the structured interviews reviewed have parent versions, consistent with the importance of including parents' perspectives in the child assessment process (Loeber, Green, & Lahey, 1990). Studies of

the reliability and validity of structured parent interviews have been conducted in tandem with evaluations of the child interviews (reviewed above). In addition, several studies have examined parent-child concordance on specific symptoms and on diagnoses (see Klein, 1991; Silverman, 1994). In general, parent-child agreement is highest for concrete, observable, and severe symptoms (e.g., Boyle et al., 1993), and lowest for subjective, internalizing symptoms, such as anxiety and depression (e.g., Edelbrock, Costello, Dulcan, Conover, & Kalas, 1986; Silverman, 1994). Similarly, parent-child concordance rates typically are better for externalizing diagnoses (e.g., conduct disorder, oppositional disorder, attention-deficit disorder) than for diagnoses of anxiety, phobias, and depression (see Edelbrock et al., 1986; Silverman, 1994). Parent-child agreement also appears to be linked to the child's age, with better agreement obtained for children age 10 and older (Edelbrock et al., 1986).

Although most agree that it is best to obtain information from both child and parent, the interview schedules reviewed differ with respect to their procedures for combining information from these two sources. When only one interview source can be used, there is general consensus that parent reports are more important for observable or objective child behavior, and child reports are more important for subjective and internal symptoms and experiences (Loeber et al., 1990; Silverman, 1994).

Conclusions Regarding Structured Diagnostic Interviews

Structured interviews have very appealing characteristics and are widely used in research to identify psychiatric symptoms and clinical diagnoses. Structured interviews also have considerable applicability in clinical settings. One concern regarding the use of structured interviews in clinical settings is that the "structure" may impede the development of rapport or be perceived negatively. However, research suggests that the vast majority of parents and children respond favorably to structured interviews (Zahner, 1991). In fact, some parents report that they appreciate the comprehensive nature of the structured interview process (W.K. Silverman, personal communication, October 6, 1998).

In selecting a structured interview to use in a clinical setting, professionals might consider two factors: the scope of the interview and the degree of training needed to administer the interview. As a rule of thumb, when skilled clinical interviewers are available and comprehensive coverage of a wide range of psychopathology is needed, interviews such as the CAS might be considered, whereas, for settings that focus on children and youth with internalizing problems, the ADIS-IV would be a good choice. When only lay interviewers are available, the DISC-2 is the best overall choice.

One issue to bear in mind regarding structured interviews is that they were specifically designed to evaluate psychiatric symptoms and clinical diagnoses. Thus, their content is strongly linked to current clinical taxonomies (e.g., *DSM-IV*). To some extent, therefore, the interviews are only as good as the diagnostic criteria that they were designed to assess. There is no gold standard to which the diagnostic interviews can be compared (see Silverman, 1994). Moreover, problems with current taxonomies and their criteria for diagnoses affect the accuracy and content of the structured interviews as well.

One further complication of designing interviews to match diagnostic criteria is that the interviews focus on symptoms and pathology more than on strengths, and do not consider the various contextual influences that affect child and adolescent behavior (e.g., family, school, peers, culture, and community). For this reason, other aspects of child and family functioning should be included in a comprehensive evaluation of children and their parents to supplement the interviews. Despite these limitations, structured interviews represent useful tools for clinical practice and research. Structured interviews are valuable for delineating specific content areas as well as specific questions to use in conducting comprehensive child and parent interviews.

Other Issues Pertinent to Child, Adolescent, and Parent Interviews

Interview Content. One appeal of structured interviews is that they cover topics relevant to evaluating children and adolescents in a comprehensive manner. For the reader's interest, Table 6.1 includes a list of content areas commonly assessed in child interviews. This list was derived from several sources (Herjanic et al., 1975; Hodges et al., 1981; Roberts, M.C., & La Greca, 1981).

Parent interviews typically cover many of the same content areas, although in more detail. In

Table 6.1   Content areas frequently assessed in child and adolescent interviews.

Area	Examples of Specific Content
Referral problem	What does the child think the main problem is? Does the child see the referral problem as a problem?
Interests	What does the child like to do (in spare time)? What does the child like to do alone? with friends? with family?
School	What does the child like best about school? least? How does the child feel about his or her teachers? What grades does the child get in school?
Peers	Who does the child like to play with? Who are the child's friends? What do they like to do together? Who does the child dislike?
Family	How does the child get along with his or her parents? What do they do that the child likes? that makes him/her angry? How does the child get along with his or her brothers and sisters?
Fears and worries	What kinds of things is the child afraid of? does the child worry about? What kinds of things make the child nervous, jumpy?
Self-image	What does the child like and dislike about himself or herself? How would the child describe himself or herself?
Mood and feelings	What kinds of things make the child feel sad? happy? mad? What does he or she do when sad? happy? mad?
Somatic concerns	Does the child have any headaches or stomach aches? Other pains? How often does this happen? What does the child usually do?
Thought disorder	Does the child hear or see things that seem funny or unusual? Describe.
Aspirations	What would the child like to do for a living when he or she gets older?
Fantasy	What kinds of things does the child daydream about? If the child could have any three wishes, what would they be?
Topics for Adolescents	
Sexuality	Is the adolescent involved in any dating activities? What kind? Are there any restrictions on the adolescent? How does he or she feel about restrictions? What sexual concerns does the adolescent have? What are his or her attitudes toward premarital sex? Do these conflict with parental views? Is the adolescent informed about contraception?
Drug and alcohol use	What has the adolescent used to get "high"? Are other friends involved in these activities?

general, more information is obtained from parents regarding the reasons for the referral, including a complete description of the presenting problem and possible contributing factors, and a history of previous attempts to remedy the problem. Other areas of inquiry include parents' methods of discipline, developmental history of the child, and medical history of the child. It is especially important to consider cultural and contextual factors when gathering information regarding child-rearing practices, as parenting practices vary widely by culture (Kelley, Power, & Wimbush, 1992; also see Greenspan & Greenspan, 1991; Semrud-Clikeman, 1995).

Although little information is available regarding interviews with adults other than parents, in clinical practice such interviews are generally problem-focused (i.e., geared toward obtaining information about the specific referral problem). Interviews with teachers and other adults also provide useful information about the child's functioning in areas outside of the home setting (e.g., school, Scouts) and offer another perspective on child and family. Teacher-report versions of behavioral checklists, such as the Teacher's Report Form of the Child Behavior Checklist (Achenbach & Edelbrock, 1986), are also very useful for assessing teachers' perspectives and have good psychometric properties.

Interview Process with Children. The importance of process considerations, such as the quality of the therapeutic relationship, has been stressed by clinicians of diverse orientations. The process of interviewing children can be complex and varies with the characteristics of the particular child (e.g., shy versus outgoing), the child's cognitive capabilities, and the age of the child. Here, we focus on several basic considerations pertinent to the child interview process (also see Stone & Lemanek, 1990). Most of these considerations (e.g., wording of questions, taking an active role in the interview) have been built into the structured interview formats described earlier.

The ability of the therapist to impart a sense of *warmth and acceptance* is important (H.P. Ginsburg, 1997; Semrud-Clikeman, 1995). Children should be encouraged to express their thoughts and feelings freely, and this can be accomplished by adopting a neutral and permissive attitude toward the child's self-expression (H.P. Ginsburg, 1997). In behavioral terms, this translates into encouraging the child to talk (rewarding verbal expression) rather than selectively attending to the kinds of things the child reports (e.g., rewarding positive statements about others but ignoring negative statements). When the purpose of the interview is assessment, the professional needs to obtain an accurate understanding of the child's perspective. Approval or disapproval of certain types of information may lead to a biased report from the child. Once treatment has been initiated, this focus may change, but at least for initial data gathering, a permissive and neutral attitude is most instrumental for obtaining an accurate report from the child.

In working with children, it is important to distinguish between verbal and behavioral expression. Whereas open *verbal* expression should be encouraged, in many cases it is necessary to impose limits on children's *behavioral* expression. For example, behaviors such as assaulting the therapist and destroying property are usually not permitted. However, more freedom should be allowed in terms of the child's verbal expression of thoughts and feelings.

Other factors that can enhance the child interview process include gearing the interview questions to the child's level of cognitive understanding; asking questions that do not overtax the child's verbal expression skills; taking an active role in guiding the interview process; and explaining the purpose or relevance of the interview to the child. In terms of *gearing the interview questions to the child's level of cognitive understanding and verbal expression,* it is important to use vocabulary that can be readily understood and to keep sentence length relatively brief (Stone & Lemanek, 1990). It may also be useful to ask more narrowly focused questions than would normally be appropriate with an adult (Bierman & Schwartz, 1986). For instance, specific questions such as "What do you like best about your mom?" may be more productive than general questions such as "How do you feel about your mom?" Rather than asking very broad questions (e.g., "What is school like for you?"), the clinician may find it more useful to ask a series of focused questions (e.g., "What is your teacher like?" "What are your favorite subjects?" ". . . least-liked subjects?"). With younger children (8 years of age or less) and those with cognitive difficulties, even more concrete questions may be needed (e.g., "What do you do in the afternoons after school?" rather than "What are your interests and hobbies?").

When working with children, the clinician needs to *take an active role in the interview process* and guide the discussion carefully. Children are more likely than adults to become off-task or to provide brief responses to questions; the interviewer should be sensitive to and prepared for these occurrences. Moreover, the interviewer should be prepared to be flexible when a child becomes distressed; for example, the interviewer may suggest that other children may feel the same way the child feels or may use pictures to facilitate communication with the child regarding his or her feelings (Hughes & Baker, 1990).

Finally, from the outset, it is important to *establish that the interview is relevant to the child.* Many children are not given adequate preparation for clinical contacts (Semrud-Clikeman, 1995). To enlist the attention and cooperation of the child, it is advisable to discuss the reasons for the interview, relating them as much as possible to the child's own concerns.

Although many of the process issues described above have been taken into account in structured diagnostic interviews, it is also important to put the child at ease and to ensure that the child understands the relevance of the interview before beginning a structured interview. The quality of the information obtained is likely to be enhanced when the child feels comfortable and ready to talk.

Interview Process with Adults. Interviews with parents and other adults are crucial for establishing positive working relationships and setting the tone for future intervention efforts. For the most part, the process of interviewing parents and other adults is very similar to the process of interviewing adult clients, and the existing literature on interviewing processes and methods can be very useful in this regard (Turkat, 1986). However, certain considerations for parent interviews warrant special attention.

During initial interviews with parents, the clinician should be sensitive to the stress and anxiety the parents may experience when discussing their child's problems with a professional (Simmons, 1987). Special care should be taken to convey respect for parents' feelings and to avoid any suggestion that they are to blame for the child's difficulties. Other rapport-enhancing skills (e.g., warmth, empathy) will also assist in laying the groundwork for a positive working relationship. Finally, it is important to include both parents (or all adult family members) in the interview process (Semrud-Clikeman, 1995); this procedure increases the accuracy of the information obtained and helps enlist the cooperation of the parents/family in the treatment process.

BEHAVIORAL OBSERVATIONS

The observation of behavior has long been an important method for assessing children. Children are generally more accessible for observations than adults, and given the situational specificity of child behavior, behavioral observations play a critical role in the child assessment and treatment process.

Until recently, direct observation of behavior in natural settings represented the hallmark of behavioral assessment. In fact, at one time, behavioral observation was considered to be synonymous with behavioral assessment (Mash & Terdal, 1997). In recent years, however, the conceptualization of behavioral assessment has broadened to include greater attention to classification and diagnosis as well as increased consideration of the roles that cognition and affect play in behavior. A stronger emphasis on diagnosis has resulted in the development of assessment schemes that vary as a function of the referral problem. Behavioral observation methodologies for children with attention deficits, for example, are very different from those used with youngsters referred for concerns regarding autism or depression.

Observational methodologies now reflect increased interest in qualitative, global, and affective aspects of behavior. Moreover, there has been growing recognition that multiple assessment methods (e.g., interviews, self-reports) are important complements to behavioral observations. For these reasons, less emphasis has been placed on the development and use of behavioral observations in child assessment.

NATURALISTIC OBSERVATIONS

Naturalistic observations of children have been conducted in a variety of settings, such as homes, classrooms, playgrounds, and outpatient clinics. With the advent of computer technologies for recording observations and statistical procedures for analyzing complex sequential interactions, it is possible to examine behaviors in ways that were impossible 20 years ago. However, from a practical standpoint, clinicians will be most interested in observation methodologies that can be used without extensive recording equipment and that do not require extensive time to train observers and to collect data.

To a large extent, the utility of behavioral observations depends on the reliability and validity of the coding systems employed. Many advantages of well-validated observational codes have been cited (Abikoff, Gittelman-Klein, & Klein, 1977; Evans & Nelson, 1977; Foster & Cone, 1986). For example, objective behavioral definitions minimize bias due to halo effects and rater expectations (Abikoff et al., 1977). This is especially important when evaluating the effects of an intervention program. Change agents (e.g., teacher, parents) may report information consistent with behavior change; objective behavioral measures offer the advantages of reducing such bias and providing a more accurate view of behavior change. A well-defined and well-validated observational code is also advantageous for providing reliable diagnostic information.

Behavioral Coding Systems
The most well-developed coding systems focus on parent-child interactions, externalizing child behavior problems, and children's fears and anxiety

Table 6.2 Selected observational coding systems.

Behavior/Authors	Type	Setting	Name
ADHD			
Abikoff, Gittelman, & Klein, 1977	Naturalistic	Classroom	——
Jacob, O'Leary, & Rosenblat, 1978	Naturalistic	Classroom	Hyperactive Behavior Code
Milich, Loney, & Landau, 1982	Structured	Clinic	Restricted Academic Playroom Situation
Conduct Problems/Aggression			
Harris, Kreil, & Orpet, 1977	Naturalistic	Classroom	Behavior Coding System
Reed & Edelbrock, 1983	Naturalistic	Classroom	Direct Observation Form
Parent-Child Interactions			
Eyberg & Robinson, 1983	Structured	Clinic	Dyadic Parent-Child Interaction Coding System
Forehand & McMahon, 1981	Structured	Clinic	Parent's Game/Child's Game
Foster & Robin, 1988	Structured	Clinic	Parent-Adolescent Interaction Coding System
Lindahl & Malick, 1996	Structured	Clinic	System for Coding Interactions and Family Functioning
Patterson, 1977	Naturalistic	Home	Family Interaction Coding System
Anxiety/Medical Distress			
Blount et al., 1997	Naturalistic	Hospital/Clinic	Child-Adult Medical Procedure Interaction Scale–Revised
Dadds et al., 1993	Structured	Clinic	Family Anxiety Coding Schedule

(see Table 6.2 for several examples). For example, Patterson (1982) developed a format for observing family interactions in a home setting, called the Family Interaction Coding System, that has been used with children referred for conduct disorders and aggressive behavior. Family members are observed for two 5-minute periods comprising 10 30-second intervals. Family interaction behaviors are coded in 29 categories, including positive (e.g., attention, approval) and negative behaviors (e.g., destructiveness, noncompliance). Because the behaviors are coded sequentially, antecedents and consequences of the child's behaviors can be evaluated and used in formulating treatment plans. Data on the reliability and validity of this observation system have been quite impressive. Thus, information obtained from this observation system can help to pinpoint family interaction difficulties, design treatment programs to remedy such difficulties, and evaluate intervention outcome (McMahon & Forehand, 1988; Patterson, 1982).

Naturalistic observations in the classroom may also facilitate the identification and treatment of child behavior problems. Abikoff and colleagues (1977) developed an observational coding system to assess children with attention-deficit/hyperactivity disorder (ADHD). Youngsters are observed during didactic teaching and independent work activities for four 4-minute periods (composed of 15-second intervals). The coding system has been found to discriminate children with ADHD from normal children. However, the identification of ADHD should not be based solely on this observational code; additional input from parents and teachers is critical. (See Barkley, 1997, for a discussion of diagnostic issues in ADHD.)

Naturalistic observations can also assist in identifying and reducing medically related pain. Blount and colleagues (1997) developed the Child-Adult Medical Procedure Interaction Scale–Revised (CAMPIS-R) to assess parent-child interactions during medical procedures. The CAMPIS-R is a six-code observational scale, focusing on behaviors from children, parents, and medical staff. The observation takes place three minutes prior to the medical procedure, during the procedure itself, and during the two minutes following the procedure. Both child behaviors (e.g., coping, distress) and adult behaviors (e.g., coping promoting, distress promoting) are coded. Interobserver reliability for the coding system has been found to be good to excellent (Blount et al., 1997). In addition, concurrent validity has been supported in a sample of preschoolers receiving routine immunizations for the categories of child coping and distress and adult coping-promoting and distress-promoting behaviors (Blount et al., 1997).

In general, complex, naturalistic behavioral coding systems, such as those described above, are most often used in clinical research. Such systems are difficult to use in clinical practice because of the large amount of time necessary for training observers and recording behaviors (Barkley, 1997).

Structured Observation Formats

Structured observation formats address the practical limitations of observing children and families in naturalistic settings. Structured observations, also referred to as analogue assessments, involve observing the child and/or family in a standard situation that has been designed to elicit the behavior(s) of interest. Despite concerns about generalization to the natural environment, structured observations have been widely used in clinical-child settings and offer a number of distinct advantages. For example, they promote efficient use of the clinician's and client's time while affording an opportunity to observe the child and/or family in a seminaturalistic manner. Naturalistic observations do not ensure that the behaviors of interest will occur during the observation period, whereas the target behaviors are much more likely to occur when structured observations are used. In addition, the frequent use of standard structured situations for observational assessment allows the clinician to establish a normative base for clinical observations, which further enhances the utility of this assessment procedure.

Structured observation formats have been designed to assess many behaviors, including parent-child interactions (Eyberg & Robinson, 1983), child activity level (Roberts, M.A., 1990), medical anxiety (Burnstein & Meichenbaum, 1979), and peer interaction skills (Gottman, Gonso, & Rasmussen, 1975). The formats differ in the extent to which they are contrived. For instance, role-play assessments are highly contrived in that the child is asked to respond to a "pretend" situation as if it were really occurring. Due to their contrived nature, concerns

about the external validity of role-play assessments have been noted (Kazdin, Matson, & Esveldt-Dawson, 1984). Despite such difficulties, role plays and other structured observations are very useful when it is not feasible or practical to observe the behaviors of interest in a natural setting. Some examples of structured observational formats are listed in Table 6.2.

Structured parent-child interactions developed for preschool and early school-aged youngsters have focused primarily on child management behaviors, such as child compliance or parental discipline methods (e.g., Eyberg & Robinson, 1983; Forehand & McMahon, 1981). For example, Forehand and associates (Forehand, King, Peed, & Yoder, 1975; Forehand et al., 1979) developed an assessment procedure that involves observing parent and child in a clinic playroom. The child's behavior is scored for compliance, noncompliance, and inappropriate behavior (e.g., whining, crying), and the parent's behavior is scored for commands (direct and vague), warnings, questions, attends, and rewards (Forehand & McMahon, 1981). Comparisons between children referred to a psychological clinic and nonreferred children (age 4–6 years) disclosed that clinic children exhibited lower rates of compliant behavior and their parents used more commands and criticisms of their child (Forehand et al., 1975). This observational system also appears to be sensitive to treatment effects (Forehand & King, 1974; Forehand et al., 1979). (See McMahon & Forehand, 1988, for further details.)

These studies suggest that this structured parent-child observation format could be used with preschool children and their parents in a clinic. The procedure requires a minimal amount of time, yet could yield clinically useful information. The Dyadic Parent-Child Interaction Coding System (Eyberg & Robinson, 1983; Robinson & Eyberg, 1981) and the Parent-Adolescent Interaction Coding System (Foster & Robin, 1988) represent other excellent examples of structured parent-child observation formats.

Parent-child observational methods are not limited to assessing behavior problems. Dadds, Ryan, and Barrett (1993) developed the Family Anxiety Coding Schedule (FACS) to evaluate the role of family processes in child anxiety. Children and their parents are separately asked to interpret ambiguous situations and describe how they would react to them. Next, the family is brought together to discuss the ambiguous situations for five minutes each. The FACS scores the anxious behavior of child and parent during the family discussion. Interrater reliability has been found to be good to excellent (Dadds, Barrett, Rapee, & Ryan, 1996).

Structured observational systems have not been limited to assessments of parent-child interactions. For example, children's interpersonal skills, such as friendship making and assertive behaviors, have been assessed using role-play formats (see Gottman et al., 1975; La Greca & Stark, 1986).

In summary, structured observational formats have been developed to assess a variety of child and family behaviors. They are particularly useful for providing information on behaviors of interest in a cost-efficient manner, although concerns regarding their external validity have been noted.

Individualized Approaches

Although empirically based observation systems may be relevant for many clinical problems, professionals often must identify, define, and measure target behaviors that are relevant to a given child or family (see Evans & Nelson 1986; Hawkins, Matthews, & Hamdan, 1999). Moreover, defining and measuring behavior is often essential in providing clinical services in a managed care environment, as it is often up to the clinician to measure progress and document change (Hawkins et al., 1999). An individualized behavioral assessment can be useful in this regard.

Generally, the first step in observational assessment is selecting appropriate target behaviors for observation. Behaviors that have *implications for treatment* are usually of primary interest (e.g., Does the behavior represent some deficit or excess that will be involved in the intervention process?). Further, it is good practice to *select behaviors for which desired goals can be specified.* Specifically, before targeting a child's temper tantrums for observation, the parents and clinician should have in mind what a desirable level of tantrum would be. If behavioral goals cannot be specified, this may not be a target behavior amenable to intervention. Finally, behaviors must be *clearly defined* so that they are observable and so that independent observers can agree on their occurrence.

Once target behaviors are selected and defined, observation should include a *situational or functional analysis of the behaviors.* To determine specific actions and events that contribute to maintaining the

behavior of concern, the observer/clinician should record the events immediately preceding the target behavior (antecedents) as well as the events immediately following the target behavior (consequences). Information on the antecedents and consequences of the target behavior should assist in the formulation of a treatment plan (Hawkins et al., 1999).

To illustrate these points, consider the example of a mother who is concerned about her 4-year-old's aggressive behavior. Initially, through interviews with the parent, it is important to establish a clear definition of the reported problem: (1) What is meant by "aggressive" (e.g., hitting, kicking, throwing objects); (2) When and where does this occur (e.g., at home, in preschool, during peer play activities); and (3) With whom does it occur (e.g., parents, siblings, teachers, peers)? Once the aggressive behavior is defined—in this case, throwing toys at a younger sibling—observations of antecedent events and consequences would be conducted. Examples of antecedent events might include the mother telling the child to play nicely or the younger child pulling the older child's hair. Consequences might include the mother moving the younger child to another room or giving a brief verbal reprimand. This functional analysis provides information needed for establishing an intervention plan; antecedent events and/or consequences may be altered in an effort to reduce the aggressive behavior. Continued observation of the target behavior (throwing toys) during treatment will help the clinician evaluate the outcome of the intervention.

In addition to conducting observations, clinicians are frequently involved in teaching others how to observe and measure behavior. For example, a teacher may be asked to keep track of a child's off-task and out-of-seat behavior in the classroom, or a parent may be taught to observe and measure a child's tantrum and noncompliant behaviors at home. Several helpful guides are available for this purpose (Hartmann & Wood, 1990; Hawkins et al., 1999).

In summary, naturalistic observations of the child and/or family provide important information for problem identification, treatment planning, and evaluating treatment outcome. However, complex coding systems are time-consuming and require trained observers. Although there are several limitations regarding their use (to be discussed later), they offer the advantages of providing objective information on behaviors of interest while minimizing some of the biases inherent in self-report assessments.

ISSUES CONCERNING BEHAVIORAL OBSERVATIONS

Although many benefits can be gained from including behavioral observations in the assessment process, several issues affect their utility. Concerns about the reliability, validity, and reactivity of observational methods have been noted. The following section reviews several psychometric and methodological issues (also see Foster & Cone, 1986; Hartmann & Wood, 1990).

Reliability
Reliability refers to the extent to which observers' recordings of behaviors correspond to the actual behavioral events. Although reliability has been confused with observer agreement (i.e., the extent to which independent observers agree on the occurrence of behaviors), these really represent two separate issues (Foster & Cone, 1986; Suen & Ary, 1989).

Several factors affect the reliability of behavioral observations. First, characteristics of the recording procedure, such as the complexity of the category definitions or the number of behaviors coded simultaneously, influence accuracy (Pelligrini, 1996; Suen & Ary, 1989). For clinical practice, it may be advisable to limit the number of behaviors being observed (to just the essentials) to optimize the accuracy of the observations. Clearly defined behavioral categories are also very important.

A second factor that influences reliability involves the characteristics of the observer (i.e., clinician, parent, trained observer). Notably, the expectancies of the observers (Foster & Cone, 1986; Pelligrini, 1996) and their prior training and experiences (Mash & McElwee, 1974) can influence accuracy. In general, when trained observers are used, expectancies for change have little effect on the behavioral recordings but significant effects on global or subjective ratings of behavior (see Kent & Foster, 1977). With untrained observers, however, greater evidence for bias in behavioral recording has been observed (Johnson & Bolstad, 1973). This suggests that relatively untrained observers, such as parents and teachers, should be provided with some instruction prior to their observation of child behaviors.

Finally, observers' prior experience can affect accuracy of behavioral recordings (Mash & McElwee, 1974). Generally, trained raters perform more accurately than those who lack experience. This suggests that clinicians, in addition to sharpening their own skills, should be prepared to teach observational recording to others who may be observing the child. Several guides may be useful here (e.g., Gelfand & Hartmann, 1984; Hartmann & Wood, 1990).

Reactivity
Reactivity refers to the extent to which the method of observation influences the behaviors of those being observed. The presence of observers in the home or classroom may affect the behavior of children, parents, and/or teachers. For instance, Johnson, Christensen, and Bellamy (1976) found that different results were obtained when parent-child interactions were recorded in an obtrusive versus an unobtrusive manner. Patterson (1977) noted that older children tend to reduce their deviancy when they are aware of being observed relative to a situation in which their behavior is observed covertly. (See Foster & Cone, 1986, and Hartmann & Wood, 1990, for a review.) Consequently, it is desirable to minimize the reactivity of the assessment procedure to obtain a realistic picture of behavior.

One way of limiting reactivity is to minimize obtrusiveness. Observations conducted behind one-way mirrors or using concealed video equipment are preferable to using in vivo observers. When observers are present, it is helpful to allow some time for the child (family, classmates) to acclimate to the observers until they are largely ignored (Pelligrini, 1996). Observations conducted by persons usually present in the child's daily environment (e.g., parent, teacher) also minimize reactivity (Bentzen, 1993).

Sometimes, reactivity is a benefit rather than a hindrance, such as when the process of observation changes the behavior in the desired direction (provided it is a lasting change). This often occurs when the individual is observing his or her own behavior, a process referred to as self-monitoring. For instance, a mother who monitors her own praising and nagging behaviors may find that praising increases and nagging decreases as a result of keeping track of these behaviors. Self-monitoring has been employed as both an assessment tool and an intervention procedure. When assessment is the goal, it is desirable to minimize reactivity; however, when intervention is the goal, reactivity can be maximized to enhance the effect of this procedure (see Bornstein, Hamilton, & Bornstein, 1986).

Validity
The validity of observational assessment is the extent to which the target behaviors reflect the construct of interest; it is often a neglected issue in behavioral research (Kazdin, 1979). For the most part, behaviors are selected for observation based on face validity and content validity. If a behavior seems relevant to the problem, it is considered to be a valid behavior for observation. Unfortunately, this approach has not always led to the selection of behaviors that are valid indicators of problems. Thus, clinicians should select behaviors for assessment and intervention that have demonstrated validity.

Normative Comparisons
When conducting behavioral observations, it is critical to obtain information on behavioral norms so that problems of an extreme nature can be recognized and those that fall within normal limits will not receive undue attention. When norms are not available, it is advisable to compare the target child with children who are not experiencing problems. In a classroom setting, for instance, this means observing at least one other child (same age, sex, and ethnic/cultural background) whom the teacher identifies as typifying normative behaviors to compare with the target child.

Issues of Diversity
Ethnic and cultural diversity issues are especially important to consider when evaluating children's problems using observations or any other means of assessment. For example, ADHD is now one of the most commonly diagnosed childhood disorders, yet there are serious concerns regarding the assessment of ADHD among culturally diverse students (Reid, 1995; Reid et al., 1998). Recently, this concern has led investigators to examine various behavior rating scales used to evaluate ADHD with culturally diverse youth (e.g., Epstein, March, Conners, & Jackson, 1998; Reid, 1995; Reid et al., 1998). Similar work with other childhood problems and with other assessment methods, including behavioral observations, is very much needed.

SUMMARY

This chapter focused on two common methods of assessment: interviews and behavioral observations. Both yield valuable information for diagnosis, treatment planning, and outcome evaluation. However, neither method is intended to be used as the sole means of assessment. In keeping with the multiperson, multimethod, developmental approach to child assessment, the combined use of interviews, observations, and other assessment strategies will be most productive in obtaining a comprehensive evaluation of the child and family. Moreover, efforts to develop interview and observation methodologies that are culturally sensitive and appropriate represent an important and essential direction for the future.

REFERENCES

Abikoff, H., Gittelman-Klein, R., & Klein, D.F. (1977). Validation of a classroom observation code for hyperactive children. *Journal of Consulting and Clinical Psychology, 45,* 772–783.

Achenbach, T.M. (1991). *Manual for the Child Behavior Checklist/4–18.* Burlington: University of Vermont, Department of Psychiatry.

Achenbach, T.M., & Edelbrock, C.S. (1986). *Manual for the Teacher's Report Form and Teacher Version of the Child Behavior Profile.* Burlington: University of Vermont, Department of Psychiatry.

Ambrosini, P.J. (1988). *Schedule for Affective Disorders and Schizophrenia for School-Aged Children–Present version.* Unpublished manuscript.

American Psychiatric Association. (1987). *Diagnostic and statistical manual of mental disorders* (3rd ed., rev.). Washington, DC: Author.

American Psychiatric Association. (1994). *Diagnostic and statistical manual of mental disorders* (4th ed.). Washington, DC: Author.

Apter, A., Orvaschel, H., Laseg, M., Moses, T., & Tyano, S. (1989). Psychometric properties of the K-SADS-P in an Israeli adolescent inpatient population. *Journal of the American Academy of Child and Adolescent Psychiatry, 28,* 61–65.

Barkley, R.A. (1997). Attention-deficit/hyperactivity disorder. In E.J. Mash & L.G. Terdal (Eds.), *Assessment of childhood disorders* (3rd ed., pp. 71–129). New York: Guilford Press.

Barrera, M., & Garrison-Jones, C.V. (1988). Properties of the Beck Depression Inventory as a screening instrument for adolescent depression. *Journal of Abnormal Child Psychology, 16,* 263–273.

Bentzen, W.R. (1993). *Seeing young children: A guide to observing and recording behavior* (2nd ed.). New York: Delmar.

Bierman, K.L., & Schwartz, L.A. (1986). Clinical child interviews: Approaches and developmental considerations. *Journal of Child and Adolescent Psychotherapy, 3,* 267–278.

Birmaher, B., Waterman, G.S., Ryan, N.D., Perel, J., McNabb, J., Balach, L., Beaudry, M.B., Nasr, F.N., Karambelkar, J., Elterich, G., Quintana, H., Williamson, D.E., & Rao, U. (1998). Randomized, controlled trial of amitriptyline versus placebo for adolescents with "treatment-resistant" major depression. *Journal of the American Academy of Child and Adolescent Psychiatry, 37,* 527–535.

Blount, R.B., Cohen, L.L., Frank, N.C., Bachanas, P.J., Smith, A.J., Manimala, R., & Pate, J.T. (1997). The Child-Adult Medical Procedure Interaction Scale–Revised: An assessment of validity. *Journal of Pediatric Psychology, 22,* 73–88.

Bornstein, P.H., Hamilton, S.B., & Bornstein, M.T. (1986). Self-monitoring procedures. In A.R. Ciminero, K.S. Calhoun, & H.E. Adams (Eds.), *Handbook of behavioral assessment* (2nd ed., pp. 176–222). New York: Wiley.

Boyle, M.H., Offord, D.R., Racine, Y.A., Sanford, M., Szatmari, P., Fleming, J.E., & Price-Munn, N. (1993). Evaluation of the Diagnostic Interview for Children and Adolescents for use in general population samples. *Journal of Abnormal Child Psychology, 21,* 663–681.

Boyle, M.H., Offord, D.R., Racine, Y.A., Szatmari, P., Sanford, M., & Fleming, J.E. (1996). Interviews versus checklists: Adequacy for classifying childhood psychiatric disorders based on adolescent reports. *International Journal of Methods in Psychiatric Research, 6,* 309–319.

Boyle, M.H., Offord, D.R., Racine, Y.A., Szatmari, P., Sanford, M., & Fleming, J.E. (1997). Adequacy of interviews versus checklists for classifying childhood psychiatric disorder based on parent reports. *Archives of General Psychiatry, 54,* 793–799.

Burnstein, S., & Meichenbaum, D. (1979). The work of worrying in children undergoing surgery. *Journal of Abnormal Child Psychology, 7,* 121–132.

Carlson, G.A., Kashani, J.H., Thomas, M.F., Vaidya, A., & Daniel, A.E. (1987). Comparison of two structured interviews on a psychiatrically hospitalized population of children. *Journal of the American Academy of Child and Adolescent Psychiatry, 26,* 645–648.

Chambers, W.J., Puig-Antich, J., Hirsch, M., Paez, P., Ambrosini, P.J., Tabrizi, M.S., & Davies, M. (1985). The assessment of affective disorders in children and adolescents by semistructured interview. *Archives of General Psychiatry, 42,* 696–702.

Costello, A.J., Edelbrock, C.S., Dulcan, M.K., Kalas, R., & Klaric, S.H. (1984). *Report on the NIMH Diagnostic Interview Schedule for Children (DIS-C).* Washington, DC: National Institute of Mental Health.

Cuffe, S.P., Addy, C.L., Garrison, C.Z., Waller, J.L., Jackson, K.L., McKeown, R.E., & Chilappagari, S. (1998). Prevalence of PTSD in a community sample of older adolescents. *Journal of the American Academy of Child and Adolescent Psychiatry, 37,* 147–154.

Dadds, M.R., Barrett, P.M., Rapee, R.M., & Ryan, S. (1996). Family process and child anxiety and aggression: An observational analysis. *Journal of Abnormal Child Psychology, 24,* 715–734.

Dadds, M.R., Ryan, S., & Barrett, P.M. (1993). *The Family Anxiety Coding Schedule.* (Available from Mark Dadds, School of Applied Psychology, Griffith University, Australia, 4111)

DiBartolo, P.M., Albano, A.M., Barlow, D.H., & Heimberg, R.G. (1998). Cross-informant agreement in the assessment of social phobia in youth. *Journal of Abnormal Child Psychology, 26,* 213–220.

DiNardo, P.A., O'Brian, G.T., Barlow, D.H., Waddell, M.T., & Blanchard, E.B. (1983). Reliability of the *DSM-III* anxiety disorder categories using a new structured interview. *Archives of General Psychiatry, 40,* 1070–1079.

Edelbrock, C., Costello, A.J., Dulcan, M.K., Conover, N.C., & Kalas, R. (1986). Parent-child agreement on child psychiatric symptoms assessed via structured interview. *Journal of Child Psychology and Psychiatry, 27,* 181–190.

Endicott, J., & Spitzer, R.L. (1978). A diagnostic interview: The Schedule for Affective Disorders and Schizophrenia. *Archives of General Psychiatry, 35,* 837–844.

Epstein, J.N., March, J.S., Conners, C.K., & Jackson, D.L. (1998). Racial differences on the Conners Teacher Rating Scale. *Journal of Abnormal Child Psychology, 26,* 109–118.

Evans, I.M., & Nelson, R.O. (1977). Assessment of child behavior problems. In A.R. Ciminero, K.S. Calhoun, & H.E. Adams (Eds.), *Handbook of behavioral assessment* (pp. 603–681). New York: Wiley.

Evans, I.M., & Nelson, R.O. (1986). Assessment of children. In A.R. Ciminero, K.S. Calhoun, & H.E. Adams (Eds.), *Handbook of behavioral assessment* (2nd ed., pp. 601–603). New York: Wiley.

Eyberg, S.M., & Robinson, E.A. (1983). Dyadic Parent-Child Interaction Coding System: A manual. *Psychological Documents, 13*(24) (MS. No. 2582). (Available from Social and Behavior Sciences Documents, Select Press, P.O. Box 9838, San Rafael, CA 94912)

Ezpeleta, L., de la Osa, N., Domenech, J.M., Navarro, J.B., Losilla, J.M., & Judez, J. (1997). Diagnostic agreement between clinicians and the Diagnostic Interview for Children and Adolescents—DICA-R—in an outpatient sample. *Journal of Child Psychology and Psychiatry, 38,* 431–440.

Fisher, P.W., Shaffer, D., Piacentini, J.C., Lapkin, J., Kafantaris, V., Leonard, H., Herzog, D.B. (1993). Sensitivity of the Diagnostic Interview Schedule for Children (DISC-2.1) for specific diagnoses of children and adolescents (2nd ed.). *Journal of the American Academy of Child and Adolescent Psychiatry, 32,* 666–673.

Forehand, R., & King, H.E. (1974). Pre-school children's noncompliance: Effects of short-term behavior therapy. *Journal of Community Psychology, 2,* 42–44.

Forehand, R., King, E., Peed, S., & Yoder, P. (1975). Mother-child interactions: Comparison of a noncompliant clinic group and a non-clinic group. *Behavior Research and Therapy, 13,* 79–84.

Forehand, R., & Kotchick, B.A. (1996). Cultural diversity: A wake-up call for parent training. *Behavior Therapy, 27,* 187–206.

Forehand, R., & McMahon, R. (1981). *Helping the noncompliant child.* New York: Guilford Press.

Forehand, R., Sturgis, E.T., McMahon, R.J., Aguar, D., Green, K., Wells, K.C., & Breiner, J. (1979). Parent behavioral training to modify child noncompliance: Treatment generalization across time and from home to school. *Behavior Modification, 3,* 3–25.

Foster, S.L., & Cone, J.D. (1986). Design and use of direct observation procedures. In A.R. Ciminero, K.S. Calhoun, & H.E. Adams (Eds.), *Handbook of behavioral assessment* (2nd ed., pp. 253–324). New York: Wiley.

Foster, S.L., & Robin, A.L. (1988). Family conflict and communication in adolescence. In E.J. Mash & L.G. Terdal (Eds.), *Behavioral assessment of childhood disorders* (2nd ed., pp. 717–775). New York: Guilford Press.

Gelfand, D.M., & Hartmann, D.P. (1984). *Child behavior: Analysis and therapy* (2nd ed.). New York: Pergamon Press.

Ginsburg, G.S., La Greca, A.M., & Silverman, W.K. (1998). Social anxiety in children with anxiety disorders: Relation with social and emotional functioning. *Journal of Abnormal Child Psychology, 26,* 175–185.

Ginsburg, H.P. (1997). *Entering the child's mind: The clinical interview in psychological research and practice.* Cambridge, England: Cambridge University Press.

Gottman, J., Gonso, J., & Rasmussen, B. (1975). Friendships in children. *Child Development, 46,* 709–718.

Greenspan, S.I., & Greenspan, N.T. (1991). *The clinical interview of the child* (2nd ed.). Washington, DC: American Psychiatric Press.

Harris, A., Kreil, D., & Orpet, R. (1977). The modification and validation of the Behavior Coding System for school settings. *Educational and Psychological Measurement, 37,* 1121–1126.

Hartmann, D.P., & Wood, D.D. (1990). Observational methods. In A.S. Bellack, M. Hersen, & A.E. Kazdin (Eds.), *International handbook of behavior modification and therapy* (pp. 107–138). New York: Plenum Press.

Hawkins, R.P., Matthews, J., & Hamdan, L. (1999). *Measuring behavioral health outcomes.* New York: Plenum Press.

Herjanic, B., Herjanic, M., Brown, F., & Wheatt, J. (1975). Are children reliable reporters? *Journal of Abnormal Child Psychology, 3,* 41–48.

Herjanic, B., & Reich, W. (1982). Development of a structured psychiatric interview: Agreement between child and parent on individual symptoms. *Journal of Abnormal Child Psychology,10,* 307–324.

Hetherington, E.M., & Martin, B. (1979). Family interaction. In H.C. Quay & J.S. Werry (Eds.), *Psychopathological disorders of childhood* (2nd ed., pp. 247–302). New York: Wiley.

Hodges, K., & Cools, J.N. (1990). Structured diagnostic interviews. In A.M. La Greca (Ed.), *Through the eyes of the child: Obtaining self-reports from children and adolescents* (pp. 109–149). Boston: Allyn & Bacon.

Hodges, K., Cools, J.N., & McKnew, D. (1986). *Child Assessment Schedule: Test-retest reliability.* Paper presented at the meeting of the American Academy of Child Psychiatry, Los Angeles.

Hodges, K., Cools, J.N., & McKnew, D. (1989). Test-retest reliability of a clinical research interview for children: The Child Assessment Schedule (CAS). *Psychological Assessment: A Journal of Consulting and Clinical Psychology, 1,* 317–322.

Hodges, K., Gordon, Y., & Lennon, M.P. (1990). Parent-child agreement on symptoms assessed via a clinical research interview for children: The Child Assessment Schedule (CAS). *Journal of Child Psychology and Psychiatry, 31,* 427–436.

Hodges, K., Kline, J., Barbero, G., & Flanery, R. (1985). Depressive symptoms in children with recurrent abdominal pain and in their families. *Journal of Pediatrics, 107,* 622–626.

Hodges, K., Kline, J., Fitch, P., McKnew, D., & Cytryn, L. (1981). The Child Assessment Schedule: A diagnostic interview for research and clinical use. *Catalogue of Selected Documents in Psychology, 11,* 56.

Hodges, K., Kline, J., Stem, L., Cytryn, L., & McKnew, D. (1982). The development of a child assessment interview for research and clinical use. *Journal of Abnormal Child Psychology, 10,* 173–189.

Hodges, K., & Saunders, W. (1989). Internal consistency of a diagnostic interview for children: The Child Assessment Schedule. *Journal of Abnormal Child Psychology, 17,* 691–701.

Hodges, K., Saunders, W.B., Kashani, J., Hamlett, K., & Thompson, R.J. (1990). Internal consistency of *DSM-III* diagnoses using the symptom scales of the Child Assessment Schedule. *Journal of the American Academy of Child and Adolescent Psychiatry, 29,* 635–641.

Hughes, J.N., & Baker, D.B. (1990). *The Clinical Child Interview.* New York: Guilford Press.

Jacob, R.G., O'Leary, K.D., & Rosenblat, C. (1978). Formal and informal classroom settings: Effects on hyperactivity. *Journal of Abnormal Child Psychology, 6,* 47–59.

Jensen, P., Roper, M., Fisher, P., Piacentini, J., Canino, G., Richters, J., Rubio-Stipec, M., Dulcan, M., Goodman, S., Davies, M., Rae, D., Shaffer, D., Bird, H., Lahey, B., & Schwab-Stone, M. (1995). Test-retest reliability of the Diagnostic Interview Schedule for Children (DISC-2.1). *Archives of General Psychiatry, 52,* 61–71.

Johnson, S.M., & Bolstad, O.D. (1973). Methodological issues in naturalistic observations: Some problems and solutions for field research. In L. Hamerlynck, L. Handy, & E. Mash (Eds.), *Behavior change: Methodology, concepts, and practice* (pp. 7–67). Champaign, IL: Research Press.

Johnson, S.M., Christensen, A., & Bellamy, G.T. (1976). Evaluation of family intervention through unobtrusive audio recordings: Experiences in "bugging" children. *Journal of Applied Behavior Analysis, 9,* 213–219.

Kazdin, A.E. (1979). Unobtrusive measures in behavioral assessment. *Journal of Applied Behavior Analysis, 12,* 713–724.

Kazdin, A.E. (1993). Treatment of conduct disorder: Progress and directions in psychotherapy research. *Development and Psychopathology, 5,* 277–310.

Kazdin, A.E., Matson, J.L., & Esveldt-Dawson, K. (1984). The relationship of role-play assessment of children's social skills to multiple measures of social competence. *Behavioral Research and Therapy, 22,* 129–139.

Kazdin, A.E., Siegel, T.C., & Bass, D. (1990). Drawing upon clinical practice to inform research on child and adolescent psychotherapy: A survey of practitioners. *Professional Psychology: Research and Practice, 21,* 189–198.

Kelley, M.L., Power, T.G., & Wimbush, D.D. (1992). Determinants of disciplinary practices in low-income Black mothers. *Child Development, 63,* 573–582.

Kent, R.N., & Foster, S.L. (1977). Direct observation procedures: Methodological issues in naturalistic settings. In A.R. Ciminero, K.S. Calhoun, & H.E. Adams (Eds.), *Handbook of behavioral assessment* (pp. 279–328). New York: Wiley.

King, N.J., Tonge, B.J., Heyne, D., Pritchard, M., Rollings, S., Young, D., Myerson, N., & Ollendick, T.H. (1998). Cognitive-behavioral treatment of school-refusing children: A controlled evaluation. *Journal of the American Academy of Child and Adolescent Psychiatry, 7,* 395–403.

Klein, R.G. (1991). Parent-child agreement in clinical assessment of anxiety and other psychopathology: A review. *Journal of Anxiety Disorders, 15,* 187–198.

Koss-Chioino, J.D., & Vargas, J.A. (1992). Through the cultural looking glass: A model for understanding culturally responsive psychotherapies. In L.A. Vargas & J.D. Koss-Chioino (Eds.), *Working with culture* (pp. 1–22). San Francisco: Jossey-Bass.

La Greca, A.M. (1990). Issues and perspectives on the child assessment process. In A.M. La Greca (Ed.), *Through the eyes of the child: Obtaining self-reports from children and adolescents* (pp. 3–17). Boston: Allyn & Bacon.

La Greca, A.M., & Hughes, J. (1999). United we stand, divided we fall: The education and training of clinical child psychologists. *Journal of Clinical Child Psychology, 28,* 435–447.

La Greca, A.M., & Lemanek, K.L. (1996). Assessment as a process in pediatric psychology. *Journal of Pediatric Psychology, 21,* 137–151.

La Greca, A.M., & Stark, P. (1986). Naturalistic observations of children's social behavior. In P. Strain, M. Guralnick, & H. Walker (Eds.), *Children's social behavior: Development assessment and modification* (pp. 181–213). New York: Academic Press.

Lahey, B.B., Applegate, B., Barkley, R.A., Garfinkel, B., McBurnett, K., Kerdyk, L., Greenhill, L., Hynd, G.W., Frick, P.J., Newcorn, J., Biederman, J., Ollendick, T., Hart, E.L., Perez, D., Waldman, I., & Shaffer, D. (1994). *DSM-IV* field trials for oppositional defiant disorder and conduct disorder in children and adolescents. *American Journal of Psychiatry, 151,* 1163–1171.

Lahey, B.B., Applegate, B., McBurnett, K., Biederman, J., Greenhill, L., Hynd, G.W., Barkley, R.A., Newcorn, J., Jensen, P., Richters, J., Garfinkel, B., Kerdyk, L., Frick, P.J., Ollendick, T., Perez, D., Hart, E.L., Waldman, I., & Shaffer, D. (1994). *DSM-IV* field trials for attention-deficit hyperactivity disorder in children and adolescents. *American Journal of Psychiatry, 151,* 1673–1685.

Lindahl, K.M., & Malik, N.M. (1996). *System for Coding Interactions and Family Functioning (SCIFF).* Coral Gables, FL, University of Miami: Authors.

Loeber, R., Green, S.M., & Lahey, B.B. (1990). Mental health professionals' perceptions of the utility of children, parents, and teachers as informants on childhood psychopathology. *Journal of Clinical Child Psychology, 19,* 136–143.

Manassis, K., & Hood, J. (1998). Individual and familial predictors of impairment in childhood anxiety disorders. *Journal of the American Academy of Child and Adolescent Psychiatry, 37,* 428–434.

Mash, E.J., & McElwee, J.D. (1974). Situational effects on observer accuracy: Behavioral predictability, prior experience, and complexity of coding categories. *Child Development, 45,* 367–377.

Mash, E.J., & Terdal, L. (1997). Assessment of child and family disturbance: A behavioral-systems approach. In E.J. Mash & L.G. Terdal (Eds.), *Assessment of childhood disorders* (3rd ed., pp. 3–69). New York: Guilford Press.

McCauley, E., Mitchell, J.R., Burke, P., & Moss, S. (1988). Cognitive attributes of depression in children and adolescents. *Journal of Consulting and Clinical Psychology, 56,* 903–908.

McMahon, R.J., & Forehand, R. (1988). Conduct disorders. In E.J. Mash & L.G. Terdal (Eds.), *Behavioral assessment of childhood disorders* (2nd ed., pp. 105–153). New York: Guilford Press.

Milich, R., Loney, J., & Landau, S. (1982). The independent dimensions of hyperactivity and aggression: A validation with playroom observation data. *Journal of Abnormal Psychology, 91,* 183–198.

Miller-Johnson, S., Lochman, J.E., Coie, J.D., Terry, R., & Hyman, C. (1998). Comorbidity of conduct and depressive problems at sixth grade: Substance use outcomes across adolescence. *Journal of Abnormal Child Psychology, 26,* 221–232.

Ollendick, T.H., Hagopian, L.P., & Huntzinger, R.M. (1991). Cognitive-behavior therapy with nighttime fearful children. *Journal of Behavior Therapy and Experimental Psychiatry, 22,* 113–121.

Orvaschel, H., Puig-Antich, J., Chambers, W., Tabrizi, M.A., & Johnson, R. (1982). Retrospective assessment of prepubertal major depression with the Kiddie-SADS-E. *Journal of the American Academy of Child Psychiatry, 21,* 392–397.

Patterson, G.R. (1977). Naturalistic observation in clinical assessment. *Journal of Abnormal Child Psychology, 5,* 309–322.

Patterson, G.R. (1982). *A social learning approach: Coercive family processes* (Vol. 3). Eugene, OR: Castalia.

Pelligrini, A.D. (1996). *Observing children in their natural worlds: A methodological primer.* New Jersey: Erlbaum.

Piacentini, J., Shaffer, D., Fisher, P., Schwab-Stone, M., Davies, M., & Gioia, P. (1993). The Diagnostic Interview Schedule for Children–Revised version (DISC-R). Concurrent criterion validity. *Journal of the American Academy of Child and Adolescent Psychiatry, 32,* 658–665.

Prescott, C.A., McArdle, J.J., Hishinuma, E.S., Johnson, R.C., Miyamoto, R.H., Andrade, N.N., Edman, J.L., Makini, G.K., Nahulu, L.B., Yuen, N.Y.C., & Carlton, B.S. (1998). Prediction of major depression and dysthymia from CES-D scores among ethnic minority adolescents. *Journal of the American Academy of Child and Adolescent Psychiatry, 37,* 495–503.

Puig-Antich, J., & Chambers, W. (1978). *The Schedule for Affective Disorders and Schizophrenia for School-Age Children (Kiddie-SADS).* New York: New York State Psychiatric Institute.

Puig-Antich, J., Perel, J.M., Lupatkin, W., Chambers, W.J., Shea, C., Tabrizi, M.D., & Stiller, B. (1979). Plasma levels of imipramine (IMI) and desmethylimipramine (DMI) and clinical response in a prepubertal major depressive disorder: A preliminary report. *Journal of the American Academy of Child and Adolescent Psychiatry, 18,* 616–627.

Reed, M.L., & Edelbrock, C. (1983). Reliability and validity of the Direct Observation Form of Child Behavior Checklist. *Journal of Abnormal Child Psychology, 11,* 521–530.

Reid, R. (1995). Assessment of ADHD with culturally different groups: The use of behavioral rating scales. *School Psychology Review, 24,* 537–560.

Reid, R., DuPaul, G.J., Power, T.J., Anastopoulos, A.D., Rogers-Adkinson, D., Noll, M.B., & Riccio, C. (1998). Assessing culturally different students for attention-deficit hyperactivity disorder using behavior rating scales. *Journal of Abnormal Child Psychology, 26,* 187–198.

Roberts, M.A. (1990). A behavioral observation method for differentiating hyperactive and aggressive boys. *Journal of Abnormal Child Psychology, 18,* 131–142.

Roberts, M.C., & Hurley, L. (1997). *Managing managed care.* New York: Plenum Press.

Roberts, M.C., & La Greca, A.M. (1981). Behavioral assessment. In C.E. Walker (Ed.), *Clinical practice of psychology: A practical guide for mental health professionals* (pp. 293–346). New York: Pergamon Press.

Robinson, E.A., & Eyberg, S.M. (1981). The Dyadic Parent-Child Interaction Coding System: Standardization and validation. *Journal of Consulting and Clinical Psychology, 9,* 245–250.

Rogers, R. (1995). *Diagnostic and structured interviewing: A handbook for psychologists.* Odessa, FL: Psychological Assessment Resources.

Rutter, M., & Graham, P. (1968). The reliability and validity of psychiatric assessment of the child: Interview with the child. *British Journal of Psychiatry, 114,* 563–579.

Schwab-Stone, M., Fisher, P., Piacentini, J., Shaffer, D., Davies, M., & Briggs, M. (1993). The Diagnostic Interview Schedule for Children–Revised version (DISC-R): II. Test-retest reliability. *Journal of the American Academy of Child and Adolescent Psychiatry, 32,* 651–657.

Semrud-Clikeman, M. (1995). *Child and adolescent therapy.* Boston: Allyn & Bacon.

Shaffer, D., Fisher, P., Dulcan, M.K., Davies, M., Piacentini, J., Schwab-Stone, M.E., Lahey, B.B., Bourdon, K., Jensen, P.S., Bird, H.R., Canino, G., & Regier, D.A. (1996). The NIMH Diagnostic Interview Schedule for Children–version 2.3 (DISC-2.3): Description, acceptability, prevalence rates, and performance in the MECA study. *Journal of the American Academy of Child and Adolescent Psychiatry, 35,* 865–877.

Shaffer, D., Schwab-Stone, M., Fisher, P., Cohen, P., Piacentini, J., Davies, M., Conners, C.K., & Regier, D. (1993). The Diagnostic Interview Schedule for Children–Revised version (DISC-R): I. Preparation, field testing, interrater reliability, and acceptability. *Journal of the American Academy of Child and Adolescent Psychiatry, 32,* 643–650.

Silverman, W.K. (1994). Structured diagnostic interviews. In T.H. Ollendick, N.J. King, & W. Yule (Eds.), *International handbook of phobic and anxiety disorders in children and adolescents* (pp. 293–315). New York: Plenum Press.

Silverman, W.K., & Albano, A.M. (1996). *Anxiety Disorders Interview Schedule for Children—DSM IV*. San Antonio, TX: Psychological Corporation.

Silverman, W.K., & Eisen, A.R. (1992). Age differences in the reliability of parent and child reports of child anxious symptomatology using a structured interview. *Journal of the American Academy of Child and Adolescent Psychiatry, 31*, 117–124.

Silverman, W.K., & Nelles, W.B. (1988). The Anxiety Disorders Interview Schedule for Children. *Journal of the American Academy of Child and Adolescent Psychiatry, 26*, 772–778.

Silverman, W.K., & Rabian, B. (1995). Test-retest reliability of the *DSM-III-R* childhood anxiety disorders symptoms using the Anxiety Disorders Interview Schedule for Children. *Journal of Anxiety Disorders, 9*, 139–150.

Simmons, J.E. (1987). *Psychiatric examination of children* (4th ed.). Philadelphia: Lea & Febiger.

Stone, W.L., & Lemanek, K.L. (1990). Developmental issues in children's self-reports. In A.M. La Greca (Ed.), *Through the eyes of the child: Obtaining self-reports from children and adolescents* (pp. 18–56). Boston: Allyn & Bacon.

Suen, H.K., & Ary, D. (1989). *Analyzing quantitative behavioral observation data*. Hillsdale, NJ: Erlbaum.

Turkat, I.D. (1986). The behavioral interview. In A.R. Ciminero, K.S. Calhoun, & H.E. Adams (Eds.), *Handbook of behavioral assessment* (2nd ed., pp. 109–149). New York: Wiley.

United States Bureau of the Census. (1996, March). *Current population survey*. Washington, DC: U.S. Government Printing Office.

Verhulst, F.C., Althaus, M., & Berden, G.F. (1987). The Child Assessment Schedule: Parent-child agreement and validity measures. *Journal of Child Psychology and Psychiatry, 28*, 455–466.

Webster-Stratton, C., & Hammond, M. (1988). Maternal depression and its relationship to life stress, perceptions of child behavior problems, parenting behaviors, and child conduct problems. *Journal of Abnormal Child Psychology, 16*, 299–315.

Weissman, M.M., Warner, V., & Fendrich, M. (1990). Applying impairment criteria to children's psychiatric diagnosis. *Journal of the American Academy of Child and Adolescent Psychiatry, 28*, 153–160.

Williamson, D.E., Birmaher, B., Frank, E., Anderson, B., Matty, M., & Kupfer, D.J. (1998). Nature of life events and difficulties in depressed adolescents. *Journal of the American Academy of Child and Adolescent Psychiatry, 37*, 1049–1057.

World Health Organization. (1992). *International classification of mental and behavioral disorders, clinical descriptions and diagnostic guidelines* (10th ed.). Geneva, Switzerland: Author.

Zahner, G.E.P. (1991). The feasibility of conducting structured diagnostic interviews with preadolescents: A community field trial of the DISC. *Journal of the American Academy of Child and Adolescent Psychiatry, 30*, 659–668.

CHAPTER 7

Assessment of Children's Intelligence

JEAN SPRUILL AND SHEILA BLACK

The assessment of children's intellectual and academic functioning probably is the most common reason for referral of a child for a psychological evaluation. The topic of intelligence has dominated the psychological literature for years and encompasses a diversity of domains within the field. The focus of this chapter is on the clinical assessment of intelligence of children. Although there are many types of "intelligence," this chapter focuses on the cognitive aspects only. It is important to remember that an intelligence test is but one aspect of a psychological evaluation and that the scores obtained must be considered in the context of the entire individual and his or her environment.

DEFINITIONS OF INTELLIGENCE

Researchers have been studying the nature of intelligence for well over a century, with still no consensus regarding the definition of the construct. There are as many definitions or conceptualizations of intelligence as there are theorists in the field. Indeed, when Sternberg and Detterman (1986) asked prominent theorists in the field to define intelligence, each person gave a somewhat different definition. Psychologists seem to know more about ways to measure some aspects of intelligence, particularly academic abilities, but less about ways to assess other aspects of intelligence such as social skills, practical knowledge, creativity, and so on. The most influential viewpoints of intelligence at the present time continue to be based on a psychometric approach, although other approaches are increasingly common. Many researchers believe there are many types of intelligence or abilities that are not captured by the psychometrically based tests; some emphasize role of culture; still others espouse a developmental approach to how children learn. With advances in technology, there seems to be a concomitant renewal of interest in the neural and biological bases of intelligence. Nevertheless, the dominant approach appears to be that of a hierarchical model of intelligence with g (general factor) at the apex, even though these same researchers often do not agree on the nature of g (Neisser et al., 1996). There is considerable diversity among researchers about the next level of the hierarchical model. Some prominent theoreticians (e.g., Cattell, 1963; Horn & Cattell, 1967) postulate that g can be subdivided into two related but different types of ability (g), called fluid and crystallized intelligence. Fluid intelligence is essentially nonverbal and culture-free and involves adaptive and new learning processes, whereas crystallized intelligence measures more of the individual's acquired skills and knowledge and is heavily dependent on the individual's educational and cultural opportunities to acquire such skills. All the mainstream intelligence tests have some subtests that measure both crystallized and fluid intelligence, although these tests may not reflect such measures explicitly. However, some tests of intelligence do reflect this division explicitly, for example, the Kaufman Adolescent and Adult Intelligence Test (KAIT; Kaufman & Kaufman, 1993) and the Stanford–Binet Intelligence Test IV (Binet IV; R.L. Thorndike, Hagen, & Sattler, 1986a).

Other approaches emphasize the theory of multiple intelligences (e.g., Gardner, 1983; Sternberg, 1986), with little or no emphasis on g. Although their theories are different, both Gardner and Sternberg believe that current psychometric tests of intelligence do not adequately measure many aspects of intelligence. Sternberg has proposed three fundamental aspects of intelligence—analytic, creative, and practical—and current tests basically measure only the analytic aspects of intelligence. Gardner includes in his theory musical ability and personal intelligences, such as personal-social abilities, neither of which appear to be measured in current intelligence tests.

Models receiving increasing attention are those based on various neuropsychological theories, the most prominent of which is that of Das, Kirby, and Jarman (1979). Their theory focuses on two types of processing of information, successive and simultaneous, and they postulate that both verbal and nonverbal tasks can involve each type of mental processing. Naglieri, Das, and Jarman (1990) and Das, Naglieri, and Kirby (1994) have proposed the PASS model (planning, attention, simultaneous, and successive cognitive processes) as an alternative view for the assessment of cognitive abilities. The Cognitive Assessment System (Naglieri & Das, 1997b), discussed later, is based on the PASS cognitive processing model of intelligence.

Information processing models of intelligence focus on the ways individuals mentally form and process representations of information. Most of these models use the way a computer processes information as a metaphor for human cognition (Kamphaus, 1993). Early researchers using the information processing model of intelligence were Campione and Brown (1978). Borkowski (1985), in his hierarchical model of intelligence, elaborated on the work of Campione and Brown. Basically, Campione and Brown's is a hierarchical theory with two levels of functioning. The first level is an architectural system, which is biologically based and refers to the properties necessary for processing information, space available for memory storage, duration of stimulus trace information, and so on. The architectural system is based on sensory input and is not thought to be influenced greatly by the person's environment. The second level, the executive system, determines how the individual solves problems and is based on such environmentally learned components as knowledge base and strategies or schemes for learning and/or retrieving already learned information. An interesting aspect of this theory is the emphasis on the continued development of both systems over the lifetime of an individual. Researchers in the field have expanded on the basic information processing model as well as other models of intelligence. Space limitations prevent further discussion here. Brief discussions of a variety of models of intelligence can be found in Kamphaus (1993), Sattler (1988), Janda (1998), and Neisser et al. (1996), as well as in many of the references for this chapter.

Although psychologists may not agree on the definition of intelligence, we do know that the current individual tests of intelligence measure, albeit in varying degrees, concepts such as the ability to reason, plan, solve problems, think abstractly, and learn quickly, and the speed at which individuals process information. There are many types of intelligence tests, but they all measure the same type of information. Research has shown that intelligence scores of people fall along a bell-shaped curve, and that the curve (with differing means) has the same shape for various ethnic groups. The bell curve for African Americans is centered around a mean of 85, for Whites around 100, for Hispanics between these two means, and for other groups (e.g., Jews and Asian) somewhat higher than for Whites. We know that the environment can influence intelligence scores, but we do not yet know how to manipulate the environment to produce lasting changes in scores. Intelligence scores are remarkably stable over time (after about age 6 years); nevertheless, when educational or other placement decisions are to be made about an individual, it is important that a current assessment be made of that individual's functioning, as changes do occur.

ASSESSMENT PROCESS

Assessment can be defined as "a process of gathering information used in screening, diagnosing, and determining eligibility, program planning and service delivery, and monitoring progress during treatment or intervention" (Vance & Awadh, 1998, p. 1). Although almost anyone can be taught the administrative skills to correctly administer a test of intelligence, the importance of clinical skills in the assessment process cannot be overemphasized. Unfortunately, clinical skills are not so easily taught. However, the validity of the IQ scores obtained often depends on the clinical skills of the examiner, particularly when testing children. It is important to remember that IQ test scores are only a sample of a child's behavior and are easily influenced by adult behavior and highly dependent on the child's motivation and cooperation. Test scores do not measure traits directly; instead, these scores allow psychologists to make inferences about traits. These inferences are only as good as the reliability and validity of the test and must take into consideration the child's cultural background and language and physical characteristics (e.g., vision, hearing, handicapping conditions). Temporary conditions, such as fatigue, anxiety, illness, and stress, also can influence the scores. Kamphaus (1993), Kaufman (1994), Sattler (1988), and Vance (1998) have excellent chapters related to the assessment process and provide many useful suggestions for both the neophyte and the experienced examiner.

A BRIEF SURVEY OF INDIVIDUAL TESTS OF INTELLIGENCE IN CHILDREN

BAYLEY SCALES OF INFANT DEVELOPMENT II (BSID-II)

The BSID-II (Bayley, 1993), an individually administered test, assesses the current developmental functioning of children in the areas of mental, motor, and behavioral functioning, from birth through 42 months. The Mental and Motor Scales assess the child's current level of cognitive, language, personal-social, and fine- and gross-motor development. The Behavioral Rating Scale assesses qualitative aspects of the child's test-taking behavior and is helpful in interpreting the results of the other scales. Because of their short attention span and activity level, very young children are often difficult to test. The Bayley makes extensive use of fun objects the child can manipulate. However, the test kit is heavy and cumbersome, and the administration is

difficult, especially when attempting to assess a hyperactive young child.

Clinically, the BSID-II most often is used to identify children who are potentially developmentally delayed and to chart the progress of these children once an intervention program has been established. The test-retest reliability coefficients for the BSID-II are acceptable (.87 for the Mental Scale and .78 for the Motor Scale) (Bayley, 1993), but not as high as typically found in individual measures of cognitive ability. There is substantial evidence supporting the validity of the BSID-II, including factor-analytic studies and correlations with other measures of ability. The BSID-II is best used as a measure of the child's current level of developmental functioning. Developmental age scores are nonlinear, as growth does not occur in equal increments from one age to the next. Children often seem to grow in spurts, to be far behind or even advanced "for his or her age" in comparison to peers. Or a particular child may never go through a certain stage or may continue with behavior other children have long outgrown. Thus, rapid developmental changes may account for the occasional low correlations between scores on the BSID-II at one age and at a later age, even when the two scores are obtained only a few months apart. Most infant measures have only modest correlations with scores obtained at a later date; however, the relationship typically is stronger after 24 months of age. Stability scores of developmentally handicapped young children are considerably better than those for nondelayed children (Goodman, 1990). The BSID-II appears to be an excellent screening device for identifying at-risk children with extreme deficits, but it has little predictive validity for children in normal ranges of intelligence.

MCCARTHY SCALES OF CHILDREN'S ABILITIES

The McCarthy Scales (McCarthy, 1972), a comprehensive battery of tests, measure the intellectual and motor development for children age 2 years 6 months to 8 years 6 months. The Verbal, Perceptual-Performance, and Quantitative Scales provide an overall measure of the child's cognitive functioning (General Cognitive Index, GCI). Two additional scales, the Memory and Motor Scales, complete the battery. The psychometric properties and the standardization (conducted in 1970–1971) of the test are good; nevertheless, the norms are quite dated.

Unless the test is revised, examiners should consider using one of the later normed tests for measures of the cognitive ability of young children. The GCI scores range from 50 to 150, making the test inappropriate for very low-functioning children. The primary advantage of the McCarthy Scales is that, in the hands of a skilled examiner, the materials are interesting enough and sufficiently varied to keep the attention of all but the most distractible children. This characteristic is lacking in many of the other tests for young children. The weaknesses of the test include insufficient ceiling for bright children (≥ age 6) and normal children (≥ age 7), as well as insufficient items to adequately measure verbal abstract reasoning, comprehension, and social judgment. However, the major drawback of the McCarthy Scales, particularly in comparison to other measures of ability for young children, is the standardization date. However, in spite of out-of-date norms, a sizable number of clinicians continue to use the McCarthy for the assessment of preschool-age children (Bracken, as cited in Kamphaus, 1993).

KAUFMAN ASSESSMENT BATTERY
FOR CHILDREN (K-ABC)

The K-ABC (Kaufman & Kaufman, 1983) is an individually administered measure of intelligence and achievement for children from age 2 years 6 months to 12 years 6 months. Intelligence, as measured by the K-ABC, is defined in terms of a child's style of information processing and solving problems. Four global scale scores are provided: Sequential Processing, Simultaneous Processing, Mental Processing Composite (MPC, a combination of Sequential plus Simultaneous Processing), and Achievement. In addition, a Nonverbal Scale score provides a measure of functioning for children with hearing or language impairment and for children whose native language is not English. Sequential Processing involves the processing of information in serial or temporal order to solve problems, and the subtests on this scale tap a variety of modalities: visual, motor, and auditory. The common theme of the subtests is the way the information must be processed (sequentially or temporally) to successfully solve the problems. Simultaneous Processing refers to the ability of the child to integrate stimuli all at once to solve a problem. The tasks may be spatial or analogic, but the unifying theme is the requirement of a

mental synthesis of the stimuli to solve the problem. Only three of the subtests are given throughout the age range covered. Thus, depending on the age of the child, composite scores are derived from different combinations of subtests. On the K-ABC, tests that traditionally have formed part of a verbal measure of intelligence (i.e., information and vocabulary) are placed on the Achievement Scale. An attractive feature of the test is the provision of sociocultural norms by socioeconomic status and race.

The standardization and psychometric properties of the K-ABC are good and comparable to other individual measures of ability in children. The factor-analytic structure of the test has been supported (mostly) by research, and the test has generated a large number of research studies. It appears that the Achievement Scale closely resembles the Verbal Scale on the Wechsler Intelligence Scale for Children (WISC) (Kamphaus & Reynolds, 1987). Unfortunately, the K-ABC has floor and ceiling effects at a number of ages, a problem that is further compounded by the use of different subtests at various ages. The lack of verbal comprehension and abstract reasoning subtests on the MPC is a major drawback; however, the use of the Achievement subtests can provide some information about these skills. Because the interpretations are so different from the more traditional tests of intelligence, examiners need to be very knowledgeable and skilled in interpreting the test. Another significant criticism of the K-ABC is that for children age 2 years 5 months to 3 years, the MPC is based on only five subtests, limiting its usefulness with these children. Clinically, the test is not recommended for assessment of mental retardation of young children or assessment of giftedness for older children. The Kaufmans are revising the test, and hopefully the revision will address many of the limitations of the current version.

STANFORD–BINET INTELLIGENCE SCALE, FOURTH
EDITION (BINET IV)

The Binet IV (R.L. Thorndike, Hagen, & Sattler, 1986b), originally developed in France in 1905 and brought to the United States shortly thereafter, is an intelligence test for children 2 years through 23 years of age. In 1912, Terman, working at Stanford University, published the first revision normed in the United States (Terman, 1916). The Binet IV is based on a three-level hierarchical model of cognitive abilities. At the top of the model is *g*, a general reasoning factor, which is subdivided into three broad factors: crystallized abilities, fluid-analytic abilities, and short-term memory. The crystallized abilities factor represents the cognitive factors necessary to acquire and use information to deal with verbal and quantitative concepts to solve problems. Crystallized abilities also represent more general verbal and quantitative problem-solving skills acquired through a variety of learning experiences, both formal (school) and informal. At the third level of the model, crystallized abilities are further divided into verbal and quantitative reasoning. The fluid-analytic abilities factor, measured by abstract/visual reasoning, represents the cognitive skills necessary to solve new problems involving nonverbal or figural stimuli. General life experiences are considered more important than formal education in the development of these abilities. Short-term memory, not further differentiated at the third level of the model, is a measure of the individual's ability to retain information until it can be stored and held in long-term memory so that the individual may use it for solving problems. Each factor is measured by varying numbers of subtests. Another important difference from the previous versions of the Binet is that instead of IQ, and mental age, the term Standard Age Score (SAS) is used.

In the first few years after publication of the Binet IV, a rash of studies attempted to determine the "true" factor structure of the test. The results of 10 factor-analytic studies published between 1988 and 1992 and one published in 1997 offer mixed support for the construct validity of the Binet IV. It appears that differing results can be found depending on the type of factor analysis used and the particular age group studied. R.M. Thorndike (1990) attempted to tie together all the factor-analytic research on the Binet IV; he concluded that the support for four factors is rather weak. The researchers who found support for four factors used confirmatory analyses, which Thorndike criticized as inappropriate. In general, all of the studies found firm support for the first level of the theory behind the Binet IV, namely, the *g* factor. However, varying degrees of support have been found for the second level of the theory, the crystallized and fluid factors. At the third level, with children under 7 years, the consensus seems to be that the memory factor is

not distinct and that the best factor solution is two factors representing primarily verbal and nonverbal skills. By age 7 years, the memory factor emerges as a separate factor. Within the age ranges of 7 to 11 and 12 to 23 years, both Sattler (1988) and R.M. Thorndike (1990) say there are solid grounds for assuming that three meaningful factors exist: verbal, abstract/visual, and short-term memory. The verbal factor includes the Vocabulary, Comprehension, and Memory for Sentences subtests in both the middle and older age ranges. However, the abstract/visual factor seems to be a combination of the Quantitative and Spatial Reasoning tasks, with differing subtests at the middle and older age ranges. The memory factor consists primarily of a Memory for Digits, supplemented to varying degrees by Memory for Objects and Sentences. Kamphaus says that Binet IV area scores "resemble the Verbal and Performance standard scores from the WISC-III when supplemented by a Digit Span subtest" (1993, p. 267).

The Binet IV has good psychometric properties with respect to reliability and validity. The adequacy of the standardization is less clear because the standardization sample contained sampling bias and the adequacy of the weighting procedure used to correct for sample bias in the data is debatable. The administration is more complicated than that of other measures of intelligence. Younger children are given 8 of the 16 subtests, and no one is given all 16 tests. Having a Composite SAS composed of different tests at different age levels makes it difficult to compare scores obtained at different age levels.

In general, the Binet IV works well for most children in the gifted range, but some subtests do not have a sufficiently high ceiling for bright adolescents or adults. All subtests appropriate for young children have inadequate subtest floors (i.e., a child 2 years 6 months who earns a raw score of 1 on all subtests appropriate for his or her age will receive a Composite SAS of 95). The lowest SAS that can be obtained for any area or composite is 36, making the test inappropriate for individuals classified in the severe or profound range of retardation. The Binet IV has not been found to be as clinically useful as the Binet Form L-M. Obringer, as cited in Kamphaus (1993), found that two years after the publication of the Binet IV, the L-M version was still used more frequently than the Binet IV. Riverside Publishing Company has begun the process of developing and standardizing the Binet V.

THE WECHSLER SCALES

The results of any survey concerning frequency of test usage always lists either the Wechsler Intelligence Scale for Children (any version) or the Wechsler Adult Intelligence Scale (any version) as the most frequently used measure of intelligence (e.g., Hutton, Dubes, & Muir, 1992; Watkins, Campbell, Nieberding, & Hallmark, 1995). The Wechsler scales appear to have become the gold standard in the arena of assessment of intelligence—the tests to which all other measures of intelligence are compared. The three versions of the Wechsler scales are discussed separately below.

Wechsler conceived of intelligence as a multifaceted, multidetermined overall, or global, entity, "the capacity of the individual to act purposefully, to think rationally, and to deal effectively with his or her environment" (1991b, p. 1). He believed that the particular types of tests used in intelligence measures were not as important as measuring or sampling a full array of cognitive abilities. Thus, he developed a wide variety of tests reflecting his multifaceted view of intelligence, but he also summed the results into one overall score, reflecting his view of intelligence as a global attribute of an individual.

The Wechsler Preschool and Primary Scale of Intelligence–Revised (WPPSI-R)

The WPPSI-R (Wechsler, 1989) is appropriate for children age 3 to 7 years and has three global scores: Verbal IQ, Performance IQ, and Full-Scale IQ. The standardization sample is excellent, matching the U.S. census data remarkably well. Research indicates that the global scores are stable and reliable and that the test has strong construct validity support from factor-analytic studies that show two factors for each age group—one composed of all verbal subtests and one composed of all performance subtests (e.g., Blaha & Wallbrown, 1991; Lo-Bello & Guelgoez, 1991). The stability coefficients for most subtest scores are inadequate (Kaufman, 1992); thus, interpreting subtest scores as representing strengths or weaknesses should be done very cautiously.

The WPPSI-R compares favorably with other measures of intellectual functioning for young children. Karr et al. (1993) found significant correlations among the scores of the WPPSI-R and the McCarthy Scales and no significant differences among the mean IQ scores. No differences were found between the Full-Scale IQ and the Composite SAS when the WPPSI-R was compared to the Binet IV (McCrowell & Nagle, 1994). Although there also were no significant differences between the Abstract/Visual Scale of the Binet IV and the Performance Scale of the WPPSI-R, there were significant differences between the Verbal Scales of the two measures.

The WPPSI-R appears to be adequate for measuring the ability of all but the brightest children at the upper age range of the test (Kaplan, 1992; Kaplan, Fox, & Paxton, 1991). However, Kaufman has criticized the emphasis on bonus points for response speed on the WPPSI-R, saying that "gifted children, as a group, don't excel quite as much in sheer speed" (1992, p. 157). At the overlapping age ranges of the WPPSI-R and WISC-III, it is recommended that the WISC-III be used for assessing bright children and the WPPSI-R be used for assessing low-functioning children. For young children, all subtests have inadequate floors, making the score an overestimate of their abilities. Other weaknesses are the emphasis on bonus points for Block Design and Object Assembly, the difficult scoring system for Geometric Design, and administration directions that are occasionally confusing for both examiner and child.

The major problem with the use of the WPPSI-R with very young children is the lengthy individual subtest format. Young children do better on brief sets of items such as those found on the Stanford–Binet Form L-M, the Bayley, and the McCarthy Scales. In addition, the lower age ranges of these tests make them preferable for very young children. The WPPSI-III is expected to have a lower age range and should be published within one or two years (David Tulsky, The Psychological Corporation, personal communication, August 21, 1999).

The Wechsler Intelligence Scale for Children III (WISC-III)

The WISC-III (Wechsler, 1991) offers the traditional Verbal and Performance Scales of the Wechsler tests and, in addition, has a new set of index scores that are essentially factor scores. The materials are colorful and easy to administer, and children seem to enjoy them. A new subtest, Symbol Search, was added to the 11 existing subtests of the WISC-R. The initial hope was that this would increase the reliability and validity of the Freedom from Distractibility Factor of the WISC-R. Instead, four factors emerged: Verbal Comprehension Index, which consists of the Information, Similarities, Vocabulary, and Comprehension subtests; Perceptual Organization Index, which consists of Picture Completion, Picture Arrangement, Block Design, and Object Assembly; Freedom from Distractibility Index, which includes the Arithmetic and Digit Span subtests; and the Processing Speed Index, which is made up of the Coding and Symbol Search subtests.

The psychometric properties of the WISC-III and the standardization sample are excellent (Kaufman, 1992). However, the test-retest or stability coefficients for many of the WISC-III subtests are not adequate. Thus, examiners need to be very cautious in interpreting strengths and weaknesses within the subtest profile. Indeed, this examiner has seen numerous cases where a child's subtest scores varied considerably from one administration to another, but where the overall Verbal and Performance IQ scores were virtually identical.

In general, correlations between scores on the WISC-III and other intelligence tests are quite high. Comparisons of mean scores, however, often produce significant differences. As would be expected from the differences in standardization dates, WISC-III scores average 4 to 5 points lower than WISC-R scores. When compared to other measures of intelligence, such as the Binet IV, WPPSI-R, K-ABC, and Woodcock–Johnson Cognitive Ability, correlations among the scores are high and the means comparable. Indeed, the WISC-III is probably the instrument of choice for the age range covered. It is the most frequently used measure for children 6 to 16 years of age (Kamphaus, 1993).

What does the WISC-III measure? In general, various factor-analytic studies have found support for the four factors of the WISC-III, although some differences in interpretation of the factors exist. Support for the four-factor model was found by Donders and Warschausky (1996); by Roid and Worrall (1997); by Tupa, Wright, and Fristad (1997); and by Kamphaus, Benson, Hutchinson, and Platt (1994). However, Kamphaus et al. point out that additional theoretical and empirical research is needed to clarify the third and fourth factors because of the lack of a theoretical base for four factors. Reynolds and Ford (1994), in comparing the WISC-R and WISC-III, found a stable and consistent three-factor solution across the age ranges of

the instrument when Symbol Search was deleted. The three factors were labeled verbal comprehension, perceptual organization, and freedom from distractibility. Keith and Witta (1997) argued against naming the third factor freedom from distractibility (FFD), suggesting instead that it may be a measure of quantitative reasoning. This interpretation is endorsed both by Carroll (1997) and by Reinecke, Beebe, and Stein (1999). The majority of Reinecke et al.'s subjects (200 children, 6–11 years of age, who had been diagnosed with attention-deficit/hyperactivity disorder) did not show a significant relative weakness on FFD factor scores, although the mean FFD scores were significantly lower than the other WISC-III factor scores. Nor did they find significant correlations between measures of sustained visual attention and FFD scores. In conclusion, it appears that whereas four factors may indeed describe the factor structure of the WISC-III, the appropriate label for the third factor may not be freedom from distractibility, and the clinical utility of the third and fourth factors is called into question. Thus, the examiner should not interpret the index scores without independent confirmation of their appropriateness for a particular child.

WOODCOCK–JOHNSON PSYCHO-EDUCATIONAL BATTERY–REVISED: TESTS OF COGNITIVE ABILITY (WJ-R COGNITIVE BATTERY)

The WJ-R Cognitive Battery (Woodcock & Johnson, 1989) is based on Cattell and Horn's model of fluid (Gf) and crystallized (Gc) intelligence and is useful for measuring cognitive ability for individuals 2 to 95+ years. The Cognitive Battery contains 21 tests of cognitive ability divided into a standard and a supplemental battery. It measures seven of the nine broad intellectual abilities or cognitive factors identified in the Gf-Gc theory: Visual Processing, Processing Speed, Long-Term Retrieval, Short-Term Memory, Auditory Processing, Comprehension-Knowledge, and Fluid Reasoning. The seven-subtest standard battery contains one subtest that measures each cognitive factor. The supplemental battery contains one to three additional measures of each cognitive factor. The eighth factor in the model, quantitative ability, is measured by two achievement subtests that are part of the achievement battery. A Broad Cognitive Ability (BCA) score is based on the seven factor scores and is best interpreted as a measure of *g*.

The WJ-R Cognitive Battery has strong psychometric properties and offers an alternative to the traditional verbal-perceptual organizational framework that might be more useful for children with learning disabilities (Tetter & Semrud-Clikeman, 1997). Factor-analytic studies have supported the eight-factor model quite well (Flanagan & McGrew, 1998; McGrew & Murphy, 1995; Woodcock, 1990). Concurrent validity studies, using the WISC-R, have found significant correlations between the BCA and WISC-R IQ scores but varying results with respect to the mean differences between the scores. Thompson and Brassard (1984) found no difference between the mean BCA score and the WISC-R Full-Scale IQ score for the normal sample, but significantly lower BCA scores in the learning disabled sample. They concluded that the achievement emphasis of the WJ-R Cognitive Battery jeopardizes its validity for assessing and classifying learning disabled students within the current achievement-ability discrepancy formula used by most school systems. Phelps, Rosso, and Falasco (1984) also found lower BCA scores than WISC-R scores, and concluded that the WJ-R Cognitive Tests are more a measure of verbal and achievement skills than of cognitive ability. Arffa, Rider, and Cummings (1984), in comparing the BCA scores with the SASs of the Binet IV, found significant correlations among the various scores, with the BCA score significantly lower than the Binet IV Composite SAS. When the WPPSI-R was compared with the WJ-R Cognitive Battery, Harrington, Kimbrell, and Dai (1992) found high correlations between the BCA and IQ scores of the WPPSI-R and a mean BCA score significantly higher (4.5 points) than the WPPSI-R Full Scale IQ Score (FSIQ). Based on the available literature, it appears that, in general, the WJ-R Cognitive BCA score is lower than other scores of intellectual ability for most clinical samples, but not necessarily for children with other disorders or with no diagnosis. Whereas the WJ-R provides an interesting and theoretically based alternative to other measures of ability, it is not recommended for diagnostic purposes, as the lower scores on the BCA may reduce its effectiveness in demonstrating an achievement-ability discrepancy necessary for a diagnosis of learning disability. The WJ-R Tests of Cognitive Ability have not attracted a lot of research attention since the mid-1980s. For example, in the literature search, there were no studies comparing it to the WISC-III. Research that compares the WJ-R Cognitive Scales to the WISC-III and WAIS-III is needed.

COGNITIVE ASSESSMENT SYSTEM (CAS)

The CAS (Naglieri & Das, 1997b) is the most recent alternative to the Binet and Wechsler Scales and is based on the PASS (planning, attention, simultaneous, and successive) cognitive processing theory of intelligence (Naglieri & Das, 1990, 1997a). According to this theory, planning is a cognitive process used by an individual to solve problems when no immediate solution is apparent; successful solutions require attention and impulse control. Attention is the process an individual uses to selectively attend to a particular stimulus and inhibit attention to a competing stimulus. Sustained focus over time is required to identify target stimuli and to avoid distractions. Simultaneous processing involves perceiving disparate stimuli as a group and interrelating the parts into a whole. Sequential processing involves solving problems in a specific serial order. More complete (and better definitions) can be found in the *CAS Interpretive Handbook* (Naglieri & Das, 1997a). A comprehensive summary of the PASS theory is presented by Das et al. (1994).

The CAS consists of 13 subtests, 12 of which constitute a standard battery and 8 of which constitute a basic battery. Eleven of the subtests are appropriate throughout the entire age range (5–17 years). In addition to the Full-Scale score (IQ), Standard scores are computed for each of the PASS abilities.

The test is well standardized and has excellent psychometric properties, with reliability scores ranging from .83 to .93 for PASS scale scores and .96 for the Full-Scale IQ score. Validity studies with special populations (mentally retarded, gifted, learning disabled, attention-deficit disordered, and those with traumatic brain injury) support the discriminant validity of the CAS (Naglieri & Das, 1997a). In addition, a subgroup of 1,600 children was administered the WJ-R Achievement Battery, which facilitates the interpretation of ability-achievement discrepancies. This is a very useful feature for aiding in the diagnosis of learning disabilities as well as facilitating academic interventions.

Factor-analytic studies have provided mixed support for the test as a measures of the PASS domains. Telzrow (1990) concludes that, although there is factor-analytic support for the tasks and scales of the CAS, the support for attention as a separate cognitive-processing construct is limited. However, in a study that compares the WISC-R third factor (freedom from distractibility) and the attention subtests of the CAS, McLarty and Das (1993) found significant positive correlations between the measures of attention. Kranzler and Keith (1999) tested the adequacy of fit provided by the PASS model with several competing models. Although they found that the CAS measures the same constructs across the 12-year span (5–17 years) and that the PASS theory provided the best fit for the data, it did not provide a particularly good fit. They suggest that the attention and planning processing factors are better interpreted as a measure of processing speed; the sequential processing factor is best interpreted as a measure of memory; and the simultaneous factor is a mixture of fluid intelligence and broad visualization. They also concluded that the use of the CAS for differential diagnosis and/or planning academic interventions was not supported. However, Naglieri (1999) responded to their critique by reviewing the empirical evidence for the CAS. He summarized data indicating that the CAS yields different profiles for children with learning disabilities and attention-deficit/hyperactivity disorder, which supports the use of the CAS for differential diagnosis. Furthermore, Naglieri concluded that the CAS predicts achievement scores better than other tests of ability.

There is not yet enough independent research available to judge the adequacy of either the Kranzler and Keith or Naglieri viewpoint. This is a promising and new way of measuring cognitive ability, and one that deserves further attention by researchers and clinicians.

LEITER INTERNATIONAL PERFORMANCE SCALE–REVISED (LIS-R)

The LIS-R (Roid & Miller, 1996) is a completely nonverbal test of intelligence and cognitive abilities. It has a "game-like" quality that holds the interest of all but the most distractible children. Because it is nonverbal, it is particularly useful for assessing children whose native language is not English and children with hearing or speech and language problems.

The revision appears to have eliminated many of the problems of the original version of the test. It also provides a more comprehensive picture of the

child's cognitive strengths and weaknesses. Emphasizing the measurement of fluid intelligence, the LIS-R provides standard scores for four domains (visualization, reasoning, memory, and attention) and also provides a composite IQ score. In general, when the original LIS was compared to other measures (WISC-R, Binet L-M, Binet IV, K-ABC), the correlations among the various scores were in the moderate to high range, but there were substantial differences in the overall IQ scores, with the LIS being larger (or smaller). Because the original version of the Leiter had many limitations, it is difficult to know if this same pattern will occur with the LIS-R. Based on the studies reported in the manual, the LIS-R has adequate content, criterion, and construct validity. Factor-analytic studies show that the test fits a hierarchical model of cognitive abilities with *g* at the top and measures of nonverbal reasoning, memory, and attention at the second level. Also, clinical samples of children show differences in IQ scores in the expected direction (e.g., gifted are higher than the standardization sample). Flemmer and Roid (1997) administered the LIS-R to a large sample of children of different ethnic origins and children with and without speech impairments. In general, there were few differences among the various ethnic or clinical groups, suggesting that the LIS-R provides an unbiased assessment for the various groups.

Clearly, the LIS-R is not the instrument of choice for the assessment of cognitive ability of the majority of children. However, the LIS-R has the potential for being very useful in the assessment of children from diverse backgrounds and with a wide variety of special needs. In the Psychology Clinic at the University of Alabama, we have found it particularly useful in assessing children with autism or pervasive developmental disorders. Often, these children are not sufficiently verbal or cooperative enough to be given more traditional measures of cognitive assessment. More research is needed to establish the utility of the LIS-R as a measure of cognitive ability in children.

SCREENING TESTS

Many of the tests discussed previously have short-form versions in which either a selected number of subtests (test reduction forms) or alternating items of all subtests (item reduction forms) are administered, and the IQ is based on these reduced subtests/items. Both techniques have been shown to provide a reasonably good estimate of their respective Full-Scale or Composite scores. However, two brief screening measures are available that were not derived from items in the full test, but were independently developed as brief measures of intellectual ability and standardized on a large national sample. Although not a substitute for more comprehensive tests of cognitive ability, both of the tests discussed below are excellent screening measures.

Kaufman Brief Intelligence Test (K-BIT)

The K-Bit (Kaufman & Kaufman, 1990) consists of two subtests: Vocabulary, which is divided into Expressive Vocabulary (naming pictures) and Definitions (defining words), and Matrices (solving visual analogies using abstract stimuli) that cover the age range 4 to 90 years. The K-BIT can be used in any situation where a screening measure of ability will suffice or as a mechanism to make referral decisions for further testing (e.g., screening for gifted or other special education programs). Administration and scoring require minimal training, thus, it can be administered by a wide variety of individuals. The standardization sample was excellent and the psychometric properties of the test are good. Correlations with other measures of ability are high, although the K-BIT may yield slightly higher or lower scores for some samples. The results of the various studies, using different populations, have found high correlations among the K-BIT Composite IQ and the various other IQ scores, but varying mean differences. For example, Prewett and McCaffery (1993) found the K-BIT IQ Composite score averaged 5.1 points lower then the Binet IV Composite SAS. Prewett (1995) found significant correlations between the K-BIT and WISC-III scores, with the K-BIT having a slightly higher Composite IQ score than the WISC-III. However, in a sample of gifted referrals, Levinson and Folino (1994) also found high correlations among K-BIT and WISC-III scores and no significant difference between the K-BIT Composite IQ and the WISC-III Full-Scale IQ. Eisenstein and Englehart (1997) found K-BIT Composite scores approximately 2 points higher than the WAIS-R Full-Scale IQ Score. The general conclusion of these studies is that the K-BIT is a promising screening instrument when time constraints prevent the use of a more comprehensive measure. The scores obtained should be considered an estimate of intellectual ability

and followed up by a more comprehensive test when necessary.

Wechsler Abbreviated Scale of Intelligence (WASI)

The WASI was "developed to meet the demands for a short and reliable measure of intelligence in clinical, psychoeducational, and research settings" (The Psychological Corporation, 1999, p. 1). It consists of four subtests: Vocabulary, Block Design, Similarities, and Matrix Reasoning, which produce Verbal, Performance, and Full-Scale IQ scores. These subtests are similar to their counterparts on the WAIS-III and WISC-III, but the item content is completely different. There are norms for the four-subtest battery and for a two-subtest battery consisting of Vocabulary and Matrix Reasoning.

The WASI is individually administered to individuals age 6 to 89 years. The standardization and psychometric properties of the WASI are good, and there are some reliability and validity studies reported in the manual. To date, there are no independent studies that compare the WASI and other tests. Based on studies reported in the manual, the WASI correlations with the WISC-III Full-Scale IQ were high (.87 for the FSIQ based on four subtests and .81 for the WASI FSIQ based on two subtests), and the mean scores differed by less than 1 point. Similar results were found when the WASI scores were compared with WAIS-III scores. WASI correlations with the WAIS-III Full-Scale IQ were .92 for the WASI FSIQ based on four subtests and .87 for the WASI FSIQ based on two subtests, and again the mean scores differed by less than 1 point. Although the WASI does have reasonable clinical utility for the cognitive screening of individuals suspected of having mental retardation, it does not have adequate ability to differentiate the degree of mental retardation. The WASI does appear to be a good measure for screening individuals for gifted programs. Clinical samples of children with ADHD, learning disabilities, and traumatic brain injury were matched with children from the standardization sample using the variables of age, race/ethnicity, sex, and parent education, and varying differences among the mean scores were found, ranging from less than 2 points for the ADHD sample to 7 to 10 points for the LD sample and 16 points for the traumatic brain injury group. Research studies indicate the four-subtest battery is slightly better than the two-subtest battery, but that both batteries are acceptable measures of ability when an estimate of intellectual ability is desired.

PUTTING IT ALL TOGETHER

It is important to remember that scores on an IQ test are just that—scores. These scores may or may not be related to many measures of daily functioning. The scores measure only part of the domain of intelligent behavior and are a measure of the extent to which a child has the basic cognitive and academic skills to function in his or her environment. In addition to reflecting basic cognitive ability, the scores also reflect personality, attitudinal, and test-taking skills. Any intellectual assessment must be accompanied by relevant background and history on the child and family as well as other tests that will aid in answering the referral question. Regardless of the reason for the assessment, the unique interpretation of the scores for a particular child is heavily dependent on the background of the child. For example, suppose that both the teacher and the mother of a 10-year-old child report problems with attention, and the examiner notes that the child answered impulsively, had great difficulty attending to certain types of items, and often asked for questions to be repeated. Certainly, attention problems are suspected in this case. However, if the symptoms are of recent origin and only began after the child fell off his bike, the clinician may begin to look for possible neurological problems. For very young children, the cornerstone of a good evaluation rests on a developmental history that allows the clinician to interpret the results obtained within a larger context (Kalesnik, 1999). Thus, a "thorough history is not just helpful—it is crucial to the proper interpretation of assessment results" (Gregory, 1999, p. 7).

WHERE DO WE GO FROM HERE?

What will the intelligence tests of the next century look like? The past century of intelligence assessment has been marked by considerable change in the tests themselves, theoretical approaches, and guidelines for test use. There is no indication from history that this pace of change is slowing; indeed,

it continues to expand rapidly. "The next century should see a change in the way we measure intelligence—based on the recent knowledge explosion in cognitive psychology, information processing and developmental psychology" (Matarazzo, 1992, p. 1012). However, "Until a new method produces better predictive validity coefficients or some other convincing evidence, the WISC-III and similar tests will likely reign supreme" (Kamphaus, 1993, p. 349).

REFERENCES

Arffa, S., Rider, L.H., & Cummings, J.A. (1984). A validity study of the Woodcock–Johnson Psycho-Educational Battery and the Stanford–Binet with Black preschool children. *Journal of Psychoeducational Assessment, 2,* 73–77.

Bayley, N. (1993). *Bayley Scales of Infant Development* (2nd ed.). San Antonio, TX: Psychological Corporation.

Blaha, J., & Wallbrown, F.H. (1991). Hierarchical factor structure of the Wechsler Preschool and Primary Scale of Intelligence–Revised. *Psychological Assessment, 3,* 455–463.

Borkowski, J.G. (1985). Signs of intelligence: Strategy generalization and metacognition. In S.R. Yussen (Ed.), *The growth of reflection in children* (pp. 105–144). Orlando, FL: Academic Press.

Campione, J.C., & Brown, A.L. (1978). Toward a theory of intelligence: Contributions from research with retarded children. *Intelligence, 2,* 279–304.

Carroll, J.B. (1997). Commentary on Keith and Witta's hierarchical and cross-age confirmatory factor analysis of the WISC-III. *School Psychology Quarterly, 12,* 108–109.

Cattell, R.B. (1963). Theory of fluid and crystallized intelligence: A critical experiment. *Journal of Educational Psychology, 54,* 1–22.

Das, J.P., Kirby, J., & Jarman, R.F. (1979). *Sequential and simultaneous cognitive processes.* New York: Academic Press.

Das, J.P., Naglieri, J.A., & Kirby, J.R. (1994). *Assessment of cognitive processes: The PASS theory of intelligence.* Needham Heights, MA: Allyn & Bacon.

Donders, J., & Warschausky, S. (1996). A structural equation analysis of the WISC-III in children with traumatic head injury. *Child Neuropsychology, 2,* 185–192.

Eisenstein, N., & Englehart, C.I. (1997). Comparison of the K-BIT with short forms of the WAIS-R in a neuropsychological population. *Psychological Assessment, 9,* 57–62.

Flanagan, D.P., & McGrew, K.S. (1998). Interpreting intelligence tests from contemporary Gf-Gc theory: Joint confirmatory factor analysis of the WJ-R and

KAIT in a non-White sample. *Journal of School Psychology, 36,* 151–182.

Flemmer, D.D., & Roid, G.H. (1997). Nonverbal intellectual assessment of Hispanic and speech-impaired adolescents. *Psychological Reports, 80,* 1115–1122.

Gardner, H. (1983). *Frames of mind: The theory of multiple intelligences.* New York: Basic Books.

Goodman, J.F. (1990). Infant intelligence: Do we, can we, should we assess it? In C.R. Reynolds & R.W. Kamphaus (Eds.), *Handbook of psychological and educational assessment of children* (pp. 183–208). New York: Guilford Press.

Gregory, R.J. (1999). *Foundations of intellectual assessment.* Needham Heights, MA: Allyn & Bacon.

Harrington, R.G., Kimbrell, J., & Dai, X. (1992). The relationship between the Woodcock–Johnson Psycho-Educational Battery–Revised (Early Development) and the Wechsler Preschool and Primary Scale of Intelligence–Revised. *Psychology in the Schools, 29,* 116–125.

Horn, J.L., & Cattell, R.B. (1967). Age differences in fluid and crystallized intelligence *Acta Psychologica, 26,* 107–129.

Hutton, J.B., Dubes, R., & Muir, S. (1992). Assessment practices of school psychologists: Ten years later. *School Psychology Review, 21,* 271–284.

Janda, L.H. (1998). *Psychological testing: Theory and application.* Boston: Allyn & Bacon.

Kalesnik, J. (1999). Developmental history. In E.V. Huttall, I. Romero, & J. Kalesnik (Eds.), *Assessing and screening preschoolers* (pp. 94–111). Needham Heights, MA: Allyn & Bacon.

Kamphaus, R.W. (1993). *Clinical assessment of children's intelligence.* Needham Heights, MA: Allyn & Bacon.

Kamphaus, R.W., Benson, J., Hutchinson, S., & Platt, L.O. (1994). Identification of factor models for the WISC-III. *Educational and Psychological Measurement, 54,* 174–186.

Kamphaus, R.W., & Reynolds, C. (1987). *Clinical and research applications of the K-ABC.* Circle Pines, MN: American Guidance Service.

Kaplan, C.H. (1992). Ceiling effects in assessing high-IQ children with the WPPSI-R. *Journal of Clinical Child Psychology, 21,* 403–406.

Kaplan, C.H., Fox, L.M., & Paxton, L. (1991). Bright children and the revised WPPSI: Concurrent validity. *Journal of Psychoeducational Assessment, 9,* 240–246.

Karr, S.K., Carvajal, H.H., Elser, D., Bays, K., Logan, R.A., & Pope, G.L. (1993). Concurrent validity of the WPPSI-R and the McCarthy Scales of Children's Abilities. *Psychological Reports, 72,* 940–942.

Kaufman, A.S. (1992). Evaluation of the WISC-III and WPPSI-R for gifted children. *Roeper Review, 14,* 154–158.

Kaufman, A.S. (1994). *Intelligent testing with the WISC-III.* New York: Wiley.

Kaufman, A.S., & Kaufman, N.L. (1983). *Kaufman Assessment Battery for Children.* Circle Pines, MN: American Guidance Service.

Kaufman, A.S., & Kaufman, N.L. (1990). *Kaufman Brief Intelligence Test.* Circle Pines, MN: American Guidance Service.

Kaufman, A.S., & Kaufman, N.L. (1993). *Kaufman Adolescent and Adult Intelligence Test.* Circle Pines, MN: American Guidance Service.

Keith, T.Z., & Witta, E.L. (1997). Hierarchical and cross-age confirmatory factor analysis of the WISC-III: What does it measure? *School Psychology Quarterly, 12,* 89–107.

Kranzler, J.H., & Keith, T.Z. (1999). Independent confirmatory factor analysis of the Cognitive Assessment System (CAS): What does the CAS measure? *School Psychology Review, 28,* 117–144.

Levinson, E.M., & Folino, L. (1994). The relationship between the WICS-III and the Kaufman Brief Intelligence. *Special Services in the Schools, 8,* 155–159.

LoBello, S.G., & Guelgoez, S. (1991). Factor analysis of the Wechsler Preschool and Primary Scale of Intelligence–Revised. *Psychological Assessment, 3,* 130–132.

Matarazzo, J.D. (1992). Psychological testing and assessment in the 21st century. *American Psychologist, 47,* 1007–1018.

McCarthy, S. (1972). *McCarthy Scales of Children's Abilities.* New York: Psychological Corporation.

McCrowell, K.L., & Nagle, R.J. (1994). Comparability of the WPPSI-R and the S-B: IV among preschool children. *Journal of Psychoeducational Assessment, 12,* 126–134.

McGrew, K., & Murphy, S. (1995). Uniqueness and general factor characteristics of the Woodcock–Johnson Tests of Cognitive Ability–Revised. *Journal of School Psychology, 33,* 235–245.

McLarty, M.L., & Das, J.P. (1993). Correlations between objective tests of attention and Third Factor in WISC-R. *Canadian Journal of School Psychology, 9,* 86–94.

Naglieri, J.A. (1999). How valid is the PASS theory and CAS? *School Psychology Review, 28,* 145–162.

Naglieri, J.A., & Das, J.P. (1990). Planning, attention, simultaneous, and successive (PASS) cognitive processes as a model for intelligence. *Journal of Psychoeducational Assessment, 8,* 303–337.

Naglieri, J.A., & Das, J.P. (1997a). *CAS interpretive handbook.* Chicago: Riverside.

Naglieri, J.A., & Das, J.P. (1997b). *Cognitive Assessment System.* Chicago: Riverside.

Naglieri, J.A., Das, J.P., & Jarman, R.F. (1990). Planning, attention, simultaneous, and successive cognitive processes as a model for assessment. *School Psychology Review, 10,* 423–442.

Neisser, U., Boodoo, G., Bouchard, T.J., Boykin, A.W., Brody, N., Ceci, S.J., Halpern, D.F., Loehlin, J.C., Perloff, R., Sternberg, R.J., & Urbina, S. (1996). Intelligence:

Knowns and unknowns. *American Psychologist, 51,* 77–101.

Phelps, L., Rosso, M., & Falasco, S.L. (1984). Correlations between the Woodcock–Johnson and the WISC-R for a behavior disordered population. *Psychology in the Schools, 21,* 442–446.

Prewett, P.N. (1995). A comparison of two screening tests (the Matrix Analogies Test–Short Form and the Kaufman Brief Intelligence Test) with the WISC-III. *Psychological Assessment, 7,* 69–72.

Prewett, P.N., & McCaffery, L.K. (1993). A comparison of the Kaufman Brief Intelligence Test (K-BIT) with the Stanford–Binet Intelligence Scale, a two-subtest short form, and the Kaufman Test of Educational Achievement (K-TEA) Brief Form. *Psychology in the Schools, 30,* 299–304.

Psychological Corporation, The. (1999). *Wechsler Abbreviated Scale of Intelligence.* San Antonio, TX: Author.

Reinecke, M.A., Beebe, D.W., & Stein, M.A. (1999). The third factor of the WISC-III: It's (probably) not freedom from distractibility. *Journal of the American Academy of Child and Adolescent Psychiatry, 38,* 322–328.

Reynolds, C.R., & Ford, L. (1994). Comparative three-factor solutions of the WISC-III and WISC-R at 11 age levels between 6½ and 16½ years. *Archives of Clinical Neuropsychology, 9,* 553–570.

Roid, G.H., & Miller, L. (1996). *The Leiter International Performance Scale–Revised.* Wood Dale, IL: Stoelting.

Roid, G.H., & Worrall, W. (1997). Replication for the Wechsler Intelligence Scale for Children–Third Edition four-factor model in the Canadian normative sample. *Psychological Assessment, 9,* 512–515.

Sattler, J.M. (1988). *Assessment of children* (3rd ed.). San Diego, CA: Author.

Sternberg, R.J. (1986). *Intelligence applied: Understanding and increasing your intellectual skills.* San Diego, CA: Harcourt, Brace.

Sternberg, R.J., & Detterman, D.K. (Eds.). (1986). *What is intelligence: Contemporary viewpoints on its nature and definition.* Norwood, NJ: Albex.

Telzrow, C.F. (1990). Does PASS pass the test? A critique of the Das–Naglieri Cognitive Assessment System. *Journal of Psychoeducational Assessment, 8,* 344–355.

Terman, L.M. (1916). *The measurement of intelligence.* Boston: Houghton Mifflin.

Tetter, P.A., & Semrud-Clikeman, M. (1997). *Child neuropsychology: Assessment and interventions for neurodevelopmental disorders.* Boston: Allyn & Bacon.

Thompson, P.L., & Brassard, M.R. (1984). Validity of the Woodcock–Johnson Tests of Cognitive Ability: A comparison with the WISC-R in LD and normal elementary students. *Journal of School Psychology, 22,* 201–208.

Thorndike, R.L., Hagen, E., & Sattler, J. (1986a). *Guide for administering and scoring the fourth edition: Stanford–Binet Intelligence Scale.* Chicago: Riverside.

Thorndike, R.L., Hagen, E., & Sattler, J. (1986b). *Stanford–Binet Intelligence Scale* (4th ed.). Chicago: Riverside.

Thorndike, R.M. (1990). Would the real factors of the Stanford–Binet Fourth Edition please come forward? *Journal of Psychoeducational Assessment, 8,* 412–435.

Tupa, D.J., Wright, M.O., & Fristad, M.A. (1997). Confirmatory factor analysis of the WISC-III with child psychiatric inpatients. *Psychological Assessment, 9,* 302–306.

Vance, H.B. (Ed.). (1998). *Psychological assessment of children: Best practices for school and clinical settings.* New York: Wiley.

Vance, H.B., & Awadh, A.B. (1998). Best practices in assessment of children: Issues and trends. In H.B. Vance (Ed.), *Psychological assessment of children: Best practices for school and clinical settings.* New York: Wiley.

Watkins, C.E., Campbell, V.L., Nieberding, R., & Hallmark, R. (1995). Contemporary practice of psychological assessment by clinical psychologists. *Professional Psychology: Research and Practice, 26,* 54–60.

Wechsler, D. (1989). *Wechsler Preschool and Primary Scale of Intelligence–Revised.* New York: Psychological Corporation.

Wechsler, D. (1991). *Wechsler Intelligence Scale for Children* (3rd ed.). New York: Psychological Corporation.

Woodcock, R.W. (1990). Theoretical foundations of the WJ-R measures of cognitive ability. *Journal of Psychoeducational Assessment, 8,* 231–258.

Woodcock, R.W., & Johnson, M.B. (1989). *Woodcock–Johnson Psycho-Educational Battery.* Chicago: Riverside.

CHAPTER 8

Educational Assessment

ELTON G. STETSON AND RANAE STETSON

Public Law 94-142, the Education for All Handicapped Children Act of 1975, and Public Law 99-457, the Individuals with Disabilities Education Act of 1986 (IDEA), which amended and strengthened PL 94-142, have had a greater effect on educational assessment and intervention than any other educational reform in modern history. In essence, these laws require: (1) a free public education for all persons with disabling conditions between 3 and 21 years of age; (2) the placement of persons with disabling conditions (or disabilities) in their least restrictive environments, including mainstreaming into regular classrooms when possible; (3) individualized educational programs (IEPs) that include a statement of ability, short- and long-range goals, and the specific means by which goals are to be met; (4) all tests and assessment instruments free of racial and cultural bias; and (5) a review of progress and a revised IEP on an annual basis. The effects of these laws on the demand for services and on the personnel required to provide services have been staggering (Wang, Reynolds, & Walberg, 1987; Yell, 1997).

Every state employs federally approved guidelines for admission, review, and dismissal (ARD) procedures for students considered for special education programs. Each local school district must comply with state standards and must make their

ARD processes known to the public. These documents are readily available from state and local agencies on request.

The purpose of this chapter is to explain the general policies and procedures followed by most school districts in carrying out the spirit of ARD routines. This examination includes an overview of the ARD procedures, a review of some of the most frequently used tests in educational assessment, discussion of assessment procedures typically used in the screening and at the more comprehensive levels of the ARD process, and a case study of one student in which a detailed psychoeducational profile is illustrated.

ADMISSION, REVIEW, DISMISSAL PROCESS

Referrals for educational assessment of children are normally based on three kinds of problems: academic, behavioral, and/or physical (Salvia & Ysseldyke, 1998). Of these, the majority are academic problems. In this case, classroom teachers usually initiate referrals when they observe students having extreme difficulties in one or more academic areas. Other students are referred for psychological testing because of behavior problems, delinquency, inability to get along with peers, withdrawal or disruptive behavior, and noncompliance. The third reason for referral, physical problems, involves students with sensory disabilities such as vision and hearing disorders, physical structure disorders such as spina bifida and cerebral palsy, and chronic health problems such as asthma and diabetes.

Although some variation may exist among school district ARD procedures, Berdine and Meyer (1987) present a five-level ARD model that typifies what a family encounters when special education services are requested. These stages are described briefly.

LEVEL I: SCREENING AND INITIAL IDENTIFICATION

The purpose of Level I screening is to determine whether the student's performance is cause for concern and whether modifying conditions within the classroom would eliminate or ameliorate the problem. At Level I, a school screening team typically consists of the classroom teacher, a school counselor or diagnostician, and a special education teacher, who collect the information. The information may come from classroom observations, samples of the student's work, standardized test scores, grades, cumulative records, parent interviews, and experimenting with modifications within the classroom to determine whether the student's performance can be affected. At this level, formal testing is often limited to screening tests.

LEVEL II: DIAGNOSIS TO ESTABLISH ELIGIBILITY

The purpose of Level II assessment is to find the student's present and potential levels of functioning, identify likely causes for the problem, determine whether the student is eligible for special education services, and select the label that best describes the student's major problem, that is, learning disabled, educable mentally retarded, emotionally disturbed, and so on. Because Level II assessment requires more sophisticated data collection than does Level I, the ARD Committee is established. The ARD Committee is a multidisciplinary team consisting of medical persons, speech and language pathologists, audiologists, school psychologists, special educators, classroom teachers, and parents. The assessment battery takes on a more

official look and involves a variety of standardized and criterion-referenced measures designed to assess factors such as intelligence; general academic achievement; language facility; diagnostic testing in reading, math, and writing; adaptive behavior; vision and hearing; and various physiological, psychological, and neurological elements. If it is determined during Level II assessment that the student does not qualify for special education services, the ARD process is terminated. If the student does qualify, the process advances to Level III.

LEVEL III: PLACEMENT AND IEP DEVELOPMENT

Using the same multidisciplinary ARD Committee, the purpose at Level III is to establish specific goals for the student, identify the individuals who will work with the student, and determine the percentage of time the student will spend in special education. It is at Level III where the federally required IEP is written by the ARD Committee and signed by all parties.

Although there are a variety of models for IEPs, they are typically two- or three-page forms specifying the following:

1. Names of the student and members of the ARD Committee.
2. Student's current level of functioning.
3. Instructional or behavioral goals to be achieved in each area for which deficiencies are identified.
4. Method for evaluating progress made toward goals.
5. List of individuals in charge of implementing the program.
6. Dates when goals are to be reached and when posttesting is to occur.
7. Signatures of parents, schools officials, and other parties involved at Level III.

LEVEL IV: INSTRUCTIONAL PLANNING

The major concerns at Level IV are instructional, that is, what skills should be learned, what environmental setting makes the most sense, and how objectives should be modified to improve the student's chances of achieving the objectives originally established at Level III.

LEVEL V: EVALUATION

The purpose of Level V assessment is to find out (1) whether goals were achieved, (2) the present level of functioning in the classroom, (3) whether special services should be continued, and if so (4) what new goals and objectives should be included in the next IEP. By law, this review must be done annually and must involve the same ARD Committee used at Levels II and III. In cases where standardized tests are repeated, alternative forms of those tests are typically used.

REVIEW OF TESTS USED IN EDUCATIONAL ASSESSMENT

There are five general domains of testing with which most schools are concerned: academic achievement, intelligence, language facility, cognitive processing, and adaptive behavior. Tests described in this chapter are limited to individually administered tests because they are used to qualify students for special education placement and most private service providers use them exclusively because they typically test individuals rather than groups.

ACADEMIC ACHIEVEMENT TESTS

Academic achievement tests assess students' current knowledge of subjects traditionally taught in schools. There are two types of achievement batteries, screening and comprehensive, and both are available for individual or group administration. Because screening and comprehensive batteries vary so much in scope and depth, it is important to know how they differ and when each is most appropriate for use with children.

Multiple-subject screening tests can be advantageous for several reasons: they are easy to administer, quick to score, and require only 15 to 45 minutes of time depending on age and ability of the child. There are also disadvantages in using screening tests: (1) they typically include only one subtest per subject area; (2) skills assessed are often at the lower level of cognition; (3) because they assess lower-level skills, inferences must be drawn to estimate how a student is likely to perform on more complex skills; (4) results rarely give insight into the cause of academic problems; and (5) additional testing is often required. Table 8.1 provides a summary of five multiple-subject screening tests that have respectable psychometric properties and are appropriate for use by educational diagnosticians and private practitioners.

The Wide Range Achievement Test (WRAT3) and Wechsler Individual Achievement Test (WIAT Screener) focus on lower-level cognitive skills. Among screening tests, they are the easiest to administer and interpret and are widely used for screening. The Hammill Multiability Achievement Test (HAMAT) and Mini Battery of Achievement (MBA) take more time to administer and are slightly more complex to score. However, both focus on higher levels of cognition in all three subject areas tested. They test for passage comprehension rather than simple word identification, and they require solving word problems in math, not just computing basic number facts. Their writing tests require sentences, not just individual words, and sentences are evaluated for punctuation as well as spelling accuracy. Finally, unlike the other screening tests, the HAMAT and MBA have subtests to evaluate factual knowledge in science, social studies, and the humanities.

When results of screening tests suggest that a problem exists in subject areas, assessment moves into Level II, where more comprehensive tests are administered. When compared to screening tests, comprehensive tests include more subject areas, assess more subskills in each subject area, and require more time to administer and score. For those who prefer to begin with comprehensive testing, initial screening can be eliminated, thus reducing achievement testing to one step instead of two. Table 8.2 summarizes the age level and subtest titles of six of the more widely used multiple-subject comprehensive achievement tests.

All tests described in Table 8.2 have moderate to strong standardization, reliability, and validity research support. Each, however, has its own unique features. The Woodcock–Johnson Revised Tests of Achievement (WJ-R ACH), Wechsler Individual Achievement Test–Comprehensive (WIAT-C), Diagnostic Achievement Battery (DAB-2), and the Diagnostic Achievement Test for Adolescents (DATA-2) have multiple subtests for reading, writing (language arts), and math. The DATA-2 and WJ-R ACH

Table 8.1 Multiple-subject screening tests.

Title and Author(s)	Age Range (yrs.)	Specific Subtests	Content Measured
Hammill Multiability Achievement Test (HAMAT) (Hammill, Hresko, Ammer, Cronin, & Quinby, 1998)	7–17	Reading	Comprehension: passages containing missing words are read and student selects correct words from list.
		Arithmetic	Computation: paper-and-pencil calculations of basic math facts through division.
		Writing	Written discourse: sentences are written from dictation and then graded for spelling and punctuation.
		Facts	Subject matter knowledge: student answers questions about science, social studies, health, and language arts.
Kaufman Test of Educational Achievement Brief Form (K-TEA-B) (N.L. Kaufman & A.S. Kaufman, 1985, 1998)	6–22	Reading	Letter identification, word decoding, reading comprehension.
		Math	Written computation and oral problem solving.
		Spelling	Spelling orally or writing from dictation.
Mini Battery of Achievement (MBA) (Woodcock, McGrew, & Werder, 1994)	4–90	Reading	Knowledge of letter names, antonyms, and passage comprehension.
		Mathematics	Basic computation and problem-solving skills.
		Writing	Knowledge of writing mechanics and proof reading.
		Factual knowledge	General knowledge of social studies, science, and the humanities.
Wechsler Individual Achievement Test–Screener (WIAT-Screener) (Psychological Corporation, 1992b)	5–19	Basic reading	Reading words in isolation.
		Mathematics reasoning	Solving mathematical problems from counting to complex sentence problems involving geometry, measurement, and statistics.
		Spelling	Spelling words from dictation.
Wide Range Achievement Test–Revision 3 (WRAT3) (Wilkinson, 1993).	5–75	Reading	Naming letters and reading words from a graded word list.
		Arithmetic	Counting, solving simple oral arithmetic, computing arithmetic problems from simple addition to decimals, fractions, and reducing fractions to lowest denominator.
		Spelling	Spelling words from dictation.

also assess competence in science, social studies, and reference skills. These are important school subjects often neglected in achievement assessments. The Kaufman Test of Educational Achievement, Comprehensive (K-TEA-C) and Peabody Individual Achievement Test, Revised (PIAT-R) have fewer subtests and are less comprehensive. The K-TEA-C has only one writing test and the PIAT-R has only one math test.

Although comprehensive multiple-subject tests provide a great deal of information about performance in several subject areas, it is not unusual to need additional diagnostic information in a particular subject for which the student is experiencing a great deal of difficulty. Many specialized tests have been developed, especially in reading, math, and writing. The most positive aspect of these tests is

Table 8.2 Multiple-subject diagnostic tests.

Title and Author(s)	Age Range (yrs.)	Specific Subtests
Diagnostic Achievement Battery, 2nd ed. (DAB-2) (Newcomer, 1990)	6–14	12 Subtests: story comprehension, characteristics, synonyms, grammatic completion, word knowledge, reading comprehension, capitalization, punctuation, spelling, written composition, mathematics reasoning, mathematics calculation.
Diagnostic Achievement Test for Adolescents, 2nd ed. (DATA-2) (Newcomer & Bryant, 1993)	12–18	13 Subtests: receptive vocabulary, expressive vocabulary, receptive grammar, expressive grammar, word identification, reading comprehension, math calculations, math problem solving, spelling, written composition, science knowledge, social studies knowledge, reference skills.
Kaufman Test of Educational Achievement–Comprehensive Form (K-TEA-C) (A.S. Kaufman & N.L. Kaufman, 1985, 1998)	6–22	5 Subtests: mathematics applications, mathematics computation, reading decoding, reading comprehension, spelling.
Peabody Individual Achievement Test, Revised (PIAT-R) (Markwardt, 1989, 1998)	5–22	6 Subtests: general information, reading recognition, reading comprehension, mathematics, spelling, written expression.
Wechsler Individual Achievement Test–Comprehensive (WIAT-C) (Psychological Corporation, 1992a)	5–19	8 Subtests: basic reading, reading comprehension, mathematics reasoning, numerical operations, listening comprehension, oral expression, spelling, written expression.
Woodcock–Johnson Revised Tests of Achievement (WJ-R ACH) (Woodcock & Johnson, 1989)	2–95	14 Subtests: letter-word identification, passage comprehension, word attack, reading vocabulary, calculation, applied problems, quantitative concepts, dictation, writing samples, proofing, writing fluency, science, social studies, humanities.

their value in identifying the specific skills that must be addressed on the IEP. Table 8.3 lists examples of single-subject comprehensive tests.

Among diagnostic reading tests, the Woodcock Reading Mastery Test–Revised (WRMT-R) is one of the most widely used and highly regarded in educational circles. The KeyMath–Revised, equally recognized, is an extensively used diagnostic math test, and, with 1998 norms now available, it will likely continue to be popular among those who are looking for more precise causes for a student's difficulty in mathematics. The Test of Written Spelling, Fourth Edition (TWS-4) can be used with confidence as a diagnostic test of spelling ability. The Test of Written Language, Third Edition (TOWL-3) provides a wealth of information about overall writing ability and those particular aspects of writing

that might contribute to a student's strengths and weaknesses.

TESTS FOR INTELLIGENCE

Experts may agree on the major attributes of intelligence, but the use of tests to measure intelligence remains one of the most controversial areas in educational assessment. It is important that professional evaluators read Jerome Sattler's (2001) cogent discussions on the use and misuse of intelligence testing before using these tests or writing diagnostic evaluations in which intelligence is discussed. Despite the controversies, let there be no doubt that in most states (1) intelligence tests are routinely administered to children referred for special education

Table 8.3 Single-subject diagnostic tests.

Title and Author(s)	Age (yrs.)/ Grade Range	Specific Subtests
Reading Tests		
Woodcock Reading Mastery Test, Revised (WRMT-R) (Woodcock, 1987, 1998)	Age 5–75	6 Subtests; visual-auditory learning, letter identification, word identification, word attack, word comprehension, passage comprehension.
Gray Oral Reading Test–Diagnostic (GORT-D) (Bryant & Wiederholt, 1991)	Age 5–12	7 Subtests: paragraph reading, decoding, word attack, word identification, morphemic analysis, contextual analysis, word ordering.
Test of Reading Comprehension, 3rd ed. (TORC-3) (V.L. Brown, Hammill, & Wiederholt, 1995)	Age 7–17	8 Subtests: general vocabulary, syntactic similarities, paragraph reading, sentence sequencing, mathematics vocabulary, social studies vocabulary, science vocabulary, reading directions of schoolwork.
Math Tests		
KeyMath–Revised (Connolly, 1988, 1998)	Grade K-9	3 Concepts Tests of numeration, rational numbers, geometry; 5 Operations Tests of addition, subtraction, division, multiplication, mental computation; and 5 Application Tests of measurement, time and money, estimation, interpreting data, problem solving.
Test of Early Mathematics Ability, 2nd ed. (TEMA-2) (Ginsburg & Baroody, 1990)	Age 3–9	Areas tested: relative magnitude, number of facts, calculating algorithms, base 10 concepts.
Test of Mathematics Ability, 2nd ed. (TOMA-2) (V. Brown, Cronin, & McEntire, 1994)	Age 8–19	5 Subtests: mathematics vocabulary, computation, general information, story problems, attitude toward math.
Spelling and Writing		
Test of Written Spelling, 4th ed. (TWS-4) (Larsen, Hammill, & Moats, 1999)	Age 6–18	Tests ability to spell predictable words (regular spellings), unpredictable words (nonregular spelling), both types of words together.
Test of Written Language, 3rd ed. (TOWL-3) (Hammill & Larsen, 1996)	Age 7–19	8 Skill Areas assessed: writing conventions; syntax, grammar, and spelling; story construction including plot and character development; vocabulary, word usage; spelling; punctuation and capitalization; logical sentence construction; sentence combining to assess use of syntax.

services; (2) children are assigned IQ scores based on test results; (3) IQ scores are used to predict students' capacity or potential to achieve; and (4) the difference between achievement and intelligence test scores is the primary factor used to determine whether students receive special education services. Table 8.4 identifies intelligence tests, divided into three categories, that are used most often for educational assessment.

Among screening tests, the Slosson Intelligence Test–Revised (SIT-R) and Hammill Multiability Intelligence Test (HAMIT) are relatively easy to administer and score, and are used primarily at Level I assessment to screen for verbal and/or nonverbal IQ. Should screening scores suggest a student might be eligible for special education services, a more comprehensive IQ test is always required. Among the comprehensive tests, the Wechsler Preschool and Primary Scale of Intelligence, Revised (WPPSI-R), the Wechsler Intelligence Scale for Children, Third Edition (WISC-III), and the Wechsler Adult Intelligence Scale, Third Edition (WAIS-III) continue to be the most popular IQ tests used in educational assessment.

Table 8.4 Intelligence tests.

Test Title and Author(s)	Age Range (yrs)	Description
Screening Tests		
Slosson Intelligence Test, Revised (SIT-R) (Slosson, Nicholson, & Hibpshman, 1990)	4–adult	Screening test of verbal ability.
Hammill Multiability Intelligence Test (HAMIT) (Hammill, Bryant, & Pearson, 1998)	6–17	3 IQ scores: verbal, nonverbal, overall.
Kaufman Brief Intelligence Test (K-BIT) (A.S. Kaufman & N.L. Kaufman, 1990)	4–90	Brief screener of verbal and nonverbal intelligence.
Comprehensive IQ Tests		
Wechsler Preschool and Primary Scale of Intelligence, Revised (WPPSI-R) (Wechsler, 1989)	3–7	12 tests yielding 3 IQ scores: verbal, performance, full-scale.
Wechsler Intelligence Scale for Children, 3rd ed. (WISC-III) (Wechsler, 1991)	6–16	13 tests yielding 3 IQ scores: verbal, performance, full-scale.
Wechsler Adult Intelligence Scale, 3rd ed. (WAIS-III) (Wechsler, 1997)	16–89	14 tests yielding 3 IQ scores: verbal, performance, full-scale.
Kaufman Assessment Battery for Children (K-ABC) (A.S. Kaufman & N.L. Kaufman, 1987)	2–12	4 IQ scores: sequential processing, simultaneous processing, mental processing composite, achievement.
Stanford–Binet Intelligence Scales, 4th ed. (Thorndike, Hagen, & Sattler, 1986)	2–adult	4 IQ scores: verbal reasoning, quantitative reasoning, abstract/visual reasoning, short-term memory.
Tests for Special Populations		
Peabody Picture Vocabulary Test, 3rd ed. (PPVT-III) (L.M. Dunn & L.M. Dunn, 1997)	2–90	Assesses nonverbal ability and requires no oral responses.
Comprehensive Test of Nonverbal Intelligence (CTONI) (Hammill, Pearson, & Wiederholt, 1996)	6–17	For individuals who are bilingual, non-English-speakers, socioeconomically disadvantaged, deaf, language disordered, motor disabled, or neurologically impaired.

For students who are challenged by or score low on verbal IQ tests, two alternative nonverbal measures used often in education are the Peabody Picture Vocabulary Test, Third Edition (PPVT-III) and the Comprehensive Test of Nonverbal Intelligence (CTONI). These tests are almost always used for children with expressive language difficulty or who experience difficulty with English, attention, hearing, fine motor acuity, and so on. Scores on these tests are then compared to scores on verbal IQ tests so that an analogy can be drawn between expressive (verbal) and receptive (nonverbal) ability.

Tests for Language Facility

In its simplest form, oral language facility (OLF) is the proficiency with which one receives and expresses language. Though simplistic in definition, OLF has a more significant impact on learning than any other skill and is at the center of all learning. There are at least two ways to assess OLF: through quantitative capabilities and through grammatical competence. In educational assessment, the initial concern is the quantitative aspects or the volume of language, which includes word knowledge, number of words known, multiple uses for words, antonyms and synonyms, storage of information previously acquired, ability to recognize similarities and differences, ability to analyze and synthesize, and short-term memory. Grammatical competence is concerned with linguistic capabilities with language, phonology or competence with speech sounds, articulation or the accuracy of producing sounds, syntax or competence with correct word order, and discrimination among sounds. Grammatical competence is

Table 8.5 Tests of language development.

Test and Author(s)	Age Range (yrs.)	Description
Receptive & Expressive Language		
OWLS: Listening Comprehension & Oral Expression (Carrow-Woolfolk, 1995)	3–21	2 Scales of receptive and expressive language: listening comprehension and oral expression.
Test of Language Development Primary, 3rd ed. (TOLD-P:3) (Newcomer & Hammill, 1997)	4–9	9 Subtests assessing syntax, semantics, speaking, listening, and spoken language.
Test of Language Development Intermediate, 3rd ed. (TOLD-I:3) (Hammill & Newcomer, 1997)	8–12	6 Subtests assessing syntax, semantics, speaking, listening, and spoken language.
Receptive Language Only		
Test of Auditory Comprehension of Language, 3rd ed. (TACL-3) (Carrow-Woolfolk, 1999)	3–90	3 Nonverbal Tests of receptive language: vocabulary, grammatical morphemes, elaborated phrases and sentences.
Peabody Picture Vocabulary Test, 3rd ed. (PPVT-III) (L.M. Dunn & L.M Dunn, 1997)	2.5–18	Entire battery assesses receptive nonverbal hearing vocabulary.
3 Wechsler Intelligence Scales (WPPSI-R, 1989; WISC-III, 1991; WAIS-III, 1997)	3–89	Picture arrangement subtest assesses nonverbal comprehension of visually presented stimuli.
Expressive Language Only		
Slosson Intelligence Test, Revised (SIT-R) (Slosson, Nicholson, & Hibpshman, 1990)	4–adult	Entire battery measures overall expressive language.
Stanford-Binet Intelligence Scales, 4th ed. (Thorndike, Hagen, & Sattler, 1986)	2–23	Entire battery measures overall expressive language.
Expressive Vocabulary Test (EVT) (Williams, 1997)	2–90	Assessment of expressive vocabulary using a test of synonyms.
3 Wechsler Intelligence Scales (WPPSI-R, 1989; WISC-III, 1991; WAIS-III, 1997)	3–89	Entire verbal battery assesses expressive language.

of particular interest to speech and language pathologists but is not typically assessed unless evidence surfaces during Level I or II assessment to suggest such disorders or deficiencies exist. Tests available to assess OLF usually focus on quantitative capabilities and tend to examine receptive OLF, expressive OLF, or both. Table 8.5 identifies various tests that can be used in part or in whole to assess one or more of these three components.

Notice that some tests of intelligence are also used to assess OLF, particularly expressive language, because the constructs of verbal intelligence and expressive language are essentially the same. However, test administrators should keep one very important assumption in mind when testing OLF: *Receptive language tends to develop more rapidly and continues to excel over expressive language.* Although adequate expressive language tends to suggest adequate receptive language, inadequate expressive language does not assume inadequate receptive language. Therefore, a diagnosis of inadequate expressive language must be followed with an assessment of receptive language to establish whether expressive language is at potential, delayed, or disordered.

TESTS FOR COGNITIVE PROCESSING

Research unquestionably supports that students have preferred styles; furthermore, learning can be impeded when those styles, popularly referred to as learning styles, are not taken into account during instruction (Butler, 1988). R. Dunn, Beaudry, and Klavas (1989) define learning style as "a biologically and developmentally imposed set of personal characteristics that make the same teaching method effective for some and ineffective for others" (p. 50). Recent studies show conclusively that:

- Seventy percent of students are affected by a perceptual preference for learning.
- Readers with a significant preference for a learning modality do better when instruction is geared toward the stronger modality (Miller & McKenna, 1989).
- When teaching strategies and learning styles are matched, achievement gains are significantly greater than when they are mismatched (R. Dunn & Griggs, 1988).

According to Hagen and Stetson (1991), the literature reveals five types of learning styles: environmental, affective or emotional, sociological, cognitive or psychological, and physiological. Of the five, physiological processing is the one with which educational assessment is most concerned. Physiological processing includes auditory processing, visual processing, and visual-motor integration.

Auditory processing is the ability to receive and understand information taken in through auditory channels. It is relatively easy to observe the quantity and quality of auditory processing in at least five domains listed in hierarchical order from lower- to higher-order skills: auditory acuity, auditory discrimination, phonological awareness, auditory comprehension, and auditory memory. Table 8.6 summarizes tests used to assess these five domains.

This hierarchical order must be taken into consideration when developing test batteries for auditory processing for the following important reasons (Stetson, 1983):

1. Strength in lower-order skills does not ensure strength in higher-order skills. For example, one may have good hearing (acuity) but poor auditory comprehension.

Table 8.6 Tests of auditory processing.

Test and Author(s)	Age Range (yrs.)	Description
Auditory Acuity		
Pure Tone Audiometer (Micro Audiometrics Corp., 1999)	All ages	Pure-tone air conduction threshold test; tests frequency levels of 250–8,000 Hz and 0–90 decibels.
Auditory Discrimination		
Test of Language Development Primary, 3rd ed. (TOLD-P:3) (Newcomer & Hammill, 1997)	4–8+	Supplemental tests of word discrimination and other phonological awareness tests.
Phonological Awareness		
Comprehensive Test of Phonological Processing (CTOP) (Wagner, Torgesen, & Rashotte, 1999)	5–24	Phonological awareness, phonological memory, and rapid naming.
Goldman–Fristoe Test of Articulation (G-FTA) (Goldman & Fristoe, 1986)	2–16+	Articulation of consonant sounds.
Auditory Comprehension		
Slosson Intelligence Test (SIT-R) (Slosson, Nicholson, & Hibpshman, 1990)	4–adult	Entire battery measures level of oral language comprehension.
3 Wechsler Intelligence Scales (WPPSI-R, 1989; WISC-III, 1991; WAIS-III, 1997)	3–89	6 Verbal Tests assess auditory or verbal comprehension.
Auditory Memory		
3 Wechsler Intelligence Scales (WPPSI-R, 1989; WISC-III, 1991; WAIS-III, 1997)	3–89	Digit span subtest measures short-term memory for numbers.
Detroit Tests of Learning Aptitude, 4th ed. (DTLA-4) (Hammill, 1998)	6–17	Reversed letters and letter sequencing.
Test of Memory and Learning (TOMAL) (Reynolds & Bigler, 1994)	5–19	Memory for stories, digits forward and backward, and letters forward and backward.
Children's Memory Scale (CMS) (Cohen, 1997)	5–16	Assesses verbal immediate, verbal delayed, and general memory.

2. Strength in higher-order skills assumes strength in lower-order skills. To have good auditory memory, one must also have good auditory comprehension, phonological awareness, discrimination, and acuity.
3. Given limitations of time, testing should begin with higher-order skills and work toward lower-order skills if deficiencies are discovered.

Jacomides's (1986) study of 400 students in grades 1 through 12 showed that 2% of the students had difficulty with auditory discrimination, 15% had difficulty with auditory comprehension, and 90% scored below average on tests of short-term auditory memory. Ironically, although most students are tested regularly for acuity, few are ever tested for auditory memory. Students who have auditory processing problems tend to do poorly in the following school-related tasks:

1. Learning phonics as a primary decoding strategy.
2. Using sound-to-letter patterns to spell.
3. Following directions when presented orally and in multiple sets.
4. Taking notes from lectures.
5. Staying on task for extended periods of time.
6. Working independently and without regular intervention by the teacher.
7. Remembering factual information, particularly who, what, where, and when answers.
8. Following through with duties and responsibilities at school or home.

Visual processing is the physiological and psychological ability to receive and understand information taken in through visual channels. Its four domains include acuity, perception, comprehension, and memory. The hierarchical nature of visual processing is similar to that of auditory processing. Visual acuity, the lowest order in the hierarchy, is not dependent on or necessarily influenced by perception, comprehension, or memory. Visual memory, the highest order in the hierarchy, is extremely dependent on and influenced by the other three domains. Table 8.7 describes the more prominent tests used in education to assess the four visual processing domains.

In the study cited earlier, Jacomides (1986) also examined visual processing abilities and found that only 4% of the 400 students tested had difficulty

with visual perception, 15% scored below average in visual comprehension, and only 10% scored below average on visual memory (90% of these same students scored below average on auditory memory tests). When comparing overall performance, auditory processing was significantly more disabling among students than visual processing. Whereas the mean auditory memory was two years below average, the mean visual memory age for these same students was average. The vast majority of students who tend to have better visual processing than auditory processing skills tend to be able to:

1. Learn to decode text more readily through visual and contextual approaches than through phonetic approaches.
2. Retain more knowledge by reading and discussing than by listening.
3. Learn lecture materials more effectively when they are taught to take good notes, mark in the margins, read along, or tape lectures.
4. Spell better when instruction focuses on use of visual memory, word structure, and mnemonics.
5. Follow directions and handle responsibilities with fewer conflicts when directions and responsibilities are in writing and posted.
6. Maintain their attention span when auditory information is reinforced with visual information.

Visual-motor integration (VMI), a subset of perceptual-motor development, is a controversial subject in education. According to Salvia and Ysseldyke (1998), visual-motor training is ineffective in improving academic performance, and the instruments designed to assess VMI are questionable. One aspect of VMI that must be set aside from this controversy, however, is handwriting. Handwriting and copying are among the most difficult and slowest forms of communication, and students spend a significant amount of time copying from chalk/white boards, books, worksheets, and/or overhead transparencies. To copy effectively, a student must possess adequate visual acuity and perception, read the information correctly, retain what is read in memory while simultaneously writing it on paper, then locate the next set of information and repeat the same process. A breakdown in any one of these skills can easily affect writing and copying. Table 8.8 identifies tests for the two major domains of VMI most closely associated with

Table 8.7 Tests of visual processing.

Test and Author(s)	Age Range (yrs.)	Description
Visual Acuity		
Keystone School Vision Test (Keystone, n.d.)	4–adult	14 Subtests cover visual acuity, depth and color perception, and binocularity.
McDowell Vision Screening Kit (McDowell & McDowell, 1996)	4–adult	Screening tests for visual acuity, perception, and binocularity.
Visual Perception		
Motor-Free Visual Perception Test (M-FVPT) (Colarusso & Hammill, 1996)	4–16	Visual discrimination, visual closure, visual memory of geometric designs, and figure-ground perception.
3 Wechsler Intelligence Scales (WPPSI-R, 1989; WISC-III, 1991; WAIS-III, 1997)	3–89	Subtests on picture completion and block design.
Visual Comprehension		
3 Wechsler Intelligence Scales (WPPSI-R, 1989; WISC-III, 1991; WAIS-III, 1997)	3–89	Subtests on object assembly and picture arrangement.
Detroit Test of Learning Aptitude, 4th ed. (DTLA-4) (Hammill, 1998)	6–17	Subtests on story construction and design reproduction.
Visual Memory		
Detroit Test of Learning Aptitude, 4th ed. (DTLA-4) (Hammill, 1998)	6–17	Subtests on design sequence and design reproduction.
Wide Range Assessment of Memory and Learning (WRAML) (Sheslow & Adams, 1990)	5–17	3 Visual Memory Tests: pictures, designs, and patterns.
Test of Memory and Learning (TOMAL) (Reynolds & Bigler, 1994)	5–19	4 Visual Memory Tests: facial memory, visual selective reminding, abstract visual memory, visual sequential memory.

Table 8.8 Tests of motor and visual-motor integration.

Test and Author(s)	Age Range (yrs.)	Description
Basic Motor Skills		
Bruininks Oseretaky Test of Motor Proficiency (Bruininks, 1978)	4–14	Screening for both gross motor (running, agility, balance, coordination, and strength with limbs) and fine motor (response speed, visual-motor control, and upper limb speed and dexterity).
Developmental Indicators for the Assessment of Learning, 3rd ed. (DIAL-3) (Mardell-Czudnowski & Goldenberg, 1998)	3–7	Screening for both gross motor (catching, jumping, hopping, and skipping) and fine motor (building with blocks, cutting, copying shapes and letters, and name writing).
Visual Motor Integration		
Developmental Test of Visual-Motor Integration, 4th ed. (DTVMI) (Berry, 1997)	3–18	Measures accuracy in drawing, copying, and overall visual-motor skills.
Test of Visual-Motor Integration (TVMI) (Hammill, Pearson, & Voress, 1996)	4–17	Assesses ability to copy increasingly complex geometric figures.
3 Wechsler Intelligence Scales (WPPSI-R, 1989; WISC-III, 1991; WAIS-III, 1997)	3–89	Subtest on coding.

handwriting: basic motor skills and visual-motor integration, that is, eye-hand coordination.

Most students can write neatly if they are motivated and take the time. A breakdown in neatness usually occurs when the student is expected to use the complex skills required in writing in a rapid-fire fashion, as is the case during note taking or copying tasks. As the amount of writing increases and the time allotted decreases, neatness deteriorates. In the vast majority of poor handwriting cases, the issue is not ability to be neat, but willingness to indulge in the time required to be neat.

TESTS OF ADAPTIVE BEHAVIOR

Because other chapters in this text include a great deal on behavior and personality, this discussion is limited to those assessment instruments typically used in school settings to assess adaptive behavior, personality, emotional development, and self-concept. The tests listed in Table 8.9 may be less sophisticated than those used by clinical psychologists because school diagnosticians are typically not trained to use the more complex projective tests.

Table 8.9 Tests of adaptive behavior, personality, emotional development, and self-concept.

Test and Author(s)	Age Range (yrs.)	Description
Adaptive Behavior & ADHD		
Scales of Independent Behavior, Revised (SIB-R) (Bruininks, Woodcock, Weatherman, & Hill, 1996)	1–80	Assessment of 14 areas of adaptive behavior and 8 areas of maladaptive behavior.
Attention-Deficit/Hyperactivity Disorder Test (ADHDT) (Gilliam, 1995)	3–23	Identifies and evaluates attention-deficit disorders.
Conners Rating Scales, Revised (CRS-R) (Conners, 1996)	3–17	Identifies children and adolescents at risk for diagnosis of ADHD.
Learning Disabilities		
Developmental Assessment for Students with Severe Disabilities, 2nd ed. (DASH-2) (Dykes & Erin, 1999)	Birth–6	Assesses language, sensorimotor skills, basic academic skills, social-emotional skills.
Learning Disabilities Diagnostic Inventory (LDDI) (Hammill & Bryant, 1998)	8–17	6 Independent Rating Scales identify processing and learning disabilities to distinguish LD from non-LD students and LD from low-achieving students.
Personal/Emotional Development		
Scale for Assessing Emotional Disturbance (SAED) (Epstein & Cullinan, 1998)	5–18	Assessment to identify children and adolescents who qualify for the federal special education category Serious Emotional Disturbance (SED).
Draw-a-Person: Screening Procedures for Emotional Disturbance (DAP:SPED) (Naglieri, McNeish, & Bardos, 1991)	3–18	Nonverbal screening of emotional and behavioral disorders.
Behavioral and Emotional Rating Scale (BERS) (Epstein & Sharma, 1998)	5–18	Assesses interpersonal strength, family involvement, intrapersonal strength, school functioning, affective strengths.
Self-Concept		
Culture-Free Self-Esteem Inventories, 2nd ed. (CFSEI-2) (Battle, 1992)	All ages	5 Areas of children's esteem: general, peers, school, parents, defensiveness; 4 Areas for adults: general, social, personal, life.
Self-Esteem Index (SEI) (Brown & Alexander, 1991)	7–18	How individuals value themselves in four areas: academic competence, family acceptance, peer popularity, personal security.

Behavior and attention-deficit disorders (ADD), particularly attention-deficit/hyperactivity disorder (ADHD), are becoming one of the most often cited reasons for teacher referral to special education. Further, this is the area among all those discussed in this chapter that almost certainly will involve a medical doctor once screening has been completed in the school setting.

INTERPRETING TEST SCORES: AN EDUCATIONAL PERSPECTIVE

Now that the reader is more familiar with commonly used tests in educational assessment, it is important to understand how test scores are used to diagnose and qualify students for special services. Test scores become magical numbers that are used to predict (1) how the student's school achievement compares with others, (2) at what level the student should be able to achieve, (3) who should receive help and through what particular program, and (4) the specific curriculum that should be delivered as written up and signed in the IEP. Therefore, a discussion of how test scores are used in educational assessment is germane, particularly the use of intelligence and achievement test scores.

USING IQ AND ACHIEVEMENT TEST SCORES TO DETERMINE ELIGIBILITY

In a Level I or II assessment, schools administer achievement tests to estimate *actual* achievement and aptitude and IQ tests to estimate *potential* achievement. Calculating the difference between actual and potential achievement is essential in educational assessment because the difference tends to be the primary determiner in qualifying a student for placement. The closer the two scores, the less likely additional academic support would be offered. The greater the difference, the more likely that the student is functioning below potential, will benefit from additional academic support, and will qualify for special placement. In most cases, the difference between potential and actual achievement must be significant, defined as more than one standard deviation (SD) between the two scores. Because most tests use standard scores with a mean of 100 and a SD of 15 points, a difference of 16 or more points between potential and actual achievement is considered significant.

A student with an IQ of 116 and a standard score of 100 on a reading achievement test is performing significantly below potential because the difference between potential (IQ = 116) and actual achievement (100) is more than 15 points. By the same token, a student with the same IQ and a standard score of 105 on a math achievement test is not functioning significantly below potential because the difference between potential (IQ = 116) and actual achievement (105) is only 11 points. The term "significant difference" drives most of the decisions relative to qualifying students for special education services. In this example, the student may be failing both reading and math but is likely to receive special help only in reading. The topic of qualifying students for special education services is discussed in more detail in the section "Level I Assessment: Establishing Eligibility."

INTERPRETING IQ SCORES

Many parents and teachers do not fully understand how to interpret an IQ score, though they may nod affirmatively when you ask if they do; helping them grasp the concept of IQ is essential. When you explain IQ in the simplest statistical terms and you know they still don't understand, you may want to be ready with a simpler explanation. Consider two explanations that always seem to make sense to parents and teachers: *percent of learning* and *months of learning*.

IQ EXPLAINED AS A PERCENT OF LEARNING

When using percent of learning to explain an IQ of 85, for example, one would say that a student with an IQ of 85 has the potential to learn approximately 85% of what the average student of the same age and grade normally learns. Likewise, a student with an IQ of 120 has the potential to learn 120% of what the average student of the same age and grade tends to learn, or 20% more than what the average student of the same age and grade tends to learn. Here are three examples using fifth-graders:

- Fifth-graders with IQs of 85 have the potential to learn 85% of what is typically learned by average fifth-graders, i.e., 85% of 5 = 4.3.
- Fifth-graders with IQs of 100 have the potential to learn 100% of what it typically learned by average fifth-graders, i.e., 100% of 5 = 5.
- Fifth-graders with IQs of 120 have the potential to achieve 120% of what is typically learned by average fifth-graders, i.e., 120% of 5 = 6.

IQ EXPLAINED AS MONTHS OF LEARNING

To explain IQ using months of learning, one must first understand that average students gain an average of 10 months of achievement for each academic year of schooling. At the beginning of the year, average third-graders with IQs of 100 normally begin the school year having attained 30 months or 3 years of achievement. At the beginning of the fourth grade, those same average students attained 40 months or 4 years of achievement. However, students with IQs of 85 have the potential to gain 8.5 months of achievement in a school year; students with IQs of 120 have the potential to gain 12 months of achievement in a school year. It is important to understand that this potential is typically realized each and every year of school. For the student with an IQ of 85, the potential is 8.5 months per year, which is 1.5 months less than average. Though a 1.5-month loss may not seem that significant in the first grade, the loss is 3 months by the end of second grade, 6 months by the fourth, and at least one full year by the end of the eighth grade.

IQ SCORES AND IQ LABELS

Most parents and many teachers are confused about the real meaning of IQ scores. It is customary to attach labels to IQ scores, and most test publishers provide tables in their test manuals to match IQ scores with appropriate labels. Because authors do not necessarily agree on categories and labels that describe them, the categories and labels presented in Table 8.10 represent a generic classification system used by many educators to label IQ scores.

Using the classification system in Table 8.10, one can easily identify, for any IQ score, the classification or label, the number of SDs from the mean, the percentage of students in the general population who fall within that range, and the approximate percentile range. For example, a student with an IQ of 135 is classified as superior, a score that is more than 2 SDs above the mean of 100, approximately 2.1% of the population score in the IQ range of 130 to 144; and students in this superior range are in the 98th to 99th percentile, meaning that only one or two students out of 100 of the same age and/or grade are likely to score higher than this range of 130 to 144.

USING IQ TO PREDICT SUCCESS IN SCHOOL

Making predictions about a student's academic success or failure is a great responsibility. One common mistake made in situations like this is to make predictions that set expectations so unrealistically high that parents and teachers place undue pressure on the student. Because students with IQs of 85

Table 8.10 Interpretation table for IQ scores.

IQ Range	Classification	Standard Deviations	Percent in Population	Percentile Equivalent
145 or above	Very Superior	+3 SD	<0.2	99th+
130–144	Superior	+2 SD	2.1	98th–99th
115–129	Above Average	+1 SD	13.6	84th–97th
100–114	Average to High Average	Within 1 SD	34.1	50th–83rd
85–99	Average to Low Average	Within 1 SD	34.1	17th–50th
70–84	Below Average	−1 SD	13.6	4th–16th
55–69	Mentally Handicapped	−2 SD	2.1	2nd–3rd
54 or below	Severely Mentally Retarded	−3 SD	<0.2	<1st

to 115 are classified as "average," too many times, parents translate this to mean that their child should be making As and Bs. Nothing could be further from the truth. Assuming all students work to their potential, which most do not, there is little chance that average students with IQs of 85 will perform to the same academic level as average students with IQs of 115. To put these two scores in better perspective, students with an 85 IQ are predicted to acquire 8.5 months of learning each year, whereas those with an IQ of 115 are predicted to acquire 11.5 months. If the curriculum targets the average learner, there is statistical evidence that students with low-average IQs (85–100) may be in academic jeopardy. One way to illustrate this concept is to draw an analogy between IQ scores and a balance beam. A student with an IQ of 100 is like the child sitting right in the middle of an academic balance beam. One can only imagine the vulnerable position of this student. Even the slightest experience with failure or success can easily thrust the student permanently toward one end of the balance beam (success) or the other (failure).

Labeling a student average and predicting the capability of A work suggests that one does not understand what average means. Table 8.11 provides what is considered realistic prediction statements for academic success based on the IQ ranges.

A comparison of the IQ ranges in Tables 8.10 and 8.11 show them to be slightly different. This is

Table 8.11 Academic predictions based on IQ scores.

IQ Range	Prediction Statements
130+	Superior to Very Superior: Upper 2% of Population 1. Little difficulty competing in average or accelerated programs. 2. Usually enrolled in gifted and talented programs. 3. Need watching to avoid boredom and lack of stimulation.
120–129	Clearly Above Average: Suited for Above-Average Programs 1. Should compete comfortably in advanced programs. 2. May lack challenge in average programs. 3. Important to maintain high level of interest and stimulation.
110–119	High Average to Above Average: A and B Student in Average Programs 1. Desired intellectual development for most average programs. 2. Capable of A and B work with reasonable effort and parental support. 3. Most exert high effort in above-average programs.
90–109	Average: B and C Student in Average Academic Programs 1. Average students are as prone to fail as they are to succeed. 2. Will experience difficulty in above-average programs. 3. Often subjected to undue pressure at home because parents usually interpret average to mean that A and B work is expected. 4. Failures often lead to poor self-concept and failure identity. 5. Response to remediation is good to guarded.
80–89	Low Average to Slow Learner: Difficulty in Average Programs 1. Achievement is often two years or more below average. 2. Qualify for some special programs. 3. Good candidates for distributive education, i.e., work-study programs; high dropout rate; not typically college-bound.
70–79	Very Slow Learner: Extreme Difficulty in Most Academic Programs 1. Experiences extreme difficulty in average academic settings. 2. Will not qualify for mentally challenged programs. 3. Gain of 6–8 months of achievement in 10 months of instruction. 4. Responds poorly to remedial procedures; high dropout rate.
Below 70	Mentally Handicapped: In Mentally Handicapped Classes Full Time 1. Qualifies for mentally handicapped programs. 2. Emphasis is on social and survival skills and on training in semiskilled labor professions.

intentional. The ranges in Table 8.10 are based on statistical differences and SDs; the ranges in Table 8.11 are based on what experienced teachers and diagnosticians have observed over time. Educational practitioners know that students with IQs in the low-average range perform very differently from students with IQs in the high-average range, and it would be misleading to let parents assume that children in either range have the same probability for performing at the same level. Use of the statements in Table 8.11 aids the psychologist in developing prediction or prognosis statements about the student's chances for success in the school in which he or she is enrolled. Notice that the prediction statement for students with average IQs takes the balance beam concept into consideration; that is, students in this range of ability are as prone to fail as they are to succeed.

CATEGORIES OF SPECIAL EDUCATION CLASSES

Public school systems offer a variety of special education classes, from classes for the trainable mentally disabled to classes for the academically talented. Larger urban school districts normally have the largest selection of special classes; smaller districts in rural settings tend to have more limited services. Few private schools have special education classes because they do not receive federal funding and are not required to comply with PL 94-142, Section 504, or IDEA. Table 8.12 identifies some more readily available classes and the criteria normally used for placement.

The eligibility criteria for the various programs are very diverse. For example, eligibility for federal- and district-funded reading improvement programs is often based on achievement test scores. IQ scores are typically not required. Students whose achievement scores in reading or mathematics are two or more years below grade placement are typically eligible, and there is no need to demonstrate the potential to do better. Admission to classes for the mentally disabled, on the other hand, is based primarily on IQ scores with little regard given to achievement. In most states, the primary criterion for placement in mentally disabled classes is an IQ score below 70.

Classes with more strict admission criteria tend to be those for the learning disabled. To be accepted, scores on both intelligence and achievement must be taken into account. Further, it must be demonstrated that potential achievement is significantly higher than actual achievement. Most schools interpret "significantly higher" to mean that standard scores on IQ tests must be at least one SD higher (+15 points) than standard scores on achievement tests. One strong justification for insisting on such criteria is that before students are

Table 8.12 Special classes available in many schools and criteria for placement.

Type of Class	IQ Criteria	Achievement Criteria	Cognitive Learning Deficiencies
Academically talented	130 & above	Typically 2 years or more above present grade level.	No requirement.
Reading & Title I	70 & above	Functioning 2 years or more below grade level.	No requirement.
Pullout resource	70 & above	Achievement is more than 1 SD below potential as measured on standardized tests.	No requirement.
Full-time learning disabled	70 & above	Achievement is more than 1 SD below potential as measured on standardized tests.	Deficiencies in one or more areas.
Educable mentally retarded	50–70	No requirement.	No requirement.
Trainable mentally retarded	Below 50	No requirement.	No requirement.

Note: Classes for the emotionally disturbed, physically handicapped, and multiple handicapped students are not included here, as the criteria have little to do with IQ, achievement, or cognitive learning styles.

given concentrated attention on their academic problems, there should be clear evidence that the student has the potential to improve.

Students with more serious learning problems are more likely to be placed in full-time self-contained classrooms as opposed to pullout programs that involve one or two periods per day. There are at least three factors that increase the probability for placement in a self-contained resource room: (1) the severity of the difference between potential and actual achievement, (2) the number of subject areas in which a student qualifies for help, and (3) the presence of significant deficits in cognitive learning abilities, that is, visual processing, auditory processing, and visual-motor integration.

Keep in mind that in spite of the many special programs available to students, the vast majority of students never receive special education services. In fact, the 96% whose IQs range from 70 to 130 find it most difficult to get special assistance except under specified circumstances. Unless schools break rules, most of these students are classified as *corrective* and are kept in their regular classroom. It is estimated that fully one-third of students who need help will be classified as corrective and thus receive no special help other than what is provided by the regular teacher.

LEVEL I ASSESSMENT: ESTABLISHING ELIGIBILITY

To qualify for special classes, students must demonstrate need through testing. Most school districts have established a two-level assessment model. At Level I, all referrals are screened to determine whether they qualify for special education services. Referrals are usually initiated by the classroom teacher who believes a student is performing significantly below classroom norms or below the student's own potential. The basic question at Level I is whether a student qualifies for special education programs or whether the student's problems can be accommodated within the regular classroom. The criteria for qualifying are often strict because many more students are referred than could possibly be taken care of in special education programs and many students who are failing in the regular classroom do not have the type of problems that warrant special education classes.

QUALIFYING FACTORS

Qualifying usually hinges on a quantitative comparison of two critical factors: potential achievement and actual achievement. Potential achievement is a hypothetical prediction statement about how well one could function academically were one achieving to one's maximum potential. Actual achievement is a measure of how well one is currently performing in academic subjects, particularly reading, math, and writing. Level I testing normally includes an intelligence test to estimate potential achievement and a standardized achievement test to determine actual achievement. Raw scores on these tests are converted to standard scores. Most IQ and achievement tests used in education have standard scores with a mean of 100 and SD of 15 points. Table 8.13 illustrates the standard scores of a Level I screening battery for a hypothetical student, Joseph, who is 11 years 1 month old and in grade 5.5. The battery consists of the Slosson Intelligence Test–Revised (SIT-R) and the K-TEA, Brief Form.

Some professionals hesitate to use the SIT-R as an intelligence screening test, preferring instead to use the Kaufman Brief Intelligence Test (K-BIT) or Hammill Multiability Intelligence Test (HAMIT), a new test that will most assuredly receive a lot of attention. Still, the SIT-R continues to show high reliability and validity, correlates highly with more sophisticated tests, and is quick to administer and

Table 8.13 Converting raw scores to standard scores.

Area Tested	Screening Tests Used	Raw Score	Standard Score
IQ	Slosson Intelligence Test, Revised (SIT-R)	M.A. 9–8	87
Reading	Kaufman Test of Educational Achievement–Brief Form (K-TEA-B)	56	85
Math	K-TEA-B	36	94
Spelling	K-TEA-B	34	79

score. The preference for the K-BIT or HAMIT is more often an issue of politics or policy than reliability or validity.

DETERMINING ELIGIBILITY USING STANDARD SCORES

Most schools require standard scores on achievement tests to be more than one SD below the student's potential to qualify for special placement (i.e., at least 16 standard points below the IQ score). Table 8.14 illustrates how standard scores are used to decide whether Joseph qualifies for special education services.

The standard scores in Column B are always 100 because 100 is what average students are expected to score on achievement tests if their progress is normal. If Joseph, who is in grade 5.5, were achieving to his grade level, his standard scores would be 100 and his actual achievement would be the same as his present grade placement. Column C, potential grade achievement, reflects his IQ of 87, and Column D contains the standard scores obtained on the three subtests of the KTEA-B. The first comparison examines the difference between actual achievement (D) and grade placement (B). The differences, recorded in Column E, show that Joseph is functioning 16 standard points below his grade level in reading, 21 points below in spelling, and 6 points below in math. He is significantly behind his peer group in two of the three subjects tested.

The second comparison examines the difference between actual achievement (D) and potential achievement (C). This comparison, shown in Column F, indicates that Joseph is functioning 3 points below potential in reading, 8 points below in spelling, and 7 points above in math. Because the criterion for special services is a difference of at least 16 standard points, this student would not qualify for special assistance. Though Joseph is clearly in academic difficulty in reading and spelling, he will not qualify for any special help outside the regular classroom. His IQ is too high for mentally disabled classes, his actual achievement is too high for resource or learning disability classes, and he is neither physically disabled nor emotionally disturbed. Joseph stays in the regular classroom and functions below his average peers. Unfortunately, the gap between Joseph's achievement and that of his peers is likely to widen each year.

LEVEL II ASSESSMENT: DIAGNOSTIC EVALUATION

Level I testing is intended to answer one basic question: Does the student qualify for special services? For those who do qualify, Level II testing is essential. It is considerably more comprehensive and designed to answer three additional and important questions:

1. What may have caused the gap between potential and actual achievement?
2. Does the student have the potential to improve, or is the student working to potential?
3. What should be done to ameliorate the problem?

Table 8.14 Using standard scores to determine eligibility.

(A)	(B)	(C)	(D)	(E)	(F)
				Standard Score Comparisons	
Subject Areas Tested	Present Grade Placement	Potential Achievement	Actual Achievement	Present Grade (B) Mnus Actual Achievement (D)[1]	Potential Achievement (C) Minus Actual Achievement (D)[2]
Reading	100	87	84	−16 pts.	−3 pts.
Math	100	87	94	−6 pts.	+7 pts.
Spelling	100	87	79	−21 pts.	−8 pts.

[1] When comparing actual achievement (D) with present grade placement (B), Joseph is functioning 1 or more SD (more than 15 pts.) below the average student in grade 5.5 in reading and spelling (E).

[2] When comparing actual achievement (D) with potential achievement (C), Joseph is functioning less than 1 SD (less than 15 pts.) below his own potential (F); therefore, Joseph is not likely to be eligible for help.

In Level II assessment, more comprehensive testing is normally done in reading, arithmetic, language facility, and cognitive processing (auditory processing, visual processing, and visual-motor integration). Properly selected instruments provide the examiner with specific details about the strengths and weaknesses in the area for which the test is designed. These diagnostic data not only provide clues to possible causes of academic difficulties, but also identify specific skills to be remediated.

One of the frustrating experiences in diagnosis is the interpretation of data. Although most professionals can administer and score the instruments identified in this chapter with minimal instruction, translating a group of scores into a meaningful diagnosis is another matter. For example, many teachers refer a child for testing because the student has trouble comprehending. The diagnostician administers a reading test and, as predicted, results verify that the student has a comprehension problem. If one is not aware that poor comprehension is a symptom rather than a cause of a reading problem, the teacher might recommend that the student receive comprehension training and fail to realize that the cause of the problem was lack of concentration, low language facility, deficient word-attack skills, or that the reading materials were written considerably above the reading level of the student. In other cases, a student may be referred because of an inability to use phonic generalizations to decode an unknown word. If the teacher does not realize that poor use of phonics is often caused by a hearing loss, inadequate discrimination, or auditory memory problems, all the phonics training available may be wasted while the teacher continues to teach phonics repeatedly, as is often done in schools, without success.

Diagnostic tests are extremely important in the design of remedial strategies. Use of a psychometric data profile can assist educational diagnosticians in displaying scores in such a way that a visual image of the student's academic performance emerges. The data profile in Table 8.15 is of Tom, age 7 years 4 months, in grade 1.6; it illustrates what the vast majority of student profiles tend to look like.

Ten different tests were administered to Tom. In Section D, note that test scores are reported in 10 different domains: intelligence, estimated potential, actual achievement, eligibility for special education classes, oral language facility, diagnostic reading tests, diagnostic math tests, auditory processing, visual processing, and visual-motor integration.

INTERPRETING A PSYCHOMETRIC DATA PROFILE

In a comprehensive data profile, such as the one in Table 8.15, all raw scores, standard scores, age equivalents, and grade equivalents will be clearly displayed. Each score is rated as below average (BA), average (A), or above average (AA) by comparing the obtained scores with the student's age or grade. In addition, scores from all subtests that assess skills within the same domain are clustered together despite the particular test in which the scores appeared. In Domain 6, for example, scores from three different tests are included to form a diagnosis in reading, the WRMT-R, the WJ-R ACH, and the WISC-III. In Domain 8, Auditory Processing, scores from four different tests contribute to the total diagnosis. This grouping procedure not only provides a complete picture of each domain, but also allows for specific strengths and weaknesses within that domain to be identified. Once completed, diagnostic statements are then generated from the profile itself. One effective method of writing diagnostic statements is to create a statement about each of the 10 domains. Listed below are sample statements about the 10 domains as they apply to Tom.

Domain 1: Intelligence
Overall intelligence is within the average range, verbal intelligence (IQ 107) is average to high average; performance intelligence (IQ 85) is low-average to below average.

Domain 2: Potential for Learning
Using verbal IQ as a predictor of potential, Tom's verbal IQ of 107 places him within the average range where students of the same potential tend to earn Bs and some Cs in their academic subjects.

Domain 3: Actual Achievement
Screening for present achievement (WJ-R ACH) indicates above average achievement in letter recognition and math calculation; average achievement in passage comprehension; and below average achievement in solving math problems and spelling dictation.

Domain 4: Eligibility for Special Education
A comparison of standard scores in achievement and intelligence indicates that there are significant deficiencies in applied problems (−16 points) and spelling dictation (−17 points). Therefore, placement

Table 8.15 Psychometric data profile.

A. Student Name, Age, School, and Purpose of Testing

Name: Tom B. Age: 7 yrs. 4 mos. (same as 7.3 yrs.) Grade: 1.6
School: Private school with high academic expectations
Purpose of Testing: Determine possible causes for school failure and frustration in the school setting.

B. Tests Administered

Name of Test	Test Code
Earscan Pure Tone Audiometer (Micro Audiometrics Corp., 1999)	Pure Tone
Detroit Test of Learning Aptitude, 4th ed. (1997); Subtests administered: word sequence, sentence imitation, letter sequence, object sequence, and design reproduction	DTLA-4
Developmental Test of Visual-Motor Integration (1997)	DTVMI-4
KeyMath, Revised (1988, 1998); All subtests	KM-R
Keystone Telebinocular Visual Survey	Keystone
Motor-Free Visual Perception Test (1996)	M-FVPT
Wechsler Intelligence Scale for Children-III (1991)	WISC-III
Test of Language Development, Primary, 3rd ed. (1997)	TOLD-P:3
Woodcock Reading Mastery Test, Revised (1987, 1998); All subtests	WRMT-R
Woodcock–Johnson Revised Tests of Achievement (1989); Subtests: letter/word identification, passage comprehension, applied calculations, problems, and dictation	W-JR-ACH

C. Abbreviations Used in Report

RS - Raw Score
SS - Standard Score*
BA - Below Average (inadequate)
A - Average (adequate)
AA - Above Average
GE - Grade Equivalent
AE - Age Equivalent

MA - Mental Age
CA - Chronological Age
GP- Grade Placement
GLP - Grade Level Potential
S - Standard Deviation

* Two Kinds of standard scores (SS)
1. Mean SS of 10 with standard deviation of ±3
2. Mean SS of 100 with standard deviation of ±15

D. Summary of Test Scores

Domain 1: Intelligence (WISC-III)

	Scores		Ratings		
	RS	SS	BA	A	AA
Verbal Subtests					
Information (WISC-III)	11	13			X
Similarities (WISC-III)	10	12		X	
Arithmetic (WISC-III)	7	9		X	
Vocabulary (WISC-III)	23	12		X	
Comprehension (WISC-III)	11	10		X	
Digit Span (WISC-III)	(5)	(6)	X		
Performance Subtests					
Picture Completion (WISC-III)	14	10		X	
Picture Arrangement (WISC-III)	17	10		X	
Block Design (WISC-III)	6	8		X	
Object Assembly (WISC-III)	11	8		X	
Coding (WISC-III)	13	3	X		
Mazes (WISC-III)					
VERBAL IQ	56	107		X	
PERFORMANCE IQ	39	85		X	
FULL-SCALE IQ	95	96		X	

(continued)

Table 8.15 (Continued)

Domain 2: Potential for Learning

a. Estimate of "Potential Achievement Age" Using IQ

$$PAA = \frac{C.A. \times Verbal\ IQ}{100} = PAA = \frac{7.3 \times 107}{100} = PAA = \frac{781.1}{100} = PAA = 7.8\ yrs.\ (7\ yrs.\ 10\ mos)$$

PAA of 7 yrs. 10 mos. Can be interpreted to mean that the student's performance on the verbal section of the WISC-R was equivalent to those students used to norm the test who were 7 yrs. 10 mos. of age.

b. Estimate of "Potential Grade Achievement" Using Verbal IQ and Current Grade Placement.

$$PGA = \frac{GP \times Verbal\ IQ}{100} \quad PGA = \frac{1.6 \times 107}{100} \quad PGA = \frac{171.2}{100} = 1.7\ Grade\ Potential$$

PGA of 1st grade 7th month can be interpreted to mean that the student's performance on the verbal section of the WISC-R was equivalent to those students used to norm the test who were in the 7th month of 1st grade.

Domain 3: Actual Achievement (WJ-R ACH)

Subtests	Scores			Ratings		
	RS	SS	GE	BA	A	AA
Letter/Word Identification (WJ-R ACH)	41	115	2.6 GE			X
Passage Comprehension (WJ-R ACH)	18	97	1.9 GE		X	
Calculations (WJ-R ACH)	24	116	2.5 GE			X
Applied Problems (WJ-R ACH)	14	91	1.2 GE	X		
Spelling Dictation (WJ-R ACH)	20	90	1.2 GE	X		
OVERALL RATING				X	⟵⟶	X

Relative strengths: letter and word identification, math computation
Relative weaknesses: silent reading comprehension, solving word problems, spelling

Domain 4: Eligibility for Special Education

(A) Subjects Tested	(B) Actual Achievement	(C) Potential Achievement	(D) Difference in Pts. (+/−)	(E) Eligible
Letter/Word Identification (WJ-R ACH)	115	107	+8	No
Passage Comprehension (WJ-R ACH)	97	107	−10	No
Calculation (WJ-R ACH)	116	107	+9	No
Applied Problems (WJ-R ACH)	91	107	−16	Yes
Spelling Dictation (WJ-R ACH)	90	107	−17	Yes

B. WJ-R ACH to assess actual achievement.
C. WISC-III to assess potential.
E. Eligibility normally requires more than 1 SD (15+ pts.) between actual achievement (B) and potential achievement (C).

Domain 5: Oral Language Facility

Subtests	Scores			Ratings		
	RS	SS	AE/GE	BA	A	AA
Information (WISC-III)	11	13	8-6 AE			X
Similarities (WISC-III)	10	12	8-6 AE		X	
Vocabulary (WISC-III)	23	12	8-2 AE		X	
Word Comprehension (WRMT-R)			1.5 GE		X	
Receptive/Expressive Language (TOLD-I:3)		110	2.0 GE			X
OVERALL RATING					X ⟵⟶	X

Relative strengths: prior experiences, word meanings, and analysis
Relative weaknesses: none

144

Table 8.15 (Continued)

Domain 6: Diagnostic Reading Tests

Subtests	Scores			Ratings		
	RS	SS	GE	BA	A	AA
Letter Identification (WRMT-R)	27	14	2.3 GE			X
Word Identification (WRMT-R)	30	14	2.4 GE			X
Word Identification (WJ-R ACH)	41	15	2.6 GE			X
Word Attack (WRMT-R)	20	8	1.0 GE	X		
Word Comprehension (WRMT-R)	28	10	1.5 GE		X	
Vocabulary (WISC-III)	33	12	1.8 GE		X	
Passage Comprehension (WJ-R ACH)	18	12	1.9 GE		X	
Passage Comprehension (WRMT-R)	24	9	1.5 GE		X	
OVERALL RATING				X	←——————→	X

Relative strengths: letter and word identification
Relative weaknesses: word attack

Domain 7: Diagnostic Mathematics Tests

Subtests	Scores			Ratings		
	RS	SS	GE	BA	A	AA
Concepts						
Numeration (KM-R)	12		2.5 GE			X
Rational Numbers (KM-R)	2		2.3 GE			X
Geometry (KM-R)	7		1.2 GE	X		
Operations						
Addition (KM-R)	6		2.0 GE		X	
Subtraction (KM-R)	3		2.0 GE		X	
Division (KM-R)	1		1.2 GE	X		
Multiplication (KM-R)	0		K.5 GE	X		
Mental Computation (KM-R)	2		2.0 GE		X	
Calculations (KM-R)	24	116	2.5 GE			X
Application						
Measurement (KM-R)	3		K.8 GE	X		
Time and Money (KM-R)	4		2.1 GE			X
Estimation (KM-R)	4		1.4 GE	X		
Interpreting Data (KM-R)	0		K.5 GE	X		
Problem Solving (KM-R)	4		1.4 GE	X		
Applied Problems (KM-R)	14	91	1.2 GE	X		
OVERALL RATING	48		2.0 GE	X	←——————→	X

Relative strengths: numeration, rational numbers, time and money, general calculations
Relative weaknesses: geometry, division, multiplication, measurement, estimation, interpreting data, problem solving, applied problems

Domain 8: Auditory Processing Skills

Subtests	Scores			Ratings		
	RS	SS	AE	BA	A	AA
Acuity, Discrimination, & Comprehension						
Acuity (Pure Tone)					X	
Word Discrimination (TOLD-P:3)	41	11			X	
Comprehension (Verbal IQ—WISC-III)	56	107	7.8 AE		X	
Memory						
Digit Memory (WISC-III)	5	6	6.2 AE	X		
Word Sequencing (DTLA-4)	20	5	5.2 AE	X		
Sentence Imitation (DTLA-4)	15	4	4.3 AE	X		
ESTIMATED AUDITORY MEMORY AGE			5 yrs. 9 mos.	X		

Relative strengths: acuity, discrimination, comprehension
Relative weaknesses: memory (probable contributor to poor word attack, literal comprehension or recall, and spelling)

(continued)

Table 8.15 (Continued)

Domain 9: Visual Processing Skills

Subtests	Scores			Ratings		
	RS	SS	AE	BA	A	AA
Acuity and Perception						
Acuity (Keystone)					X	
Perception without motor (MVPT)	26		7.3 AE		X	
Perception with motor						
(WISC-III Block Design)	6	8	6.5 AE	X		
Visual Comprehension						
Picture Arrangement (WISC-III)	17	10	7.3 AE		X	
Object Assembly (WISC-III)	11	8	6.7 AE	X		
Visual Memory						
Letter Sequencing (DTLA-4)	4-1		7.5 AE		X	
Object Sequencing (DTLA-4)	15		7.4 AE		X	
ESTIMATED VISUAL MEMORY AGE			7 yrs. 0 mos.	X		

Relative strengths: acuity, visual comprehension, memory
Relative weaknesses: perception, object assembly

Domain 10: Visual Motor Integration (VMI)

Subtests	Scores			Ratings		
	RS	SS	AE	BA	A	AA
Untimed VMI						
Design Reproduction (DTLA-4)	14		7.1 AE		X	
Visual-Motor Integration (DTVMI-4)	14		7.2 AE		X	
Timed VMI						
Coding (WISC-III)	13		6.2 AE	X		
ESTIMATED VMI AGE–TIMED			6 yrs. 8 mos.	X		

Relative strengths: capable of accuracy and neatness when motivated, short assignments, and not hurried
Relative weaknesses: accuracy and neatness not so likely when not motivated, assignments get longer, or under pressure

in special education resource rooms to receive special help in these areas appears warranted.

Domain 5: Oral Language
Expressive language facility is average to above average in all areas tested.

Domain 6: Reading
Overall reading is estimated to be low to mid-first-grade level, which is (1) slightly below present grade level, (2) clearly below potential, (3) considerably below the expected achievement levels of the private school Tom attends, and (4) lower than the readability levels of most of the textbooks used in first-grade classes. Strengths in reading include above average letter recognition and sight vocabulary with average word meaning and comprehension. The primary weakness in reading is ineffective use of decoding skills, particularly phonics analysis, which is nonfunctional at this time.

Domain 7: Mathematics
Overall math ability is estimated to be grade level 2.0, which at first glance is adequate. However, examination of the weaker subtests suggests otherwise for two reasons. First, the particular deficiencies involve computational and application skills and are among the more critical domains in math. Second, the expectations of the private school are somewhat higher than the test results indicate. Remediation in math should include instruction in the skill areas in Domain 7 identified as below average. These include geometry, division, multiplication, and most of the skills associated with application, that is, measurement, estimation, interpreting data, problem solving, and applied problems.

Domain 8: Auditory Processing
Although hearing, discrimination, and comprehension of auditory stimuli appear to be adequate, there are severe deficiencies in auditory memory; Tom's

estimated auditory short-term memory age is 5 years 9 months, about 1.5 years below his present chronological age. Serious deficits in auditory memory are often associated with (1) poor short-term memory, (2) incompatibility with phonics instruction, (3) distractibility, (4) difficulty remembering information, (5) poor memory for basic number facts, (6) problems working independently and for long periods of time, and (7) forgetting directions in school and at home. The significant variance of 22 points between the Verbal IQ of 107 and the Performance IQ of 85 (Domain 1) and the 1.5-year deficiency in estimated auditory memory will classify the student as learning disabled in many school districts, provided actual achievement is also deficient.

Domain 9: Visual Processing

Visual processing is better developed than auditory processing. The average visual processing age is 7 years 0 months, which is more than a year higher than the mean auditory processing age.

Domain 10: Visual-Motor Integration

Higher scores on untimed tests of VMI suggest that handwriting and copying can be adequate when assignments are short in duration and when time pressures are not imposed. The low score on the timed VMI task suggests that handwriting will likely deteriorate when assignments are long, when adequate time is not provided, and when the teacher places importance on neatness.

In summary, the prognosis for Tom's success in the private school with an accelerated environment is guarded without constant supervision, intervention, and special assistance in and out of the school. Chances for success will increase dramatically as the academic expectations match the student's capabilities.

INSTRUCTIONAL PLANNING IN REMEDIAL EDUCATION

It is not possible to give adequate attention to planning remedial education in a chapter such as this because the law requires each student to have an IEP and there are as many different IEPs as there are individuals receiving special services. What is typically done in writing IEPs, however, is to look at the diagnostic data in the Level II testing battery and, for each deficiency, write an objective to correct the

problem. In the test data for Tom in Table 8.15, for example, the educational diagnostician would likely write the IEP with input from other members of the ARD Committee. It might look something like this:

1. According to achievement screening (Domain 3), Tom is functioning at or above average in reading and math calculations but below average in applied math and spelling.
2. According to eligibility criteria (Domain 4), Tom is eligible for special assistance with the resource teacher for math and spelling.
3. In math, instruction is to be provided in geometry, division, multiplication, measurement, estimation, interpreting data, and solving sentence problems (see weaknesses in Domain 7).
4. In writing, instruction is to be provided in spelling, sentence dictation, and punctuation (see Dictation in Domain 3).
5. Although Tom did not qualify for reading instruction, if time permits, instruction should be provided in word attack skills, i.e., phonics and structural analysis (see Word Attack in Domain 6).
6. Due to the weakness in auditory memory (Domain 8) and strength in visual memory (Domain 9), teachers will write directions on the board, write homework assignments on index cards to send home, and ask Tom to repeat directions that are given orally to ensure that they are heard correctly.
7. To accommodate Tom's problem with writing and copying (see Coding in Domain 10), teachers will limit his writing assignments to 15 minutes at any one period of time and will focus grading on content more than neatness.
8. Retesting is to occur before the end of the year. By that time, it is expected that Tom's achievement scores in the specific skills tested in math and dictation will be up to grade level, i.e., grade equivalent 2.0.
9. Consideration for retention or dismissal in special education will be reviewed at the end of the current school year.

As one can readily tell, the variations in IEPs are endless. It should be noted, however, that the list of objectives for Tom represents what is considered a deficit model of remediation: locate the deficiencies, ameliorate them, and the student will be working to potential. The deficit model is highly controversial, as is the practice of removing students from the regular classroom for remedial education. A growing number of experts suggest that instruction for reading and learning disabled students (1) take place in the regular classroom; (2) be developed on a strength model, not a deficit model; (3) be stepped up and intensified; and (4) avoid adjusting instruction to the level of the slower learners.

CONCLUSION

The purpose of this chapter was to provide some insight into the theory and practice of quality educational assessment. Although some schools may not operate at the level of sophistication presented here, educational assessment is becoming more of a science and more involved with the law. The procedures for admitting, retaining, and dismissing students from special education services, though somewhat quantitatively based, is an attempt to provide services to those in greatest need and to return to the classroom those who can function effectively with whatever attention the classroom teacher is able to provide.

To supplement this chapter and provide valuable information not included here, a few important additional references are recommended. First, a copy of the aforementioned legislative acts (PL 94-142; IDEA; Section 504), available through most local school districts, provides a full explanation of the law governing the education of all handicapped children. Second, the textbooks *Assessment in Special and Remedial Education*, fourth edition (Salvia & Ysseldyke, 1998) and the third edition of *Educational Evaluation* (Popham, 1992) provide important descriptions of the assessment instruments discussed here and summarize the latest empirical research related to validity and reliability factors. Finally, *Section 504 and the Public Schools* (Smith & Patton, 1998) provides practical guidelines for determining eligibility, developing accommodation plans, and documenting compliance.

Special education is charged with providing services for students with a wide variety of needs, from the mentally disabled to the gifted. Yet, there is a large group of students who are average in every respect who have significant problems that keep them from success, but whose problems fall outside the purview of special education. These are the slow learners for whom there are no services and those whose academic failures are not significant enough to warrant special classes. The psychologist will become very active in helping some students qualify for special services and helping others who do not qualify to search for alternatives. It is a big responsibility. If clinical psychologists are to work effectively with schools, it will be important for schools to believe the psychologist has credibility. This can be accomplished by understanding school officials' language, communicating with them in their terms, and even using some of their assessment instruments in the diagnostic process.

REFERENCES

Battle, J. (1992). *Culture-Free Self-Esteem Inventories (CF/SEI-2)* (2nd ed.). Odessa, FL: Psychological Assessment Resources.

Berdine, W.H., & Meyer, S.A. (1987). *Assessment in special education.* Boston: Scott Foresman.

Berry, K.E. (1997). *Developmental Test of Visual-Motor Integration (DTVMI-4).* Parsippany, NJ: Modern Curriculum Press.

Brown, L., & Alexander, J. (1991). *Self-Esteem Index (SEI).* Odessa, FL: Psychological Assessment Resources.

Brown, V.L., Hammill, D.D., & Wiederholt, J.L. (1995). *Test of Reading Comprehension (TORC-3)* (3rd ed.). Austin, TX: ProEd.

Brown, V.L, Cronin, M., & McEntire, E. (1994). *Test of Mathematical Abilities (TOMA-2)* (2nd ed.). Austin, TX: ProEd.

Bruininks, R. (1978). *Bruininks Oseretsky Test of Motor Proficiency.* Circle Pines, MN: American Guidance Service.

Bruininks, R., Woodcock, R., Weatherman, R., & Hill, B. (1996). *Scales of Independent Behavior (SIB-R).* Itasca, IL: Riverside.

Bryant, B.R., & Wiederholt, J.L. (1991). *Gray Oral Reading Test–Diagnostic (GORT-D).* Austin, TX: ProEd.

Butler, K.A. (1988, November/December). How kids learn: What theorists say. *Learning 88,* 28–43.

Carrow-Woolfolk, E. (1995). *Oral and Written Language Scales (OWLS): Listening Comprehension & Oral Expression.* Circle Pines, MN: American Guidance Service.

Carrow-Woolfolk, E. (1999). *Test for Auditory Comprehension of Language (TACL-3)* (3rd ed.). Austin, TX: ProEd.

Cohen, M. (1997). *Children's Memory Scale (CMS).* San Antonio, TX: Psychological Corporation.

Colarusso, R.P., & Hammill, D.D. (1996). *Motor-Free Visual Perception Test–Revised.* Austin, TX: ProEd.

Conners, K. (1996). *Conners Rating Scales, Revised (CRS-R)*. Austin, TX: ProEd.

Connolly, A.J. (1988). *KeyMath–Revised*. Circle Pines, MN: American Guidance Services.

Connolly, A.J. (1998). *KeyMath–Revised Normative Update manual*. Circle Pines, MN: American Guidance Service.

Dunn, L.M., & Dunn, L.M. (1997). *Peabody Picture Vocabulary Test (PPVT-III)* (3rd ed.). Circle Pines, MN: American Guidance Services.

Dunn, R., Beaudry, J.S., & Klavas, A. (1989). Survey of research on learning styles. *Educational Leadership, 46*(6), 50–58.

Dunn, R., & Griggs, S.A. (1988). *Learning styles: Quiet revolution in American secondary schools*. Reston, VA: National Association of Secondary School Principals.

Dykes, M., & Erin, J. (1999). *Developmental Assessment for Students with Severe Disabilities (DASH-2)*. Austin, TX: ProEd.

Education for All Handicapped Children Act, Pub. L. No. 94-142, 20 U.S.C. § 1401 (1975).

Epstein, M., & Cullinan, D. (1998). *Scale for Assessing Emotional Disturbance (SAED)*. Austin, TX: ProEd.

Epstein, M., & Sharma, J. (1998). *Behavioral and Emotional Rating Scale (BERS)*. Austin, TX: ProEd.

Gilliam, J.E. (1995). *Attention-Deficit/Hyperactivity Disorder Test (ADHDT)*. Austin, TX: ProEd.

Ginsburg, H.P., & Baroody, A.J. (1990). *Test of Early Mathematics Ability (TEMA-2)* (2nd ed.). Austin, TX: ProEd.

Goldman, R., & Fristoe, M. (1986). *Goldman–Fristoe Test of Articulation (G-FTA)*. Circle Pines, MN: American Guidance Service.

Hagen, R., & Stetson, E.G. (1991, January 24–26). *Learning styles and the teaching of reading*. Paper presented to the 1991 Southwest Educational Research Association annual meeting, San Antonio, TX.

Hammill, D.D. (1998). *Detroit Tests of Learning Aptitude (DTLA-4)* (4th ed.). Austin, TX: ProEd.

Hammill, D.D., & Bryant, B.R. (1998). *The Learning Disabilities Diagnostic Inventory (LDDI)*. Austin, TX: ProEd.

Hammill, D.D., Bryant, B.R., & Pearson, N.A. (1998). *Hammill Multiability Intelligence Test (HAMIT)*. Austin, TX: ProEd.

Hammill, D.D., Hresko, W., Ammer, J., Cronin, M., & Quinby, S. (1998). *Hammill Multiability Achievement Test (HAMAT)*. Austin, TX: ProEd.

Hammill, D.D., & Larsen, S. (1996). *Test of Written Language (TOWL-3)* (3rd ed.). Austin, TX: ProEd.

Hammill, D.D., & Newcomer, P. (1997). *Test of Language Development, Intermediate Level (TOLD-I:3)*. Austin, TX: ProEd.

Hammill, D.D., Pearson, N.A., & Voress, J. (1996). *Test of Visual Motor Integration (TVMI)*. Austin, TX: ProEd.

Hammill, D.D., Pearson, N.A., & Wiederholt, J.L. (1996). *Comprehensive Test of Nonverbal Intelligence (C-TONI)*. Austin, TX: ProEd.

Jacomides, V. (1986). *The relationship between auditory and visual memory and specified academic skills in reading and written spelling among remedial students in grades 1–6*. Unpublished doctoral dissertation, University of Houston, TX.

Kaufman, A.S., & Kaufman, N.L. (1985). *Kaufman Test of Educational Achievement–Comprehensive Form (K-TEA-Comprehensive)*. Circle Pines, MN: American Guidance Services.

Kaufman, A.S., & Kaufman, N.L. (1987). *Kaufman Assessment Battery for Children (K-ABC)*. Circle Pines, MN: American Guidance Service.

Kaufman, A.S., & Kaufman, N.L. (1990). *Kaufman Brief Intelligence Test (K-BIT)*. Circle Pines, MN: American Guidance Service.

Kaufman, A.S., & Kaufman, N.L. (1998). *Kaufman Test of Educational Achievement–Comprehensive Form Normative Update manual*. Circle Pines, MN: American Guidance Service.

Kaufman, N.L., & Kaufman, A.S. (1985). *Kaufman Test of Educational Achievement–Brief Form (K-TEA, Brief Form)*. Circle Pines, MN: American Guidance Service.

Kaufman, N.L., & Kaufman, A.S. (1998). *Kaufman Test of Educational Achievement–Brief Form Normative Update manual*. Circle Pines, MN: American Guidance Service.

Keystone View Company. (n.d.). *Keystone School Vision Tests*. Davenport, IA: Author.

Larsen, S., Hammill, D.D., & Moats, L. (1999). *Test of Written Spelling (TWS-4)* (4th ed.). Austin, TX: ProEd.

Mardell-Czudnowski, C., & Goldenburg, D. (1998). *Developmental Indicators for the Assessment of Learning (DIAL-3)* (3rd ed.). Circle Pines, MN: American Guidance Service.

Markwardt, F.C. (1989). *Peabody Individual Achievement Test, Revised (PIAT-R)*. Circle Pines, MN: American Guidance Service.

Markwardt, F.C. (1998). *Peabody Individual Achievement Test, Revised Normative Update manual*. Circle Pines, MN: American Guidance Service.

McDowell, P.M., & McDowell, R.L. (1996). *McDowell Vision Screening Kit*. Los Angeles: Western Psychological Services.

Micro Audiometrics Corporation. (1999). *Earscan Microprocessor Pure Tone Audiometer*. Murphy, NC: Author.

Miller, J.W., & McKenna, M. (1989). *Teaching reading in the elementary classroom*. Scottsdale, AZ: Gorsuch Scarisbrick.

Naglieri, J.A., McNeish, T.J., & Bardos, A.N. (1991). *Draw-a-Person: Screening Procedures for Emotional Disturbance (DAP:SPED)*. Austin, TX: ProEd.

Newcomer, P.L. (1990). *Diagnostic Achievement Battery (DAB-2)* (2nd ed.). Itasca, IL: Riverside.

Newcomer, P.L., & Bryant, B.R. (1993). *Diagnostic Achievement Test for Adolescents (DATA-2)* (2nd ed.). Itasca, IL: Riverside.

Newcomer, P.L., & Hammill, D.D. (1997). *Test of Language Development, Primary Level (TOLD-P:3)*. Austin, TX: ProEd.

Popham, W.J. (1992). *Educational evaluation* (3rd ed.). New York: Allyn & Bacon.

Psychological Corporation. (1992a). *Wechsler Individual Achievement Test, Comprehensive (WIAT-Comprehensive)*. San Antonio, TX: Author.

Psychological Corporation. (1992b). *Wechsler Individual Achievement Test, Screener (WIAT-Screener)*. San Antonio, TX: Author.

Reynolds, C.R., & Bigler, E.D. (1994). *Test of Memory and Learning (TOMAL-R)* (Rev.). Austin, TX: ProEd.

Salvia, J., & Ysseldyke, J.E. (1998). *Assessment* (7th ed.). Boston: Houghton Mifflin.

Sattler, J.M. (2001). *Assessment of children: Cognitive Applications* (4th ed.). San Diego, CA: Author.

Sheslow, D., & Adams, W. (1990). *Wide Range Assessment of Memory and Learning (WRAML)*. Austin, TX: ProEd.

Slosson, R.L., Nicholson, C.L., & Hibpshman, T.H. (1990). *Slosson Intelligence Test–Revised (SIT-R)*. Austin, TX: ProEd.

Smith, T.E., & Patton, J.R. (1998). *Section 504 and the public schools*. Austin, TX: ProEd.

Snyderman, M., & Rothman, S. (1987). Survey of expert opinion on intelligence and aptitude testing. *American Psychologist, 42*, 137–144.

Stetson, E.G. (1983). Assessment of word analysis and processing skills. In D. Phelps-Terasaki, T. Phelps-Gunn, & E. Stetson (Eds.), *Remediation and instruction in language: Oral language, reading, and writing*. Austin, TX: ProEd.

Thorndike, R.L., Hagen, E., & Sattler, J. (1986). *Stanford–Binet Intelligence Scale* (4th ed.). Itasca, IL: Riverside.

Wagner, R., Torgesen, J., & Rashotte, C. (1999). *Comprehensive Test of Phonological Processing (CTOPP)*. Austin, TX: ProEd.

Wang, M., Reynolds, M., & Walberg, H. (1987). *Handbook of special education: Research and practice*. Oxford, England: Pergamon Press.

Wechsler, D. (1989). *Wechsler Preschool and Primary Scale of Intelligence, Revised (WPPSI-R)*. San Antonio, TX: Psychological Corporation.

Wechsler, D. (1991). *Wechsler Intelligence Scale for Children (WISC-III)* (3rd ed.). San Antonio, TX: Psychological Corporation.

Wechsler, D. (1997). *Wechsler Adult Intelligence Scale (WAIS-III)* (3rd ed.). San Antonio, TX: Psychological Corporation.

Wilkinson, G.S. (1993). *Wide Range Achievement Test, Revision 3 (WRAT-3)*. Wilmington, DE: Jastak Associates.

Williams, K. (1997). *Expressive Vocabulary Test (EVT)*. Circle Pines, MN: American Guidance Service.

Woodcock, R.W. (1987). *Woodcock Reading Mastery Tests, Revised (WRMT-R)*. Circle Pines, MN: American Guidance Service.

Woodcock, R.W. (1998). *Woodcock Reading Mastery Test, Revised Normative Update manual*. Circle Pines, MN: American Guidance Service.

Woodcock, R.W., & Johnson, M.B. (1989). *Woodcock–Johnson, Revised, Tests of Achievement (WJ-R-ACH)*. Itasca, IL: Riverside.

Woodcock, R.W., McGrew, K.S., & Werder, J.K. (1994). *Woodcock, McGrew, Werder Mini-Battery of Achievement (MBA)*. San Antonio, TX: Psychological Corporation.

Yell, M.L. (1997). *The law and special education*. New York: Prentice Hall.

CHAPTER 9

Neuropsychological Assessment of the Child

MICHELLE L. BENGTSON AND THOMAS J. BOLL

PURPOSE OF NEUROPSYCHOLOGICAL ASSESSMENT OF THE CHILD

The purpose of neuropsychological assessment varies according to the population involved. Parents of pediatric patients often view the purpose of neuropsychological assessment for their child as a means for directing and strengthening discussions with school administrators regarding academic accommodations. Parents whose children are ill view the assessment as a direct line to diagnosis and treatment recommendations. Physicians at times view neuropsychological assessment as a means for diagnostic confirmation and at other times emphasize the importance of deficit documentation or remediation. The goal of any individual neuropsychological assessment varies according to the patient, referral source, or reimbursement party. It may range from diagnosis to treatment effectiveness evaluation or implementation, prognosis determination, or intervention. The core of neuropsychological assessment is depicting brain-behavior relationships through comprehension, explanation, screening, evaluation, identification and determination of the nature of the problem, prediction of current as well as future abilities and limitations, and suggestions. This underlying goal surfaces in both clinical service and research, which work in concert, for "without clinical questions, research would lose its meaning; without systematic review of practice, science would be static" (Boll, 1993, p. 142).

It is commonly misperceived that the "be-all and end-all" role of the neuropsychologist is to diagnose brain damage while discounting the importance of normal development of brain function and organization. The primary goal of neuropsychology is to provide a description of the relationship between brain function and human behavior, utilizing what is known about normal functioning. The legitimacy and reliability inherent in neuropsychological assessment for determining brain-behavior relationships provides the basis for description that, in turn, is the largest portion of clinical neuropsychological practice. The neuropsychologist determines the patient's level of functioning and explains ramifications that can then be used for detailing prognosis, management, and treatment options and recommendations.

The role of neuropsychology is more than a binary decision-making process documenting the presence or absence of neurobehavioral deficits. The numerical outcome from neuropsychological assessment holds inherent interest for the scientific community, but perhaps more important, it must also be useful in enhancing the patient's functional competence. The pursuit of documentation of central nervous system disruption falls short of the mark. Little service is provided to a patient if the assessment documents brain damage but fails to help the patient in understanding, clarification, and recommendation for changes or assistance to improve on the quality of daily living as compared to preevaluation levels. Determination of deficiencies needs to be of value to the patient clinically. The aim of scientific neuropsychological investigation should be to further understanding while providing a platform to assist in the determination of appropriate and effective remediation and management techniques. In the end, the evaluation can be considered complete only when it has helped guide the formulation of a comprehensive treatment framework with ecological validity that will prove beneficial as the patient attempts to meet the demands of daily life (Lezak, 1995; Rourke, Bakker, Fisk, & Strang, 1983; Taylor, 1986). Following the documentation of neurocognitive dysfunction, neuropsychological evaluation can prove useful in tracking the course of recovery (Boll & Barth, 1981; Hammock, Milhorat, & Baron, 1976; Levin et al., 1987). Serial assessment allows the patient, family, teachers, and medical staff to be given feedback that can be useful in the development and modification of strategies for management, adjustment, and rehabilitation and will serve to promote success and limit frustration and disappointment.

Neuropsychological evaluation can provide an indication of a patient's day-to-day functioning. The patient may present in such a way as to appear generally neurocognitively intact on neurological examination and may be deemed essentially "normal" when positive neuroradiologic findings are lacking. This can be misleading and ultimately detrimental to the patient when the outward manifestation of recovery, fluctuation, and deterioration of central nervous system disease does not fully parallel findings on physical neurological examination. Complicating matters is the fact that neurocognitive sequelae generally persist long after anomalies depicted by physical or neuroradiological examinations recover. Conversely, neuropsychological assessment can also be used to quantify residual skill or ability despite positive neuroradiological findings. Abnormalities in brain appearance as seen on CT-scan, MRI, or PET do not necessarily translate into functional loss of ability. Without neuropsychological quantification of ability, such results could have unnecessary deleterious effects on the patient's presumed prognosis and even livelihood. In some cases, neuroradiological abnormality is the result of a life-long aberration or progressive but subjectively undetectable process that has little bearing on day-to-day functioning.

Referral for pediatric neuropsychological assessment can result from numerous different presenting questions and concerns. Commonly, children are referred for neuropsychological assessment secondary to known or suspected organic disease with potential neurocognitive sequelae. At other times, children are referred when skills deteriorate or fail to develop at age-appropriate rates. Referral for neuropsychological evaluation is often made when children exhibit complex learning or behavioral problems. Children who present for neuropsychological evaluation may suffer the consequences of developmental disorders such as chromosomal or genetic disorders, structural anomalies, pre- or postnatal infection, anoxic episodes, traumatic brain injury, convulsive disorders, or focal neurological disorders. They could also present with disturbances of function including but not limited to language, auditory, visual, or motor disorders, attentional disturbances, learning disorders, or psychiatric disorders. Putnam and DeLuca (1990) reported that the most frequent conditions referred for assessment included brain tumor, seizure disorder, traumatic brain injury, learning disability, and psychiatric disorder. Similar results were obtained by Yeates, Ris, and Taylor (1995), with attention-deficit disorder, mental retardation, phenylketonuria, acute lymphocytic leukemia, encephalitis, and various metabolic disorders being other common diagnostic referral categories in a hospital setting. Two separate studies (Sweet & Moberg, 1990; Yeates et al., 1995) reported that pediatric neuropsychological assessment referrals most commonly came from neurologists, neurosurgeons, physiatrists, pediatricians, psychiatrists, psychologists, or the child's parents or family. Other typical referral sources include attorneys and school personnel.

The scientific literature has recurrently attested to the validity of psychological/behavioral assessment (Boll, 1974; Filskov & Boll, 1981; Hammock et al., 1976; Reitan, 1974; Reitan & Davidson, 1974; Wright, Schaefer, & Solomons, 1979). Studies have demonstrated the diversity of behavioral expressions of central nervous system dysfunction in children, including head injury (Klonoff, Low, & Clark, 1977; Levin & Eisenberg, 1979), anoxia (Graham, Ernhart, Craft, & Berman, 1963), muscular dystrophy (Knights, Hinton, & Drader, 1973), posterior fossa tumors (Knights & Hinton, 1973), and epilepsy (O'Leary, Seidenberg, Berent, & Boll, 1981; Seidenberg, O'Leary, Giordani, Berent, & Boll, 1981). Neuropsychological assessment of children differs from traditional psychological assessment in that it emphasizes a broader range of abilities, largely cognitive in nature, and focuses on brain-behavior relationships.

GOALS OF THE PEDIATRIC NEUROPSYCHOLOGICAL EVALUATION

The overriding goal of pediatric neuropsychological assessment is to evaluate the degree of compromised and preserved neurocognitive function that will bear on prognosis for the management of daily living tasks. The identification of cognitive and problem-solving ability is a subgoal that looks at overall intellectual capacity, memory functioning, abstract reasoning, and verbal and nonverbal problem-solving ability. Particularly with children, attention is paid to the evaluation of academic strengths and weaknesses in the areas of reading, spelling, writing, and arithmetic. Other abilities are analyzed through a variety of perceptual modalities including visual, auditory, and motoric functioning. Language and communication ability or deficit is evaluated as another subgoal during the assessment process and is considered through oral and written as well as receptive and expressive modalities. Finally, another subgoal of neuropsychological assessment of children is to assess the child's and perhaps the family's social and emotional functioning through a variety of means including but not limited to clinical interview with the child and the child's parents, behavioral observation, measures of self-help and adaptive functioning, parent and/or teacher rating forms, and projective evaluation.

In addition to the more purely neurocognitive domains, complete neuropsychological evaluations appraise disruptions in physical, adaptive, and emotional well-being. "Children with known brain impairment cannot be considered to have received the best care if the behavioral correlates of their disorder have not been carefully and explicitly addressed in a manner integral to the overall management of the patient" (Boll, 1993, p. 143). The ultimate outcome of the pediatric neuropsychological evaluation is the provision of compensatory techniques, behavioral management, and individualized

educational programs, which must emphasize attention, self-control, and thought organization. Compensatory techniques, behavioral management, and strategies for improved community and interpersonal integration can be provided to the patient, family, and other caretakers (Boll, 1988).

At one time, pediatric neuropsychological assessment was primarily utilized for the substantiation of acquired neurocognitive and psychological impairments coupled with documentation of improvement through an inspection of changes between repeated assessments. Although this is still the case in some neuropsychological referrals, there has been a movement toward assimilating information regarding etiological processes for varying pathologies and integrating multidisciplinary perspectives on the utility of preserved function and the impact of deficits on the patient's ability to meet environmental demands. Knowledge of neurocognitive deficits in and of themselves is not sufficient for determining long-term impact on improvement and adaptation. A knowledge of elements integrally related to the central nervous system disorders, including the nature, location, duration, and severity of the actual injury, may aid in understanding the impact of the other dimensions of the overall equation. These include the patient's level of functioning and general adaptive abilities prior to the injury, the quality of the patient's environment, and any additional support accessible to ensure treatment and perpetuate improvement through rehabilitation (Boll, 1983).

NEUROPSYCHOLOGICAL APPROACHES TO ASSESSMENT OF CHILDREN

Neuropsychological assessment must utilize measures that are both broad and detailed enough to allow for the development of a thorough understanding of patient strengths and weaknesses. A picture of both preserved and impaired function is derived through a comparison of actuarial performance to expected performance. The use of actuarial and clinical approaches is believed to most adequately provide descriptive and diagnostic information (Boll, 1983; Filskov & Goldstein, 1974; S.G. Goldstein, Deysach, & Kleinknecht, 1973; Mathews, Shaw, & Klov, 1966; Reitan & Boll, 1973; Selz & Reitan, 1979a). Within the neuropsychological evaluation, sufficient breadth of assessment is required to cover both content and process. Whereas the evaluation needs to be long enough to cover all areas of concern, brevity is also of interest to minimize fatigue and boredom.

> Content includes language, perception, motor, and sensory functions, as well as variations within these major content areas both of modality (visual, auditory, tactile) and of material (figure or symbol). Processes such as attention, memory, learning, and problem solving are central to human day-to-day competence. Mental processes and content interact to define the core of human behavioral repertoire that is the focus of neuropsychological evaluation. (Boll, 1993, p. 142)

There are generally considered to be three primary pediatric neuropsychological assessment approaches: the fixed battery approach, the flexible battery approach, and the process approach. The fixed battery approach utilizes the same assessment battery for each child, regardless of the referral question or presenting complaint, although it may vary according to age groups, with younger children (5–8 years old) utilizing one battery, and older children (9–15 years old) another. The work of Reitan and his colleagues contributed greatly to the fixed battery approach of neuropsychological assessment, with the Reitan–Indiana Neuropsychological Test Battery being used for younger children, 5 to 8 years old, and the Halstead–Reitan Neuropsychological Test Battery for older children, 9 to 14 years old (Boll, 1974; Reitan, 1969, 1974; Reitan & Wolfson, 1992a, 1992b). Another fixed battery for use with children 8 to 12 years of age is the Luria–Nebraska Neuropsychological Battery for Children, published by Golden (1981). Generally speaking, the fixed battery approach emphasizes quantifiable differentiation between patients and normal children.

The flexible battery, or eclectic approach, relies on a core battery of standardized test procedures, but remains flexible in test selection to orient the evaluation of the child to specifically address the referral question and anticipated deficits (Rourke, Fisk, & Strange, 1986). This approach has the advantage of allowing flexibility in test selection, which, in many cases, may minimize the time required to complete the assessment while providing for similar factor structure of the traditional fixed battery approach. On the other hand, potential disadvantages of this approach are that the

particular selection of tests may not assess all areas of strength and deficiencies, and the data compared across varying normative samples may provide only an estimate of the child's relative performance.

The process approach, quite similar to the flexible battery approach, utilizes standardized tests to provide a profile of patient strengths and weaknesses, but proceeds to attempt to determine specific processing deficiencies responsible for weak performances, providing both nomothetic and ideographic information. This approach has the advantage of providing possibly more useful information and applicable remediation and deficit management once the patient's primary processing deficits are elucidated, although its potential strength can yield the potential weakness of inaccurate recommendations if the evaluation of patient strengths and weaknesses is imprecise (Williams & Boll, 1997). It is also the case that this potential advantage has yet to be scientifically validated.

Many factors, including the referral question, the patient population, the assessment setting, and more, contribute to the selection of a particular assessment approach by a neuropsychologist. Lezak (1995) suggests that "general guidelines for the examination can be summed up in the injunction: *'Tailor the examination to the patient's needs, abilities, and limitations'* in order to answer the examination questions most fully at the least cost with the greatest benefit to the patient" (p. 110). More specific advice was espoused by Boll (1993), who indicated that practical-technical factors as well as issues of validity would most significantly impact the clinician's testing approach. For example, there are many factors inherent in the test construction that could ultimately significantly impact the instrument's utility (e.g., alternate forms for serial assessments, scope of instrument, availability of normative comparison, objective versus subjective scoring, potential for false negatives or false positives).

THE NEUROPSYCHOLOGICAL ASSESSMENT PROCESS

Neuropsychological assessment of a child can be considered a hypothesis-driven process. Perhaps the best assessment is one that begins with the consideration of the child, rather than the particular assessment battery to be used. Consideration of the referral question prompting the assessment should lead to hypotheses that may explain the presenting symptoms. These are the hypotheses that will be systematically tested throughout the course of the assessment, keeping in mind the general developmental process. Data to support or refute such hypotheses are acquired through three separate avenues and include background information acquired largely through the clinical interview process and questionnaires designed to elicit historical information, behavioral observations obtained during the actual neuropsychological evaluation or in the patient's home or school environment, and test data accumulated during the quantitative portion of the neuropsychological assessment. The conclusion of the assessment then will yield not only information about the likely etiology and neurocognitive manifestations of the child's disorder, but a pattern of strengths and weaknesses that will likely drive treatment recommendations and potential intervention.

A comprehensive neuropsychological evaluation provides only a sample of capacities required of the patient for successful daily living. An accurate personal history and clinical interview will significantly improve the reliability of the interpretation of neuropsychological performance. The clinical interview provides the best opportunity to derive relevant information pertaining to the child's prior and current levels of functioning, in addition to eliciting potentially key historical events in the child's past that may have a bearing on current functioning and future prognosis. A good clinical interview will address not only current complaints but also historical data.

A thorough clinical interview will typically address 10 to 12 different domains, ranging from current complaints to the child's medical, behavioral, and educational history. Pertinent information should be obtained to allow for easy access at a future date with the child's parents, teachers, and perhaps even physicians with parental permission. Familial history holds several important pieces of information. It is essential to learn not only with whom the child resides, but also information regarding parental educational attainment and any history of difficulty, including special education, remediation, or other assistance, in addition to current occupational standing. One of the best predictors of a child's ultimate cognitive ability is the mother's functioning, which is often best deduced by direct intellectual assessment (this can be done

briefly or with the full Wechsler Scale) and by her educational attainment. Similarly, the academic ability demonstrated by siblings who live in the child's home can provide a window into the child's own expected level of functioning. Of course, these are not deterministic measures, but merely statistical correlations. Also in terms of familial history, it is important to investigate any familial psychiatric diagnoses and treatment, as many are often inherited and could serve to adversely impact a child's overall level of neurocognitive functioning. A good clinical interview should also investigate educational, medical, and psychiatric histories of extended family members.

A clinical interview will also address the patient's birth and developmental history. It is important to assess the "normalcy" of the mother's pregnancy, with questions pertaining to any substances and prescribed medications used by the mother during her pregnancy, in addition to the course, labor, and delivery. Perinatal history investigates the patient's birth weight, APGAR scores, required special or intensive care, as well as any noted birth defects.

Questions pertaining to the child's infancy and early childhood provide an understanding of the patient's developmental milestones with respect to motor, language, social, and adaptive functioning. This is also the time to determine the child's early childhood temperament, social interaction, and abnormal behaviors or concerns if any were present.

The child's medical history potentially bears great weight on current neuropsychological performance and for this reason will be investigated in depth. Areas to be addressed include any significant illnesses, hospitalizations, surgery, accidents, injuries, loss of consciousness, or medications. This is also an apt time to find out about any vision or hearing testing. It is also during this time that the interviewer is likely to determine if the child has ever before been diagnosed with attention-deficit/hyperactivity disorder.

Perhaps equally important as the child's medical history is information pertaining to the child's behavioral and mental health history. Specific areas warranting discussion are any behaviors of concern to the child's parents or teachers in addition to any particularly traumatic or stressful events in the child's past. Information regarding the child's current personality and behavior traits is also of significant value.

Another important domain to evaluate during the clinical interview pertains to the child's educational history. This includes information on the child's current academic placement and associated performance. Further, it is vital to assess any history of special education, tutoring, learning disability assessment and treatment, or any other treatment in an academic setting. It is often also feasible to obtain signed releases of information to receive academic information from the child's school and teachers.

Finally, in addition to a thorough clinical history, it is vital to discuss with the child's parents what current complaints have brought them to seek medical and/or psychological assistance. Presenting problems take various forms, ranging from the desire for presurgical baseline assessments to concerns regarding deterioration in academic performance to assessments for the purpose of satisfying criteria for gifted program placement. Whatever the reason for referral, a thorough understanding of the referral question or current complaint is vital for steering the direction of the neuropsychological assessment, recommendations, potential treatment, and follow-up.

RECENT ADVANCES IN NEUROPSYCHOLOGICAL ASSESSMENT MEASURES

Despite the varying approaches to pediatric neuropsychological assessment, most child neuropsychologists design their test battery to adequately sample several core neurocognitive domains, including general intellectual functioning, academic achievement, memory, language, attention and executive functioning, visuospatial ability, sensorimotor skill, and social, emotional, and adaptive functioning. Our purpose here is not to review every possible pediatric neuropsychological assessment tool available to the child neuropsychologist, as such reviews are available elsewhere (Anderson, 1994; Taylor & Fletcher, 1990; Williams & Boll, 1997; Wilson, 1986; Ylvisaker et al. 1990). Rather, we highlight several of the more recent additions to the pediatric neuropsychologists' bag of tricks.

There are several options for the assessment of overall intellectual functioning, but two of the more common are the Wechsler Intelligence Scale for Children, third edition (WISC-III) (Wechsler, 1991)

and the Stanford–Binet Intelligence Scale, fourth edition (SB4) (Thorndike, Hagen, & Sattler, 1986). The WISC-III was published in 1991 and is an updated version of its predecessor, the WISC-R (Wechsler, 1974). It has retained the basic design of Wechsler's original instrument, but has more up-to-date norms. All of the WISC-R subtests have been retained in the current version, with one additional supplementary subtest, Symbol Search. The SB4 has been available since 1986, as an updated version of the Stanford–Binet Intelligence Scale–Form LM edition. The SB4 has generally retained the earlier format, but now provides four separate domain scores—verbal reasoning, quantitative reasoning, abstract/visual reasoning, and short-term memory—in addition to the global index score.

Just as with updated measures of global intelligence, changes and additions have been made to better assess academic achievement in the pediatric population. The Wide Range Achievement Test–Revised was updated with a third edition in 1993 (WRAT-3) (Wilkinson, 1993). The purpose of this instrument has remained consistent with its earlier version: to provide a relatively brief assessment of academic achievement in the areas of reading, spelling, and mathematics while providing normative data for persons 5 to 74 years of age. The 1977 version of the Woodcock–Johnson Psycho-Educational Battery was revised in 1989 (Woodcock & Johnson, 1989) and consists of a Test of Academic Achievement and a Test of Cognitive Ability, with norms ranging from 2 to 90+ years of age. A new academic achievement measure has emerged on the scene: the Wechsler Individual Achievement Test (WIAT) (Wechsler, 1992) assesses eight areas of academic performance (reading, mathematics reasoning, spelling, reading comprehension, numerical operations, listening comprehension, oral expression, and written expression) for children 5 to 19 years 11 months of age. This particular instrument has two primary advantages over the previous two that were discussed in that it was conormed with three of the Wechsler Intelligence Tests (Wechsler Preschool and Primary Scale of Intelligence–Revised [WPPSI-R], WISC-III, and the Wechsler Adult Intelligence Scale–Revised [WAIS-R]), and it can be used to assess all areas of learning disabilities under the Education for All Handicapped Children Act (Public Law 94-142; Federal Register, 1976).

One of the newest pediatric neuropsychological assessment tools to become available for assessment of a broad range of neurocognitive functions is the NEPSY, a developmental neuropsychological assessment (Korkman, Kirk, & Kemp, 1998). The NEPSY was designed for use with children age 3 to 12 to assess five core domains (attention/executive, language, sensorimotor, visuospatial, and memory) with either a one-hour initial core test battery or an extended evaluation that provides numerous supplemental scores including auditory attention, visual attention, design fluency, speeded naming, verbal fluency, fingertip tapping, visuomotor precision, imitating hand positions, memory for faces, narrative memory, memory for names, and list learning. The expanded assessment serves to further delineate a problem determined by deficits noted during the core assessment. The NEPSY also provides for quantification of qualitative observations including but not limited to off-task behavior, requests for repetition, voice volume, misarticulation, and tremor. Another advantage of the NEPSY is that it was normed on over 1,000 American children, with separate norms for children from Finland, Sweden, and Denmark. Because it covers all core cognitive competencies, it is appropriate for use in diagnosing acquired and developmental disabilities, although it does not purport to be a substitute for an overall measure of intellectual ability.

Several independent measures have been designed in the past decade to assess children's memory rather than relying on scaled-down versions of adult memory measures: the California Verbal Learning Test for Children (CVLT-C) (Delis, Kramer, Kaplan, & Ober, 1994), the Children's Memory Scale (CMS) (Wechsler, 1995), the Test of Memory and Learning (TOMAL) (Reynolds & Bigler, 1994), and the Wide Range Assessment of Memory and Learning (WRAML) (Sheslow & Adams, 1990). The CVLT-C (Delis et al., 1994) is generally identical to the adult format except that each list consists of three five-word categories. It was designed for use with children from 5 years to 16 years 11 months of age who present with learning and memory problems and provides multiple measures of learning processes and learning problems. Scoring can be done either by hand or through a computerized scoring program. The CMS was one of the first internationally standardized measures of learning and memory. It was created for assessment of auditory/verbal, visual/nonverbal, and attention/concentration processes in children 5 to 16 years of age, with separate forms for use with chil-

dren 5 to 8 and 9 to 16 years old. It was conormed with the Children's Category Test (Boll, 1993), a measure of nonverbal learning efficiency. It was also linked to the WISC-III and WIAT, and provides information in the manual for interpreting the three instruments conjointly. The instrument can be scored either individually or with the aid of a computerized program. The TOMAL was designed to assess both verbal and nonverbal memory proficiency of children age 5 to 19. It comprises 14 subtests and provides for a composite memory index, as well as a delayed recall index. The authors of the instrument (Reynolds & Bigler, 1994) reported that four distinct factors resulted from a factor analysis: a complex memory factor score, a sequential recall factor score, a backwards recall factor score, and a spatial memory factor score. The WRAML is another instrument designed to assess verbal memory, visual memory, and learning in children 5 to 17 years of age. The test consists of nine individual subtests and provides a means for a shorter screening battery, as well as for assessment of delayed recall. The instrument provides scaled scores for each subtest and standardized scores and percentiles for each index score.

Relatively few new measures have been published to better assess children's language functioning, visual-spatial and constructional ability, somatosensory and motor skill, attention, and problem solving, although comprehensive evaluation using the NEPSY assesses all of these areas quite nicely for children in the 3- to 12-year age range.

RECENT CHANGES IN *DSM* DIAGNOSES AND THEIR ROLE IN NEUROPSYCHOLOGY

One of the principal changes between the *DSM-III-R* and *DSM-IV* affecting neuropsychologists is the deletion of organic mental disorders are the addition of diagnostic criteria for cognitive disorder NOS and mental disorders due to a general medical condition. These classifications may offer a better explanation of acquired difficulties than other, more developmentally based diagnoses, particulary when personality and neurocognitive alterations seemed to be direct sequelae of acquired brain lesions.

Neuropsychologists assess patients with a variety of neurologic conditions, including closed head injury, cerebral neoplasms, cerebral vascular accidents, seizure disorders, and many others. They are also relied on to assist in the diagnosis of a variety of neuropsychiatric syndromes that are largely neurocognitive in nature, including specific learning disabilities, attention-deficit/hyperactivity disorder, and pervasive developmental disorder. They also see patients with psychiatric symptoms as primary presenting complaints. In many cases, neuropsychologists rely not only on objective standardized assessment measures but on diagnostic criteria set forth by the American Psychiatric Association. In 1994, the APA updated the revised third edition (APA, 1987) and published the fourth edition of the *Diagnostic and Statistical Manual of Mental Disorders (DSM)*. The fourth edition of the *DSM* contains many changes over the revised third edition, many of which pertain to the diagnosis of children and are briefly identified here. Learning disorders cited in the *DSM-IV* are comparable to the *DSM-III-R* academic skills disorders and are diagnosed when the child's achievement on individually administered standardized tests of reading, spelling, written expression, or arithmetic is substantially lower (generally considered to be a discrepancy of 1 to 2 standard deviations between achievement and IQ scores) than the child's expected performance based on the child's age, educational attainment, and overall level of intellectual functioning. The *DSM-III-R* learning disorders were listed as developmental disorders (developmental arithmetic disorder, developmental expressive writing disorder, developmental reading disorder). Although *DSM-IV* gives more consideration to expected levels of functioning based on the child's age, no real diagnostic criteria have changed, despite minor changes in the diagnostic labels (mathematics disorder, disorder of written expression, reading disorder).

Within the *DSM-IV* prescribed communication disorders (*DSM-III-R* language and speech disorders) exist expressive language disorder (previously developmental expressive language disorder), phonological disorder (formerly developmental articulation disorder), stuttering (classified the same in *DSM-III-R* but under speech disorders not elsewhere classified), a new entry, the mixed receptive-expressive language disorder, and communication disorder NOS. The diagnostic criteria for the communication disorders in the *DSM-IV* has remained largely the same as those set forth in the revised third edition, with the additional criteria of disturbed academic, occupational, or social functioning as a result of speech sound production difficulties for the diagnosis of phonological disorder. The criteria required for a diagnosis of stuttering are also much more explicit and expanded in the *DSM-IV* as compared to its earlier counterpart, and among other things, require that the stuttering significantly interfere with academic, occupational, and/or social functioning. Further, the *DSM-III-R* provided for a diagnosis of developmental receptive language disorder, which does not appear as a diagnosis in the fourth edition, and the fourth edition provides for a diagnosis of mixed receptive-expressive language disorder, which was not an option using the *DSM-III-R*. A diagnosis of mixed receptive-expressive language disorder is in order when the child's performance on standardized tests tapping both receptive and expressive language functioning is significantly below scores obtained on tasks assessing nonverbal intellectual ability and markedly interfere with academic, occupational, and/or interpersonal functioning. The earlier *DSM* version did, however, provide for a diagnosis of developmental receptive language disorder, which does not appear as an option in the more recent version. No changes in diagnostic labels or criteria were made within the motor skills disorders, which include developmental coordination disorder.

In addition to learning disorders, pediatric neuropsychologists also often assess children whose diagnoses come under the diagnostic realm of pervasive developmental disorders. Aside from minor verbiage changes, there were generally no changes in diagnostic criteria between the revised third and subsequent fourth editions of the *DSM* for diagnosis of autistic disorder. There are several new diagnoses in *DSM-IV* under the heading of pervasive developmental disorder, including Rett's disorder, childhood disintegrative disorder, and Asperger's disorder.

Several changes were made in the *DSM-IV* to diagnoses under the attention-deficit and disruptive behavior disorders subgroup. Whereas the *DSM-III-R* provided for severity classification of attention-deficit hyperactivity disorder, the *DSM-IV* no longer provides an option for severity rating. The *DSM-IV* does, however, provide for subclassification of the disorder into predominantly hyperactive-impulsive type, predominantly inattentive type, and combined type, and breaks down diagnostic criteria into symptoms of inattention, hyperactivity, and impulsivity. The other change in the later *DSM* edition is the additional criterion that the disorder must significantly interfere with academic, occupational, or social functioning.

HINDRANCES TO NEUROPSYCHOLOGICAL ASSESSMENT OF CHILDREN

Neuropsychological assessment of children is similar to neuropsychological assessment of adults in that its foundation is grounded on a knowledge of the functioning of a normal, mature brain in addition to knowledge of basic neuroanatomy. Assessment of children differs from assessment of adults, however, in several ways. Neuropsychological assessment of children emphasizes developmental neuroanatomy, which includes factors such as understanding the development of hemispheric specialization, generally considered complete by the time an individual reaches adulthood. Neuropsychological assessment of children relies on a more developmental approach as opposed to the oft-used pathological approach in adult assessment. Further, the assessment instruments used in child neuropsychological evaluations ideally are entities of their own, as opposed to scaled-down versions of adult batteries, and rely on age-appropriate pediatric norms.

We must make mention of particular problems encountered in the neuropsychological assessment of children. Children represent a population for neuropsychological assessment vastly different from adults. Yet, too often, many of the instruments available for use with this younger population are simply scaled-down versions of adult tests, with little consideration of developmental issues related to the pediatric population. Further, many of the pediatric instruments used today have poor norms or poor psychometric qualities. This makes accurate comparison and conclusions difficult to render. Another problem often encountered in child neuropsychological assessment, which is typically not an issue with the adult population, is the difficulty of ascertaining a reasonably accurate estimate of premorbid state. Conclusions regarding the impact of current functioning are more readily ascertained and greatly aided if current performance can be compared to preinjury performance. Yet, children's brain development is not yet complete, and without prior records to provide an indication of premorbid

ability, we have little to compare assessment results. Yeates and Taylor (1997) provided evidence to suggest that premorbid neuropsychological functioning can be predicted in children, particulary traumatically brain injured (TBI) children, but that the precision of the prediction is much lower than would prove useful in a clinical context. Another problem encountered in the assessment of children is the potential for greater sensitivity to examiner effects. Similar to neuropsychological assessment of adults, assessment of children must incorporate knowledge of factors that influence test performance before conclusions can be reached regarding the significance of assessment findings. Such factors include but are not limited to the child's age, education, gender, ethnicity, overall socioeconomic standing, anxiety and nervousness, potential medication side effects such as fatigue and altered attentional capacities, sensory disabilities, motivation, premorbid capacities, practice effects, and potential preevaluation priming, particularly on the part of the child's parents or legal representatives. For example, in a study looking at the relationship among several factors, including motivation, ability to perform, ability to learn, and eagerness to participate, several researchers (Adelman, Lauber, Nelson, & Smith, 1989; Deci & Chandler, 1986; Licht & Kistner, 1986) found that motivation plays an integral role in assessing the validity of diagnostic assessment with patients presenting with learning difficulties.

It is common practice in neuropsychological assessment to rely on standardized measures that have normative data to which individual patient performances can be compared, keeping in mind that significant deviation from such norms is not necessarily an indication of central nervous system dysfunction, but may at times be attributed to patient or examiner characteristics that impinge on an otherwise generally objective evaluation. After considering such potential interference factors, however, patient performances can be statistically compared to the reference group. Documentation of either neurocognitive decline or recovery is reliant on repeat evaluations with identical or alternate-form instruments.

Some researchers and clinicians have sought to determine statistical ways of predicting premorbid levels of functioning in children to which post–brain injury performance could be compared. Such research has been met with inconsistency.

One approach is using demographic variables such as educational attainment and familial socioeconomic status that correlate with intelligence. Such attempts demonstrated significant findings for both children and adults (Barona, Reynolds, & Chastain, 1984; Karzmark, Heaton, Grant, & Matthews, 1985; Klesges & Sanchez, 1980; Reynolds & Gutkin, 1979). Yeates and Taylor (1997) sought to predict premorbid functioning for children with acquired TBI through the use of regression equations derived from orthopedic controls, but found that although premorbid neuropsychological functioning could be predicted for TBI children, it was less accurate than would be clinically useful. Two other methods of predicting premorbid functioning, the use of skills such as reading ability (which are related to intelligence but thought to be relatively resistant to brain impairment) (Blair & Spreen, 1989) and regression analysis (combining sociodemographic variables and measures of skills) (Karekan, Gur, & Saykin, 1995; Krull, Scott, & Sherer, 1995), have been applied exclusively to adult populations. Aside from the study by Yeates and Taylor using retrospective parental ratings, demographic variables, and a task of reading skill to predict premorbid functioning in TBI children, we know of no other studies that use demographic variables and measures of concurrent skills to predict premorbid neuropsychological functioning in children. Still another means of approximating premorbid functioning is through the collection of retrospective data such as parental report, school records, and teacher ratings (Levin & Eisenberg, 1979; Richardson, 1963), although this can be hampered by selective memory, lack of quantifiable data, and inadequate definition of standards. All of this underscores the value of assessment of parental intellectual level as one available baseline with documented relationship to a child's expected level of functioning.

The detection of differences between expected performance and actual performance can be useful and informative, particularly in the assessment of children. "The precision and sensitivity of neuropsychological measurement techniques make them valuable tools for investigation of small, sometimes quite subtle behavioral alterations" (Lezak, 1995, p. 14). Neuropsychological assessment efforts with children must contend with factors not generally present in neuropsychological assessment of adults. Abnormal brain functioning in children may be the result of aberrant brain development or early brain injury, either of which may stem from any number of etiological conditions that are beyond the scope of this chapter.

Prior to beginning the evaluation, it is important to determine the best time to conduct an assessment. The primary reason for this concern is the fact that early assessment of brain damage provides an incomplete picture of issues that will arise at a later time. Several studies have suggested that a neuropsychological assessment conducted early in a child's development may be incapable of providing a clear picture of the extent of future deficits at a time when the emergence of additional skills and demands occur (Banich, Cohen-Levine, Kim, & Huttenlocher, 1990; Goldman, 1974; Goldman-Rakic, Isseroff, Schwartz, & Bugbee, 1983; Kolb & Whishaw, 1989). As a result of the complex changes experienced by a child during the course of development, it is often difficult to fully determine associated brain injury sequelae until a later date, when the child begins to learn new information and experiences difficulty in the acquisition or application of such information and when additional behavioral disturbances begin to surface. Such a point was made by Kolb and Fantie (1997) when they suggested that little valuable information would be gained from the assessment of language deficit in a young infant. Several studies have documented the delayed emergence of neurocognitive sequelae following early prefrontal lesions (Eslinger, Grattan, Damasio, & Damasio, 1992; Grattan & Eslinger, 1991; Mateer & Williams, 1991; Mills, Coffey, & Neville, 1994). Ylvisaker (1993) concluded that "persisting communication challenges are often secondary to cognitive and psychosocial disturbances and may coexist with good scores on standardized tests of speech and language development. These problems, often associated with frontal lobe injury, may worsen as the child ages and experiences new developmental challenges" (p. 383).

There is little support for the myth of the unitary pathognomonic deficit. It can be misleading to use the results of a single test or finding evaluated against a fixed scale as an absolute yes-or-no determination of the presence of neuropathology. In addition, the search for a pathognomonic deficit can lead to the conceptualization of potential pathology as what Boll and La Marche (1993) described as a "unitary entity" or a single functional unit. Most pathology cannot be diagnosed or conceptualized using a single neuropsychological instrument. Accurate diagnosis and conceptualization requires confirmatory evidence from multiple measures.

MISPERCEPTIONS ABOUT PEDIATRIC NEUROPSYCHOLOGICAL ASSESSMENT

No chapter on neuropsychological assessment would truly be complete without helping to dispel some of the common misperceptions perpetuated in the field by ill-informed practitioners and laypersons. These misperceptions mislead our patients and potentially circumvent effective intervention priorities and strategies. It is only in the scientific investigation of these misperceptions that truth can be elucidated, and it is here that we can better see the importance of the marriage of both clinical service and research in neuropsychological assessment.

A previous edition of this chapter (Boll & La Marche, 1993) presented information regarding myths of neuropsychological assessment. To spare the reader, the current version provides a summary account of such information with appropriate references and updated material, but refers the reader to the previous edition for a more complete account of this subject matter.

Boll (1993) suggested several distinct "myths" or misperceptions of pediatric neuropsychological assessment that all generally relate to the misperception that children will react, respond, behave, and recover in predictable fashion following brain damage. This myth can be broken down into several discrete but interrelated categories. First, it is often inaccurately assumed that all brain damaged children will experience predictable changes in cognition and behavior. This misperception fails to acknowledge that in reality, brain damage serves to increase the variability of behavior rather than making "life after brain damage" routine and mundane. Numerous studies have attempted to characterize stable patterns of neurocognitive deficits related to brain damage. Yet, just as there were several factors noted above that serve to influence test performance, these same factors (e.g., age, education, and ethnicity), coupled with factors intrinsic to the acquisition of brain damage (including age at injury, location, etiology, severity of injury, and chronicity), all have an impact on the child's neurocognitive functioning

and contribute to between-patient variability. Many studies have demonstrated that brain damage does not contribute to a predictable change in cognition or behavior (Adelman et al., 1989; Boll, 1974, 1978, 1981; Boll & Barth, 1981; Dall'Oglio, Bates, Volterra, Di Capua, Pezzini, 1994; Eide & Tysnes, 1992; Ernhart, Graham, Eichman, Marshall, & Thurston, 1963; Fletcher & Taylor, 1984; Gardner, 1976; Graham et al., 1963; Klonoff & Low, 1974; Klonoff & Paris, 1974; Lezak, 1976, 1995; H.B.C. Reed, Reitan, & Klove, 1965; Smith, 1975, 1981; Taylor, 1986). In fact, "the only commonality in brain injured patients is an increase in behavioral variability" (Boll & La Marche, 1993, p. 134).

The diversity of previously mentioned referral diagnoses provides a window into the various brain injury etiologies and subsequent unending potential neurocognitive and behavioral manifestations. In the earlier days of neuropsychology, there were attempts to classify a patient as either "brain damaged" or "not brain damaged" on the basis of performances on screening instruments such as the Bender Visual Motor Gestalt Test (Bender, 1938) or the Shipley Institute of Living Scale (Zachary, 1986). More recent investigations have indicated the inappropriateness of this practice (Bigler & Ehrfurth, 1981; Phay, 1990). Lezak (1995) suggested, "Two rules should never be broken when conducting a neuropsychological examination: (1) *Treat each patient as an individual*; (2) *Think about what you are doing*" (p. 110). She went on to suggest that, contrary to the one-test screening method espoused earlier in the development of neuropsychological practice, the variety of neurological conditions, individual patient deficits, and referral expectations lead to great variability in the assessment, interpretation, recommendations, and treatment for each patient given a neuropsychological assessment.

Perhaps the research demonstrating the inconsistencies in diagnosis of learning disabled children (Adelman et al., 1989; Dangel & Ensminger, 1988; Reynolds, 1985; Rivers & Smith, 1988) lends further support to the notion that brain injury does not yield reliable, predictable changes in cognition or behavior even within discrete diagnostic categories. If all children with learning disabilities presented with precisely the same clinical profile, consistent diagnosis of the disability could be taken for granted. The rules and regulations for the diagnosis of learning disability are clearly specified in PL 94-142 of the Federal Register (1977) and require that to qualify for learning disability class placement, a student demonstrate a severe discrepancy between aptitude and achievement in at least one of seven permitted achievement domains and that the discrepancy is due to a learning disability and not the result of a sensory handicap, emotional disturbance, or environmental, cultural, or economic disadvantage. Despite the rules and regulations stipulated for a learning disability diagnosis, much variability continues to exist in the diagnostic process. In one study, it was found that in more than half the cases of students not meeting the severe discrepancy cutoff, the student was placed in LD classes anyway (Dangel & Ensminger, 1988). These authors suggested that when making a diagnosis, clinicians relied on professional judgment to place a nonqualifying student into an LD class, but relied less heavily on professional judgment to exclude a qualifying student from services. Hence, it appears that clinicians have a tendency to subjectively prefer to make false-positive diagnostic decisions than false-negative, at least under circumstances affecting the ability of a child to obtain services perceived as helpful (Reynolds, 1985).

We cannot expect unitary behavioral presentations of neurocognitive deficit in the brain injured population, and in fact can expect little predictive power in trying to determine who will experience long-range complaints and decreased adaptive functioning on the basis of neuroradiological findings. Many factors contribute to the variance in neurocognitive presentation, such as the type of lesion, variability in the rate of skill acquisition in the normal population, and extra-individual factors like familial adjustment and adaptation. Eide and Tysnes (1992) suggested that the type of brain lesion identified through CT scans can help determine early outcome in head injured patients, with multifocal brain contusions producing greater neurocognitive deficits and decreased adaptive and social functioning than focal contusions or brain concussion. When there is considerable variability in the rate and ability of skill acquisition in the normal pediatric population (Bates, Dale, & Thal, 1994; Fenson et al., 1993), how then can we expect less variability in the performances of brain damaged children, particularly when we have little in the way of premorbid indices available for comparison (Dall'Oglio et al., 1994)? Taylor (1986) also made the point that brain injury may lead to behavioral deviance on the part of the patient's family and friends, which may

consequently lead to altered behavior on the part of the patient rather than as a direct consequence of brain injury.

While it has been impossible to establish a single or unitary pattern of cognitive and behavioral change following pediatric brain injury, several guidelines can aid in the understanding and interpretation of pediatric neuropsychological assessment performance following brain injury. The potential impact of TBI on pediatric neurocognitive functioning can range from imperceptible to very severe and is reliant on a number of factors. Given any number of combination of factors, certain neurocognitive skills will remain intact while others become significantly impaired. Age at time of injury can have a dramatic impact on neurocognitive functioning and interpretation thereof: younger children may experience neurocognitive decline secondary to brain injury and must then in essence divide cognitive resources to aid in the recovery of such damaged functions while at the same time attempt to continue the normal neurocognitive maturation process, whereas older children will have more established skills and be able to devote more neurocognitive capacity to the recovery process in full (F.C. Goldstein, Levin, Boake, & Lohrey, 1990; Thompson et al., 1994). Particular neurocognitive domains may be more vulnerable to brain injury: neurocognitive compromise is most likely to occur in the more vulnerable complex processes, with attention, mental speed, concept formation, visuoperception, auditory nonverbal perception, tactile form perception, and motor functioning affected more or less in this order (Boll, 1972, 1983; Dreifus, 1975).

To interpret individual neurocognitive sequelae of acquired brain damage with any degree of certainty, one must consider the patient's expected performance based on level of preinjury neurocognitive functioning. Further, consideration must be given to normal expected developmental patterns (Ernhart et al., 1963; Graham et al., 1963). Research has suggested that those patients with better premorbid abilities experience the most significant neurocognitive deficits secondary to injury (Mayes, Pelco, & Campbell, 1989).

The second in a series of misperceptions about the impact of brain injury on children posits that brain injury predictably causes hyperactive motor behavior in children (Boll & La Marche, 1993; Weinberg & Brumback, 1992). This misperception flies in the face of studies that have demonstrated quite the opposite to be true, with either reduced motor speed, strength and coordination, or normal motor skills following pediatric brain injury (Boll, 1974; Klonoff & Low, 1974; Reitan, 1974; Rutter, Graham, & Yule, 1970; Schulman, 1965). Hyperactive features have been found to be somewhat rare in children who have suffered fetal anoxia (Graham, Ernhart, Thurston, & Craft, 1962), head injury (Shaffer, Chadwick, & Rutter, 1975), and cerebral palsy (Seidel, Chadwick, & Rutter, 1975).

The idea of brain damage characteristically causing increased motor behavior and hyperactivity in a uniform pattern is in conflict with findings that suggest that if and when motor impairment occurs following traumatic brain injury, it is more likely to occur in infants and toddlers than in older children (Mahoney et al., 1983; Raimondi & Hirschauer, 1984; Ylvisaker, 1993). Further, Tramontana and Hooper (1997) posited that although hyperactive motor behavior may be a presenting complaint following neurologic disorder, it may also occur in psychiatric or behavioral disorders when no neurologic disorder is present.

Given the possibility that learning disorders, inattention, and hyperactivity can all result from factors in the psychological environment, it is inconceivable that all such sequelae will be direct results of brain damage (Taylor, 1986). Along this line, Weinberg and Brumback (1992) asserted that ADHD really comprises a symptom complex that can be best explained by numerous specific disease conditions and that the symptoms of inattention or hyperactivity should alert the investigator of potential underlying psychiatric conditions such as depression, mania, and narcolepsy. In fact, they posit that "comorbidity and concurrent diagnoses are explainable as a consequence of interactions between affected brain centers" (p. 442).

The effect of brain damage on motoric behavior varies according to the etiology and severity of the damage and may be exhibited by an increase or decrease in preferred behavior. Research seems to refute expectation that there will be behavioral manifestation of change in motoric function secondary to brain injury.

It is commonly believed that children are better able to recover and/or compensate for brain injury than are similarly injured adults. This theory is intricately related to plasticity theory, which suggests the brain's ability to change and compensate for loss of function following damage. Some believe that a child's brain can shift functioning so that the uninjured areas compensate for the decreased functioning of the damaged areas, whereas the neurocognitive organization of adults is inflexible and rigid, leading to the belief that adult brains are less able to compensate for lost abilities in damaged areas. If one follows this theory, then it might be believable that brain injured adults will present with more neurocognitive symptomatology than would children secondary to the loss of function and reorganization capabilities.

Plasticity theory is largely based on the work of Kennard (1936, 1938), who was the first to look at such theories in primate studies. Kennard reported the effects of lesions in the motor cortex and the ultimate recovery of motor function. She also reported that some primates seemingly developed certain symptoms at a later stage but to a lesser degree than adult primates with similar lesions. Yet, despite these reports, those who promulgate the misconception that children possess better neurocognitive recovery processes than adults seem to forget that even Kennard never espoused a general sparing of capacity in young brain injured primates, but rather reported significant deficits following prefrontal injury in very young as opposed to older primates (Dennis, 1991; Finger, 1991; Kennard & Fulton, 1942).

Lenneberg (1967), however, found some supporting evidence for the theory of plasticity as it relates to the neurodevelopment of children. Plasticity theory holds that whereas gross anatomical development of the brain occurs prenatally, the development of neurological functioning occurs during the maturational process in children. Lenneberg concluded that greater recovery rates among children were due to the ongoing maturational process in the still developing brains of children.

Plasticity theory predicts that prognosis is inversely related to age; the younger the patient at the time of injury, the better the likelihood of recovery. However, there is little scientific support for the misperception that younger patients enjoy greater recovery and prognosis following brain injury. Recently, Levin and colleagues (Levin et al., 1993) reported support for the work of Brink, Garrett, Hale, Woo-Sam, and Nickel (1970) and Levin, Eisenberg, Wigg, and Kobayashi (1982), indicating that head injury severity may have a more adverse impact on the intellectual ability of young children (6–10 years of age) than of older children and adolescents.

Levin and colleagues postulated that the young brain has not fully developed centers of focus for cognitive abilities. Because of this, developmental neuropathologies tend to be less focal and more diffuse in their ramifications. Isaacson (1975) questioned the differences in causality of brain injury in adults versus children and suggested that these differences contribute to differential outcomes. Isaacson identified numerous ramifications of TBI and used these to suggest that brain injury is complexly related to brain structure, not age of onset.

Thompson et al. (1994) reported that older children experience more rapid neurocognitive recovery than do younger children, and suggested that this might be attributed either to an interaction between age and recovery, leading to a more protracted recovery period for younger children, or to the increased skill development demands on younger children in addition to the necessary recovery process, whereas older children have neared developmental performance plateaus, necessitating only recovery to premorbid levels of functioning. They described flatter recovery curves for younger children; the recovery curves of older children and adults would initially be steep but then flat, indicative of less maturation and quicker recovery. Perhaps an unexpected finding was that although more severely injured children recovered at a slower rate than less severely injured young children, there was no significant difference in the rate of recovery between severely injured and less severely injured adolescents. There have also been reports of no significant performance differences across age groups (Chadwick, Rutter, Shaffer, & Shrout, 1981).

There is some indication that older brain injured children recover from motor impairment more quickly than do infants and toddlers (Mahoney et al., 1983; Raimondi & Hirschauer, 1984). Research looking at preschoolers has found slower recovery on intellectual, language, and motor measures for younger versus older preschoolers with similar injuries (Ewing-Cobbs, Miner, Fletcher, & Levin, 1989). When looking at language recovery in children who experienced prolonged unconsciousness, children with closed head injuries were more likely to regain language than were children who had experienced crushing or penetrating head injuries. Those children who experienced the greatest improvement in language were older at the time of injury (Kriel, Krach, Luxenberg, & Chun, 1995). Finally, there have been numerous studies that

suggest that neurocognitive recovery of young school-aged children is slower or at the very least comparable to but not faster than that of older adolescents (Brink et al., 1970; Chadwick et al., 1981; Ewing-Cobbs, Levin, Eisenberg, & Fletcher, 1987; Klonoff et al., 1977; Levin et al., 1982; Ylvisaker, 1993).

The Kennard principle is intuitive. We would like to believe that the younger the child, the better the prognosis, but this intuition and the assumptions behind it have actually not been borne out. A review of the literature indicates that a preponderance of scientific studies refute the Kennard principle. Studies in support of the principle, particularly as it relates to neurocognitive functioning, are hard to find and tend to date back several decades, with little in the way of recent verification. The Kennard principle, however, must be recognized for its historical significance: it established the need to consider the state of the organism as one of the defining factors related to neuropathological deficits.

Yet another misconception related to pediatric neuropsychological assessment is the expectation that brain damage causes serious emotional disturbance. It has been estimated that approximately 30% to 35% of brain damaged children experience subsequent emotional disturbance. Although this figure is significantly higher than that for non–brain damaged children, there is no documentation of a causal relationship between brain injury and emotional disturbance, nor has there been any characteristic behavior or syndrome identified (Boll, Berent, & Richards, 1977; Ernhart et al., 1963; Rutter, 1977; Shaffer, 1974; Tramontanta & Hooper, 1997). Organic mental syndromes and disorders for adults, delineated by the American Psychiatric Association (1987) in the *DSM-III-R*, are now subsumed under delirium, dementia, amnestic disorders, and other cognitive disorders (e.g. cognitive disorder NOS) diagnostic headings in the fourth edition (American Psychiatric Association, 1994), but are not clearly specified for, nor necessarily relevant to, acquired TBI. Some provision is now made for a diagnosis of mental disorders due to a general medical condition. This diagnostic problem is even greater for children in whom a neurological condition interacts more actively with the developmental situation cognitively, socially, and emotionally. Diagnostic categorization is virtually always required to obtain third-party reimbursement. Whereas previous etiology-free classifications for children such as developmental disorders of academic skills and/or pervasive developmental disorder not otherwise specified may have missed the difference between developmental and acquired disorders, the new provision for disorders secondary to a general medical condition may begin to fill the gap. The natural history of developmental versus acquired brain abnormalities is quite different, and therefore, the diagnosis and treatment appropriate for one may be very inappropriate for the other.

Several factors may interact and contribute to personality changes following brain injury, including aberrant brain activity, cognitive deficits impacting independent functioning and self-awareness, fatigue and decreased stamina, medication effects, and reduced frustration tolerance, social perceptiveness, self-control, learned social behavior, and the appropriate temperance of emotions (Livingston, 1990; Rutter, 1977). In fact, it has been suggested that attention to and treatment of emotional distress in the brain injured patient may have the potential benefits of improving recovery rate and minimizing postinjury confusion (Livingston, 1990; Prigatano et al., 1984). Whereas the *DSM-III-R* didn't provide for a diagnostic acknowledgment and/or validation of postinjury emotional sequelae, the *DSM-IV* allows for a diagnosis based on personality disturbances secondary to a general medical condition. Although this may not diminish potential social stigma or personal frustration, it allows the patient to accept the changes as a manifestation of injury as opposed to adopting an internal locus of control for such seemingly uncontrollable postinjury experiences.

Although many patients may experience some degree of subclinical emotional sequelae secondary to brain injury, many may find the secondary difficulties in academic and social adjustment more pervasive and perhaps more directly troublesome (Gulbrandsen, 1984). The lack of a stereotypical psychiatric syndrome in no way negates the potential for behavioral and emotional ramifications of brain injury. There are many potential emotional sequelae secondary to brain injury, ranging from emotional lability to temper outbursts and decreased anger management to irritability, social withdrawal, and boredom (Boll, 1983). The potential exists for adjustment difficulties not only for the brain injured patient but for the patient's family as well (Jacobs, 1984). Several studies have been conducted in an attempt to elucidate the impact of pediatric craniocerebral trauma on familial adjustment (Tarter, 1990). These have suggested that

greater stress is experienced by families and parents of brain injured children who exhibit greater behavioral and emotional disturbance. It was suggested that parents and other family members be included in rehabilitative efforts to enhance their own understanding, self-investment, and adjustment strategies in addition to the child's overall adaptive outcome, which will have long-term implications for adjustment into adulthood.

It has been said that "knowledge is power" and this holds true for the ultimate adjustment of the pediatric brain injured patient and family. While the patient experiences postinjury confusion and foreign emotional disturbance, the patient's family too experiences confusion, concern, and at times frustration regarding "normal," anticipated, and expected sequelae secondary to brain injury. Without appropriate education and explanation, patients, families, and other caretakers are left to make inaccurate assumptions and potentially detrimental causal attributions. In the case of pediatric brain injury, a little knowledge can assist patients and their families in understanding and adjusting to the ramifications of a brain injury.

Another common misperception is the belief that "intact" or average neuropsychological performance on neurocognitive measures equates with "normal" abilities in the real world. Caution must be taken in the interpretive process, as performance in the average range does not necessarily represent normalcy for any one specific patient. An example of this was provided by Bruel and Albee (1962) and Russell (1976) in case studies demonstrating the possible acquisition of test scores in the average range for hemispherectomized patients (possessing only one cerebral hemisphere). Many studies in both the pediatric and adult neuropsychological literature support the notion that patients may in fact demonstrate intact performance on any number of measures, including those that assess intellectual capacity and language, following frontal lobe injury; however, inspection of academic or daily functional adaptation suggests that there is some degree of neurocognitive compromise (Benton, 1991; Bigler, 1988; Dennis, 1991; Eslinger & Damasio, 1985; Grattan & Eslinger, 1991; Mateer & Williams, 1991; Stuss & Benson, 1986; Welsh, Pennington, & Grossier, 1991). Fletcher, Ewing-Cobbs, Miner, and Levin (1990) found significant behavioral adjustment difficulties in young closed head injured children and adolescents despite demonstration on tests of good neurocognitive ability. Ylvisaker

(1993) studied the recovery of speech and language in children and adolescents who had sustained a TBI. He concluded that as a whole, these children experienced much greater success in the midst of tightly controlled conditions but experienced much greater difficulty and at times unsuitable public behavior. Ylvisaker suggested that this argues for "pragmatic analysis based on contextually more realistic and less highly structured interactions" (p. 375). Perrott, Taylor, and Montes (1991) also looked at the outcome of pediatric TBI patients, but provided an interesting control of environmental factors and genetic variability through the use of a sibling control group. Although they found no significant differences between the injured and non-injured sibling groups on eventual neuropsychological functioning, the TBI group demonstrated significantly greater behavior problems, poorer academic performance, greater parent-child interaction difficulties, and, in general, considerably greater challenge coping with daily living demands.

Even the use of standardized norms for comparison purposes does not ensure accurate diagnostic or descriptive labels: standardized norms represent typical or average performances for the population tested, but any individual patient may have started out with more or less skill or ability prior to cranio-cerebral trauma than represented in the standardization sample. What can be considered "normal" for a patient is actually a composite of individual assets and deficiencies. Less than average performances may occur due to several factors other than or in addition to the specific injury and may include premorbid traits, individual biases, or response to damage (Boll, 1983).

Conversely, at least in some instances, the presence of "atypical" scores does not necessarily imply aberrant performance. Fletcher and Taylor (1984) referred to the assumption that poor performance on assessment measures is verification of brain dysfunction without regard for other potential sources of variability (such as experiential, socioeducational, or emotional factors) as the "brain-behavior isomorphism fallacy." Such is the potential case for normal, non–brain injured children who demonstrate scattered performances within or between tests (Kaufman, 1981). In reality, little evidence has been found for significant differences in subtest scatter on instruments such as the WISC-R (Wechsler, 1974) between learning disabled and nondisabled children (Ackerman, Peters, & Dykman, 1971; Anderson, Kaufman, & Kaufman, 1976).

Fletcher and Taylor (1984) described other misunderstandings that taint an accurate understanding of the association between a child's neuropsychological test performance and the concomitant structural integrity of the brain. The differential-sensitivity assumption implies that test findings ascribed to brain injury in adults is commensurate with what would be expected in brain injured children. Rather, it must be acknowledged that measures derived for use with adults may not be sensitive neurobehavioral measures in children. The similar-skills assumption posits that neuropsychological measures intended for use with adults measure similar domains in children, hence the use of stepped-down age norms from traditional adult measures mentioned previously. Evidence to the contrary was provided by Fletcher and Taylor (1984), who referenced studies demonstrating age-based differences between children and adults on neuropsychological processes including language (Segalowitz, 1983), memory (Kail, 1984), and reading (Bakker, 1984). The special sign assumption refers to the tendency of either inferring brain damage from specific test behaviors (pathognomonic signs, if you will) or relying on signs of brain dysfunction in adults as valid indicators of brain dysfunction in children despite the lack of evidence for comparable behavioral pathologies in both adults and children secondary to similar etiological conditions (Boll & La Marche, 1993; Fletcher & Taylor, 1984).

CONCLUSION

Much work has been done in the field of pediatric neuropsychological assessment since the original version of this chapter was written. New test development and increased scientific investigation have helped further the understanding not only of neuropsychological functioning in children, but also of the contribution that clinical child neuropsychologists can make in diagnosis, treatment, and management of pediatric neurologic disorders in addition to the rehabilitation and adaptation of the pediatric patient and family. The recent advances have provided greater support for neuropsychological truths while helping to further dispel the common misperceptions in the field. Pediatric neuropsychology has been shown to make a contribution to the overall health and well-being of pediatric patients through diagnosis, description, clarification, treatment, and rehabilitation. Continued clinical service and scientific investigation will help solidify the ability of pediatric neuropsychology to contribute to the pediatric multidisciplinary health care service.

REFERENCES

Ackerman, P.T., Peters, J.E., & Dykman, R.A. (1971). Children with specific learning disabilities: WISC profiles. *Journal of Learning Disabilities, 4*(3), 33–49.

Adelman, H.S., Lauber, B.A., Nelson, P., & Smith, D.C. (1989). Toward a procedure for minimizing and detecting false positive diagnoses of learning disability. *Journal of Learning Disabilities, 22*(4), 234–244.

American Psychiatric Association. (1987). *Diagnostic and statistical manual of mental disorders* (3rd ed., rev.). Washington, DC: Author.

American Psychiatric Association. (1994). *Diagnostic and statistical manual of mental disorders* (4th ed.). Washington, DC: Author.

Anderson, K., Kaufman, A., & Kaufman, N. (1976). Use of the WISC-R with a learning disabled population: Some diagnostic implications. *Psychology in the Schools, 23*(4), 381–386.

Anderson, R.M. (1994). *Practitioner's guide to clinical neuropsychology.* New York: Plenum Press.

Bakker, D.J. (1984). The brain as a dependent variable. *Journal of Clinical Neuropsychology, 6*(1), 1–16.

Banich, M.T., Levine, S.C., Kim, H., & Huttenlocher, P. (1990). The effects of developmental factors on IQ in hemiplegic children. *Neuropsychologia, 28*(1), 35–47.

Barona, A., Reynolds, C.R., & Chastain, R. (1984). A demographically based index of premorbid intelligence for the WAIS-R. *Journal of Consulting and Clinical Psychology, 52,* 885–887.

Bates, E., Dale, P., & Thal, D. (1994). Individual differences and their complications in language development. In P. Fletcher & B. MacWhinney (Eds.), *Handbook of language acquisition.* Oxford, England: Oxford University Press.

Bender, L.A. (1938). Visual Motor Gestalt Test and its clinical use. *American Orthopsychiatric Association Research Monograph* (No. 3). New York: American Orthopsychiatric Association.

Benton, A. (1991). Prefrontal injury and behavior in children. *Developmental Neuropsychology, 7*(3), 275–281.

Bigler, E.D. (1988). Frontal lobe damage and neuropsychological assessment. *Archives of Clinical Neuropsychology, 3,* 279–297.

Bigler, E.D., & Ehrfurth, J.W. (1981). The continued inappropriate singular use of the Bender Visual Motor Gestalt Test. *Professional Psychology, 12*(5), 562–569.

Blair, J.R., & Spreen, O. (1989). Predicting premorbid IQ: A revision of the National Adult Reading Test. *Clinical Neuropsychologist, 3,* 129–136.

Boll, T.J. (1972). Conceptual vs. perceptual vs. motor deficits in brain-damaged children. *Journal of Clinical Psychology, 28,* 157–159.

Boll, T.J. (1974). Behavioral correlates of cerebral damage in children aged 9–14. In R.M. Reitan & L.A. Davison (Eds.), *Clinical neuropsychology: Current status and applications.* Washington, DC: Winston.

Boll, T.J. (1978). Diagnosing brain impairment. In B.B. Wolman (Ed.), *Clinical diagnosis of mental disorders.* New York: Plenum Press.

Boll, T.J. (1981). The Halstead–Reitan Neuropsychology Battery. In S.B. Filskov & T.J. Boll (Eds.), *Handbook of clinical neuropsychology.* New York: Wiley.

Boll, T.J. (1983). Neuropsychological assessment of the child: Myths, current status, and future prospects. In C.E. Walker & M.C. Roberts (Eds.), *Handbook of clinical child neuropsychology* (pp. 107–127). New York: Wiley.

Boll, T.J. (1988). Neuropsychological assessment of children. In P. Karoly (Ed.), *Handbook of child health assessment: Biopsychosocial perspectives.* New York: Wiley.

Boll, T.J. (1993). *Children's Category Test.* San Antonio: Psychological Corporation.

Boll, T.J., & Barth, J. (1981). Neuropsychology of brain damaged children. In S.B. Filskov & T.J. Boll (Eds.), *Handbook of clinical neuropsychology.* New York: Wiley.

Boll, T.J., Berent, S., & Richards, H. (1977). Tactile perceptual functions as a factor in general psychological abilities. *Perceptual and Motor Skills, 47,* 491–495.

Boll, T.J., & La Marche, J.A. (1993). Neuropsychological assessment of the child: Myths, current status, and future prospects. In C.E. Walker (Ed.), *Handbook of clinical child psychology.* New York: Wiley.

Brink, J.D., Garrett, A.L., Hale, W.R., Woo-Sam, J., & Nickel, V.L. (1970). Recovery of motor and intellectual function in children sustaining severe head injuries. *Developmental Medicine and Child Neurology, 12,* 565–571.

Bruel, J.H., & Albee, G.W. (1962). Higher intellectual functions in a patient with hemispherectomy for tumors. *Journal of Consulting Psychology, 15,* 281–285.

Chadwick, O.F.D., Rutter, M., Shaffer, D., & Shrout, P.E. (1981). A prospective study of children with head injuries, IV: Specific cognitive deficits. *Journal of Clinical Neuropsychology, 3,* 101–120.

Dall'Oglio, A.M., Bates, E., Volterra, V., DiCapua, M., & Pezzini, G. (1994). Early cognition, communication and language in children with focal brain injury. *Developmental Medicine and Child Neurology, 36*(12), 1076–1098.

Dangel, H.L., & Ensminger, E.E. (1988). The use of a discrepancy formula with LD students. *Learning Disability Focus, 4*(1), 24–31.

Deci, E.L., & Chandler, C.L. (1986). The importance of motivation for the future of the LD field. *Journal of Learning Disabilities, 19*(10), 587–594.

Delis, D.C., Kramer, J., Kaplan, E., & Ober, B.A. (1994). *California Verbal Learning Test–Children's Version.* New York: Psychological Corporation.

Dennis, M. (1988). Language and the young damaged brain. In T.J. Boll & B.K. Bryant (Eds.), *Clinical neuropsychology and brain function: Research, measurement and practice*. Washington, DC: American Psychological Association.

Dreifus, F.P. (1975). The pathology of central communicative disorders in children. In D.B. Tower (Ed.), *The nervous system: Human communication and its disorders* (Vol. 3). New York: Raven Press.

Eide, P.K., & Tysnes, O.B. (1992). Early and late outcome in head injury patients with radiological evidence of brain damage. *Acta Neurologica Scandinavica, 86*, 194–198.

Ernhart, C.B., Graham, F.K., Eichman, P.L., Marshall, J.M., & Thurston, D. (1963). Brain injury in the preschool child: Some developmental considerations: II. Comparison of brain-injured and normal children. *Psychological Monographs, 77*(Whole No. 574), 17–33.

Eslinger, P.J., & Damasio, A.R. (1985, December). Severe disturbance of higher cognition after bilateral frontal lobe ablation: Patient EVR. *Neurology, 35*(12), 1731–1741.

Eslinger, P.J., Grattan, L.M., Damasio, H., & Damasio, A.R. (1992). Developmental consequences of childhood frontal lobe damage. *Archives of Neurology, 49*(7), 764–769.

Ewing-Cobbs, L., Levin, H.S., Eisenberg, H.M., & Fletcher, J.M. (1987, October). Language functions following closed-head injury in children and adolescents. *Journal of Clinical and Experimental Neuropsychology, 9*(5), 575–592.

Ewing-Cobbs, L., Miner, M.E., Fletcher, J.M., & Levin, H.S. (1989, December). Intellectual, motor, and language sequelae following closed head injury in infants and preschoolers. *Journal of Pediatric Psychology, 14*(4), 531–547.

Federal Register. (1976). v. 41, pp. 52404–52407. Washington, DC, ISSN: 0097–6326.

Federal Register. (1977). v. 42, p. 42478. Washington, DC, ISSN: 0097–6326.

Fenson, L., Dale, P., Reznick, S., Thal, D., Bates, E., Hartung, J., Pethick, S., & Reily, J. (1993). *MacArthur Communicative Development Inventories: Technical manual*. San Diego, CA: Singular Press.

Filskov, S.B., & Boll, T.J. (1981). *Handbook of clinical neuropsychology*. New York: Wiley.

Filskov, S.B., & Goldstein, S.G. (1974). Diagnostic validity of the Halstead–Reitan neuropsychological battery. *Journal of Consulting and Clinical Psychology, 42*, 383–388.

Finger, S. (1991). Brain damage, development, and behavior: Early findings. *Developmental Neuropsychology, 7*(3), 261–274.

Fletcher, J.M., Ewing-Cobbs, L., Miner, M.E., Levin, H.S., & Eisenberg, H.M. (1990). Behavioral changes after closed head injury in children. *Journal of Consulting and Clinical Psychology, 58*(1), 93–98.

Fletcher, J.M., & Taylor, H.G. (1984, February). Neuropsychological approaches to children: Toward a developmental neuropsychology. *Journal of Clinical Neuropsychology, 6*(1), 39–56.

Gardner, L. (1976). Review: Is brain damage a useful concept? *Child Care, Health and Development, 2*(6), 395–411.

Golden, C.J. (1981). The Luria–Nebraska Children's Battery: Theory and formulation. In G.W. Hynd & J.E. Obrzut (Eds.), *Neuropsychological assessment and the school-age child: Issues and perspectives* (pp. 277–302). New York: Grune & Stratton.

Goldman, P.S. (1974). An alternative to developmental plasticity: Heterology of CNS structures in infants and adults. In D.G. Stein, J.J. Rosen, & N. Butters (Eds.), *Plasticity and recovery of function in the central nervous system* (pp. 149–174). New York: Academic Press.

Goldman-Rakie, P.S., Isseroff, A., Schwartz, M.L., & Bugbee, N.M. (1983). The neurobiology of cognitive development. In P. Mussen (Ed.), *Handbook of child psychology: Biology and infancy development* (pp. 281–344). New York: Wiley.

Goldstein, F.C., Levin, H.S., Boake, C., & Lohrey, J.H. (1990). Facilitation of memory performance through closed head injury. *Journal of Clinical and Experimental Neuropsychology, 12*, 286–300.

Goldstein, S.G., Deysach, R.E., & Kleinknecht, R.A. (1973). Effect of experience and amount of information on identification of cerebral impairment. *Journal of Consulting and Clinical Psychology, 41*, 30–34.

Graham, F.K., Ernhart, C.B., Craft, M., & Berman, P.W. (1963). Brain injury in the preschool child: Some developmental considerations: I. Performance of normal children. *Psychological Monographs, 77*(Whole No. 573), 1–16.

Graham, F.K., Ernhart, C.B., Thurston, D., & Craft, M. (1962). Development three years after perinatal anoxia and other potentially damaging newborn experiences. *Psychological Monographs, 76*(Whole No. 522).

Grattan, L.M., & Eslinger, P.J. (1991). Frontal lobe damage in children and adults: A comparative review. *Developmental Neuropsychology, 7*(3), 283–326.

Gulbrandsen, G.B. (1984). Neuropsychological sequelae of light head injuries in older children six months after trauma. *Journal of Clinical Neuropsychology, 6*(3), 257–268.

Hammock, M.K., Milhorat, T.H., & Baron, I.S. (1976). Normal pressure hydrocephalus in patients with myelomeningocele. *Developmental Medicine in Child Neurology, 18*(Suppl. 37), 55–68.

Isaacson, R.L. (1975). The myth of recovery from early brain damage. In N. Ellis (Ed.), *Aberrant development in infancy*. London: Wiley.

Jacobs, H.E. (1984). The family as a therapeutic agent: Long-term rehabilitation for traumatic head injury patients. *Final Report*. Los Angeles: National Institute of Handicapped Research.

Kail, R., & Nippold, M.A. (1984). Unconstrained retrieval from semantic memory. *Child Development, 55*(3), 944–951.

Karekan, D.A., Gur, R.C., & Saykin, A.J. (1995). Reading on the Wide Range Achievement Test–Revised and parental education as predictors of IQ: Comparison with the Barona formula. *Archives of Clinical Neuropsychology, 10*, 147–157.

Karzmark, P., Heaton, R.K., Grant, I., & Matthews, C.G. (1985). Use of demographic variables to predict Full Scale IQ: A replication and extension. *Journal of Clinical and Experimental Neuropsychology, 7*, 412–420.

Kaufman, A.S. (1981, November). The WISC-R and learning disabilities assessment: State of the art. *Journal of Learning Disabilities, 14*(9), 520–526.

Kennard, M.A. (1936). Age and other factors in motor recovery from precentral lesions in monkeys. *American Journal of Physiology, 115*, 138–146.

Kennard, M.A. (1938). Reorganization of motor function in the cerebral cortex of monkeys deprived of motor and premotor areas in infancy. *Journal of Neurophysiology, 1*, 477–496.

Kennard, M.A., & Fulton, J.F. (1942). Age and reorganization of central nervous system. *Mt. Sinai Journal of Medicine, 9*, 594–606.

Klesges, R.C., & Sanchez, V.C. (1980). Cross-validation of an index of premorbid intellectual functioning in children. *Journal of Consulting and Clinical Psychology, 49*, 141.

Klonoff, H., & Low, M. (1974). Disordered brain function in young children and early adolescents: Neuropsychological and electroencephalographic correlates. In R.M. Reitan & L.A. Davison (Eds.), *Clinical neuropsychology: Current status and applications* (pp. 121–178). Washington, DC: Winston.

Klonoff, H., Low, M.D., & Clark, C. (1977). Head injuries in children: A prospective five-year follow-up. *Journal of Neurology, Neurosurgery and Psychiatry, 40*, 1211–1219.

Klonoff, H., & Paris, R. (1974). Immediate, short-term and residual effects of acute head injuries in children: Neuropsychological and neurological correlates. In R.M. Reitan & L.A. Davison (Eds.), *Clinical neuropsychology: Current status and applications* (pp. 179–210). Washington, DC: Winston.

Knights, R.M., & Hinton, G.G. (1973). *Neuropsychological test results in children of posterior fossa tumors* (Research Bulletin No. 7). Ottawa, Canada: Carleton University, Department of Psychology.

Knights, R.M., Hinton, G.G., & Drader, D. (1973). *Changes in intellectual ability with Duchenne Muscular Dystrophy* (Research Bulletin No. 8). Ottawa, Canada: Carleton University, Department of Psychology.

Kolb, B., & Fantie, B. (1997). Development of the child's brain and behavior. In C.R. Reynolds & E. Fletcher-Janzen (Eds.), *Handbook of clinical child neuropsychology* (2nd ed., pp. 17–41). New York: Plenum Press.

Kolb, B., & Wishaw, I.Q. (1989). Plasticity in the neocortex: Mechanisms underlying recovery from early brain damage. *Progress in Neurology, 32*, 235–276.

Korkman, M., Kirk, U., & Kemp, S. (1998). *NEPSY: A developmental neuropsychological assessment*. New York: Psychological Corporation.

Kriel, R.L., Krach, L.E., Luxenberg, M., & Chun, C. (1995). Recovery of language skills in children after prolonged unconsciousness. *Journal of Neurologic Rehabilitation, 9*(3), 145–150.

Krull, K.R., Scott, J.G., & Sherer, M. (1995). Estimation of premorbid intelligence from combined performance and demographic variables. *Clinical Neuropsychologist, 9*, 83–88.

Lenneberg, E. (1967). *Biological foundations of language*. New York: Wiley.

Levin, H.S., & Eisenberg, H.M. (1979). Neuropsychological outcome of closed-head injury children and adolescents. *Journal of Pediatric Psychology, 4*, 389–402.

Levin, H.S., Eisenberg, H.M., Wigg, N.R., & Kobayashi, K. (1982). Memory and intellectual ability after head injury in children and adolescents. *Neurosurgery, 11*, 668–673.

Levin, H.S., Mattis, S., Ruff, R.M., Eisenberg, H.M., Marshall, L.F., & Tabaddor, K. (1987). Neurobehavioral outcome of minor head injury: A three-center study. *Journal of Neurosurgery, 66*, 234–243.

Lezak, M.D. (1976). *Neuropsychological assessment*. New York: Oxford University Press.

Lezak, M.D. (1995). *Neuropsychological assessment* (3rd ed.). New York: Oxford University Press.

Licht, B.G., & Kistner, J.A. (1986). Motivational problems of learning disabled children: Individual differences and their implications for treatment. In J. Torgesen & B.Y.L. Wong (Eds.), *Psychological and educational perspectives on learning disabilities* (pp. 225–255). Orlando, FL: Academic Press.

Livingston, M.G. (1990). Effects on the family system. In M. Rosenthal, E.R. Griffith, M.R. Bord, & J.D. Miller (Eds.), *Rehabilitation of the adult and child with traumatic brain injury*. Philadelphia: F.A. Davis.

Mahoney, W.J., D'Souza, B.J., Haller, J.A., Rogers, M.C., Epstein, M.M., & Freeman, J.M. (1983). Long-term outcome of children with severe head trauma and prolonged coma. *Pediatrics, 71*, 756–761.

Mateer, C.A., & Williams, D. (1991). Effects of frontal lobe injury in childhood. *Developmental Neuropsychology, 7*(2), 359–376.

Mathews, C.G., Shaw, D.J., & Klov, H. (1966). Psychological test performances in neurologic and "pseudoneurologic" subjects. *Cortex, 2,* 244–253.

Mayes, S.D., Pelco, L.E., & Campbell, C.J. (1989). Relationships among pre- and post-injury intelligence, length of coma and age in individuals with severe closed head injuries. *Brain Injury, 3,* 301–313.

Mills, D., Coffey, S., & Neville, H. (1994). Changes in cerebral reorganization in infancy during primary language acquisition. In G. Dawson & K. Fischer (Eds.), *Human behavior and the developing brain* (pp. 427–455). New York: Guilford Press.

O'Leary, D.S., Seidenberg, M., Berent, S., & Boll, T.J. (1981). The effect of age on onset of tonic-clonic seizures on neuropsychological performance in children. *Epilepsia, 22,* 197–204.

Phay, A.J. (1990). Shipley Institute of Living Scale: Part 2–Assessment of intelligence and cognitive deterioration. *Medical Psychotherapy, 3,* 17–35.

Prigatano, G.P., Fordyce, D.J., Zeiner, H.K., Roueche, J.R., Pepping, M., & Wood, M.C. (1984). Neuropsychological rehabilitation after closed head injury in young adults. *Journal of Neurology, Neurosurgery, and Psychiatry, 47,* 505–513.

Putnam, S.H., & DeLuca, J.W. (1990). The TCN Professional Practice Survey: I. General practices of neuropsychologists in primary employment and private practice settings. *Clinical Neuropsychologist, 4*(3), 199–243.

Raimondi, A.J., & Hirschauer, J. (1984). Head injury in the infant and toddler: Coma Scoring and Outcome Scale. *Child's Brain, 11*(1), 12–35.

Reed, H.B.C., Reitan, R.M., & Klove, H. (1965). Influence of cerebral lesions on psychological test performance of older children. *Journal of Consulting Psychology, 29,* 247–251.

Reitan, R.M. (1969). *Manual for administration of neuropsychological test batteries for adults and children.* Indianapolis, IN: Author.

Reitan, R.M. (1974). Psychological effects of cerebral lesions in children of early school age. In R.M. Reitan & L.A. Davison (Eds.), *Clinical neuropsychology: Current status and applications.* Washington, DC: Winston.

Reitan, R.M., & Boll, T.J. (1973). Neuropsychological correlates of minimal brain dysfunction. *Annals of New York Academy of Science, 205,* 65–88.

Reitan, R.M., & Davison, L.A. (Eds.). (1974). *Clinical neuropsychology: Current status and applications.* New York: Wiley.

Reitan, R.M., & Wolfson, D. (1992a). *Neuropsychological evaluation of older children.* Tucson, AZ: Neuropsychology Press.

Reitan, R.M., & Wolfson, D. (1992b). *Neuropsychological evaluation of young children.* Tucson, AZ: Neuropsychology Press.

Reynolds, C.R. (1985, Winter). Critical measurement issues in learning disabilities. *Journal of Special Education, 18*(4), 451–476.

Reynolds, C.R., & Bigler, E. (1994). *Tests of Memory and Learning.* Los Angeles: Western Psychological Services.

Reynolds, C.R., & Gutkin, T.B. (1979). Prediction of the premorbid intellectual status of children using demographic data. *Clinical Neuropsychology, 1,* 36–38.

Richardson, F. (1963). Some effects of severe head injury: A follow-up study of children and adolescents after protracted coma. *Developmental Medicine and Child Neurology, 5,* 471–482.

Rivers, D., & Smith, T.E. (1988). Traditional eligibility criteria for identifying students as specific learning disabled. *Journal of Learning Disabilities, 21*(10), 642–644.

Rourke, B.P., Bakker, D.J., Fisk, J.L., & Strang, J.D. (1983). *Child neuropsychology: An introduction to theory, research and practice.* New York: Guilford Press.

Rourke, B.P., Fisk, J.L., & Strange, J.D. (1986). *Neuropsychological assessment of children: A treatment-oriented approach.* New York: Guilford Press.

Russell, E.W. (1976). The Bender–Gestalt and the Halstead–Reitan Battery: A case study. *Journal of Clinical Psychology, 32,* 355–361.

Rutter, M. (1977). Brain damage syndromes in childhood: Concepts and findings. *Journal of Child Psychology and Psychiatry, 18,* 1–21.

Rutter, M., Graham, P., & Yule, W. (1970). A neuropsychiatric study in childhood. *Clinics and Developmental Medicine* (Nos. 35 and 36). London: Simp/Seineman.

Satz, P., & Fletcher, J.M. (1981). Emergent trends in neuropsychology: An overview. *Journal of Consulting and Clinical Psychology, 49,* 851–865.

Schulman, J.L. (1965). *Brain damage and behavior.* Springfield, IL: Thomas.

Segalowitz, S. (Ed.). (1983). *Language functions and brain organization.* New York: Academic Press.

Seidel, U.P., Chadwick, O.F.D., & Rutter, M. (1975). Psychological disorders in crippled children: A comparative study of children with and without brain damage. *Developmental Medicine and Child Neurology, 17,* 563–573.

Seidenberg, M., O'Leary, D.S., Giordani, B., Berent, S., & Boll, T.J. (1981). Test-retest IQ changes of epilepsy patients: Assessing the influence of practice effects. *Journal of Clinical Neuropsychology, 3,* 237–255.

Selz, M., & Reitan, R.M. (1979). Neuropsychological test performance of normal, learning disabled, and brain damaged children. *Journal of Nervous and Mental Disease, 167,* 298–302.

Shaffer, D. (1974). Suicide in childhood and early adolescence. *Journal of Child Psychology and Psychiatry, 15,* 275–291.

Shaffer, D., Chadwick, O., & Rutter, M. (1975). Psychiatric outcome of localized head injury in children. *Ciba Foundation Symposium, 34,* 191–213.

Sheslow, D., & Adams, W. (1990). *Wide Range Assessment of Memory and Learning.* Wilmington, DE: Jastak Associates.

Smith, A. (1975). Neuropsychological testing in neurological disorders. In W.J. Friedlander (Ed.), *Advances in Neurology, 7,* New York: Raven Press.

Smith, A. (1981). Principles underlying human brain functions in neuropsychological sequelae of different neuropathological processes. In S.B. Filskov & T.J. Boll (Eds.), *Handbook of clinical neuropsychology.* New York: Wiley.

Stuss, D.T., & Benson, D.F. (1986). *The frontal lobes.* New York: Raven Press.

Sweet, J.J., & Moberg, P.J. (1990). A survey of practices and beliefs among ABPP and non-ABPP clinical neuropsychologists. *Clinical Neuropsychologist, 4,* 101–120.

Tarter, S.B. (1990). Factors affecting adjustment of parents of head trauma victims. *Archives of Clinical Neuropsychology, 5*(1), 15–22.

Taylor, E. (1986). Brain disorder as a cause of behavior change. *Maladjustment and Therapeutic Education, 4*(1), 13–19.

Taylor, H.G., & Fletcher, J.M. (1990). Neuropsychological assessment of children. In G. Goldstein & M. Hersen (Eds.), *Handbook of psychological assessment* (pp. 228–255). New York: Pergamon Press.

Thompson, N.M., Francis, D.J., Stuebing, K., Fletcher, J.M., Ewing-Cobbs, L., Miner, M.E., Levin, H.S., & Eisenberg, H.M. (1994). Motor, visual-spatial, and somatosensory skills after head injury in children and adolescents: A study of change. *Neuropsychology, 8*(3), 333–342.

Thomsen, I.V. (1989). Do young patients have worse outcomes after severe blunt head injury? *Brain Injury, 3,* 157–162.

Thorndike, R.L., Hagen, E.P., & Sattler, J.M. (1986). *Stanford–Binet Intelligence Scale* (4th ed.). Chicago: Riverside.

Tramontana, M.G., & Hooper, S.R. (1997). Neuropsychology of child psychopathology. In V.R. Reynolds & E. Fletcher-Janzen (Eds.), *Handbook of clinical child neuropsychology* (2nd ed., pp. 120–139). New York: Plenum Press.

U.S. Department of Education. (1985). *Seventh annual report to Congress on the implementation of Pub. L. 94-142: The Education for All Handicapped Children Act.* Washington, DC: U.S. Office of Special Education.

Wechsler, D. (1974). *Wechsler Intelligence Scale for Children–Revised.* New York: Psychological Corporation.

Wechsler D. (1991). *Wechsler Intelligence Scale for Children* (3rd ed.). New York: Psychological Corporation.

Wechsler, D. (1992). *Wechsler Individual Achievement Test.* New York: Psychological Corporation.

Wechsler, D. (1995). *Children's Memory Scale.* San Antonio, TX: Psychological Corporation.

Weinberg, W.A., & Brumback, R.A. (1992). The myth of attention deficit-hyperactivity disorder: Resulting from multiple causes. *Journal of Child Neurology, 7*(4), 431–445.

Welsh, M.C., Pennington, B.F., & Grossier, D.B. (1991). A normative-developmental study of executive function: A window on prefrontal function in children. *Developmental Neuropsychology, 7*(2), 131–149.

Wilkinson, G.S. (1993). *The Wide Range Achievement Test* (3rd ed.). Wilmington, DE: Jastak Associates.

Williams, M.A., & Boll, T.J. (1997). Recent developments in neuropsychological assessment of children. In G. Goldstein & T. Incagnoli (Eds.), *Contemporary approaches to neuropsychological assessment* (pp. 231–276). New York: Plenum Press.

Wilson, B.C. (1986). An approach to the neuropsychological assessment of the preschool child with developmental deficits. In S.B. Filskov & T.J. Boll (Eds.), *Handbook of clinical neuropsychology.* New York: Wiley.

Woodcock, R.W., & Johnson, M.B. (1989). *Woodcock–Johnson Psycho-Educational Battery–Revised.* Allen, TX: DLM Teaching Resources.

Wright, L., Schaefer, A.B., & Solomons, G. (1979). *Encyclopedia of pediatric psychology.* Baltimore: University Park Press.

Yeates, K.O., Ris, M.D., & Taylor, H.G. (1995). Hospital referral patterns in pediatric neuropsychology. *Child Neuropsychology, 1*(1), 56–62.

Yeates, K.O., & Taylor, H.G. (1997). Predicting premorbid neuropsychological functioning following pediatric traumatic brain injury. *Journal of Clinical and Experimental Neuropsychology, 19,* 825–837.

Ylvisaker, M. (1986). Language and communication disorders following pediatric head injury. *Journal of Head Trauma Rehabilitation, 1,* 48–56.

Ylvisaker, M. (1993). Communication outcome in children and adolescents with traumatic brain injury: Issues in the neuropsychological rehabilitation of children with brain dysfunction [Special issue]. *Neuropsychological Rehabilitation, 3*(4), 367–387.

Ylvisaker, M., Chorazy, A.J.L., Cohen, S.B., Mastrilli, J.P., Molitor, C.B., Melson, J., Szekeres, S.F., Valko, A.S., & Jaffee, K.M. (1990). Rehabilitative assessment following head injury in children. In M. Rosenthal, E.R. Griffith, M.R. Bond, & J.D. Miller (Eds.), *Rehabilitation of the adult and child with traumatic brain injury.* Philadelphia: Davis.

Zachary, R.A. (1986). *Shipley Institute of Living Scale–Revised manual.* Los Angeles: Western Psychological Services.

CHAPTER 10

Projective Testing with Children and Adolescents

JAMES H. KLEIGER

Referred to as *projection* in psychological circles, the process of creating or interpreting external stimuli in a manner that gives expression to aspects of internal experience is a part of our everyday life. Perhaps best stated by the novelist Samuel Butler (Hammer, 1986, quoting Butler),

> Every man's work, whether it be literature or music or pictures or architecture, or anything else, is always a portrait of himself, and the more he tries to conceal himself, the more clearly will his character appear in spite of him. (p. 239)

This general principle of human behavior has been used strategically by psychologists in the study of personality processes and functioning. In addition to assessing personality objectively by asking direct questions about one's experience and functioning in the world, psychodiagnositicians have also relied on *projective techniques* to assess an individual's internal world. Projective methods have become part of the child psychologist's standard diagnostic armamentarium for evaluating personality organization and dynamics in youngsters and adolescents. There currently are over 20 different projective methods organized across several major categories that are employed in clinical diagnostic settings with younger patients (Rabin, 1986). Before reviewing the most widely used of these procedures, it is helpful to define the essential nature of the projective hypothesis and then trace the development of this concept in the field of personality assessment.

THE PROJECTIVE HYPOTHESIS

The projective hypothesis in personality assessment derives from Freud's defense mechanism of projection. As protection from anxiety arising from an internal conflict, projection enables an individual to attribute unacceptable thoughts, feelings, and impulses to someone or something else. However, beyond its defensive context, projection has a much broader meaning. Projection is understood as a common aspect of mental life, whereby one externalizes mental contents (thoughts, wishes, motives, feelings, attitudes about oneself and others) and attributes these to the environment.

Murray (1938) was one of the first psychologists to recognize the importance of the concept of projection for psychological assessment. The developer of the Thematic Apperception Test (TAT), Murray indicated that people have a tendency to interpret an ambiguous human situation in conformity with their past experience and present needs and wishes. As one of the first to utilize the term "projective methods," Frank (1948) concluded that projective techniques are valuable because they evoke things that are expressive of a subject's private internal world and unique personality makeup. Lindzey (1961) offered a more complete definition of projective methods in testing that addressed the complexity of the techniques:

> A projective technique is an instrument that is considered especially sensitive to covert or unconscious aspects of behavior, it permits or encourages a wide variety of subject responses, is highly multidimensional, and it evokes unusually rich and profuse response data with a minimum of subject awareness concerning the purpose of the test. (p. 45)

Regarding the nature of the projective stimulus and the process of interpretation, Lindzey wrote:

> The stimulus material presented by the projective test is ambiguous, interpreters of the test depend on holistic analysis, the test evokes fantasy responses, and there are no correct or incorrect responses to the test. (p. 45)

Lindzey's comprehensive definition introduces a number of characteristics that define the essence of projective testing. The ambiguity of the projective stimuli lends itself to myriad interpretations that identify a subject's uniqueness. Although it is true that some answers might be "better" or more appropriate than others, "there are no correct or incorrect responses." Through their sensitivity to "covert or unconscious aspects of behavior," projective techniques tell us what the patient cannot. Whereas objective or interview methods of assessment tell us, in large part, what the subject chooses for us to know, projective techniques allow for the expression of psychological issues that exist beyond the subject's immediate awareness. Because the data are gathered "with a minimum of subject awareness," projective methods sidestep defensiveness and particular response sets. Finally, because projective techniques "permit and encourage a wide variety of subject responses" and "evoke unusually rich and profuse response data," they allow for the graphic symbolic representation of internal representations of self and other; motivational issues; affect, wishes, and defense configurations; and significant areas of conflict.

It should be noted that Lindzey's definition limits the scope to the assessment of the "contents of the mind." In other words, by stating that projective techniques "evoke fantasy responses," Lindzey emphasizes mental content and dynamics over form and structure. However, inferences from projective methods should not be limited to mental content (e.g., wishes, motivation, affects and defenses, and self and object representations) but can also be directed to formal aspects of personality. For example, in using projective storytelling, inkblot, or drawing techniques, psychologists pay attention not only to *what* the story, inkblot, or drawing is about but also *how* it was told, seen, or drawn, or in other words, its coherence and degree of organization.

Another problem with Lindzey's definition is that it restricts interpretation to "holistic analysis," implying that systematic and quantitative approaches to evaluating projective test responses are nonexistent. Although it is true that some projective techniques do not have formal scoring systems, many of these techniques have systems for analyzing responses that are not widely used. For example, over the years, different scoring systems have been proposed for the TAT and human figure drawing tests, but these have typically yielded to holistic evaluation of thematic content and gestalt analysis. In other cases, formal scoring is considered an essential part of response analysis. This is nowhere clearer than in the Rorschach Inkblot Test, in which formal scoring systems have always been considered a standard part of test analysis.

Two other related characteristics of the testing stimuli should be added to a comprehensive definition of projective techniques. To maximize chances for projection to occur, the stimuli should be *ambiguous* and *unstructured*. Ambiguous stimuli lack clarity and can be taken to mean almost anything. Although ambiguous stimuli typically have some clues inherent in the testing item, subjects are given maximum reign to "read in" whatever meaning they choose. The concept of structure is also important in understanding projective techniques. Structured tests are inherently clear with built-in directions that guide the subject in making his or her response. In contrast, unstructured tasks lack the directional clarity inherent in structured or objective tests and, as such, require subjects to impose their own direction or internal road map. To create structure for a test that lacks external structure, subjects must turn inward and rely on their own ideas, images, memories, and fantasies. According to Rapaport, Gill, and Schafer (1946), the individual "actively and spontaneously structures unstructured material, and in so doing reveals . . . the principles of his psychological structure" (p. 225).

Finally, it should be noted that some projective methods are circumscribed in their scope, focusing on some narrow area of personality functioning. Others are more comprehensive, taking the whole personality as a subject of inquiry. Both types of projective tests may be given in a battery of tests designed to assess the breadth and depth of a child's personality functioning.

Projective techniques can be categorized in several ways. In this chapter, they are grouped according to whether they are drawing methods, storytelling methods, or inkblot methods. A final miscellaneous projective category is also presented.

PROJECTIVE FIGURE DRAWING TECHNIQUES

Interest in the link between creative expression and psychology has become part of our cultural milieu. Literary and art critics write that artistic expression tells us something about the artist's internal psychological experience. Thus, it is widely accepted that Van Gogh's stormy emotional life and Hemingway's preoccupation with the definition of masculinity found expression in their artistic products. Van Gogh even observed that artists paint things not as they are, but as they *feel* them. In their subjective interpretations, artists may (though not always, depending on the artist's intentions) reveal something about their internal worlds.

Psychologists interested in understanding the workings of the mind developed these observations into clinical techniques for assessing personality functioning. The projective graphic techniques that followed were predicated on the belief that figure drawings, especially the drawing of human figures, express something about the subject that the individual cannot express verbally. The French novelist Sauraute (1984) eloquently pointed out how language shapes, transforms, and, in some cases, squelches emotional life. Words are more distant from experience than are feelings. Language, according to Sauraute, "dries out" one's experiences. Before the advent of language, we experienced the world in pictorial images that retain the essence or "juice" of feelings. Because one picture may be worth a thousand words, in terms of conveying emotional experience, projective drawing techniques may be especially

well-suited for children and adolescents who express things through drawings that they are unable to express in words. This is consistent with Hammer's (1986) conclusion that children and adolescents put more of themselves into graphic versus verbal techniques.

DEVELOPMENT OF PROJECTIVE DRAWING TECHNIQUES

Goodenough (1926) developed the first systematic approach to using human figure drawings to assess children's intelligence. Her test involved instructing children to draw a person to assess the child's mental age and IQ based on the number of details the child included. It was believed that the child's intelligence and developmental level were associated with the number of details drawn. Harris (1963) revised Goodenough's Draw-a-Person (DAP) procedure by requesting the subject to make three drawings, one of a male, one of a female, and one of "yourself." As with the original method, Harris relied on scales and normative data for evaluating the male and female drawings.

Others in the field (Hammer, 1958; Koppitz, 1968; Machover, 1949) believed that the diagnostic use of human figure drawings should not be limited to the evaluation of intellectual or maturational level. Machover, in particular, expanded Goodenough's evaluation method to include personality variables, and Koppitz developed a developmental scoring system that had indicators for emotional difficulties.

Buck (1948) developed the House-Tree-Person test (HTP) specifically for the purpose of assessing personality adjustment. This technique was later elaborated by Jolles (1952) to include three separate procedures involving achromatic pencil drawings and an inquiry phase, followed by chromatic crayon drawings. More contemporary methods involve having the subject draw a house, tree, and person either on separate pages or all on the same page. Originally designed to be used with children, the technique has generally been used with subjects of all ages.

Projective drawing techniques were subsequently employed in the evaluation of a child's perceptions of his or her family (Hulse, 1952). To Hulse's original direction for the child to "Draw a picture of your family," Burns and Kaufman (1970, 1982) added the instruction "Draw a picture of your family *doing something."* Called the Kinetic Family Drawing (KFD), the addition of movement emphasizes perceived relationships and interactions in a more dynamic, versus static, context. Aspects elicited regarding self and family interactions are those of intimacy and distance, emotional tone, and alliances and conflicts between subjects and their family members.

ADMINISTRATION

The DAP, HTP, and KFD all require the same basic tools and setting. Each is started by giving the child sheets of $8\frac{1}{2} \times 11$ unlined paper and some sharpened No. 2 pencils with erasers. The child is seated comfortably with sufficient room for arms and legs. The writing surface should be flat and smooth.

Although specific instructions for each procedure may vary slightly, the examiner tells the child to either draw a picture of a person (DAP); a house, followed by a tree and a person (HTP); or the subject's family doing something (KFD). With each test, little more is said, even if the subject asks more questions about the procedure. As with all projective techniques, the examiner resists the subject's request for additional structure, thereby maximizing the projective nature of the task by providing as little information as possible. Adults and children sometimes protest that they cannot draw very well. To this, the examiner may respond, "This is not a test of artistic ability. I'm not concerned with how good of an artist you are. Just do the best you can do" (Handler, 1985, p. 174).

DAP
A single sheet of paper is placed in front of the child in the vertical position with the specific instruction "Draw a picture of a person." If older children and adolescents draw an incomplete person or stick figure, the examiner gives them another sheet of paper and says, "This time, I'd like you to draw the entire person" (or "a non-stick figure"). When the drawing is complete, the child is given another sheet of paper and asked to "Draw a picture of the opposite sex." For younger children, some additional explanation may be necessary, such as "You just drew a woman (girl), now draw a man (boy)." The examiner should indicate the order in which each picture was drawn.

After both drawings have been completed, the examiner presents the first drawing to the child and asks him or her to make up a story about the person drawn. If the youngster is reticent or unable to make up a story, a series of prompts may be given. Any questions that help the child associate to the drawing can be used. For example, the child may be asked such questions as How old is this person? What does he (she) do for a living? How does this person feel? and What is he (she) thinking? Other questions might include What will happen to this person in the future? and What makes him (her) angry (happy, sad, scared)?

HTP
Like the DAP, the administration of the HTP is a simple matter. In the standard method proposed by Buck (1948), the child is presented with four pieces of blank paper and asked to "Draw as good a house as possible," followed by the same instruction for a tree, a person, and a person of the opposite sex. The pencil drawings are then taken away and the child is asked to repeat the procedure with a crayon. In clinical practice, only the pencil drawings are typically used. Following the drawings, the child may be asked a series of questions designed to increase the projective yield of each of the drawings.

KFD
The specific instruction recommended by Burns and Kaufman (1970) is "Draw a picture of everyone, including you, and your family *doing* something." The child is not told to draw everyone doing something *together,* because it is left to the child to decide how much "togetherness," closeness, and reciprocal interaction is a part of his or her family. As with the other projective drawing techniques, the child may be asked to describe the drawing so that the examiner can understand each of the family members, their relationships, and what they are all doing.

INTERPRETATION

In attempting to understand meanings connected with projective drawings, psychologists focus on three aspects of each drawing: (1) the form of the drawing, or formal characteristics; (2) the content, details, or themes conveyed by the drawings; and (3) the subject's behavior while carrying out the task. Inferences drawn from each of these areas may reflect something about personality structure, traits, dynamics, or conflicts.

Formal aspects of the drawings describe how the figures were drawn. Dimensions such as which gender is drawn first, size of the figures, placement on the page, line quality, and erasure may all potentially reflect something about the subject's ego or cognitive functioning, coping ability, and possible areas of conflict. The content domain includes the kind of figures drawn, their posture, facial expressions, as well as the nature of the individual elements (e.g., mouth, eyes, hair, clothes, hands). Personality issues and developmental level may be assessed from this domain. Developmental variables are reflected in the features of the drawing, including integration of the figure, number of elements included, line quality, frequency of erasure, and perspective. Finally, the behavior of the subject while drawing the figures is a third source of valuable information for making inferences about the subject's psychological structure and functioning. Here, the examiner takes note of the subject's attitude toward the task and instructions. The subject's pace of work and reaction to the drawings are important to observe. Do subjects utter comments about the figures they drew? Are they disparaging and devaluing of their efforts?

Groth-Marnat (1984) recommended that the interpreter first consider each drawing in its totality. Instead of focusing on isolated details, the examiner can begin by viewing the entire picture and assessing what feeling or tone is conveyed. From the initial intuitive "feel" of the drawing, the interpreter can then analyze specific details, using empirical data to support any inferences made. Instead of inventorying each element of the drawing and attaching an interpretation to these (the sign approach), the interpreter should pay particular attention to discontinuities or anomalies such as intense scribbles or erasures, unusual size or placement of the figure on the page. Attending to such features helps the interpreter discern some important psychological meaning or issue expressed in the drawing.

Human figure drawings are primarily understood as representations of the self (and members of the opposite sex). The ways the subject draws the head, hair, facial features, eyes, ears, nose, mouth, neck, arms, hands, legs, trunk, feet, and clothing may reveal something about the individual's self-image, ego functioning, or area of conflict.

Koppitz (1968) compiled a list of 30 features she called emotional indicators (EIs) found to be uncommon in the drawings of normal children. These features have been shown to occur more often in the drawings of emotionally disturbed children (Chandler & Johnson, 1991; Koppitz, 1968). EIs include three general categories: (1) qualitative features such as poor integration of body parts, gross asymmetry, and transparencies; (2) inclusion of certain elements such as clouds, birds, teeth, and rain; and (3) omission of common elements such as eyes, hands, or legs. Each of the EIs is thought to be associated with one or more personality traits such as impulsivity, aggressivity, insecurity, or anxiety. The appearance of a single EI in a drawing is unlikely to have significant clinical implications. Only when these signs begin to cluster together in the child's drawings should they be given strong interpretive significance.

The HTP test can be interpreted in terms of attitudes about significant people in the subject's life or feelings directed toward the self. Houses are viewed as a reflection of the person, even though in reality they may be drawn to represent the individual's personal or childhood house. In children, the house may reflect their attitudes toward their family and relationships to parents and siblings (Hammer, 1985). Trees are generally considered to reflect something about the self in relation to the environment, but some believe that tree drawings reflect unconscious feelings about the self (Groth-Marnat, 1984; Hammer, 1985). In contrasting drawings of trees and people, Hammer indicated that the tree reflects the subject's deeper and unconscious feelings about the self, whereas the drawn person is the vehicle for the more conscious (or, possibly, preferred) views of the self. The view that the tree elicits more unconscious core aspects of self-representation is supported by the finding that the tree is less susceptible to change on retesting (Hammer, 1985).

Children may express feelings of worth and belonging within the family in their KFD drawings. When the child omits the self from the KFD, it suggests a perception of not belonging to the family in a meaningful way (Chandler & Johnson, 1991). The same can be inferred for omissions of significant family members from the child's KFD. Omissions of parents or siblings may represent the child's feelings of alienation, rejection, or anger toward the missing family member.

Age Considerations
It is critical that the interpreter be aware of developmental considerations when trying to understand the drawings of younger children. Two-year-olds

will typically scribble when presented with paper and pencil. Three-year-olds may be able to make lines, circles, loops, and arcs in an attempt to draw human figures. At the age of 4, the child can draw a more complete figure, consisting of loops and circles and lines for arms and legs. These drawings may be recognizable as human figures. The average 5-year-old has matured to the point where he or she can produce a human figure that includes a head and body with extremities coming from the body. The head is typically too large and details are scant. It is not until the ages of 6 to 8 that the child can draw more elaborate figures and represent movement in drawings. Human figures are less frequently stick figures but take on the shape of real people. Pressure is often heavy and erasures are frequent. By age 8, the average child can plan drawings in advance and incorporate perspective and appropriate proportion into drawings. Ten-year-olds tend to include realistic body positions, clothing, motion, and perspective in their drawings, which are often neat, orderly, and detailed.

EMPIRICAL SUPPORT

The empirical support for projective drawing techniques has been equivocal. Recent surveys of the literature by Falk (1981), Kahill (1984), and Handler and Habenicht (1994) all report that the evidence for the differential diagnostic use of figure drawing tests has been rather thin. Although Falk presented some research in support of the DAP as a diagnostic tool, he reported that numerous investigations have concluded that diagnosing emotional disturbances on the basis of the DAP is not scientifically valid. In particular, the DAP was not shown to be successful in differentiating clinical groups from nonpsychiatric groups or from each other. In her review of the adult DAP literature, Kahill found limited support for many of Machover and Hammer's hypotheses regarding the psychological meaning of formal and content variables. Handler and Habernicht reported similar findings with the KFD. Falk and Kahill both reported that the literature has identified artistic ability as a significant confounding variable, making it more difficult to interpret the drawings of more artistically talented subjects.

Falk (1981) noted that there are relatively few studies on the use of the DAP with children. This is surprising because the technique was originally devised to assess intelligence and developmental in children. Hammer (1986) reported that validity studies of children's drawings have generally revealed more positive findings than those with adults (Koppitz, 1966; Springer, 1941; Vane & Eisen, 1962). Falk discussed reasons why the DAP may be uniquely suited to children, even more so than for adults, who tend to be more defensive and perhaps resistant to projection in drawing tasks.

Although Falk (1981), Kahill (1984), and Handler and Habenicht (1994) concluded that the research has not clearly supported many of the premises on which interpretation of projective drawings are based, all agree that the methodology of many of these studies has been flawed, asking inappropriate questions that go beyond what should be expected of projective techniques. For example, both Falk and Handler and Habernicht emphasized that much of the research reporting negative findings has employed projective drawings to make categorical diagnostic decisions. They correctly point out that as projective techniques, figure drawing tasks are intended to tell us something about the child's internal world or views of self and family. It is both misguided and unfair to expect that these techniques should predict behavior or membership in diagnostic categories. Furthermore, many studies have looked only at formal and content variables without inquiring into the subjects' pictures, observing their behavior while carrying out the task, or integrating drawings with other test findings. These methodological practices are inconsistent with how projective figure drawings are used in clinical practice. Falk concluded that future research should no longer focus on proving or disproving the validity of human figure drawings but, instead, on what aspects of drawings are helpful in understanding patients. Kahill concluded something similar by encouraging clinicians and researchers to view the DAP as a "rich and potentially valuable clinical tool that can provide working hypotheses and a springboard for discussion with the patient" (p. 288).

In sum, all reviewers found projective drawing techniques valuable for children but cautioned against taking a rigid, formulized sign approach. Instead of a cookbook approach, principles of disciplined inference making should be used. Thus, the use of single features to derive a list of static personality traits or differential diagnoses is considered to be an invalid procedure. On the other hand, viewing the drawings in a holistic and integrated way that may help generate hypotheses about the child's ego functioning and self and object representations is recommended. Such an approach that employs global ratings of health/sickness may also help identify vulnerable children (Tharinger & Stark, 1990). One final cautionary note regarding the interpretation of any kind of drawing is that the subject's responses constitute an ambiguous stimulus onto which examiners may project their own idiosyncratic interpretations (G. Walker, personal communication, April 2, 1999).

PICTURE-STORYTELLING TECHNIQUES

Occupying an important place in the testing battery with children and adolescents are techniques that involve making up stories to a series of ambiguous pictures. The projective nature of these techniques is obvious; the subject is simply given the instruction to make up a story, one with a beginning, middle, and end. The way the child chooses to tell the stories and the themes or content of the stories are left up to the child. As with all projective methods, the child's responses can be analyzed through the lenses of response structure, content, and behavior or patient-examiner interaction. Three projective picture-storytelling techniques are widely used in clinical practice. These are the Thematic Apperception Test (TAT), the Children's Apperception Test (CAT), and the less well-known Michigan Picture Test–Revised (MPT-R).

THEMATIC APPERCEPTION TEST (TAT)

The TAT was developed by Murray (1938) as a tool to study his personality theory. Murray emphasized the biopsychosocial determinants of behavior. At the heart of his personality theory lay the concept of *needs* and *presses.* Needs are significant determinants of behavior residing within the individual; presses refer to environmental determinants that elicit behavior or trigger needs from the individual. Murray developed the TAT to evaluate and assess the relative strength of the individual's specific psychological needs and perceived environmental presses acting on him or her. In all, Murray listed 26 needs under four separate categories. By subjects telling stories to the ambiguous TAT pictures, Murray believed that past experience and present needs could be mobilized.

Although used primarily with adults, the TAT may be used with older children and adolescents. The TAT spawned other picture-storytelling techniques with younger children, including the CAT, the Children's Apperception Test–Human Forms (CAT-H), and the MPT-R. With cross-cultural issues in mind, TAT card sets have been developed for African American (Dlepu & Kimbrough, 1982; Triplett & Brunson, 1982) and Native American children (Henry, 1947).

Murray's original set of cards included 31 pictures, with different cards designated for different age groups. Certain cards were designated for boys/males (BM) and others for girls/females (GF). There are two additional adult cards (12M and 12F), three children's cards (12BG, 13B, 13G), and a blank card (16) to be used with subjects of all ages. Cards 1 to 10 were supposed to be less ambiguous and reflect everyday situations, whereas cards 11 to 20 were designed to be more ambiguous, dramatic, and unusual.

Administration
The TAT is not a standard psychometric instrument with a single agreed upon set of verbatim instructions or specified number of cards that must be administered to all subjects. Typically, the subject is asked to make up a story that includes a description of (1) the characters and what they are doing; (2) what led up to the events or situation in the picture; (3) what might happen in the future; (4) the feelings and thoughts of the characters, and (5) how the story will end. The examiner makes a verbatim recording (either written or tape-recorded) of each story and may ask questions to clarify aspects of the story that are unclear or omitted (e.g., "How does this story end?" or "What is he (she) feeling or thinking?"). Instructions for children and adolescents should be informal and adhere to the general instructions.

Murray used 20 cards over two separate testing sessions. Contemporary methods include smaller card sets. Dana (1986) suggested Cards 2, 3, 4, 6 (BM or GF), 7, and the blank card be used for adolescents, and Cards 1, 8BM, 12, BG, 13B, 13G, and 19 for younger children. Gerver (1946) reported that 5- to 10-year-olds were responsive to Cards 7GF, 18GF, 3 GF, and 8GF.

Normative length of stories for children and adolescents has been determined to be 29 words for 5- to 7-year-olds and 63 words for 8- to 15-year-olds

(Friedman, 1972). Gender differences were apparent only in the 8- to 11-year-old group, in which girls produced longer stories. Length of stories is also apparently confounded by need for achievement, with higher-achievement adolescents giving longer and more verbally fluent stories (Schaible, 1975).

Scoring and Interpretation

Perhaps one of the biggest drawbacks of the TAT is the lack of any widely used and consensually agreed upon scoring system. Murray devised his own system, and a number of others have proposed quantitative methods for scoring the TAT. However, none has developed a popular following, and according to Vane's (1981) review of alternative scoring systems, all have had significant shortcomings. Thus, most interpreters analyze story content with their subjective norms in mind.

Although not offering a specific scoring system, Dana (1986) proposed interpretative guidelines for the use of the TAT with adolescents and adults. According to Dana, each story can be analyzed from five distinct perspectives: (1) compliance with stimulus demands, (2) needs and motives, (3) sex-role development, (4) story content, and (5) subject's control over story content. Dana suggested that each of these domains corresponds to a specific interpretative area. Compliance with stimulus demands is related to ego strength. Ego strength is assessed by attending to how well the subject conforms to the instructions to tell a story with a beginning, middle, and end and how congruent the story is with the stimulus nature of the picture. Thought organization and reality testing can be inferred from the quality of the subject's verbalization. The presence of peculiar verbalizations, parapraxes, incoherence, condensation, and autistic logic suggest disturbances in thought organization. Reality-testing problems may be reflected in distortions or omissions of stimulus elements in the card.

Motives and needs can be assessed from each story. Murray rated needs on a five-point scale for intensity, duration, frequency, and importance. Different cards may elicit different needs. A large body of literature has determined that needs can be scored reliably (Dana, 1968).

The sex-role development dimension has to do with examining whether the subject's stories are more or less consistent with those expected by same-aged males or females. By age 6, females typically tell stories containing negative experience (deprivation) followed by positive emotion, whereas the pattern is reversed in boys. According to Dana, adolescents who do not demonstrate this pattern may be at a higher risk for psychopathology or problems in sex-role development.

Content themes can be viewed from a developmental perspective. At different phases of adolescence, subjects are expected to emphasize different content characteristics. Dana (1986) reviewed studies that provide information about thematic content that might be expected at different age levels. Significant deviations from developmentally appropriate content may alert examiners to the possibility of psychopathology.

Paying attention to the subject's efforts to exert control over his or her story reveals something about defenses. What the subject allows into the story may or may not be present in actual behavior. Subjects can exert control over their stories by withholding or censoring needs or fantasies. The defense of projection, whereby the subject attributes unacceptable traits to others, is more typically seen in males. In these cases, the TAT stories that reveal projected needs or impulses are more likely to be congruent with overt behavior. On the contrary, repression may result in the avoidance of unacceptable or threatening content. More typically seen in females, repression may result in bland and constricted stories that do not mirror the psychological issues with which the subject may be struggling.

More recently, Westen and his colleagues (Westen, Lohr, Silk, Kerber & Goodrich, 1989) developed a Social Cognition and Object Relations Scale (SCORS) to measure four dimensions of an individual's object relational capacity based on TAT stories. Developed for use with adults, more recent revisions of the SCORS have been successfully applied to adolescents and latency-aged and younger children. The four dimensions of object relational capacity determined from TAT stories are (1) complexity of human representation, (2) affect tone of relational paradigms, (3) capacity for emotional investment in relationships, and (4) understanding of social causality.

Empirical Support

Empirical support for systematic scoring systems has been lacking. Using a sample of nearly 1,400 youngsters between the ages of 12 and 17, Neuman and colleagues (Neuman, Neuman, & Sellers, 1974) compared 31 TAT scores, reflecting structural and content variables that emerged from various scoring manuals, to criterion measures for school, emotional, and social adjustment. They found no significant association between any of the TAT measures and these criterion variables. However, the newer SCORS approach described above may be a valid and potentially useful scale for assessing structural dimensional of internalized object relations.

McGrew and Teglasi (1990) used the TAT with males aged 6 to 12 to assess formal characteristics of storytelling ability. On the basis of formal structural characteristics of TAT stories, the researchers found that they could correctly classify 85% of emotionally disturbed boys and 95% of the comparison group. The emotionally disturbed group differed from the comparison group on the following structural dimensions: adequacy of story (internal logic); characteristics of verbalization (perceptual personalization, inappropriate or bizarre comments, and inadequacy); adequacy of judgment (positive action and outcome); and hostility to less aggressive cards.

Dana (1968, 1986) argued for better normative data on particular scores that assess structural and content dimensions. He reasoned that until more comprehensive normative data on a wider array of scoring dimensions are provided, the TAT will remain an extremely useful, but limited, idiographic technique for studying personality.

CHILDREN'S APPERCEPTION TEST
(CAT, CAT-H, AND CAT-S)

Bellak and Bellak (1952) developed the CAT for use with children ages 3 to 10. The original test consisted of 10 cards with pictures of animals engaged in human behaviors. The cards depict animals in humanlike activities or situations representing a variety of parent-child and peer relationship situations symbolic of developmental issues and conflicts. For example, Card 3 shows a lion with a pipe and cane, sitting on a throne with a little mouse in the background. Card 10 shows a puppy lying across the knees of an adult dog in the bathroom.

In 1952, the Bellaks published a supplemental form of the test (CAT-S) designed for very young children. The CAT-S consists of 10 cards mounted on heavy cardboard, again depicting animals engaged in family and peer activity of a human

nature. Surmising that the animal figures might be inappropriate for older children, the Bellaks developed a CAT version with human figures (CAT-H) in 1966. The CAT-H essentially parallels the CAT, in that each card depicts human children engaged in activities or situations analogous to those of the animals on each CAT card.

Administration
As with most techniques, it is optimal to have the child seated next to the examiner at a small desk or table. The cards are placed face down on the table/desktop and handed to the child one by one. The cards are given to the child in proper order because they are designed to have sequential impact. Specific instructions vary according to the child's age and capacity to understand. Although the CAT was designed for children 3 to 10 years of age, Chandler and Johnson (1991) found best results when used with children between the ages of 5 and 9.

The CAT is introduced as a storytelling game. The child is asked (urged, cajoled) to look at each card and make up a story. Instructions may include questions such as "What might be going on in this picture?" and "What led up to it, and how will it turn out?" As with all inquires of this sort, it is important to limit the number of questions and not lead the child in any direction. For particularly resistant children, the examiner may need to prompt the child by beginning the story with a familiar phrase, such as "Once upon a time . . . " The examiner may even have to model a response by telling a story of his or her own. This strategy should, however, be used only once.

Scoring and Interpretation
Chandler and Johnson (1991) recommended analyzing stories in terms of developmental issues, current concerns, needs and threats (motivations), and perception of self, others, and the world. Four principles guide inference making: (1) developmental level, (2) manifest content of each card (card pull), (3) repetitive themes, and (4) background and context. Interpretation is always tempered by an awareness of the child's developmental status and age-appropriate concerns. Each card depicts more or less specific situations and tends to elicit certain themes. Like the TAT, the content of the pictures of the CAT is not neutral. We are less interested, for example, if a child tells a story with oral themes to a

card that pulls for these kinds of themes, but more with how the child manages this stimulus pull. The repeated presence of a theme across several stories carries more interpretative weight than a single occurrence. Finally, interpretation should always take into account the child's current family situation as well as past history and traumas. The CAT can be useful in determining the impact these experiences had on the child; for example, what do they emphasize repeatedly, or what do they omit from their stories?

Some researchers have developed forms to use for summarizing responses in terms of ego psychological issues such as drives, anxieties, defenses, conflicts, superego and ego manifestations, identity, relationships with others, and regression (Bellak, 1954; Haworth, 1965). Haworth developed a Schedule of Adaptive Mechanisms in CAT Responses for evaluating the relative use of different defensive mechanisms. The schedule was designed for qualitative analysis of the stories but could be used quantitatively as well.

CAT-H

Developed for children approaching the upper age limits of appropriateness for the CAT and for younger children with superior intelligence, the CAT-H is administered and interpreted in the same manner as the CAT. Haworth (1986) has given both forms to children and found few differences in terms of adequacy of defenses. She also analyzed stories of children who had taken both forms and found that oral-dependent and oedipal themes were more common in the animal stories, and oppositional tendencies were observed more frequently in the human stories. Haworth recommended using the CAT-H when it is known that the child has experienced some traumatic interpersonal event because the human cards may elicit more information about anxiety and coping associated with the trauma. By contrast, such youngsters may give rather bland and unrevealing stories to the animal cards.

CAT-S

The supplemental form of the CAT is designed for very young children or older children with intellectual impairment. Ten cards (different from the CAT) are mounted on heavy cardboard. Cards are presented to the youngster one at a time or simply given to the child to play with. Some children spontaneously tell stories to the cards. Generally, however, the examiner must prompt the child to tell a story. The pictures seem to elicit themes about peer play, school activities, mother-child relationships, and trips to the doctor.

Empirical Support

Between ages 6 and 10, children demonstrate no preference for animal or human figures. After age 10, they prefer animals in natural form over animals engaged in human activity (Simmons, 1967). Other studies have shown little difference in projective power between the CAT and CAT-H. However, little research has been done with the CAT-S.

Studies have also looked at factors that facilitate storytelling in younger children. Passman and Lautmann (1982) found that the presence of a parent for half a testing session improves storytelling productivity more than does the presence of a security blanket. Erikson and Rorosgaard (1979) proposed a method of actively facilitating storytelling by play-acting the characters in the stories.

Few normative and longitudinal studies have been conducted with the CAT. Bradfer-Blomart (1970) found few gender differences between the CAT responses of 8-year-old boys and girls, except that boys were less likely to oppose adult control than were girls. In addition to describing research on psychiatric groups, Haworth (1986) presented diagnostic studies on stutterers (Porterfield, 1969) and intellectually and orthopedically handicapped children (Bose & Benerjee, 1969). The CAT has been widely studied and adapted for use in many cultures and countries, including Japan, India, the Phillipines, and Czechoslovkia.

MICHIGAN PICTURE TEST–REVISED (MPT-R)

Originally developed by Hartwell, Hutt, Andrew, and Walton (1951) as a rapid screening device to differentiate emotionally disturbed from well-adjusted children, the MPT was subsequently updated and revised by Hutt (1980). The revised form of the test (MPT-R) consists of 15 picture cards and one blank card. Norms are available for grades 3 through 9.

Administration

The administration typically takes 10 to 20 minutes, and scoring usually can be done in 5 minutes once the scoring criteria are mastered. The examiner may administer only the four core cards or as many of the other cards as desired. The cards are given one at a time, in order, and the child is asked to make up a story about each picture. Asking the child to elaborate a beginning, middle, and end and to describe the feelings of the characters follows the procedure of the TAT and CAT.

The core cards (Cards 1, 5, 8, and 11) are intended to provide a rapid, nonthreatening examination that produces an objective score related to degree of emotional adjustment or areas of conflict, including interpersonal relations with peers and family, achievement and failure, sexual wishes and anxieties, school attitudes and phobias, reactions to authority figures, identity problems, and feelings about the body.

Scoring, Interpretation, and Empirical Support

Three formal test variables or scores were found to discriminate between healthy and emotionally disturbed youngsters (Hartwell et al., 1951): tension, verb tense, and direction of forces. The tension index is based on the frequency with which seven defined needs (love, extrapunitiveness, intropunitiveness, succor, achievement, submissiveness, and personal adequacy) are expressed in the child's stories. Poorly adjusted children express more needs than do their well-adjusted counterparts. Verb tense is determined by a straightforward count of the tense of verbs in the stories. In general, the well-adjusted students tend to use more past and future tense verbs than do the poorly adjusted children. Direction of forces is determined by gauging whether the central figure is directing force outward (centrifugal), having force directed upon him or her (centripetal), or neither (neutral). This score was shown to discriminate well-adjusted and poorly adjusted children at each grade level. Hutt (1986) reported that interscorer reliability for these variables has ranged from .87 to .98.

INKBLOT METHODS

Long before television or video games, children used to entertain themselves by playing parlor games with inkblots. Called *Klecksographie* in nineteenth-century Europe, the game involved making shapes from inkblots. Hermann Rorschach,

reportedly nicknamed Klex as a child, may have first have become interested in the scientific used of inkblots through playing with them as a child (Ellenberger, 1954). Even before Rorschach developed his inkblot test (1921), psychologists had been interested in using inkblots to study personality structure and developmental trends in children (Kirkpatrick, 1900; Parsons, 1917; Pyle, 1915).

Inkblot methods have occupied a prominent place in the diagnostic armamentarium of child and adolescent psychologists. Because of their uniquely unstructured nature, inkblot techniques tend to maximize projective tendencies and allow for a graphic representation of structural and dynamic issues. Compared to projective picture-storytelling and drawing techniques, both of which involve more or less familiar stimuli, inkblot methods present children with the most unfamiliar and ambiguous stimuli to interpret. Because the answers are not present in the stimuli themselves, child and adolescent subjects must turn inward and rely on their internal resources to structure their responses.

It is somewhat of a mistake to think of inkblot methods as simply projective techniques that reveal the subject's wishes, anxieties, and conflicts. Both the Rorschach and Holtzman inkblot tests are complex problem-solving tests that assess the subject's cognitive, perceptual, and representational capacities. Although there is some controversy regarding whether these methods are psychometrically sound tests or simply clinically useful techniques, the two major inkblot methods presented here have been subjected to rigorous empirical investigations.

RORSCHACH INKBLOT TEST

In addition to his earlier interest in Klecksographie, Rorschach apparently decided to pursue the psychological study of inkblots after learning of a report of grade school children's reactions to them (Leichtman, 1996). Although he applied his test primarily to adults, Rorschach was interested in developmental changes in children's Rorschach responses. In the decades between the development of the test (Rorschach, 1921) and World War II, practitioners and researchers began to investigate the use of the Rorschach with preschoolers. Most of the Rorschach pioneers, including Klopfer, Beck, Hertz, and Piotrowski, were interested in how children responded to the Rorschach. Two works presenting normative data for youngsters were published in the 1940s and 1950s (Ames, Learned, Metraux, & Walker, 1952; Ford, 1946). In the 1970s to 1990s, Exner (Exner & Weiner, 1982, 1995) honed his psychometrically sophisticated Comprehensive Rorschach System and applied it to children and adolescents. Perhaps Exner's greatest contribution was an extensive developmental database that included norms for youngsters age 5 through 16.

Leichtman (1996) discussed two key issues in using the Rorschach with children. One involves methodology, or how the Rorschach should be administered, scored, and interpreted with children. The other involves psychological development, or how to understand normal developmental trends in children's Rorschach protocols. Leichtman stated that both of these issues are critical for the clinical application of the Rorschach with children.

Methodological issues are to be explored first, followed by a discussion of developmental considerations.

Administration

The Rorschach Inkblot Test consists of 10 cards, 5 of which are achromatic and 5 with varying degrees of color. All 10 cards are presented to the subject in order. Unlike the storytelling apperception tests, the procedure is standardized and remains more or less the same for subjects of all ages. Exner and Weiner (1982) stressed the importance of collecting the data properly. To do so, the test must be administered according to standard specifications. Although different methods of administration have existed over time, Exner's (1993) Comprehensive System is generally accepted as the standard methodology.

The examiner is situated beside and slightly behind the subject. Both are seated at a table. For younger children, it is permissible, and in some cases perhaps advisable, to sit on the floor or in some less formal setting. Following a brief introduction in which subjects are told that they will be shown inkblots and asked to say what they look like, the child is handed the first card with the simple question, "What might this be?" or "What does it look like?" If the child needs more reassurance before beginning, the examiner may indicate "Kids see all kinds of different things; there are no right or wrong answers." Children frequently ask questions about the nature of the inkblots or the test itself. Simple brief answers are appropriate in such cases. The child's responses are recorded verbatim. Following the presentation of the 10 cards, the examiner asks the child to indicate where he or she saw the percepts or images and what about the inkblot made it look like the percepts that were seen. This inquiry phase may be introduced with a statement such as "Now I want to be able to see things just like you do and find out where you saw these things and what about the card made them seem that way to you."

Scoring, Interpretation, and Empirical Support

Unlike most other projective techniques that lack rigorous scoring systems, different Rorschach approaches have always included elaborate scoring or coding rules. One of Exner's key contributions was to consolidate and systematize the disparate scoring rules of the different systems and subject them to empirical tests. Scoring variables have been shown to be reliable and valid measures of a range of psychological functions (Exner, 1993; Exner & Weiner, 1982, 1995). Each response is coded according to its location (the area of the blot chosen), the determinants (what aspect of the inkblot determined the response, e.g., form, color, shading), the content of the response, and any special verbalizations. The degree to which the response is integrated or organized, its form level (or perceptual accuracy), and conventionality are also scored. The Rorschachs of children are scored in the same way as those of adults.

According to Exner and Weiner (1982), "Rorschach behavior means what it means regardless of the age of the subject" (p. 14). By this, they mean that the meaning of Rorschach variables is the same, no matter if the subject is a child, adolescent, or adult. Although the interpretation of scores remains the same despite the age of the subject, the actual meaning of the scores depends on developmental factors. It is critical, then, to refer to normative data when attempting to ascertain the meaning of the scores.

Regarding the role of development in Rorschach records, Exner and Weiner (1982) noted a number of changes that occur between the ages of 5 and 16. Younger children give briefer records with more whole (W) than detail responses (D, Dd). They give few synthesis responses (DQ+) and a greater incidence of special scores that would be suggestive of disordered thinking in adolescents and adults. Human movement responses (M) and form-dominated color responses (FC) also increase with age. However, there are no normative differences in perceptual accuracy (F+%, X+%) among children, adolescents, and adults.

Developmental Progression

Clinicians and researchers have questioned how old a child must be to be able to take the Rorschach. The norms in the Comprehensive System begin at age 5, suggesting that this is the lowest age level for which the test can be given. Observing a relative lack of literature on Rorschach responses among preschoolers, Leichtman (1996) proposed a developmental progression based on the developmental theory of Heinz Werner (1961). Werner's orthogenetic principle proposed that development always proceeds from a global and undifferentiated state to an increasingly differentiated, integrated, and articulated state. Using Werner's model as a backdrop, Leichtman described how children progress through three stages in their capacities to master the Rorschach task. According to Leichtman, each stage is characterized by shifts in how the Rorschach is given and taken. Each stage is also associated with different test-taking behavior and test responses. Finally, each progressive stage incorporates aspects of the earlier stages. Leichtman called his three stages perseverative approaches to the Rorschach (in which the same response is given repeatedly), confabulatory approaches to the Rorschach (in which youngsters embellish their responses with storylike themes or details that cannot be justified by concrete aspects of the inkblots themselves), and "The Rorschach." His stages are defined by specific patterns, not ages per se. Leichtman noted that his stages are of heuristic value in that they clarify the steps in a developmental progression.

Stage I: Perseverative Approaches to the Rorschach.
Leichtman (1996) pointed out that when one is bold enough to attempt to get 2-year-olds to focus on the Rorschach, their responses tend to be characterized by perseveration and absurdity. Leichtman notes that researchers have long observed that toddlers respond to the 10 cards as if there is little difference between them (Klopfer & Margulies, 1941). Additionally, examiners have concluded that the basis for the toddler's response is frequently unclear (Ford, 1946; Klopfer & Margulies, 1941).

Leichtman elaborated on the views of Klopfer and Margulies (1941) by pointing out that this perseverative pattern may be an adaptive problem-solving solution for the toddler. Presented with a difficult and unfamiliar task such as the Rorschach, the youngster may arbitrarily seize on the first response and then stick, for the remainder of the test, with what apparently seemed to work for him or her in the beginning.

Just before turning 3, the toddler may exhibit a bit of a shift in his or her perseverative pattern. Although absurd perseverations may still prevail, toddlers at this age may either try to refuse some of the cards or give new responses to others.

Stage II: Confabulatory Approaches to the Rorschach.
Three- and four-year-olds take the Rorschach in a qualitatively different manner. Now the youngster may give different responses to each blot, which serves as a springboard for often idiosyncratic fantasy. The child's Rorschach may take a more familiar form and may even reveal something about the child's personality functioning. Although the form level of most responses is better than that of the perseverating toddler, most of the responses of 3- to 4-year-olds are confabulatory wholes. The child has become enamored with ideas, which take precedence over perceptual reality. The boundary between reality and fantasy is permeable, and affect states that tend to influence perception.

As children transition from stage II to III, there is an increase in the number of responses and large-detail responses (as opposed to wholes). Klopfer, Spiegelman, and Fox (1956) believed that this transition period was also marked by the introduction of "confabulatory combinations," which they defined as essentially thematically embellished incongruous combinations. Other researchers (Ames et al., 1952) noted that the Rorschachs of 5-year-olds are characterized less by confabulations and more by incongruous combinations.

Stage III: "The Rorschach." At the age of 7, the child is able to move from confabulated-whole responses (DW) to conventional detail responses (D) and to exclude incongruous details that would spoil an otherwise adequate response. At this point, Leichtman (1996) notes that the Rorschach has become a reliable test for the subject and can be taken in the same way that adults take the test. The child is now capable of more successful integration between perceptual and associative components of the response process. Leichtman states that confabulations are more uncommon at this age and can be taken as a sign of ideational disturbance.

The Holtzman Inkblot Test

Originally developed to overcome the psychometric limitations of the pre–Comprehensive System Rorschach, the Holtzman Inkblot Test (HIT) has been used with subjects of all ages. Published in 1961 by Holtzman, Thorpe, Swartz, and Herron, the HIT has spawned hundreds of studies (Holtzman, 1986) and developed a normative database, which includes norms on over 800 children. Even though its popularity is overshadowed by the Rorschach, the HIT is reported to be a viable projective alternative for use with children.

Administration

Several differences distinguish the HIT from the Rorschach. First, Holtzman's test includes 45 cards; however, the subject is limited to one response per card. A brief inquiry, similar to the Rorschach, is conducted after each response. As with the Rorschach, the instructions and administrative format may be modified to suit the needs of younger children.

Scoring and Interpretation

The HIT includes 22 quantitative scoring variables that cover many of the important scoring categories contained in the Rorschach. Most of the major location, determinant, and content scores are included, along with some other scores that measure other useful psychological constructs. Variables are weighted to make quantitative analysis of scores easy.

MISCELLANEOUS PROJECTIVE TECHNIQUES

A number of additional projective tests have been developed for use with adults and children in particular. Although not as widely accepted as the standard procedures described thus far, these other techniques often find their way into the assessment batteries of child and adolescent psychodiagnosticians. Several are worth mentioning.

Sentence Completion Tests

Sentence completion tests (SCTs) are less ambiguous and unstructured than most other projective tests. They are extremely economical techniques that can be given in brief periods of time, either individually or in groups. As a self-report form, SCTs can be given to subjects to complete on their own. It is useful, however, to be aware of how much time a subject spends completing the items.

A variety of SCTs exist, some of which assess general personality issues and others that are developed to assess more specific areas of functioning. Most SCTs typically contain anywhere from 25 to 75 sentence stems. Subjects are asked to complete each incomplete sentence with the first answer that comes to mind.

Responses are usually subjected to two forms of qualitative analysis. Formal aspects of responses are viewed as pertinent sources of data. The length of the response, presence of unexpected grammatical errors, coherence, intrusion of personal pronouns, neatness, and organization may all reveal something about cognitive or ego functioning. Content may be evaluated in terms of interpersonal perceptions, self-experience, attitudes, wishes, and fears.

SCTs are popular projective tools for assessing personality functioning in children and adolescents. Zlotogorski and Wiggs (1986) reviewed several techniques that have yielded significant empirical findings related to identifying school behavior, fear of failure, feelings of deprivation, aggression, stress tolerance, and ego development.

The Hand Test

Wagner (1962) developed the Hand Test to assess the action tendencies of the individual. Instead of focusing on broad features of personality organization, Wagner intended for his test to be used as a focal technique for assessing action potentials that are close to the surface and may be expressed in behavior.

The Hand Test consists of 10 cards that show drawings of hands in different positions; the last card is blank. Subjects are asked to state what the hands look like they are doing. For the blank card, the subject is asked to imagine a hand that would be doing something and to report what it would be doing. The entire procedure takes about 10 minutes. Responses are recorded and scored according to criteria provided in the test manual. Protocols can be analyzed both qualitatively and quantitatively.

Wagner (1986) indicated that the test is well suited for children; the instructions are simple and can be used as part of a game with the child. Because children are often referred for testing because of questions about their behavior, a test that assesses action tendencies can be useful. Disadvantages include its inappropriateness for children under the age of 6 and the rather limited information it reveals about a child's personality functioning.

Norms have been developed for over 1,700 children, including normals, juvenile delinquents, brain-damaged, schizophrenics, and dyslexics, as well as children from different cultures. Most of the research using the Hand Test has focused on acting-out behavior. A number of studies have reported its effectiveness in predicting aggressive behavior (Bricklin, Piotrowski, & Wagner, 1962; Wagner & Hawkins, 1964).

ANIMAL PREFERENCE TEST

The Animal Preference, or Choice, Test (APT) capitalizes on children's natural predilection for projecting or displacing unacceptable attributes onto or identifying with animals. The test is simple, brief, and easy to administer and can be incorporated into most clinical interviews. The APT usually takes about 5 to 10 minutes to administer. There are no materials, only a series of questions posed to the child. The child is asked "What animal would you most like to be like?" and why. Next, the examiner asks "What animal would you least like to be like?" and why. Other versions of the technique involve asking what animal the subject's mother/father/ siblings are most/least like and why.

Another simple projective procedure that is often used in conjunction with the APT is the "three wishes technique," in which the child is asked "If you had three wishes, what would they be?" The projective implications of the child's selected wishes may help illuminate aspects of the youngster's personality functioning.

Research has shown the positive APT choice to be more indicative of a conscious, rational, and intellectual process, whereas the negative choice is a less rational and more idiosyncratic representation of the child's personality (David & Leach, 1957; Rojas & Tuber, 1991). Rojas and Tuber also found that children who disown animals on the basis of nurturing, pleasing, and aesthetic qualities tend to exhibit more aggressive and depressed behavior as reported by their parents.

THE USEFULNESS OF PROJECTIVE TECHNIQUES WITH CHILDREN

Despite general acceptance of projective testing in the diagnostic testing battery, its validity and usefulness in the assessment of children and adolescents have been questioned (Gittelman-Klein, 1988). Citing research that she feels has not supported the promise of projective testing, Gittelman-Klein concluded that, as a whole, projective testing does not provide sufficient valid information to justify its use in psychodiagnostic work with children. In particular, she objected to the term "test" for these procedures, which she said was misleading and inaccurate.

Questions of the wholesale validity of any category of testing are best viewed through a more refined lens. Certainly, it is true that the literature always presents a mixed picture. Some studies support the use of a particular procedure; others do not. Given this reality ubiquitous in social science research, it seems wiser to frame questions of validity in more specific ways. The question is better phrased not "Is this a valid test?" but "Which aspects of the test are useful for understanding which aspects of personality functioning?" Some tests are not helpful and yield meaningless results for some subjects but reveal important information about others. Research should be directed to answering questions about why this is so.

Gittelman-Klein does have a valid point when it comes to whether we call these procedures tests or techniques. The field of personality assessment has long struggled with how to integrate idiographic and nomothetic methods for studying personality. It seems that many of the projective methods presented here should best be considered clinical techniques and not psychometric tests, although this distinction does not apply to all of the procedures reviewed here. In the end, the fundamental issue remains which of these tests or techniques, if given with other assessment procedures, can help generate useful inferences that can be weighed against inferences from other perspectives to form a complete and in-depth picture of a child's internal world.

REFERENCES

Ames, L.B., Learned, J., Metraux, R.W., & Walker, R.N. (1952). *Children's Rorschach responses* (2nd ed.). New York: Brunner/Mazel.

Bellak, L. (1954). *The TAT and CAT in clinical use.* New York: Grune & Stratton.

Bellak, L., & Bellak, S.S. (1952). *Manual for the supplement to the Children's Apperception Test (CAT-S).* Larchmont, NY: C.P.S.

Bellak, L., & Bellak, S.S. (1966). *CAT-H: Children's Apperception (human figures) manual.* Larchmont, NY: C.P.S.

Bose, S., & Benergee, S.N. (1969). A resolution on the personality make-up of some institutionalized physically handicapped children by the Children's Apperception Test (CAT-H). *Journal of Psychological Researches, 13,* 32–36.

Bradfer-Blomart, J. (1970). Analyse des thèmes fournis au CAT par des garçons de huit ans: Comparaison des recits d'un groupe des garçons et des filles du même age [An analysis of themes on the CAT of eight-year-old boys: A comparison of responses of boys and girls of the same age]. *Enfance, 2,* 215–234.

Bricklin, B., Piotrowski, A.A., & Wagner, E.E. (1962). The Hand Test with special reference to the prediction of overt aggressive behavior. In M. Harrower (Ed.), *American lecture series in psychology.* Springfield, IL: Thomas.

Buck, J.N. (1948). The House-Tree-Person technique, a qualitative and quantitative scoring manual. *Journal of Clinical Psychology, 4,* 317–396.

Burns, R., & Kaufman, S. (1970). *Kinetic Family Drawing (KFD): An introduction to understanding children through kinetic drawing.* New York: Brunner/Mazel.

Burns, R., & Kaufman, S. (1982). *Self-growth in families: Kinetic Family Drawings (KFD) research and application.* New York: Brunnel/Mazel.

Chandler, L.A., & Johnson, V.J. (1991). *Using projective techniques with children: A guide to clinical assessment.* Springfield, IL: Thomas.

Dana, R.H. (1968). Thematic techniques and clinical practice. *Journal of Projective Techniques and Personality Assessment, 32,* 204–214.

Dana, R.H. (1986). Thematic Apperception Test used with adolescents. In A.I. Rabin (Ed.), *Projective techniques for adolescents and children* (pp. 12–36). New York: Springer.

David, H., & Leach, W.W. (1957). The projective question: Further studies. *Journal of Projective Techniques, 21,* 3–9.

Dlepu, O., & Kimbrough, C. (1982). Feeling tone and card preferences of Black elementary children for the TCB and TAT. *Journal of Non-White Concerns in Personnel and Guidance, 10,* 50–56.

Ellenberger, H. (1954). The life and work of Hermann Rorschach. *Bulletin of the Menninger Clinic, 18,* 171–222.

Erikson, H., & Rorosgaard, O. (1979). An alternative way of administering the CAT. *Tidsskrift for Norsk Psykologforering, 16,* 484–492.

Exner, J.E. (1993). *The Rorschach* (Vol. 1, 3rd ed.). New York: Wiley.

Exner, J.E., & Weiner, I.B. (1982). *The Rorschach* (Vol. 3). New York: Wiley.

Exner, J.E., & Weiner, I.B. (1995). *The Rorschach* (Vol. 3, 2nd ed.). New York: Wiley.

Falk, J.D. (1981). Understanding children's art: An analysis of the literature. *Journal of Personality Assessment, 45,* 465–472.

Ford, M. (1946). *The application of the Rorschach Test to younger children.* Minneapolis: University of Minnesota.

Frank, L. (1948). *Projective methods.* Springfield, IL: Thomas.

Freud, S. (1913). *Totem and taboo.* New York: Moffatt, Yard & Co.

Friedman, R.J. (1972). TAT story length in children. *Psychology in the Schools, 9,* 413–414.

Gerver, J.M. (1946). *Level of interpretation of children on the Thematic Apperception Test.* Unpublished master's thesis, Ohio State University at Columbus.

Gittelman-Klein, R. (1988). Questioning the clinical usefulness of projective psychological tests for children. In S. Chess, A. Thomas, & M. Hertzig (Eds.), *Annual progress in child psychiatry and child development 1987* (pp. 451–461). New York: Brunner/Mazel.

Goodenough, F. (1926). *Measurement of intelligence in drawings.* New York: World Book.

Groth-Marnat, G. (1984). *Handbook of psychological assessment.* New York: Van Nostrand-Reinhold.

Hammer, E.F. (1958). *The clinical application of projective drawings.* Springfield, IL: Thomas.

Hammer, E.F. (1985). The House-Tree-Person Test. In C.S. Newmark (Ed.), *Major psychological assessment instruments* (pp. 135–164). Boston: Allyn & Bacon.

Hammer, E.F. (1986). Graphic techniques with children and adolescents. In A.I. Rabin (Ed.), *Projective techniques for adolescents and children* (pp. 239–263). New York: Springer.

Handler, L. (1985). The clinical use of the Draw-a-Person Test (DAP). In C.S. Newmark (Ed.), *Major psychological assessment instruments* (pp. 165–216). Boston: Allyn & Bacon.

Handler, L., & Habenicht, D. (1994). The Kinetic Family Drawing Technique: A review of the literature. *Journal of Personality Assessment, 62,* 440–464.

Harris, D.B. (1963). *Children's drawings as a measure of intellectual maturity.* New York: Harcourt Brace.

Hartwell, S.W., Hutt, M.L., Andrew, G., & Walton, W.E. (1951). The Michigan Picture Test: Diagnosis and therapeutic possibilities of a new projective test in child guidance. *American Journal of Orthopsychiatry, 21,* 124–137.

Haworth, M.R. (1965). *A schedule of adaptive mechanisms in CAT responses.* Larchmont, NY: C.P.S.

Haworth, M.R. (1986). Children's Apperception Test. In A.I. Rabin (Ed.), *Projective techniques for adolescents and children* (pp. 37–72). New York: Springer.

Henry, W. (1947). The scoring and analysis of the Thematic Apperception Test. *Journal of Psychology, 24,* 319–330.

Holtzman, W.H. (1986). Holtzman Inkblot Technique with children and adolescents. In A.I. Rabin (Ed.), *Projective techniques for adolescents and children* (pp. 168–192). New York: Springer.

Holtzman, W.H., Thorpe, J.S., Swartz, J.C., & Herron, E.W. (1961). *Inkblot perception and personality.* Austin: University of Texas.

Hulse, W. (1952). Childhood conflict expressed through family drawings. *Journal of Projective Techniques, 16,* 66–79.

Hutt, M.L. (1980). *Michigan Picture Test–Revised.* New York: Grune & Stratton.

Hutt, M.L. (1986). The Michigan Picture Test–Revised. In A.I. Rabin (Ed.), *Projective techniques for adolescents and children* (pp. 73–84). New York: Springer.

Jolles, I.A. (1952). *A catalog for the qualitative interpretation of the House-Tree-Person Test.* Beverly Hills, CA: Western Psychological Services.

Kahill, S.A. (1984). Human figure drawing in adults: An update of the empirical evidence, 1967–1982. *Canadian Psychology/Psychologie Canadienne, 25,* 269–292.

Kirkpatrick, E.A. (1900). Individual tests of school children. *Psychological Review, 7,* 274–280.

Klopfer, B., & Margulies, H. (1941). Rorschach reactions in early childhood. *Rorschach Research Exchange, 5,* 1–23.

Klopfer, B., Spiegelman, M., & Fox, J. (1956). The interpretation of children's records. In B. Klopfer (Ed.), *Developments in the Rorschach Technique* (Vol. 2, pp. 22–44), New York: Harcourt Brace.

Koppitz, E. (1966). Emotional indicators in human figure drawings of children: A validation study. *Journal of Clinical Psychology, 22,* 313–315.

Koppitz, E. (1968). *Psychological evaluation of children's human figure drawings.* New York: Grune & Stratton.

Leichtman, M. (1996). *The Rorschach: A developmental perspective.* Hillsdale, NJ: Analytic Press.

Lindzey, G. (1961). *Projective techniques and cross-cultural research.* New York: Appleton-Century-Crofts.

Machover, K. (1949). *Personality projection in the drawings of the human figure.* Springfield, IL: Thomas.

McGrew, M.W., & Teglasi, H. (1990). Formal characteristics of Thematic Apperception Test stories as indices of emotional disturbance in children. *Journal of Personality Assessment, 54,* 639–655.

Murray, H. (1938). *Explorations in personality.* New York: Oxford University Press.

Neuman, R.S., Neuman, J., & Sellers, S.B. (1974). *Language and adjustment scales for the Thematic Apperception Test for youths 12–17 years* (DHEW Publication No. HRA 75–1336). Rockville, MD: National Center for Health Statistics.

Parsons, C.J. (1917). Children's interpretation of inkblots. *British Journal of Psychology, 9,* 151–156.

Passman, R.H., & Lautmann, L.A. (1982). Fathers', mothers', and security blankets' effects on the responsiveness of young children during projective testing. *Journal of Clinical and Consulting Psychology, 50,* 310–312.

Porterfield, C.L. (1969). Adaptive mechanisms of young disadvantaged stutterers and nonstutterers. *Journal of Projective Techniques and Personality Assessment, 33,* 372–375.

Pyle, W.H. (1915). A psychological study of bright and dull pupils. *Journal of Educational Psychology, 6,* 151–156.

Rabin, A.I. (1986). Concerning projective techniques. In A.I. Rabin (Ed.), *Projective techniques for adolescents and children* (pp. 3–13). New York: Springer.

Rapaport, D., Gill, M., & Schafer, R. (1946). *Diagnostic psychological testing.* Chicago: Yearbook.

Rojas, E.B., & Tuber, S. (1991). The Animal Preference Test and its relationship to behavioral problems in young children. *Journal of Personality Assessment, 57,* 141–148.

Rorschach, H. (1921). *Psychodiagnostik [Psychodiagnostics]* (E. Bircher, Trans.) (6th ed.). New York: Grune & Stratton.

Sauraute, N. (1984). *Childhood.* London: John Calder.

Schaible, M. (1975). Analysis of noncontent TAT variables in a longitudinal sample. *Journal of Personality Assessment, 39,* 480–485.

Simmons, D.D. (1967). Children's preferences for humanized versus natural animals. *Journal of Projective Techniques and Personality Assessment, 31,* 39–41.

Springer, N.N. (1941). A study of the drawings of maladjusted and adjusted children. *Journal of Genetic Psychology, 58,* 131–138.

Tharinger, D., & Stark, K. (1990). A qualitative versus quantitative approach to evaluate the Draw-a-Person and Kinetic Family Drawing: A study of mood- and anxiety-disorder children. *Psychological Assessment, 2,* 365–375.

Triplett, S., & Brunson, P. (1982). TCB and TAT response characteristics in Black males and females: A replication. *Journal of Non-White Concerns in Personnel and Guidance, 10,* 50–56.

Vane, J.R. (1981). The Thematic Apperception Test: A review. *Clinical Psychology Review, 1,* 319–336.

Vane, J.R., & Eisen, V.W. (1962). The Goodenough Draw-a-Man Test and signs of maladjustment in kindergarten children. *Journal of Clinical Psychology, 18,* 276–279.

Wagner, E.E. (1962). *Hand Test: Manual for administration, scoring, and interpretation.* Los Angeles: Western Psychological Services.

Wagner, E.E. (1986). Hand Test interpretation for children and adolescents. In A.I. Rabin (Ed.), *Projective techniques for adolescents and children* (pp. 279–305). New York: Springer.

Wagner, E.E., & Hawkins, R. (1964). Differentiation of assaultive delinquents with the Hand Test. *Journal of Projective Techniques and Personality Assessment, 28,* 363–365.

Werner, H. (1961). *Comparative psychology of mental development.* New York: Science Editions.

Westen, D., Lohr, N., Silk, K., Kerber, K., & Goodrich, S. (1989). *Object relations and social cognition TAT scoring manual* (14th ed.). Unpublished manuscript, University of Michigan, Ann Arbor.

Zlotogorski, Z., & Wiggs, E. (1986). Story- and sentence-completion techniques. In A.I. Rabin (Ed.), *Projective techniques for adolescents and children* (pp. 195–211). New York: Springer.

CHAPTER 11

Standardized Rating Scales in the Assessment of Children's Behavioral and Emotional Problems

PAUL J. FRICK AND RANDY W. KAMPHAUS

Standardized rating scales have long played a prominent role in the assessment of both adult's and children's psychological adjustment. There is a long history of using self-report inventories to assess personality dimensions in adults (e.g., Hathaway & McKinley, 1942). Having adults rate their attitudes, emotions, and behaviors using a standardized format (e.g., standard questions, standard response format) results in very reliable information that can be collected in a time-efficient manner. Both the reliability and time-efficiency of these ratings enable them to be used widely in research, thus allowing for the validity of these ratings in predicting clinically important criteria (e.g., degree of impairment, response to treatment, risk for arrest or hospitalization) to be tested. Also, the ease of administration allows standardized rating scales to be given to large samples of individuals in a community so that an individual's ratings can be compared to those of others in the general population.

All of these characteristics of adult self-report rating scales make them appealing for use in the assessment of children and adolescents, especially the ability to compare a child's ratings with those from large normative samples. Given children's rapid passage through many developmental stages, it is important that a child's emotional and behavioral functioning be compared to others of approximately the same developmental level. Unfortunately, the unfolding development of the child presents additional problems for the use of self-report inventories in youth. For example, the limited reading ability of many young children makes it hard to construct inventories on which children can accurately report on their own attitudes, emotions, and behavior. In addition, children's developing cognitive capacities make it difficult for many of them to accurately perceive and describe their own emotional states and behaviors, irrespective of their reading ability. As result, standardized rating scales for children, especially young children (before the age of 8 or 9), often are completed by knowledgeable others in a child's environment, such as parents and teachers.

With these developmentally appropriate modifications, standardized rating scales possess many characteristics that make them indispensable in the clinical assessment of children and adolescents. They provide reliable information on many aspects of a child's psychological adjustment in a time-efficient manner. Furthermore, they often provide normative information so that the ratings of a child

Table 11.1 Summary of selected comprehensive rating scales used in the assessment of children and adolescents.

Scale/Authors	Publisher	Age Range (yrs.)	Domains Assessed	Informant	Quality of Normative Data
Behavioral Assessment System for Children (BASC; Reynolds & Kamphaus, 1992)	American Guidance Service	4–18	Adaptability, aggression, anxiety, attention problems, conduct problems, atypicality, depression, hyperactivity, leadership, learning problems, social skills, somatization, study skills, withdrawal, attitude to school, attitude to teachers, interpersonal relations, locus of control, relations with parents, self-esteem, self-reliance, sensation seeking, sense of inadequacy, social stress	Parent, teacher, and child (ages 8–18)	E
Child Behavior Checklist (CBCL; Achenbach, 1991)	Author, University of Vermont	4–18	Withdrawal, somatic complaints, anxiety/depression, social problems, thought problems, attention problems, aggressive behavior, delinquency	Parent, teacher, and child (ages 11–18)	F
Children's Symptom Inventory 4 (CSI-4; Gadow & Sprafkin, 1994)	Check-mate Plus	5–14	Attention-deficit/hyperactivity disorder, oppositional defiant disorder, conduct disorder, generalized anxiety disorder, social phobia, separation anxiety disorder, major depressive disorder, dysthymic disorder, autistic disorder, schizophrenia, tic disorder	Parent and teacher	P
Conners' Rating Scales (Conners, 1997)	Multi-Health Systems	3–17	Cognitive problems, oppositionality, hyperactivity, anxious-shy, perfectionism, social problems, psychosomatic, family problems, anger control problems	Parent, teacher, and child	G
Minnesota Multiphasic Personality Inventory for Adolescents (MMPI-A; Butcher et al., 1992)	National Computer Systems	14–18	Hypochondriasis, depression, hysteria, psychopathic deviate, masculinity-femininity, paranoia, psychasthenia, schizophrenia, hypomania, social introversion	Child	P
Personality Inventory for Children–Revised (PIC-R; Lachar & Gruber, 1991)	Western Psychological Services	9–18	Achievement, intellectual screening, development, somatic concerns, depression, family relations, withdrawal, anxiety, psychosis, hyperactivity, delinquency, social skills, reality distortion	Parent and child	G

Note: Evaluation of the scales' normative base as either poor (P), fair (F), good (G), or excellent (E) is taken from Kamphaus & Frick (1996), with the exception of the CSI-4 and the Conners' Rating Scales, which were not included in this text. Some of the domains assessed are not included on all forms completed by the different informants.

can be compared to the ratings of other children of a similar developmental level. However, standardized rating scales also possess a number of limitations as well. One of the key limitations of standardized ratings is that they assess a rater's *perceptions* of his or her own or other's emotions and behaviors. As such, these perceptions can be affected by a host of factors, such as intentional or unintentional biases, imperfect knowledge of a child's behavior, inaccuracies in perceptions due to an immature cognitive level, and differences in raters' standards for judging the severity of behavior.

A second limitation is that there are substantial variations in how rating scales are constructed, leading to substantial variability in how psychological constructs are assessed across the scales. To illustrate this variability, items on the Attention Problems scale of the Child Behavior Checklist (Achenbach, 1991) include such items as "nervous or high-strung" and "nervous movements and twitching," as well as items that are more traditionally associated with inattention such as "can't pay attention for long" and "daydreams." Also, this scale includes items assessing hyperactivity, such as "can't sit still," and impulsivity, such as "impulsive or acts without thinking." In contrast, the Attention Problems scale of the Behavior Assessment System for Children (C.R. Reynolds & Kamphaus, 1992), despite having the same name, includes items that are focused only on inattention, such as "is easily distracted" and "completes work on time." Given these differences in items, scores on the two subscales with the same name may result from very different behaviors (see Kamphaus & Frick, 1996, for other examples). As a result, assessors must be well informed on the items that are included on subscales of behavior rating scales and make interpretations based on the specific item content.

Recognizing both the strengths and limitations of standardized rating scales is critical for using them appropriately in the clinical assessment of children and adolescents. As a result, these issues are revisited in many sections throughout this chapter. In the next two sections, an overview of some of the more commonly used standardized rating scales is provided. First, comprehensive rating scales that assess a wide range of emotional and behavioral problems are reviewed; this section is followed by a review of scales that assess more circumscribed domains of functioning. Given that there are hundreds of standardized rating scales in use, this is obviously a very selective review and is designed to provide examples of how to evaluate the critical characteristics of standardized scales. Also, this brief overview of individual scales should not take the place of the more detailed information provided in the manuals that accompany most of these rating scales (see also Kamphaus & Frick, 1996, for more comprehensive reviews of most scales). Finally, Table 11.1 on page 191 provides a brief summary of the key characteristics of the comprehensive rating scales that are reviewed in this chapter.

COMPREHENSIVE RATING SCALES

BEHAVIOR ASSESSMENT SYSTEM FOR CHILDREN (BASC)

Description
The BASC rating scales (Reynolds & Kamphaus, 1992) were designed to provide a multi-informant assessment of a wide range of emotional and behavioral problems, as well as to assess many types of adaptive behaviors (e.g., social skills, leadership, adaptability, and study skills). All forms of the BASC have multiple rating forms that are specific to certain age groups. The Self-Report of Personality (SRP) has a form for children ages 8 to 11 and another one for adolescents ages 12 to 18. All items on the SRP are rated by the child as being either true or false. The Parent Rating Scales (PRS) and Teacher Rating Scales (TRS) have three formats, one for preschool children (4–5), a second for elementary school-age children (6–11), and a third for middle/high school-age children (12–18). The behavioral descriptors on the PRS and TRS scales are rated by parents and teachers on a four-point scale, ranging from never to almost always. The length of the BASC across all of the formats ranges from 109 items to 186 items. The BASC also includes a parent interview form, the Structured Developmental History (SDH), and a classroom observation scale, the Student Observation System (SOS).

The content of the TRS and PRS versions of the BASC are fairly similar, with the main difference being that teachers also rate behavior indicative of learning problems and study skills. The content of the SRP, however, is quite different. For example, the child does not rate his or her own level of behavioral (e.g., aggression and conduct problems) or attentional problems. Instead, the SRP focuses largely on ratings of a child's or adolescent's emotional functioning, attitudes toward parents and teachers, self-concept, and social relationships. The BASC also includes several validity scales to assess whether there were any obvious response patterns that would make the assessor suspect the validity of the child's, parent's, or teacher's responses. For example, it has a scale checking the consistency of responses, a scale assessing the use of a socially desirable response set, and a scale assessing the tendency of a rater to portray the child in a particularly deviant way. Although such validity scales are common in self-report instruments, their inclusion on ratings by parents and teachers is somewhat unique.

The BASC scales are relatively lengthy, taking approximately 15 to 20 minutes to complete. There are both hand-scoring and computer formats that allow for easy calculation of norm-referenced scores (T-scores and percentile ranks) to aid in interpreting the scales. These scores are based on very large samples of children (ranging from $n = 2,401$ for the SRP to $n = 3,483$ for the PRS) spanning 116 sites across the United States and Canada. The sampling procedures were designed to ensure an adequate representation of ethnic minorities; in fact, the sample had a slightly larger representation of African-American and Hispanic children than would be expected based on 1986 to 1988 U.S. population figures. However, norm-referenced scores are statistically weighted to approximate census data.

The manual for the BASC (Reynolds & Kamphaus, 1992) provides evidence for various types of reliability (e.g., internal consistency, test-retest reliability, and interrater reliability) for the subscales. With very few exceptions, the subscales proved to be quite reliable in the standardization sample. For example, across all the estimates of internal consistency for the BASC scales, only one, the Conduct Problems scale for girls ages 6 to 7, had questionable internal consistency (coefficient alpha = .48). The manual provides factor analytic support for the construct validity of the scales as well, and provides correlations between the BASC scales and several other commonly used rating scales. Also, whereas the scale content was guided by factor analyses, rational decisions were also made to ensure that the content of the scales were somewhat homogeneous and correspond to current conceptualizations of most constructs.

Overall Evaluation

The BASC scales cover the major domains of behavioral and emotional functioning, as well as assessing many aspects of adaptive behavior (adaptability, leadership, social skills, and study skills). The content seems to reflect current conceptualizations of childhood psychopathology in many important respects, such as including separate anxiety and depression scales and separate hyperactivity and attention scales. The BASC scales were developed to have fairly homogeneous item content on the subscales, which greatly facilitates interpretation of scale scores. Also, the BASC includes validity indices for all formats across age and informants. The PRS and TRS versions have a preschool version for children ages 4 to 5 (with new norms for ages 2–6 through 3–11), an age group often not included in many other rating scales, and the self-report version was standardized to a younger age (i.e., age 8) than many other scales. Finally, and perhaps most important, the BASC has a large nationwide normative sample, allowing an assessor to confidently make many norm-referenced interpretations.

All these considerations make the BASC one of the most useful rating scale systems for the assessment of children and adolescents. One weakness, however, is that because the BASC was published more recently than many of the other scales reviewed in this chapter, there is less research on the validity of its scales. The manual reports encouraging initial findings on the validity of the scales, especially the factor analytic support for its scale structure. Early studies of the use of the BASC for the diagnosis of ADHD are encouraging (Doyle, Ostrander, Skare, Crosby, & August, 1997; Vaughn, Riccio, Hynd, & Hall, 1997). However, the use of the BASC in clinical populations needs further testing to more firmly establish its validity for various purposes.

CHILD BEHAVIOR CHECKLIST (CBCL)

Description

The CBCL (Achenbach, 1991) has a long and prominent history for assessing children's emotional and behavioral functioning and may be one of the most widely used rating scale systems reviewed in this chapter. The Parent Report Form (PRF) was designed for children ages 4 to 18, whereas the Teacher Report Form was designed for school-aged children (5–18).

The Youth Self-Report (YSR) of the CBCL was designed for ages 11 to 18. The content of the 113 items across the three assessment formats is identical, as are the subscales, all of which greatly facilitates interpreting information across different raters. All CBCL items are rated as being not true, somewhat true or sometimes true, or very true or often true, and these items cover a broad array of both internalizing (e.g., anxiety, depression, somatic complaints) and externalizing (antisocial behavior, aggression, oppositionality) behaviors.

The CBCL can typically be completed in about 10 to 15 minutes and both hand-scoring and computer-scoring options are available. The computer-scoring system converts raw scores to norm-referenced scores appropriate for the child's age and gender. The normative sample for the CBCL involves a large (n = 2,368) nationwide sample that is geographically representative of the U.S. population. Yet, although it includes representation of African-American and Hispanic children that approximates the U.S. population, there is an overrepresentation of middle to upper socioeconomic classes. Also, the normative sample excluded children who had received mental health services or special remedial school classes within the preceding 12 months. Therefore, the sample should be considered a normal comparison group rather than one that is normative and representative of the general population.

The CBCL manual presents several types of reliability estimates for the subscales, and generally these scales have proven to be reliable across most age groups. The one notable exception was the Thought Problems scale, which tended to have somewhat low internal consistency and poor test-retest reliability in girls. The manual provides factor analytical support for the subscales. As mentioned previously, the scales were largely based on the results of the factor analyses with the only modifications made to ensure consistent subscales across informants, ages, and gender. No attempts were made to ensure homogeneous item content, making some subscales quite heterogeneous.

The CBCL has been widely used in research, and these studies generally support the validity of the scales in (1) differentiating clinic-referred children from nonclinic children, (2) being correlated with classroom observations of children's behavior, and (3) being correlated with independent clinical diagnoses (see Achenbach, 1991; Piacentini, 1993). One note of caution, however, is that most of these stud-

ies on the CBCL have focused primarily on the externalizing scales (i.e., the Aggressive Behavior and Delinquency scales) and the Attention Problem scale, with much less information being available on the validity of the internalizing scales.

Overall Evaluation

The CBCL is one of the most widely used of all the rating scales reviewed in this chapter. Therefore, there is a large literature showing correlations between CBCL scales and important clinical criteria, especially for the externalizing scales. The scale content of the CBCL is consistent across informants, which greatly aids in assessing cross-informant consistency in the ratings of a child's adjustment. The geographical and ethnic representativeness of the normative sample is a great improvement over that of the original CBCL, although there are still several problematic areas. For example, the normative sample is somewhat weighted toward children from upper socioeconomic strata and it excluded children who had received mental health or special education services. Finally, the subscales of the CBCL tend to have heterogeneous item content, which needs to be considered when interpreting scores. However, the computer-scoring program provides a summary of how each individual item was rated, which greatly aids in this interpretation. Finally, because the items on the CBCL were originally developed in the 1970s, some of the content does not match current conceptualizations of childhood psychopathology, leading to some difficulty in making some specific distinctions among types of childhood problems. For example, there are single scales combining anxious with depressive behaviors and attentional problems with overactivity.

CHILDREN'S SYMPTOM INVENTORY 4 (CSI-4)

Description

The CSI-4 (Gadow & Sprafkin, 1994) is a standardized rating scale designed to assess the symptoms of over a dozen childhood disorders. This content is unique from other rating scales in several respects. First, it is the only omnibus rating scale to be explicitly tied to the diagnostic criteria specified in the *Diagnostic and Statistical Manual of Mental Disorders,* fourth edition (*DSM-IV;* American Psychiatric Association [APA], 1994). Therefore, its content reflects the research that went into developing these diagnostic criteria, which is excellent for some disorders but more suspect for others (Widiger et al., 1998). Second, it covers many symptom domains that are not assessed by other rating scales (e.g., tic disorders), especially symptoms of more severe types of childhood psychopathology (e.g., obsessive-compulsive disorder, posttraumatic stress disorders, schizophrenia, and autism). As a result, the CSI-4 may be especially useful in the assessment of more severely disturbed children.

The CSI-4 has both parent and teacher report versions that contain analogous scale content and were designed for use with children ages 5 to 14. There is an analogous Adolescent Symptom Inventory 4 (ASI-4; Gadow & Sprafkin, 1995) that has both parent and teacher versions as well, but also includes an adolescent self-report checklist. Also, in 1997, the Early Childhood Inventory 4 (ECI-4; Gadow & Sprafkin, 1997) was published to assess preschool children. The 97 items on the CSI-4 are rated on a 0 (never) to 3 (very often) scale. Like other rating scales, quantitative scale scores corresponding to each diagnostic category (e.g., conduct disorder) can be determined by simply summing the ratings across items; this score is called the symptom severity index. However, a symptom count score can be used to more closely approximate the *DSM-IV* method of considering symptoms as either present or absent. Using this method, any item rated as being present often or very often is considered to indicate a symptom as being present, and any item rated as never or sometimes is considered to indicate the absence of the symptom.

Given its explicit link to the *DSM-IV*, which bases its classification on levels of "impairment" rather than on normative cutoffs, there is only limited normative data on the CSI-4. Therefore, norm-referenced interpretations should not be made from the CSI-4. The main evidence for the reliability of the CSI-4 scores comes from a six-week test-retest study of 75 boys between the ages of 6 and 10. In general, the test-retest estimates were higher using the symptom severity scoring method and were all above .60, with the exception of the items assessing major depressive disorder ($r = .56$), dysthymic disorder ($r = .54$), and schizophrenia ($r = .37$). From the validity evidence provided in the manual, the CSI-4 scales are effective in differentiating normal control children from clinic children.

The content of the CSI-4 scales was not based on factor analyses but were designed to assess symptoms contained in the *DSM-IV* diagnostic categories. Therefore, the most important information on its validity is how well it corresponds to *DSM-IV* categories. Evidence for this correspondence is provided by Gadow and Sprafkin (1998). In a clinic sample of 101 referrals to an outpatient child psychiatry service (6–12 years), the correspondence between CSI-4 diagnostic cutoffs and clinical diagnoses made by mental health professionals was assessed using conditional probability indices (sensitivity and specificity). These indices for each CSI-4 scale are provided in Table 11.2. A couple of issues are important for interpreting these indices. First, these are quite conservative tests in clinic-referred samples because even those children who do not have a given diagnosis often have other forms of psychopathology. Therefore, these indices reflect the ability of the CSI-4 to differentiate *within* psychiatric disorders, and such differential validity has been very difficult to prove for many standardized rating scales. Second, the estimates of sensitivity and specificity are highly influenced by a number of factors, such as the base rate of the diagnoses in the sample and the level of severity used to determine cutoff scores on the CSI-4 (see Frick et al., 1994). Therefore, it is difficult to provide a single estimate that would be stable across samples. However, these rates are very informative as to the correspondence between ratings on the CSI-4 and a clinical diagnosis. For example, a sensitivity of .80 for ADHD indicates that of those in the sample who had a clinical diagnosis of ADHD, 80% crossed the screening cutoff for a diagnosis on the CSI-4. The specificity of .74 indicates that of those without the diagnosis of ADHD in the sample, 74% did not cross the screening cutoff on the CSI-4. Evident from these estimates, the sensitivity rates for the CSI-4 were typically enhanced when a combination of parent and teacher reports on the CSI-4 were used.

Overall Evaluation
The CSI-4 is unique in its attempt to assess content that directly corresponds to *DSM-IV* classifications of childhood psychopathology. This focus on diagnostic classification allows for the assessment of a number of behavior domains, especially those indicative of more severe forms of psychopathology, that are not covered by other standardized rating scales. However, because of its attempt to correspond to *DSM-IV*, there was minimal focus on developing normative data for the CSI-4; therefore, norm-referenced

Table 11.2 Agreement between screening cutoff scores on the CSI-4 and clinical diagnoses in a sample of clinic-referred children ($n=101$).

CSI-4 Category	Parent		Teacher		Parent or Teacher	
	Sen	Spe	Sen	Spe	Sen	Spe
Attention-Deficit/Hyperactivity	.80	.74	.60	.86	.87	.65
Oppositional Defiant	.69	.75	.71	.80	.89	.55
Conduct	NA	.83	NA	.80	NA	NA
Generalized Anxiety	.38	.95	.38	.71	.93	.71
Specific Phobia	NA	.63	NA	.81	NA	.89
Obsessive-Compulsive	NA	.73	NA	.68	NA	.89
Posttraumatic Stress	NA	.72	NA	.77	NA	.94
Social Phobia	.43	.83	.50	.94	.87	.81
Separation Anxiety	NA	.95	NA	NA	NA	NA
Depressive Disorder	.81	.73	.61	.83	.88	.59
Tic Disorder	.89	.63	.89	.62	1.00	.40
Schizophrenia	NA	.97	NA	.99	NA	NA
Pervasive Developmental	.64	.99	.86	.93	1.00	.92
Elimination Disorder	1.00	.64	NA	NA	NA	NA

Note: Information is taken from Gadow and Sprafkin (1998). Sen=Sensitivity and Spe=Specificity. No estimates are calculated (NA) when there were too few children with a diagnosis to calculate conditional probability estimates.

interpretations should not be made from this rating scale system. The correspondence between CSI-4 scores and clinical diagnoses is quite good, especially when a combination of parent and teacher ratings are used. However, these figures are based on only one moderately sized sample and clearly more data are needed from other samples. Also, as explicitly stated in the manual for the CSI-4, this scale (or any other assessment technique) should not be used as the sole criterion for making a clinical diagnosis, which should instead be based on a combination of many sources of information (Kamphaus & Frick, 1996).

CONNERS RATING SCALES (CRS)

Description

The CRS (Conners, 1997) has a long history of use in the assessment of childhood psychopathology. It was originally developed to assess the effectiveness of medication trials for hyperactive children (Conners, 1969). The 10-item Conner's Global Index (CGI; formerly called the Hyperactivity Index) remains one of the best-validated measures for this purpose. Through much of the first three decades in which it was used, there were many different versions of the CRS, each with different content and psychometric properties. The most recent version,

published by Multi-Health Systems in 1997, has parent and teacher versions for assessing children and adolescents ages 3 through 17 and a self-report version for ages 12 through 17. Each report format has both long (ranging from 59 to 87 items) and short (ranging from 27 to 28 items) forms, with the long forms taking between 15 and 20 minutes to complete and the short forms taking from 5 to 10 minutes to complete.

Items on the CRS are rated on a 0 (not true at all) to 3 (very much true) scale. The item content and scale structure is fairly similar for the parent and teacher versions. Both versions assess externalizing (oppositional, hyperactivity) and internalizing behaviors (anxious-shy, perfectionism), and they assess social problems and behaviors indicative of learning difficulties. The only difference between the teacher and parent versions of the CRS is the presence of a Psychosomatic subscale on the parent version. The adolescent self-report version of the CRS includes scales assessing the adolescent's perception of family functioning and the presence of anger control problems. Unlike the revisions done by many other rating scales, the content of the newest version of the CRS was not solely driven by items contained on earlier versions of the scale, and, as a result, the content is fairly reflective of current conceptualizations of childhood emotional and behavior problems. Also, the method of scale construction led to fairly homogeneous scale content that greatly facilitates interpretation.

The CRS has both hand-scoring and computer-scoring formats that allow for easy calculation of norm-referenced scores. The most important advance of the 1997 revision is its normative sample. This sample consisted of children from 45 states and 10 provinces throughout the United States and Canada, ranging in size from 3,394 for the adolescent report formats to 1,973 for the teacher formats. Despite the improvement in the size of the normative sample from previous version of the CRS, a number of fairly important weaknesses remain. Most important, the manual is unclear about the representativeness of the normative sample in terms of ethnicity and socioeconomic status, although it is reported that such data were collected. Furthermore, the sample eliminated children currently enrolled in special education classes, making it a "normal" sample rather than a representative normative sample.

Internal consistency coefficients for the CRS subscales in the standardization sample were uniformly high. Further support for the reliability of the scales comes from test-retest (6–8 weeks) reliability coefficients reported in the CRS manual, based on a sample of 50 children and adolescents. In general, these coefficients were also quite high, with only the Anxious-Shy scale from parent report ($r = .47$) and the Cognitive Problems scale from teacher report ($r = .47$) showing somewhat low test-retest reliability. The justification for the factor structure of all versions of the CRS is also provided in its manual and is quite impressive. However, other evidence for the validity of the subscales is minimal. There are correlations between the CRS scales and the Children's Depression Inventory (CDI; Kovacs, 1992) in several small samples (ranging from $n = 27$ to $n = 33$). The correlations with CDI total score ranged from $r = .23$ for the parent report Perfectionism scale to $r = .82$ for the parent report Oppositional scale. In fact, the correlation between the CDI and parent report Oppositional scale was higher than the correlation between the CDI and the adolescent report of Emotional Problems scale ($r = .76$), which calls into question the ability of the CRS scales to distinguish between different types of emotional and behavioral problems.

Also in the manual are analyses comparing the CRS subscales across children diagnosed with attention-deficit/hyperactivity disorder (ADHD), children diagnosed with "emotional problems" by a child psychologist or psychiatrist, and a normal control sample. In general, most CRS scales not only differentiated ADHD children from the normal control group but also differentiated ADHD children from the group with emotional problems. However, several aspects of these analyses also call into question the divergent validity of CRS scales. The Anxious-Shy scale of the parent and teacher versions of the CRS and the Emotional Problems scale of the CRS did not differentiate between the clinical groups. Also, the teacher version of the Hyperactivity scale of the CRS was not significantly different between the ADHD and Emotional Problems groups.

Overall Evaluation

The revised CRS updated its content so that it more closely corresponds to current conceptualizations of childhood psychopathology, while still maintaining some of its best-validated content, such as the CGI. Also, its method of scale formation led to scales with fairly homogeneous item content, and there is good correspondence across scales on the parent and teacher versions, which facilitates comparisons in a multi-informant assessment. Despite the improved item content on the CRS, however, there are still some notable weaknesses. Specifically, only oppositional types of conduct problems are assessed and not more serious conduct problems (e.g., stealing, lying, vandalism). Also, there is fairly minimal coverage of depression items, especially on parent and teacher versions, and there is no assessment of attentional difficulties on the main forms of the CRS. The normative sample, although large and geographically diverse, is suspect in its representation of ethnic minorities. Finally, there is only minimal evidence at present for the external validity of many of the CRS scales. Because the content is substantially revised from previous versions, evidence from past versions of the scale are not likely to be applicable to the new CRS scales.

MINNESOTA MULTIPHASIC PERSONALITY INVENTORY–ADOLESCENT (MMPI-A)

Description

The MMPI-A (Butcher et al., 1992) has its roots in the original work of Hathaway and McKinley

(1942), who developed the adult version of the MMPI and the later revision of this scale, the MMPI-2 (Butcher et al., 1992). The MMPI-A contains the 5 validity scales and 10 clinical scales that are the hallmark of the adult MMPI scales. However, the MMPI-A also contains 15 content scales specifically designed for adolescents. These scales are Anxiety, Obsessiveness, Depression, Health Concerns, Alienation, Bizarre Mentation, Anger, Cynicism, Conduct Problems, Low Self-Esteem, Low Aspirations, Social Discomfort, Family Problems, School Problems, and Negative Treatment Indicators. Besides being designed specifically for adolescents, making their content somewhat more age-appropriate, the content scales were developed in a different fashion from the original clinical scales and, as a result, have much more homogeneous item content. The MMPI-A is unusually lengthy in comparison to other self-report inventories designed for children and adolescents, containing 478 true-false questions necessary to obtain the validity scales, clinical scales, and content scales.

The normative sample for the MMPI-A was obtained in eight states in the continental United States and contains 805 males and 815 females ages 14 to 18. The distribution of the sample by variables such as gender, age, grade, and parental education and occupation are given in the manual. These variables were not, however, used as stratification variables in order to match U.S. Census or other criteria. The Hispanic population, for example, is clearly undersampled, constituting only 2.2% of the female sample and 2% of the male sample. Similarly, the SES distribution seems to be skewed toward higher levels of SES than the national population. The age distribution of the sample is also highly variable. For example, at age 18, only 42 male cases and 45 female cases were collected.

There are distinct differences in the internal consistency estimates for the MMPI-A across scales. Some of the clinical scales have typical and respectable estimates, whereas others, such as the Masculinity-Femininity scale, have reliability coefficients well below what would be considered acceptable (i.e., internal consistency estimates of .43 for boys and .40 for girls). The internal consistency estimates for the content scales of the MMPI-A are generally better than those for the original clinical scales, supporting a greater attention to these scales in the interpretation of scores for many adolescents. Also, studies of the clinical scales of the MMPI-A

have generally found 4 factors rather than 10, labeled general anxiety, overcontrol or repression, social introversion, and masculinity-femininity (Butcher et al., 1992). In contrast to the clinical scales, there is a wealth of available evidence for the external validity of many of the MMPI-A content scales (see Butcher et al., 1992). For example, the Depression content scale has been correlated with measures of suicidal ideation and suicidal gestures and a history of clinical depression.

Overall Evaluation

The MMPI-A's long history is simultaneously its greatest asset and greatest liability. The loyalty to the original MMPI structure is untenable; it assumes that all of the original clinical scales have been the beneficiary of strong validation support and that research on adolescent psychopathology and personality has not progressed since the inception of the scales. On the other hand, it leads to a familiar structure to a large group of devoted users. Furthermore, its validity scales are some of the most studied of any method of detecting obvious response sets, and there are numerous books and chapters devoted to the MMPI that offer highly sensible guidance for interpreting profiles of scale elevations. Furthermore, the content scales of the MMPI-A appear to have great promise in the assessment of adolescents. These scales, however, are embedded in a very lengthy test in which a number of scales are not internally consistent and have minimal factor analytic support. Furthermore, there is little evidence that the normative sample matches well the demographics of the U.S. population, which calls into question the interpretation of norm-referenced scores. Finally, the MMPI-A, with its direct link to the adult personality assessment tradition that has typically relied on self-report, does not have forms to collect analogous information from other informants.

PERSONALITY INVENTORY FOR CHILDREN–REVISED (PIC-R) AND THE PERSONALITY INVENTORY FOR YOUTH (PIY)

Description

The PIC-R (Wirt, Lachar, Klinedinst, & Seat, 1990), is one of the oldest of the parent rating scales. The original development of the PIC was conducted in the 1950s as a childhood equivalent of the MMPI.

However, given the skepticism concerning young children's ability to provide reliable information on their behavioral and emotional functioning, it was designed to be a parent-report inventory. Recently, the authors of the PIC have published a child self-report form, the PIY, for children and adolescents age 9 through 19 years (Lachar & Gruber, 1995). The PIC-R was designed to assess children and adolescents age 3 to 16.

Both the PIC-R and PIY are quite comprehensive, making them quite long, with the PIC-R containing 420 items and the PIY 269 items. However, there are short forms of both inventories. Both have behavioral descriptions that are answered in a true-false format and contain several validity indices designed to detect certain response sets by the parent or child. The content of both inventories covers problem areas that are typical of most standardized rating scales, such as externalizing behavior problems (e.g., conduct problems, hyperactivity), internalizing emotional problems (e.g., anxiety and depression), and problems in social interactions. However, these inventories also contain subscales that assess behaviors that can be indicative of cognitive and learning problems, and they contain scales that assess global indicators of family dysfunction. Although the general content covered by the PIC-R and PIY is similar, the subscales that are derived from each measure are different, making it difficult to compare scores across parent and child report. Furthermore, there is no teacher-report format of this rating scale system, which further limits its usefulness in a multi-informant assessment battery.

The PIC item pool developed in the 1950s served as the basis for developing items for the PIY. In fact, only a few new items were added in the development of PIY. As a result, in some cases, the item content does not reflect more current conceptualizations of the psychological domains being assessed. Despite the shared item pool, the method of scale construction was different across the two rating scales, which led to the differences in scale structure. The PIC-R used a type of empirical item keying in which items were put through a multistep iterative process designed to select items with the highest correlations with specified criterion measures (e.g., measures of delinquency). This process of scale construction leads to subscales that have very heterogeneous content. In contrast, the PIY items were first divided into nine clinical scales based on the original PIC-R scales. The items were

then tested by their item-total correlations with each subscale and through factor analyses. The authors explicitly note that clinical and rational decisions were made in determining scale content. However, the emphasis on the original PIC-R scales to determine initial scale content and the reliance on item intercorrelations to largely determine subscale content still resulted in somewhat heterogeneous subscales. For example, the item "Money is my biggest interest" is placed on the Distractibility/Overactivity subscale, and the item "Several times I have said I wanted to kill myself" is included on the Sleep Disturbance subscale.

Like most of the other standardized rating scales reviewed in this chapter, the PIY and PIC-R have both hand-scoring and computer-scoring options. Both options allow raw scores to be converted to T-scores that are specific to a child's age and gender. The PIC-R normative sample for ages 6 to 16 consists of 2,390 children and adolescents from schools in the Minneapolis area. SES data were collected for only a subset of the sample (n = 600), and ethnicity of the sample was not reported. Based on these considerations, the representativeness of the norming sample is quite questionable. The PIY norming sample consists of 2,327 "regular education" students tested in five states. The sample was stratified to meet U.S. Census Bureau statistics for ethnicity, parental educational level (SES), and community size. There was a slight undersampling of African-American children, but otherwise, the quality of the PIY norms is much better than that for the PIC-R.

Internal consistency coefficients and test-retest reliability of the PIY and PIC-R subscales are provided in the test manuals and are generally quite good. Much of the external validation of the PIC-R has focused on identifying clinical case history correlates of 12 core profiles. That is, 12 distinct profiles of PIC-R clinical scales have been identified, and these have been correlated with concurrent variables such as intelligence, achievement, and special education placement (e.g., LaCombe, Kline, Lachar, Butkus, & Hillman, 1991). The PIC-R manual provides guidance on these profile correlates to be used in clinical interpretations of the scale. The validity of the PIY has focused more on the correlations of individual scales with analogous scales from other self-report inventories. For example, a study of 152 adolescents who took the PIY and the original MMPI produced modest relationships between the scales from the two inventories, with the majority of correlations falling in the .20 to .50 range (Lachar & Gruber, 1995). Another study correlated the PIY Psychological Discomfort scale with the State-Trait Anxiety Inventory ($r = .51$) and the Reynolds Adolescent Depression Scale ($r = .70$), suggesting that this scale may measure more depressive than anxious symptomatology. Several samples were also used to assess the factor invariance of the PIY by gender and ethnicity and were generally supportive of consistent factor structure across groups (Lachar & Gruber, 1995).

Overall Evaluation

Both the PIC-R and the PIY have manuals that summarize a wealth of research providing external validation of scale profiles and individual scale elevations that are very helpful in making clinical interpretations. Both of these inventories assess a large number of psychological domains leading to rather lengthy but also very comprehensive rating scales. Following in the MMPI tradition, their validity scales provide good screenings of informant response sets to aid in the interpretation of the scales. The content of these scales, though comprehensive, is also somewhat outdated and does not correspond to current conceptualizations of childhood emotional and behavioral problems in many cases. Also, the method of scale construction led to quite heterogeneous item content on many scales, which complicates the interpretation of scale elevations. The lack of correspondence in the scale structure across the two inventories and the absence of a teacher version also leads to difficulty in making cross-informant comparisons. Finally, the PIY nationwide norming sample seems to be adequate for making many norm-referenced interpretations. However, the geographically limited normative sample of the PIC-R, without sufficient data on the racial and socioeconomic status of the sample, makes use of its norm-referenced scores questionable.

SINGLE-DOMAIN RATING SCALES

The review of standardized rating scales in this chapter has largely focused on comprehensive scales that assess multiple domains of functioning. There are also numerous specialized rating scales that focus specifically on a single psychological dimension. As a result, they provide more in-depth

yet focused assessments of some specific area of functioning. Because of their focused nature, these single-domain scales may not be as uniformly used across many situations as the comprehensive scales reviewed above. However, in some testing situations, they can be used to supplement these broad rating scales. One additional issue that is important in considering these single-domain rating scales is the fact that most of them have not been standardized on large representative samples that allow for good norm-referenced interpretations. Most have emphasized more criterion-based methods of interpretation, such as determining when a score on a depression inventory predicts the presence of a major depressive disorder.

A common focus of single-domain rating scales is a child's or adolescent's level of anxiety and depression. Typically, these scales are based on a child's self-report of level of emotional distress. Three examples of these scales are the 27-item Children's Depression Inventory (CDI; Kovacs, 1992), the 30-item Reynolds Depression Scales for children and adolescents (RADS, RCDS; W.M. Reynolds, 1986, 1989), and the 37-item Revised Children's Manifest Anxiety Scale (RCMAS; C.R. Reynolds & Richmond, 1985). Both the CDI and RCMAS are based on measures used to assess emotional distress in adults but have been modified for use with children. The RCMAS is noteworthy in that it has a fairly large normative sample ($n = 4,972$) collected in 13 states in the United States.

Given how common the assessment of ADHD is in many child mental health clinics, it is not surprising that there are a number of single-domain rating scales that focus on behaviors indicative of this disorder. Unlike the scales for the assessment of anxiety and depression, however, these scales often rely on ratings of parents and teachers. For example, the Attention Deficit Disorders Evaluation Scale (ADDES; McCarney, 1989) has both parent and teacher forms containing either 46 (parent) or 60 (teacher) items all assessing the inattentive, impulsive, and overactive behaviors associated with this diagnosis. The ADDES also has a fairly large normative sample, with the teacher version being normed on over 4,876 students throughout the United States with fairly good representation of gender, ethnicity, and parental occupation.

There are also a few scales that provide a more in-depth assessment into the types and severity of conduct problems exhibited by children and adolescents. Brown, Atkins, Osborne, and Milnamow

(1996) have developed a 28-item rating scale, the Teacher Ratings of Aggression (TRA), that is completed by classroom teachers. This scale assesses multiple behaviors indicative of both reactive (i.e., in response to perceived provocation) and proactive (i.e., for dominance or for instrumental gain) aggression. Similarly, Frick, Barry, and Bodin (in press; see also Frick, 1998a) used a parent and teacher rating scale, the Psychopathy Screening Device (PSD), to assess a child's callous and unemotional interpersonal style (e.g., lacking guilt, lacking empathy, emotional constrictedness), narcissism (e.g., child thinks he or she is more important than others), and poor impulse control (e.g., acts without thinking of consequences). Both the PSD and the TRA assess dimensions of antisocial behavior that could be important for defining distinct subgroups of children with conduct disorders (Frick, 1998b). However, both scales are in their early stages of development.

An increasingly popular focus of standardized rating scales is in the assessment of the level of impairment that a child or adolescent is experiencing, rather than the assessment of the type and severity of emotional and behavioral problems. One example of this type of rating scale is the Child Global Assessment Scale (CGAS; Setterberg, Bird, & Gould, 1992), which asks a parent, teacher, or clinician to rate on a 0 (extremely impaired) to 100 (no impairment) scale the child's lowest level of functioning within the past month, taking into account how the child functions at home, at school, with friends, and during leisure time. Every group of 10 points on the scale is anchored by a behavioral descriptor. For example, between the scores of 61 and 70 is the descriptor "Some Problems—most people who do not know the child very well would not notice the problems, but people who know him/her well would be concerned." Another example of an impairment-oriented rating scale is the Home and School Situations Questionnaire (Barkley & Edelbrock, 1987). On these questionnaires, parents or teachers rate up to 12 situations (e.g., during individual desk work, at recess) in which a child may have problems. The informant rates each situation as either being a problem or not for the child; then, for all situations rated as problematic, the level of problem severity in that situation is rated on a 1 to 9 scale. As a result, rather than assessing the type and severity of problem behavior experienced by a child, these questionnaires assess the pervasiveness of the child's problem behavior.

INTERPRETATION

BASIC PSYCHOMETRIC ISSUES

One feature of standardized rating scales that makes them so important to most clinical assessments of children and adolescents is the fact that they are easy to administer and score. Unfortunately, many professionals also assume that the interpretation of scores from these scales is also relatively simple. There are, in fact, many important issues that should influence how one interprets these scores. Many issues are unique to the individual rating scales based on how they were developed and standardized; therefore, assessors should always be familiar with the technical manual of a behavior rating scale before using one in a clinical assessment. However, there are a few important interpretive issues that are critical in the use of any standardized rating scale.

The first critical issue is that, with the exception of the CSI-4, most behavior rating scales are designed to be interpreted based primarily on *norm-referenced scores*. Typically, a child's raw score on a behavior rating scale is converted to a standardized score, most often a T-score with a mean of 50 and standard deviation of 10. This standardized score reflects where the child's score falls in the distribution of scores from the normative sample. For example, a T-score of 70 on the Aggressive Behavior scale of the CBCL-91 indicates that a child's score fell at 2 standard deviations above the mean of the normative sample. Typically, 2 standard deviation units above the mean is considered a conservative cutoff for judging something to be *clinically significant*. Often, scores of between 65 and 70 are considered *suggestive* of problematic behavior. Although this interpretative process seems straightforward, there are a number of issues that can affect how one should interpret these scores for individual tests.

Obviously, a critical factor for interpreting these scores is the adequacy of the normative samples on which the standard score conversions were based. Over the past decade, there have been substantial improvements in the adequacy of normative samples for most of the most widely used rating scales. Despite many improvements in the normative samples, there remains significant variability in the size and composition (e.g., ethnic representation) across rating scales, making it important for assessors to carefully evaluate the sample on which scores are being based. One important source of variability in the composition of normative samples is whether children in special education categories or children who have been seen by a professional for emotional and behavior problems are eliminated. This procedure, which is used by most of the comprehensive rating scales reviewed in this chapter (i.e., CBCL, CRS, PIY), actually creates a "normal" sample by eliminating the upper end of the distribution of scores. As a result, a child's score may look more deviant when compared to a normal sample in which the upper end of the distribution is eliminated but less deviant when compared to a normative sample in which the upper end of the distribution is maintained. In contrast, the normative sample of the BASC maintains representation of children in special education classes.

Another issue that is important for interpreting norm-referenced scores is whether a child's scores should be compared to all other children within a specified age group or to only those of the same sex. This is a critical issue because many types of emotional and behavior problems experienced by children and adolescents show clear sex differences in their prevalence. In essence, using sex-specific comparisons equates for these differences in prevalence. Although sex-specific comparison is probably the most common norm-referenced score provided by most rating scales and, in fact, is the only one that can be obtained on some scales (i.e., the CBCL, CRS, PIY), the theoretical rationale for this use is debatable. For example, if one has a scale assessing impulsive and overactive behaviors in children, boys are quite likely to be rated higher on these behaviors than girls. Using sex-specific norms, this difference in prevalence is "removed" because a child is considered to have a clinically significant level of behavior if his or her scores are deviant compared to others of the same sex. If these differences reflect true sex differences in the trait being assessed in the normal population, the rationale for removing such differences is unclear.

Another issue when interpreting norm-referenced scores, such as T-scores, is whether or not the distribution of the normative sample was altered prior to creating the standard scores. For example, many dimensions of emotional and behavioral problems are not normally distributed (i.e., the distribution forms a normal curve) in the general population, with most dimensions showing a positive skewness. That is, most individuals in the general population do not

show high levels of these problems. Furthermore, the level of skewness is often different across the various types of emotional and behavioral problems assessed by rating scales. Because of these skewed distributions, some rating scales (e.g., CBCL) statistically create a normal distribution of scores prior to creating standardized scores. This procedure has some interpretive advantages in that most psychologists are familiar with the normal curve and can intuitively interpret standard score units. However, the disadvantage of this procedure is that it creates an artificial distribution of scores for the dimension being assessed that does not correspond to the actual distribution of raw scores in the general population. In very skewed distributions, this practice forces a certain percentage of scores to the extreme ends of the distribution. Thus, an alternative is to use linear transformations into standard scores that maintain the shape of the distribution in the normative sample, which is done by the BASC and CRS scales. However, use of these nonnormalized scores makes it important to not only interpret T-scores, but also to interpret the percentile ranks associated with these T-scores.

One final issue for interpreting scores from a behavior rating scale is the need to consider which items on a scale led to elevations on a subscale. For example, if a child scores above a T-score of 70 on the Anxious/Depressed scale of the CBCL, it is important to then investigate which items led to this elevation to better interpret its meaning. Given the unreliability of individual items, one should primarily interpret individual items that are on subscales that reach a significant level. The exception is in the interpretation of certain critical items that, by themselves, can indicate the need for further assessment and possibly treatment (e.g., "I have thought of killing myself"). However, it is important to inspect individual items on elevated subscales for two reasons. First, as mentioned previously, the way subscales are formed on many rating scales leads to very heterogeneous item content, and, as a result, very different subsets of items can lead to scale elevations. Second, the names of some subscales may not fully capture the construct being assessed by the items. For example, the Aggressive Behavior scale of both the CBCL and the BASC primarily focus on oppositional, defiant, and argumentative behaviors rather than physical aggression itself. By knowing which items led to the elevation on the Aggressive Behavior subscale, one can better describe the types of behaviors being exhibited by the child or adolescent.

INTEGRATING INFORMATION ACROSS INFORMANTS

As mentioned at the beginning of the chapter, one difficulty of interpreting scores on behavior rating scales is the fact that they measure a rater's *perceptions* of a child's adjustment, and these perceptions can be influenced by a number of factors. Some rating scales include items designed to detect specific types of biased responding. However, these validity scales often detect only certain types of response sets (e.g., inconsistent responding, a tendency to respond in a socially desirable manner). A better solution is to collect information from multiple informants, thereby obtaining many different perceptions of a child's adjustment. The interpretive problem with this approach, however, is in determining what to do with the information from different informants when it is not consistent. Research suggests that this is the rule, rather than the exception, in assessing childhood psychopathology. For example, Achenbach, McConaughy, and Howell (1987) reviewed 119 studies assessing childhood psychopathology and found that the average correlations among different informants were between .22 and .28.

The most common explanation for this low rate of agreement is to attribute it to the presence of idiosyncratic biases that influence the perceptions of different informants in rating a child's behavior. However, Achenbach et al. (1987) provided convincing data that at least some of the low cross-informant consistency could reflect *real differences* in a child's behavior across different settings. Specifically, the average correlation between the ratings of informants that see a child in different settings (e.g., parent and teacher) was .28, whereas the average correlation between different informants who see a child in the same setting (e.g., mothers and fathers or pairs of teachers) was .60. Therefore, there is much higher cross-informant consistency from persons who see the child in similar contexts. The potential difference in a child's adjustment across contexts has important implications for the use and interpretation of behavior rating scales. First, it highlights the need to assess a child's adjustment in many different contexts. Second, it suggests the need to understand the contextual demands that might influence a child's behavior in different settings.

SUMMARY

Standardized behavior rating scales provide reliable information on a child or adolescent's psychological adjustment in a time-efficient manner. As a result, many different aspects of a child's psychosocial adjustment can be assessed from the perceptions of many different informants. Also, most behavior rating scales allow for a child's score to be compared to the scores of children of similar ages from large normative samples, providing an important developmental reference for a child's emotional and behavioral functioning. All of these characteristics make standardized rating scales an integral part of most clinical assessments of childhood psychopathology. Given their importance in the assessment process, it is not surprising that there are a significant number of standardized rating scales that are readily available, are easily scored, and assess a wide range of emotional and behavioral problems of children and adolescents.

A key focus of this chapter was to illustrate that, although these scales are often relatively easy to administer and score, interpretation of them is not quite so simple. The interpretation of rating scales requires a knowledge of the important differences in how the various scales were developed. Also, there are a number of important psychometric issues (e.g., how norm-referenced scores were formed) that should influence the interpretations one makes from these scales. Also, the fact that rating scales measure the perceptions of various persons who see the child in different contexts also must be considered. All of these issues converge to suggest that scores from any single rating scale are rarely informative in isolation from other information on the child and his or her psychosocial context. However, the same could be said for all methods for assessing childhood psychopathology. Therefore, standardized rating scales should be viewed as an important and informative part of a comprehensive clinical assessment of a child's or adolescent's psychosocial adjustment.

REFERENCES

Achenbach, T.M. (1991). *Manual for the Child Behavior Checklist/4–18 and 1991 profile*. Burlington: University of Vermont, Department of Psychiatry.

Achenbach, T.M., McConaughy, S.H., & Howell, C.T. (1987). Child/adolescent behavioral and emotional problems: Implications of cross-informant correlations for situational specificity. *Psychological Bulletin, 101,* 213–232.

American Psychiatric Association. (1994). *The diagnostic and statistical manual of mental disorders* (4th ed.). Washington, DC: Author.

Barkley, R.A., & Edelbrock, C.S. (1987). Assessing situational variation in children's problem behaviors: The home and school situations questionnaires. In R.J. Prinz (Ed.), *Advances in behavioral assessment of children and families* (Vol. 3, pp. 157–176). New York: JAI Press.

Brown, K., Atkins, M.S., Osborne, M.L., & Milnamow, M. (1996). A revised teacher rating scale for reactive and proactive aggression. *Journal of Abnormal Child Psychology, 24,* 473–480.

Butcher, J.N., Williams, C.L., Graham, J.R., Archer, R.P., Tellegen, A., Ben-Porath, Y.S., & Kaemmer, B. (1992). *MMPI-A, Minnesota Multiphasic Personality Inventory–Adolescent: Manual for administration, scoring, and interpretation.* Minneapolis: University of Minnesota Press.

Conners, C.K. (1969). A teacher rating scale for use in drug studies with children. *American Journal of Psychiatry, 126,* 884–888.

Conners, C.K. (1997). *Conners Rating Scales–Revised manual.* New York: Multi-Health Systems.

Doyle, A., Ostrander, R., Skare, S., Crosby, R.D., & August, G.J. (1997). Convergent and criterion-related validity of the Behavior Assessment System for Children–parent rating scale. *Journal of Clinical Child Psychology, 26,* 276–284.

Frick, P.J. (1998a). Callous-unemotional traits and conduct problems: A two-factor model of psychopathy in children. In R.D. Hare, D.J. Cooke, & A. Forth (Eds.), *Psychopathy: Theory, research, and implication for society* (pp. 161–187). Dordrecht, The Netherlands: Kluwer Press.

Frick, P.J. (1998b). *Conduct disorders and severe antisocial behavior.* New York: Plenum Press.

Frick, P.J., Barry, C.T., & Bodin, S.D. (2000). Applying the concept of psychopathy to children: Implications for the assessment of antisocial children. In C.B. Gacono (Ed.), *The clinical and forensic assessment of psychopathy* (pp. 3–24). Mahwah, NJ: Erlbaum.

Frick, P.J., Lahey, B.B., Applegate, B., Kerdyck, L., Ollendick, T.H., Hynd, G.W., Garfinkel, B., Greenhill, L., Biederman, J., Barkley, R.A., McBurnett, K., Newcorn, J., & Waldman, I. (1994). *DSM-IV* field trials for the disruptive behavior disorders: Use of symptom utility estimates. *Journal of the American Academy of Child and Adolescent Psychiatry, 33,* 529–539.

Gadow, K.D., & Sprafkin, J. (1994). *Child Symptom Inventory 4 manual.* Stony Brook, New York: Checkmate Plus.

Gadow, K.D., & Sprafkin, J. (1995). *Adolescent Symptom Inventory 4 manual.* Stony Brook, New York: Checkmate Plus.

Gadow, K.D., & Sprafkin, J. (1997). *Early Childhood Inventory 4 manual.* Stony Brook, New York: Checkmate Plus.

Gadow, K.D., & Sprafkin, J. (1998). *Child Symptom Inventory 4 Screening manual.* Stony Brook, New York: Checkmate Plus.

Hathaway, S.R., & McKinley, J.C. (1942). *Minnesota Multiphasic Personality Inventory.* Minneapolis: University of Minnesota Press.

Kamphaus, R.W., & Frick, P.J. (1996). *Clinical assessment of child and adolescent personality and behavior.* Boston: Allyn & Bacon.

Kovacs, M. (1992). *The Children's Depression Inventory manual.* New York: Multi-Health Systems.

Lachar, D., & Gruber, C.P. (1995). *Personality Inventory for Youth (PIY).* Los Angeles: Western Psychological Services.

LaCombe, J.A., Kline, R.B., Lachar, D., Butkus, M., & Hillman, S.B. (1991). Case history correlates of a Personality Inventory for Children (PIC) profile typology. *Psychological Assessment, 3,* 678–687.

McCarney, S.B. (1989). *The Attention Deficit Disorders Evaluation Scale–home version technical manual.* Columbia, MO: Hawthorne Educational Services.

Piacentini, J.C. (1993). Checklists and rating scales. In T.H. Ollendick & M. Hersen (Eds.), *Handbook of child and adolescent assessment* (pp. 82–97). Boston: Allyn & Bacon.

Reynolds, C.R., & Kamphaus, R.W. (1992). *Behavior Assessment System for Children (BASC).* Circle Pines, MN: American Guidance Service.

Reynolds, C.R., & Richmond, B.O. (1985). *Revised Children's Manifest Anxiety Scale (RCMAS).* Los Angeles: Western Psychological Services.

Reynolds, W.M. (1986). *Reynolds Adolescent Depression Scale.* Odessa, FL: Psychological Assessment Resources.

Reynolds, W.M. (1989). *Reynolds Child Depression Scale.* Odessa, FL: Psychological Assessment Resources.

Setterberg, S., Bird, H., & Gould, M. (1992). *Parent and interviewer versions of the Children's Global Assessment Scale.* New York: Columbia University Press.

Vaughn, M.L., Riccio, C.A., Hynd, G.W., & Hall, J. (1997). Diagnosing ADHD subtypes: Discriminant validity of the Behavior Assessment System for Children (BASC) and the Achenbach parent and teacher rating scales. *Journal of Clinical Child Psychology, 26,* 349–357.

Widiger, T.A., Frances, A.J., Pincus, H.A., Ross, R., First, M.B., Davis, W., & Kline, M. (1998). *DSM-IV sourcebook* (Vol. 4). Washington, DC: American Psychiatric Association.

Wirt, R.D., Lachar, D., Klinedinst, J.K., & Seat, P.S. (1990). *Personality Inventory for Children, 1990 edition.* Los Angeles: Western Psychological Services.

PROBLEMS OF EARLY LIFE

CHAPTER 12

Genetic Influences on Behavior and Development

JEAN C. ELBERT, THOMAS W. SEALE, AND ELISABETH MCMAHON

Rapid progress in the field of behavioral genetics in general, and molecular genetics in particular, is allowing us to view both normal and abnormal behavior from a more biologically based perspective. The intent of this chapter is to survey current understanding of the role of inheritance in the development of both normal and abnormal behavior. Ultimately, human behavior genetics will help us to better define both inherited and environmental factors that affect behavioral risk and/or resilience. Following an introduction to perspectives from the field of behavioral genetics, the role of genotype in intelligence and specialized cognitive abilities is reviewed. Selected genetically determined developmental disorders (Fragile X, Prader-Willi, Turner, and Kleinfelter syndromes) with broad spectrum effects on cognition and behavior are discussed next, followed by a discussion devoted to relatively circumscribed effects on cognition (specific learning disabilities). The second major section begins with a survey of the genetic influence on temperament and personality, followed by sections related to genetic influence on selected child psychiatric disorders (attention-deficit/hyperactivity disorder, disruptive behavior disorders, anxiety disorders, and depression). Developments in the field of genetics are also playing an important role in bridging formerly independent research areas of temperament, personality, and abnormal child psychology and their respective integration in the emerging field of developmental psychopathology. Finally, several caveats are necessary. In view of the vast behavioral genetics literature, our comments are necessarily selective, and breadth necessarily limits the depth to which each topic can be explored. Rapid progress in the areas of quantitative and molecular genetics dictates that a review is necessarily an emerging story likely to become quickly obsolete.

BEHAVIORAL GENETICS AND THE IMPACT OF RECENT ADVANCES

The human genome consists of approximately 100,000 genes, some 30% to 40% of which are selectively expressed in the nervous system and devoted to its differentiation, development, function, and maintenance. Thus, tens of thousands of genes conceivably contribute to the neuroanatomical and neurophysiological substrates in the central nervous system (CNS) that underlie human behaviors. These genes do not act in isolation. The expression of a given gene at the molecular and behavioral phenotypic levels depends on both the genetic milieu in which it is placed and its interaction with the environment. Different genes, and their mutations, may be nonidentically expressed in individuals with different genetic backgrounds, or who are exposed to nonidentical environments. This axiom of behavioral genetics can be formally stated in the following way:

$$V_T = V_G + V_E + V_G \cdot V_E$$

V_T, the total phenotypic variance, equals V_G, the component of variance due to genetic factors plus V_E, the component of phenotypic variance due to environmental factors, plus a component of variance, which reflects specific gene-environment interactions. Environmental factors can be pre- or postnatal, acute or chronic, single, additive, or multiplicative, biochemical or social in nature. These would include such important variables affecting behavioral development as parenting styles, family interaction, peer interaction, and education (reviewed in other chapters of the present volume). It should not be surprising, then, that both nongenetic and inherited forms of behavioral abnormalities can occur, and that among inherited forms, there can exist a high degree of complexity and heterogeneity with regard to both genetic transmission and phenotypic expression. In this light, genotype (an individual's genetic constitution) should be considered a risk factor rather than an absolute determinant of behavioral abnormalities.

Behavioral traits are typically quantitative in nature; that is, the phenotype is a continuum rather than a discrete, quantal entity (e.g., albino or black; presence or absence of catalytic activity of the enzyme phenylaline hydroxylase in phenylketonuria) that typifies classic Mendelian traits. In clinical diagnosis, the parallel would be "categorical" diagnosis, such as the *DSM-IV* (APA, 1994), as opposed to "dimensional" diagnosis, in which "abnormality" is determined by exceeding or falling below an empirically derived point on a scale. Quantitative traits are polygenically inherited, meaning that multiple genes contribute to the phenotype. Polygenic traits exhibit non-Mendelian patterns of inheritance, heterogeneity in severity of the clinical presentation, and significant gene-environment interactions. Individual genes contributing to a polygenically determined trait may have nonidentical effect sizes (i.e., some may have large effects on the phenotype, whereas others have only small effects). Phenotypic

effects of some genes may be independent of other genes (causing additive effects), whereas others are nonadditive (with their effect depending on their interaction with other genes). In addition to polygenic traits, all of the other modes of genetic transmission have been implicated in CNS abnormalities leading to behavioral dysfunction.

Quantitative genetic research concentrates on individual differences and assumes, first, that proper theory should account for how individuals are similar as well as different, and second, that individual variation is the basis for evolutionary change (Loehlin, 1996). Traditional methods of quantitative behavior genetics have included twin, adoption, and family studies, all directed to partitioning the observed variation of behavioral traits into components associated with various categories of genetic and environmental influence. Environmental influence in turn is divided into shared (e.g., with other family members) and unshared types (e.g., individually distinct experience). Such work has developed a strong case for the importance of genetic factors in the complex behaviors/traits involved in normal and abnormal cognition and behavior.

In contrast to purely quantitative genetic analyses of behavior, molecular genetic studies focus on locating individual genes on specific chromosomes and mapping them relative to other genes on that chromosome. Once specific genes are localized they can be isolated and cloned and their function determined. Earlier molecular genetic studies relied largely on a reductionistic, single-gene, single-disorder approach. It is now apparent that such single-gene alterations are likely to be uncommon, because multiple genes generally contribute to complex behavioral traits. Consequently, interest now focuses on individual genes that act in sets, each member of which contributes a part of the genetically determined variance of the trait. Such loci are referred to as quantitative trait loci (QTLs) because each contributes quantitatively, and in varying degrees, to the variance in a behavioral trait. Identification of QTLs begins by finding statistically significant associations between genetic markers at particular chromosomal regions and the variance in the phenotype of interest. In practice, current resolving power is about 15% of the behavioral variance due to genotype; that is, potentially up to six genes contributing equally to the phenotype can be resolved. In practice, some genes make small contributions to the phenotype and are difficult to identify, whereas others make larger contributions (e.g., accounting for 50% of the phenotypic variance) and are more readily resolved. Once a QTL for a given chromosomal region is identified, the search is then narrowed by first investigating the potential involvement of candidate genes that reside in that chromosomal region. Candidate genes are ones whose map positions and functions are known and for which the function of the gene can be plausibly related to the behavior in question (e.g., genes encoding receptors for neurotransmitters through which therapeutic drugs for a psychiatric disorder are known to act). Positional cloning of the chromosomal region of interest is then undertaken with the goal of determining how mutant alleles in the gene of interest alter the function of its product, which in turn alters brain function. This approach, merging quantitative and molecular genetics, promises to open new windows to pathways and processes important to cognitive neuroscience (Rimoin, Connor, & Pyeritz, 1996). The Human Genome Project is markedly accelerating this process. Begun in 1991, this worldwide research effort has the goal of determining the location of the estimated 100,000 human genes, beginning to understand the heredity instructions, and decoding the exact sequence of all 3 billion nucleotide bases that make up our genome (Collins et al., 1998). Sequencing of the entire genome is expected to be completed by 2003.

This explosion of genetic research has generated high interest in the public media as well as considerable controversy in the scientific and clinical communities, for example, refueling the nature-nurture debate and charges that such work vastly oversimplifies extremely complex social behavior (e.g., Billings, Beckwith, & Alper, 1992). Concerns about public misconception and society's misapplication of conclusions drawn from human behavior genetics research have prompted statements from professional societies such as the American Psychological Association and the American Society of Human Genetics (Neisser et al., 1996; Sherman et al., 1997).

THE ROLE OF INHERITANCE IN COGNITIVE ABILITIES

INTELLIGENCE

More behavior genetic studies of intelligence have been conducted than of any other behavioral trait.

The mass of evidence points to a heritability (h^2) (e.g., the standardized proportion of phenotypic variance or individual differences in a population due to genetics) of about .50. This indicates powerful effects of *both* genetic and environmental influences (Plomin & Craig, 1997). Although much of the traditional work in exploring the inheritance of intelligence had assumed a dichotomous view of nature versus nurture (i.e., partitioning the variance into genetic and environmental effects), recent work reflects the use of more sophisticated models that better account for the complexity of the interaction. Quantitative genetic studies of cognitive ability have addressed both *general* ability (general intelligence, or *g*, the unrotated principal component, typically indexed by global IQ scores) and *specific* abilities (e.g., verbal, spatial, perceptual speed, memory). Much of the quantitative research involving twin and adoption studies has spanned many years, and results are derived from studies of monozygotic (MZ) twins raised apart (e.g., Bouchard, Lykken, McGue, Segal, & Tellegren, 1990), and from adoption studies (e.g., DeFries, Plomin, & Fulker, 1994). Additional questions relate to the findings for extreme levels of ability; for example, if heritability of IQ varies with age, does it also vary with the level of cognitive ability? Finally, there is both interest and controversy in the molecular genetics studies of cognitive abilities.

Controversy regarding the interpretation of quantitative genetic studies of intelligence prompted the American Psychological Association to produce an authoritative report, including the relative importance of genes and environment in shaping intelligence (Neisser et al., 1996). A major conclusion of this report was the finding that the heritability of IQ changes from infancy to adulthood, with quotients of about .45 found in childhood and .75 by adolescence. Conversely, shared environment decreases, with estimates approximating .35 in childhood, declining to near 0 by adolescence. This discovery in the 1980s that genetic influence on IQ increases with age was contrary to the widely held belief that environmental influences accumulate with age and, thus, are expected to decrease the contribution of inheritance to the variance in IQ. Though at first sight this may appear counterintuitive, gene effects on the same behaviors at different ages tend to be the same, whereas environmental effects are often different. As a consequence, there are more opportunities for genetic effects to be cumulative. Meta-analyses of the accumulating data sets from twin studies (e.g., Bouchard, 1996) confirmed the robustness of heritability of IQ throughout most of adulthood. From early childhood to late adulthood, IQ correlations from MZ twins continuously increase throughout life, whereas those for dizygotic (DZ) twins decline after adolescence. The proportion of individual variation in IQ associated with shared environmental factors is relatively constant (~30%) until early adulthood, but then declines to zero. Thus, their transactions with the environment are increasingly influenced by the characteristics they bring to those environments, with less influence of the family of origin and social surroundings (Neisser et al., 1996). Aside from these general findings, there are more subtle developmental differences. For example, although genotype apparently accounts for age-specific, persistent effects in twin studies, siblings' shared environmental effects are constant from age 1 to 9. In addition, although there is no new genetic variation at age 4, at age 7, new variation arises, attributed by some to reflect the novel demands of school entry (Rose, 1995).

OTHER SPECIALIZED COGNITIVE ABILITIES

In addition to investigations of general cognitive abilities (g), interest has also focused on the heritability of specialized abilities; for example, are there genes selectively influencing verbal abilities that do not also affect spatial, memory, and perceptual speed abilities? In contrast to the greater consistency among measures of general IQ, studies of specialized abilities are less congruent, and relatively little is known about the continuity and change of genetic and environmental influences on specific abilities in childhood. Data from the Colorado Adoption Project addressed this question in a longitudinal study of children whose testing at ages 3, 4, 7, and 9 included measures of verbal, spatial, perceptual speed, and memory abilities. At age 7, there were moderate genetic loadings for all special ability factors, suggesting shared genetic influence on g; however, by age 9, shared environment effects emerged for spatial and perceptual speed abilities. Additional evidence of genetic influence has been found for speed of information processing, including reaction time (Baker, Vernon, & Ho, 1991). Twin studies of the major special mental abilities (verbal, spatial, perceptual speed, memory) indicate heritability estimates of about .50 and modest estimates of common environmental influence, with evidence that the spatial domain appears to yield the highest heritability, and memory the lowest (Bouchard, 1998). However, with the exception of verbal ability, which continued to show independent influence, the specialized ability components appeared to combine into a more common genetic factor. Such results strongly indicate that specific abilities are more than just simple subsets of general intelligence. Additional genetic findings support specific memory domains, with a significant influence of genotype for learning, probe recall, and memory for names and faces, but not for digit span and picture memory (Thapar, Petrill, & Thompson, 1994). Taken together, such findings suggest that specialized mental abilities appear to be somewhat less heritable than general cognitive ability, with heritability of approximately .50 and a modest shared environment (McGue & Bouchard, 1998).

An additional question of interest is whether heritability of IQ is consistent across groups with different levels of cognitive ability. Studies of 14- to 36-month-old children suggest a genetic explanation for the stability of low general cognitive ability over time (Petrill et al., 1997). In samples of school-aged children (6–12 years), those with lower ability showed higher levels of heritability and lower influence of shared environment. This suggests a genotype-environment correlation in which higher-ability persons seek out better environments (Detterman, Thompson, & Plomin, 1990). In contrast, however, other investigators found no evidence for a linear or quadratic effect of level of cognitive ability on estimates of heritability or shared environment (Cherney, Cardon, Fulker, & DeFries, 1992).

Given substantial evidence of the genetic contribution to cognitive ability, the next challenge has been to locate and identify the genes involved. Several reviews address the controversial issue of whether molecular genetic research on IQ can or should be done (e.g., Daniels, McGuffin, & Owen, 1996). As mentioned previously, cognitive ability involves a continuous or quantitative trait, which is polygenic, that is, involving the combined effect of many genes. Molecular genetic studies of quantitative traits have found that different gene loci (e.g., QTL) have different effect sizes, and that often, the genetic variance can be explained by a small number of loci. An application of this methodology to cognitive ability is illustrated in an ongoing project investigating QTL for IQ that involves four twin study sites in the United States and Britain (Plomin et al., 1994). In the first phase, work focused on DNA markers in which there is variation near or at genes of neurological relevance (potential "candidate genes"). At least 100 gene markers have been examined, 3 of which were significantly associated with IQ: an *HLA-A* (B) allele, *CTG-B33* (a brain-expressed trinucleotide repeat), and *ESTOOO83* (a mitochondrial polymorphism). However, a significant QTL for *g* has not yet emerged from this work. DNA markers associated with high and low IQ have also been examined in the QTL project. In the first report of this research, two markers were found that yielded significant allelic frequency differences between the high- and low-IQ groups, thus locating a new *HLA* marker for a gene unique to the human species and a new brain-expressed triplet repeat marker (*CTGB33*). Molecular genetic methods are also being used to determine inheritance of specialized abilities. Following a finding of significantly reduced visuospatial performance in children with the *TAQI A1* allele of the *D2* dopamine receptor gene, Petrill and colleagues (1997) used eight DNA markers to predict the following cognitive factors: verbal, spatial, perceptual speed, and memory, together with Wechsler Intelligence Scale for Children–Revised subtest scores. Four markers showed similar effects across scales (suggesting a relationship to *g*); however, three markers continued to be significantly associated with specific scales after the effects of *g* had been removed (Petrill et al., 1997).

Finally, these molecular genetic studies of IQ have not progressed without significant debate regarding whether they *should* occur (i.e., concerns about self-fulfilling prophecy if QTLs for IQ are known). Despite caution regarding the oversimplification and/or exaggeration of such research by the popular media, such research is likely to continue unabated (Daniels et al., 1996).

GENETICALLY DETERMINED DISORDERS OF COGNITION

Discussion now shifts from the role of genotype in the normal variation in cognition to genetically determined disorders affecting cognition. These disorders are subdivided into two categories: (1) generalized disruptions in the development of cognition, involving forms of mental retardation (MR), and (2) circumscribed impairment resulting in specific disorders of learning. Although the genetic mechanisms for many disorders have been known previously, recent molecular genetic findings provide important implications: understanding the mechanistic bases underlying the neurobiology of impaired cognition; rapid, accurate, and early laboratory diagnosis; assessment of recurrence risk in families; prevention; and, finally, the potential for development of novel intervention strategies. This review is necessarily highly selective, with several disorders whose behavioral phenotypes are of particular interest for clinical child psychologists chosen for discussion. For a more extended discussion of neurogenetic disorders, the reader is referred to additional sources (Goldstein & Reynolds, 1999; Phelps, 1998).

BROAD SPECTRUM DISORDERS

In the field of MR, a two-category distinction has traditionally been drawn between severe *(pathological)* and mild *(familial, cultural-familial, or sociocultural)* MR, each associated with assumptions regarding etiology (Zigler & Hodapp, 1986). The pathological type is typically consistent with a categorical/diagnostic model of MR in which the origin of the CNS insult is known (e.g., genetic disorders, pre-, peri-, or postnatal insults, other biologically based etiologies). In contrast, the mild MR types are often associated with a dimensional model, in which mild retardation is assumed to reflect the low end of a normal distribution of IQ and/or reflects increased incidence in kindreds, suggesting a higher emphasis on environmental influences. Although this distinction has generally held up, the dichotomy between severe and mild MR is overly simplistic and must be modified in light of newer information (Simonoff, Bolton, & Rutter, 1998). For example, certain severe forms of MR can be familial in the genetic sense (i.e., multiple individuals in several generations of a kindred can be affected). Correspondingly, contrary to previous thinking, some 10% of cases of severe retardation have no identifiable organic pathology.

In a substantial fraction of individuals with mild MR (up to 30%–50%), epilepsy, cerebral palsy, or other readily identifiable neuropathological condition indicates the presence of a rather global and nonspecific CNS insult. Second, in some types previously regarded as familial, the primary neurochemical basis of an inherited neuropathological disorder is now known. However, in general, the relative contribution of genetic and environmental factors in mild MR is not well-known, because there are as yet no comprehensive, reliable epidemiological data. It is also likely that heredity and environment differentially affect aspects of cognition. For example, environment may play a larger role in the social deficits accompanying low IQ than in the variation of IQ per (Simonoff, Bolton, et al., 1998). Clearly, IQ is not immutably set by genotype at all levels of cognitive ability, and studies have demonstrated consistently that major environmental variations *do* affect cognitive performance in children from psychosocially at-risk backgrounds, indicating that both parental biological factors and rearing have approximately equal effects on IQ (Rutter, 1994). In addition, modification of the environment

via prevention/early intervention has been shown to result in modest IQ change, a finding that serves to question previous concepts regarding the immutability of low IQ (Ramey & Ramey, 1999).

Genetic etiologies of MR traditionally have been subdivided into two primary groups: those associated with a single gene (Mendelian) and those associated with chromosomal abnormalities (see Table 12.1, which provides an overview of genetically influenced disorders affecting cognition either globally or more narrowly). Among the single gene forms, some 300 different types of inherited conditions involving intermediary metabolism are known to produce MR as one of their sequelae, underscoring the sensitivity of the developing brain to metabolic insults. However, because many such insults are nonselective in their toxicity and do not have readily identifiable clinical phenotypes, they typically are not the focus of attention when considering single gene effects in MR. Instead, the emphasis is typically on those genes that directly contribute to the cognitive deficit, for example, phenylketonuria.

Table 12.1 Current knowledge regarding genetically determined disorders affecting cognition.

Diagnosis	Incidence	Involved Chromosome	Type of Mutation	Chromosome Region Known	Candidate Gene(s) Identified	Gene Known
Mental Retardation						
Chromosomal Abnormalities						
Down syndrome	1/1,000	21	trisomy	2 regions 1 arm	MHBH	No
Prader-Willi syndrome	1/10,000	15	microdeletion*	15q11-q13	—	SNRP
Angelman syndrome	1/15,000	15	microdeletion*	15q11-q13	—	UBE3A
DiGeorge syndrome	1/4,000	22	microdeletion	22q11.2	ES2, PNUTL1	No
Williams syndrome	1/20,000	7	microdeletion	7q11.23	LIMK1, FZD3	No
Single Gene Abnormalities						
Fragile X syndrome	1/1,250 males	X	triplet repeat expansion	Xq27.3	—	FMR-1
Phenylketonuria	1/10,000	12	base changes	12q22	—	PAH
Selective Cognitive Alterations						
Kleinfelter syndrome	1/1,000 males	X	XXY combination	No	No	No
Turner syndrome	1/2,500 females	X	monosomy X	No	No	No
Dyslexia	†	6,15, other	single gene	6p23-p21	GABAB	No

*Microdeletions are the predominant type of mutation, but other types including uniparental disomy and single gene defects also occur.

†Although the incidence of these disorders has been estimated, the fraction that has an inherited basis is imprecisely known but generally believed to be frequent.

In contrast, although polygenic forms of MR do exist, they have yet to be characterized in detail. The sections that follow review the more recent genetic and phenotypic findings in *selected* types of MR, particularly as they relate to the neurobiological mechanisms that underlie MR. The descriptions include a discussion of the genetic mechanisms involved in each disorder, together with the cognitive and behavioral phenotypes.

Fragile X Syndrome
Syndromes involving cognitive deficits linked to genes on the X chromosome occur in about 1/600 live births and are believed to account for 20% to 30% of all such abnormalities (Feldman, 1996). Fragile X syndrome (FXS) is the most frequent of these; it represents approximately 30% of all X-linked forms of MR, is the most commonly occurring single gene form of MR (see Table 12.1), and occurs in 1/1,250 males and 1/2,500 females. Males with FXS usually have MR and often exhibit characteristic physical features and behavior; affected females exhibit a similar but usually less severe phenotype (Warren & Nelson, 1994).

Since discovery of the Fragile X gene *(FMR1)* in 1991, there has been a virtual explosion of research investigating both the complex genetic mechanisms and the cognitive and behavioral phenotypes for FXS. FXS involves a chromosome abnormality, which is characterized by a marker for an unusual type of mutation, rather than the direct cause of the deficit. It is the loss of function of a single mutated gene *(Xq27.3),* located in a fragile site *(FRAXA)* on the distal portion of the long arm of the X chromosome that produces MR in FXS. Although FXS is transmitted as an X chromosome-linked trait, two phenomena associated with this syndrome remained puzzling for many years. First, 20% of male obligate carriers of the mutation are unaffected, yet transmit the trait to their grandsons. Second, penetrance (the degree to which a trait is expressed in each generation) is dependent on position in the pedigree and appears to increase in successive generations. The latter phenomenon, termed "anticipation," is associated with decreased age of onset and increased severity of certain inherited diseases. The phenomenon of anticipation is uniquely associated with an unusual type of gene mutation termed triplet (or trinucleotide) repeat expansion mutations (Gusella & MacDonald, 1996). Triplet repeat expansion mutations in different genes are now

known to cause 14 different diseases involving the nervous system. The nature of the triplet repeat expansion and its consequences leading to FXS are described below. Further details regarding the molecular bases of this form of inherited MR can be found in reviews by Warren and Nelson (1994) and deVries, Halley, Oostra, and Niemeijer (1998).

In 1991, the gene responsible for FXS, *FMR1,* was isolated and cloned. The mutation associated with both the MR phenotype and the associated fragility of the X chromosome bearing it was found to consist of an increased number of a normally repetitive three-base sequence (the triplet *CGG:* cytosine, guanine, guanine) in a proximal portion of the *FRM1* gene not translated into a protein product. Normal individuals possess 6 to 42 tandem *CGG* repeats with an average of about 30 repeats. Expansion of the *CGG* repeat number to > 200, termed a "full mutation," is invariably associated with MR in males; in some individuals, thousands of *CGG* repeats occur in this region of the *FMR1* gene. Because this disorder involves the X (sex) chromosome, there are major gender differences in phenotype among individuals having the full mutation, with males being more severely affected than females. This results from males having only a single copy of genes on the X chromosome, whereas females receive two X chromosomes and have one mutant and one nonmutant allele when they receive the full *FMR1* mutation. Approximately 20% of males carrying the FXS abnormal gene are unaffected, but these "normal transmitting" males pass on the mutation, relatively unchanged in size, to all of their daughters.

In females, one of the two X chromosomes is inactivated permanently during early embryogenesis. Cells receiving the inactivated chromosome express none of the genes carried on that chromosome; this process is random with regard to the maternal or paternal origin of the X chromosome. Therefore, females heterozygous for a full mutation will be mosaics. By chance, some females will have greater numbers of cells in which the nonmutant X chromosome is inactivated; others will have higher populations of cells in which the X chromosome bearing the *FMR1* full mutation is inactivated. Approximately 50% to 70% of females who have the full mutation exhibit milder intellectual deficits and specific learning disabilities, with IQ in the borderline to mild MR range. In contrast, females with *CGG* repeat numbers in the range of 43 to 199 may be phenotypically normal but are carriers of the

FXS "premutation." This premutation can be transmitted without alteration in repeat number, but often expands to the full mutation when transmitted to the next generation. The risk of a Fragile X premutation carrier transmitting the full mutation to his or her children is dependent on gender; that is, expansion to a full mutation occurs much more frequently when the carrier is female, and is proportional to the CGG repeat number.

With regard to diagnosis, although the fragile site (FRAXA) can be detected in significantly affected individuals by standard cytogenetic testing, standard karyotyping does not typically identify unaffected carriers of the FMR1 gene. Newer molecular methods employing polymerase chain reaction (PCR) technology now make it possible to genotype individuals both pre- and postnatally for their CGG repeat number in the FMR1 gene. Thus, those with a family history of FXS (though they may have tested negative on standard cytogenetic testing) should be reevaluated with the more recent DNA method to determine possible carrier status.

How does expansion of the CGG repeat region cause MR? The FMR1 gene is now known to encode a protein that appears to play a crucial role in the production of adequate amounts of proteins derived from a subset of genes expressed in the brain during fetal development. The FMR1 protein binds messenger RNAs from specific genes and can also bind to proteins on the large subunit of ribosomes (the organellar sites for protein synthesis). FMR1 protein is found both in the nucleus and cytoplasm. It is hypothesized that the FMR1 gene product acts as a shuttle to move specific mRNAs from the nucleus into the cytoplasm and facilitates their binding to ribosomes for translation into proteins. Thus, it can be viewed as a kind of translation factor for the expression of a family of products from different genes. It is now experimentally established that the expansion of the CGG region beyond 200 repeats stops the production of the FMR1 protein. Full mutations cause chemical alteration (methylation) of the DNA in a region of the FMR1 gene (the promoter), which prevents its transcription into messenger RNA. This type of mutation accounts for nearly all FXS individuals. Thus, the loss of the FMR1 gene product leads to a relative deficiency of other gene products during prenatal development of the brain, which in turn results in MR. Investigations of brain anatomy have further elucidated FXS; imaging studies have typically shown greater brain volume in FXS adults (e.g.,

Hagerman & Cronister, 1996), with increased volume of the hippocampus, caudate nucleus, thalamus, and in males, the lateral ventricles. Such findings are likely associated with such behavioral characteristics as hyperarousal and problems with executive functioning.

Our review of the physical, cognitive, and behavioral characteristics of individuals with FSX must necessarily be brief, and we refer the reader to more comprehensive reviews of this topic (e.g., Dykens, Hodapp, & Leckman, 1994; Hagerman & Cronister, 1996).

Most phenotype studies have focused on males with the full mutation. Facial features in males often include a long, narrow face, prominent ears, and frequently prominent forehead and jaw; however, some of these features, in addition to macroorchidism (enlarged testes) are frequently not observable until middle childhood or puberty. Other related features include connective tissue dysplasia, cardiac mitral valve prolapse (heart murmur), recurrent otitis media, flat feet, and hyperextendible joints. Variability in growth curves is frequently observed, with leveling of height and increase in weight at adolescence. Females with either the full mutation or the premutation have few of the physical features seen in males, except for the occasional presence of prominent ears. A Physical Index (PI) has been developed to assess the number of physical features present in an individual with FXS, and this has been found to correlate with the degree of involvement in the DNA and the level of FMR1 gene protein measured in the blood (Tassone et al., 1999).

Sensory and/or sensory integration difficulty has been noted in many FXS children, including hypersensitivity to sound, light, or texture, tactile defensiveness, and associated feeding and sleeping problems. As mentioned previously, IQ is related to both type of mutation (full or premutation) and gender, and ranges from borderline/low average (10%) to mild/moderate MR (60%) and severe MR (30%) (Santos, 1992). Females with the full mutation and normal IQ typically demonstrate learning disabilities, particularly in math, and often have poor attention and organizational abilities.

Dykens et al. (1994) described what appears to be a specific cognitive profile in FXS children, with specific weaknesses in sequential, as opposed to simultaneous processing on the Kaufman Assessment Battery for Children (Naglieri, 1985). Such associated weaknesses in sensorimotor and auditory processing may be consistent with related speech and language problems, including word retrieval, dysfluency, and perseveration/echolalia, as well as delayed development of syntactic, semantic, and pragmatic features of language. A particular interest related to the FXS cognitive phenotype is the question of cognitive decline with age: mental age in FXS appears to level off, with consequent decline in IQ. However, such reported changes in the developmental trajectory of FXS individuals remain somewhat controversial because of methodological problems inherent in these studies (combining data across different intelligence tests; the occurrence of specific cognitive deficits that may be confounded with the task demands of particular IQ tests at particular ages) (Hay, 1994). Because most investigations of this question involve retrospective studies, a multisite, prospective, longitudinal study by Fisch and colleagues (1996) is of particular interest. Of males (age 3 to 15) who were evaluated with the Stanford–Binet (fourth edition) and Vineland Adaptive Behavior Scales, declines in IQ scores were found in 75%, with 4 showing no change. Though adaptive scores were higher than IQ scores (83%), declines in adaptive (DQ) scores were also noted (92%). Decreases in IQ scores appeared to follow a well-defined, negatively decelerating function, with steeper declines in DQ suggesting a slower rate of development rather than a regression of intellectual and social skills.

Numerous behavioral studies of males have suggested poor self-control, including symptoms of short attention span and hyperactivity (though not more frequently than in other MR individuals). Problems with social relatedness, shyness, and characteristic gaze avoidance are frequent, and such socialization problems have suggested some degree of overlap with the autistic spectrum disorders. Although a number of studies in the 1980s attempted to determine whether FXS may represent a genetic etiology of autism, most such studies were plagued with methodological weaknesses (Dykens et al., 1994). Several studies have examined populations of autistic individuals for the Fragile X chromosome or the *FMR1* mutation. Overall, approximately 6% of males with autism are positive for FXS, with 15% of males with FXS fulfilling *DSM-III* criteria for autism (Hagerman & Lampe, 1999), underscoring the importance of DNA studies for FXS in individuals with autism of unknown etiology. Currently, the evidence suggests that, although a large fraction of FXS males exhibit various combinations of autisticlike

behaviors and traits (i.e., rocking, hand flapping, perseveration), such behaviors often decrease in frequency or severity and have been shown to be qualitatively different from matched autistic controls. Thus, most FXS individuals *do* relate to others, *are* attached to their caregivers, *do not* show the profound indifference to people that is characteristic of autism, yet most show more subtle problems of social relatedness. With regard to females, many show emotional vulnerabilities both similar to and different from males. The characteristic shyness is frequently observed in carrier females with average IQ, who have been found to have a personality pattern of internalizing disorders and withdrawal. Aside from the internalizing symptoms seen in males, some studies have indicated a higher incidence of anxiety disorders, lability of mood, and depression in adult females with the premutation, suggesting a possible biological predisposition for internalizing problems in these individuals as well.

Clinical management of individuals with FXS clearly involves the integration of medical, behavioral, and educational approaches, underscoring the need for multidisciplinary services. For the young child with tantrums, hyperactivity, and labile mood, stimulant medications have been beneficial in some, but exacerbate problems in others (Hagerman & Lampe, 1999). Speech and language services are often needed to address such problems as perseveration, word retrieval, and dysfluency, and sensory integration and occupational therapy can be helpful in decreasing hyperarousal. Children with FXS can often be educated in an inclusion setting in the regular classroom, with special education support. The nature of the generalized delays, coupled with specific difficulty with auditory sequential processing, typically require targeted approaches to instruction. Techniques involving simultaneous processing strategies, for example, whole word approaches used initially in reading instruction, have been recommended. Psychological interventions would typically also be targeted toward educating parents and educational personnel about both cognitive and psychosocial characteristics (see Hagerman & Lampe, 1999; Harris-Schmidt & Fast, 1998, for additional information regarding management).

Prader-Willi Syndrome

This disorder was chosen for discussion for several reasons. First, the behavioral phenotype of Prader-Willi syndrome (PWS) is quite distinctive among the syndromes involving MR, and psychologists are likely to be involved in developing intervention/ management strategies for some of the unique problems these children present. Second, from a genetic standpoint, PWS exemplifies two genetic phenomena, which are likely to become increasingly important in the genetics of MR: the phenomena of imprinting and microdeletions (Simonoff, Bolton, et al., 1998). Finally, although PWS occurs relatively infrequently, its incidence (approximately 1/10,000 live births) is similar to that of phenylketonuria (see Table 12.1).

PWS, together with the genetically related Angelman syndrome (AS), involves mutations in a limited region of the long arm of chromosome 15 (15q11-q13) involving about 2 million base pairs. (The cognitive and behavioral phenotypes of PWS and AS are quite different, with AS individuals characterized by severe intellectual impairment. AS is not discussed in this review.) This region of chromosome 15 is of general interest because genes here are subject to *genomic imprinting*. This phenomenon pertains to a process by which paternally and maternally derived alleles of specific genes, or specific chromosome regions, are marked molecularly during gametogenesis (see review by Mannens & Alders, 1999). Imprinting involves differential chemical alteration (the addition of methyl groups) of bases in DNA. The result of this molecular marking is differential expression of the paternally or maternally derived genes or chromosomal regions during embryonic development. Genomic imprinting leads to the nonidentical phenotypic expression of alleles based on their parent of origin. The latter situation differs from Mendelian transmission of traits in which the parental origin of an allele has no effect on the phenotype it produces. (For a detailed molecular discussion of this phenomenon in PWS and AS, see Nicholls, Saitoh, & Horsthemke, 1998.) Within the *15q11-q13* region, eight different genes have been shown to be sensitive to imprinting. The maternally derived chromosome 15 fails to express seven of these eight genes. All but one of the paternally derived genes in this region are expressed in the brain. The gene that is not expressed by the paternally derived chromosome 15 is the one expressed by the maternally derived gene. Most PWS cases are sporadic, but familial forms can also occur. The types of mutations occurring in the *q11-q13* region of chromosome 15, which cause both PWS and AS, are primarily small deletions in this region. These microdeletions are not normally visible in conventional Giemsa banded karyotypes, but they are readily identified by the FISH technique employing specific DNA sequence probes complementary to this region. Such deletions occur in about 70% of both PWS and AS cases. However, deletions in the *paternally* derived chromosome produce PWS, and those in the *maternally* derived chromosome produce AS. An additional unusual feature of PWS is that most children without karyotype abnormalities (25% of PWS cases) result from a uniparental disomy in which the affected individual receives two structurally normal copies of chromosome 15 from the mother and none from the father. A fourth type of mutation involving the mechanisms of imprinting occurs in ≤5% of PWS cases. The type of mutation observed has important implications for risk of recurrence in subsequent pregnancies and has been important in understanding the molecular underpinnings of PWS. Rapid, accurate methods based on PCR technology are available to provide molecular diagnosis of PWS and AS (Muralidhar & Butler, 1998).

For some years, it had been conjectured that PWS was caused by the loss of function of multiple genes carried on and expressed from the paternal chromosome 15. Recent evidence indicates that disrupting the function of a single gene, *SNRPN*, results in the spectrum of abnormalities characteristic of PWS (Kuslich, Kobori, Mohapatra, Gregorio-King, & Donlon, 1999). The *SNRPN* gene encodes a small nucleoriboprotein that appears to play a key role in erasing the inherited imprint status of genes in the PWS/AS region of chromosome 15 and establishing a new imprint pattern that is itself expressed in the human preimplantation embryo (Huntriss, Daniels, Bolton, & Monk, 1998). *SNRPN* belongs to a family of genes whose protein products are important in processing of messenger RNAs in the nucleus before they are exported for protein synthesis in the cytoplasm. A reduction in the amount of the product of the *SNRPN* gene could influence the relative ability to express the protein products of many brain proteins during embryological development. Thus, the PWS deficit is in some way mechanistically analogous to that which occurs in Fragile X syndrome.

PWS has a recognizable pattern of changed growth and development. The syndrome is characterized by two stages, the first involving prenatal development through infancy until age 2 years. Following a prenatal history of minimal fetal movement and frequent breech presentation at birth, infants are often born preterm, with low birthweight, failure to thrive, hypotonia, poor sucking reflex, weak cry, and delayed development. The second stage, coinciding with late-developing walking, is typified by one of the most distinctive characteristics of PWS: compulsive, indiscriminate, and insatiable appetite (hyperphagia), coupled with rapid weight gain. Such a behavioral change is often difficult for parents, who usually are initially pleased that the child has begun to thrive and gain weight. Morbid obesity is thus a major risk factor for PWS, with adults reaching 300 to 400 pounds without appropriate intervention (Daniel & Gridley, 1998). Moreover, the characteristic hyperphagia appears to be a unique aspect of PWS that does not occur to the same degree in other individuals with MR who show a propensity for being overweight and is apparently not related to IQ (Dykens & Cassidy, 1999).

The physical phenotype for PWS has been well-established, with the following features typically used as clinical criteria for the syndrome: hypotonia at birth; characteristic facial features (narrow face, almond-shaped eyes, small-appearing mouth, down-turned corners of mouth); hypogonadism (delayed or incomplete pubertal development); excessive appetite; short stature; small hands and/or feet; eye abnormalities (crossed eyes, myopia); speech articulation defects; and thick, viscous saliva. An unusual body composition has been reported, with greater fat composition at limbs and reduced lean mass especially in the limbs (Brambilla et al., 1997). Hair pulling (trichotillomania) and excessive scratching and picking of the skin are also apparent in many PWS individuals. Delays in gross and fine motor skills, speech, and the risk of bone fracture are associated with the hypotonia (Curfs, 1992). Additional risk is associated with the time of diagnosis: the later in life the child is diagnosed, the more likely poor eating habits have become deeply ingrained, leading to a shortened life span. Because normal gonadotropic hormones are not produced, the PWS adolescent does not develop secondary sex characteristics or experience puberty and remains short in stature.

The cognitive phenotype for PWS is often associated with global developmental delays. IQ is typically found to be in the mild to moderate range of MR, with various studies reporting IQ ranges of 12 to 91. IQ data extrapolated from > 500 subjects suggest 34% in the mild MR range, 27% in the

moderate range, and 6% in the severe/profound range (Curfs, 1992). Specific weaknesses in short-term memory, sequential processing, and auditory-verbal abilities have been reported (van Lieshout, de Meyer, Curfs, & Fryns, 1998), with corresponding strengths in visual perception and organization, for example, an unusual facility with jigsaw puzzles. Individuals with PWS also typically exhibit speech and language deficits, including problems with voice quality (high pitch, nasality), speech production, and certain aspects of language (grammar, comprehension). Although language development is typically delayed, expressive language and vocabulary may eventually emerge as strengths for many PWS children. (Akefeldt, Akefeldt, & Gillberg, 1997).

Beyond the physical and cognitive limitations, social and psychological difficulties are frequent, and associated behavioral problems become increasingly apparent with age (Dykens, Hodapp, Walsh, & Nash, 1992). During the early preschool years, these children often display an easy temperament, including affectionate, gentle, and good-natured qualities. However, beginning at about age 4 years, a temperament change typically occurs, characterized by traits of stubbornness, negativity, emotional lability, and temper outbursts; such behavioral changes may be related to the chronic frustrated appetite. More frequent and severe maladaptive behaviors have been reported in children with PWS when matched with both DS and other mentally retarded peers, with particular elevations in the following behaviors: hyperactivity, skin picking, fatigue, obsessions, impulsivity, speech problems, and compulsive talking (Dykens & Kasari, 1997). In addition to compulsive eating, other obsessions and compulsive behaviors often include hoarding, redoing, persistent questioning, and ordering/arranging. Despite their verbal and socially engaging behavior, PWS individuals are also often highly argumentative and display poor judgment, low impulse control, irritability, and temper tantrums (Sulzbacher, 1988). Such negative and immature behaviors also result in considerable peer teasing and rejection and lead to significant levels of parental stress (van Lieshout et al., 1998). Parents' descriptions of the most problematic behaviors they encounter included temper tantrums, repetitive speech, mood lability, self-injury, disobedience, and inactivity (Clarke & Boer, 1998). Psychosis has been reported in 6.3% of a sample of 95

PWS adults (D. Clark, 1998), and case studies of psychotic symptoms were noted in adults with a paternal deletion on chromosome 15. In contrast, co-occurring diagnoses of autism or pervasive developmental disorder in individuals with maternal UPD of chromosome 15 have suggested that comorbid psychiatric symptoms may be related to PWS genotype.

The array of problems exhibited by PWS children require multifaceted management. In terms of medical interventions, the short stature and growth problems are often treated with growth hormones to promote developmental changes during puberty. Nutritional counseling and the early establishment of an exercise routine are equally important in management, as is regular monitoring by physicians and other specialists. Important social and psychological interventions include anger control and devising behavioral strategies to reduce preoccupations and perseveration, such as skin picking in children with PWS. Because coping skills are weak in these individuals, interventions that work to diminish problem behaviors but also build or reinforce appropriate coping strategies are important (Dykens et al., 1992). Studies have shown that early diagnosis and parental guidance programs have been successful in reducing problem behaviors; likewise, establishing support programs to deal with the greater stress of parenting these children is important in reducing anger and promoting optimal adjustment (van Lieshout et al., 1998). Additional management concerns involve school placement. The majority of these children are placed in special education programs, with fewer (20%) included with general education peers. Issues such as establishing a general intelligence level, including speech/language therapy, implementing goals for specialized physical education and exercise, limiting caloric intake, and managing associated behavior problems (tantrums, skin picking) are part of the need for school management (Daniel & Gridley, 1998; Sulzbacher, 1988). Finally, recent improvements in care and management have contributed to increased life span in PWS, leading to an increased need to integrate adults with PWS into the community. Given the nature of the behavioral phenotype, a group home specifically tailored to the needs of PWS, coupled with sheltered employment, is increasingly recommended (Greenswag & Alexander, 1995).

Klinefelter Syndrome

Klinefelter syndrome (KS), characterized by an extra X chromosome, is one of the most frequent sex chromosome abnormalities seen in males, with an estimated occurrence rate in the general population of 1/1,000 males (Batshaw, 1997). The most common observed karyotype is the 47, XXY pattern, although mosaic and variant (i.e., XXXY) karyotypes also exist in a small fraction of cases (10%) (Mandoki & Sumner, 1991). Approximately 50% of KS cases occur during maternal meiosis, with a significant fraction of these reported to show effects of maternal age. In contrast to the other syndromes previously described, to date there have not been dedicated and systematic attempts to identify genes or regions on the X chromosome, whose copy number of two in the presence of a Y chromosome contributes to the KS phenotype.

Because of the relatively common occurrence of this syndrome, together with discovery of the genetic mechanism of the extra X chromosome in the 1950s, KS is by now a well-studied disorder, with large-scale prospective studies of developmental outcome (e.g., Berch & Bender, 1991). In KS, physical features may not be apparent at birth, physical development is typically normal, and, though clinical evaluation of hypospadias and microphallus may lead to early diagnosis (Schwartz & Root, 1991), many individuals may not be diagnosed until adolescence. Characteristics of the syndrome are typically noted with delayed puberty (e.g., lower testosterone production, small testes, breast enlargement, absent or diminished growth of hair, absence of voice changes) (Mandoki & Sumner, 1991). In addition to the genital abnormalities, KS males tend to be taller than their cohorts with proportionately longer legs and have smaller head circumferences and slightly altered craniofacial structure (Rovet, Netley, Keenan, Bailey, & Stewart, 1996). Additional features include poor weight gain through childhood; delays in gross and fine motor skills, coordination, speed, dexterity, and strength; impaired hearing thought to be associated with frequent childhood respiratory tract infections; and insulin resistance, with associated higher risk of diabetes (see reviews by Mandoki & Sumner, 1991; Mandoki, Sumner, Hoffman, & Riconda, 1991).

In contrast to autosomal chromosome abnormalities such as Down syndrome, the sex chromosome disorders typically have a much less profound effect on cognitive development, and MR, if present, tends to be mild. However, genotypes including >2 X chromosomes occur rarely, and, as the number of X chromosomes increase beyond 2, the likelihood of mental retardation and its severity increases. Most KS males have low average to normal intelligence, although global IQ is typically lowered due to decreased verbal abilities (Mandoki & Sumner, 1991). Sorensen (1992) reports a mean Full-Scale IQ of 95.6 for these males (Verbal IQ mean of 91 and Performance IQ of 101), illustrating the characteristic weakness in verbal abilities seen in KS. This cognitive phenotype also includes language deficits and significant academic difficulties. Speech and language delays as well as associated language-based learning disabilities are characteristic of KS. A prospective, 20-year longitudinal study of achievement indicated grade repetition in the majority, special education for 60% to 80%, and increased rates of specific learning disabilities in most KS males, particularly in reading, spelling, and written language (Rovet et al., 1996). Frequently reported auditory processing difficulty and poor short-term memory impact the amount and accuracy of information acquired and underscore the specific learning impairments. Although many of these males graduate from high school, by the end of high school, they may remain as much as five years behind their peers in math and reading skills.

With regard to the behavioral phenotype in KS, it should be underscored that much of the research on personality types prior to 1980 presented a significantly flawed characterization of KS males as having increased aggressiveness, criminal behavior, and psychotic tendencies (based on studies of institutionalized individuals). More recent and methodologically improved studies suggest such features as low activity levels, low endurance and drive, diminished self-confidence and self-esteem, dependence on parents, emotional immaturity, shyness and reticence, passivity, low sexual activity, anxiety, and social stress (Mandoki & Sumner, 1991; Sorensen, 1992). The most common presenting problems of KS males are poor peer relationships, underachievement in school, impulsivity, aggressiveness, withdrawal, apathy, and immaturity (Mandoki & Sumner, 1991). Reports of inattention, difficulty concentrating, and decreased motivation have suggested either comorbid attention-deficit disorder or, conversely, a more basic difficulty in

processing auditory information (Rovet et al., 1996). Finally, based on their prospective study, Berch and Bender (1991) suggest a high-risk profile for children with sex chromosome disorders, including difficulty communicating with peers, low achievement, behavioral immaturity, and social isolation, often as a function of teasing by peers. Although sexual identity is typically male, their differences in psychosexual development place adolescent KS boys at risk for associated problems with body image and social withdrawal.

Because a large proportion of KS boys are not diagnosed early, many come to attention because of their school-related difficulties. Thus, males exhibiting characteristic learning difficulty, together with KS physical features, should be referred for genetic workup, as early diagnosis and multidisciplinary intervention plans are important for optimal outcome in these boys. Treatment with testosterone has resulted in KS males being less tired, having improved mood, experiencing more drive, and having an increased ability to work and concentrate (Sorensen, 1992). Psychological intervention is often warranted in individuals because of their lowered self-esteem, social withdrawal, and adjustment difficulties. Finally, guidelines for educational management include speech and language and special education services to include emphasis on vocabulary, sentence structure, comprehension, and word finding, as well as the related reading and written language difficulties (Rovet et al., 1996).

Turner Syndrome

Turner syndrome (TS) is a fairly common sex-linked chromosomal abnormality observed in 1/2,500 to 1/5,000 live female births. One of the two X chromosomes is either absent or abnormal in cells from TS individuals. A variety of distinct karyotype abnormalities produce this syndrome, the most commonly occurring of which is monosomy X (45,X), which occurs in more than 50% of cases. In approximately 70% of the 45,X cases, the single X is of maternal origin; in the remaining 30%, it is of paternal origin. An estimated 99% of 45,X conceptions are spontaneously aborted. Some 15% of TS individuals have structural abnormalities: partial deletions of the X chromosome, X isochromosomes, or ring chromosomes (Pasaro-Mendez, Fernandez, Goyanes, & Mendez, 1994; Skuse et al., 1997). Mosaicism in TS (having cells with nonidentical genotypes, e.g.,

45,X/46,XX or 45,X/XY) occurs relatively frequently (15%–40% of cases), and those females who have the mosaic type are often less severely affected. The 45,X/XY mosaics (which occur in about 5% of cases) are of special importance because they have a 20% risk of malignancy of the dysgenic gonad.

Because the genetic mechanism involved in TS has been known since the 1950s, there is now considerable information regarding the phenotype in females with the most common 45,X genotype. The impetus of more recent studies has been to examine phenotypic variability as a function of parental origin of the X chromosome, the less frequent mosaic forms, and deletions. In addition, systematic attempts to utilize partial X monosomies to identify the gene(s) contributing to each aspect of the TS phenotype have only recently been initiated (Zinn et al., 1998); however, these have not focused on cognitive or behavioral features. The most common physical characteristics of TS include short stature (height typically 4 to < 5 feet in adult females), short webbed neck, stocky bold build, broad chest with widely spaced nipples, absence of secondary sexual characteristics, lack of spontaneous puberty, and infertility. These and other less common features occur in a range of degrees (Epstein, 1990). Similar to KS, girls with TS are often not diagnosed until late adolescence, when they fail to begin puberty.

Although a distinctive cognitive phenotype exists in TS, it contrasts with that of KS: TS females typically are of average intelligence; however, verbal IQ is typically significantly higher than nonverbal IQ (Rovet, 1990, 1995), the degree of verbal/nonverbal difference varying across studies. A consistent finding in TS is characteristic difficulty with both visuospatial processing and math, a constellation consistent with nonverbal, or right hemisphere, learning disabilities, a finding supported by electrophysiologic studies (Rovet, 1995; Shucard, Shucard, Clopper, & Schacter, 1992). Such deficits are apparent in the performance of TS females on a variety of visuospatial and constructional tasks requiring perceptual organization, with more recent work suggesting that the core deficit may be in visuospatial working memory, a phenotypic trait found to be related to gene dosage (Buchanan, Pavlovic, & Rovet, 1998). Other specific nonverbal deficits include difficulties with visuomotor coordination, motor learning, spatiotemporal processing,

poor sense of direction, and poor perceptual stability. Consistent with nonverbal learning disorders, a specific learning disability in the area of mathematics is also well-known in TS (Rovet, 1995; Siegel, Clopper, & Stabler, 1998). Recent investigations of phenotypic differences suggest that, as a rule, the mosaic form of TS results in fewer cognitive and visuospatial difficulties than the more common 45,X type (El Abd, Turk, & Hill, 1995).

Although female gender identity and gender role behavior develop normally and TS females appear to have a generally adequate adjustment, social immaturity and poor self-esteem often occur and are apparently not mediated by such factors as socioeconomic status or IQ scores (McCauley, Ross, Kushner, & Cutler, 1995). In childhood, most girls appear to cope well with looking younger and appearing less socially immature. However, as in KS, the beginning of puberty often dramatically increases the psychological risks in TS girls, who often begin to fall behind their female peers in psychological maturation. Social isolation, anxiety disorders, behavior problems, anorexia nervosa, and a tendency toward withdrawal are not uncommon. As adults, they often experience continued difficulty with social interaction, appearing less socially mature, and they are less likely to leave home or to marry when compared to controls in the general population (Downey & Erhardt, 1990).

Refinement in karotyping techniques has prompted investigation of the genotype-phenotype relationship in TS, that is, differences between paternally and maternally derived forms of 45,X. Although characteristic impairment in nonverbal/visuospatial abilities occurs in both types of TS, those with the maternally derived X chromosome have been shown to have significantly lower verbal intelligence, more frequently require special education services, demonstrate significant social difficulties, and lack flexibility and responsiveness in social interactions. Such differences suggest an imprinted genetic locus at which gene(s) influencing social adjustment are expressed only from the paternally derived X chromosome; if confirmed, this may also explain why males are markedly more vulnerable to pervasive developmental disorders affecting social adjustment and language (e.g., autism) (Skuse et al., 1997).

Additional studies related to genotype have shown more frequent delays in motor and speech development in monosomic X girls than the other karyotypes. In contrast, monosomic X girls have been shown to be more sociable and extroverted, more even-tempered, and more emotionally stable than girls of the mosaic type (Pasaro-Mendez et al., 1993).

The relative prevalence of TS, as well as the considerable impact of this syndrome on a TS female's life, highlight the importance of effective interventions. Medical management of short stature and the development of secondary sexual characteristics typically involves both growth hormone and estrogen replacement therapy. Data from the National Cooperative Growth Study including > 2,500 TS females have shown very significant gains in growth, with adult height attained in some girls (Plotnick, Attic, Blethen, & Sy, 1998). Related studies of psychosocial functioning of a subset of these females suggested reduction in ratings on both internalizing and externalizing scales, with specific recommendations that the comprehensive treatment of TS females should include educational and behavioral interventions (Siegel et al., 1998). Estrogen replacement therapy has also become standard in medical management, with some reports that it may have positive effects on nonverbal processing speed and motor function (Ross, Roeltgen, Feuillan, Kushner, & Cutler, 1998), but with additional evidence that it may be associated with the occurrence of anorexia nervosa in some young adult TS females. Although most TS women are infertile, pregnancy is possible in about 2% of cases with particular genotypes (Tarani et al., 1998). Visuospatial deficits and accompanying learning disability need to be addressed through the use of special education services; such educational management should optimally occur before difficulties develop at school. The frequent problems with social interaction likely reflect social cognitive deficits, difficulty reading social cues, and not knowing how to interact with others (Siegel et al., 1998), suggesting the need for intervention. Support involving both same-age girls and opportunities to meet older TS females as "mentors" may assist adjustment, as well as provide support to parents. Finally, with the development of newer, more sophisticated karotyping techniques, the ability to target girls at heightened risk for specific symptoms (speech delays in monosomic X; social difficulties in mosaics) exists and should lead to more effective early intervention.

NARROW SPECTRUM DISORDERS

In contrast to those disorders whose genotypes influence a broad spectrum of effects involving physical, cognitive, and behavioral phenotypes, the following section describes one of the *specific learning disabilities (SLD)*. These very frequently occurring neurobehavioral disorders involve more circumscribed deficits in cognition, learning, and/or attention (Lyon, 1996). Despite numerous attempts to define homogeneous phenotypic subtypes of SLD, based on patterns of neuropsychological strengths and weaknesses (e.g., Hooper & Willis, 1989), SLD remain a very heterogeneous group of disorders. The inherent difficulty in finding agreement on definition of the phenotype(s) has plagued studies of these children since the inception of the diagnostic label in the 1970s. However, a long-held distinction between SLD and the disorders described previously is the cardinal assumption that the difficulties with aspects of academic learning are *not* a result of generalized cognitive delay (MR), sensory deficits, or environmental effects, but rather, are presumed to be the result of *specific CNS dysfunction*. Given that impaired reading is the most frequently reported characteristic of SLD children, it is not surprising that the overwhelming majority of studies investigating genetic etiology have focused on this aspect of the phenotype, with a very limited number of studies beginning to investigate specific mathematics disorders (Alarcon, DeFries, Light, & Pennington, 1997) and specific language impairment (SLI) (Rice, 1996). Attention-deficit/hyperactivity disorder (ADHD) is also a very frequently occurring neurobehavioral disorder (involving significant co-occurrence with SLD). However, because genetic studies have tended to focus more on the behavioral phenotype of impulsive and hyperactive behavior than on the cognitive phenotype of impaired attention, ADHD disorder will be discussed in the section devoted to child psychopathology.

Dyslexia

In contrast to the heterogeneous group of SLD, developmental dyslexia (used synonymously with specific reading disability) has been recently defined as "a specific language-based disorder of constitutional origin, characterized by difficulties in single word decoding, usually reflecting insufficient phonological processing. These difficulties... are often unexpected in relation to age and other cognitive and academic abilities; they are not the result of generalized developmental disability or sensory impairment" (Lyon, 1995, p. 9). This common neurobehavioral disorder has prevalence rates estimated to range from 5% to 10% of the school population. Contrary to previous thinking that dyslexia occurs predominantly in males, more recent epidemiologic studies carried out by investigators in the NICHD-sponsored Learning Disabilities Research Network have shown this to be an artifact of ascertainment, with males and females (1.4:1) being approximately equally affected (Shaywitz, 1998). Such prevalence figures differ from the excess of males identified as having a learning disability in public schools, where comorbid ADHD and behavioral problems clearly bias the ascertainment rates. In addition, longitudinal investigations confirm a chronic, persistent condition that does not represent a "developmental lag" (Shaywitz, 1998).

Interest in the biological bases of specific reading disability/dyslexia has existed for the better portion of this century, with research directed to determining genetic etiology spanning the past 50 years (see reviews by DeFries & Gillis, 1993; Pennington, 1995; Pennington & Gilger, 1996; Smith, Kelly, & Brower, 1998). Several major issues have plagued genetic investigations of dyslexia: (1) whether impaired reading reflects a homogeneous phenotype, or involves multiple phenotypes; (2) whether dyslexia represents a discrete disorder with a distinct etiology; and (3) whether it represents the tail end of a normal distribution of reading ability, thus caused by the same factors that influence normal variation in reading (e.g., Pennington & Gilger, 1996).

In spite of these major conceptual issues, genetic investigations of dyslexia have progressed in a methodical fashion for the past 50 years. By now, there is extensive evidence that dyslexia is familial, with numerous pedigree (e.g., Elbert & Seale, 1988) and family studies (e.g., Gilger, Pennington, & DeFries, 1991) indicating familial aggregation. Results from methodologically sound family studies (summarized in Pennington & Gilger, 1996) suggest the following: (1) the increase in risk to a child having an affected parent is approximately 8 times the population risk; (2) recurrence rates for first-degree relatives (with varying estimates ranging between 35% and 45%) approach the value expected (50%) under

a simple autosomal dominant mode of transmission; and (3) there is corresponding evidence against a simple autosomal recessive model. Because familial occurrence of dyslexia suggests but does not confirm genetic heritability of dyslexia, investigation proceeded to systematic twin concordance studies, followed by segregation analyses, chromosomal linkage studies, and, most recently, gene localization studies.

Twin studies conducted in the 1960s and 1970s have consistently found significantly greater concordance in MZ twins (concordance ranging between 32% and 100%) than in DZ twins (concordance ranging between 21% and 42%). Perhaps the current gold standard, the Colorado Twin Study of Reading Disability, begun in 1982, is a methodologically well-controlled study of > 200 twin pairs, in which pairwise concordance rates for reading disability for MZ and same-sex DZ twins were 66% and 43%, respectively (DeFries & Gillis, 1993). These investigators have also systematically explored several aspects of the phenotype, finding, for example, that deficits in reading, spelling, and nonword reading were substantially heritable whereas deficits in orthographic coding (recognition of a word through such visual characteristics as spelling patterns) were not significantly heritable but, rather, were found to be significantly influenced by common family environment (e.g., type of instruction). Finally, in contrast to previous twin studies involving dichotomous variables (e.g., dyslexia present or absent), more powerful multiple regression models treat reading scores as a continuous variable and predict scores of DZ twins to show greater regression toward the test standardization and/or control group mean. In this large-scale and ongoing study, the Colorado investigators have shown that MZ twins regressed only .24 standard deviation units toward the mean, whereas DZ twins regressed .87 standard deviations, suggesting that approximately 50% of the observed deficit in the reading disabled twins could be accounted for by inheritance (DeFries & Gillis, 1993).

Subsequent complex segregation analyses of the pattern of transmission have suggested that the modes of transmission in a large fraction of families may include autosomal dominant or additive types, as well as sex-influenced types (the latter explaining the slight excess of males). In contrast, however, classic X-linked transmission, maternal inheritance, and an imprinting effect on either rate or severity of dyslexia were rejected. Moreover, the major dominant gene would also appear to have incomplete penetrance, indicating that not all of the individuals receiving a copy of the defective allele will demonstrate significantly impaired reading performance. Finally, the considerable evidence for genetic heterogeneity has reduced the likelihood of a single gene producing dyslexia (e.g., Pennington & Gilger, 1996).

A critical element for progress in understanding the genetic mechanisms of dyslexia is better consensus regarding the phenotype. There has been a growing interface between developmental cognitive neuroscience and behavioral genetics, with critical research aimed at defining the behavioral phenotype(s) of dyslexia prior to molecular genetic investigations (Pennington, 1997). Such research has generated converging evidence for core deficits underlying reading impairment: *phonological awareness* (the ability to detect individual speech sounds within words) and/or *phonological coding* (the ability to segment and manipulate these sounds). Such findings have clearly implicated the auditory system in dyslexia and have guided the more recent molecular studies. Through investigation of visual cognitive mechanisms in dyslexia continues to expand (e.g., Chase, 1996; Eden, VanMeter, Rumsey, & Zeffiro, 1996), such aspects of the phenotype have not been as rigorously studied as the phonological mechanisms (e.g., orthographic coding). One such investigation is a twin study of two dyslexia subtypes: phonological dyslexia (characterized by poor nonword reading) and surface dyslexia (characterized by difficulty in reading irregular words). Reading deficits were found to be significantly heritable in both subgroups; however, the genetic contribution to the group reading deficit was much greater in the phonological dyslexics (Castles, Datta, Gayan, & Olson, 1999).

An important related finding from genetic studies is that familiality, heritability, and transmission for *normal variation* in reading skill are not clearly different from dyslexia, suggesting that the gene locus/loci likely represents a *susceptibility* rather than a *disease* locus (i.e., dyslexics would have more of the unfavorable alleles at these loci and/or additional environmental risk factors, so that their reading scores are pushed beyond the cutoff for dyslexia). Related support of this notion comes from the Connecticut Longitudinal Study, which provides strong evidence for a dimensional model, that is, that dyslexia occurs along a continuum,

with reading disability representing the lower tail of a normal distribution (Shaywitz, Escobar, Shaywitz, Fletcher, & Makuch, 1992). Thus, reading disability likely is not an "all-or-none" phenomenon, but occurs in degrees and across a continuum of normally distributed reading scores. This notion that dyslexia may not be qualitatively different from the "garden variety poor reader" (those with no discrepancy between reading performance and general IQ) has created considerable controversy and a rethinking of the long-held assumption of the distinctiveness of dyslexia. It has also become increasingly apparent that the core phonological processing deficit in dyslexia affects basic single-word reading/decoding, whereas more complex reading comprehension also involves multiple systems, including higher-order language and cognitive abilities.

Advances in molecular genetic approaches have begun to identify the specific genetic mechanisms responsible for inherited forms of dyslexia, with current focus on chromosomes 15 and 6. The first report of a gene locus was a linkage study of nine families in which dyslexia had apparently been transmitted in an autosomal dominant fashion and in which a chromosome 15p locus was suggested (Smith, Kimberling, Pennington, & Lubs, 1983). However, subsequent analysis using the improved technology of DNA markers from the centromic and proximal long arm of chromosome 15 did not confirm linkage to dyslexia (Smith et al., 1998). A subsequent study using 21 families found two markers on the long arm of chromosome 15 but further suggested that only a small fraction of families may have this particular locus (Smith, Pennington, Kimberling, & Ing, 1990). An important follow-up study (Grigorenko et al., 1997) utilized a broader array of five theoretically derived dyslexia phenotypes, including both global criteria (i.e., single-word reading; discrepancy between intelligence and reading ability) as well as the component processes likely involved in reading (e.g., phonological awareness, phonological decoding, and rapid automatized naming) and found a significant association of the single-word reading phenotype with chromosome 15 markers.

Evidence for a QTL (6p23-21.3) has also been reported for chromosome 6 (Cardon et al., 1994) from two independent sib pair studies and an independent sample of DZ twin pairs, with stronger evidence for the QTL found in the more severely affected twins. Grigorenko et al. (1997) subsequently investigated chromosome 6 using the five theoretically derived phenotypes and found significant linkage of the phonological awareness phenotype with five adjacent markers on the short arm of chromosome 6. Interestingly, the least compelling results were found for single-word reading. This latter investigation represents the first finding that cognitively dissociable and hierarchical components of the reading process may be separately genetically controlled. The Colorado group has reported another study using an independent sample of 126. In this study, the QTL on chromosome 6 was found to affect *both* phonological and orthographic skills and was not specific to phoneme awareness, as suggested by previous studies (Gayan et al., 1999). A promising candidate gene, *GABA(B)*, which encodes a receptor for the inhibitory neurotransmitter gamma-aminobutyric acid (GABA), maps at chromosomal locus 6p21.3 (Goei et al., 1998). This GABA receptor differs in properties from the better known GABA(A) receptors through which benzodiazepines such as Valium act, and has a different distribution among brain regions. GABA(B) receptors have been shown recently to play an important role in learning and memory in animals. Although compounds that activate GABA receptors impair learning and memory in animals, antagonists selective for this receptor enhance these functions (Getova & Bowery, 1998). If mutant alleles in the GABA(B) receptor gene actually underlie the inherited form of dyslexia mapping on chromosome 6, then such mutations might be expected to cause an increase in sensitivity to their natural substrate, GABA, or a hyperresponsiveness on binding this neurotransmitter. In principle, such an abnormality might respond to selective pharmacotherapy. However, it must be noted that not all molecular genetic studies are in agreement with regard to the phenotypic effects of gene(s) located in this region. An independent investigation of chromosome 6 markers in 79 families having at least two siblings affected with phonological coding dyslexia failed to find linkage to chromosome 6, suggesting that previous analytic methods may have resulted in false positives (Field & Kaplan, 1998). The chromosomal mapping of QTLs for genes that increase the risk for dyslexia is a crucial first step that must be unambiguously established before the systematic search for candidate genes on particular chromosomes can be undertaken.

Pennington and Smith (1997) have commented on the difficulty in interpreting findings from molecular studies, suggesting that considerable interdisciplinary collaboration will need to occur before clinical implications are fully apparent. For example, there is apparent incongruence between genetic findings of the separability of single-word reading and phonological awareness, because the latter is increasingly viewed as a separate but essential component skill in the more complex skill of single-word reading. Additional research will need to address the apparent inconsistency in findings related to the heritability of orthographic (i.e., surface dyslexia) coding processes. The robustness of the phonological processing deficits found in dyslexia has begun to impact practice, as research in intervention has clearly shown evidence for the success of methods of reading instruction involving systematic phonemic awareness and phonological decoding over orthographic or "sight" approaches (e.g., Lyon, 1995 or Torgesen, Wagner, & Rashotte, 1997). Current research clearly suggests (1) that dyslexia is genotypically heterogeneous, with multiple genetic profiles accounting for impaired performance, and (2) within a single individual, the component processes in reading may be influenced by different and multiple genes at multiple loci.

It is clear that dyslexia is frequently comorbid with a variety of other neurodevelopmental disorders, including other SLD, ADHD, developmental communication disorders of speech and language, and some of the behavioral disorders. Mathematics disability has also been found to be significantly heritable, with concordance rates for MZ and DZ twins being .73 and .56, respectively (Alarcon et al., 1997). The comorbidiy between mathematics and reading disability has also been found to be due in part to genetic influences (Knopik, Alarcon, & DeFries, 1997). Finally, the link between language disorder and dyslexia has been documented in longitudinal studies of early language delay in young preschool children who become dyslexic (e.g., Scarborough, 1990). Whether speech and/or language disorders will be shown to be included in one or more multiple dyslexia phenotypes awaits further genetic study.

PERSONALITY AND TEMPERAMENT

The focus now shifts, first, to a review of selected research investigating genetic influence on development and variability of personality and temperament, followed by a discussion of emerging genetic investigations in developmental psychopathology. Personality, temperament, and psychopathology in both adults and children have traditionally represented distinct areas of study, in which genetic research typically emphasized the partitioning of heritable and environmental variance. Historically, temperament has been viewed as a set of narrower, biologically based characteristics, whereas personality is believed to represent the later elaboration of development with experience and more socially determined characteristics. Both areas have involved trait models, and convergence of the two is recent, with interest in whether the domains of temperament map onto personality traits. The emergence of the paradigm of developmental psychopathology, together with the application of multivariate biometric models to behavioral genetic data, has ushered in a second phase of integrated research in these domains. This integration reflects a move away from more simplistic models to more complex and sophisticated approaches that consider two models for psychopathology: first, the more traditional categorical method represented by discrete clinical diagnosis (e.g., *DSM-IV*; APA, 1994), and second, the dimensional approach, which begins to define psychopathology as extremes of a normally distributed temperament or personality trait. Thus, mapping of dimensional liability-threshold models of psychopathology and evaluating empirically the categorical versus dimensional etiology of traits and disorders has been an important step forward in understanding childhood disorders. The following review of these areas is highly selective, and the reader is referred to more detailed reviews (Nigg & Goldsmith, 1998; Rende & Plomin, 1995; and Rothbart, Posner, & Hershey, 1995).

PERSONALITY

The adult personality literature contains extensive quantitative genetic data drawn from a large number of twin and adoption studies, which form a considerable body of information regarding inheritance of personality. In comparison to the work on the genetics of intelligence, however, it should be pointed out that summarizing data on the contribution of genes and environment to differences in personality traits is considerably more complex (Loehlin, 1996). First, personality varies over a number of dimensions whose measurement is far

from standardized. Second, intelligence is measured behaviorally, whereas personality is typically measured by self-report and, only more recently, by objective ratings of behavior. Thus, determining equivalencies from study to study or from age to age within a study are difficult to establish. However, on balance, results appear similar to IQ research.

The study of personality has emerged on the basis of a wide variety of behavioral or personality traits originating initially from early theoretical work from psychoanalysis (e.g., introversion and extroversion), followed by a generation of factor-analytic studies, typically developed via self-report questionnaires. Such research assumes that personality is hierarchically organized, with broad band, higher-order traits such as neuroticism and extroversion comprising narrower, more homogeneous traits. Among the array of proposed traits encompassing adult personality, there is consensus that at least five independent personality factors exist: the "Big Five" (Loehlin, 1996). These are labeled somewhat differently by different investigators, but most agree on the following adjectives: *extroversion, agreeableness, conscientiousness, neuroticism,* and *openness to experience.* Loehlin (1992) has been a major figure in interpreting the large number of quantitative genetic studies of personality with his important reanalysis of data on the Big Five factors from international studies using behavioral genetic designs. In spite of problems related to differing methodologies, the data fit two models, one involving additive genes, genetic epistasis, and shared twin/sibling environments, the other involving additive genes, special MZ twin environments, and shared environments of DZ twins and other siblings. Additive effects under either model fell generally in the moderate range, 22% to 46%; shared family environmental effects were small, 0% to 11%; and the ambiguous third factor, nonadditive or special MZ twin environments, was intermediate at 11% to 19%. The remaining variation, 44% to 55%, presumably represents some combination of environmental effects unique to the individual, genotype-environment interaction, and measurement error.

McCartney and colleagues have summarized much of the quantitative genetic analyses of personality traits in their meta-analysis of personality traits across approximately 103 twin studies published between 1967 and 1985 (McCartney, Harris, & Bernieri, 1990). Correlations across eight personality traits (activity-impulsivity, aggression, anxiety, dominance, emotionality, masculinity-femininity, sociability, task orientation) declined with age for both MZ and DZ twins, and about equally so (in contrast to an increase for MZ and decrease for DZ twins in correlations for IQ), implying a more or less stable influence over time for heredity of personality and a decline in the effect of shared family environment. In general, both MZ and DZ personality correlations were lower (by 20 points or so) than IQ correlations (suggesting more residual variance and the greater magnitude of measurement error in personality studies). These data suggest that, as individuals grow older, there is a shift away from a relatively greater degree of shared family environmental influences in the earlier years to more distinctive environments as the twins get older. However, studies are not all consistent in this finding, leading some to conclude that the evidence for inheritability of personality over the life span is equivocal, and certainly much less clear than for intelligence.

Adoption studies confirm a moderate effect of genes and little enduring effect of shared environment on personality traits, as measured later in life by personality traits (Loehlin, 1996). From the Minnesota project, average correlations among personality traits were .20 for biological siblings and .07 for adopted siblings; in Loehlin's Texas study, the correlation for biological siblings was .22 and .01 for adopted siblings. In this latter study, changes in means over a 10-year interval suggested that adopted children as a group tended to shift in the direction of their birth parents, as one would expect if personality is increasingly affected by genes.

In summary, existing research suggests (1) a moderate genetic influence on individual differences that emerges in childhood, peaks in young adulthood, and after a slight drop, continues stable until fairly late in life; (2) an influence of shared family environment that decreases over time at least until late adolescence; (3) nonadditive genetic effects or some special twin environmental factor that tends to decrease DZ relative to MZ resemblance; and (4) nonshared environmental effects, gene-environment interactions, and random developmental variation (Loehlin, 1996, p. 47).

TEMPERAMENT

Thomas and Chess (1977), who were instrumental in developing the formal discipline of temperament,

regarded it as the *how* of behavior. Rowe (1997) described temperament as the first expression of personality in the very young, whereas others regard temperament as forming the core—primarily affective and innately biological—around which broader personality dimensions develop (Clark, Watson, & Mineka, 1994). Although investigation of individual differences in behavior is common to personality and temperament research, temperament has come to be regarded as representing traits present in infancy or early childhood and that to some degree are biologically based. Contemporary theorists differ with regard to whether "biological" should be equated with genetic. Those in the biological camp argue that temperament reflects a limited number of constitutionally determined, biologically based characteristics that are demonstrably heritable (Plomin & Dunn, 1986). In contrast, adherents to a biosocial model of temperament argue that heritability should *not* form part of the definition of temperament for several reasons: (1) genetic effects change with age and context of development; (2) heritability estimates are difficult to quantify; and (3) peri- and postnatal experiences as well as learning potential may well confound (Prior, 1992). Given these fundamentally different definitions of temperament, it follows that methods for assessing essential temperamental traits have similarly differed. Goldsmith et al. (1987) chose categories on the basis of basic emotions; Buss and Plomin (1984) identified three broad temperaments: emotionality (general arousal, fear, anger), activity (total motoric activity: amount of movement, pacing, running), and sociability (preference for social interactions with others, as opposed to being alone). Thomas and Chess, in the New York Longitudinal Study (NYLS), originally defined nine categories: activity level, threshold, mood, rhythmicity, approach/ withdrawal, intensity, adaptability, distractibility, and attention span/persistence. Recent research has supported distilling the NYLS list to four dimensions: negative emotionality (identified by some investigators as fear and/or irritability/frustration), positive affect/approach (associated with curiosity, eagerness, energy, and mastery, but when not controlled, shows a failure of self-regulation), attention span (including effortful control and persistence), and activity level (Rothbart & Bates, 1998).

Emerging evidence from twin studies has generally supported the heritability of basic temperaments. In the Louisville Twin Study, temperament differences in twins were assessed by parent interviews and laboratory behavioral ratings. On temperament ratings by laboratory personnel at 9 and 11 months, there was little if any resemblance for MZ versus DZ twins, but by 2 years, MZs were being rated as more and DZ as less alike on the four traits. By middle childhood (age 7 to 10), differences were substantially larger, although shifts in traits measured and methods of measurement make comparisons difficult (Riese, 1990).

Nigg and Goldsmith's (1998) review of other twin studies concluded the following: (1) minimal heritability for traits in the neonatal period; (2) increasing heritability of traits through infancy and into childhood; (3) heritabilities of major child temperament traits approaching .50, with slightly increasing heritability later in life; (4) environmental variance generally of the nonshared (within-family) type; and (5) shared experience (between-family variance) contributing little to variation in these traits. However, to date, such findings have not been supported by adoption studies, which are sparse. Thus, reliable conclusions about heritability of temperament await continuing research.

Two recent areas of interest in the genetics of temperament research include developmental variation and change in the expression of temperament. Emerging findings underscore the dynamic nature of genetic influence across development. For example, stability of inhibition may be due to genetic factors, whereas shared environment has been shown to influence change in shyness. Shared environmental factors also appear to affect positive affectivity during the toddler period, and genetic influences were strong for variation in attentional capacities and effortful control. To the extent that such traits are important risk factors for later psychopathology, these findings have begun to underscore the dynamic nature of genetic influence across development (Nigg & Goldsmith, 1998).

Consistent with the rapidly expanding molecular genetic studies, there has been considerable interest in the search for gene loci for temperament traits known to have significant heritability. A cornerstone of interest for both temperament and psychopathology is *novelty seeking*. Ebstein and colleagues (1996) reported that individuals with this characteristic were significantly associated with the 7-repeat allele (the long form of an exon 3 polymorphism, *DRD4*7R)* of the dopamine receptor locus

DRD4 in a sample of 124 adult Israeli subjects. The finding was subsequently replicated in a sample of 315 American subjects, using a different measure of novelty seeking (Benjamin et al., 1996). In addition, *neuroticism* and *harm avoidance* have been linked in some studies to the serotonin transporter promoter region (STPR). In neonates, a significant association for *D4DR* was found across four behavioral clusters pertinent to temperament, including orientation, motor organization, range of state, and regulation of state, as well as a significant interaction between *D4DR* and STPR (Ebstein et al., 1996). Such findings have generated a flurry of attempts at replication, with conflicting results and concerns about methodology, suggesting that the role of *DRD4* in novelty seeking is presently controversial and inconclusive at best (Alsobrook & Pauls, 1998; Paterson, Sunohara, & Kennedy, 1999).

These recent molecular studies attempting to link a personality trait with a specific genetic locus provide transition and integration with research in developmental psychopathology, for example, efforts to associate the trait of novelty seeking with substance abuse, antisocial behavior, and ADHD. The past decade has seen greatly increasing interest in pursuing the relationship of extremes in temperament to later clinical problems in children, for example, the association of such temperamental traits as withdrawal from new stimuli, low adaptability, high intensity, and negative mood with externalizing disorders of oppositional, conduct, and attentional disorders (Maziade, Caron, Cote, Boutin, & Thivierge, 1990). Another aspect of temperament showing evidence of stability/continuity is behavioral *inhibition*, a well-characterized trait involving wary, avoidant, and fearful responses to the unfamiliar (Kagan, Reznick, & Snidman, 1988). Added to the considerable evidence for physiological differences (salivary cortisol levels and vagal tone) between behaviorally inhibited and noninhibited young children, data from the MacArthur Longitudinal Twin Studies support a substantial heritability factor for inhibition (Plomin et al., 1993). Although longitudinal studies have not as yet provided evidence of the continuity of this temperament trait, cross-sectional studies of school-age children identified as behaviorally inhibited have revealed a higher incidence of psychiatric disorders, including anxiety disorders, when compared to noninhibited controls (Biederman et al., 1990). In a Norwegian twin study of temperament and behavior problems, Gjone and Stevenson (1997) assessed the longitudinal covariance between temperament traits of emotionality, activity, and sociability and later anxious/depressed behavior, attention problems, and aggressive and delinquent behavior. High emotionality was found to predict anxious/depressed behavior, attention problems, delinquent behavior, and aggressive behavior. Similar predictive validity for behavioral inhibition was found for children who develop internalizing disorders. Two different groups, young children of parents with panic disorder and agoraphobia and an epidemiologically derived sample of children, had increased risk for multiple anxiety, overanxious, and phobic disorders (Biederman et al., 1990).

Finally, the issue of variability in personality traits and the relationship of extremes in such traits to psychopathology are best illustrated in the application of the reported findings regarding the trait of novelty seeking (associated with impulsive, exploratory, and quick-tempered behavior) to ADHD, whose clinical symptoms of inattention, impulsivity, and hyperactivity intuitively appear to be closely linked. Additional discussion of the role of temperamental predisposition to psychopathology and its inheritance follows in our discussion of the major internalizing and externalizing disorders of childhood: ADHD, conduct disorder, depression, and anxiety.

DEVELOPMENTAL PSYCHOPATHOLOGY

Reflecting the rapid developments in molecular genetics, the literature now includes a number of theoretical papers on the implications for psychiatry of behavioral genetic research in general (e.g., Alsobrook & Pauls, 1998; Rutter, 1994; Rutter & Plomin, 1997) and molecular genetics, in particular (e.g., Henderson, Jorm, Jacomb, Korten, & Easteal, 1997; McInnes, Reus, & Freimer, 1998; Owen & Craddock, 1996). By comparison with the well-circumscribed and more homogeneous disorders described in our section on genetically influenced disorders of cognition, it is important to underscore the increased difficulty posed by psychiatric disorders for genetic research for at least the following reasons: (1) heterogeneity, resulting in a given behavioral phenotype exhibiting different genetic pathways in different individuals; (2) pliotropy

(different behavioral manifestations of the same genotype); (3) genetic complexity, arising from multiple genes acting in combination; (4) populations derived by differing methods: categorical (meeting clinical diagnostic criteria) or dimensional criteria (degree of symptom or trait severity); (5) as yet unvalidated subtypes of current diagnostic categories; (6) multiple neurotransmitters undoubtedly involved in each disorder; and (7) primary neurotransmitters and their receptors (identified by response to medication) involved in multiple complex pathways. Finally, Plomin and Rutter (1998) have suggested three key issues for the molecular genetics investigations of normal and abnormal child development: (1) focusing on the continuities and discontinuities in development, (2) understanding the meanings of patterns of psychopathology, and (3) the complexity of gene-environment interaction.

Prior to a discussion of individual, clinically defined disorders, we briefly note heritability of the more global patterns of effects across selected broad band child problem dimensions. Recent investigations have used Achenbach's (1991) Child Behavior Checklist, an empirically derived behavior rating scale including the two higher-order factors: *internalizing* (depressed, anxious, withdrawn) and *externalizing* (aggressive, defiant, and overactive) behaviors. Significant heritability was found for externalizing behavior, but shared environment effects and somewhat lower heritability for delinquency in adolescence. Consistent and high heritabilities have been shown in younger children for both internalizing and externalizing behaviors; however, heritability for internalizing behaviors tends to *decrease* with age, whereas shared environment effects *increase*, particularly as children approached adolescence. Such results suggest that the developmental pattern of causal effects on psychopathology in children (decreasing heritability for internalizing behaviors, important shared environment effects for comorbid problems and for adolescent difficulties) are sometimes different from the generally accepted pattern of results in the temperament and personality literature (Nigg & Goldsmith, 1998).

The following sections are devoted to a discussion of how genetic studies have contributed to our understanding of the etiology and developmental progression of several of the major diagnostic categories of childhood. General descriptions of the clinical behavioral phenotypes of these disorders are not provided, as they are reviewed in other chapters in the present volume or elsewhere (e.g., Mash & Barkley, 1996). Studies examining the genetic versus environmental influences on psychopathology take several forms: in addition to twin and adoption studies, other types of family studies evaluating continuity and discontinuity and developmental pathways involve top-down approaches (examining the existence/prevalence of symptoms and/or psychopathology in children of parents with a psychiatric disorder) and bottom-up approaches (prevalence of psychopathology in parents of diagnosed children).

EXTERNALIZING DISORDERS

Attention-Deficit/Hyperactivity Disorder (ADHD)

ADHD is the most common psychiatric/behavioral disorder of childhood, with current prevalence estimates ranging from 3% to 5% of the childhood population (APA, 1994). Our choice to discuss ADHD in this section deserves brief comment, because the high rate of comorbidity with SLD clearly links ADHD to the primary disorders of cognition. Barkley (1998a) has argued that ADHD is appropriately classified as a mental disorder in *DSM-IV* (1994), as opposed to a disorder of development, in view of the significant risks for behavioral maladjustment. However, although "underachievement" is not synonymous with SLD, it is clear that ADHD is frequently comorbid with reading disorders (8%–39%), math disorders (12%–30%), and spelling disorders (12%–27%) (Frick et al., 1991). Second, as will be seen subsequently, not all ADHD subgroups are associated with externalizing disorders.

Investigations of the etiology of ADHD abound, including both genetic and environmental factors. Although such nongenetic etiologies as head trauma, intrauterine exposure to toxins, and intrauterine infections have been documented in individual cases of ADHD (Barkley, 1998a), it is apparent that in the majority of cases, no environmental etiology has been verified.

Our discussion of the evidence for genetic etiology of ADHD is drawn from several sources (Alsobrook & Pauls, 1998; Barkley, 1998a, 1998b; Hechtman, 1994; Thapar, Holmes, Poulton, & Harrington, 1999). The current *DSM-IV* (APA, 1994) clinical diagnostic criteria identify three subtypes: primarily inattentive type (without hyperactivity),

hyperactive-impulsive type, and combined type (see Barkley, 1998a, for a comprehensive review). Given the critical importance of a well-defined phenotype for genetic studies, ADHD presents particular difficulty. Diagnostic criteria have changed over various editions of the *DSM*, the diagnostic classification is based on reported symptoms rather than biochemical abnormalities or quantitative measures, and clinical diagnoses (as opposed to severity of behavioral traits) may not represent genetic validity.

A particularly important issue for genetic investigation of ADHD is whether there is genetic validation of the clinical subtypes. Barkley (1998a) has raised critical issues as to whether the predominantly inattentive type is actually a *subtype* of ADHD, as there are clearly important qualitative phenotypic differences between this subtype and the two hyperactive subtypes (e.g., problems in focused/selective attention and sluggish information processing, greater frequency of comorbidity with internalizing disorders, greater frequency in females in the primarily inattentive subtype vs. problems of persistence of effort and distractibility, greater frequency of comorbidity with externalizing disorders, and greater frequency in males in the hyperactive types). Second, it is unclear whether there are valid differences between the two hyperactive subtypes. The *DSM* field trial found that the predominantly hyperactive-impulsive subtype consisted primarily of preschool-age children, and the two subtypes may actually turn out to be different developmental stages of the same type (Barkley, 1998a). In addition, Thapar et al. (1999) noted the differences in phenotype across varying diagnostic nosologies: *DSM-IV* versus *ICD-10* (World Health Organization [WHO], 1992).

Thus, although the genetics of ADHD has been the subject of intensive study, in addition to the subtype issues, research has also been hampered by nonidentical diagnostic criteria in different countries, whether categorical or dimensional definitions are used to establish who is affected and to test genetic models, and the lack of objective measures such as physical features or biochemical markers. These issues are not unique to ADHD, but apply to other psychiatric diagnoses as well (Thapar et al., 1999).

First, there is ample evidence that ADHD can be familial (Hechtman, 1996). Research suggests that between 10% and 35% of the immediate family members of children with ADHD are also likely to have the disorder, with the risk to siblings being about 32%, and an even more striking 57% risk for the child of a parent with ADHD. For simple autosomal dominant inheritance with complete penetrance, the sibling risk should be 50%, as should the risk to a child if the parent is affected. Although ADHD has high rates of comorbidity with other internalizing and externalizing disorders, the rates of hyperactivity remain high in families without co-occurring disorders (Biederman et al., 1992). However, evidence that relatives of ADHD probands with comorbid conduct disorder are at greater risk for ADHD suggests that this may represent a separate familial subtype. Further evidence suggests that individuals with ADHD and depression may be etiologically different from those comorbid with either anxiety or learning disorders (Thapar et al., 1999).

A widening array of twin studies has provided considerable evidence for a high degree of heritability. Hechtman's (1994) review of the available twin studies indicated greater concordance in MZ than DZ twins, with concordance rates ranging from 68% to 84% for MZ twins, and from 29% to 32% for DZ twins. Although these studies used respectable sample sizes (50 to 100 twin pairs), a more recent study is notable in view of its large sample size and the interest in investigating the categorical (diagnostic) versus dimensional aspects of ADHD (Levy, Hay, McStephen, Wood, & Waldman, 1997). This Australian study investigated 1,938 4- to 12-year old twins from the Australian national twin registry, making it the largest genetic study of ADHD to date. When a diagnostic symptom criterion (DSM-III) was used, concordance rates for MZ twins were 82%, in comparison to 37% to 46% for DZ twins. A subsequent quantitative approach was used to determine heritability when the proband group was selected on the basis of extreme scores (e.g., a dimensional model). Results indicated that ADHD has an exceptionally high rate of heritability (.91 vs. .12) compared with other behavior disorders. The finding was robust in that heritability was determined to be high whether a continuous (e.g., quantitative trait) or discrete (e.g., categorical/diagnostic) approach is used to define ADHD. Moreover, the finding that ADHD was not significantly more heritable for the disorder (minimal symptom criteria) than the trait lends further support to the argument

that ADHD may represent the extreme of a continuum rather than a discrete group. In addition, genetic studies have been generally consistent in showing little evidence for the effect of shared environment in contributing to ADHD, typically accounting for 0% to 13% of the variance among individuals (Barkley, 1998b).

Given that evidence for genetic influence in ADHD has existed for some time and has been strengthened by such large-scale studies as Levy et al. (1997), there has obviously been much interest in the mode of inheritance and the search for gene loci. At the time of Hechtman's (1994) review, segregation analyses suggested a single major gene locus and polygenic transmission; however, a definitive mode of inheritance had not been established. Soon thereafter, Cook et al. (1995) examined the dopamine transporter as a primary gene locus for ADHD, reasoning that the stimulant medications used to treat ADHD serve to inhibit the dopamine transporter. In a sample of 48 families of ADHD probands and 8 probands with ADD (without hyperactivity), a significant association was found with the dopamine transporter allele (DAT1). A subsequent replication similarly found this allele to be associated with ADHD (Gill, Daly, Heron, Hawi, & Fitzgerald, 1997), suggesting that further molecular analyses of this gene may identify mutations that increase the susceptibility to ADHD. The dopamine D4 receptor is also of major interest because of the high degree of functionally relevant variability in its gene (DRD4) and, as discussed previously, the association of this gene with the behavioral trait of novelty seeking. Other laboratories have focused attention on this gene, with several published studies to date indicating that the DRD4 gene may be associated with a refined phenotype of ADHD (e.g., Swanson et al., 1998). However, reportedly, only a fraction (approximately 29%) of individuals with ADHD diagnosis or symptoms have this repeat allele, suggesting that it is not the major gene for ADHD (Barkley, 1998b). Because other investigators have failed to replicate these findings (e.g., Castellanos et al., 1998) and, given the prevalence and clinical importance of this disorder, it is clear that the search for the ADHD gene(s) can be expected to accelerate.

Finally, the high degree of comorbidity of ADHD with other internalizing and externalizing disorders clearly complicates genetic investigations of

ADHD. The most common condition comorbid with ADHD appears to be conduct disorder, with studies suggesting that from 54% to 67% of ADHD children and adolescents will meet full criteria for oppositional or conduct disorder (Barkley, 1998a). Thus, ADHD with and without antisocial disorders may be etiologically and genetically distinct disorders. Faraone and colleagues propose that ADHD, ADHD with oppositional defiant disorder, and ADHD with conduct disorder fall along a continuum of increasing levels of environmental (family) factors in both the etiology and severity of ADHD (Faraone, Biederman, Keenan, & Tsuang, 1991). Similarly, ADHD families with antisocial disorders show the greatest risk for depression; however, familial risk for depression exists in ADHD families independent of antisocial disorder. This suggests that environmental factors are also important in the occurrence of depression in ADHD individuals. Co-occurrence of ADHD with bipolar disorder has also suggested this may likewise be a specific subtype of the same familial condition (Faraone, Biederman, Mennin, & Russell, 1998). An additional issue complicating such studies of comorbidity is the question of multiple ADHD phenotypes, that is, whether the primarily inattentive groups are included. In view of the complexity of these associations, molecular genetic studies have to date not been attempted to explain the comorbidity.

Disruptive Behavior Disorders
First, there is both ample and convincing evidence of genetic risk factors in the etiology and development of disruptive behavior (including the *DSM-IV* diagnoses of oppositional defiant disorder and conduct disorder in children and adolescents, and the more severe antisocial personality disorder in adults). Such evidence is derived from multiple lines of research: continuity of temperament traits in early childhood, heritability of aggressiveness per se, genetic predisposition to antisocial behaviors, and the impact of other comorbid disorders on the development of disruptive behavior disorders. It is also apparent that children with maladaptive behaviors involving noncompliance, aggression, and/or other antisocial behaviors are known to be phenotypically heterogeneous, and likely represent several distinct subtypes (i.e., property violations, status violations, oppositional behavior, aggression)

(Simonoff, Pickles, Meyer, Silberg, & Maes, 1998), each of which may have different degrees of genetic influence, and indicating genetic heterogeneity. For example, there is a convergence of evidence confirming the phenotypic differences between adults who have a childhood onset of symptoms and those whose antisocial behaviors developed during adolescence (Rutter, Bolton, et al., 1990; Rutter, Macdonald, et al., 1990), with the former child-onset group being at more serious risk for chronic antisocial difficulties. Moffitt (1993a) coined the term "adolescent-limited" to reflect the findings from numerous longitudinal studies that those youth whose conduct problems begin in adolescence are much less likely to persist in their antisocial behavior into adulthood.

Both twin and adoption studies have contributed a considerable body of evidence for the importance of inheritance in antisocial behavior and conduct disorders. Several longitudinal twin studies have suggested that shared environmental influences may be more important in early childhood than in middle childhood, whereas the reverse holds for genetic influences (Schmitz, Fulker, & Mrazek, 1995). Shared environment is also clearly shown to be important in studies of juvenile delinquency in adolescent twins. DiLalla and Gottesman (1991) have shown that differences in weighted concordance rates for delinquent juvenile MZ twins (51%) and DZ twins (72%) were not remarkable and did not implicate a genetic predisposition, suggesting that a shared environmental effect may be the mutual influence within twin pairs, that is, siblings who model delinquent behavior for one another. However, in the case of adoption studies, importance of heredity is underscored; large-scale adoption studies have shown that having at least one biological parent with a history of antisocial behavior significantly increases the rate of conduct disorder in children (Caspi & Moffitt, 1995).

Another line of evidence involves the heritability of aggression, a hallmark characteristic of many antisocial individuals. Evidence supports both a genetic role in criminality and a physiological basis for violent behavior, complementing what is known about intergenerational transmission of violent behaviors (Cadoret, Leve, & Devor, 1997). Moreover, a strong overall genetic effect may account for up to 50% of the variance in aggression that increases with age (Miles & Carey, 1997).

The link between early temperament and conduct disorder is of increasing interest, because "difficult children" with negative mood, poor adaptability to change, and high intensity to new stimuli are likely to show behavioral problems concurrently or to develop these problems later, and are subsequently referred for treatment for aggressive behaviors (Kazdin, 1996). Such early negative emotionality may also predict depression, whereas impulsivity shows a stronger prediction for conduct disorder, perhaps indicating the increased risk in children with comorbid ADHD and conduct disorder. Longitudinal data suggest that the heritability of such temperamental traits appears to be stronger for inhibition than for anger or negative emotion, which, in contrast, appears to reflect greater genetic influence in adolescence and adulthood. Similarly, those neuropsychological risk factors, or markers, that characterize many children with conduct disorders (i.e., deficits in verbal learning, verbal fluency, memory, verbal IQ) are believed to be neuropsychological underpinnings of conduct disorders which may also reflect genetic influence (Moffitt, 1993b).

Molecular studies of disruptive behavior disorders are beginning to appear and, given the increased rate of both aggression and conduct disorder in males, initial interest has focused on the X chromosome. A pedigree study of a large Dutch kindred, in which probands were characterized by violent, episodic aggression, identified a region on the X chromosome containing genes for monoamine oxidase (MAO) enzymes, with a resulting locus for the disorder assigned to the monoamine oxidase Type A (MAOA) locus of X (Brunner, Nelen, Breakfield, Ropers, & Van Oost, 1993). Investigations of this region by additional groups represent the increasing interest in searching for QTLs for aggressive behavior.

Finally, it is as yet unclear what it is that is inherited: temperamental attributes leading to later aggression, hyperactivity combined with aggression (known to be one of the best predictors of persistent antisocial behaviors), inherited cognitive deficits involving executive function, verbal ability, behavioral inhibition, and/or some combination of these factors interacting in a complex way with important environmental influences. Complex biosocial interactions are clearly involved, in which genotype might influence the broader dispositional characteristics of the child, which, in turn, act as a mediating link in interacting with important environmental influences to produce patterns of persistent antisocial behavior.

Internalizing Disorders

Depression

As with other psychiatric disorders, there are major methodological problems facing genetic studies of depression, including phenotypic heterogeneity (e.g., bipolar vs. unipolar, child vs. adult onset, simple vs. comorbid, chronic vs. nonchronic, variable age of onset). Identified individuals may thus compose multiple phenotypic definitions, for example depressed mood, a constellation of symptoms forming a syndrome, or a set of symptoms meeting criteria for a formal diagnosis of depression (Hammen & Rudolph, 1996). Disagreement about clinical definition reflects differing perspectives on development, an illustration being disagreement over the proposed criteria for identification of mood disorder in infancy (e.g., Zero to Three/National Center for Clinical Infant Programs, 1994). Such issues present daunting problems for the study of the genetic etiology of depression.

Given such caveats, genetic studies have consistently indicated familial aggregation of depression (a finding that may reflect both genetic and environmental factors). Fivefold greater odds of a lifetime depressive disorder have been found in family members of children/adolescents with childhood-onset depressive disorder (primarily first-degree and female), suggesting that juvenile and adult-onset depression may share the same diathesis (Kovacs, Devlin, Pollock, Richards, & Mukerji, 1997). Correspondingly, children of bipolar parents have been shown to have a fivefold higher risk for having an affective disorder diagnosis, with evidence that the distribution of affective disorder diagnoses is compatible with the presence of important genetic factors contributing to early-onset affective disorder (Todd et al., 1996).

Despite the methodological difficulties discussed, evidence from quantitative genetic studies of adult depression is quite strong. Reviews suggest strong evidence from twin studies for a genetic factor, particularly in the more severe forms of depression: a clearly higher concordance in MZ twins (.67 to .69 for bipolar disorder, compared with .13 to .20 for DZ twins) and averaged results of earlier studies for which the overall MZ concordance was .69

compared with .13 for DZ (McGuffin & Katz, 1989, 1993). However, evidence from adoption studies is less consistent, with some studies finding increased rates of affective disorder in biological relatives and not in adopted relatives, and others suggesting evidence for substantial nonshared environmental influence (Eley, Deater-Deckard, Fombonne, Fulker, & Plomin, 1998). In addition, the role of inheritance clearly differs with respect to the categorization of depression into bipolar and unipolar types: family members of unipolar index cases tend toward an excess of *only* unipolar disorder, whereas family members of patients with bipolar disorder are at increased risk for *both types* of mood disorder, with risk for affective disorder greater in the relatives of individuals with bipolar disorder (McGuffin & Katz, 1989, 1993).

Environmental precursors such as stressful life events clearly contribute to development of clinical depression in many cases, and the subjective distress associated with such events appears to be familial. It is clear that there are high levels of disruption and stress in families with depressed members, suggesting that children may inherit environmental risk factors as well as genetic predisposition. Evidence from a recent twin study designed to examine this question indicates that depressive symptoms and some life events share a common genetic influence; however, at least part of the association is mediated by familial factors that include both genes and shared environment (Thapar, Harold, & McGuffin, 1998).

An increasing number of studies have examined temperament and developmental pathways to depression, both unipolar and bipolar disorders of child or adolescent onset, providing some preliminary evidence for the interaction of temperament and gender in clinical outcome of depression. Hyperthymic temperament appears to be more common in males and may be one pole of an attenuated form of bipolar disorder; that is, those with this temperament had high rates of bipolar family history. The depressive temperament, more prevalent in females, was correlated with earlier onset and higher number of depressive episodes, suggesting that temperamental dysregulations may be an intermediate step between predisposing genetic factors and gender-related clinical expressions of mood disorders (Akiskal, 1995).

Bipolar disorder in children presents major difficulties with respect to accurate differential diagnosis, with symptoms often similar to and/or comorbid with ADHD, panic disorder, conduct disorder, sexual and substance abuse, or childhood schizophrenia (Weller, Weller, & Fristad, 1995). The current state of knowledge about childhood bipolar disorder has been likened to that of major depression 20 years ago, when the notion of "masked" depression in children was prominent (B. Geller & Luby 1997). Despite a need for much further research, evidence regarding the risk for children of bipolar parents has begun to accumulate, with meta-analyses indicating a 4 to 5 times greater risk of their developing an affective disorder (Lapalme, Hodgins, & LaRoche, 1997).

Finally, molecular genetic research in depression has greatly accelerated, primarily for bipolar disorder. As with other affective disorders, efforts to understand the mechanisms of inheritance in bipolar disorder (apparently non-Mendelian modes of transmission) have been hindered by the complexity of the phenotype, which may range from benign mood swings to chronic psychosis. Genetic linkage has been reported in 14 different chromosomal regions with subsequent replications of linkage on 18 and 21 (McGue & Bouchard, 1998). Considerable interest has focused on chromosome 18 as a possible site, with international collaborators identifying four potential loci (Van Broeckhoven & Verheyen, 1999), suggesting the likelihood of a susceptibility gene of some modest effect. In view of the genetic complexity of bipolar disorder, many of the loci reported to be linked may confer susceptibility in some families and not others, making replication a challenge and requiring large sample sizes.

ANXIETY DISORDERS

With the high prevalence rate of anxiety disorders—15% in adults, 17% in adolescents, and 9% in children—the investigation of genetic etiology has been of particular interest, yet has lagged behind that for other psychiatric disorders (Bernstein, Borchardt, & Perwien, 1996). Similar to the situation in other psychiatric disorders, methodological problems in genetic studies of anxiety involve, first, lack of agreement as to what distinguishes clinical anxiety disorders from transient, developmentally appropriate anxieties, and, second, the heterogeneous nature of the phenotype(s) for the clinical diagnostic categories of anxiety, both of which are critical first steps in identifying susceptibility genes. Illustrative of the heterogeneity, anxiety disorders range between generalized anxiety and the more circumscribed phobic symptoms, with panic and agoraphobia disorders in adults, separation and social anxiety in children, and considerable comorbidity (e.g., with depression). Given such issues regarding the phenotype(s), there is clearly a need for longitudinal studies of at-risk children to better understand continuity and discontinuity of anxiety in children and adults.

Considerable evidence now exists for the familial aggregation of anxiety, both for generalized and specific anxiety disorders (Silverman, Cerny, & Nelles, 1986). In general, relatives of children with anxiety disorders show a significantly higher rate of anxiety disorders when compared with controls, and additional studies confirm familial aggregation for specific diagnostic categories. Separation anxiety, panic, and generalized anxiety disorder have been shown to cluster in parents and siblings of child probands (Silove, Manicavasagar, O'Connell, & Morris-Yates, 1995; Skre, Onstad, Edvardsen, Torgersen, & Kringlen, 1994), and children of parents with social phobia have been shown to be at risk for this disorder (23%) or another type of anxiety disorder (49%) (Mancini, van Ameringen, Szatmari, Fugere, & Boyle, 1996), with significantly higher lifetime risks of panic disorder and simple phobias in first-degree relatives.

An important issue regarding heritability of anxiety disorders is whether a child may inherit a broad vulnerability to anxiety disorders in general, as opposed to disorder-specific genetic predisposition. Current evidence from twin studies suggests a genetic risk factor leading to vulnerability for anxiety disorders in general, the specific expression of which may be modified by unique experience (Albano, Chorpita, & Barlow, 1996). However, research bearing on this issue is at best sparse. From twin and adoption studies, heritability estimates for various anxiety disorders have been reported: .44 for panic disorder, .39 for agoraphobia, .32 for generalized anxiety disorder, .32 for animal phobias, .30 for social phobia, and minimal to no genetic component for situational phobias. Reviews are generally consistent, with estimates of genetic contribution ranging between 40% and 60% of the variance for anxiety disorders in general, and panic disorders in particular (Lesch et al., 1996). Similar to parallel studies in depression, childhood anxiety symptoms (by parent rating) are often best explained by an additive genetic model, with heritability estimated at .59 (Thapar & McGuffin, 1996). However, this was not the case for adolescents, for whom shared environmental factors were found to be more salient. Anxiety types may also differ with regard to the importance of shared environmental factors; when self-reported symptoms were evaluated in a large community twin sample, shared environment was more influential in separation anxiety disorder, whereas additive genetic variation contributed to symptoms of overanxious disorder (Topolski et al., 1997). However, despite various complex theoretical models developed to explain the integration of genetic predisposition with psychosocial variables, data are limited to primarily cross-sectional studies, and research findings have not as yet been integrated with the similarly strong evidence for environmental/ psychosocial factors involved in the development of anxiety disorders.

Based on more complex developmental models of psychopathology, a growing body of research has concentrated on the relationship between personality and temperament traits or features that predict development of anxiety disorders—the search for "anxiety diathesis." *Neuroticism, harm avoidance, anxiety sensitivity,* and behavioral *inhibition* are anxiety-related traits receiving considerable interest to date. A phobic-anxious temperament has been associated with panic disorder without agoraphobia in adults (Perugi et al., 1998), and, though retrospective, such data support the continuity of subclinical to clinical manifestations of temperament, panic, phobic, and avoidant phases in the development of the adult disorder. Other studies have shown a link between the trait neuroticism and anxiety symptoms, with adverse life events important in predicting the variability of symptoms (Mackinnon, Henderson, & Andrews, 1990).

The trait of behavioral inhibition (characterized by caution, shyness, avoidance, and more reactive sympathetic nervous systems) has also received considerable research attention. In a series of prospective studies, Rosenbaum and colleagues (1993) clearly identified this trait as a robust predictor of later anxiety disorders: children of parents with anxiety disorders had a higher risk for being behaviorally inhibited; children who are behaviorally inhibited have a greater occurrence of childhood anxiety disorders; behaviorally inhibited children have more relatives who are behaviorally inhibited; and children with the most stable and consistent behavioral inhibition were more likely to have a family history of anxiety disorders and to develop an anxiety disorder.

Heritability estimates for behavioral inhibition and neuroticism (characterized by anxiety, worry, or depression) have each been shown to approximate .50 (Smoller & Tsuang, 1998). Anxiety sensitivity involves the tendency to amplify fears and other anxiety reactions because the individual

fears the bodily sensations associated with anxiety (Taylor & Cox, 1998) and has been shown to be a strong predictor of the severity of anxiety disorders.

Finally, molecular genetic studies of anxiety have to date been sparse. However, based on the emerging evidence for the association between temperament traits and later clinical manifestations of anxiety, investigations of possible loci associated with these traits have begun. A locus on chromosome 17 (17q12) involving the gene for regulating

Table 12.2 Current knowledge regarding genetic influences on child psychopathology.

Diagnosis	Heritability Indicated by Twin or Adoption Studies (adults only[a])	Chromosomal Region(s) Identified[a]/Investigated[b]	Candidate Genes under Investigation
Internalizing Disorders			
Anxiety Disorders			
Panic disorder	Yes[a]	13q; 17	CCK-B; 5-HT2A(13q); 5HT2A(17)
Personality traits:			
Harm avoidance	—	8p21–23[b]; 17q12[b]	5HT1 (17)
Neuroticism	—	17q12[b]	5HT1 (17)
Affective Disorders			
Major depressive disorder	Yes[a]	X4p[b]; X6p[b]; X13q[b]; X15q[b];	No
Bipolar disorder	Yes[a]	Xq26[a]; 4pter[a]; 11p15[a]; 18p11[a]; 18q21[a]; 18q22[a] 6[b]; 11p[b]; 15[b]; 13[b]; 15[b]; 18[b]; 21[b]; 22[b]	Golf(18p11); IMPA2 (18p11)
Personality Traits:			
Neuroticism	—	17q12[b]	No
Externalizing Disorders			
Attention-deficit/hyperactivity disorder	Yes	5p; 11p; 11q22–23	DAT1(5p); RD4(11p); DRD2(11q22–23)
Personality traits:			
Novelty seeking	—	11p; 11q22–23	DRD4(11p); DRD2(11q22–23)
Conduct disorder	Yes	X[b]	MAOA (X)
Personality traits:			
Aggression	—	X[a]	MAOA (X)
Other Childhood Disorders			
Autism	Yes	X[a]; 2q[a]; 7q[a]; 15q11–13[a] 6p[a]; 17[a]	FMR1 (X); GABRB3 (15)
Obsessive-compulsive disorder	Yes	X[b]; 11p[b]; 22q11[b]	COMT (22q11); MAOA (X); SLC6A4; DRD4 (11p)
Tourette's syndrome	Yes	X[b]; 2[b]; 3p[b]; 5p[b]; 5q[b]; 6p[b]; 8q[b]; 11q[b]; 14q[b]; 20q[b]; 21q[b]	DAT2(5p); 5HT1A (5q); DRD2 (11q)

Note: For disorders in which multiple chromosomes have been investigated and/or identified, the chromosomal locus for the respective candidate gene is included in parentheses.

serotonin *(5-HTT)* accounted for 7% to 9% of the genetic variance in individuals high in neuroticism and harm avoidance (Lesch et al., 1996). Additional support was found for a locus on chromosome 8 (8p21-23), which accounted for 20% to 30% of the genetic variance for the trait harm avoidance (Cloninger et al., 1998). Given the recent interest, it is likely that molecular genetic studies of anxiety, like those for depression, will continue the search for susceptibility genes (Smoller & Tsuang, 1998).

Table 12.2 on page 235 represents an overview of current quantitative and molecular genetic investigations of selected psychiatric disorders, as well as examples of temperament/personality traits under investigation for their potential link to the disorders. It should be underscored, first, that much of this work represents genetic investigations of the *adult* phenotype of these disorders, with issues of continuity and discontinuity between child and adult disorders not yet well understood. Second, the rapidly expanding work in molecular genetics dictates that any such summary is tentative. Third, it is apparent that the same candidate genes are being investigated in phenotypically different disorders (i.e., *FMR1* in Fragile X syndrome and autism; DRD4 in ADHD, obsessive-compulsive disorder, and novelty seeking). This may indicate that different allelic forms change the gene products in different ways (i.e., "hyper" vs. "hypo" functionality) and/or that these genes become significant in causing a particular disorder by interaction with other genes. Finally, included in Table 12.2 are three additional childhood disorders that were not discussed in this chapter (autism, obsessive-compulsive disorder, and Tourette's syndrome), but for which there has been considerable interest in establishing the genetic mechanisms in their respective etiologies. For reviews of these areas, see Cook (1998) and Szatmari (1998) on autism; D. Geller, Biederman, Jones, Schwartz, and Park (1998) on obsessive compulsive disorder; and Alsobrook and Pauls (1997) on Tourette's syndrome.

CONCLUSIONS AND FUTURE DIRECTIONS

The findings summarized in this chapter make clear the compelling evidence now available that genotype plays a significant role in both normal and abnormal development and behavior in children. The power of molecular genetics is begin-ning to identify the genetically based mechanisms by which such behaviors unfold. We are at the threshold of a major revolution in understanding how the neuroanatomical, neurophysiological, and neurochemical levels of brain development, organization, and function interact with environment and experience to influence normal and abnormal development and behavior. For neurodevelopmental disorders whose genetic etiology has been long established, further insight into the mechanisms involved and how gene products affect phenotype can be expected, as illustrated by the further elucidation of Fragile X syndrome. However, even apparently very simple behaviors are highly complex when viewed in terms of their component parts and the processes that underlie them, suggesting that many genes must be involved in the functions underlying even simple behaviors. The interdisciplinary collaboration of behavior and molecular genetics is poised to begin analyses of the component processes/behavioral elements of normal and abnormal behaviors. We have discussed the probability of multiple genes being involved in psychiatric disorders. New, molecularly based methodologies now make the identification of these genes feasible. Within the next three years, the entire gene sequence of the human genome will be known. How specific genes affect the brain and behavior can then be investigated systematically by what has been termed "reverse genetics," that is, mutating individual genes in experimental animals and examining their effects on brain structure and behavior. Much additional research will be needed, first, to empirically establish clinical risk associated with particular combinations of alleles and subsets of genes for each behavioral component contributing to a behavioral disorder, and second, to determine the interaction of specific environmental stressors with particular genotypes in modifying behavior.

A likely general contribution of behavioral genetics to our understanding of normal and abnormal child development and behavior is its potential to clarify a number of fundamental clinically relevant questions. First, identifying susceptibility genes will in turn greatly aid in the delineation of environmental risk factors and how gene-environment interactions can produce differences in sensitivity to stressful life experience or increased selection of environments contributing to psychopathology (e.g., chaotic homes, antisocial peers). This will also shed considerable light on the issue of the continuity of childhood and adult disorders (i.e., from ADHD to conduct disorder to antisocial personality disorder) (Plomin & Rutter, 1998). Second, identification of genes whose neurobiological functions contribute in significant ways to specific behaviors should directly lead to improved and etiologically appropriate diagnostic criteria, thus allowing significant refinement of current diagnostic categories. Third, such information should lead to better appreciation for the variability of phenotypic expression associated with a single specific inherited deficit. This has particular relevance for the issue of comorbidity and the pattern of psychopathology. As molecular genetic markers for behavioral disorders become available, it should be possible to determine whether a particular genotype affecting brain development always gives rise to the same spectrum of behavioral abnormalities, or whether the qualitative type and/or degree of the abnormality can be influenced by chance events during brain development or by environmental variables. Certain mutant genes/gene combinations may cause abnormal brain development or dysregulations in such a way that they predispose toward multiple behavioral abnormalities. By knowing the genotype of individuals with a particular disorder, it may be possible to identify whether comorbid symptom development is an intrinsic feature of the underlying genetic defect or is influenced by indirectly related genetic, environmental, or experiential factors. Fourth, the ability to identify high- and low-risk genotypes in presymptomatic individuals should have major implications for the design of both biologically based and psychosocial interventions for at-risk children. Understanding the mechanisms of susceptibility genes should lead to the development of major new pharmacotherapies to prevent the onset of and/or treat behaviors that arise from neurochemical abnormalities and that respond to drug treatment. And independently, or in combination with newer, more targeted drug therapies, further refinements of efficacious psychosocial treatments are likely to be enhanced (Lonigan, Elbert, & Bennet-Johnson, 1998). Last, gene therapy for a variety of disorders of the central nervous system is being actively considered (e.g., see de la Cruz & Friedmann, 1995). At present, however, this presents many practical problems, not the least of which is that many inherited behavioral disorders may reflect irreversible neuropathological changes that originate in the early stages of brain development. In closing this chapter, we want to remind the reader that "knowledge is not synonymous with wisdom." Certainly, the ethical and social issues concerning practical application of appropriate usage of behavior genetic testing and manipulation of human behavior are great. These issues must remain the subject of debate and thoughtful consideration both by the professional community and by our society as a whole.

REFERENCES

Achenbach, T.M. (1991). *Manual for the Child Behavior Checklist.* Burlington: University of Vermont, Department of Psychiatry.

Akefeldt, A., Akefeldt, B., & Gillberg, C. (1997). Voice, speech and language characteristics of children with Prader-Willi syndrome. *Journal of Intellectual Disabilities Research, 41,* 302–311.

Akiskal, H.S. (1995). Developmental pathways to bipolarity: Are juvenile-onset depressions pre-bipolar? *Journal of the American Academy of Child and Adolescent Psychiatry, 34*(6), 754–763.

Alarcon, M., DeFries, J.C., Light, J.G., & Pennington, B.F. (1997). A twin study of mathematics disability. *Journal of Learning Disabilities, 30*(6), 617–623.

Albano, A.M., Chorpita, B.F., & Barlow, D.H. (1996). Childhood anxiety disorders. In E.J. Mash & R.A. Barkley (Eds.), *Child psychopathology* (pp. 196–241). New York: Guilford Press.

Alsobrook, J.P., II, & Pauls, D.L. (1997). The genetics of Tourette syndrome. *Neurology Clinics, 15*(2), 381–393.

Alsobrook, J.P., II, & Pauls, D.L. (1998). Molecular approaches to child psychopathology. *Human Biology, 70*(2), 413–432.

American Psychiatric Association. (1994). *Diagnostic and statistical manual of mental disorders* (4th ed.). Washington, DC: Author.

Baker, L.A., Vernon, P.A., & Ho, H.Z.H. (1991). The genetic correlation between intelligence and speed of information processing. *Behavior Genetics, 21,* 351–367.

Barkley, R.A. (1998a). *Attention deficit hyperactivity disorder: A handbook for diagnosis and treatment* (2nd ed.). New York: Guilford Press.

Barkley, R.A. (1998b). Gene linked to ADHD verified. *ADHD Report, 6*(3), 1–5.

Batshaw, M.L. (Ed.). (1997). *Children with disabilities* (4th ed.). Baltimore: Brookes.

Benjamin, J., Li, L., Patterson, C., Greenberg, B.D., Murphy, D.L., & Hamer, D.H.

Benjamin, J.L., Lin, C., Patterson et al. (1996). Population and familial association between the D4 dopamine receptor gene and measures of novelty seeking. *Nature Genetics, 12,* 81–84.

Berch, D.B., & Bender, B.G. (Eds.). (1991). *Sex chromosome abnormalities and human behavior.* Boulder, CO: Westview Press.

Bernstein, G.A., Borchardt, C.M., & Perwien, A.R. (1996). Anxiety disorders in children and adolescents: A review of the past 10 years. *Journal of the American Academy of Child and Adolescent Psychiatry, 35*(9), 1110–1119.

Biederman, J., Faraone, S.V., Keenan, K., Benjamin, J., Krifcher, B., Moore, C., Sprich-Buckminster, S., Ugaglia, K., Jellinek, M.S., Steingard, R., Spencer, T., Norman, D., Kolodny, R., Kraus, I., Perrin, J., Keller, M.B., & Tsuang, M.T. (1992). Further evidence for family-genetic risk factors in attention deficit hyperactivity disorder: Patterns of comorbidity in probands and relatives in psychiatrically and pediatrically referred samples. *Archives of General Psychiatry, 49,* 728–738.

Biederman, J., Rosenbaum, J.F., Hirshfeld, D.R., Faraone, S.V., Bolduc, E.A., Gersten, M., Meminger, S.R., Kagan, J., Snidman, N., & Reznick, J.S. (1990). Psychiatric correlates of behavioral inhibition in young children of parents with and without psychiatric disorders. *Archives of General Psychiatry, 47*(1), 21–26.

Billings, P.R., Beckwith, J., & Alper, J.S. (1992). The genetic analysis of human behavior: A new era? *Social Sciences and Medicine, 35,* 227–238.

Bouchard, T.J., Jr. (1996). Behaviour genetic studies of intelligence, yesterday, and today: The long journey from plausibility to proof. *Journal of Biosocial Science, 28,* 527–555.

Bouchard, T.J., Jr. (1998). Genetic and environmental influences on adult intelligence and special mental abilities. *Human Biology, 70,* 257–279.

Bouchard, T.J., Jr., Lykken, D.T., McGue, M., Segal, N.L., & Tellegen, A. (1990). Sources of human psychological differences: The Minnesota study of twins reared apart. *Science, 250,* 223–228.

Brambilla, P., Bosio, L., Manzoni, P., Pietrobelli, A., Beccaria, L., & Chiumello, G. (1997). Peculiar body composition in patients with Prader-Labhart-Willi syndrome. *American Journal of Clinical Nutrition, 65,* 1369–1374.

Brunner, H.G., Nelen, M., Breakfield, X.O., Roppers, H.H., & Van Oost, B.A. (1993). Abnormal behavior associated with a point mutation in the structural gene for a monoamine oxidase A. *Science, 262,* 578–580.

Buchanan, L., Pavlovic, J., & Rovet, J. (1998). A reexamination of the visuospatial deficit in Turner syndrome: Contributions of working memory. *Developmental Neuropsychology, 14*(2–3), 341–367.

Buss, A.H., & Plomin, R. (1984). *Temperament: Early developing personality traits.* Hillsdale, NJ: Erlbaum.

Cadoret, R.J., Leve, L.D., & Devor, E. (1997). Genetics of aggressive and violent behavior. *Psychiatric Clinics of North America, 20*(2), 301–322.

Cardon, L.R., Smith, S.D., Fulker, D.W., Kimberling, W.J., Pennington, B.F., & DeFries, J.C. (1994). Quantitative trait locus for reading disability on chromosome 6. *Science, 266*(5183), 276–279.

Caspi, A., & Moffitt, T.E. (1995). The continuity of maladaptive behavior: From description to understanding in the study of antisocial behavior. In D. Cicchetti & D.J. Cohen (Eds.), *Developmental psychopathology: Risk, disorder, and adaptation* (Vol. 2, pp. 472–511). New York: Wiley.

Castellanos, F.X., Lau, E., Tayebi, N., Lee, P., Long, R.E., Giedd, J.N., Sharp, W., March, W.L., Walter, J.M., Hamburger, S.D., Ginns, E.I., Rapoport, J.L., & Sidransky, E. (1998). Lack of an association between dopamine-4 receptor polymorphism and attention-deficit/hyperactivity disorder: Genetic and brain morphometric analyses. *Molecular Psychiatry, 3*(5), 431–434.

Castles, A., Datta, H., Gayan, J., & Olson, R.K. (1999). Varieties of developmental reading disorder: Genetic and environmental influences. *Journal of Experimental Child Psychology, 72*(2), 73–94.

Chase, C.H. (1996). A visual deficit model of developmental dyslexia. In C.H. Chase, G.D. Rosen, & G.F. Sherman (Eds.), *Developmental dyslexia: Neural, cognitive, and genetic mechanisms* (pp. 127–156). Baltimore: York Press.

Cherny, S.S., Cardon, L.R., Fulker, D.W., & DeFries, J.C. (1992). Differential ability across levels of cognitive ability. *Behavior Genetics, 22,* 153–162.

Clark, D. (1998). Prader-Willi syndrome and psychotic symptoms: 2. A preliminary study of prevalence using the Psychopathology Assessment Schedule for Adults with Developmental Disability Checklist. *Journal of Intellectual Disability Research, 42*(Pt. 6), 451–454.

Clark, L.A., Watson, D., & Mineka, S. (1994). Temperament, personality and the mood and anxiety disorders. *Journal of Abnormal Psychology, 103*(1), 103–116.

Clarke, D.J., & Boer, H. (1998). Problem behaviors associated with deletion Prader-Willi, Smith-Magenis, and cri du chat syndromes. *American Journal of Mental Retardation, 103,* 264–271.

Cloninger, C.R., Van Eerdewegh, P., Goate, A., Edenberg, H.J., Blangero, J., Hesselbrock, V., Reich, T., Nurnberger, J., Jr., Schuckit, M., Porjesz, B., Crowe, R., Rice, J.P., Foroud, T., Przybeck, T.R., Almasy, L., Bucholz, K., Wu, W., Shears, S., Carr, K., Crose, C., Willig, C., Zhao, J., Tischfield, J.A., Li, T.K., Conneally, P.M. et al. (1998). Anxiety proneness linked to epistatic loci in genome scan of human personality traits. *American Journal of Medical Genetics, 81,* 313–317.

Collins, F.S., Patrinos, A., Jordan, E., Chakravarti, A., Gesteland, R., Walters, L., & The members of the DOE and NIH planning groups. (1998). New goals for the U.S. human genome project: 1998–2003. *Science, 282,* 682–689.

Cook, E.H. (1998). Genetics of autism. *Mental Retardation and Developmental Disabilities Research Reviews, 4*(2), 113–120.

Cook, E.,H., Stein, M.A., Krasowski, M.D., Cox, N.J., Olkon, D.M., Kieffer, J.E., & Leventhal, B.L. (1995). Association of attention-deficit disorder and the dopamine transporter gene. *American Journal of Human Genetics, 56*(4), 993–998.

Curfs, L.M.G. (1992). Psychological profile and behavioral characteristics in the Prader-Willi syndrome. In S.B. Cassidy (Ed.), *Prader-Willi syndrome and other chromosome 15q deletion disorders* (pp. 211–222). Berlin, Germany: Springer-Verlag.

Daniel, L.L., & Gridley, B.E. (1998). Prader-Willi syndrome. In L. Phelps (Ed.), *Health-related disorders in children and adolescents* (pp. 534–540). Washington, DC: American Psychological Association.

Daniels, J., McGuffin, P., & Owen, M.J. (1996). Molecular genetic research on IQ: Can it be done? Should it be done? *Journal of Biosocial Science, 28,* 491–507.

DeFries, J.C., & Gillis, J.J. (1993). Genetics of reading disability. In R. Plomin & G.E. McClearn (Eds.), *Nature and nurture* (pp. 121–145). Washington, DC: American Psychological Association.

DeFries, J.C., Plomin, R., & Fulker, D.W. (1994). *Nature, nurture during middle childhood.* Cambridge, MA: Blackwell.

de la Cruz, F., & Friedmann, T. (Guest Eds.). (1995). Gene therapy. *Mental Retardation and Developmental Disabilities Research Reviews, 1*(1).

Detterman, D.K., Thompson, L.A., & Plomin, R. (1990). Differencies in resistability across groups differing in ability. *Behavior Genetics, 20,* 369–384.

deVries, B.B., Halley, D.J., Oostra, B.A., & Niemeijer, M.F. (1998). The Fragile X syndrome. *Journal of Medical Genetics, 35,* 576–589.

DiLalla, L.F., & Gottesman, I.I. (1991). Biological and genetic contributors to violence: Widom's untold tale. *Psychological Bulletin, 109*(1), 125–129.

Downey, J., Elken, E.J., Ehrhardt, A.A., Meyer-Bahlburg, H.F.L., Ball, J.J., & Morishima, A. (1991). Cognitive ability and everyday functioning in women with Turner syndrome. *Journal of Learning Disabilities, 24,* 32–39.

Dykens, E.M., & Cassidy, S.B. (1999). Prader-Willi syndrome. In S. Goldstein, & C.R. Reynolds (Eds.), *Handbook of neurodevelopmental and genetic disorders in children* (pp. 525–553). New York: Guilford Press.

Dykens, E.M., Hodapp, R.M., & Leckman, J.F. (1994). *Behavior and development in Fragile X syndrome.* Thousand Oaks, CA: Sage.

Dykens, E.M., Hodapp, R.M., Walsh, K., & Nash, L.J. (1992). Profiles, correlates, and trajectories of intelligence in Prader-Willi syndrome. *Journal of the American Academy of Child and Adolescent Psychiatry, 31,* 1125–1130.

Dykens, E.M., & Kasari, C. (1997). Maladaptive behavior in children with Prader-Willi syndrome, Down syndrome, and nonspecific mental retardation. *American Journal of Mental Retardation, 102,* 228–237.

Ebstein, R.P., Novick, O., Umansky, R. Priel, B., Osher, Y., Blaine, D., Bennett, E.R., Nemanov, L., Katz, M., & Belmaker, R.H. (1996). Dopamine D4 receptor (D4DR) exon III polymorphism associated with the human personality trait of novelty seeking. *Nature Genetics, 12,* 78–80.

Eden, G.F., VanMeter, J.W., Rumsey, J.M., & Zeffiro, T.A. (1996). The visual theory of developmental dyslexia. *Neuroimage, 4,* S108–S117.

El Abd, S., Turk, J., & Hill, P. (1995). Annotation: Psychological characteristics of Turner sundrome. *Journal of Child Psychology and Psychiatry, 36*(7), 1109–1125.

Elbert, J.E., & Seale, T.W. (1988). Complexity of the cognitive phenotype in an inherited form of learning disability. *Developmental Medicine and Child Neurology, 30,* 181–189.

Eley, T.C., Deater-Deckard, K., Fombonne, F., Fulker, D.W., & Plomin, R. (1998). An adoption study of depressive symptoms in middle childhood. *Journal of Child Psychology and Psychiatry, 39*(3), 337–345.

Epstein, C.J. (1990). The consequences of chromosomal imbalance. *American Journal of Medical Genetics, 7*(Suppl.), 31–37.

Faraone, S.V., Biederman, J., Keenan, K., & Tsuang, M.T. (1991). Separation of *DSM-III* attention deficit disorder and conduct disorder: Evidence from a family-genetic study of American child psychiatric patients [Abstract]. *Psychol. Med., 21*(1), 109–121.

Faraone, S.V., Biederman, J., Mennin, D., & Russell, R. (1998). Bipolar and antisocial disorders among relatives of ADHD children: Parsing familial subtypes of illness. *American Journal of Medical Genetics, 81*(1), 108–116.

Feldman, E.J. (1996). The recognition and investigation of X-linked learning disability syndromes. *Journal of Intellectual Disability Research, 40,* 400–411.

Field, L.L., & Kaplan, B.J. (1998). Absence of phonological coding dyslexia to chromosome 6p23-p21.3 in a large family data set. *American Journal of Human Genetics, 63*(5), 1448–1456.

Fisch, G.S., Simensen, R., Tarleton, J., Chalifoux, M., Holden, J.J., Carpenter, N., Howard-Peebles, P.N., & Magdalena, A. (1996). Longitudinal study of cognitive abilities and adaptive behavior levels in fragile X males: A prospective multicenter analysis. *American Journal of Medical Genetics, 64,* 356–361.

Frick, P.J., Kamphaus, R.W., Lahey, B.B., Loeber, R., Christ, M.A.G., Hart, E.L., & Tannenbaum, L.E. (1991). Academic underachievement and the disruptive behavior disorders. *Journal of Consulting and Clinical Psychology, 59,* 289–294.

Gayan, J., Smith, S.D., Cherny, S.S., Cardon, L.R., Fulker, D.W., Brower, A.M., Olson, R.K., Pennington, B.F., & DeFries, J.C. (1999). Quantitative-trait locus for specific langauge and reading deficits on chromosome 6p. *American Journal of Human Genetics, 64*(1), 157–164.

Geller, B., & Luby, J. (1997). Child and adolescent bipolar disorder: A review of the past 10 years. *Journal of the American Academy of Child and Adolescent Psychiatry, 36*(9), 1168–1176.

Geller, D.A., Biederman, J., Jones, J., Schwartz, S., & Park, K.S. (1998). Obsessive-compulsive disorder in children and adolescents. *Harvard Review of Psychiatry, 5*(5), 260–273.

Getova, D., & Bowery, N.G. (1998). The modulatory effects of high affinity GABA (B) receptor antagonists in an active avoidance learning paradigm in rats. *Psychopharmocology, 137,* 369–373.

Gilger, J.W., Pennington, B.F., & DeFries, J.C. (1991). Risk for reading disabilities as a function of parental history of reading problems: Data from three samples of families demonstrating genetic transmission. *Reading and Writing, 3,* 205–217.

Gill, M., Daly, G., Heron, S., Hawi, Z., & Fitzgerald, M. (1997). Confirmation of association between attention deficit hyperactivity disorder and a dopamine transporter polymorphism. *Molecular Psychiatry, 2*(4), 311–313.

Gjone, H., & Stevenson, J. (1997). A longitudinal twin study of temperament and behavior problems: Common genetic or environmental influences? *Journal of the American Academy of Child and Adolescent Psychiatry, 36*(10), 1448–1456.

Goei, V.L., Choi, J., Ahn, J., Bowlus, C.L., Raha-Chowdhury, R., & Gruen, J.R. (1998). Human gamma-aminobutyric acid B receptor gene: Complementary DNA cloning, expression, chromosomal location, and genomic organization. *Biological Psychiatry, 44*(8), 659–666.

Goldsmith, H.H., Buss, A.H., Plomin, R., Rothbart, M.K., Thomas, A., Chess, S., Hinde, R.A., & McCall, R.M. (1987). Roundtable: What is temperament? Four approaches. *Child Development, 58,* 505–529.

Goldstein, S., & Reynolds, C.R. (Eds.). (1999). *Handbook of neurodevelopmental and genetic disorders in children.* New York: Guilford Press.

Greenswag, L.R., & Alexander, R.A. (Eds.). (1995). *Management of Prader-Willi syndrome* (2nd ed.). New York: Springer-Verlag.

Grigorenko, E.L., Wood, F.B., Meyer, M.S., Hart, L.A., Speed, W.C., & Shuster, A. (1997). Susceptibility loci for distinct components of developmental dyslexia on chromosomes 6 and 15. *American Journal of Human Genetics, 60,* 27–39.

Gusella, J.F., & MacDonald, M.E. (1996). Trinucleotide instability: A repeating theme in human inherited disorders. *Annual Review of Medicine, 47,* 201–209.

Hagerman, R.J., & Cronister, A.J. (Eds.). (1996). *Fragile X syndrome: Diagnosis, treatment, and research.* Baltimore: Johns Hopkins University Press.

Hagerman, R.J., & Lampe, M.E. (1999). Fragile X syndrome. In S. Goldstein & C.R. Reynolds (Eds.), *Handbook of neurodevelopmental and genetic disorders in children* (pp. 298–316). New York: Guilford Press.

Hammen, C.H., & Rudolph, K.D. (1996). Childhood depression. In E.J. Mash & R.A. Barkley (Eds.), *Child psychopathology* (pp. 153–195). New York: Guilford Press.

Harris-Schmidt, G., & Fast, D. (1998). Fragile X syndrome: Genetics, characteristics, and educational implications. In A. Rotatori, J. Schwenn, & S. Burkhardt (Eds.), *Advances in special education* (Vol. 11, pp. 187–222). Greenwich, CT: JAI Press.

Hay, D.A. (1994). Does IQ decline with age in Fragile X? A methodological critique. *American Journal of Medical Genetics, 51*(4), 358–363.

Hechtman, L. (1994). Genetic and neurobiological aspects of attention deficit hyperactivity disorder: A review. *Journal of Psychiatry and Neuroscience, 19*(3), 193–201.

Hechtman, L. (1996). Families of children with attention deficit hyperactivity disorder: A review. *Canadian Journal of Psychiatry, 41*(6), 350–360.

Henderson, S., Jorm, A., Jacomb, P., Korten, A., & Easteal, S. (1997). Molecular genetics and the epidemiology of common mental disorders: New opportunities. *Epidemiologia e Psichiatria Social, 6*(3), 167–172.

Hershko, A., & Ciechanover, A. (1998). The ubiquitin system. *Annual Review of Biochemistry, 67,* 425–479.

Hooper, S.R., & Willis, W.G. (1989). *Learning disability subtyping: Neuropsychological foundations, conceptual models, and issues in clinical differentiation.* New York: Springer-Verlag.

Huntriss, J., Daniels, R., Bolton, V., & Monk, M. (1998). Imprinted expression of SNRPN in human preimplantation embryos. *American Journal of Medical Genetics, 63,* 1009–1014.

Kagan, J., Reznick, J.S., & Snidman, N. (1988). Biological bases of childhood shyness. *Science, 240,* 167–173.

Kazdin, A.E. (1996). *Conduct disorders in childhood and adolescence* (2nd ed.). Thousand Oaks, CA: Sage.

Knopik, V.S., Alarcon, M., & DeFries, J.C. (1997). Comorbidity of mathematics and reading deficits: Evidence for a genetic etiology. *Behavior Genetics, 27*(5), 447–453.

Kovacs, M., Devlin, B., Pollock, M., Richards, C., Mukerji, P. (1997). A controlled family history study of childhood-onset depressive disorder. *Archives of General Psychiatry, 54*(7), 613–623.

Kuslich, C.D., Kobori, J.A., Mohapatra, G., Gregorio-King, C., & Donlon, T.A. (1999). Prader-Willi syndrome is caused by disruption of the SNRPN gene. *American Journal of Human Genetics, 64,* 70–76.

Lapalme, M., Hodgins, S., & LaRoche, C. (1997). Children of parents with bipolar disorder: A meta-analysis of risk for mental disorder. *Canadian Journal of Psychiatry, 42*(6), 623–631.

Lesch, K.P., Bengel, D., Heils, A., Sabol, S.Z., Greenberg, B.D., Petri, S., Benjamin, J., Muller, C.R., Hamer, D.H., & Murphy, D.L. (1996). Association of anxiety-related traits with a polymorphism in the serotonin transporter gene regulatory region. *Science, 274,* 1527–1531.

Levy, F., Hay, D.A., McStephen, M., Wood, C., & Waldman, I. (1997). Attention-deficit hyperactivity disorder: A category or a continuum? Genetic analysis of a large-scale twin study. *Journal of the American Academy of Child and Adolescent Psychiatry, 36,* 737–744.

Loehlin, J.C. (1992). *Genes and environment in personality development.* Newbury Park, CA: Sage.

Loehlin, J.C. (1996). Genes and environment. In D. Magnusson (Ed.), *The lifespan development of individuals: Behavioral, neurobiological, and psychosocial perspectives* (pp. 38–51). New York: Cambridge University Press.

Lonigan, C., Elbert, J.C., & Bennet-Johnson, S. (Guest Eds.). (1998). Empirically validated interventions for children [Special issue]. *Journal of Clinical Child Psychology, 27*(2).

Lyon, G.R. (1995). Toward a definition of dyslexia. *Annals of Dyslexia, 45,* 3–27.

Lyon, G.R. (1996). Learning disabilities. In E.J. Mash & R.A. Barkley (Eds.), *Child psychopathology* (pp. 390–435). New York: Guilford Press.

Mackinnon, A.J., Henderson, A.S., & Andrews, G. (1990). Genetic and environmental determinants of the lability of trait neuroticism and the symptoms of anxiety and depression. *Psychological Medicine, 20*(3), 581–590.

Mancini, C., van Ameringen, M., Szatmari, P., Fugere, C., & Boyle, M. (1996). A high-risk pilot study of the children of adults with social phobia. *Journal of the American Academy of Child and Adolescent Psychiatry, 35,* 1511–1517.

Mandoki, M.W., & Sumner, G.S. (1991). Klinefelter syndrome: The need for early identification and treatment. *Clinical Pediatrics, 30,* 161–164.

Mandoki, M.W., Sumner, G.S., Hoffman, R.P., & Riconda, D.L. (1991). A review of Klinefelter's syndrome in children and adolescents. *Journal of the American Academy of Child and Adolescent Psychiatry, 30,* 160–172.

Mannens, M., & Alders, M. (1999). Genomic imprinting: Concept and clinical consequences. *Annals of Medicine, 31,* 4–11.

Mash, E.J., & Barkley, R.A. (Eds.). (1996). *Child psychopathology.* New York: Guilford Press.

Maziade, M., Caron, C., Cote, R., Boutin, P., & Thivierge, J. (1990). Extreme temperament and diagnosis: A study in a psychiatric sample of consecutive children. *Archives of General Psychiatry, 47*(5), 477–484.

McCartney, K., Harris, M.J., & Bernieri, F. (1990). Growing up and growing apart: A developmental meta-analysis of twin studies. *Psychological Bulletin, 107,* 226–237.

McCauley, E., Ross, J.L., Kushner, H., & Cutler, G., Jr. (1995). Self-esteem and behavior in girls with Turner syndrome. *Journal of Developmental Behavior and Pediatrics, 16,* 82–88.

McGue, M., & Bouchard, T.J. (1998). Genetic and environmental influences on human behavioral differences. *Annual Review of Neuroscience, 21,* 1–24.

McGuffin, P., & Katz, R. (1989). The genetics of depression and manic-depressive illness. *British Journal of Psychiatry, 155,* 294–304.

McGuffin, P., & Katz, R. (1993). Genes, adversity, and depression. In R. Plomin & G.E. McClearn (Eds.), *Nature, nurture and psychology* (pp. 217–230). Washington, DC: American Psychological Association.

McInnes, L.A., Reus, V.I., & Freimer, N.B. (1998). Mapping genes for psychiatric disorders and behavioral traits. *Current Opinion in Genetics and Development, 8*(3), 287–292.

Miles, D.R., & Carey, G. (1997). Genetic and environmental architecture of human aggression. *Journal of Personality and Social Psychology, 72*(1), 207–217.

Moffitt, T.E. (1993a). Adolescence-limited and life-course persistent antisocial behavior: A developmental taxonomy. *Psychological Review, 100,* 674–701.

Moffitt, T.E. (1993b). The neuropsychology of conduct disorder. *Development and Psychopathology, 5,* 135–151.

Muralidhar, B., & Butler, M.G. (1998). Methylation PCR analysis of Prader-Willi syndrome, Angelman syndrome, and control subjects. *American Journal of Medical Genetics, 63,* 1009–1014.

Naglieri, J.A. (1985). Use of the WISC-R and K-ABC with learning disabled, borderline, mentally retarded, and normal children. *Psychology in the Schools, 22,* 133–141.

Neisser, U., Gwyneth, B., Bouchard, T.J., Boykin, A.W., Brody, N., Ceci, S.J., Halpern, D.F., Loehlin, J.C., Perloff, R., Sternberg, R.J., & Urbina, S. (1996). Intelligence: Knowns and unknowns. *American Psychologist, 51,* 77–101.

Nicholls, R.D., Saitoh, S., & Horsthemke, B. (1998). Imprinting in Prader-Willi and Angelman syndromes. *Trends in Genetics, 14,* 194–200.

Nigg, J.T., & Goldsmith, H.H. (1998). Developmental psychopathology, personality, and temperament: Reflections on recent behavioral genetics research. *Human Biology, 70,* 387–412.

Owen, M.J., & Craddock, N. (1996). Modern molecular genetic approaches to complex traits: Implications for psychiatric disorders. *Molecular Psychiatry, 1*(1), 21–26.

Pasaro-Mendez, E.J., Fernandez, R.M., Goyanes, V., & Mendez, J. (1993). Turner's syndrome: A behavioral and cytogenetic study. *Journal of Genetic Psychology, 154,* 433–447.

Paterson, A.D., Sunohara, G.A., & Kennedy, J.L. (1999). Dopamine D4 receptor gene: Novelty or nonsense? *Neuropsychopharmacology, 21*(1), 3–16.

Pennington, B.F. (1995). Genetics of learning disabilities. *Journal of Child Neurology, 10*(Suppl. 1), S69–S77.

Pennington, B.F. (1997). Using genetics to dissect cognition. *American Journal of Human Genetics, 60,* 13–16.

Pennington, B.F., & Gilger, J.W. (1996). How is dyslexia transmitted? In C.H. Chase, G.D. Rosen, & G.F. Sherman (Eds.), *Developmental dyslexia: Neural, cognitive, and genetic mechanisms* (pp. 41–61). Baltimore: York Press.

Pennington, B.F., & Smith, S.D. (1997). Genetic analysis of dyslexia and other complex behavioral phenotypes. *Current Opinion in Pediatrics, 9,* 636–641.

Perugi, G., Toni, C., Benedetti, A., Simonetti, B., Simoncini, M., Torti, C., Musetti, L., & Akiskal, H.S. (1998). Delineating a putative phobic-anxious temperament in 126 panic-agoraphobic patients: Toward a rapprochement of European and U.S. views. *Journal of Affective Disorders, 47,* 11–23.

Petrill, S.A., Plomin, R., McClearn, G.E., Smith, D.L., Vignetti, S., Chorney, M.J., Chorney, K., Thompson, L.A., Detterman, D.K., Benbow, C., Lubinski, D., Daniels, J., Owen, M., & McGuffin, P. (1997). No association between general cognitive ability and the A1 allele of the Dr dopamine receptor gene. *Behavior Genetics, 27,* 29–31.

Phelps, L. (Ed.). (1998). *Health-related disorders in children and adolescents.* Washington, DC: American Psychological Association.

Plomin, R., & Craig, I. (1997). Human behavioural genetics of cognitive abilities and disabilities. *Bioessays, 19,* 1117–1124.

Plomin, R., & Dunn, J. (1986). *The study of temperament: Changes, continuities, and challenges.* Hillsdale, NJ: Erlbaum.

Plomin, R., Emde, R.N., Braungart, J.M. et al. (1993). Genetic change and continuity from fourteen to twenty months: The MacArthur Longitudinal Twin Study. *Child Development, 64,* 1354–1376.

Plomin, R., McClearn, G.E., Smith, D.L., Vignetti, S., Chorney, M.J., Chorney, K., Venditti, C.P., Kasarda, S., Thompson, L.A., Detterman, D.K., Daniels, J., Owen, M., & McGuffin, P. (1994). DNA markers associated with high versus low IQ: The IQ Quantitative Trait Loci (QTL) project. *Behavior Genetics, 24,* 107–118.

Plomin, R., & Rutter, M. (1998). Child development, molecular genetics, and what to do with genes once they are found. *Child Development, 69*(4), 1223–1242.

Plotnick, L., Attie, K.M., Blethen, S.L., & Sy, J.P. (1998). Growth hormone treatment of girls with Turner syndrome: The National Cooperative Growth Study experience. *Pediatrics, 102*(2, Pt. 3), 479–481.

Prior, M. (1992). Childhood temperament. *Journal of Child Psychology and Psychiatry, 33*(1), 249–279.

Ramey, S.L., & Ramey, C.T. (1999). Early experience and early intervention for children "at risk" for developmental delay and mental retardation. *Mental Retardation and Developmental Disabilities Research Reviews, 5*(10), 1–10.

Rende, R., & Plomin, R. (1995). Nature, nurture, and the development of psychopathology. In D. Cicchetti & D.J. Cohen (Eds.), *Developmental psychopathology* (Vol. 1, pp. 291–314). New York: Wiley.

Rice, M.L. (Ed.). (1996). *Toward a genetics of language.* Mahwah, NJ: Erlbaum.

Riese, M.L. (1990). Neonatal temperament in monozygotic twins and dizygotic twin pairs. *Child Development, 61*(45), 1230–1237.

Rimoin, D.L., Connor, J.M., & Pyeritz, R.E. (Eds.). (1996). *Emery and Rimoin's principles and practice of medical genetics* (3rd ed.). New York: Churchill Livingstone.

Rose, R.J. (1995). Genes and human behavior. *Annual Review of Psychology, 46,* 625–654.

Rosenbaum, J.F., Biederman, J., Bolduc-Murphy, E.A., Faraone, S.V., Chaloff, J., Hirshfeld, D.R., & Kagan, J. (1993). Behavioral inhibition in childhood: A risk factor for anxiety disorders. *Harvard Review of Psychiatry, 1,* 2–16.

Ross, J.L., Roeltgen, D., Feuillan, P., Kushner, H., & Cutler, G.B. (1998). Effects of estrogen on nonverbal processing speed and motor function in girls with Turner's syndrome. *Journal of Clinical Endocrinology and Metabolism, 83*(9), 3198–3204.

Rothbart, M.K., & Bates, J.E. (1998). Temperament. In W. Damon (Series Ed.) & N. Eisenberg (Vol. Ed.), *Handbook of child psychology: Social, emotional, and personality development* (Vol. 3, 5th ed., pp. 105–176). New York: Wiley.

Rothbart, M.K., Posner, M.I., & Hershey, K.L. (1995). Temperament, attention, and developmental psychopathology. In D. Cicchetti & D.J. Cohen (Eds.), *Developmental psychopathology* (Vol. 1, pp. 315–340). New York: Wiley.

Rovet, J. (1990). The cognitive and neuropsychological characteristics in children with Turner syndrome. In D. Berch & B. Bender (Eds.), *Sex chromosome abnormalities and human behavior: Psychological studies* (pp. 38–77). Boulder, CO: Westview Press.

Rovet, J. (1995). Turner syndrome. In B.P. Rourke (Ed.), *Syndrome of nonverbal learning disabilities: Neurodevelopmental manifestations* (pp. 351–371). New York: Guilford Press.

Rovet, J., Netley, C., Keenan, M., Bailey, J., & Stewart, D. (1996). The psychoeducational profile of boys with Klinefelter syndrome. *Journal of Learning Disabilities, 29,* 180–196.

Rowe, D.C. (1997). Genetics, temperament, and personality. In R. Hogan, J. Johnson, & S. Briggs (Eds.), *Hand-

book of personality psychology (pp. 369–386). San Diego, CA: Academic Press.

Rutter, M. (1994). Psychiatric genetics: Research challenges and pathways forward. *American Journal of Medical Genetics (Neuropsychiatric Genetics), 54,* 185–198.

Rutter, M., Bolton, P., Harrington, R., Le Couteur, A., Macdonald, H., & Simonoff, E. (1990). Genetic factors in child psychiatric disorders: I. A review of research strategies. *Journal of Child Psychology and Psychiatry, 31*(1), 3–37.

Rutter, M., Macdonald, H., Le Couteur, A., Harrington, F.R., Bolton, P., & Abiley, A. (1990). Genetic factors in child psychiatric disorders: II. Empirical findings. *Journal of Child Psychology and Psychiatry, 31*(1), 39–83.

Rutter, M., & Plomin, R. (1997). Opportunities for psychiatry from genetic findings. *British Journal of Psychiatry, 171,* 209–219.

Santos, K. (1992). Fragile X syndrome: An educator's role in identification, prevention, and intervention. *Remedial and Special Education, 13,* 32–39.

Scarborough, H.S. (1990). Very early language deficits in dyslexic children. *Child Development, 61*(6), 1728–1743.

Schmitz, S., Fulker, D.W., & Mrazek, D.A. (1995). Problem behavior in early and middle childhood: An initial behavior genetic analysis. *Journal of Child Psychology and Psychiatry, 36*(8), 1443–1458.

Schwartz, I.D., & Root, A.W. (1991). The Klinefelter syndrome of testicular dysgenesis. *Endocrinology and Metabolism Clinics of North America, 20*(1), 153–163.

Sewillen, A., Devriendt, K., Legius, E., Eyskens, B., Dumoulin, M., Gewillig, M., & Fryns, J.P. (1997). Intelligence and psychosocial adjustment in velocardiofacial syndrome: A study of 37 children and adolescents with VCFS. *Journal of Medical Genetics, 34*(6), 453–458.

Shaywitz, S.E. (1998). Dyslexia. *New England Journal of Medicine, 338*(5), 307–312.

Shaywitz, S.E., Escobar, M.D., Shaywitz, B.A., Fletcher, J.M., & Makuch, R. (1992). Evidence that dyslexia may represent the lower tail of a normal distribution of reading ability. *New England Journal of Medicine, 326*(3), 145–150.

Sherman, S.L., DeFries, J.C., Gottesman, I.I., Loehlin, J.C., Meyer, J.M., Pelias, M.Z., Rice, J., & Waldman, I. (1997). Behavioral genetics '97: ASHG statement. Recent developments in human behavioral genetics: Past accomplishments and future directions. *American Journal of Human Genetics, 60,* 1265–1275.

Shucard, D.W., Shucard, J.L., Clopper, R.R., & Schacter, M. (1992). Electrophysiological and neuropsychological indices of cognitive processing deficits in Turner syndrome. *Developmental Neuropsychology, 18,* 299–323.

Siegel, P.T., Clopper, R., & Stabler, B. (1998). The psychological consequences of Turner syndrome and review of the National Cooperative Growth Study psychological substudy. *Pediatrics, 102,* 488–491.

Silove, D., Manicavasagar, V., O'Connell, D., & Morris-Yates, A. (1995). Genetic factors in early separation anxiety: Implications for the genesis of adult anxiety disorders. *Acta Psychiatrica Scandinavica, 92,* 17–24.

Silverman, W.K., Cerny, J.A., & Nelles, W.B. (1986). The familial influence in anxiety disorders: Studies on the offspring of patients with anxiety disorders. In B.B. Lahey & A.E. Kazdin (Eds.), *Advances in clinical child psychology.* New York: Plenum Press.

Simonoff, E., Bolton, P., & Rutter, M. (1998). Genetic perspectives on mental retardation. In J.A. Burack, R.M. Hodapp, & E. Zigler (Eds.), *Handbook of mental retardation and development* (pp. 41–79). New York: Cambridge University Press.

Simonoff, E., Pickles, A., Meyer, J., Silberg, J., & Maes, H. (1998). Genetic and environmental influences on subtypes of conduct disorder behavior in boys. *Journal of Abnormal Child Psychology, 26*(6), 495–509.

Skre, I., Onstad, S., Edvardsen, J., Torgersen, S., & Kringlen, E. (1994). A family study of anxiety disorders: Familial transmission and relationship to mood disorder and psychoactive substance use disorder. *Acta Psychiatrica Scandinavica, 90,* 366–374.

Skuse, D.H., James, R.S., Bishop, D.V.M., Coppin, B., Dalton, P., Aamodt-Leeper, G., Bacarese-Hamilton, M., Creswell, C., McGurk, R., & Jacobs, P.A. (1997). Evidence from Turner's syndrome of an imprinted X-linked locus affecting cognitive function. *Nature, 387,* 705–708.

Smith, S.D., Kelley, P.M., & Brower, A.M. (1998). Molecular approaches to the genetic analysis of specific reading disability. *Human Biology, 70*(2), 239–256.

Smith, S.D., Kimberling, W.J., Pennington, B.F., & Lubs, H.A. (1983). Specific reading disability: Identification of an inherited form through linkage analysis. *Science, 219,* 1345–1347.

Smith, S.D., Pennington, B.F., Kimberling, W.J., & Ing, P.S. (1990). Familial dyslexia: Use of genetic linkage data to define subtypes. *Journal of the American Academy of Child and Adolescent Psychiatry, 29,* 204–213.

Smoller, J.W., & Tsuang, M.T. (1998). Panic and phobic anxiety: Defining phenotypes for genetic studies. *American Journal of Psychiatry, 155,* 1152–1162.

Sorensen, K. (1992). Physical and mental development of adolescent males with Klinefelter syndrome. *Hormone Research* (Suppl. 3), 55–61.

Sulzbacher, S. (1988). Psychological and behavioral management. In L.R. Greenswag & R.C. Alexander (Eds.), *Management of Prader-Willi syndrome* (pp. 99–112). New York: Springer-Verlag.

Swanson, J.M., Sunohara, G.A., Kennedy, J.L., Regino, R., Fineberg, E., Wigal, T., Lerner, M., Williams, L., LaHoste, G.J., & Wigal, S. (1998). Association of the dopamine receptor D4 (DRD4) gene with a refined type of attention deficit disorder. *Molecular Psychiatry, 3*(1), 38–41.

Szatmari, P. (1998). Heterogeneity and the genetics of autism. *Journal of Psychiatry and Neuroscience, 24*, 159–165.

Tarani, I., Lampariello, S., Raguso, G., Colloridi, F., Pucasrelli, I., Pasquino, A.M., & Bruni, L.A. (1998). Pregnancy in patients with Turner's syndrome: Six new cases and review of the literature. *Gynecological Endocrinology, 12*(2), 83–87.

Tassone, F., Dyer, P.D., Lampe, M., Willemsen, R., Oostra, B., Hagerman, R.J., & Taylor, A.K. (1999). FMRP expression as a potential prognostic indicator in Fragile X syndrome. *American Journal of Medical Genetics, 84*, 250–261.

Taylor, S., & Cox, B.J. (1998). An expanded anxiety sensitivity index: Evidence for a hierarchic structure in a clinical sample. *Journal of Anxiety Disorders, 12*, 463–483.

Thapar, A., Harold, G., & McGuffin, P. (1998). Life events and depressive symptoms in childhood: Shared genes or shared adversity? A research note. *Journal of Child Psychology and Psychiatry, 39*(8), 1153–1158.

Thapar, A., Holmes, J., Poulton, K., & Harrington, R. (1999). Genetic basis of attention deficit and hyperactivity. *British Journal of Psychiatry, 174*, 105–111.

Thapar, A., & McGuffin, P. (1996). The genetic etiology of childhood depressive symptoms: A developmental perspective. *Developmental and Psychopathology, 8*(4), 751–760.

Thapar, A., Petrill, S.A., & Thompson, L.A. (1994). The heritability of memory in the Western Reserve twin project. *Behavior Genetics, 24*, 155–160.

Thomas, A., & Chess, S. (1977). *Temperament and development and behavior disorders in children.* New York: New York University Press.

Todd, R.D., Reich, W., Petti, T.A., Joshi, P., DePaulo, J.R., Nurnberger, J., & Reich, T. (1996). Psychiatric diagnoses in the child and adolescent members of extended families identified through adult bipolar affective disorder probands. *Journal of the American Academy of Child and Adolescent Psychiatry, 35*(5), 664–671.

Topolski, T.D., Hewitt, J.K., Eaves, L.J., Meyer, J.M., Pickles, A., & Simonoff, E. (1997). Genetic and environmental influences on child reports of manifest anxiety and symptoms of separation anxiety and over anxious disorders: A community-based twin study. *Behavior Genetics, 27*, 15–28.

Torgesen, J.K., Wagner, R.K., & Rashotte, C.A, (1997). Approaches to the prevention and remediation of phonologically based reading disabilities. In B.A. Blachman (Ed.), *Foundations of reading acquisition and dyslexia* (pp. 287–304). Mahwah, NJ: Erlbaum.

Van Broeckhoven, C., & Verheyen, G. (1999). Report of the chromosome 18 workshop. *American Journal of Medical Genetics, 1888*(3), 263–270.

van Lieshout, C.F., de Meyer, R.E., Curfs, L.M., & Fryns, J.P. (1998). Family contexts, parental behaviour, and personality profiles of children and adolescents with Prader-Willi, Fragile-X, or Williams syndrome. *Journal of Child Psychology and Psychiatry, 39*, 699–710.

Warren, S.T., & Nelson, D.L. (1994). Advances in molecular analysis of Fragile X syndrome. *Journal of the American Medical Association, 271*, 536–542.

Weller, E.B., Weller, R.A., & Fristad, M.A. (1995). Bipolar disorder in children: Misdiagnosis, underdiagnosis, and future directions. *Journal of the American Academy of Child and Adolescent Psychiatry, 34*(6), 709–714.

World Health Organization. (1992). *The tenth edition of the International Classification of Diseases and Related Health Problems (ICD-10).* Geneva, Switzerland: Author.

Zero to Three: National Center for Clinical Infant Programs. (1994). *Diagnostic classification of mental health and developmental disorders of infancy and early childhood.* Arlington, VA: Author.

Zigler, E., & Hodapp, R. (1986). *Understanding mental retardation.* Cambridge, England: Cambridge University Press.

Zinn, A.R., Tonk, V.S., Chen, Z., Flejter, W.L., Gardner, H.A., Guerra, R., Kusher, H., Schwartz, S., Sybert, V.P., Van Dyke, D.L., & Ross, J.L. (1998). Evidence for a Turner syndrome locus or loci on Xp11.2-p22.1. *American Journal of Human Genetics, 63*, 1757–1766.

CHAPTER 13

Clinical Problems of Birth, the Neonate, and the Infant

GLEN P. AYLWARD

In the neonatal and infancy periods, the velocity of neuromaturational and behavioral change is greater than at any other time. Subsequent development of children exposed to pre-, peri-, and postnatal problems is the result of an interchange among normal developmental processes, recovery of function (either physical or neurodevelopmental), and environmental influences.

Psychologists who work with neonates and infants are advised to consider several general guidelines. First is the concept of risk. Risk refers to influences that have a potential negative effect on the infant's development. Tjossem (1976) delineated three categories of risk: *established*, *biological*, and *environmental*. Established risks are medical disorders of a known etiology whose developmental outcome is well documented (e.g., Down syndrome, human immunodeficiency virus [HIV], Tay-Sachs). Biological risks include exposure to potentially noxious pre-, peri-, or postnatal events such as asphyxia, intraventricular hemorrhage, periventricular leukomalacia, or low birthweight (LBW). Environmental risks include the quality of the mother-infant interaction, opportunities for developmental/cognitive stimulation, and health care. Practitioners must consider all three categories of risk, acknowledging that biological and environmental risks often occur together, as children from poor socioeconomic circumstances and poverty are also exposed to medical risk factors such as inadequate prenatal care, LBW, environmental toxins, poor nutrition, drugs, and limited access to medical care. This combination of risks is referred to as *double jeopardy* or *double hazard* (Escalona, 1982; Parker, Greer, & Zuckerman, 1988). In such situations, nonoptimal biological and environmental factors work in a synergistic fashion to affect outcome negatively.

Second, behavioral/developmental (intrinsic), medical/biologic, and environmental/psychosocial risk *and* protective factors should be considered routinely when working with infants (Aylward & Kenny, 1979). Whereas risk factors are associated with developmental and mental health vulnerability, protective factors, in contrast, refer to attributes or situations that would enhance the infant's resilience or resistance to negative influences. The balance between risk and protective factors and the magnitude of each will determine the infant's ultimate level of adaptation. For example, the infant's intrinsic biologic vulnerability can be moderated to some degree by the influence of extrinsic (environmental) protective factors.

A third consideration is that *bidirectional* influences occur between the infant and the environment. More specifically, the infant can influence the caretaker just as the caretaker can influence the infant. Such influences can be risk-producing or protective in nature (Wolraich, Felice, & Drotar, 1996).

Hence, there is a transaction over time between the infant and the environment, with the infant bringing certain behavioral predispositions (e.g., temperament) to such transactions. Moreover, genetic/ constitutional factors can drive development by influencing the infant's early responses to the environment in terms of eliciting interaction and seeking experiences.

Our understanding of how various risks and protective factors work to influence development during infancy and early childhood has evolved over the past four decades. In the "continuum of reproductive casualty" (Pasamanick & Knobloch, 1961), the severity of developmental problems (e.g., cerebral palsy, epilepsy, mental retardation, behavioral disorders, and learning problems) is influenced by the degree of perinatal complications. A more serious condition such as cerebral palsy is associated with more obstetric and perinatal complications than is a milder disorder such as a reading problem. Essentially, the greater the degree of perinatal complications, the greater the later deviancy. However, studies such as the Kauai Longitudinal Project (Werner, 1986), which underscore the role of the environment, do not support this biologically driven model. The "transactional approach" (Sameroff & Chandler, 1975) is more widely endorsed and assumes that a degree of plasticity is inherent in both the child and the environment. The child is constantly reorganizing and self-righting; a poorly stimulating environment would interfere with this self-righting, and the probability of a disrupted child-environment transaction increases. Conversely, more positive environmental circumstances are assumed to enhance the child's resiliency. This approach has led to the concept of the "continuum of caretaking casualty." The more specific effects of established, biological, and environmental risks are outlined below.

ESTABLISHED AND BIOLOGICAL RISKS

Approximately 3% of children born in the United States show evidence of major malformations, and 11% are born prematurely (i.e., < 37 weeks gestational age) (Paneth, 1995). Many etiological agents produce problems in neonates and infants, including genetic, nutritional, traumatic, infectious, metabolic, intoxicant, maternal disease, anoxic-hypoxic, neoplastic, environmental, and idiopathic factors (Risser & Edgell, 1988). The timing of exposure to these etiologic agents is important (Aylward, 1997a). A "critical period" is the time during which the action of a specific internal or external influence is necessary (critical) for *normal* developmental progress (e.g., Capone, 1996). A "sensitive period" is the time during which the central nervous system (CNS) is highly susceptible to the effects of harmful or deleterious internal or external conditions. Therefore, a critical period occurs when certain conditions are necessary for the CNS to develop normally; a sensitive period is the time in which damage to the CNS can lead to alterations, reorganization, and potential aberrations of the system. Critical periods are very circumscribed; sensitive periods are more flexible.

CRITICAL PERIODS

In the prenatal period, problems in the *dorsal induction phase* of CNS development (closure of neural tube; 3–4 weeks gestation) result in neural tube problems such as anencephaly, encephalocele, myelomeningocele (spina bifida), or hydrocephalus. Problems in the *ventral induction phase* (major portions of the brain are formed; 5–6 weeks gestation) result in abnormalities of the face or brain and include holoprosencephaly or Dandy Walker malformation. Disruptions in the *proliferation phase* (production of nerve cells; 2–4 months) produce aberrations in the number of neurons, causing conditions such as microcephaly or megalencephaly (macrocephaly). Disruptions in the *migration phase* (movement of nerve cells from site of origin to final position; 3–5 months gestation) are associated with anomalous formation of the cortical plate, resulting in disorders such as schizencephaly, lissencephaly, pachygyria, polymicrogyria, heterotopias, and agenesis of the corpus callosum. Problems in *organization/ differentiation* of the brain (dendritic, axonal, and synaptic development; peak age 6 months gestation through the third postnatal year) result in disorders in neural differentiation or in the development of synapses, thereby causing aberrant cortical circuitry. Finally, *myelination* disruptions (myelination occurs over a prolonged period, beginning at 6 months gestation and proceeding into adulthood) result in nerve conduction problems and include cerebral white matter hypoplasia. In addition, amino acid deficits (e.g., phenylketonuria), inborn errors of metabolism, degenerative diseases (e.g., adrenoleukodystropy), and early malnutrition can negatively affect myelin development. Whereas the dorsal induction, ventral induction, and proliferation stages occur prenatally, the migration stage may occur postnatally in preterm infants. Organization/differentiation and myelination phases occur prenatally and postnatally in all babies (see Aylward, 1997a). Established or biological risks can affect any of these stages.

LOW BIRTHWEIGHT

LBW children compose a heterogeneous group and include preterm infants (born < 37 weeks gestational age) as well as babies born at term but who are below normal in weight due to abnormal maternal or fetal conditions. Biologically at-risk LBW populations, therefore, consist largely, but not exclusively, of babies born prematurely. Moreover, many of these preterm infants have also experienced intrauterine growth retardation (IUGR) to varying degrees and are classified as small for gestational age (SGA; < 3rd percentile). Infants classified as SGA typically have a higher gestational age than babies of similar birthweights, are more mature, yet have smaller size and more developmental problems later. Full-term SGA infants often have been exposed to intrauterine infections such as herpes, cytomegalovirus, or toxoplasmosis (described subsequently).

In 1950, the World Health Organization defined LBW as < 2,500 g (5 pounds, 8 ounces). Subsequently, due to advances in neonatal care, in the 1960s interest shifted to infants weighing < 1,500 g (termed very low birthweight; VLBW) and in the late 1970s, to those with birthweights of < 1,000 g (extremely low birthweight; ELBW). More recently, interest has focused on those born at < 750 g (Hack & Fanaroff, 1999). However, in the 1990s, there was an emerging consensus that maturity of the infant at birth, as measured by gestational age, is a better predictor of outcome than is birthweight. This is due in part to the birthweight issues discussed previously, coupled with availability of better methods to estimate gestational age.

In general, rates of major handicapping conditions (e.g., cerebral palsy, epilepsy, severe mental retardation, and neurosensory deficits) are inversely related to birthweight or gestational age, ranging from 5% to 20%. The rate of major handicapping conditions in normal birthweight infants is 5%. Although *percentages* of disabilities are higher in smaller babies, in *real numbers*, there are more normal birthweight babies who have developmental problems (e.g., VLBW babies represent only 1.2% of live births). Similarly, with regard to gestational age, 18% to 40% of surviving babies born at 23 to 25 weeks gestational age have major handicaps, with percentages decreasing with longer gestational ages (23–24 weeks gestational age is considered the limit of viability). In addition, there is an increased incidence of high-prevalence/low-severity dysfunctions (attention, learning, and behavior problems) in infants born ≤ 1,500 g, with some estimates being as high as 50% to 70%. As a result, although there may not be significant differences among LBW groups in terms of intelligence (Aylward, Pfeiffer, Wright, & Verhulst, 1989), there is a much higher likelihood of later special education placement with lower birthweights. Other considerations that affect these outcome percentages include maternal complications, antenatal steroid use, surfactant therapy, assisted ventilation, and the medical risk status of infants determined by use of one of the existing biological risk scores (e.g., lung disease, seizures, retinopathy of prematurity, sepsis).

ASPHYXIA

The spectrum of CNS disorders following perinatal insults is determined by the nature and severity of the insult and by the brain's maturational stage at the time of the insult (Aylward, 1997b; Hill & Volpe, 1989). Although asphyxia traditionally has been indexed as a low Apgar score (range 0–10, based on heart rate, respiration, muscle tone, reflex irritability, and color), this score has been misused. A low 1-minute Apgar score does not correlate with later outcome (American Academy of Pediatrics, 1996; Aylward, 1993), and even a 5-minute Apgar score of 0 to 3 has limited predictive utility. Therefore, Apgar scores are best considered as simply indicating the infant's condition during and immediately after the birth process. In actuality, *perinatal asphyxia* is defined as a disturbed exchange of oxygen and carbon dioxide caused by an interruption of respiration. Oxygen deficiency *(hypoxemia)* and carbon dioxide excess *(hypercarbia)* result in metabolic changes and a decrease in blood pH. Decreased blood pressure causes decreased blood flow to the brain *(ischemia)*. The combined effects of hypoxemia and ischemia cause the condition known as *hypoxic-ischemic encephalopathy* (HIE). Asphyxia is the precipitating event for HIE, and perinatal HIE is the major cause of neurodevelopmental morbidity in the neonatal period (Volpe, 1998). In full-term babies, HIE causes cell death in the cerebral cortex, diencephalon, brain stem, and cerebellum. Injury to the basal ganglia and thalamus also occurs more frequently in full-term than in preterm infants. With moderate and severe HIE in term babies, there is a high incidence of cognitive and motor dysfunction, including microcephaly, mental retardation, epilepsy, and cerebral palsy.

HIE in the preterm infant causes cell death deeper within the brain, namely, in the white matter behind and to the side of the lateral ventricles (*periventricular leukomalacia*) and is more often associated with spasticity and neurosensory and motor problems than with cognitive deficits. *Periventricular/intraventricular hemorrhage* (PVH/IVH) occurs in 35% to 45% of infants < 32 weeks gestational age and involves bleeding into the subependymal germinal matrix (site of cell proliferation). HIE, respiratory distress, or circulatory problems can produce PVH/IVH, and obstructive hydrocephalus is a frequent result. IVH is graded (I–IV), with the incidence of neurodevelopmental problems increasing with grade (e.g., 5%–20% with Grade II, 35%–50% with Grade III, and 90% with Grade IV).

In general, clinical features associated with cerebral injury in full-term neonates include hypotonia, seizures, lethargy, irritability, decreased primitive reflexes, and motor abnormalities. In preterm babies, clinical features include irritability, hypertonia (particularly of the lower extremities), increased neck extensor tone, poor feeding, and seizures. In terms of subsequent clinical management of babies affected by established and/or biological risks, in addition to standard cognitive and neurological outcomes, *functional outcomes* in several areas need to be addressed.

Infections of the CNS

Cytomegalovirus (CMV) is the most common viral disease transmitted in utero that negatively affects developmental functioning. CMV results in IUGR, microcephaly, seizures, mental retardation, prematurity, retinal problems, and hearing loss, particularly if symptoms are evident at birth (90% are asymptomatic at birth).

Toxoplasmosis is caused by a protozoan parasite, often introduced by cats as the host. Mothers are asymptomatic and transfer the parasite to their fetus after the second month of gestation. Approximately 10% of infants exposed to toxoplasmosis are symptomatic in the newborn period; resultant problems include prematurity, microcephaly, hydrocephalus, seizures, CNS calcifications, and eye damage (chorioretinitis).

Congenital *rubella* is characterized by IUGR, cataracts and other eye problems, microcephaly, hearing deficits, and other organ involvement. Approximately 25% of infants have neurological symptoms at birth, and 33% to 40% display psychomotor retardation by the end of the first year. Timing of infection is critical, with more severe problems occurring before 12 weeks gestation.

Herpes simplex virus (HSV) problems are related to HSV type 2. The fetus is at risk in the first half of pregnancy (first 20 weeks) and particularly at birth. Severe brain abnormalities, mental retardation, and seizures can occur.

With *human immunodeficiency virus* (HIV), transmission to the fetus occurs in 30% of all cases, and vertical transmission (prenatal, perinatal, or postnatal mother-child transmission) accounts for the largest number of new cases. Virtually all infants born to HIV-positive mothers will test positive for the virus at birth, but may actually not be infected. This is due to the fact that infants passively acquire maternal antibodies in utero via the placenta, and these persist throughout the first year of life. In infants who are indeed infected, encephalopathy and other infections result, with many dying by 12 to 18 months. Survival time after diagnosis appears to depend on a number of factors: timing of infection, premature birth, route of transmission (vertical or horizontal), and type of other acquired infectious agents (Johnson, 1993). The terms HIV encephalopathy or neuroaids are used to refer to children with delayed motor and/or mental milestones, abnormal motor signs, weakness, disordered brainstem function, ataxia, blindness, secondary microcephaly, and seizures (Diamond & Cohen, 1992). Three patterns of developmental decline emerge: (1) infants who demonstrate symptoms very early (onset in the first several months after birth), with a progressive decline and relentless loss of developmental milestones; (2) those who develop deterioration in early childhood or at school age (median age approximately 6 years), with academic and attentional difficulties being markers of a deteriorating course; and (3) children who display a more subacute course, interrupted by plateaus, with milestone acquisition being initially slow followed by protracted plateau without further new acquired skills, and accompanied by mild spasticity. The developmental course is affected by pharmacological treatment including AZT, DDI (dideoxyinosine), and DDC (dideoxycytidine).

Other infections, such as *Haemophilis influenzae Type b* (Hib meningitis) may cause damage later in infancy. This disorder is the most common bacterial infection of meningeal tissues, resulting in ischemia and direct compression of the brain as the primary cause of damage (Taylor, Schatschneider, & Rich, 1992). Sequelae include mental retardation, hearing loss, seizures, hemiparesis/motor dysfunction, and frequent learning disorders.

OTHER TERATOGENS

A variety of drugs can disrupt the development and function of the CNS in fetuses and infants. Unfortunately, there are serious methodological problems in the existing literature on drug effects and specific outcomes. Most often, confounding variables vitiate the data in clinical studies.

Cocaine hydrochloride readily crosses the placenta and affects nerve endings and chemical messenger transmission. Fetal injury from maternal cocaine ingestion can take place directly and indirectly. Indirect injury occurs as a result of drug effects on maternal physiology. Direct effects involve the influence of the drug on fetal and peripheral nervous system development. With prolonged exposure to cocaine, dopamine depletion occurs, which can adversely affect the developmental outcome of the infant exposed in utero. Other physiological changes include a marked rise in maternal and fetal systolic blood pressure, reduction in uterine blood flow, and decreased fetal oxygenation. The concentration of the drug in the fetus's brain can be as much as 20 times higher than in maternal plasma. Cocaine can therefore affect the regions of the brain crucial for learning, memory, behavioral, and cognitive functions (Phillips, Sharma, Premachandra, Vaughn, & Reyes-Lee, 1996). In infants, problems in state modulation, an increase in irritability, poor habituation, and later attention and behavior problems (arousal, emotional control) have been reported fairly consistently (Bendersky & Lewis, 1998). A trend toward decreased intelligence scores is found, as are structural abnormalities. The mechanism of the teratogenic effects is unclear, although the destructive

neural effects may be secondary to the drug's vasoconstrictive effect. Timing, amount, and duration of drug exposure as well as subsequent nutrition and environment determine outcome.

Ethanol exposure can lead to fetal alcohol syndrome (FAS), more subtle fetal alcohol effects (FAE), or alcohol-related neurodevelopmental disorder (ARND) (Sampson et al., 1997). The effects should be considered as occurring on a continuum, with FAE occurring more than twice as frequently as FAS. Ethanol exposure may affect all organ systems and may induce fetal hypoxia. The diagnosis of FAS is made when a recognizable pattern of malformation is noted, which includes specific facial abnormalities, somatic growth failure, and organic brain dysfunction. The typical facial abnormalities are found in a T-shaped area of the central facial region: short palpebral fissures (small eyes), epicanthal folds, premaxillary overgrowth with resultant flat, smooth philtrum, thin upper lip, and flattening of the medial midface. Many infants are SGA. In infancy, 75% show irritability, tremulousness, difficulties with sucking, and weak muscle tone (hypotonia). Microcephaly and behavioral/cognitive deficits such as learning disabilities, perceptual problems, mild mental retardation, delayed adaptive behavior, ADHD, and behavior problems also occur. Again, amount, timing, duration and use of other drugs in conjunction with alcohol determine the type and severity of dysfunction. Cell proliferation, migration, development of synapses, myelination, and neurotransmitter function are affected by ethanol.

Some antiepileptic medications (phenytoin [Dilantin], barbiturates [Phenobarbitol], carbamazepine [Tegretol], sodium valproate [Depakote]) can cause CNS malformations, IUGR, and later behavioral and cognitive changes. Narcotics (heroin, codeine, methadone) produce fetal growth retardation, premature birth, withdrawal symptoms, and microcephaly. Infants exposed to phencyclidine (PCP) often initially are hypertonic and jittery and later have problems in fine motor function.

SUMMARY

Brain injury in the neonate and young infant can be caused by genetic disturbances, trauma, hemorrhage, stroke, infection, metabolic changes, lack of oxygen, and toxins. Each directly and indirectly destroys some portion of the brain or prevents normal development and maturation. There also is a very large number of potential problems of a subtle nature. Subtle metabolic and chemical changes occur, which may add to the insult, cause the dysfunction, and/or interfere with recovery. Conversely, some changes may actually promote recovery. This explains why developmental deficits are variable in neonates and infants with the same apparent CNS insult.

ENVIRONMENTAL RISKS

Environmental risk also is a powerful determinant of development in infancy. It is well established that infants raised in at-risk environments are later overrepresented in special education classes and that 75% of children with mild mental retardation come from lower socioeconomic households. Yet, one cannot identify all infants of low socioeconomic status (SES) as being at risk for subnormal intelligence, as most subsequently demonstrate normal, versus deficient, intellectual development (Aylward, 1996).

SES, the environmental measure that is employed most frequently, is represented by maternal education and occupational status. Social support is more difficult to operationalize, because it includes tangible components (e.g., housing, financial assistance) and intangible components (e.g., attitudes, encouragement, guidance). Moreover, environment contains both process and status features. The former are specific aspects that are experienced most directly (objects, persons, events). Status factors are broader and are experienced more indirectly (social class, location of residence). Process factors are more proximal, in that they involve the child and caretakers on a regular basis (e.g., mother-infant interaction), whereas status factors are distal, meaning they are secondary and more peripheral (e.g., SES). Process factors are more predictive of developmental outcome early on, whereas more generalized distal measures (SES, social support) are more predictive later. Therefore, measurement of occupational status or other distal variables alone may not accurately reflect the type of parenting to which a child is exposed (Aylward, 1990, 1992). Such measurement also does not provide appreciation of everyday stresses or day-to-day positive aspects of the environment that may serve to buffer the infant from negative factors associated with global environmental risk (measured by SES). Conversely, the overwhelming negative effects of status factors such as poverty may minimize any process protective factors.

Isolated or single environmental factors have a small, incremental effect on later cognitive function. The accumulation of risk factors is the major contributor to developmental morbidity (Sameroff, Seifer, Barocas, Zax, & Greenspan, 1987). A large number of variables influence parents' ability to meet their infant's developmental needs. As a result, quality of parenting is determined by multiple issues: child characteristics, parents' personal characteristics, situational factors, community characteristics, and broader sociocultural factors (Aylward, 1996). The interrelatedness of these factors causes them to mediate each other. However, the presence of poverty increases the likelihood that personal or situational determinants of parenting will become risk rather than protective factors in the infant's life (Rutter, 1987). Stress is estimated to be two to four times greater for mothers having low income than for those with more financial resources. This stress is particularly high for poor women with infants and preschoolers, and it most likely inhibits positive interaction and attachments. Thus, the chronic and pervasive influence of poverty increases the probability that the negative impact of early risk factors will accumulate and persist over time and intensify the strong draw toward poor outcome. The broader status variable of poverty minimizes the naturally occurring protective factors in these risk environments because it has such a pervasive effect on the parents' basic capacity to parent.

The effects of status environmental variables such as SES and maternal education become increasingly apparent between 18 and 36 months, with 24 months being cited frequently (Aylward, 1990, 1992). As a result, infants from poor or nonstimulating households tend to display a decline in cognitive performance over time. However, environmental effects are apparent even during the first year of life, particularly when parent-infant interaction measures are combined with environmental quality (Aylward, Verhulst, & Bell, 1989). Process, proximal environmental variables (HOME scores, mother-infant interactions) are better early predictors of outcome; distal (status) measures (SES, social support) are more predictive if measured later.

Therefore, biologic risk factors seem to determine whether a given dysfunction or deficit will occur, and environmental risks have a tempering effect and determine severity (Hunt, Cooper, & Tooley, 1988). The worst-case scenario, identified in multiple outcome studies, is the infant who has been exposed to severe perinatal stress and who then is raised in a poor environment. By adolescence, these individuals are 10 times more likely to have serious learning and behavior problems than peers who have had similar perinatal stress but who were not living in poverty (Werner, 1986). Without doubt, clinicians must consider environmental influences and how these interact with biological factors, vis-à-vis the transactional approach discussed earlier.

INTERVENTION

Interventions can occur while the infant is still hospitalized, over the first 5 years, or both. The former typically is offered to infants who have had pre-, peri-, or postnatal problems; the latter is provided to infants at biological and/or environmental risk.

NURSERY INTERVENTIONS

The initial task facing infants at biological risk is stabilization of the medical condition and physiologic processes. However, because long periods of hospitalization are required for growth and recovery, it is not unusual for an infant to remain hospitalized two or more months after birth, this being particularly true for ELBW babies. The nervous system is developing over this time, and the infant is exposed to a variety of disorganized sensory stimuli from caregivers and their physical surroundings. As a result, these infants also require "developmental care" (Gorski, 1991).

Studies of infant sleep and wake states (High & Gorski, 1985) have indicated that the caregiving environment alternately provides an overabundance of stimulation due to different caregivers and procedures and deprivation of frequent patterns of contact and direct observation from human caregivers (High & Gorski, 1985). As a result, three perspectives on nursery stimulation have been delineated: (1) the neonatal intensive care unit (NICU) environment deprives infants of necessary stimulation, (2) the NICU bombards infants with continuous overstimulation, and (3) this environment lacks contingent patterns

of stimulation organized around maturationally determined physiologic or behavioral cues from the infants (Gorski, 1991). Depending on which perspective one endorses, the resultant intervention approach can vary significantly.

Those who take the perspective that the NICU environment deprives the infant adopt a "do something" tactic in which visual, auditory, tactile, vestibular-kinesthetic, or combined input is provided. Massaging, rocking, oscillatory waterbeds, music boxes, mobiles, and recorded heart beats are techniques that are often applied. In the second perspective, that NICUs provide overstimulation, the motto is "protection," and decreased handling, reduced traffic, quiet, and dimmed lighting are emphasized. In the contingency-based approach, caretakers are taught to use cues emitted by the infant (e.g., facial movements, activity, irritability, sleep and wake states, heart rate, respiration) as signals of the infant's needs.

In actuality, each of these approaches has some merit, depending on the infant's medical condition, conceptional age (chronologic age minus number of weeks of prematurity), duration of hospitalization, and level of CNS maturity. The best approach to in-hospital stimulation is individualized, functional, modifiable, and responsive to the neurodevelopmental and autonomic states of the infant (Gorski, 1991). Without doubt, parent involvement is critical.

INTERVENTION OVER INFANCY AND EARLY CHILDHOOD

Early intervention (EI) services are federally mandated by Public Law (Amendments to the Individuals with Disabilities Education Act, 1997; PL No.105-17, Part C). EI is typically directed toward infants with identified disabilities or economic disadvantage. Positive effects of early intervention have been documented in meta-analytic studies (Bennett & Guralnick, 1991; Shonkoff & Hauser-Cram, 1987), but simply extracting a child from his or her environment to provide intervention activities is not productive, and a broader approach is more appropriate.

C. Ramey and Ramey (1998) have postulated a "zone of modifiability" with regard to EI efforts. More specifically, there is a band of possible improvement that lies between a given infant's current, delayed developmental trajectory and a so-called typical developmental trajectory. Where in this band the infant's ultimate developmental course falls depends on many factors. For example, interventions that begin earlier (infancy) and continue longer produce greater benefit. Programs that are more intensive (e.g., more home visits per week, full-day program) are more influential, and children who receive direct intervention services show greater benefit than those who receive indirect intervention (e.g., parent training). Interventions that provide more comprehensive services and use multiple routes to enhance development (e.g., health and social services, transportation, help in family crises, therapies, parent services/training) have larger positive effects (S. Ramey & Ramey, 1992).

The severity of the biological insult is a significant issue and, in conjunction with family involvement, may explain why some infants show positive effects from EI and others do not. In fact, severity of disability can account for 50% to 70% of variance in developmental changes (Bennett & Guralnick, 1991). Those infants with the most severe problems require the most intensive intervention, yet the actual change in the aforementioned zone of modifiability may be minimized because of a biological "ceiling."

The tempering effects of biological factors on intervention effects is most recently exemplified in the Infant Health and Development Program (IHDP), an eight-site, randomized, controlled trial of the effect of early intervention on the development of LBW preterm infants from 40 weeks to 8 years of age (McCormick, McCarton, Brooks-Gunn, Belt, & Gross, 1998). A total of 985 infants were enrolled in either an intervention group or an intensive follow-up group, the interventions lasting from 40 weeks to 36 months. The intervention and follow-up groups were subdivided into babies with birthweights ≤ 2,000 g and those 2,001 to 2,500 g.

Data from the IHDP indicated that children in the intervention group had higher 3-year IQ scores than did controls, and the frequency of problem behaviors decreased (Brooks-Gunn, McCarton, & Casey, 1994; Infant Health and Development Program, 1990). However, intervention effects varied by birthweight; the mean difference in infants 2,001 to 2,500 g was 13.2 IQ points, and in the ≤ 2,000 g babies, the mean difference was 6.6 IQ points. There were no group differences at 12 months, but differences began to emerge by 24 months (9.75 points).

There was a decline in test scores over time for both intervention and control groups; however, the drop was more pronounced between 12 and 24 months than between 24 and 36 months. Change over time was less evident in the intervention than in the routine follow-up group. At 5 years of age, the overall intervention group had scores similar to controls. However, in the heavier birthweight group, children in the intervention program had higher Full-Scale IQ scores (3.7 points) and higher verbal IQ scores (4.2 points) than matched controls; no differences were noted in the lower birthweight group. Similar results were obtained at 96 months, with no difference found in overall cognitive scores. Again, in subgroup analyses, 2,001 to 2,500 g (heavier LBW group) infants had a 4-point advantage, whereas no difference between intervention and control children was found in the lower birthweight group (McCarton, Brooks-Gunn, and Wallace, 1997). Actual participation of the family, measured by the Family Participation Index (C. Ramey et al., 1992), was predictive of 3-year scores. The index consisted of the sum of frequencies of home visits, attendance at parent group meetings, days of attendance at parent group meetings, and days of attendance at the child development center. Risk and protective factors were indicated to predict 3-year IQ: birthweight, maternal IQ, maternal education (risk factors), and intensive early intervention (protective factor) all contributed significantly to the regression model. These data suggest that intervention generally appeared to prevent decline rather than enhance development (Aylward, 1996).

SUMMARY

For infants at environmental risk, intervention programs generally do not enhance early intellectual development to the above-average range, but instead prevent the slow decline away from average. Interventions are more effective for children in lower SES circumstances who reside in communities where intervention resources are not provided routinely. Intervention programs should be multifaceted and include home visits, parent involvement, and provision of structured curricula that begin in the first or second year of life. In addition to evaluating gains in IQ or academic achievement, one must consider less tangible and perhaps more important outcomes such as improvement in social competence, family functioning, and parental empowerment that result from intervention services. Efficacy of early intervention is enhanced if enrollment is in the first year of life and the degree of developmental delay is not severe (Aylward, 1996). Finally, one must consider child-family as well as programmatic issues in intervention programs.

EVALUATION

There are several levels of evaluation during the newborn and infancy periods (Aylward, 1997a). *Screening* is the process of testing whole populations of infants to identify those at high risk for unsuspected deviations from normal. The goal is to detect babies whose development is at risk and who otherwise would not be identified. Screening is indicative and flags children who need further assessment (e.g., the Bayley Infant Neurodevelopmental Screener; Aylward, 1995).

Assessment is a more detailed evaluation or estimation of development, the end product being a clinical decision as to what intervention would be appropriate to facilitate development. As assessment is conclusive and incorporates data from multiple sources, it results in a definitive "diagnosis" (Aylward, 1994).

However, screening techniques are often misapplied, as they are used in situations where the clinician already suspects a developmental delay and simply uses the screening test to verify these concerns. Moreover, in many pediatric offices, patient volume, time, and reimbursement issues make screening difficult. Therefore, the concept of *prescreening* has been forwarded (Squires, Nickel, & Eisert, 1996). Prescreening is a two-step process in which the parent or caretaker completes a questionnaire or developmental survey such as the Parents' Evaluation of Developmental Status (Glascoe, 1997), the Ages and Stages Questionnaire (Bricker, Squires, & Mounts, 1995), or the Child Developmental Inventories (Ireton, 1992). Prescreening is estimated to have sensitivity and specificity figures in the 75% to 80% range and is quite efficient, given that 25% of infants will fail a screening test, and of these, approximately 10% will have a confirmed developmental delay.

The terms *sensitivity* and *specificity* are heavily emphasized in developmental screening and assessment. The former (true positive rate) measures the proportion of babies with a developmental problem who are also identified by the test. Specificity (true negative rate) measures the proportion of infants who have no developmental problems and whom the test identifies as normal. However, because there are no true gold standards in developmental screening and assessment with the screening test being compared to a reference test, the terms *copositivity* and *conegativity* are more appropriate (Aylward, 1997b).

Development during infancy can be conceptualized as falling into four areas or streams (Aylward, 1997a):

- Motor (gross, fine).
- Language (receptive, expressive, articulation).
- Cognitive (problem solving, imitation, object permanency, planning, understanding cause-effect relationships).
- Adaptive/personal-social (interactions, self-help skills).

Cognitive and language domains are better predictors of later functioning than are motor or adaptive/personal-social areas. For example, it has been estimated that as many as 80% of children who are later found to have mild mental retardation (IQ 55–70) have normal motor milestones. Similarly, as many as 50% of those with moderate mental retardation will have normal or only slightly deviant motor milestones (Hreidarsson, Shapiro, & Capute, 1983). It is useful to consider patterns of congruence in developmental levels between the different streams or areas of function. For example, if delays are found in language and cognitive and adaptive functioning, but not in motor abilities, the practitioner may consider mental retardation as a potential cause. Conversely, if delays are found solely in the language area (and cognitive functioning is normal), the possibility of a specific language disorder is raised (Aylward, 1997b).

It is not the individual developmental function nor ability per se that is most important in the evaluation of infants. Rather, the *integration* of abilities and the functional units of the brain that control these abilities is critical and provides the best window through which to view and predict the infant's developmental level (Aylward, 1997a, 1997b). An individual function such as visual perception of a pellet is not in itself very predictive of later cognitive functioning. However, if the infant attempted to reach the pellet, bring it to his or her mouth, or dump it from a container, visual perception is combined with intentionality, reasoning, and goal-directedness. Such tasks involve the integration of various abilities and underlying neural units and reflect a process.

There is growing dissatisfaction with the use of normative assessments such as the Bayley Scales of Infant Development II (Bayley, 1993). These tests are designed to discriminate among children on a linear scale, by comparing the child's performance to a reference group on which the test was normed, and are administered on a single occasion. The end result of normative assessment is a diagnosis. Critics of this approach endorse a "new vision" and emphasize that intervention strategies cannot be readily extrapolated from this procedure (Greenspan & Meisels, 1996; Meisels, 1996). Because of the natural linkage between assessment and intervention, emphasis is placed on assessments that rely on criterion-referenced (proportion of skills in an area that the infant has mastered) and curriculum-based (specific objectives to be achieved) approaches. In the former, the score the child obtains measuring a developmental domain criterion (e.g., language, gross motor skills) indicates the proportion of the domain the child has mastered. The individual items reflect specific levels of competence that are arranged on a developmental sequence or continuum. Curriculum-based assessment focuses less on developmental hierarchies and more on specific objectives or skills that are to be achieved by the child. These techniques provide an absolute criterion against which a child's performance can be evaluated (level of mastery based on achievement of a specified number of successes) and involve observation by a team of evaluators on multiple occasions. Rather than have testing occur in an office or clinic, evaluation has moved into more familiar, naturalistic surroundings such as homes, child care locations, and intervention programs. How this new approach will affect the practice and impact of developmental screening is not clear at this time.

INFANT CHARACTERISTICS

TEMPERAMENT

Temperament is defined as behavioral style, or the "how" of behavior (Thomas & Chess, 1977). It con-

cerns the way a child behaves, spontaneously and in reaction to situations. The infant is born with a specific temperament, and it is likely that temperament characteristics are derived from genetic factors that interact with the environment and the child's physical state (Aylward, 1992). These traits are relatively stable but are not entirely fixed, again underscoring the bidirectional nature of caretaker-infant interaction. Measurement of temperament can be accomplished by parental interview, questionnaires (Carey & McDevitt, 1995b; Medloff-Cooper, Carey, & McDevitt, 1995), and the clinician's own behavioral observations (Aylward, 1992; Carey & McDevitt, 1995a). The interest in temperament was derived from the 1956 New York Longitudinal Study (NYLS) (Thomas & Chess, 1977). From infant behavioral records in the NYLS, nine categories of temperament were established: activity level, rhythmicity (regularity), approach/withdrawal, adaptability, threshold of responsiveness, intensity of reaction, quality of mood, distractibility, and attention span/persistence. From these nine temperament categories, three constellations of temperament have been identified. The *easy child* constellation, found in 40% of the population, is characterized by regularity, positive approach and responses to new stimuli, good adaptability to change, and a predominantly positive mood. At the opposite end of the continuum is the *difficult child*, comprising approximately 10% of the population. Characteristics include irregularity in biological functions, negative withdrawal responses to new stimuli or people, poor adaptability to change, and primarily negative mood expressions that are intense (although even laughing is loud and excessive). The *slow-to-warm-up* child temperament was found in 15%, and consists of negative responses of a mild intensity to new stimuli, slow but eventual adaptability, and a tendency toward irregularity of biologic function. Approximately 35% of infants do not fit these three constellations, having different combinations of behavioral traits.

A difficult temperament should not be considered pathologic. However, the difficult child is more prone to behavior problems in early and middle childhood, with 70% of these children from the NYLS manifesting behavioral problems before 10 years of age. These infants and toddlers require more effort by parents to deal with tantrums, crying, and oppositional behavior, and a difficult temperament in conjunction with other child risk factors such as developmental delays, language disorders, or physical handicaps may be particularly demanding on parents. Parents react by feeling inadequate, intimidated, threatened, and anxious, or by resenting and blaming the infant. Slow-to-warm-up infants are often stressed by parental insistence that they adapt quickly to a new situation (e.g., day care), food, or a peer play activity. When an infant with an easy temperament develops a behavioral concern, the clinician should look to situational stresses or parenting issues as causative factors.

Studies seeking to further understand the contributions of biological and genetic factors to temperament involve salivary cortisol (Gunnar, 1990), vagal tone (Porges, 1992), EEG activation, and twin studies such as the MacArthur Longitudinal Twin Study. Particular emphasis has been placed on infants and young children with behavioral inhibition. Moreover, investigations of the relationship between temperament and attachment (see below) have suggested an association between the pattern of mother-infant attachment and the infant's biological responses to stress (Nachmias, Gunnar, Mangelsdorf, Parritz, & Buss, 1996).

ATTACHMENT

Attachment refers to proximity/contact-seeking behavior, and intensifies at age 6 to 7 months. Infants vary in the degree of attachment shown to caretakers. Experimental work on attachment has yielded three basic attachment types (Ainsworth, Blehar, Waters, & Wall, 1978), and behavioral indicators of these types are often evident in informal office observation. In *secure attachment*, the infant uses the mother as a secure base from which to explore the environment. The child may initially be wary of strangers, tends to become upset if the mother leaves, and is very happy on her return. Mothers of these infants deal promptly and appropriately with their baby's needs, with the mother being "tuned in" to her infant. *Insecurely attached* babies fall into two groups: *insecure-ambivalent* and *insecure-avoidant*. In the former, infants sometimes approach and cling to the mother, yet at other times push away. They may ask for help but then become angry when it is offered. These babies often resist their parents' attempts to console them. On separation, their reaction to being reunited with the mother varies, with aggression occasionally being evident.

Mothers of insecure-ambivalent children are typically inconsistent in their responses; at times, they ignore the infant's cues, and at others they respond. Responsivity depends on the mother's needs and mood. Insecure-avoidant children often fail to seek proximity with their caretaker and display very independent behavior. They do not cry when separated from the mother and on reunion frequently ignore the mother altogether. The mothers are highly insensitive to the baby's signals and avoid close contact with the child, rarely showing affection or emotional expression. Neglected and maltreated infants often develop insecure attachments. Another attachment status, *disorganized attachment*, has been identified. These babies demonstrate more disorganized, often bizarre conflict behaviors directed toward caregivers, especially during stress. They also may have one of the other attachment classifications as a primary underlying pattern. In general, attachment patterns are relationship-specific versus traitlike, meaning that the infant can have different attachments to mothers than to fathers (Steele, Steele, & Fonagy, 1996).

ASSESSMENT OF EMOTIONAL AND BEHAVIORAL PROBLEMS IN INFANCY

Emotional and behavioral concerns in infancy range from the obvious (failure to thrive [FTT], pervasive developmental disorder [PDD]) to the very subtle (excessive irritability). However, in infancy and early childhood, there are many adverse psychological symptoms or situations of a more "subclinical" nature that do not meet the criteria for a specific mental disorder as specified in the *Diagnostic and Statistical Manual for Mental Disorders IV* (DSM-IV; American Psychiatric Association, 1994). Nonetheless, these concerns require intervention (Wolraich et al., 1996). Examples of such include the "vulnerable child syndrome" (Green & Solnit, 1964), parental overprotectiveness (Thomasgard, Shonkoff, Metz, & Edelbrock, 1995), the child who bites, and the whining infant. This emphasis has led to development of new diagnostic frameworks such as the American Academy of Pediatrics' *Diagnostic and Statistical Manual for Primary Care (DSM-PC), Child and Adolescent Version* (Wolraich et al., 1996). Caretaker and environmental factors are extremely influential in this age range, with symptoms falling on a continuum from normal developmental variations, to problems, to disorders. Developmental variations are within the range of expected behaviors and can be handled with reassurance. The second category involves behaviors that are sufficiently problematic as to disrupt the infant's functioning within the family, yet are not severe enough to warrant the diagnosis of a mental disorder. Disorders, constituting the last category, are more extreme and warrant referral to mental health clinicians.

In the *DSM-PC, child (infant) characteristics* such as physical health, temperament, developmental status, emotional health, sociability, and reaction to stress are considered. In addition, *situational or environmental factors* must be weighed. These include parent competence, family resources, quality/stability/safety of the environment, family relationships, emotional/physical support, emotional/physical health of caregivers, caregiver reaction to stress, and community support. Moreover, V-codes for situations that could adversely affect an infant's emotional well-being are emphasized. These include challenges to the primary support group (attachment, death of parent, marital discord, divorce, domestic violence), changes in caregiving (foster care, adoption, abuse, neglect, mental/physical disorder in caregiver, caregiver substance abuse), community or social challenges, and educational, occupational, housing, economic, or legal problems (Wolraich et al., 1996).

Similarly, the American Academy of Child and Adolescent Psychiatry has published *Practice Parameters for the Psychiatric Assessment of Infants and Toddlers (0–36 Months)* (American Academy of Child and Adolescent Psychiatry [AACAP] 1997, 1998). Again, emphasis is placed on a developmental perspective. The concern about "goodness of fit" between the infant and environmental expectations warrants evaluation of the infant in the context of the caregiving unit (AACAP, 1997, 1998). In infancy, problems are typically found in "dysregulation of physiological function," feeding and sleeping problems, and failure to thrive. With toddlers, the breadth of problems broadens to include aggression, defiance, impulsivity, and overactivity. Therefore, recommended assessment involves family interview, parent account of the presenting complaints, developmental history, family relations history, clinical observation (parent-child, interactive play), use of standardized instruments (e.g., Bayley

Infant Behavior Record; Bayley, 1993), and interdisciplinary input. Use of the Infant and Toddler Mental Status Examination (ITMSE; AACAP, 1998) is recommended. The ITMSE includes traditional categories of the mental status examination adopted for infants and toddlers and adds sensory and state regulation and individual and interactive behaviors. The resulting diagnostic formulation is the product of the clinician's "synthesis of the biopsychosocial and cultural influences that contribute to, maintain, or ameliorate the infant's or toddler's difficulties" (AACAP, 1998, p. 132).

A final diagnostic classification scheme is the *Diagnostic Classification: 0–3* (DC: 0–3) (*Diagnostic Classification of Mental Health and Developmental Disorders of Infancy and Early Childhood;* Zero to Three: National Center for Clinical Infant Programs, 1994). The *DC: 0–3* is designed to complement existing frameworks such as the *DSM-IV,* and characterizes emotional and behavioral patterns that represent significant deviations from normative development in the earliest years of life, the goal being to develop a *diagnostic profile* of the infant. Axis I disorders include traditional standards such as mood disorders, reactive attachment disorders, and adjustment disorders, but also include regulatory disorders and multisystem developmental disorders. The former are constitutionally and maturationally based sensory, sensorimotor, or organizational processing problems that produce difficulties in regulating behavior (hypersensitive, underreactive, motorically disorganized, impulsive). Multisystem developmental disorders provide an alternative to the diagnosis of pervasive developmental disorders for youngsters who have significant problems relating and significant motor and sensory processing difficulties, yet who maintain some potential for closeness (Patterns A–C, ranging from "aimless/unrelated" to "avoids continuous relations/can be reactive"). Axis II is Relationship Classification and describes relationship disorders or patterns with each significant parent figure or caregiver (e.g., overinvolved, underinvolved, abusive). Whereas Axes III and IV are comparable to the *DSM-IV,* Axis V, Functional Emotional Developmental Level, assesses the infant's capacity to organize experience (mutual engagement, interactive intentionality). The major premise of the *DC: 0–3* format is that the diagnostic formulation better describes a given infant's problems, taking into consideration predisposing factors, current precipitants, and contributions of different areas assessed, thereby allowing development of a comprehensive treatment or intervention plan.

SUMMARY

Clinicians working with neonates and infants must consider infant characteristics, biological influences, environmental factors, and caretaker-infant interactions in the context of developmental change, recovery, and maturation. Development is dynamic, and as such, the infant is constantly rearranging and reorganizing cognitively, behaviorally, and emotionally in a transactional matrix. Risk factors that may disrupt development can be of an established, biological, or environmental nature. Conversely, protective factors may be infant- and/or environmentally based. The vast numbers of permutations and combinations of these risk and protective influences, superimposed on a given infant's constitutional and behavioral predispositions, help to explain individuality. Early identification of an infant's problems *and* strengths is critical to afford comprehensive intervention and maximize development.

REFERENCES

Ainsworth, M.D.S., Blehar, M.C., Waters, E., & Wall, S. (1978). *Patterns of attachment: A psychological study of the Strange Situation.* Hillsdale, NJ: Erlbaum.

American Academy of Child and Adolescent Psychiatry. (1997). Practice parameters for the psychiatric assessment of infants and toddlers (0–36 months). *Journal of the Academy of Child and Adolescent Psychiatry, 36,* 21S–36S.

American Academy of Child and Adolescent Psychiatry. (1998). Summary of the practice parameters for the psychiatric assessment of infants and toddlers (0–36 months). *Journal of the American Academy of Child and Adolescent Psychiatry, 37,* 127–132.

American Academy of Pediatrics, Committee on Fetus and Newborn. (1996). Use and abuse of the Apgar Score. *Pediatrics, 98,* 141–142.

American Psychiatric Association. (1994). *Diagnostic and statistical manual of mental disorders* (4th ed.). Washington, DC: Author.

Aylward, G.P. (1990). Environmental influences on developmental outcome of children at risk. *Infants and Young Children, 2,* 1–9.

Aylward, G.P. (1992). The relationship between environmental risk and developmental outcome. *Journal of Developmental and Behavioral Pediatrics, 13,* 222–229.

Aylward, G.P. (1993). Perinatal asphyxia: Effects of biologic and environmental risks. *Clinics in Perinatology, 20,* 433–449.

Aylward, G.P. (1994). *Practitioner's guide to developmental and psychological testing.* New York: Plenum Medical Books.

Aylward, G.P. (1995). *The Bayley Infant Neurodevelopmental Screener manual.* San Antonio, TX: Psychological Corporation.

Aylward, G.P. (1996). Environmental risk, intervention and developmental outcome. *Ambulatory Child Health, 2,* 161–170.

Aylward, G.P. (1997a). *Infant and early childhood neuropsychology.* New York: Plenum Press.

Aylward, G.P. (1997b). Conceptual issues in developmental screening and assessment. *Journal of Developmental and Behavioral Pediatrics, 18,* 340–349.

Aylward, G.P., & Kenny, T.J. (1979). Developmental follow-up: Inherent problems and a conceptual model. *Journal of Pediatric Psychology, 4,* 331–343.

Aylward, G.P., Pfeiffer, S.I., Wright, A., & Verhulst, S.J. (1989). Outcome studies of low birthweight infants published in the last decade: A meta-analysis. *Journal of Pediatrics, 115,* 515–520.

Aylward, G.P., Verhulst, S.J., & Bell, S. (1989). Correlation of asphyxia, other risk factors, and outcome: A contemporary view. *Developmental Medicine and Child Neurology, 31,* 329–340.

Bayley, N. (1993). *The Bayley Scales of Infant Development II.* San Antonio, TX: Psychological Corporation.

Bendersky, M., & Lewis, M. (1998). Arousal modulation in cocaine-exposed infants. *Developmental Psychology, 34,* 555–564.

Bennett, F.C., & Guralnick, M.J. (1991). Effectiveness of developmental intervention in the first five years of life. *Pediatric Clinics of North America, 38,* 1513–1528.

Bricker, D., Squires, J., & Mounts, L. (1995). *Ages and Stages Questionnaires: A parent-completed, child monitoring system.* Baltimore: Brookes.

Brooks-Gunn, J., McCarton, C.M., & Casey, P.H. (1994). Early intervention in low-birthweight premature infants: Results through age 5 years from the Infant Health and Development Program. *Journal of the American Medical Association, 272,* 1257–1262.

Capone, G.T. (1996). Human brain development. In A.J. Capute & P.J. Accardo (Eds.), *Developmental disabilities in infancy and childhood. Neurodevelopmental diagnosis and treatment* (2nd ed., Vol. 1, pp. 25–75). Baltimore: Brookes.

Carey, W.B., & McDevitt, S.C. (1995a). *Coping with children's temperament.* New York: Basic Books.

Carey, W.B., & McDevitt, S.C. (1995b). *Revised Infant Temperament Questionnaire (RITQ).* Scottsdale, AZ: Behavioral-Developmental Initiatives.

Diamond, G., & Cohen, H. (1992). Developmental disabilities in children with HIV infection. In A. Crocker,

H. Cohen, & T. Kastner (Eds.), *HIV infection and developmental disabilities* (pp. 33–43). Baltimore: Brookes.

Escalona, S.K. (1982). Babies at double hazard: Early development of infants at biologic and social risk. *Pediatrics, 70,* 670–676.

Glascoe, F.P. (1997). Parents' concerns about children's development: Prescreening technique or screening test? *Pediatrics, 99,* 522–528.

Gorski, P.A. (1991). Developmental interventions during neonatal hospitalization: Critiquing the state of the science. *Pediatric Clinics of North America, 38,* 1469–1480.

Green, M., & Solnit, A.J. (1964). Reactions to the threatened loss of a child: A vulnerable child syndrome. *Pediatrics, 34,* 58–66.

Greenspan, S.I., & Meisels, S.J. (1996). Toward a new vision for the developmental assessment of infants and young children. In S.J. Meisels & E. Fenichel (Eds.), *New visions for the developmental assessment of infants and young children* (pp. 11–26). Washington, DC: Zero to Three: National Center for Infants, Toddlers, and Families.

Gunnar, M.R. (1990). The psychobiology of infant temperament. In J. Colombo & J. Fagan (Eds.), *Individual differences in infancy: Reliability, stability, prediction* (pp. 387–409). Hillsdale, NJ: Erlbaum.

Hack, M., & Fanaroff, A.A. (1999). Outcomes of children of extremely low birthweight and gestational age in the 1990s. *Early Human Development, S3,* 193–218.

High, P.C., & Gorski, P.A. (1985). Womb for improvement: A study of preterm development in an intensive care nursery. In A.W. Gottfried & J.L. Gaiter (Eds.), *Infant stress under intensive care* (pp. 131–155). Baltimore: University Park Press.

Hill, A., & Volpe, J.J. (1989). Perinatal asphyxia: Clinical aspects. *Clinics in Perinatology, 16,* 435–457.

Hreidarsson, S.J., Shapiro, B.K., & Capute, A.J. (1983). Age of walking in the cognitively impaired. *Clinical Pediatrics, 22,* 248–252.

Hunt, J.V., Cooper, B.A.B., & Tooley, W.H. (1988). Very low birthweight infants at 8 and 11 years of age: Role of neonatal illness and family status. *Pediatrics, 82,* 596–603.

Infant Health and Development Program. (1990). Enhancing the outcome of low birthweight, premature infants: A multisite, randomized trial. *Journal of the American Medical Association, 262,* 3035–3042.

Ireton, H. (1992). *Child Development Inventories manual.* Minneapolis, MN: Behavioral Science Systems.

Johnson, C.B. (1993). Developmental issues: Children infected with the human immunodeficiency virus. *Infants and Young Children, 6,* 1–10.

McCarton, C.M., Brooks-Gunn, J., & Wallace, I.F. (1997). Results at age 8 years of early intervention for low birth-weight, premature infants: The Infant Health and Development Program. *Journal of the American Medical Association, 277,* 126–132.

McCormick, M.C., McCarton, C., Brooks-Gunn, J., Belt, P., & Gross, R.T. (1998). The Infant Health and Development Program: Interim summary. *Journal of Developmental and Behavioral Pediatrics, 19,* 359–370.

Medloff-Cooper, B., Carey, W.B., & McDevitt, S.C. (1995). *Early Infant Temperament Questionnaire (EITQ).* Scottsdale, AZ: Behavioral-Developmental Initiatives.

Meisels, S.J. (1996). Charting the continuum of assessment and intervention. In S.J. Meisels & E. Fenichel (Eds.), *New visions for the developmental assessment of infants and young children* (pp. 27–52). Washington, DC: Zero to Three: National Center for Infants, Toddlers, and Families.

Nachmias, M., Gunnar, M.R., Mangelsdorf, S., Parritz, R.H., & Buss, K. (1996). Behavioral inhibition and stress reactivity: Moderating role of attachment security. *Child Development, 67,* 508–522.

Paneth, N.S. (1995). The problem of low birthweight. *Future of Children, 5,* 11–34.

Parker, S., Greer, S., & Zuckerman, B. (1988). Double jeopardy: The impact of poverty on early child development. *Pediatric Clinics of North America, 35,* 1227–1240.

Pasamanick, B., & Knobloch, H. (1961). Epidemiologic studies on the complications of pregnancy and the birth process. In G. Caplan (Ed.), *Prevention of mental disorders in children.* New York: Basic Books.

Phillips, R.B., Sharma, R., Premachandra, B.R., Vaughn, A.J., & Reyes-Lee, M. (1996). Intrauterine exposure to cocaine: Effect on neurobehavior of neonates. *Infant Behavior and Development, 19,* 71–81.

Porges, S.W. (1992). Vagal tone: A physiologic marker of stress vulnerability. *Pediatrics, 90,* 498–504.

Ramey, C.T., Bryant, D.M., Wasik, B.H., Sparling, J.J., Fandt, K.H., & La Vange, L.M. (1992). Infant Health and Development Program for low birthweight, premature infants: Program elements, family participation, and child intelligence. *Pediatrics, 89,* 454–465.

Ramey, C.T., & Ramey, S.L. (1998). Early intervention and early experience. *American Psychologist, 53,* 109–120.

Ramey, S.L., & Ramey, C.T. (1992). Early educational intervention with disadvantaged children: To what effect? *Applied and Preventive Psychology, 1,* 131–140.

Risser, A.H., & Edgell, D. (1988). Neuropsychology of the developing brain: Implications for neuropsychological assessment. In M. Tramontana & S. Hooper (Eds.), *Assessment issues in child neuropsychology* (pp. 41–65). New York: Plenum Press.

Rutter, M. (1987). Psychosocial and protective mechanisms. *American Journal of Orthopsychiatry, 57,* 316–331.

Sameroff, A.J., & Chandler, M.J. (1975). Reproductive risk and the continuum of caretaking casualty. In F.D. Horowitz (Ed.), *Review of child development research* (Vol. 4, pp. 157–243). Chicago: University of Chicago Press.

Sameroff, A.J., Seifer, R., Barocas, R., Zax, M., & Greenspan, S. (1987). Intelligence quotient scores of

4-year-old children: Social environmental risk factors. *Pediatrics, 79,* 343–349.

Sampson, P.D., Streissguth, A.P., Bookstein, F.L., Little, R.E., Clarren, S.K., Dehaene, P., Hanson, J.W., & Graham, J.M. (1997). Incidence of fetal alcohol syndrome and prevalence of alcohol-related neurodevelopmental disorder. *Teratology, 56,* 317–326.

Shonkoff, J.P., & Hauser-Cram, P. (1987). Early intervention for disabled infants and their families: A quantitative analysis. *Pediatrics, 80,* 650–658.

Squires, J., Nickel, R.E., & Eisert, D. (1996). Early detection of developmental problems: Strategies for monitoring young children in the practice setting. *Journal of Developmental and Behavioral Pediatrics, 17,* 420–427.

Steele, H., Steele, M., & Fonagy, P. (1996). Associations among attachment classifications in mothers, fathers, and their infants. *Child Development, 67,* 541–555.

Taylor, H.G., Schatschneider, C., & Rich, D. (1992). Sequelae of Haemophilis Influenzae meningitis: Implications for the study of brain disease and development. In M.G. Tramontana & S.R. Hooper (Eds.), *Advances in child neuropsychology* (Vol. 1, pp. 50–108). Berlin, Germany: Springer-Verlag.

Thomas, A., & Chess, S. (1977). *Temperament and development.* New York: Brunner/Mazel.

Thomasgard, M., Shonkoff, J.P., Metz, W.P., & Edelbrock, C. (1995). Parent-child relationship disorders. Part II. The vulnerable child syndrome and its relations to parental overprotection. *Journal of Developmental and Behavioral Pediatrics, 16,* 251–256.

Tjossem, T. (1976). *Intervention strategies for high risk infants and young children.* Baltimore: University Park Press.

Volpe, J.J. (1998). Neurologic outcome of prematurity. *Archives of Neurology, 55,* 297–300.

Werner, E.E. (1986). A longitudinal study of perinatal risk. In D.C. Farran & J.D. McKenny (Eds.), *Risk in intellectual and psychosocial development* (pp. 3–27). New York: Academic Press.

Wolraich, M.L., Felice, M.E., & Drotar, D. (1996). *The classification of child and adolescent mental diagnoses in primary care. Diagnostic and statistical manual for primary care (DSM-PC), child and adolescent version.* Elk Grove, IL: American Academy of Pediatrics.

Zero to Three: National Center for Clinical Infant Programs. (1994). *Diagnostic classification: 0–3. Diagnostic classification of mental health and developmental disorders of infancy and early childhood.* Arlington, VA: Author.

CHAPTER 14

Clinical Problems of the Preschool Child

CAROLYN S. SCHROEDER AND BETTY N. GORDON

The preschool years (age 2–5) are considered to be one of the most important developmental periods of childhood. It is during this period that the foundation for later competence in many areas is laid. The emergence of language, self-awareness, peer relationships, autonomy and independence, and the increasing complexity of cognitive, play, social, and motor skills all set the stage for new and often intense interactions between children and their environments. As children's capacity to interact with the environment increases, so do the concerns of their parents. Yet, many of the problems seen in the preschool years, such as temper tantrums, overactivity, noncompliance, and aggression as well as problems with separation anxiety, shyness, sleep, toileting, feeding/eating, tics, headbanging, and more, can reflect transitory age-appropriate difficulties that will resolve with time. Nonetheless, some of these behaviors predict problems that will persist into later childhood or even adulthood. Understanding the factors that place children at risk for significant problems and why some children are able to overcome early difficulties and others continue to suffer is important for planning prevention and early intervention strategies.

This chapter focuses on behavior problems and their relationship to development in the preschool years. Further, some of the influences that affect the trajectory of these problems and the development of child psychopathology are considered. The first part of the chapter speaks to the methods used to diagnose problems during the preschool years. The prevalence of problems is also discussed and child, parent, and environmental factors that influence children's risk of developing persistent problems are reviewed. This is followed by discussion of the assessment issues that are important for this age range, including a brief review of developmental milestones, areas to assess, and assessment methods. Last, an overview of some common but troublesome behavior problems that occur during the preschool years is given and intervention strategies are discussed.

DIAGNOSTIC METHODS

The most commonly used classification system in the United States is the *Diagnostic and Statistical Manual of Mental Disorders* (*DSM-IV*; American Psychiatric Association [APA], 1994). *DSM-IV* is a categorical classification system in which an individual meets or does not meet criteria for a particular disorder. This method of classification is particularly problematic when talking about preschool children because their rapid development makes it difficult to determine which behaviors are transient developmental problems and which will be clinically significant (Campbell, 1990). Although the recent *DSM* revision encourages the clinician to view individuals with a particular disorder as heterogeneous and to gather information that goes beyond the diagnosis, it still does not provide adequate guidelines for determining the developmental and clinical significance of those symptomatic behaviors that define a problem during the preschool years. In addition, parent-child relationships are very important in diagnosing problems among preschoolers and, although both parent-child and sibling relational problems can be coded as "other conditions that may be the focus of clinical intervention" (APA, 1994, p. 675), the diversity of these problems are not adequately taken into account (Volkmar & Schwab-Stone, 1996).

Despite these continuing concerns about the use of the *DSM-IV* with preschool children, it is widely used in clinical practice. It is, therefore, worthwhile to review the disorders that specifically have their onset during infancy, childhood, or adolescence. Table 14.1 provides a summary of these disorders. As shown in Table 14.1, eight of these childhood *DSM-IV* disorders have an age of onset during the preschool years. With the exception of enuresis, which is not actually considered a disorder until age 5, the problems listed are uncommon and do not reflect the range of behavioral concerns seen by most child clinicians, especially during the preschool years. Nonetheless, clinicians are encouraged to use the *DSM-IV* V-codes for insurance purposes. These codes cover problems or conditions that may be the focus of clinical attention, such as parent-child relational problem or sibling relational problem (APA, 1994), when a mental disorder is not present.

The American Academy of Pediatrics (Wolraich, Felice, & Drotar, 1996) recently published the *Diagnostic and Statistical Manual for Primary Care (DSM-PC)*. Their goal was to develop a diagnostic system that was comprehensive and developmentally appropriate to help primary care pediatricians recognize, manage, and refer a wide spectrum of children's behavioral and developmental problems as well as stressful family and environmental situations (Drotar, 1999). Some of the critical underlying assumptions of this system include (1) symptoms viewed along a continuum from normal variations to severe mental disorders that is divided into clinically meaningful graduations; (2) the quality of children's environment recognized as having a critical impact on their mental health and taken into

account in assessing problems; (3) children's expression of symptoms and response to stressful environmental situations varies as a function of age and level of development; and (4) the system is based on objective data where possible and professional consensus in cases where data are not yet available. In addition, the system was developed to be fully compatible with *DSM-IV* (APA, 1994) and the *International Classification of Diseases (ICD-10;* World Health Organization [WHO], 1992). Although this system is currently not yet in wide clinical use and much research must be done to support it, it holds promise in describing not only problem behavior but its significance within a particular developmental and environmental context.

Another approach to classification is quantitative or dimensional. This approach assumes that behavior occurs along a continuum rather than dichotomously (i.e., either you have a disorder or you do not). Differences in types of problems are examined statistically through methods such as factor analysis (Achenbach, 1991, 1992; Achenbach & Edelbrock, 1978). Dimensional diagnosis allows one to describe multiple behavior patterns for any individual child. Dimensional systems do not lead to a statement that a child has a particular disorder but rather describe the degree to which one or more behavioral characteristics are present. Cutoff scores are used to determine the clinical significance of specific behaviors for different age groups. Although normative developmental considerations can more readily be taken into account with dimensional systems, they generally do not address important relational and cross-situational issues, the length of time the behavior has occurred, or how the behavior impairs functioning.

Arend, Lavigne, Rosenbaum, Binns, and Christoffell (1996) examined the *DSM* approach to diagnosis and a dimensional one based on the Child Behavior Checklist and profile (CBCL; Achenbach, 1991, 1992). Focusing on disruptive disorders in 510 2- to 5-year-olds selected from pediatric primary care settings, they compared *DSM-III-R* (APA, 1987) diagnoses derived from semistructured parent interviews, parent questionnaires, play observations, and developmental testing with parent responses to the CBCL. The greatest convergence between the two approaches was found when there was clearly no problem. Children who received scores below the clinical cutoff on the CBCL but were given a *DSM* diagnosis were compared with those who

Table 14.1 *DSM-IV disorders usually first diagnosed in infancy, childhood, or adolescence.*

Disorders	Age of Onset	Prevalence
Mental Retardation	Birth	1%
Learning Disorders		
Reading disorder	6–9 years	4%
Mathematics disorder	6–10 years	1%
Written expression disorder	7–? years	Unknown
Motor Skills Disorders		
Developmental coordination	Preschool	6% of 5–11-year-olds
Communication Disorders		
Expressive language disorder, developmental type	3 years	3%–5% school-age children
Mixed receptive-expressive language disorder	Before 4 years	3% school-age children
Phonological disorder	Preschool	2%–3% of 6–7-year-olds; 0.5% of 17-year olds
Stuttering	2–7 years	1% preadolescents; 0.8% adolescents
Pervasive Developmental Disorders		
Autistic disorder	Before 3 years	2–5 cases per 10,000
Rett's disorder	5–48 months	Uncommon, only females
Childhood disintegrative disorder	Before 10 years	Very rare
Asperger's disorder	Preschool to early school age	Unknown
Attention-Deficit and Disruptive Behavior Disorders		
Attention-deficit/hyperactivity disorder	Before 7 years	3%–5% school-age
Conduct disorder	Pre- and early adolescence	6%–16% males < 18 years 2%–9% females 18 years
Oppositional defiant disorder	Before age 8–not later than early adolescence	2%–16% of children
Feeding and Eating Disorders		
Pica	Infancy (?)	Unknown
Rumination disorder	3–12 months	Unknown
Feeding disorder of infancy and early childhood	Before 6 years	0.5%–2.5% of pediatric hospital admissions
Tic Disorders		
Tourette's disorder	Before 18 years	4–5 per 10,000
Chronic motor or vocal tic	Before 18 years	4–5 per 10,000
Transient tic disorder	Before 18 years	4–5 per 10,000
Elimination Disorders		
Encopresis	At least 4 years	1% of 5-year-olds
Enuresis	At least 5 years	Age 5: 7% male, 3% female Age 10: 3% male, 2% female Age 18: 1% male
Other Disorders		
Separation anxiety disorder	Before 18 years	4% of children and adolescents
Selective mutism	Before 5 years	Rare: < 1% of children seen in mental health setting
Reactive attachment disorder	Before 5 years	Very uncommon
Stereotypic movement disorder	All ages	2%–3% of children and adolescents with MR living in community settings; 25% of adults with severe or profound MR in institutions

were below the CBCL cutoff but did not receive a diagnosis. These two groups differed in the severity of their behavior and in the number of situations in which the behavior occurred. Arend et al. also found that children's lack of cooperation across settings indicated a greater likelihood of more severe behavior problems. So, the addition to the CBCL of questions regarding the cross-situational nature of the child's behavior or having both the teacher and the parent complete the CBCL would enhance the utility of the CBCL dimensional diagnostic system in identifying children with significant problems that might otherwise be missed.

It is remarkable that 28 different *DSM-III-R* diagnoses were used with this sample of preschoolers (Arend et al., 1996). This raises the question of the ability of the *DSM* categories to differentiate children in this preschool group. Not surprisingly, problems appeared to be better differentiated among the 4- to 5-year-olds than among the 2- to 3-year-olds. Although the authors indicate that interviewing may allow for a greater amount and richness of information with which to make a categorical diagnosis, they also point out that the utility of the study depends on the validity of the *DSM-III-R* diagnosis. This is an important cautionary note, particularly with preschool children who exhibit a significant number of problem behaviors that are age-appropriate and transient. Although the authors indicate that they have few data to recommend either the categorical or dimensional approach over the other, it appears that clinical judgment is enhanced when information is gathered through multiple methods and sources and across situations.

PREVALENCE

The prevalence of problems in preschool children is difficult to determine due to the variety of nonstandardized criteria used to identify the presence of a particular problem as well as the varying labels and definitions of problem behavior. In addition, the wide variability in development and behavior among children during the preschool years makes it difficult to say that a certain behavior or set of behaviors represents a clinical disorder except in extreme cases, for example, mental retardation or autism.

Table 14.1 indicates prevalence rates for the *DSM-IV* disorders that have their onset during in-

fancy, childhood, or adolescence. More generally, large-scale studies in health care settings indicate that 5% to 25% of all children seen in primary health care evidence significant behavioral or emotional problems (Costello et al., 1988; Goldberg, Regier, McInery, Pless, & Roghmann, 1984; Goldberg, Roghmann, McInery, & Burke, 1984; Starfield et al., 1980). In the Arend et al. (1996) study discussed previously, over 21.4% of the preschool-age participants had *DSM* disorders and 9.1% had severe disorders. In a follow-up study, these authors found that a substantial number of these children's problems persisted over 42 to 48 months (Lavigne et al., 1999).

Other large-scale surveys estimate that 7% to 14% of preschoolers have serious behavioral problems (Achenbach, Edelbrock, & Howell, 1987; Richman, Stevenson, & Graham, 1982; Rose, Feldman, Rose, Wallace, & McCarton, 1992). Richman, Stevenson, and Graham (1975), for example, interviewed mothers of 3-year-old children in London and estimated that 7% of the children had moderate-to-severe problems and 15% had mild problems. Furthermore, 66% of the children with problems continued to present problems a year later, compared with 15% of the control group (Richman et al., 1982). Hooks, Mayes, and Volkmar (1988) examined records of 193 children less than 5 years of age who were seen during a two-year-period at the Yale Child Study Center. The *DSM-III* diagnoses for those children included 10.9% parent-child problems, 17.1% pervasive developmental delay, 32.1% emotional disorders, 4.1% disruptive behavior disorder, 22.3% specific developmental delay, and 6.3% global developmental delay; 29% had no diagnostic label. It is interesting to note that 59% of the children were experiencing severe to extreme psychosocial stresses, which is consistent with other studies (e.g., Earls, 1982; Lee, 1987).

Other work indicates that the prevalence of problems may vary depending on the age or developmental status of the child. Jenkins, Bax, and Hart (1980), for example, found that the percentage of parents who worried about their preschoolers was highest when the children were 3 years old (23%). The problems reported included difficulty in management, demanding too much attention, and temper tantrums. Although food fads and poor appetite were more common at the age of 3, parents did not view these as significant problems. Mesibov, Schroeder, and Wesson (1977) found similar results in a study of parental concerns reported to a consultation service in a pediatric office. The greatest number of concerns was among the parents of 2- and 3-year-olds, with negative behavior, toileting, and developmental delays being the most frequent problems/concerns.

Overall, prevalence studies indicate that behavior problems are relatively common in the preschool years and are most often associated with a particular developmental period. Thus, issues with toileting, sleep, and eating are more likely to occur during the first three years, and struggles for independence and autonomy at age 3 often result in increased disobedience and defiance. For most children, these problems are transient and decrease in meaningful and predictable ways with development, yet some appear to persist and may even worsen (Campbell, 1997). Understanding the factors that predict increased severity is important for assessment and treatment of these children.

RISK/PROTECTIVE FACTORS

The factors that place children at risk for continuing and/or severe emotional and behavioral problems have received increasing attention in the past 10 years. One way of categorizing risk factors is to view them as (1) established risk factors, such as a frank genetic disorder (i.e., Fragile X syndrome or Down syndrome); (2) biological risk factors, such as poor prenatal care, drug and/or alcohol abuse by the mother during pregnancy, prematurity, anoxia, and low birthweight; and (3) environmental risk factors, such as poor responsivity or lack of sensitivity by the mother to her child, low level of language stimulation, or family socioeconomic status (SES) (Odom & Kaiser, 1997). It is recognized that it is the dynamic and complex interplay of these factors (e.g., the individual child, his or her developmental status, the social background, and the cultural context) that ultimately determines the child's risk for developmental and/or behavior problems (Haggerty, Sherrod, Garmezy, & Rutter, 1996). Rutter (1996) points out that it is not the isolated life event or stressor but rather the aggregated accumulation of events that contributes to psychological vulnerability for the individual child. Conversely, it is recognized that protective factors are also on a continuum, and when accumulated and present across time, these factors can increase the probability of a positive outcome for children in

high-risk situations (Goodyer, 1990). Even for children with known genetic disorders, the negative effects associated with the disability can be reduced through early and ongoing intervention programs that focus on both the child and his or her family. Though this chapter primarily focuses on environmental risk/protective factors, it is important to recognize that it is the interplay of genetic, biological, and environmental factors over time that ultimately determines the developmental trajectory of the child.

TYPE AND SEVERITY OF EARLY CHILDHOOD PROBLEMS

Externalizing behaviors, such as inattention, aggression, and noncompliance, have received the greatest amount of attention regarding their stability and durability when the age of onset is in the preschool years. Longitudinal studies show that about half of these hard-to-manage children identified as preschoolers continue to have significant behavioral difficulties at follow-up periods of 1 to 13 years (Campbell & Ewing, 1990; Campbell, Ewing, Breaux, & Szumowski, 1986; Campbell, Szumowski, Ewing, Gluck, & Breaux, 1982; Egeland, Kalkoske, Gottesman, & Erickson, 1990; Pierce, Ewing, & Campbell, 1999; Richman et al., 1982). Factors associated with persistent externalizing problems include early onset; initial problem severity; cognitive deficits; parenting that is uninvolved, rejecting, and harsh; and ongoing family adversity, especially low SES, that is associated with less stable, supportive, and involved caretaking in early childhood (Campbell, 1995). According to Campbell, the children showing a combination of hyperactivity and aggression/noncompliance appear to have the most severe and pervasive problems with the worst prognosis, in part because they tend to live in the most dysfunctional families and have a very early onset of problems.

Other work has shown that externalizing problems in combination with low IQ may result in more persistent problems (Sonuga-Barke, Lamparelli, Stevenson, Thompson, & Henry, 1994). Clearly, this combination of problems places children at risk for even greater difficulties as they enter school. Further, children rated by both teachers and parents as having significant externalizing problems have been observed to be more difficult to handle when interacting with peers, teachers, and parents in both structured and unstructured situations (Campbell, Pierce, March, Ewing, & Szumowski, 1994; Schaughency & Fagot, 1993). This further increases the risk for both learning and peer-relationship problems.

PARENT-CHILD INTERACTION AND SOCIALIZATION

For preschool children, the quality of parenting seems to be an especially important factor, as these youngsters are "both vulnerable and dependent on their families for nurturance, guidance and support" (Campbell, 1996, p. 375). Parenting behavior and parent-child interaction have been associated with a variety of child behavior problems. For example, maternal behavior that is arbitrary, inconsistent, negative, or uninvolved is associated with noncompliance and low internal control in preschoolers (Webster-Stratton, 1990). Conversely, maternal responsiveness to child requests and a history of a warm, positive relationship appear to be important for the development of mother-child reciprocity and later prosocial behavior with peers (Sroufe & Fleeson, 1986). Further, mothers of preschool children with behavior problems have been observed to initiate a smaller proportion of activities, make fewer contributions to keeping the activity going, and be less responsive to the child's contributions during spontaneous joint play (Gardner, 1994). In contrast to control children, problem children play a greater role than their mothers in initiating and maintaining activities (Gardner, 1994). So, maternal involvement in play may be an important factor in the development of behavior problems.

The nature of the parent-infant attachment relationship has also been shown to be an important risk factor for preschool children. There is ongoing work demonstrating that the quality of early attachment relationships bears directly on adaptation during the preschool years (M. Greenberg, Cicchetti, & Cummings, 1990). Secure attachments have been found "to foster favorable self-images, satisfying relationships outside the family, and a stable basis for exploring the environment and mastering new developmental tasks" (Easterbrooks & Goldberg, 1990, p. 238). Conversely, insecure parent-infant attachments can place the preschool child at risk for problems with motivation, emotional regulation, and peers, especially if the environment continues to be unstable over time

(Sroufe & Fleeson, 1986; see Greenberg et al. for a review of attachment in the preschool years).

FAMILY

Children in families coping with adverse circumstances such as low SES, single or stepparenting, conflicted family relationships (including disagreement over child rearing), or parent psychopathology (especially maternal depression) are at increased risk of behavior problems (Campbell, 1995). In a study of the relative impact of maltreatment, SES level, physical health problems, cognitive ability, and the quality of parent-child interaction on behavioral dysfunction, 206 children were assessed at both preschool and school age (Herrenkohl, Herrenkohl, Rupert, Egolf, & Lutz, 1995). The results indicated that socioeconomic level and the family climate in which the child was raised were strongly related to children's behavioral functioning. Interestingly, physical and emotional maltreatment were significant but less powerful influences on behavior. SES appeared to be the most critical factor in predicting behavioral functioning. It was associated with patterns of teaching, communicating with, stimulating, and guiding children, as well as with the resources available to families for support in facilitating children's development. The next most important construct associated with child dysfunction was the quality of the mother's interaction with the child, including the degree of rejection, hostility, and control exhibited (Herrenkohl et al., 1995). Conversely, a supportive family environment, less invasive control, and greater amounts of encouragement given to independence and experimentation in problem solving was associated with better behavior functioning among the children. Other studies support the impact of low SES on parent-child interactions (Herrenkohl, Herrenkohl, Toedter, & Yanushefski, 1984), cognitive maturity, and the encouragement of autonomy and independence in the child (Trickett, Aber, Carlson, & Cicchetti, 1991).

The relationship between SES and behavioral functioning appears to be a linear one, with the risk of behavior problems increasing linearly with decreasing SES. Dodge, Pettit, and Bates (1994), found that SES was significantly negatively correlated with eight factors in the child's socialization and social context: harsh discipline, lack of maternal warmth, exposure to aggressive adult models, maternal aggressive values, family life stresses, mother's lack of social support, peer group instability, and lack of cognitive stimulation. These factors accounted for over half of the total effect of SES on outcomes that, in turn, significantly predicted teacher-rated externalizing problems and peer-nominated aggression (over 60% of low SES children received a score in the clinical risk range sometime during elementary school). Thus, the effect of SES on children's externalizing behavior problems may be mediated by status-related socializing experiences. These studies clearly indicate that being a preschooler in a family living in poverty can have far-reaching negative effects on development.

MATERNAL DEPRESSION

Maternal depression has long been known to be a risk factor for child development. In a recent review, however, Cummings and Davies (1994) conclude that the effects of maternal depression on development cannot be viewed independently of the family's psychosocial circumstances as a whole. Although parental (especially maternal) depression increases the likelihood of family discord, impairments in parenting, marital conflict, and, consequently, child disturbance, the effects of these adverse family circumstances have a similar effect in families without depression. Thus, although maternal depression is one risk factor, it is actually a combination of risk factors that predict child disturbance. Leadbeater and Bishop (1994) find support for this conclusion in a study of 83 disadvantaged Afro-American and Puerto Rican adolescent mothers of 28- to 36-month-old children. They found that maternal depressive symptoms in the first year were predictive of significant behavior problems in 13% of the children. However, those depressed mothers who had higher levels of emotional support and lived with maternal grandparents had children with fewer behavior problems.

INTELLIGENCE LEVEL

A few studies of children prior to or at entry into school have shown a relationship between behavioral problems, such as aggression and disruptiveness, and lower IQ (Campbell, 1994; Richman et al., 1982). Cole, Usher, and Cargo (1993), for example, found that preschoolers with lower intellectual functioning were more likely to be rated by their parents or teachers as showing moderate to high levels of externalizing behaviors than were children who had average or above-average intellectual functioning. Furthermore, low verbal and visuospatial scores were associated with above-average behavioral difficulty and greater problems with behavioral regulation.

Dietz, Lavigne, Arend, and Rosenbaum (1997) examined the relationship between intelligence and psychopathology in a nonclinical sample of 510 children, age 2 to 5 years. Both the CBCL (Achenbach, 1991, 1992) and the *DSM-III-R* (APA, 1987) were used to measure psychopathology. Results indicated that lower McCarthy (McCarthy, 1972) general, verbal, and perceptual performance IQ scores were associated with various types of psychopathology. Similarly, Sanson, Prior, and Smart (1996) conducted a large (1,251 children) longitudinal study of children from infancy to 6 years and found that at age 7 years, children with a combination of reading and behavior problems differed from a group of children with only reading problems from infancy onwards. For boys especially, difficult temperament and behavior, poor mother-child relationship, lower educational stimulation, and relative social disadvantage increased the risk of developing behavior problems and later emergence of reading disabilities. These results are consistent with those of clinical samples of preschool children. Hyperactive preschoolers have lower IQs than nonhyperactive preschoolers (Sonuga-Barke et al., 1994), and children with speech and language delay are at risk for ADHD, oppositional defiant disorder, and anxiety (Cantwell, Baker, & Mattison, 1979; Love & Thompson, 1988). Finally, Campbell (1994), using a mixed clinical and school-based sample of preschool boys, found that lower IQ predicted persistent problems two years later.

The pathway for the association between cognitive deficits and psychopathology is not clear. It could be that cognitive deficits cause psychopathology, or vice versa, or they may share a common cause such as neural system damage (Goodman, 1993).

In summary, the literature on behavior problems during the preschool years suggests that isolated problem behaviors or a constellation of mild symptoms are likely to disappear with development. Constellations of more severe problems in early childhood, particularly externalizing problems, may signify difficulties that are likely to persist at least to middle childhood. Further, low SES, low intelligence, ongoing family disruption, and poor mother-child relationships are often associated with continued difficulties, especially among boys who are hyperactive and aggressive. Although there is increasing evidence to support the continuity of preschoolers' behavior problems, only in rare cases can the clinician identify causal mechanisms in the development of disorders in children. Furthermore, predicting future outcome and delineating the specific factors that contribute to or mediate outcome remains difficult (Campbell, 1990).

ASSESSMENT ISSUES

Assessment of problems in the preschool years is a complex task. To begin the process, it is important to have knowledge of the developmental processes and what would be expected of the "typically" developing child. This, in combination with knowledge of risk and protective factors, sets the stage for developing hypotheses about the origins of the behavior of concern and planning intervention strategies. This section covers some important developmental milestones, areas that should be assessed, and assessment methods.

DEVELOPMENTAL MILESTONES

Previously, the importance given to any aspect of development during the preschool years depended to a great extent on one's theoretical perspective. Psychoanalytic theory, for example, emphasizes the emergence of independence and psychosexual development, and social learning theory focuses on the development of self-control and self-efficacy. However, the failure of any one theory to adequately explain the complexity of development across areas has led to general acceptance of a transactional and/or ecological perspective that attempts to account for factors within the child, family, and society that influence development either directly or indirectly (Campbell, 1990; Mash & Terdal, 1997). Within this perspective, developmental gains in each area (social, cognitive, motor, language, etc.) are thought to be related to progress in other areas. Further, competencies or problems in

any area of development early in life are seen as setting the stage for later development.

In considering developmental milestones, inter- and intra-individual differences should be kept in mind. Individual differences in the rate of development are nowhere more apparent than during the preschool years. Some children, for example, have extensive language before the age of 2, whereas other, "normal" children do not acquire speech until 3 years of age. An individual child's rate of development in various areas can vary as much as the rate of development between children. Some of these inter- and intra-individual differences are primarily the result of genetic-organic factors, and others seem to be more the result of environmental influences. It is, of course, the unique interaction of these two factors—the child and the environment—that ultimately determines each child's developmental progress. This section briefly touches on some of the important developmental milestones that occur during the preschool years. The reader is referred to Davies (1999) and Lyman and Hembree-Kigin (1994) for more in-depth reviews of preschool development.

Motor Development

In an article on a new synthesis of motor development, Esther Thelen (1995) states that recent work "restores the primacy of perception and action in the evolving mental and social life of the child" (p. 80). She describes how even young infants possess dynamic systems that can integrate information from all their senses. It is through the process of exploration and selection that infants gain the ability to generate behavior that provides a variety of perceptual-motor experiences and to differentially retain those correlated actions. So, repeated cycles of perception and action, which are primary to the developing child, give rise to emergent new forms of behavior that is the link between "the simple activities of the infant and the growing life of the mind" (p. 93). There is strong support for this view, and it changes the long-held views on the unfolding developmental process and especially of the importance of motor behavior in that process. Although further discussion of this view of development is beyond the scope and purpose of this chapter, it would be remiss to not mention this important work. For our purposes, we restrict this section to simply describing motor behaviors that most children accomplish during the preschool years.

By the age of 2 years, children can walk, run, and jump smoothly and their balance is improving. They like to pull and ride toy vehicles and roll, bounce, and catch a ball. By age 3, they can stand on either foot for a brief period of time and are beginning to hop. They can also throw and catch a ball and pedal a tricycle. Four-year-olds like to climb, hop, skip, and dance. They can also play simple ball games and respond to a sequence of motor directions. By age 5, most children are strong and confident in their movements, can move in many ways, quickly following directions, and may be riding a bicycle with training wheels. Motor development is essential for active exploration, learning, and mastery of the environment, and as preschoolers become stronger and more coordinated, they seem to thrive on physical activity. This increased activity often increases parental concerns about overactivity (Campbell, 1990). Activity level for most children, however, peaks at age 3 and then begins to decrease around age 5, when expectations to sit and listen increase (Routh, Schroeder, & O'Tuma, 1974).

Improving eye-hand coordination promotes cutting with scissors, drawing circles and squares, and, by age 5, drawing a recognizable human figure. Between 4 and 5 years, most children are able to dress themselves, including managing buttons, zippers, and Velcro.

Cognitive Development
The area of cognitive development is so complex that only a brief discussion is possible in this chapter. Cognitive development involves qualitative changes in the ability to reason about environmental and social events and is driven by the motivation to explore and experience the environment (Flavell, 1977; Thelen, 1995). Children's cognitive processing skills are ever-changing, as shown by recent work on developmental changes in speed of information processing. The speed at which children are able to process information follows a global developmental trend, with speed increasing with age in relatively simple nonverbal and verbal tasks (Miller & Vernon, 1997).

In contrast to Thelen's (1995) dynamic systems theory described previously, Piaget (Piaget & Inhelder, 1969) proposed that children progress through a universal sequence of stages in understanding the physical world. Piaget described preschool children as preoperational; they are beginning to think representationally or symbolically and to understand cause-and-effect relationships. Preschoolers lack the ability to take another's perspective (described as egocentric), have trouble coordinating information from more than one source, and cannot attend to more than one dimension of a stimulus array at a time (i.e., they classify according to one dimension). Other work, however, suggests that Piaget underestimated the capabilities of preschoolers (Gelman & Baillargeon, 1983). When tasks and materials are familiar and do not require sophisticated language skills, children appear less egocentric and better able to reason.

Recent research indicates that children as young as 3 and 4 years have the ability to understand mental representation as demonstrated in studies of pretense and reality (Golomb & Galasso, 1995). Even though they can be deeply engaged in pretend play and its elaboration, many preschoolers differentiate it from reality and describe it as "thoughts" versus reality. Likewise, preschool children have demonstrated that they have considerable ability in reasoning about permission rules (e.g., you may go outside if you wear a coat). By the ages of 3 and 4, it has been demonstrated that children know when rules have been violated and can give reasons for the violations (Harris & Nunez, 1996). Thus, there is the clear implication that when most children at these ages violate a permission rule, they do it knowingly.

Other theories and research in cognitive development have viewed social influences as having a major impact on cognitive development, with the parent-child interaction seen as the primary arena for the development of cognitive skills (Fagot & Gauvain, 1997; Hart & Risley, 1995, 1999; Vygotsky, 1978). During early childhood, much of children's problem-solving efforts are done in social situations under the guidance and supervision of their parents, who structure and model ways to solve problems (Rogoff, 1990). Through these interactions, the parents provide the child with cognitive opportunities that encourage and support learning and growth. The history of these interactions as well as the characteristics that both the child and parent bring to these interactions have been shown to predict the child's cognitive problem-solving skills over time and the cognitive outcomes, as measured by IQ tests, at age 5 years (Fagot & Gauvain, 1997). These authors found that children whose parents gave limited assistance to their problem-solving tasks were more likely to be rated by teachers at age 5 years as having learning problems.

Other work points to the importance of maternal social support networks for children's cognitive development. Melson, Ladd, and Hsu (1993) found that both the size and quality of the maternal network during preschool years directly predicted the cognitive performance of the child. Larger, more supportive networks have been associated with a less restrictive, less intrusive style of interaction and warmer and more nurturant parenting (Jennings, Stagg, & Conners, 1991).

Children who do not evidence normal cognitive development are commonly identified during the preschool years. Frequently, these children are referred for evaluation because of slow or atypical language development, behavior problems such as noncompliance, short attention span or distractibility, because a preschool teacher or day care worker senses that "something is not quite right," or because parents become concerned that the child will not be ready to start school. The resulting diagnosis is often mental retardation.

At the opposite end of the spectrum from the child with mental retardation, but no less exceptional, is the gifted child. Gifted children are also most often identified during the preschool years because they go beyond developmental expectations. Robinson (1987) suggests that precocious development of language or reading skills is an important marker in the identification of gifted children. Although gifted children have been thought to be at risk for adjustment problems, some work indicates that this is not necessarily the case. Chamrad and Robinson (1986), for example, report that young gifted children often have higher self-esteem and more energy, enthusiasm, and curiosity than average children.

Language Development
The period between 2 and 6 years of age represents a time of enormous growth in children's language abilities, with acquisition of word meanings as the hallmark of the preschool years. Rapin (1996), in a synopsis of language development in the first 6 years of life, states that in the first year, infants go from cooing vowel sounds to producing repetitive consonant/vowel syllables such as "mama" or "baba" to producing meaningful but imperfect words. In the second year, words are initially acquired, one by one, and then vocabulary takes off.

After they acquire a few dozen words, children start to produce two-word utterances. These utterances are the root for grammar, which allows children to understand and produce meaningful sentences. In the third year, vocabulary increases to hundreds of words and syntactic knowledge from the production of two-word utterances to full sentences. From then on, language acquisition involves the comprehension and production of ever more complex sentences such as passive and embedded grammatical constructions and increased vocabulary to thousands of words; by school age, children start to master written language. Rice (1989) states that without explicit teaching, preschoolers acquire as many as 14,000 new word meanings as they encounter them in meaningful situations and conversations, and that this phenomenon is the foundation for later reading skills. It is during the preschool years that children begin to be able to use language to develop cognitive skills, to facilitate their understanding of the world, to aid their remembering, and to organize their thoughts (Rice, 1989).

Hart and Risley's (1995, 1999) two volumes of meticulously collected data from a longitudinal study of the development of language in 42 children demonstrates the profound effect that responsive parenting has on a child's acquisition of language and on intellectual performance. They found that children living in poverty, children born into middle-class families, and children with professional parents all had the same kind of language experience. However, the children born into homes with fewer economic resources had fewer of these experiences. In other words, the amount or frequency of talking the parents engaged in was a crucial factor in the later development of these children. This increased frequency provided greater language diversity through lots of talk, increased proportional amounts of encouragement and discouragement, and provided greater opportunity for symbolic emphasis on names, relations, and recall. Hart and Risley also documented the importance of a parental guidance style that focused on asking rather than demanding and a responsiveness that stressed the importance of the child's behavior during interactions. Thus, children whose parents talked a lot had far more experience with every quality feature of language and interaction. These findings suggest far-reaching recommendations for early intervention programs and the importance of talking by parents and children in children's overall development.

Given the importance of language development in mediating cognitive and social development (e.g., Hart & Risley, 1995, 1999; Simon, Larson, & Lehrer, 1988), it seems evident that delays or disorders of language will impede development in other areas. Any of the major categories of speech and language disorders can be seen in preschool youngsters, and these are also often significantly associated with other disabilities, such as mental retardation, externalizing and internalizing disorders (particularly hyperactivity and attention problems), peer rejection, and learning problems (Benasich, Curtiss, & Tallal, 1993). In fact, it is often because parents are concerned that their preschool child is not developing language as expected that they seek professional help. Table 14.2 outlines the ages and indicators for referral to a communication specialist (Wang & Baron, 1997).

Social Development
In the area of social development, the tasks for the preschooler are to learn social skills, prosocial behaviors, and values and to learn how to play with peers and develop friendships (Davies, 1999). Research in the area of social development has focused more recently on the cognitive and emotional factors that regulate or inhibit prosocial actions, with agreement that children can exhibit prosocial behavior early in life (Hay, 1994). There is research to support a genetic basis for temperamental differences in sociability and extroversion (Plomin, 1989), and there is also research to support the importance of a child's experiences in early caregiving relationships (M. Greenberg et al., 1990; Hartup, 1989; Rubin & Stewart, 1996) as well as later peer relationships (Bukowski, Newcomb, & Hartup, 1996) in developing social competence.

Reasoning about the physical world is thought to provide the basis for reasoning about the social world. Thus, the constraints in preschoolers' understanding of the characteristics of the environment also apply to their understanding of social situations and relationships (Crick & Dodge, 1994). Social competence is dependent, for example, on the development of specific cognitive skills such as representational or symbolic thinking and social perspective taking (Howes, 1987). It is also dependent on past experience with the family and parents, who serve as models for children's developing

Table 14.2 Indications for speech-language evaluation.

Age at Which Referral Is Indicated	*Indication for Referral*
Birth–6 months	No response to environmental sounds and voices.
3–4 months	No cooing or comfort sounds, crying only.
1 year	No response to the sound of people talking.
	No babbling or stopped babbling.
2 years	No comprehension when spoken to.
	Fewer than 10–20 words.
2½ years	No phrases of two or more words.
	Very limited vocabulary.
	Not beginning to answer simple questions.
	Speech entirely unintelligible.
3 years	No short sentences.
	Not engaging in simple conversation.
	Speech largely unintelligible.
4 years	Difficulty learning new concepts.
	Difficulty explaining events.
	No complete sentences.
	Difficulty following two-step directions.
	Still echoing speech.
	Speech unclear.

Source: P.P. Wang & M.A. Baron (1997). Language: A code for communication. In M.L. Batshaw (Ed.), *Children with disabilities* (4th ed., p. 286). Baltimore: Brooks.

relationships with others (Parke & Ladd, 1992). For example, healthy infant-parent attachment is important to later development of children's "working models" of themselves and others (Greenberg et al., 1990). Also, parents who provide warmth, nurturance, and clear limits encourage the development of similar prosocial behaviors and values (Davies, 1999). Peer relationships also play a critical role during the preschool years in fostering the development of more complex and effective social behavior (Bierman & Welsh, 1997).

Peer relationships begin to develop around age 2 as solitary play decreases and parallel play increases. Gradually, play becomes more cooperative and reciprocal between 3 and 5 years, and by age 5 or 6, most children enjoy simple, competitive, rule-governed play activities with other children. Friendships that involve reciprocity, liking, affection, and fun also begin to develop during the preschool years (Bukowski et al., 1996). Having friends is clearly a "developmental advantage" (Hartup, 1989), as social rejection in childhood is consistently found to be related to later adjustment problems (Boivin, Hymel, & Bukowski, 1995; Coie, 1990).

Personality and Emotional Development
Temperament, or the behavioral style of a child's interaction with the environment, is an important aspect of early personality development. The work of Thomas and Chess (1977) demonstrated individual differences in temperament as early as the first few weeks of life, and other research in behavioral genetics suggests that many aspects of personality may be inborn (H. Goldsmith, Buss, & Lemery, 1997). Temperamental characteristics of infants and preschoolers have been related to the development of behavior problems, adjustment to preschool and kindergarten, peer relationships, IQ scores, and academic achievement (Earls & Jung, 1987; Keogh & Burstein, 1988; Palisin, 1986; Schmitz & Fulker, 1994; Skarpness & Carson, 1987). Thomas, Chess, and Birch (1968) derived a cluster of traits (irregularity of biological functions, withdrawal from novel stimuli, slow to adapt, intense responses, and predominantly negative in mood), called "difficult temperament," that has been shown to be clinically significant. The "difficult" child is harder to parent and at higher risk for developing behavior problems (J. Goldsmith et al., 1987). In a sample of 350 preschool children, McDevitt and Carey (1978) found almost 19% to be difficult. Not all difficult children develop adjustment problems, however, and Thomas et al. also introduced the idea of "goodness-of-fit" to account for this phenomenon. Goodness-of-fit describes the interrelationship between the child's characteristics and environmental demands and expectations. A "good fit" facilitates optimal development; a "poor fit" interferes with it. Thus, a difficult infant born to a highly stressed, unresponsive mother would be considered at higher risk than a difficult infant born to a responsive, sensitive, calm mother (Campbell, 1990; Davies, 1999).

Another important aspect of personality development during the preschool years is the development of the self-system, which includes self-concept, self-control, and self-esteem (Harter, 1983). Although the self-system is only just beginning to emerge during the preschool years, it is central to later social-emotional adjustment (Achenbach & Edelbrock, 1978; Pope, McHale, & Craighead, 1988). For preschoolers, identifying with their parents is a primary means of identifying themselves (Davies, 1999; M. Greenberg et al., 1990). Consistent with their cognitive developmental level, the self-concept of preschool children consists primarily of concrete attributes such as physical characteristics and possessions. Preschoolers also tend to think of themselves in either/or terms, that is, as nice or mean, good or bad (Pope et al., 1988). Increasingly with age, self-concept is derived from comparisons with peers. Not surprisingly, preschoolers are very much aware of how other children behave and how they are treated.

In large part, how preschool children perceive of and evaluate themselves (self-esteem) is the result of the perceptions and behavior of significant adults. Clearly, a sense of mastery over environmental events also contributes to self-esteem, but during the preschool years, this too is mediated by significant adults (Davies, 1999). As Campbell (1990) states, adults can provide or thwart opportunities for children to explore the environment and experience mastery, and they can reward, punish, or ignore successful experiences, thus influencing the child's perceptions of self.

The expression of emotion during the preschool years is usually uninhibited because the child is in the process of learning how to express emotions in a socially acceptable way. Anger is usually expressed physically in response to an immediate stimulus by biting, scratching, or kicking, but is typically short-lived (Davies, 1999). Temper outbursts occur most often around 2 to 3 years of age and then gradually diminish during the later preschool years (Mesibov et al., 1977). Children's ability to label emotions, to talk about emotions, and to use language about emotions to guide their own behavior increases during the preschool years (Davies, 1999; Kopp, 1989). This ability, however, is greatly influenced by family practices, which can accelerate or impede the child's appreciation of the privacy of emotion (Harris, 1994). In a review of the literature on children's understanding of the subjectivity of emotions, Harris found that individual differences were influenced by the emotional atmosphere of the home, the amount of discussion about emotions, the availability of a sibling close in age, and the involvement in pretend play.

This ability to regulate emotions or self-control is related both directly and indirectly to self-esteem (Davies, 1999; Pope et al., 1988). Children who have good self-control feel better about themselves and also receive more positive feedback from adults. Further, the authoritative parenting style that has been shown to be related to the development of self-control in children also fosters self-esteem.

A number of studies have focused on the attachment of preschoolers to a soft object or "transitional object" and the importance of this behavior to the development of separation-individuation and emotional regulation (S. Brody, 1980; Kopp, 1989). Recent work demonstrates that a secure, healthy mother-infant relationship is an important condition that leads to the later attachment to a soft object versus some other object such as a pacifier (Lehman, Denham, Moser, & Reeves, 1992). Kopp proposes that the use of transitional objects can function as a mechanism for young children to gain control over stress and emotional arousal, with the soft object providing the soothing and comfort previously given by the mother. Passman (1987) suggests that transitional objects serve to reduce anxiety or arousal for the child because they are associated with positive consequences. Thus, it is generally accepted that the use of transitional soft objects has positive value in the child's move to greater independence and is not associated with maladjustment or insecurity.

ASSESSMENT PROCESS

The task of the child clinician is to identify and treat those children who suffer from emotional and/or behavioral problems that significantly interfere with their development or functioning and are likely to persist. The assessment process can help the clinician determine which problems are clinically significant and which are only annoying but transient behaviors. Campbell (1990) suggests five criteria to help identify those children who are exhibiting potentially significant difficulties or disorders: (1) the presence of a pattern or constellation of problem behaviors (e.g., aggression, hyperactivity, attention deficit, and noncompliance, or withdrawal, anxiety, and sadness); (2) a pattern of problem behavior that persists beyond a transient adjustment to stress or change, such as entry into school or the hospitalization of a parent; (3) a

cluster of symptoms that occur across settings and people; (4) behaviors that are relatively severe; and (5) behaviors that interfere with the child's ability to handle developmental transitions or impair functioning.

In addition to determining if particular behaviors are clinically significant, the assessment process must also determine factors contributing to the behavior problems and target areas for intervention. Therefore, the assessment of preschoolers must take into account the developmental level of the child and potential biological influences, as well as broader ecological (familial, social, cultural) factors that interact with children's characteristics. In assessing problems of the preschool child, the following general areas should be covered:

1. The presenting problem should be described in detail, including an objective description of the type of behavior; the severity, frequency, and situation specificity of the behavior (i.e., does it occur in only one setting or across settings); the persistence of the behavior; changes from previous behavior; and if the behavior is isolated or part of a cluster of behaviors.
2. The developmental status of a child's physical, cognitive, emotional, and social behavior should be determined. Is the child functioning at the expected level in each area?
3. Familial factors should be reviewed, including a history of medical, learning/intellectual problems or psychopathology, parental attitudes and expectations for child development, ethnic and cultural issues, marital adjustment, parenting style, and social support system.
4. Environmental factors such as socioeconomic level, sociocultural setting, and life circumstances should be reviewed.
5. The consequences of the presenting problem behavior for the child, his or her family, and their community should be determined.

Methods to assess these variables are necessarily multimodal and may include (1) interviews with parents and/or other significant adults in the child's life; (2) parent questionnaires; (3) direct observation of the child in the clinic, home, day care, or any other setting in which the child spends time; (4) observation and objective measurement of parent-child interaction in free play and structured settings; (5) standardized developmental tests and rating scales; and (6) referral to an allied health professional for further assessment of a specific area, such as language or motor development.

Gathering general background information and ratings on standardized scales from the parents before interviewing them can be very helpful in planning the assessment process. This information allows the clinician to be more specific in the interview. It also alerts the clinician to potential problems in the parent-child relationship and the possible need for additional assessment methods such as a home visit, observation of the child with the teacher or other caregiver, use of standardized developmental instruments, or further assessment of parental characteristics. Samples of general parent questionnaires that gather demographic, developmental, medical, and behavioral information and are useful for the preschool child can be found in Culbertson and Willis (1993) and Schroeder and Gordon (1991). Three age-appropriate, standardized, and reliable parent rating scales are recommended for use with preschool children. The Child Behavior Checklist (CBCL; Achenbach, 1991, 1992) provides multiple behavior-problem scales derived separately for boys and girls in different age groups, starting with 2-year-olds. The Eyberg Child Behavior Inventory (ECBI; Eyberg, 1999) is a 36-item behavioral inventory of conduct problems for children age 2 to 16 years. The Parenting Stress Index (PSI; Abidin, 1995) contains 126 items divided into two major domains that focus on child and parent characteristics; the items reflect stress in the parent-child relationship. When completed by both parents, the CBCL and the ECBI give a good picture of the similarities and differences in parents' perceptions of their child's adjustment, how this perception relates to that of parents of similar-age children, and if the behavior is in a clinically significant range. The PSI allows a broader look at the context of the parent-child relationship and the potential stresses on that relationship.

Interviewing parents is an essential part of the assessment process; for a guide, the reader is referred to Schroeder and Gordon (1998). For preschool children, an unstructured interview is recommended as this allows the clinician more freedom to explore the nature and context of a particular problem as well as the opportunity to investigate contributing factors, such as parental expectations and environmental conditions. In addition to the previously mentioned areas to be covered, the parent interview should include (1) a clarification of the referral question (so there is a mutual understanding of the concerns to be addressed); (2) a determination of the social context of the problem (e.g., who is concerned and why; ways they have tried to handle the problem; their expectations, hopes, and fears in seeking help); and (3) a determination of areas for intervention or plans for further evaluation.

Direct observations of the child in his or her environment (home and/or preschool or day care) and observation of parent-child interaction in both a structured and unstructured play setting are especially important for preschool children. These observations can provide information on possible etiologies and/or factors in the environment that maintain problems (Crowell, Feldman, & Ginsberg, 1988; Sattler, 1988). Observation can, thus, give a wealth of information about intervention strategies. The assessment of the preschool child in a free play situation can give information about the child's intellectual, emotional, social, and language development, and fantasy play may reflect current concerns and anxieties. It also allows observation of how a child uses his or her time and organizes play activities. Eyberg and colleagues have developed a coding system for parent-child interactions that is very helpful in both the assessment and treatment process (Eyberg, Bessmer, Newcomb, Edwards, & Robinson, 1994).

Standardized assessment of the preschool child is often necessary when there is a question of developmental problems. Doing this work involves special training not only in the administration and interpretation of the instruments but also in learning to interact with the child so as to maximize his or her performance. The reader is referred to Culbertson and Willis (1993) and Nuttall, Romero, and Kalesnik (1999) for information on the specific assessment instruments and techniques available for assessing preschool children.

In summary, assessment of problems during the preschool years is a complex task that requires a knowledge base cutting across a number of areas and disciplines. Questions should include: Is it a developmental problem? Is the expected behavior absent or occurring at a rate that is too high or too low? Are parental expectations, attitudes, or beliefs appropriate for the social situation, the age, and the developmental level of the child? Are parental characteristics and/or marital discord contributing to the problem or to the perception of the behavior? Are child-rearing styles appropriate for the child in question? Are environmental conditions contributing to the behavior problem or to the perceptions of the behavior? What are the setting conditions for the behavior? Will the behavior cause the child, parents, or others to suffer now or in the future? Should a referral to an allied health professional be made to determine a possible physical or organic problem? Data gathered in the assessment process should answer these questions, giving information on the nature of the behavior problem, the target of intervention, and the selection of appropriate intervention strategies.

COMMON BEHAVIOR PROBLEMS

During the course of the preschool years, children are sure to exhibit behavior problems at one time or another. Although it is true that most of these problems are transitory and may require little or no intervention, recent research has shown clearly that many can set the stage for later, more serious difficulties. As a result, treatment approaches to problems in the preschool years often emphasize prevention of later problems. In our experience, the concerns of parents of preschool children are most often about sleep, toileting, eating, fears, noncompliance and aggression, habits, and sibling rivalry. Child maltreatment, including neglect and physical, sexual, and psychological abuse, is also a major problem during the preschool years. Given that the National Center on Child Abuse and Neglect (NCCAN, 1996) in a review of 41 states found that nearly 80% of the perpetrators of child maltreatment were parents (as cited in Reppucci, Britner, & Woolard, 1997), the consequences of maltreatment for preschool children can be particularly devastating to their cognitive, social-emotional, and language development. The reader is referred to the chapter on maltreatment in this volume for more information on this important social problem. This section briefly reviews some of the common problems as they manifest during the preschool years. Most, if not all, of the problem behaviors covered in this chapter are covered in depth in other chapters in this volume.

SLEEP PROBLEMS

The sleeping patterns of children change with age, and consequently, the types of sleep problems seen in children vary along developmental lines. During the preschool years, sleep problems are often initiated by a transient difficulty such as an ear infection or other illness, traveling, or overnight visitors and then are maintained or exacerbated by parental management to the extent that professional consultation and/or intervention may be required.

It is estimated that as many as 25% of preschoolers evidence significant sleep disturbances of one type or another (Mindell, 1993; Pollock, 1994). The significance of these problems is illustrated by recent research that indicates that early sleep disturbance can be associated with a variety of other difficulties, including behavior management problems, parental depression, attention-deficit disorder, and difficult temperament (Lyman & Hembree-Kigin, 1994; Stores, 1996). Moreover, in the absence of intervention, the continuity between early and later sleep problems has been documented (Butler & Golding, 1986; Pollock, 1994). Although treatment will vary depending on the specific problem, assessment of sleep problems typically involves having parents complete a sleep diary/log for one to two weeks (see Schroeder & Gordon, 1991, for an example). This information should include 24 hours of data on eating and sleeping schedules and routines, time and characteristics of the sleep disturbance, and parents' responses to the child's behavior. The importance of prevention through establishment of consistent bedtime routines is emphasized in the literature (Lyman & Hembree-Kigin, 1994; Stores, 1996), and efforts to prevent sleep problems through parent training during early infancy have been effective (Wolfson, Lacks, & Futterman, 1992). Sleep problems during the preschool years most often include fear of the dark and/or of sleeping alone (discussed in the section on fears), nightmares, and sleep terrors and other confusional arousals such as sleep walking, sleep apnea, refusal to go to bed, and night waking.

Nightmares

Children's nightmares usually begin to occur between the ages of 3 and 6 years. In contrast to sleep terrors, nightmares are associated with REM sleep (irregular pulse and respiratory rate, rapid eye movements, and waking/drowsy sleep pattern) and typically happen during the last third of the sleep cycle, when REM sleep is predominant (Anders & Eiben, 1997). Nightmares are vivid, elaborate, and usually clearly remembered. Chronic nightmares are generally thought to result from emotional stress, either ongoing, such as marital conflict, birth of a sibling, or toilet training, or a specific traumatic event, such as an accident or injury (Lyman & Hembree-Kigin, 1994; Stores, 1996). Treatment of nightmares is typically focused on physical comfort and reassurance of the child in the child's own room/bed, some explanation of the nature of dreams geared to the child's level of understanding, and reduction of stresses in the child's life (Ferber, 1985; Lyman & Hembree-Kigin, 1994). Severe cases may require individual and/or family psychotherapy. Behavior therapy (including contingency management, relaxation therapy, and systematic desensitization) and bibliotherapy (reading stories about children who have nightmares) can also be useful in dealing with children's nightmares (Barclay & Whittington, 1992; Greening & Dollinger, 1989).

Sleep Terrors and Confusional Arousals
Sleep terrors and other confusional arousals such as sleep walking occur during the first one to three hours of sleep during transitions from deep sleep or NREM to REM sleep (Anders & Eiben, 1997). They are thought to be manifestations of central nervous system arousal and are more common in boys than girls. Sleep terrors occur in about 3% of children age 18 months to 6 years and only rarely in older children (Anders & Eiben, 1997). In sleep terrors, the child sits up in bed or cowers in a corner, has a glassy stare, screams or cries inconsolably, and cannot be awakened. Other signs of autonomic arousal, such as tachycardia, rapid breathing, and sweating, are often present (Lyman & Hembree-Kigin, 1994). In contrast to nightmares, the child typically has no memory of the event the next morning.

Confusional arousals are thought to be more common than sleep terrors, with almost all preschool children experiencing a mild form every now and then (Ferber, 1989). Confusional arousals typically begin with some movement and crying out, but instead of looking terrified as in sleep terrors, the child appears confused and agitated. Sleep

walking is a form of confusional arousal wherein the child wanders around the house, may attempt to leave the house, and may engage in unusual behavior such as urinating in an inappropriate place. Similar to sleep terrors, the child who is experiencing confusional arousal cannot be awakened and does not remember the episode.

Sleep terrors and confusional arousals are not associated with emotional or behavioral disturbance and typically disappear without intervention (Ferber, 1985). Thus, treatment is usually a brief parent consultation in which parents are reassured and given information about sleep and development. Safety precautions may be recommended in cases of sleep walking. In severe cases, systematic waking 15 to 30 minutes before the typical time of sleep walking or sleep terrors for up to one month has been shown to be effective in reducing the incidence of this problem (Frank, Spirito, Stark, & Owens-Stively, 1997; Lask, 1988).

Resistance to Sleeping and Night Waking
Bedtime struggles and waking during the night are very common among preschool children, with estimates of prevalence ranging from 25% to 50% of 1- to 3-year-olds (Anders & Eiben, 1997; Johnson, 1991; Pollock, 1994). Bedtime rituals and routines that promote relaxation and drowsiness are very important at this age and, when used consistently, can often prevent bedtime problems from developing (Stores, 1996). When the child resists sleep despite these routines, firmness and consistency in not responding to cries is usually all that is needed. Older preschoolers respond well to the addition of a story to let the child know what is expected and what the parent is going to do (ignore), plus a sticker in the morning for good nighttime behavior (Schroeder & Gordon, 1991). Although this extinction approach can be difficult for parents, it is very effective in eliminating bedtime struggles and night wakings. Further, there is no evidence that it results in detrimental effects on the child's emotional well-being (France, 1992). Ferber (1985) and Lawton, France, and Blampied (1991) describe more gradual approaches to extinction.

Sleep Apnea
Sleep apnea is the one sleep disorder seen in preschool children that results from physical abnormality: a blockage of the airways that prevents

passage of oxygen (Hansen & Vandenberg, 1997). Apnea episodes can occur once or twice or hundreds of times a night and last from 10 seconds to 2 minutes. Obviously, frequent or lengthy episodes can have serious consequences for the young child. Specifically, daytime difficulties that interfere with the child's cognitive, social, and emotional functioning, including irritability especially upon awakening, difficult behavior, impaired attention, memory, and visual-motor performance, and poor progress in school have been documented (Stores, 1996).

The primary symptom of sleep apnea is snoring. However, up to 10% of children snore, yet only 1% to 2% actually have sleep apnea. Other symptoms include mouth breathing, profuse sweating, and unusual sleeping positions, especially with the neck extended (Stores, 1996). Evaluation of sleep apnea is recommended for children who are experiencing learning and/or behavioral problems, especially those that are similar to attention-deficit disorder (Hansen & Vandenberg, 1997). Assessment may involve physical examination with special attention to tonsils and adenoids as well as a sleep history. Typical treatment is removal of tonsils and adenoids.

EATING PROBLEMS

Feeding difficulties are among the most common concerns of parents of preschool children, with estimates of prevalence ranging from 24% to 45% of 2- to 4-year-olds (Beautrois, Fergusson, & Shannon, 1982; Bentovim, 1970). Specific problems most common to this age group include food refusal, obesity, failure to thrive, and pica.

Food Refusal
Of all the feeding problems seen in preschool children, food refusal is the most common. It can range from simple picky eating to total food refusal resulting in life-threatening malnutrition. Food refusal can be a consequence of medical procedures that interfere with normal eating development, but more typically, parent-child interaction around mealtimes is implicated (Sanders, Patel, LeGrice, & Shepherd, 1993). Assessment of food refusal problems requires information about the interplay of environmental, physical, and behavioral factors. Observation of parent-child interaction during mealtimes is considered critical (Lyman &

Hembree-Kigin, 1994). Even severe cases of food refusal can be successfully treated with behavioral methods, including differential attention to appropriate behavior, shaping, reinforcement contingent on desired behavior, and gradual exposure/desensitization (Lyman & Hembree-Kigin, 1994).

Obesity
It is estimated that 5% to 10% of preschoolers are obese, and these rates appear to be increasing despite the well-known health risks (Maloney & Klykylo, 1983). Obesity in the preschool years is highly associated with obesity in adulthood. Furthermore, there is a strong correlation between parent and child obesity that suggests a genetic link. Research shows, however, that this association is primarily due to family eating and activity patterns (Lyman & Hembree-Kigin, 1994). Most cases of obesity occur in the absence of family dysfunction or psychopathology, although if the condition persists into later childhood and adolescence, children can develop significant problems with self-esteem and peer relations. Behavioral methods have been most successful in treating obesity, and parent involvement is necessary in treating preschoolers. These methods include self-monitoring, stimulus control, reinforcement procedures (including response cost and contingency contracting), and cognitive restructuring (Lyman & Hembree-Kigin, 1994). Also important are exercise programs and nutritional information.

Failure to Thrive
Failure to thrive is defined as failure to gain weight or weight loss with adequate nutrition. The etiology of failure to thrive is not entirely clear, although parental and family factors such as low SES, lack of nutritional knowledge, improper feeding, alcoholism, and stress have been implicated. Others suggest that characteristics of the infant such as prematurity, difficult temperament, and cognitive deficits play a role. Lyman and Hembree-Kigin (1994) conclude, "It appears that both organismic and environmental variables are significant in the interaction that produces the failure-to-thrive syndrome" (p. 70). Treatment most frequently involves hospitalization; altering parent-child interactions, particularly around feeding; role-modeling appropriate feeding techniques; nutritional education; and environmental intervention to reduce levels of stress (Lyman & Hembree-Kigin, 1994).

Pica

Although most young children mouth objects during the early years of life, some persist in this behavior beyond the age of 18 months and actually eat inedible substances, resulting in a diagnosis of pica (Lyman & Hembree-Kigin, 1994). Pica is more common among children from lower socioeconomic backgrounds and those with mental retardation and tends to disappear by age 4 or 5 in those with normal intelligence. Pica is a serious disorder because of its association with accidental poisoning, especially lead poisoning, which can lead to neurological damage and cognitive deficits. Treatment of pica typically involves parent education and behavioral methods such as overcorrection (brushing with mouthwash) and differential reinforcement of other, more appropriate behaviors (Lyman & Hembree-Kigin, 1994).

FEARS

During the preschool years, fears are an almost inevitable occurrence, although some children may be predisposed to be more fearful than others as a result of temperamental characteristics or family history of anxiety (Stevenson-Hinde & Shouldice, 1995). In a parent survey done through a pediatrician's office, parents perceived fears as a "problem" most often in their 2-year-olds and less often in their 3- to 5-year-old children (Schroeder & Wool, 1979). The types of stimuli evoking fear reactions in children is clearly linked to the development of cognitive skills such as the ability to differentiate reality from fantasy. Two-year-olds, for example, tend to be afraid of concrete objects (animals, trains) or loud noises (thunder, vacuum cleaners), whereas 3- to 5-year-olds increasingly develop more abstract fears of imaginary creatures, being alone in the dark, and bad dreams (Marks, 1987).

Most childhood fears are transitory (Marks, 1987), and it typically is not possible to determine the origins of a child's specific fear. It is, however, very easy for parents to inadvertently reinforce fearful behavior in the attempt to comfort and support the child. If fears persist, generalize, or intensify to the extent that they interfere with the child's functioning and/or development, professional intervention may be indicated. Among other types of general information, assessment of preschool fears should include a family history of anxiety and

observations (if possible) or descriptions of the parents' response to the child's behavior.

Behavioral techniques are most effective in treating intense fear in preschool children. The literature suggests that modeling (with models that closely match the child's age, gender, and fear level) and in vivo desensitization are the most effective methods. Parents can easily be taught to conduct desensitization programs in the home (Klesges, Malott, & Ugland, 1984; Matson, 1983), although they may need support and encouragement to make their child confront the feared stimulus directly—a critical and necessary component of successful treatment. Other useful treatment methods include contingency management with rewards for interacting with the feared stimulus and symbolic modeling through stories or doll play of how to cope with fears.

Separation Anxiety

Separation anxiety is typical during the course of normal development at around 12 to 20 months of age and may reappear between 2 and 4 years as children go off to preschool or day care. This type of separation anxiety usually resolves successfully among securely attached children who have had the opportunity to experience repeated parental separation and reunion and have learned to cope with parental absence. Campbell (1990) notes that it is difficult to distinguish "excessive" separation anxiety from that which is adaptive in preschoolers. She states that preschool children may be most vulnerable to separation anxiety during those times when it is normative developmentally and an "attachment altering event" (e.g., death, divorce, move) occurs.

Assessment of separation anxiety should focus on early attachment history, patterns of caregiving behavior (specifically, inconsistent or unresponsive caregiving), and observation of parent-child interaction including reactions to separation (Lyman & Hembree-Kigin, 1994). Treatment typically will involve behavioral techniques such as gradual exposure to separation while engaged in an anxiety-reducing behavior (eating ice cream, watching cartoons, etc.) and reinforcement of good separation behavior (Lyman & Hembree-Kigin, 1994). Parent counseling and parent-child interaction training may also be included if the problem is related to attachment issues. Medication for separation anxiety in preschoolers is controversial because of potential serious side effects and lack of adequate research (Last & Francis, 1988).

Preschool Refusal

Much has been written about school refusal or school phobia among older children, but there is little regarding preschoolers who refuse to go to preschool or day care. There is general agreement that preschool refusal is related to either separation anxiety, specific fears related to the preschool or day-care center, or part of a generalized pattern of conduct problems (Lyman & Hembree-Kigin, 1994). Children whose refusal to attend preschool is related to separation anxiety will typically have difficulty separating from parents in other contexts, whereas those who have a specific fear related to some aspect of the preschool environment will not. Children who resist going to preschool as part of a general pattern of negative behavior usually settle down and do well once the parent has left. Treatment of preschool refusal will obviously depend on which type the child manifests and may involve procedures described for specific fears and/or separation anxiety. If the fear is specific to the preschool or day care situation, the parent should investigate for possible problems in the setting. Children who have conduct-related problems can benefit from parent-training interventions.

NEGATIVE BEHAVIOR

One of the most frequent complaints from parents of preschool children is that of negative behavior or conduct problems. Negative behavior consists of a variety of aversive behaviors, including noncompliance, verbal and physical aggression, whining, temper tantrums, talking back, taunting and teasing, cursing, overactivity, destructive behavior, and deliberate cruelty. Although all preschool children engage in some of these negative behaviors at one time or another, most develop without difficulty. Some children, however, with severe conduct problems during the preschool years evidence behavior disorders, substance abuse, and legal problems later in childhood and adolescence (Campbell & Ewing, 1990; Pierce et al., 1999). Determining which children will continue to evidence conduct problems requires an understanding of the transactional nature of development and the many risk and protective factors that are both constitutional and environmental (Eyberg, Schuhmann, & Rey, 1998). Children who grow up in more adverse family circumstances, have more negative mother-child relationships, and demonstrate clusters of negative behaviors across multiple settings are particularly at risk for continuing conduct problems.

Developmentally, negative behavior probably first appears as characteristics of difficult temperament (difficult to soothe, irritable, irregular, intense reactivity). In contrast, parents' earliest concerns about negative behavior revolve around overactivity, which is seen by 1 to 2 years (Loeber, Green, Lahey, Christ, & Frick, 1992). Stubbornness and noncompliance increase from age 2 and peak at about 3 years. This trend reflects the development of autonomy and independence and pressures of socialization. As language sophistication and social and emotional maturity develop, direct defiance ("No!") decreases and negotiation strategies increase (Kinzynski, Kochanska, Radke-Yarrow, & Girnius-Brown, 1987). Parent and sibling responses to and modeling of negative behavior give the child clear feedback about the efficacy of these behaviors, especially aggression, and serve to maintain or exacerbate the problem (Stormont-Spurgin & Zentall, 1995).

Although preschool children are still strongly influenced by parenting style and environmental conditions, their peers also increasingly influence them. Recent research has found that preschool children are selective in their affiliation with peers who have a behavioral style and social competence level similar to themselves and that child behavior is subsequently shaped within those close affiliative relationships (Farver, 1996; Snyder, Horsch, & Childs, 1997). Snyder et al. found that aggressive preschool children appear to have more difficulty establishing affiliations, and they tend to select other aggressive children as strong peer affiliates. Further, the interactions of these aggressive children are characterized by frequent and lengthy conflict and by higher levels of escalation in aggressive behavior. Even relatively nonaggressive children became more aggressive as the amount of time they spent with aggressive peers increased. Treatment for aggression should thus go beyond the individual child and focus on the larger peer group (Farver, 1996). The teacher, for example, could change the composition of the children's "cliques" for particular activities to create opportunities for new friendships, peer alliances, and networks. The use of cooperative versus competitive games in the classroom has also been shown to increase cooperative behaviors and decrease aggressive behaviors (Bay-Hinitz, Peterson, & Quilitch, 1994). Training children through videotapes and practice in dealing with interpersonal problems has also been found successful in reducing aggression and, when combined with parent training, gives even more significant improvements in child behavior at one-year follow-up (Webster-Stratton & Hammond, 1997).

Parent management training and parent-child interaction training programs are the most frequent and successful treatments for preschool children with negative behavior problems (Brestan & Eyberg, 1998; Foote, Schuhmann, Jones, & Eyberg, 1998). Parent management training focuses on teaching parents basic principles of learning so that they can modify their child's behavior by targeting specific behaviors for reinforcement or punishment. In contrast, parent-child interaction training focuses on the relationship between parent and child using a two-step program that teaches parents positive interaction skills and use of time-out for inappropriate behavior. Some studies (Patterson & Fleischmann, 1979; Wahler, 1990) have found a lack of long-term effectiveness of both types of parent training for some families, particularly low-income, socially isolated, multiproblem families. In a recent review, however, Eyberg, Edwards, Boggs, and Foote (1998) provide evidence for the efficacy of various methods designed to ensure the long-term effectiveness of treatment, especially for these difficult families.

Habits

Children display a number of "habits" throughout the preschool years. Most of these habits, however, seem to appear in the normal sequence of development and only become problems when (1) the behavior continues longer than is typical (into school age, for example); (2) the behavior becomes severe or chronic enough to cause physical damage; and/or (3) the behavior is engaged in so frequently that it interferes with ongoing physical, social, and/or cognitive development.

Nervous Habits
The prevalence estimates of "nervous habits" such as thumb sucking, nail biting, chewing on objects, hair twirling, and picking at lips, sores, and

elsewhere vary depending on the sample and criteria used, but they are frequently seen in typically developing preschoolers. Thumb sucking is reported in approximately 21% to 31% of preschoolers (Foster, 1998; Troster, 1994; Werry, Carlielle, & Fitzpatrick, 1983); nail biting in 12% to 23%; and hair twisting in 3% to 16% of preschoolers (Foster, 1998; Troster, 1994). Foster found that parents as compared to teachers reported almost double the number of these behaviors in a nonclinical sample of 100 preschoolers, with the most frequent behaviors being thumb sucking and nail biting. In addition, the nervous habits were expressed 69% of the time when the child was in a negative mood (e.g., nervous, upset, angry, etc.), were never reported when the child was in a positive mood, and occurred almost exclusively in structured situations. It would thus seem important for parents and teachers to consider the circumstances and functions of the behaviors before trying to stop the child from engaging in them, especially because these behaviors are reported to significantly decrease in age without intervention (Foster, 1998; Klackenberg, 1949). Although parents may be concerned about malocclusion, Popovich and Thompson (1973) found that the incidence of malocclusion did not increase if thumb sucking was stopped by age 6.

The systematic use of a bad-tasting substance placed on the thumb or fingers along with positive reinforcement for not sucking (Friman & Leibowitz, 1990) has been found to be a very effective intervention strategy. Friman (1988) also eliminated thumb-sucking in a 5-year-old girl by preventing a covarying response (holding a favorite doll).

Body Rocking and Head Banging
Body rocking and head banging are common in children under 3 years and decrease with age but are quite likely to be distressing to parents. Body rocking was found to occur in 4% to 19% of young children (Foster, 1998; Troster, 1994) Head banging occurs three times more often in boys, peaking at age 12 to 17 months (Sallustro & Atwell, 1978; Werry et al., 1983), and rarely results in serious injury, although parents are cautioned to pad and anchor the crib (Yancy, 1981). Different hypotheses have been posited regarding the function of these behaviors, including extra stimulation of the vestibular system, anxiety, and boredom (Sallustro & Atwell, 1978; Thelen, 1981; Troster, 1994; Werry et al., 1983), with Foster finding negative mood state

and structured activities significantly related to the behavior. As with nervous habits, it is important to try to determine the function of the behavior before planning an intervention program.

Padding the child's crib, tightening the screws to eliminate squeaking, and placing a soft rug under the crib may sufficiently reduce noise and movement to cause the child to "lose interest" in rocking, at least in the crib. More direct approaches to body rocking, if its severity has been determined to be a significant problem for the child and/or parents, include reassurance, consultation with parents, alternative activities, positive attention (at times other than when rocking or banging) to provide extra stimulation/enrichment (N. Greenberg, 1964), and overcorrection (Strauss, Rubinoff, & Atkeson, 1983).

Rituals, Sameness, and Perfectionism
Young children engage in a significant number of rituals and compulsive-like behaviors, such as insisting on the "exact" same bedtime routine, wanting the same story read over and over, insisting that food be presented in the same way, or wearing only certain clothes, all of which appear to be a part of their normal behavioral repertoire. Evans et al. (1997), using a parent-report questionnaire with 1,488 parents of 8-month to 6-year-old children, found a developmental trend of over 75% of the 2- to 4-year-old children engaging in these behaviors. Repetitive, compulsive-like behaviors usually begin around 18 to 21 months, and the more perfectionistic behaviors around 24 months. Prevalence studies done in childhood and adolescence with estimates of 1% to 3% (Flament, Whitaker, Rapoport, Davies, & Zaremba Berg, 1988; Rutter, Tizard, & Whitmore, 1970) indicate that these behaviors significantly decrease after the preschool years; thus, it appears that they serve some adaptive purpose for the preschooler. Kopp (1989), for example, states that they serve a child's emotional and social needs to gain a sense of self-control and to regulate emotional states. Evans et al. suggest that they might be similar to repetitive, fixed-action behaviors found in other species and, therefore, have biological or biochemical origins.

Although these behaviors may be annoying to parents, it appears that the best approach is to make reasonable accommodations to the child's needs, as the behaviors will likely decrease with time. However, given that these behaviors are very similar to those seen in obsessive-compulsive disorders, if

they persist in an overly rigid manner into the school-age years, an assessment of the child may be appropriate.

Sibling Rivalry

Sibling rivalry appears to be a near-universal phenomenon that is more apparent during the preschool years than at almost any other time. Researchers (G. Brody, Stoneman, & Burke, 1987; Kowal & Kramer, 1997; Stocker, Dunn, & Plomin, 1989) have found that child temperament, maternal behavior, and age of siblings (because of rapid changes in cognitive and social development) all have some influence on sibling relationships. A number of studies have demonstrated a link between the presence of parental differential treatment (PDT) and the quality of sibling relationships. Stocker et al., for example, have found that PDT is related to competition and controlling behaviors between siblings. Kowal and Kramer, however, found that PDT does not have to adversely affect sibling relationships if the children are able to interpret the differential treatment as justified (e.g., that a sibling needs more attention or that age differences require different treatment). In fact, 75% of the children who acknowledged that differential treatment was occurring in their home did not find this to be "unfair." This points to the importance of birth order and developmental level for understanding children's perspectives on complex family relationships. Older children were better able to understand their parents' objectives and intentions in treating them differently from their siblings, which, in turn, was related to the amount of warmth, closeness, or conflict in their sibling relationships. It is thus understandable that preschoolers who may not have the verbal and cognitive skills to understand these differential processes are more likely to have conflicted sibling relationships. Parents should try to be fair and equitable in the treatment of their children, but it also appears that openly discussing their differential treatment will help children understand and accept their parents' behavior and, consequently, decrease this as a source of sibling rivalry.

Children's immediate reactions to the birth of a new baby are described as ambivalent at best. Preschool children, especially, experience some adjustment problems, although positive reactions such as increased maturity and independence are also noted (Campbell, 1990; Stewart, Mobley, Van Tuyl, & Salvador, 1987). Faber and Mazlish (1987) stress the importance of supporting and listening to older siblings' feelings, no matter how negative, while setting limits on acting out those feelings in ways that hurt others. Dunn and Kendrick (1982) suggest that mothers can encourage positive sibling relationships by involving the older child in the care of the infant and modeling respect for the infant as a person with needs and feelings.

CONCLUSION

Child clinicians entering the twenty-first century have a better understanding of development and the technology to implement more and better intervention programs for children and their families. Prevention, however, should also be an important focus, especially for those who work with preschool children. The child development and child clinical literature provide evidence for certain parental styles and practices and other factors such as SES that facilitate children's development and those that make children more vulnerable to problems. A goal of the child clinician should be to apply this information from the empirical literature to programs focused on the prevention of significant problems in the preschool years and the enhancement of the intellectual, emotional, and social development of all children. This will involve moving from the consulting room to the political arena where policy/funding decisions are made about the importance of children and parents in our society. Parents can be provided with information about child development, behavior management techniques, parent-child interaction training, and methods of providing appropriate intellectual and social stimulation. Children and families living in poverty and unstable families, however, will need far more support to effectively use this information. To be effective, prevention and intervention programs must take into account the individual needs and characteristics of each family and provide the necessary supports as the child continues to develop and the family's needs change.

REFERENCES

Abidin, R.R. (1995). *Parenting Stress Index manual* (3rd ed.). Odessa, FL: Psychological Assessment Resources.

Achenbach, T.M. (1991). *Manual for the Child Behavior Checklist/4–18 and 1991 profile.* Burlington: University of Vermont.

Achenbach, T.M. (1992). *Manual for the Child Behavior Checklist/2–3 and 1992 profile.* Burlington: University of Vermont.

Achenbach, T.M., & Edelbrock, C. (1978). The classification of childhood pathology: A review and analysis of empirical efforts. *Psychological Bulletin, 85,* 1273–1301.

Achenbach, T.M., Edelbrock, C., & Howell, C.T. (1987). Empirically based assessment of the behavioral/emotional problems of 2- and 3-year-old children. *Journal of Abnormal Child Psychology, 15,* 629–650.

American Psychiatric Association. (1987). *Diagnostic and statistical manual of mental disorders* (3rd ed., rev.). Washington, DC: Author.

American Psychiatric Association. (1994). *Diagnostic and statistical manual of mental disorders* (4th ed.). Washington, DC: Author.

Anders, T.F., & Eiben, L.A. (1997). Pediatric sleep disorders: A review of the past 10 years. *Journal of the American Academy of Child and Adolescent Psychiatry, 36,* 9–19.

Arend, R., Lavigne, J.V., Rosenbaum, D., Binns, H.J., & Christoffell, K.K. (1996). Relation between taxonomy and qualitative diagnostic systems in preschool children: Emphasis on disruptive disorders. *Journal of Clinical Child Psychology, 25,* 288–307.

Barclay, K.H., & Whittington, P. (1992, Spring). Night scares: A literature-based approach for helping children. *Childhood Education,* 149–154.

Bay-Hinitz, A.K., Peterson, R.F., & Quilitch, H.R. (1994). Cooperative games: A way to modify aggressive and cooperative behaviors in young children. *Journal of Applied Behavior Analysis, 27,* 435–446.

Beautrois, A.L., Fergusson, D.M., & Shannon, F.T. (1982). Family life events and behavioral problems in preschool-aged children. *Pediatrics, 70,* 774–779.

Benasich, A.A., Curtiss, S., & Tallal, P. (1993). Language, learning, and behavioral disturbances in children: A longitudinal perspective. *Journal of the American Academy of Child and Adolescent Psychiatry, 32,* 585–594.

Bentovim, A. (1970). The clinical approach to feeding disorders of childhood. *Journal of Psychosomatic Research, 14,* 267–276.

Bierman, K.L., & Welsh, J.A. (1997). Social relationship deficits. In E.J. Mash & L.G. Terdal (Eds.), *Assessment of childhood disorders* (pp. 328–365). New York: Guilford Press.

Boivin, M., Hymel, D., & Bukowski, W.M. (1995). The role of social withdrawal, peer rejection, and victimization by peers in predicting loneliness and depressed mood in childhood. *Development and Psychopathology, 7,* 765–785.

Breston, E., & Eyberg, S.M. (1998). Effective psychosocial treatments for children and adolescents with disruptive disorders: 29 years, 82 studies and 5,275 kids. *Journal of Clinical Child Psychology, 27,* 180–189.

Brody, G., Stoneman, L., & Burke, M. (1987). Child temperaments, maternal differential behavior, and sibling relationships. *Developmental Psychology, 23,* 354–362.

Brody, S. (1980). Transitional objects: Idealization of a phenomenon. *Psychoanalytic Quarterly, 49,* 561–605.

Bukowski, W.M., Newcomb, A.F., & Hartup, W.W. (Eds.). (1996). *The company they keep: Friendships in childhood and adolescence.* New York: Cambridge University Press.

Butler, N.R., & Golding, J. (Eds.). (1986). *From birth to five.* Oxford, England: Pergamon Press.

Campbell, S.B. (1990). *Behavior problems in preschool children.* New York: Guilford Press.

Campbell, S.B. (1994). Hard-to-manage preschool boys: Externalizing behavior, social competence, and family context at 2-year follow-up. *Journal of Abnormal Psychology, 22,* 147–166.

Campbell, S.B. (1995). Behavior problems in preschool children: A review of recent research. *Journal of Child Psychology and Psychiatry, 36,* 113–149.

Campbell, S.B. (1996). Young children at risk for psychopathology: Developmental and family perspectives. *Journal of Clinical Child Psychology, 25,* 372–375.

Campbell, S.B. (1997). Behavior problems in preschool children: Developmental and family issues. In T.H. Ollendick & R.J. Prinz (Eds.), *Advances in clinical child psychology* (Vol. 19, pp. 1–26). New York: Plenum Press.

Campbell, S.B., & Ewing, L.J. (1990). Hard-to-manage preschoolers: Adjustment at age nine and predictors of continuing symptoms. *Journal of Child Psychology and Psychiatry, 31,* 871–889.

Campbell, S.B., Ewing, L.J., Breaux, A.M., & Szumowski, E.K. (1986). Parent-referred problem three-year-olds: Follow-up at school entry. *Journal of Child Psychology and Psychiatry, 27,* 473–488.

Campbell, S.B., Pierce, E., March, C., Ewing, L.J., & Szumowski, E.K. (1994). Hard-to-manage preschool boys: Symptomatic behavior across contexts and time. *Child Development, 65,* 836–851.

Campbell, S.B., Szumowski, E.K., Ewing, L.J., Gluck, D.S., & Breaux, A.M. (1982). A multidimensional assessment of parent-identified behavior problem toddlers. *Journal of Abnormal Child Psychology, 10,* 569–592.

Cantwell, D.P., Baker, L., & Mattison, R.E. (1979). The prevalence of psychiatric disorder in children with speech and language disorder. *Journal of the American Academy of Child Psychiatry, 18,* 450–461.

Chamrad, D.L., & Robinson, N.M. (1986). Parenting the intellectually gifted preschool child. *Topics in Early Childhood Special Education, 6,* 74–87.

Coie, J.D. (1990). Toward a theory of peer rejection. In S.R. Asher & J.D. Coie (Eds.), *Peer rejection in childhood* (pp. 365–401). New York: Cambridge University Press.

Cole, P.M., Usher, B.A., & Cargo, A.P. (1993). Cognitive risk and its association with risk for disruptive disorder in preschoolers. *Journal of Clinical Child Psychology, 22,* 154–164.

Costello, E.J., Costello, A.J., Edelbrook, C., Burns, B.J., Dulcan, M.K., Brent, D., & Janiszewski, S. (1988). Psychiatric disorders in pediatric primary care: Prevalence and risk factors. *Archives of General Psychiatry, 45,* 1107–1116.

Crick, N.R., & Dodge, K.A. (1994). A review and reformulation of social information-processing mechanisms in children's social adjustment. *Psychological Bulletin, 115,* 74–101.

Crowell, J.A., Feldman, S.S., & Ginsberg, N. (1988). Assessment of mother-child interaction in preschoolers with behavior problems. *Journal of the American Academy of Child and Adolescent Psychiatry, 27,* 303–311.

Culbertson, J.L., & Willis, D.J. (Eds.). (1993). *Testing young children.* Austin, TX: ProEd.

Cummings, E.M., & Davies, P.T. (1994). Maternal development and child development. *Journal of Child Psychology and Psychiatry, 35,* 73–112.

Davies, D. (1999). *Child development: A practitioner's guide.* New York: Guilford Press.

Dietz, K.R., Lavigne, J.V., Arend, R., & Rosenbaum, D. (1997). Relation between intelligence and psychopathology among preschoolers. *Journal of Clinical Child Psychology, 26,* 99–107.

Dodge, K.A., Pettit, G.S., & Bates, J.E. (1994). Socialization mediators of the relation between socioeconomic status and child conduct problems. *Child Development, 65,* 649–665.

Drotar, D. (1999). The diagnostic and statistical manual for primary care (DSM-PC), child and adolescent version: What pediatric psychologists need to know. *Journal of Pediatric Psychology, 24,* 369–380.

Dunn, J., & Kendrick, C. (1982). *Siblings: Love, envy, and understanding.* Cambridge, MA: Harvard University Press.

Earls, F. (1982). Application of *DSM-III* in an epidemiology study of preschool children. *American Journal of Psychiatry, 139,* 242–243.

Earls, F., & Jung, K.G. (1987). Temperament and home environment characteristics as causal factors in the early development of childhood psychopathology. *Journal of the American Academy of Child and Adolescent Psychiatry, 26,* 491–498.

Easterbrooks, M.A., & Goldberg, W.A. (1990). Security of toddler–parent attachment: Relation to children's sociopersonality functioning during kindergarten. In M.T. Greenberg, D. Cicchetti, & E.M. Cummings (Eds.), *Attachment in the preschool years: Theory, research and intervention* (pp. 221–224). Chicago: University of Chicago Press.

Egeland, B., Kalkoske, M., Gottesman, N., & Erickson, M.F. (1990). Preschool behavior problems: Stability and factors accounting for change. *Journal of Child Psychology and Psychiatry, 31,* 891–909.

Evans, D.W., Leckman, J.F., Carter, A., Reznick, J.S., Henshaw, D., King, R.A., & Pauls, D. (1997). Ritual, habit, and perfectionism: The prevalence and development of compulsive-like behavior in normal young children. *Child Development, 68,* 58–68.

Eyberg, S.M. (1999). *Eyberg Child Behavior Inventory: Professional manual.* Odessa, FL: Psychological Assessment Resources.

Eyberg, S.M., Bessmer, J., Newcomb, K., Edwards, D., & Robinson, E. (1994). *Manual for the Dyadic Parent-Child Interaction Coding System-II* (Social & Behavioral Sciences Documents, Ms. No. 2897). (Available from Select Press, P.O. Box 9838, San Rafael, CA 94912)

Eyberg, S.M., Edwards, D., Boggs, S.R., & Foote, R. (1998). Maintaining the treatment effects of parent training: The role of booster sessions and other maintenance strategies. *Clinical Psychology: Science and Practice, 5,* 544–554.

Eyberg, S.M., Schuhmann, E.M., & Rey, J. (1998). Child and adolescent psychotherapy research: Developmental issues. *Journal of Abnormal Child Psychology, 26,* 71–81.

Faber, A., & Mazlish, E. (1987). *Siblings without rivalry.* New York: Norton.

Fagot, B.I., & Gauvain, M. (1997). Mother-child problem solving: Continuity through the early childhood years. *Developmental Psychology, 33,* 480–488.

Farver, J.A.M. (1996). Aggressive behavior in preschoolers' networks: Do birds of a feather flock together? *Early Childhood Research Quarterly, 11,* 333–350.

Ferber, R. (1985). *Solve your child's sleep problems.* New York: Simon & Schuster.

Ferber, R. (1989). Sleepwalking, confusional arousals, and sleep terrors in the child. In M.H. Kryger, T. Roth, & W.C. Dement, (Eds.), *Principle and practice of sleep medicine* (pp. 633–639). Philadelphia: Saunders.

Flament, M., Whitaker, A., Rapoport, J.L., Davies, M., & Zaremba Berg, C. (1988). Obsessive-compulsive disorder in adolescence: An epidemiological study. *Journal of the American Academy of Child and Adolescent Psychiatry, 27,* 764–771.

Flavell, J. (1977). *Cognitive development.* Englewood Cliffs, NJ: Prentice-Hall.

Foote, R.C., Schuhmann, E.M., Jones, M.L., & Eyberg, S.M. (1998). Parent-child interaction therapy: A guide for clinicians. *Clinical Child Psychology and Psychiatry, 3,* 361–373.

Foster, L.G. (1998). Nervous habits and stereotyped behaviors in preschool children. *Journal of the American Academy of Child and Adolescent Psychology, 37,* 711–717.

France, K.G. (1992). Behavior characteristics and security in sleep-disturbed infants treated with extinction. *Journal of Pediatric Psychology, 17,* 467–475.

Frank, N.C., Spirito, A., Stark, L., & Owens-Stively, J. (1997). The use of scheduled awakening to eliminate childhood sleepwalking. *Journal of Pediatric Psychology, 22,* 345–353.

Friman, P. (1988). Eliminating chronic thumbsucking by preventing a covarying response. *Journal of Behavior Therapy and Experimental Psychiatry, 87,* 87–90.

Friman, P., & Leibowitz, J.M. (1990). An effective and acceptable treatment alternative for chronic thumb- and finger-sucking. *Journal of Pediatric Psychology, 15,* 57–65.

Gardner, F.E.M. (1994). The quality of joint activity between mothers and their children with behaviour problems. *Journal of Child Psychology and Psychiatry, 35,* 935–948.

Gelman, R., & Baillargeon, R. (1983). A review of some Piagetian concepts. In J.H. Flavell & E.M. Markman (Eds.), P. Mussen (Series Ed.), *Handbook of child psychology: Cognitive development* (Vol. 3, pp. 167–230). New York: Wiley.

Goldberg, I.D., Regier, D.A., McInery, T.K., Pless, I.B., & Roghmann, K.J. (1984). The role of the pediatrician in the delivery of mental health services to children. *Pediatrics, 63,* 898–909.

Goldberg, I.D., Roghmann, K.J., McInery, T.K., & Burke, J.D. (1984). Mental health problems among children seen in pediatric practice: Prevalence and management. *Pediatrics, 73,* 278–293.

Goldsmith, H.H., Buss, K.A., & Lemery, K.S. (1997). Toddler and childhood temperament: Expanded content, stronger genetic evidence, new evidence for the importance of the environment. *Developmental Psychology, 33,* 891–905.

Goldsmith, J.J., Buss, A.H., Plomin, R., Rothbart, M.K., Thomas, A., Chess, S., Hinde, R.A., & McCall, R.B. (1987). Roundtable: What is temperament? Four approaches. *Child Development, 58,* 505–529.

Golomb, C., & Galasso, L. (1995). Make believe and reality: Explorations of the imaginary realm. *Developmental Psychology, 31,* 800–810.

Goodman, R. (1993). Brain abnormalities and psychological development. In D.F. Hay & A. Angold (Eds.), *Precursors and causes in development and psychopathology* (pp. 51–86). Chichester, England: Wiley.

Goodyer, I.M. (1990). *Life experience, development and child psychopathology.* Chichester, England: Wiley.

Greenberg, M.T., Cicchetti, D., & Cummings, E.M. (Eds.). (1990). *Attachment in the preschool years: Theory, research and intervention.* Chicago: University of Chicago Press.

Greenberg, N.H. (1964). Origins of head-rolling (spasmus mutans) during early infancy: Clinical observations and theoretical implications. *Psychosomatic Medicine, 26,* 162–171.

Greening, L., & Dollinger, S.J. (1989). Treatment of a child's sleep disturbance and related phobias in the family. In M.C. Roberts & C.E. Walker (Eds.), *Casebook of child and pediatric psychology* (pp. 94–111). New York: Guilford Press.

Haggerty, R.J., Sherrod, L.R., Garmezy, N., & Rutter, M. (Eds.). (1996). *Stress, risk and resilience in children and adolescents: Processes, mechanisms, and interventions.* Cambridge, England: Cambridge University Press.

Hansen, D.E., & Vandenberg, B. (1997). Neuropsychological features and differential diagnosis of sleep apnea syndrome in children. *Journal of Clinical Child Psychology, 26,* 304–310.

Harris, P.L. (1994). The child's understanding of emotion: Developmental change and family environment. *Journal of Child Psychology and Psychiatry, 35,* 3–28.

Harris, P.L., & Nunez, M. (1996). Understanding of permission rules by preschool children. *Child Development, 67,* 1572–1591.

Hart, B., & Risley, T.R. (1995). *Meaningful differences in the everyday experience of young American children.* Baltimore: Brookes.

Hart, B., & Risley, T.R. (1999). *The social world of children: Learning to talk.* Baltimore: Brookes.

Harter, S. (1983). Developmental perspective on the self system. In E.M. Hetherington (Ed.), P. Mussen (Series Ed.), *Handbook of child psychology: Socialization, personality, and social development* (Vol. 4, pp. 275–385). New York: Wiley.

Hartup, W.W. (1989). Social relationships and their developmental significance. *American Psychologist, 44,* 120–126.

Hay, D.F. (1994). Prosocial development. *Journal of Child Psychology and Psychiatry, 35,* 29–71.

Herrenkohl, E.C., Herrenkohl, R.C., Rupert, L.J., Egolf, B.P., & Lutz, J.G. (1995). Risk factors for behavioral dysfunction: The relative impact of maltreatment, SES, physical health problems, cognitive ability, and quality of parent-child interaction. *Child Abuse and Neglect, 19,* 191–203.

Herrenkohl, E.C., Herrenkohl, R.C., Toedter, L., & Yanushefski, A.M. (1984). Parent-child interactions in abusive and non-abusive families. *Journal of the American Academy of Child and Adolescent Psychiatry, 23,* 641–648.

Hooks, M.Y., Mayes, L.C., & Volkmar, F.R. (1988). Psychiatric disorders among preschool children. *Journal of the American Academy of Child and Adolescent Psychiatry, 27,* 623–627.

Howes, C. (1987). Social competence with peers in young children: Developmental sequences. *Developmental Review, 7,* 252–272.

Jenkins, S., Bax, M., & Hart, H. (1980). Behaviour problems in preschool children. *Journal of Child Psychology and Psychiatry, 21,* 5–18.

Jennings, K.D., Stagg, V., & Conners, R.E. (1991). Social networks and mothers' interactions with their preschool children. *Child Development, 62,* 966–978.

Johnson, M. (1991). Infant and toddler sleep: A telephone survey of parents in one community. *Journal of Developmental Behavioral Pediatrics, 12,* 108–114.

Keogh, B.K., & Burstein, N.D. (1988). Relationship of temperament to preschoolers' interactions with peers and teachers. *Exceptional Children, 54,* 456–461.

Kinzynski, L., Kochanska, G., Radke-Yarrow, M., & Girnius-Brown, O. (1987). A developmental interpretation of young children's noncompliance. *Developmental Psychology, 23,* 799–806.

Klackenberg, G. (1949). Thumbsucking: Frequency and etiology. *Pediatrics, 4,* 418–423.

Klesges, R., Malott, J., & Ugland, M. (1984). The effects of graded exposure and parental modeling on the dental phobias of a four-year-old girl and her mother. *Journal of Behavior Therapy and Experimental Psychiatry, 15,* 161–164.

Kopp, C. (1989). Regulation of distress and negative emotions: A developmental view. *Developmental Psychology, 25,* 343–354.

Kowal, A., & Kramer, L. (1997). Children's understanding of parental differential treatment. *Child Development, 68,* 113–126.

Lask, B. (1988). Novel and nontoxic treatment of night terrors. *British Medical Journal, 297,* 592.

Last, C.G., & Francis, G. (1988). School phobia. In B.B. Lahey & A.E. Kazdin (Eds.), *Advances in clinical child psychology* (Vol. 11, pp. 193–222). New York: Plenum Press.

Lavigne, J.V., Gibbons, R.D., Arend, R., Rosenbaum, D., Binns, H., & Christoffell, K.K. (1999). Toward rational service planning in pediatric primary care: Continuity and change in the occurrence of psychopathology among young children enrolled in pediatric practices. *Journal of Pediatric Psychology, 24,* 393–403.

Lawton, C., France, K.G., & Blampied, N.H. (1991). Treatment of infant sleep disturbance by graduated extinction. *Child and Family Behavior Therapy, 13,* 39–56.

Leadbeater, B.J., & Bishop, S.J. (1994). Predictors of behavior problems in preschool children of inner-city Afro-American and Puerto Rican adolescent mothers. *Child Development, 65,* 638–648.

Lee, B.J. (1987). Multidisciplinary evaluation of preschool children and its demography in a military psychiatric clinic. *Journal of the American Academy of Child and Adolescent Psychiatry, 26,* 313–316.

Lehman, E.B., Denham, S.A, Moser, M.H., & Reeves, S.L. (1992). Soft object and pacifier attachments in young children: The role of security attachment to the mother. *Journal of Child Psychology and Psychiatry, 33,* 1205–1215.

Loeber, R., Green, S.M., Lahey, B.B., Christ, M.A., & Frick, P.J. (1992). Developmental sequences in the age of onset of disruptive child behaviors. *Journal of Child and Family Studies, 1,* 21–41.

Love, A.J., & Thompson, M.G. (1988). Language disorders and attention deficit disorders in young children referred for psychiatric services: Analysis of prevalence and a conceptual synthesis. *American Journal of Orthopsychiatry, 58,* 52–64.

Lyman, R.D., & Hembree-Kigin, T.L. (1994). *Mental health interventions with preschool children.* New York: Plenum Press.

Maloney, M.F., & Klykylo, W.M. (1983). An overview of anorexia nervosa, bulimia and obesity in children and adolescents. *Journal of the American Academy of Child Psychiatry, 22,* 99–107.

Marks, I. (1987). The development of normal fear: A review. *Journal of Child Psychiatry, 28,* 667–697.

Mash, E.J., & Terdal, L.G. (Eds.). (1997). *Assessment of childhood disorders.* New York: Guilford Press.

Matson, J.L. (1983). Exploration of phobic behavior in a small child. *Journal of Behavior Therapy and Experimental Psychiatry, 14,* 257–259.

McCarthy, D.A. (1972). *Manual for the McCarthy Scales of Children's Abilities.* San Antonio, TX: Psychological Corporation.

McDevitt, S.C., & Carey, W.B. (1978). The measurement of temperament in 3–7 year old children. *Journal of Child Psychology and Psychiatry, 19,* 245–253.

Melson, G.F., Ladd, G.W., & Hsu, H-C. (1993). Maternal support networks, maternal cognitions, and young children's social and cognitive development. *Child Development, 64,* 1401–1417.

Mesibov, G.B., Schroeder, C.S., & Wesson, L. (1977). Parental concerns about their children. *Journal of Pediatric Psychology, 2,* 13–17.

Miller, L.T., & Vernon, P.A. (1997). Developmental changes in speed of information processing in young children. *Developmental Psychology, 33,* 549–554.

Mindell, J.A. (1993). Sleep disorders in children. *Health Psychology, 12,* 151–162.

Nuttall, E.V., Romero, I., & Kalesnik, J. (Eds.). (1999). *Assessing and screening preschoolers: Psychological and educational dimensions* (2nd ed.). Needham Heights, MA: Allyn & Bacon.

Odom, S.I., & Kaiser, A.P. (1997). Prevention and early intervention during early childhood: Theoretical and empirical bases for practice. In W.E. McLean, Jr. (Ed.), *Ellis' handbook of mental deficiency, psychological, theory and research* (pp. 137–172). Hillsdale, New Jersey: Erlbaum.

Palisin, H. (1986). Preschool temperament and performance of achievement tests. *Developmental Psychology, 22,* 766–770.

Park, R.D., & Ladd, G.W. (1992). *Family-peer relationships: Models of linkage.* Hillsdale, NJ: Erlbaum.

Passman, R.H. (1987). Attachments to inanimate objects: Are children who have security blankets insecure? *Journal of Consulting and Clinical Psychology, 55,* 825–830.

Patterson, G.R., & Fleischmann, M.J. (1979). Maintenance of treatment effects: Some considerations concerning family systems and follow-up data. *Behavior Therapy, 10,* 168–185.

Piaget, J., & Inhelder, B. (1969). *The psychology of the child.* New York: Basic Books.

Pierce, E.W., Ewing, L.J., & Campbell, S.B. (1999). Diagnostic status and symptomatic behavior of hard-to-manage preschool children in middle childhood and early adolescence. *Journal of Clinical Child Psychology, 28,* 44–57.

Plomin, R. (1989). Environment and genes: Determinants of behavior. *American Psychologist, 44,* 105–111.

Pollock, J.I. (1994). Night-waking at five years of age: Predictors and prognosis. *Journal of Child Psychology and Psychiatry, 35,* 699–708.

Pope, A.W., McHale, S.M., & Craighead, W.E. (1988). *Self-esteem enhancement with children and adolescents.* New York: Pergamon Press.

Popovich, F., & Thompson, G.W. (1973). Thumb- and finger-sucking: Its relation to malocclusion. *American Journal of Orthodontics, 63,* 148–155.

Rapin, I. (1996). Practitioner review: Developmental language: A clinical update. *Journal of Child Psychology and Psychiatry, 37,* 643–655.

Reppucci, N.D., Britner, P.A., & Woolard, J.L. (1997). *Preventing child abuse and neglect through parent education.* Baltimore: Brookes.

Rice, M.L. (1989). Children's language acquisition. *American Psychologist, 44,* 149–156.

Richman, N., Stevenson, J., & Graham, P. (1975). Prevalence of behaviour problems in three-year-old children: An epidemiological study in a London borough. *Journal of Child Psychology and Psychiatry, 26,* 272–287.

Richman, N., Stevenson, J., & Graham, P. (1982). *Preschool to school: A behavioural study.* London: Academic Press.

Robinson, N.M. (1987). The early development of precocity. *Gifted Child Quarterly, 31,* 161–168.

Rogoff, B. (1990). *Apprenticeship in thinking.* New York: Oxford University Press.

Rose, S.L., Feldman, J.F., Rose, S.A., Wallace, I.F., & McCarton, C. (1992). Behavior problems at 3 and 6 years: Prevalence and continuity in full-terms and preterms. *Development and Psychopathology, 4,* 361–374.

Routh, D.K., Schroeder, C.S., & O'Tuma, L.A. (1974). Development of activity level in children. *Developmental Psychology, 10,* 163–168.

Rubin, K.H., & Stewart, S.L. (1996). Social withdrawal. In E.J. Mash & R.A. Barkley (Eds.), *Child psychopathology* (pp. 277–310). New York: Guilford Press.

Rutter, M. (1996). Stress research: Accomplishments and tasks ahead. In R.J. Haggerty, C.R. Sherrod, N. Garmezy, & M. Rutter (Eds.), *Stress, risk and resiliency in children and adolescents: Processes, mecha-*

nisms, and interventions. New York: Cambridge University Press.

Rutter, M., Tizard, J., & Whitmore, K. (1970). *Education, health and behavior.* London: Longmans.

Sallustro, F., & Atwell, C.W. (1978). Body rocking, head banging, and head rolling. *Journal of Pediatrics, 93,* 704–708.

Sanders, M.R., Patel, R.K., LeGrice, B.L., & Shepherd, R.W. (1993). Children and persistent feeding difficulties: An observational analysis of the feeding interactions of problem and non-problem eaters. *Health Psychology, 12,* 64–73.

Sanson, A., Prior, M., & Smart, D. (1996). Reading disabilities with and without behaviour problems at 7–8 years: Prediction from longitudinal data from infancy to 6 years. *Journal of Child Psychology and Psychiatry, 37,* 259–241.

Sattler, J.P. (1988). *Assessment of children* (3rd ed.). San Diego, CA: Author.

Schaughency, E.C., & Fagot, B.I. (1993). The prediction of adjustment at age 7 from activity level at age 5. *Journal of Abnormal Child Psychology, 21,* 29–50.

Schmitz, S., & Fulker, D.W. (1994). Continuation and change in the etiology of problem behaviors between early and middle childhood. *Behavior Genetics, 24,* 528.

Schroeder, C.S., & Gordon, B.N. (1991). *Assessment and treatment of childhood disorders: A clinician's guide.* New York: Guilford Press.

Schroeder, C.S., & Gordon, B.N. (1998). Interviewing parents. In G.P. Koocher, J.C. Norcross, & S.S. Hill, III (Eds.), *Psychologist's desk reference* (pp. 73–79). New York: Oxford University Press.

Schroeder, C.S., & Wool, R. (1979, March). Parental concerns for children one month to 10 years and the informational sources desired to answer the concerns. Paper presented at the meeting of the Southeastern Psychological Association, New Orleans, LA.

Simon, J., Larson, C., & Lehrer, R. (1988). Preschool screening: Relations among audiometric and developmental measures. *Journal of Applied Developmental Psychology, 9,* 107–123.

Skarpness, L.R., & Carson, D.K. (1987). Correlates of kindergarten adjustment: Temperament and communicative competence. *Early Childhood Research Quarterly, 2,* 367–376.

Snyder, J., Horsch, E., & Childs, J. (1997). Peer relationships of young children: Affiliative choices and the shaping of aggressive behavior. *Journal of Clinical Child Psychology, 26,* 145–156.

Sonuga-Barke, E.J.S., Lamparelli, M., Stevenson, J., Thompson, M., & Henry, A. (1994). Behaviour problems and preschool intellectual attainment: The associations of hyperactivity and conduct problems. *Journal of Child Psychology and Psychiatry, 35,* 949–960.

Sroufe, L.A., & Fleeson, J. (1986). Attachment and the construction of relationships. In W. Hartup & Z. Rubin (Eds.), *The nature and development of relationships.* Hillsdale, NJ: Erlbaum.

Starfield, B., Gross, E., Wood, M., Pantell, R., Allen, C., Gordon, B., Moffatt, P., Drachman, R., & Katz, H. (1980). Psychosocial and psychosomatic diagnoses in primary care of children. *Pediatrics, 66,* 159–167.

Stevenson-Hinde, J., & Shouldice, A. (1995). 4.5 to 7 years: Fearful behaviour, fears and worries. *Journal of Child Psychology and Psychiatry, 36,* 1027–1038.

Stewart, R.B., Mobley, L.A., Van Tuyl, S.S., & Salvador, R.A. (1987). The first born's adjustment to the birth of a sibling: A longitudinal assessment. *Child Development, 58,* 341–355.

Stocker, C., Dunn, J., & Plomin, R. (1989). Sibling relationship: Links with child temperament, maternal behavior, and family structure. *Child Development, 60,* 715–727.

Stores, G. (1996). Practitioner review: Assessment and treatment of sleep disorders in children and adolescents. *Journal of Child Psychology and Psychiatry, 37,* 907–925.

Stormont-Spurgin, M., & Zentall, S.S. (1995). Contributing factors in the manifestation of aggression in preschoolers with hyperactivity. *Journal of Child Psychology and Psychiatry, 36,* 491–509.

Strauss, C., Rubinoff, A., & Atkeson, B. (1983). Elimination of nocturnal headbanging in a normal seven-year-old girl using overcorrection plus rewards. *Journal of Behavior Therapy and Experimental Psychiatry, 14,* 269–273.

Thelen, E. (1981). Rhythmical behaviors in infancy: An ethnological perspective. *Developmental Psychology, 17,* 237–257.

Thelen, E. (1995). Motor development: A new synthesis. *American Psychologist, 50,* 79–95.

Thomas, A., & Chess, S. (1977). *Temperament and development.* New York: Brunner/Mazel.

Thomas, A., Chess, S., & Birch, H.B. (1968). *Temperament and behavior disorders in children.* New York: University Press.

Trickett, P.K., Aber, L.W., Carlson, V., & Cicchetti, D. (1991). Relationship of socioeconomic status to the etiology and development sequelae of physical child abuse. *Developmental Psychology, 27,* 148–158.

Troster, H. (1994). Prevalence and functions of stereotyped behaviors in non-handicapped children in residential care. *Journal of Abnormal Child Psychology, 22,* 79–97.

Volkmar, F.R., & Schwab-Stone, M. (1996). Annotation: Childhood disorder of *DSM-IV. Journal of Child Psychology and Psychiatry, 37,* 779–784.

Vygotsky, L.S. (1978). *The mind in society: The development of higher psychological processes.* Cambridge, MA: Harvard University Press.

Wahler, R.G. (1990). The insular mother: Her problems in parent-child treatment. *Journal of Applied Behavior Analysis, 13,* 207–219.

Wang, P.P., & Baron, M.A. (1997). Language: A code for communicating. In M.L. Batshaw (Ed.), *Children with disabilities* (4th ed.). Baltimore: Brookes.

Webster-Stratton, C. (1990). Stress: A potential disrupter of parent perceptions and family interactions. *Journal of Clinical Child Psychology, 4,* 301–312.

Webster-Stratton, C., & Hammond, M. (1997). Treating children with early-onset conduct problems: A comparison of child and parent training interventions. *Journal of Consulting and Clinical Psychology, 65,* 93–109.

Werry, J., Carlielle, J., & Fitzpatrick, J. (1983). Rhythmic motor activities (stereotypies) in children under five: Etiology and prevalence. *Journal of the American Academy of Child Psychiatry, 22,* 329–336.

Wolfson, A., Lacks, P., & Futterman, A. (1992). Effects of parent training on infant sleeping patterns, parents' stress and perceived parental competence. *Journal of Consulting and Clinical Psychology, 60,* 41–49.

Wolraich, M.L., Felice, M.E., & Drotar, D. (Eds.). (1996). *The manual for primary care (DSM-PC), child and adolescent version.* Elk Grove, IL: American Academy of Pediatrics.

World Health Organization. (1992). *ICD-10: The ICD classification of mental and behavioral disorder: Clinical description and diagnostic guidelines.* Geneva, Switzerland: Author.

Yancy, W.S. (1981). Repetitive movements. In S. Gabel (Ed.), *Behaviour problems of childhood* (pp. 317–324). New York: Brunner/Mazel.

CHAPTER 15

Fear and Anxiety in Children

ANNE MARIE ALBANO, DAVID CAUSEY, AND BRYAN D. CARTER

As for you, my fine friend, you're a victim of disorganized thinking. You are under the unfortunate delusion that simply because you run away from danger, you have no courage. You're confusing courage with wisdom.

—The Wizard of Oz, addressing the Cowardly Lion (1939)

Fear and anxiety are expected, normal, and basic emotions experienced by all humans throughout the course of a lifetime. As noted by prominent clinical scientists, fear serves the valuable and essential role of alerting an individual to imminent danger, focusing attention and physical resources to prepare to fight or flee, and subsequently consolidating the experience into memory for use in future, similar situations (cf. Barlow, 1988). Repeated experiences with fear-provoking situations and cues provide an individual with opportunities to learn appropriate cognitive and behavioral responses for mastering these situations, along with learning to differentiate true threat from false or more innocuous situations. For children, the experience of fear is an essential part of normal development. However, for some children and adolescents, excessive and intense fears and anxiety can occur, resulting in disruption of the child's daily activities and quality of life. In this chapter, we examine current issues relevant to the study and understanding of nonclinical and clinical manifestations of fear and anxiety in youth.

FEAR AND ANXIETY DEFINED

Contemporary scientists define fear as an emotion arising directly from the fight-or-flight system of the autonomic nervous system (Barlow, Chorpita, & Turovsky, 1996; cf. Gray, 1982). Fear is an immediate alarm reaction to present danger or life-threatening situations. This alarm reaction, called the "fight-or-flight response," involves activation of the autonomic nervous system coupled with a focusing of attention on either escaping the situation or fighting the potential threat. The response of the autonomic nervous system involves a number of physiological sensations, such as pounding heart, rapid breathing, sweating, muscle tension, hot or cold flashes, and nausea. These sensations are harmless and viewed as adaptive. For example, the pounding heart and rapid breathing result from more efficient and increased circulation of blood and oxygen to the large muscles of the body. Thus, sensations are a result of the alarm system's readying the body to either fight or flee. An individual experiencing an alarm reaction is likely to be thinking "This situation can hurt me now, so I've got to get out of here or fight for my life." Children and adolescents will respond with an alarm reaction to perceived threatening situations and stimuli, such as the sight of the doctor, an approaching dog, flying insects, thunderstorms, costumed characters, unfamiliar persons, and the dark.

In contrast to the immediate alarm reaction associated with fear, anxiety is a mood state or emotion characterized by negative affect and the somatic symptoms of tension, along with apprehension that some future negative event, situation, or misfortune will occur (Barlow, 1988). Thus, in contrast to the immediacy of the fear response, anxiety is a state of dread, unease, worry, or apprehension about an upcoming or anticipated situation. Although anxiety may not be a pleasant experience, the purpose of anxiety is to assist with planning and managing future events. Anxiety has been termed the "shadow of intelligence" by psychologist Howard Liddell (1949), because humans can anticipate and plan for future events, allowing one to prepare for any number of consequences or scenarios. The physiological symptoms accompanying anxiety may involve fidgeting, increased heart rate, and muscle tension. In proper or moderate amounts, anxiety serves the function of motivating an individual and enhancing performance in various situations. This finding was demonstrated by Yerkes and Dodson (1908), who found that moderate levels of anxiety enhanced performance, whereas too little or too much anxiety interfered with task performance. Anxiety may be characterized by some degree of "what if" thinking, such as "What if I fail that upcoming test?"; "What if no one talks to me at the party?"; or "What if Mom and Dad get divorced?" Children and adolescents may have anxiety focused on academic performance, social relationships, athletic competence, and family issues.

THREE-COMPONENT MODEL

Whether confronted with an immediate danger or worrying about an upcoming stressful situation, fear and anxiety are expressed through three distinct yet interactive components. The *physiological component* is composed of an individual's physical reactions, such as the sensations of the fight-or-flight response or the experience of tension, sleep disturbance, and impaired concentration; the *cognitive component* involves all the thoughts, images, beliefs, interpretations, and attributions about the situation and its expected outcomes; and the *behavioral component* is comprised of motor reactions that typically involve taking action, avoidance, or escape. Understanding anxiety and fear from this perspective allows a clinician to present a concrete and straightforward explanation of the nature of a client's symptoms and distress, along with providing a framework for understanding the choice of treatment procedures.

THE CONCEPT OF NEGATIVE AFFECT

Investigators have long wrestled with the question of whether anxiety and fear represent unique psychological constructs, or whether these emotions are manifestations of a larger, more diffuse construct of negative affect. As such, anxiety and fear are hypothetical constructs, inferred from multiple methods of assessment including self-report, physiological monitoring, and behavioral indicators. As noted above, anxiety and fear share many features within the three-component model. The main difference between the constructs relates to the interpretation of threat as immediate or in the future, and the nature of the physiological arousal as an alarm reaction or an elevated level of tension and apprehension. Confounding the distinction of anxiety and fear is the consistent finding that anxiety and depression are highly correlated (Lonigan, Carey, & Finch, 1994; Norvell, Brophy, & Finch, 1985; Wolfe et al., 1987). For example, Norvell et al., in a study of self-reported anxiety and depression in an inpatient sample, found a correlation of .70 for the constructs. These results suggested a unitary model of anxiety and depression, which the authors explained as a "complex relationship" warranting further study. Extending this research, Wolfe et al. examined the relationship among anxiety, depression, and anger in a larger study of inpatient children. Using a multitrait multimethod analysis (MTMM), correlations for anxiety and depression ranged from .36 to .56, with correlations with anger as high as .28.

Further investigation in the realm of childhood emotions supported the association of anxiety and depression (e.g., Lonigan et al., 1994; Ollendick & Yule, 1990; Tannenbaum, Forehand, & McCombs-Thomas, 1992), although the structure of negative affect in youth remained unclear. Chorpita, Albano, and Barlow (1998) identified several problems with the extant literature examining negative affect in youth. First, investigations were constricted by measurement error inherent in self-report, particularly with regard to construct validity. Second, the MTMM approach became outdated, and more sophisticated models for testing latent constructs had advanced the field of adult emotional disorders, yet this methodology was infrequently applied to studies with children. Third, the diagnostic reliability found in prior studies using inpatient samples was questioned. Finally, the research on adults supported the discriminability of the components of negative emotions into a general factor and specific factors (Barlow et al., 1996; Clark & Watson, 1991; Watson et al., 1995). In general, three discriminable factors are proposed to constitute negative affect in adults: *fear,* consisting of the symptoms of autonomic arousal and fear/panic; *anxiety,* corresponding to tension, worry, apprehension, and general distress; and *depression,* consisting of low positive affect, anhedonia, and hopelessness.

In an effort to address the aforementioned limitations, Chorpita and colleagues (1998) utilized a structural equation modeling technique based in confirmatory factor analysis. Such advanced statistical methods are better suited to accounting for measurement effects (unreliability of self-report) in model testing. Moreover, this investigation involved a large sample of children and adolescents diagnosed with an empirically derived and reliable structured diagnostic interview method. Diagnostic reliability ensured that anxiety and mood disorders were highly represented in the participants. Of the 216 participants, 111 (51.4%) were female, and the mean age was 12.53 years (*SD* = 2.85; range 6–17). All participants were assigned a *DSM-III-R* diagnosis of an anxiety disorder, with 48 (22%) also assigned a comorbid mood disorder. In addition to the diagnostic interview, children and their parents completed several measures of childhood fear, anxiety, and depression. Results supported a three-factor solution for children with clinical anxiety disorders. Fear, anxiety, and depression were found to be three distinct yet correlated latent constructs. These results were consistent with the models proposed for adults. That is, anxiety was found to correspond to general distress; depression corresponded to low positive affect; and fear corresponded to heightened physiological arousal. The authors caution that further research is necessary to examine negative affect in relation to other

emotions (e.g., anger, mania) and in samples incorporating children with other well-defined clinical syndromes (e.g., ADHD). Most notably, the authors caution that many existing self-report measures of anxiety and depression may be outdated, thus accounting for the high correlation between measures of different constructs. As such, items should be generated that specifically tap empirically established factors of negative affect and its components.

DEVELOPMENTAL TRENDS

FEARS IN CHILDREN AND ADOLESCENTS

Dating back to 1935 with the work of Jersild and Holmes, the commonality of fears and anxiety in children has been well documented. Since that time, research has shown that children and adolescents may experience 9 to 13 excessive fears or worries at a given time in their development (Lapouse & Monk, 1959; Ollendick, 1983). In addition, these fears may be characterized by children as being frequent, intrusive, and difficult to control (Muris, Meesters, Merckelbach, Sermon, & Zwakhalen, 1998). The complexity of fears in children appears to increase around the age of 8, corresponding to cognitive development that involves an increased capacity to reason and elaborate on possible negative consequences and future outcomes (Vasey, 1995). Also, the primary source of anxiety changes relative to developmental stages of life (Berensen, 1993; Reed, Carter, & Miller, 1990). In their study of a community sample of 210 children, Kashani and Orvaschel (1990) found that, when compared to children 12 years of age and younger, adolescents showed lower rates of fear regarding strangers and separation and higher rates of fear related to social and interpersonal concerns and personal inadequacy. A summary of common fears and anxieties for children and adolescents is presented in Table 15.1. In addition to the types of fears identified by children, a number of stable and consistent findings occur throughout the developmental literature. As noted above, fears are common in children (e.g., Ollendick, 1983). With increasing age, the number of fears reported by children declines and the focus of the fear changes. Girls consistently report a greater number of fears than do boys, a finding that is consistent across cultures (see Albano, Chorpita, & Barlow, 1996, for a review).

Table 15.1 Fears and anxieties associated with different age levels in youth.

Age	Focus of Fear or Anxiety
0–6 Months	Loss of support, loud noises, excessive sensory stimuli.
6–9 Months	Strangers; sudden or unexpected stimuli (e.g., noise).
1 Year	Separation from caretakers, injury, toilet, strangers.
2 Years	A variety of fears including loud noises (e.g., sirens, thunder), animals, imaginary creatures, dark, separation from caretakers.
3 Years	Animals, masks, being alone, separation from caretakers.
4 Years	Darkness, animals, noises.
5 Years	Animals, "bad" people, dark, separation from caretakers.
6 Years	Monsters, ghosts and other supernatural creatures, bodily injury, thunder and lightening, sleeping alone, separation from caretakers (e.g., going to school).
7–8 Years	Monsters, ghosts and other supernatural creatures (e.g., those found in movies or books), extraordinary events exposed in the media (e.g., bombings, war, kidnappings), staying alone, injury.
9–12 Years	Tests, oral reports, answering questions aloud, and similar school situations (school performance and evaluation by others), peer bullying or teasing, rejection.
13–18 Years	Social alienation, embarrassment or humiliation, failure, school performance, death, injury or serious illness, natural or man-made disasters.

Source: Agras, Chapin, & Oliveau, 1972; Eme & Schmidt, 1878; Hampe, Noble, Miller, & Barrett, 1973; Jersild & Holmes, 1935; Jones & Jones, 1928; Ollendick, 1983.

CLINICAL MANIFESTATION OF FEAR AND ANXIETY

Based on the developmental literature, it stands to reason that children and adolescents may be more vulnerable to experiencing different fears or anxieties at various points in their development. Yet, what distinguishes a normal, developmental fear or anxiety reaction from a clinical phobia or anxiety disorder? Clinicians utilize a number of guidelines to distinguish normal, transient fear reactions from pathological anxiety conditions. These guidelines are based on the current psychiatric classification system and information gained through the study of normative and psychopathological conditions (see American Psychiatric Association [APA], 1994; Marks, 1969; Miller, Barrett, & Hampe, 1974). Youth with actual anxiety disorders tend to differ from normal youth in terms of the intensity, frequency, content, timing, and/or manifestation of anxiety-based symptoms (Albano et al., 1996):

1. The *intensity* of the fear reaction is out of proportion to the actual demands or threat of the situation. For example, a child may be considered phobic if he or she screams, flails, kicks, and has to be held down by several adults to be examined by a doctor.

2. The fear reaction occurs with increased *frequency* and cannot be reasoned away through information or reassurance. Many parents complain that no amount of reassurance will allay their child's fear.

3. The *content* of the fear reaction is focused on a rather innocuous situation or stimulus, that is, something that is not likely to cause harm. Such stimuli include the fear of going to school, riding in elevators, costumed characters, and noises such as from a siren or vacuum.

4. The fear reaction appears to be *spontaneous* and beyond the voluntary control of the child.

5. The fear reaction leads to *escape or avoidance* of the situation. For example, a child is considered to have a specific phobia of thunderstorms if he or she refuses to leave the house at the threat of a rainstorm.

Clinicians also evaluate whether the fear reaction persists over time, as opposed to a child's gaining courage and mastery of his or her anxiety with repeated exposure to the situation or stimulus. Moreover, phobic reactions and pathological anxiety conditions are not age- or stage-specific. For example, as opposed to the expected fears of a young child, adolescents may present with phobias of the dark or sleeping alone and older children may worry about separating from their parents. Finally, the degree of interference in the child and family's functioning is evaluated to determine whether a fear or anxiety response is at the disorder level (APA, 1994). Crying or tantrums, sleep disturbance, change in appetite, somatic complaints, concentration difficulties, and mood disturbances can accompany a clinical level of anxiety. In addition, interference may be noted in school and academic activities and progress, social relationships, and family functioning.

ANXIETY DISORDERS IN YOUTH

In recent years, there has been an increase in efforts to better delineate developmental trends in the symptom manifestations of anxiety disorders in children and adolescents (Last, Hansen, & Franco, 1997). Much of the available literature has been limited by methodological constraints such as small sample sizes, cross-sectional designs, and inadequate follow-up assessments (Albano et al., 1996). Nevertheless, this research, along with an increasing number of studies using prospective designs, provides important insights that can assist the clinician to better understand and more accurately identify and treat anxiety disorders in children.

Research on childhood anxiety disorders has consistently indicated that the age of onset as well as the natural course and outcome will vary according to the specific anxiety-based disorder being examined (Albano et al., 1996). A number of prospective studies have examined the course and outcome of anxiety disorders (e.g., Berg et al., 1989; Cantwell & Baker, 1989; Last, Perrin, Hersen, & Kazdin, 1996). The culmination of evidence from this research seems to suggest that anxiety disorders diagnosed in children are likely to show moderate to high rates of recovery over time; however, anxiety disordered children appear to be at a higher risk of developing other types of anxiety and/or psychiatric disorders. In a recent eight-year prospective study by Last et al. (1997), follow-up data was collected on 101 young adults with a history of diagnosed childhood anxiety disorders. Interestingly, they found that youngsters who did not show comorbid depression in childhood were functioning relatively similarly to normal controls once they reached adulthood, whereas those with previous comorbid depression continued to experience considerable adjustment difficulties into adulthood.

On the subject of age of onset, in their study of 188 child and adolescent patients presenting to an anxiety-disorders clinic, Last, Perrin, Hersen, and Kazdin (1992) found the age of onset to be early childhood for separation anxiety disorder (SAD) (7.5 years), simple phobias (SP) (8.4 years), and overanxious disorder (OAD) (8.8 years). In contrast, age of onset for obsessive-compulsive disorder and social phobia occurred somewhat later in childhood (10.8 and 11.3 years, respectively), and panic disorders were characterized by an even later age of onset, the early teen years (14.1 years). This study seemed to highlight the importance of age and developmental stages in understanding anxiety disorders and provided useful diagnostic information for clinicians to consider.

CORE FEATURES AND TRENDS OF ANXIETY DISORDERS

Separation anxiety disorder (SAD) is the only childhood anxiety disorder identified in the fourth edition of the *Diagnostic and Statistical Manual of Mental Disorders* (APA, 1994). Although children and adolescents can be diagnosed with any of the "adult" anxiety diagnoses, SAD retains its status as a disorder of childhood because of its unique age of onset, prior to age 18. SAD is characterized by excessive anxiety focused on separating from home or primary attachment figures (parents). Children with SAD may evidence crying and distress in anticipation of or at the occasion of separation. These children often fear that some untoward event will occur to cause the separation (e.g., fear of being kidnapped or getting lost). Children with SAD are reluctant to be alone and often try to sleep with their parents or refuse to leave the house. In extreme cases, children with SAD will "shadow" their parents and refuse to be alone at any time.

SAD can be seen at any age up to young adulthood, but is most commonly diagnosed in prepubertal children (Bell-Dolan & Brazeal, 1993). Kashani and Orvaschel (1990) found that the occurrence of SAD was significantly higher in 8-year-old children compared to 12- or 17-year-olds. Moreover, expression of SAD varies with age, in that younger children are more likely to manifest clinging or shadowing behaviors, whereas older children with this disorder are likely to struggle with separation involving greater time and space, such as staying away from home overnight. In addition, younger children (age 5–8) most commonly express associated concerns regarding nightmares, fear of loss of loved ones, and school refusal. Preadolescents (9–12) indicate more common concerns regarding emotional distress at separation, and adolescents (13–16) express concerns related to somatic difficulties and school refusal (Francis et al., 1987). Most often, the onset of SAD is acute and typically occurs following a significant change and/or major life event (e.g., moving, death in the family, prolonged illness) (Last, 1989). However, SAD may also correspond to developmental transitions, such as entering school for the first time or beginning middle or junior high school (Albano et al., 1996). Recurrence of SAD also appears to be tied to such events as prolonged illness, school holidays, or periods of increased demands and stress. Youngsters with SAD have been shown to be at considerable risk of also developing social phobia, and both disorders share a characteristic symptom of school refusal (Albano et al., 1996). Research suggests that the quantity of absenteeism in children displaying school refusal increases with age (Berg, 1970; Francis et al., 1987). This may reflect the heightened developmental complexity of older children and young adolescents, along with an increased capacity to cognitively and physically challenge authority (Hansen et al., 1998).

Specific phobias, in contrast to normal fears of childhood, reflect fears that are excessive, lead to avoidance of the feared object, are persistent and maladaptive, and are perceived as being uncontrollable by the child (Miller et al., 1974). Common phobias in childhood may include excessive fears of animals, storms, darkness, needles, and high places (Silverman & Rabian, 1993; Strauss & Last, 1993). Phobias are evident in children and adolescents of all ages, can begin at early ages of childhood, and are not necessarily tied to traumatic precipitating events (Marks & Gelder, 1966; Öst, 1987). Prospective empirical research regarding the course of childhood phobias is lacking, and thus many conclusions in this area are based on retrospective studies with adults (e.g., Öst, 1987). Nevertheless, both prospective (e.g., Agras, Chapin, & Oliveau, 1972; Hampe, Noble, Miller, & Barrett, 1973) and retrospective studies suggest that some phobias may resolve without specific intervention. Improvement is more rapid in children compared to adults; however, for a considerable portion of children and adolescents, phobias can persist over time and continue to interfere with daily functioning (Albano et al., 1996).

Social phobia is characterized by excessive fear in social or evaluative situations where the child is exposed to unfamiliar people or to possible evaluation by others. Individuals with social phobia are excessively self-conscious and shy and may be nonassertive. Children and adolescents with social phobia are overly concerned about social failure and negative evaluation and fear embarrassment or humiliation. In extreme cases, selective mutism may become evident, a condition whereby the child refuses to speak outside of the home. Selective mutism is considered an extreme form of social phobia (Black & Uhde, 1994). The onset of social phobia occurs in early adolescence (11.3 years), although children as young as 3 years may manifest selective mutism. Moreover, refinements in the diagnostic criteria for social phobia, along with advances in diagnostic assessment, are resulting in a greater number of identified cases of young school-age children (Beidel & Turner, 1988). However, the finding that social phobia is more common in adolescence corresponds to the developmental age-related increase in social fears found in normal, nonreferred youth. Social phobia rarely remits and is the third most common mental disorder among adults (Kessler et al., 1994). In child samples, social phobia is represented equally in males and females (Last et al., 1992; Vasey, 1995).

It is not uncommon for children to exhibit normal, age-related obsessive-compulsive behaviors, which often correspond to developmentally relevant issues, including mastery and control (March & Mulle, 1998). Examples may include an insistence on order with possessions or maintaining an extensive bedtime ritual. These types of developmentally appropriate rituals are consistent with younger childhood (i.e., 4–8 years of age) and help to promote mastery and increased socialization (Berensen, 1993). In contrast, the compulsive, ritualistic behaviors that characterize children with **obsessive-compulsive disorder** (OCD) tend to emerge later in childhood (i.e., 10 years of age) and are severe, incapacitating, bizarre, and often lead to disrupted socialization and isolation (March & Mulle, 1998). Research indicates that boys may have a younger age of onset (9 years) compared to girls, whose average age of onset occurs around the time of puberty (11 years) (Leonard et al., 1993). Leonard et al. also note that younger children, age 6 to 8 years, diagnosed with OCD may be characterized by having elaborate washing or checking rituals, but may lack the cognitive obsessions that often accompany compulsions in older children. OCD in children and adolescents fluctuates in severity, and patterns of specific symptom constellations tend to be inconsistent over time (Rettew et al., 1992). Unfortunately, evidence regarding childhood OCD reflects the chronicity and intractability of this disorder. In their longitudinal study, Berg et al. (1989) found that a relatively high proportion of subjects (31%) maintained a diagnosis of OCD at a two-year follow-up. Even when criteria for a diagnosis of OCD is no longer met, it is rare to observe complete remission of all obsessive-compulsive symptoms.

Perhaps one of the more controversial anxiety disorders of childhood is that of **panic disorder.** Individuals with panic disorder fear the internal sensations of the fight-or-flight system. That is, the individual with panic disorder misinterprets as dangerous symptoms such as palpitations, breathlessness, tingling and numbing sensations, tightness of the chest, and muscle tension. Cognitive misinterpretations include fears of dying, going crazy, or losing control, and individuals with panic often develop elaborate avoidance behaviors to prevent a panic attack from occurring. In children, avoidance may involve refusing to attend school or ride the school bus. Panic disorder is diagnosed when the occurrence of at least one panic attack is followed by a minimum of one month or more of persistent fear of future attacks, worry about the implications of the attack or its consequences, or a significant change in behavior (APA, 1994).

Until fairly recently, many thought that panic disorder did not exist in children (Black & Robbins, 1990). Moreau and Follett (1993) conducted an extensive literature review that highlights the numerous empirical and case studies that confirm the occurrence of panic disorder in children. In their review, they note that panic attacks have been diagnosed in children as young as 7 years of age, with a symptom profile that parallels that seen in adults. Although children do experience panic attacks, there is evidence that panic attacks are more common in adolescents, with a higher frequency of occurrence and a peak age of onset in adolescence (Hayward et al., 1992; Ollendick, Mattis, & King, 1994). Interestingly, rates of panic attacks appear to increase with developing sexual maturity, and this increase is not accounted for specifically by increasing age (Hayward et al., 1992). Symptoms most often described in children and adolescents with panic disorder include trembling and shaking, palpitations, dizziness or faintness, shortness of breath, sweating, and fears of dying or losing control (Kearney, Albano, Eisen, Allan, & Barlow, 1997). Depersonalization, however, may occur less commonly in children, as it has been rarely described in prepubertal youngsters and may involve a cognitive concept that is not yet adequately developed in younger children (Moreau & Follett, 1993). Accurate diagnosis of panic disorder has become increasingly important, with mounting evidence indicating a higher likelihood of psychiatric disturbance in adults with a history of this disorder (Black & Robbins, 1990). When age of onset occurs prior to 18 years, there is a significantly higher likelihood of problems in adulthood such as alcohol abuse, suicidal thoughts and gestures, and emergency room visits (Weissman, 1989).

Generalized anxiety disorder (GAD), often considered the basic anxiety disorder, is characterized by the pervasive and diffuse subjective feelings of tension, worry, and apprehension. The diagnosis of GAD applies when an individual experiences excessive and uncontrollable anxiety and worry about a number of events and situations. Children and adolescents may worry about the future, competency in academics and social functioning, health concerns, family matters, and events going on in the world. These worries must occur more days than not for at least six months and be accompanied by at least one physiological symptom (APA, 1994).

To date, GAD has not been well researched in children and adolescents, and the developmental course of the disorder in this age group demands investigation. Recent conclusions regarding GAD in children are often based on research examining overanxious disorder (OAD), which was excluded from *DSM-IV* and subsumed under GAD (American Academy of Child and Adolescent Psychiatry [AACAP], 1997). Although the link between GAD and OAD in children has been questioned (Last, 1993), recent research suggests a high degree of overlap between *DSM III-R* OAD and *DSM-IV* GAD in children (Tracey, Chorpita, Douban, & Barlow, 1997). Research regarding OAD in children suggests that the disorder may be somewhat unstable (Albano et al., 1996). Longitudinal studies have shown that symptoms of OAD are likely to remit over time (e.g., Cantwell & Baker, 1989; Last et al., 1996). In a three- to four-year follow-up study of 84 children diagnosed with anxiety disorders, approximately 80% of those diagnosed with OAD did not meet criteria for this disorder at follow-up (Last et al., 1996). However, children with OAD showed a relatively high likelihood of developing a new psychiatric disorder (35%) at follow-up. Also, compared to other anxiety disorders, symptoms of OAD may take longer to remit (Last et al., 1996). Cohen and colleagues (Cohen, Cohen, & Brook, 1993) found that, in a sample of nonreferred children and adolescents, almost half of those diagnosed with severe overanxious disorder at baseline were rediagnosed 2.5 years later. In terms of additional developmental issues, youth diagnosed with OAD have shown high comorbidity with other psychiatric diagnoses. Specifically, Strauss et al. (1988) found that younger children (5–11 years) more often experienced comorbid SAD and ADD, and older children (12–19 years) more often showed comorbid depression and specific phobia. It is also noteworthy that older youth with OAD have been shown to experience significantly more symptoms than younger children with this disorder (McGee et al., 1990; Strauss et al., 1988).

SCHOOL REFUSAL BEHAVIOR

The concept of school refusal behavior replaces the antiquated term "school phobia" and represents an empirical approach to understanding this serious concomitant of childhood emotional disorders (Kearney & Silverman, 1996). School phobia was often used to describe children who refused to attend school due to fears or anxiety, but the term was broadly and loosely applied without clear definition or distinction. For example, the use of the term "phobia" implied a clinical fear of some object or situation in or about the school. However, this terminology was insufficient and improper in describing all youth refusing to attend all or part of a school day, such as those refusing due to separation anxiety or truancy. Kearney and Silverman (1993, 1996) developed the current approach to understanding school refusal behavior, through a combination of an empirically derived categorical and dimensional system of classification. In this system, school refusal behavior refers to substantial, child-motivated refusal to attend or stay in school and/or difficulties remaining in class for an entire day. School refusal is viewed on a spectrum that includes youngsters who rarely miss school but

attend under duress, as well as those who always miss school. Although children age 5 to 17 years may be identified as manifesting school refusal behavior, most youngsters who refuse are 10 to 13 years old (Kearney & Albano, 2000). The problem peaks at times of school transitions (ages 5–6 and 14–15) as children enter new school environments.

In the functional approach to school refusal behavior outlined by Kearney and Silverman (1993, 1996), the problem is hypothesized to occur due to one or a combination of the following four reasons: (1) avoidance of situations or activities arousing negative affectivity (e.g., anxiety, fear, depression); (2) escape from aversive social and evaluative situations (e.g., social anxiety due to peer evaluation, oral reports, tests); (3) attention-seeking behavior (e.g., secondary gains of separation anxiety); and (4) positive tangible reinforcement (e.g., watching television, sleeping late). Children refusing for reasons 1 or 2 are motivated by negative reinforcement; those refusing for reasons 3 and 4 are motivated by positive reinforcement paradigms. This approach to understanding and classifying school refusal behavior also provides for the prescriptive treatment of the problem. On conducting a functional assessment of the motivating conditions for the school refusal behavior, the child is prescribed a specific treatment approach that is supported by empirical research to address this type of problem (see Kearney & Albano, 2000). This system provides an empirically sound connection between assessment and treatment planning and represents the current climate of clinical care, where utilization of scientifically sound and proven methods for addressing complex emotional problems are applied in clinical practice.

ANXIETY AND ATTENTION-DEFICIT DISORDERS

With the increasing popularity of attention-deficit/hyperactivity disorder (ADHD), a frequent differential diagnostic question posed to child clinicians is whether behavioral disturbance is due to deficits in attention or the presence of anxiety. It is often assumed by nonclinicians that these conditions are mutually exclusive, whereas in fact, they may co-occur with considerable frequency. In fact, comorbidity in general is more common than not in psychopathological conditions in childhood (Silverman & Rabian, 1993). A number of studies have demonstrated that up to 22% of school-age children who meet diagnostic criteria for an anxiety disorder have a comorbid diagnosis of attention-deficit disorder (ADD; Bird, Gould, & Staghezza, 1993; Bradley & Hood, 1993). Adolescents with an anxiety disorder have been estimated to have even higher levels, with over 50% being found to have comorbid ADD in some studies (August & Garfinkle, 1993; Biederman, Newcorn, & Sprich, 1991; Bird et al., 1993; Bradley & Hood, 1993). In a population of 73 patients seen at a children's anxiety disorder clinic, ADD was diagnosed in only 2 of the subjects, suggesting only a 3% comorbidity (Last, Strauss, & Francis, 1987). This is in contrast to the findings in an inpatient child psychiatric setting, in which comorbid anxiety and behavior disorder, including ADHD, was seen in over 50% of the study sample (Woolston et al., 1989). There are no data to suggest which condition, anxiety disorder or ADHD, predates the other. Anecdotally, in some cases, anxiety may be considered secondary and is seen to develop, along with depressive symptoms, in response to the academic failure and peer rejection experienced by many children with an impulse control disorder such as ADHD.

Others (Perrin & Last, 1996) have argued that both anxiety disorders and ADHD tend to be seen more frequently in families, yet are transmitted independently. This is based on the observations that male children with a mother reporting anxiety are at increased risk for having a diagnosis of ADHD (Perrin & Last, 1996; Sylvester, Hyde, & Reichsler, 1987). Anxiety disorder is much more likely to appear in the first-degree relatives of children with anxiety disorders than in children with ADHD and healthy controls (Last, Hersen, Kazdin, Orvaschel, & Perrin, 1991). In general, symptoms of anxiety are more frequently associated with depression than with externalizing behavior disorders (Last et al., 1992), with a number of studies showing approximately a one-third prevalence of anxiety symptoms in both referred and nonreferred youth with ADHD (Biederman, Faraone, et al., 1993; Last et al., 1992). There is some indication that children with comorbid anxiety disorder and ADHD may be less impulsive and more overactive than children with only the ADHD diagnosis (Pliszka, 1992) and less likely to develop a conduct disorder (Pliszka, 1989). Indeed, it has been suggested that children with comorbid ADHD and anxiety disorder and comorbid

ADHD and aggressive conduct disorder represent unique subtypes with different etiologies and developmental course (Jensen, Martin, & Cantwell, 1997).

TEMPERAMENTAL PREDISPOSITIONS AND ANXIETY

Investigators are focusing increasing attention on the observation that individuals who manifest psychopathological conditions often possess pre-existing tendencies or traits for those particular conditions, especially when exposed to certain experiences and environmental stimuli (Biederman, Rosenbaum, et al., 1993). Some of these notions came out of the developmental studies on shyness and behavioral inhibition of Kagan and his colleagues at the Harvard Infant Study laboratory (Kagan, 1989; Kagan & Reznick, 1984). Shyness is depicted as feelings of discomfort in social situations but not nonsocial situations, whereas behavioral inhibition reflects a propensity to react with inhibition to both social and nonsocial novel situations (Van Ameringen, Mancini, & Oakman, 1998). Infants and children with behavioral inhibition are described as being wary around unfamiliar people, excessively timid in situations that contain risk of harm, and highly cautious in situations that involve risk of failure (Kagan & Reznick, 1986; Kagan, Snidman, & Arcus, 1993). It has been estimated that up to 10% to 15% of White American children are born with a behavioral predisposition toward irritability as infants, shyness and fearfulness as toddlers, and cautiousness and introversion at school age (Kagan, Reznick, & Snidman, 1988). Kagan and colleagues' longitudinal studies of toddlers classified as either behaviorally inhibited or uninhibited reveal dramatic behavioral consistencies several years later, suggesting that a child's tendency to approach or withdraw from novelty is an enduring temperamental trait that predisposes them toward certain pathological conditions. Indeed, the inhibited children in their study manifested such difficulties as avoidant behavior on attending school as well as frequent symptoms consistent with separation anxiety (Gersten, 1986). These traits may predict such specific behaviors as presurgical distress (Quinonez, Santos, Boyar, & Cross, 1997).

From a parent-child dynamic perspective, in some situations, childhood anxiety may be related to disruptions in attachment. In a study of 172 child-parent dyads assessed with Ainsworth's Strange Situation Procedure at 12 months of age, anxious/resistant attachment was found to be related to meeting diagnostic criteria for anxiety disorder on a structured diagnostic interview at 17.5 years of age (S.L. Warren, Huston, Egeland, & Sroufe, 1997). Consistent with the hypothesis of the genetic transmission of these traits is the observation that the parents of children with stable behavioral inhibition over several years had higher rates of multiple childhood anxiety disorders and continuing anxiety disorder in adulthood (Hirshfield et al., 1992). Although mothers of children with SAD do not show an increased history of this disorder, up to 83% of mothers of children with SAD or GAD had a lifetime history of anxiety disorders (Last, Phillips, & Statfeld, 1987). However, it has been suggested that attachment may play a more primary role than parental anxiety and temperament (S.L. Warren et al., 1997).

In their proposed etiological pathway for the development of social phobia in children and adolescents, Beidel and Morris (1995) speculate a sequential process progressing from inborn temperamental inhibition leading to an insecure attachment between mother and child due to the child's highly reactive and difficult-to-soothe qualities. This pattern of anxious-insecure attachment is likely to lead the child to withdraw from peer interaction, further impairing her or his development of social skills needed to form supportive peer relationships (Vernberg et al., 1992). Biological factors may be pivotal here, as Kagan (1989) and others have noted that behaviorally inhibited children who remain inhibited in later childhood (beyond 7 years of age) had strong physiological reactions in early childhood suggesting overexcitability of the amygdala-hypothalamic circuit. Yet, the mediating role of attachment, experience, and parent-child interaction are obviously in need of further investigation.

ASSESSMENT OF FEAR AND ANXIETY IN YOUTH

In general, the strategies and types of assessment methods used to evaluate childhood anxiety disorders is dependent on the goals of the assessment (i.e., research, screening, diagnosis) (Silverman & Ginsburg, 1998). As with other forms of psychiatric

disorders, the assessment of anxiety disorders often relies on reports of parents, teachers, and other significant individuals in the child's life (Michael & Merrel, 1998). However, internal distress experienced by children may not be overtly identified by others, and thus reports of the child regarding his or her inward experiences is vital to assessing anxiety problems (Flanery, 1990). Indeed, it has been noted that children with internalizing pathology are better at reporting symptoms than their parents, whereas the reverse is generally true in regard to externalizing disorders (Achenbach, McConaughy, & Howell, 1987; Jensen et al., 1988). There is consensus that relying on multiple methods and informants is preferred for most accurately determining the presence, type, and severity of anxiety disorders in children (Bell-Dolan & Brazeal, 1993). This approach helps to minimize the impact of confounding factors (e.g., response bias) that may compromise the validity and reliability of an assessment. A thorough assessment of anxiety disorders includes a clinical interview, clinical rating scales, and self-report questionnaires (March & Albano, in press). These assessment methods may provide a broadened evaluation of overall psychiatric impairment and symptomatology, whereas others may be more focused on specific aspects of anxiety (Bell-Dolan & Brazeal, 1993). Moreover, the combination of assessment tools utilized should have the capacity to delineate the behavioral, subjective, and physiological manifestations of anxiety in children (Reed et al., 1990).

INTERVIEWS

The clinical interview has been the most commonly used and relied upon tool for the assessment of psychiatric pathology. The development of semistructured clinical interviews emerged due to concerns that unstructured interviews are vulnerable to missed and/or unreliable diagnosis (Bell-Dolan & Brazeal, 1993). The advent of semistructured interviews has helped to increase the standardization and reliability of the diagnosis of anxiety disorders in children. The Schedule for Affective Disorders and Schizophrenia in School-Age Children (K-SADS) (Puig-Antich & Chambers, 1978) is a commonly utilized semistructured interview that has undergone several revisions and has been widely researched (e.g., Kaufman et al., 1997). Similarly, the Child Assessment Schedule (CAS; Hodges & Fitch, 1979) has been used as a broad-based semistructured interview of psychiatric disorders in children. Both diagnostic tools assess the full range of psychiatric diagnostic categories in children, including anxiety disorders. To a limited degree, clinicians have freedom to choose questions to elicit *DSM* relevant diagnostic information. Thus, both interviews require use by trained clinicians to help ensure reliability in diagnosis. Furthermore, parent and child versions are available for both interviews. In general, recent research has indicated that both the K-SADS and CAS provide valid and reliable assessments of psychiatric disorders, including anxiety disorders, when used by trained clinicians (e.g., Hodges, McKnew, Burbach, & Roebuck, 1987).

Contrary to the K-SADS and CAS, the Anxiety Disorders Interview Schedule for Children (ADIS-C; Silverman & Nelles, 1988) is a semistructured interview specifically designed to evaluate anxiety disorders in children and adolescents. The ADIS-C was recently modified to incorporate *DSM-IV* criteria (Silverman & Albano, 1996) and is recommended for inclusion in evaluations designed to differentiate among anxiety disorders in youth (AACAP, 1997). The ADIS-C has parent and child versions, which also include sections for assessing mood and externalizing symptoms to delineate comorbidity of other disorders. Detailed, verbatim questions focus on situational cues for anxiety, extent of avoidance, intensity of anxiety, precipitating events, and problem history. Some clinical judgment is required in the administration of both the parent and child interviews to establish essential criteria for and to differentiate among disorders. Research on both the original and modified versions of the ADIS-C support its utility in reliably diagnosing anxiety disorders in youth (e.g., Silverman & Rabian, 1995).

The Yale–Brown Obsessive Compulsive Scale (YBOCS; Goodman et al., 1989) uses a semistructured interview format and specifically assesses obsessions and compulsions in individuals suspected of having OCD. The YBOCS initially relies on a comprehensive symptom checklist to account for specific obsessive/compulsive symptoms, and is followed by an assessment of obsessions and compulsions separately according to time consumed, related distress, interference, degree of resistance, and associated control (March, Leonard, & Swedo,

1995). The YBOCS has been used in numerous studies for the purpose of assessing treatment outcome and OCD phenomenology (e.g., March & Mulle, 1995; March et al., 1995) and is considered to be the primary assessment instrument for diagnosing OCD in youth (March & Mulle, 1998).

CLINICAL QUESTIONNAIRES

In contrast to interviews that are used to determine specific diagnoses, the purpose of most clinical questionnaires is to assess the severity and frequency of symptoms in youngsters (Michael & Merrell, 1998). Among the more common questionnaires completed by parents and teachers to assess symptoms in children are the Child Behavior Checklist (CBCL; Achenbach & Edelbrock, 1983) and the Conner's Parent/Teacher Rating Scale (CPRS, CTRS; Goyette, Conners, & Ulrich, 1978). Each of these measures assesses a multitude of emotional and behavioral symptoms and specific adjustment problem domains (e.g., anxiety, hyperactivity, inattention). Both sets of questionnaires have been widely researched and have been found to be valid and reliable as clinical tools in determining adjustment difficulties in youth, including anxiety. However, these tools may be somewhat limited in thoroughly assessing anxiety symptoms in children secondary to the internalized, subjective nature of many anxiety symptoms (Michael & Merrell, 1998).

A third, more recently developed questionnaire that also assesses multiple symptom domains in children is the Behavioral Assessment System for Children (BASC; Reynolds & Kamphaus, 1992). The BASC also includes parent and teacher forms and assesses both externalizing (e.g., conduct problems) and internalizing (e.g., anxiety, depression) domains of maladjustment. With its relatively recent development, research is limited with the BASC, and thus conclusions regarding its utility in assessing anxiety problems have not been adequately determined. However, early studies have suggested adequate reliability and validity in assessing internalizing and externalizing problems in youth (Vaughn, Riccio, Hynd, & Hall, 1997).

The Child Symptom Inventory 4 (CSI-4; Gadow & Sprafkin, 1995a) and the Adolescent Symptom Inventory 4 (ASI-4; Gadow & Sprafkin, 1995b) represent additional multidomain assessment instruments based on parent and teacher reports. These questionnaires are unique from those described above in that informants basically respond to a checklist of items that parallel *DSM-IV* symptoms. Indeed, the primary purpose in the initial development of these measures was to develop a structure for collecting information leading to the categorization of children's adjustment problems into conventional psychiatric diagnoses (Gadow & Sprafkin, 1995a). Informants indicate the frequency with which specific symptoms are observed in the child (i.e., never, often, very often), and symptom endorsements are then counted and compared to *DSM-IV* criteria. Initial research with these instruments indicates good reliability and validity in assessing adjustment problems in youth. However, evidence regarding their utility in the identification of psychiatric disorders in youth, including anxiety disorders, is somewhat mixed. Although the ASI-4 and the CSI-4 have shown adequate sensitivity in terms of differentiating psychiatric diagnoses among youth, they may also yield somewhat high numbers of false negatives or false positives in identifying *DSM-IV* disorders. The authors note that sensitivity and specificity of these instruments increase when information from both teacher and parent reports are taken into account (Gadow & Sprafkin, 1995a, 1995b). Finally, it is important to note that these instruments are not intended to be used alone for the purpose of diagnosis, but may best be utilized as a screening device to help guide information gathering in the assessment process.

SELF-REPORT MEASURES OF ANXIETY

Self-report measures of anxiety provide a time-efficient way to assess the internal, subjective experience of anxiety in children. Such measures are particularly useful for screening for the existence of anxiety and for identifying and quantifying symptoms (Silverman & Ginsburg, 1998). Though useful in the assessment of anxiety problems in children, self-report measures are susceptible to methodological limitations that may include underreporting (Glennon & Weisz, 1978), demographic influences (e.g., age) (Ollendick, Matson, & Helsel, 1985), and questionable validity in terms of differentiating anxiety disorders from other psychiatric disorders in children (Perrin & Last, 1992). Nevertheless, self-report measures can contribute to the clinician's capacity to more accurately determine subjective,

covert anxiety symptoms experienced by the child and thus enhance overall diagnostic accuracy.

Several self-report measures have been widely used in research and clinical practice in assessing anxiety in children. Among the most popular is the Revised Children's Manifest Anxiety Scale (RCMAS: Reynolds & Richmond, 1985). This is a 37-item measure made up of four subscales (Physiological Anxiety, General Worry, Social/Interpersonal Concerns, and Lie subscales). Children respond either yes or no to items describing various anxiety symptoms, and the number of yes responses are summed to yield a total anxiety score and subscale scores. The Lie subscale is a useful feature in terms of permitting an assessment of social desirability in the child's response style. Psychometric properties of the RCMAS have been examined, and reliability for the measure has been well established (e.g., Witt, Heffer, & Pfeiffer, 1990). Although the RCMAS clearly assesses anxiety-related distress in youth, research with this measure has not supported its usefulness in differentiating among anxiety disorders and other forms of psychiatric disorders, such as depression (e.g., Mattison & Bagnoto, 1987). Thus, it has been suggested that the RCMAS may best be used as an index of general distress in youngsters (March & Albano, in press).

The revised Fear Survey Schedule for Children (FSSC-R; Ollendick, 1983) is another widely used self-report assessment of anxiety symptoms in children that was adapted from the original Fear Survey for Children developed by Scherer and Nakamura (1968). The FSSC-R contains 80 items assessing five domains of fear: fear of failure and criticism, fear of the unknown, fear of injury and small animals, fear of danger and death, and medical fears. Normative data are available for youth age 7 to 18 years and is also separated by gender (Ollendick et al., 1985). Adequate internal consistency, test-retest reliability, and criterion validity have been established for this measure (Ollendick, 1983). In a study by Last, Francis, and Strauss (1989), the capacity of the measure to differentiate among various anxiety disorders in a group of children being seen in an anxiety disorders clinic was examined. In terms of quantitative indices, they found that the FSSC-R did not differentiate among anxiety disorders in subjects when using the standard total score or any of the five-factor scores. However, qualitative analyses (i.e., examining patterns of intense fear) did indicate that the diagnostic groups (SAD, OAD, SP) differed in regard to their most prevalent fears. Thus, the authors concluded that the measure may be most useful in identifying specific fear sensitivities in youths.

The State-Trait Anxiety Scale for Children (STAIC), or "How I Feel Questionnaire," is yet another, relatively well-known self-report instrument used to assess anxiety symptoms in children (Speilberger, 1973). The measure consists of two 20-item scales that assess state anxiety and trait anxiety. State anxiety refers to varying or fluctuating aspects of anxiety that may change relative to a given situation, whereas trait anxiety refers to the more enduring, chronic anxiety that an individual may experience irrespective of specific circumstances. The STAIC has generally shown adequate internal consistency, but the validity of the state-trait distinction has been questioned (Johnson & Melamed, 1979). Moreover, research with the STAIC has shown limited capacity to differentiate among anxiety disorders in children (Hoehn-Saric, Maisami, & Weigand, 1987). Thus, the overall utility of this measure in assessing and diagnosing specific anxiety disorders in youth appears to be limited.

In response to psychometric weaknesses in the above-mentioned self-report instruments, several empirically derived self-report measures have been recently developed. The Multidimensional Anxiety Scale for Children (MASC; March, Parker, Sullivan, Stallings, & Conners, 1997) is a newly developed, 45-item self-report measure assessing four factors and six subfactors covering anxiety domains in youth age 8 to 17 years. These factors, which were generally supported by factor-analytic procedures, include physical anxiety (tense/restless and somatic/autonomic), harm avoidance (perfectionism and anxious coping), social anxiety (humiliation fears and performance anxiety), and separation anxiety. The Screen for Child Anxiety-Related Emotional Disorders (SCARED; Birmaher et al., 1997) assesses five factors in youth age 9 to 18 years: somatic/panic, generalized anxiety, separation anxiety, social phobia, and school phobia. Items for both the MASC and SCARED were developed to reflect symptoms consistent with anxiety disorders described in *DSM-IV*. Analyses of psychometric properties of these instruments indicates good internal and test-retest reliability. Convergent and divergent validity has also been assessed and supported for both measures in that total scores for each measure were most closely associated with measures of anxiety, but were less or not at all significantly associated with measures of depression or externalizing problems. Furthermore,

the SCARED showed the capacity to differentiate among individual anxiety disorders including panic disorder, GAD, and SAD. Although additional research is needed with these relatively new self-report instruments, they appear to show excellent psychometric rigor as empirically derived, multi-domain measures of anxiety in youth.

In addition to the instruments described above, a number of self-report instruments have also been developed to assess more specific aspects of anxiety symptomatology in youth. The Social Phobia and Anxiety Inventory for Children (Beidel, Turner, & Morris, 1995) is an empirically derived self-report measure that assesses specific somatic symptoms (e.g., fast heartbeat), cognitions (e.g., What if I make a mistake?), and behavior (e.g., avoidance) regarding a variety of fear-producing situations. The Social Anxiety Scale for Children–Revised (SASC-R; La Greca & Stone, 1993) is a 22-item measure that assesses symptoms related to social anxiety, including generalized social avoidance and distress, social avoidance and distress in new situations, and fear of negative evaluation. The Social Anxiety Scale includes versions for children, adolescents, and corresponding parent versions. The Leyton Obsessional Inventory–Child Version (LOI-CV; Berg et al., 1988) is a 20-item self-report measure of four factors of obsessive-compulsive symptomatology in youth: general obsessive, dirt/contamination, numbers/luck, and school-related symptoms. An additional self-report measure, the Childhood Anxiety Sensitivity Index (CASI; Silverman, Fleisig, Rabian, & Perteseon, 1991) is an 18-item measure used essentially to delineate the fear of anxiety as reflected by children's beliefs about anxiety symptoms that they experience (e.g., It scares me when I feel nervous). In general, studies examining the psychometric properties and sensitivity of these measures in assessing specific aspects of anxiety in children have supported their usefulness (e.g., Chorpita, Albano, & Barlow, 1996; Weems, Hammond-Laurence, Silverman, & Ginsburg, 1998).

OBSERVATIONAL ASSESSMENT

All of the assessment instruments described above rely on descriptions and item ratings provided by informants (e.g., teacher, parent, child) and, thus, are vulnerable to response bias that may compromise their usefulness. Clinical observation of children's fear and anxiety behaviors in a natural environment provides a means for obtaining a wealth of information that may not be otherwise available (Bell-Dolan & Brazeal, 1993). Observational coding schemes have been developed for the purpose of standardizing naturalistic observation regarding the manifestation of children's anxiety in their everyday environments. Unfortunately, naturalistic observation is rarely practical for clinicians due to time constraints and the possibility that fear-producing situations may not readily occur at the time of observation; thus, the use of analogue observational procedures may be preferable to most clinicians (Silverman & Ginsburg, 1998). Such procedures essentially involve setting up anxiety-producing situations for children and observing behavioral responses. Behavioral avoidance tasks, separation from parents, and confronting feared stimuli are examples of tasks that can be arranged and observed (Kendall, 1994). An example of a standardized observation measure is the Observation of Separation-Relevant Play (Milos & Reiss, 1982). Using this measure, a trained observer can monitor and count the number of anxiety-related behaviors exhibited by a child, resulting in an overall separation anxiety score. Observational measures such as this appear to show good interrater reliability and are considered useful in identifying the presence and/or intensity of anxiety symptoms in children that may otherwise be missed (Glennon & Weisz, 1978).

PHYSIOLOGICAL MEASURES

Physiological measures of anxiety have an extensive research history and can be obtained from many areas of autonomic function, including blood pressure, heart rate, muscular tension, and sweating (Reed et al., 1990). In addition to self-report instruments that may inquire about some physiological symptoms of anxiety experienced by youth, instruments are available for obtaining measures of autonomic responses when the subject is presented with the feared stimulus or a verbal/imagined description of the stimulus. Some research has indicated that children with varying anxiety disorders show differences on measures of pulse rate and blood pressure (Bell-Dolan & Brazeal, 1993). For example, Beidel (1988) found that children with social phobia showed significantly higher increases in pulse rate compared to children with OAD and

normal controls when presented with taking a test or reading in front of a group. Unfortunately, the area of physiological assessment of anxiety in children has been relatively understudied (Beidel, 1988). Moreover, the questionable validity of these types of measures, individual differences in physiological development of children, and sensitivity to influence unrelated to anxiety limit the usefulness of the physiologic instruments in assessing anxiety in youth (Reed et al., 1990).

TREATMENT OF ANXIETY DISORDERS IN CHILDREN

By far the most empirically supported psychological interventions for anxiety disorders in children and adolescents, as well as for adults, are the behavioral and cognitive-behavioral therapies (Kazdin & Weisz, 1998; Ollendick & King, 1998). Among the behavioral therapy (BT) interventions are in vivo (real life) desensitization/exposure, flooding and implosive therapy, operant conditioning and contingency management, modeling (live, filmed, and participant), and multimodal approaches. Cognitive-behavioral therapy (CBT) methods include such interventions as self-monitoring, imaginal desensitization and emotive imagery, and the teaching of specific coping skills such as positive self-talk, verbal self-instructional procedures, thought stopping, distraction, self-reinforcement, and progressive relaxation (Kronenberger & Meyer, in press). BT interventions focus primarily on exposure methods that control the child's engagement in avoidance behavior. This allows for counterconditioning to take place, in which the child is exposed to anxiety/fear-producing stimuli while engaging in incompatible behaviors/responses. Reinforcement for graduated successful mastery is a frequent component to such interventions, to make engagement in the behaviors that are incompatible with fear/anxiety more likely. CBT interventions focus on teaching the child to identify specific anxiety cues and then apply specific cognitive and behavioral coping responses, and are thus more appropriate for older children and adolescents. They are designed to alter the child's perceptions, images, thoughts, and beliefs via the restructuring of presumed maladaptive and distorted cognitions (Ollendick & King, 1998). In addition, the use of parents/caregivers as surrogate therapists and the employment of family therapy, in cases where the boundaries and roles of family members are instrumental in maintaining symptoms, is often recommended to enhance treatment outcome (Bernstein, 1990; Ollendick & King, 1998). Finally, group-based interventions focusing on the integration of exposure with specific skill remediation (e.g., for youth with social phobias; Albano, Marten, Holt, Heimberg, & Barlow, 1995; Beidel & Turner, 1998) may also be employed.

BEHAVIORAL THERAPY INTERVENTIONS

BT interventions, particularly in the acute stage of development of an anxiety disorder, may be as simple as suggesting to parents that they impose firm rules and limits about behaviors that may lead to more severe avoidance on the part of the child. For example, Black (1995) found that in the acute stage (less than 2–4 months duration) of a child's first episode of SAD, symptoms are often abated if the parents impose firm rules about separation behavior, while programmatically reinforcing appropriate separation behavior and removing incidental reinforcements for avoidance. However, more intense and programmatic behavioral interventions are often needed for more severe cases of longer duration (Kronenberger & Meyer, in press).

In vivo systematic desensitization/exposure is one of the most frequently employed treatments for a variety of anxiety disorders, particularly SAD and specific phobias. This treatment consists of a graduated exposure of the child to the feared stimulus/situation (e.g., a dog, separation from the parent). Progression through a hierarchy of stimuli or situations, from the least to the most anxiety-provoking, is employed to expose the child to gradually increased levels of threatening stimuli.

For example, in the case of a child with a severe fear of vomiting, the initial goal may be for the child to talk about observing another child vomiting. Next, it may involve having the child view videotape of someone vomiting. Gradually, the treatment regimen would involve the child looking at vomitus (typically, a concoction of purchased foods that produce the look and smell of vomit) in a realistic setting (e.g., on a bathroom sink or toilet), and perhaps even pouring the vomit concoction into the toilet bowl themselves. Throughout the treatment process, the child is coached in strategies to reduce anxiety, such as slow chest breathing and relaxation and self-talk strategies to reinforce mastery, and reinforcement contingencies are set for accomplishment of the various stages in the hierarchy.

The efficacy of in vivo desensitization is generally supported and superior to no-treatment control conditions (Ollendick & King, 1998; Ultee, Griffioen, & Schellekens, 1982) with children with anxiety disorders. The support for imaginal systematic desensitization is less well established (Miller, Barrett, Hampe, & Noble, 1972; Ollendick & King, 1998) and has been found in at least one study (Ultee et al., 1982) to be inferior to in vivo desensitization. Emotive imagery (Lazarus & Abramowitz, 1962), a variant of systematic desensitization in which the child is coached in the use of an imagined exciting story involving a favorite superhero as an anxiety inhibitor, has received some preliminary support. Cornwall, Spence, and Schotte (1997) treated darkness phobia in twenty-four 7- to 10-year-old children using a between-group design. Subjects were randomly assigned to either the emotive imagery treatment group or a waiting-list control group. The treatment condition was superior in reducing general fearfulness, trait anxiety, observable anxious behaviors during a darkness tolerance test, child fear thermometer ratings, and parental ratings of their child's fearfulness after treatment.

Flooding and implosive therapies involve continuous exposure, either in vivo or in imagination, to the anxiety-provoking situation or object until the child's anxiety level decreases or dissipates. Whereas flooding procedures employ actual exposure to the feared stimuli, implosive therapy uses imaginal exposure. Flooding has been employed with SAD when there is a primary problem with school avoidance, and involves requiring the child to attend school for the full day. Child complaints and attempts to resist separation from the parent are handled with firmness. Obviously, parental and school cooperation are crucial to enforcement of the treatment plan (Kearney & Albano, 2000). In flooding, there is no gradual exposure to the anxiety-provoking situation, unlike in systematic desensitization, and thus this technique must be used with caution with children with high levels of anxiety who may become overwhelmed.

Modeling is a procedure based in social learning theory (Bandura, 1981) involving the process of observational learning to overcome fear and anxiety. In its various forms, it may involve the use of live models, filmed models, and participant modeling by the child. Extinction of the child's avoidance responses is thought to occur via the child's observation of the model confronting the anxiety-provoking stimuli while demonstrating both nonfearful behavior and a more adaptive and appropriate response to the situation (Ollendick & King, 1998). In general, the greater the similarity between the child and the model and the situation depicted, the better the outcome. The efficacy of modeling in the treatment of children with SAD is well documented. It is helpful for the model to initially show some difficulty with separation, followed by gradual mastery, to facilitate the child's ability to identify with the model. There are indications that assisted child participation by the therapist along with viewing a model may be more effective than modeling alone in reducing avoidance behaviors (Blanchard, 1970; Lewis, 1974); this can be either child-initiated or therapist-initiated (Murphy & Bootzin, 1973). Indeed, participant modeling may be more effective than the passive observation of a model alone (Ritter, 1968). Empirical studies of the efficacy of modeling have been conducted on children with fear of dogs (Bandura & Menlove, 1968), fear of snakes (Bandura, Blanchard, & Ritter, 1969; Ritter, 1968), and avoidant behavior toward water activities (Lewis, 1974).

Contingency management methods focus on identifying the inadvertent rewards and reinforcers that may be serving to maintain the child's anxious, fearful, and avoidant behavior. Based on principles of operant conditioning, contingency management procedures attempt to alter fearful behavior by manipulating its consequences (King & Ollendick, 1997). Operant techniques assert that the child's acquisition of approach behaviors alone is sufficient for change, without focusing on anxiety reduction. The most frequently employed contingency management procedures with childhood anxiety and phobic conditions include positive reinforcement, extinction, and shaping (Ollendick & King, 1998).

Common positive reinforcers that often help to maintain a child's separation anxiety symptoms include increased parental attention and interaction with the parent, freer access to food, television, and toys throughout the day, and being able to sleep late (Kearney & Albano, 2000). Negative reinforcers, or conditions that reward avoidant behavior, may include avoidance of aversive peer interactions, avoidance of the fear that harm will come to the parent in the child's absence, avoiding fear of failure in school, avoidance of the anxiety inherent in separation from the parent and the achievement of separation and independence. In such a clinical situation, a thorough evaluation of the positive and negative reinforcers that the child may receive when displaying separation anxiety is a crucial first step. These existing reinforcers must be eliminated and new reinforcers of behaviors that are incompatible with SAD must be identified and applied. In the example of a child with SAD, this might involve taking the child to the doctor for examination if he or she is to be allowed to remain home from school, having the child remain in bed with minimal interaction with the parent and no access to TV, and setting up specific rewards for school attendance. Contingency management procedures are often enhanced when combined with desensitization (Kearney & Albano, 2000).

Contingency management procedures have been demonstrated to be effective in helping children overcome the fear of riding a bus (Obler & Terwilliger, 1970), fear of dogs (Obler & Terwilliger, 1970), fear of the dark (Sheslow, Bondy, & Nelson, 1983), and fear of water (Menzies & Clark, 1993). In fact, some studies have found reinforced practice to be superior to live adult modeling of the behavior (Menzies & Clark, 1993), as well as to the use of verbal coping skills (Sheslow et al., 1983).

COGNITIVE-BEHAVIORAL THERAPY

In anxiety disorders, it is assumed that the child's maladaptive cognitions lead to the use of maladaptive avoidant behaviors. Treatment focuses on producing cognitive changes that, in turn, will produce behavior changes incompatible with anxious or phobic symptomatology. Supporting this key assumption is the finding that youth experiencing significant test-taking anxiety report engaging in frequent negative self-evaluations, infrequent positive self-evaluations, and off-task thoughts that distract them from the test-taking tasks (Beidel & Turner, 1988; M.K. Warren, Ollendick, & King, 1996). CBT methods teach the child skills at identifying anxiety cues and to apply specific coping responses (Kendall, Kane, Howard, & Siqueland, 1992). A typical CBT treatment regimen begins with instructing children in self-monitoring tasks, such as keeping a daily diary of anxiety-provoking situations and cues, as well as their affective, cognitive (thinking, self-talk), and behavioral response (avoidance vs. coping and mastery). The self-monitoring stage teaches the child to identify the cues that lead to anxiety (e.g., separation from caretaker or getting up to speak in class). The next stage involves teaching the child a variety of coping skills to be employed in anxiety-provoking situations, such as positive self-talk, distraction, self-reinforcement, emotive imagery, and relaxation. The child then applies the skills in vivo. There is considerable clinical and research support for this approach (Kazdin & Weisz, 1998; Ollendick & King, 1998).

Kendall (1994) employed a comprehensive CBT regimen in treating a mixed group of children with anxiety disorders including SAD, GAD, and social phobia. Called "The Coping Cat" program (Kendall et al., 1992), this 16-week protocol included teaching the children to recognize their somatic reactions and anxious feelings, to become aware of the accompanying anxiety-related cognitions, and to develop a coping plan involving *positive self-talk* and problem-solving skills. In addition, youth were taught to evaluate their coping responses and apply *self-reinforcement* for adaptive coping behaviors. Both *imaginal* and *in vivo* exposure were employed in the treatment protocol. A workbook and in- and extrasession activities were employed to reinforce subjects' use of their skills. One- and three-year follow-ups revealed maintenance of the treatment gains compared to waiting-list controls, and controls who were given the CBT treatment later showed similar gains (Kendall & Southam-Gerow, 1996). The program has also proven effective over the long term in an Australian adaptation (Barrett, Dadds, & Rapee, 1996).

Parent Intervention and Family Therapy

It is common for parents to be involved in their child's treatment program because the child's anxiety is often centered in his or her relationship with the primary caretaker and the child's symptoms may have a profound impact on family interactions and dynamics (Kronenberger & Meyer, in press). At a minimum, this may involve educating the parents about the etiology, symptoms, and treatment of their child's anxiety disorder. In many cases, for example, the treatment of SAD, school avoidance, and social phobia, the parent may be directly involved on a daily basis in both monitoring the child's behavior and performance of treatment tasks, as well as in implementing treatment procedures. Parents also need to be apprised of the role their behaviors may play in inadvertently reinforcing the child's avoidance behaviors, as well as the role of environmental stresses on both child and family. Parents may also require considerable support due to feelings of guilt and doubtfulness as to the limits they may be posing on their child during the treatment process. It is a continual process of motivating the parents to adhere to the treatment process and following through with recommendations.

Family therapy is occasionally needed in cases where the parent may be overreliant on the child and reinforcing him or her for excessively dependent and avoidant behavior (Meyer, 1993). Parents in such a situation may be unmotivated to implement therapeutic recommendations or even openly sabotage intervention (Kronenberger & Meyer, in press). The child's avoidant symptoms may actually serve a role in the family environment. Family therapy may be needed as an adjunct to behavioral and cognitive-behavioral therapies to address issues of boundaries and roles of family members as well as more general systemic issues such as child-parent boundaries and proper family hierarchy (Bernstein, 1990). The therapist may need to actively intervene in structural family issues and openly explain how the child is using the avoidant behavior to exercise control in the relationship or to avoid independent roles and behaviors (Kaplan & Sadock, 1988).

A recent review of empirically supported treatments for anxiety disorders in children suggests that involving the family in behavioral and cognitive treatments can enhance the effectiveness of these treatments (Ollendick & King, 1998). Family members are often trained to ignore (*extinction*) overanxious or fearful behavior, deliver reinforcements for goal attainment (both verbal praise and tangible rewards), and to serve as models for effective coping and management of anxiety-producing situations. Often, parental anxiety and worries, as well as expectations regarding the child's performance, are contributors to the child's anxiety. In such situations, adjunctive treatment for the parent may be indicated, particularly if parental psychopathology is felt to be contributing to the child's symptoms.

Summary

Behavioral and cognitive-behavioral therapies have become a virtual therapeutic mainstay in the treatment of childhood anxiety disorders. As such, it is surprising that there are so few controlled between-group design studies of the efficacy of these interventions (Ollendick & King, 1998). Although a number of single-case design studies have supported the efficacy of these treatment methods (Eisen & Silverman, 1993; Hagopian, Weist, & Ollendick, 1990; Ollendick, 1995), more comprehensive, controlled between-group design studies utilizing manualized treatment procedures, such as Kendall's (Kendall et al., 1992; Kendall, 1994) "Coping Cat" treatment program for anxious youth, are needed. Much more methodically rigorous research is needed to firmly establish the efficacy of these treatments with clinical populations (Ollendick & King, 1998).

Pharmacologic Interventions

A common question of most parents seeking help for their anxious children is whether medication will be a part of the treatment regimen. Indeed, many parents selectively seek treatment with a mental health professional based on their biases for or against the use of medication. Biases against medication may result from negative information and stories portrayed in the popular press, religious beliefs, personal preferences, and safety concerns, along with the knowledge that relatively little information is known about the long-term use of psychotropic medications in youth. However, with increased attention to the study of anxiety disorders in children, the field of psychopharmacology and clinical trials are advancing daily with regard to this issue. In addition to research on the efficacy, safety, and specific use of medications for youth, investigators are focused on developing guidelines for the practice of pharmacotherapy alone and in combination with CBT (see, e.g., March, Frances, Kahn, & Carpenter, 1997). To date, few empirical studies of the efficacy of specific medications for anxious youth have been conducted, with the exception of medications for the treatment of OCD. In fact, many of the medications used in the treatment of childhood anxiety disorders are the result of clinical experience rather than empirical testing

(March & Albano, in press). In response to the dearth of controlled pharmacologic trials, the National Institute of Mental Health has established the Research Units in Pediatric Pharmacology (RUPP), a division focused on the controlled evaluation of psychotropic medications for use in children younger than 18 years. RUPP investigations focus on testing the efficacy of specific compounds for the range of emotional and behavioral disorders in youth.

Most pediatric psychiatrists agree that treatment of anxious youth should begin with or be initiated in conjunction with CBT. It is unusual and not recommended for medication to be considered as the sole treatment for anxious youth (AACAP, 1997). Clinicians may use the following guidelines in deciding to include medication in the child's treatment regimen (Klee & Hack, 1999; March & Albano, in press):

1. Has CBT or other psychosocial treatments been tried and found ineffective?
2. Can these symptoms respond to pharmacotherapy?
3. Do the symptoms cause significant distress and interference in functioning?
4. Is the parent asking for medication intervention?
5. Does the comorbidity pattern suggest more aggressive intervention?
6. Is the child or adolescent suicidal?
7. Are the symptoms of significant severity to warrant exposing the child to the potential risks of taking a specific medication?
8. Despite past trials of CBT, does the child evidence a relapse pattern of increasing frequency and severity?

Although empirical data are limited outside of the use of medications for OCD, the selective serotonin reuptake inhibitors (SSRIs) are gaining increasing empirical support for their use in the long-term management of child anxiety (Birmaher et al., 1994; Manassis & Bradley, 1994). To date, only open-label trials have been reported in the literature, although several controlled trials are underway. This class of medication is generally well tolerated by patients and relatively safe if overdosing occurs (Riddle et al., 1989). Side effects of the SSRIs are typically minimal and may include gastrointestinal upset, sedation or insomnia, activation, and headaches. Older adolescents and adults may

Table 15.2 Medications used in the treatment of child and adolescent anxiety disorders.

Class of Medication	Drug	Brand Name	Therapeutic Focus
Tricyclic antidepressants	Imipramine Nortriptyline Desipramine	Tofranil Pamelor Norpramin Anafranil	Typically used for separation anxiety, school refusal, generalized anxiety, and panic disorder. Not commonly used for treating OCD and specific phobias. Note: This class of medication is used increasingly less often, due to side effect profiles.
	Clomipramine		(Clomipramine is the only TCA used for OCD.)
Serotonin reuptake inhibitors	Citalopram Fluoxetine Fluvoxamine Paroxetine Sertraline	Cilexia Prosac Luvox Paxil Zoloft	Controlled studies of the SRIs are underway, with preliminary support suggesting efficacy for all anxiety disorders except specific phobias.
Benzodiazepines	Alprazolam Clonazepam Lorezapam	Xanax Klonopin Ativan	This class of medication is used sparingly in children, due to the side effect of sedation and the potential for habit formation. Benzodiazepines are useful in the treatment of situation and anticipatory anxiety across all anxiety disorders, but most often for panic disorder, generalized anxiety disorder, and phobia.
Other drugs	Buspirone Bupropion	Buspar Wellbutrin	Generalized Anxiety Disorder.
	Propolanol	Inderal	Non-generalized social phobia, such as public speaking anxiety.
	Venlafaxine Nefazodone Mitrazapine	Effexor Serzone Remeron	New medications under study for use in anxiety; Little data in children.

Source: Klee & Hack, 1998; March & Albano (in press).

experience sexual dysfunction. For short-term and more immediate relief, the high-potency benzodiazepines may be used, although these medications are habit-forming and many patients report discontinuation difficulties with long-term use. Side effects of this class of medication include sedation, dizziness, and cognitive blunting. In addition, reports of behavioral disinhibition have been reported (Graae, Milner, Rizzotto, & Klein, 1994; Reiter & Kutcher, 1991). Tricyclic antidepressants in general have little empirical support and high potential for serious side effects, including orthostatic hypotension and EKG changes. Table 15.2 presents a summary of medications used to treat anxiety disorders. For a complete review of the indications and use of medications for anxious children, the reader is referred to the published practice parameters outlined by the American Academy of Child and Adolescent Psychiatry (AACAP, 1997).

SUMMARY AND CONCLUSION

In this chapter, we reviewed a wide range of conceptual, methodological, and clinical considerations relating to the study and treatment of fears and anxiety in youth. It is clear that advances have occurred on a number of fronts. Sophisticated statistical modeling procedures are providing investigators with more refined and precise means of evaluating theoretical constructs, although this area of study is relatively new to the child arena. The field of developmental psychopathology is advancing, with increased knowledge of the timing for onset and course of symptoms of fear and anxiety in both normative and clinical samples. The integration of information gained through model testing and epidemiological research is leading investigators to propose algorithms for predicting risk, vulnerability, and protective factors, which may inform efforts in the areas of identification and prevention of diagnostic syndromes. Indeed, the past two decades have witnessed a burgeoning of scientifically sound and effective cognitive-behavioral intervention methods, with the field of psychopharmacology advancing at a steady pace. At present, clinical scientists are moving toward evaluating the integration of cognitive-behavioral methodologies with medication. Toward this end, multimodal, multicenter clinical trials are being proposed to evaluate the effectiveness of the psychosocial and pharmacological treatment regimens by themselves and in combination. The goals of such research, beyond establishing efficacy and effectiveness, are to advance practice guidelines and parameters for the treatment of children and adolescents with anxiety disorders and to disseminate these guidelines widely.

REFERENCES

Achenbach, T.M., & Edelbrock, C. (1983). *Manual for the Child Behavior Checklist and Revised Child Behavior Profile.* Burlington: University of Vermont, Department of Psychology.

Achenbach, T.M., McConaughy, S.H., & Howell, C.T. (1987). Child/adolescent behavioral and emotional problems: Implications of cross-informant correlations for situational specificity. *Psychological Bulletin, 101,* 213–232.

Agras, W.S., Chapin, H.S., & Oliveau, D.C. (1972). The natural history of phobia. *Archives of General Psychiatry, 26,* 315–317.

Albano, A.M., Chorpita, B.F., & Barlow, D.H. (1996). Childhood anxiety disorders. In E.J. Mash & R.A. Barkley (Eds.), *Child psychopathology* (pp. 196–241). New York: Guilford Press.

Albano, A.M., Marten, P.A., Holt, C.S., Heimberg, R.G., & Barlow, D.H. (1995). Cognitive-behavioral group treatment for social phobia in adolescents: A preliminary study. *Journal of Nervous and Mental Disease, 183,* 685–692.

American Academy of Child and Adolescent Psychiatry. (1997). Practice parameters for the assessment and treatment of children and adolescents with anxiety disorders. *Journal of the American Academy of Child and Adolescent Psychiatry, 36,* 69–84.

American Psychiatric Association. (1994). *Diagnostic and statistical manual of mental disorders* (4th ed.). Washington, DC: Author.

August, G.J., & Garfinkle, B.D. (1993). The nosology of attention-deficit hyperactivity disorder. *Journal of the American Academy of Child and Adolescent Psychiatry, 32,* 155–165.

Bandura, A. (1981). In search of pure unidirectional determinants. *Behavior Therapy, 12,* 30–40.

Bandura, A., & Menlove, F.L. (1968). Factors determining vicarious extinction of avoidance behavior through symbolic modeling. *Journal of Personality & Social Psychology, 3,* 99–108.

Bandura, A., Blanchard, B., & Ritter, B. (1969). Relative efficacy of desensitization and modeling: Approaches for inducing behavioral, affective, and attitudinal changes. *Journal of Personality & Social Psychology, 13,* 173–199.

Barlow, D.H. (1988). *Anxiety and its disorders.* New York: Guilford Press.

Barlow, D.H., Chorpita, B.F., & Turovsky, J. (1996). Fear, panic, anxiety, and the disorders of emotion. In D.A. Hope (Ed.), *Nebraska Symposium on Motivation: Perspectives on anxiety, panic, and fear* (Vol. 43, pp. 251–328). Lincoln: University of Nebraska Press.

Barrett, P.M., Dadds, M.R., & Rapee, R.M. (1996). Family intervention for child anxiety: A controlled trial. *Journal of Consulting and Clinical Psychology, 64,* 333–342.

Beidel, D.C. (1988). Psychophysiological assessment of anxious emotional states in children. *Journal of Abnormal Child Psychology, 97,* 80–82.

Beidel, D.C., & Morris, T.L. (1995). Social phobia. In J. March (Ed.), *Anxiety disorders in children and adolescents.* New York: Guilford Press.

Beidel, D.C., & Turner, S.M. (1998). *Shy children, phobic adults: Nature and treatment of social phobia.* Washington, DC: American Psychological Association Press.

Beidel, D.C., & Turner, S.M. (1988). Comorbidity of test anxiety and other anxiety disorders in children. *Journal of Abnormal Child Psychology, 24,* 187–203.

Beidel, D.C., Turner, S.M., & Morris, T.I. (1995). A new inventory to assess childhood social anxiety and phobia: The Social Phobia and Anxiety Inventory for Children. *Psychological Assessment, 7,* 73–79.

Bell-Dolan, D., & Brazeal, T.J. (1993). Separation anxiety disorder, overanxious disorder, and school refusal. *Child and Adolescent Psychiatric Clinics of North America, 2,* 563–580.

Berensen, C.K. (1993). Evaluation and treatment of anxiety in the general pediatric population. *Child and Adolescent Psychiatric Clinics of North America, 4,* 727–747.

Berg, C. (1970). A follow-up study of school phobic adolescents admitted to an inpatient unit. *Journal of Child Psychology and Psychiatry, 11,* 37–47.

Berg, C., Rapoport, J.L., Whitaker, A., Davies, M., Leonard, H.L., Swedo, S.E., Braiman, S., & Lenane, M. (1989). Childhood obsessive compulsive disorder: A two-year prospective follow-up of a community sample. *Journal of the American Academy of Child and Adolescent Psychiatry, 28,* 528–533.

Berg, C.Z., Whitaker, A., Davies, M., Flament, M.F., & Rapoport, J.L. (1988). The survey form of the Leyton Obsessional Inventory–Child Version: Norms from an epidemiological study. *Journal of the American Academy of Child and Adolescent Psychiatry, 27,* 759–763.

Bernstein, G.A. (1990). Anxiety disorders. In B.D. Garfinkel, G.A. Carlson, & E.V. Weller (Eds.), *Psychiatric disorders in children and adolescents.* Philadelphia: Saunders.

Biederman, J., Faraone, S.V., Spencer, T., Wilens, T., Norman, D., Lapey, K.A., Mick, E., Lehman, B.K., & Doyle, A. (1993). Patterns of psychiatric comorbidity, cognition, and psychosocial functioning in adults with attention deficit hyperactivity disorder. *American Journal of Psychiatry, 150,* 1792–1798.

Biederman, J., Newcorn, J., & Sprich, S. (1991). Comorbidity of attention deficit hyperactivity disorder with conduct, depressive, anxiety and other disorders. *American Journal of Psychiatry, 148,* 564–577.

Biederman, J., Rosenbaum, J.F., Bolduc-Murphy, E.A., Faraone, S.V., Chaloff, J., Hirshfield, D.R., & Kagan, J. (1993). Behavioral inhibition as a temperamental risk factor for anxiety disorders. *Child and Adolescent Psychiatric Clinics of North America, 2,* 667–684.

Bird, H.R., Gould, M.S., & Staghezza, B. (1993). Patterns of diagnostic comorbidity in a community sample of children aged 7 through 16 years. *Journal of the American Academy of Child and Adolescent Psychiatry, 32,* 361–368.

Birmaher, B., Khetarpal, S., Brent, D., Marlane, C., Balach, L., Kaufman, J., & McKenzie, S. (1997). The Screen for Child Anxiety-Related Emotional Disorders (SCARED): Scale construction and psychometric characteristics. *Journal of the American Academy of Child and Adolescent Psychiatry, 36,* 545–553.

Birmaher, B., Waterman, G.S., Ryan, N., Cully, M., Balach, L., Ingram, J., & Brodsky, M. (1994). Fluoxetine for childhood anxiety disorders. *Journal of the American Academy of Child and Adolescent Psychiatry, 33,* 993–999.

Black, B. (1995). Separation anxiety disorder and panic disorder. In J.S. March (Ed.), *Anxiety disorders in children and adolescents* (pp. 212–234). New York: Guilford Press.

Black, B., & Robbins, D.R. (1990). Panic disorder in children and adolescents. *Journal of the American Academy of Child and Adolescent Psychiatry, 29,* 36–44.

Black, B., & Uhde, T.W. (1994). Treatment of elective mutism with fluoxetine: A double blind, placebo-controlled study. *Journal of the American Academy of Child and Adolescent Psychiatry, 33,* 1090–1094.

Blanchard, E.B. (1970). Relative contributions of modeling, informational influences, and physical contact in extinction of phobic behavior. *Journal of Abnormal Psychology, 76,* 55–61.

Bradley, S.J., & Hood, J. (1993). Psychiatrically referred adolescents with panic attacks: Presenting symptoms, stressors, and comorbidity. *Journal of the American Academy of Child and Adolescent Psychiatry, 32,* 826–829.

Cantwell, D.P., & Baker, L. (1989). Stability and natural history of *DSM-III* childhood diagnoses. *Journal of the American Academy of Child and Adolescent Psychiatry, 29,* 691–700.

Chorpita, B.F., Albano, A.M., & Barlow, D.H. (1996). The Childhood Anxiety Sensitivity Index: Considerations for children with anxiety disorders. *Journal of Clinical Child Psychology, 25,* 77–82.

Chorpita, B.F., Albano, A.M., & Barlow, D.H. (1998). The structure of negative emotions in a clinical sample of children and adolescents. *Journal of Abnormal Psychology, 107,* 74–85.

Clark, L.A., & Watson, D. (1991). Tripartite model of anxiety and depression: Psychometric evidence and taxonomic implications. *Journal of Abnormal Psychology, 100,* 316–336.

Cohen, P., Cohen, J., & Brook, J.S. (1993). An epidemiological study of disorders in late childhood and adolescence: II. Persistence of disorders. *Journal of Child Psychology and Psychiatry, 34,* 867–875.

Cornwall, E., Spence, S.H., & Schotte, D. (1997). The effectiveness of emotive imagery in the treatment of darkness phobia in children. *Behaviour Change, 13,* 223–229.

Eisen, A.R., & Silverman, W.K. (1993). Should I relax or change my thoughts? A preliminary examination of cognitive therapy, relaxation training, and their combination with overanxious children. *Journal of Cognitive Psychotherapy: An International Quarterly, 7,* 265–280.

Eme, R., & Schmidt, D. (1978). The stability of children's fears. *Child Development, 49,* 1277–1279.

Flanery, R.C. (1990). Methodological and psychometric considerations in child reports. In A.M. La Greca (Ed.), *Through the eyes of a child: Obtaining self-reports from children and adolescents* (pp. 57–82). Boston: Allyn & Bacon.

Francis, G., Last, C.G., & Strauss, C.C. (1987). Expression of separation anxiety disorder: The roles of age and gender. *Child Psychiatry and Human Development, 18,* 82–89.

Gadow, K.D., & Sprafkin, J. (1995a). *Manual for the Child Symptoms Inventories.* Stony Brook, NY: Checkmate Plus.

Gadow, K.D., & Sprafkin, J. (1995b). *Adolescent supplement to the manual for the Child Symptom Inventories.* Stony Brook, NY: Checkmate Plus.

Gersten, M. (1986). *The contribution of temperament to behavior in natural contexts.* Unpublished doctoral dissertation, Harvard Graduate School of Education, Cambridge, MA.

Glennon, B., & Weisz, J.R. (1978). An observational approach to the assessment of anxiety in young children. *Journal of Consulting and Clinical Psychology, 46,* 1246–1257.

Goodman, W.K., Price, L.H., Rasmussen, S.A., Mazure, C., Delgado, P., Heninger, G.R., & Charney, D.S. (1989). The Yale-Brown Obsessive Compulsive Scale: Vol. II. Validity. *Archives of General Psychiatry, 46,* 1012–1016.

Goyette, C.H., Conners, C.K., & Ulrich, R.F. (1978). Normative data on revised Conner's Parent and Teacher Ratings Scales. *Journal of Clinical Child Psychology, 6,* 221–236.

Graae, F., Milner, J., Rizzotto, L., & Klein, R.G. (1994). Clonazepam in childhood anxiety disorders. *Journal of the American Academy of Child and Adolescent Psychiatry, 33,* 372–376.

Gray, J.A. (1982). *The neuropsychology of anxiety.* New York: Oxford University Press.

Hagopian, L.P., Weist, M.D., & Ollendick, T.H. (1990). Cognitive-behavior therapy with an 11-year-old girl fearful of AIDS infection, other diseases, and poisoning: A case study. *Journal of Anxiety Disorders, 4,* 457–465.

Hampe, E., Noble, M., Miller, L.C., & Barrett, C.L. (1973). Phobic children at two years post-treatment. *Journal of Abnormal Psychology, 82,* 446–453.

Hansen, D.J., Nangle, D.W., & Meyer, K.A. (1998). Enhancing the effectiveness of social skills interventions with adolescents. *Education and Treatment of Children, 21,* 489–513.

Hayward, C., Killen, J.D., Hammer, L.D., Litt, I.F., Wilson, D.M., Simmonds, B., & Taylor, C.B. (1992). Pubertal stage and panic attack history in sixth- and seventh-grade girls. *American Journal of Psychiatry, 149,* 1239–1243.

Hirshfield, D.R., Rosenbaum, J.F., Biederman, J., Bolduc, E.A., Faraone, S.V., Snidman, N., Reznick, J.S., & Kagan, J. (1992). Stable behavioral inhibition and its association with anxiety disorder. *Journal of the American Academy of Child and Adolescent Psychiatry, 31,* 103–111.

Hodges, K., & Fitch, P. (1979). Development of a mental status examination interview for children. Paper presented at the meeting of the Missouri Psychological Association, Kansas City, MO.

Hodges, K., McKnew, D., Burbach, D.J., & Roebuck, L. (1987). Diagnostic concordance between the Child Assessment Schedule (CAS) and the Schedule for Affective Disorders and Schizophrenia for School-Age Children (K-SADS) in an outpatient sample using lay interviewers. *Journal of the American Academy of Child and Adolescent Psychiatry, 26,* 654–661.

Hoehn-Saric, E., Maisami, M., & Weigand, D. (1987). Measurement of anxiety in children and adolescents using semi-structured interviews. *Journal of the American Academy of Child and Adolescent Psychiatry, 28,* 541–545.

Jensen, P.S., Martin, D., & Cantwell, D.P. (1997). Comorbidity in ADHD: Implications for research, practice, and *DSM-V. Journal of the American Academy of Child and Adolescent Psychiatry, 36,* 1065–1079.

Jensen, P.S., Traylor, J., Xenakis, S.N., & Davis, H. (1988). Child psychopathology rating scales and interrater agreement: Vol. I. Parents' gender and psychiatric symptoms. *Journal of the American Academy of Child and Adolescent Psychiatry, 27,* 442–450.

Jersild, A.T., & Holmes, F.B. (1935). Children's fears. *Child Development Monograph, No. 20.*

Johnson, S.B., & Melamed, B.G. (1979). Assessment and treatment of children's fears. In B.B. Lahey & A.E. Kazdin (Eds.), *Advances in clinical child psychology* (Vol. E, pp. 108–139). New York: Plenum Press.

Kagan, J. (1989). *Unstable ideas.* Cambridge, MA: Harvard University Press.

Kagan, J., & Reznick, S.J. (1986). Shyness and temperament. In W.H. Jones, J.M. Cheek, & S.R. Briggs (Eds.), *Shyness: Perspectives on research and treatment* (pp. 81–90). New York: Plenum Press.

Kagan, J., & Reznick, J.S. (1984). Behavioral inhibition to the unfamiliar. *Child Development, 55,* 2212–2220.

Kagan, J., Reznick, J.S., & Snidman, N. (1988). Biological bases of childhood shyness. *Science, 240,* 167–175.

Kagan, J., Snidman, N., & Arcus, D. (1993). On the temperamental categories of inhibited and uninhibited children. In K.H. Rubin & J.B. Asendorpf (Eds.), *Social withdrawal, inhibition and shyness in childhood* (pp. 19–28). Hillsdale, NJ: Erlbaum.

Kaplan, H.I., & Sadock, B.J. (1988). *Synopsis of psychiatry: Behavioral sciences and clinical psychiatry* (5th ed.). Baltimore: Williams & Wilkins.

Kashani, J.H., & Orvaschel, H. (1990). A community study of anxiety in children and adolescents. *American Journal of Psychiatry, 147,* 313–318.

Kaufman, J., Birmaher, B., Brent, D., Rao, U., Flynn, C., Moreci, P., Williamson, D., & Ryan, N. (1997). Schedule for Affective Disorders and Schizophrenia for School-Age Children–Present and Lifetime Version (K-SADS-PL): Initial reliability and validity data. *Journal of the American Academy of Child and Adolescent Psychiatry, 36,* 980–988.

Kazdin, A.E., & Weisz, J.R. (1998, February). Identifying and developing empirically supported child and adolescent treatments. *Journal of Consulting and Clinical Psychology, 66*(1), 19–36.

Kearney, C.A., & Albano, A.M. (2000). *Therapist's guide for the prescriptive treatment of school refusal behavior.* San Antonio, TX: Psychological Corporation.

Kearney, C.A., Albano, A.M., Eisen, A.R., Allan, W.D., & Barlow, D.H. (1997). The phenomenology of panic disorder in youngsters: An empirical study of a clinic sample. *Journal of Anxiety Disorders, 11,* 49–62.

Kearney, C.A., & Silverman, W.K. (1993). Measuring the function of school refusal behavior: The School Refusal Assessment Scale. *Journal of Clinical Child Psychology, 22,* 85–86.

Kearney, C.A., & Silverman, W.K. (1996). The evolution and reconciliation of taxonomic strategies for school refusal behavior. *Clinical Psychology: Science and Practice, 3,* 339–354.

Kendall, P.C. (1994). Treating anxiety disorders in children: Results of a randomized clinical trial. *Journal of Consulting and Clinical Psychology, 62,* 100–110.

Kendall, P.C., Kane, M.T., Howard, B.L., & Siqueland, L. (1992). *Cognitive-behavioral therapy for anxious children: Treatment manual (The Coping Cat).* Philadelphia: Temple University.

Kendall, P.C., & Southam-Gerow, M.A. (1996). Long-term follow-up of a cognitive-behavior therapy for anxiety-disordered youth. *Journal of Consulting and Clinical Psychology, 64,* 724–730.

Kessler, R.C., McGonagle, K., Zhao, S., Nelson, C.B., Hughes, M., Eshleman, S., Wittchen, H-U., & Kendler, K.S. (1994). Lifetime and 12-month prevalence of *DSM-III-R* psychiatric disorders in the United States. *Archives of General Psychiatry, 51,* 8–19.

King, N.J., & Ollendick, T.H. (1997). Annotation: Treatment of childhood phobias. *Journal of Child Psychology and Psychiatry, 38,* 389–400.

Klee, B., & Hack, S. (1999, March/April). Child and adolescent psychopharmacology at a glance. In H.S. Koplewicz (Ed.), *Child study letter.* New York: NYU School of Medicine.

Kronenberger, W.G., & Meyer, R.G. (in press). *The child clinicians's handbook* (2nd ed.). Needham Heights, MA: Allyn & Bacon.

La Greca, A.M., & Stone, W.L. (1993). The Social Anxiety Scale for Children–Revised: Factor structure and concurrent validity. *Journal of Clinical Child Psychology, 22,* 17–27.

Lapouse, R., & Monk, M.A. (1959). Fears and worries in a representative sample of children. *American Journal of Public Health, 48,* 1134–1144.

Last, C.G. (1989). Anxiety disorders of childhood or adolescence. In C.G. Last & M. Hersen (Eds.), *Handbook of child psychiatric diagnosis* (pp. 156–169). New York: Wiley.

Last, C.G. (Ed.). (1993). Introduction. *Anxiety across the lifespan: A developmental perspective* (pp. 1–7). New York: Springer.

Last, C.G., Francis, G., & Strauss, C.C. (1989). Assessing fears in anxiety-disordered children with the Revised Fear Survey Schedule for Children (FSSC-R). *Journal of Clinical Child Psychology, 18,* 137–141.

Last, C.G., Hansen, C., & Franco, N. (1997). Anxious children in adulthood: A prospective study of adjust-ment. *Journal of the American Academy of Child and Adolescent Psychiatry, 36,* 645–652.

Last, C.G., Hersen, M., Kazdin, A.E., Orvaschel, H., & Perrin, S. (1991). Anxiety disorders in children and their families. *Archives of General Psychiatry, 48,* 928–934.

Last, C.G., Perrin, S., Hersen, M., & Kazdin, A.E. (1992). *DSM-III-R* anxiety disorders in children: Sociodemographic and clinical characteristics. *Journal of the American Academy of Child and Adolescent Psychiatry, 31,* 1070–1076.

Last, C.G., Perrin, S., Hersen, M., & Kazdin, A.E. (1996). A prospective study of childhood anxiety disorders. *Journal of the American Academy of Child and Adolescent Psychiatry, 35,* 1502–1510.

Last, C.G., Phillips, J.E., & Statfeld, A. (1987). Childhood anxiety disorders in mothers and their children. *Child Psychiatry and Human Development, 18,* 103–112.

Last, C.G., Strauss, C.C., & Francis, G. (1987). Comorbidity among childhood anxiety disorders. *Journal of Nervous and Mental Diseases, 175,* 726–730.

Lazarus, A.A., & Abramowitz, A. (1962). The use of "emotive imagery" in the treatment of children's phobias. *Journal of Mental Science, 108,* 191–195.

Leonard, H.L., Swedo, S.E., Lenane, M.C., Rettew, D.C., Hamburger, S.D., Bartko, J.J., & Rapoport, J.L. (1993). A 2- to 7-year follow-up study of 54 obsessive-compulsive children and adolescents. *Archives of General Psychiatry, 50,* 429–439.

Lewis, S. (1974). A comparison of behavior therapy techniques in the reduction of fearful avoidance behavior. *Behavior Therapy, 5,* 648–655.

Liddell, H. (1949). The role of vigilance in the development of animal neuroses. In P. Hoch & J. Zubin (Eds.), *Anxiety.* New York: Grune & Stratton.

Lonigan, C.J., Carey, M.P., & Finch, A.J. (1994). Anxiety and depression in children and adolescents: Negative affectivity and the utility of self-report. *Journal of Consulting and Clinical Psychology, 62,* 1000–1008.

Manassis, K., & Bradley, S. (1994). Fluoxetine in anxiety disorders [Letter]. *Journal of the American Academy of Child and Adolescent Psychiatry, 33,* 761–762.

March, J.S., & Albano, A.M. (in press). Anxiety disorders in children and adolescents. In D. Stein (Ed.), *Textbook of anxiety disorders.* Washington, DC: APA Press.

March, J., Frances, A., Kahn, D., & Carpenter, D. (1997). Expert consensus guidelines: Treatment of obsessive-compulsive disorder. *Journal of Clinical Psychiatry, 58,* 1–72.

March, J.S., & Mulle, K. (1995). Manualized cognitive-behavioral psychotherapy for obsessive-compulsive disorder in childhood: A preliminary single case study. *Journal of Anxiety Disorders, 9,* 175–184.

March, J.S., & Mulle, K. (1998). *OCD in children and adolescents: A cognitive-behavioral treatment manual.* New York: Guilford Press.

March, J.S., Leonard, H.L., & Swedo, S.E. (1995). Obsessive-compulsive disorder. In J.S. March (Ed.), *Anxiety disorders in children and adolescents* (pp. 251–275). New York: Guilford Press.

March, J.S., Parker, J., Sullivan, K., Stallings, P., & Conners, K. (1997). The Multidimensional Anxiety Scale for Children (MASC): Factor structure, reliability, and validity. *Journal of the American Academy of Child and Adolescent Psychiatry, 36*, 554–565.

Marks, I.M. (1969). *Fears and phobias.* New York: Academic Press.

Marks, I.M., & Gelder, M.G. (1966). Different ages of onset in varieties of phobia. *American Journal of Psychiatry, 123*, 218–221.

Mattison, R.E., & Bagnoto, S.J. (1987). Empirical measurement of overanxious disorder in boys 8 to 12 years old. *Journal of the American Academy of Child and Adolescent Psychiatry, 26*, 536–540.

McGee, R., Feehan, M., Williams, S., Partridge, F., Silva, P.A., & Kelly, J. (1990). *DSM-III disorders in a large sample of adolescents. Journal of the American Academy of Child and Adolescent Psychiatry, 29*, 611–619.

Menzies, R.G., & Clark, J.C. (1993). A comparison of in vivo and vicarious exposure in the treatment of childhood water phobia. *Behavior Research and Therapy, 31*, 9–15.

Meyer, R.G. (1993). *The clinician's handbook* (3rd ed.). Boston: Allyn & Bacon.

Michael, K.D., & Merrell, K.W. (1998). Reliability of children's self-reported internalizing symptoms over short to medium-length time intervals. *Journal of the American Academy of Child and Adolescent Psychiatry, 37*, 194–201.

Miller, L.C., Barrett, C.L., & Hampe, E. (1974). Phobias of childhood in a prescientific era. In A. Davids (Ed.), *Child personality and psychopathology: Current topics* (pp. 89–174). New York: Wiley.

Miller, L.C., Barrett, C.L., Hampe, E., & Noble, H. (1972). Comparison of reciprocal inhibition, psychotherapy, and waiting list control for phobic children. *Journal of Abnormal Psychology, 79*, 269–279.

Milos, M.E., & Reiss, S. (1982). Effects of three play conditions on separation anxiety in young children. *Journal of Consulting and Clinical Psychology, 50*, 389–395.

Moreau, D., & Follett, C. (1993). Panic disorder in children and adolescents. *Child and Adolescent Psychiatric Clinics of North America, 2*, 581–602.

Muris, P., Meesters, C., Merckelbach, H., Sermon, A., & Zwakhalen, S. (1998). Worry in normal children. *Journal of the American Academy of Child and Adolescent Psychiatry, 37*, 703–710.

Murphy, C.M., & Bootzin, R.R. (1973). Active and passive participation in the contact desensitization of snake fear in children. *Behavior Therapy, 4*, 203–211.

Norvell, N., Brophy, C., & Finch, A.J. (1985). The relationship of anxiety to childhood depression. *Journal of Personality Assessment, 49*, 150–153.

Obler, M., & Terwilliger, R.F. (1970). Pilot study on the effectiveness of systematic desensitization with neurologically impaired children with phobic disorders. *Journal of Consulting and Clinical Psychology, 34*, 314–318.

Ollendick, T.H. (1983). Reliability and validity of the revised Fear Survey Schedule for Children (FSSC-R). *Behaviour Research and Therapy, 21*, 395–399.

Ollendick, T.H. (1995). Cognitive behavioral treatment of panic disorder with agoraphobia in adolescents: A multiple baseline design analysis. *Behavior Therapy, 26*, 517–531.

Ollendick, T.H., & King, N.J. (1998). Empirically supported treatments for children with phobic and anxiety disorders. *Journal of Clinical Child Psychology, 27*, 156–167.

Ollendick, T.H., Matson, J., & Helsel, W.J. (1985). Fears in children and adolescents: A review. *Journal of Child Psychology and Psychiatry, 35*, 113–134.

Ollendick, T.H., Mattis, S.G., & King, N.J. (1994). Panic in children and adolescents: A review. *Journal of Child Psychology and Psychiatry, 35*, 113–134.

Ollendick, T.H., & Yule, W. (1990). Depression in British and American children and its relationship to fear and anxiety. *Journal of Consulting and Clinical Psychology, 58*, 126–129.

Öst, L. (1987). Age of onset of different phobias. *Journal of Abnormal Psychology, 96*, 123–145.

Perrin, S., & Last, C.G. (1992). Do childhood anxiety measures measure anxiety? *Journal of Abnormal Child Psychology, 20*, 567–578.

Perrin, S., & Last, C.G. (1996). Relationship between ADHD and anxiety in boys: Results from a family study. *Journal of the American Academy of Child and Adolescent Psychiatry, 35*, 988–996.

Pliszka, S.R. (1989). Effect of anxiety on cognition, behavior, and stimulant response in ADHD. *Journal of the American Academy of Child and Adolescent Psychiatry, 28*, 882–887.

Pliszka, S.R. (1992). Comorbidity of attention-deficit hyperactivity disorder and overanxious disorder. *Journal of the American Academy of Child and Adolescent Psychiatry, 31*, 197–203.

Puig-Antich, J., & Chambers, W. (1978). *The Schedule for Affective Disorders and Schizophrenia for School-Aged Children.* New York: New York State Psychiatric Institute.

Quinonez, R., Santos, R.G., Boyar, R., & Cross, H. (1997). Temperament and trait anxiety as predictors of child behavior prior to general anesthesia for dental surgery. *Pediatric Dentistry, 19*, 427–431.

Reed, L.J., Carter, B.D., & Miller, L.C. (1990). Fear and anxiety in children. In C.E. Walker & M.C. Roberts. (Eds.), *Handbook of clinical child psychology* (2nd ed., pp. 237–260). New York: Wiley.

Reiter, S., & Kutcher, S. (1991). Disinhibition and anger outbursts in adolescents treated with clonazepam [Letter]. *Journal of Clinical Psychopharmacology, 11,* 268.

Rettew, D.C., Swedo, S.E., Leonard, H.L., Lenane, M.C., & Rapoport, J.L. (1992). Obsessions and compulsions across time in 79 children and adolescents with obsessive-compulsive disorder. *Journal of the American Academy of Child and Adolescent Psychiatry, 31,* 1050–1056.

Reynolds, C.R., & Kamphaus, R.W. (1992). *Behavior Assessment System for Children manual.* Circle Pines, MN: American Guidance Services.

Reynolds, C.R., & Richmond, B.O. (1985). *Revised Children's Manifest Anxiety Scale (RCMAS) manual.* Los Angeles: Western Psychological Services.

Riddle, M., Brown, N., Dzubinski, D., Jetmalani, A.N., Law, Y., & Woolston, J.L. (1989). Case study: Fluoxetine overdose in an adolescent. *Journal of the American Academy of Child and Adolescent Psychiatry, 28,* 587–588.

Ritter, B. (1968). The group desensitization of children's snake phobias using vicarious and contact desensitization procedures. *Behaviour Research and Therapy, 6,* 1–6.

Scherer, M.W., & Nakamura, C.Y. (1968). A Fear Survey Schedule for Children (FSS-FC): A factor analytic comparison with manifest anxiety (CMAS). *Behaviour Research and Therapy, 6,* 173–182.

Sheslow, D.V., Bondy, A.S., & Nelson, R.O. (1983). A comparison of graduated exposure, verbal coping skills, and their combination in the treatment of children's fear of the dark. *Child and Family Behavior Therapy, 4,* 33–45.

Silverman, W.K., & Albano, A.M. (1996). *The Anxiety Disorders Interview Schedule for DSM-IV: Child and parent versions.* San Antonio, TX: Psychological Corporation.

Silverman, W.K., & Ginsburg, G.S. (1998). Anxiety disorders. In T.S. Ollendick & M. Hersen (Eds.), *Handbook of child psychopathology* (3rd ed.). New York: Plenum Press.

Silverman, W.K., & Nelles, W.B. (1988). The Anxiety Disorders Interview Schedule for Children. *Journal of the American Academy of Child and Adolescent Psychiatry, 27,* 772–778.

Silverman, W.K., & Rabian, B. (1993). Simple phobias. *Child and Adolescent Psychiatric Clinics of North America, 2,* 603–622.

Silverman, W.K., & Rabian, B. (1995). Test-retest reliability of the *DSM-III-R* anxiety disorders symptoms using the Anxiety Disorders Interview Schedule for Children. *Journal of Anxiety Disorders, 9,* 1–12.

Silverman, W.K., Fleisig, W., Rabian, B., & Peterson, R.A. (1991). Childhood Anxiety Sensitivity Index. *Journal of Clinical Child Psychology, 20,* 162–168.

Speilberger, C.D. (1973). *Manual for the State-Trait Anxiety Inventory for Children.* Palo Alto, CA: Consulting Psychologists Press.

Strauss, C.C., Lahey, B.B., Frick, P., Frame, C.L., & Hynd, G.W. (1988). Peer social status of children with anxiety disorders. *Journal of Consulting and Clinical Psychology, 56,* 137–141.

Strauss, C.C., & Last, C.G. (1993). Social and simple phobias in children. *Journal of Anxiety Disorders, 2,* 141–152.

Sylvester, C.E., Hyde, T.S., & Reichsler, R.J. (1987). The Diagnostic Interview for Children and Personality Inventory for Children in studies of children at risk for anxiety disorders or depression. *Journal of the American Academy of Child and Adolescent Psychiatry, 26,* 668–675.

Tannenbaum, L.F., Forehand, R., & McCombs-Thomas, A. (1992). Adolescent self-reported anxiety and depression: Separate constructs or a single entity. *Child Study Journal, 22,* 61–72.

Tracey, S.A., Chorpita, B.F., Douban, J., & Barlow, D. (1997). Empirical evaluation of the *DSM-IV* generalized anxiety disorder criteria in children and adolescents. *Journal of Clinical Child Psychology, 26,* 404–414.

Ultee, C.A., Griffioen, D., & Schellekens, J. (1982). The reduction of anxiety in children: A comparison of the effects of "systematic desensitization in vitro" and "systematic desensitization in vivo." *Behaviour Research and Therapy, 20,* 61–67.

Van Ameringen, M., Mancini, C., & Oakman, J.M. (1998). The relationship of behavioral inhibition and shyness to anxiety disorder. *Journal of Nervous and Mental Diseases, 186,* 425–431.

Vasey, M.W. (1995). Social anxiety disorders. In A.R. Eisen, C.A. Kearney, & C.A. Schaefer (Eds.), *Clinical handbook of anxiety disorders in children and adolescents* (pp. 131–168). Northvale, NJ: Jason Aronson.

Vaughn, M.L., Riccio, C.A., Hynd, G.W., & Hall, J. (1997). Diagnosing ADHD (predominantly inattentive and combined type subtypes): Discriminant validity of the Behavior Assessment System for Children and the Achenbach Parent and Teacher Rating Scales. *Journal of Clinical Child Psychology, 26,* 349–357.

Vernberg, E.M., Abwender, D.A., Ewell, K.K., & Beery, S.H. (1992). Social anxiety and peer relationships in early adolescence: A prospective analysis. *Journal of Clinical Child Psychology, 21,* 189–196.

Warren, M.K., Ollendick, T.H., & King, N.J. (1996). Test anxiety in children and adolescents: A clinical-developmental analysis. *Behaviour Change, 13,* 157–170.

Warren, S.L., Huston, L., Egeland, B., & Sroufe, L.A. (1997). Child and adolescent anxiety disorders and early attachment. *Journal of the American Academy of Child and Adolescent Psychiatry, 36,* 637–644.

Watson, D., Clark, L.A., Weber, K., Assenheimer, J.S., Strauss, M., & McCormick, R.A. (1995). Testing a tripartite model: I. Evaluating the convergent and discriminant validity of anxiety and depression symptom scales. *Journal of Abnormal Psychology, 104,* 3–14.

Weems, C.F., Hammond-Laurence, K., Silverman, W.K., & Ginsburg, G.S. (1998). Testing the utility of the anxiety and sensitivity construct in children and adolescents referred for anxiety disorders. *Journal of Clinical Child Psychology, 27,* 69–77.

Weissman, M.M. (1989, May 6). *The epidemiology of panic disorder in adolescents: Implications for diagnosis.* Paper presented at the annual meeting of the American Society for Adolescent Psychiatry, San Francisco.

Witt, J.C., Heffer, R.W., & Pfeiffer, J.P. (1990). Structured rating scales: A review of self-report and informant rating processes, procedures, and issues. In C.R.

Reynolds & R.W. Kamphaus (Eds.), *Handbook of psychological and educational assessment of children: Personality, behavior, and context* (pp. 364–394). New York: Guilford Press.

Wolfe, V.V., Finch, A.J., Saylor, C.F., Blount, R.L., Pallmeyer, T.P., & Carek, D.J. (1987). Negative affectivity in children: A multitrait-multimethod investigation. *Journal of Consulting and Clinical Psychology, 55,* 245–250.

Woolston, J., Rosenthal, S.L., Riddle, M.A., Sparrow, S.S., Cicchetti, C., & Zimmerman, J. (1989). Childhood comorbidity of anxiety/affective disorders and behavioral disorders. *Journal of the American Academy of Child and Adolescent Psychiatry, 28,* 707–713.

Yerkes, R.M., & Dodson, J.D. (1908). The relation of strength of stimulus to rapidity of habit formation. *Journal of Comprehensive Neurology and Psychology, 18,* 459–482.

CHAPTER 16

Evaluation and Treatment of Sleep Disorders in Children

J. CATESBY WARE, WILLIAM C. ORR, AND TOM BOND

Most new parents quickly learn that "sleeping like a baby" means more than they thought it did. Getting up periodically to feed and calm an infant not inclined to stay asleep, walking the floor at night with an awake infant, and arising early in the morning to diaper an infant may discourage even the most prepared parent. To make matters worse, knowledge of the sudden infant death syndrome (SIDS) may create anxiety even during quiet periods of the night. Fortunately, we now understand much more about sleep than we did just a few years ago and can use this knowledge to help parents and children sleep better.

Although sleep difficulties may be transient and developmentally related, a sleep disturbance also may reflect early signs of pathology or poor parenting. Perhaps reassurance may be all that a parent needs. Usually, treatment for difficulties such as falling asleep or staying asleep in an otherwise healthy child is quite successful, often by teaching parents the consistent application of behavioral techniques along with sleep hygiene principles. In some cases, assessment and treatment need a multidisciplinary approach to deal with potential psychological, psychiatric, pulmonary, neurologic, and family-related problems (Rosen, 1997).

When dealing with sleep problems, one needs to determine the following. Does the problem stem from the parents rather than the child? Common but not trivial examples of this are letting the child drink caffeinated beverages in the evening, exciting the child by playing roughly immediately before bed, using going to bed as a punishment, or reinforcing the child's crying during the night with attention. Does the complaint reflect a lack of parental experience and knowledge rather than a true sleep problem? Are they expecting the child to sleep 12 hours from 7 P.M. to 7 A.M., not knowing that 10 hours is the average time in bed for 5-year-olds? Do they expect their 4-year-old to take a regular nap? Do the parents inappropriately attribute certain behaviors to poor sleep, as was the case with a mother who believed incorrectly that her 14-year-old healthy daughter's slow swim lap times must be the result of poor sleep? Is the child normal but creating stress that the parents are not dealing with adequately, or are the parents actually complaining about their own problem rather than the child's? One mother who was awake much of the night herself following separation from her husband sought consolation for her son's frequent awakenings at night rather than her own. Nearly half of the mothers of children who wake at night have a sleep problem themselves, and half of the mothers of children who talked or rocked in their sleep had sleep problems or nightmares (Salzarulo et al., 1980). Often, both the parents and the child need treatment, with the parents often the focus of interventions. Even 1-month-old infants of depressed mothers have different sleep and EEG patterns than those of normal mothers (Jones, Field, Fox, Lundy, & Davalos, 1997).

NORMAL STRUCTURE OF SLEEP

To deal most effectively with sleep complaints, knowledge of normal sleep and how it changes with age is essential. Behaviorally, sleep is relatively homogeneous to the casual observer, seasoned here and there with a few jerks, twitches, and larger body movements. However, under the calm exterior of a sleeping child there is a rich complexity of physiological activity that unfolds in closely inspected recordings of brain waves, eye movements, muscle tension, and other physiological activity. A polysomnogram (PSG) is the simultaneous recording of a number of parameters during the night. The alternating cycles of physiological quiescence and activation that are the dominant motif of sleep. This pattern and its repetitions normally make up each sleep period from birth to death. Complexity develops when activity in one physiological system occurs during quiescence in another.

Non-rapid-eye-movement (NREM) sleep increases from approximately 50% of sleep at birth to 70% of the sleep of 3- to 5-year-olds, to 75% of 13- to 15-year-olds, and finally to 80% of adult sleep. Sleep stages 1 through 4 compose NREM sleep. These stages signify changes from very light (Stage 1) to very deep sleep (Stage 4). Light and deep sleep are behavioral terms indicating the ease with which a person awakens from sleep. A parent peeking into the room during Stage 1 sleep is likely to awaken a child. In Stage 4 sleep, a child may roll off the bed, crash onto the floor, and remain asleep. If awakened from Stage 4, the child may exhibit confusion because it is at this time that the activity in the cortex is at its lowest level.

Rapid-eye-movement (REM) sleep, a period of intense brain activation, eye movements, and muscle atonia, composes the rest of sleep. Tonic and phasic components also compose REM sleep. The phasic events (e.g., bursts of eye movements) occur within a background of fairly stable electroencephalographic (EEG) activity. Humans awaken from REM sleep about as easily as they do from

Stage 2 (Rechtschaffen, Hauri, & Zeitlin, 1966). However, the sensation on awakening from REM sleep may be that of total relaxation because the antigravity muscles that allow us to sit and stand actually are paralyzed during REM sleep. This paralysis keeps children and adults from acting out their dreams.

A typical child in a sleep center will fall asleep in 15 to 20 minutes and reach deep sleep 15 to 20 minutes after falling asleep (Williams, Karacan, & Hursch, 1974). One to two hours after sleep onset, the first REM period will begin. Although the first REM period may last only 5 minutes, REM periods are usually 15 to 20 minutes long. Following the first REM period, NREM sleep will begin again and the NREM–REM cycle will repeat itself approximately every 90 minutes. The longer a child has been asleep, the less likely there will be deep sleep (Stages 3 and 4) during NREM sleep.

BRAIN WAVES, EYE MOVEMENTS, AND MUSCLE TENSION

A variety of brain wave patterns occur during sleep. When awake but relaxed with eyes closed, alpha waves (regular 8–12 Hz waves of moderate amplitude) occur, and children and adults will easily respond to the clicks, flashes, and bells of a laboratory setting. As the person becomes drowsy, alpha waves disappear along with any consistent response to a stimulus. This is Stage 1 (or transition) sleep. The Stage 1 EEG is a low-voltage, mixed frequency pattern often dominated by theta (4–7 Hz) activity. Less than five minutes later, Stage 2 sleep begins. Stage 2 is characterized by 1-second bursts of 14 Hz waves called sleep spindles and large-amplitude biphasic waves called K-complexes. In most cases, a noise will also elicit these K-complexes. In the progression from Stage 2 sleep to Stages 3 and 4, delta waves begin to appear that are slow in frequency (<4 Hz) with high amplitudes (>75 microvolts). Delta waves composing 20% to 50 % in the EEG tracing characterize Stage 3 sleep; when the percentage of delta waves reaches 50 or more, Stage 4 sleep begins. As from any NREM stage of sleep, it is possible to awaken the sleeper only to hear the claim that he or she was not asleep but lying peacefully thinking. This sleep state misperception is most common when awakening from Stage 1 sleep and least common when awakening from deep sleep.

In the 1950s, Nathaniel Kleitman's graduate student, Eugene Aserinsky, noticed that sometimes during apparent Stage 1 sleep, the infant's eyes moved rapidly under closed eyelids (Aserinsky & Kleitman, 1953). Further observation established that this was not Stage 1 sleep but REM sleep, a period of sleep with Stage-1-like EEG accompanied by a host of what was previously thought to be nonsleeplike activities (Aserinsky & Kleitman, 1955). Because of atonal (paralyzed) antigravity muscles during this phase of sleep, major behavioral responding to dreams normally does not occur. Although muscle tension reduces at sleep onset and may get very low during deep sleep, the actual inhibition that occurs in REM sleep is not present in any other stage.

Other Physiological Systems

Many physiological systems have circadian (approximately 24 hours) or ultradian (shorter than 24 hours) rhythms associated with sleep and waking cycles. Some hormonal cycles are ultradian and may follow the NREM-REM cycle of sleep. During NREM sleep, particularly during Stage 4 sleep, growth hormone secretion occurs (Veldhuis & Iranmanesh, 1969). Cycles longer than a day (infradian) such as the menstrual cycle can also affect sleep. Seasonal changes in the light-dark cycle may affect sleep in both children and adults. Sleep time tends to increase in winter and decrease in summer.

Heart rate and respiratory rate typically slow during NREM sleep. In a well-conditioned athlete, a heart rate in the 40s is not unusual. In REM sleep, heart and respiratory rate generally increase while becoming more irregular. During an eye movement burst in REM sleep, respiration may halt for several seconds, particularly in infants. Penile erections and analogous changes in females also occur in REM sleep after the age of 3 months (Korner, 1968).

Core body temperature also fluctuates in relation to sleep and wakefulness. Throughout the 24-hour day, body temperature may change 1.5 to 2 degrees, with the low point in the late phase of sleep around awakening time and the peak body temperature in the late afternoon. In REM sleep, body temperature is more likely to track room temperature (one becomes poikilothermic). Although body temperature and the sleep-wake cycle may become out of phase and cause sleep problems, they typically are closely related. Bed selection times, self-rated alertness, the amount of time after sleep onset to REM onset (REM latency), and the duration of the sleep period are related to body temperature (Czeisler, Weitzman, Moore-Ede, Zimmerman, & Kranauer, 1980). For example, in an experimental environment devoid of time cues, going to sleep near the body temperature minimum results in a shorter sleep period than if sleep onset occurs at the maximum of the temperature cycle.

Ontogeny of Sleep

Although the NREM-REM cycling occurs throughout one's life, sleep continues to change from the earliest recordings (in utero) to death. Understanding age-related changes is necessary to understand sleep complaints. During the first few days of life, an infant sleeps on the average of 16 to 17 hours out of each 24-hour period, broken into periods of sleep typically less than four hours in duration (Parmelee, Schulz, & Disbrow, 1961). By the sixth month of life, total sleep per 24-hour period averages 13 to 14 hours (Kleitman & Englemann, 1953). However, there is considerable variability among infants. Soon after birth, infants respond to certain time cues or *zeitgebers*, bodily functions begin to establish a circadian rhythm, and sleep becomes more consolidated. Seventy percent of infants are quiet (settle) for a five-hour stretch at night by the age of 3 months and 83% by 6 months (T. Moore & Ucko, 1957). However, less than half actually sleep throughout the night, as many "settled" children will awaken during the night without crying or calling for parents (Anders, 1979).

Newborns spend approximately 50% of their sleep time in REM sleep, and their REM-NREM cycles are shorter than the 90-minute cycle seen in adults (Roffwarg, Muzio, & Dement, 1966). Because their sleep is fragmented and because they have a higher percentage of REM sleep, an observer is more likely to notice an early or sudden onset of REM sleep; that is, REM sleep occurs almost immediately after sleep onset rather than being buffered from waking by 90 minutes of NREM sleep as it is in adults. The term "indeterminate sleep" describes about 10% to 15% of sleep in infants under 3 months (Anders, Emde, & Parmelee, 1971). Although the infant is behaviorally asleep, the particular EEG sleep stage is unclear, hence indeterminate.

Table 16.1 Selected sleep parameters from normals subjects.

Age (yrs.)	Time in Bed (hrs.)	Total Sleep Time (hrs.)	Sleep Latency (mins.)	Time Asleep in Bed (%)
3–5	10.3	9.9	14	96
6–9	10.0	9.7	12	97
10–12	9.8	9.3	17	95
13–15	8.4	8.1	16	96
16–19	8.0	7.5	18	95

Note: Data are from the mean of the second and third consecutive nights recorded from healthy children without sleep complaints sleeping in a sleep center (Williams, Karacan, & Hursch, 1974).

An early sleep milestone occurs around the age of 3 months. At this time, sleep spindles begin to appear (Lenard, 1970; Metcalf, 1970), making sleep stages more easily classifiable. At about the same time, other indices of nervous system maturation occur during sleep. Normally, there are bursts of autonomic activity resulting in electrodermal activity (EDA; Johnson & Lubin, 1966). In adults, these bursts of EDA activity occur primarily in NREM sleep and may reflect the regulation of the intensity of deep sleep by the sympathetic nervous system (Ware & Pittard, 1990). However, in newborn infants, EDA occurs more in REM than in NREM sleep. Concurrent with sleep spindle appearance, EDA changes to the adult pattern of occurring predominantly in NREM sleep (Curzi-Dascalova & Dreyfus-Brisac, 1976). As EDA moves to NREM sleep, penile erections move to REM sleep. In addition, around the age of 3 months, the prevalence of sudden infant death decreases, perhaps related to a change in the arousal response. Normally, a stimulus produces a highly consistent arousal response in sleeping infants. The first two to four seconds consist of a sigh, followed by a sleep startle, followed by stereotyped thrashing. This response, follows, for example, the covering of the infant's airway (Thach & Lijowska, 1996). The duration of this arousal response becomes shorter up to the age of 6 years, at least in REM sleep (Kohyama, Shimohira, & Iwakawa, 1997).

Both respiration rate and variability decline up to 3 months of age and then stabilize (Hoppenbrouwers, Harper, Hodgman, Sterman, & McGinty, 1978). Respiratory pauses contribute to the variability in respiratory rate in normal infants. These pauses are primarily a result of lack of respiratory effort rather than a blockage of airflow. They occur maximally among children 6 and 12 weeks of age, and by the end of the first year cluster primarily in REM sleep (Guilleminault, 1980). Typically, their duration is less than 15 seconds (Hoppenbrouwers et al., 1977). Normally, less than one apnea event per hour of sleep should occur in infants. Respiratory rate and variability measured continuously across states in infants are greatest when awake, lowest when in NREM sleep, and intermediate when in REM sleep (Hoppenbrouwers et al., 1978). In infants during NREM sleep, heart rate drops from approximately 135 bpm at 1 month to approximately 115 bpm at 6 months of age (Harper, Leake, Hodgman, & Hoppenbrouwers, 1982). A momentary slowing of the heart (or an asystole) is also not uncommon. Table 16.1 illustrates changes in some sleep parameters after infancy until the teenage years.

SLEEP DISORDERS

A survey of nearly 1,000 parents of 5- to 12-year-olds found five common sleep-related complaints: bedtime resistance (27%), morning wake-up problems (17%), fatigue (17%), sleep-onset delays (11%), and night waking (6.5%) (Blader, Koplewicz, Abikoff, & Foley, 1997). Napping and irregular bedtimes correlated with these problems and to some extent psychiatric and medical conditions. In French adolescents, sleep complaints occurred in relation to various personal and family disorders (Vignau et al., 1997). Tracking down the causes to complaints leads to the most focused and successful treatment.

SLEEP-WAKE SCHEDULE DISORDERS

All infants have a schedule disorder, because initially, their sleep pattern is sporadic in relation to the 24-hour day. To diagnose a true schedule disorder, the child must be well into the age at which sleep and waking periods normally synchronize with clock time. This usually happens within the first year. Infants who suffer from certain perinatal problems, for example, anoxia, will typically settle later (T. Moore & Ucko, 1957). Parents may affect settling by how they respond to the child when he or she does awaken and by the daily consistency in the child's schedule. Once an infant has settled, waking at night may reappear as a result of a variety of factors, including illness, environmental changes, and emotional trauma.

Delayed Sleep Phase Syndrome

Adolescents may complain that it is difficult for them to fall asleep at night and equally difficult to wake up on time in the morning. However, their total sleep time may not be outside the expected range. They sleep well once asleep, and they function well once awake on their own schedule. Partly because of this delayed sleep pattern (delayed in relation to clock time), some school systems have the older children start school later. Even controlling for total sleep, fifth-grade students starting school at 7:10 complained more about daytime fatigue, sleepiness, and concentration difficulties in school than those starting school at 8:00 (Epstein, Chillag, & Lavie, 1998).

For most children, a strict bedtime and waking schedule keeps the sleep period from drifting later into the day. The zeitgebers of bright light (Lewy, Sack, & Singer, 1984), social contact, exercise, and eating reset the circadian clock to that of the 24-hour clock. By far the most powerful zeitgeber is bright light. Because of this, phototherapy (administering bright light pulses at appropriate times of the day) is helpful in treating circadian rhythm disorders (Campbell et al., 1995). Of the 10% to 20% of adolescents complaining of a sleep disturbance, a large percentage reported problems of falling asleep and feeling tired during the day (Anders, Carskadon, & Dement, 1980). These complaints are prime clues to the existence of a circadian rhythm disturbance. For the most part, circadian rhythm disturbances in children should be relatively transient. A shift in time zones and other sleep disturbances as a result of medical or psychological problems may additionally result in a schedule disturbance that will be self-correcting after eliminating the cause and establishing regular bed and arising times. However, although there may be a physiological basis, not getting up in time for school may be part of the teenager-parent power struggle and therefore easily fixed with bright light and regular arising times.

THE PARASOMNIAS

During NREM sleep, particularly in the first half of the night when there is a concentration of Stage 4 sleep, "all hell may break loose" behaviorally with the occurrence of night terrors and sleepwalking. Bed-wetting, teeth grinding, and sleep rocking are examples of parasomnias not as closely related to one particular sleep stage. In terms of frequency of complaints, the parasomnias may be the most common and are often the most misunderstood. They are often the attention-getters in children's sleep disorders, although, like sleep talking, they are usually benign in the sense that they generally are not signs of more serious pathology (Pareja, de Pablos, Caminero, Millan, & Dobato, 1999).

Many children experience a parasomnia at least once. Often, there is no clear etiology, although stress may be an exacerbating factor. For most, the frequency of occurrence is relatively rare and the problem disappears with maturation. Treatment often consists of providing information and support and treating any secondary problem that may arise, for example, the enuretic child's self-image. Nevertheless, in some situations, the complaint of a parasomnia may indicate significant pathology, most notably seizures.

Sleep Terrors (Pavor Nocturnus)

Sleep terrors usually occur within the first few hours of going to bed, often while parents are still awake and can fully appreciate the sudden and frightening occurrence. In the classic case, the child sits up and lets out a loud, panic-stricken scream followed by several inconsolable minutes. Pulse rates climb well above 100 beats per minute. Subsequently, the child is totally amnesic for an event that the parents are unlikely to forget. These behaviors may vary, however, from agitation to screaming. In some cases, children get out of bed and move around.

A sleep terror, like sleepwalking, is a NREM phenomenon usually occurring out of Stage 4 sleep. Sleep terrors as a rule are not associated with any particular pathology, although a febrile illness may precipitate sleepwalking (J.D. Kales, Kales,

Soldatos, Chamberlin, & Martin, 1979). Also, the first event of sleep talking, screaming, or walking may occur after a disaster or psychic trauma (Dollinger, 1986). They generally occur infrequently, and except in the case of posttraumatic stress disorders, any treatment is more likely to be for the benefit of the family members rather than the child.

Treatment consists of first eliminating exacerbating factors. Sleep deprivation may increase deep sleep and thus provide increased opportunity for night terrors. Reduce caffeine or other stimulants that may fragment sleep. Make sure the bedroom is quiet, dark, and relatively stimulus-free. During an event, it is generally not only futile but also counterproductive to turn on the lights and try to comfort the child. Keep external stimulation to a minimum during the event. Discussing the episode with the child in the morning does nothing more than increase anxiety. If simple interventions are ineffective for frequent events, a benzodiazepine medication (e.g., diazepam) appears to attenuate the problem for reasons that are not entirely clear (C. Fisher, Kahn, Edwards, & Davis, 1973). Diazepam, as any benzodiazepine medication, tends to reduce Stage 4. Diazepam may decrease arousability of the child to the triggering stimulus. Diazepam may also decrease anxiety that may fuel the severity of arousal. However, before any drug treatment, compare the potential beneficial effects against the known side effects (daytime sedation, alteration of normal sleep) and the possible unknown effects of a sedative on a developing nervous system. Education and reassurance alone are often successful.

Sleepwalking (Somnambulism)

Sleepwalking is also a NREM phenomenon usually occurring in Stage 4 sleep during the first third of the sleep period. It may be similar to and part of a night terror attack. The movements or walking may last a few seconds to several minutes. Usually, the sleepwalker walks with eyes open and arms at sides with a blank, distant expression. At the beginning of the first movements, the EEG is still indicative of deep sleep, often with unusually large delta waves. In those predisposed to sleepwalking, a sharp noise or standing them on their feet may precipitate an episode (Broughton, 1968). Thus, minimizing environmental stimuli during sleep is important. Sleepwalking occurs in 10% to 15% of schoolchildren (B.E. Fisher & Wilson, 1987). It is possible that other

sleep pathologies, such as a sleep apnea, will trigger an episode of sleepwalking. One way to view sleepwalking and night terrors is as disorders of arousal (Broughton, 1968). Apparently, arousal from the brain stem triggers movements during deep sleep when there is not sufficient cortical activity to inhibit the behavior.

The fact that sleepwalking usually disappears by adulthood may reflect a maturational factor perhaps related to the decrease in the amount of deep sleep. The mean age of onset is 5 to 6 years, and there often is a family history of sleepwalking (A. Kales, Soldatos, & Bixler, et al., 1980). There is a high incidence of other parasomnias in sleepwalkers, suggesting a common pathophysiological substrate. Recollection of the episodes and purposeful speech or actions are unusual and suggest the possibility of a psychological problem or malingering rather than a parasomnia. Sleepwalking in the early morning hours when there is less Stage 4 sleep suggests a problem other than true somnambulism, for example, a seizure disorder.

We have seen two examples of sleepwalking associated with seizure disorders in young females. One college student had infrequent periods of sleepwalking but scheduled an evaluation after an episode where she drove five miles out of town before "awakening." Because of its occurrence at 3 A.M., the diagnostic polysomnogram included an all-night clinical EEG. Abnormal EEG activity occurred from the temporal lobe area. The second case would sleepwalk two to four nights per week and had been a sleepwalker and talker for most of her life. These events occurred in the first part of the night, and she did not remember them the next morning. While sleepwalking, she had a blank expression and was moderately uncoordinated. She had frequent traumas during these episodes, including two teeth-breaking accidents and one coccyx fracture after falling downstairs. Her father had been a sleepwalker his entire life. Her family's solution had been to tie her in bed at night. Although laboratory tests, a CT scan, and a waking EEG were normal, the PSG with a clinical EEG montage indicated significant EEG abnormalities. An anticonvulsant medication eliminated her sleepwalking (Dervent, Karacan, Ware, & Williams, 1978).

In spite of these examples, a large majority of children experiencing sleepwalking and night terrors do not have a seizure disorder and will respond to nonpharmacological treatments (Guilleminault,

1987a). Most treatments of night terrors also are applicable for somnambulism, particularly increasing total sleep time. Therefore, making sure the child is getting enough sleep is usually the first treatment step. Because stress, anxiety, and other factors may exacerbate sleepwalking and night terrors, psychological assessment of children can help. Behavioral therapy including relaxation, family therapy, hypnosis, and psychotherapy, where appropriate, can be effective even in children also treated pharmacologically. Although hypnotism is unlikely to eliminate the sleep arousals, giving the child a hypnotic suggestion to awaken when the feet hit the floor may prevent wandering through the house or neighborhood. For some, alarms on doors, gates in front of stairs, bureaus in front of windows, and bedrooms on the first floor may be necessary. Because injuries during these episodes are not unusual, parents should remove objects that may injure the child. In unusually severe cases, locking the room's door to keep the child from wandering out of the house may be necessary. Putting the mattress on the floor makes falling out of bed less injurious; also, it requires more effort to get up. Such added effort may produce enough awareness to stop the episode. Waking the child just before the typical time of sleepwalking (which may be before the parents go to bed) may eliminate the problem (Frank, Spirito, Stark, & Owens-Stively, 1997).

Nightmares

Nightmares are different from sleep terrors. Nightmares are a REM sleep–related phenomenon. Therefore, unlike the sleep terror, patients recall a considerable amount of complicated dream content. Because of the suppression of muscle tone in REM sleep, major movements are minimal. Virtually all children have nightmares at one time or another; nightmares per se are not pathological. They may create a disturbance in the child's sleep and concern over going to bed. For reoccurring nightmares, the suggestion by M. Moore (1945) to have the patient tell and retell the nightmare may act as an effective desensitization method. Some children respond to the suggestion that they can control the outcome by flying away or use magical powers to destroy dream monsters. Rehearsing an alternative dream ending may be helpful. Alternatively, reassurance (e.g., "Try not to worry, you just had a bad dream. They can't hurt you"), and normalization (e.g., "Everybody has them") may help. Relaxation training at bedtime helps some children. Nightmares may also be a symptom of some significant psychopathology that may need more in-depth psychotherapy. However, when such is the case, there are often daytime signs that point to a psychological disturbance.

REM Sleep Behavior Disorder

The excitement generated by the usually benign sleepwalker in Stage 4 sleep with somewhat uncoordinated, nonpurposeful behavior pales when compared to a person acting out a dream by diving out of bed to attack the nightstand turned monster. The disorder can occur in children (Sheldon & Jacobsen, 1998), with the youngest case reported being a 22-month-old (Herman, Blaw, & Steinberg, 1989). Most commonly, however, REM sleep behavior disorder (RBD) occurs in middle-age or older males (Schenck, Bundlie, Ettinger, & Mahowald, 1986). Our first such patient came to us after his wife refused to sleep with him after he slugged her in the chin one night with enough force to knock her out of bed. This was the most violent of many behaviors he had experienced during sleep for a number of years. She finally agreed to return to his bed only if he would wear an elaborate harness that allowed her to strap him securely in bed each night.

The behaviors occur as a result of loss of the muscle paralysis that normally occurs in REM sleep, therefore allowing the acting out of dreams. In normal sleepers, twitches and jerks briefly interrupt this paralysis but not long enough to result in sustained behaviors. In those patients with clear RBD, approximately 60% have some identifiable neuropathology on a careful neurological workup that includes MRI (Mahowald & Schenck, 1989). Treatment with a benzodiazepine medication (usually clonazepam) is effective in 80% of the cases.

Bedwetting (Enuresis)

Enuresis occurs in approximately 10% of children past potty-training age and is more likely to occur in males. Enuresis can be primary (the child has never had a significant dry period) or secondary, where the child learns control of bladder function and later begins having problems with incontinence. Although primary enuresis may be a developmental delay, it also may occur in response to sleep apnea, sleep deprivation, diabetes, urinary tract infection, epilepsy, emotional problems, or food substances. One 6-foot, 200-pound 16-year-old who had only one to two dry nights per month responded to the elimination of the approximately

250 mg of caffeine from two liters of cola every afternoon after school. Although psychological factors may trigger secondary enuresis, a small percentage (< 5%) may have an organic etiology (Guilleminault & Anders, 1976). Salmon (1975) gives an interesting historical account of the problem. Although there was little understanding of the cause, there was no lack of treatment procedures, which varied from eating boiled mice and wood lice to strychnine injections into the perineum and cauterization of the urinary meatus with silver nitrate.

Enuresis is not specifically sleep-stage-related and may even occur when the child is awake at night. Enuretic children often have a family history of the problem. Their sleep may be deeper than that of nonenuretics (Finley, 1971), resulting in an elevated or abnormal arousal threshold (Neveus, Lackgren, Stenber, Tuvemo, & Hetta, 1998). Often, parents of enuretic children are surprised by how difficult their child is to awaken to urinate before an accident occurs. Some physiological data do support the idea of an arousal disorder (Kawauchi et al., 1998). Other etiological theories have focused on physical immaturity, psychological immaturity, psychopathology, and failure to learn an appropriate response to bladder cues (Werry & Cohrssen, 1965).

If a physical evaluation is negative, the next step can be no treatment, behavioral treatment, or drug treatment. A spontaneous remission rate of 15% occurs yearly (De Jonge, 1973). When giving no treatment other than supporting the patient and family in dealing with the problem, the underlying assumption is that the problem is primarily developmental. This, however, is easier to accept in a 5-year-old than in a teenager. If there is a family history of enuresis, the age at which enuresis stopped in the parent may be helpful in predicting when the episodes will end.

Behavioral treatment with a bell that rings when the child urinates assumes that the underlying etiology is either a disorder of arousal (Broughton, 1968; Finley, 1971) or a failure to attend and respond to the appropriate cues for another reason. With its use, the child wakes up sooner and sooner after a micturition episode begins, resulting in smaller and smaller wet spots that eventually disappear altogether (Finley, Besserman, Bennett, Clapp, & Finley, 1973). The child learns to respond appropriately to the cues for the need to urinate by either awaking to urinate or increasing bladder sphincter tone to compensate for bladder contractions. Unfortunately, parents may need to supplement the alarm when it does not awaken the child. Bladder capacity increases in responders and nonresponders during bell-and-pad treatment, and thus is not significantly related to success or failure (Oredsson & Jorgensen, 1998).

Pediatricians often treat enuresis with medications. In the past, the most commonly used was a low dose of the drug imipramine. The decision to treat with imipramine is an easy one to make on a purely pragmatic basis because on average, it reduces the number of episodes by about half (A. Kales, Kales, Jacobson, Humphrey, & Soldatos, 1977). However, not all children are responders (Mikkelsen & Rapoport, 1980). Also, it does not cure the problem because the relapse rate is high after drug discontinuation. The mechanism of its action is probably to increase spincter tone. A potential overdose problem occurs if a child reasons "1 pill helps, 20 should stop it altogether," particularly when planning to spend a night away from home. An overdose of imipramine can be lethal due to slowing the conduction of the heart.

Some enuretic children during sleep are deficient in the antidiuretic hormone vasopressin (Rittig, Knudsen, Norgaard, Pedersen, & Djurhuus, 1989). Treatment with desmopressin (DDAVP) will correct enuresis in up to 65% of children (Klauber, 1989). Dryness continues after withdrawal at a higher rate than if there had been no treatment (Lackgren, Lilja, Neveus, & Stenberg, 1998).

Sleep Rocking and Head Banging (Jactatio Capitus Nocturnal)

Rhythmical sleep rocking can be from side to side, back and forth on knees and elbows, or slamming one's head into the pillow (head banging). It initially occurs around the age of 6 months (Evans, 1961), often beginning just prior to sleep. Like enuresis, sleep rocking may occur in all stages of sleep (Baldy-Moulinier, Levy, & Passouant, 1979; Gagnon & DeKonick, 1985). Sleep rocking may be maturational and, therefore, self-limiting. Head banging declines with age. Besides maturational processes, researchers suggest a variety of factors, ranging from relief of sleep-associated anxiety to epilepsy.

How vigorously to pursue treatment depends on the severity. Parents of otherwise healthy children who have observed the behavior and incidentally reported it simply need to be told what is known about the phenomenon. Although unusual, injury may occur. In these cases, evaluations for psychological and physiological pathology are appropriate, as well as instituting protective measures against injury such as the addition of extra pillows and a helmet. We have evaluated two children, 10 and 12 years old, who had excessively intrusive and protective caretakers dominating their home life. Therapy with one child dealing with control issues eliminated the rocking (Bond, Ware, & Hoelscher, 1989).

Sleep Paralysis

As is easily imagined, waking up unable to move is a terrifying experience for a child or an adult. It sounds so bizarre that parents may not take a child's complaint seriously, attributing it to a dream. Adults often will not complain if it happens to them for fear of being labeled "crazy." This phenomenon is even more unusual and frightening when it is accompanied by hallucinations. Some adults have had these "terrifying" experiences since childhood and told no one but their most trusted friend. Sleep paralysis is a dissociation of the REM sleep phenomenon. The dreamer awakens, but the loss of muscle tone that accompanies REM sleep remains. Some patients try to return to sleep and wake up again. Others move their eyes quickly back and forth and produce enough arousal to break the paralysis. Finally, most patients can moan during a paralysis episode. If the bed partner touches the patient, the paralysis will often disappear due to the additional arousal stimulus. Because the experience may be common to several generations of family members, particular names and stories develop around the phenomenon. One expression we hear in reference to the occurrence is "The witches were riding last night."

Sleep paralysis may occur in association with narcolepsy (discussed later), and the clinician must be careful not to overlook the possible existence of this condition. For true familial sleep paralysis, there is no cure, although there is no real danger except for the anxiety produced by its occurrence. Just recognizing and naming the problem is helpful.

Sleep Bruxism

Sleep bruxism rivals snoring in its ability to disturb the sleep of others because of the distinct loud noise resulting from rhythmically grinding and gnashing teeth. Bruxism occurs in all ages but has its maximum incidence in children and adolescents. Fifteen percent of those 3 to 17 years of age have a history of bruxism (Reding, Rubright, & Zimmerman, 1966). For most children, bruxism is benign. In some severe cases, the patient may complain of fatigue or sleepiness during the day, probably related to arousals from sleep. Those adults who grind their teeth in REM sleep appear more likely to damage teeth and temporomandibular joints (Ware & Rugh, 1988).

Anatomical, neurological, and genetic factors may contribute to bruxism. Psychological trait factors do not play a strong role, although anxiety and stress do increase bruxism (Clark, Rugh, & Handelman, 1980; Vanderas, Menenakou, Kouimtzis, & Papagiannoulis, 1999). Because the etiology in children is unknown and the condition tends to alleviate with time, treatment in severe cases consists of the fitting of a tooth-protecting prosthesis. Behavioral treatments focusing on stress reduction/relaxation may be successful in adults, although there is little evidence to suggest that these are beneficial in children.

EXCESSIVE DAYTIME SLEEPINESS

The symptom of sleepiness in children may be less clear-cut than in adults. Besides the fact that adults are more likely to say "I'm sleepy," adults spend more time in sedentary activities (e.g., reading, driving) that are compatible with the onset of sleepiness. In children, the first sign of sleepiness may be behavior changes such as increased activity, a shorter attention span, reduced coordination, or fussiness. Although a variety of disorders and environmental conditions may result in excessive sleepiness, including the parasomnias if they sufficiently disturb sleep, we limit our discussion to narcolepsy and sleep-related respiratory disorders.

Narcolepsy

Narcolepsy, a specific disorder whose major symptom is the inability to maintain consistent periods of wakefulness, is generally diagnosed in adulthood. However, one-third date the onset of their sleepiness to adolescence (Anders et al., 1980). Although frequently unrecognized, excessive sleepiness and other signs of narcolepsy do occur in preadolescents (Guilleminault & Pelayo, 1998; Young, Zorick, Wittig, Roehrs, & Roth, 1988).

Narcolepsy is not a form of epilepsy. There are no abnormal electrical discharges in the EEG. Narcoleptic symptoms occur when the sleep system, particularly the REM sleep system, is uncontrolled. This can produce (in addition to inappropriate sleepiness) cataplexy, hypnagogic hallucinations, and sleep paralysis. Episodes of muscle weakness (cataplexy), most often associated with emotion-evoking events, are experienced by 68% to 88% of narcoleptics (Anders et al., 1980). However, cataplexy may not develop until years after sleepiness becomes a problem. Particularly in adolescents, parents or teachers may misinterpret the narcoleptic's sleepiness as laziness or even psychopathology. REM sleep often occurs within 15 minutes of sleep onset in narcoleptic patients instead of the normal 90 minutes. Also, narcoleptics are more likely to have disturbed sleep.

Because, at the present time, narcolepsy is not curable, clinicians should not give the diagnosis lightly. An incorrect diagnosis of narcolepsy may prevent further evaluation that may reveal a correctable problem. In addition to a PSG to rule out other sleep problems, a multiple sleep latency test (MSLT), consisting of five naps at two-hour intervals during the day, is usually necessary for a correct diagnosis. Typically, narcoleptics will fall asleep within five minutes and enter REM sleep within a few minutes on at least two of the five naps. The sleep latency of normal subjects is typically 10 minutes or longer (Richardson et al., 1978), and REM sleep appears only rarely within the first 15 minutes of sleep.

Hypnagogic hallucinations occur in approximately 50% to 60% of narcoleptics (Young et al., 1988) and may be either auditory or visual. Most patients find them to be disturbing if not frightening but typically are able to differentiate between reality and the hallucinations. These may be vivid, dreamlike experiences that occur as the patient is falling asleep. They are secondary to the occurrence of sleep-onset REM periods. The sleep paralysis of narcolepsy is essentially no different from the sleep paralysis discussed earlier except for its association with other narcoleptic symptoms. It occurs in 30% to 60% of narcoleptics (Young et al., 1988).

In Caucasians, approximately 3 out of every 10,000 have narcolepsy (Hublin et al., 1994). Having a first-degree relative with narcolepsy increases the likelihood about 18-fold (Guilleminault, Mignot, & Grumet, 1989). Mignot and colleagues recently identified a narcolepsy canine gene (Lin et al.,

1999). This gene and one identified in mice (Chemelli et al., 1999) control the hypocretin/orexin neuropeptide system with neurons located in the lateral and posterior hypothalamus. These findings offer hope for the development of specific medications for the treatment of narcolepsy.

Medications now used suppress narcoleptic symptoms sufficiently to improve performance but do not eliminate narcolepsy. Narcoleptics may do poorly in school because of sleepiness resulting in inattentiveness. However, stimulants must be used with caution. Regular use may not only result in tolerance but may result in a sleep disturbance that further increases the daytime sleepiness. Often, a small dose 30 minutes before the maximum period of sleepiness (e.g., the school period right after lunch) and none on the weekend will be sufficient to overcome the major episodes of sleepiness and retard the development of tolerance. Short naps (10–15 minutes) in place of the stimulant may work. Narcoleptics characteristically experience some relief of sleepiness after a nap. Unfortunately, special naptime in school for a 15-year-old is difficult to arrange. If cataplexy is a problem, medications that are effective REM sleep suppressants usually will reduce the episodes.

It is important to give the child, the parents, and the teachers a thorough explanation of the problem. With a better understanding of the problem, patients can learn to organize their lives, in conjunction with pharmacotherapy, to cope with narcolepsy. Still, most present with depressive symptoms in reaction to narcolepsy at some time. Surprisingly, teachers may not acknowledge narcolepsy as a medical problem, and many families refuse referrals to support and counseling groups (Guilleminault & Pelayo, 1998).

Sleep Apnea
Due to reduction of muscle tone and decreased sensitivity to carbon dioxide, sleep can exacerbate known respiratory problems such as asthma and create specific sleep breathing problems. Sleep apnea, the most common of the latter category, refers to the cessation of breathing during sleep. In infants, central apnea events often occur; there is no attempt to breathe. In older children and adults, an obstruction of the upper airway is more likely to cause apnea events. The reduced muscle tone of sleep and negative pressure caused by inspiratory efforts contribute to a collapse of the upper airway. Though once thought to be rare, 14% of patients

evaluated in a pediatric sleep disorders clinic received a primary diagnosis of sleep apnea (Feber, Boyler, & Belfer, 1981).

In children, large tonsils and adenoids are perhaps the most common causes of obstructive sleep apnea. Obesity and features such as retrognathia, micrognathia, and macroglossia are other risk factors. Children with enlarged tonsils can have hundreds of apnea periods during sleep that markedly disturb sleep and alter daytime behavior.

Tonsillectomy and adenoidectomy on these children improve the sleep-related breathing disturbance. One study examined first-grade children in the lowest 10th percentile for sleep apnea. Of 297 children, 18% has a positive screening. Twenty-four were treated with a tonsillectomy and adenoidectomy; the parents of 30 decided against treatment. A follow-up of the children in the second grade indicated an increase in grade point average of 0.43, while there was essentially no change in those not treated or in those without sleep apnea (Gozal, 1998). Although hypertrophied tonsils may be an indication for a tonsillectomy, treatment decisions must take into account the frequency of the apnea periods, the degree of the sleep disturbance, the severity of the oxygen desaturations, the presence of cardiac arrhythmias, and the presence of behaviors (e.g., fatigue, sleepiness, grouchiness, and enuresis) that are likely to be secondary to sleep apnea (Marcus, 1997).

Any anomaly that reduces the diameter of the upper airway may cause obstructive sleep apnea, such as a large tongue in Down syndrome children. The profound retrognathia associated with Pierre-Robin syndrome (a congenital defect in the prenatal development of the mandible) results in a posterior displacement of the base of the tongue that reduces upper airway size. Repairing a cleft palate by rotating a pharyngeal flap to close the palate may result in a constriction, making the upper airway more susceptible to occlusion during sleep (Abramson, Marrinan, & Mulliken, 1997). In one case, a respiratory arrest after surgery resulted in an emergency tracheostomy. A subsequent study with the tracheostomy closed indicated that the cleft palate repair resulted in over 400 apnea episodes during the night (Orr, Levine, & Buchanan, 1987). Finally, offspring of sleep apnea patients may inherit subtle defects that may contribute to the problem (Pillar, Schnall, Peled, Oliven, & Lavie, 1997).

Sleep apneic children may present in a variety of ways that may be different from adult sleep apnea patients. A number of behavioral manifestations may underlie this potentially lethal condition. Most frequently, the parent will note restless sleep associated with loud snoring and sternal retractions. The parent may even have noted episodes of cyanosis associated with a cessation of breathing. The profound sleepiness in association with obstructive sleep apnea in adults is a less consistent finding in children. It is more likely that the child will present with complaints of lethargy, daytime fatigue, extreme difficulty waking in the morning, or even failure to thrive. Diagnosis of sleep apnea without a PSG is not reliable (Nieminen et al., 1997).

OTHER DISORDERS

Sudden Infant Death Syndrome (SIDS)

The sudden and unexplained demise of an ostensibly healthy infant is the sine qua non of SIDS. Death in nearly all instances occurs in a presumably sleeping infant. The incidence of SIDS has decreased since the campaign began to have infants sleep on their back. One explanation of this success is that soft bedding no longer covers the external airways (Scheers, Dayton, & Kemp, 1998). However, this may not be the complete story; position may have other effects. For example, because auditory arousal thresholds are higher when infants sleep in the prone position (Franco et al., 1998), the arousal threshold to clear an obstructed airway may also be higher. Other risk factors for SIDS include a gestational age of less than 37 weeks, repeated episodes of apnea, a family history of SIDS, low parental social and education level, poor postnatal care, and maternal smoking during pregnancy (Kohlendorfer, Kiechl, & Sperl, 1998).

Although there is no consistent abnormality common to all infants who have succumbed to SIDS, they are not completely normal infants. Subtle neurological abnormalities occur in infants considered to be at high risk for SIDS (Korobkin & Guilleminault, 1979). Pathologic apnea is a popular hypothesis used to explain the mechanism in SIDS (Guilleminault, 1987b; Guilleminault, Peraita, Souquet, & Dement, 1975). However, apnea and even cardiac arrhythmias do not predict an increased risk for SIDS in newborn infants discharged from an intensive care unit (Southall, Richards, & Rhoden, 1982).

For SIDS victims, heart rate is higher over all states at less than 1 month of age and higher in

REM sleep after 1 month of age compared to control groups (Schechtman et al., 1988). In infants with recurrent apnea and aborted SIDS, induction of transient mild hypoxemia results in increased frequency and duration of apneic spells (Brady et al., 1978). No change in the parameters occurred in the control group. In addition, Shannon, Kelly, and O'Connell (1977) demonstrated decreased carbon dioxide sensitivity in a group of aborted SIDS infants. This suggests, at least in some cases of SIDS, aberrant chemical control of breathing.

Although there are other plausible notions concerning the etiology of SIDS that are related to behavioral development in the neonatal period (Lipsitt, 1979), the alterations in the control of breathing and cardiac function during sleep must be given priority as factors important in identifying not only the etiology of SIDS but also in identifying the high-risk infant.

Munchausen's Syndrome by Proxy

Just when SIDS became recognized and parents of healthy children who died in their sleep were not looked at suspiciously, a bizarre form of child abuse was recognized as more common than previously thought (Botash, Blatt, & Meguid, 1998). Baron von Munchausen was a renowned German adventurer and storyteller who lived in the 18th century. In honor of his wild tales and widely ranging travels, patients who manufacture symptoms and carry them from doctor to doctor are referred to as having Munchausen's syndrome. *The Diagnostic and Statistical Manual of Mental Disorders* (DSM-IV, American Psychiatric Association [APA], 1994) lists this disorder under the heading of factitious disorders. When patients manufacture the symptoms in their children, it is referred to as Munchausen's syndrome by proxy or factitious disorder by proxy.

We have recorded on videotape from an infrared-lit room a mother choking her 10-month-old child. While she was in the presence of others, she acted appropriately. Approximately monthly, hospitalizations occurred throughout the child's short life as a result of apparent apnea spells requiring resuscitation. Apnea spells had also occurred while he was hospitalized, but only when the mother was alone with the child. Other sleep centers have recorded similar events (Griffith & Slovik, 1989; Rosen et al., 1983).

We know of no way to detect such cases conclusively other than by observing the event surreptitiously.

However, in otherwise healthy infants who have undocumented repeated events or who have unusual symptom clusters in the presence of normal laboratory and diagnostic evaluations, the possibility of parentally induced symptoms exists.

INSOMNIA

Insomnia is a symptom with multiple causes and not a disorder itself. A survey by Bixler, Kales, and Soldatos (1979) found that physicians estimated 30% of their patients had a sleep complaint. When broken down according to specialties, obstetrician-gynecologists estimated that 19% and child psychiatrists estimated that 60% of their patients had a sleep complaint, with insomnia and nightmares the two most common complaints. In evaluating a group of 129 children (1–19 years) presenting with sleep complaints, Ferber et al. (1981) gave a psychiatric diagnosis to only 14% but noted the additional presence of psychological factors in many patients. *The International Classification of Sleep Disorders: Diagnostic and Coding Manual* (ICSD, 1997) discusses the diagnostic categories described below in detail.

Otherwise healthy infants and children with difficulty going to sleep or staying asleep fall into several categories. Children who "misbehave" at night are also more likely to have behavior problems during the day (Zuckerman, Stevenson, & Bailey, 1987). Our experience and that of others is that the large majority of these children respond in less than a month if the parents follow appropriate recommendations. Treatment of insomnia complaints in adults is less successful than in children, perhaps due to the fact that adults do not have someone to control their environment and behavior to the degree that infants do. In older children, problems can arise from a disagreement between parent and child as to when the sleep period should begin and end. For many highly motivated parents, reading the book *Solve Your Child's Sleep Problems* (Ferber, 1985) and following the recommendations produce a better-sleeping child.

Inadequate Sleep Hygiene

Sleep hygiene factors are the important and sometimes subtle factors that can improve or disturb sleep (Hauri, 1982; Kleitman, 1963). Poor sleep hygiene often goes unrecognized. Correcting sleep hygiene alone may cure the problem or greatly increase how quickly other treatments restore good sleep.

The development of a stable prebed routine is important. Presleep behavioral patterns usually evolve from the age of 2 to 5 years and consist of ritualistic behaviors (e.g., saying prayers, being read stories, putting toy animals to bed) that serve the purpose of avoiding sleep-related anxiety and calming the child. Although regular exercise benefits sleep, a calm transition period between hard play and bed is important. A certain amount of anxiety associated with sleep is not unusual because the child may equate going to sleep with leaving his or her parents and a relatively predictable environment to contend with the strange places and frightening characters of dreams. Part of the prebed routine is to have a set bedtime. Regular bed and arising times also prevent schedule disorders by resulting in well-entrained circadian rhythms. Therefore, sleep latency tends to be shorter and awakenings fewer. In a number of cases, a frustrating and unpleasant prebed routine develops. The child organizes the routine more than the parents do. The crying of infants and the distracting and delaying tactics of older children can be surprisingly regular. Night after night, these behaviors can exhaust all involved. An understanding of the situation, a plan to change it, and a consistent response from mother and father over a period of one to two weeks are often all that it takes to turn bedtime into a pleasant experience.

Often unrecognized are the bedtime demands of the parents. These may be unrealistic and contribute to the problem. Some adults, despite numerous sensors and a strange environment, fall asleep more easily in a sleep center than they do at home. One explanation for this is that at home, they "try hard" to go to sleep, often unsuccessfully. The bedroom becomes an arousal stimulus after frequent pairings with the unpleasant experience of not being able to go to sleep. Once in the sleep center, the patients plan to demonstrate how they suffer through each night and thus do not try to go to sleep. However, lying quietly with eyes closed in a darkened, sound-attenuated room is more compatible with sleep than the arousal produced by "trying hard" at home in the presence of a conditioned arousal response to the bedroom. The same situation occurs in some children. The child hears "It's time to go to sleep." The lights go off with instructions to "go to sleep." Unfortunately, the harder a

child tries, the less likely sleep will come, and the more likely he or she will associate the bed and bedroom with failure and anxiety.

Naps may be a blessing for the afternoon caregiver but a problem when they prevent sleep from occurring at night. A child's total daily sleep requirements decrease from over 15 hours in the infant to less than 10 in the adolescent. Insistence on the daytime nap, particularly if late, will produce delayed and perhaps disturbed sleep. The more children sleep during the day, the less they sleep at night. Typically, the three-nap 3-month-old becomes a one-nap 1-year old, then a no-nap 3-year-old, though the child may still lie down without actually going to sleep.

Environmental disturbances may be present for the child but not the parents, in part depending on the location of the bedroom. Parents may overlook traffic noise, lights, pets, the television, room temperature, siblings, and the actual bed as sleep-disturbing factors. When comparing groups of children with and without a sleep disturbance, 34% of the sleep disturbed children slept with a sibling or parent, whereas only 16% of the control group were "cosleepers" (Kataria, Swanson, & Trevathan, 1987). Parents sharing a bed with infants can be controversial, but contrary to popular perception, it is not uncommon. The effects on sleep appear modest. The deep sleep of infants 11 to 15 weeks old is slightly less and arousals are elevated when bed-sharing with a parent (Mosko, Richard, & McKenna, 1997). One benefit may be increased opportunity to monitor the infant. No studies have compared older children sleeping with and without a parent. However, the sleep of kibbutz children in communal sleeping houses improved after moving to familial sleep (Epstein, Herer, Tzischinsky, & Lavie, 1997). The authors attributed this to an increased sense of security when sleeping with their families.

Sleep-Onset Association Disorder
This disorder develops out of problems with the bedtime routine. The routine may be wonderfully effective for getting the child to sleep, but, when the child later awakens, he or she reasonably expects the same set of circumstances to fall asleep again. If children associate rocking, drinking juice, or back rubbing with sleep onset, they do what they can to recreate the circumstances. This usually means crying for a parent. The solution is to have the child initially fall asleep in the set of circumstances that will

330 PROBLEMS OF CHILDHOOD

be present during an awakening. If using a relaxation tape helps children go to sleep, instruct them to play the tape again if they awaken. Also, reward them for not waking their parents (G. Walker, personal communication, 1999).

Limit-Setting Sleep Disorder
Once a child becomes mobile enough to climb out of a crib and leave the bedroom, this problem can develop. Finding a parent and requesting a drink of water, a snack, or a story may become routine. If the parents become immune to these simple requests, a complaint of monsters in the bedroom or the need to go to the bathroom will usually get attention. An hour or more of complying with midnight requests is not unusual with this disorder. Although the problem may be infrequent enough to be benign, it can occur sufficiently to curtail by one to two hours the child's total sleep. Sleep patterns may become irregular enough to contribute to the development of a circadian rhythm disturbance that further disturbs the child's sleep and daytime functioning. Finally, more complex issues are raised in terms of the development of parent-child interactions. The situation can evolve so innocently that parents do not think of the situation as a disorder. Treatment is usually straightforward, consisting of explaining the situation and applying behavioral methods to shape the child's nocturnal responding.

Eating or Drinking at Night
After the age of 6 months, most children have the capability to make it through the night without a feeding. A child that has difficulty maintaining sleep, awakens to eat or drink, and returns to sleep and sleeps normally afterwards likely suffers from this problem. Although the child may have true hunger cues, food intake is well beyond any necessary nutritional needs. There is no associated pathology other than the conditioning that has taken place. However, these feedings can affect circadian, digestive, and endocrine rhythms as well as distort the parents' sleep. Just telling a caring parent not to feed an apparently hungry child during the night usually will not solve the problem. Education and gradually altering the behavior of parent and child over a period of several days to weeks is needed for successful treatment outcome.

Sleep State Misperception
Early in their careers, sleep specialists learn that the complaint of too little sleep or insomnia often

does not correspond to the amount of sleep a patient actually obtains. Not only may judgment of time be poor while lying awake in bed, but the cues that one may use to judge the quality or quantity of sleep (e.g., next-day aches, fatigue, bags under eyes) may be entirely unrelated to sleep. Guilleminault and Anders (1976) give an example of a 12-year-old boy who from the age of 6 months was a poor sleeper. He had received a variety of treatments, including phenobarbital to put him to sleep and dextroamphetamine to keep him awake. When the authors initially saw him at 12 years of age, parents and patient indicated that he was sleeping no more than 4 hours per night. However, objective monitoring revealed a normal sleep pattern of 448 minutes (nearly 7.5 hours) in duration. Usually, an accurate understanding of the amount and type of sleep that the patient is getting can be a prerequisite for successful treatment.

Psychopathology
Typically, depressed patients have reduced total sleep time and longer sleep latencies, awaken more often, stay awake longer, and have REM sleep earlier in the night (Reynolds & Kupfer, 1987). However, the variability among patients is large, and the data on sleep in depressed children do not paint a clear picture. In some cases, depressed patients spend more time in bed. This may be particularly true for adolescents, who have a normal tendency for increased sleepiness (Carskadon et al., 1980). Generally, a sleep center is not the place to begin if depression alone is suspected as the cause of disturbed sleep.

Drug Use
Like psychological problems, almost any medical problem (e.g., ear infections) may result in a sleep disturbance. For the most part, parents and pediatricians detect the cause-effect relationship. However, there are several problems that are difficult to detect. One of these is the consequence of drug use.

There are few, if any, indications for using a sleeping pill (hypnotic) in healthy children or infants. Chronic use of sedative/hypnotic medications is likely to create more problems. Although a sleep disturbance secondary to stimulant use is not unexpected, sedative/hypnotics may also produce insomnia as well as daytime sleepiness. They usually do not restore normal sleep patterns. Hypnotics can suppress REM sleep and deep sleep. Tolerance develops with chronic use resulting in the need for a higher dose to be effective. Because some hypnotics have a relatively long half-life, they may impair daytime alertness and school performance. A sudden stopping of the drug can produce a rebound insomnia that can last from a day to weeks.

Drugs with hypnotic effects are used for other reasons, for example, to treat epilepsy. Lairy and associates (Lairy, Catani, Findjii, & Laird, 1980) reported on five children from 2.5 to 10.5 years old with behavioral or school problems who were on barbiturates for epilepsy. Presenting complaints were school retardation, passivity, sleep disturbances, daytime sleep attacks, and frequent awakenings at night. Careful withdrawal produced a consistent increase of deep sleep, improvement or elimination of the sleep disturbances, and improvement of the behavioral problems.

If children must use hypnotics for sleep, a period of days rather than months is a reasonable trial. During this time, dealing with identified insomnia causes should begin. One exception may be in some mentally retarded children with pronounced sleep problems who may need sedation for longer periods and larger doses. Besides stimulants and hypnotics, other medications may result in disturbed sleep; these include sympathomimetic amines used for allergic disorders and theophylline and its derivatives used as an antiasthmatic agent.

Childhood-Onset Insomnia

The large majority of children with insomnia complaints have normal sleep systems that are disrupted by a variety of factors. The phrase "childhood-onset insomnia" describes some adult insomnia patients. Although such a diagnosis implies that there are children who sleep poorly because of inadequate sleep systems, they have yet to be identified except in children with clear neurological deficits. However, even moderate prenatal exposure to alcohol and marijuana can increase movements during sleep and decrease NREM sleep soon after birth (Scher, Richardson, Coble, Day, & Stoffer, 1988).

Gastroesophageal Reflux

Gastroesophageal reflux (GER), the flow of gastric contents from the stomach into the esophagus, can disturb sleep. This reflux may produce multiple sleep arousals or nocturnal wheezing in asthmatics (Wilson, Charette, Thomson, & Silverman, 1985). GER is common in both adults and children and occurs with myriad symptom complaints and complications (Richter, Bradley, & Castell, 1989). The most

common symptom in children and adults is heartburn, but in infants, the most common symptom is regurgitation and/or failure to thrive. GER can be a source of sleep apnea and other respiratory complications such as the exacerbation of bronchial asthma, chronic cough and hoarseness, and pulmonary aspiration (Gonzalez & Castell, 1988).

Heartburn is not a consistent clinical complaint with GER, and its absence should never rule out the possibility of GER in the pathogenesis of symptoms such as wheezing or multiple arousals from sleep. There is a high incidence of reflux events in infants presenting primarily with respiratory symptoms (Jolley, Herbst, & Johnson, 1981). Elimination of reflux in these patients markedly improves the sleep-related symptoms and respiratory complications.

Food Allergy Insomnia

Food allergies are blamed for many undesired behaviors, including sleep disturbance. The number of substances that may cause a reaction is immense and, as a group, poorly studied. Evidence does exist that a cow's milk allergy may cause a chronic sleep disturbance in infants independent of GER (Kahn et al., 1988). The problem often begins within the first two years of life. Removing cow's milk normalized the sleep in Kahn's patients by increasing total sleep time and decreasing the fragmentation of sleep Stages 2 and 3.

Although not associated with allergies, certain other foods are consistently likely to disturb sleep. Caffeinated beverages, chocolate (with its caffeine-like properties), and peppermint that is likely to increase GER are best avoided.

EVALUATION OF SLEEP DISORDERS

The following information is helpful when dealing with children with sleep problems.

Description

If possible, interview parents and child separately. Each often has a different tale to tell. Particularly for insomnia complaints, a description of sleep and wakefulness behaviors for the whole 24-hour day is important. A late afternoon nap and a cola at the sitter's before being picked up by parents after work may cause the bedtime battles. The ideal time to assess sleep hygiene problems is while obtaining a description of the daily routine of the child.

The First Occurrence
What was happening in the child's environment? Were there changes in the bedroom, family members, or daytime activities? Was there a particularly stressful event, such as loss of friends, divorce, or a death in the family? Had the child been healthy? Had he or she been on, or recently removed from, medication? Sleep problems can begin following a particular event that has long vanished. Knowing the precipitating event may make finding the source presently feeding the sleep disturbance easier.

Time and Frequency of Occurrence
If the problem occurs only in the first part of the night, is that because the parents are awake only then to notice it? The time of occurrence often gives a clue to the sleep stage from which it is occurring. If the problem is one of inability to sleep, is it more likely to be a problem initiating sleep, maintaining sleep, or waking up too early in the morning? What is the frequency of occurrence? Is the problem occurring with increasing frequency? If nightly, how many times per night?

Description of the Behavior(s)
What does the child do while awake during the night? Just as important, how do the parents respond? How anxious is the family about the problem? Has the child's problem significantly increased the amount of attention he or she is getting? Does the child's anxiety over the problem match that of the parents? In parasomniacs, are the movements repetitive? Are they purposeful? Has an injury occurred? Can the child remember the events or thought content at the time of occurrence?

The Other Sleep Parameters
Is the present problem isolated, or are there other sleep problems? Did the child settle normally? Is his or her total bedtime within the normal range for his or her age? How easily awakened is the child in the morning? From a nap? What was the actual event that caused the parents to seek help? Why are they seeking a consult now?

Child's Daytime Performance
Has there been a change in the child's attention span, fussiness, school performance, and interactions with others? Significant psychopathology does not rule out the possibility that a disorder such as

sleep apnea precipitated the performance changes, the psychopathology, and the sleep complaint.

Family Sleep History
Did the parents have a similar sleep problem? If so, was its course similar to that of their child? How was it treated? How did/do the parents react to their own sleep problem? It may be that the parents' own experience with a similar sleep problem does not help them deal with the child's problem. For example, with an enuretic, the parent may want the child to excel where he or she failed, or the parent may believe (incorrectly) that his or her problem was due to laziness and project the same cause onto the child's enuresis.

Medical History
The evaluation should be multidimensional. Particularly important is a history of medication use. Medical disorders commonly occur with disturbed sleep, including allergies (McColley, Carroll, Curtis, Loughlin, & Sampson, 1997), asthma (Stores, Ellis, Wiggs, Crawford, & Thomson, 1998), ADHD (Chervin, Dillon, Bassetti, Ganoczy, & Pituch, 1997), atopic eczema (Bartlet, Westbroek, & White, 1997), autism (Taira, Takase, & Sasaki, 1998), fibromyalgia syndrome in children and adolescents (Siegel, Janeway, & Baum, 1998), and juvenile rheumatoid arthritis (Zamir, Press, Tal, & Tarasiuk, 1998).

Referral to a Sleep Disorders Center
Generally, consultation with a sleep disorders center is helpful (1) when narcolepsy or sleep apnea is suspected, or (2) for any problem affecting sleep sufficiently to impair daytime performance, or (3) when the problem is long-standing and severe enough for the child to have an unsuccessful treatment history.

CONCLUSIONS

Most complaints of sleep problems are not occult and have identifiable factors. Appropriate assessment can discover the etiologies. Undoubtedly, the key to successful treatment is an accurate diagnosis that begins with a careful history. Because a combination of factors may contribute to a sleep disorder, the evaluation needs to be comprehensive and the treatment often eclectic, keeping in mind that time and reassurance best treat some childhood sleep disorders. However, the recognition that sleep problems may result in significant medical and psychological problems has contributed to the current interest in and concern over sleep disorders.

REFERENCES

Abramson, D.L., Marrinan, E.M., & Mulliken, J.B. (1997). Robin sequence: Obstructive sleep apnea following pharyngeal flap. *Cleft Palate Craniofacial Journal, 34,* 256–260.

American Psychiatric Association. (1994). *Diagnostic and statistical manual of mental disorders* (4th ed.). Washington, DC: Author.

Anders, T. (1979). Night waking in infants during the first year of life. *Pediatrics, 63,* 860–864.

Anders, T., Carskadon, M.A., & Dement, W.C. (1980). Sleep and sleepiness in children and adolescents. *Pediatric Clinics of North America, 27,* 29–42.

Anders, T., Emde, R., & Parmelee, A., Jr. (Eds.). (1971). *A manual of standardized terminology, techniques and criteria for scoring states of sleep and wakefulness in newborn infants.* Los Angeles: UCLA Brain Information Service, NINDS.

Aserinsky, E., & Kleitman, N. (1953). Regularly occurring periods of eye motility, and concomitant phenomena during sleep. *Science, 118,* 273–274.

Aserinsky, E., & Kleitman, N. (1955). A motility cycle in sleeping infants as manifested by ocular and gross bodily activity. *Journal of Applied Physiology, 8,* 11–18.

Baldy-Moulinier, M., Levy, M., & Passouant, P. (1979). A study of jactatio capitis during night sleep. *Electroencephalography and Clinical Neurophysiology, 23,* 87.

Bartlet, L.B., Westbroek, R., & White, J.E. (1997). Sleep patterns in children with atopic eczema. *Acta Dermato-Venereologica, 77,* 446–448.

Bixler, E.O., Kales, A., & Soldatos, C.R. (1979). Sleep disorders encountered in medical practice: A national survey of physicians. *Behavioral Medicine, 6,* 1–6.

Blader, J.C., Koplewicz, H.S., Abikoff, H., & Foley, C. (1997). Sleep problems of elementary school children: A community survey. *Archives of Pediatrics and Adolescent Medicine, 151,* 473–480.

Bond, T., Ware, J.C., & Hoelscher, T.J. (1989). Therapeutic interventions for sleep rocking and headbanging [Abstract]. *Sleep Research, 18,* 112.

Botash, A.S., Blatt, S., & Meguid, V. (1998). Child abuse and sudden infant death syndrome. *Current Opinion in Pediatrics, 10,* 217–223.

Brady, J., Chir, B., Ariagno, R., Watts, J., Goldman, S., & Dumpit, F. (1978). Apnea, hypoxemia, and aborted sudden infant death syndrome. *Pediatrics, 62,* 686–691.

Broughton, R. (1968). Sleep disorders: Disorders of arousal. *Science, 159,* 1070–1078.

Campbell, S.S., Eastman, C.I., Terman, M., Lewy, A.J., Boulos, Z., & Dijk, D.J. (1995). Light treatment for sleep disorders: Consensus report I. Chronology of seminal studies in humans. *Journal of Biological Rhythms, 10,* 105–109.

Carskadon, M.A., Harvey, K., Duke, P., Anders, T.F., Litt, I.F., & Dement, W.C. (1980). Pubertal changes in daytime sleepiness. *Sleep, 2,* 453–460.

Chemelli, R.M., Willie, J.T., Sinton, C.M., Elmquist, J.K., Scammell, T., Lee, C., Richardson, J.A., Williams, S.C., Xiong, Y., Kisanuki, Y., Fitch, T.E., Nakazato, M., Hammer, R.E., Saper, C.B., & Yanagisawa, M. (1999). Narcolepsy in orexin knockout mice: Molecular genetics of sleep regulation. *Cell, 98,* 437–451.

Chervin, R.D., Dillon, J.E., Bassetti, C., Ganoczy, D.A., & Pituch, K.J. (1997). Symptoms of sleep disorders, inattention, and hyperactivity in children. *Sleep, 12,* 1185–1192.

Clark, G.T., Rugh, J.D., & Handelman, S.L. (1980). Nocturnal masseter muscle activity and urinary catecholamine levels in bruxers. *Journal of Dental Research, 59,* 1571–1576.

Curzi-Dascalova, L., & Dreyfus-Brisac, C. (1976). Distribution of skin potential responses according to state of sleep during the first month of life in human babies. *Electroencephalography and Clinical Neurophysiology, 41,* 399–407.

Czeisler, C.A., Weitzman, E.D., Moore-Ede, M.C., Zimmerman, J.C., & Kranauer, R.S. (1980). Human sleep: Its duration and organization dependent on its circadian phase. *Science, 210,* 1264–1267.

De Jonge, G.A. (1973). Epidemiology of enuresis: A survey of the literature. In I. Kolvin, R.C. MacKeith, & S.R. Meadow (Eds.), *Bladder control and enuresis* (pp. 39–46). Philadelphia: Saunders.

Dervent, A., Karacan, I., Ware, J.C., & Williams, R.L. (1978). Somnambulism: A case report [Abstract]. *Sleep Research, 7,* 220.

Dollinger, S.J. (1986). The measurement of children's sleep disturbances and somatic complaints following a disaster. *Child Psychiatry and Human Development, 16,* 148–153.

Epstein, R., Chillag, N., & Lavie, P. (1998). Starting times of school: Effects on daytime functioning of fifth-grade children in Israel. *Sleep, 21,* 250–256.

Epstein, R., Herer, P., Tzischinsky, O., & Lavie, P. (1997). Changing from communal to familial sleep arrangements in the kibbutz: Effects on sleep quality. *Sleep, 20,* 334–339.

Evans, J. (1961). Rocking at night. *Journal of Child Psychology, 2,* 71–85.

Ferber, R. (1985). *Solve your child's sleep problems.* New York: Simon & Schuster.

Ferber, R., Boyle, M.P., & Belfer, M. (1981). Initial experience of a pediatric sleep disorders clinic [Abstract]. *Sleep Research, 10,* 194.

Finley, W.W. (1971). An EEG study of the sleep of enuretics at three age levels. *Clinical Electroencephalography, 2,* 35–39.

Finley, W.W., Besserman, R.L., Bennett, L.F., Clapp, R.K., & Finley, P.M. (1973). The effect of continuous, intermittent, and "placebo" reinforcement on the effectiveness of conditioning treatment for enuresis nocturna. *Behavior Research and Therapy, 11,* 289–297.

Fisher, B.E., & Wilson, A.E. (1987). Selected sleep disturbances in school children reported by parents: Prevalence, interrelationships, behavioral correlates and parental attributions. *Perceptual and Motor Skills, 64,* 1147–1157.

Fisher, C., Kahn, E., Edwards, A., & Davis, N. (1973). A psychophysiological study of nightmares and night terrors: The suppression of stage 4 night terrors with diazepam. *Archives of General Psychiatry, 28,* 252–259.

Frank, N.C., Spirito, A., Stark, L., & Owens-Stively, J. (1997). The use of scheduled awakenings to eliminate childhood sleepwalking. *Journal of Pediatric Psychology, 22,* 345–353.

Franco, P., Pardou, A., Hassid, S., Lurquin, P., Groswasser, J., & Kahn, A. (1998). Auditory arousal thresholds are higher when infants sleep in the prone position. *Journal of Pediatrics, 132,* 240–243.

Gagnon, P., & DeKonick, J. (1985). Repetitive head movements during REM sleep. *Biological Psychiatry, 20,* 176–178.

Gonzalez, E.R., & Castell, D.O. (1988). Respiratory complications of gastroesophageal reflux. *American Family Journal of Physicians, 37,* 169–172.

Gozal D. (1998). Sleep-disordered breathing and school performance in children. *Pediatrics, 102,* 616–620.

Griffith, J.L., & Slovik, L.S. (1989). Munchausen syndrome by proxy and sleep disorders medicine. *Sleep, 12,* 178–183.

Guilleminault, C. (1980). Sleep and respiration in infants. In L. Popoviciu, B. Asgian, & G. Badiu (Eds.), *Sleep* (pp. 133–137). Basel, Switzerland: Karger.

Guilleminault, C. (1987a). Disorders of arousal in children: Somnambulism and night terrors. In C. Guilleminault (Ed.), *Sleep and its disorders in children* (pp. 243–252). New York: Raven Press.

Guilleminault, C. (Ed.). (1987b). *Sleep and its disorders in children* (pp. 195–211). New York: Raven Press.

Guilleminault, C., & Anders, T. (1976). Sleep disorders in children: Part II. *Advances in Pediatrics, 22,* 151–174.

Guilleminault, C., Mignot, E., & Grumet, F.C. (1989). Familial patterns of narcolepsy. *Lancet, 2,* 1376–1379.

Guilleminault, C., & Pelayo, R. (1998). Narcolepsy in prepubertal children. *Annals of Neurology, 43,* 135–142.

Guilleminault, C., Peraita, R., Souquet, M., & Dement, W.C. (1975). Apneas during sleep in infants: Possible relationship with sudden infant death syndrome. *Science, 190,* 677–679.

Harper, R.M., Leake, B., Hodgman, J.E., & Hoppenbrouwers, T. (1982). Developmental patterns of heart rate and heart rate variability during sleep and waking in normal infants and infants at risk for the sudden infant death syndrome. *Sleep, 5,* 28–38.

Hauri, P. (1982). *The sleep disorders.* Kalamazoo, MI: Upjohn.

Herman, J.H., Blaw, M.E., & Steinberg, J.B. (1989). REM behavior disorder in a two-year-old male with evidence of brainstem pathology [Abstract]. *Sleep Research, 18,* 242.

Hoppenbrouwers, T., Harper, R.M., Hodgman, J.E., Sterman, M.B., & McGinty, D.J. (1978). Polygraphic studies of normal infants during the first six months of life. II. Respiratory rate and variability as a function of state. *Pediatric Research, 12,* 120–125.

Hoppenbrouwers, T., Hodgman, J.E., Harper, R.M., Hofman, E., Sterman, M.B., & McGinty, D.J. (1977). Polygraphic studies of normal infants during the first six months of life, III. Incidence of apnea and periodic breathing. *Pediatrics, 60,* 418–425.

Hublin, C., Kaprio, J., Partinen, M., Koskenvuo, M., Heikkila, K., Koskimies, S., & Guilleminault, C. (1994). The prevalence of narcolepsy: An epidemiological study of the Finnish twin cohort. *Annals of Neurology, 35,* 709–716.

International Classification of Sleep Disorders (ICSD). (1997). *Diagnostic and coding manual, revised.* Rochester, MN: American Sleep Disorders Association.

Johnson, L.C., & Lubin, A. (1966). Spontaneous electrodermal activity during waking and sleeping. *Psychophysiology, 3,* 8–17.

James, D., & Ma, L. (1997). Mandibular reconstruction in children with obstructive sleep apnea due to micrognathia. *Plastic Reconstructive Surgery, 100,* 1131–1137.

Jolley, S.G., Herbst, J.J., & Johnson, D.G. (1981). Esophageal pH monitoring during sleep identifies children with respiratory symptoms from gastroesophageal reflux. *Gastroenterology, 80,* 1501–1506.

Jones, N.S., Field, T., Fox, N.A., Lundy, B., & Davalos, M. (1997). EEG activation in 1-month-old infants of depressed mothers. *Developmental Psychopathology, 9,* 491–505.

Kahn, A., Francois, G., Sottiaux, M., Rebuffat, E., Nduwimana, M., Mozin, M.J., & Levit, J. (1988). Sleep characteristics in milk-intolerant infants. *Sleep, 11,* 291–297.

Kales, A., Kales, J.D., Jacobson, A., Humphrey, F.J., & Soldatos, G.R. (1977). Effects of imipramine on enuretic frequency and sleep stages. *Pediatrics, 60,* 431–436.

Kales, A., Soldatos, C., Bixler, E., Ladda, R., Charney, D., Weber, G., & Schweitzer, P. (1980). Hereditary factors in sleepwalking and night terrors. *British Journal of Psychiatry, 137,* 111–118.

Kales, A., Soldatos, C., Caldwell, A., Kales, J., Humphrey II, F., Charney, D., & Schweitzer, P. (1980). Somnambulism. *Archives of General Psychiatry, 37,* 1406–1410.

Kales, J.D., Kales, A., Soldatos, C.R., Chamberlin, K., & Martin, E.D. (1979). Sleepwalking and night terrors related to febrile illness. *American Journal of Psychiatry, 136,* 1214–1215.

Kataria, S., Swanson, M.S., & Trevathan, G.E. (1987). Persistence of sleep disturbances in preschool children. *Behavioral Pediatrics, 110,* 642–646.

Kawauchi, A., Imada, N., Tanaka, Y., Minami, M., Watanabe, H., & Shirakawa, S. (1998). Changes in structure of sleep spindles and delta waves on electroencephalography in patients with nocturnal enuresis. *British Journal of Urology, 81,* 72–75.

Klauber, G.T. (1989). Clinical efficacy and safety of desmopressin in the treatment of nocturnal enuresis. *Journal of Pediatrics, 114,* 719–722.

Kleitman, N. (1963). *Sleep and wakefulness.* Chicago: University of Chicago Press.

Kleitman, N., & Englemann, T.G. (1953). Sleep characteristics of infants. *Journal of Applied Physiology, 6,* 269–282.

Kohlendorfer, U., Kiechl, S., & Sperl, W. (1998). Sudden infant death syndrome: Risk factor profiles for distinct subgroups. *American Journal of Epidemiology, 147,* 960–968.

Kohyama, J., Shimohira, M., & Iwakawa, Y. (1997). Maturation of motility and motor inhibition in rapid eye-movement sleep. *Journal of Pediatrics, 130,* 117–122.

Korner, A. (1968). REM organization in neonates. *Archives of General Psychiatry, 19,* 330–340.

Korobkin, R., & Guilleminault, C. (1979). Neurological abnormalities in near miss for sudden infant death syndrome infants. *Pediatrics, 64,* 369–374.

Kupfer, D.J., Himmelhoch, G.R., Swarzburg, M., Anderson, C.M., Byck, R., & Detre, T.P. (1972). Hypersomnia in manic-depressive disease (a preliminary report). *Diseases of the Nervous System, 33,* 720–724.

Lackgren, G., Lilja, B., Neveus, T., & Stenberg, A. (1998). Desmopressin in the treatment of severe nocturnal enuresis in adolescents: A 7-year follow-up study. *British Journal of Urology, 81,* 17–23.

Lairy, C.G., Catani, P., Findjii, F., & Laird, C. (1980). Contribution of sleep recordings to the control of anticonvulsant withdrawal. In L. Popoviciu, B. Asyian, & G. Badiu (Eds.), *Sleep* (pp. 87–103). Basel, Switzerland: Karger.

Lenard, H.G. (1970). The development of sleep spindles in the EEG during the first two years of life. *Neuropaediatrie, 1,* 264–276.

Lewy, A.J., Sack, R.A., & Singer, C.L. (1984). Assessment and treatment of chronobiologic disorders using plasma melatonin levels and bright light exposure: The clock-gate model and the phase response curve. *Psychopharmacology Bulletin, 20,* 5651–5655.

Lin, L., Faraco, J., Li, R., Kadotani, H., Rogers, W., Lin, X., Qiu, X., de Jong, P.J., Nishino, S., & Mignot, E. (1999). The sleep disorder canine narcolepsy is caused by a mutation in the hypocretin (orexin) receptor 2 gene. *Cell, 98,* 365–376.

Lipsitt, L. (1979). Infants at risk: Perinatal and neonatal factors. *International Journal of Behavioral Development, 2,* 23–42.

Mahowald, M.W., & Schenck, C.H. (1989). REM sleep behavior disorder. In M.H. Kryger, T. Roth, & W.C. Dement (Eds.), *Principles and practice of sleep medicine.* Philadelphia: Saunders.

Marcus, C.L. (1997). Management of obstructive sleep apnea in childhood. *Current Opinions in Pulmonary Medicine, 3,* 464–469.

McColley, S.A., Carroll, J.L., Curtis, S., Loughlin, G.M., & Sampson, H.A. (1997). High prevalence of allergic sensitization in children with habitual snoring and obstructive sleep apnea. *Chest, 1,* 170–173.

Metcalf, D.R. (1970). EEG sleep spindle ontogenesis. *Neuropaediatrie, 1,* 428–433.

Mikkelsen, E.J., & Rapoport, T.L. (1980). Enuresis: Psychopathology, sleep stage, and drug response. *Urologic Clinics of North America, 7,* 361–377.

Moore, M. (1945). Recurrent nightmares: A simple procedure for psychotherapy. *Military Surgeon, 97,* 281–285.

Moore, T., & Ucko, C. (1957). Night waking in early infancy: Part I. *Archives of Diseases of Children, 33,* 333–342.

Mosko, S., Richard, C., & McKenna, J. (1997). Maternal sleep and arousals during bedsharing with infants. *Sleep, 20,* 142–150.

Neveus, T., Lackgren, G., Stenber, A., Tuvemo, T., & Hetta, J. (1998). Sleep and night-time behaviour of enuretics and non-enuretics. *British Journal of Urology, 81,* 67–71.

Nieminen, P., Tolonen, U., Lopponen, H., Lopponen, T., Luotonen, J., & Jokinen, K. (1997). Snoring children: Factors predicting sleep apnea. *Acta Otolaryngology, 529*(Suppl.), 190–194.

Oredsson, A.F., & Jorgensen, T.M. (1998). Changes in nocturnal bladder capacity during treatment with the bell and pad for monosymptomatic nocturnal enuresis. *Journal of Urology, 160,* 166–169.

Orr, W.C., Levine, N.S., & Buchanan, R.T. (1987). The effect of cleft palate repair and pharyngeal flap surgery on upper airway obstruction during sleep. *Journal of Plastic and Reconstructive Surgery, 80,* 226–232.

Pareja, J.A., de Pablos, E., Caminero, A.B., Millan, I., & Dobato, J.L. (1999). Native language shifts across sleep-wake states in bilingual sleeptalkers. *1999, 22,* 243–247.

Parmelee, A.H., Schulz, H.R., & Disbrow, M.A. (1961). Sleep patterns of newborns. *Journal of Pediatrics, 58,* 241–250.

Pillar, G., Schnall, R.P., Peled, N., Oliven, A., & Lavie, P. (1997). Impaired respiratory response to resistive loading during sleep in healthy offspring of patients with obstructive sleep apnea. *American Journal of Respiratory and Critical Care Medicine, 155*, 1602–1608.

Rechtschaffen, A., Hauri, P., & Zeitlin, M. (1966). Auditory awakening thresholds in REM and NREM sleep stages. *Perceptual and Motor Skills, 22*, 927–942.

Reding, G.R., Rubright, L., & Zimmerman, W.C. (1966). Incidence of bruxism. *Journal of Dental Research, 45*, 1198–1204.

Reynolds, C.F., & Kupfer, D.J. (1987). Sleep research in affective illness: State of the art circa 1987. *Sleep, 10*, 199–215.

Richardson, G., Carskadon, M., Flagg, W., van Den Hoed, J., Dement, W.C., & Mitler, M.M. (1978). Excessive daytime sleepiness in man: Multiple sleep latency measurement in narcoleptic and control subjects. *Electroencephalography and Clinical Neurophysiology, 45*, 621–627.

Richter, J.E., Bradley, L.A., & Castell, D.O. (1989). Esophageal chest pain: Current controversies in pathogenesis, diagnosis and therapy. *Annals of Internal Medicine, 110*, 66–78.

Rittig, S., Knudsen, U.B., Norgaard, J.P., Pedersen, E.B., & Djurhuus, J.C. (1989). Abnormal diurnal rhythm of plasma vasopressin and urinary output in patients with enuresis. *American Journal of Physiology, 256*, F664–F671.

Roffwarg, H., Muzio, J., & Dement, W. (1966). Ontogenetic development of the human sleep-dream cycle. *Science, 152*, 604.

Rosen, C.L. (1997). Sleep disorders in infancy, childhood, and adolescence. *Current Opinions in Pulmonary Medicine, 3*, 449–455.

Rosen, C.L., Frost, J.D., Bricker, T., Tarnow, J.D., Gillette, P. L. C., & Dunlavy, S. (1983). Two siblings with recurrent cardiorespiratory arrest: Munchausen syndrome by proxy of child abuse. *Pediatrics, 71*, 714–720.

Salmon, M.A. (1975). An historical account of nocturnal enuresis and its treatment. *Proceedings of the Royal Society of Medicine, 68*, 443–445.

Salzarulo, P., Chevalier, A., Colvez, A., Brunel, M., Sender, C., Kastler, B., & Roc, M. (1980). Child sleep problems: Parental attitude and recourse: An approach by survey. In L. Popoviciu, B. Asgian, & G. Badiu (Eds.), *Sleep* (pp. 595–598). Basel, Switzerland: Karger.

Schechtman, V.L., Harper, R.M., Kluge, K.A., Wilson, A.J., Hoffman, H.J., & Southall, D.P. (1988). Cardiac and respiratory patterns in normal infants and victims of the sudden infant death syndrome. *Sleep, 11*, 413–424.

Schenck, C.H., Bundlie, S.R., Ettinger, M.G., & Mahowald, M.W. (1986). Chronic behavioral disorders of human REM sleep: A new category of parasomnia. *Sleep, 9*, 293–308.

Scheers, N.J., Dayton, C.M., & Kemp, J.S. (1998). Sudden infant death with external airways covered: Case-comparison study of 206 deaths in the United States. *Archives of Pediatrics and Adolescent Medicine, 152*, 540–547.

Scher, M., Richardson, G.A., Coble, P.A., Day, N.L., & Stoffer, D.S. (1988). The effects of prenatal alcohol and marijuana exposure: Disturbances in neonatal sleep cycling and arousal. *Pediatric Research, 24*, 101–105.

Shannon, D., Kelly, D., & O'Connell, K. (1977). Abnormal regulation of ventilation in infants at risk for sudden infant death syndrome. *New England Journal of Medicine, 297*, 747–784.

Sheldon, S.H., & Jacobsen, J. (1998). REM-sleep motor disorder in children. *Journal of Child Neurology, 13*, 257–260.

Siegel, D.M., Janeway, D., & Baum, J. (1998). Fibromyalgia syndrome in children and adolescents: Clinical features at presentation and status at follow-up. *Pediatrics, 101*, 377–382.

Stokes, D., McBride, T., Wall, M., Erba, G., & Strieder, D. (1980). Sleep hypoxemia in young adults with cystic fibrosis. *American Journal of Diseases of Childhood, 134*, 741–743.

Stores, G., Ellis, A.J., Wiggs, L., Crawford, C., & Thomson, A. (1998). Sleep and psychological disturbance in nocturnal asthma. *Archives of Diseases in Children, 78*, 413–419.

Southall, D.P., Richards, J.M., & Rhoden, K.J. (1982). Prolonged apnea and cardiac arrhythmias in infants discharged from neonatal intensive care units: Failure to predict an increased risk for sudden infant death syndrome. *Pediatrics, 70*, 844–851.

Thach, B.T., & Lijowska, A. (1996). Arousals in infants. *Sleep, 19*, S271–S273.

Taira, M., Takase, M., & Sasaki, H. (1998). Sleep disorder in children with autism. *Psychiatry and Clinical Neurosciences, 52*, 182–183.

Vanderas, A.P., Menenakou, M., Kouimtzis, T., & Papagiannoulis, L. (1999). Urinary catecholamine levels and bruxism in children. *Journal of Oral Rehabilitation, 26*, 103–110.

Veldhuis, J.D., & Iranmanesh, A. (1969). Physiological regulation of the human growth hormone (GH)-insulin-like growth factor type I (IGF-I) axis: Predominant impact of age, obesity, gonadal function, and sleep. *Sleep, 19*, S221–S224.

Vignau, J., Bailley, D., Duhamel, A., Vervaecke, P., Beuscart, R., & Collinet, C. (1997). Epidemiologic study of sleep quality and troubles in French secondary school adolescents. *Journal of Adolescent Health, 21*, 343–350.

Ware, J.C., & Pittard, J.T. (1990). Increased deep sleep after trazodone use: A double blind placebo controlled study in healthy young adults. *Journal of Clinical Psychiatry, 51S*, 18–22.

Ware, J.C., & Rugh, J.D. (1988). Destructive bruxism: Sleep stage relationship. *Sleep, 11*, 172–181.

Werry, J.S., & Cohrssen, J. (1965). Enuresis: An etiologic and therapeutic study. *Journal of Pediatrics, 67*, 423–431.

Wilson, N.M., Charette, L., Thomson, A.H., & Silverman, M. (1985). Gastroesophageal reflux and childhood asthma: The acid test. *Thorax, 40*, 592–597.

Williams, R.L., Karacan, I., & Hursch, C.J. (1974). *EEG of human sleep: Clinical applications.* New York: Wiley.

Young, D., Zorick, F., Wittig, R., Roehrs, T., & Roth, T. (1988). Narcolepsy in a pediatric population. *American Journal of Diseases of Childhood, 142*, 210–213.

Zamir, G., Press, J., Tal, A., & Tarasiuk, A. (1998). Sleep fragmentation in children with juvenile rheumatoid arthritis. *Journal of Rheumatology, 6*, 1191–1197.

Zuckerman, B., Stevenson, J., & Bailey, V. (1987). Sleep problems in early childhood: Continuities, predictive factors, and behavioral correlates. *Pediatrics, 80*, 664–671.

CHAPTER 17

Tics, Stereotypic Movements, and Habits

LEE H. MATTHEWS, JANET R. MATTHEWS, AND J. MICHAEL LEIBOWITZ

This chapter focuses on tic disorders, including Tourette's, stereotypic movement disorders, and several habit disturbances commonly seen during a child's developing years. Most of these motor movement behaviors relate primarily to the American Psychiatric Association's *Diagnostic and Statistical Manual of Mental Disorders* (*DSM-IV*, 1994), but several common behavioral habits that often are of concern to parents are also reviewed. In 1992, the World Health Organization (WHO) published *The Classification of Mental and Behavioural Disorders: Clinical Descriptions and Diagnostic Guidelines (ICD-10)*, which uses many of the same basic categories of descriptions. Tics and other motor movements that primarily occur in individuals with psychoses, mental retardation, or other disorders are discussed only to the extent required by the surrounding text.

TIC DISORDERS

The major defining characteristic of tic disorders is abnormality in the child's motor movement or vocalization. These disorders include Tourette's, chronic motor or vocal tic disorder, transient tic disorder, and tic disorder not otherwise specified. The last category appears to be used primarily (in the research literature) for tics with an onset in adulthood, although tics lasting less than four weeks are also classified as such. Conclusive evidence is lacking on whether these classifications represent distinct problems or a continuum of severity of the same problem (Golden, 1987). Tics are likely to contribute to such feelings as shame, self-consciousness, depression, and anxiety. The child with severe tics may be excluded from activities and thus lag behind the peer group in social development. Because of the extensive research on Tourette's, it is covered in a separate section.

DEFINITION

A tic is defined by *DSM-IV* (APA, 1994) as a "sudden, rapid, recurrent, nonrhythmic, stereotyped motor movement or vocalization" (p. 100). Although both motor and vocal tics may be classified as simple or complex, there is disagreement as to what constitutes such a division. Simple motor tics include eye blinking, facial grimacing, neck jerking, and shoulder shrugging. Complex motor tics are echokinesis (mimicking the movements of someone who is being observed), facial gestures, grooming behaviors, jumping, self-biting or -hitting, smelling objects, stamping, and touching. Simple vocal tics include barking, coughing, grunting, throat clearing, sniffing, and snorting. Complex vocal tics are coprolalia (use of obscene or unacceptable words), echolalia (repeating the last-heard word, phrase, or sound of another person or a last-heard sound), palilalia (repeating one's own sounds or words), and repeating words or phrases out of context. Keshavan (1988) reported 10 cases of tics of the ear. Tics increase during stress and markedly diminish in sleep. In some instances, the individual is aware of the mannerism, but in most cases, they are automatic and unconscious (Carson, Butcher, & Mineka, 1998; Woody & Laney, 1986).

INCIDENCE

Although incidence rates vary, Golden and Hood (1982) indicate that tics are the most common movement disorder of childhood. Tics are most common in the 8- to 12-year age range (Berkow, 1992), with onset at 5 to 7 years. Chronic tics do not seem to occur in children under age 5 (Werry, Carlielle, & Fitzpatrick, 1983); transient tics are the most common type and are most frequent between the ages of 4 and 5 (WHO, 1992). The male:female ratio is approximately 3:1. Some have found a higher incidence among children of Jewish and other Eastern European ancestry (Shapiro & Shapiro, 1982), but another researcher (Comings, 1994) has disputed the higher rate in Jewish children. Retrospective studies (Matthews & Barabas, 1985) suggest spontaneous recovery within one month to over a year, with a recovery rate of at least 50% after 2 to 15 years. However, some evidence exists that tics may recur in later adult life (Klawans & Barr, 1985).

DIAGNOSIS

In the chronic tic, both multiple motor and at least one vocal tic must be present, but not both at the same time. The tics occur nearly every day, many times per day, or occur intermittently throughout a period of more than one year. Often, the tics occur in clusters. The critical feature in the differential diagnosis of this disorder is the presence at any one time of either motor tics or vocal tics, but not both. Tourette's, by contrast, requires the existence of both multiple motor tics and one or more vocal tics at the same time.

The primary feature of a transient tic disorder is its temporary nature. There will be a single or multiple motor and/or vocal tic that occurs many times each day for at least four weeks but less than one year. The tic may be suppressed for a few minutes or even hours. Multiple tics may occur sequentially, simultaneously, or randomly. Stress may precipitate a relapse. Variability of symptoms can be expected over time. The most common form is the eye blink or other facial tic, but the entire head or the torso may be involved. Other features are the same as for Tourette's, but the severity and magnitude of the symptoms are usually much less. The diagnostic criteria have changed slightly from *DSM-III-R* (APA, 1987), in that the length of time the tic must be present has increased from two weeks to four weeks.

Tics must be differentiated from other movement disorders such as dyskinesia, spasms, and chorea. Tics are most frequently confused with chorea, although patients with tics usually have a longer asymptomatic period between movements and always perform the movements in the same stereotyped manner. Although it may be possible to easily distinguish between a simple motor tic such as a blinking eye (a tic) and picking at the skin (a stereotypic movement), it may be more difficult to differentially diagnose that same stereotypic behavior from a more complex motor tic, such as grooming behaviors or facial gestures (Cohen, Leckman, & Towbin, 1989). Stereotypic movements (to be covered later in this chapter), although rhythmic, are viewed as intentional behaviors, as are compulsions (Golden, 1987).

ETIOLOGY

There is disagreement as to the causes and conditions associated with ticing behavior. Several authors have noted a relationship to learning disabilities (Clementz, Lee, & Barclay, 1988; Lerer, 1987) and other psychological factors (Keshavan, 1988), including auditory hallucinatory experiences (Kerbeshian & Burd, 1985), posttraumatic stress (Fahn, 1982), and obsessive-compulsive disorder (Swedo & Leonard, 1994). However, Shapiro and Shapiro (1992), in a methodological review of 21 articles, discussed problems with many of these studies, such as adequacy of clinical and control samples, definitions, and diagnostic procedures. Although noting the considerable clinical indications for such an association, the evidence from the studies reviewed does not adequately support such an association.

Behavioral

Theoretical models based on both operant and respondent learning techniques have been suggested related to the onset of ticing. Early models emphasized a drive-reducing conditioned response paradigm. Most behavioral explanations have suggested that unwitting reinforcement by increased attention or stress serve to maintain ticing behavior (Azrin & Nunn, 1973). Another hypothesis is that tics begin as purposeful movements in response to specific stimuli, but eventually, similar movements are carried out automatically in a purposeless fashion. For example, a neck tic may have its origin in a collar that was too tight or otherwise annoying (Bachman, 1972).

Traditional/Psychodynamic

Psychodynamic and psychoanalytic theories stress that tics are repressed conflicts expressed in a symbolic manner. As such, they are often viewed as hysterical reactions to ward off danger, manifestations of unresolved oedipal conflicts, and a substitution for angry feelings, revealed by tics resembling a hitting motion (Cavenar, Spaulding, & Sullivan, 1979). Mahler (1949) presents perhaps the classic review of formulations based on psychodynamic theory. She and other authors suggested that tics serve many different functions, which fall into various categories. One type, systematic tics (such as transient tics), indicate tension phenomena; an example is eye twitches experienced under strong emotional stress. A second category is the tic as a sign of primarily reactive behavior disorders on the verge of internalization. For example, the tic is an indicator of a reaction to what was originally a situational stressor (in the same way that anger might be a reaction to being sexually abused). However, such responses (anger or tic) begin to become internalized (incorporated) into the child's view of self. The end result is that the tic becomes part of the child's body-self image. A third category is the tic as a symptom or symptom substitute of neurosis or psychosis. That is, the tic either serves as an indicator of underlying psychopathology or is the manifestation of an internal psychic conflict that in other children would be expressed in a variety of psychological disorders such as depression, anxiety, or psychosis. Mahler also said that the unconscious fantasies producing the tics are concerned with movement or paralysis. Cavenar et al. (1979) cited unresolved oedipal conflicts as the etiology for tics.

Silber (1981) reported the case of a tic associated with a recurrent dream stimulated by observation of the primal scene. Other factors cited include a background of emotional tension (Bakwin & Bakwin, 1972), home conflicts, and psychiatrically ill parents (A.L. Miller, 1970). However, Abe and Oda (1980) found no more psychological symptoms in mothers of 3-year-old ticers who themselves had tics in childhood than in a control sample of 1,000 mothers.

Organic

Genetic or other familial factors may play a role in the onset of tics (Clementz et al., 1988), in that a family history of tics is found in about 10% to 30% of all cases. Abe and Oda (1980) found that children of parents who had tics in childhood had a prevalence rate of 20% to 25% compared to 10% in controls. Soft neurological signs have been reported in 87% of children studied, suggesting a single autosomal dominant genetic transmission (Elston, Granje, & Lees, 1989; Golden, 1990). Abnormality of CNS dopamine metabolism as a factor in the development of tics has been reported, as have tics caused or exacerbated by anticonvulsant or stimulant medications, which may not remit with discontinuation of the treatment (Chandler, Barnhill, Gualtieri, & Patterson, 1989; Clementz et al., 1988).

TREATMENT

Regardless of the model of treatment used, a careful review of associated problems should be undertaken. A review by Peterson, Campise, and Azrin (1994) of approximately 350 articles on tics and habit disturbances indicated that these disorders could be effectively controlled by behavioral and pharmacological methods.

Behavioral

A variety of behavioral techniques have been successfully employed in reducing or eliminating tics (Azrin & Peterson, 1989). Carr (1995) presented a table defining competing response treatment methods of various types for tics that were reported in the literature from 1973 to 1990. He also included a brief history of the competing response practice treatment as well as a basic explanation of the procedure.

Perhaps the most widely used of the behavioral techniques is habit reversal, where the focus is on practicing muscular movements opposite the tic

(Azrin & Nunn, 1973; Pray, Kramer, & Lindskog, 1986). In their original study, Azrin and Nunn presented data on 12 patients with various ticlike symptoms. Marked decreases in the targeted behaviors occurred within one day, with an average percentage reduction below base rate of 95%, going to 99% after three weeks.

A recent article by Woods and Miltenberger (1995) reviews the research on habit reversal and noted that use of these methods results in rapid and long-lasting treatment. Further component analysis identified the use of awareness training to help the patient identify the occurrence of the tic as well as the use of a competing response as the two primary factors in treatment effectiveness. Several variations on this method have been used, including self-monitoring, awareness training, competing response practice, and social support procedures using family members (Finney, Rapoff, Hall, & Christophersen, 1983; Pray et al., 1986; Zikis, 1983).

Other behavioral techniques that have been effective include operant conditioning (Schulman, 1974), negative or massed practice (Teichman & Eliahu, 1986), self-monitoring (Carr, 1995), and reciprocal inhibition techniques by autogenic training (Uchiyama, 1976). Self-monitoring procedures have been observed to be tic inhibiting with rates of 50% to 100% reduction and associated with long-lasting remission of symptoms (Ollendick, 1989). Biofeedback, desensitization, and other relaxation and feedback methods have also been used successfully (Azrin & Peterson, 1989; Poth & Barnett, 1983). Schulman (1974) successfully removed multiple tics by reducing parental attention. Aversive techniques have included the use of electric shock, avoidance of a loud noise, incompatible responses, and response cost (Bachman, 1972; Singh, 1981). Although effective, such methods should be used only after all other positive procedures have been attempted.

Traditional/Psychodynamic

Therapies have included brief analytic outpatient family therapy, dream analysis, hypnosis, oedipal conflict resolution, psychoanalysis, play therapy, and structured family therapy (Cavenar et al., 1979; Goldenson, 1970; Teichman & Eliahu, 1986). However, Matesevac (1993) indicated that psychotherapy is not effective as a primary treatment but may have supportive value for the parents or the child, and can be of help with the interpersonal consequences of these disorders. She also points out some of the limitations in using only single-focus interventions (medication only, behavioral only) rather than a more global biopsychosocial perspective.

Organic

Several authors have reviewed psychotropic medications and reported a 50% to 90% reduction in the frequency of ticing and reductions of 70% to 85% with haloperidol in ticers (Shapiro & Shapiro, 1996; Towbin & Cohen, 1996). Although this medication is associated with a high incidence of side effects, most if not all the symptoms seen in both chronic tics and Tourette's can be suppressed. In addition, over time, lower doses may be effective in obtaining the same clinical results (Cohen, Riddle, & Leckman, 1992).

Goetz, Tanner, and Klawans (1984) successfully treated 21 patients with fluphenazine hydrochloride who were intolerant of haloperidol. Polak, Molcan, and Dimova (1985), in a study of 30 children, found that penfluridol was somewhat superior to haloperidol, but both were more effective than thioridazine. Leung and Fagan (1989) say that drugs should not be used unless the tic is seriously disabling, due to possible risks and lack of curative value. Troung, Bressman, Shale, and Fahn (1988) suggest the use of chlorpromazine or clonazepam, later combined with clonidine, followed by the use of haloperidol only if other medications fail. This recommendation was made because of the risk of tardive dyskinesia with haloperidol.

CONCLUSIONS

A review of the chronic and transient tic literature indicates that transient tics may well be the most frequently seen movement disorder in children. There are few psychoanalytic treatment studies in which the data were collected in a systematic manner regarding either etiology or treatment. The increase in behavioral articles points to the interest in this area of research and also demonstrates effective treatment and data-based cure rates. Medications have been noted to be highly effective in reducing both the frequency and the intensity of ticing, especially in those children with chronic tic disorder. Although pharmacologic intervention may facilitate early reduction in rates of ticing, concerns are still frequently made regarding possible side effects, such as tardive dyskinesia.

TOURETTE'S DISORDER

DEFINITION

Tourette's disorder (TD) falls under the *DSM-IV* (APA, 1994) classification of tic disorders. Variously called Tourette's syndrome, or Gilles de la Tourette syndrome, it has been recognized for well over 100 years. Gilles de la Tourette, a pupil of Charcot, wrote an extensively detailed account describing chronic tics of the face and body accompanied by speech aberrations in one patient (referred to as Miss X or Miss de M) in a two-part paper published in 1885 (Kolb & Whishaw, 1990). This disorder often includes echolalia (repeating words or phrases) and coprolalia (shouting obscenities). This patient had episodes of echolalia including "barking like a dog." On one occasion, "a dog came and barked under the window of her room. She immediately began involuntarily to echo the dog's barking." The patient apparently continued this behavior for several hours, unable to sleep until early in the morning, due to "her body being wracked by muscular spasms that accompanied the noisy barking, exactly like the dog's." Miss X, who was described as a 15-year-old female "belonging to an upper-class family," also displayed coprolalia, to the obvious distress of the family, as "one had to wonder how and where she picked up the words she continually uttered" (Kolb & Whishaw, 1990, pp. 300–301). Other, less detailed early cases were described by Itard (1825), Beard (1880), and several other authors prior to the turn of the 20th century. They saw the syndrome as either an undifferentiated chorea or a symptom of hysteria and gave it a variety of names depending on the country of observation. Although one of the rarer of the movement disorders, its unusual and oftentimes bizarre presentation has resulted in considerable interest in its etiology and treatment (Robertson, 1994).

One of the earliest accounts of an apparent victim of TD was Prince deConde, who served in the seventh-century French court of King Louis XIV. He was seized by "barking attacks" at royal receptions, and so made it a practice to stand next to a window so he could stuff curtains in his mouth. Retrospective studies suggest that Samuel Johnson, the noted English writer, exhibited a number of the signs of TD, including tics of the mouth, torso, and feet; he was also noted for making unusual vocalizations ("Medical Mystery: Tourette's," 1981). Recently, it has been suggested that author Leo Tolstoy's description of the character Nikolai in the novel *Anna Karenina* incorporates many of the features of TD. Mahmood Abdul-Rauf, an NBA starting professional basketball player, is considered quite competitive despite continuing treatment for TD; at various times in his career, his medication has had to be adjusted to control the symptomatology (Hurst & Hurst, 1994).

Additional symptoms seen in TD include mimicking the movements of others, compulsive touching of persons or objects, and periodic displays of jumping, self-mutilation, or aggressive behavior (Eisenhauser & Woody, 1987). Compulsive thoughts occur in some patients, and about 50% of these children suffer from diagnosable learning disabilities (Lerer, 1987).

INCIDENCE

Using 1994 census estimates of 260 million individuals in the United States, current estimates of TD range between 130,000 (0.05%) and 4.16 million individuals (1.6%) (Ollendick, 1989). Prevalence rates as low as 1 per 1 million to as high as 1 per 1,000 have been reported (APA, 1994; Erenberg, 1988; Ollendick, 1989). The disorder is three times more common in males than in females. The marked difference in reported rates is likely associated with misdiagnosis, which may be due to the erratic course of TD or because transient tics, which occur in approximately 5% of all children, may be diagnosed as TD. Several authors (Golden, 1990; Lacey, 1986; Shapiro & Shapiro, 1982) have noted the difficulty of accurate diagnosis and the frequent delay between onset of symptoms and diagnosis. Many patients suffer the affliction for 10 years before the illness is properly diagnosed. The throat-clearing grunts frequently seen with the disorder are often mistaken for allergic rhinitis.

A variety of other physical conditions and behavioral problems have been associated with TD. About 50% of children with TD suffer from diagnosable learning disabilities (Singer, Schuerholz, & Denckla, 1995).

The genes associated with TD also appear to be associated with a broad spectrum of psychiatric disorders that include obsessive-compulsive and schizoid behaviors (Comings, 1994). It was suggested in *DSM-III-R* (APA, 1987) that obsessive-compulsive disorders are more common in first-degree biologic relatives of TD patients and these symptoms are thought to be an expression of the same underlying dysfunction. Sensory sensations have also been described (Kurlan, Lichter, & Hewitt, 1989) as part of TD.

Diagnosis

The diagnosis of TD requires the presence of both motor and vocal tics. There must be at least two motor and one or more vocal tics, although these do not have to be present at the same time. The tics must occur several times per day and be present for more than a year in duration, without any lapse in symptoms longer than three months (APA, 1994, p. 103). These tics usually include head movements, although other parts of the body are also involved in many cases.

Coprolalia or other vocal disturbances occur in up to 60% of the cases. Vocalizations include "sounds such as clicks, grunts, yelps, barks, sniffs, snorts, and coughs" (APA 1994, p. 102). Additional symptoms include mimicking the movements of others, compulsive touching of persons or objects, and periodic displays of jumping or aggressive behavior (A. Martin, 1977). Studies of sign language incorporated into tic behavior suggest that obscenities vocalized in TD are due to "a random generation of high-probability sequences of phonemes" (Lang, Consky, & Sandor, 1993).

In 50% of cases, TD starts with a single tic of the eyes, head, or face. The tic may include throat clearing, snorting, sniffling, hacking, tongue protrusion, barking, or some other noise. Some patients present with two to eight of these signs initially, but all eventually have involuntary movements and some vocal tics (Cohen, Brunn, & Leckman, 1988). Complex motor tics such as touching, deep knee bends, squatting, or twirling when walking often occur. Symptoms appear between the ages of 2 and 15, typically around 7 or 8 years of age, although some symptoms may occur as early as 1 year of age.

Etiology

Genetic
TD is reportedly transmitted as an autosomal dominant gene (Eapen, Pauls, & Robertson, 1993). The possibility of a single autosomal dominant transmission for TD was proposed over 10 years ago (Comings, 1994). The role of dopamine receptors and metabolizing enzyme abnormalities remains unclear, as linkage analyses suggest that these

abnormalities do not appear to have a major effect on the etiology of the disease (Brett, Curtis, Robertson, & Gurling, 1995a). In a related study, the serotonin 1A receptor and tryptophan oxygenase genes were excluded from causing susceptibility to TD and chronic multiple tics (Brett, Curtis, Robertson, & Gurling, 1995b).

Golden and his associates (Golden, 1990; Golden & Hood, 1982) noted the strong family history of tics in TD patients. In a recent twin study (Hyde, Fitzcharles, & Weinberger, 1993), 16 of 18 twin pairs with one ticer were concordant for TD, and the twin with the earliest onset of a vocal tic had the more severe course of the disease.

Behavioral
Most behavioral conceptualizations have stressed the importance of reinforcement through increased attention or a release of tension; thus, the response is reinforced and learned. A chronic need for tension reduction is also assumed to increase anxiety and produces a recurrent cycle (Cohen et al., 1988).

Traditional/Psychodynamic
Ascher (1948) suggested that both a hereditary disposition and an emotional stress must be present for the disorder to manifest itself. Specific environmental stressors such as removal of teeth, tonsillectomy, birth of siblings, starting school, automobile accident, parental illness, parental quarreling, stopping thumbsucking, attack by a dog, and separation from parents or siblings may initiate the disorder. Lake (1978) suggested that perinatal recall of birth trauma may point to the origin of TD. A variety of other etiologies have been cited as the cause for TD (Shapiro & Shapiro, 1982; Zahner, Clubb, Leckman, & Pauls, 1988). As recently as 10 years ago, medical texts still frequently listed it as a psychoneurotic disorder. Other theories emphasize parental relationships, preoedipal issues, and emotional suppression (Sperling & Sperling, 1978). There is occasionally misdiagnosis based on a formulated psychodynamic basis for the symptoms. For example, Comings and Comings (1993) reported on the case of a 7-year-old boy with TD who was diagnosed mistakenly as having been sexually abused by his father.

Organic
Many studies have reported aberrant physiological findings in TD. Up to half of TD patients show abnormal EEGs (Bergen, Tanner, & Wilson, 1982).

Diseases that have been considered of etiological importance range from mumps and measles to chicken pox, whooping cough, and cholera (Boshes, 1976; Surwillo, Shafii, & Barrett, 1978). Another explanation is the dopamine receptor hypothesis (Jankovic, Glaze, & Frost, 1984). Boshes (1976) reported postmortem examinations showing changes in the basal ganglia of the brain, and A.K. Shapiro and Shapiro (1982) suggested some organic dysfunction of the central nervous system.

The use of stimulants has been associated with apparent drug-related onset of tics when used to treat other behavior disorders (Chandler et al., 1989). Even when medication was discontinued, the disorder often remained or reappeared later.

TREATMENT

Behavioral

The application of behavioral techniques to verbal tics was first reported by Clark (1966), who produced complete elimination of obscenities in two of three subjects by instructing them to repeat the obscenities until they could no longer do so. This use of negative or massed practice on both motor and verbal tics has been successful in numerous other studies (Cohen et al., 1988; Lahey, McNees, & McNees, 1973). Other methods include self-monitoring, EEG sensorimotor rhythm biofeedback, and reinforcement of incompatible behaviors (Ostfeld, 1988). Although behavioral techniques are successful, concerns have been raised over the possibility of unwanted side effects. Several of these articles appear to be based on theoretical orientation and the possibility of "symptom substitution." However, some studies do indicate that under certain circumstances, behavioral applications are not effective. Savicki and Carlin (1972) reported an unsuccessful attempt to teach self-monitoring and self-regulation methods. Failure was attributed to lack of appropriate behavior cueing and reinforcement within the family.

Traditional/Psychodynamic

The bizarre symptoms of TD have in turn resulted in some unusual treatments. Exorcism has been used in an attempt to rid individuals of a supposed possession by the devil. Other, more enlightened treatments have included hot and cold hydrotherapy, hot mustard plasters, tonsillectomy, chiropractic adjustment for extra nerves in the spine, and slowly sipping water for an hour at a time, 12 hours a day (Wright, Schaefer, & Solomons, 1979).

Because of the historical focus on this disorder as a manifestation of repressed emotions, id-ego conflict resolution treatments such as psychoanalysis (Stern, 1983), hypnotherapy (Culbertson, 1989), sleep therapy, and psychoanalytic family therapy (Goldenson, 1970) have been used. However, such therapies have had limited success (Ollendick, 1989).

Organic

Because of the effectiveness of low doses of antipsychotic agents, especially haloperidol, in treating TD and other tic disorders (Gelenberg, Bassuk, & Schoonover, 1991), interest in both causative factors and treatment has centered on dopaminergic-based agents. Although many of these can be excluded as causative agents, they are clearly affected in dopamine-blocking studies with drugs effective in treating TD, even when dopamine receptor availability is not shown to be abnormal (George, Robertson, Costa, & Ell, 1994). The use of clonidine has proven effective in some children with TD, as have other drugs such as chlorpromazine, pimozide, diazepam, imipraimine, methylphenidate, and phenothiazines that include clonazepam, s-blockers, desipramine, and calcium-channel blockers (Gelenberg et al., 1991). Other psychopharmacological agents used in treatment include over 100 major chemicals used with varying success, including almost every stimulant, anticonvulsant, vitamin, antiparkinsonian, and antidepressant drug available (Jankovic et al., 1984; Kerbeshian & Burd, 1994).

The use of stimulant medication remains controversial. Price, Leckman, Pauls, Cohen, and Kidd (1986) noted that up to 24% of patients treated with stimulants had persistent exacerbation of tics or were not helped, whereas Erenberg (1988), in a review of 200 children, suggested that stimulant therapy was beneficial to many patients.

Frequently, high levels of haloperidol are necessary to maintain good therapeutic dosages. Inability to tolerate high levels is a chief cause of therapeutic failure, and significant side effects may include cognitive impairment, hypersomnia, extreme anxiety, and depression (Golden & Hood, 1982). Parkinson-like effects such as drooling, tremors, rigidity, and loss of associated movements have been reported. Although these reactions are often temporary, usually disappearing after three or four months, additional use of antiparkinsonian agents is usually suggested (Surwillo et al., 1978).

Other treatments that have been reported as effective include marijuana (Hemming & Yellowlees, 1993) and the use of weak electromagnetic fields (Sandyk, 1995).

Psychosurgical procedures have been used as last resort measures to relieve tics. These include ligature of various prefrontal nerves, leukotomy, and lobotomy (Carson et al., 1998). Rauch, Baer, Cosgrove, and Jenike (1995) presented the theoretical rationale for such procedures and critically reviewed 36 cases with a variety of operational sites. They concluded that there was no evidence that any procedure was superior to all others, with the exception that cingulotomy seemed to be ineffective in alleviating tics.

CONCLUSIONS

Significant advances are being made in understanding the etiology, diagnosis, and treatment of TD. Psychological counseling to help patients and their families adjust to the social stresses associated with manifestations of this disorder is frequently used. Special clinics devoted to TD research and treatment are maintained at medical centers around the United States, and there are many local, state, and regional associations, as well as a national organization for these children and their parents.

STEREOTYPIC MOVEMENT DISORDERS

DEFINITION

A wide variety of repetitive motor behaviors that are nonfunctional in nature (appearing to serve no constructive purpose) are classified as stereotypic movement disorders in *DSM-IV* (APA, 1994). The previous category in *DSM-III-R* (APA, 1987) was stereotypy/habit disorder. Examples of such behaviors include head banging, body rocking, a variety of self-hitting behaviors, self-biting, mouthing of objects, and self-picking at skin or body openings.

Sprague and Newell (1996) indicated that although stereotypy has been reported for centuries in clinical observations, there has been little or no integration of the behavioral and biomedical

approaches to these disorders. These authors also suggest that until recently, there has not been any coherent theoretical or empirical explanation of these behaviors, which they say are actually conceptually related.

The occurrence of these behaviors has been described in the clinical and research literature as self-injurious behavior (Tate & Baroff, 1966) and self-mutilation (Phillips & Muzaffer, 1961). The term self-injurious behavior (SIB) will be used in this chapter to cover all of these disorders.

INCIDENCE

Motor habits such as head rolling, head banging, and bed rocking are common, occurring in 15% to 20% of pediatric clinic patients. Although usually transitory, about 5% of children have symptoms for months or even years, usually disappearing at 2.5 to 3 years of age. Such behaviors are 3.5 times more common in boys than in girls (Bakwin & Bakwin, 1972). Head rolling or head rocking may begin as early as 2 to 3 months of age; incidence rates increase up to 6 to 7 months. Rocking of the body and head banging usually first appear after 8 months of age. Body rocking is often a repetitive movement in a seated position and frequently begins or becomes more intense when a child goes from the sitting to the standing stage, although the rocking may occur anytime a child is passing from one developmental phase to another (Brody, 1960).

In normal children from the ages of 9 months to 6 years, SIB of various unspecified forms is frequently observed (DeLissovoy, 1961). It occurs in 11% to 17% at age 9 to 18 months, in 9% at 2 years of age, and by 5 years of age is virtually absent.

Head banging occurs in approximately 3.5% of infants of normal intellect and is about 3.5 times as common in boys as in girls (Kravitz, Rosenthal, Teplitz, Murphy, & Lesser, 1960). Onset is between 5 and 11 months and lasts about 17 months. About 67% of head bangers also rock. The usual duration is approximately 15 minutes but may continue for an hour or more. The frontal-parietal region is most frequently struck, and such banging may lead to soft tissue swelling. The most common position is for the child to be on knees and hands in the crib. DeLissovoy (1961) found an incidence rate as high as 15.2% in the normal population between 19 and 32 months of age, with a 22.3% rate in boys as opposed to 7.4% in girls. Abe, Oda, and Amatomi (1984), in a five-year follow-up of a large number of children who were head bangers at age 3, found that only three still had the symptom.

DIAGNOSIS

A stereotypic movement disorder diagnosis is given only when the behavior either causes (or has the potential to cause) physical injury to the child or markedly interferes with normal activities.

If the motor movements are considered a feature of a pervasive developmental disorder, schizophrenia, an obsessive-compulsive disorder, or hair pulling (trichotillomania), they are usually not diagnosed separately. In extreme cases, however, a dual diagnosis may be warranted. For example, if a diagnosis of mental retardation has been made, these behaviors would be diagnosed separately if the severity of the symptoms were such as to require specialized treatment. Severe stereotypic behaviors may even involve mutilation and life-threatening injuries. For example, eye damage can occur as the result of head banging.

Whereas tics are considered to be involuntary, stereotypic disorders are thought by many authors to be at least partially voluntary in origin. Differential diagnosis should exclude self-stimulating behaviors such as rocking and thumb sucking, which are common in normal infants.

Information should be obtained regarding onset, duration, and the situations in which the behavior occurs. A precise behavioral description, parental responses, associated behaviors, and some measure of whether the child's functioning has been impaired or whether the behavior is an indication of severe emotional disturbance or deprivation should also be obtained.

Wright et al. (1979) state that the presence of SIB is more likely to be an indication of severe disturbance than body rocking or other repetitive movements. In general, these behaviors occur more often in developmentally delayed populations and are associated with sensory handicaps.

Body rocking and head banging are both monotonous, repetitive movements that occur with a set rhythm (Thelen, 1981). Differential diagnosis is important, as Duchowny, Resnick, Deray, and Alvarez (1988) point out that stereotypic behavior may appear to be seizures. In a study of 60 children under 10 years of age referred for EEG testing, 40% had pseudoseizures consisting of rhythmic movements or staring episodes.

ETIOLOGY

Behavioral

Bachman (1972) and others (Thelen, 1981) suggested that SIB may develop if the behavior leads to the avoidance of even more aversive consequences (the avoidance hypothesis). Another possibility is that an aversive event might be paired with a positive reinforcer that maintains a given activity (the discriminative stimulus-conditioned reinforcer hypothesis). Because SIB seems to occur only in the presence or absence of specific stimuli and is often maintained by social reinforcement, it appears that it may be a learned operant under the control of environmental stimuli. As support for this position, Pyles, Riodan, and Bailey (1997) noted that the stereotypy analysis (a partial-interval recording of the occurrence of certain targeted behaviors in the presence/absence of specific environmental events) was effective in determining interventions for hand mouthing and body rocking in children with moderate to profound developmental disabilities.

Green (1978) describes an abuse case where SIB developed as an avoidance response to parental attack. Money, Wolff, and Annecillo (1972) cite higher rates of SIB in abused children than in neglected or normal children as further support for this hypothesis. An alternative explanation might be that the behavior is due to mild organic dysfunction often associated with such abuse.

Traditional/Psychodynamic

A variety of psychodynamic explanations for these behaviors have been presented in the psychodynamic literature (Kennedy & Moran, 1984). These include maternal deprivation, an anxiety-reducing response, repression of hostility, disturbed narcissism, libidinal fixation, and displaced genital damage and self-aggression as a result of oral fixation (Kohut, 1972).

Organic

The increased rates of body rocking and head banging in children with intellectual or sensory handicaps (Cantwell & Baker, 1980) suggest CNS involvement in these behaviors. Ridley and Baker

(1982) suggest that stereotypy is associated with cognitive inflexibility and social and sensory isolation due to some deficit in CNS regulatory function. Gedyre (1989) found associations between stereotyped movement and the presence of desynchronized EEG activity, often frontal lobe in location.

Thelen (1981) suggested that the amount of vestibular stimulation was a critical factor in the etiology of rocking (although such activities were also associated with being in close proximity to a caregiver). He found an inverse relationship between the amount of holding, moving, and touching of the child and the amount of stereotyped behavior. Cocchi (1997) suggested that rocking may be a metabolic stabilizing function. Rocking is hypothesized to stimulate glutaminergic cerebellar areas of the brain as a way of increasing glutamate turnover, thus reducing the cerebellar hypoplasia often seen in autistic patients.

TREATMENT

Behavioral
A variety of behavioral techniques have been used for the elimination of self-stimulatory and self-injurious behaviors (Bachman, 1972; Rincover, 1986). These methods include differential reinforcement (Carr, 1995), aversive techniques (Baroff & Tate, 1968; R.D. Martin & Conway, 1976), extinction and overcorrection (Strauss, Rubinoff, & Atkeson, 1983), and time-out (Tate & Baroff, 1966).

Traditional/Psychodynamic
Therapeutic strategies include distracting stimulation, such as reading; sensory stimulation by playing music; and vestibular stimulation to reduce rocking rates (Lasich & Bassa, 1985). Harris (1968) used psychoanalytic play therapy. Kohut (1972) investigated the relationship of narcissism and aggression and suggested that psychoanalysis was of value in taming narcissistic rage manifested by self-mutilation.

Organic
Tranquilizing or sedative drugs, such as naloxone and clonidine, have been successfully used for chronic SIB (Richardson & Zaleski, 1983). Manni and Tartara (1997) used low doses of clonazepam to treat head banging and body rocking occurring at sleep

onset and during sleep in two cases. Sprague (1977), in a review of psychopharmacology in children, indicated that although neuroleptics reduce bizarre or stereotypical behavior, there is also the possibility that they may suppress learning performance.

CONCLUSIONS

Although there are a variety of etiologic factors associated with the occurrence of stereotypic movement disorders, especially body rocking and head banging, including some genetically determined diseases, the most effective methods of controlling these behaviors in both normal and behaviorally disordered children has been the use of operant conditioning techniques. The increase in the literature of intervention techniques for normal children and the ease with which many parents can successfully apply behavioral procedures suggest that the focus on these procedures will increase in the future.

HABITS

The following habits or mannerisms are not currently diagnosed in the *DSM-IV* (APA, 1994). However, several of them were included under the stereotypic/habit disorders in the previous edition, and all are behaviors that frequently elicit parental questions or concerns. Topics to be covered are nail biting, teeth grinding, and thumb sucking.

NAIL BITING

Definition
Nail biting, or onychophagy, is one of the most common habit disturbances among children and is no longer classified as a stereotypic movement disorder. This behavior consists of biting on or chewing the nails of the hand. Once seen as an indicator of extreme psychopathology, nail biting has become a more normally accepted habit or mannerism. Demographic research has shown that large numbers of nail-biting children are neither psychopathological nor do they appear to have unresolved complexes.

Incidence
This behavior is reported by Foster (1998) as the second most frequent habit (at 23%) in preschool

children age 30 to 82 months. These data appear to be in marked contrast to data from approximately 50 years ago, when it was noted to rarely occur before 4 years of age. At around 6 years, there is a marked increase; then the incidence rate seems to remain constant from 6 years until puberty, when the highest incidence occurs (Ilg & Ames, 1955). It is unclear if the behavior is more frequent in boys or girls. The difference in incidence may be developmental, as girls and boys seem equally prone to this habit during the early years, but males outnumber females at a later age (Carson et al., 1998). Warme (1977) indicated that 40% of children between the ages of 5 and 18 bite one or more nails, and 18% bite all 10 nails severely and persistently. In contrast to other authors, he stated that the incidence peaks in boys at age 12 to 13 and in girls at 8 to 9. However, other studies of nail-biting rates in preadolescent children range from 33% to 50%, dropping to around 24% by 17 to 18 years of age and progressively declining after age 40 (Westling, 1988).

Diagnosis

Diagnosis and measurement of nail biting can be accomplished based on reports by the child or parent and by visual inspection of the nails. The length of the nail can be measured over a period of time, and severity of biting can be determined in this way (Westling, 1988).

Etiology

Behavioral. Several behavioral explanations have been advanced for nail biting, but the most widely accepted is tension or anxiety reduction. The behavior is a learned habit that provides a physical outlet; thus, it relieves anxiety. It is most pronounced during periods of stress (Carson et al., 1998; Pierce, 1972; Warme, 1977).

Traditional/Psychodynamic. Goldenson (1970) states that nail biters as a group are more anxious and intropunitive than other children. Deardoff, Finch, and Royall (1974) administered the Children's Anxiety Scale to 90 students in the seventh and eighth grades and found that the percentage of nail biters was only 12.2. In addition, although nail biters reported more anxiety than nonbiters, the difference was not found to be significant. Other psychodynamic explanations have considered it as a substitute for masturbation, an indication of low self-confidence, a fixation at the oral-aggressive

stage of development, or an outlet for hostile or sexual impulses (Gilleard, Eskin, & Savasir, 1988).

Organic. Studies suggest both familial and genetic components, in that monozygotic twins were found to have rates of nail biting four times that of dizygotic twins. Up to two-thirds of monozygotic twins and one-third of dizygotic twins were found to be concordant for nail biting in some studies (Bakwin & Bakwin, 1972).

Treatment

Behavioral. Carson et al. (1998) suggest that physical restraint and the use of bitter-tasting materials are ineffective and indicated that behavior therapy was more effective. Smith (1957) used a massed practice technique and helped 50% of the subjects in his study. The use of competing responses or reinforcing alternative behaviors has been successful (Adesso, Vargas, & Siddall, 1979; Azrin & Nunn, 1973), with a treatment package consisting of self-monitoring plus regularly scheduled nail measurements the most effective in producing a reduction in nail biting. Many of these authors note that aversive procedures will reduce the frequency of nail biting, but do not seem adequate for total suppression of the behavior. In contrast, Allen (1996) compared the use of mild aversion (in the form of a bitter-tasting liquid on the nail) to a competing response technique and to a self-monitoring control group and reported that the mild aversion was the most effective.

Traditional/Psychodynamic. Warme (1977) suggested that generally no intervention is indicated, to ignore the behavior if it is infrequent, but that severe nail biting is a symptom of some underlying disorder, for which the child and the family may need to receive treatment. Goldenson (1970) suggested that persistent nail biting be treated by reducing stressful family situations and having the child talk over tensions. He advocated using tranquilizing drugs as an adjunct to these approaches during periods of special strain and tension, but stated that the use of punishment, such as forcing the child to wear gloves or applying a bitter-tasting substance to the nails, is not recommended as it produces few positive results. Bakwin and Bakwin (1972) noted that other treatment procedures include an appeal to the child's vanity, softening of the cuticles with olive oil, wearing white cotton mittens at night as a reminder not to bite the nails, and using a bitter substance or adhesive tape on the nails, but they did not indicate the effectiveness of such interventions.

Organic. No specific drugs have been recommended for the treatment of nail biting. However, when the nail biting behavior is assumed, from a psychodynamic point of view, to be a symptom of an underlying disorder such as obsessive-compulsive neurosis or acute anxiety, the drug of choice for each of these disorders has been used. Examples include chlorpromazine for obsessive-compulsive neurosis (Grimshaw, 1965) and imipramine hydrochloride for anxiety (Mendel & Klein, 1969). In a novel approach, Wright et al. (1979) suggest the possibility of providing minor tranquilizers to parents who are unable to ignore nail biting in their child.

Conclusions

Nail biting is a common habit disturbance in children. The use of behavioral techniques, especially a shaping program for growing first a single nail, then the others, seems to be the best approach if the habit is distressing to the child or the parents. It is recommended that the nail-biter always carry a nail file, as a rough nail is an invitation to biting behavior.

TEETH GRINDING

Definition

Teeth grinding, or bruxism, refers to any habitual gnashing, grinding, clicking, or clenching of the teeth and may occur either nocturnally or diurnally. This habit has been listed under a variety of terms throughout the centuries. It is mentioned in the Bible and was called bruxomania by Marie and Pietkiewicz in 1907 (Wright et al., 1979). Historically, the term "occlusal neurosis" was used for neurotic grinding and "bruxism" for nonneurotic nocturnal grinding. Today, the term bruxism is used to describe all forms of teeth-gnashing behavior.

Incidence

Reding, Rubright, and Zimmerman (1966) report rates of bruxism between 5% and 18%. Bruxism appears somewhat dependent on dental articulation. Both males and females with poor dental alignment have higher rates of bruxism than those with good dental articulation. The male:female ratio is

approximately 3:1 in most studies. The onset of bruxism most commonly occurs prior to the age of 3 years, usually is nocturnal, is more frequent in older children and adolescents, and persists into adult life in about 35% of cases (Cash, 1988).

Diagnosis

The initial diagnosis of the condition is usually made by a dentist. The gnashing of the teeth may at times be so loud that parents or others around the child can hear it. Any grinding that occurs for over one hour per day should be considered bruxism (Cash, 1988). Psychological evaluation should include both the child and parents, with data obtained on personality factors, frequency and time of occurrence, events or factors associated with increases or decreases in frequency, and recent family stressors (Berkow, 1992).

Etiology

Behavioral. The most widely accepted behavioral formulation is that bruxism is a learned behavior associated with a response to excessive stress (Cash, 1988; Rugh & Harlan, 1988).

Traditional/Psychodynamic. Most psychodynamic formulations suggest that bruxism results from a fixation at oral-aggressive/oral-sadistic stages or is a symptom of repression or self-aggression (Walsh, 1965). However, some studies (Frisch, Katz, & Ferreira, 1960; Reding et al., 1966) found no correlation between bruxism and aggression. Anxiety has been associated with bruxism (S.C. Miller, Thaller, & Sobermark, 1956).

Organic. A variety of dental problems or other medical conditions may be significant factors in bruxism. Included may be malocclusion, missing or rough teeth, oral or systemic infections, allergies, and malnutrition (Egermark, Carlsson, & Magnusson, 1987; Marks, 1980). Genetic and familial aspects have been postulated as being associated with the occurrence of bruxism, with higher incidence in parents and siblings of bruxists than in the normal population (Reding et al., 1966), especially when both parents exhibited the behavior.

Treatment

Behavioral. Because bruxism is associated with increased anxiety, relaxation techniques or massed practice may be useful. Biofeedback using a tone when bruxism occurs, with electrodes attached to the jaw, has been successful (Cassisi, McGlynn, & Belles, 1987) in reducing facial pain.

Traditional/Psychodynamic. Psychodynamic treatments have been directed at unmet oral and dependency needs using brief psychotherapy or hypnosis aimed at verbally releasing hostility or other pent-up feelings (Goldenson, 1970).

Organic. Medical and dental treatments of bruxism have focused on improvements of malocclusion or an appliance such as a bite block to reduce damage to the teeth. The use of drugs has included diazepam and methocarbamol, with some reduction in both frequency and severity (Berkow, 1992).

Conclusions

Medical research is being undertaken into conditions associated with bruxism, such as allergies. At the same time, the cost of dental injury resulting from bruxism continues to increase. Several behavioral techniques, especially biofeedback, have the potential to rapidly reduce the incidence of this habit.

THUMB SUCKING

Definition

Thumb sucking includes not only the sucking of one or both thumbs, but also may include finger and fist sucking. Historically, interpretation of this behavior has shifted in the past century from being a sign of placidity, to a symptom of infant sexuality and possible neurosis, to a habit disturbance. In contrast, Wolfenstein (1972), in a study of trends of severity in handling children's impulse disorders, noted that between 1914 and 1951, the severity in handling thumb sucking showed a consistently declining curve, even though thumb sucking became a diagnosed psychiatric condition.

Incidence

Thumb sucking is a common behavior in children. Age of onset is between 3 and 4 months of age in 20% of cases, with 15% between 6 and 9 months. Only 10% start after 9 months (Ilg & Ames, 1955). The behavior most often occurs immediately after feeding. After a reduction in the amount of sucking, there is an increase around 18 months of age. By 2.5

to 3 years of age, thumb sucking occurs less during the day, and at night may be associated with the child's holding some other object, such as a favorite blanket. Foster (1998) noted that in preschoolers age 30 to 82 months, the most common habit was thumb sucking, with 25% of her sample engaging in the behavior. By 3.5 years, most daytime sucking is stimulated by activities such as watching television. By age 5, sucking often happens only with sleep. Approximately 45% of all 2-year-olds, 42% of all 3-year-olds, 36% of all 4-year-olds, 20% to 30% of all 5-year-olds, 21% of all 6-year-olds, but only approximately 5% of 11-year-olds engage in these behaviors (Lichstein & Kachmarik, 1980).

Traisman and Traisman (1958) reported that 46% of children from birth to 16 years suck their thumbs. Specific data on the male:female ratio are lacking, with Palermo (1956) reporting it as more frequent in males and Bakwin and Bakwin (1972) saying it occurs more often in females. Studies have indicated that the incidence of emotional disturbance is no higher among thumb-suckers than non-thumb-suckers, and some indicate positive effects, in that the child may cry less, be less destructive of objects, get through teething easier, and sleep much better (Lapouse & Monk, 1959; Traisman & Traisman, 1958).

Diagnosis

The diagnosis of this habit is relatively simple, involving the observation of the child with his or her thumb or fingers in the mouth. Because it is often impractical to do continuous observations of children, a time sampling procedure may be utilized at appropriate intervals. The habit often occurs when the child is hungry, sleepy, frustrated, or fatigued. The child may pull an ear, pat the head, twist or pull the hair, suck a blanket or diaper, rub a cheek with a pillow, or pull a blanket in front of the face (Bakwin & Bakwin, 1972).

Etiology

Behavioral. Thumb sucking is described as being maintained because of its pleasurable associations with feeding and alleviation of hunger in a classic conditioning pairing (Bakwin & Bakwin, 1972), and as a conditioned response for tension reduction to stress (Lichstein & Kachmarik, 1980; Palermo, 1956; Pierce, 1972).

Traditional/Psychodynamic. Psychoanalytic theorists view thumb sucking either as one of the origins of autoerotic functioning occurring in the fetal stage of development (Schalin, 1995; Whitewood, 1997) or as an expression of the oral stage of psychosexual development (Freud, 1965). Whitewood reported a case in which a 5-year-old in therapy remembered the onset of thumb sucking as a 2-month-old fetus. Questioning of the mother indicated that this event began when she told the father of the pregnancy and he had expressed anger.

In psychoanalytic theory, the mouth is viewed as an erotic zone, and adequate stimulation is considered essential if the child's sexual and character development is to proceed normally. The individual who successfully goes through the oral stage has the capacity for oral satisfaction and continues getting "sucking satisfaction" not only from thumb sucking but, in later life, from activities such as gnawing on pencils, biting the lips, and sucking on a pipe or cigar (the latter a high-frequency behavior with Freud himself). Concerns are frequently raised over the stopping of thumb sucking if it is a symptom of underlying psychopathology. Ottenbacher and Ottenbacher (1981) present a case in which decreases in thumb sucking were associated with a marked increase in enuretic episodes. Although similar psychodynamic hypotheses are often stated for associations with other deviant behaviors, there is little direct evidence for these conclusions (Haryett, Hansen, & Davidson, 1970; Palermo, 1956), especially those adult behaviors related to inadequate sucking in infancy.

Thumb sucking has been associated with psychiatric illness, family disruption, especially after 4 years of age, and medical/dental disorders (Geis & Piarulle, 1988; Newson, Newson, & Mahalski, 1982). At times, thumb sucking has been viewed as habit related to masturbation, in that the behavior can serve as an erotic gratification or as a means of reducing tension or anxiety. Although such assumptions (or myths) exist, there are no data available indicating that children who suck their thumbs masturbate more often at a later age than others who do not suck their thumbs (Bakwin & Bakwin, 1972).

Sears and Wise (1950) suggested that excessive breast or bottle sucking leads to thumb sucking. Support for this view or a biological need to exercise the sucking mechanism comes from observations that sucking serves a soothing function when a child is sleepy, frustrated, or upset. Thumb sucking has been related to object-attachment relationships and is also advanced as the explanation for

older children and even adults reverting to thumb sucking under stress.

Organic. Differential rates of malocclusion and other jaw or dental problems are reported as both causative and outcome factors in thumb suckers (Rubel, 1986) and have even been identified in skulls from A.D. 1000 to 1500 (Larsson & Dahlin, 1985; Traisman & Traisman, 1958). In a review, Haryett et al. (1970) noted that malocclusion rates ranged from a low of 14% to a high of 87%, with little permanent damage, providing that the habit is discontinued prior to the age of 4 years. However, Modeer, Odenrick, and Lindner (1982) found that damage occurs if thumb sucking continues after 2 years of age. Although the relationship between thumb sucking and malocclusion is of concern to dentists, many hesitate to treat the habit because of the possibility of psychological trauma to the child.

Recently, concerns have been raised over rotational deformity damage to the thumb from this habit (Bloem, Kon, & deGraaf, 1988). Minimal research has been undertaken into the genetic or familial aspects of thumb sucking. Bakwin and Bakwin (1972), in a study of twins, failed to find a genetic predisposition to thumb sucking persisting after 3 years of age. Willmot (1984) presented a case of monozygotic twins, only one of whom thumbsucked, and reported significant dental differences.

Treatment

Behavioral. A variety of behavioral techniques have been successfully applied to reduce or eliminate thumb sucking. Methods include positive reinforcement (Knight & McKenzie, 1974), use of edible reinforcers such as hard candy (Hughes, Hughes, & Dial, 1979), self-recording (Cohen, Monty, & Williams, 1980), modeling and a token program using an older sibling (D. Martin, 1974), response cost using removal of cartoons, reading material, or a toy (Baer, 1962; Rolider & Van Houten, 1988), overcorrection, and time-out (Azrin & Nunn, 1973; Clowes & King, 1982; Knight & McKenzie, 1974). Of special interest is Doke and Epstein's (1975) research, which used an overcorrection procedure (toothbrushing with an oral antiseptic) in which the treatment suppressed the thumb sucking of the child and also another child who witnessed the procedure.

Differential reinforcement of other responses (DRO) programs at home and school have been used (Christensen & Sanders, 1987; Lichstein &

Kachmarik, 1980), with reduction in thumb-sucking rates up to 92% in the first weeks. Another author has raised questions regarding the use of such programs (van Norman, 1985).

The use of bandages as a form of treatment (see "Traditional/Psychodynamic" section) has recently been labeled as response prevention and, along with fading techniques, has been effective (Luciano, 1988; Rolider & Van Houten, 1988).

Azrin and Peterson (1989) did a controlled comparison with a bitter-tasting substance on the finger and produced a reduction in sucking of only 35%. Earlier attempts to reduce thumb sucking by making the thumb or finger taste unpleasant with substances such as quinine, mustard, vinegar, and commercial preparations such as Red Hot and Finger Tip had been reported as ineffective. However, more recent studies (Friman, Barone, & Christophersen, 1986; Friman & Leibowitz, 1990) found that a bitter-tasting liquid combined with extrinsic reinforcers was effective in significantly reducing finger sucking.

Hughes et al. (1979) used a "behavioral seal" in which a small amount of litmus paper was affixed to the fingernail or thumbnail as a means of obtaining a reliable measure of the presence or absence of thumb sucking over long periods of time. These authors suggest that this procedure eliminates the possibility of overlooking and/or inadvertently reinforcing the occurrence of the target behavior between observations. It also enjoys the advantage of being an economic, highly reliable observation technique.

Traditional/Psychodynamic. The use of paradoxical intention, from a logotherapy framework, was reported by Yoder (1983) as being effective after only three sessions. Whitewood (1997) reported success with a single session of hypnosis with age regression in a 5-year-old. A hypnotic suggestion of being loved by the parents resulted in no thumb sucking being reported on follow-up several years after treatment.

Duke and Nowicki (1979) remarked that foul-tasting preparations that were smeared on children's fingers were used in an attempt to make the behavior "distasteful," but many of the children soon liked the taste because of its association with the pleasurable act of thumb sucking. Recent modifications of this method (see "Behavioral" section) have proven effective. The use of threats, nagging, and restrictive devices, such as mittens, gloves,

cages, or plastic splints for the thumbs, elbow braces (so the child cannot bend the arms), and bandages (Lassen & Flubt, 1978; Lewis, Shilton, & Fuqua, 1981), have been successful. The more recent studies are often described in behavioral terms but use the same methods found in the earlier traditional literature.

Dental. In the early 1900s, a number of devices to halt thumb sucking were developed. Dentists have advocated the use of a variety of methods, including pacifiers as an alternative. Unattractive oral devices or a palatal crib that has spurs so that thumb insertion in the mouth produces a painful sensation have also been used successfully (Engelmeier, 1985; Haryett et al., 1970; Norton & Gellin, 1968; Wehbe, 1982). However, though producing a reduction in the rate of thumb sucking, especially in those who had the appliance in for more than six months, sucking did recur in some of these children following removal of the device.

Conclusions

Thumb sucking is a mannerism that often produces ridicule from others around the child. Of all the habits, it may be the most misunderstood, and also the mannerism for which virtually everyone has an opinion as to its cause and cure. Authors have generally suggested ignoring the behavior (Bakwin & Bakwin 1972; Goldenson, 1970), especially in preschool-age children. Ignoring the behavior, however, is often difficult in a world where everyone from the neighbors to grandparents may comment in tones ranging from mild disapproval to horror about the child's thumb sucking. Thus, parents have resorted to threats, nagging, and restrictive devices such as elbow braces. These methods have been largely ineffective. Behavioral procedures produce immediate and often lasting results, but foul-tasting liquids placed on the thumb without other techniques are often ineffective unless combined with behavioral techniques.

REFERENCES

Abe, K., & Oda, N. (1980). Incidence of tics in the offspring of childhood tiquers: A controlled follow-up study. *Developmental Medicine and Child Neurology,* 22(5), 649–653.

Abe, K., Oda, N., & Amatomi, M. (1984). Natural history and predictive significance of head-banging, head-rolling, and breath-holding spells. *Developmental Medicine and Child Neurology, 26*(5), 644–648.

Adesso, V.J., Vargas, J.M., & Siddall, J.W. (1979). The role of awareness in reducing nail-biting behavior. *Behavior Therapy, 10*,148–154.

Allen, K.W. (1996). Chronic nailbiting: A controlled comparison of competing response and mild aversion treatments. *Behavioural Research and Therapy, 34*(3), 269–272.

American Psychiatric Association. (1987). *Diagnostic and statistical manual of mental disorders* (3rd ed., rev.). Washington, DC: Author.

American Psychiatric Association. (1994). *Diagnostic and statistical manual of mental disorders* (4th ed.). Washington, DC: Author.

Ascher, E. (1948). Psychodynamic considerations in Gilles de la Tourette's disease with a report of five cases and discussion of the literature. *American Journal of Psychiatry, 105*, 267–275.

Azrin, N.H., & Nunn, R.G. (1973). Habit reversal: A method of eliminating nervous habits and tics. *Behavior Research and Therapy, 11*, 619–628.

Azrin, N.H., & Peterson, A.L. (1989). Reduction of an eye tic by controlled blinking. *Behavior Therapy, 20*(3), 467–473.

Bachman, J.A. (1972). Self-injurious behavior: A behavioral analysis. *Journal of Abnormal Psychology, 80*, 211–224.

Baer, D.M. (1962). Laboratory control of thumb-sucking in three young children by withdrawal and re-presentation of positive reinforcement. *Journal of the Experimental Analysis of Behavior, 5*, 525–528.

Bakwin, H., & Bakwin, R.M. (1972). *Behavior disorders in children* (4th ed.). Philadelphia: Saunders.

Baroff, G.S., & Tate, B.G. (1968). The use of aversive stimulation in the treatment of chronic self-injurious behavior. *Journal of the American Academy of Child Psychiatry, 7*, 454–470.

Beard, G. (1880). Experiments with the "jumpers" or "jumping Frenchmen" of Maine. *Journal of Nervous and Mental Diseases, 7*, 487.

Bergen, D., Tanner, C.M., & Wilson, R. (1982). The electroencephalogram in Tourette syndrome. *Annuals of Neurology, 11*(4), 382–385.

Berkow, R. (Ed.). (1992). *The Merck manual of diagnosis and therapy* (16th ed.). Rahway, NJ: Merck, Sharp, & Dohme Research Laboratories.

Bloem, J.J., Kon, M., & deGraaf, F.H. (1988). Rotational deformity of the index finger caused by reversed finger sucking. *Annual of Plastic Surgery, 21*(6), 597–600.

Boshes, L.D. (1976). Gilles de la Tourette's syndrome. *American Journal of Nursing, 76*, 1637–1638.

Brett, P.M., Curtis, D., Robertson, M.M., & Gurling, H. (1995a). Exclusion of the 5-HT1A serotonin neuroreceptor and tryptophan oxygenase genes in a large British kindred multiply affected with Tourette's syndrome, chronic motor tics, and obsessive-compulsive behavior. *American Journal of Psychiatry, 152*, 437–440.

Brett, P.M., Curtis, D., Robertson, M.M., & Gurling, H. (1995b). The genetic susceptibility to Gilles de la Tourette syndrome in a large multiply affected British kindred: Linkage analysis excludes a role for the genes coding for dopamine D1, D2, D3, D4, D5 receptors, dopamine beta hydroxylase, tyrosinase, and tyrosine hydroxylase. *Biological Psychiatry, 37*, 533–540.

Brody, S. (1960). Self-rocking in infancy. *Journal of the American Psychoanalytic Association, 7*, 464–491.

Cantwell, D.P., & Baker, L. (1980). Psychiatric and behavioral characteristics of children with communication disorders. *Journal of Pediatric Psychology, 5*, 161–178.

Carr, J.E. (1995). Competing responses for the treatment of Tourette syndrome and tic disorders. *Behavior Research and Therapy, 33*(4), 455–466.

Carson, R.C., Butcher, J.N., & Mineka, S. (1998). *Abnormal psychology and modern life* (10th ed.). New York: Addison-Wesley.

Cash, R.C. (1988). Bruxisim in children: Review of the literature. *Journal of Periodontics, 12*(2), 107–127.

Cassisi, J.E., McGlynn, F.D., & Belles, D.R. (1987). EMG activated feedback alarms for the treatment of nocturnal bruxism: Current status and future directions. *Biofeedback and Self-Regulation, 12*(1), 13–30.

Cavenar, J.O., Spaulding, J.G., & Sullivan, J.L. (1979). Child's reaction to mother's abortion: Case report. *Military Medicine, 144*, 412–413.

Chandler, M.L., Barnhill, J.L., Gualtieri, C.T., & Patterson, D.R. (1989). Tryptophan antagonism of stimulant induced tics. *Journal of Clinical Psychopharmacology, 9*(1), 69–70.

Christensen, A.P., & Sanders, M.R. (1987). Habit reversal and differential reinforcement of other behavior in the treatment of thumb-sucking: An analysis of generalization and side-effects. *Journal of Child Psychology and Psychiatry, 28*(2), 281–295.

Clark, D.F. (1966). Behavior therapy of Gilles de la Tourette's syndrome. *British Journal of Psychiatry, 112*, 771–778.

Clementz, G.L., Lee, R.L., & Barclay, A.M. (1988). Tic disorders of childhood. *American Family Physician, 38*(2), 163–170.

Clowes, H., & King, N. (1982). Parents and siblings as behavior modifiers in the control of a common developmental problem (thumbsucking). *Journal of Clinical Child Psychology, 11*(3), 231–233.

Cocchi, R. (1997). Rocking as consummatory behavior against a glutamate excess? *Italian Journal of Intellective Impairment, 10*(1), 7–12.

Cohen, D.J., Brunn, R.D., & Leckman, J.F. (1988). *Tourette's syndrome and tic disorders: Clinical understanding and treatment.* New York: Wiley.

Cohen, D.J., Leckman, J.F., & Towbin, K.E. (1989). Tic disorders. In American Psychiatric Association, *Treatments of psychiatric disorders: A task force report of the American Psychiatric Association* (Vol. 1–3 & Index Vol., pp. 687–714). Washington, DC: Author.

Cohen, D.J., Monty, H., & Williams, D. (1980). Management of thumbsucking using self-recording with parent as observer and experimenter. *Perceptual and Motor Skills, 50,* 136.

Cohen, D.J., Riddle, M.A., & Leckman, J.F. (1992). Pharmacotherapy of Tourette's syndrome and associated disorders. *Psychiatric Clinics of North America, 15,* 109–129.

Comings, D.E. (1994). Tourette syndrome: A hereditary neuropsychiatric spectrum disorder. *Annals of Clinical Psychiatry, 6,* 235–247.

Comings, D.E., & Comings, B.G. (1993). Sexual abuse or Tourette's syndrome? *Social Work, 38,* 347–350.

Culbertson, F.M. (1989). A four-step hypnotherapy model for Gilles de la Tourette's syndrome. *American Journal of Clinical Hypnosis, 31*(4), 252–256.

Deardoff, P.A., Finch, A.J., & Royall, L.R. (1974). Manifest anxiety and nail-biting. *Journal of Clinical Psychology, 30,* 378.

DeLissovoy, V. (1961). Head-banging in early childhood: A study of incidence. *Journal of Pediatrics, 58,* 803–805.

Doke, L.A., & Epstein, L.H. (1975). Oral overcorrection: Side effects and extended applications. *Journal of Experimental Child Psychology, 20,* 496–511.

Duchowny, M.S., Resnick, T.J., Deray, M.J., & Alvarez, L.A. (1988). Video EEG diagnosis of repetitive behavior in early childhood and its relationship to seizures. *Pediatric Neurology, 4*(3), 162–164.

Duke, M., & Nowicki, S., Jr. (1979). *Abnormal psychology: Perspectives on being different.* Belmont, CA: Wadsworth.

Eapen, V., Pauls, D.L., & Robertson, M.M. (1993). Evidence for autosomal dominant transmission in Tourette's syndrome: United Kingdom cohort study. *British Journal of Psychiatry, 162,* 593–596.

Egermark, E.I., Carlsson, G.E., & Magnusson, T. (1987). A long-term epidemiologic study of the relationship between occlusal factors and mandibular dysfunction in children and adolescents. *Journal of Dental Research, 66*(1), 67–71.

Eisenhauser, G.L., & Woody, R.C. (1987). Self-mutilation and Tourette's disorder. *Journal of Child Neurology, 2*(4), 265–267.

Elston, J.S., Granje, F.C., & Lees, A.J. (1989). The relationship between eye-winking tics, frequent eye-blinking and blepharospasm. *Journal of Neurology, Neurosurgery and Psychiatry, 52*(4), 477–480.

Engelmeier, R.L. (1985). Technique for constructing custom thumb-chewing guards. *Journal of Prosthetic Dentistry, 54*(1), 154–155.

Erenberg, G. (1988). Pharmacologic therapy of tics in childhood. *Pediatric Annals, 17*(6), 395–404.

Fahn, S. (1982). A case of post-traumatic tic syndrome. *Advances in Neurology, 35,* 349–350.

Finney, J.W., Rapoff, M.A., Hall, C.L., & Christophersen, E.R. (1983). Replication and social validation of habit reversal treatment for tics. *Behavior Therapy, 14*(1), 116–126.

Foster, L.G. (1998). Nervous habits and stereotyped behaviors in preschool children. *Journal of the American Academy of Child and Adolescent Psychiatry, 37*(7), 711–717.

Freud, A. (1965). *Normality and pathology in childhood.* New York: International Universities Press.

Friman, P.C., Barone, V.J., & Christophersen, E.R. (1986). Aversive taste treatment of finger and thumb sucking. *Pediatrics, 78*(1), 174–176.

Friman, P.C., & Leibowitz, J.M. (1990). An effective and acceptable treatment alternative for chronic thumb and finger sucking. *Journal of Pediatric Psychology, 15,* 57–65.

Frisch, J., Katz, L., & Ferreira, A.J. (1960). A study of the relationship between bruxism and aggression. *Journal of Periodontics, 31,* 409–412.

Gedyre, A. (1989). Extreme self-injury attributed to frontal lobe seizures. *American Journal of Mental Retardation, 94,*(1), 20–26.

Geis, A.H., & Piarulle, D.H. (1988). Psychological aspects of prolonged thumbsucking habits. *Journal of Clinical Orthodontry, 22*(8), 492–495.

Gelenberg, A.J., Bassuk, E.L., & Schoonover, S.C. (1991). *The practitioner's guide to psychoactive drugs* (3rd ed.). New York: Plenum Press.

George, M.S., Robertson, M.M., Costa, D.C., & Ell, P.J. (1994). Dopamine receptor availability in Tourette's syndrome. *Psychiatry Research: Neuroimaging, 55,* 193–203.

Gilleard, E., Eskin, M., & Savasir, B. (1988). Nailbiting and oral aggression in a Turkish student population. *British Journal of Medical Psychology, 61*(2), 197–201.

Goetz, C.G., Tanner, C.M., & Klawans, H.L. (1984). Fluphenazine and multifocal tic disorders. *Neurology, 41*(3), 271–272.

Golden, G.S. (1987). Tic disorders in childhood. *Pediatric Review, 8*(8), 229–234.

Golden, G.S. (1990). Tourette syndrome: Recent advances. *Neurologic Clinics, 8*(3), 705–714.

Golden, G.S., & Hood, O.J. (1982). Tics and tremors. *Pediatric Clinics of North America, 29*(1), 95–103.

Goldenson, R.M. (1970). *The encyclopedia of human behavior: Psychology, psychiatry and mental health* (Vol. 2). Garden City, NY: Doubleday.

Green, A.H. (1978). Self-destructive behavior in battered children. *American Journal of Psychiatry, 135,* 579–582.

Grimshaw, L. (1965). The outcome of obsessional disorder: A follow-up study of 100 cases. *British Journal of Psychiatry, 111,* 1051–1056.

Harris, M. (1968). The child psychotherapist and the patient's family. *Journal of Child Psychotherapy, 2,* 50–63.

Haryett, R.D., Hansen, F.C., & Davidson, P.O. (1970). Chronic thumbsucking: A second report on treatment and its psychological effects. *American Journal of Orthodontics, 57,* 164–177.

Hemming, M., & Yellowlees, P.M. (1993). Effective treatment of Tourette's syndrome with marijuana. *Journal of Psychopharmacology, 7,* 389–391.

Hughes, H., Hughes, A., & Dial, H. (1979). Home-based treatment of thumbsucking: Omission training with edible reinforcers and behavioral seal. *Behavior Modification, 3,* 179–186.

Hurst, M.J., & Hurst, D.L. (1994). Tolstoy's description of Tourette syndrome in *Anna Karenina. Journal of Child Neurology, 9*(4), 366–367.

Hyde, T.M., Fitzcharles, E.K., & Weinberger, D.R. (1993). Age-related prognostic factors in the severity of illness of Tourette's syndrome in monozygotic twins. *Journal of Neuropsychiatry and Clinical Neurosciences, 5,* 178–182.

Ilg, F.L., & Ames, L.B. (1955). *Child behavior.* New York: Harper & Row.

Itard, J.M.G. (1825). Memories of some involuntary functions of the appearance of movement, grasp, and voice. *Archives of General Medicine, 8,* 358.

Jankovic, J., Glaze, D.G., & Frost, J.D. (1984). Effect of tetrabenazine on tics and sleep of Gilles de la Tourette's syndrome. *Neurology, 34*(5), 688–692.

Kennedy, H., & Moran, G.S. (1984). The developmental roots of self-injury and response to pain in a 4-year-old boy. *Psychoanalytic Study of Children, 39,* 195–212.

Kerbeshian, J., & Burd, L. (1985). Auditory hallucinosis and atypical tic disorder: Case reports. *Journal of Clinical Psychiatry, 46*(9), 398–399.

Kerbeshian, J., & Burd, L. (1994). Tourette's syndrome: A developmental psychobiological view. *Journal of Developmental and Physical Disabilities, 6*(3), 203–218.

Keshavan, M.S. (1988). The ear wigglers: Tics of the ear in 10 patients. *American Journal of Psychiatry, 145*(11), 1462–1463.

Klawans, H.L., & Barr, A. (1985). Recurrence of childhood multiple tic in late adult life. *Archives of Neurology, 42*(11), 1079–1080.

Knight, M.F., & McKenzie, H.S. (1974). Elimination of bedtime thumbsucking in home settings through contingent reading. *Journal of Applied Behavior Analysis, 7,* 33–38.

Kohut, H. (1972). Thoughts on narcissism and narcissistic rage. *Psychoanalytic Study of the Child, 27,* 360–400.

Kolb, B., & Whishaw, I.Q. (1990). *Fundamentals of human neuropsychology.* New York: Freeman.

Kravitz, H., Rosenthal, V., Teplitz, Z., Murphy, J., & Lesser, R. (1960). A study of head banging in infants and children. *Diseases of the Nervous System, 21,* 203–208.

Kurlan, R., Lichter, D., & Hewitt, D. (1989). Sensory tics in Tourette's syndrome. *Neurology, 39*(5), 731–734.

Lacey, D.J. (1986). Diagnosis of Tourette syndrome in childhood. *Clinical Pediatrics of Philadelphia, 25*(9), 433–435.

Lahey, B.B., McNees, M.P., & McNees, M.C. (1973). Control of an obscene "verbal tic" through timeout in an elementary school classroom. *Journal of Applied Behavior Analysis, 6,* 101–104.

Lake, F. (1978). Treating psychosomatic disorders related to birth trauma. *Journal of Psychosomatic Research, 22,* 227–238.

Lang, A.E., Consky, E., & Sandor, P. (1993). "Signing tics": Insight into the pathophysiology of symptoms in Tourette's syndrome. *Annals of Neurology, 33,* 212–215.

Lapouse, R., & Monk, M.A. (1959). Fears and worries in a representative sample of children. *American Journal of Orthopsychiatry, 29,* 803–818.

Larsson, E.F., & Dahlin, K.G. (1985). The prevalence and the etiology of the initial dummy- and finger-sucking habit. *American Journal of Orthodontics, 87*(5), 432–435.

Lasich, A.J., & Bassa, F. (1985). Stereotyped movement disorder of rocking. *Journal of Nervous and Mental Disease Disorders, 173*(3), 187–190.

Lassen, M.K., & Flubt, N.R. (1978). Elimination of nocturnal thumbsucking by glove wearing. *Journal of Behavior Therapy and Experimental Psychiatry, 9,* 85.

Lerer, R.J. (1987). Motor tics, Tourette syndrome, and learning disabilities. *Journal of Learning Disabilities, 20*(5), 266–270.

Leung, A.K., & Fagan, J.E. (1989). Tic disorders in childhood (and beyond). *Postgraduate Medicine, 86*(1), 251–252, 257–261.

Lewis, M., Shilton, P., & Fuqua, R.W. (1981). Parental control of nocturnal thumbsucking. *Journal of Behavioral Therapy and Experimental Psychiatry, 12*(1), 87–90.

Lichstein, K.L., & Kachmarik, G. (1980). A non-aversive intervention for thumbsucking: Analysis across settings and time in the natural environment. *Journal of Pediatric Psychology, 5,* 405–414.

Luciano, M.C. (1988). A systematic replication of response prevention to eliminate nocturnal thumbsucking. *Child and Family Behavior Therapy, 10*(2–3), 69–75.

Mahler, M.S. (1949). A psychoanalytic evaluation of tics in psychopathology of children: Symptomatic tic and tic syndrome. *Psychoanalytic Study of the Child, 3/4,* 279–310.

Manni, R., & Tartara, A. (1997). Clonazepam treatment of rhythmic movement disorders. *Sleep, 20*(9), 812.

Marks, M.B. (1980). Bruxism in allergic children. *American Journal of Orthodontics, 77,* 48–59.

Martin, A. (1977). Tourette's syndrome. *Children Today, 6,* 26–27.

Martin, D. (1974). A six-year-old "behaviorist" solves her sibling's chronic thumb-sucking problem. *Corrective and Social Psychiatry and Journal of Applied Behavior Technology, 21*, 19–21.

Martin, R.D., & Conway, J.B. (1976). Aversive stimulation to eliminate infant nocturnal rocking. *Journal of Behavior Therapy and Experimental Psychiatry, 7*, 200–201.

Matesevac, H. (1993). Treatment of impulse disorders: Tic, OCD and ADHD. In L.F. Koziol, C.E. Stout, & D.H. Ruben (Eds.), *Handbook of childhood impulse disorders and ADHD: Theory and practice.* Springfield, MA: Thomas.

Matthews, W., & Barabas, G. (1985). Recent advances in developmental pediatrics related to achievement and social behavior. *School Psychology Review, 14*(2), 182–187.

Mendel, J.G.C., & Klein, D.F. (1969). Anxiety attacks with subsequent agoraphobia. *Comprehensive Psychiatry, 10*, 190–195.

Miller, A.L. (1970). Treatment of a child with Gilles de la Tourette's syndrome using behavior modification techniques. *Journal of Behavior Therapy and Experimental Psychiatry, 1*, 319–321.

Miller, S.C., Thaller, J.L., & Soberman, A. (1956). The use of the Minnesota Multiphasic Personality Inventory in periodontal disease. *Journal of Periodontology, 27*, 44–46.

Modeer, T., Odenrick, L., & Lindner, A. (1982). Sucking habits and their relation to posterior cross-bite in 4-year-old children. *Scandinavian Journal of Dental Research, 90*(4), 323–328.

Money, J., Wolff, G., & Annecillo, C. (1972). Pain agnosia and self-injury in the syndrome of reversible somatotropin deficiency (psychosocial dwarfism). *Journal of Autism and Childhood Schizophrenia, 2*, 127–139.

Newson, J., Newson, E., & Mahalski, P.A. (1982). Persistent infant comfort habits and their sequelae at 11 and 16 years. *Journal of Clinical Child Psychology and Psychiatry, 23*(4), 421–436.

Norton, L.A., & Gellin, M.E. (1968). Management of digital sucking and tongue thrusting in children. *Dental Clinics of North America, 12*, 363–382.

Ollendick, D.G. (1989). Tics and Tourette's disorder. In T.H. Ollendick, & M. Hersen (Eds.), *Handbook of child psychopathology* (2nd ed., pp. 277–290). New York: Plenum Press.

Ostfeld, B.M. (1988). Psychological interventions in Gilles de la Tourette's syndrome. *Pediatric Annuals, 17*(6), 417–421.

Ottenbacher, K., & Ottenbacher, M. (1981). Symptom substitution: A case study. *American Journal of Psychoanalysis, 41*(2), 173–175.

Palermo, D.S. (1956). Thumbsucking: A learned response. *Pediatrics, 17*, 392–399.

Peterson, A.A., Campise, R.L., & Azrin, N.H. (1994). Behavioral and pharmacological treatments for tic and habit disorders: A review. *Journal of Developmental and Behavioral Statistics, 15*(6), 430–441.

Phillips, R.H., & Muzaffer, A. (1961). Some aspects of self-mutilation in the general population of a large psychiatric hospital. *Psychiatric Quarterly, 35*, 421–423.

Pierce, C.M. (1972). Nail-biting and thumb-sucking. In A.M. Freedman & H.I. Kaplan (Eds.), *The child: His psychological and cultural development: I. Normal development and psychological assessment* (pp. 210–213). New York: Atheneum.

Polak, L., Molcan, J., & Dimova, N. (1985). Butyrophenons are superior to thioridazine in the treatment of tic in children. *Activitas Nervosa Superior, 27*(1), 46–47.

Poth, R., & Barnett, D.W. (1983). Reduction of a behavioral tic with a preschooler using relaxation and self-control techniques across settings. *School Psychology Review, 12*(4), 472–476.

Pray, B., Kramer J.J., & Lindskog, R. (1986). Assessment and treatment of tic behavior: A review and case study. *School Psychology Review, 15*(3), 418–429.

Price, R.A., Leckman, J.F., Pauls, D.L., Cohen, D.J., & Kidd, K.K. (1986). Gilles de la Tourette's syndrome: Tics and central nervous system stimulants in twins and nontwins. *Neurology, 36*(2), 232–237.

Pyles, D.A.M., Riodan, M.M., & Bailey, J.S. (1997). The stereotypy analysis: An instrument for examining environmental variables associated with differential rates of stereotypic behavior. *Research in Developmental Disabilities, 18*(1), 11–38.

Rauch, S.L., Baer, L., Cosgrove, G.R., & Jenike, M.A. (1995). Neurosurgical treatment of Tourette's syndrome: A critical review. *Comprehensive Psychiatry, 36*(2), 141–156.

Reding, G.R., Rubright, W.C., & Zimmerman, S.O. (1966). Incidence of bruxism. *Journal of Dental Research, 45*, 1198–1204.

Richardson, J.S., & Zaleski, W.A. (1983). Naloxone and self-mutilation. *Biological Psychiatry, 18*(1), 99–101.

Ridley, R.M., & Baker, H.F. (1982). Stereotypy in monkeys and humans. *Psychological Medicine, 12*(1), 61–72.

Rincover, A. (1986). Behavioral research in self-injury and self-stimulation. *Psychiatric Clinics of North America, 9*(4), 755–766.

Robertson, M.M. (1994). Gilles de la Tourette syndrome: An update. *Journal of Child Psychology and Psychiatry and Allied Disciplines, 35*(4), 597–611.

Rolider, A., & Van Houten, R. (1988). The use of response prevention to eliminate daytime thumbsucking. *Child and Family Behavior Therapy, 10*(2/3), 135–142.

Rubel, I. (1986). Atypical root resorption of maxillary primary central incisors due to digital sucking: A report of 82 cases. *Journal of Dentistry for Children, 53*(3), 201–204.

Rugh, J.D., & Harlan, J. (1988). Nocturnal bruxism and temporomandibular disorders. *Advances in Neurology, 49*, 329–341.

Sandyk, R. (1995). Improvement of right hemispheric functions in a child with Gilles de la Tourette's syndrome by weak electromagnetic fields. *International Journal of Neuroscience, 81*, 199–213.

Savicki, V., & Carlin, A.S. (1972). Behavioral treatment of Gilles de la Tourette syndrome. *International Journal of Child Psychotherapy, 1*, 97–109.

Schalin, L.J. (1995). On autoerotism and object relations in the psycho-sexual development: Some viewpoints on Freud's drive theories. *Scandinavian Psychoanalytic Review, 18*(1), 22–40.

Schulman, M. (1974). Control of tics by maternal reinforcement. *Journal of Behavior Therapy and Experimental Psychiatry, 5*, 95–96.

Sears, R.R., & Wise, G.W. (1950). Relation of cup feeding to thumbsucking and the oral drive. *American Journal of Orthopsychiatry, 20*, 123–128.

Shapiro, A.K., & Shapiro, E. (1982). An update on Tourette syndrome. *American Journal of Psychotherapy, 36*(3), 379–390.

Shapiro, A.K., & Shapiro, E. (1992). Evaluation of the reported association of obsessive-compulsive symptoms of disorder with Tourette's disorder. *Comprehensive Psychiatry, 33*(3), 152–165.

Shapiro, A.K., & Shapiro, E. (1996). Treatment of tic disorders with neuroleptic drugs. In M.A. Richardson & G. Haugland (Eds.), *Use of neuroleptics in children: Clinical practice* (No. 37; pp. 137–170). Washington, DC: American Psychiatric Press.

Silber, A. (1981). A tic, a dream and the primal scene. *International Journal of Psychoanalysis, 62*(3), 259–269.

Singer, H.S., Schuerholz, L.J., & Denckla, M.B. (1995). Learning difficulties in children with Tourette syndrome. *Journal of Child Neurology, 10*, 58–61.

Singh, N.N. (1981). Current trends in the treatment of self-injurious behavior. *Advances in Pediatrics, 28*, 377–440.

Smith, M. (1957). Effectiveness of symptomatic treatment of nailbiting in college students. *Psychological Newsletter, 8*, 219–231.

Sperling, M., & Sperling, O.E. (1978). *Psychosomatic disorders in childhood.* New York: Jason Aronson.

Sprague, R.L. (1977). Psychopharmacotherapy in children. In M. McMillan (Ed.), *Child psychiatry: Treatment and research* (pp. 130–149). New York: Brunner/Mazel.

Sprague, R.L., & Newell, K.M. (Eds.). (1996). *Stereotyped movements.* Washington, DC: American Psychological Association.

Stern, L.S. (1983). The modern psychoanalytic treatment of a case of Gilles de la Tourette's Syndrome. *Modern Psychoanalysis, 8*(1), 93–101.

Strauss, C.C., Rubinoff, A., & Atkeson, B.N. (1983). Elimination of nocturnal headbanging in a normal seven-year-old girl using overcorrection plus rewards.

Journal of Behavior Therapy and Experimental Psychiatry, 14(3), 269–273.

Surwillo, W.W., Shafii, M., & Barrett, C.L. (1978). Gilles de la Tourette syndrome: A 20-month study of the effects of stressful life events and haloperidol on symptom frequency. *Journal of Nervous and Mental Disease, 166*, 812–816.

Swedo, S.E., & Leonard, H.H. (1994). Childhood movement disorders and obsessive compulsive disorder. *Journal of Clinical Psychiatry, 55*(Suppl. 3), 32–37.

Tate, B.G., & Baroff, G.S. (1966). Aversive control of self-injurious behavior in a psychotic boy. *Behavior Research and Therapy, 4*, 281–287.

Teichman, Y.E., & Eliahu, D. (1986). A combination of structural family therapy and behavior techniques in treating a patient with two tics. *Journal of Clinical Child Psychology, 15*(4), 311–316.

Thelen, E. (1981). Kicking, rocking and waving: Contextual analysis of rhythmical stereotypies in normal human infants. *Animal Behavior, 29*(1), 3–11.

Towbin, K.E., & Cohen, D.J. (1996). Tic disorders. In J.M. Wiener (Ed.), *Diagnosis and psychopharmacology of childhood and adolescent disorders* (2nd ed., pp. 349–374). New York: Wiley.

Traisman, A.S., & Traisman, H.S. (1958). Thumb and finger sucking: A study of 2,650 infants and children. *Journal of Pediatrics, 52*, 566–572.

Troung, D.D., Bressman, S., Shale, H., & Fahn, S. (1988). Clonazepam, haloperidol, and clonidine in tic disorders. *Southern Medical Journal, 81*(9), 1103–1105.

Uchiyama, K. (1976). Effects of reciprocal inhibition through autogenic training relaxation on psychogenic tics. *Bulletin of Clinical and Consulting Psychology, 15*, 1–10.

van Norman, R.A. (1985). Digit sucking: It's time for an attitude adjustment or a rationale for the early elimination of digit-sucking habits through positive behavior modification. *International Journal of Orofacial Myology, 11*(2), 14–21.

Walsh, J.P. (1965). The psychogenesis of bruxism. *Journal of Periodontology, 36*, 417–420.

Warme, G. (1977). Childhood developmental problems. In P.D. Steinhauer & Q. Rae-Grant (Eds.), *Psychological problems of the child and his family* (pp. 100–125). Toronto, Canada: Macmillan.

Wehbe, M.A. (1982). An orthopaedic solution to thumbsucking. *Journal of the Iowa Medical Society, 72*(10), 412–413.

Werry, J.S., Carlielle, J., & Fitzpatrick, J. (1983). Rhythmic motor activities (stereotypies) in children under five: Etiology and prevalence. *Journal of the American Academy of Child Psychiatry, 22*(4), 329–336.

Westling, L. (1988). Fingernail biting: A literature review and case reports. *Journal of Cranio-Mandibular Process, 6*(2), 182–187.

Whitewood, G. (1997). Hypnotic intervention in the breaking of a thumb sucking habit. *Australian Journal of Clinical Hypnotherapy and Hypnosis, 18*(1), 1–4.

Willmot, D.R. (1984). Thumb sucking habit and associated dental differences in one of monozygous twins. *British Journal of Orthodontics, 11*(4), 195–199.

Wolfenstein, M. (1972). Trends in infant care. In S. Harrison (Ed.), *Childhood psychopathology* (pp. 176–188). New York: International Universities Press.

Woods, D.W., & Miltenberger, R.G. (1995). Habit reversal: A review of applications. *Journal of Behavior Therapy and Experimental Psychiatry, 26*(2), 123–131.

Woody, R.C., & Laney, M. (1986). Tics and Tourette's syndrome: A review. *Journal of Arkansas Medical Society, 83*(1), 53–55.

World Health Organization. (1992). *The ICD-10 classification of mental and behavioural disorders: Clinical descriptions and diagnostic guidelines.* Geneva, Switzerland: Author.

Wright, L., Schaefer, A.B., & Solomons, G. (1979). *Encyclopedia of pediatric psychology.* Baltimore: University Park Press.

Yoder, J. (1983). A child, paradoxical intention, and consciousness. *International Forum for Logotherapy, 6*(1), 19–21.

Zahner, G.E.P., Clubb, M.M., Leckman, J.F., & Pauls, D.L. (1988). The epidemiology of Tourette's syndrome. In D.J. Cohen, R.D. Brunn, & J.F. Leckman (Eds.), *Tourette's syndrome and tic disorders: Clinical understanding and treatment* (pp. 79–87). New York: Wiley.

Zikis, P. (1983). Treatment of an 11-year-old obsessive-compulsive ritualizer and tiqueur girl with in vivo exposure and response prevention. *Behavioural Psychotherapy, 11*(1), 75–81.

CHAPTER 18

Psychosomatic Problems in Children

THOMAS J. KENNY AND JENNIFER WILLOUGHBY

The past two decades have seen a significant change in the relationship between psychology and medicine. The psychologist's role is expanding beyond that of a mental health subspecialist who relates primarily to the psychiatrist. Increasingly, psychology has become involved in primary health care through the emerging subspecialties of pediatric and health psychology. The involvement in health care has been stimulated by changing conceptualizations of illness and by the positive role psychology has played in the treatment of psychosomatic disorders. In this chapter, the term *psychosomatic disorder* is used in a broad sense to include any problem that has both physical and psychological components. The traditional concept of a mind-body separation in conceptualizing psychosomatic disorders has been discarded, replaced by a model that takes into account the combined effects of biological, psychological, and social influences on childhood illness. The aims of this chapter are (1) to examine relevant historical and theoretical concepts leading to the current conceptualization of psychosomatic illness; (2) to describe a biopsychosocial model of psychosomatic disorders, including consideration of developmental level; and (3) to discuss issues relevant to the assessment and treatment of psychosomatic disorders in children.

We wish to acknowledge the contribution of Edward Arndt and Valarie Kager to the earlier version of this chapter.

HISTORY AND CONCEPTUALIZATION

Examination of the history of psychosomatic disorders reveals a trend from conceptualizing these conditions as resulting from a singular cause, either physical or psychological, to a more integrated and multifactorial approach that considers multiple levels and paths of causality and illness maintenance. Historically, psychoanalytic theory dominated thinking regarding psychosomatic disorders. Freud was the first to use the term *conversion* in reference to the substitution of a somatic symptom for a repressed idea (Jones, 1953). Treatment involved the production of a catharsis in the patient, which allowed repressed ideas to become conscious, thereby alleviating the somatic symptoms. Freud's success in treating such conversion disorders produced several results. First, it thrust Freud to the forefront of the emerging field of psychiatry, but in an associative manner, it also set the theory of psychosomatic illness in a position where the illness was a manifestation of the mind. This tenet was so strong that it suggested that the body had little or no part in the illness, resulting in the treatment of affected patients as mentally and not physically ill.

The psychoanalytic conceptualization of psychosomatic disorders led to a limited treatment approach, characterized by a mind-body dualism, whereby physical illness had to be excluded before a psychosomatic illness could be considered. If no physical basis was found, it was presumed that a specific, unresolved conflict accounted for the illness and the physical symptoms were disregarded. Thus, the psychoanalytic approach generally ignored proximal causation, including psychosocial factors, and failed to account for such contributory factors as genetic, immunologic, infectious, and traumatic variables in the pathogenesis of disease (Leight & Reiser, 1977). The consistent lack of empirical validation of the psychoanalytic approach was also troublesome (Lipowski, 1988).

The first major change in the theory of conversion and psychosomatic disorders came about through the postulation of a relation between psychological and physical symptoms (Alexander, 1950; Selye, 1956). Alexander's specific conflict theory linked unresolved, unconscious conflicts with specific somatic disorders. However, the physical symptom was still viewed as being symbolic of the underlying conflict. In the mid-1950s, Selye focused even more attention on the physical symptom with the specific vulnerability theory. Stress and psychological conflicts were presumed to lead to autonomic arousal of a particularly vulnerable target organ through physiological mechanisms. Such psychological conflicts were proposed to serve a major role in the etiology and development of such disorders as rheumatoid arthritis, bronchial asthma, essential hypertension, and peptic ulcer. However, Selye failed to consider the role of cognitive/affective variables in the initiation of the stress response. This early work on the influence of stress on illness led to a significant amount of research on the stress-illness relationship in adults and, recently, more in children and adolescents (e.g., Compas, 1987a, 1987b; Compas & Harding, 1998; Compas, Worsham, & Ey, 1992; Walker, Garber, & Greene, 1993).

AN INTEGRATIVE MODEL OF CHILDHOOD PSYCHOSOMATIC DISORDERS

As is evident from the preceding discussion, psychosomatic disorders were once believed to have a unified etiology. This view has been progressively replaced by a more comprehensive conceptualization, and contemporary theory includes the consideration of the complex interaction of factors that may contribute to psychosomatic disorders. The biopsychosocial model (Engel, 1977; Everly, 1986; Fabrega & Van Egeren, 1976) provides a useful framework for considering the etiology, assessment, and treatment of these disorders. The biopsychosocial conceptualization, as applied to psychosomatic disorders, maintains that the interaction of psychological, social, and biological factors may produce psychosomatic symptoms. In contrast to earlier theories, this approach stresses that although individuals may display similar symptoms, the factors that contribute to these symptoms differ across people. Fabrega and Van Egeren also emphasize the systemic nature of the biopsychosocial model, referring to the reciprocal causality both across and within levels of the model. Sameroff (1975) proposed that development problems be viewed as on a continuum that reacts to the effects of illness, environment, and society. Aylward (this volume) describes these issues in his examination of the factors involved in the outcome of high-risk infants and proposes the concept of "risk routes" that are able to exert both negative and positive change on outcome. Accordingly, developmental and social psychological researchers, in particular, have begun to move from linear causal explanations to examination of the reciprocal relationships of people and their environments (e.g., Bandura, 1977; Fagot, 1977; Sameroff, 1975). In the following pages, each component of the biopsychosocial model will be discussed as it applies to the etiology and maintenance of psychosomatic disorders in children. For the sake of clarity, each area—psychological, social, and biological—will be reviewed separately.

PSYCHOLOGICAL FACTORS

Developmental considerations have been largely ignored in the explanation of psychosomatic disorders in children. However, developmental level is perhaps the most important factor to consider, because it influences and is influenced by every other aspect of the child's life, including social interactions, biological processes, and other intraindividual factors. The lack of attention to developmental factors in psychosomatic disorders has resulted, in part, from a more general tendency to examine children's psychological disorders under adult models. The following discussion highlights relevant developmental research, including studies of the child's understanding of illness and its treatment, adherence to the treatment regimen, and the development of natural capacities to cope with stress. Developmental changes in children's conceptions of illness have received a great deal of research attention in the general childhood illness literature, but they have not yet been extended to the understanding of disorders in children with medical and psychological components. However, research findings suggest that children's ideas about illness may add to the understanding of the development, maintenance, and treatment of psychosomatic disorders. For example, developmental changes in children's beliefs about how illnesses are transmitted may provide clues regarding the manifestation of psychosomatic symptoms. Further, because many of these children are referred for adverse treatment reactions, knowledge of children's misconceptions about treatment could support particular psychological interventions and be used to aid families in explaining particular aspects of treatment to their children.

Children's conceptions of illness have been shown to have a developmental progression corresponding generally to cognitive development, as measured by Piagetian tasks (see Varni, 1983, for review). Young children's understanding of illness causality is influenced by magical qualities or observable events that are temporally or spatially related to the illness (Bibace & Walsh, 1980). At this age, clinical observations suggest that many children believe that the illness itself and resulting treatment are punishment for some misdeed (Brewster, 1982; Peters, 1978; Varni, 1983). However, research does not support this contention (e.g., Ross & Ross, 1984). Rather, it appears that younger children simply do not understand the link between the treatment and the illness, which results in distortions and misattributions (Willis, Elliott, & Jay, 1982), leading to increased fear and anxiety surrounding treatment. During the elementary school years, children's illness conceptions tend to be concrete, based on rotely learned facts (e.g., germs cause illness) but lacking in more abstract causal understanding (Bibace & Walsh, 1980). Further, as children get older, health rules gain importance as children realize their own role in preventing illness (La Greca & Schuman, 1995). Pain tolerance also increases with age. Jay, Ozokins, Elliott, and Caldwell (1983), in an observational study of children's distress during painful medical procedures, found that children less than 7 years of age displayed distress rating 5 to 10 times higher than those older than 7

years. In adolescence, the emergence of more logical, conceptual thought leads to an understanding of the physiological mechanisms that cause illness and the biological mechanisms by which illness is treated (Bibace & Walsh, 1980). More developmentally advanced children also have an understanding of the role of psychological factors in illness causation and the exacerbation of existing illness. In adolescence, despite the decrease in reactivity to pain, there is an increase in attention to bodily sensations, precipitated by pubertal changes (Barsky, 1979).

The developmental progression of children's adherence to treatment has received insufficient research attention (La Greca & Schuman, 1995; Thompson, Dahlquist, Koening, & Bartholomew, 1995). However, the child's level of development has implications for adherence behavior. La Greca and Schuman suggest that adherence behavior must be understood in the context of the child's social-emotional development, which determines the type and extent of adherence problems that may arise. Younger children, who are dependent on parents for implementing treatment regimens, may present with adherence problems because of parental inadequacies or behavioral difficulties that make care difficult. Adolescents, on the other hand, are sensitive to peer evaluation and may find that their treatment regimen makes them different from peers, resulting in neglect of treatment such as self-management in diabetes. Holmes (1986) also suggests that certain chronic disorders may foster dependency on parents, which may lead to adherence difficulties when adolescents move toward independence. In this context, mismanagement may be seen as the child's attempt to maintain dependence.

The child's developmental level also influences important individual factors that may promote or deter the development, progression, and treatment of psychosomatic disorders. One such characteristic, which has received increasing research attention, is the child's coping skills. The understanding of developmental changes in coping is important for several reasons. First, when evaluating a particular child's natural responses to stress, it is useful to know how he or she compares to other children of the same age. Further, with regard to treatment, knowledge of the natural development of coping may suggest appropriate and inappropriate means of treatment. Finally, the evaluation of responses to stress may be important for an individual child, as the particular means of coping may be part of the psychosomatic symptomatology (Lipowski, 1988). In fact, coping and individual personality styles may partially explain the preliminary evidence of a developmental continuum in psychosomatic disorders. Researchers have found in retrospective studies that adulthood somatization disorder is many times preceded by recurrent abdominal pain in childhood (Coryell & Norton, 1981). Empirical study of this area is in its infancy, but developmental researchers are beginning to systemically address children's coping (Band & Weisz, 1988; Compas et al., 1992; Drotar, Angle, Eckl, & Thompson, 1996; Rossman, 1990).

SOCIAL FACTORS

The three most well-researched areas pertaining to social influences on psychosomatic disorders in children are studies of the relationship between stress and illness, research on family processes, and family patterns of psychosomatic disorders. In this chapter, psychosomatic disorders are viewed as those disorders with both a physiological and psychological component. Therefore, two areas of the childhood stress literature are applicable: the relationship between stress and physiological symptoms and the impact of disease-related stress on psychological adjustment. Several authors have reported a link between stress and illness onset. Jacobs and Charles (1980) assessed this relationship retrospectively with children diagnosed with cancer. They found that previous life changes, as reported by the parents, were significantly greater for the cancer patients than for a control group, indicating that stress may play some role in the onset of this illness. Boyce et al. (1976) also found a relationship between parent-reported stress and both severity ($r = .18$) and duration ($r = .40$) of upper respiratory infections in children. Gad and Johnson (1980) used a self-report scale of stress to assess the relationship between stress and health status in adolescents. The results suggested a positive relationship between self-reported stress and recurrent abdominal and chest pain in adolescents. Hodges, Kline, Barbero, and Flanery (1984) obtained similar results with children's stress and recurrent abdominal pain using parent report.

Investigations of the relationship between illness-related stress and psychological adjustment are pertinent, as children with chronic physical conditions are frequently referred for emotional difficulties related to their illness. Research in this area has taken two general approaches: the examination of the relationship between illness variables (e.g., severity) and psychological symptoms and the comparison of ill and healthy children on measures of psychological well-being. Research on the relationship between illness severity and psychological adjustment has produced varying results. McAnarney, Pless, Satterwhite, and Friedman (1974) found an inverse relationship between functional disability and adjustment in children with juvenile rheumatoid arthritis, whereas Ivey, Brewer, and Giannini (1981) found no such relationship in the juvenile arthritis group they studied.

Investigations of the chronic illness-adjustment relationship have also produced inconsistent results. In a frequently cited study, Pless and Roghmann (1971) presented data based on three epidemiological surveys. These authors reported that compared with healthy children, those with chronic physical disorders exhibited more behavioral and psychological problems, including higher rates of truancy, school problems, and social isolation. Some later studies have also found that children with chronic conditions have a higher incidence of psychological problems. For example, Hurtig and White (1986) assessed the adjustment of children and adolescents with sickle cell disease. The authors found that these children, especially adolescent males, displayed more behavioral and social adjustment problems when compared with normative data. On the other hand, several authors have found that the psychological well-being of children with chronic conditions is no different from that of healthy children. Tavormina, Kastner, Slater, and Watt (1976) administered several standardized measures to a sample of 144 children with one of the following conditions: diabetes, asthma, cystic fibrosis, or a hearing impairment. In general, these children showed little deviance from the norms on measures of pathology. The only exception was children in the hearing-impaired group who showed problems in several areas. Other studies have reported positive adaptation of children with cancer, cardiologic disorders, diabetes, cystic fibrosis, nephrotic conditions, and rheumatological disorders (Zeltzer, Kellerman, Ellenberg, Dash, & Rigler, 1980); diabetic children (Jacobson et al., 1986); children with hypopituitarism (Drotar, Owens, & Gotthold, 1980); and those with sickle cell anemia (Lemanek, Moore, Gresham, Williamson, & Kelley, 1986).

The marginal relationships found between stress and illness in children and the inconsistent findings in the childhood chronic illness literature stem from several problems, including research design and the use of different measures across studies. In addition, the study of stress in children was prompted by significant findings in the relationship between stress and illness in adults. Research, therefore, has been geared toward the downward extension of adult theory to children. This has resulted in the development of inappropriate or inadequate assessment devices, the lack of a developmental perspective, and, to some extent, emphasis on major stressful events (which are the focus of adult literature) to the exclusion of chronic stressors and daily hassles (which may be more relevant for children) (Compas, 1987a, 1987b; Compas et al., 1992). The unidirectional nature of stress studies also has impeded the understanding of the relationship between stress and illness. Most studies assume that stress *causes* illness, but the few prospective studies that have investigated the relationship between stress and psychological adjustment suggest that, in children and adolescents, psychological symptoms precede rather than follow stressful events. This highlights the importance of a developmental perspective, as well as the need to use more complex research designs and statistical analyses in examining these relationships. The unclear relationships found between stress and illness also emphasize the need to examine factors that may mediate or moderate this relationship. Accordingly, Compas, Malcarne, and Fondacaro (1988) advocate the use of a "transactional developmental model," which concurrently considers the child's individual characteristics, stress and coping processes, and the reciprocal influences of the child and his or her social system.

Several studies have identified an increased incidence of psychosomatic and other psychological disorders in family members of children diagnosed with psychosomatic disorders. Early studies of adult hysteria linked this disorder with alcoholism, sociopathy, and depression in family members (e.g., Ljundberg, 1957; Minuchin, 1974; Slater, 1961). Case studies (e.g., Kriechman, 1987; Orr, 1986) have indicated that psychopathology is common in families of children with psychosomatic disorders. Well-designed, controlled studies have supported family

patterns in certain psychosomatic disorders. Routh and Ernst (1984) examined familial incidence of somatization disorder, alcoholism, personality disorder, and hysteria in families of children with functional abdominal pain, in comparison with a control group of children with organic abdominal pain. Semistructured diagnostic interviews were used to arrive at diagnoses, and interviewers were blind to the child's diagnosis. The results showed that the children with functional abdominal pain had a significantly greater number of relatives with somatization disorder; half (10) of the study children had one or more relatives with this disorder, compared with only one of the children with organic pain. Children with functional pain also had significantly more relatives diagnosed with attention-deficit disorder, alcoholism, and antisocial or conduct disorder, compared with the children with organic disease. Further, the two groups differed significantly on the Somatization scale of the Child Behavior Checklist (Achenbach, 1978; Achenbach & Edelbrock, 1979). Another study (Hodges et al., 1984) investigated whether depressive symptoms are more common in children with recurrent abdominal pain and/or their parents. Two comparison groups were used: healthy children and those referred to an outpatient psychiatric clinic. The study children did not differ from the healthy children either on a measure of self-reported depression or in level of depression on a structured diagnostic interview.

Family interaction patterns have also been implicated in the development of psychosomatic disorders. Minuchin et al. (1975) developed a conceptually based model to explain the interaction of family influences and psychosomatic disorders in children. In this model, patterns of family functioning are believed to influence the development and maintenance of psychosomatic symptoms, and these symptoms are assumed to contribute to the homeostasis of the family. Three factors are considered necessary for the development of severe psychosomatic disorders: specific organ vulnerability, family dysfunction, and the centralization of the sick child to avoid family conflict, which, in turn, reinforces the sick role. Studies examining the relationship between family factors and psychosomatic symptoms have supported this theory. Minuchin, Rosman, and Baker (1978) compared three groups of families during a series of stress interviews: those with a child with diabetes-related psychosomatic symptoms, those with a behaviorally disordered child, and those with a nonreferred child. The results indicated that the diabetic children were much more likely to be used as a detour in parental conflicts. Negative physiological changes were documented in the child as a result of parental conflict, as well as when the child was used by family members to decrease parental stress. This seems to support the concept of enmeshment described by Minuchin (1974) and suggests family therapy as a treatment.

BIOLOGICAL FACTORS

The interface of biological and psychological factors is most clearly demonstrated in two areas: studies of physiological responses to stress and research on diabetes heritability. Current conceptualizations of responses to stress point to three major physiological pathways: the autonomic nervous system, the neuroendocrine system, and the endocrine system (Everly & Rosenfeld, 1981). The neural response, which is the initial physiological response to stress, consists of the activation of the sympathetic and parasympathetic nervous systems. The neuroendocrine system sustains this initial response through release of the hormones epinephrine and norepinephrine, which have effects such as increased heart rate and muscle tension and decreased blood flow to the kidneys and gastrointestinal system. Finally, if stress is prolonged, the body stimulates the endocrine system to release various hormones, some of which may suppress immune function, increase cholesterol, and increase serum glucose levels (Everly & Rosenfeld, 1981; Zegans, 1982). Also of importance is the individual's reactivity to stressful stimuli, although such reactivity is not well understood. Recent theorists have begun to examine individuals' interpretations of stressful events, coping strategies, and the mediating impact of these cognitive functions. Zegans states, "It is the way in which the organism handles perceived stressors—the defenses it mobilizes and the alarm reactions ignited—that constitutes the true nature of stress" (p. 140). In addition to cognitive processes, research has pointed to personality styles, such as the Type A pattern, that predispose individuals to more intense physiological responses to stress. These physiological responses to stress have particular implications for psychosomatic disorders. There is evidence that certain childhood physical disorders

and conditions are induced or exacerbated by stress. These include asthma (Milkich, Rewey, Weiss, & Kolton, 1973), diabetes (Chase & Jackson, 1981; Stabler, Morris, Litton, Feinglos, & Surwit, 1986), and pain (Holm, Holroyd, Hursey, & Penzien, 1986). Stress may also be related to physiological changes (e.g., immunosuppression) that can have serious health implications for those with certain disorders (e.g., cancer, HIV infection).

There is a body of research implicating genetic factors in the development of some psychosomatic disorders (see Farber, 1982, for review). Preliminary evidence exists for genetic predisposition to migraine headaches (e.g., Farber, 1981; Holden, 1980; McKusick, 1978), ulcerative colitis (e.g., Roberts & Pembry, 1978), and asthma (Farber, 1981). However, many of the studies in this area suffer from poor methodology or the reliance on inadequately controlled twin research or case studies. Therefore, more biological research is needed to determine the exact nature of the genetic transmission, as well as the interaction of genetic and environmental factors.

ASSESSMENT AND TREATMENT OF PSYCHOSOMATIC DISORDERS

The central tenet of this chapter is that psychosomatic difficulties represent a multitude of disorders, with each instance representing a unique constellation of causal and maintaining factors. This conceptualization has several implications for assessment and treatment. The individuality of manifestations and causes requires clinicians to consider the particular characteristics of each presenting problem by carefully assessing the individual, interpersonal, and biological contributors. The interface of physiological and psychological causes make it likely that treatment will be multimodal and will include both medical and psychological components. A common problem in the assessment and treatment of psychosomatic difficulties results from the residual effects of the mind-body distinction. Specifically, children are usually referred for evaluation of emotional and behavioral difficulties only after receiving multiple medical work-ups. For some disorders, consultations with several different specialists are common. The energy, cost, and time expended on hospitalizations and tests leave all parties feeling frustrated, and when a referral to a mental health professional is finally made, neither the patient, the family, nor the physician is in a constructive state of mind. This is commonly complicated by the lack of adequate preparation of the family for such a referral. This exclusionary model has been increasingly replaced as physicians and specialists realize that combined approaches are more successful in the treatment of psychosomatic disorders. This has resulted in the integration of psychologists into subspecialty medical treatment teams. The introduction of behavioral/mental health specialists in this way normalizes psychological evaluation and treatment and reduces the resistance often encountered when consultations are requested. This union has proven especially fruitful in specialties that commonly encounter psychosomatic difficulties, such as neurology, adolescent medicine, hematology-oncology, and endocrinology.

Assessment of Psychosomatic Problems

The *Diagnostic and Statistical Manual, 4th Edition* (*DSM-IV*, American Psychiatric Association [APA], 1994) appears to sustain the problems associated with the early concepts of psychosomatic illness. It continues to imply a mind-body dichotomy and it uses adult concepts of psychosomatic illness with children. The *DSM-IV* divides psychosomatic illness into three different types of disorders: somatoform disorders, factitous disorders, and psychological factors affecting medical conditions. The *DSM-IV* diagnostic criteria for these disorders were established for adults and, as is often the case, were applied to children despite a lack of research on these disorders in children (Fritz, Fritsch, & Hagino, 1997). A description of each of the *DSM-IV* categories ensues, including discussion of how each category applies to children and adolescents.

Somatoform disorders include disorders that present as physical symptoms indicative of a general medical condition that cannot be fully explained by a general medical condition, the overt effects of a substance, or another mental disorder. There are five specific somatoform disorders described in *DSM-IV*, and of the five only one, conversion disorder, is usual in children; the other four (somatization disorder, pain disorder, hypochondriasis, and body dysmorphic disorder) are rarely seen in children.

Another category of *DSM-IV* disorders that may present as a medical disorder is factitious disorders. These disorders refer to the presentation of symptoms that are intentionally feigned to assume a sick role. They are divided into three types: those with predominantly psychological symptoms, those with predominantly physical symptoms, and those with combined psychological and physical symptoms. A related disorder more specific to children presented in the *DSM-IV* as a category for further study is factitious disorder by proxy, or Munchausen by proxy. This disorder refers to the deliberate production or feigning of symptoms in another person who is under the individual's care in order to receive attention from medical providers. Typically, the victim is a young child, and the perpetrator is the child's mother. Although this diagnosis applies to the individual producing the symptoms, the diagnosis is often made in the pediatric setting when a child repeatedly presents with symptoms that do not fit a typical clinical course. This syndrome can be very dangerous to the child, but is extremely difficult to diagnose (Bryk & Siegel, 1997).

A final *DSM-IV* category of psychosomatic illness, as conceptualized in this chapter, includes psychological factors affecting medical conditions. This category includes a wide array of psychological and behavioral factors that adversely affect a general medical condition. These factors may include a mental disorder, psychological symptoms, personality traits or coping style, maladaptive health behaviors (such as smoking), and stress-related physiological responses. This category applies to adults and children alike and addresses the importance of considering the contribution of psychological and social influences to physical illness.

Within the biopsychosocial framework, the interaction of developmental, personality, familial, social, and biological factors produce, and are affected by, the presenting psychosomatic problems. In this vein, the evaluation process must take place at several levels. Assessment should not merely be seen as a starting point from which treatment begins, but as an ongoing process that allows frequent monitoring and the ability to evaluate change. Whether the clinician is working with a child with a recurrent pain syndrome or a chronic illness, an assessment of cognitive and personality functioning is essential for developing a treatment plan. Knowledge of intellectual level as a gross indicator of developmental functioning can help to focus the treatment, assess the child's understanding of his or her disorder, and detect learning difficulties that may contribute to the symptoms. The child's responsibilities with regard to a treatment regimen also need to be consistent with his or her developmental understanding and skills. The assessment of personality factors is also important, as particular traits may predispose children and adolescents to psychosomatic symptoms. When assessing children with recurrent pain syndromes, such as pediatric headaches, recurrent abdominal pain (RAP), or arthritis, emotional factors may initiate or exacerbate the child's pain (McGrath, 1987). Psychological testing can provide descriptive information about the child's self-image, locus of control, and personality characteristics. Such information can also provide keys to understanding the child's characteristic ways of coping with stress that may precipitate or exacerbate the psychosomatic symptoms. Compas (1987a) points out that children and adolescents may differ in the personal and social resources they have available for managing or overcoming stress, and they may differ in the ways they try to deal with stress. The child's resources for coping and coping behaviors are valuable in distinguishing the child who can effectively handle stressors from the child who may be less successful.

Evaluation of the child's current adaptation is also important. Children may respond quite differently to treatment despite having similar illnesses or pain complaints. Therefore, an assessment of current behavioral and emotional adjustment is useful to determine how the particular disorder is affecting day-to-day functioning. Certain objective measures may be useful in assessing psychosomatic symptoms in children and adolescents. The Somatic Complaints subscale of the Child Behavior Checklist has been found to distinguish between children with functional abdominal pain and those whose pain has a physiological basis (Routh & Ernst, 1984). Conversely, the usefulness of the Somatoform scale of the Personality Inventory for Children in differentiating between children with psychologically and those with physically based disorders has been questioned (Pritchard, Ball, Culbert, & Faust, 1988) because it failed to distinguish between children with neurological conditions and those diagnosed with somatoform disorder. In addition to more general measures of child functioning, several specialized assessment instruments exist that may be helpful in evaluating children with psychosomatic

difficulties. Many measures of children's pain now include consideration of emotional and situational variables (e.g., Children's Comprehensive Pain Questionnaire; McGrath, 1987; Varni/Thompson Pediatric Pain Questionnaire; Varni, Thompson, & Hanson, 1987) that may aid in determining the focus of treatment. In addition, research on children and adolescents with eating disorders has led to the development of scales designed to assess particular aspects of these psychosomatic difficulties (e.g., Eating Disorders Inventory; Garner, Olmsted, & Polivy, 1983; Diagnostic Schedule for Eating Disorders; C. Johnson, 1984). In the pediatric psychology literature, numerous scales have been developed that focus on how children and families adapt to particular aspects of chronic physical conditions (e.g., Coping Health Inventory for Parents; McCubbin et al., 1983; Kidcope; Spirito, Stark, & Williams, 1988; Parent Diabetes Opinion Survey; S.B. Johnson, Silverstein, Cunningham, & Carter, 1985). Researchers have also developed scales assessing illness-specific adjustment (e.g., Diabetes Adjustment Scale; Sullivan, 1979).

Evaluation of parental and sibling responses to the child's illness may provide relevant information for the selection of appropriate treatment by revealing family behavior patterns that may prolong symptoms. McGrath (1987) points out that parents often become protective and overly solicitous toward a child with a recurrent pain complaint, with the consequence that the child's household responsibilities are minimized and special attention is provided to alleviate pain and suffering. Pain behavior is thus reinforced through the child's receiving additional emotional support combined with lowered parental demands and expectations (Mansdorf, 1981). Parental perceptions of the implications of their child's illness may also influence how the parents respond to their child (Dahlquist, Power, & Carlson, 1995, Drotar, 1997a; Silver, Westbrook, & Stein, 1998). For example, Bergman and Stamm (1967) found that the parents' perception of implications of their child's heart murmur greatly influenced what they allowed their child to do.

There is some evidence to suggest that particular psychosomatic symptoms may serve a specific function in the family (Minuchin et al., 1978). It is important, therefore, to gain an understanding of how family dynamics may relate to the etiology and maintenance of symptoms. In the Minuchin et al. study, families with children with intractable asthma or juvenile-onset diabetes showed characteristics of enmeshment, overprotectiveness, rigidity, lack of conflict resolution, and the use of the child's symptoms as a conflict-deterring mechanism. Within the framework proposed by Minuchin et al., assessment consists of identifying patterns in the family and extrafamily environment that tend to exacerbate and maintain the symptoms.

The role of the health care system in contributing to the adaptation of the chronically ill or pain-disordered child and the family has only been partially explored (Anderson & Auslander, 1980; Coyne & Anderson, 1988). Coyne and Anderson point out that the treatment of juvenile diabetes is characterized by an almost immediate transfer of responsibility from health care professionals to the family. Treatment often complicates normal tasks of family living, requiring major readjustments by the entire family. In the midst of these major changes, families may feel unsupported by health care professionals. Therefore, understanding the family's relationship with and attitude toward the health care system is essential in addressing the needs of the child with a chronic illness or pain disorder (Drotar, 1997a, 1997b; S.B. Johnson, 1994).

TREATMENT APPROACHES

Because of the reliance on psychodynamic conceptualizations of psychosomatic difficulties, treatment has been dominated by individual insight-oriented approaches, focused on uncovering the psychic conflict leading to particular symptoms. However, proponents of psychodynamic approaches have been unable to demonstrate the theoretical or clinical efficacy of such approaches (see Weiner, 1977, for a review). With the emergence of the fields of behavioral medicine, health psychology, and pediatric psychology, and the treatment success of these disciplines in applied settings, traditional approaches have been increasingly replaced by more multifaceted, individualized methods. The underlying assumption, with regard to treatment, is that for each individual case, a different combination of individual and family treatment approaches may be indicated and, depending on the particular physical problems, may be combined with different degrees of medical treatment. The following treatment approaches have been found useful with a variety of childhood psychosomatic disorders.

For more extensive reviews of these approaches, please see other relevant chapters in this *Handbook*.

Behavioral approaches have been particularly useful in the treatment of psychosomatic symptoms in children. The rapid symptom relief afforded by these approaches is especially useful, because it serves to persuade the family that nonphysical factors may contribute to the child's disorder. Further, especially within a medical system, prompt symptom relief is valued. Several studies have reported the effectiveness of behavioral approaches with psychosomatic problems, including control of asthma attacks (Creer, Harm, & Marion, 1988), treatment adherence (Greenan-Fowler, Powell, & Varni, 1984), pediatric headaches (Holden, Deichmann, & Levy, 1999), food refusal (Linscheid, Tarnowski, Rasnake, & Brams, 1987), and other eating disorders (Epstein, Wing, Steranchak, Dickson, & Michelson, 1980). Relaxation training and hypnosis have been used increasingly in pediatric problems; they have been found especially useful in pain management (Varnie, 1981a, 1981b) and in decreasing distress during painful medical procedures (Kellerman, Zeltzer, Ellenberg, Dash, & Rigler, 1980; Zeltzer & LeBaron, 1982). Relaxation and hypnotic techniques have many similarities, including limited activity and sensory intake and restricted attention (Paul, 1969). The primary difference is the method that is used to produce these experiences. Relaxation techniques focus on the alleviation of muscular tension, whereas hypnotic approaches make use of mental imagery (Bernstein & Borkovec, 1973). In practice, these distinctions become blurred; most clinicians believe that relaxation is necessary for trance induction (Conners, 1983), and mental imagery is generally used as part of relaxation techniques. The study of these approaches in the pediatric cancer literature has been especially fruitful. Zeltzer and LeBaron (1982) tested the effectiveness of hypnosis and nonhypnotic distraction in 33 children (aged 6–17) undergoing bone marrow aspirations and spinal taps. Both self-report and observer ratings indicated the superiority of hypnotic techniques. Larsson, Melin, Lamminen, and Ullstedt (1987) also found self-help relaxation to be particularly useful in control of headaches in an adolescent sample.

Cognitive-behavioral techniques, which represent an array of different methods, have also gained popularity. These procedures have proved quite useful in preparing children for medical treatment (Peterson & Shigetomi, 1981), in decreasing treatment-related distress (Jay, Elliott, Katz, & Siegel, 1987), and in treating specific psychosomatic disorders such as bulimia (Fairburn, 1985). Jay et al. (1987) compared the use of a package of cognitive behavioral methods, the use of Valium, and an attention-control technique in alleviating distress of children during bone marrow aspiration. The results indicated that, during the procedure, the cognitive-behavioral package was most effective.

Individual play therapy may be used in conjunction with other approaches. Phillips (1988) reviewed the literature on the use of play therapy in health care settings. Four assumptions regarding the effectiveness of play therapy were evaluated: improves mastery, autonomy, and control; aids in cooperation and communication; helps children cope with anxiety and fear; and provides opportunity for education and information giving. The author concluded that the only promising findings are in the areas of anxiety reduction and information giving, suggesting that traditional play therapy may not provide children with the control and coping skills purported, at least in medical settings. However, one study (Rae, Worchel, Upchurch, Sanner, & Daniel, 1989) found play therapy to have positive effects on hospitalized children. In particular, children participating in a nondirective play therapy group reported significantly more reduction in hospital-related fears than those who received either verbal supportive therapy or nontherapeutic play or who were in a control group. Interestingly, children in the nondirective play therapy group showed an increase in somatic complaints compared with the other three groups. Clearly, more research is needed to determine the therapeutic components of play.

The use of family therapy with children who have psychosomatic disorders has been stimulated by the work of Minuchin and his colleagues. The results of studies on a range of clinical disorders has been very positive. Liebman, Minuchin, and Baker (1974), for example, used this group's systemic approach to treat a group of children with intractable asthma. They contend that intractable asthma represents a psychosomatic disorder in which the primary allergic disorder has been complicated by emotional factors, especially chronic, unresolved family conflicts. The stress precipitated by these conflicts is assumed to precipitate acute attacks and perpetuate the severity of the asthma. Weekly family therapy sessions focused on alleviating symptoms and identifying and changing the structure

and functioning of the family system. A low dropout rate and high success rates have been reported for this and other psychosomatic disorders (Hodas & Liebman, 1978; Liebman et al., 1974; Minuchin et al., 1978).

Another model for the treatment of psychosomatic disorders is consultation. The traditional method of consultation is direct patient contact through referral by a physician (Drotar, 1995; Hamlett & Stabler, 1995; Roberts & Wright, 1982; Stabler, 1988). The goal of the consult is generally limited, and usually takes the form of psychological evaluation, diagnostic assessment, or brief intervention. For example, a pediatrician may request psychological testing to determine the role of psychological factors in a child's headache. Although any consultation offers the opportunity for education of and collaboration with medical professionals, this particular type of consultation may be limiting, as minimal face-to-face interaction is required (Stabler, 1988). It may, however, facilitate entry into a particular medical subspecialty, allowing for further interaction. Another model of consultation, which offers more opportunity for innovation on the part of the psychologist, is the "shared caregiving" approach (Stabler, 1988), in which patients are seen jointly with physicians, with continual contact between the psychologist and the health care provider. Disorders such as anorexia nervosa would be optimally treated by such a collaboration. Consultation to programs is also becoming a role of the psychologist. In this case, the psychologist offers no direct service. Rather, physicians and other health care providers are educated regarding the detection of psychological and behavioral difficulties, and particular programmatic changes may be incorporated to aid in this detection. For example, a battery of screening instruments may be given to all children when they are diagnosed with migraine headaches to determine how psychological and behavioral variables might be contributing to their disorder.

In some instances, psychosomatic disorders may not be treatable on an outpatient basis. Reasons for this may include life-threatening symptoms, such as in severe anorexia or noncompliance in diabetes; symptoms that may lead to further medical complications, such as possible contractures in some conversion disorders; and family difficulties that will not allow improvement while the child remains in the home. Inpatient hospitalization is indicated in such problems to implement intensive intervention procedures. Many hospitals now offer comprehensive treatment programs for children with psychosomatic disorders that combine many of the approaches outlined in this chapter.

The increasing prevalence of managed care plans such as health maintenance organizations (HMOs) can have a significant impact on the treatment of psychosomatic disorders. Whereas managed care programs enlist panels of medical specialists to provide services to their patients, mental health services are often handled in a different manner. Mental health services are frequently made what is called a "carve out," in which an outside group of mental health providers contract to provide mental health services to the HMO's members. This practice re-creates an old criticism of mental health providers: detachment from the primary care provider, which leads to diminished communication and coordination. The biopsychosocial model presented in this chapter emphasizes the interaction of physical and psychological factors in psychosomatic disorders as well as the close coordination of care between physicians and mental health care providers. The potential separation of the care providers could also reduce referrals to appropriate psychological care for the patient. This could take place because of a more complicated referral system or because of an emphasis on cost containment. This would affect the quality of care and would also likely prove to be a false economy. Appropriate use of psychological services usually results in lowering the utilization of medical services, resulting in better care and lower costs.

REFERENCES

Achenbach, T.M. (1978). The Child Behavior Profile: I. Boys aged 6–11. *Journal of Consulting and Clinical Psychology, 46,* 478–488.

Achenbach, T.M., & Edelbrock, C.S. (1979). The Child Behavior Profile: II. Boys aged 12–16 and girls aged 6–11 and 12–16. *Journal of Consulting and Clinical Psychology, 47,* 223–233.

Alexander, F. (1950). *Psychosomatic medicine.* New York: Norton.

American Psychiatric Association. (1994). *Diagnostic and statistical manual of mental disorders* (4th ed.). Washington, DC: Author.

Anderson, B.J., & Auslander, W.A. (1980). Research on diabetes management and the family: A critique. *Diabetes Care, 2,* 696–702.

Aylward, G.P., & Kenny, T.J. (1979). Developmental follow-up: Inherent problems and a conceptual model. *Journal of Pediatric Psychology, 4,* 331–343.

Band, E.B., & Weisz, J.R. (1988). How to feel better when it feels bad: Children's perspectives on coping with everyday stress. *Developmental Psychology, 24,* 247–253.

Bandura, A. (1977). *Social learning theory.* Englewood Cliffs, NJ: Prentice-Hall.

Barsky, A.J. (1979). Patients who amplify bodily sensations. *Annals of Internal Medicine, 9,* 63–70.

Bergman, A.B., & Stamm, S.J. (1967). The morbidity of cardiac non-disease in school children. *New England Journal of Medicine, 276,* 1008–1116.

Bernstein, D.A., & Borkovec, T.D. (1973). *Progressive relaxation training for the helping professions.* Champaign, IL: Research Press.

Bibace, R., & Walsh, M.E. (1980). Development of children's concepts of illness. *Pediatrics, 66,* 912–917.

Boyce, T.W., Jensen, E.W., Cassell, J.C., Collier, A.M., Smith, A.H., & Rainey, C.T. (1976). Influence of life events and family routines on childhood respiratory tract illness. *Pediatrics, 60,* 608–615.

Brewster, A.B. (1982). Chronically ill hospitalized children's concepts of their illness. *Pediatrics, 69,* 355–362.

Bryk, M., & Siegel, P.T. (1997). My mother caused my illness: The story of a survivor of Munchausen by Proxy syndrome. *Pediatrics, 100,* 1–7.

Chase, H.P., & Jackson, G.G. (1981). Stress and sugar control in children with insulin-dependent diabetes mellitus. *Journal of Pediatrics, 98,* 1011–1013.

Compas, B.E. (1987a). Coping with stress during childhood and adolescence. *Psychological Bulletin, 101,* 393–403.

Compas, B.E. (1987b). Stress and life events during childhood and adolescence. *Clinical Psychology Review, 7,* 275–302.

Compas, B.E., & Harding, A. (1998). Competence across the lifespan: Lessons from coping with cancer. In D. Pushkar & W.M. Bukowski (Eds.), *Improving competence across the lifespan: Building interventions based on theory and research* (pp. 9–26). New York: Plenum Press.

Compas, B.E., Malcarne, V.L., & Fondacaro, K.M. (1988). Coping with stressful events in older children and young adolescents. *Journal of Consulting and Clinical Psychology, 56,* 405–411.

Compas, B.E., Worsham, N.L., & Ey, S. (1992). Conceptual and developmental issues in children's coping with stress. In A.M. La Greca, L.J. Siegel, J.L. Wallander, & C.E. Walker (Eds.), *Stress and coping in child health: Advances in pediatric psychology* (pp. 7–24). New York: Guilford Press.

Conners, C.K. (1983). *Psychological management of the asthmatic child.* New York: Elsevier.

Coryell, W., & Norton, S.G. (1981). Briquet's syndrome (somatization disorder) and primary depression: Comparison of backgrounds and outcome. *Comprehensive Psychiatry, 22,* 249–256.

Coyne, J.C., & Anderson, B.J. (1988). The psychosomatic family reconsidered: Diabetes in context. *Journal of Marital and Family Therapy, 14*(2), 113–123.

Creer, T.L., Harm, D.L., & Marion, R.J. (1988). Childhood asthma. In D.K. Routh (Ed.), *Handbook of pediatric psychology* (pp. 162–189). New York: Guilford Press.

Dahlquist, L.M., Power, T.G., & Carlson, L. (1995). Physician and parent behavior during invasive pediatric cancer procedures: Relationship to child behavioral distress. *Journal of Pediatric Psychology, 20,* 477–490.

Drotar, D. (1995). *Consulting with pediatricians: Psychological perspectives.* New York: Plenum Press.

Drotar, D. (1997a). Intervention research: Pushing back the frontiers of pediatric psychology. *Journal of Pediatric Psychology, 22,* 593–606.

Drotar, D. (1997b). Relating parent and family functioning to the psychological adjustment of children with chronic health conditions: What have we learned? What do we need to know? *Journal of Pediatric Psychology, 22,* 149–165.

Drotar, D., Angle, D.P., Eckl, C.L., & Thompson, P.A. (1996). Brief report: Impact of expressive personality style on the measurement of psychological distress in children and adolescents with chronic illness: An example from hemophilia. *Journal of Pediatric Psychology, 21,* 283–293.

Drotar, D., Owens, R., & Gotthold, J. (1980). Personality adjustment of children and adolescents with hypopituitarism. *Child Psychiatry and Human Development, 11,* 59–66.

Engel, G. (1977). The need for a new medical model: A challenge for biomedicine. *Science, 196,* 129–136.

Epstein, L.H., Wing, R.R., Steranchak, L., Dickson, B., & Michelson, J. (1980). Comparison of family-based behavior modifications and nutrition education for childhood obesity. *Journal of Pediatric Psychology, 5,* 25–36.

Everly, G. (1986). A biopsychosocial analysis of psychosomatic disease. In T. Milton & G.L. Klerman (Eds.), *Contemporary directions in psychopathology: Toward the DSM-IV* (pp. 535–551). New York: Guilford Press.

Everly, G., & Rosenfeld, R. (1981). *The nature and treatment of the stress response.* New York: Plenum Press.

Fabrega, H., & Van Egeren, L.A. (1976). A behavioral framework for the study of human disease. *Annals of Internal Medicine, 84,* 200–208.

Fagot, B.I. (1977). Consequences of moderate cross-gender behavior in preschool children. *Child Development, 48,* 902–907.

Fairburn, C.G. (1985). Cognitive-behavioral treatment for bulimia. In D.M. Garner and P.E. Garfinkel (Eds.), *Anorexia nervosa and bulimia* (pp. 160–192). New York: Guilford Press.

Farber, S.L. (1981). *Identical twins reared apart: A reanalysis.* New York: Basic Books.

Farber, S.L. (1982). Genetic diversity and differing reactions to stress. In L. Goldberger & S. Breznitz (Eds.), *The handbook of stress: Therapeutic and clinical aspects.* New York: Free Press.

Fritz, G.K., Fritsch, S.L., & Hagino, O. (1997). Somatoform disorders in children and adolescents: A review of the past 10 years. *Journal of the American Academy of Child and Adolescent Psychiatry, 36,* 1329–1338.

Gad, M.T., & Johnson, J.H. (1980). Correlates of adolescent life stress as related to race, sex, and levels of perceived social support. *Journal of Clinical Child Psychology, 9,* 13–16.

Garner, D.M., Olmstead, M.P., & Polivy, J. (1983). *Eating Disorders Inventory.* Odessa, FL: Psychological Assessment Resources.

Greenan-Fowler, E., Powell, C., & Varnie, J.W. (1984). Behavioral therapy of adherence to therapeutic exercise by children with hemophilia. *Archives of Physical Medicine and Rehabilitation, 68,* 846–849.

Hamlett, K.W., & Stabler, B. (1995). The developmental progress of pediatric psychology consultation. In M.C. Roberts (Ed.), *Handbook of pediatric psychology* (2nd ed., pp. 39–54). New York: Guilford Press.

Hodas, G.R., & Liebman, R. (1978). Psychosomatic disorders in children: Structural family therapy. *Psychosomatics, 19,* 709–719.

Hodges, K., Kline, J.J., Barbero, G., & Flanery, R. (1984). Life events occurring in families of children with recurrent abdominal pain. *Journal of Psychosomatic Research, 28,* 185–188.

Holden, C. (1980). Twins reunited. *Science, 7,* 55–59.

Holden, E.W., Deichmann, M.M., & Levy, J.D. (1999). Empirically supported treatments in pediatric psychology: Recurrent pediatric headache. *Journal of Pediatric Psychology, 24,* 91–109.

Holm, J.E., Holroyd, K.A., Hursey, K.G., & Penzien, M.S. (1986). The role of stress in recurrent tension headache. *Headache, 26,* 160–167.

Holmes, D.M. (1986). The person and diabetes in psychosocial context. *Diabetes Care, 9,* 194–206.

Hurtig, A.L., & White, L. (1986). Psychosocial adjustment in children and adolescents with sickle cell disease. *Journal of Pediatric Psychology, 11,* 411–427.

Ivey, J., Brewer, E.J., & Giannini, E.H. (1981). Psychosocial functioning in children with juvenile rheumatoid arthritis. *Arthritis and Rheumatism, 24,* S100.

Jacobs, T.J., & Charles, E. (1980). Life events and the occurrence of cancer in children. *Psychosomatic Medicine, 42,* 11–24.

Jacobson, A.M., Hauser, S.T., Wertlieb, D., Wolfsdorf, J.L., Orleans, J., & Vieyra, M. (1986). Psychological adjustment of children with recently diagnosed diabetes mellitus. *Diabetes Care, 9,* 323–329.

Jay, S.M., Elliott, C.H., Katz, E., & Siegel, S.E. (1987). Cognitive-behavioral and pharmacologic interventions for children's distress during painful medical procedures. *Journal of Consulting and Clinical Psychology, 55,* 860–865.

Jay, S.M., Ozokins, M., Elliott, C.H., & Caldwell, S. (1983). Assessment of children's distress during painful medical procedures. *Health Psychology, 2,* 133–148.

Johnson, C. (1984). Initial consultation for patients with bulimia and anorexia nervosa. In D.M. Garner & P.E. Garfinkel (Eds.), *Handbook of therapy for anorexia nervosa and bulimia.* New York: Guilford Press.

Johnson, S.B. (1994). Health behavior and health status: Concepts, methods, and applications. *Journal of Pediatric Psychology, 19,* 129–142.

Johnson, S.B., Silverstein, J., Cunningham, W., & Carter, R. (1985). *The development and current status of the Diabetes Opinion Survey (DOS) and the Parent Diabetes Opinion Survey.* Unpublished manuscript, University of Florida, North Florida Regional Diabetes Program, Gainesville.

Jones, E. (1953). *The life and work of Sigmund Freud.* New York: Basic Books.

Kellerman, J., Zeltzer, L., Ellenberg, L., Dash, J., & Rigler, D. (1980). Psychological effects of illness in adolescents: I. Anxiety, self-esteem, and perception of control. *Journal of Pediatric Medicine, 97,* 126–131.

Kriechman, A.M. (1987). Siblings with somatoform disorders in childhood and adolescence. *Journal of the American Academy of Child and Adolescent Psychiatry, 26,* 226–231.

La Greca, A.M., & Schuman, W.B. (1995). Adherence to prescribed medical regimens. In D.K. Routh (Ed.), *Handbook of pediatric psychology* (pp. 55–83). New York: Guilford Press.

Larsson, B., Melin, L., Lamminen, M., & Ullstedt, E. (1987). A school-based treatment of chronic headaches in adolescents. *Journal of Pediatric Psychology, 12,* 553–566.

Leight, H., & Reiser, M.F. (1977). Major trends in psychosomatic medicine: The psychiatrist's evolving role in medicine. *Annals of Internal Medicine, 87,* 233–239.

Lemanek, K., Moore, S., Gresham, F., Williamson, D., & Kelley, H. (1986). Psychosocial adjustment of children with sickle cell anemia. *Journal of Pediatric Psychology, 11,* 397–410.

Liebman, D., Minuchin, S., & Baker, L. (1974). The use of structural family therapy in the treatment of intractable asthma. *American Journal of Psychiatry, 131,* 5.

Linscheid, T.R., Tarnowski, K.J., Rasnake, L.K., & Brams, J.S. (1987). Behavioral treatment of food refusal in a child with short-gut syndrome. *Journal of Pediatric Psychology, 12,* 451–459.

Lipowski, Z.J. (1988). Somatization: The concept and its clinical application. *American Journal of Psychiatry, 145,* 1358–1368.

Ljundberg, L. (1957). Hysteria: A clinical, prognostic and genetic study. *Acta Psychiatrica Scandinavica, 32,* 1–162.

Mansdorf, I.J. (1981). Eliminating somatic complaints in separation anxiety through contingency management. *Journal of Behavior Therapy and Experimental Psychiatry, 12,* 73–75.

McAnarney, E.R., Pless, I.B., Satterwhite, B., & Friedman, S.B. (1974). Psychological problems of children with chronic juvenile arthritis. *Pediatrics, 53,* 523–528.

McCubbin, H.I., McCubbin, M.A., Patterson, J.M., Cauble, A.E., Wilson, L.R., & Warwick, W. (1983). CHIP: Coping Health Inventory for Parents: An assessment of parental coping patterns in the care of the chronically ill child. *Journal of Marriage and the Family, 45,* 359–370.

McGrath, P.A. (1987). The multidimensional assessments and management of research pain syndrome in children. *Behavioral Research and Therapy, 25*(4), 251–262.

McKusick, V.A. (1978). *Mendelian inheritance in man.* Baltimore: Johns Hopkins University Press.

Milkich, D.R., Rewey, H.H., Weiss, J.H., & Kolton, S. (1973). A preliminary investigation of psychophysiological response to stress among different subgroups of asthmatic children. *Journal of Psychosomatic Research, 17,* 1–8.

Minuchin, S. (1974). *Families and family therapy.* Cambridge, MA: Harvard University Press.

Minuchin, S., Baker, L., Rossman, B.L., Liebman, R., Milman, L., & Todd, T.C. (1975). A conceptual model of psychosomatic illness in children: Family organization and family therapy. *Archives of General Psychiatry, 32,* 1031–1038.

Minuchin, S., Rosman, B., & Baker, L. (1978). *Psychosomatic families: Anorexia nervosa in context.* Cambridge, MA: Harvard University Press.

Orr, D. (1986). Adolescence, stress, and psychosomatic symptoms. *Journal of Adolescent Health Care, 7,* 97S–108S.

Osborne, R.B., Hatcher, J.W., & Richtsmeier, A.J. (1989). The role of social modeling in unexplained pediatric pain. *Journal of Pediatric Psychology, 14,* 43–61.

Paul, G. (1969). Physiological effects of relaxation training and hypnotic suggestion. *Journal of Abnormal Psychology, 74,* 425–437.

Peters, B.M. (1978). School-aged children's beliefs about causality of illness: A review of the literature. *MCN: American Journal of Maternal Child Nursing, 7,* 143–154.

Peterson, L., & Shigetomi, C. (1981). The use of coping techniques to minimize anxiety in hospitalized children. *Behavior Therapy, 12,* 1–14.

Phillips, R.D. (1988). Play therapy in health care settings. Promises never kept? Play in health care settings [Special issue]. *Children's Health Care, 16*(3), 182–187.

Pless, I.B., & Roghmann, K.J. (1971). Chronic illness and its consequences: Observations based on three epidemiologic surveys. *Journal of Pediatrics, 79*, 351–359.

Pritchard, C.T., Ball, J.D., Culbert, J., & Faust, D. (1988). Using the Personality Inventory for Children to identify children with somatoform disorders: MMPI findings revisited. *Journal of Pediatric Psychology, 13*, 237–245.

Rae, W.A., Worchel, F.F., Upchurch, J., Sanner, J.H., & Daniel, C.A. (1989). The psychosocial impact of play on hospitalized children. *Journal of Pediatric Psychology, 14*, 617–627.

Roberts, J., & Pembry, M.E. (1978). *An introduction to medical genetics*. New York: Oxford University Press.

Roberts, M.C., & Wright, L. (1982). The role of the pediatric psychologist as consultant to pediatricians. In J.M. Tuma (Ed.), *Handbook for the practice of pediatric psychology*. New York: Wiley.

Ross, D.M., & Ross, S.A. (1984). Childhood pain: The school-aged child's viewpoint. *Pain, 20*, 179–191.

Rossman, B.B.R. (1990). *Children's perception of coping with distress: Assessment, developmental differences, and moderation of adjustment*. Unpublished manuscript, University of Denver at Denver, CO.

Routh, D.K., & Ernst, A.R. (1984). Somatization disorder in relatives of children and adolescents with functional abdominal pain. *Journal of Pediatric Psychology, 9*, 427–437.

Sameroff, A.J. (1975). Early influences on development: Fact or fancy? *Merrill-Palmer Quarterly, 21*, 267–294.

Selye, H. (1956). *The stress of life*. New York: McGraw-Hill.

Silver, E.J., Westbrook, L.E., & Stein, R.E.K. (1998). Relationship of parental psychological distress to consequences of chronic health conditions in children. *Journal of Pediatric Psychology, 23*, 5–15.

Slater, E. (1961). The 35th Mosley lecture. *Journal of Mental Sciences, 107*, 359–381.

Spirito, A., Stark, L.J., & Williams, C. (1988). Development of a brief checklist to assess coping in pediatric patients. *Journal of Pediatric Psychology, 13*, 555–574.

Stabler, B. (1988). Pediatric consultation-liaison. In D.K. Routh (Ed.), *Handbook of pediatric psychology*. New York: Guilford Press.

Stabler, B., Morris, M.A., Litton, J., Feinglos, M.N., & Surwit, R.S. (1986). Differential glycemic response to stress in Type A and Type B individuals with IDDM. *Diabetes Care, 9*, 550–551.

Sullivan, B. (1979). Adjustment in diabetic girls: I. Development of the Diabetic Adjustment Scale. *Psychosomatic Medicine, 41*, 119–126.

Tavormina, J.B., Kastner, L.S., Slater, P.M., & Wyatt, S.L. (1976). Chronically ill children: A psychologically and emotionally deviant population? *Journal of Abnormal Child Psychology, 4*, 99–110.

Thompson, S.M., Dahlquist, L.M., Koening, G.M., & Bartholomew, L.K. (1995). Adherence facilitating behaviors of a multidisciplinary pediatric rheumatology staff. *Journal of Pediatric Psychology, 20*, 291–298.

Varni, J.W. (1981a). Behavioral medicine in hemophilia arthritic pain management: Two case studies. *Archives of Physical Medicine and Rehabilitation, 61*, 183–187.

Varni, J.W. (1981b). Self-regulation techniques in the management of chronic arthritic pain in hemophilia. *Behavior Therapy, 12*, 185–194.

Varni, J.W. (1983). *Clinical behavioral pediatrics: An interdisciplinary biobehavioral approach*. New York: Pergamon Press.

Varni, J.W., Thompson, K.L., & Hanson, V. (1987). The Varni/Thompson Pediatric Pain Questionnaire: I. Chronic musculoskeletal pain in juvenile rheumatoid arthritis. *Pain, 28*, 27–38.

Walker, L.S., Garber, J., & Greene, J.W. (1993). Somatic complaints in pediatric patients: A prospective study of the role of negative life events, child social and academic competence, and parental somatic symptoms. *Journal of Consulting and Clinical Psychology, 62*, 1213–1221.

Weiner, H. (1977). *Psychobiology and human disease*. New York: Elsevier.

Willis, D., Elliott, C., & Jay, S. (1982). Psychological effects of physical illness and its concomitants. In J. Tuma (Ed.), *Handbook for the practice of pediatric psychology*. New York: Wiley.

Zegans, L.S. (1982). Stress and the development of psychosomatic disorders. In L. Goldberger & S. Breznitz (Eds.), *The handbook of stress: Therapeutic and clinical aspects*. New York: Free Press.

Zeltzer, L., Kellerman, J., Ellenberg, L., Dash, J., & Rigler, D. (1980). Psychological effects of illness in adolescents: II. Impact of illness in adolescents: Crucial issues and coping styles. *Journal of Pediatrics, 97*, 132–138.

Zeltzer, L., & LeBaron, S. (1982). Hypnosis and nonhypnotic techniques for reduction of pain and anxiety during painful procedures in children and adolescents. *Journal of Pediatrics, 101*, 1032–1035.

CHAPTER 19

Depression in Preadolescents

LEONARD S. MILLING

Do preadolescent children become clinically depressed? At one time, mental health professionals commonly recited the dogma that preadolescents were incapable of experiencing a genuine depressive disorder. However, an alliance of clinical experience and empirical research has revealed that a small but consequential number of preadolescent children suffer from serious depression. The purpose of this chapter is to provide a selective review of the literature on the epidemiology, assessment, diagnosis, and treatment of preadolescent depression that will be of utility to child clinicians and researchers who seek to understand and help these troubled youngsters.

Many scholars of child psychopathology suggest that our understanding of depression in preadolescent children has evolved through at least three conceptual stages over the past 40 years (see Carlson & Garber, 1986; Craighead, Curry, & McMillian, 1994; Hammen & Rudolph, 1996; Harrington, 1993; Speier, Sherak, Hirsch, & Cantwell, 1995). Early on, it was believed that depression simply did not exist in preadolescents. Psychoanalytic theorists argued that depression was a product of anger turned against the self by the superego (Mahler, 1961; Rie, 1966; Rochlin, 1959). Consequently, genuine depression could not emerge until the superego was adequately developed, which was said to occur no earlier than adolescence. A second conceptualization, often referred to as "masked depression,"

contended that preadolescents could become depressed, but that the clinical presentation might be vastly different from that of adults (Cytryn & McKnew, 1972, 1980; Glaser, 1968; Toolan, 1962). Indeed, a common criticism of this model was that almost any symptom of psychopathology could be considered a manifestation of depression, thereby obscuring distinctions between this problem and other childhood disorders. A third and most recent viewpoint asserts that preadolescents do experience clinical depression and that the associated symptoms are very similar (although not identical) to those of depression in adolescents and adults. Beginning with the publication of the third edition of the *Diagnostic and Statistical Manual of Mental Disorders* (*DSM-III*; American Psychiatric Association [APA], 1978), essentially the same criteria have been employed to diagnose depressive disorder in preadolescents, adolescents, and adults. At the current time, there appears to be substantial consensus among scholars of child psychopathology that preadolescents do indeed become clinically depressed and that the symptoms of preadolescent, adolescent, and adult depression are quite similar. (At the same time, these scholars tend to emphasize that there are likely to be some important differences among preadolescents, adolescents, and adults in the symptoms, etiology, and treatment of depression as a function of development.) This most recent model has provided the theoretical underpinning for much of the empirical research on preadolescent depression that has burgeoned over the past 20 years.

CONCEPTUAL AND METHODOLOGICAL ISSUES

There are at least three important conceptual and methodological issues that may be useful to consider when exploring the empirical literature on depression in preadolescents. The first issue concerns the definition of depression. Leading authorities in child psychopathology note that the term "depression" can refer to three different phenomena: symptom, syndrome, and disorder (Carlson & Cantwell, 1980; Craighead et al., 1994; Hammen & Rudolph, 1996; Kazdin & Marciano, 1998). A symptom refers to a subjective indicator of a pathological condition that is typically reported by the patient. When spoken of as a single symptom, depression most commonly means sad affect. A child who is described as depressed in this sense might appear despondent, "blue," melancholy, or unhappy. In contrast, a syndrome is a group of symptoms and signs (i.e., an objective indicator of a pathological condition typically observed by the examiner) frequently occurring together that may reflect an underlying cause or process. Thus, as a syndrome, depression would encompass not only sad affect but also lack of pleasure, sleep disturbance, lethargy, difficulty concentrating, as well as other symptoms. For example, self-report depression scales such as the Child Depression Inventory (Kovacs, 1985) are measures of syndromal depression. Finally, a disorder is a syndrome consisting of particular signs and symptoms contained within a diagnostic classification system such as the fourth edition of the *Diagnostic and Statistical Manual of Mental Disorders* (*DSM-IV*; APA, 1994) or the 10th edition of the *International Classification of Diseases* (*ICD-10*; World Health Organization, 1992). Each diagnostic system organizes signs and symptoms in its own way to form the criteria for various depressive disorders. For example, major depressive disorder and dysthymic disorder are two depressive disorders (each with its own criteria) appearing in *DSM-IV* that are commonly applied to preadolescent children. Any discussion of depression will have vastly different implications depending on whether the phenomena of interest are symptoms, syndromes, or disorders.

A second conceptual issue involves the use of generic terms such as child, childhood, youth, youngsters, and so on throughout much of the empirical literature on this topic. It is often unclear what age group is meant by these nonspecific terms. Some investigators seem to mean only the preadolescent years (i.e., ages 6–12). Other authors appear to be referring to both preadolescents and adolescents. Still others seem to mean the entire age range between birth and 18. As we shall see later in this chapter, the nature of depression changes as the individual develops. To ascribe certain characteristics to "childhood" depression is to conceal these important developmental distinctions. Of course, it would be cumbersome to completely avoid the use of terms such as children and youngsters. However, to elucidate developmental aspects of depression, we need to move beyond these broad labels and to specify symptoms, etiologies, useful treatments, and other facets of depression associated with narrower, clearly defined age groups. The current chapter focuses on preadolescent depression. Accordingly, as much as possible, research conducted with youngsters in the 6- to 12-year-old age range serves as the knowledge base for this review.

A third issue that might be helpful to keep in mind when evaluating the empirical literature on preadolescent depression is methodological in nature. It concerns informant variability in the assessment of childhood psychopathology. The term "informant" refers to the source of information about the pathology. Conceivably, in assessing child psychopathology, information could be obtained from the child himself or herself, parents, teachers, clinicians, and peers, to name the most common sources. In what has become a classic meta-analytic review of informant variability, Achenbach, McConaughy, and Howell (1987) observed that correlations among different informants on a range of child behavioral and emotional problems was surprisingly weak, averaging less than 9% of shared variance overall. The lack of correspondence was especially pronounced between the child (i.e., self-reports) and other informants, as well as for overcontrolled (e.g., depression) versus undercontrolled problems. Similarly, Kazdin (1994) cogently elucidates the substantial lack of correspondence among different informants in studies of childhood depression.

There are many possible explanations for the lack of convergence among informants. Compared with adult observers, preadolescents may lack the cognitive skills and maturity to accurately evaluate their own behavior. On the other hand, adult observers do not have direct access to the child's thoughts, feelings, and other private experiences that would seem crucial in assessing an internalizing problem such as depression. Additionally, the child's behavior is likely to vary systematically from situation to situation, but adult observers typically view the child's behavior in only a limited number of those situations. For example, parents may see one set of behaviors at home, whereas teachers witness a very different set of behaviors in the classroom. These factors can contribute to the considerable variability among informants that, in turn, may have a profound impact on findings of studies of any aspect of preadolescent depression (e.g., prevalence, comorbidity, treatment outcome). For example, in studying prevalence, obtaining information from the children about whether they are depressed is likely to produce higher prevalence rates than asking parents or teachers for the same information (Kashani, Orvaschel, Rosenberg, & Reid, 1989; Polaino-Lorente & Domenech, 1993). Thus, in evaluating any study of preadolescent depression, it may be wise to keep in mind who it was that provided information about depression.

CLASSIFICATION

At the current time, the most popular system for diagnosing depressive disorders in preadolescent children is *DSM-IV* (APA, 1994). Unlike some other disorders (e.g., anxiety), no special provisions are made in *DSM-IV* for classifying the symptoms of depression experienced by youngsters under the section entitled "Disorders Usually First Diagnosed in Infancy, Childhood, or Adolescence." Rather, the same criteria used to diagnose adult depression are applied to children, with the main exception being that irritability often is seen in place of depressed affect among young people. Within *DSM-IV*, there are at least seven disorders that could be used to classify depression symptoms exhibited by preadolescents. Of these, the two diagnoses most commonly employed with young children seem to be major depressive disorder and dysthymic disorder.

Major depressive disorder (MDD) is a severe form of unipolar depression characterized by at least one major depressive episode in the absence of manic or hypomanic symptomatology. In turn, to qualify for a major depressive episode, a preadolescent must experience depressed/irritable mood or a loss of interest/pleasure in most activities for a period of at least two weeks. Simultaneously, the preadolescent must suffer from at least four of the following symptoms on a persistent basis: (1) appetite disturbance, significant weight loss or gain, or failure to make expected weight gains; (2) sleep disturbance; (3) feeling agitated/restless or slowed down; (4) loss of energy; (5) feelings of worthlessness or guilt; (6) difficulty concentrating or indecisiveness; and (7) thoughts of death or suicidal ideation. These symptoms must cause significant distress or impaired functioning in social, occupational, or other important domains. Further, the condition must not be the result of a medical problem or drug. Similarly, symptoms must not be due to bereavement (i.e., death of a loved one) or meet the criteria for mixed episode (i.e., the person simultaneously evidences symptoms of a major depressive episode and a manic episode).

In contrast to MDD, dysthymic disorder (DD) is a somewhat less severe but more chronic condition characterized by long-standing depressed mood. Specifically, to qualify for DD, a preadolescent must experience a period of one year in which his or her mood is predominantly depressed or irritable. Simultaneously, the preadolescent must suffer from at least two of the following symptoms: (1) appetite disturbance; (2) sleep disturbance; (3) loss of energy; (4) low self-esteem; (5) difficulty concentrating or indecisiveness; and (6) hopelessness. Like MDD, these symptoms must cause substantial distress or dysfunction. DD should not be diagnosed if, during the one-year period in question, depressive symptoms remit for more than two months. Likewise, if the individual has ever displayed manic or hypomanic symptomatology consistent with bipolar disorder, if the symptoms occur only as part of a chronic psychotic condition, or if the symptoms are due to a drug or medical condition, DD should not be diagnosed. Similarly, if the person qualifies for a diagnosis of MDD during the first year of the disturbance, DD should not be diagnosed. However, if the symptoms of MDD arise after the first year of DD, both diagnoses can be given (i.e., the so-called double depression).

MDD and DD are typically the two most common diagnoses employed with preadolescents displaying depressive symptomatology. However, there are at least five other classifications that may be appropriate for youngsters complaining of depressed affect. These classifications are briefly summarized here. An adjustment disorder with depressed mood is a short-term reaction that can be used to classify dysphoric mood, tearfulness, or hopelessness that arises within three months of a stressor. Similarly, an adjustment disorder with mixed anxiety and depressed mood is a comparable short-term reaction characterized by a combination of depression and anxiety symptoms. Depressive disorder not otherwise specified can be used to diagnose depressive symptoms that do not squarely fit the criteria for MDD, DD, or an adjustment disorder. The various forms of bipolar disorder (e.g., bipolar I disorder, bipolar II disorder, cyclothymic disorder) involve the cycling of manic features (predominated by elevated or expansive mood) with depressive symptomatology. In adults, the most common form of bipolar disorder involves sustained manic symptomatology that immediately precedes or follows a depressive episode, although in about one-third of cases, the manic and depressive episodes are separated by a period of normal functioning. In contrast, Geller and Luby (1997) observe that preadolescent bipolar disorder is characterized by brief, ongoing episodes in which the child rapidly cycles from manic to depressed behavior without any improvement in between. Thus, bipolar disorder in preadolescents is distinguished by the rapidity of the cycling (and is probably very rare in this age group). Finally, bereavement is a V-code employed to classify depressive symptoms that may arise for up to two months after the loss of a significant other.

PREVALENCE

In their benchmark review of epidemiological research on childhood depressive disorders, Fleming and Offord (1990) found that there had been very few large-scale prevalence studies of preadolescent children drawn from the general population where operational diagnostic criteria were employed. Large samples of nonpatients increase the likelihood that obtained results will be representative of the general preadolescent population. Operational diagnostic criteria enhance the reliability of classifications.

In one large-scale epidemiological study, the primary diagnostic information was obtained only from the children. Puura et al. (1997) randomly sampled 5,686 eight- to nine-year-olds in Finland and assessed them with self-report questionnaire measures of depression and a structured interview measure of general psychopathology. Prevalence rates of 0.48% for MDD and 0.06% for DD were obtained regardless of whether *DSM-III, DSM-III-R,* or *DSM-IV* criteria were employed to make the diagnoses.

Other large-scale studies have combined information obtained from both parents and children to arrive at a single prevalence rate. Cohen et al. (1993) studied 10- to 20-year-olds drawn from 776 households randomly sampled from two counties in upstate New York. Among the 10- to 13-year-olds, *DSM-III-R* diagnoses of MDD derived from structured interviews with parents and children produced a prevalence rate of 2%.

Similarly, Kashani et al. (1983) conducted a longitudinal study of 641 9-year-olds drawn from a cohort of approximately 1,000 children who had been born at a single hospital in New Zealand between April 1972 and March 1973. Depression rating scales were completed by children as well as their parents and teachers. Also, structured interviews were administered to the children. *DSM-III* criteria produced a current prevalence rate of 1.8% for MDD and 2.5% for minor depression. Two years later, Anderson, Williams, McGee, and Silva (1987) studied 792 children, then age 11, drawn from the same cohort. Based on structured interviews with the children and rating scales completed by parents and teachers, *DSM-III* criteria yielded a prevalence of .5% for MDD and 1.7% for DD during the previous 12-month period.

Two studies have reported separate prevalence rates based on information provided by parents versus children. Kashani et al. (1989) administered structured interviews to 210 children drawn from public school lists of 4,810 children and adolescents living in a single Midwestern county. Children's parents were also interviewed. Among both the 8-year-olds and 12-year-olds, prevalence rates for depressive disorder, according to *DSM-III* criteria, were 1.5% based on child interviews. In contrast, for parent interview information, prevalence rates were 0% for 8-year-olds and 1.4% for 12-year-olds.

Additionally, Polaino-Lorente and Domenech (1993) studied 6,432 children, age 8 to 11, from four cities and two rural areas in Spain. Diagnoses using *DSM-III* criteria were based on a self-report questionnaire, a clinician rating scale, a peer nomination scale, and a newly constructed teacher rating scale. Based on information supplied by the children themselves, prevalence rates were 1.8% for MDD and 6.4% for DD. In contrast, material provided by all other informants produced prevalence rates of 0.6% for MD and 3% for DD.

The findings of these latter two studies indicate that children consistently acknowledge more depressive symptomatology than is reported by other informants. This pattern underscores the need to carefully consider who is supplying the information when interpreting the results of any study of preadolescent depression. Overall, these large-scale studies suggest that MDD is uncommon among preadolescents, with no studies reporting a prevalence greater than 3%. In comparison, the one-year prevalence of MDD in adults is about 8% for males and 13% for females (Kessler et al., 1994). As for DD in preadolescents, there would seem to be too few data to arrive at a reliable prevalence estimate.

Generally, epidemiological studies have found that the prevalence of depression is approximately equal in preadolescent boys and girls (e.g., Kashani et al., 1983), although Anderson et al. (1987) showed that the rates were greater for male than female 11-year-olds. Conversely, Polaino-Lorente and Domenech (1993) reported a significant sex difference in the prevalence of DD (but not MDD) among 8- to 11-year-olds, with more girls than boys evidencing disorder. Socioeconomic status has been found to be unrelated to prevalence in one study of preadolescents (Kashani et al., 1983), but neither this variable nor race have been well studied in the preadolescent age group.

COURSE

The most common age of onset of depressive disorder among youth appears to be mid- to late adolescence for MDD and late preadolescence for DD (Burke, Burke, Regier, & Rae, 1990; Lewinsohn, Hoberman, & Rosenbaum, 1988). Indeed, in a classic longitudinal study of referred children between the ages of 8 and 13 years, Kovacs and her colleagues found that among those diagnosed with a depressive disorder (via parent and child structured interviews), the mean age of onset of DD was significantly lower than the mean age of onset of MDD (Kovacs, Feinberg, Crouse-Novak, Paulauskas, & Finkelstein, 1984a). The modal age of onset for DD in this sample was in the 7- to 8-year-old age range, whereas the modal age of onset for MDD was in

the 11- to 12-year-old age range. Indeed, there was greater variability in age of onset among the children diagnosed with DD, with some experiencing dysfunction as early as age 6. In contrast, no cases of MDD had an onset earlier than age 8. Generally, there seems to be some disagreement among authorities about whether a poorer prognosis is associated with an age of onset that is earlier (Hammen & Rudolph, 1996; Kovacs et al., 1984a) or later (Harrington, Fudge, Rutter, Pickles, & Hill, 1990; Ryan et al., 1987).

For the most part, preadolescents who are diagnosed with depressive disorder can expect to experience symptoms for an extended period. According to Kovacs and her colleagues (Kovacs et al., 1984a), among preadolescents, initial episodes of MDD continued for an average of 32 weeks, whereas initial episodes of DD lasted an average of about three years.

Over the short run, the prognosis for preadolescents diagnosed with depressive disorder is good. Many of these children can expect remission of the disorder. For example, Kovacs et al. (1984a) reported 59% of preadolescents diagnosed with MDD had recovered within 9 to 12 months of onset and a maximum recovery rate of 92% was achieved by 18 to 21 months. In contrast, DD is a much more protracted disorder. Of those diagnosed with DD, 58% had recovered within 48 to 54 months of onset and a maximum recovery rate of 89% was not achieved until 78 to 84 months.

Unfortunately, the long-term prognosis is not quite as bright. A substantial number of recovered children will experience a recurrence of the disorder. For example, Kovacs, Feinberg, Crouse-Novak, Paulauskas, and Finkelstein (1984b) found that within two years of recovery from an initial episode of MDD or DD, 35% of children had experienced a recurrence/occurrence of MDD. Within five years, 72% of those initially diagnosed with MDD had suffered a relapse. Similarly, in a three-year longitudinal study of 11- to 12-year-olds, current depression was found to be significantly associated with the occurrence of later depression as measured by a self-report scale (Garrison, Jackson, Marsteller, McKeown, & Addy, 1990). Other longitudinal studies of preadolescents have shown a similar high rate of recurrence (e.g., Poznanski, Krahenbuhl, & Zrull, 1976). Indeed, a long-term retrospective study found that an initial episode of depression during preadolescence or adolescence was associated with increased risk for some form of depressive disorder approximately 18 years later, during adulthood (Harrington et al., 1990).

Thus, there seems to be some continuity among preadolescent, adolescent, and adult depression. Preadolescents who are diagnosed with depressive disorder can expect to experience depressive symptoms during adolescence and into adulthood. However, there do seem to be some important developmental differences in symptomatology. The prevalence of depressive disorder seems to increase markedly in early to mid-adolescence (Angold & Rutter, 1992; Cohen et al., 1993; Hankin et al., 1998). Furthermore, the clinical features of adolescent depression are somewhat different from those of depressed preadolescents. For example, in a study of referred preadolescents and adolescents assessed via parent and child structured interviews, Ryan et al. (1987) found that adolescents were significantly more likely to evidence hopelessness, anhedonia, hypersomia, weight disturbance, and lethality of suicide attempt. On the other hand, prepubertal children were more likely to display depressed appearance, somatic complaints, psychomotor agitation, separation anxiety, phobias, and hallucinations.

COMORBIDITY

Comorbidity refers to the co-occurrence of two or more disorders. Maser and Cloninger (1990) describe three kinds of comorbidity. First, diagnostic comorbidity entails the co-occurrence of several disorders because of shared criteria for making classifications. For example, some clinicians believe that the substantial co-occurrence of MDD and DD is simply a product of the considerable overlap of the *DSM* diagnostic criteria for these two disorders. (However, others view DD as a very distinct disorder from MDD; see Kovacs, Akiskal, Gatonis, & Parrone, 1994, for a discussion of this issue.) Many symptoms in the *DSM* are not specific to a single disorder, thereby increasing the likelihood of diagnostic comorbidity. Second, pathogenic comorbidity refers to a situation in which one disorder causes another. For example, some children with attention-deficit/hyperactivity disorder (ADHD) may later develop symptoms of depression in response to the social and academic difficulties resulting from an inability to regulate and inhibit impulses. Third, prognostic comorbidity is a circumstance in which a single underlying pathology

emerges in the form of one disorder early on and as another disorder later. For example, because anxiety disorders occur on average at an earlier age than depressive disorders (Brady & Kendall, 1992) and because both disorders often develop in the same person, it has been argued that these frequently co-occurring sets of symptoms are part of a single underlying pathogenic process referred to by Watson and Clark (1984) as "negative affectivity." Indeed, some researchers point out that anxiety and depression in children cannot be separated empirically and contend that there is no real distinction between these disorders, at least among young people (Achenbach, 1991a; Finch, Lipovsky, & Casat, 1989).

Reviews of the empirical literature suggest that among the various disorders arising in preadolescence, depression evinces one of the highest rates of comorbidity with other psychiatric conditions (Angold & Costello, 1993; Brady & Kendall, 1992; Hammen & Compas, 1994). The two most common comorbid conditions with depression are anxiety disorders and conduct/oppositional disorders. With regard to the former, large-scale studies of preadolescent children drawn from the general population have generally shown a substantial overlap between anxiety and depression. For example, in the longitudinal study of children, then 11 years old, born at a single hospital in New Zealand, Anderson et al. (1987) found that of all children diagnosed with some form of depressive disorder, 71% had a co-occurring anxiety disorder. Similarly, in the longitudinal study of 10- to 20-year-olds from families living in two counties of upstate New York, Cohen et al. (1993) reported that 43% of the youngsters diagnosed with depressive disorder also met criteria for some form of anxiety disorder. Although these findings are based on the entire group of 10- to 20-year-olds, the authors indicated that this general pattern of comorbidity was comparable among preadolescents, younger adolescents, and older adolescents.

Clinical samples of preadolescents show a similar high comorbidity rate between depression and anxiety. In Kovac's classic study of depressed preadolescents, 33% of the youngsters with MDD and 36% of those with DD also suffered from some form of anxiety disorder (Kovacs et al., 1984a). Likewise, among the depressed preadolescents in Ryan's investigation of clinically referred preadolescents and adolescents, 58% of preadolescents suffered from separation anxiety disorder and 45% met criteria for phobias with avoidance (Ryan et al., 1987). More-over, the rates of comorbid anxiety problems among the preadolescents were substantially higher than those observed among the adolescent subsample. Additionally, in a clinical sample of 95 children age 7 to 17 years who had been diagnosed with MDD via structured interviews with parents and children, Mitchell, McCauley, Burke, and Moss (1988) found that 42% of the preadolescents met criteria for separation anxiety disorder, 18% for generalized anxiety disorder, 11% for phobia, and 2% for obsessive-compulsive disorder. Studies of combined groups of referred preadolescents and adolescents support the contention that depressed children are especially likely to experience the entire range of anxiety symptoms, except possibly panic symptoms (Biederman, Faraone, Mick, & LeLon, 1995; Hershberg, Carlson, Cantwell, & Strober, 1982).

As for conduct disorders, large-scale epidemiological studies of children from the general population show a substantial overlap between depression and conduct problems, rivaling comorbidity rates with anxiety difficulties. For example, among the depressed 11-year-olds in Anderson et al. (1987), 79% suffered from concurrent conduct and oppositional disorders. (Indeed, 71% of the depressed preadolescents in this study were simultaneously diagnosed with conduct and anxiety disorders!) Likewise, Cohen et al. (1993) reported that among the depressed youngsters sampled from two counties in upstate New York, 62% also met the criteria for what was termed a disruptive disorder (i.e., conduct disorder, oppositional disorder, plus ADHD). Studies of clinical samples demonstrate a comparably high rate of overlap. For example, Ryan et al. (1987) found that 38% of the depressed preadolescents in his referred sample evidenced conduct symptoms (whereas only 25% of depressed adolescents demonstrated these behaviors). Mitchell et al. (1988) noted that 16% of the depressed preadolescents in his clinical sample were also conduct disordered. Finally, Kovacs et al. (1984a) reported that 7% of the preadolescents with MDD and 11% of the children with DD also met criteria for conduct disorder. Overall, the findings of research on the comorbidity of preadolescent depression suggest that depressive disorders in this age group are very likely to be accompanied by other serious symptomatology, typically conduct or anxiety problems, and that "pure" cases of depression among preadolescents are probably the exception rather than the rule.

THEORIES OF ETIOLOGY

Generally, theories regarding the causes of preadolescent depression are downward extensions of etiological models of adult depression. Little if any attention has been devoted to theories of causation specific to preadolescents. This section briefly describes the predominant models that have been applied to understanding the causes of depression in preadolescents.

BIOLOGICAL THEORIES

A variety of biological causes have been implicated in the etiology of depression, including genetic and neuroendocrine factors. With regard to genetics, it is well-known that depression tends to run in families. Indeed, family studies tend to show a higher than expected rate of affective disorder among the first-degree relatives of depressed preadolescents (e.g., Puig-Antich, Goetz, et al., 1989), but these investigations fail to control for environmental transmission of causative factors. There is little in the way of data from twin and adoption studies that can substantiate a genetic etiology in preadolescent-onset depression. For example, Thapar and McGuffin (1994) administered depression rating scales to the parents of 411 monzygotic and dyzygotic twin pairs 8 to 16 years old who were born in a single county in Wales. Depression symptoms were heritable only among adolescents. Shared environmental factors accounted for all of the variability in depression ratings of preadolescents. Thus, the findings of this study suggest that the influence of genetic factors in the etiology of depression may be more important among adolescents than among preadolescents.

As for neuroendocrine studies, this research has focused on the functioning of the hypothalamic-pituitary-adrenal (HPA) axis in depressed children. Specifically, investigations in preadolescents of levels of cortisol, a hormone secreted in response to stress, have failed to show reliable differences between depressed and nondepressed youngsters (Puig-Antich, Dahl, et al., 1989). Furthermore, studies of the dexamethasone suppression test (DST), a challenge test in which depressed youngsters are administered dexamethasone to temporarily suppress the production of cortisol, have been unable to demonstrate that depressed preadolescents respond differently from their nondepressed counterparts (e.g., Puig-Antich, Dahl, et al., 1989). Unfortunately, the DST lacks specificity and tends to identify many false positives who are ultimately found not to be depressed. Consequently, it is no longer viewed as a reliable tool for diagnosing depression in preadolescents. Many other biologic factors have been suggested as having a role in preadolescent depression, including growth hormones, melatonin, and sleep. For a thorough review of these factors, the interested reader is referred to Ryan and Dahl (1993).

PSYCHODYNAMIC THEORIES

There are several psychodynamic models of depression. According to S. Freud (1950), depressed affect is caused by aggressive drives turned against the self by the superego. (However, classical psychoanalysts also claimed that depression could not exist in preadolescents because they lacked a fully developed superego.) Bibring (1965) describes a similar model revolving around loss of self-esteem that results from feelings of helplessness produced by an inability to satisfy the ego ideal. Finally, attachment theorists postulate that object loss due to separation from and disruption of relations with primary attachment figures can predispose a child to depression later in life (Bowlby, 1980; Spitz, 1946).

BECK'S COGNITIVE THEORY

According to Beck and his colleagues (Beck, Rush, Shaw, & Emery, 1979), depression results from faulty cognitions or schemas about the self and world through which the individual filters events. These schemas are said to develop in childhood. In a healthy person, schemas accurately reflect the world, whereas in people prone to depression, the schemas are distorted. These distortions can include selective abstraction (i.e., focusing on negative elements of an event and ignoring positive elements), overgeneralization (i.e., drawing a general rule from a single negative event), personalization (drawing conclusions about oneself based on unrelated events), and dichotomous thinking (understanding the world in terms of two categories rather than seeing shades of gray), all of which can contribute to depression. Additionally, in a person prone to depression, schemas come to include negative core beliefs about the self, the world, and the future (i.e., negative cognitive triad).

LEARNED HELPLESSNESS

According to Seligman (1975), exposure to inescapable or uncontrollable aversive events results in general expectations of noncontingency and helplessness. In turn, these expectations produce the cognitive, motivational, and emotional symptoms of depression. The learned helplessness model was the theoretical springboard from which the attributional and hopelessness models of depression were developed.

HOPELESSNESS THEORY

According to this cognitive theory, hopelessness, or a general expectation of negative outcomes, is the cause of some types of depression (Abramson, Metalsky, & Alloy, 1989). In turn, hopelessness results from the kinds of inferences a person makes about a significant negative life event. These inferences can involve the causes of the event, the consequences of the event, or the self. Hopelessness is more likely to occur if the event is attributed to causes that are stable over time and global in effect across many situations. Also, hopelessness is more probable if negative consequences are seen as likely to result from the negative event. Finally, hopelessness is more likely if the individual responds to the event by making negative inferences about himself or herself. A generalized tendency to draw pathogenic inferences about causes, consequences, and self increases the likelihood that the person will make such inferences about the specific event in question. A generalized tendency to make depressive inferences about causes of events was originally referred to as the attributional model of depression (Abramson, Seligman, & Teasdale, 1978).

REHM'S SELF-CONTROL THEORY

According to Rehm (1977), depression is a function of faulty self-monitoring, self-evaluation, and self-reinforcement. Self-monitoring problems result from a tendency to focus on negative events and not positive ones, as well as attending to the immediate but not delayed outcomes of behavior. Self-evaluation difficulties include setting overly stringent standards for success and a tendency to attribute positive outcomes to external factors. Disturbances in self-reinforcement involve providing high rates of self-punishment for negative outcomes and low rates of self-reinforcement for positive outcomes.

LEWINSOHN'S BEHAVIORAL THEORY

According to this model, lack of reinforcement from positive events, particularly events that are contingent on the behavior of the individual, predispose the person to depression (Lewinsohn, 1974). The lack of positive reinforcers in the environment can contribute to depression, but the amount of social skill that the person possesses and a willingness to use those skills are also important determinants of who becomes depressed and who does not. Finally, an inability to appreciate the positive reinforcers that are present can predispose an individual to depression.

ASSESSMENT

As a result of the considerable variability among informants in measuring preadolescent depression (Kazdin, 1994), a thorough assessment would seem to require information from multiple sources, including the child himself or herself as well as adult informants such as parents and clinicians. There are a multitude of good child, parent, teacher, clinician, and peer measures of preadolescent depression. A review of all these instruments is beyond the scope of this chapter. Instead, this section selectively reviews assessment tools that, because of their outstanding psychometric properties, are especially suitable for assessing depression in both research and clinical situations.

SELF-REPORT QUESTIONNAIRES

A self-report measure of preadolescent depression appropriate for both research and clinical practice should possess not only evidence of reliability and validity but also a test manual and normative information. Clinical norms should be based on a sizable, representative sample against which the scores of any single child can be compared. Ideally, norms should include cutoff scores indicating clinical levels of dysfunction. Two self-report measures of preadolescent depression seem to fulfill these requirements: the Children's Depression Inventory

(CDI) and the Reynolds Child Depression Scale (RCDS). There are many other reliable and valid self-report measures of preadolescent depression that may not be appropriate for use in clinical situations. The interested reader is referred to Reynolds (1994) for more information.

Children's Depression Inventory

The CDI is a 27-item self-report measure of the severity of depression symptoms. It was designed for use with 9- to 15-year-olds as a downward extension of the Beck Depression Inventory (Kovacs, 1979, 1992). It is the most popular self-report measure of childhood depression for research and clinical purposes. The scale requires approximately a third-grade reading level. Scale items operationalize various symptoms of depression, with each item consisting of three statements that vary the severity of the symptom in question. From among each of the three statements, the child selects the one that best describes him or her over the past two weeks. A manual is available for the CDI that presents norms apparently based on a sample of second- to eighth-graders (Kovacs, 1992). Normative data based on other large samples of children are available as well (e.g., Smucker, Craighead, Craighead, & Green, 1986). Kovacs (1980/1981) has recommended a cutoff score of 19 to identify clinical levels of depression, which distinguishes approximately 10% of a sample of school-age children.

Reviews of research employing the CDI suggest that the scale typically produces internal consistency coefficients of .70 or higher and yields test-retest reliability coefficients that are quite variable, although not inappropriate to the measurement interval and the nature of the construct (Curry & Craighead, 1993; Reynolds, 1994). Furthermore, these reviews tend to support the construct validity of the scale in that the CDI has been shown to correlate with related constructs such as anxiety, self-esteem, attributional style, and hopelessness (Curry & Craighead, 1993).

Reynolds Child Depression Scale

The RCDS is a 30-item self-report measure of the severity of depression symptoms (Reynolds, 1989). It was designed for youngsters 8 to 13 years old, and there is a corresponding version for adolescents. Respondents rate items according to the frequency of their occurrence during the previous two weeks along a 4-point scale ranging from "almost never" to "all the time." Thus, it may be somewhat easier for cognitively limited children to use the RCDS than the CDI. Seven items are reverse-keyed, thereby providing some control for acquiescence response set. A manual for the RCDS presents normative information based on a sample of over 1,600 preadolescents. There is a cutoff score indicating clinical levels of symptom severity.

Reviews of research utilizing the RCDS suggest that the scale typically produces internal consistency coefficients of .80 and substantial test-retest reliability coefficients (Reynolds, 1994). The RCDS test manual (Reynolds, 1989) as well as reviews of empirical research employing the scale (Reynolds, 1994) provide evidence of the scale's construct validity, indicating that it is correlated with other self-report and interview measures of depression and is sensitive to change resulting from treatment.

CLINICAL INTERVIEWS

Structured interviews are perhaps the most common assessment method for establishing diagnoses of depressive disorder. Whereas self-report measures and rating scales can measure symptom severity, they cannot yield diagnoses. Clinical interviews can perform both tasks. In addition to the psychometric attributes required of a satisfactory self-report measure, a clinical interview appropriate for both research and clinical uses will evidence a standardized method of administration that helps to produce a high level of interrater reliability when interviewers make clinical judgments. Two instruments currently appear to fulfill these requirements: the Schedule for Affective Disorders and Schizophrenia for School-Age Children (K-SADS) and the Child Assessment Schedule (CAS). There are many other structured interviews that have stimulated much interest in the child clinical community and seem to have much potential, but these instruments do not as yet possess the necessary empirical evidence of reliability and validity to make them a prudent choice for all research and clinical purposes. The interested reader may wish to consult Hodges (1994) for a description and evaluation of these other measures.

Schedule for Affective Disorders and Schizophrenia for School-Age Children
The K-SADS is a semistructured interview measure of general child psychopathology, including affective, psychotic, and anxiety symptomatology (Puig-Antich & Chambers, 1978). There are separate versions of the K-SADS for parents and children, as well as separate versions for the current episode (K-SADS-P) and an epidemiologic version for past episodes (K-SADS-E) (Orvaschel, Puig-Antich, Chambers, Tabrizi, & Johnson, 1982). The K-SADS is probably the most popular structured interview measure of child psychopathology.

In the K-SADS assessment process, parents are interviewed first, followed by the child. In each of the interviews, the examiner asks a series of semistructured questions about symptom onset, duration, chronicity, and severity. The interviewer then makes a series of summary ratings based on both interviews. Because of the semistructured nature of the interview process, the K-SADS is intended for use only by mental health professionals and not by lay interviewers.

The K-SADS has good evidence of reliability. Interrater reliability of ratings of videotaped interviews produced coefficients exceeding .85 for depression summary scales and .75 for depression diagnoses (Ambrosini, Metz, Prabrucki, & Lee, 1989). In a reliability study of a clinical sample of preadolescents and adolescents interviewed twice over a 72-hour period, test-retest reliability coefficients ranged from .67 to .81 for the four depression summary scales and exceeded .70 for diagnoses of minor depression and .54 for major depression (Chambers et al., 1985). Internal consistency coefficients were all greater than .68 for the depression summary scales. The K-SADS also possesses satisfactory evidence of validity. For example, K-SADS diagnoses of affective disorder have been shown to correlate with the CDI as well as diagnoses of depression produced by other interview measures (Hodges, McKnew, Burbach, & Roebuck, 1987; McCauley, Mitchell, Burke, & Moss, 1988).

Child Assessment Schedule
The CAS is a standardized, semistructured clinical interview measure of general child psychopathology that produces *DSM* diagnoses and symptom scores, including one for depression. There are separate versions for children and parents. The original CAS was developed in 1978 for use with 5- to 7-year-olds (Hodges, 1983). The second version, published in 1986, is intended for 7- to 12-year-olds (Hodges, 1986). A third version, which appeared in 1990, is designed for adolescents (Hodges, 1990a).

The CAS is constructed to resemble a traditional clinical interview in that questions are grouped around 11 topic areas (e.g., school, family, peers, hobbies, self-image, mood) rather than symptom clusters. The first part of the interview comprises questions that address these topic areas. The second part consists of questions about the onset and duration of symptoms that the child mentions in the first section. The third part involves ratings of the child's presentation and behavior during the interview (e.g., grooming, insight, activity level). Unlike some other clinical interviews (e.g., Diagnostic Interview Schedule for Children; Diagnostic Interview for Children and Adolescents), the semistructured nature of the CAS requires that it be used only by professionals and not by lay examiners. The interview produces scale scores for content areas, symptom clusters, and total psychopathology. A diagnostic algorithm produces *DSM* categories including MDD and DD. The CAS has available not only a test manual but also computer algorithms for generating scale scores and *DSM* diagnoses.

The CAS has been extensively researched and there is ample evidence of its reliability and validity. For example, interrater reliability of videotaped interviews was reported to be .90 for total symptoms and .84 for mood symptoms (Hodges, Kline, Stern, Cytryn, & McKnew, 1982). Test-retest reliabilities of MDD and DD diagnoses in child psychiatric inpatients were shown to be greater than .70 over approximately a nine-day period (Hodges, Cools, & McKnew, 1989). The internal consistency of items yielding MDD and DD diagnoses was found to exceed .80 (Hodges, Saunders, Kashani, Hamlett, & Thompson, 1990). CAS scores correlate with corresponding Child Behavior Checklist scores and global clinical ratings (Hodges et al., 1982). CAS diagnoses of mood disorders correlate with self-report measures of depression (Hodges, 1990a) and show a high level of agreement with diagnoses produced by other commonly used structured scales (Hodges et al., 1987). The CAS is the most thoroughly researched of all the structured interviews and is a prudent choice for most clinical and research purposes.

RATING SCALES

Rating scales are typically completed by adult informants such as clinicians, parents, or teachers to produce scores reflecting severity of symptomatology. Rating scales have the advantage of being relatively brief and easily administered, but they do not produce diagnoses of depression. Rather, they are best viewed as measures of the severity of syndromal depression. There are many rating scales that can be used to assess depression. Two of the most judicious choices from a psychometric point of view seem to be the Children's Depression Rating Scale (CDRS) and the Child Behavior Checklist (CBCL). For a discussion of other measures, the reader may wish to see Clarizo (1994).

Children's Depression Rating Scale–Revised
The CDRS-R is a clinician-rated 15-item scale for children 6 to 12 years old that yields severity of depression scores (Poznanski, 1990). It is a downward extension of the Hamilton Depression Rating Scale (Hamilton, 1960). The clinician asks a series of questions and then rates the child's response along a 7-point scale. Three of the items address observations of the child's nonverbal behavior. There is a cutoff score indicating levels of symptomatology equivalent to clinical depression (Poznanski et al., 1984). The scale takes only 20 minutes to complete.

The CDRS-R has not been researched as extensively as some of the other measures described in this chapter, but it does seem to be a reliable and valid measure of syndromal depression. For example, interrater reliability of the original scale was reported to be at least .80 across several studies (Poznanski, Cook, & Carroll, 1979; Poznanski, Cook, Carroll, & Corzo, 1983). Test-retest reliability over two weeks with an outpatient sample was found to be .86 (Poznanski et al., 1984). The revised scale was shown to be highly correlated ($r = .87$) with clinician's global depression ratings of outpatients, and it discriminates children diagnosed with depression versus those not so diagnosed (Poznanski et al., 1984).

Child Behavior Checklist
The CBCL is a 118-item parent-completed measure of the severity of general child psychopathology for children 4 to 18 years old (Achenbach, 1991a). The 118 items yield eight syndrome scales, including an Anxious/Depressed scale composed of 14 items. The eight syndrome scales were derived via factor analysis. The Anxious/Depressed scale is not a pure measure of depression and is consistent with

the view that among preadolescents, anxiety and depression are not separate constructs but rather are a single syndrome often referred to as "negative affectivity" (Watson & Clark, 1984). There are separate norms for males and females at two age levels: 4 to 11 years and 12 to 18 years. To complete the CBCL, parents rate each of the 118 items on a 3-point scale according to how often the child has displayed each over the past six months.

In addition to the 118 problem items measuring symptomatic behavior, the CBCL contains 40 items that measure social competence. The CBCL takes about 20 minutes to complete and requires a fifth-grade reading level. One advantage of the CBCL is that there are corresponding measures for preadolescents that are completed by other informants such as teachers (Teacher Report Form; Achenbach, 1991b) and trained observers (Direct Observation Form; Achenbach; 1991a).

The CBCL is one of the most extensively researched measures of child psychopathology. It has an excellent test manual and extensive normative information, including cutoff scores indicating normal, borderline, and clinical levels of functioning. According to the test manual, alpha for the Anxious/Depressed scale is .87 for both the male and female versions of the 4- to 11-year-old profiles, indicating excellent internal consistency. One-week test-retest reliability coefficients on these scales are .87 for boys and .85 for girls. As for validity, according to the manual, the Anxious/Depressed scale correlated .78 with the Anxiety-Withdrawal scale of the Quay-Peterson Revised Behavior Problem Checklist in a study of 6- to 11-year-olds seen in outpatient clinics. Discriminant analysis indicated that the Anxious/Depressed scale could significantly distinguish referred and nonreferred 6- to 11-year old boys and girls. In addition to the psychometric information described in the test manual, there is a wealth of data in the empirical literature attesting to the validity of the current and previous versions of the CBCL (Achenbach, 1994). For example, in a study of 325 six- to sixteen-year-olds from an outpatient sample, the Anxious/Depressed scale significantly predicted *DSM* diagnoses of MDD and DD established via the Diagnostic Interview Schedule for Children (Kasius, Ferdinand, van den Berg, & Verhulst, 1997). Overall, the existing evidence suggests that the CBCL Anxiety/Depression scale is a robust parent-report measure of negative affectivity in children.

TREATMENT

Common treatments for preadolescent depression encompass a range of pharmacological and psychological intervention. This section summarizes these interventions, including empirical evidence of efficacy.

MEDICATION

Tricyclic Antidepressants (TCAs)

Traditionally, the class of antidepressants most commonly prescribed for preadolescents is the TCAs. These medications include imipramine (Tofranil), desipramine (Norpramin), nortriptyline (Pamelor), and amitriptyline (Elavil). The therapeutic effect of these medications is produced by increasing the amount of available serotonin and norepinephrine that results from blocking the reuptake (i.e., reabsorption) of these neurotransmitters into presynaptic axons from which they were released. Because response to any of the antidepressants is delayed rather than immediate (e.g., two weeks), it is generally believed that the therapeutic effect does not directly result from changes in levels of neurotransmitters, but rather is caused by the body's adaptation to the presence of additional neurotransmitters in the synapse (e.g., the number of receptor sites is increased). Depending on the particular TCA, neurotransmitter systems other than serotonin and norepinephrine are affected, typically producing a wide range of side effects such as dry mouth, sedation, and alterations in cardiac function. In addition to these side effects, there have been four cases of sudden death reported with the use of desipramine (Riddle, Geller, & Ryan, 1993) and one case with imipramine (Saraf, Klein, Gittelman-Klein, & Groff, 1974).

Of all the antidepressants employed with preadolescents, the most popular and most thoroughly investigated is imipramine, perhaps because it is the only antidepressant approved by the FDA for use with children (to treat enuresis, not depression). Generally, placebo-controlled, double-blind studies of depressed preadolescents treated with imipramine (Petti & Law, 1982; Puig-Antich et al., 1987) as well as amitriptyline (Kashani, Shekim, & Reid, 1984) and nortriptyline (Geller, Cooper, Graham, Fetner, & Marsteller, 1992; Geller, Cooper, McCombs, Graham, & Wells, 1989) have failed to show that any of these compounds are significantly more effective than a placebo in relieving the symptoms of depression. However, Puig-Antich et al. (1987) reported that response to the medication was correlated with plasma levels of imipramine and desipramine. Because children metabolize these drugs faster than do adolescents and adults, it may be especially important to monitor and titrate the blood levels of antidepressants to achieve a therapeutic effect. Indeed, Preskorn, Weller, Hughes, Weller, and Boltke (1987) found that with plasma levels of imipramine carefully monitored and kept within a therapeutic range, this medication was significantly more effective than a placebo in treating depression in 6- to 12-year-olds.

Selective Serotonin Reuptake Inhibitors (SSRIs)
The popularity of the SSRIs for treating adult depression has exploded since the introduction of Prozac several years ago. In addition to fluoxetine (Prozac), this class of medication includes sertraline (Zoloft), paroxetine (Paxil), and fluvoxamine (Luvox). These medications achieve their therapeutic action by blocking the reuptake of serotonin. Other neurotransmitter systems are not affected, thereby resulting in fewer side effects than the TCAs. There are no double-blind, placebo-controlled studies of the efficacy of the SSRIs for preadolescent depression.

Monoamine Oxidase Inhibitors (MAOIs)
The MAOIs are not often used to treat preadolescent depression. This class of medication includes phenelzine (Nardil), tranylcypromine (Parnate), and isocarboxazid (Marplan). These agents achieve their therapeutic effect by blocking the action of monoamine oxidase, an enzyme that metabolizes serotonin and norepinephrine, thereby increasing the amount of these neurotransmitters at the receptor. The MAOIs require strict adherence to a special diet (i.e., free of thyamine) or the individual is at risk for cerebrovascular complications. Because preadolescents are less likely to adhere to such diets, MAOIs are rarely used in this age group. There are no controlled, double-blind studies of the use of MAOIs with preadolescents.

PSYCHOTHERAPY

Play Therapy
Among dynamically oriented clinicians, play therapy is often the treatment of choice for depressed preadolescent children. For the young child, play is a natural medium of self-expression and communication with other children and adults (Axline, 1947). Therapists of many theoretical orientations recognize that a child's play has meaning of some kind and can represent an attempt to address the problems of life. Play may serve many functions, including expressing feelings, gaining a sense of control, coping with difficult situations, communicating with others, and developing relationships. In therapy, the clinician can use play to promote a trusting relationship with the child. Furthermore, play may allow the therapist to understand the child better, as psychological themes emerge in the content and style of the youngster's play activities. Some analytically oriented play therapists take an active role in interpreting the meaning of children's play behavior (e.g., A. Freud, 1928; Klein, 1932), whereas nondirective therapists use play as a vehicle for empathic relating (Axline, 1947). It is common for behavioral and family-oriented therapists to integrate some form of play into their work when a preadolescent is involved. Aside from case material, there are no published data on the effectiveness of play therapy for treating depressed preadolescents.

Rational-Emotive Therapy (RET)
This cognitive approach to therapy is a downward extension of the work of Albert Ellis with adults (Ellis & Bernard, 1983). It focuses on the emotional consequences of irrational beliefs. In RET, children are trained to see that emotions such as sadness can be the result of irrational beliefs that are activated by unpleasant events. Through therapy, children learn to recognize these irrational beliefs, to dispute them, and to replace them with more rationale alternatives. Therapy sessions consist of discussion and role playing where the clinician helps the child to identify and challenge irrational cognitions. Additionally, children are given homework assignments to practice these cognitive skills in the real world. At present, there are no empirical studies of the efficacy of RET for treating preadolescent depression.

Beck's Cognitive Therapy
Beck's cognitive therapy is designed to correct negative core beliefs about the self, the world, and the future (i.e., negative cognitive triad), as well as distortions in thinking such as selective abstraction,

overgeneralization, personalization, and dichotomous thinking (Beck et al., 1979). Stark (1990) adapted Beck's model for use with preadolescents in a multicomponent intervention program. First, children are taught to recognize and label various feeling states. Second, children are trained to monitor daily events, feelings, and behavioral responses. Third, the clinician helps the child to identify cognitive distortions. Finally, child and clinician together challenge distorted cognitions and substitute more adaptive beliefs. Homework assignments are provided to enhance generalization of cognitive skills to the real world.

Lewinsohn's Behavioral Therapy

This behaviorally oriented model was originally developed for adults (Lewinsohn, Antonuccio, Steinmetz, & Terr, 1984; Lewinsohn, Sullivan, & Grosscup, 1980) and was extended downward for use with adolescents (Lewinsohn, Clarke, Hops, & Andrews, 1990). According to Lewinsohn's model, depression can result from a high frequency of aversive events and from a lack of contingency between adaptive behaviors and positive events. Furthermore, the model contends that one of the key variables that determines how much positive reinforcement individuals receive from the environment is the amount of social skill they possess to elicit social reinforcement.

According to the adolescent program, treatment is delivered in 14 two-hour group sessions provided separately to adolescents and their parents (Lewinsohn et al., 1990; Lewinsohn, Hoberman, & Clarke, 1989). Youngsters are taught methods for controlling irrational thoughts, increasing pleasant events, and improving social skills. The family component emphasizes communication and conflict resolution skills to minimize reciprocally punishing interactions. Although this treatment was originally designed for adults and then extended downward for use with adolescents, its effectiveness has been studied with older preadolescents (Kahn, Kehle, Jensen, & Clarke, 1990), and the approach could easily be modified for use with preadolescents of any age.

Self-Control Therapy

This cognitive therapy is designed to help depressed children repair deficits in self-monitoring, self-evaluation, self-reinforcement, and self-punishment (Kaslow & Rhem, 1983; Rehm, 1977). There are several components to this treatment approach, which are often provided in a group format. First, children

are helped to see that they may be attending to negative events and ignoring positive ones. They are coached to monitor positive experiences and the pleasant mood that accompanies them. Second, children are helped to differentiate between the short-term and long-term consequences of a behavior and to understand that positive aftereffects may not be evident over the short run. Third, youngsters are taught to develop realistic goals for themselves, to identify intermediate steps along the way to their goals, and to provide themselves with self-reinforcement for attainment of the intermediate steps. Homework assignments are often provided to help patients generalize their new cognitive skills to the real world.

Problem-Solving Therapy

In this cognitive approach, children are taught skills that will enable them to generate solutions to interpersonal problem situations. Based on the work of D'Zurilla and Goldfried (1971), Spivack and Shure (1974), and others, the therapist works with the child to help him or her identify a problem situation and alternative solutions to the problem. The child is then trained to evaluate the potential consequences of each solution and to select the one with the optimal expected outcome. Finally, the child is encouraged to implement and evaluate the preferred solution.

Interpersonal Family Therapy

Family treatment approaches are based on the premise that the family is a system and depressive symptomatology in a preadolescent reflects dysfunction in the entire family system (see Haley, 1987; Minuchin, 1974). Accordingly, the family system is in need of intervention. Although many approaches to family therapy are compatible with the treatment of preadolescent depression, one method merits special attention because it was conceptualized with depressed youngsters in mind. Interpersonal family therapy is a specific type of family intervention utilizing systems, cognitive-behavioral, and object relations theory to help restructure the interactions of members of families in which there is a depressed child (Kaslow & Racusin, 1988; Racusin & Kaslow, 1991; Schwartz, Kaslow, Racusin, & Carton, 1998). Interpersonal family therapy is an exciting development for clinicians who work with the families of depressed youngsters, but as yet, there have been no outcome studies of this treatment with children.

Studies of Psychotherapy Outcome with Preadolescent Depression

Despite the considerable interest in childhood affective disorders, there have been only a handful of controlled studies of the efficacy of psychosocial interventions for preadolescent depression. In an initial study of treatments for depressed preadolescents, Butler, Miezitis, Friedman, and Cole (1980) compared cognitive restructuring, role playing, attention-placebo, and no-treatment control conditions to treat 56 depressed fifth- and sixth-graders. These youngsters were identified as depressed by completing a battery of self-report measures of depression, locus of control, and self-concept in their school classrooms and through consultation with their teachers. The cognitive restructuring intervention, drawing on RET and Beck models, focused on identifying irrational cognitions, improving listening and social skills, as well as understanding relations between thoughts and feelings. The role-playing treatment, presumably based on the work of D'Zurilla and Goldfried (1971), emphasized social problem-solving skills. Treatments were provided in 10 one-hour small group sessions. Unfortunately, complete between-group statistical comparisons were not made, but the investigators concluded that both active treatments were more effective than control conditions in reducing self-reported symptoms of depression.

Stark, Reynolds, and Kaslow (1987) compared self-control, problem-solving, and waiting-list control conditions for preadolescents age 9 to 12 years who had been identified as depressed by completing the CDI at their elementary school. The self-control therapy, based on Rehm's model (Kaslow & Rehm, 1983; Rehm, 1977), was designed to help children set more realistic standards and subgoals for behavior, reinforce themselves more, and punish themselves less. The problem-solving therapy emphasized interpersonal problem-solving skills. Treatments were provided in 12 fifty-minute sessions delivered in group format. The self-control treatment was significantly more effective than the control condition at posttreatment in reducing self-reported depression symptoms. These differences vanished at the eight-week follow-up. However, at follow-up, children in the self-control condition were significantly less depressed than children in the problem-solving group, as measured by a clinician depression rating scale. The authors concluded that both treatments appeared to be of benefit to these moderately depressed youngsters.

In a similar study, Stark, Rouse, and Livingston (1991) compared a cognitive-behavioral intervention against traditional counseling to treat depressed fourth- to seventh-graders who had been screened using the CDI. The cognitive-behavioral intervention included training in self-control, social skills, relaxation, and cognitive restructuring. The traditional counseling group was taught how to understand their feelings. Intervention was provided for about 25 sessions over about a 14-week period. Following treatment, the cognitive-behavioral group showed significantly less depressive symptomatology, but this difference was not maintained at a seven-month follow-up.

Finally, Kahn et al. (1990) evaluated the effectiveness of three treatments for reducing depression in seventh- and eighth-graders: cognitive-behavioral, self-modeling, and relaxation. A control group was included for comparison purposes. Children were screened for participation using self-report and interview measures. The cognitive-behavioral intervention was based on Lewinsohn's behavioral model, described above. The self-modeling condition employed training in enacting nondepressed behaviors (e.g., smiling). The relaxation intervention utilized progressive muscle relaxation. Treatments were provided in 12 fifty-minute sessions. All three of the treatments were significantly more effective than the control condition in reducing depression as assessed by self-report and interview measures at posttreatment and at one-month follow-up, but there was no difference among the three treatments in effectiveness.

Overall, compared with research in other areas of preadolescent depression (e.g., prevalence, comorbidity), the empirical literature on treatments for this disorder appears to be in a relatively underdeveloped state. The handful of placebo-controlled, double-blind studies of antidepressant medications thus far shows these agents to be no more effective than placebos, but additional research in which plasma levels are carefully monitored may help clarify the benefits of these medications for depressed preadolescents. There have been too few studies of psychosocial interventions for depressed preadolescents to draw any meaningful conclusions at this time, except perhaps to say that any downward extension of an intervention proven successful with depressed adults or adolescents might be more helpful than no treatment at all. The small size of research samples and a failure to employ clinically referred youngsters are serious limitations of the existing literature. Clinical experience suggests that depressed preadolescents benefit from many forms of psychotherapy. Consequently, outcome studies of these psychotherapies seem to be sorely needed and much in demand.

SUMMARY

Despite early claims to the contrary, it is now well-known that small numbers of preadolescents suffer from depressive disorder. Large-scale epidemiological studies have shown that major depressive disorder affects about 3% or fewer of preadolescents. On average, those so diagnosed will endure symptoms for less than a year, followed by a remission, and then a later recurrence of the disorder. A large number of preadolescents can expect recurrences throughout adolescence and into adulthood. However, there seem to be meaningful discontinuities between preadolescent and adolescent depression. Depressed preadolescents tend to present with symptoms different from those of depressed adolescents. Also, prevalence rates of depression increase dramatically around midadolescence, and at this time, the sex ratio of those afflicted shows a clear shift, with depressed females for the first time outnumbering males. Additionally, depression in preadolescence is usually accompanied by comorbid diagnoses; this is not nearly as common in adolescent depression. Furthermore, the existing evidence reveals a genetic etiological component to depression symptoms during adolescence, but not during preadolescence. All in all, there may be some important differences between preadolescent-onset depression and depressions that arise later in life. Finally, clinical experience suggests that several different medications and psychotherapies may be helpful to depressed preadolescents, but unfortunately, there is little in the way of scientific evidence that would help child clinicians choose one treatment over another.

REFERENCES

Abramson, L.Y., Metalsky, G.I., & Alloy, L.B. (1989). Hopelessness depression: A theory-based subtype of depression. *Psychological Review, 96,* 358–372.

Abramson, L.Y., Seligman, M.E.P., & Teasdale, J.D. (1978). Learned helplessness in humans: Critique and reformulation. *Journal of Abnormal Psychology, 87,* 49–74.

Achenbach, T.M. (1991a). *Manual for the Child Behavior Checklist/4–18 and 1991 profile.* Burlington: University of Vermont, Department of Psychiatry.

Achenbach, T.M. (1991b). *Manual for the Teacher's Report Form and 1991 profile.* Burlington: University of Vermont, Department of Psychiatry.

Achenbach, T.M. (1994). Child Behavior Checklist and related instruments. In M.E. Maruish (Ed.), *The use of psychological testing for treatment planning and outcome assessment* (pp. 517–549). Hillsdale, NJ: Erlbaum.

Achenbach, T.M., McConaughy, S.H., & Howell, C.T. (1987). Child/adolescent behavioral and emotional problems: Implications of cross-informant correlations for situational specificity. *Psychological Bulletin, 101,* 213–232.

Ambrosini, P.J., Metz, C., Prabrucki, K., & Lee, J. (1989). Videotape reliability of the third revised edition of the K-SADS. *Journal of the American Academy of Child and Adolescent Psychiatry, 28,* 723–728.

American Psychiatric Association. (1978). *Diagnostic and statistical manual of mental disorders* (3rd ed.). Washington, DC: Author.

American Psychiatric Association. (1994). *Diagnostic and statistical manual of mental disorders* (4th ed.). Washington, DC: Author.

Anderson, J.C., Williams, S., McGee, R., & Silva, P. (1987). *DSM-III* disorders in preadolescent children. *Archives of General Psychiatry, 44,* 69–76.

Angold, A., & Costello, E.J. (1993). Depressive comorbidity in children and adolescents: Empirical, theoretical, and methodological issues. *American Journal of Psychiatry, 150,* 1779–1791.

Angold, A., & Rutter, M. (1992). Effects of age and pubertal status on depression in a large clinical sample. *Development and Psychopathology, 4,* 5–28.

Axline, V. (1947). *Play therapy.* New York: Ballantine.

Beck, A.T., Rush, A.J., Shaw, B.F., & Emery, G. (1979). *Cognitive therapy of depression.* New York: Guilford Press.

Bibring, E. (1965). The mechanism of depression. In P. Greenacre (Ed.), *Affective disorders* (pp. 13–48). New York: International Universities Press.

Biederman, J., Faraone, S., Mick, E., & LeLon, E. (1995). Psychiatric comorbidity among referred juveniles with major depression: Fact or artifact. *Journal of the American Academy of Child and Adolescent Psychiatry, 34,* 579–590.

Bowlby, J. (1980). *Attachment and loss: Vol. 3. loss.* New York: Basic Books.

Brady, E.U., & Kendall, P.C. (1992). Comorbidity of anxiety and depression in children and adolescents. *Psychological Bulletin, 111,* 244–255.

Burke, K.C., Burke, J.D., Regier, D.A., & Rae, D.S. (1990). Age at onset of selected mental disorders in five community populations. *Archives of General Psychiatry, 47,* 511–518.

Butler, L., Miezitis, S., Friedman, R., & Cole, E. (1980). The effects of two school-based intervention programs on depressive symptoms in preadolescents. *American Educational Research Journal, 17,* 111–119.

Carlson, G., & Cantwell, D. (1980). Unmasking masked depression. *American Journal of Psychiatry, 137,* 445–449.

Carlson, G., & Garber, J. (1986). Developmental issues in the classification of depression in children. In M. Rutter, C.E. Izzard, & P.B. Read (Eds.), *Depression in young people: Developmental and clinical perspectives* (pp. 399–434). New York: Guilford Press.

Chambers, W.J., Puig-Antich, J., Hirsch, M., Paez, P., Ambrosini, P.J., Tabrizi, M.A., & Davies, M. (1985). The assessment of affective disorders in children and adolescents by semi-structured interview: Test-retest reliability of the Schedule for Affective Disorders and Schizophrenia for School-Age Children, present episode version. *Archives of General Psychiatry, 42,* 696–702.

Clarizo, H.F. (1994). Assessment of depression in children and adolescents by parents, teachers, and peers. In W.M. Reynolds & H.F. Johnston (Eds.), *Handbook of depression in children and adolescents* (pp. 235–248). New York: Plenum Press.

Cohen, P., Cohen, J., Kasen, S., Velez, C.N., Hartmark, C., Johnson, J., Rojas, M., Brook, J., & Streuning, E.L. (1993). An epidemiological study of childhood disorders in late childhood and adolescence: I. Age and gender-specific prevalence. *Journal of Child Psychology, Psychiatry and Allied Health Disciplines, 34,* 851–867.

Craighead, W.E., Curry, J.F., & McMillan, D.K. (1994). Childhood and adolescent depression. In L.W. Craighead, A.E. Kazdin, & M.J. Mahoney (Eds.), *Cognitive and behavioral interventions* (pp. 301–312). Boston: Allyn & Bacon.

Curry, J.F., & Craighead, W.E. (1993). Depression. In T.H. Ollendick & M. Hersen (Eds.), *Handbook of child and adolescent assessment* (pp. 251–268). Boston: Allyn & Bacon.

Cytryn, L., & McKnew, D.H. (1972). Proposed classification of childhood depression. *American Journal of Psychiatry, 129,* 149–155.

Cytryn, L., & McKnew, D.H. (1980). Diagnosis of depression in children: A reassessment. *American Journal of Psychiatry, 137,* 22–25.

D'Zurilla, T.J., & Goldfried, M.R. (1971). Problem solving and behavior modification. *Journal of Abnormal Psychology, 78,* 107–126.

Ellis, A., & Bernard, M. (1983). *Rational-emotive approaches to the problems of children.* New York: Plenum Press.

Finch, A.J., Lipovsky, J.A., & Casat, C.D. (1989). Anxiety and depression in children and adolescents: Negative affectivity or separate constructs? In P.C. Kendall & D. Watson (Eds.), *Anxiety and depression: Distinctive and overlapping features.* New York: Academic Press.

Fleming, J.E., & Offord, D.R. (1990). Epidemiology of childhood depressive disorders: A critical review. *Journal of the American Academy of Child and Adolescent Psychiatry, 29,* 571–580.

Freud, A. (1928). *Introduction to the technique of child analysis.* Washington, DC: Nervous and Mental Disease.

Freud, S. (1950). Mourning and melancholia. In J. Strachey (Ed.), *The standard edition of the complete psychological works of Sigmund Freud* (Vol.. 4, pp. 152–172). London: Hogarth Press.

Garrison, C.Z., Jackson, K.L., Marsteller, F., McKeown, R., & Addy, C. (1990). A longitudinal study of depressive symptomatology in young adolescents. *Journal of the American Academy of Child and Adolescent Psychiatry, 29,* 581–585.

Geller, B., Cooper, T.B., Graham, D.L., Fetner, H.H., & Marsteller, F.A. (1992). Pharmokinetically designed double-blind placebo-controlled study of nortriptyline in 6- to 12-year olds with major depressive disorder. *Journal of the American Academy of Child and Adolescent Psychiatry, 31,* 34–44.

Geller, B., Cooper, T.B., McCombs, H.G., Graham, D., & Wells, J. (1989). Double-blind, placebo-controlled study of nortriptyline in depressed children using a "fixed plasma level" design. *Psychopharmacology Bulletin, 25,* 101–108.

Geller, B., & Luby, J. (1997). Child and adolescent bipolar disorder: A review of the past 10 years. *Journal of the American Academy of Child and Adolescent Psychiatry, 36,* 1168–1176.

Glaser, K. (1968). Masked depression in children and adolescents. *Annual Progress in Child Psychiatry and Child Development, 1,* 345–355.

Haley, J. (1987). *Problem-solving therapy.* San Francisco: Jossey-Bass.

Hamilton, M. (1960). A rating scale for depression. *Journal of Neurology, Neurosurgery, and Psychiatry, 23,* 56–62.

Hammen, C., & Compas, B.E. (1994). Unmasking masked depression in children and adolescents: The problem of comorbidity. *Clinical Psychology Review, 14,* 585–603.

Hammen, C., & Rudolph, K.D. (1996). Childhood depression. In E.J. Mash & R.A. Barkley (Eds.), *Child psychopathology* (pp. 153–195). New York: Guilford Press.

Hankin, B.L., Abramson, L.Y., Moffitt, T.E., Silva, P.A., McGee, R., & Angell, K. (1998). Development of depression from preadolescence to young adulthood: Emerging gender differences in a 10-year longitudinal study. *Journal of Abnormal Psychology, 107,* 128–140.

Harrington, R. (1993). Similarities and dissimilarities between child and adult disorders: The case of depression. In C.G. Costello (Ed.), *Basic issues in psychopathology* (pp. 103–124). New York: Guilford Press.

Harrington, R., Fudge, H., Rutter, M., Pickles, A., & Hill, J. (1990). Adult outcomes of childhood and adolescent depression I. *Archives of General Psychiatry, 47,* 465–473.

Hershberg, S.G., Carlson, G.A., Cantwell, D.P., & Strober, M. (1982). Anxiety and depressive disorders in psychiatrically disturbed children. *Journal of Clinical Psychiatry, 43,* 358–361.

Hodges, K. (1983). *Guidelines to aid in establishing interrater reliability with the Child Assessment Schedule.* Unpublished manuscript.

Hodges, K. (1986). *Guidelines to aid in establishing interrater reliability with the Child Assessment Schedule* (2nd ed.). Unpublished manuscript.

Hodges, K. (1990a). Depression and anxiety in children: A comparison of self-report questionnaires to clinical interview. *Psychological Assessment: A Journal of Consulting and Clinical Psychology, 2,* 376–381.

Hodges, K. (1990b). *Guidelines to aid in establishing interrater reliability with the Child Assessment Schedule* (3rd ed.). Unpublished manuscript.

Hodges, K. (1994). Evaluation of depression in children and adolescents using diagnostic clinical interviews. In W.M. Reynolds & H.F Johnston (Eds.), *Handbook of depression in children and adolescents* (pp. 183–208). New York: Plenum Press.

Hodges, K., Cools, J., & McKnew, D. (1989). Test-retest reliability of a clinical research interview for children: The Child Assessment Schedule. *Psychological Assessment: A Journal of Consulting and Clinical Psychology, 1,* 317–322.

Hodges, K., Kline, J., Stern, L., Cytryn, L., & McKnew, D. (1982). The development of a child assessment schedule for research and clinical use. *Journal of Abnormal Child Psychology, 10,* 173–189.

Hodges, K., McKnew, D., Burbach, D.J., & Roebuck, L. (1987). Diagnostic concordance between the Child Assessment Schedule (CAS) and the Schedule for Affective Disorders and Schizophrenia for school-age children (K-SADS) in an outpatient sample using lay interviewers. *Journal of the American Academy of Child Psychiatry, 26,* 654–661.

Hodges, K., Saunders, W., Kashani, J., Hamlett, K., & Thompson, R. (1990). Internal consistency of *DSM-III* diagnoses using the symptom scales of the Child Assessment Schedule (CAS). *Journal of the American Academy of Child and Adolescent Psychiatry, 26,* 654–661.

Kahn, J.S., Kehle, T.J., Jensen, W.R., & Clarke, E. (1990). Comparisons of cognitive-behavioral, relaxation, and self-modeling interventions for depression among middle-school students. *School Psychology Review, 19,* 196–211.

Kashani, J.H., McGee, R.O., Clarkson, S.E., Anderson, J.C., Walton, L.A., Williams, S., Silva, P.A., Robins, A.J., Cytryn, L., & McKnew, D.H. (1983). Depression in a sample of 9-year-old children: Prevalence and associated characteristics. *Archives of General Psychiatry, 40,* 1217–1223.

Kashani, J.H., Orvaschel, H., Rosenberg, T.K., & Reid, J.C. (1989). Psychopathology in a community sample of children and adolescents: A developmental perspective. *Journal of the American Academy of Child and Adolescent Psychiatry, 28,* 701–706.

Kashani, J.H., Shekim, W.O., & Reid, J.C. (1984). Amitriptyline in children with major depressive disorder: A double-blind crossover pilot study. *Journal of the American Academy of Child and Adolescent Psychiatry, 23,* 348–351.

Kasius, M.C., Ferdinand, R.F., van den Berg, H., & Verhulst, F.C. (1997). Associations between different diagnostic approaches for child and adolescent psychopathology. *Journal of Child Psychology and Psychiatry and Allied Health Disciplines, 38,* 625–632.

Kaslow, N.J., & Racusin, G.R. (1988). Assessment and treatment of depressed children and their families. *Family Therapy Today, 3,* 39–59.

Kaslow, N.J., & Rehm, L.P. (1983). Childhood depression. In R.J. Morris & T.R. Kratochwill (Eds.), *The practice of child therapy* (pp. 27–51). New York: Pergamon Press.

Kazdin, A.E. (1994). Informant variability in the assessment of childhood depression. In W.M. Reynolds & H.F. Johnston (Eds.), *Handbook of depression in children and adolescents* (pp. 249–271). New York: London.

Kazdin, A.E., & Marciano, P. (1998). Childhood and adolescent depression. In E.J. Mash & R.A. Barkley (Eds.), *Treatment of childhood psychopathology* (pp. 211—248). New York: Guilford Press.

Kessler, R.C., McGonagle, K.A., Zhao, S., Nelson, C.B., Hughes, M., Eshleman, S., Wittchen, H.U., & Kendler, K.S. (1994). Lifetime and 12-month prevalence of *DSM-III-R* psychiatric disorders in the United States: Results from the National Comorbidity Survey. *Archives of General Psychiatry, 51,* 8–19.

Klein, M. (1932). *The psycho-analysis of children.* New York: Norton.

Kovacs, M. (1979). *Children's Depression Inventory.* University of Pittsburgh (PA) School of Medicine: Author.

Kovacs, M. (1980/1981). Ratings scales to assess depression in school-age children. *Acta Paedopsychiatrica, 46,* 305–315.

Kovacs, M. (1985). The Children's Depression Inventory. *Psychopharmacology Bulletin, 25,* 995–998.

Kovacs, M. (1992). *Children's Depression Inventory manual.* North Tonawanda, NY: Multi-Health Systems.

Kovacs, M., Akiskal, H.S., Gatonis, C., & Parrone, P.L. (1994). Childhood-onset dysthymic disorder: Clinical features and prospective naturalistic outcome. *Archives of General Psychiatry, 51,* 365–374.

Kovacs, M., Feinberg, T.L., Crouse-Novak, M.A., Paulauskas, S.L., & Finkelstein, R. (1984a). Depressive disorders in childhood I. *Archives of General Psychiatry, 41,* 229–237.

Kovacs, M., Feinberg, T.L., Crouse-Novak, M.A., Paulauskas, S.L., & Finkelstein, R. (1984b). Depressive disorders in childhood II. *Archives of General Psychiatry, 41,* 643–649.

Lewinsohn, P. (1974). A behavioral approach to depression. In R. Friedman & M. Katz (Eds.), *The psychology of depression: Contemporary theory and research.* Washington, DC: U.S. Government Printing Office.

Lewinsohn, P., Antonuccio, D., Steinmetz, J., & Terr, L. (1984). *The coping with depression course.* Eugene, OR: Castalia.

Lewinsohn, P.M., Clarke, G., Hops, H., & Andrews, J. (1990). Cognitive-behavioral treatment for depressed adolescents. *Behavior Therapy, 21,* 385–401.

Lewinsohn, P.M., Hoberman, H.M., & Clarke, G.N. (1989). The coping with depression course: Review and future directions. *Canadian Journal of Behavioral Science, 21,* 470–493.

Lewinsohn, P.M., Hoberman, H.M., & Rosenbaum, M. (1988). A prospective study of risk factors for unipolar depression. *Journal of Abnormal Psychology, 97,* 251–264.

Lewinsohn, P.M., Sullivan, J.M., & Grosscup, S.J. (1980). Changing reinforcing events: An approach to the treatment of depression. *Psychotherapy: Theory, Research and Practice, 17,* 322–334.

Mahler, M.S. (1961). On sadness and grief in infancy and childhood. *Psychoanalytic Study of the Child, 16,* 332–354.

Maser, J.D., & Cloninger, C.R. (1990). Comorbidity of anxiety and mood disorders. In J.D. Maser & C.R. Cloninger (Eds.), *Comorbidity of mood and anxiety disorders* (pp. 3–12). Washington, DC: American Psychiatric Press.

McCauley, E., Mitchell, J.R., Burke, P., & Moss, S. (1988). Cognitive attributes of depression in children and adolescents. *Journal of Consulting and Clinical Psychology, 56,* 903–908.

Minuchin, S. (1974). *Families and family therapy.* Cambridge, MA: Harvard University Press.

Mitchell, J., McCauley, E., Burke, P.M., & Moss, S.J. (1988). Phenomenology of depression in children and adolescents. *Journal of the American Academy of Child and Adolescent Psychiatry, 27,* 12–20.

Orvaschel, H., Puig-Antich, J., Chambers, W., Tabrizi, M.,A., & Johnson, R. (1982). Retrospective assessment of prepubertal major depression with the Kiddie-SADS-E. *Journal of the American Academy of Child Psychiatry, 21,* 392–397.

Petti, T.A., & Law, W., III. (1982). Imipramine treatment of depressed children: A double-blind pilot study. *Journal of Clinical Psychopharmacology, 2,* 107–110.

Polaino-Lorente, A., & Domenech, E. (1993). Prevalence of childhood depression: Results of the first study in Spain. *Journal of Child Psychology, Psychiatry and Allied Health Disciplines, 34,* 1007–1017.

Poznanski, E.O. (1990). *Children's Depression Rating Scale* (Rev. ed.) Unpublished manuscript.

Poznanski, E.O., Cook, S.C., & Carroll, B.J. (1979). A depression rating scale for children. *Pediatrics, 64,* 442–450.

Poznanski, E.O., Cook, S.C., Carroll, B.J., & Corzo, H. (1983). Use of the Children's Depression Rating Scale in an inpatient psychiatric population. *Journal of Clinical Psychiatry, 44,* 200–203.

Poznanski, E.O., Grossman, J.A., Buchsbaum, Y., Banegas, M., Freeman, L., & Gibbons, R. (1984). Preliminary studies of the reliability and validity of the Children's Depression Rating Scale. *Journal of the American Academy of Child Psychiatry, 23,* 191–197.

Poznanski, E.O., Krahenbuhl, V., & Zrull, J.P. (1976). Childhood depression: A longitudinal perspective. *Journal of the American Academy of Child Psychiatry, 15,* 491–501.

Preskorn, S., Weller, E., Hughes, C., Weller, R., & Boltke, K. (1987). Depression in prepubertal children: Dexamethasone nonsupression predicts differential response to imipramine versus placebo. *Psychopharmacology Bulletin, 23,* 128–133.

Puig-Antich, J., & Chambers, W. (1978). *The Schedule for Affective Disorders and Schizophrenia for school-age children (K-SADS).* New York: New York State Psychiatric Institute.

Puig-Antich, J., Dahl, R., Ryan, N., Novacenko, H., Goetz, D., Twomey, J., & Klepper, T. (1989). Cortisol secretion in prepubertal children with major depressive disorder. *Archives of General Psychiatry, 46,* 810–809.

Puig-Antich, J., Goetz, R., Davies, M., Kaplan, T., Davies, S., Ostrow, L., Asnis, L., Twomey, J., Iyengar, S., & Ryan, N.D. (1989). A controlled family history of prepubertal major depressive disorders. *Archives of General Psychiatry, 46,* 406–418.

Puig-Antich, J., Perel, J.M., Lupatkin, W., Chambers, W.J., Tabrizi, M.A., King, J., Goetz, R., Davies, M., & Stiller, R.L. (1987). Imipramine in prepubertal major depressive disorders. *Archives of General Psychiatry, 44,* 81–89.

Puura, K., Tamminen, T., Almqvist, F., Kresanov, K., Kumpulainen, K., Moilanen, I., & Koivisto, A.M. (1997). Should depression in young school children be diagnosed with different criteria? *European Child and Adolescent Psychiatry, 6,* 12–19.

Racusin, G.R., & Kaslow, N.J. (1991). Assessment and treatment of childhood depression. In P.A. Keller & S.R. Heyman (Eds.), *Innovations in clinical practice: A sourcebook* (Vol. 10, pp. 223–243). Sarasota, FL: Professional Resource Exchange.

Rehm, L.P. (1977). A self-control model of depression. *Behavior Therapy, 8,* 787–804.

Reynolds, W.M. (1989). *Reynolds Child Depression Scale: Professional manual.* Odessa, Fl: Psychological Assessment Resources.

Reynolds, W.M. (1994). Assessment of depression in children and adolescents by self-report questionnaires. In W.M. Reynolds & H.F Johnston (Eds.), *Handbook of depression in children and adolescents* (pp. 209–234). New York: Plenum Press.

Riddle, M.A., Geller, B., & Ryan, N. (1993). Another sudden death in a child treated with desipramine. *Journal of the American Academy of Child and Adolescent Psychiatry, 32,* 792–797.

Rie, H.E. (1966). Depression in childhood: A survey of some important contributors. *Journal of the American Academy of Child and Adolescent Psychiatry, 5,* 653–685.

Rochlin, G. (1959). The loss complex. *Journal of the American Psychoanalytic Association, 7,* 299–316.

Ryan, N.D., & Dahl, R.E. (1993). The biology of depression in children and adolescents. In J.J. Mann & D.J. Kupfer (Eds.), *Biology of depressive disorders: Part B.* New York: Plenum Press.

Ryan, N.D., Puig-Antich, J., Ambrosini, P., Rabinovich, H., Robinson, D., Nelson, B., Iyengar, S., & Twomey, J. (1987). The clinical picture of major depression in children and adolescents. *Archives of General Psychiatry, 44,* 854–861.

Saraf, K.R., Klein, D.F., Gittelman-Klein, R., & Groff, S. (1974). Imipramine side effects in children. *Psychopharmacologia, 37,* 265–274.

Schwartz, J.A., Kaslow, N.J., Racusin, G.R., & Carton, E.R. (1998). Interpersonal family therapy for childhood depression. In V. Van Hasselt & M. Hersen (Eds.), *Handbook of psychological treatment protocols for children and adolescents* (pp. 109–151). Mahwah, NJ: Erlbaum.

Seligman, M.E.P. (1975). *Learned helplessness.* San Francisco: Freeman.

Smucker, M.R., Craighead, W.E., Craighead, L.W., & Green, B.J. (1986). Normative and reliability data for the Children's Depression Inventory. *Journal of Abnormal Child Psychology, 14,* 25–39.

Speier, P.L., Sherak, D.L., Hirsch, S., & Cantwell, D.P. (1995). Depression in children and adolescents. In E.E. Beckham & W.R. Leber (Eds.), *Handbook of depression* (pp. 467–493). New York: Guilford Press.

Spitz, R.A. (1946). Anaclitic depression. *Psychoanalytic Study of the Child, 11,* 313–342.

Spivack, G., & Shure, M.B. (1974). *Social adjustment of young children: A cognitive approach to solving real life problems.* San Francisco: Jossey-Bass.

Stark, K.D. (1990). *Childhood depression: School-based intervention.* New York: Guilford Press.

Stark, K.D., Reynolds, W.M., & Kaslow, N.J. (1987). A comparison of the relative efficacy of self-control therapy and a behavioral problem-solving therapy for depression in children. *Journal of Abnormal Child Psychology, 15,* 91–113.

Stark, K.D., Rouse, L.W., & Livingston, R. (1991). Treatment of depression during childhood and adolescence: Cognitive behavioral procedures for the individual and family. In P.C. Kendall (Ed.), *Child and adolescent therapy: Cognitive-behavioral procedures* (pp. 165–208). New York: Guilford Press.

Thapar, A., & McGuffin, P. (1994). A twin study of depressive symptoms in childhood. *British Journal of Psychiatry, 165,* 259–265.

Toolan, J.H. (1962). Depression in children and adolescents. *American Journal of Orthopsychiatry, 32,* 404–414.

Watson, D., & Clark, D.A. (1984). Negative affectivity: The disposition to experience aversive emotional states. *Psychological Bulletin, 96,* 465–490.

World Health Organization. (1992). *International classification of diseases and health-related problems* (10th ed.). Geneva, Switzerland: Author.

CHAPTER 20

Aggressive, Antisocial, and Delinquent Behavior in Childhood and Adolescence

JAMES H. JOHNSON, JOHN W. MCCASKILL IV, AND BRANLYN E. WERBA

Children who come to the attention of mental health professionals display a range of problems that create difficulties for themselves, their parents, or those around them. Some show evidence of mental retardation, others of neurological impairment, and still others display problems of relatedness, cognition, and behavior to such a degree that they are judged psychotic. A range of other childhood problems can be subsumed under the headings of internalizing and externalizing syndromes (Achenbach, 1985; Achenbach & McConaughy, 1987). Under the heading of internalizing syndromes are a variety of problems reflective of depression, withdrawal, anxiety, obsessions, and somatic complaints. Generally, children with such problems seem to suffer more than others in their environment as a result of their difficulties. These problems are most closely associated with the traditional categories of neurotic and psychophysiological (psychosomatic) disorders and are considered under various headings elsewhere in this book.

Under externalizing syndromes are included several other types of behavioral problems. These difficulties can be distinguished from the ones listed above by the fact that they are primarily reflected in the child's conflicts with the environment rather than childhood distress, although this may also be present. Most frequently considered under this heading are problems such as hyperactive, aggressive, and oppositional behaviors as well as more serious rule violations that can bring the child or adolescent into contact with the juvenile justice system. In this chapter, we focus primarily on the problems of aggressive behavior and delinquency. Although aggression and delinquency are sometimes related, they often are not, and separate literatures related to these two problems have evolved. For these reasons, they are considered separately, at the same time, acknowledging the fact that the two problems often coexist.

CHILDHOOD AGGRESSION

Although aggressive behavior is more frequently seen in males than in females (Herbert, 1987), almost all children display aggressive behavior to some degree at some point in their development. Fortunately, in the case of most children, aggressive behaviors are of relatively low intensity and frequency and do not constitute a serious problem. In other cases, however, children may display

The authors wish to acknowledge the contributions of Dr. Eileen Fennell to an earlier edition of this chapter.

aggressive behaviors that are of such a high intensity/ high frequency that they demand a response from parents, teachers, or sometimes mental health professionals. Thus, aggressive behavior seems to constitute both a common and sometimes serious problem of childhood that may have important implications for the development of conduct disordered and delinquent behavior. For example, childhood aggression has been identified as one of the strongest predictors of delinquency and drug use during both the adolescent (Brook, Whiteman, & Finch, 1992; Roff, 1992) and adult years (Brook, Whiteman, Finch, & Cohen, 1996.

THEORETICAL FORMULATIONS OF AGGRESSIVE BEHAVIOR

There are a variety of theoretical perspectives on aggressive behavior which emphasize different variables as possible causal factors (see Bandura, 1973; Herbert, 1987). Classical psychoanalytic views tend to regard aggression as resulting from a dynamic interplay of life and death instincts and as result of biologically based instinctual drives. Ethological views (Lorenz, 1966) have emphasized the role of instincts toward aggressive behavior that are elicited by "releasing stimuli" from the environment. Other views have postulated that aggression results from the frustration that comes from having one's access to goals blocked. More recent versions of this original frustration-aggression hypothesis (Dollard, Doob, Miller, Mower, & Sears, 1939) suggest that, while frustration does not always result in aggression, it may result in "aggressive inclinations" which, in concert with other factors, increase the probability of aggressive responding (Berkowitz, 1989).

More recent perspectives include social learning and social information processing views of aggression. Social learning views highlight the essential role of learning in the development and maintenance of aggressive behavior (Bandura, 1973). High levels of aggressive behavior are seen as resulting from experiences where the child has been directly reinforced for aggressive responding, or from vicarious learning where the child has observed models such as parents, peers, or others who may have been reinforced for engaging in aggressive behavior. Aggressive behavior, however learned, is seen as being maintained by the reinforcement of this behavior

by the natural environment. Social information processing views (Dodge, 1986; Dodge & Schwartz, 1997) focus on cognitive operations that mediate the relationship between aggressive cues and behavioral responses to these cues. For example, a child's aggressive behavior in response to social stimuli is seen as being mediated by a series of mental operations such as the encoding of social cues, the interpretation of cues, the clarification of goals, response construction, response evaluation, and behavioral enactment (Dodge & Schwartz, 1997). It can be noted that this perspective, which emphasizes the role of cognitive factors in aggression, is not necessarily at odds with certain of the other views presented above; current formulations of both social learning theory (Bandura, 1983) and frustration-aggression views (Berkowitz, 1989) have acknowledged the role of cognitive processes in aggressive behavior.

SUBTYPES OF AGGRESSION

Research on childhood aggression has typically made global comparisons between aggressive and nonaggressive children. Recently, emphasis has been placed on the heterogeneity among aggressive children to enhance increased understanding of the etiology of aggressive behavior and determine the efficacy of treatments for different types of aggressors. One typology that is gaining increasing empirical support distinguishes between reactive and proactive aggressors. Reactive aggression is seen as aggressive behavior that occurs as a defensive reaction to a perceived threat (Dodge & Coie, 1987). Proactive aggression is defined in terms of goal-directed aggressive behaviors that are deliberate, planned, and accompanied by relatively little emotion (Dodge & Coie, 1987)

Aspects of both the frustration-aggression model and social learning theory have been implicated in making the distinction between children who display reactive and those who display proactive aggression (see Dodge, 1991; Dodge, Lochman, Harnish, Bates, & Petit, 1997). The frustration-aggression model supports the notion of reactive aggression where aggression is viewed as an angry reaction to frustration. Social learning theory focuses on the proactive aspects of aggression, conceptualizing aggression as goal-directed, instrumental behavior controlled by patterns of reinforcement.

Several distinctions have been made between youth who display reactive versus proactive aggression, using either teacher checklists (Dodge & Coie, 1987; Dodge et al., 1997) or juvenile court records (Dodge et al., 1997). Early stressful life events, such as a history of physical abuse, have been associated with reactive rather than proactive aggression (Dodge et al., 1997). Reactive aggressors have also been found to display more social problems in elementary school than do children who are proactive aggressors (Day, Bream, & Pal, 1992; Dodge, Price, Bachorowski, & Newman, 1990; Price & Dodge, 1989). In an additional study of elementary school children, both reactive and pervasive aggressors (who were high on measures of proactive *and* reactive aggression) were found to be characterized by lower peer social preference ratings and more social problems than either proactive aggressors or nonaggressive children (Dodge et al., 1997). Social information processing mechanisms have also been implicated in the distinction between proactive and reactive aggression. For example, Dodge (1991) hypothesized that early stages of processing, such as encoding, would be related to reactive aggression, whereas later stages, such as response evaluation, would be more closely related to proactive aggression. Related to these hypotheses, hostile attribution biases, which are believed to occur during the early stages of information processing (encoding), have been found to be characteristic of reactive aggressors (Dodge & Coie, 1987; Dodge et al., 1997) but not proactive aggressors. Positive outcome expectancies for aggressive behavior, which are believed to occur during later stages of processing (response evaluation), have been found to be more characteristic of children who display proactive aggression than those whose behavior is characterized primarily by reactive aggression (Crick & Dodge, 1996; Dodge et al., 1997).

Although research has suggested that aggressive children may display aspects of both types of aggression, it is possible to distinguish between these groups by considering which type of aggressive behavior is most predominant (Cornell et al., 1996; Dodge et al., 1997). Although making distinctions between aggressive subtypes is of obvious importance, more research in this area is needed to pursue the goal of understanding the etiologies of different types of aggression and reaching the point of matching appropriate interventions to specific aggressive subtypes.

THE DEVELOPMENT AND MAINTENANCE OF AGGRESSIVE BEHAVIOR TEMPERAMENT

Temperment

Child temperament has been postulated as an individual difference variable that may relate to increased aggressive behavior in both children and adolescents. For example, some research findings have suggested that undercontrolled temperament characteristics (e.g., low response threshold with heightened emotional reactivity, intense emotional responses, low soothability, heightened activity level) displayed by children at 3 years of age is related to self-reported levels of impulsivity, recklessness, aggressiveness, and social alienation at 18 years of age, whereas indices of a more inhibited temperament style are related to fewer problems in these areas (Caspi & Silva, 1995). With reference to specific subtypes of aggression, it has been suggested that chronic physiological underarousal may underlie instrumental aggression, whereas overarousal or physiological overreactivity may underlie emotional/reactive aggression (Scarpa & Raine, 1997).

A larger body of research suggests that an interaction between child temperament and parental/familial factors is more strongly predictive of developmental outcomes. For instance, preschoolers' easy temperaments have been associated with fewer behavioral problems, regardless of family environment; but the combination of difficult child temperament and a highly expressive and conflictual family environment has been linked to an increased likelihood of childhood aggression (Tschann, Kaiser, Chesney, Alkon, & Boyce, 1996). Here, it is noteworthy that neither difficult temperament nor a conflictual family environment alone was predictive of heightened aggressiveness and that easy temperament was related to fewer behavior problems irrespective of family/parental factors. These findings suggest that children's temperament may function as either a risk factor or a protective factor, depending on the quality of their caregiving environment. Children's emotion-regulation capabilities (e.g., abilities to regulate affective arousal via attentional processes, communication skills, and behavioral coping) have also been postulated as key variables mediating the relationship between physiological arousal/temperament processes and behavioral outcomes (Fabes, Eisenberg, Karbon, Troyer, & Switzer, 1994; Wilson & Gottman, 1996). The development of effective and adaptive emotion-regulation capabilities has been strongly linked with parental factors (e.g., modeling, teaching, reinforcement) and the overall quality of parent-child interaction patterns. Moreover, poor emotion regulation abilities have been linked with both children's attachment insecurity and an increased risk of engaging in aggressive behaviors.

The Role of Attachment

Attachment theory has emerged as a dominant perspective for understanding the development of parent-child interactional problems and child psychopathology. Based on the work of Ainsworth and Bowlby (1991), attachment theory has continued to develop and accumulate solid empirical support over the past three decades. Briefly, attachment theory states that over the course of the first years of life, children come to rely on primary caregivers to meet their needs for comfort, support, and safety. Through this process, children come to internalize a model of their attachment figure's availability and style of providing for their needs. Securely attached children tend to demonstrate more positive inter actions with their caregivers and, when distressed, are more readily soothed by their caregivers (Ainsworth, Blehar, Waters, & Wall, 1978). Insecurely attached children either ignore their caregivers when distressed or express high levels of anger toward caregivers, and have more difficulty being soothed when distressed. They generally have trouble using their relationship with their caregiver to regulate their needs for security and autonomy, particularly in stressful situations.

A central tenet of attachment theory is that attachment security develops out of a history of receiving sensitive, contingent care, wherein significant caregivers are responsive to their child's cues and needs. Increased risk of developing an insecure attachment has been repeatedly linked with parenting factors (e.g., parental psychopathology, substance abuse), factors that can negatively affect the quality of caregiving via reduced parental sensitivity and responsiveness to child needs, or by reduced availability due to competing demands placed on the parent (Belsky & Isabella, 1988; Goldsmith & Alansky, 1987; van Ijzendoorn, Goldberg, Kroonenberg, & Frenkel, 1992). Socioenvironmental stressors (e.g., poverty, single parenthood, lower parental educational level, higher frequency of stressful life events) that have the potential to compromise the quality of caregiving

have been inconsistently linked to an increased risk of developing an insecure attachment (Easterbrooks & Goldberg, 1990). Current findings suggest that the relationship between socioenvironmental stressors and quality of attachment is mediated by parenting sensitivity (Belsky, 1984; Belsky & Isabella, 1988). Indeed, the development of attachment security appears to reflect a history of more or less optimal matching between child needs and parenting styles, or the "goodness-of-fit" between child characteristics and parent caregiving styles (Belsky & Isabella, 1988).

The development of a secure attachment involves the internalization of a view that others are available for care and comfort and, therefore, plays an important role in promoting socioemotional adaptation. Research has shown that securely attached children are more socially competent, better behaviorally adjusted, and better able to regulate emotions than those with insecure attachments (Cicchetti, Ganiban, & Barnett, 1991; Lamb, Thompson, Gardner, & Charnov, 1985; Sroufe, 1983). On the other hand, insecure attachment has been linked to increased risk of child maladjustment, including higher rates of aggressive behaviors, fewer prosocial behaviors, and more emotion-regulation difficulties during the preschool years (Greenberg & Speltz, 1988).

In particular, atypical insecure attachments in the infant/toddler years have been found to predict increased rates of aggressive behaviors with peers at 5 years of age (Lyons-Ruth, Alpern, & Repacholi, 1993). Additionally, maternal psychopathology during a child's infant/toddler years has been found to independently predict children's aggressive behaviors at age 5 years apart from attachment insecurity (Lyons-Ruth et al., 1993). In another study, atypical attachments at 12 months of age and maternal perceptions of toddlers as being difficult to manage during their second year of life have been found to conjointly predict increased levels of aggressive behaviors at age 5 (D.S. Shaw, Owens, Vondra, & Keenan, 1996). Most strikingly, the combination of atypical attachment at 12 months, along with maternal psychopathology and parental disagreements about child rearing at 24 months, predicted children's aggressive behaviors at age 5 years as well as did children's level of aggression at age 3.

Although attachment refers to a child's relationship with a significant caregiver, parental factors have consistently been found to correlate more highly than child factors with attachment security (Belsky & Isabella, 1988; van Ijzendoorn et al., 1992). Constantino (1996) has found parents' insecure mental representations of attachments (i.e., attitudes regarding self, significant others, and social interaction patterns) to be linked with increased rates of child aggressive behaviors in the preschool years. In this same study, maternal education, family income, parental abuse histories, and other family history variables did not discriminate aggressive from nonaggressive children. Thus, parental attitudes regarding parenting and parent-child relationships, and expectations for children's behavior, appear to play a strong role in the development of children's aggressive behaviors via caregiving and parent-child interaction patterns.

The Modeling of Aggression
In support of a social learning formulation, a number of laboratory-based studies have provided data suggesting that aggressive behavior can be learned and facilitated by the individual's vicarious learning experiences (Bandura, 1965; Bandura, Ross, & Ross, 1961, 1963).

Support for the relationship between modeling experiences and aggressive behavior has also been demonstrated in more naturalistic studies such as those dealing with the effects of television violence. Of note are the results of longitudinal research that have suggested that the amount of violent TV watched by males during childhood is a significant predictor of aggressive behavior in later adolescence (see Eron & Huesmann, 1984). A separate study observed increases in aggressive behavior and concurrent decreases in prosocial behaviors in 4- to 6-year-olds after viewing a violent cartoon or playing a violent video game (Silvern & Williamson, 1987). More recently, observational learning principles have been extended to the learning of cognitions. Here, it has been suggested that viewing violent images in the mass media may contribute to lasting cognitive schemas that mediate future aggressive behavior (see Huesmann, Moise, & Podolski, 1997). Taken together, findings from laboratory and naturalistic studies provide strong support for the role of vicarious learning in the development of aggressive modes of responding. It seems important to point out, however, that although the results of such studies suggest that aggressive behaviors can be acquired through observation, the performance of aggressive behaviors

may be importantly related to the consequences that are later made contingent on these behaviors.

Aggressive Behaviors as Operants
Other studies have also demonstrated a relationship between contingent reinforcement and continued aggressive responding. Geen (1976), for example, has noted that several laboratory studies have demonstrated increased aggressive behavior when such behaviors are followed by verbal approval. Walters and Brown (1963) have shown that it is possible, by reinforcing children for displaying aggressive responses toward a plastic Bobo doll, to increase aggressive behavior even when assessed several days later. The effects of reinforcement on aggression have also been demonstrated in observational research by Patterson, Littman, and Bricker (1967). Here, children whose aggressive behaviors were usually followed by reinforcement (submission, crying, etc., on the part of the victimized child) displayed the highest levels of aggression. More recently, research comparing preschoolers identified as displaying either high or low rates of aggression during interactions with their mothers has found both aversive parenting behaviors and the functional utility of child aggressive behaviors (e.g., in terminating conflictual parent-child interactions) to be predictive of overall child aggression (Snyder & Patterson, 1995).

Taken together, the findings concerning the learning and maintenance of aggressive behavior are quite in line with the social learning position presented earlier.

THE MODIFICATION OF AGGRESSIVE BEHAVIOR

Several approaches have been successfully employed in attempting to modify aggressive child behavior. A variety of studies have found that it is possible to reduce aggressive behavior by exposing the child to nonaggressive models or models whose aggressive behaviors are disapproved of or punished (see Bandura, 1973; Kirkland & Thelen, 1977).

An additional procedure shown to be effective in dealing with aggressive behavior is time-out. As there are several excellent discussions of time-out procedures in the published literature (Gelfand & Hartmann, 1984; Gross & Wixted, 1987; Herbert, 1987; A.O. Ross, 1981), research findings related to this procedure will not be reviewed here. Suffice it to say that a range of studies has suggested the use-fulness of time-out in dealing with aggressive child behavior.

Time-out procedures can often be combined with other procedures in such a way as to further enhance effectiveness. For example, time-out procedures can be combined with direct reinforcement of other behavior (DRO) procedures where the child is not only placed in time-out contingent on aggressive behavior but is also rewarded for engaging in behaviors other than the one that is judged problematic. Alternatively, one might combine time-out with reward for some specific behavior that is incompatible with aggression (Gelfand & Hartmann, 1984). Such a combined approach teaches the child not only which behaviors are undesirable (through time-out) but also which behaviors are judged to be more appropriate (through positive reinforcement). In most instances, such an approach is judged to be preferable to the use of time-out alone (Johnson, Rasbury, & Siegel, 1997).

Because aggressive behavior often occurs within the home (and may be accompanied by other behavioral difficulties), intervention with younger children is often carried out within the context of structured parent-child training programs. These programs typically involve training the parent(s) to use behavioral principles such as reinforcement, extinction, and punishment (e.g., time-out, response cost) to decrease aggressive and other problem behaviors and to increase prosocial behaviors. Although parent-child training programs have met with considerable success (Foote, Eyberg, & Schuhmann, 1998; Kazdin, 1987a, 1987b), in recent years, it has become apparent that it may be necessary to combine parent training methods with attempts to remediate social skills deficits that the child may display. Likewise, less-structured interventions designed to enhance family-based communication and to improve parent-child relationships are usually considered to be important as well. Such interventions with multiple foci appear to hold promise for preventing future problems of children who show early aggressive antisocial modes of responding (Patterson, DeBaryhe, & Ramsey, 1989).

It can be noted that at least two specific behavior management programs, which include behavioral techniques such as those described here, have received sufficient empirical support to be considered examples of Empirically Supported Treatments (Brestan & Eyberg, 1998). These programs, which

are designed to reduce conduct disordered behaviors, including aggression, are based on Patterson and Guillion's (1968) book/manual *Living with Children* and Videotape Modeling Parent Training (Webster-Stratton, 1984, 1990, 1994). Patterson's training program relies primarily on the use of operant techniques such as reinforcement, extinction, and time-out to teach parents effective behavior management skills. Videotape Parent Training employs modeling to teach basic principles of parent training originally described by Hanf (1969) in a group format along with therapist-led discussions. Consistent with the designation of Empirically Supported Treatments, both approaches have been found to be highly effective in reducing aggression and other conduct disordered behaviors when evaluated within the context of well controlled empirical studies.

JUVENILE DELINQUENCY

Delinquency is a legal term referring to a juvenile (usually under 18 years of age) who is brought to the attention of the juvenile justice system by virtue of committing a criminal act or displaying a variety of other behaviors not specified under criminal law. These "other behaviors" are usually referred to as status offenses and include truancy, curfew violations, running away from home, and the use of alcohol. Offenses such as these are violations of the law only as a result of the child's age and his or her status as a minor (White, 1989).

Considered within the framework of *DSM-IV* (APA, 1994), the concept of delinquency overlaps with the broader spectrum of problems classified as conduct disorders. These disorders are characterized by a persistent pattern of conduct in which the rights of others and major age-appropriate norms or rules are violated. Specifically, as Kazdin (1987a) has noted, the term conduct disorder refers to instances where the child or adolescent displays a pattern of antisocial behavior that involves a significant impairment in daily functioning and where these behaviors are seen as unmanageable by significant others. Thus, conduct disorders involve antisocial behavior that is *clinically significant* and *beyond the bounds of normal functioning* (Kazdin, 1987a). Although many delinquents meet the criteria for a diagnosis of conduct disorder, many youths who come into contact with the juvenile justice system and who are considered legally delinquent do not show the pattern of seriously antisocial behavior that is associated with the diagnosis of conduct disorder. Likewise, many conduct disordered youth are never considered delinquent, as their illegal behaviors escape detection. As Kazdin has noted, "Although a distinction can be drawn, many of the behaviors of delinquents and conduct disordered youths overlap and fall under the general rubric of antisocial behavior" (p. 23). The seriousness of the problem is suggested by national statistics documenting the persistent problem of juvenile crime and a growing body of evidence from longitudinal studies on the poor outcomes of children identified as "at risk" for conduct disorders or identified by the mental health or judicial system as antisocial (Loeber, 1990; Loeber & Stouthamer-Loeber, 1987).

THE CLASSIFICATION OF DELINQUENCY

Given that juvenile delinquency is essentially a legal category used to designate those who have committed any of numerous offenses, one might expect children or adolescents labeled delinquent to represent a very heterogeneous group. In spite of this, research studies have often focused on the causes, correlates, and treatment of delinquency without taking this variability into account. This tendency to treat delinquency as a unitary construct has often led to unreplicated findings and inconclusive results.

As a result of the observed variability within the delinquent population, some researchers have considered the possibility that various dimensions of delinquency may exist and have attempted to study correlates of these dimensions. Most prominent in this regard is the work of Quay (1964, 1987).

Quay (1964) is generally credited with developing the most widely cited empirically based classification scheme for delineating dimensions of delinquent behavior. In this early research, factor analyses of ratings of behavioral traits obtained from the case histories of institutionalized male delinquents yielded four independent groupings: socialized-subcultural delinquency, unsocialized-psychopathic delinquency, disturbed-neurotic delinquency, and inadequate-immature delinquency.

Delinquents who scored high on the socialized-subcultural dimensions were defined by such traits as having strong allegiance to selected peers, being

accepted by a delinquent subgroup, having bad companions, staying out late at night, and having low ratings on shyness and seclusiveness. Unsocialized-psychopathic delinquents, in contrast, were described as solitary rather than group-oriented delinquents who were rated high on such traits as inability to profit from praise or punishment, defiance of authority, quarrelsomeness, irritability, verbal aggression, impudence, and assaultiveness. Disturbed-neurotic delinquents were described as unhappy, shy, timid, and withdrawn, and prone to anxiety, worry, and guilt over their behavior. The final group, the inadequate-immature group, was described as not usually accepted by delinquent peers, passive and preoccupied, picked on by others, and easily frustrated. Quay (1987) later characterized this fourth group of youngsters as being relatively inadequate in their functioning and often unable to cope with environmental demands because of a poorly developed behavioral repertoire.

Although often given different labels (see Quay, 1987), these four dimensions have been replicated in a number of other factor analytic studies of delinquent behavior, and variables associated with these subtypes have been examined. As much of the research related to the correlates of these dimensions has been reviewed by Quay and will be alluded to at later points in this chapter, it will not be considered in detail here. However, the results of this research strongly argue for the distinction among subgroups. Unfortunately, studies that attempt to determine antecedents and correlates of delinquency or that attempt to develop treatments of delinquency, considering delinquency as a unitary construct, are still prominent in the research literature.

THE MAGNITUDE OF THE JUVENILE CRIME PROBLEM

Although arrest rates of juveniles increased dramatically between 1960 and 1973 (138% for juveniles as opposed to 16% for adults) and although there was a similar increase in the rates of youth seen by the juvenile courts (a 250% increase between 1950 and 1974), the actual rates of delinquent behavior seemed to level off from the mid-1970s through the mid-1980s (Loeber, 1990; White, 1989). However, juvenile crime remains a significant social problem and has been on the rise since the mid- to late 1980s. Between 1985 and 1994, the number of delinquency cases processed by U.S. juvenile courts increased 41%. Somewhere between 4% and 5% of the adolescent population were being seen by the juvenile courts for delinquent offenses through the 1980s, a figure that stood in contrast with the figure of 2%, which represented the proportion of the juvenile population that was seen in juvenile courts in 1960 (U.S. Department of Justice, 1978). However, 7.7% of the total juvenile population were taken into police custody in 1995, and 5.8% of the U.S. juvenile population were arrested in 1996 (U.S. Department of Justice, 1996). Between 1985 and 1994, the number of person offense cases (e.g., robbery, assault) processed by the juvenile courts increased 93%, with drug offense cases up 62%, public order offenses up 50%, and property offenses up 22% (Butts, Snyder, Aughenbaugh, & Poole, 1996). Most disturbing was the increase in juvenile weapons violations, which increased 156% from 1985 through 1994.

Delinquency has often been characterized as a male problem, but the number of female delinquents has increased over the years with the present sex ratio being around 3 or 4 to 1. Between 1985 and 1994, the volume of delinquency cases involving males increased by 38%, and the number of cases involving females increased 54% (Butts et al., 1996). Historically, there have also appeared to be important sex differences regarding type of delinquent behavior most characteristically displayed. Specifically, more males than females have been arrested for violent crimes and crimes against property, whereas females typically have been more likely to be charged with offenses such as sexual promiscuity, running away from home, truancy, and violation of liquor laws (White, 1989). However, whereas males were involved in 79% of the delinquency cases handled by juvenile courts in 1994, the offense characteristics of the male and female juvenile cases were similar (Butts et al., 1996).

Other data regarding the occurrence of delinquent behavior have come from studies of "normal" individuals responding to anonymous questionnaires. Results of these studies suggest that a great deal of antisocial and delinquent behavior goes undetected, the so-called hidden delinquency. For example, an early study by Offer, Sabshin, and Marcus (1965) found that as many as 75% of their respondents admitted to acts that would be labeled delinquent if detected. Likewise, other investigations obtaining anonymous self-reports of delinquent behavior have suggested that 80% to 90% of adolescents display delinquent behavior that does not come to the attention of the juvenile justice system (Gibbons & Krohn, 1986; Jefferson & Johnson, 1991).

As can be seen from these findings, whether one considers official crime statistics or self-report surveys of normal individuals, an alarming percentage of young people admit to, or are charged with, antisocial and/or delinquent acts.

ETIOLOGICAL PERSPECTIVES ON DELINQUENCY

Biological Views

Biological views of delinquency typically highlight the influence of genetic, neuropsychological, or psychophysiological factors in the development of delinquency. Although there are numerous studies documenting the role of genetic factors in the development of antisocial behavior, perhaps some of the best data have come from a recent large-scale meta-analysis of twin and adoption studies conducted by Mason and Frick (1994). Results of this study suggest a significant genetic contribution. Indeed, some 50% of the variance in antisocial behavior was found to be directly attributable to genetic factors.

Regarding neuropsychological and neurophysiological characteristics, Hooper and Tramontana (1997) note that a variety of studies have reported abnormal neurological findings. Electrophysiological studies have found evidence for increased frequencies of sleep abnormalities, specific types of seizure activity (which may relate to recurrent and unprovoked aggression), and frontal lobe paroxysmal activity in antisocial adolescents with a history of assaultive behavior. Hooper and Tramontana also cite studies that have found juvenile offenders to show a variety of impairments on neuropsychological tests. Prominent in these findings are language-related difficulties and deficits in executive functions. Here executive function deficits refer to deficits in self-directed actions: in the organization of behavior; in the use of self-directed speech, rules, or plans; in the inability to delay gratification; or in the carrying out of future-oriented, purposeful, goal-directed, or intentional actions (Barkley, 1997). Studies focusing on other biological factors have found conduct disordered children to have lowered levels of certain neurotransmitters such as serotonin and epinephrine and higher levels of the male hormone testosterone. Such children have likewise been found to display abnormalities in autonomic responding (e.g., showing reduced autonomic reactivity on psychophysiological measures) (Frick, 1998).

Although findings such as these are suggestive, it is difficult to draw firm conclusions because of methodological limitations inherent in most published studies. And it is unlikely that the neuropsychological, neurochemical, and psychophysiological differences described above are characteristic of all children with antisocial behavior.

Sociological Views

Sociological or sociocultural theories have emphasized a wide range of social factors in the development of delinquency (Rogers & Mays, 1987; White, 1989). For example, specific theories have dealt with the cultural transmission of delinquency (C.R. Shaw & McKay, 1969), group delinquency (Thrasher, 1963), and middle-class delinquency (Vaz, 1967), among other factors. The inability of an individual to obtain socially valued goals (property, status) through legitimate means has been proposed by some as a major variable in the development of antisocial behavior. Merton (1957), for instance, has suggested that when social constraints do not permit members of the lower socioeconomic classes to obtain desired goals, they often resort to delinquent behavior to reach them. A somewhat similar formulation is presented by the "opportunity structure theory" (Cloward & Ohlin, 1969). This suggests that lower-socioeconomic-class youths blame society for their lack of opportunity to reach desired goals and become disenchanted and alienated by society's failure to meet their needs. By affiliating with a delinquent subculture, their needs for status and material gains are met along with the opportunity to act on their feelings of frustration and alienation. Recognition of the role of limited education and job opportunities among the lower income groups in the United States led to the development of such federally subsidized training programs as the Job Corps.

Psychological Views

Two broad classes of psychological theories are evident: those that emphasize intrapsychic conflict and those that stress the effects of learning. Psychodynamic theories often emphasize the role of individual intraspychic factors or family conflicts in the development of delinquency. From this point of view, antisocial behavior is seen as a form of psychopathology, frequently symptomatic of an underlying defect in personality, underlying conflict, or a characterological disorder. In general, dynamic theories have tended to view inadequate or faulty early life interpersonal relations between child and parent as crucial to the development of antisocial behaviors. These behaviors are seen as developing out of the neurotic need to assuage guilt through punishment or out of displaced hostility or anxiety that results in the individual's acting out against society.

In contrast, learning-based perspectives generally view antisocial behavior as resulting largely from environmental influences. For example, Bandura (1973) outlined a social learning theory of delinquency based on two learning principles: (1) delinquent behavior can be learned either through direct experience or through the observation of others who display such behaviors, and (2) delinquent behavior, like all behavior, is influenced and maintained by environmental factors that include both the opportunity for delinquent behavior and the consequences that follow the behavior. Similarly, A.O. Ross (1974) has conceptualized delinquency as reflecting the failure to have learned essential controls over deviant behavior typically acquired during the course of childhood.

VARIABLES ASSOCIATED WITH JUVENILE DELINQUENCY

Delinquency and Social Class

The apparent relationship between juvenile delinquency and lower socioeconomic classes has gained credence from official delinquency statistics that show delinquency rates to be somewhat higher among youth from lower social classes (Schwartz & Johnson, 1985). However, this relationship seems to hold only for urban areas. Studies from rural areas and small towns have generally not shown greater delinquency rates among youth from the lower socioeconomic classes. Furthermore, when one examines the rates of so-called hidden or undetected delinquency among young people, the relationship between social class and antisocial behavior is even less clear. Employing anonymous self-report surveys, a number of investigators have shown that a high proportion of children from all social classes admit to antisocial behavior (Empey, 1978; Gold & Petronio, 1980).

Although the results of these self-report studies suggest that delinquent behavior is unrelated to socioeconomic status, such a conclusion has been questioned by studies that have assessed both the *rate* and the *severity* of delinquent offenses in addition to their occurrence. Reviews of this literature (Elliot & Ageton, 1980; Rutter & Giller, 1984) have suggested that although self-report studies have found the majority of youths from various socioeconomic backgrounds reporting "delinquent" behavior, many of the offenses reported are not especially serious ones. Elliot and Ageton found that when both the rate and severity of offenses are considered in self-report studies, social class is inversely related to indicators of "severe" delinquency. These findings seem to indicate that although juveniles from the upper social classes (as a group) may engage in delinquent activities, these illegal acts, on the whole, are less severe and less frequent than those displayed by lower-socioeconomic-status youth (as a group).

Family Variables

Numerous investigations have suggested a link between family variables and delinquent behavior. For example, in a now classic study, Glueck and Glueck (1950; see also Glueck & Glueck 1968) sought to delineate differences between 500 male delinquents and 500 nondelinquents from high-delinquency areas. As a group, parents of delinquents were found to more often display serious physical problems as well as emotional, intellectual, and behavioral disturbances. There was also more evidence of alcoholism, criminal behavior, and "immorality" among these parents than among parents of nondelinquents. The relationships between parents and delinquent children were characterized by more conflict and incompatability than were the families of nondelinquents, and, as might be expected, families of delinquents were more often characterized by separation, divorce, and prolonged absence of a parent from the home.

As regards parent-child attitudes, parents of delinquents were found to be much less likely to show warmth, sympathy, and affection toward their children. Mothers of delinquents were found to be far more permissive than mothers of nondelinquents.

Fathers of delinquents tended to be stricter in their discipline than were fathers of nondelinquents and more often resorted to the use of physical punishment. Also, inconsistent discipline was more than twice as prominent among fathers of delinquent boys. Finally, families of delinquents were found to display less regularity in general family routine and a higher degree of disorganization than families of nondelinquents.

More recent investigations have also focused on family factors that may be related to the development of delinquency among "high-risk" children and adolescents. Such investigations have suggested that, although impoverished living conditions (e.g., stress related to low SES, living in neighborhoods with higher rates of violent crime) seem related to an increased likelihood of delinquent behavior, family structural factors may mediate the effects of poverty on delinquent behavior. Noteworthy in this regard, Sampson and Laub (1994) identified patterns of erratic, threatening, and harsh disciplinary practices by parents, low levels of parental supervision of adolescent behaviors, and poor quality parent-child relationships as being important mediating variables in determining the likelihood of adolescent delinquency in low SES living conditions. A number of other studies have explored the relationship between family variables and delinquency. As much of this research has been described in detail elsewhere (Moore & Arthur, 1983; Snyder & Patterson, 1987), only a brief overview will be provided here.

In general, studies have found parents of delinquents to display lower levels of moral judgment, to be more extreme in terms of discipline (permissiveness-restrictiveness), to be more hostile and rejecting, to be more likely to use physical punishment, to be more erratic and inconsistent in discipline, to show higher levels of parental conflict, and to display higher rates of antisocial behavior. It may be noted that the majority of these findings are consistent with the earlier results of the Glueck and Glueck studies.

Unfortunately, most studies that have found differences in the families of delinquent versus nondelinquent children have treated delinquents as a homogeneous group, failing to consider the relationship between the various subtypes of delinquency and different child-rearing practices or family interactions that may characterize these groups.

Personality Correlates

A sizable number of studies have compared delinquents to nondelinquents on a variety of personality measures, including interviews, projective tests (e.g., Rorschach Inkblot Test), and objective personality measures (e.g., Minnesota Multiphasic Personality Inventory, MMPI) as well as on measures designed to assess specific personality constructs (e.g., time orientation, impulsivity, locus of control, self-concept). Results of such studies are often found to be inconsistent, with few clear patterns emerging (see Arbuthnot, Gordon, & Jurkovic, 1987, for an overview of much this research).

It is noteworthy that few studies have investigated personality characteristics of delinquents classified according to the subtypes cited earlier (Quay, 1964, 1987). When correlates of subtypes have been investigated, interesting findings have often emerged. For example, Genshaft (1980) compared the MMPI profiles of a group of juvenile delinquents classified according to Quay's (1964) scheme. When the groups were compared with regard to profile characteristics, significant differences were found. For example, the mean 2-point code type for the neurotic-delinquent group was 4-8/8-4 (Pd, Sc), whereas the predominant 2-point code for the psychopathic-delinquent group was 8-9/9-8 (Sc, Ma). The mean code type for the socialized-delinquent group was 4-5/5-4 (Pd, Mf). The fact that these results were replicated in a subsequent cross-validation study provides additional support for the notion that the findings represent reliable differences among delinquent subtypes.

Likewise, research by Ellis (1982) dealing with the relationship between delinquency and empathy has supported the need to consider the variability within the delinquent population. Here, Ellis found delinquents as a group to show lower levels of empathy than nondelinquents. However, further analyses that assessed subgroup differences in empathy found disturbed-neurotic delinquents to be the least empathic, followed by unsocialized-psychopathic delinquents and socialized-subcultural delinquents (who did not differ from nondelinquents). Each of these three delinquent groups was found to differ significantly from the others. Again, these findings suggest the importance of making distinctions among types of delinquents in personality research.

One additional variable worthy of discussion could also be considered under the earlier heading of biological factors and delinquency. This is the variable of sensation seeking (Zuckerman, 1979). Sensation seeking can be defined as the tendency to engage in a variety of exciting, stimulating, and novel behaviors that are assumed to result in increased arousal (e.g., race car driving, skydiving). It has been suggested that tendencies toward sensation seeking result from a biologically determined deficit whereby the person displays a less-than-optimal level of arousal. Sensation seekers are thus seen as engaging in behaviors that will raise their level of stimulation to some more optimal state.

Regarding such behaviors, it may be pointed out that there are numerous antisocial acts that may be quite stimulating when engaged in (e.g., trying to get away with stealing a car, experimenting with certain drugs). It seems reasonable to assume that, if socially acceptable ways of increasing stimulation are not readily available, the high-sensation seeker may engage in delinquent behavior that does provide stimulation. Although the exact relationship between sensation seeking and delinquent behavior is unclear, Farley and Sewell (1976) found higher sensation seeking scores among delinquents than among nondelinquents. Farley and Farley (1972) also found institutionalized female delinquents scoring high in sensation seeking to show more aggressive behavior, to make more escape attempts, and to disobey supervisors more often than low-scoring delinquents. Indices of sensation seeking have also been found to relate to drug usage and to extent and variety of sexual behavior (Zuckerman, 1979). Although tendencies toward sensation seeking have been linked to delinquency per se, it seems likely that sensation seeking may be primarily characteristic of unsocialized-psychopathic delinquency, as laboratory studies have found unsocialized-psychopathic delinquents to differ from other delinquent subgroups in terms of stimulation-seeking behaviors (Quay, 1987).

DELINQUENCY AND OTHER CHILDHOOD BEHAVIOR PROBLEMS

Academic Underachievement and Learning Problems

There is a sizable literature that suggests increased rates of academic underachievement and learning disabilities in conduct disordered and antisocial youth (Frick, 1998; Hinshaw & Anderson, 1996). Investigators have reported estimates of learning problems among adjudicated delinquents that are, in some cases, as high as 90% (Zinkus & Gottlieb, 1977). Frick (1998) has cited more recent findings that somewhere between 20% and 25% of conduct disordered children display evidence of actual learning disability. Keilitz and Dunivant (1986), in a study of some 1,943 adolescent males from public schools, juvenile courts, and correctional facilities, have also found learning disabled males to have significantly higher rates of violence, substance abuse, arrests, and adjudication than non-learning disabled males.

Despite data that support a link between various types of learning problems and antisocial behavior, many questions remain unanswered. For example, are learning problems and academic underachievement contributors to the development of delinquency and antisocial behavior, or are they a consequence of problems associated antisocial behavior such as poor school attendance, disruptive classroom behavior that interferes with learning, and so forth? Such question are important, as different treatment foci may result from different etiologic assumptions. Although the precise nature of the frequently documented relationship between child and adolescent antisocial behavior and learning difficulties remains unclear, reviews of this literature by Hinshaw (Hinshaw, Heller, & McHale, 1992; Hinshaw & Anderson, 1996) have led to some tentative conclusions. Here, it has been suggested that the nature of the relationship between these variables may vary as a function of age. With young children, the association between conduct disorder and academic problems is seen as resulting mainly from the fact that ADHD is a commonly occurring comorbid condition in conduct disordered children *and* is significantly associated with learning problems; the link between antisocial behavior and learning problems thus results from their joint association with ADHD. Indeed, somewhere between 19% and 26% of children with ADHD show diagnosable learning disabilities (Barkley, 1996), and many more display less serious problems of academic underachievement. The relationship between delinquency and learning difficulties may be somewhat different in those with adolescent-onset antisocial behavior. Among this group, academic deficits frequently appear *prior* to the onset of antisocial behavior, perhaps suggesting a causal relationship whereby academic problems contribute to the development of antisocial behavior (Hinshaw &

Anderson, 1996). Clearly, additional research is needed in this area.

Problems of Attention and Hyperactivity
There is considerable evidence for an association between hyperactive attention disordered behavior and antisocial modes of responding (Barkley, 1996, 1997; Rutter & Giller, 1984). For example, in contrast to the prevalence of this disorder in the general population, where estimates range from 3% to 5% (APA, 1994; Rapport, 1987), figures as high as 30% have been suggested for juvenile offenders (Taylor & Watt, 1977). Symptoms of restlessness, distractibility, and irritability have been found in the case histories of adult criminals and in the early developmental histories of children brought before the juvenile court system (Cantwell, 1978; D.M. Ross & Ross, 1976).

A link between juvenile delinquency and hyperkinesis has also gained credence through studies of later life outcome for hyperactive children. Studies of children diagnosed hyperkinetic in childhood suggest that many of these children later have multiple police and court contacts (Stewart, Mendelson, & Johnson, 1973), are often institutionalized for antisocial behavior (Huessy, Metayer, & Townsend, 1974), and are more likely to show evidence of substance abuse (Barkley, 1996, 1997; Hinshaw & Anderson, 1996).

An additional line of evidence comes from the positive response of some delinquents to stimulant drugs employed in the treatment of hyperkinesis (Maletsky, 1974). Most noteworthy in this regard are recent findings of Hinshaw et al., (1992), which indicated that children with ADHD were more likely to engage in both stealing and cheating than were control children, but that stimulant medication brought about a reduction in both stealing and property destruction. The link between ADHD and antisocial behavior is also suggested by the fact that hyperkinetic children and at least certain delinquents appear to show similar types of response to stimulation (e.g., smaller autonomic responses, slower habituation to stimuli) (Hastings & Barkley, 1978; Satterfield & Schell, 1984). Reasoning that such delinquents may suffer from an abnormally low level of arousal, which stimulant drugs may raise (not unlike the condition seen in hyperkinetic children), Cantwell (1978) has proposed that organically based defects in physiological arousal may account for the frequently observed continuity between hyperkinesis and later delinquency.

Whatever the degree to which such arousal deficits account for the behavioral problems of antisocial children, it is clear that many hyperkinetic children do not engage in serious antisocial behavior and that many delinquents do not manifest hyperactive symptoms. Current research suggests that these variables may turn out to operate most potently with unsocialized-psychopathic delinquents who display hyperactivity in childhood and who, as adolescents and adults, are described as "stimulation seekers" (Quay, 1965).

Alcohol Abuse
Alcohol usage has been identified as a potential moderating variable that interacts with other factors related to an increased likelihood of violent criminal behaviors in adolescent males. Specifically, it has been found that although alcohol usage does not seem to be independently related to violent crime, it does appear to interact with deviant social attitudes and propensity toward aggression/hostility in increasing the likelihood of violent criminal activity (Zhang, Wieczorek, & Welte, 1997).

LATER LIFE OUTCOMES AND PROGNOSIS

In a major study related to the prognosis of delinquency, Glueck and Glueck (1968) conducted an extensive follow-up of 500 delinquent and 500 nondelinquent males who had participated in their earlier study (Glueck & Glueck, 1950) who (at follow-up) were in their mid-twenties and early thirties. The overall outcome for the delinquents was much worse than for the nondelinquents on almost all measures considered. For example, 84% of the former delinquents had had court convictions. Although the number of serious offenses committed did decline with increasing age, frequent arrests involving vagrancy, drunk and disorderly conduct, assault, and desertion of family persisted into adult life. In contrast, the nondelinquents generally remained out of the court systems and had more stable marriages and better educational and employment records.

Similar later life outcomes for children displaying early antisocial behavior have been reported by Robins (1966), who found that, at follow-up, 82% of

male subjects had been arrested for a nontraffic offense, 70% of female subjects had been married early to men with high rates of criminal arrests and had been divorced, and both groups had higher rates of unemployment and poor work records. About 25% had been on public assistance and had a very high rate of alcohol abuse.

Another study by Henn, Bordwell, and Jenkins (1980) addressed the issue of different adult life outcome for different subtypes of delinquents. Case records of a large sample of delinquents treated in the Iowa State Training School for Boys were examined, and three subgroups were identified: undersocialized aggressive, undersocialized unaggressive, and socialized delinquents. The groups differed significantly in the number of subsequent adult arrests for violent crimes as well as in the number of criminal convictions and incarcerations. The investigators concluded that there was a tendency for the hostile, confrontive behavior of the undersocialized aggressive males and the runaway, sneaky activity of the undersocialized unaggressive males to continue into adult life. Again, it is important to note that many of the boys successfully negotiated return to their homes and had no further contact with the criminal justice system. Nevertheless, the fact that almost 53% of the undersocialized aggressives were subsequently jailed for crimes, including crimes of violence, suggests that the continual search for effective treatment is necessary. Follow-up statistics such as those just discussed suggest a generally unfavorable outlook for juveniles who become known to legal authorities for antisocial behavior. Whether this is characteristic of adjudicated delinquents as a group or the prognosis for specific subgroups, such as those defined by Quay (1964, 1987), is better than for others is an important question. Generally, the prognosis would seem to be the poorest for those juveniles who engage in seriously delinquent acts of a varied nature and whose antisocial behaviors began as preadolescents (Moore & Arthur, 1983).

THE MODIFICATION OF DELINQUENT BEHAVIOR

Given the seriousness of the problem, it is not surprising that a variety of treatment approaches have been developed to deal with children and adolescents who display delinquent behaviors. These approaches have ranged from probation to institutionalization to the development of community-based programs of various sorts.

Historically, one popular approach for dealing with delinquent youth has been institutionalization. Most states have one or more institutions referred to as detention centers, training schools, or reform schools that are designed specifically for the treatment of delinquents. These institutions vary widely along the custodial-rehabilitative dimension. Some have active treatment programs; others primarily serve a custodial role of keeping the juvenile offender separated from society. For the most part, institutional treatment is reserved for those youths who are most committed to crime and who have been convicted of the most serious offenses (Binder, 1988). Unfortunately, institutions that are adequate to meet the rehabilitation needs of these types of residents are probably in the minority.

Stumphauzer (1986) has suggested that rather than being a place where youths are rehabilitated, juvenile correctional institutions often provide a fertile environment within which youths learn new modes of antisocial behaviors and where delinquent behaviors are maintained through reinforcement provided by peers and inadvertently by staff who respond inconsistently to antisocial behaviors.

The high recidivism rates of those who have been incarcerated suggest that standard institutional treatment is generally not highly successful. Early studies have shown that, at least among males, as many as 70% to 80% of juveniles who are institutionalized are likely to be rearrested within a year or so following their release (Cohen & Filipczak, 1971; Gibbons, 1976).

Because of the lack of success resulting from traditional institutional treatment, several innovative treatment programs have been developed that have been carried out both within and outside of the institutional setting. Of those programs that have been carried out within correctional institutions, two are the most notable. These are the Contingencies Applicable to Special Education (CASE) project, conducted by Cohen and Filipczak (1971), and the Cascadia project, conducted by Sarason and Ganzer (1971).

In the CASE program, the focus was on developing academic skills, because a lack of such skills was assumed to preclude the individual from finishing school and finding meaningful employment and indirectly to increase the likelihood of future delinquency. The program involved developing a token economy whereby residents were reinforced for engaging in a range of desirable academic behaviors and for improved academic performance. Participants were found to make rapid improvement in terms of both academic and social behaviors. During the two-year period after release, participants were found to have a recidivism rate much below that of juveniles who received the usual institutional treatment. These changes were not, however, found to be maintained at a three-year follow-up. Thus, although the program effected significant change, these effects were less durable than one would wish. To bring about more long-lasting change, it may be necessary to modify contingencies, not only within the institution but in the natural environment as well.

Sarason and colleagues (Sarason, 1968; Sarason & Ganzer, 1971), in a large-scale study conducted at the Cascadia Juvenile Reception and Diagnostic Center in Tacoma, Washington, had residents observe models who depicted behaviors appropriate to a wide range of situations that they might encounter in the future (e.g., how to resist temptation, how to delay gratification). They were then asked to discuss the contents of these scenes and role-play what they had observed. The program, which lasted for 16 sessions, was based on the assumption that juvenile offenders are deficient in many of the skills necessary for functioning in a socially acceptable manner and that such skills can be learned through modeling and role-playing procedures. Residents receiving this modeling treatment were compared with others who participated in a discussion group who did not observe models or engage in role playing and with a group who received the usual institutional treatment. After a five-year period, residents who had participated in treatment (modeling, discussion group) were shown to have a recidivism rate less than half that of the control group receiving institutional treatment. These findings strongly suggest that such an approach is likely to be useful in teaching adaptive prosocial behaviors to juvenile offenders and that the learning of such behaviors may relate to a decreased likelihood of repeat offenses.

Along with those treatment programs conducted within institutions, there have been others based in community settings. This move toward community-based interventions has been partly due to the fact that such treatments are usually less costly than treatment within an institution. The assumption underlying community-based treatment programs is that changes made within the context of these programs are more likely to generalize to the youth's home environment. Further, it is often assumed that there is no need for the youth to be institutionalized in cases where the offender is not considered dangerous. Finally, since the mid-1970s, the push for deinstitutionalization has been spurred on by the passage of the Juvenile Justice and Delinquency Act, which prohibits the institutionalization of status offenders who have not committed illegal acts.

Because a detailed overview of community-based programs is beyond the scope of this chapter, we have chosen to discuss in some detail one of the better-known and more well-researched community programs, Achievement Place, and to briefly describe one additional recent and very promising approach to the modification of delinquent behaviors, multisystemic therapy.

The Achievement Place program (Phillips, 1968), which was originally developed in conjunction with the Department of Human Development at the University of Kansas, probably represents the most sophisticated community-based application of behavioral principles to the treatment of delinquency. Like the CASE project, Achievement Place is based on a token economy. Rather than being carried out within the institution, however, the program is conducted by trained houseparents in a homelike residence suitable for housing up to eight juveniles at a time. Residents attend school, have assigned work responsibilities, and are generally allowed home visits on weekends and holidays. Residents are rewarded with points for engaging in appropriate behaviors (and fined for displaying inappropriate behaviors), and these points can be cashed in for a wide variety of backup reinforcers.

The primary targets for modification are behaviors leading to development of more adaptive skills and decreases in inappropriate behaviors (e.g., completing homework assignments, modifying aggressive statements and behaviors). Points earned for engaging in such behaviors can be cashed in for a wide variety of backup reinforcers such as snacks, permission to watch TV or go to town by themselves, and so forth.

As a major problem with token economies has been that changed behavior often does not generalize to the natural environment (Kazdin, 1977), attempts have been made in the Achievement Place

program to enhance the generalization and maintenance of behavior change. For example, in the program, residents are moved from a program that involves a highly structured token economy (where points are earned or lost daily) to one where points are earned or lost on a weekly basis and finally to a merit system. On the merit system, privileges residents once had to earn through obtaining points are freely available, and backup reinforcers, which had once been give to maintain desirable behaviors, are replaced by social reinforcers such as approval and praise. From the merit system, residents are gradually moved back into their home environment.

A number of studies have shown that this program is effective in modifying a range of desirable and undesirable behaviors. Further, there are some studies comparing juveniles treated at Achievement Place with those treated elsewhere (but who were judged to have been acceptable for treatment in the Achievement Place program) that have indicated recidivism rates at follow-up that were well below those of juveniles receiving institutional treatment (Gross & Brigham, 1980). It should be noted that, despite these positive findings, a review of 13 Achievement Place programs by Kirigin, Braukmann, Atwater, and Wolf (1982) suggested that, although these specific programs resulted in reductions in antisocial behavior during treatment, recidivism rates at one-year follow-up were not significantly different from the rates for youths living in standard group homes. Such findings suggest that, despite the many positive attributes of the Achievement Place model, issues of generalizability and durability of treatment still require attention. It is noteworthy that, since its original development, the Achievement Place model, which is applicable to groups other than delinquents, has been subsumed under a more general integrated service delivery system, the Teaching Family Model, which is now employed in over 250 group homes across the United States and Canada (Blase, Fixen, Freeborn, & Jaeger, 1989). For a more comprehensive description of the Teaching Family Model, see Kirigin and Wolf (1998).

Another relatively new, noninstitutional approach to treatment is multisystemic therapy (MST). This family- and home-based treatment for serious juvenile offenders appears to be one of the most promising, empirically validated treatment approaches for this extremely hard to treat population. Designed to address the role of multiple, interconnected systems in which the adolescent is embedded, MST recognizes the potential importance of family, school, work, peer, community, and cultural institutions on adolescents' functioning (Henggeler & Borduin, 1990; Henggeler, Melton, Brondino, Scherer, & Hanley, 1997).

Based on family systems (Minuchin, 1974) and social-ecological (e.g., Bronfenbrenner, 1979) models of behavior, therapists employ empirically based treatment techniques, including those used in structural family therapy and cognitive-behavioral therapy, to tailor interventions to the needs and strengths of each family (Henggeler et al., 1997). Although specific therapeutic techniques are flexible, therapists abide by nine treatment principles, such as "Focus on systemic strengths," and "Interventions should be developmentally appropriate" (Henggeler, Schoenwald, Borduin, Rowland, & Cunningham, 1998). MST averages between 13 and 17 sessions, which may vary across sites.

In contrast to many past intervention approaches in which treatment gains have not held at follow-up, MST has been shown to result in long-term reduction in criminal activity (Henggeler, Melton, & Smith, 1992; Henggeler, Melton, Smith, Schoenwald, & Hanley, 1993). For example, in a longitudinal investigation of treatment efficacy with chronic juvenile offenders at risk for incarceration, MST improved family cohesion, reduced the number of incarcerations at a 59-week follow-up, and reduced peer-related aggression (Henggeler et al., 1992). Rearrest rates were also reduced at a 2.4-year follow-up (Henggeler et al., 1993). In another study, MST reduced violent and criminal activity at a four-year follow-up (Borduin et al., 1995). Other promising aspects of this treatment include its efficacy with ethnic minority populations (Brondino, Henggeler, Rowland, & Pickrel, 1997) and its cost-effectiveness in comparison to incarceration.

In addition to the above, many other treatment approaches have been tried with juvenile delinquents. Redner, Snellman, and Davidson (1983) for example, have reviewed a range of additional behaviorally oriented programs similar to those presented here. More traditional approaches to individual and group psychotherapy have also been employed, as have various forms of family therapy, in addition to MST (Alexander & Parsons, 1973). Other approaches such as reality therapy (Glasser, 1965) and transactional analysis (Jesness, 1975) have likewise been used in the treatment of delinquents. Although there are relatively good data on

the effectiveness of certain behavioral approaches and on MST and some support for the effectiveness of other family therapy approaches (Chamberlain & Rosicky, 1995), firm empirical support for the effectiveness of some of these other approaches is lacking. Further, mental health professionals know little regarding the effectiveness of most approaches with different types of delinquents. Research of this type would seem to be an important task for the future.

REFERENCES

Achenbach, T.M. (1985). *Assessment and taxonomy of child and adolescent psychopathology.* Newbury Park, CA: Sage.

Achenbach, T.M., & McConaughy, S.H. (1987). *Empirically based assessment of child and adolescent psychopathology.* Newbury Park, CA: Sage.

Ainsworth, M.D., Blehar, M.C., Waters, E., & Wall, S. (1978). *Patterns of attachment.* Hillsdale, NJ: Erlbaum.

Ainsworth, M.D., & Bowlby, J. (1991). An ethological approach to personality development. *American Psychologist, 46,* 333–341.

Alexander, J.F., & Parsons, B.V. (1973). Short-term behavioral intervention with delinquent families: Impact on family process and recidivism. *Journal of Abnormal Psychology, 81,* 219–225.

American Psychiatric Association. (1994). *Diagnostic and statistical manual of mental disorders* (4th ed.). Washington, DC: Author.

Arbuthnot, J., Gordon, D.A., & Jurkovic, G.J. (1987). Personality. In H.C. Quay (Ed.), *Handbook of juvenile delinquency* (pp. 139–183). New York: Wiley.

Bandura, A. (1965). Influence of models' reinforcement contingencies on the acquisition of imitative responses. *Journal of Personality and Social Psychology, 11,* 589–595.

Bandura, A. (1973). *Aggression: A social learning analysis.* Englewood Cliffs, NJ: Prentice-Hall.

Bandura, A. (1983). Psychological mechanisms of aggression. In R. Geen & E. Donnerstein (Eds.), *Aggression: Theoretical and empirical reviews, Vol. 1. Theoretical and methodological issues* (pp. 1–40). New York: Academic Press.

Bandura, A., Ross, D.M., & Ross, S.A. (1961). Transmission of aggression through limitation of aggressive models. *Journal of Abnormal and Social Psychology, 63,* 525–582.

Bandura, A., Ross, D., & Ross, S. (1963). Imitation of film-mediated aggressive models. *Journal of Abnormal and Social Psychology, 66,* 3–11.

Barkley, R.A. (1996). Attention-deficit/hyperactivity disorder. In E. Mash & R. Barkley (Eds.), *Child Psychopathology* (pp. 63–112). New York: Guilford Press.

Barkley, R.A. (1997). *ADHD and the nature of self-control.* New York: Guilford Press.

Belsky, J. (1984). The determinants of parenting: A process model. *Child Development, 55,* 83–96.

Belsky, J., & Isabella, R. (1988). Maternal, infant, and social-contextual determinants of attachment security. In J. Belsky & T. Nezworski (Eds.), *Clinical implications of attachment* (pp. 41–94). Hillsdale, NJ: Erlbaum.

Berkowitz, L. (1989). Frustration-aggression hypothesis: Examination and reformulation. *Psychological Bulletin, 106,* 59–73.

Binder, A. (1988). Juvenile delinquency. *Annual Review of Psychology, 39,* 253–282.

Blase, K.A., Fixen, D., Freeborn, K., & Jaeger, D. (1989). The behavioral model. In R.D. Lyman, S. Prentice-Dunn, & S. Gaber (Eds.), *Residential and inpatient treatment of children and adolescents* (pp. 43–58). New York: Plenum Press.

Borduin, C.M., Mann, B.J., Cone, L., Hengeller, S.W., Fucci, B.R., Blaske, D.M., & Williams, R.A. (1995). Multisystemic treatment of serious juvenile offenders: Long-term prevention of criminality and violence. *Journal of Consulting and Clinical Psychology, 63,* 569–578.

Brestan, E.V., & Eyberg, S.M. (1998). Effective psychosocial treatments of conduct-disordered children and adolescents: 29 years, 82 studies, and 5,272 kids. *Journal of Clinical Child Psychology, 27*(2), 180–189.

Brondino, M.J., Henggeler, S.W., Rowland, M.D., & Pickrel, S.G. (1997). Application and practice in health psychology. In D.K. Wilson & J.R. Rodrigue (Eds.), *Health-promoting and health-compromising behaviors among minority adolescents* (pp. 229–250). Washington, DC: American Psychological Association.

Bronfenbrenner, U. (1979). *The ecology of human development: Experiments by nature and design.* Cambridge, MA: Harvard University Press.

Brook, J.S., Whiteman, M.M., & Finch, S.J. (1992). Childhood aggression, adolescent delinquency, and drug use: A longitudinal study. *Journal of Genetics & Psychology, 153,* 369–383.

Brook, J.S., Whiteman, M.M., Finch, S.J., & Cohen, P. (1996). Young adult drug use and delinquency: Childhood antecedents and adolescent mediators. *Journal of the American Academy of Child and Adolescent Psychiatry, 35,* 1584–1592.

Butts, J.A., Snyder, H.N., Aughenbaugh, A.L., & Poole, S. (1996). *Juvenile court statistics: 1994.* Washington, DC: U.S. Department of Justice, Office of Juvenile Justice and Delinquency Prevention.

Cantwell, D.P. (1978). Hyperactivity and antisocial behavior. *Journal of the American Academy of Child Psychiatry, 17,* 252–262.

Caspi, A., & Silva, P.A. (1995). Temperamental qualities at age three predict personality traits in young adulthood: Longitudinal evidence from a birth cohort. *Child Development, 66,* 486–498.

Chamberlain, P., & Rosicky, J.G. (1995). The effectiveness of family therapy in the treatment of adolescents with conduct disorder and delinquency. *Journal of Marital and Family Therapy, 21,* 441–459.

Cicchetti, D., Ganiban, J., & Barnett, D. (1991). Contributions from the study of high-risk populations to understanding the development of emotion regulation. In J. Garber & K. Dodge (Eds.), *The development of emotion regulation and dysregulation* (pp. 15–48). New York: Cambridge University Press.

Cloward, R., & Ohlin, L. (1969). *Delinquency and opportunity.* Glencoe, IL: Free Press.

Cohen, H., & Filipczak, J. (1971). *A new learning environment.* San Francisco: Jossey-Bass.

Constantino, J.N. (1996). Intergenerational aspects of the development of aggression: A preliminary report. *Journal of Developmental and Behavioral Pediatrics, 17,* 176–182.

Cornell, D.G., Warren, J., Hawk, G., Stafford, E., Oram, G., & Pine, D. (1996). Psychopathy in instrumental and reactive violent offenders. *Journal of Consulting and Clinical Psychology, 64*(4), 783–790.

Crick, N.R., & Dodge, K.A. (1996). Social information-processing mechanisms in reactive and proactive aggression. *Child Development, 67,* 993–1002.

Day, D.M., Bream, L.A., & Pal, A. (1992). Proactive and reactive aggression: An analysis of subtypes based on teacher perceptions. *Journal of Clinical Child Psychology, 21*(3), 210–217.

Dodge, K.A. (1986). A social information processing model of social competence in children. In M. Perlmutter (Ed.), *The Minnesota Symposium on Child Psychology* (Vol. 18, pp. 77–125). Hillsdale, NJ: Erlbaum.

Dodge, K.A. (1991). The structure and function of reactive and proactive aggression. In D.J. Pepler & K.H. Rubin (Eds.), *The development and treatment of childhood aggression* (pp. 201–218). Hillsdale, NJ: Erlbaum.

Dodge, K.A., & Coie, J.D. (1987). Social information processing factors in reactive and proactive aggression in children's peer groups. *Journal of Personality and Social Psychology, 53,* 1146–1158.

Dodge, K.A., Lochman, J.E., Harnish, J.D., Bates, J.E., & Petit, G.S. (1997). Reactive and proactive aggression in schoolchildren and psychiatrically impaired chronically assaultive youth. *Journal of Abnormal Psychology, 106*(1), 37–51.

Dodge, K.A., Price, J.M., Bachorowski, J., & Newman, J.M. (1990). Hostile attributional biases in severely aggressive adolescents. *Journal of Abnormal Psychology, 99,* 385–392.

Dodge, K.A., & Schwartz, D. (1997). Social information processing mechanisms in aggressive behavior. In S.M. Stoff, J. Breiling, & J.D. Maser (Eds.), *Handbook of antisocial behavior* (pp. 171–180). New York: Wiley.

Dollard, J., Doob, L.W., Miller, N.E., Mower, O.H., & Sears, R.R. (1939). *Frustration and aggression.* New Haven, CT: Yale University Press.

Easterbrooks, M.A., & Goldberg, W.A. (1990). Security of toddler-parent attachment: Relation to children's sociopersonality functioning during kindergarten. In M.T. Greenberg, D. Cicchetti, & E.M. Cummings (Eds.), *Attachment in the preschool years: Theory, research and intervention* (pp. 221–244). Chicago: University of Chicago Press.

Elliot, D.S., & Ageton, S.S. (1980). Reconciling race and class differences in self-reported and official estimates of delinquency. *American Sociological Review, 45,* 45–110.

Ellis, P.L. (1982). Empathy: A factor in antisocial behavior. *Journal of Abnormal Child Psychology, 10,* 123–134.

Empey, L.T. (1978). *American delinquency: Its meaning and construction.* Homewood, NJ: Dorsey Press.

Eron, L.D., & Huesmann, L.R. (1984). The role of television in the development of prosocial and antisocial behavior. In D. Olweus, J. Block, & M. Rradke-Yarrow (Eds.), *Development of antisocial and prosocial behavior* (pp. 285–314). New York: Academic Press.

Fabes, R.A., Eisenberg, N., Karbon, M., Troyer, D., & Switzer, M. (1994). The relations of children's emotion regulation to their vicarious emotional responses and comforting behaviors. *Child Development, 65,* 1678–1693.

Farley, F.A., & Farley, S.V. (1972). Stimulus seeking motivation and delinquent behavior among institutionalized delinquent girls. *Journal of Consulting and Clinical Psychology, 39,* 94–97.

Farley, F., & Sewell, T. (1976). Test of an arousal theory of delinquency: Stimulation seeking in delinquent and non delinquent Black adolescents. *Criminal Justice and Behavior, 3,* 315–320.

Foote, R., Eyberg, S., & Schuhmann, E. (1998). Parent-child interaction approaches to the treatment of child behavior problems. In T. Ollendick & R. Prinz (Eds.), *Advances in clinical child psychology* (Vol. 20, pp. 125–151). New York: Plenum Press.

Frick, P.J. (1998). *Conduct disorders and severe antisocial behavior.* New York: Plenum Press.

Geen, R.G. (1976). *Personality: The science of behavior.* St. Louis, MO: Mosby.

Gelfand, D.M., & Hartmann, D.P. (1984). *Child behavior analysis and therapy* (2nd ed.). New York: Pergamon Press.

Genshaft, J.L. (1980). Personality characteristics of delinquent subtypes. *Journal of Abnormal Child Psychology, 8,* 279–283.

Gibbons, D.C. (1976). *Delinquent behavior* (2nd ed.). Englewood Cliffs, NJ: Prentice-Hall.

Gibbons, D.C., & Krohn, M.D. (1986). *Delinquent behavior* (4th ed.). Englewood Cliffs, NJ: Prentice-Hall.

Glasser, W. (1965). *Reality Therapy.* New York: Harper & Row.

Glueck, S., & Glueck, E. (1950). *Unraveling juvenile delinquency.* New York: Commonwealth Fund.

Glueck, S., & Glueck, E. (1968). *Delinquents and nondelinquents in perspective.* Cambridge, MA: Harvard University Press.

Gold, M., & Petronio, R.J. (1980). Delinquent behavior in adolescence. In J. Adelson (Ed.), *Handbook of adolescent psychology* (pp. 495–535). New York: Wiley.

Goldsmith, H.H., & Alansky, J. (1987). Maternal and infant temperamental predictors of attachment: A meta-analytic review. *Journal of Consulting and Clinical Psychology, 55,* 805–816.

Greenberg, M.T., & Speltz, M.L. (1988). Attachment and the ontogeny of conduct problems. In J. Belsky & T. Nezworski (Eds.), *Clinical implications of attachment* (pp. 177–218). Hillsdale, NJ: Erlbaum.

Gross, A.M., & Brigham, T.A. (1980). Behavior modification and the treatment of juvenile delinquency: A review and proposal for future research. *Corrective and Social Psychiatry, 26,* 98–106.

Gross, A.M., & Wixted, J.T. (1987). Oppositional behavior. In M. Hersen & V. Van Hasselt (Eds.), *Behavior therapy with children and adolescents* (pp. 301–324). New York: Wiley.

Hanf, C.A. (1969). *A two-stage program for modifying maternal controlling during mother-child interaction.* Paper presented at the meeting of the Western Psychological Association, Vancouver, B.C.

Hastings, J.E., & Barkley, R.A. (1978). A review of psychophysiological research with hyperkinetic children. *Journal of Abnormal Child Psychology, 6,* 413–447.

Henggeler, S.W., & Borduin, C.M. (1990). *Family therapy and beyond.* Pacific Grove, CA: Brooks/Cole.

Henggeler, S.W., Melton, G.B., Brondino, M.J., Scherer, D.G., & Hanley, J.H. (1997). Multisystemic therapy with violent and chronic juvenile offenders and their families: The role of treatment fidelity in successful dissemination. *Journal of Consulting and Clinical Psychology, 65,* 821–833.

Henggeler, S.W., Melton, G.B., & Smith, L.A. (1992). Family preservation using multisystemic therapy: An effective alternative to incarcerating serious juvenile offenders. *Journal of Consulting and Clinical Psychology, 60,* 953–961.

Henggeler, S.W., Melton, G.B., Smith, L.A., Schoenwald, S.K., & Hanley, J.H. (1993). Family preservation using multisystemic treatment: Long-term follow-up to a clinical trial with serious juvenile offenders. *Journal of Child and Family Studies, 4,* 283–293.

Henggeler, S.W., Schoenwald, S.K., Borduin, C.M., Rowland, M.D., & Cunningham, P.B. (1998). *Multisystemic treatment for antisocial behavior in youth.* New York: Guilford Press.

Henn, F., Bordwell, R., & Jenkins, R.L. (1980). Juvenile delinquents revisited. *Archives of General Psychiatry, 37,* 1160–1163.

Herbert, M. (1987). *Conduct disorders of childhood and adolescence* (2nd ed.). Chichester, England: Wiley.

Hinshaw, S.P., & Anderson, C.A. (1996). Conduct and oppositional defiant disorders. In E. Mash & R. Barkley (Eds.), *Child psychopathology* (pp. 113–149). New York: Guilford Press.

Hinshaw, S.P., Heller, T., & McHale, J.P. (1992). Covert antisocial behavior in boys with attention-deficit/hyperactive disorder: External validation and effects of methylphenidate. *Journal of Consulting and Clinical Psychology, 60,* 274–281.

Hooper, S.R., & Tramontana, M.G. (1997). Advances in the neuropsychological bases of child and adolescent psychopathology: Proposed models, findings, and ongoing issues. In T. Ollendick & R. Prinz (Eds.), *Advances in clinical child psychology* (Vol. 19, pp. 138–157). New York: Plenum Press.

Huesmann, L.R., Moise, J.F., & Podolski, C. (1997). The effects of media violence on the development of antisocial behavior. In S.M. Stoff, J. Breiling, & J.D. Maser (Eds.), *Handbook of Antisocial Behavior* (pp. 181–193). New York: Wiley.

Huessy, H., Metoyer, M., & Townsend, M. (1974). 8–10 year follow-up of 84 children treated for behavior disorders in rural Vermont. *Acta Paedopsychiatrica, 10,* 230–235.

Jefferson, T.W., & Johnson, J.H. (1991). The relationship of hyperactivity and sensation seeking to delinquent subtypes. *Criminal Justice and Behavior, 18,* 195–201.

Jesness, C. (1975). Comparative effectiveness of behavior modification and transactional analysis programs for delinquents. *Journal of Consulting and Clinical Psychology, 43,* 758–779.

Johnson, J.H., Rasbury, W.C., & Siegel, L.J. (1997). *Approaches to child treatment: Introduction to theory, research and practice* (2nd ed.). Needham, MA: Allyn & Bacon.

Jurkovic, G.J. (1980). The juvenile delinquent as a moral philosopher: A structural-developmental perspective. *Psychological Bulletin, 88,* 709–727.

Kazdin, A.E. (1977). *The token economy: A review and evaluation.* New York: Plenum Press.

Kazdin, A.E. (1987a). *Conduct disorders in childhood and adolescence.* Newbury Park, CA: Sage.

Kazdin, A.E. (1987b). Treatment of antisocial behavior of children: Current status and future directions. *Psychological Bulletin, 102,* 187–203.

Keilitz, I., & Dunivant, N. (1986). The relationship between learning disabilities and juvenile delinquency. *Remedial and Special Education, 7,* 18–26.

Kirigin, K.A., Braukmann, C.J., Atwater, J.D., & Wolf, M.M. (1982). An evaluation of teaching-family (Achievement Place) group homes for juvenile offenders. *Journal of Applied Behavior Analysis, 15*(1), 1–16.

Kirigin, K.A., & Wolf, M.M. (1998). Application of the teaching-family model to children and adolescents with conduct disorder. In V.B. Van Hasselt & M. Hersen (Eds.), *Handbook of psychological treatment protocols for children and adolescents. The LEA series in personality and clinical psychology* (pp. 339–380). Mahwah, NJ: Erlbaum.

Kirkland, K.D., & Thelen, M.H. (1977). Uses of modeling in child treatment. In B. Lahey & A. Kazdin (Eds.), *Advances in clinical child psychology,* (Vol. 1, pp. 302–328). New York: Plenum Press.

Lamb, M.E., Thompson, R.A., Gardner, W., & Charnov, E.L. (1985). *Infant-mother attachments: The origins and developmental significance of individual differences in Strange Situation behavior.* Hillsdale, NJ: Erlbaum.

Loeber, R. (1990). Development and risk factors of juvenile antisocial behavior and delinquency. *Clinical Psychology Review, 10,* 1–42.

Loeber, R., & Stouthamer-Loeber, M. (1987). Prediction. In H.C. Quay (Ed.), *Handbook of juvenile delinquency* (pp. 325–382). New York: Wiley.

Lorenz, K. (1966). *On aggression.* New York: Basic Books.

Lyons-Ruth, K., Alpern, L., & Repacholi, B. (1993). Disorganized infant attachment classification and maternal psychosocial problems as predictors of hostile-aggressive behavior in the preschool classroom. *Child Development, 64,* 572–585.

Maletsky, B.M. (1974). D-amphetamine and delinquency. *Diseases of the Nervous System, 35,* 543–547.

Mason, D.A., & Frick, P.J. (1994). The heritability of antisocial behavior: A meta-analysis of twin and adoption studies. *Journal of Psychopathology and Behavioral Assessment, 16,* 301–323.

Merton, R.K. (1957). *Social theory and social structure.* New York: Free Press.

Minuchin, S. (1974). *Families and family therapy.* Cambridge, MA: Harvard University Press.

Moore, D.R., & Arthur, J.L. (1983). Juvenile delinquency. In T. Ollendick & M. Hersen (Eds.), *Handbook of child psychopathology* (2nd ed., pp. 197–217). New York: Plenum Press.

Offer, D., Sabshin, M., & Marcus, D. (1965). Clinical evaluation in normal adolescents. *American Journal of Psychiatry, 121,* 864–872.

Patterson, G.R., DeBaryshe, B.D., & Ramsey, E. (1989). A developmental perspective on antisocial behavior. *American Psychologist, 44,* 329–335.

Patterson, G.R., & Guillion, M.E. (1968). *Living with children: New methods for parents and teachers.* Champaign, IL: Research Press.

Patterson, G.R., Littman, R.A., & Bricker, W. (1967). Assertive behavior in children: A step toward a theory of aggression. *Monographs of the Society for Research in Child Development, 32* (No. 113).

Phillips, E.L. (1968). Achievement Place: Token reinforcement procedures in a homestyle rehabilitation setting for "pre-delinquent" boys. *Journal of Applied Behavior Analysis, 1,* 213–223.

Price, J.M., & Dodge, J.A. (1989). Reactive and proactive aggression in childhood: Relations to peer status and social context dimension. *Journal of Abnormal Child Psychology, 17,* 455–471.

Quay, H.C. (1964). Dimensions of personality in delinquent boys as inferred from factor analysis of case history data. *Child Development, 35,* 479–484.

Quay, H.C. (1965). Psychopathic personality as pathological stimulation seeking. *American Journal of Psychiatry, 122,* 180–183.

Quay, H.C. (1987). Patterns of delinquent behavior. In H.C. Quay (Ed.), *Handbook of juvenile delinquency* (pp. 118–138). New York: Wiley.

Rapport, M. (1987). Attention deficit disorder with hyperactivity. In M. Hersen & V. Van Hasselt (Eds.), *Behavior therapy with children and adolescents.* New York: Wiley.

Redner, R., Snellman, L., & Davidson, W.S. (1983). Juvenile delinquency. In R.J. Morris & T.R. Kratochwill (Eds.), *The practice of child therapy* (pp. 193–220). New York: Pergamon Press.

Robins, L.N. (1966). *Deviant children grown up: A sociological and psychiatric study of sociopathic personality.* Baltimore: Williams & Wilkins.

Roff, J.D. (1992). Childhood aggression, peer status, and social class as predictors of delinquency. *Psychological Reports, 70,* 31–34.

Rogers, J.W., & Mays, G.L. (1987). *Juvenile delinquency and juvenile justice.* New York: Wiley.

Ross, A.O. (1974). *Psychological disorders of children: A behavioral approach to theory, research and therapy.* New York: McGraw-Hill.

Ross, A.O. (1981). *Child behavior therapy.* New York: Wiley.

Ross, D.M., & Ross, S.A. (1976). *Hyperactivity: Theory, research and action.* New York: Wiley.

Rutter, M., & Giller, H. (1984). *Juvenile delinquency: Trends and perspectives.* London: Guilford Press.

Sampson, R.J., & Laub, J.H. (1994). Urban poverty and the family context of delinquency: A new look at structure and process in a classic study. *Child Development, 65,* 523–540.

Sarason, I.G., & Ganzer, V.J. (1971). *An approach to the rehabilitation of juvenile offenders.* (Report to the Social and Rehabilitation Service.) Washington, DC: U.S. Department of Health, Education and Welfare.

Satterfield, J.H., & Schell, A.M. (1984). Childhood brain function differences in delinquent and nondelinquent hyperactive boys. *Electroencephalography and Clinical Neurophysiology, 57,* 199–207.

Scarpa, A., & Raine, A. (1997). Psychophysiology of anger and violent behavior. *Psychiatric Clinics of North America, 20,* 375–394.

Schwartz, S., & Johnson, J.H. (1985). *Psychopathology of childhood* (2nd ed.). New York: Pergamon Press.

Shaw, C.R., & McKay, H.D. (1969). *Juvenile delinquency in urban areas.* Chicago: University of Chicago Press.

Shaw, D.S., Owens, E.B., Vondra, J.I., & Keenan, K. (1996). Early risk factors and pathways in the development of early disruptive behavior problems. *Development and Psychopathology, 8,* 679–699.

Silvern, S.B., & Williamson, P.S. (1987). The effects of video game play on young children's aggression, fantasy, and prosocial behavior. *Journal of Applied Developmental Psychology, 8,* 453–462.

Snyder, J., & Patterson, G. (1987). Family interaction and delinquent behavior. In H.C. Quay (Ed.), *Handbook of Juvenile Delinquency.* New York: Wiley.

Snyder, J.J., & Patterson, G.R. (1995). Individual differences in social aggression: A test of a reinforcement model of socialization in the natural environment. *Behavior Therapy, 26,* 371–391.

Sroufe, L.A. (1983). Infant-caregiver attachment and patterns of adaptation in preschool: The roots of maladaptation and competence. In M. Perlmutter (Ed.), *Minnesota Symposium in Child Psychology* (No. 16, pp. 14–83). Minneapolis: University of Minnesota Press.

Stewart, M.A., Mendelson, W.B., & Johnson, N.E. (1973). Hyperactive children as adolescents: How they describe themselves. *Child Psychiatry and Human Development, 4,* 3–11.

Stumphauzer, J.S. (1986). *Helping delinquents change.* New York: Haworth Press.

Taylor, T., & Watt, D.C. (1977). The relation of deviant symptoms and behavior in a normal population to subsequent delinquency and maladjustment. *Psychological Medicine, 7,* 163–169.

Thrasher, F.M. (1963). *The gang* (Rev. ed.). Chicago: University of Chicago Press.

Tschann, J.M., Kaiser, P., Chesney, M., Alkon, A., & Boyce, W.T. (1996). Resilience and vulnerability among preschool children: Family functioning, temperament, and behavior problems. *Journal of the American Academy of Child and Adolescent Psychiatry, 35*(2), 184–192.

U.S. Department of Justice. (1978). *Sourcebook for criminal justice statistics: 1977.* Washington, DC: Author.

U.S. Department of Justice. (1996). *Sourcebook for criminal justice statistics: 1996.* Washington, DC: Author.

van Ijzendoorn, M.H., Goldberg, S., Kroonenberg, P.M., & Frenkel, O.J. (1992). The relative effects of maternal and child problems on the quality of attachment: A meta-analysis of attachment in clinical samples. *Child Development, 63,* 840–858.

Vaz, E.W. (1967). *Middle-class delinquency.* New York: Harper & Row.

Walters, R.H., & Brown, M. (1963). Studies of reinforcement of aggression, III: Transfer of responses to an interpersonal situation. *Child Development, 34,* 563–571.

Webster-Stratton, C. (1984). Randomized trial of two parent-training programs for families with conduct-disordered children. *Journal of Consulting and Clinical Psychology, 52,* 666–678.

Webster-Stratton, C. (1990). Enhancing the effectiveness of self-administered videotape parent training for families with conduct-problem children: Comparison with two cost-effective treatments and a control group. *Journal of Consulting and Clinical Psychology, 56,* 558–566.

Webster-Stratton, C. (1994). Advancing videotape parent training: A comparison study. *Journal of Consulting and Clinical Psychology, 62,* 583–593.

White, J.L. (1989). *The troubled adolescent.* New York: Pergamon Press.

Wilson, B.J., & Gottman, J.M. (1996). Attention—The shuttle between emotion and cognition: Risk, resiliency, and physiological bases. In E.M. Hetherington & E.A. Blechman (Eds.), *Stress, coping and resiliency in children and families. Family research consortium: Advances in family research* (pp. 189–228). Mahwah, NJ: Erlbaum.

Zhang, L., Wieczorek, W.F., & Welte, J.W. (1997). The nexus between alcohol and violent crime. *Alcoholism: Clinical and Experimental Research, 21,* 1264–1271.

Zinkus, P.W., & Gottlieb, M.I. (1977). Learning disabilities and juvenile delinquency. *Clinical Pediatrics, 17,* 775–780.

Zuckerman, M. (1979). *Beyond the optimal level of stimulation.* Hillsdale, NJ: Erlbaum.

CHAPTER 21

Neurotic Disorders in Children: Obsessive-Compulsive, Somatoform, Dissociative, and Posttraumatic Stress Disorders

BRENDA O. GILBERT, LEILANI GREENING, AND STEPHEN J. DOLLINGER

Our purpose in this chapter is to review the current status of definition, conceptualization, and treatment of several childhood and adolescent disorders that traditionally were called the childhood neuroses. The term originally was used by clinicians who viewed personal distress and dysfunction in terms of internalized unconscious conflict stemming from early childhood trauma. The common underlying theme of anxiety gave some coherence to the clustering of such problems as obsessive-compulsive, somatoform, and dissociative disorders. However, developments since 1980, not the least of which are three versions of the *Diagnostic and Statistical Manual of Mental Disorders* (*DSM-III, DSM-III-R, DSM-IV*; American Psychiatric Association, 1980, 1987, 1994), have shifted the term neurosis to a descriptive rather than a formal usage. At the same time that the term neurotic has been deleted from classification systems, it has been used increasingly in the field of personality psychology to describe one of the five most commonly found factors of personality (Wiggins, 1996). This factor, also called negative affectivity (Watson & Clark, 1984), has also been reported with children (Wolfe et al., 1987).

The former childhood neuroses now fall under new systems of classification. The current primary methods of categorizing children's psychological disorders are via the *DSM-IV* and factor analytically derived measures, for example, the Child Behavior Checklist (Achenbach, 1993). The *DSM-IV* classification system was developed by committees of experts, who gathered authoritative opinion and research findings to construct an atheoretical classification system of child and adult mental disorders. Factor analytic approaches depend on statistical methods intercorrelating symptoms, behaviors, and problems to determine related patterns of behavior. Information from statistical as well as other research can be incorporated into *DSM-IV* diagnostic classification, but the two are not synonymous.

Theories about the etiology of these so-called neurotic disorders include the psychodynamic (where symptomatic behavior is taken as a mere surface manifestation of underlying conflict and defense), behavioral (where symptoms reflect excesses and deficits acquired through learning processes), cognitive-social learning (taking into account the influence of behavioral examples and thought processes, such as attention and self-perception, as well as reward contingencies), temperament and neurobiological factors, and family systems (where a disorder is the symptom of family dysfunction).

OBSESSIVE-COMPULSIVE DISORDER OF CHILDHOOD

Obsessive-compulsive disorder (OCD) is thought to be relatively infrequent in childhood. An estimated incidence of 0.2% was found in one study (Hollingsworth, Tanguary, Grossman, & Pabst, 1980). In a survey of the high school population of a New Jersey county, a prevalence rate for OCD of 0.33% was found (Flament, Rapoport, Whitaker, Berg, & Sceery, 1985). Wolff and Rapoport (1988) argue that the tendency toward secrecy of youngsters with this disorder and the potential of measures to miss OCD diagnoses make it likely that current studies underreport the true rate. This is important because childhood OCD frequently continues into adulthood (Berg et al., 1989; Hollingsworth et al., 1980). In a similar vein, one-third to one-half of adults with OCD experience onset of the disorder by the age of 15 years (Wolff & Rapoport, 1988).

The behavioral presentation of OCD is highly similar in adults and children. Swedo, Rapoport, Leonard, Lenane, and Cheslow (1989) found that these children often have both rituals and obsessions, with "pure" obsessors being relatively rare. Washing was the most common ritual, present in 85% of the youngsters. Repeating and checking rituals also were frequently presented, with 51% and 46% of the children exhibiting these symptoms. The major theme of obsessions centered around dirt and germs, but other strong themes included danger to self or loved ones, symmetry, or "meticulous" religiosity. These researchers pointed out two striking broad themes arising from their data: "a preoccupation with and/or rituals for cleanliness, grooming, and averting danger, and a pervasive doubt or inability to 'know' that one is right" (p. 337). They concluded that underlying all of the rituals, including repetitions and counting, is a sense that "it didn't feel right yet." Similar findings have been found by Riddle, Scahill, and King (1992).

OCD appears to have a persistent course. Warren's (1960) study of children seven years postdiagnosis reported a majority of these individuals still experiencing significant symptoms. More recent follow-up studies have found that only minorities

of those diagnosed with OCD in childhood or adolescence are diagnosis-free several years later. For example, Thomsen and Mikkelsen (1995) reported that 1.5 to 5 years postreferral, 50% of the children and adolescents diagnosed with OCD retained their diagnosis, with about one-third having an episodic course and two-thirds a chronic course. Comparable findings emerged from the work of Flament et al. (1990) and Leonard, Swedo, and Lenane (1993).

ASSOCIATED CHARACTERISTICS

OCD has been identified in children as young as 3 years old (Adams, 1973; Swedo et al., 1989). Relative to girls, a higher rate of boys have the disorder, and boys also tend to have earlier onsets. However, in the older age groups, the disparity in the ratio declines until adulthood, when the numbers of men and women with OCD are similar (Swedo et al., 1989). Evidence from several sources suggests a relationship between abnormal neurological function and OCD; for example, Behar et al. (1984), in a comparison between adolescents with OCD and a matched control group, found that the OCD group had a mean ventricular-brain ratio (VBR) significantly higher than the controls. Similarly, this group showed spatial-perceptual deficits similar to those found in individuals with frontal lobe lesions. Other sources of evidence for neurological abnormalities include such findings as an increased incidence of Gilles de la Tourette's syndrome and other repetitive disorders, a high rate of abnormal birth events, and a positive response to chlomipramine among those with OCD (Capstick & Selfrup, 1977; Elkins, Rapoport, & Lipsky, 1980; Flament, Rapoport, Berg, et al., 1985).

Youngsters with OCD appear similar to peers on measures of intelligence (Swedo et al., 1989). There is, however, a high rate of specific developmental disability (e.g., reading or language delay) in these children; for example, Swedo et al. found that 24% of their sample had a coexisting developmental disability. In addition to the aforementioned neurological and learning-cognitive dysfunctions, children with OCD have high rates of associated psychological disorders. Swedo et al. found that only 26% of their sample were free of other psychiatric diagnoses, whereas 35% suffered from depression either currently or in their past. Forty percent had anxiety disorders, with simple phobia (17%) and overanxious disorder (16%) composing the largest diagnostic groups. Other disorders included oppositional disorder (11%), attention-deficit disorder (10%), and conduct disorder (7%). Of note, Last, Perrin, Hersen, and Kazdin (1992) found that almost half their OCD children and adolescents had a history of simple phobia. However, in the Swedo et al. sample, only 11% of the youngsters met the criteria for compulsive personality disorder. This finding is in contrast to many early adult studies that reported high rates of obsessional traits (e.g., A. Black, 1974). In a pattern that resembles the Swedo et al. findings, however, D. Black, Yates, Noyes, Pfohl, and Reich (1988) did not find this high rate of compulsive personality disorder in OCD adults but did find higher rates of other personality disorders.

FAMILY CHARACTERISTICS

Several authors have commented on the degree of psychological disorder in the families of obsessive-compulsive children (e.g., Swedo et al., 1989). In particular, the parents of such children frequently show OCD themselves. Swedo et al. found a family history of OCD in approximately 25% of their sample, with father-son pairs most frequent

TREATMENT

Treatment for children with OCD most frequently is a multifaceted package involving several components such as psychodynamic, behavioral, family, and pharmacotherapy. From a more or less traditional psychodynamic framework, Adams (1973, 1985) recommended a variety of therapeutic strategies in individual therapy. These strategies directly follow from and challenge the obsessive child's values. Specifically, Adams recommended encouraging the child to (1) give examples and communicate clearly; (2) focus on day-to-day concerns; (3) participate in a relationship with the therapist that "can be talked about, discussed and questioned . . . [and that] will end"; (4) experience and label affects (the "feelings are in" strategy); (5) be frank and truthful; (6) "Keep it clean," that is, state his or her thoughts simply and directly (when necessary, Adams suggests that the clinician restate in simple terms what the child has said obsessively); (7) take a chance,

take risks, and (8) use language that describes what needs "to be cured"—phrases such as "at ease," "natural," and "letting loose." In a 1985 article, Adams highlighted clear shifts he discerned in the OCD child psychotherapy literature since 1973. His appraisal included the trends: (1) dropping libido theory from discussions of OCD; (2) placing less emphasis on anxiety, anger, and rage as usual dynamisms in OCD of children; (3) emphasizing learning and culture as potential ameliorative agents; (4) bringing in a family group focus, seeing the family as a potent learning milieu; (5) stressing parental empathy as the needed corrective to reduce overconformity and rectitude in the child's symptom picture; and (6) placing greater emphasis on the self, the self-concept, and self-regard. These shifts, in Adams's opinion, "make it easier for the practitioner, even if thoroughly dynamo-verbal in preference, to be flexible and to offer more multimodal treatments, to welcome biologic methods certainly, to adopt behavioral and cognitive approaches surely" (pp. 303–304). Although Adams (1973) does not present results quantitatively, he noted a number of qualitative changes across his 49 patients, including reduction in obsessive-compulsive symptoms, changes in other related behaviors indicative of greater spontaneity, increased self-esteem and ego strength, superego changes (in the direction of more personalized values), and improved interpersonal relations.

The behavioral techniques utilized in the treatment of childhood OCD include graded and prolonged exposure, response prevention, thought-stopping, cognitive restructuring, differential reinforcement of other behavior (DRO), modeling, shaping, operant techniques, systematic desensitization, and disruption of behavioral chain (see Franklin et al., 1998; March, 1995). In a majority of the reports, family members are involved as cotherapists and record keepers. Likewise, the behavior of family members is frequently a focus of treatment. For example, Stanley (1980) attempted to change parental behavior that accommodated and/or inadvertently reinforced an 8-year-old girl's OCD rituals.

The more commonly reported behavioral approaches include response prevention and graded exposure. These approaches, as evidenced with adults, may have special utility for OCD children (Franklin et al., 1998; March, 1995). Furthermore, Wolff and Rapoport (1988) cited anecdotal examples of "spontaneous" remission in which OCD adolescents appeared to treat themselves successfully with methods similar to graded exposure and response prevention. Similarly, in the 2- to 10-year follow-up of the Flament, Rapoport, Whitaker, et al. (1985) study, several adolescents described efforts in which they forced themselves to tolerate abhorrent ideas, resist compulsions to perform rituals, or avoid feared objects, resulting in gradual improvement.

Studies are beginning to emerge comparing treatment components of several OCD treatment programs. For example, although all 15 participants in the March, Muller, and Herbel (1994) study were provided a protocol-based cognitive-behavioral therapy (CBT) intervention, most also were treated pharmacologically. These researchers reported that all patients improved posttreatment and that these improvements were maintained over an 18-month follow-up period. Six became asymptomatic and six were able to discontinue medication. Moreover, these researchers reported that the average magnitude of improvement was greater and relapse rates lower than usually found with medication alone (March, 1995). Thus, CBT and medication together may be superior for many OCD children and adolescents than when used separately. However, this comparison is only suggestive. These findings argue strongly for increased research comparing the utility of CBT, pharmacotherapy, and combined treatment for OCD in child and adolescent populations.

Franklin et al. (1998) assessed two components of March's CBT protocol in the treatment of OCD and the value of intensive or weekly treatment. They compared the exposure/response prevention component alone or in combination with the anxiety management training component in the treatment of 14 children and adolescents. They also looked at the intensity of treatment (about 18 90-minute sessions provided in one month versus about 16 60-minute sessions conducted weekly). They found that including anxiety management training added little to overall improvement and no differences emerged between the intensive and the weekly treatment schedules. These findings suggest that exposure and response prevention are the active components in ameliorating OCD symptoms and that weekly therapy is as effective as intense therapy. Moreover, the levels of improvement were comparable to those of March et al. (1994) and, as found by March et al., more impressive than those found in studies using medication alone.

Two other examples of combining behavioral methods with other treatments include the work of Fine (1973) and Kellerman (1981). Fine effectively treated two boys, age 11 and 9, for a variety of rituals and compulsions, using symptom interruption within a broader framework of family therapy. Kellerman successfully employed thought-stopping and covert reinforcement in combination with hypnosis and a variant of "prescribing the symptom" for a 12- year-old boy exhibiting a variety of ritualized behavior with cognitive-behavioral and insight-oriented psychotherapy treatments.

Some clinicians have noted resistance by patients to behavioral methods (e.g., Apter, Bernhout, & Tyano, 1984). In this regard, Harris and Wiebe (1992) recommend that the therapist may elect graded versus flooded exposure and response prevention with the patient selecting treatment targets. These methods seem less aversive and better at engaging the client's cooperation in the therapy process. An important challenge to the therapist is to gain the active support of the child/adolescent and family members by helping them understand the nature of OCD, recognize the continual costs to the OCD sufferer and the family, and help them understand the treatment options and their potential value in reducing OCD symptoms. Using a CBT protocol incorporating most of these suggestions, March et al. (1994) treated 15 consecutive children and adolescents with OCD; none refused treatment and only two cases withdrew prematurely, neither due to the child's objections to the therapy process.

Chlomipramine and fluoxetine have been demonstrated to be effective treatments for OCD in children (Flament, Rapoport, Berg, et al., 1985; Geller, Biederman, Reed, Spencer, & Wilens, 1995; Leonard et al., 1991). In the well-designed study by Flament, Rapoport, Berg, et al., 74% of the OCD children and adolescents age 6 to 18 showed at least moderate improvements on chlomipramine. Among those who improved, 32% showed much improvement and 10% were symptom-free. Boys tended to show greater improvement. Prior levels of depression, anxiety, or OCD severity were unrelated to response rate. A better response was obtained for those who were primarily ritualizers compared with those who were obsessors. Side effects of this medication were primarily anticholinergic symptoms associated with tricyclic medications (dry mouth, tremoring, dizziness). Relapse tends to occur from three days to two weeks after chlomipramine treatment is withdrawn. Geller et al. found comparable results with fluoxetine.

CHILDHOOD SOMATOFORM AND DISSOCIATIVE DISORDERS

Although conversion, dissociative disorders, and "hysteria" have enjoyed a special place in the history of medical psychology (Veith, 1977), their low incidence and prevalence plus changes in terminology and diagnostic schemes currently classify such problems as somatoform or dissociative disorders. Descriptively, somatoform disorders imply the presence of physical symptoms suggestive of a medical condition that cannot be explained by organic or other mental disorders (APA, 1994). They include such problems as seizures; loss of hearing, vision, or speech; anesthesias; motor unsteadiness; and generalized or specific pain. These symptoms are often associated with vomiting, headaches, abdominal pain, nausea, and dizziness. Dissociative disorders are characterized by disruptions in the normal integration of memory, consciousness, and identity and include such problems as amnesia, feelings of depersonalization, and dissociative identity disorder (APA, 1994).

From a psychodynamic viewpoint, these symptoms have the important function of symbolically expressing the core, intrapsychic conflict— the forbidden sexual or aggressive impulse and the defense against this impulse. Within this framework, the symptom serves multiple purposes: primary gain is achieved by the controlling or binding of anxiety associated with the conflict; secondary gain is achieved in the attention directed by family members and others to the child's physical ailment. Learning theory would view these behaviors as acquired and maintained as a function of modeling, environmental contingencies, and biological inheritance.

FAMILY CHARACTERISTICS

Information on the family characteristics of children and adolescents with somatoform and dissociative disorders continues to emerge. Routh and Ernst (1984) compared the families of children with functional abdominal pain (no organic basis for the abdominal pain) with those of children reporting abdominal pain with an identified medical cause. The families of those children with functional abdominal pain had significantly higher rates of alcoholism, antisocial or conduct disorder, attention-deficit disorder, or somatization disorder. In fact, 50% of the children with functional abdominal pain had at least one relative with somatization disorder, compared to 5% of the organic group. These family members with somatization disorder were predominantly women.

Other researchers studying those diagnosed with dissociative disorders have noted from clinical observations and case histories the common finding that other family members demonstrate high rates of dissociative disorders as well (Braun, 1985; Mann & Sanders, 1994). For example, in the families of those identified as having a dissociative disorder, Braun identified an average of over four family members with dissociative experiences.

Yates and Steward (1976) commented on the generalized inhibition of anger within the family and considered this to be an important clue for differential diagnosis. Laitman (1981) has commented that the family system of children with these disorders tends to have enmeshed boundaries between parent and child and that the children are commonly "triangulated" by the parents, that is, forced into cross-generational alliances as a function of parent or spouse subsystem problems. Obviously, one of the weaknesses of some of the aforementioned family descriptors is their dependence on clinician opinion alone. Finally, demographically, cases of conversion disorder are more common in lower social economic strata and rural families (Steinhausen, Aster, Pfeiffer, & Gobel, 1989).

DIAGNOSIS OF SOMATAFORM DISORDERS

Friedman (1973) has emphasized an important diagnostic rule in possible cases of somatoform reactions: Base the diagnosis on positive criteria rather than the mere absence of physical laboratory findings. There is always the possibility that an unidentified organic/physiological reason for the physical problem exists (Scharff, 1997). Another consideration sometimes used in the diagnosis of conversion disorder is the child's apparent lack of concern about his or her illness, the classic *la belle indifférence.* However, some authors have failed to find evidence of this attitude in their patient sample (Goodyer, 1981). Extrapolating from the extant literature, Rock (1971) suggests that three conditions are needed for a positive diagnosis: (1) a prominent somatic symptom lacking anatomic or physiological basis, (2) onset with or exacerbated by a significant emotional event, and (3) evidence that the symptom serves an emotional need. *DSM-IV* provides specific criteria for the individual disorders.

Conversion Disorder with Seizures or Convulsions
One form of conversion disorder, seizures, is occasionally classified as a conversion reaction and occasionally as a dissociative reaction. Apparently, this variation in diagnostic practice is a function of whether the disorder mimics a grand mal seizure or resembles a petit mal disorder. The latter is more likely to be diagnosed as a dissociative reaction and the former as a conversion reaction.

Conversion disorder seizures have been most frequently reported in adolescent girls, often in association with sexual pressure or exploitation (Bernstein, 1969; Dollinger, 1983; LaBarbera & Dozier, 1980), rape or incestuous rape (Goodwin, Simms, & Bergman, 1979; Gross, 1979), and attempted homosexual rape (Caldwell & Stewart, 1981). Indeed, Anthony (1981) has noted with some surprise that the two psychoanalytic reports of childhood hysteria-related seizures provide evidence of actual seduction in their social history, "almost as if they had set out to confirm Freud's older theory" (p. 8). At this point, the clinical literature is certainly highly suggestive if not definitive; the clinician should seriously consider the possibility of exploitation or similar dynamics in adolescent girls who present with these nonorganically based seizures. It should be noted however, that such dynamics have not been mentioned in the case reports of younger children with psychogenic seizures. Additionally, Linder (1973) presented the case of an adolescent (and one adult) in which the need to cope with aggressive feelings seemed to be the predominant dynamic factor. Finally, there is evidence of cultural influences, including cases of mass hysteria (e.g., in a community of Canadian Indian children; Armstrong & Patterson, 1975).

Treatment. Treatment from the psychodynamic viewpoint involves the uncovering, interpretation, and working through of the conflictual emotion, thereby eliminating the need for the symptom.

Useful material from a psychodynamic perspective has been presented by Gilpin and Mattes (1981) and Rock (1971). Guidelines for the short-term management and therapy of conversion reactions have also been offered (Brooksbank, 1984; Dubowitz & Herson, 1976; Leaverton, Rupp, & Poff, 1977; Schulman, 1988).

A social learning or behavioral framework starts with similar observations but construes these observations differently. From this perspective, we note that the child presenting somatoform symptomatology has important models for sick role behavior and receives considerable reinforcement from multiple sources while actively engaged in the sick role. Therefore, within this framework, the clinician attends to the observable elements of the clinical picture. Rather than ascribing a tendency to mimic or imitate, the therapist concentrates attention to behavioral models; rather than focusing on unconscious secondary gain, the rewards for sick role behavior are changed. A focus on such observable and manipulable components leads to treatment strategies involving differential reinforcement of nonsick behavior combined with efforts to change the reinforcing patterns of family members. Useful adjuncts can include relaxation training and self-control strategies. Such methodologies have been successfully employed in the treatment of children with hysterical contracture (Hendrix, Thompson, & Rau, 1978), paralysis (Delamater, Rosenbloom, Conners, & Hertweck, 1983), paralysis and anesthesia (McKinlay, Kelly, & Collum, 1977), psychogenic habit cough (Gay et al., 1987), and motor unsteadiness following a minor gym accident (Dollinger & Cotter, 1980). These procedures have as their major advantage that the presenting symptom is resolved fairly quickly. A major disadvantage in rapid symptom relief may be a tendency of the child's family to resist the working through of what is important for maintaining therapeutic gains (i.e., the correction or reduction of familial contingencies contributing to the problem in the first place). Thus, several authors have noted a tendency of families to drop out of treatment after the symptom is removed (Dollinger & Cotter, 1980; Hendrix et al., 1978). This problem is not specific to behavior therapies; others have noted this tendency for parents to challenge psychological interpretations of their child's problem or continually to ask if an organic basis of the problem had been discovered (Dollinger & Cotter, 1980; Friedman, 1973; Rock,

1971). In this regard, it may be most appropriate to include family members as well as the identified patient in the treatment. Successful treatment approaches for psychogenic seizures have included behavior therapy (Caldwell & Stewart, 1981) and behavioral procedures combined with hypnotherapy (Williams, Spiegel, & Mostofsky, 1978).

Dissociative Disorders

The dissociative disorders share a disruption in the usually integrated functions of memory, consciousness, identity, or perception of the environment (APA, 1994). In children, a dissociative reaction may take the form of feelings of depersonalization, hallucinations, and seizure-like absences or "spells." Examples of such disorders include dissociative amnesia, fugue, dissociative identity disorder (formerly, multiple personality disorder), and depersonalization disorders. One of the first cases of a dissociative disorder described was that of an 11-year-old girl whose treatment was reported by the physician Antoine Despine in the mid-1800s (Ellenberger, 1970). Even so, such problems originally were thought to be rare in children. More recently, paralleling the growth of knowledge about child physical and sexual abuse, increased reports of dissociative identity disorders (DID) in children have occurred (e.g., Anderson, Yasenik, & Ross, 1993; Briere & Zaidi, 1989; Malinosky-Rummell & Hoier, 1992). For example, articles have appeared suggesting that DID in children is underrecognized and undertreated even though it is more amenable to intervention than in adults (Coons, Bowman, & Milstein, 1988; Kluft, 1985).

Although dissociative disorders have long been described in the literature (i.e., Gmelin's report of the personality changes of a German woman in the French Revolution, in Greaves, 1993), interest waned in the mid-1900s. The disorder was viewed as rare and of minor importance and often its validity was questioned (see Wallach & Dollinger, 1999). More recently, it has been argued that DID is an artifact of personality (Putnam, 1989) that can be produced in specific situations where suggestibility is high (e.g., under hypnosis; Spanos, Weekes, & Bertrand, 1985). New "personalities" can be created by hypnosis as well as "memories" of events that never occurred. As a result of this new information, clinicians treating dissociative disorders need to carefully avoid highly suggestive treatments that may operate to exacerbate the disorder (Yapko, 1994). The possibility that one can create "new

personalities" through hypnosis suggests some of the important processes that may operate in its development. For example, retrospective adult accounts of DID onset include self-hypnoticlike experiences (Routh, Ernst, & Harper, 1988). These experiences sometimes produced an alter ego to deal with highly stressful situations such as physical or sexual abuse. Such accounts put the onset of DID as early as 4 to 6 years of age.

Currently, models of dissociative disorders are based on the proposition that the disorders arise as a coping response to significant, severe, traumatic events, for example, in children who have experienced profound physical, sexual, and/or emotional abuse (Putnam, 1989; Terr, 1991). A new body of work has emerged describing a continuum of dissociative behavior ranging from normative to pathological experiences in children and adolescents (e.g., Putnam, Helmers, & Trickett, 1993). A normal dissociative experience may include overinvolvement in an activity or daydreaming, whereas maladaptive experiences involve extreme alterations in identity and memory (Putman, 1989). Braun and Sachs (1985) suggest several key predisposing factors contributing to DID, including innate dissociative ability, hypnotic susceptibility, high intelligence, and exposure to severe trauma in childhood. The disorder is maintained when dissociation continues to be the preferred way to cope with stressful life events.

DID rarely is diagnosed early in the referral process. In fact, Coons et al. (1988) note a seven-year gap between initial contact and a diagnosis of DID. Previous diagnoses cover the full range of internalizing and externalizing disorders and personality disorders (in the teenage years) as well as schizophrenia, often to explain hallucinations (Dell & Eisenhower, 1990; Putnam, 1989). In contrast to the pattern in adults, children who experience hallucinations are typically showing a dissociative rather than a psychotic disorder (Bender & Lipkowitz, 1940; Kessler, 1972; Putnam, 1989). Kessler summarizes one of her own cases in which an adolescent girl experienced an auditory hallucination of a whistling sound, which the girl called a "warning signal." Kessler concludes that the signal expressed the girl's conflicting wish for sexual attractiveness (hence, to receive "wolf" whistles) and a warning about the dangers of sexuality. Egdell and Kolvin (1972) have suggested that at least some childhood hallucinations are related to stress. For example, a fourth-grade girl seen by one of this chapter's authors (Dollinger) reported that the devil "put a stew in her mind" shortly after her parents divorced. This bizarre bedtime-associated experience developed into visual and auditory hallucinations of the devil during the daytime. Thus, it appeared that the child experienced hypnagogic and hypnopompic hallucinations at a time of family stress. As a function of her active imagination and fantasy-oriented reading interests, she construed her experience in demonic terms. Brief strategic treatment eliminated the hallucination. Equally interesting is that this young girl was easily hypnotizable, and in a hypnotic session months after the last hallucination, she recalled reading a comic book about the devil given to her by a family friend around the time of her parents' separation, offering one possible contributing link. A similar case of comic-book-mediated delusions was treated behaviorally by Waye (1979). In this case, the child's Sunday School teacher had emphasized "spiritual shrinking as a consequence to not being good." After seeing comics about a shrinking man, this 5-year-old girl reported that her own body parts were shrinking.

Treatment. At this point, the empirical study of treatment outcomes for dissociative disorders in children and adolescents is minimal. Generally, those treating these disorders have relied on a therapeutic approach emphasizing the development of a therapeutic alliance with the child and family, providing education about the disorder to both, and identifying the current problem areas of the child (and family) and devising procedures to deal with them. These problems are likely multifaceted and span most areas of the child's functioning, including school, peer relationships, family life, emotional and behavioral functioning, and preferred coping strategies (see Wallach & Dollinger, 1999). The decision to use hypnosis or other suggestive techniques should be made cautiously, avoiding potential iatrogenic effects (e.g., producing new personalities, creating false memories, or reinforcing dissociative phenomena). In the treatment by one of the authors (Gilbert) and her student of one 10-year-old girl reporting several different personalities, treatment was focused on a series of identified problem areas, including (1) the resolution of severe conduct problems at school and home, by using primarily behavioral procedures; (2) modifying dysfunctional interpersonal behavior and cognitions that put her at risk for abuse by adults and predisposed her to a deviant lifestyle, by using primarily social skills and cognitive-behavioral

approaches; (3) assisting her in coming to terms with/accepting and moving beyond the severe emotional trauma she had experienced, by using supportive and cognitive behavioral approaches; and (4) dealing with her different "personalities" in a matter-of-fact way, by discussing them as parts of her whole self and drawing attention to appropriate ways of meeting different contingencies that did not require a "different personality." These efforts resulted in clear and clinically relevant improvement in each of the identified problem areas.

POSTTRAUMATIC STRESS DISORDER

Once referred to as war neurosis, posttraumatic stress disorder (PTSD) involves the kinds of negative emotionality traditionally associated with neurosis. Currently, defined in the *DSM-IV* (APA, 1994), PTSD is a constellation of symptoms that occurs in response to an event involving death, or actual or perceived threat of harm or injury to oneself or others. The symptoms are organized into three broad categories: reexperiencing symptoms, avoidance/general numbing, and hyperarousal. Trauma survivors plagued by reexperiencing symptoms may report intrusive thoughts, recurrent distressing dreams, intense psychological and/or physiological reactivity in response to trauma-related cues, and act or feel as if the event were recurring. In an attempt to manage these symptoms, survivors may avoid trauma-related stimuli. Alternatively, they may show other avoidant symptoms, including amnesia for aspects of the traumatic event, detachment, diminished interest and participation in significant activities, a sense of foreshortened future, and a restricted range of affect. Hyperarousal is characterized by physiological arousal and can be manifested as sleep disturbances, irritability, difficulty concentrating, hypervigilance, or exaggerated startle response. If a child exhibits a requisite number of symptoms from each category and shows significant impairment in his or her psychosocial functioning as a result, then the symptoms are considered diagnostic of PTSD. Children who are personally distressed by posttraumatic symptoms but who do not show significant impairment in their psychosocial functioning may still benefit from clinical interventions.

Although primarily based on clinical observations of adult victims, factor analytic research confirms the application of the core symptoms described in *DSM-IV* to younger populations (Sack, Seeley, & Clarke, 1997). Children may exhibit symptoms from any of the three broad categories, but tend to report reexperiencing symptoms more often than avoidance/numbing and hyperarousal after a major disaster (Garrison et al., 1995; Goenjian et al., 1995; La Greca, Silverman, Vernberg, & Prinstein, 1996; Schwarz & Kowalski, 1991; Vernberg, La Greca, Silverman, & Prinstein, 1996; Vogel & Vernberg, 1993). Individual symptoms may be manifested differently across age groups. Young children, for example, are more likely to engage in posttraumatic play than to report intrusive thoughts because of their limited verbal skills. Terr (1981) observed a group of children using posttrauma play to work through their traumatic experience of being kidnapped from their school bus and buried in a tractor trailer before escaping. Developmental differences in symptom expression raise serious questions about the universal application of standard diagnostic criteria to all age groups.

The *DSM-IV* outlines discrete, episodic behaviors or experiences that occur as a result of trauma exposure, but neglect the more subtle characterological effects of exposure (Brett, 1996). Terr (1991) has proposed that characterological problems are more likely to develop following chronic (Type II) stressors, whereas survivors of infrequent, acute (Type I) traumas tend to exhibit classic PTSD symptoms. Type II traumas (e.g., sexual abuse) are more likely to be associated with enduring personality changes because of the betrayal of trust and violation of belief systems involved in such events. Other conceptualizations of posttraumatic stress reactions include Herman's (1992) disorders of extreme stress not otherwise specified (DESNOS) and the *ICD-10*'s enduring personality changes after catastrophic experience (van der Kolk, 1996). Both of these disorders include characterological sequelae as essential features of their diagnostic categories.

PREVALENCE

Prevalence rates for PTSD in children range from as low as 5% to 13% following exposure to hurricanes, pediatric burns, physical abuse, and cancer treatment (Deblinger, McLeer, Atkins, Ralphe, & Foa, 1989; Garrison et al., 1995; La Greca et al.,

1996; Shannon, Lonigan, Finch, & Taylor, 1994; Stoddard, Norman, Murphy, & Beardslee, 1989; Stuber et al., 1996), to as high as 43% to 70% following sexual abuse, a schoolyard sniper attack, and war trauma (Kinzie, Sack, Angell, Clarke, & Ben, 1989; Macksound & Aber, 1996; McLeer, Callaghan, Henry, & Wallen, 1994; Pynoos et al., 1987). Rates tend to be higher for events involving exposure to life threats to self or others, destruction, loss, and Type II traumas. Exposure to Type II traumas are more likely to produce PTSD symptoms that reach clinical significance because of the chronicity of these events. Less is known about prevalence rates in nonclinical community samples. Giaconia et al. (1995) estimated 6.3% of adolescents met criteria for PTSD but because their community sample included largely older adolescents, this rate is not generalizable to younger children.

The rate of PTSD tends to be high soon after trauma exposure but generally declines as time passes (La Greca et al., 1996; Shaw, Applegate, & Schorr, 1996; Shaw et al., 1995). Approximately 25% of adolescents living near Three Mile Island reported acute psychological distress two months after a nuclear accident (Davidson & Baum, 1990). However, their symptoms subsided rapidly thereafter. Similarly, rates declined from 30% three months after a widely destructive hurricane, Hurricane Andrew, to 12.5% 10 months later (La Greca et al., 1996).

ETIOLOGY

Perspectives on the underlying causes of PTSD include cognitive, behavioral, and neurobiological explanations. Horowitz (1980) provides a primarily cognitive theory in which human cognition has an innate completion tendency. Experiences are repeatedly worked through until they can be assimilated into a person's view of the self and the world. However, individuals attempt to avoid traumatizing memories because of their distressing nature. Thus, accommodation to the traumatization is hampered, and unwelcome memories continue to intrude (Haugaard & Reppucci, 1988). This model helps explain why more developmentally appropriate activities, emotions, and cognitions are thwarted in these children. Their attention and energy are tied up in the largely unproductive activity of attempting both to assimilate and to avoid the traumatic event.

Other cognitive theorists focus on attributions for the traumatic event (Janoff-Bulman, 1985). Victims may assume personal responsibility for their trauma experiences, which can generate negative feelings, especially if the child believes in the just world hypothesis, "You get what you deserve." This theory can explain many PTSD symptoms, including physiological arousal, hypervigilance, and negatively altered future expectations. However, self-blame may be a symptom of posttraumatic stress rather than a cause (Downey, Silver, & Wortman, 1990; Joseph, Brewin, Yule, & Williams, 1993). In a study of children struck by lightning, survivors making any attributions for the event were more distressed than the children who did not make attributions (Dollinger, 1986), suggesting that making attributions may be a function of emotional distress.

People generally tend to feel invulnerable to negative life events, and when this illusion is shattered, they become more aware of their vulnerability to future negative events (Gibbs, 1989; Greening, 1997; Greening & Dollinger, 1992; March & Amaya-Jackson, 1993; McCormack, Burgess, & Hartman, 1988). Being in a heightened state of alertness elicits a chain of physiological reactions, manifested as re-experiencing and hyperarousal symptoms. People may then develop avoidant behaviors to prevent contact with anxiety-provoking stimuli.

Behavioral theorists explain posttraumatic stress with the classical conditioning theory. That is, trauma survivors are conditioned to respond to trauma-related stimuli with physiological arousal because of the initial pairing of the event and hyperarousal (Charney, Deutch, Krystal, Southwick, & Davis, 1993). Operant conditioning theory can explain children's developing avoidant behaviors to prevent experiencing uncontrollable states of arousal associated with trauma-related stimuli. Although avoidant behaviors are reinforcing because of the reduction in distressing hyperarousal symptoms, they can be detrimental if children's social and academic activities are restricted as a result.

Neurobiological explanations for PTSD have evolved from research on the fear conditioning model. Fear is an adaptive emotion that elicits a chain of reactions for responding to an impending threat. However, under prolonged or traumatic stress, the body can sustain long-standing neurobiological sequelae that have been linked to PTSD

symptoms. Neurochemical disturbances and dysregulation of the control center for stress reactions—the hypothalamic-pituitary-adrenal axis—have been the subject of much of the research on the neurobiology of PTSD. Only recently has this research been extended to children, most of which has been with abused children. Compared to matched control groups, a small sample of sexually abused children ($N = 26$) exhibited significantly higher levels of urinary catecholamines (stress hormones) and their metabolites (De Bellis, Lefter, Trickett, & Putnam, 1994). Although only one girl was diagnosed with PTSD, the elevated catecholamine levels resembled the physiological pattern seen in Vietnam combat veterans diagnosed with PTSD. An extensive discussion of the neurobiological underpinnings of PTSD are beyond the scope of this chapter; the reader is referred to De Bellis (1997) and van der Kolk (1988) for further discussion.

ASSESSMENT

One of the most widely used self-report measures of PTSD is the Children's Posttraumatic Stress Reaction Index (RI; Frederick, 1985a; Frederick, Pynoos, & Nader, 1988). The form can be administered as either an interview or as a self-report rating scale. The interview approach is typically preferred for assessing the nature, extent, and severity of symptomatology (Green, 1991). Revised over the past decade, the current form provides a weighted count of 20 PTSD symptoms derived from the three broad categories of symptoms outlined in *DSM-IV*. The RI does not provide a diagnosis of PTSD. However, 90% of children classified in the severe range or above (≥ 40) after a major earthquake met *DSM-III-R* (APA, 1987) criteria for PTSD (Pynoos et al., 1993). Frederick (1985b) reported a high correlation between the RI sum score and clinical cases of PTSD among children. Total scores also have been linked to the level of trauma exposure and to the extent of bereavement (Lonigan, Shannon, Finch, Daugherty, & Taylor, 1991; Nader, Pynoos, Fairbanks, & Frederick, 1990; Pynoos et al., 1987, 1993). The measure has been used across cultures (Pynoos et al., 1993) and for children as young as 5 years (Pynoos et al., 1987).

Horowitz's Impact of Event Scale (Horowitz, Wilner, & Alvarez, 1979) is another commonly used self-report measure that was developed to assess intrusion and avoidance symptoms. Other self-report scales include the Children's Posttraumatic Stress Disorders Inventory (Saigh, 1989a), the Posttraumatic Stress Disorder Index (Llabre & Hadi, 1997), and the Posttraumatic Stress Reaction Checklist (Macksound & Aber, 1996). Although these measures appear to be promising, further research on their psychometric properties is necessary. Measures designed for more specific populations include the Children's Impact of Traumatic Events Scale–Revised (Wolfe, Gentile, Michienzi, Sas, & Wolfe, 1991), a measure that was developed for child victims of sexual abuse.

Scales incorporated within structured interview measures that assess PTSD symptoms include PTSD modules of the Structured Clinical Interview for Diagnosis (Pelcovitz et al., 1994; Spitzer, Williams, & Gibbon, 1987), the Diagnostic Interview Schedule for Children (DISC) (Fisher & Kranzler, 1990), and supplemental questions in the Diagnostic Interview for Children and Adolescents (DICA) (Reich & Welner, 1990). These structured measures offer the benefit of being multi-informant measures (parent and child). Questions have been raised about the sensitivity of the DICA–R for measuring PTSD (Vogel & Vernberg, 1993), and the DISC might be difficult for preadolescents (Edelbrock, Costello, Dulcan, Kalas, & Conover, 1985).

COMORBIDITY

Some of the more common comorbid disorders of PTSD include anxiety and depression. Children exposed to chronic traumas may show more generalized anxiety, whereas victims of *acute* traumas may be more likely to exhibit specific phobias. Being a victim of a traffic accident, for example, has been associated with fears of riding in a vehicle or of event-related stimuli (Di Gallo, Barton, & Parry-Jones, 1997). Similarly, Dollinger, O'Donnell, and Staley (1984) observed storm-related fears in children exposed to a lightning-strike disaster that left a 10-year-old soccer player dead and two others wounded. A meaningful generalization gradient was obtained whereby death-related fears were also exacerbated. Although vulnerable to anxiety, most young survivors generally do not score in the clinical range (Lonigan et al., 1991; Lonigan, Shannon, Taylor, Finch, & Sallee, 1994;

March, Amaya-Jackson, Terry, & Costanzo, 1997; Shannon et al., 1994).

Depression has been found to be a comorbid disorder following highly traumatic and destructive events. Goenjian et al. (1995) observed higher rates of depressive symptoms several years after a fatal earthquake in Armenia that killed over 20,000 people. The relation may be explained by higher rates of losses in fatal disasters. However, Goenjian et al. found severity of depressive symptoms related to the severity of PTSD symptoms even after controlling for the extent of loss and trauma exposure. This finding suggests that depressive symptoms might develop as a result of PTSD symptoms, and not simply in response to losses (Goenjian et al., 1995).

RISK FACTORS

Exposure to high levels of trauma including life threat, witnessing deaths and destruction, and losing a friend or relative has been identified as a significant risk factor for PTSD. These were found to be significant even after controlling for demographic variables and time since exposure (Garrison et al., 1995; Green et al., 1991; Llabre & Hadi, 1997; Lonigan et al., 1991; Macksound & Aber, 1996; March et al., 1997; Pynoos et al., 1987, 1993; Rossman, Bingham, & Emde, 1997; Vernberg et al., 1996). Some studies suggest that the disruption in the child's family life is a stronger predictor of symptomatology than the level of trauma exposure (Garrison et al., 1995; McFarlane, Policansky, & Irwin, 1987), whereas others report that greater symptomatology is linked to both post-disaster disruption and threatening experiences during the event (Lonigan et al., 1991, 1994). The differential findings are likely explained by the varying degrees of life threat and disruption that occur across events. In situations involving equally high levels of life threat and loss/disruption, both variables have contributed to PTSD. Children's subjective experience and understanding can be more predictive of symptomatology than the actual life threat and loss caused by traumatic events (Green et al., 1991; Lonigan et al., 1994; Pynoos et al., 1987).

Although girls and young children tend to report more PTSD symptoms (Garrison et al., 1995; Green et al., 1991; Lonigan et al., 1991, 1994; Macksound & Aber, 1996; Pynoos et al., 1993; Rossman et al., 1997; Shannon et al., 1994; Vernberg et al., 1996), not all reports document age and gender differences

(Pynoos et al., 1987, 1993; Rossman et al., 1997; Sack et al., 1997; Shaw et al., 1995; Vernberg et al., 1996). Some even suggest that older children may be more vulnerable to PTSD symptoms than younger children (Garrison et al., 1995; Stuber et al., 1996). Whatever differences exist seem to dissipate with time (La Greca et al., 1996).

Ethnicity has emerged recently as a significant predictor of PTSD in children following acute events (Garrison et al., 1995; Lonigan et al., 1991; March et al., 1997; Shannon et al., 1994). Among the victims of Hurricane Andrew, African-American and Hispanic children were significantly more likely to show PTSD symptomatology 3, 7, and 10 months later (La Greca et al., 1996). Limited availability of financial resources for disaster recovery might have increased their risk.

In one of the few studies on intrapersonal risk factors, Vernberg et al. (1996) found coping strategies to account for 21% of the variance in PTSD after controlling for the effects of exposure to Hurricane Andrew, demographic variables, and social support. Blaming oneself or others and being angry about the hurricane accounted for a sizable percentage (13%) of the variance explained by the strategies. Although high levels of positive and negative coping were associated with more symptoms three months after the hurricane, only negative coping strategies predicted symptomatology 10 months after the disaster (La Greca et al., 1996).

The availability of social support was one of the best buffers against stress for the young survivors of Hurricane Andrew (La Greca et al., 1996; Vernberg et al., 1996). Similar effects were observed among children exposed to traumatic events in other countries, with girls benefiting more than boys (Llabre & Hadi, 1997). Although parents are typically children's primary sources of support in times of crisis, they may be too preoccupied with postdisaster recovery efforts or with their own distress to be available to their children. In such situations, other sources of support including peers and teachers can buffer postdisaster stress for children (Garrison et al., 1995; La Greca et al., 1996; Vernberg et al., 1996).

TREATMENT

Various treatment protocols have been described for use with trauma survivors (Pynoos & Eth, 1986;

Pynoos & Nader, 1988; Vogel & Vernberg, 1993), but few have been evaluated empirically. They all share in common emotional expression under controlled conditions, decreasing cognitive distortions regarding the safety of oneself and others, correcting erroneous attributions for the disaster, normalizing emotional reactions, and education about the recovery process (Pynoos & Nader, 1988). Although immediate service may seem warranted, Yule (1993) cautions against introducing treatment too soon after trauma exposure, when survivors may be too numb to benefit from debriefing. He suggests that children would be more responsive to interventions 7 to 14 days after exposure. This suggestion does not override the possibility that some children might benefit from immediate assistance (Pynoos & Eth, 1986).

It is important to bear in mind that some treatments are limited in scope. Family therapies, for example, may be too limited for treating paranormal experiences and perceiving a foreshortened future (Terr, 1989). Other treatment approaches focus less on emotional expression and more on trauma-related phobic symptoms. In his treatment of young wartime survivors, Saigh (1989b) used a behavioral treatment approach that is based on the principle of extinction and involves prolonged exposure to imaginal aversive stimuli. Relaxation exercises are incorporated to help children cope with exposure to such anxiety-provoking stimuli during treatment sessions. Saigh reports successfully treating four children with treatment gains lasting as long as six months posttreatment. Although psychoactive medications may be therapeutic for treating comorbid symptoms (e.g., depression) in children with PTSD, further research on their efficacy for more trauma-specific symptoms is warranted (Vogel & Vernberg, 1993). A multimodal approach is likely the most effective, with medication being one component of treatment.

CONCLUDING REMARKS

In updating this chapter, we were struck by the level of activity that has transpired in the past 10 years on these child and adolescent disorders. Simultaneously, we were struck by the enormous gaps in knowledge, the paucity of research in assessment and treatment outcomes, and the ongoing debates that continue to characterize the literature. It makes for an exciting time in which the field can expect new empirically derived information to emerge on a regular basis and growing opportunities for scientifically oriented child clinicians to contribute to this area. Even so, mental health professionals are too often left with having to make decisions based on their best judgment or theoretical predisposition and training, never fully comfortable that they are making the best choices. As described by Eisenberg (1975), too often clinicians are "acting in uncertainty."

Some diagnostic areas have more literature development than others (e.g., OCD compared to DID). Controversy is more prominent in some of the diagnostic areas than in others (e.g., DID compared to OCD). Actually, comparisons across disorders become problematic to the extent that each *DSM* edition moves them apart. Their former unifying element ("neurosis") is gone, and it is not clear that all would be grouped under internalizing disorders although they will generally correlate more with anxiety and depression than with anger or disobedience.

Across the disorders a common therapeutic theme of engendering mastery seems to materialize. Children and adolescents are asked to actively face and engage in processes that ameliorate their symptomotology. They become responsible and successful in acquiring new self-control and social skills and clearer ways of thinking about their problems. In these ways, mastery becomes an underlying and important psychological element of recovery.

REFERENCES

Achenbach, T.M. (1993). Implications of multiaxial empirically based assessment for behavior therapy with children. *Behavior Therapist, 24,* 91–116.

Adams, P.L. (1973). *Obsessive children.* New York: Brunner/Mazel.

Adams, P.L. (1985). The obsessive child. *American Journal of Psychotherapy, 39,* 301–313.

American Psychiatric Association. (1980). *Diagnostic and statistical manual of mental disorders* (2nd ed.). Washington, DC: Author.

American Psychiatric Association. (1987). *Diagnostic and statistical manual of mental disorders* (3rd ed., rev.). Washington, DC: Author.

American Psychiatric Association. (1994). *Diagnostic and statistical manual of mental disorders* (4th ed.). Washington, DC: Author.

Anderson, G., Yasenik, L., & Ross, C.A. (1993). Dissociative experiences and disorders among women who identify themselves as sexual abuse survivors. *Child Abuse and Neglect, 17,* 677–686.

Anthony, E.J. (1981). The flowers of mankind. In E.J. Anthony & D.C. Gilpin (Eds.), *Three further clinical faces of childhood* (pp. 1–10). New York: Spectrum.

Apter, A., Bernhout, E., & Tyano, S. (1984). Severe obsessive-compulsive disorder in adolescence: A report of eight cases. *Journal of Adolescence, 7,* 349–358.

Armstrong, H., & Patterson, P. (1975). Seizures in Canadian Indian children: Individual, family, and community approaches. *Canadian Psychiatric Association Journal, 20,* 247–255.

Behar, D., Rapoport, J., Berg, C., Denckla, M., Mann, L., Cox, C., Fedio, P., Zahn, T., & Wolfman, M. (1984). Computerized tomography and neuropsychological test measures in adolescents with OCD. *American Journal of Psychiatry, 141*(3), 363–368.

Bender, L., & Lipkowitz, H.H. (1940). Hallucinations in children. *American Journal of Orthopsychiatry, 10,* 471–490.

Berg, C.Z., Rapoport, J.L., Whitaker, A., Davies, M., Leonard, H.L., & Lenane, M. (1989). Childhood OCD: A two-year prospective follow-up of a community sample. *Journal of the American Academy of Child and Adolescent Psychiatry, 28,* 528–523.

Bernstein, N.R. (1969). Psychogenic seizures in adolescent girls. *Behavioral Neuropsychiatry, 1,* 31–34.

Black, A. (1974). The natural history of obsessional neurosis. In H.R. Beech (Ed.), *Obsessional states* (pp. 19–54). New York: Methuen.

Black, D., Yates, W., Noyes, R., Pfohl, B., & Reich, J. (1988, May 12). *Personality disorder in obsessive-compulsives.* Paper presented at the 137th meeting of the American Psychiatric Association, Montreal, Canada.

Braun, B.G. (1985). The transgenerational incidence of dissociation and multiple personality disorder. In R.P. Kluft (Ed.), *Childhood antecedents of multiple personality* (pp. 127–150). Washington, DC: American Psychiatric Press.

Braun, B.G., & Sachs, R.G. (1985). The development of multiple personality disorder. In R.P. Kluft (Ed.), *Childhood antecedents of multiple personality* (pp. 37–64). Washington, DC: American Psychiatric Press.

Brett, E.A. (1996). The classification of posttraumatic stress disorder. In B.A. van der Kolk, A.C. McFarlane, & L. Weisaeth (Eds.), *Traumatic stress: The effects of overwhelming experience on mind, body, and society* (pp. 117–128). New York: Guilford Press.

Briere, J., & Zaidi, L.Y. (1989). Sexual abuse histories and sequelae in female psychiatric emergency room patients. *American Journal of Psychiatry, 146,* 1602–1606.

Brooksbank, D.J. (1984). Management of conversion reaction in five adolescent girls. *Journal of Adolescence, 7,* 359–376.

Caldwell, T.A., & Stewart, R.S. (1981). Hysterical seizures and hypnotherapy. *American Journal of Clinical Hypnosis, 23,* 294–298.

Capstick, N., & Selfrup, J. (1977). Obsessional states. *Acta Psychiatrica Scandinavia, 56,* 427–439.

Charney, D.S., Deutch, A.Y., Krystal, J.H., Southwick, S.M., & Davis, M. (1993). Psychobiologic mechanisms of posttraumatic stress disorder. *Archives of General Psychiatry, 50,* 294–305.

Coons, P.M., Bowman, E.S., & Milstein, V. (1988). Multiple personality disorder: A clinical investigation of 50 cases. *Journal of Nervous and Mental Disease, 176,* 519–527.

Davidson, L.M., & Baum, A. (1990). Posttraumatic stress in children following natural and human-made trauma. In M. Lewis & S.M. Miller (Eds.), *Handbook of developmental psychopathology* (pp. 251–259). New York: Plenum Press.

De Bellis, M.D. (1997). Posttraumatic stress disorder and acute stress disorder. In R.T. Ammerman & M. Hersen (Eds.), *Handbook of prevention and treatment with children and adolescents* (pp. 455–494). New York: Wiley.

De Bellis, M.D., Lefter, L., Trickett, P.K., & Putnam, F.W. (1994). Urinary catecholamine excretion in sexually abused girls. *Journal of the American Academy of Child and Adolescent Psychiatry, 33,* 320–327.

Deblinger, E., McLeer, S.V., Atkins, M.S., Ralphe, D., & Foa, E. (1989). Post-traumatic stress in sexually abused, physically abused, and nonabused children. *Child Abuse and Neglect, 13,* 403–408.

Delamater, A.M., Rosenbloom, N., Conners, C.K., & Hertweck, L. (1983). The behavioral treatment of hysterical paralysis in a ten-year-old boy. *Journal of the American Academy of Child Psychiatry, 22,* 73–79.

Dell, P.F., & Eisenhower, J.W. (1990). Adolescent multiple personality disorder. *Journal of the American Academy of Child and Adolescent Psychiatry, 29,* 359–366.

Di Gallo, A., Barton, J., & Parry-Jones, W. (1997). Road traffic accidents: Early consequences in children and adolescents. *British Journal of Psychiatry, 170,* 358–362.

Digman, J.M. (1990). Personality structure: Emergence of the five-factor model. *Annual Review of Psychology, 41,* 417–440.

Dollinger, S.J. (1983). A case report of dissociative neurosis (depersonalization disorder) in an adolescent treated with family therapy and behavior modification. *Journal of Consulting and Clinical Psychology, 51,* 479–484.

Dollinger, S.J. (1986). The need for meaning following disaster: Attributions and emotional upset. *Personality and Social Psychology Bulletin, 12,* 300–310.

Dollinger, S.J., & Cotter, P.D. (1980). Behavioral and cognitive-control strategies in the elimination of an 11-year-old boy's psychogenic pain. *Behavioral Disorders, 6,* 36–40.

Dollinger, S.J., O'Donnell, J.P., & Staley, A.A. (1984). Lightning-strike disaster: Effects on children's fears and worries. *Journal of Consulting and Clinical Psychology, 52,* 1028–1038.

Downey, G., Silver, R.C., & Wortman, C.B. (1990). Reconsidering the attribution-adjustment relation following a major negative event: Coping with the loss of a child. *Journal of Personality and Social Psychology, 59,* 925–940.

Dubowitz, V., & Herson, L. (1976). Management of children with non-organic (hysterical) disorders of motor function. *Developmental Medicine and Child Neurology, 18,* 358–368.

Edelbrock, C., Costello, A.J., Dulcan, M.K., Kalas, R., & Conover, N.L. (1985). Age differences in the reliability of the psychiatric interview of the child. *Child Development, 56,* 265–275.

Egdell, H.G., & Kolvin, I. (1972). Childhood hallucinations. *Journal of Child Psychology and Psychiatry, 13,* 279–287.

Eisenberg, L. (1975). The ethics of intervention: Acting amidst ambiguity. *Journal of Child Psychology and Psychiatry, 16,* 93–104.

Elkins, R., Rapoport, J.L., & Lipsky, A. (1980). Obsessive-compulsive disorder of childhood and adolescence: A neurobiological viewpoint. *Journal of the American Academy of Child Psychiatry, 19,* 511–524.

Ellenberger, H.F. (1970). *The discovery of the unconscious.* New York: Basic Books.

Fine, S. (1973). Family therapy and a behavioral approach to childhood obsessive-compulsive neurosis. *Archives of General Psychiatry, 28,* 695–697.

Fisher, P., & Kranzler, E. (1990). *Post-traumatic stress disorder: Supplemental module for the DISC-2.1.* New York: New York Psychiatric Institute, Division of Child and Adolescent Psychiatry.

Flament, M., Koby, E., Rapoport, J., Berg, C., Zahn, T., Cox, C., Denckla, M., & Lenane, M. (1990). Childhood obsessive-compulsive disorder: A prospective follow-up study. *Journal of Child Psychology and Psychiatry, 31,* 363–380.

Flament, M., Rapoport, J., Berg, C., Sceery, W., Kilts, C., Mellstrom, B., & Linnoila, M. (1985). Clomipramine treatment of childhood obsessive-compulsive disorder. *Archives of General Psychiatry, 42,* 977–983.

Flament, M., Rapoport, J., Whitaker, A., Berg, C., & Sceery, W. (1985). OCD in adolescence. Paper presented at the 32nd meeting of the American Academy of Child Psychiatry, San Antonio, TX.

Franklin, M.E., Kozak, M.J., Cashman, L.A., Coles, M.E., Rheingold, A.A., & Foa, E.B. (1998). Cognitive-behavioral treatment of pediatric OCD. *Journal of the American Academy of Child and Adolescent Psychiatry, 37*(4), 412–419.

Frederick, C.J. (1985a). Children traumatized by catastrophic situations. In S. Eth & R.S. Pynoos (Eds.),

PTSD in children (pp. 73–99). Washington, DC: American Psychiatric Press.

Frederick, C.J. (1985b). Selected foci in the spectrum of posttraumatic stress disorders. In J. Laube & S. Murphy (Eds.), *Perspectives on disaster recovery* (pp. 110–130). Norwalk CT: Appleton-Century-Crofts.

Frederick, C.J., Pynoos, R.S., & Nader, K.O. (1988). *Child Post-Traumatic Stress–Reaction Index.* Los Angeles: Prevention Intervention Program in Trauma.

Friedman, S.B. (1973). Conversion symptoms in adolescents. *Pediatric Clinics of North America, 20,* 873–882.

Frischholz, E.J., Lipman, L.S., Braun, B.G., & Sachs, R.G. (1992). Psychopathology, hypnotizability, and dissociation. *American Journal of Psychiatry, 149,* 1521–1525.

Garrison, C.Z., Bryant, E.S., Addy, C.L., Spurrier, P.G., Freedy, J.R., & Kilpatrick, D.G. (1995). Posttraumatic stress disorder in adolescents after Hurricane Andrew. *Journal of the American Academy of Child and Adolescent Psychiatry, 34,* 1193–1201.

Gay, M., Blager, F., Bartsch, K., Emery, C., Rosenstiel-Gross, A., & Spears, J. (1987). Psychogenic habit cough: Review and case reports. *Journal of Clinical Psychiatry, 48,* 483–486.

Geller, D., Biederman, J., Reed, E., Spencer, T., & Wilens, T. (1995). Similarities in response to fluoxetine in the treatment of children and adolescents with OCD. *Journal of the American Academy of Child and Adolescent Psychiatry, 34*(1), 36–44.

Giaconia, R.M., Reinherz, H.Z., Silverman, A.B., Pakiz, B., Frost, A.K., & Cohen, E. (1995). Traumas and posttraumatic stress disorder in a community population of older adolescents. *Journal of the American Academy of Child and Adolescent Psychiatry, 34,* 1369–1380.

Gibbs, M.S. (1989). Factors in the victim that mediate between disaster and psychopathology: A review. *Journal of Traumatic Stress, 2,* 489–514.

Gilpin, D.C., & Mattes, K. (1981). Psychotherapy of the hysterical. In E.J. Anthony & D.C. Gilpin (Eds.), *Three further clinical faces of childhood* (pp. 59–65). New York: Spectrum.

Goenjian, A.K., Pynoos, R.S., Steinberg, A.M., Najarian, L.M., Asarnow, J.R., Karayan, I., Ghurabi, M., & Fairbanks, L.A. (1995). Psychiatric comorbidity in children after the 1988 earthquake in Armenia. *Journal of the American Academy of Child and Adolescent Psychiatry, 34,* 1174–1184.

Goodwin, J., Simms, M., & Bergman, R. (1979). Diagnosis and management of hysterical seizures: A sequel to incest. *American Journal of Orthopsychiatry, 49,* 698–703.

Goodyer, I. (1981). Hysterical conversion reaction in childhood. *Journal of Child Psychiatry, 22,* 179–188.

Greaves, G.G. (1993). A history of multiple personality disorder. In R.P. Kluft & C.G. Fine (Eds.), *Clinical perspectives on multiple personality disorder* (pp. 355–380). Washington, DC: American Psychiatric Press.

Green, B.L. (1991). Evaluating the effects of disasters. *Psychological Assessment, 3,* 538–546.

Green, B.L., Korol, M., Grace, M.C., Vary, M.G., Leonard, A.C., Gleser, G.C., & Smitson-Cohen, S. (1991). Children and disaster: Age, gender, and parental effects on PTSD symptoms. *Journal of the American Academy of Child and Adolescent Psychiatry, 30,* 945–951.

Greening, L. (1997). Risk perception following exposure to a job-related electrocution accident. *Acta Psychologica, 95,* 267–277.

Greening, L., & Dollinger, S. (1992). Illusions (and shattered illusions) of invulnerability. *Journal of Traumatic Stress, 5,* 63–75.

Gross, M. (1979). Incestuous rape: A cause of hysterical seizures in four adolescent girls. *American Journal of Orthopsychiatry, 49,* 704–708.

Harris, D., & Wiebe, D. (1992). An analysis of response prevention and flooding procedures in the treatment of adolescent OCD. *Journal of Behavior Therapy and Experimental Psychiatry, 23,* 107–115.

Haugaard, J., & Reppucci, N. (1988). *The sexual abuse of children.* San Francisco: Jossey-Bass.

Hendrix, E.M., Thompson, L.M., & Rau, B. (1978). Behavioral treatment of an "hysterically" clenched fist. *Journal of Behavior Therapy and Experimental Psychiatry, 9,* 273–276.

Herman, J.L. (1992). Complex PTSD: A syndrome in survivors of prolonged and repeated trauma. *Journal of Traumatic Stress, 5,* 377–391.

Hollingsworth, C.E., Tanguary, P.E., Grossman, L., & Pabst, P. (1980). Long-term outcome of obsessive-compulsive disorder in childhood. *Journal of the American Academy of Child Psychiatry, 19,* 134–144.

Hornstein, N., & Tyson, S. (1991). Inpatient treatment of children with multiple personality/dissociative disorders and their families. *Psychiatric Clinics of North America, 14*(3), 631–648.

Horowitz, M.J. (1980). Psychological response to serious life events. In V. Hamilton & D. Warburton (Eds.), *Human stress and cognition* (pp. 249–275). New York: Wiley.

Horowitz, M., Wilner, N., & Alvarez, W. (1979). Impact of event scale: A measure of subjective stress. *Psychosomatic Medicine, 41,* 209–218.

Janoff-Bulman, R. (1985). The aftermath of victimization. In C. Figley (Ed.), *Trauma and its wake* (pp. 15–35). New York: Brunner/Mazel.

Joseph, S.A., Brewin, C.R., Yule, W., & Williams, R. (1993). Causal attributions and posttraumatic stress in adolescents. *Journal of Child Psychology and Psychiatry, 34,* 247–253.

Kellerman, J. (1981). Hypnosis as an adjunct to thought-stopping and covert reinforcement in treatment of homicidal obsessions in a twelve-year-old boy. *International Journal of Clinical and Experimental Hypnosis, 29,* 128–135.

Kessler, J.W. (1972). Neurosis in childhood. In B.B. Wolman (Ed.), *Manual of child psychopathology* (pp. 387–435). New York: McGraw-Hill.

Kinzie, J.D., Sack, W.H., Angell, R., Clarke, G.N., & Ben, R. (1989). A three-year follow-up of Cambodian young people traumatized as children. *Journal of the American Academy of Children and Adolescent Psychiatry, 28*, 501–504.

Kluft, R. (Ed.). (1985). *Childhood antecedents of multiple personality.* Washington, DC: American Psychiatric Association.

LaBarbera, J.D., & Dozier, J.E. (1980). Hysterical seizures: The role of sexual exploitation. *Psychosomatics, 21*, 897–903.

La Greca, A.M., Silverman, W.K., Vernberg, E.M., & Prinstein, M.J. (1996). Symptoms of posttraumatic stress in children after Hurricane Andrew: A prospective study. *Journal of Consulting and Clinical Psychology, 64*, 712–723.

Laitmen, R.J. (1981). A family therapy perspective on hysterical dynamics in childhood. In E.J. Anthony & D.C. Gilpin (Eds.), *Three further clinical faces of childhood* (pp. 85–94). New York: SP Medical and Scientific Books.

Last, C., Perrin, S., Hersen, M., & Kazdin, A. (1992). *DSM-III-R* anxiety disorders in children: Sociodemographic and clinical characteristics. *Journal of the American Academy of Child and Adolescent Psychiatry, 31*, 1070–1076.

Leaverton, D.R., Rupp, J.W., & Poff, M.G. (1977). Brief therapy for monocular hysterical blindness in childhood. *Child Psychiatry and Human Development, 7*, 254–263.

Leonard, H.L., Goldberger, E.L., Rapoport, J.L., Cheslow, D.L., & Swedo, S.E. (1990). Childhood rituals: Normal development or obsessive-compulsive symptoms. *Journal of the American Academy of Child and Adolescent Psychiatary, 29*, 17–23.

Leonard, H., Swedo, S., & Lenane, M. (1993). A two to seven year follow-up study of 54 OCD children and adolescents. *Archives of General Psychiatry, 50*, 429–439.

Leonard, H., Swedo, S., Lenane, M., Rettew, D., Cheslow, D., Hamburger, S., & Rapoport, J. (1991). A double-blind desipramine substitution during long-term clomipramine treatment in children and adolescents with OCD. *Archives of General Psychiatry, 48*, 922–927.

Linder, H. (1973). Psychogenic seizure states: A psychodynamic study. *International Journal of Clinical and Experimental Hypnosis, 21*, 261–271.

Llabre, M.M., & Hadi, F. (1997). Social support and psychological distress in Kuwaiti boys and girls exposed to the Gulf crisis. *Journal of Clinical Child Psychology, 26*, 247–255.

Lonigan, C.J., Shannon, M.P., Finch, A.J., Jr., Daugherty, T.K., & Taylor, C.M. (1991). Children's reactions to a natural disaster: Symptom severity and degree of exposure. *Advances in Behaviour Research and Therapy, 13*, 135–154.

Lonigan, C.J., Shannon, M.P., Taylor, C.M., Finch, A.J., Jr., & Sallee, F.R. (1994). Children exposed to disaster: II. Risk factors for the development of post-traumatic symptomatology. *Journal of the American Academy of Child and Adolescent Psychiatry, 33*, 94–105.

Macksound, M.S., & Aber, J.L. (1996). The war experiences and psychosocial development of children in Lebanon. *Child Development, 67*, 70–88.

Malinosky-Rummell, R., & Hoier, T. (1992). Validating measures of dissociation in sexually abused and nonabused children. *Behavioral Assessment, 13*(3), 341–357.

Mann, B., & Sanders, S. (1994). Child dissociation in a family context. *Journal of Abnormal Child Psychology, 3*, 373–387.

March, J.S. (1995). Cognitive-behavioral psychotherapy for children and adolescents with OCD. *Journal of the American Academy of Child and Adolescent Psychiatry, 34*, 1265–1273.

March, J.S., & Amaya-Jackson, L. (1993, Fall). Post-traumatic stress in children and adolescents. *The National Center for Post-Traumatic Stress Disorder Research Quarterly, 4*, 1–3.

March, J.S., Amaya-Jackson, L., Terry, R., & Costanzo, P. (1997). Posttraumatic symptomatology in children and adolescents after an industrial fire. *Journal of the American Academy of Child and Adolescent Psychiatry, 36*, 1080–1088.

March, J.S., Muller, K., & Herbel, B. (1994). Behavioral psychotherapy for children and adolescents with OCD. *Journal of the American Academy of Child and Adolescent Psychiatry, 33*(3), 333–341.

McCormack, A., Burgess, A.W., & Hartman, C. (1988). Familial abuse and post-traumatic stress disorder. *Journal of Traumatic Stress, 1*, 231–242.

McFarlane, A.C., Policansky, S.K., & Irwin, C. (1987). A longitudinal study of the psychological morbidity in children due to a natural disaster. *Psychiatric Medicine, 17*, 727–738.

McKinlay, T., Kelly, J.A., & Collum, J.M. (1977). The multi-modal treatment of conversion reactions in adolescence: A case study. *Journal of Clinical Child Psychology, 6*, 66–68.

McLeer, S.V., Callaghan, M., Henry, D., & Wallen, J. (1994). Psychiatric disorders in sexually abused children. *Journal of the American Academy of Child and Adolescent Psychiatry, 33*, 313–319.

Nader, K.O., Pynoos, R.S., Fairbanks, L.A., & Frederick, C.J. (1990). Children's PTSD reactions one year after a sniper attack at their school. *American Journal of Psychiatry, 147*, 1526–1530.

Pelcovitz, D., Kaplan, S., Goldenberg, B., Mandel, F., Lehane, J., & Guarrera, J. (1994). Post-traumatic stress disorder in physically abused adolescents. *Journal of the American Academy of Child and Adolescent Psychiatry, 33,* 305–312.

Putnam, F.W. (1989). *Diagnoses and treatment of multiple personality disorder.* New York: Guilford Press.

Putnam, F., Helmers, K., & Trickett, P. (1993). Development, reliability, and validity of a child dissociation scale. *Child Abuse and Neglect, 17,* 731–741.

Pynoos, R.S., & Eth, S. (1986). Witness to violence: The child interview. *Journal of the American Academy of Child Psychiatry, 25,* 306–319.

Pynoos, R.S., Frederick, C.J., Nader, K.O., Arroyo, W., Steinberg, A., Eth, S., Nunez, F., & Fairbanks, L.A. (1987). Life threat and posttraumatic stress disorder in school-age children. *Archives of General Psychiatry, 44,* 1057–1063.

Pynoos, R.S., Goenjian, A.K., Tashjian, M., Karakashian, M., Manjikian, R., Manoukian, G., Steinberg, A.M., & Fairbanks, L.A. (1993). Post-traumatic stress reactions in children after the 1988 Armenian earthquake. *British Journal of Psychiatry, 163,* 239–247.

Pynoos, R.S., & Nader, K.O. (1988). Psychological first aid and treatment approach to children exposed to community violence: Research implications. *Journal of Traumatic Stress, 1,* 445–473.

Reich, W., & Welner, Z. (1990). *Diagnostic Interview for Children and Adolescents–Revised.* St. Louis: Washington University School of Medicine.

Riddle, M., Scahill, L., & King, R. (1992). Double-blind, cross-over trial of fluoxetine and placebo in children and adolescents with OCD. *Journal of the American Academy of Child and Adolescent Psychiatry, 31,* 1062–1069.

Rock, N.L. (1971). Conversion reaction in childhood: A clinical study on childhood neuroses. *Journal of the American Academy of Child Psychiatry, 10,* 65–93.

Rossman, B.B.R., Bingham, R.D., & Emde, R.N. (1997). Symptomatology and adaptive functioning for children exposed to normative stressors, dog attack, and parental violence. *Journal of the American Academy of Child and Adolescent Psychiatry, 36,* 1089–1097.

Routh, D., & Ernst, A. (1984). Somatization disorders in relatives of children and adolescents with functional abdominal pain. *Journal of Pediatric Psychology, 9,* 427–437.

Routh, D., Ernst, A., & Harper, D. (1988). Recurrent abdominal pain in children and somatization disorder. In D. Routh (Ed.), *Handbook of pediatric psychology* (pp. 492–504). New York: Guilford Press.

Sack, W.H., Seeley, J.R., & Clarke, G.N. (1997). Does PTSD transcend cultural barriers? A study from the Khmer adolescent refugee project. *Journal of the American Academy of Child and Adolescent Psychiatry, 36,* 49–54.

Saigh, P.A. (1989a). The development and validation of the Children's Posttraumatic Stress Disorder Inventory. *International Journal of Special Education, 4,* 75–84.

Saigh, P.A. (1989b). The use of an in vitro flooding package in the treatment of traumatized adolescents. *Journal of Developmental and Behavioral Pediatrics, 10,* 17–21.

Scharff, L. (1997). Recurrent abdominal pain in children. *Clinical Psychology Review, 17,* 145–166.

Schulman, J.L. (1988). Use of a coping approach in the management of children with conversion reactions. *Journal of the American Academy of Child and Adolescent Psychiatry, 27,* 785–788.

Schwarz, E.D., & Kowalski, J.M. (1991). Malignant memories: PTSD in children and adults after a school shooting. *Journal of the American Academy of Child and Adolescent Psychiatry, 30,* 936–944.

Shannon, M.P., Lonigan, C.J., Finch, A.J., Jr., & Taylor, C.M. (1994). Children exposed to disaster: I. Epidemiology of post-traumatic symptoms and symptom profiles. *Journal of the American Academy of Child and Adolescent Psychiatry, 33,* 80–93.

Shaw, J.A., Applegate, B., & Schorr, C. (1996). Twenty-one-month follow-up study of school-age children exposed to Hurricane Andrew. *Journal of the American Academy of Child and Adolescent Psychiatry, 35,* 359–364.

Shaw, J.A., Applegate, B., Tanner, S., Perez, D., Rothe, E., Campo-Bowen, A.E., & Lahey, B.L. (1995). Psychological effects of Hurricane Andrew on an elementary school population. *Journal of the American Academy of Child and Adolescent Psychiatry, 34,* 1185–1192.

Spanos, N., Weekes, J., & Bertrand, L. (1985). Multiple personality: A social-psychological perspective. *Journal of Abnormal Psychology, 94,* 361–376.

Spitzer, R.L., Williams, J.B., & Gibbon, M. (1987). *Structured clinical interview for DSM-III-R.* New York: New York State Psychiatric Institute.

Stanley, L. (1980). Treatment of ritualistic behavior in an eight-year-old girl by response prevention. *Journal of Child Psychology and Psychiatry, 21,* 85–90.

Steinhausen, H.C., Aster, M., Pfeiffer, E., & Gobel, D. (1989). Comparative studies of conversion disorders in childhood and adolescence. *Journal of Child Psychology and Psychiatry, 30,* 615–621.

Stoddard, F.J., Norman, D.K., Murphy, J.M., & Beardslee, W.R. (1989). Psychiatric outcome of burned children and adolescents. *Journal of the American Academy of Child and Adolescent Psychiatry, 28,* 589–595.

Stuber, M.L., Nader, K.O., Houskamp, B.M., & Pynoos, R.S. (1996). Appraisal of life threat and acute trauma response in pediatric bone marrow transplant patients. *Journal of Traumatic Stress, 9,* 673–686.

Swedo, S., Rapoport, J., Leonard, H., Lenane, M., & Cheslow, D. (1989). Obsessive-compulsive disorder in children and adolescents. *Archives of General Psychiatry, 46,* 335–341.

Terr, L.C. (1981). Psychic trauma in children: Observations following the Chowchilla school-bus kidnapping. *American Journal of Psychiatry, 138,* 14–19.

Terr, L.C. (1989). Treating psychic trauma in children: A preliminary discussion. *Journal of Traumatic Stress, 2,* 3–20.

Terr, L.C. (1991). Childhood traumas: An outline and overview. *American Journal of Psychiatry, 148,* 10–20.

Thomsen, P., & Mikkelsen, H. (1995). Course of OCD in children and adolescents. *Journal of the American Academy of Child and Adolescent Psychiatry, 34*(11), 1432–1440.

van der Kolk, B.A. (1988). The traumatic spectrum: The interaction of biological and social events in the genesis of the trauma response. *Journal of Traumatic Stress, 1,* 273–290.

van der Kolk, B.A. (1996). The complexity of adaptation to trauma: Self-regulation, stimulus discrimination, and characterological development. In B.A. van der Kolk, A.C. McFarlane, & L. Weisaeth (Eds.), *Traumatic stress: The effects of overwhelming experience on mind, body, and society* (pp. 182–213). New York: Guilford Press.

Veith, I. (1977). Four thousand years of hysteria. In M.J. Horowitz (Ed.), *Hysterical personality* (pp. 7–93). New York: Aronson.

Vernberg, E.M., La Greca, A.M., Silverman, W.K., & Prinstein, M.J. (1996). Prediction of posttraumatic stress symptoms in children after Hurricane Andrew. *Journal of Abnormal Psychology, 105,* 237–248.

Vogel, J.M., & Vernberg, E.M. (1993). Part 1: Children's psychological responses to disasters. *Journal of Clinical Child Psychology, 22,* 464–484.

Wallach, H.R., & Dollinger, S.J. (1999). Dissociative disorders in childhood and adolescence. In S. Netherton, D. Holmes, & C. Walker (Eds.), *Child and adolescent disorders: A comprehensive handbook* (pp. 344–366). New York: Oxford University Press.

Warren, W. (1960). Some relationships between the psychiatry of children and adolescents. *Journal of Mental Science, 106,* 815–826.

Watson, D., & Clark, L.A. (1984). Negative affectivity: The disposition to experience aversive emotional states. *Psychological Bulletin, 96,* 465–490.

Waye, M.F. (1979). Behavioral treatment of a child displaying comic-book mediated fear of hand shrinking. *Journal of Pediatric Psychology, 4,* 43–47.

Wiggins, J. (1996). *The five-factor model of personality: Theoretical perspectives.* New York: Guilford Press.

Williams, D.T., Spiegel, H., & Mostofsky, D.I. (1978). Neurogenic and hysterical seizures in children and adolescents: Differential diagnostic and therapeutic considerations. *American Journal of Psychiatry, 135,* 82–86.

Wolfe, V.V., Finch, A.J., Jr., Saylor, C.F., Blount, R.L., Pallmeyer, T., & Carek, D.J. (1987). Negative affect in children: A multitrait-multimethod investigation. *Journal of Consulting and Clinical Psychology, 55,* 245–250.

Wolfe, V.V., Gentile, C., Michienzi, T., Sas, L., & Wolfe, D.A. (1991). The Children's Impact of Traumatic Events Scale. *Behavioral Assessment, 13,* 359–383.

Wolfe, V.V., Gentile, C., & Wolfe, D.A. (1989). The impact of sexual abuse on children: A PTSD formulation. *Behavior Therapy, 20,* 215–228.

Wolff, R., & Rapoport, J. (1988). Behavioral treatment of childhood obsessive-compulsive disorder. *Behavior Modification, 12*(2), 252–266.

Yapko, M. (1994). *Suggestions of abuse.* New York: Simon & Schuster.

Yates, A., & Steward, M. (1976). Conversion hysteria in childhood. *Clinical Pediatrics, 15,* 379–382.

Yule, W. (1993). Technology-related disasters. In C.F. Saylor (Ed.), *Children and disasters* (pp. 105–121). New York: Plenum Press.

CHAPTER 22

Autism

JULIE OSTERLING, GERALDINE DAWSON, AND JAMES MCPARTLAND

HISTORICAL CONTEXT

Autism was first described by Kanner in 1943. He included the following features in his description: an inability to relate to people, language deviance characterized by delayed acquisition, echolalia, occasional mutism, pronoun reversals, literalness, excellent rote memory, repetitive and stereotyped play activities, and an obsessive desire for maintenance of sameness in the environment. Kanner also noted that the children began experiencing difficulties during infancy. The children's lack of obvious physical anomalies and good rote memory led Kanner to conclude that they were endowed with normal cognitive potential.

DISTINCTION BETWEEN AUTISM AND CHILDHOOD SCHIZOPHRENIA

During the next few decades following Kanner's (1943) article, clinicians and researchers disagreed on whether autism was a form of childhood schizophrenia. This disagreement was related in part to Kanner's use of the term autism, which many investigators confused with Bleuler's (1950) descriptions

of "autistic withdrawal from reality" found in patients with schizophrenia. Verification of differences between autism and childhood schizophrenia came from studies (e.g., Kolvin, 1971a) showing that the distribution of the onset of "childhood psychosis," which included autism, is markedly bipolar, falling most frequently either before 3 years of age or in early adolescence. In addition, Kolvin (1971b) found differences between early- and late-onset childhood psychosis in parental social class, family history of schizophrenia, frequency of cerebral dysfunction, speech patterns, and intelligence quotient (IQ) level. Also, remissions and relapses were much more characteristic of late-onset childhood psychosis (i.e., schizophrenia). People with autism also rarely develop the delusions and hallucinations that are hallmarks of schizophrenia.

EARLY THEORIES

Along with other researchers, Kanner asserted that autism was caused by an interaction between an innate abnormality and family environment (Eisenberg & Kanner, 1956). Based on Kanner's initial assertions, early theories postulated that autism has, in part, a psychogenic basis. Some theories stressed unusual personality traits in parents and posited that autism results from the child's response to the parents (Meyers & Goldfarb, 1961). Others suggested

The writing of this chapter was supported by the National Institute of Child Health and Human Development and the National Institute on Deafness and Communication Disorders (PO1HD34565).

that autism is the result of a pathological parent-child interaction consisting of either poor maternal communication (Goldfarb, Levy, & Myers, 1966), too much or too little stimulation (Tinbergen & Tinbergen, 1972), or early parental rejection or separation (Bettelheim, 1967). Studies conducted in the 1960s and 1970s found no evidence of abnormal parental personality characteristics or maladaptive parent-child interactions (Allen, DeMyer, Norton, Pontius, & Yang, 1971). Thus, there is no evidence to support parenting as a factor in the origin of autism (Schopler, 1971).

DIAGNOSIS, EPIDEMIOLOGY, AND PROGNOSIS

Autism and related disorders are defined similarly by the *Diagnostic and Statistical Manual of Mental Disorders*, fourth edition (*DSM-IV*; American Psychiatric Association [APA], 1994) and the *International Classification of Diseases*, tenth edition (*ICD-10*; World Health Organization, 1992). These diagnostic systems view autism as existing under the broader category of pervasive developmental disorders. Autistic spectrum is another term used to characterize the broad range of disorders in this category.

All pervasive developmental disorders involve impairments in social interaction. However, these impairments take many forms across individuals and across the development of each individual. Social impairments include difficulties in the use of nonverbal social behaviors such as eye contact, facial expressions, and gestures. Impairments can also pertain to how readily the individual shares personal interests with others and how skillfully the person relates with others, particularly peers. In addition to social impairments, individuals with a pervasive developmental disorder display delays or atypical behaviors in communication and restricted/repetitive behaviors. The presentation of symptoms in each of these categories is described in detail below.

It is important to note that there is a great deal of heterogeneity within the category of pervasive developmental disorders in terms of the severity of symptoms within each category (social, communication, restricted/repetitive behaviors), cognitive abilities, temperament, and adaptive functioning. For instance, a young child with autism who is also mentally retarded might be nonverbal, make little eye contact, rarely initiate social interactions with others, and engage in repetitive motor behaviors. In contrast, an older child with autism who has an IQ in the average range might make consistent eye contact, use exaggerated gestures and facial expressions, and initiate interaction frequently with others to talk repetitively about specific interests. The older child may be interested in making friends but have difficulty knowing how to do so.

DIAGNOSTIC CATEGORIES

Autistic Disorder
Autism is considered the most prototypic form of pervasive developmental disorder. Individuals with autism display six symptoms across three categories, with at least two symptoms in the social category, one in the communication category, and one in restrictive/repetitive behaviors category. These symptoms must be present before 3 years of age, and symptoms are not accounted for by Rett's syndrome or childhood disintegrative disorder. Almost all individuals with this diagnosis have some type of language delay in early childhood; however, some higher-functioning individuals may not. Cognitive abilities range from severe levels of mental retardation to those with above-average or even superior abilities.

Asperger Syndrome
Around the same time that Kanner was describing autism, Asperger (1944) was identifying a group of children who had higher levels of cognitive and language ability, but who nevertheless had social impairments. Over the next few decades, Asperger syndrome became further characterized by normal or near normal formal language ability (e.g., vocabulary) along with difficulties in the social use of language, social awkwardness, marked impairment in nonverbal expressiveness, idiosyncratic and engrossing interests, and motor clumsiness (Tantam, 1988). A Swedish epidemiological survey (C. Gillberg & Gillberg, 1983) found that Asperger syndrome was more common than classic autism (2.6–3 per 1,000 children with Asperger syndrome). Diagnostic criteria for Asperger syndrome involve at least two symptoms in the social category and one symptom in the repetitive/restricted behavior category. Individuals cannot display clinically significant delays in intellectual, adaptive, and language abilities.

Until 1994, Asperger syndrome was not listed in the *DSM.* Accordingly, the research on Asperger syndrome before that time did not use consistent diagnostic criteria. However, in the past five years, the literature involving Asperger syndrome has increased significantly. Interestingly, research examining motor and neuropsychological skills in individuals with Asperger syndrome versus high-functioning autism has not consistently supported the validity of a distinction between these two syndromes (Ozonoff & Griffith, 2000).

Rett Syndrome

Rett syndrome involves a progressive deterioration of functioning; cases have been reported only in females. A diagnosis of Rett syndrome requires normal pre- and perinatal development, normal psychomotor development through the first 5 months, and normal head circumference at birth. Generally, girls with Rett's syndrome develop normally until 6 to 28 months. This period is followed by a period of decelerated head growth between the ages of 5 and 48 months and progressive loss of motor and then cognitive skills. There is also a loss of social engagement, but often, social interaction will develop later. Impairments in motor skills are characterized by the loss of purposeful hand movements, development of stereotypic hand movements such as hand wringing, and poorly coordinated gait. Rett syndrome is associated with severe to profound mental retardation (Van Acker, 1991).

Childhood Disintegrative Disorder

Childhood disintegrative disorder (CDD), previously referred to as Heller's syndrome, is characterized by normal development for the first two years of life, followed by a clinically significant loss of skills in at least two of the following areas: (1) expressive or receptive language skills, (2) social or adaptive skills, (3) bowel or bladder control, (4) play, and (5) motor skills. In addition, the individual must display impairments in two of the three symptom categories: social, communication, and restricted/repetitive behavior. Although this regression can occur anytime before 10 years of age, it typically occurs between 36 and 48 months. A diagnosis of CDD is rare, with Volkmar, Klin, Marans, and Cohen (1997) reporting no more than 100 cases.

Approximately 1 in 5 children with autism are reported to have a course of ostensibly normal development until 18 to 24 months of age that is followed by a regression in language and social skills.

In these cases, children are classified as having a late-onset course of autism rather than receiving a diagnosis of CDD because the regression occurred prior to 24 months of age. Information regarding variations in early course of development has come from either parent report or a review of medical records. Recently, Osterling and Dawson (1999) examined home videotapes of children reported to have late-onset autism and found that, indeed, these children displayed typical social and communication behaviors at 1 year. There is evidence suggesting that late-onset autism is associated with epileptiform EEGs (Tuchman & Rapin, 1997).

Pervasive Developmental Disorder, Not Otherwise Specified (PDD, NOS)

This category of symptom is also referred to as atypical autism. This diagnosis is given when a child demonstrates clinically significant impairments in social interaction and communication and restricted/repetitive behaviors, but does not meet criteria for any of the diagnoses mentioned above because of too few symptoms or subthreshold severity of symptoms. There is great variability of symptom severity and cognitive ability encompassed in this category.

DIFFERENTIAL DIAGNOSIS BETWEEN AUTISM AND CLOSELY RELATED DISORDERS

Autism and Mental Retardation

Several studies have made comparisons between children with autism and children with mental retardation. Children with autism often exhibit a cognitive pattern that is different from those with only retardation, consisting of high scores on tests of visual-spatial skills and auditory rote memory combined with a low score on verbal comprehension (Lockyer & Rutter, 1970). Approximately 25% of children with autism are not mentally retarded. The prognosis for children with autism tends to be worse than for children with mental retardation in terms of language skills, employability, and independence. Thus, it is generally agreed that autism and mental retardation constitute two different (though overlapping) syndromes. Research also has identified differences between children with autism and children with mental retardation in motor imitation, social behavior, attachment, use of affective communication, and nonverbal communication. This work is discussed in the following sections.

Autism and Developmental Language Disorder

Children with autism differ in important ways from those with developmental receptive dysphasia (Bartak, Rutter, & Cox, 1975). Children with autism generally have more deviant language, including more frequent occurrences of pronoun reversal, echolalia, stereotyped utterances, metaphorical language, and inappropriate remarks. They make less use of language for social purposes, tend to use nonverbal communication less effectively, and show less symbolic play. However, there are less pronounced differences in the two groups in their use of repetitive behaviors and of spontaneous joint attention (Lord & Pickles, 1996). Children with autism and children with dysphasia have not been found to differ in mean utterance length and grammatical complexity of speech; children with autism have been found to have better articulation and visual word recognition skills (Bartak et al., 1975).

Early Identification

Usually, children with autism are diagnosed around 3 to 4 years of age (Siegel, Pliner, Eschler, & Elliot, 1988). There have been a number of important developments in the early identification of autism in the past five years. Recent prospective research in the area of early identification indicates that the symptoms of autism are present much earlier and that children with an autistic spectrum disorder often can be reliably diagnosed at 18 months of age (Baron-Cohen et al., 1996). It also appears that a diagnosis in the autistic spectrum at 18 to 20 months is quite stable into childhood (Lord, 1995b; Stone et al., 1999). However, the stability of a specific diagnosis (e.g., autism vs. PDD, NOS) is not as strong, particularly for a diagnosis of PDD, NOS. Stone (1998) suggests that the social and communication impairments are stronger diagnostic symptoms in children under 3 years of age, and that restricted, repetitive, and stereotyped activities and behaviors do not appear as consistently in very young children with autism. These behaviors appear later in the development of children, generally around the third birthday.

Another promising area of research involves the retrospective use of home videotape recordings to study early development in autism. Using this method, investigators can essentially go back in time and examine the development of infants who later receive a diagnosis of autism. This type of research has indicated that by at least 12 months of age, there are significant differences in the social, communication, and sensorimotor development of infants with autism when compared with infants who are typically developing (Mars, Mauk, & Dowrick, 1998; Osterling & Dawson, 1994) and infants with mental retardation (Baranek, 1999; Osterling & Dawson, 1999).

Epidemiological Findings and Prognosis

Using a broader definition of autism, recent studies have estimated prevalence rates of approximately 1 case per 1,000 and possibly even higher rates (Bryson, 1996). This is a higher rate than previous studies indicated (Rutter, 1978). The increased rate of prevalence is generally attributed to both changes in diagnostic criteria and a broadening of the definition of autism. However, it is not entirely understood if there are other factors involved.

Although Kanner's (1943) emphasis on peak skills led many to believe that these children have the potential for normal intellectual functioning, current estimates are quite different. Rates of mental retardation in autism range from 76% to 89% (Steffenburg & Gillberg, 1986). Studies based on nonbiased samples have shown that the social class distribution of families of children with autism is similar to that of the general population (Steffenburg & Gillberg, 1986; Wing & Gould, 1979). The ratio of males to females in autism is approximately 3 or 4 to 1 (Kolvin, 1971b; Rutter & Lockyer, 1967). Volkmar, Szatmari, and Sparrow (1993) reported that a greater proportion of females with autism were severely mentally retarded and that males with autism were approximately nine times more likely to have normal intelligence. Research suggests that females with autism may have more severe symptoms as a consequence of this lower intellectual ability (Konstantareas, Homatidis, & Busch, 1989). For individuals with autism who fall within a normal range of intellectual ability, females may be less symptomatic (McLennan, Lord, & Schopler, 1993).

For the overwhelming majority of individuals with autism, social, communication, and behavioral impairments persist throughout their lives. In general, approximately 60% to 70% of individuals with autism require a high level of support in adulthood, and 5% to 15% show very positive outcomes. These high-functioning individuals are able to maintain some social relationships and perform acceptably in a job setting (Nordin & Gillberg, 1998). IQ is the single best predictor of outcome, with higher IQ predicting higher levels of educational and vocational performance (Bartak & Rutter, 1971; Lockyer & Rutter, 1969). An IQ below 50 is associated with low levels of adaptive skills. A lack of communicative language ability at 5 to 6 years is a strong predictor of poorer prognosis on average. At the individual level, however, there is more variability, with some individuals displaying marked language improvement beyond their preschool years (Nordin & Gillberg, 1998). In adolescence, a portion of individuals displays increased aggressive behavior and deterioration of cognitive, social, and communication skills, especially those with seizure disorders and lower IQs (C. Gillberg & Steffenburg, 1987). Piven, Harper, Palmer, and Arndt (1996) found a trend toward improvement of social and communication symptoms in a sample of high-functioning people with autism and found less improvement in restricted/repetitive behaviors.

SYMPTOM PRESENTATION

Children with autism have impairments in areas of functioning that usually develop between birth and 2 years of age. By the age of 2 years, the typically developing toddler has skills in social awareness and interaction, imitation, symbolic play, and communication through gestures and language. The typically developing 2-year-old also has a basic sense of self as different from others and the ability to express a wide variety of emotions and some understanding of the emotions of others. Many of these aspects have been found to be disturbed in children with autism.

SOCIAL COGNITION

Social Orienting

By six months of age, infants typically exhibit an orienting response to stimuli that are mildly novel and unpredictable in nature, particularly social stimuli such as facial expressions and speech (Trevarthen, 1979). Children with autism tend to exhibit anomalies in this orienting response. Osterling and Dawson's (1994, 1999) studies of home videotapes of infants' first birthday parties indicated that this failure to orient to social stimuli was evident in 12-month-old infants with autism but not in age-matched infants with mental retardation. When comparing children with autism to developmentally matched children with developmental delays, children with autism more frequently failed to orient to both social and nonsocial stimuli, but their performance is markedly worse for social stimuli (Dawson, Meltzoff, Osterling, & Brown, 1998). An impairment in "social orienting" may be one of the earliest emerging impairments in autism (Dawson, Meltzoff, Osterling, & Brown 1998).

Motor Imitation

Studies demonstrating that neonates are able to imitate facial expressions (e.g., Meltzoff & Moore, 1977) suggest that this is an innate ability. Numerous studies (e.g., Sigman & Ungerer, 1984; Stone, Ousley, & Littleford, 1997) have shown that children with autism show marked delays in both immediate and deferred motor imitation. It appears that imitation skills in children with autism are associated with the development of social and language learning; specifically, it appears that body imitation and object imitation represent distinct skills, the former predicting expressive language skills and the latter predicting play skills (Stone et al., 1997). Indeed, a failure to imitate, particularly social imitative play, may be a fundamental impairment in autism, interfering with the development of reciprocity, joint attention, and awareness of emotional and mental states in self and others (Dawson, 1991; Meltzoff & Gopnick, 1993; Rogers & Pennington, 1991).

Joint Attention Behavior

By about 10 months of age, normal infants begin to share attention with others by pointing, showing, or making eye contact while holding an object or watching an interesting event (Klinnert, Campos, Sorce, Emde, & Svejda, 1983). Children with autism have been found to use joint attention behaviors less often than typical, mentally retarded, or language-delayed children across a number of studies (e.g., McArthur & Adamson, 1996). Furthermore, these impairments in joint attention behaviors, or protodeclarative gestures, seem to be much more severe than impairments in the use of gestures to make requests, known as protoimperative gestures (Mundy, Sigman, & Kasari, 1990). Research suggests that joint attention impairments are fundamental to autistic disorders and, as such, are reliable early diagnostic indicators (see Mundy & Crowson, 1997, for a review), even at 20 months of age (Charman et al., 1998). Mundy, Sigman, and Kasari (1994) found that level of functioning among children with autism was related to degree of impairment in joint attention behaviors. Based on such findings, joint attention has been posited to be a pivotal skill on which the development of more complex abilities, such as pretend play, language, and theory of mind, may depend (Charman, 1997; Mundy & Crowson, 1997; Sigman, 1997).

Theory of Mind

By preschool age, normally developing children begin to understand that others have feelings, beliefs, and intentions that are separate from their own (Wellman, 1993). Some believe that a cognitive impairment in theory of mind is fundamental and specific to autism and that this leads to the difficulties in social interaction and communication that characterize the disorder (Baron-Cohen, Leslie, & Frith, 1985). For example, in an experiment by Baron-Cohen et al., 86% of Down syndrome and normal subjects were able to attribute beliefs to a puppet that differed from their own, compared with only 20% of the children with autism. Burack (1992) has posited that theory of mind skills are qualitatively deviant, not just delayed, in individuals with autism. This idea is supported by the finding that nonretarded adolescents with autism followed over a three-year period did not exhibit improvements in theory of mind abilities (Ozonoff & McEvoy, 1994). Some have suggested that impairments in theory of mind may be related to language impairments and even prelinguistic skills. Ozonoff and McEvoy found theory of mind test performance to be related to verbal IQ and verbal mental age. Mundy and Sigman (1989) suggest that the development of theory of mind ability may hinge on early joint attention experiences.

Emotion Perception and Expression

Hobson (1989) and others have argued that autism involves a basic impairment in the perception of emotions. Children with autism have been found to perform worse than developmentally delayed children on tasks requiring recognition and matching of emotional faces and responding to the emotional displays of others (Dawson, Meltzoff, Osterling, & Rinaldi, 1998; Loveland et al., 1997; Sigman, Ungerer, Mundy, & Sherman, 1987).

Children with autism also have been found to exhibit atypical patterns of emotional expression. Kasari, Sigman, Yirmiya, and Mundy (1993) reported that facial expressions of children with autism were frequently negative and composed of unusual blends of emotions. Young children with autism generally display less positive affect in social interaction with adults than do matched mentally retarded children, and their positive affect was less likely to be expressed toward their social partner (Dawson & Galpert, 1990). Children with autism display similar numbers of attention-directing and goal-requesting gestures but fewer social-affective gestures than do developmentally delayed children (Attwood, Frith, & Hermelin, 1988).

LANGUAGE AND PLAY DEVELOPMENT

Communication and Language Abilities

Approximately 25% of people with autism remain mute their entire lives. Of those who do develop language, onset typically is delayed and language usage is deviant. The level of communicative ability eventually achieved varies widely from one-word or echolalic speech to only subtle impairments in the social usage of language.

Individuals with autism often do not display the same level of impairments in articulation, morphology, syntax, and phonology (Bartolucci & Pierce, 1977; Tager-Flusberg, 1996) as mental-age-matched children with mental retardation. However, they do exhibit deviancies in prosody (i.e., intonation, loudness, rhythm, stress, and speech quality) that persist into adulthood despite improvements in other aspects of language use. For some individuals with autism, the acquisition of general word categories or meanings and syntactic structure is commensurate with what would be expected based on their mental ages (Swisher & Demetras, 1985; Tager-Flusberg, 1985). A majority of individuals with autism who develop speech exhibit immediate or delayed echolalia, or the repetition of previously heard words or phrases, especially early in development. Echolalia can be used to make requests, to self-regulate, to protest, and to convey affirmation (Prizant & Rydell, 1984).

Verbal children with autism do not readily use language to share information (Howlin, 1984; Tager-Flusberg, 1993). Koegel and Koegel (1995) have posited that this phenomenon is attributable to a lack of curiosity. Children with autism have difficulties with initiating and maintaining topics in conversation, conversational turn taking, and maintaining an appropriate level of detail (Eales, 1993), as well as having difficulties with speaker-listener relations and pronominal reversal (Lee, Hobson, & Chiat, 1994). Individuals with autism also have more difficulty on tests that require the completion of jokes than of nonhumorous narratives (Ozonoff & Miller, 1996) and are more likely than mentally retarded or typical controls to create shorter narrative accounts that omit descriptions of casual relationships among events in a story (Tager-Flusberg, 1995). Thus, many language impairments in people with autism pertain to the social use of language (pragmatics). This fact has led some investigators to relate at least some of the language problems found in autism to impairments in social relatedness (Tager-Flusberg, 1989) or lack of comprehension of speaker-listener conversational rules (Tager-Flusberg, 1993).

Symbolic Play

Based on comparisons with mental-age-matched mentally retarded, developmentally delayed, and typical children, the ability of children with autism to engage in symbolic play has been found to be absent or delayed (Charman et al., 1998; Mundy, Sigman, Ungerer, & Sherman, 1987; Wing & Gould, 1979). Ungerer and Sigman (1981) found that when symbolic play was used by children with autism, it was less diverse than that of mentally retarded and typical children. However, one study indicated that when prompts were provided, children with autism and those with mental retardation did not differ in their functional or symbolic play (Charman & Baron-Cohen, 1997).

RESTRICTED AND REPETITIVE BEHAVIORS

Approximately half of children with autism are reported to display stereotypic motor movements, the most common of which are rocking; toe walking; arm, hand, and finger flapping; and spinning. As a result of these behaviors, 85% of a sample of parents of children with autism reported their child to be excessively active (Volkmar, Cohen, & Paul, 1986). These stereotypes are more prevalent in children with autism who are young or low-functioning,

with higher-functioning children with autism exhibiting more complex repetitive behaviors (Wing, 1988; Wing & Gould, 1979). These ritualistic activities may include the repeated arrangement or ordering of objects, engagement in a complicated yet seemingly arbitrary sequence of motor movements, or an insistence on sameness in terms of physical environment, sequence of events in the course of a day or a given procedure, or eating habits. Individuals with autism may tend to exhibit restricted behavior in terms of particularly intense, circumscribed interests or preoccupations with unusual subject matter (Wing, 1988). These individuals may perseverate on these topics and are likely to exhibit encyclopedic knowledge of pertinent factual information. Baranek, Foster, and Berkson (1997) found that restricted and repetitive behaviors were related to tactile defensiveness, or aversive responsiveness to sensory stimulation.

NEUROPSYCHOLOGICAL THEORIES AND FINDINGS

Neuropsychological impairments in autism are broad, affecting executive functions, language, memory, and attention. Although problems with certain aspects of executive function seem common to an overwhelming majority of individuals with autism (Dawson, 1996; Ozonoff, Pennington, & Rogers, 1991), large individual differences are found in impairments related to memory, language, and attention.

INTELLECTUAL ABILITY

Between 76% and 89% of individuals with autism have IQs that fall into the range of mental retardation, that is, below 70 (Steffenburg & Gillberg, 1986). One longitudinal study that examined children with autism beginning in preschool found that both intelligence and developmental quotients were overall stable and predictive of later functioning (Lord & Schopler, 1989). However, a portion of the children initially assessed as moderately to severely retarded made disproportionate advances over time. Individuals with autism characteristically exhibit substantial differences in skill level on measures of verbal and nonverbal abilities, with relative proficiency in the latter category (Lockyer & Rutter, 1970).

MEDIAL TEMPORAL LOBE DYSFUNCTION

The impairments in social ability and memory led some investigators to consider the medial temporal lobe, including the hippocampus and the amygdala, as a region of dysfunction in autism (Dawson, 1996; Fein & Waterhouse, 1985). Evidence from animal models (Bachevalier, 1994) and human lesion studies suggests that there exists a system that is specialized for social cognition and certain aspects of memory (declarative), which involves the medial temporal and orbital frontal lobes, including the amygdala, hippocampus, and entorhinal cortex (Allman & Brothers, 1994; Damasio, 1994). Interestingly, some autopsy studies (Bauman & Kemper, 1994) have revealed reduced neuronal cell size and increased cell packing density in the hippocampus, amygdala, and adjacent limbic regions. These brain structures, especially the amygdala, mediate basic brain functions that may be required for skills in which persons with autism are typically impaired, such as motor imitation, joint attention, and social orienting (Dawson, Meltzoff, Osterling, & Rinaldi, 1998; Mundy, Sigman, Ungerer, & Sherman, 1986; Osterling & Dawson, 1994; Smith & Bryson, 1994). There is evidence to suggest that the individual differences in symptom severity may correspond to varying degrees of dysfunction in these brain regions (Bachevalier, 1994; Dawson, Meltzoff, Osterling, & Rinaldi, 1998).

FRONTAL LOBE AND EXECUTIVE FUNCTIONS

Damasio and Maurer (1978) proposed that a number of the symptoms of children with autism may be related to dysfunction of the medial frontal lobe regions and related limbic structures. These authors argued that many of the motor disturbances common in autism, such as problems in initiating or controlling motor activity, resemble neurological symptoms of adult patients with dysfunction of the basal ganglia and associated regions of the frontal and temporal lobes. Other autistic symptoms, including a lack of initiative to communicate and lack of orientation to relevant stimuli, have been linked to frontal regions. Several other investigators have argued that autism is best characterized as a disorder of the prefrontal cortex (Minshew & Goldstein, 1993; Rogers & Pennington, 1991). Some studies have demonstrated impairments in executive functioning in individuals with autism (Ozonoff, 1995; Ozonoff, Strayer, McMahon, & Filloux, 1994; Prior & Hoffmann, 1990), although it appears that some frontal functions are more impaired than others in autism.

Rogers and Pennington (1991) have suggested that the core behavioral impairments of autism are a combination of social cognitive and executive functions that may be linked to frontal brain areas. Executive function refers to the cognitive abilities involved in maintaining information online while working toward an overarching objective (i.e., working memory, impulse control, inhibition of non-task-related responses, and planning). Furthermore, it has been hypothesized that the variability in symptom expression in autism is related to degree of impairment in prefrontal functioning. Research has shown a correlation between executive function skill and higher-order autistic impairments, such as the ability to understand the mental states of others (theory of mind) (McEvoy, Rogers, & Pennington, 1993). Individual differences in frontal functioning have been found to relate to joint attention and social interaction skills (McEvoy et al., 1993).

CEREBELLAR DYSFUNCTION

Courchesne and colleagues have stressed the role of the cerebellum in the symptoms of autism (Courchesne, Chisum, & Townsend, 1994). Reduced numbers of Purkinje or granule cells in the cerebellum is not uncommon in autism (see Courchesne, 1989). Courchesne hypothesized that granule cell loss results in major disruptions in the functioning of the cerebellum, which mediates several basic behavioral functions such as attention, motor functions, and associative learning. Furthermore, Courchesne proposed that Purkinje cell loss may result in an excitatory interference to brain stem and thalamic systems that mediate arousal and attention. Abnormalities in autonomic regulation and attention have been found in persons with autism (Dawson & Lewy, 1989). Hypotheses of cerebellar dysfunction are not incompatible with those involving the medial temporal or frontal lobe. Courchesne, Chisum, et al. (1994) have suggested that early impairments in cerebellar functioning might affect later development of limbic regions.

NEUROBIOLOGICAL FINDINGS

PRENATAL AND PERINATAL COMPLICATIONS

Several studies of birth histories of children with autism found an increase in the incidence of prenatal and perinatal complications as compared to control groups (Lobascher, Kingerlee, & Gubbay, 1970). More frequent complications include bleeding during pregnancy, meconium in amniotic fluid, and use of physician-prescribed drugs, including hormones (Deykin & MacMahon, 1980; C. Gillberg & Gillberg, 1983). Some studies have suggested an association between autism and maternal age greater than 35 (Tsai, 1987). Autism and autistic-like behaviors also have been found to occur in association with central nervous system diseases and disorders, including viral infection (Chess, 1971), tuberous sclerosis (Lotter, 1974), congenital syphilis (Rutter & Lockyer, 1967), and metabolic disturbances (Knobloch & Pasamanick, 1975). Lord, Mulloy, Wendelboe, and Schopler (1991) found that, compared to typical controls, high-functioning children with autism differed only in having a higher incidence of being first- or later-than-fourth-born and a gestational age greater than 42 weeks. Most evidence suggests that obstetric difficulties are attributable to extant fetal abnormalities (Bolton et al., 1994).

MINOR NEUROLOGICAL SIGNS

Many children with autism exhibit neurological "soft" signs (Gubbay, Lobascher, & Kingerlee, 1970). Epidemiological studies have reported associated central nervous system conditions in 28% (Cialdella & Mameile, 1989) to 33% (Bryson, Clark, & Smith, 1988) of persons with autism. Epileptic seizures are frequently observed among approximately 20% to 33% of individuals with autism, and they most frequently begin in adolescence or young adulthood (C. Gillberg & Steffenburg, 1987; Goode, Rutter, & Howlin, 1994; Rutter, 1970; Volkmar & Nelson, 1990). Some research suggests a greater likelihood

of seizure activity among extremely low-functioning individuals with autism (Rutter, 1984; Volkmar & Nelson, 1990), but results have not been wholly consistent (Goode et al., 1994). Studies have found atypical electroencephalogram (EEG) activity in approximately half of individuals with autism sampled (Minshew, 1991), and the phenomenon was more likely to be observed among individuals with low intellectual ability. There is no clear pattern in terms of lateralization or brain region in these observed EEG abnormalities (Tsai, Tsai, & August, 1985).

ORIENTING AND AROUSAL

Research has demonstrated abnormal autonomic response patterns to the presentation of novel stimuli in children with autism (Dawson & Lewy, 1989). Findings include accelerations in heart rate, reductions in rate of habituation (Palkowitz & Wiesenfeld, 1980), a failure to habituate (James & Barry, 1980), and a failure to reinstate to novelty when habituation occurs (Bernal & Miller, 1971). Most studies of electrodermal responses to novel, repetitive stimuli have reported some abnormality, including reduced response to the first trials (Bernal & Miller, 1971; van Engeland, 1984), reduced or absent habituation (Stevens & Gruzelier, 1984), and higher mean level of skin conductance (Palkowitz & Wiesenfeld, 1980). Studies of tonic heart rate levels in children with autism suggest that some of these children have difficulty in the regulation of autonomic arousal (Hutt, Forrest, & Richer, 1975), which may help to explain their difficulty in coping with unpredictable information and changes in their environments.

BRAIN-IMAGING STUDIES

Magnetic Resonance Imaging (MRI)
MRI studies have documented that ventricular enlargement is relatively common in autism (Damasio, Maurer, Damasio, & Chue, 1980). Studies have found that brain volume among individuals with autism is greater than in individuals with typical development, mental retardation, and developmental language disorders (Filipek et al., 1992; Piven et al., 1995). Studies have also found cortical abnormalities in the brains of individuals with autism

or Asperger's syndrome (Courchesne, Townsend, & Saitoh, 1994). The various malformations are not consistent in terms of brain hemisphere but have included predominantly the parietal, temporal, and frontal cortices. Neuronal migration anomalies have also been detected in individuals with autism (Schifter et al., 1994). The lack of consistency in the results of the above neuroimaging studies may be partly attributable to inconsistency in both subjects with autism and controls, disparities in protocols for MRI scanning, and the combination of quantitative and qualitative methods without uniformity of anatomical definitions (Filipek, 1996).

Positron Emission Tomography (PET)
The PET scan, which is a measure of regional glucose metabolism reflecting brain activity, has been used in several studies to examine distribution of brain activity among individuals with autism. Horowitz, Rumsey, Grady, and Rappoport (1988) found lower correlations between measures of brain activity derived from the frontal and parietal regions and between certain subcortical regions and the frontal and parietal regions in individuals with autism as compared to control subjects. Other studies have found atypical asymmetries in the basal ganglia and temporal and frontal lobes, hypofrontality and hyperfrontality, and lower correlation of patterns of activity between the frontal region and other areas (Rumsey et al., 1985). Additional research has found decreased temporal and frontal lobe perfusion and slower maturation of the frontal cortex (I. Gillberg, Biure, Uvebrant, Vestergren, & Gillberg, 1993). These data suggest that brain dysfunction in autism is best characterized by disruption of distributed brain systems involving several brain structures.

Electrophysiological Studies
Measures of brain activity using EEG methods during information processing have revealed two types of abnormalities in individuals with autism. First, using both alpha-blocking and event-related potential EEG methods, Dawson and her colleagues have found that a large majority of individuals with autism exhibit an atypical pattern of lateralized brain activity during left-hemisphere-mediated tasks, including language and motor imitation tasks (Dawson, Finley, Phillips, & Galpert, 1986). Studies that examined children with autism not in the context of a particular task found left

hemisphere lateralized differences consisting of reduced EEG power in the temporal and frontal regions but typical power in the parietal region (Dawson, Klinger, Panagiotides, Lewy, & Castelloe, 1995).

The second cortical abnormality found in autism is a reduced P3 component of the event-related potential (ERP) (Courchesne, Lincoln, Kilman, & Galambos, 1985; Dawson, Finley, Phillips, Galpert, & Lewy, 1988). ERPs are a measure of the brain's electrical activity in response to discrete, repeated stimuli. The P3 component of this response is associated with the detection of novel, unpredictable stimuli. In individuals with autism, reductions in the P3 component of the ERP have been reliably found for auditory stimuli and less reliably found for other types of stimuli, such as visual and musical stimuli. The data, thus far, suggest that even high-functioning persons with autism have attentional difficulties when presented with unpredictable auditory information. This idea is consistent with the findings of Courchesne et al. (1994), who detected anomalous ERPs in individuals with autism performing tasks that required shifting of attention between different sensory modalities. Minshew (1996) reviewed the findings of ERP studies and reported consistent abnormalities in cognitive potentials and in the integrity of early and middle latency potentials.

NEUROCHEMICAL FINDINGS: SEROTONIN

Although many neurotransmitters have been studied in autism, thus far, the only consistent finding is elevated blood serotonin levels. Serotonin is a neurotransmitter related to diverse behavioral and physiological processes, including appetite, learning, memory, sleep, motor function, and pain and sensory perception (Volkmar & Anderson, 1989). Since Schain and Freedman (1961) first reported that some individuals with autism have elevated blood serotonin concentrations, mean levels of serotonin in persons with autism have been observed to be 17% to 128% higher than in control groups (G.M. Anderson & Hoshino, 1987). From 30% to 50% of individuals with autism are hyperserotonemic (having serotonin levels in the upper 59% of the normal distribution). Elevated levels of serotonin also have been detected in first-degree relatives of individuals with autism (Leboyer et al., 1999). Because mentally retarded individuals without autism have also shown increased serotonin levels (Anderson & Hoshino, 1987), it is uncertain whether elevated serotonin is a specific biological marker for autism.

Recent technological advances have enabled researchers to investigate levels of serotonin in the brain itself. Chugani et al. (1997) examined seven boys with autism using PET scans and found unilateral decreases in the synthesis of serotonin in the thalamus and frontal cortex. This pattern was associated with increased synthesis of serotonin in the contralateral dentate nucleus of the cerebellum.

GENETIC STUDIES

The familiality of autism is supported by evidence that the rate of autism in siblings of individuals with autism is about 50 to 100 times the prevalence in the general population, or between 3% and 5% (Smalley, Asarnow, & Spence, 1988). If the broader range of pervasive developmental disorders is considered, the prevalence rate among siblings is estimated to be about 5% (Szatmari et al., 1993). The heritability of autism is supported by twin studies indicating a much greater concordance rate for autism in monozygotic than in dizygotic twins. Such studies have estimated the concordance rate among monozygotic twins to range between 36% and 91% (Bailey et al., 1995). The heritability of autism is estimated to between 91% and 93%, depending on the assumed base rate (Bailey et al., 1995). There also is evidence for an aggregation of other disorders and deviancies in families of children with autism. Research has found that 15% to 25% of siblings of children with autism exhibited some form of cognitive or social impairment (Bolton & Rutter, 1990).

The "broader phenotype of autism" includes characteristics that are similar to individuals with autism, but in less severe forms. The broader phenotype can include problems with social functioning, communication disorders, cognitive impairments, affective or anxiety disorders, and obsessive-compulsive or excessively rigid patterns of behavior. Higher rates of broader phenotype characteristics have been found in some family members of individuals with autism. These characteristics include social and communication impairments (Piven, Palmer, Jacobi, Childress, & Arndt, 1997), relatively higher verbal and nonverbal IQ scores, lower executive functioning (Fombonne, Bolton, Prior, Jordan, & Rutter, 1997; Piven & Palmer, 1997), and personality characteristics such as hypersensitivity and anxiousness (Piven, Palmer, Landa, et al., 1997).

Possible genetic subtypes in autism include autosomal recessive inheritance, multifactorial inheritance, X-linked inheritance, and nonfamilial chromosomal anomalies. Autism has been associated with various single-gene disorders, including Fragile X syndrome, untreated phenylketonuria (PKU), and possibly tuberous sclerosis and neurofibromatosis, and genetic heterogeneity is believed to be present in autism (Szatmari, Jones, Zwaigenbaum & MacLean, 1998). Fragile X syndrome is present in approximately 8% of individuals with autism, but it is more likely associated with mental retardation than with autism (Smalley et al., 1988). It is currently believed that autism is a result of the interaction of multiple genes on several different chromosomes. Although studies have shown associations between autism or autistic behavior and each of the chromosomes, excluding Chromosomes 14 and 20, the most promising areas for further study involve Chromosome 15 and the sex chromosomes (C. Gillberg, 1998). In light of the evidence indicating a genetic role in the transmission of autism, several have acknowledged the importance of genetic counseling and have provided guidelines for the genetic counseling of parents whose child has been diagnosed as having autism (Folstein & Rutter, 1987).

TREATMENT

BIOLOGICAL INTERVENTIONS

A range of biological interventions has been explored for use with individuals with autism. Currently, there are no pharmacological treatments specifically for autism, that is, one that targets social and communication impairments. However, a number of studies indicate that pharmacological interventions can be used to address some autistic symptoms and related conditions, such as obsessive, aggressive, or repetitive behaviors. To determine the degree of efficacy and the individuals for whom these medications are most useful, more studies are needed that implement double-blind, placebo-controlled protocols.

The most promising classes of medications are those that influence serotonin; these drugs have been found to have effects on restricted/repetitive behaviors and anxiety. Fluoxetine has been found to reduce repetitive behaviors and increase sociability and language use in adults with autism in a double-blind, placebo-control study by McDougle and colleagues (1996). It is likely that the subjects became more sociable due to the decrease in repetitive behavior. Clomipramine has also been shown in double-blind, placebo-control studies to reduce obsessive-compulsive, repetitive behaviors in some individuals with autism (Gordon, State, Nelson, Hamburger & Rapoport, 1993; McDougle et al., 1992). It should be noted, however, that there can be serious cardiovascular side effects in some patients and that caution and close monitoring is needed. At one time, flenfluramine was thought to have significant positive effects on autistic symptomology through influence of the serontenergic system (Ritvo, Freeman, Geller, & Yuwiler, 1983). However, later studies found insignificant results (see Holm & Varley, 1989, for a review).

Other drugs have been found to effect specific symptoms. Several studies have found reduced levels of self-injurious behaviors among individuals with autism who are administered opiate agonists (Campbell, Overall, Small, & Sokol, 1989; Walters, Barrett, Feinstein, Mercurio, & Hole, 1990). A later study conducted by Campbell et al. (1993) did not support these results. Among 41 children with autism, an administered opiate agonist was associated with a nonsignificant decrease in self-injurious behavior. Neuroleptics have shown efficacy in some cases, especially in reducing aggressive, hyperactive, and stereotypic behaviors. Because of the potential serious side effects of tardive dyskenesia, these drugs are typically administered in more serious cases of behavioral disturbance and with close monitoring.

In some cases of autism, a metabolic abnormality is seen (e.g., high excretion of uric acid or hippuric acid), and some individuals may have gut pathology evidenced by excretion of unusual peptides. Although systematic research is lacking, in some anecdotal cases, removal of dietary proteins has resulted in improvement of autistic symptoms (Page, 1999). Megavitamin therapy, particularly B_6 and magnesium, has been used by some individuals with autism; however, there is a lack of studies employing rigorous methodology. Thus, a definitive conclusion cannot be drawn regarding their efficacy (Pfeiffer, Norton, Nelson, & Shott, 1995).

EARLY BEHAVIORAL INTERVENTION

Recent reviews of the literature suggest that early behavioral intervention is very effective for young children with autism (Rogers, 1998). Dawson and Osterling (1996) reviewed the outcomes of children receiving specialized intervention during their preschool years. These programs were characterized by high teacher-child ratios, an average of 27 hours of intervention per week, and systematic instruction focusing on the development of social, communication, adaptive, and academic skills. Approximately 50% of children who received these services were placed in regular education classrooms, with varying levels of support. In the programs that measured IQ, average IQ gains for children ranged from 19 to 30 points (Handleman & Harris, 1994; Lovaas, 1987). In addition, studies have indicated that children with autism who received intervention by 2 to 3 years of age tend to have more positive outcomes than those who receive intervention later in their preschool years (Simeonsson, Olley, & Rosenthal, 1987).

Thus, evidence is mounting that children with autism benefit most from intervention programs that begin early and that are characterized by a high level of structure, predictability, systematized instruction, and intensity (Dawson & Osterling, 1996; Rogers, 1998). Applied behavior analysis is one approach that clearly meets these criteria. Questions still remain regarding which type of approach is most effective, what is the optimal level of intensity, and what setting is most appropriate for intervention.

TYPES OF BEHAVIORAL INTERVENTION

Applied Behavior Analysis

Very positive and long-term results have been reported for 40 hour per week, one-to-one behavioral intervention that occurred throughout children's preschool years (Lovaas, 1987). This type of approach utilizes the principles of applied behavior analysis (ABA), including operant conditioning, to teach children compliance, communication, social, adaptive, and academic skills. Because skills are initially taught in a highly structured environment, great effort is devoted to the generalization of skills to more natural environments. Several preschool intervention model programs have incorporated ABA approaches into center-based treatment in various ways. Modifications include providing one-to-one behavioral training to establish basic attending and compliance skills before a child is placed in a classroom environment (S.R. Anderson, Campbell, & Cannon, 1994; Handleman & Harris, 1994), providing behavioral training in various settings with various instructors (McClannahan & Krantz, 1994), and implementing behavioral principles of ABA within the context of a developmentally appropriate preschool classroom (Strain & Cordisco, 1994). R. Koegel and Koegel (1995) have modified traditional ABA approaches to include a range of naturalistic activities that foster child initiative, motivation, and the development of "pivotal" skills (i.e., skills that can lead to changes in a wide range of contexts).

ABA techniques also have been used to bring the challenging behaviors of children with autism (e.g., self-abusive, self-stimulatory, and aggressive behaviors) under control (Carr, Newsom, & Binkoff, 1980; Lovaas & Simmons, 1969). More recently, behavioral interventions have stressed the pragmatic aspect of these behaviors (Donnellan, Mirenda, Mesaros, & Fassbender, 1984). Difficult behaviors are often viewed as an attempt by the child to communicate with others. Thus, instead of attempting to simply eliminate the behaviors, a pragmatic approach emphasizes teaching the child alternative communicative behaviors to replace challenging behaviors and modification of the child's environment (Donnellan et al., 1984).

Psychoeducational Programs: "Structured Teaching"
Psychoeducational treatments usually are carried out in the classroom, but also have been used in the home. One example of a successful psychoeducational approach, the Treatment & Education for Autistic & Related Communication for Handicapped Children (TEACCH) program, has been developed by Eric Schopler and colleagues (Schopler, Mesibov, Shigley, & Bashford, 1984). In this program, the classroom is structured to be as predictable and comprehensible as possible, to ease transitions from one activity to another, to maximize generalization of communication and other skills, and to promote independence. Structure is often provided to children in forms that are most easily understood, which is often a visual-spatial format. Examples of these strategies are the use of picture schedules to give individuals information about what they can expect to happen and

the use of work systems that help children attend and persevere during tasks. Other strategies have incorporated TEACCH principles in various ways, for example, by emphasizing the use of visual and spatial cues to increase an individual's ability to comprehend, remember, and exchange information. For instance, visual cues and other kinds of environmental supports can be used flexibly to decrease problem behaviors (Dalrymple, 1995).

Specific Interventions Targeting Language and Social Skills
Recent language and communication interventions emphasize the social context in which early communication develops and the need to promote preverbal communicative skills as a prerequisite to spoken language (Greenspan, Wieder, & Simons, 1998; Wetherby & Prizant, 1999). In addition, emphasis is placed on promoting the child's intrinsic motivation to communicate and increasing the child's ability to communicate actively and spontaneously (L. Koegel & Koegel, 1996). Often, principles of applied behavior analysis are used in more child-directed, play-based settings (R. Koegel & Koegel, 1995). Previous studies underscored the importance of utilizing treatment contexts most closely resembling natural linguistic settings (Hart, 1985; R. Koegel & Johnson, 1989). Prizant and colleagues have stressed the need to respond positively to the unusual language of individuals with autism; they have demonstrated that echolalia serves a communicative function and should be viewed as an early stage of language development for children with autism (Prizant & Rydell, 1984).

Many children with autism improve their social interactions with adults as they grow older (Baltaxe & Simmons, 1983), but interactions with peers typically remain impaired (Lord & Hopkins, 1986). Peer-directed play has been used to teach social skills to children with autism (Lord, 1984; Strain, Kohler, & Goldstein, 1996). If normal peers are specially trained to initiate, to persist in initiating, and to reinforce the actions of children with autism, they can produce almost immediate increased rates of interaction with the children with autism. However, Lord (1984) found that these increases in interaction do not always generalize to untrained peers. The use of a one-to-one peer tutor in elementary-age children has been described by Lord (1995a). In addition, visual supports can be provided to children for them to learn social skills (Gray, 1995; Hodgdon, 1995).

Vocational Skills and Residential Living Programs

Awareness of the special needs of adolescents and adults with autism has led to a strong focus on vocational and adaptive living skills training in as normalized a setting as possible (Schopler & Mesibov, 1983). Individuals with autism often function best with a job that involves a concrete and linear process (Sugiyama & Takahasi, 1996) in an area of their particular interest and with continued job support (Mathews, 1996). It is important to note that individuals with autism are sometimes not motivated by commitment to their employer or the approval of others, and other systems of reinforcement may be needed by them.

CONCLUSION

Determining the exact causes and nature of brain dysfunction in autism will have to await future research. Similarly, we have much to learn about how we can help people with autism and their families. However, since the previous edition of this *Handbook* was published almost a decade ago, we have achieved important gains in our understanding of this puzzling and challenging disorder. Several large-scale genetic studies are currently underway, and we are almost certain to make great strides in discovering the genetic cause of autism in the next decade. Hopefully, such discoveries will lead to important clues regarding the neuropathology and medical treatment of autism. New techniques for assessing brain anatomy and function continue to offer intriguing clues. The roles of the frontal lobe, the limbic system, and the cerebellum will continue to be a focus of future research. As the result of numerous studies on the social and emotional functioning of individuals with autism, we now know that autism involves, among other impairments, specific difficulties in imitation, affective expression and sharing, joint attention, and comprehension of the mental states of others. Such research has led to better and earlier diagnosis of autism. In the area of treatment, we have yet to discover an effective pharmacological intervention for autism, but we have been steadily improving our psychoeducational interventions, which increasingly are focusing on the social behaviors of people with autism. We now realize that early intensive intervention promises positive outcomes for a large proportion of children with autism. Moreover, many programs for assisting people with autism throughout the life span now exist. We look forward to improving resources for adult persons with autism while, at the same time, recognizing the paramount need for comprehensive early intervention programs for young children with autism and their families.

REFERENCES

Allen, I.A., DeMyer, M.K., Norton, A., Pontius, W., & Yang, E. (1971). Intellectuality in parents of psychotic, subnormal, and normal children. *Journal of Autism and Childhood Schizophrenia, 1,* 311–326.

Allman, J., & Brothers, L. (1994). Faces, fear, and the amygdala. *Nature, 372,* 613.

American Psychiatric Association. (1994). *Diagnostic and statistical manual of mental disorders* (4th ed.). Washington, DC: Author.

Anderson, G.M., & Hoshino, Y. (1987). Neurochemical studies of autism. In D.J. Cohen & A. Donnellan (Eds.), *Handbook of autism and pervasive developmental disorders* (pp. 164–191). New York: Wiley.

Anderson, S.R., Campbell, S., & Cannon, B.O. (1994). The May Center for early childhood education. In S. Harris & J. Handleman (Eds.), *Preschool education program for children with autism* (pp. 15–36). Austin, TX: ProEd.

Asperger, H. (1944). Die "autistischen psychopathen" im kindesalter. *Archiv fur Psychiatrie und Nervenkrankheiten, 117,* 76–136.

Attwood, A., Frith, U., & Hermelin, B. (1988). The understanding and use of interpersonal gesture by autistic and Down's syndrome children. *Journal of Autism and Developmental Disorders, 18,* 241–258.

Bachevalier, J. (1994). Medial temporal lobe structures and autism: A review of clinical and experimental findings. *Neuropsychologia, 32,* 627–648.

Bailey, A., LeCouteur, A., Gottesman, I., Bolton, P., Simonoff, E., Yuzda, E., & Rutter, M. (1995). Autism as a strongly genetic disorder: Evidence from a British twin study. *Psychological Medicine, 25,* 63–77.

Baltaxe, C.A.M., & Simmons, J.Q. (1983). Communication deficits in the adolescent and adult autistic. *Seminars in Speech and Language, 4,* 27–42.

Baranek, G.T. (1999). Autism during infancy: A retrospective video analysis of sensory-motor and social behaviors at 9–12 months of age. *Journal of Autism and Developmental Disorders.*

Baranek, G.T., Foster, L., & Berkson, G. (1997). Tactile defensiveness and stereotyped behaviors. *American Journal of Occupational Therapy, 51,* 91–95.

Baron-Cohen, S., Cox, A., Baird, G., Swettenham, J., Nightingale, N., Morgan, K., Drew, A., & Charman, T. (1996). Psychological markers in the detection of autism in infancy in a large population. *British Journal of Psychiatry, 168,* 1–6.

Baron-Cohen, S., Leslie, A.M., & Frith, U. (1985). Does the autistic child have a "theory of mind"? *Cognition, 21,* 37–46.

Bartak, L., & Rutter, M. (1971). Educational treatment of autistic children. In M. Rutter (Ed.), *Infantile autism: Concept, characteristics and treatment* (pp. 304–370). London: Churchill.

Bartak, L., Rutter, M.L., & Cox, A. (1975). A comparative study of infantile autism and specific developmental language disorder: I. The children. *British Journal of Psychiatry, 126,* 127–145.

Bartolucci, G., & Pierce, S.J. (1977). A preliminary comparison of phonological development in autistic, normal, and mentally retarded subjects. *British Journal of Disorders of Communication, 12,* 134–147.

Bauman, M., & Kemper, A.T. (1994). Neuroanatomic observations of the brain in autism. In M.L. Bauman & T.L. Kemper (Eds.), *The neurology of autism* (pp. 119–145). Baltimore: Johns Hopkins University Press.

Bernal, M.E., & Miller, W.H. (1971). Electrodermal and cardiac responses of schizophrenic children to sensory stimuli. *Psychophysiology, 7,* 155–168.

Bettelheim, B. (1967). *The empty fortress: Infantile autism and the birth of the self.* New York: Free Press.

Bleuler, E. (1950). *Dementia praecox or the group of schizophrenias.* New York: International Universities Press. (Original work published 1911)

Bolton, P., MacDonald, H., Pickles, A., Rios, P., Goode, S., Crowson, M., Bailey, A., & Rutter, M. (1994). A case control family history study of autism. *Journal of Child Psychology and Psychiatry and Allied Disciplines, 35,* 877–900.

Bolton, P., & Rutter, M. (1990). Genetic influences in autism. *International Review of Psychiatry, 2,* 67–70.

Bryson, S. (1996). Brief report: Epidemiology of autism. *Journal of Autism and Developmental Disorders, 26,* 165–167.

Bryson, S.E., Clark, B.S., & Smith, I.M. (1988). First report of a Canadian epidemiological study of autistic syndromes. *Journal of Child Psychology and Psychiatry, 29,* 433–445.

Burack, J.A. (1992). Debate and argument: Clarifying developmental issues in the study of autism. *Journal of Child Psychology and Psychiatry, 33,* 617–621.

Campbell, M., Anderson, L.T., Small, A.M., Adams, P., Gonzalez, N.M., & Ernst, M. (1993). Naltrexone in autistic children: Behavioral symptoms and attentional learning. *Journal of the American Academy of Child and Adolescent Psychiatry, 32,* 1283–1291.

Campbell, M., Overall, J.E., Small, A.M., & Sokol, M.S. (1989). Naltrexone in autistic children: An acute open dose range tolerance trial. *Journal of the American Academy of Child and Adolescent Psychiatry, 28,* 200–206.

Carr, E.G., Newsom, C.D., & Binkoff, J. (1980). Escape as a factor in the aggressive behavior of two retarded children. *Journal of Applied Behavior Analysis, 13,* 101–112.

Charman, T. (1997). The relationship between joint attention and pretend play in autism. *Development and Psychopathology, 9,* 1–16.

Charman, T., & Baron-Cohen, S. (1997). Brief report: Prompted pretend play in autism. *Journal of Autism and Developmental Disorders, 27,* 325–332.

Charman, T., Swettenham, J., Baron-Cohen, S., Cox, A., Baird, G., & Drew, A. (1998). An experimental investigation of social-cognitive abilities in infants with autism: Clinical implications. *Infant Mental Health Journal, 19,* 260–275.

Chess S. (1971). Autism in children with congenital rubella. *Journal of Autism and Childhood Schizophrenia, 1,* 33–47.

Chugani, D.C., Muzik, O., Rothermel, R., Behen, M., Chakraborty, P., Mangner, T., da Silva, E.A., & Chugani, H.T. (1997). Altered serotonin synthesis in the dentatothalamocortical pathway in autistic boys. *Annals of Neurology, 42,* 666–669.

Cialdella, P., & Mamelle, N. (1989). An epidemiological study of infantile autism in a French department (Rhone): A research note. *Journal of Child Psychology and Psychiatry, 30,* 165–175.

Courchesne, E. (1989). Neuroanatomical systems involved in infantile autism: The implications of cerebellar abnormalities. In G. Dawson (Ed.), *Autism: Nature, diagnosis, and treatment* (pp. 234–289). New York: Guilford Press.

Courchesne, E., Chisum, H., & Townsend, J. (1994). Neural activity-dependent brain changes in development: Implications for psychopathology. *Development and Psychopathology, 6,* 697–722.

Courchesne, E., Lincoln, A.J., Kilman, B.A., & Galambos, R. (1985). Event-related brain potential correlates of the processing of novel visual and auditory information in autism. *Journal of Autism and Developmental Disorders, 15,* 55–75.

Courchesne, E., Townsend, J., & Saitoh, O. (1994). The brain in infantile autism: Posterior fossa structures are abnormal. *Neurology, 44,* 214–223.

Dalrymple, N. (1995). Environmental supports to develop flexibility and independence. In K. Quill (Ed.), *Teaching children with autism* (pp. 166–200). New York: Delmar.

Damasio, H. (1994). *Descartes' error: Emotion, reason, and the human brain.* New York: Putnam.

Damasio, H., & Maurer, R.G. (1978). A neurological model for childhood autism. *Archives of Neurology, 35,* 777–786.

Damasio, H., Maurer, R.G., Damasio, A.R., & Chue, H.C. (1980). Computerized tomographic scan findings in patients with autistic behavior. *Archives of Neurology, 37,* 504–510.

Dawson, G. (1991). A psychobiological perspective on the early socioemotional development of children with autism. In D. Cicchetti & S. Toth (Eds.), *Developmental psychopathology* (Vol. 3, pp. 207–234). Hillsdale, NJ: Erlbaum.

Dawson, G. (1996). Brief report: Neuropsychology of autism: A report on the state of the science. *Journal of Autism and Developmental Disorders, 26,* 179–184.

Dawson, G., Finley, C., Phillips, S., & Galpert, L. (1986). Hemispheric specialization and the language abilities of autistic children. *Child Development, 57,* 1440–1453.

Dawson, G., Finley, C., Phillips, S., Galpert, L., & Lewy, A. (1988). Reduced P3 amplitude of the event-related brain potential: Its relationship to language ability in autism. *Journal of Autism and Developmental Disorders, 18,* 493–504.

Dawson, G., & Galpert, L. (1990). Mother's use of imitative play for facilitating social responsiveness and toy play in young autistic children. *Development and Psychopathology, 2,* 151–162.

Dawson, G., Klinger, L.G., Panagiotides, H., Lewy, A., & Castelloe, P. (1995). Subgroups of autistic children based on social behavior display distinct patterns of brain activity. *Journal of Abnormal Child Psychology, 23,* 569–583.

Dawson, G., & Lewy, A. (1989). Arousal, attention, and the socioemotional impairments of individuals with autism. In G. Dawson (Ed.), *Autism: Nature, diagnosis, and treatment* (pp. 49–74). New York: Guilford Press.

Dawson, G., Meltzoff, A.N., Osterling, J., & Brown, E. (1998). Children with autism fail to orient to social stimuli. *Journal of Autism and Developmental Disorders, 28,* 479–485.

Dawson, G., Meltzoff, A.N., Osterling J., & Rinaldi, J. (1998). Neuropsychological correlates of early symptoms of autism. *Child Development, 69,* 1276–1285.

Dawson, G., & Osterling, J. (1996). Early intervention in autism. In M. Guralnick (Ed.), *The effectiveness of early intervention* (pp. 307–326). Baltimore: Brookes.

Deykin, E.Y., & MacMahon, B. (1980). Pregnancy, delivery, and neonatal complications among autistic children. *American Journal of Diseases of Children, 134,* 860–864.

Donnellan, A.M., Mirenda, P.L., Mesaros, R.A., & Fassbender, L.L. (1984). Analyzing the communicative functions of aberrant behavior. *Journal of the Association for Persons with Severe Handicaps, 9,* 201–212.

Eales, M.J. (1993). Pragmatic impairments in adults with childhood diagnoses of autism or developmental receptive language disorder. *Journal of Autism and Developmental Disorders, 23,* 593–617.

Eisenberg, L., & Kanner, L. (1956). Early infantile autism. *American Journal of Orthopsychiatry, 26,* 556–566.

Fein, D., & Waterhouse, L. (1985, June). *Infantile autism: Delineating the key deficits.* Paper presented at a meeting of the Interventional Neuropsychology Society, North Berwick, Scotland.

Filipek, P.A. (1996). Brief report: Neuroimaging in autism: The state of the science 1995. *Journal of Autism and Developmental Disorders, 26,* 211–215.

Filipek, P.A., Richelme, C., Kennedy, D.N., Rademacher, J., Pitcher, D.A., Zidel, S.Y., & Caviness, V.S. (1992). Morphometric analysis of the brain in developmental language disorders and autism [Abstract]. *Annals of Neurology, 32,* 475.

Folstein, S., & Rutter, M. (1987). Autism: Familial aggregation and genetic implications. In E. Schopler & G.B. Mesibov (Eds.), *Neurobiological issues in autism* (pp. 83–106). New York: Plenum Press.

Fombonne, E., Bolton, P., Prior, J., Jordan, H., & Rutter, M. (1997). A family study of autism: Cognitive patterns and levels in parents and siblings. *Journal of Child Psychology and Psychiatry and Allied Disciplines, 38,* 667–683.

Gillberg, C. (1998). Chromosomal disorders and autism. *Journal of Autism and Developmental Disorders, 28,* 415–425.

Gillberg, C., & Gillberg, I.C. (1983). Infantile autism: A total population study of reduced optimality in the pre-, peri-, and neonatal periods. *Journal of Autism and Developmental Disorders, 13,* 153–166.

Gillberg, C., & Steffenburg, S. (1987). Outcome and prognostic factors in infantile autism and similar conditions. *Journal of Autism and Developmental Disorders, 17,* 271–285.

Gillberg, I.C., Bjure, J., Uvebrant, P., Vestergren, E., & Gillberg, C. (1993). SPECT (Single photon emission computed tomography) in 31 children and adolescents with autism and autistic-like conditions. *European Child and Adolescent Psychiatry, 2,* 50–59.

Goldfarb, W., Levy, D.M., & Myers, D.I. (1966). The verbal encounter between the schizophrenic child and his mother. In G. Goldman & D. Shapiro (Eds.), *Developments in psychoanalysis at Columbia University* (pp. 89–176). New York: Hetner.

Goode, S., Rutter, M., & Howlin, P. (1994). *A twenty-year follow-up of children with autism.* Paper presented at the 13th biennial meeting of ISSBD, Amsterdam, The Netherlands.

Gordon, C., State, R., Nelson, J., Hamburger, S., & Rapoport, J. (1993). A double blind comparison of clomipramine, desimipramine, and placebo in the treatment of autistic disorder. *Archives of General Psychiatry, 50*(6), 441–447.

Gray, C. (1995). Teaching children with autism to "read" social situations. In K. Quill (Ed.), *Teaching children with autism.* New York: Delmar.

Greenspan, S.I., Wieder, S., & Simons, R. (1998). *The child with special needs: Encouraging intellectual and emotional growth.* Reading MA: Addison-Wesley.

Gubbay, S.S., Lobascher, M., & Kingerlee, P. (1970). A neurological appraisal of autistic children: Results of a Western Australian survey. *Developmental Medicine and Child Neurology, 12,* 422–429.

Handleman, J., & Harris, S. (1994). The Douglass Developmental Disabilities Center. In S. Harris & J. Handleman (Eds.), *Preschool education programs for children with autism* (pp. 71–86). Austin, TX: ProEd.

Hart, B.M. (1985). Naturalistic language training techniques. In S.F. Warren & A.K. Rogers-Warren (Eds.), *Teaching functional language* (pp. 63–88). Baltimore: University Park Press.

Hobson, P. (1989). Beyond cognition: A theory of autism. In G. Dawson (Ed.), *Autism: Nature, diagnosis, and treatment* (pp. 22–48). New York: Guilford Press.

Hodgdon, L. (1995). Solving social-behavioral problems through the use of environmental supports. In K. Quill (Ed.), *Teaching children with autism.* New York: Delmar.

Holm, V.A., & Varley, C.K. (1989). Pharmacological treatment of autistic children. In G. Dawson (Ed.), *Autism: Nature, diagnosis, and treatment* (pp. 386–404). New York: Guilford Press.

Horowitz, B., Rumsey, J., Grady, C., & Rappoport, S. (1988). The cerebral metabolic landscape in autism: Intercorrelations of regional glucose utilization. *Archives of Neurology, 4,* 749–755.

Howlin, P. (1984). The acquisition of grammatical morphemes in autistic children: A critique and replication of the findings of Bartolucci, Pierce, and Streiner, 1980. *Journal of Autism and Developmental Disorders, 14,* 127–136.

Hutt, S.J., Forrest, S.J., & Richer, J. (1975). Cardiac arrhythmia and behavior in autistic children. *Acta Psychiatrica Scandinavica, 51,* 361–372.

James, A., & Barry, R.J. (1980). Respiratory and vascular responses to simple visual stimuli in autistics, retardates, and normals. *Psychophysiology, 17,* 541–547.

Kanner, L. (1943). Autistic disturbances of affective contact. *Nervous Child, 2,* 217–250.

Kasari, C., Sigman, M., Yirmiya, N., & Mundy P. (1993). Affective development and communication in children with autism. In A.P. Kaiser & D.B. Gray (Eds.), *Enhancing children's communication: Research foundations for intervention* (pp. 201–222). Baltimore: Brookes.

Klinnert, M.D., Campos, J.J., Sorce, J.F., Emde, R.N., & Svejda, M. (1983). Emotions as behavior regulators: Social referencing in infancy. In R. Plutchik & H. Kellerman (Eds.), *Emotion: Theory, research and experience* (Vol. 2). New York: Academic Press.

Knobloch, H., & Pasamanick, B. (1975). Some etiologic and prognostic factors in early infantile autism and psychosis. *Pediatrics, 55,* 182–191.

Koegel, L.K., & Koegel, R.L. (1996). The child with autism as an active communicative partner: Child-initiated strategies for improving communication and reducing behavior problems. In E.D. Hibbs & P.S. Jensen (Eds.), *Psychosocial treatments for child and adolescent disorders* (pp. 553–572). Washington, DC: American Psychological Association.

Koegel, R., & Koegel, L. (1995). *Teaching children with autism.* Baltimore: Brookes.

Koegel, R.L., & Johnson, J. (1989). Motivating language use in autistic children. In G. Dawson (Ed.), *Autism: Nature, diagnosis, and treatment.* New York: Guilford Press.

Kolvin, I. (1971a). Psychoses in childhood: A comparative study. In M. Rutter (Ed.), *Infantile autism: Concepts, characteristics and treatment.* Edinburgh, Scotland: Churchill Livingstone.

Kolvin, I. (1971b). Studies in childhood psychoses: I. Diagnostic criteria and classification. *British Journal of Psychiatry, 118,* 381–384.

Konstantareas, M.M., Homatidis, S., & Busch, J. (1989). Cognitive, communication, and social differences between autistic boys and girls. *Journal of Applied Developmental Psychology, 10,* 411–424.

Leboyer, M., Phillipp, A., Bouvard, M., Guilloud-Bataille, M., Bondoux, D., Tabuteau, F., Feingold, J., Mouren-Simeoni, M., & Launay, J. (1999). Whole blood serotonin and plasma beta-endorphins in autistic probands and their first-degree relatives. *Biological Psychiatry, 45,* 158–163.

Lee, A., Hobson, R.P., & Chiat, S. (1994). I, you, me, and autism: An experimental study. *Journal of Autism and Developmental Disorders, 24,* 155–176.

Lobascher, M.E., Kingerlee, P.E., & Gubbay, S.D. (1970). Childhood autism: Etiological factors in 25 cases. *British Journal of Psychiatry, 117,* 525–529.

Lockyer, L., & Rutter, M. (1969). A five to fifteen year follow-up study of infantile psychosis: III. Psychological aspects. *British Journal of Psychiatry, 115,* 865–882.

Lockyer, L., & Rutter, M. (1970). A five to fifteen year follow-up study of infantile psychosis: IV. Patterns of cognitive ability. *British Journal of Social and Clinical Psychology, 9,* 1952–1963.

Lord, C. (1984). The development of peer relations in children with autism. In F.J. Morrison, C. Lord, & D.P. Keating (Eds.), *Applied developmental psychology* (pp. 165–229). New York: Academic Press.

Lord, C. (1995a). Facilitating social inclusion: Examples from peer intervention programs. In E. Schopler & G. Mesibov (Eds.), *Learning and cognition in autism* (pp. 221–239). New York: Plenum Press.

Lord, C. (1995b). Follow-up of two-year-olds referred for possible autism. *Journal of Child Psychology and Psychiatry and Allied Disciplines, 36,* 1365–1382.

Lord, C., & Hopkins, J.M. (1986). The social behavior of autistic children with younger and same-age nonhandicapped peers. *Journal of Autism and Developmental Disorders, 16,* 449–462.

Lord, C., Mulloy, C., Wendelboe, M., & Schopler, E. (1991). Pre- and perinatal factors in high-functioning females and males with autism. *Journal of Autism and Developmental Disorders, 21,* 197–209.

Lord, C., & Pickles, A. (1996). Language level and nonverbal social-communicative behaviors in autistic and language delayed children. *Journal of the American Academy of Child and Adolescent Psychiatry, 35*(11), 1542–1550.

Lord, C., & Schopler, E. (1989). The role of age at assessment, developmental level, and test in the stability of intelligence scores in young autistic children. *Journal of Autism and Developmental Disorders, 19,* 483–499.

Lotter, V. (1974). Factors related to outcome in autistic children. *Journal of Autism and Childhood Schizophrenia, 4,* 263–267.

Lovaas, O.I. (1987). Behavioral treatment and normal educational and intellectual functioning in young autistic children. *Journal of Consulting and Clinical Psychology, 55,* 3–9.

Lovaas, O.I., & Simmons, J.Q. (1969). Manipulation of self-destruction in three retarded children. *Journal of Applied Behavioral Analysis, 2,* 143–157.

Loveland, K.A., Tunali-Kotoski, B., Chen, Y.R., Ortegon, J., Pearson, D.A., Brelsford, K.A., & Gibbs, M.C. (1997). Emotion recognition in autism: Verbal and nonverbal information. *Development and Psychopathology, 9,* 579–593.

Mars, A.E., Mauk, J.E., & Dowrick, P.W. (1998). Symptoms of pervasive developmental disorders as observed in prediagnostic home videos of infants and toddlers. *Journal of Pediatrics, 132,* 1–5.

Mathews, A. (1996). Employment training and the development of a support model within employment for adults who experience Asperger's syndrome and autism: The Gloucestershire Group Homes model. In H. Morgan (Ed.), *Adults with autism: A guide to theory and practice* (pp. 163–184). Cambridge, England: Cambridge University Press.

McArthur, D., & Adamson, L.B. (1996). Joint attention in preverbal children: Autism and developmental language disorder. *Journal of Autism and Developmental Disorders, 26,* 481–495.

McClannahan, L., & Krantz, P. (1994). The Princeton Child Development Institute. In S. Harris & J. Handleman (Eds.), *Preschool education programs for children with autism* (pp. 107–126). Austin, TX: ProEd.

McDougle, D., Price, L., Volkmar, F., Goodman, W., Ward-O'Brien, D., Nielsen, J., Bregman, J., & Cohen, D. (1992). Clomipramine in autism: Preliminary evidence of efficacy. *Journal of the American Academy of Child and Adolescent Psychiatry, 31,* 746–750.

McEvoy, R.E., Rogers, S.J., & Pennington, B.F. (1993). Executive function and social communication deficits in young autistic children. *Journal of Child Psychology and Psychiatry, 34,* 563–578.

McLennan, J.D., Lord, C., & Schopler, E. (1993). Sex differences in higher functioning people with autism. *Journal of Autism and Developmental Disorders, 23,* 217–227.

Meltzoff, A., & Moore, M. (1977). Imitation of facial and manual gestures by human neonates. *Science, 198,* 75–78.

Meltzoff, A.N., & Gopnick, A. (1993). The role of imitation in understanding persons and developing a theory of mind. In S. Baron-Cohen, H. Tager-Flusberg, & D.J. Cohen (Eds.), *Understanding other minds: Perspectives from autism* (pp. 335–366). Oxford, England: Oxford University Press.

Meyers, D., & Goldfarb, W. (1961). Studies of perplexity in mothers of schizophrenic children. *American Journal of Orthopsychiatry, 31,* 551–561.

Minshew, N. (1991). Indices of neural function in autism: Clinical and biological implications. *Pediatrics, 31,* 774–780.

Minshew, N. (1996). Brief report: Brain mechanisms in autism: Functional and structural anomalies. *Journal of Autism and Developmental Disorders, 26,* 205–209.

Minshew, N.J., & Goldstein, G. (1993). Is autism an amnesic disorder? Evidence from the California Verbal Learning Test. *Neuropsychology, 7,* 209–216.

Mundy, P., & Crowson, M. (1997). Joint attention and early social communication: Implications for research on intervention with autism. *Journal of Autism and Developmental Disorders, 27,* 653–675.

Mundy, P., & Sigman, M. (1989). The theoretical implications of joint-attention deficits in autism. *Development and Psychopathology, 1,* 173–183.

Mundy, P., Sigman, M., & Kasari, C. (1990). A longitudinal study of joint attention and language development in autistic children. *Journal of Autism and Developmental Disorders, 20,* 115–128.

Mundy, P., Sigman, M., & Kasari, C. (1994). Joint attention, developmental level, and symptom presentation in autism. *Development and Psychopathology, 6,* 389–401.

Mundy, P., Sigman, M., Ungerer, J., & Sherman, T. (1986). Defining the social deficits of autism: The contribution of nonverbal communication measures. *Journal of Child Psychology and Psychiatry, 27,* 657–669.

Mundy, P., Sigman, M., Ungerer, J., & Sherman, T. (1987). Nonverbal communication and play correlates of language development in autistic children. *Journal of Autism and Developmental Disorders, 17,* 349–364.

Nordin, V., & Gillberg, C. (1998). The long-term course of autistic disorders: Update on follow-up studies. *Acta Psychiatrica Scandinavica, 97,* 99–108.

Osterling, J., & Dawson, G. (1994). Early recognition of children with autism: A study of first birthday home videotapes. *Journal of Autism and Developmental Disorders, 24,* 247–257.

Osterling, J., & Dawson, G. (1999, April). *Early recognition of infants with autism versus mental retardation.* Poster presented at the biennial meeting of the Society for Research in Child Development. Albuquerque, New Mexico.

Ozonoff, S. (1995). Executive function impairments in autism. In E. Schopler & G. Mesibov (Eds.), *Learning and cognition in autism* (pp. 199–220). New York: Plenum Press.

Ozonoff, S., & Griffith, E.M. (2000). Neuropsychological function and the external validity of Asperger syndrome. In A. Klin, F.R. Volkmar, & S.S. Sparrow (Eds.), *Asperger syndrome.* New York: Guilford Press.

Ozonoff, S., & McEvoy, R. (1994). A longitudinal study of executive function and theory of mind development in autism. *Development and Psychopathology, 6,* 415–431.

Ozonoff, S., & Miller, J.N. (1996). An exploration of right-hemisphere contributions to the pragmatic impairments in autism. *Brain and Language, 52,* 411–434.

Ozonoff, S., Pennington, B., & Rogers, S. (1991). Executive function deficits in high-functioning autistic individuals: Relationship to theory-of-mind. *Journal of Child Psychology and Psychiatry, 32,* 1081–1105.

Ozonoff, S., Strayer, D.L., McMahon, W.M., & Filloux, F. (1994). Executive function abilities in autism and Tourette syndrome: An information processing approach. *Journal of Child Psychology and Psychiatry, 35,* 1015–1032.

Page, T. (1999). *Metabolic treatments of autism.* Paper presented at NIH Conference on Treatment for People with Autism, Besthesda, MD.

Palkowitz, R.W., & Wiesenfeld, A.R. (1980). Differential autonomic responses of autistic and normal children. *Journal of Autism and Developmental Disorders, 10,* 347–390.

Pfeiffer, S.I., Norton, J., Nelson, L., & Shott, S. (1995). Efficacy of vitamin B_6 and magnesium in the treatment of autism: A methodology review and summary of outcomes. *Journal of Autism and Developmental Disorders, 25*(5), 481–493.

Piven, J., Arndt, S., Bailey, J., Havercamp, S., Andreasen, N.C., & Palmer, P. (1995). An MRI study of brain size in autism. *American Journal of Psychiatry, 152,* 1145–1149.

Piven, J., Harper, J., Palmer, P., & Arndt, S. (1996). Course of behavioral change in autism: A retrospective study of high-IQ adolescents and adults. *Journal of the American Academy of Child and Adolescent Psychiatry, 35,* 523–529.

Piven J., & Palmer, P. (1997). Cognitive deficits in parents from multiple-incidence autism families. *Journal of Child Psychology and Psychiatry and Allied Disciplines, 38,* 1011–1021.

Piven, J., Palmer, P., Jacobi, D., Childress, D., & Arndt, S. (1997). Broader autism phenotype: Evidence from a family history study of multiple-incidence autism families. *American Journal of Psychiatry, 154,* 185–190.

Piven, J., Palmer, P., Landa, R., Santangelo, S., Jacobi, D., & Childress, D. (1997). Personality and language characteristics in parents from multiple-incidence autism families. *American Journal of Medical Genetics, 74,* 398–411.

Prior, M., & Hoffmann, W. (1990). Brief report: Neuropsychological testing of autistic children through an exploration with frontal lobe tests. *Journal of Autism and Developmental Disorders, 20,* 581–590.

Prizant, B.M., & Rydell, P.J. (1984). An analysis of the functions of delayed echolalia in autistic children. *Journal of Speech and Hearing Research, 27,* 183–192.

Ritvo, E., Freeman, B., Geller, E., & Yuwiler, A. (1983). Effects of fenfluramine on 14 outpatients with the syndrome of autism. *Journal of the American Academy of Child Psychiatry, 22,* 549–558.

Rogers, S. (1998). Empirically supported comprehensive treatments for young children with autism. *Journal of Clinical Child Psychology, 27,* 168–179.

Rogers, S., & Pennington, B. (1991). A theoretical approach to the deficits in infantile autism. *Development and Psychopathology, 3,* 137–162.

Rumsey, J., Duara, R., Grady, C., Rapoport, J.L., Margolin, R.A., Rappoport, S.I., & Cutler, N.R. (1985). Brain metabolism in autism: Resting cerebral glucose utilization rates as measured with positron emission tomography. *Archives of General Psychiatry, 42,* 44–45.

Rutter, M. (1970). Autistic children: Infancy to adulthood. *Seminars in Psychiatry, 2,* 435–450.

Rutter, M. (1978). Diagnosis and definition. In M. Rutter & E. Schopler (Eds.), *Autism: A reappraisal of concepts and treatment* (pp. 1–25). New York: Plenum Press.

Rutter, M. (1984). Autistic children growing up. *Developmental Medicine and Child Neurology, 26,* 122–129.

Rutter, M., & Lockyer, L. (1967). A five to fifteen year follow-up study of infantile psychosis: I. Description of sample. *British Journal of Psychiatry, 113,* 1169–1182.

Schain, R.J., & Freedman, D. (1961). Studies on 5hydroxyindole metabolism in autistic and other mentally retarded children. *Journal of Pediatrics, 58*(31), S320.

Schifter, T., Hoffman, J.M., Hatten J.P., Jr., Hanson, M.W., Coleman, R.E., & DeLong, G.R. (1994). Neuroimaging in infantile autism. *Journal of Child Neurology, 9,* 155–161.

Schopler, E. (1971). Parents of psychotic children as scapegoats. *Journal of Contemporary Psychotherapy, 4,* 17–22.

Schopler, E., & Mesibov, G.B. (Eds.). (1983). *Autism in adolescents and adults.* New York: Plenum Press.

Schopler, E., Mesibov, G.B., Shigley, H., & Bashford, A. (1984). Helping autistic children through their parents: The TEACCH model. In E. Schopler & G. Mesibov (Eds.), *The effects of autism on the family* (pp. 65–81). New York: Plenum Press.

Siegel, B., Pliner, C., Eschler, J., & Elliot, G.R. (1988). How children with autism are diagnosed: Difficulties in identification of children with multiple developmental delays. *Developmental and Behavioral Pediatrics, 9,* 199–204.

Sigman, M. (1997). The Emmanuel Miller Memorial Lecture 1997: Change and continuity in the development of children with autism. *Journal of Child Psychology and Psychiatry, 39,* 817–827.

Sigman, M., & Ungerer, J. (1984). Cognitive and language skills in autistic, mentally retarded, and normal children. *Developmental Psychology, 20,* 293–302.

Sigman, M., Ungerer, J.A., Mundy, P., & Sherman, T. (1987). Cognition in autistic children. In D.J. Cohen & A. Donnellan (Eds.), *Handbook of autism and pervasive developmental disorders.* New York: Wiley.

Simeonsson, R.J., Olley, J.G., & Rosenthal, S.L. (1987). Early intervention for children with autism. In M.J. Guraloick & F.C. Bennet (Eds.), *The effectiveness of early intervention for at-risk and handicapped children.* New York: Academic Press.

Smalley, S.L., Asarnow, R.F., & Spence, A. (1988). Autism and genetics: A decade of research. *Archives of General Psychiatry, 45,* 953–961.

Smith, I.M., & Bryson, S.E. (1994). Imitation and action in autism: A critical review. *Psychology Bulletin, 116,* 259–273.

Steffenburg, S., & Gillberg, C. (1986). Autism and autistic-like conditions in rural and urban areas: A population study. *British Journal of Psychiatry, 149,* 81–87.

Stevens, S., & Gruzelier, J. (1984). Electrodermal activity to auditory stimuli in autistic, retarded, and normal children. *Journal of Autism and Developmental Disorders, 14,* 245–260.

Stone, W. (1998). *Early behavioral indicators of autism.* Paper presented at the NIH meeting on the State of the Science in Autism: Screening and Diagnosis, Washington, DC.

Stone, W.L., Lee, E.B., Ashford, L., Brissie, J., Hepburn, S.L., Coonrod, E.E., & Weiss, B.H. (1999). Can autism be diagnosed accurately in children under three years? *Journal of Child Psychology and Psychiatry and Allied Disciplines, 40,* 219–226.

Stone, W.L., Ousley, O.Y., & Littleford, C.D. (1997). Motor imitation in young children with autism: What's the object? *Journal of Abnormal Child Psychology, 25,* 475–485.

Strain, P., Kohler, F., & Goldstein, H. (1996). Learning experiences: An alternative program: Peer-mediated interventions for young children with autism. In E.D. Hibbs & P.S. Jensen (Eds.), *Psychosocial treatments for child and adolescent disorders* (pp. 573–587). Washington, DC: American Psychological Association.

Strain, P.S., & Cordisco, L.K. (1994). LEAP preschool. In S. Harris & J. Handleman (Eds.), *Preschool education programs for children with autism* (pp. 225–244). Austin, TX: ProEd.

Sugiyama, T., & Takahasi, O. (1996). Employment of autistics. *Japanese Journal of Child and Adolescent Psychiatry, 37*(1), 19–25.

Swisher, L., & Demetras, M.J. (1985). The expressing language characteristics of autistic children compared with mentally retarded or specific language-impaired children. In E. Schopler & G.B. Mesibov (Eds.), *Communication problems in autism* (pp. 147–162). New York: Plenum Press.

Szatmari, P., Jones, M.B., Tuff, L., Bartolucci, G., Fisman, S., & Mahoney, W. (1993). Lack of cognitive impairment in first-degree relatives of children with pervasive developmental disorders. *Journal of the American Academy of Child and Adolescent Psychiatry, 32,* 1264–1273.

Szatmari, P., Jones, M.B., Zwaigenbaum, L., & MacLean, J.E. (1998). Genetics of autism: Overview and new directions. *Journal of Autism and Developmental Disorders, 28,* 351–368.

Tager-Flusberg, H. (1985). Psycholinguistic approaches to language and communication in autism. In E. Schopler & G.B. Mesibov (Eds.), *Communication problems in autism* (pp. 69–87). New York: Plenum Press.

Tager-Flusberg, H. (1989). A psycholinguistic perspective on language development in the autistic child. In G. Dawson (Ed.), *Autism: Nature, diagnosis, and treatment* (pp. 92–118). New York: Guilford Press.

Tager-Flusberg, H. (1993). What language reveals about the understanding of minds in children with autism. In S. Baron-Cohen, H. Tager-Flusberg, & D.J. Cohen (Eds.), *Understanding other minds: Perspectives from autism* (pp. 138–157). Oxford, England: Oxford University Press.

Tager-Flusberg, H. (1995). "Once upon a ribbit": Stories narrated by autistic children. *British Journal of Developmental Psychology, 13,* 45–59.

Tager-Flusberg, H. (1996). Brief report: Current theory and research on language and communication in autism. *Journal of Autism and Developmental Disorders, 26,* 169–172.

Tantam, D. (1988). Asperger's syndrome. *Journal of Child Psychology and Psychiatry, 29*(3), 245–255.

Tinbergen, E.A., & Tinbergen, N. (1972). Early childhood autism: An ethological approach. In *Advances in Ethology, 10*[Suppl.]. Berlin, Germany: Verlag.

Trevarthen, C. (1979). Communication and cooperation in early infancy: A description of primary intersubjectivity. In M. Bullowa (Ed.), *Before speech: The beginnings of interpersonal communication.* Cambridge, England: Cambridge University Press.

Tsai, L. (1987). Pre-, peri-, and neonatal factors in autism. In E. Schopler & G. Mesibov (Eds.), *Neurobiological issues in autism* (pp. 17–189). New York: Plenum Press.

Tsai, L.Y., Tsai, M.C., & August, G.J. (1985). Brief report: Implication of EEG diagnoses in the subclassification of infantile autism. *Journal of Autism and Developmental Disorders, 15,* 339–344.

Tuchman, R.F., & Rapin, I. (1997). Regression in pervasive developmental disorders: Seizures and epileptiform electroencephalogram correlates. *Pediatrics, 99,* 560.

Ungerer, J., & Sigman, M. (1981). Symbolic play and language comprehension in autistic children. *Journal of the American Academy of Child Psychiatry, 20,* 318–337.

Van Acker, R. (1991). Rett syndrome: A review of current knowledge. *Journal of Autism and Developmental Disorders, 21,* 381–406.

van Engeland, H. (1984). The electrodermal orienting response to auditive stimuli in autistic children, normal children, mentally retarded children, and child psychiatric patients. *Journal of Autism and Developmental Disorders. 14,* 261–279.

Volkmar, F., & Anderson, G. (1989). Neurochemical perspectives on infantile autism. In G. Dawson (Ed.), *Autism: Nature, diagnosis, and treatment* (pp. 208–224). New York: Guilford Press.

Volkmar, F., & Nelson, I. (1990). Seizure disorders in autism. *Journal of the American Academy of Child and Adolescent Psychiatry, 29,* 127–129.

Volkmar, F.R., Cohen, D.J., & Paul, R. (1986). An evaluation of *DSM-III* criteria for infantile autism. *Journal of the American Academy of Child Psychiatry, 25,* 190–197.

Volkmar, F.R., Klin, A., Marans, W., & Cohen, D.J. (1997). Childhood disintegrative disorder. In D.J. Cohen & F.R. Volkmar (Eds.), *Handbook of autism and pervasive developmental disorders* (2nd ed.). New York: Wiley.

Volkmar, F.R., Szatmari, P., & Sparrow, S.S. (1993). Sex differences in pervasive developmental disorders. *Journal of Autism and Developmental Disorders, 23,* 579–591.

Walters, A.S., Barrett, R.P., Feinstein, C., Mercurio, A., & Hole, W.T. (1990). A case report of naltrexone treatment of self-injury and social withdrawal in autism. *Journal of Autism and Developmental Disorders, 20,* 169–176.

Wellman, H.M. (1993). Early understanding of mind: The normal case. In S. Baron-Cohen, H. Tager-Flusberg, & D.J. Cohen (Eds.), *Understanding other minds: Perspectives from autism* (pp. 10–39). Oxford, England: Oxford University Press.

Wetherby, A.M., & Prizant, B. (1999). Enhancing language and communication development in autism: Assessment and intervention guidelines. In D. Berkell (Ed.), *Autism: Identification, education, and treatment* (2nd ed., pp. 141–174). Hillsdale, NJ: Erlbaum.

Wing, L. (1988). The continuum of autistic characteristics. In E. Schopler & G. Mesibov (Eds.), *Diagnosis and assessment in autism* (pp. 91–110). New York: Plenum Press.

Wing, L., & Gould, J. (1979). Severe impairments of social interaction and associated abnormalities in children: Epidemiology and classification. *Journal of Autism and Developmental Disorders, 9,* 11–29.

World Health Organization. (1992). *International classification of diseases* (10th ed.). Geneva, Switzerland: Author.

CHAPTER 23

Toileting Problems in Children

EDWARD R. CHRISTOPHERSEN AND PATRICIA C. PURVIS

All parents must decide when and how to toilet train their offspring. The section of this chapter that deals with toilet training discusses procedures available for reducing or minimizing difficulties that stem from toilet training. The rest of the chapter deals with the problems most often associated with toilet training or the lack thereof, including children who refuse to use the toilet (no reliable estimates of occurrence available), encopresis (roughly 3% of the general pediatric population; Levine, 1975), and enuresis (roughly 25% of all 4-year-olds; Cohen, 1975). Within each section, the available literature on etiology, developmental concerns, history and physical examination, and treatment will be discussed. General recommendations to clinicians who see children with toileting problems also will be discussed.

TOILET TRAINING

The mastery of bowel and bladder control is a major milestone in the physical and social development of children. By the age of 36 months, most children have achieved diurnal bowel and bladder control, although occasional accidents may occur through 5 years of age (Simonds, 1977).

Brazelton (1962) suggested that coercive toilet training is a primary factor in the development of problems such as encopresis and enuresis. Although much importance has been placed on this developmental task, little evaluative research has been done. Several reasons for the paucity of research have been suggested: (1) toilet training has been viewed as a taboo subject for study; (2) data collection on children under 3 years of age is difficult, as they are usually at home and not as accessible as children in preschool; (3) the amount of time necessary to study the toilet training process can be prohibitive (Pumroy & Pumroy, 1965); and (4) toileting problems do not fare well in national health research priorities compared with cancer, heart disease, accidents, and AIDS. Another possible deterrent to research may be the lack of established procedures available for systematic evaluation.

Surveys have shown that parents may have unrealistic expectations about when toilet training should begin (Carlson & Asnes, 1974). Of a sample of 69 mothers of firstborn children surveyed, 50% of them planned to initiate toilet training before their children were 16 months of age and 55% expected to have their children trained by 24 months of age (Stephens & Silber, 1971). A follow-up questionnaire was sent to this same sample of mothers several years later. Of the 57 mothers who responded, 58% reported initiating toilet training before their child's second birthday (Stephens & Silber, 1974). Most mothers (51%) sought advice about toilet training from a friend or relative, 30% consulted

Baby and Child Care (Spock, 1976), 26% sought advice from their physicians, and 21% consulted with their husbands.

Central to the task of toilet training children is the concept of readiness. Brazelton (1962) has suggested several physiological and psychological readiness criteria. Physiological readiness criteria include reflex sphincter control, which can be elicited as early as 9 months, and mylinization of pyramidal tracts, which is completed between 12 and 18 months. Psychological readiness criteria include (1) established motor milestones of sitting and walking, (2) some verbal understanding, (3) positive relationships with caregivers as evidenced in the desire to please, (4) identification with and imitation of parents and significant others, and (5) the desire to be autonomous and master primitive impulses. Brazelton suggests that readiness appears to peak for most children between 18 and 30 months of age.

Azrin and Foxx (1974) suggested several readiness criteria similar to Brazelton's. These include (1) bladder control (the child should empty his or her bladder completely when voiding, stay dry for several hours, and indicate that he or she is about to urinate or defecate by facial expressions or posturing); (2) physical readiness (the child should exhibit enough fine and gross motor coordination to pick up objects easily, walk well without assistance, and dress and undress enough for toileting); and (3) instruction readiness (the child should have enough receptive language to follow one-stage and two-stage directions). Table 23.1 provides a toilet training readiness checklist based on Azrin and Foxx that can be a helpful guideline for parents and professionals when determining if a youngster is realistically prepared to learn this process.

Azrin and Foxx (1974) state that most children over 20 months can usually meet these criteria. Christophersen (1994, 1998) has suggested that parents wait three months after their children have met the Azrin and Foxx readiness criteria before beginning training. This means that training with most children would be initiated between 24 and 30 months of age. This is the same age that Brazelton (1962) reported the average parent reported beginning to toilet train. Additionally, it may be helpful to wait until warmer months of the year, eliminating the need to remove or wash extra clothing. Brazelton et al. (1999) provide a detailed discussion of the factors that influence a child's readiness for toilet training.

Table 23.1 Toilet training readiness checklist.

1. Does your child urinate a good deal at one time rather than dribbling through the day?
   Yes _____ No _____

2. Does your child stay dry for several hours at a time?
   Yes _____ No _____

3. Does your child have enough finger and hand coordination to pick up objects easily?
   Yes _____ No _____

4. Does your child walk from room to room easily without help? Yes _____ No —

5. Can your child carry out the following instructions when asked?
   a. Point to his or her nose? Yes _____ No _____
   b. Point to his or her eyes? Yes _____ No _____
   c. Point to his or her mouth? Yes _____ No _____
   d. Point to his or her hair? Yes_____ No _____
   e. Sit down on a chair? Yes _____ No _____
   f. Stand up? Yes _____ No _____
   g. Walk to a specific place in another room?
      Yes _____ No _____
   h. Imitate you in a simple task, such as playing patty-cake? Yes _____ No _____
   i. Bring you a familiar toy? Yes _____ No _____
   j. Put one familiar object with another, such as putting a doll in a wagon? Yes _____ No _____

Scoring

If your answers to Questions 1 and 2 are "Yes," your child has the necessary bladder control to begin toilet training. If your answers to Questions 3 and 4 are "Yes," your child has the physical skills to begin toilet training. If your child can follow 8 of the 10 instructions in Question 5, your child has the verbal and social skills to begin toilet training.

If your child does not meet all of these criteria, you should delay toilet training until he or she can meet them.

Source: Based on H.H. Azrin & R.M. Foxx *Toilet Training in Less Than a Day.* 1974.

Until recently, a major source of information about toilet training has been child-rearing books written for lay audiences (e.g., Spock, 1976). Several direct attempts to expedite the toilet training process have been reported in the literature, based on operant conditioning principles such as reinforcement and stimulus control. These studies have been done with normal (Brown & Brown, 1974; Pumroy & Pumroy, 1965) and handicapped children (Giles & Wolf, 1966; VanWagenen, Meyerson, Kerr, & Mahoney, 1969) and both normal and handicapped children (Mahoney, VanWagenan, & Meyerson, 1971). These studies have all yielded positive results; however, the sample sizes were small, which limits the generalizability of the findings. One group study compared several training procedures with a no-treatment control group (Madsen, Hoffman, Thomas, Koropsat, & Madsen, 1969). The study was designed to compare the effectiveness of different techniques over a six-week period including one week of baseline, four weeks of training, and one week of posttraining follow-up. Therefore, it was expected that not all of the children would be completely trained. The investigators found that children treated in the reinforcement and reinforcement plus buzzer-pants groups were trained more successfully when compared with the parent method, control, and buzzer-pants alone groups. Although the reinforcement and the reinforcement plus buzzer group did not differ significantly, the buzzer apparatus did decrease the number of accidents. The investigators concluded that reinforcement procedures combined with scheduling and a buzzer apparatus (which alerts trainers to accidents) can enhance toilet training in normal children.

Brazelton (1962) has suggested a method of toilet training that is often cited in the pediatric literature. This approach emphasizes minimal guidance by the parent because the child is allowed to proceed through several phases at his or her own pace. The parent begins by acclimating the child to the presence of a potty chair (by taking the child to the potty chair and having him or her sit on it completely clothed). Next, the child sits without a diaper on the potty chair. Then he or she sits on the potty chair after having soiled the diaper; the diaper is removed and placed in the potty chair under the child to show the eventual function of the potty chair. Next, the potty chair is prominently placed and the child is taken to it several times each day, with diaper off, and is encouraged to use the potty chair independently. This gradually progresses to the point where the child is eliminating in it. Brazelton reviewed the patient office records of 1,170 primarily upper-middle-class children in 10 years of pediatric practice and reported, from the parents comments during well-child office visits, that 80.3% of these children were completely trained (daytime and nighttime) by 3 years of age. The average age for day training was 28.5 months and for day and night training, 33.3 months. Among this group of children, Brazelton reported a lower incidence of residual symptoms such as enuresis and encopresis as compared to the general population. Although there is much surface appeal to this approach, Brazelton gathered his

data by retrospective chart audit (he went through children's medical records in his office to find when the mothers reported that their child was successfully trained). An actual evaluation, using reliable data as well as some type of a control group (which would allow for a comparison with simple maturation combined with general methods used by parents), would facilitate making decisions about whether to adopt this method.

Foxx and Azrin (1973a) reported on a rapid and effective program for toilet training normal children that has been popularized in book form for parents (Azrin & Foxx, 1974). This method was first tested with retarded children (Azrin & Foxx, 1971; Foxx & Azrin, 1973b) and later was extended to normal children. There are at least 16 major characteristics of this training program that include practice and reinforcement in dressing skills, immediacy of reinforcement for correct toileting, required practice in toilet approach after accidents by utilizing positive practice trials, and learning by imitation. The original study with normal children (Foxx & Azrin, 1973a) included a sample of 34 children with a mean age of 25 months. The training was conducted in the natural home or in the home of the trainer with family members absent. All 34 children were trained in an average of 3.9 hours, with a range of 30 minutes to 14 hours. Accidents within the first posttraining week had decreased by 97% (to 0.2 accidents per day per child, about one a week). Accidents remained at a near zero level during four months of follow-up. Foxx and Azrin (1973a) concluded that virtually all healthy children 20 months and older can be trained within a few hours. They do caution that, because the program relies heavily on verbal, instructional, and symbolic procedures, rapid training may not be possible with less verbal children. Although these results are the most impressive published to date, replications by other investigators are important to establish the generalizability of the effectiveness of the program.

Two studies have been published that involve the Azrin and Foxx program. Butler (1976) reported on a group training effort based on the Azrin and Foxx book (1974). Following a three-session training program for parents that included attending lectures, receiving written instructions, and reading the Azrin and Foxx book, there was a significant reduction in the frequency of accidents among the children as compared with pretraining levels. Butler reported that parents found it difficult to deal with their children's negative reactions to the positive practice trials that involve having the child go back and forth to the bathroom 10 times from various locations in the house following an accident. Some parents also found it difficult to avoid prompting their child to go to the toilet after their child began to self-initiate going to the toilet. The other study utilizing the Azrin and Foxx program sought to determine if parents could successfully train their children without professional assistance (Matson & Ollendick, 1977). Mothers of 10 normal children were randomly assigned to a book-only group or book plus supervision group, with five mothers in each group. Mothers in the book-only group were given a copy of the book and trained their children without supervision. The mothers in the book plus supervision group were given the book and an experienced trainer was available during the actual training to supervise the mother's efforts. Only one child of the mothers in the book-only group was successfully trained. In contrast, four of the five children of mothers in the book plus supervision group were successfully trained. Knowledge of the program was assessed by questionnaire and was found to be comparable between the two groups. All of the mothers in this study reported emotional side effects with their children, including tantrums and avoidance behaviors. Matson and Ollendick noted that their study questions the usefulness of the program when conducted by parents without professional supervision. Matson (1975) has noted that parents may experience problems with the Azrin and Foxx method, including negative reactions of their children (such as tantrums). In addition, parents may not have the necessary self-control to manage the program and may become frustrated when training is not accomplished as quickly as the book's title suggests (Kimmel, 1974).

From either an empirical or clinical perspective, the clinician has few options for suggesting a particular approach to training. Brazelton's approach is appealing in that it involves little intensive effort for parents. However, the program components are not as clearly specified as with the Azrin and Foxx method. In addition, some children may not possess sufficient motivation to progress at a reasonable pace. This may lead to impatience and coercive attempts by the parents to accelerate the pace of training, thus making a more structured approach desirable.

The Azrin and Foxx method has been more systematically studied, but the few replications that have been done suggest that parent-mediated training may be problematic. The program is quite intensive and may be too demanding for some parents. If a child is generally noncompliant, compliance training may be indicated before toilet training is begun. In our experience, the Azrin and Foxx method has been successful with professional supervision. Children 24 months and older can realistically be trained within three days to one week and be accident-free within three to six months. Parents frequently need specific instructions on how to deal with avoidance and tantrum behaviors exhibited by their children during training (e.g., using time-out).

Parents can take several steps to facilitate toilet training that were not mentioned by either Brazelton or Azrin and Foxx. First, parents should place two small steps on the sides of the toilet. The steps usually enable children to get up on the toilet more easily and to sit much more securely. By placing their feet on the steps, children gain considerable leverage to use in defecating. Second, parents can collect interesting books and small toys that can be played with only when sitting on the toilet. This can make sitting on the toilet for a brief period of time (no more than five minutes) enjoyable and desirable.

Surveys suggest that parents obtain advice about toilet training by asking relatives or friends or by reading books (Carlson & Asnes, 1974; Stephens & Silber, 1971). Parents generally do not seek professional assistance, but when they do, they are likely to consult with their pediatrician (Stephens & Silber, 1974). Psychologists working outside of pediatric settings are not likely to be consulted very often about normal toilet training. Psychologists who are working with pediatric health care providers can assist them in offering sound advice to parents regarding toilet training. Table 23.2 provides a guideline for psychologists to use when providing advice for parents who are beginning to address toilet training.

Toilet training can create unnecessary conflicts between parents and children. Clinicians can minimize potential conflicts by giving parents advice about when to begin training (which frequently means the clinician encourages the parents to wait until the child is ready to be trained) and how to conduct training. The rapidity with which training is accomplished may not be as important to parents as how smoothly training proceeds. It is fortunate that most children have been able to master toileting, like walking, with minimal prompts and social

Table 23.2 Toilet training checklist.

_____ 1. Age of child at least 24–30 months.

_____ 2. Child completes all activities on toileting readiness checklist confidently.

_____ 3. General behavioral compliance is good. If not, address this first by teaching strategies of effective instruction giving, time-in, and time-out.

_____ 4. Parents purchase new books/small toys/games that stay in the bathroom.

_____ 5. Parents purchase footstool to go at base of adult-sized toilet or use junior chair.

_____ 6. Parents have some type of timer device available to regularly remind them to take the child to the bathroom for toilet sits.

_____ 7. Assistance of day care or other caregivers has been obtained so that all caregivers have agreed to begin working on this process at the same time.

_____ 8. Warm weather requiring lighter clothing is preferable.

reinforcement. Both Brazelton (1962) and Azrin and Foxx (1974) tend to sidestep the issue of bowel versus bladder training. Whereas Brazelton seems to assume that the training will occur simultaneously, Azrin and Foxx state that the parent should concentrate on the bladder training because, in their experience, formal bowel training is usually not necessary.

TOILETING REFUSAL

Only recently have articles begun appearing in the published literature on the topic of toileting refusal. The present authors routinely encounter questions about it from parents. Typically, these children are around 3 years old and will have regular bowel movements in their pants or in a diaper but refuse to defecate in the toilet. One common variation of toileting refusal is children in training pants who will ask a parent for a diaper so that they can have a bowel movement. As soon as they get the diaper on, they will usually walk into another room and promptly have a bowel movement in their diaper.

The only etiological factor that we've been able to identify in toileting refusal is a history of hard stools or constipation. Taubman (1997), in a prospective study of 482 children, reported that 22%

experienced at least one month of stool toileting refusal. Taubman also reported that there was an association between the presence of a younger sibling and parental inability to set limits for the child and stool toileting refusal. Blum, Taubman, and Osborne (1997), Luxem, Christophersen, Purvis, and Baer (1997), and Taubman (1997) have reported that children with toileting refusal often have histories of constipation and/or painful defecation.

Blum et al. (1997) also reported that children with stool toileting refusal were not found to have more behavior problems than matched children who were toilet trained. This is consistent with the findings of Friman, Mathews, Finney, Christophersen, and Leibowitz (1988) for children with encopresis. Often, children with stool toileting refusal have tried to have a bowel movement on the adult-size toilet and either were unable to or did so with some degree of discomfort. As mentioned earlier, the placement of two small steps at the base of the toilet can enable the child to sit more securely and allow for leverage when defecating.

For children who are already refusing to defecate in the adult toilet, the first step is to make certain that the stools are soft and formed. This can usually be accomplished over a period of a couple of weeks by suggesting changes in diet, use of medication, or both. The dietary changes include the addition of more dietary fiber to moisten and soften the stools and, in cases where the child is consuming an excess of dairy products, reducing the number and amount of dairy products that are offered or are available. A small amount of mineral oil (one tablespoon), mixed with 7-Up, Sprite, or other liquid will often be all that is necessary to soften the stools.

If the child whose stools are soft and formed is still reluctant to defecate in the toilet, the pediatrician can recommend the use of glycerine rectal suppositories for a period up to one week. The suppositories, when given just prior to a meal (the meal closest to when the child typically has a bowel movement), help to produce a movement. Several bowel movements in the toilet without discomfort are usually all that is necessary to encourage the child to begin having stools in the toilet. The softening up of the child's stools should always precede any attempts to get the child to use the toilet.

By treating toileting refusal at an early age, the health care provider may be able to avoid later episodes of encopresis. Many parents of children who present with encopresis will report that their

Table 23.3   Toileting refusal checklist.

_____	1. Are bowel movements of an appropriate consistency?
_____	2. What is the frequency of bowel movements?
_____	3. When was toilet training started?
_____	4. What is the child's current behavior when he or she is ready to eliminate (asks for a diaper, hides in another room, etc.)?
_____	5. Are all caregivers in agreement that this is the time to address this problem?
_____	6. Have any previous interventions been attempted (suppositories, mineral oil)?
_____	7. What type of toilet seat is being used (child-size or regular seat with appropriate footrests)?
_____	8. Does the child eat a balanced diet (need to limit dairy, increase fiber)?
_____	9. Is compliance an issue? If so, start with parent management training while working on softening stools.
_____	10. Is sitting on the toilet an issue? If so, a toilet sit shaping technique should be used first.

children had problems with constipation, toileting refusal, or both at an earlier age. It is interesting to note that the first research paper that documented normal stooling habits in children didn't appear in the literature until 1984 (Weaver & Steiner). They report that the average 1-year-old child has one or two stools per day and that, by 4 years of age, the majority of children have one stool a day, although it is still not uncommon for 4-year-olds to have two stools per day. Constipation would be considered if stool frequency is less than three times per week (Loening-Baucke, 1996). Table 23.3 provides a list of appropriate information necessary to the clinician when gathering a history of toileting refusal.

CONSTIPATION AND ENCOPRESIS

Approximately 3% of the general pediatric population are encopretic (Levine, 1975). About 80% of encopretic children seen by pediatricians present with a history of fecal retention and/or constipation. The formal definition of encopresis requires that four criteria be met: (1) repeated passage of feces into inappropriate places whether involuntary or intentional; (2) at least one such event a month for at least

three months; (3) chronological age is at least 4 years (or equivalent developmental level); and (4) the behavior is not due exclusively to the direct physiological effects of a substance or a general medical condition except through a mechanism involving constipation (American Psychiatric Association, 1994). _The Diagnostic and Statistical Manual of Mental Disorders IV_ (1994) describes two types of encopresis: a "primary type," in which the child has never had fecal continence, and a "secondary type," in which incontinence occurs after the child has been completely continent for a period of time. Both diurnal and nocturnal encopresis can be present, although nocturnal encopresis is rare (Walker, Kenning, & Faust-Campanile, 1989). The etiology and treatment of constipation is discussed first, followed by a brief discussion of additional considerations for the management of encopresis.

A basic working knowledge of the physiology of the colon or large intestine is important in any discussion of constipation. The colon serves two major functions, which may be interrelated. One is the storage of feces until expulsion through defecation is completed. The purpose of toilet training is to acquaint the child with the proprioceptive feedback from the colon and to coordinate the relaxing of the external anal sphincter with the appropriate positioning over a potty chair or a toilet. The internal anal sphincter is stretched or distended by the presence and pressure of feces from the sigmoid colon. Afferent neural pathways signal the brain when the sigmoid colon is distended and defecation can occur volitionally.

While the final products of digestion pass through the colon, its second major function is the absorption of water back into the body (cf. Wright, Schaeffer, & Solomons, 1979). In this way, the contents of the colon are gradually dehydrated until they assume the consistency of normal feces or can even become quite hard. If the motility of the colon is reduced, either involuntarily due to insufficient bulk or roughage or too many bland foods in the diet, or voluntarily due to the child's retention of feces in the colon for abnormal lengths of time, then excess quantities of water can be drawn off. When this happens, the feces becomes dryer than normal, and colonic motility is reduced or slowed down. It is this cycle—the retention of feces, which then has more water extracted than is optimal with a resulting decrease in motility—that can result in constipation and fecal incontinence. Partin, Hamill,

Fischel, and Partin (1992) documented that the vast majority of children with encopresis have histories of problems with constipation.

Although there are no known studies of fecal moisture and constipation in children, Graham, Moser, and Estes (1982) reported that the addition of bran to the patient's diet significantly reduced problems with constipation in adult women. Interestingly, O'Regan, Yazbeck, Hamberger, and Schick (1986) reported that a significant number of enuretic children who presented with histories of constipation evidenced a significant decrease in their enuresis after their constipation had been eliminated.

Although the etiology for this constipation/soiling cycle can rarely be accurately identified, several factors have a known causative role. These include (1) insufficient roughage or bulk; (2) a bland diet, too high in dairy products and cheeses, which results in reduced colonic motility; (3) insufficient oral intake of fluids, which allows the normal reabsorption of water from the colon to dehydrate the feces too much, or dehydration stemming from many activities that increase loss of fluids from sweating; (4) fecal retention by the child; (5) medications (such as some drugs used to control seizures or hyperactivity and narcotics used to control pain) that may have a side effect of promoting constipation; and (6) the child's emotional state. Any of these factors, singly or in some combination, can result in constipationlike symptoms or actual constipation. Loening-Baucke, Cruikshand, and Savage (1987) found that the persistence of encopresis at 6-month and 12-month follow-up was not related to social competence, but was significantly related to the inability to defecate and the inability to relax the external anal sphincter during defecation attempts.

When a child with a history of uncomfortable or painful bowel movements feels the "call to stool" or the urge to defecate, he or she may associate that urge with similar symptoms at some earlier date that were followed by a painful or uncomfortable bowel movement. In an attempt to prevent a recurrence of the painful bowel movement, the child may voluntarily retain feces, thus exacerbating the condition. If constipation results from one of the preceding factors, then the child may become lethargic, which in turn reduces activity level with a resultant decrease in colonic motility, and the constipation is perpetuated. Also, more severe constipation may result in a decreased appetite. The child may

develop a fecal impaction, which is a large blockage caused by the collection of hard dry stool.

If a child with constipation continues to consume a diet that is compatible with constipation, then the whole symptom complex can be exacerbated. Not infrequently, these children will experience seepage around the fecal impaction that results from prolonged constipation, producing what has been termed "paradoxical diarrhea," that is, although the child is actually constipated or impacted, symptomatically, he or she appears as though he or she has diarrhea, producing numerous watery, foul-smelling stools each day. Occasionally, these bouts of paradoxical diarrhea will result in the passage of huge amounts of feces that can even cause problems with the plumbing in the child's home. A period of inactivity of the bowel follows, during which there is no fecal soiling until the colon gets distended again and the constipation returns, followed by the paradoxical diarrhea. Some parents will attempt to treat this type of diarrhea with over-the-counter antidiarrheal agents, an approach that, though well intentioned, will only exacerbate the condition.

MEDICAL EVALUATION OF ENCOPRESIS

Levine (1975) reported on 102 children with encopresis who were seen in a general pediatric outpatient clinic. Of these children, 81 were found to have stool impaction at the time of the first visit. Of these, 39 were treated for constipation in infancy. This fact by itself, if replicated by other investigators, seriously undermines any general discussion of a psychosocial etiology for encopresis. In most cases, the parents need to be assured that this is not their fault and is not caused by a psychological disturbance.

Children with encopresis should be examined by a physician prior to implementing a treatment procedure. Although most physicians will examine a child prior to referring him or her to another practitioner, this is not always true; the psychologist should always ask the parents if a physical examination and full history were done by the referring physician. The physician will typically take a thorough medical, dietary, and bowel history. In addition, an abdominal examination and rectal examination are often necessary to check for either large amounts of stool or very dry stool in the rectal vault and to check for poor sphincter tone. Approximately 70% of constipation can be determined on physical exam; 90% is apparent from viewing a KUB (X-ray of kidneys, ureter, and bladder) (Barr, Levine, & Watkins, 1979). A plain abdominal film is helpful in determining encopresis when a fecal mass is not detected during a physical exam, and in difficult to treat children such as those who refuse a rectal exam or are obese (Loening-Baucke, 1996).

Some medical conditions (e.g., Hirschsprung's disease), if identified, may preclude referral to a behavioral practitioner. Levine (1981) provides an excellent tabular comparison for the clinician to use in differentiating encopresis from Hirschsprung's disease (the most common organic cause for bowel dysfunction that is present from birth on). Table 23.4 lists the symptoms of Hirschsprung's that would mandate referral to a physician for management. Additionally, the absence of weight gain in a child who is below the growth curve for weight may be suggestive of one of the variety of malabsorption syndromes that are known to be present in a small percentage of children (cf. Barr et al., 1979).

If the child is severely impacted, the physician will usually prescribe a regimen for relieving the impaction prior to, or at the same time as, referral to a behavioral practitioner. Davidson (1958) and Davidson, Kugler, and Bauer (1963) described what has come to be called the pediatric approach to constipation or encopresis. Davidson recommends starting a child on a daily dose of mineral oil (which acts both as a stool softener and as a lubricant) and increasing the dosage until regular bowel functioning is established. To aid in the establishment of bowel functioning, Davidson also recommends cutting back (when indicated) on the amount of milk and milk products ingested and increasing ingestion of fruits. Davidson et al. reported a high success rate (90%) with 119 pediatric patients placed on this regimen.

Levine and Bakow (1976) followed 110 encopretic children for one year. At first, the authors described formal intestinal function to the parents in an attempt to demystify the child's presenting problem (this demystification is described in detail in Levine, 1982). The parents were instructed to use enemas and suppositories to get the child's bowel well cleaned out. Then the children started a daily mineral oil regimen that was to last for at least six months. In addition, the children were asked to sit on the toilet for at least 10 minutes, twice each day. Of the patients, 78% fell into the two most successful outcome groups (either marked improvement or some improvement).

Wright (1973) and Wright and Walker (1977) describe a slightly different approach designed to accomplish the same purpose of establishing normal bowel functioning. They recommend initially

Table 23.4   Comparison of encopresis and Hirschsprung's disease.

Parameter	Encopresis	Hirschsprung's Disease
Fecal incontinence	Always	Rare
Constipation	Common, sometimes intermittent	Always
Symptoms as newborn	Rare	Almost always
Infant constipation	Sometimes	Common
Late onset (after 3)	Common	Rare
Difficult bowel training	Common	Rare
Avoidance of toilet	Common	Rare
Failure to thrive	Rare	Common
Anemia	None	Common
Obstructive symptoms	Rare	Common
Stool in ampula	Common	Rare
Tight sphincter	Rare	Common
Large-caliber stools	Common	Never
Preponderance of males	86%	90%
Incidence	1.5% at age 7–8	1:25,000 births
Anal manometry	Sometimes abnormal	Always abnormal

Source: M.D. Levine, "The Schoolchild with Encopresis," *Pediatrics in Review,* 1981, 2(9). Copyright 1981 by John Wiley and Sons. Used with permission.

cleaning out any constipated or impacted stool, instituting a high-fiber diet, devising a program to reward bowel movements in the toilet, and giving mild punishment (e.g., temporary loss of TV privileges) for toileting accidents. The contingencies are such that unassisted (i.e., without a suppository or an enema) and appropriate bowel movements are heavily rewarded, minimally assisted bowel movements (with a suppository) are given a smaller reward, and passively induced bowel movements (with an enema) receive no reward. Wright and Walker recommend using social praise or reinforcement for bowel movements in the toilet.

Christophersen and Rainey (1976) and Christophersen and Berman (1978) offer variations of Wright's (1973) procedure, with more emphasis on dietary intake, increased fluid intake, and no punishment for soiling episodes beyond having the child clean out his or her own pants and cleaning off his or her own buttocks. In more recalcitrant cases, positive practice (cf. Azrin & Foxx, 1974) is recommended for soiling accidents. O'Brien, Ross, and Christophersen (1986) documented the efficacy of this treatment regimen with objective, reliable outcome data.

Recently, the present authors have added even more emphasis on dietary intake by using a handout for parents that lists by brand name a number of high-roughage foods and foods that have either a natural laxative effect (honey, prunes) or a lubricating effect (butter, fried-foods, margarine). We also now recommend encouraging the child to ingest six to eight glasses of fluid daily (other than milk) and encourage more vigorous activities for those children who tend to sit around or watch TV. In cases in which the youngster is able to read, the authors provide an individual list of recommendations (jobs) that are written on the child's reading level including suggestions that will help him or her to eliminate more easily and not have as many accidents. In this manner, the child is included in the process and has information about what is expected.

To date, no research studies have been done that compare the mineral oil regimens with the suppository regimens. The mineral oil has the advantage that parents do not have to administer the rectal suppository. The suppository regimen offers the advantage that parents are better able to time the child's bowel movement and, because the colon is usually evacuated in the morning prior to departure to school, there is less likelihood of the child's

soiling at school. A common misconception was explored by Clark, Russell, Fitzgerald, and Nagamori (1987), who examined the long-standing assumption that oral intake of mineral oil would interfere with the absorption of some vitamins. They concluded that treatment with mineral oil had no adverse effects on the children in the study. Tolia, Lin, and Elitsur (1993) examined the use of gastric lavage and mineral oil therapy and reported a positive outcome with no negative side effects of the treatment. McClung et al. (1993) also demonstrated the efficacy and lack of negative effects of combination therapy (high-fiber, laxative, and lubricants) for encopresis.

All of the preceding regimens involve two basic strategies: (1) to eliminate any constipation or impaction that may be impairing intestinal functioning; and (2) to stimulate regular bowel functioning long enough to establish bowel regularity without the use of any medications. Each of the regimens includes some form of fading to withdraw medications gradually. The Wright and Christophersen regimens also include components to improve parents' compliance with the behavioral medical regimen. Both Wright and Christophersen have the parents mail in recording forms or phone the therapist periodically.

There are times when the use of laxatives are employed as part of the intervention with the sole purpose of softening the stool to allow for comfortable emptying of the lower bowel on a daily basis. Coordination with the child's pediatrician may be necessary when deciding on appropriate medication. Lactulose, sorbitol (both nonabsorbable carbohydrates), and senna are products that can be used. Laxatives are generally used on a shorter-term basis (approximately three months), but in some cases may be used for much longer periods of time to induce soft stools (Loening-Baucke 1996).

By definition, constipation always includes episodic retention of feces. However, approximately 20% of encopretics do not have a history of constipation or fecal impaction. For these children, complete reduction of the soiling episodes is usually much more difficult to achieve. In the child who presents with encopresis with no history of constipation, several distinct possibilities exist. One is that the child has been incompletely toilet trained. These children usually have a normal stool on a regular basis but soil their pants. Frequently, either a positive practice regimen for soilings or a brief trial with daily glycerine suppositories or a combination will yield rather rapid results.

Although numerous case studies have been published that anecdotally report successes with both traditional and behavioral psychotherapeutic approaches, a child who is impacted or severely constipated deserves to have this medical condition treated prior to, or in addition to, attempts to address either the child's underlying problem or his or her lack of adequate reinforcement for appropriate toileting. With such a high percentage of encopretic children presenting with a history of constipation, treatment of possible constipation must be an initial part of a treatment regimen.

Since the publication of the Davidson (1958) paper on the pediatric management of constipation and encopresis, much less emphasis has been placed on the psychodynamic view of these clinical entities. In the opinion of the present authors, a child with constipation and/or encopresis should be seen by a professional trained in dealing with the physical and psychological aspects of constipation. Table 23.5 provides a guideline for practitioners working with the diagnosis of encopresis.

One issue discussed in the psychodynamic literature concerns the hypothesis that treatment of the mere symptoms of encopresis can have undesirable results, so-called symptom substitution. Levine, Mazonson, and Bakow (1980) demonstrated that, although encopresis may have psychological implications, it is a specific disease entity that can be treated without fear of symptom substitution. Levine et al. used a behavioral inventory to compare (before and after treatment and at three-year follow-up) a group of encopretic children who were cured with a group who were not cured to determine whether any significant symptom substitution occurred in children cured of encopresis. They concluded:

> There was no consistent trend toward acquisition of any specific symptom or cluster in the cured group. In no case did a child's condition deteriorate to the point where he or she was hospitalized for emotional difficulties, arrested by the police, suspended from school, or said to have developed highly troublesome new symptoms such as fire setting, school phobia, or stealing. (p. 667)

Two studies have examined the incidence of behavioral disorders in children who present with encopresis (Friman et al., 1988; Loening-Baucke et al.,

Table 23.5 Practitioner's guidelines for treatment of encopresis.

_____ 1. A pediatric medical exam has been completed to confirm encopresis.

_____ 2. A thorough history has been conducted. Along with a thorough psychological history, it should include information about the child's behavior (lethargic, shows loss of appetite, child reports no sensation when stooling), information about the stools (foul-smelling, large, hard in consistency), diet history, exercise history, and family history of bowel problems.

_____ 3. The issue of behavioral compliance should be addressed. If compliance is a problem, the first step is to help establish effective behavior management.

_____ 4. Education and demystification about the disorder is conducted with the parents and the child.

_____ 5. A step-by-step protocol for the process of evacuation and maintenance of an empty bowel is explained and provided.

_____ 6. A list of dietary suggestions is provided.

_____ 7. An abbreviated form of the protocol is provided for the child on the child's reading level.

_____ 8. Recording sheets are provided to document bowel habits before beginning the protocol and during treatment.

1987). Both have concluded that, although some children with encopresis also have behavioral problems, the incidence is simply not high enough even to suggest a causal relationship between the two conditions. Rather, the encopresis and the emotional problems may have to be dealt with separately. The actual presenting symptoms would determine the degree to which these problems were addressed.

NOCTURNAL ENURESIS

Enuresis can be defined as persistent, uncontrolled passage of urine in the day or night in the absence of urological, neurological, and psychological pathology and beyond the age when most children are continent (McKendry, Stewart, Khana, & Netteg, 1975). The diagnostic criteria from *DSM-IV* (1994) states that four criteria are necessary for the diagnosis of enuresis: (1) repeated voiding of urine into bed or clothes; (2) the behavior is clinically significant as manifested by either a frequency of twice a week for at least three consecutive months or the presence of clinically significant distress or impairment in social, academic, or other important areas of functioning; (3) chronological age is at least 5 years; and (4) the behavior is not due exclusively to the direct physiological effect of a substance or a general medical condition. This discussion will be limited to nocturnal enuresis, or bedwetting.

Approximately 40% of children wet the bed at 3 years of age, 22% at 5 years, 10% at 10 years, and 3% at 15 years (Bindelglas, 1975). A positive history of enuresis in family members of enuretic children has been frequently noted. When both parents were enuretic, 77% of children are enuretic; when one parent was enuretic, 42% of children are enuretic; and when neither parent had a history of enuresis, only 15% of children are enuretic (Cohen, 1975). Enuresis is generally a self-limiting condition with a spontaneous cure rate of 12% to 15% per year (Bindelglas, 1975). Shelov and participants (1981) reported on a survey of parents and pediatricians that asked when children should be dry at night. Parents thought that children should be dry at night at a much younger age than did the physicians (2.75 years vs. 5.13 years).

A number of etiologic factors have been proposed for enuresis, including food allergies, deep sleep, small bladder capacity, developmental delays, and faulty training habits (Cohen, 1975; McKendry & Stewart, 1974; Simonds, 1977). Houts (1991) suggested that current leading hypotheses focus on deficiencies in nocturnal ADH (antidiuretic hormone) secretion and on deficiencies in muscular responses necessary to inhibit urination. However, no definitive cause of enuresis has been identified. There is general agreement that enuresis is not primarily a psychopathological disorder (Olness, 1975; Perimutter, 1976; Werry & Cohrssen, 1965). However, secondary emotional and behavioral problems may develop as a result of having to cope with being enuretic, and eliminating the problem can only contribute to more positive social adjustment.

Numerous treatments for enuresis have been suggested, including diet restrictions, psychotherapy, retention control training, drugs, and behavioral methods. Assuming that enuretics have a smaller bladder capacity than nonenuretic children, it has been suggested that small bladder capacity may be due to spasms of the smooth muscle in the bladder wall. This spasm may have an allergic basis

and, therefore, removal of substances that irritate the bladder wall may arrest enuresis. Esperanca and Gerrard (1968) recommended the elimination of milk and dairy products, eggs, citrus fruits and juices, tomatoes and tomato products, cocoa and chocolate, carbonated beverages containing coloring agents, and other soft drinks for 50 enuretic children. Defining a cure as no more than one wet bed in two weeks, they found dietary restrictions to be effective in 15% of the cases. However, it is impossible to separate the effects of imipramine (drug treatment) and dietary restrictions because both treatments were used in the study. In general, dietary restrictions have been found to be effective with only a small percentage of enuretic children and have been suggested only for children with a history of allergies (McKendry & Stewart, 1974; McKendry et al., 1975; Perimutter, 1976).

Short-term psychotherapy has been recommended by some clinicians for treatment of enuresis (Sperling, 1965). However, the few comparative studies that have been done have shown that short-term psychotherapy is no more effective than no treatment, and that more direct methods (such as use of a urine alarm) are more effective (DeLeon & Mandell, 1966; Werry & Cohrssen, 1965). Psychotherapy may be indicated in those few cases where significant psychopathology is suspected in addition to the fact that the child is enuretic (Cohen, 1975; Lovibond, 1964). A recent study (Friman, Handwerk, Swearer, McGinnia, & Warzak, 1998) failed to demonstrate any more behavior problems in children with enuresis compared to control children who did not have enuresis.

Cohen (1975) and Muellner (1960) suggested that enuretic children had smaller functional bladder capacities when compared with nonenuretic children. Based on this assumption, urine retention training has been recommended as a treatment for enuresis (cf. Starfield & Mellits, 1968). Retention control training generally involves having the child delay urination (when he or she feels the urge) for increasingly longer time intervals throughout the day up to a maximum duration of 30 minutes (cf. Doleys, 1977). In addition, the child is instructed to stop and start his or her urine stream when voiding. With repeated practice, it is expected that the enuretic child will increase his or her bladder capacity and be able to sleep through the night without the need to void. Some clinicians have reported success in reducing the frequency of

bedwetting by retention control training (Kimmel &
Kimmel, 1970; Paschalis, Kimmel, & Kimmel, 1972;
Starfield & Mellits, 1968). However, well-controlled
studies have failed to demonstrate both the efficacy
of retention control training for enuresis and the relationship between bedwetting frequency and bladder capacity (Doleys, Ciminero, Tollison, Williams,
& Wells, 1977; Harris & Purohit, 1977).

Historically, the drug most commonly used to
treat enuresis was imipramine (Tofranil), a tricyclic
antidepressant. In general, this drug stops enuresis
completely in 40% to 50% of enuretic children, and
another 10% to 20% show considerable improvement
(Perlmutter, 1976). The relapse rate after the drug is
discontinued is high, however, with about two-thirds
of enuretics resuming wetting frequently enough
to warrant further treatment (Bindelglas, 1975;
Marshall & Marshall, 1973; McKendry & Stewart,
1974). The FDA has recommended that imipramine
be used only as "temporary adjunctive therapy" for
enuretic children 6 years of age and older (*Physicians'
Desk Reference,* 1997). Like any other powerful pharmacological agent, imipramine has potentially serious side effects and should be reserved for those
cases where more conventional therapies are not
practical or effective (Gaultieri, 1977).

Recently, the efficacy and safety of the use of
desmopressin (DDAVP, a hormone nasal spray used
to treat diabetes insipidus) for nocturnal enuresis
has been examined, with an improvement noted in
from 10% to 60% of the patients, typically with
an increase in enuresis after discontinuation of the
medication (Klauber, 1989). However, there has
been significant controversy associated with the use
of desmopressin for enuresis ("Desmopressin,"
1990). Besides the level of controversy associated
with the use of desmopressin, it is considerably
more expensive, has potentially more side effects
(some serious), and is less effective than dry-bed or
urine alarm training. Thus, practitioners might best
learn how to teach parents to use the dry-bed or
urine alarm training procedures until such time as
pharmacological management becomes a more viable alternative. Because, at present, pharmacological management takes less time for the physician
hardly justifies the increased risk and cost to the
patient. (See Moffatt, Harlos, Kirshen, & Burd, 1993,
for a review of the literature on the use of DDAVP to
treat enuresis.)

For more than four decades, the standard behavioral treatment for enuresis has been the urine

alarm or bell-and-pad procedure originally investigated by Mowrer and Mowrer (1938). This procedure involves placing an apparatus on the child's
bed that has a sensing mechanism that activates
an alarm when urine is passed. When the alarm
sounds, the child is awakened, turns off the alarm,
finishes voiding in the toilet, and changes his or her
bedding. (For a more detailed description of this
procedure, the reader is referred to Dische, 1973,
and Turner, 1973.) In general, studies have shown
that the urine alarm treatment initially eliminates
enuresis in approximately 75% of enuretics, with
treatment duration ranging from a mean of 5 weeks
to 12 weeks (Doleys et al., 1977). Relapse rates are
generally high and occur on the average in 46% of
cases, although reinstatement of the procedures
usually results in a complete cure (Taylor & Turner,
1975). The urine alarm treatment has also been
shown to be superior to no treatment, short-term
psychotherapy, and imipramine (DeLeon &
Mandell, 1966; McKendry et al., 1975; Werry &
Cohrssen, 1965). Houts (1991) found children
who wet the bed multiple times each night typically
take longer to respond to this method than children
who wet only one time nightly. Possible disadvantages of this treatment include the time necessary to
effect a cure, the inconvenience of waking during
the night, and malfunctions of the urine alarm
(Christophersen & Rapoff, 1978; Doleys, 1977).

One variation of urine alarm training that has reportedly had a very high success rate is the dry-bed
training program developed by Azrin and his colleagues (see Azrin, Sneed, & Foxx, 1974, for the
original program description). Dry-bed training
combines a number of behavioral procedures, including cleanliness training, positive practice,
nighttime waking, retention control training, and
positive reinforcement.

Table 23.6 provides a comparison of the various
treatment procedures for enuresis (Christophersen
& Rapoff, 1978). Several procedural changes have
been suggested for dry-bed training since the original study, including omission of the use of a urine
alarm, having parents conduct the training with
minimal direct supervision, and instruction in an
office versus home setting (Azrin, Thienes-Hontos,
& Besalel-Azrin, 1979; Besalel-Azrin, Azrin,
Thienes-Hontos, & McMorrow, 1980; Bollard &
Nettelbeck, 1982; Nettelbeck & Langeluddecke,
1979). Dry-bed training has been adapted for use by
nurses in an inpatient child psychiatric unit (Kolko,

Table 23.6 Comparison of enuresis treatment procedures.

	Effectiveness (% of cases)	Relapse Rate (% of cases)	Cost and Length of Treatment	Immediacy of Treatment Effects	Long-Term Treatment Effects
Dry-bed training	+	+	+	+	+
Self-hypnosis	+	+	−	+	0
Urine alarm	0	−	+	−	+
Drugs (imipramine)	0	−	+	+	−
Urine retention	−	−	+	−	−
Dietary restrictions	−	−	+	−	−
Psychotherapy	−	−	−	−	−

Source: Adapted from E.R. Christophersen and M.A. Rapoff (1978). "Enuresis Treatment." *Issues in Comprehensive Pediatric Nursing,* 2, 35–52.

Key: + Better than average
      0 Average
      − Less than average

1987). Although several studies have shown that dry-bed training was superior to the urine alarm treatment, retention control training, and no-treatment controls (Azrin et al., 1974; Azrin & Thienes, 1978; Bollard & Woodroffe, 1977; Doleys et al., 1977), more research is needed before a definitive answer is available. Relapse rates with dry-bed training range from 7% to 29% with a mean of 18% (see Table 23.6). However, as with urine alarm treatment, relapsed children were cured when the training procedures were reinstated. Considering degree of effectiveness, relapse rates, rapidity of remission of symptoms, and potential side effects, the clinician may want to consider the office-based dry-bed training program or the use of urine alarm as the treatment of choice. The training procedures for dry-bed training have been described in a self-help book written for parents (Azrin & Besalel-Azrin, 1979). The standard urine alarm procedures are described in the literature that accompanies the alarm when purchased from the original retailer. In our experience, alarms that are placed on the child's bed and that use a large external buzzer are preferable to the alarms that have a sensor in the child's underwear with a buzzer on the child's waist or shoulder. In most cases, parent participation is an integral part of the intervention. Parents are more likely to hear the external buzzer and respond to assist with the protocol than they would with the smaller alarm. Drug treatment and retention control training might be reserved for those cases where dry-bed training or urine alarm procedures are not practical or available.

Olness (1977) reports an 80% success rate with the use of a self-hypnosis procedure, after having treated more than 200 children. However, these results have not been replicated. The interested reader is referred to Luxem and Christophersen (1999), Walker (1978), and Walker, Milling, and Bonner (1988) for more detailed discussions of toileting problems in children.

Houts and Liebert (1984) developed a behavioral treatment package titled *Full Spectrum Home Training.* The package includes bell-and-pad treatment with cleanliness training, retention control training, and an overlearning technique. The initial training is provided in one-hour group sessions attended by parents and children. Follow-up phone calls are then made biweekly to answer questions. Success criterion is met when the child has been dry for 14 consecutive nights (Houts, Liebert, & Padawer, 1983). Initial studies utilizing this multiple component intervention resulted in lower relapse rates at one-year follow-up (23.9%) than rates reported by Doleys (1977) and supported the success of group training. Further attempts at evaluating the delivery of group training looked at filmed delivery versus delivery by a live trainer (Houts, Whelan, & Peterson, 1987). It was concluded that filmed delivery was not sufficient to obtain the optimal outcome.

RECOMMENDATIONS

Toilet training, toileting refusal, constipation, encopresis, and enuresis usually involve a complex interplay of the child's gastrointestinal and/or genital-urinary system with a variety of environmental inputs. Practitioners interested in treating these conditions would be well advised to acquaint themselves with normal physiological functioning prior to embarking on a vigorous treatment program. In the majority of toileting problems, the child should be evaluated by a competent physician with appropriate medical treatment as indicated. Behavioral treatment should begin only after such screening has been completed.

Obviously, the child's developmental status also plays an important part in determining whether to institute a treatment approach. For a parent to begin toilet training before a child has matured sufficiently is inviting failure and disappointment. If a parent requests treatment for a child's toileting problem (e.g., enuresis) when the child is too young (e.g., below 3 years of age), the clinician should consider trying to persuade the parent to wait until the child is maturationally ready. A discussion with parents about developmental norms would be helpful in pointing out to parents that failure to achieve continence of urine and feces is not considered a problem (i.e., is not considered abnormal) until a child reaches an age when most of his or her peers have achieved continence.

Because toileting problems are often a source of enormous frustration for parents, a carefully prepared and supervised treatment program can be very rewarding for clinicians. Clinicians who seem to have the best success rates and who are most capable of dealing with occasional treatment failures are the ones who have been trained to recognize possible organic causes, who refer to appropriate medical staff when organicity is suspected, and who use experimentally validated procedures to treat children for whom organicity has been ruled out.

REFERENCES

American Psychiatric Association. (1994). *Diagnostic and statistical manual of mental disorders* (4th ed.). Washington, DC: Author.

Azrin, N.H., & Besalel-Azrin, V. (1979). *A parent's guide to bedwetting control: A step-by-step method.* New York: Simon & Schuster.

Azrin, N.H., & Foxx, R.M. (1971). A rapid method of toilet training the institutionalized retarded. *Journal of Applied Behavior Analysis, 4,* 89–99.

Azrin, N.H., & Foxx, R.M. (1974). *Toilet training in less than a day.* New York: Simon & Schuster.

Azrin, N.H., Sneed, T.J., & Foxx, R.M. (1974). Dry-bed training: Rapid elimination of childhood enuresis. *Behaviour Research and Therapy, 12,* 147–156.

Azrin, N.H., & Thienes, P.M. (1978). Rapid elimination of enuresis by intensive learning without a conditioning apparatus. *Behavior Therapy, 9,* 342–354.

Azrin, N.H., Thienes-Hontos, P., & Besalel-Azrin, V. (1979). Elimination of enuresis without a conditioning apparatus: An extension by office instruction of the child and parents. *Behavior Therapy, 10*(1), 14–19.

Barr, R.G., Levine, M.D., & Watkins, J.B. (1979). Recurrent abdominal pain due to lactose intolerance. *New England Journal of Medicine, 300*(26), 1449–1452.

Besalel-Azrin, V., Azrin, N.H., Thienes-Hontos, P., & McMorrow, M. (1980). Evaluation of parent's manual for training enuretic children. *Behaviour Research and Therapy, 18*(4), 358–360.

Bindelglas, P.M. (1975). The enuretic child. *Journal of Family Practice, 2*(5), 375–380.

Blum, N.J., Taubman, B., & Osborne, M.D. (1997). Behavioral characteristics of children with stool toileting refusal. *Pediatrics, 99,* 50–53.

Bollard, R.J., & Nettelbeck, T. (1982). A component analysis of dry-bed training for treatment for bedwetting. *Behaviour Research and Therapy, 20*(4), 383–390.

Bollard, R.J., & Woodroffe, P. (1977). The effect of parent-administered dry-bed training on nocturnal enuresis in children. *Behaviour Research and Therapy, 15*(2), 159–165.

Brazelton, T.B. (1962). A child-oriented approach to toilet training. *Pediatrics, 29,* 121–128.

Brazelton, T.B., Christophersen, E.R., Filmer, R.B., Frauman, A.C., Gorski, P.A., Poole, J.M., Stadtler, A.C., & Wright, C.L. (1999). Instruction, timeliness, and medical influences affecting toilet training. *Pediatrics, 103*(6), 1353–1358.

Brown, R.M., & Brown, N.L. (1974). The increase and control of verbal signals in the bladder training of a seventeen month old child: A case study. *Journal of Child Psychology and Psychiatry, 15,* 105–109.

Butler, J.F. (1976). The toilet training success of parents after reading *Toilet Training in Less Than a Day. Behaviour Therapy, 7,* 185–191.

Carlson, S.S., & Asnes, R.S. (1974). Maternal expectations and attitudes toward toilet training: A comparison between clinic mothers and private practice mothers. *Journal of Pediatrics, 84,* 148–151.

Christophersen, E.R. (1994). *Pediatric compliance: Guidelines for the primary care physician.* New York: Plenum Press.

Christophersen, E.R. (1998). *Little people: Guidelines for commonsense child rearing* (4th ed.). Shawnee Mission, KS: Overland Press.

Christophersen, E.R., & Berman, R. (1978). Encopresis treatment. *Issues in Comprehensive Pediatric Nursing, 3*(4), 51–66.

Christophersen, E.R.. & Rainey, S. (1976). Management of encopresis through a pediatric outpatient clinic. *Journal of Pediatric Psychology, 1,* 38–41.

Christophersen, E.R., & Rapoff, M.A. (1978). Enuresis treatment. *Issues in Comprehensive Pediatric Nursing, 2,* 35–52.

Clark, J.H., Russell, G.J., Fitzgerald, J.F., & Nagamori, K.E. (1987). Serum beta-carotine, retinol, and alpha-tocopherol levels during mineral oil therapy for constipation. *American Journal of Diseases of Children, 141,* 1210–1212.

Cohen, M.W. (1975). Enuresis. *Pediatric Clinics of North America, 22,* 545–560.

Davidson, M. (1958). Constipation and fecal incontinence. *Pediatric Clinics of North America, 5,* 749–757.

Davidson, M., Kugler, M.M., & Bauer, C.H. (1963). Diagnosis and management in children with severe and protracted constipation and obstipation. *Journal of Pediatrics, 62,* 261–275.

DeLeon, G., & Mandell, W. (1966). A comparison of conditioning and psychotherapy in the treatment of functional enuresis. *Journal of Clinical Psychology, 22*(3), 326–330.

Desmopressin for nocturnal enuresis. (1990, April 6). *The Medical Letter,* pp. 38–39.

Dische, S. (1973). Treatment of enuresis with an enuresis alarm. In I. Kolvin, R.C. MacKeith, & S.R. Meadow (Eds.), *Bladder control and enuresis* (pp. 211–230). Philadelphia: Lippincott.

Doleys, D.M. (1977). Behavioral treatments for nocturnal enuresis in children: A review of the recent literature. *Psychological Bulletin, 84*(1), 30–54.

Doleys, D.M., Ciminero, A.R., Tollison, J.W., Williams, D.L., & Wells, K.C. (1977). Dry-bed training and retention control training: A comparison. *Behavior Therapy, 8*(4), 541–548.

Esperanca, M., & Gerrard, J.W. (1968). Nocturnal enuresis: Comparison of the effect of imipramine and dietary restriction on bladder capacity. *Canadian Medical Association Journal, 101,* 721–724.

Foxx, R.M., & Azrin, N.H. (1973a). Dry pants: A rapid method of toilet training children. *Behaviour Research and Therapy, 11,* 435–442.

Foxx, R.M., & Azrin, N.H. (1973b). *Toilet training the retarded.* Champaign, IL: Research Press.

Friman, P.C., Handwerk, M.L., Swearer, S.M., McGinnis, J.C., & Warzak, W.J. (1998). Do children with primary nocturnal enuresis have clinically significant behavior problems? *Archives of Pediatrics and Adolescent Medicine, 152,* 537–539.

Friman, P.C., Mathews, J.R., Finney, J.W., Christophersen, E.R., & Leibowitz, J.M. (1988). Do encopretic children have clinically significant behavior problems? *Pediatrics, 82*(3), 407–409.

Gaultieri, C.T. (1977). Imipramine and children: A review and some speculations about the mechanism of drug action. *Diseases of the Nervous System, 38,* 368–375.

Giles, D.K., & Wolf, M.M. (1966). Toilet training institutionalized, severe retardates: An application of operant behavior modification techniques. *American Journal of Mental Deficiency, 70,* 766–780.

Graham, D.Y., Moser, S.E., & Estes, M.K. (1982). The effect of bran on bowel function in constipation. *American Journal of Gastroenterology, 77,* 599–603.

Harris, L.S., & Purohit, A.P. (1977). Bladder training and enuresis: A controlled trial. *Behaviour Research and Therapy, 15,* 485–490.

Houts, A.C. (1991). Nocturnal enuresis as a biobehavioral problem. *Behavior Therapy, 22,* 133–151.

Houts, A.C., & Liebert, R.M. (1984). *Bedwetting: A guide for parents and children.* Springfield, IL: Thomas.

Houts, A.C., Liebert, R.M., & Padawer, W. (1983). A delivery system for the treatment of primary enuresis. *Journal of Abnormal Child Psychology, 11,* 513–520.

Houts, A.C., Whelan, J.P., & Peterson, J.K. (1987). Filmed versus live delivery of full-spectrum home training for primary enuresis: Presenting the information is not enough. *Journal of Consulting and Clinical Psychology, 55,* 902–906.

Kimmel, H.D. (1974). Toilet training in less than a day: How to do it [Book review]. *Journal of Behaviour Therapy and Experimental Psychiatry, 5,* 113.

Kimmel, H.D., & Kimmel, E. (1970). An instrumental conditioning method for the treatment of enuresis. *Journal of Behaviour Therapy and Experimental Psychiatry, 1,* 121–123.

Klauber, G.T. (1989). Clinical efficacy and safety of desmopressin in the treatment of nocturnal enuresis. *Journal of Pediatrics, 114,* 719–722.

Kolko, D.J. (1987). Simplified inpatient treatment of nocturnal enuresis in psychiatrically disturbed children. *Behavior Therapy, 18,* 99–112.

Levine, M.D. (1975). Children with encopresis: A descriptive analysis. *Pediatrics, 56,* 412–416.

Levine, M.D. (1981). The schoolchild with encopresis. *Pediatrics in Review, 2*(9), 285–290.

Levine, M.D. (1982). Encopresis: Its potentiation, evaluation, and alleviation. *Pediatric Clinics of North America, 29,* 315–331.

Levine, M.D., & Bakow, H. (1976). The schoolchild with encopresis: A treatment outcome study. *Pediatrics, 58,* 845–852.

Levine, M.D., Mazonson, P., & Bakow, H. (1980). Behavioral symptom substitution in children cured of encopresis. *American Journal of Diseases of Children, 134,* 663–667.

Loening-Baucke, V. (1996). Encopresis and soiling. *Pediatric Clinics of North America, 43*(1), 279–298.

Loening-Baucke, V., Cruikshand, B., & Savage, C. (1987). Defecation dynamics and behavior profiles in encopretic children. *Pediatrics, 80*(5), 672–679.

Lovibond, S.H. (1964). *Conditioning and enuresis*. Oxford, England: Pergamon Press.

Luxem, M.C., & Christophersen, E.R. (1999). Elimination disorders. In S.D. Netherton, D. Holmes, & C.E. Walker (Eds.), *Child and adolescent psychological disorders: A comprehensive textbook* (pp. 195–233). New York: Oxford University Press.

Luxem, M.C., Christophersen, E.R., Purvis, P.C., & Baer, D.M. (1997). Behavioral-medical treatment of pediatric toileting refusal. *Journal of Development and Behavioral Pediatrics, 18,* 34–41.

Madsen, C.H., Hoffman, M., Thomas, D.R., Koropsat, E., & Madsen, D.K. (1969). Comparisons of toilet training procedures. In D.M. Gelfand (Ed.), *Social learning in childhood* (pp. 104–112). Belmont, CA: Brooks/Cole.

Mahoney, K., VanWagenen, R.K., & Meyerson, L. (1971). Toilet training of normal and retarded children. *Journal of Applied Behavior Analysis, 4*(3), 173–181.

Marshall, S., & Marshall, H.H. (1973). A practical approach to nonorganic enuresis. *Medical Times, 101,* 58–61.

Matson, J.L. (1975). Some practical considerations for using the Foxx and Azrin rapid method of toilet training. *Psychological Reports, 37,* 350.

Matson, J.L., & Ollendick, T.H. (1977). Issues in toilet training normal children. *Behavior Therapy, 8,* 549–553.

McClung, H.J., Boyne, L.J., Linsheid, T., Heitlinger L.A., Murray, R.D., Fyda, J., & Li, B.U.K. (1993). Is combination therapy for encopresis nutritionally safe? *Pediatrics, 91,* 591–594.

McKendry, J.B., & Stewart, D.A. (1974). Enuresis. *Pediatric Clinics of North America, 21,* 1019–1020.

McKendry, J.B., Stewart, D.A., Khana, F., & Netteg, C. (1975). Primary enuresis: Relative success of three methods of treatment. *Canadian Medical Association Journal, 113,* 953–955.

Moffatt, M.E., Harlos, S., Kirshen, A.J., & Burd, L. (1993). Desmopressin acetate and nocturnal enuresis: How much do we know? *Pediatrics, 92,* 420–425.

Mowrer, O.H., & Mowrer, W.M. (1938). Enuresis: A method for its study and treatment. *American Journal of Orthopsychiatry, 8,* 436–459.

Muellner, S.R. (1960). Development of urinary control in children: A new concept in cause, prevention, and treatment of primary enuresis. *Journal of Urology, 84,* 714–716.

Nettelbeck, T., & Langeluddecke, P. (1979). Dry-bed training without an enuresis machine. *Behaviour Research and Therapy, 17,* 403–404.

O'Brien, S., Ross., L.V., & Christophersen, E.R. (1986). Primary encopresis: Evaluation and treatment. *Journal of Applied Behavior Analysis, 19,* 137–145.

Olness, K. (1975). The use of self-hypnosis in the treatment of childhood enuresis. *Clinical Pediatrics, 14,* 273–279.

Olness, K. (1977, September 30). How to help the wet child and the frustrated parents. *Modern Medicine,* 42–46.

O'Regan, S., Yazbeck, S., Hamberger, B., & Schick, E. (1986). Constipation a commonly unrecognized cause of enuresis. *American Journal of Diseases of Children, 140*(3), 260–261.

Partin, J.C., Hamill, S.K., Fischel, J.E., & Partin, J.S. (1992). Painful defecation and fecal soiling in children. *Pediatrics, 89,* 1007–1009.

Paschalis, A., Kimmel, H.D., & Kimmel, E. (1972). Further study of diurnal instrumental conditioning in the treatment of enuresis nocturna. *Journal of Behaviour Therapy and Experimental Psychiatry, 3,* 253–256.

Perimutter, A.D. (1976). Enuresis. In T.P. Kelalis & L.R. King (Eds.), *Clinical pediatric urology* (pp. 166–181). Philadelphia: Saunders.

Physicians' desk reference. (1997). Oradell, NJ: Medical Economics.

Pumroy, D.K., & Pumroy, S.S. (1965). Systematic observation and reinforcement technique in toilet training. *Psychological Report, 16,* 467–471.

Shelov, S.P., Gundy, J., Weiss, J.C., McIntire, MS., Olness, K., Staub, H.P., Jones, D.J., Haque, M., Ellerstein, N.S., Heagarty, M.C., & Starfield, B. (1981). Enuresis: A contrast of attitudes of parents and physicians. *Pediatrics, 67*(5), 707–710.

Simonds, S.D. (1977). Enuresis: A brief survey of current thinking with respect to pathogenesis and management. *Clinical Pediatrics, 16,* 79–82.

Sperling, M. (1965). Dynamic considerations and treatment of enuresis. *Journal of the American Academy of Child Psychiatry, 4,* 19–31.

Spock, B. (1976). *Baby and child care* (Rev. ed.). New York: Pocket Books.

Starfield, B., & Mellits, E.D. (1968). Increase in functional bladder capacity and improvements in enuresis. *Journal of Pediatrics, 72,* 483–487.

Stephens, J.A., & Silber, D.L. (1971). Parental expectations in toilet training. *Pediatrics, 48*(4), 451–454.

Stephens, J.A., & Silber, D.L. (1974). Parental expectations versus outcome in toilet training. *Pediatrics, 54,* 493–495.

Taubman, B. (1997). Toilet training and toileting refusal for stool only: A prospective study. *Pediatrics, 99,* 54–58.

Taylor, P.D., & Turner, R.K. (1975). A clinical trial of continuous intermittent and overlearning "bell and pad" treatments for nocturnal enuresis. *Behaviour Research and Therapy 3,* 281–293.

Tolia, V., Lin, C.H., & Elitsur, Y. (1993). A prospective randomized study with mineral oil and oral lavage solution for treatment of faecal impaction in children. *Alimentary Pharmacology and Therapeutics, 7,* 523–529.

Turner, R.K. (1973). Conditioning treatment of nocturnal enuresis. In I. Kolvin, R.C. MacKeith, & S.R. Meadows (Eds.), *Bladder control and enuresis* (pp. 195–210). Philadelphia: Lippincott.

VanWagenen, R.K., Meyerson, L., Kerr, M.J., & Mahoney, K. (1969). Field trials of a new procedure for toilet training. *Journal of Experimental Child Psychology, 8*(1), 147–159.

Walker, C.E. (1978). Toilet training, enuresis, encopresis. In P.R. McGrab (Ed.), *Psychological management of pediatric problems* (Vol. 1, pp. 129–189). Baltimore: University Park Press.

Walker, C.E., Kenning, M., & Faust-Campanile, J. (1989). Enuresis and encopresis. In E.J. Mash & R.A. Barkley (Eds.), *Treatment of childhood disorders* (pp. 423–448). New York: Guilford Press.

Walker C.E., Milling, L.S., & Bonner, B.L. (1988). Incontinence disorders: Enuresis and encopresis. In D.K. Routh (Ed.), *Handbook of pediatric psychology* (pp. 363–397). New York: Guilford Press.

Weaver, L.T., & Steiner, H. (1984). The bowel habits of young children. *Archives of Diseases in Childhood, 59,* 649–652.

Werry, S.S., & Cohrssen, J. (1965). Enuresis: An etiologic and therapeutic study. *Journal of Pediatrics, 67,* 423–431.

Wright, L. (1973). Handling the encopretic child. *Professional Psychology, 4,* 137–144.

Wright, L., Schaeffer, A.B., & Solomons, G. (Eds.). (1979). *Encyclopedia of pediatric psychology.* Baltimore: University Park Press.

Wright, L., & Walker, E. (1977). Treatment of the child with psychogenic encopresis. *Clinical Pediatrics, 16,* 1042–1045.

CHAPTER 24

Attention-Deficit/Hyperactivity Disorder

ARTHUR D. ANASTOPOULOS AND STEPHANIE D. SHAFFER

During the past 10 years, attention-deficit/ hyperactivity disorder (AD/HD; American Psychiatric Association [APA], 1994) has received a tremendous amount of clinical and research attention. Over this same period, there has been a virtual explosion of media and public interest in AD/HD. Although such trends have served to increase our awareness and knowledge of AD/HD, there remains much confusion and misunderstanding about the disorder. Thus, there continues to be a need for up-to-date, comprehensive, scientifically based discussions of AD/HD.

This chapter attempts to provide such a discussion. To achieve this goal, we begin with a brief review of the history of AD/HD. This is followed by a description of its defining features and of the criteria that are currently used to establish an AD/HD diagnosis. Next, a detailed discussion of its etiology, epidemiology, developmental aspects, clinical presentation, impact on psychosocial functioning, and associated features is presented. Against this background, many of the commonly used assessment procedures and treatment strategies are discussed. Throughout this review, every effort is made to discuss AD/HD from a developmental perspective. In so doing, we hope to provide readers with an overview of AD/HD that calls attention to its impact across the life span.

HISTORY

There is little justification for claiming that AD/HD is "just the disorder of the '90s." A more accurate characterization would be to say that it is the most recent in a long line of diagnostic labels that have been used to describe children who display developmentally inappropriate levels of inattention, impulsivity, and/or hyperactivity. Although confusing to some, this periodic relabeling has not been without purpose. On the contrary, each diagnostic term has reflected shifts in the way this disorder has been conceptualized at different points in time.

Two major trends characterize the history of this disorder in North America. The first of these pertains to the issue of diagnostic uniformity. From Still's (1902) earliest account until the late 1960s, there was very little agreement within the field as to what to call this condition. Thus, at various times, what is now known as AD/HD was referred to as postencephalitic behavior disorder (Hohman,

470

1922), organic driveness (Kahn & Cohen, (1934), brain-injured child syndrome (Strauss & Lehtinen, 1947), minimal brain damage syndrome (Strauss & Kephart, 1955), minimal brain dysfunction (MBD; Clements & Peters, 1962), and hyperactive child syndrome (Chess, 1960). As it became increasingly more apparent that the use of multiple labels would seriously limit scientific progress, many clinicians and researchers began to acknowledge the need for a common diagnostic terminology. The arrival of the second edition of the *Diagnostic and Statistical Manual of Mental Disorders* (DSM-II; APA, 1968) afforded the first real opportunity for this to occur, through its presentation of hyperkinetic reaction of childhood. Since that time, this commitment to diagnostic uniformity has gained widespread acceptance, with most professionals now using the same diagnostic language in their descriptions of this disorder.

The other major historical trend pertains to the manner in which this disorder has been labeled. With the exception of Still's (1902) account, most of the early descriptions of this condition, such as postencephalitic behavior disorder (Hohman, 1922), reflected its presumed etiology. During the mid-1930s, a competing trend began to emerge in the form of various symptom-based descriptions, which included such terms as restlessness syndrome (Levin, 1938). Although both trends remained in evidence for the next three decades (Chess, 1960; Clements & Peters, 1962), they eventually began taking very different directions, with etiologically based descriptions declining in importance and symptom-based descriptions gaining in acceptance. When hyperkinetic reaction of childhood appeared in *DSM-II*, it marked the beginning of a new era in which only symptom-based descriptions were used as labels for this disorder. Such a tradition remained in place for the third edition of the *Diagnostic and Statistical Manual* (DSM-III; American Psychiatric Association, 1980), which used attention deficit disorder with or without hyperactivity as its diagnostic terms. This was also evident in DSM-III-R, (APA, 1987), which employed attention-deficit hyperactivity disorder and undifferentiated attention deficit disorder. As will be seen shortly, this same tradition continues to be an integral part of the current diagnostic guidelines.

Given the relatively large number and variety of terms that historically have been applied to what is now known as AD/HD, it is no wonder that confusion about this disorder so often exists. If nothing else, what the history of AD/HD teaches us is that its assessment is a very dynamic, rather than static, process.

CURRENT DIAGNOSTIC CRITERIA

In North America, child health care professionals and educators have traditionally diagnosed AD/HD following the *DSM* guidelines set forth by the American Psychiatric Association (APA). In most other parts of the world, the classification system of the World Health Organization (WHO) has been adopted. Although it is beyond the scope of this text to present a detailed discussion of global thinking on this matter, it remains important for readers to have a better understanding of how the current APA system differs from that used elsewhere. Thus, a brief description of the diagnostic criteria set forth by the WHO will be provided, following a discussion of the current *DSM* guidelines.

DSM-IV

The currently accepted criteria for making an AD/HD diagnosis appear in *DSM-IV* (APA, 1994). At the heart of this decision-making process are two 9-item symptom listings, one pertaining to inattention symptoms, the other to hyperactivity-impulsivity concerns. Included among the inattention symptoms are not listening when spoken to, not finishing assigned work, distractibility, and difficulties organizing tasks. The hyperactive-impulsive list includes six hyperactive symptoms (e.g., fidgeting, difficulties remaining seated, talking excessively) along with three symptoms of impulsivity (e.g., interrupting others, difficulties waiting for turn). Parents and/or teachers must report the presence of at least six of nine problem behaviors from either list to warrant consideration of an AD/HD diagnosis. Such behaviors must have an onset prior to 7 years of age, a duration of at least six months, and a frequency above and beyond that expected of children of the same mental age. Furthermore, they must be evident in two or more settings, have a clear impact on psychosocial functioning, and not be due to other types of mental health or learning disorders that might better explain their presence.

As is evident from these criteria, the manner in which AD/HD presents itself clinically can vary from child to child. For some children with AD/HD, symptoms of inattention may be of relatively greater concern than impulsivity or hyperactivity problems. For others, impulsivity and hyperactivity difficulties may be more prominent. Reflecting these possible differences in clinical presentation, the new *DSM-IV* criteria not only allow for but *require* AD/HD subtyping. For example, when more than six symptoms are present from both lists and all other criteria are met, a diagnosis of AD/HD, combined type is in order. If six or more inattention symptoms are present but fewer than six hyperactive-impulsive symptoms are evident, and all other criteria are met, the proper diagnosis is AD/HD, predominantly inattentive type. Those familiar with prior diagnostic classification schemes will quickly recognize these *DSM-IV* categories as similar, but not exact, counterparts to what previously was known as attention-deficit hyperactivity disorder and undifferentiated attention deficit disorder in *DSM-III-R* (APA, 1987) and attention deficit disorder with or without hyperactivity in *DSM-III* (APA, 1980). Appearing for the first time in *DSM-IV*, however, is the subtyping condition known as AD/HD, predominantly hyperactive-impulsive type, which is the appropriate diagnosis whenever six or more hyperactive-impulsive symptoms arise, fewer than six inattention concerns are evident, and all other criteria are met.

Along with these major subtyping categories, *DSM-IV* also makes available two additional classifications that have primary bearing on adolescents and adults. For example, a diagnosis of AD/HD, in partial remission, may be given to individuals who have clinical problems resulting from AD/HD symptoms that currently do not meet criteria for any of the above subtypes, but nonetheless were part of a documented AD/HD diagnosis at an earlier point in time. In similar cases where an earlier history of AD/HD cannot be established with any degree of certainty, a diagnosis of AD/HD, not otherwise specified, would instead be made.

ICD-10

Although educators and child health care professionals in Europe and in many other parts of the world certainly agree that symptoms of inattention and/or hyperactivity-impulsivity constitute a diagnostic condition, they would not refer to it as AD/HD nor would they follow *DSM-IV* guidelines in deciding whether or not a diagnosis was present. If any diagnosis was to be made at all, it would be hyperkinetic disorder, the criteria for which appear in the tenth edition of the *International Classification of Diseases* (*ICD-10*; World Health Organization [WHO], 1993). Somewhat akin to *DSM-IV*, *ICD-10* uses separate symptom listings, encompassing a total of 18 symptoms. Unlike *DSM-IV*, however, *ICD-10* utilizes a 9-item inattention list, a 5-item hyperactivity list, and a 4-item list of impulsivity symptoms, each of which also differs in the symptom cut-points they employ. For example, at least six inattention symptoms, three hyperactivity symptoms, and one impulsivity symptom must be present before considering a hyperkinetic disorder diagnosis. *ICD-10* further requires that these symptoms (1) have an early childhood onset no later than 7 years of age, (2) have a duration of at least six months, (3) be developmentally deviant, and (4) not be due to pervasive developmental disorder or certain other psychiatric conditions (e.g., mood disorder).

SUMMARY

Although *DSM-IV* and *ICD-10* share many similarities, significant differences exist. Perhaps the most important of these is that *ICD-10* does not allow for any diagnostic subtyping involving the primary features of hyperkinetic disorder. Thus, any comparisons between *DSM-IV* and *ICD-10* must necessarily be limited to a consideration of AD/HD, combined type, and hyperkinetic disorder, respectively. A related concern is that with only one form of hyperkinetic disorder available for consideration, fewer individuals can be expected to receive this type of clinical diagnosis. Another important difference between *ICD-10* and *DSM-IV* is found among their exclusionary criteria. In *ICD-10*, the co-occurring presence of a depressive episode or an anxiety disorder automatically precludes making a diagnosis of hyperkinetic disorder. Although *DSM-IV* recognizes that such conditions can preclude an AD/HD diagnosis, it also allows for the possibility that they might instead be comorbid with AD/HD.

ETIOLOGY

Dating back to Still's (1902) earliest account, there has been a tremendous amount of scientific and public interest in what causes AD/HD. For the most part, biological explanations have dominated discussions of this topic. Less frequently, psychological and psychosocial conceptualizations have been put forth as well. Despite the fact that such efforts have increased our awareness of what might cause AD/HD, the exact manner in which this disorder arises is not well understood. Thus, what we currently know about the etiology of AD/HD lies more in the domain of theoretical speculation than established fact.

BIOLOGICAL EXPLANATIONS

Neurochemistry

Among professionals and laypersons, it is commonly assumed that AD/HD is caused by chemical imbalances in the brain. Although intuitively appealing, the validity of this assumption has not been well established empirically. Relatively few investigations have actually addressed this matter. Among those that have, inconsistent findings have emerged. In some studies, there have been reports of abnormalities in one of the monoaminergic systems, involving either dopamine (Raskin, Shaywitz, Shaywitz, Anderson, & Cohen, 1984) or norepinephrine (Arnsten, Steere, & Hunt, 1996). In others, serotonin deficiencies have been implicated (Halperin et al., 1997).

Due to the variable manner in which AD/HD was defined, it is very likely that the samples in the above studies differed in their clinical presentation. Such differences may provide an explanation for the discrepancies in the neurochemical findings (Halperin et al., 1997). According to one recently proposed model (Pliszka, McCracken, & Maas, 1996), norepinephrine dysregulation might be expected in samples whose primary difficulties are attentional in nature, whereas dopamine deficiencies are predicted for samples in which hyperactivity and impulsivity are prominent. In addition to these subtyping considerations, certain comorbidity differences may come into play. This point was recently emphasized by Halperin and his associates, who detected serotonin abnormalities in an AD/HD sample, but only when co-occurring aggressive features were present (Halperin et al., 1997).

Neuroanatomical Systems

Abnormalities in the structure and function of the brain have also been suspected of causing AD/HD (Zametkin & Rapoport, 1987). Among studies using high-resolution magnetic resonance imaging (MRI) devices, differences in brain structure have emerged, but not in any consistent fashion. There have been reports that children with AD/HD have a smaller corpus callosum than do normal children (Baumgardner et al., 1996), but some investigators have failed to find this anatomical distinction (Castellanos et al., 1996). MRI studies have also raised the possibility that the caudate nucleus and other prefrontostriatal areas may be smaller among children with AD/HD (Castellanos et al., 1996; Hynd et al., 1993). Whether or not these anatomical differences are functionally important has not been adequately addressed. Preliminary findings suggest that they probably are, given that the size of the prefrontostriatal area has been shown to be significantly correlated with performance on a psychological test of behavioral inhibition (Casey et al., 1997).

As for the brain functioning of children with AD/HD, this has been addressed primarily in the context of cerebral blood flow (CBF) and positron emission tomography (PET) studies. Although small in number, CBF investigations have consistently found decreased blood flow in the prefrontal regions of the brain and in the various pathways connecting these regions to the limbic system, including the caudate nucleus (Lou, Henriksen, & Bruhn, 1984; Sieg, Gaffney, Preston, & Hellings, 1995). What makes these findings even more theoretically meaningful is that these deficits were reversed when stimulant medication was administered. In PET scans that have been done with adults, there has been evidence of diminished cerebral glucose metabolism in the prefrontal and cingulate regions, as well as in the caudate and in other subcortical structures (Zametkin et al., 1990). Similar PET results were initially reported for adolescent girls with AD/HD (Ernst et al., 1994; Zametkin et al., 1993), but recent efforts to replicate this finding have not been successful (Ernst, Cohen, Liebenauer, Jons, & Zametkin, 1997). Likewise, PET scan abnormalities have yet to be found among adolescent boys (Zametkin et al., 1993).

Genetics

Assuming for a moment that neurochemical, neuroanatomical, and/or neurophysiological abnormalities exist, it becomes necessary to ask the question: How did these arise? At present, the best answer seems to be that multiple pathways are involved, among which genetic mechanisms very likely play a prominent role.

Findings consistent with a genetic hypothesis have emerged from comparisons between biological and adopted relatives of children with AD/HD (Deutsch, 1987; Morrison & Stewart, 1973). High rates of AD/HD have also been detected among the immediate and extended biological relatives of children with AD/HD (Biederman et al., 1987). Among biological siblings, anywhere from 11% to 32% may have this disorder themselves (Levy, Hay, McStephen, Wood, & Waldman, 1997). An even higher degree of concordance exists for twins, with rates ranging from 29% to 38% for dizygotic pairs and 51% to 82% for monozygotic pairs (Gilger, Pennington, & DeFries, 1992; Levy et al., 1997). Further analyses of these twin data have yielded consistently high heritability estimates, ranging from .64 to .91 (Edelbrock, Rende, Plomin, & Thompson, 1995; Levy et al., 1997). Additional genetic support comes from research that took a somewhat different family perspective, namely, the point of view of the parent. In particular, what such research has shown is that when one parent has AD/HD, there is a 50% chance that at least one of the offspring will also have this condition (Biederman et al., 1995).

Some investigators have speculated that a single gene may account for the expression of this disorder (Faraone et al., 1992). Although single-gene defects have been identified in the studies that have thus far addressed this matter, different locations have been implicated. These include a dopamine transporter gene on Chromosome 5 (Cook et al., 1995), a dopamine D4 receptor gene on Chromosome 11 (LaHoste et al., 1996), and the HLA site on Chromosome 6 (Cardon et al., 1994). Why there would be such discrepancies is presently unclear. Procedural variation once again may account for some of these differences. Alternatively, these differences may be an indication that multiple genes are involved, with different genes or combinations of genes leading to the expression of different AD/HD subtypes.

Prenatal Complications

Another possible mechanism by which the chemistry, structure, and functioning of the brain may be altered is through prenatal complications. Such a possibility stems from a consideration of research findings showing that there is an increased incidence of AD/HD among the offspring of pregnancies complicated by excessive maternal consumption of alcohol and/or nicotine (Streissguth, Bookstein, Sampson, & Barr, 1995), independent of whether or not maternal AD/HD was present (Milberger, Biederman, Faraone, Chen, & Jones, 1996). As was the case for the genetic findings, these prenatal results are highly correlational in nature, which limits any etiological inferences that can be drawn.

Other Biological Factors

There have been reports that damage to certain parts of the brain, such as the prefrontal-limbic areas, can lead to AD/HD (Heilman & Valenstein, 1979). Because less than 5% of the AD/HD population is likely to have a history of this type of problem (Rutter, 1983), brain damage is generally not considered to be a major cause of this disorder. Investigators have also found a relatively higher incidence of AD/HD among children with elevated lead levels (Gittelman & Eskinazi, 1983). Unfortunately, the physiological mechanisms responsible for this association have yet to be identified. Moreover, most children with AD/HD do not have histories of lead poisoning, suggesting that elevated lead levels are at best a minor cause of this disorder. Despite their widespread public appeal, there is also little support for the assertions of Feingold (1975) and others that the ingestion of sugar or other food substances directly causes AD/HD (Wolraich, Wilson, & White, 1995).

PSYCHOLOGICAL CONCEPTUALIZATIONS

Over the years, numerous psychological theories have been put forth to explain the manner in which AD/HD affects psychosocial functioning. Early accounts implicated core deficiencies in the regulation of behavior to situational demands (Routh, 1978), in self-directed instruction (Kendall & Braswell, 1985), and in the self-regulation of arousal to environmental demands (Douglas, 1983). Though differing somewhat, each of these views shared the belief that poor executive functioning was a central problem. Building on what is now known about the biology of AD/HD, more recent theories have taken on a distinctive neuropsychological flavor, emphasizing the impulsivity features of this disorder. Quay (1997), for example, has proposed that AD/HD stems from an impairment in a neurologically based behavioral inhibition system. In an extensive elaboration of this same theme, Barkley (1998) has also contended that a deficit in behavioral inhibition is central to understanding the cognitive, behavioral, and social deficits observed in AD/HD populations. Many others in the field share the view that deficits in behavioral inhibition lie at the core of many AD/HD problems (Schachar, Tannock, & Logan, 1993; Sergeant, 1995).

Psychosocial Conceptualizations

Although a few environmental theories have been proposed to explain AD/HD (Block, 1977; Jacobvitz & Sroufe, 1987; Willis & Lovaas, 1977), there is little empirical justification for claiming that poor parenting, chaotic home environments, or poverty *cause* AD/HD. The results of twin studies in particular have highlighted this limited role, by showing that less than 5% of the variance in AD/HD symptomatology can be accounted for by environmental factors (Levy et al., 1997; Sherman, McGue, & Iacono, 1997; Silberg et al., 1996). When AD/HD is found among children who come from such family circumstances, one might reasonably speculate that the parents of such children may themselves be individuals with childhood and adult histories of AD/HD. If so, this would help to explain why their homes are so chaotic and, at the same time, provide support for a genetic explanation for the child's AD/HD condition. Under this same scenario, the resulting chaos in the home might then be viewed as a factor exacerbating, rather than causing, the child's preexisting, inborn AD/HD condition.

Summary

Several lines of evidence point toward biological factors being involved in the etiology of AD/HD. In particular, research has suggested that abnormalities in brain chemistry, structure, and/or function may play an important role. Multiple pathways presumably lead to these abnormalities. Among these, genetic mechanisms and certain pregnancy complications very likely account for the largest percentage of children who have AD/HD. For some children, AD/HD may be acquired after birth, resulting from head injury, elevated lead levels, and other biological complications.

EPIDEMIOLOGY

According to the *DSM-IV*, the overall prevalence of AD/HD among children—that is, the sum total of all subtyping categories—is 3% to 5% (APA, 1994). Higher global estimates have been reported for community samples, ranging from 7.5% to 21.6% for both parent- and teacher-generated samples (Baumgaertel, Wolraich, & Dietrich, 1995; DuPaul, Anastopoulos, et al., 1998; Gaub & Carlson, 1997). That these would be higher than the 3% to 5% prevalence described in *DSM-IV* is not at all surprising, given that the community rates were derived primarily on the basis of the AD/HD symptom frequency requirement alone. Thus, such estimates very likely represent upper limits on the true prevalence of AD/HD in the general population.

Among clinic samples, the combined type appears to be the most commonly encountered subtype category (Lahey et al., 1994), whereas the inattentive type occurs most often in community samples (DuPaul, Power, et al., 1998). According to teachers, younger children display the combined subtype most often, whereas older children and adolescents are much more likely to be identified with the inattentive classification. Similar findings have emerged from parent ratings of older children and adolescents, but parents are much more likely to identify very young children as having the hyperactive-impulsive subtype (DuPaul, Anastopoulos et al., 1998). Of additional interest is that the overall prevalence of *DSM-IV*-defined AD/HD—that is, the total for all three major subtypes—seems to decline with age. In terms of gender issues, boys outnumber girls across all subtypes, with ratios ranging from 1.3:1 to 3.3:1, depending on the informant and subtype under consideration (APA, 1994). Because mixed results have emerged with respect to the moderating influence of ethnicity, few conclusions can be drawn about this matter. Likewise, not much can be said about the impact of socioeconomic factors, due to the dearth of research on this topic.

DEVELOPMENTAL CONSIDERATIONS

One of the most consistent findings to emerge from the preceding discussion is that age seems to have a significant impact on the prevalence of AD/HD and its major subtypes. This implies that the manner in which AD/HD expresses itself across development is a dynamic rather than static process. To the extent that it is dynamic in nature, it becomes important to know how and when these developmental changes occur.

ONSET

Most of what is known about the onset of AD/HD symptoms comes from research using *DSM-III* and *DSM-III-R* guidelines. In one such study, the mean age of onset for a group of 158 hyperactive children was 3.5 years (Barkley, Edelbrock, & Smallish, 1990). In a similar investigation involving 177 clinic-referred boys, the mean age of onset was 6 years, with hyperactive-impulsive symptoms appearing somewhat earlier than inattentive symptoms (Green, Loeber, & Lahey, 1991). Recognizing that there can be a great deal of variability around group means, McGee, Williams, and Feehan (1992) conducted an individual analysis of their onset data. About a third of their sample had an onset before 3 years of age, which is consistent with prior research (Hartsough & Lambert, 1985). Another third of their sample first showed symptoms prior to 5 or 6 years; the remaining third first displayed their symptoms sometime between 6 and 7 years.

At face value, the above findings suggest that AD/HD symptoms do indeed arise in early childhood, thereby justifying *DSM*'s requirement of an onset prior to 7 years of age. Although long-standing and widely held, such an assumption has recently been challenged by some investigators (Barkley & Biederman, 1997), who contend that existing data are insufficient for rigidly imposing a 7-year cut-point.

COURSE

According to most experts in the field, AD/HD is a chronic condition that persists across the life span (Barkley, 1998; Weiss & Hechtman, 1986). Although this might suggest constancy in its clinical presentation, long-term follow-up studies have consistently shown that no more than 50% to 80% of the children identified as AD/HD will continue to meet diagnostic criteria for this condition as adolescents (Barkley et al., 1990).

To account for this apparent decline in the number of children who carry an AD/HD diagnosis into adolescence, it is first necessary to consider what might be going on at the level of the symptoms themselves. In one of the few longitudinal investigations addressing this matter, Hart and her associates (Hart, Lahey, Loeber, Applegate, & Frick, 1995) annually evaluated a sample of 106 clinic-referred boys with AD/HD over a four-year period. Their results indicated that the frequency of parent- and teacher-reported hyperactive-impulsive symptoms declined with age, especially during late childhood and early adolescence. Although slight age-related reductions in the frequency of inattention symptoms were also detected, these did not reflect any real developmental change. Similar findings have emerged from a recently completed cross-sectional investigation using teacher ratings of a nationwide community sampling of children between 5 and 18 years (DuPaul, Power, et al., 1997). In that study, 11- to 13-year-old children displayed significantly fewer hyperactive-impulsive symptoms as compared to children 5 to 10 years of age. Of additional interest is that 14- to 18-year-olds exhibited significantly fewer hyperactive-impulsive symptoms, relative to children 13 years of age and younger. As was the case in the Hart et al. study, no significant developmental changes were detected in the frequency of inattention symptoms.

Given that children seem to display fewer hyperactive-impulsive symptoms as they get older, it stands to reason that when they are teenagers, they will be less likely to receive either the combined subtype or the hyperactive-impulsive subtype classification. Coupled with the fact that inattention symptoms remain relatively constant over time, it becomes easier to understand why the overall prevalence of AD/HD, encompassing all subtyping classifications, decreases from childhood into adolescence. This may also help to explain why, if a teenager is to receive any AD/HD diagnosis at all, he or she is most likely to be identified with a predominantly inattentive subtype diagnosis, which is consistent with recently reported cross-sectional findings (DuPaul, Anastopoulos, et al., 1997; DuPaul, Power, et al., 1997).

Very little is known about the manner in which AD/HD unfolds from adolescence into adulthood. What evidence is available has suggested that no more than 30% of those who were identified as children or adolescents with AD/HD will continue to meet diagnostic criteria for this condition as adults (Gittelman, Mannuzza, Shenker, & Bonagura, 1985; Mannuzza, Klein, Bessler, Malloy, & La Padula, 1993). Up to 50% of these individuals, however, will continue to exhibit subclinical levels of these symptoms, which interfere with daily functioning (Weiss & Hechtman, 1993).

One additional point bears mentioning. All the aforementioned developmental changes assume that the same *DSM-IV* symptom listing is appropriate for use with individuals of all ages. In point of fact, the content of the *DSM-IV* items was determined largely on the basis of what is known about school-age children with AD/HD, with relatively few modifications being made to accommodate preschoolers, adolescents, or adults. Thus, many of the *DSM-IV* items may not be developmentally appropriate for such individuals. This may mean a lower ceiling for adolescents and adults on the number of possible symptoms that might be endorsed. If so, this would artificially reduce the overall number of symptoms that adolescents or adults report, thereby creating an illusion of a downward developmental trend, when in fact none existed. Additional research is obviously needed to clarify this situation.

Summary

Current findings suggest that most individuals with AD/HD begin to display their symptoms in early childhood, with hyperactive-impulsive difficulties typically preceding inattention. Most often,

such symptoms appear around 3 to 4 years, but they can also surface during infancy or on school entrance. The question of whether or not AD/HD symptoms can have an onset after 7 years of age is a matter now being debated (Barkley & Biederman, 1997).

On reaching late childhood and early adolescence, many children with AD/HD begin to display significantly fewer hyperactive-impulsive symptoms. Some may also show a reduction in their overall level of inattention, but to a much lesser degree. Little is known about the course that AD/HD symptoms follow from adolescence into adulthood. Potentially complicating this situation is that childhood estimates are based on parent and teacher reports, whereas adult estimates stem from self-report.

CLINICAL PRESENTATION

The exact manner in which AD/HD symptoms are expressed can vary a great deal, in large part as a function of the child's age. Another important determinant of AD/HD symptom expression is the nature of the situational demands placed on an individual.

DEVELOPMENTAL CHANGES

Inattention
Some parents retrospectively report that their child's earliest displays of inattention occurred during infancy. Descriptions of such infants typically involve comments such as "He could never entertain himself. Somebody always had to be there keeping him busy." The same is true for many toddlers and preschoolers with AD/HD, some of whom may shift excessively from one activity center to another in day care or preschool settings. Entrance into the early elementary grades typically brings with it a variety of new demands for self-regulation, thereby greatly increasing the number of opportunities in which inattentiveness can occur. For a child with AD/HD, this might mean doing tasks incorrectly because of not listening to teacher instructions, or perhaps finishing only 5 of 10 assigned math problems due to daydreaming or being distracted by the movements of other students in the classroom. At home, many of these

same children might forget to do what they were told, fail to remember where they left their shoes, misplace favorite toys, or lose hats and gloves when playing outside.

As children get older, even greater demands for self-regulation and responsibility arise. During the middle and high school years, many students with AD/HD have a great deal of difficulty remembering to bring books home or to turn in homework assignments. Just finishing such assignments is perhaps the biggest challenge, especially when such tasks are long term in nature and require careful planning and organization. College entrance exams pose additional problems for many teens with AD/HD who can't pay attention long enough to do well or who perform poorly because they lose track of where they are and fill in the wrong circles on the answer sheet. Other problems exhibited by this age group include forgetting to show up for work and getting into automobile accidents as a result of not paying sufficient attention to their driving (Barkley, Guevremont, Anastopoulos, DuPaul, & Shelton, 1993).

Impulsivity

As was the case for inattentiveness, the exact manner in which impulsivity is expressed is subject to developmental influences. When something of interest captures a preschooler's attention, he or she may go after it with little regard for what might be in the way; often, this can lead to injuries from bumping into tables, chairs, or other objects. In elementary school settings, teachers frequently observe children with AD/HD cutting in front of other children in line, beginning tasks before directions are completed, or blurting out inappropriate remarks that lead to the well-deserved reputation of being the class clown. Careless mistakes in schoolwork are of additional concern, often resulting from a preference for speed over accuracy and/or a failure to stop and check work. When at home, elementary school-age children have an especially difficult time refraining from interrupting a parent who is on the phone, making dinner, reading a newspaper, or visiting with company.

By the time they reach the middle school and high school years, many teens with AD/HD have become quite adept at playing the role of class clown. Impulsively talking back to parents,

teachers, friends, and employers is yet another problem likely to surface during the adolescent years. Other ways in which they might not thoroughly think through the consequences of their actions may be seen in terms of various risk-taking behaviors, including sexual indiscretions and reckless experimentation with alcohol or illicit drugs (Mannuzza et al.,1993).

Hyperactivity

Developmental factors also exert a powerful influence over the manner in which hyperactivity symptoms appear. According to one mother, "all hell broke loose" when her infant son learned how to walk, because he was into everything and required constant monitoring. Additional problems with hyperactivity can occur in day care or preschool settings, where young children with AD/HD very often cannot sit in one place for circle time or lie down on a mat for the duration of rest time. Walking in line can pose major challenges for elementary school-age children with AD/HD. So too can remaining seated at the dinner table or at a desk for the duration of a school day. Of all the places where remaining seated is required, the one that perhaps poses the greatest challenge of all is the one that occurs on the bus ride both to and from school. Even when able to remain seated, many children continue to exhibit hyperactivity, albeit in a different form. This might include noisily tapping fingers on a desk, swinging feet to and fro, or rocking a chair back and forth to the point where it tips over, spilling the child onto the floor.

For a variety of reasons, not the least of which is likely to be developmental maturity, most teens with AD/HD do not display as many of these physical features of hyperactivity as do younger children. When such symptoms are present, they typically appear in the form of restless leg movements or finger tapping. Even when there are no obvious signs of motor restlessness, some teens may still experience subjective feelings of restlessness, often described in terms of racing thoughts. Clinical experience also suggests that many teens are more inclined to exhibit verbal rather than physical forms of hyperactivity. Thus, it is not uncommon to hear complaints regarding incessant talking in class and not letting others get in a word edgewise during social conversations.

SITUATIONAL VARIABILITY

Implicit in the preceding discussion is that AD/HD is not an all-or-none phenomenon, either always present or never present. Instead, it is a condition whose primary symptoms show significant fluctuations in response to different situational demands (Zentall, 1985). AD/HD symptoms are much more likely to occur in situations that are highly repetitive, boring, or familiar versus those that are novel or stimulating (Barkley, 1977). Significant AD/HD problems are also much more likely to arise when others place demands or set rules for behavior versus in free-play situations (Luk, 1985). Group settings pose far more problems for children with AD/HD than is the case in one-to-one situations. There is also an increased likelihood for AD/HD symptoms to arise in situations where feedback is dispensed infrequently and/or on a delayed basis (Douglas, 1983).

In view of this tendency for AD/HD symptoms to be subject to situational variability, it should come as no great surprise that children with AD/HD often display tremendous inconsistency in their task performance, in terms of both productivity and accuracy (Douglas, 1972). Although it may be argued that all children display a certain amount of variability in these areas, it is clear from clinical experience and research findings that children with AD/HD exhibit this to a much greater degree. Thus, instead of reflecting laziness, as some might contend, the inconsistent performance of children with AD/HD may represent yet another manifestation of this disorder.

PSYCHOSOCIAL IMPACT AND ASSOCIATED FEATURES

Having AD/HD does not automatically lead to psychosocial difficulties. Having AD/HD does, however, place an individual at higher risk for such problems to occur, not only during childhood but throughout the life span. Unfortunately, most of the research that has examined the psychosocial impact of AD/HD has focused almost exclusively on elementary school-age children. Very little research has been done with preschool or adolescent AD/HD populations; even less exists for AD/HD adults.

Despite these limitations, it is possible to begin the process of discussing the psychosocial impact of AD/HD across development.

EARLY CHILDHOOD

Academic Functioning
Although taking on a more active approach to learning is considered normal at this stage of development, preschoolers with AD/HD take this to an extreme. Research has shown, for example, that they engage in more transitional behavior and are less attentive and cooperative during group activities (Alessandri, 1992; McIntosh & Cole-Love, 1996). They also seem to have greater difficulty with motor control and persistence during tasks requiring working memory (Mariani & Barkley, 1997). Because they often have difficulty sitting still while looking at a book, many preschoolers with AD/HD seem immature and do not perform well in formal preschool or kindergarten settings. For those who do not acquire necessary readiness skills from these early educational experiences, there is an increased risk that more serious academic difficulties will arise in middle childhood.

Family Functioning
For many parents of preschool children with AD/HD, daily self-care activities become a test of wills, because these children often lack the patience to complete such tasks independently and have the activity level and impulsivity necessary for fueling long chases around the house. In response to their preschooler's frequent displays of negative and noncompliant behavior (Campbell, 1995), many parents resort to the use of aversive, coercive, and controlling parenting strategies to keep things in check (Pisterman et.al., 1992). Over time, such battles very likely contribute to the increased parenting stress and marital discord that so often occur among these families (Barkley, Shelton, et al., in press; Shelton et al., 1999).

Social Functioning
Preschoolers with AD/HD also behave more aggressively toward their peers (Campbell, 1990). As a result of such negative interactions, many of these children may encounter peer rejection and therefore

find themselves engaged in solitary play much more often than they might like (Alessandri, 1992).

Middle Childhood

Behavioral Functioning

At this stage of development, children with AD/HD commonly display secondary features of aggression as well as comorbid diagnoses of oppositional-defiant disorder and conduct disorder (Jensen, Martin, & Cantwell, 1997). In clinic-referred samples of children with AD/HD, up to 60% will meet criteria for a secondary diagnosis of oppositional-defiant disorder, with another 25% meeting criteria for conduct disorder (Barkley, 1998). Somewhat lower rates have been noted in community samples, with oppositional-defiant disorder and conduct disorder occurring up to 32% and 12% of the time, respectively (August, Realmuto, MacDonald, Nugent, & Crosby, 1996). Although applicable to the AD/HD population as a whole, these comorbidity rates are clearly subject to the influence of demographics and subtyping considerations. As noted recently by Gaub and Carlson (1997), girls with AD/HD tend to exhibit relatively less aggression than do boys with this same condition. The risk for secondary externalizing problems also seems to be greater when hyperactive-impulsive features are prominent. This was shown recently in a study that found oppositional-defiant disorder in 48% of the children with a combined type AD/HD diagnosis versus 19% of those with a predominantly inattentive subtyping classification (Eiraldi, Power, & Nezee, 1997).

Academic Functioning

Due to their difficulties in sustaining attention (Hooks, Milich, & Lorch, 1994), children with AD/HD often fail to complete assigned tasks. Over time, this failure to produce satisfactory amounts of work takes its toll in terms of limiting practice opportunities, which are essential for learning to occur. Although most children with AD/HD do not show deficits in their storage and recall of simple information (Cahn & Marcotte, 1995), many have significant difficulties when asked to memorize complex information, especially when it requires organization and deliberate rehearsal strategies (Douglas & Benezra, 1990).

Such learning deficits provide a basis for understanding why so many children with AD/HD experience difficulties in school. Depending on the exact definition used, anywhere from 18% to 53% of the population will be academic underachievers, that is, performing academically at a level that is significantly below what one would predict based on a consideration of intelligence (Barkley, 1998; Frick et al., 1991). Although younger children with AD/HD can display significant academic underachievement, many do not because they have not been in school long enough for this type of problem to develop. They may, however, show clear evidence of deficiencies in the *amount* of work they produce, which often serves as a red flag for later academic underachievement (DuPaul & Stoner, 1994). Along with age, subtyping considerations may have an impact on academic achievement, with academic problems occurring more often among children with either a combined or predominantly inattentive classification, versus those with a predominantly hyperactive-impulsive presentation (Gaub & Carlson, 1997).

For some children with AD/HD, there may be additional academic complications in the form of comorbid learning disorders. The reported incidence of such difficulties in the AD/HD population has ranged from 10% to 50%, depending on the type of learning disorder under consideration and the manner in which it is defined (August & Garfinkel, 1990; Barkley, 1998; Frick et al., 1991). Of the various comorbid learning problems that can arise, reading disorders seem to occur most often (August & Garfinkel, 1990). Language-based disabilities have also been found fairly consistently, surfacing most often as pragmatic deficits (i.e., the organization, monitoring, and use of language) rather than as deficits in speech production, semantics, or syntax (Tannock et al., 1990). There have also been reports that children with AD/HD may be at increased risk for central auditory processing disorders (Riccio, Hynd, Cohen, Hall, & Malt, 1994) as well as deficits in their visual-motor functioning (Barkley, 1998).

As a group, children with AD/HD score slightly lower on standardized intelligence tests than do normal controls (McGee, Williams, Moffitt, & Anderson, 1989). Whether these findings represent real differences in intellectual functioning, differences in achievement, or just differences in test-taking behavior is unclear. Relatively more certain is the fact that AD/HD can be found across all levels of intelligence (Barkley, 1998), with slightly higher rates of occurrence (i.e., 9%–18%) reported for children with mental retardation (Epstein, Cullinan, & Polloway, 1986).

Family Functioning

As was true for parents of preschoolers with AD/HD, parents of school-age children with AD/HD may become overly directive and negative in their parenting style (Cunningham & Barkley, 1979). Not being able to control their child's behavior may lead many parents to the conclusion that they are less skilled and less knowledgeable in their parenting roles (Mash & Johnston, 1990). For similar reasons, they may experience considerable stress in their parenting roles, especially when comorbid oppositional-defiant features are present (Anastopoulos, Guevremont, Shelton, & DuPaul, 1992; Johnston, 1996). Of additional clinical concern is that many parents of children with AD/HD become depressed, abuse alcohol, and experience marital difficulties (Cunningham, Benness, & Siegel, 1988; Lahey et al., 1988; Pelham & Lange, 1993). For the most part, it has been assumed that such parental problems were the direct result of raising a child with AD/HD. Recently, however, it has become increasingly more apparent that not all of the blame should fall on the child's shoulders, because many of these same difficulties could potentially stem from the parents themselves having adult AD/HD (Murphy & Barkley, 1996).

Social Functioning

During interactions with peers, many children with AD/HD impulsively jump into conversations, are not able to wait for a turn in a game, or quit play activities prematurely due to boredom (Pelham & Bender, 1982). This inability to control behavior in social situations can at times complicate the process of establishing new friendships (Grenell, Glass, & Katz, 1987). More often than not, however, these inappropriate behaviors serve to alienate existing friends and acquaintances, who in turn respond with social rejection or avoidance (Cunningham & Siegel, 1987). Such problems seem to occur more often among children with a combined type classification versus those with a predominantly inattentive presentation (Lahey, Carlson, & Frick, 1997). Due to the absence of any systematic research in this area, little is known about the manner in which age, gender, and other demographic factors affect the social relations of children with AD/HD.

Emotional Functioning

Children with AD/HD have fewer success opportunities and therefore receive more negative feedback than do most other children. Such circumstances may help to explain, at least in part, why as many as 13% to 51% of the AD/HD child population may have secondary emotional disorders (Jensen et al., 1997). In both clinic-referred and community samples, up to 30% of the children with AD/HD have been found to have a secondary mood disorder, with major depression and dysthymic disorder occurring most often (August et al., 1996; Biederman, Newcorn, & Sprich, 1991). Co-occurring anxiety disorders are common as well, affecting as many as 34% of the AD/HD population (August et al. 1996). There have also been reports, albeit controversial, that up to 11% of children with AD/HD may carry a secondary diagnosis of bipolar disorder (Biederman et al., 1996). As noted by some investigators, such mood and anxiety disorders are not likely to be present when they are the only comorbid diagnoses. Among children with AD/HD who have only one other diagnosis, only 3% were found to have a mood disorder, with another 6% having anxiety problems (August et al., 1996). In contrast, rates of depression and anxiety rose to 30% and 34%, respectively, among children with AD/HD who also had a diagnosis of oppositional-defiant disorder or conduct disorder (August et al., 1996). Thus, the additional presence of a secondary externalizing disorder seems to increase the risk for developing depression or anxiety problems.

ADOLESCENCE

Behavioral Functioning

In comparison with normal teens, adolescents with AD/HD are much more likely to display extreme forms of defiance and noncompliance with rules, often warranting a secondary diagnosis of oppositional defiant disorder (Barkley, Anastopoulos, Guevremont, & Fletcher, 1991). For similar reasons, teens with AD/HD are also more inclined to engage in thefts and to exhibit other features of conduct disorder (Barkley et al., 1991).

Academic Functioning

Many adolescents with AD/HD experience significant difficulties in school. Such difficulties include lower grades on report cards and greater utilization of special education services (Barkley, Guevremont, Anastopoulos, & Fletcher, 1992). Teens with AD/HD are also more likely to repeat a grade, to be suspended from school, to drop out of high school, and to become employed after graduating from high school rather than attend college (Klein & Mannuzza, 1991).

Family Functioning

Adolescents with AD/HD are much more likely to encounter problems in their family relations, in terms of more frequent and more intense interpersonal conflicts with parents (Barkley, Anastopoulos, Guevremont, & Fletcher, 1992). Perhaps as a consequence of such conflicts, parents of these teens are also at greater risk of being psychologically distressed and less satisfied in their marriages, especially when comorbid oppositional-defiant disorder features are present (Barkley et al., 1992).

Social Functioning

The overall social adjustment of adolescents with AD/HD is often impaired (Taylor, Chadwick, Heptinstall, & Danckaerts, 1996). This may be manifested as having fewer friends and engaging in fewer social activities (Barkley et al., 1991). Although some studies have not found higher rates of substance abuse or cigarette smoking (Biederman et al., 1997; Taylor et al., 1996), others have (Barkley et al., 1990; Klein & Mannuzza, 1991). Furthermore, teens with AD/HD have been shown to be at increased risk for becoming involved in automobile accidents and for engaging in various traffic violations, especially speeding (Barkley et al., 1993).

Emotional Functioning

Although teens with AD/HD seldom report higher rates of internalizing problems, ratings completed by their parents and teachers very often point their being at risk for such emotional difficulties (Barkley et al., 1991). This risk is even greater for those adolescents who also have histories of learning difficulties requiring special education assistance (Barkley et al., 1990). Implicit in this latter finding is the possibility that the emotional problems experienced by adolescents with AD/HD are not entirely due to their diminished capacity for

regulating emotions. At least in part, such problems may be the result of a long-standing history of repeated failure and frustration, not only in academics but also in terms of social and family functioning.

SUMMARY

Having AD/HD puts children at risk for a multitude of psychosocial difficulties across the life span. In addition to being affected by its primary symptoms, children with AD/HD are also at increased risk for secondary or comorbid diagnoses, especially other disruptive behavior disorders. Such comorbid conditions increase the overall severity of psychosocial impairment that children with AD/HD experience, thereby making for a less favorable prognosis.

ASSESSMENT

Despite the existence of relatively clear diagnostic guidelines (APA, 1994), establishing an AD/HD diagnosis remains a difficult matter. One factor contributing to this situation is the availability of an enormous number and variety of clinical assessment procedures on the market. Because detailed information about the reliability and validity of such measures is not always readily available, clinicians frequently have little to go on in trying to determine how best to obtain a representative sample of a child's or adolescent's real-life behavior. The special nature of the AD/HD population also presents many other assessment obstacles. An especially important consideration is the degree to which AD/HD symptoms vary as a function of situational demands. Recognizing that this occurs, clinicians must try to obtain information from individuals who observe identified children across different settings. At the very least, this should include input from parents and teachers. When appropriate, other significant caretakers, such as day-care providers, should provide similar input. Another critical factor affecting the evaluation process is the increased likelihood that children with AD/HD will display comorbid conditions. In view of this possibility, clinicians must incorporate assessment methods that address not only primary AD/HD symptoms, but also other aspects of the identified child's psychosocial functioning. Of additional importance is the need to gather assessment data pertaining to parental, marital, and family functioning. Although this type of information may not shed much light on whether or not an AD/HD diagnosis is present, it nevertheless provides a context for understanding how problem behaviors may be maintained. Moreover, such information often serves as a basis for determining how likely it is that parents and other caretakers will implement recommended treatment strategies on behalf of their child.

Implicit in the preceding discussion is that clinical evaluations of AD/HD must be comprehensive and multidimensional in nature, so as to capture its situational variability, its comorbid features, and its impact on home, school, and social functioning (Barkley, 1998). This multimethod assessment approach may include not only the traditional methods of parent and child interviews, but also standardized child behavior rating scales, parent self-report measures, direct behavioral observations of AD/HD symptoms in natural or analogue settings, and clinic-based psychological tests.

INTERVIEWS

Given their flexibility, unstructured and semistructured interviews with parents and children can yield a wealth of information pertaining to a child's psychosocial functioning. They do not, however, allow for accurate normative comparisons, which complicates the process of documenting developmental deviance. An alternative to these traditional approaches is the structured interview. In addition to avoiding the above problems, structured interviews allow for standardized administration across children, which facilitates data collection and research. Among the many procedures of this sort that have been employed in AD/HD research and clinical practice are the Diagnostic Interview Schedule for Children (DISC; Costello, Edelbrock, Kalas, Kessler, & Klaric, 1982) and the Diagnostic Interview for Children and Adolescents (DICA; Herjanic, Brown, & Wheatt, 1975), both of which can now be administered via computer in a format compatible with *DSM-IV*. Though offering many advantages, structured interviews nevertheless possess certain limitations (Edelbrock & Costello, 1984), which may make them cumbersome to employ in typical clinical situations.

BEHAVIOR RATING SCALES

Standardized behavior checklists and rating scales are often an indispensable part of the assessment of children and adolescents with AD/HD. Their convenience, their applicability to multiple informants, their ability to gather information collapsed across long time intervals, and their provision of normative references have led to their widespread application in clinical practice. Among those having documented diagnostic utility with AD/HD as defined by *DSM-IV* are the Behavior Assessment System for Children (Reynolds & Kamphaus, 1992), the recently revised Conners Parent and Teacher Rating Scales (Conners, Sitarenios, Parker, & Epstein, 1998), the Child Behavior Checklist (Achenbach, 1991), and the ADHD Rating Scale IV (DuPaul, Anastopoulos, et al., 1998; DuPaul, Power, et al., 1997). A particular strength of these measures is their provision of norms, which allows for statistical comparison of identified children against normal children of the same age and gender. This, of course, facilitates documentation of the degree to which primary AD/HD symptoms, as well as other symptoms of concern, deviate from developmental expectations.

In view of the relatively high incidence of parenting stress, marital discord, and psychopathology that exists among parents of children with AD/HD, clinicians often must also incorporate parent self-report measures into the assessment process. This may include, but certainly is not limited to, such measures as the Symptom Checklist 90–Revised (SCL 90-R; Derogatis, 1986), the Parenting Stress Index (Abidin, 1983), the Beck Depression Scale (Beck, Rush, Shaw, & Emery, 1979), and the Locke–Wallace Marital Adjustment Scale (Locke & Wallace, 1959).

CLINIC-BASED MEASURES

Laboratory measures of sustained attention and impulsivity are commonly included in AD/HD evaluations. Perhaps the most widely used instrument for assessing these particular AD/HD features is the continuous performance test (CPT). Numerous versions of the CPT exist, including the Conners (Conners, 1994), the Test of Variables of Attention (Greenberg & Waldman, 1993), and the Gordon Diagnostic System (Gordon, 1983). One possible reason for their widespread usage is the degree to which they have been successful in differentiating groups of children with AD/HD from normal controls. Despite such success at a group level, many of these measures produce unacceptably high false negative rates when applied to individual children or adolescents (DuPaul, Anastopoulos, Shelton, Guevremont, & Metevia, 1992; Matier-Sharma, Perachio, Newcorn, Sharma, & Halperin, 1995). Although the exact reasons for this discrepancy are unclear, one possible explanation stems from a consideration of the fact that these procedures are typically administered in clinic settings under relatively novel, one-to-one, high-feedback conditions, which greatly reduces the likelihood of eliciting AD/HD symptomatology.

Direct Observation

Also available are various observational assessment procedures, which more directly assess the behavior problems of children with AD/HD as well as their interactions with others. Among these are systems for observing behavior in classroom settings (Abikoff, Gittelman-Klein, & Klein, 1977; Jacob, O'Leary, & Rosenblad, 1978), systems for examining child behavior in clinic-analogue situations (Roberts, 1987), and systems for assessing the clinic-based interactions between AD/HD children and others (Mash & Barkley, 1987). Many of these coding systems target behaviors reflecting specific AD/HD concerns, such as off-task behavior, fidgeting, and so on. Due to the fact that they attempt to capture behavior under conditions more representative of real-life circumstances, such procedures often are more reliable and valid than clinic-based assessment devices.

Other Procedures

Information about intellectual functioning, level of academic achievement, and learning disabilities status needs to be incorporated into the assessment of children and adolescents suspected of having AD/HD. Due to the fact that school personnel and other professionals very often address such concerns prior to the AD/HD referral, such information usually can be obtained through review of school and medical records. If for some reason

this is not available at the time of the AD/HD work-up, additional testing of this sort must then be conducted.

TREATMENT

Many of the same factors that complicate the assessment process can affect treatment outcome as well. Foremost among these are the cross-situational pervasiveness of primary AD/HD symptoms and the relatively high incidence of co-occurring or comorbid conditions. Such circumstances make it highly unlikely that any singular treatment approach can satisfactorily meet all of the clinical management needs of children with AD/HD. For this reason, clinicians must often employ multiple treatment strategies in combination, each of which addresses a different aspect of the child's psychosocial difficulties.

Among those treatments that have received adequate or, at the very least, preliminary empirical support are pharmacotherapy, parent training/counseling, classroom applications of contingency management techniques, and cognitive-behavioral training (Pelham, Wheeler, & Chronis, 1998). Despite such support, these interventions should not be viewed as curative of AD/HD. Instead, their value lies in their temporary reduction of AD/HD symptom levels and in their reduction of related behavioral or emotional difficulties. When these treatments are removed, AD/HD symptoms very often return to pretreatment levels of deviance. Thus, their effectiveness in improving prognosis presumably rests on their being maintained over long periods of time.

Pharmacotherapy

For many years, clinicians and researchers have employed medications in their management of children with AD/HD. The rationale for doing so rests on the assumption that neurochemical imbalances are involved in the etiology of this disorder. Although the exact neurochemical mechanisms underlying their therapeutic action remain unclear, research has shown that at least two classes of medication, stimulants and antidepressants, can be helpful in reducing AD/HD symptomatology.

Numerous studies have consistently demonstrated that stimulant medications are highly effective in the management of AD/HD symptoms in a large percentage of the children and adolescents who take them (Greenhill, Halperin, & Abikoff, 1999). According to some estimates, as many as 80% to 90% will respond favorably, with a majority of these displaying behavior that is relatively normalized (Rapport, Denney, DuPaul, & Gardner, 1994). Somewhat lower response rates have been reported for preschoolers. In addition to bringing about improvements in primary AD/HD symptomatology, these medications very often can lead to increased child compliance and decreased aggressive behavior (Hinshaw, Henker, & Whalen, 1984). Although certain side effects can arise from their use (e.g., decreased appetite), these tend to be mild in nature, and most children tolerate them without great difficulty, even over extended periods of time (Zeiner, 1995). For reasons such as these, many child health care professionals have incorporated stimulant regimens into their clinical practices.

Historically, Ritalin, Dexedrine, and Cylert have been the most commonly prescribed stimulants. Of these, Ritalin has most often been the medication of choice. In its standard form, Ritalin acts rapidly, producing effects on behavior within 30 to 45 minutes after oral ingestion and peaking in its therapeutic impact within 2 to 4 hours. Its utility in managing behavior, however, typically dissipates within 3 to 7 hours, even though minuscule amounts of the medication may remain in the blood for up to 24 hours. More often than not, it is prescribed in twice-daily doses, but adding a third dose to the daily regimen can be tolerated fairly well by most children. Although many children take this medication exclusively on schooldays, it can also be used on weekends and during school vacations, especially in cases where AD/HD symptoms seriously interfere with home functioning.

A major disadvantage of using Ritalin in its standard form is that it must be administered multiple times over the course of a day. Although a sustained release version has been available for many years, its use has not been adopted widely, primarily due to concerns about its failure to deliver therapeutic benefits for a full 6- to 8-hour duration, as intended. Partially in response to this situation, a new stimulant medication, adderall, was recently put on the market. Preliminary research findings have suggested that adderall delivers therapeutic benefits evenly over the course of its 6- to 8-hour duration (Swanson et al., 1998). An additional advantage to using this medication is that it comes in a variety of doses, thereby allowing physicians the opportunity to tailor medication regimens more precisely to the needs of individual children and adolescents.

Despite their overall utility, stimulants may not be appropriate for some children with AD/HD who nevertheless require a medication component in their overall clinical management. As a way of meeting the needs of such children, child health care professionals have recently turned to the use of tricyclic antidepressants, such as imipramine and Wellbutrin. Most often, these medications are employed in situations where certain side effects (e.g., motor tics), known to be exacerbated by stimulants, are present, or where significant mood disturbances accompany AD/HD symptomatology (Pliszka, 1987). As a rule, antidepressants are given twice daily, usually in the morning and evening. Because they are longer-acting than stimulants, it takes more time to evaluate the therapeutic value of any given dose (Rapoport & Mikkelsen, 1978). Despite this limitation, recent research has suggested that low doses of these medications can produce increased vigilance and decreased impulsivity, as well as reductions in disruptive and aggressive behavior. Mood elevation may also occur, especially in children with significant pretreatment levels of depression or anxiety (Pliszka, 1987). Such treatment effects, however, can diminish over time. Thus, antidepressants frequently are not the medication of choice for long-term management of AD/HD.

PARENT TRAINING

As discussed earlier, AD/HD is now conceptualized as a condition characterized by deficiencies in behavioral inhibition (Barkley, 1997; Quay, 1997). Stated somewhat differently, children with AD/HD have difficulty regulating their behavior in response to situational demands. Such demands include not only the stimulus properties of the settings in which children function, but also the consequences for their behavior. To the extent that these situational parameters can be modified, one might reasonably anticipate corresponding changes in AD/HD symptomatology. Assuming this to be valid provides ample justification for utilizing various behavior therapy techniques in the clinical management of children with AD/HD.

Despite the plethora of research on parent training in behavior modification, very few studies have examined the efficacy of this approach with children specifically identified as having AD/HD. What few studies exist can be interpreted with cautious optimism as supporting the use of behavioral parent training with such children (Anastopoulos, Shelton, DuPaul, & Guevremont, 1993; Pelham et al., 1988; Pisterman, McGrath, Firestone, & Goodman, 1989). Most of these interventions involved training parents in general contingency management tactics, such as positive reinforcement, response cost, and/or time-out strategies. Some, however, combined contingency management training with didactic counseling aimed at increasing parental knowledge and understanding of AD/HD (Anastopoulos et al., 1993). In addition to producing changes in child behavior, parent training interventions have also led to improvements in various aspects of parental and family functioning, including decreased parenting stress and increased parenting self-esteem (Anastopoulos et al., 1993; Pisterman et al., 1989).

CLASSROOM MODIFICATIONS

For reasons similar to the rationale given for parent training, another clinically appropriate method for treating children and adolescents with AD/HD is through classroom modifications. In comparison with the parent training literature, relatively more research has addressed the use of behavior management methods for children with AD/HD in the classroom. Such studies suggest that the contingent use of positive reinforcement alone can produce immediate, short-term improvements in classroom behavior, productivity, and accuracy (DuPaul & Stoner, 1994). For most children with AD/HD, secondary or tangible reinforcers seem to be more effective in improving behavior and academic performance than teacher attention or other types of social reinforcement (Pfiffner, Rosen, & O'Leary, 1985). The combination of positive reinforcement with various punishment strategies, such as response cost, typically leads to even greater improvements in behavior than either alone (Pfiffner & O'Leary, 1987).

Despite the promising nature of such findings, many of these reported treatment gains subside when treatment is withdrawn (Barkley, Copeland, & Sivage, 1980). Of additional concern is that these

improvements in behavior and performance seldom generalize to settings where treatment is not in effect. In response to this situation, researchers recently have directed their attention to the development of interventions that have greater potential for generalization. In an elaboration of the above behavioral themes, Barkley (1998) noted that children with AD/HD usually respond well to daily report card systems, which involve having teachers rate two or three target behaviors multiple times throughout the day, and then having parents convert these ratings into tangible reinforcers. Zentall (1985) has also found benefits to altering the properties of educational stimuli presented to children, such as when written instructions are highlighted with color. Recognizing that it is not always possible to make classroom modifications for only one child, DuPaul and his associates (DuPaul, Ervin, Hook, & McGoey, 1998) recently demonstrated that classwide peer tutoring is an effective, nondisruptive way to bring about academic and behavioral improvements in children with AD/HD.

COGNITIVE-BEHAVIORAL THERAPY

Over the past 20 years, clinicians and researchers have employed a large number and variety of cognitive-behavioral interventions with children manifesting AD/HD symptomatology. Included among these are various self-monitoring, self-reinforcement, and self-instructional techniques. Much of the appeal for their clinical application stems from their apparent focus on some of the primary deficits of AD/HD, including impulsivity, poor organizational skills, and difficulties with rules and instructions. Also contributing to their popularity is their presumed potential for enhancing treatment generalization above and beyond that achieved through more traditional contingency management programs.

Research on self-monitoring has shown that it can improve on-task behavior and academic productivity in some children with AD/HD (Shapiro & Cole, 1994). The combination of self-monitoring and self-reinforcement can also lead to improvements in on-task behavior and academic accuracy, as well as in peer relations (Hinshaw, Henker, & Whalen, 1984). As for self-instructional training, the picture is less clear, with many recent studies (Abikoff & Gittelman, 1985) failing to replicate earlier reported successes (Meichenbaum & Goodman, 1971).

Readily apparent in these recent studies are several potential limitations. For example, to achieve desired treatment effects in the classroom, children with AD/HD must be reinforced for utilizing self-instructional strategies. Hence, contrary to initial expectations, this form of treatment apparently does not free children from control by the social environment. Instead, it seems to shift such external control to a slightly less direct form. Another limitation is that treatment effects seldom generalize to settings where self-instructional training is not in effect or to academic tasks that are not specifically part of the training process (Barkley et al., 1980). In this regard, self-instructional training apparently does not, as had been hoped, circumvent the problem of situation specificity of treatment effects, which has plagued the use of contingency management methods for many years.

COMBINED INTERVENTIONS

What should be evident from the preceding discussion is that singular treatment approaches—whether pharmacological, behavioral, or cognitive-behavioral—are not, by themselves, sufficient to meet all of the clinical management needs of children with AD/HD. In response to this situation, many child health care professionals have recently begun to employ multiple AD/HD treatments in combination.

Despite the intuitive appeal of this clinical practice, there presently exists little empirical justification for utilizing such combinations. Although limited in number, studies generally have shown that regardless of which combination is used, the therapeutic impact of the combined treatment package typically does not exceed that of either treatment alone. This would certainly seem to be the case when stimulant medication therapy is combined with classroom contingency management (Gadow, 1985). Similar findings have emerged from studies examining the use of stimulant regimens in combination with cognitive-behavioral interventions (Hinshaw et al., 1984).

From a somewhat different perspective, there have been attempts to evaluate, retrospectively, the long-term effects of individualized multimodality intervention on AD/HD outcome (Satterfield, Satterfield, & Cantwell, 1980). Such multimodal interventions included medication, parent training, individual counseling, special education, family therapy, and other treatments as needed by the individual. The obtained results suggested that an individualized program of combined treatments, when continued over a period of several years, can produce improvements in the social adjustment of children with AD/HD, in their rates of antisocial behavior, and in their academic achievement. Similar prospective multimodal intervention research is currently nearing completion under the sponsorship of the Child and Adolescent Branch of the National Institutes of Mental Health. Thus, in the not too distant future, additional light will be shed on this matter.

ADJUNCTIVE PROCEDURES

Discussed in the preceding sections were numerous treatment strategies directly targeting the needs of children with AD/HD. Not covered was the manner in which various comorbid features are typically addressed. When certain types of comorbid features, such as aggression, are present, very often they too will diminish in frequency and severity when targeted AD/HD symptoms come under the control of various interventions. This does not always occur, however. Moreover, there are numerous occasions when secondary emotional or behavioral features arise independent of the primary AD/HD diagnosis and therefore are unresponsive to AD/HD interventions. In situations such as these, it becomes necessary to consider the use of adjunctive intervention strategies. For example, individual therapy may be appropriate for children or adolescents to assist them in their adjustment to parental divorce.

Due to the increased incidence of various psychosocial difficulties among the parents of such children, clinicians must sometimes recommend that they too receive therapy services, such as individual or marital counseling. In addition to providing therapeutic benefits for the parents themselves, these adjunctive procedures can produce indirect benefits for their children. For example, when parental distress is reduced, parents very often become better able to implement recommended treatment strategies, such as parent training, on behalf of their child. Although intuitively appealing and sound on the basis of clinical experience, the use of such adjunctive procedures in an AD/HD population has yet to be addressed empirically. Thus, this would seem to be an area fertile for further, clinically meaningful research.

CONCLUSIONS

Although researchers and clinicians have been well aware of AD/HD for nearly 100 years, there is no question that there has been a surge of professional and public interest in this disorder over the past decade. The exact details of what causes AD/HD are not well understood, but there has been a recent convergence of theory and empirical findings, pointing toward a combination of genetic, neurochemical, and other neurobiological factors being involved. Due to the highly variable manner in which epidemiological research has been conducted, the exact prevalence of AD/HD has been difficult to determine, but probably lies in the 3% to 5% range for children and in a somewhat lower range for adolescents and adults, with males outnumbering females by wide margins across the life span. AD/HD symptoms typically arise in early childhood and persist across the life span, with hyperactivity-impulsivity symptoms diminishing somewhat over time. Of additional clinical importance is that AD/HD symptoms can vary a great deal in their presentation, partly as a function of age and various situational demands. At least in clinic-referred populations, AD/HD is often accompanied by secondary behavioral, academic, social, emotional, and family complications, which increase the overall severity of psychosocial impairment and increase the risk for negative outcomes.

Given the complexity of AD/HD in its clinical presentation, multiple assessment procedures are usually necessary for establishing an accurate picture of the disorder and its associated features. Likewise, multiple treatments must be used in combination to bring about optimal therapeutic benefits. Unfortunately, little research has been conducted to date addressing the question of which combinations of treatments should be used for which children. Until such research is conducted, clinicians must rely on their own clinical judgment to guide them in putting together multimodal treatment plans to meet the needs of individual children and their families. When doing so, clinicians should also make every effort to include in their multimodal interventions treatments for which there is at least some modicum of empirical validation. Among the many treatments available for dealing with this disorder, stimulant medication therapy is perhaps the one used most often and most effectively. Although not yet empirically validated, combining stimulant medication therapy with other types of treatments, such as parent training and classroom modifications, is regarded as acceptable and desirable clinical practice.

REFERENCES

Abidin, R.R. (1983). *The Parenting Stress Index.* Charlottesville, VA: Pediatric Psychology Press.

Abikoff, H., & Gittelman, R. (1985) Hyperactive children treated with stimulants: Is cognitive training a useful adjunct? *Archives of General Psychiatry, 42,* 953–961.

Abikoff, H., Gittelman-Klein, R., & Klein, D. (1977). Validation of a classroom observation code for hyperactive children. *Journal of Consulting and Clinical Psychology, 45,* 772–783.

Achenbach, T.M. (1991). *Manual for the Child Behavior Checklist/4–18 and 1991 profile.* Burlington: University of Vermont, Department of Psychiatry.

Alessandri, S.M. (1992). Attention, play, and social behavior in ADHD preschoolers. *Journal of Abnormal Child Psychology, 20,* 289–302.

American Psychiatric Association. (1968). *Diagnostic and statistical manual of mental disorders* (2nd ed.). Washington, DC: Author.

American Psychiatric Association. (1980). *Diagnostic and statistical manual of mental disorders* (3rd ed.). Washington, DC: Author.

American Psychiatric Association. (1987). *Diagnostic and statistical manual of mental disorders* (3rd ed., rev.). Washington, DC: Author.

American Psychiatric Association. (1994). *Diagnostic and statistical manual of mental disorders* (4th ed.). Washington, DC: Author.

Anastopoulos, A.D., Guevremont, D.C., Shelton, T.L., & DuPaul, G.J. (1992). Parenting stress among families of children with attention deficit hyperactivity disorder. *Journal of Abnormal Child Psychology, 20,* 503–520.

Anastopoulos, A.D., Shelton, T., DuPaul, G.J., & Guevremont, D.C. (1993). Parent training for attention deficit hyperactivity disorder: Its impact on parent functioning. *Journal of Abnormal Child Psychology, 21,* 581–596.

Arnsten, A.F.T., Steere, J.C., & Hunt, R.D. (1996). The contribution of alpha2 noradrenergic mechanism to prefrontal cortical cognitive function. *Archives of General Psychiatry, 53,* 448–455.

August, G.J., & Garfinkel, G.D. (1990). Comorbidity of ADHD and reading disability among clinic-referred children. *Journal of Abnormal Child Psychology, 18,* 29–45.

August, G.J., Realmuto, G.M., MacDonald, A.W., Nugent, S.M., & Crosby, R. (1996). Prevalence of ADHD and comorbid disorders among elementary school children screened for disruptive behavior. *Journal of Abnormal Child Psychology, 24,* 571–595.

Barkley, R.A. (1977). The effects of methylphenidate on various measures of activity level and attention in hyperkinetic children. *Journal of Abnormal Child Psychology, 5,* 351–369.

Barkley, R.A. (1997). *ADHD and the nature of self-control.* New York: Guilford Press.

Barkley, R.A. (1998). *Attention deficit hyperactivity disorder: A handbook for diagnosis and treatment* (2nd ed.). New York: Guilford Press.

Barkley, R.A., Anastopoulos, A.D., Guevremont, D.C., & Fletcher, K.E. (1991). Adolescents with AD/HD: Patterns of behavioral adjustment, academic functioning, and treatment utilization. *Journal of the American Academy of Child and Adolescent Psychiatry, 30,* 752–761.

Barkley, R.A., Anastopoulos, A.D., Guevremont, D.C., & Fletcher, K.E. (1992). Adolescents with attention deficit hyperactivity disorder: Mother-adolescent interactions, family beliefs and conflicts, and maternal psychopathology. *Journal of Abnormal Child Psychology, 20,* 263–288.

Barkley, R.A., & Biederman, J. (1997). Towards a broader definition of the age of onset criterion for attention deficit hyperactivity disorder. *Journal of the American Academy of Child and Adolescent Psychiatry, 36,* 1204–1210.

Barkley, R.A., Copeland, A.P., & Sivage, C. (1980). A self-control classroom for hyperactive children. *Journal of Autism and Developmental Disorders, 10,* 75–89.

Barkley, R.A., Fischer, M., Edelbrock, C.S., & Smallish, L. (1990). The adolescent outcome of hyperactive children diagnosed by research criteria: I. An 8 year prospective follow-up study. *Journal of the American Academy of Child and Adolescent Psychiatry, 29,* 546–557.

Barkley, R.A., Guevremont, D.C., Anastopoulos, A.D., DuPaul, G.D., & Shelton, T.L. (1993). Driving-related risks and outcomes of attention deficit hyperactivity disorder in adolescents and young adults: A 3- to 5-year follow-up survey. *Pediatrics, 92,* 212–218.

Barkley, R.A., Guevremont, D.C., Anastopoulos, A.D., & Fletcher, K.E. (1992). A comparison of three family therapy programs for treating family conflicts in adolescents with attention deficit hyperactivity disorder. *Journal of Consulting and Clinical Psychology, 60,* 450–462.

Barkley, R.A., Shelton, T.L., Crosswait, C.R., Moorehouse, M., Fletcher, K., Barrett, S., Jenkins, L., & Metevia, L. (in press). Multi-method psycho-educational intervention for preschool children with aggressive and hyperactive-impulsive behavior. *Child Psychology and Psychiatry.*

Baumgaertel, A., Wolraich, M.L., & Dietrich, M. (1995). Attention deficit disorders in a German elementary school-aged sample. *Journal of the American Academy of Child and Adolescent Psychiatry, 34,* 629–638.

Baumgardner, T.L., Singer, H.S., Denckla, M.B., Rubin, M.A., Abrams, M.T., Colli, M.J., & Reiss, A.L. (1996). Corpus callosum morphology in children with Tourette syndrome and attention deficit hyperactivity disorder. *Neurology, 47,* 477–482.

Beck, A.T., Rush, A.J., Shaw, B.F., & Emery, G. (1979). *Cognitive therapy for depression.* New York: Guilford Press.

Biederman, J., Faraone, S.V., Mick, E., Spencer, T., Wilens, T., Kiely, K., Guite, J., Ablon, J.S., Reed, E., & Warburton, R. (1995). High risk for attention deficit hyperactivity disorder among children of parents with childhood onset of the disorder: A pilot study. *American Journal of Psychiatry, 152,* 431–435.

Biederman, J., Faraone, S.V., Milberger, S., Curtis, S., Chen, L., Marrs, A., Duellette, C., Moore, P., & Spencer, T. (1996). Predictors of persistence and remission of ADHD into adolescence: Results from a four-year prospective follow-up study. *Journal of the American Academy of Child and Adolescent Psychiatry, 35,* 343–351.

Biederman, J., Munir, K., Knee, D., Armentano, M., Autor, S., Waternaux, C., & Tsuang, M. (1987). High rate of affective disorders in probands with attention deficit disorders and in their relatives: A controlled family study. *American Journal of Psychiatry, 144,* 330–333.

Biederman, J., Newcorn, J., & Sprich, S. (1991). Comorbidity of attention deficit hyperactivity disorder with conduct, depressive, anxiety, and other disorders. *American Journal of Psychiatry, 152,* 1652–1658.

Biederman, J., Wilens, T.E., Mick, E., Faraone, S.V., Weber, W., Curtis, S., Thornell, A., Pfister, K., Jetton, J.G., & Soriano, J. (1997). Is ADHD a risk for psychoactive substance use disorders? Findings from a four-year prospective follow-up study. *Journal of the American Academy of Child and Adolescent Psychiatry, 36,* 21–29.

Block, G.H. (1977). Hyperactivity: A cultural perspective. *Journal of Learning Disabilities, 110,* 236–240.

Cahn, D.A., & Marcotte, A.C. (1995). Rates of forgetting in attention deficit hyperactivity disorder. *Child Neuropsychology, 1,* 158–163.

Campbell, S.B. (1990). *Behavior problems in preschoolers: Clinical and developmental issues.* New York: Guilford Press.

Campbell, S.B. (1995). Behavior problems in preschool children: A review of recent research. *Journal of Child Psychology and Psychiatry, 36,* 113–149.

Cardon, L.R., Smith, S.D., Fulker, D.W., Kimberling, W.J., Pennington, B.F., & DeFries, J.C. (1994). Quantitative trait locus for reading disability in chromosome 6. *Science, 266*, 276–279.

Casey, B.J., Castellanos, F.X., Giedd, J.N., Marsh, W.L., Hamburger, S.D., Schubert, A.B., Vauss, Y.C., Vaituzis, A.C., Dickstein, D.P., Sarfatti, S.E., & Rapoport, J.L. (1997). Implication of right frontostriatial circuitry in response inhibition and attention-deficit/hyperactivity disorder. *Journal of the American Academic of Child and Adolescent Psychiatry, 36*, 374–383.

Castellanos, F.X., Giedd, J.N., Marsh, W.L., Hamburger, S.D., Vaituzis, A.C., Dickstein, D.P., Sarfatti, S.E., Vauss, Y.C., Snell, J.W., Lange, N., Kaysen, D., Krain, A.L., Ritchhie, G.F., Rajapakse, J.C., & Rapoport, J.L. (1996). Quantitative brain magnetic resonance imaging in attention-deficit hyperactivity disorder. *Archives of General Psychiatry, 53*, 607–616.

Chess, S. (1960). Diagnosis and treatment of the hyperactive child. *New York State Journal of Medicine, 60*, 2379–2385.

Clements, S.D., & Peters, J.E. (1962). Minimal brain dysfunctions in the school age child. *Archives of General Psychiatry, 6*, 185–197.

Conners, C.K. (1994). *The continuous performance test (CPT): Use as a diagnostic tool and measure of treatment outcome.* Paper presented at the annual meeting of the American Psychological Association, Los Angeles.

Conners, C.K., Sitarenios, G., Parker, J.D., & Epstein, J.N. (1998). Revision and restandardization of the Conners Teacher Rating Scale (CTRS-R): Factor structure, reliability, and criterion validity. *Journal of Abnormal Child Psychology, 26*, 279–291.

Cook, F.H., Stein, M.A., Krasowski, M.D., Cox, N.J., Olkon, D.M., Kieffer, J.E., & Leventhal, B.L. (1995). Association of attention deficit disorder and the dopamine transporter gene. *American Journal of Human Genetics, 56*, 993–998.

Costello, A., Edelbrock, C., Kalas, R., Kessler, M., & Klaric, S. (1982). *The NIMH Diagnostic Interview Schedule for Children (DISC).* Pittsburgh, PA: Author.

Cunningham, C.E., & Barkley, R.A. (1979). The interactions of hyperactive and normal children with their mothers during free play and structured task. *Child Development, 50*, 217–224.

Cunningham, C.E., Benness, B.B., & Siegel, L.S. (1988). Family functioning, time allocation, and parental depression in the families of normal and ADDH children. *Journal of Clinical Child Psychology, 17*, 169–177.

Cunningham, C.E., & Siegel, L.S. (1987). Peer interactions of normal and attention-deficit disordered boys during free-play, cooperative task, and simulated classroom situations. *Journal of Abnormal Child Psychology, 15*, 247–268.

Derogatis, L. (1986). *Manual for the Symptom Checklist 90 Revised (SCL-90R).* Baltimore: Author.

Deutsch, K. (1987). *Genetic factors in attention deficit disorders.* Paper presented at symposium on Disorders of Brain and Development and Cognition, Boston.

Douglas, V.I. (1972). Stop, look, and listen: The problem of sustained attention and impulse control in hyperactive and normal children. *Canadian Journal of Behavioural Science, 4*, 259–282.

Douglas, V.I. (1983). Attention and cognitive problems. In M. Rutter (Ed.), *Developmental neuropsychiatry.* New York: Guilford Press.

Douglas, V.I., & Benezra, E. (1990). Supraspan verbal memory in attention deficit disorder with hyperactivity, normal, and reading disabled boys. *Journal of Abnormal Child Psychology, 18*, 617–638.

DuPaul, G.J., Anastopoulos, A.D., Power, T.J., Reid, R., Ikeda, M.J., & McGoey, K.E. (1998). Parent ratings of attention-deficit/hyperactivity disorder symptoms: Factor structure and normative data. *Journal of Psychopathology and Behavioral Assessment, 20*, 83–102.

DuPaul, G.J., Anastopoulos, A.D., Shelton, T.L., Guevremont, D.C., & Metevia, L. (1992). Multi-method assessment of ADHD: The diagnostic utility of clinic based tests. *Journal of Clinical Child Psychology, 21*, 394–402.

DuPaul, G.J., Ervin, R.A., Hook, C.L., & McGoey, K.E. (1998). Peer tutoring for children with attention deficit hyperactivity disorder: Effects on classroom behavior and academic performance. *Journal of Applied Behavior Analysis, 31*, 579–592.

DuPaul, G.J., Power, T.J., Anastopoulos, A.D., Reid, R., McGoey, K.E., & Ikeda, M.J. (1997). Teacher ratings of attention-deficit/hyperactivity disorder symptoms: Factor structure and normative data. *Psychological Assessment, 9*, 436–444.

DuPaul, G.J., & Stoner, G. (1994). *ADHD in the schools: Assessment and intervention strategies.* New York: Guilford Press.

Edelbrock, C., & Costello, A. (1984). Structured psychiatric interviews for children and adolescents. In G. Goldstein & M. Hersen (Eds.), *Handbook of psychological assessment* (pp. 276–290). New York: Pergamon Press.

Edelbrock, C.S., Rende, R., Plomin, R., & Thompson, L. (1995). A twin study of competence and problem behavior in childhood and early adolescence. *Journal of Child Psychology and Psychiatry, 36*, 775–786.

Eiraldi, R.B., Power, T.J., & Nezee, C.M. (1997). Patterns of comorbidity associated with subtypes of attention-deficit/hyperactivity disorder among 6- to 12-year-old children. *Journal of the American Academy of Child and Adolescent Psychiatry, 36*, 503–514.

Epstein, M.H., Cullinan, D., & Polloway, E.A. (1986). Patterns of maladjustment among mentally retarded children and youth. *American Journal of Mental Deficiency, 91,* 127–134.

Ernst, M., Cohen, R.M., Liebenauer, L.L., Jons, P.H., & Zametkin, A.J. (1997). Cerebral glucose metabolism in adolescent girls with attention-deficit/hyperactivity disorder. *Journal of the American Academy of Child and Adolescent Psychiatry, 36,* 1399–1406.

Ernst, M., Liebenauer, L.L., King, A.C., Fitzgerald, G.A., Cohen, R.M., & Zametkin, A.J. (1994). Reduced brain metabolism in hyperactive girls. *Journal of the American Academy of Child and Adolescent Psychiatry, 33,* 858–868.

Faraone, S.V., Biederman, J., Chen, W.J., Krifcher, B., Keenan, K., Moore, C., Sprich, S., & Tsuang, M.T. (1992). Segregation analysis of attention deficit hyperactivity disorder. *Psychiatric Genetics, 2,* 257–275.

Feingold, B. (1975). *Why your child is hyperactive.* New York: Random House.

Frick, P.J., Kamphaus, R.W., Lahey, B.B., Loeber, R., Christ, M.A.G., Hart, E.L., & Tannenbaum, L.E. (1991). Academic underachievement and the disruptive behavior disorders. *Journal of Consulting and Clinical Psychology, 59,* 289–294.

Gadow, K.D. (1985). Relative efficacy of pharmacological, behavioral, and combination treatments for enhancing academic performance. *Clinical Psychology Review, 5,* 513–533.

Gaub, M., & Carlson, C.L. (1997). Gender differences in ADHD: A meta-analysis and critical review. *Journal of the American Academy of Child and Adolescent Psychiatry, 36,* 1036–1045.

Gilger, J.W., Pennington, B.F., & DeFries, J.C. (1992). A twin study of the etiology of comorbidity: Attention-deficit hyperactivity disorder and dyslexia. *Journal of the American Academy of Child and Adolescent Psychiatry, 31,* 343–348.

Gittelman, R., & Eskinazi, B. (1983). Lead and hyperactivity revisited. *Archives of General Psychiatry, 40,* 827–833.

Gittelman, R., Mannuzza, S., Shenker, R., & Bonagura, N. (1985). Hyperactive boys almost grown up: I. Psychiatric status. *Archives of General Psychiatry, 42,* 937–947.

Gordon, M. (1983). *The Gordon Diagnostic System.* Boulder, CO: Clinical Diagnostic Systems.

Green, S.M., Loeber, R., & Lahey, B.B. (1991). Stability of mothers' recall of the age of onset of their child's attention and hyperactivity problems. *Journal of the American Academy of Child and Adolescent Psychiatry, 30,* 131–137.

Greenberg, L.M., & Waldman, I.D. (1993). Developmental normative data on the Test of Variables of Attention (TOVA). *Journal of Child Psychology and Psychiatry and Allied Disciplines, 34,* 1019–1030.

Greenhill, L.L., Halperin, J.M., & Abikoff, H. (1999). Stimulant medications. *Journal of the American Academy of Child and Adolescent Psychiatry, 38,* 503–512.

Grenell, M.M., Glass, C.R., & Katz, K.S. (1987). Hyperactive children and peer interaction: Knowledge and performance of social skills. *Journal of Abnormal Child Psychology, 15,* 1–13.

Halperin, J.M., Newcorn, J.H., Kopstein, I., McKay, K.E., Schwartz, S.T., Siever, L.J., & Sharma, V. (1997). Serotonin, aggression, and parental psychopathology in children with attention-deficit hyperactivity disorder. *Journal of the American Academy of Child and Adolescent Psychiatry, 36,* 1391–1398.

Hart, E.L., Lahey, B.B., Loeber, R., Applegate, B., & Frick, P.J. (1995). Developmental changes in attention-deficit hyperactivity disorder in boys: A four-year longitudinal study. *Journal of Abnormal Child Psychology, 23,* 729–750.

Hartsough, C.S., & Lambert, N.M. (1985). Medical factors in hyperactive and normal children: Prenatal, developmental, and health history findings. *American Journal of Orthopsychiatry, 55,* 190–201.

Heilman, K.M., & Valenstein, E. (1979). *Clinical neuropsychology.* New York: Oxford University Press.

Herjanic, B., Brown, F., & Wheatt, T. (1975). Are children reliable reporters? *Journal of Abnormal Child Psychology, 3,* 41–48.

Hinshaw, S.P., Henker, B., & Whalen, C.K. (1984). Self-control in hyperactive boys in anger-inducing situations: Effects of cognitive-behavioral training and of methylphenidate. *Journal of Abnormal Child Psychology, 12,* 55–77.

Hohman, L.B. (1922). Post-encephalitic behavior disorders in children. *Johns Hopkins Hospital Bulletin, 33,* 372–375.

Hooks, K., Milich, R., & Lorch, E.P. (1994). Sustained and selective attention in boys with attention deficit hyperactivity disorder. *Journal of Clinical Child Psychology, 23,* 69–77.

Hynd, G.W., Hern, K.L., Novey, E.S., Eliopulos, D., Marshall, R., Gonzalez, J.J., & Voeller, K.K. (1993). Attention-deficit hyperactivity disorder and asymmetry of the caudate nucleus. *Journal of Child Neurology, 8,* 339–347.

Jacob, R.G., O'Leary, K.D., & Rosenblad, C. (1978). Formal and informal classroom settings: Effects on hyperactivity. *Journal of Abnormal Child Psychology, 6,* 47–59.

Jacobvitz, D., & Sroufe, L.A. (1987). The early caregiver-child relationship and attention-deficit disorder with hyperactivity in kindergarten: A prospective study. *Child Development, 58,* 1488–1495.

Jensen, P.S., Martin, D., & Cantwell, D.P. (1997). Comorbidity of ADHD: Implications for research, practice, and *DSM-V. Journal of the American Academy of Child and Adolescent Psychiatry, 36,* 1065–1079.

Johnston, C. (1996). Parent characteristics and parent-child interactions in families of nonproblem children and ADHD children with higher and lower levels of oppositional-defiant behavior. *Journal of Abnormal Child Psychology, 24,* 85–104.

Kahn, E., & Cohen, L.H. (1934). Organic driveness: A brain stem syndrome and an experience. *New England Journal of Medicine, 210,* 748–756.

Kendall, P.C., & Braswell, L. (1985). *Cognitive-behavioral therapy for impulsive children.* New York: Guilford Press.

Klein, R.G., & Mannuzza, S. (1991). Long-term outcome of hyperactive children: A review. *Journal of American Academy of Child and Adolescent Psychiatry, 30,* 383–387.

Lahey, B.B., Applegate, B., McBurnett, K., Biederman, J., Greenhill, L., Hynd, G.W., Barkley, R.A., Newcorn, J., Jensen, P., Richters, J., Garfinkel, B., Kerdyk, L., Frick, P.J., Ollendick, T., Perez, D., Hart, E.L., Waldman, I., & Shaffer, D. (1994). *DSM-IV* field trials for attention deficit/hyperactivity disorder in children and adolescents. *American Journal of Psychiatry, 151,* 1673–1685.

Lahey, B.B., Carlson, C.L., & Frick, P.J. (1997). Attention deficit disorder without hyperactivity: A review of research relevant to *DSM-IV.* In T.A. Wideger, A.J. Frances, H.A. Pincus, et al. (Eds.), *DSM-IV sourcebook* (Vol. 3, pp. 189–209). Washington, DC: American Psychiatric Association.

Lahey, B.B., Pelham, W.E., Schaughency, E.A., Atkins, M.S., Murphy, H.A., Hynd, G.W., Russo, M., Hartdagen, S., & Lorys-Vernon, A. (1988). Dimensions and types of attention deficit disorder with hyperactivity in children: A factor and cluster-analytic approach. *Journal of the American Academy of Child and Adolescent Psychiatry, 27,* 330–335.

LaHoste, G.J., Swanson, J.M., Wigal, S.B., Glabe, C., Wigal, T., King, N., & Kennedy, J.L. (1996). Dopamine D4 receptor gene polymorphism is associated with attention deficit hyperactivity disorder. *Molecular Psychiatry, 1,* 121–124.

Levin, P.M. (1938). Restlessness in children. *Archives of Neurology and Psychiatry, 39,* 764–770.

Levy, F., Hay, D.A., McStephen, M., Wood, C., & Waldman, I. (1997). Attention-deficit hyperactivity disorder: A category or a continuum? Genetic analysis of a large-scale twin study. *Journal of the American Academy of Child and Adolescent Psychiatry, 36,* 737–744.

Locke, H.J., & Wallace, K.M. (1959). Short marital adjustment and prediction tests: Their reliability and validity. *Journal of Marriage and Family Living, 21,* 251–255.

Lou, H.C., Henriksen, L., & Bruhn, P. (1984). Focal cerebral hypoperfusion in children with dysphasia and/or attention deficit disorder. *Archives of Neurology, 41,* 825–829.

Luk, S. (1985). Direct observation studies of hyperactive behaviors. *Journal of the American Academy of Child Psychiatry, 24,* 338–344.

Mannuzza, S., Klein, R.G., Bessler, A., Malloy, P., & LaPadula, M. (1993). Adult outcome of hyperactive boys: Educational achievement, occupational rank, and psychiatric status. *Archives of General Psychiatry, 45,* 13–18.

Mariani, M., & Barkley, R.A. (1997). Neuropsychological and academic functioning in preschool children with attention deficit hyperactivity disorder. *Developmental Neuropsychology, 13,* 111–129.

Mash, E.J., & Barkley, R.A. (1987). Assessment of family interaction with the response class matrix. In R. Prinz (Ed.), *Advances in behavioral assessment of children and families* (Vol. 2, pp. 29–67). Greenwich, CT: JAI Press.

Mash, E.J., & Johnston, C. (1990). Determinants of parenting stress: Illustrations from families of hyperactive children and families of physically abused children. *Journal of Clinical Child Psychology, 19,* 313–328.

Matier-Sharma, K., Perachio, N., Newcorn, J.H., Sharma, V., & Halperin, J.M. (1995). Differential diagnosis of ADHD: Are objective measures of attention, impulsivity, and activity level helpful? *Child Neuropsychology, 1,* 118–127.

McGee, R., Williams, S., & Feehan, M. (1992). Attention deficit disorder and age of onset of problem behaviors. *Journal of Abnormal Child Psychology, 20,* 487–502.

McGee, R., Williams, S., Moffitt, T., & Anderson, J. (1989). A comparison of 13-year-old boys with attention deficit and or reading disorder on neuropsychological measures. *Journal of Abnormal Child Psychology, 17,* 37–53.

McIntosh, D.E., & Cole-Love, A.S. (1996). Profile comparisons between ADHD and non-ADHD children on the Temperament Assessment Battery for Children. *Journal of Psychoeducational Assessment, 14,* 362–372.

Meichenbaum, D., & Goodman, J. (1971). Training impulsive children to talk to themselves: A means of developing self-control. *Journal of Abnormal Psychology, 77,* 115–126.

Milberger, S., Biederman, J., Faraone, S.V., Chen, L., & Jones, J. (1996). Is maternal smoking during pregnancy a risk factor of attention deficit hyperactivity disorder in children? *American Journal of Psychiatry, 153,* 1138–1142.

Morrison, J., & Stewart, M. (1973). The psychiatric status of the legal families of adopted hyperactive children. *Archives of General Psychiatry, 28,* 888–891.

Murphy, K., & Barkley, R.A. (1996). Prevalence of *DSM-IV* symptoms of ADHD in adult licensed drivers: Implication for clinical diagnosis. *Journal of Attention Disorders, 1,* 147–161.

Pelham, W.E., & Bender, M.E. (1982). Relationships in hyperactive children: Description and treatment. *Advances in Learning and Behavioral Disabilities, 1,* 365–436.

Pelham, W.E., & Lang, A.R. (1993). Parental alcohol consumption and deviant child behavior: Laboratory studies of reciprocal effects. *Clinical Psychology Review, 13*, 763–784.

Pelham, W.E., Schnedler, R.W., Bender, M.E., Nilsson, D.E., Miller, J., Budrow, M.S., Ronnel, M., Paluchowski, C., & Marks, D.A. (1988). The combination of behavior therapy and methylphenidate in the treatment of attention deficit disorders: A therapy outcome study. In L. Bloomingdale (Ed.), *Attention deficit disorders* (Vol. 3). New York: Spectrum.

Pelham, W.E., Wheeler, T., & Chronis, A. (1998). Empirically supported psychosocial treatments for attention deficit hyperactivity disorder. *Journal of Clinical Child Psychology, 27*, 190–205.

Pfiffner, L.J., & O'Leary, S.G. (1987). The efficacy of all-positive management as a function of the prior use of negative consequences. *Journal of Applied Behavior Analysis, 20*, 265–271.

Pfiffner, L.J., Rosen, L.A., & O'Leary, S.G. (1985). The efficacy of an all-positive approach to classroom management. *Journal of Applied Behavior Analysis, 18*, 257–261.

Pisterman, S., Firestone, P., McGrath, P., Goodman, J., Webster, I., & Mallory, R. (1992). The role of parent training in the treatment of preschoolers with attention deficit disorder with hyperactivity. *American Journal of Orthopsychiatry, 62*, 397–408.

Pisterman, S., McGrath, P., Firestone, P., & Goodman, J.T. (1989). Outcome of parent-mediated treatment of preschoolers with attention deficit disorder with hyperactivity. *Journal of Consulting and Clinical Psychology, 57*, 636–643.

Pliszka, S.R. (1987). Tricyclic antidepressants in the treatment of children with attention deficit disorder. *Journal of the American Academy of Child and Adolescent Psychiatry, 26*, 127–132.

Pliszka, S.R., McCracken, J.T., & Maas, J.W. (1996). Catecholamines in attention-deficit hyperactivity disorder: Current perspectives. *Journal of the American Academy of Child and Adolescent Psychiatry, 35*, 264–272.

Quay, H.C. (1997). Inhibition and attention deficit hyperactivity disorder. *Journal of Abnormal Child Psychology, 25*, 7–13.

Rapoport, J., & Mikkelsen, E. (1978). Antidepressants. In J. Werry (Ed.), *Pediatric psychopharmacology* (pp. 208–233). New York: Brunner/Mazel.

Rapport, M.D., Denney, C., DuPaul, G.J., & Gardner, M.J. (1994). Attention deficit disorder and methylphenidate: Normalization rates, clinical effectiveness, and response prediction in 76 children. *Journal of the American Academy of Child and Adolescent Psychiatry, 33*, 882–893.

Raskin, L.A., Shaywitz, S.E., Shaywitz, B.A., Anderson, G.M., & Cohen, D.J. (1984). Neurochemical correlates of attention deficit disorder. *Pediatric Clinics of North America, 31*, 387–396.

Reynolds, C.R., & Kamphaus, R.W. (1992). *BASC: Behavior Assessment System for Children manual.* Circle Pines, MN: American Guidance Service.

Riccio, C.A., Hynd, G.W., Cohen, M.J., Hall, J., & Molt, L. (1994). Comorbidity of central auditory processing disorder and attention-deficit hyperactivity disorder. *Journal of the American Academy of Child and Adolescent Psychiatry, 33*, 849–857.

Roberts, M.A. (1987). How is playroom behavior observation used in the diagnosis of attention deficit disorder? In J. Loney (Ed.), *The young hyperactive child: Answers to questions about diagnosis, prognosis, and treatment* (pp. 65–74). New York: Haworth Press.

Routh, D.K. (1978). Hyperactivity. In P. Magrab (Ed.), *Psychological management of pediatric problems* (pp. 3–48). Baltimore: University Park Press.

Rutter, M. (1983). Introduction: Concepts of brain dysfunction syndromes. In M. Rutter (Ed.), *Developmental neuropsychiatry* (pp. 1–14). New York: Guilford Press.

Satterfield, J.H., Satterfield, B.T., & Cantwell, D.P. (1980). Three-year multimodality treatment study of 100 hyperactive boys. *Journal of Pediatrics, 98*, 650–655.

Schachar, R.J., Tannock, R., & Logan, G. (1993). Deficient inhibitory control in attention deficit hyperactivity disorder. *Journal of Abnormal Child Psychology, 23*, 411–438.

Sergeant, J.A. (1995). Hyperkinetic disorder revisted. In J.A. Sergeant (Ed.), *Eunnethydis: European approaches to hyperkinetic disorder* (pp. 7–17). Amsterdam, The Netherlands: Author.

Shapiro, E.S., & Cole, C.L. (1994). *Behavior change in the classroom: Self-management interventions.* New York: Guilford Press.

Shelton, T., Barkley, R., Crosswait, C., Moorehouse, M., Fletcher, K., Barrett, S., Jenkins, L., & Metevia, L. (1999). Psychiatric and psychological morbidity as a function of adaptive disability in preschool children with aggressive and hyperactive-impulsive-inattentive behavior. *Journal of Abnormal Child Psychology, 26*, 475–494.

Sherman, D.K., McGue, M.K., & Iaconon, W.G. (1997). Twin concordance for attention deficit hyperactivity disorder: A comparison of teachers' and mothers' reports. *American Journal of Psychiatry, 154*, 532–535.

Sieg, K.G., Gaffney, G.R., Preston, D.F., & Hellings, J.A. (1995). SPECT brain imaging abnormalities in attention deficit hyperactivity disorder. *Clinical Nuclear Medicine, 20*, 55–60.

Silberg, J., Rutter, M., Meyer, J., Maes, H., Hewitt, J., Simonoff, E., Pickles, A., Loeber, R., & Eaves, L. (1996). Genetic and environmental influences on the covariation between hyperactivity and conduct disturbance in juvenile twins. *Journal of Child Psychology and Psychiatry, 37*, 803–816.

Still, G.F. (1902). Some abnormal psychical conditions in children. *Lancet, i,* 1008–1012, 1077–1082, 1163–1168.

Strauss, A.A., & Kephart, N.C. (1955). *Psychopathology and education of the brain-injured child: Vol. 2. Progress in theory and clinic.* New York: Grune & Stratton.

Strauss, A.A., & Lehtinen, L.E. (1947). *Psychopathology and education of the brain-injured child.* New York: Grune & Stratton.

Streissguth, A.P., Booksetin, F.L., Sampson, P.D., & Barr, H.M. (1995). Attention: Prenatal alcohol and continuities of vigilance and attentional problems from 4 through 14 years. *Development and Psychopathology, 7,* 419–446.

Swanson, J., Wigal, S., Greenhill, L., Browne, R., Waslick, B., Lerner, M., Williams, L., Flynn, D., Agler, D., Crowley, K., Fineberg, E., Baren, M., & Cantwell, D. (1998). Analog classroom assessment of Adderall (R) in children with ADHD. *Journal of the American Academy of Child and Adolescent Psychiatry, 37,* 519–526.

Taylor, E., Chadwick, O., Heptinstall, E., & Danckaerts, M. (1996). Hyperactivity and conduct problems as risk factors for adolescent development. *Journal of the American Academy of Child and Adolescent Psychiatry, 35,* 1213–1226.

Weiss, G., & Hechtman, L. (1986). *Hyperactive children grown up.* New York: Guilford Press.

Weiss, G., & Hechtman, L. (1993). *Hyperactive children grown up* (2nd ed.). New York: Guilford Press.

Willis, T.J., & Lovaas, I. (1977). A behavioral approach to treating hyperactive children: The parent's role. In J.B. Millichap (Ed.), *Learning disabilities and related disorders* (pp. 119–140). Chicago: Yearbook Medical.

Wolraich, M.L., Wilson, D.B., & White, J.W. (1995). The effect of sugar on behavior or cognition in children: A meta-analysis. *Journal of the American Medical Association, 274,* 1617–1621.

World Health Organization. (1993). *The ICD-10 classification of mental and behavioral disorders: Diagnostic criteria for research.* Geneva, Switzerland: Author.

Zametkin, A.J., Liebenauer, L.L., Fitzgerald, G.A., King, A.C., Minkunas, D.V., Herscovitch, P., Yamada, E.M., & Coher, R.M. (1993). Brain metabolism in teenagers with attention-deficit hyperactivity disorder. *Archives of General Psychiatry, 50,* 333–340.

Zametkin, A.J., Nordahl, T.E., Gross, M., King, A.C., Semple, W.E., Rumsey, J., Hamburger, S.D., & Coher, R.M. (1990). Cerebral glucose metabolism in adults with hyperactivity of childhood onset. *New England Journal of Medicine, 323,* 1361–1366.

Zametkin, A.J., & Rapoport, J.L. (1987). Neurobiology of attention deficit disorder with hyperactivity: Where have we come in 50 years? *Journal of the American Academy of Child and Adolescent Psychiatry, 26,* 676–686.

Zeiner, P. (1995). Body growth and cardiovascular function after extended (1.75 years) with methylphenidate in boys with attention deficit hyperactivity disorder. *Journal of Child and Adolescent Psychopharmacology, 5,* 129–138.

Zentall, S.S. (1985). A context for hyperactivity. In K.D. Gadow & I. Bialer (Eds.), *Advances in learning and behavioral disabilities* (Vol. 4, pp. 273–343). Greenwich, CT: JAI Press.

CHAPTER 25

Sexual Problems of Children

BETTY N. GORDON AND CAROLYN S. SCHROEDER

ew topics are more difficult to discuss or engender more controversy in our society than sex, especially children and sex. Public debate, often quite heated, has centered around issues such as the rise in teen pregnancy, the pros and cons of abortion, the morality of homosexuality, increases in sexually transmitted diseases among adolescents, provision of sex education, including what should be taught and who should teach it, and, most recently, children's access to sexually explicit material on the Internet. In the midst of this debate, we often lose sight of the fact that sexuality is a normal and important part of child development. Thus, broad knowledge of normal sexual development, as well as where things can go wrong, is essential, as it is only through this knowledge that the clinician can come to a complete understanding of a presenting problem involving issues of sexuality.

Although some childhood sexual problems may require referral to a medical or mental health professional who specializes in this area, many can be successfully managed in the context of a general clinical child practice. Indeed, early identification and treatment of sexual problems can often prevent development of adult sexual disorders that are very distressing and difficult to treat (Borneman, 1994).

Portions of this chapter were previously published in B.N. Gordon and C.S. Schroeder (1995). *Sexuality: A Developmental Approach to Problems*. New York: Plenum Press. Reprinted by permission.

The child clinician should be aware of developmental norms for sexual behavior and knowledge, the precursors of adult sexual problems, the etiology of specific sexual problems, and the symptoms or manifestations of these problems at different developmental stages. This chapter provides the child clinician with empirically based information about the complex area of childhood sexuality. First, what is known about normal sexual development is reviewed. This is followed by a discussion of issues related to sex education, including sexual abuse prevention. Finally, sexual problems of childhood other than sexual abuse are discussed. Child sexual abuse is not included in this discussion, as this topic is covered in Chapter 50 of this volume.

NORMAL SEXUAL DEVELOPMENT

The study of sexual development is influenced by cultural attitudes and values about sexuality in general, about children and sexuality specifically, and by a variety of methodological factors. Much of the research in this area has come from European countries, especially Scandinavia, where attitudes toward sexuality are more permissive than in the United States. Further, methodological issues have led to inconsistencies across the results of various studies. Studies that rely on parental report of children's sexual behavior, for example, provides lower estimates of the frequency and nature of children's sexual experiences than studies that include self-reports. This inconsistency simply reflects the fact that much of children's sexual behavior, particularly after the preschool years, is undiscovered by adults. Further, the participants involved in studies of sexuality typically are White and from higher socioeconomic backgrounds. Thus, the results reported may not represent the full range or frequency of sexual behaviors exhibited by children from different ethnic or social class families. With these problems in mind, the next sections examine what is known about physical sexual development and the development of sexual knowledge and behaviors.

PHYSICAL ASPECTS OF SEXUAL DEVELOPMENT

Although a child's genetic sex is determined at conception, differentiation into male or female does not begin until about the sixth or seventh week of pregnancy. Money (1994) outlines the process of fetal sexual development as follows: (1) Genetic or chromosomal sex is determined at conception by the contribution of an X chromosome from the mother and either an X or a Y chromosome from the father; (2) next, undifferentiated fetal gonads develop in both male and female fetuses: testes at about 6 weeks and ovaries at about 12 weeks; (3) between the third and fourth month of gestation, if the baby is to be a boy, the testes begin to secrete male hormones, androgen and antimullerian hormone, which prod the development of male sexual anatomy and inhibit development of female anatomy, respectively; the lack of these male hormones results in female development regardless of the chromosomal sex of the fetus; (4) finally, also stimulated by the secretion or lack of secretion of male hormones, differentiated external sex organs develop. Many of the sexual problems seen among children that are covered in a later section of this chapter originate during these early stages of development.

At the time of a child's birth, it is generally recognized that the physiology for sexual arousal and orgasm and the capacity for a variety of sexual behaviors are present. We know, for example, that newborn male babies have penile erections and female babies are capable of vaginal lubrication

(Martinson, 1981). There are few if any physical changes in sexual development during infancy and early childhood and no developmental milestones have been clearly identified. For both boys and girls, hormone production is limited and there is little growth in the gonads until adolescence (Tanner, 1962). In contrast to the lack of physical changes in childhood, the changes that occur during adolescence are tremendous. These changes happen over a relatively lengthy period of time (4–5 years for boys and 3–4 years for girls) and include growth of testes and penis in boys, breasts in girls, and pubic hair and a growth spurt in both sexes, resulting in adult height. There is considerable variation in the age at which puberty begins. In boys, for example, the age of pubertal onset ranges between about 12 and 16 years but can occur as early as 9.5 years, with the average age of first ejaculation at about 14 years (range = 10–16 years) (Mazur & Cherpak, 1995). For girls, the average age of menarche is between 12 and 13 years, with a range of from 10.5 to 15.5 years; however, breast development may begin earlier (between 8 and 13 years) (Mazur & Cherpak, 1995). The many psychosocial factors associated with the age at which puberty occurs are discussed in the section on precocious and delayed puberty.

CHILD SEXUAL BEHAVIOR

Despite the lack of physical changes prior to adolescence, much important development in the psychosexual arena occurs during early childhood. Research on the type and frequency of sexual behaviors shown by children is inconsistent, however, reflecting methodological differences among studies. Nonetheless, it is clear that children engage in a surprising variety of overt sexual behaviors. In a survey of U.S. parents of normally developing children age 2 to 12 years, for example, Friedrich, Grambsch, Broughton, Kuiper, and Beilke (1991) found that although some behaviors were reported to occur relatively rarely (e.g., puts mouth on sex parts, inserts objects in vagina/anus, imitates intercourse, masturbates with object), all of the 44 sexual behaviors listed on their questionnaire were shown by at least some children. The types of sexual behaviors that are to be expected at different ages are summarized in Table 25.1.

Table 25.1 Normal sexual development.

Sexual Knowledge	Sexual Behavior
Birth to 2 Years	
Origins of gender identity.	Genital exploration.
Origins of self-esteem.	Penile erections and vaginal lubrication.
Learns labels for body parts, including genitals.	Experiences genital pleasure.
Uses slang labels.	Touches other's sex parts.
	Enjoys nudity, takes clothes off in public.
3–5 Years	
Gender permanence is established.	Masturbates for pleasure; may experience orgasm.
Gender differences are recognized.	Sex play with peers and siblings: exhibits genitals, exploration of own and other's genitals, attempted intercourse.
Limited information about pregnancy and childbirth.	
Knows labels for sexual body parts but uses elimination functions for sexual parts.	Enjoys nudity, takes clothes off in public.
	Uses elimination words with peers.
6–12 Years	
Genital basis of gender is known.	Sex games with peers and siblings: role plays and sex fantasy, kissing, mutual masturbation, simulated intercourse, playing "doctor."
Knows correct labels for sex parts but uses slang.	
Sexual aspects of pregnancy are known.	Masturbation in private.
Increasing knowledge of sexual behavior: masturbation, intercourse.	Shows modesty, embarrassment: hides sex games and masturbation from adults.
Knowledge of physical aspects of puberty by age 10.	Body changes begin: girls may begin menstruation, boys may experience wet dreams.
	May fantasize or dream about sex.
	Interested in media sex.
	Uses sexual language with peers.
13–18 Years	
Sexual intercourse.	Pubertal changes continue: most girls menstruate by age 16; most boys are capable of ejaculation by age 14.
Contraception.	Dating begins.
Sexually transmitted diseases.	Sexual contacts are common: mutual masturbation, kissing, petting.
Date rape and sexual exploitation.	Sexual fantasy and dreams.
	Sexual intercourse may occur in up to ⅓.

Source: This table was previously published in B.N. Gordon and C.S. Schroeder (1995). *Sexuality: A Developmental Approach to Problems.* New York: Plenum Press. Reprinted by permission

Masturbation

Masturbation is probably the most common sexual behavior seen in young children (Routh & Schroeder, 1981). It has been observed in infants as young as 7 months (Martinson, 1981), and evidence suggests that even children as young as 2 or 3 (males especially) are capable of experiencing orgasm as a result of masturbation (Gundersen, Melas, & Skar, 1981). During the first two years of life, masturbation appears largely related to general curiosity about one's body and is most appropriately thought of as "pleasure seeking" rather than sexual. Gradually, however, children discover that genital stimulation results in particularly pleasurable sensations and masturbation begins to take on a decidedly erotic aspect.

Although there is a great deal of individual variation, boys are generally observed to masturbate earlier and more frequently than girls. Boys also are more likely to masturbate socially, in groups of two or more, whereas girls tend to engage in this behavior alone. There is some disagreement among researchers about developmental trends in the incidence of masturbation. Masturbation is reported by some to increase among boys and girls in the years preceding puberty (although the rates are thought to be somewhat lower among girls) (Martinson, 1981; Rutter, 1970); others (e.g., Friedrich et al., 1991) report a decline in sexual behavior in general, and masturbation in particular, with age. It is likely that these conflicting results reflect the fact that older children are more aware of societal views about the acceptability of sexual behavior and exercise restraint in where and when they engage in these behaviors.

Despite the fact that masturbation is such a common sexual behavior among children, many parents react negatively to it and may even punish their children if they are caught touching themselves (Calderone & Johnson, 1983). Parents who accept masturbation in their preschool children may become uncomfortable with this behavior as, with age, it assumes a more adult sexual quality (Klein & Gordon, 1991). Yet, there is no evidence that masturbation is harmful. Rather, it is seen by many as a viable sexual activity throughout the life span and by some as an important developmental step in becoming reliably orgasmic in adult partner sex (Haroian, 1991).

Because it is inherently pleasurable, the key clinical question regarding masturbation among children is not *why* they masturbate, but *how much* and *where* masturbation occurs. Clearly, it can be considered abnormal when a child masturbates to the extent that it interferes with other activities or causes physical harm, and careful assessment regarding the causes of this behavior is warranted. In other instances, whether or not masturbation constitutes a "problem" is, in large part, a function of family, societal, and cultural attitudes. There is agreement among professionals that the best way to handle childhood masturbation is to teach the child where and when it is appropriate to engage in this "private" behavior (Petty, 1995).

Child-Child Sexual Interaction
The age at which children first become aware of sexual behavior as an interpersonal phenomenon is unclear. Obviously, cultural attitudes and values greatly influence our understanding of this issue. Nonetheless, it is common knowledge that preschool children are very curious about their own and others' bodies and that, given the opportunity, they will engage in sexual exploration with other children.

Sexual play with peers is reported to be very common among preschool and school-age children and may involve relatively adultlike sexual activities such as genital fondling, oral-genital contact, insertion of objects in genitals, or attempts at sexual intercourse (Lamb & Coakley, 1993). In contrast, sex play between siblings appears to occur much less frequently than between friends. Estimates of the prevalence of sibling sexual encounters range from 9% (Lamb & Coakley, 1993) to 13% of children (Finkelhor, 1981). It is likely that the lower rate of sex between siblings reflects in part the age differential that typically exists between them. In a survey of college students, Finkelhor found that the majority of sibling sexual encounters (67%) reported were initiated by older brothers with the average age difference between participants reported to be 2.9 years.

Sexual encounters between siblings appear to be similar to those between friends in the types of activities involved, the motivations associated with the interactions, the ages at which they occur, and the perception of the experiences as relatively positive or normal. Although most childhood sexual experiences with peers or siblings are viewed positively, some involve coercion (persuasion, manipulation, or force) of some type. Not surprisingly, the more coercion reported, the less likely the experience is perceived positively (Finkelhor, 1981; Lamb & Coakley, 1993).

Finkelhor (1981) examined the extent to which sexual play in childhood affects later adjustment. He found that the women who reported having had sexual experiences with a sibling, regardless of the nature of the experience (e.g., positive or negative), were more likely to be sexually active than those who had not had this type of sexual encounter. Positive sexual experiences with siblings, particularly those that occurred later (i.e., after age 9), had apparently healthy effects on sexual self-esteem. These women reported being more comfortable with their sexuality as adults. In contrast, sexual experiences that involved a significant age differential between the siblings, especially those that occurred before age 9, were associated with lower sexual self-esteem.

Taken together, the work on sibling and peer sexual encounters suggests that "normal" sexual contact among children occurs on a continuum and that the differentiation between sexual play and sexual abuse is not always clear. Children's sexual games can range from reciprocal encounters that are motivated by curiosity, are positively perceived, and are associated with better self-esteem and later sexual functioning, to coercive encounters, often involving the use of physical force, that are associated with poorer adjustment.

Child-Adult Sexual Interaction
Although the data on sexual play among children may not be surprising, it also has been demonstrated that nonabusive sexual encounters between children and adults are quite common. Many sensual and possibly erotic encounters between the infant and mother (and other caregivers) occur in the context of nurturant caregiving, beginning at birth and continuing throughout the early years. Indeed, these early experiences of touching and physical affection are essential for the healthy development of the child. Research also indicates that nonabusive sexual interaction occurs with surprising frequency between older children and their parents and that these experiences do not necessarily have a negative or damaging effect on the children or other family members involved (Nelson, 1981; Rosenfeld, Bailey, Siegel & Bailey, 1986; Symonds, Mendoza, & Harrell, 1981). Issues of relative power and freedom of choice appear to be important in determining how these experiences are perceived.

Taken together, this research indicates that sexual contact between children, siblings, and adults is relatively common, that much of this contact is motivated by children's curiosity about their own bodies and those of others and may be perceived positively or negatively. Thus, the important clinical issue is to determine when children's sexual interactions are developmentally appropriate and when they are inappropriate and/or abusive. The next section addresses this issue.

NORMAL VERSUS ABNORMAL CHILD SEXUAL BEHAVIOR

Several sources are available to clinicians that are helpful in distinguishing normal sex play from that which might indicate a more serious problem. Gil (1993), for example, provides a framework that focuses assessment of sexual behaviors on factors such as age, size, and relative status or authority

differences, consistency with developmental norms, and presence or absence of coercion. Johnson and Friend (1995) provide criteria for determining when a child's sexual behavior falls outside the norm, including:

1. Sexual behaviors engaged in by children who do not have an ongoing mutual play relationship.
2. Sexual behaviors that interfere with other aspects of the child's life.
3. Sexual knowledge that is greater than expected for the child's age.
4. Sexual behaviors that occur in public places and/or persist in spite of frequent requests to stop.
5. Behaviors that are embarrassing or annoying and elicit complaints from other children or adults.
6. Sexual behaviors that increase in intensity, frequency, or intrusiveness.
7. Sexual behaviors that are associated with negative emotions such as fear, anxiety, intense guilt or shame, or anger.
8. Sexual behaviors that cause physical or emotional pain or discomfort to self or others.
9. Sexual behaviors that are associated with aggression, coercion, force, bribery, manipulation, or threats.

Johnson and Friend (1995) also provide a very useful table of the sexual behaviors that can be expected of preschool or early elementary school-age children, when these behaviors are of concern, and when they indicate the need for professional help. Preschool children, for example, can be expected to touch the genitals or breasts of familiar adults or children. This behavior would be of concern if the child touches the genitals or breasts of adults not in the family or of unfamiliar children or asks to be touched himself or herself. Professional help should be sought when the child "sneakily touches adults, makes others allow touching or demands touching of self" (p. 60). Similarly, early elementary school-age children can be expected to play doctor, inspecting each other's bodies. It is of concern when a child frequently engages in this behavior or gets caught after being told no. Professional help should be sought when a child forces another to play doctor or to take his or her clothes off.

ADOLESCENT SEXUAL BEHAVIOR

Although there is limited research on sexual development in young children, adolescent sexuality has received a great deal of attention, largely because of concerns about early pregnancy and sexually transmitted diseases, especially HIV infection. The issue of greatest concern to parents and professionals in the area of adolescent sexuality is the age at which teens begin to engage in sexual intercourse. Estimates of the age at which adolescents become sexually active vary greatly across studies, depending on the characteristics of the sample (e.g., rural vs. urban, ethnicity, and gender), the time the research was done, and even how questions were asked. It is generally accepted, however, that the average age at which adolescents become sexually active has decreased rapidly in recent years, with some adolescents first engaging in sexual intercourse as early as age 12 (Scott-Jones & White, 1990). Moreover, the vast majority of teenagers (79%–91%) are sexually active by age 19 (Jensen, deGaston, & Weed, 1994; White & DeBlassie, 1992).

In addition to an increased risk of HIV infection and/or pregnancy, the early onset of sexual intercourse is problematic because of its effect on children's psychosocial development. Early onset of sexual activity is associated with greater involvement in delinquent behavior (Elliott & Morse, 1989). Moreover, teens who engage in sexual intercourse earlier are less likely to use effective methods of birth control and thus are at higher risk for unintended pregnancy and a variety of sexually transmitted diseases than those who wait until they are older (Scott-Jones & White, 1990). Further, teenage parents are more likely to drop out of school, thus setting up a series of long-term economic disadvantages and other negative life consequences (White & DeBlassie, 1992). Because research has shown that these events appear to be causally related, Rutter and Rutter (1993) refer to early sexual activity among teenagers as a "turning point" that can significantly shift the course of one's life trajectory. Thus, it is clear that understanding the factors that predict early sexual activity among teens is important for planning both prevention and intervention programs.

A variety of factors have been shown to be associated with the onset of sexual activity among teenagers. Scott-Jones and White (1990) found that among teenagers between 12.5 and 15.5 years of age, those most likely to be sexually active (1) had less highly educated mothers; (2) had a boyfriend or girlfriend; (3) had lower educational expectations (i.e., did not intend to go to college); and (4) were at the upper end of the age range. In addition to these factors, White and DeBlassie (1992) indicate that circumstances related to family functioning such as authoritarian parenting, poor communication about sexuality, and having older siblings who are sexually active also may be important in the prediction of early sexual activity.

It is assumed that sex education programs can prevent much early sexual activity, and it is commonly accepted that teenagers desperately need sex education. Yet, parents and professionals continue to argue about what sex education should consist of and, perhaps more important, who should be responsible for teaching it. Information about what children of different ages know and do not know about sexuality can help to inform this debate.

SEXUAL KNOWLEDGE

The fact that children are known to engage in sexual behavior alone and in interaction with others from an early age does not necessarily mean that they have knowledge or understanding of sexual facts. Again, research in this area is inevitably biased by the culture in which it is conducted. It is important to note that the research reviewed in this section primarily was conducted in the United States and therefore reflects the prevailing attitudes (considered to be relatively restrictive) in this country. Sexual knowledge that can be expected at different ages is summarized in Table 25.1.

Early studies of children's knowledge of sexuality focused on the development of gender identity (e.g., Slaby & Frey, 1975) and the extent of children's understanding of pregnancy and birth (e.g., Bernstein & Cowen, 1975). In general, these studies have found a developmental progression in children's understanding of gender and the birth process, with younger children having incomplete and inaccurate knowledge and older children having a more accurate understanding of these topics. Studies of the concept of gender identity, for example, suggest that children first understand that gender is permanent (i.e., a girl always was and always will be a girl) and only later understand that gender is determined by one's genitalia (McConaghy, 1979).

More recent work indicates that even very young children can be quite knowledgeable about many aspects of sexuality (e.g., body parts and functions, gender differences), whereas knowledge about other areas (e.g., sexual intercourse, pregnancy, and birth) may be lacking even in older children (B.N. Gordon, Schroeder, & Abrams, 1990a; Waterman, 1986). Moreover, these age differences may vary depending on the area of sexuality assessed, the sex of the child, the sexual attitudes of the parents, and the socioeconomic status of the family (Bem, 1989; B.N. Gordon et al., 1990a).

Knowledge about sexuality also varies by age and gender among adolescents. Winn, Roker, and Coleman (1995) found that knowledge increased more between 11 and 14 years than between 14 and 16 years and that girls knew more at all ages than did boys. Moreover, some 15- to 16-year-olds lacked sufficient information about contraception to prevent unwanted pregnancy.

The relationship between children's sexual knowledge and their sexual behavior is not clear. At least two studies (B.N. Gordon, Schroeder, & Abrams, 1990b; Gundersen et al., 1981) suggest that sexual experience does not always lead to increased sexual knowledge/understanding, although the reasons why this is the case are not clear. It is possible that the relationship between knowledge and experience is mediated by parental attitudes toward sexuality. In the B.N. Gordon et al. (1990a) study, for example, children with less knowledge had parents who reported more restrictive attitudes about sexuality and had done less sex education with their children.

Studies of teenagers' knowledge and use of contraceptives suggest that attitudes are important in understanding the relationship between sexual knowledge and behavior. Scott-Jones and White (1990) found that although the majority of their sample of young adolescents knew which contraceptive methods were most effective (i.e., the pill and condoms vs. withdrawal), those who were sexually active tended *not* to use these more effective methods; 31% of those who were sexually active reported using withdrawal, an obviously noneffective method. Other work indicates that those adolescents who are at highest risk for unwanted

pregnancies (i.e., those who are sexually active at younger ages) are least likely to perceive a responsibility to use effective contraception (Morrison, 1989; Reis & Herz, 1989).

In summary, the research reviewed indicates that across childhood and adolescence, sexual experience and behavior typically precede knowledge and understanding. The fact that children engage in sexual behavior before they have a clear understanding of what it is all about places them at very high risk for a variety of adverse experiences that can impact negatively on their development. Conversely, although many adolescents have sexual knowledge, this knowledge does not always influence their behavior. The discrepancy between knowledge and behavior indicates that we have much to learn about how to effectively educate children about sexuality. The next section examines issues related to the topics of sex education and sexual abuse prevention.

SEX EDUCATION

Sexuality education in its broadest sense involves communication of attitudes, values, and feelings about being male or female, as well as teaching the anatomical parts and functions of the body. Children also must be taught the skills to enable them to make good decisions in the sexual arena and to recognize and avoid dangerous and/or exploitive situations. Although most parents do not talk with their children about sex until preschool or early school-age, sex education actually begins with the birth of the infant and is most appropriately thought of as an ongoing process that continues throughout one's lifetime. Children begin to learn about sexuality as parents communicate their feelings about different body parts through caregiving behaviors (e.g., breast-feeding, changing diapers, bathing). As the infant begins to exhibit exploratory sexual behaviors, parental reactions to these behaviors send clear positive or negative messages to the child about sexuality. This early nonverbal communication sets the stage for teaching sexual values and attitudes that will be important influences on the child's behavior later in life.

Parents are the primary sex educators for their children, especially in the early years, even if they do not actively provide information. Moreover, most teenagers view their parents as influential in determining their attitudes and values about sexuality and prefer sex education to come from parents (Sanders & Mullis, 1988). Thus, children's knowledge of and values about sexuality are clearly going to be related to the information provided by parents. Many parents, however, are uncomfortable discussing sexual matters with their children, and most do not discuss all aspects of sexuality with their children. These two factors may lead to the consistently low correlation found between the extent to which parents believe they have communicated with their children about sex and the information children perceive their parents as having provided (Jaccard, Dittus, & Gordon, 1998).

Most commonly, parents talk with children about sexual anatomy, puberty, pregnancy, and the birth process but do not discuss sexual intercourse, sexually transmitted diseases, birth control, or sexual abuse, the very topics about which children, especially adolescents, need information. When parents do not provide their children with sexual information, children are likely to get it from siblings, peers, and public media such as television, magazines, movies, and advertising (Ansuini, Fiddler-Woite, & Woite, 1996). Unfortunately, this information is likely to be inaccurate and confusing and may even be damaging to the child's self-perception.

Parents may be uncomfortable talking about sex with their children for a number of reasons, including their own attitudes about sexuality and their own experiences with sex education as children. Many parents of adolescents have been found to lack sufficient understanding of sexual development to teach their children or to reinforce what is taught in school (Hockenberry-Eaton, Richman, Dilorio, Rivero, & Maibach, 1996). Klein and Gordon (1991) suggest that two prevailing myths about sex education influence parents' decision not to provide information about sexuality to their children: (1) Knowledge is harmful and will overstimulate children to participate in more sexual activity at earlier ages, and (2) Children already know all there is to know, so why teach them? The empirical evidence contradicts both of these myths. Provision of sexual information is actually associated with postponement of sexual activity by teenagers and with more responsible sexual behavior when they do become sexually active (Coley & Chase-Lansdale, 1998). Moreover, research clearly indicates that both children and adolescents often do

not understand many important aspects of sexuality despite the fact that they may be engaging in a variety of sexual behaviors (Hockenberry-Eaton et al., 1996).

Although some parents and professionals may be concerned about giving children too much information too early, this is difficult to do. If children are told more than they want to know or are given information that they do not understand, they will simply "tune out" (Klein & Gordon, 1991). Conversely, children also will seek out (although not necessarily from parents) and assimilate information when they are interested in and ready to learn about a particular topic. In general, we believe it is better to err in the direction of giving more rather than less information.

For a variety of reasons, many children do not initiate conversations about sex, so parents must respond to behavioral cues that their children are "ready" for sexual information. Answering children's questions and responding to their sexual behavior in a simple, nonjudgmental manner that is appropriate to the child's developmental level can serve to satisfy curiosity about sex and decrease the need for sexual experimentation (S. Gordon & Snyder, 1983).

By understanding normal sexual development (see Table 25.1), parents and clinicians can more easily determine what information is needed by children as they grow and develop. Suggestions for what to teach children at different ages are outlined in Table 25.2. In reviewing the information in Table 25.2, it is important to note that it is not sufficient to teach the facts about sex. Parents need to communicate clearly and repeatedly with their children, especially during adolescence, their views about sexuality and especially premarital sex. Research has shown that parents tend to underestimate the extent of children's sexual activity and that teenagers tend to misperceive parents' disapproval of premarital sex (Jaccard et al., 1998). It is particularly important that parents view sex education as an ongoing process rather than a one-time effort and gear the information to the child's developmental level.

Evaluation of sexuality education programs has shown mixed results. Many programs have demonstrated increases in knowledge of sexual facts but have not shown changes in behavior among teenagers (Buysse & Van Oost, 1997). Programs that teach only abstinence but do not provide information

Table 25.2 Information for parents to teach children at different ages.

Birth to 2 Years

Body Parts and Functions
Provide correct labels for body parts, including male or female genitalia, when child is touching or parent is pointing to each part. Provide simple information about basic body functions. Allow child to explore all his or her body parts.

Gender Identity
Learning about gender begins at birth, when baby boys are dressed in blue and girls in pink. Parents provide guidance about this topic by their choices of toys, clothing, activities, and the behaviors of the child they choose to notice. Gender stereotypes are pervasive in our culture, but flexibility is healthy. It's OK for boys to play with dolls and girls to play with trucks. Begin to teach the child what is special about being a girl or a boy.

Sexual Abuse Prevention
Children must first learn about body parts and functions before they can learn to protect themselves from exploitation. The best prevention at this age is close supervision.

3–5 Years

Body Parts and Functions
Continue to use proper labels for body parts, including male and female genitalia. Teach child about functions of genitalia, including both elimination and reproduction. This is a good age to begin talking about sexual intercourse, as children are naturally curious about pregnancy and often have a new brother or sister.

Gender Identity
Talk about the physical differences between boys and girls. Reinforce the idea that each child is special and has unique characteristics, including being a girl or a boy. Talk about what is special about being male or female.

Sexual Abuse Prevention
Genitalia are private parts, and no one should touch them for purposes other than health or hygiene. Children should not touch anyone else's private parts. Explain that these rules apply to friends and relatives as well as strangers. Teach the child to say, "No, my parents told me not to do that," and to get away if someone tries to touch his or her private parts. Teach the child to tell someone if this happens and keep telling until someone who will help is found. Have the child make a list of who to tell. Practice saying no and telling. Allow your child to say no in other situations that are uncomfortable. Children should know not to go with a stranger under any circumstances. Explain why and make sure the child knows what a stranger is. Practice "what would you do if" role plays.

Sexual Behavior
Don't overreact if child is caught in sex play with another child. Use it as a "teachable moment." Explain that insertion of objects into body openings may be harmful and is prohibited. Child should learn that masturbation is a "private" behavior. Teach about appropriate and inappropriate words.

6–12 Years

Body Parts and Functions
Children should have complete understanding of sexual, reproductive, and elimination functions of body parts, including sexual intercourse. Discuss changes that will come with puberty for both sexes, including menstruation and wet dreams.

Gender Identity
Gender identity is fixed by this age. Encourage both boys and girls to pursue individual interests and talents regardless of gender stereotypes.

Sexual Abuse Prevention
Discuss the child's conceptualization of an abuser and correct misperceptions. Identify abusive situations, including sexual harassment by peers. Practice assertiveness and problem-solving skills in troublesome social situations. Explain how abusers, including friends, relatives, and strangers, may manipulate children.

Sexual Behavior
Talk about making good decisions in the context of potentially sexual relationships. Provide information about birth control and sexually transmitted diseases (including AIDS).

(continued)

Table 25.2   (Continued)

13–18 Years

Body Parts and Functions
Discuss health and hygiene. Provide more information about contraceptives and sexually transmitted diseases, especially AIDS. Provide access to gynecological exam for girls if sexually active.

Gender Identity
Although boys and girls are able to do many of the same things, reinforce the idea that there are special aspects of being male or female. Talk about the differences between girls and boys in social perception. Males tend to perceive social situations more sexually than girls and may interpret neutral cues (e.g., clothing, friendliness) as sexual invitations.

Sexual Abuse Prevention
Teach teens to avoid dangerous situations (e.g., walking alone at night, avoiding certain parts of town). Discuss dating relationships, in particular date/acquaintance rape and its association with alcohol and drug use. Let your teenager know you are available for a ride home *anytime* he or she is in a difficult or potentially dangerous situation. Enroll your child in a self-defense class.

Sexual Behavior
Share your attitudes and values regarding premarital sex. Provide access to contraceptives, if necessary. Accept your teenager's need and desire for privacy. Set clear rules about dating and curfews.

Source: This table was previously published in B.N. Gordon and C.S. Schroeder (1995). *Sexuality: A Developmental Approach to Problems.* New York: Plenum Press. Reprinted by permission.

about contraceptive use, an increasingly popular approach for school-based programs, have had little effect on reducing sexual activity or pregnancy among teenagers (Kirby, 1994). The most successful programs include both these topics *and* provide access to condoms for those teens who are already sexually active (Frost & Forrest, 1995). In addition, an innovative program that is more broadly focused on preventing multiple diverse problem behaviors among adolescents has recently been shown to reduce teenage pregnancy as well as school failure (J.P. Allen, Philliber, Herrling, & Kupermine, 1997). This program involved teens in highly structured volunteer activities that were linked to class work on life choices, career options, and relationship decision making.

Despite the mixed effectiveness of sexuality education programs, the importance of providing children with accurate information about sexuality cannot be overemphasized. Lack of adequate sexual education is seen as a primary cause for the two most troublesome sexual problems of the 1990s: (1) increases in rates of teenage pregnancy; and (2) the number of teenagers who are HIV positive (Petty, 1995). Moreover, with the increased reports of child sexual abuse, teaching children personal safety skills has become an increasingly important aspect of sex education. Children today are bombarded with sexual messages from films, advertising, TV situation comedies and soap operas, and

even the nightly news report! Sex education can help to put sexuality into proper perspective, assist children in making sense out of these confusing messages, and increase the chances that they will behave responsibly with regard to their own sexuality.

SEXUAL PROBLEMS

A wide variety of sexual problems are seen among children and adolescents, including physical/anatomical abnormalities that have an impact on later psychological and social development, "public or semipublic behaviors that cause adults (usually the parents) embarrassment and concern because they are a departure from society's expectations" (Haroian, 1991, p. 432), and aggressive or abusive sex. In this section, we begin with a description of physical sexual problems, followed by a review of recent research in the areas of precocious or delayed puberty, gender identity disorder, and homosexuality. Finally, oversexualized and sexually aggressive behavior problems are discussed.

SEX ERRORS OF THE BODY

When a baby is born, the first information received by parents is whether the infant is a boy or a girl. This information sets in motion a chain of events and behaviors that, over the course of development, will influence the child's understanding of himself or herself as masculine or feminine. For most families, the news about the sex of the child is part of a joyous occasion. For others, however, fetal development is incomplete or abnormal at birth and the sex of the child is an issue that parents and physicians must resolve. A full discussion of the physiology and anatomy of these sex errors of the body is beyond the scope of this chapter, but the reader is referred to an easily understandable book, *Sex Errors of the Body and Related Syndromes: A Guide to Counseling Children, Adolescents, and Their Families,* by John Money (1994). The following discussion is based on this work.

Sex errors of the body can originate at any of the stages of fetal development and can include abnormalities of the sex chromosomes, gonads, fetal hormones, or internal and/or external sex organs. Each of these abnormalities can result in variations of hermaphroditism or intersexuality, of which three types have been defined: (1) true hermaphroditism, in which both ovarian and testicular tissue is present and external genitalia are ambiguous; (2) female hermaphroditism, in which external genitalia are masculine but ovaries are present; and (3) male hermaphroditism, in which external genitalia are female but female internal organs are missing or malformed. There are also abnormalities of the external genitalia that do not involve hermaphroditism, such as lack of a penis (penile agenesis), a very small penis (micropenis), or insufficient or lack of a vaginal orifice (vaginal atresia). Money (1994) provides detailed descriptions of the etiology and clinical manifestations of each of these abnormalities (see also Mazur & Dobson, 1995). A summary of these disorders is shown in Table 25.3.

Sex errors of the body are relatively rare but are more often found in males than in females, probably due to the greater complexity of male fetal development. For both sexes, the extent of abnormality of the external genitalia varies, but the assignment of sex is usually a central clinical issue. Because reconstruction of male external genitalia may not be very satisfactory, sex assignment often is female. When sex reassignment is an issue, the first step in treatment is to determine what sex the child is to be. This decision is usually made shortly after birth with subsequent surgical, hormonal, and social interventions aimed at concordance between assigned sex and gender identity and gender role. The assignment of sex is extremely complex, however,

and there does not appear to be consensus on which of multiple factors are most important (Money, 1994). Factors that should be considered include the child's genetic sex, the nature of the internal sex organs, the external genitalia, and potential hormonalization at puberty. The question of how this child will function best sexually as an adult should be asked. Sometimes, despite everyone's best efforts, gender identity and gender role develop inconsistently with assigned sex. These cases must be evaluated very carefully, as sex reassignment after the toddler age is difficult (see section on gender identity disorder).

Counseling with the family typically begins at the infant's birth and continues aperiodically throughout development, involving parents, the child, and his or her siblings. Money (1994) provides some excellent suggestions for clinicians. He states that a helpful way to describe these children to parents and other family members is as having been born "sexually unfinished." The focus of medical intervention is, thus, one of finishing the task that nature left unfinished. Open discussion with parents about the child's physical condition, the necessary medical interventions, and their feelings regarding the sex of their child is essential. Parents who are not comfortable (for whatever reason) with the assigned sex of the child will be less able to carry out the necessary but often complicated medical and behavioral recommendations. Open communication with other family members also is critical when sex reassignment is an issue. Siblings, for example, may hold the misguided belief that their sex might be reassigned as well. Moreover, grandparents and others who will be caring for the infant need to be prepared for the child's unusual appearance.

Children born with sex errors of the body need a variety of information as they grow and develop. Because many parents are unable or unwilling to discuss these sensitive issues with their children, this task often falls to professionals. Information must be geared to the child's ability to understand but should include the etiology (e.g., chromosomal or hormonal) and prognosis (e.g., prospects for fertility or sexual intercourse) specific to the child's abnormality and basic sexuality education, including the physiology and anatomy of reproduction as well as the psychological and sociological aspects of sexuality. Further, these children often have difficulty with self-image and self-esteem, particularly as they approach adolescence, and for some,

Table 25.3 Sex errors of the body.

Sex Chromosome Abnormalities

Triple X syndrome (47,XXX)	Associated with mental retardation, although many appear normal and are not detected. The more extra X chromosomes, the greater the mental retardation.
Supernumerary syndrome (47,XYY)	Associated with criminality/aggression, but many in normal population have this syndrome. Associated with high impulsivity, which causes school/learning and behavioral problems. Average to high IQ and height over 6 ft. are typical.
Klinefelter syndrome (47,XXY)	Typically diagnosed in males at puberty with swelling of breasts, small testicles, small penis, insufficient masculinization. Associated with sterility, low sex drive, language and reading problems. Mental retardation is seen in some.
Turner syndrome (45,X)	Short stature, missing or abnormal ovaries or testicles, female external genitalia. May have other physical anomalies. Uterus is present and menstruation may occur. Associated with a variety of learning problems, especially low nonverbal IQ. 45X/46XY is a variation that includes male or ambiguous external genitalia.

Gonadal Abnormalities

Undescended testicles	Very common and usually self-corrects at puberty. May signal some other abnormality, e.g., lack of testicles.
Swyer syndrome (46,XY)	Failure to develop either ovaries or testicles because of missing gene on short arm of Y chromosome. Fetus develops as female without ovaries because of lack of male hormone secretion. Uterus is present. Diagnosed in females at puberty because of lack of breast development and menstruation.

Fetal Hormonal Anomalies

Androgen insensitivity syndrome (46,XY)	A form of male hermaphroditism. Caused by defective gene on X chromosome that interferes with absorption of androgen. Testes are formed and secrete male hormones, so female internal organs do not develop. External genitalia are female because androgen is not absorbed. Breasts develop because the testicles secrete small amounts of estrogen. Often diagnosed at puberty with lack of menstruation. Sex assignment is female. Treatment involves removal of testicles and female hormone replacement therapy.
Persistent mullerian duct syndrome (46,XY)	Failure to secrete or absorb antimullerian hormone, which inhibits development of female organs. External genitalia are male, internal are both male and female. May be infertile. Treatment involves removal of female organs.
Congenital adrenal hyperplasia syndrome (46,XX)	A form of female hermaphroditism. Excess androgen secreted when external genitalia are formed. Results in female internal organs and male or ambiguous external organs. Masculinization continues at puberty if untreated. External genitalia are unsuitable for sexual intercourse unless surgically corrected. Sex assignment is typically female and hormone treatment is lifelong.
True hermaphroditism (typically 46XX but can be 46XY or 46XX/46XY)	Thought to be caused when male-deterring material from Y chromosome splices onto X chromosome. The result is an ovary on one side of body and testicle on the other. External genitalia are ambiguous. Sex assignment depends on prospects for sexual intercourse and fertility in adulthood.

Nonhermaphroditic External Anomalies

Hypospadias (46,XY)	Urinary opening is misplaced along the penis instead of at tip. May be mild or severe. Corrected surgically. Associated with undescended or missing testicles. May be caused by poorly done circumcision.
Epispadias (46XX or 46,XY)	Malformation of urinary and/or defecatory systems. Surgical repair may result in incontinence. Male penis may be abnormal and best reassigned as female.
Micropenis (46XY), Penile agenesis	Missing or very small penis. When extreme, typically reassigned as female. Treatment involves surgical correction at birth, gender identity training, hormone therapy, and surgery for vaginal construction in adolescence.
Vaginal atresia (46,XX or 46XY)	Insufficient or lack of vaginal orifice. Can be caused by androgen insensitivity syndrome in 46,XY males or Meyer-Rokitansky-Kuster syndrome in 46,XX females. Ovaries usually present, but uterus and vagina are malformed. Often diagnosed at puberty with lack of menstruation.

Source: Previously published in B.N. Gordon and C.S. Schroeder (1995). *Sexuality: A Developmental Approach to Problems.* New York: Plenum Press. Reprinted by permission.

sexual preference and/or gender identity may also be central issues. The nature and timing of any necessary surgery is particularly important to discuss with children and parents. Surgery to correct external and internal abnormalities can interact with issues of development such as adolescent sexual identity.

Money (1994) describes an approach called "the parable technique," which is designed to help open discussion with the child about sexual matters. The therapist tells a story based on the child's own experience and medical history that deals with issues likely to be important for the child, such as reconstructive genital surgery, fear of rejection, telling peers or siblings, gender issues, and so forth. The story communicates to the child that it is OK to talk about any of these difficult topics and allows for further questioning and discussion in a nonjudgmental atmosphere. Through education and support of their sexuality, children with sex errors of the body can be helped to develop along the normal continuum.

DELAYED OR PRECOCIOUS PUBERTY

The onset of puberty is a time of dramatic physical changes. Along with large increases in height and weight and the development of secondary sex characteristics, adolescents often experience increases in activity level and emotional lability as a function of changes in the endrocrine system (Rekers, 1991). It should not be surprising that this period of rapid development is associated with adjustment problems in a number of areas, such as self-image, body image, peer relations, and parental relations, even among normally developing teens (Brooks-Gunn & Warren, 1988).

The age at which children normally reach puberty ranges from 10 to 13 years among girls and 11 to 15 years among boys. Puberty is considered to be precocious or delayed if it occurs outside this normal range (Mazur & Cherpak, 1995; Sonis et al., 1986). The age at which puberty is reached appears to have a significant impact on adjustment, although the problems experienced as a result of delayed or precocious puberty are different for boys and girls (Rutter, 1970; Rutter & Rutter, 1993). Adolescents who are early or late maturing are at risk for problems with peer acceptance, but boys tend to suffer more from delayed puberty, whereas girls experience more problems associated with early or precocious puberty.

Precocious puberty is caused by increased levels of sex steroids, which can have a variety of etiologies, including (1) central nervous system lesions, such as hydrocephalous; (2) being part of an identified syndrome, such as neurofibromatosis; (3) genetic disorders; and (4) a premature signal from the hypothalamic-pituitary biological clock (Money, 1994). Most cases (up to 80%) of precocious puberty in girls are idiopathic or of unknown origin (and may be considered extreme variations of normal), whereas the majority of cases (approximately 65%) among boys involve an organic disorder such as congenital adrenal hyperplasia (Mazur & Cherpak, 1995).

Regardless of its cause, the early onset of puberty clearly interacts with other social and psychological factors in ways that have the potential to alter a child's developmental course. For boys, distinct advantages come with early maturation. Increases in height and weight, for example, enhance boys' ability to compete in athletics. As a result, early-maturing boys often receive more positive feedback from adults and may be considered more attractive by their peers than those who mature later. These advantages result in higher self-esteem, greater self-confidence, and social maturity (Rekers, 1991). In contrast, boys who mature late tend to be less popular, less confident, and more withdrawn, and these effects may persist into adulthood (Rutter, 1970).

For girls, the impact of the timing of puberty is quite different from that of boys. Late-maturing girls are more in step with the boys in their peer groups and thus are not as likely to experience significant adjustment problems associated with onset of puberty. In contrast, girls who mature very early are at risk for a number of behavior problems, both internalizing and externalizing. Sonis et al. (1986) found that girls with precocious puberty exhibited 10 times more behavior problems in the areas of social withdrawal, depression, aggression, and social competence than did a group of matched controls. Although some girls who mature early may withdraw and consequently become less popular among their peer group (Rekers, 1991), others have been shown to engage in a range of precocious sexual behaviors, including sexual intercourse (Meyer-Bahlburg et al., 1985). The reason for this early sexual behavior may be that girls who mature early appear older than their peers and may be exposed to sexual advances that are not appropriate for their chronological age and level of social and emotional development.

Treatment of precocious or delayed puberty should include a thorough medical evaluation to determine the cause and rule out dangerous conditions (e.g., a brain tumor). Hormonal therapy may be indicated to slow down or stop the process of puberty and allow for normal bone growth when onset is exceedingly premature, or to precipitate the onset of puberty when it is quite delayed (Money, 1994). Psychological intervention is likely to involve issues of self-esteem and social relations. Rekers (1991) suggests that group treatment with other children who are late or early to mature can focus on empathy and social skills. The clinician can help parents understand the potential lability in the child's moods and encourage them to provide the child with opportunities for age-appropriate activities. Finally, sex education with an emphasis on the bodily changes that are occurring and the potential for sexual exploitation is essential for these children.

GENDER IDENTITY DISORDER

The development of a sense of oneself as male or female and the value one places on being a member of one's sex, or gender identity, begins very early in life. Hospital personnel, parents, and families typically begin to influence the development of gender identity at birth by providing blue or pink clothing and masculine or feminine names. Same-sex preferences, or gender-role behaviors (e.g., choice of toys, games, playmates, clothing), typically begin by the age of 2 years, and these stereotypic behaviors increase up to age 4 or 5 years (Bradley & Zucker, 1997). Boys appear to develop same-sex preferences earlier and more consistently than do girls (Rutter, 1975), probably reflecting differential societal attitudes toward sex-typed behaviors for boys and girls. It is not clear whether gender identity (e.g., choice of toys, games, playmates, clothing) precedes gender-typed behavior ("I am a girl, therefore I want to do girl things"; Zucker & Green, 1992, p. 110) or vice versa ("I like to do girl things, therefore I must be a girl," p. 110).

Whatever the developmental process, most children engage in behaviors and have preferences that

are consistent with their physical sex beginning in the preschool years. For some children, however, there is a significant incongruity between their biological sex and their preferred gender. These children express a strong desire to be (or a belief that they are) the opposite sex, and are preoccupied with activities that are strongly associated with the opposite sex. The intensity of their desire and belief differentiates these children from those who are simply "tomboys" or "sissies," and often results in a diagnosis of gender identity disorder (GID).

Diagnostic Issues

In the fourth edition of the *Diagnostic and Statistical Manual of Mental Disorders* (*DSM-IV*; APA, 1994), the diagnostic criteria for GID include two central features: (1) "strong and persistent cross-gender identification," as manifested in a desire to be or belief that one is the opposite sex, and preferences for stereotypical cross-gender clothing, activities or playmates, and roles in fantasy or make-believe play; and (2) "persistent discomfort" with one's own sex, as manifested in aversion to one's own genitalia or sex-typed behavior, activities, or clothing.

Symptoms of GID typically appear between 2 and 4 years of age (Zucker & Bradley, 1995). Zucker and Bradley describe several behaviors that are diagnostic for GID: (1) identity statements indicating that one is or wishes to be a member of the opposite sex; (2) cross-dressing, which may occur in public and can have an obsessive or driven quality resulting in tantrums when prohibited; (3) cross-sex toy and role play; (4) preference for opposite-sex peers and avoidance of same-sex peers; (5) cross-sex mannerisms and voice quality; (6) anatomic dysphoria, wherein the child expresses dislike of or tries to hide his or her genitalia; and (7) preference for (among girls) or avoidance of (among boys) rough-and-tumble play. Many of these symptoms appear to be age-dependent, at least for boys; less is known about the course of the disorder in girls. Cross-gender behavior and explicit statements about wishing to be the opposite sex, for example, decrease with age among boys, probably because of the social stigma associated with these behaviors (Zucker, 1990a). Thus, few boys who are diagnosed with GID in childhood will continue to meet the *DSM-IV* criteria in adolescence or adulthood (APA, 1994).

GID in both boys and girls often co-occurs with other forms of psychopathology, particularly internalizing disorders (Coates & Person, 1985). Older children and adolescents with GID appear to have higher rates of comorbid psychopathology than do younger children (Zucker, 1990b; Zucker & Bradley, 1995), which may reflect the cumulative effects of peer rejection and social isolation that almost inevitably accompany GID. Zucker and Green (1992) argue for a comprehensive assessment for all children and especially for adolescents who are suspected of having gender identity problems. The assessment should include objective as well as projective measures to ensure that covert wishes or fantasies about being the opposite sex are noted even when little overt cross-gender behavior is evident. See Zucker and Bradley (1995) for examples of a clinical behavioral rating form and child interview protocol.

Epidemiology

Although the definitive epidemiological study remains to be done, there is some agreement that GID is a relatively rare disorder (Zucker & Bradley, 1995). Instances of cross-gender behavior among preschool children are quite common, but it is not known how many of these children would actually fulfill all the criteria for a *DSM-IV* diagnosis of GID (Achenbach & Edelbrock, 1983). Higher rates of cross-sex-typed behaviors are typically found in clinic samples, although less so for girls than for boys (Bradley & Zucker, 1997).

Referral rates for GID are much higher for boys than for girls (6–7:1), raising the question of whether the prevalence of GID is actually higher for boys than for girls (Bradley & Zucker, 1997; Zucker & Bradley, 1995). It may be that boys are more vulnerable to GID because masculine development is dependent on prenatal androgen secretion, whereas feminine development occurs in the absence of prenatal androgens (Money & Ehrhardt, 1972). Alternatively, the higher referral rates for boys may be due to the fact that society has less tolerance for cross-gender behavior in boys (Bradley & Zucker, 1997). Interestingly, Bradley and Zucker report that referral rates for adolescent boys and girls with gender disturbance are much more similar (1.4:1).

Etiology

Zucker and his colleagues (Bradley & Zucker, 1997; Zucker & Bradley, 1995; Zucker & Green, 1992) summarize the research related to various theories about the etiology of GID. They conclude that there is some evidence (based on studies of adults with GID, of homosexual men and women, and of individuals with hormonal abnormalities) that biological factors, particularly prenatal hormone secretion, may predispose children to problems with gender identity. Variations in prenatal hormone exposure (i.e., increases or decreases in androgens) have been shown to influence later behavior (without altering external genital structures) of both animals and humans (Money & Ehrhardt, 1972). Female fetuses exposed to androgens prenatally exhibit behaviors more typical of males after birth, whereas male fetuses that are not exposed to sufficient levels of androgens exhibit more typically feminine behaviors. Studies of temperament in children with GID have shown similar results (Bradley & Zucker, 1997). The causes of variations in hormone secretion during pregnancy are not yet well understood. In rats, prenatal maternal stress has been linked to decreased androgen secretion and later demasculinized behavior in male offspring (Ward, 1984). To date, however, there have been no definitive studies that replicate this particular phenomenon in humans.

Further evidence for a biological contribution to GID is found in studies indicating that boys with GID are more likely to be later born and have more brothers than sisters when compared to boys without GID (Blanchard, Zucker, Bradley, & Hume, 1995; Blanchard, Zucker, Cohen-Kettenis, Gooren, & Bailey, 1996). It is hypothesized (but not proven) that antibodies to one or more of the hormones needed for sexual differentiation (including testosterone) produced by the mother of a male fetus may reduce the biological activity of these hormones and that this effect might increase over several pregnancies involving a male fetus (Blanchard et al., 1995).

Finally, boys with GID are judged to be more physically attractive than control boys (Green, 1987), whereas GID girls are judged to be less attractive (Fridell, Zucker, Bradley, & Maing, 1996). It is suggested that certain physical characteristics, such as facial features, elicit behavior from adults that reinforces feminine or masculine behavior independent of the child's physical gender (Stoller, 1975; Zucker & Green, 1992).

Psychosocial Factors

Rekers and Kilgus (1995) argue that the lack of evidence for abnormal chromosome numbers, external genitalia, and hormone levels among adults with gender disturbance indicates that the etiology of gender deviance is found in psychological development variables and social learning within the family environment rather than in biological factors. Evidence for the role of the social environment in GID is found in studies that show successful formation of gender identity in children born with ambiguous genitalia and assigned to one sex or another shortly after birth (Money, Devore, & Norman, 1986; Money & Norman, 1987; Quattrin, Aronica, & Mazur, 1990). Other research demonstrates higher rates of parental and family dysfunction for children with GID than for controls (see, e.g., Marantz & Coates, 1991). Moreover, clinical experience indicates that parents of children with GID often respond neutrally or positively to their children's early cross-gender behavior, thus potentially increasing this behavior through differential reinforcement (Zucker & Green, 1992).

Taken together, research on etiology of GID suggests that this disorder probably results from an interaction between biological and environmental factors. Money and Russo (1979) suggest that fetal sex hormones influence brain development, which subsequently mediates behavior. This process creates a predisposition to behave as a male or a female. The social environment then functions to reinforce or discourage cross- or same-gender behavior and identification. This view suggests that the co-occurrence of other forms of psychopathology with gender disturbances may be the result of the social consequences (peer rejection, social isolation, and poor self-esteem) of engaging in cross-gender behavior.

Long-Term Prognosis

Although GID is relatively rare, its significance as a clinical problem lies in the strong relationship between early cross-gender behavior and later homosexuality. This link has been shown in both prospective and retrospective studies for boys and in retrospective studies for girls (for a summary, see Bailey & Zucker, 1995). Prospective work indicates that a substantial majority (60%–80%) of boys with GID have a homosexual or bisexual orientation as adults (Bailey & Zucker, 1995; Green, 1987). Similarly, in an analysis across 41 retrospective studies, Bailey and Zucker found that adult male and female homosexuals consistently recalled more cross-gender behavior in childhood than did heterosexuals,

although the effect was larger for men than for women. It is important to note that the association between cross-gender behavior in childhood and later homosexuality is not absolute; a substantial minority of homosexual adults do not recall engaging in cross-gender behavior during childhood, and some children with gender disturbance do not adopt a homosexual orientation as adults. Nonetheless, it seems safe to assume that, at least for many children, cross-gender identity may be a precursor of homosexuality, or that cross-gender identity and homosexuality may be two different manifestations of the same underlying phenomenon, with cross-gender behavior more salient early in development and homosexual behavior seen later. This latter hypothesis is supported by the fact that deviant gender identity for most boys with GID normalizes with development and by the fact that most adult homosexuals do not demonstrate gender identity or gender role problems as adults (Zucker & Green, 1992). The reason gender identity appears to normalize with development is not yet clear. It may be, however, that gender identity problems are resolved through the process of determining one's sexual orientation.

It would be reasonable to expect a similar strong association between GID and transsexualism (adults who have persistent gender identity problems and wish to undergo sex reassignment); however, research indicates a somewhat different picture. Although retrospective studies show that almost all adult transsexuals (both male and female) recall cross-gender behavior as children (e.g., Blanchard, Clemmensen, & Steiner, 1987), prospective studies of children with GID indicate that very few become transsexuals as adults (Green, 1987; Money & Russo, 1979). Zucker and Green (1992) propose three explanations for these findings: (1) base rates for transsexualism are so low that large numbers of childhood GID cases would be needed to find any adult transsexuals; (2) transsexuals come from families in which cross-gender behavior is condoned, and thus these children never come to the attention of mental health or research professionals; and (3) assessment for research studies and subsequent treatment may alter the natural course of GID, thus preventing the development of transsexualism. Zucker and Bradley (1995) suggest that the transition from childhood to adolescence may be a critical time for the development of transsexualism. They note that those children who maintain a consistent cross-gender identification as they move through adolescence are most at risk for transsexualism.

Transvestism (male heterosexuals who cross-dress for purposes of sexual arousal) does not appear to be related to GID, and in fact, the clinical picture for this disorder is quite different from that of GID. Transvestites typically do not have gender problems as children and are usually quite securely masculine as adults. Moreover, they clearly demonstrate masculine gender roles (Blanchard, 1990). The function of cross-dressing appears to distinguish potential transvestism from GID. Cross-dressing among gender-disturbed boys is done for the purpose of enhancing identification with the opposite sex (typically employing outer clothing) as opposed to a soothing or erotic function (typically involving female underwear) for transvestism (Zucker & Green, 1992).

To summarize, a strong association between cross-gender disturbances in children and homosexual behavior in adults has been clearly demonstrated. Children who evidence severe gender disturbance and those whose symptoms persist into adolescence are most likely to be diagnosed as transsexuals. There appears to be little relationship between transvestism and GID.

Treatment
Treatment of gender problems in children has generated a considerable amount of controversy. One view argues that treatment reinforces a sexist view of child rearing (Zucker, 1990c), and therefore it is inappropriate to try to change the child's discordant gender identity. According to this view, rigid sex-typed behavior is undesirable, and it would be more appropriate to change societal attitudes about which behaviors are labeled deviant. This, in turn, might decrease the extent to which other psychopathology accompanies gender disturbances (Winkler, 1977). Others have questioned the ethics of treating GID in the attempt to prevent homosexuality (although it is not clear that treatment is effective in this regard) and argue that the treatment could, in effect, cause more harm than good by focusing on the idea that homosexuality is undesirable (Green, 1987).

An alternative view proposes that early treatment of GID could at least alleviate the peer relationship and self-esteem problems that typically

accompany the disorder and may be effective in resolving the gender identity disturbance, thus preventing transsexualism in adulthood (Rekers, Kilgus, & Gosen, 1990; Zucker, 1990c; Zucker & Bradley, 1995). This view supports early intervention to eliminate cross-gender behaviors and to replace them with behaviors that are consistent with the child's physical sex. This approach might speed up the natural developmental process of cross-gender behavior (i.e., a decrease with age) and prevent the development of other forms of psychopathology that typically result from peer rejection.

A third approach is to acknowledge and affirm the child's cross-gender preference and then help the child learn how to express this preference in a manner that allows for good peer relations while maintaining a positive self-image. According to this view, cross-gender behaviors are seen as problematic only in reference to where and when they are expressed.

Given that the research on treatment of children born with ambiguous sex organs indicates that gender identity can be successfully taught, at least early in life (e.g., Money & Norman, 1987; Money et al., 1986; Quattrin et al., 1990), it would seem reasonable for clinicians to intervene to replace cross-gender with same-gender behavior in preschool children. Because gender identity and gender roles are firmly established by age 7, intervention with the goal of changing cross-gender identity is less likely to be effective after this age. Therefore, for preadolescent children whose gender identity is persistently of the opposite sex, an approach that helps them accept themselves as they are while recognizing and adapting to societal norms may be appropriate.

A behavioral approach to treatment of GID in children is most common (but see Lim & Bottomley, 1983; Soutter, 1996; Sugar, 1995, for alternatives). This approach assumes that cross-gender behavior is learned and therefore can be changed by manipulating the consequences for cross- and same-gender behavior (Meyer-Bahlburg, 1985; Zucker, 1990c). Behavioral treatment provides opportunities and positive reinforcement for engaging in gender-appropriate behavior and choosing gender-appropriate games and toys. Verbal feedback is given about appropriate and inappropriate gender behavior, and cross-gender behavior is extinguished by ignoring (Rekers & Lovaas,

1974; Schaefer & Millman, 1981). Zucker (1990c) suggests "that parents disallow cross-dressing, discourage cross-gender role play and fantasy play, restrict playing with cross-sex toys, tell the child that they value him as a boy (or her as a girl), encourage same-sex peer relations, and help the child engage in more sex-appropriate or neutral activities" (p. 38). For example, the clinician might instruct the parents of a 4-year-old girl who insists on playing only the male role in make-believe play to reply, "This time, I want to play the prince and you play Cinderella." If the child persists, the parent can be instructed to say that he or she does not want to play that game today (Zucker, 1990c).

Self-esteem enhancement focused on gender-related issues is also an important component of treatment in most cases of GID (Pope, McHale, & Craighead, 1988). For example, the clinician can instruct parents to describe positively the specific gender-related attributes of the child ("You are such a strong young man. I really appreciate your carrying in the groceries. You are getting to be just like your Dad.").

Parental involvement is essential to the success of treatment, both to provide parents with insight into their contribution to the problem (if any) and so they can assist with the treatment program. Parents can participate in treatment by ensuring that the program is implemented consistently across settings and people. However, treatment of any accompanying parental or family psychopathology is essential to maximize the effectiveness of the treatment program.

Homosexuality

Homosexuality is a difficult topic to discuss because the current political climate is so polarized and lacking in objectivity. Despite the fact that homosexuality is no longer considered a psychological disorder (APA, 1994), child clinicians must have some knowledge of this important area because it remains an issue of concern for parents and adolescents. Moreover, homosexuality places young people at very high risk of a number of psychological, emotional, and physical problems, including substance abuse, sexually transmitted diseases (especially HIV infection), suicide, school problems, peer rejection, and social isolation (Lundy & Rekers, 1995).

The prevalence of homosexuality is estimated to be 1.5% of females and between 1% and 5% of males (Bailey, Bobrow, Wolfe, & Mikach, 1995), and these rates appear to be relatively stable over time. With regard to etiology, there is growing consensus that there are probably multiple pathways, both biological and psychosocial/environmental, leading to an adult homosexual orientation. That is, no one explanation can account for all cases of homosexuality. The preponderance of evidence appears to favor a biological etiology, at least in the sense of a strong predisposition to become homosexual. The various hypotheses regarding etiology of homosexuality can be summarized as follows:

1. Prenatal hormones influence neurological structures in the brain, particularly the hypothalamus, leading to cross-sex-typed behaviors in childhood and later homosexual orientation. Evidence for this hypothesis is provided by several different types of research: (a) structural differences in the brains of homosexual and heterosexual men have been found (e.g., L.A. Allen & Gorski, 1992; LeVay, 1991); (b) women with congenital adrenal hyperplasia (CAM), a disorder that results in prenatal exposure to high levels of androgens, or who have been exposed to DES (a synthetic estrogen used to prevent spontaneous abortion in high-risk pregnancies) prenatally, are reported to have increased rates of bisexuality and homosexuality (e.g., Dittman, Kappes, & Kappes, 1992; Meyer-Bahlburg et al., 1995); and (c) numerous animal studies indicate that prenatal injection of male or female sex hormones predicts cross-sex-typed social behavior (see Adkins-Regan, 1988, for a review).

2. There is a genetic basis for homosexuality. Recent research has identified a marker for homosexuality on the X chromosome of some but not all homosexual males (Hamar, Hu, Magnuson, Hu, & Pattatucci, 1993). Further, twin studies have shown concordance rates of 52% for MZ twins, 22% for DZ twins, 11% for adopted brothers, and 9% for sons of homosexual fathers (Bailey & Pillard, 1991; Bailey et al., 1995).

3. There may be a maternal immune response, similar to that seen in Rh incompatible pregnancies, to prenatal excretion of testosterone by male fetuses that reduces the hormone's biological activity. Male homosexuals have been reliably shown to have more male siblings and later birth order than male heterosexuals, suggesting that the maternal immune

response builds with successive pregnancies involving male fetuses (Blanchard et al., 1995).

4. Identification with the opposite-sex parent rather than the same-sex parent is a precursor to homosexuality. In retrospective studies, male homosexuals recall their fathers being unavailable/distant/hostile, and lesbians tend to report poorer relations with their mothers (e.g., Bell, Weinberg, & Hammersmith, 1981).

5. Differential socialization, by which parents selectively reinforce or extinguish behaviors that increase the probability of homosexual versus heterosexual orientation, predicts sexual orientation. There is little or no research that directly addresses this hypothesis.

Homosexual Parents

Another issue of concern to child clinicians is that of the adjustment of children raised by gay or lesbian parents. It is estimated that between 6 million and 14 million children have gay or lesbian parents. The majority of these children are born in the context of a heterosexual relationship in which one parent subsequently comes out as a homosexual. However, there also are an increasing number of lesbian and gay couples who seek to adopt children, provide foster homes, or use artificial insemination to have children. Thus, clinicians are increasingly being asked about the impact on children of living in these "nontraditional" households.

Historically, the legal system has been hostile to gay and lesbian parents based on an assumption that growing up in such a household will have a negative impact on children's development, placing them at increased risk for aberrant psychosexual development, including problems with gender identity, gender role behaviors, and especially sexual orientation, isolation from or rejection by peers, and other emotional or behavioral problems. Although research addressing these questions is limited, the data overwhelmingly indicate that children raised by homosexuals are at no greater risk for these problems than children growing up in more "traditional" households (Bailey et al., 1995; Golombok & Tasker, 1996).

In a review of studies that evaluated over 300 children of gay or lesbian parents in 12 different samples, C.J. Patterson (1992) found that these children did not exhibit significant problems in their psychosexual development. The children were happy with the sex to which they belonged, had no wish to be members of the opposite sex, and their interests in and preferences for activities were no different from those of other children. Further, there was no evidence that the number of children raised by gay or lesbian parents who as adults identified themselves as homosexual exceeded that expected in the population at large. Children of gay and lesbian parents were also found to have normal relationships both with their peers and with adults of both sexes. Finally, there was no evidence to support the fear that children with homosexual parents are more vulnerable to being sexually abused either by the parent or the parent's acquaintances than are children with heterosexual parents.

Not surprisingly, the quality of the relationships within the family seems to be more important than the sexual orientation of the parents in influencing children's development. If parents are open about their sexual orientation, for example, and this is accepted by other significant people, the mental health of both parents and children is likely to be improved (Rand, Graham, & Rawlings, 1982). Furthermore, unless there is some reason to highlight parental sexuality (e.g., a divorced parent remarries), most children do not think of their parents as sexual beings and the significance of a sexual relationship is not fully understood until adolescence.

Children's ability to accept their parent's homosexuality is influenced by when they first learn about it. It is not surprising that children who are first told in early to middle adolescence have the most difficulty, as these children are in the process of exploring their own sexual identity (Schulenberg, 1985). In general, we have found that the acceptance of the parent's homosexuality by significant adults in the child's life, particularly the other parent, helps the child understand and accept the parent's sexual orientation. When discussing sexual orientation with children, it is important to emphasize relationships rather than sexual behavior per se. As with any stressful life event, it can be helpful for children to have the opportunity to talk with other children who have had similar experiences. Thus, participation in groups with other children who have gay or lesbian parents can promote the child's adjustment. A book by Rafkin (1990) shares stories by children growing up in lesbian families, and another by Russ (1990) is helpful for the professional working with families with homosexual parents.

OVERSEXUALIZED AND SEXUALLY AGGRESSIVE BEHAVIOR

Although all children display interest in and curiosity about sexuality at various times during their development, some appear to be overly focused and preoccupied with sexual matters beyond what is expected for their age. The behavior of these children may vary a great deal, ranging from compulsive, public masturbation to coercive or aggressive sexual interactions with other children, but for the most part, the behavior is unresponsive to parental limit-setting, interferes with other age-appropriate activities, and may be indicative of serious psychopathology. In adolescents, these behaviors may lead to adjudication as a juvenile sex offender.

Lucy Berliner (cited in Friedrich, 1990) has described three levels of sexualized behavior: (1) coercive sexual behavior where physical force, verbal threats, or social coercion are used to gain another child's compliance; (2) developmentally precocious sexual behavior, such as noncoercive attempted or completed intercourse; and (3) inappropriate sexual behavior, including persistent, public masturbation, sexualization of nonsexual situations, or repeatedly exhibiting genitalia. Behaviors at levels 2 and 3 are not necessarily considered indicators of psychopathology but would suggest the need for evaluation and would be considered serious if they were found to be frequent, persistent, and pervasive across many situations, or to interfere with the child's development or be accompanied by other disturbed behavior (Friedrich, 1990).

Sexualized Behavior

Sexualized behavior is often thought to be an indication that a child has been sexually abused, and indeed, many sexual behaviors (e.g., asks to engage in sex acts, puts mouth on sex parts, masturbates with objects) have been shown to occur more frequently among children who have been sexually abused than in those who have not (Friedrich et al., 1992). But not all children who exhibit these types of behavior have been sexually abused, and conversely, many children who have been abused do not exhibit sexualized behavior. Nonetheless, sexualized behavior that occurs to the extent that it interferes with other age-appropriate activities is a warning signal that a child may have other problems. Thus, the clinician needs to make a comprehensive assessment of these children and their

families. This assessment should cover the child's psychological/emotional status, the home situation, and a review of the child's daily routines, including interactions with children and adults in the extended family and community. The possibility that the child may have been sexually abused should be explored but, if possible, without raising unnecessary concern. Problems discovered in any of the assessed areas need to be addressed before treating the sexual behaviors themselves. Indeed, as these other problems are treated, the sexual behavior may cease to be an issue.

Because sexual behaviors (especially masturbation) are inherently pleasurable, they may continue to be a problem even after successful treatment of associated problems. For these children, the clinician may find that a behavioral approach is relatively simple and effective in eliminating the problem. Using masturbation as an example, a first step is to identify times and places when the child is most likely to masturbate and the consequences of the behavior. The child can then be reinforced for engaging in behaviors that are incompatible with masturbation (playing with or holding a toy or other object) at these times and while in public places. The idea that masturbation is OK in private is easily understood even by very young children ("I know it feels good to touch your penis/vulva, but you are only allowed to do that in your bedroom"). In addition to teaching alternative behaviors, reinforcement can be provided for increasing amounts of time not spent masturbating.

Ryan (1997b) suggests that all sexual behaviors exhibited by children, especially those that verge on the deviant, require some adult response. Because children inevitably look to adults for guidance, failure to respond to sexualized behaviors can easily be interpreted by the child as acceptance or approval. Ryan notes that the response to these behaviors should encompass three primary goals so as to teach the child important skills and promote healthy development: (1) communication: label the behavior nonjudgmentally; (2) empathy: tell the child how this behavior makes you and/or others feel; and (3) accountability: teach the child that he or she is responsible for controlling his or her behavior in the future.

Sexualized behavior that is associated with a history of sexual abuse is considered "reactive" to the abuse and is taken as an indication that the child has not resolved the abuse experience. Treatment for these children must include attention to issues related to sexual abuse as well as teaching the child more appropriate ways to behave in public and/or to interact with others (for further discussion, see Chapter 50, this volume).

Preadolescent Sexual Aggression

Sexually aggressive behaviors among children are never normal and always warrant careful assessment and treatment by the clinician. These behaviors tend to be part of a larger picture of conduct problems and typically reflect significant psychopathology in the child and/or family (Friedrich, 1990). The clinical picture for children who engage in sexually aggressive behavior appears to vary depending on age and gender. For instance, a history of sexual abuse has been found in almost all cases of sexually aggressive behavior in preadolescent girls (Johnson, 1989). These girls can be distinguished from others who have been abused but do not engage in sexually aggressive behaviors in that they typically have been more severely and frequently abused, have a close relationship to the perpetrator, and tend to come from very dysfunctional families that have not provided support following disclosure of the abuse (Johnson, 1989). In contrast to girls, preadolescent boys who engage in sexually aggressive behavior may or may not have a history of sexual abuse, although the majority come from dysfunctional families (Johnson, 1988). It is suspected that those boys who do not have a history of sexual abuse have been exposed to deviant sexuality of some sort.

Treatment of children who engage in sexually aggressive behaviors is very complex and must necessarily be multifaceted, involving individual, group, and family intervention. The clinician can easily be overwhelmed by these difficult cases, but Friedrich (1990) suggests that a good place to start treatment is with a careful analysis of the needs and issues of the individual child and family. These can then be prioritized and treatment planned to deal with each in turn. Among the issues that are likely to be important for the clinician to address are those related to the child's experience of sexual abuse or exposure to deviant sexuality, the child's own abusive sexual behavior, and parental management of the child's conduct disordered behavior.

Friedrich (1990) notes that many factors can interfere with individual therapy for sexually aggressive youngsters, including lack of support and participation in treatment by a primary parent figure, lack of protection of the child from further victimization, and a therapist who is unwilling or unable to be goal-oriented and directive.

Because of the co-occurrence of sexual aggression and conduct disorder, the approach outlined by G.R. Patterson, Reid, Jones, and Conger (1975) for delinquent and aggressive youth is also an appropriate treatment model to help parents gain better control over their child's sexual and nonsexual aggressive behaviors. This approach assumes that aggressive behavior (including sexual aggression) is learned and involves teaching parents to use systematic rewards (tokens) and punishments (removal of tokens and time-out) for appropriate and inappropriate behaviors. Excellent detailed descriptions of other treatment approaches for sexually aggressive children are provided by Friedrich (1990) and Gil and Johnson (1993).

Adolescent Sexual Offenders

Sexual offenses committed during adolescence are recognized to be a very serious problem. Adolescents accounted for 20% of the arrests for sexual offenses in the United States in 1981 (Brown, Flanagan, & McLeod, 1984) and 15% of forcible rapes in 1990 (Ryan, Miyoshi, Metzner, Krugman, & Fryer, 1996). Further, it has been estimated that adolescent males are responsible for up to 50% of child sexual abuse cases, and it is suspected that this may underrepresent the actual incidence because of a reluctance to report these young offenders (Kempton & Forehand, 1992; Ryan, 1997a).

The victims of adolescent sex offenders are most likely to be younger children; it is estimated that over 60% are under 9 years of age, typically 6 to 8 years old (Fehrenbach, Smith, Monastersky, & Deisher, 1986; Ryan 1997c). Rates of repeated offenses among these teenagers are very high; the average number of victims reported in a national survey was 7.7, with more offenses committed by older teens (Ryan, 1997c; Ryan et al., 1996). At the time of initial contact with authorities, however, these teenagers are not likely to have prior convictions for sexual assault, although the majority have been arrested for other nonsexual offenses (e.g., shoplifting, theft, burglary, assault, vandalism) (Ryan et al., 1996). Research on the nature of the assaults committed by adolescents against children indicates that up to two-thirds involve penetration and/or oral-genital contact (Ryan et al., 1996).

Other offenses include noncontact behaviors such as exhibitionism, obscene telephone calls, and voyeurism, which may precede actual assaults or may occur in between assaults (Ryan, 1997c; Ryan et al., 1996).

Who are these sexually aggressive youngsters? The characteristics of a national sample of 1,600 adolescents referred for evaluation or treatment following a sexual offense are described by Ryan et al. (1996) and indicate some common features in their histories. Consistent with other research, the vast majority of adolescent sexual offenders are male (97.4% vs. 2.6% female). The low number of females in this population may be due to the fact that girls are less likely to come to the attention of mental health or law enforcement professionals either because their numbers are very small or because of societal biases about male and female sexual roles (i.e., males are aggressive, females are passive). It also is possible that the sexual acting-out of girls occurs with peers or in the form of prostitution rather than abuse of younger children.

Child maltreatment and neglect also is common in the histories of these youth, and according to Ryan et al. (1996), few of these incidents result in criminal charges. Matthews, Hunter, and Vuz (1997) report that girls are more likely than boys to have experienced extensive and severe maltreatment with exposure to interpersonal aggression by females as well as males. Other characteristics of sexually aggressive adolescents include the experience of some form of family violence, living in a broken home, and loss of a parent or other important person, indicating significant disruptions in caregiving.

There is general agreement that relative to their nonoffending peers, these adolescents lack maturity, empathy, and a sense of self-worth as a result of feeling inadequately loved and cared for emotionally (Martinson, 1997). Moreover, they have been found to lack appropriate information about sexuality and to externalize blame for their actions. The fact that they engage in sexual deviance versus some other form of inappropriate behavior is thought possibly to stem from early exposure to deviant sexuality through actual sexual abuse or other inappropriate stimuli.

In an effort to understand the unique characteristics of adolescents who commit sexual offenses, O'Brien and Bera (1986) have identified seven categories of adolescent offenders:

1. *Naïve experimenter.* An adolescent who has little sexual experience or knowledge and engages in a few isolated incidences of sexual contact with younger children.
2. *Undersocialized child exploiter.* A socially isolated adolescent who uses manipulation, trickery, or rewards to entice a child to engage in sexual activity. This type of offender may be motivated by an attempt to increase self-esteem.
3. *Pseudosocialized child exploiter.* An older adolescent with good social skills but who lacks meaningful peer relations. Sexual behavior is typically highly rationalized and the offender shows little remorse.
4. *Sexual aggressive.* This type of offender typically comes from a dysfunctional and abusive family. There is often a history of antisocial behaviors, poor impulse control, and drug abuse.
5. *Sexual compulsive.* A youngster who engages in repetitive, sexually arousing behavior (usually nontouching: peeping, exposure, phone calls, etc.) of an addictive nature.
6. *Disturbed impulsive.* This type engages in a single unpredictable, uncharacteristic act or a pattern of bizarre acts that may be the result of thought disorder or substance abuse. There may be a history of severe family problems, substance abuse, or significant learning problems.
7. *Group-influenced.* A younger adolescent whose offense is committed in the context of a peer group as a result of peer pressure or an attempt to gain group approval, attention, or leadership.

Although the clinical utility of these categories has yet to be demonstrated, it seems clear that personality variables play an important role in the deviant sexual behavior of these adolescents. There is some consensus that youngsters who commit sexual offenses are characteristically socially isolated and have significant school/learning problems and psychopathology, including both internalizing and externalizing disorders (Awad & Saunders, 1989; Katz, 1990). Unfortunately, few studies have employed adequate control groups, so it is not yet possible to determine whether these characteristics differentiate adolescents who commit sexual offenses from those who commit nonsexual offenses.

Because adolescent boys who molest children are a diverse group, treatment must be preceded by careful assessment of the individual adolescent and family. The clinician should determine the nature of the sexual offense, the precipitating factors, and the sexual history of the adolescent and members of the immediate family (Gilby, Wolf, & Goldberg, 1989). The clinician also should assess the youngster's intellectual, social, and personality functioning. Becker and Hunter (1997) provide an excellent description of their approach to assessment including an interview format and some objective measures. They recommend caution in the use of phallometric assessment, as their research indicates a weak relationship between arousal patterns and clinical characteristics among adolescents (Hunter & Becker, 1994).

Davis and Leitenberg (1987) suggest that the most important treatment issues include (1) accepting responsibility for the sexual offense; (2) increasing recognition of the impact of the abuse on the victim; (3) gaining insight into the motives that led to the abuse; (4) dealing with the adolescent's own experience of sexual abuse, if this has occurred; (5) sex education; (6) cognitive restructuring with regard to beliefs and myths about sexuality; (7) social skills training with a focus on dating relationships; (8) training in assertiveness skills and anger control; (9) techniques to eliminate deviant arousal patterns; and (10) family therapy to promote effective parenting. The reader also is referred to Sgroi (1989) and Ryan (1997b) for a description of other approaches.

Coercive Sexuality among Adolescents
Coercive sexuality among peers (as opposed to younger children) during adolescence also is a significant problem. A large number of girls report some unwanted sexual contact in the context of dating relationships, and many boys report that they have used coercion to gain sexual contact with girls. Various studies estimate that 50% to 80% of girls have experienced some form of unwanted sexual contact, with 10% to 30% reporting unwanted attempted or completed intercourse (Craig, 1990). Furthermore, 15% to 25% of boys indicate that they have coerced a girl to engage in sexual intercourse against her will (Craig, 1990), and when a broad definition is used (including unwanted kissing), over 57% of college men admit to coerced sexual activity (Muehlenhard & Linton, 1987)!

Girls who experience coerced sex in a dating relationship are at risk for a number of psychological problems that can have long-term consequences, including depression, self-blame, somatic symptoms, posttraumatic stress disorder, and relationship problems. Despite this, it is likely that many girls who experience coerced sex do not seek treatment because of their own and society's tendency to "blame the victim."

Considerable research has been devoted to determining characteristics that distinguish sexually coercive males from those who are noncoercive. Craig (1990) summarizes this work:

> Sexually coercive males appear to be more aggressive, hold beliefs that relationships with women are adversarial in nature, and are supportive of rape myths and stereotypical ideas about sex roles. They tend to be more sexually experienced, but less sexually satisfied than noncoercive men, and have a family history of violence. Peer approval also plays a role, where sex is emphasized as a status symbol. Sexually coercive men are also more sexually aroused by the use of force. (p. 411)

Further, sexually coercive boys actively create dating situations in which sexual contact is likely to occur and misperceive girls' behavior as provocative or insincere. Alcohol or other forms of intoxication are highly likely to be involved in these coercive situations (Muehlenhard & Linton, 1987).

It is not clear whether boys who engage in coercive sex in dating relationships are from the same population of teenagers who are arrested for sex offenses. It is possible that individuals in both groups represent a continuum of coercive behaviors, with juvenile sex offenders engaging in more serious sexual behaviors that bring them to the attention of law enforcement agencies. It may also be the case that one or more subtypes of juvenile sex offenders may represent the extreme of those boys who engage in coercive sex in dating relationships. Among O'Brien and Bera's (1986) seven categories of juvenile sex offenders, the sexual aggressive category includes boys who engage in coercive sexual behavior in dating relationships. These youngsters are described as having good social skills but poor impulse control. Moreover, they are likely to abuse alcohol and/or other chemicals and engage in other antisocial behaviors. The motivation for coerced sex for these youngsters is to experience personal power and/or to humiliate the victim.

Although many adolescent boys who engage in coercive sex with peers may never come to the attention of mental health professionals (i.e., their behavior is never reported by the victims), intervention for more severe cases is important because recidivism rates are very high and these youngsters are at high risk for becoming adult sexual offenders. Treatment in these cases often consists of referral to a residential sex offender program. It also seems important to attempt to prevent coercive sex in dating relationships by including this topic in sex education programs for school-age children and adolescents. Information should be presented that describes how boys and girls perceive social situations and behaviors differently (i.e., boys tend to have a more sexualized perception of interpersonal relations and social cues than do girls) (Craig, 1990). Further, role plays can help teenagers avoid sexual conflict and exploitive situations.

REFERENCES

Achenbach, T.M., & Edelbrock C.S. (1983). *Manual for the Child Behavior Checklist and revised Child Behavior Profile.* Burlington: University of Vermont, Department of Psychiatry.

Adkins-Regan, E. (1988). Sex hormones and sexual orientation in animals. *Psychobiology, 16,* 335–347.

Allen, J.P., Philliber, S., Herrling, S., & Kupermine, G.P. (1997). Preventing teen pregnancy and academic failure: Experimental evaluation of a developmentally based approach. *Child Development, 64,* 729–742.

Allen, L.A., & Gorski, R.A. (1992). Sexual orientation and the size of the anterior commissure in the human brain. *Proceedings of the National Academy of Sciences, USA, 89,* 7199–7202.

American Psychiatric Association. (1994). *Diagnostic and statistical manual of mental disorders* (4th ed.). Washington, DC: Author.

Ansuini, C.G., Fiddler-Woite, J., & Woite, R.S. (1996). The source, accuracy, and impact of initial sexuality information on lifetime wellness. *Adolescence, 31,* 283–289.

Awad, G.A., & Saunders, E.B. (1989). Adolescent child molesters: Clinical observations. *Child Psychiatry and Human Development, 19,* 195–206.

Bailey, J.M., Bobrow, D., Wolfe, M., & Mikach, S. (1995). Sexual orientation of adult sons of gay fathers. *Developmental Psychology, 31,* 124–129.

Bailey, J.M., & Pillard, R.C. (1991). A genetic study of male sexual orientation. *Archives of General Psychiatry, 48,* 1089–1096.

Bailey, J.M., & Zucker, K.J. (1995). Childhood sex-typed behavior and sexual orientation: A conceptual analysis and quantitative review. *Developmental Psychology, 31,* 43–55.

Becker, J.V., & Hunter, J.A. (1997). Understanding and treating child and adolescent sexual offenders. In T.H. Ollendick & R.J. Prinz (Eds.), *Advances in clinical child psychology* (Vol. 19, pp. 177–197). New York: Plenum Press.

Bell, A.P., Weinberg, M.S., & Hammersmith, S.K. (1981). *Sexual preference: Its development in men and women.* Bloomington: Indiana University Press.

Bem, S.L. (1989). Genital knowledge and gender constancy in preschool children. *Child Development, 60,* 649–662.

Bernstein, A.C., & Cowen, P.A. (1975). Children's concepts of how people get babies. *Child Development, 46,* 77–91.

Blanchard, R. (1990). Gender identity disorders in adult men. In R. Blanchard & B.W. Steiner (Eds.), *Clinical management of gender identity disorders in children and adults* (pp. 47–76). Washington, DC: American Psychiatric Press.

Blanchard, R., Clemmensen, L.H., & Steiner, B.W. (1987). Heterosexual and homosexual gender dysphoria. *Archives of Sexual Behavior, 16,* 139–152.

Blanchard, R., Zucker, K.J., Bradley, S.J., & Hume, C.S. (1995). Birth order and sibling sex ratio in homosexual male adolescents and probably prehomosexual feminine boys. *Developmental Psychology, 31,* 22–30.

Blanchard, R., Zucker, K.J., Cohen-Kettenis, P.T., Gooren, L.J.G., & Bailey, J.M. (1996). Birth order and sibling sex ratio in two samples of Dutch gender-dysphoric homosexual males. *Archives of Sexual Behavior, 25,* 495–514.

Borneman, E. (1994). *Childhood phases of maturity: Sexual developmental psychology.* Amherst, NY: Prometheus Books.

Bradley, S.J., & Zucker, K.J. (1997). Gender identity disorder: A review of the past 10 years. *Journal of the American Academy of Child and Adolescent Psychiatry, 36,* 872–880.

Brooks-Gunn, J., & Warren, M.P. (1988). The psychological significance of secondary sexual characteristics in nine- to eleven-year-old girls. *Child Development, 59,* 1061–1069.

Brown, E., Flanagan, T., & McLeod, M. (Eds.). (1984). *Sourcebook of criminal justice statistics 1983.* Washington, DC: Bureau of Justice Statistics.

Buysse, A., & Van Oost, P. (1997). Impact of a school-based prevention programme on traditional and egalitarian adolescents' safer sex intentions. *Journal of Adolescence, 20,* 177–188.

Calderone, M.A., & Johnson, E.W. (1983). *The family book about sexuality* (Rev. ed.). New York: Bantam Books.

Coates, S., & Person, E.S. (1985). Extreme boyhood femininity: Isolated behavior or pervasive disorder? *Journal of the American Academy of Child and Adolescent Psychiatry, 24,* 702–709.

Coley, R.L., & Chase-Lansdale, L. (1998). Adolescent pregnancy and parenthood: Recent evidence and future directions. *American Psychologist, 53,* 152–166.

Craig, M.E. (1990). Coercive sexuality in dating relationships: A situational model. *Clinical Psychology Review, 10,* 395–423.

Davis, G.E., & Leitenberg, J. (1987). Adolescent sex offenders. *Psychological Bulletin, 101,* 417–427.

Dittman, R.W., Kappes, M.E., & Kappes, M.H. (1992). Sexual behavior in adolescent and adult females with congenital adrenal hyperplasia. *Psychoneuroendocrinology, 17,* 153–170.

Elliott, D.S., & Morse, B.J. (1989). Delinquency and drug use as risk factors in teenage sexual activity. *Youth and Society, 21,* 32–57.

Fehrenbach, P.A., Smith, W., Monastersky, C., & Deisher, R.W. (1986). Adolescent sexual offenders: Offender and offense characteristics. *American Journal of Orthopsychiatry, 56,* 225–233.

Finkelhor, D. (1981). Sex between siblings: Sex play, incest, and aggression. In L.L. Constantine & F.M. Martinson (Eds.), *Children and sex: New findings, new perspectives* (pp. 129–149). Boston: Little, Brown.

Fridell, S.R., Zucker, K.J., Bradley, S.J., & Maing, D.M. (1996). Physical attractiveness of girls with gender identity disorder. *Archives of Sexual Behavior, 25,* 17–31.

Friedrich, W.N. (1990). *Psychotherapy of sexually abused children and their families.* New York: Norton.

Friedrich, W.N., Grambsch, P., Broughton, D., Kuiper, J., & Beilke, R.L. (1991). Normative sexual behavior in children. *Pediatrics, 88,* 456–464.

Friedrich, W.N., Grambsch, P., Damon, L., Koverola, C., Wolfe, V., Hewitt, S., Lang, R., & Broughton, D. (1992). The Child Sexual Behavior Inventory: Normative and clinical comparisons. *Psychological Assessment, 4,* 303–311.

Frost, J.J., & Forrest, J.D. (1995). Understanding the impact of effective teenage pregnancy prevention programs. *Family Planning Perspectives, 27,* 188–195.

Gil, E. (1993). Age-appropriate sex play versus problematic sexual behaviors. In E. Gil & T.C. Johnson (Eds.), *Sexualized children: Assessment and treatment of sexualized children and children who molest.* Rockville, MD: Launch Press.

Gil, E., & Johnson T.C. (1993). *Sexualized children: Assessment and treatment of sexualized children and children who molest.* Rockville, MD: Launch Press.

Gilby, R., Wolf, L., & Goldberg, B. (1989). Mentally retarded adolescent sex offenders: A survey and pilot study. *Canadian Journal of Psychiatry, 34,* 542–548.

Golombok S., & Tasker, F. (1996). Do parents influence the sexual orientation of their children? Findings from a longitudinal study of lesbian families. *Developmental Psychology, 32,* 3–11.

Gordon, B.N., & Schroeder, C.S. (1995). *Sexuality: A developmental approach to problems.* New York: Plenum Press.

Gordon, B.N., Schroeder, C.S., & Abrams, J.M. (1990a). Age and social-class differences in children's knowledge of sexuality. *Journal of Clinical Child Psychology, 19,* 33–43.

Gordon, B.N., Schroeder, C.S., & Abrams, J.M. (1990b). Children's knowledge of sexuality: A comparison of sexually abused and nonabused children. *American Journal of Orthopsychiatry, 60,* 250–257.

Gordon, S., & Snyder, S.V. (1983). Sex education. In C.E. Walker & M.C. Roberts (Eds.), *Handbook of clinical child psychology* (pp. 1154–1173). New York: Wiley.

Green, R. (1987). *The "sissy boy syndrome" and the development of homosexuality.* New Haven, CT: Yale University Press.

Gundersen, B.H., Melas, P.S., & Skar, J.E. (1981). Sexual behavior of preschool children. In L.L. Constantine & F.M. Martinson (Eds.), *Children and sex: New findings, new perspectives* (pp. 45–72). Boston: Little, Brown.

Hamar, D.H., Hu, S., Magnuson, V.L., Hu, N., & Pattatucci, A. (1993). A linkage between DNA markers on the X chromosome and male sexual orientation. *Science, 261,* 321–327.

Haroian, L.M. (1991). Sexual problems of children. In C.E. Walker & M.C. Roberts (Eds.), *Handbook of clinical child psychology* (2nd ed., pp. 431–450). New York: Wiley.

Hockenberry-Eaton, M., Richman, M., Dilorio, C., Rivero, T., & Maibach, E. (1996). Mother and adolescent knowledge of sexual development: The effects of gender, age, and sexual experience. *Adolescence, 31,* 35–47.

Hunter, J.A., & Becker, J.V. (1994). The role of deviant sexual arousal in juvenile sexual offending: Etiology, evaluation, and treatment. *Criminal Justice and Behavior, 21,* 132–149.

Jaccard, J., Dittus, P.J., & Gordon, V.V. (1998). Parent-adolescent congruency in reports of adolescent sexual behavior and in communications about sexual behavior. *Child Development, 69,* 247–261.

Jensen, L.C., deGaston, J.R., & Weed, S.E. (1994). Sexual behavior of nonurban students in grades 7 and 8: Implications for public policy and sex education. *Psychological Reports, 75,* 1504–1506.

Johnson, T.C. (1988). Child perpetrators: Children who molest other children: Preliminary findings. *Child Abuse and Neglect, 12,* 219–229.

Johnson, T.C. (1989). Female child perpetrators: Children who molest other children. *Child Abuse and Neglect, 13,* 571–585.

Johnson, T.C., & Friend, C. (1995). Assessing young children's sexual behaviors in the context of child sexual abuse evaluations. In T. Ney (Ed.), *True and false allegations of child sexual abuse: Assessment and case management* (pp. 49–72). New York: Brunner/Mazel.

Katz, R.C. (1990). Psychosocial adjustment in adolescent child molesters. *Child Abuse and Neglect, 14,* 567–575.

Kempton, T., & Forehand, R. (1992). Juvenile sex offenders: Similar to, different from other incarcerated delinquent offenders? *Behavior Research and Therapy, 30,* 533–536.

Kirby, D. (1994). *Sex education in the schools.* Menlo Park, CA: Henry J. Kaiser Family Foundation.

Klein, M., & Gordon, S. (1991). Sex education. In C.E. Walker & M.C. Roberts (Eds.), *Handbook of clinical child psychology* (2nd ed., pp. 933–949). New York: Wiley.

Lamb, S., & Coakley, M. (1993). "Normal" childhood sexual play and games: Differentiating play from abuse. *Child Abuse and Neglect, 17,* 515–526.

LeVay, S. (1991). A difference in hypothalamic structure between heterosexual and homosexual men. *Science, 253,* 1034–1037.

Lim, M.H., & Bottomley, V. (1983). A combined approach to the treatment of effeminate behaviour in a boy: A case study. *Journal of Child Psychology and Psychiatry, 24,* 469–479.

Lundy, M.S., & Rekers, G.A. (1995). Homosexuality: Development, risks, parental values, and controversies. In G.A. Rekers (Ed.), *Handbook of child and adolescent sexual problems* (pp. 290–312). New York: Lexington Books.

Marantz, S., & Coates, S. (1991). Mothers of boys with gender identity disorder: A comparison of matched controls. *Journal of the American Academy of Child and Adolescent Psychiatry, 30,* 310–315.

Martinson, F.M. (1997). Sexual development in infancy and childhood. In G. Ryan & S. Lane (Eds.), *Juvenile sexual offending: Causes, consequences and correction* (pp. 36–58). San Francisco: Jossey-Bass.

Martinson, F.M. (1981). Eroticism in infancy and childhood. In L.L. Constantine & F.M. Martinson (Eds.), *Children and sex: New findings, new perspectives* (pp. 23–35). Boston: Little, Brown.

Matthews, R., Hunter, J.A., & Vuz, J. (1997). Juvenile female sexual offenders: Clinical characteristics and treatment issues. *Sexual Abuse: Journal of Research and Treatment, 9,* 187–199.

Mazur, T., & Cherpak, R.L. (1995). Psychologic issues of adjustment in precocious, normal, delayed, and incongruent puberty. In G.A. Rekers (Ed.), *Handbook of child and adolescent sexual problems* (pp. 55–80). New York: Lexington Books.

Mazur, T., & Dobson, K. (1995). Psychologic issues in individuals with genetic, hormonal, and anatomic anomalies of the sexual system: Review and treatment considerations. In G.A. Rekers (Ed.), *Handbook of child and adolescent sexual problems* (pp. 101–134). New York: Lexington Books.

McConaghy, M.J. (1979). Gender permanence and the genital basis of gender: Stages in the development of constancy of gender identity. *Child Development, 50,* 1223–1226.

Meyer-Bahlburg, H.R.L. (1985). Gender identity disorder of childhood: Introduction. *Journal of the American Academy of Child Psychiatry, 24,* 681–683.

Meyer-Bahlburg, H.R.L., Ehrhardt, A.A., Bell, J.J., Cohen, S.F., Healey, J.M., Feldman, J.F., Morishima, A., Baker, S.W., & New, M.I. (1985). Idiopathic precocious puberty in girls. *Journal of Youth and Adolescence, 14,* 339–353.

Meyer-Bahlburg, H.R.L., Ehrhardt, A.A., Rosen, L.R., Gruen, R.S., Veridiano, N.P., Vann, F.H., & Neuwalder, H.F. (1995). Prenatal estrogens and the development of homosexual orientation. *Developmental Psychology, 31,* 12–21.

Money, J. (1994). *Sex errors of the body and related syndromes: A guide to counseling children, adolescents, and their families* (2nd ed.). Baltimore: Brookes.

Money, J., Devore, H., & Norman, B.F. (1986). Gender identity and gender transposition: Longitudinal study of 32 male hermaphrodites assigned as girls. *Journal of Sex and Marital Therapy, 12,* 165–181.

Money, J., & Ehrhardt, A.A. (1972). *Man and woman, boy and girl: The differentiation and dimorphism of gender identity from conception to maturity.* Baltimore: Johns Hopkins University Press.

Money, J., & Norman, B.F. (1987). Gender identity and gender transposition: Longitudinal outcome study of 24 male hermaphrodites assigned as boys. *Journal of Sex and Marital Therapy, 13,* 75–92.

Money, J., & Russo, A.J. (1979). Homosexual outcome of discordant gender identity/role in childhood. *Journal of Pediatric Psychology, 4,* 29–41.

Morrison, D. (1989). Predicting contraceptive efficacy: A discriminant analysis of three groups of adolescent women. *Journal of Applied Social Psychology, 19,* 1431–1452.

Muehlenhard, C., & Linton, M. (1987). Date rape and sexual aggression in dating situations: Incidence and risk factors. *Journal of Counseling Psychology, 34,* 186–196.

Nelson, J.A. (1981). The impact of incest: Factors in self-evaluation. In L.L. Constantine & F.M. Martinson (Eds.), *Children and sex: New findings, new perspectives* (pp. 163–174). Boston: Little, Brown.

O'Brien, M., & Bera, W. (1986). Adolescent sexual offenders: A descriptive typology. *Preventing Sexual Abuse, 1,* 1–4.

Patterson, C.J. (1992). Children of lesbian and gay parents. *Child Development, 63,* 1025–1042.

Patterson, G.R., Reid, J.B., Jones, R.R., & Conger, R.E. (1975). *A social learning approach to family intervention. Vol. 1: Families with aggressive children.* Eugene, OR: Castalia.

Petty, D.L. (1995). Sex education toward the prevention of sexual problems. In G.A. Rekers (Ed.), *Handbook of child and adolescent sexual problems* (pp. 31–54). New York: Lexington Books.

Pope, A.W., McHale, S.M., & Craighead, W.E. (1988). *Self-esteem enhancement with children and adolescents.* Elmsford, NY: Pergamon Press.

Quattrin, R., Aronica, S., & Mazur, T. (1990). Management of male pseudohermaphroditism: A case report spanning twenty-one years. *Journal of Pediatric Psychology, 15,* 699–709.

Rafkin, L. (1990). *Different mothers: Sons and daughters of lesbians talk about their lives.* San Francisco: Cleis Press.

Rand, C., Graham, D.L.R., & Rawlings, E.I. (1982). Psychological health and factors the court seeks to control in lesbian mother custody trials. *Journal of Homosexuality, 8,* 27–39.

Reis, J., & Herz, E. (1989). An examination of young adolescents' knowledge of and attitude toward sexuality according to perceived contraceptive responsibility. *Journal of Applied Social Psychology, 19,* 231–250.

Rekers, G.A. (1991). Development of problems of puberty and sex roles in adolescence. In C.E. Walker & M.C. Roberts (Eds.), *Handbook of clinical child psychology* (2nd ed., pp. 607–622). New York: Wiley.

Rekers, G.A., & Kilgus, M.D. (1995). Differential diagnosis and rationale for treatment of gender identity disorders and transvestitism. In G.A. Rekers (Ed.), *Handbook of child and adolescent sexual problems* (pp. 225–289). New York: Lexington Books.

Rekers, G.A., Kilgus, M.D., & Gosen, A.C. (1990). Long-term effects of treatment for childhood gender disturbance. *Journal of Psychology and Human Sexuality, 3,* 121–153.

Rekers, G.A., & Lovaas, O.I. (1974). Behavioral treatment of deviant sex-role behaviors in a male child. *Journal of Applied Behavior Analysis, 7,* 173–190.

Rosenfeld, A., Bailey, R., Siegel, B., & Bailey, G. (1986). Determining incestuous contact between parent and child: Frequency of children touching parents' genitals in a nonclinical population. *Journal of the American Academy of Child Psychiatry, 25,* 481–484.

Routh, D.K., & Schroeder, C.S. (1981). Masturbation and other sexual behaviors. In S. Gabel (Ed.), *Behavior problems of childhood* (pp. 387–392). New York: Grune & Stratton.

Rutter, M. (1970). Normal psychosexual development. *Journal of Child Psychology and Psychiatry, 11,* 259–283.

Rutter, M. (1975). *Helping troubled children.* New York: Plenum Press.

Rutter, M., & Rutter, M. (1993). *Developing minds: Challenge and continuity across the life span.* New York: Basic Books.

Ryan, G. (1997a). Incidence and prevalence of sexual offenses committed by juveniles. In G. Ryan & S. Lane (Eds.), *Juvenile sexual offending: Causes, consequences and correction* (pp. 10–18). San Francisco: Jossey-Bass.

Ryan, G. (1997b). Perpetration prevention: Primary and secondary. In G. Ryan & S. Lane (Eds.), *Juvenile sexual offending: Causes, consequences and correction* (pp. 433–456). San Francisco: Jossey-Bass.

Ryan, G. (1997c). Sexually abusive youth: Defining the population. In G. Ryan & S. Lane (Eds.), *Juvenile sexual offending: Causes, consequences and correction* (pp. 3–9). San Francisco: Jossey-Bass.

Ryan, G., Miyoshi, T.J., Metzner, J.L., Krugman, R.D., & Fryer, G.E. (1996). Trends in a national sample of sexually abusive youths. *Journal of the American Academy of Child and Adolescent Psychiatry, 35,* 17–25.

Sanders, G., & Mullis, R. (1988). Family influences on sexual attitudes and knowledge as reported by college students. *Adolescence, 23,* 837–845.

Schaefer, C.E., & Millman, H.L. (1981). *How to help children with common problems.* New York: Van Nostrand-Reinhold.

Schulenberg, J. (1985). *Gay parenting: A complete guide for gay men and lesbians with children.* Garden City, NY: Anchor Books.

Scott-Jones, D., & White, A.B. (1990). Correlates of sexual activity in early adolescence. *Journal of Early Adolescence, 10,* 221–238.

Sgroi, S. (Ed.). (1989). *Vulnerable populations: Sexual abuse treatment for children, adult survivors, offenders, and persons with mental retardation* (Vol. 2). Lexington, MA: Lexington Books.

Slaby, R.G., & Frey, K.S. (1975). Development of gender constancy and selective attention to same-sex models. *Child Development, 46,* 849–856.

Sonis, W.A., Comite, R., Pescovitz, O.H., Hench, K., Rahn, C.W., Cutler, G.B., Loriaus, D.L., & Klein, R.P. (1986). Biobehavioral aspects of precocious puberty. *Journal of the American Academy of Child Psychiatry, 25,* 647–679.

Soutter, A. (1996). A longitudinal study of three cases of gender identity disorder of childhood successfully resolved in the school setting. *School Psychology International, 17,* 49–57.

Stoller, R.J. (1975). *Sex and gender: The transsexual experiment* (Vol. 2). London: Hogarth Press.

Sugar, M. (1995). A clinical approach to childhood gender identity disorder. *American Journal of Psychotherapy, 49,* 260–281.

Symonds, C.L., Mendoza, M.J., & Harrell, W.C. (1981). Forbidden sexual behavior among kin. In L.L. Constantine & F.M. Martinson (Eds.), *Children and sex: New findings, new perspectives* (pp. 151–162). Boston: Little, Brown.

Tanner, J.M. (1962). *Growth at adolescence* (2nd ed.). Oxford, England: Blackwell.

Ward, I.L. (1984). The prenatal stress syndrome: Current status. *Psychoneuroendocrinology, 9,* 3–11.

Waterman, J. (1986). Developmental considerations. In K. MacFarlane & J. Waterman (Eds.), *Sexual abuse of young children: Evaluation and treatment* (pp. 15–29). New York: Guilford Press.

White, S.D., & DeBlassie, R.R. (1992). Adolescent sexual behavior. *Adolescence, 27,* 183–191.

Winkler, R.C. (1977). What types of sex-role behavior should behavior modifiers promote? *Journal of Applied Behavior Analysis, 10,* 549–552.

Winn, S., Roker, D., & Coleman, J. (1995). Knowledge about puberty and sexual development in 11–16 year olds: Implications for health and sex education in the schools. *Educational Studies, 21,* 187–201.

Zucker, K.J. (1990a). Gender identity disorders in children. In R. Blanchard & B.W. Steiner (Eds.), *Clinical management of gender identity disorders in children and adults* (pp. 3–23). Washington, DC: American Psychiatric Press.

Zucker, K.J. (1990b). Psychosocial and erotic development in cross-gender identified children. *Canadian Journal of Psychiatry, 35,* 487–495.

Zucker, K.J. (1990c). Treatment of gender identity disorders in children. In R. Blanchard & B.W. Steiner (Eds.), *Clinical management of gender identity disorders in children and adults* (pp. 27–45). Washington, DC: American Psychiatric Press.

Zucker, K.J., & Bradley, S.J. (1995). *Gender identity disorder and psychosexual problems in children and adolescents.* New York: Guilford Press.

Zucker, K.J., & Green, R. (1992). Psychosexual disorders in children and adolescents. *Journal of Psychology and Psychiatry, 33,* 107–151.

CHAPTER 26

Eating Problems in Children

THOMAS R. LINSCHEID AND L. KAYE RASNAKE

Feeding is the first area of parent-child inter-action in which the child's cooperation is re-quired. Whereas initially, the child's responses are reflexive in nature, very quickly the unique na-tures of both feeder (usually parent) and infant begin to affect each other's behavior in the feeding situation and help to set the stage for adaptive or maladaptive interactional patterns inside and out-side of feeding.

In this chapter, we describe the incidence and na-ture of children's eating problems, the development of normal feeding skills and patterns in children, and a framework for diagnosis and remediation of eating problems in children. Physical and develop-mental factors are stressed.

INCIDENCE AND NATURE OF CHILDREN'S EATING PROBLEMS

A standard classification system for childhood feed-ing disorders does not exist (e.g., Linscheid, 1998). This is due, in part, to the wide variety of feeding problems and the wide variety of disciplines addressing the problems. A continued lack of com-monality in diagnostic criteria and professional in-volvement has made the goal of determining incidence figures somewhat futile. A best-guess estimate based on reports from a variety of settings suggests that 20% to 50% of children exhibit recognized or reportable eating problems (Forsyth, Leventhal, & McCarthy, 1985; Hagekull & Dahl, 1987; Lindberg, Bohlin, & Hagekull, 1991) and that 1% to 3% of infants and children show severe and long-standing eating problems resulting in im-paired growth (Lindberg et al., 1991). More re-cently, Wolraich, Felice, and Drotar (1996) reported that 1% to 5% of all pediatric hospital admissions are due to failure to gain expected weight, and ap-proximately half of these admissions are not due to a predisposing medical condition.

Although estimates of prevalence rates of up to 20% to 50% may seem high, it is possible that this rate actually underestimates the true population prevalence. Rates reported are largely based on cases where help was sought by parents or guardians. Many parents whose children are having problems in other areas will fail to report eating problems. In fact, a survey of a nonclinical sample of 413 parents of infants and toddlers suggests that feeding prob-lems are a common concern for parents. Mealtime difficulties was rated 8th on a list of 20 daily hassles encountered in parenting; 33% of parents endorsed the food refusal item on the Child Behavior Inven-tory, and 35% identified a need for additional infor-mation about nutrition and feeding (M. O'Brien, 1996). In a different sample of 42 children identified as a control group, 55% of the mothers reported ex-perience of some kind of feeding problem (Hagekull & Dahl, 1987). Further, the true incidence of eat-ing problems may be hidden by the tendency to report more general diagnostic labels such as oppositional disorder (*Diagnostic and Statistical Manual of Mental Disorders*, 4th ed. [*DSM-IV*], American Psychiatric Association [APA], 1994), which may well include food refusal or significant mealtime behavior problems.

Recent formal classification systems have recognized the importance of identifying eating problems in very young children. Classification of feeding/eating problems by *DSM-IV* represents a major advancement over *DSM-III-R* (Kerwin & Berkowitz, 1996). The new system offers two broad diagnostic categories: feeding and eating disorders of infancy and early childhood, and eating disorders. This distinction acknowledges that the feeding/eating problems of infants and very young children are characteristically different from those of older children and adolescents. In addition, the requirement that underlying physiological causes be ruled out mandates involvement of necessary medical professionals.

In their book on childhood feeding disorders, Kedesdy and Budd (1998) offer an "integrated multidimensional classification" system. This system includes both descriptive and causal information. The descriptive categories are intended to reflect a definition of feeding disorder characterized as "deviations of ingestive behavior with significant clinical consequences" (p. 13). The eight causal constructs include diet, physical competence, appetite, illness, interaction/management, child constitution, caregiver competence, and systemic. This system augments other systems with the inclusion of caregiver competence (i.e., parent mental illness, maladaptive nutrition beliefs, nonnurturant parenting) and systemic (i.e., poverty, family stressors, multiple feeders) etiologies.

Although these classification systems have good features, we prefer a modified system proposed originally by Palmer, Thompson, and Linscheid (1975) that considers the specific nature of the problems and the probable causes. Under the original system the major problems are (1) mealtime tantrums, (2) bizarre food habits, (3) multiple food dislikes, (4) prolonged subsistence on pureed foods, (5) delay or difficulty in sucking, chewing, or swallowing, and (6) delay in self-feeding. Possible causes for these problems are (1) behavioral mismanagement, (2) neuromotor dysfunction, and (3) mechanical obstructions. Several of the major problems may have one or more of the primary causes; for example, delays in self-feeding may be due to behavioral mismanagement, neuromotor dysfunction, and/or mechanical obstruction. Although the Palmer et al. 1975 system was a good start, it needed expansion to include more problems and an additional category of possible causes. In an earlier edition of this chapter, an expansion of the classification system as shown in Table 26.1 was offered.

Table 26.1 An expansion of the Palmer, Thompson, and Linscheid (1975) classification system for childhood feeding problems.

Major Problems	Possible Causes			
	Behavioral Mismanagement	Neuromotor Dysfunction	Medical or Mechanical Obstruction	Genetic Abnormality
Mealtime tantrums		X		
Bizarre food habits	X			X
Multiple food dislikes	X			X
Prolonged subsistence on pureed foods	X	X	X	
Delay or difficulty in chewing, sucking, or swallowing		X	X	
Delay in self-feeding	X	X	X	
Pica	X			X
Excessive overeating	X			X
Pronounced underintake of food	X	X	X	X
Rumination	X	X		X

The major problems that were added to the original system are (1) pica, (2) overeating, (3) undereating, and (4) rumination. To the list of possible causes, medical and genetic abnormalities were added so that allergies, rare but important disturbances in taste and smell, and genetically related disturbances in appetite (e.g., Prader-Willi syndrome) can be included. In light of recent research that describes the nature and treatment of several feeding problems related to specific medical conditions (e.g., short gut syndrome, dysphagia) or produced by necessary medical treatment that interferes with the normal development of feeding skills and food preferences (cf. Ginsberg, 1988; Linscheid, Tarnowski, Rasnake, & Brams, 1987), addition of a medical category was warranted.

As a possible cause, the term "behavioral mismanagement" was chosen specifically to suggest that the behaviors in question are the result of a failure to teach the child more appropriate and productive feeding patterns. It suggests that the feeding problem is modifiable by environmental contingencies as opposed to medical or surgical treatment. The clinical child psychologist most often will be involved with those problems that have behavioral mismanagement as their cause. It is very important to reiterate, however, that of the problems listed in Table 26.1 that have behavioral mismanagement as a possible cause, eight have other possible causes as well. In reality, most problems will have multiple causes. For example, a problem may originate from a medical condition and be maintained or exacerbated through behavioral mismanagement. Thus, the important need to consult other specialists (e.g., nutritionists, physicians) before embarking on a psychological or behavioral treatment is emphasized.

DEVELOPMENT OF NORMAL FEEDING PATTERNS

Anyone who works with children is acutely aware that knowledge of normal development is crucial to understanding a particular child's problems. This is especially true in diagnosing and treating eating problems in children because there are almost always physical, emotional, developmental, and nutritional factors that must be considered. Birch (1990) edited a special section on eating behavior in the journal *Developmental Psychology* that includes papers on the development of taste preferences, the role of suckling in feeding and attachment, and the effects of environment on food acceptance. This special section is required reading for clinicians and researchers who work with early feeding problems. In addition, a recent book by Capaldi (1996) contains two chapters of particular relevance to child clinicians. Mennella and Beauchamp (1996) provide information on the early development of flavor preferences, and Birch and Fisher (1996) discuss the role of experience in the development of children's eating behavior.

Infants double their weight in the first five months and triple it by the end of the first year (Hoekelman, Blatman, Brunell, Friedman, & Seidel, 1978). This is a period in which growth and intake of food are among the primary concerns of the parents and the pediatrician. At each well child visit, the infant is weighed and measured and his or her growth compared to normative charts. How feeding is going and preparation for changes in feeding schedules or types of food are common topics of discussion during these visits. Parents come to rely a great deal on these visits for feedback on how both they and their infant are doing.

Initially, the child's feeding behavior is controlled exclusively by reflexes and the physiological distress induced by hunger. Current pediatric practice suggests allowing the child to feed on demand for the first few months, with gradual structuring of a feeding schedule by the middle of the first year of life (Satter, 1990b). Nighttime feedings are the rule during the first month but usually are eliminated by the infant during the second month.

Most pediatricians and nutritionists recommend breast-feeding as a first choice, provided the mother is convinced that she wants to breast-feed. A target of 75% of infants being breast-fed at hospital discharge in the year 2000 was established (U.S. Department of Health and Human Services [DHHS], 1990). The advantages of breast-feeding are that the infant receives a balanced and nutritionally adequate diet and has a significantly reduced incidence of gastrointestinal, respiratory, and allergy problems (Cheraskin, 1994). Also, mother-child interaction and bonding are enhanced (but not guaranteed) because of the close physical contact required in breast-feeding. Evidence suggests, however, that bottle-fed babies given proper vitamin and mineral supplements grow and develop normally (AAP Committee of Nutrition, 1976). A major concern in bottle-feeding is that parents will not hold their infants during feedings. This may lead to problems in parent-infant bonding because the opportunity to associate physical contact with need fulfillment is reduced. In fact, even if parents always hold the infant during bottle-feeding, it has been demonstrated that bottle-feeding is a significantly faster form of feeding than breast-feeding. If feeding time represents an important opportunity for social integration and communicative development, as some believe, the difference between breast-fed and bottle-fed babies deserves further evaluation (Paul, Dittrichova, & Papousek, 1996). Also, dental problems, ear infections, and difficulty in weaning have been traced to the practice of putting a baby to bed with a bottle (Bernick, 1971).

Solid foods in the form of infant cereal and pureed foods are started between 4 and 6 months of age, with chopped or table foods added around 8 months of age or when teeth begin to appear (Christophersen & Hall, 1978). Weaning from the breast or bottle usually occurs between 6 and 18 months. Effective feeding during the second six months of life involves selecting foods that the child can readily manipulate. Parents should be present in the feeding situation but restrained sufficiently to allow the child to initiate feeding behaviors (Satter, 1990b).

By the end of this first year, the infant is eating three meals a day with one or two light snacks interspersed. A clear feeding schedule is established, as the child is able to wait for food. The effective parent plans mealtimes and snack delivery so that the child is hungry when foods are offered (Satter, 1990b). Finger feeding, which begins sometime in the sixth or seventh month, is still occurring, and self-feeding with a spoon is often possible by the twelfth month. By 15 months, the infant should be totally capable of self-feeding (Christophersen & Hall, 1978). Further, meals typically should take no longer than 30 minutes. Children who require more than 30 minutes to complete a meal are considered outside of the normal range (Reau, Senturia, Lebailly, & Christoffel, 1996).

After 1 year of age, an infant's appetite and interest in food decrease dramatically. Whereas the infant has gained 12 to 18 pounds in the first year, he or she will experience weight gains of only about 5 pounds per year over the next three to four years (Smith, 1977). This is an especially crucial time for

the development of eating problems because parents who have been primarily concerned with quantity and consistency of intake are now faced with a child whose appetite becomes erratic with changing interests and food likes and dislikes (Schwartz, 1958). Parental anxiety over their child's eating is often greatest during this stage.

Further, during the toddler period, children show an increasing willingness to assert their independence and will. Often, noncompliant behaviors emerge as a result. Some developmentalists argue that these episodes of noncompliance provide the opportunity for children to develop strategies to express their autonomy in socially acceptable ways (e.g., Kuczynski, Kochanski, Radke-Yarrow, & Girius-Brown, 1987). Thus, noncompliant behaviors occurring in the feeding situation and in nonfeeding situations are expected and represent an opportunity for children to mature socially. A caregiver's understanding of and response to these overlapping developments (i.e., changes in appetite and eating patterns and social-emotional maturation) can have a significant impact on the feeding situation. For example, at the same time the quest for autonomy is emerging, the onset of self-feeding and establishment of food preferences are expected. The feeding situation changes from one in which a parent has primary control to one of required shared control between feeder and child (Linscheid, Budd, & Rasnake, 1995).

When the child reaches school-age, a more consistent appetite returns and dietary habits are now the result of patterns learned during the years 1 to 6 and the modeling of the family's eating habits. Foods associated with positive adult interactions become preferred foods (Birch, Zimmerman, & Hind, 1980). The main concerns during this period arise from the likely increase in nonnutritious food as a result of peer pressure and the family's decreased ability to supervise the child's consumption (Christophersen & Hall, 1978).

PREVENTION OF EATING PROBLEMS

Psychologists are playing an increasing role in the psychological management of pediatric problems (cf. Roberts, 1995) and in advising parents, either directly or through consultation to pediatricians and nurses, in the prevention or early remediation of behavioral or emotional problems, many of which are related to eating. Prevention and treatment of feeding problems/disorders in children and adolescents have been aided by recent research on the development of food preferences, feeder-child interactions, and learned feeding habits (e.g., Birch, 1990; Capaldi, 1996).

There are two major avenues to prevention of eating problems in children. The first is to ensure that the child is exposed to the types of food that are developmentally appropriate, thereby providing the child the opportunity to experience different textures and quantities and to practice self-feeding when appropriate. Illingworth and Lister (1964) suggested that the age of 7 to 10 months constitutes a critical period for the introduction of solids, and children who are not introduced to solids during this time will have difficulty learning to chew and swallow solids later. Parents should be educated about the importance of successful introduction of textured foods at this age, as many parents are inclined to revert to pureed foods when their child initially rejects or gags on a new, more textured food. Once introduction of solid food is completed, the parents need to be counseled to provide their child with the full range of textures and food groups so that the child learns to eat a balanced diet.

The second major avenue to prevention of eating problems is to ensure that parents have sufficient knowledge and appropriate techniques to deal with feeding-related behaviors in their child (Satter, 1990a). This is especially important during the ages 1 to 5 years, when the child's appetite and taste preferences become variable and when the drive for independence is demonstrated through denial of parental authority (Bakwin & Bakwin, 1972; Linscheid et al., 1995).

ASSESSMENT OF EATING PROBLEMS IN CHILDREN

The proper assessment of feeding/eating problems requires information from three main areas: medical history and status, nutritional history and status, and behavioral assessment. Two of the three areas are outside of the expertise of the clinical psychologist; however, medical and nutritional assessment is extremely important, and the psychologist who works with feeding problems must be

prepared and willing to develop close working relationships with other disciplines.

MEDICAL ASSESSMENT

Medical conditions that can affect diet or reduce weight gain must be ruled out. These include such conditions as food allergies, thyroid or other endocrine function anomalies, and congenital anomalies of the gastrointestinal tract. Any medical condition affecting central nervous system functioning must be assessed as well. Most frequently, these conditions affect neuromotor functioning and may interfere with responses needed for proper eating. In the past several years, use of videofluoroscopy to study the suck-swallow response has increased. For infants with impaired swallow responses, behavioral attempts to induce swallowing may be dangerous because of the potential for aspiration. Medical history can also reveal conditions that, even though no longer active, may have had a significant effect on the development of the present problem. Children who were seriously ill as infants, especially those who spent a great deal of time in hospitals, may have been prevented from progressing through the normal feeding stages. Sometimes, it is not the medical complication itself that prevented the acquisition of normal feeding skills but the fact that normalizing eating habits and skills in the infant or child was considered of much less importance in light of his or her medical condition.

NUTRITIONAL ASSESSMENT

Nutritional assessment determines the adequacy of intake in relation to age, height, and weight. Specific deficiencies or excesses in nutrients, vitamins, or calories are established, and laboratory tests or biochemical analyses are conducted as needed. Nutritional assessment is extremely important in treatment planning. First, the seriousness of a child's nutritional status is used in determining the intensity of treatment that may be needed. Some authors (e.g., Linscheid et al., 1995; Satter, 1990b) have advised that nutritional status be considered a major criterion when deciding to treat on an outpatient or inpatient basis. Second, nutritional deficits are used to establish treatment goals.

BEHAVIORAL ASSESSMENT

Behavioral assessment has three major purposes: (1) assessment of preferences, (2) assessment of current intake, and (3) assessment of eating-related behaviors. The assumption underlying behavioral assessment is that feeding and eating involve a series of behaviors on the part of the child who is eating (or not eating) and on the part of the individual who is responsible for that child's eating. These eating behaviors can be defined in objective terms, and they can be measured using common behavior assessment techniques and strategies (Linscheid & Rasnake, 1986).

Assessment of Preference
Nutritionists often use food records to assess nutritional status (Ekvall, 1978). These records usually cover a three- to seven-day period and are kept by the child's parent or caregiver. The parent simply writes down what and how much the child ate at each meal. Food records can be used in the determination of a child's preferred and nonpreferred foods; however, they may be misleading in that the range of foods offered by the caregiver may be limited to those he or she knows the child will likely accept. This is especially true if the record is kept for only a few days.

To test whether reported likes and dislikes are accurate, several authors have reported presenting a variety of foods to the child during assessment/baseline sessions and allowing the child to eat what he or she desires (e.g., Linscheid, Oliver, Blyler, & Palmer, 1978; Munk & Repp, 1994). No direct attempt to influence food choice via contingent approval or disapproval or other procedures is used during these sessions. The behavioral reaction (e.g., acceptance, rejection, expulsion, negative behaviors) to each type or texture of food can be recorded. This is especially important if a child is to be treated outside the home or by someone other than his or her usual feeder. Commonly, a child will readily eat a food that was reported by a parent as disliked.

Assessment of Present Intake
As in the assessment of preference, food records kept by the child's parent or caregiver can be helpful in determining a child's intake. Quantity of food consumed is seldom actually weighed or measured, but is usually listed as an estimate, for example, a half a cup of juice or a glass of milk. The food record kept by parents can supply a general estimate of intake but should not be considered highly reliable.

Published reports of feeding treatments have used several methods for assessing intake. The most simple and straightforward method, of course, is to weigh the food before and after eating (cf. Riordan, Iwata, Wohl, & Finney, 1980). Other authors have used number of bites of food or sips of liquid as a measure of intake (Lamm & Greer, 1988; Riordan et al., 1980). The drawback of using bites or sips as a measure of intake, of course, lies in the variability of the amount of food or liquid that can be taken in on any single bite or sip. Riordan et al. (1980) defined a bite as when "the child moved a piece of food from the tray/container so that at least $\frac{1}{2}$ tsp. or $\frac{1}{4}$ in. square piece of food was deposited in the mouth" (p. 99).

An indirect measure of intake is the child's weight. This indirect method of assessing intake has been used most extensively when the presenting problem is obesity or anorexia nervosa but has also been used in assessing intake in infants and younger children (Cunningham & Linscheid, 1976; Lamm & Greer, 1988).

Assessment of Eating-Related Behaviors
The actual consumption of food itself is often a small part of a child's eating problems. The behavior during the feeding session related to the child's reluctance or inability to feed himself or herself may be of more concern than the amount of food consumed. These behaviors fall into two categories: those that are disruptive to or interfere with the consumption of food and those that need to be learned for self-feeding to be possible. Examples of behaviors in the first category are mealtime tantrums, excessive crying, and the spitting out of food. Examples of behaviors in the second category are the absence of spoon use or the fear of swallowing. Observations of eating behaviors can be made directly in the clinic, home, or school, or can be made indirectly through viewing videotapes (Stark et al., 1993; Wherle, Murphy, & Budd, 1993).

Behaviors that interfere with eating have been defined and assessed in various ways. G.A. Thompson, Iwata, and Poynter (1979) assessed tongue thrusting in a youngster with severe mental retardation by defining two separate behaviors that interfered with feeding: "tongue out" and "food expulsion." Assessment of these behaviors was conducted using an interval scoring method and provided the authors with an empirical measure of the rate of the behaviors and the observation that these two behaviors did not always occur simultaneously.

Other behaviors that interfere with eating (e.g., crying, leaving the table) have been assessed. In two studies, crying during the feeding session was assessed by simply recording the duration of crying and then transforming this to a percentage of crying per session by dividing the actual time spent crying by the total length of the feeding session (R.J. Thompson, 1977; R.J. Thompson & Palmer, 1974). F. O'Brien and Azrin (1972) defined inappropriate responses as any response or behavior that would be deemed improper if performed by a customer in a restaurant. A somewhat similar system was used by Barton, Guess, Garcia, and Baer (1970).

When the presenting problem is lack of self-feeding, assessment of pretreatment behavior is done by carefully defining what the appropriate behavior should be and then observing the child in an eating setting in which it is possible to perform the correct eating behavior. No assistance is given to the child during this time. This allows the clinician or therapist to observe what the child will do when entirely on his or her own.

Assessment of Child-Feeder Behaviors

An individual's behavior in any situation is determined not so much by the individual but by his or her interaction with the present environment, especially other individuals in that environment. In any behavioral assessment, observation of the child in the eating situation with the feeder is crucial. Few published studies have reported data on the behavior of the feeder or on the interaction between feeder and child. In a series of reports by Thompson and his colleagues (R.J. Thompson & Linscheid, 1976; Thompson, Palmer, & Linscheid, 1977), they described the adaptation of the mother-child interaction scale procedure originally developed by Moustakas, Segel, and Schalock (1956). Their adaptation was designed to incorporate concepts of operant conditioning and to make the scale applicable to the feeding situation. The scale generated useful data on the nature of the mother-child interaction but was cumbersome to use and required more time

than was realistically possible (or would be available) in the average clinical setting. Subsequently, other infant-feeder interaction scales have been developed and proven useful in the assessment of feeding problems (cf. Stark et al., 1993).

Assessment of Parental Attitudes about Eating and Nutrition

Americans, who have become increasingly concerned about health and diet, are continually exposed to information about nutrition and the positive and negative effects of foods and food additives. The impact of this blitz of information was assessed by Rozin, Ashmore, and Markwith (1996). In an interesting series of studies, they identified a trend for adults to dichotomize foods (i.e., either good or bad) and to show "dose insensitivity" (i.e., "If something is harmful in large amounts, it is also harmful in small amounts"; p. 445). Recently, research has noted increasing parental concern about obesity and about children becoming "junk food addicts," leading to growth failure problems (Birch, 1990). The appropriate concern for healthier diets currently in vogue in this country can have detrimental effects on infants if parents are not aware of infant and child growth needs and how they may differ from adult nutritional needs. For example, some parents show the monotonic thinking described by Rozin et al., believing that an ideal diet is one that contains no fat or sugar, when in reality, the rapid rate of growth during the first year of life necessitates these components. Failure-to-thrive has become more common among middle-class families in which parents overrestrict calorie intake based on fears of obesity (Pugliese, Weyman-Daum, Moses, & Lifshitz, 1987).

For these reasons, assessment of parental attitudes and beliefs about nutrition, obesity, and growth as well as the parents' own eating habits is essential. Interestingly, in the past several years, we have seen two cases of infants with growth failure whose mothers had anorexia nervosa or were recovering from this disease. This clinical experience has been substantiated empirically by Russell, Treasure, and Eisler (1998), who found that children of mothers with anorexia nervosa showed growth failure. The authors reported that all mothers were concerned about their children and had no intention of abusing them; however, the mothers reported fears that their children might become fat.

TREATMENT OF CHILDREN'S EATING PROBLEMS

There is an emerging body of literature on the treatment of eating problems in children. However, most literature has addressed primarily the eating problems of children or adults with developmental disabilities or the problem of childhood obesity from the viewpoint of a weight reduction strategy. In the past 10 years, several studies have documented treatment of feeding problems stemming directly from medical conditions or medical treatment (cf. Babbitt et al., 1994; Stark et al., 1993).

The treatment strategies to be outlined in the remainder of this chapter are direct intervention approaches calling for specific actions or behaviors on the part of the parent, therapist, or child. The issue of the uncooperative parent is often raised when the direct approach is suggested. It is true that parental cooperation, support, and follow-through are needed if feeding treatments are to be successful. The child clinician must assume responsibility for fostering a cooperative, working relationship.

The treatment of eating problems falls into three main categories. The first category of eating problems and their treatment contains those that are best treated within the feeding situation itself. These are most often problems for which quantity of intake is not the major issue because the child is showing normal growth and weight gain. The second category contains those eating problems for which direct treatment during eating may take place but for which treatment outside of the actual feeding situation is also a major component of the overall treatment plan. Quantity of intake, either excessive or insufficient, leading to abnormal growth and weight gain is a major concern in this type of problem. The third category addresses those eating problems occurring in medically compromised infants and children. Although these children may be showing normal growth and weight gain, this is usually maintained via artificial feeding and treatment is needed to create a developmentally and socially normal feeding situation.

Although not the focus of this chapter, a major decision to be made in the treatment of eating problems in infants and young children is where the treatment is to be conducted. Linscheid et al. (1995) discussed the important factors to be considered in making this decision. Briefly, inpatient treatment is generally recommended if (1) the child's medical status is poor, (2) outpatient therapy has been unsuccessful, (3) the parent-child interaction has become so impaired as to preclude effective home-based treatment, or (4) the treatment technique may require medical monitoring. Outpatient treatment is advocated when the child's medical status is stable and the caregivers are available and supportive of the treatment recommendations.

TREATMENT OF EATING PROBLEMS IN CHILDREN WITH NORMAL GROWTH AND WEIGHT GAIN

Non-quantity-related eating problems are those in which the child continues to ingest sufficient (or near sufficient) quantities of food to maintain growth within normal limits. The problem arises because of food type, texture, or variety, or because of specific mealtime conduct problems. In the classification scheme proposed in Table 26.1, these problems include mealtime conduct problems, prolonged subsistence on pureed foods, bizarre food habits, multiple food dislikes, and delays in self-feeding.

Despite adequate intake for weight maintenance, these problems are potentially very serious. For example, children with multiple food dislikes or bizarre food habits may be lacking in or receiving excessive quantities of certain essential vitamins or minerals that could cause serious and irreversible physical complications if allowed to continue. In fact, Marchi and Cohen (1990) found "picky" eating in childhood to be predictive of anorexia nervosa in adolescence. Further, prolonged subsistence on pureed food can cause abnormalities in gums and teeth, and delays in self-feeding can lead to problems in socialization and independence despite a nutritionally adequate diet.

The feeding situation is especially amenable to the use of behavior modification procedures as a remedy for this category of eating problems (Rasnake & Linscheid, 1987). The eating process is made up of objectively definable and quantifiable behaviors; thus, spelling out specific procedures and contingencies is relatively easy. Hunger is a natural source of motivation that can be increased, if necessary, by withholding food (within limits) prior to a treatment session. Linscheid et al. (1995) summarized issues to consider when manipulating appetite, but generally recommend restricting between-meal intake to water only. Although appetite manipulation is a common component of inpatient treatment, it may be more difficult to use this tool in an outpatient treatment program. The child's medical condition and current weight are important determinants of the extent to which access to food is restricted.

Planning for a behaviorally based feeding treatment program should include the following elements. First, the treatment goals in behavioral and nutritional terms should be specified. A second requirement is to establish a measurement system designed to accurately reflect progress toward treatment goals. The reliability of this measurement system must be empirically determined (see Hersen & Bellack, 1976, for a description of observational measurement strategies and reliability determinations). If the therapist has done a good job of pretreatment assessment, these measures have most probably been developed by the time treatment is to begin, and often, the pretreatment behavioral assessment may serve as the baseline against which to compare treatment effects. A third requirement is that behavioral treatment procedures must be spelled out, including a description of what the feeder will do in response to the child's behavior. Empirically supported procedures or ones based on operant or respondent conditioning principles are recommended.

Review of Common Behavioral Treatment Procedures

Positive Reinforcement. The use of positive reinforcement procedures involves the delivery of a desired stimulus contingent on the occurrence of a predetermined behavior. Several studies have reported the use of positive reinforcement to increase the consumption of foods that were previously refused (e.g., Linscheid et al., 1987; Rasnake & Linscheid, 1987; Riordan et al., 1980; Stark, Bowen, Tyc, Evans, & Passero, 1990; Stark et al., 1993). The procedure typically involves the identification of a preferred food, a small portion of which is delivered to the child, along with social praise contingent on the child's consuming a bite of a nonpreferred food. Reinforcement via social interaction or tangible reinforcers is used as well. Foods that are classified as nonpreferred initially often become preferred foods after treatment is initiated

(R.J. Thompson et al., 1977) and hence become positive reinforcers themselves.

Negative Reinforcement. In negative reinforcement, the probability of a response is increased by that response's termination of an ongoing aversive situation or by the avoidance of an aversive situation. The term "negative reinforcement" is often confused with the behavioral term "punishment." In reality, they are very different processes. Negative reinforcement results in an increase in the probability of a response, whereas punishment decreases the probability of a response. Negative reinforcement is the opposite of positive reinforcement only in that the reason for the increase in the rate of behavior is due to a termination of an aversive situation in one (negative reinforcement) and by the addition of a desired stimulus into a nonaversive situation (positive reinforcement) in the other.

Allowing the child to escape an ongoing aversive situation has been used to increase food acceptance (e.g., Ahearn, Kerwin, Eicher, Shantz, & Swearingin, 1996, Babbitt et al., 1994; Hoch, Babbitt, Coe, Krell, & Hackbert, 1994). For example, Hoch et al. presented food to the child with the verbal prompt to eat. If the food was not accepted, the utensil with the food was kept in contact with the child's lip until it was accepted. Assuming that the child finds the presence of the food-filled utensil aversive, escape is possible by opening the mouth and accepting the food. Negative reinforcement is most often used with positive reinforcement.

Time-Out from Positive Reinforcement. Time-out is a punishment technique designed to reduce the probability of a specific behavior or set of behaviors. Punishment as a behavioral term should not be interpreted to mean a procedure or event that is physically painful. Punishment in behavioral terminology refers to the reduction in the probability of a response because of a contingent stimulus event. Time-out from positive reinforcement is just what it suggests: a time period during which no positive reinforcement is available. If time-out is made contingent on a specific behavior and that behavior decreases in frequency, then time-out is a punisher. In feeding treatment, time-out has been used in a variety of ways (e.g., Barton et al., 1970; Linscheid et al., 1978, 1987).

Time-out can be a very effective procedure, especially if it is revealed during the assessment phase that the child uses food refusal to increase social interaction with the feeder. In one case, it was observed prior to treatment that the child's food refusals induced increased verbalizations from his mother. Quantitative analysis revealed that the rate of verbalization during the feeding session was 2.6 words per second. The decision to include the withdrawal of social interaction (time-out) for food refusal and the contingent delivery of social praise and verbal interaction (positive reinforcement) based on acceptance of nonpreferred foods was an easy one. The case was successfully treated in a very short time.

Extinction. Extinction is the reduction in the probability of a response when that response is no longer reinforced. In the feeding situation, extinction is used to decrease the probability of an undesirable response if pretreatment analysis makes it possible to identify the source of reinforcement for that response. For example, a child who is dawdling over food may be doing so to induce his or her mother to interact with him or her.

Specifically, the parent is instructed to pay no attention to the child when the child is not actively eating. If the child's dawdling had been reinforced by the mother's attention, we would expect dawdling to decrease when it is no longer reinforced. Extinction (ignoring), in this case, may sound very similar to a time-out procedure. Extinction and time-out, however, are really quite different procedures. Time-out requires an overt act such as turning away from the child, removing the child's food, or removing the child from the feeding situation. Time-out also imposes a time period during which the child can receive no positive reinforcement, regardless of behavior. With the use of extinction, no specific behavior on the part of the feeder is required. The only requirement is that the feeder pay no attention to a specific behavior; that is, the feeder acts as if totally unaware that the child is engaged in the behavior. Extinction is not based on time and does not rule out the possibility of providing reinforcement for desirable responses.

Although extinction seems on the surface to be a simple and straightforward concept, it is often ineffective in the treatment of feeding disorders. Two major difficulties are encountered when ignoring is used. First, it is usually impossible for a parent or feeder to ignore a behavior completely. The slightest bit of annoyance or distress shown on a parent's face while attempting to ignore a feeding behavior may be enough reinforcement for the child to ensure that the behavior continues. Second, if ignoring is chosen as a treatment procedure, the parent or feeder must be willing to go all the way and not attend to the behavior even though it may increase in frequency or intensity (Drabman & Jarvie, 1977).

In summary, ignoring (extinction) is a simple procedure conceptually, but a very difficult procedure to implement and should be used only in limited situations. Kanner (1957) warned against the use of ignoring, reasoning that the parent's underlying inability to ignore the child's behavior may be a major contributor to the problem in the first place. In our experience, this certainly is true, and it is much better to recommend a more active rather than passive treatment role for parents.

Shaping. Shaping, or the method of successive approximations, is used to teach new behaviors that are not presently in the child's repertoire of responses. In a shaping procedure, the behavior to be taught is broken down into its components. The frequency or probability of each of the components is then increased through contingent reinforcement in a sequential manner, beginning with the component most removed from the final behavior and ending with the component that is the final stage of the total behavior.

Linscheid and colleagues (1978) used a modification of the shaping procedure to teach a 3-year-old with severe mental retardation to accept spoon feeding. Prior to treatment, the child ate only from a bottle. Attempts to place anything other than a bottle with nipple near his mouth resulted in his screaming, kicking, and placing his hands in his mouth. The spoon was gradually brought closer to the child's mouth in a series of preplanned steps until he was required to allow it to touch his lips before reinforcement was delivered.

Fading or Manual Guidance. With children, this procedure has been used most frequently to train proper self-feeding skills (Azrin & Armstrong, 1973; F. O'Brien, Bugle, & Azrin, 1972). The procedure involves the feeder manually guiding the child through the entire behavior to be learned and then gradually withdrawing his or her physical control.

The withdrawal of control begins at the end of the behavior and is removed in a backward manner until only a slight physical prompt is needed to initiate the entire behavior response. The procedure does require skill in the systematic withdrawal of control by the trainer, and unless this is carefully monitored, the results can be that the child effectively trains the trainer to do it for him or her (i.e., feed him or her).

TREATMENT OF EATING PROBLEMS IN CHILDREN WITH ABNORMAL GROWTH AND WEIGHT GAIN

Childhood Obesity

Parents, physicians, school personnel, and psychologists have become increasingly concerned about childhood obesity (e.g., Epstein, Saelens, Myers, & Vito, 1997; Epstein, Valoski, Wing, & McCurley, 1994). Data suggest that 20% to 25% of children and adolescents (6–18 years of age) are overweight (e.g., Troiana, Flegal, Kuczmanski, Campbell, & Johnson, 1995). Alarmingly, Deitz (1988) reported a 54% and 39% increase in the prevalence of obesity in 6 to 11 and 12 to 17-year-olds, respectively, over the past 20 years.

Childhood obesity can be a serious problem. Obese children are more likely to be obese adults. Stunkard and Burt (1967) reported that the odds against obese 13-year-olds becoming normal-weight adults were 4:1. If they are still obese when they reach adolescence, the odds increase to 28:1. There are increased medical risks associated with obesity (Wolf & Colditz, 1996). Obese children and adolescents may suffer from psychological and social problems in the areas of peer acceptance, discrimination from adults, and disturbed body image and self-concept (Foreyt & Goodrick, 1988).

There are likely many causes of obesity in children. Genetics are obviously involved, as it has been shown that if one parent is obese, the incidence of obesity in children increases from 10% to 25%. If both parents are obese, the incidence of obesity in their children has been estimated to be 50% or higher (Deutscher, Epstein, & Kjelsberg, 1966).

Behaviorally oriented therapists have been involved in the treatment of obesity, initially with adults and subsequently with children. The two most direct causes of obesity, overintake of food and lack of exercise, have habit components, and thus the behavioral model, with its emphasis on assessment of behavior and direct behavior change, is uniquely appropriate for the treatment of obesity.

Treatment of obesity in children can best be described in two categories: direct and indirect. Indirect treatments address underlying factors thought to be causes of obesity and assume if the underlying causes of obesity are alleviated, then weight loss will naturally occur (Bruch, 1957). With this approach, the emotional concerns and adjustment of the child rather than eating behavior and habits are the subject of therapy. This approach to treating obesity, which has generally not been successful, has two major drawbacks. First, emotional problems seen in children are not always the cause or the effect of the obesity. Second, there is no guarantee that the child will automatically lose weight, even if an indirect treatment is successful. Habits and food preferences learned while the child is obese are not easily changed, even if the desire to lose weight is strong and genuine.

At present, the most promising direct approach to the reduction of weight in obese children is through behavior modification procedures originally developed for use with adults (cf. Powers, "Behavior Therapy," in this volume). There are now a significant number of studies documenting weight loss in obese children using behavior modification procedures (cf. Brownell & Stunkard, 1978; Epstein, McCurley, Wing, & Valoski, 1990; Epstein, et al., 1994; Epstein & Wing, 1987). Factors related to the long-term maintenance of weight loss have only recently been documented (Epstein et al., 1990, 1994).

The major components of the behavioral approach have been described by Brownell and Stunkard (1978) and are summarized below. Many of the procedures used in behavioral weight loss programs are the same as or similar to those used with adults.

Self-Monitoring/Stimulus Control. The child is required to write down or in some other way record daily his or her food intake and its caloric value and weight, his or her activity level, and any occurrences that are felt to affect his or her moods or intake. One result of self-monitoring is the documentation of where the child eats, with whom he or she eats, and how he or she is feeling. The assumption is that if the child frequently eats in a specific location, then that location will come to acquire the property of eliciting the desire to eat. Stimulus situations that signal eating can be identified and then avoided or changed so that they no longer elicit the desire to eat. Epstein and Squires (1988) developed a "stoplight" diet for children in which the colors green, yellow, and red are used to classify foods. Green or "go" foods are those that are low in calories and high in nutritional value; yellow foods are those for which the child should exercise caution; and red foods are high in calories and low in nutritional value. Children can use this signaling or stimulus control system to assist in food selection.

Slowing the Act of Eating. Most obese adults eat faster than nonobese adults. This pattern has been documented in children as well (Drabman, Hammer, & Jarvie, 1977). Drabman et al. also observed that obese children chewed less than nonobese children. To slow the speed of eating, several techniques have been employed. One requires the child to set his or her utensils down between bites. Another technique requires the counting of each bite. A third introduces a delay of a set amount of time between helpings. Slower eating allows the initial absorption of food to send physiological messages of fullness before all the food is eaten.

Reinforcement. Reinforcement for weight loss or for behaviors incompatible with overeating constitutes a major component of most programs. This is easily accomplished with children because it is usually easy to identify and deliver reinforcers. Older children should be included in designing their own reinforcement system. Reinforcement for parental habit changes is also very important in the attainment and maintenance of child weight loss. This reinforcement can be provided by the child to the parent and vice versa (Epstein et al., 1990, 1994).

Cognitive Restructuring. This is a form of self-control in which less productive thoughts or feelings are controlled through supplying the child with legitimate counterarguments. For example, a child who relates that he or she often thinks "I'll never be able to lose 20 pounds" may be instructed to think "My goal this week is only one pound. I can make that." Cognitive restructuring requires that the child be able to identify his or her own internal statements and be able to verbalize them accurately. For this reason, this technique may be more useful with the older child.

Exercise. Increasing exercise and physical activity is an important component of any treatment of childhood obesity. Although exercise alone is usually not sufficient, combined with diet, an increase in physical activity has been associated with successful weight loss and weight control (cf. Epstein, 1992). Further, Epstein, Wing, Koeske, Ossip, and Beck (1982) showed that reinforcement of lifestyle exercise changes was superior to programmed aerobic exercises for weight loss and fitness. Lifestyle changes were defined as habit changes that increase energy expenditure outside of specific exercise programs, for example, walking home for lunch rather than staying at school during lunch break. In their 10-year follow-up report, Epstein et al. (1994) provided clear support for the importance of exercise in the treatment of obesity in children (58% of the children in the aerobic group and 64% of those in the lifestyle exercise group maintained a weight decrease of 20% as compared to an increase of 20% in the calisthenics control group).

In summary, to use a behavioral approach to treatment of obesity in children, the clinician must carefully assess the child's eating patterns and cognitive style. An initial assessment phase detailing current habits, nutritional knowledge, and attitudes toward eating and weight is vitally important when planning an individualized program (cf. McKenzie, Klein, Epstein, & McCurley, 1993). Perhaps more important is the inclusion of the parent(s)/family in the treatment process. When only child behaviors are targeted, without involvement of the parent, there is little evidence of weight loss maintenance (Epstein et al., 1990, 1994).

Nonorganic Failure to Thrive

Nonorganic failure to thrive (NOFTT) has traditionally described a condition in which an infant or child demonstrates physical growth failure in the absence of a specific medical condition. Diagnosis is made by ruling out medical causes of growth retardation and is often confirmed by the success of behavioral interventions or when it is observed that the infant gains weight when removed from the environment in which the NOFTT was observed. The fourth edition of the *DSM* (APA, 1994) includes a diagnostic category called feeding disorder of infancy and early childhood that reflects the traditional definition of NOFTT. Diagnostic criteria include persistent failure to eat adequate amounts leading to significant failure to gain weight at an expected rate, absence of a medical cause, onset before age 6 years, and the disorder is not accounted for by another mental disorder such as rumination.

Prevalence rates range from 6% to 35%, suggesting a fairly common disorder (Linscheid & Bennett Murphy, 1999). The wide prevalence estimate range reflects historical problems with definition and provides a reminder that NOFTT is not really a diagnosis but, more accurately, a description of a state of nutrition.

Numerous etiological factors have been proposed. Linscheid and Rasnake (1986) proposed two types of NOFTT. Type I occurs in infants usually below 8 months of age and is related to deficiencies in contingency experiences for both infant and mother. Type II occurs in children over 1 year of age and is related more to behavioral mismanagement of feeding and difficulties in achieving independent feeding. Although NOFTT has often been linked to environmental deprivation (cf. Drotar, 1985), it is interesting to note, as reported earlier, that Pugliese et al. (1987) documented NOFTT based solely on overconcern by parents about the amount of fat and calories in their infant's diet. Thus, the etiological factors remain unclear (see Linscheid & Bennett Murphy, 1999, for an extended discussion of theoretical models of NOFTT).

Palmer and Kim (1978) argued that an interdisciplinary team made up of a nutritionist, physician, social worker, psychologist, and public health nurse is essential to the successful treatment of NOFTT and should be involved from the very beginning of treatment. Treatment has included direct behavioral approaches, as discussed in this chapter, as well as psychological and psychoeducational interventions (Drotar, 1995).

Rumination

Rumination is the voluntary regurgitation of food or liquid. The food or liquid is either allowed to run from the mouth or is rechewed and reswallowed. It can occur in individuals at any age but seems to be found most often in two separate groups: normal infants between 4 months and 1 year of age and children and adults with mental retardation. Flanagan (1977), in reviewing the literature during the 20 years prior to his paper, found only 23 reported cases in infants. The incidence for the population of individuals with mental retardation is much higher. Although rare in nondisabled populations, rumination, especially in infants, is a

potentially fatal behavior. Kanner (1957) found that, of 53 cases reviewed, 11 had died as a result of malnutrition and other complications directly attributable to rumination.

The diagnosis of rumination is made only after all potential medical explanations for the vomiting have been ruled out. Observation of the child while he or she is ruminating is important when initially considering the diagnosis. One component of rumination mentioned by several authors is the observable pleasure or self-satisfaction that the infant appears to derive from rumination. For this reason, observation of the child can help to establish the diagnosis and can differentiate rumination from other sources of psychogenic vomiting that may be caused by stress, desire for attention, or spite (Bakwin & Bakwin, 1972).

Several explanations have been advanced for the cause of rumination in infants. Richmond, Eddy, and Green (1958) suggested that the cause of rumination is faulty mothering. They described the mothers of ruminating infants as unable to relate to their babies, fearful of their infant's death, and immature, with an accompanying incapacity to want, accept, and give to their baby. However, when analyzing the interaction between mother and infant, one must be careful not to confuse cause and effect. It is important to keep in mind that the interaction between mother and infant can be significantly changed due to the prolonged occurrence of ruminating with resulting hospitalization. What would be the normal response of a mother whose infant is in serious medical danger due to excessive self-initiated vomiting of unknown cause?

Behaviorally oriented authors have suggested that the basic causes of rumination for both infants and individuals with mental retardation are pleasurable self-stimulation and the attention that the behavior may elicit from others (Linscheid & Cunningham, 1977; Scheinbein, 1975). With this explanation, the crucial variable is not parental psychopathology itself but the lack of attention that may be given to the infant as a result. Any situation leading to reduced stimulation or attention can lead to the development of rumination. Once the act of ruminating begins, it may be maintained by its pleasant, self-stimulatory properties and become a habit.

Treatment of rumination can include two components. First, providing the infant with a warm, caring, and stimulating environment, sometimes requiring a mother substitute, is recommended (Berline, McCullough, Lisha, & Szurek, 1957; Richmond et al., 1958). Second, in severe cases, behavioral treatment of rumination has employed aversive procedures with a great deal of success. Lang and Melamed (1969) were the first to use electric shock as an aversive stimulus and were successful in eliminating rumination in an infant within nine days of treatment. Subsequently, other authors have reported comparable success with infants over short periods using mild electric shock as the aversive stimulus (Cunningham & Linscheid, 1976; Linscheid & Cunningham, 1977; Toister, Colin, Worley, & Arthur, 1975). The procedure has been used with ruminators who are mentally retarded as well (Luckey, Watson, & Musick, 1968).

Pica

Pica is the name given to the ingestion of inedible substances. Mouthing and occasional swallowing of nonfood items are common in all children before they begin to walk but usually disappear spontaneously. The problem is more likely to be found in children with mental retardation. Estimates of prevalence in institutionalized populations range from approximately 4% (Harden & Sahl, 1997) to approximately 26% (Danford & Huber, 1982). In children who engage in pica after they begin walking, the habit is especially difficult to break (Bakwin & Bakwin, 1972). The dangers from pica do not derive from the act itself but from the type of substances consumed. Common substances ingested are paint, soot, chalk, dirt, plaster, tobacco, and cloth. The most serious result of pica is the potential for lead poisoning, which occurs when substances such as paint or plaster are consumed. Lead poisoning can lead to neurological impairment and mental retardation.

The reduction of pica-related lead poisoning can occur through the elimination of the potential for lead ingestion by removing the sources of lead in the child's environment. Most urban communities have programs to warn parents of these dangers. In addition, there is some evidence that enriching the child's physical and emotional environment may indeed be an appropriate treatment for pica (Madden, Russo, & Cataldo, 1980).

In addition, general behavioral principles have been found effective in treatment packages for pica. Discrimination training packages have been shown to be particularly efficacious. For example, Bogart,

Piersel, and Gross (1995) reported a multiphase intervention to teach discrimination of edible from nonedible items to an institutionalized 21-year-old woman with profound mental retardation. First, a collection of medically approved nonfood items was identified. This was an essential feature of the intervention, as "baiting" was used to establish the connection between punishment and nonedibles. Then, using verbal reprimands, handheld restraints, and facial screening as consequences of consumption of nonfood items, pica was reduced to slightly over one incident per month. The authors note that although the behavior was managed successfully, an extensive allocation of staff resources was necessary. Other behavioral techniques have been used successfully to treat pica, such as negative practice (Duker & Nielen, 1993) and habit reversal (Woods, Miltenberger, & Lumley, 1996). One interesting alternative to punishment strategies was described by Hirsch and Myles (1996). A 10-year-old child with diagnoses of autism and pica was provided with a "pica box" containing alternatives to the inedible items selected by the child. The box contained edible (e.g., raisins, jerky, crackers) and inedible (e.g., washcloth, plastic toy, multicolored handkerchief) items selected to resemble in appearance and texture items the child had shown preferences for in the past. Using an ABAB design, the authors reported a significant drop in pica attempts when the pica box was available. The authors do note that the box provides a safe alternative but does not "cure" the behavior.

Often, children diagnosed with pica are placed in mechanical restraints in an effort to reduce the risks associated with ingestion of inedible items (Rojahn, Schroeder, & Mulick, 1980). In an interesting case study, LeBlanc, Piazza, and Krug (1997) determined that "the use of restraints did not decrease the amount of supervision and effort required to maintain" the safety of a 4-year-old child with severe retardation. The child had more attempts at pica when not in restraints; however, she did not have a higher frequency of ingestion of inedibles. The authors proposed a process to be used for making decisions about the need for mechanical restraints during treatment for pica. This process involves the consideration of a number of variables (e.g., play behaviors, negative vocalizations, pica attempts, therapist effort), weighing the concerns for safety and the intrusiveness of the restraints. Given the potential negative impact of restraints (i.e., reduced social interactions, restriction of movement), additional work in this area seems warranted.

Recently, the relation of pica and obsessive-compulsive disorder (OCD) has been considered. Responding to a report by Zeitlin and Polivy (1995), Luiselli (1996) pondered the likelihood of pica's being a manifestation of OCD in persons with developmental disabilities. He suggested that combined behavioral and pharmacological treatment interventions (i.e., selective serotonin reuptake inhibitors) should be examined.

TREATMENT OF EATING PROBLEMS IN MEDICALLY COMPROMISED INFANTS AND CHILDREN

With the advancement of medical and surgical technology, many children with severe prematurity or medical complications at birth are now surviving into childhood and adolescence. To save these children, artificial feedings are often necessary. The need for artificial feeding often precludes the normal development of sucking, swallowing, and chewing, and these children are at risk for developing feeding problems once the medical condition is stable and the artificial feedings are no longer medically necessary (Ginsberg, 1988). The most common problems to develop as a result of prolonged artificial feedings are disturbances in appetite and dysphagia, or fear of swallowing (Handen, Mandell, & Russo, 1986; Lamm & Greer, 1988).

Behavioral procedures described earlier have been successfully used to treat these problems. For example, Linscheid et al. (1987) taught a 6-year-old with short gut syndrome to chew and swallow using positive reinforcement, punishment, and shaping. Blackman and Nelson (1985) reported the use of a forced feeding procedure to treat food refusal in children maintained on G-tubes. A technique developed by Iwata and colleagues (Iwata, Roirdan, Wohl, & Finney, 1982) also used forced feeding but gave the individuals two seconds to accept the food prior to placing it in their mouths.

The treatment of medically related feeding problems in infants and children will surely become one of the major concerns for pediatric psychologists as more and more children with severe medical problems are successfully treated. Additionally, because of the child's precarious medical condition, treatment is most often conducted in an inpatient pediatric or specialized hospital unit. Research into the effects of early artificial feeding on appetite regulation, swallowing, and feeding skill development is still in its infancy.

CONCLUDING REMARKS

Eating and feeding problems in children are common and varied and may have multiple etiologies. The impact of a feeding problem on a child's physical growth and development and on parent-child interaction can be dramatic and long-lasting. As discussed, the complexity of feeding problems is reflected in the difficultly in developing an agreed upon classification system sufficiently broad to encompass the diversity of feeding and eating difficulties. A classification system utilizing both etiology and problem presentation is proposed.

Adequate assessment of feeding problems includes nutritional, medical, and behavioral approaches. Interventions are generally behaviorally based when assessment indicates that the problem is due to faulty or inadequate learning or poor behavior management in the feeding situation. Increasingly, the impact of early medical conditions has been recognized as an etiological factor in feeding problems. Awareness of the interaction between medical condition and normal development of feeding skills is critical for the successful treatment of many feeding disorders.

The best and most appropriately planned treatment is not better than its implementation (Linscheid, 1998). The main threats to program integrity are the complexity of the program, the number and type of people involved, the setting in which the program is to be carried out, the child's medical condition, and the willingness of parents or caregivers to be involved and to follow through.

REFERENCES

American Academy of Pediatrics Committee on Nutrition. (1976). Commentary on breast-feeding and infant formulas, including proposed standards for formulas. *Pediatrics, 57*(2), 278–285.

Ahearn, W.H., Kerwin, M.E., Eicher, P.S., Shantz, J., & Swearingin, W. (1996). An alternating treatments comparison of two intensive interventions for food refusal. *Journal of Applied Behavior Analysis, 29,* 321–332.

American Psychiatric Association. (1994). *Diagnostic and statistical manual of mental disorders* (4th ed.). Washington, DC: Author.

Azrin, N.H., & Armstrong, P.M. (1973). The "mini-meal": A method of teaching eating skills to the profoundly retarded. *Mental Retardation, 11*(1), 9–13.

Babbitt, R.L., Hoch, T.A., Coe, D., Cataldo, M.F., Kelly, K., Stackhouse, C., & Perman, J. (1994). Behavioral assessment and treatment of pediatric feeding disorders. *Journal of Behavioral and Developmental Pediatrics, 15*, 278–291.

Bakwin, H., & Bakwin, R.M. (1972). *Behavioral disorders in children.* Philadelphia: Saunders.

Barton, E.S., Guess, D., Garcia, E., & Baer, D.M. (1970). Improvement of retardates' mealtime behaviors by time-out procedures using multiple baseline techniques. *Journal of Applied Behavior Analysis, 3*, 77–84.

Berlin, I.N., McCullough, G., Lisha, E.S., & Szurek, S. (1957). Intractable episodic vomiting in a three year old child. *Psychiatric Quarterly, 31*, 228–249.

Bernick, S.M. (1971). What the pediatrician should know about children's teeth. *Clinical Pediatrics, 10*, 243–244.

Birch, L.L. (1990). Development of food acceptance patterns. *Developmental Psychology, 26*, 515–519.

Birch, L.L., & Fisher, J. (1996). The role of experience in the development of children's eating behavior. In E. Capaldi (Ed.), *Why we eat what we eat: The psychology of eating* (pp. 113–141). Washington, DC: American Psychological Association.

Birch, L.L., Zimmerman, S., & Hind, H. (1980). The influence of social-affective context on preschool children's food preference. *Child Development, 51*, 856–861.

Blackman, J.A., & Nelson, C. (1985). Reinstituting oral feedings in children fed by gastrostomy tube. *Clinical Pediatrics, 24*, 434–438.

Bogart, L.C., Piersel, W.C., & Gross, E.J. (1995). The long-term treatment of life-threatening pica: A case study of a woman with profound mental retardation living in an applied setting. *Journal of Developmental and Physical Disabilities, 7*(1), 39–50.

Brownell, K.D., & Stunkard, A.J. (1978). Behavioral treatment of obesity in children. *American Journal of Diseases in Children, 132*, 403–412.

Bruch, H. (1957). *The importance of overweight.* New York: Norton.

Capaldi, E. (1996). *Why we eat what we eat: The psychology of eating.* Washington, DC: American Psychological Association.

Cheraskin, E. (1994). The myths of milk. *Journal of Orthomolecular Medicine, 9*, 151–156.

Christophersen, E.R., & Hall, C.L. (1978). Eating patterns and associated problems encountered in normal children. *Issues in Comprehensive Pediatric Nursing, 3*, 1–16.

Cunningham, C.E., & Linscheid, T.R. (1976). Elimination of chronic infant ruminating by electric shock. *Behavior Therapy, 7*, 231–234.

Danford, E.E., & Huber, M. (1982). Pica among mentally retarded adults. *American Journal of Mental Deficiency, 87*, 141–146.

Deitz, W.H. (1988). Metabolic aspects of dieting. In N.A. Krasnegor, G.D. Grave, & N. Kretchmer (Eds.), *Childhood obesity: A biobehavioral perspective* (pp. 173–182). Caldwell, NJ: Telford Press.

Deutscher, S., Epstein, F.H., & Kjelsberg, M.O. (1966). Familial aggregation of factors associated with coronary heart disease. *Circulation, 33*, 911–924.

Drabman, R.S., & Jarvie, G. (1977). Counseling parents of children with behavior problems: The use of extinction and time-out techniques. *Pediatrics, 59*(1), 78–85.

Drabman, R.S., Hammer, D., & Jarvie, G.J. (1977). Eating styles of obese and nonobese Black and White children in a naturalistic setting. *Addictive Behaviors, 2*, 83–86.

Drotar, D. (Ed.). (1985). *New directions in failure-to-thrive: Implications for research and practice.* New York: Plenum Press.

Drotar, D. (1995). Failure to thrive (growth deficiency). In M.C. Roberts (Ed.), *Handbook of pediatric psychology* (2nd ed., pp. 516–536). New York: Guilford Press.

Duker, P.C., & Nielen, M. (1993). The use of negative practice for the control of pica behavior. *Journal of Behavior Therapy and Experimental Psychiatry, 24*, 249–253.

Ekvall, S. (1978). Assessment of nutritional status. In S. Palmer & S. Ekvall (Eds.), *Pediatric nutrition in developmental disorders* (pp. 502–526). Springfield, IL: Thomas.

Epstein, L.H. (1992). Exercise and obesity in children. *Journal of Applied Sport Psychology, 4*, 120–133.

Epstein, L.H., McCurley, J., Wing, R.R., & Valoski, A. (1990). Five-year follow-up of family-based behavioral treatments for childhood obesity. *Journal of Consulting and Clinical Psychology, 58*, 661–664.

Epstein, L.H., Saelens, R.E., Myers, M., & Vito, D. (1997). Effects of decreasing sedentary behavior on activity choice in obese children. *Health Psychology, 16*, 107–113.

Epstein, L.H., & Squires, S. (1988). *The stoplight diet for children.* Boston: Little, Brown.

Epstein, L.H., Valoski, A., Wing, R.R., & McCurley, J. (1994). Ten-year outcomes of behavioral family-based treatment to childhood obesity. *Health Psychology, 13*, 373–383.

Epstein, L.H., & Wing, R.R. (1987). Behavioral treatment of childhood obesity. *Psychological Bulletin, 101*, 91–95.

Epstein, L.H., Wing, R.R., Koeske, R., Ossip, D.O., & Beck, S. (1982). A comparison of lifestyle change and programmed aerobic exercise on weight and fitness changes in obese children. *Behavior Therapy, 13*, 91–95.

Flanagan, C.H. (1977). Rumination in infancy—past and present. *American Academy of Psychiatric Services for Children, 38,* 140–149.

Foreyt, J.P., & Goodrick, G.K. (1988). Childhood obesity. In E.J. Mash & L.G. Terdal (Eds.), *Behavioral assessment of childhood disorders* (2nd ed., pp. 528–551). New York: Guilford Press.

Forsyth, B.W., Leventhal, J.M., & McCarthy, P.L. (1985). Mother's perceptions of problems of feeding and crying behaviors. *American Journal of Diseases of Childhood, 139,* 269–272.

Ginsberg, A. (1988). Feeding disorders in the developmentally disordered population. In D.C. Russo & J.H. Kadesty (Eds.), *Behavioral medicine with the developmentally disabled* (pp. 21–39). New York: Plenum Press.

Hagekull, B., & Dahl, M. (1987). Infants with and without feeding difficulties: Maternal experiences. *International Journal of Eating Disorders, 6,* 83–98.

Handen, D., Mandell, F., & Russo, D.C. (1986). Feeding induction in children who refuse to eat. *American Journal of Diseases in Children, 140,* 52–54.

Harden, A., & Sahl, R. (1997). Psychopathology in children and adolescents with developmental disorders. *Research in Developmental Disabilities, 18,* 369–382.

Hersen, M., & Bellack, A.S. (Eds.). (1976). *Behavioral assessment: A practical handbook.* New York: Pergamon Press.

Hirsch, N., & Myles, B.S. (1996) The use of a pica box in reducing pica behavior in a student with autism. *Focus on Autism and Other Developmental Disabilities, 11,* 222–225, 234.

Hoch, T.A., Babbitt, R.L., Coe, D., Krell, D., & Hackbert, L. (1994). Contingency contacting: Combining positive reinforcement and escape extinction procedures to treat persistent food refusal. *Behavior Modification, 18,* 106–128.

Hoekelman, R.A., Blatman, S., Brunell, P.A., Friedman, S.B., & Seidel, H.M. (Eds.). (1978). *Principles of pediatrics: Health care of the young.* New York: McGraw-Hill.

Illingworth, R.S., & Lister, J. (1964). The critical or sensitive period, with special reference to certain feeding problems in infants and children. *Journal of Pediatrics, 65,* 834–851.

Iwata, B.A., Roirdan, M.M., Wohl, M.K., & Finney, J.W. (1982). Pediatric feeding disorders: Behavior analysis and treatment. In P.J. Accardo (Ed.), *Failure to thrive in infancy and early childhood: A multi-disciplinary team approach* (pp. 296–329). Baltimore: University Park Press.

Kanner, L. (1957). *Child psychiatry* (3rd ed.). Springfield, IL: Thomas.

Kedesdy, J., & Budd, K. (1998). *Childhood feeding disorders: Biobehavioral assessment and intervention.* Baltimore: Brookes.

Kerwin, M.E., & Berkowitz, R.I. (1996). Feeding and eating disorders: Ingestive problems of infancy, childhood, and adolescence. *School Psychology Review, 25,* 316–328.

Kuczynski, L., Kochanski, G., Radke-Yarrow, M., & Girius-Brown, O. (1987). A developmental interpretation of young children's noncompliance. *Developmental Psychology, 23,* 799–806.

Lamm, N., & Greer, R. (1988). Induction and maintenance of swallowing responses in infants with dysphagia. *Journal of Applied Behavior Analysis, 21,* 143–156.

Lang, P.J., & Melamed, B.G. (1969). Avoidance conditioning therapy of an infant with chronic ruminative vomiting. *Journal of Abnormal Psychology, 74,* 139–142.

LeBlanc, L.A., Piazza, C.C., & Krug, M.A. (1997). Comparing methods for maintaining the safety of a child with pica. *Research in Developmental Disabilities, 18,* 215–220.

Lindberg, L., Bohlin, G., & Hagekull, B. (1991). Early feeding problems in a normal population. *International Journal of Eating Disorders, 10,* 395–405.

Linscheid, T.R. (1998). Behavioral treatment of feeding disorders in children. In T.S. Watson & F.M. Gresham (Eds.), *Behavioral treatment of childhood disorders* (pp. 357–368). New York: Plenum Press.

Linscheid, T.R., & Bennett Murphy, L. (1999). Feeding disorders of infancy and early childhood. In S.D. Notherton & C.E. Walker (Eds.), *Child and adolescent psychological disorders: A comprehensive textbook* (pp. 139–155). New York: Oxford University Press.

Linscheid, T.R., Budd, K., & Rasnake, L.K. (1995). Pediatric feeding disorders. In M.C. Roberts (Ed.), *Handbook of pediatric psychology* (2nd ed., pp. 501–515). New York: Guilford Press.

Linscheid, T.R., & Cunningham, C.E. (1977). A controlled demonstration of the effectiveness of electric shock in the elimination of chronic infant rumination. *Journal of Applied Behavior Analysis, 10,* 500.

Linscheid, T.R., Oliver, J., Blyler, E., & Palmer, S. (1978). Brief hospitalization for the behavioral treatment of feeding problems in the developmentally disabled. *Journal of Pediatric Psychology, 3,* 72–76.

Linscheid, T.R., & Rasnake, L.K. (1986). Behavioral approaches to the treatment of failure to thrive. In D. Drotar (Ed.), *New directions in failure to thrive: Implications for research and practice* (pp. 279–294). New York: Plenum Press.

Linscheid, T.R., Tarnowski, K.J., Rasnake, L.K., & Brams, J.S. (1987). Behavioral treatment of food refusal in a child with short-gut syndrome. *Journal of Pediatric Psychology, 12,* 451.

Luckey, R.E., Watson, C.M., & Musick, J.N. (1968). Aversive conditioning as a means of inhibiting vomiting and rumination. *American Journal of Mental Deficiency, 733,* 139–142.

Luiselli, J.K. (1996). Pica as obsessive-compulsive disorder. *Journal of Behavior Therapy and Experimental Psychiatry, 27,* 195–196.

Madden, N., Russo, D.C., & Cataldo, M.F. (1980). Environmental influences on mouthing in children with lead intoxication. *Journal of Pediatric Psychology, 5,* 207–216.

Marchi, M., & Cohen, P. (1990). Early childhood eating behaviors and adolescent eating disorders. *Journal of the American Academy of Child and Adolescent Psychiatry, 29,* 112–117.

McKenzie, S.J., Klein, K.R., Epstein, L.H., & McCurley, J. (1993). Effects of setting and number of observations on generalizability of parent-child interactions in childhood obesity treatment. *Journal of Psychopathology and Behavioral Assessment, 15*(2), 129–139.

Mennella, J., & Beauchamp, G. (1996). The early development of human flavor preferences. In E. Capaldi (Ed.), *Why we eat what we eat: The psychology of eating* (pp. 83–112). Washington, DC: American Psychological Association.

Moustakas, C.E., Segel, I.E., & Schalock, H.D. (1956). An objective method for the measurement and analysis of adult-child interaction. *Child Development, 27,* 109–134.

Munk, D., & Repp, A.C. (1994). Behavioral assessment of feeding problems of individuals with severe disabilities. *Journal of Applied Behavior Analysis, 27,* 241–250.

O'Brien, F., & Azrin, N.H. (1972). Developing proper mealtime behaviors in the institutionalized retarded. *Journal of Applied Behavior Analysis, 4,* 389–399.

O'Brien, F., Bugle, C., & Azrin, N.H. (1972). Training and maintaining a retarded child's proper eating. *Journal of Applied Behavior Analysis, 5,* 67–72.

O'Brien, M. (1996). Child-rearing difficulties reported by parents of infants and toddlers. *Journal of Pediatric Psychology, 21,* 433–446.

Palmer, S., & Kim, M. (1978). Failure to thrive. In S. Palmer & S. Ekvall (Eds.), *Pediatric nutrition in developmental disorders* (pp. 95–100). Springfield, IL: Thomas.

Palmer, S., Thompson, R.J., Jr., & Linscheid, T.R. (1975). Applied behavior analysis in the treatment of childhood feeding problems. *Developmental Medicine and Child Neurology, 17,* 333–339.

Paul, K., Dittrichova, J., & Papousek, H. (1996). Infant feeding behavior: Development in patterns and motivation. *Developmental Psychobiology, 29,* 563–576.

Pugliese, M.T., Weyman-Daum, M., Moses, N., & Lifshitz, F. (1987). Parental health beliefs as a cause of non-organic failure to thrive. *Pediatrics, 80,* 175–182.

Rasnake, L.K., & Linscheid, T.R. (1987). A behavioral approach to the treatment of pediatric feeding problems. *Journal of Pediatric and Perinatal Nutrition, 1,* 75–82.

Reau, N.R., Senturia, Y.D., Lebailly, S., & Christoffel, K.K. (1996). Infant and toddler feeding patterns and problems: Normative data and a new direction. *Developmental and Behavioral Pediatrics, 17,* 149–153.

Richmond, J.B., Eddy, E., & Green, M. (1958). Rumination: A psychosomatic syndrome of infancy. *Pediatrics, 22,* 49–55.

Riordan, M.M., Iwata, B.A., Wohl, M.K., & Finney, J.W. (1980). Behavioral treatment of food refusal and selectivity in developmentally disabled children. *Applied Research in Mental Retardation, 1,* 95–112.

Roberts, M.C. (Ed.). (1995). *Handbook of pediatric psychology* (2nd ed.). New York: Guilford Press.

Rojahn, J., Schroeder, S.R., & Mulick, J.A. (1980). Ecological assessment of self-protective devices in three profoundly retarded adults. *Journal of Autism and Developmental Disorders, 10,* 59–66.

Rozin, P., Ashmore, M., & Markwith, M. (1996). Lay American conceptions of nutrition: Dose insensitivity, categorical thinking, contagion, and the monotonic mind. *Health Psychology, 15,* 438–447.

Russell, G.F.M., Treasure, J., & Eisler, I. (1998). Mothers with anorexia nervosa who underfeed their children: Their recognition and management. *Psychological Medicine, 28,* 93–108.

Satter, E. (1990a). *Childhood feeding problems: Feelings and their medical significance.* Columbus, OH: Ross Laboratories.

Satter, E. (1990b). The feeding relationship: Problems and interventions. *Journal of Pediatrics, 117,* 181–189.

Scheinbein, M. (1975). Treatment for the hospitalized infant ruminator. *Clinical Pediatrics, 14*(8), 719–724.

Schwartz, A.S. (1958). Eating problems. *Pediatric Clinics of North America, 5,* 595–611.

Smith, D.W. (1977). *Introduction to clinical pediatrics.* Philadelphia: Saunders.

Stark, L.J., Bowen, A., Tyc, V.L., Evans, S., & Passero, M.A. (1990). A behavioral approach to increasing calorie consumption in children with cystic fibrosis. *Journal of Pediatric Psychology, 15,* 309–326.

Stark, L.J., Knapp, L., Bowen, A., Powers, S.W., Jelalian, E., Evans, S., Passero, M., Mulvihill, M., & Hovell, M. (1993). Increasing calorie consumption in children with cystic fibrosis: Replication with 2-year follow-up. *Journal of Applied Behavior Analysis, 26,* 435–450.

Stunkard, A.J., & Burt, V. (1967). Obesity and body image: II. Age at onset of disturbances in body image. *American Journal of Psychiatry, 123,* 1443–1447.

Thompson, G.A., Jr., Iwata, B.A., & Poynter, H. (1979). Operant control of pathological tongue thrust in spastic cerebral palsy. *Journal of Applied Behavior Analysis, 12,* 325–333.

Thompson, R.J., Jr. (1977). Applied behavior analysis in the treatment of mealtime tantrums and delay in self-feeding in a multi-handicapped child. *Journal of Clinical Child Psychology, 6,* 52–54.

Thompson, R.J., Jr., & Linscheid, T.R. (1976). Adult-child interaction analysis: Methodology and case application. *Child Psychiatry and Human Development, 7*(1), 719–724.

Thompson, R.J., Jr., & Palmer, S. (1974). Treatment of feeding problems: A behavioral approach. *Journal of Nutrition Education, 6,* 63–66.

Thompson, R.J., Jr., Palmer, S., & Linscheid, T.R. (1977). Single subject design and interaction analysis in the behavioral treatment of a child with a feeding problem. *Child Psychiatry and Human Development, 8,* 43–53.

Toister, R.P., Colin, J., Worley, L.M., & Arthur, D. (1975). Faradic therapy of chronic vomiting in infancy: A case study. *Journal of Behavior Therapy and Experimental Psychiatry, 6*(1), 55–59.

Troiana, R.P., Flegal, K.M., Kuczmanski, R.J., Campbell, S.M., & Johnson, C.I. (1995). Overweight prevalence and trend for children and adolescents. *Archives of Pediatric and Adolescent Medicine, 149,* 1085–1091.

U.S. Department of Health and Human Services. (1990). *Healthy people 2000: National health promotion/disease prevention objectives.* Washington, DC: U.S. Government Printing Office.

Wherle, M., Murphy, T., & Budd, K.S. (1993). Treating chronic food refusal in young children: Home-based parent training. *Journal of Applied Behavior Analysis, 26,* 421–433.

Wolf, A.M., & Colditz, G.A. (1996). The social and economic effects of body weight in the United States. *American Journal of Clinical Nutrition, 63,* 466S-469S.

Wolraich, M., Felice, M., & Drotar, D. (1996). *The classification of child and adolescent mental diagnoses in primary care: Diagnostic and statistical manual for primary care (DSM-PC), child and adolescent version.* Elk Grove, IL: American Academy of Pediatrics.

Woods, D.W., Miltenberger, R.G., & Lumley, V.A. (1996). A simplified habit reversal treatment for pica-related chewing. *Journal of Behavior Therapy and Experimental Psychiatry, 27,* 257–262.

Zeitlin, S.B., & Polivy, J. (1995). Coprophagia as a manifestation of obsessive-compulsive disorder: A case report. *Journal of Behavior Therapy and Experimental Psychiatry, 26,* 57–63.

CHAPTER 27

Mental Retardation

WILLIAM E. MACLEAN, JR., MICHAEL L. MILLER, AND KAREN BARTSCH

ental retardation is a developmental disability characterized by inadequate adaptation to societal demands. This disability is typically diagnosed in early childhood, when a discrepancy is recognized between a child's level of functioning and that of peers of the same chronological age. The American Association on Mental Retardation (AAMR) has served as the premier authority on matters of definition and classification for mental retardation since 1876. The *Diagnostic and Statistical Manual of Mental Disorders (DSM)*, published by the American Psychiatric Association (APA), incorporated the AAMR definition beginning in 1968. The current AAMR (Luckasson, 1992) and *DSM-IV* (APA, 1994) definitions have three criteria that must be met for a diagnosis of mental retardation: significantly subaverage intelligence, concurrent deficits or impairments in adaptive functioning, and onset before 18 years of age.

The definition of mental retardation has historically emphasized deficient intellectual functioning as the primary diagnostic criterion. The cutoff score defining mental retardation has typically been set at a point 2 standard deviations below the mean on a standardized measure of intelligence. However, the cutoff score has been a matter of some debate given the inherent measurement error in psychological tests and respect for clinical judgment in instances where a child may have an IQ that exceeds the cutoff but would clearly benefit from access to specialized services. As a result, there is not a fixed IQ cutoff; rather, a range of 70 to 75 or below has been the demarcation. This lack of precision has been a source of great concern for researchers and administrators. Given the presumed normal distribution of intelligence, even a 5-point difference in IQ would alter prevalence rates significantly. For example, if the cutoff score is set at an IQ score below 70, the potential prevalence of mental retardation would be 2.28%. However, if the cutoff score is set at an IQ below 75, the prevalence would more than double to 4.75% (MacMillan & Reschly, 1997). Researchers argue that the lack of a firm diagnostic criterion makes it difficult to compare results among research studies. Moreover, such an apparently small difference in cutoff score would also have profound administrative and economic ramifications regarding eligibility for services.

Although limitations in adaptive functioning have been considered an important historical aspect of mental retardation, this criterion was not a formal aspect of the AAMR definition until the 1970s. Earlier AAMR definitions used the term "associated" to link deficits in intellectual and adaptive functioning. The terminology "existing concurrently" was added to the AAMR definition in 1973 and incorporated into *DSM-III* in 1980. The current AAMR and *DSM* definitions indicate that limitations must be evident in "two or more of the applicable adaptive skill areas: communication, self-care, home living, social/interpersonal skills, use of community resources, self-direction, functional academic skills, work, leisure, health and safety" (APA, 1994, p. 46).

The definition of mental retardation also holds that onset must occur prior to age 18, establishing the limit of the developmental period. Although a case could be made for other ages, a chronological age of 18 as the beginning of adulthood is consistent with various legal, social, and developmental perspectives (Luckasson, 1992).

Beyond the criterion of deficient general intellectual functioning, limitations in adaptive behavior functioning, and onset during the developmental period, the *DSM-IV* adheres to previous definitions in describing degrees of severity of mental retardation. In the *DSM-IV*, severity is based on the level of intellectual impairment only. Four levels of severity are specified, corresponding to standard deviation units: mild, moderate, severe, and profound. The mild range is between 2 and 3 standard deviations below the mean, the moderate range between 3 and 4 standard deviations, the severe range between 4 and 5 standard deviations, and the profound range is greater than 5 standard deviations below the mean.

In 1992, the AAMR published a revision of its classification manual that represented a fairly radical departure from earlier editions (Luckasson, 1992). This version presents a multidimensional classification system that distinguishes among people on the basis of supports needed to function optimally in four areas of living: (1) intellectual functioning and adaptive skills; (2) psychological and emotional considerations; (3) physical, health, and etiological considerations; and (4) environmental considerations. Reasons for this change include the belief that the previous classification system had limited relevance for treatment and the recognized heterogeneity among individuals classified according to IQ levels alone. Similarly, it has been recognized that "specific adaptive limitations often coexist with strengths in other adaptive skills or other personal capabilities" (p. 6). The change also reflects the view that the functioning of a person with mental retardation will generally improve if appropriate supports are provided over a sustained period. Support functions are defined as befriending, financial planning, employee assistance, behavioral support, in-home living assistance, community access and use, and health assistance. According to the new system, levels of

support are intermittent, limited, extensive, and pervasive, depending on both duration and intensity. By assessing needed supports across the four dimensions, the AAMR fosters the perspective that mental retardation influences all aspects of a person's life and, therefore, that assessment and treatment should address this pervasive influence. It remains to be seen whether the 1992 AAMR definition and multidimensional classification system will be incorporated into general practice.

Clinicians are often reluctant to assign a diagnosis of mental retardation to a very young child, particularly if the child's intelligence and adaptive behavior scores are near the 2 standard deviation cutoff. The diagnosis of developmental delay is often used in such cases until greater certainty is attained through serial assessments. Deferral of a mental retardation diagnosis may be based on the nature of the assessment instrument and its predictive validity, the possibility that a child has another medical condition that reduces his or her ability to communicate and thus suggests intellectual impairment, or that the child may be in adverse social conditions (Fotheringhan, 1983).

PREVALENCE

The prevalence of mental retardation is greatest during the school-age years. During this time, many children with mild mental retardation are identified and receive services. Prevalence declines in later adolescence and adulthood because many persons with mild mental retardation are no longer identified or receive special services and because of reduced life expectancy for some particular etiologies. Overall, the prevalence of mental retardation among children and adolescents is believed to be less than 2% (Reschly, 1992). No definitive prevalence data are available; rather, estimates are frequently drawn from statistics provided by state departments of education. Prevalence rates vary across states given legal decisions regarding the suitability of intelligence tests for diagnosis of learning problems in children from minority backgrounds. Educator referral and diagnostic practices also affect prevalence rates (MacMillan, Gresham, Siperstein, & Bocian, 1996). MacMillan and colleagues cite data from the U.S. Department of Education showing that between 1976 to 1977 and 1992 to 1993, the number of children served as learning disabled increased by 207% and the number of children served as mentally retarded decreased by 38%. They provide a convincing case that some children who meet the diagnostic criteria for mild mental retardation are actually classified as learning disabled in the educational system (MacMillan, Gresham, & Bocian, 1998). Beyond the issues of potential stigmatization, overrepresentation of minority children with labels of mild mental retardation, and the concern regarding the use of intelligence tests in the evaluation of children from minority backgrounds, there is some question regarding the value of the mild mental retardation classification in the educational setting (MacMillan et al., 1996). Moreover, MacMillan et al. suggest that IQ-based distinctions may not be instructionally relevant and that educators rely on behavior and achievement in making recommendations for special education.

ASSESSMENT

INTELLIGENCE

General intellectual functioning is determined by an individually administered, standardized intelligence test. Measures frequently used include the Bayley Scales of Infant Development II, Wechsler Preschool and Primary Test of Intelligence–Revised, Wechsler Intelligence Scale for Children III, Stanford–Binet fourth edition, and Kaufman Assessment Battery for Children. Chapter 6 in this *Handbook* provides a thorough discussion of the psychological base for these measures and their psychometric qualities. Rather than repeating that discussion here, we will elaborate specific issues relevant to the use of intelligence tests in establishing a diagnosis of mental retardation.

First, test selection should be based on the child's developmental level. Chronological age-appropriate tests should be used for children who appear to have minor delays. Children with severe delays may be below the basal level of a particular test and little information regarding relative strengths and weaknesses will be obtained. Preassessment screening with measures such as the Batelle or the Brigance may be needed to determine which intellectual functioning measure is appropriate.

Second, sensory and motor capabilities should be taken into account because there is significant co-occurrence of sensory impairments and motor limitations among children with mental retardation (Batshaw & Shapiro, 1997). Children with sensory impairments or motor limitations may require alternative assessment devices. For example, the Leiter International Performance Scale–Revised is a nonverbal intelligence test appropriate for children with hearing impairments. Children with limited motor ability may require modification in administration of test measures or reliance on verbal measures to gain an estimate of overall intellectual ability (Sattler, 1992).

Third, some children with mental retardation are nonverbal and require specialized intellectual assessment measures. Again, the Leiter and the Test of Nonverbal Intelligence 2 are specifically designed for this purpose.

Fourth, children with mental retardation may have a comorbid condition such as autism that requires special accommodations. Volkmar and Cohen (1997) provide an excellent discussion of developmentally based assessments for children with autism and related conditions. Children with mental retardation may also have behavior problems that require management in the setting to obtain a valid assessment. A good discussion of behavioral management approaches can be found in Sattler (1992).

ADAPTIVE BEHAVIOR

In contrast to professional understanding of intelligence, there has been little agreement on a definition of adaptive behavior. Most definitions emphasize social responsibility and personal independence as cardinal features. Some definitions embed adaptive behavior in a broader context of personal or social competence (Greenspan & Granfield, 1992). Despite theoretical and definitional arguments, measures have been developed and incorporated into diagnostic evaluations. The Vineland Adaptive Behavior Scales, the AAMR Adaptive Behavior Scale second edition, and the Scales of Independent Behavior–Revised are commonly used instruments. Although the specific content of the measures vary, most adaptive behavior measures assess social and interpersonal skills, communication and language skills, gross and fine motor skills, and independent functioning in daily living skills.

Adaptive behavior deficits are readily apparent among people with intellectual abilities in the severe to profound range of mental retardation. Such deficits are less apparent among people with mild mental retardation. In part, this variation is related to social and contextual factors that influence environmental complexity and thus the demands that are presented (Hickson, Blackman, & Reis, 1995). Hickson et al. suggest interpreting adaptive behavior scores in relation to the overall environmental context, including such dimensions as demand and level of family and school support.

ETIOLOGY

Over the past 40 years, tremendous strides have been made in our understanding of mental retardation, diagnostic procedures, assessment techniques, intervention, and prevention strategies. The net effect of these efforts has been the recognition that mental retardation is associated with a number of conditions and can no longer be considered a unitary phenomenon. The field has now begun to focus greater attention on etiologic conditions, particularly those of genetic origin, which have mental retardation as an associated feature. There is general agreement that the timing of an insult is important in establishing etiology. The

current AAMR system, illustrated in Table 27.1, is organized by prenatal, perinatal, and postnatal influences.

There is a clear relation between level of mental retardation and the determination of disease-specific etiologies. Matilainen, Airaksinen, Mononen, Launiala, and Kaariainen (1995) compared the causes of severe and mild mental retardation in birth cohorts of Finnish children born during the period 1969 to 1972. Prenatal causes were identified in 60% of the group with severe mental retardation as compared with 22% of the group with mild mental retardation. Perinatal and postnatal causes were identified in 9% versus 1% and 8% versus 3% of the groups with severe or mild mental retardation, respectively. Perhaps most important was the unknown etiology category, which contained 23% of the group with severe mental retardation and 74% of the group with mild retardation. This difference was due in large part to the number of chromosomal conditions associated with IQ scores in the severe range of mental retardation. Given the advances in molecular genetics, it is reasonable to predict that the number of cases of mental retardation due to unknown origin has decreased steadily in recent years.

Table 27.1 Representative etiologies associated with mental retardation.

I. Prenatal Causes	
Chromosomal disorders	Trisomy 21, Fragile X syndrome
Syndrome disorders	Neurofibromatosis, tuberous sclerosis
Inborn errors of metabolism	Phenylketonuria, congenital hypothyroidism
Developmental disorders of brain formation	Neural tube defect, porencephaly
Environmental influences	Fetal alcohol syndrome, maternal malnutrition
II. Perinatal Causes	
Intrauterine disorders	Premature labor, toxemia
Neonatal disorders	Intracranial hemorrhage, meningitis
III. Postnatal Causes	
Head injuries	Cerebral concussion
Infections	Encephalitis, meningitis
Demyelinating disorders	Acute disseminated encephalomyelitis
Degenerative disorders	Rett's syndrome, Tay-Sachs syndrome
Seizure disorders	Epilepsy
Toxic-metabolic disorders	Reye syndrome, lead intoxication
Malnutrition	Kwashiorkor, marasmus
Environmental deprivation	Psychosocial disadvantage, child abuse
Hypoconnection syndrome	Reduced dendritic elaboration and connectivity

Source: Adapted from Luckasson (1992, pp. 81–91). Copyright 1992 by the American Association on Mental Retardation. Adapted by permission.

Norman Ellis (1969) observed that "rarely have behavioral differences characterized different etiological groups" (p. 561). Subsequent research suggests otherwise, and today a great deal of effort is being directed toward defining phenotypic descriptions of genetic etiologies (Dykens, 1995). In fact, there is ample evidence that etiology explains profound differences in various aspects of cognitive, language, and social functioning as well as maladaptive behaviors among people with mental retardation. With this distinction in mind, the following sections consider functional domains from the viewpoints of typical development and mental retardation and then use etiologic distinctions as a way to illustrate the diversity of functional outcomes.

COGNITIVE ASPECTS

TYPICAL DEVELOPMENT

Cognitive development was recently defined as "the development over time of the ability to understand the world in which we live" (Lutz & Sternberg, 1999, p. 275). From birth, changes occur in cognitive content, such as concepts and categories, and processes, including attention, memory, and strategy use.

Attention developments are noted by parents and teachers, who observe that younger, as compared to older, children spend shorter times involved in tasks, struggle to focus on details, and are easily distracted. As sustained attention improves over the elementary school years, children get better at deliberately and selectively focusing on situational aspects that are relevant to their task goals while ignoring other aspects. Relatedly, children become increasingly able to shift their attention to relevant information when their task changes. As attentional resources typically increase from early to middle childhood, so does the use of efficient attentional strategies.

Equally impressive are the normal developments of memory and information processing. With age, children become more likely to encode the gist of an event as opposed to verbatim representations, at least partly because of an increasing knowledge base (Brainerd, Reyna, Howe, & Kingma, 1990). Memory storage also develops; most 5-year-olds can recall lists of four digits but not longer ones, whereas most adults can recall lists of seven digits.

Even if they can initially recall as much as older children, younger children are more likely to forget material over long periods of time (Brainerd & Reyna, 1995). Relatedly, the speed of information processing increases with age as does information retrieval, with young children tending to underreport what happened unless prompted (Saywitz, Goodman, Nichols, & Moan, 1991).

Typical development involves changes in memory strategies. Some strategies, such as pointing to a location that needs to be remembered, are observed in 2-year-olds (DeLoache, 1991). However, younger children's memory strategies, like their attention strategies, are characterized by production, control, and utilization deficiencies. For example, asked to remember a series of pictures of objects, more 10-year-olds than 6-year-olds spontaneously rehearse the names of the objects. Even when younger children are trained to rehearse, they tend to abandon the strategy on a later test. Similar developments occur in organizational strategies (Best & Ornstein, 1986) and, later in childhood, elaboration strategies (Schneider & Pressley, 1989).

CHILDREN WITH MENTAL RETARDATION

Studies of cognitive abilities in people with mental retardation were an attempt to break the circularity evident in the observation that people with mental retardation have difficulty learning because they have low intelligence (Bray, Fletcher, & Turner, 1997). Early studies showed that people with mental retardation performed poorly because they had difficulty attending to tasks. Others indicated that short-term memory was deficient and this interfered with learning. Still others suggested that people with mental retardation had learning deficits because they did not use rehearsal strategies effectively. Recent efforts to understand the cognitive abilities of people with mental retardation have adopted a strategy of studying competencies (as opposed to deficits) and have yielded evidence that people with mental retardation have considerable strategy competency. Indeed, developmental studies indicate that there are age-related increases in memory performance and strategy use in individuals with mental retardation. Nonetheless, it is true that people with mental retardation do not perform as well as people without mental retardation, and the difference seems to emerge from functional limitations in the capacity of working memory. In other words, their basic cognitive abilities are similar to those of many nonretarded people. The difference occurs when their information-processing abilities are taxed.

A review of the attention literature generated a similar conclusion (Tomporowski & Tinsley, 1997). That is, people with mental retardation are more affected by increased information-processing demands than their typically developing counterparts. However, these authors suggest that decreased attentional capacity and suboptimal allocation of attention has something to do with the observed differences. Additionally, metacognitive abilities may be less adequate and motivational factors may play a significant role.

Careful studies conducted over 30 years have revealed that the poor learning of people with mental retardation emerges in part from slowed speed of information processing (Nettelbeck & Wilson, 1997), implicating structural differences that cannot be remediated through practice or increased knowledge of the tasks. Research concerning the role of maturation in the increased processing speed observed in typical development is consistent with these findings. At a given age, children who are more physically mature (i.e., a greater percentage of height than would be expected from their parents' height) process information more quickly (Eaton & Ritchot, 1995), an ability unlikely to be due to practice effects. Kail (1991) reports that the best-fitting mathematical function for describing the increase in processing speed with age differs from the one that best describes the improvements that come with practice.

Relatively little is known about specific cognitive deficits or competencies with regard to particular etiologies. The predominant experimental design has been one that matches participants on IQ, mental age, or chronological age regardless of etiology. Reports of decreases in the IQ scores of children with Down syndrome or Fragile X syndrome over time will undoubtedly fuel research on specific cognitive abilities and investigation of neuropathology that may play a role in these and other etiologies.

LANGUAGE ASPECTS

TYPICAL DEVELOPMENT

Early competencies are evident in language perception. Even before birth, infants can distinguish foreign languages from the language spoken by their mother (Werker & Tees, 1992). The production of speech sounds also begins at birth in the form of crying and then follows a predictable course of development, with cooing emerging at 1 to 2 months, simple articulation at about 3 months, babbling by 6 months, and patterned speech at about 1 year (Kent & Miulo, 1995). Full phonological competence is not typically acquired until about school age.

Word learning similarly follows a predictable course. By 1.5 years of age, a typical vocabulary of 3 to 100 words includes mostly words referring to concrete objects and actions interesting to the child, such as "doggie" and "ball" (Siegler, 1998). Between about 1.5 and 2 years, children often experience a vocabulary spurt (Goldfield & Resnick, 1990). By preschool age, they acquire new words at the astonishing rate of about one every two hours (Pinker, 1994). By 2.5 years, the average vocabulary is about 600 words; by 5 or 6, it is about 15,000 words. Through middle childhood, vocabulary continues to increase at the rate of 5,000 to 10,000 words per year (Anglin, 1993).

Other rapid developments occur in children's ability to put words together in sentences. In the first half-year of speech, single words are often used to convey larger meanings, for example, "ball" may mean "Give me the ball." Shortly thereafter, children construct two-word phrases, such as "Mommy sock," and do so in ordered ways that appear to reflect basic grammatical rules. Between roughly 2 and 3 years of age, a grammar explosion occurs. Children use past tenses, plurals, auxiliary verbs, and prepositions. They add inflections, ask questions, and invoke negatives (e.g., "I not crying"). A particularly intriguing phenomenon is overregularization—when young children create new regularized forms of words (e.g., "goed"), consistent with the claim that they use rules of grammar rather than merely imitate what they hear. Children then learn exceptions to the rules one by one. Complex sentences, such as "Where did you say you put my doll?" appear in the speech of children age 2.5 to 4 years (de Villiers & de Villiers, 1992). Later developments include the construction of even more complex sentences and the elimination of overregularization errors (Bowerman, 1985).

Children's use of speech to communicate with others—the pragmatic aspect of language—similarly involves both early competencies and measurable development. At 1.5 years, children talking to a parent typically show adultlike gaze patterns

(Rutter & Durkin, 1987). As early as age 2, children adapt the form of their language to their situation or their audience. Four-year-olds use simpler language when talking to 2-year-olds than when talking to adults (Tomasello & Mannle, 1985). First-graders explain things more fully to a stranger than to a friend (Sonnenschein, 1986).

Children's remarkable early language achievements have inspired strong theoretical claims. The possibility of a critical period for grammar acquisition has been suggested. Although some research has refuted a strong version of this hypothesis (Chapman, 1995), other research has supported a weaker claim that there is an optimal period (Newport, 1990). The underlying notion that changes may be associated with brain developments, such as decreasing synapse density after about age 4, has received some support (Bates, Thal, & Marchman, 1991; Warren & Yoder, 1997).

CHILDREN WITH MENTAL RETARDATION

Children with mental retardation typically achieve language milestones at later ages, develop language at a slower rate, and achieve a lower level of communicative competence than typically developing children (Rosenberg & Abbeduto, 1993). Both receptive and expressive language are affected. Although children with mild to moderate mental retardation may communicate in full sentences, children with severe mental retardation may be limited to brief phrases or single words. Children with profound mental retardation may be nonverbal. Rosenberg and Abbeduto point out that there is considerable variation in the language development of children with mental retardation. This variation may be explained by genetic differences linked with specific etiologies (Warren & Yoder, 1997).

Research on language development in children with Down syndrome has revealed weaknesses in grammar and expressive skills coexisting with strengths in receptive language, pragmatics, and vocabulary (Chapman, 1995; Fowler, 1990). Moreover, Chapman, Schwartz, and Kay-Raining Bird (1991) found that differences between lexical and syntactic comprehension abilities among children with Down syndrome increase with age. Other researchers report that children with Fragile X syndrome display a variety of problems with speech and language functioning (Lachiewicz, Spiridigliozzi, Gullion, Ransford, & Rao 1994; Sudhulter, Cohen, Silverman, & Wolf-Schein, 1990). The speech of males with Fragile X has been described as echolalic, cluttered, and perseverative (Sudhalter et al., 1990). In contrast, females with Fragile X have relative strength in verbal processing and language, although they may exhibit odd communication patterns, including tangential speech. Children with Williams syndrome are often very social, display large, complex vocabularies, and have grammatical and pragmatic skills much greater than what would be expected based on their intellectual abilities (Bellugi, Bihrle, Neville, Jernigan, & Doherty, 1992). This discrepancy challenges the prevailing belief that cognitive development paves the way for language development (Warren & Yoder, 1997). In contrast, individuals with Angelman syndrome display deficits in language much greater than what would be expected based on their intellectual abilities (Penner, Johnston, Faircloth, Irish, & Williams, 1993).

SOCIAL ASPECTS

TYPICAL DEVELOPMENT

Immersed from birth in a social world, children arrive with capacities that facilitate their interactions with others. They typically go on to develop specific concepts, emotions, and skills that enhance their social functioning. Three areas of important developments are relationships, prosocial behavior, and social cognition.

Attachment theorists, such as Bowlby (1969), have drawn attention to infants' first relationships. Initially, infants emit various proximity-promoting behaviors that are not directed at specific persons (Ainsworth, 1989). Eventually, infants develop specific relationships with their caregivers and others as indicated by proximity-seeking as well as proximity-promoting behaviors. Shortly thereafter, children begin to engage in social referencing (Walden, 1991), that is, looking at a parent's expression when presented with a novel situation and reacting accordingly. By age 2 or 3, attachment behaviors are less visible, and by about age 4, children can be quite independent; Bowlby suggests that children now understand that their relationship with their caregiver continues to exist even when the partners are apart.

Children eventually develop relationships with peers as well as parents. They may show interest in each other as early as 6 months of age. By 14 to 18 months, children will play side by side, and from about 18 months they may begin to chase or imitate each other, exhibiting some of the first signs of individual friendships (Howes, 1987). By 3 or 4, children typically prefer to play with peers, play is more cooperative and coordinated, and many children show signs of stable friendships. Shared play interests continue to form the basis of friendships among school-age children. In adolescence, mixed-sex groups begin to replace the sex-segregated groups typical of middle childhood, and friendships become increasingly intimate and long-lasting.

As children develop relationships, they typically show improvements in prosocial behavior: "intentional, voluntary behavior intended to benefit another" (Eisenberg, 1992, p. 3). Certainly as early as 2 or 3 years, children will offer to help another child who is hurt, offer a toy, or try to comfort a distressed stranger. With age, children are increasingly likely to offer to share objects or money with others and to provide physical and verbal assistance to someone in need (Eisenberg, 1992). As prosocial behaviors and verbal skills increase, aggressive behaviors typically decrease between toddlerhood and adolescence; in most cultures, this means that anger is increasingly disguised and controlled (Underwood, Coie, & Herbsman, 1992).

Contributing to normal development in relationships and prosocial behavior are changes in how children understand themselves and others. The social referencing typical of 10-month-olds involves using the emotional expressions of adults as information to evaluate a novel situation. As early as 18 months, children can "read" and respond to the intentions of others. Between 4 and 5 years, children typically acquire an ability to reason about a person's false belief, for example, to predict that a person will look in an empty location where he or she believes a desired candy to be (Wimmer & Perner, 1983). Like children's understanding of beliefs, their understanding of emotions undergoes development into the school years. Happiness and sadness are apparently both experienced and recognized by babies, but social emotions such as guilt and shame emerge at around ages 2 and 3 (Lewis, Sullivan, Stanger, & Weiss, 1989). Reasoning about emotions in others also develops in early childhood. Predicting that a child who wants and gets a puppy will be happy is easy for a 2-year-old (Wellman & Woolley, 1990), but predicting that a child will be both happy and sad when his lost dog returns home with a cut ear is difficult even for a 6-year-old (Harris, 1989).

However, by age 10, children successfully predict a mixed emotional reaction.

CHILDREN WITH MENTAL RETARDATION

In contrast, children with mental retardation often show delays and/or deficits in social development. Children with mental retardation may have greater difficulty recognizing and responding to the emotions of others, reading social cues, taking another's perspective, understanding social context and social inference, recognizing and responding to affective stimuli, and making friends (Greenspan & Love, 1997; Kasari & Bauminger, 1998). Although social difficulties vary with etiology, the abilities to absorb information from the interpersonal realm and use it to achieve interpersonal goals are commonly deficient in people with mental retardation (Greenspan & Love, 1997). It follows, then, that social insight and social communication are negatively affected, depressing social competence more generally (Gresham, 1986).

Social skills difficulties are a pervasive problem in children with mental retardation. In fact, mental retardation is defined by impairments in adaptive/social behavior and intellectual limitations. Social skills difficulties have been linked to a variety of additional problems, including juvenile delinquency, substance abuse, depression, and aggression. Moreover, social skills may influence such factors as the level of integration an individual has with his or her community and an individual's response to emotional difficulties. However, the nature and degree of the social impairment may vary from etiology to etiology (Kasari & Bauminger, 1998).

Most research pertaining to social abilities within specific etiologies of mental retardation has focused on Down syndrome. Children with Down syndrome are often described as friendly and outgoing, perhaps because of their tendency to make adequate eye contact with others and exhibit social smiles (Gibson, 1978). However, in comparison to typically developing children, children with Down syndrome may exhibit brief smiles and less frequent positive affect (Brooks-Gunn & Lewis, 1982; Kasari, Mundy, Yirmiya, & Sigman, 1990).

Children with Fragile X syndrome display significant social difficulties. In particular, children with Fragile X are marked by their avoidant manner, lack of eye contact, shyness, and social anxiety

(Mazzocco, Pennington, & Hagerman, 1994). Moreover, males with Fragile X may have difficulties similar to those found in children with autism, such as recognizing emotions in others and taking the perspective of others. However, emotional recognition and perspective-taking limitations were not found in a sample of female carriers of the Fragile X gene with typical intelligence (Mazzocco et al., 1994). Individuals with Angelman syndrome are marked by the presence of mental retardation, epilepsy, a "puppetlike" gait, lack of speech, and excessive laughter. Research on children with Angelman syndrome indicates that these children have social difficulties that are often more pronounced than their level of mental retardation. In a study involving six adults and one child with Angelman syndrome, Penner et al. (1993) found that only one subject exhibited the joint skills of attending to and acting on an object, as well as the turn-taking skills necessary for one-on-one interaction. In contrast, these skills are present in typically developing infants and may serve as building blocks for social communication.

Children with Prader-Willi syndrome exhibit social performance deficits that may be linked to behavioral problems. Parents of children with Prader-Willi syndrome report greater behavioral disturbances than parents of children with Down syndrome (Dykens & Kasari, 1997). Relatedly, Mitchell and Cook (1987) reported that staff members trained to work with individuals with Prader-Willi syndrome identified failures to take turns in conversations, failure to listen to others, emotional outbursts, verbal assaults, inappropriate expressions of displeasure, and violations of personal space as the major social skills difficulties in this population.

Socially, children with Williams syndrome are described as friendly and outgoing. These children exhibit verbal abilities that are greater than what would be expected based on their level of intelligence, perceptual abilities, and motor skills (Udwin, 1990); however, their language is often repetitive and contains numerous "catch phrases." Many children with Williams syndrome have poor relationships with their peers. In a study involving 119 adolescents and adults with Williams syndrome, approximately 66% had difficulties making and/or sustaining friendships with similar-aged peers (Udwin, 1990). Moreover, 66% of the sample were described as socially isolated by their parents. Over 90% had difficulty

organizing their leisure time, which may increase feelings of social isolation (Udwin, 1990).

Social skills problems are common among school-age children with mental retardation and can have detrimental effects on the levels of acceptance from peers and teachers (Gresham, 1983; Guralnick, 1992). As children move into mainstream educational settings, expectations for skillful behaviors likely increase (Greenspan & Love, 1997). However, research on children with mental retardation in mainstreamed settings suggests that they have few sustained interactions with their typically developing peers (Guralnick, 1984), engage in high levels of aggressive and attention-seeking behaviors (Sinson & Wetherick, 1981), and have few typically developing friends (Field, 1984). Because of the strong focus on inclusion and the high comorbidity rates of mental retardation and behavioral/emotional problems, it is not surprising that research has focused on social skills training (Hamilton & Matson, 1992).

TEMPERAMENT

TYPICAL DEVELOPMENT

Seminal work conducted by Chess and colleagues over 30 years ago established nine parameters of temperament: activity level, rhythmicity, approach or withdrawal, adaptability, intensity of reaction, threshold of responsiveness, quality of mood, distractibility, and attention span and persistence (Chess & Thomas, 1989). Although each can be addressed individually, the manner in which certain traits cluster together is often more helpful in understanding a child's temperament (Chess & Korn, 1970a). The typology of "easy," "difficult," and "slow to warm up" is based on a clustering of various temperament parameters. Beyond this basic typology, children with challenging temperaments often display higher activity levels, greater sensitivity to changes in their environment, shorter attention spans, higher degrees of distractibility, and less persistence (Whitman, O'Callaghan, & Sommer, 1997).

Temperament is generally believed to have a genetic origin. However, environmental variables such as the responses provided by primary caregivers likely influence the role temperament plays in later personality development. With maturation, children become more capable of regulating their behavior during stressful situations and gain a sense of self-efficacy (Whitman et al., 1997).

At school, temperament influences the child's ability to concentrate on a lesson, to remain focused on the task at hand, to adjust to different instructors, and to make adequate transitions from class to class. In addition, a teacher's perception of how intelligent a child is may be influenced by the child's performance along these dimensions (Chess & Korn, 1970a). Thus, children with challenging temperaments may have traits that not only interfere with learning but may influence what their teacher believes they are capable of learning. In these situations, children with challenging temperaments may benefit from emotional and cognitive support provided through verbal prompts, modeling, breaking tasks down into smaller components, breaks, and skill building. These interventions allow for the child to spend increasing amounts of time in the classroom while gaining confidence through accomplishing academic goals.

CHILDREN WITH MENTAL RETARDATION

Although, as a group, children with mental retardation may not vary significantly from normative populations on the various temperament parameters, they are more likely than their typically developing peers to have "difficult" temperaments (Chess & Korn, 1970b). Moreover, children with mental retardation and difficult temperament are more likely to be described as behavior disordered than control groups.

As with typically developing children, temperament traits vary considerably among children with mental retardation. This variability is likely seen both between and within specific etiologies of mental retardation. However, few researchers have examined the relationship between temperament and specific etiologies of mental retardation. Moreover, most research in this area has focused on children with Down syndrome. Historically, children with Down syndrome have been reported to have easy temperaments. Subsequent studies have shown that this is not universally the case. In studies of gender and age effects, it is the younger female subjects who receive endorsements of easy temperament. Studies have revealed a subset of people with Down syndrome who are aggressive and very difficult to handle.

Kerby and Dawson (1994) compared the temperament traits of nine males with Fragile X syndrome to nine males with other etiologies of mental retardation. Temperament was assessed using the Emotionality, Activity, and Sociability Temperament Scale (Buss & Plomin, 1984), which yielded scores on scales of emotionality, activity, sociability, and shyness. Results indicated that males with Fragile X syndrome were more emotional, more socially withdrawn, more shy, and less active than their peers of similar IQ, chronological age, and living environment.

Tomc, Williamson, and Pauli (1990) compared the temperament of children with Williams syndrome to typically developing children. As a group, children with Williams syndrome exhibited higher activity, lower rhythmicity, greater approach, less adaptability, more intensity, more negative mood, less persistence, higher distractibility, and lower threshold to arousal than typically developing children. In a similar study, Plissart, Borghgraef, and Fryns (1996) found trends for greater intensity, less persistence, and lower threshold to arousal for individuals with Williams syndrome compared to individuals of similar IQ but differing etiologies.

Although children with challenging temperaments are more likely to have behavioral and/or learning problems, how much temperament characteristics negatively impact development is likely dependent on how people in their home, academic, and social environments respond to them. Environments that are structured, flexible, cognizant of individual variation, and accommodating are more likely to foster development (Whitman et al., 1997). Moreover, Chess and Thomas (1989) suggest that environmental responses to a child's temperament strongly influence such factors as personality development, self-concept, and academic functioning. Thus, an appropriate intervention that considers temperament may have positive effects on a child's self-esteem, mood, social competence, adaptability, persistence, and motivation to achieve.

MOTOR DEVELOPMENT

TYPICAL DEVELOPMENT

The attainment of motor milestones such as rolling over, sitting independently, standing, and walking is often used as a primary index of developmental progress. Infant assessment instruments, such as the Bayley II, often include a motor scale composed of various fine and gross motor skills. Early motor development has been characterized by Capute et al. (1984) as having three basic components. As children develop, primitive reflexes such as the asymmetric tonic neck reflex and Moro reflex gradually disappear by 12 months of age. Second, there is a progressive acquisition of various postural adjustment reactions that assist the child in maintaining posture and moving in space. Third, there are several important motor skills or milestones that are attained during the first 12 months. Taken together, most children are independently sitting by 6 months of age and walking by 12 months. Attainment of motor skills continues throughout childhood and includes more precise fine motor skills and more complex gross motor abilities than assessed at earlier ages. Frequently employed measures of motor development include the Peabody Developmental Motor Scales and the Bruininks-Oseretsky Test of Motor Proficiency.

CHILDREN WITH MENTAL RETARDATION

Although not a defining aspect of mental retardation, the early motor development of mentally retarded children is frequently delayed in comparison with their chronological age and typically developing peers. Delay is apparent in attainment of motor milestones, disappearance of the earliest or primitive reflexes, and acquisition of postural adjustment reactions. It is presumed that there is a neurological basis for the delayed development. Most children with mental retardation eventually walk, although their balance and coordination may continue to be impaired.

Although motor delay can be explained readily in cases of neuromuscular dysfunction (e.g., cerebral palsy), there is a high incidence of delay among children of other etiologic groups. For example, children with Down syndrome walk alone at 19 months on average, as compared with 12 months for typically developing children. Delay in these cases may be attributed to abnormal muscle tone (either hypotonia or hypertonia), decreased strength, lack of coordination, or abnormalities in deep tendon reflexes associated with the maintenance of posture.

Thelen (1979) provided evidence that repetitive motor behaviors are also crucial to early motor development. She showed that repetitive motor behavior evolves in a predictable sequence and is integrally associated with preambulatory motor development. MacLean, Ellis, Galbreath, Halpern, and Baumeister (1991) demonstrated that children with delayed development manifest these motor behaviors at appropriate motor ages. In this longitudinal study, children with Down syndrome and children with demonstrable motor impairment were compared to children without disability. Despite differences in chronological age and developmental rate, each group exhibited repetitive motor behavior of the sort reported in previous studies of preambulatory children. Many of these repetitive motor behaviors are topographically similar to stereotyped behaviors exhibited by older children and adults with mental retardation, leading some to speculate that these repetitive motor behaviors may serve as a precursor to the stereotyped behavior exhibited by older children and adolescents with mental retardation. Thus far, no definitive study has been conducted on this question.

Although considerable emphasis has been placed on the remediation of cognitive, academic, and social deficits characteristic of children with mental retardation, relatively little attention has been directed toward intervening in their delayed motor development. There is some reason to believe that early intervention directed at motor development might have implications for other aspects of development. For example, if one subscribes to the view that environmental exploration facilitates cognitive development, then increased mobility would help.

COMORBIDITY

Many children with mental retardation manifest associated, or comorbid, conditions that further affect their adaptation and development. These conditions include cerebral palsy, seizure disorders, sensory impairment, and psychological disorders. The following sections address the prevalence and nature of these comorbid conditions. Given the primary emphasis of this volume, somewhat greater attention is directed toward comorbid psychological disorders.

CEREBRAL PALSY

This term refers to a disorder of movement and posture that has its origin early in development. A variety of etiologies have been described, each producing some perturbation of the developing brain that leads to a nonprogressive form of brain damage (Pellegrino, 1997). The resulting motor abnormalities and functional impairments are termed cerebral palsy. In some etiologies, both the intellectual impairment and cerebral palsy may result from the same destructive process as in the case of perinatal anoxia. For children with a genetic condition associated with mental retardation, cerebral palsy may be the result of an additional pathologic event. Approximately 10% of children with mental retardation also have cerebral palsy, and level of mental retardation is related to prevalence (Kiely, 1987). For example, in a study conducted in Sweden, children with mild mental retardation had a cerebral palsy prevalence rate of 7% as compared with 19% for children with severe mental retardation. By contrast, 50% to 66% of children with cerebral palsy also have mental retardation. Type of cerebral palsy seems related to the risk for mental retardation. Children with cerebral palsy involving the entire body are the most likely to have an additional diagnosis of mental retardation.

Seizure Disorders

Approximately 8% of U.S. children have at least one seizure by 15 years of age (O'Donohoe, 1994). Only half that number have a second seizure. Thus, the number of children who have repeated, unprovoked seizures, or epilepsy, is very small (Brown, 1997). Epidemiological studies show a greater prevalence of seizure disorders among children with mental retardation; some studies range as high as 16% (Wallace, 1990). As with cerebral palsy, there is a relation between the prevalence of seizure disorders and level of mental retardation. In the same Swedish study cited above, 36% of children with severe mental retardation had epilepsy as compared with 18% of the children with mild mental retardation.

Sensory Impairments

Sensory handicaps are also quite prevalent among children with mental retardation. Many of the etiologies involve sensory systems as well as the cortex. Epidemiologic studies yield widely varying prevalence estimates of visual and auditory

impairment. These differences are most likely related to the definitional criteria employed in defining "impairment." For example, if the criterion is blindness, the prevalence would probably be on the order of 10%. However, if you consider a less stringent criterion, estimates would be as high as 48% to 75% (Menacker & Batshaw, 1997). The picture is similar for auditory impairments. Again, particular etiologies seem to have a greater association with auditory impairment than others.

Psychological-Behavioral

A broad review of mental retardation research suggests that psychiatric disorders are four to five times more common in children with mental retardation compared to children with typical intellectual and adaptive functioning (MacLean, 1993). Moderate to severe cases of psychiatric disorders are seen as much as seven times more often in children with mental retardation. However, prevalence estimates of psychopathology among persons with mental retardation vary widely, depending on the type of diagnostic criteria employed in the study, the age and gender of the subjects, the severity of the mental retardation, the nature of the sample, and the method of psychiatric evaluation (MacLean, 1993). In general, more severe behavior problems correspond to greater degrees of mental retardation (Jacobson, 1982).

In a study of 30,578 individuals with mental retardation, Jacobson (1982) found the prevalence rate of psychiatric disorders to be 11.6%. He found that aggression, self-injurious behavior, affect problems, and hyperactivity commonly co-occurred with mental retardation. In another study, Fee, Matson, and Benavidez (1994) discovered that conduct disorder, anxiety problems, social withdrawal, and attention-deficit disorder were common among elementary school boys with mental retardation. In fact, children with mental retardation had higher ratings of anxiety than children with typical intellectual abilities.

Reiss (1993) found that impaired social skills were the most prevalent problem among a sample of people with mental retardation. Approximately 37% of the sample had ratings indicating that their impaired social skills created problems in their lives. Researchers also found that individuals with mental retardation may have difficulties regulating their behavior and controlling their impulses. For example, Coe and Matson (1993) found that people with mental retardation may often be at risk for hyperactivity, impulse control problems, and tic disorders. Finally, individuals with mental retardation are also at risk for sexual disorders, including exhibitionism, public masturbation, and inappropriate sexual advances toward others.

In a literature review, Thomas (1994) reported that 10% to 39% of persons with mental retardation in various studies also had an additional mental disorder. Children with mental retardation have higher prevalence rates of behavioral and emotional problems, stereotypic behaviors, self-injurious behaviors, and pica compared to children without a developmental disability (Johnson, Lubetsky, & Sacco, 1995). However, in a recent study of 169 preschoolers with developmental disabilities, investigators found that noncompliance, aggression, and attention-deficit/hyperactivity disorder (ADHD)

were more readily identified in children with mild mental retardation or average intelligence compared to children with lower levels of cognitive ability. In addition, children with less cognitive ability displayed higher levels of stereotypic behavior, seizure disorders, and cerebral palsy (Johnson et al., 1995).

Children with mental retardation are generally considered at risk for a variety of other problems, thus requiring early intervention. However, prevalence rates for particular disorders may be derived from faulty assessment procedures that employed tools with no experimental basis for use with persons with mental retardation. In addition, Dykens (1995) argues that psychiatric illness in individuals with mental retardation is often overlooked because of diagnostic overshadowing, or the tendency to attribute maladaptive behavior to lower intelligence. Thus, the presence of problem behaviors in

Table 27.2 Etiologies associated with mental retardation and their associated features.

Type	Timing	Prevalence	Typical IQ	Associated Features
Down syndrome	Prenatal	1/1,000	50–60	Conduct disorder, oppositional behaviors, temper tantrums, depression.
Fragile X	Prenatal	1/2,000 (males) 1/4,000 (females)	25–40 (males) 60–85 (females)	Males: ADHD, PDD, self-injurious behaviors, autisticlike behaviors. Females: anxiety, depression, schizoid personality, attention problems.
Fetal alcohol syndrome	Prenatal	1–2/1,000	50–85	ADHD, oppositional and defiant behavior.
Prader-Willi syndrome	Prenatal	1/25,000	60	Obesity, hoarding and storing food, skin picking, whining and complaining.
Williams syndrome	Prenatal	1/10,000	50–60	Excessive anxiety, ADHD.
Cytomegalovirus	Prenatal	5–25/1,000	Variable	Hearing and motor impairment.
Meningitis	Postnatal	2–10/1,000	Variable	Learning problems, seizures, hearing loss, cerebral palsy.
Rett's syndrome	Postnatal	1/10,000 – 1/15,000	< 40	Stereotypic hand-washing movements, autisticlike behaviors, seizures, dementia, neurological and developmental declines in infancy and early childhood.
Traumatic brain injury	Postnatal	1/500 children per year	Cognitive declines vary with the extent of the injury	ADHD, irritability, aggression, emotional lability, social withdrawal, low frustration tolerance, adaptive abilities may decrease depending on severity of the injury.

persons with mental retardation may be greater than initially thought.

Investigation of psychological and behavioral problems associated with particular etiologies has been a highly productive enterprise. Careful study has shown that children with particular etiologies have increased rates of ADHD, conduct disorder, depression, anxiety, skin picking, aggression, and pervasive developmental disorder among other disorders. Table 27.2 provides a sampling of this literature for comparison.

Finally, it should be pointed out that approximately 75% of children with autism also have mental retardation. A chapter on autism is included in this volume.

IDEA

In 1975, Congress passed the Education for All Handicapped Children Act (PL 94-142), which required a free, appropriate education to all children with disabilities. This law established that children should receive educational services in the least restrictive environment, that their education be guided by an individualized education plan (IEP), that they have the right to due process, and that placement should be based on nondiscriminatory testing (Hickson et al., 1995).

In 1986, the Handicapped Children's Protection Act (PL 99–457) was passed; it provided funds for early intervention services for infants and toddlers with disabilities from birth through 2 years of age. Through the use of "child find" projects involving attempts to increase public awareness of developmental disabilities, infants and toddlers with or at risk for developmental disabilities can be served at a greater rate than before. For identified children and families, an individualized family service plan (IFSP) is developed. An IFSP must consist of (1) a statement regarding the child's current developmental level; (2) a statement of the family's concerns, the issues that are important to the family, and their resources for enhancing the child's development; (3) a statement concerning how progress will be defined and monitored, a time line regarding progress, and expected outcomes; (4) the early intervention services required to meet the needs of the child and the family, how long these services will be administered, the frequency of the services, and the intensity of the services; (5) the service

coordinator's name; and (6) the procedures that will be followed to assist the child's transition into preschool programs (Batshaw & Shapiro, 1997).

In 1990, the Education for All Handicapped Children Act was officially renamed the Individuals with Disabilities Education Act (IDEA; PL 101–476). With this legislation, autism and traumatic brain injury were added to the list of disabilities served by special education. In addition, a transition plan was mandated to be added to every child's IEP by the age of 16. The legislation emphasized an accurate assessment of and quality intervention for minorities with disabilities. Finally, the availability of technological devices in the classroom was expanded.

In 1997, IDEA was amended (IDEA-97; PL 105–17). The implementation of this law has made sweeping changes in the procedures that must be followed. States must now conduct "child find" programs that include private as well as public schools. In addition, IDEA-97 expanded eligibility requirements by allowing for children ages 3 to 9 with developmental delays to receive services. Thus, children can now receive services that are directly related to their needs without being diagnosed with a specific disability that may not adequately describe their limitations.

States and local education agencies may also look to outside sources such as Medicaid to help pay for noneducational services necessary for the child to successfully complete the goals described in the IEP. However, educational agencies are still responsible for the adequate and timely delivery of such services. New requirements mandate that paraprofessionals and assistants working with children with disabilities be appropriately trained and supervised according to state law. In addition, performance goals for children with disabilities must be established along with reliable indicators to measure progress. Moreover, parents of children with disabilities must receive feedback on their child's performance at least as often as parents of typically developing children. Children with disabilities must also participate in statewide and districtwide assessments of student progress. For children who cannot participate in such assessments, alternative assessments must be developed and implemented by July 1, 2000.

In the area of assessment, children with disabilities are required to be reevaluated every three years. However, IDEA-97 stipulates that for some children with more pronounced delays, a reevaluation for the presence of a disability is not necessary. Instead, the reevaluation process should focus on gathering new information on how to teach the child or enhance his or her likelihood for learning. Beginning at age 14, children with disabilities should have a statement in their IEP regarding transition service needs such as advance courses for potential college placement or vocational services for a marketable skill.

In the area of discipline, IDEA-97 mandates that children with disabilities must not be removed from their primary educational setting for a period longer than 10 school days. During this period of time, children with disabilities must be placed in an alternative setting that is capable of both meeting their educational goals and addressing their behavioral problems. Nonetheless, IDEA-97 states that removing a child from his or her primary educational setting is not permissible if the child's behavior problems can be addressed in that setting. Similarly, if the child's actions were a result of his or her disability and were not controllable, then the child should not be subject to disciplinary action. However, if a child with disabilities carries a weapon to school or possesses, uses, or sells a controlled substance while at school, then that child is subject to the same punishment a typically developing child would incur, up to a maximum of 45 days. For serious behavioral offenses, the school district can request a hearing for a longer placement if there is substantial evidence to suggest that maintaining the child in the primary setting will likely result in injury to the child or others.

Prior to the IDEA legislation, approximately one million children with disabilities were denied an education. Since its inception, the number of children with developmental disabilities residing in state institutions has decreased by nearly 90%. In addition, enrollment in postsecondary education by adults with developmental disabilities has tripled. Moreover, unemployment rates for young adults with developmental disabilities are almost half that of older adults with developmental disabilities. Currently, approximately 5.5 million children are receiving special education services to assist them in meeting their educational needs. Although educational achievement for children with disabilities is showing improvement, acceptable levels have yet to be reached. For example, children with disabilities tend to have difficulty passing courses and are nearly twice as likely to drop out of school compared to students without disabilities. To combat this problem, IDEA-97 provides funding to several programs responsible for personnel training, program development and improvement, research on disabilities, research on interventions, parent training, and technological assistance.

FAMILY ISSUES

The birth of a child with a serious congenital malformation is not an expected outcome of pregnancy. Although the availability and widespread use of prenatal screening methods has the potential to prepare for such eventualities, many parents discover at birth that their child has a diagnosable condition associated with mental retardation. Drotar, Baskiewicz, Irvin, Kennel, and Klaus (1975) provided an understanding of the "normal" reactions of having a child with a serious congenital malformation such as mental retardation. They described a series of adaptational stages reported by parents after the birth of an affected child. According to this model, reactions at diagnosis included shock, disbelief, and a sense of loss. This reaction seemed to be precipitated by the realization that the child was not the one expected. In a sense, there is a grief reaction in which the "ideal" child must be put to rest given the presence of a child who might not meet parental expectations for independent living, academic success, grandchildren, or the like. Following this period, depression, anger, and acceptance follow. There has been some argument that not all parents pass through the stages in sequence and that some parents may go back and forth between stages before moving on. It is certainly possible that not all parents ever really accept that their child has mental retardation. Similarly, there is the belief that parents may cycle back through these stages as new developmental tasks are encountered. Sadness and anger may reappear as parents realize that they may not have experiences shared by other families.

Studies of families who have children with mental retardation provide compelling evidence that mental retardation has an effect on parents, siblings, grandparents, and other members of the extended family. The additional demands presented by a child with mental retardation can require considerable coping resources. Common stressors encountered by families include physical and time demands on parents, management of challenging behavior, children's sleep problems, difficulties balancing child care with job and career responsibilities, financial burdens, family strain related to parenting siblings, and interactions with various educational and helping service agencies, to name only a few. Coping is often affected by previous life experiences, religious and cultural background, and family members' attitudes toward mental retardation (Stoneman, 1997). It has been a consistent finding that social support provides an important buffer against the effects of stress. Support may be obtained from extended family members, friends, and siblings in the case of older caregivers (Stoneman, 1997). Professionals, service agencies, and parent groups are also sources of social support.

Mothers and fathers have different reactions to the presence of a child with mental retardation in the family. Moreover, they employ different coping strategies. For example, fathers may employ problem-focused coping strategies, whereas mothers may use emotion-focused coping strategies to a greater degree. These differences are normal and probably reflect gender differences and already established roles within the family. Strong marital relationships have also been shown to buffer the effects of stress and to enhance family functioning overall. Similarly, single-parent families with a child with mental retardation have been shown to have a greater risk for compromised functioning. Parents who have good parenting and problem-solving skills cope better. Social support and financial stability are also related to coping effectiveness.

Siblings are also affected by the presence of a child with a disability in the family. There is no one universal reaction: effects vary with gender, age, birth order, and temperament of the sibling. Sibling adjustment is related in part to parental coping. Siblings fare best when their parents' marriage is stable and supportive, when feelings are discussed openly, when the disability is explained completely, and when they are not overburdened with child care responsibilities. Sibling adjustment can also be enhanced through participation in sibling support groups and interaction with other siblings through Internet pages and chat rooms sponsored by various helping agencies.

REFERENCES

Ainsworth, M.D.S. (1989). Attachments beyond infancy. *American Psychologist, 44,* 709–716.

American Psychiatric Association. (1994). *Diagnostic and statistical manual of mental disorders* (4th ed.). Washington, DC: Author.

Anglin, J.M. (1993). Vocabulary development: A morphological analysis. *Monographs of the Society for Research in Child Development, 58*(10, Serial No. 238).

Bates, E., Thal, D., & Marchman, V. (1991). Symbols and syntax: A Darwinian approach to language development. In N. Krasnegor, D. Rumbaugh, R.L. Schiefelbusch, & M. Studdert-Kennedy (Eds.), *Biological and behavioral determinants of language development* (pp. 67–88). Hillsdale, NJ: Erlbaum.

Batshaw, M.L., & Shapiro, B.K. (1997). Mental retardation. In M.L. Batshaw (Ed.), *Children with disabilities* (4th ed., pp. 335–359). Baltimore: Brookes.

Bellugi, U., Bihrle, A., Neville, H., Jernigan, T., & Doherty, S. (1992). Language, cognition, and brain organization in a neurodevelopmental disorder. In M. Gunnar & C. Nelson (Eds.), *Developmental behavioral neuroscience* (pp. 201–232). Hillsdale, NJ: Erlbaum.

Best, D.L., & Ornstein, P.A. (1986). Children's generation and communication of mnemonic organizational strategies. *Developmental Psychology, 22,* 845–853.

Bowerman, N. (1985). Beyond communicative adequacy: From piecemeal knowledge to an integrated system in the child's acquisition of language. In K.E. Nelson (Ed.), *Children's language* (Vol. 5, pp. 369–398). Hillsdale, NJ: Erlbaum.

Bowlby, J. (1969). *Attachment and loss: Vol. 1. Attachment.* New York: Basic Books.

Brainerd, C.J., & Reyna, V.F. (1995). Learning rate, learning opportunities, and the development of forgetting. *Developmental Psychology, 31,* 251–262.

Brainerd, C.J., Reyna, V.F., Howe, M.L., & Kingma, J. (1990). The development of forgetting and reminiscence. *Monographs of the Society for Research in Child Development, 55*(3–4, Serial No. 222).

Bray, N.W., Fletcher, K.L., & Turner, L.A. (1997). Cognitive competencies and strategy use in individuals with mental retardation. In W.E. MacLean Jr. (Ed.), *Ellis' handbook of mental deficiency, psychological theory and research* (3rd ed., pp. 197–217). Mahwah, NJ: Erlbaum.

Brooks-Gunn, J., & Lewis, M. (1982). Affective exchanges between normal and handicapped infants and their mothers. In T. Field & A. Fogel (Eds.), *Emotion and early interaction* (pp. 161–212). Hillsdale, NJ: Erlbaum.

Brown, L.W. (1997). Seizure disorders. In M.L. Batshaw (Ed.), *Children with disabilities* (4th ed., pp. 553–593). Baltimore: Brookes.

Buss, A.H., & Plomin, R. (1984). *Temperament: Early developing personality traits.* Hillsdale, NJ: Erlbaum.

Capute, A.J., Palmer, F.B., Shapiro, B.K., Wachtel, R.C., Ross, A., & Accardo, P.J. (1984). Primitive reflex profile: A quantification of primitive reflexes in infancy. *Developmental Medicine and Child Neurology, 26,* 375–383.

Chapman, R.S. (1995). Language development in children and adolescents with Down syndrome. In P. Fletcher & B. MacWhinney (Eds.), *Handbook of child language* (pp. 641–663). Oxford, England: Blackwell.

Chapman, R.S., Schwartz, S.E., & Kay-Raining Bird, E. (1991). Language skills of children and adolescents with Down syndrome: I. Comprehension. *Journal of Speech and Hearing Research, 34,* 1106–1120.

Chess, S., & Korn, S. (1970a). The influence of temperament on education of mentally retarded children. *Journal of Special Education, 4,* 13–27.

Chess, S., & Korn, S. (1970b). Temperament and behavior disorders in mentally retarded children. *Archives of General Psychiatry, 23,* 122–130.

Chess, S., & Thomas, A. (1989). Temperament and its functional significance. In S.I. Greenspan & G.H. Pollack (Eds.), *The course of life* (Vol. 2, pp. 163–227). Madison, CT: International Universities Press.

Coe, D.A., & Matson, J.L. (1993). Hyperactivity and disorders of impulse control. In J.L. Matson & R.P. Barrett (Eds.), *Psychopathology in the mentally retarded* (pp. 253–271). Boston: Allyn & Bacon.

DeLoache, J.S. (1991). Symbolic functioning in very young children: Understanding of pictures and models. *Child Development, 62,* 736–752.

de Villiers, P.A., & de Villiers, J.G. (1992). Language development. In M.H. Bornstein & M.E. Lamb (Eds.), *Developmental psychology: An advanced textbook* (3rd ed., pp. 337–418). Hillsdale, NJ: Erlbaum.

Drotar, D., Baskiewicz, A., Irvin, N., Kennel, J., & Klaus, M. (1975). The adaptation of parents to the birth of an infant with a congenital malformation: A hypothetical model. *Pediatrics, 56,* 710–717.

Dykens, E.M. (1995). Measuring behavioral phenotypes: Provocations from the "new genetics." *American Journal on Mental Retardation, 99,* 522–532.

Dykens, E.M., & Kasari, C. (1997). Maladaptive behavior in children with Prader-Willi syndrome, Down syndrome, and nonspecific mental retardation. *American Journal on Mental Retardation, 102,* 228–237.

Eaton, W.O., & Ritchot, K.F.M. (1995). Physical maturation and information processing speed in middle childhood. *Developmental Psychology, 31,* 967–972.

Eisenberg, N. (1992). *The caring child.* Cambridge, MA: Harvard University Press.

Ellis, N.R. (1969). A behavioral research strategy in mental retardation: Defense and critique. *American Journal on Mental Deficiency, 73,* 557–566.

Fee, V.E., Matson, J.L., & Benavidez, D.A. (1994). Attention-deficit hyperactivity disorder among mentally retarded children. *Research in Developmental Disabilities, 15,* 67–79.

Field, T. (1984). Play behaviors of handicapped children who have friends. In T. Field, J.L. Roopnarine, & M. Segal (Eds.), *Friendships in normal and handicapped children* (pp. 153–163). Norwood, NJ: Albex.

Fotheringhan, J.B. (1983). Mental retardation and developmental delay. In K.D. Paget & B.A. Bracken (Eds.), *The psychoeducational assessment of preschool children* (pp. 207–223). New York: Grune & Stratton.

Fowler, A. (1990). Language abilities in children with Down syndrome: Evidence for a specific syntactic delay. In D. Cicchetti & M. Beeghly (Eds.), *Children with Down syndrome: A developmental perspective* (pp. 302–328). Cambridge, England: Cambridge University Press.

Gibson, D. (1978). *Down's syndrome: The psychology of mongolism.* Cambridge, England: Cambridge University Press.

Goldfield, B., & Resnick, J.S. (1990). Early lexical acquisition: Rate, content, and the vocabulary spurt. *Journal of Child Language, 17,* 171–183.

Greenspan, S., & Granfield, J.M. (1992). Reconsidering the construct of mental retardation: Implications of a model of social competence. *American Journal on Mental Retardation, 96,* 442–453.

Greenspan, S., & Love, P.F. (1997). Social intelligence and developmental disorder: Mental retardation, learning disabilities, and autism. In W.E. MacLean Jr. (Ed.), *Ellis' handbook of mental deficiency, psychological theory and research* (3rd ed., pp. 311–342). Mahwah, NJ: Erlbaum.

Gresham, F.M. (1983). Social skills assessment as a component of mainstreaming placement decisions. *Exceptional Children, 49,* 331–338.

Gresham, F.M. (1986). Conceptual issues in the assessment of social competence in children. In P.S. Strain, M.J. Guralnick, & H.M. Walker (Eds.), *Children's social behavior: Development, assessment, and modification* (pp. 143–179). Orlando, FL: Academic Press.

Guralnick, M.J. (1984). The peer interactions of young developmentally delayed children in specialized and integrated settings. In T. Field, J.L. Roopnarine, & M. Segal (Eds.), *Friendships in normal and handicapped children* (pp. 139–152). Norwood, NJ: Albex.

Guralnick, M.J. (1992). A hierarchical model for understanding children's peer-related social competence. In S.L. Odom, S.R. McConnell, & M.A. McAvoy (Eds.), *Social competence in young children with disabilities* (pp. 37–64). Baltimore: Brookes.

Hamilton, M., & Matson, J.L. (1992). Mental retardation. In S.M. Turner, K.S. Calhoun, & H.E. Adams (Eds.),

Handbook of clinical behavior therapy (2nd ed., pp. 317–336). New York: Wiley.

Harris, P.L. (1989). *Children and emotion: The development of psychological understanding.* Oxford, England: Blackwell.

Hickson, L., Blackman, L.S., & Reis, E.M. (1995). *Mental retardation: Foundations of educational programming.* Boston: Allyn & Bacon.

Howes, C. (1987). Social competence with peers in young children: Developmental sequences. *Developmental Review, 7,* 252–272.

Jacobson, J.W. (1982). Problem behavior and psychiatric impairment within a developmentally disabled population I: Behavior frequency. *Applied Research in Mental Retardation, 3,* 121–129.

Johnson, C.R., Lubetsky, M.J., & Sacco, K.A. (1995). Psychiatric and behavioral disorders in hospitalized preschoolers with developmental disabilities. *Journal of Autism and Developmental Disorders, 25,* 169–182.

Kail, R. (1991). Developmental changes in speed of processing during childhood and adolescence. *Psychological Bulletin, 109,* 490–501.

Kasari, C., & Bauminger, N. (1998). Social and emotional development in children with mental retardation. In J.A. Burack & R.M. Hodapp (Eds.), *Handbook of mental retardation and development* (pp. 411–433). New York: Cambridge University Press.

Kasari, C., Mundy, P., Yirmiya, N., & Sigman, M. (1990). Affect and attention in children with Down syndrome. *American Journal on Mental Retardation, 95,* 55–67.

Kent, R.D., & Miulo, G. (1995). Phonetic abilities in the first year of life. In P. Fletcher & B. MacWhinney (Eds.), *The handbook of child language.* Cambridge, MA: Blackwell.

Kerby, D.S., & Dawson, B.L. (1994). Autistic features, personality, and adaptive behavior in males with Fragile X syndrome and no autism. *American Journal on Mental Retardation, 98,* 455–462.

Kiely, M. (1987). The prevalence of mental retardation. *Epidemiology Reviews, 9,* 194–218.

Lachiewicz, A.M., Spiridigliozzi, G.A., Gullion, C.M., Ransford, S.N., & Rao, K. (1994). Aberrant behaviors of young boys with Fragile X syndrome. *American Journal on Mental Retardation, 98,* 567–579.

Lewis, M., Sullivan, M.W., Stanger, C., & Weiss, M. (1989). Self-development and self-conscious emotions. *Child Development, 60,* 146–156.

Luckasson, R. (Ed.). (1992). *Mental retardation: Definition, classification, and systems of support.* Washington, DC: American Association on Mental Retardation.

Lutz, D.J., & Sternberg, R.J. (1999). Cognitive development. In M.H. Bornstein & M.E. Lamb (Eds.), *Developmental psychology: An advanced textbook* (4th ed., pp. 275–311). Mahwah, NJ: Erlbaum.

MacLean, W.E. (1993). Overview. In J.L. Matson & R.P. Barrett (Eds.), *Psychopathology in the mentally retarded* (pp. 1–15). Boston: Allyn & Bacon.

MacLean, W.E., Ellis, D.N., Galbreath, H.N., Halpern, L.F., & Baumeister, A.A. (1991). Rhythmic motor behavior of preambulatory motor impaired, Down syndrome, and nondisabled children: A comparative analysis. *Journal of Abnormal Child Psychology, 19,* 319–330.

MacMillan, D.L., Gresham, F.M., & Bocian, K.M. (1998). Discrepancy between definitions of learning disabled and what schools use: An empirical investigation. *Journal of Learning Disabilities, 31,* 314–326.

MacMillan, D.L., Gresham, F.M., Siperstein, G.N., & Bocian, K.M. (1996). The labyrinth of IDEA: School decisions on referred students with subaverage intelligence. *American Journal on Mental Retardation, 101,* 161–174.

MacMillan, D.L., & Reschly, D.J. (1997). Issues of definition and classification. In W.E. MacLean Jr. (Ed.), *Ellis' handbook of mental deficiency, psychological theory and research* (3rd ed., pp. 47–74). Mahwah, NJ: Erlbaum.

Matilainen, R., Airaksinen, E., Mononen, T., Launiala, K., & Kaariainen, R. (1995). A population-based study on the causes of mild and severe mental retardation. *Acta Paediatrica, 84,* 261–266.

Mazzocco, M.M., Pennington, B.F., & Hagerman, R.J. (1994). Social cognition skills among females with Fragile X. *Journal of Autism and Developmental Disorders, 24,* 473–485.

Menacker, S.J., & Batshaw, M.L. (1997). Vision. In M.L. Batshaw (Ed.), *Children with disabilities* (4th ed., pp. 211–239). Baltimore: Brookes.

Mitchell, W., & Cook, K.V. (1987). Social skills training of Prader-Willi staff. *American Journal of Medical Genetics, 28,* 907–913.

Nettelbeck, T., & Wilson, C. (1997). Speed of information processing and cognition. In W.E. MacLean Jr. (Ed.), *Ellis' handbook of mental deficiency, psychological theory and research* (3rd ed., pp. 245–274). Mahwah, NJ: Erlbaum.

Newport, E. (1990). Maturational constraints on language learning. *Cognitive Science, 14,* 11–28.

O'Donohoe, N.V. (1994). *Epilepsies of childhood* (3rd ed.). Oxford, England: Butterworth-Heinemann.

Pellegrino, L. (1997). Cerebral palsy. In M.L. Batshaw (Ed.), *Children with disabilities* (4th ed., pp. 499–528). Baltimore: Brookes.

Penner, K.A., Johnston, J., Faircloth, B.H., Irish, P., & Williams, C.A. (1993). Communication, cognition, and social interaction in the Angelman syndrome. *American Journal of Medical Genetics, 46,* 34–39.

Pinker, S. (1994). *The language instinct: How the mind creates language.* New York: Morrow.

Plissart, L., Borghgraef, M., & Fryns, J.P. (1996). Temperament in Williams syndrome. *Genetic Counseling, 7,* 41–46.

Reiss, S.R. (1993). Assessment of psychopathology in persons with mental retardation. In J.L. Matson & R.P. Barrett (Eds.), *Psychopathology in the mentally retarded* (pp. 17–40). Boston: Allyn & Bacon.

Reschly, D.J. (1992). Mental retardation: Conceptual foundation, definitional criteria, and diagnostic operations. In S.R. Hynd & R.E. Mattison (Eds.), *Assessment and diagnosis of child and adolescent psychiatric disorders: Vol. II. Developmental disorders* (pp. 23–67). Hillsdale, NJ: Erlbaum.

Rosenberg, S., & Abbeduto, L. (1993). *Language and communication in mental retardation: Development, processes, and intervention.* Hillsdale, NJ: Erlbaum.

Rutter, D.R., & Durkin, K. (1987). Turn-taking in mother-infant interaction: An examination of vocalizations and gaze. *Developmental Psychology, 23,* 54–61.

Sattler, J.M. (1992). *Assessment of children* (3rd ed.). San Diego, CA: Author.

Saywitz, K., Goodman, G., Nichols, G., & Moan, S. (1991). Children's memory of a physical examination involving genital touch: Implications for reports of child sexual abuse. *Journal of Consulting and Clinical Psychology, 59,* 682–691.

Schneider, W., & Pressley, M. (1989). *Memory development between 2 and 20.* New York: Springer-Verlag.

Siegler, R.S. (1998). *Children's thinking* (3rd ed.). Upper Saddle River, NJ: Prentice Hall.

Sinson, J.C., & Wetherick, N.E. (1981). The behavior of children with Down syndrome in normal playgroups. *Journal of Mental Deficiency Research, 25,* 113–120.

Sonnenschein, S. (1986). Development of referential communication skills: How familiarity with a listener affects a speaker's production of redundant messages. *Developmental Psychology, 22,* 549–552.

Stoneman, Z. (1997). Mental retardation and family adaptation. In W.E. MacLean Jr. (Ed.), *Ellis' handbook of mental deficiency, psychological theory and research* (3rd ed., pp. 405–437). Mahwah, NJ: Erlbaum.

Sudhulter, V., Cohen, I., Silverman, W., & Wolf-Schein, E. (1990). Conversational analyses of males with Fragile X, Down syndrome, and autism: Comparison of the emergence of deviant language. *American Journal on Mental Retardation, 94,* 431–441.

Thelen, E. (1979). Rhythmical stereotypies in normal human infants. *Animal Behavior, 27,* 699–715.

Thomas, J.R. (1994). Quality care for individuals with dual diagnosis: The legal and ethical imperative to provide qualified staff. *Mental Retardation, 32,* 356–361.

Tomasello, M., & Mannle, S. (1985). Pragmatics of sibling speech to one-year-olds. *Child Development, 56,* 911–917.

Tomc, S.A., Williamson, N.K., & Pauli, R.M. (1990). Temperament in Williams syndrome. *American Journal of Medical Genetics, 36,* 345–352.

Tomporowski, P.D., & Tinsley, V. (1997). Attention in mentally retarded persons. In W.E. MacLean Jr. (Ed.), *Ellis' handbook of mental deficiency, psychological theory and research* (3rd ed., pp. 219–244). Mahwah, NJ: Erlbaum.

Udwin, O. (1990). A survey of adults with Williams syndrome and idiopathic infantile hypercalcemia. *Developmental Medicine and Child Neurology, 32,* 129–141.

Underwood, M.K., Coie, J.D., & Herbsman, C.R. (1992). Display rules for anger and aggression in school-age children. *Child Development, 63,* 366–380.

Volkmar, F.R., & Cohen, D.J. (1997). Developmentally based assessments. In D.J. Cohen & F.R. Volkmar (Eds.), *Handbook of autism and pervasive developmental disorders* (2nd ed., pp. 411–447). New York: Wiley.

Walden, T.A. (1991). Infant social referencing. In J. Garber & K.A. Dodge (Eds.), *The development of emotion regulation and dysregulation* (pp. 69–88). Cambridge, England: Cambridge University Press.

Wallace, S.J. (1990). Risk of seizures (Annotation). *Developmental Medicine and Child Neurology, 32,* 645–649.

Warren, S.F., & Yoder, P.J. (1997). Communication, language, and mental retardation. In W.E. MacLean Jr. (Ed.), *Ellis' handbook of mental deficiency, psychological theory and research* (3rd ed., pp. 379–403). Mahwah, NJ: Erlbaum.

Wellman, H.M., & Woolley, J.D. (1990). From simple desires to ordinary beliefs: The early development of everyday psychology. *Cognition, 35,* 245–275.

Werker, J.F., & Tees, R.C. (1992). The organization and reorganization of human speech perception. *Annual Review of Neuroscience, 15,* 377–402.

Whitman, T.L., O'Callaghan, M., & Sommer, K. (1997). Emotion and mental retardation. In W.E. MacLean Jr. (Ed.), *Ellis' handbook of mental deficiency, psychological theory and research* (3rd ed., pp. 77–98). Mahwah, NJ: Erlbaum.

Wimmer, H., & Perner, J. (1983). Beliefs about beliefs: Representation and constraining function of wrong beliefs in young children's understanding of deception. *Cognition, 13,* 103–128.

CHAPTER 28

School Problems of Children

JOSEPH A. DURLAK

CURRENT STATUS

At first glance, school problems can seem overwhelming. Between 15% and 22% of young people have mental health problems that meet criteria for a clinical disorder, and a similar percentage probably have less serious problems that nevertheless interfere with their general growth and development. Youth bring their psychological problems into schools instead of leaving them at the door, and their ability to profit from school is thus impaired to varying degrees.

The academic performance of American schoolchildren leaves much to be desired, and some would say is downright embarrassing. A startling half of all students will either drop out of school or graduate from high school with less than adequate reading, math, writing, and thinking skills. Some studies suggest that four out of five American youth cannot adequately summarize the main points of a newspaper article, calculate the correct change for a retail purchase, or understand a bus schedule. Businesses spend an estimated $25 billion annually training their workers in basic reading, writing, and reasoning skills that should have been acquired in school (Murphy, 1990).

Discipline and misbehavior continue to be major concerns for many teachers, and academic development is jeopardized when students are apathetic, inattentive, or disruptive. One out of five parents has been called to school because of their first- or second-grade child's behavioral problems; a little over 1 of every 10 teachers indicates that student conduct has negatively affected their ability to teach; and approximately 11% of eighth-graders have been suspended from school at least once (U.S. Department of Education, 1997).

Finally, violence occurs too frequently in schools. About 10% of schoolchildren are bullied by their peers (Olweus, 1994). Up to 11% of youth do not feel safe at their school, and 6% have stayed home from school at least once out of fear for their personal safety (Kingery, Coggeshall, & Alford, 1998).

WHY IS ALL THIS HAPPENING?

It has been easy to point the finger of blame for different problems. Sometimes, society blames the victim. A medical model conceptualizes adjustment problems in terms of disease states. A concomitant reliance on individual psychotherapy suggests that the source and resolution of problems often reside in the child.

For some teachers and principals, the fault also lies with students who are lazy and unmotivated to learn and who have little respect for teachers, their school, or education in general. Some teachers also blame parents for not supporting their child's education or not raising their children effectively. Some

561

teachers blame principals or other administrators for lack of support and effective guidance, poor leadership, or political cowardice in times of controversy. Schools cannot be improved in the face of ineffectual leadership.

At the same time, some parents blame teachers and the schools. Some teachers are incompetent and should not be in the classroom. Schools do not really want parental input, do not do enough to assist parents, and do not try hard enough to motivate and teach all students, especially those who are in some way "different" from the mainstream.

In their defense, students complain that schools are not a stimulating or nurturing environment. Students are often bored in school and feel frequently "put down" by teachers who fail to offer support or listen to what students have to say.

Local taxpayers can also be blamed. Most of the financial support for schools comes through local taxes and bond issues, resulting in marked disparities in pupil expenditures and basic services across school districts. In the mid-1990s, it was estimated that over $112 *billion* was immediately needed to repair and upgrade school facilities to meet minimal safety standards and improve the learning environment (U.S. Government Accounting Office, 1995). Taxpayers will not foot such a large bill.

Finally, society in general is to blame. There is too much poverty and drug use, too many broken homes, and a general complacency over violence, sex, morality, and basic values. American society has deserted its children and its schools, and makes no firm commitment to child welfare.

REASON FOR HOPE

There are many problems in American schools, but assigning blame for their existence does not lead to very productive attempts at problem solving. The main point of this chapter is that there is reason for hope. A dedicated cadre of individuals has demonstrated that schools can be highly effective. Examples abound that rates of behavioral and social problems can be greatly reduced, levels of academic performance can be substantially enhanced, and strong working relationships and close personal bonds can form among teachers, students, and parents.

Schools are highly complex social organizations and bureaucracies. As a result, professionals do not know precisely which factors are most responsible

for the success of different efforts, how best to tailor initiatives to fit the characteristics of each local setting, and how the very best programs can be effectively replicated on a broad scale. Nonetheless, a picture is slowly emerging regarding which approaches offer the most potential.

Many interventions that have reduced problems and improved school functioning share five common, related themes: they (1) intervene proactively to prevent later problems; (2) think holistically about child development and adjustment; (3) recognize that because most outcomes are multidetermined, multidimensional solutions are needed; (4) adopt an ecological perspective; and (5) focus on the positive.

In brief, these themes emphasize that it is possible to prevent many serious school adjustment problems: that psychological, social, academic, and physical development cannot be easily separated, and each domain influences the others; that there are multiple interacting risk and protective factors affecting outcomes, so it is important to intervene at multiple levels to modify as many factors as possible (i.e., to involve peers, parents, teachers, and the local community in interventions); that behavior cannot be viewed apart from the context in which it occurs; and, finally, that people are the school's most valuable resources. The key is to develop programs that maximize the positive contributions that teachers, students, and parents can make to improve schools (see Durlak, 1995, 1997, 1998; Institute of Medicine, 1994; Trickett & Schmidt, 1993). The next sections discuss successful school-based interventions that illustrate these themes.

ACADEMIC PERFORMANCE

Although topics such as learning disabilities and mental retardation are important (see chapters by Rourke and MacLean in this volume), together they affect only about 10% of the school population. This section discusses approaches to enhance the academic performance and prevent general learning problems for all schoolchildren.

CENTRAL ROLE OF SCHOOL SUCCESS

Good academic performance is a major protective factor in children's lives. Children who do well in school have fewer behavioral and social problems, better peer relations, less drug use and delinquency, and heightened psychological well-being (self-esteem, self-efficacy, and life satisfaction). Furthermore, children who do well in school graduate with cognitive skills that prepare them for later life challenges. Conversely, poor academic performance is a major risk factor for many behavioral and social problems, such as acting-out, delinquency, drug use, poor peer relations, teenage pregnancy, depression, and dropping out of school with poor cognitive and social skills. Therefore, professionals should do everything they can to ensure that as many children as possible experience success in school.

GETTING OFF TO A GOOD START

In general, the best estimate of future school performance is current performance. Unfortunately, many children display early learning problems. In 1998, 70% of fourth-graders did not possess all the grade-level reading skills they needed, and only 7% of children demonstrated above-grade-level skills (U.S. Department of Education, 1999). Most of the 70% with insufficient skills will not outgrow their problems without active efforts at remediation; therefore, it is important to discuss the types of academic interventions that are the least and most likely to be helpful for young schoolchildren.

What Probably Will Not Work
The three most common programmatic responses that schools make to help children with learning problems in general or reading deficiencies in particular are grade retention, placement in special education, and remedial Chapter I programs. However, none of these strategies is very effective (Kauffman, 1999; Slavin, Karweit, & Madden, 1989; Tanner & Galis, 1997). For instance, the sad fact is that once a child has flunked a grade or has been placed in special education, the odds are that child will never catch up academically to his or her peers. Chapter I programs constitute the largest single source of federal funding for education and target academically at-risk low-income children. Over 5 million students have been served in Chapter I programs. Unfortunately, analyses suggest that the remediation given low-performing children through Chapter I is neither extensive nor intensive enough to help most youngsters in need (Slavin et al., 1989). In summary, the usual approaches that schools take to help those in academic trouble miss the mark for many children.

What Does Work
Slavin and his colleagues (Slavin, Karweit, & Wasik, 1994; Slavin et al., 1989) have reviewed several types of effective reading programs. Successful programs share three common themes: early intervention, a direct focus on academic skills, and individualizing the learning process as much as possible. Successful programs begin as early as possible (sometimes in preschool, as discussed below), and they work intensively with students on an individual and small group basis until mastery is achieved. These programs also incorporate many other elements discussed in this chapter. Thus, schools usually have to reorient their resources toward ensuring early academic competency and train and support teachers in learning new instructional and classroom management skills. Many programs also enlist the active support of parents and guide them in how to promote learning at home.

For example, Successful For All (SFA) is one effective program used in several school districts to help children read and acquire other basic academic competencies. SFA is based on the premise "that the school must *relentlessly continue with every child until that child is succeeding*" (Slavin et al., 1994, p. 176; original italics).

SFA is an intensive approach that emphasizes (1) early intervention (in preschool, kindergarten, or, at the very latest, first grade); (2) one-on-one tutoring to develop reading skills; and (3) active parent participation. The preschool intervention emphasizes both academic readiness and social development. First-graders receive intensive tutoring in reading from adult tutors. Additional cooperative learning programs are also provided for skill development in other subjects such as writing and arts. Finally, family support teams are created at each school to monitor the school performance and behavior of children and assist teachers and parents as needed. SFA has increased the percentage of children reading at grade level by 49, reduced the percentage who were falling significantly behind by 41, and reduced the need for placement in special education classes by over 50% (Slavin et al., 1994).

Early Childhood Programs
For some children, intervention must occur *before* elementary school. An estimated one-third of U.S. children do not begin first grade ready to learn

(Lewit & Baker, 1995). School readiness is a multidimensional concept that generally refers to the developmental maturation of linguistic, cognitive, and social skills that allow children to take advantage of a formal educational curriculum. Children from low-income households are the group at greatest risk for low levels of school readiness and later poor school performance. For a variety of reasons, many poor children do not receive enough social and cognitive stimulation to prepare them for formal schooling.

Fortunately, there is now a growing database confirming the long-term value of early childhood programs for poor, academically at-risk children. The Perry Preschool Program (PPP) has received the most attention (Schweinhart & Weikart, 1988). PPP was an intensive intervention for African American, inner-city families that combined an up to two-year-long, five-day-a-week preschool curriculum with a home-based parent stimulation and development program. A 14-year follow-up indicated that children in PPP were superior to controls on academic outcomes such as grades, grade retentions, rates of mental retardation (15% vs. 35%), and proportion of high school graduates (67% vs. 49%), and on social outcomes such as arrest rates (31% vs. 51%) and employment status (50% vs. 32%).

PPP is not alone in demonstrating the positive long-term effects of early childhood programs for low-income children. Several carefully evaluated programs conducted in the United States (Barnett, 1990) and throughout the world support the general conclusion that early intervention "can have strong positive effects on children's school readiness and their subsequent academic performance" (Boocock, 1995, p. 103).

IMPROVING GENERAL ACADEMIC PERFORMANCE

In addition to specific programs such as SFA and early childhood interventions, academic performance in general can be enhanced by focusing on three aspects of school life: specific teaching practices, the classroom environment, and the overall school environment.

Specific Teaching Practices
There is fairly good consensus that the principles summarized in Table 28.1 represent "best practices" in teaching and are applicable for most

Table 28.1   Effective teaching practices.

1. Establish a positive learning environment characterized by order, a focus on learning goals, and emotional support.
2. Clearly communicate standards and consequences for student behavior and learning.
3. Have high expectations for students.
4. Directly teach academic skills. Avoid focusing on indirect methods, such as perceptual or motor processing.
5. Allocate as much time as possible to productive academic learning time (PALT).
6. Use multiple instructional strategies and emphasize active forms of learning (e.g., answering questions, doing group projects, discussing issues, and using relevant resources such as workbooks, exercise sheets, and media).
7. Establish step-by-step learning goals.
8. Provide quick help to students who are struggling with the material.
9. Present material suited to students' ability levels.
10. Continually monitor student progress and adjust instructional pace to accommodate individual learning styles.
11. Reinforce and support students for both effort and mastery.
12. Value student diversity.

Source: Drawn from Doyle (1986) and Good and Brophy (1994).

instructional situations. That is, with only a few modifications, primarily for such things as children's developmental level and specific pedagogic goals, effective teaching looks remarkably the same wherever it occurs.

Space does not permit a complete discussion of each point presented in Table 28.1, but some brief comments are in order. For instance, teachers with high expectations for students (principle 3) usually teach so that students are able to meet their expectations. In other words, teachers who expect their children to do well spend more time on instruction, help those who initially struggle, and give more feedback and praise. Teachers with low expectations tend to do just the opposite: they spend less time on instruction and give less praise, support, and assistance to their students.

Productive academic learning time (PALT) refers to the amount of time students are engaged with material that is suited to their ability level (principle 5). PALT is one of the most important bellwethers of effective teaching (Gettinger, 1990). In general, higher levels of PALT are associated with better student performance regardless of the student's prior achievement and is an important element in helping underachieving students improve their performance.

Principles 7 to 12 reflect the importance of individualizing instruction as much as possible. This can be the most challenging aspect of teaching, given the many students and range of abilities usually present in classrooms. It is not uncommon to find classes in which student abilities span five different grades! With heavy demands on their time, teachers must be resourceful and creative in teaching to each student's ability. Two helpful instructional strategies in this regard have been cooperative learning and peer tutoring.

Cooperative Learning. Cooperative learning refers to students working together in small groups to promote each other's learning. For maximum effectiveness, the class should be divided into small groups, making sure students of different ability levels are spread out across the groups. Students in each group then receive rewards such as extra free time or special activities provided all group members master and learn the material. This contingency prevents freeloaders from doing little and benefiting from others' work.

Cooperative learning has been very successful in improving achievement, peer relationships, and attitudes toward school, and reducing misconduct, and is suitable for both lower- and higher-level cognitive tasks and with students who are heterogeneous with respect to ability level, socioeconomic, racial, and ethic status, and gender. Therefore, cooperative learning is applicable for most classrooms (Johnson & Johnson, 1991).

Tutoring. After reviewing the research, Slavin et al. (1994) noted, "One-on-one tutoring is the most effective form of instruction known" (p. 178). Tutoring has been successfully accomplished by college students, adult community volunteers, teachers, and parents, and its intensity and duration can be varied to suit each learner's needs. Peer tutoring includes cross-age tutoring, in which older students tutor younger ones, and reciprocal tutoring procedures in which tutors and tutees from the same class or instructional group switch roles. Both cross-age and reciprocal tutoring interventions have been effective (see Cohen, Kulik, & Kulik, 1982; Slavin et al., 1994, for reviews).

One of the more impressive findings on classroomwide reciprocal tutoring was reported by Greenwood, Delquadri, and Hall (1989). This study involved over 400 low-income students and 94 teachers from grades 1 through 4 in 15 different schools. Two comparison groups were used to evaluate the impact of peer tutoring: an untutored low-income control group and a selected group of children from high-income homes who served as a local standard for good academic performance. Children participating in the experimental reciprocal tutoring program did significantly better than control students in reading, mathematics, and language studies, and their achievement was not significantly different from the high-performing comparison group. In other words, peer tutoring brought the performance of low-income students to within the levels of the best students at participating schools.

THE CLASSROOM ENVIRONMENT

Note that the first practice related to effective teaching in Table 28.1 involves establishing a positive learning environment. Research confirms that the classroom environment must be taken into account when trying to understand students' school adjustment (Fraser & Walberg, 1991; Moos, 1979).

A positive classroom learning environment refers to a setting in which three related features are prominent: warm and supportive interpersonal relationships, a strong focus on learning, and well-organized and structured yet flexible daily routines and policies. The types of outcomes that have been associated with these classroom features include higher academic motivation and achievement, better peer relations, stronger attachment to school and education, less misconduct, less student stress, depression, and anxiety, more prosocial behavior, and enhanced psychological well-being (Fraser & Walberg, 1991; Moos, 1979). Many of these findings have been replicated in several countries around the world, across different educational levels, and with a diversity of teachers and students.

Interpersonal Relationships

Although the relationships that form among students are important, the level of personal support and encouragement the teacher provides to students often sets the emotional tone in a classroom.

Students try harder, perform better, are better behaved, are more helpful to each other, and generally enjoy school more when their teachers are supportive and caring. Early positive relationships with teachers increase the likelihood of later good school performance and may be a major protective factor for academically at-risk children (Pianta, Steinberg, & Rollins, 1995). Close relationships with teachers are also helpful to adolescents negotiating the simultaneously stressful experiences of puberty and transition into junior high school (Roeser & Eccles, 1998).

Learning Goals

Heightened student learning in more academically oriented classrooms is consistent with the previous discussion on the importance of PALT. However, research also indicates that it is often more beneficial for students if teachers create a learning environment that stresses a *task goal structure* (or mastery structure) rather than an *ability goal structure* (Eccles et al., 1993).

In a task goal structure, personal *mastery* is most important, and students receive messages that their continual effort and improvement is critical. When this type of learning atmosphere is combined with teacher support, students are consistently praised for their relative improvement. Goals and social rewards are individualized: "You are improving, getting better. Keep at it."

In contrast, students come to perceive that demonstration of their personal ability is important when an ability goal structure is emphasized. This often creates a competitive learning atmosphere as social comparisons become salient and students tend to believe that how they stand in comparison to others is a crucial aspect of their success. In ability goal classrooms, social comparisons are further fostered by grading on a curve, and there is more likely to be differential treatment of students depending on their accomplishments. Teachers tend to offer more rewards and supports for those who do better than others.

In most cases, a task goal structure is associated with more positive attitudes toward school, more effort and higher levels of motivation, and higher self-concept of ability than is an ability goal structure. An ability goal structure can also create more stress and performance anxiety among students and often penalizes lower-performing students, who quickly learn that they cannot compete effectively for academic rewards and will not receive much teacher support. Under such circumstances, more academic disengagement and behavioral problems may occur (Roeser & Eccles, 1998).

Order, Organization, and Flexibility

Well-organized and structured classrooms provide a good setting for student growth. At the same time, effective teachers are not domineering or completely controlling. As students progress through school, their classroom environments should encourage more independence and self-direction. This is not only consistent with developmental needs for greater personal autonomy and independence with advancing age, but also encourages students' self-responsibility as learners. High school students, for instance, often want their teachers to have less control in the classroom and they desire more input and control (Moos & Trickett, 1974). Effective teachers recognize this and allow their students meaningful input into classroom activities.

Changing Classroom Environments

Classroom environments that are not conducive to student growth can be modified through schoolwide efforts at restructuring (as discussed later), on an individual classroom-by-classroom basis, and through structured teacher inservice training workshops (Evertson, 1985; Fraser & Walberg, 1991; Moos, 1979). In summary, there is growing consensus in the field of education that the classroom environment influences students' learning *and* their personal and social adjustment.

THE SCHOOL ENVIRONMENT

Many studies also confirm that the schoolwide environment has a strong influence on students' learning and their personal and social adjustment. In one classic demonstration of school effects, substantial differences emerged across 12 London schools in daily attendance, school dropout rates, appropriate classroom behavior, delinquency, and achievement that could not be explained solely by students' socioeconomic status or incoming academic abilities (Rutter, Maughan, Mortimore, Ouston, & Smith, 1979). For instance, in 6 of the 12 schools, students' exam grades tended to be close to their predicted grades (that is, within 5%–15%). For the other 6 schools, however, students' examination scores departed markedly from predictions. Students in two schools did *very much better* than expected (exam scores were 55% or 70% higher than expected), whereas pupils in four schools *did much more poorly* than expected (exam scores were between 26% and 50% lower than predicted).

There is no single feature that makes a school effective; at this point, research has identified at least 11 characteristics of effective schools, which are listed in Table 28.2.

In general, effective schools produce good outcomes in most students in three areas: general achievement, attitudes and values, and personal and social behavior. That is, effective schools help *most* of the student body, not just a select population of students, and effective schools tend to produce good results in multiple domains of adjustment.

Making Schools More Effective

Professionals do not know which aspects of school life are the most important or how different features interact and vary across settings. Changing an entire school is a systemic, ecological effort directed at modifying organizational structures, policies, and procedures. This process is often called school reform or school restructuring in the educational literature. Schools are complex social institutions whose bureaucracies can resist or sabotage real change. Nevertheless, there is evidence that dramatic improvements can occur in schools, including those that previously were characterized by disillusioned staff, poor overall student performance, and apathetic parents (Henderson & Milstein, 1996; Sergiovanni, 1994).

Table 28.2 Characteristics of effective schools.

1. An orderly and safe school environment.
2. A shared sense of purpose and values among staff.
3. Strong leadership and administrative support.
4. High expectations for student achievement.
5. A demanding and well-coordinated curriculum.
6. Frequent monitoring of student progress and consistent reinforcement for good performance.
7. Positive relationships among the principal, teachers, students, and parents.
8. A high level of positive parent involvement.
9. A staff development program in place that is sensitive to teachers' professional and personal needs.
10. Needed community support.
11. A positive sense of community.

For example, the Yale–New Haven Project is one prototype for an effort at school reform that has been used in over 100 schools and has come to be called the Comer model after the psychiatrist who developed this approach (Comer, 1980). The usual strategy for school reform in the Comer model is to develop a school planning and management team (SPMT) composed of the principal, teachers, parents, and both professional (e.g., psychologist, social worker) and nonprofessional school staff (e.g., secretaries, janitors). The basic job of the SPMT is to improve the overall school climate by improving interpersonal relationships among all participants and by launching and evaluating new school programs that attend to students' emotional and academic needs. The SPMT operates according to a collaborative process that enlists the support of other teachers, parents, and school staff and students. Comer schools have focused their attention primarily on inner-city schools serving low-income African-American students and other minorities.

Schools as Communities

The school environment is greater than the sum of each teacher's pedagogy, each student's behavior, and each classroom's environment. Each school develops its own culture or climate. Several authors are now using the term "sense of community" (SOC) in reference to the school environment. In general, a school's SOC is reflected by the extent to which its students experience a sense of belonging and connection to the school, perceive caring and support in the school environment, believe they have opportunities to influence school life, and are generally satisfied with how the school responds to their personal needs. SOC varies across schools even within similar socioeconomic neighborhoods and also varies among the teachers and students within a school.

SOC has been linked to many different outcomes, such as students' relationships with teachers and peers, academic achievement, educational aspirations, psychological well-being, and problem behaviors (Battistich, Solomon, Kim, Watson, & Schaps, 1995; Roeser & Eccles, 1998; Solomon, Watson, Battistich, Schaps, & Delucchi, 1996). It is not hard to see the benefits of a positive SOC: "students who experience the school as a caring and supportive environment in which they actively participate and have opportunities to exercise influence will feel attached to the school community and will, therefore, come to accept its norms and values" (Battistich et al., 1995, p. 649). SOC may be particularly important for students who otherwise experience stressful lives due to familial or neighborhood influences. In such cases, schools can be opportunities for support and mastery and buffer other life stresses.

Although outcome studies have not always included a specific assessment of SOC or measured it in similar ways, many successful efforts at school reform can be viewed as interventions affecting SOC for both students and teachers. Other studies indicate that positive changes in student adjustment often correspond to positive changes in SOC (Roeser & Eccles, 1998).

PARENT INVOLVEMENT

Data provided by a large sample of parents who had a child in elementary school provide a perspective on how schools try to involve parents in their child's school life (National Opinion Research Center, 1998). Two major findings were: (1) there was tremendous variability in schools' efforts to involve parents, and (2) regardless of the school's activities, most parents wanted more information and assistance from schools about how to support their child's education.

In brief, the National Opinion Research Center (1998) survey found that whereas some schools frequently encourage involvement by inviting parents to attend workshops (26%), serve on committees (54%), or volunteer at school (61%), many schools make minimal or no efforts in these areas (44%–75%). Likewise, although most parents think teachers listen to them (85%), these same parents (77%) also feel that teachers could learn more about involving parents. Other areas for improvement include soliciting parental opinions about how the school could foster more involvement (38%), keeping more parents informed about children's achievement and successful work at school (60%), and offering more guidance on how parents can foster their child's academic achievement at home (35%).

On the one hand, reviews suggest that only about 20% of families are knowledgeable and active partners with their children's schools (Epstein & Lee, 1995). On the other hand, many studies indicate that more effective school-home partnership programs can be formed and that the more actively parents participate in their child's education, the better the child's school performance. This finding "is as impressive as any in the field of educational change" (Fullan, 1992, p. 228). Most important, parental involvement improves children's school performance regardless of the child's level of school, from preschool through high school, and irrespective of the family's socioeconomic, racial, or ethnic status.

One important characteristic of an effective school (see Table 28.2) is a high level of parent involvement. Most of the successful interventions discussed in this chapter have components that promote more parental involvement in schools. The key seems to be the school's initiative in encouraging parents. Parents who feel welcome, accepted, and supported by school staff participate more actively in their child's educational development.

This chapter concludes by discussing three more topics: (1) school violence; (2) school transitions; and (3) improving the work environment for teachers. The first of these topics has received much attention in the public media, but the latter two are often overlooked.

SCHOOL VIOLENCE

Although children are more likely to be physically injured in their homes or neighborhoods, physical violence is also a problem in many schools. School violence includes fighting, peer bullying, petty and major crimes against persons and school property, and school shootings. Since 1995, 44 students have committed multiple acts of homicide on school property ("Multiple Shootings," 1999). Minor discipline problems can also escalate into more serious instances of violence that result in physical assault and injury.

It is informative to contrast two divergent strategies for dealing with school violence: the "get tough" approach and the positive approach (Noguera, 1995). The major philosophy behind a get-tough approach is that serious problems must be countered with strict and immediate force and punishment. This philosophy leads to such tactics as metal detectors at school, zero-tolerance policies, and corporal punishment for rule infractions where permitted by law. Paddling of students is allowed in 23 states, and in 1994 an estimated 470,000 schoolchildren were subjected to physical punishment (Lang, 1998).

In contrast, a positive approach emphasizes that students cannot be forced to learn and behave; they must be motivated to learn and conform to school norms, and they are more likely to do so if they perceive the school community as a caring and supportive setting. For this to occur, however, all school staff must act positively toward students as much as possible and work to enhance children's social and academic competencies. A positive strategy stresses the need for several different actions, all of which are intended to create a more supportive social environment for students and to teach children positive social behaviors. Student accomplishments are praised, teachers' skills at classroom management are enhanced, and schoolwide policies promoting prosocial and condemning antisocial behavior are clearly communicated and systematically enacted. Children are actively taught and rewarded for using effective methods of problem solving, conflict resolution, or behavioral self management. This approach stresses that children must be taught how to behave appropriately and that social interactions occurring throughout the school day are opportunities for learning new skills. Punitive strategies (but not corporal punishment) are used only as a last resort for the most serious problems.

Although some school officials and many in the general public believe that a get-tough policy is the best strategy to deal with school violence and discipline problems, there are *no* controlled research data confirming its effectiveness (Noguera, 1995). Moreover, a get-tough strategy runs the risk of alienating students and creating an oppressive school environment that breeds mistrust and fear and may increase misbehavior. There is also the issue of social inequity; members of low-income and minority groups may be disproportionately the targets of punitive strategies undertaken by schools. In contrast, there is growing empirical evidence that a positive approach to discipline and violence can reduce these problems on a schoolwide basis.

For instance, Gottfredson (1987) reported that an organizational development approach undertaken to improve the overall school climate by rewarding students' prosocial behavior and academic efforts and increasing teacher support for students significantly reduced serious behavioral problems in a problem-plagued inner-city junior high school. This intervention also encouraged more parent participation in school activities and increased the local community's support and advocacy for the program school. Program students not only demonstrated fewer serious acting-out problems, but also reported a stronger sense of belonging and attachment to their school and had higher academic expectations than controls. Teachers' morale also improved significantly. Moreover, when a similar intervention was conducted in another school district that had previously and unsuccessfully used a get-tough educational strategy, the positive approach significantly improved student conduct (Gottfredson, Gottfredson, & Hybl, 1993).

Because serious adolescent behavioral problems can be an exacerbation of less serious difficulties present at earlier ages, it makes sense to intervene with young school populations to preclude the later development of more severe problems. This approach has also been effective in several cases. For instance, Lewis, Sugai, and Colvin (1998) describe the success of a proactive schoolwide effort to teach elementary schoolchildren social skills as a way to reduce or eliminate discipline problems. Teachers delivered social skills training in their first-through fifth-grade classrooms, and this instruction was accompanied by an explanation of new school rules describing what positive behaviors were expected. Children were rewarded for following the prescribed rules, and the generalization of the program throughout the school was assessed by collecting behavioral data in the cafeteria, playground, and school hallways. A multiple baseline design indicated that problem behaviors were significantly reduced in each school setting, and this improvement was maintained at three-month follow-up.

In summary, there is no easy solution to the problem of school violence. Although some may be moved to use a punitive approach, research has indicated that positive strategies are much more effective in the long run. Positive strategies ultimately aim to improve the overall school environment and create a positive sense of community for schoolchildren and teach them how to resolve interpersonal differences and frustrations through prosocial means.

PEER BULLYING

One frequently overlooked form of interpersonal violence in many schools is peer bullying (also called peer victimization). Peer bullying refers to teasing, harassment, or aggression intentionally directed at peers. Overall, boys are more likely to bully than girls and are more likely to use physical aggression or verbal assaults and threats. Girls are more likely to be social or relational bullies and make critical remarks, spread rumors or gossip about others, or actively shun or exclude others from social groups.

Bullying is a significant problem that involves up to 15% of schoolchildren as victims or bullies (Olweus, 1994). Peer bullying can begin in preschool (Crick, Casas, & Ku, 1999) and is both an immediate problem in its own right and a risk factor in the later lives of both bullies and victims. Child bullies are at risk for a variety of later problems, such as poor school performance, substance abuse, and antisocial activities, and they may continue to victimize others through dating and domestic violence (Crick et al., 1999). Victims are at risk for heightened levels of loneliness and anxiety and lowered self-esteem; these qualities may be present before the victimization begins but are exacerbated with continued bullying (Kochenderfer & Ladd, 1996). Victims also may develop negative attitudes toward school and show more voidance of school, so that their academic performance may suffer. Peer bullying is a relatively stable phenomenon; thus, intervention is needed to disrupt this otherwise continuing destructive pattern of peer behavior.

Antibullying Programs
Olweus (1994) has developed an effective school-based prevention program for bullying that has gained widespread acceptance in Scandinavian countries. The intervention is multilevel and contains components for individuals, parents, peers, and school staff.

The typical program usually begins by educating school staff and parents about the extent and seriousness of bullying to motivate them to take some action. This is done through the use of educational materials, school workshops, and reporting the results of an anonymous survey regarding bullying completed by students at the target school.

Then school staff are encouraged to formulate and enforce schoolwide policies against bullying. These policies are generally designed to promote and reinforce prosocial peer behavior and actively discourage bullying and other forms of negative and hostile peer behavior. Teachers also develop similar policies for their classrooms and are instructed on how to hold classwide meetings and develop class rules to deal with bullying. Schoolwide and classroom policies serve to foster prosocial, antibullying norms. Children are also encouraged to come to the aid of those who are bullied. Peer intervention is important because having friends who will stand up for you is one protective factor against bullying (Hodges, Malone, & Perry, 1997). Schools also develop effective methods to monitor child behavior throughout the school campus, especially on the playground and in the cafeteria, where negative incidents often occur. Finally, individual children who continue to bully receive counseling and their parents receive guidance in child management as needed.

Programs following the general model described above have been very effective in reducing rates of bullying by 50% or more and also reducing other problem behaviors such as vandalism, stealing, and fighting. The school environment also changes for the better: more order and discipline is observed in classrooms, more positive attitudes toward school develop, and relationships among peers improve (Olweus, 1994).

SEXUAL HARASSMENT/DATING VIOLENCE

During adolescence, peer bullying can be transformed into sexual harassment, which appears to be more prevalent than peer bullying. For instance, in one survey, 87% of high school females and 71% of males reported being sexually harassed by another student; in another survey, 66% of males and 52% of females admitted harassing someone else (see Fineran & Bennett, 1998).

There have not been many programs targeting youthful sexual harassment and dating violence. One schoolwide intervention, however, called Safe Dates (Foshee et al., 1998), was evaluated in a large-sample, randomized experiment and has reported promising results. Safe Dates was a program for eighth- and ninth-graders attending 14 different public schools. The intent of the intervention was to change gender stereotyping, improve conflict management and communication skills, and develop prosocial dating norms. A structured classroom curriculum was supplemented by schoolwide events and involvement of community-based agencies to promote appropriate dating behavior. At a one-month follow-up, there was 25% less sexual violence, 60% less physical violence, and 25% less psychological abuse occurring on dates among students who participated in the Safe Dates program compared to controls.

SCHOOL TRANSITIONS

Approximately six million children between the ages of 6 and 13 change schools each year, and multiple school transitions are common for many children. Many enroll at four different schools on their way to high school graduation (elementary, middle, junior high, and high school), and this does not count the one out of five families who move each year, necessitating still another school change.

The above figures are cause for concern because school transitions are associated with such negative consequences as lower grades, less participation in school activities, lowered school attendance, poorer peer and teacher relationships, decreases in self-esteem, heightened anxiety, and feelings of isolation and disconnection (Hirsch & DuBois, 1992; Siedman, Aber, Allen, & French, 1996). Negative effects do not appear in all children, but temporary problems are not unusual, and some students never seem to recover completely from a very difficult transition. Unfortunately, most school districts do not have any formal mechanism to help students negotiate school transitions.

Because school transitions can be stressful, one important way to protect students from potential negative consequences is through the mechanism of social support. Most interventions that have been developed to ease the passage of students during school transitions have emphasized mobilizing social support from teachers, parents, and peers, and these programs have been successful (see Durlak & Wells, 1997).

One particularly effective intervention is the School Transition Project (STP; Jason et al., 1992). STP follows an ecological model by emphasizing that individual and environmental characteristics interact to affect the adjustment of transfer students and takes specific steps to identify and help those most at risk. STP examines students' prior academic and emotional adjustment and their current coping skills to identify those who are more likely to have a difficult time in their new school. STP operates on several levels. First, there is a special orientation program for all new transfer students that is conducted by peer leaders at the new school. The orientation helps transfer students learn about the new school and its rules and procedures. Peer buddies are selected so that each incoming student has at least one supportive peer relationship.

Second, STP administers both a school- and home-based tutoring program and also uses undergraduate college students to serve as advocates for transfer students and to help parents become involved in school activities. STP students show improved levels of academic achievement following their school transfer, and teachers report less inattentiveness and social withdrawal compared to controls. Evaluations also indicate that a high proportion of at-risk children demonstrate acceptable to good levels of adjustment during follow-up. In other words, STP seems able to ease the passage of children through a potentially difficult school transition and is effective for those most in need.

IMPROVING TEACHERS' WORK ENVIRONMENT

More resources must be devoted to improving the work environment of teachers. Schools cannot flourish as growth-enhancing environments for students unless teachers' needs are addressed. Teaching is a demanding and stressful occupation in several ways. The profession of teaching is not necessarily highly valued or respected in the United States. Teachers' salaries vary substantially across districts, and it is not unusual to find dental hygienists and sanitation workers who are paid more than teachers. The average beginning teacher's salary in 1996 was only $25,167 (U.S. Department of Education, 1997).

Several other factors make teaching stressful. In a national survey, only 16% of teachers felt they received sufficient support from parents, about 30% indicated that administrative duties and paperwork interfered with their teaching, only 37% said their school had adequate pedagogical materials, and only 35% reported that the teachers at their school worked cooperatively with each other (U.S. Department of Education, 1997). Teachers also commonly report limited opportunities for professional growth and that they do not have enough authority to make necessary changes in how children are instructed. Finally, other major sources of teacher stress come from negative interactions with students that result in discipline or management problems in the classroom, large class sizes, substantial variability in student ability levels, and the role demands that are increasingly being placed on teachers to be personal counselors and developmental specialists as well as educators.

Prolonged stress places teachers at risk for emotional and physical health problems and diminishes teaching effectiveness. Teachers under more stress tend to be more negative and less positive with their students, less focused on learning goals and tasks, less effective in managing and organizing the classroom, and less sensitive to students' personal needs (Wisniewski & Gargiulo, 1997). In other words, students suffer some of the brunt of teacher stress and the classroom environment is negatively affected.

The above issues should be viewed in relation to the basic, everyday job demands of a teacher. The average elementary school teacher has over 500 individual exchanges with students daily, emits at least 4 behaviors per minute (or around 1,500 per day), manages about 30 different activities each day (e.g., seatwork, recitation, reading circles), and must instruct a large class of diverse students (Doyle, 1986). Teaching requires considerable initiative, energy, patience, and persistence.

HIGH TEACHER TURNOVER AND ATTRITION

One indication of the stressful character of teaching is the high rate of teacher turnover and attrition. Turnover refers to leaving one job for another in a different school or school district, whereas attrition refers to teachers quitting the profession. Work-related stress leading to job dissatisfaction and professional burnout play a major role in both teacher turnover and attrition, which affects over 300,000 teachers annually (Boe, Bobbitt, & Cook, 1997). High attrition and turnover are costly to schools in several ways. Time and expense must be devoted to hiring and training new teachers, and the continuity of the school curricula can be negatively affected when many new staff are added each year. Finally, there is concern that the field of education is losing some of its most talented teachers through attrition.

COMBATING TEACHER STRESS

Although the few stress management programs developed for teachers have been helpful (Cecil & Forman, 1990), the philosophy behind such programs is reactive; that is, help is offered after problems appear. Over the long term, it is more productive to adopt a proactive, preventive strategy and try to eliminate or modify the factors that produce stress in the first place. Interventions at two points in time are needed. First, teacher education programs must be improved. Teachers who are better trained are more effective and experience less stress on the job. Many professionals now agree that new teachers are not being adequately prepared for their teaching roles (Reynolds, 1992; Tomlinson et al., 1997). In general, there is a need for more hands-on practical training on how to successfully manage and instruct large groups of diverse students.

After teachers begin their jobs, there is a continuing need for effective professional development programs. It is no secret in the profession that many mandatory in-service teacher training programs offered to satisfy state board of education bureaucratic requirements are dull, largely irrelevant to daily practice, and a general waste of time. In contrast, actions that have galvanized the most teachers have been those that include them in meaningful decision making and organizational change (e.g., effective efforts at school change and restructuring that have occurred). In other words, successful efforts to improve school quality have often focused on fostering the professional development of teachers. In fact, there has probably not been a single school that has undergone a significant improvement in its functioning that has not drawn on the leadership, expertise, and initiative of its teachers. Professional development programs for teachers are a win-win strategy for schools. Teachers benefit because their work environment is less stressful and more personally satisfying, and students benefit from improvement in school practices.

CONCLUDING COMMENTS

There will always be a need for therapeutic and remedial services for schoolchildren with the most serious behavioral and academic problems. Furthermore, school-based therapy programs have been effective in helping children with a variety of adjustment problems (Durlak, 1992; Prout & Prout, 1998). The major limitation regarding traditional therapeutic and remedial services, however, is that these reactive approaches will never stem the tide of future problems. There will always be too many to serve and too few resources to go around if we wait for difficulties to appear before intervening.

For example, few schools have the necessary mental health resources to respond adequately to students' needs: 45% of public schools have no counselors, 59% have no psychologists, 79% have no social workers, and 98% have no psychiatrists on staff even on a part-time basis (Davis, Fryer, White, & Igoe, 1995). Moreover, *most* parochial and private schools have no mental health staff whatsoever even on a part-time basis.

Therefore, this chapter has highlighted proactive efforts to improve the overall adjustment of school-children. School success is a protective factor for many important developmental outcomes, and school failure is a risk factor for many negative outcomes (Durlak, 1998). School success is not a panacea. Nevertheless, interventions that increase opportunities for students to maximize their skills and talents have the potential to promote healthy development and reduce the future incidence of problems for millions of young people.

REFERENCES

Barnett, W.S. (1990). Benefits of compensatory preschool education. *Journal of Human Resources, 27,* 279–312.

Battistich, V., Solomon, D., Kim, D., Watson, M., & Schaps, E. (1995). Schools as communities, poverty levels of student populations, and students' attitudes, motives, and performance: A multilevel analysis. *American Educational Research Journal, 32,* 627–658.

Boe, E.E., Bobbitt, S.A., & Cook, L.H. (1997). Whither didst thou go? Retention, reassignment, migration, and attrition of special and general education teachers from a national perspective. *Journal of Special Education, 30,* 371–389.

Boocock, S.S. (1995). Early childhood programs in other nations: Goals and outcomes. *Future of Children, 5,* 94–114.

Cecil, M.A., & Forman, S.G. (1990). Effects of stress inoculation training and coworker support groups on teachers' stress. *Journal of School Psychology, 23,* 105–118.

Cohen, P.A., Kulik, J.A., & Kulik, C.C. (1982). Educational outcomes of tutoring: A meta-analysis of findings. *American Educational Research Journal, 19,* 237–248.

Comer, J.P. (1980). *School power: Implications of an intervention project.* New York: Free Press.

Crick, N.R., Casas, J.F., & Ku, H.C. (1999). Relational and physical forms of peer victimization in preschool. *Developmental Psychology, 35,* 376–385.

Davis, M., Fryer, G.E., White, S., & Igoe, J.B. (1995). *A closer look: A report of select findings from the National School Health Survey 1993–1994.* Denver, CO: Office of School Health, University of Colorado Health Sciences Center.

Doyle, W. (1986). Classroom organization and management. In M.C. Wittrock (Ed.), *Handbook of research on teaching* (3rd ed., pp. 392–431). New York: Macmillan.

Durlak, J.A. (1992). School problems of children. In C.E. Walker & M.C. Roberts (Eds.), *Handbook of clinical child psychology* (2nd ed., pp. 497–510). New York: Wiley.

Durlak, J.A. (1995). *School-based prevention programs for children and adolescents.* Thousand Oaks, CA: Sage.

Durlak, J.A. (1997). *Successful prevention programs for children and adolescents.* New York: Plenum Press.

Durlak, J.A. (1998). Common risk and protective factors in successful prevention programs. *American Journal of Orthopsychiatry, 68,* 512–520.

Durlak, J.A., & Wells, A.M. (1997). Primary prevention mental health programs for children and adolescents: A meta-analytic review. *American Journal of Community Psychology, 25,* 115–152.

Eccles, J.S., Midgely, C., Wigfield, A., Buchanan, C.M., Reuman, D., Flanagan, C., & Mac Iver, D. (1993). Development during adolescence: The impact of stage-environment fit on young adolescents' experiences in schools and in families. *American Psychologist, 48,* 90–101.

Epstein, J., & Lee, S. (1995). National patterns of school and family connections in the middle grades. In B.A. Ryan, G.R. Adams, T.P. Gullotta, R.P. Weissberg, & R.L. Hampton (Eds.), *The family-school connections: Theory, research and practice* (pp. 108–154). Thousand Oaks, CA: Sage.

Evertson, C.M. (1985). Training teachers in classroom management: An experimental study in secondary school classrooms. *Journal of Educational Research, 79,* 51–58.

Fineran, S., & Bennett, L. (1998). Teenage peer sexual harassment: Implications for social work practice in education. *Social Work, 43,* 55–64.

Foshee, V.A., Bauman, K.E., Arriaga, X.B., Helms, R.W., Koch, G.G., & Linder, G.F. (1998). An evaluation of Safe Dates, an adolescent dating violence prevention program. *American Journal of Public Health, 88,* 45–50.

Fraser, B.J., & Walberg, H.J. (1991). *Educational environments: Evaluation, antecedents and consequences.* New York: Pergamon Press.

Fullan, M.G. (1992). *Successful school improvement: The implementation perspective and beyond.* Philadelphia: Open University Press.

Gettinger, M. (1990). Best practices in increasing academic learning time. In A. Thomas & J. Grimes (Eds.), *Best practices in school psychology II* (pp. 393–405). Washington, DC: National Association of School Psychologists.

Good, T.L., & Brophy, J.E. (1994). *Looking in classrooms* (6th ed.). New York: HarperCollins.

Gottfredson, D.C. (1987). An evaluation of an organization development approach to reducing school disorder. *Evaluation Review, 11,* 739–763.

Gottfredson, D.C., Gottfredson, G.D., & Hybl, L.G. (1993). Managing adolescent behavior: A multiyear, multischool study. *American Educational Research Journal, 30,* 179–215.

Greenwood, C.R., Delquadri, J.C., & Hall, R.V. (1989). Longitudinal effects of classwide peer tutoring. *Journal of Educational Psychology, 81,* 371–383.

Henderson, N., & Milstein, M.M. (1996). *Resiliency in schools: Making it happen for students and educators.* Thousand Oaks, CA: Corwin Press.

Hirsch, B.J., & DuBois, D.L. (1992). The relation of peer social support and psychological symptomatology during the transition to junior high school: A two-year longitudinal analysis. *American Journal of Community Psychology, 20,* 333–347.

Hodges, E.V.E., Malone, M.J., & Perry, D.G. (1997). Individual risk and social risk as interacting determinants of victimization in the peer group. *Developmental Psychology, 33,* 1032–1039.

Institute of Medicine. (1994). *Reducing risks for mental disorders: Frontiers for preventive intervention research.* Washington, DC: National Academy Press.

Jason, L.A., Weine, A.M., Johnson, J.H., Warren-Sohlberg, L., Filippelli, L.A., Turner, E.Y., & Lardon, C. (1992). *Helping transfer students: Strategies for educational and social readjustment.* San Francisco: Jossey-Bass.

Johnson, D.W., & Johnson, R.J. (1991). Cooperative learning and classroom and school climate. In B.J. Fraser & H.J. Walberg (Eds.), *Educational environments: Evaluation, antecedents and consequences* (pp. 55–74). New York: Pergamon Press.

Kauffman, J.M. (1999). Commentary: Today's special education and its messages for tomorrow. *Journal of Special Education, 32,* 244–254.

Kingery, P.M., Coggeshall, M.B., & Alford, A.A. (1998). Violence at school: Recent evidence from four national surveys. *Psychology in the Schools, 35,* 247–258.

Kochenderfer, B.J., & Ladd, G.W. (1996). Peer victimization: Cause or consequence of school maladjustment? *Child Development, 67,* 1305–1317.

Lang, J. (1998, May 3). Student paddling persists in U.S. *Chicago Sun-Times,* p. A22.

Lewis, T.J., Sugai, G., & Colvin, G. (1998). Reducing problem behavior through a school-wide system of effective behavioral support: Investigation of a school-wide social skills training program and contextual interventions. *School Psychology Review, 27,* 446–459.

Lewit, E.M., & Baker, L.S. (1995). School readiness. *Future of Children, 5,* 128–139.

Moos, R.H. (1979). *Evaluating educational environments.* San Francisco: Jossey-Bass.

Moos, R.H., & Trickett, E.J. (1974). *Classroom environment scale manual.* Palo Alto: CA: Consulting Psychologists Press.

Multiple shooting deaths in U.S. schools, 1995 to present. (1999, April 25). *Chicago Tribune,* Sec. 2, p. 1.

Murphy, J. (Ed.). (1990). *The educational reform movement of the 1980s.* Berkeley, CA: McCutchan.

National Opinion Research Survey. (1998). *Family involvement in education: A national portrait.* Washington, DC: U.S. Government Printing Office.

Noguera, P.A. (1995). Preventing and producing violence: A critical analysis of responses to school violence. *Harvard Educational Review, 65,* 189–212.

Olweus, D. (1994). Bullying at school: Basic facts and effects of a school-based intervention program. *Journal of Child Psychology and Psychiatry, 35,* 1171–1190.

Pianta, R.C., Steinberg, M.S., & Rollins, K.B. (1995). The first two years of school: Teacher-child relationships and deflections in children's classroom adjustment. *Development and Psychopathology, 7,* 295–312.

Prout, S.M., & Prout, H.T. (1998). A meta-analysis of school-based studies of counseling and psychotherapy: An update. *Journal of School Psychology, 36,* 121–136.

Reynolds, A. (1992). What is competent beginning teaching? A review of the literature. *Review of Educational Research, 62,* 1–35.

Roeser, R.W., & Eccles, J.S. (1998). Adolescents' perceptions of middle school: Relation to longitudinal changes in academic and psychological adjustment. *Journal of Research on Adolescence, 8,* 123–154.

Rutter, M., Maughan, B., Mortimore, P., Ouston, J., & Smith, A. (1979). *Fifteen thousand hours: Secondary schools and their effects on children.* Cambridge, MA: Harvard University Press.

Schweinhart, L.J., & Weikart, D.B. (1988). The High Scope/Perry Preschool Program. In R.H. Price, E.L. Cowen, R.P. Lorion, & J. Ramos-McKay (Eds.), *14 ounces of prevention: A casebook for practitioners* (pp. 53–65). Washington, DC: American Psychological Association.

Sergiovanni, T.J. (1994). *Building community in schools.* San Francisco: Jossey-Bass.

Siedman, E., Aber, J.L., Allen, L., & French, S.E. (1996). The impact of the transition to high school on the self-esteem and perceived social context of poor urban youth. *American Journal of Community Psychology, 24,* 489–515.

Slavin, R.E., Karweit, N.L., & Madden, N.A. (1989). *Effective programs for students at risk.* Needham Heights, MA: Allyn & Bacon.

Slavin, R.E., Karweit, N.L., & Wasik, B.A. (1994). *Preventing early school failure.* Needham Heights, MA: Allyn & Bacon.

Solomon, D., Watson, M., Battistich, V., Schaps, E., & Delucchi, K. (1996). Creating classrooms that students experience as communities. *American Journal of Community Psychology, 24,* 719–748.

Tanner, C.K., & Galis, S.A. (1997). Student retention: Why is there a gap between the majority of research findings and school practice? *Psychology in the Schools, 34,* 107–114.

Tomlinson, C.A., Callahan, C.M., Tomchin, E.M., Eiss, N., Imbeau, M., & Landrum, M. (1997). Becoming architects of communities of learning: Addressing academic diversity in contemporary classrooms. *Exceptional Children, 63,* 269–282.

Trickett, E.J., & Schmidt, K.D. (1993). The school as a social context. In P.H. Tolan & B.N. Cohler (Eds.), *Handbook of clinical research and practice with adolescents* (pp. 173–202). New York: Wiley.

U.S. Department of Education. (1999). *National assessment of educational progress 1998.* Washington, DC: Author.

U.S. Department of Education, National Center for Education Statistics. (1997). *The condition of education 1997.* Washington, DC: U.S. Government Printing Office.

U.S. Government Accounting Office. (1995). *School facilities: Condition of America's schools* (HEHS–95–61). Washington, DC: Author.

Wisniewski, L., & Gargiulo, R.M. (1997). Occupational stress and burnout among special educators: A review of the literature. *Journal of Special Education, 31,* 325–346.

CHAPTER 29

Learning Disabilities: A Neuropsychological Perspective

BYRON P. ROURKE AND JEREL E. DEL DOTTO

This chapter is designed to introduce the child clinical psychologist to research and practice that relates to children with learning disabilities (LD). It is organized in terms of a frankly neuropsychological approach to the topic because, in our view, this constitutes the most comprehensive perspective from which to structure this field.

A summary and critique of the various viewpoints regarding research and professional practice within the field of LD is not presented because these have been summarized many times elsewhere (e.g., Benton, 1975; Ceci, 1986, 1987; Gaddes, 1985; Rourke, 1978a, 1985, 1991; Rourke & Del Dotto, 1994), and it was deemed advantageous for the reader to be introduced to what we consider to be a coherent, comprehensive, and cohesive view of the field. The organizational format for this chapter is quite simple: It begins with a brief historical overview, continues with an explication of an approach to the specification of subtypes of LD, and concludes with clinical considerations. References for the interested reader who may wish to pursue these topics in greater depth are provided within each section.

Some sections of this chapter have been adapted, with the permission of Guilford Press, from Rourke (1989).

GENERAL HISTORICAL BACKGROUND

LEARNING DISABILITIES AS A UNIVOCAL, HOMOGENEOUS DISORDER

Early work in the neuropsychology of LD focused almost exclusively on the study of reading disability (Benton, 1975; Rourke, 1978a). With a few notable exceptions, this research was characterized by the "contrasting-groups" or "comparative populations" (Applebee, 1971) investigative strategy that was the almost exclusive approach adopted by North American and European researchers. Studies involving comparisons of groups of children with LD and groups of age- and otherwise-matched "normal" controls were employed to determine *the* deficit(s) that characterize the neuropsychological ability structure of *the* learning-disabled child (Doehring, 1978). The use of this method for the determination of the neuropsychological abilities and deficits of children with LD assumed, implicitly or explicitly, that such children formed a univocal, homogeneous diagnostic entity.

This approach was also characterized by rather narrow samplings of areas of human performance that were thought to be related to the learning (primarily reading) disability. For example, some researchers who were convinced that a deficiency in memory formed the basis for LD in youngsters followed a rather straightforward research tack; that is, they measured and compared "memory" in groups of children with LD and matched control children. Almost without fail, the conclusion of such a research effort was that children with LD were deficient in memory; this led to the inference that it was this deficient memory that was the cause of LD. In fact, the only crucial variable that typically influenced the results of such studies was the severity of the learning deficit of the children with LD studied: The more severe the learning deficit, the more likely it was that the contrasting groups would differ (see Brandys & Rourke, 1991, for an alternative strategy for studying memory in children with LD).

Such research was periodically seen as somewhat shortsighted and inconclusive when it could be demonstrated, for example, that disabled learners were more deficient in "auditory memory" than in "visual memory." This constituted something of an advance in the field, because a rather more comprehensive sampling of skills and abilities was undertaken in this sort of study. However, there remained the commitment to the contrasting-groups methodology, and there was one other complicating factor that crept into the considerations of investigators in the field. This factor can best be described as the developmental dimension. Specifically, it became clear to some that one "obtained" significant differences between contrasting groups of disabled and normal readers on some variables and not on others as an apparent function of the age at which the children were studied. Thus, an example of the next advance that took place in this research tradition was to compare groups of younger and older children on auditory and visual memory tasks to determine if the main effects (for auditory and visual memory) and the interactions (with age) were significant.

Even with these advances, however, there remained the reluctance of those who adopted this essentially narrow nomothetic approach to engage in the analysis of the abilities and deficits of individual children with LD. For example, it was rarely the case that investigators would report results of individual cases in their studies of auditory and visual memory, even though this is very simply accomplished (see Czudner & Rourke, 1972; Rourke & Czudner, 1972, for examples of how individual results can be reported in such studies). Thus,

researchers were left with group results that may not reflect how all individuals within the group performed. Some critics of this nomothetic approach to the understanding of LD in children adopted a position that was quite antithetical to it, one that is best described as an "idiosyncratic" or "idiographic" approach to the field.

LEARNING DISABILITIES AS AN IDIOSYNCRATIC DISORDER

As was the case in the history of the study of frank brain damage in youngsters, there have long been investigators in the field of learning disabilities who maintained that persons so designated exhibit very unique, idiosyncratic, nongeneralizable origins, characteristics, and reactions and, as such, must be treated in an idiographic manner. Investigators of this ilk suggested that the single-case study is the only viable means for discovering valid scientific information. They also argued that the important dimensions of this disorder are individualized to the extent that meaningful generalizations are virtually impossible.

It is clear that this point of view contrasts sharply and in almost all respects with the contrasting-groups position outlined above. This nomothetic/idiographic debate is not unique to the study of LD and frankly brain-damaged individuals. (A particularly poignant and insightful characterization of this nomothetic/idiographic controversy in the entire field of clinical neuropsychology has been presented by Reitan, 1974.)

CRITIQUE OF THE CONTRASTING-GROUPS AND IDIOSYNCRATIC APPROACHES

Contrasting-Groups Approach

As suggested above, studies within this tradition served to do little more than produce a lengthy catalogue of variables that differentiate so-called learning-disabled from normal children (Rourke, 1978a). Considered as a whole, the results of this corpus of research made it abundantly evident that virtually any single measure of perceptual, psycholinguistic, or higher-order cognitive skill could be used to illustrate the superiority of normal children over comparable groups of children diagnosed as having LD.

However, there are many who persist in comparative populations or contrasting-groups methodology, with all of the limitations that such a methodology involves, not only with respect to research findings but also with respect to model building and theory development. This mode of approach to research—aimed at the identification of *the* supposed cognitive and other correlates of children with LD—has not been terribly contributory: for example, the results of many studies are trivial, contradictory to one another, and not supported in replication attempts; there is little to suggest that the factors identified as "characteristic" of children with LD in these studies are related to one another in any meaningful fashion (Rourke, 1985). In sum, the evidence regarding perceptual, cognitive, and other forms of functioning that emerges from the contrasting-groups approach to research is, at best, equivocal. A coherent and meaningful pattern of neuropsychological characteristics of children with LD does not emerge from this literature. We maintain that this is the case because such a univocal pattern does not obtain (more on this point below).

In any event, there appear to be at least four major reasons why the results of these studies have not been very contributory to the testing of important hypotheses relating to the neuropsychological integrity of youngsters with LD. These, together with some brief comments on alternative approaches, follow.

Lack of a Conceptual Model. In the vast majority of studies that can be characterized in terms of the comparative-populations or contrasting-groups rubric, there is an obvious absence of a comprehensive conceptual model that could be employed to elucidate the skills involved in perception, learning, memory, and cognition and that are deficient in children with LD. Most models that have been developed in this genre of research bear the marks of either post hoc theorizing about a very limited spectrum of skills and abilities or "pet" theories derived from what are characterized as more "general" models of perception, learning, memory, and cognition. Research that is cast in terms of these very limited, narrow-band models and, a fortiori, research that is essentially atheoretical in nature are virtually certain to yield a less than comprehensive explanation of LD.

As an example of an alternative to this conceptually limited approach, a componential analysis of academic and other types of learning should sensitize the researcher to the possibility that, whereas some subtypes of children with LD may experience learning problems because of deficiencies in certain perceptual, cognitive, or behavioral skills, others may manifest such problems as a more direct result of attitudinal/motivational or vastly different perceptual, cognitive, or behavioral difficulties. It should also be clear that different patterns of perceptual, cognitive, and behavioral assets and deficits may encourage different types or degrees of learning difficulties. Several theories that emphasize this type of comprehensive, componential approach to the design of developmental neuropsychological explanatory models in this area have emerged (e.g., Fletcher & Taylor, 1984). Our own efforts in this regard (Rourke, 1982a, 1987, 1988b, 1989, 1995; Rourke & Fisk, 1988; Rourke & Fuerst, 1991, 1992, 1996) are described in subsequent sections of this chapter.

Definition of LD. There has been no consistent formulation of the criteria for LD in the contrasting-groups genre of study. For example, most studies of this ilk employ vaguely defined or even undefined groups, and others use the ratings of teachers and other school personnel that remain otherwise unspecified. Some even employ the guidelines of a particular political jurisdiction to define LD! It is obvious that this lack of clarity and consistency has had a negative impact on the generalizability of the (limited) findings of such studies.

Clear definitions that are amenable to consensual validation are urgently needed in this area of investigation. In this connection, it seems patently obvious that the very definitions themselves should be a *result* of sophisticated subtype analysis rather than the starting point of such inquiry (Fletcher et al., 1989, 1994; Fletcher, Francis, Rourke, Shaywitz, & Shaywitz, 1992, 1993; Francis, Fletcher, Shaywitz, Shaywitz, & Rourke, 1996; Morris & Fletcher, 1988; Rourke, 1983a, 1983b, 1985, 1995; Rourke & Gates, 1981).

Developmental Considerations. Part and parcel with the contrasting-groups approach to the study of youngsters with LD is a gross insensitivity to age differences and developmental considerations. Several studies offer support for the notion that the nature and patterning of the skill and ability deficits of (some subtypes of) children with LD vary with age (e.g., Fisk & Rourke, 1979; Fletcher & Satz, 1980; McKinney, Short, & Feagans, 1985; Morris, Blashfield, & Satz, 1986; Ozols & Rourke, 1988; Rourke, Dietrich, & Young, 1973). Because it seems reasonable to infer that the neuropsychological functioning of (some subtypes of) children with LD varies as a function of age (considered as one index of developmental change), the aforementioned inconsistencies in contrasting-groups research results could reflect differences in the ages of the subjects employed.

Although this possibility is sometimes acknowledged by investigators who employ this type of methodology, such a realization has, until quite recently, been the exception rather than the rule. Be that as it may, it is abundantly clear that more cross-sectional and longitudinal studies are necessary to clarify the nature of those developmental changes that appear to take place in some children with LD. It is also clear that attention to the issues involved in the study of developmental changes in children with LD are an almost direct function of the sophistication in subtype analysis exhibited by the neuropsychological investigators in this area (see Morris et al., 1986, for an especially good example of perspicacious sensitivity to such issues). Unfortunately, those who pay little or no attention to subtypal analysis also demonstrate little or no regard for the changes in the neuropsychological ability structures of children with LD that may transpire during the course of development.

Treatment Considerations. Practical experience with children who exhibit marked LD suggests clearly that only some of these individuals respond positively to particular forms of treatment. It is also the case that some forms of treatment for some children with LD are actually counterproductive (Rourke, 1981, 1982b). Once again, it is the case that subtypal analysis of children with LD helps to clarify a situation created by the application of the results of contrasting-groups methodology. For example, Lyon (1985) has demonstrated that specific subtypes of disabled readers respond very differently to synthetic phonics and "sight-word" approaches to reading instruction. Sweeney and Rourke (1985) also demonstrated what appeared to be an overreliance of phonetically accurate disabled spellers on the phonetic analysis of individual words—to the apparent detriment of their reading speed.

The Idiosyncratic Approach

A strictly individualistic standpoint in this field, although attractive from some clinical perspectives, is viable on neither practical (applied/clinical) nor theoretical grounds. It is patently obvious that persons with LD are unique. It is also the case that most of them can be classified into homogeneous subtypes on the basis of sets of shared relative strengths and deficiencies in neuropsychological skills and abilities. That is, they have enough in common to be grouped (i.e., subtyped) for the purpose of some important aspects of treatment as well as for specific model-testing purposes. The fact that models based on subtype analysis can, in fact, be shown to be internally consistent and externally (including ecologically) valid (see Rourke, 1985, 1989, 1991, 1995) suggests strongly that one need not adopt a position that maintains that each and every individual child with LD is so implacably unique that nothing can be said about his or her development, prognosis, and preferred mode of intervention/treatment. That treatment effects such as those demonstrated by Lyon (1985) is also sufficient proof that strict individualism is not necessary.

To accomplish the very desirable goals of scientific and clinical generalizability while ensuring the individual applicability of the "general" results of studies in this area, it is necessary to be able to demonstrate that each individual who falls within a particular LD subtype exhibits a very close approximation to the pattern of neuropsychological assets and deficits that characterizes the subtype as a whole. This should satisfy the individualistic criterion while maintaining the generalizability of treatment and hypothesis-testing imperatives of scientific investigations within this area (Rourke, 1995). The possibility of obtaining this degree of individuation of group results will be particularly apparent when we examine such issues in relationship to the nonverbal learning disabilities (NLD) subtype.

We turn now to a brief historical overview of the "subtype" approach to the investigation of children with LD.

LD AS A HETEROGENEOUS GROUP OF DISORDERS (SUBTYPES)

Scientific investigation of LD subtypes emerged primarily from careful clinical observations of children who were assessed because they were thought to be experiencing perceptual disabilities and/or LD. Astute observers of children with LD, such as Johnson and Myklebust (1967), noted that there are very clear differences in patterns of assets and deficits exhibited by such children, and that specific variations in developmental problems (e.g., learning to read) appeared to stem from these very different patterns of assets and deficits. In other words, equally impaired *levels* of learning appeared to result from quite different "etiologies," as suggested in patterns of relative perceptual and cognitive strengths and weaknesses.

The search for subtypes of LD took on added importance when it was inferred that these potentially isolatable patterns of perceptual and cognitive strengths and weaknesses (that were thought to be responsible for learning difficulties) might be more or less amenable to different modes of intervention. Indeed, the "subtype by treatment interaction" hypothesis—that is, the notion that the tailoring of specific forms of treatment to the underlying abilities and deficits of children with LD would be advantageous—was alive and well very early in the history of the LD field (e.g., Kirk & McCarthy, 1961). This constituted a second clinical issue that encouraged researchers to seek a determination of subtypal differences among such children. Indeed, many researchers and professionals in the field virtually *assumed* that the matching of interventions/treatments to the underlying strengths and weaknesses of the child who is experiencing outstanding difficulties in learning would be the most efficient and effective therapeutic course to follow.

Positions of this sort were mirrored in the studies conducted by Johnson and Myklebust (1967) and later by Mattis, French, and Rapin (1975). These investigators employed an essentially "clinical" approach to the identification of subtypes of LD. This rather important thrust to research, involving as it did an emphasis on subtypal patterns, was accompanied in the late 1970s by that of investigators who sought to isolate reliable subtypes of children with LD through the use of statistical algorithms such as Q-type factor analysis and cluster analysis (e.g., Doehring & Hoshko, 1977; Doehring, Hoshko, & Bryans,1979; Fisk & Rourke, 1979; Petrauskas & Rourke, 1979).

At this juncture, it is sufficient to point out that the use of statistical algorithms to assist in the generating of subtypes of LD was well underway in the 1980s (e.g., Fisk & Rourke, 1979; Joschko & Rourke, 1985; Morris, Blashfield, & Satz, 1981). There are clear indications that this type of systematic search for reliable subtypes of children with LD has begun to have a profoundly positive effect on investigative efforts in this area (see Rourke,1985, 1991, 1995, for many examples of this). Furthermore, systematic attempts at establishing the concurrent, predictive, and construct validity of such subtypes have been proceeding apace (e.g., Dool, Stelmack, & Rourke, 1993; Fletcher, 1985; Lyon, 1985; Rourke, 1991, 1993; Rourke & Conway, 1997; Rourke & Fisk, 1992; Rourke & Tsatsanis, 1996; Stelmack, Rourke, & van der Vlugt, 1995).

A SYSTEMATIC DEVELOPMENTAL NEUROPSYCHOLOGICAL APPROACH TO THE STUDY OF LD

We turn now to a developmental neuropsychological approach to the study of LD that seeks to understand problems in learning by studying developmental change in behavior as seen through the perspective of brain-behavior models. It is an approach that combines the study of brain development with the study of behavior development. This approach involves research strategies that pay as much attention to the development of an individual's approach to material-to-be learned as they do, say, to the electrophysiological correlates at the level of the cerebral hemispheres that accompany that approach. In a word, it is a systematic attempt to fashion a complete understanding of brain-behavior relationships as these are mirrored in the development of central processing abilities and deficits throughout the life span.

Unfortunately, the utilization of a neuropsychological framework such as this for the investigation of LD in children has often been misinterpreted as reflecting an emphasis on static, intractable (and, therefore, limited) notions of the effects of brain impairment on behavior. Indeed, although specific statements to the contrary have been made on many occasions (e.g., Rourke, 1975, 1978a, 1978b, 1981, 1995), many otherwise competent researchers and clinicians persist in the notion that such an approach *assumes* that brain damage, disorder, or dysfunction lies at the basis of LD. Nothing could be further from the truth, because the thrust of much work in this area (see Benton, 1975; Rourke, 1975, 1978a, 1989, 1991, 1995; Taylor & Fletcher, 1983) has been to *demonstrate* whether and to what extent such might be the case.

Be that as it may, the emphasis that we have brought to this enterprise is one that attempts to integrate dimensions of individual and social development on the one hand with relevant central processing features on the other—all of this in order to fashion useful models with which to study crucial aspects of perceptual, cognitive, and other dimensions of human development. That models and explanatory concepts developed with this aim in mind (e.g., Rourke, 1976, 1982b, 1983b, 1987, 1988b, 1989, 1995) contain explanations that are thought to apply both to some children with frank brain damage as well as to some types of children with LD and to some aspects of normal human development should come as no surprise, because maximum generalizability is one goal of any scientific model or theory. Specifically with respect to the child with LD, the aspects of these concepts and models that are most relevant are those that have to do with proposed linkages between patterns of central processing abilities and deficits that may predispose a youngster to predictably different patterns of social as well as academic LD. In addition, these models are designed to encompass developmental change and outcome in patterns of learning and behavioral responsivity.

In the neuropsychology of LD, the important relationships to bear in mind are those that obtain between *patterns* of performance and *models* of developmental brain-behavior relationships. This is not meant to imply something as trite as that LD are the *result* of brain damage or dysfunction. Indeed, the illogical leap of such an implication (assumption) is only one of its shortcomings. More important is the notion that, even were such a cause-effect (i.e., brain damage/dysfunction → LD) relationship shown to be the case, it would carry few, if any, corollaries for the understanding of developmental brain-behavior relationships or for their treatment.

This is not to say that brain-behavior relationships are of little or no importance in the study of LD. Rather, it is simply the case that we currently understand much more about developmental neuro*psychological*-performance interactions than we do about developmental-*neuro*psychological

performance interactions. The patterns of interaction among brain, development, and behavior that have, from time to time, been exquisitely hypothesized are, unfortunately, still largely unexplored and must be the subject of rigorous scientific test (Taylor, 1983). Recent attempts to address this issue (e.g., as summarized in Dool et al., 1993; Stelmack et al., 1995) have suggested rather strongly that specific types of brain function/dysfunction/difference play rather important roles in the manifestations of some subtypes of LD.

We turn now to a discussion of selected investigations carried out in our laboratory that serve to illustrate the heuristic properties of this framework. For a compendium of our efforts in this area, see Rourke (1985, 1989, 1991, 1995).

THE WINDSOR STUDIES

The focus of the studies to be discussed in this section is on the academic and psychosocial dimensions of LD; the perspective employed is one that has emerged from our study of these and related problems over some 30 years in the University of Windsor Laboratory.

To appreciate the main issues involved in this presentation, it is necessary to reflect on the crucial historical issues that bear on them as well as the relationships that obtain between LD on the one hand and deficits in academic and psychosocial functioning on the other. In this connection, it should be clear from the outset that the principal hypothesis that we have attempted to test in our work is the following: LD are manifestations of basic neuropsychological assets and deficits; the subtypes of LD in question may lead to problems in academic functioning and/or psychosocial functioning; and the relationships among neuropsychological deficits, LD, and academic and social learning deficits can be understood fully only within a neurodevelopmental framework that takes into consideration the changing nature of the academic, socioemotional, and vocational demands confronting humans in a particular sociocultural milieu.

To illustrate the research and model development strategy employed in our laboratory that speaks to the issues of concern in this chapter, we describe in some detail the nature of two of the subtypes of children with LD who have been the subject of intensive investigation in our laboratory.

Two Subtypes of LD

Although several subtypes of LD have been isolated in our investigations, we have been particularly interested in the study of two of these. Children in one group—referred to as those with a Basic Phonological Processing Disorder (BPPD; Rourke, 1989)—are those who exhibit many relatively poor psycholinguistic skills in conjunction with very well-developed visual-spatial-organizational, tactile-perceptual, psychomotor, and nonverbal problem-solving skills. They exhibit very poor reading and spelling skills and significantly better, though still impaired, mechanical arithmetic competence. The other group—those with Nonverbal Learning Disabilities (NLD, Rourke, 1989)—exhibits outstanding problems in visual-spatial-organizational, tactile-perceptual, psychomotor, and nonverbal problem-solving skills, within a context of clear strengths in psycholinguistic skills such as rote verbal learning, regular phoneme-grapheme matching, amount of verbal output, and verbal classification. Children who exhibit the syndrome of NLD experience their major academic learning difficulties in mechanical arithmetic, while exhibiting advanced levels of word recognition and spelling. Both of these subtypes of children with LD—especially the second subtype of child, characterized as having NLD (Myklebust, 1975; Rourke, 1989)—have been the subject of much scrutiny in our laboratory (for reviews, see Rourke, 1975, 1978b, 1982a, 1987, 1988b, 1989, 1995; Rourke & Strang, 1983; Strang & Rourke, 1983, 1985a, 1985b).

An examination of Figures 29.1 and 29.2 will elucidate the models that we have used in our attempts to explain the developmental dynamics of the neuropsychological and adaptive dimensions of these two subtypes of LD. For example, the summaries of the assets and deficits of the NLD subtype should be viewed within a specific context of cause-effect relationships; that is, the primary neuropsychological assets and deficits are thought to lead to the secondary neuropsychological assets and deficits, and so on within the four categories of neuropsychological dimensions; and the foregoing are seen as causative vis-à-vis the academic and socioemotional/adaptive aspects of this subtype. In this sense, the latter dimensions are, essentially, *dependent* variables (i.e., effects rather than causes) in the NLD subtype. The same applies, mutatis mutandis, to the summary of the assets and deficits of the BPPD subtype.

Specific Comparisons of BPPD and NLD

In a series of studies (e.g., Rourke & Finlayson, 1978; Rourke & Strang, 1978; Strang & Rourke, 1983), we have investigated the neuropsychological assets and deficits of these two subtypes of children with LD. Based on these and related analyses (Ozols & Rourke, 1988, 1991), the following specific conclusions apply to these two subtypes. (In the following, "older" refers to 9–14-year-old children, "younger" to 7–8-year-old children.)

1. Older children with BPPD exhibit some (often no more than mild) deficiencies in the more rote aspects of psycholinguistic skills, such as the recall of information and word definitions; those with NLD exhibit average to superior skills in these areas.

2. Older children with BPPD exhibit outstanding deficiencies in the more complex semantic-acoustic aspects of psycholinguistic skills such as sentence memory and auditory analysis of common words. Children with NLD exhibit less than normal performances in these areas, but their levels of performance are superior to those with BPPD. Children with NLD tend to perform least well on those tests of semantic-acoustic processing that place an emphasis on the processing of novel, complex, and/or meaningful material.

3. Older children with BPPD exhibit normal levels of performance on visual-spatial-organizational, psychomotor, and tactile-perceptual tasks; children with NLD have outstanding difficulties on such tasks. The deficiencies exhibited by children with NLD on tactile-perceptual and psychomotor tasks are in evidence bilaterally; when there is evidence of lateralized impairment on such tasks for the child with NLD, it is almost always a relative deficiency in performance on the left side of the body. In general, the more novel the visual-spatial, psychomotor, and tactile-perceptual task, the more impairment, relative to age-based norms, that is exhibited by the child with NLD.

4. Older children with BPPD perform normally on nonverbal problem-solving tasks. They have no difficulty benefiting from experience with such tasks. They are particularly adept at utilizing nonverbal informational feedback to modify their performance to meet the demands of such tasks. Children with NLD exhibit moderate to severe problems on nonverbal problem-solving tasks. They benefit very little from informational feedback and continued experience with such tasks, even when

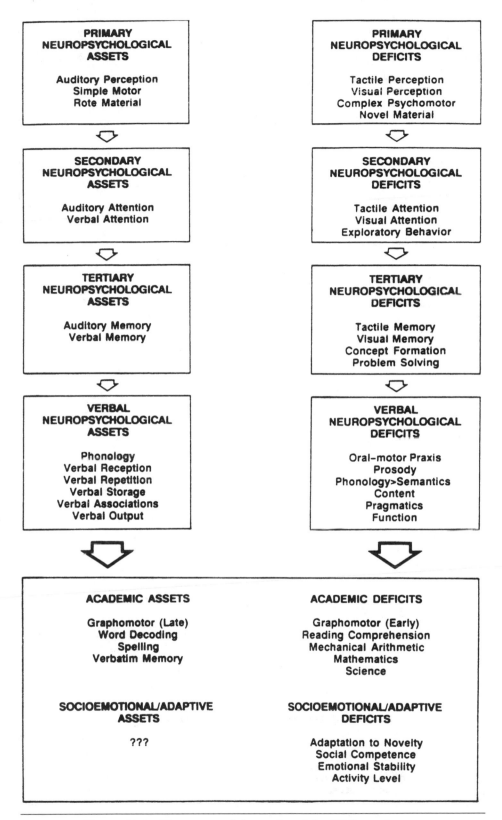

Figure 29.1 Elements and dynamics of the NLD syndrome.

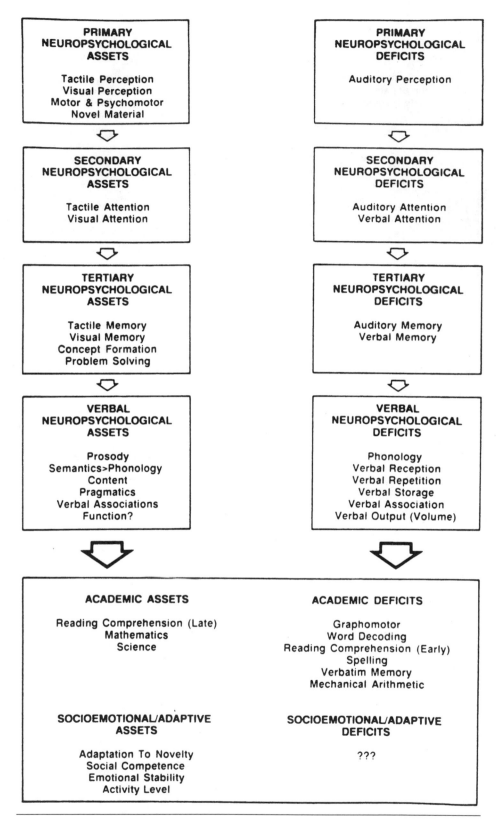

Figure 29.2 Elements and dynamics of the Group BPPD.

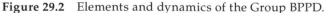

the information provided would be expected to be well within estimates based on their largely rote verbal learning capacity (Fisher, DeLuca, & Rourke, 1997).

5. Younger children with BPPD and those with NLD exhibit inter- and intragroup patterns of relative abilities and deficits on automatic (rote) verbal, semantic-acoustic, and visual-spatial-organizational tasks that are similar to those exhibited by older children in these two groups. The exception is that the more rote aspects of verbal skills tend to be more deficient relative to age-based norms in younger than in older children with BPPD.

6. Differentiations in terms of psychomotor and tactile-perceptual skills and abilities are less marked in younger than in older children of these two groups.

7. Although there is some evidence to suggest that younger children with NLD have more difficulty adapting to novel problem-solving situations than do their BPPD counterparts, the precise measurement of such suspected difficulties has yet to be completed.

8. The adaptive implications of the relative assets and deficits of older children with BPPD and NLD extend well beyond the confines of the academic setting. For example, children with BPPD tend to fare far better in social situations than do children with NLD (Rourke & Fisk, 1981). More precise delineations of these extra-academic learning considerations are contained in Rourke (1989) and in other investigations (Del Dotto, Fisk, McFadden, & Rourke, 1991; Fuerst & Rourke, 1995; Loveland, Fletcher, & Bailey, 1990; Ozols & Rourke, 1985, 1991; Rourke & Fuerst, 1991; Tsatsanis, Fuerst, & Rourke, 1997).

Note on Research Methodology. These conclusions and generalizations should be sufficient to make the desired point: namely, that children with LD chosen solely on the basis of specific variations in patterns of academic performance (with adequate controls for age, Full-Scale IQ, and other important attributes) can be shown to exhibit very different patterns of neuropsychological abilities and deficits. In this connection, it should be noted that both of the subtypes under consideration exhibited deficient mechanical arithmetic performance. Thus, members of each of these groups could have been included in the "learning disabled" sample of a contrasting-groups type of study that is designed to compare

"arithmetic disabled" and "normal" children. It should be clear, from the above conclusions and generalizations, that such an "arithmetic disabled" group could be made up of at least two very distinct arithmetic-disabled subtypes. It is also the case that (1) these subtypes of children share virtually nothing in common, from a neuropsychological standpoint, with each other; (2) their similarly deficient levels of performance in mechanical arithmetic reflect these quite different "etiologies"; and (3) their needs for academic habilitation/rehabilitation with respect to mechanical arithmetic differ markedly from one another (see Rourke 1989, 1993; Rourke & Conway, 1997; Rourke & Strang, 1983; Strang & Rourke, 1985a, 1985b, for a discussion of these issues).

A PROPOSED CLASSIFICATION OF LD SUBTYPES

As a final attempt to provide the reader with some structure regarding the subtyping efforts in the LD field, the following definitions and classification system are presented for perusal. No claim is made for the perspicacity of the formulations that follow: they are proffered as apparently reasonable generalizations that fit with our review of the reasonably well-controlled studies that have appeared in the neuropsychological subtyping literature over the past 25 or so years.

A note on definitions: If there are reliable and valid differences between LD subtypes, and we still wish to retain the term LD as a generic descriptor of this heterogeneous group of disorders, then there are at least two issues with which we must deal:

1. There is a need for a generic definition. The current one(s) will probably do quite nicely; however, it might be well to focus the generic definition on the common content of this group of disorders, namely, difficulties in learning in one or more areas.
2. There is a need for specific definitions of specific subtypes. Some of these (e.g., NLD, BPPD) can be formulated now; others will need to wait on further research.

Generic Definition
The following modification of the National Joint Committee on Learning Disabilities (January 30, 1981) definition appears appropriate:

Learning disabilities is a generic term that refers to a heterogeneous group of disorders manifested by significant difficulties in the mastery of one or more of the following: listening, speaking, reading, writing, reasoning, mathematical, and other skills and abilities that are traditionally referred to as "academic." The term learning disabilities is also appropriately applied in instances where persons exhibit significant difficulties in mastering social and other adaptive skills and abilities. In some cases, investigations of learning disabilities have yielded evidence that would be consistent with hypotheses relating central nervous system dysfunction to the disabilities in question. Even though a learning disability may occur concomitantly with other handicapping conditions (e.g., sensory impairment, mental retardation, social and emotional disturbance) or environmental influences (e.g., cultural differences, insufficient/inappropriate instruction, psychogenic factors), it is not the direct result of those conditions or influences. However, it is possible that emotional disturbances and other adaptive deficiencies may arise from the same patterns of central processing assets and deficits that generate the manifestations of academic and social learning disabilities.

Specific Definitions (Subtypes)

All of the following subtypes are characterized in terms of the specific patterns of neuropsychological assets and deficits that are thought to be responsible for the particular patterns of learning assets and deficits exhibited by children within the subtype. Issues such as inadequate or inappropriate motivation or a mismatch between learning history and the specific demands of the academic environment are not dealt with. There are two dimensions emphasized, namely, the impact of the specific learning disability subtype (i.e., the specific pattern of neuropsychological assets and deficits) on (1) academic learning in the elementary school years and (2) socioemotional adaptation. With the exception of (B) below, these subtypal definitions have received very little investigative attention; they are more in the nature of hypotheses that could (and, we think, should) be investigated.

In proposing the patterns of neuropsychological assets and deficits that characterize these hypothesized LD subtypes, reference will be made to Figures 29.1 and 29.2. These subtypes constitute rather well-defined entities and should serve as exemplars for the type of dynamic analysis that we feel should be determined for each LD subtype.

(A) Learning Disabilities Characterized Primarily by Disorders of Linguistic Functioning.
   (i) BPPD
      Figure 29.2 contains a description of this subtype. As a summary of the assets and deficits that characterize this subtype, the following is offered.

Neuropsychological Assets: Tactile-perceptual, visual-spatial-organizational, psychomotor, and nonverbal problem-solving and concept-formation skills and abilities are developed to an average to above-average degree. The capacity to deal with novelty and the amount and quality of exploratory behavior are average. Attention to tactile and visual input is normal.

Neuropsychological Deficits: Disordered phonemic hearing, segmenting, and blending are paramount. Attention to and memory for auditory-verbal material are clearly impaired. Poor verbal reception, repetition, and storage are evident. Amount and quality of verbal associations are clearly underdeveloped. There is a less than average amount of verbal output.

Rules of classification for BPPD have been developed (Pelletier, Ahmad, & Rourke, in press).

Prognoses:

Academic. Reading and spelling are affected as are those aspects of arithmetic performance that require reading and writing. The symbolic aspects of writing are affected. The nonverbal aspects of arithmetic and mathematics are unaffected. The prognosis for advances in reading and spelling and the verbal-symbolic aspects of writing and arithmetic must be very guarded.

Psychosocial. Psychosocial disturbance may occur if parents, teachers, and other caretakers establish unattainable goals for the child and/or if antisocial models and lifestyles hold reinforcing properties for the child that the school is unable to provide. When psychopathology occurs, it may be of the externalizing variety; other possibilities include mild anxiety (Pelletier et al., in press).

   (ii) Phoneme-Grapheme Matching Disorder (PGMD)
      With reference to Figure 29.2 and the description of the BPPD subtype, the

following assets, deficits, and prognoses appear to apply.

Neuropsychological Assets: Identical to the BPPD subtype, except that phonemic hearing, segmenting, and blending are normal.

Neuropsychological Deficits: Phoneme-grapheme (most often, grapheme → phoneme) matching problems are paramount.

Prognoses:

Academic. Written spelling of words known "by sight" may be average or better; written spelling of words not known "by sight" is as poor as in the BPPD subtype. Word recognition is much better than that exhibited by the BPPD subtype, although still at an impaired level. Word-decoding skills may be as poor as for the BPPD subtype. Arithmetic and mathematics performances may rise to average or above-average levels when the words involved in performance on problems in this domain are minimized or learned "by sight." The prognosis for advances in reading and spelling is fair, and much better than that for the BPPD subtype. Prognoses for advancement in arithmetic and mathematics are good under the conditions mentioned above. Writing of unfamiliar words continues to be problematic.

Psychosocial. The prognosis for socioemotional disturbance is the same as that for the BPPD subtype, but with somewhat less risk.

(iii) Word-Finding Disorder (WFD)

This subtype is characterized by outstanding problems in word-finding and verbal expressive skills within a context of a wide range of intact neuropsychological skills and abilities.

Neuropsychological Assets: Identical to those of the PGMD subtype, except that phoneme-grapheme matching skills are intact.

Neuropsychological Deficits: The only outstanding deficit is difficulty in accessing a normal store of verbal associations.

Prognoses:

Academic. Reading and spelling are very poor during early school years, with near-average or average performances in these areas emerging toward the end of the elementary school period (i.e., at approximately grade 6–8). Arithmetic and mathematics

are seen as early strengths. Writing of words that can be expressed and writing from a model are average to good.

Psychosocial. Prognosis for socioemotional functioning is virtually normal, but with the added minor risk factor of early failure in school.

(B) Learning Disabilities Characterized Primarily by Disorders of Nonverbal Functioning

The NLD Syndrome (see Figure 29.1)

Neuropsychological Assets: Auditory-verbal perception, attention, and memory become well developed. Simple motor and tasks that can be learned by rote are well accomplished. Good phonological skills are seen fairly early in development. Verbal reception, repetition, storage, and associations are evident from the early school years onward. A high volume of verbal output characterizes this subtype.

Neuropsychological Deficits: Tactile and visual perception deficits are evident early in development; these include attention to and memory for material delivered through these modalities. Complex psychomotor tasks, except those that can be learned through extensive repetition, are poorly performed. An aversion for novel experiences, with consequent negative impact on exploratory behavior, characterizes this subtype. Problems in age-appropriate concept formation and problem solving are especially evident. The principal deficits in linguistic skills are those relating to the content and pragmatic dimensions of language. In addition, language is often used for inappropriate purposes.

Rules of classification for BPPD have been developed (Pelletier et al., under review).

Prognoses:

Academic. Word decoding and spelling often develop to superior levels. Verbatim memory, especially for material of an auditory-verbal nature, becomes very well developed. Areas of emerging and continuing concern include reading comprehension, mechanical arithmetic, mathematics, and science. Some dimensions of "science" and "mathematics" can be learned if the material is presented and practiced in a rote fashion; difficulties become apparent when reasoning, deduction, and the like are required.

Psychosocial. Basic problems in perception, judgment, problem solving, and reasoning lead to difficulties in social competence. Risk for moderate to severe psychopathology, especially of the internalized variety, is high. Activity level tends to decline to hypoactive levels by late childhood. Long-term prognosis for psychosocial development is very guarded (Pelletier et al., in press).

(C) Learning Disabilities Characterized Primarily by Output Disorders in All Modalities

This subtype is similar to the WFD subtype with respect to neuropsychological assets and deficits. Within the academic realm, there are added problems of deficient output in the writing of words and written arithmetic.

Neuropsychological Assets: Identical to WFD subtype.

Neuropsychological Deficits: Identical to WFD subtype, with the additional difficulty of organizing, directing, and orchestrating all aspects of behavioral expression.

Prognoses:

Academic. Rather severe problems in oral and written output are prominent in early school years. Marked advances in word recognition, word decoding, and reading comprehension are evident in the middle school years. Written work remains poor, as does the capacity to deliver verbal descriptions and answers to questions.

Psychosocial. Such children are often characterized as having "acting-out" disorders in early school years. They are also at risk for social withdrawal and depression. This may develop into full-blown externalized and/or internalized forms of psychopathology if management by the child's principal caretakers is inappropriate.

A number of broad, general conclusions appear warranted on the basis of the results of the intensive investigations of LD subtypes in our own and others' laboratories that have been carried out over the past three decades. These include generalizations that relate to academic performance as well as to psychosocial/adaptive functioning.

CONCLUSIONS AND GENERALIZATIONS

With respect to the role of subtyping pursuits in the field of LD, it appears that the following conclusions and generalizations are warranted:

1. There is no single, unitary pattern of neuropsychological assets and deficits displayed by children with LD. Indeed, distinct subtypes of LD have been isolated in a reliable fashion in a number of studies (see Rourke, 1985, 1991, for several examples of these).

2. There is an emerging body of evidence attesting to the content, concurrent, predictive, construct, and clinical validity of some subtypes of youngsters with LD (e.g., Casey & Rourke, 1991; Casey, Rourke, & Picard, 1991; Harnadek & Rourke, 1994; Stelmack et al., 1995).

3. No single, unitary pattern of personality characteristics, psychosocial adaptation, social competence, self-concept, locus of control, or other facet of socioemotional functioning that we have examined is characteristic of all children with LD (Fuerst, Fisk, & Rourke, 1989, 1990; Porter & Rourke, 1985; Rourke, 1988a). For a fuller discussion of these issues and for a review of the studies that support this conclusion and those in 4 through 11 below, see Fuerst and Rourke, 1993, 1995.

4. Some children with LD experience mild to severe disturbance of psychosocial functioning. However, most children with LD appear to achieve adequate psychosocial adaptation (Rourke & Fuerst, 1991, 1995; Tsatsanis et al., 1997).

5. There are distinct types of psychosocial disturbance and behavior disorder that may be displayed by children with LD. These various manifestations of emotional and behavioral disorder may be more frequent among children with LD than among their normally achieving peers; our knowledge about the precise types and incidence of emotional and behavioral problems in children with LD is becoming quite precise (e.g., Fuerst & Rourke, 1995; Rourke & Fuerst, 1991; Tsatsanis et al., 1997).

6. One pattern of central processing abilities and deficits in nonverbal learning disabilities (NLD) appears to lead to the following: a particular configuration of academic achievement (well-developed word recognition and spelling as compared to significantly poorer mechanical arithmetic); increased risk of psychopathology; and a tendency to develop an internalized form of psychosocial disturbance

(Rourke, 1989, 1995). Other patterns of central processing abilities and deficits (those marked by outstanding difficulties in psycholinguistic skills) appear to lead to particular patterns of academic achievement (striking problems in reading and spelling and varying levels of performance in mechanical arithmetic), with some correlative, although relatively minor, effect on the incidence of psychopathology but with no particular effect on its specific manifestations (Pelletier et al., under review).

7. There is no conclusive evidence that children with LD are prone to developing problems with substance abuse, truly antisocial behavior, or delinquency. Carefully conducted longitudinal research suggests that, as a group, children with LD are no more likely to develop these problems than are youngsters free of such disabilities (Rourke & Fuerst, 1991).

8. There is no conclusive evidence that children with LD, as a group, tend to become more prone to psychosocial disturbance with advancing age relative to normally achieving peers (Fuerst & Rourke, 1995; Tsatsanis et al., 1997).

9. One exception to item 8 is the worsening in the manifestations of psychopathology and the increasing discrepancies between assets and deficits exhibited by children and adolescents with NLD (Rourke, Young, & Leenaars, 1989; Rourke, Young, Strang, & Russell, 1986). This is the case in spite of the fact that the *pattern* of neuropsychological assets and deficits and the specific manifestations of psychopathology in such individuals remain quite stable over time (Rourke, Del Dotto, Rourke, & Casey, 1990).

10. Developmental differences in the manifestations of LD appear to obtain for some subtypes of LD. For example (see 9 above), there appears to be a worsening of the manifestations of psychopathology and the increasing discrepancies between assets and deficits exhibited by children with NLD (Casey et al., 1991; Rourke, Young, et al., 1986).

11. At least one subtype of learning disability (i.e., NLD) is evident within groups of children who are suffering from various types of neurological disease, disorder, and dysfunction (e.g., Klin, Volkmar, Sparrow, Cicchetti, &

Rourke, 1995; Rourke, 1995). This should encourage the search for reliable patterns of central processing abilities and deficits among other groups that are typically excluded from such scrutiny (e.g., the mentally retarded).

12. Efforts to clarify the relationships between LD and patterns of neuropsychological assets and deficits should eschew the "contrasting groups/unitary deficit" approach in favor of research efforts that deal adequately with the heterogeneity of the LD population, both with respect to their patterns of abilities and deficits and with respect to their distinctive forms and manifestations of psychopathology. Model developments (e.g., Fletcher & Taylor, 1984; Rourke, 1982; 1987, 1988b, 1989, 1995; Rourke & Fisk, 1988) must be sufficiently complex and sophisticated to encompass and illuminate these heterogeneous patterns of central processing abilities/disabilities among children with LD. Continuing to carry out essentially atheoretical, correlational studies of matched groups of youngsters with LD and those who learn in a normal manner to address the important theoretical and clinical issues in this area is counterproductive.

NEUROPSYCHOLOGICAL ASSESSMENT PROCEDURES FOR CHILDREN WITH LD

CONTENT AND RATIONALE

Extensive treatments of the neuropsychological assessment procedures that we have found useful for children and adolescents can be found in Rourke (1976, 1981, 1994), Rourke, Bakker, Fisk, and Strang (1983, especially Chapter 5), and Rourke, Fisk, and Strang (1986, especially Chapters 1 and 2). Only a few points will be emphasized here.

Comprehensiveness

A neuropsychological assessment of a child who is thought to have LD should be comprehensive in nature. Our experience with procedures that aim simply to "screen" for LD is that they typically do more harm than good. Even disregarding for the moment the very high levels of false positives and false negatives that such procedures typically generate, it should be pointed out that it is rarely, if ever, useful to know simply that a child does or does not have LD. In fact, such knowledge, especially when a positive "diagnosis" of LD is made on the basis of such an assessment procedure, may very well be counterproductive for the child. This is so because there are patterns of assets and deficits evident in various subtypes of children with LD that differ very markedly from one another (see, e.g., Figures 29.1 and 29.2 for a comparison of the NLD and BPPD profiles). Thus, lumping them under the common rubric of LD may lead to gross misunderstanding on the part of professionals and other caretakers involved with the child, not to mention the potentially dramatic negative ramifications that such a homogeneous designation might have for treatment.

Additionally, it is usually essential to know at least as much about what a child with LD *can* do as what he or she *cannot* do if one's goal is to design an appropriate treatment/intervention plan for the youngster. A designation of LD very often accentuates the disabilities and deficits that the child exhibits while virtually ignoring the assets and strengths that are probably going to be useful in compensatory intervention strategies. Most treatment plans for children with LD usually involve a combination of direct "attack" on the deficits and the exploitation of the child's assets for compensatory modes of adaptation. In general, the older and the more impaired the child, the more likely it is that compensatory techniques accentuating the use of the child's assets will be found to be effective and will tend to dominate the treatment picture. Comprehensive neuropsychological assessment procedures are designed with this "accentuate the positive" rule in mind.

But what constitutes a comprehensive assessment? As explained in detail in the references cited above, a comprehensive neuropsychological assessment is one that involves the measurement of the principal skills and abilities thought to be subserved by the brain. Thus, a fairly broad sampling of tasks involving sensory, perceptual, motor/psychomotor, attentional, mnestic, linguistic, and concept-formation/problem-solving/hypothesis-testing would need to be employed. In addition, it would be well to vary the levels of complexity of such tasks (from quite simple to quite complex) and to present tasks that vary along the dimensions of rote and novel requirements. Inclusion of tasks that

vary from those that involve information processing within a single modality to those that involve the coordination and execution of response requirements within several modalities is also desirable. It is clear that the aforementioned continua of tests and measures are not mutually exclusive. Finally, it is often important in the analysis of children with LD to have available fairly comprehensive personality and "behavioral" data on the child. Standardized tests of important dimensions of psychopathology, activity level, and common problem behaviors are often useful—sometimes essential—for this purpose.

A collection of tests and measures that includes these dimensions would meet the minimal requirements for comprehensiveness. For a list of the tests that fulfill such criteria and that we use routinely in our evaluation of children referred for neuropsychological assessment, the interested reader should examine the appendix of Rourke et al. (1983) or Rourke, Fisk, and Strang (1986). Some specification of these procedures is contained in the next section of this chapter.

Standardized Administration Procedures and the Availability of Norms

We have found that testing procedures that are standardized and that have norms available are essential in the study of children who exhibit LD and any number of other neuropsychological difficulties. This is so for a variety of reasons, not the least of which is the fact that the manifestations of LD may change in many ways over time; the predictability that can be seen to obtain in such circumstances is best couched in terms of deviations from age-expected performances that either decline, remain stable, or increase over time. For example, without the availability of developmental norms and standardized tests, it would not have been possible to determine the predictable developmental manifestations of the NLD syndrome. Furthermore, the use of unstandardized procedures would have made it all but impossible to assess its fulminations, responses to therapy, and other aspects of its course in the individual patient. In the last analysis, standardized assessment procedures and their attendant benefits make it possible to translate clinical lore into rigorous, testable clinical generalizations (e.g., the NLD syndrome and model).

Procedures Amenable to a Variety of Methods of Inference

The methods of inference for comprehensive neuropsychological assessment procedures first proposed by Reitan (1966) are as important now as they were when he articulated them. It is crucial that one (1) be able to apply *level of performance* interpretations (especially within the context of developmental norms as outlined in the preceeding paragraph; (2) have a sufficiently broad sample of performances so that *pathognomonic signs* of brain impairment may emerge; (3) have data in a variety of realms that are amenable to the *differential score* approach; and (4) be able to carry out systematic *comparisons of performance on the two sides of the body* (Rourke, 1975). In the analysis of the NLD and other LD subtypes, all of these methods of inference are employed, as the data spread in the previous section dealing with hypothesized subtypes illustrates.

There are a number of other features of comprehensive, systematic neuropsychological assessment that are important considerations in the analysis of the behavior of children with LD (e.g., Rourke & Adams, 1984). Some of these arise in the next section. More comprehensive treatments of such issues are contained in the references cited above.

A DEVELOPMENTAL NEUROPSYCHOLOGICAL REMEDIATION/ HABILITATION MODEL

Figure 29.3 contains a modification of a remediation/habilitation model that was developed by Rourke et al. (1983) and Rourke, Fisk, et al. (1986) for general neuropsychological assessment. It is modified slightly in Figure 29.3 to take into consideration the special dimensions of LD. Note that the model is couched in terms of "steps." In explaining the content and dynamics of the model, we consider each step in order.

STEP 1: LEVELS AND PATTERNS OF ASSETS AND DEFICITS

This step appears, at first blush, to be quite simple. However, it is meant to imply a number of dimensions that are fairly complex and sometimes difficult to determine in the assessment process. In general, the pictorial representation of this step is meant to imply that the levels and patterns of neuropsychological assets and deficits that constitute the child's LD may have a differential impact on the child's capacities for academic and social learning. The impact may be small or large, it may be in academic and not in social areas, it may have more impact on some areas of academic functioning than on others, and so on. Furthermore, it is taken for granted that factors other than LD may have a bearing on academic and social learning. Thus, the initial goal of the assessment process is to make a determination of whether and to what extent LD impact on various academic and social learning/adaptation capacities.

To accomplish this purpose, it should go without saying that the neuropsychological assessment procedures should be reliable (Brown, Rourke, & Cicchetti, 1989) and valid (Rourke, 1991). The principal dimensions of validity in the consideration of the clinical dimensions of assessment are those relating to content, concurrent, predictive, and ecological/clinical validity. The issues of content (or coverage) and concurrent validity are discussed just below; issues surrounding predictive validity are particularly relevant in the context of Steps 2 and 3; ecological/clinical validity is basic to all of the steps, but most specifically to considerations relevant to Steps 4 through 7.

Content validity—what we prefer to view as "coverage"—is a simple concept, but one with far-reaching ramifications. Simply put, a neuropsychological assessment has adequate content validity or coverage to the extent that it meets the following criteria: (1) the skill and ability domains tapped are sufficient to mirror the principal areas of functioning that are thought to be mediated by the brain; and (2) the data gathered are sufficient to deal with the clinical (sometimes the referral) problems presented by the child. Failure to meet these criteria— that is, having poor content/coverage validity—can, and often does, severely limit our knowledge regarding the child's present neuropsychological status (concurrent validity), his or her probable prognosis with and without intervention (predictive validity), and the impact of the child's neuropsychological status on a reasonably broad spectrum of his or her developmental/adaptive task demands (ecological validity).

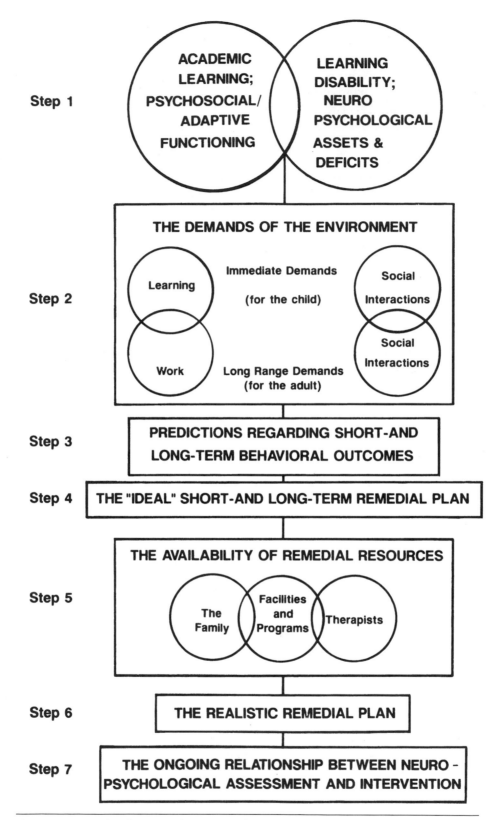

Figure 29.3 A developmental neuropsychological remediation/habilitation model.

If the clinician is interested merely in determining if a child has LD, the particular approach to assessment advocated by us is, for the most part, irrelevant. Adopting a more reasonable perspective—for example, one that invokes criteria of probable therapeutic relevance for determining the validity of a neuropsychological assessment—places the evaluation of coverage within a vastly different, and potentially more exciting, framework. Thus, the evaluation of content/coverage validity within the context of ecological validity is tantamount to requiring that the content of the neuropsychological assessment (assuming for the moment that such content is adequately interpreted) must be fairly broad, pervasive, and comprehensive. It should be clear that such a goal will be achieved only through a reasonably painstaking analysis of a wide variety of functions, with attention given to their interrelatedness and their dissociations.

To this end, we propose that the ability and skill areas outlined in Table 29.1 constitute a bare minimum with respect to the dimensions that must be addressed to provide reasonable, relevant, and comprehensive answers to developmentally important clinical questions for children with LD. The reader should bear in mind that the specific tests and measures mentioned in Table 29.1 are of secondary importance. The crucial issues in the present context are related to the ability and skill domains that are sampled and developmental considerations that bear on levels of performance and complexity; the actual tests and measures employed must be evaluated vis-à-vis these issues and considerations. We should be quick to add that this categorization of skills and abilities lacks a firm scientific basis. However, the continuation of our work regarding the construct validity (dimensionality) of this test battery (Francis, Fletcher, & Rourke, 1988; Francis, Fletcher, Rourke, & York, 1992) is expected to yield such a basis.

STEP 2: THE DEMANDS OF THE ENVIRONMENT

It is clear and evident that the results and dimensions of the neuropsychological assessment described above—no matter how thorough and insightful—remain virtually useless until such time as they are related in a meaningful way to the developmental demands (behavioral tasks, skill developments) that the child faces. This necessitates an appreciation on the part of the assessor of the social-historical-cultural milieu within which the child is expected to function. In North American society and, for the most part, that of Europe, the demands for learning in both academic and extra-academic milieux are quite well-known. Some of these are immediate (short-term, in the model), some more far-flung (long-term, in the model). Some have to do with formal learning environments such as the schoolroom, others with informal learning situations such as play. All are important; hence, all four sectors within the matrix associated with Step 2 (see Figure 29.3) need to be addressed. Failure to do so can, and often does, lead to terribly limited and even counterproductive forms of intervention for the child. (For examples of such outcomes, see Rourke, Fisk, et al., 1986, especially Chapters 1, 5, and 6.)

STEP 3: PREDICTIONS REGARDING SHORT- AND LONG-TERM BEHAVIORAL OUTCOMES

This step involves, essentially, the formulation of prognostications for the individual child that flow from a melding of the conclusions arrived at in Steps 1 and 2. Thus, the child's neuropsychological assessment results are viewed within the context of the short- and long-term developmental demands that he or she is expected to face so that the relative ease or difficulty of these demands for the child can be seen within the context of the particular neuropsychological assets and deficits exhibited by the youngster. The formulation of confident prognostic statements is a complicated step that requires considerable experience with (1) those deficits in children at different ages that are expected to diminish or increase with the passage of time, with and without treatment, and (2) the relative impact of various forms of treatment on those deficits. It should be clear that the processes involved at this level of the model are intimately connected with those required to deal effectively with the next step in the process.

STEP 4: THE IDEAL SHORT- AND LONG-TERM REMEDIAL PLANS

Although seldom possible to put into practice, the formulation of ideal remedial plans offers an

Table 29.1 Tests included in neuropsychological test battery.

Tactile-Perceptual

Reitan–Kløve Tactile-Perceptual and Tactile-Forms Recognition Test
    Tactile Imperception and Suppression
    Finger Agnosia
    Fingertip Number-Writing Perception (9–15 yr)
    Fingertip Symbol-Writing Recognition (5–8 yr)
    Coin Recognition (9–15 yr)
    Tactile-Forms Recognition (5–8 yr)

Visual Perceptual

Retain–Kløve Visual-Perceptual Tests
Target Test
Constructional Dyspraxia Items, Halstead-Wepman Aphasia Screening Test
WISC Picture Completion, Picture Arrangement, Block Design, Object Assembly subtests
Trial Making Test for Children, Part A (9–15 yr)
Color Form Test (5–8 yr)
Individual Performance Test (5–8 yr)
Progressive Figures Test (5–8 yr)
    Matching Figures
    Star Drawing
    Matching Vs
    Concentric Squares Drawing

Auditory-Perceptual and Language Related

Reitan–Klove Auditory-Perceptual Test
Seashore Rhythm Text (9–15 yr)
Auditory Closure Test (Kass, 1964)
Auditory Analysis Test (Rosner & Simon, 1970)
Peabody Picture Vocabulary Test (Dunn, 1965)
Speech-Sounds Perception Test
Sentence Memory Test (Strong, 1963)
Verbal Fluency Test (Strong, 1963)
WISC Information, Comprehension, Similarities, Vocabulary, Digit Span subtests
Aphasia Items, Aphasia Screening Test

Problem Solving, Concept Formation, Reasoning

Halstead Category Test
Children's Word-Finding Test (Rourke & Fisk, 1976)
WISC Arithmetic subtest
Matching Pictures Test (5–8 yr)

Motor and Psychomotor

Reitan–Klove Lateral Dominance Examination
Dynamometer
Finger Tapping Test
Foot Tapping Test
Klove–Matthews Motor Steadiness Battery
    Maze Coordination Test
    Static Steadiness Test
    Grooved Pegboard Test

Other

Underlining Test (Doehring, 1968; Rourke & Gates, 1980; Rourke & Petrauskas, 1978)
WISC Coding subtest
Tactual Performance Test
Trail Making Test for Children, Part B (9–15 yr)

Note: Unless otherwise indicated, these measures are described in Reitan and Davison (1974) or Wechsler (1949, 1974). They are described extensively in Rourke et al. (1986) and Rourke (1989).

opportunity to "flesh out" the implications of Steps 1, 2, and 3. More important from a clinical perspective is the necessity to formulate a prognosis that fits the neuropsychological status of the child. For example, it might be anticipated that a particular form of intervention (say, the institution of a synthetic phonics approach to single-word reading) would be beneficial in the short-term but counterproductive over the long haul. Such prognoses regarding the advisability of starting and stopping of appropriate treatments/interventions at particular times are often essential to the judgment of treatment efficacy. This approach to this phase of the assessment process also implies that the assessor will proffer some advice regarding the necessity for the type of assessment process that should be applied to determine whether a change of therapeutic/intervention tack would be advisable. Such an assessment could be as simple as the application of a standardized achievement test or as complex as a comprehensive examination (see Step 7).

STEP 5: THE AVAILABILITY OF REMEDIAL RESOURCES

The best therapeutic plans in the world cannot be applied without appropriate therapeutic resources. Hence, it is necessary for the psychologist to be able to evaluate the therapeutic/intervention resources of the family, specialized "therapists," and the community. By evaluation we mean the fairly precise specification of the types of therapies and forms of intervention that the child with a specific subtype of LD needs and the likelihood that particular families, therapists, and other caregivers can and will provide.

Perhaps the importance of this principle is best seen in an example of its breach: Very often, in our experience, the conclusions of standard psychoeducational assessments read like excerpts from the services offered by a particular school district. Suggestions like the following are common: placement in a Specific Learning Disabilities (SLD) class; phonics training; referral to a speech pathologist. The results of any and, indeed, of all such recommendations may turn out to be quite productive. But it is far more common that such recommendations—lacking, as they do, specifications regarding precise modes of intervention, intensity, goals, and prognoses—form a very poor guide for

the caregiver. What usually happens is that the therapists (e.g., teacher, speech pathologist, physiotherapist) must carry out their own assessment and relate those findings to what they view as their own therapeutic facilities. This is a very unproductive state of affairs, as it is wasteful of time, effort, and resources, and—far more important—causes unnecessary delays in the application of efficacious modes of intervention. Even worse, such shilly-shallying can lead to grossly inappropriate modes of intervention being applied.

STEP 6: THE REALISTIC REMEDIAL PLAN

The differences between Step 4 and Step 5 constitute the broad outline for the realistic remedial plan. When such differences are consistently large and/or consistently within one particular area (e.g., speech/language therapy), they constitute parts of a "laundry list" of services required to address the needs of children with LD.

STEP 7: THE PERSISTING RELATIONSHIP BETWEEN NEUROPSYCHOLOGICAL ASSESSMENT AND INTERVENTION

In view of the changes that maturation and formal and informal learning experiences can effect, it is necessary to point out that neuropsychological and other forms of comprehensive assessment are not "one-shot" affairs. It should come as no surprise that repeated neuropsychological assessments are often required to fine-tune, or even grossly alter, remedial plans for children with LD.

Follow-up neuropsychological assessments also afford an opportunity to evaluate the effectiveness of particular modes of remedial intervention. Given our current (fairly abysmal) state of knowledge regarding the therapeutic efficacy of various forms of intervention for children with LD, a rigorous, objective, comprehensive, standardized assessment appears to be a minimum requirement for any protocol designed to assess the effectiveness of these complex undertakings.

With these issues regarding assessment as background, we turn now to a consideration of issues relating to prognosis and treatment for the child who exhibits the NLD syndrome (subtype). We present these general principles as an example of the sort of treatment program that can emerge from the systematic, comprehensive analysis of children who exhibit a specific subtype of LD.

TREATMENT PROGRAMS FOR CHILDREN WITH DIFFERENT SUBTYPES OF LD

The identification of subtypes of LD in combination with the intensive and comprehensive neuropsychological examination of the children with LD should provide insight into their disposition and treatment. One of the main objectives of subtyping efforts is to delineate with more precision the sorts of deficiencies that may account for a child's inability to acquire normal reading, spelling, arithmetic, or psychosocial skills so that these might be addressed in a treatment program. The comprehensive neuropsychological assessment further individualizes this process. The aim of this double-barreled process is to fashion remedial programs tailored to the individual's specific assets and deficits. Indeed, it has been our clinical experience that a remedial management intervention that fails to "fit" the neurocognitive ability makeup of the child can, in effect, be counterproductive in respect to the acquisition of basic academic-related and psychosocial skills (Rourke, Fisk, et al., 1986).

Subtyping methods have an additional long-term economy in permitting the use of multivariate classification schemes that have some hope of being replicated in other clinical and research settings. In our experience, such a systematic collection of data has proven to be helpful in the design, implementation, and validation of various treatment approaches. Some of the reasons for failure to replicate findings by independent investigators are that there has not been sufficient denotation of the measurement operations or that the investigators have used different sets of performance measures. One can hardly expect to develop efficacious and generalizable treatment procedures when the assessment data have been collected by one-of-a-kind techniques.

The problem of translating neuropsychological assessment data into viable and effective educational and therapeutic procedures is not a simple one and has not yet been satisfactorily solved. Although a lack of experimental verification of treatment approaches is partly responsible for this state of affairs, there has also been the tendency for the educational community to favor the more traditional psychoeducational assessment for purposes of remedial planning. Unfortunately, children who have been subjected to remedial regimens prescribed by this approach often make gains in skills that they practice and yet exhibit little or no transfer-of-training to the classroom situation (Taylor, 1989).

As we have suggested in the past (Rourke, 1981), perhaps one of the main problems in bridging the gap between assessment information and intervention strategies lies in the lack of a sophisticated method for determining distinct groups of individual differences among youngsters with LD that would allow for an adequate test of the presumed relationship between patterns of abilities and deficits and patterns of failure and success in the classroom. In the absence of any reliable and valid model of the child's cognitive ability structure, it is no wonder that most, if not all, academic remedial prescriptions can be viewed as speculative and having little hope of enjoying the luxury of a definitive empirical test. To complicate matters further, many educators seem to be more attached to the defense of professional turf than to the progress of scientific knowledge.

Still another factor of considerable importance in the treatment of children with LD involves the relationship between the child's ability-related strengths and weaknesses and his or her adaptive capacities. There has been a tendency in the design of remedial programs to focus almost exclusively on the immediate demands of the academic milieu. Most often, scant attention is paid to the child's capacities to adapt to informal learning situations (e.g., play), social relationship requirements (within the family and with age-mates), and long-term learning and social developmental demands (Rourke, Fisk, et al., 1986). It is not enough simply to focus on promoting the child's academic growth while giving short shrift to issues of personal integration and psychosocial adjustment and adaptation.

Although there are a number of treatment programs for LD reported in the literature, very few have been demonstrated to be effective in well-controlled and replicated research (Taylor, 1989; Torgeson, 1997). An excellent summary of several of the factors critical in assessing the interaction between instructional methods and outcome for children with LD has been provided by Lyon and Flynn (1991). According to these investigators, the degree of relationship between LD subtype, instructional treatment method, and outcome is difficult to interpret because of variations and/or limitations in variables such as the following: (1) measuring adherence to or compliance with a particular treatment strategy; (2) teacher-related variables, such as preparation or style; (3) specific classroom climate; and (4) the learning-disabled child's previous and concurrent instructional experiences. To complicate matters further, limited follow-up compliance, initial refusal to "experiment" with any given form of instruction, and delayed recognition of the effects of remediation pose additional problems when measuring the efficacy of remedial efforts. At the same time, the work of Fiedorowicz and Trites (1991) as well as Bakker (1986, 1990) and his associates (Bakker, Licht, & Van Strien,1991) seems to hold some promise in the effective treatment of subtypes of reading disorders in particular.

Our own work in this area has employed more in the way of clinical inferential rather than empirically based investigative strategies. For example, several single-case follow-up examinations of distinct subgroups of reading- and spelling-disordered children have shown them to be less amenable to instructional strategies that tend to be more "deficit-driven" than "compensatory" in nature. This appears to be the case in children who exhibit marked deficits in phonologic, symbolic, sequential, and/or mnemonic processing. In addition, neither age nor sex of the child appears to be a contributing factor in differentiating outcome. Although the results of relevant research to date (e.g., Fuerst et al., 1989, 1990; Fuerst & Rourke, 1995; Loveland et al., 1990; Ozols & Rourke, 1985, 1991; Porter & Rourke, 1985; Rourke & Fuerst, 1991; Tsatsanis et al., 1997) suggest that children whose LD seem due primarily to auditory-perceptual and/or psycholinguistic-related processing deficiencies (i.e., BPPD) tend to be generally well adjusted, those children who do experience some degree of emotional maladjustment seem to profit little from verbally biased psychotherapeutic techniques. This condition most likely reflects compromised verbal comprehension competencies and may very well lead such children to avoid situations that are verbally interactive. Nevertheless, the fact remains that the deficits that such children exhibit do not have a necessary negative impact on psychosocial functioning (Fuerst & Rourke, 1995; Rourke & Fuerst, 1991; Tsatsanis et al., 1997).

As is the case of the psycholinguistically impaired youngster, most of the habilitational considerations for children with NLD are garnered from single-case follow-up investigations and reflect general principles of treatment intervention. We have attempted to relate the unique pattern of neuropsychological assets and deficits of such children to modes of intervention that are primarily, although not exclusively, compensatory in nature.

Our formulation of treatment strategies with children with NLD is based, in part, on a model of brain functioning that implicates the involvement of white matter disease or dysfunction in its manifestation (Rourke, 1989, 1995). This is of both theoretical and clinical importance in selecting the appropriate "mode" of intervention. For example, the earlier in development that white matter disease occurs, the more propitious it would be to utilize a treatment approach that attacks the deficits. This notion is predicated on the assumption that such an approach will serve to stimulate the functioning of the remaining white matter to foster the development of centers of gray matter. On the other hand, the longer the NLD syndrome persists and the later its psychosocial manifestations, the more likely that compensatory techniques will prove to be efficacious in pursuit of a therapeutic nature. For a complete explication of the specifics of this particular program, the interested reader is referred to Rourke (1989, 1995).

DIRECTIONS FOR FUTURE STUDY

Although some of the shortcomings of existing theoretical formulations and experimental procedures in the study of LD are beginning to be understood, it is clear that the investigations conducted to date represent at best only a small fraction of the work yet to be done in this area. The results of multivariate classification studies have made us cognizant of the fact that LD in children can be analyzed at a number of levels and with rather sophisticated statistical precision. Ultimately, we hope for an integration of these findings with other levels of analyses such as those provided by more in-depth educational, psychosocial, and neuropsychological models. To accomplish this, the following areas of investigation appear to be of considerable importance.

First, there remains a state of confusion regarding the definition of LD. There are those who continue to "diagnose" LD, and yet professionals vary greatly when asked to state what it is they are diagnosing. In a climate of definitional and, as one consequence, etiologic confusion, it is easy to see why the determination of the types of intervention that would be most appropriate for different subtypes of children with LD has been elusive. We have proposed some specific definitions above and are in the process of determining their validity. The goal of this exercise is to arrive at consensually validated characterizations of LD.

With the exception of NLD, subtypal definitions have received very little investigative attention. Although there has been an increasing amount of empirical study aimed at the determination of the reliability and validity of LD (see several chapters in Rourke, 1991, 1995, for a review of these investigations), there is still much that needs to be done to relate these to considerations of ecological validity (e.g., areas of psychosocial and adaptive functioning). We feel that there has been sufficient work in this area to this point (e.g., Fuerst et al., 1989, 1990; Fuerst & Rourke, 1995; Rourke, 1988a, 1989; Rourke & Fuerst, 1991; Russell & Rourke, 1991; Tsatsanis et al., 1997) to justify some optimism with respect to the fruitfulness of research in this area.

Also, there is the issue of comparisons of subtypes of LD with comorbid conditions, such as attention-deficit disorder (e.g., Casey, Rourke, & Del Dotto, 1996), and the generalizability of psychosocial subtypes of LD to other areas of neuropsychological interest, such as traumatic brain injury (Butler, Rourke, Fuerst, & Fisk, 1997). Even more generally, the incidence of subtypes of LD, such as NLD, in conditions such as Asperger's syndrome (e.g., Klin et al., 1995) as well as a host of other neurological syndromes (Rourke, 1995) is an area that is ripe for neuropsychological investigation (Tsatsanis & Rourke, 1995).

Finally, it is clear that we need to establish whether and to what extent the specificity of subtype identification leads to specificity of efficacious treatments. Vapid debates regarding the relative utility of deficit- or compensatory-driven strategies at different stages of development will continue to be the rule until we make considerably more headway in this area. To this end, we need to focus on investigations in which preferred modes of intervention are deduced from models of neuropsychological relationships that have been shown to have concurrent and predictive validity. The work of Bakker and his associates (e.g., Bakker, 1986, 1990; Bakker et al., 1991) is one example of this approach; that of Lyon and associates (e.g., Lyon &

Flynn, 1991) is another. Both of these approaches have shown considerable promise, and we can expect to see more developments along these lines in the near future.

CAUTIONARY NOTE

In this chapter, we have attempted to describe and explain in some detail a particular approach to the understanding, assessment, and treatment of LD. The neuropsychological approach adopted is comprehensive and, in our view, efficacious. Some disagree with this stance, but that is of little importance in the present context. What is important is that the reader understand a coherent framework from which to view this very complex field. We hope that our aim of sensitizing the reader to some or all of these issues has been achieved. At the same time, we should emphasize that we do not think that, without appropriate training and supervision, even otherwise duly qualified child clinical psychologists should engage in the type of neuropsychological assessment procedures that are reviewed in this chapter. Guidelines for the training that would qualify one to do this are readily available (Reports of the INS-Division 40 Task Force, 1987). Be that as it may, we hope that the material contained in this chapter is of sufficient interest to whet the reader's appetite for further investigation in this complex area.

REFERENCES

Applebee, A.N. (1971). Research in reading retardation: Two critical problems. *Journal of Child Psychology and Psychiatry, 12,* 91–113.

Bakker, D.J. (1986). Electrophysiological validation of L- and P-type dyslexia. *Journal of Clinical and Experimental Neuropsychology, 8,* 133.

Bakker, D.J. (1990). *Neuropsychological treatment of dyslexia.* New York: Oxford University Press.

Bakker, D.J., Licht, R., & Van Strien, J. (1991). Biopsychological validation of L- and P-type dyslexia. In B.P. Rourke (Ed.), *Neuropsychological validation of learning disability subtypes* (pp. 124–139). New York: Guilford Press.

Benton, A.L. (1975). Developmental dyslexia: Neurological aspects. In W.J. Friedlander (Ed.), *Advances in neurology* (Vol. 7, pp. 1–41). New York: Raven Press.

Brandys, C.F., & Rourke, B.P. (1991). Differential memory capacities in reading- and arithmetic-disabled children. In B.P. Rourke (Ed.), *Neuropsychological validation of learning disability subtypes* (pp. 73–96). New York: Guilford Press.

Brown, S.J., Rourke, B.P., & Cicchetti, D.V. (1989). Reliability of tests and measures used in the neuropsychological assessment of children. *The Clinical Neuropsychologist, 3,* 353–368.

Butler, K., Rourke, B.P., Fuerst, D.R., & Fisk, J.L. (1997). A typology of psychosocial functioning in pediatric closed-head injury. *Child Neuropsychology, 3,* 98–133.

Casey, J.E., & Rourke, B.P. (1991). Construct validation of the nonverbal learning disabilities syndrome and model. In B.P. Rourke (Ed.), *Neuropsychological validation of learning disability subtypes* (pp. 271–292). New York: Guilford Press.

Casey, J.E., Rourke, B.P., & Del Dotto, J.E. (1996). Learning disabilities in children with attention deficit disorder with and without hyperactivity. *Child Neuropsychology, 2,* 83–98.

Casey, J.E., Rourke, B.P., & Picard, E.M. (1991). Syndrome of nonverbal learning disabilities: Age differences in neuropsychological, academic, and socioemotional functioning. *Development and Psychopathology, 3,* 331–347.

Ceci, S.J. (1986). *Handbook of cognitive, social, and neuropsychological aspects of learning disabilities* (Vol. 1). Hillsdale, NJ: Erlbaum.

Ceci, S.J. (1987). *Handbook of cognitive, social, and neuropsychological aspects of learning disabilities* (Vol. 2). Hillsdale, NJ: Erlbaum.

Czudner, G., & Rourke, B.P. (1972). Age differences in visual reaction time in "brain-damaged" and normal children under regular and irregular preparatory interval conditions. *Journal of Experimental Child Psychology, 13,* 516–526.

Del Dotto, J.E., Fisk, J.L., McFadden, G.T., & Rourke, B.P. (1991). Developmental analysis of children/adolescents with nonverbal learning disabilities: Long-term impact on personality adjustment and patterns of adaptive functioning. In B.P. Rourke (Ed.), *Neuropsychological validation of learning disability subtypes* (pp. 293–308). New York: Guilford Press.

Doehring, D.G. (1978). The tangled web of behavioral research on developmental dyslexia. In A.L. Benton & D. Pearl (Eds.), *Dyslexia: An appraisal of current knowledge* (pp. 125–135). New York: Oxford University Press.

Doehring, D.G., & Hoshko, I.M. (1977). Classification of reading problems by the Q-technique of factor analysis. *Cortex, 13,* 281–294.

Doehring, D.G., Hoshko, I.M., & Bryans, B.N. (1979). Statistical classification of children with reading problems. *Journal of Clinical Neuropsychology, 1,* 5–16.

Dool, C.B., Stelmack, R.M., & Rourke, B.P. (1993). Event-related potentials in children with learning disabilities. *Journal of Clinical Child Psychology, 22,* 387–398.

Fiedorowicz, C.A.M., & Trites, R.L. (1991). From theory to practice with subtypes of reading disabilities. In B.P. Rourke (Ed.), *Neuropsychological validation of learning disability subtypes* (pp. 243–266). New York: Guilford Press.

Fisher, N.J., DeLuca, J.W., & Rourke, B.P. (1997). Wisconsin Card Sorting Test and Halstead Category Test performances of children and adolescents who exhibit the syndrome of nonverbal learning disabilities. *Child Neuropsychology, 3,* 61–70.

Fisk, J.L., & Rourke, B.P. (1979). Identification of subtypes of learning-disabled children at three age levels: A neuropsychological, multivariate approach. *Journal of Clinical Neuropsychology, 1,* 289–310.

Fletcher, J.M. (1985). External validation of learning disability typologies. In B.P. Rourke (Ed.), *Neuropsychology of learning disabilities: Essentials of subtype analysis* (pp. 187–211). New York: Guilford Press.

Fletcher, J.M., Espy, K.A., Francis, D.J., Davidson, K.C., Rourke, B.P., & Shaywitz, S.E. (1989). Comparisons of cutoff score and regression-based definitions of reading disabilities. *Journal of Learning Disabilities, 22,* 334–338.

Fletcher, J.M., Francis, D.J., Rourke, B.P., Shaywitz, S.E., & Shaywitz, B.A. (1992). The validity of discrepancy-based definitions of reading disabilities. *Journal of Learning Disabilities, 25,* 555–561.

Fletcher, J.M., Francis, D.J., Rourke, B.P., Shaywitz, S.E., & Shaywitz, B.A. (1993). Classification of learning disabilities: Relationships with other childhood disorders. In G.R. Lyon, D.B. Gray, J.F. Kavanagh, & N.A. Krasnegor (Eds.), *Better understanding learning disabilities: New views from research and their implications for education and public policies* (pp. 27–55). Baltimore: Brookes.

Fletcher, J.M., & Satz, P. (1980). Developmental changes in the neuropsychological correlates of reading achievement: A six-year longitudinal follow-up. *Journal of Clinical Neuropsychology, 2,* 23–37.

Fletcher, J.M., Stuebing, K.K., Shaywitz, B.A., Shaywitz, S.E., Rourke, B.P., & Francis, D.J. (1994). Validity of the concept of dyslexia: Alternative approaches to definition and classification. In K.P. van den Bos, L.S. Siegel, D.J. Bakker, & D.L. Share (Eds.), *Current directions in dyslexia research* (pp. 31–43). Amsterdam, The Netherlands: Swets & Zeitlinger.

Fletcher, J.M., & Taylor, H.G. (1984). Neuropsychological approaches to children: Toward a developmental neuropsychology. *Journal of Clinical Neuropsychology, 6,* 39–56.

Francis, D.J., Fletcher, J.M., & Rourke, B.P. (1988). Discriminant validity of lateral sensorimotor measures in children. *Journal of Clinical and Experimental Neuropsychology, 10,* 779–799.

Francis, D.J., Fletcher, J.M., Rourke, B.P., & York, M.J. (1992). A five-factor model for motor, psychomotor, and visual-spatial tests used in the neuropsychological assessment of children. *Journal of Clinical and Experimental Neuropsychology, 14,* 625–637.

Francis, D.J., Fletcher, J.M., Shaywitz, B.A., Shaywitz, S.E., & Rourke, B.P. (1996). Defining learning and language disabilities: Conceptual and psychometric issues with the use of IQ tests. *Language, Speech, and Hearing Sciences in Schools, 27,* 132–143.

Fuerst, D.R., Fisk, J.L., & Rourke, B.P. (1989). Psychosocial functioning of learning-disabled children: Replicability of statistically derived subtypes. *Journal of Consulting and Clinical Psychology, 57,* 275–280.

Fuerst, D.R., Fisk, J.L., & Rourke, B.P. (1990). Psychosocial functioning of learning-disabled children: Relations between WISC Verbal IQ–Performance, IQ discrepancies, and personality subtypes. *Journal of Consulting and Clinical Psychology, 58,* 657–660.

Fuerst, D.R., & Rourke, B.P. (1993). Psychosocial functioning of children: Relations between personality subtypes and academic achievement. *Journal of Abnormal Child Psychology, 21,* 597–607.

Fuerst, D.R., & Rourke, B.P. (1995). Psychosocial functioning of children with learning disabilities at three age levels. *Child Neuropsychology, 1,* 38–55.

Gaddes, W.H. (1985). *Learning disabilities and brain function* (2nd ed.). New York: Springer-Verlag.

Harnadek, M.C.S., & Rourke, B.P. (1994). Principal identifying features of the syndrome of nonverbal learning disabilities in children. *Journal of Learning Disabilities, 27,* 144–154.

Johnson, D.J., & Myklebust, H.R. (1967). *Learning disabilities.* New York: Grune & Stratton.

Joschko, M., & Rourke, B.P. (1985). Neuropsychological subtypes of learning-disabled children who exhibit the ACID pattern on the WISC. In B.P. Rourke (Ed.), *Neuropsychology of learning disabilities: Essentials of subtype analysis* (pp. 65–88). New York: Guilford Press.

Kirk, S.A., & McCarthy, J.J. (1961). The Illinois Test of Psycholinguistic Abilities: An approach to differential diagnosis. *American Journal of Mental Deficiency, 66,* 399–412.

Klin, A., Volkmar, F.R., Sparrow, S.S., Cicchetti, D.V., & Rourke, B.P. (1995). Validity and neuropsychological characterization of Asperger syndrome: Convergence with nonverbal learning disabilities syndrome. *Journal of Child Psychology and Psychiatry, 36,* 1127–1140.

Loveland, K.A., Fletcher, J.M., & Bailey, V. (1990). Nonverbal communication of events in learning-disability subtypes. *Journal of Clinical and Experimental Neuropsychology, 12,* 433–447.

Lyon, G.R. (1985). Educational validation studies of learning disability subtypes. In B.P. Rourke (Ed.), *Neuropsychology of learning disabilities: Essentials of subtype analysis* (pp. 257–280). New York: Guilford Press.

Lyon, G.R., & Flynn, J.M. (1991). Educational validation studies with subtypes of learning-disabled readers. In B.P. Rourke (Ed.), *Neuropsychological validation of learning disability subtypes* (pp. 223–242). New York: Guilford Press.

Mattis, S., French, J.H., & Rapin, I. (1975). Dyslexia in children and young adults: Three independent neuropsychological syndromes. *Developmental Medicine and Child Neurology, 17,* 150–163.

McKinney, J.D., Short, E.J., & Feagans, L. (1985). Academic consequences of perceptual-linguistic subtypes of learning-disabled children. *Learning Disabilities Research, 1,* 6–17.

Morris, R., Blashfield, R., & Satz, P. (1981). Neuropsychology and cluster analysis: Potentials and problems. *Journal of Clinical Neuropsychology, 3,* 79–99.

Morris, R., Blashfield, R., & Satz, P. (1986). Developmental classification of reading-disabled children. *Journal of Clinical and Experimental Neuropsychology, 8,* 371–392.

Morris, R.D., & Fletcher, J.M. (1988). Classification in neuropsychology: A theoretical framework and research paradigm. *Journal of Clinical and Experimental Neuropsychology, 10,* 640–658.

Myklebust, H.R. (1975). Nonverbal learning disabilities: Assessment and intervention. In H.R. Myklebust (Ed.), *Progress in learning disabilities* (Vol. 3, pp. 85–121). New York: Grune & Stratton.

Ozols, E.J., & Rourke, B.P. (1985). Dimensions of social sensitivity in two types of learning-disabled children. In B.P. Rourke (Ed.), *Neuropsychology of learning disabilities: Essentials of subtype analysis* (pp. 281–301). New York: Guilford Press.

Ozols, E.J., & Rourke, B.P. (1988). Characteristics of young learning-disabled children classified according to patterns of academic achievement: Auditory-perceptual and visual-perceptual disabilities. *Journal of Clinical Child Psychology, 17,* 44–52.

Ozols, E.J., & Rourke, B.P. (1991). Classification of young learning-disabled children according to patterns of academic achievement: Validity studies. In B.P. Rourke (Ed.), *Neuropsychological validation of learning disability subtypes* (pp. 97–123). New York: Guilford Press.

Pelletier, P.M., Ahmad, S., & Rourke, B.P. (in press). *NLD and BPPD: Rules for classification and a comparison of psychosocial subtypes.*

Petrauskas, R.J., & Rourke, B.P. (1979). Identification of subtypes of retarded readers: A neuropsychological, multivariate approach. *Journal of Clinical Neuropsychology, 1,* 17–37.

Porter, J.E., & Rourke, B.P. (1985). Personality and socioemotional dimensions of learning disabilities in children. In B.P. Rourke (Ed.), *Neuropsychology of learning disabilities: Essentials of subtype analysis* (pp. 257–280). New York: Guilford Press.

Reitan, R.M. (1966). A research program on the psychological effects of brain lesions in human beings. In N.R. Ellis (Ed.), *International review of research in mental retardation* (Vol. 1, pp. 153–218). New York: Academic Press.

Reitan, R.M. (1974). Methodological problems in clinical neuropsychology. In R.M. Reitan & L.A. Davison (Eds.), *Clinical neuropsychology: Current status and applications* (pp. 19–46). New York: Wiley.

Reports of the INS-Division 40 Task Force on Education, Accreditation, and Credentialing. (1987). Guidelines for doctoral training programs in clinical neuropsychology. *The Clinical Neuropsychologist, 1,* 29–34.

Rourke, B.P. (1975). Brain-behavior relationships in children with learning disabilities. *American Psychologist, 30,* 911–920.

Rourke, B.P. (1976). Issues in the neuropsychological assessment of children with learning disabilities. *Canadian Psychological Review, 17,* 89–102.

Rourke, B.P. (1978a). Neuropsychological research in reading retardation: A review. In A.L. Benton & D. Pearl (Eds.), *Dyslexia: An appraisal of current knowledge* (pp. 141–171). New York: Oxford University Press.

Rourke, B.P. (1978b). Reading, spelling, arithmetic disabilities: A neuropsychologic perspective. In H.R. Myklebust (Ed.), *Progress in learning disabilities* (Vol. 4, pp. 97–120). New York: Grune & Stratton.

Rourke, B.P. (1981). Neuropsychological assessment of children with learning disabilities. In S.B. Filskov & T.J. Boll (Eds.), *Handbook of clinical neuropsychology* (pp. 453–478). New York: Wiley-Interscience.

Rourke, B.P. (1982). Central processing deficiencies in children: Toward a developmental neuropsychological model. *Journal of Clinical Neuropsychology, 4,* 1–18.

Rourke, B.P. (1983a). Outstanding issues in research on learning disabilities. In M. Rutter (Ed.), *Developmental neuropsychiatry* (pp. 564–574). New York: Guilford Press.

Rourke, B.P. (1983b). Reading and spelling disabilities: A developmental neuropsychological perspective. In U. Kirk (Ed.), *Neuropsychology of language, reading, and spelling* (pp. 209–234). New York: Academic Press.

Rourke, B.P. (Ed.). (1985). *Neuropsychology of learning disabilities: Essentials of subtype analysis.* New York: Guilford Press.

Rourke, B.P. (1987). Syndrome of nonverbal learning disabilities: The final common pathway of white-matter disease/dysfunction? *The Clinical Neuropsychologist, 1,* 209–234.

Rourke, B.P. (1988a). Socioemotional disturbances of learning-disabled children. *Journal of Consulting and Clinical Psychology, 56,* 801–810.

Rourke, B.P. (1988b). The syndrome of nonverbal learning disabilities: Developmental manifestations in neurological disease, disorder, and dysfunction. *The Clinical Neuropsychologist, 2,* 293–330.

Rourke, B.P. (1989). *Nonverbal learning disabilities: The syndrome and the model.* New York: Guilford Press.

Rourke, B.P. (Ed.). (1991). *Neuropsychological validation of learning disability subtypes.* New York: Guilford Press.

Rourke, B.P. (1993). Arithmetic disabilities, specific and otherwise: A neuropsychological perspective. *Journal of Learning Disabilities, 26,* 214–226.

Rourke, B.P. (1994). Neuropsychological assessment of children with learning disabilities: Measurement issues. In G.R. Lyon (Ed.), *Frames of reference for the assessment of learning disabilities: New views on measurement issues* (pp. 475–514). Baltimore: Brookes.

Rourke, B.P. (1995). The science of practice and the practice of science: The scientist-practitioner model in clinical neuropsychology. *Canadian Psychology, 36,* 259–287.

Rourke, B.P., & Adams, K.M. (1984). Quantitative approaches to the neuropsychological assessment of children. In R.E. Tarter & G. Goldstein (Eds.), *Advances in clinical neuropsychology* (Vol. 2, pp. 79–108). New York: Plenum Press.

Rourke, B.P., Bakker, D.J., Fisk, J.L., & Strang, J.D. (1983). *Child neuropsychology: An introduction to theory, research, and clinical practice.* New York: Guilford Press.

Rourke, B.P., & Conway, J.A. (1997). Disabilities of arithmetic and mathematical reasoning: Perspectives from neurology and neuropsychology. *Journal of Learning Disabilities, 30,* 34–46.

Rourke, B.P., & Czudner, G. (1972). Age differences in auditory reaction time in "brain-damaged" and normal children under regular and irregular preparatory interval conditions. *Journal of Experimental Child Psychology, 14,* 372–378.

Rourke, B.P., & Del Dotto, J.E. (1994). *Learning disabilities: A neuropsychological perspective.* Thousand Oaks, CA: Sage.

Rourke, B.P., Del Dotto, J.E., Rourke, S.B., & Casey, J.E. (1990). Nonverbal learning disabilities: The syndrome and a case study. *Journal of School Psychology, 28,* 361–385.

Rourke, B.P., Dietrich, D.M., & Young, G.C. (1973). Significance of WISC verbal-performance discrepancies for younger children with learning disabilities. *Perceptual and Motor Skills, 36,* 275–282.

Rourke, B.P., & Finlayson, M.A.J. (1978). Neuropsychological significance of variations in patterns of academic performance: Verbal and visual abilities. *Journal of Abnormal Child Psychology, 6,* 121–133.

Rourke, B.P., & Fisk, J.L. (1981). Socio-emotional disturbances of learning disabled children: The role of central processing deficits. *Bulletin of the Orton Society, 31,* 77–88.

Rourke, B.P., & Fisk, J.L. (1988). Subtypes of learning-disabled children: Implications for a neurodevelopmental model of differential hemispheric processing. In D.L. Molfese & S.J. Segalowitz (Eds.), *Developmental implications of brain lateralization* (pp. 547–565). New York: Guilford Press.

Rourke, B.P., & Fisk, J.L. (1992). Adult presentations of learning disabilities. In R.F. White (Ed.), *Clinical syndromes in adult neuropsychology: The practitioner's handbook* (pp. 451–473). Amsterdam, The Netherlands: Elsevier.

Rourke, B.P., Fisk, J.L., & Strang, J.D. (1986). *Neuropsychological assessment of children: A treatment-oriented approach.* New York: Guilford Press.

Rourke, B.P., & Fuerst, D.R. (1991). *Learning disabilities and psychosocial functioning: A neuropsychological perspective.* New York: Guilford Press.

Rourke, B.P., & Fuerst, D.R. (1992). Psychosocial dimensions of learning disability subtypes: Neuropsychological studies in the Windsor Laboratory. *School Psychology Review, 21,* 360–373.

Rourke, B.P., & Fuerst, D.R. (1995). Cognitive processing, academic achievement, and psychosocial functioning: A neuropsychological perspective. In D. Cicchetti & D. Cohen (Eds.), *Developmental psychopathology* (Vol. 1, pp. 391–423). New York: Wiley.

Rourke, B.P., & Fuerst, D.R. (1996). Psychosocial dimensions of learning disability subtypes. *Assessment, 3,* 277–290.

Rourke, B.P., & Gates, R.D. (1981). Neuropsychological research and school psychology. In G.W. Hynd & J.E. Obrzut (Eds.), *Neuropsychological assessment and the school-age child: Issues and procedures* (pp. 3–25). New York: Grune & Stratton.

Rourke, B.P., & Strang, J.D. (1978). Neuropsychological significance of variations in patterns of academic performance: Motor, psychomotor, and tactile-perceptual abilities. *Journal of Pediatric Psychology, 3,* 62–66.

Rourke, B.P., & Strang, J.D. (1983). Subtypes of reading and arithmetical disabilities: A neuropsychological analysis. In M. Rutter (Ed.), *Developmental neuropsychiatry* (pp. 473–488). New York: Guilford Press.

Rourke, B.P., & Tsatsanis, K.D. (1996). Syndrome of nonverbal learning disabilities: Psycholinguistic assets and deficits. *Topics in Language Disorders, 16,* 30–44.

Rourke, B.P., Young, G.C., & Leenaars, A. (1989). A childhood learning disability that predisposes those afflicted to adolescent and adult depression and suicide risk. *Journal of Learning Disabilities, 21,* 169–175.

Rourke, B.P., Young, G.C., Strang, J.D., & Russell, D.L. (1986). Adult outcomes of central processing deficiencies in childhood. In I. Grant & K.M. Adams (Eds.), *Neuropsychological assessment in neuropsychiatric disorders: Clinical methods and empirical findings* (pp. 244–267). New York: Oxford University Press.

Russell, D.L., & Rourke, B.P. (1991). Concurrent and predictive validity of phonetic accuracy of misspellings in normal and disabled readers and spellers. In B.P. Rourke (Ed.), *Neuropsychological validation of learning disability subtypes* (pp. 57–72). New York: Guilford Press.

Stelmack, R.M., Rourke, B.P., & van der Vlugt, H. (1995). Intelligence, learning disabilities, and event-related potentials. *Developmental Neuropsychology, 11,* 445–465.

Strang, J.D., & Rourke, B.P. (1983). Concept-formation/non-verbal reasoning abilities of children who exhibit specific academic problems with arithmetic. *Journal of Clinical Child Psychology, 12,* 33–39.

Strang, J.D., & Rourke, B.P. (1985a). Adaptive behavior of children with specific arithmetic disabilities and associated neuropsychological abilities and deficits. In B.P. Rourke (Ed.), *Neuropsychology of learning disabilities: Essentials of subtype analysis* (pp. 302–328). New York: Guilford Press.

Strang, J.D., & Rourke, B.P. (1985b). Arithmetic disability subtypes: The neuropsychological significance of specific arithmetical impairment in childhood. In B.P. Rourke (Ed.), *Neuropsychology of learning disabilities: Essentials of subtype analysis* (pp. 167–183). New York: Guilford Press.

Sweeney, J.E., & Rourke, B.P. (1985). Spelling disability subtypes. In B.P. Rourke (Ed.), *Neuropsychology of learning disabilities: Essentials of subtype analysis* (pp. 147–166). New York: Guilford Press.

Taylor, H.G. (1983). MBD: Meanings and misconceptions. *Journal of Clinical Neuropsychology, 5,* 271–287.

Taylor, II.G. (1989). Learning disabilities. In E.J. Mash & R.A. Barkley (Eds.), *Behavioral treatment of childhood disorders* (pp. 347–380). New York: Guilford Press.

Taylor, H.G., & Fletcher, J.M. (1983). Biological foundations of specific developmental disorders: Methods, findings, and future directions. *Journal of Clinical Child Psychology, 12,* 46–65.

Torgeson, J.K. (1997). The prevention and remediation of reading disability: Evaluating what we know from research. *Journal of Academic Language Therapy, 1,* 11–47.

Tsatsanis, K.D., Fuerst, D.R., & Rourke, B.P. (1997). Psychosocial dimensions of learning disabilities: External validation and relationship with age and academic functioning. *Journal of Learning Disabilities, 30,* 490–502.

Tsatsanis, K.D., & Rourke, B.P. (1995). Conclusions and future directions. In B.P. Rourke (Ed.), *Syndrome of nonverbal learning disabilities: Neurodevelopmental manifestations* (pp. 476–496). New York: Guilford Press.

CHAPTER 30

Disorders of Communication: Developmental Language Disorders and Cleft Palate

LYNN C. RICHMAN AND MICHELE J. ELIASON

The psychological aspects of language and speech disorders in children are relatively new considerations for many clinical child psychologists. Few child psychologists specialize in communication disorders, and much of the clinical information available is found in the speech and language or neuropsychological literature. Speech and language clinicians usually treat speech problems such as developmental articulation errors, primary stuttering, and voice disorders. However, with recent research in neuropsychology, language disorders, learning disabilities, and pediatric psychology, there are increasing requests for the clinical child psychologist to diagnose and treat children with language or communication disorders.

Child psychologists are usually not trained to evaluate children with communication disorders. A language-disordered child may be misdiagnosed as unmotivated when learning problems are not identified or as emotionally disturbed when unusual language associations are observed. There are several manifestations of communication disorder that require psychological expertise. Childhood attention deficits, behavioral problems, and anxiety may be related to subtle speech or language disorders, and some thought disorders might be secondary to language disorders.

The purpose of this chapter is to review psychological research on communication disorders to provide the child psychologist with a clinical perspective on diagnosis and treatment of such children. Two general groups of communication-disordered children are examined as examples: those with language disorders and those with cleft palate. Language disorders occur in an extremely high number of children with learning, behavior, and emotional disorders. Cleft palate is one of the most frequently occurring congenital anomalies in children, and children with cleft palate frequently have speech and language problems as well as facial disfigurement.

LANGUAGE DISORDERS

A developmental language disorder exists when there is a deficiency in expressing or understanding verbal communication that is not due primarily to mental retardation, hearing loss, or defect in the oral mechanism. The term "language" is used to refer to the symbolic system used for human communication purposes. Speech is the verbal articulation of language expression, and verbal mediation is the use of the symbolic language system in thinking. There are primary language disorders and secondary language disorders, which are due to other conditions such as cleft palate and brain injury. Gilger (1997) reviewed genetic aspects of language disorders and Rapin (1996) reviewed neurological and biological aspects of language disorders. Language disorders may be accompanied by speech disorders. For an extensive review of disorders related to speech articulation, phonological processing, verbal apraxia, and aphasia, see Aram (1984), Korkman and Hakkinen-Rihu (1994), and Ludlow (1980).

Possible etiologies of childhood language disorder include genetic factors (Gilger, 1997), atypical cerebral lateralization of language functions (Geschwind & Galaburda, 1987), and impairment of left hemisphere functions (Rapin, 1996). However, given present knowledge and technology, most children with developmental language disorders must be assessed and treated without confirmation of genetic or neurological etiology. Language disorders have been reported in approximately 5% to 10 % of the childhood population (Cantwell & Baker, 1991).

Montgomery, Windsor, and Stark (1991) pointed out the pervasive nature of language-based learning disabilities associated with dyslexia. Some specific aspects of impaired linguistic functioning that have been found in reading-disabled populations include verbal labeling or disnomia, auditory perception or comprehension, and phonological production or dyspraxia (Korkman & Hakkinen-Rihu, 1994). There is increasing evidence that many different types of language deficits should be considered when assessing the child with a learning disability. Furthermore, it has been shown that reading disability may be only one symptom of an underlying language disorder. It has also been suggested that subtyping language disorders, similar to what has been done in the subtyping studies of learning disorders, may provide more definitive clinical groupings (Wilson & Risucci, 1986). However, until more research is accomplished in this area, the clinician must rely on present diagnostic models.

The current diagnostic nomenclature for psychological diagnosis of developmental language disorders (DLDs) is the *Diagnostic and Statistical Manual of Mental Disorders* (*DSM-IV*; APA, 1994). This manual distinguishes three primary types of DLD: expressive, phonological, and mixed receptive-expressive. The diagnosis of DLD is made only if the impairment negatively affects academic achievement. Expressive types of DLD generally have a better prognosis than receptive types. Many children with mild expressive DLD develop out of the disorder by school age, but approximately 40% do not (Aram & Hall, 1989). Children with receptive or mixed DLD have an even more variable prognosis, with some affected for life. The primary objective criterion most often used to diagnose DLD is a discrepancy in standard test scores, such as significantly lower scores on a test of language (receptive or expressive) than on an individually administered nonverbal IQ test.

A high frequency of behavioral and psychiatric diagnoses coexist in children with DLD. The rate of other psychiatric disorders has been reported as 45% for children with speech and language disorders and over 90% for children with "pure" language disorders (Cantwell & Baker, 1991). These same investigators found that 25% were diagnosed with behavior disorder and 20% received a diagnosis of an emotional disorder. For a more detailed review of behavior and emotional disorders in children with DLD, see Piacentini (1987).

INTELLECTUAL AND COGNITIVE SYMPTOMS

The lack of an agreed upon, empirically derived classification system for identifying subgroups of language-disordered children has limited the study of intellectual characteristics of homogeneous samples of DLD children. There is disagreement regarding what intelligence test should be used to test children with DLD. Johnson and Myklebust (1967) recommended use of both Verbal and Performance IQ on the Wechsler Intelligence Scale for Children (WISC), although they cautioned that the Full-Scale IQ should not be used if there is a significant discrepancy between the two. Eisenson (1972) recommended the use of intelligence tests that do not require oral language or verbal mediation. He suggested the Leiter International Performance Scale and Raven's Progressive Matrices to eliminate verbal mediation and the Peabody Picture Vocabulary Test to eliminate oral response. However, even when only a nonverbal IQ test was used to identify average intelligence, this disqualified over 50% of the children in classes for the language impaired (Ludlow, 1980). It is important to evaluate language functions beyond that provided on a standard intelligence test in assessing children with DLD.

ASSESSMENT

The child psychologist is frequently involved in diagnostic assessment of DLD children because educational placement and treatment decisions are based on laws and guidelines requiring assessment of intellectual ability. Questions may arise after the psychologist has administered a standard intelligence test such as the WISC-III to a language-disordered child. Some common intellectual patterns and related clinical questions are listed below:

1. All three IQ scores (Verbal, Performance, Full-Scale) are significantly below average:
    a. Is the child more generally mentally retarded than language-disordered?
    b. What if the child has a receptive language problem that results in confusion of directions even on the Performance section?
    c. What if the child has a developmental motor dyscoordination with a motor speech deficit, lowering Verbal IQ, and an eye-hand motor deficit, lowering Performance IQ?
2. Verbal IQ is significantly below Performance IQ, by 15 points or more, and Performance IQ is 90 or above:
    a. Does the lower Verbal Scale indicate a language disorder?
    b. If the answer to 2a is yes, is the language disorder general or specific?
3. Both Verbal IQ and Performance IQ are greater than 90 and are not significantly different:
    a. Does this suggest that the child does not have a language disability?
    b. What other tests should be administered to answer 3a?

A review of the research on commonly occurring cognitive deficits of language-disordered children provides some direction related to psychological assessment. As recommended by Korkman and Hakkinen-Rihu (1994), currently derived subtypes of children with DLD should not be considered as clear diagnostic subgroups, but as providing specific dimensions of language that should be assessed. Because there is very little agreement regarding discrete subtypes of language-disordered children, this section reviews specific language symptoms within the context of developmental aphasia. The terms "childhood aphasia" and "developmental aphasia" have been used to refer to children with delayed or disordered language development even though definitive neurological evidence is lacking. The term "dysphasia" is frequently used to indicate a delay in acquisition of language function, as distinct from aphasia, which is loss of a previously acquired language function. Some of the most frequently reported symptoms of children with developmental dysphasia or language disorder include the following:

1. *Auditory perception deficit:* Inability to discriminate phonetic sounds and to synthesize phonetic units into words (Tallal, Stark, & Mellitis, 1985).
2. *Naming and labeling deficits:* Inability to name common objects or pictures (Denkla & Rudel, 1976; Wilson & Risucci, 1986).
3. *Auditory memory deficit:* Memory deficits for isolated content, meaningful material (e.g., sentences), and verbally mediated memory—even when stimulus and response are non-aural (Lindgren & Richman, 1984; Wilson & Risucci, 1986).
4. *Serial-order processing deficit:* Errors in sequence or order rather than in memory span per se (Torgesen, 1982; Wood, Richman, & Eliason, 1989).
5. *Verbal concept formation and language association deficit:* Categorization of words and verbal association (Korkman & Hakkinen-Rihu, 1994; Lindgren, Richman, & Eliason, 1986; Richman & Kitchell, 1981; Richman & Lindgren, 1980; Vellutino, 1979; Wood & Richman, 1988).

There are comprehensive neuropsychological language test batteries developed or normed specifically for children, such as the Illinois Test of Psycholinguistic Abilities (McCarthy & Kirk, 1961), the Neurosensory Center Comprehensive Examination for Aphasia (Crockett, 1974; Spreen & Benton, 1969), the Reynell Developmental Language Scale (Reynell, 1969), the Hiskey–Nebraska Test of Learning Aptitude (Hiskey, 1966), and the Detroit Tests of Learning Aptitude (Hammill, 1985). However, further work is needed in development and standardization of language assessment batteries for children with DLD (Ludlow, 1980; Ludlow & Cooper, 1983). Recent development of assessment includes the Neuropsychological Investigation for Children (Korkman, Kirk, & Kemp, 1998). At the present time, the child psychologist must rely on a combination of intellectual, neuropsychological, and language assessment techniques in assessing the child with language disorder. It is recommended that the examiner select tests from various batteries with proven clinical usefulness and adequate psychometric properties. Selected subtests in the areas of verbal fluency, auditory memory, associative language, and auditory processing are usually useful in the diagnosis of subtypes of language disorders (Richman, 1983).

During the evaluation, the psychologist should be alert to symptoms that might suggest a language disorder. Some speech articulation errors may be associated with underlying language disorders (Rapin, 1996). The clinician should also note other signs of language disorder that may be detected during assessment:

1. Word-finding or naming problems.
2. Telegraphic speech (omission of articles, connectives, and prepositions, yet maintaining meaning).
3. Circumlocutions (roundabout explanations that do not quite answer the question).
4. Delayed verbal response (long latencies before responding or answering a previous question during the response to a later question).

These symptoms should be recorded and alert the examiner to the possibility of a language disorder; however, they may not be reflected in the actual test scores.

There are numerous tests of each language area, and the choice of a specific test may be less critical than making sure several tests of each area are administered (Wilson & Risucci, 1986). The tests in Table 30.1 have proven useful in our research and clinical evaluation of children with language disorders. The Hiskey–Nebraska Test of Learning Aptitude has assisted in identifying three separate subgroups of children with language-based learning disability and a low Verbal/high Performance WISC profile (Richman, 1983; Richman & Lindgren, 1980).

Table 30.1 Test to evaluate differential language functions.

Associative Language – Expressive
  Similarities: Wechsler Intelligence Scale for Children (WISC-R)
  Auditory Association: Illinois Test of Psycholinguistic Ability (ITPA)
  Word Fluency: Neurosensory Center Comprehensive Examination for Aphasia (NCCEA)

Associative Language – Receptive or Mediational
  Picture Association: Hiskey–Nebraska Test of Learning Aptitude
  Visual Association: ITPA
  Token Test: Multilingual Aphasia Battery (MLAB)

Naming and Word Finding
  Visual Naming: MLAB
  Boston Naming Test
  Rapid Automatized Naming

Sequencing-Memory (auditory, vocal)
  Digit Span: WISC-R
  Rey Auditory Verbal Learning Test
  Sentence Repetition: NCCEA

Sequencing-Memory (verbally mediated, nonvocal)
  Memory for Color: Hiskey
  Visual Attention Span: Hiskey

Intramodal and Intermodal Memory
  Color Span Test (Richman & Lindgren, 1984)

Auditory Processing
  Sound Blending: ITPA
  Dichotic Listening
  Phoneme Discrimination

Because the Hiskey allows evaluation of verbal mediation skills (even though stimulus and response can be nonvocal), it is well suited for children with DLD. A factor analysis of WISC and Hiskey scores identified three separate subgroups of DLD children with deficits in sequencing-memory, associative reasoning, or both (Richman & Lindgren, 1980). This test is currently being renormed by the Psychological Corporation.

Based on this battery of selected tests, several patterns of language strengths and weaknesses usually emerge. If there are no weaknesses in any of the areas assessed, other factors may have been overlooked and a primary language disorder should not be diagnosed. Emotional or environmental problems are the most frequent factors that might produce symptoms similar to a primary language disorder.

EDUCATIONAL CONSIDERATIONS FOR LANGUAGE DISORDER SUBTYPES

Some children will demonstrate deficits on all of the subtests of the language battery. When this occurs, the child is most likely diagnosed as having a general language disorder. These children usually will show deficits in all areas of academic achievement. If there are deficiencies in both memory and associative language functions and in both receptive and expressive modalities, the child likely will require some type of self-contained learning program such as classes for children with communication disorders or learning disabilities. However, many language-disordered children display differential strengths and weaknesses in expressive language, associative language, and memory functions. When this occurs, it is important to relate the language strength or weakness to differential learning styles and provide a comprehensive treatment program. We have developed clinical and statistical language disability subtypes through several research studies and clinical investigations from which the following clinical observations and recommendations are made (Eliason & Richman, 1988a; Lindgren & Richman, 1984; Richman, 1979, 1983; Richman & Lindgren, 1980; Richman & Wood, 1999; Wood & Richman, 1988; Wood et al., 1989).

Language Disorder: Expressive (LDE)

These children perform relatively well on most language tests except for those requiring rapid word-finding, such as Verbal Fluency, Visual Naming, and Boston Naming. They demonstrate adequate associative language functions on most tests; however, when there is a requirement of spontaneous vocal response, they may show problems (e.g., in comprehension or vocabulary). These children usually display variable performance on auditory memory tests not because of a memory span deficit per se, but usually due to difficulty in automatic verbal rehearsal or spontaneous vocal responding. Children with LDE typically show difficulties in sequencing and temporal order rather than in specific memory capacity. A useful clinical technique is to ask this child to tell a simple story out loud because this will permit consideration of the oral expressive difficulties related to halting speech, word-finding difficulty, and telegraphic speech. It is important for the clinician to determine whether an expressive language problem may be masked by children who give no response or an "I don't know" response to verbal test questions.

Educational considerations for the LDE child include making sure the child is not mistakenly held back in reading due to the expressive deficit. These children usually will have slightly below average word recognition skills and slow reading rates. Their reading pattern is usually a combination of phonetic and sight word errors, but they often have better reading comprehension. However, their expressive problems in oral reading may affect comprehension. They may show better comprehension on silent reading tests. Educational strategies beneficial to children with LDE include the following:

1. Reading rate may be increased by practicing speed reading on easy passages.
2. Use of flash cards and other visual aids is usually helpful (although this is not the case with most other language-disordered children).
3. Mnemonic strategies to assist these children with their word-finding difficulties.
4. Spelling is usually impaired, although this is secondary to the reading problem, and giving them extra time on spelling tests is beneficial.
5. Severe cases should receive individual or small-group expressive language therapy using procedures similar to those for expressive aphasia.

Language Disorder: Memory (LDM)

These children typically do well on language tasks that require verbal associations in reasoning and do poorly on sequencing and memory tasks. They may be identified by a WISC and Hiskey pattern that includes low Verbal/high Performance, along with higher scores on Similarities and Block Design (WISC) as well as Picture Association and Block Patterns (Hiskey). They also typically have lower scores on Arithmetic, Digit Span, and Hiskey memory tasks. Further information on identification is elaborated in several studies (Richman, 1979; Richman & Lindgren, 1980; Wood et al., 1989).

The primary educational problems of LDM children are related to memory and sequencing difficulties. They have difficulty remembering words by sight and may show impaired conversational skills (e.g., poor word recall, verbal labeling problems, and delayed verbal response). Problems in mathematics are frequently identified, especially in automatic, rapid recall of math facts. The sequencing and memory deficiency is also expressed in poor spelling skills. Sometimes, memory deficits appear to be reading comprehension deficits because the child cannot remember what was read. Asking conceptual rather than factual questions may be helpful. Most teachers and parents consider children with LDM to be bright due to their good associative reasoning skills. However, they are often considered to be lazy or unmotivated when the memory problem is not diagnosed. Remedial procedures with LDM children that have been beneficial include the following:

1. Emphasize their good associative language skills and de-emphasize rote recall through teaching for meaning.
2. Use phonetic strategies in reading and teach "rules of reading" to use in word attack strategies.
3. Teach the principles of mathematical computation and do not require timed tests of math facts.
4. Use visual and auditory associations to enhance recall of isolated content.

Language Disorder: Associative Deficit (LDA)
Children with LDA have primary deficiencies in receptive language, verbal abstractions, and verbal logical processing. They may not be identified in early elementary grades because some have an isolated ability in automatic rote recall (Richman, 1983). The intellectual-cognitive pattern for children with LDA is a low Verbal/high Performance WISC profile with relatively better scores on Arithmetic, Picture Arrangement, and Coding, along with low scores on Similarities and Block Design (Richman & Lindgren, 1980). The Hiskey pattern includes lower scores on associative tasks (Picture Association and Block Patterns), with higher scores on memory subtests. Because children with LDA have difficulty following the logical progression of conversation, they often make statements that are unrelated to the topic or show lack of understanding. Sometimes, they form tangential associations.

The educational problems of children with LDA are more pervasive and severe than for those with LDE or LDM. Reading assessment of these children should not rely solely on simple word-recognition skills. It is important to evaluate oral reading in

context and reading comprehension, as these skills are usually deficient. Reading symptoms for children with LDA usually also include deficient phonetic segmentation and synthesis. Boder's (1973) description of the dysphonetic reader is consistent with the reading pattern of the LDA child. The primary educational remediations for children with LDA include the following:

1. Language therapy should focus on language categorization and concept formation.
2. Reading assistance should stress comprehension by having children read a short passage and retell it in their own words.
3. The clinician should be alert to the superficial word-calling ability of these children even though understanding may be deficient. They should not be advanced in reading based on this inflated word calling.
4. Recent approaches to remediation of deficient phonemic awareness by using delayed auditory feedback appear promising. This is based on work on the temporal aspects of sounds (Tallal, 1988).
5. Children with LDA are extremely variable in their educational and behavioral functioning, making them quite difficult to diagnose (Eliason & Richman, 1988b; Richman & Lindgren, 1980, 1981; Richman & Wood, 1999).

RELATIONSHIP OF LANGUAGE DISORDERS AND BEHAVIOR/PERSONALITY

Luria (1966) provided comprehensive examinations of the possible relationship among language development, verbal mediation, and self-regulation of behavior. The findings provided evidence that children's deficiencies in verbal mediation (i.e., labeling, rehearsal, self-guiding speech, etc.) are associated with impulsivity, inattention, and lack of self-control of activity level. Luria suggested that deficiency in higher cortical language functions such as associative logic may impair the development of internalized self-control of behavior. More recent studies have stressed the importance of verbal mediation in the development, maintenance, and modification of abnormal behavior (Meichenbaum, 1977), aggression and impulsivity (Camp, 1977; Richman & Lindgren, 1981), and delinquency (Lindgren, Harper, Richman, & Stehbens, 1986).

There are extensive reviews of the relationship of language disorders to aggressive behaviors (Hogan & Quay, 1984) and the role language plays in general behavior and psychiatric disorders (Cantwell & Baker, 1991; Piacentini, 1987). A summary of the relationship between language disorders and behavior disorders suggests that children with DLD show more general psychiatric problems, attention deficit with/without hyperactivity, delinquency, somatic complaints, oppositional disorders, and conduct disorders. Piacentini reviewed problems in methodology, etiology, and primacy of disorder (language vs. behavioral), emphasizing the importance of the interrelationship of language and emotional behavior disorders.

Clinicians treating behavioral and emotional symptoms of children with language disorders should consider how language-based cognitive deficits such as expressive and memory deficits can affect behavior and how verbal mediation deficiency can interfere with self-control of behavior. There is evidence that language-deficient children display excessive aggression and impulsivity (Camp, 1977). Although excessive expression of impulse may be related to deficient verbal mediation, it has been shown that this may be the case for only a subset of language-disordered children who have a primary deficiency in language association skills (Richman & Lindgren, 1981). It is also becoming increasing apparent that there is a relationship of language impairment and attention-deficit/hyperactivity disorder, although the etiology remains unclear.

Specific subtypes of language-disordered children are characterized by different types of behaviors. Children with LDE usually show excessive internalization, low self-esteem, and frustration, which may be related to their verbal expression deficit (Eliason & Richman, 1988b). Treatment approaches that include supportive, patient understanding by parents, teachers, and clinicians are recommended. Sometimes, children with severe LDE demonstrate acting-out frustration responses, although they usually show remorse for this, unlike children with primary conduct disorders.

Children with LDM frequently appear inattentive because they do not remember what to do. Therefore, they may be erroneously labeled lazy or unmotivated. Because children with LDM usually appear bright due to good associative language functions, teachers and parents may punish them for underachievement if their memory disability is undiagnosed. Children with LDM are often assumed to have attention-deficit disorder without hyperactivity (ADD) due to their difficulty in recalling directions and assignments. Although they do show a mild elevation in errors of selective attention or vigilance (Eliason & Richman, 1987), their difficulty can be treated by teaching memory strategies; medication for ADD is often not necessary.

The most severe behavioral and emotional problems in subgroups of language-disordered children usually are related to associative language deficits. Children with LDA show excessive conduct disorder based on objective checklists (Richman & Lindgren, 1981), and some show significant attention deficit and hyperactivity, which may be related to delayed development of rule-governed behavior and self-control (Barkley, 1981; Luria, 1966). Children with LDA often act impulsively without the verbal mediation skills to consider the consequences of their behavior. Thus, they often appear confused or bewildered when reprimanded. In severe cases, their behavior problems and odd responses may lead to diagnoses of emotional disturbance, autism, or thought disorder. Unfortunately, traditional behavioral and psychotherapy approaches do not seem to be effective with these children. Usually, more direct treatment of LDA through language therapy is needed. Social skills training through cognitive behavior modification approaches is sometimes useful in conjunction with language therapy.

CLEFT PALATE

Cleft palate is one of the most frequently occurring congenital anomalies, affecting 1 out of 750 live births. Clefts can be complete or incomplete, bilateral or unilateral, and involve the lip, hard palate, and/or soft palate. Approximately 50% of all clefts involve the lip and palate, 25% the palate only, and 25% the lip only (Jones, 1988). There are over 50 recognized syndromes of which cleft palate is one feature, but each of these syndromes is relatively rare. Approximately 30% have recognized genetic syndromes such as Sticklers or velocardiofacial syndromes, or teratogenic exposures such as fetal alcohol effects or fetal hydantoin syndrome. An additional 71% of individuals with cleft lip and palate (CLP) and 85% of individuals with cleft palate only

(CPO) have minor physical anomalies (not recognized as syndromic), with females more likely than males to show other defects (Cook, Harding, Krogman, Mazaheri, & Millard, 1979).

The incidence of cleft palate varies according to race and sex. American Blacks have a relatively low incidence (1 per 2,000 births), and Asians have a relatively high rate of occurrence (2 per 1,000). Clefts occur more frequently in males than in females by a 6:4 ratio. More males exhibit CLP, and in general, males have more severe defects than females. Females are more likely to develop CPO than are males. Cook et al. (1979) proposed a difference in fetal developmental time sequences for the sexes to account for this uneven sex distribution.

The cause of any individual case of cleft palate is largely speculative. About one-third of the cases have a family history of clefts (Drillien, Ingram, & Wilkinson, 1966). Nonfamilial clefts have many hypothesized causes, including prenatal exposure to viral infections, toxic substances, metabolic deficiencies, endocrine imbalances, radiation, and hypoxia. Cook et al. (1979) reported a significant correlation between the presence of a nonfamilial cleft and impaired reproductive capacity of the mother (including severe menstrual disturbances, abnormal outcome of other conceptions, and difficulty conceiving).

Children with cleft have a higher incidence of hearing disorders, hearing loss, and middle ear disease than the general population. Otitis media is universal in infants with cleft and persists in over 50% of children and adults with cleft. The hearing loss associated with otitis can be unilateral or bilateral and is more likely to be conductive than sensorineural. There are conflicting data as to whether cleft type, CLP or CPO, is associated with a greater degree of hearing loss. Because children with cleft frequently have fluctuating hearing losses with few outward symptoms, it is often difficult to identify without close monitoring.

Children with cleft have a high frequency of speech problems in two primary areas: nasal voice quality and articulation errors. Vocal resonance, which determines voice quality, depends on the shape and size of the oral cavity and normal movement of the palate. When the palate is too short or immobile, it may not reach the back of the pharynx during certain speech sounds, allowing air to leak through the nose and resulting in a nasal voice quality. Articulation errors in children with cleft are usually related to abnormal dentition or incorrect learning of speech sounds before the cleft treatment has been completed. The child with cleft lip and/or palate often requires extensive speech therapy to relearn speech sounds after treatment. Interrelated factors such as intermittent hearing loss, nasal voice quality, and faulty articulation complicate the speech therapy process. Thus, speech therapy for children with cleft may be less effective than for children with other speech disorders.

INTELLECTUAL AND COGNITIVE DEVELOPMENT

Early studies found that the average IQ of samples of children with cleft was slightly below that of the general population. However, the validity of these studies is questionable because most compared subjects who had been given different intelligence tests and/or the studies failed to use control groups (Richman & Eliason, 1986). Even when control groups and standard intelligence tests were utilized, studies found slightly lower IQs in children with cleft. There is increasing evidence that the slightly lower Full-Scale IQ is primarily due to decreased verbal scores. In a survey of over 200 children with cleft lip and/or palate, Richman and Eliason found that over 30% of the children had lower Verbal/higher Performance IQ discrepancies greater than 12 points.

Several factors confound the relationship between cleft palate and intelligence, such as type and severity of cleft, age, and sex. Children with CPO tend to have lower IQs than children with CLP, which may be related to the higher incidence of other congenital anomalies. Richman (1980) found that males with CPO had more severe language deficits than any other cleft-by-sex-type group. However, studies by Eliason and Richman (1985) and Heineman-DeBoer (1985) failed to identify sex-by-cleft-type interactions.

There are several possible reasons for the lower Verbal IQ found in most studies of children with cleft. The deficit may be due to less language stimulation in the home, hearing loss, or the quality of speech. Any of these could cause depressed scores on tests of intelligence. More recent research has examined the possibility that children with cleft may have verbal-language learning disabilities.

Only a few studies have attempted to delineate specific cognitive abilities of cleft children. Brennan and Cullinan (1974) found that a sample of children with cleft scored lower than controls on object naming and word recognition tasks. Richman (1980) studied 57 children with cleft who displayed low Verbal/high Performance IQ patterns and identified two subgroups of language deficiency. One group (46%) displayed a verbal expressive deficit, and the other group showed a more general language disorder characterized by deficits in associative reasoning and categorization. Richman and Eliason (1984) found that children with CLP were more likely to display the verbal expressive deficit, whereas children with CPO were more likely to have generalized language deficiencies. The two groups were similar on measures of visual perception and word recognition, but differed on language and memory measures, reading comprehension, and types of oral reading errors.

Preschool-age children with cleft also show different cognitive patterns than noncleft children. Eliason and Richman (1990) studied 65 children with cleft (ages 4, 5, and 6) on a variety of language, memory, and perceptual-motor tasks. The sample as a whole showed normal vocabulary development, language reasoning, and short-term memory span, but displayed a deficit in verbal mediation. Several comprehensive reviews provide more extensive information on psychological aspects of cleft in children (Eder, 1995; Richman & Eliason, 1993). A recent paper also reviews the status of current research in this area (Speltz & Richman, 1997).

ASSESSMENT AND TREATMENT OF
COGNITION AND LANGUAGE

Research data suggest that, in general, the cleft palate population approximates the normal curve in general intellectual ability, but with an increased incidence of specific verbal expressive deficit or a more general language disorder. Therefore, assessment of children with cleft should always include measures of verbal cognitive skills. Particular attention should be given to differentiation of verbal expression versus symbolic language mediation abilities. (See details of this type of assessment in the previous section on language disorders.) If a significant verbal deficit is present, a nonverbal test that assesses associative reasoning, categorization, and memory skills should be utilized. The Hiskey, which has been useful in this respect, includes norms for

both hearing-impaired and normal-hearing children (Richman, 1980).

The Peabody Picture Vocabulary Test (PPVT), although frequently used in clinical evaluations of children, has not been particularly useful in assessing language skills in children with cleft (McWilliams, 1974) or language disorder (Richman, 1979). McWilliams found poor predictive validity among the PPVT, the Stanford–Binet, and the Illinois Test of Psycholinguistic Ability (ITPA). Richman suggested that the PPVT does not necessarily assess the symbolic component of language but may be only a simple paired-associate learning test and tends to overestimate reading and cognitive abilities. Conversely, the Hiskey assesses sequential memory and abstract reasoning skills that are important variables in reading and language development.

If a verbal deficit, whether specific or general, is discovered, the child will probably benefit from language therapy. Those cleft children with general language deficits need extensive language therapy focusing on abstract reasoning and categorization. Children with more specific deficits in verbal expression, along with intact verbal mediation skills, will usually need only traditional speech therapy. Because children with cleft may not be reinforced for vocalizations as much as children without cleft, parents and teachers should be encouraged to reward early vocalization, even when articulation errors and/or hypernasality make utterances unintelligible or difficult to understand. For toddlers and preschool-age children, early language stimulation should be provided via home programs or parent training to ensure ample verbal interaction (Endriga & Speltz, 1997).

EDUCATIONAL CONSIDERATIONS

Children with cleft are at risk for speech problems, hearing loss, facial disfigurement, and specific verbal language deficits; thus, the possibility of school achievement deficits is quite high (Broder, Richman, & Matheson, 1998). Children with cleft have been found to score significantly lower than controls on standardized group achievement tests (Richman, 1976; Richman & Harper, 1978). Richman (1980) reported that over 50% of children with cleft who had average IQs exhibited significantly below average reading and math skills on the Wide Range Achievement Test.

Richman, Eliason, and Lindgren (1988) found a high rate of reading disability in a sample of 172 elementary school-age children with cleft (94 with CLP and 78 with CPO). Children with CPO had a higher overall rate of reading disability across all age groupings. The rate was highest in the early grades (53%), but declined to 33% by grades 5 to 6. Children with CLP also had a high rate of reading problems in the early grades (49%), but by grades 5 to 6, the rate had dropped to 8%. These findings supported the authors' earlier work, suggesting that children with CPO have generalized language learning disabilities, whereas children with CLP are more likely to show transitory verbal expressive deficits.

Richman (1978a) found that teachers rated children with more noticeable facial disfigurement as having lower intelligence than measured by individual intelligence tests, although they are more accurate in estimating intelligence of children with relatively normal appearance. Teachers also rated children with cleft as more inhibited and withdrawn in the classroom than parents viewed them at home (Richman, 1978b). It was suggested that teachers' perceptions of the child may have a detrimental influence on school achievement. Thus, facial disfigurement (and probably speech impairment as well) may adversely affect school achievement, compounding problems caused by verbal language disabilities.

The clinician should be alert to the possibility that children with cleft may have lower achievement levels than one would expect based on parent interview. Parents may have lower expectations for their children and not report lower achievement. Teachers may also underestimate the child's ability and expect less. Therefore, it is important to evaluate each child's individual levels of ability and achievement.

Children with specific or general language disorders are at risk for reading disabilities. A major problem in assessing reading is that many of the available tests are based solely on oral reading errors. For children with cleft, one must determine whether reading errors are due to faulty articulation, language disorder, or reading disability. Children with poor speech or some form of verbal language disorder may rely only on sight word strategies of reading, thus failing to benefit from phonetic sound-blending methods. Tests of sight word recognition may overestimate the child's reading ability, whereas tests of phonics skills may

underestimate reading ability. Therefore, a reading comprehension test, which would evaluate understanding of reading, should always be administered to obtain an accurate assessment of reading level. A sample of written language should also be obtained because spelling and grammatical patterns may reveal further information about phonics and language skills and may aid in diagnosing an underlying language disorder.

It is important to determine whether the educational expectations of parents and teachers are realistic based on the child's abilities. When adult expectations do not match the child's abilities, barriers to academic achievement may arise. When expectations are too low, the child may increasingly underachieve; when expectations are too high, the child may achieve adequately but suffer secondary emotional damage. In addition to unrealistic expectations, another barrier to academic achievement is behavioral inhibition; the resulting lack of competitiveness and assertiveness may interfere with classroom work. For example, inhibited children who do not hear all of the directions may avoid asking the teacher for help because they fear calling attention to themselves. When treating educational problems in children with cleft, the effects of behavioral inhibition, including low self-esteem and anxiety, must be considered as well as intellectual and cognitive factors.

BEHAVIOR AND PERSONALITY DEVELOPMENT

Attempts to document a "syndrome-specific" personality type for children with cleft have failed to identify unique personality traits. However, a wide variety of "mild" adjustment issues have been identified. Spriestersbach (1973) found that parents perceived their children with cleft as less confident, less aggressive, and less independent than other children. Richman (1976) used teacher ratings of cleft and matched control groups on the Quay-Peterson Behavior Problem Checklist and found that children with cleft scored high on the internalizing factors, showing an excessive inhibition of impulse. Richman and Harper (1979), using the Missouri Child's Picture Series (a nonverbal personality test), also found greater behavioral inhibition in children with cleft. Harper, Richman, and Snider (1980) found a difference in behavior according to severity of impairment; children with mild facial disfigurement displayed greater inhibition than more severely impaired children. Longitudinal analysis of children with cleft over nine years provided evidence of long-term behavioral inhibition (Richman & Millard, 1997).

Parenting characteristics may have an influence on the behavior of children with clefts. Tobiasen and Hiebert (1984) found that parents of children with cleft were more tolerant of acting-out behavior than parents of noncleft children. They suggested that this may reflect parental overprotectiveness. Richman and Harper (1978) found that males with cleft complained that their mothers were too intrusive, also suggesting some degree of overprotectiveness.

Adolescents with a cleft palate showed behavioral inhibition, self-concern, and ruminative self-doubts over interpersonal interactions on a Minnesota Multiphasic Personality Inventory (MMPI) profile analysis (Harper & Richman, 1978). Females with cleft showed a greater dissatisfaction with their life situation than did males, possibly related to a greater emphasis on physical appearance in females. These MMPI profiles did not suggest emotional maladjustment but rather variations of normal behavior. Researchers suggest that children with cleft do not display a unique personality trait related to their condition, nor is there indication of a high incidence of psychopathology. However, they are more likely to be inhibited, shy, and less independent than noncleft peers.

Adolescents with cleft frequently express patterns of excessive inhibition with feelings of anxiety and self-consciousness in social situations. Excessive inhibition may create feelings of social alienation for the male with cleft because adolescent males typically display increased levels of impulsive behavior. Females with cleft frequently experience low self-esteem and feelings of alienation due to increased physical appearance concerns. The clinician working with cleft adolescents should be alert to these concerns and provide supportive counseling in this regard.

EFFECTS OF FACIAL DISFIGUREMENT/ SPEECH IMPAIRMENT

Most judgments of attractiveness are based predominantly on facial features. Social psychologists have shown a "beautiful is good" phenomenon, whereby "attractive" persons are rated as likable, intelligent, successful, fun, and so on. Those who are considered unattractive or facially different are perceived negatively. Research on the social desirability of children with cleft supports these findings. In a study by Schneiderman and Harding (1984), schoolchildren rated slides of children with unilateral and bilateral cleft and with no cleft. The children with bilateral cleft were rated most negatively, followed by the children with unilateral cleft. The noncleft group received positive ratings on the adjective checklist (clean, friendly, smart, happy, etc.). Tobiasen (1987) also found that children with facial disfigurement were rated more negatively on personality characteristics than children without disfigurement. Females with disfigurement were rated more negatively than males with disfigurement, supporting other research that suggests that appearance is a more salient social cue for females than for males (e.g., Styczynski & Langlois, 1977). Because much of a social message is conveyed by nonverbal cues such as facial expression and tone of voice (which may be altered by speech difficulties), children with cleft are at a social disadvantage.

Some researchers have found that ratings of speech impairment were affected by facial appearance. Podol and Salvia (1976) found that hypernasality of speech was more likely to be rated as problematic when coupled with a photograph of a child with a cleft. Richman, Holmes, and Eliason (1985) found that adolescents with cleft who were considered poorly adjusted by their parents rated themselves unrealistically on speech and appearance measures. There appears to be a complex interrelationship between the cleft palate variables (such as speech and appearance) and social/emotional adjustment. Other researchers have examined the influence of speech impairment on social desirability. Sinko and Hedrick (1982) found that adults rated speech impairment more severely than facial disfigurement in individuals with cleft. McKinnon, Hess, and Landry (1986) found that college students rated speakers with speech disorders (including hypernasal speech) as less valued, less understandable, and as producing anxiety in the listener. Speech disorders can be socially stigmatizing and contribute to academic underachievement. Thus far, little attention has been paid to the possible interactive effects of facial disfigurement and speech impairment. Clinicians need to be alert to the social effects of speech problems and recommend speech interventions as early as possible.

Identifying potential biases due to facial difference or disfigurement is difficult. However, research indicates that teachers, peers, and significant others in a child's life may hold negative attitudes or lower expectations for the child solely on the basis of appearance. These negative attitudes and lower expectations can affect the child's behavior, resulting in low self-esteem, social isolation, and shy, withdrawn behavior. Academic underachievement and peer problems may be the end result. Psychologists can be instrumental in studying the phenomenon of facial stigmatization and can offer educational programs to teachers and children, stressing the value of interpersonal judgments based on more than appearance.

CONCLUSION

This chapter has focused on research and clinical aspects of communication disorders of children using two representative groups: developmental language disorders and cleft palate. Because there remain conflicting psychological research findings on communication disorders, many clinical decisions must be made without an extensive or consistent database. There is promise, however, in the increased attention to children with communication disorders brought about by the Education for All Handicapped Children Act, which emphasized educational placement in the least restrictive environment. Because many children with speech and language disorders are receiving more careful diagnostic scrutiny, there is increased responsibility for the clinical child psychologist to make accurate diagnoses of these disorders. The child psychologist evaluating and/or treating a child with a language disorder should have knowledge of the aphasia literature and be able to employ procedures adopted from neuropsychology. There are also important relationships between language deficiency and behavior that have clinical importance. Cleft palate may be one of the most neglected of the congenital anomaly groups in terms of psychological involvement. However, the research findings suggest that there is a need to overcome the subtle social influences and "hidden" learning disorders, which may result in less than optimal academic progress and lowered self-esteem.

This chapter has emphasized diagnostic considerations because many of the psychological problems experienced by children with communication disorders are often overlooked. The child who sustains brain injury or disease and related aphasic symptoms comes to the attention of many professionals and is likely to receive extensive evaluation and rehabilitation treatment. However, the child with a DLD is often undiagnosed or misdiagnosed as "slow," as having attention-deficit disorder or behavior disorder, or as emotionally disturbed. These children are often competing in regular classrooms without adequate support services. Children with cleft palate rarely receive the consideration necessary to identify their problems. They frequently experience subtle reading, speech, or language disorders, along with behavioral inhibition secondary to social aspects of facial disfigurement. It is important for the child psychologist to be aware of the interacting factors of speech impairment, language disorder, and facial disfigurement on behavior and achievement.

Although there is increasing research documentation of some of the unique intellectual, cognitive, and educational problems of children with communication disorders, there is a dearth of information regarding the behavioral and emotional adjustment of these children. This chapter has attempted to describe some of the more frequently identified adjustment concerns. It is important for the child psychologist evaluating and treating children with communication disorders to be aware of the complex interactions and relationships of communication disorders with learning, attention, behavioral, and emotional symptoms.

REFERENCES

American Psychiatric Association. (1994). *Diagnostic and statistical manual of mental disorders* (4th ed.). Washington, DC: Author.

Aram, D.M. (Ed.). (1984). Assessment of treatment of developmental apraxia. *Seminars in Speech and Language, 5,* 2.

Aram, D.M., & Hall, N.E. (1989). Longitudinal follow-up of children with preschool communication disorders: Treatment implications. *School Psychology Review, 18,* 487–501.

Barkley, R.A. (1981). *Hyperactive children.* New York: Guilford Press.

Boder, E. (1973). Developmental dyslexia: A diagnostic approach based on three atypical reading patterns. *Developmental Medicine and Child Neurology, 15,* 663–687.

Brennan, D., & Cullinan, W. (1974). Object identification and naming in cleft palate children. *Cleft Palate Journal, 11,* 188–195.

Broder, H.L., Richman, L.C., & Matheson, P. (1998). Learning disability, school achievement and grade retention among children with cleft: A two center study. *Cleft Palate–Craniofacial Journal, 35,* 127–131.

Camp, B.W. (1977). Verbal mediation in young aggressive boys. *Journal of Abnormal Psychology, 86,* 145–153.

Cantwell, D.P., & Baker, L. (1991). *Psychiatric and developmental disorders in children with communication disorder.* Washington, DC: American Psychiatric Press.

Cook, H., Harding, R., Krogman, W., Mazaheri, M., & Millard, R. (1979). *Cleft palate and cleft lip: A team approach to clinical management and rehabilitation of the patient.* Philadelphia: Saunders.

Crockett, D.J. (1974). Component analysis within correlations of language-skills tests in normal children. *Journal of Special Education, 8,* 361–375.

Denkla, M., & Rudel, R. (1976). Rapid automatized naming (RAN): Dyslexia differential from other learning disabilities. *Neuropsychologia, 14,* 471–479.

Drillien, C., Ingram, T., & Wilkinson, E. (1966). *The causes and natural history of cleft lip and palate.* Baltimore: Williams & Wilkins.

Eder, R.A. (Ed.). (1995). *Craniofacial anomalies: Psychological perspectives.* New York: Springer-Verlag.

Eisenson, J. (1972). *Aphasia in children.* New York: Harper & Row.

Eliason, M.J., & Richman, L.C. (1985). *Sex and cleft type influences on intellectual development in children with cleft.* Miami, FL: American Cleft Palate Association.

Eliason, M.J., & Richman, L.C. (1987). The continuous performance test in learning disabled and nondisabled children. *Journal of Learning Disabilities, 20,* 614–619.

Eliason, M.J., & Richman, L.C. (1988a). Behavior and attention in LD children. *Learning Disability Quarterly, 11,* 360–369.

Eliason, M.J., & Richman, L.C. (1988b). *Guide to learning disabilities.* (Available from EAMS Publications, P.O. Box 1151, Iowa City, IA 52244.)

Eliason, M.J., & Richman, L.C. (1990). Language development in preschool children with cleft. *Developmental Neuropsychology, 6,* 173–182.

Endriga, M.C., & Speltz, M.L. (1997). Face to face interaction between infants with orofacial clefts and their mothers. *Journal of Pediatric Psychology, 22,* 439–453.

Geschwind, N., & Galaburda, A.M. (1987). *Cerebral lateralization: Biological mechanisms, associations, and pathology.* Cambridge, MA: MIT Press.

Gilger, J. (1997). Behavioral genetics: Concepts for research and practice in language development and disorders. *Journal of Speech and Hearing Disorders, 40,* 1126–1142.

Hammill, D. (1985). *Detroit Tests of Learning Aptitude.* Austin, TX: ProEd.

Harper, D.C., & Richman, L.C. (1978). Personality profiles of physically impaired adolescents. *Journal of Clinical Psychology, 34,* 636–642.

Harper, D.C., Richman, L.C., & Snider, B. (1980). School adjustment and degree of physical impairment. *Journal of Pediatric Psychology, 5,* 377–383.

Heineman-DeBoer, J.A. (1985). *Cleft palate children and intelligence.* Lisse, The Netherlands: Swets & Zeitlinger.

Hiskey, M.S. (1966). *Hiskey–Nebraska Test of Learning Aptitude.* Lincoln, NE: Union College Press.

Hogan, A.E., & Quay, H.C. (1984). Cognition in child and adolescent behavior disorders. In B.B. Lahey & A.E. Kazdin (Eds.), *Advances in clinical child psychology* (Vol. 7, pp. 1–34). New York: Plenum Press.

Johnson, D.J., & Myklebust, H.R. (1967). *Learning disabilities: Educational principles and practices.* New York: Grune & Stratton.

Jones, M.C. (1988). Etiology of facial clefts: Prospective evaluation of 428 patients. *Cleft Palate Journal, 25,* 16–20.

Korkman, M., & Hakkinen-Rihu, P. (1994). A new classification of developmental language disorders. *Brain and Language, 47,* 96–116.

Korkman, M., Kirk, U., & Kemp, S. (1998). *NEPSY: A developmental neuropsychological assessment.* San Antonio: Harcourt Brace.

Lindgren, S.D., Harper, D.C., Richman, L.C., & Stehbens, J.A. (1986). Mental imbalance and the prediction of recurrent delinquent behavior. *Journal of Clinical Psychology, 42,* 821–825.

Lindgren, S.D., & Richman, L.C. (1984). Immediate memory functions of verbally deficient reading disabled children. *Journal of Learning Disabilities, 17,* 222–225.

Lindgren, S.D., Richman, L.C., & Eliason, M.J. (1986). Memory processes in reading disability subtypes. *Developmental Neuropsychology, 2,* 173–181.

Ludlow, C.L. (1980). Children's language disorders: Recent research advances. *Annals of Neurology, 7,* 497–507.

Ludlow, C.L., & Cooper, J.A. (1983). *Genetic aspects of speech and language disorders.* New York: Academic Press.

Luria, A.R. (1966). *Higher cortical functions in man.* New York: Basic Books.

McCarthy, J.J., & Kirk, S.A. (1961). *Illinois Test of Pyscholinguistic Ability.* Urbana: University of Illinois.

McKinnon, S.L., Hess, C.W., & Landry, R.G. (1986). Reactions of college students to speech disorders. *Journal of Communication Disorders, 19,* 75–82.

McWilliams, B.J. (1974). Clinical use of the Peabody Picture Vocabulary Test with cleft palate preschoolers. *Cleft Palate Journal, 11,* 439–442.

Meichenbaum, D. (1977). *Cognitive-behavior modification: An integrative approach.* New York: Plenum Press.

Montgomery, J.W., Windsor, J., & Stark, R.E. (1991). Specific speech and language disorders. In J. Obrzut &

G. Hynd (Eds.), *Neuropsychological foundations of learning disabilities* (pp. 573–601). San Diego, CA: Academic Press.

Piacentini, J.C. (1987). Language dysfunction and childhood behavioral disorders. In B. Lahey & A. Kazdin (Eds.), *Advances in clinical child psychology* (Vol. 10, pp. 259–287). New York: Plenum Press.

Podol, J., & Salvia, J. (1976). Effects of prepalatal cleft on the evaluation of speech. *Cleft Palate Journal, 13,* 361–366.

Rapin, I. (1996). Practitioner review: Developmental language disorders. *Journal of Child Psychology and Psychiatry, 37,* 643–655.

Reynell, J. (1969). *Reynell Developmental Language Scales.* Windsor, England: NFER Publishing.

Richman, L.C. (1976). Behavior and achievement of the cleft palate child. *Cleft Palate Journal, 13,* 4–10.

Richman, L.C. (1978a). The effects of facial disfigurement on teachers' perceptions of ability in cleft palate children. *Cleft Palate Journal, 15,* 155–160.

Richman, L.C. (1978b). Parents and teachers: Differing views of behavior of cleft palate children. *Cleft Palate Journal, 15,* 360–364.

Richman, L.C. (1979). Language variables related to reading ability of children with verbal deficits. *Psychology in the Schools, 16,* 299–305.

Richman, L.C. (1980). Cognitive patterns and learning disabilities in cleft palate children with verbal deficits. *Journal of Speech and Hearing Research, 23,* 447–456.

Richman, L.C. (1983). Language-learning disability: Issues, research, and future directions. In M. Wolraich & D. Routh (Eds.), *Advances in developmental and behavioral pediatrics* (Vol. 4, pp. 87–107). Greenwich, CT: JAI Press.

Richman, L.C., & Eliason, M.J. (1984). Type of reading disability related to cleft type and neuropsychological patterns. *Cleft Palate Journal, 21,* 1–6.

Richman, L.C., & Eliason, M.J. (1986). Development in children with cleft lip and/or palate. *Seminars in Speech and Language, 7,* 225–239.

Richman, L.C., & Eliason, M.J. (1993). Psychological characteristics associated with cleft palate. In K. Moller & C. Starr (Eds.), *Cleft palate: Interdisciplinary issues and treatment* (pp. 356–380). Austin, TX: ProEd.

Richman, L.C., Eliason, M.J., & Lindgren, S.D. (1988). Reading disability in children with cleft lip and/or palate. *Cleft Palate Journal, 25,* 21–25.

Richman, L.C., & Harper, D.C. (1978). School adjustment of children with observable disabilities. *Journal of Abnormal Child Psychology, 6,* 11–18.

Richman, L.C., & Harper, D.C. (1979). Self-identified personality patterns of children with facial or orthopedic disfigurement. *Cleft Palate Journal, 16,* 257–261.

Richman, L.C., Holmes, C.S., & Eliason, M. (1985). Adolescents with cleft lip and palate: Self-perceptions of appearance and behavior related to personality adjustment. *Cleft Palate Journal, 22,* 93–96.

Richman, L.C., & Kitchell, M. (1981). Hyperlexia as a variant of developmental language disorder. *Brain and Language, 12,* 203–212.

Richman, L.C., & Lindgren, S.D. (1980). Patterns of intellectual ability in children with verbal deficits. *Journal of Abnormal Child Psychology, 8,* 65–81.

Richman, L.C., & Lindgren, S.D. (1981). Verbal mediation deficits: Relation to behavior and achievement in children. *Journal of Abnormal Child Psychology, 90,* 99–104.

Richman, L.C., & Lindgren, S.D. (1984). *The Color Span Test.* (Available from EAMS Publications, 3043 Westberry, Iowa City, IA 52240)

Richman, L.C., & Millard, T. (1997). Brief report: Cleft lip and palate: Longitudinal behavior and relationships of cleft conditions to behavior and achievement. *Journal of Pediatric Psychology, 22*(4), 487–494.

Richman, L.C., & Wood, K.M. (1999). Psychological assessment and treatment of communication disorders: Childhood language subtypes. In S. Netherton, D. Holmes, & C.G. Walker (Eds.), *Child and adolescent psychological disorders: A comprehensive textbook.* New York: Oxford University Press.

Schneiderman, C.R., & Harding, J.B. (1984). Social ratings of children with cleft lip by school peers. *Cleft Palate Journal, 21,* 219–223.

Sinko, G.R., & Hedrick, D.L. (1982). The interrelationships between ratings of speech and facial acceptability in persons with cleft palate. *Journal of Speech and Hearing Research, 25,* 402–407.

Speltz, M.L., & Richman, L.C. (1997). Editorial: Progress and limitations in the psychological study of craniofacial anomalies. *Journal of Pediatric Psychology, 22,* 433–438.

Spreen, D., & Benton, A. (1969). *Neurosensory Center Comprehensive Examination of Aphasia.* Victoria, Canada: University of Victoria.

Spriestersbach, D.C. (1973). *Psychosocial aspects of the "cleft palate problem"* (Vols. 1–2). Iowa City: University of Iowa Press.

Styczynski, L., & Langlois, J.H. (1977). The effects of familiarity on behavioral stereotypes associated with physical attractiveness in young children. *Child Development, 48,* 1137–1141.

Tallal, P. (1988). Developmental language disorders. In J.F. Kavanagh & T.J. Truss (Eds.), *Learning disabilities: Proceedings of the national conference.* Parkton, MD: York Press.

Tallal, P., Stark, R.E., & Mellitis, E.D. (1985). Identification of language-impaired children on the basis of rapid perception and production skills. *Brain and Language, 25,* 314–322.

Tobiasen, J.M. (1987). Social judgments on facial deformity. *Cleft Palate Journal, 24,* 323–327.

Tobiasen, J.M., & Hiebert, J. (1984). Parents' tolerance for the conduct problems of the child with cleft lip and palate. *Cleft Palate Journal, 21,* 82–85.

Torgesen, J.K. (1982). The study of short term memory in learning disabled children. In K. Gadow & I. Bailer (Eds.), *Advances in learning and behavioral disorders* (Vol. 1, pp. 117–149). Greenwich, CT: JAI Press.

Vellutino, F.R. (1979). *Dyslexia: Theory and research.* Cambridge, MA: MIT Press.

Wilson, B.C., & Risucci, P.A. (1986). A model for clinical-quantitative classification. Generation I: Application to language-disordered preschool children. *Brain and Language, 27,* 281–309.

Wood, K.M., & Richman, L.C. (1988). Developmental trends within memory-deficient reading-disability subtypes. *Developmental Neuropsychology, 4,* 261–274.

Wood, K.M., Richman, L.C., & Eliason, M.J. (1989). Immediate memory functions in reading disability subtypes. *Brain and Language, 36,* 181–192.

PROBLEMS OF ADOLESCENCE

CHAPTER 31

Common Teen-Parent Problems

WILLIAM A. RAE

When I was a boy of fourteen, my father was so ignorant I could hardly stand to have the old man around. But when I got to be twenty-one, I was astonished at how much the old man had learned in seven years.

—Attributed to Mark Twain

Most referrals to a clinical child psychologist for teen-parent problems address one of three issues. First, the teenager might be manifesting specific behavioral or emotional problems (e.g., alcohol use, violation of curfew, emotional withdrawal, anxiety, depression, falling grades) that concern parents. Second, the teenager and parents might have escalating teen-parent conflict and discord (e.g., arguing with parents, temper outbursts to parental rules, poor communication) independent of any behavioral or emotional problem. Finally, the teen-parent problem could include a combination of teen behavioral or emotional problems and escalating teen-parent conflicts. Obviously, the focus of treatment depends on the psychologist's assessment of the impact the maladaptive teen-parent conflict has on either causing and/or maintaining the problem behaviors (Foster & Robin, 1998).

Adolescent storm and stress appears to be a real phenomenon characterized by conflict with parents, mood disruptions, and risk behavior (Arnett,

1999). In addition, parents often have difficulty differentiating between developmentally normal adolescent behavior and disordered adolescent behavior. Well-trained psychologists know that the cause of adolescent behavior problems or teen-parent conflict can be a temporary emotional or behavioral turmoil rather than the result of true psychopathology. However, if psychological intervention is delayed because of the psychologist's attribution of the teen's behavior to temporary adolescent turmoil, the problem might deteriorate, resulting in greater psychopathology (Masterson, 1968). Psychologists should be very cognizant of their own values and biases as these can affect their ability to render an objective assessment of the teen-parent problem. The clinical child psychologist must be cautious about not overdiagnosing or underdiagnosing psychopathology in teenagers.

The purpose of this chapter is to describe common behavior problems of teenagers and typical conflicts that occur between teenagers and their parents. Many of the teen-parent problems referred to a clinical child psychologist are not disorders that fit the diagnostic criteria of the fourth edition of the *Diagnostic and Statistical Manual of Mental Disorders* (*DSM-IV*; American Psychiatric Association, 1994). Rather, the referral to the psychologist is made because parents are concerned about an escalation of discord and conflict between themselves and their teenager or because their teenager has begun behaving in potentially negative, inappropriate, or destructive ways that alarm the parents. Obviously, the clinical child psychologist should carefully assess the nature, duration, degree, and chronicity of the presenting complaint to be sure that a diagnosable *DSM-IV* disorder does not exist. If a diagnosable disorder is found, the psychologist should identity and treat the disorder accordingly. Certain kinds of behavior necessitate immediate intervention. Symptoms such as sexual promiscuity, delinquent or criminal acts, excessive or chronic drug abuse, excessive or chronic alcohol abuse, and suicidal or homicidal behaviors should be aggressively treated. Although problematic adolescent behaviors that can lead to pathological conditions will be described, this chapter will not focus on specific mental disorders. For the most part, this chapter describes nonpathological behavioral and emotional problems that are commonly the focus of treatment by a clinical child psychologist.

PARENTAL REACTIONS DURING ADOLESCENCE

Although a major task of adolescence is to develop autonomy from parents and other authority figures, parents often expect these changes to occur much later than they actually do (Feldman & Quatman, 1988). Separating from parents is necessary if the adolescent is to take on the adult role. To become autonomous, the teenager must risk leaving the security and stability of the family unit where behavioral expectations are well defined and enter a life stage where rules are shifting. Many teenagers are overwhelmed by the disequilibrium precipitated by their emerging adolescence and separate in an awkward manner. Some teenagers may develop inappropriately intense interpersonal attachments with peers as a way of separating from parents. Alternatively, some teenagers may retreat into the comfort of an overly dependent relationship with their parents because of fear of their impending autonomy. To have an appropriate and healthy separation, the teenager must develop an independent peer support group (Erikson, 1963). Peer relationships and support are crucial to breaking away from the dependence on parents.

The rigid, polarizing responses between parents and their teenager can lead to greater conflict and escalating anger in interpersonal interactions.

Conflicted interchanges also encourage the teenager to withdraw from parents and develop inappropriate interactions with peers. Foster and Robin (1998) suggest that negative, irrational attributions play a role in how family members respond to the teenager. That is, parents react in a manner consistent with their own stereotypes of teenagers. For example, if parents perceive teenagers as being powerful, aggressive victimizers, they will try to restrict the teenager's behavior, but if parents perceive teenagers as being passive, impotent victims, they will be much more nurturing. Younger parents tend to perceive their teenagers more negatively than older parents, especially for their first-born children (M. Cohen, Adler, Beck, & Irwin, 1986). If parents are warm and supportive, interpersonal conflicts are maintained at a low to moderate level during early adolescence and even decrease as the teenager gets older (Rueter & Conger, 1995).

If parents are hostile and coercive to their teenager, interpersonal conflict can escalate and become progressively worse throughout early to middle adolescence. Interaction between parents and their teenager that is characterized by negative emotion and poor communication can lead to ineffectual behavior management (Lantz, 1975). Parents are often ambivalent about giving up the control of their teenager. In some ways, parents want their teenager to become autonomous and independent, which they recognize as being developmentally appropriate. In other ways, parents want to protect their teenager from potentially damaging influences and, as a result, they place greater restrictions and behavioral controls on their teenager. Because of the ongoing conflict and fear that they will have another negative interchange, parents sometimes shy away from placing appropriate restrictions on their teenager. This parental retreat is often misinterpreted by the teenager as tacit consent for his or her inappropriate behavior.

Good parenting yields a positive, supportive environment where problems between parent and teenager can be solved. The effectiveness of teen-parent problem solving appears to be directly related to the child-rearing strategy of the parents (Rueter & Conger, 1998). If parents are skilled at accurately perceiving their teen's thoughts and feelings during a disagreement, they tend to have successful outcomes with less conflict because they tailor their disciplinary interventions to the emotional needs of their teen (Hastings & Grusec,

1997). In contrast, if a parent is perceived as being hostile and angry, teenagers tend to increase acting-out. When parents manifest depressed mood and are less able to respond to their teenagers, the teenager shows significant problems in internalizing, externalizing, and cognitive domains (Thomas & Forehand, 1991). Thus, it appears that good listening skills, good communication skills, good problem-solving skills, and realistic expectations are crucial to mitigating conflict and avoiding major teen-parent problems.

TYPICAL AREAS OF TEEN-PARENT PROBLEMS

Most teenagers find various ways of expressing their individuality as they separate from parents. Testing limits is the way teenagers rebel against parental authority, separate from parental standards, develop independent competency, and develop an independent value system. Erikson (1968) states that during the adolescent stage, the teenager develops a unique self-identity by assimilating past experiences and applying them to new situations. Mood swings, social alienation, peer overidentification, and rebellious behavior result from a role diffusion that accompanies the testing of new roles. These excessive behaviors are the teenager's method for discovering whether the new role will or will not fit his or her emerging self-identity.

Teenagers also tend to engage in risk-taking behavior. Obviously, these behaviors can compromise the developmental integrity of the teenager and can result in negative life outcomes in well-being, health, and life course. No single explanation accounts for teenage risk taking, but it is recognized that both risk factors and protective factors exert an influence. The teenager's social and perceived environment can influence the course and outcome of risk-taking behaviors (Jessor, 1998). For example, if a teenager is supported by a cohesive family and by other interested adults, the teenager could be protected from engaging in risk-taking behaviors. When a teenager does engage in risk-taking behaviors, parents can be instrumental in moderating their negative effects. The psychologist helping the family deal constructively with parent-teen problems avoids alienating the teenager from parents, thus enhancing interpersonal protective factors.

The following are some typical problem situations precipitating referrals to a clinical child psychologist. An attempt is made to provide a brief overview of salient issues that should be known by the practitioner within each of these domains. This listing should not be regarded as exhaustive, but rather is designed to orient the practitioner to these normal variants of adolescent and parent problem behaviors. The psychologist must be cognizant of the fact that these teen-parent problems have the potential for becoming seriously pathological, especially if the frequency, intensity, or duration of the behavior increases. The psychologist must deal with these problems effectively and efficiently if serious difficulties are to be avoided.

TESTING LIMITS AS A CHALLENGE TO PARENTAL AUTHORITY AND VALUES

Parents and teens frequently disagree as to the nature and extent of parental authority. At the same time, the majority of teens are generally not anti-authority (Murray & Thompson, 1985). Teenagers view parents as being more extreme in their parenting styles (i.e., more permissive or more authoritarian) than parents view themselves. At the same time, parents view themselves as more authoritative than do teenagers (Smetana, 1995). Typical conflicts between teens and parents usually center around such mundane issues as spending money, using the phone, selecting clothes, and completion of home chores, with most of the conflicts with mothers rather than fathers (Ellis-Schwabe & Thornburg, 1986). Responses from the teenager to parental authority can range from passive resistance to more assertive refusals accompanied by anger directed toward the parent. In response, parents often resort to verbal aggression directed to their teenager. Unfortunately, teens who experienced frequent verbal aggression from their parents exhibited higher rates of physical aggression, delinquency, and interpersonal problems than teens who were not the target of verbal aggression (Vissing, Straus, Gelles, & Harrop, 1991).

Parents understandably can become very upset when their teenager does not comply with their requests and rules. When this occurs, parents often attribute negative qualities to the teenager (e.g., "He's rude," "She's lazy"). Because the parents feel that they have lost control, many will try to exert more control, thus becoming more authoritarian. As a result, the teenager feels more intruded upon, which tends to heighten the teen-parent discord (Ellis-Schwabe & Thornburg, 1986). Even if the parents use only psychological control mechanisms, the teenager is more prone to adjustment problems and to diminished self-confidence (Conger, Conger, & Scaramella, 1997). In addition, parents can become very confused at the seemingly inconsistent behavior of their teenager. At times, their teenager can be compliant, pleasant, and good-natured; at other times, he or she can be rude, uncompromising, and rebellious. Some adolescents show few signs of overtly challenging parental authority. The degree of challenge can be proportionate to the degree of emotional enmeshment that the teenager has with the parents. Strong negative affect and rebellion is sometimes needed to break the overly close bonds with parents. Even when rebellion appears to be extreme, it is not necessarily an indicator of genuine hostility toward authority or true psychopathology.

Teenagers often covertly rebel from parental influence and values by rejecting conventional lifestyle choices endorsed by their parents. The teenager may endorse hairstyle, grooming, clothing, music, and motion picture preferences that are unacceptable to parents. Teenagers often get into conflicts with parents about how they decorate or maintain the cleanliness of their room. In the same way, teenagers and parents often have substantial disagreements on topics such as politics, sex, drugs, alcohol, and religion. These value disagreements are a covert form of challenging parental values and further serve to facilitate the appropriate separation from the parents.

DEPRESSION AND WITHDRAWAL GESTURES

Depressed, sad, irritable, and withdrawing behaviors are very common for teenagers and are often the cause of parent-teen conflict. In one survey, nearly 30% of teenagers and young adults endorsed at least one depressive symptom, although only a small portion actually received a formal diagnosis of depression (R.E. Roberts, Lewinsohn, & Seeley, 1995). Unfortunately, the symptoms of depression and sadness often go unnoticed by parents (Stivers, 1988). In fact, parents often misinterpret the meaning of adolescent irritability even though it is a common symptom of adolescent depression as

described in the *DSM-IV* (American Psychiatric Association, 1994). Longitudinal studies have shown that teenagers are at risk for depression if there is a family history of depression and recent stressful events (Kazdin & Marciano, 1998), but depressive symptoms have also been noted in families with poor family cohesion (Feldman, Rubenstein, & Rubin, 1988). Other factors influencing the expression of depression for a teenager include a lower degree of maternal acceptance (Garber, Robinson, & Valentiner, 1997), exposure to urban violence (Pastore, Fisher, & Friedman, 1996), and low self-esteem (Overholser, Adams, Lehnert, & Brinkman, 1995). This subclinical sad, irritable, and depressed symptom pattern often can precipitate distressing behavioral changes that are very upsetting to parents. For example, parents typically are distressed even by mild forms of social withdrawal (e.g., wanting to be alone, avoiding parent interaction, not talking to parents).

Teenagers who report depressive symptoms are at risk for continued irritable or depressive symptoms over time. In addition, teenagers who experience continued depression report lower self-esteem, higher anxiety, and higher levels of acting-out behavior (DuBois, Felner, Bartels, & Silverman, 1995). Males tend to externalize their depression through acting out, whereas females tend to internalize their depression through a negative self-concept (Donnelly & Wilson, 1994). Parents do not always recognize the underlying depressive symptoms of their teenagers and may exacerbate the problem by responding only to the externalizing, irritable, acting-out behaviors that fuel the teen-parent conflicts.

One common acting-out behavior is running away. Running away appears to have different meanings for adolescent boys and girls. For boys, running away tends to be associated with passive avoidance and internalization, whereas for girls, running away tends to be associated with a mixed pattern of simultaneously expressing withdrawal and overt deviancy (De Man, Dolan, Pelletier, & Reid, 1994). When an adolescent runs away from home, it is often seen as an expression of a need for help, fear of parental rejection, or unhappiness and dissatisfaction with a destructive or conflict-filled home situation (Jones, 1988). In addition, many runaways leave home because of physical or sexual abuse (Warren, Gary, & Moorhead, 1994). The threat or completion of running away by a teenager should be perceived by parents as a serious indication of distress and should be dealt with quickly.

Suicidal ideation is common for teenagers. In a survey of high school students, over 12% thought about killing or hurting themselves, and over 7% had actually tried to kill themselves at one time (Lewinsohn, Rohde, & Seeley, 1996). In another survey of junior and senior high school students, more than 33% reported suicidal thoughts, with significantly more girls than boys reporting these thoughts (Chartier & Lassen, 1994). Obviously, a diagnosable affective disorder using *DSM-IV* criteria (American Psychiatric Association, 1994) or a bona fide suicide attempt requires immediate intervention. At the same time, even the normal teenager can make statements such as "I wish I was dead" or "I wish I wasn't here." This type of statement often expresses a desire to obtain help from others to transcend their unsatisfactory life situation. Assessment of potentially suicidal behavior is beyond the scope of this chapter, but each instance of self-destructive ideation and behavior must be taken seriously and thoroughly evaluated.

SEXUALITY AND INTIMACY

Intimacy is very important to teenagers because they are slowly breaking away emotionally from their parents. Teenagers are notoriously prone to "falling in love" as a way of helping to define who they are by seeing themselves reflected in someone else (Erikson, 1968). With the onset of puberty and sexual development, teenagers can become very confused. In fact, although boys seem to have poorer awareness of physical changes as compared to girls, boys seem to deal better with their accompanying autonomy and individuality than do girls (Zani, 1991). Although clearly influenced by the onset of puberty, sexual behavior is also influenced by significant nonsexual psychological and social needs of the teenager (Hajcak & Garwood, 1988). The development of a sexual identity occurs both prior to and after the initiation of sexual intercourse, but it is recognized that the initiation of sexual behavior clearly influences the course of sexual identity. Most clinicians recognize that young teenagers are not psychologically prepared to deal with the interpersonal aspects of intense romantic relationships and the potential for untoward events occurring from nonmarital sexual intercourse.

Conflicts occur during adolescence between parents and teenagers regarding dating, sexualized behavior, and sexual values. Many times, the teenager's values reflect what he or she has learned from parents. Parents often have difficulty talking to their teenagers about sexual matters for fear of a negative interaction or for fear that increased sexual knowledge will lead to more sexualized behavior (Petty, 1995). Because parents avoid talking about sexual matters, the teenager can be subjected to misinformation from peers. Major predictors of having an open discussion about sexuality with parents is different for mothers and fathers, but openness in general family communication is clearly an important factor (Fisher, 1990). The clinical child psychologist can facilitate communication between the teenager and his or her parents regarding sexual matters and values and help to reduce areas of potential conflict.

The frequency of sexual activity of teenagers has risen over the past several decades. Currently, for unmarried women after the onset of menarche, 21% have had sexual intercourse by age 15, 38% by age 16, 50% by age 17, and 63% by age 18. Most of these unmarried women had older male partners, but the vast majority of the women had intercourse within the context of a committed relationship with their partners (e.g., "going steady" or being engaged) (Centers for Disease Control, 1997). For males, the onset of sexual behavior tends to occur at a somewhat younger age with relatively more partners than is typical for females. Once teenagers have initiated sexual intercourse, they are likely to engage in continued sexual behavior in the future. Factors associated with increased premarital sexual activity include permissive attitudes of the teenager, dating frequency at a young age, permissive parenting styles, intercourse at an early age, history of sexual abuse, lower educational aspirations or attainment, friends being sexually active, lower religiosity, poor parent support, nonintact family background, lower social class, drug use, and delinquency (Olson, Huszti, & Youll, 1995; Schumm, 1995).

Teenagers often experience conflict and distress regarding their sexual behavior. Each teenager must make a choice about how to express his or her sexuality, ranging from abstinence and suppression of sexual feelings to immediate gratification of sexual impulses. Obviously, the reasons a teenager chooses to become sexually active and/or engages in potentially risky sexual behaviors are multifaceted.

Females are clearly more committed to abstinence than males; females also see sexual activity as being detrimental to future goal attainment (De Gaston, Weed, & Jensen, 1996). Risky, indiscriminate sexual behavior can be an indicator of poor self-image because immature teenagers equate a sexual relationship with being a worthy person. In the same way, immature teenagers might believe their sexual relationship is a way of emancipating themselves from parental control or even of exacting revenge against parents. Teenagers often feel invulnerable to the consequences of their behavior, allowing them to disregard potentially risky situations such as sexually transmitted diseases and pregnancy (Olson et al., 1995). Teenagers clearly represent a high-risk group for acquired immunodeficiency syndrome and other health problems because of their predisposition for drug and sexual experimentation and their inclination to ignore the dangers of potentially risky situations (Olson, Huszti, Mason, & Seibert, 1989). Each teenager appears to have a particular sexual style and tolerance for sexual risk-taking, which must be understood if appropriate intervention is to take place (Buzwell & Rosenthal, 1996).

Some teenagers show considerable confusion about sexual orientation. The teenager with lesbian, gay, or bisexual inclinations or behavior can have considerable difficulty dealing with parents. Some teenagers are aware of their sexual preference in early adolescence and are at risk for lowered self-esteem, harassment from peers, engaging in self-injurious behavior, and discrimination in school environments. As a result of this vulnerability, the American Psychological Association (1993) developed a resolution on lesbian, gay, and bisexual youths in schools advocating for their rights and dignity, for their fair and safe treatment, and encouraging appropriate intervention by psychologists. Even though many teenagers may have confusion about their sexual preferences, most parents are not ambivalent about wanting their teenager to have a heterosexual orientation. The clinical child psychologist must recognize that many teenagers may not have a fully developed sexual identity and, as a result, great care must be taken to not inappropriately influence the teenager. At the same time, because of the profound impact any potentially impulsive behavior might have on future choices, it has been recommended that clinicians should offer advice that the teenager postpone any sexual choices until a certain modicum of wisdom has been obtained. Usually occurring with greater maturity, this increased wisdom is seen as expanding both the quality and quantity of decisions for the teenager (Lundy & Rekers, 1995). The clinical child psychologist must help the teenager make an appropriate choice without unduly influencing the decision process by a preconceived bias of sexual partner gender preferences, by parental attitude, or by societal notions of appropriate sexual behavior, whether positively or negatively predisposed to homosexuality. In addition, the focus of attention should be to help deal with any distressing and conflicting feelings of the teenager or in the teen-parent interaction. In addition, Lundy and Rekers believe that the major goal of a quick and effective intervention is to expand the nature and quality of future choices for the teenager. This is accomplished by focusing attention on potential health risks associated with onset of sexual behavior, on the emotional issues surrounding an early sexual lifestyle, and on the risks of premature sexual involvement regardless of sexual orientation.

Alcohol, Tobacco, and Drug Use

The use of alcohol, tobacco, and drugs is very common during the teenage years. For the past two decades, the Monitoring the Future study has annually surveyed high school seniors as to their alcohol, tobacco, and drug use (National Institute on Drug Abuse, 1998). Clearly, alcohol remains the intoxicant of choice for teenagers. Among the high school seniors of the class of 1997, more than 81% admitted to alcohol use at some time during their lifetime, but nearly 75% admitted to alcohol use within the past year and 53% admitted to getting drunk within the past year. The statistics on alcohol use have remained fairly stable over the past several years in spite of numerous public service campaigns trying to discourage teenage drinking. In the same way, illicit drug use is also common with teenagers. In the survey of the class of 1997, over 54% reported illicit drug use sometime during their lifetime and over 42% reported drug use within the past year. The modal illicit drug used is marijuana or hashish, with over 38% of the teenagers admitting using it within the past year (National Institute on Drug Abuse, 1998). Although this represents a deceleration of the increase of marijuana use over the past six years, the admission by teenagers of marijuana or hashish use within the past year has always been fairly high, fluctuating between 21% and 51% between 1975 and 1997. In fact, the historic changes in marijuana use appear most likely related to the perceived risks and disapproval of the drug, which tends to change over time (Bachman, Johnston, & O'Malley, 1998). Lifetime prevalence reported by the class of 1997 indicated that 17% have used stimulants, 16% have used inhalants, 15% have used hallucinogens, 9% have used cocaine, 9% have used sedatives, and 2% have used heroin (National Institute on Drug Abuse, 1998). In the same survey, over 60% of teenagers have tried cigarettes sometime during their school-age years. Among the class of 1997, more than 24% of seniors report daily cigarette use, with more than half of those students smoking more than a half-pack of cigarettes per day (National Institute on Drug Abuse, 1998).

The vast majority of teenagers use alcohol, tobacco, or drugs on an intermittent and casual basis. In fact, most teenagers are able to control their use of alcohol or drugs. On the other hand, the habitual use of tobacco can have long-term health effects that are not fully recognized by teenagers. Unfortunately, the potential always exists for teenagers who use drugs or alcohol on an indiscriminate, impulsive, or frequent basis to significantly harm themselves. A teenage pattern of drug or alcohol abuse can lead to significant adult substance abuse patterns. The teenagers who appear to engage in risky, out-of-control drug and alcohol use are clearly in need of immediate psychological intervention.

Alcohol, tobacco, and/or illicit drug use by a teenager usually precipitates teen-parent conflicts. Parents do not comprehend why their teenager does not appreciate the inherent risks of drug, tobacco, or alcohol use. If parents are helped to understand the developmental basis for this behavior, the resulting teen-parent conflict can sometimes be reduced. Teenagers use drugs, alcohol, and tobacco for several divergent reasons. First, teenagers use these substances as a way of experimenting with life. Getting drunk, smoking your first cigarette, or experiencing substance intoxication in some circles is regarded as a rite of passage for teenagers. Second, drug or alcohol use is often related to intensified peer interaction and/or identification with a peer subculture. The use of drugs or alcohol can foster teen camaraderie because it is social activity

and/or is a way of instantly identifying with their peer subgroup (e.g., heads or goths). In the same way, tobacco use can help to define a teenager's social group. Third, drug, alcohol, or tobacco use can represent an overt rebellion from parental values. Because most parents do not want their teenagers to engage in drug, alcohol, or tobacco use, teenagers can functionally defy their parents and assert their independence from parental values. Finally, drug, alcohol, and tobacco use can be a method by which teenagers deal with emotional distress. Many teenagers report that smoking a cigarette helps them to "calm down." In addition, alcohol and certain drugs can provide self-medication for adolescent depression and anxiety. Regardless of the reason, parents who can understand why their teenager uses alcohol, tobacco, or drugs will be in a better position to provide appropriate intervention.

SCHOOL DIFFICULTIES

Schools can be very stressful places for teenagers. In recent years, violence toward persons and property has taken place in schools with greater frequency. School violence can include bullying, victimization, noncompliance with rules, vandalism, fighting, and, in extreme cases, shootings. Unfortunately, a violence-laden school environment can lead to untoward effects on teenagers, such as precipitating dropping out, increasing bullying and harassment, increasing drug and alcohol abuse, promoting gang membership, and increasing suicidal incidence (Stephens, 1997). This kind of educational environment erodes a sense of school belonging that has been significantly associated with academic motivation-related measures, including expectancy for success, valuing schoolwork, general school motivation, and self-reported academic effort (Goodenow & Grady, 1993). In addition, secondary school environments, especially those in urban settings, are often characterized as overcrowded and understaffed, which adds to the overall stress. Although most schools do not present a significant threat to the safety and security of students, it is recognized that the aggression and violence in our society affect schools in both subtle and substantive ways (Goldstein & Conoley, 1997). The clinical child psychologist must be aware of the pressures inherent in the teenager's school environment and how these may affect that particular teenager.

Many other stresses contribute to the potential that a teenager may have poor academic performance. Adolescent rebellion and acting-out may be manifested in the school environment by disobeying school rules, not completing school assignments, fighting with peers, or truancy. In fact, some teachers report a marked increase in problem behaviors after developmental transitions such as onset of puberty. In the same way, the transition from primary to secondary school can be stressful for teenagers because more emphasis is placed on academic competition that requires organization and time management. Obviously, these transitions and problem behaviors can have very negative effects on academic performance. In the same way, social standing and popularity in a peer group is often a preoccupation for the adolescent. Teenagers commonly report that they like school because they can see their friends; their primary motivation is not on the academic work, but on the opportunity to interact with peers. Unfortunately, preoccupation with being socially popular at school is not always conducive to adolescent mental health. A study of teenagers who perceived themselves as unpopular revealed that they experienced emotional and behavioral distress about their status (E. Cohen, Reinherz, & Frost, 1994). Regardless of the source of stress, the clinical child psychologist must be sensitive to the developmental changes that affect teenagers.

At the same time that school-based and peer-based stresses can erode academic performance, parents become more preoccupied with the importance of above-average academic performance when college admission looms in the future. The educational goals articulated by parents are strongly transmitted to the teenager. In addition, teenagers tend to have even higher college expectations than parents do for them (Trusty & Pirtle, 1998), which places even more stress on the teenager. Even though teenagers usually have a desire similar to their parents' to perform well in school, academic underachievement and failure do occur. Academic failure appears to increase teen-parent conflicts in that teenagers become more demanding and negative toward parents and parents become more disapproving and punishing of the teenager (Repetti, 1996). The clinical child psychologist must assess the reasons for poor academic performance and determine whether it is caused by an emotional, behavioral, or learning deficit. Remediation of school-related problems is often successful if the problems are identified early by the clinical child psychologist.

RULE-BREAKING AND ANTISOCIAL BEHAVIORS

Many teenagers have minimal regard for rules and social customs. Rule-breaking and antisocial behaviors such as lying, fighting, and stealing seem to peak in midadolescence, with boys being more accepting of antisocial acts than are girls (Keltikangas-Jaervinen & Lindeman, 1997). Along with their proclivity toward taking greater risks, teenagers seem to be predisposed to break rules. Most teenage rule-breaking is not extreme enough to be diagnosable as a mental disorder in the *DSM-IV*, such as oppositional defiant disorder or conduct disorder (American Psychiatric Association, 1994). At the same time, inappropriate or antisocial behaviors cause parental concern and can be the focus of treatment by clinical child psychologists.

Cheating and lying are common adolescent behaviors (Stouthamer-Loeber, 1986). Teenagers cheat especially in school environments where grade performance is more highly valued than mastery and improvement (Anderman, Griesinger, & Westerfield, 1998). High levels of dishonest behavior have been seen with both secular and religious high school students; cheating does not appear to be related to a lack of moral reasoning (Bruggeman & Hart, 1996). Lying is seen by most parents and teachers as a serious behavioral transgression, especially because chronic lying has been linked to delinquency and adult maladjustment (Stouthamer-Loeber, 1986). Lying frequency has been shown to decrease with age. The frequency of lying seems to increase in families when mothers do not adequately supervise their teens, when teens are rejected, and when parents do not get along or live together (Stouthamer-Loeber & Loeber, 1986). Parents need to understand that lying and deception can be strategic ways for the teenager to avoid punishment or conflict. In fact, infrequent and mild forms of lying may be a method by which the teenager can assure privacy and independence by thwarting parental access to information. In this regard, lying can serve a developmental function of aiding in the separation from parent control.

Teenagers also engage in stealing, which often takes the form of shoplifting. Many adolescent thefts are an act of bravado and not necessarily predictive of adult stealing behavior. The tendency to shoplift is generally not related to socioeconomic status. Teenagers appear to shoplift for excitement, although peer pressure may have some influence (Lo, 1994). Involvement in shoplifting has also been shown to be strongly influenced by the teen's beliefs regarding the morality of the behavior, attachment to parents, and friends' shoplifting behavior (Cox, Cox, Anderson, & Moschis, 1993). Stealing may serve as an initiating ritual, as a way of establishing peer group membership (Meeks, 1979). For similar reasons, some teenagers engage in vandalism and destruction of property. Teen vandalism in schools is associated with younger teenagers, with higher-status families, and with being absent less often from schools (Tygart, 1988). The thoughtless destruction of property can also be the result of the impulsive expression of adolescent anger.

Regardless of the kind of rule-breaking behavior displayed, the clinical child psychologist should try to understand why this behavior occurs. Nonpathological, normal variants of rule-breaking behavior can easily escalate into more serious pathological, antisocial behavior. Obviously, if the rule-breaking behaviors become chronic, intense, and/or persistent, more frequent and intense intervention will be necessary. Rule-breaking behavior must be treated because it can damage the teen-parent relationship, which otherwise can be a protective factor to moderate further adolescent risk taking and antisocial behavior (Jessor, 1998).

THERAPEUTIC CONSIDERATIONS FOR ADOLESCENTS AND PARENTS

THERAPEUTIC ALLIANCE WITH TEENAGERS AND PARENTS

Even normal teenagers are often uncommunicative and aloof toward adults, but for the teenager who has been compelled by parents to obtain psychotherapy, there can be severe resistance to treatment. For the most part, adolescents have a high frequency of missed sessions, tardiness, distractibility during sessions, and premature termination of treatment. Teenagers often overtly express anger about being forced to attend therapy. This can lead to unpredictable or rebellious behavior during therapy, which can functionally sabotage the therapeutic process. Resisting therapy can be another mechanism whereby the teenager can inappropriately express independence. When a teenager does not cooperate with therapy, parents become upset, which in turn can escalate the preexisting teen-parent conflict. Although the psychologist might be tempted to aggressively confront the teenager's resistance to therapy, it is rarely a constructive solution. When resistance is discovered, the psychologist should acknowledge its presence and then help the teenager try to understand why it happened (Semrud-Clikeman, 1995).

The therapeutic alliance is the centerpiece of any successful psychotherapy with teenagers. Without a nonjudgmental, supportive relationship, the teenager will have trouble dealing with the difficult, sensitive issues that emerge in therapy. This stable, positive relationship can buffer a teenager's acting-out and resistance to treatment. Beginning with the initial session, the psychologist should listen carefully to the teenager's concerns. The psychologist should indicate that the purpose of therapy is to help the teenager improve his or her life, but the teenager must define his or her own needs for treatment if there is to be investment in the therapeutic process. During initial sessions, some teenagers may not admit to emotional or behavioral symptoms (e.g., depression, anxiety, conduct problems) because doing so would be tantamount to "having a problem" or "being crazy." Even so, most teenagers will readily admit to anger, unhappiness, worry, being in trouble, or conflict with parents. By tapping into the teenager's distress and dissatisfaction, the psychologist can improve treatment motivation.

Parents can also be helpful in improving motivation and cooperation for treatment. They can provide their teenager with incentives for participation and/or with gentle coercion against nonparticipation during the first few sessions. For example, the teenager could be given a valued gift or selected privileges at home if he or she attends a specific number of therapy sessions. In the same way, the teenager could be prohibited from attending a special social function if he or she does not attend therapy. This approach is suggested only for the first few sessions of treatment to overcome any initial inhibition. For sustained cooperation and motivation in therapy, the teenager must feel that therapy participation is in his or her own best interest and is independently valuable without any external incentives.

A psychologist who appears uninterested, uncommitted, or indifferent rarely evokes a positive response from a teenager. In the same way, a psychologist who moralizes or parrots parental prohibitions is not appreciated. Most teenagers appreciate supportive, nonjudgmental interactions with adults. Teenagers who feel treated fairly are rarely uncooperative. In fact, even though most teenagers are ambivalent and protest attending therapy, they will work productively and regularly attend sessions if a good therapeutic alliance has been established. The teenager must believe that the psychologist is an advocate for the teenager's point of view and that there is hope of a positive treatment outcome. Even when the teenager challenges the psychologist's authority, the psychologist must continue to be accepting and uncritical so that trust can develop.

During the first session, parents and teenager should be seen together briefly. The psychologist should describe therapy as a shared undertaking where problems can be addressed by either the parents or the teenager. At this point, teenagers often deny that they have a problem. The psychologist should acknowledge the teenager's point of view, but also point out that if the parents believe that there is a problem, then that in itself is a problem for the teenager. Even if the teenager does not indicate any emotional or behavioral problem, the teenager will usually acknowledge disagreements with parents. Articulating a problem that parents and teenager share in common (e.g., teen-parent conflict) is helpful for setting the tone for a cooperative endeavor. The consent/assent form that includes a description of the limits of confidentiality is usually completed during this initial contact. Although not a legal requirement, the teenager should sign the form indicating agreement. At this point during this initial session, parents and teenager should be allowed to decide who should be seen first in private. By observing this decision process, the psychologist can develop insights into how parents and teenager interact. If they cannot reach a decision, the teenager should be seen first because that choice communicates commitment to the teenager.

During this initial private visit, the psychologist can hear the teenager's concerns without intrusion from parents. The teenager's point of view should be acknowledged and supported. The psychologist must reassure the teenager that he or she will be treated fairly and not be thought of as "crazy." The psychologist should also indicate that the teenager's problems are not solely caused by the teenager alone, but should be understood as a complex interaction of several factors (e.g., teenager behavior, parent behavior, peer influences, school, extended family). At the end of the private session, the present author suggests that the teenager fill out a sentence completion test or other paper-and-pencil task (e.g., structured questionnaire, diary, or essay). If the teenager refuses, the psychologist should not compel the teenager to complete the task. Written assignments can yield important supplemental information because teenagers often write down important information that they might be unwilling to express in face-to-face interaction.

If there is sufficient time during the first visit, the parents should also be seen in private. Parents should be allowed to express their concerns, feelings, and complaints with few restrictions. Using the common problem articulated in the initial session as a starting point, the psychologist can describe the factors contributing to the family's problems. The psychologist must not reveal information from the private conversation with the teenager unless there has been prior agreement. The psychologist should assure the parents that their teenager's problems are common to adolescence, but the psychologist must also not guarantee a particular outcome. During this interaction, the psychologist can assess family dynamics that contribute to the teen-parent problem. The parents should be warned that during the family sessions, the psychologist might appear to take sides against the parents in favor of the teenager. The parents need to understand that by supporting the teenager, trust and communication will be encouraged, which are necessary precursors to successful treatment.

The teenager and parents should be seen together at the end of the initial session. The psychologist should reiterate the common goals for parents and teenager (i.e., eliminating conflict, distress, and/or interpersonal discord) as a way of helping parents and teenager stay motivated for treatment. As issues are being recapitulated, the psychologist must not breach confidences from the private interviews. A tentative treatment plan should be articulated, but only after the teenager has provided significant input. The teenager should not be coerced into accepting a plan. Because teenagers can functionally sabotage treatment, accommodations may have to be made if their cooperation is to be maintained. As long as the teenager believes that the psychologist is an advocate, he or she usually continues to be motivated.

CONFIDENTIALITY ISSUES

The clinical child psychologist must maintain confidentiality consistent with the Ethical Principles of Psychologists and Code of Conduct of the American Psychological Association (1992). Ensuring confidentiality is a frequent ethical dilemma for psychologists treating teenagers and their parents. If not assured of nearly complete confidentiality, teenagers would probably refuse treatment, fearing that private information will be divulged to parents. Teenagers are often suspicious of parental intentions and motives because they were most likely forced to attend therapy by their parents. Therapists very often make treatment conditional on the fact that confidentially is maintained from parents even though there is no legal basis for doing so (Gustafson & McNamara, 1987). By keeping information confidential, open communication is encouraged during treatment.

During the initial session, confidentiality should be discussed with the parents and the teenager together. Misunderstandings can be avoided if a consent/assent form that includes a description of the limits of confidentiality between parents and teenager is signed at that session. This description should stipulate that no written or oral information will be communicated to schools, mental health agencies, physicians, insurance providers, and/or others without the written approval of the parents. The parents and the teenager should also be informed that cases are sometimes discussed among colleagues, but only information necessary to achieve the purposes of the consultation will be discussed. The legal limits of confidentiality should also be explained, including those circumstances when confidentiality must be broken either by ethical guidelines (e.g., danger to self or others) or by statute (e.g., child abuse reporting laws).

Parents and teenagers often have radically different expectations about how confidential information should be handled. Teenagers often believe that whatever they say should be totally confidential. In the same way, parents often believe that the psychologist should reveal information about the teenager to them because they are the parents and have the teenager's best interests at heart. The psychologist must clarify any divergent expectations of confidentiality between parents and teenager at the first session. The psychologist should negotiate an agreement between the parents and teenager that stipulates clear guidelines for handling confidential information. Even when the psychologist has clarified confidentiality, parents may still expect to be treated preferentially. For example, some parents may try to telephone the psychologist in an attempt to obtain information about what was discussed during therapy. The psychologist must also be clear with parents about how the parents' confidential information will be handled. For example, during a private session, a parent may admit to past or present inappropriate behavior (e.g., illicit drug use, extramarital affairs) that the parent does not want the teenager to know. As a way of reassuring the teenager, parents sometimes agree not to have any private sessions or phone calls with the psychologist, which ensures against any compromise of confidentiality.

Confidentiality must be broken to protect the teenager and/or parents from harm to self or others. The clinical child psychologist must assess the potential of danger to self or others and disclose that information to appropriate professional workers, public authorities, the potential victim, and/or the family of the teenager. In most clinical situations, it is very difficult to determine if the teenager or family presents a bona fide risk of danger to self or others. The decision to break confidentiality is affected by the psychologist's own values and how he or she interprets the degree of risk for that teenager. For example, some psychologists might break confidentiality if a teenager casually experiments with an illicit drug or alcohol, but other psychologists might break confidentiality only if the teenager chronically abuses drugs or alcohol and, in their opinion, presents a substantial risk. This lack of consensus regarding breaking confidentiality and adolescent risk taking has been illustrated in a survey of pediatric psychologists on topics such as alcohol or drug use, sexual behavior, criminal or illegal behavior, and suicidal or homicidal intentions (Rae & Worchel, 1991). To eliminate any potential confusion, the psychologist should fully inform the teenager regarding the kinds of risky behaviors that the psychologist considers sufficient to break confidentiality. Before the decision is made to break confidentiality, the psychologist should also be familiar with relevant state statutes and be willing to consult with attorneys and other professional colleagues as needed (Gustafson & McNamara, 1987). In addition, the psychologist must be aware that by breaking confidentiality, the therapeutic alliance with the teenager could be compromised, which might precipitate premature termination.

Because of the nature of the presenting problems and the importance of using a joint interview and treatment formats, parents and teenagers should always be encouraged to discuss their concerns about confidentiality during the sessions. Because many teenagers view their parents as being intrusive and meddling, the psychologist can help teenagers understand that their parents' concerns are a sincere expression of caring for them. In the same way, because many parents feel that their teenager's behavior is deviant, the psychologist can help the parents understand that the behavior is typical. The psychologist must be careful not to take sides while confidentiality is discussed, but should encourage open communication and mutual respect for privacy. Openly discussing confidentiality can help parents and teenager to gain further understanding of each other and aid in the resolution of teen-parent problems.

MODALITY OF THERAPEUTIC INTERVENTION

Although not always logistically possible, both parents should be involved in treatment with their teenager. The necessity of parental participation is dictated by the nature of the presenting problem. For example, if the teen-parent problem concerns primarily the teenager's having an emotional problem (e.g., depressive symptoms), individual sessions with the teenager may be preferable. In contrast, if the teen-parent problem concerns teenage behavior that is unacceptable to the parents (e.g., breaking rules) or ongoing discord in the family, sessions with the parents and teenager may be preferable. The teenager's age and/or maturity will also influence the level of parental involvement. Younger or more immature teenagers who are more dependent on parents for financial and emotional support necessitate involvement of parents in treatment. On the other hand, nearly emancipated teenagers (e.g., an 18-year-old attending college) may not require as much direct parent participation.

The clinical child psychologist treating teen-parent problems must be flexible in the treatment approach utilized. Treatment usually focuses on the teenager, on the parents (family), and/or on a combination of parents and teenager. For treating teenagers, a variety of outpatient interventions such as individual, group, and family psychotherapy can be useful, but the psychologist must choose the approach that best fits the presenting problem. Individual therapy is an obvious treatment of choice for teenagers who have internalized emotional problems (e.g., depression, poor self-concept, anxiety). Group therapy is the treatment of choice for teenagers who have problems with peers (e.g., poor peer acceptance, poor social skills, lack of appropriate assertiveness). Group therapy allows the teenager to appropriately deal with peer influences and constructively assert independence from parents. Group therapy can also be helpful with resistant teenagers because teenagers are more likely to listen to another teenager than to a psychologist. Family therapy is the treatment of choice when participation by parents and/or other family members is necessary to resolve interpersonal conflicts. Inpatient, residential, and other equally restrictive treatments (e.g., boarding school placement, living with a relative) are usually unnecessary for nonpathological teen-parent problems and should only be considered as a treatment of last resort.

For treating parents, a variety of outpatient interventions such as individual, couples, group, and family psychotherapy can be used. The therapist must assess how useful each approach might be in resolving the teen-parent problems. For example, couples therapy might be helpful if significant discord occurs between the parents themselves and/or significant marital difficulties exist. In a similar way, group therapy might be helpful for parents who are aided by the support and experience of other parents having similar teen-parent conflicts. Finally, family therapy is useful in helping all family members understand the characteristic interaction patterns among and between family members. Family therapy is especially useful in elucidating family pathology and helps family members change structural relationships, which will eventually help resolve teen-parent problems.

Before engaging in any treatment, the clinical child psychologist must choose how to best approach the teen-parent problem. If the teenager is manifesting specific behavioral or emotional symptoms, the specific symptom should be treated directly. Although this chapter discusses only nonpathological problems, a variety of empirically supported interventions used to treat clinical disorders may be helpful in ameliorating specific behavioral and emotional symptoms. For example, if the teenager is experiencing depressive symptoms, cognitive-behavioral treatment might be helpful (Kaslow & Thompson, 1998). (Treatment approaches for specific disorders are described in other chapters in this *Handbook*.) Regardless, treatment must focus on the teen-parent conflict because it is always a central part of the parents' referral concern.

A MULTIMODAL APPROACH TO RESOLVING TEEN-PARENT CONFLICT

Before beginning treatment of a teen-parent conflict, the psychologist should determine the general goals of treatment. Foster and Robin (1998) state that therapy usually includes one or more of three basic goals. First, the specific inappropriate teen behaviors that trigger teen-parent arguments should be addressed. Second, the therapist should make improvements in interactions of family members by decreasing family arguments. Third, the therapist should help all family members be more satisfied with relationships in the family. Foster and Robin have provided a comprehensive review of the empirical literature pertaining to the treatment of teen-parent conflict, including such areas as problem-solving and communication skills, beliefs and cognitive distortions, angry affect, and structural factors of family interaction. In any treatment of teen-parent conflict and discord, these elements must be addressed, but the psychologist must choose which areas of dysfunction actually require remediation for that particular family. Obviously, the psychologist must assess the importance of each of these areas, tailoring the

treatment plan to that particular teenager and his or her family.

Treatment of teen-parent conflicts are best accomplished using a multimodal approach. Usually, treatment falls into three discrete domains. First, the psychologist should educate the parents about normal adolescent behavior and development. Second, the psychologist should help the teenager, parents, and other family members to improve communication, interaction, and understanding of each other. Finally, the psychologist should help the parents develop skills in managing the teenager's behavior. In addition, because of the advent of managed care, the psychologist should use time-limited modalities during treatment (M.C. Roberts & Hurley, 1997).

EDUCATION ABOUT ADOLESCENT DEVELOPMENT

Parents often do not understand what constitutes normal adolescent behavior and, as a result, misunderstandings can occur. When parents understand adolescent development, they can anticipate potential areas of conflict and can interpret the teenager's behavior within that context. The psychologist can use a didactic approach to help parents decrease inappropriate expectations of their teenager and to help them understand their teenager's motivations. During this stage of therapy, the psychologist can dissuade parents from overreacting to typical teenage outlandish behavior and emotional reactivity. For example, parents can be helped to understand that their teenager's secrecy is not an oppositional, sneaky behavior, but actually is a developmentally appropriate way for the teenager to separate from them. As another example, increasing parents' knowledge about teens' usual expressions of anger can be helpful. Parents have a tendency to take anger expression as personal affronts to them and their authority rather than seeing anger expression in the larger context of normal adolescent development. In the context of describing adolescent development, the psychologist can address major misattributions and cognitive distortions that affect parents' ability to respond appropriately to their teenager (Robin & Foster, 1989). In addition, in the context of talking about normal developmental issues, the psychologist can address structural issues of family functioning through a process of multisystemic or functional family therapy (Foster & Robin, 1998).

COMMUNICATION AND PROBLEM-SOLVING SKILLS TRAINING

Interpersonal communication and problem-solving skills are often lacking when a teen-parent conflict exists. Although the parents and the teenager purport to be communicating with each other, their communication is prone to significant distortions. The psychologist can improve communication in the family by role playing and didactic instruction. Communication training usually involves elements such as development of listening skills, accurate expression of feelings, practice in expressing positive or affectionate comments, providing rationales, giving feedback, topic persistence, being straightforward in communication, congruence of verbal and nonverbal communications, and avoiding attributions. In addition, psychologists can train parents and teenager in problem-solving and negotiating skills. Problem-solving training usually involves elements such as problem definition, solution listing, evaluation, implementation, and reevaluation (Barkley, Edwards, & Robin, 1999; Foster & Robin, 1998). The empathic understanding of parents and teenager can help reduce conflict within the family.

During the process of communication training, the psychologist can identify other areas of interpersonal functioning that may require intervention. More specifically, other family members may be identified as contributors to the family dysfunction. By teaching skills and processing communication during therapy sessions, family members will be better able to understand and cope with negative affect. It is hoped that all family members will develop the skills to solve problems using each other as positive resources. This process should improve mutual respect and acceptance for each other's point of view and help to facilitate more constructive interpersonal interactions.

BEHAVIOR MANAGEMENT AND CONTRACTING

Parents often complain about their teenager's inappropriate behaviors. When the teenager's behavior has been improved, many of the teen-parent conflicts dissolve. Barkley et al. (1999) describe a comprehensive approach to dealing with defiant and oppositional teens. In this manualized program based on empirically supported research, parents are taught basic principles of behavior modification and behavior management. Parents are helped to understand how their reactions can inadvertently reinforce an inappropriate behavioral pattern between them and their teenager. In addition, parents and teenager are helped to develop a behavioral contract based on contingency management principles (Barkley et al., 1999).

The psychologist must mediate between parents and teenager during behavioral contracting so that both sides can reach a settlement. Accomplishing this goal is sometimes difficult because teenagers often become angry when restrictions are put on their behavior and parents often fear losing control if they agree to negotiate. The psychologist must actively arbitrate between teenager and parents to develop a workable behavioral contract. The psychologist should indicate that neither the teenager nor the parents will get exactly what they want in the behavioral contract. Parents must understand that most teenagers are capable of sabotaging a behavioral contract if they cannot be persuaded that the contract is for their benefit. The teenager's active participation is mandatory if a behavioral contract is to be effective. On the other hand, teenagers must understand that parents are still morally and legally responsible for their behavior and, as a result, they must exert appropriate parental control. Because teenagers and parents often have intransigent points of view, compromise can be very difficult. This mediation can be very stressful for the psychologist because the discussion of these concrete issues recapitulates the teen-parent discord.

Observing this discord during the sessions helps the psychologist understand the family's interaction patterns and can lead to specific clinical interventions. For example, during the session, the psychologist can identify misconceptions or misattributions that interfere with the compromise process. In particular, the parents might believe that granting the teenager a later curfew is allowing the possibility of untoward events such as pregnancy, drug use, and antisocial behaviors. In a similar way, the teenager might believe that not having a later curfew is equated with having no friends and being unpopular. The psychologist must facilitate a mutually agreeable contract between parents and teenager.

The behavior contract should always be in written form because this forces parents and teenager to be explicit. The more detail the contract has, the less likely there will be misunderstandings. The contract should have positive consequences specified for compliance and negative consequences for noncompliance. The psychologist can help parents and teenager to develop a contract that is beneficial to all of them. For example, the teenager might be willing to come home by curfew if his or her allowance is increased. In the same way, the parents might agree to a later curfew if the teenager has been compliant with curfew for several weeks.

CONCLUSIONS

Teenagers are usually referred to a clinical child psychologist because of parental concern about emotional or behavioral problems and/or about conflicts with parents. Because they tend to resist psychological treatment, teenage patients are regarded as challenging by therapists. Many of the teen-parent problems and conflicts described in this chapter should be viewed as a normal part of growing up for a teenager. Although teenagers and their families can be difficult for the clinical child psychologist, often substantive progress can be made in a relatively short period of time. Empirically supported treatments can be provided that are effective in ameliorating specific behavioral and emotional symptoms for the teenager. By developing a collaborative alliance with teenager and parents, the psychologist can effectively treat teen-parent conflicts by teaching specific problem-solving, communication, and behavior management skills. This can serve to ameliorate the presenting issues, and the skills learned may facilitate resilience in parents and teenager alike.

REFERENCES

American Psychiatric Association. (1994). *Diagnostic and statistical manual of mental disorders (4th ed.).* Washington, DC: Author.

American Psychological Association. (1992). Ethical principles of psychologists and code of conduct. *American Psychologist, 47,* 1597–1611.

American Psychological Association. (1993). *Policy statements on lesbian, gay, and bisexual concerns: Resolution on lesbian, gay, and bisexual youths in schools.* Washington, DC: Author.

Anderman, E.M., Griesinger, T., & Westerfield, G. (1998). Motivation and cheating during adolescence. *Journal of Educational Psychology, 90,* 84–93.

Arnett, J.J. (1999). Adolescent storm and stress, reconsidered. *American Psychologist, 54,* 317–326.

Bachman, J.G., Johnston, L.D., & O'Malley, P.M. (1998). Explaining recent increases in students' marijuana use: Impacts of perceived risks and disapproval, 1976 through 1996. *American Journal of Public Health, 88,* 887–892.

Barkley, R.A., Edwards, G.H., & Robin, A.L. (1999). *Defiant teens: A clinician's manual for assessment and family intervention.* New York: Guilford Press.

Bruggeman, E.L., & Hart, K.J. (1996). Cheating, lying, and moral reasoning by religious and secular high school students. *Journal of Educational Research, 89,* 340–344.

Buzwell, S., & Rosenthal, D. (1996). Constructing a sexual self: Adolescents' sexual self-perceptions and sexual risk-taking. *Journal of Research on Adolescence, 6,* 489–513.

Centers for Disease Control. (1997). *Fertility, family planning, and women's health: New data from the 1995 national survey of family growth* (DHHS Publication No. PHS 97–1995). Washington DC: U.S. Government Printing Office.

Chartier, G.M., & Lassen, M.K. (1994). Adolescent depression: Children's Depression Inventory norms, suicidal ideation, and (weak) gender effects. *Adolescence, 29,* 859–864.

Cohen, E., Reinherz, H.Z., & Frost, A.K. (1994). Self-perceptions of unpopularity in adolescence: Links to past and current adjustment. *Child and Adolescent Social Work Journal, 11,* 37–52.

Cohen, M., Adler, N., Beck, A., & Irwin, C.E. (1986). Parental reactions to the onset of adolescence. *Journal of Adolescent Health Care, 7,* 101–106.

Conger, K.J., Conger, R.D., & Scaramella, L.V. (1997). Parents, siblings, psychological control, and adolescent adjustment. *Journal of Adolescent Research, 12,* 113–138.

Cox, A.D., Cox, D., Anderson, R.D., & Moschis, G.P. (1993). Social influences on adolescent shoplifting: Theory, evidence, and implications for the retail industry. *Journal of Retailing, 69,* 234–246.

De Gaston, J.F., Weed, S., & Jensen, L. (1996). Understanding gender differences in adolescent sexuality. *Adolescence, 31,* 217–231.

De Man, A., Dolan, D., Pelletier, R., & Reid, C. (1994). Adolescent running away behavior: Active or passive avoidance? *Journal of Genetic Psychology, 155,* 59–64.

Donnelly, M., & Wilson, R. (1994). The dimensions of depression in early adolescence. *Personality and Individual Differences, 17,* 425–430.

DuBois, D.L., Felner, R.D., Bartels, C.L., & Silverman, M.M. (1995). Stability of self-reported depressive symptoms in a community sample of children and adolescents. *Journal of Clinical Child Psychology, 24,* 386–396.

Ellis-Schwabe, M., & Thornburg, H.D. (1986). Conflict areas between parents and their adolescents. *Journal of Psychology, 120,* 59–68.

Erikson, E.H. (1963). *Childhood and society* (2nd ed.). New York: Norton.

Erikson, E.H. (1968). *Identity: Youth and crisis.* New York: Norton.

Feldman S.S., & Quatman, T. (1988). Factors influencing age expectations for adolescent autonomy: A study of early adolescents and parents. *Journal of Early Adolescence, 8,* 325–343.

Feldman, S.S., Rubenstein, J.L., & Rubin, C. (1988). Depressive affect and restraint in early adolescents: Relationships with family structure, family process, and friendship support. *Journal of Early Adolescence, 8,* 279–296.

Fisher, T.D. (1990). Characteristics of mothers and fathers who talk to their adolescent children about sexuality. *Journal of Psychology and Human Sexuality, 3,* 53–70.

Foster, S.L., & Robin, A.L. (1998). Parent-adolescent conflict and relationship discord. In E.J. Mash & R.A. Barkley (Eds.), *Treatment of childhood disorders* (2nd ed., pp. 601–646). New York: Guilford Press.

Garber, J., Robinson, N.S., & Valentiner, D. (1997). The relation between parenting and adolescent depression: Self-worth as a mediator. *Journal of Adolescent Research, 12,* 12–33.

Goldstein, A.P., & Conoley, J.C. (1997). Student aggression: Current status. In A.P. Goldstein & J.C. Conoley (Eds.), *School violence intervention: A practical handbook* (pp. 3–19). New York: Guilford Press.

Goodenow, C., & Grady, K.E. (1993). The relationship of school belonging and friends' values to academic motivation among urban adolescent students. *Journal of Experimental Education, 62,* 60–71.

Gustafson, K.E., & McNamara, J.R. (1987). Confidentiality with minor clients: Issues and guidelines for therapists. *Professional Psychology: Research and Practice, 18,* 503–508.

Hajcak, F., & Garwood, P. (1988). What parents can do to prevent pseudo-hypersexuality in adolescents. *Family Therapy, 15,* 99–105.

Hastings, P., & Grusec, J.E. (1997). Conflict outcome as a function of parental accuracy in perceived child cognitions and affect. *Social Development, 6,* 76–90.

Jessor, R. (1998). New perspectives on adolescent risk behavior. In R. Jessor (Ed.), *New perspectives on adolescent risk behavior* (pp. 1–10). New York: Cambridge University Press.

Jones, L.P. (1988). A typology of adolescent runaways. *Child and Adolescent Social Work Journal, 5,* 16–29.

Kaslow, N.J., & Thompson, M.P. (1998). Applying the criteria for empirically supported treatments to studies of psychosocial interventions for child and adolescent depression. *Journal of Clinical Child Psychology, 27,* 146–155.

Kazdin, A.E., & Marciano, P.L. (1998). Childhood and adolescent depression. In E.J. Mash & R.A. Barkley (Eds.), *Treatment of childhood disorders* (2nd ed., pp. 211–248). New York: Guilford Press.

Keltikangas-Jaervinen, L., & Lindeman, M. (1997). Evaluation of theft, lying, and fighting in adolescence. *Journal of Youth and Adolescence, 26,* 467–483.

Lantz, J.E. (1975). The rational treatment of parental adjustment reaction to adolescence. *Clinical Social Work Journal, 3,* 100–108.

Lewinsohn, P.M., Rohde, P., & Seeley, J.R. (1996). Adolescent suicidal ideation and attempts: Prevalence, risk factors, and clinical implications. *Clinical Psychology: Science and Practice, 3,* 25–46.

Lo, L. (1994). Exploring teenage shoplifting behavior: A choice and constraint approach. *Environment and Behavior, 26,* 613–639.

Lundy, M.S., & Rekers, G.A. (1995). Homosexuality: Development, risks, parental values, and controversies. In G.A. Rekers (Ed.), *Handbook of child and adolescent sexual problems* (pp. 290–312). New York: Lexington Books.

Masterson, J.F. (1968). The psychiatric significance of adolescent turmoil. *American Journal of Psychiatry, 124,* 1549–1554.

Meeks, J.E. (1979). Behavioral and antisocial disorders. In J.D. Noshpitz (Ed.), *Basic handbook of child psychiatry* (Vol. 2, pp. 482–530). New York: Basic Books.

Murray, C., & Thompson, F. (1985). The representation of authority: An adolescent viewpoint. *Journal of Adolescence, 8,* 217–229.

National Institute on Drug Abuse. (1998). *National survey results on drug use from the Monitoring the Future Study, 1975–1997. Volume I: Secondary school students* (NIH Publication No. 98–4345). Rockville, MD: Author.

Olson, R.A., Huszti, H.C., Mason, P.J., & Seibert, J.M. (1989). Pediatric AIDS/HIV infection: An emerging challenge to pediatric psychology. *Journal of Pediatric Psychology, 14,* 1–21.

Olson, R.A., Huszti, H.C., & Youll, L.K. (1995). Sexual behaviors and problems of adolescents. In M.C. Roberts (Ed.), *Handbook of pediatric psychology* (2nd ed., pp. 327–341). New York: Guilford Press.

Overholser, J.C., Adams, D.M., Lehnert, K.L., & Brinkman, D.C. (1995). Self-esteem deficits and suicidal tendencies among adolescents. *Journal of the American Academy of Child and Adolescent Psychiatry, 34,* 919–928.

Pastore, D.R., Fisher, M., & Friedman, S.B. (1996). Violence and mental health problems among urban high school students. *Journal of Adolescent Health, 18,* 320–324.

Petty, D.L. (1995). Sex education toward the prevention of sexual problems. In G.A. Rekers (Ed.), *Handbook of child and adolescent sexual problems* (pp. 31–51). New York: Lexington Books.

Rae, W.A., & Worchel, F.F. (1991). Ethical beliefs and behaviors of pediatric psychologists: A survey. *Journal of Pediatric Psychology, 16,* 727–745.

Repetti, R.L. (1996). The effects of perceived daily social and academic failure experiences on school-age children's subsequent interactions with parents. *Child Development, 67,* 1467–1482.

Roberts, M.C., & Hurley, L.K. (1997). *Managing managed care.* New York: Plenum Press.

Roberts, R.E., Lewinsohn, P.M., & Seeley, J.R. (1995). Symptoms of *DSM-III-R* major depression in adolescence: Evidence from an epidemiological survey. *Journal of the American Academy of Child and Adolescent Psychiatry, 34,* 1608–1617.

Robin, A.L., & Foster, S.L. (1989). *Negotiating parent-adolescent conflict: A behavioral–family systems approach.* New York: Guilford Press.

Rueter, M.A., & Conger, R.D. (1995). Antecedents of parent-adolescent disagreements. *Journal of Marriage and the Family, 57,* 435–448.

Rueter, M.A., & Conger, R.D. (1998). Reciprocal influences between parenting and adolescent problem-solving behavior. *Developmental Psychology, 34,* 1470–1482.

Schumm, W.R. (1995). Nonmarital sexual behavior. In G.A. Rekers (Ed.), *Handbook of child and adolescent sexual problems* (pp. 381–423). New York: Lexington Books.

Semrud-Clikeman, M. (1995). *Child and adolescent therapy.* Boston: Allyn & Bacon.

Smetana, J.G. (1995). Parenting styles and conceptions of parental authority during adolescence. *Child Development, 66,* 299–316.

Stephens, R.D. (1997). National trends in school violence: Statistics and prevention strategies. In A.P. Goldstein & J.C. Conoley (Eds.), *School violence intervention: A practical handbook* (pp. 72–90). New York: Guilford Press.

Stivers, C. (1988). Parent-adolescent communication and its relationship to adolescent depression and suicide proneness. *Adolescence, 23,* 291–295.

Stouthamer-Loeber, M. (1986). Lying as a problem behavior in children: A review. *Clinical Psychology Review, 6,* 267–289.

Stouthamer-Loeber, M., & Loeber, R. (1986). Boys who lie. *Journal of Abnormal Child Psychology, 14,* 551–564.

Thomas, A.M., & Forehand, R. (1991). The relationship between paternal depressive mood and early adolescent functioning. *Journal of Family Psychology, 4,* 260–271.

Trusty, J., & Pirtle, T. (1998). Parents' transmission of educational goals to their adolescent children. *Journal of Research and Development in Education, 32,* 53–65.

Tygart, C. (1988). Public school vandalism: Toward a synthesis of theories and transition to paradigm analysis. *Adolescence, 23,* 187–200.

Vissing, Y.M., Straus, M.A., Gelles, R.J., & Harrop, J.W. (1991). Verbal aggression by parents and psychosocial problems of children. *Child Abuse and Neglect, 15,* 223–238.

Warren, J.K., Gary, F., & Moorhead, J. (1994). Self-reported experiences of physical and sexual abuse among runaway youths. *Perspectives in Psychiatric Care, 30,* 23–28.

Zani, B. (1991). Male and female patterns in the discovery of sexuality during adolescence. *Journal of Adolescence, 14,* 163–178.

CHAPTER 32

Emotional Problems of Adolescents

MARY BETH LOGUE

The topic of adolescent emotional problems has received renewed attention in recent years as professionals and the lay public search for answers to why today's teenagers engage in highly publicized acts of violence. The widespread publicity and shocking nature of these events give the impression that prior to the mid-1990s little thought was given to adolescent emotional problems or how to solve them. This is an inaccurate impression, however. Writers through the ages have focused on the nature of adolescence and the apparent difficulties experienced by young people. From the ancient philosophers and teachers such as Aristotle and Plato, to twentieth-century physicians and psychiatrists such as G. Stanley Hall and Anna Freud, adolescent emotional problems have been considered and analyzed. In the final quarter of this century, there has been a marked increase in empirical research on adolescents, meriting the founding of several scientific journals and scores of textbooks and other academic and professional publications dedicated to understanding adolescent phenomena.

This chapter presents research and theory about adolescent emotional problems. First will be discussed the nature and assumptions inherent in the phrase "adolescent emotional problems," presenting a historical view of adolescence and a summary of the development of attitudes and beliefs about adolescent problems. Next, the literature that describes prevalence rates for adolescent problems will be critiqued and reviewed. This is followed by a description of an integrated approach to the study of adolescent emotional problems that takes into account multiple factors that influence risk for, resilience to, and onset of development and course of these problems.

ADOLESCENT EMOTIONAL PROBLEMS: A HISTORICAL PERSPECTIVE

Any study of adolescent emotional problems requires a review of several assumptions and the literature relevant to those assumptions. The phrase "adolescent emotional problems" is likely to conjure notions of troubled teens, generation gaps, and problems presented by puberty's onset. This chapter explores these notions and assumptions, presents research about the general base rates of serious emotional problems in adolescents, provides a developmental perspective to understanding those problems, and reviews the literature on adolescent coping. Other chapters in this volume address in detail specific problems such as depression and suicide, eating disorders, anxiety, substance abuse, and family problems.

There is a long-standing assumption that adolescence is generally a time of great emotional turmoil. From the writings of Aristotle (cited by Fox, 1977) to present-day commentary about adolescent mental health by mental health providers (Hughes & Brand, 1993), writers have commented on their observations of the troubles and difficulties that young people appear to experience as a function of the developmental stage of adolescence. Perhaps the writing that has most deeply influenced present-day thought about adolescent development comes from G. Stanley Hall, the "father of adolescent psychology," whose 1904 treatise served as the seminal work on adolescent development. Hall's work covered all aspects of development pertinent to the times (physical, emotional, and cognitive) and also provided a review of the adolescent in literature. He is the first scientific writer to amass information to support the assumption that adolescence is a difficult time of development. Hall asserted, "Psychoses and neuroses abound in early adolescent years more than at any other period of life" (p. 266). His use of the phrase *Sturm und Drang* or "storm and stress" (Hall, 1916) to characterize the expected course of adolescent development influenced, for over half a century, professionals' thinking about adolescence as a time during which turmoil and upheaval are commonplace. Later, the writing of psychodynamic theorists proclaimed the necessity of emotional upheaval for the development of a healthy adult personality.

In 1958, Anna Freud wrote a paper about adolescence in the context of psychoanalytic theory. This paper outlined current thought and guided theoretical thinking about adolescence for years. Based on clinical observation and the writings of other psychoanalytic theorists, Freud addressed several questions of the day about the inevitability and predictability of "the Adolescent Upset" (p. 264). She described the personality stability and developmental gains of children who have passed latency period as "preliminary only and precarious" (p. 264), and she noted that further development of the personality over the course of adolescence came about as a product of continued internal conflict between the ego and the id. According to Freud, the behavior problems seen in her patients were external manifestations of the internal id-ego conflict. Freud went on to assert that this conflict and the behavioral upheaval that accompanies it are so necessary that children who do not experience this may need therapy to develop healthy adult personalities. Regarding psychopathology in adolescence, Freud stated that

"adolescence constitutes by definition an interruption of peaceful growth which resembles in appearance a variety of other emotional upsets and structural upheavals . . . the differential diagnosis between the adolescent upsets and true pathology becomes a difficult task" (p. 267). Given this assessment of the situation of adolescents, it would seem that Freud advocated therapy for all adolescents. This, however, is not the case. She commented that it is perhaps the parents of the adolescents, rather than the adolescents themselves, who may need therapy to cope with this difficult but normal time.

More contemporary psychodynamic writers have tempered Freud's and Hall's assertions. Stein, Golombek, Marton, and Korenblum (1991) examined changes in personality functioning across the years of adolescence. As part of a longitudinal study of a school-based sample of teenagers, they interviewed the youths at the ages of 16 and 18 years, using a semistructured interview based on object relations theory. These authors looked at several aspects of personality functioning (maintaining an internal sense of identity, reality testing, relatedness, verbal communication, self-esteem, identity, and role adequacy). They also used clinician ratings to assess attitudes and affective functioning in the sample. In general, these researchers found that adolescence progressed without significant difficulty for most of the adolescents. About a quarter of the sample was rated as having some disturbance in personality functioning at both ages 16 and 18. Problems in personality functioning were related to the clinician-rated display of the attitude "hate." Those who had improved over time were distinguished from the rest of the group by decreases in clinician-reported displays of depression. In sum, this study, which took a psychodynamic and dimensional approach, lends support to the notion that adolescence is a troubling time for only a minority of youths and that attitudes and dysphoria can identify those for whom adolescence will be difficult in early adolescence.

Siegel and Shaughnessy (1995) suggested that adolescence may be considered a stormy time because it is a time of firsts. Unlike childhood, when firsts are experienced under the guidance and supervision of parents, adolescents' move from family-centered spheres of influence to peer-centered spheres of influence may leave them without the perspective that is tempered by the ability to take a long-term perspective. They posited that the emotional experience of adolescents may be perceived as more dramatic because the adolescent lacks a true future orientation: "As adolescents they can perceive a future, but the future they perceive may be identical to the present" (p. 218).

The idea that adolescence is a difficult time continues to influence clinicians' thinking today. Writing in response to an article entitled "Debunking the Myths of Adolescence: Findings from Recent Research," Hughes and Brand (1993) argued that adolescence is a time of significant difficulties and that "it has been our experience that there is a certain amount of turmoil inherent in any developmental phase especially adolescence" (p. 1077). Responding to the critique, Offer and Schonert-Reichl (1993) cited their research, suggesting that mental health professionals may have a view of adolescents that is overly pathological because of sampling biases (i.e., clinicians may deal only with disturbed individuals; Offer, Ostrov, & Howard, 1981).

This notion of adolescence as a typically difficult time has passed from the writings of theorists and professionals to colloquial wisdom and is often found today in textbooks and magazine articles about negotiating the transition from childhood to adulthood. Casual conversation about adolescent development also posits the normalcy of difficult problems during this transition. How have these notions persisted? One possible explanation is ascertainment bias: people tend to look for confirmation of what they believe to be true. Clinicians' tendency to overgeneralize psychopathology or other difficulties may result from their limited contact with a truly representative population of adolescents: It is only the teenagers with difficulties that are referred to treatment. Parents' generalized views of adolescents as troubled teens may arise from their sensitivity to and focus on problems that require parental attention and mediation rather than normal or adaptive functioning that does not require them to intervene.

In writing about adolescent emotional problems, the first task is to review the empirical basis of the assumptions that abound. To do so requires first a brief overview of the general concept of adolescence as a developmental stage separate from childhood and adulthood. Adolescence, as currently understood, is a fairly recent concept. The industrialization of society in the late nineteenth and early twentieth centuries had profound influences on how adolescence is perceived and how long this stage of development lasts. In less industrialized societies, the advent of adulthood was marked by rites of passage or events that occurred in conjunction with the physical changes of puberty. There were distinct economic benefits to quickly moving children who were developing mature bodies, into productive, adult roles. In an industrialized society, however, there are economic benefits to prolonging youth. Not only do life expectancies lengthen, making it important to delay entry into the work world, but also entering the work world in an industrial society requires more education and training. Thus, the period of transition from childhood to adulthood lengthens to accommodate these needs. At the same time that entry into the adult world is delayed in an industrial society, physiological maturation occurs earlier than it did in previous centuries. This creates a time when physiologically mature individuals are placed in an intermediate phase of life: no longer fully dependent children, but not yet fully independent adults. This prolonged transition during which expectations and roles are not as precisely defined as in either childhood or adulthood may have given rise to some of the early- and mid-twentieth-century writers' positions about the difficulties of adolescence. However, the statements in and the assumptions of these writings have not been supported in full by empirical research conducted in the past 20 years.

Summarizing the burst of research in the 1980s about adolescents, Offer and Schonert-Reichl (1992) addressed head-on the notion that many myths linger about adolescent development and emotional turmoil. They noted that years of psychoanalytic theorizing and clinical observations have instilled the idea that adolescence is a time of turmoil, and that idea has permeated the colloquial understanding of adolescence in our society. Their review of empirical studies of nonclinical populations indicated that although adolescence can be a time of serious disturbance for some, most adolescents pass this time with good relationships with family and peers (Offer & Schonert-Reichl, 1992).

A review of empirical studies will indicate the best estimates of prevalence of emotional problems and mental disorders in adolescents. Unlike studies of adult psychopathology, there have been no comprehensive, inclusive studies of adolescents. Indeed, point prevalence investigations (which indicate numbers of individuals experiencing a disorder at a given time) or lifetime prevalence investigations (which indicate numbers of individuals who have ever experienced a disorder) are more difficult to conduct in adolescents than in adults. Some writers question the validity and utility of diagnoses of adolescents. These issues are addressed in the next section about prevalence estimates.

CURRENT PREVALENCE ESTIMATES OF ADOLESCENT EMOTIONAL PROBLEMS

A CRITIQUE OF THE RESEARCH

Understanding adolescent emotional problems is hampered by the limits of current conceptualizations of psychopathology and the constraints of research methodology. How problems are organized for research (e.g., categorical vs. dimensional approaches), the extent to which the approach is truly developmental, and the reliability and appropriateness of the research tools and methods all contribute to the current limitations of prevalence research and our understanding of adolescent emotional problems.

A review of the *DSM-IV* (*Diagnostic and Statistical Manual of Mental Disorders*, 4th edition; American Psychiatric Association [APA], 1994) indicates that many mental disorders begin in adolescence. Researchers of adult psychopathology also note the early onset of many disorders. Burke and her colleagues (Burke, Burke, Regier, & Rae, 1990) used life table survival analysis methods to estimate the age of onset of depressive disorders, anxiety disorders, and substance use/abuse disorders from data collected in the Epidemiologic Catchment Area (ECA) Program studies (see Eaton et al., 1984; Regier et al., 1984 for a description of the ECA Program). Their review of the ECA's retrospective data suggests that people are at greatest risk for developing these disorders during adolescence and young adulthood. Indeed, this study reported that the greatest likelihood of age of onset is younger than that suggested by the *DSM* that was current at the time.

Estimating prevalence of particular disorders that occur during adolescence is difficult for a number of reasons. The first difficulty arises from philosophical issues related to the nature of classification and the use of categorical versus dimensional

systems to understand emotional or behavioral problems. Cantwell (1996) argued that dimensional systems may be more appropriate for assessing psychopathology in children and adolescents. He raised the following points: Categorical systems such as the *DSM-IV* APA (1994), or the *Classification of Mental and Behavioural Diseases* (ICD-10; World Health Organization [WHO], 1992) group symptoms of psychopathology into discrete categories, with cutoffs for criteria for assigning a diagnosis. Because they assign a generally agreed-upon label to a specific group of symptoms, categorical systems can make communication about a particular patient or a group of patients with similar symptoms easier. These approaches are limited by the categories they include and may not show an appropriately complex picture of an individual's symptoms and phemonemology of psychopathology. Furthermore, people with a particular diagnosis may have very different symptom patterns, leading to heterogeneous groups within a diagnostic category. Cutoff points for numbers and types of symptoms may be arbitrary and thus create an artificial two-tiered system of diagnosis: "clinically significant" versus "subclinical" levels of a disorder.

Dimensional approaches to psychopathology (e.g., the Child Behavior Checklist [CBCL], Achenbach & Edelbrock, 1991, or the Behavioral Assessment System for Children [BASC], Reynolds & Kamphaus, 1992) allow for the description of multiple symptoms in one individual that occur at various levels. This can be useful when several symptoms co-occur but may not be part of the same diagnostic category (e.g., depressed mood and obsessive, but not mood-congruent thoughts).

These arguments for dimensional approaches notwithstanding, categorical systems for classification of clinical decision making about children and adolescents are used more than dimensional systems. The *DSM* has undergone great changes in the past 30 years, including how child and adolescent diagnoses are handled. For example, in *DSM-III-R* (APA, 1987), children who had symptoms of generalized anxiety with somatic complaints were diagnosed with overanxious disorder, but not generalized anxiety disorder. In the *DSM-IV* (APA, 1994), overly anxious children are diagnosed as having generalized anxiety disorder. These changes in nosology impede research directed toward identifying prevalence rates. Furthermore, the custom of separating diagnoses that are thought to begin in childhood or adolescence from those thought to begin in adulthood can have effects on the estimates of prevalence. Clinicians may be reluctant to use "adult" diagnoses in children, even when the reported symptoms match the diagnostic category (Logue, 1996). Also, dividing diagnoses into categories by age may lead to prevalence underestimates of disorders that cover the life span but have changes in symptoms that might accompany aging. For example, the hallmark symptom of depression (disturbed affect) may be displayed more as irritable rather than depressed mood in children and adolescents.

Cantwell (1996) presented another problem with the diagnosis of disorder in children and adolescents. The comorbid or co-occurring symptoms are a bigger problem in adolescent diagnosis than in adult diagnosis. Several researchers have noted that there is greater continuity across symptoms and syndromes as age increases (e.g., Giaconia et al., 1994; Nottelmann & Jensen, 1995). Also, diagnosis is more reliable as age increases. Reliability of a diagnostic interview increases with age (Edelbrock, Costello, Dulcan, Kalas, & Conover, 1985). This also may mean that diagnosis stability increases with age. Cantwell (1996) stated that comorbidity of symptoms in children and adolescents does not necessarily reflect co-occurrence of disorders; it may represent general, nonspecific psychopathology that does not "crystallize" (p. 5) until adulthood. Thus, the earlier one assesses psychopathology, the more likely one should expect fluctuation in the diagnosis over time.

This fluctuation may be due to a number of factors. First, the cognitive abilities used in reporting symptoms develop and change over time. Interviewing requires communicating complex concepts of symptoms to the interviewee to assess presence or absence of symptoms. Interpreting the responses is at times an inexact science, and reliability of answers must be assessed with changing cognitive abilities in mind.

Second, diagnostic categories for mental illness, for the most part, have been developed for adult psychopathology and then extended downward for children. This may appear to be a developmental approach to psychopathology. However, by beginning with adult symptoms and "working backwards," phenomenology unique to childhood and adolescence may be overlooked. Although the downward extension approach has served as an initial means

for establishing diagnostic criteria, the changes in the *DSM* from version III to III-R and IV are instructive: We do not have a good classification system for children and adolescents at the present time.

The comorbidity of symptoms and diagnoses also makes it more difficult to make definite classifications of emotional problems in adolescents. Cantwell (1996) suggested that what appears to be comorbidity of disorders in a discrete, categorical diagnostic system may confuse the phenomenology of symptom expression that is unique to younger people. For example, the well-reasoned debate about whether some attention-deficit disorder is bipolar disorder in children and adolescents raises the issue that these discrete diagnostic categories do not accurately capture the phenomenology of impulsive and hyperactive behavior in children and adolescents (Beiderman, Klein, Pine, & Klein, 1998). It is possible that some children and adolescents experience a combination of symptoms of the two disorders and cannot accurately be diagnosed as having either attention-deficit disorder or bipolar disorder.

The pervasiveness of categorical systems and the press to use time-efficient research methods has led to a compromise in research that may yield overly simplistic results. Studies often use symptom checklists (e.g., the CBCL or the BASC) or nondiagnostic questionnaires (e.g., the Children's Depression Inventory, Kovacs, 1985; or the Revised Children's Manifest Anxiety Scale, Reynolds & Richmond, 1978) and draw conclusions based on clinically recommended cutoff scores. However, in the absence of a "gold standard" clinical interview, these can only be symptom reports and are indications of emotional problems, not necessarily of psychopathology (see chapter by La Greca in this volume).

Current research and clinical practice rely on categorical systems, and assessment and diagnostic practices have been developed accordingly. Each method has characteristics that may influence prevalence rates. A number of standardized interviews have been developed, such as the Child Assessment Schedule (CAS; Hodges, McKnew, Cytryn, Stern, & Kline, 1982), the Diagnostic Interview for Children and Adolescents (DICA; Herjanic & Reich, 1982), and the Schedule for Affective Disorders and Schizophrenia in Children and Adolescents (K-SADS; Puig-Antich & Chambers, 1983). Each has its strengths and weaknesses. For example, some standardized diagnostic interviews may not be comprehensive or include all possible disorders for adolescents in particular. It may be difficult to estimate severity or degree of impairment due to symptoms with some interviews that use a rating system that may merely assess the presence or absence of a symptom (e.g., the DICA or the CAS). Other interviews that have broader ranges of symptom report (e.g., the K-SADS) make judging the relative severity of symptoms easier. Some interviews are more structured than others. The DISC and DICA are highly structured, leaving little freedom for the interviewer to stray from the questions as written. The CAS and the K-SADS are semistructured interviews and require clinical judgment on the part of the interviewer, while allowing freedom to explore unclear answers more fully. Prevalence rate differences across interviews or interview types have not been tested; thus, it is not possible to say whether semistructured or structured, clinician-rated or lay-rated diagnosis rates differ.

Another issue salient to the estimation of problems in adolescents is the source of the report of problems. Self-report about internalizing symptoms has greater reliability than parent report, and parent report of externalizing symptoms is greater than self-report of those symptoms (La Greca, 1990; see also La Greca chapter in this volume). If two sources of information are used, the interviewer must decide how much weight to give to each reporter of conflicting information. Inclusive approaches (counting symptoms from either reporter as present) tend to overestimate problems, whereas exclusive approaches (requiring congruence between reporters to count a symptom) may underestimate problems.

Numerous authors have recommended that a measure of impairment caused by the reported symptoms be used to make a diagnosis (Bird et al., 1988; Brandenburg, Friedman, & Silver, 1990; Cantwell, 1996; Kashani et al., 1987). Two types of systems can be used: the Children's Global Assessment Scale (CGAS; Shaffer et al., 1983), which rates functioning on a scale from 0 to 100 with behavioral anchors for each decile; or a clinician rating of the necessity for intervention for symptoms (Kashani et al., 1987). Rates of diagnosis tend to be greater in studies that do not require some sort of estimate of impairment than in studies that require such measures.

Related to this is the question of subthreshold disorders. There are cases when there are insufficient

symptoms present to warrant a categorical diagnosis, but there is functional impairment in one or more areas (e.g., home, school, peers). These cases represent significant pathology that is difficult to categorize. Adolescents with problems like this may be more likely to present to primary care providers than mental health professionals (Cantwell, 1996). This may be reflected in the findings that many adolescents who seek help for emotional problems may visit medical providers rather than mental health providers (Offord et al., 1987).

Cantwell (1996) recommended considering factors beyond phenomenology in assessing psychopathology (e.g., biology, psychosocial correlates, familiality, treatment response, and natural history). Failure to consider these broader contexts may lead to overdiagnosis or inaccurate assessment of the problems and the meaning that adolescents may ascribe to the problem. Roberts and colleagues (Roberts, Attkisson, & Rosenblatt, 1998) discussed several methodological issues that must be addressed in future research to increase the accuracy of prevalence estimates: sampling, case ascertainment, case definition, data analysis, and presentation. Typically in studies of adolescent emotional problems, samples have tended to be small, assess a number of diagnoses, and cover a wide range of ages. If studies are to examine occurrence of rare events (e.g., disorders that in the adult population occur in fewer than 5% of the population) in a comprehensive investigation (e.g., all anxiety, mood, and behavior disorders in the *DSM*) across a large age span (e.g., 12–18 years), great numbers of participants are required to produce stable estimates. Few samples are representative of the population from which the sample was drawn. For example, clinic-based samples would likely overestimate prevalence because they include only disturbed or referred children. Community-based school survey samples would likely underestimate prevalence because they exclude adolescents who had dropped out of school and who may be likely to have different rates of psychopathology.

How cases are defined and ascertained is also a concern. As noted above by Cantwell (1996), the use of categorical or dimensional systems for identifying cases, the choice of reporters, and the evaluation of impairment by reported symptoms impact prevalence estimates. Case ascertainment that uses multistage methods (e.g., using a sensitive symptom screen such as the CBCL followed by a specific measure such as a structured clinical interview) tends to produce lower prevalence rate estimations than studies that use single-stage methods of ascertainment. And, because all estimates of prevalence include some measurement error, Roberts et al. (1998) recommended reporting the confidence intervals around the stated estimates. They also recommended presenting prevalence rates as odds ratios for subgroups from the sample based on age, gender, ethnicity, or other relevant factors that are likely to affect prevalence rates.

Finally, current methods of conceptualizing adolescent emotional problems and measuring the prevalence of problems may lack external validity and utility for severe and dangerous outcomes. Neither categorical systems such as the *DSM* nor dimensional systems such as the BASC can sufficiently predict specific behavioral outcomes. For example, a *DSM* diagnosis of depression or an elevated score on a depression questionnaire such as the Children's Depression Inventory (Kovacs, 1985) is insufficient information to make predictions about problem course or outcome. Furthermore, a single outcome can arise from a number of diagnoses or dimensions. For example, suicide is noted to be a risk in depression, schizophrenia, and substance abuse. The high-profile cases of teen shootings at the close of this century have led laypeople and professionals alike to ask about causes and explanations for violent behavior. No current diagnostic or dimensional system can explain, let alone predict, such violent behavior. Thus, the practical utility of the present way of looking at adolescent emotional problems is minimal for these critical but rare events.

BEST ESTIMATES OF PREVALENCE

To date, no study of adolescent emotional problems has adequately addressed the preceding conceptual or methodological issues. Nevertheless, some cautious conclusions about psychopathology in adolescents can be drawn. Beginning with studies reviewed in Roberts et al. (1998), the mean prevalence of any psychopathology in adolescents is estimated as 16.5% (range: 6.2%–41.3%). The 52 studies reviewed by these authors were conducted over a 30-year period, included both children and adolescents, and defined psychopathology in a wide variety of ways, including using interviews with parents and/or children and self-report or parent-report questionnaires. Sample sizes (for studies that included adolescents) ranged from 58 to 8,462. The age ranges in the studies were quite broad, and Roberts and colleagues did not report different general prevalence rates for younger versus older adolescents. They did, however, address whether or not prevalence rates of psychopathology are increasing over time. These authors' analysis suggested that generally, limits of the data notwithstanding, prevalence rates have not changed during the past 40 years.

Brandenburg et al. (1990) reviewed eight studies of children and adolescents (ages ranging from 4 to 19 years). Four studies included adolescents and were not included in the Roberts et al. (1998) review. All four of these studies used multistage assessment techniques (e.g., screening questionnaire followed by clinical interview for a subset of the sample). Prevalence rates for *DSM* psychopathology in adolescents ranged from 7% to 18.7%. The samples were all community- or school-based. All these studies included some measurement of impairment (e.g., CGAS, clinician's rating of "moderate or severe" impairment, or symptom report in excess of two standard deviations above the mean).

Neither of these two reviews provided information about the prevalence of specific disorders identified in the studies reviewed. What follows here is a summary of prevalence rates from seven studies (see Table 32.1 for a summary of study characteristics) that meet the more stringent criteria proposed by Roberts et al. (1998), Brandenburg et al. (1990), and Cantwell (1996). Although this is not a comprehensive review of all investigations of all *DSM* diagnoses in adolescents, it does provide an indication about the rates and types of psychopathology that have been identified in adolescents. Excluded from this review are studies that investigated only one disorder (e.g., panic disorder) or one type of disorder (e.g., depressive disorders) in adolescents. The studies reviewed here assessed a range of emotional and behavior problems in adolescents. They assessed disorders from at least three types of problems (e.g., depressive disorders, anxiety disorders, and substance use disorders). Looking at several disorder groups in a single sample is important because it gives an indication of the overlap in symptoms experienced by adolescents. All were community-based samples. Several used screening procedures to target a specific subset of a large

Table 32.1 Summary of reviewed studies of psychopathology in adolescents.

Author	Total N	Age	Prevalence	Diagnostic Criteria	Interview	Diagnostic Methods	Severity Rating
Offord et al. (1987); Boyle et al. (1987)	1,674	4–16	6-month	DSM-III	CBCL-derived scales	Stratified random sample with parent and child interviews	Psychiatrist rating of impairment
Kashani et al. (1987)	150	14–16	point	DSM-III	DICA	Interview with a stratified random sample of adolescents attending public school	Clinician-rated need of treatment
Kashani et al. (1989)	210	8, 12, 17	point	DSM-III	CAS	Community-based sample; child and parent interview	Dimensional CAS scores
Bird et al.	777	4–16	6-month	DSM-III	DISC	CBCL/TRF followed by interviews with a random sample of 386 families (parent and child interview)	CGAS
Whitaker et al. (1990)	5,108	High school students	lifetime	DSM-III	DSM-based interview	Screening questionnaires and adolescent interview of select sample of 356	CGAS
Giaconia et al. (1994); Reinherz et al. (1993)	386	18	lifetime	DSM-III-R	DIS-III-R	Adolescent interview of participants in a longitudinal study	CBCL Total Problem Scale
Feehan et al. (1993)	988	15, 18	1-year	DSM-III	DISC	Adolescent self-report and significant other questionnaire from a longitudinal study	5-point scale of life functioning

sample for more in-depth assessment. Before reporting prevalence estimates that have been abstracted across the studies, we briefly review each study's methodology.

Offord and colleagues (Boyle et al., 1987; Offord et al., 1987) assessed children ages 4 to 16 years from a Canadian population-based survey using items from the CBCL (Achenbach & Edelbrock, 1981). Four scales were derived from these items: hyperactivity, emotional disorder, conduct disorder, and somatization. Psychiatrists used these scales to interview the children, their parents, and their teachers to determine the presence or absence of clinically significant symptoms. Severity of disorder was measured using Rutter and Graham's (1968) criteria. These authors found a six-month prevalence rate of 18.1% for any of the four derived problem scales. Of note is the fact that fewer than 18% of the children and adolescents who were diagnosed had sought mental health or social services in the previous six months. Over half of the study participants had seen an ambulatory care medical provider. This suggests that mental health providers may not be the most sought-out source of help for those with emotional or behavioral problems. These authors recommended that it would be helpful to integrate mental health services into the schools and agencies that have daily contact with students.

Kashani's group conducted two studies that are included in this review. Both used similar sampling techniques, but the interview techniques (and the subsequently observed rates of pathology) were quite different. The earlier study (Kashani et al., 1987) used a fairly conservative approach to identifying cases by applying a rating of dysfunction and need for treatment by the interviewer. In this study, adolescents age 14 to 16 were interviewed using a structured diagnostic interview (DICA; Herjanic & Reich, 1982) with a clinician-rated scale of dysfunction and need for treatment to identify adolescents who had *DSM-III* disorders. Sixty-two (42.3%) of the 150 interviewed met criteria for at least one *DSM-III* disorder. However, when the authors measured dysfunction to identify true cases, only 28 (18.7%) adolescents were considered to have psychopathology severe enough to warrant treatment. In the second study, Kashani, Orvaschel, Rosenberg, and Reid (1989) looked at a sample of three cohorts of adolescents (ages 8, 12, and 17) and their parents to identify patterns and trends in psychopathology that could help explain age differences in the rates of psychopathology across adolescence. This study assessed problems using the CAS (Hodges et al., 1982), a semistructured interview organized around spheres of functioning (e.g., family, peer relations, school performance). The CAS not only provides *DSM* diagnoses, but also includes dimensional scores for level of functioning in each of the spheres and each of the diagnostic categories. Symptom complex scores were used as measures of severity of disorder in this study. Over 34% of this sample met criteria for some *DSM-III* disorder, with anxiety disorder having the highest prevalence (21%). Kashani et al. (1989) found that problems reported by adolescents and their parents differed by cohort, suggesting that there is a developmental progression of symptoms experienced by adolescents. Specifically, anxiety symptoms decrease with age, conduct problems increase with age for males, and affective disorders increase with age for females.

Bird and colleagues (Bird et al., 1988) conducted a population-based study of psychopathology in Puerto Rican children age 4 to 16. Over one-third of the 777 children and adolescents in the sample met *DSM-III* criteria for one or more types of disorders, grouped into four general domains (anxiety, conduct/oppositional, attention-deficit disorders, or affective disorders). Trained psychiatrists used a Spanish version of the DISC (Costello, Edelbrock, Kalas, Kessler, & Klaric, 1982). All five *DSM* axes were specified and the severity of symptoms was rated using the CGAS (Shaffer et al., 1983). Forty-six percent of these children and adolescents fell into two or more domains of diagnoses. However, only 17.9% met criteria for a disorder with the required impairment (a score lower than 61 on the CGAS). This study used a fairly inclusive rule for identifying cases, which may have led to an overestimate of psychopathology before the severity scores were applied.

Whitaker and colleagues (1990) screened 5,108 ninth- through twelfth-graders in public and private high schools in one county in New Jersey. They first used a screening questionnaire to assess symptoms of a number of disorders, including eating disorders, depression, obsessive-compulsive disorder, panic disorder, and substance use disorders. They then selected 356 students to participate in the interview stage of the study. The select sample was a stratified random sample that was designed to over-select potential cases at various levels of symptom severity because of the presumed rarity of these disorders in adolescents. The semistructured interview developed by these researchers was based on *DSM-III* criteria for lifetime occurrence of the disorders that were included in the study. Clinicians used the CGAS to rate impairment in all children interviewed in the sample. Only 54% of high school students with lifetime major diagnoses were rated as impaired (10.6% of those without diagnoses were rated as impaired). Lifetime prevalence of any disorder plus impairment (CGAS < 71) was about 5%. Girls had higher rates of disorder than boys for all disorders except obsessive-compulsive disorder. Only 35% of those with disorders had used some sort of counseling services (e.g., psychologist, psychiatrist, physician, social worker, minister, guidance or agency counselor). These authors concluded that the second-stage interview process of the study revealed serious emotional problems in a significant number of youth. Three key points are illustrated in this study. First, screening instruments that are designed to be highly sensitive, taken by themselves, may lead to overestimates of problems. Second, diagnostic criteria alone are not enough in evaluating psychopathology; a specific measure of impairment is also essential to identify serious problems. Third, only about half of those who experience impairment from diagnosable psychopathology seek help from professionals who are typically in positions to help. Thus, it is clear that mental health professionals may not be reaching those who need help.

A longitudinal study conducted by Giaconia et al. (1994; Reinherz, Giaconia, Lefkowitz, Pakiz, & Frost, 1993) assessed six *DSM-III-R* disorders in adolescents at age 15 and then later at age 18 using the NIMH Diagnostic Interview Schedule Version III Revised (*DIS-III-R*; Robins, Helzer, Cottler, & Goldring, 1989). Several measures of general behavioral and emotional functioning were also included. The authors found that adolescents with *DSM-III-R* diagnoses at the first assessment had poor functioning (which varied by diagnosis) at the later assessment, regardless of whether they were currently experiencing symptoms of the earlier diagnosed disorder. This finding suggests that when adolescents have identifiable problems that impair functioning, functioning is likely to be impaired for a substantial period of time. This interpretation argues for early intervention with youth that have diagnoses and impairment.

Feehan, McGee, and Williams (1993) reported on psychopathology in a cohort of 988 adolescents from New Zealand who were participating in a longitudinal study followed from birth as a part of the Dunedin Multidisciplinary Health and Development Study. These authors assessed the youth at age 15 using the DISC (Costello et al., 1982) with *DSM-III* criteria, and at age 18 using the DIS-III-R (Robins et al., 1989) with *DSM-III-R* criteria. Impairment was rated on a five-point scale of severity or judged by reports of involvement with the police or a history of having sought treatment for symptoms. One-year prevalence rates were established and compared across time. At age 15, 191 adolescents (19.3%) were diagnosed with one or more disorders; at age 18, 121 (12.2%) were diagnosed with one or more disorders. The purpose of this study was to examine the course of disorder in adolescents. These authors found that two-thirds of the sample having disorder at age 15 had disorder at age 18. This study was unable to differentiate factors that might predict which adolescents would have transient versus enduring problems.

This series of studies using somewhat varied methodology gives a general view about adolescent emotional and behavior problems. All of the studies used *DSM* criteria and a structured or semistructured interview (e.g., the DIS-III-R or the CAS) to assess psychopathology. All included some indication of impairment (e.g., CGAS or evidence of help-seeking for diagnosed problems). Two studies reported lifetime prevalence of disorder (Giaconia et al., 1994; Whitaker et al., 1990). The rest report point prevalence ranging from 6 months to 1 year. None of the studies assessed all *DSM* disorders; thus, the prevalence rates are abstracted from the seven studies reviewed here. Together, the studies assessed mood disorders, anxiety, substance abuse, eating disorders, disruptive behavior disorders, elimination disorders, somatization, and adjustment disorders.

Mood Disorders

Fewer than 10% of adolescents have mood disorders that are serious enough to require treatment or interfere with daily functioning. Lifetime prevalence rates of major depression ranged from 2.2% (Giaconia et al., 1994) to 7.4% (Whitaker et al., 1990). Whitaker and colleagues were the only researchers to assess dysthymia as a separate disorder and found 6.5% lifetime prevalence. Two studies (Bird et al., 1988; Kashani et al., 1987) combined depression and dysthymia and established prevalence rates in 8% and 5.9%, respectively.

Combining the two disorders in the latter two studies likely accounts for relatively higher rates of disorder than those reported by the other research groups. Only one study assessed mania (Kashani et al., 1987) and reported the point prevalence to be 0.7% in their sample of 14- to 16-year-old.

Anxiety Disorders

Across all of the reviewed studies, the entire range of *DSM* anxiety disorders was assessed. Three studies looked at anxiety disorders as a group and reported prevalence rates for any anxiety disorder in the sample. Rates for any anxiety disorder ranged from a low of 6.3% (Feehan et al., 1993) to a high of 21.4% (Kashani et al., 1989). Feehan and colleagues used the DISC to diagnose anxiety disorders, and Kashani's group used the CAS. One possible explanation for the apparently large difference in prevalence rates is related to constraints placed on the administration of the different interviews. The DISC is a highly structured interview and the CAS is semistructured. The DISC is organized by diagnosis and includes skip-out questions, which if answered in the negative lead the interview to a new diagnostic section. The CAS is organized according to domains of functioning (e.g., school, home, peer relations). The interviewer assesses functioning within a domain and is not bound by skip-out questions. The interviewer may be able to ask more questions that lead to more information about symptoms that tend to be more situation-specific and thus not elicited by a broad question about symptoms in general. This may be the case, for example, with simple phobias, which would result in higher prevalence rates than in other interviews. Support for this hypothesis comes from Kashani's own later work. In a study using the DICA, an interview structured similarly to the DISC, Kashani's group (1987) found 8.7% of 14- to 16-year-olds to have any anxiety disorder, a rate similar to Feehan et al.'s and much lower than Kashani's 1989 study.

Two studies reported rates for simple phobia. Bird et al. (1988) used an interview based on items from the CBCL to derive *DSM-III* diagnoses and found 2.1% of this sample to have a 6-month prevalence of simple phobias. Giaconia and colleagues (1994) used the DIS-III-R and found a lifetime prevalence of 13.7% for simple phobia. These two studies had different ages of children and adolescents: Bird's study included children 4 though 16, and Giaconia's study included only 18-year-olds who were part of a longitudinal study. Different types of prevalence reporting (point versus lifetime) as well as differences in the age ranges in the samples may account for the apparent differences in prevalence rates of simple phobias.

Unfortunately, among the seven studies reviewed here, the following disorders were assessed in only one investigation each. Thus, we can make no comparisons across studies about prevalence rates. Giaconia et al. (1994) found a lifetime prevalence of 13.7% for social phobia and 6.3% for PTSD. Whitaker et al. (1990) found a lifetime prevalence of 5.6% for obsessive-compulsive disorder, 5.6% for generalized anxiety disorder, and 2% for panic disorder in high school students. Whitaker's large sample ($N = 5,108$) was screened using questionnaires that assess particular symptoms and disorders. Subsequent interviews were undertaken prior to the development of standardized interviews such as the DISC or DICA. The authors developed an interview based on *DSM* diagnostic criteria, which was then used by trained clinicians. These estimates are all consistent with the other estimates of anxiety disorders in children.

Emotional Problems, Somatization, and Adjustment Disorders

Offord et al. (1987) used diagnostic categories based on symptom clusters from the CBCL (Achenbach & Edelbrock, 1981). Symptoms in these clusters overlap with the cognitive and somatic symptoms of depression and anxiety, and thus may represent an estimate of problems that resemble depression and anxiety but that do not easily fit into *DSM* categories. These authors reported the incidence of general emotional problems to be 4.9% for boys and 13.6% for girls ages 12 to 16. They also reported rates of somatization in the same age group of boys and girls to be 4.5% and 10.7%, respectively. Only one study assessed *DSM-III* adjustment disorder (Bird et al., 1988). The 6-month prevalence rate for adjustment disorder in children 4 through 16 was 4.2%.

Substance Abuse

Rates of substance use, abuse, and dependence are difficult to interpret across studies. Four studies reported prevalence rates for substance use problems. Several studies combined alcohol and drug problems and reported only combined substance problem rates. These found between 3% and 6% 1-year prevalence rates of either drug or alcohol misuse.

Reinherz et al. (1993) combined abuse and dependence problems in their reporting of 386 18-year-old adolescents. Lifetime prevalence rates for both kinds of use problems were higher in males than females (alcohol: 37.6% in males and 26.8% in females; drugs: 10.8% in males and 8.9% in females). These rates are considerably higher than the studies that report point prevalence for either drug or alcohol misuse.

Eating Disorders

Whitaker et al. (1990) and Kashani ct al. (1987) assessed eating disorders in adolescents according to *DSM-III* criteria. Kashani's group found no eating disorders in their sample of 150 14- to 16-year-olds using the DICA. Whitaker and colleagues found lifetime rates of anorexia (1.7%) and bulimia (5.1%) in females only.

Elimination Disorders

Bird et al. (1988) assessed functional enuresis in children and adolescents age 4 to 16 years and found a 6-month prevalence of 4.7%. Kashani et al. (1987) found enuresis in only 0.07% of their sample of 14- to 16-year-olds.

Disruptive Behavior Disorders

Disruptive behavior disorders include attention-deficit disorder, oppositional defiant disorder, and conduct disorder. Rates of these problems in adolescents varied considerably across studies. Attention-deficit disorders (ADD) occurred in 1.4% of Kashani's group (1989) sample and in 9.5% of Bird's group (1988) sample. Two other studies assessed ADD: Offord et al. (1987) and Kashani et al. (1987) found rates of 5.3% and 2%, respectively. Oppositional defiant disorder, assessed in two studies, was found in 6.7% of Kashani's group (1989) sample and in 9.9% of Bird's group (1988) sample. It should be noted here, as above, that Bird's sample embraced a wider range of ages (4–16) than Kashani's (14–16), and the inclusion of younger children may explain the difference in point prevalence rates in these two studies. Finally, conduct disorder rates were assessed in five of the studies. Rates varied widely, from < 1% (Feehan et al., 1993) to 11.4% (Kashani et al., 1989). All five studies were estimating point prevalence or 1-year prevalence. Lower prevalence rates were found in studies that used more stringent criteria for functional impairment in case ascertainment.

ANOTHER PERSPECTIVE

The preceding was a review of epidemiological research about psychopathology and emotional problems in adolescence. These studies have been conducted by internationally recognized research groups using state-of-the-art methodology with the most contemporary understanding of psychopathology of the times. In sum, this research suggests that there is a wide range of problems experienced by a minority of adolescents. Longitudinal research, such as that done by Feehan et al. (1993), indicates that when problems exist, they endure and cause difficulties. This is consistent with Offer and Schonert-Reichl's (1992) assessment of the situation of adolescent psychopathology. All of the research cited heretofore has been researcher-driven, based on current classification schemes of psychopathology. Another way to look at adolescent emotional problems is to use a constituent-focused approach and ask the adolescents themselves to assess the problem.

Kutcher and colleagues (1996) did just this in their unique approach to assessing adolescents' mental health problems. They asked high school students to develop a mental health survey questionnaire that assessed issues pertinent to adolescent mental health. Independent of the authors, these selected adolescents developed a one-page survey that was then administered to 486 students in grades 9, 11, and 13 from four Toronto high schools. The results from the adolescents' survey outlined mental health issues that adolescents believe are important rather than relying on assessment of the quantity and severity of symptoms that fit empirically or theoretically based categories (e.g., *DSM* or psychoanalytic theories of psychopathology). Responses to the survey support this: fewer than 20% of adolescents surveyed reported experiencing significant life stress, and many of those that do experience stress (over 40%) use healthy ways of coping (e.g., exercise, seeking personal support). The authors recognize the methodological limitations of this study, but concluded that there are several points to be made. First, they pointed out that what the adolescents *do not* ask is as important as what they *do* ask. The adolescents did not develop a survey of epidemiology that assessed what researchers and clinicians identify as common in adolescent-onset psychopathology. Rather, the adolescents labeled their mental health issues as "stress." In the words of one adolescent survey developer, "Mental health is about stress and how we cope. What's mental illness got to do with it?" (p. 9).

The authors suggested that this thinking may represent a form of denial of problems that are commonly seen in adolescence, as evidenced by epidemiologic studies. However, it is intriguing to note that the number of adolescents experiencing "significant life stress" is quite similar to those identified as having any kind of psychopathology in the epidemiologic studies (Brandenburg et al., 1990; Offer & Schonert-Reichl, 1992).

SUMMARY

In the studies reviewed thus far, it is apparent that psychopathology occurs in a minority of adolescents. Rates for any mental health problem are about 20% to 25% of the adolescent population. Some problems are more severe than others and are likely to have longer-term and more serious consequences than others. For example, early-onset depression increases the risk of relapse and life-long maladjustment, whereas specific phobias appear to be age-limited and may be so circumscribed as to have only modest negative effects on the individual's quality of life. There are clear and predictable gender differences in types of problems experienced by adolescents. For example, more boys than girls have conduct problems, and, as they enter middle and late adolescence, more girls than boys are depressed. Yet, chronological age and gender alone do not explain the complex variation in adolescent emotional problems. More comprehensive models are needed to increase the ability to predict which adolescent will have what type of problem at what period in his or her life.

PREDICTING PROBLEMS IN ADOLESCENCE: AN INTEGRATED APPROACH

Compas, Hinden, and Gerhardt (1995) present a comprehensive analysis of research that supports an integrative model for understanding adolescent emotional problems. In keeping with Cantwell (1996), they asserted that any satisfactory model should include biological, environmental, person-

ological, social, and societal contributions to problem development. Biological contributions include genetic influences (e.g., family history of disorder) and the sequelae of medical problems (e.g., history of a closed head injury or a chronic illness such as diabetes). Environmental contributions are stressors that demand a coping response. Compas, Orosan, and Grant (1993) defined stressors as being environmental events, the consequences of those events, and the individual's appraisal of the impact and meaning of the event. Stressors can be generic and normative; that is, they are expected to occur to anyone (e.g., the onset of puberty or transitioning from junior high to high school). They can be acute, traumatic events (e.g., the illness or death of a parent or experiencing a disaster such as a tornado), and they can be enduring or chronic (e.g., poverty, the long-term effects of the loss of a parent). Personological factors that have been demonstrated to be related to different rates of problems include traits related to temperament, extroversion and introversion, locus of control, and attachment. Social contributions to comprehensive models of psychopathology include family and peer relations. Societal factors include socioeconomic status, culture, and availability of resources. When the different effects of these variables are taken into account, gender and developmental differences in the experience of emotional problems are more clearly understood. Compas et al. (1993, 1995) presented research from a variety of disciplines that helps to explain age and gender differences in rates of aggressive and antisocial behavior and depression.

FIVE TRAJECTORIES DESCRIBE VARIABILITY

It is easy to see that there is considerable variability of rates of problems experienced by adolescents. Clearly, not all adolescents experience the same type of problems or the same course of difficulty through these problems. Prognosis is quite variable. Compas et al. (1995) outlined five developmental trajectories that describe the pathways to and through adolescent psychopathology. These trajectories may explain the observed variability in adolescent emotional problems. These pathways are defined by multiple factors that influence development: environment, genetic predisposition, interpersonal functioning, parental stress and skill, and social influences. These influences impact both risk for problems as well as resilience to stressors during adolescent development. Two trajectories are defined by stable functioning that continues from childhood through adolescence to adulthood; three trajectories are defined by fluctuating functioning.

The first of the five trajectories is one of stable, adaptive functioning that characterizes most of adolescent development. These adolescents show good coping and adaptation in childhood, which continues through adolescence to adulthood. This trajectory likely applies to most adolescents (Offer & Schonert-Reichl, 1992).

The second trajectory is that of stable maladaptive functioning that begins early in childhood and continues throughout adolescence and adulthood. These adolescents typically cope poorly with environmental stressors and find themselves in environments that inadvertently support continued maladaptive coping.

The third trajectory is that of good functioning in childhood, with a decline during adolescence that continues through adulthood. This path may be a result of poor coping to a traumatic environmental change during adolescence (e.g., parental divorce or death) from which the adolescent never recovers adequate functioning.

The fourth trajectory is that of poor functioning during childhood, followed by a move to good functioning during adulthood. Compas et al. (1995) referred to this as a "turnaround or recovery" (p. 272), in which an environmental change provokes adaptive coping and functioning. By way of example, they describe the troubled adolescent who is able to acquire good coping skills in the military.

The final trajectory is that of temporary maladaptive development that begins and ends during adolescence. Examples of this include the transitory antisocial behavior displayed by some adolescent males (Moffitt, 1993).

Compas et al. (1993) described substantial empirical support for these five trajectories and an integrative model for understanding both aggression and depression in adolescents. These authors emphasized the importance of looking at comprehensive, longitudinal research to understand the causes and courses of adolescent emotional problems. Integrating an understanding of biological risk factors (e.g., familial alcoholism, antisociality, or depression) with coping-style differences and individual response to environmental factors is essential to developing predictive models of adolescent emotional problems and prevention and treatment programs.

GENDER AND COPING

In addition to looking at the descriptive pathways that define adolescent problems, Compas et al. (1993, 1995) summarized research that may help to explain why there are differential rates of certain types of emotional and behavior problems in adolescence. They drew from a wide body of research on stress, coping, and gender differences in adult coping styles and the impact of puberty to explain the different rates of aggression and depression in adolescents.

Boys and girls experience stress in different ways. Girls experience more stress in general than boys (Peterson, Sarigiani, & Kennedy, 1991) and more interpersonal stress than boys (Wagner & Compas, 1990). Although stress is related to depression, this alone does not fully account for increased rates of depression in adolescent girls.

Different coping styles used by males and females may help to explain the divergent increases in rates of problems among adolescents. Gender-specific styles have been found in the way adults cope with stressors (Nolen-Hoeksema, 1991): women tend to use more emotion-focused coping that includes dwelling on the stressor and emotions related to the problem. This response style may lead to increased levels of depression and hopelessness. Men tend to use more avoidant or instrumental styles of coping, thus avoiding rumination or negative thinking about stressors. Avoidant styles in male adolescents may explain increased rates of conduct problems such as substance abuse or antisocial behavior (Compas et al., 1993).

Coping styles also change with age. Age-related coping styles can be divided into two types: (1) problem-focused coping (trying to change the stressor or solve the problem); and (2) emotion-focused coping (trying to change affect or attitude toward the problem). A number of studies have demonstrated that problem-focused coping develops in middle childhood and continues throughout adolescence, and that emotion-focused coping develops in middle and later adolescence (see Compas et al., 1993, for a review of this literature). The increase in emotion-focused coping in middle and later adolescence, combined with the particular style of emotion-focused coping (e.g., ruminative vs. avoidant) may increase the risk of depression for females and of conduct problems in males (Compas et al., 1995).

THE IMPACT OF PUBERTY

The onset of puberty has often been thought to herald emotional and personality changes in adolescents. It is not uncommon for a clinician to hear problem behavior in adolescents explained by the parental exclamation: "Hormones." Puberty is marked by great changes in endocrine functioning and accompanying physical changes that in more traditional societies marked the transition from childhood to adulthood. This uneven rate of change (e.g., physical changes occurring faster than social role changes) is exacerbated by the fact that children experience puberty at younger and younger ages and the assumption of adult social roles (e.g., age of majority, assumption of self-supporting work, entering into long-term intimate relationships) occurs later and later. If adolescence is defined as beginning at puberty and ending when adult roles are adopted and integrated into the individual's life, then adolescence in America today can last from age 12 to 25 years. In traditional societies, puberty signals the individual's readiness to adopt adult roles. In contemporary societies, puberty is less likely to signal the onset of adulthood. Rather, it signals the onset of a "betwixt and between" state of existence wherein adolescents have rapidly maturing physical bodies, quickly evolving social roles and expectations, and more slowly maturing expectations for individual responsibilities. This apparent dyssynchrony in adolescent development gives rise to the notion that puberty causes the difficulties that some adolescents experience during this developmental phase. Moffitt (1993) suggested that it is just this disjointed development of physique and social role that plays a significant role in the development of conduct problems in adolescence.

However, more than just the fact that puberty occurs and youths in contemporary society experience longer periods of adolescence, how puberty evolves has an impact on adolescent development and the rise of emotional problems. Alsaker (1996) provided a cogent review of research relevant to the impact of puberty, key points of which are summarized here. She noted that the timing of pubertal changes (the time at which an individual experiences the physiological and physical changes relative to peers) rather than the changes themselves have the greatest influence on adolescent coping. Changes in hormone levels are weak predictors of behavior. However, the chronological age at which the changes occur can make big differences in emotional and behavioral functioning. In general, early maturation (i.e., before 90% of peers) predicts internalizing and externalizing problems for girls. The effects of pubertal timing on boys are less clear. The only robust effects appear to be that boys who mature off-time (either later or earlier than 90% of their peers) may be at greater risk for developing alcohol problems than boys whose maturation is in step with their age-mates. As puberty progresses, parental influence on the adolescent decreases and peer influence increases. This is typically a normal adjustment made with little difficulty. However, pubertal timing influences peer relationships. Alsaker noted that early maturing girls tend to have older friends who may have a wider repertoire of behaviors (e.g., more adultlike behaviors such as having a job, engaging in sexual relationships, smoking, drinking) that are seen as problematic for the younger but more physically mature girl. This may be the source of stress between the girl and her family, rather than the physical maturation of puberty itself. This effect is not seen in boys; early maturation has either a positive influence or no influence at all on dating and intimate relationships.

Alsaker (1996) discussed the impact of off-time maturation on the normal developmental tasks of puberty. She emphasized a developmental task model that takes into account not only the particular task (e.g., developing independent peer relationships) but also the individual and social context of the task. The individual's perception of the task, how he or she is coping with it and progressing relative to peers, and others' perceptions of the individual's process through the developmental task have more influence on the process than the nature of the task itself. She noted that those who mature earlier than their peers may lack role models and may be unprepared for the changes, and others around them may be unprepared for the early maturation. Later maturers will likely have models and will be prepared for the change. Regarding social influences on off-time maturation, Alsaker notes that others around the early maturer may be unprepared for those changes as well, whereas those around the late maturer may express concern over the off-time development. The perceptions of others about an individual have powerful influences on the individual's self-perception and behavior. Off-time maturers must cope not only with the changes of puberty that all experience, but also with their own and others' reactions to the nonnormative timing of the changes.

Finally, pulling together these lines of research, Compas and colleagues (1993) suggested that girls experiencing pubertal changes coincidentally with other stressors (e.g., changing schools) may be at greater risk for depressive problems than boys because of gender-linked ways of emotion-focused coping. Boys presumably would be at greater risk for substance use problems or delinquency. The considerable comorbidity and symptom overlap in adolescent psychopathology suggests that the model would have utility in explaining and predicting other disorders. Although Compas and colleagues (1995) summarized the literature that is supportive of these predictions for depressive and conduct disorders, research has yet to demonstrate the utility of this model in other types of psychopathology in adolescents.

IMPLICATIONS FOR RESEARCH, PREVENTION, AND TREATMENT

The lines of research and theory presented thus far have implications for prevention and treatment of adolescent emotional problems. The first order of business is to establish accurate rates of problems in adolescents. The debate about the use of categorical versus dimensional schemes for evaluating problems has largely been determined by clinical practice and, for more practical purposes, reimbursement requirements by third-party payers. Nevertheless, the extent to which problems experienced by adolescents overlap and fluctuate over time suggests that empirically derived dimensional rating systems are useful to track problems over time. These systems are more flexible and can help to identify truly developmentally determined variants of emotional and behavioral problems that might be missed in a categorical system. To date, there has been no comprehensive study of adolescents that encompasses all pertinent categories of psychopathology. Thus, current estimates are merely extrapolations across studies and

are subject to biases inherent in the interpretation of studies. Most individuals will move through the period of adolescence with few if any difficulties. Although most will experience some difficulties at some time during their adolescence, most individuals will cope quite well. There is a significant minority that will experience disruptive disorder; best estimates suggest that severe psychopathology occurs in about 20% of adolescents sometime during their youth. There is considerable overlap among disorders, and longitudinal studies indicate that there is also considerable fluctuation across symptom types.

Appropriate models of assessment need to be developed to adequately account for the complexities of developmental psychopathology. Any model of assessment should include known variables related to rates of problems. In addition to counting the number of symptoms and diagnoses that occur at what ages and in which gender, research should include historical assessment of stressors, coping, family variables, physiological maturation, and the trajectory or course of the observed problems. Longitudinal research that uses such complex models will help us to develop an understanding of these factors. This in turn will be useful in developing predictive models that can be used for targeted prevention and treatment.

Prevention and treatment efforts may be directed toward early identification and treatment using techniques or modalities that are specific and empirically supported. Prevention efforts should take into account known risk factors: biological risk for disorder (e.g., family history of disorder, medical problems that increase risk for depression), gender-specific response to stressors, and family, social, and environmental problems. Intervention can be tied directly to these known risks. Assessing environmental stressors and their perceived impact on the individual and family will help to determine the level and type of coping skills that need to be developed to buffer the stressor. Understanding the relative differences between boys and girls in the kinds of stressors that are problematic is essential in developing specific coping mechanisms that will be useful. As the drive to demonstrate treatment efficacy continues, understanding the specific and relative contributions of predictive factors will become increasingly important. For example, in targeting depression in girls, treatment protocols may be developed based on differences in coping styles and the effects of ruminative thinking. Using cognitive-behavioral techniques to decrease negative thoughts might lead to more instrumental responses that would decrease depressive symptoms. Similarly, in boys, using emotion-focused therapy to decrease avoidant or distracting responses to dysphoria could impact rates of conduct and substance use problem. Theory-driven treatment evaluation studies can help increase the predictive value of classification systems for adolescent problems.

Professionals' understanding of adolescent emotional problems has come a long way from Hall's *Sturm und Drang* to Compas's complex models of factors that contribute to the development and maintenance of psychopathology. Although adolescence is generally a time devoid of serious problems, for a significant minority of adolescents problems occur and persist. Future research should focus on three things: (1) identifying more specifically who is at risk for what type of symptom or disorder and how to ameliorate those risks; (2) creating a truly developmental approach to emotional and behavior problems in childhood and adolescence; and (3) developing effective treatment programs targeted to particular groups of individuals that share common risk factors and symptoms.

REFERENCES

Achenbach, T.M., & Edelbrock, C. (1991). *Manual for the Child Behavior Checklist/4–18 and 1991 profile.* Burlington: University of Vermont, Department of Psychiatry.

Achenbach, T.M., & Edelbrock, C.S. (1981). Behavioral problems and competencies reported by parents of normal and disturbed children aged 4 through 16. *Monographs in Social Research and Child Development, 46*(1, Whole No. 188), 1–78.

Alsaker, F.D. (1996). Annotation: The impact of puberty. *Journal of Child Psychology and Psychiatry and Allied Disciplines, 37*, 249–258.

American Psychiatric Association. (1987). *Diagnostic and statistical manual of mental disorders* (3rd ed., rev.). Washington, DC: Author.

American Psychiatric Association. (1994). *Diagnostic and statistical manual of mental disorders* (4th ed.). Washington, DC: Author.

Beiderman, J., Klein, R.G., Pine, D.S., & Klein, D.F. (1998). Resolved: Mania is mistaken for ADHD in prepubertal children. *Journal of the American Academy of Child and Adolescent Psychiatry, 37*, 1091–1096.

Bird, H.R., Canino, G., Rubio-Stipec, M., Gould, M.S., Ribera, J., Sesman, M., Woodbury, M., Huertas-Goldman, S., Pagan, A., Sanchez-Lacay, A., & Moscoso, M. (1988). Estimates of the prevalence of childhood maladjustment in a community survey in Puerto Rico: The use of combined measures. *Archives of General Psychiatry, 45*, 1120–1126.

Boyle, M.H., Offord, D.R., Hofmann, H.G., Catlin, G.P., Byles, J.A., Cadman, D.T., Crawford, J.W., Links, P.S., Rae-Grant, N.I., & Szatmari, P. (1987). Ontario child health study: I. Methodology. *Archives of General Psychiatry, 44*, 826–831.

Brandenburg, N.A., Friedman, R.M., & Silver, S.E. (1990). The epidemiology of childhood psychiatric disorders: Prevalence findings from recent studies. *Journal of the American Academy of Child and Adolescent Psychiatry, 29*, 76–83.

Burke, K.C., Burke, J.D., Regier, D.A., & Rae, D.S. (1990). Age of onset of selected mental disorders in five community populations. *Archives of General Psychiatry, 47*, 511–518.

Cantwell, D.P. (1996). Classification of child and adolescent psychopathology. *Journal of Child Psychology and Psychiatry and Allied Disciplines, 37*, 3–12.

Compas, B.E., Hinden, B.R., & Gerhardt, C.A. (1995). Adolescent development: Pathways and processes of risk and resilience. *Annual Review of Psychology, 46*, 265–293.

Compas, B.E., Orosan, P.G., & Grant, K.E. (1993). Adolescent stress and coping: Implications for psychopathology during adolescence. *Journal of Adolescence, 16*, 331–349.

Costello, A., Edelbrock, C., Kalas, R., Kessler, M., & Klaric, S.A. (1982). *Diagnostic Interview Schedule for Children (DISC)* (Contract RFP-DB-81–0027). Bethesda, MD: National Institute of Mental Health.

Eaton, W.W., Holzer, C.E., VonKorff, M., Anthony, J.C., Helzer, J.E., George, L., Burnam, A., Boyd, J.H., Kessler, L.G., & Locke, B.Z. (1984). The design of the Epidemiologic Catchment Area surveys: The control and measurement of error. *Archives of General Psychiatry, 41*, 942–948.

Edelbrock, C., Costello, A.J., Dulcan, M.K., Kalas, R., & Conover, N.C. (1985). Age differences in the reliability of the psychiatric interview of the child. *Child Development, 56*, 265–275.

Feehan, M., McGee, R., & Williams, S.M. (1993). Mental health disorders from age 15 to 18 years. *Journal of the American Academy of Child and Adolescent Psychiatry, 32*, 1118–1126.

Fox, V. (1977). Is adolescence a phenomenon of modern times? *Journal of Psychohistory, 1*, 271–290.

Freud, A. (1958). Adolescence. *Psychoanalytic Study of the Child, 13*, 255–278.

Giaconia, R.M., Reinhertz, H.Z., Silverman, A.B., Pakiz, B., Frost, A.K., & Cohen, E. (1994). Ages of onset of psychiatric disorders in a community population of older adolescents. *Journal of the American Academy of Child and Adolescent Psychiatry, 33,* 706–717.

Hall, G.S. (1904). *Adolescence* (Vol. 1). New York: Appleton.

Hall, G.S. (1916). *Adolescence* (Vol. 2). New York: Appleton.

Herjanic, B., & Reich, W. (1982). Development of a structured psychiatric interview for children: Agreement between child and parent on individual symptoms. *Journal of Abnormal Child Psychology, 10,* 307–324.

Hodges, K.K., McKnew, D., Cytryn, L., Stern, L., & Kline, J. (1982). The Child Assessment Schedule (CAS) diagnostic interview. *Journal of the American Academy of Child Psychiatry, 21,* 468–473.

Hughes, D.D., & Brand, M. (1993). Myths or truths of adolescence [Letter and comment]. *Journal of the American Academy of Child and Adolescent Psychiatry, 32,* 1077–1078.

Kashani, J.H., Beck, N.C., Hoeper, E.W., Fallahi, C., Corcoran, C.M., McAllister, J.A., Rosenberg, T.K., & Reid, J.C. (1987). Psychiatric disorders in a community sample of adolescents. *American Journal of Psychiatry, 144,* 584–589.

Kashani, J.H., Orvaschel, H., Rosenberg, T.K., & Reid, J.C. (1989). Psychopathology in a community sample of children and adolescents: A developmental perspective. *Journal of the American Academy of Child and Adolescent Psychiatry, 28,* 701–706.

Kovacs, M. (1985). The Children's Depression Inventory. *Psychopharmacology Bulletin, 21,* 995–998.

Kutcher, S., Ward, B., Hayes, D., Wheeler, K., Brown, F., & Kutcher, J. (1996). Mental health concerns of Canadian adolescents: A consumer's perspective. *Canadian Journal of Psychiatry, 41,* 5–10.

La Greca, A.M. (Ed.). (1990). *Through the eyes of the child: Obtaining self-reports from children and adolescents.* Needham Heights, MA: Allyn & Bacon.

Logue, M.B. (1996). *Panic disorder in an outpatient pediatric cardiology sample.* Unpublished doctoral dissertation, University of Missouri at Columbia, Department of Psychology.

Moffitt, T.E. (1993). Adolescence-limited and life-course-persistent antisocial behavior: A developmental taxonomy. *Psychological Review, 100,* 674–701.

Nolen-Hoeksema, S. (1991). Responses to depression and their effects on the duration of depressive episodes. *Journal of Abnormal Psychology, 100,* 569–582.

Nottelmann, E.D., & Jensen, P.S. (1995). Comorbidity of disorders in children and adolescents: Developmental perspectives. *Advances in Clinical Child Psychology, 17,* 109–155.

Offer, D., Ostrov, E., & Howard, K.I. (1981). The mental health professional's concept of the normal adolescent. *Archives of General Psychiatry, 38,* 149–152.

Offer, D., & Schonert-Reichl, K.A. (1992). Debunking the myths of adolescence: Findings from recent research. *Journal of the American Academy of Child and Adolescent Psychiatry, 31,* 1003–1014.

Offer, D., & Schonert-Reichl, K.A. (1993). The authors reply: Response to myths of adolescence. [Comment]. *Journal of the American Academy of Child and Adolescent Psychiatry, 32,* 1077–1078.

Offord, D.R., Boyle, M.H., Szatmari, P., Rae-Grant, N.I., Links, P.S., Cadman, D.T., Byles, J.A., Crawford, J.W., Blum, H.M., Byrne, C., Thomas, H., & Woodward, C.A. (1987). Ontario Child Health Study: II. Six-month prevalence of disorder and rates of service utilization. *Archives of General Psychiatry, 44,* 832–836.

Peterson, A.C., Sarigiani, P.A., & Kennedy, R.E. (1991). Adolescent depression: Why more girls? *Journal of Youth and Adolescence, 20,* 247–271.

Puig-Antich, J., & Chambers, W.J. (1983). *Schedule for Affective Disorders and Schizophrenia for School-Aged Children.* Unpublished interview schedule, Pittsburgh, PA, Western Psychiatric Institute and Clinic.

Regier, D.A., Myers, J.K., Kramer, M., Robins, L.N., Blazer, D.G., Hough, R.L., Eaton, W.W., & Locke, B.Z. (1984). The NIMH Epidemiologic Catchment Area program: Historical context, major objectives, and study population characteristics. *Archives of General Psychiatry, 41,* 934–941.

Reinherz, H.Z., Giaconia, R.M., Lefkowitz, E.S., Pakiz, B., & Frost, A.K. (1993). Prevalence of psychiatric disorders in a community population of older adolescents. *Journal of the American Academy of Child and Adolescent Psychiatry, 32,* 369–377.

Reynolds, C.R., & Kamphaus, R.W. (1992). *Behavior Assessment System for Children manual.* Circle Pines, MN: American Guidance Service.

Reynolds, C.R., & Richmond, B.O. (1978). What I think and feel: A revised measure of children's manifest anxiety. *Journal of Abnormal Child Psychology, 6,* 271–280.

Roberts, R.E., Attkisson, C.C., & Rosenblatt, A. (1998). Prevalence of psychopathology among children and adolescents. *American Journal of Psychiatry, 155,* 715–725.

Robins, L., Helzer, J., Cottler, L., & Goldring, E. (1989). *NIMH Diagnostic Interview Schedule–Version III, Revised.* St. Louis, MO: Washington University, Department of Psychiatry.

Rutter, M., & Graham, P. (1968). The reliability and validity of the psychiatric assessment of the child: I. Interview with the child. *British Journal of Psychiatry, 114,* 563–576.

Shaffer, D., Gould, M.S., Brasic, J., Ambrosini, P., Fisher, P., Bird, H.R., & Aluwahlia, S. (1983). A Children's Global Assessment Scale (CGAS). *Archives of General Psychiatry, 40,* 1228–1231.

Siegel, J., & Shaughnessy, M.F. (1995). There's a first time for everything: Understanding adolescence. *Adolescence, 30,* 217–221.

Stein, B.A., Golombek, H., Marton, P., & Korenblum, M. (1991). Consistency and change in personality characteristics and affect from middle to late adolescence. *Canadian Journal of Psychiatry, 36,* 16–20.

Wagner, B.M., & Compas, B.E. (1990). Gender, instrumentality, and expressivity: Moderators of the relation between stress and psychological symptoms during adolescence. *American Journal of Community Psychology, 18,* 383–406.

Whitaker, A., Johnson, J., Shaffer, D., Rapoport, J.L., Kalikow, K., Walsh, B.T., Davies, M., Braiman, S., & Dolinsky, A. (1990). Uncommon troubles in young people: Prevalence estimates of selected psychiatric disorders in a nonreferred adolescent population. *Archives of General Psychiatry, 47,* 487–496.

World Health Organization. (1992). *ICD-10: Classification of mental and behavioural disorders: Clinical descriptions and diagnostic guidelines.* Geneva, Switzerland: Author.

CHAPTER 33

Depression and Suicide in Adolescence

PETER L. SHERAS

In the latter part of the 1990s, depression among adolescents has become a widely publicized phenomenon. Looking only at such events as the suicide of teen idol Kurt Cobain of the rock group Nirvana and the school shootings in Jonesboro, Arkansas, Springfield, Oregon, West Paducah, Kentucky, Bethel, Alaska, Pearl, Mississippi, and Littleton, Colorado, one comes to the conclusion that depression and suicide are a common occurrence for this generation of adolescents. Even though an examination of suicide rates for this age group will show that the dramatic increases in the 1970s and 1980s have begun to level off, major declines in suicidal behaviors do not appear to be occurring, and depression appears to be ever-present.

DEPRESSION IN ADOLESCENCE

Only in the 1980s was depression clearly acknowledged as a clinical phenomenon occurring in children and adolescents (Matson, 1989). This acknowledgment occurred primarily with the advent of more behavioral indices of depressive symptoms. Prior to that time, there was controversy as to whether children and adolescents suffered from such a syndrome as depression and how to view depressive symptoms shown by these affected individuals.

CLINICAL FEATURES

According to Matson (1989), there exists a continuum of opinions related to the diagnosis of depression in children and adolescence. At one end appears the most conservative approach reported by Lefkowitz and Burton (1978). They believe that depression cannot be diagnosed if "depressed" behaviors are also prevalent in normal children and if such behaviors disappear over time without treatment. At the other end of the spectrum is the contention that many behaviors in children and adolescents are symptoms of "masked depression." Cytryn and McKnew (1974), Lesse (1974), and Curran (1987), as well as many other authors, discuss this concept at length. Although masked depression is no longer a popular concept and has been criticized in the literature (Bemporad, 1978), the alternative explanation for such symptoms appears to be the co-occurrence of depression with other disorders. Weller and Weller (1990) cited a number of studies of the comorbidity of depression and attention-deficit disorders, anxiety disorders, and conduct disorders in their review. In many ways, the preceding taxonomy attempts to distinguish whether symptoms manifested by adolescents constitute depression. Symptoms that adolescents manifest, however, need to be acknowledged due to their potential for dysfunction or self-destructiveness, not just because of their significance in terms of diagnostic formulation. It is for this reason that it is important to examine a variety of observed symptoms before deciding whether or not they are masking depression. As Toolan (1975) pointed out, and others have asserted (Curran, 1987), there is rarely a clear and focused picture of depression in the adolescent. Clinicians working with such populations must often spend a great deal of time assessing how the adolescent presents in a variety of contexts. Does a depressed symptom observed at home but not at school or with peers constitute justification for a diagnosis of depression? There is often a need, therefore, to assess a person's functioning in a variety of settings through the eyes of a number of observers, including the individual's own view. It is characteristic of adolescents, however, to sometimes disguise their own perceptions or color them when speaking with adults.

Common Syndromes

Notwithstanding this confusion, Nissen (1983) described a study of depressed adolescents in which he differentiated three common depressive syndromes: quietness and resignation, retardation and loss of drive, and agitation and anxiety. Symptoms of quietness and resignation can include grief, overadjustment, shyness, self-isolation, enuresis, nail biting, unmotivated weeping, bouts of aggressiveness, and suicidal behavior. Retardation and loss of drive might cause symptoms of psychomotor sluggishness, apathy, insecurity, difficulty in learning, mutism, and passivity. Symptoms of agitation and anxiety may feature auto- and heteroaggressiveness, insecurity, compulsive eating, unmotivated weeping, and suicidal behavior. There is considerable overlap in the symptoms in the three groups, partially because the symptoms of depression may vary widely from one adolescent to another.

Curran (1987), in his description of symptomatology, believed that adolescents desire or are able to mask depressive affect for a number of reasons, including capacity for denial, tendency to act out feelings, and avoidance of dependence and helplessness (e.g., running away, sexual acting-out, boredom and restlessness, disturbance of concentration, aggressive behavior, delinquency). Curran held that these symptoms can be especially unhealthy because they may actually obscure the level of distress experienced by the adolescent from adults, other peers, and themselves.

It may be the case that some adolescents are unable to clearly articulate their experiences because they do not have mature language skills, or their environment has not taught them the use of a more vivid vocabulary, or their language is heavily influenced by slang or the vernacular of their peers or pop culture. The words "depressed" or "suicidal" may represent "cool" or highly accepted characteristics of the social group and not have the same connotation as for the adult interviewer or observer.

Kazdin (1989), in his review of literature on childhood depression, concluded that the essential features of depression are similar for children, adults, and adolescents. In other words, the criteria for identifying affective disorders appear to be applied independent of age. This conclusion makes considerable sense given that some of the symptoms of masked depression may remit with age. Kazdin pointed out that depressive symptoms do seem to appear with progressive development and that these symptoms, though fitting within the diagnostic rubric of adult depression or affective disorder, may not be identical for each developmental group. Kazdin and others have pointed out the need to differentiate a depressive symptom from a syndrome or mood disorder. The former may be transitory or developmentally determined, whereas the latter may be part of a larger group of symptoms. Strategies for treatment may depend on a clinician's ability to explore this distinction adequately.

This clinical picture of the depressed adolescent, therefore, may be varied and complex. It includes symptoms characteristic of adult depressions and mood disorders and those of children (if such depressions do, indeed, exist). Briefly summarized, the inclusion criteria for major depressive episode in the *Diagnostic and Statistical Manual of Mental Disorders* (*DSM-IV*; American Psychiatric Association, 1994) are depressed mood, markedly diminished interest or pleasure in almost all activities, significant weight loss or weight gain, insomnia or hypersomnia, psychomotor agitation or retardation, fatigue or loss of energy nearly every day, feelings of worthlessness or excessive guilt, diminished ability to concentrate or think, and recurrent thoughts of death or suicidal ideation nearly every day. In addition, reference to disorders or syndromes other than major depressive disorder are made in the *DSM-IV* under categories of uncomplicated bereavement, separation anxiety disorder, adjustment reaction with depressed mood, and dysthymia. The *DSM-IV* also indicates that in the case of adolescents, depressive episodes frequently are associated with other disorders, including disruptive behavior disorders, anxiety disorders, eating disorders, substance-related disorders, and attention-deficit disorders.

Depressive symptoms for adolescents appear in a variety of contexts, including peer relations and school settings. Poland (1989) listed symptoms of adolescent depression as withdrawal from friends and activities, loss of joy in life and bleak outlook, changes in eating and sleeping habits, risk-taking or reckless behavior, preoccupation with death, increased somatic complaints, problems concentrating on schoolwork, frequent mood changes, uncharacteristic emotional or rebellious outbursts, low self-esteem and lack of confidence in abilities or decision-making capabilities, significant weight loss or gain, and decreased attention to physical appearance. In addition, depressed adolescents may evidence increase in substance abuse, rapidly falling grades, and hostile attitudes.

PREVALENCE

Adolescents with severe psychiatric disorders have demonstrated rates of mood disorder from 27% in an inpatient/outpatient sample (Carlson & Cantwell, 1979) to 40% (Hudgens, 1974; King & Pittman, 1969). Young people suffering from medical disorders, especially those with orthopedic problems and diagnosed cancer, showed rates of depression in some studies of 23% and 17%, respectively (Kashani & Hakami, 1982; Kashani, Venzke, & Millar, 1981).

Normal populations show varied rates of depression. In a large study of 13 to 19-year-olds using a self-report measure, Kandel and Davies (1982) reported rates of major depression of 13% to 28% depending on the cutoff scores used. In a review of depression in children and adolescents, Hammen and Rudolph (1996) report prevalence rates from 3.4% to 7.8% depending on the age group and *DSM* diagnostic category. Additionally, in a study of junior and senior high school students, Kaplan, Hong, and Weinhold (1984) used the Beck Depression Inventory with a cutoff of 16 and found the occurrence of depression to be 8.6%, or approximately that found in adult populations. In that same study,

22.1% of the sample had scores over 10, which is a level nearly identical to that reported by Rutter, Graham, and Chadwick (1976) using their self-report measure. Pfeffer (1985) also noted the prevalence of depression in adolescents to be 8.6%. Carlson (1979) reported a 16% occurrence rate of severe depression in a pediatric population, whereas Earls (1984) confirmed an increase in the rates of depression from middle childhood through the life cycle to adulthood. The incidence of adolescent depression has also been linked in a number of studies with the occurrence of depression and other psychiatric disorders in parents and family members (Strober, 1984; Strober & Carlson, 1982; Weissman, Prusoff, & Gammon, 1984). Weller and Weller (1990) reviewed 18 additional epidemiological studies of depression in children and adolescents from 1970 to 1987. Only one of these studies, however, examined normal adolescents, and they demonstrated a depression rate of only 4.7%.

Common wisdom leads people to believe that the incidence of depression is higher among adolescent girls than boys. In a number of reviews and studies, gender differences in depressive symptoms were indeed found using scores on common measures of depression. Occurrence rates were consistently higher for females than for males (Campbell, Byrne, & Baron, 1992; Fleming & Offord, 1990; Lewinsohn, Hops, Roberts, Seeley, & Andrews, 1993; McGee, Feehan, Williams, & Anderson, 1992; Nolen-Hoeksema & Girgus, 1994; Reinherz, Giaconia, Lefkowitz, Pakiz, & Frost, 1993).

ETIOLOGY

Models to account for behavior have been posited in most areas of psychological functioning, psychopathology, and psychological development. Adolescents' depression is no exception. No less than eight major models and many minor ones have been described in the literature. This work has been reviewed thoroughly by both Kazdin (1989) and Weller and Weller (1990).

Psychodynamic

At the root of the psychodynamic formulation of depression was Freud's (1917/1957) idea of the actual or perceived loss of the love object. This loss was followed by self-rejection and self-criticism, the anger toward the parent turned inward. Narcissistic cravings, oral fixation, loss of self-esteem stemming from unsatisfied affection needs, and feelings of helplessness are manifestations of this condition. The child's inability to achieve an ego ideal was for some the cause of depression.

Cognitive

Cognitively based theories of depression examine the nature of attributions and perceptions. Seligman (1975) introduced the concept of "learned helplessness," positing that when people cannot influence events in their lives, that very experience or expectation produces depression. Beck (1976) emphasized negative cognitions that affect a person's judgment about the social environment and the world. Three types of negative thinking—negative views of the self, of the world, and of the future—create systematic errors in thought or cognitive distortions that may produce depression.

Behavioral

Behavioral formulations of depression are based on the notion that depressed symptoms are learned in interaction with the environment. Social skills deficits as well as other skill deficiencies may be a function of reinforcement histories. Clarizio (1985) and Clarkin and Glazer (1981) examined learning, skill acquisition (or deficit), and environmental consequences in relation to depression. Depressive symptoms may also occur because of a lack of reinforcers in the environment, a loss of access to such major reinforcers, or a progressive thinning of reinforcement. Rehm (1977) attempted to relate the occurrence of depression to maladaptive self-control mechanisms, including self-monitoring, self-evaluation, and self-reinforcement. Those with self-control deficits are likely to set very high and unobtainable standards for themselves and focus more on failures or negative events and on short-term rather than long-term consequences.

Life Stresses/Socioenvironmental

Most research demonstrates that stressful life events are more frequently reported by depressed persons (Paykel, 1982), and the occurrence and number of stressors appear to be positively related to depression in children (Mullins, Siegel, & Hodges, 1985). Family interaction and the parent-child relationship are also topics beginning to appear in the literature

on depression (Weller & Weller, 1990). VanWicklin (1990) indicated that the loss of social support and control was a primary determinant of depressive symptoms.

Biological/Biochemical

There has been an increasing interest in biological models of depression, especially biochemical models. Identification of neurotransmitters related to depression has been undertaken, but the results are still very preliminary (Usdin, Asberg, Bertilsson, & Sjoqvist, 1984). Again, very few studies have been directed toward adolescents as a population; most work has been performed with adults. This research has examined a number of neurotransmitters and neuroendocrine abnormalities. The major implicated transmitters are monoamines. Indoleamines and catecholamines have also been implicated, with indication that deficits in these agents will produce depression and excesses will produce mania (Zis & Goodwin, 1982).

Neuroendocrine studies have suggested that depression often includes disturbances in sex drive, appetite, sleep, and autonomic activity as well as mood and may be related to hypothalamic dysfunction (Sachar, 1982). Noradrenalin, acetylcholine, and serotonin in certain levels have all been indicated as present in those suffering from depression. These agents regulate neuroendocrine levels controlling hormone production and in some cases pituitary functioning (Carroll, 1983). Other biological markers in childhood and adolescent depression have been discussed by McConville and Bruce (1985).

Genetics

Research has demonstrated that there are genetic influences on the occurrence of depressive disorders. Studies have examined concordance for a number of subtypes of affective disorders. The strength of the concordance appears to depend on the particular type of depression examined. In general, studies demonstrated that in the case of affective disorders, monozygotic twins have a 65% concordance rate compared with 14% for dizygotic twins (Gershon, Targum, Kessler, Mazure, & Bunney, 1997). Studies of adoptees have also demonstrated strong familial links to affective disorders (Morrison, 1983). Strober (1984) and Strober and Carlson (1982) were able to demonstrate that, in the cases of depressed adolescents, 35% of parents and 20% of second-degree relatives were depressed; an even larger percentage were depressed when adolescents were bipolar by diagnosis.

ASSESSMENT

Currently, there are many methods to assess depression in adolescents. In most cases, it appears that a comprehensive approach, including a number of methods, is indicated. The five major components appear to be clinical interview; direct observation by clinicians; observations by significant others; self-reports, checklists, and inventories; and biochemical/physiological measures. Each of these areas is worthy of elaborate explication, as provided by the reviews, but are merely mentioned here (Costello & Angold, 1988; Kazdin, 1989; Matson, 1989; McConville & Bruce, 1985).

Clinical Interviews

These techniques include both structured and unstructured methods. Unstructured methods are the most commonly employed, though not necessarily the most efficient. Palmer (1983), for instance, believes that three major issues need to be addressed in an unstructured interview: (1) the child's own view of his or her complaints, symptoms, and stressors; (2) the child's view of his or her environment and current level of functioning; and (3) the child's view of his or her developmental history. Most of the unstructured approaches employ open-ended questioning to obtain information.

Structured interviews have been described in a number of reviews (e.g., Kazdin, 1989; Matson, 1989; Weller & Weller, 1990). The most frequently identified instruments in the literature are the Schedule for Affective Disorders and Schizophrenia in School-Age Children (Kiddie-SADS; Puig-Antich & Chambers, 1978), including parent and child forms; the Diagnostic Interview for Children and Adolescents (DICA), described by Herjanic and Campbell (1977); and the NIMH Diagnostic Interview Schedule for Children (DISC), including child and parent interview forms (Costello, Edelbrock, Dulcan, & Kalas, 1984). The latter two interview schedules concentrate more on pathology.

Observations

Observations of adolescents can be made by clinicians or by significant others. Matson (1989), in reviewing observational studies by clinicians, suggests observing and examining behaviors in three categories when attempting to assess depression: (1) social activity such as talking and interacting with others and participating in group activities; (2) solitary behavior; and (3) affect-related expression, such as frowning, smiling, complaining, and arguing. Obviously, much of the clinical observation takes place in the context of the clinical interview and interviews with parents.

Checklists and Inventories

A variety of inventories and checklists are available to examine depression in adolescents. Kazdin (1989), Matson (1989), and others list a large number of such instruments. Perhaps the best known and most often used behavioral observational instrument is the Child Behavior Checklist (CBCL). This instrument is designed to isolate a number of problem behavior areas (Achenback & Edelbrock, 1983). Other frequently used tools are the Children's Depression Inventory (CDI; Kovacs, 1981; Kovacs & Beck, 1977), designed to assess cognitive, behavioral, and affective signs of depression; the Beck Depression Inventory (BDI), modified for adolescents (described in Chiles, Miller, & Cox, 1980); and the Reynolds Adolescent Depression Scale (RADS; Reynolds, 1986). These latter two scales have been well studied (Atlas & DiScipio, 1992; Campbell, Byrne, & Baron, 1994) and show useful factor structure and at least moderate correlations to one another. Other instruments receiving some attention in the literature are the Children's Depression Scale (Tisher & Lang, 1983), the Children's Depression Adjective Checklist (Sokoloff & Lubin, 1983), the Children's Depression Rating Scale (Proznanski, Cook, & Carroll, 1979), and the Stress Index for Parents of Adolescents (Sheras & Abidin, 1998), which measures parents' perceptions of their adolescent's mood.

Biochemical and Physiological Measures

Biological measures of depression as described earlier have to do with measurement of dexamethasone suppression. The Dexamethasone Suppression Test (DST) has been controversial for some time, however. It does not always appear accurate or predictive of depression; Carroll (1982) reported that it is accurate only 25% to 60% of the time. There have been numerous reports of its usefulness as well, reported by Matson (1989).

INTERVENTION

Strategies to treat depressed adolescents are as varied as the models to describe depression and the methods to assess it. In general, treatments that combine more than one approach are most supported in the literature. Marcotte (1997) reviewed seven studies of cognitive behavioral programs, including problem-solving skills, relaxation, cognitive restructuring, communication, and self-control training. Kazdin (1989) provided summaries of treatments that include cognitive therapy, increase in pleasant activities, social skills training, self-control therapy, and interpersonal psychotherapy. His review, however, focuses primarily on work with children. Matson (1989) emphasized cognitive therapies that include both behavioral interventions and more cognitive ones. He listed the major treatment components discussed in a number of studies as self-monitoring, activity schedules, cognitive restructuring, attribution retraining, self-evaluation, and self-reinforcement. These approaches highlight a controversy reviewed by Beidel and Turner (1986) that attempts to differentiate between the operant and social learning theorists. Learning theorists consider cognitions to be private and unobservable events, whereas cognitive psychologists see cognitions as behaviors capable of modification by the laws of learning. Social skills training, behavioral techniques (including systematic desensitization), cognitive strategies (including problem-solving therapies), and psychopharmacological intervention are seen as the major treatments for depression in children and adolescents.

Psychopharmacological studies using such drugs as imipramine (Petti, 1983) and monoamine oxidase inhibitors (Elkins & Rappaport, 1983) are reviewed by McConville and Bruce (1985), Kazdin, (1989) and Matson (1989). There is very little review of such modes of therapy as working with the individual adolescent, with the family, group treatment, or use of these in some combination. Clearly, group therapy is a method of choice more for adolescents than for younger children, and social skills training is best accomplished in a group modality. Outcome studies of a number of treatments leave the picture somewhat clouded at best. Treatment appears to combine those used for adults and those with children, which focus mostly on behavior modification, cognitive restructuring, and/or drug therapy.

Insight-oriented or psychodynamic therapies are less frequently reviewed.

SUICIDE AND PARASUICIDE IN ADOLESCENCE

Despite an increase in the suicide rate among adolescents in the past 30 years and a concomitant rise in the amount of research in the area, it is still easy to agree with students of adolescent suicide (e.g., Diekstra & Moritz, 1987; Haim, 1974) who state that our understanding of why adolescents choose to kill themselves is limited. At the outset, it is important to assert that suicide is *not a syndrome but a symptom*. Like other symptoms, it can be the manifestation of a number of underlying problems, not necessarily just depression. A particular suicidal act can result from a variety of circumstances, including:

1. Depression.
2. Reaction to stress.
3. Loss or grief.
4. Unresolved conflict.
5. Substance use.
6. Unexpressed anger or rage.
7. Social pressure.
8. Lack of problem-solving skills.
9. Poor conflict resolution.
10. Hopelessness or frustration.
11. Escape from chronic victimization.
12. The desire for respect.
13. The need to avoid embarrassment or humiliation.
14. The desire to be visible and noticed.
15. Mental illness other than depression.

Each of these circumstances may be a function of a variety of causes, creating a multifactoral etiologic model discussed by Goldman and Beardslee (1999) and others.

A number of comprehensive works attempt to examine thoroughly the occurrence, treatment, and prevention of adolescent suicide (Curran, 1987; Diekstra & Hawton, 1987; Goldman & Beardslee, 1999; Peck, Farberow, & Litman, 1985; Pfeffer, 1989). The reader is encouraged to examine these or other works for a more in-depth treatment of this complicated subject.

PREVALENCE

The occurrence of suicidal behaviors can be divided into behaviors that are successful in ending life (completed suicides) and those that for one reason or another fail at ending life (suicide attempts or parasuicides). Prevalence of suicide is now well documented in the national statistics and literature (Berman, 1986; Curran, 1987; Fremouw, dePerczel, & Ellis, 1990; Hicks, 1990; Lewis, Walker, & Mehr, 1990; Mash, 1989; McIntosh, 1998; Peters & Murphy, 1998; Roberts, 1990; Shaw, Sheehan, & Fernandez, 1987). Information on current suicide rates can be seen in Table 33.1 and Figure 33.1.

In general, the consensus appears to be that nearly 5,000 adolescents will commit suicide this year in the United States. As an example, statistics for 1996 report that 313 children 5 to 14 years and 4,146 individuals 15 to 24 years committed suicide (National Center for Health Statistics, 1998). Suicide is currently the third leading cause of death in adolescence, after accident and homicide. Statistics demonstrate an increase in the rate of suicide over the past generation in most categories. People age 15 to 24 represent 13.7% of the current U.S. population and committed 14.1% of the suicides in 1996 (Peters et al., 1998). An average of one person under

age 25 commits suicide every 1 hour and 53 minutes (McIntosh, 1998). In 1996, suicide ranked as the third leading cause of death for those aged 15 to 24 and the fifth for 10- to 14-year-olds.

Many researchers believe that even this current high rate of suicide among the adolescent and young adult population, 10 to 24 years of age, may be significantly higher because of underreporting errors (Holinger, 1979; Marks & Haller, 1977; J.P. Miller, 1975; Seiden, 1969; Toolan, 1975). This

Table 33.1 Suicide rates/100,000 U.S. population for sample years by age group and gender.

| | Age Group | | | | | |
| | 10–14 yrs. | | 15–19 yrs. | | 20–24 yrs. | |
Year	M	F	M	F	M	F
1960	0.9	0.2	5.6	1.6	11.5	2.9
1965	0.9	0.2	6.1	1.9	13.8	4.3
1970	0.9	0.3	8.8	2.9	19.3	5.7
1975	1.2	0.4	12.2	2.9	26.4	6.8
1980	1.2	0.3	13.8	3.0	26.7	5.5
1987	2.3	0.6	16.2	4.2	26.1	4.4
1993	2.4	0.9	17.6	3.8	26.8	4.4
1996	2.3	0.8	15.6	3.5	24.8	3.7

Source: Data compiled from National Center for Health Statistics, U.S. Department of Health and Human Services.

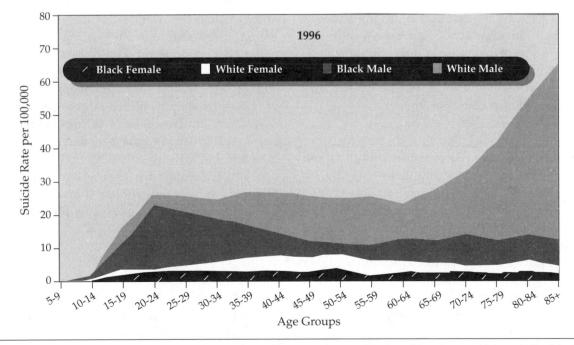

Figure 33.1 U.S. suicide rates by age, gender, and racial group. *Source:* National Institute of Mental Health. *Data:* Centers for Disease Control and Prevention, National Center for Health Statistics.

underestimation may be the result of reticence by family physicians or emergency room officials to state suicide as a cause of death on the death certificate. In an attempt to be compassionate or avoid stigma for the family, suicide may not be listed. It may be the case that some suicides (e.g., single vehicle accidents) are being reported as accidents even though circumstances are suspicious. It may also be the case that some cases reported as homicides were circumstances where adolescents placed themselves at high risk for death as a function of suicidal intent (e.g, confronting people with guns, trying to fight a gang by oneself).

Rates for parasuicide or attempted suicide are significantly higher than for suicide. Curran (1987) and many others report a sharp increase in attempted suicides over the past 20 years. Early studies indicated attempt success ratios ranging from 4:1 to 10:1. Farberow and Schneidman (1961) reported a rate of 8:1. More recently, however, studies indicate that the ratio might be significantly higher. McIntire, Angle, and Schlicht (1980) reported a ratio of 220:1 in their study of adolescents under the age of 19. In a study of 15- to 24-year-olds, Angle, O'Brien, and McIntire (1983) reported a 200:1 ratio, and Curran (1987) reported a ratio of 312:1 in a sample of 15- to 18-year-olds. Consider also the reporting difficulties in this area. Many attempts are never reported or occur as "silent" attempts confided only to friends or even parents. Suicide attempts, unlike accomplished suicides, also occur on a continuum from mild to severe depending on the circumstances and the intent. A handful of swallowed aspirin may constitute an attempt to a young person when it may not be perceived as such by parents.

Age

It is clear from the data presented in Table 33.1 and Figure 33.1 that the rate of completed suicides increases from early to late adolescence. Safer (1997) reported that, although adolescent and adult suicides are similar in terms of gender ratio, the use of guns, and the rates of completion on first attempts, adolescents have a greater rate of attempts, a higher percentage of successful suicides per attempt, and lower rates of completion following psychiatric hospitalizations than their adult counterparts.

Gender and Sexual Orientation

In the case of suicide, males have historically killed themselves at a ratio of 3:1 over females (Curran,

1987). In a study by McIntosh and Jewell (1986), it was suggested that this ratio may be increasing. A variety of studies (reviewed in Curran, 1987) show ratios ranging from 3:1 to 10:1 of female over males. It is important to note that attempted suicides are not merely milder forms of accomplished suicide but may, in some instances, represent an entirely different clinical picture (Seiden, 1969; Sheras, 1983).

The study of the relationship of sexual orientation and gender identity to suicidality is still very young. Few data are available, although it is reported anecdotally by Remafedi, Farrow, and Deisher (1993) that completion rates are higher than expected for lesbian and gay populations. It is hypothesized that such elevations may be a result of increased stress and feelings of alienation and loneliness relating to the process of "outing," or revealing oneself to the outside world.

Race and Ethnicity

There are differences in the suicide rates of minority groups in the United States. The Report of the Secretary's Task Force on Youth Suicide to the Secretary of the U.S. Department of Health and Human Services (1989) reported that the suicide rate for Blacks is half that of Whites, with males outnumbering females at a ratio of 4:1. A number of sources do report a recent increase in the suicide rate among Blacks (Curran, 1987; Gibbs, 1988). There are few studies to be found regarding attempting suicide in this population. Figure 33.1 depicts the fact that African-American men and women have lower suicide rates than their White peers.

Native American suicide rates are reported to be more than double those of Whites, with the peak rate at a slightly younger age. Suicide rates among Hispanics in a study of residents of the southwestern United States are lower than those of non-Hispanic Whites but higher than those of Blacks (U.S. Department of Health and Human Services, 1989).

METHODS

The methods selected for suicide vary with age group and availability. Table 33.2 presents a breakdown of methods by age and sex from a sample year for adolescents and young adults. It is obvious that methods for attempted suicides are weighted more

Table 33.2   Suicides by Firearms and Other Means in the United States, 1996.

	Firearms			Other Means[1]		
	Number	*Rate*[2]	*% Total*	*Number*	*Rate*[2]	*% Total*
Total USA	18,166	6.8	58	12,737	4.8	41.2
Ages 15–24	2,724	7.5	62.5	1,634	4.5	37.5
All Males	15,808	12.2	63.2	9,190	7.1	36.8
All Females	2,358	1.7	39.9	3,547	2.6	60.1

Source: K.D. Peters, K.D. Kochanek, & S.L. Murphy. (1998). Deaths: Final data for 1996. *National Vital Statistics Report, 47*(9). Hyattsville, MD: National Center for Health Statistics. (DHHS Publication No. PHS 99-1120).

[1] Other means include poison and strangulation.
[2] Rates are per 100,000.

toward passive and less lethal means. Therefore, firearms and explosives are more prevalent methods for suicides than poisoning (most frequently, drug or medication overdose) and are most prevalent among suicide attempters, males and females (Curran 1987; McKenry, Tishler, & Kelley, 1983).

CLINICAL PICTURE

The clinical picture of suicidal adolescents varies. Schneidman (1986) believed that there are a number of approaches to the understanding of suicide. These include a personal and literary document approach; a philosophical and theoretical approach; a sociological approach; a dyadic and familial approach; a psychodynamic approach; a psychiatric mental illness approach; a constitutional and genetic approach; a biological and biochemical approach; a legal and ethic approach; a systems theory approach; a political, global, supernational approach; and, of course, a psychological approach. Schneidman identifies 10 commonalities in accomplished suicides despite their tendency to be individualized and idiosyncratic events:

1. The common purpose of suicide is to seek a solution.
2. The common goal of suicide is the cessation of consciousness.
3. The common stimulus in suicide is intolerable psychological pain.
4. The common stressor in suicide is frustrated psychological needs.
5. The common emotion in suicide is hopelessness-helplessness.
6. The common negative state in suicide is ambivalence.
7. The common perceptual state in suicide is constriction.
8. The common action in suicide is egression (to depart from the region of distress).
9. The common interpersonal act in suicide is communication of intention.
10. The common consistency in suicide is with lifelong coping patterns.

Types

A number of theorists and researchers have tried to classify suicidal behaviors into some typology. Schneidman (1968) provided one of the most cited characterizations of suicidal behaviors. He describes three types of suicide: egotic, dyadic, and ageneratic.

Egotic suicides result from intrapsychic conflict and struggle. This type produces a suicide that is seemingly independent of situational circumstances, that is, where the impact on others seems less important than a person's disturbed ideation, withdrawal, or impulsivity. These suicides often appear "irrational," magical, or nihilistic.

Dyadic suicides appear to be a result of incomplete or problematic interpersonal relationships. Such relationships may be with peers, boyfriends or girlfriends, parents, or significant others. An interpersonal event such as rejection or the breakup of a relationship often precipitates this type of suicide or suicide attempt.

In ageneratic suicides, adolescents experience a displacement in their place in the appropriate generation. They may be "promoted" prematurely to adult roles as a result of deaths of parents or change in the family structure, or they may be infantilized by family dynamics. These people may very well feel they have lost their place in the appropriate generation and feel isolated, empty, or disengaged.

Stages

One set of clinical features discussed in the literature has to do with temporal characteristics of suicidal behaviors. Examples of such theories are stage theories. Perhaps the most useful described in the current literature were proposed by Teicher and Jacobs (1966), Jacobs (1971), and Teicher (1973). Based on case studies, it is believed that a suicidal adolescent progresses through a series of discrete periods that can be detected if looked for.

The first stage, according to these theorists, is a *history of problems.* Such problems may exist throughout childhood or in the recent past. Examples of such problems include parents or close friends who have committed suicide or attempted suicide; one or both biological parents missing from the home; dealing with an unwanted stepparent; parents with multiple marriages or relationships; primary parents working; an average of 10 serious problem-causing environmental changes; alcoholic parent(s); living with people other than parents; and frequent residential moves and/or school changes (Teicher, 1973).

The second stage in this theory is the *escalation of problems.* The problems may escalate as a result of developmental changes occurring with the onset of adolescence. Such changes occur in the individual's social, psychological, and physiological development, but may also be a function in the changes of perception and expectation of those in the youth's environment. Escalation can produce behavior problems, mood changes, rebelliousness, withdrawal, and the like. Such symptoms are probably designed (perhaps unconsciously) to gain attention or help.

Following the escalation of problems, adolescents reach the third stage, in which there is a *failure of coping* (Jacobs, 1971). Strategies to deal with the escalation of problems begin to fail (e.g., an adolescent may cope with progressive school failure by skipping school, a strategy that fails when the student is discovered).

Failures to cope lead directly to the fourth stage, *loss of hope.* Such loss of hope may be manifested by social withdrawal, loss of future orientation, dropping out of school, increase in substance abuse and/or high-risk behaviors, or loss of general motivation for any activities. This hopelessness is a hallmark of almost all suicidal behaviors.

Finally, when hope is lost, according to Jacobs (1971), there occurs for the adolescent a *justification.* During this time, the person moves from thought to action. The justifying event may appear trivial (e.g., breaking up with a boyfriend, failing a test, social rejection), but because of withdrawal from peer relationships or supports, the person feels without options or support.

RISK FACTORS

It is most parsimonious to view predispositions, etiology, and symptoms under one heading called "risk factors." Combining these categories captures the prevailing notion that suicidal behavior has multiple causation. A number of authors and researchers have attempted to isolate or review risk factors (Aoki & Turk, 1997; Curran, 1987; Diekstra & Moritz, 1987; Farberow, 1985; Fremouw et al., 1990; Goldman & Beardslee, 1999; Pfeffer, 1989; Sheras, 1983; U.S. Dept. of Health and Human Services, 1989). Some risk factors may be developmental in nature, others are historical or situational, and still others are seen to be psychological. Some of these factors are preexisting (e.g., predispositions), some are behaviors (such as symptoms), and others appear to be of undetermined causality (such as substance abuse or access to firearms or other lethal means). There are certainly developmental considerations regarding adolescence and its impact on the tendency for suicidal behaviors. Fremouw et al. write about two important considerations: the young person's concept of death and his or her language development; the latter may make it difficult to communicate clearly to others. Construction of identity and other developmental tasks may also confuse a young person's feelings of order and potency and produce the sort of ambivalence described by Schneidman (1968). This turmoil may contribute to the selection of suicide as a solution. In addition, Hafen (1972) believed that adolescence magnified some suicidal elements, such as guilt, rage, impulsivity, feelings of inadequacy, the desire for revenge or vindication, suggestibility, loneliness, anxiety, and sensitivity.

Historical and Developmental Factors

There are a number of historical and developmental risk factors. *Medical or physiological problems* represent such a factor. Chronic illness or certain biochemical imbalances (e.g., low concentrations of serotonin metabolite, 5-hydroxyindoleacetic acid [5-HIAA], and homovanillic acid [HVA] in cerebrospinal fluid) may be responsible for an increase in suicidal behaviors. *Concepts of death* may differ for adolescents, especially in the younger age ranges. They may view death as temporary or act without an understanding of consequences. *Family systems and dynamics* is another risk factor. Problems in such families might include disorganization, discord, enmeshment, and poor communication and problem-solving skills. Some theorists have examined parent-child role reversal (Meeks, 1971) and the stress it creates on children who are asked to take on adult roles prematurely. Sibling order has also been shown to be a factor in suicidal behaviors (Cantor, 1972; Lester, 1967; Toolan, 1962). *Parental psychopathology* may also increase the risk of suicide (Pfeffer, 1986; Tishler & McHenry, 1982). *Family history of suicide* has long been a major factor for adolescents; this "exposure" factor is considered to be one of the major predictors of suicidality.

Situational Factors

Many situational factors are related to an increase in suicidal behavior. Most encompass the increase in stress on the adolescent, but some have additional power. Adolescents may feel stress as a function of *skill deficits,* especially in the interpersonal area. They may have inadequate problem-solving ability to generate alternatives to the solution of suicide. *Academic and school stress* is also considered to be a risk factor. Ironically, it now appears that stress affects not only the underachieving student but those who perform well in school. Such students feel pressure to continue to succeed and may become suicidal from fear of potential future failures. McBride and Siegel (1997) examined the role of learning disabilities in suicidal behaviors. They showed that 89% of suicide notes showed significant deficits in spelling and handwriting, indicative of learning disabilities.

General *life stress* can be a risk factor as well. Cohen-Sandler, Berman, and King (1982) demonstrated that suicidal children had significantly more life stress than nonsuicidal children. *Changes in social and cultural dynamics* may also play a role in suicide, such as popular valuation of youth, violence, and success. In addition, current culture has made *access to lethal means* a significant risk factor. Lethal drugs and firearms are often available to even the youngest children and adolescents. Finally, the effect of the media on suicidal behavior is notable. Media coverage of suicides and self-destructive behaviors constitutes another method of exposure further glorifying such behaviors. Such coverage may be responsible for imitative suicides or the development of suicide clusters (Gould, Wallentstein, & Davidson, 1989).

Parental influence and family structure have been examined by a number of researchers. Allison, Pearce, Martin, Miller, and Long (1995) demonstrated that suicidal youth perceived their parents to be more critical, more overprotective, and less caring than nonsuicidal youth. *Alcohol and drug abuse* have also been examined as factors that contribute to suicidal risk (Jones, 1997).

Psychosocial Factors

Harter and Marold (1994) examined a broad range of psychosocial risk factors contributing to suicidal ideation. They looked at such factors as negative self-evaluation, parental support, peer support, and physical appearance.

A number of risk factors are primarily psychological. Some appear to be predispositions or preexisting determinants, whereas others appear to be effects. Such factors include *depression; personality disorders,* especially borderline disorders and disorders related to impulsivity (Finch & Poznanski, 1971); and certain forms of *psychosis,* especially where high levels of distortion are present. *Eating disorders,* usually bulimia, are associated with self-destructive impulses and may increase suicide risk (Chiles, 1986). *Loss and separation* (Brent, Perper, Moritz, & Liotus, 1994a, 1994b) as well as exposure to recent suicides may also be major contributing factors. Adolescents frequently must deal with loss, whether it is the death of a grandparent or the loss associated with changing schools, peer groups, or boyfriends/girlfriends. Identity construction is predicated on the notion of creating the new and letting go of the old.

Finally, one of the least understood risk factors is *substance abuse and chemical dependency.* It is unclear whether substance abuse increases suicidal behavior or is a manifestation of such behavior. Suffice it to say, it is clearly a risk factor to be considered. In addition, a number of effects or behaviors seem to be clear warnings of suicidal intention. Among these are the experience of helplessness, development of a suicide plan, making final arrangements including giving away possessions, social or interpersonal withdrawal, aggression or vindictive behaviors, increased imitation of others, and the appearance of an "I don't care" attitude.

It is difficult to summarize all of the preceding factors. For many adolescents, suicidal behavior is an attempt to solve the problem of having no control in life. As such, it is designed to attract attention. Some observers (Sheras, 1983) note that the experience of *invisibility* may be a metadeterminant of suicidality. Desires to avoid domination and escape humiliation may also be significant reasons but are related to the individual's attempts to control his or her life ultimately, and desperately, by taking it.

CLINICAL ACTIONS

Four basic clinical actions regarding suicide in adolescents are discussed in the literature: assessment, prevention, intervention, and postvention. It is usually the case that assessment and intervention occur first in any sequence, followed by postvention (dealing with the aftermath of a suicide or suicide attempt) and, finally, prevention. Somewhat ironic is the fact that prevention is usually undertaken last. Perhaps it is human nature that we never act until it is too late. And so, each suicide may become the next prevention opportunity.

Assessment

Assessment of suicidality is often accomplished in an interview with a teacher, parent, school counselor, or family physician. There are instruments (discussed earlier) that assess suicidality as part of depression. They are useful if there is occasion to give them. In inpatient settings, suicide assessment measures and depression scales may be helpful in assessing the depth of depression or the imminence of suicidal behavior, but most suicides and suicide attempts occur outside the hospital setting. Such instruments, then, in the larger scheme of things may not be very useful. Curran (1987) summarized well the goals of assessment, taking into account a number of key factors: sex

and age, history of attempts, other self-destructive behaviors, substance abuse, status of adaptive strategies, chronicity of problems, experience of loss, support systems, relations with parents and others, state of mind, openness to communication, perturbation, and attitude toward death. Some studies attempt to distinguish between those who think about suicide (ideators) and those who make attempts (attempters). An analysis of this approach was conducted by Negron, Piacentini, Graae, Davies, and Shaffer (1997).

Intervention

Interventions and treatments are discussed widely with regard to adolescent suicide and parasuicide. A number of authors describe the basic assumptions underlying treatment of a suicidal adolescent (Berman & Jobes, 1991; Curran, 1987; Fremouw et al., 1990; Hicks, 1990; Peck et al., 1985). Motto (1985) wrote of the importance of the establishment of the therapeutic relationship, the stimulation of emotional growth, and the diminution of the dependent aspects of the relationship as key steps in the therapeutic process. Curran identified the following therapeutic issues as important when treating a suicidal adolescent: therapist activity versus passivity, object loss and dependency needs, sensitivity to rejection or separation, ambivalence, low self-esteem, aggression, hopelessness, constriction, and termination.

Reviews of particular schools of therapy (Fremouw et al., 1990; Hicks, 1990; Pfeffer, 1986; Sheras, 1983) or particular techniques run the gamut, including individual (Spirito, 1997b); group and family work (Spirito, 1997a; Henry, Stephenson, Hanson, & Hargett, 1994); intervention in the home, in the school (Kirk, 1993), or in the hospital; and use of psychodynamic, behavioral, and biochemical systems. What emerges most clearly from these studies and reviews is:

1. All suicide attempts should be taken seriously.
2. Developing a relationship with the client is essential.
3. Enhanced communication among all parties is necessary.
4. Continual monitoring and support are needed.
5. Acknowledgment of the client's pain and existence is very important.
6. Provision must be made for the person's reentry into his or her previous environment.

Postvention

Postvention is the process of dealing with the aftermath of a suicide or a suicide attempt. Sometimes, it involves working with the suicide attempter in recovering; sometimes, it means helping a system or family deal with and adapt to the loss of an adolescent. Postventions may involve community members helping in schools (Sheras, 1990) or school systems developing plans in the aftermath of a suicide (Hicks, 1990; Phi Delta Kappa, 1988). Some postventions involve families or even peer groups. The key to postvention is the establishment of a network of personnel to facilitate the expressions of grief and loss of those directly affected by the suicide or attempt and also to identify and support all others for whom this event has reactivated unresolved grief. The ultimate goal of postvention is to establish prevention programs by resolving the issue of loss that suicide engenders.

Prevention

With the increase in adolescent suicides and the increased awareness of the problem, more energy has been directed toward establishing suicide prevention programs. Many of these programs are designed for school systems (Curran, 1987; Hicks, 1990; D.N. Miller & DuPaul, 1996; Peach & Reddick, 1991; Poland, 1989), and some are for other sectors of the community (U.S. Department of Health and Human Services, 1989). Most clinicians, however, feel that given the number of risk factors involved, some prevention can be done on an ongoing basis in a number of settings.

Berman and Jobes (1995) used a compelling population perspective to examine suicide prevention. They wrote of primary, secondary, and tertiary prevention efforts and the "second generation" of prevention efforts required to effectively address the problem of adolescent suicide. It does seem clear, however, that prevention programs cannot succeed without support from the schools and the communities in which they are designed to work. Parents must be willing partners along with community workers, school personnel, and local governments. Programs can likely be most effective if they include the following components:

1. Contact points for adolescents to communicate with the system.
2. Outreach programs in schools and communities to find adolescents at risk.
3. Routine enrichment, stress management, and counseling for adolescents in schools.
4. Public education to heighten awareness of the need to communicate with one another and identify those who might be in need of support.

REFERENCES

Achenbach, T.M., & Edelbrock, C.S. (1983). *Manual for the Child Behavior Checklist and Revised Child Behavior profile.* Burlington: University of Vermont, Department of Psychiatry.

Allison, S., Pearce, C., Martin, G., Miller, K., & Long, R. (1995). Parental influence, pessimism and adolescent suicidality. *Archives of Suicide Research, 1,* 229–242.

American Psychiatric Association. (1994). *Diagnostic and statistical manual of mental disorders* (4th ed.). Washington, DC: Author.

Angle, C., O'Brien, T., & McIntire, M. (1983). Adolescent self-poisoning: A nine-year follow-up. *Developmental and Behavioral Pediatrics, 4*(2), 83–87.

Aoki, W.T., & Turk, A.A. (1997). Adolescent suicide: A review of risk factors and implications for practice. *Journal of Psychology and Christianity,16,* 273–279.

Atlas, J.A., & DiScipio, W. (1992). Correlations of Beck Depression Inventory and Reynolds Adolescent Depression Scale. *Psychological Reports, 70,* 621–622.

Beck, A.T. (1976). *Cognitive therapy and the emotional disorders.* New York: Guilford Press.

Beidel, D.C., & Turner, S.M. (1986). A critique of the theoretical bases of cognitive-behavioral theories and therapy. *Clinical Psychology Review, 6,* 177–197.

Bemporad, J. (1978). Manifest symptoms of depression in children and adolescents. In S. Arieti & J. Bemporad (Eds.), *Severe and mild depression: The psychotherapeutic approach* (pp. 87–100). New York: Basic Books.

Berman, A.L. (1986). Adolescent suicide: Issues and challenges. *Seminars in Adolescent Medicine, 2*(4), 269–277.

Berman, A.L., & Jobes, D.A. (1991). *Adolescent suicide.* Washington, DC: American Psychological Association.

Berman, A.L., & Jobes, D.A. (1995). Suicide prevention in adolescents (age 12–18). *Suicide and Life-Threatening Behavior, 25,* 143–154.

Brent, D.A., Perper, J.A., Moritz, G., & Liotus, G. (1994a). Familial risk factors for adolescent suicide: A case-control study. *Acta Psychiatrica Scandinavica, 89,* 52–58.

Brent, D.A., Perper, J.A., Moritz, G., & Liotus, G. (1994b). Major depression or uncomplicated bereavement? A follow-up of youth exposed to suicide. *Journal of the American Academy of Child and Adolescent Psychiatry, 33,* 231–239.

Campbell, T.L., Byrne, B.M., & Baron, P. (1992). Gender differences in the expression of depressive symptoms in early adolescents. *Journal of Early Adolescence, 12,* 326–338.

Campbell, T.L., Byrne, B.M., & Baron, P. (1994). The Reynolds Adolescent Depression Scale: An exploratory factor analytic study. *European Review of Applied Psychology, 44,* 319–325.

Cantor, P. (1972). The adolescent attempter: Sex, sibling position and family constellation. *Suicide and Life-Threatening Behavior, 2*(4), 252–261.

Carlson, G. (1979). Affective disorders in adolescence. *Psychiatric Clinics of North America, 2,* 513–526.

Carlson, G., & Cantwell, D. (1979). A survey of the depressive symptoms in a child and adolescent population. *Journal of the American Academy of Child Psychiatry, 18,* 587–599.

Carroll, B.J. (1982). The dexamethasone suppression test for melancholia. *British Journal of Psychiatry, 140,* 292–304.

Carroll, B.J. (1983). Neuroendocrine diagnosis of depression: The dexamethasone suppression test. In P.J. Clayton & J.E. Barrett (Eds.), *Treatment of depression* (pp. 1–30). New York: Raven Press.

Chiles, J.A. (1986). *Teenage depression and suicide.* New York: Chelsea House.

Chiles, J.A., Miller, M.L., & Cox, G.B. (1980). Depression in an adolescent delinquent population. *Archives of General Psychiatry, 37,* 1179–1184.

Clarizio, H.F. (1985). Cognitive-behavioral treatment of childhood depression. *Psychology in the Schools, 22,* 308–322.

Clarkin, J.F., & Glazer, H.I. (Eds.). (1981). *Depression: Behavioral and directive intervention strategies.* New York: Garland Press.

Cohen-Sandler, R., Berman, A.L., & King, R. (1982). A follow-up study of hospitalized suicidal children. *Journal of the American Academy of Child Psychiatry, 21,* 398–403.

Costello, E.J., & Angold, A. (1988). Scales to assess child and adolescent depression: Checklists, screens, and nets. *Journal of the American Academy of Child and Adolescent Psychiatry, 27,* 726–737.

Costello, E.J., Edelbrock, C.S., Dulcan, M.K., & Kalas, R. (1984). *Testing of the NIMH Interview Schedule for Children (DISC) in a clinical population.* Final report to the Center for Epidemiological Studies, National Institute for Mental Health. Pittsburgh, PA: University of Pittsburgh.

Curran, D.K. (1987). *Adolescent suicidal behavior.* New York: Hemisphere.

Cytryn, L., & McKnew, D. (1974). Factors influencing the changing clinical expression of the depressive process in children. *American Journal of Psychiatry, 129,* 149–155.

Diekstra, R.F.W., & Hawton, K. (Eds.). (1987). *Suicide in adolescence.* Dordrecht, The Netherlands: Martinus Nijhoff.

Diekstra, R.F.W., & Moritz, B.J.M. (1987). Suicidal behaviour among adolescents: An overview. In R.F.W. Diekstra & K. Hawton (Eds.), *Suicide in adolescence* (pp. 7–24). Dordrecht, The Netherlands: Martinus Nijhoff.

Earls, F. (1984). The epidemiology of depression in children and adolescents. *Pediatric Annual, 13,* 23–31.

Elkins, R., & Rappaport, J. (1983). Psychopharmacology of adult and childhood depression: An overview. In D. Cantwell & G. Carlson (Eds.), *Affective disorders in childhood and adolescence: An update* (pp. 363–374). New York: Spectrum Press.

Farberow, N.L. (1985). Youth suicide: A summary. In M.L. Peck, N.L. Farberow, & R.E. Litman (Eds.), *Youth suicide* (pp. 191–203). New York: Springer.

Farberow, N., & Schneidman, E. (1961). *The cry for help.* New York: McGraw-Hill.

Finch, S.M., & Poznanski, E.O. (1971). *Adolescent suicide.* Springfield, IL: Thomas.

Fleming, J.E., & Offord, D.R. (1990). Epidemiology of childhood depressive disorders: A critical review. *Journal of the American Academy of Child and Adolescent Psychiatry, 29,* 571–580.

Fremouw, W.J., dePerczel, M., & Ellis, T.E. (1990). *Suicide risk: Assessment and response guidelines.* New York: Pergamon Press.

Freud, S. (1957). Mourning and melancholia. In J. Strachey (Ed. and Trans.), *The standard edition of the complete psychological works of Sigmund Freud* (Vol. 14, pp. 243–258). London: Hogarth Press. (Original work published 1917)

Gershon, E.S., Targum, S.D., Kessler, L.R., Mazure, C.M., & Bunney, W.E., Jr. (1997). Genetic studies and biologic strategies in the affective disorders. *Progress in Medical Genetics, 2,* 101–164.

Gibbs, J.T. (1988). Conceptual, methodological, and socio-cultural issues in Black youth suicide: Implications for assessment and early intervention. *Suicide and Life-Threatening Behavior, 18*(1), 73–89.

Goldman, S., & Beardslee, W.R. (1999). Suicide in children and adolescents. In D.G. Jacobs (Ed.), *The Harvard Medical School guide to suicide assessment and intervention* (pp. 417–442). San Francisco: Jossey-Bass.

Gould, M.S., Wallenstein, S., & Davidson, L. (1989). Suicide clusters: A critical review. *Suicide and Life-Threatening Behavior, 19*(1), 17–29.

Hafen, B.Q. (Ed.). (1972). *Self-destructive behavior.* Minneapolis MN: Burgess.

Haim, A. (1974). *Adolescent suicide.* New York: International Universities Press.

Hammen, C., & Rudolph, K.D. (1996). Childhood depression. In E.J. Mash & R.A. Barkley (Eds.), *Child psychopathology* (pp. 153–195). New York: Guilford Press.

Harter, S., & Marold, D.B. (1994). Psychosocial risk factors contributing to adolescent suicidal ideation. In G.G. Noam & S. Borst (Eds.), *Children, youth and suicide: Developmental perspectives* (pp. 71–91). San Francisco: Jossey-Bass.

Henry, C.S., Stephenson, A.L., Hanson, M.F., & Hargett, W. (1994). Adolescent suicide and families: An ecological approach. *Family Therapy, 21,* 63–80.

Herjanic, B., & Campbell, W. (1977). Differentiating psychiatrically disturbed children on the basis of a structured interview. *Journal of Abnormal Child Psychology, 51,* 127–134.

Hicks, B.B. (1990). *Youth suicide: A comprehensive manual for prevention and intervention.* Bloomington, IN: National Educational Service.

Holinger, P.C. (1979). Violent deaths among the young: Recent trends in suicide, homicide, and accidents. *American Journal of Psychiatry, 136,* 1144–1147.

Hudgens, R. (1974). *Psychiatric disorders in adolescents.* Baltimore: Williams & Wilkens.

Jacobs, J. (1971). *Adolescent suicide.* New York: Wiley.

Jones, G.D. (1997). The role of drugs and alcohol in urban minority adolescent suicide attempts. *Death Studies, 21,* 189–202.

Kandel, D.B., & Davies, M. (1982). Epidemiology of depressive mood in adolescents. *Archives of General Psychiatry, 39,* 1205–1212.

Kaplan, S.L., Hong, G.K., & Weinhold, C. (1984). Epidemiology of depressive symptomatology in adolescents. *Journal of the American Academy of Child Psychiatry, 23,* 91–98.

Kashani, J., & Hakami, N. (1982). Depression in children and adolescents with malignancy. *Canadian Journal of Psychiatry, 27,* 474–477.

Kashani, J., Venzke, R., & Millar, E. (1981). Depression in children admitted to hospital for orthopaedic procedures. *British Journal of Psychiatry, 138,* 21–25.

Kazdin, A.E. (1989). Childhood depression. In E. Mash & R. Barkley (Eds.), *Childhood disorders* (pp. 135–166). New York: Guilford Press.

King, L., & Pittman, G. (1969). A six-year follow-up study of sixty-five adolescent patients: Predictive value of presenting clinical picture. *British Journal of Psychiatry, 115,* 1437–1441.

Kirk, W.G. (1993). *Adolescent suicide: A school-based approach to assessment and intervention.* Champaign, IL: Research Press.

Kovacs, M. (1981). Rating scales to assess depression in school-aged children. *Acta Paedopsychiatrica, 46,* 305–315.

Kovacs, M., & Beck, A.T. (1977). An empirical clinical approach toward a definition of childhood depression. In J.G. Schulterbrandt & A. Raskin (Eds.), *Depression in children: Diagnosis, treatment, and conceptual models* (pp. 1–25). New York: Raven Press.

Lefkowitz, M.M., & Burton, N. (1978). Childhood depression: A critique of the concept. *Psychological Bulletin, 85,* 716–726.

Lesse, S. (1974). Depression masked by acting out behavior patterns. *American Journal of Psychotherapy, 28,* 352–361.

Lester, D. (1967). Sibling position and suicidal behavior. *Journal of Individual Psychology, 22,* 204–207.

Lewinsohn, P.M., Hops, H., Roberts, R.E., Seeley, J.R., & Andrews. J.A. (1993). Adolescent psychopathology: Prevalence and incidence of depression and other *DSM-III-R* disorders in high school students. *Journal of Abnormal Psychology, 102,* 133–144.

Lewis, R., Walker, B.A., & Mehr, M. (1990). Counseling with adolescent suicidal clients and their families. In A.R. Roberts (Ed.), *Crisis intervention handbook* (pp. 44–62). Belmont, CA: Wadsworth.

Marcotte, D. (1997). Treating depression in adolescence: A review of the effectiveness of cognitive behavioral treatments. *Journal of Youth and Adolescence 26,* 273–283.

Marks, P.A., & Haller, D.L. (1977). Now I lay me down for keeps: A study of adolescent suicide attempts. *Journal of Clinical Psychology, 33,* 390–400.

Mash, E.J. (1989). Treatment of child and family disturbance: A behavioral-systems perspective. In E.J. Mash & R.A. Barkley (Eds.), *Treatment of childhood disorders* (pp. 3–36). New York: Guilford Press.

Matson, J.L. (1989). *Treating depression in children and adolescents.* New York: Pergamon Press.

McBride, H.E., & Siegel, L.S. (1997). Learning disabilities and adolescent suicide. *Journal of Learning Disabilities, 30,* 652–659.

McConville, B.J., & Bruce, R.T. (1985). Depressive illnesses in children and adolescents: A review of current concepts. *Canadian Journal of Psychiatry, 30,* 119–129.

McGee, R., Freehan, M., Williams, S., & Anderson, J. (1992). *DSM-III* disorders from age 11 to age 15 years. *Journal of the American Academy of Child and Adolescent Psychiatry, 31,* 50–59.

McIntire, M., Angle, C., & Schlicht, M.L. (1980, February). Suicide and self-poisoning in pediatrics. *Resident and Staff Physician,* 72–85.

McIntosh, J., & Jewell, B. (1986). Sex difference trends in completed suicide. *Suicide and Life-Threatening Behavior, 16,* 16–27.

McIntosh, J.L. (1998). *Suicide data page.* Washington, DC: American Association of Suicidology.

McKenry, D., Tishler, C., & Kelley, C. (1983). The role of drugs in adolescent suicide attempts. *Suicide and Life-Threatening Behavior, 13*(3), 166–175.

Meeks, J.E. (1971). *The fragile alliance: An orientation to the outpatient psychotherapy of the adolescent.* Baltimore: Williams & Wilkins.

Miller, D.N., & DuPaul, G.J. (1996). School-based prevention for adolescent suicide: Issues, obstacles, and recommendations for practice. *Journal of Emotional and Behavioral Disorders, 4,* 221–230.

Miller, J.P. (1975). Suicide in adolescence. *Adolescence, 10,* 11–24.

Morrison, H.L. (Ed.). (1983). *Children of depressed parents: Risk, identification, and intervention.* New York: Grune & Stratton.

Motto, J.A. (1985). Treatment concerns in preventing youth suicide. In M.L. Peck, N.L. Farberow, & R.E. Litman (Eds.), *Youth suicide* (pp. 91–111). New York: Springer.

Mullins, L.L., Siegel, L.J., & Hodges, K. (1985). Cognitive problem-solving and life event correlates of repressive symptoms in children. *Journal of Abnormal Child Psychology, 13,* 305–314.

National Center for Health Statistics, U.S. Department of Health and Human Services. (1998a). Advance report of final mortality statistics, 1986. *Monthly vital statistics report* (Vol. 37, No. 6, Supp. DHHS Publication No. PHS 88–1120). Hyattsville, MD: Public Health Service.

National Center for Health Statistics, U.S. Department of Health and Human Services. (1998b). *Vital statistics of the United States.* Hyattsville, MD: Public Health Service.

Negron, R., Piacentini, J., Graae, F., Davies, M., & Shaffer, D. (1997). Microanalysis of adolescent suicide attempters and ideators during the acute suicidal episode. *Journal of the American Academy of Child and Adolescent Psychiatry, 36,* 1512–1519.

Nissen, G. (1983). Depression in adolescence: Clinical features and developmental aspects. In H. Golombek & B. Garfinkel (Eds.), *The adolescent and mood disturbance* (pp. 167–178). New York: International Universities Press.

Nolen-Hoeksema, S., & Girgus, J.S. (1994). The emergence of gender differences in depression during adolescence. *Psychological Bulletin, 115,* 424–443.

Palmer, J.O. (1983). *The psychological assessment of children.* New York: Wiley.

Paykel, E.S. (1982). Life events and early environment. In E.S. Paykel (Ed.), *Handbook of affective disorders* (pp. 146–161). New York: Guilford Press.

Peach, L., & Reddick, T.L. (1991). Counselors can make a difference in preventing adolescent suicide. *School Counselor, 39,* 107–110.

Peck, M.L., Farberow, N.L., & Litman, R.E. (Eds.). (1985). *Youth suicide.* New York: Springer.

Peters, K.D., & Murphy, S.L. (1998). Deaths: Final data for 1996. *National Vital Statistics Report* 47(9, DHHS Publication No. PHS 99–1120). Hyattsville, MD: National Center for Health Statistics.

Petti, T. (1983). Imipramine in the treatment of depressed children. In D. Cantwell & G. Carlson (Eds.), *Affective disorders in childhood and adolescence: An update* (pp. 375–416). New York: Spectrum Press.

Pfeffer, C.R. (1985). Feelings and their medical significance. *Ross Laboratories, 27,* 1–4.

Pfeffer, C.R. (1986). *The suicidal child.* New York: Guilford Press.

Pfeffer, C.R. (Ed.). (1989). *Suicide among youth: Perspectives on risk and prevention.* Washington, DC: American Psychiatric Press.

Phi Delta Kappa Task Force on Suicide in the Schools. (1988). *Responding to adolescent suicide.* Bloomington, IN: Phi Delta Kappa.

Poland, S. (1989). *Suicide intervention in the schools.* New York: Guilford Press.

Proznanski, E., Cook, S., & Carroll, B. (1979). A depression rating scale for children. *Pediatrics, 64,* 442–450.

Puig-Antich, J., & Chambers, W. (1978). *Schedule for Affective Disorders and Schizophrenia for School-Aged Children (6–16 years) (Kiddie-SADS).* New York: New York State Psychiatric Institute.

Rehm, L.P. (1977). A self-control model of depression. *Behavior Therapy, 8,* 787–804.

Reinherz, H.Z., Giaconia, R.M., Lefkowitz, E.S., Pakiz, B., & Frost, A.K. (1993). Prevalence of psychiatric disorders in a community population of older adolescents. *Journal of the American Academy of Child and Adolescent Psychiatry, 32,* 369–377.

Remafedi, G., Farrow, J.A., & Deisher, R.W. (1993). Risk factors in attempted suicide in gay and bisexual youth. In L.D. Garnets & D.C. Kemmel (Eds.), *Psychological perspectives on lesbian and gay studies* (pp. 486–499). New York: Columbia University Press.

Reynolds, W.M. (1986). A model for screening and identification of depressed adolescents in school settings. *Professional School Psychology, 1,* 117–129.

Roberts, A.R. (1990). *Crisis intervention handbook.* Belmont, CA: Wadsworth.

Rutter, M., Graham, P., & Chadwick, F. (1976). Adolescent turmoil: Fact or fiction. *Journal of Child Psychology and Psychiatry, 17,* 35–56.

Rutter, M., Izard, C.E., & Read, P.B. (Eds.). (1986). *Depression in young people: Developmental and clinical perspectives.* New York: Guilford Press.

Sachar, E.J. (1982). Endocrine abnormalities in depression. In E.S. Paykel (Ed.), *Handbook of affective disorders* (pp. 191–201). New York: Guilford Press.

Safer, D.J. (1997). Adolescent/adult differences in suicidal behavior and outcome. *Annals of Clinical Psychiatry, 9,* 61–66.

Schneidman, E.S. (1968). Orientation toward cessation: A reexamination of current modes of death. *Journal of Forensic Sciences, 13,* 33–45.

Schneidman, E.S. (1986). A psychological approach to suicide. In G.R. Vandenbos & B.K. Bryant (Eds.), *Cataclysms, crises, and catastrophes: Psychology in action*. Washington, DC: American Psychological Association.

Seiden, R.H. (1969). Suicide among youth: A review of the literature 1900–1967. *Bulletin of Suicidology* (Suppl.).

Seligman, M.E.P. (1975). *Helplessness: On depression, development, and death*. San Francisco: Freeman.

Shaw, K.R., Sheehan, K.H., & Fernandez, R.C. (1987). Suicide in children and adolescents. *Advances in Pediatrics, 34*, 313–334.

Sheras, P.L. (1983). Suicide in adolescence. In C.E. Walker & M.C. Roberts (Eds.), *Handbook of clinical child psychology*. New York: Wiley.

Sheras, P.L. (1990). *Developing a school crisis network*. Paper presented at the meeting of the American Psychological Association, Boston.

Sheras, P.L., & Abidin, R.R. (1998). *The Stress Index for Parents of Adolescents (SIPA)*. Sarasota, FL: PAR.

Sokoloff, R.M., & Lubin, B. (1983). Depressive mood in adolescents, emotionally disturbed females: Reliability and validity of an adjective checklist (C-DACL). *Journal of Abnormal Child Psychology, 11*, 531–536.

Spirito, A. (1997a). Family therapy techniques with adolescent suicide attempters. *Crisis, 18*, 106–109.

Spirito, A. (1997b). Individual therapy techniques with adolescent suicide attempters. *Crisis, 18*, 62–64.

Strober, M. (1984). Familial aspects of depressive disorder in early adolescence. In E.B. Weller & R.A. Weller (Eds.), *Current perspectives on major depressive disorders in children* (pp. 38–48). Washington, DC: American Psychiatric Press.

Strober, M., & Carlson, G. (1982). Bipolar illness: I. Adolescents with major depression: Clinical, genetic, and psychopharmacologic predictors in a three- to four-year prospective follow-up investigation. *Archives of General Psychiatry, 39*, 549–555.

Teicher, J.D. (1973). A solution to the chronic problem of living: Adolescent attempted suicide. In J.C. Schoolar (Ed.), *Current issues in adolescent psychiatry* (pp. 129–147). New York: Brunner/Mazel.

Teicher, J.D., & Jacobs, J. (1966). Adolescents who attempt suicide: Preliminary findings. *American Journal of Psychiatry, 122*, 1246–1257.

Tisher, M., & Lang, M. (1983). The Children's Depression Scale: Review and further developments. In D.P. Cantwell & G.A. Carlson (Eds.), *Affective disorders in childhood and adolescence: An update* (pp. 181–203). New York: SP Medical and Scientific Books.

Tishler, C.L., & McHenry, P.C. (1982). Parental negative self and adolescent suicide attempts. *Journal of the American Academy of Child Psychiatry, 21*, 404–408.

Toolan, J.M. (1962). Depression in children and adolescents. *American Journal of Orthopsychiatry, 32*, 404–414.

Toolan, J.M. (1975). Suicide in children and adolescents. *American Journal of Psychotherapy, 29*(3), 339–344.

U.S. Department of Health and Human Services, Public Health Service. (1989). *Report to the Secretary's Task Force on Youth Suicide* (DHHS Publication No. ADM 89–1621). Washington, DC: U.S. Government Printing Office.

Usdin, E., Asberg, M., Bertilsson, J., & Sjoqvist, B. (Eds.). (1984). *Advances in biochemical psychopharmacology: Vol. 39. Frontiers in biochemical and pharmacological research in depression*. New York: Raven Press.

VanWicklin, J.E. (1990). Adolescent depression: A systematic overview. *Journal of Psychology and Christianity, 9*, 5–14.

Weissmen, M.M., Prusoff, B.A., & Gammon, G.D. (1984). Psychopathology in the children (ages 6–18) of depressed and normal parents. *Journal of the American Academy of Child Psychiatry, 23*, 78–84.

Weller, E.B., & Weller, R.A. (1990). Depressive disorders in children and adolescents. In B.D. Garfinkel, G.A. Carlson, & E.B. Weller (Eds.), *Psychiatric disorders in children and adolescents* (pp. 3–23). Philadelphia: Saunders.

Zis, A.P., & Goodwin, F.K. (1982). The amine hypothesis. In E.S. Paykel (Ed.), *Handbook of affective disorders* (pp. 175–190). New York: Guilford Press.

CHAPTER 34

Development of Problems of Puberty and Sex Roles in Adolescence*

GEORGE A. REKERS

Knowledge regarding the psychological and physiological impact of puberty and normal sex-role development provides the clinician the context for diagnostically differentiating normal needs for sex education and guidance in heterosocial development and sex-role socialization from special needs for therapeutic intervention for adjustment problems in adolescence (Mazur & Cherpak, 1995; Rekers, 1992; Rekers & Kilgus, 1997).[†] Differentiating normal adjustment phases in

* Appreciation is expressed to my colleague, Dr. Jane Littmann, clinical psychologist and Associate Professor at the University of South Carolina School of Medicine, for her helpful review and critique of a draft of this chapter, and to Josephine Evans, Diane McLaughlin, and Ansley D. Roberts for word processing the various drafts of this manuscript.
[†] The prior editions of this chapter (Rekers & Jurich, 1983; Rekers, 1992) and the more recent *Handbook of Child and Adolescent Sexual Problems* (Rekers, 1995c, which can be ordered directly from Jossey-Bass Publishers at 1-800-956-7739) together constitute a much lengthier review of the earlier clinical research studies on adolescent sex-role, sexual, and pubertal development. The studies covered by these previous publications are hereby cited as further documentation for the specific statements and conclusions made in this present summary chapter. Specific references to the numerous studies cited in my earlier reviews were largely omitted from this present chapter for the sake of brevity and for the purpose of providing the reader with a concise overview of the most recent research studies presented in the context of a broad summary of the findings of selected classic literature in this area.

psychosexual development from psychological disturbances (Arndt, 1995; Culley & Flanagan, 1995; Rekers, 1995c) is complicated by the fact that normal adolescents must make a wide range of developmental adjustments pertaining to their socially ascribed sex roles (Alsaker, 1996) and their bodily process of sexual maturation across the years just before and during puberty (Mazur & Cherpak, 1995). This chapter provides an overview of the range of clinical issues pertaining to problems of puberty and sex roles in adolescence together with references to key journal articles and selected recent literature reviews on the detailed clinical assessment and treatment procedures that have been developed for both common and rare disorders.

PROBLEMS ASSOCIATED WITH PUBERTAL CHANGES

ADAPTING TO THE PHYSICAL GROWTH SPURT

The increase in skeletal size and muscular strength is especially salient for the social lives of boys, who gain 50% more muscle mass during their growth spurt than do girls. However, for girls, the growth spurt starts on the average around 9.6 years, whereas for boys it begins around 11.7 years. The peak of growth occurs around 12 years for girls and 14 years for boys. Because of this two-year lag of boys behind girls, the early adolescent girl is typically taller than the male, contradicting the American cultural stereotype of a taller, stronger male. This sets the stage for adjustment problems among some early adolescent males who may resent their earlier maturing female counterparts and aggressively act out to compensate for their felt inadequacy (Mazur & Cherpak, 1995; Rekers, 1992).

As a group, adolescent males with lower levels of physical strength have more generalized tensions, physical symptoms, inferiority feelings, and lowered social prestige (Rekers, 1992). Clinicians need to be alert to these tendencies and help such adolescents to adjust better and to overcome further avoidance of physical and group activities that can cause isolation and potential deficits in normal physical skill acquisition.

RELATIONSHIP CONFLICTS RELATED TO HEIGHTENED ENERGY LEVEL AND MOOD CHANGES

In some North American families, pubertal maturation is associated with increased emotional distance between adolescents and their parents (Steinberg, 1987). Many adolescents experience an increased energy level as a function of rapid changes in their endocrine system (Petersen & Taylor, 1980). This heightened energy level typically occurs around the time of a spurt in muscular development and may create new difficulties for the teenager who needs to conform to adult expectations for remaining still. Some parents and teachers become annoyed by the increased adolescent activity level. Thus, some highly energized adolescents have greater difficulty pleasing parents and teachers than they did when younger; they may tend to rush from activity to activity, thereby spending less time keeping neat and clean. Even after cleaning up, their high activity level may quickly undo their neat appearance. Clinicians can explain these new physical sources for greater physical activity to teens and the adults around them, and therapeutically assist the adolescent in learning self-control in appropriate settings.

Some parents become concerned about this pubertal increase in energy level and associated changes in the adolescent's emotional life. Adolescent girls experiencing pubertal changes report more nervousness and negative moods, more variability in moods, heightened energy, and restlessness than do prepubertal girls (Buchanan, 1991). Some individuals experience greater depression and aggressive affect during puberty, which may reflect hormonal changes (Brooks-Gunn, Graber, & Paikoff, 1994). Based on an accurate diagnostic assessment, the clinician can appropriately intervene either to treat a psychological disorder per se or to help concerned parents understand, emotionally support, and affirm their teenager, who is learning to cope with a new intensity of energy and some new fluctuations in mood state.

ADJUSTMENT TO THE MATURATION OF PRIMARY SEX ORGANS

Shortly after the growth spurt is initiated, the same hormonal trigger increases production of androgens and estrogens that stimulate the maturation of the reproductive organs (Mazur & Chepak, 1995). Pubertal changes have a different impact on body image and peer relations for boys compared to girls (Rodriguez, Bariaud, Cohen-Zardi, & Delmas, 1993). In males, first the testes, then the penis and internal accessory structures grow, and ultimately the reproductive glands produce motile sperm and seminal fluid. Episodic secretion of luteinizing hormone during sleep leads to a first ejaculation (semenarche), typically between the ages of 12 and 13, and to nocturnal emissions between the ages of 12 and 16 (Mazur & Cherpak, 1995); common reactions to semenarche include surprise, pleasure, curiosity, confusion, and even fear, particularly in males who are unprepared by sex education in advance (Stein & Reiser, 1994).

The external and internal genitalia of the pubescent female begin to grow at about 11 to 12 years of age, coinciding with the first vaginal secretions and a widening of the pelvic diameter. Menarche typically occurs late in the pubescent female's growth spurt and after the beginning of breast development, at a mean age of 12 to 13.5, with a range from 10 to 16.5 years (Mazur & Cherpak, 1995; Petersen & Taylor, 1980). Environmental stress may trigger earlier menarche in that girls from divorced families or families with more conflict have an earlier onset of menarche than girls from intact families and families with less conflict (Wierson, Long, &

Forehand, 1993). Full reproductive capacity is typically not achieved until a few years after menarche.

The young adolescent who is unprepared for these changes can suffer adjustment problems. Experiencing his first nocturnal emission, an ill-informed boy may conclude that he has an infection, is enuretic, or is physically abnormal. The initially menstruating girl may conclude that she is physically injured or ill (Logan, 1980). As adolescents develop physically during puberty, they need to integrate their maturing genitals into their body image (Jongbloed-Schurig, 1997). Clinicians working with a prepubertal adolescent need to inquire of parents regarding the youngster's preparation for puberty; thus, preventive intervention should be offered to the preadolescent, and developmental information provided to adolescents, to enhance their adjustment to the maturation of their genitals (Mayekiso & Twaise, 1993).

PROBLEMS SECONDARY TO PUBERTY RELATED TO SOCIAL APPEARANCE AND SELF-IMAGE

Because the peer group culture emphasizes physical attributes for social and sexual attractiveness, any perceived physical abnormality can lead to embarrassment, self-concept problems, and potential behavior disorders or substance abuse in adolescents (Slap, Khalid, Paikoff, & Brooks-Gunn, 1994). During puberty, a major task for the adolescent is to examine and restructure the elements of identity. The major changes in physical characteristics brought about by puberty can contribute to a psychological crisis for an adolescent, particularly for the chronically ill adolescent (Sinnema, 1986). The changes in physical appearance and body odors prompt changes in the teenager's body image (Petersen & Taylor, 1980). The onset of puberty typically is less surprising for boys because their gonads and genitals are more visible, but the initial pubertal events for girls (budding of breasts and appearance of straight pubic hair) can be just as easily observed by girls as the initial pubertal events for boys (scrotum and testes growth, appearance of straight pubic hair, and penile growth) (Rekers, 1992).

Physical changes during puberty are so comprehensive and rapid that the adolescent may have difficulty assimilating them. Boys may vacillate between impulses to exhibit and conceal their erections. Girls may vacillate between dressing to flatten or to make their breasts appear bigger (Rekers, 1992), and most express embarrassment over the purchase of a bra (Brooks-Gunn, Newman, Holderness, & Warren, 1994).

Most adolescents scrutinize their attitudes and feelings about their developing body and focus on the discrepancy between ideal and actual body characteristics (Petersen & Taylor, 1980). Some adolescent male athletes illegally use steroids to enhance their muscular development, but steroid users not only have significantly greater muscular density and hardness, they also experience significantly more bloating, gynecomastia, acne, depression, anger, vigor, and other mood disturbances compared to other male adolescent athletes and nonathletes (Burnett & Kleiman, 1994). These dangers should be explained by the psychologist or physician to adolescent boys on steroids. The adolescent's self-image must incorporate bodily changes, developing sexuality, and the roles involved in love, marriage, and potential parenthood.

The special adjustment issues faced by adolescents with physical abnormality of their sexual anatomy have been preliminarily studied (e.g., Bradley, Oliver, Chernick, & Zucker, 1998; Zucker et al., 1996), and available data have been reviewed in terms of their clinical implications by Mazur and Dobson (1995). Similarly, clinical interventions for the obstacles to sexual adjustment of adolescents with disabilities have been reviewed by Warzak, Kuhn, and Nolten (1995).

REACTIONS TO THE DEVELOPMENT OF SECONDARY SEX CHARACTERISTICS

The initial sign of secondary sex characteristics (typically, straight pubic hair) usually occurs between 8 and 13 in girls and a year or two later in boys (Mazur & Cherpak, 1995). Pubic hair becomes a valued social indicator of pubescence. For adolescent males, the subsequent (i.e., later in the maturational sequence) appearance of facial hair is an even more significant badge of sexual maturity than their earlier pubic hair development (see review by Rekers, 1992). In some females, the growth of dark, course terminal hairs on the face may create a major adjustment problem necessitating clinical psychological intervention (Mazur & Cherpak, 1995).

Testosterone stimulates a rapid rate of growth in the adolescent male's larynx (Petersen & Taylor, 1980), which can occur faster than the boy's capacity to gain skill in controlling his "voicebox." Thus, a pubescent boy's voice will typically "crack" during this period, causing him some potential psychological distress and embarrassment.

The most socially conspicuous secondary sex characteristic of girls is breast development, beginning as early as age 9 and typically taking two to three years to complete (Mazur & Cherpak, 1995). Breast development is an important symbol of sexual maturity for most adolescent girls, and change in breast size is positively associated with adjustment scores (Slap et al., 1994). Because she has no control over it, the extent of her development compared with that of her peers often becomes cause for concern. Self-conscious about breast development, some girls withdraw from athletics or stop wearing bathing suits or certain tight-fitting clothes. On the other hand, many girls at this age wear more revealing clothing or attempt to make it appear that they have more breast development than has actually occurred by padding their bras or by wearing special uplift bras.

Some boys may be fearful that feminine characteristics are developing when a slight breast enlargement (gynecomastia) and nipple sensitivity take place during puberty. When such concerns are brought to the attention of a clinical psychologist, the boy should be sensitively evaluated for potential gender insecurities, hostile teasing by peers, and/or social isolation. Boys may need to be reassured about the common transience of these phenomena or referred for a physician's evaluation for potential medical intervention in cases of severe breast development (Mazur & Cherpak, 1995).

Secondary sex characteristics are significant for adolescents as indicators of mature masculinity and femininity. They are more socially visible than the primary sex organs and therefore play a major role in the peer group's definition of social attractiveness.

ADJUSTMENTS TO THE TIMING OF PUBERTY

Normal adolescents differ greatly in the age of the onset of their puberty and in the time from onset to completion of the pubertal changes. Both early- and late-maturing adolescents can feel disadvantaged

with respect to peer acceptance. Early maturers tend to be taller, heavier, and more stout than later maturers, and they grow faster during their growth spurts (Mazur & Cherpak, 1995). Early-maturing boys generally get a better reception from adults because they are usually treated on the basis of their physical, not chronological, age (Rekers, 1992, 1995c). They also excel in athletics due to advanced muscle development. These advantages contribute to a higher self-esteem, greater confidence, and social maturity. Although early maturation is related to more positive self-evaluations in boys, late maturation is associated with greater amounts of negative self-evaluation (Alsaker, 1992). But early pubertal maturation is also related to increased risk for sexual activity and for delinquency in both males and females (Flannery, Rowe, & Gulley, 1993). By contrast, the early-maturing girl is viewed as more "out of step" with both her male and female peers (see reviews by Rekers, 1992, 1995c). Many early-maturing girls become self-conscious about their bodies, develop poor body images with global negative self-evaluations, tend to withdraw socially, develop internalizing psychological disorders, and ultimately become less popular among their peers (Alsaker, 1992; Hayward, Killen, Wilson, & Hammer, 1997).

Although late maturers finally achieve the same height as their earlier maturing age-mates, they tend to be thinner. The late-maturing boy must overcome feelings of physical inferiority and inadequacy (see review by Rekers, 1992), particularly in the school locker room, where he is visually aware of his peers' greater genital size compared with his own, which can become a source of embarrassment and feelings of masculine inadequacy. Some boys react by engaging in bravado or conduct disorder, some become relatively more shy and socially withdrawn, and others develop a more flexible style of adaption and adjust normally.

The early-maturing girl is more often perceived as "different" from her late-maturing counterpart, in that the late-maturing girl is more in synchrony with the development of boys her age who experience onset of puberty two years later than girls on the average. The late-maturing girl is typically rated by her peers as being attractive, expressive, prestigious, and socially aware.

Thus, early-maturing boys and late-maturing girls are generally thought to have the fewest psychological liabilities (see also further discussion in the review by Mazur & Cherpak, 1995). Early-maturing girls and late-maturing boys often have the highest risk for adjustment problems because they are the most socially conspicuous and potentially more self-conscious about their difference from their peers (see reviews by Mazur & Cherpak, 1995; and Rekers, 1992).

In rare pathological cases, the adolescent either has an extremely early or an extremely late puberty (Mazur & Dobson, 1995). These children typically have severe body image problems, stemming from peer teasing and their self-doubt regarding normalcy, which may lead to a poor self-concept and social adjustment problems. Referral for a comprehensive medical evaluation is recommended, together with assessment for a potential need for psychotherapy. In some cases of extremely delayed puberty, the adolescent's physician may find that hormonal intervention is indicated (Mazur & Dobson, 1995).

In the management of cases of late or early puberty, the clinician must help the adolescent cope with the fact that the cause of the pubertal timing (in the vast majority of cases) is beyond the control of the individual, his or her physician, and the psychotherapist. The clinician should assess and address the emotional needs of the individual adolescent and refer the adolescent for medical evaluation, rather than reiterating the simplistic prescription to wait that well-meaning parents often offer adolescents with extremely late puberty (Rekers & Jurich, 1983). The psychologist should address the discomfort associated with coping with an advanced or retarded puberty. Group therapy with early or late maturers and their peers can focus on social skills and empathy for peers at different levels of pubertal development. Family therapy and/or parent counseling can address potential secondary problems and promote family cohesiveness as a mutual support system. For example, many parents of youngsters with precocious puberty assume that their child will become sexually active or promiscuous simply as a result of early sexual maturation. But biological precociousness actually has less influence on their actual behavior than psychological, religious, and social influences (Petty, 1995; Rekers & Hohn, 1998). Therefore, parents often need reassurance that their active nurturing support, effective communication, and moral guidance of their adolescent will assist the young person to avoid unwise sexual involvement.

MANAGING ADOLESCENT OBESITY AND EATING DISORDERS

Shortly after the adolescent's maximum growth spurt, it is common for the pubescent boy or girl to accumulate fat tissue (Tanner, 1974). Obesity is often clinically defined as 20% more than the expected body weight for the individual's height. Although affecting the adjustment of both males and females, the obese adolescent girl is even more likely than the obese adolescent boy to suffer from a disturbed body image, to feel unattractive, to be stigmatized, and to withdraw from social interactions (Regan, 1996; Steen, Wadden, Foster, & Andersen, 1996).

The psychological management of the obese adolescent depends on the clinician's diagnosis of the genesis and maintenance of the obesity (Brooks-Gunn, Graber, et al., 1994). If the etiology of the obesity is a biological abnormality, the psychologist may need to focus intervention on self-acceptance, social skill development, and/or coping with the physical ailment. However, if the adolescent's obesity is diagnosed as psychogenic in etiology, the psychologist should explore the specific factors that contribute to this condition in the individual. Comprehensive behavioral interventions are the treatment of choice in the management of a proper dietary and exercise regimen for weight reduction (Haddock, Shadish, Klesges, & Stein, 1994; Riva, 1996). Family support and positive parental expectations for weight loss in the adolescent are significantly related to weight loss response (Uzark, Becker, Dielman, & Rocchini, 1988).

An adolescent may consciously seek weight loss as a reaction to the gain in fat tissue during puberty. Normal pubertal increases in fat tissue and weight are associated with the initial development of eating-related concerns in some adolescents; however, the subsequent psychological reaction to these bodily changes, particularly the acquisition of a more negative body image, is more significant in the etiology of eating disorders (Cattarin & Thompson, 1994; Jagstaidt, Golay, & Pasini, 1996; Koff & Rierdan, 1993; Thompson, Coovert, Richards, & Johnson, 1995). Although eating disorders occur in males with poor body image or with sexual and identity conflicts (Keel, Fulkerson, & Leon, 1997), the occurrence of anorexia nervosa is more frequent in females and may have a later age of onset than in males (Shisslak, Crago, & Yates, 1989; Steiger, 1989). Adolescent females who are delayed in sexual milestones developmentally are at higher risk for anorexia nervosa (Schmidt, Evans, & Treasure, 1995). Body dissatisfaction and negative emotionality are related to greater risk of eating disorders in female adolescents (Leon, Fulkerson, Perry, & Cudeck, 1993). As the adolescent becomes obsessed with weight reduction, physical health and survival can be threatened. Clinicians should also be aware that there are ethnic differences in body dissatisfaction in adolescents; for example, among those in the leanest quartile, Asian and Hispanic adolescent girls report significantly more body dissatisfaction than White adolescent girls (Robinson, Killen, Litt, & Hammer, 1996). Sexual and physical abuse may increase risk for anorexia nervosa and bulimia nervosa (Douzinas, Fornai, Goodman, & Sitnick, 1994).

The clinician must assess the motivations that maintain the adolescent's eating disorder. Striegel-Moore (1995) theorized that female gender-role socialization places adolescent females at risk for binge eating. Intervention may consist of individual psychotherapeutic or behavioral techniques, including readjustment of expectations and modified behavioral patterns. Psychotherapy, hospital day care, and family therapy have been used to treat anorexia nervosa in adolescence (Danziger, Carel, Tyano, & Mimouni, 1989). Family therapy is particularly important in light of research indicating that adolescent girls' positive relationships with both mother and father are associated with healthier eating (Swarr & Richards, 1996). Further information on clinical interventions for eating disorders is presented elsewhere in this *Handbook.*

Adjustment Issues with Acne

Facial blemishes are the most frequently voiced concerns of adolescents, with acne conditions found in 75% to 90% of the adolescent population. This great concern over facial appearance may cause the adolescent to withdraw from social activities, thereby contributing to self-concept problems. This is exacerbated by parents and teachers if they fail to understand the level of adolescent concern.

Psychotherapy can be directed toward self-acceptance and the development of social skills to minimize the potential self-esteem problems. Medical treatment of the acne can produce beneficial psychological effects. Without effective

medical treatment, the adolescent may feel powerless over his or her complexion, which could generate depression.

SEXUAL BEHAVIOR PROBLEMS IN ADOLESCENCE

In adjusting to a new body image, pubescent adolescents must transform their self-image from that of a child to that of an adult sexual being (see review by Rekers, 1992). The physiological changes in puberty potentiate increased sexual thoughts, feelings, and behaviors in the adolescent (Mazur & Cherpak, 1995). Frequency of masturbation increases, particularly in boys. Whereas the vast majority of adolescent males have masturbation experience, the majority of adolescent girls have not masturbated, and girls report feeling more guilt after masturbation than do boys (deSouza, deAlmeida, Wagner, & Zimmerman, 1993; Raboch, Zverina, Raboch, & Sindlar, 1994). Boys who do masturbate have three times the frequency rate of girls who masturbate (Leitenberg, Detzer, & Srebyik, 1993). Although myths that masturbation causes health problems are no longer commonly held, clinicians need to assess for harmful forms of masturbation, such as masturbation with physical objects, with deviant pornography, or with induced asphyxia (Hucker & Blanchard, 1992). Masturbation associated with various physical objects can lead to obligatory dependence on that equipment to achieve orgasm; masturbation fixation occurs when masturbation becomes the preferred sexual outlet (Slosarz, 1992). Also, the exploration of heterosexual and homosexual behaviors increases (Lundy & Rekers, 1995b). Sexual fantasies, masturbation, and nonmarital sexual interactions produce considerable guilt, shame, and fear of parental discovery in many adolescents (Sharma, Sharma, Dave, & Chauhan, 1996).

Adolescents will be potentially better adjusted to the transitions of puberty if they have close relationships and good communication with parents (Petty, 1995; Rekers, 1984) and are provided accurate information regarding the adolescent growth spurt, primary sex organ changes, and the development of secondary sex characteristics prior to their actual occurrence (Mazur & Cherpak, 1995). This education on the biology of sexual development and change is often introduced into the health education curriculum in schools for the preadolescent and adolescent; for some groups of adolescents, their parents are the major source of information on such topics (Rekers & Hohn, 1998; Tucker, 1989). In addition, various authors contend that adolescents benefit from knowledge about sexually transmitted diseases, including acquired immunodeficiency syndrome (AIDS) (Seibert & Olson, 1989), society's laws regulating sexual behavior and marriage (MacNamara & Sergrin, 1977), courtship relationships (McDowell, 1987; Petty, 1995; Rekers & Hohn, 1998), and the ethical and moral dimensions of sexuality (Lundy & Rekers, 1995a; McDowell, 1987; Rekers & Hohn, 1998) provided by their parents, church, school, and/or clinician with parental consent (Allen-Meares, 1989; McDowell, 1987; Petty, 1995; Rekers, 1984; Rekers & Hohn, 1998). Nonmarital coitus in adolescence and a low frequency of contraceptive use (deSouza et al., 1993; Rekers & Hohn, 1998) result in the major social problems of sexually transmitted diseases, teen pregnancies (often with poor prenatal care), and high abortion rates (Rekers & Hohn, 1998; Schumm, 1995). Sexual intercourse between adolescents is more likely when the male drinks alcohol (Cooper & Orcutt, 1997). The level of sexual risk taking (including unprotected oral and anal sexual activity) is associated with illicit substance use, even in adolescents who do not participate in vaginal intercourse (Schuster, Bell, & Kanouse, 1996).

DEVIANT SEXUAL DEVELOPMENT

The etiology of many cases of sexual deviation has been traced to the adolescent period of development (Arndt, 1995; Rekers, 1995c, 1998). The problems of transsexualism, transvestism, and homosexuality will be reviewed in the following section on sex-role development. A more extensive review of specific treatments for sexual problems in adolescence is offered by Rekers (1995c), and clinicians often need to treat not only the adolescent but also the family. Here, it is only briefly noted that clinical psychological treatment procedures have been reported for a variety of adolescent sexual adjustment problems (Rekers, 1995b, 1995c), including exhibitionism (MacCulloch, Williams, & Birtles, 1971; Veenhuizen, Van Strien, & Cohen-Kettenis, 1992), sadistic sexual behavior (Woods, 1993), and promiscuous sexual behavior (Simon,

1989). Other adolescent sexual problems that have been reported in the clinical literature include excessive or public masturbation (Lundervoid & Young, 1992; Stirt, 1940), hypersexual behavior (Adams, McClellan, Douglass, & McCurry, 1995), sexual asphyxias and autoerotized repetitive hangings (the practice of self-induced cerebral anoxia, usually by hanging, strangulation, or suffocation, during masturbation) (Blanchard & Hucker, 1991; Burch, Case, & Turgeon, 1995; Friedrich & Gerber, 1994; Hucker & Blanchard, 1992), fetishism (Weinberg, Williams, & Calhan, 1995), the dehumanizing experiences of male and female prostitution (Boyer, 1989; Burgess & Hartman, 1995a; Coleman, 1989; deSouza, deOliveria, Wagner, & Vinciprova, 1996; Kunawararak, Beyrer, Natpratan, & Feng, 1995; Tremble, 1993; Widom & Kuhns, 1996), and sex offenses (Bradford, Motayne, Gratzer, & Pawlak, 1995; Richardson, Kelly, & Graham, 1997), including exhibitionism (Adams et al., 1995; Veenhuizer et al., 1992), sexual assault (Veenhuizen et al., 1992), obscene phone calls (Arndt, 1995), and sexual homicide (Lowenstein, 1992; Myers, 1994; Myers, Scott, Burgess, & Burgess, 1995).

SEXUAL VICTIMIZATION

Clinical psychologists also encounter adolescents who have been victims of various forms of sexual abuse (Faller, 1995; Rekers, 1996), including sexual coercion (Anderson, Reis, & Stephens, 1997; Poitras & Lavoie, 1995), acquaintance or date rape (Karp, Silber, Holmstrom, & Stock, 1995; Vicary, Klingaman, & Harkness, 1995), and involvement in pornography production and sex rings (Burgess & Hartman, 1995b). Adjustment problems have been reported in cases where the minor is exposed to the observation of certain adult sexual behavior or pornography (Burgess & Hartman, 1995a; Effa, 1996) and where minors have been victims of sexual seduction (Bagley, 1995). Adolescents with a history of sexual abuse are at risk for health-compromising behavior (Neumark, Story, French, & Resnick, 1997). Various treatment approaches have been reported for adolescent victims of sexual abuse and incest (Cuffe & Frick-Helms, 1995; Trepper & Barrett, 1986). See other chapters in this *Handbook* for further information on clinical interventions for sexual abuse.

SEX-ROLE PROBLEMS IN ADOLESCENT BOYS

Although sex typing and sex-role development begin in the preschool years (Rekers & Kilgus, 1995, 1998; Rekers & Mead, 1979), sex roles are further developed in the adolescent years, and clear sex differences have been observed among adolescents (Rekers, Sanders, Rasbury, Strauss, & Morey, 1989). As children move toward adolescence, they become increasingly aware of the socially defined components of sex roles and learn to make finer discriminations between masculine and feminine sex-typed behaviors in themselves and others (Rekers & Kilgus, 1995). In some cases, this poses a particular diagnostic problem for the clinical child psychologist in that some adolescents, unlike young children, may conceal certain covert deviant patterns of sex typing or sexual identity problems (Rekers & Kilgus, 1997).

HYPERMASCULINITY

One type of sex-role problem in adolescent males is a syndrome of excessive hypermasculinity. This pattern is seen in some teenage boys who are destructive, interpersonally violent, belligerent, uncontrolled, high in vengeance, and who lack kindness, gentleness, self-control, and socially sensitive behaviors (Hutt, Iverson, Bass, & Gayton, 1997; Rekers, 1992). These exaggeratedly "supermasculine" boys have adopted a "macho" caricature of the masculine social role, have greater anger and less empathy than nonhypermasculine adolescents, have greater risk of sexually aggressive behavior (O'Donohue, McKay, & Schewe, 1996; Vass & Gold, 1995), have greater alcohol consumption (Davidoff, Mallya, & Blacker, 1996), and thereby require psychotherapeutic intervention.

Some cases of conduct disorder have their etiology in such a sex-role development problem (Rekers, 1992). A careful psychological assessment of the adolescent boy is necessary to ascertain the functional characteristics of the conduct disorder and its potential relationship to a psychosexual disorder (Rekers, 1995c; Rekers & Morey, 1989b). Based on this individual assessment, treatment may be required for the conduct disorder itself and/or for an underlying gender disturbance (Rekers, 1995a).

GENDER IDENTITY DISORDER IN ADOLESCENTS

A cross-gender identity is manifested in adolescent boys if their behavior pattern includes either (1) repeatedly labeling themselves as female, as evidenced by a stated intense desire to be a girl or woman or by excessively and persistently passing as a female or expressing inner convictions that one has the typical reactions or feelings of females, sometimes including fantasies of bearing children and of breast-feeding infants; and/or (2) discomfort with male sexuality or gender role, including pronounced aversion toward masculine activities or clothing, or anatomic dysphoria, sometimes expressed in requests by the adolescent boy to have his penis removed or to have other sex reassignment medical procedures performed (Barlow, Abel, & Blanchard, 1979; Barlow, Reynolds, & Agras, 1973; Bradley & Zucker, 1997; Rekers, 1992, 1995a). Boys with cross-gender identification have been typically found to be normal physically according to current methods of biomedical assessment and to have disturbed family relationships (Rekers & Kilgus, 1995, 1998). Patients diagnosed with gender identity disorder in adolescence have a negative self-image (Bodlund & Armelius, 1994).

In the case of an adolescent boy referred for a potential cross-gender identification problem, a complete psychological assessment of the major dimensions of sex and gender should be conducted (see Rekers, 1995a; Rekers & Kilgus, 1995, 1997, 1998). Some clinicians speculate that radical surgical and hormonal sex reassignment procedures are required for the adolescent in the pretranssexual or transsexual condition (Bradley & Zucker, 1997; Cohen-Kettenis & Gooren, 1992; Gooren & Delemarre vande Waal, 1996), and hormonal and surgical sex reassignment has been practiced recently for some adolescents with gender identity disorder at Utrecht University Hospital in the Netherlands (Cohen-Kettenis & vanGoozen, 1997). However, longitudinal follow-up studies of operated and unoperated adult transsexuals found no significant change in the adjustment scores of the operated transsexuals and found up to 31% regretting surgical sex change, which has led many clinicians to doubt that medical sex reassignment is a legitimate treatment (Lindemalm, Korlin, & Uddenberg, 1986; Meyer & Reter, 1979). Furthermore, research studies using intrasubject replication designs have demonstrated that a combination of behavioral treatment procedures are effective in normalizing the gender identity and sexual arousal patterns of adolescent and young adult transsexuals (e.g., Barlow et al., 1973). Because all other approaches to the treatment of cross-sex identification have failed, many clinicians consider the behavioral treatment procedures developed by Barlow and his colleagues and Rekers and his colleagues to be the only ethically responsible approach to the clinical management of adolescent cases of cross-sex identification (see the discussions by Bradley et al., 1978; Rekers, 1995a; Rekers, Bentler, Rosen, & Lovaas, 1977; Rekers, Kilgus, & Rosen, 1990; Rekers & Mead, 1980). The only other form of intervention that has resulted in an empirically demonstrated and comprehensive change in gender identification and homosexual orientation has been religious conversion and associated spiritual development (Barlow, Abel, & Blanchard, 1977; Pattison & Pattison, 1980; see discussion by Rekers, 1997).

CROSS-GENDER BEHAVIOR DISORDER

Without manifesting a complete cross-gender identity, some adolescents have a history of cross-gender stereotypic behavior that can be traced back to as young an age as 3 years old (Doorn, Poortinga, & Verschoor, 1994; Rekers, 1995a). The earlier childhood behavioral history of such an adolescent boy includes a combination of some of the following: (1) chronic aversion toward or avoidance of peer activities with other boys or preoccupation with feminine sex-typed activities and games; (2) repeated actual or improvised cross-dressing in feminine clothing; (3) chronic use of feminine-appearing mannerisms, behavioral gestures, or gait; (4) repeated actual use or play-acting the use of feminine cosmetics articles; (5) repeated use of a high femininelike vocal inflection and/or predominantly feminine speech content; (6) taking a feminine role in play on frequent occasions; and (7) associated courtship disorder in adolescence (Rekers & Kilgus, 1995; Rekers & Morey, 1989a, 1989b, 1990).

For some adolescent males, cross-sex role behavior patterns take the form of habitual sexual relations with other boys, including oral and anal receptive intercourse, which places the adolescent

at high risk of acquiring AIDS (Calhoun & Weaver, 1996; Coleman, 1989; Crofts, Marcus, Meade, & Sattier, 1995; Green, 1987; Rekers, 1998; Sussman & Duffy, 1996; Wadsworth, Hickman, Johnson, & Wellings, 1996; Zuger, 1989). Interventions involving social skills and behavioral self-management training with social support and stress/coping assistance have been effective in reducing high-risk same-sex anal and oral sexual behaviors (Rotheram-Borus, Reid, Rosario, & Kasen, 1995). Drug abuse is highly associated with risky homosexual behavior in adolescents, which points to the need to provide drug abuse interventions to this population (Winters, Remafedi, & Chan, 1996).

The psychological assessment of cross-gender behavior disorders should be designed to include procedures that measure all of the relevant psychosexual dimensions, including social sex assignment (the history of the obstetrician's and parents' assignment of the child as boy or girl), sexual identification (normal identification with sexual morphology, or cross-gender identity, or bisexual or homosexual identity), sex-role self-labeling ("feminine," "masculine," "boy," "girl," "man," "woman," "queen," "fag," "queer," "gay," etc.), sex-role behavioral adjustment (feminine, masculine, androgynous, or undifferentiated), masturbation fantasy (with or without specific types of pornography or objects; content of fantasy accompanying self-stimulation), sexual arousal patterns (magnitude and frequency to male and female, adult and child stimuli; to objects; to animal[s]; and to visual or fantasized stimuli), and genital behaviors (masturbatory pattern, male and/or female human partner[s], inanimate objects used; animal partner[s], intrusive vs. receptive behavior) (Billingham & Hockenberry, 1987; see Rekers, 1995a, for an overview of diagnostic procedures).

The treatment of cross-gender behavior disorders in adolescence (see reviews by Rekers, 1995a) may involve psychotherapy and specific behavior therapy procedures developed for transvestic behavior, fetishistic patterns, or problems with homosexual behavior (Arndt, 1995; Barlow, Agras, Abel, Blanchard, & Young, 1975; Canton-Dutari, 1974; Lundy & Rekers, 1995c; McConaghy, 1975; Moberly, 1983; Nicholosi, 1991; Wilson, 1988).

Primarily since the 1980s, there has been some controversy among mental health professionals with respect to whether or not gender disorders, transvestism, transsexualism, homosexuality, and "victimless" paraphilias should be considered forms of deviance or psychopathology and whether they should be regarded as appropriate conditions for treatment (e.g., see Bayer, 1981; Coates & Person, 1985; Feder, 1997; Green, 1987; Lindemalm et al., 1986). One body of literature considers such gender and sexual conditions valid personal choices or preferences within a broader range of "normality" (e.g., Feder, 1997; Fontaine & Hammond, 1996; MacDonald, 1985; Radkowsky & Siegel, 1997; Serbin, 1980). Other clinicians and research investigators make a case for conceptualizing these conditions as either psychopathology or, if not a mental disorder, then still a condition for which an individual and/or parents can legitimately request and receive treatment (Barlow et al., 1975, 1979; Lief & Kaplan, 1986; Lundy & Rekers, 1995a, 1995b, 1995c; Moberly, 1983; Nicholosi, 1991; Pattison & Pattison, 1980; Rosen, Rekers, & Bentler, 1978; Smith, 1985; Socarides, 1988; Stoller, 1975, 1978; Wilson, 1988).

DEVELOPMENTAL COURSE OF SEX-ROLE PROBLEMS IN MALES

The adolescent boy's peers are highly likely to label his feminine behavior homosexual ("sissy," "queer," or "fag"), and adult men or other adolescent boys may make sexual advances toward the adolescent boy with sex-role deviance. Such social experiences, in turn, have an impact on the adolescent boy's identification and sexual development (Arndt, 1995; Rekers, 1995c, 1998; Rosen, Rekers, & Bentler, 1978). The available prospective longitudinal data indicate that effeminate behavior in boys and young adolescents is fairly predictive of adult male homosexuality and is retrospectively reported by adult male homosexuals, adult male transvestites, and adult male transsexuals. Compared to male heterosexual adolescents, significantly more male homosexual adolescents report a poor body image, frequent dieting, and binge eating or purging behaviors (French, Story, Remafedi, & Resnick, 1996). Cross-gender behavior and cross-dressing begins in early boyhood and persists (in the absence of treatment) into the adolescent years for the majority of adult transsexuals and transvestites (see Green, 1987; Rekers, 1992; Rekers & Kilgus, 1995; Whitam & Mathy, 1991).

The various prospective studies of essentially untreated gender-disturbed boys predict a deviant sexual outcome in 40% to 75% of the cases. For example, Zuger's (1978, 1989) long-term prospective follow-up of a sample of untreated gender-disturbed boys found that 20 years later, 65% were homosexual, 6% were transvestite, 6% were transsexual, and 12% were heterosexual; 25% had attempted suicide, and 6% had committed suicide. By contrast, the long-term effects of family and behavior therapy for gender-disturbed children reevaluated by an independent clinical psychologist during the adolescent years documented successful normalization of the cross-gender identity (Rekers, 1995a, 1998; Rekers et al., 1990). Thus, the severe maladjustment of a gender identity disorder has been shown to be treatable in childhood; furthermore, treatment in adolescence not only has reversed a cross-gender identity but also has changed an adolescent homosexual orientation to a heterosexual one (Barlow et al., 1973, 1975, 1977, 1979). More research is needed on the long-term adult outcomes of treatment interventions in the childhood and adolescent years.

SEX-ROLE PROBLEMS IN ADOLESCENT GIRLS

The detection of sex-role behavior problems in adolescent girls is a much more complex task because of the relatively greater sex-role flexibility allowed girls in childhood and early adolescent development. Also, there is greater social acceptance of masculinelike clothing and behavior in girls as contrasted with the acute social concerns in our society about boys wearing dresses, for example (Rekers & Mead, 1980). Therefore, the clinical psychologist's task of assessing sex-role problems in light of the broader range of acceptable behaviors in girls poses even more complex issues than the parallel assessment for boys (Rekers & Mead, 1979).

GENDER IDENTITY DISORDER IN ADOLESCENTS

Tomboyism is often a normal, healthy part of feminine development that involves an adaptive flexibility to engage in a wide range of activities and clothing styles. In rare cases, however, excessive, compulsive, and rigidly narrow masculine behavior develops in an adolescent girl as a chronic pattern, in association with a gender identity disorder, in which the adolescent girl rigidly rejects feminine sex-role activity and clothing and rejects or denies her female body.

Joan was a 14-year-old White female from a rural background whose home life included two divorces, 15 moves in the past six years, and little affection from an adult male figure. When she first appeared in our clinic, she was wearing a masculine shirt, a black leather jacket, blue jeans, and cowboy boots. She claimed that no one could force her to wear a dress. Joan reported feeling like and wanting to be a boy all her life, and she had made repeated requests for sex reassignment surgery. Her manner of speech, gestures, and mannerisms were hypermasculine. She reported a strong sexual interest in the same sex. Her social interactions were limited largely to boys, and she indicated her cross-sex identification by referring to this male group and herself as "we." At school, she repeatedly received Fs in physical education for refusing to participate because the coach would not allow her to play on the boys' team. She preferred to be called Paul. Joan reacted negatively to her physical maturation as a woman. She wore a jacket or an overshirt to hide her developing breasts, refused to wear a bra, and would not tell her mother when she needed feminine hygiene articles. Joan was rejected by the majority of her peers. She was very unhappy with her situation, experiencing frequent depressive episodes accompanied by suicidal ideation. She stated that she sometimes felt that she would rather be dead than remain a female (Rekers & Mead, 1980, p. 199).

A DEVIANT TYPE OF TOMBOY BEHAVIOR

Adolescent girls such as Joan have a childhood history including the following masculine sex-role behaviors at high frequency rates: (1) rigid rejection of and dissatisfaction with female primary and secondary sexual characteristics and a strong desire to have male anatomy; (2) chronic avoidance of female peer activities and preoccupation with playing exclusively with boys, often with the expressed desire to be considered one of the boys; (3) rigid and chronic insistence on wearing masculine sex-typed clothing, coupled with chronic rejection of dresses, skirts, cosmetic articles, and feminine jewelry; (4) repeated use of masculine-appearing behavioral gestures, postures, and gait, to the exclusion of fem-

inine mannerisms; (5) repeated use of an artificially induced low voice inflection; and (6) repeated requests to be called by a boy's name or nickname (Blanchard & Freund, 1983; Rekers & Mead, 1980).

Although the transient phase of taking on the tomboy role appears to be part of adaptive behavioral development in many girls, a small percentage of such tomboys are genuinely unhappy about their anatomic status as a female (Green, 1987). For this small minority, the girl's masculine sex-role behavior patterns are combined with a rigid rejection of most feminine sex-role activity and clothing styles and reflect her cross-gender identification; a comprehensive psychological evaluation (that is informed by the psychological literature) is necessary to make this diagnostic distinction.

DEVELOPMENTAL COURSE OF SEX-ROLE PROBLEMS IN GIRLS

In contrast to the normal progression of the tomboy phase, the gender-disturbed adolescent girl persists with predominantly masculine activities and interests from the childhood period into adolescence. This chronicity of a predominantly masculine behavior pattern, coupled with indices of a cross-gender identification, is predictive of adult transsexualism or homosexuality in the female (Saghir & Robins, 1973). Stoller (1975) has reported a distinction between the "masculine female," who progresses from psychological development to a period of "secondary masculinity" that is combined with her primary feminine identification, and the development of female transsexuals, who are more typically and uniformly masculine in their development from an early age onward, often beginning as early as 3 to 4 years old.

Nearly all female transsexuals retrospectively report that they desired to be a member of the opposite sex from their earliest recollected childhood (Pauly, 1974a). In the sample of 13 female adult transsexuals reported by Walinder, for example, 92% were tomboys in childhood and adolescence, and 100% felt as though they belonged to the opposite sex prior to the onset of puberty. In the majority of cases of female transsexualism in adolescence and adulthood, the cross-gender behavior began before the age of 3 and the process of cross-sex identification appears to be completed by age 7 or 8 (see Pauly's 1974b review of the literature). Most of the adolescent and adult female transsexuals reported that they had not engaged in doll play as children, and they preferred boys' toys (Pauly, 1974a). During their childhood and adolescent years, the majority identified with their father rather than with their mother (Pauly, 1974a; Rekers & Mead, 1980).

TRAUMA OF PUBERTY IN GENDER-DISTURBED GIRLS

The experience of puberty is reported to be traumatic for female transsexuals. During adolescence, virtually all were repulsed by their own breast development (Pauly, 1974a), and many reacted by binding their breasts with clothing to appear male (Pauly, 1974a). Similarly, in adolescence these girls were repulsed by menstruation, disliked their own sexual anatomy, and typically requested sex reassignment surgery (Landen, Walinder, & Lundstrom, 1996; Pauly, 1974a). In early adolescence, most of these girls experience sexual attraction to very feminine females (Pauly, 1974a).

DIFFERENTIAL DIAGNOSIS OF NORMAL TOMBOYISM FROM PREHOMOSEXUALITY AND PRETRANSSEXUALISM

The retrospective reports of adult female homosexuals and adult female transsexuals suggest both some similarities and some differences in the developmental course of female homosexuality as compared with female transsexualism. Although nearly all of the female transsexuals reported being tomboys in their childhood and youth, approximately 66% of adult female homosexuals and 16% of the heterosexual control group report having been tomboys as children (Saghir & Robins, 1973; see also Phillips & Over, 1995; Whitam & Mathy, 1991). The pattern of tomboyish desire to portray a male role and rejection of traditional femininity persisted into adolescence and adulthood (Cooper, 1990) for about half of the homosexual females but for none of the heterosexual females (who returned to many of their earlier feminine interests) (Saghir & Robins, 1973). Another difference reported by Saghir and Robins was that female homosexuals who reported a tomboy phase also reported definite disliking and avoidance of doll play, whereas the female heterosexual control subjects who were tomboys had a wider behavioral repertoire that included many sports activities, for example, but they felt no particular aversion to doll play (which they might engage in occasionally if invited to by other girls).

Because approximately 16% to 19% of normal adolescent girls have had a childhood history in which they expressed a preference for masculine activities (Saghir & Robins, 1973), the presence or existence of a given pattern of masculine and feminine activities in a girl at any particular point in time cannot be taken by itself to define a sex-role development problem. Instead, the intensity, clustering, chronicity, and cultural context of a particular combination of stereotypic "masculine" and "feminine" behaviors must all be considered together in making a clinical diagnosis of female gender disturbance in adolescents (Cooper, 1990; see the extended discussion by Rekers & Mead, 1980).

The psychological assessment of an adolescent girl with potential gender behavior disturbance or a cross-gender identity problem should include measures of all the major dimensions of sex and gender, as reviewed by Rekers and Kilgus (1995) and Rekers and Mead (1980). Very little has been published on psychological treatment for gender disturbances in adolescent girls (Bradley & Zucker, 1997; Rekers, 1995a), even though early identification and early psychotherapeutic intervention to prevent adulthood transvestism, transsexualism, and egodystonic homosexuality are commonly held to be the preferred clinical strategy (Pauly, 1974a, 1974b; Wilson, 1988).

REFERENCES

Adams, J., McClellan, J., Douglass, D., & McCurry, C. (1995). Sexually inappropriate behaviors in seriously mentally ill children and adolescents. *Child Abuse and Neglect 5*, 555–568.

Allen-Meares, P. (1989). Adolescent sexuality and premature parenthood. *Journal of Social Work and Human Sexuality, 8*, 133–142.

Alsaker, F.D. (1992). Pubertal timing, overweight, and psychological adjustment. *Journal of Early Adolescence, 12*, 396–419.

Alsaker, F.D. (1996). Annotation: The impact of puberty. *Journal of Child Psychology and Allied Disciplines, 37*(3), 249–258.

Anderson, V., Reis, J., & Stephens, Y. (1997). Male and female adolescents' perceived interpersonal communication skills according to history of sexual coercion. *Adolescence, 32*(126), 419–427.

Arndt, W.B. (1995). Deviant sexual behavior in children and adolescents. In G.A. Rekers (Ed.), *Handbook of child and adolescent sexual problems* (pp. 424–445). New York: Lexington Books.

Bagley, C. (1995). Early sexual experience and sexual victimization of children and adolescents. In G.A. Rekers (Ed.), *Handbook of child and adolescent sexual problems* (pp. 135–163). New York: Lexington Books.

Barlow, D.H., Abel, G.G., & Blanchard, E.B. (1977). Gender identity change in transsexuals: An exorcism. *Archives of Sexual Behavior, 6,* 387–395.

Barlow, D.H., Abel, G.G., & Blanchard, E.B. (1979). Gender identity change in transsexuals. *Archives of General Psychiatry, 36,* 1001–1007.

Barlow, D.H., Agras, W.S., Abel, G.G., Blanchard, E.B., & Young, L.D. (1975). Biofeedback and reinforcement to increase heterosexual arousal in homosexuals. *Behavior Research and Therapy, 13,* 45–50.

Barlow, D.H., Reynolds, E.J., & Agras, W.S. (1973). Gender identity change in a transsexual. *Archives of General Psychiatry, 28,* 569–576.

Bayer, R. (1981). *The politics of diagnosis: Homosexuality and American psychiatry.* New York: Basic Books.

Billingham, R.E., & Hockberry, S.L. (1987). Gender conformity, masturbation fantasy, infatuation, and sexual orientation. *Journal of Sex Research, 23,* 368–374.

Blanchard, R., & Freund, K. (1983). Measuring masculine gender identity in females. *Journal of Consulting and Clinical Psychology, 51,* 205–214.

Blanchard, R., & Hucker, S.J. (1991). Age, transvestism, bondage, and concurrent paraphillic activities in 117 fatal cases of autoerotic asphyxia. *British Journal of Psychiatry, 159,* 371–377.

Bodlund, O., & Armelius, K. (1994). Self-image and personality traits in gender identity disorders. *Journal of Sex and Marital Therapy, 20*(4), 303–317.

Boyer, D. (1989). Male prostitution and homosexual identity. *Journal of Homosexuality, 17,* 151–184.

Bradford, J.M.W., Motayne, G., Gratzer, T., & Pawlak, A. (1995). Child and adolescent sex offenders. In G.A. Rekers (Ed.), *Handbook of child and adolescent sexual problems* (pp. 446–475). New York: Lexington Books.

Bradley, S.J., Oliver, G.D., Chernick, A.B., & Zucker, K.J. (1998). Experiment of nurture. *Pediatrics, 102,* 1–5.

Bradley, S.J., Steiner, B., Zucker, K., Doering, R.W., Sullivan, J., Finegan, J.D., & Richardson, M. (1978). Gender identity problems of children and adolescents. *Canadian Psychiatric Association Journal, 23,* 175–183.

Bradley, S.J., & Zucker, K.J. (1997). Gender identity disorder: A review of the past 10 years. *Journal of the Academy of Child and Adolescent Psychiatry, 36,* 872–880.

Brooks-Gunn, J., Graber, J.A., & Paikoff, R.L. (1994). Studying links between hormones and negative affect. *Journal of Research on Adolescence, 4*(4), 469–486.

Brooks-Gunn, J., Newman, D.L., Holderness, C.C., & Warren, M.P. (1994). The experience of breast development and girls' stories about the purchase of a bra. *Journal of Youth and Adolescence, 23*(5), 539–565.

Buchanan, C.M. (1991). Pubertal status in early-adolescent girls. *Journal of Early Adolescence, 11*(2), 185–200.

Burch, P.M., Case, M.E.S., & Turgeon, R. (1995). Sexual asphyxiation: An unusual case involving four male adolescents. *Journal of Forensic Sciences, 40*(3), 490–491.

Burgess, A.W., & Hartman, C.R. (1995a). Adolescent runaways and juvenile prostitution. In G.A. Rekers (Ed.), *Handbook of child and adolescent sexual problems* (pp. 187–208). New York: Lexington Books.

Burgess, A.W., & Hartman, C.R. (1995b). Child and adolescent sex rings and pornography. In G.A. Rekers (Ed.), *Handbook of child and adolescent sexual problems* (pp. 164–186). New York: Lexington Books.

Burnett, K.F., & Kleiman, M.E. (1994). Psychological characteristics of adolescent steroid users. *Adolescence, 29*(113), 81–89.

Calhoun, T.C., & Weaver, G. (1996). Rational decision making among male street prostitutes. *Deviant Behavior, 17*(2), 209–227.

Canton-Dutari, A. (1974). Combined intervention for controlling unwanted homosexual behavior. *Archives of Sexual Behavior, 3,* 367–371.

Cattarin, J.A., & Thompson, J.K. (1994). A three year longitudinal study of body image, eating disturbance, and general psychological functioning in adolescent females. *Eating Disorders: The Journal of Treatment and Prevention, 2*(2), 114–125.

Coates, S., & Person, E.S. (1985). Extreme boyhood femininity: Isolated behavior or pervasive disorder? *Journal of the American Academy of Child Psychiatry, 24,* 702–709.

Cohen-Kettenis, P.T., & Gooren, L.J. (1992). The influence of hormone treatment of psychological functioning of transsexuals. *Journal of Psychology and Human Sexuality, 5*(4), 55–67.

Cohen-Kettenis, P.T., & vanGoozen, S.H.M. (1997). Sex reassignment of adolescent transsexuals: A follow-up study. *Journal of the American Academy of Child and Adolescent Psychiatry, 36*(2), 263–271.

Coleman, E. (1989). The development of male prostitution activity among gay and bisexual adolescents. *Journal of Homosexuality, 17,* 131–149.

Cooper, M. (1990). Rejecting "femininity." *Deviant Behavior, 11*(4), 371–380.

Cooper, M.L., & Orcutt, H.K. (1997). Drinking and sexual experience on first dates among adolescents. *Journal of Abnormal Psychology, 106*(2), 191–202.

Crofts, N., Marcus, L., Meade, J., & Sattier, G. (1995). Determinants of HIV risk among men who have homosexual sex and inject drugs. *AIDS Care, 7*(5), 647–655.

Cuffe, S.P., & Frick-Helms, S.B. (1995). Treatment interventions for child sexual abuse. In G.A. Rekers

(Ed.), *Handbook of child and adolescent sexual problems* (pp. 232–251). New York: Lexington Books.

Culley, D.C., & Flanagan, C.H., Jr. (1995). Assessment of sexual problems in childhood and adolescence. In G.A. Rekers (Ed.), *Handbook of child and adolescent sexual problems* (pp. 14–30). New York: Lexington Books.

Danziger, Y., Carel, C.A., Tyano, S., & Mimouni, M. (1989). Is psychotherapy mandatory during acute refeeding period in the treatment of anorexia nervosa? *Journal of Adolescent Health Care, 10,* 328–331.

Davidoff, S., Mallya, K., & Blacker, D. (1996). Gender roles, aggression, and alcohol use in dating relationships. *Journal of Sex Research, 33*(1), 47–55.

deSouza, R.P., deAlmeida, A.B., Wagner, M.B., & Zimmerman, I.I. (1993). A study of sexual behavior of teenagers in South Brazil. *Journal of Adolescent Health, 14*(4), 336–339.

deSouza, R.P., deOliveira, J.S., Wagner, M.B., & Vinciprova, A.R. (1996). Sexual behavior of teenagers. *Journal of Adolescent Health, 18*(3), 166–167.

Doorn, C.D., Poortinga, J., & Verschoor, A.M. (1994). Cross gender identity in transvesities and male transsexuals. *Archives of Sexual Behavior, 23*(2), 185–201.

Douzinas, N., Fornai, V., Goodman, B., & Sitnick, T. (1994). Eating disorders and abuse. *Child and Adolescent Psychiatric Clinic of North America, 3*(4), 777–796.

Effa, H.G. (1996). The influence of media pornography on adolescents. *IFE Psychologia: An International Journal, 4*(1), 80–90.

Faller, K.C. (1995). Assessment and treatment issues in child sexual abuse. In G.A. Rekers (Ed.), *Handbook of child and adolescent sexual problems* (pp. 209–232). New York: Lexington Books.

Feder, E.K. (1997). Disciplining the family. *Philosophical Studies, 85,* 195–211.

Flannery, D.J., Rowe, D.C., & Gulley, B.L. (1993). Impact of pubertal status, timing and age on adolescent sexual experience and delinquency. *Journal of Adolescent Research, 8*(1), 21–40.

Fontaine, J.H., & Hammond, N.L. (1996). Counseling issues with gay and lesbian adolescents. *Adolescence, 31*(124), 817–830.

French, S.A., Story, M., Remafedi, G., & Resnick, M.D. (1996). Sexual orientation and prevalence of body dissatisfaction and eating disordered behaviors: A population based study of adolescents. *International Journal of Eating Disorders, 19*(2), 119–126.

Friedrick, W.N., & Gerber, P.N. (1994). Autoerotic asphyxia. *Journal of the American Academy of Child and Adolescent Psychiatry, 33*(7), 970–974.

Gooren, L.J., & Delemarre vande Waal, H. (1996). The feasibility of endocrine interventions in juvenile transsexuals. *Journal of Psychology and Human Sexuality, 8*(4), 69–74.

Green, R. (1987). *The "sissy boy syndrome" and the development of homosexuality.* New Haven, CT: Yale University Press.

Haddock, C.K., Shadish, W.R., Klesges, R., & Stein, R.J. (1994). Treatment for childhood and adolescent obesity. *Annals of Behavioral Medicine, 16*(3), 235–244.

Hayward, C., Killen, J.D., Wilson, D.M., & Hammer, L.D. (1997). Psychiatric risk associated with early puberty in adolescent girls. *Journal of the American Academy of Child and Adolescent Psychiatry, 36*(2), 255–262.

Hucker, S.J., & Blanchard, R. (1992). Death scene characteristics in 118 cases of autoerotic asphyxia compared with suicidal asphyxia. *Behavioral Sciences and the Law, 10*(4), 509–523.

Hutt, M.J., Iverson, H.L., Bass, H., & Gayton, W.F. (1997). Further validation of the Vengeance Scale. *Psychological Reports, 80*(3, Pt. 1), 744–746.

Jagstaidt, V., Golay, A., & Pasini, W. (1996). Sexuality and bulimia. *New Trends in Experimental and Clinical Psychiatry, 12*(1), 9–15.

Johnson, T.P., Aschkenasy, J.R., Herbers, M.R., & Gillenwater, S.A. (1996). Self-reported risk factors for AIDS among homeless youth. *AIDS Education and Prevention, 8*(4), 308–322.

Jongbloed-Schurig, U. (1997). Schicksale pathologischer identifizienrungen in der Adoleszenz von Madchen. *Zeitschrift fur Psychoanalytische Theorie und Praxis, 12*(1) 58–73.

Karp, S.A., Silber, D.E., Holmstrom, R.W., & Stock, L.J. (1995). Personality of rape survivors as a group and by relation of survivor to perpetrator. *Journal of Clinical Psychology, 51*(5), 587–593.

Keel, P.K., Fulkerson, J.A., & Leon, G.R. (1997). Disordered eating precursors in pre- and adolescent girls and boys. *Journal of Youth and Adolescence, 26*(2), 203–216.

Koff, E., & Rierdan, J. (1993). Advanced pubertal development and eating disturbance in early adolescent girls. *Journal of Adolescent Health, 14*(6), 433–439.

Kunawararak, P., Beyrer, C., Natpratan, C., & Feng, W. (1995). The epidemiology of HIV and syphilis among male commercial sex workers in Northern Thailand. *AIDS, 9*(5), 517–521.

Landen, M., Walinder, J., & Lundstrom, B. (1996). Incidence and sex ratio of transsexualism in Sweden. *Acta Psychiatrica Scandinavica, 93*(4), 261–263.

Leitenberg, H., Detzer, M.J., & Srebyik, D. (1993). Gender differences in masturbation and the relation of masturbation experience in preadolescence and/or early adolescence to sexual behavior and sexual adjustment in young adulthood. *Archives of Sexual Behavior, 22*(2), 87–98.

Leon, G.R., Fulkerson, J.A., Perry, C.L., & Cudeck, R. (1993). Personality and behavioral vulnerabilities associated with risk status for eating disorders in adolescent girls. *Journal of Abnormal Psychology, 102*(3), 438–444.

Lief, H.I., & Kaplan, H.S. (1986). Ego-dystonic homosexuality. *Journal of Sex and Martial Therapy, 12,* 259–266.

Lindemalm, G., Korlin, D., & Uddenberg, N. (1986). Long-term follow-up of "sex change" in 13 male-to-female transsexuals. *Archives of Sexual Behavior, 15,* 187–210.

Logan, D.D. (1980). The menarche experience in twenty-three foreign countries. *Adolescence, 15,* 253–256.

Lowenstein, L.F. (1992). The psychology of the obsessive compulsive. *Criminologist, 16*(4), 26–38.

Lundervoid, D.A., & Young, L.G. (1992). Treatment acceptability ratings for sexual offenders. *Research in Developmental Disabilities, 13*(3), 229–237.

Lundy, M., & Rekers, G.A. (1995a). Homosexuality in adolescence: Interventions. In G.A. Rekers (Ed.), *Handbook of child and adolescent sexual problems* (pp. 341–377). New York: Lexington Books.

Lundy, M., & Rekers, G.A. (1995b). Homosexuality: Development, risks, parental values and controversies. In G.A. Rekers (Ed.), *Handbook of child and adolescent sexual problems* (pp. 290–312). New York: Lexington Books.

Lundy, M., & Rekers, G.A. (1995c). Homosexuality: Presentation, evaluation and clinical decision making. In G.A. Rekers (Ed.), *Handbook of child and adolescent sexual problems* (pp. 313–340). New York: Lexington Books.

MacCulloch, M.J., Williams, C., & Birtles, C.J. (1971). The successful application of aversion therapy to an adolescent exhibitionist. *Journal of Behavior Therapy and Experimental Psychiatry, 2,* 61–66.

MacDonald, A.P., Jr. (1985). Reactions to issues concerning sexual orientations, identities, preferences, and choices. *Journal of Homosexuality, 10,* 23–27.

MacNamara, D.E.J., & Sergrin, E. (1977). *Sex, crime, and the law.* New York: Free Press.

Mayekiso, T.V., & Twaise, N. (1993). Assessment of parental involvement in imparting sexual knowledge to adolescents. *South African Journal of Psychology, 23*(1), 21–23.

Mazur, T., & Cherpak, R.L. (1995). Psychologic issues of adjustment in precocious, normal, delayed, and incongruent puberty. In G.A. Rekers (Ed.), *Handbook of child and adolescent sexual problems* (pp. 55–80). New York: Lexington Books.

Mazur, T., & Dobson, K. (1995). Psychologic issues in individuals with genetic, hormonal, and anatomic anomalies of the sexual system: Review and treatment considerations. In G.A. Rekers (Ed.), *Handbook of child and adolescent sexual problems* (pp. 101–131). New York: Lexington Books.

McConaghy, N. (1975). Aversive and positive conditioning treatments of homosexuality. *Behavior Research and Therapy, 13,* 309–319.

McDowell, J. (1987). *How to help your child say "no" to sexual pressure.* Waco, TX: Word Books.

Meyer, J.K., & Reter, D.J. (1979). Sex reassignment: Follow-up. *Archives of General Psychiatry, 36,* 1010–1015.

Moberly, E. (1983). *Psychogenesis.* Boston: Routledge & Kegan Paul.

Myers, W.C. (1994). Sexual homicide by adolescents. *Journal of the American Academy of Child and Adolescent Psychiatry, 33*(7), 962–969.

Myers, W.C., Scott, K., Burgess, A.W., & Burgess, A.G. (1995). Psychopathology, biopsychosocial factors, crime characteristics and classification of 25 homicidal youths. *Journal of the American Academy of Child and Adolescent Psychiatry, 34*(11), 1483–1489.

Neumark, S.D., Story, M., French, S.A., & Resnick, M.D. (1997). Psychosocial correlates of health-compromising behaviors among adolescents. *Health Education Research, 12*(1), 37–52.

Nicholosi, J. (1991). *Reparative therapy of male homosexuality.* Northvale, NJ: Aronson.

O'Donohue, W., McKay, J.S., & Schewe, P.A. (1996). Sexual abuse. *Journal of Research and Treatment, 8*(2), 133–141.

Pattison, E.M., & Pattison, M.L. (1980). Ex-gays: Religiously mediated change in homosexuals. *American Journal of Psychiatry, 137,* 1553–1562.

Pauly, I.B. (1974a). Female transsexualism: Part I. *Archives of Sexual Behavior, 3,* 487–507.

Pauly, I.B. (1974b). Female transsexualism: Part II. *Archives of Sexual Behavior, 3,* 509–526.

Petersen, A.C., & Taylor, B. (1980). The biological approach to adolescence. In J. Adelson (Ed.), *Handbook of adolescent psychology* (pp. 117–155). New York: Wiley.

Petty, D.L. (1995). Sex education toward the prevention of sexual problems. In G.A. Rekers (Ed.), *Handbook of child and adolescent sexual problems* (pp. 31–51). New York: Lexington Books.

Phillips, G., & Over, R. (1995). Differences between heterosexual, bisexual, and lesbian women in recalled childhood experiences. *Archives of Sexual Behavior, 24*(1), 1–20.

Poitras, M., & Lavoie, F. (1995). A study of the prevalence of sexual coercion in adolescent heterosexual dating relationships in a Quebec sample. *Violence and Victims, 10*(4), 299–313.

Raboch, J.J., Zverina, J., Raboch, J., & Sindlar, M. (1994). Masturbacni chovani dospivajicion. *Cesko Slovenska Pschiatrie, 90*(2), 97–100.

Radkowsky, M., & Siegel, L.J. (1997). The gay adolescent: Stressors, adaptations, and psychosocial interventions. *Clinical Psychology Review, 17*(2), 191–216.

Regan, P.C. (1996). Sexual outcasts: The perceived impact of body weight and gender on sexuality. *Journal of Applied Social Psychology, 26*(20), 1803–1815.

Rekers, G.A. (1984). Adolescent sexuality and family well-being. In *Hearings before the Subcommittee on*

Family and Human Services, Committee on Labor and Human Resources, United States Senate, on parental involvement with their adolescents in crisis. Washington, DC: U.S. Government Printing Office.

Rekers, G.A. (1992). Development of problems in puberty and sex roles in adolescence. In C.E. Walker & M.C. Roberts (Eds.), *Handbook of clinical child psychology* (2nd ed., pp. 606–622). New York: Wiley.

Rekers, G.A. (1995a). Assessment and treatment methods for gender identity disorder and transvestism. In G.A. Rekers (Ed.), *Handbook of child and adolescent sexual problems* (pp. 272–289). New York: Lexington Books.

Rekers, G.A. (1995b). Early detection and treatment of sexual problems. In G.A. Rekers (Ed.), *Handbook of child and adolescent sexual problems* (pp. 3–31). New York: Lexington Books.

Rekers, G.A. (Ed.). (1995c). *Handbook of child and adolescent sexual problems.* New York: Lexington Books.

Rekers, G.A. (1996). *Susan Smith: Victim or murderer.* Lakewood, CO: Glenbridge.

Rekers, G.A. (1997). Escaping the bondage of early environment. In R. McQuilkin (Ed.), *Free and fulfilled* (pp. 166–183). Nashville, TN: Thomas Nelson.

Rekers, G.A. (1998). The development of homosexual orientation. In C. Wolfe (Ed.), *Homosexuality and American public life* (pp. 62–84). Dallas, TX: Spence.

Rekers, G.A., Bentler, P.M., Rosen, A.C., & Lovaas, O.I. (1977). Child gender disturbances. *Psychotherapy: Theory, Research and Practice, 14,* 2–11.

Rekers, G.A., & Hohn, R. (1998). Sex education. In J. Sears & J. Carper (Eds.), *Curriculum, religion, and public education* (pp. 139–160). New York: Teachers College Press.

Rekers, G.A., & Jurich, A.P. (1983). Development of problems of puberty and sex-roles in adolescence. In C.E. Walker & M.C. Roberts (Eds.), *Handbook of clinical child psychology* (pp. 785–812). New York: Wiley.

Rekers, G.A., & Kilgus, M.D. (1995). Differential diagnosis and rationale for treatment of gender identity disorders and transvestism. In G.A. Rekers (Ed.), *Handbook of child and adolescent sexual problems* (pp. 255–271). New York: Lexington Books.

Rekers, G.A., & Kilgus, M.D. (1997). Cross-sex behavior problems. In R.A. Hoekelman, S.B. Friedman, N.M. Nelson, H.M. Seidel, M.L. Weitzman, & M.E.H. Wilson (Eds.), *Primary pediatric care* (3rd ed., pp. 718–721). St Louis, MO: Mosby.

Rekers, G.A., & Kilgus, M.D. (1998). Practical issues in the diagnosis and treatment of gender identity disorders in children and adolescents. In L. VandeCreek (Ed.), *Innovations in clinical practice: A source book* (pp. 127–141). Sarasota, FL: Professional Resources Press.

Rekers, G.A., Kilgus, M.D., & Rosen, A.C. (1990). Long-term effects of treatment for childhood gender

disturbance. *Journal of Psychology and Human Sexuality, 3*(2), 121–153.

Rekers, G.A., & Mead, S.L. (1979). Early intervention for female sexual identity disturbances. *Journal of Abnormal Child Psychology, 7,* 405–423.

Rekers, G.A., & Mead, S.L. (1980). Female sex-role deviance. *Journal of Clinical Child Psychology, 8,* 199–203.

Rekers, G.A., & Morey, S.M. (1989a). Personality problems associated with childhood gender disturbance. *Italian Journal of Clinical Psychology, 1,* 85–90.

Rekers, G.A., & Morey, S.M. (1989b). Relationship of maternal report of feminine behavior and extroversion to the severity of gender disturbance. *Perceptual and Motor Skills, 69,* 387–394.

Rekers, G.A., & Morey, S.M. (1989c). Sex-typed body movements as a function of severity of gender disturbance in boys. *Journal of Psychology and Human Sexuality, 2,* 183–196.

Rekers G.A., & Morey, S.M. (1990). The relationship of measures of sex-typed play with clinician ratings on degree of gender disturbance. *Journal of Clinical Psychology, 46,* 28–34.

Rekers, G.A., Sanders, J.A., Rasbury, W.C., Strauss, C.C., & Morey, S.M. (1989). Differentiation of adolescent activity participation. *Journal of Genetic Psychology, 150,* 323–335.

Richardson, G., Kelly, T.P., & Graham, F. (1997). Group differences in abuser and abuse characteristics in a British sample of sexually abusive adolescents. *Sexual Abuse Journal of Research and Treatment, 9*(3), 239–257.

Riva, G. (1996). The role of emotional and socio-cognitive patterns in obesity. *Psychological Reports, 79*(1), 35–46.

Robinson, T.N., Killen, J.D., Litt, I.F., & Hammer, L.D. (1996). Ethnicity and body dissatisfaction. *Journal of Adolescent Health, 19*(6), 384–393.

Rodriguez, T.H., Bariaud, F., Cohen-Zardi, M.F., & Delmas, C. (1993). The effects of pubertal changes on body image and relations with peers of the opposite sex in adolescence. *Journal of Adolescence, 16*(3), 421, 428.

Rosen, A.C., Rekers, G.A., & Bentler, P.M. (1978). Ethical issues in the treatment of children. *Journal of Social Issues, 34,* 122–136.

Rotheram-Borus, M.J., Reid, H., Rosario, M., & Kasen, S. (1995). Determinants of safer sex patterns among gay/bisexual male adolescents. *Journal of Adolescence, 18*(1), 3–15.

Saghir, M.T., & Robins, E. (1973). *Male and female homosexuality.* Baltimore: Williams & Wilkins.

Sanders, G.L. (1996). Recovering from paraphilla. *Journal of Child and Youth Care, 11*(1), 43–54.

Saunders, E.B., & Awad, G.A. (1991). Male adolescent sexual offenders. *Child Psychiatry and Human Development, 21*(3), 169–178.

Schmidt, U., Evans, K., & Treasure, J. (1995). Puberty, sexual milestones and abuse. *Psychological Medicine, 25*(2), 413–417.

Schumm, W.R. (1995). Nonmarital heterosexual behavior. In G.A. Rekers (Ed.), *Handbook of child and adolescent sexual problems* (pp. 381–423). New York: Lexington Books.

Schuster, M.A., Bell, R.M., & Kanouse, D.E. (1996). The sexual practices of adolescent virgins. *American Journal of Public Health, 86*(11), 1570–1576.

Seibert, J.M., & Olson, R.A. (Eds.). (1989). *Children, adolescents, and AIDS.* Lincoln: University of Nebraska Press.

Serbin, L.A. (1980). Sex-role socialization. In B.B. Lahey & A.E. Kazdin (Eds.), *Advances in clinical child psychology* (Vol. 3, pp. 41–96). New York: Plenum Press.

Sharma, V., Sharma, A., Dave, S., & Chauhan, F. (1996). Sexual behavior of adolescent boys. *Sexual and Marital Therapy, 11*(2), 147–151.

Shisslak, C.M., Crago, M., & Yates, A. (1989). Typical patterns in atypical anorexia nervosa. *Psychosomatics, 30*, 307–311.

Simon, A. (1989). Promiscuity as sex difference. *Psychological Reports, 64*, 802.

Sinnema, G. (1986). The development of independence in chronically ill adolescents. *International Journal of Adolescent Medicine and Health, 2*, 1–14.

Slap, G.B., Khalid, N., Paikoff, R.L., & Brooks-Gunn, J. (1994). Evolving self-image, pubertal manifestations, and pubertal hormones. *Journal of Adolescent Health, 15*(3), 327–325.

Slosarz, W. (1992). Masturbation fixation and the problem of adaptation to heterosexual partnerships. *Sexual and Marital Therapy, 7*(3), 275–281.

Smith, J. (1985). The treatment of ego-dystonic homosexuality. *Journal of the American Academy of Psychoanalysis, 13*, 299–412.

Snow, B., & Sorensen, T. (1990). Ritualistic child abuse in a neighborhood setting. *Journal of Interpersonal Violence, 5*(4), 474–487.

Socarides, C.W. (1988). Sexual politics and scientific logic. In P.F. Fagan (Ed.), *Hope for homosexuality* (pp. 46–64). Washington, DC: Free Congress Foundation.

Steen, S.N., Wadden, T.A., Foster, G.D., & Andersen, R.E. (1996). Are obese adolescent boys ignoring an important health risk? *International Journal of Eating Disorders, 20*(3), 281–286.

Steiger, H. (1989). Anorexia nervosa and bulimia in males. *Canadian Journal of Psychiatry, 34*, 419–424.

Stein, J.H., & Reiser, L.W. (1994). A study of White middle-class adolescent boys' responses to "semenarche." *Journal of Youth and Adolescence, 23*(3), 373–384.

Steinberg, L. (1987). Impact of puberty on family relations. *Developmental Psychology, 23*, 451–460.

Stirt, S.S. (1940). Overt mass masturbation in the classroom. *American Journal of Orthopsychiatry, 40*, 801–804.

Stoller, R.J. (1975). *Sex and gender.* New York: Aronson.

Stoller, R.J. (1978). Boyhood gender aberrations: Treatment issues. *Journal of the American Psychoanalytic Association, 26*, 541–558.

Striegel-Moore, R. (1995). Psychological factors in the etiology of binge eating. *Addictive Behaviors, 20*(6), 713–723.

Sullivan, T.R. (1996). The challenge of HIV prevention among high-risk adolescents. *Health and Social Work, 21*(1), 58–66.

Sussman, T., & Duffy, M. (1996). Are we forgetting about gay male adolescents in AIDS-related research and prevention? *Youth and Society, 27*(3), 379–393.

Swarr, A.E., & Richards, M.H. (1996). Longitudinal effects of adolescent girls' pubertal development, perceptions of pubertal timing, and parental relations on eating problems. *Developmental Psychology, 32*(4), 636–646.

Tanner, J.M. (1974). Sequence and tempo in the somatic changes in puberty. In M.M. Grumbach, G.D. Grave, & F.E. Mayer (Eds.), *Control of the onset of puberty.* New York: Wiley.

Thompson, J.K., Coovert, M.D., Richards, K.J., & Johnson, S. (1995). Development of body image, eating disturbance, and general psychological functioning in female adolescents. *International Journal of Eating Disorders, 18*(3), 221–236.

Tremble, B. (1993). Prostitution and survival: Interviews with gay street youth. *Canadian Journal of Human Sexuality, 2*(1), 39–45.

Trepper, T.S., & Barrett, M.J. (1986). *Treating incest.* New York: Haworth Press.

Tucker, S.K. (1989). Adolescent patterns of communication about sexually related topics. *Adolescence, 24*, 269–278.

Uchiyama, A. (1989). A study of juvenile victims sexually abused. *Reports of National Research Institute of Police Science, 30*(2), 151–164.

Uzark, K.C., Becker, M.H., Dielman, T.E., & Rocchini, A.P. (1988). Perceptions held by obese children and their parents. *Health Education Quarterly, 15*(2), 185–198.

Vass, J.J., & Gold, S.R. (1995). Effects of feedback on emotion in hypermasculine males. *Violence and Victims, 10*(3), 217–226.

Veenhuizen, A.M., Van Strien, D.C., & Cohen-Kettenis, P.T. (1992). The combined psychotherapeutic and lithium carbonate treatment of an adolescent with exhibitionism and indecent assault. *Journal of Psychology and Human Sexuality, 5*(3), 53–64.

Vicary, J.R., Klingaman, L.R., & Harkness, W.L. (1995). Risk factors associated with date rape and sexual assault of adolescent girls. *Journal of Adolescence, 18*(3), 289–306.

Wadsworth, J., Hickman, M., Johnson, A.M., & Wellings, K. (1996). Geographic variation in sexual behavior in Britain. *AIDS, 10*(2), 193–199.

Warzak, W.J., Kuhn, B.R., & Nolten, P.W. (1995). Obstacles to the sexual adjustment of children and adolescents with disabilities. In G.A. Rekers (Ed.), *Handbook of child and adolescent sexual problems* (pp. 81–100). New York: Lexington Books.

Weinberg, M.S., Williams, C.J., & Calhan, C. (1995). "If the shoe fits . . .": Exploring male homosexual foot fetishism. *Journal of Sex Research, 32*(1), 17–27.

Whitam, F.L., & Mathy, R.M. (1991). Childhood cross-gender behavior of homosexual females in Brazil, Peru, the Philippines, and the United States. *Archives of Sexual Behavior, 20*(2), 151–170.

Widom, C.S., & Kuhns, J.B. (1996). Childhood victimization and subsequent risk for promiscuity, prostitution and teenage pregnancy: A prospective study. *American Journal of Public Health, 36*(11), 1607–1612.

Wierson, M., Long, P.J., & Forehand, R.L. (1993). Toward a new understanding of early menarche. *Adolescence, 22*(112), 913–924.

Wilson, E.D. (1988). *Counseling and homosexuality.* Waco, TX: Word Books.

Winters, K.C., Remafedi, G., & Chan, B.Y. (1996). Assessing drug abuse among gay-bisexual young men. *Psychology of Addictive Behaviors, 10*(4), 228–236.

Woods, P. (1993). Overview of an adolescent sadistic sex offender. *Issues in Criminological and Legal Psychology, 19,* 33–36.

Zucker, K.J., Bradley, S.J., Oliver, G.D., Blake, J., Fleming, S., & Hood, J. (1996). Psychosexual development of women with congenital adrenal hyperplasia. *Hormones and Behavior, 30,* 300–318.

Zuger, B. (1978). Effeminate behavior present in boys from childhood: Ten additional years of follow-up. *Comprehensive Psychiatry, 19,* 363–369.Zuger, B. (1989). Homosexuality in families of boys with early effeminate behavior. *Archives of Sexual Behavior, 18,* 155–166.

Zuger, B. (1989) Homosexuality in families of boys with early effeminate behavior. *Archives of Sexual Behavior, 18,* 155–166.

CHAPTER 35

Treatment of Eating Disorders in Adolescents

DAVID M. GARNER AND DECLAN BARRY

The increased recognition of eating disorders among adolescent and young adult women as well as the dangerous physical and psychological consequences of eating disorders have resulted in a rapid increase in theoretical formulations and research involving pathogenesis and treatment. This research has led to a divergence in etiological viewpoints as well as a convergence of opinion with regard to the usefulness of practical intervention strategies. Although current knowledge has yet to lend support for any one theoretical viewpoint, one of the most enduring theoretical orientations for understanding eating disorders has been a risk-factor model that accounts for the development and maintenance of symptoms through the interaction of cultural, biological, and psychological predisposing factors (Garner & Garfinkel, 1980). According to the risk-factor model, these features are manifested differently within the context of a heterogeneous patient population (Garfinkel & Garner, 1982). This heterogeneity must be appreciated to fully understand and to competently treat this group of patients.

The aim of this chapter is to first provide background regarding diagnostic and prevalence of eating disorders in adolescents and then to discuss the risk-factor model, including major cultural, biological, and psychological factors that have been hypothesized to predispose to eating disorders. This is followed by an overview of the major perpetuating factors that need to be understood in treating eating disorders. Finally, empirically supported treatments, including family therapy, cognitive-behavioral, interpersonal, and pharmacological therapies, are discussed along with a rationale for integrating and sequencing interventions.

DIAGNOSIS

ANOREXIA NERVOSA

The current requirements for a diagnosis of anorexia nervosa according to the *Diagnostic and Statistical Manual of Mental Disorders*, (*DSM-IV*; American Psychiatric Association [APA], 1994) are summarized as follows: (1) refusal to maintain a body weight over a minimally normal weight for age and height; (2) intense fear of gaining weight or becoming fat, even though underweight; (3) disturbance in the way body weight, size, or shape is experienced; and (4) amenorrhea in females (absence of at least three consecutive menstrual cycles). The *DSM-IV* suggests that weight loss leading to maintenance of a body weight 15% below norms and failure to achieve expected weight gain during a period of growth are also indicative of anorexia nervosa. The failure to achieve expected weight gain during a period of growth is particularly important in addressing anorexia nervosa in adolescents whose growth and development may have been interrupted by the onset of their disorder. Severe dieting because of a fear of fatness has been shown to lead to short-stature syndrome and delayed puberty in a subgroup of young children (Puglifse, Lifshitz, Grad, Fort, & Marks-Katz, 1983). Weight loss or active weight suppression may lead to a cessation of normal growth and menstruation as well as osteoporosis, scoliosis and vulnerability to fractures, and stunting of growth (Grinspoon, Herzog, & Klibanski, 1997; Warren, Brooks-Gunn, Hamilton, Warren, & Hamilton, 1986).

The *DSM-IV* (APA, 1994) divides anorexia nervosa into two diagnostic subtypes: restricting type and binge eating/purging type. The restricting type is defined by rigid restriction of food intake without bingeing or purging. The binge eating/purging type is defined by stringent attempts to limit intake, punctuated by episodes of binge eating as well as self-induced vomiting and/or laxative abuse. This diverges from previous conventions in which anorexia nervosa was subdivided simply on the basis of the presence or absence of binge eating. The rationale for dividing anorexia nervosa patients on the basis of bingeing *and* purging rather than binge eating alone rests on two observations. First, there are significant medical risks associated with compensatory behaviors such as self-induced vomiting and laxative abuse. Second, recent research has indicated that patients who purge, even if they do not engage in objective episodes of binge eating, display significantly more psychosocial disturbance than nonpurging patients (Garner, Garner, & Rosen, 1993). Patients who regularly engage in bulimic episodes report greater impulsivity, social/sexual dysfunction, substance abuse, general impulse control problems (e.g., lying and stealing), family dysfunction, and depression as part of a general picture of more conspicuous emotional disturbance when compared to patients with the restricting subtype of anorexia nervosa (Garner et al., 1993). In contrast, restricting anorexia nervosa patients have been described as being overly compliant but at the same time obstinate, perfectionistic, obsessive-compulsive, shy, introverted, interpersonally sensitive, and stoical.

BULIMIA NERVOSA

The criteria for diagnosis of bulimia nervosa according to the *DSM-IV* (APA, 1994) are summarized as follows: (1) recurrent episodes of binge eating (a sense of lack of control over eating a large amount of food in a discrete period of time, which would be considered unusual under similar circumstances); (2) recurrent inappropriate compensatory behavior(s) to prevent weight gain (e.g., vomiting; abuse of laxatives, diuretics, or other medications; fasting or excessive exercise); (3) a minimum average of two episodes of binge eating and inappropriate compensatory behaviors per week for the past three months; (4) self-evaluation unduly influenced by body shape and weight; and (5) the disturbance does not occur exclusively during episodes of anorexia nervosa. Bulimia nervosa patients are further divided into purging and nonpurging subtypes based on the regular use of self-induced vomiting, laxatives, or diuretics (APA, 1994). Although binge eating is the key symptom identifying bulimia nervosa, agreement has not been reached on the definition of this behavior in the disorder. For example, the requirement that binges must be "large" is inconsistent with research indicating that a significant proportion of "binges" reported by bulimia nervosa patients involve small amounts of food (cf. Garner, Shafer, & Rosen, 1992).

EATING DISORDERS NOT OTHERWISE SPECIFIED

The *DSM-IV* (APA, 1994) delineates a large and heterogeneous diagnostic category, eating disorder, not otherwise specified (EDNOS), for individuals with clinically significant eating disorders who fail to meet all of the diagnostic criteria for anorexia nervosa or bulimia nervosa. However, the specific terminology of this diagnostic category may result in misinterpretations regarding the clinical significance of such eating problems, as they may mistakenly be perceived as being of less importance. This view is inaccurate, as the clinical picture for individuals diagnosed with EDNOS can be as highly complex and serious as those who meet the diagnostic criteria for anorexia nervosa and bulimia nervosa (Walsh & Garner, 1997).

BINGE EATING DISORDER

Binge eating disorder (BED) is included in the *DSM-IV* as a category requiring further study. Although there is merit in adopting BED into the diagnostic nomenclature, it is critical to remain aware of the fact that binge eating and associated psychological symptoms, particularly in the obese, may be attributed to standard weight loss treatments (cf. Garner & Wooley, 1991). BED has been proposed to apply to individuals who suffer from serious distress or impairment as a result of binge eating, but who do not qualify for a diagnosis of bulimia nervosa because they do not regularly engage in inappropriate compensatory behaviors such as self-induced vomiting and the abuse of laxatives and/or medications. Despite those differences, individuals who fit into the separate *DSM-IV* categories also share many common features, especially pertaining to the degree of emphasis placed on body weight in self-assessment.

The *DSM-IV* criteria in qualifying for BED diagnosis include the following: (1) eating a quantity of food that most people would consider large under similar circumstances within a specific period of time, which is associated with (2) a sense of loss of control with regard to eating behavior. Additionally, it must occur within the context of three of the five subsequent items: (1) eating quickly, (2) eating beyond the point of satiety, (3) eating for reasons other than physical hunger, (4) eating in isolation due to self-consciousness regarding the quantity of food consumed, or (5) experiencing self-depreciating, depressive, or guilty feelings after overeating. Marked distress as a result of binge eating must be present, and the binge eating should occur for two days per week for a duration of six months (APA, 1994).

Relationship among Different Eating Disorders

There is extraordinary variability within each of the diagnostic subgroups in terms of demographic, clinical, and psychological variables (Welch, Hall, & Renner, 1990). Patients with anorexia and bulimia nervosa have been observed to move between diagnostic categories at different points in time (Russell, 1979). For example, patients move between the two subtypes of anorexia nervosa (restricting and binge eating/purging types); however, the tendency is for restricters to move toward bulimia (and purging) more often than bulimic anorexics move to an exclusively abstaining mode (Garner et al., 1993). Kreipe, Churchill, and Strauss (1989) reported that whereas only 6 of 49 adolescent anorexia nervosa patients (13%) had a

history of binge eating before hospitalization, 22 (45%) initiated the symptom during the mean 6.5-year follow-up period. Diminishing the probability of binge eating developing is one aim of treatment.

Even though distinctions among diagnostic subgroups have been emphasized in the research literature, it is important to recognize that these subgroups tend to share many features in common. For example, even though anorexia nervosa patients are differentiated into restricter and binge eating/purging subtypes, it must be remembered that virtually all eating disorder patients restrict their food intake, diet, and probably fast for abnormally long periods of time. Some do this in association with binge eating, some with vomiting and/or purgation, and some with none of these symptoms. For some, this occurs at a statistically normal body weight (bulimia nervosa), and for others, it occurs well over the body weight norms (e.g., BED).

Differential Diagnosis

Patients without anorexia nervosa, bulimia nervosa, or some variant can superficially resemble patients with an eating disorder diagnosis. Patients with a severe affective disorder can display marked weight loss (due to loss of appetite) or hyperphagia. Schizophrenia can present with an aversion to eating and occasionally binge eating or purging. Vomiting and weight loss also can be associated with what has been described as a conversion disorder (Garfinkel, Garner, Kaplan, Rodin, & Kennedy, 1983). A range of physical illnesses producing weight loss (e.g. inflammatory bowel disease, chronic hepatitis, Addison's disease, Crohn's disease, undiagnosed cystic fibrosis, diabetes mellitus, hyperthyroidism, tuberculosis, malignancies, malabsorption diseases, or other wasting diseases) should be ruled out as the primary diagnosis (Powers, 1997).

Childhood Eating Disorders

Case reports of anorexia nervosa in young children exist (Fosson, Knibbs, Bryant-Waugh, & Lask, 1987), but there is agreement that it is very rare in this age group (Jaffe & Singer, 1989). However, many children present with subclinical variants of eating disorders that fail to meet the strict *DSM-IV* criteria (Bryant-Waugh & Lask, 1995). Whereas cases of anorexia nervosa in prepubertal children have been well documented, the occurrence of bulimia nervosa in this group is very rare (Lask & Bryant-Waugh, 1997). Lask and Bryant-Waugh delineate childhood eating problems and disorders that have been well researched but that are not included in the *DSM-IV* or *ICD-10*, including food avoidance emotional disorder (Higgs, Goodyer, & Birch, 1989), selective eating (Lask & Bryant-Waugh, 1997), and pervasive refusal syndrome (Lask, Britten, Kroll, Magagna, & Tranter, 1991). Food avoidance emotional disorder comprises a cluster of symptoms including food avoidance and affective symptoms, such as anxiety and depression, and may represent a childhood partial syndrome of anorexia nervosa. Children diagnosed with selective eating tend to prefer a very restrictive range of food that is often carbohydrate-based, and often demonstrate deficits in social but not physical functioning. Pervasive refusal syndrome may be life-threatening and is characterized by a refusal to eat, drink, walk, or engage in activities that are basic to survival and growth.

INCIDENCE AND PREVALENCE

Incidence rates are defined as the number of new cases in the population per year; prevalence rates refers to the actual number of cases in the population at a certain point in time. Data on incidence and prevalence rates of eating disorders have been limited, as many estimates have been derived exclusively from self-report instruments and on samples that may not reflect demographic differences in base rates. Estimates of incidence based on detected cases in primary care practices yielded rates of 8.1 per 100,000 persons per year for anorexia nervosa and 11.5 for bulimia nervosa (Hoek et al., 1995). The most sophisticated prevalence studies using strict diagnostic criteria report rates of about 0.3% for anorexia nervosa and about 1% for bulimia nervosa among young females in the community (Fairburn & Beglin, 1990; Hoek, 1993). This compares to surveys using questionnaires that find that as many as 19% of female students reporting bulimic symptoms. Nonetheless, there is consensus that anorexia nervosa and bulimia nervosa occur in 1% to 4% of female high school and college students (cf. Fairburn & Beglin, 1990; Kreipe, 1995). Subclinical variants of eating disorders are represented in

certain subgroups, where there is increased pressure to diet or maintain a thin shape. Research demonstrates a high incidence of suspected and actual cases among ballet dancers, professional dancers, wrestlers, swimmers, skaters, and gymnasts (cf. Garner, Rosen, & Berry, 1998).

RISK FACTORS FOR EATING DISORDERS

PREDISPOSING FACTORS

A comprehensive understanding of anorexia and bulimia nervosa involves examining those factors that predispose individuals to each of the eating disorders, and theory should be able to depict the range of developmental experiences that interact with those factors to initiate symptom expression and the maintaining variables (biological, psychological, and interpersonal) in their various clinical presentations. Although the current models fail to stipulate these features in detail, the quality and quantity of research and clinical observations have augmented the understanding of eating disorders, resulting in more specific treatment recommendations.

In the past few decades, the conceptualization of eating disorders as multidetermined has taken the place of single-factor causal theories (Garner, 1993). Symptomatic patterns denote the final common pathways resulting from the interchange of the three broad categories of predisposing factors depicted in Figure 35.1. This model stipulates that cultural, individual (psychological and biological), and familial causal factors interact with each other in various ways, leading to the development of eating disorders. Less is known about the precipitating factors, except that dieting is customarily an early element. The most useful advancements in treatment have been derived from a heightened appreciation of the perpetuating effects of starvation with its psychological, emotional, and physical consequences.

CULTURAL FACTORS

A complete understanding of eating disorders requires attention to the cultural forces selectively impinging on young girls and women over the past several decades. One of the most pernicious has been the intense pressure to diet and to engage in

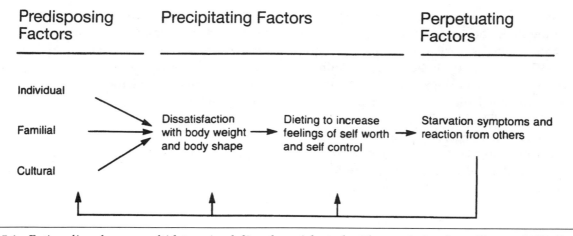

Figure 35.1   Eating disorders as multidetermined disorders. Adapted with permission from Garner, 1997. Copyright 1997 by Guilford Press.

strict weight control to meet unrealistic standards for thinness (Garner, Garfinkel, Schwartz, & Thompson, 1980). Young women today are totally immersed in the cultural admiration of a physical form for women that has little to do with the actual shape of most women in our society. The disconcerting result is a norm for which women report being dissatisfied with their shapes and feeling guilty about eating even reasonable amounts of food. A strong concern about physical appearance seems to predate the onset of eating disorders (Rastam, 1992). Research has shown that dieting to lose weight and fear of fatness are common in girls as young as 7 years old; these attitudes and behaviors escalate significantly during adolescence, particularly among those at the heavier end of the weight spectrum (Button, Loan, Davies, & Sonuga-Barke, 1997; Edlund, Halvarsson, & Sjödén, 1995). It has been shown that the risk of developing an eating disorder is eight times higher in dieting than in nondieting 15-year-old girls (Patton, Johnson-Sabine, Wood, Mann, & Wakeling, 1990). In Western culture, those exposed to more pressure to diet, such as athletes participating in sports that emphasize leanness for performance or appearance, are at greater risk of eating disorders (Garner et al., 1998).

In 1990, 44% of female high school students were trying to lose weight, compared to 15% of male students (Serdula et al., 1993). An additional 26% of female students and 15% of male students were trying to keep from gaining more weight. In a study of 1,410 students in grades 9 through 12 (mean age 16.5 years), Timmerman, Wells, and Chen (1990) reported that 2% of the girls and .14% of the boys

met all of the diagnostic criteria for bulimia nervosa ascertained through an anonymous self-report instrument. In a more recent study of 140 children age 7 to 12 years, Tiggemann and Wilson-Barrett (1998) found that, regardless of age, girls reported their current figure as substantially larger than their ideal figure, whereas boys reported no significant difference between ideal and current figure ratings. Body weight concerns have been reported in children age 8 to 12 in the United States, Israel, and Australia (Rolland, Farnill, & Griffiths, 1997). It has been increasingly recognized that dieting can play a direct role in causing a range of symptoms, including binge eating and mood disturbances (Garner, 1997). The values surrounding slenderness have become sufficiently embedded in our cultural value system that many of the symptoms required for eating disorders are not viewed as unusual or abnormal by members of the general public (Huon, Brown, & Morris, 1988). Although traditionally it was believed that eating disorders were culture-specific to White, middle-class women (Silber, 1986), more recent studies have documented eating problems and disorders in minority populations (e.g., Smith & Krejci, 1991; Story, Hauck, Broussard, White, & Resnick, 1994). In North America, disordered eating patterns appear to be equally common among Caucasian and Hispanic females, less common among Black and Asian females, and most common among Native Americans (Crago, Shisslak, & Estes, 1996). Evans, Dolan, and Toriola (1997), among others, have drawn attention to intra- and cross-cultural methodological considerations in measuring eating attitudes and behaviors. Increasing Westernization and globalization has been implicated in the development of eating disorders in non-Western countries (Abou-Saleh, Younis, & Karim, 1998). There is even some evidence that eating disorders may have developed a positive social stereotype and, in some instances, may be spread by social contagion (Bruch, 1973; Chiodo & Latimer, 1983).

Recognition of the impact of cultural factors on norms related to dieting and weight control has led to the conclusion that eating disorders may develop in those without underlying personality disturbances or family dysfunction, although secondary disruption in both of these areas may be present by the time the person presents for an assessment (Garner, 1997). Much of current psychological theorizing related to eating disorders may be criticized for not accounting for these cultural factors or, when they are mentioned, not specifying the details of how they must be integrated into the understanding of the psychology of the disorder. In the case of ethnic minorities and immigrants in the United States, the notion of Westernization could be more usefully operationalized in terms of ethnic identity, acculturation, and self-construal (Barry, 1997).

Athletes exposed to more pressure to diet by participating in sports that emphasize leanness for performance or appearance, are at greater risk of eating disorders (Garner et al., 1998).

INDIVIDUAL FACTORS

During the past decade, there has been intense interest in the relationship between eating disorders and personality disorders. A number of recent reports have indicated that almost two-thirds of eating disordered patients receive a concurrent diagnosis of personality disorder, with borderline personality disorder being reported as particularly common (Bulik, Sullivan, Joyce, & Carter, 1995; Cooper et al., 1988; Gillberg, Rastam, & Gillberg, 1995; Johnson, Tobin, & Dennis, 1990; Levin & Hyler, 1986). Levin and Hyler (1986) assessed 24 bulimia nervosa patients and found that 15 (63%) met diagnostic criteria for personality disorder, with 6 (25%) fulfilling the diagnosis for borderline personality disorder. Similarly, Bulik et al. (1995) found at least one personality disorder in 63% of a sample of 76 women with bulimia nervosa: 51% of the personality disorders were in cluster C (specifically,

avoidant, obsessive-compulsive, or dependent personality disorders), 41% in cluster B (particularly borderline or histrionic), and 33% in cluster A (paranoid, schizoid, or schizotypal). In an earlier evaluation of 35 patients with eating disorders, Gartner, Marcus, Halmi, and Loranger (1989) found that 57% met the *DSM-III-R* diagnostic criteria for at least one form of personality disorder, with borderline, self-defeating, and avoidant being the most common. Two or more Axis II diagnostic criteria were met by 40% of the patients, and 17% fulfilled all of the criteria for five to seven personality disorder diagnoses. Wonderlich, Swift, Slotnick, and Goodman (1990) interviewed 46 eating disordered patients and reported that 72% met criteria for at least one personality disorder. Obsessive-compulsive personality disorder was common among restricting anorexic patients; histrionic and borderline personality disorder diagnoses were common among bulimic groups. Johnson et al. (1990) followed patients one year after an initial assessment and found that those who initially scored above a threshold on the self-report Borderline Syndrome Index had a worse prognosis in terms of eating behavior and general psychiatric symptoms. Gillberg et al. (1995) found that obsessive-compulsive and avoidant personality disorders were particularly common in a study comparing 51 anorexia nervosa patients with an age-matched community sample.

Arguing that borderline assessment measures are confounded by certain eating symptoms, Pope and Hudson (1989) challenged the interpretation that borderline personality disorder is overrepresented among eating disorders. For example, bulimic eating patterns may be used to satisfy the *DSM-III-R* poor impulse control criterion for borderline personality disorder, making the association between disorders tautological. Nevertheless, the tendency toward poor impulse regulation has been identified as a negative prognostic sign in eating disorders (e.g., Hatsukami et al., 1986; Sohlberg, Norring, Holmgren, & Rosmark, 1989).

Results from research on the incidence and prevalence of personality disorders in anorexia nervosa are inconsistent. Some studies indicate remarkably high rates, with avoidant personality disorder occurring in as many as 33% of anorexic restricters and borderline personality disorder occurring in almost 40% of anorexic bulimic patients (Piran, Lerner, Garfinkel, Kennedy, & Brouilette, 1988). Other studies suggest that personality disorders are relatively uncommon in anorexia ner-vosa (Herzog et al., 1992; Pope & Hudson, 1989). Im-pulse control problems, such as self-mutilation, suicide attempts, and stealing, are reported in a subgroup of anorexia nervosa patients, particularly those with purging and/or bulimic symptoms (Gar-ner et al., 1993). Although personality disturbances are not uniform in eating disorders, their presence suggests meaningful subtypes that may be relevant to treatment planning and prognosis.

There has been considerable interest and contro-versy in recent years regarding the role of sexual abuse as a risk factor for the development of eating disorders. Clinical accounts and the observation in some studies of a high incidence of sexual abuse in eating disordered patient samples (Oppenheimer, Howells, Palmer, & Chaloner, 1985) were followed by further clinical reports and numerous empirical studies yielding conflicting findings (Fallon & Wonderlich, 1997). Fallon and Wonderlich summa-rized the literature and concluded that (1) childhood sexual abuse appears to be positively associated with bulimia nervosa; (2) there is less evidence for this as-sociation in anorexia nervosa; (3) childhood sexual abuse does not appear to be a specific risk factor for eating disorders (i.e., it is no higher for eating disor-ders than in psychiatric controls); (4) childhood sex-ual abuse does appear to be associated with greater levels of comorbidity among those with eating disor-ders; however, there is not strong evidence that it pre-dicts a more severe eating disorder; and (5) a more complex approach to the definition of sexual abuse has led to better prediction of later disturbances in eating. In a study of 77 girls between the ages of 14 and 18, Moyer, DiPietro, Berkowitz, and Stunkard (1997) found that psychological variables, including depression and weight satisfaction, were more pre-dictive of binge eating than was childhood sexual abuse. Moyer et al. defined childhood sexual abuse as any unwanted contact or noncontact sexual activ-ity between the subject and perpetrator, regardless of any age differential. Furthermore, the proposed relationship between childhood sexual abuse and disordered eating may not be linear or static. Kenardy and Ball (1998), for example, reported that childhood sexual abuse was predictive of disordered eating, but not dieting or weight satisfaction, for a middle-aged female sample ($N = 268$) who ranged in age from 45 to 49 years. However, childhood sexual abuse was predictive of weight dissatisfaction but not dieting or disordered eating for the 201 young women, age 18 to 22 years, who participated in the same study. It is indisputable that a significant sub-group of women from some clinical eating disorder samples have a history of sexual abuse and that care-ful assessment and treatment is important in the process of dealing with resulting feelings of shame, distrust, and anger (Fallon & Wonderlich, 1997).

DEVELOPMENTAL AND FAMILIAL FACTORS

From the earliest descriptions, there has been agree-ment that anorexia nervosa is a disorder primarily of adolescence and that the core psychopathology often relates to conflicts that emerge with pubertal changes in body shape. Theander (1996) reviewed the topic of age of onset and concluded that the aver-age age of onset is usually found to be about 17 years, with about 30% of cases with an onset at 14 years or younger. Selection bias yields younger age at onset in pediatric treatment facilities. Theander summarizes the distribution of age at onset as fol-lows: (1) there are occasional patients with an early age of onset (7–10 years); (2) the number of cases rises steeply at age 11 and 12; (3) most patients develop the disorder in the teenage years, 13 to 19; (4) there is a gradual decline in onset from 20 to 30 years; and (5) there are fewer cases with an onset after 30. Some have found that age of onset tends to be a bit younger for males than females; however, this point remains controversial (Theander, 1996).

The age of onset of anorexia nervosa is paralleled by data on body dissatisfaction and dieting in non-clinical populations, again supporting developmen-tal vulnerability. As mentioned earlier, feeling fat and restricting food intake are common among schoolchildren and adolescents. Low self-esteem and frequency of maternal dieting may be predic-tive of dieting awareness in young girls (Hill & Pallin, 1998).

The role of the family and its relative contribu-tion to the development of eating disorders has been depicted in some of the earliest descriptions of the disorder (cf. Garfinkel & Garner, 1982). Regard-less of their theoretical orientations, writers have examined the potential familial contribution to the development of both anorexia nervosa and bulimia nervosa (cf. Garner & Garfinkel, 1997). The struc-tural approach, conceived by Minuchin and his col-leagues (Minuchin, Rosman, & Baker, 1978), was considered a significant progression in the domain of family therapy. These theorists specified many characteristics representative of the interactions occurring in eating disorder families, including enmeshment, overprotectiveness, rigidity, and poor conflict resolution. In a controlled trial examining the efficacy of family therapy for anorexia nervosa, Russell, Szmukler, Dare, and Eisler (1987) found that family therapy was superior to individual therapy for younger patients. This study as well as clinical experience suggest that family therapy should be routinely employed as the treatment of choice for young eating disordered patients.

A number of psychodynamic writers have suggested that eating disorders evolve from particular developmental experiences. These accounts have been based primarily on clinical experience; however, they have been very popular in guiding clinical interventions with eating disorders. Early psychodynamically oriented writings on eating disorders accentuated the viewpoint that eating disorders represent a repudiation of adult femininity. Crisp (1965), who expanded and refined this theme, maintains that fear of the psychological and biological experiences related to an adult weight pertains to the core psychopathology of anorexia nervosa and bulimia nervosa. Following this viewpoint, starvation is used as the main mechanism to prevent psychobiological maturity because it results in a return to prepubertal appearance and hormonal status.

Some developmental theorists have conceptualized eating disorders as resulting from differing types of parenting failures. Both Bruch (1973) and Selvini-Palazzoli (1974) provided a developmental paradigm suggesting that the mother superimposes her own inaccurate perceptions of the child's needs onto the child, invalidating the child's experiences. Accordingly, this results in an arrest of cognitive development, which is manifest in debilitating feelings of ineffectiveness that appear later in adolescent struggles for autonomy and control of the body. Bruch theorized that these early parenting failures produce basic deficits in self-awareness, including the manner in which the body is perceived and experienced. Attachment styles have also been hypothesized to play a role in the development of eating disorders. Certain attachment styles may prime the development of weight concerns, which in turn may predispose individuals to develop eating disorders (Sharpe et al., 1998).

Goodsitt (1997) has used a self-psychology perspective to explain eating disorders as a reflection of developmental arrest in the separation-individuation process. In accordance with this conceptualization, the eating disordered individual's lack of a cohesive sense of self is a consequence of the primary caregiver's failure to provide essential functions (mirroring, tension regulation, and integration) during development. The overconcern with eating and repeated episodes of bingeing and purging provide the individual with organizing and tension-regulating mechanisms to assist in managing essential deficits in "self-structures." The symptomatic behaviors displayed by the eating disordered individual serve to organize events and provide extreme stimulation to help anesthetize the suffering and void that permeate the eating disordered individual's life.

Strober (1997) has intertwined developmental theory, psychobiology, and personality genetics to provide a meaningful understanding of the adaptive mechanisms responsible for the spectrum of symptoms observed among eating disordered patients. He synthesizes current psychoanalytic concepts of development with constructs denoting (1) that individual differences may be expected in the internal regulators of arousability or temperament that organize self-experiences, and (2) that heritable personality traits, and their presumed biological substrata, set limits within which behavior patterns are expressed.

There is some evidence of genetic vulnerablity to eating disorders, particularly for anorexia nervosa. Studies of approximately 100 twin pairs culled from selected twin case report summaries and from twin studies indicate concordance rates of more than 50% for monozygotic twin pairs compared to less than 10% for dizygotic twins (Garfinkel & Garner, 1982; Holland, Sicotte, & Treasure, 1988). These studies suggest that there may be a genetic component to the transmission of anorexia nervosa; however, it is not at all clear what is inherited. Is it the specific disorder, a particular personality trait associated with the disorder, or a general vulnerability to psychiatric disturbance? Moreover, the concordance data on twins reared together do not conclusively distinguish between genetic and environmental transmission (Holland et al., 1988).

PERPETUATING FACTORS

It may not be apparent from an initial assessment whether depression, low self-esteem, psychological distress, personality features, and social maladjustment reported by eating disordered patients signal fundamental emotional deficits or are secondary elaborations resulting from weight loss and chaotic dietary patterns. These and other symptoms identified in human semistarvation studies and in research on the consequences of dieting may perpetuate eating disorders (Garner, 1997). Findings from these studies indicate that striking changes in personality traits can occur with relatively small reductions in body weight, and these may perpetuate eating disorders by making coping more difficult or by aggravating preexisting psychopathology.

The therapist needs to carefully review the array of starvation symptoms identified in a well-known

Table 35.1 Effects of starvation.

Attitudes and Behavior toward Food
    Food preoccupation
    Collection of recipes, cookbooks, and menus
    Unusual eating habits
    Increased consumption of coffee, tea, and spices
    Gum chewing
    Binge eating

Emotional and Social Changes
    Depression
    Anxiety
    Irritability, anger
    Lability
    "Psychotic" episodes
    Personality changes on psychological tests
    Decreased self-esteem
    Social withdrawal

Cognitive Changes
    Decreased concentration
    Poor judgment
    Apathy

Physical Changes
    Sleep disturbances
    Weakness
    Gastrointestinal disturbances
    Hypersensitivity to noise and light
    Edema (water retention, particularly in ankles)
    Hypothermia and feeling cold
    Paresthesia
    Decreased metabolic rate
    Decreased sexual interest
    Dry skin
    Hair loss
    Lanugo (fine, soft hair on face and elsewhere)

Source: From Garner and Bemis, 1985, and Garner, Vitousek, and Pike, 1997, with permission. Copyright 1997 by Guilford Press.

study of the effects of starvation derived from studies with normal volunteers (see Table 35.1). The description of the "starvation state" as normal physiological consequences of weight suppression can mitigate guilt or defensiveness about what may have been perceived as "primary psychopathology." It also introduces the notion that the current starved state seriously impedes the assessment of personality. This implies that restoring biological equilibrium is required to change fundamental emotional problems. Trying to make meaningful psychological changes in this starved state is analogous to trying to address underlying issues with the alcoholic patient who is intoxicated. This concept must be presented sensitively to avoid minimizing the patient's current experiences and the need for treatment despite the distortions imposed by starvation. Moreover, patients with bulimia nervosa report depression, general psychological distress, and personality disturbance, including traits that would indicate borderline personality disorder on initial assessment; however, the speed of the marked improvement in these psychological features once eating symptoms have been brought under control with treatment suggests that they may be secondary to the eating disorder rather than indicative of enduring emotional deficits (Garner et al., 1990).

ASSESSMENT

Assessment should be considered integral to the ongoing treatment process. Various approaches to information gathering have been developed for eating disorders, including standard clinical interviews, semistructured interviews, behavioral observation, standardized self-report measures, symptom checklists, clinical rating scales, self-monitoring procedures, and standardized tests. There are three broad areas of focus in the assessment process: (1) the assessment of specific symptom areas that allow the diagnosis of the eating disorder; (2) the measurement of other attitudes or behaviors characteristic of eating disorders; and (3) the identification and measurement of associated psychological and personality features that are indicative of overall psychosocial functioning (Crowther & Sherwood, 1997).

Assessment should include careful questioning regarding the duration and frequency of binge eating, as well as extreme measures designed to control body weight such as vomiting, laxative abuse, and excessive exercise. It should also cover weight controlling behaviors such as other drug or alcohol use to control appetite, chewing and spitting food out before swallowing, prolonged fasting, and vigorous exercise for the purpose of controlling body weight. Diabetic patients may manipulate insulin levels to control weight, and patients taking thyroid replacement may alter their dosage to control their weight (Garfinkel & Garner, 1982).

Marked personality changes mimicking primary personality disorders may actually stem from prolonged undernutrition. Thus, the assessment should include a careful evaluation of premorbid personality features. Patients may recall being sociable and more confident prior to the onset of the disorder; as the disorder has progressed, they may have become more sullen and isolated from others. Other patients describe a passive, compliant, and reserved premorbid personality style. Formal personality testing may be useful in some cases; however, the confounding of primary and secondary symptoms is a concern (Crowther & Sherwood, 1997; Garner, 1997). When primary personality disturbance is identified, it usually means a longer duration of therapy with a more difficult course. Adaptations are required for patients whose disorder is complicated by substance, physical, or sexual abuse.

In many cases, standardized self-report measures can be efficient in gathering information regarding eating behavior and other symptoms common in those with eating disorders. Self-report measures have the advantages of being relatively economical, brief, easily administered, and objectively scored. They are not susceptible to bias from interviewer-subject interactions and can be administered anonymously. The major disadvantage of self-report measures is that they are less accurate than interview methods, particularly when assessing ambiguous behaviors such as binge eating. The Eating Disorder Inventory 2 (EDI-2; Garner, 1991) is a standardized, multiscale measure that adds three subscales to the original EDI. The EDI-2 is specifically aimed at assessing a range of psychological characteristics clinically relevant to eating disorders, and it consists of three subscales for tapping attitudes and behaviors relating to eating, weight, and shape (Drive for Thinness, Bulimia, Body Dissatisfaction), in addition to eight subscales assessing more general organizing constructs or psychological traits clinically relevant to eating

disorders (Ineffectiveness, Perfection, Interpersonal Distrust, Interoceptive Awareness, Maturity Fears, Asceticism, Impulse Regulation, and Social Insecurity). In clinical settings, the EDI-2 is designed to provide information helpful in understanding the patient, planning treatment, and assessing progress. In nonclinical settings, the EDI-2 is intended as an economical means of identifying individuals who have subclinical eating problems or those who may be at risk for developing eating disorders.

The different methods for assessing psychopathology in eating disorders have different aims, strengths, and weaknesses. The strategy adopted should be guided by the aims of the assessment, and, whenever possible, convergent methods should be employed. Regardless of the assessment techniques used, assessment and treatment of children with eating problems should be conducted by clinicians who have expertise in developmental issues as well as in eating disorders.

In the assessment interview, it is often useful to provide the adolescent patient with a tentative and more abstract formulation of the personal "meaning" of the disorder, making it clear that it is usually much more than dieting that has spiraled out of control (Garner, Vitousek, & Pike, 1997). If the patient describes specific premorbid fears and conflicts at this point, then these can be integrated into the tentative understanding of the function of symptoms. If specific fears are denied, then it is possible to present a generic and hypothetical scenario with the suggestion that the functional nature of the disorder often becomes more clear during the course of recovery. This approach avoids direct confrontation and resulting defensiveness but at the same time informs the patient of the therapist's commitment to addressing fears exposed during the process of recovery. Relying on an adaptation of Crisp's (1980) well-known developmental diagram (Figure 35.2), we have recommended an approach to illustrate the multilevel adaptive function of symptoms (Garner & Bemis, 1985; Garner et al., 1997).

Figure 35.2 can be used to (1) underscore the concurrent physiological and psychological adaptation occurring with weight loss; (2) illustrate the range of potential adaptive functions; (3) explain how and why the adaptation might lead to resistance to change at particular points in the recovery process, highlighting the rationale for the therapist's commitment to helping the patient deal with psychological

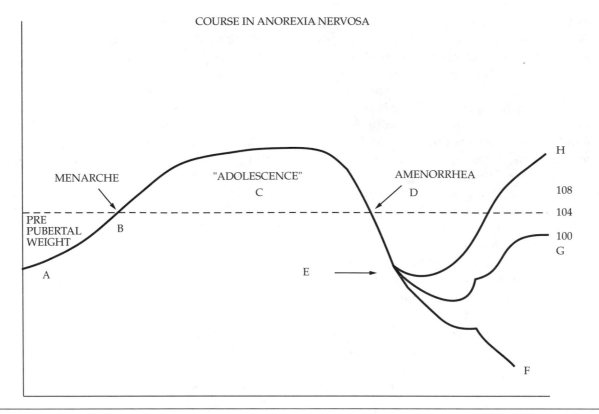

COURSE IN ANOREXIA NERVOSA

Figure 35.2   The weight course in anorexia nervosa. The dotted line represents the "menstrual weight threshold," which is approximately 47 kg (104 pounds) for a woman 163 cm (5'4") tall (Frisch & McArthur, 1974). A represents the natural process of weight gain into adolescence; B indicates the menarche; C represents normal adolescence; D indicates the normal menstrual weight threshold; E represents further weight loss; F indicates still further weight loss and possible death; G represents pseudo-recovery; and H represents full recovery. The two arrows at E and D represent weights at which anorexia nervosa patients typically express panic: at the initiation of weight gain and when they approach the menstrual weight threshold. Adapted with permission from Garner and Bemis, 1985, and Garner, Vitousek, and Pike, 1997. Copyright 1997 by Guilford Press.

distress that may *follow* weight restoration; and (4) imply that recovery and maintenance of a suboptimal (submenstrual) weight are mutually exclusive events. Thus, weight gain and changed eating behaviors are placed in the context of achieving other personal goals such as contentment, happiness, competence, and interpersonal skills. The following therapist monologue illustrates the key points:

> This is a diagram illustrating your weight history and the way that anorexia nervosa can change your life to resolve certain problems but, unfortunately, at great personal cost. The problems solved aren't the same for everyone, and later we will want to understand the details of this process as it has applied to you. This is the natural process of weight gain into adolescence (pointing to A on the diagram). In addition to the

obvious physical changes that occur as a girl enters into puberty, research has shown that there are important changes in thinking and overall experience that occur with menarche (B) and puberty. Entering adolescence can produce new challenges and problems. It is not uncommon for young women to feel insecure or distressed during this time (pointing to D) and to decide that dieting and weight loss might be a solution. Weight loss of the magnitude seen in anorexia nervosa causes changes in physical appearance, hormonal functioning, and general experience that turn back the developmental clock in some ways. Discomfort and conflicts associated with the move to adulthood no longer seem relevant and are replaced by feelings of control and confidence (elaborating then on the specific positive and negative reinforcement contingencies that seem at this point to be relevant to this particular patient). Amenorrhea develops, and this is a biological watershed: It means that here at E, you are now more as you were back at A, in terms of shape, hormones, and perhaps even thinking, than you were at C. Thus, achieving a subpubertal weight and shape appear to "resolve" a host of potential developmental concerns. Further weight loss (E) becomes like "money in the bank," keeping you at a distance from the shape and the experiences that have had negative associations and maybe even allaying certain unexpressed fears in parents (pointing to C). From this point on, the course of the disorder becomes variable, with some doing poorly (F), others trying to walk the biological tightrope (G), never really resuming biological and psychological maturity (elaborating on the biological significance of normal menstrual functioning, if necessary) and others recovering (H). Recovery does not mean simply gaining weight. It requires addressing the issues at C that may have made weight loss, with its biopsychosocial regression (to A), attractive. If you were to become involved in therapy, these issues at C, if they indeed exist (because some patients deny problems at this juncture), will become an important focus of treatment. Thus, you can see why weight gain is necessary, but clearly not the only concern. You will need guidance to address other important issues that may be uncovered along the way.

Many patients readily appreciate this interpretation of their disorder as having psychological and developmental meaning. Although the foregoing is based on Crisp's (1980) "phobic" response to perceived demands of adulthood and its consequent reversal of the normal hormonal substrate, it is remarkably similar to observations of others arguing from very different theoretical perspectives. Some patients are immediately able to recognize that there is a particular weight that they fear most, and this translates into a weight threshold for the return of the menses and associated normalization of hypothalamic-pituitary functioning. They sometimes seize this opportunity to elaborate on fears of "growing up"; however, it must be emphasized that this theme is relevant only to a subset of patients and disregards the powerful influence of positively reinforcing aspects of anorexic symptomatology described earlier.

At this point, the patient needs to acknowledge in general terms that *recovery* from the eating disorder is the goal. Typically, the devil is in the details, but it is essential to establish that recovery is the theoretically desired outcome, even though any decision is tentative and experimental at this point. The *goal* of treatment is defined in general and

nonthreatening terms at this juncture, with the understanding that it will be revisited in greater detail once there has been some change in body weight, eating behavior, and other symptoms. The following illustrates the first step in this process:

THERAPIST: Let's talk about some specific goals for treatment. At this point, what kind of problems, other than eating and weight, do you think are at the heart of the problem?
PATIENT: I feel disgusted about feeling fat.
THERAPIST: Tell me more. What does being fat mean to you?
PATIENT: It means I am a slob—I don't feel confident. I do not like myself very much.
THERAPIST: So you don't feel confident except when you are in control of your weight?
PATIENT: Yes.
THERAPIST: If treatment is to make any sense, priority must be given to help you find ways to feel confident other than weight control. This is important—let me write this goal down. What about other goals? What about relationships with your family?
PATIENT: My family is fine. It is me that is the problem.
THERAPIST: O.K. But if we should find later that you have concerns about your family or if there are other issues that we need to address, we will add them to the list then.

The therapist purposely stopped at this general goal rather than press for a clearer operational definition of the patient's negative feelings. Clarification will be pursued in subsequent meetings; the purpose here is to establish that this non-weight-related subject domain will be a priority in therapy and that other similar issues, including emergent family concerns, can be added later.

EMPIRICALLY SUPPORTED INTERVENTIONS

The quantity of psychotherapeutic options accessible to eating disordered patients has proliferated in the past decade, and the principal approaches to psychotherapy have been explained well and have been accompanied by development of alternative treatment choices (Garner & Garfinkel, 1997). The wisdom of considering integration of different psychotherapeutic procedures is increasingly evident with the demonstrated effectiveness of different forms of treatment (Garner & Needleman, 1997). There has been recent interest in stepped-care, decision-tree, and integration models, which rely on standard rules for the delivery of the various treatment options (Garner & Needleman, 1997). Figure 35.3 illustrates a tentative decision-making paradigm for sequencing and integration of treatments for

people with eating disorders. Various treatment options (hospitalization, family therapy, self-help, and individual therapy) are represented by the sharp-cornered boxes, and pertinent questions (those associated with symptoms, patient characteristics, responses to previous treatments) related to deciding the type of treatment are characterized by curved-cornered boxes. Although all existing treatment alternatives are not incorporated in Figure

DECISION GUIDELINES FOR
TREATING EATING DISORDERS

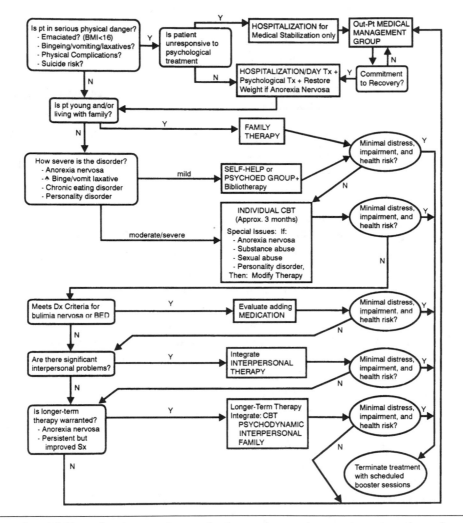

Figure 35.3   General guidelines for integration and sequencing major treatment options for eating disordered patients. Begin in the upper left corner with the question "Is the patient in serious physical danger?" Further criteria for decision making, including symptom areas, patient characteristics, and response to previous treatments, are indicated by boxes with rounded corners (mostly on the left side of the figure). The treatment options are represented by boxes with sharp corners (hospitalization, family therapy, self-help, individual therapy, etc.). The figure does not delineate all treatment alternatives or all considerations for decision making. However, it does include the main interventions for which there is good clinical and/or empirical support and key variables to consider in determining the most appropriate type and intensity of treatment. Adapted with permission from Garner and Needleman, 1997. Copyright 1997 by Guilford Press.

35.3, it focuses on those that are supported both clinically and empirically.

FAMILY THERAPY

Family therapy is the initial treatment choice for patients who are young and/or living at home (see Figure 35.3). As mentioned earlier, Russell et al. (1987) found that family therapy was superior to individual therapy for younger patients. Family therapy is an essential component of treatment for patients who are young and/or living at home, and should also be strongly considered as a therapeutic adjunct for older patients (living outside of the home) who experience family discord. The recommendation of family therapy for young patients is based on both a practical and a theoretical rationale. Practically, parents are responsible for the well-being of the patient and can serve as powerful agents of change by providing guidance and assistance to facilitate the implementation and achievement of treatment goals because they reside within the child's physical environment. Family members also need therapeutic direction in learning how to cope with the eating disordered patient and deal with their own feelings in an effective manner.

Family therapists have persuasively maintained their stance that eating disorders may be indicative of discord, dysfunctional roles, or disturbed interactional patterns within the family context (Dare & Eisler, 1997; Minuchin et al., 1978; Selvini-Palazzoli, 1974). The list provided below depicts some of the most common problematical themes:

1. The parents and identified patient may display denial regarding the seriousness of the eating disorder and will require assistance in accurately labeling the eating disorder without minimizing or maximizing the importance of behavioral symptoms.
2. Parents of younger patients might need assistance in establishing an effective parenting style, as feelings of guilt and fear may have prevented them from maintaining firm and clear behavioral guidelines consistent with recovery. Unless unrealistic parental expectations are directly related to the problem, it is suggested that parents maintain their expectations in those areas that are unrelated to food and eating (i.e., bedtime, chores, language, treatment of siblings/parents). Treatment

interventions should be developmentally appropriate for the child and should be within the boundaries of the family's value system.
3. Parents will need help in understanding and respecting the patient's need for autonomy and self-expression through traits, interests, and values that may differ from expectations set by the family.
4. Parental attitudes regarding weight, shape, thinness, or fitness may be inappropriate at times, and unsuitable eating patterns, beliefs about food, eating, and exercise should be identified and addressed using practical interventions to interrupt any possible problem areas.
5. An eating disorder can deflect members of the family away from potentially threatening developmental expectations emergent in the transition to puberty. It can function as a maladaptive solution to the adolescent's struggle to achieve autonomy in a family where any move toward independence is perceived as a threat to family unity. It can also become a powerful diversion enabling the parents and the child to avoid major sources of conflict.
6. The identified patient's symptoms may be functional in a disturbed family context, and the meaning systems that underlie the resulting interactional patterns need to be identified and corrected. Problematic family interactional patterns that need to be addressed include enmeshment, overprotectiveness, inadequate mechanisms for resolving conflicts, and inappropriate parent-child allegiances that undermine the marital relationship. (Minuchin et al., 1978)

It is essential for parents to consider the following factors when their child is being treated for an eating disorder, as they bear moral and legal responsibilities for the child's welfare. Lask and Bryant-Waugh (1997) describe four critical factors to prevent the maintenance of the child's eating disorder: cohesion, consistency, communication, and conflict resolution. In addition to providing parents with basic education and information, it is important that the parents maintain cohesiveness and present a unified front to best help the child. Parents must also remain consistent in their interactions so that the child knows what to expect. Finally, the integration of family therapy with long-term individual therapy must be strategic in addressing physical and sexual abuse in the family (Andersen, 1985; Garner, Garfinkel, & Bemis, 1982).

COGNITIVE-BEHAVIORAL THERAPY

Cognitive-behavioral therapy (CBT) has become the standard treatment for bulimia nervosa and forms the theoretical base for much of the treatment of anorexia nervosa. As indicated in Figure 35.3, CBT should be considered the treatment of choice for patients whose age does not mandate family therapy and whose symptoms range from moderate to severe. The CBT for bulimia nervosa developed by Fairburn and colleagues (Fairburn, 1985; Fairburn, Marcus, & Wilson, 1993) has the following major points of emphasis: (1) self-monitoring of food intake, bingeing, and purging episodes as well as thoughts and feelings that trigger these episodes; (2) regular weighing; (3) specific recommendations such as the introduction of avoided foods and meal planning designed to normalize eating behavior and curb restrictive dieting; (4) cognitive restructuring directed at habitual reasoning errors and underlying assumptions that are relevant to the development and maintenance of the eating disorder; and (5) relapse prevention.

There have now been more than 25 controlled treatment studies of bulimia nervosa and they provide very encouraging findings (McKisack & Waller, 1997; Mitchell, Raymond, & Specker, 1993). In a long-term prospective follow-up of 91 eating disordered patients from two randomized controlled trials involving CBT, behavior therapy (BT), and focal interpersonal therapy (FIT), Fairburn et al. (1995) found that those who received BT did poorly, whereas bulimia nervosa patients who received CBT or FIT did markedly better. Compared to subjects in the BT condition, those in the FIT were twice as likely to be in remission (defined as no longer meeting a *DSM-IV* diagnosis for an eating disorder), and those in the CBT condition were more than three times as likely to be in remission. Similarly, about 50% of the patients who received CBT or FIT were completely abstinent from all key behavioral symptoms such as binge eating, vomiting, and laxative and diuretic abuse, compared to 18% of those receiving BT.

In the case of anorexia nervosa, CBT has been recommended largely on clinical grounds (Garner, 1986; Garner & Bemis, 1982, 1985; Garner & Rosen, 1990; Garner et al., 1997; Vitousek &

Orimoto, 1993). Case studies and preliminary research provide some grounds for optimism (Channon, DeSilva, Hemsley, & Perkins, 1989; Cooper & Fairburn, 1984); however, current data are insufficient to warrant meaningful conclusions regarding effectiveness.

There are many areas of overlap between the versions of CBT offered for anorexia and bulimia nervosa; however, there are also important differences that have implications for clinical care (Garner et al., 1997). A major focus for both disorders is the patient's underlying assumption that "weight, shape, or thinness can serve as the sole or predominant referent for inferring personal value or self-worth" (Garner & Bemis, 1982, p. 142). Fear of body weight gain is a central theme for both anorexia and bulimia nervosa; however, most bulimia nervosa patients can be reassured that treatment will probably result in little weight gain. In contrast, in anorexia nervosa, therapeutic strategies must be aimed at actual weight gain in the face of the implacable wish to maintain a low weight. Establishing a sound and collaborative therapeutic relationship is particularly important in anorexia nervosa because it becomes a fulcrum for gradually helping the patient to relinquish the myriad of ego-syntonic symptoms. As indicated in Figure 35.3, CBT is modified for anorexia nervosa; it is typically longer in duration, and the targets for cognitive interventions are broad, encompassing a wider range of personal and interpersonal subject domains than is typical for bulimia nervosa (Garner et al., 1997). This is to address the marked deficits impeding normal psychosocial functioning in many of these patients. Thus, cognitive interventions are aimed not only at beliefs that maintain extreme dieting and chronic weight suppression but also at fundamental assumptions associated with interpersonal conflicts, feelings of ineffectiveness, struggles with autonomy, and fears associated with psychosocial developmental (Garner & Bemis, 1982; Garner et al., 1997). Components of interpersonal therapy and family therapy are often integrated into longer-term CBT for anorexia nervosa (see Figure 35.3). In the subset of anorexia nervosa patients who do not engage in binge eating and those who show no obvious serious physical complications, there may be extraordinary resistance to complying with the therapeutic objectives of weight gain. However, as long as there is gradual improvement in symptoms (see Figure 35.3), outpatient therapy is recommended; however, if the patient's condition deteriorates, hospitalization must be considered. Outpatient medical management (groups) should be considered if there is a protracted therapeutic impasse. This often takes the form of apparent psychological insights that invariably fail to translate into symptomatic change.

INTERPERSONAL THERAPY

For almost a decade, the prevailing view was that CBT's effectiveness with eating disorders was tied to cognitive and behavioral methods aimed specifically at overconcern about weight and shape that are responsible for restrictive dieting and extreme weight controlling behaviors. Changing these attitudes presumably relaxed restrictive dieting and relieved the biological tension created by chronic attempts to suppress body weight. However, a series of studies using interpersonal psychotherapy (IPT) adapted to bulimia nervosa has prompted reexamination of earlier speculations regarding the specific mechanisms of action in the treatment of binge eating (Fairburn et al., 1995). This is because IPT does not directly focus on eating problems; it was originally proposed by Klerman, Weissman, Rounsaville, and Chevron (1984) as a short-term treatment for depression. The IPT treatment process is divided into three stages (Fairburn, 1997). The first stage involves the identification of the interpersonal problems that led to the development and maintenance of the eating problems. The second stage consists of a therapeutic contract for working on these interpersonal problems. The final stage addresses issues related to termination. Fairburn et al. (1991) found IPT somewhat less effective than CBT at the end of treatment; however, patients who received IPT gradually improved during the follow-up period so that after one year, both treatments were equally effective (Fairburn, Jones, Peveler, Hope, & O'Connor, 1993). These findings are maintained over the longer term with patients receiving CBT or IPT doing significantly better than those receiving BT (Fairburn et al., 1995). This pattern of improvement during follow-up was not found in a study of another, very different form of interpersonally oriented therapy, supportive-expressive therapy (Garner et al., 1993). These findings suggest that the interpersonal therapies offered in the Oxford trials contain specific therapeutic ingredients that facilitate change. Further support for the effectiveness of IPT comes from

Wilfley et al. (1993) in a study of nonpurging bulimic patients, many of whom presented with obesity. They found both CBT and IPT equally effective in reducing binge eating assessed both at the end of treatment and at one-year follow-up.

The evidence that certain interpersonal therapies are as effective with binge eating as CBT has implications for the decision process illustrated in Figure 35.3. It could be argued that there should be no priority for either IPT or CBT as the initial treatment of choice for bulimia nervosa because both treatments are equally effective in the long term. Certainly, a therapist well trained in one of the interpersonal therapies described by Fairburn and colleagues should not be encouraged to abandon this form of treatment in favor of CBT. However, we are still inclined to recommend CBT as the preferred initial treatment at this time because it has been shown to have a more rapid effect on symptoms. Moreover, the efficacy of IPT for bulimia nervosa has been demonstrated in just one center compared to many studies in support of CBT. If the findings from the Oxford trials are replicated in other centers, then IPT may become another standard initial treatment for bulimia nervosa. At this time, there is no empirical basis for suggesting that IPT should be differentially applied to patients on the basis of premorbid features such as interpersonal conflicts. However, integrating IPT into treatment should be considered for bulimia nervosa patients who fail to respond favorably to an initial course of CBT when interpersonal conflicts predominate according to Figure 35.3. The IPT orientation should also be a leading candidate for integration into longer-term psychotherapy for anorexia nervosa patients and for others with persistent symptoms.

PHARMACOTHERAPY

As depicted in Figure 35.3, medication is generally not indicated for anorexia nervosa, although it should be considered for those patients with bulimia nervosa or binge eating disorder who fail an initial trial of CBT. After reviewing the research in this area, Raymond, Mitchell, Fallon, and Katzman (1994) suggested that medication should not be "the primary mode of therapy with patients with bulimia nervosa" (p. 241). This conclusion is based on the following observations: (1) psychological interventions have been shown to be very effective;

(2) high dropout rates are reported in most medication studies; (3) there are risks of drug side effects; and (4) data suggest high relapse rates with drug discontinuation. In a meta-analysis using 9 double-blind, placebo-controlled medication trials (870 subjects) and 26 randomized psychosocial studies (460 subjects), Whittal, Agras, and Gould (1999) reported that CBT produced significantly larger-weighted effect sizes for all indices of treatment outcome.

Tricyclic antidepressants may be considered as an alternative for some patients failing a course of fluoxetine, but side effects such as high dropout rates and greater lethality with overdose may be a source of concern when treating some patients (Leitenberg et al., 1994). Similarly, monoamine oxidase inhibitors (MAOIs) may be useful in a small minority of patients who fail using fluoxetine and tricyclics. There is some evidence that patients who fail on one tricyclic may benefit from changing to an alternative medication (see Mitchell et al., 1993). Importantly, the specific decision to *not prescribe* medication may be therapeutic (Raymond et al., 1994).

There is still little evidence for change in the early recommendations that pharmacotherapy has a very limited value with emaciated anorexia nervosa patients and should never be the sole treatment modality (Garfinkel & Garner, 1982). Occasionally, patients may benefit from medication to deal with overwhelming anxiety, severe depression, or intolerable gastric discomfort after meals, but this applies to only a small minority of patients (Andersen, 1985; Garfinkel & Garner, 1982; Garfinkel & Walsh, 1997).

Thus, in the decision-tree approach for treating eating disorders, antidepressant medication should be considered as an adjunct or possibly an alternative for bulimia nervosa patients who fail to respond to psychosocial therapies or for those whose affective symptoms are clearly impeding progress in other forms of treatment. Drug treatments have generally not proven effective for anorexia nervosa.

INTEGRATING AND ADAPTING INTERVENTIONS

A major premise in this chapter has been that eating disorders are multidetermined and heterogeneous syndromes resulting from the interplay of biological, psychological, familial, and sociocultural predisposing factors. In this sense, they are probably best understood as final common pathways that appear to have different psychological points of entry. In this overall context, this chapter has selectively reviewed diagnostic issues, major etiological formulations, and associated psychopathology applied to eating disorders. An important direction for future research will be the clearer specification of the relative contribution of particular biological, psychological, and interpersonal predisposing features considered relevant to eating disorders. It is to be hoped that the extraordinary clinical and research interest in personality disorders, depression, sexual abuse, and addictive behaviors as related to eating disorders will continue to lead to improved understanding. Further research is clearly needed to determine the precise nature and the significance of the observed associations. If past research is any indication of future findings, the within-diagnostic-group variability will continue to be as noteworthy as the between-group differences.

MANAGED CARE CONSIDERATIONS WITH EATING DISORDERS

During the 1980s, there was a convergence of extraordinary economic incentives for inpatient care, surging demands for clinical services, and widespread misinformation regarding optimal treatment that led to the unnecessary hospitalization of many eating disordered patients who could easily have been managed at a less intensive level of care. The earlier abuse of inpatient treatment led to an understandable backlash by insurers, resulting in denial of hospital coverage or extreme limitations of coverage for eating disordered patients, putting many at unnecessary risk for chronic illness or death. This has created a major problem in the treatment of eating disorders, as it is well established in the treatment literature that even the most ambitious treatment for patients with severe eating disorders requires more time and expense than is routinely allowed in the benefits packages of many patients. If insufficient time is devoted to treatment, few patients recover, and this has very negative economic consequences for insurers as well as sufferers. Research has shown that discharging anorexia nervosa patients before they achieve a reasonable goal weight is associated with relapse (Baran, Weltzin, & Kaye, 1995). Even though this is a time-consuming and expensive process, it is an economical alternative if it leads to recovery, for a chronic eating disorder incurs a heavy price, in both monetary and emotional terms. There has been a growing trend to treat eating disorders in specialized treatment settings (as apposed to general hospital wards) because experienced staff may be able to manage more severely disturbed patients at a lower level of care than traditional hospitalization (i.e., partial hospitalization or intensive day treatment). We have found intensive day treatment (seven hours a day, five days a week) to be preferable to inpatient care because it provides structure around meal times as well as the possibility for intensive therapy that is sufficient for most patients to make behavioral changes, without requiring them to be totally disengaged from the supports and therapeutic challenges outside of the hospital.

SUMMARY

It is now evident that certain patients respond relatively quickly to brief interventions, in contrast to others who require more intensive and protracted treatments. Perhaps the most significant goal for future research will be the identification of traits, personality features, and background factors that predict differential response to treatment. Even better would be a taxonomy yielding an accurate match between patient characteristics and treatment type. Recent advances in research on psychopathology and treatment efficacy warrant genuine optimism with regard to bulimia nervosa. Less is known about personality and response to treatment for anorexia nervosa because of the relative absence of controlled treatment research with this eating disorder. It is hoped that controlled treatment research will assume a high priority and that the results will generate the same level of progress that is now evident with bulimia nervosa.

REFERENCES

Abou-Saleh, M.T., Younis, Y., & Karim, L. (1998). Anorexia nervosa in an Arab culture. *International Journal of Eating Disorders, 23,* 207–212.

Agras, W.S., Rossiter, E.M., Arnow, B., Schneider, J.A., Telch, C.F., Raeburn, S.D., Bruce, B., Perl, M., & Koran, L.M. (1992). Pharmacologic and cognitive-behavioral treatment for bulimia nervosa: A controlled comparison. *American Journal of Psychiatry, 149,* 82–87.

American Psychiatric Association. (1994). *Diagnostic and statistical manual of mental disorders* (4th ed.). Washington, DC: Author.

Andersen, A.E. (1985). *Practical comprehensive treatment of anorexia nervosa and bulimia.* Baltimore: Johns Hopkins University Press.

Baran, S.A., Weltzin, T.E., & Kaye, W.H. (1995). Low discharge weight and outcome in anorexia nervosa. *American Journal of Psychiatry, 152,* 1070–1072.

Barry, D. (1997). *Strangers in a foreign land: Acculturation, ethnic identity, self-construal, and self-esteem in male Arab immigrants in the United States.* Unpublished master's thesis, University of Toledo, OH.

Bruch, H. (1973). *Eating disorders: Obesity, anorexia nervosa and the person within.* New York: Basic Books.

Bryant-Waugh, R., & Lask, B. (1995). Annotation: Eating disorders in children. *Journal of Child Clinical Psychiatry, 36,* 191–202.

Bulik, C., Sullivan, P., Joyce, P., & Carter, F. (1995). Temperament character, and personality disorder in bulimia nervosa. *Journal of Nervous and Mental Disease, 183*(9), 593–598.

Button, E.J., Loan, P., Davies, J., & Sonuga-Barke, E.J.S. (1997). Self-esteem, eating problems, and psychological well-being in a cohort of schoolgirls age 15–16: A questionnaire and interview study. *International Journal of Eating Disorders, 21,* 39–47.

Channon, S., DeSilva, P., Hemsley, D., & Perkins, R. (1989). A controlled trial of cognitive-behavioral and behavioral treatment of anorexia nervosa. *Behavioral Research and Therapy, 27,* 529–535.

Chiodo, J., & Latimer, P.R. (1983). Vomiting as a learned weight-control technique in bulimia. *Journal of Behavior Therapy and Experimental Psychiatry, 14,* 131–135.

Cooper, P.J., & Fairburn, C.G. (1984). Cognitive-behavioral treatment for anorexia nervosa: Some preliminary findings. *Journal of Psychosomatic Research, 28,* 493–499.

Cooper, J.L., Morrison, T.L., Bigman, O.L., Abramowitz, S.I., Levin, S., & Krener, P. (1988). Mood changes and affective disorder in the bulimic binge-purge cycle. *International Journal of Eating Disorders, 7,* 469–474.

Crago, M., Shisslak, C.M., & Estes, L.S. (1996). Eating disturbances among American minority groups: A review. *International Journal of Eating Disorders, 19,* 239–248.

Crisp, A.H. (1965). Clinical and therapeutic aspects of anorexia nervosa: Study of 30 cases. *Journal of Psychosomatic Research, 9,* 67–78.

Crisp, A.H. (1980). *Anorexia nervosa.* New York: Grune & Stratton.

Crowther, J., & Sherwood, N. (1997). Assessment. In D.M. Garner & P.E. Garfinkel (Eds.), *Handbook of treatment for eating disorders* (pp. 34–49). New York: Guilford Press.

Dare, C., & Eisler, I. (1997). Family therapy for anorexia nervosa. In D.M. Garner & P.E. Garfinkel (Eds.), *Handbook of treatment for eating disorders* (pp. 307–326). New York: Guilford Press.

Davies, E., & Furnham, A. (1986). The dieting and body shape concerns of adolescent females. *Journals of Child Psychology and Psychiatry, 3,* 417–428.

Edlund, B., Halvarsson, K., & Sjödén, P. (1995). Eating behaviours, and attitudes to eating, dieting, and body image in a 7-year-old Swedish girl. *European Eating Disorders Review, 3,* 111–114.

Evans, C., Dolan, B., & Toriola, A. (1997). Detection of intra- and cross-cultural non-equivalence by simple methods in cross-cultural research: Evidence from a study of eating attitudes in Nigeria and Britain. *Eating and Weight Disorders, 2,* 67–78.

Fairburn, C.G. (1985). Cognitive-behavioral treatment for bulimia. In D.M. Garner & P.E. Garfinkel (Eds.), *Handbook of psychotherapy for anorexia nervosa and bulimia* (pp. 160–192). New York: Guilford Press.

Fairburn, C.G. (1997). Interpersonal psychotherapy for bulimia nervosa. In D.M. Garner & P.E. Garfinkel (Eds.), *Handbook of treatment for eating disorders* (pp. 278–294). New York: Guilford Press.

Fairburn, C.G., & Beglin, S.J. (1990). Studies of the epidemiology of bulimia nervosa. *American Journal of Psychiatry, 147,* 401–408.

Fairburn, C.G., Jones, R., Peveler, R.C., Carr, S.J., Solomon, R.A., O'Connor, M.E., Burton, J., & Hope, R.A. (1991). Three psychological treatments for bulimia nervosa: A comparative trial. *Archives of General Psychiatry, 48,* 463–469.

Fairburn, C.G., Jones, R., Peveler, R.C., Hope, R.A., & O'Connor, M. (1993). Psychotherapy and bulimia nervosa: The longer-term effects of interpersonal psychotherapy, behavior therapy and cognitive-behavior therapy. *Archives of General Psychiatry, 50,* 419–428.

Fairburn, C.G., Marcus, M.D., & Wilson, G.T. (1993). Cognitive-behavioral therapy for binge eating and bulimia nervosa. In C.G. Fairburn & G.T. Wilson (Eds.), *Binge eating: Nature, assessment and treatment* (361–404). New York: Guilford Press.

Fairburn, C.G., Norman, P.A., Welch, S.L., O'Connor, M.E., Doll, H.A., & Peveler, R.C. (1995). A prospective study of outcome in bulimia nervosa and the long-term effects of three psychological treatments. *Archives of General Psychiatry, 52,* 304–312.

Fallon, P., & Wonderlich, S. (1997). Sexual abuse and other forms of trauma. In D.M. Garner & P.E. Garfinkel (Eds.), *Handbook of treatment for eating disorders* (pp. 394–414). New York: Guilford Press.

Fosson, A., Knibbs, J., Bryant-Waugh, R., & Lask, B. (1987). Early onset anorexia nervosa. *Archives of Disease in Childhood, 62,* 114–118.

Frisch, R., & McArthur, J. (1974). Menstrual cycles: Fatness as a determinant of minimum weight for height necessary for their maintenance and onset. *Science, 185,* 941–951.

Garfinkel, P.E., & Garner, D.M. (1982). *Anorexia nervosa: A multidimensional perspective.* New York: Brunner/Mazel.

Garfinkel, P.E., Garner, D.M., Kaplan, A.S., Rodin, G., & Kennedy, S. (1983). Differential diagnosis of emotional disorders that cause weight loss. *Canadian Medical Association Journal, 129,* 939–945.

Garfinkel, P.E., & Walsh, B. (1997). Drug therapies. In D.M. Garner & P.E. Garfinkel (Eds.), *Handbook of treatment for eating disorders* (pp. 229–247). New York: Guilford Press.

Garner, D.M. (1986). Cognitive therapy for anorexia nervosa. In K.D. Brownell & J.P. Foreyt (Eds.), *Handbook of eating disorders* (pp. 301–327). New York: Basic Books.

Garner, D.M. (1991). *Eating Disorder Inventory: Professional manual* (2nd ed.). Odessa, FL: Psychological Assessment Resources.

Garner, D.M. (1993). Pathogenesis of anorexia nervosa. *Lancet, 341,* 1631–1635.

Garner, D.M. (1997). Psychoeducational principles in treatment. In D.M. Garner & P.E. Garfinkel (Eds.), *Handbook of treatment for eating disorders* (pp. 145–177). New York: Guilford Press.

Garner, D.M., & Bemis, K.M. (1982). A cognitive-behavioral approach to anorexia nervosa. *Cognitive Therapy and Research, 6,* 123–150.

Garner, D.M., & Bemis, K.M. (1985). Cognitive therapy for anorexia nervosa. In D.M. Garner & P.E. Garfinkel (Eds.), *Handbook of psychotherapy for anorexia nervosa and bulimia* (pp. 107–146). New York: Guilford Press.

Garner, D.M., & Garfinkel, P.E. (1980). Socio-cultural factors in the development of anorexia nervosa. *Psychological Medicine, 10,* 647–656.

Garner, D.M., & Garfinkel, P.E. (1997). *Handbook of treatment for eating disorders.* New York: Guilford Press.

Garner, D.M., Garfinkel, P.E., & Bemis, K.M. (1982). A multidimensional psychotherapy for anorexia nervosa. *International Journal of Eating Disorders, 1,* 3–46.

Garner, D.M., Garfinkel, P.E., Schwartz, D.M., & Thompson, M.M. (1980). Cultural expectations of thinness in women. *Psychological Reports, 47,* 483–491.

Garner, D.M., Garner, M.V., & Rosen, L.W. (1993). Anorexia nervosa "restricters" who purge: Implications for subtyping anorexia nervosa. *International Journal of Eating Disorders, 13,* 171–185.

Garner, D.M., & Needleman L. (1997). Sequencing and integration of treatments. In D.M. Garner & P.E. Garfinkel (Eds.), *Handbook of treatment for eating disorders* (pp. 50–66). New York: Guilford Press.

Garner, D.M., Olmsted, M.P., Davis, R., Rockert, W., Goldbloom, D., & Eagle, M. (1990). The association between bulimic symptoms and reported psychopathology. *International Journal of Eating Disorders, 9,* 1–15.

Garner, D.M., & Rosen, L.W. (1990). Anorexia nervosa and bulimia nervosa. In A.S. Bellack, M. Hersen, & A.E. Kazdin (Eds.), *International handbook of behavior modification and therapy* (pp. 805–817). New York: Plenum Press.

Garner, D.M., Rosen, L., & Barry, D. (1998). Eating disorders in athletes. *Child and Adolescent Psychiatric Clinics of North America, 7,* 839–857.

Garner, D.M., Shafer, C.L., & Rosen, L.W. (1992). Critical appraisal of the *DSM-III-R* personality diagnostic criteria for eating disorders. In S.R. Hooper, G.W. Hynd, & R.E. Mattison (Eds.), *Child psychopathology: Diagnostic criteria and clinical assessment* (pp. 261–303). Hillsdale, NJ: Erlbaum.

Garner, D.M., Vitousek, K., & Pike, K. (1997). Cognitive-behavioral therapy for anorexia nervosa. In D.M. Garner & P.E. Garfinkel (Eds.), *Handbook of treatment for eating disorders* (pp. 94–144). New York: Guilford Press.

Garner, D.M., & Wooley, S.C. (1991). Confronting the failure of behavioral and dietary treatments for obesity. *Clinical Psychology Review, 11,* 729–780.

Gartner, A.F., Marcus, R.N., Halmi, K., & Loranger, A.W. (1989). *DSM-III-R* personality disorders in patients with eating disorders. *American Journal of Psychiatry, 146,* 1585–1591.

Gillberg, G., Rastam, M., & Gillberg, C. (1995). Anorexia nervosa 6 years after onset: Part I. Personality disorders. *Comprehensive Psychiatry, 36,* 61–69.

Goodsitt, A. (1997). Eating disorders: A self psychological perspective. In D.M. Garner & P.E. Garfinkel (Eds.), *Handbook of treatment for eating disorders* (pp. 205–228). New York: Guilford Press.

Grinspoon, S., Herzog, D., & Klibanski, A. (1997). Mechanisms and treatment options for bone loss in anorexia nervosa. *Psychopharmacology Bulletin, 33*(3), 399–404.

Hatsukami, D., Mitchell, J.E., Eckert, E.D., & Pyle, R. (1986). Characteristics of patients with bulimia only, bulimia with affective disorder, and bulimia with substance abuse problems. *Addictive Behaviors, 11,* 399–406.

Herzog, D.B., Keller, M.B., Sacks, N.R., Yeh, C.J., & Lavori, P.W. (1992). Psychiatric morbidity in treatment-seeking anorexics and bulimics. *Journal of the American Academy of Child and Adolescent Psychiatry, 31,* 810–818.

Higgs, J., Goodyer, I., & Birch, J. (1989). Anorexia nervosa and food avoidance emotional disorder. *Archives of Disease in Childhood, 64,* 515–524.

Hill, A.J., & Pallin, V. (1998). Dieting awareness and low self-worth: Related issues in 8-year-old girls. *International Journal of Eating Disorders, 24,* 405–413.

Hoek, H.W. (1993). Review of the epidemiological studies of eating disorders. *International Review of Psychiatry, 5,* 61–74.

Hoek, H.W., Bartelds, A., Bosveld, J., Graff, Y., Limpens, V., Maiwald, M., & Spaij, C. (1995). Impact of urbanization on detection rates of eating disorders. *American Journal of Psychiatry, 152*(9), 1272–1278.

Holland, A.J., Sicotte, N., & Treasure, J. (1988). Anorexia nervosa: Evidence for a genetic basis. *Journal of Psychosomatic Research, 32,* 561–571.

Huon, G.F., Brown, L., & Morris, S. (1988). Lay beliefs about disordered eating. *International Journal of Eating Disorders, 7,* 239–252.

Jaffe, A.C., & Singer, L.T. (1989). Atypical eating disorders in young children. *International Journal of Eating Disorders, 8,* 575–582.

Johnson, C., Tobin, D.L., & Dennis, A. (1990). Differences in treatment outcome between borderline and non-borderline bulimics at one-year follow-up. *International Journal of Eating Disorders, 9,* 617–627.

Kenardy, J., & Ball, K. (1998). Disordered eating, weight dissatisfaction and dieting in relation to unwanted childhood sexual experiences in a community sample. *Journal of Psychosomatic Research, 44,* 327–337.

Killen, J.D., Hayward, C., Wilson, D.M., Taylor, C.B., Hammer, L.D., Litt, I., Simmonds, B., & Haydel, F. (1994). Factors associated with eating disorder symptoms in a community sample of 6th and 7th grade girls. *International Journal of Eating Disorders, 15,* 357–367.

Klerman, G.L., Weissman, M.M., Rounsaville, B.J., & Chevron, E. (1984). *Interpersonal psychotherapy for depression.* New York: Basic Books.

Kreipe, R.E. (1995). Eating disorders among children and adolescents. *Pediatrics in Review, 16,* 370–379.

Kreipe, R.E., Churchill, B.H., & Strauss, J. (1989). Long-term outcome of adolescents with anorexia nervosa. *American Journal of Diseases of Children, 143,* 1322–1327.

Lask, B., Britten, C., Kroll, L., Magagna, J., & Tranter, M. (1991). Pervasive refusal in children. *Archives of Diseases in Childhood, 66,* 866–869.

Lask, B., & Bryant-Waugh, R. (1997). Pre-pubertal eating disorders. In D.M. Garner & P.E. Garfinkel (Eds.), *Handbook of treatment for eating disorders* (pp. 476–483). New York: Guilford Press.

Leitenberg, H., Rosen, J.C., Wolf, J., Vara, L.S., Detzer, M.J., & Srebnik, D. (1994). Comparison of cognitive-behavior therapy and desipramine in the treatment of bulimia nervosa. *Behavior Research and Therapy, 32,* 37–45.

Levin, A.P., & Hyler, S.E. (1986). *DSM-III* personality diagnosis in bulimia. *Comprehensive Psychiatry, 27,* 47–53.

Maloney, M.J., McGuire, J.B., & Daniels, S.R. (1988). Reliability testing of a children's version of the Eating Attitudes Test. *Journal of the American Academy of Child and Adolescent Psychiatry, 27,* 541–543.

McKisack, C., & Waller, G. (1997). Factors influencing the outcome of group psychotherapy for bulimia nervosa. *International Journal of Eating Disorders, 22,* 1–13.

Minuchin, S., Rosman, B.L., & Baker, L. (1978). *Psychosomatic families: Anorexia nervosa in context.* Cambridge, MA: Harvard University Press.

Mitchell, J.E., Pyle, R.L., Eckert, E.D., Hatsukami, D., Pomeroy, C., & Zimmerman, R. (1990). A comparison study of antidepressants and structured intensive group psychotherapy in the treatment of bulimia nervosa. *Archives of General Psychiatry, 47,* 149–157.

Mitchell, J.E., Raymond, N., & Specker, S. (1993). A review of the controlled trials of pharmachotherapy and psychotherapy in the treatment of bulimia nervosa. *International Journal of Eating Disorders, 14,* 229–247.

Moyer, D.M., DiPietro, L., Berkowitz, R.I., & Stunkard, A.J. (1997). Childhood sexual abuse and precursors of binge eating in an adolescent female population. *International Journal of Eating Disorders, 21,* 23–30.

Oppenheimer, R., Howells, K., Palmer, R.L., & Chaloner, D.A. (1985). Adverse sexual experience in childhood and clinical eating disorders: A preliminary description. *Journal of Psychiatric Research, 19,* 357–361.

Patton, G.C., Johnson-Sabine, E., Wood, K., Mann, A.H., & Wakeling, A. (1990). Abnormal eating attitudes in London schoolgirls: A prospective epidemiological study: Outcome at 12 month follow-up. *Psychological Medicine, 20,* 383–394.

Piran, N., Lerner, P., Garfinkel, P.E., Kennedy, S.H., & Brouilette, C. (1988). Personality disorders in anorexia patients. *International Journal of Eating Disorders, 5,* 589–599.

Pope, H.G., & Hudson, J.I. (1989). Are eating disorders associated with borderline personality disorder? A critical review. *International Journal of Eating Disorders, 8,* 1–9.

Powers, P. (1997). Management of patients with comorbid medical conditions. In D.M. Garner & P.E. Garfinkel (Eds.), *Handbook of treatment for eating disorders* (pp. 424–436). New York: Guilford Press.

Puglifse, M.T., Lifshitz, F., Grad, G., Fort, P., & Marks-Katz, M. (1983). Fear of obesity: A cause of short stature and delayed puberty. *New England Journal of Medicine, 309,* 513–518.

Rastam, M. (1992). Anorexia nervosa in 51 Swedish adolescents: Premorbid problems and comorbidity. *Journal of the American Academy of Child and Adolescent Psychiatry, 31,* 819–829.

Raymond, N.C., Mitchell, J.E., Fallon, P., & Katzman, M.A. (1994). A collaborative approach to the use of medication. In P. Fallon, M. Katzman, & S.C. Wooley (Eds.), *Feminist perspectives on eating disorders* (pp. 231–250). New York: Guilford Press.

Rolland, K., Farnill, D., & Griffiths, R.A. (1997). Body figure perceptions and eating attitudes among Australian schoolchildren aged 8 to 12 years. *International Journal of Eating Disorders, 21,* 273–278.

Russell, G.F.M. (1979). Bulimia nervosa: An ominous variant of anorexia nervosa. *Psychological Medicine, 9,* 429–448.

Russell, G.F.M., Szmukler, G.I., Dare, C., & Eisler, I. (1987). An evaluation of family therapy in anorexia nervosa and bulimia nervosa. *Archives of General Psychiatry, 44,* 1047–1056.

Sands, R., Tricker, J., Sherman, C., Armatas, C., & Maschette, W. (1997). Disordered eating patterns, body image, self-esteem, and physical activity in preadolescent school children. *International Journal of Eating Disorders, 21,* 159–166.

Selvini-Palazzoli, M.P. (1974). *Self-starvation.* London: Chaucer.

Serdula, M.K., Collins, M.E., Williamson, D.F., Anda, R.F., Pamuk, E.R., & Byers, T.E. (1993). Weight control practices of U.S. adolescents and adults. *Annals of Internal Medicine, 119,* 667–671.

Sharpe, T.M., Killen, J.D., Bryson, S.W., Shisslak, C.M., Estes, L.S., Gray, N., Crago, M., & Taylor, C.B. (1998). Attachment style and weight concerns in preadolescent and adolescent girls. *International Journal of Eating Disorders, 23,* 39–44.

Silber, T.J. (1986). Anorexia nervosa in Blacks and Hispanics. *International Journal of Eating Disorders, 5,* 121–128.

Sohlberg, S., Norring, C., Homgren, S., & Rosmark, B. (1989). Impulsivity and long-term prognosis of psychiatric patients with anorexia nervosa/bulimia nervosa. *Journal of Nervous and Mental Disease, 177,* 249–258.

Smith, J.E., & Krejci, J. (1991). Minorities join the majority: Eating disturbances among Hispanic and Native American youth. *International Journal of Eating Disorders, 10,* 179–186.

Story, M., Hauck, F.R., Broussard, B.A., White, L.L., & Resnick, M.D. (1994). Weight perceptions and weight control practices in American Indian and Alaska Native adolescents: A national survey. *Archives of Pediatric Adolescent Medicine, 148,* 567–571.

Strober, M. (1997). Consultation and therapeutic engagement in severe anorexia nervosa. In D.M. Garner & P.E. Garfinkel (Eds.), *Handbook of treatment for eating disorders* (pp. 229–247). New York: Guilford Press.

Swift, W.J., & Letven, R. (1984). Bulimia and the basic fault. *Journal of the American Academy of Child and Adolescent Psychiatry, 23,* 489–497.

Telch, C.F., Agras, W.S., Rossiter, E.M., Wilfley, D., & Kenardy, J. (1990). Group cognitive-behavioral treatment for the non-purging bulimic: An initial evaluation. *Journal of Consulting and Clinical Psychology, 58,* 629–635.

Theander, S. (1996). Anorexia nervosa with an early onset: Selection, gender, outcome, and results of a long-term follow-up study. *Journal of Youth and Adolescence, 25,* 419–429.

Tiggemann, M., & Wilson-Barrett, E. (1998). Children's figure ratings: Relationship to self-esteem and negative stereotyping. *International Journal of Eating Disorders, 23,* 83–88.

Timmerman, M.G., Wells, L.A., & Chen, S. (1990). Bulimia nervosa and associated alcohol abuse among secondary school students. *American Academy of Child and Adolescent Psychiatry, 29,* 118–122.

Vitousek, K.B., & Ewald, L.S. (1993). Self-representation in eating disorders: A cognitive perspective. In Z. Segal & S. Blatt (Eds.), *The self in emotional disorders: Cognitive and psychodynamic perspectives* (pp. 221–257). New York: Guilford Press.

Vitousek, K.B., & Orimoto, L. (1993). Cognitive-behavioral models of anorexia nervosa, bulimia nervosa, and obesity. In P. Kendal & K. Dobson (Eds.), *Psychopathology and cognition* (pp. 191–142). New York: Academic Press.

Walsh, B.T., & Garner, D.M. (1997). Diagnostic issues. In D.M. Garner & P.E. Garfinkel (Eds.), *Handbook of treatment for eating disorders* (2nd ed., pp. 25–33). New York: Guilford Press.

Walsh, B.T., Hadigan, C.M., Devlin, M.J., Gladis, M., & Roose, S.P. (1991). Long-term outcome of antidepressant treatment for bulimia nervosa. *American Journal of Psychiatry, 148,* 1206–1212.

Wardle, J., & Beales, S. (1986). Restraint, body image and food attitudes in children from 12 to 18 years. *Appetite, 7,* 209–217.

Warren, M.P., Brooks-Gunn, J., Hamilton, L.H., Warren, F., & Hamilton, W.G. (1986). Scoliosis and fractures in young ballet dancers: Relation to delayed menarche and secondary amenorrhea. *New England Journal of Medicine, 314,* 1348–1353.

Welch, G.W., Hall, A., & Renner, R. (1990). Patient subgrouping in anorexia nervosa using psychologically-based classification. *International Journal of Eating Disorders, 9,* 311–322.

Wertheim, E.J., Paxton, S.J., Maude, D., Szmukler, G.I., Gibbons, K., & Hiller, L. (1992). Psychosocial predictors of weight loss behaviors and binge eating in adolescent girls and boys. *International Journal of Eating Disorders, 12,* 151–160.

Whittal, M.L., Agras, W.S., & Gould, R.A. (1999). Bulimia nervosa: A meta-analysis of psychosocial and pharmacological treatments. *Behavior Therapy, 30,* 117–135.

Wilfley, D.E., Agras, W.S., Telch, C.F., Rossiter, E.M., Schneider, J.A., Cole, A.G., Stifford, L., & Raeburn, S.D. (1993). Group cognitive-behavioral therapy and group interpersonal psychotherapy for the nonpurging bulimic individual: A controlled comparison. *Journal of Consulting and Clinical Psychology, 2,* 296–305.

CHAPTER 36

School Problems of Adolescents

Beeman N. Phillips

This chapter reviews school problems of adolescents, focusing on a developmental and ecological perspective.* Current evidence about different types of school problems is summarized, and approaches to intervening are presented. Overall, the chapter takes a conceptual and descriptive rather than a prescriptive view of school problems.

UNDERSTANDING SCHOOL PROBLEMS OF ADOLESCENTS: AN APPLIED DEVELOPMENTAL FRAMEWORK

Adolescence is not an isolated phenomenon. For example, Blos (1979) has argued that the adolescent must rework certain intrapsychic tensions initially faced in childhood. As further evidence, it has been found that childhood behavior disorders influence later adjustment. A longitudinal study by Shedler and Block (1990) is a case in point. They followed a group of children from preschool through age 18 and found that psychological differences among adolescent frequent drug users, experimenters, and abstainers could be traced to the earliest years of childhood. In another important longitudinal study, Cass and Thomas (1979) followed 200 children seen in a child guidance center during the

early 1960s who were then interviewed at 18 and 27 years of age. At the time they were seen in the clinic, they averaged 9 years of age, and the vast majority were boys. One of the best predictors of adult psychopathology was poor *school* adjustment, although a number of childhood indices were significant predictors.

There also is a need to reflect on the purpose in isolating such phenomena for special consideration. Presumably such a focus facilitates a clear understanding of the unique aspects of school problems that are not generalizable to other students in other developmental periods. For example, the consideration of adolescent drug use or adolescent pregnancy suggests that there is something unique about adolescence in relation to these problems. Although sexual activity is likely to begin in adolescence and drug use intensifies during the teen years, the clinician who focuses too narrowly on that period is apt to not fully realize the similarities and differences in such behaviors across developmental periods.

Adolescence can also be viewed from a social psychological, psychodynamic, evolutionary, cognitive, or normative perspective. Examining adolescence in different cultures adds still another perspective and leads to the realization that there are different paths from childhood to adulthood. Further, within the period of adolescence, it is possible to postulate subperiods corresponding to early adolescence (12–15 years) and late adolescence (15–18 years). Such a breakdown has some arbitrariness, but it is useful

---

*Portions of this chapter are based on Phillips (1992).

because it permits positing important developmental and secondary school events on a scale of time. For example, early adolescence is a crucial period of cognitive, psychosexual, and affective development (see Block, 1971; Blos, 1979; Gholson & Rosenthal, 1984). Gender differences also appear to be important in these developmental sequences (see Compas & Wagner, 1991; Rutter, 1980). For example, adolescent boys with psychological difficulties are likely to have problems in childhood; girls, in contrast, are more likely to manifest psychological difficulties in adolescence.

In essence, the perspective in this chapter sees the adolescent as moving through a *cumulative set* of determining experiences. The young person passes through a series of chained options that give direction to outcome. At many points, new experiences, feedback, or exposure to new role models may redirect the teenager's development. Secondary school experiences are important in this general developmental model, as, for example, when the adolescent who establishes a pattern of high achievement in secondary school then has the option of pursuing higher education. This further schooling, in turn, allows for the possibility of certain careers that then have personal, economic, lifestyle, and cultural implications.

A PROBLEM OF PERCEPTION?

To some extent, labeling certain behaviors "school problems" is a perennial problem in itself. To what extent, for example, is there an objective reality to school problems? Or is a label a value choice of the teacher or school? A focus on the primary "diagnostic" agent (i.e., the classroom teacher) allows the argument that identification of certain behaviors as school problems reflects only deviation from the dominant values of the school. For example, there is a greater tendency to associate school problems with Black or low socioeconomic status adolescents. This general situation may support the idea that the judgments of school professionals are influenced by their own backgrounds, educational values, assumptions about schooling, and expectations for certain groups.

A second level of reality in school problem identification focuses on whether the school's perception of the student parallels perceptions in other ecological contexts such as the family and peer group.

The attitudes of teachers, for example, may be divergent from those of peers, and this raises the question of whether there is less tendency to label behavior deviant when there is congruence. In addition, schools must deal with adolescents in a variety of confrontational situations, and in such situations it is important to distinguish between normal adolescent behavior and behavior that may indicate serious psychological difficulties. Furthermore, a school problem may be manifested differently among different groups of adolescents. In the upper-middle class, for example, there is a tendency toward passive behavior as opposed to the more active manifestation of developmental disorders in the lower class.

Schools also must deal with public perceptions of the problems of the schools. For example, in annual Gallup polls on education sponsored by Phi Delta Kappa, lack of discipline was viewed in the 1970s as the biggest problem with which public schools must deal, but in the 1980s, lack of discipline was displaced by drug abuse (e. g., Gallup & Elam, 1988). As a consequence, some schools rushed to promote programs to end drug abuse at the risk of becoming fertile ground for the entrepreneurship that often accompanies a rising public interest in a school problem. However, by the mid-1990s, lack of discipline had again overtaken drug abuse, although drug abuse still ranked third in seriousness (Rose, Gallup, & Elam, 1997).

DEFINITION OF SCHOOLS AND SCHOOLING MAKES A DIFFERENCE

How one defines schools and schooling also has an effect on how one defines school problems. Those who think of schooling as narrowly defined will suggest a different agenda for school problem identification and intervention than will those who seek to expand the role of schools. That is, there are different ways of framing school problems that depend on how one defines the purpose and nature of schooling. For example, Cremin (1988) claims that Americans are asking too much of schools and challenges the belief that public schools have the power to solve the social and economic problems that beset American society.

Others, however, ask much more of the public schools, for example, that they reduce teenage drug addiction and pregnancies, combat the spread of

AIDS, lead America to a more just and equal society, and restore/maintain American preeminence in the world economy. One example of this expanded view is the Hogg Foundation for Mental Health School of the Future project (Holtzman, 1992). Essential features of this conception of schooling include (1) the integration of a broad spectrum of human services (including physical and mental health services); (2) full involvement of parents and teachers in program activities; and (3) involvement of both public and private sectors of the community.

AN ECOLOGICAL PERSPECTIVE

School adjustment, broadly defined, is the interplay between the student and the school environment, although in this chapter, we are preoccupied with school problems, where there is a lack of adjustment. In both cases, however, there is a need to assess relationships between the school environment and student outcomes. However, until recently, such relationships remained tangled, and few school effects were shown, in spite of extensive research. Best known among these studies is that by Coleman et al. (1966). This large-scale survey indicated that schools had little effect, although the appropriateness of this and similar studies has been questioned, partly because of the limited variables used to evaluate school impact.

More recently, research has focused more directly on school process and ecological influence. Rutter, Maughan, Mortimore, and Ouston (1979), for example, considered not only achievement outcomes but student behaviors as well. The total pattern of their findings suggests that students' school experiences influence their behaviors in secondary schools. Many other indications of the potential of schools to influence student outcomes are reported by Walberg, Schiller, and Haertel (1979). They examined hundreds of studies and concluded that certain school conditions consistently produce positive effects on student outcomes. Good and Weinstein (1986) also examined evidence that "schools make a difference."

Another approach to this question is to investigate the opinions and understandings of young adults about their secondary school experiences, and Project TALENT makes this possible. In a report by Flanagan (1978) of life history interviews

acquired in 1975 from 1,000 30-year-old participants in this longitudinal project, five types of educational factors were identified as having a lasting impact: personal support and counseling, individualization, vocational guidance, quality of teaching, and curriculum. The overall results clearly indicated that memories were overwhelmingly negative for all areas except quality of teaching. The most common theme of dissatisfaction with high school was its lack of relevance to later life. This was followed by lack of concern for the individual and his or her mental health. Training for leisure time also is reported to have been inadequate, and evidently the curriculum contributed little to later employment possibilities.

In light of such results, we must avoid an overly simplistic view of school problems because their etiology is complex. Secondary schools operate as intricate social settings, and there are multiple patterns of student dysfunction that interfere with and impede school performance. The secondary school may serve as an antecedent in the sense that something that happens there precedes the onset of a school problem; it may function as a determinant that shapes the nature of a school problem, or events in the secondary school may be the occasions in which underlying causes are activated or manifested. But the secondary school is not usually the cause of a school problem in the sense of providing the conditions or circumstances that effectively and inevitably call forth the problem.

For these reasons, it is advantageous, and even necessary, to view school problems of adolescents from an ecological perspective. In this connection, one of Bronfenbrenner's (1979) more interesting ideas is that of developmental contexts. He believes that typical analyses of environmental influences on development do little more than identify the environments from which students come. For example, studies regularly show that family background is an important factor in school achievement (see Coleman, 1987). But such studies explain little about the processes involved, even where there is a focus on interpersonal factors—as in studies of parent-child relationships—because they lack generalizability across settings and contexts. What is necessary, he maintains, is to have concepts and data that go beyond the dyadic level and relate to transcontextual factors.

To apply Bronfenbrenner's general thesis, the environments in which adolescents live, and the processes through which these environments affect the course of development, are crucial to an understanding of their school problems. For example, the classroom could be considered a key primary developmental context. On the other hand, many extracurricular activities fit the concept of a secondary developmental context. Furthermore, the extent to which a principal supports his or her teachers is illustrative of the role of third parties, and supportive links between the family and secondary school is an example of the last principle.

Carrying this ecological perspective further, the changes that occur in school developmental contexts may be critical. For example, according to a report by Goodlad (1984), by the senior high school level, the frequency of encouraging behaviors and positive interaction by teachers has dropped to 50% of what is reported in elementary school. But whether such changes are related to organizational factors, instructional factors, or other school differences has yet to be determined. Another equally important consideration is the linkage between peer groups and the school. For example, when secondary students in the same study were asked to respond to the "one best thing about their school," 35% said their friends. Sports and good student activities were the next most popular type of response. The classes they were taking, the variety of course offerings, and teachers were less often mentioned. Adding to the significance of these results, students with lower self-concepts didn't participate as much in extracurricular aspects of secondary schooling and tended to have less satisfactory relations with peers.

As another illustration of the need for an ecological perspective, in many secondary schools there are various forms of academic tracking, the most common being vocational and college-bound tracks. According to Goodlad's (1984) findings, such segregation probably influences the character of both in-class and out-of-class experiences. His findings further suggest that the nature and quality of developmental contexts vary from high school to high school.

IMPLICATIONS OF *DSM-IV* FOR UNDERSTANDING SCHOOL PROBLEMS OF ADOLESCENTS

In the past, the American Psychiatric Association's diagnostic system, the *Diagnostic and Statistical Manual of Mental Disorders (DSM)*, has not been used in the assessment of school problems of adolescents (McConaughy & Achenbach, 1990). On occasion, some psychologists working in schools have found some utility in the *DSM* in recognizing a treatable disorder or for communicating with professionals in other settings. The newest version of the diagnostic system, *DSM-IV* (American Psychiatric Association [APA], 1994), faced the same challenges of limited relevance, although the situation has changed in recent years. One factor that has helped to bring this about is the trend toward providing more mental health services in schools (Carlson, Paavola, & Talley, 1995). Another is that the *DSM-IV* is more a product of empirical analysis and has greater theoretical sophistication than prior editions.

A special advantage of the *DSM-IV* is that it can serve an important function in mapping the developmental course of disruptive and other behavior disorders. For example, the emergence of oppositional patterns of behavior in the elementary school years often presages more serious antisocial behaviors later in adolescence (Patterson, Reid, & Dishion, 1992). Similarly, *DSM-IV* guidelines may help psychologists to better understand the needs of adolescents who demonstrate highly complex social and communication problems, and to thereby be in a position to develop more comprehensive assessment and intervention plans.

A further advantage of the *DSM-IV* as a framework for considering the school problems of adolescents is that it presents multiple explanations to account for a set of behavioral symptoms and suggests factors that need to be considered to test clinical hypotheses. For example, an adolescent's symptoms of generalized anxiety disorder (GAD) can be explained by one of several hypotheses, including anxiety due to a medical condition or anxiety induced by substance abuse, depression, or posttraumatic stress. Understanding these distinctions can be useful to psychologists in assessing the needs of anxious adolescents and collaborating, for example, with teachers and other school professionals in developing effective intervention plans.

Still another advantage is that mental health disorders are often linked with impairment of adolescents' functioning in the school environment. For example, students with conduct disorder (CD) are low achievers with poor relations with teachers and peers (Kazdin, 1987). As one more example, students with *DSM-IV* symptoms of anxiety and depression manifest impaired peer relationships, social withdrawal, somatic complaints, and negative self-statements (Jolly et al., 1994; Stark, 1990).

However, one limitation of the *DSM-IV* as an approach to evaluating and intervening in the school problems of adolescents, particularly in school settings, is that, at the general level, the *DSM-IV* emphasizes the medical model. That is, it explicitly characterizes problematic behavior as representing a disorder within the student. As a result, school environmental and other external factors that often play a significant role in behavior difficulties of students are unlikely to receive sufficient attention. In addition, it is one thing to understand the mechanics of *DSM-IV* and to learn to screen for a particular disorder, but it is quite another to develop competence in differential diagnosis of the disorders in the *DSM-IV*. As a case in point, although *DSM-IV* is explicit about how to combine symptoms and other criteria to make a diagnosis, it provides little guidance about how to gather the information needed to determine if the symptoms are present (Blashfield & Livesley, 1991). For example, informants (teachers, parents, and students) vary in their ability to provide reliable information about symptom presence, and weighing and combining the reports of informants can become a complex and difficult process. Finally, questions have been raised about the treatment validity of the *DSM-IV* by some investigators (see McBurnett, 1996). Nevertheless, *DSM-IV* diagnosis does provide substantial direction for selecting treatment, and, in some cases, there is direct evidence of treatment validity. For example, a Division 12 Task Force (1995, 1996) has identified a variety of successful treatments for *DSM-IV* behavior disorders, although many of these treatments would be difficult to use in school-based interventions.

INTERVENING IN SCHOOL PROBLEMS: THE SECONDARY SCHOOL AS A SOCIAL SITUATION

The "situation," as a social-psychological concept, can be used to unify the different methods of intervening in the school problems of adolescents. Based on the work of Gump (1980) and Sarason and Klaber (1985), the school situation is viewed as an arena where social, educational, and psychological forces converge. There is the further premise

in a situational view of school problems that understanding must go beyond characteristics of students. For example, in analyses of structures of social relations, the professional must move beyond conventional sociometric methods and instead utilize less atomistic analysis with more emphasis on the complexity and multideterminate situation underlying social relations. In this process, it also is important to take into account variables close to the school (e.g., the coping strategies that adolescents bring to the school setting) as well as societal features (e.g., inequality of the power and resources of the families of adolescents).

However, the concept of situation is, in some aspects of school problems, only a sensitizing one because it is not in itself a clearly defined phenomenon. That is, it is necessary to have a better understanding of relevant situations if we are to have a strong research base capable of yielding school interventions. In this connection, the review of the school as a social situation by Gump (1980) pointed out that physical milieu, participants, and program factors are the basic components of school settings. Barker and his colleagues (1978), in their groundbreaking efforts, also examined these features of behavior settings in a variety of environments, and have traced the ways that settings have consequences for participants.

Additional perspectives on the secondary school as a social situation are provided by newer conceptions of learning that have entered the psychological literature. The various forms of constructionism, such as cognitive constructionism, as well as sociocultural approaches to school learning that emphasize the interdependence of social and individual educational processes are of particular note (Marshall, 1996).

SYSTEMS OF PSYCHOLOGICAL INTERVENTION

It also is important that those who are concerned about intervening in the school problems of adolescents not think about intervention as if it were a single, unified process. As one manifestation of that complexity, it is important that efforts to intervene in school problems of adolescents include competence-building interventions in addition to pathology-fighting strategies. One good example of this competence-building approach is provided by Strayhorn (1988). In addition to identifying competencies that adolescents need to develop, he also identifies methods of promoting these competencies.

Despite the complexity of the intervention process, considerable progress has been made in developing efficacious interventions. For example, Lipsey and Wilson (1993) concluded, from their broad review of the results of 302 meta-analyses reported in the past 20 years, that there are many psychological, educational, and behavioral interventions that have generally positive effects on intended outcomes. Another example of progress is the book edited by Thomas and Grimes (1995) that offers advice on "best practices" the psychologist in the schools can implement. Egan's (1986) book is further evidence that the helping skills domain has progressed far. Although Egan's book has a strong client-centered orientation throughout, he gives significant attention to other theoretical insights (and related helping strategies) and thus expands awareness of the complexity possible in any helping relationship, in secondary schools and other settings.

It is important to also point out that numerous studies show that *some* adolescents can successfully change their school problem behavior without the help of professional intervention. Nevertheless, the puzzle of how adolescents *intentionally* change their behavior without professional intervention has not been well solved, and the need to concentrate more on the phenomenon of intentional change has not been well recognized in efforts to change the school problem behavior of adolescents. One step toward understanding this phenomenon has occurred, however, through the work of Prochaska, DiClemente, and Norcross (1992), who have developed a promising model of intentional behavior change.

As to the future, practice guidelines that fully incorporate empirically supported interventions may well become prominent in tomorrow's psychological services landscape. To illustrate what is beginning to happen, the APA Division of Clinical Psychology (Division 12 Task Force, 1995, 1996) has identified many well-established or probably efficacious treatments for a substantial number of different *DSM-IV* behavior disorders. There is the need, however, to draw a distinction between the efficacy of an intervention and its generalizability and utility in real-life settings. Although available practice guidelines are not yet very useful to psychologists concerned with the school problems of adolescents, they have the potential to enhance future efforts to intervene with and help such students.

THE SOCIAL PSYCHOLOGY OF SECONDARY EDUCATION

The psychologist who works with school problems of adolescents also needs to become familiar with research on the social psychology of education. One example of this task is to ask the question: What does it mean for an adolescent to be "competent" in the classroom? Traditionally, classroom competence has been defined in terms of student variables such as performance on standardized tests, or in terms of stimulus variables such as word recognition and task-structure variables. However, these two approaches to defining classroom competence have been challenged, one good example being the work reported by Wilkinson (1982). The contributors to this book emphasize that, in addition to meaning in the stimulus and student, classroom competence involves meaning in the social situation. That is, classroom competence is a social phenomenon as well as a psychological and linguistic phenomenon. In essence, such research provides the psychologist with a new definition of classroom competence that has important implications for efforts to help adolescents.

Another example is cooperative learning. This refers to instructional methods in which students work together to learn academic material. Slavin (1983) reviewed 45 elementary and secondary school field experiments that evaluated achievement effects of such strategies, and for those interested in the practical side of cooperative learning, Bohlmeyer and Burke (1987) presented a schema for categorizing cooperative learning techniques that can be utilized by psychologists consulting with teachers. The classification scheme they proposed will facilitate the matching of cooperative learning strategies with the classroom teacher's instructional objectives and teaching style.

In addition, if psychologists who work with the school problems of adolescents are to provide instructional consultation, as advocated by Rosenfield (1987), they need to be conversant with teachers and teaching. For grounding in these matters, there is no better resource than the *Handbook of Research on Teaching* (Wittrock, 1986). However, to put work with teachers into a broader context, a useful resource is *How Students Learn* (Lambert & Mc-Combs, 1998). In addition to examining current research on how students learn, this volume offers perspectives on learner-centered classrooms, assessment systems, needs of teachers, and successful school reform.

SPECIFIC AND NONSPECIFIC EFFECTS OF INTERVENTIONS

To better understand the place of interventions in secondary schools and schooling, it also is helpful to distinguish between specific and nonspecific effects. An intervention's effectiveness may be due primarily to its nonspecific effects, and various combinations of specific and nonspecific effects produce different outcomes (see Schopler, 1987). To concretize the situation, specific effects are effects that are inherently and directly related to the intervention and that are demonstrated when well-designed interventions are experimentally compared with no or a control intervention. In contrast, nonspecific effects are related to external factors that are present in or generated by the use of the intervention in natural settings. These effects are not inherently related to the intervention itself, nor, in most cases, do they depend on the efficacy (in the specific effects sense) of the intervention. A highly efficacious intervention may generate negative rather than positive nonspecific effects, so that overall outcomes of the intervention, applied in a secondary school or other natural setting, are minimal.

One set of nonspecific effects relates to theoretical interpretations of the problem at which intervention is aimed. Schopler (1987) illustrates this in his discussion of intervention programs for autistic children and adolescents. Autism is sometimes explained psychodynamically as social withdrawal from cold, hostile, and rejecting parents, so that parents of such children and adolescents see themselves as the cause of the disorder and feel responsible, blamed, and misunderstood. An alternative view is to interpret the disorder in biological terms, thus making the parents, like their children, victims of the disorder. The point, of course, is that an intervention based on this latter theory is likely to be more enthusiastically received and to enlist more active parental support, thus generating more positive nonspecific effects that, in turn, might be

critical to the success of the intervention. The enthusiastic response of other constituencies, such as teachers and other school professionals, parents, and the adolescents themselves (who manifest the school problems for which intervention is done), also is important. For a review of these and other acceptability factors, readers should consult Elliott (1986); Levy-Leboyer (1988); Reimers, Wacker, and Koeppl (1987); and Witt (1986).

But what holds these diverse elements together is the critical importance of school settings. Too often, applications of interventions in schools are not really that. They are interventions with adolescents in settings that happen to include secondary schools, and in most such efforts, it is not important that adolescents be in schools. Nevertheless, it is essential that psychologists use interventions in ways that capitalize on the unique opportunities provided by the secondary school. This calls for better understanding of secondary school settings and for the conception and planning of interventions based on that knowledge.

LINKING SCHOOL ADJUSTMENT PROBLEMS WITH INTERVENTION

A wide array of school adjustment problems occur in relation to secondary schools and schooling. Although in some instances, these can be serious, they more often are only bothersome to teachers and other students. Other school adjustment problems are more serious and are discussed in the following sections.

VIOLENCE IN SECONDARY SCHOOLS

In discussing violence in secondary schools, there is an initial problem in agreeing on what should be called violence. It certainly is not a unidimensional problem. Acts against students and teachers are different from such victimless crimes as vandalism.

As to the incidence of school violence and vandalism, Gottfredson and Gottfredson (1985) analyzed the considerable data in the national Safe Schools–Violent Schools survey (National Institute of Justice, 1978) that was conducted in 4,000 public junior and senior high schools. One conclusion is that there is a substantial amount of disruption and disorder in those schools. For example, in an average month, 12% of the pupils surveyed reported having more than $1 stolen from them, and 50% of the teachers reported being the target of swearing or obscene gestures. Although this might not seem extraordinary, most people not learning or working in schools are probably not subjected to the same levels of affront or victimization.

However, there are few good, large-scale studies of the prevalence of school violence, which has led some to question whether there is a problem with violence in schools and to advocate reviewing any set of statistics about school violence with skepticism. Nevertheless, school violence is a major concern of the public and of many groups of professionals. For example, in the 1997 Phi Delta Kappa/Gallup Poll of the public's attitudes toward the public schools, fighting/violence/gangs was ranked as the fourth biggest problem with which the public schools must deal (Rose et al., 1997). In addition, there has been a major survey of weapons possession by adolescents on school campuses (Callahan & Rivara, 1992). In response to these concerns, recommendations have been made by the National Center for Disease Control and Prevention for multiagency involvement in community-based programs to reduce violence (Rosenberg, O'Carroll, & Powell, 1992).

Schools, of course, are searching for solutions. Many are standing up to violence by trying everything from enacting new school suspension policies to using closed-circuit television on school buses and adopting "zero tolerance" policies for possession of weapons or any kind of violent behavior. More importantly, schools are trying to confront the issue of violence by introducing antiviolence curricula, conflict resolution, and conflict management programs and by collaborating with social service agencies to address underlying causes of violence (see Morrison et al., 1994; Sautter, 1995). Sautter also includes a "resource guide for action" that would be useful to psychologists interested in becoming involved in programs to reduce school violence.

At this point, social scientists have not contributed much substantive knowledge about the "whys" of various kinds of violence in secondary schools. However, there are many sources of authoritative coverage of traditional theories of aggression (see, e.g., Berkowitz, 1993). In these books, general theoretical perspectives on aggression are framed in terms of antecedent conditions, mediating factors, and anticipated consequences, and for purposes of treatment, aggression is conceptualized along a continuum encompassing a tendency to aggress. There also is the realization that the search for a primary causal factor or a primary treatment strategy is likely to be futile. Beyond this, theories of aggression imply that major changes in secondary schools are a necessary step to reduce violence significantly. In addition, restructuring the family, work settings, and the stratification system of society ultimately would be required.

GENDERED VIOLENCE AND BULLYING

Gendered violence, which is another aspect of the school violence situation, can take various forms. Frequently, it is the result of dating problems. Ex-boyfriends and ex-girlfriends cause a lot of anger and hate because what sounds like a minor issue to a grownup—the breakup of a two-week relationship, losing a date to a dance—feels like a crisis to the early adolescent that can precipitate violent behavior. In addition, many adolescents experience other forms of violent behavior, such as slapping, shoving, and shouting, from dating partners. Gendered violence can also take the form of sexual harassment and abuse of students by other students (Horton, 1996; Johnson, 1992). Less common is the verbal, and sometimes physical, abuse directed toward gay and lesbian students.

Sexual abuse of students by school personnel is another important dimension of the problem. However, the extent of such abuse is not precisely known, although surveys of students indicate that sexual harassment is a problem for a significant number of students. One such survey of high school graduates in North Carolina (Wishnietsky, 1991) found that 82% of females and 18% of males reported sexual harassment by school staff during their school career. In another survey (American Association of University Women, 1993), 25% of females and 10% of males in grades 8 through 11 said they had been sexually harassed by school faculty or staff. To deal with such problems, Shakeshaft and Cohan (1995) pointed out that school districts need strong and clear policies on sexual harassment. School districts also need to make sure all employees and students know what these policies are and how to make complaints. In addition, school districts need to educate students, faculty, and staff members about sexual harassment and what to do if harassment occurs.

Bullying is another facet of violence in schools that needs special mention. Although most research has been conducted in Scandinavian countries, studies done on bullying in the United States have produced similar results (Batsche & Knoff, 1994). Bullying can be physical (hitting, kicking, etc.) and it can be verbal (name calling, threats, gossiping, ignoring); it can involve girls as well as boys, although the bullying that takes place among boys tends to be more physical. In some cases, bullying can lead to serious injuries, and occasionally a student who can't get over the persistent fear and humiliation will take another student's and/or his own life. Bullying also is occurring more frequently and in more serious forms now than in the past, and follow-up studies of bullies don't paint a positive picture. For example, two-thirds of the boys identified as bullies in grades 6 to 9 in one Scandinavian study had one or more criminal convictions by the time they were 24 years old (cited in Batsche & Knoff, 1994). For these reasons, bullying must be directly addressed by school systems. Remedies deemed to be effective in dealing with bullying, including school-based interventions, are described by Batsche and Knoff (1994) and Barone (1997).

IN-SCHOOL TRUANCY

A problem that particularly plagues urban high schools is in-school truancy (Teachman, 1979). Teachman reports, for example, that absence from classes in which students were enrolled in the Detroit Public Schools during 1977 to 1979 was nearly 20%. But this was only the official rate. Teachers' attendance figures suggest that the rate was actually closer to 30%.

Although this is an in-class problem, students in the building but not in class are the source of other problems. For example, most of the violence in high schools occurs outside the classroom. Interestingly, in-school truancy in the Detroit high schools was highest in the ninth grade, during the first and second hours of the school day, and for all classes after lunch (Teachman, 1979).

These data suggest that it is not just whether classes are relevant and interesting that determines the incidence of in-school truancy. Student characteristics, as well as teaching effectiveness, attendance policies, and other school factors enter in. As an indication of the importance of both student and school factors, Teachman (1979) points out that official in-school truancy rates varied from 33.5% at one high school to a low 6.9% at another that had a selected student body.

ACCIDENT PREVENTION

With more explicit concern about school and other environmental contexts, the ground is set for a perspective that can be brought to bear on accident behavior of adolescents and the important school concern for student safety. According to Baker, O'Neill, and Karph (1984), motor vehicle collisions are the leading cause of adolescent deaths from injury. In addition, males are at far greater risk than females, particularly for serious injury, as are poor and African-American adolescents. However, the ways injuries occur to adolescents are not, as some might think, "accidents," that is, random, uncontrollable acts of fate. They are understandable, predictable, and preventable. Avoidable injuries also result in great economic costs as well as lost school days and inestimable psychological costs for adolescents. For these reasons, injury prevention programs that can be implemented in secondary schools, such as those described by Peterson (1988), are critical, including comprehensive programs aimed at both environmental and behavioral intervention.

DELINQUENCY

Juvenile delinquency is a pervasive phenomenon in many areas of the country. The FBI's *Uniform Crime Reports* (U.S. Department of Justice, 1990) show that 50% of all arrests for property offenses involve persons under 18. More than one million youngsters are accused of delinquent and/or criminal behavior annually and appear in the juvenile court system. In terms of the expectations that the public has for its schools, it is safe to assume that the school has some responsibility for the out-of-school life of its students, so that there is a broad relationship between the schools and delinquency. Further, because delinquency is a legal concept, the point of contact between the adolescent and delinquency is the juvenile justice system. Juvenile justice is intrinsically tied, therefore, to the schools.

Generally, studies of delinquency provide glimmers of hope that it is preventable, but no more than that (see Burchard & Burchard, 1987). Programs may have had only modest success, however, because they do not address the most important causes of delinquency, which might be considered to be social, economic, organizational, and political. From their analyses, it also seems clear that early intervention holds out more hope for modest reductions in delinquency than later treatment. In addition, a list of the important causes of delinquency would ordinarily also include poor parenting and school failure, which need to be more effectively addressed in delinquency prevention programs. Peer and community prevention programs also need special attention.

CHRONIC ACTING-OUT ADOLESCENTS

A major characteristic of aggressive adolescents is their own difficulty in perceiving and accepting responsibility for their acts. Unfortunately, the educational system serving them can often mirror a similar inability to accept responsibility for them. Because of the direct and indirect harm they inflict on others, and because of the chronicity of their problems, aggressive, acting-out adolescents often insidiously become increasingly neglected and shunned by others in the secondary school environment. There is the need, therefore, to increase the response of school systems toward these youth, and the clinician can, among other things, be an advocate for the needs of acting-out adolescents, especially in school settings. The responsibilities of secondary schools are made more difficult, however, because of the wide variety of problems that occur in an overlapping manner in these adolescents, including school failure, delinquency, substance abuse, teen pregnancy, family violence, and repeated relocations and changes in living arrangements. As a result, intervention needs to be multidisciplinary and involve active coordination of school efforts and those of social and mental health systems. For school-based efforts, there is a range of effective programs, including social problem-solving and cognitive-behavioral interventions as

well as behavioral training programs for teachers and parents (see Hughes & Hall, 1989; Kazdin, 1987; Kratochwill & Morris, 1993).

PREGNANT ADOLESCENTS

Each year, more than one million teenage girls in the United States become pregnant; more than 400,000 get abortions, and 500,000 others—the majority of whom are unmarried—give birth (National Research Council, 1987). This is a very serious problem because, among other things, many pregnant teenagers drop out of school. In addition, disciplinary, academic, and other school problems tend to increase. Teenagers who give birth during their adolescent years also tend to function less effectively in numerous other realms than their peers who delay childbearing (Chase-Lansdale & Brooks-Gunn, 1994).

As public and political attention has become increasingly focused on teenage childbearing, efforts to prevent teenage pregnancy and to ameliorate its consequences have proliferated. Of particular note, the National Research Council report (1987) concluded that programs and policies designed to address adolescent pregnancy should make pregnancy prevention their highest priority. Although a specific role for schools is not addressed, many of the approaches suggested can be or are already being carried out by secondary schools. For examples of these programs, the reader should consult surveys by the Education Research Group (1987) and the Children's Defense Fund (1986) and the review of sex education in public schools by Kirby (1994). The problem is extreme, however, and secondary schools can only ameliorate some aspects; coordinated community, governmental, and broad societal efforts are needed. Such broad-based efforts are addressed by Brooks-Gunn and Furstenberg (1989), who review what is known about adolescent sexual behavior, and by Furstenberg, Brooks-Gunn, and Chase-Landsdale (1989), who review changing patterns of childbearing among adolescents and the impact of premature parenthood. More recent detailed reviews of efforts to prevent the occurrence of teenage pregnancy and to ameliorate its consequences also are available (see Frost & Forrest, 1995; Maynard, 1995). The evidence in both of these recent articles gives additional strong support to the importance of increasing the availability of services to adolescents and the need for more integrated school and community services.

ADOLESCENT SUICIDAL BEHAVIOR

Adolescent suicidal behavior is a growing problem for secondary schools. As the numbers of sublethal attempts and committed suicides increase, school professionals are forced to accept the seriousness of this behavior. The literature pertaining to suicidal youth is reviewed by Smith (1990) and more recently by Mazza (1997), who attempt to make a coherent picture out of what seems, at least superficially, to be a confusing literature. In contrast, Poland (1989) has provided a concise, practice-oriented volume that provides a focused and prescriptive account of school-based techniques for changing suicidal youths' behavior. Another reference that provides useful information on suicidal behavior of adolescents has been written by Curran (1987). The final portion (Chapters 8, 9, 10), which addresses assessment, treatment, and prevention of suicidal behavior, will be of particular interest to clinicians working at the school-community interface. In light of the association between depression and suicidal behaviors, school-based interventions that focus on depressive tendencies (such as those presented by Stark, 1990) also would be helpful.

As to concrete recommendations on what can be done in secondary schools to prevent suicidal behavior, one strategy is to help adolescents do things for themselves. They need to be able to monitor themselves, to recognize when they are under stress and when they are beginning to feel depressed. Instead of letting the pressure build up, they can then seek help earlier. In other words, youngsters need to learn to recognize and admit to being troubled. However, girls are more willing than boys to say they're depressed and to seek help, a difference that prevention programs need to take into account.

Another intervention strategy is to help teenagers understand coping styles and coping mechanisms (see Phillips, 1993). This way, they will be better able to adapt to stress and feelings of depression. Intervention techniques also need to teach them to replace ineffective coping styles with more effective ones. Assertive, direct, and clear communication is a central goal of intervention efforts. Once these adolescents are able to communicate their feelings and are willing to share them, the aim of intervention is to help them become logical problem solvers, so that, when personal problems arise, they can sort them out logically and try to arrive at reasonable solutions.

Teachers also can be helped to take a number of steps. First, teachers should not try to handle such a burden alone. They should be urged to tell the school psychologist, school counselor, or school social worker. Helping to establish such a support network in secondary schools is one of the first things that should be done. Second, with one of these other professionals, the teacher should confront the student to discuss what is causing him or her to contemplate suicide. If the student recognizes the need for help, the family should be alerted. The principal and mental health professional should sit down with the family and discuss the concerns of the school staff about the student. It also is essential that the school maintain monitoring and follow-up. Just asking how things are going and showing interest and concern may be all that is required. But if things are not getting better, the school should again alert the family.

If the student does not recognize the need for help, there are additional ethical and legal considerations (Fischer & Sorenson, 1996). The law presumes that most adolescents are incompetent to know what is best for themselves, and that parents possess what the adolescent lacks in maturity, experience, and capacity or judgment. The situation is further complicated by the special relation of schools to their students and parents. Perhaps the best approach to take is to inform the student of the limits of confidentiality, while at the same time attempting to secure the student's agreement to involve his or her parents. It also would be important to obtain the agreement of the parents to cooperate with the school in the course of intervention and to help protect their child's potential benefit from the treatment.

PHYSICAL APPEARANCE AND SOCIAL RECEPTION

Physical appearance is especially important to adolescents because of its impact on social reception. Thus, it ultimately can affect school learning and behavior and be the source of significant school problems. Adolescents feel and behave toward others as a function of physical appearance, and personality is shaped by these social responses to appearance. For example, teenagers who are overweight might be perceived as lazy. Also, better-looking adolescents seem to be more socially skilled than less attractive youngsters. These are factual matters, yet why is it that physical appearance has such impact? A possible answer is that physically attractive adolescents are expected to be more competent. This expectation causes other teenagers to behave toward attractive peers as if they were competent, and this, in turn, leads to a self-fulfilling prophecy. Much of the book edited by Herman, Zanna, and Higgins (1986) addresses matters of this sort. Concerned with the interrelated topics of appearance, deviance, and social stigmatization, their book can play a major role in calling attention to the importance of physical appearance. However, the psychologist who wants to intervene directly in these problems will need additional resources that deal with specific assessment and intervention matters. For example, for work with eating disorders, the article by Phelps and Bajorek (1991) and the handbooks edited by Garner and Garfinkel (1985) and Brownell and Foreyt (1986) are particularly useful. In treating eating disorders, it is important to emphasize that collaboration between psychologist and physician is necessary. Another significant feature of such treatment programs has been the extent to which significant persons in the adolescent's environment, such as parents and teachers, have been utilized as change agents.

FAMILY AS A RELATIONAL CONTEXT FOR SCHOOL PROBLEMS

Youniss and Smollar (1985) present a theoretical formulation concerning the role of adolescents' relationships with parents that has important implications for educators and psychologists. In addition to their important theoretical statements, Youniss and Smollar also present the results of eight descriptive, exploratory studies in which parent-adolescent relationships come to life and which might provide helpful insights to educators and psychologists working with adolescents' school problems. As a case in point, adolescents' relationships with their mother and father are very different, and this has important implications for dealing with adolescents in single-parent families. The seriousness of

the single-parent family as an influence on school problems is further indicated by U.S. Census Bureau projections that almost 50% of children born in 1980 will live a considerable time with only one parent before they reach 18 years of age (Brown, 1980). Moreover, research by the Kettering Foundation (Brown, 1980) and meta-analyses by Amato and Keith (1991a, 1991b) show that adolescents from divorced and remarried families, in comparison with those from two-parent, nondivorced families, are at greater risk for developing problems in adjustment. As to the school-based differences, results for absenteeism, suspensions, truancy, expulsions, dropouts, tardiness, and discipline problems all show an advantage to the two-parent family. Of course, one-parent families are more often in the low-income category, but the disparities still exist when this and related background factors are controlled.

Adolescence also coincides with certain types of parental crisis, including concerns about midlife transitions, aging, marital deficiencies, and anticipation of the empty nest. A further point is that intrapsychic changes associated with the adolescent "passage" require systematic external influence, mainly by parents. This puts additional strains on the family, which may already be in crisis. In addition, the developmental tasks that are commonly recognized as important to adolescence cannot be achieved without significant conflict with parents. For example, the sense of autonomy is important to adolescence, and the adolescent must give up the dependency characteristic of preadolescence to make the passage to adolescence successfully. But many aspects of the situation make parents want to hang on or even increase the controls, and much ambivalence about the adolescent's growing sense of independence occurs. Such conflicts can add to the parents' own developmental crises and their reactions can be counterproductive. The adolescent's need for understanding and guidance as well as autonomy and parental confidence, therefore, are not met, with the result that the adolescent's school adjustment often suffers. Although the problems are complex, there are a number of parent education programs (see Fine, 1980) that might be useful in such situations. However, credible evidence is lacking on their success, even though some programs, such as the very popular Parent Effectiveness Training (PET) program, have reached thousands of parents.

DRUG USE AND ABUSE

In the past two decades, public concern about non-medical drug use has stimulated much research. As to the prevalence of drug use in the adolescent age range, a survey conducted by the U.S. Department of Health and Human Services (1987) reported that approximately 90% of high school seniors had tried alcohol at least once, 67% had used alcohol in the previous month, and 37% reported instances of heavy drinking (five or more alcoholic drinks in a row) within the previous two weeks. Among high school seniors, 57% also had tried other illicit drugs, and 2% reported using marijuana daily. In addition, 20% reported daily cigarette smoking. These data, which are typical of the findings of other surveys, indicate high levels of substance use and abuse among adolescents. As things now stand, it is easy to be against substance abuse but very difficult to develop and implement intervention programs in secondary schools. Nevertheless, secondary schools provide important grounds for such interventions because most adolescents can be reached in this setting, and school personnel have or can be trained to have the requisite knowledge and skills for developing and implementing intervention programs.

Drug education has been the most widely used approach, despite the lack of evidence of its efficacy (see Glynn, Leukefeid, & Ludford, 1983a; Tobler, 1986). Peer pressure, which often has been cited as a significant cause of substance abuse, is the basis of other intervention programs. These programs focus on teaching adolescents the necessary social skills to resist peer pressure and to handle social situations in which substance use is problematic (see Glynn, Leukefeid, & Ludford, 1983b). In addition to structured training in the recognition of peer pressure and the development of assertiveness techniques, such programs involve role playing in social situations common to substance use. Other correlates of substance use and abuse, such as impulsivity, external locus of control, and poor self-concept, are the basis of a broad spectrum of interventions that focus on general personal and social coping skills (see Forman & Linney, 1988; Gilchrist & Schinke, 1985).

In contrast to these largely preventive interventions, there is minimal research and few intervention activities with students at high risk, that is, students who have already begun to experiment with drugs and those who manifest poor school attendance, poor grades, and other precursors of substance use. In future efforts, approval and commitment from secondary school personnel and other implementation issues also need special attention. There also should be multilevel, multifactor intervention approaches that take into account the variety of personal, social, and ecological variables leading to substance use and abuse (see Shedler & Block, 1990).

Nevertheless, some adolescents can modify problem drug use without the benefit of formal intervention, and there is a need to give special attention to the phenomenon of *intentional* change in problem drug use. A first step in that direction has already been made in studies of self-initiated and professionally facilitated change of addictive behavior (Prochaska et al., 1992). In this research, done primarily with young adults, a promising stages-and-processes model of intentional behavior change has been developed that has implications for changing problem drug use by adolescents.

LINKING SCHOOL ACHIEVEMENT PROBLEMS WITH INTERVENTION

Secondary schools educate the intellect as well as the emotions, and education takes place in a variety of settings other than the place called secondary school. In essence, many components of American society have a role to play in dealing with the intellectual development of adolescents (see Goodlad, 1984; Mullis, Campbell, & Farstrup, 1993; National Commission on Excellence in Education, 1983; Ravitch & Finn, 1987; Sizer, 1984). Overall, the cumulative effect of these reports, and others like them in the 1980s and 1990s, has been a clearer recognition of an expanded national interest in improved schooling for adolescents.

ACADEMIC UNDERACHIEVEMENT

Such recognition is important because the public generally and many educators believe that American adolescents are academic underachievers. The best data on adolescent underachievement come from the National Assessment of Educational Progress (NAEP), which has monitored the academic achievement of the nation's youth at ages 9, 13, and 17 annually or biannually since 1969. With these data, it is possible to track the academic achievement of the same cohort of students, first at age 9, then at age 13, and then at age 17. This way, achievement growth can be ascertained. What has been found in the reading, science, and mathematics areas is that many adolescents score no higher at age 17 than many of their peers did at age 9, despite the fact that they differ by eight years of schooling (Ralph, Keller, & Crouse, 1994). Ralph et al. further point out that other national studies (e.g., High School and Beyond, the Longitudinal Study of America's Youth, and Project TALENT) have produced academic growth estimates for adolescents that are quite similar to those found in the NAEP studies.

International comparisons also help to document the general academic underachievement of adolescents in American public schools. For example, the Third International Mathematics and Science Study (TIMSS) report shows that American twelfth-graders, when compared to students in other countries, perform poorly in mathematics and science (Forgione, 1998). However, there are critics of such international comparisons (Baker, 1997).

As a measured response to this contentious situation, it can be argued that, despite our nation's extensive efforts to improve public schooling, achievement trends in reading, mathematics, and science have been relatively flat since at least the 1970s (Stedman, 1993). It also can be argued that academic achievement levels of American adolescents are not what they need to be to meet the challenges of the coming decades. That is, arguments about whether the academic achievement of our adolescents has declined over time miss the point. The crucial question is whether our secondary schools are good enough to stand up to future competitive challenges.

School Dropouts

There is a common assumption that the nation's dropout rate is going down. According to the National Center for Education Statistics (1995), only 10% of the population segment between ages 16 and 24 were high school dropouts, defined as persons who are not high school graduates and who are not enrolled in school. However, evidence abounds that school districts and even some states report inaccurate dropout information. In particular, understating the dropout problem, which is common in big school districts, has concealed the crisis in urban schools, where as many as half of the students either drop out or graduate without basic skills (Fossey, 1996).

However, addressing the dropout problem involves more than designing a better student-tracking system. We need more useful strategies for helping potential dropouts be successful. To help remedy that situation, Hahn, Danzberger, and Lefkowitz (1987) provide a comprehensive overview of the nature of the problem and the kinds of programs that schools either have adopted or could adopt to combat this problem. They review what social scientists say are the major risk factors indicating that a student might be in danger of dropping out. One of these is being behind in grade level and older than classmates. For example, about one-third of all high school students are behind the modal grade by one to two years. Poor academic performance is another indicator. In California, for example, 41,000 out of 98,000 students left twelfth grade because they failed graduation examinations or courses they needed to graduate. Another reason for dropping out is dislike of school; in urban high schools, students may feel tremendous insecurity. A substantial number of high school dropouts also have been suspended or placed in detention before dropping out. In addition, most girls who become pregnant in high school drop out. Dropouts also are much more likely than high school graduates to come from families that receive welfare, and for youngsters having trouble in school, the world of work sometimes seems to be the only alternative. The literature also links dropping out to undiagnosed and unattended to learning disabilities and emotional problems.

Hahn et al. (1987) also report on programs that have been instituted to help keep teenagers in school. The strands of these in-school reforms include (1) mentorships and intensive, sustained counseling for troubled youngsters; (2) an array of social services, including health care, family planning education, and infant care facilities for adolescent mothers; (3) concentrated remediation using individualized instruction and competency-based curriculum; (4) improved incentives, including financial rewards for completing high school; (5) year-round schools and alternative schools; (6) an effective school-business collaboration that provides access to the mainstream economy; (7) heightened accountability for dropout rates at all levels of the system of public education; and (8) involvement of parents and community organizations in dropout prevention.

Failure to Meet the Problem of Student Differences

Individual differences among students present a pervasive and profound problem to secondary school educators, and adaptations that are responsive to individual differences will help provide better educational opportunities for secondary as well as elementary students. As a case in point, Cuban (1989) argues that we must reexamine the institution of the graded school. It is a primary source of the high rates of academic failure among at-risk students, and it is ill-equipped to overcome the educational disadvantages of at-risk students. He does recognize, however, that redesigning schools and schooling is extremely difficult, and he suggests that incremental change, rather than complete redesign, is more feasible. As examples of such incremental change, he briefly discusses grouping across age and ability, team teaching, core curricula, and cooperative learning. However, creating a culture of change is more important than the specific alternatives or implementation strategies chosen (Oakes & Lipton, 1992).

The size of secondary schools is a related issue. Barker and Gump (1964) and later Wicker (1968) and Baird (1969) have traced the consequences of "undermanning" and "overmanning" in secondary schools. This theory states that as high schools become larger, the number of students rises faster than the number of settings, resulting in more students per setting in larger high schools. With more students available, there are fewer pressures and opportunities to become actively involved in setting operations. When applied to extracurricular activities, for example, students in smaller high schools experience more opportunities to participate and take responsibility and are more likely to perform leadership and other supportive roles. A consequence of this increased involvement is more satisfaction with such activities, which is important to school satisfaction generally. Such satisfactions not only are related to feelings of competence and success (Barker & Gump, 1964), there also is a

"promotion effect" in that participants are more often pushed into leadership roles (Gump, 1980). Of special interest, it has been found that these effects may be greater for academically marginal students (Willems, 1967). In summary, analyses of over- and undermanning have indicated some of the disadvantages of large high schools, which are typical of urban areas. Adolescents enrolled in such schools are less likely to experience feelings of responsibility and importance. This lack of needs-environment fit can influence achievement and other school problems.

School reform efforts in the 1980s and early 1990s have moved in still other directions in attempts to better meet the needs of an increasingly diverse student population. Examples of these school reforms include school-site management (Clune & Witte, 1990); choice plans (Raywid, 1989); accountability for outcomes (Finn, 1990); the effective schools model (Bancroft & Lezotte, 1985); partnership or collaborative relationships between business and schools (Kearns & Doyle, 1988); and computer technology and integrated instructional systems (Collins, 1991).

However, a more radical approach for dealing with the increasing diversity in the public schools involves a number of proposals for restructuring general education and special education in both elementary and secondary schools. If this were carried out, virtually all handicapped students—as well as students currently served in compensatory and remedial elementary and secondary education programs and students who need special help but are not eligible for any type of categorical assistance—could be served within a single, adaptive system of public education (see Gartner & Lipsky, 1987; Hallahan, Kauffman, Lloyd, & McKinney, 1988; M.C. Reynolds, Wang, & Walberg, 1987). These authors also provide qualitative reviews of the research literature on some of the instructional strategies that have reemerged in the 1980s (e.g., cooperative learning, mastery learning, peer-mediated instruction, cognitive-behavioral training, and cognitive strategy instruction), all of which they consider in place of traditional special education practices. Although nearly all the research included is empirical, the problem is that there are few attempts to use theory to explain findings. In addition, the issue of cost is rarely raised. The emphasis in these discussions has also been on the elementary school, but without more attention to the secondary school—its ecology, the interdependence of its students and the schooling environment, and the diverse needs of its students—regular education initiatives will not achieve their full potential. The more troubling aspect of this situation, however, is that there is little or no evidence to indicate that educating students with disabilities in the regular classroom really works (Zigmond et al., 1995).

DIFFICULTIES IN CLASSROOM DISCOURSE

Much teaching in secondary schools takes place through the medium of spoken language, and it is the medium in which students demonstrate much of what they have learned. In addition, secondary schools include teachers and students from different linguistic backgrounds. There is general agreement, therefore, on the importance of spoken language in the process of secondary education. When teachers do not take these differences into proper account, stereotyping and inappropriate differential treatment can occur, and classroom learning can suffer as a result. By studying how discourse affects thought processes and thereby the nature of what is and is not learned, foundations are laid for appropriate interventions (see Cazden, 1986). The effect of success, however, may be to cause a disjunction among the school, family, and community for students with different linguistic backgrounds. Ultimately, whether differential treatment is helpful individualization or detrimental bias is an important question in interventions with such adolescents.

SPECIAL PROGRAMS FOR GIFTED SECONDARY STUDENTS

Two surveys of 1970s and 1980s programs for the gifted were conducted by Mitchell (1984) and Gallagher, Weiss, Oglesby, and Thomas (1983). They show a general consensus that programs for the gifted should be an integral part of the school system, although a trend away from enrichment in the regular classroom as the primary way of meeting the needs of gifted students is evident. Instead, acceleration, mentoring, self-directed and independent study, individual education plans, special schools, Saturday and summer programs, and community-based programs have become more

popular. In addition, an enormous amount of instructional material was created for use with gifted students. In such programs, special attention also was given to the disadvantaged and culturally different and the learning-disabled gifted as well as gifted girls. For a thorough summary of such developments, the reader should consult Torrance (1986). More recently, there also has been an interest in the role of mentors, role models, and heroes in the education of gifted high school students (Pleiss & Feldhusen, 1995).

In contrast to these earlier developments, there is now a growing movement to disband such programs, and instead of calling for more of the existing programs, Winner (1997) argues that standards first should be raised for all students. If this is done, many more of the moderately gifted would be appropriately challenged in regular classrooms, and only those who still remain unchallenged would receive advanced classes, special classrooms, or special schools. If implemented, fewer students would be identified as being in need of special services, and those identified would be the more profoundly gifted students, who would receive the strongest kind of intervention.

ISSUES IN MEETING VOCATIONAL NEEDS OF SECONDARY STUDENTS

The widespread interest in vocational education in secondary schools is understandable. Vocational education is a logical way to integrate those students at the bottom of the economic heap into the mainstream. It helps solve economic problems. Vocational education also provides a curriculum for the 50% of high school students not suited to the academic, college preparatory curriculum. It also is an important tool in tackling the "youth problem," which is manifested in such symptoms as gang activity, crime, and teenage pregnancy.

As to the quality and effects of vocational education, it often is claimed that such programs keep students in school longer. But the literature on this matter is inconclusive (see National Institute of Education, 1981). However, there is some evidence that vocational education students do better in the labor market than students who have graduated from general programs, although the initial benefits drop off with time. This NIE-sponsored study also concluded that comprehensive high schools are consistently inferior to specialized vocational high schools. They attribute this to the greater depth of programming, the ability to employ more experienced staff, closer relations with business and industry, and the higher priority specialized vocational high schools place on vocational training.

Recent developments, however, have changed the overall picture in significant ways (Hamilton & Hamilton, 1997). In particular, a greater range of work-based learning options is now available, including visits to workplaces, youth-run enterprises, service training, youth jobs, subsidized employment training programs, youth apprenticeships, and cooperative education programs. Educators and psychologists in the schools who are working to create school-to-work opportunities should consider all these types of work-based learning and try to provide a wide range of options for students in a manner that situates each program in a comprehensive school-to-work system.

Career development is a related issue because making wise career decisions is one of the critical problems of late adolescence. One problem is career indecision. For example, Noeth (1983) studied 2,000 high school juniors longitudinally but found that assessments of career development and future plans did not successfully predict the criterion, which was what occupation was held two years after completing high school. Sex roles are another consideration. For example, Farmer (1985) has proposed a model of career achievement for men and women. She put her model to the test, examining 2,000 high school students, and found that career aspirations, occupational knowledge, and career commitment are significantly related to students' background and to personal and environmental factors. In another study, Farmer (1983) found that high school girls have higher career aspirations than boys; that boys endorse a life plan reflecting an expectation that they will share parenting and career roles with their spouses; and that more girls than boys endorse statements suggesting that their future careers will be central to their adult roles. However, this finding is inconsistent with what really happens and may reflect a lack of realism in high school students.

Vocation indecision is not necessarily a unitary trait, however, and it is likely that different factors are associated with such difficulties. For example, Noeth, Roth, and Prediger (1975) studied a large national sample of high school students, and found

that even eleventh-graders couldn't answer most of the items on the occupational knowledge test that was used. In the same survey, more than half of the eleventh-graders also reported that they received little help from their high schools with career plans and problems. Overall, career maturity tends to show developmental progress over the adolescent years. Those higher in career maturity, for example, have been more successful in resolving crises represented in the first six psychological stages of Erikson's theory (Munley, 1975). In addition, career maturity is correlated with various aspects of school performance and personal characteristics of adolescents (see Kahn & Alvi, 1983). Nevertheless, there is the suggestion in the literature that it is difficult to change what happens in the career development of male and female high school students. For example, Brooks, Holahan, and Galligan (1985) found that a five-week intervention teaching nontraditional career options to secondary school girls did not significantly change preferences for nontraditional occupations. It would seem that interventions designed to influence career development must start earlier than secondary school.

USE AND MISUSE OF STANDARDIZED TESTS IN SECONDARY SCHOOLS

The idea of using tests to assess the effects of secondary schooling is hardly new. Student performance on achievement tests has played an important role in secondary education since the 1920s. But in recent years, the role of secondary school testing has expanded. For example, student certification for a high school diploma has included minimum competency testing requirements in an increasing number of states and local school districts around the country. The current emphasis on national standards and national tests as a strategy for education reform is another example (Ravitch, 1995). However, in both of these situations, it is important that the standardized achievement tests used have content validity (i.e., provide an estimate of learning that has occurred in a subject), curricular validity (i.e., provide an indication of opportunity to learn that actually occurs), and instructional validity (i.e., provide an indication of whether the material was actually taught). Tests have also become a major factor in special education placement in secondary as well as elementary schools. In addition, there has been expanded use of tests in making instructional decisions. For example, professionals are increasingly turning to curriculum-based assessment, although this work has focused on elementary schools (see Shapiro & Derr, 1990).

With this extraordinary emphasis on standardized testing, it is not surprising that the use and potential misuse of tests is a major concern of minorities and other groups. They not only point to abuses of tests in the early years of the testing movement but also insist that test misuse is painfully obvious today. Objections that have been raised to standardized educational and psychological tests include, according to Reynolds (see C.R. Reynolds, 1982; C.R. Reynolds & Kaiser, 1990), inappropriate content, inappropriate standardization samples, examiner and language bias, inequitable educational and social consequences, measurement of different constructs, and differential predictive validity. Of these, the most pertinent to this chapter's focus is inequitable educational and social consequences because inappropriate diagnostic and intervention activities are likely to have a disproportionate impact on minority students. Such deleterious outcomes are compounded by the concomitant effects of labeling, teacher expectancy effects, and special class placement.

Nevertheless, standardized testing will continue to have a prominent role in sorting secondary school students for placement and certification and for evaluating the effectiveness of secondary education programs. Indeed, in many of the secondary education reforms taking place, there is great reliance on standardized tests. Yet, despite substantial scientific and technical advances in testing, there still are unresolved issues concerning the appropriate use and interpretation of tests (see Linn, 1986; Suzuki & Valencia, 1997). Achieving the goal of using tests in the interests of the students tested will require a better understanding of the processes and outcomes that tests measure, as well as a better understanding of the consequences of the uses of test results, especially in terms of instruction and other forms of educational and psychological intervention.

CONCLUDING COMMENT

A great deal of data support the view that not only are school problems of adolescents on the increase but much adolescent school failure can be characterized as symptomatic of societal problems. The data therefore raise important questions about the continuing vitality of American society because that vitality ultimately depends on the effectiveness of secondary schools in helping adolescents to mature into competent adults.

In an eloquent response to this situation, Bronfenbrenner (1974, 1978) has described the school as an increasingly insular setting, isolated from the home and community. To some extent, the size of secondary schools, their resultant distance from the neighborhood, and the concomitant size of staffs are factors in this process. This insularity is further magnified by segregation into academic, vocational, and other "tracks," and by a curriculum that is highly compartmentalized, with students moving from class to class during the school day. There is the additional age-grading of students, so that they are thrown together primarily with their own peers, which contributes to the disruptive forces at work in the secondary school environment. In many communities, cross-town busing has added to these disintegrative pressures.

Although there is an absence of hard data, the escalation of school problems of adolescents in the past three decades appears to be the result of these converging trends, and many of the school problems of adolescents reflect their alienation. It may be further argued that such alienation has led to the decline in academic achievement and, in its more acute forms, is the source of rising delinquency, drug use, suicide, and other serious problems. Another indication of alienation is rising school violence and vandalism, which is a pattern of destructive behavior that is no longer confined to urban, inner-city areas.

With such a perspective, concepts that point to the systemic character of secondary schools become important. As Sarason (1982) has eloquently explained, schools have their own cultures, an idea that focuses attention on the total pattern of behavior in secondary school settings. The things to be examined and understood and, if necessary, changed, therefore, are those found in the context of secondary schools. Ecological theory, which is necessarily grounded in contextual data, then becomes increasingly appealing to those who see major reform of secondary schools as a critical factor in coping with school problems of adolescents.

Building on this broad ecological thesis, there is an obvious need to begin with the basic environmental unit, which is the behavior setting. In the secondary school, the classroom is the major behavior setting, and within this setting, the behaviors of students and teachers and arrangements of the physical space are highly coordinated. The classroom, however, is linked to other school and nonschool behavior settings, and these linkages require extensive exploration. Apart from the need to understand both school and nonschool behavior settings of adolescents and their linkages, there is the need for a wide range of ecologically oriented intervention strategies to improve setting functioning and to increase the well-being and satisfaction of the adolescents in those settings. To achieve such benefits, deliberate use of behavior-setting technology should be advocated. In addition, in development of such a technology, it is important to include key strategic components of the community because they are part of the total ecological matrix of the adolescent.

One can also make the point that allocation of energies and resources in secondary schools must go increasingly to building wellness and lifetime competence rather than just struggling to contain the school problems of adolescents. The factors and conditions that define well-being and the relative strength of forces that promote it differ, of course, for different groups of adolescents. In the perspective of this chapter, it also is assumed that secondary schools represent a potentially powerful but not well-harnessed force for advancing the educational, mental, and physical wellness of adolescents. However, anyone who is committed to improving secondary schools and who tries to effect fundamental changes in secondary schooling should read Sarason (1990). In his commonsense approach combined with a strategic planner's vision, Sarason reminds us that the fundamental reality of school reform is that power shapes schools and schooling, and that those who would restructure this institution must understand and use that authority well.

Finally, a theme that pervades the whole chapter is that school problems of adolescents present a serious challenge to psychologists. There are different views of "school" problems, and such differences can provoke prolonged discussion and debate. Furthermore, these issues are compounded by the paucity of knowledge on adolescence, which, in contrast to childhood, has been a relatively unstudied period in the public schools. For psychologists who share a commitment to the scientific study of school problems of adolescents and intervention and innovation that can enrich and improve adolescents' lives in school, there is much to do.

REFERENCES

Amato, P.R., & Keith, B. (1991a). Parental divorce and adult well-being: A meta-analysis. *Journal of Marriage and the Family, 53,* 43–58.

Amato, P.R., & Keith, B. (1991b). Parental divorce and the well-being of children: A meta-analysis. *Psychological Bulletin, 110,* 26–46.

American Association of University Women. (1993). *Hostile hallways.* Washington, DC: AAUW Educational Foundation.

American Psychiatric Association. (1994). *Diagnostic and statistical manual of mental disorders* (4th ed.). Washington, DC: Author.

American Psychological Association. (1993). *Youth & violence: Psychology's response. Vol. I: Summary report of the American Psychological Association Commission on Violence and Youth.* Washington, DC: Author.

Baird, L.L. (1969). Big school, small school. *Journal of Educational Psychology, 60,* 253–260.

Baker, D.P. (1997). Surviving TIMSS: Or, everything you blissfully forgot about international comparisons. *Phi Delta Kappan, 79,* 295–300.

Baker, S.P., O'Neill, B., & Karph, R.S. (1984). *The injury fact book.* Lexington, MA: Lexington Books.

Bancroft, B.A., & Lezotte, L.W. (1985). Growing use of effective schools model for school improvement. *Educational Leadership, 42,* 23–27.

Barker, R.G., & Associates. (1978). *Habitats, environments and human behavior.* San Francisco: Jossey-Bass.

Barker, R.G., & Gump, P.V. (1964). *Big school, small school.* Palo Alto, CA: Stanford University Press.

Barone, F. (1997). Bullying in school: It doesn't have to happen. *Phi Delta Kappan, 79,* 80–82.

Batsche, G.M., & Knoff, H.M. (1994). Bullies and their victims: Understanding a pervasive problem in the schools. *School Psychology Review, 23,* 165–174.

Berkowitz, L. (1993). *Aggression: Its causes, consequences, and control.* New York: McGraw-Hill.

Blashfield, R.K., & Livesley, W.J. (1991). Metaphorical analysis of psychiatric classification as a psychological test. *Journal of Abnormal Psychology, 100,* 262–270.

Block, J. (1971). *Lives through time.* Berkeley, CA: Bancroft.

Blos, P. (1979). *The adolescent passage.* New York: International Universities Press.

Bohlmeyer, E.M., & Burke, J.P. (1987). Selecting cooperative learning techniques: A consultative strategy guide. *School Psychology Review, 16,* 336–349.

Bronfenbrenner, U. (1974). The origins of alienation. *Scientific American, 231,* 53–61.

Bronfenbrenner, U. (1978). Who needs parent education? *Teachers College Record, 79,* 767–787.

Bronfenbrenner, U. (1979). *The ecology of human development.* Cambridge, MA: Harvard University Press.

Brooks, L., Holahan, W., & Galligan, J. (1985). The effects of a nontraditional role-modeling intervention on sex-typing of occupational preferences in career salience in adolescent females. *Journal of Vocational Behavior, 26,* 264–276.

Brooks-Gunn, J., & Furstenberg, F.F., Jr. (1989). Adolescent sexual behavior. *American Psychologist, 44,* 249–257.

Brown, B.F. (1980). A study of the school needs of children from one-parent families. *Phi Delta Kappan, 61,* 537–540.

Brownell, K.D., & Foreyt, J.P. (1986). *Handbook of eating disorders.* New York: Basic Books.

Burchard, J.D., & Burchard, S.N. (Eds.). (1987). *Prevention of delinquent behavior.* Newbury Park, CA: Sage.

Callahan, C.M., & Rivara, F.P. (1992). Urban high school youth and guns: A school-based survey. *Journal of the American Medical Association, 267,* 3071–3072.

Carlson, C., Paavola, J., & Talley, R. (1995). Historical, current, and future models of schools as health care delivery settings. *School Psychology Quarterly, 10,* 184–202.

Cass, L.K., & Thomas, C.B. (1979). *Childhood pathology and later adjustment: The question of prediction.* New York: Wiley.

Cazden, C.B. (1986). Classroom discourse. In M.C. Wittrock (Ed.), *Handbook of research on teaching* (3rd ed., pp. 432–463). New York: Macmillan.

Chase-Lansdale, P.L., & Brooks-Gunn, J. (1994). Correlates of adolescent pregnancy and parenthood. In C.B. Fisher & R.M. Lerner (Eds.), *Applied developmental psychology* (pp. 207–236). New York: McGraw-Hill.

Children's Defense Fund. (1986). *Preventing adolescent pregnancy: What schools can do.* Washington, DC: Author.

Clune, W.H., & Witte, J.F. (Eds.). (1990). *Choice and control in American education.* Philadelphia: Falmer Press.

Coleman, J.S. (1987). Families and schools. *Educational Researcher, 16,* 32–38.

Coleman, J.S., Campbell, E.Q., Hobson, C.J., McPartland, J., Mood, A.M., Weinfeld, F.D., & York, R.L. (1966). *Equality of educational opportunity.* Washington, DC: U.S. Government Printing Office.

Collins, A. (1991). The role of computer technology in restructuring schools. *Phi Delta Kappan, 73,* 28–36.

Compas, B.E., & Wagner, B.M. (1991). Psychosocial stress during adolescence: Intrapersonal and interpersonal processes. In M.E. Colton & S. Gore (Eds.), *Adolescent stresses: Causes and consequences* (pp. 67–85). New York: Aldine de Gruyter.

Cremin, L.A. (1988). *American education: The metropolitan experience, 1876–1980.* New York: Harper & Row.

Cuban, L. (1989). The "at-risk" label and the problem of urban school reform. *Phi Delta Kappan, 70,* 780–784, 799–801.

Curran, D.K. (1987). *Adolescent suicidal behavior.* Washington, DC: Hemisphere.

Division 12 Task Force. (1995). Training in and dissemination of empirically validated psychological treatments: Report and recommendations. *Clinical Psychologist, 48,* 3–23.

Division 12 Task Force. (1996). An update on empirically validated therapies. *Clinical Psychologist, 49,* 5–18.

Education Research Group. (1987). *Teen pregnancy: Impact on the schools.* Alexandria, VA: Capitol.

Egan, G. (1986). *The skilled helper: A systematic approach to effective helping* (3rd ed.). Monterey, CA: Brooks/Cole.

Elliott, S.N. (1986). Children's acceptability of classroom interventions for misbehavior: Findings and methodological considerations. *Journal of School Psychology, 24,* 23–25.

Farmer, H.S. (1983). Career and homemaking plans for high school youth. *Journal of Counseling Psychology, 30,* 40–45.

Farmer, H.S. (1985). Model of career and achievement motivation for women and men. *Journal of Counseling Psychology, 32,* 363–390.

Fine, M.J. (Ed.). (1980). *Handbook on parent education.* New York: Academic Press.

Finn, C.E. (1990). The biggest reform of all. *Phi Delta Kappan, 71,* 584–592.

Fischer, L., & Sorenson, G.P. (1996). *School law for counselors, psychologists, and social workers* (3rd ed.). White Plains, NY: Longman.

Flanagan, J.C. (Ed.). (1978). *Perspectives on improving education: Project TALENTS's young adults look back.* New York: Praeger.

Forgione, P.D., Jr. (1998). Responses to frequently asked questions about 12th-grade TIMSS. *Phi Delta Kappan, 79,* 769–772.

Forman, S.G., & Linney, J.A. (1988). School-based prevention of adolescent substance abuse: Programs, implementation, and future directions. *School Psychology Review, 17,* 550–558.

Fossey, R. (1996). School dropout rates: Are we sure they are going down? *Phi Delta Kappan, 78,* 140–144.

Frost, J.J., & Forrest, J.D. (1995). Understanding the impact of teenage pregnancy prevention programs. *Family Planning Perspectives, 27,* 188–195.

Furstenberg, F.F., Brooks-Gunn, J., & Chase-Lansdale, L. (1989). Teenaged pregnancy and childbearing. *American Psychologist, 44,* 313–320.

Gallagher, J.J., Weiss, P., Oglesby, K., & Thomas, T. (1983). *The status of gifted/talented education.* Ventura, CA: Ventura County Superintendent of Schools Office.

Gallup, A.M., & Elam, S.M. (1988). The 20th annual Gallup poll of the public's attitudes toward the public schools. *Phi Delta Kappan, 70,* 33–45.

Garner, D.M., & Garfinkel, P.E. (Eds.). (1985). *Handbook of psychotherapy for anorexia nervosa and bulimia.* New York: Guilford Press.

Gartner, A., & Lipsky, D.K. (1987). Beyond special education: Toward a quality system for all students. *Harvard Educational Review, 57,* 367–395.

Gholson, B., & Rosenthal, T.L. (Eds.). (1984). *Applications of cognitive-developmental theory: Developmental psychology series.* Orlando, FL: Academic Press.

Gilchrist, L.D., & Schinke, S.P. (1985). Preventing substance abuse with children and adolescents. *Journal of Consulting and Clinical Psychology, 53,* 121–135.

Glynn, T.J., Leukefeid, C.G., & Ludford, J. (Eds.). (1983a). *Preventing adolescent drug abuse.* Rockville, MD: National Institute on Drug Abuse.

Glynn, T.J., Leukefeid, C.G., & Ludford, J. (Eds.). (1983b). *Preventing adolescent drug abuse: Intervention strategies.* Rockville, MD: National Institute on Drug Abuse.

Good, T.L., & Weinstein, R.S. (1986). Schools make a difference: Evidence, criticisms, and new directions. *American Psychologist, 41,* 1090–1097.

Goodlad, J.I. (1984). *A place called school: Prospects for the future.* New York: McGraw-Hill.

Gottfredson, G.D., & Gottfredson, D.C. (1985). *Victimization in schools: Law, society, and policy* (Vol. 2). New York: Plenum Press.

Gump, P.V. (1980). The school as a social situation. *Annual Review of Psychology, 31,* 553–582.

Hahn, A., Danzberger, J., & Lefkowitz, B. (1987). *Dropouts in America: Enough is known for action.* Washington, DC: Institute for Educational Leadership.

Hallahan, D.P., Kauffman, J.M., Lloyd, J.W., & McKinney, J.D. (1988). Questions about the regular education initiative. *Journal of Learning Disabilities, 21,* 3–5.

Hamilton, S.F., & Hamilton, M.A. (1997). When is learning work-based? *Phi Delta Kappan, 78,* 677–681.

Herman, C.P., Zanna, M.P., & Higgins, E.T. (Eds.). (1986). *Physical appearance, stigma, and social behavior: The Ontario Symposium* (Vol. 3). Hillsdale, NJ: Erlbaum.

Holtzman, W.H. (Ed.). (1992). *The school of the future.* Austin, TX: Hogg Foundation for Mental Health and the American Psychological Association.

Horton, C.B. (1996). Children who molest other children: The school psychologist's response to the sexually aggressive child. *School Psychology Review, 25,* 540–557.

Hughes, J.N., & Hall, R.J. (Eds.). (1989). *Cognitive-behavioral psychology in the schools: A comprehensive handbook.* New York: Guilford Press.

Hyman, I.A., & Perone, D.C. (1998). The other side of school violence: Educator policies and practices that may contribute to student misbehavior. *Journal of School Psychology, 36,* 7–27.

Johnson, T.C. (1992). *Sexualized children and children who molest.* Walnut Creek, CA: Launch Press.

Jolly, J.B., Wherry, J.N., Wiesner, D.C., Reed, D.H., Rule, J.C., & Jolly, J.M. (1994). The mediating role of anxiety in self-reported somatic complaints of depressed adolescents. *Journal of Abnormal Child Psychology, 22,* 691–702.

Kahn, S.B., & Alvi, S.A. (1983). Educational, social, and psychological correlates of vocational maturity. *Journal of Vocational Behavior, 22,* 357–364.

Kazdin, A.E. (1987). Treatment of antisocial behavior in children: Current status and future directions. *Psychological Bulletin, 102,* 187–203.

Kearns, D.T., & Doyle, D.P. (1988). *Winning the brain race.* San Francisco: Institute for Contemporary Studies.

Kirby, D. (1994). *Sex education in the schools.* Menlo Park, CA: Henry J. Kaiser Family Foundation.

Kratochwill, T.R., & Morris, R.J. (Eds.). (1993). *Handbook of psychotherapy with children and adolescents.* Boston: Allyn & Bacon.

Lambert, N.M., & McCombs, B.L. (1998). *How students learn: Reforming schools through learner-centered education.* Washington, DC: American Psychological Association.

Levy-Leboyer, C. (1988). Success and failure in applying psychology. *American Psychologist, 43,* 779–785.

Linn, R.L. (1986). Educational testing and assessment: Research needs and policy issues. *American Psychologist, 41,* 1153–1160.

Lipsey, M.W., & Wilson, D.B. (1993). The efficacy of psychological, educational, and behavioral treatment. *American Psychologist, 48,* 1181–1209.

Marshall, H.H. (1996). Clarifying and implementing contemporary psychological perspectives. *Educational Psychologist, 31,* 29–34.

Maynard, R. (1995). Teenage childbearing and welfare reform: Lessons from a decade of demonstration and evaluation research. *Children and Youth Services Review, 17,* 309–332.

Mazza, J.J. (1997). School-based suicide prevention programs: Are they effective? *School Psychology Review, 26,* 382–396.

McBurnett, K. (1996). Development of the *DSM-IV:* Validity and relevance for school psychologists. *School Psychology Review, 25,* 259–273.

McConaughy, S.H., & Achenbach, T.M. (1990). Contributions of developmental psychopathology to school services. In T.B. Gutkin & C.R. Reynolds (Eds.), *The handbook of school psychology* (2nd ed., pp. 244–268). New York: Wiley.

Mitchell, B.M. (1984). An update on gifted/talented education in the U.S. *Roeper Review, 6,* 161–163.

Morrison, G.M., Furlong, M.J., & Morrison, R.L. (1994). School violence to school safety: Reframing the issue for school psychologists. *School Psychology Review, 23,* 236–256.

Mullis, I.V.S., Campbell, J.R., & Farstrup, A.E. (1993). *NAEP 1992 reading report card.* Princeton, NJ: Educational Testing Service.

Munley, P.H. (1975). Erik Erikson's theory of psychosocial development and vocational behavior. *Journal of Counseling Psychology, 22,* 314–319.

National Center for Education Statistics. (1995). *Digest of education statistics 1995.* Washington, DC: U.S. Department of Education.

National Commission on Excellence in Education. (1983). *A nation at risk: The imperative for educational reform.* Washington, DC: National Institute of Education.

National Institute of Education. (1981). *The vocational education study: The final report.* Washington, DC: Author.

National Institute of Justice, U.S. Department of Health, Education, and Welfare. (1978). *Safe schools–violent schools: The safe school study report to Congress.* Washington, DC: U.S. Government Printing Office.

National Research Council. (1987). *Risking the future: Adolescent sexuality, pregnancy, and childbearing.* Washington, DC: National Academy Press.

Noeth, R.J. (1983). The effects of enhancing expressed vocational choice with career development measures to predict occupational field. *Journal of Vocational Behavior, 22,* 365–375.

Noeth, R.J., Roth, J.D., & Prediger, D.J. (1975). Student career development: Where do we stand? *Quarterly of Vocational Guidance, 25,* 210–218.

Oakes, J., & Lipton, M. (1992). Detracking schools: Early lessons from the field. *Phi Delta Kappan, 73,* 448–454.

Patterson, G.R., Reid, J.B., & Dishion, J.J. (1992). *Antisocial boys.* Eugene, OR: Castalia Press.

Peterson, L. (1988). Preventing the leading killer of children: The role of the school psychologist in injury prevention. *School Psychology Review, 17,* 593–600.

Phelps, L., & Bajorek, E. (1991). Eating disorders of the adolescent: Current issues in etiology, assessment, and treatment. *School Psychology Review, 20,* 9–22.

Phillips, B.N. (1992). School problems of adolescents. In C.E. Walker & M.C. Roberts (Eds.), *Handbook of clinical child psychology* (2nd ed., pp. 643–660). New York: Wiley.

Phillips, B.N. (1993). *Educational and psychological perspectives on stress in students, teachers and parents.* Brandon, VT: Clinical Psychology.

Pleiss, M.K., & Feldhusen, J.F. (1995). Mentors, role models, and heroes in the lives of gifted children. *Educational Psychologist, 30,* 159–169.

Poland, S. (1989). *Suicide intervention in the schools.* New York: Guilford Press.

Prochaska, J.O., DiClemente, C.C., & Norcross, J.C. (1992). In search of how people change: Applications to addictive behavior. *American Psychologist, 47,* 1102–1114.

Ralph, J., Keller, D., & Crouse, J. (1994). How effective are American schools? *Phi Delta Kappan, 76,* 144–150.

Ravitch, D. (1995). *National standards in American education.* Washington, DC: Brookings Institute Press.

Ravitch, D., & Finn, C.E., Jr. (1987). *What do our 17-year-olds know?* New York: Harper & Row.

Raywid, M.A. (1989). *The case for public schools of choice.* Bloomington, IN: Phi Delta Kappa Educational Foundation.

Reimers, T.M., Wacker, D.P., & Koeppl, G. (1987). Acceptability of behavioral interventions: A review of the literature. *School Psychology Review, 16,* 212–227.

Reynolds, C.R. (1982). The problem of bias in psychological assessment. In C.R. Reynolds & T.B. Gutkin (Eds.), *The handbook of school psychology* (pp. 178–208). New York: Wiley.

Reynolds, C.R., & Kaiser, S.M. (1990). Test bias in psychological assessment. In T.B. Gutkin & C.R. Reynolds (Eds.), *The handbook of school psychology* (2nd ed., pp. 487–525). New York: Wiley.

Reynolds, M.C., Wang, M.C., & Walberg, H.J. (1987). The necessary restructuring of special and general education. *Exceptional Children, 53,* 391–398.

Rose, L.C., Gallup, A.M., & Elam, S.M. (1997). The 29th annual Phi Delta Kappa/Gallup poll of the public's attitudes toward the public schools. *Phi Delta Kappan, 79,* 41–56.

Rosenberg, M.L., O'Carroll, P.W., & Powell, K.E. (1992). Let's be clear: Violence is a public health problem. *Journal of the American Medical Association, 267,* 3071–3072.

Rosenfield, S.A. (1987). *Instructional consultation.* Hillsdale, NJ: Erlbaum.

Rutter, M. (1980). *Changing youth in a changing society: Patterns of adolescent development and disorder.* Cambridge, MA: Harvard University Press.

Rutter, M., Maughan, B., Mortimore, P., & Ouston, J. (with Smith, A.). (1979). *Fifteen thousand hours: Secondary schools and their effects on children.* Cambridge, MA: Harvard University Press.

Sarason, S.B. (1982). *The culture of the school and the problem of change* (2nd ed.). Boston: Allyn & Bacon.

Sarason, S.B. (1990). *The predictable failure of educational reform: Can we change course before it's too late?* San Francisco: Jossey-Bass.

Sarason, S.B., & Klaber, M. (1985). The school as a social system. *Annual Review of Psychology, 36,* 115–140.

Sautter, R.C. (1995). Standing up to violence [Special Report]. *Phi Delta Kappan, 76,* K1–K12.

Schopler, E. (1987). Specific and nonspecific factors in the effectiveness of a treatment system. *American Psychologist, 42,* 376–383.

Shakeshaft, C., & Cohan, A. (1995). Sexual abuse of students by school personnel. *Phi Delta Kappan, 76,* 513–520.

Shapiro, E.S., & Derr, T.F. (1990). Curriculum-based assessment. In T.B. Gutkin & C.R. Reynolds (Eds.), *The handbook of school psychology* (2nd ed., pp. 365–387). New York: Wiley.

Shedler, J., & Block, J. (1990). Adolescent drug use and psychological health: A longitudinal study. *American Psychologist, 45,* 612–630.

Sizer, T. (1984). *Horace's compromise: The dilemma of the American high school.* Boston: Houghton Mifflin.

Slavin, R.E. (1983). When does cooperative learning increase student achievement? *Psychological Bulletin, 94,* 429–445.

Smith, K. (1990). Suicidal behavior in school-aged youth. *School Psychology Review, 19,* 186–195.

Stark, K.D. (1990). *Childhood depression: School-based intervention.* New York: Guilford Press.

Stedman, L.C. (1993). The condition of education: Why school reformers are on the right track. *Phi Delta Kappan, 75,* 215–225.

Strayhorn, J.M. (1988). *The competent child: An approach to psychotherapy and preventive mental health.* New York: Guilford Press.

Suzuki, L.A., & Valencia, R.R. (1997). Race-ethnicity and measured intelligence: Educational implications. *American Psychologist, 52,* 1103–1114.

Teachman, G.W. (1979). In-school truancy in urban schools: The problem and a solution. *Phi Delta Kappan, 61,* 203–205.

Thomas, A., & Grimes, J. (Eds.). (1995). *Best practices in school psychology: III.* Washington, DC: National Association of School Psychologists.

Tobler, N.S. (1986). Meta-analysis of 143 adolescent drug prevention programs: Quantitative outcome results of program participants compared to a control or comparison group. *Journal of Drug Issues, 16,* 537–568.

Torrance, E.P. (1986). Teaching creative and gifted learners. In M.C. Wittrock (Ed.), *Handbook of research on teaching* (3rd ed., pp. 630–647). New York: Macmillan.

U.S. Department of Health & Human Services. (1987). *Drug use among American high school students, college students, and other young adults.* Washington, DC: U.S. Government Printing Office.

U.S. Department of Justice, Federal Bureau of Investigation. (1990). *Uniform Crime Reports for the United States, 1989.* Washington, DC: U.S. Government Printing Office.

Walberg, H.J., Schiller, D., & Haertel, G.D. (1979). The quiet revolution in educational research. *Phi Delta Kappan, 61,* 179–183.

Wicker, A.W. (1968). Undermanning, performances, and students' subjective experiences in behavior settings of large and small high schools. *Journal of Personality and Social Psychology, 10,* 255–261.

Wilkinson, L.C. (Ed.). (1982). *Communicating in the classroom.* New York: Academic Press.

Willems, E.P. (1967). Sense of obligation to high school activities as related to school size and marginality of student. *Child Development, 38,* 1247–1260.

Winner, E. (1997). Exceptionally high intelligence and schooling. *American Psychologist, 52,* 1070–1081.

Wishnietsky, D.H. (1991). Reported and unreported teacher-student sexual harassment. *Journal of Educational Research, 3,* 164–169.

Witt, J.C. (1986). Teachers' resistance to the use of school-based interventions. *Journal of School Psychology, 24,* 37–44.

Wittrock, M.C. (1986). *Handbook of research on teaching* (3rd ed.). New York: Macmillan.

Youniss, J., & Smollar, J. (1985). *Adolescent relations with mothers, fathers, and friends.* Chicago: University of Chicago Press.

Zigmond, N., Jenkins, J., Fuchs, L., Deno, S., Fuchs, D., Baker, J., Jenkins, L., & Couthino, M. (1995). Special education in restructured schools: Findings from three multi-year studies. *Phi Delta Kappan, 76,* 531–540.

CHAPTER 37

Vocational Development: Assessment and Intervention in Adolescent Career Choice

MARTIN HEESACKER, GREG J. NEIMEYER, AND SACHA E. LINDEKENS

Across the ages, people have worked for a wide variety of reasons. The need to sustain life, to produce essential goods and services, to structure time, to attain personal fulfillment, and to improve society have all occupied important forces behind occupational pursuits (Task Force on Work, 1973). These shifting values associated with the world of work highlight two aspects of vocational choice that have occupied an important place in contemporary vocational theory and research. The first of these aspects underscores the cultural contingency of career concerns and the second addresses their developmental nature. This chapter briefly outlines both of these features and then turns toward a consideration of problems related to the developmental nature of vocational choice and satisfaction. Attention then turns toward assessment, emphasizing accessible means of measuring career-relevant variables. Finally, we consider issues of intervention, outlining some of the dominant methods of assisting in solving vocational problems. Annual reviews of recent developments in this literature can be found in Fouad (1994a), Stoltz-Loike (1996), and Niles (1997).

CULTURAL CONTINGENCY AND CAREER DEVELOPMENT

Researchers have long respected the interrelationship between personal and cultural work values. On the one hand, cultural values serve as the backdrop from which the individual derives and instantiates his or her personal work values. Even as they inform personal values, cultural and social forces can also restrict their implementation, as when processes of socialization and stratification enforce cultural limitations on fulfilling occupational preferences and ambitions (Gottfredson & Becker, 1981; Roberts, 1977). Whether these restrictions are imposed extrinsically by prevailing social prohibitions (Swanson & Woitke, 1997) or intrinsically by processes of self-selection (as in the case of math anxiety among women; see Betz & Fitzgerald, 1987, for a review), personal, cultural, and social processes interact in determining the course and outcome of career development.

The recognition of the interdependence among these forces dates back at least to the founding of the Vocational Guidance Bureau in 1907, when

738 PROBLEMS OF ADOLESCENCE

Parsons (1909) firmly established the link between occupational choice and personal development. Variants on this long-standing position pervade the contemporary literature, echoing Osipow's (1973) observation, "The process of career choice is so deeply embedded in cultural and economic factors that it is unreasonable to try to develop a theory of vocational development without including these variables" (p. 293). Most contemporary career theories present extensions of this basic premise. Recognizing the boundaries imposed by social factors, they consider vocational development in terms of its implementation of the self-concept within available occupational domains (e.g., Kidd, 1984; Roe, 1956; Super, 1957).

Of course, the personal and occupational domains are not so easily separable. At least since Super's (1951) early formulation, vocational development has been viewed as a form of self-expression, a means through which the individual implements, fulfills, and extends aspects of the self, a position that has been supported by considerable research (e.g., Blocker & Schultz, 1961; Oppenheimer, 1966). Even within lower socioeconomic levels, where it is usually presumed that processes of social stratification eclipse self-expression, research has demonstrated the impact of self-concept on occupational selection (Kidd, 1984). Most current career theories, therefore, advance developmental accounts, where development is understood as the "process of growth and learning which underlies the sequence of vocational behavior" (Super et al., 1957, p. vii).

The assumption here is that, in expressing an occupational preference, an individual is translating into occupational terms important personal values. Even as the individual's personal values influence occupational selection and satisfaction, however, so too does the occupation influence personal values. In this way, occupational and personal arenas are largely interrelated, with each exerting substantial influence on the other. As Havighurst (1982) has commented regarding the importance of work to the individual's sense of self, "Its influences extend beyond the actual work life of the individual. We also find that the part of his/her adult life not spent in work is, nonetheless, affected . . . in short, the job in our society exerts an influence which pervades the whole of the adult life span" (p. 580). The interdependence of personal and occupational domains suggests that changes in either one would carry implications for the other. Consistent

with this perspective, one form of vocational counseling is a matter of encouraging sufficient personal and occupational exploration and then effecting a suitable "match" between the individual's current self views and the occupational values. The success of this match between one's self-concept and occupational values is largely contingent on the successful development of the self-concept, of course, and for that reason vocational theories should be informed by larger developmental accounts of personal identity formation (Blustein, Devenis, & Kidney, 1989; Raskin, 1989; Vondracek, 1993).

Only recently, however, has research turned to address the cultural contingency of these developmental processes. Earlier research assumed uniformity in those processes associated with the development of the self-concept. But recent work has begun to question this assumption. A growing literature now supports the role of distinctive cultural features in self-development, creating a tension between developing conceptualization and available forms of intervention.

One reflection of this tension has been documented by Ramirez, Wassef, Paniagua, and Linsky (1996). Despite evidence suggesting that the probability of inappropriate intervention increases significantly in the absence of cultural considerations, few clinicians feel qualified on this account. Ramirez et al. reported a substantial discrepancy between the perceived importance of cultural factors on the one hand, and practitioners' effectiveness in attending to these factors on the other. In their study, they noted that 71% of the practicing mental health professionals in their sample acknowledged differences between the ways majority and minority clients express emotional distress, and a substantial majority (89%) viewed these variations as vital to effective case conceptualization and intervention. Surprisingly, however, only 49% indicated any success in making such cultural assessments, with many practitioners regarding themselves as either uncertain (25%) or unsuccessful (25%) in this regard. This growing gap between cultural awareness and culture-adapted interventions has fueled an ongoing reappraisal of theoretical, conceptual, and practical work in the area of career counseling.

At the broadest level, cross-cultural scholars have begun to redress the "need for theoretical models to guide counseling and conceptualize career assessment with culturally different clients" (Leong &

Hartung, 1997, p. 183). As Ibrahim, Ohnishi, and Wilson (1994, p. 276) note, "The changing demographics in our society demand that we attend to culture and gender issues in our services to clients," and they are joined by a growing array of scholars, researchers, and practitioners who are dedicated to that goal. Much of this research is culture-specific, as in research that tests the validity of common career assessment measures for African-American, Asian, Hispanic, and Native American populations (Fouad 1994b; Martin, 1991; Swanson & Bowman, 1994; Westbrook & Sanford, 1991). Additional research focuses on the development of culture-specific intervention programs with, for example, inner-city African Americans (D'Andrea & Daniels, 1992), Native Americans living on reservations (Martin, 1991), Asian Americans (Leong & Leung, 1994; Martin, & Farris, 1994), and Latinos/Hispanics (Fouad, 1994b). Likewise, special developmental processes and needs have been linked to lesbian, gay, and bisexual individuals (Prince, 1997), gifted students (Achter, Benbow, & Lubinski, 1997; Hollinger & Fleming, 1993; Kerr & Fisher, 1997), and people with disabilities (Klein, Wheaton, & Wilson, 1997), among others (Lehr & Jeffery, 1996; Swanson & Woitke, 1997). Common ties that bind these otherwise diverse expressions include Fouad's (1993, p. 12) observation that "culture plays a very large role in vocational counseling," underscoring the growing conviction that, to be effective, "career counselors must understand the client's cultural identity" (Ibrahim et al., 1994, p. 277).

PERSONAL IDENTITY AND VOCATIONAL DEVELOPMENT

As Blustein et al. (1989) have noted in their review of career development theories, "two prevalent developmental tasks emerge consistently across various theoretical approaches" (p. 196). The first concerns the task of active exploration of the self and the occupational environment (Harren, 1979; Jordaan, 1963; Super, 1957); the second concerns processes of commitment to specific career paths (Harren, 1979; Super, 1957). These two processes can be viewed as derivatives of Erikson's (1968) life-stage theory of psychosocial development.

Erikson (1968) viewed the individual as progressing through a series of eight distinct psychosocial stages. Each stage presents a particular task or challenge that requires resolution. Vocational concerns are reflected most acutely in early school and adolescent stages. It is during school age that the child is faced with developing a sense of industry and the capacity to derive enjoyment and satisfaction from work. Failure to achieve this results in a sense of inferiority. During adolescence, the major developmental task is personal identity formation; this is the period that has received the greatest attention in the vocational literature. This attention follows from the important role that Erikson accorded occupational processes, observing that it is "the inability to settle on an occupational identity which most disturbs young people" (p. 132).

James Marcia's (1966) derivative conceptualization of identity development provided a major impetus for subsequent work by establishing a framework that has sustained a vibrant empirical literature for more than 30 years. According to this framework, identity development can be viewed as progressing along two different dimensions: commitment and crisis. Commitment refers to the degree to which an individual has attained stable values and beliefs in specific life domains (e.g., occupational), whereas crisis refers to the individual's level of active exploration in seeking and determining these identity commitments. The primary task of adolescence from this perspective is to develop a sense of ego identity that provides integration and continuity to the self rather than perpetuating a sense of uncertainty and confusion. The occupational domain provides an important arena for the development of the self.

According to Marcia's paradigm, four different identity statuses can develop, each reflecting the presence or absence of exploration and commitment. Diffuse individuals have not yet successfully negotiated the tasks of vocational identity development because they lack both a stable system of commitments and any active process of exploration directed at achieving them. In contrast, foreclosed individuals have resolved this process by prematurely co-opting available, often parental, value systems. The adolescent boy follows the uncritical pursuit of engineering, for example, largely because his father is an engineer and would support his development along similar occupational lines. In this case, strong vocational commitments occur in the absence of any active self-exploration or crisis. Moratorium individuals, on the other hand, are actively involved in the struggle to explore alternative beliefs but have not yet attained firm occupational commitments. Finally, achieved individuals have settled on a stable set of occupational values following an active period of exploration and crisis.

Considerable research now supports the validity of this status paradigm for investigating differences in vocational development (see Archer, 1989; Berzonsky, 1990; Blustein et al., 1989; Raskin, 1989, 1994). At the broadest level, for example, researchers have found support for the covariation between processes of occupational and personal development (Blustein et al., 1989; Neimeyer, Nevill, Probert, & Fukuyama, 1985; Nevill, Neimeyer, Probert, & Fukuyama, 1986). In their study of 99 undergraduates, for instance, Blustein et al. concluded that "empirical support has been demonstrated for the proposition that the exploration and commitment processes that characterize one's identity formation are closely related to an analogous set of career development tasks" (p. 200), a proposition that has received independent support elsewhere in the literature (Berzonsky & Neimeyer, 1994; Neimeyer & Metzler, 1987; Nevill et al., 1986).

Beyond this general level of support for the interrelationship between personal and vocational development, other researchers have documented specific differences among the four identity statuses along various career-relevant variables. For example, Neimeyer, Prichard, Berzonsky, and Metzler (1991) noted that participants with high-crisis status (i.e., achievement and moratorium) engaged in less-biased vocational hypothesis testing, at least when they were considering relatively neutral occupations that they had not previously judged to be either highly relevant or irrelevant to their occupational interests. Similarly, Blustein et al. (1989) adduced evidence in favor of the notion that high-crisis statuses are associated with greater vocational exploration (cf. Neimeyer et al., 1985; Nevill et al., 1986), a finding that is generally consistent with the positive relationship between vocational identity development and career decision-making self-efficacy (Neimeyer & Metzler, 1987).

Other research has documented differences in the selection of college majors as a function of identity development and corresponding differences in work-role salience (Fannin, 1979). For example, Waterman (1982) noted that moratorium individuals changed college majors more frequently than those in other statuses, a finding that is consistent with their higher levels of exploration in the absence of stable identity commitments. Other researchers have noted that individuals who had attained the identity achievement status tended to select the most difficult college majors, whereas diffuse individuals gravitated toward the least demanding majors (Marcia & Friedman, 1970; Matteson, 1974).

Implicit in this work is the belief that the specific nature of career concerns should vary as a result of vocational identity development (see Raskin, 1989, for specific suggestions for career interventions based on each of the identity statuses). So, for example, vocational indecision is a more likely concomitant of identity moratorium than it is of foreclosure or achievement. Likewise, insufficient career exploration is more likely to typify foreclosed individuals than those in the midst of moratorium. In this way, some of the specific difficulties in vocational choice and satisfaction might be linked to developmental features of occupational identity. Recent developments in this literature have been summarized in the reviews of Stoltz-Loike (1996) and Niles (1997).

PROBLEMS IN VOCATIONAL DEVELOPMENT

Efforts to locate vocational difficulties within traditional theories of psychosocial development are relatively recent. Despite this emerging trend, theories of psychosocial development and theories of vocational development have mostly developed independently (Raskin, 1985, 1989, 1994). Neither psychosocial nor vocational theories of development have reflected particular familiarity with, or interest in, the conceptual agendas of the other (Vondracek, 1993; Vondracek, Lerner, & Schulenberg, 1983, 1986). In a sense, however, these two different orientations are gradually converging on one another. Even as the developmental literature begins to integrate vocational concerns, the vocational area is gradually attending to the larger developmental literature (see Osipow & Fitzgerald, 1996, chap. 5).

The vocational work that follows from Erikson's (1963) development theory offers the twin advantages of situating vocational development within a larger theory of development and at the same time retaining fidelity to the epistemological assumptions of its parent (ego-analytic) theory. But this work is just beginning. For example, there is one psychometrically sound measure specifically designed for assessing vocational ego-identity development (Melgosa, 1987; see "Career Development Assessment," below), and only a few published investigations (e.g., Berzonsky & Ferrari, 1996; Neimeyer et al., 1991) highlighting the largely promissory nature of this line of work. In contrast to the recency of this line of work, the field of vocational psychology offers its own long-standing developmental theories. Focusing predominantly on vocational processes, these models understandably have attended less to larger cognitive and psychosocial processes that constitute the cornerstone of developmental psychology (Vondracek, 1993; Vondracek et al., 1983). Counterbalancing this, however, is their long-standing responsiveness to the pragmatic needs of the vocational client, highlighting stages and processes of vocational development and maturation and suggesting methods of intervention.

Super's (1957, 1990) developmental model of vocational behavior is the most strongly empirically supported and most widely employed vocational development theory (Osipow & Fitzgerald, 1996). This life span theory holds as its central postulate that vocational development is the process of developing and implementing one's self-concept in the work world. Super has identified two stages (growth and exploration) of this process as occurring in children and adolescents, and three stages (establishment, maintenance, and decline) occurring in adulthood (for an alternative perspective to vocational development, see review by Jepson, 1984).

In Super's (1957) growth stage, which he suggested lasts until approximately age 14, children are developing their self-concepts as well as their own understanding of work, its meaning, and purpose. In the exploration stage, which occurs, according to Super, between the ages of 14 and 24, a wide array of career-related developments occur. These include recognizing and accepting the need to make career-related decisions, obtaining information regarding careers, relating one's interests and abilities to work opportunities, identifying specific fields and levels of aspiration harmonious with one's interests and abilities, securing training to prepare for entry into a specific career, and entering a career. The ages associated with each of these stages are approximate, but clearly cover the adolescent period. These two earliest of Super's five stages account for a large and crucially important group of career tasks.

Vocational development can be slowed or arrested at various points along this developmental path. The sources of slowed vocational development are varied and complex.

PROBLEMS IN THE GROWTH STAGE (BIRTH TO AGE 14)

For clarification of vocational problems affecting children and early adolescents, the work of Herr and Cramer (1992), who have used Super's (1957) theory to identify age-appropriate career-related issues, is particularly useful. Herr and Cramer have identified four discrete temporal substages within Super's growth stage, which last from birth to age 14. In the first of these substages, from birth to 4 years old, later vocational problems can arise from a developmental failure in any of the following areas: self-concept, self-help behaviors, social interaction skills, self-direction, industry, goal setting, and persistence. Problems in the second substage, labeled fantasy (age 4–10), arise from the child's not engaging in work-related and other types of role-playing fantasies. In the third substage, labeled interest (age 11–12), problems can occur if the child's own preferences are not the major determinant of his or her aspirations and activities. In the fourth and final substage of the growth stage, labeled capacity (age 13–14), vocational problems can occur if children do not consider their own abilities and the requirements of jobs in their vocationally related thoughts. The crucial overall tasks in the growth stage are developing a self-concept and developing an understanding of work's meaning (Herr & Cramer, 1992).

PROBLEMS IN THE EXPLORATION STAGE (AGE 15–24)

Super (1957) has divided his exploration stage into three substages. In the tentative substage (age 15–17), the adolescent's needs, interests, values, and opportunities are all held tentatively. Tentative career choices are "tried out" in various life arenas, such as discussions, classes, and work. The key task of this stage is to crystallize one's vocational preference (Herr & Cramer, 1992).

In the transition substage (age 18–21), real-world factors are given more importance in vocational decision making, as one is typically entering either the work world or choosing specific, postsecondary education. The general preferences of the tentative substage become more specific. The primary task of this substage is to develop specific vocational preferences (Herr & Cramer, 1992).

In the uncommitted trial substage (age 22–24) of the exploration stage, typically an occupation has been found, and the person is trying out the job as a potential life's work. If the person finds the work unsatisfying, he or she may return to earlier substages. The primary task of this substage is to implement the vocational choice developed in the previous substage (Herr & Cramer, 1992).

Campbell and Cellini (1981) have employed Super's theory of vocational development as the primary basis for their taxonomy of career problems. This taxonomy is a useful framework for understanding adolescent career problems within the exploration stage of Super's stage taxonomy. Campbell and Cellini identified four problem categories relevant to adolescents: (1) decision making, (2) implementing plans, (3) performing career tasks, and (4) adapting to work settings.

The first category highlights problems in vocational decision making. They further subdivide the category into four problem categories: (1) getting started; (2) gathering information; (3) generating, evaluating, and selecting alternatives; and (4) formulating plans for decision implementation. Vocational psychology research on career decision making and indecision (see reviews by Mitchell & Krumboltz, 1984; Slaney, 1988; Spokane & Jacob, 1996) and career maturity (see Betz, 1988; Crites & Savickas, 1996) illuminates important issues associated with this problem category. The second Campbell–Cellini diagnostic category highlights problems in implementing one's career plans. The focus in this category is on characteristics of both the person and the environment. Vocational psychology research on career barriers to women (see Fitzgerald, Fassinger, & Betz, 1995), racial minorities (see Leong, 1995), and people with physical and intellectual handicaps (see Zunker, 1998) illuminates issues associated with this problem category. The third Campbell–Cellini diagnostic category highlights performance problems in educational or work settings. They further divide this category into performance problems based on (1) deficiencies in skills, abilities, or knowledge; (2) personal factors, such as feeling unchallenged by a job; and (3) deficiencies in the work environment,

such as ambiguous job requirements. The final Campbell–Cellini diagnostic category involves problems adapting to the work setting, excluding performance problems, which are included in the prior category. These problems include "difficulties in adjusting to organizational policies, regulations, rules, decorum, administrative structure, and to other members of the organization" (1981, p. 187). Campbell and Cellini subdivide this category into problems occurring (1) initially (which are clearly relevant to adolescent career problems), (2) over time, and (3) in interpersonal relationships.

The task of the career counselor is to identify the locus of the client's particular difficulty and to develop an effective treatment plan to guide intervention. Theoretical understanding of career difficulties can be aided by conceptually and psychometrically sound assessment devices.

ASSESSMENT

Vocational assessment is designed to assist the career counselor in diagnosing career concerns and in performing the multiple functions of vocational counseling. As the definition of vocational counseling has expanded over time, however, methods of assessment have proliferated correspondingly. Originally conceived as the process of helping the individual to select and prepare for an occupation, vocational counseling owes historical allegiance to a model of trait-factor matching. This model assumes that the role of the counselor is to assist the individual in identifying his or her inherent interests, aptitudes, values, and the like, and then to match those to occupations that promise to maximize the realization of those features in the world of work. As a result, most early assessment devices focused on assessing occupational abilities, interests, aptitudes, and values.

With the redefinition of vocational counseling initiated by Super (1951), the tasks of the counselor turned decidedly toward processes and away from exclusive attention to matching outcome. Emphasis shifted from a focus on the choice to a focus on the chooser (Kapes & Mastie, 1988). With this shift came discussion of career preparedness, uncertainty, maturity, self-efficacy, decision making, and other topics central to measuring readiness for effectively undertaking the process of career exploration and commitment.

These and many other characteristics in the career domain have been operationalized in assessment instruments. Kapes, Mastie, and Whitfield (1994) provide critical reviews of 52 of these and schematic coverage of 245 additional measures (see Kapes & Vacha-Haase, 1994, for these additional measures). Although career assessment devices vary widely in their design and function, a number of researchers have pointed to their common purposes. Herr and Cramer (1992), for example, argued that career assessments are designed to fulfill at least one of four functions: prediction, discrimination, monitoring, and evaluation. The predictive function is aimed at helping clients to determine how competitive they might be in relation to specific careers and to forecast their likelihood of success, satisfaction, and upward mobility. The discrimination function assists clients in determining how well they match the dominant values and requisite abilities of the occupations considered. Monitoring functions are served by assessing the individual's readiness to choose, the status of his or her occupational identity development, career maturity, and decision-making skills. Finally, assessment devices provide indices of both programmatic and individual change. They permit the counselor to evaluate the outcome of the career interventions and to chart the individual's progress along relevant vocational dimensions.

Any one instrument may effectively target one or more of these goals, of course, and one of the tasks of the vocational counselor is to determine the instrument(s) best suited to the client's needs (see "Selecting Suitable Assessments," below). Because excellent reviews of various career assessments are available elsewhere (e.g., Kapes et al., 1994), this chapter highlights only a few of the most accessible and widely used instruments to reflect the diversity of devices available to the practicing career counselor. Measures are considered as they fit into one of four broad categories: measures of work values, vocational interests, career decision making, and career development.

WORK VALUES

As Zytowski (1988) has noted, "Practicing career counselors know what many career theorists do not: that people vary widely in their attraction to the idea of working" (p. 151). Super's (1980) recognition

of this possibility has been translated into an instrument designed to tap the differential value placed on a variety of life roles. Named the Salience Inventory (Nevill & Super, 1986), this instrument assesses a person's degree of participation, commitment, and value expectation in relation to five life roles: academic study, work, homemaking, leisure, and community service. The self-administered instrument requires approximately 35 minutes to complete and is amenable to hand or computer scoring.

The Salience Inventory has undergone a large-scale norming process. Developed on a sample of 2,000 adolescents and adults in the United States, it has been applied as well to samples of Australians, Belgians, Canadians, Croatians, Italians, Japanese, Poles, Portuguese, South Africans, and Yugoslavians (Nevill & Calvert, 1996). The instrument's psychometric properties are sound, with internal consistency reliabilities above .80, appropriate test-retest reliability, and data from several investigations, some from the scale's authors and most from others, providing evidence in support of the inventory's construct validity. Further critique and details of the instrument can be found in Zytowski (1988), Nevill and Super (1986), Osberg (1992), and more recently in Nevill and Calvert.

VOCATIONAL INTERESTS

The Strong Interest Inventory (SII; Harmon, Hansen, Borgen, & Hammer, 1994) has long occupied an important place in career assessment. Now entering its ninth decade, the recent revisions of this instrument command even greater respect because they provide sex-balanced scales, the substantial addition of occupational scales geared toward noncollege populations, and a large-scale renorming. The instrument is designed for ages 14 and up, requires about 30 minutes to complete, and provides computer-based scoring and output along a series of three major scales, each organized according to Holland's (1985) six personality types (realistic, investigative, artistic, social, enterprising, and conventional).

The general occupational themes are the most global of the SII scales, followed by the basic interest scales, which provide more detailed feedback about interest matching. More specific still are the over 200 occupational scales, each offering information concerning the levels of interest shared by an individual and a large sample of successful individuals who occupy that vocation. Finally, the profile furnishes a variety of special scales measuring introversion-extroversion, academic comfort, and overall response tendencies, such as missing or unusual responses.

As Fouad (1994a) has noted, "The Strong Interest Inventory (SII) has continued to be the interest inventory that attracts the most scientific investigation" (p. 155). These investigations reveal that the SII is psychometrically sound. The average two-week test-retest reliabilities for the occupational scales were over .90, for example, with the other scale averages ranging in the .80 to .90 range. Longer-term retests support the stability of these measures and can be found in Harmon et al. (1994). Predictive validity, based on longitudinal sampling across substantial periods of time, has been the cornerstone of the SII's validity assessments. Long-term predictive validity tests have indicated that 60% to 75% of college student samples enter occupations that were predictable from prior testing (e.g., Borgen, 1988). Concurrent and discriminant validity estimates are also detailed in the instrument's most current manual (Harmon et al., 1994).

CAREER DECISION MAKING

Several aspects of career decision making have been the object of instrument design. Broad emphasis has been placed on two different aspects of career decision making: the outcome (i.e., the degree of commitment, certainty, or decidedness) and the process (i.e., emphasizing how the decisions are made).

The Career Decision Scale (CDS; Osipow, 1980) is a 19-item, self-administered outcome measure of career indecision appropriate for high school and college populations (see Hartman, Utz, & Farnum, 1979, for an extension of the instrument to graduate student populations). The first two items measure level of comfort with and decidedness regarding choices of career and academic major. Items 3–18 sum to form an omnibus measure of career indecision, and item 19 is a free-response item.

Psychometric properties of this brief instrument support its utility. Beginning with its first published report (Osipow, Carney, & Barak, 1976; Osipow, Carney, Winer, Yanico, & Koschier, 1976) and continuing through factor analytic (Osipow, 1980), predictive validity, and concurrent and construct validity assessments (W.B. Rogers & Westbrook, 1983), the CDS has demonstrated sound psychometric qualities. Two-week test-retest reliabilities, for example, range from .82 to .90, and factor analytic studies revealed four indecision factors that accounted for 81% of the instrument's total variance, though Osipow prefers to use the CDS as a single scale. Reviews by Allis (1984), Slaney (1988), and more recently Hackett and Watkins (1995) give generally positive evaluations of the CDS, along with details regarding its uses and properties.

Beyond measures of decision outcome, other instruments are designed to address the *processes* that undergird career decision making. One approach has been to emphasize the perceived self-efficacy related to career decision making, for example, and this has given rise to the Career Decision-Making Self-Efficacy Scale (CDMSES; Hackett & Betz, 1981). The term "career self-efficacy" refers to generic efficacy expectancies in relation to the variety of behaviors necessary to career adjustment and choice (Betz & Hackett, 1986; Hackett & Betz, 1981). The CDMSES provides a total decision-making self-efficacy score that is comprised of the sum of five subscale scores pertaining to the areas of goal selection, occupational information, problem solving, planning, and self-appraisal.

The CDMSES has demonstrated highly satisfactory psychometric properties (Luzzo, 1995). Studies of basic scale reliabilities (Hackett & Betz, 1981), concurrent validity (R.W. Lent, Brown, & Larkin, 1984), and predictive validity (Neimeyer & Metzler, 1987; Taylor & Betz, 1983) point to the instrument's essential psychometric soundness (see Betz & Luzzo, 1996). Finally, as Betz and Hackett (1986, p. 287) have indicated, "The most important test of the career self-efficacy construct will come in studies investigating the effectiveness of theory-based interventions," and data along these lines provide further support for the instrument's utility in the context of career counseling (e.g., Fukuyama, Probert, Neimeyer, Nevill, & Metzler, 1988). Most recently, Osipow and Temple (1996) have introduced a task-specific short form of the instrument. The purpose of this adaptation, as noted by the authors, is "to generate an instrument that would be useful across a broad spectrum of occupationally related activities yet, at the same time, be sufficiently specific to apply to any given individual career situation (p. 447).

CAREER DEVELOPMENT

A number of measures have been designed to assess developmental features of vocational identity formation. Instruments such as the Career Development Inventory (Super, Thompson, Lindeman, Jordaan, & Myers, 1981), the Assessment of Career Decision Making (Harren, 1980), the Career Maturity Inventory (Crites & Savickas, 1996), and My Vocational Situation (Holland, Daiger, & Powers, 1980) have all been directed at measuring features of vocational development.

One measure along these lines is the Occupational Identity Scale (OIS; Melgosa, 1987). Patterned after successful (and broader) measures of ego identity development (i.e., the Extended Objective Measure of Ego-Identity Development; Adams, Shea, & Fitch, 1979; Grotevant & Adams, 1984), the 28-item, self-administered OIS is derived from Erikson's (1950) conceptualizations of identity formation. Following Marcia's translation of this theory into operational terms, Melgosa's (1987) measure assesses levels of occupational exploration and commitment, furnishing continuous scores along each of the four status designations discussed earlier in this chapter: diffusion, foreclosure, moratorium, and achievement.

Estimates of the instrument's psychometric properties are positive, but incomplete. For example, factor analytic studies support the instrument's portrayal of four primary clusters, reflecting each of the four identity statuses. Internal reliability coefficients range from .70 to .87, and concurrent validity estimates show significant but moderate relationships with conceptually similar measures, ranging from .38 to .79 (Melgosa, 1987). Although not as widely employed as measures reflecting vocational psychology's traditional perspectives on development, Melgosa's measure offers the advantages associated with the articulation of occupational identity formation within the larger developmental literature (see Raskin, 1985, 1989, 1994).

SELECTING SUITABLE ASSESSMENTS

For the practitioner interested in selecting suitable instruments for career assessment, useful guidelines are available. Extensive evaluations of various career counseling–relevant instruments can assist in navigating the sea of available assessment measures. Frazier (1988), for example, has provided brief synopses of 126 career guidance instruments. As mentioned earlier, Kapes et al. (1994) have more recently edited a particularly useful volume in which 52 major career assessment tools are individually evaluated. An additional chapter in their volume briefly describes and categorizes 245 additional instruments (Kapes & Vacha-Haase, 1994). Appendix D in that same volume provides in tabular form useful information regarding each of the 247 instruments discussed in the book, including the target of measurement (e.g., aptitudes, interests, career development, or personality) and populations of interest (e.g., elementary, high school, college, postgraduate, or disabled).

Squarely addressing the complexity associated with sorting through the multitude of available assessment tools, Womer (1988) has provided a practical step-by-step procedure for assessing and selecting suitable career counseling instruments. A useful adjunct to this can be found in a chapter by Prediger and Garfield (1988), who provide a checklist of counselor competencies to assist the practitioner in determining his or her own suitability to administer, score, and interpret career assessment devices. Taken together, these resources can be valuable assets to the practitioner, who is otherwise faced with the unwieldy task of selecting the most suitable instruments from a complex array of career assessment tools varying widely in their targeted intent and populations as well as their conceptual and psychometric sophistication.

TREATMENT OF PROBLEMS IN VOCATIONAL DEVELOPMENT

Career problems, including those occurring in adolescents, have received a great deal of attention in the literature. Admittedly less research has been done assessing treatment process and outcome in the career arena than has been done within the realm of traditional psychotherapy (Swanson, 1995). Nonetheless, a wide array of interventions has been developed in response to the career-related concerns of adolescent and adult clients, with the empirical evidence clearly supporting the efficacy of career interventions of various types (see meta-analysis by Whiston, Sexton, & Lasoff, 1998). Typically, children in later adolescence seek counseling for career concerns more than do younger children, so the section that follows is aimed primarily at this client age group. The career-related issues of children and younger adolescents are typically addressed via school-based career guidance (see Herr & Cramer, 1992).

Lunneborg (1983) has divided career treatment into three broad areas: individual career counseling, group career counseling, and counselor-free career problem treatment. In addition, increasing attention in the field is being drawn to conceptualizing career concerns in the context of broader life issues, including an awareness of a wide array of social roles (e.g., Super, 1980) as well as an awareness of the relationship between work and leisure in the overall well-being of the client (D.J. Tinsley & Schwendener-Holt, 1992; H.E.A. Tinsley & Tinsley, 1988). Moreover, in recent years, attention has begun to focus on a common factors approach to career counseling (e.g., Savickas & Lent, 1994), similar to the now well-established common factors approach to psychotherapy.

INDIVIDUAL CAREER COUNSELING

Crites (1981) has developed a taxonomy of individual career counseling that is reminiscent of taxonomies of traditional individual psychotherapy. Use of Crites's taxonomy can facilitate the understanding of career counseling among practitioners more well-versed in traditional psychotherapy theories. Moreover, use of this taxonomy in helping practitioners bridge from traditional psychotherapy to career counseling instantiates one of the most important recent themes among scholars of vocational psychology, namely, that career counseling should no longer be divorced from psychotherapy and personal counseling (Betz & Corning, 1993; Blustein & Spengler, 1995; Richardson, 1996). Crites has identified five major approaches to individual career counseling: trait-and-factor, client-centered, psychodynamic, developmental, and behavioral. Table 37.1 details how these various approaches differ with respect to diagnosis, process, outcome, interviewing techniques, test interpretation, and use of occupational information.

Trait-and-factor career counseling posits that clients with differentiating traits can be fitted to different vocations with differentiating factors to optimize the fit between person and work environment. Trait-and-factor counseling focuses on individual differences psychology applied to the world of work. These approaches enjoy the most widespread use of vocational approaches by psychologists and vocational counselors. John Holland's (1985; Holland & Gottfredson, 1990) vocational theory is the most widely researched and practiced of the trait-and-factor approaches (see review by Osipow & Fitzgerald, 1996, ch. 4; see Swanson, 1996, for a response to critics and an update of this approach).

Client-centered vocational counseling has its roots in Carl Rogers's client-centered therapy (1942), although the primary theorist for client-centered vocational therapy, Patterson (1974), has argued that specialized vocational training is required beyond basic client-centered skills. The core of client-centered vocational counseling is the understanding that vocational problems result from a lack of congruence between the self and the world of work. This approach is markedly different from the trait-and-factor approach because it eschews assessment and diagnosis and focuses on common human processes rather than on individual differences. E. Lent (1996) has provided an informative overview of this approach, including a brief case study.

Psychodynamic career counseling as the name suggests, has a psychoanalytic heritage, having been influenced by Freud, Rank, and Erikson. However, Bordin (1968, 1990), the primary theorist of this approach, developed psychodynamic career counseling as a framework for integrating trait-and-factor and client-centered approaches, hoping to provide increased complexity regarding normative human experiences as well as an improved diagnostic system, based on more psychological concepts than trait-and-factor theory. Bordin and Kopplin (1973) have described a diagnostic system with seven problem categories: (1) synthetic difficulties, in which the client simply has had difficulty achieving cognitive clarity regarding careers; (2) identity difficulties, in which client career problems are associated with the need to form a viable sense of self; (3) gratification conflicts, in which the client has limited gratification from work activities; (4) change orientation, in which vocational choice issues reflect deeper dissatisfaction with self; (5) overt pathology, in which the client's psychopathology hinders vocational behavior and must be

Table 37.1 Summary of major approaches to individual career counseling.

	Trait-and-Factor	Client-Centered	Psychodynamic	Developmental	Behavioral
Diagnosis	Different courses of treatment stem from a determination of what is wrong with the client.	Rogers and Patterson consider diagnosis as disruptive of the client/counselor relationship; instead, they determine whether or not the client has a "vocational problem."	Bordin stipulates that diagnosis must form the basis for the choice of treatment; wants more psychologically based constructs (choice anxiety, dependence, self-conflict) to be used in diagnosis.	Super coins "appraisal" rather than diagnosis; delineates three types that focus on the client's potentialities and problems; (1) problem appraisal, (2) person appraisal, (3) prognostic appraisal; client is active in the appraisal process.	Goodstein, in his behavioral-theoretic approach, attributes a central role to anxiety in the diagnosis of behavioral and career-choice problems; Krumboltz and Thoresen focus fully on behavioral analysis or problem identification in the specification of goals for counseling. In this behavioral-pragmatic approach, they do not focus on anxiety or diagnosis.
Process M O D E L S	Involves largely the counselor in gathering and interpreting data on the client; client assists only in the actual determination of treatment or counseling to effect desired adjustment, and in follow-up.	Patterson sees the process as encompassing Rogers' highest stage of personal adjustment in psychotherapy; the adjustment level of a client following psychotherapy approximates that of a vocational client before counseling when he/she is finding out who he/she is and what his/her needs are.	Bordin defines three states of process: (1) exploration and contract setting state; (2) critical decision states in which client decides what facets of personal adjustment other than just vocational he/she would pursue; (3) "working for change" stage in which increased understanding of self is aimed at in counseling.	The immediate objective is to facilitate the client's career development; Super states that the broader goal is to bring about improvements in the individual's general personal adjustment (represents a synthesis of trait-and-factor and client-centered orientations).	According to Goodstein, process varies with the etiology of the client's problem: antecedent anxiety necessitates counterconditioning and instrumental learning; consequent anxiety necessitates only the latter. Krumboltz and Thoresen, on the other hand, aim at the elimination of nonadjustive behavior patterns.
Outcomes	Immediate goal is to resolve the presenting problem of client; longer-term objective is to help him/her better understand and manage his/her own assets and liabilities, so he/she can solve future problems.	Goal is to facilitate the clarification and implementation of the self-concept in a compatible occupational role at whatever point the client is; relates to psychotherapy's overall outcome of an individual's reorganized self that can accept and convert into reality a picture of himself/herself and role in the work world.	Results are twofold: (1) assist the client in career decision making and (2) in broader terms, to effect some positive change in the client's personality.	The process of career development progresses from orientation and readiness for career choice to decision making and reality testing; the counselor initiates counseling at that point in the process that the client has reached.	Goodstein's theoretic outcomes are (1) elimination of antecedent and consequent anxiety and (2) acquisition of decision-making skills. Krumboltz and Thoresen's pragmatic goals involve skill acquisition: altering maladaptive behavior, learning decision-making process, and preventing problems.

(continued)

Table 37.1 (Continued)

	Trait-and-Factor	Client-Centered	Psychodynamic	Developmental	Behavioral
Interview Techniques	Involves a pragmatic technological method of establishing rapport, cultivating self-understanding, advising a program of action, carrying out a plan, and referring the client to other personnel for more assistance.	Counselor will make responses during the interview geared to helping the client experience and implement the self-concept in an occupational role.	Bordin enumerates three interpretive counselor response categories that can be used: (1) clarification, to focus the client's thinking and verbalizations; (2) comparisons; and (3) the interpretation of "wish-defense" systems; represents a synthesis of psychoanalytic practices, trait-and-factor, client-centered approaches.	Super's "cyclical" approach is to respond directly to content statements by the client and nondirectly to expressions of feeling.	Goodstein proposes techniques of psychotherapy for the alleviation of anxiety; he joins with Krumboltz and Thoresen in their pragmatic stance that the counselor should reinforce desired client responses, encourage social modeling, and teach discrimination learning in the acquisition of decision-making skills.
Test Interpretation	Involves the counselor, who makes authoritative interpretations of the test results and draws conclusions and recommendations from them for the client's deliberation.	Counselor proposes that tests be used primarily for the client's edification and as needed and requested by client; use only as needed and requested by client; termed by Super "precision testing."	Bordin defines three major uses: (1) that the client be an active participant in selecting the tests (as in the client-centered approach); (2) that the tests provide diagnostic information for counselor to give client and stimulate self-exploration; and (3) that the counselor verbally present the test interpretation. Introduce as needed rather than presenting it all at once as in trait-and-factor.	The most appropriate information is the description of career patterns in different occupational pursuits; Super observes that there are approximately six types of descriptive data on career patterns that are needed for this approach.	Test use, in either a theoretical or pragmatic stance, is almost negligible as they measure individual differences in behavior rather than reflect individual-environment interaction, a primary concern to a behavioral counselor; objective indices of behavior are therefore gathered.
Use of Occupational Information	Counselor provides this information to either confirm a choice already made or resolve indecision between two equally attractive options; may help a client readjust an inappropriate choice; also used to involve the client actively in the decision-making process.	Introduced when there is a recognized need on the part of the client; counselor must recognize that such information has personal meanings to the client, which must be understood and explored within the context of needs and values and objective reality.	Information that is based on a "need analysis" of job duties and tasks is needed; resembles the trait-and-factor approach of matching individuals and jobs, but differs in that variables are personality needs and gratifying work conditions, rather than static characteristics of the individual and occupation.	The purpose is to maximize the value of tests in decision making by administering them in a discriminating way, and by involving the client in each phase of the process; represents "precision" testing rather than "saturation" testing as in the trait-and-factor approach.	Behavioral counselors have developed "career kits" that are more useful in stimulating further career exploration and decision making than simply printed information.

M E T H O D S

Source: From J.O. Crites, Career Counseling: Models, Methods, and Materials. Copyright 1981, by McGraw-Hill, Inc. Reproduced with permission of McGraw-Hill, Inc.

treated before vocational counseling will be effective; (6) client motivational problems that are otherwise unclassifiable; and (7) vocational problems not otherwise diagnosable.

Developmental career counseling is based on Super's (1957) developmental model of vocational behavior, a part of which has already been detailed. The core of this approach is the notion that vocational behavior is part of a larger human developmental process. Vocational problems occur as a result of arrested developmental processes or failures in development at the current or previous stage. Super's approach involves assessing whether the client is suffering from developmental deficits regarding vocational behavior, called "career immaturity," and seeks to redress the deficits by focusing on earlier stages (see Betz, 1988; Savickas, 1994, for reviews of career maturity research). In addition to the stages of growth and exploration, which have already been detailed, Super described the stages of establishment (age 25–44), in which the chief tasks are to achieve occupational competence and to advance and improve status; maintenance (age 45–65), in which the chief tasks are to preserve work skills and to develop plans and means for retirement; and decline (age 65 and older), in which the tasks are to adapt work to one's changing physical capacity and to sustain independence through resource management (see review by Osipow & Fitzgerald, 1996, chap. 5).

Behavioral career counseling is, like client-centered and psychodynamic approaches, derived from traditional psychotherapy. The central theorist regarding behavioral career counseling is John Krumboltz (e.g., 1996; Krumboltz & Baker, 1973), whose model applies operant and social learning principles to problems in (1) the development of preferences in education and career, (2) learning to make vocational decisions, and (3) entry into training or work. Theorizing by Goodstein (1972) complements the work of Krumboltz by conceptualizing the role and the treatment of anxiety in vocational problems, and by clarifying the distinction between vocational indecision, from which anxiety results, and indecisiveness, a chronic state caused by anxiety (Crites, 1981). The social learning approach, arguably an outgrowth of behavioral career counseling just as cognitive behaviorism can be viewed as an outgrowth of behaviorism, is now a burgeoning area of growth in career counseling (see review by Osipow & Fitzgerald, 1996, chap. 6).

GROUP CAREER COUNSELING

Lunneborg (1983) described several group approaches to vocational counseling. She suggested that vocational groups share a common trait of reliance on the group leader or counselor as an expert who determines what happens in the group, in contrast to some psychotherapy groups. Vocational counseling groups vary widely on the dimension of outcome orientation versus process orientation, with, for example, behavioral and trait-and-factor groups being outcome oriented and client-centered career groups more process-oriented. Five of the seven group approaches described by Lunneborg correspond with the five individual career counseling approaches just described (trait-and-factor, client-centered, psychodynamic, developmental, and behavioral; readers are referred to Lunneborg for details about example groups). Two additional group approaches described by Lunneborg deserve additional detail. Systematically organized vocational groups reflect the growing trend toward highly structured psychoeducational groups and workshops. Often offered in colleges and universities (sometimes for course credit), these group experiences emphasize learning vocational information (e.g., myths about careers and knowledge about occupations) and acquiring specific career-relevant skills (e.g., goal setting and resume writing). Finally, Lunneborg has described a novel form of vocational group counseling, the nontraditional career group. The nontraditional group differs from other groups in two respects. First, it is not based on an explicit theoretical approach to group counseling, such as behaviorism or psychoeducation. Second, nontraditional groups are developed in direct response to specific needs as perceived by constituent groups. This approach stands in contrast to most vocational counseling groups in which groups are developed in response to needs perceived by vocational counselors and psychologists. As an exemplar of nontraditional group vocational counseling, Lunneborg described a preretirement group. The group agenda was determined by collecting responses from potential members regarding their perceived informational needs and their personal priorities with respect to retirement planning.

COUNSELOR-FREE TREATMENT OF VOCATIONAL PROBLEMS

Counselor-free treatment refers to service modalities in which a counselor or psychologist is not directly involved in the provision of psychological services. Vocational psychology has been at the forefront of applied psychology in the development of alternative service modalities. These alternative modalities represent a rapidly growing and changing segment of vocational counseling (Taylor, 1988). This stems in part from a disparity between client demand for vocational counseling, which is high, and the willingness and ability of psychologists to offer such services, which are relatively low (Crites, 1981, p. 13; Fitzgerald & Osipow, 1986, 1988). Counselor-free methods of providing career counseling include self-help books and exercises, computerized vocational counseling, and career resource centers.

Vocational self-help books, like their counterparts in psychotherapeutic bibliotherapy, have proliferated and range widely in quality, focus, and style. Craighead, McNamera, and Horan (1984) found very little research evaluating the efficacy of even the most popular vocational self-help books, such as *What Color Is Your Parachute?* (Bolles, 1999). However, one notable exception to this lack of evaluation of self-help books comes from Santrock, Minnett, and Campbell (1994), who enlisted the help of over 500 counseling and clinical psychologists in evaluating over 1,000 self-help books, including a section devoted to career development. Readers interested in evaluations of self-help books in vocational psychology are referred to Santrock et al.'s excellent and much needed guide.

Another noteworthy exception to the lack of information supporting the efficacy of these books and materials is research on Holland's (1985) Self-Directed Search (SDS). The SDS is a paper-and-pencil self-help exercise developed to aid in the selection of postsecondary training and careers by clarifying client career interest. For example, Krivatsy and Magoon (1976) demonstrated that clients randomly assigned to use the SDS with no contact with psychologists scored the same as clients in traditional vocational counseling and significantly better than members of a no-treatment control group on a host of outcome measures (including satisfaction). Reardon, Lenz, and Straussberger (1996) found that career counselors were able to give more efficient service to college students who used the SDS first, especially when the students initially believed they lacked sufficient self-knowledge to match personal characteristics to career choices.

Computerized vocational counseling is probably the area of most rapid advance in the delivery of vocational counseling services over the past two decades. Computerized vocational counseling is clearly distinguishable from computerized administration and scoring of assessment instruments by the former's emphasis on computer-client interaction and on providing usable career-relevant information to the client immediately. Taylor (1988) identified and reviewed in detail no fewer than 12 commercially available vocational counseling packages. Of these 12, only two packages were said to provide comprehensive computerized services: DISCOVER and SIGI (System of Interactive Guidance and Information). Taylor also identified nine other published reviews of vocational computer software. DISCOVER and SIGI were reviewed most often, DISCOVER by all reviewers and SIGI by all but one reviewer. More recently, Sampson et al. (1994) have evaluated 15 of these packages, again including DISCOVER and SIGI. One useful feature of Sampson et al.'s evaluation is a separate evaluation of computer packages focused on junior high/middle school clients. In their comparisons of both college/adult and junior high/middle school packages, the DISCOVER packages emerge as particularly strong. In addition, Luzzo and Pierce (1996) performed an experiment on middle school students that revealed that DISCOVER led to increased career maturity over a control condition. Zunker (1998), among others, has provided guidelines for selecting a computerized vocational counseling package.

DISCOVER consists of four basic parts. The first involves a series of client assessments regarding vocational interests, self-assessment of abilities, and values. The second part provides the client with a flexible variety of ways to search for specific occupations, including via inputting the results of the most widely used vocational interest assessment instruments. The third part allows the client to retrieve detailed information regarding specific occupations. The fourth part allows the client to retrieve detailed information regarding thousands of technical schools, colleges, and graduate schools.

SIGI has six basic parts. The Values part provides clients with an opportunity to clarify their vocationally relevant values. In the Locate part, occupations consistent with client values are listed: Clients have the opportunity to see the effect of changing the importance of specific values on career selection. In the Compare part of SIGI, clients can compare up to three selected careers on such dimensions as required training, income, and working conditions. In the Prediction part, locally provided information from a college, university, or technical school informs clients of their probability of success in a given field of study. In the Planning part, clients learn specific steps to gain employment in a chosen field. Finally, the Strategy part teaches decision-making skills to clients (see Peterson, Ryan-Jones, Sampson, & Reardon, 1994, for a comparison of DISCOVER, SIGI, and SIGI Plus; see Reardon, Peterson, Sampson, & Ryan-Jones, 1992, for a comparison of SIGI and SIGI PLUS).

Though still in its infancy, career counseling via the Internet is beginning to receive attention from scholars of vocational psychology (Stevens & Lundberg, 1998). We uncovered no documentation by scholars in the field of useful Web sites for career counseling of children and adolescents, but we can readily imagine a bright future for this modality.

One important and innovative approach to counselor-free treatment of vocational problems is the career resources center. Far more than a library of career-relevant books and publications, the career resources center is a hub of numerous vocationally related self-help activities. These centers can be located in communities, in such places as shopping centers, but also most commonly in community colleges and universities (Lunneborg, 1983). Although the director of such a center is likely to be a psychologist or a master's-level vocational counselor, the line staff is typically composed of indigenous paraprofessionals. Resource centers are tailored to meet local vocational needs, but typical features include descriptions of occupations; projections regarding employment opportunities in specific occupations; information regarding colleges, universities, and technical schools; information regarding government and military employment; information regarding internships and apprenticeships; information regarding resource or contact persons associated with particular occupations; vocationally relevant information for special populations; and information regarding financial aid for postsecondary education (see Zunker, 1998, for a detailed overview of career resource centers).

CONCLUSION

Successful career counseling involves a range of conceptual and technical skills. At the conceptual level, the field's predominant developmental orientation calls attention to the need to situate the presenting career problem within an individual's own autobiographical trajectory. For example, the same presenting concern (e.g., vocational indecision) may carry implications for very different interventions depending on whether it occurs in early adolescence or in young adulthood.

Likewise, development occurs along multiple fronts simultaneously, though not necessarily in lockstep cadence to a common beat (cf. Adams et al., 1979; Blustein et al., 1989; Raskin, 1989). For this reason, the vocational counselor should attend concurrently to the processes of identity formation, psychosocial maturation, and vocational development in assessing and intervening in career concerns. This assessment and intervention is aided considerably by an assortment of instruments and procedures designed to clarify and surmount liabilities to career development. Treatment modality (individual, group, counselor-free) can be tailored to the particular client once the nature of the career problem has been specified. Career difficulties during adolescence may be located in early growth or later exploration stages and may reflect a wide spectrum of potential problems, ranging from deficits in early identity development through difficulties with career exploration, indecision, or implementation.

In vocational counseling, as elsewhere, effective intervention depends on effective prior conceptualization, a point that is reminiscent of Vondracek et al.'s (1983) caveat that "one should not intervene to promote vocational role development along an inadequately idealized and studied developmental pathway" (p. 184). As vocational and developmental literatures continue their productive interface, career counselors will have access to models of increasing sophistication, models that reflect both an understanding of broader developmental processes and a sensitivity to the practical concerns of vocational counseling.

REFERENCES

Achter, J.A., Benbow, C., & Lubinski, D. (1997). Rethinking multipotentiality among the intellectually gifted: A critical review and recommendations. *Gifted Child Quarterly, 41,* 5–15.

Adams, G.R., Shea, J., & Fitch, S. (1979). Toward the development of an objective assessment of ego-identity status. *Journal of Youth and Adolescence, 8,* 223–237.

Allis, M.R. (1984). Career Decision Scale. *Measurement and Evaluation in Counseling and Development, 17,* 98–100.

Archer, S.C. (1989). Gender differences in identity development: Issues of process, domain, and timing. *Journal of Adolescence, 12,* 117–138.

Berzonsky, M.D. (1990). Self-construction over the lifespan: A process perspective on identity formation. In G. Neimeyer & B. Neimeyer (Eds.), *Advances in personal construct psychology* (pp. 155–186). Greenwich, CT: JAI Press.

Berzonsky, M.D., & Neimeyer, G.J. (1994). Ego identity status and identity processing orientation: The moderating role of commitment. *Journal of Research in Personality, 28,* 425–435.

Berzonsky, M.D., & Ferrari, J.R. (1996). Identity orientation of decisional strategies. *Personality and Individual Differences, 20,* 597–606.

Betz, N.E. (1988). The assessment of career development and maturity. In W.B. Walsh & S.H. Osipow (Eds.), *Career decision making* (pp. 77–136). Hillsdale, NJ: Erlbaum.

Betz, N.E., & Corning, A.F. (1993). The inseparability of "career" and "personal" counseling. *Career Development Quarterly, 42,* 137–142.

Betz, N.E., & Fitzgerald, L.F. (1987). *The career psychology of women.* Orlando, FL: Academic Press.

Betz, N.E., & Hackett, G. (1986). Applications of self-efficacy theory to understanding career choice behavior. *Journal of Social and Clinical Psychology, 4,* 279–289.

Betz, N.E., & Luzzo, D.A. (1996). Career assessment and the Career Decision-Making Self-Efficacy Scale. *Journal of Career Assessment, 4,* 413–428.

Blocker, D.H., & Schultz, R.A. (1961). Relationships among self-descriptions, occupational stereotypes, and vocational preferences. *Journal of Counseling Psychology, 8,* 314–317.

Blustein, D.L., Devenis, L.E., & Kidney, B.A. (1989). Relationship between the identity formation process and career development. *Journal of Counseling Psychology, 36,* 196–202.

Blustein, D.L., & Spengler, P.M. (1995). Personal adjustment: Career counseling and psychotherapy. In W.B. Walsh & S.H. Osipow (Eds.), *Handbook of vocational psychology: Theory, research, and practice* (2nd ed., pp. 295–329). Mahwah, NJ: Erlbaum.

Bolles, R.N. (1999). *What color is your parachute?* Berkeley, CA: Ten Speed Press.

Bordin, E.S. (1968). *Psychological counseling.* New York: Appleton-Century-Crofts.

Bordin, E.S. (1990). Psychodynamic models of career choice and satisfaction. In D. Brown & L. Brooks (Eds.), *Career choice and development: Applying contemporary theories to practice* (2nd ed., pp. 102–144). San Francisco: Jossey-Bass.

Bordin, E.S., & Kopplin, D.A. (1973). Motivational conflict and vocational development. *Journal of Counseling Psychology, 20,* 154–161.

Borgen, F.H. (1988). Review of Strong-Campbell Interest Inventory. In J.T. Kapes & M.M. Mastie (Eds.), *Counselor's guide to career assessment instruments* (pp. 121–126). Alexandria, VA: National Career Development Association.

Campbell, R.E., & Cellini, J.V. (1981). A diagnostic taxonomy of adult career development problems. *Journal of Vocational Behavior, 19,* 175–190.

Craighead, L.W., McNamera, K., & Horan, J.J. (1984). Perspectives on self-help and bibliotherapy: You are what you read. In S.D. Brown & R.W. Lent (Eds.), *Handbook of counseling psychology* (pp. 878–929). New York: Wiley.

Crites, J.O. (1981). *Career counseling: Models, methods, and materials.* New York: McGraw-Hill.

Crites, J.O., & Savickas, M.L. (1996). Revision of the Career Maturity Inventory. *Journal of Career Assessment, 4,* 131–138.

D'Andrea, M., & Daniels, J. (1992). A career development program for inner-city Black youth. *Career Development Quarterly, 42,* 272–280.

Erikson, E.H. (1950). Growth and crises of the "healthy personality." In M.J.E. Senn (Ed.), *Symposium on the healthy personality.* (pp. 73–94). New York: Josiah Macy Jr. Foundation.

Erikson, E.H. (1963). *Childhood and society* (2nd ed.). New York: Norton.

Erikson, E.H. (1968). *Identity: Youth and crisis.* New York: Norton.

Fannin, P.M. (1979). The relation between ego-identity status and sex-role attitude, work-role salience, atypicality of major and self-esteem in college women. *Journal of Vocational Behavior, 14,* 12–22.

Fitzgerald, L.F., Fassinger, R.E., & Betz, N.E. (1995). Theoretical advances in the study of women's career development. In W.B. Walsh & S.H. Osipow (Eds.), *Handbook of vocational psychology: Theory, research, and practice* (2nd ed., pp. 67–109). Mahwah, NJ: Erlbaum.

Fitzgerald, L.F., & Osipow, S.H. (1986). An occupational analysis of counseling psychology: How special is the speciality? *American Psychologist, 41,* 535–544.

Fitzgerald, L.F., & Osipow, S.H. (1988). We have seen the future, but is it us? *Professional Psychology: Research and Practice, 19,* 575–583.

Fouad, N.A. (1993). Cross-cultural vocational assessment. *Career Development Quarterly, 42,* 4–13.

Fouad, N.A. (1994a). Annual review 1991–1993: Vocational choice, decision-making, assessment, and intervention. *Journal of Vocational Behavior, 45,* 125–176.

Fouad, N.A. (1994b). Career assessment with Latinos/Hispanics. *Journal of Career Assessment, 2,* 226–239.

Frazier, N. (1988). Additional career assessment instruments. In J.T. Kapes & M.M. Mastic (Eds.), *Counselor's guide to career assessment instruments* (pp. 287–312). Alexandria, VA: National Career Development Association.

Fukuyama, M.A., Probert, B.S., Neimeyer, G.J., Nevill, D.D., & Metzler, A.E. (1988). Effects of DISCOVER on career self-efficacy and decision making of undergraduates. *Career Development Quarterly, 37,* 56–62.

Goodstein, L.D. (1972). Behavioral views of counseling. In B. Stefflre & W.H. Grant (Eds.), *Theories of counseling* (pp. 243–286). New York: McGraw-Hill.

Gottfredson, L.S., & Becker, H.J. (1981). A challenge to vocational psychology: How important are aspirations in determining male career development? *Journal of Vocational Behavior, 18,* 121–137.

Grotevant, H.D., & Adams, G.R. (1984). Development of an objective measure to assess ego identity in adolescence: Validity and replication. *Journal of Youth and Adolescence, 11,* 33–47.

Hackett, G., & Betz, N.E. (1981). A self-efficacy approach to the career development of women. *Journal of Vocational Behavior, 18,* 326–339.

Hackett, G., & Watkins, C.E., Jr. (1995). Research in career assessment: Abilities, interests, decision making, and career development. In W.B. Walsh & S.H. Osipow (Eds.), *Handbook of vocational psychology: Theory, research, and practice* (2nd ed., pp. 181–215). Mahwah, NJ: Erlbaum.

Harmon, L.W., Hansen, J.C., Borgen, F.H., & Hammer, A.L. (1994). *Strong Interest Inventory: Applications and technical guide.* Palo Alto, CA: Consulting Psychologists Press.

Harren, V.A. (1979). A model of career decision-making for college students. *Journal of Vocational Behavior, 14,* 119–133.

Harren, V.A. (1980). *Assessment of career decision-making (ACDM): Counselors instruction guide.* Unpublished manuscript, Southern Illinois University, Carbondale.

Hartman, B.W., Utz, P.W., & Farnum, S.O. (1979). Examining the reliability and validity of an adapted scale of educational-vocational undecidedness in a sample of graduate students. *Journal of Vocational Behavior, 15,* 224–230.

Havighurst, R.J. (1982). The world of work. In B.B. Wolman (Ed.), *Handbook of developmental psychology* (pp. 771–787). Englewood Cliffs, NJ: Prentice-Hall.

Herr, E.L., & Cramer, S.H. (1992). *Career guidance and counseling through the life span: Systemic approaches* (4th ed.). Boston: Little, Brown.

Holland, J.L. (1985). *Making vocational choices* (2nd ed.). Englewood Cliffs, NJ: Prentice-Hall.

Holland, J.L., Daiger, D.C., & Powers, P.G. (1980). Some diagnostic scales and signs for the selection of vocational treatments. *Journal of Personality and Social Psychology, 39,* 1191-1200.

Holland, J.L., & Gottfredson, G.D. (1990). *An annotated bibliography for Holland's theory of vocational personalities and work environments.* Baltimore: Johns Hopkins University Press.

Hollinger, C.L., & Fleming, E.S. (1993). Project CHOICE: The emerging roles and careers of gifted women. *Roeper Review, 15,* 156–160.

Ibrahim, F.A., Ohnishi, H., & Wilson, R.P. (1994). Career assessment in a culturally diverse society. *Journal of Career Assessment, 2,* 276–288.

Jepson, D. (1984). The developmental perspective on vocational behavior: A review of theory and research. In S.D. Brown & R.W. Lent (Eds.), *Handbook of counseling psychology* (pp. 178–215). New York: Wiley.

Jordaan, J.P. (1963). Exploratory behavior: The formation of self and occupational concepts. In D.E. Super (Ed.), *Career development: Self-concept theory* (pp. 42–78). New York: College Entrance Examination Board.

Kapes, J.T., & Mastie, M.M. (Eds.). (1988). *Counselor's guide to career assessment instruments.* Alexandria, VA: National Career Development Association.

Kapes, J.T., Mastie, M.M., & Whitfield, E.A. (Eds.). (1994). *A counselor's guide to career assessment instruments* (3rd ed.). Alexandria, VA: National Career Development Association.

Kapes, J.T., & Vacha-Haase, T. (1994). A counselor's guide user's matrix: An alphabetical listing of career assessment instruments by category and type of use. In J.T. Kapes, M.M. Mastie, & E.A. Whitfield (Eds.), *Counselor's guide to career assessment instruments* (3rd ed., pp. 473–489). Alexandria, VA: National Career Development Association.

Kerr, B., & Fisher, T. (1997). Career assessment with gifted and talented students. *Journal of Career Assessment, 5,* 239–251.

Kidd, J.M. (1984). The relationship of self and occupational concepts to the occupational preferences of adolescents. *Journal of Vocational Behavior, 24,* 48–65.

Klein, M.A., Wheaton, J.E., & Wilson, K.B. (1997). The career assessment of persons with disabilities: A review. *Journal of Career Assessment, 5*, 203–211.

Krivatsy, S.E., & Magoon, T.M. (1976). Differential effects of three vocational counseling treatments. *Journal of Counseling Psychology, 23*, 112–118.

Krumboltz, J.D. (1996). A learning theory of career counseling. In M.L. Savickas & W.B. Walsh (Eds.), *Handbook of career counseling theory and practice* (pp. 55–80). Palo Alto, CA: Davies-Black.

Krumboltz, J.D., & Baker, R.D. (1973). Behavioral counseling for vocational decision. In H. Borow (Ed.), *Career guidance for a new age* (pp. 235–283). Boston: Houghton Mifflin.

Lent, E. (1996). The person focus in career theory and practice. In M.L. Savickas & W.B. Walsh (Eds.), *Handbook of career counseling theory and practice* (pp. 109–120). Palo Alto, CA: Davies-Black.

Lent, R.W., Brown, S.D., & Larkin, K.C. (1984). Relation of self-efficacy expectations to academic achievement and persistence. *Journal of Counseling Psychology, 31*, 356–362.

Lehr, R., & Jeffery, G. (1996). Career support needs of youth: A qualitative analysis of the rural perspective. *Canadian Journal of Counselling, 30*, 240–253.

Leong, F.T.L. (1995). *Career development and vocational behavior of racial and ethnic minorities.* Mahwah, NJ: Erlbaum.

Leong, F.T.L., & Hartung, P. (1997). Career assessment with culturally different clients: Proposing an integrative-sequential conceptual framework for cross-cultural career counseling research and practice. *Journal of Career Assessment, 5*, 183–202.

Leong, F.T.L., & Leung, S.A. (1994). Career assessment with Asian-Americans. *Journal of Career Assessment, 2*, 240–257.

Lunneborg, P.W. (1983). Career counseling techniques. In W.B. Walsh & S.H. Osipow (Eds.), *Handbook of vocational psychology: Applications* (Vol. 2, pp. 41–76). Hillsdale, NJ: Erlbaum.

Luzzo, D.A. (1995). A psychometric evaluation of the Career Decision-Making Self-Efficacy Scale. *Journal of Counseling and Development, 74*, 276–279.

Luzzo, D.A., & Pierce, G. (1996). Effects of DISCOVER on the career maturity of middle school students. *Career Development Quarterly, 45*, 170–172.

Marcia, J.E. (1966). Development and validation of ego identity status. *Journal of Personality and Social Psychology, 3*, 551–558.

Marcia, J.E., & Friedman, M.L. (1970). Ego identity status in college women. *Journal of Personality, 38*, 249–263.

Martin, W.E., Jr. (1991). Career development of American Indians living on reservations: Cross-cultural factors to consider. *Career Development Quarterly, 39*, 269–278.

Martin, W.E., Jr., & Farris, K.K. (1994). A cultural and contextual decision path approach to career assessment with Native Americans: A psychological perspective. *Journal of Career Assessment, 2*, 258–275.

Matteson, D.R. (1974). *Alienation vs. exploration and commitment: Personality and family corollaries of adolescent identity status* (Project Rep.). Copenhagen, Denmark: Danmarks Laerhojskole.

Melgosa, J. (1987). Development and validity of the Occupational Identity Scale. *Journal of Adolescence, 10*, 385–397.

Mitchell, L.K., & Krumboltz, J.D. (1984). Research on human decision making: Implications for career decision making and counseling. In S.D. Brown & R.W. Lent (Eds.), *Handbook of counseling psychology* (pp. 238–282). New York: Wiley.

Neimeyer, G.J., Nevill, D.D., Probert, B.S., & Fukuyama, M.A. (1985). Cognitive structures in vocational development. *Journal of Vocational Behavior, 27*, 191–201.

Neimeyer, G.J., & Metzler, A.E. (1987). The development of vocational structures. *Journal of Vocational Behavior, 30*, 26–32.

Neimeyer, G.J., Prichard, S., Berzonsky, M.D., & Metzler, A.E. (1991). Vocational hypothesis testing: The role of occupational relevance and identity orientation. *Journal of Vocational Behavior, 38*, 318–332.

Nevill, D.D., & Calvert, P.D. (1996). Career assessment and the Salience Inventory. *Journal of Career Assessment, 4*, 399–412.

Nevill, D.D., Neimeyer, G.J., Probert, B.S., & Fukuyama, M.A. (1986). Cognitive structures in vocational information processing and decision making. *Journal of Vocational Behavior, 28*, 110–122.

Nevill, D.D., & Super, D.E. (1986). *Manual for the Salience Inventory.* Palo Alto, CA: Consulting Psychologists Press.

Niles, S.G. (1997). Annual review: Practice and research in career counseling and development: 1996. *Career Development Quarterly, 46*, 115–141.

Oppenheimer, E.A. (1966). The relationship between criteria self constructs and occupational preferences. *Journal of Counseling Psychology, 13*, 191–197.

Osberg, T.M. (1992). Review of the Salience Inventory. In J.J. Kramer & J.C. Conoley (Eds.), *Eleventh mental measurements yearbook* (pp. 778–779). Lincoln: University of Nebraska-Lincoln.

Osipow, S.H. (1973). *Theories of career development.* Englewood Cliffs, NJ: Prentice Hall.

Osipow, S.H. (1980). *Manual for the Career Decision Scale.* Columbus, OH: Marathon Consulting Press.

Osipow, S.H., & Fitzgerald, L.F. (1996). *Theories of career development* (4th ed.). Needham Heights, MA: Allyn & Bacon.

Osipow, S.H., & Temple, R.D. (1996). Development and use of the Task-Specific Occupational Self-Efficacy Scale. *Journal of Career Assessment, 4*, 445–456.

Osipow, S.H., Carney, C.G., & Barak, A. (1976). A scale of educational-vocational undecidedness: A typological approach. *Journal of Vocational Behavior, 9*, 233–243.

Osipow, S.H., Carney, C.G., Winer, J., Yanico, B., & Koschier, M. (1976). *Career Decision Scale.* Columbus, OH: Marathon Consulting Press.

Parsons, F. (1909). *Choosing a vocation.* Boston: Houghton Mifflin.

Patterson, C.H. (1974). *Relationship counseling and psychotherapy.* New York: Harper & Row.

Peterson, G.W., Ryan-Jones, R.E., Sampson, J.P., & Reardon, R.C. (1994). A comparison of the effectiveness of three computer-assisted career guidance systems: DISCOVER, SIGI and SIGI Plus. *Computers in Human Behavior, 10*, 189–198.

Prediger, D.J., & Garfield, N.J. (1988). Testing competencies and responsibilities: A checklist for counselors. In J.T. Kapes & M.M. Mastie (Eds.), *Counselor's guide to career assessment instruments* (pp. 49–54). Alexandria, VA: National Career Development Association.

Prince, J.P. (1997). Career assessment with lesbian, gay, and bisexual individuals. *Journal of Career Assessment, 5*, 225–238.

Ramirez, S.Z., Wassef, A., Paniagua, F.A., & Linsky, A.O. (1996). Mental health providers' perceptions of cultural variables in evaluating ethnically diverse clients. *Professional Psychology: Research and Practice, 27*, 284–288.

Raskin, P.M. (1985). Identity and vocational development [Special issue]. *New Directions for Child Development, 30*, 25–42.

Raskin, P.M. (1989). Identity status research: Implications for career counseling. *Journal of Adolescence, 12*, 375–388.

Raskin, P.M. (1994). Identity and the career counseling of adolescents: The development of vocational identity. In S.L. Archer (Ed.), *Interventions for adolescent identity development* (pp. 141–176). Thousand Oaks, CA: Sage.

Reardon, R., Lenz, J., & Straussberger, S. (1996). Integrating theory, practice and research with the Self-Directed Search: Computer Version Form R. *Measurement and Evaluation in Counseling and Development, 28*, 211–218.

Reardon, R.C., Peterson, G.W., Sampson, J.P., & Ryan-Jones, R.E. (1992). A comparative analysis of the impact of SIGI and SIGI Plus. *Journal of Career Development, 18*, 315–322.

Richardson, M.S. (1996). From career counseling to counseling/psychotherapy and work, jobs, and career. In M.L. Savickas & W.B. Walsh (Eds.), *Handbook of career counseling theory and practice* (pp. 347–360). Palo Alto, CA: Davies-Black.

Roberts, K. (1977). The social conditions, consequences and limitations of career guidance. *British Journal of Counseling and Guidance, 5*, 1–9.

Roe, A. (1956). *The psychology of occupations.* New York: Wiley.

Rogers, C.R. (1942). *Counseling and psychotherapy: Newer concepts in practice.* Boston: Houghton Mifflin.

Rogers, W.B., & Westbrook, B.W. (1983). Measuring career indecision among college students: Towards a valid approach for counseling practitioners and researchers. *Measurement and Evaluation in Guidance, 16*, 78–85.

Sampson, J.P., Jr., Reardon, R.C., Wilde, C.K., Norris, D.S., Peterson, G.W., Strausberger, S.J., Garis, J.W., Lenz, J.G., & Saunders, D.E. (1994). A comparison of the assessment components of fifteen computer-assisted career guidance systems. In J.T. Kapes, M.M. Mastie, & E.A. Whitfield (Eds.), *Counselor's guide to career assessment instruments* (3rd ed., pp. 373–379). Alexandria, VA: National Career Development Association.

Santrock, J.W., Minnett, A.M., & Campbell, B.D. (1994). *The authoritative guide to self-help books.* New York: Guilford Press.

Savickas, M.L. (1994). Measuring career development: Current status and future directions. *Career Development Quarterly, 43*, 54–62.

Savickas, M.L., & Lent, R.W. (1994). *Convergence in career development theories.* Palo Alto, CA: CPP Books.

Slaney, R.B. (1988). The assessment of career decision making. In W.B. Walsh & S.H. Osipow (Eds.), *Career decision making* (pp. 33–76). Hillsdale, NJ: Erlbaum.

Spokane, A.R., & Jacob, E.J. (1996). Career and vocational assessment 1993-1994: A biennial review. *Journal of Career Assessment, 4*, 1–32.

Stevens, D.T., & Lundberg, D.J. (1998). The emergence of the Internet: Enhancing career counseling education and services. *Journal of Career Development, 24*, 195–208.

Stoltz-Loike, M. (1996). Annual review: Practice and research in career development and counseling: 1995. *Career Development Quarterly, 45*, 99–140.

Super, D.E. (1951). Vocational adjustment: Implementing a self-concept. *Occupations, 30*, 88–92.

Super, D.E. (1957). *Psychology of careers.* New York: Harper & Row.

Super, D.E. (1980). A life-span, life-space approach to career development. *Journal of Vocational Behavior, 16*, 282–298.

Super, D.E. (1990). A life-span, life-space approach to career development. In D. Brown & L. Brooks (Eds.), *Career choice and development* (2nd ed., pp. 197–261). San Francisco: Jossey-Bass.

Super, D.E., Crites, J.D., Hummel, R.C., Moser, H.P., Overstreet, P.L., & Warnath, C.F. (1957). *Vocational development: A framework for research.* New York: Columbia University, Bureau of Publications, Teachers College.

Super, D.E., Thompson, A.S., Lindeman, R.H., Jordaan, J.P., & Myers, R.A. (1981). *The Career Development*

Inventory. Palo Alto, CA: Consulting Psychologists Press.

Swanson, J.L. (1995). The process and outcome of career counseling. In W.B. Walsh & S.H. Osipow (Eds.), *Handbook of vocational psychology: Theory, research, and practice* (2nd ed., pp. 217–259). Mahwah, NJ: Erlbaum.

Swanson, J.L. (1996). The theory *is* the practice: Trait-and-factor/person-environment fit counseling. In M.L. Savickas & W.B. Walsh (Eds.), *Handbook of career counseling theory and practice* (pp. 93–108). Palo Alto, CA: Davies-Black.

Swanson, J.L., & Bowman, S.L. (1994). Career assessment with African-American clients. *Journal of Career Assessment, 2*, 210–225.

Swanson, J.L., & Woitke, M.B. (1997). Theory into practice in career assessment for women: Assessment and interventions regarding perceived career barriers. *Journal of Career Assessment, 5*, 443–462.

Task Force on Work. (1973). *Work in America.* Cambridge, MA: MIT Press.

Taylor, K.M. (1988). Advances in career-planning systems. In W.B. Walsh & S.H. Osipow (Eds.), *Career decision making* (pp. 137–211). Hillsdale, NJ: Erlbaum.

Taylor, K.M., & Betz, N.E. (1983). Applications of self-efficacy theory to the understanding and treatment of career indecision. *Journal of Vocational Behavior, 22*, 63–81.

Tinsley, D.J., & Schwendener-Holt, M.J. (1992). Retirement and leisure. In S.D. Brown & R.W. Lent (Eds.), *Handbook of counseling psychology* (2nd ed., pp. 627–662). New York: Wiley.

Tinsley, H.E.A., & Tinsley, D.J. (1988). An expanded context for the study of career decision making, development, and maturity. In W.B. Walsh & S.H. Osipow (Eds.), *Career decision making* (pp. 213–264). Hillsdale, NJ: Erlbaum.

Vondracek, F.W. (1993). Promoting vocational development in early adolescence. In R.M. Lerner (Ed.), *Early adolescence: Perspectives on research policy and intervention* (pp. 277–292). Hillsdale, NJ: Erlbaum.

Vondracek, F.W., Lerner, R.M., & Schulenberg, J.M. (1983). The concept of development in vocational theory and intervention. *Journal of Vocational Behavior, 23*, 179–202.

Vondracek, F.W., Lerner, R.M., & Schulenberg, J.M. (1986). *Career development: A life-span approach.* Hillsdale, NJ: Erlbaum.

Waterman, A.S. (1982). Identity development from adolescence to adulthood: An extension of theory and a review of research. *Developmental Psychology, 10*, 387–392.

Westbrook, B.W., & Sanford, E.E. (1991). The validity of career maturity attitude measures among Black and White high school students. *Career Development Quarterly, 39*, 199–208.

Whiston, S.C., Sexton, T.L., & Lasoff, D.L. (1998). Career-intervention outcome: A replication and extension of Oliver and Spokane (1988). *Journal of Counseling Psychology, 45*, 150–165.

Womer, F.B. (1988). Selecting an instrument: Chore or challenge? In J.T. Kapes & M.M. Mastie (Eds.), *Counselor's guide to career assessment instruments* (pp. 27–35). Alexandria, VA: National Career Development Association.

Zunker, V.G. (1998). *Career counseling: Applied concepts of life planning* (5th ed.). Pacific Grove, CA: Brooks/Cole.

Zytowski, D.G. (1988). Review of Salience Inventory. In J.T. Kapes & M.M. Mastie (Eds.), *Counselor's guide to career assessment instruments* (pp. 150–154). Alexandria, VA: National Career Development Association.

CHAPTER 38

Adolescent Alcohol and Drug Abuse

SANDRA A. BROWN, GREGORY A. AARONS, AND ANA M. ABRANTES

Alcohol and drug abuse among adolescents has become a major health and social problem in the United States. In a national survey, more than five million adolescents (age 12 to 17) acknowledged drinking at least monthly. Alcohol and drug use and abuse continues to be prevalent in the teenage population (Johnston, O'Malley, & Bachman, 1998).

This chapter provides an overview of adolescent alcohol and drug abuse problems and assessment and intervention strategies. Because major differences exist between substance abuse among adults and alcohol and drug abuse among adolescents, prominent theories highlighting developmental factors and prevalence patterns of teen drug abuse are reviewed.

PREVALENCE

Estimates of the prevalence of alcohol and drug abuse among adolescents vary with the definition of adolescent "problem drinking" and "problem drug use." Most commonly, prevalence estimates have been based on measures of consumption such as quantity consumed, frequency of use, frequency of intoxication, or binge drinking. For example, as of 1998, 49.1% of high school seniors report marijuana use, 22.8% report use within the past month, and 5.6% report daily use (Johnston et al., 1998).

Additionally, 29.4% of seniors report past use of one or more hard drugs, 81.4% acknowledge using alcohol some time in their life, and 32.9% report being drunk in the past 30 days. This survey also indicates that 3.9% of high school seniors drink daily.

Much of what is currently understood about the progression of adolescent alcohol and drug abuse comes from longitudinal studies of school samples. Such research implicates peer, family, sociocultural, and personality factors in the onset of drinking, heavy consumption, and later problems with alcohol and drugs. Evidence from longitudinal studies (e.g., Aarons et al., 1999; Kandel, Davies, Karus, & Yamaguchi, 1986; Newcomb & Bentler, 1988) also suggests that drug use during adolescence has important consequences during young adulthood, including delinquent behavior, physical and psychological disturbances, unstable work patterns, and higher divorce rates. Interestingly, drinking patterns may vary markedly from adolescence to young adulthood, and the consequences of alcohol consumption during adolescence appear to be less severe than that of hard drug use.

Although research utilizing school samples provides important information about adolescent substance use and its consequences, these studies may underestimate the true frequency and severity of the problem. Teens with the most disruptive alcohol and drug use patterns are underrepresented in school samples, as they often fail to attend school

757

and experience frequent suspension or expulsion (e.g., Brown, Vik, & Creamer, 1989). Additionally, an early onset of drug and alcohol problems of sufficient severity to merit treatment suggests that there may be differences in the course of abuse or consequences for those entering treatment compared to teens who remain in school (Brown, Mott, & Myers, 1990). Keeping in mind these differences, the next section discusses major risk factors for adolescent alcohol and drug abuse.

RISK FACTORS

BIOLOGICAL VARIABLES

Family, twin, and adoption studies document the importance of genetic factors in lifetime risk for alcohol dependence, especially in males (e.g., Schuckit, 1985). It has been argued (Cloninger, Bohman, & Sigvardsson, 1981) that the clinical course is different for adult alcoholics with a family history of alcoholism compared to alcoholics without such a family history. Family studies consistently find an elevated prevalence of alcohol dependence in the first-degree relatives of alcoholics (Sher, 1987). In a review of 39 studies, Cotton (1979) found that adult alcoholics were more than six times as likely as nonalcoholic nonpsychiatric individuals, and more than two times as likely as nonalcoholic psychiatric patients, to report parental alcoholism. Twin studies demonstrate a concordance of 60% or higher for the identical twin of an alcoholic but only 30% or less if the relationship is fraternal. Adoption studies (e.g., Cloninger et al., 1981; Goodwin et al., 1974) find a fourfold increased risk for lifetime alcoholism in offspring separated from their biological parents in infancy and raised without knowledge of the parents' drinking problem. Alcohol problems in biologic relatives have also been associated with drug abuse in adopted offspring (Cadoret, Troughton, O'Gorman, & Heywood, 1986), though the importance of genetic risk for other drug abuse is less consistent.

Differences between nonalcoholic offspring of alcoholics (family history positive, FHP) and matched offspring of nonalcoholics (family history negative, FHN) have been identified on a variety of behavioral, cognitive, and neurological measures. Compared to FHN teens, FHP adolescents and young adults demonstrate more disturbed school

careers, impulsivity, rebelliousness, and nonconformity (Knop, Teasdale, Schulsinger, & Goodwin, 1985); poorer neuropsychological performance (Tarter & Edwards, 1988); and significantly lower amplitude in P300 brain waves, which are believed to measure selective attention (Begleiter, Porjesz, Bihari, & Kissin, 1984). Further, following ingestion of alcohol, sons of alcoholics report less body sway and less subjective intoxication (Schuckit, 1988), higher levels of flushing (Schuckit & Duby, 1982), and decreased P300 amplitudes when performing difficult tasks (Polich & Bloom, 1987).

Not all individuals with a family history of alcohol dependence become alcohol and/or drug abusers, however, and genetics alone cannot account for the transmission of alcoholism and drug abuse (Cadoret et al., 1986). Among both FHP and FHN adolescents, a number of potential environmental and personal factors moderate alcohol and drug use.

ENVIRONMENTAL RISK FACTORS

Modeling
Environmental factors may operate independently as well as in interaction with biological factors in producing risk for the development of substance abuse (Sher, 1987). The effects of modeling and social reinforcement on the initiation of adolescent alcohol and drug use seem indisputable (e.g., Donovan & Jessor, 1985; Hundleby & Mercer, 1987). For example, the majority of adolescents drink alcohol for the first time with parents or relatives at home (Braucht, Brakarsh, Follingstad, & Berry, 1973), and parental modeling has a significant impact on the adolescent's attitude toward alcohol (Capuzzi & Lecoq, 1983). Further, peer support and instruction are responsible for a substantial portion of initial adolescent marijuana use (e.g., Brook, Whiteman, & Gordon, 1983) as well as decisions to continue to use after initiation (Capuzzi & Lecoq, 1983).

Family Functioning
Family environment also appears to be related to adolescent substance use. Children who report a lack of closeness, support, and affection from their parents are more likely to begin to use drugs and to maintain the abuse of those drugs (Kandel, 1978). Other family factors associated with adolescent

substance abuse include parent-adolescent conflict (Needle, Glynn, & Needle, 1983) and lack of family cohesiveness (Hundleby & Mercer, 1987). Sadava (1987) summarized the available evidence by noting three major areas of disturbance among families of adolescent problem drinkers: parental deviance or antisocial behavior, parental disinterest and lack of involvement with their child; and lack of affectionate and supportive interaction between parents and children. Conversely, a positive, loving bond between parent and child is linked to a reduced likelihood of the child's drug use (Hundleby & Mercer, 1987). Thus, family functioning appears to be important in initiation of substance use and progression from use to abuse.

Psychosocial Stress
Although most studies documenting a relationship between stressful life events and alcohol or drug abuse have been conducted with adults, psychosocial stress is also associated with adolescent alcohol and drug abuse (Pandina & Schuele, 1983). Higher levels of stress may actually precipitate alcohol and drug abuse by adolescents (Duncan, 1977). A significant correlation between the extent of life stress experienced by the family and adolescent substance abuse has been found, even after controlling for substance-related stress (McCubbin, Needle, & Wilson, 1985). Further, in a series of studies (Brown, 1985, 1987, 1989), Brown found that adolescents in drug abuse treatment and nonabusing teens with an alcoholic parent have more negative life experiences, and subjectively rated those events as less desirable, than nonabusing teens from nonalcoholic families.

Social Support
Over the past two decades, research has established that the availability of social relationships is related to health status, personal adjustment, and social behavior, including risk for adolescent alcohol and drug abuse. In the absence of adequate social supports, modeling, and reinforcing alternative coping efforts, some teens begin to use alcohol and other drugs to cope with stress (Holden, Brown, & Mott, 1988; Tucker, 1982). Adolescents with a substance-abusing parent may be especially likely to use drugs as a coping technique. The combined experience of parental alcohol abuse and dysfunctional social modeling may lead to inadequacies in social functioning, including impaired ability or willingness to solicit support from persons within and outside the family (Holden et al., 1988). Additionally, adolescents with social support networks composed of alcohol or drug abusers not only acquire behavior patterns consistent with their resource network, but also develop beliefs and values consistent with a drug-use lifestyle.

PERSONAL RISK FACTORS

Temperament and Personality
The major personality correlates of adolescent drug use cluster into rebelliousness, autonomy striving, liberalism, willingness to try new experiences, and independence (Segal, Huba, & Singer, 1980). Other personality or temperament characteristics associated with substance use include high sensation seeking (e.g., Cloninger, Sigvardsson, & Bohman, 1988), low self-esteem (Kaplan, 1977), low impulse control (Victor, Crossman, & Eiserman, 1973), behavioral disinhibition (McGue, Slutske, Taylor, & Iacono, 1997) and nonconventionality (Brook et al., 1983). Longitudinal studies (e.g., Labouvie & McGee, 1986) suggest that these characteristics precede drug use and act as risk factors for alcohol and drug abuse.

Emotional Health
Adolescent substance abuse is associated with a variety of deviant behaviors, including several forms of psychopathology (Brown, Gleghorn, Schuckit, Myers, & Mott, 1996; Donovan & Jessor, 1985). For example, alcohol- and drug-abusing adolescents commonly display symptoms of depression, including suicidal ideation, anxiety, and anger. Further, adolescent alcohol and drug abuse often appears as one of a constellation of disruptive problem behaviors. Researchers (e.g., Brown et al., 1996; Rydelius, 1983) have found a relationship between drug consumption and criminality, including stealing, assault, and malicious damage. The association of substance abuse and conduct disorder–type behaviors persists even when deviant acts related to substance use (e.g., stealing while under the influence) are excluded (e.g., Myers, Stewart, & Brown, 1998).

Drug Expectancies
Another personal variable that predicts onset of adolescent substance involvement and progression to problematic use is effect expectancies. Alcohol expectancies consist of those effects attributed to

alcohol that the individual anticipates experiencing when drinking. Alcohol effect expectancies play a mediational role in the development of use patterns by influencing drinking decisions (Christiansen, Goldman, & Brown, 1985). These anticipated consequences, acquired through multiple sources (i.e., peers, family, media, personal experiences) explain in part the process whereby distal risk factors (e.g., family history of alcoholism) influence evolving drinking behavior of youth. Expectancies of adolescents (particularly global positive effects, social changes, and enhancement of cognitive and motor performance) are most closely related to teen drinking patterns (Brown, Creamer, & Stetson, 1987) and predict alcohol abuse as adolescents mature (Christiansen, Smith, Roehling, & Goldman, 1989). Although expectancy research on other drugs of abuse such as marijuana and cocaine is less developed, evidence to date suggests that drug effect expectancies are also linked to personal drug use patterns (e.g., Schafer, McQuaid, & Brown, 1989).

COMORBIDITY

The study of comorbid psychopathology in substance-abusing individuals has become an important area of clinical research. The comorbidity of a substance use disorder and a psychiatric disorder has been given considerable attention in the adult literature, but it has not been explored to the same extent with adolescents. Recent studies have shown high prevalence rates of psychiatric disorders among substance-abusing adolescents both in community and inpatient samples. Lewinsohn, Rhode, and Seeley (1995) examined lifetime comorbid psychiatric disorders in a community sample of adolescents age 14 to 18 years. They found that 66% of adolescents who met criteria for a *Diagnostic and Statistical Manual of Mental Disorders* (*DSM-III-R;* American Psychiatric Association [APA], 1987) substance use disorder also met criteria for at least one other Axis I disorder. The Methods for the Epidemiology of Child and Adolescent Mental Disorders (MECA) study obtained similar rates with a community sample of 1,285 children and adolescents (9–18 years old) (Kandel et al., 1997). Of those who used illicit drugs three or more times in the past year, 85% of females and 56% of males met criteria for at least one psychiatric disorder.

Rates of psychiatric disorders in inpatient substance-abusing adolescents tend to be higher than those of community samples. Stowell and Estroff (1992) reported that 82% of adolescents entering inpatient treatment for a substance use disorder also met *DSM-III-R* criteria for an Axis I disorder. Rates were also high in a sample of substance-abusing American Indian adolescents (Novins, Beals, Shore, & Manson, 1996), where 68% of the adolescents also had a comorbid mental disorder.

Substance use disorders are prevalent in adolescent psychiatric inpatients as well. Deas-Nesmith, Campbell, and Brady (1998) studied adolescents in an acute care psychiatric inpatient unit and found that 33% met criteria for a substance abuse or dependence. Similarly, Grilo et al. (1995) found a rate of substance use disorders in 50% of adolescent psychiatric inpatients. This rate is the same as that obtained in a large epidemiological study of a community sample of 776 adolescents (P. Cohen et al., 1993). With respect to adolescent psychiatric outpatients, rates of substance use disorders have been found to be lower (11%) than in the previously mentioned populations (Wilens, Biederman, Abrantes, & Spencer, 1997).

The most common co-occuring psychiatric disorders in substance-abusing adolescents are conduct, mood, anxiety, and attention-deficit/hyperactivity disorders. Yet, the lack of a systematic approach in assessing psychiatric comorbidity in these individuals has made it difficult to determine rates of individual mental disorders and patterns of co-occurance of multiple disorders. Not surprisingly, rates of mental disorders differ based on the type of population studied. For example, estimates of rates of mood disorders in substance-abusing adolescents involved in a psychiatric inpatient program range from 20% to 85% (Grilo, Becker, Fehon, Edell, & McGlashon, 1996; Grilo et al., 1995; Kaminer, Tarter, Bukstein, & Kabene, 1992). Anxiety disorders were present in 9% to 49% of inpatient samples, conduct disorder in 42% to 75%, and ADHD in 26% to 82% of the substance-abusing adolescents.

Consistently high but variable rates of mental disorders have also been reported for psychiatric outpatient samples of substance-abusing youth as well as community samples. Among psychiatric outpatients, mood disorders have been reported for 47% to 76%, anxiety for 26% to 37%, conduct for 50% to 70%, and ADHD for 20% to 61% of these substance-abusing adolescents (Tarter, Kirisci, &

Mezzich, 1997; Wilens et al., 1997). Studies on community samples have found 53% occurrence of depression, 16% anxiety, 22% disruptive disorders, with substance-abusing youth being almost 10 times more likely to have conduct disorder and 8 times more likely to have ADHD than non-substance-abusing adolescents (P. Cohen et al., 1993; Lewinsohn et al., 1995).

INTERACTIONIST THEORIES OF ADOLESCENT SUBSTANCE ABUSE

Adolescent alcohol and drug abuse has been conceptualized from a number of different perspectives; the most prevalent models consider the development of substance abuse as a complex process with many interacting risk factors, including biological predisposition, environmental risks, and personal vulnerabilities (Sadava, 1987). Support for the interactionist perspective comes from the pioneering work of Jessor and colleagues (e.g., Jessor, Chase, & Donovan, 1980; Jessor & Jessor, 1975), who view alcohol and drug involvement as one of a series of problem or deviant behaviors of adolescents. Their problem behavior theory holds that adolescent problem behavior, including problem drinking and drug use, can be explained by three major sources of psychosocial variation: personality (e.g., lower value on academic achievement, higher value on independence; greater alienation, less religiosity); perceived environment (e.g., less parental control, greater friends' approval and lower parental disapproval of problem behavior); and behavior patterns (e.g., higher actual involvement in various problem behaviors). Within this framework, the problem behaviors have consistently been found to have high rates of co-occurrence, and the best predictors of future problem behaviors appear to be combinations of motivationally oriented personality and situational variables. Further, teens who mature out of problem drinking as young adults demonstrate a change in personal and environmental factors toward greater conventionality (Jessor, 1985).

A second interactive developmental theory of substance involvement (Huba, Wingard, & Bentler, 1980) specifies that biological, interpersonal, intrapersonal, and sociocultural characteristics influence personal behavior directly or indirectly (Sadava, 1987). The biological influences consist of

genetically determined characteristics as well as the status of the organism (e.g., acute or chronic states of health or illness). Psychological status, cognitive style, and personality traits constitute the intrapersonal system. Features of the interpersonal system influencing substance involvement include intimate support, modeling factors, social reinforcement, and one's sense of identity and belonging. Finally, the sociocultural domain molds social expectations and sanctions and environmental stressors. A dimension of time is implicit in the framework, such that various patterns of causal influence can be expected at different stages of use (e.g., initiation vs. maintenance vs. abuse vs. cessation vs. relapse) and at different stages of development before, during, and after adolescence.

The third major developmental interactionist position (Zucker, 1979; Zucker & Gomberg, 1986) has primarily been used to understand adolescent alcohol use but can be extrapolated to account more generally for substance involvement. Zucker and his colleagues have delineated a model including direct and indirect influences: sociocultural and community (e.g., social class, ethnic and religious influences, neighborhood values); family and peer (e.g., personalities and interaction patterns of parents and peers, child-rearing patterns, peer socialization, and parental/peer modeling of alcohol use); and intraindividual (e.g., genetic predispositions, cognitive and personality variables) (Ellis, Zucker, & Fitzgerald, 1997; Loukas, Twitchell, Piejack, Fitzgerald, & Zucker, 1998;). Drinking is seen as influenced directly only by intraindividual factors. These in turn are influenced by the social variables (directly through intimate groups and both indirectly and directly by the sociocultural and community environment). Conversely, drinking behavior is expected to influence intraindividual attributes, which will in turn influence other domains.

When considering a model for adolescent substance abuse, it is important to incorporate differential effects of factors in relation to the developmental stage of the adolescent. The relative contribution of factors included in interactions and theories vary as youth progress through adolescence and into young adulthood. For example, peer group influences are more important in adolescence than during childhood, whereas parental influences may become increasingly indirect. Similarly, personality characteristics and drug effect expectancies may become more stable with increasing experience with evolving social roles and may consequently have a greater impact on substance abuse during later adolescence. Also, experimentation with substances may markedly alter (expand or contract) opportunities to gain experience with the diverse new roles and tasks unfolding over the course of adolescence.

In the remainder of this chapter, we review the most common drugs of abuse for adolescents, drug effects and withdrawal symptoms, current prevalence, and methods of assessment and intervention.

ABUSE AND DEPENDENCE CONCEPTS

Any substance that alters mood, perception, or brain functioning might be considered a drug of abuse (Schuckit, 1989). Generally, abused drugs are self-administered to produce a change in affective state or consciousness. All abused substances can lead to psychological dependence, in which the user experiences the subjective feeling of needing the drug to adequately function or to maintain a sense of well-being. Extended use of some drugs can lead to physical dependence, with physiological adaptation to the drug's presence. One aspect of this physical dependence is tolerance: as nervous system cells adapt to the presence of a drug, higher and higher doses of the drug are required to achieve the same effect. Drugs of the same class (based on predominant nervous system effects) usually show cross-tolerance such that if tolerance to a particular drug has developed, it will be evident when another drug of the same class is administered. However, the picture is different if the two drugs are administered at the same time. In this case, the drugs potentiate each other. This is an important concern, as teens frequently use several drugs in concert (Stewart & Brown, 1995) and such use can and does lead to unintentional overdose and death.

Another important aspect of physical dependence is withdrawal, in which physical symptoms appear when a drug is abruptly removed from the body. There are characteristic symptoms of withdrawal for each drug class. Although the withdrawal syndrome may be less prevalent than among adults (Chassin, 1984), withdrawal symptoms are common (Stewart & Brown, 1995). Affective and cognitive features, rather than physiological

symptoms, predominate among adolescents during acute withdrawal from multiple substances. Therefore, the clinician should not rely on signs of physical dependence in assessing adolescent drug abuse or dependence.

Isolated instances of adolescent alcohol or drug use do not necessarily imply abuse or dependence. The *DSM-IV* (APA, 1994) identifies the following problems as indicative of substance dependence: marked tolerance, characteristic withdrawal symptoms, substance use to avoid or relieve withdrawal symptoms, taking the drug in large amounts or over longer periods than intended, desire and/or unsuccessful efforts to cut down on use, a great deal of time spent obtaining, using, and recovering from the substance, giving up or reducing important activities because of substance use, and continued use despite knowledge of problems.

DSM-III-R (APA, 1987) criteria for dependence involved possessing any three of the above symptoms persistent over a month long. *DSM-IV* has changed this to three or more problems occurring at any time in the same 12-month period. The more general diagnosis of substance abuse indicates a maladaptive pattern of use, including continued use despite knowledge of problems or recurrent use in dangerous situations.

Such categorical distinctions are useful, though the *DSM-IV* criteria are based on adult symptoms. Recent studies of *DSM-IV* abuse and dependence criteria among adolescents suggest a stage or sequence model at the development of substance dependence (Martin & Winters, 1998). Further, because youth experiencing alcohol and/or drug related problems who are entering treatment do not uniformly meet criteria for *DSM-IV* abuse or dependence diagnosis, an alternative diagnostic structure ultimately may be advantageous for youth. Examination of contingencies and the topography of substance involvement and typical negative consequences may be more useful in the evaluation process of substance-abusing teens. For example, the nature of the responsibilities of adolescents vary from that of adults, and many manage to avoid drug-related interference with activities typically to diagnose adults. On the other hand, even socially acceptable substance use by adults (e.g., social drinking) is illegal for adolescents, and a gradual deterioration in performance and participation in school are common consequences of involvement. A careful consideration of drug use and its impact (e.g., on school, family, emotional and social functioning) is called for.

Although there are no pathognomonic symptoms of drug use or abuse, clinicians are often asked to help parents or responsible institutions assess potential drug problems among adolescents. In general, increasing the knowledge of authorities with regard to symptoms of intoxication, withdrawal, and abuse/dependence for commonly used drugs is the first step in this process. The second step is to identify abnormal behaviors and their time course that give rise to concern for the youth. Because drug abuse may produce psychiatric symptoms (e.g., depression, anxiety, mania, delusions, and paranoia), drug problems are often misdiagnosed as psychiatric disorders. Abrupt symptom onset and marked alterations in symptoms (e.g., mood extremes) suggest that drug use may be involved. Common indicators of child and adolescent drug use are presented in Table 38.1.

The following section summarizes effects of the predominant substances of abuse for youth. Several cautionary notes are in order, however. As previously noted, physiological withdrawal symptoms are less pronounced among adolescents. Most street drugs are not pure and a portion do not contain the supposed major substance. Also, physical

Table 38.1 Indicators of child and adolescent drug use.

Physical Changes
- Eyes bloodshot; extremely large or small pupils; watery, with blank stares or nystagmus.
- Deterioration in physical appearance; rapid weight loss; evidence of unexplained injury (e.g., cuts, bruises); unusual breath or body odors.

Emotional Changes
- Extremes of energy and lethargy; insomnia and excessive sleep or fatigue; dramatic appetite fluctuation.
- Marked or rapid changes in school grades, social activities, or peer groups; irresponsibility with money.
- Clinically significant levels of depression or anxiety, or onset of multiple deviant behaviors not evident in childhood.

Health Changes
- Chronic coughing, sniffing, black phlegm.
- Evidence of intravenous drug use (needle tracks) or inhalation (perforated nasal septum).
- Skin boils or sores; nasal bleeding.

and behavioral effects of a drug can vary a great deal with factors such as health, length of use, dose, and environment. Finally, adolescent drug abusers commonly use more than one substance, thereby complicating the clinical picture.

DRUGS OF ABUSE

DEPRESSANTS

The depressants include alcohol, hypnotics, and antianxiety drugs. These drugs all derive their major effects from depression of central nervous system (CNS) activity. They produce a similar "high" or euphoria and display a similar pattern of other effects. Depressants show cross-tolerance, and because many have high potential for lethal overdose in themselves, the combination of alcohol with another depressant presents an especially dangerous situation, where accidental overdose and death can occur.

Alcohol
The psychological effects of this, the most commonly used substance by adolescents, can include euphoria, disinhibition, and self-confidence. With increasing dose, effects include slowed thought, poor judgment, mood swings, confusion, and memory losses. Irritation and violence are not uncommon with intoxication. Even after modest doses, when the blood alcohol content (BAC) is decreasing, most people feel sad, anxious, or irritated. At higher doses, the acute physical effects of alcohol include impaired coordination or ataxia, slowed reaction time, slurred speech, nausea and vomiting, anesthesia, and, potentially, respiratory failure, coma, and death. Depression and anxiety, which are also common problems for those who are alcohol-dependent, can closely resemble a major psychiatric syndrome, but generally clear within three weeks of abstinence (Brown, Irwin, & Schuckit, 1991; Brown & Schuckit, 1988). Alcohol produces sleep problems, including frequent awakenings, reduced REM latency, and reduced sleep efficiency, both during drinking and for up to six months after drinking stops (Gillin et al., 1990). The medical problems that can develop with alcoholism are extensive and well-known; however, they appear to be less prevalent among adolescents than among adults. Among heavy alcohol adolescent users, the most commonly reported withdrawal

symptoms include nausea, vomiting, depression/irritability, and muscle aches (Stewart & Brown, 1995).

Sedative-Hypnotics

This general term includes hypnotics such as barbiturates (e.g., pentobarbital, secobarbital), methaqualone (Quaalude), glutethimide (Doriden), and chloral hydrate (Noctec). Also included are most antianxiety drugs (the benzodiazepines), including Valium, Librium, Dalmane, and Ativan. These preparations, taken at the common dosage for intoxication, produce effects very similar to alcohol intoxication. Greater doses can also produce hallucinations or paranoid delusions. Like alcohol, impaired judgment and ataxia can lead to the improper operation of automobiles, accidents, and loss of life. Sedation is dose-dependent, ranging from lethargy, sleepiness, and decreased heart and respiratory rate, to increasing anesthesia, deep sleep, coma, and death due to depression of heart and respiratory functioning. In particular with children, sedative-hypnotics can produce a "paradoxical reaction," including excitement, fright, anger, panic, excessive energy, and inability to sleep (Schuckit, 1989).

The severity of depressant withdrawal depends on the strength of the drug and the degree of tolerance that has developed. Symptoms can include restlessness, gastrointestinal upset, muscle aches, increased heart and respiratory rate, tremor, and more severe problems of confusion, disorientation, convulsions, and hallucinations. Benzodiazepines were thought not to lead to physical dependence, but it is now well-known that these drugs have a high risk for dependence (File & Pellow, 1990). Withdrawal symptoms can also include anxiety, insomnia, headaches, and fatigue. Severe withdrawal can be as serious as that seen with other depressants.

STIMULANTS

The major stimulants of abuse include the amphetamines ("crystal" methamphetamine, Benzedrine, Dexadrine, and others) and all forms of cocaine, including crack. (A widely used stimulant, nicotine, is discussed later.) All of these drugs produce a euphoria, increased energy, decrease in fatigue and appetite, and possibly increased sexual drive.

Cocaine

Cocaine has most commonly been obtained in powder form and "snorted" (inhaled through the nose). Cocaine is also available in a crystallized form known as "crack," which is typically smoked. Crack (sometimes termed "rock") is more purified and more potent than other forms of cocaine. It produces the same effects as inhaled cocaine, but the effects are more rapid and intense.

Psychologically, cocaine produces euphoria and a sense of well-being. Increased doses also produce restlessness, emotional lability, irritability, aggression, and insomnia. A number of severe problems can develop, including a panic reaction, which might involve feeling as though one is having a heart attack, or fear of going crazy or losing control; suspiciousness and paranoia; and visual, auditory, or tactile hallucinations.

Physical effects include hand tremor, increased heart rate and blood pressure, nausea, dry mouth, increased body temperature, and sweating. Cocaine is dangerous in overdose, with the possibility of convulsions, heart attack, and death. Tolerance to stimulants, in particular cocaine, develops rapidly (within hours to days). The "crash" when coming off the drug includes intense craving, agitation, depression, decreased appetite, fatigue, and insomnia, with a gradual reduction in these symptoms. Violence is not uncommon during cocaine withdrawal.

Amphetamines

These drugs are usually taken orally, intravenously (IV), or through inhalation. Crystal is a smokable form of methamphetamine. Like crack, its effects can be quite rapid and intense. The predominant effects of the various amphetamines and amphetamine-like substances are similar to those of cocaine. These include the sought after effects of euphoria, sense of well-being, alertness, energy, and self-confidence. Higher doses can lead to agitation, anxiety, talkativeness, and disorganized thought. Panic reactions, delusions of persecution, and hallucinations can also develop shortly after amphetamine ingestion. Physical symptoms include nervous system stimulation (increased heart rate and blood pressure, raised body temperature, and pupil dilation). Headache, bruxism, and dizziness are also possible.

Withdrawal from these substances may involve depression, irritability, anxiety, fatigue, agitation, sleep disturbance, and possibly violence or aggression; hallucinations are also possible. The refractory depression usually begins three to five days following withdrawal and may last for several weeks.

Marijuana

Marijuana is undoubtedly the most widely used illicit drug among adolescents. Although it induces less physiological and psychological change than most other abused drugs and so has been considered safe or harmless by some, it is clear that there are potential dangers from acute as well as chronic use. Delta-9-tetrahydrocannabinol (THC) content, the psychologically active element in marijuana, has significantly increased since the 1970s, and addictive properties have been documented. Desired effects of marijuana include relaxation, euphoria, and changes in perception. Time seems to pass more slowly, and odors and sounds seem enhanced. The euphoria is followed by sleepiness. Concentration and short-term memory are also impaired. Anxiety and suspiciousness are possible, with panic reactions, confusion, paranoia, and hallucinations (usually visual) at higher doses.

Physical effects of marijuana can include a fine tremor, impaired coordination and decreased muscle strength, hunger, bloodshot eyes, dry mouth, and increased heart and respiratory rate. Chronic marijuana use poses a number of health threats, including lung damage, impaired sperm production and decreased size of the prostate and testes in males, and blocked ovulation in females. Chronic use is also associated with an "amotivational syndrome" (S. Cohen, 1981; McGlothin & West, 1968), characterized by apathy, social withdrawal, decreased self-awareness, and slowed thinking. Recent studies indicate that extended use during adolescence is associated with a deterioration in neurocognitive functioning, particularly attention (Tapert & Brown, 1999).

Opiates

This classification of drugs refers to those derivatives of the opium poppy, which include heroin, morphine, opium, and codeine; altered poppy products such as Percodan and Dilaudid; and opiate-like synthetics, including Darvon, Demerol, and Talwin. Tolerance develops rapidly and markedly to most of the substances and all have analgesic effects and depress functioning of most activities of the human body (Gilman, Goodman, & Gilman, 1980). Opiates are taken orally, snorted, smoked (especially opium), or injected (especially heroin).

At the common dosage taken for intoxication, the user will experience an intense, euphoric feeling or "rush" that lasts briefly, followed by a floating feeling, extreme relaxation, and drowsiness. Apathy, poor judgment, and impaired attention or memory are also possible. Other effects include a slowed respiratory rate, slurred speech, constricted pupils, and constipation. Extended opiate use is associated with depression (Kosten & Rounsaville, 1988). Overdose with opiates is a significant danger, with the possibility of respiratory depression or cardiac arrest, and death. With timely attention, the reaction can be controlled with the administration of Narcan or another opiate antagonist. Another problem is the use of unclean needles for injection, which can lead to tetanus, malaria, blood poisoning, hepatitis, skin or muscle infections, HIV infection, and other problems.

Withdrawal from opiates, though not fatal, can be particularly painful, with muscle pains and spasms, tremor, weakness, nausea, vomiting, and diarrhea. Other flulike symptoms are prevalent, including sweating, tearing, yawning, and runny nose. Craving and irritability are also common.

Hallucinogens

This classification consists of substances that produce an intense change in sensation or perception (illusions or hallucinations). These include lysergic acid diethylamide (LSD), mescaline (contained in peyote), psilocybin (from mushrooms), dimethyltryptamine (DMT), 2,5-dimethoxy-4-methylamphetamine (STP), methylene dioxyamphetamine (MDA), and methylene dioxymethamphetamine (MDMA or "ecstasy"). Most commonly, these drugs are taken orally, though they are also injected or smoked. Hallucinogens produce an intense awareness of the senses, visual hallucinations (colors, lights, and geometric shapes), detachment, euphoria, and feelings of enhanced thought. Labile emotion, anxiety, and sadness are also reported. Hallucinogens induce increased heart rate and blood pressure, dilated pupils, flushing, tremor, increased body temperature, and possible nausea and vomiting.

Hallucinogen intoxication may include panic, with marked anxiety and fear of going crazy. Confusion, paranoid delusions, and significant depression are possible. Deaths have resulted from acting on delusional beliefs such as an ability to fly or immortality. Another problem associated with hallucinogens is the reexperiencing of past drug experiences, or flashbacks. Flashback episodes usually involve euphoria, detachment, and visual illusions or hallucinations, as well as significant distress among some individuals. Flashbacks are apparently triggered by a stressful situation or other drug use (e.g., marijuana) and can be reoccurring, but generally will remit gradually over a period of weeks.

PHENCYCLIDINE (PCP)

PCP was developed as an anesthetic but found to produce agitation and hallucinations. It is now obtained "on the street" under many different names, and is usually smoked or taken orally. Additionally, PCP is often substituted for other, more expensive drugs.

Psychological effects of PCP include a dissociative or floating feeling, euphoria, relaxation, intensification of emotion and perception, and hallucinations. More intense reactions include hyperactivity, panic, paranoia with hallucinations, and confusion. Hostility and violence can occur during PCP intoxication and flashbacks may follow use.

The physical effects of PCP include anesthesia, loss of coordination, sweating, dizziness, and slurred speech. Higher doses can lead to increased heart rate and blood pressure, numbness in the extremities, and muscle rigidity or a catatoniclike state. Overdose is a serious concern, with the possibility of convulsions, respiratory depression, coma, and death.

INHALANTS

The inhalants include industrial substances such as glues, aerosol sprays, gasoline, paints, paint thinners, nail polish remover, and typewriter corrector fluid. Nitrous oxide, which is used as a dental anesthesia and propellant in aerosol-packaged food products, is included in this category. These substances are predominantly abused by children and young adolescents, presumably due to high availability and low cost. They are commonly sniffed or drunk from a soaked rag. The desired effects last anywhere from minutes to one hour, and include initial euphoria with a floating sensation, a buzzing noise in the ears, possibly visual hallucinations, and distortion of time. There can also be confusion and disorientation, irritability, anxiety, and panic attacks. Butyl nitrate may be taken during sexual intercourse to produce a subjective experience of extended orgasm (S. Cohen, 1978). Physical symptoms include loss of coordination, slurred speech, dizziness, abdominal pain, loss of energy, nausea and vomiting, and diarrhea. Headache is common during and following intoxication.

Abuse of these volatile substances can lead to serious medical problems. Inhaling is irritating to the eyes, nose, throat, and upper respiratory system and can cause damage to the kidney, liver, heart, gastrointestinal tract, and nervous system (Morton, 1990). Loss of consciousness can occur during intoxication. There are also instances of death from heart arrhythmias or suffocation by the plastic bag containing the substance. Long-range effects such as elevated cancer risk may not be evident for 10 to 30 years (Hect, 1980), and protracted use is associated with impairment in neurocognitive functioning. There does not appear to be a significant physical withdrawal syndrome associated with inhalants, but craving and anxiety may be prominent.

TOBACCO

Use of tobacco products is second only to alcohol use among adolescents. Despite well-known adverse health effects, the use of tobacco is widespread, especially among teens who use other drugs. Up to 87% of adolescents entering treatment for alcohol and drug abuse are current smokers (Myers & Brown, 1990a). Although stress and environmental cues contribute to the amount of tobacco used, nicotine is a major factor in maintaining the habit (Balfour, 1990).

Smokers often experience enhanced alertness, thinking, and concentration after tobacco use. Symptoms of withdrawal (which can last up to several weeks) include craving, irritability, frustration, anxiety, poor concentration, restlessness, and decreased heart rate. Although not tested among adolescents, nicotine containing chewing gum (e.g., Nicorette Gum) is sometimes used to reduce nicotine withdrawal symptoms when quitting and increases the likelihood of abstinence when used as part of adult smoking-cessation programs (Lam, Sacks, Sze, & Chalmers, 1987). Relapse rates for tobacco use appear to be comparable to rates for alcohol and other drugs.

Persistence of regular cigarette smoking once initiated during adolescence has been demonstrated (Pierce, Choi, Gilpin, Farkas, & Berry, 1998). Similarly, Myers and Brown (1997) found that among substance abusers, 80% of adolescent smokers continued smoking four years later, even if they abstained from alcohol and other illicit drugs. Although one would not expect smoking-related health problems to be evident in adolescent smokers, there is evidence that they may indeed begin to occur at this stage. Rates of respiratory problems among substance-abusing adolescents has been associated with greater quantity and frequency of smoking when assessed over a two-year period (Myers & Brown, 1994).

EPIDEMIOLOGY

Table 38.2 indicates drug use trends in high school seniors over a 10-year period, from 1986 to 1996

(NIDA, 1998). Here, the use of stimulants, opiates, sedatives, and tranquilizers refers to the nonmedical use of these drugs. Although use of some drugs has remained fairly stable (e.g., opiates, inhalants), most substances have seen a slight decrease in use over this period. One important example of decline is alcohol, with past month use dropping from a high of 65.3% in 1986 to 51% in 1993. Past month cocaine use fell from 6.2% in 1986 to 2% in 1996. However, part of this decrease may have to do with increases in the use of crack cocaine.

Downward trends in drug use are promising, but there is still substantial involvement with drugs among young people in the United States: 50.8% of seniors reported they had used an illicit drug at some time in their life, and 24.6% had done so in the prior 30 days. Table 38.3 presents information from another recent national survey (NHSDA–NIDA, 1998), showing prevalence of adolescent substance use (ages 12–17). As expected, alcohol, cigarettes, and marijuana are most commonly used, and the relative popularity of inhalant abuse is also apparent. Almost 40% in this age group have used alcohol, 32.7% have drunk alcohol in the past year, and 18.8% drink at least monthly. Of note, one-third (31.3%) of seniors surveyed reported being drunk within the past month, and 3.7% reported drinking daily. A large proportion of American teens are still using cigarettes, with 22.2% of the 1996 seniors classified as daily smokers, the majority smoking half a pack or more (NIDA, 1998).

Table 38.2 Trends in prevalence (percentage) of substance use by high school seniors, 1986–1996.

Substance	Lifetime Prevalence (Ever Used)						Used in Past Month					
	1986	1988	1990	1992	1994	1996	1986	1988	1990	1992	1994	1996
Alcohol*	91.3	92.0	89.5	87.5	80.4	79.2	65.3	63.9	57.1	51.3	50.1	50.8
Marijuana	50.9	47.2	40.7	32.6	38.2	44.9	23.4	18.0	14.0	11.9	19.0	21.9
Stimulants	23.4	19.8	17.5	13.9	15.7	15.3	5.5	4.6	3.7	2.8	4.0	4.1
Cocaine	16.9	12.1	9.4	6.1	5.9	7.1	6.2	3.4	1.9	1.3	1.5	2.0
Hallucinogens	11.9	9.2	9.7	9.4	11.7	14.0	3.5	2.3	2.3	2.3	3.2	n/a
Heroine	1.1	1.1	1.3	1.2	1.2	1.8	0.2	0.2	0.2	0.3	0.3	0.5
Other opiates	9.0	8.6	8.3	6.1	6.6	8.2	2.0	1.6	1.5	1.2	1.5	2.0
Sedatives	10.4	7.8	7.5	6.1	7.3	n/a	2.2	1.4	1.4	1.2	1.8	n/a
Tranquilizers	10.9	9.4	7.2	6.0	6.6	7.2	2.1	1.5	1.2	1.0	1.4	2.0
Inhalants	20.1	17.5	18.5	17.0	18.3	n/a	3.2	3.0	2.9	2.5	2.9	n/a
Cigarettes	67.6	66.4	64.4	61.8	62.0	63.5	29.6	28.7	29.4	27.8	31.2	34.0

Source: Taken from NIDA Capsule—Monitoring the Future Study, 1998.

* Alcohol questions for lifetime prevalence changed in 1993 and subsequent years, resulting in lower percentage relative to previous years.

n/a = data not available.

Table 38.3 Prevalence of substance use (percentage) among adolescents 12–17 in national survey and drug treatment programs.

Substance	Ever Used	Past Year	Past Month
*National Survey**			
Alcohol	38.8	32.7	18.8
Marijuana	16.8	13.0	7.1
Stimulants	2.2	1.5	0.5
Cocaine	1.9	1.4	0.6
Hallucinogens	5.6	4.3	2.0
Analgesics	5.5	3.7	1.5
Sedatives	1.1	0.4	0.2
Tranquilizers	1.7	1.0	0.2
Inhalants	5.9	4.0	1.7
Cigarettes	36.3	24.2	18.3
Drug Treatment Sample†			
Alcohol	100.0	99.3	63.8
Marijuana	100.0	98.0	71.1
Amphetamines	96.6	94.6	65.1
Cocaine	72.5	66.4	22.8
Hallucinogens	67.8	60.4	12.8
Opiates	17.4	13.4	2.7
Barbiturates	20.1	14.1	3.3
Inhalants	43.0	28.2	8.1
Cigarettes	90.6	87.2	83.9

*Taken from 1996 National Household Survey on Drug Abuse (NIDA, 1998).
†N=149.

In contrast to the above trends, Table 38.3 also displays drug use patterns by adolescents entering alcohol and drug abuse treatment programs in San Diego County, California. The majority (61%) of these teens were not attending school prior to admission to treatment. Although prevalence rates for specific substances vary with geographic location, extensive and diversified drug use is evident. Alcohol and marijuana, which are typically considered gateway drugs, have been used by all of the teens in the treatment sample. Two of three teens report regular use of three or more drugs (excluding cigarettes); 73.8% of adolescents were classified as regularly (at least weekly) using marijuana prior to treatment. Adolescents in treatment also abuse common medical preparations. In this sample, 19.5% report using a medication over the prescribed dosage or acquiring prescription medication for recreational use. The most often abused medications include codeine and other pain relievers, but there are also instances of Valium, antihistamines, and caffeine pills. Thus, teens in treatment for drug abuse commonly use several drugs on a regular basis and in significantly greater quantities than teens in school samples.

ASSESSMENT

As noted previously, adolescent alcohol and drug abuse results in different symptoms and consequences than does adult addiction. Emotional distress, school difficulties, and family conflicts are prevalent among youth with substance use disorders. Further, alcohol-related automobile accidents are the leading cause of injury and death among 15 to 24-year-olds, and substance involvement is considered a major risk factor for teen suicide (Garfinkel & Golombek, 1983). Thus, adolescent alcohol and drug abuse assessment efforts should focus on alcohol and other drug use patterns and prevalent symptoms and features typical of addictive behaviors during this developmental period.

Adolescence is a time of considerable emotional disruption and behavioral diversity even in the most stable, supportive environments and in the absence of drug use. Body changes, including pubertal development and increased physical size resulting from hormonal changes (e.g., gonadotropin-releasing hormones, follicular-stimulating hormones, and luteinizing hormones), are accompanied by an acceleration in negative affect (Brooks-Gunn & Warren, 1989). Changes in social behavior, including increased interest in sexual involvement, heightened involvement with one's peer group, and decreased investment in parent-child relationships, vary tremendously during adolescence. Thus, the escalation of deviant and oppositional behaviors, a hallmark of adolescent development, may reflect normal attempts to master the psychosocial tasks of adolescence rather than consequences of early alcohol and drug abuse.

A variety of emotional and behavioral changes that are produced by adolescent alcohol and drug use may also reflect other behavior problems that antedate or co-occur with teen drug abuse. Table 38.4 outlines common behavioral correlates of teen drug abuse. These behaviors are typical of a variety of behavioral disorders of adolescence (most notably, conduct disorder and oppositional defiant disorder), and no specific behavioral change is pathognomic of addiction. However, teens who

Table 38.4 Assessing teen alcohol and drug abuse: common behavioral correlations of abuse.

Domain of Functioning	*Behavioral Correlates Change*
School	Attendance: truancy, suspension, expulsion.
	Academic performance: decreased grades, decreased comprehension.
	Behavioral problems: conflict with authorities and peers.
Family	Withdrawal: decreased contact and expressiveness.
	Conflict: arguments, running away, lying.
Social	Behavior: fights, decreased communication.
	Peer group: change in friends or peer drug use.
	Sexuality: promiscuity, teen pregnancy.
Activities	Work: absenteeism, firing, walking off job.
	School activities: decreased participation.
	Illegal behavior: theft, property damage.
	Reckless behavior: speeding while driving.
Health	Physical: accidents, injury, withdrawal symptoms.
	Emotional: emotional lability, anxiety, depression or anger; suicidal ideation, psychotic thoughts, decreased motivation.

report certain behaviors (i.e., cruelty to people or animals, starting fights, setting illegal fires, and theft with victim confrontation) while not under the influence of alcohol or other drugs are more likely to have an independent conduct disorder diagnosis (Brown et al., 1996). By some estimates, up to three-quarters of clinical samples of drug-abusing teens have a co-existing disorder, most typically conduct disorder (50%), affective disorder (20%), and attention-deficit disorder (20%) (Brown et al., 1990; Winters, 1990). Although comorbidity estimates may be inflated due to assessment during recent drug use periods and failure to exclude behaviors directly or indirectly related to drug use, coexisting disorders may be as prevalent among adolescent alcohol and drug abusers as among adult abusers.

Given these potential confounds, it is difficult to assess adolescent alcohol and drug abuse and dependence separate from the functional impairment of coexisting disorders. Several procedures may enhance diagnostic accuracy with adolescents:

1. Initiate assessment in areas in which the adolescent is most concerned or motivated rather than substance use specifically.
2. Inquire about substance use separately from questions of problem behaviors and current difficulties.
3. Determine onset of symptoms and problem behaviors in relation to drug involvement by constructing a time line (i.e., which behaviors or symptoms occurred before drug use or during periods of extended abstinence).
4. Gather the same information from a resource person (i.e., parent) to confirm sequence of difficulties, symptoms, and drug use.
5. Utilize biochemical verification (e.g., using toxicology screen, hair samples).
6. Assess symptoms on several occasions to ensure symptoms were not transient consequences of drug use.

In addition to the issues noted above, the recent development of adolescent-tailored instruments has improved clinical and research measurement of adolescent substance use disorders. Instruments vary in purpose and format and should be selected to meet the needs of the stage of the assessment. Sequence of assessment can be done beginning with screening, followed by detailed assessment and diagnosis. The Problem Oriented Screening Instrument for Teenagers (Gruenwald & Klitzner, 1991) is designed to identify potential problems in 10 functional areas, including substance use and abuse and delinquency. The Customary Drinking and Drug Use Record (Brown et al., 1998) provides a detailed assessment of substance use patterns and abuse and dependence symptoms, including diagnostic information that can be used to derive *DSM-IV* diagnoses. The Teen-Addiction Severity Index (T-ASI; Kaminer, Wagner, Plummer, & Siefer, 1993) provides more global measures of substance use but focuses on drug-related functional impairment in seven domains. The Personal Experiences Inventory (PEI; Winters & Henley, 1989) assesses not only substance use, but also psychological variables and adolescent's perceptions of family and peer functioning that may impact substance use. For a comprehensive discussion of substance use measures for youth and adults, see Allen and Columbus (1995).

INTERVENTION

Results of the assessment of alcohol and drug use and consequences should guide decisions regarding intervention. Even prior to drug use or in cases of minimal experimentation, prevention and early intervention efforts can deter or reduce certain types of drug use. For example, cigarette and marijuana use has been reduced among seventh- and eighth-graders following prevention efforts focusing on coping skill resistance training and knowledge of the impact of drugs on daily lives and social relations (Ellickson & Bell, 1990). Reduction in cigarette use is more easily attained than for other classes of drugs, and the impact of many prevention efforts appear short-lived, yet community-based prevention efforts (e.g., school-based, mass media, parent education, health policy) can reduce use of all three gateway drugs: cigarettes, alcohol, and marijuana (Johnson et al., 1990).

Once substance involvement progresses to regular (weekly) use, involvement of major supportive systems is critical to produce and maintain lifestyle changes associated with abstinence. Family, peers, and school staff can be particularly helpful in addressing the behavioral, social, and psychological consequences of drug use. Typically, youth are poorly motivated to terminate alcohol or drug use, because problems are often perceived as a consequence of other external factors (e.g., family conflict) and long-term consequences of drug use are not viewed as personally applicable. Thus, attending to the concerns of the adolescent as well as presenting problems can facilitate motivation for change.

There are several practical avenues for early intervention, depending on the resources available to the professionals and the parents of teens. Realistic, nonthreatening education about drug use effects, including short- and long-term consequences for affective state, cognitive skills, peer relations, identity development, and family functioning, allows this topic to be discussed as is any other issue that is important to adolescent development. A functional analysis of the contingencies and reinforcement

associated with drug use can help clinicians and parents, in conjunction with the adolescent, develop alternative activities supportive of a drug-free lifestyle and conducive to a positive self-image. Involvement in sports, hobbies, recreational activities, or personal development efforts can enhance teen self-efficacy and interpersonal competence and facilitate individuation in a nondestructive manner. New activities that position the adolescent in a positive, respected role (e.g., volunteer activities with children or elderly) may be particularly useful in altering self-image and self-esteem.

Additionally, support of and intervention with the family system may be particularly important, as the majority of adolescents entering treatment report considerable family disruption (Brown, 1993). Family therapy for adolescent substance abuse is based on the causative role of family relationships in the formulation and continuation of the disorder (Liddle & Dakof, 1995). It has been increasingly used as a primary or adjunctive treatment for adolescent substance abuse with consistently positive results (Liddle & Dakof, 1995). Family therapy can be helpful in reducing problem behaviors associated with drug abuse and improvement in school performance and provides continuity of effort, which is critical to maintenance of behavior change (Brown, 1993; Friedman & Granick, 1990). In cases where insufficient support is available, efforts to provide more environmental structure (e.g., extended summer camps) and parent effectiveness training are in order. Despite positive results, family interventions are inconsistently used.

Like family therapy, multisystemic therapy (MST) is based on systems theory. This framework moves beyond suggesting that substance abuse problems reflect family relationships to incorporate other interconnected systems, such as peers, schools, and community (Pickrel & Henggeler, 1996). MST is a high-intensity intervention conducted in the adolescent's natural environment, including home, school, and community settings. Thus far, MST has been successful in reducing substance use and criminal behavior over extended periods for adolescent delinquents.

Although alcohol and drug treatment programs for adolescents flourished in the 1980s, managed health care has fostered outpatient rather than inpatient programs in recent years. A significant portion of hospital-based programs have shut down, but others have restructured their programs to meet state-mandated coverage. Within the current health care climate, substance-abusing adolescents tend to receive episodic and fragmented treatment. Inpatient and outpatient programs typically include: (1) a detoxification/crisis management phase with primary focus on medical management and problem identification; (2) a rehabilitation phase focusing on coping skills training, environmental management, and alterations in social networks; and (3) a maintenance phase involving ongoing contact with treatment aftercare, extended residential treatment, self-help groups (e.g., Alcoholics Anonymous), or drug use monitoring (e.g., urinalysis, antabuse). Relapse rates are quite high for adolescents (e.g., Brown et al., 1989), suggesting that continuity of intervention efforts may be the critical feature in long-term outcome.

Heretofore, adolescent alcohol and drug treatment has received less evaluation than adult treatment. Large-scale descriptive studies suggest that programs are successful in reducing drug use and associated deviant behaviors and in increasing productivity (e.g., employment and education), but that effectiveness varies with types of drugs used and length and type of treatment (Brown et al., 1990). Relapse rates for adolescents appear to be comparable to those of adults, but the precursors to teen relapse are primarily social, whereas negative emotional states and interpersonal conflict play a greater role as immediate precursors in adult relapse (Brown et al., 1989). Further, whereas cognitive coping efforts (e.g., thinking of negative consequences of alcohol/drug use) are associated with better adult treatment outcome, successful adolescents report a greater use of behavioral coping strategies (e.g., avoidance of situations, utilization of social supports) in high-risk situations (Myers & Brown, 1990b).

Adolescent development influences the appropriateness and effectiveness of intervention strategies. For example, teens conceptualize and evaluate coping in a different fashion than adults do (Brown & Stetson, 1988). In general, teen drug abusers respond best in highly structured environments with immediate and personally relevant reinforcement. Thus, most inpatient programs use a token economy system with rewards of increased freedom and personal responsibility. Strategies that encourage personal responsibility (e.g., participating in decision making) and independence (e.g., choosing from a list of options of self-esteem-enhancing activities) are more acceptable and facilitate mastery of major social-emotional tasks of adolescence. Further, given the priority of peer relations during adolescence, peer modeling and group discussion may be more acceptable therapeutic approaches for youth than adult directives. Because alcohol and drug abuse interferes with major developmental tasks (e.g., school completion, individuation), adolescent treatment programs are designed not only to terminate drug abuse but to facilitate social, educational, and emotional development.

SUMMARY

Adolescent alcohol and drug abuse is a major problem in the United States, with 60% of high school seniors having used illicit drugs and approximately three million problem-drinking teens. Numerous biological, psychological, social, and environmental risk factors for teen drug abuse have been identified, yet diagnosis is often difficult due to confounds of normal developmental deviations and concomitant psychopathology. Assessment and intervention with adolescents should recognize both the prominent developmental issues and differences in drug use patterns and symptomatology between adolescents and adults. Although comprehensive intervention evaluation is emerging, clearly, the most cost-effective approach to teen drug abuse is prevention.

REFERENCES

Aarons, G.A., Brown, S.A., Coe, M.T., Myers, M.G., Garland, A.F., Ezzet-Lofstram, R., Hazen, A.L., & Hough, R.L. (1999). Adolescent alcohol and drug abuse and health. *Journal of Adolescent Health, 24,* 412–421.

Allen, J.P., & Columbus, M. (1995). *Assessing alcohol problems: A guide for clinicians and researchers.* Bethesda, MD: National Institute on Alcohol Abuse and Alcoholism.

American Psychiatric Association. (1987). *Diagnostic and statistical manual of mental disorders* (3rd ed., rev.). Washington, DC: Author.

American Psychiatric Association. (1994). *Diagnostic and statistical manual of mental disorders* (4th ed.). Washington, DC: Author.

Balfour, D.J.K. (1990). Nicotine as the basis of the smoking habit. In D.J.K. Balfour (Ed.), *Psychotropic drugs of abuse* (pp. 453–481). New York: Pergamon Press.

Begleiter, H., Porjesz, B., Bihari, B., & Kissin, B. (1984). Event-related brain potentials in boys at risk for alcoholism. *Science, 225*, 1493–1496.

Braucht, G.N., Brakarsh, D., Follingstad, D., & Berry, K.L. (1973). Deviant drug use in adolescence: A review of psychosocial correlates. *Psychological Bulletin, 70*(2), 92–106.

Brook, J.S., Whiteman, M., & Gordon, A.S. (1983). Stages of drug use in adolescence: Personality, peer, and family correlates. *Developmental Psychology, 19*(2), 269–277.

Brooks-Gunn, J., & Warren, M.P. (1989). Biological and social contributions to negative affect in young adolescent girls. *Child Development, 60*, 40–55.

Brown, S.A. (1985). *Stress and alcohol use: Family patterns.* Paper presented at the Western Psychological Association annual convention, San Jose, CA.

Brown, S.A. (1987). Alcohol use and type of life events experienced during adolescence. *Psychology of Addictive Behaviors, 1*(2), 104–107.

Brown, S.A. (1989). Life events of adolescents in relation to personal and parental substance abuse. *American Journal of Psychiatry, 146*(4), 484–489.

Brown, S.A. (1993). Recovery patterns in adolescents. In S. Baer & A. Marlatt (Eds.), *Addictive behaviors across the lifespan: Prevention, treatment, and policy issues* (pp. 161–183). Newbury Park, CA: Sage.

Brown, S.A., Creamer, V.A., & Stetson, B.A. (1987). Adolescent alcohol expectancies in relation to personal and parental drinking patterns. *Journal of Abnormal Psychology, 96*(2), 117–121.

Brown, S.A., Gleghorn, A.A., Schuckit, M.A., Myers, M.G., & Mott, M.A. (1996). Conduct disorder among adolescent alcohol and drug abusers. *Journal of Studies on Alcohol, 57*, 314–324.

Brown, S.A., Irwin, M., & Schuckit, M.A. (1991). Changes in anxiety among abstinent male alcoholics. *Journal of Studies on Alcohol, 52*, 55–61.

Brown, S.A., Mott, M.A., & Myers, M.G. (1990). Adolescent alcohol and drug treatment outcome. In R.R. Watson (Ed.), *Drug and alcohol abuse prevention* (pp. 373–403). Clifton, NJ: Humana Press.

Brown, S.A., Myers, M.G., Lippke, L., Tapert, S.F., Stewart, D.G., & Vik, P.W. (1998). Psychometric evaluation of the Customary Drinking and Drug Use Record (CDDR): A measure of adolescent alcohol and drug involvement. *Journal of Studies on Alcohol, 59*, 427–438.

Brown, S.A., & Schuckit, M.A. (1988). Changes in depression among abstinent alcoholics. *Journal of Studies on Alcohol, 49*, 412–417.

Brown, S.A., & Stetson, B.A. (1988). Coping with drinking pressures: Adolescent versus parent perspectives. *Adolescence, 23*(90), 297–301.

Brown, S.A., Vik, P.W., & Creamer, V.A. (1989). Characteristics of relapse following adolescent substance abuse treatment. *Addictive Behaviors, 14*, 291–300.

Cadoret, R.J., Troughton, E., O'Gorman, T.W., & Heywood, E. (1986). An adoption study of genetic and environmental factors in drug abuse. *Archives of General Psychiatry, 43*, 1131–1136.

Capuzzi, D., & Lecoq, L.L. (1983). Social and personal determinants of adolescent use and abuse of alcohol and marijuana. *Personnel Guidance Journal, 62*(4), 199–205.

Chassin, L. (1984). Adolescent substance use and abuse. *Advances in Child Behavioral Analysis and Therapy, 3*, 99–152.

Christiansen, B.A., Goldman, M.S., & Brown, S.A. (1985). The differential development of adolescent alcohol expectancies may predict adult alcoholism. *Addictive Behaviors, 10*, 299–306.

Christiansen, B.A., Smith, G.T., Roehling, P.V., & Goldman, M.S. (1989). Using alcohol expectancies to predict adolescent drinking behavior after one year. *Journal of Consulting and Clinical Psychology, 57*(1), 93–99.

Cloninger, C.R., Bohman, M., & Sigvardsson, S. (1981). Inheritance of alcohol abuse: Cross-fostering analysis of adopted men. *Archives of General Psychiatry, 38*, 861–868.

Cloninger, C.R., Sigvardsson, S., & Bohman, M. (1988). Childhood personality predicts alcohol abuse in young adults. *Alcoholism: Clinical and Experimental Research, 12*(4), 494–505.

Cohen, P., Cohen, J., Kasen, S., Velez, C.N., Hartmark, C., Johnson, J., Rojas, M., Brook, J., & Streuning, E.L. (1993). An epidemiological study of disorders in late childhood and adolescence: I. Age- and gender-specific prevalence. *Journal of Child Psychology and Psychiatry, 34*(6), 851–867.

Cohen, S. (1978). Amyl nitrite rediscovered. *Drug Abuse and Alcoholism Newsletter, 7*(1), 1–3.

Cohen, S. (1981). Cannabis: Impact on motivation, Part I. *Drug Abuse and Alcoholism Newsletter, 10*(1), 1–3.

Cotton, N.S. (1979). The familial incidence of alcoholism: A review. *Journal of Studies on Alcohol, 40*(1), 89–116.

Deas-Nesmith, D., Campbell, S., & Brady, K.T. (1998). Substance use disorders in an adolescent inpatient psychiatric population. *Journal of the National Medical Association, 90*, 233–238.

Donovan, J.E., & Jessor, R. (1985). Structure of problem behavior in adolescence and young adulthood. *Journal of Consulting and Clinical Psychology, 53*, 890–904.

Duncan, D.F. (1977). Life stress as a precursor to adolescent drug dependence. *International Journal of the Addictions, 12*(8), 1047–1056.

Ellickson, P.L., & Bell, R.M. (1990). Drug prevention in junior high: A multisite longitudinal test. *Science, 247*, 1299–1305.

Ellis, D.A., Zucker, R.A., & Fitzgerald, H.E. (1997). The role of family influences in development and risk. *Alcohol Health and Research World, 21*, 218–226.

File, S.E., & Pellow, S. (1990). Behavioral pharmacology of minor tranquilizers. In D.J.K. Balfour (Ed.), *Psychotropic drugs of abuse* (pp. 147–172). New York: Pergamon Press.

Freidman, A.S., & Granick, S. (Eds.). (1990). *Family therapy for adolescent drug abuse.* Lexington, MA: Lexington Books.

Garfinkel, B.D., & Golombek, H. (1983). Suicidal behavior in adolescence. In B.D. Garfinkel & G.H. Golombek (Eds.), *The adolescent and mood disturbance* (pp. 189–217). New York: International Universities Press.

Gillin, J.C., Smith, T.L., Irwin, M.R., Kripke, D.F., Brown, S.A., & Schuckit, M.A. (1990). Short REM latency in primary alcoholics with secondary depression. *American Journal of Psychiatry, 147*(1), 106–109.

Gilman, A.G., Goodman, L.S., & Gilman, A. (1980). *Goodman and Gilman's: The pharmacological basis of therapeutics* (6th ed.). New York: Macmillan.

Goodwin, D.W., Schulsinger, F., Moller, N., Hermansen, L., Winokur, G., & Guze, B. (1974). Drinking problems in adopted and nonadopted sons of alcoholics. *Archives of General Psychiatry, 31,* 164–169.

Grilo, C.M., Becker, D.F., Fehon, D.C., Edell, W.S., & McGlashan, T.H. (1996). Conduct disorder, substance use disorder, and coexisting conduct and substance use disorders in adolescent inpatients. *American Journal of Psychiatry, 153*(7), 914–920.

Grilo, C.M., Becker, D.F., Walker, M.L., Levy, K.N., Edell, W.S., & McGlashan, T.H. (1995). Psychiatric comorbidity in adolescent inpatients with substance use disorder. *Journal of the American Academy of Child and Adolescent Psychiatry, 34*(8), 1085–1091.

Gruenwald. P.J., & Klitzner, M. (1991). Results of a preliminary POSIT analyses. In E. Radhert (Ed.), *Adolescent assessment: Referral system manual* (DHHS Publication No. ADM 91–1735). Washington, DC: U.S. Government Printing Office.

Hect, A. (1980). Quick route to danger. *FDA Consumer* (Order No. 1980–254/72)

Holden, M.G., Brown, S.A., & Mott, M.A. (1988). Social support network of adolescents: Relation to family alcohol abuse. *American Journal of Drug and Alcohol Abuse, 14*(4), 487–498.

Huba, G.J., Wingard, J.A., & Bentler, P.M. (1980). Framework for an interactive theory of drug use. In D.J. Lettieri, M. Sayers, & H.W. Pearson (Eds.), *Theories on drug abuse* (pp. 95–101). Rockville, MD: National Institute on Drug Abuse.

Hundleby, J.D., & Mercer, G.W. (1987). Family and friends as social environments and their relationship to young adolescents' use of alcohol, tobacco, and marijuana. *Journal of Marriage and the Family, 49,* 151–164.

Jessor, R. (1985). Adolescent problem drinking: Psychosocial aspects and developmental outcomes. In

L.H. Towle (Ed.), *Proceedings: NIAAA-WHO Collaborating Center Designation Meeting and Alcohol Research Seminar* (pp. 104–143). Washington, DC: Public Health Service.

Jessor, R., Chase, J.A., & Donovan, J.E. (1980). Psychosocial correlates of marijuana use and problem drinking in a national sample of adolescents. *American Journal of Public Health, 70,* 604–613.

Jessor, R., & Jessor, S.L. (1975). Adolescent development and the onset of drinking. *Journal of Studies of Alcohol, 36,* 27–51.

Johnson, C.A., Pentz, M.A., Weber, M.D., Dwyer, J.H., Baer, N., Mackinnon, D.P., & Hansen, W.B. (1990). Relative effectiveness of comprehensive community programming for drug abuse prevention with high-risk and low-risk adolescents. *Journal of Consulting and Clinical Psychology, 58*(4), 447–456.

Johnston, L.D., O'Malley, P.M., & Bachman, J.G. (1998). *National survey results on drug use from the Monitoring the Future study, 1975–1997. Volume I: Secondary school students* (NIH Publication No. ADM 98–4345). Rockville, MD: National Institute on Drug Abuse.

Kaminer, Y., Tarter, R.E., Bukstein, O.G., & Kabene, M. (1992). Comparison between treatment completers and noncompleters among dually diagnosed substance-abusing adolescents. *Journal of the American Academy of Child and Adolescent Psychiatry, 31*(6), 1046–1049.

Kaminer, Y., Wagner, E., Plummer, B., & Siefer, R. (1993). Validation of the Teen Addiction Severity Index (T-ASI): Preliminary findings. *American Journal on Addictions, 2,* 250–254.

Kandel, D. (1978). Convergences in prospective longitudinal surveys of drug use in normal populations. In D. Kandel (Ed.), *Longitudinal research in drug use: Empirical findings and methodological issues.* Washington, DC: Hemisphere.

Kandel, D.B., Davies, M., Karus, D., & Yamaguchi, K. (1986). The consequences in young adulthood of adolescent drug involvement. *Archives of General Psychiatry, 43,* 746–754.

Kandel, D.B., Johnson, J.G., Bird, H.R., Canino, G., Goodman, S.H., Lahey, B.B., Regier, D.A., & Schwab-Stone, M. (1997). Psychiatric disorders associated with substance use among children and adolescents: Findings from the Methods for the Epidemiology of Child and Adolescent mental disorders (MECA) study. *Journal of Abnormal Psychology, 25*(2), 121–132.

Kaplan, H.B. (1977). Antecedents of deviant responses: Predicting from a general theory of deviant behavior. *Journal of Youth and Adolescence, 7,* 253–277.

Knop, J., Teasdale, T.W., Schulsinger, F., & Goodwin, D.W. (1985). A prospective study of young men at high risk for alcoholism: School behavior and achievement. *Journal of Studies on Alcohol, 46*(4), 273–278.

Kosten, T.R., & Rounsaville, B.J. (1988). Suicidality among opioid addicts. *American Journal of Drug and Alcohol Abuse, 14,* 357–369.

Labouvie, E.W., & McGee, C.R. (1986). Relation of personality to alcohol and drug use in adolescence. *Journal of Consulting and Clinical Psychology, 54*(3), 289–293.

Lam, W., Sacks, H.S., Sze, P.C., & Chalmers, T.C. (1987). Meta-analysis of randomized controlled trials of nicotine chewing-gum. *Lancet, 2,* 27–30.

Lewinsohn, P.M., Rhode, P., & Seeley, J.R. (1995). Adolescent psychopathology III: The clinical consequences of comorbidity. *Journal of the American Academy of Child and Adolescent Psychiatry, 34*(4), 510–519.

Liddle, H., & Dakof, G. (1995). Efficacy of family therapy for drug abuse: Promising but not definitive. *Journal of Marital and Family Therapy, 21,* 511–543.

Loukas, A., Twitchell, G., Piejak, L., Fitzgerald, H., & Zucker, R.A. (1998). The family as a unity of interacting personalities. In L. L'Abate (Ed.), *Family psychopathology: The relational roots of dysfunctional behavior* (pp. 35–59). New York: Guilford Press.

Martin, C.S., & Winters, K.C. (1998). Diagnosis and assessment of alcohol use disorders among adolescents. *Alcohol Health and Research World, 22,* 95–105.

McCubbin, H.I., Needle, R.H., & Wilson, M. (1985). Adolescent health risk behaviors: Family stress and adolescent coping as critical factors. *Family Relations, 34,* 51–62.

McGlothin, W.H., & West, L.J. (1968). The marijuana problem: An overview. *American Journal of Psychiatry, 125,* 1126–1134.

McGue, M., Slutske, W., Taylor, J., & Iacono, W. (1997). Personality and substance use disorders: I. Effects of gender and alcoholism subtype. *Alcoholism: Clinical and Experimental Research, 21,* 513–520.

Morton, H.G. (1990). Occurrence and treatment of solvent abuse in children and adolescents. In D.J.K. Balfour (Ed.), *Psychotropic drugs of abuse* (pp. 431–451). New York: Pergamon Press.

Myers, M.G., & Brown, S.A. (1990a). *Cigarette smoking and health in adolescent substance abusers.* Paper presented at the annual meeting of the Society of Behavioral Medicine, Chicago.

Myers, M.G., & Brown, S.A. (1990b). Coping and appraisal in potential relapse situations among adolescent substance abusers following treatment. *Journal of Adolescent Chemical Dependency, 1*(2), 95–115.

Myers, M.G., & Brown, S.A. (1994). Smoking and health in substance abusing adolescents: A two year follow-up. *Pediatrics, 93,* 561–566.

Myers, M.G., & Brown, S.A. (1997). Cigarette smoking four years following treatment for adolescent substance abuse. *Journal of Child and Adolescent Substance Abuse, 7,* 1–15.

Myers, M.G., Stewart, D.G., & Brown, S.A. (1998). Progression from conduct disorder to antisocial personality disorder following treatment for adolescent substance abuse. *American Journal of Psychiatry, 155,* 479–485.

National Institute on Drug Abuse. (1998). *National household survey on drug abuse: Main findings.* Rockville, MD: Author.

Needle, R.H., Glynn, T.J., & Needle, M.P. (1983). Drug abuse: Adolescent addictions and the family. In R. Figley & H.I. McCubbin (Eds.), *Stress and the family* (pp. 37–52). New York: Brunner/Mazel.

Newcomb, M.D., & Bentler, P.M. (1988). *Consequences of adolescent drug use: Impact on the lives of young adults.* Newbury Park, CA: Sage.

Novins, D.K., Beals, J., Shore, J.H., & Manson, S.M. (1996). Substance abuse treatment of American Indian adolescents: Comorbid symptomatology, gender differences, and treatment patterns. *Journal of the American Academy of Child and Adolescent Psychiatry, 35*(12), 1593–1601.

Pandina, R.J., & Schuele, J.A. (1983). Psychosocial correlates of alcohol and drug use of adolescent students and adolescents in treatment. *Journal of Studies on Alcohol, 44*(6), 950–973.

Pickrel, S.G., & Henggeler, S.W. (1996). Multisystemic therapy: Adolescent substance abuse and dependence. *Child and Adolescent Psychiatric Clinics of North America, 5,* 201–211.

Pierce, J.P., Choi, W.S., Gilpin, E.A., Farkas, A.J., & Berry, C.C. (1998). Tobacco industry promotion of cigarettes and adolescent smoking. *Journal of the American Medical Association, 279,* 511–515.

Polich, J., & Bloom, F.E. (1987). P300 from normals and adult children of alcoholics. *Alcohol, 4,* 301–305.

Rydelius, P.A. (1983). Alcohol-abusing teenage boys: Testing a hypothesis on the relationship between alcohol abuse and social background factors, criminality and personality in teenage boys. *Acta Psychiatrica Scandinavica, 63,* 368–380.

Sadava, S.W. (1987). Interactionist theories. In H.T. Blane & K.E. Leonard (Eds.), *Psychological theories of drinking and alcoholism* (pp. 90–130). New York: Guilford Press.

Schafer, J., McQuaid, J.R., & Brown, S.A. (1989). *Drug effect expectancies discriminate patterns of marijuana and cocaine use.* Paper presented at the annual meeting of the American Psychological Association, New Orleans, LA.

Schuckit, M.A. (1985). Genetics and the risk for alcoholism. *Journal of the American Medical Association, 254*(18), 2614–2617.

Schuckit, M.A. (1988). Reactions to alcohol in sons of alcoholics and controls. *Alcoholism: Clinical and Experimental Research, 12*(4), 465–470.

Schuckit, M.A. (1989). *Drug and alcohol abuse: A clinical guide to diagnosis and treatment* (3rd ed.). New York: Plenum Press.

Schuckit, M.A., & Duby, J. (1982). Alcohol-related flushing and the risk for alcoholism in sons of alcoholics. *Journal of Clinical Psychiatry, 43,* 415–418.

Segal, B., Huba, G.J., & Singer, J.L. (1980). *Drugs, daydreaming, and personality: A study of college youth.* Hillsdale, NJ: Erlbaum.

Sher, K.J. (1987, December 2). *What we know and do not know about COAs: A research update.* Paper presented at the MacArthur Foundation meeting on Children of Alcoholics, Princeton, NJ.

Stewart, D.G., & Brown, S.A. (1995). Withdrawal and dependency symptoms among adolescent alcohol and drug abusers. *Addiction, 90,* 627–635.

Stowell, R.J., & Estroff, T.W. (1992). Psychiatric disorders in substance-abusing adolescent inpatients: A pilot study. *Journal of the American Academy of Child and Adolescent Psychiatry, 31*(6), 1036–1040.

Tapert, S.F., & Brown, S.A. (1999). Neuropsychological correlates of adolescent substance abuse: Four year outcomes. *Journal of the International Neuropsychological Society, 5,* 475–487.

Tarter, R.E., & Edwards, K. (1988). Psychological factors associated with the risk for alcoholism. *Alcoholism: Clinical and Experimental Research, 12*(4), 471–480.

Tarter, R.E., Kirisci, L., & Mezzich, A. (1997). Multivariate typology of adolescents with alcohol use disorder. *American Journal of Psychiatry, 6,* 150–158.

Tucker, M.B. (1982). Social support and coping: Applications for the study of female drug abuse. *Journal of Social Issues, 38*(2), 117–137.

Victor, H.R., Crossman, J.C., & Eiserman, R. (1973). Openness to experience and marijuana use in high school students. *Journal of Consulting and Clinical Psychology, 41*(1), 78–85.

Wilens, T.E., Biederman, J., Abrantes, A.M., & Spencer, T.J. (1997). Clinical characteristics of psychiatrically referred adolescent outpatients with substance use disorder. *Journal of the American Academy of Child and Adolescent Psychiatry, 36*(7), 941–947.

Winters, K. (1990). Clinical considerations in the assessment of adolescent chemical dependency. *Journal of Adolescent Chemical Dependence, 1,* 31–52.

Winters, K.C., & Henly, G.A. (1989). *The Personal Experiences Inventory (PEI) manual.* Los Angeles: Western Psychological Service.

Zucker, R.A. (1979). Developmental aspects of drinking through the adult years. In H.T. Blane & M.E. Chafetz (Eds.), *Youth, alcohol, and social policy* (pp. 91–146). New York: Plenum Press.

Zucker, R.A., & Gomberg, E.S.L. (1986). Etiology of alcoholism reconsidered: The case for a biopsychosocial process. *American Psychologist, 41,* 783–793.

CHAPTER 39

Delinquency and Criminal Behavior

MARK JAMES JOHNSON and WILLIAM JAMES SHAW

Juvenile delinquency is defined as illegal behavior committed by a minor. Although this definition is rather simple, the tremendous volume of literature that exists on delinquency and the many disciplines that have contributed to this body of literature, including criminology, law, sociology, and psychology, indicate that the issue itself is complex.

Delinquent behavior is a relative concept: it has meaning only in relation to the laws that apply to a given population at a specific point in time. This makes discussion of the incidence of delinquency virtually meaningless, because what defines a behavior as delinquent can vary from time to time, culture to culture, and even state to state (Lunden, 1964). Wootton (1959) noted that a single change in the law could make many behaviors illegal or make previously illegal behavior legal. This makes the study of delinquency, or antisocial behavior, very difficult. The most accurate statistics are compiled by agencies that can control for the variations in legislation and criminal justice practices. Therefore, the reader wishing such data is referred to the annual reports published by the U.S. Department of Justice and state and local law enforcement agencies.

As Cressey (1960) pointed out, the most precise study of delinquency and criminal antisocial behavior is drawn from the psychological and sociological literature. The President's Commission on Law Enforcement and Administration of Justice (1967) correctly noted that the complexities of

human psychology are such that any attempt to find the cause of crime in human motivation alone is pointless. Sobel (1979) expressed a similar view relative to the inadequacies of traditional theories of personality development and the understanding of the delinquent offender. The sociological literature on delinquency is vast but lacks sufficient depth by itself to explain the etiology of particular delinquent patterns or to spell out the steps necessary to control or correct these patterns.

Statistics compiled on the prevalence of juvenile delinquency indicate that juvenile violence and crime have significantly increased throughout the past decade. A report provided by the American Psychological Association's Commission on Violence and Youth (1993) highlights the increasing problem of youth and violence while also providing a message of hope for change. However, not everyone shares the optimism of the American Psychological Association. In 1989, the Task Force on Juvenile Delinquency of the New Jersey State Supreme Court stated, "The conditions of modern society are such that delinquency has intensified in terms of the number involved and in the seriousness of the crimes charged" (Supreme Court of the State of New Jersey, 1989, p. 2). This increase in juvenile crime prompted many lawmakers to draft propositions that would place juvenile antisocial behavior on the same level as adult antisocial behavior. For example, on February 19, 1997, Senator John

Ashcroft (Missouri) publicly stated, "Violent juvenile criminals should be handled as adult criminals, not as candidates for counseling and social work." The economics of illicit drug traffic have undoubtedly contributed significantly to the changes in patterns of juvenile delinquency. Illegal and violent behavior, perpetrated both individually and in gangs, represent major problems, particularly in larger urban areas. The role of illicit drugs cannot be underestimated. Much of the violence relates to the sale and distribution of these drugs, and much of the violence perpetrated by juveniles against society occurs when these juveniles are under the influence of alcohol or illicit drugs. We also know that the suicide rate among adolescents and young adults has continued to rise. There is every reason to believe that this may parallel an increasingly violent society and may, in part, be another manifestation of the violence that exists within adolescent groups. A frighteningly high percentage of crimes in general, and violent crimes in particular, are now being committed by juveniles, making juvenile delinquency one of the most critical problems threatening to disrupt the internal order of this country.

To provide as complete a report as possible of the historical and contemporary views on delinquency, this chapter reviews some of the significant work in both the sociological and psychological fields. In addition, the efforts of scholars and clinicians to integrate the most promising work are presented. Finally, some examination of the interplay between the criminal justice system and other institutions within our society is examined in terms of their role in combating the problem of juvenile delinquency.

THEORIES OF DELINQUENCY

A vast amount of research and writing has been done on the subject of juvenile delinquency. Despite the difficulties in determining exact causes of antisocial behavior, much of the work has attempted to locate individual factors that would account for delinquency. However, today, most experts in the field believe in multiple causation, that is, the probability that, in any particular case, a combination of factors is responsible for delinquent behavior. Furthermore, three spheres of influence are seen as playing a major part in the development

of personality and behavioral patterns, including delinquency. These spheres of influence are home and family, peer group and community, and psychological and biological factors.

THE INFLUENCE OF HOME AND FAMILY

Although there are many different factors to consider in the development of antisocial behavior, the influence of the family is significant. The influence of the family on juvenile delinquency was examined in early reports by Powers and Witmer (1951) and McCord and McCord (1958). Glueck and Glueck (1950) believed that the influence of the home and the family far outweighs cultural or socioeconomic influences in the development of delinquent behavior. These respected investigators stated that an inadequate home life was a major contributor to delinquency, increasing the chances that a child would become delinquent to 98 out of 100. They believed that a child in a good home had fewer than 3 chances in 100 of becoming delinquent. Homes judged as inadequate by Glueck and Glueck were those where separation and/or divorce had occurred, where parents demonstrated a consistent avoidance of responsibility, and in which criminal history, significant health problems, or alcohol abuse were noted. Other researchers have found a similar pattern. Robins, West, and Herjanic (1975) found a correlation between children's conduct problems and parental antisocial personality traits. This study also found that parental antisocial behavior preceded the child's antisocial behavior.

Studies have indicated that there is a significant correlation between externalizing behavior problems in infancy and behavior problems when the child reaches school age and beyond (Farrington, 1997). Behavior problems in children are associated with depressed mothers (Mash & Johnston, 1983), manifest marital conflict (Katz & Gottman, 1993), the early loss of a close family member (Bowlby, 1951; Earle & Earle, 1961), and growing up in fatherless homes (Toman, 1969).

Recent models addressing the precursors of antisocial behavior highlight the interaction/transaction that occurs between children and their environment, including the child's home and family (D. Shaw & Winslow, 1997). To simply state that the family exerts influence on the child ignores the complexity of the interactions that occur between parent and child. The social interaction hypothesis of antisocial behavior, as defined by Dishion and Peterson (1997), stresses that "antisocial behavior has a function within the individual's immediate environment" (p. 205). This model suggests that children may engage in a number of different behaviors (e.g., whining, noncompliance, arguing) to either get their parent's attention or reduce parents' intrusions into their lives. Parents who do not respond to their child's needs in a prosocial manner may actually be reinforcing antisocial behavior. Therefore, the child learns to control family interactions with aversive behavior. When this pattern is frequently repeated, parents may feel a sense of defeat and give up on the child. Therefore, there is less likelihood that the parents will adequately supervise their child as he or she matures (Dishion & Patterson, 1997).

Toby (1967) reported on two separate processes that have been suggested to account for the relationship between parental inadequacy and juvenile delinquency. First, the developing personality of the child is impaired by parental rejection and neglect. The child becomes poorly socialized and lacks impulse control. As a result, the child reacts violently to trivial provocation, and the behavior of the child lacks purpose. The second process also begins with parental inadequacy and neglect. The parents absolve themselves of control of the family and direct the child away from the family, toward the peer group. Then the family and peer group become competitors for the allegiance of the child. If the peer group is delinquent, the child's need for acceptance forces him or her also to engage in delinquent activities.

The American Psychological Association, through its task force on Violence in the Family, has thoroughly investigated the topic of violence in the family. The task force published a report that includes conclusions regarding the effect of violence in the family (American Psychological Association, 1996). One specific area of familial influence that has received attention in recent years is the effect of maltreatment on behavior problems in children and adolescents.

EFFECTS OF MALTREATMENT

Studies have shown that there is a connection between child maltreatment and delinquent/antisocial behavior. For example, 35% of juveniles in a Florida detention center reported having been sexually abused (Dembo, Getrev, Washburn, Wish, & Schemeidler, 1988), and 58% of males and 90% of females in a Colorado detention center reported being sexually abused (Colorado Division of Youth Services, 1985). Longitudinal studies indicate that 20% to 30% of children who have been maltreated will engage in antisocial behavior, and being maltreated as a child increased a person's risk to engage in antisocial behavior by nearly 50% (26% vs. 17%) (Widom, 1997). These statistics indicate that although the majority of maltreated children did not engage in antisocial behavior, being abused or neglected placed the individual at increased risk for future antisocial behavior. A number of studies have indicated that children who are maltreated exhibit more behavior problems than children who were not maltreated (Friedrich, Einbender, & Luecke, 1987; Kolko, Moser, & Weldy, 1990).

Research regarding aggressive responses to others indicates that there are two very different types of aggression. Instrumental aggression is the type considered antisocial. This aggression is described as "methodical and nonemotional, appears oriented toward attaining resources or achieving dominance among peers" (Shields & Cicchetti, 1998, p. 382). Reactive aggression is "associated with a high degree of sympathetic arousal and angry reactivity and is thought to be motivated by a desire to protect oneself from real or perceived threat" (p. 382). A recent study by Shields and Cicchetti indicated that maltreated children have significant difficulty regulating their emotions and therefore are prone to increased behavior problems, including reactive aggression. Although further research is needed in this area to determine the eventual effect this may have on delinquency in adolescence, it is possible that being maltreated as a child may continue to have a negative effect on affect regulation, and subsequently aggressive behavior, throughout adolescence and adulthood.

THE INFLUENCE OF COMMUNITY

The school is an important community influence in the etiology and maintenance of delinquency (Hunt & Hardt, 1965; Silverberg & Silverberg, 1971). Truancy is probably the most obvious and common school-related behavior demonstrated by delinquents. A disproportionately high number of delinquents are poor readers, inattentive, impulsive, and concrete in their thinking. Although these conditions correlate with delinquency, they do not seem to play a causative role.

A disturbing trend in juvenile violence is the epidemic of school violence. In the past decade, the incidence of school violence, even in rural communities, has increased in frequency and number of deaths associated with each incidence. These incidents have resulted in society and Congress engaging in a national debate regarding gun control and limiting children's access to guns and information on how to make other weapons (including information on the Internet on how to manufacture bombs). As the author was preparing this chapter, two students in Littleton, Colorado, stormed their high school, killing 12 students and one teacher using guns and homemade bombs. A few weeks later, a 15-year-old student entered his school with two guns, shooting and wounding 6 students. Since 1993, over 43 students were killed in school shootings in 14 incidents, prompting many to describe the increase in school killings as epidemic.

Many experts believe that negative experiences in school may lead youth to follow delinquent styles. School is seen as a source of frustration, a constant embarrassment to children or adolescents who are unable or unwilling to succeed (Schafer & Polk, 1967, pp. 222–227). Yochelson and Samenow (1976) noted a tendency for the delinquent child to develop deviant behavior patterns (e.g., sneaky, attention seeking, disobedient, marginal adjustment to school, etc.) at approximately 10 years of age, although these behaviors may not be serious violations of school rules. The description by Yochelson and Samenow is of a child who is self-centered, uninterested in scholastic activities, sensation seeking, and resistant to external authority. Although there is little empirical evidence regarding violence in rural school settings, Sleek (1998) interviewed some of the leading experts in the area of school violence. These experts indicated that some similarities among the episodes of school shootings include a tendency to kill and injure multiple victims in a single incident; the absence of a secondary motive (such as robbery); perpetrators younger than the average age of most juvenile delinquents; and perpetrators' tendency to have a history of social problems.

The issue of school shootings also prompted a discussion on the impact the media has on children and adolescents. In a review of the literature, Huesmann, Moise, and Podolski (1997) indicate that studies do support the sentiment that viewing violence on television increases aggressive and antisocial behavior. According to Huesmann et al., these findings have been supported in field studies, longitudinal studies, and meta-analyses. Furthermore, exposure to violence in music videos and video games was also related to an increase in violent attitudes and behavior. Exposure to violence as parts of news programs has not been conclusively linked to an increase in violent attitudes, but the authors note that additional research is needed in this area.

The community influence on the evolution of delinquency most often involves the neighborhood, specifically the role of socioeconomic class and the relative impact of the slum and inner city. In fact, for years, the standard explanations and discussions of delinquency focused on the impact of overcrowding, poverty, and substandard housing (Block & Flynn, 1956; C. Shaw, 1938). Substance abuse, influenced by both personal and community factors (i.e., peer pressure, gang involvement, etc.), also plays a part in juvenile delinquency. Studies indicate that 70% to 95% of juvenile delinquents in treatment or rehabilitation have used alcohol or other drugs (Colorado Division of Youth Services, 1985; Dembo et al., 1988).

Law enforcement agents are an important community influence. Their role in the prevention and control of criminal activity is obvious. However, some authorities in the field of criminology believe that criminal and delinquent behavior may actually be reinforced by apprehension, arrest, and confinement. It has been further suggested that the criminal justice process actually serves as a catalyst for budding delinquent careers (Becker, 1963; Cloward & Ohlin, 1960; Tannenbaum, 1938). Little has been done to fully study these hypotheses relative to the juvenile offender. The need for research in this area is great.

Crime and delinquency are not limited to one class in society, nor is it restricted to the inner-city environment. Miller (1958) reported on gang delinquency as a function of a lower socioeconomic status (SES). Miller sees certain realities existing in lower SES communities that contribute to the violation of legal and social standards. First, certain basic, common practices found in lower SES communities are automatically violations of certain laws. These practices often allow a person to achieve or acquire something desirable quicker and more easily than more lawful means, even when lawful means are readily available. Some unique situations occur regularly in lower SES neighborhoods. There are specific ways of responding to such situations that are not merely accepted—they are required. Because the law does not address solutions to such situations in ways that are accepted by the neighborhood, these required responses are usually illegal. However, insofar as we equate lower SES communities of society with poverty, we must be careful not to perpetuate the now apparently erroneous notion that poverty causes crime. It is obvious that there are many millions of poor people throughout this country, the vast majority of whom never commit a felony. However, certain other problems are likely to occur in the lower SES communities and may occur as a function of poverty: overcrowding, abandonment and single parenting, dissolution of the family, financial crises, health concerns, and so forth. The small fraction of juveniles from lower SES communities who do commit crimes tend to commit them repeatedly, and therefore, a large percentage of crimes is the result of the action of a surprisingly small number of juveniles. This repetitive criminal pattern, however, cannot be explained satisfactorily by the various problems just cited, such as financial problems. Kramer (1988) and Samenow (1984), among others, agree that the repetitive criminal pattern has more to do with the psychology of individual offenders than the social or cultural pressures with which they must deal.

Although the presence of crime and delinquency in lower SES communities is clear, Vaz (1967) specifically addressed the problem of delinquency in the middle class. A fundamental point is stressed: As long as delinquency remains faithful to the values of a particular class, it will tend to advance the social status of the child or adolescent and will become more firmly rooted in the individual and in that level of society. Similar theories have been offered by Clark and Wenninger (1962), Erickson and Empey (1965), and Polk (1967, Appendix R, pp. 343–347). Of particular note is the work by Erickson and Empey.

Erickson and Empey found strong indications that the degree of commitment to peers may vary from class to class and may be more predictive of delinquency than social class alone. The evidence in their study pointed to middle-class youth as having the strongest commitment to peers, followed by lower SES youth, and finally, by higher SES youth, who are the least committed to peer groups. The question of whether peer group influence is more critical than SES certainly warrants further study.

Delinquents are often thought to have adopted deviant standards of a nondominant portion of society that differs from the values of the dominant society. Sykes and Matza (1957) have proposed an alternative process whereby the person becomes delinquent by first learning the moral implications of a particular act according to the standards of the dominant society. However, the delinquent learns to neutralize the moral implications of the act. Although social class may play a role, the key in this explanation is that the moral imperative followed by the juvenile delinquent is consistent with a deviant culture rather than the standards of mainstream society.

A significant sociological concept dealing with the norms, or lack of norms, in the prevailing culture is called "anomie" (Cloward, 1959; Durkheim, 1930/1951; A. Cohen, 1965; Merton, 1957). The theory is based on the interactions between the norms that exist in a society and the goals to which the society encourages its youth to aspire. The key element is the opportunity that the society offers its youth to accomplish these goals. A basic premise in the theory is that some special systems exert pressure on certain members to engage in deviant behavior. This occurs when the society prescribes certain goals or aspirations for its members but fails to support the prescribed means for reaching these goals. Those aspiring to the goals, generally the youth of the society, will identify the most efficient means of reaching these goals, and, whether legal or not, these means will be followed. The social structure becomes unsteady as a result of the failure by society to provide its members with legal means to achieve the goals that the society itself values. This basic flaw in a society encourages and maintains delinquent and criminal behavior.

Some theories (e.g., control theory) suggest that association with delinquent peers is simply a by-product of exhibiting delinquent behavior rather than an influential force in the development and maintenance of delinquent behavior (i.e., Birds of a feather flock together) (Hirschi, 1969). However, a contrasting theory advanced by Sutherland (1939) has received a great deal of attention and support. His differential association theory is essentially a learning model that incorporates genetic and sociological elements. The crux of Sutherland's theory is: "A person becomes delinquent because of an excess of definitions favorable to violations of the law over definitions unfavorable to violations of the law" (Sutherland & Cressey, 1966, p. 78). Sutherland believed this would explain all criminal patterns of behavior. Subsequent work has yielded mixed results. In their reformation of Sutherland's theory, Burgess and Akers state:

> Criminal behavior is a function of norms which are discriminative for criminal behavior, the learning of which takes place when such behavior is more highly reinforced than non-criminal behavior.... The strength of criminal behavior is a direct function of the amount, frequency, and probability of its reinforcement. (1966, pp. 143–144)

When this model is applied to juvenile delinquents and the influence of peers on delinquent behavior, the theory suggests that association with deviant peers will influence the adolescent to develop deviant beliefs. These deviant beliefs, then, will result in deviant behavior. Empirical evidence, gathered from a number of different sources and time periods, support the differential association theory premise that association with delinquent peers is linked to delinquent behavior (see Agnew, 1991; Elliott, Huizinga, & Ageton, 1985; LaGrange & White, 1983; Short, 1960). In a review of the literature on peer influence on juvenile drug use and other deviant behaviors, Thornberry and Krohn (1997) present findings indicating that association with deviant peers is directly related to the increase in deviant behavior.

Revisions to the differential association theory focus more on the process by which the delinquent chooses to model his or her behavior after others in his or her life and to incorporate established learning principles. In many ways, these attempts have helped sociology use the theory of differential association to clarify the manner in which individual delinquent patterns emerge as well as those patterns that are descriptive of group behavior. Furthermore, this theory has helped pull the sociological and psychological perspective more closely together, especially in those formulations based on learning theory.

BIOLOGICAL INFLUENCES

During the Middle Ages, demonic possession was the explanation offered most frequently for delinquent and criminal behavior (Lowry, 1944). In the early twentieth century, hereditary "moral insanity" held forth as the most widely accepted theory (Tredgold, 1915). In 1911, Lombroso advanced a theory that criminals had certain physical characteristics that distinguished them from noncriminals. It was believed that these physical characteristics were indicative of a criminal predisposition. The notion of inherited predisposition has been considered by many to be firmly established (Bandura & Walters, 1963; Gibbens, 1963; Glueck & Glueck, 1956; Sheldon, 1949). The classic studies of the Jukes (Dugdale, 1877) and Kallikaks (Goddard, 1912) also had a profound impact on the possibility of a link between heredity and crime.

Subsequent studies have continued to provide evidence that biological, genetic, and neurological factors impact antisocial/delinquent behavior. In a review of the literature on genetic influences on antisocial behavior, Carey and Goldman (1997) note that most studies have found evidence for a genetic effect on antisocial behavior. One study (Grove et al., 1990) found that similar symptoms of antisocial personality disorder were evident in identical twins even when the twins were reared apart.

One interesting finding from this literature review is that all of the studies reviewed indicated that genetics did not explain all of the variance and that the environment also played an important part in the development of antisocial behavior. Moffitt (1993), describing a life-course-persistent offender theory, notes that biological/neuropsychological deficits (caused by either prenatal, perinatal, or postnatal injuries/neglect/trauma) interact with environmental factors to place individuals at significantly increased risk to engage in antisocial/delinquent behavior. The interaction effect between biological and environmental influences, also called transactional influence (Sameroff & Chandler, 1975), explains how biological or environmental trauma/deficits experienced in one developmental stage *may* impact the individual's ability to successfully negotiate subsequent developmental stages. Longitudinal studies investigating the effects of prenatal and perinatal trauma/insult (Broman, Nichols, & Kennedy, 1975; Drillien, 1964) indicate that most children will not experience continued difficulties. However, if there is more than one form of insult, subsequent insults provide an additive effect on eventual outcome. Furthermore, the child's environment can either be beneficial or detrimental to the eventual outcome for the child (Brennan & Mednick, 1997).

Multiple studies provide evidence of juvenile delinquents performing more poorly on verbal-based tests compared to performance-based tests. Studies show that juvenile delinquents exhibit difficulties with executive functioning, typically a frontal lobe function that includes:

> sustaining attention and concentration; abstract reasoning and concept formation; formulating goals; anticipating and planning; programming and initiating purposive sequences of behavior; self-monitoring and self-awareness; inhibiting unsuccessful, inappropriate, or impulsive behaviors; and interrupting ongoing behavior patterns in order to shift to a more adaptive alternative behavior. (Henry & Moffitt, 1997, p. 281)

As can be seen from this list, deficits in executive functioning are descriptive of the problems exhibited by many juvenile delinquents. Blackburn (1993) has noted that testosterone may be related to aggressive or antisocial behavior due to its inhibitory effect of the neurotransmitter metabolite monoamine oxidase. Studies have also provided evidence that serotonin and cortisol levels have an impact on aggressive behavior in children (Loeber & Stouthamer-Loeber, 1998).

Despite the multitude of studies providing evidence of biological influences on delinquent behavior, however, the data clearly suggest that biological factors play an interactive role with environmental, cultural, and psychological factors.

PSYCHOLOGICAL THEORIES

Thus far, sociology and psychology have played pivotal roles in the study of delinquency. Although no one discipline has been able to fully analyze this complex area, the contributions of psychology have been important.

Juvenile delinquency was a proper area of interest of the early psychoanalysts; a fine summary of their position can be found in Feldman (1964). The psychoanalytic explanation is that delinquency and criminal behavior are used to maintain psychic equilibrium. In early analytic thinking, criminality was viewed as a form of neurosis that, rather than taking the symbolic form of symptoms, took the form of overt acting out against others (Blos, 1961; Ilg & Ames, 1955). The criminal was seen as wishing to be punished so as to retrieve the guilt arising from poorly sublimated sexual drives. Healey and Bronner (1926, 1936) described delinquency as a symptom of disturbance that reflects a need to escape, to compensate, to gain recognition, or to seek punishment. Delinquency was thus defined as being a meaningful experience for the individual in terms of his or her personal drives and needs being acted out in the environment. This position has also been reflected in the work of Aichhorn (1935) and Lindner (1944). Blos pointed out that the exclusive use of antisocial solutions directed against the environment is an element of criminal behavior and juvenile delinquency that set them apart from other failures to adjust and adapt.

Because of the nature and consequences of delinquent behavior, it was logical for behavior therapists and learning therapists to investigate delinquency from their theoretical positions. The idea that child/adolescent delinquent behavior is related to learning was proposed by the early proponents of learning theory (Dollard, Doob, Miller, Mowrer, & Sears, 1939). These early learning theories (such as the frustration/aggression theory) (Dollard et al., 1939) were developed in response to the psychoanalytic theory of delinquency. Social learning theorists emphasized the influence of the child's environment through modeling and vicarious learning (Bandura, 1973; Bandura & Walters, 1963). Current learning theorists integrate the findings from cognitive psychology into their conceptualizations (Eron, 1997).

One of the major psychodynamic notions that the behavior therapists have investigated is the paradoxical idea that guilt, often seen as an agent of self-control, causes antisocial behavior. Research reported by Bandura and Walters (1963) fails to support the assertion that the antisocial personality is either guilt-free or guilt-ridden. Bandura and Walters take the position that the intermittent reinforcement of criminal activity is substantial and far outweighs the inhibitory effects of punishment or the possibility of punishment. These punishments generally are some form of social sanction: suspension from school, arrest and criminal charges, fines, jail sentences, and so forth. When delinquent behavior occurs in spite of these sanctions, it is not necessarily true that the delinquent is unsocialized, if unsocialized is taken to mean that he or she does not understand the norms of society and is unable to anticipate the consequences of his or her behavior. An alternative explanation, in light of the work of Bandura and Walters, is that, regardless of the delinquent's level of understanding of social norms, the habitual delinquent's learning or reinforcement history is such that the incentive to secure rewards through delinquent behavior is stronger than the incentive to comply with social codes.

The theory of socialization (Eysenck, 1957, 1964; Mowrer, 1950; Trasler, 1962) examines how children learn conformity to social rules. This theory states that there is a difference between the way certain skills or behaviors, such as walking, are learned and the way values are learned. The child is taught skilled forms of behavior that are rewarded and approved by society. This is fairly straightforward. However, when we consider values, some of society's rules may be in conflict with the child's natural urges and impulses. Society must train the child to conform to certain rules seen as necessary for the preservation of society. This training involves a conditioning to fear, and, as a result, anxiety is aroused as the child approaches the undesirable act. This conditioned fear then inhibits the act as soon as it begins to occur. Physical punishment and withdrawal of parental approval are the means by which the anxiety and fear are conditioned to the early stages of the behavior. For the behavior to be fully self-regulated, the values must be internalized; that is, the child must develop a conscience. The major contribution of this theory is its consideration of individual differences in degrees of socialization and how they are produced. Conformity is a function of the interaction between conditionability and the amount and severity of training. The ability to be conditioned is seen as dependent on the child's individual resources. Socialization occurs when fear responses are conditioned that inhibit the tendency to perform delinquent behaviors.

Several studies have been conducted on delinquents using this theory (Peterson, Quay, & Tiffany, 1961; Quay, 1964, 1966; Quay & Blumen, 1963; Quay, Peterson, & Consalvi, 1960; Quay & Quay, 1965; Randolph, Richardson, & Johnson, 1961). Based on these, three types of delinquent have been identified: the unsocialized, psychopathic delinquent; the neurotic delinquent with acting-out tendencies; the socialized, subcultural adolescent. The unsocialized psychopathic delinquent is the classic psychopathic individual who tends to commit crimes against people and/or property while experiencing no remorse. The neurotic/acting-out delinquent has

a sense of behaviors that are right and wrong, and the antisocial behavior is directly related to anxiety or depressive symptoms. These individuals may exhibit symptoms commonly referred to as masked symptoms of depression or anxiety. Finally, the socialized subcultural adolescent has socialized into a subculture where delinquent behavior is accepted and expected. Therefore, the individual adopts the norms of the gang, neighborhood, or subculture in which he or she is a member. When removed from this subculture, this individual may no longer exhibit delinquent behavior.

In the context of social-learning theory, modeling and reinforcement are important in the acquisition and maintenance of aggressive, antisocial behavior patterns (Bandura, 1969, 1973; Bandura, Ross, & Ross, 1961, 1963; Hayes, Rincover, & Volosin, 1980). The study by Hayes et al., showed that modeling influences are significant in the acquisition of aggressive behaviors, whereas sensory reinforcement determines the maintenance of the behaviors. It is likely that acquisition of delinquent patterns can be explained in similar ways through the influence of modeling with continuous or frequent reinforcement and the maintenance of delinquent patterns through intermittent reinforcement, thus making the behaviors more resistant to extinction (Bandura, 1969; Bandura & Walters, 1963).

Proponents of social-learning and behavior theories also believe that these approaches allow more resources within the community to be involved in solving the problem of juvenile delinquency. They believe that these theories reduce dependence on the traditional clinical approaches and increase the ability of resources such as law enforcement agencies, schools, and residential facilities to play a part in resolving the problems associated with juvenile delinquency on an individual as well as communitywide basis.

Although her work is more descriptive than explanatory, Kramer (1988) addresses the characterological component of juvenile delinquency and, therefore, places it in a psychological context. In the juvenile justice system in New York, she observed that juvenile delinquents do not specialize in a particular type of violent or nonviolent crime: They tend to get involved in a variety of illegal behaviors and therefore demonstrate a characterological way of relating to other people and to their own social responsibilities. She cites several professionals from the juvenile justice system in New York who state that juvenile delinquents, particularly violent ones, are fully responsible for their own actions and that their actions are a function of choices they make. These conscious, deliberate choices result from their using a set of rules that completely disregards the rights of other people. Seeing no obligation to respect the rights of others, they believe that they are completely and totally free to behave toward other people and property in whatever fashion suits their immediate needs. Furthermore, they believe society has neither the right nor the capacity to hold them responsible for the consequences of their actions. This failure to recognize any ability on the part of society to sanction them, coupled with their own lack of any internal standards or sense of responsibility to anyone other than themselves, allows for the development of a decidedly antisocial behavior pattern that may know no limits in terms of its severity. According to Kramer, projection is seen as a very common defense mechanism for these adolescents, who are able to hold others responsible for any punishment, however slight, they may incur. Therefore, they may have to spend a short time in custody as a result of the actions of a police officer, judge, or some other individual, but they deny any responsibility for their own behavior and, although totally disregarding the rights of others, are surprisingly forceful in protesting when they perceive that their rights have been violated.

Stanton Samenow, a psychologist who has studied criminal behavior in juveniles and adolescents for many years, also sees crime and delinquent behavior as largely a psychological process. Noting that behavior is significantly influenced by thinking, Samenow (1984) pointed out that criminals, including juvenile delinquents, think differently from responsible people and want different things from life. Far from accepting criminals or juvenile delinquents as "sick" or psychologically disturbed, Samenow views delinquents as very deliberate and measured in their actions. Although they subscribe to a system of rules that is highly egocentric and largely inconsistent with the fundamental philosophies of our society, criminals and delinquents are unusually logical and controlled when it comes to adhering to their own distorted values and thought processes.

Samenow believes that detailed analysis of the lives of criminals reveals that these individuals are liars, cheaters, destructive toward property, and aggressive toward other people even at a very young age. Setting aside the idea that children become

delinquent because their parents reject them, Samenow insists that it is the criminal, even as a child, who rejects his or her parents. Samenow examined a variety of explanations often provided for criminal behavior and basically dismisses them in favor of his psychological theories as to the etiology of such patterns. Samenow says it is the delinquent who rejects school, jobs, churches, and noncriminal friendships rather than the reverse. He believes that it is a serious error to attribute criminal behavior to the influence of peers, school, and so forth because this takes away what he sees as being the critical element in the etiology of criminal and delinquent behavior, that is, the choice that the delinquent or the adult criminal makes to reject school, gainful employment, socially acceptable friends, parental values, and a whole host of things that are more consistent with noncriminal patterns of behavior. He challenges the notion, for example, of delinquents being learning disabled or educationally handicapped. He notes that in many cases, criminals exhibit extraordinary intelligence, forethought, and restraint as they plan and execute their criminal activities. Therefore, the pivotal feature in the etiology of delinquent behavior, as Samenow sees it, is the deviant thinking patterns of the juvenile delinquent.

Yochelson and Samenow (1976) note that the delinquent often commits thinking errors. The delinquent then progresses from deviant thinking to deviant behavior. For example, they note that delinquents are highly sensitive to being "put down," due to a fear that if one appears weak, one will be reduced to nothing. Therefore, delinquents retaliate if put down because they fear that if they bend (allow this put-down to go without retaliation), they will break (not be perceived as a person with strength). In addition, the delinquent individual may not be able to understand another person's perspective. For example, even though delinquents may verbalize that it is wrong to lie, they may accept lies as part of life. In their mind, only a fool would tell the truth when it may result in unpleasant consequences.

IDENTIFICATION AND ASSESSMENT OF JUVENILE DELINQUENCY

The psychologist seeking to assess child and adolescent antisocial behavior must be aware that a high percentage of delinquent behaviors and juvenile crimes are committed by nondelinquents, that is, youngsters for whom there is no persistent, serious pattern of unlawful activity. McCandless and Evans (1973, p. 475) refer to this as the distinction between true delinquency and pseudodelinquency. A persistent, regular pattern of illegal activity is the most critical difference between the true delinquent and the one-time offender or the nonoffender. For this reason, anyone evaluating juvenile delinquents should not rely on court records. Court records report the most serious offenses committed but, by their nature, cannot address the pattern, either in its regularity or its severity (Erickson & Empey, 1963).

Recent developments in the assessment of antisocial behavior in children and adolescents have emphasized the need to broaden the assessment process beyond the individual child/adolescent to include multiple risk factors (such as individual genetic/neurological/characterological determinants and comorbidity of ADHD or learning disabilities) and environmental factors (such as SES, family environment, history of maltreatment, and deviant peer relationships or gang involvement) (Hinshaw & Zupan, 1997). Hinshaw and Zupan indicate that psychologists assessing children/adolescents for antisocial/delinquent behavior, should keep the following in mind:

1. The necessity of adopting a developmental approach.
2. The relevance of identifying specific subtypes of antisocial individuals and behaviors.
3. The importance of reliably detecting and defining comorbid conditions.
4. The challenges involved in amalgamating multi-informant data acquired across multiple settings (p. 37).

The clinician must be careful not to "diagnose delinquency." As mentioned earlier, delinquency is a phenomenological (Blos, 1961) and legal term. Because it does not clarify a "pathological condition," it is not a diagnostic term. The advent of the *Diagnostic and Statistical Manual of Mental Disorders* (*DSM-I*; American Psychiatric Association, 1952) provided the clinician with discrete diagnostic categories to be used in the differentiation of various psychiatric disorders. The most recent edition, *DSM-IV* (American Psychiatric Association, 1994), has several distinct disorders in which antisocial behavior of children and adolescents may

be classified. These include oppositional defiant disorder (ODD), conduct disorder (CD), and child or adolescent antisocial behavior (this diagnosis is ascribed when the child/adolescent exhibits isolated antisocial behaviors absent a pattern of antisocial behavior). In a recent review of the literature, Lahey and Loeber (1997), indicate that the diagnosis of attention-deficit/hyperactivity disorder (ADHD) often occurs comorbidly with ODD and CD. Furthermore, research indicates that the co-occurrence of ADHD and ODD/CD exacerbates the amount and severity of antisocial behavior (Lahey & Loeber, 1997; The reader is referred to the *DSM-IV* for a thorough description of each of the disorders). One potential problem with the checklist method of diagnosing using the *DSM-IV* is that the same diagnosis may mean very different things. For instance, to meet criteria for the diagnosis of CD, the child/adolescent must meet at least 3 of 15 potential criteria. This means there are over 455 potentially different combinations of CD symptoms (Gacono & Meloy, 1994).

Though the use of discrete diagnostic categories has been useful in describing and studying antisocial/delinquent behavior as it is exhibited in childhood/adolescence, experts in the field emphasize the need to also assess developmental and dimensional aspects (e.g., Robins & McEvoy, 1990; Rutter, 1997). Specifically, these authors and others underscore the need to assess for continuity or discontinuity of antisocial/delinquent behavior exhibited during different developmental stages (e.g., Loeber, 1988; Moffitt, 1993).

An evaluation of a juvenile exhibiting antisocial behavior must start with a complete history. This history should be drawn from various sources for the purpose of verification. The complete history is extremely important when an assessment is being conducted at the request of a court or in conjunction with court proceedings. One of the major concerns of juvenile courts is the living situation of the delinquent: how it contributes to the criminal pattern and what resources may be available to correct this pattern. The other major concern of a court requesting psychological evaluation is an assessment of the character structure of the delinquent (Piliavin & Briar, 1964).

In reference to an assessment of the character structure of the delinquent, courts are not looking for elaborate descriptions of the learning history or psychodynamic patterns of the delinquent. Instead, the courts are concerned with the degree to which the delinquent is a threat to the safety of the community. Potential for rehabilitation is, of course, an important concern, but satisfactory psychological evaluation of a delinquent will always weigh the potential for rehabilitation against the risks that are incurred by society in providing rehabilitation opportunities. For example, Miller (1958) identified six basic concerns of juveniles, particularly those from lower SES. In assessing the delinquent potential of a juvenile, Miller urges careful evaluation of the positive or negative valence that the youngster displays in each of these areas. Miller contends that such an evaluation will greatly improve the understanding of the juvenile's motivations and his or her orientation toward society and its values.

According to Miller (1958), the first concern to be evaluated as part of any assessment is the relative importance of staying out of trouble versus the degree to which trouble is welcomed as an opportunity to prove oneself. The definition of trouble is not absolute. It may refer to conflicts with peers or with family; however, in its most extreme form, trouble is defined as conflict with the law and other recognized social authorities. The second concern of juveniles that requires evaluation is the importance that the youngster places on being tough. In its most extreme form, being tough is seen as a sign of bravery and accomplishment. Third, intelligence is a concern for juvenile delinquents, but not in the traditional sense. A great deal about the youth can be learned by understanding the degree to which intelligence is believed to be the ability to outsmart people, to "run games." Sensation seeking is a fourth common concern of juveniles; many incidents of pseudodelinquency are, in fact, done for the excitement and thrill. Fifth, adolescents often see life as beyond their control; They see themselves as victims of fate with little or no sense of responsibility for what they do or what happens to them. Finally, authority is a basic concern of the adolescent. An adolescent's tendency to rebel against authority is common and is often pointed out in evaluation reports. However, it is important for an evaluation to assess the degree to which the youth rejects external authority as something that stands in the way of "getting what's coming to me."

Describing the process of risk assessment in corrections, a specific application of psychological evaluation in the criminal justice system, Eber presented a framework that would be useful in applying principles of psychological testing to the evaluation of the delinquent (Eber, 1976). First, the outcome of the evaluation should be uncontaminated by subjective data or by any data other than that necessary to determine which test should be used and how the results should be analyzed and reported. Additional information known to be useful should be determined, such as age at first arrest, number of prior arrests, disposition of previous cases, severity of offense, and social-family support systems.

Second, the evaluation should focus on those personal characteristics that are changeable as a function of maturity or intervention. To the degree possible, the evaluation should lead to recommendations based on the amount of change needed, the probability of such change occurring, the means by which such change can be brought about, and the risk involved to society.

The psychologist should have a systematic approach to the assessment of delinquents, making alterations in the procedure only when necessary. As much as possible, objective, empirically derived tests should be used. The procedures should be clear and easily explained to appropriate laypersons. The research supporting the procedures should also be understandable by those not necessarily familiar with psychological terminology. The recommendations should be clearly linked to the procedures used and the findings reported. Recommendations should be clear, observable, and measurable. As much as possible, the use of available resources should be stressed rather than scarce professional resources.

A fourth need is for some of the techniques of assessment, if not all, to be available when necessary and not be contingent on the availability of experts. There is often need for these techniques in rural areas, county jails, and other settings in which psychologists are not readily available. This need could be addressed through the use of paraprofessionals trained in the administration of psychological tests or by making certain screening tools available. Of course, the psychologist has the ethical obligation to ensure that these tools and techniques are used with appropriate consultation and supervision.

Finally, the adequacy of a procedure should be continually evaluated in terms of its accuracy and its errors. It is especially important to analyze the errors, that is, inaccurate assessments or inappropriate recommendations. This allows for the identification of systematic bias or other errors of measurement.

Monahan (1981) provided an outline for the clinical examination of potentially violent persons. Because acting-out behavior, both violent and nonviolent, is a primary concern in such an evaluation, Monahan's outline is appropriate as a model for the psychological evaluation of juvenile delinquents. The procedure is essentially a multimethod, multisource approach; that is, it uses a variety of psychological techniques and draws data from a variety of sources.

The best evaluations are those that break down complex problems into simpler questions. The psychologist must clarify the reason for the referral, the questions to be answered, and the purposes to which the report will be put. Before beginning the evaluation, the psychologist must determine if he or she is being asked to evaluate the adolescent with an emphasis on overall personality functioning, psychopathology, specific delinquent patterns, or a combination of all three. The emphasis may vary depending on the source of the referral and how the report will be used.

The multimethod, multisource approach suggests that the evaluation could consist of a standard interview as well as one or more self-report or behavioral checklists (e.g., the Child Behavior Checklist [CBCL]; Achenbach, 1991). Standardized interviews provide a more objective framework for gathering data. Significant people in the adolescent's life should be interviewed to give a complete description of the adolescent in a variety of experiences and settings. In the process of gathering this data, the psychologist should pay special attention to the circumstances and settings in which the delinquency or other behavior in question has occurred. For example, a method of assessment often used in controlled settings such as schools, penal institutions, and residential facilities is applied behavioral analysis (Bassett, Blanchard, & Koshland, 1975; H. Cohen & Filipczak, 1971; Winett & Winkler, 1972). Types of observations carried out in applied behavioral analysis can most easily be done in controlled settings. However, psychological evaluation of delinquents should include behavior analysis in any setting where the target behaviors can be clearly specified and where reliable measurement of these behaviors can be obtained. Utilizing behavior analysis, the psychologist gains a better understanding of the stresses to which the adolescent is subject and the characteristic behaviors, especially delinquent behaviors, that are exhibited in response to that stress. The gains that maintain the antisocial behavior can then be clarified.

Therefore, leaving the selection of individual tests to the psychologist, a sound battery consists of the following: an interview with the adolescent and significant others from whom data can be obtained; self-report measures for the adolescent and behavioral checklists to be completed by the adolescent and by significant others; a sound, standardized intelligence test; an empirically derived measure of psychopathology with norms appropriate for the individual being tested; an empirically derived test of personality that focuses on the assessment of dimensions of normal personality functioning rather than emphasizing psychopathology; observation of the adolescent's behavior in the natural environment; and miscellaneous screening instruments or tests to address questions specific to an individual case.

Unfortunately, psychological tests are not good predictors of violence, a reality that must be stressed because assessment of the potential for violence is often the reason for referral. Although several tests may aid in assessing the presence or absence of pathology that may contribute to violent acting-out, sole reliance on these scales will lead to drastic overprediction of violence. This not only risks clinical error but may lead to unnecessary legal restraints and sanctions being imposed, possibly to the point of violation of due process rights. Given the difficulty of predicting violence/antisocial behavior, Heilbrun (1999) differentiates between risk assessment to predict future antisocial behavior and risk assessment to manage the juvenile during treatment.

According to Heilbrun (1999), risk assessment focusing on prediction of antisocial behavior is concerned with what type of harm the individual may perpetrate over a specified time frame. This type of prediction is worded in terms of relative probability statements rather than dichotomous (yes/no) predictions. The assessment focusing on management of an individual emphasizes dynamic rather than static factors of the individual and environment. Heilbrun indicates that assessment of risk needs to bear in mind the base rates for a specific outcome for a specific population. The base rates are calculated from statistics gathered by the Office of Juvenile Justice and Delinquency Prevention, as well as other studies and sources. Based on these studies and statistics, a list of risk factors can be compiled that is useful in determining the potential risk for violence and so on. Of note, these risk factors are additive: the more risk factors present, the greater the likelihood of violent/antisocial behavior. For juveniles, the list of risk factors (Cornell, Peterson, & Richards, 1999; Farrington & Hawkins, 1991; Hawkins & Catalano, 1992; Office of Juvenile Justice and Delinquency Prevention [OJJDP], 1995) is consistent with the influential factors noted earlier in this chapter, and they include:

- Age at first referral or adjudication.
- Number of prior arrests.
- Number of out-of-home placements or institutional commitments.
- Academic achievement.
- School behavior and attendance.
- Substance abuse.
- Anger problems.
- Family stability.
- Parental control.
- Peer relationships.

Finally, Heilbrun (1999) provides some important suggestions for conducting an evaluation or risk assessment of a juvenile. Suggestions not covered elsewhere in this section include (p. 19 of handout):

- Ask the individual direct questions regarding:
  —Current thoughts, feelings, fantasies regarding violence.
  —History of violent behavior, including details of circumstances.
  —History of thoughts, feelings, fantasies regarding violence.
- Ask about experiences both as a victim and as a perpetrator.
- Use language that is understandable and less likely to increase defensiveness.
- "Push and back off" on questions regarding violence potential. (Be careful not to push the person to the point where he or she may become violent or defensive.)
- Ask the most problematic questions at the end of the overall evaluation, including confrontation regarding inconsistencies.

Certainly, there is a place for traditional clinical instruments in the evaluation of delinquents. These must be used with due regard for their limitations. Although there is no evidence that traditional instruments can clearly predict violent or dangerous behavior, results from evaluations using these instruments may be very helpful in devising a treatment/rehabilitation plan (Heilbrun, 1997). Recent advances in the field of psychological evaluation are pertinent to the evaluation of delinquent/antisocial behavior in children and adolescents. Some of the traditional instruments that have been revised to specifically address juveniles include the Minnesota Multiphasic Personality Inventory–Adolescent version (MMPI-A), Millon Adolescent Clinical Inventory (MACI), and research regarding the responses children and adolescents with conduct behavior problems provide on the Rorschach. One instrument that has been designed to specifically assess the element of psychopathy in individuals, the Psychopathy Checklist–Revised (PCL-R), is also reviewed.

MMPI-A/MMPI-2

Despite criticisms, the MMPI has been used to assess adolescents for delinquency and pathology for a number of years. Adolescent norms were developed for the original instrument. The MMPI-A (Butcher et al., 1992) was developed using adolescent subjects from both normative and clinical samples (Butcher et al., 1992; Williams, Butcher, Ben-Porath, & Graham, 1992) and separated by gender (Butcher & Williams, 1996). A distinct advantage for clinicians and researchers is that the normative distribution for both the MMPI-A and the MMPI-2 are the same. Therefore, comparisons can be made between MMPI-A scores collected when the subject was an adolescent and MMPI-2 scores collected as an adult (Butcher & Williams, 1996). A sixth-grade reading level is required for self-administration, but a standardized tape recording of the items is available from the publisher (NCS Assessments).

As with any assessment instrument, it is important that the entire protocol be used in any interpretation; however, MMPI-A standard scales noted to assess behaviors associated with delinquency are scale 4 (Psychopathic Deviate), scale 6 (Paranoia), and scale 9 (Mania) (Pena, Megargee, & Brody, 1996). Specifically, high scores on scale 4 are associated with a higher incidence of externalizing behavior (cheating, stealing, etc.), running away, and physical abuse (boys) or sexual abuse (girls) (Butcher & Williams, 1996). High scores on scale 9 are associated with school problems, drug use, and possible poor motivation for treatment/rehabilitation (Butcher & Williams, 1996). Like the MMPI-2, the MMPI-A also includes content scales (devised of face-valid items that assess a specific content area) that inform the clinician about problem areas. Examples of content scales that are specifically pertinent to the assessment of delinquency are conduct problems, family problems, school problems, anger, and negative treatment indicators.

MACI

Another objective personality measure that has been redesigned and normed to specifically assess adolescents is MACI (McCann 1997; Millon, 1993). The MACI is a 160-item objective personality inventory that is appropriate for adolescents age 13 to 19, based on Theodore Millon's theory of personality and psychiatric disorders as described in *DSM-IV*. As with the MMPI-A, a sixth-grade reading level is required for self-administration, but a standardized tape recording of the items is available from the publisher (NCS Assessments). Several scales specifically assess for delinquent and aggressive behaviors. Some of these scales include 6A, which assesses the tendency to engage in impulsive, antisocial behavior; 6B, which assesses the tendency to engage in aggressive and sadistic behavior; 8A, which assesses the tendency to engage in oppositional-defiant behavior; and a clinical syndrome scale called the Delinquency Predisposition Scale, which assesses the adolescent's propensity to engage in delinquent behavior. Given the relative newness of the MACI as an assessment instrument, little research has been completed with the instrument.

RORSCHACH

Gacono and Meloy (1994) have completed research regarding the use of the Rorschach Inkblot Test in the assessment of antisocial/psychopathic personality. Utilizing a combination of structural systems—Exner's Comprehensive System (Exner, 1994), the Mutuality of Autonomy scale to assess for object relations within Rorschach records (Urist,

1977), and content interpretation of Rorschach records—they have combined the psychostructural (Exner system) aspects of the test with the psychodynamic aspects of the individual. Building on Cleckley's (1976/1941) and Hare's (1991) description of a psychoapathic personality, they have identified several factors in the Rorschach that may be useful in the assessment of children and adolescents with antisocial behavior. Although additional research is needed, Gacono and Meloy report that children with CD differ from normal controls in the following ways:

- Conduct disordered children and adolescents have more difficulty regulating their emotions (Affective ratio).
- Aggressive responses are actually lower for CD children and adolescents (indication that AG scores on the Rorschach should not be used to predict future aggression for this population).
- Conduct disordered children tend to perceive reality differently from others (fewer Popular responses; X+% and F+% significantly below average).
- Conduct disordered children and adolescents do not expect cooperation with others (COP = 0 for 60% of CD children compared to COP = 0 for 3% of normal control children; COP = 0 for 39% and 48% of adolescent males and females, respectively, compared to COP = 0 for only 11% of the normal population).
- Conduct disordered children and adolescents (especially adolescent females) compare themselves negatively to other children (Egocentricity < .33 in 72% of the cases).
- Conduct disordered children tend to produce "significantly more narcissistic, malevolent, and destructive object relational precepts on the Rorschach, suggesting that their internal representations of self and others are governed by these same troublesome and psychopathological characteristics" (p. 32).

PCL-R

The PCL-R is an instrument devised for the clinical assessment of adult males in forensic settings. Recent research has been completed that validates the

PCL-R for adolescent male offenders (Forth, Hart, & Hare, 1990). Administration of the PCL-R includes a semistructured interview and collateral information (Hare, 1991). The interview and administration of the instrument take approximately 60 minutes. The modified version of the PCL-R used in the above study had 18 items. (The adult version has 20 items.) Responses to the questions included in the interview are scored as per the guidelines in the manual. Studies have shown that individuals scoring in the severe range (≥ 30) have committed more illegal/violent offenses, are less likely to respond to treatment/intervention, and are more likely to reoffend (Christian, 1996). Heilbrun (1999) indicates that the PCL-R is the one instrument that is shown to have some credibility in predicting future violence/antisocial behavior.

TREATMENT AND REHABILITATION OF THE DELINQUENT

There is virtually unanimous agreement that effective treatment and rehabilitation (assuming "rehabilitation" is the appropriate term) of juvenile delinquents is a complex process involving a variety of individuals and institutions, including, but not limited to, the courts, including juvenile court, family court, district court, federal court; social service and mental health agencies, including welfare departments and mental health departments; law enforcement agencies; schools, including regular junior high and high school programs as well as vocational and technical schools; corrections departments, both juvenile corrections and adult corrections; and a wide assortment of professionals from a variety of disciplines who provide services through these public facilities and through the private sector.

Because juvenile delinquency is a legal concept, effective treatment and rehabilitation of juvenile delinquents of necessity involves the court system. In recent years, a number of changes have taken place around the country in courts that deal with juvenile offenders. In virtually every state, laws have been passed that give special consideration to the actions of juveniles, usually defined as those 15 years of age and younger. The theory behind this change may have been praiseworthy, but in its practical application, many of the changes that

have resulted in the court system as a result of these laws have made it extremely difficult, and in some cases impossible, to deal effectively with juvenile delinquency.

Kramer (1988) analyzes some of these developments in detail. She notes that many of these laws were meant, philosophically, not to determine guilt or punishment for juvenile offenders but rather to emphasize the age of the alleged offender over the nature and quality of the act. This led, according to Kramer, to an emphasis on, first of all, protecting the legal rights of the juveniles and affording due process of law. The second effect was to emphasize benevolent and nonpunitive treatment of juveniles so that all decisions reached would be "in the best interest of the child." Furthermore, any treatment or punishment given by society to the juvenile because of his or her actions was to be carried out in the "least restrictive environment."

Many experts believe that the most significant change in the system as a result of these efforts has not been improvement in the protection of the juveniles, nor in the protection of society, but rather the introduction of defense lawyers and all of the resulting complications. The defense lawyers enter the proceedings with the sole intended purpose of "getting my client off." This has led to a host of legal maneuvers that slow down the legal proceedings. The juvenile courts now closely resemble the adult courts. Many cases never come to trial because they are thrown out on technicalities. Many acts that are considered felonies if committed by an adult are dealt with in an entirely different fashion when the perpetrator is a juvenile. Juveniles are frequently remanded to the custody of their parents, which results merely in a return to the environment that has already become the setting for a pattern of criminal behaviors. In many jurisdictions, the previous records of juveniles are closed after disposition of a particular case, so courts trying subsequent cases are often unaware of the seriousness of a given juvenile's criminal behavior pattern. As a result, these juveniles often are released back to the streets or to some facility with inadequate supervision and security. Anyone who has dealt with juvenile delinquents with any frequency is aware that many of them believe they have nothing to fear from the legal system, that "you can't do nothing to me because of my age." No one would deny that excessive punishment of juvenile delinquents is counterproductive. However, it is Kramer's contention, and that of many in the field, that the "best interest of the child" has, in practice, been protected at the expense of the best interest of society.

The Task Force on Juvenile Delinquency of the Supreme Court of the State of New Jersey (1989) also acknowledges significant judicial problems in dealing with juvenile delinquency:

> Societal and familial problems which produce abhorrent juvenile behavior, including delinquency, will soon overwhelm both the Judiciary and the State and local government agencies associated with the courts—if present trends continue. . . . the Division's records show thousands of troubled youngsters with deeply-rooted problems not likely to be ameliorated by the approaches and resources being applied. (p. 1)

The report cites four reasons the current Code of Juvenile Justice in New Jersey has not fulfilled expectations. The similarity of statutes in other states makes these conclusions seem relevant for other jurisdictions as well. First, the Task Force concluded that courts must deal with juveniles in isolation and notes the reluctance of judges to exercise the necessary authority to order parental involvement and to impose sanctions for failure to comply. Second, various state departments have often failed to develop the necessary services for juvenile offenders with special needs. This is especially true in the public sector. Third, various jurisdictions differ widely in the dispositions handed down in juvenile delinquency cases, particularly with respect to juvenile sex offenders. Finally, states have failed to adopt appropriate legislation or establish services for developmentally disabled juveniles who are delinquent, although the statutes in many states prohibit these youngsters from being incarcerated. This is an area in which the deference to the age of the offender over the nature of the offense is very apparent.

Therefore, a major issue to be confronted is the difficulty that courts now experience in making proper disposition of delinquent youngsters. If legal maneuvering fails to "get the kid off," the range of options available to the courts, particularly in the public sector, usually fails to meet the needs of the population. Even in those cases where children age 12 or 13 years have deliberately and repeatedly engaged in violent, even hideous, crimes against persons, the courts often find themselves unable to properly remand the child because of a lack of resources, lack of access to the child's prior records,

or a host of other safeguards that, unfortunately, have served to make the juvenile delinquent almost immune to prosecution rather than to further "the best interest of the child."

A number of noble, but ineffective, untested, even ill-conceived solutions have been offered. Some fundamental issues seem to repeatedly escape lawmakers and policymakers. For example, several years ago, programs were developed along the "Scared Straight" model in which potential offenders were brought into maximum security adult facilities and required to face adult inmates. These inmates, using the language of the streets, told the youngsters their own histories and what it was like to be "behind the walls." The thinking was that such an experience would discourage a significant percentage of these youngsters from engaging in delinquent behaviors. In recent years, talk shows have confronted adolescents on TV, taken them to boot camps, the morgue, and so forth, in an attempt to "shock" them into changing their behavior. However, studies have failed to prove that these type of programs (others include boot camps and mock incarceration) have the desired deterrent effect (Lipsey, 1992). Many of the youngsters, rather than being intimidated by the inmates, were impressed by their own ability to stand face to face with them. In addition, many of the juveniles decided that prison life was not so bad and "if they can take it, so can I." In a sense, the ability to withstand such an experience was almost the measure of the child's masculinity or toughness.

However, the overriding problem is simply that juveniles see no reason to fear punishment, no matter how severe, if they can beat the system. Many juveniles, especially those most in need of adjudication, namely, the habitual offenders, know how to beat the system by legal maneuvering, feigned remorse, and a host of other measures. In fact, many of the most violent offenders are so adept at beating the system that they are more likely to avoid incarceration or other serious punishment than less serious offenders. Kramer (1988) reports a study undertaken by an attorney in a New York family court in 1985. Examining the first three-month period of 1985, she found that only 44% of juveniles convicted of having committed a serious felony, such as homicide, rape, robbery, sexual abuse, or sodomy, were institutionalized. However, during the same period of time, 58% of those convicted of less serious crimes, such as larceny or robbery without violence, were institutionalized.

Therefore, an important step in addressing the problem of juvenile delinquency will involve looking at the laws defining juvenile crime and the sanctions for these crimes. In addition, attention must be paid to the internal workings of the courts that deal with juvenile offenders. The availability of resources will be of little use if laws do no permit judges to assign those juveniles in need of higher levels of security to an appropriate level of security. No other vehicle in society—schools, psychologists, families—can effectively address juvenile delinquency without appropriate legal support. A variety of proposals have been offered, including sentencing guidelines that remove discretion and put forth mandatory sentences for certain offenses. There are many objections to these, some of which are quite valid. However, it is important for us to reevaluate our current methods of bringing juveniles to justice. Specifically with respect to psychological treatment, the voluntary treatment versus coerced treatment issue is an important one, and a dialogue between the legislative and psychological community is imperative to implement appropriate standards and procedures.

Individual therapy with juvenile delinquents is extremely difficult, requiring not merely skill but extreme patience. Many of the traditional psychological models, based on psychopathology and abnormal psychology, do not adequately explain juvenile delinquency. For example, Rogerian therapy, or client-centered therapy, makes certain assumptions that, although clinically appropriate with many populations, may have exactly the opposite effect with juvenile delinquents. "Unconditional positive regard," a necessary clinical stance for the therapist using client-centered therapy, is often seen by delinquents not as acceptance, but as gullibility, a weakness or naïveté to be exploited. On the other hand, many advocates of behavior therapy have said that we, as a clinical community, should avoid theoretical positions and hypotheses about juvenile delinquent behavior and should deal strictly with the behavior. One of the many underlying assumptions is that effective control of the contingencies allows for the control of behavior. Many delinquents, however, have shown themselves to be remarkably resistant and resilient when it comes to withstanding behavioral techniques involving extinction, punishment, or positive and negative reinforcement.

Samenow (1984) believes that juvenile delinquents cannot be rehabilitated because they have never been "habilitated." He believes that juvenile delinquents are individuals who have engaged in a repetitive pattern of offenses, some serious and others less so, over a period of years. Based on his work, Samenow insists that patterns of delinquent behavior, even those predictive of adult criminal behavior, are well ingrained before the age of 13 or 14. According to Samenow, juvenile delinquents have a completely different set of values, think according to a completely different set of rules, and are fundamentally uninterested in living cooperatively according to society's norms. He was very critical of traditional clinical models regarding such things as insight, stating that insight not only permits further criminal behavior but frequently becomes a rationalization or justification for continuation of the criminal patterns, even while in residential therapy settings.

Recognizing the significant contributions to his own thinking by his mentor, Samuel Yochelson, Samenow insists that the behavior of criminals can change only with a dramatic alteration in their thinking. Delinquents must be challenged to accept that their lives have been a pattern of self-centered and criminal behavior, based on a desire to be slick enough to fool others and to get away with anything and everything possible. It is necessary to change delinquents' notion of themselves as victim to that of victimizer. Efforts to "change" must be challenged as efforts merely to look good rather than to make substantial improvement. Samenow describes a method of intervention that is confrontive and challenging and that essentially attempts to defeat every attempt by delinquents to rationalize or justify their behavior or to project responsibility onto anyone else or any event. It is meant to force delinquents to assume more responsibility for their behavior and to accept that the problem rests not in society or the clinician's failure to understand them, but rather in their failure to understand the clinician and society. The clinician continually confronts the delinquent with a picture of himself or herself as a liar, a manipulator, and a person constantly in a state of turmoil due to fear, insecurity, and self-doubt. Samenow challenges the notion that the delinquent is someone who is irrational, impulsive, or unable to think clearly. Rather, he believes that delinquents are usually very calculating in their execution of their plans and demonstrate an ability to think very clearly when it comes to the commission of their acts or to constructing a defense. Samenow acknowledges that individual therapy can play an important part, but also stresses the importance of milieu-type therapies for some of the more hard-core offenders who are unable or unwilling to profit from any therapy unless the security and restraints are powerful.

Unlike Samenow, Dodge, and Schwartz (1997) contend that delinquent behavior is the result of problems in the social information processing (SIP) mechanisms of the juvenile delinquent. When the child/adolescent has not learned to effectively process social information, maladaptive behavior results. The SIP theory asserts that there are six stages involved in the processing of social information (Dodge & Schwartz, 1997, p. 172):

1. *Encoding of social cues into short term memory.* At this stage, the child attends to those cues that seem important to the immediate situation. If experience has taught the child to be leery of situations such as the one he is in, he may only attend to social cues which are confirming to a view that the situation is threatening.
2. *Interpretation of social cues.* At this stage, the attributions that the child/adolescent places on the situation become important. He attempts to determine the motives of the individuals involved in the situation. He may perceive a non-threatening situation as threatening.
3. *Clarification of goals for the current situation.* Next, the child/adolescent determines what the goals are for the current situation. These may be mediated by past experience or current feeling states.
4. *Response access or construction.* The child/adolescent then processes how he has handled similar situations in the past. He may consider, "What type of past responses may be appropriate for this current situation?"
5. *Response evaluation and decision.* At this stage, the child/adolescent considers all of the options for behaving available to him. At this stage, morality or expected outcomes for the situation will be considered.
6. *Behavioral enactment.* The child/adolescent acts upon the chosen response.

Treatment and prevention programs that have been developed based on the SIP model attempt to impact the attributions through the teaching of social skills, development of problem-solving skills, and anger management. Experts in the field suggest that the maximum benefit of these programs would be actualized as a preventive treatment. Some studies have found that teaching these skills resulted in a 24% lower recidivism rate for those youngsters receiving skills training compared to a control group that did not receive the training (Lipsey, 1992). Lending support to Samenow's contention that juvenile delinquents need habilitation rather than rehabilitation, Kazdin (1995) indicated that even with skills training, many juvenile delinquent youth will still not possess the same level of skills as youth from a normative sample.

Building on social learning theory, Webster-Stratton (1996) developed an intervention and prevention program that uses observations of models on videotape and role playing to intervene with parents of oppositional and conduct disordered children. Webster-Stratton also developed a modeling/role play intervention to increase the social skills of the children as well. Combined, these interventions have been shown to significantly reduce behavior problems, while increasing prosocial behaviors (Webster-Stratton, 1996). Kazdin (1996) also describes a combined Problem Solving Skills Training (PSST) for conduct disordered children with a Parent Management Training (PMT). Results of Kazdin's studies concur with results from Webster-Stratton that programs that address skill development in both children and parents are more effective than programs that address only either children or parents.

Realizing that there are multiple factors/influences affiliated with the development and maintenance of delinquent/antisocial behavior among adolescents, Henggeler et al. (1994) developed a model that simultaneously impacts the various systems relevant to an adolescent's life (i.e., school, legal, family, peers, neighborhood, individual, and other community agencies/institutions). Henggeler's Multi-Systemic Treatment (MST) model is designed to intervene in each, or all, of these relevant settings for the adolescent. Therefore, MST provides a model of intervention for the adolescent in his or her "world." The therapist and the adolescent's family derive relevant and appropriate treatment goals.

Therapists utilizing MST are held accountable for the progress of their clients and are encouraged to "do whatever it takes" to engage their clients and the families in treatment (Henggeler et al., 1994). Studies have shown that MST is effective in reducing the recidivism rate of adolescent antisocial/delinquent behavior (Henggeler, Schoenwald, Borduin, Rowland, & Cunningham, 1998).

MST is based on nine principles outlined in detail in the treatment manual (Henggeler et al., 1994):

1. The primary purpose of assessment is to understand the fit between the identified problems and their broader systemic context.
2. Therapeutic contacts should emphasize the positive and use systemic strengths as levers for change.
3. Interventions should be designed to promote responsible behavior and decrease irresponsible behavior among family members.
4. Interventions should be present-focused and action-oriented, targeting specific and well-defined problems.
5. Interventions should target sequences of behavior within or between multiple systems.
6. Interventions should be developmentally appropriate and fit the development needs of youth.
7. Interventions should be designed to require daily or weekly effort by family members.
8. Intervention efficacy is evaluated continuously from multiple perspectives.
9. Interventions should be designed to promote treatment generalization and long-term maintenance of therapeutic change.

At times, the juvenile's behavior problems will be so severe that he or she will not be able to be maintained at home, but not so severe that he or she will need to be placed in a juvenile detention center. Chamberlain (1996) describes an Intensified Foster Care (IFC) program based on some of the same principles as Henggeler's MST. Foster parents are specially trained to address the adolescent's needs and behavior. Case managers and therapists consult with the foster parents and school personnel on a daily basis to address any problems encountered during the placement. Results indicate that this program has been effective in reducing the recidivism rate for participants, and a cost-benefit analysis indicated that when compared to the monetary cost of treating control subjects through conventional treatment means, IFC treatment realized significant savings by reducing recidivism rates and allowing the adolescents to be treated at a less restrictive level of care.

Needless to say, other approaches to individual and group therapy of juvenile delinquents draw on a variety of other theoretical orientations to psychotherapy and psychopathology. Psychoanalysts have addressed the etiology and treatment of juvenile delinquency. Blos (1961) reported that insight is inaccessible to delinquents because their acting-out is ego-syntonic. If the delinquent behaviors start in adolescence following a period of latency, Blos believes the prognosis is favorable. The goal in this psychoanalytic approach is to make the delinquent behavior a neurotic symptom rather than a symptom equivalent. As the resulting conflicts emerge, they can be treated through psychoanalysis. However, numerous studies over several decades have failed to confirm the effectiveness of psychoanalysis as a treatment modality for delinquent behavior.

Because family influences are important in the evolution of juvenile delinquency, family therapy is an important tool in the rehabilitative process (Alexander, Barton, Schiavo, & Parsons, 1976). In addition to MST described above, Bell (1975) offered four reasons in support of the value of traditional family therapy in the rehabilitation of the delinquent. First, the family is the smallest, most important social group of which the delinquent is a member. Second, the family plays a basic role in the etiology of delinquent patterns of behavior and provides a vehicle through which the problem can be addressed at one of its sources. Third, family therapy provides the opportunity to reduce the pressure within the family that elicits criminal responses on the part of the adolescent. Finally, the family can help supply the delinquent with the motivation and strength necessary to change behaviors. An important contribution of Bell's work is his discussion of the role of family therapy in the rehabilitation of the institutionalized offender, a situation that is common but unfortunately often overlooked.

Family therapy can provide a means of prevention as well as rehabilitation. Klein, Alexander, and Parsons (1977) offered a model of prevention using family therapy that was intended to reduce recidivism and sibling delinquency. Delinquency was defined as a function of the disintegration of the family system in which the delinquent resides. This disintegration is likely to facilitate the development of a criminal pattern in several of the children, particularly in those families where one child has already engaged in extensive delinquent activity. The goal of therapy in these cases is to improve the disrupted patterns of communication that are seen as contributing to the disintegration of the family. It is anticipated that improving the clarity of communication within the family will make communicating the values of society and in reinforcing compliance with these values more effective.

The family's role in a treatment and rehabilitation process is important in ways other than through participating in family therapy. Kramer (1988) noted a tendency growing progressively worse in the latter half of this century for families to presume that some other entity, usually one supported by public funds, should be responsible for the failure of delinquents to live within the law or to be effectively treated and rehabilitated. Kramer documents many instances in which parents and others held "the system" responsible for the delinquent behavior of juveniles, stating that the delinquency occurred because the youth was unable to get the help that he or she needed. This tendency of many families, especially parents, to hold failures of the system, rather than themselves, responsible for the problems of their children may parallel the progressive deterioration in the family unit as the fundamental and basic unit of society. Many people interested in addressing the problem of delinquency bemoan the absence of any single agency or institution capable of helping those children who find it difficult to cope with the responsibilities of life in modern society, such as lawful behavior and school attendance.

Kramer (1988) suggested that such an institution does exist—the intact family. However, Kramer added that the intact family has unfortunately become unavailable to larger numbers of children. Thus, whether it is through family therapy or other means, it is absolutely necessary to take steps at all levels to turn the tide of disintegration of families and to reestablish the family as the most fundamental unit of society and the one with the primary responsibility of teaching children and adolescents to live within the law. The Task Force on Juvenile Delinquency of the Supreme Court of the State of New Jersey (1989) agreed, noting that

40% of juvenile delinquents are victims of family neglect, including substance abuse and criminality. Stressing the responsibility of the family for seeing that delinquent behavior is corrected, the Task Force went on to suggest that the court can order treatment and, in the case of families with adequate resources, can demand that the families rather than the state bear the cost of treatment.

Some factors, however, must be considered when attempting to enlist the aid of the family in dealing with juvenile delinquents. A very common problem experienced by professionals dealing with juvenile delinquents is the frustration of parents with the juvenile and the resulting unwillingness of these parents to cooperate in therapeutic attempts. There is increasing agreement that parents should not be allowed to walk away from such responsibilities by turning the care and custody of their adolescent children over to the state or to other public agencies. The Task Force said:

> The court should view the family from two perspectives: (a) to understand how the family contributes to the child's development; and (b) to determine the family's capacity to control and care for the juvenile. . . . A major hypothesis of the Task Force is that if and when New Jersey data concerning juvenile delinquents are developed, their families will also be found at many points along the similar continuum of health-pathology or function-dysfunction. Virtually every family can be a productive partner with the court, service agencies, and others in addressing their family problems. . . . A growing number of studies has proposed that the familial experience can prevent or contribute to juvenile delinquency; or if a child is already engaging in delinquent behavior, the family can successfully intervene and deter the child from future delinquent acts. Family, then, is recognized as the primary institution responsible for protecting, disciplining, and nurturing children. (1989, p. 25)

Noting that states cannot "parent" the thousands of juvenile delinquents confronted annually, a major objective of the juvenile justice reforms carried out in New Jersey involved the extension of the family's responsibilities. The New Jersey Code of Criminal Justice is cited, in which the court is given the authority to:

> order the parents or guardian of the juvenile to participate in appropriate programs or services when the court has found either that such person's omission or conduct was a significant contributing factor towards

the commission of the delinquent act, or, under its authority to enforce litigant's rights that such person's omission or conduct has been a significant contributing factor towards the ineffective implementation of a court order previously entered in relation to the juvenile. (1989, p. 26)

The report of the Task Force repeatedly asserted the critical and essential role to be played by parents and family in all programs and services for juvenile delinquents. The report said that refusal by parents, guardians, and other family members to comply with court orders requiring parental involvement in all programs and services related to juveniles manifests disrespect for the court and thwarts the juvenile's rehabilitation. Therefore, the Task Force urged that courts be given the authority to bring the full force of the law to bear on such individuals who refuse to comply and encouraged empowering courts to monitor compliance closely. When compliance is not demonstrated, the Task Force recommended that courts be given the authority to use civil or even criminal contempt procedures to assure parental involvement and that violation of a parental involvement order be considered by the court to be a separate disorderly person's offense committed by the parent or guardian in the case at hand.

The experience of many therapists is that therapy can be effective. However, many therapists have concerns about requiring people to participate in therapy. Psychologists and others in the mental health field must recognize that there is increasing pressure to deal with social problems. If our current psychotherapeutic techniques do not permit effective work with individuals who were coerced into therapy, even if those individuals pose serious threats to society, then we must turn our efforts to the development of such techniques that will work.

At this point, it is useful to note that, even in poorly socialized families, few authorities categorically advocate breaking ties between the delinquent and the family. However, in those instances where it becomes impossible to keep the delinquent with his or her family, halfway houses or group-living homes are thought to be more capable of providing supportive and therapeutic environments than the more traditional large institutions. The halfway houses and group-living homes represent attempts to emphasize a family model of interdependence and mutual support in a clearly defined program.

Such programs often utilize a token economy model that stresses that bad behavior has bad consequences (i.e., punishment) and does not necessarily require an assumption of pathology needing clinical intervention (Fersch, 1979).

Residential treatment is not new. It represented one of the first extensions of psychoanalysis following World War I. Aichhorn (1935) based this model on the belief that delinquents failed to learn delayed gratification (a common psychoanalytic theory, as noted earlier) and that deficiencies in superego controls resulted. The goal of treatment was to allow the delinquents to gratify impulses with no restrictions and to allow them to suffer the consequences of their own actions.

The current approaches, stressing the token economy (Allyon & Milan, 1979; Phillips, Phillips, Fixsen, & Wolf, 1973) and social skills training (Freedman, Rosenthal, Donahoe, Schlundt, & McFall, 1978), are well-known. These programs are based on social learning and behavior therapy approaches. Just as modeling is thought to facilitate the acquisition of deviant behavior, so too these influences, with appropriate reinforcement and punishment, are thought to be capable of modifying the deviant patterns of behavior. Critical variables involved in the development of such social learning programs include not merely the modeling of appropriate behaviors, but the identification of circumstances in which these appropriate behaviors are to be demonstrated. In addition, the ability of the delinquent to identify with the role model is critical. Thus, staff members who have more credibility include those of social and ethnic backgrounds similar to the delinquent's, those who have had similar juvenile experiences, and those who are able to help the delinquent make the cognitive connection between certain situational variables and the appropriate and inappropriate behaviors to be demonstrated. It is very important that such programs emphasize the contingencies that arise from the demonstration of appropriate and inappropriate behaviors and allow the delinquent to be exposed, as much as possible, to these consequences. An integral part of such social learning programs is, of course, the influence of peers relative to the demonstration of appropriate behavior patterns and even the vicarious learning that can take place by observing the consequences of certain patterns of behavior in peers.

Samenow (1984) also advocates group therapy. These groups, however, are much more structured than usual therapy groups and are highly directed in that the therapist, not the group members, runs the meetings. As might be expected, greater emphasis is placed on the exposition of thoughts and sequences of thoughts into understandable patterns. Group members, many of whom are at varying points in the change process, are then asked to comment on and discuss the specific thoughts as well as the patterns and to draw the connection between these thoughts and the specific behaviors that might be appropriate or inappropriate within the societal context. The leader, however, does not permit freewheeling discussion but vigorously engages in challenging and correcting errors in thinking for the person speaking as well as for the entire group. Samenow notes that the challenges and standards in these groups, specifically citing those conducted by his late colleague, Samuel Yochelson, are far more strict and confrontive than almost anything the delinquent could expect to find in the community. Specific attention is paid to the criminal tendency to lie; consequently, therapists in residential facilities and in groups must constantly look for objective verification of what the criminal reports.

A great deal of work remains to be done in the development of effective treatment programs for juvenile delinquents. A variety of techniques exist. At the present time, however, it seems that the most profitable research will focus on attempting to match the delinquents to variables such as age, sex, and offense, as well as to types of therapies, settings, qualifications of therapists, and length of treatment (Kazdin, 1996). In fact, the introduction of psychotherapy, in its traditional sense, as a means of treating juvenile delinquency or adult criminality may actually have backfired. Clinicians who have treated delinquents or criminals in reasonably large numbers can attest that many of these individuals have learned to exploit the theories of psychopathology and personality and to cite significant events in their past as causes of the behaviors for which they are incarcerated. Delinquents and criminals can rationalize their criminal patterns of behavior because parents were too strict or too lenient, they were overindulged or deprived, their parents were overprotective or negligent, they were too influenced by peer pressure, or they had too few friends and were alienated as youths. Criminals and delinquents have often used these theoretical concepts to explain away their own decisions to

engage in criminal patterns of behavior. Yochelson and Samenow went directly to the heart of this issue by asserting that the criminal who had no excuses or cause for his or her actions before being in psychotherapy would, after psychotherapy, have many causes, excuses, and justifications for such actions. Certainly, psychology, as a study of behavior, has much to contribute to the understanding of juvenile delinquent patterns. However, we must rethink our current theories and techniques, encourage the development of new theories and techniques, and submit these to critical examination.

CONCLUSION

It may be idealistic to hope for a society free of crime and delinquency. Some degree of deviation in the form of crime and delinquency may be inevitable and part of the natural order of things in a free and democratic society. Furthermore, for the most part, crime and delinquency are not absolutes, but are highly determined by factors that change over time as a result of modifications in the law and changes in social customs. Only time will yield the truth, if any truth exists, and history will have to be the ultimate judge of how well we in the twentieth century studied, understood, and effectively responded to crime and delinquency.

Some simple facts do appear to be evident. First, the steps that we have taken in recent decades to control juvenile delinquency have not worked. Not only has there been no decrease in the incidence of juvenile delinquency, but the severity of crimes being committed by progressively younger juveniles has increased dramatically. Violence perpetrated by juveniles is no less serious or lethal than the violence perpetrated by adults. Regular news reports frequently remind us of this fact. Reports of gang violence and school shootings, often thought to be related to the ready availability of firearms, also remind us of the increasing seriousness of juvenile crimes of violence against both property and people.

Kramer (1988) notes that the few violent youngsters who are responsible for most of these serious crimes start their criminal careers early, come from broken homes and are frequently born of teenage mothers, have been victims of child abuse, and have grown up with serious psychological disorders that our present therapies do not effectively address.

Unfortunately, with many of these young people, nothing that has been tried has been shown to work in terms of rehabilitating them, although such an admission may be abhorrent to our collective mentality and our desire to maintain our view of the "innocent child." In addition, efforts to change the basic attitudes of violent juveniles, to increase their empathy or consideration of social codes, do not necessarily improve the ability of these juveniles to control their impulses, a critical feature of controlling violent behavior. Consequently, for many of these young people, the only deterrent to impulsively engaging in criminal activity is the certainty of swift sanctions perceived as punishment directly linked to their offensive behavior. Because there is evidence that certain incapacitation through incarceration has some effect on deterring and reducing crime, the Justice Department's Office of Juvenile Justice and Delinquency Prevention recommended in 1986 that state legislatures adopt a system of fixed penalties for convicted juveniles. The punishment would fit the crime and would also be predictable and fair, doing away with what many have perceived to be the irrational discrepancies resulting from the judge's powers of discretion in disposition. Marvin Wolfgang, a well-known student of crime and criminal behavior, strongly endorses the notion that it is the seriousness of the crime, not the age of the criminal, that should dictate the punishment. Wolfgang strongly opposes special treatment for juvenile offenders who commit violent and serious offenses (Tracy, Wolfgang, & Figlio, 1985). Of course, the implications of such a step are significant. It involves consideration of such delicate and controversial issues as a death sentence or life sentence for juveniles, mandatory sentences of predetermined length regardless of factors often thought to be mitigating circumstances, such as family background, clinical history, and environmental factors. And yet, the data make clear that many serious adult offenders are juvenile offenders who "got away" with several very serious offenses prior to the age of 16, 17, or 18 simply because of their "innocent age." Kramer and the New Jersey State Supreme Court's Task Force on Juvenile Delinquency (1989) both give a great deal of attention to the role of the schools and education in the rehabilitation of juvenile delinquents. Although Yochelson and Samenow (1976) and Samenow (1984) may well be right in their assertion that the delinquent is not the victim of an inferior school system, but rather is

responsible for his or her school failures, nonetheless the data show that high dropout rates are positively correlated with high rates of delinquency. Steps taken to lower the dropout rate have frequently been shown to have a beneficial effect on the incidence of delinquent behavior in given communities. This may be because increased educational responsibilities give delinquents less time on the streets, or it may be because it gives the school greater opportunity to teach acceptable social values. Certainly, keeping juveniles in school gives them the educational preparation to pursue alternatives to criminal acts. Having a marketable skill or sound preparation for college does not itself turn juveniles away from criminal acts. For those juveniles who do wish to turn away from delinquent behavior patterns, however, the availability of such alternatives makes the transition easier. Therefore, as a society, we must address our educational needs far more vigorously than we seem to be doing at present. Nationally, education remains notoriously underfunded amid a flurry of political rhetoric about how important education really is. The value of education must be emphasized through appropriate levels of funding and through the passage of laws that give the school and other agencies sufficient authority to carry out their mission safely and effectively by bringing appropriate pressure to bear on students and parents. Furthermore, as we consider the necessary punishments or sanctions for delinquent behavior, we must include consideration of the educational resources necessary in juvenile residential facilities or juvenile correctional facilities and give these educational resources priority commensurate with their importance in the rehabilitation of juvenile offenders.

In all probability, no one discipline has all of the answers. We may find that delinquency and crime result from causes and determinants that are quite broad and varied, including significant social problems, such as poverty, and psychological and learning factors as well as physiological and biological causes. A final basic point must be stressed: Although the pressure to provide services, to "counsel" or "rehabilitate," is great, the need for continuing research, thought, and study is paramount. Our present methods of assessment and intervention are inadequate. A basic reason for this inadequacy is that we do not yet fully understand the problem. The answers cannot be found either in extreme permissiveness or in a punitive mentality of vigilantism. The simplicity of these options makes them very attractive to some who are frustrated by rising crime rates and perceived disruption in the social system. It is necessary for a society to ensure that its responses to crime and delinquency are based on reason, and this reason must be drawn from careful, thoughtful analysis of the problem in its fullest dimensions, apart from political considerations and considerations born out of vested "turf" issues.

REFERENCES

Achenbach, T.M. (1991). *Manual for the Child Behavior Checklist/4–18 and 1991 profiles.* Burlington: University of Vermont, Department of Psychiatry.

Agnew, R.S. (1991). The interactive effect of peer variables on delinquency. *Criminology, 29,* 47–72.

Aichhorn, A. (1935). *Wayward youth.* New York: Viking.

Alexander, J.F., Barton, C., Schiavo, R.S., & Parsons, B.V. (1976). Systems-behavioral intervention with families of delinquents: Therapist characteristics, family behavior, and outcome. *Journal of Consulting and Clinical Psychology, 44,* 656–664.

American Psychiatric Association. (1952). *Diagnostic and statistical manual of mental disorders.* Washington, DC: Author.

American Psychiatric Association. (1994). *Diagnostic and statistical manual of mental disorders* (4th ed.). Washington, DC: Author.

American Psychological Association. (1993). *Violence and youth: Psychology's response: Vol. I: Summary report of the American Psychological Association Commission on Violence and Youth.* Washington, DC: Author.

American Psychological Association. (1996). *Violence and the family: Report of the American Psychological Association Presidential Task Force on Violence and the Family.* Washington, DC: Author.

Andrew, J.M. (1978). Laterality on the Tapping Test among legal offenders. *Journal of Clinical Child Psychology, 7,* 149–150.

Ashton, J. (1997). Statement on juvenile crime legislation [online]. Available from http://www.senate.gov/washcroft/2-19-97.htm.

Ayllon, T., & Milan, M. (1979). *Correctional rehabilitation and management: A psychological approach.* New York: Wiley.

Bandura, A. (1969). *Principles of behavior modification.* New York: Holt, Rinehart, and Winston.

Bandura, A. (1973). *Aggression: A social learning analysis.* Englewood Cliffs, NJ: Prentice-Hall.

Bandura, A., & Walters, R.H. (1963). *Adolescent aggression.* New York: Holt, Rinehart, and Winston.

Bandura, A., Ross, D., & Ross, S.A. (1961). Transmission of aggression through imitation of aggressive models. *Journal of Abnormal and Social Psychology, 63,* 575–582.

Bandura, A., Ross, D., & Ross, S.A. (1963). Imitation of film-mediated aggressive models. *Journal of Abnormal and Social Psychology, 66,* 3–11.

Bassett, J.E., Blanchard, E.B., & Koshland, E. (1975). Applied behavioral analysis in a penal setting: Targeting "free world" behaviors. *Behavior Therapy, 6,* 639–648.

Becker, H.S. (1963). *Outsiders: Studies in the sociology of deviance.* New York: Free Press.

Bell, J.E. (1975). *Family therapy.* New York: Aronson.

Bender, L. (1953). *Aggression, hostility and anxiety in children.* Springfield, IL: Thomas.

Blackburn, R. (1993). *The psychology of criminal conduct.* Chichester, England: Wiley.

Block, H.A., & Flynn, F.T. (1956). *Delinquency.* New York: Random House.

Blos, P. (1961). Delinquency. In S. Lorand & H.I. Schneer (Eds.), *Adolescents: Psychoanalytic approach to problems and therapy.* New York: Dale.

Bowlby, J. (1951). *Maternal care and mental health* [Monograph]. Geneva, Switzerland: World Health Organization.

Brandon, S. (1960). *An epidemiological study of male adjustment in childhood.* Unpublished doctoral dissertation, University of Durham, England.

Brennan, P.A., & Mednick, S.A. (1997). Medical histories of antisocial individuals. In D.M. Stoff, J. Breiling, & J.D. Maser (Eds.), *Handbook of Antisocial Behavior* (pp. 269–279). New York: Wiley.

Broman, S.H., Nichols, P.L., & Kennedy, W.A. (1975). *Preschool IQ: Prenatal and early developmental correlates.* Hillsdale, NJ: Erlbaum.

Burgess, R.L., & Akers, R.L. (1966). A differential association-reinforcement theory of criminal behavior. *Social Problems, 14*(2), 128–147.

Burt, C. (1925). *The young delinquent.* New York: Appleton.

Butcher, J.N., & Williams, C.L. (1996). *Essentials of MMPI-2 and MMPI-A interpretation.* Minneapolis: University of Minnesota Press.

Butcher, J.N., Williams, C.L., Graham, J.R., Archer, R.P., Tellegen, A., Ben-Porath, Y.S., & Kaemmer, B. (1992). *MMPI-A (Minnesota Multiphasic Personality Inventory for Adolescents): Manual for administration, scoring, and interpretation.* Minneapolis: University of Minnesota Press.

Carey, G., & Goldman, D. (1997). The genetics of antisocial behavior. In D.M. Stoff, J. Breiling, & J.D. Maser (Eds.), *Handbook of antisocial behavior* (pp. 243–254). New York: Wiley.

Chamberlain, P. (1996). Intensified foster care: Multilevel treatment for adolescents with conduct disorders in out-of-home care. In E.D. Hibbs & P.S. Jensen (Eds.), *Psychosocial treatments for child and adolescent disorders: Empirically based strategies for clinical practice* (pp. 475–495). Washington, DC: American Psychological Association.

Christian, R.E., (1996). The use of Hare's revised Psychopathy Checklist with adolescents. *Child Assessment News, 5*(4), 1–5.

Clark, J.P., & Wenninger, E.P. (1962). Socioeconomic class and area as correlates of illegal behavior among juveniles. *American Sociological Review, 27,* 826–834.

Cleckley, H. (1976). *The mask of sanity* (5th ed.). St. Louis, MO: Mosby. (Original work published 1941)

Cloward, R.A. (1959). Illegitimate means, anomie, and deviant behavior. *American Sociological Review, 24,* 164–176.

Cloward, R.A., & Ohlin, L.E. (1960). *Delinquency and opportunity: A theory of delinquent gangs.* Glencoe, IL: Free Press.

Cohen, A.K. (1965). The sociology of the deviant act: Anomie theory and beyond. *American Sociological Review, 30,* 5–14.

Cohen, H.L., & Filipczak, J. (1971). *A new learning environment.* San Francisco: Jossey-Bass.

Coie, J.D., & Dodge, K.A. (1998). Aggression and antisocial behavior. In W. Damon & N. Eisenberg (Eds.), *Handbook of child psychology: Vol. 3. Social, emotional and personality development* (5th ed., pp. 779–862). New York: Wiley.

Colorado Division of Youth Services. (1985). *The relationship between drug use, delinquency, and behavioral adjustment problems among committed juvenile offenders: A report to the Colorado Alcohol and Drug Abuse Division.* Denver: Colorado Division of Youth Services.

Cornell, D., Peterson, C., & Richards, H. (1999). Anger as a predictor of aggression among incarcerated adolescents. *Law and Human Behavior, 15,* 655–665.

Cressey, D.R. (1960). Epidemiology and individual conduct: A case from criminology. *Pacific Sociological Review, 3,* 47–58.

Dembo, R., Getrev, A., Washburn, M., Wish, E.D., & Schemeidler, J. (1988). The relationship between physical and sexual abuse and illicit drug use: A replication among a new sample of youth entering a juvenile detention center. *International Journal of the Addictions, 23,* 1101–1123.

Dishion, T.J., & Patterson, G.R. (1997). The timing and severity of antisocial behavior: Three hypotheses within an ecological framework. In D.M. Stoff, J. Breiling, & J.D. Maser (Eds.), *Handbook of antisocial behavior* (pp. 205–217). New York: Wiley.

Dodge, K.A., & Schwartz, D. (1997). Social information processing mechanisms in aggressive behavior. In D.M. Stoff, J. Breiling, & J.D. Maser (Eds.), *Handbook of antisocial behavior* (pp. 171–180). New York: Wiley.

Dollard. K., Doob, L.W., Miller, N.E., Mowrer, O.H., & Sears, R.R. (1939). *Frustration and aggression.* New Haven, CT: Yale University Press.

Dugdale, R. (1877). *The Jukes: A study in crime, pauperism, disease and heredity.* New York: Putnam.

Durkheim, E. (1951). *Suicide.* (J.A. Spaulding & G. Simpson, Trans.). Glencoe, IL: Free Press. (Original work published 1930)

Earle, A.M., & Earle, B.V. (1961). Early maternal deprivation and later psychiatric illness. *American Journal of Orthopsychiatry, 31,* 181–186.

Eber, H. (1976). *Some psychometric correlates of inmate behavior.* Unpublished manuscript (Available from H. Eber, PhD, Psychological Resources, 74 14th St., NW, Atlanta, GA 30309)

Elliott, D.S., Huizinga, D., & Ageton, S.S. (1985). *Explaining delinquency and drug use.* Beverly Hills, CA: Sage.

Erickson, M.L., & Empey, L.T. (1963). Court records, undetected delinquency, and decision making. *Journal of Criminal Law, Criminology, and Police Science, 54,* 456–469.

Erickson, M.L., & Empey, L.T. (1965). Class position, peers, and delinquency. *Sociology and Social Research, 49,* 268–282.

Eron, L.D. (1997). The development of antisocial behavior from a learning perspective. In D.M. Stoff, J. Breiling, & J.D. Maser (Eds.), *Handbook of antisocial behavior* (pp. 140–158). New York: Wiley.

Exner, J.E., Jr. (1994). *The Rorschach: A comprehensive system. Vol. 1: Basic foundations* (3rd ed.). New York: Wiley.

Eysenck, H.J. (1957). *The dynamics of anxiety and hysteria.* London: Routledge & Kegan Paul.

Eysenck, H.J. (1964). *Crime and personality.* London: Routledge & Kegan Paul.

Farrington, D.P. (1997). A critical analysis of research on the development of antisocial behavior from birth to adulthood. In D.M. Stoff, J. Breiling, & J.D. Maser (Eds.), *Handbook of antisocial behavior* (pp. 234–240). New York: Wiley.

Farrington, D.P., & Hawkins, D. (1991). Predicting participation, early onset and later persistence in officially recorded offending. *Criminal Behavior and Mental Health, 1,* 1–33.

Feldman, D. (1964). Psychoanalysis and crime. In B. Rosenberg, I. Gerver, & F.W. Howton (Eds.), *Mass society in crisis.* New York: Macmillan.

Fersch, E.A. (1979). *Law, psychology and the courts.* Springfield, IL: Thomas.

Forth, A.E., Hart, S.D., & Hare, R.D. (1990). Assessment of psychopathy in male young offenders. *Psychological Assessment: A Journal of Consulting and Clinical Psychology, 2,* 342–344.

Freedman, B.J., Rosenthal, L., Donahoe, C.P., Schlundt, D.G., & McFall, R.M. (1978). A social-behavioral analysis of skill deficits in delinquent and nondelinquent adolescent boys. *Journal of Consulting and Clinical Psychology, 46,* 1448–1462.

Friedrich, W., Einbender, A.J., & Luecke, W.J. (1987). Cognitive and behavioral characteristics of physically abused children. *Journal of Consulting and Clinical Psychology, 51,* 313–314.

Gacono, C.B., & Meloy, J.R. (1994). *The Rorschach assessment of aggressive and psychopathic personalities.* Hillsdale, NJ: Erlbaum.

Gibbens, T.C.N. (1963). *Psychiatric studies of Borstal boys.* London: Oxford University Press.

Glueck, S., & Glueck, E. (1950). *Unraveling juvenile delinquency.* Cambridge, MA: Commonwealth Fund.

Glueck, S., & Glueck, E. (1956). *Physique and delinquency.* New York: Harper.

Goddard, H. (1912). *The Kallikak family: A study of the heredity of feeblemindedness.* New York: Macmillan.

Grove, W.M., Eckert, E.D., Heston, L.L., Bouchard, T.J., Jr., Segal, N., & Lykken, D.T. (1990). Heritability of substance abuse and antisocial behavior: A study of monozygotic twins raised apart. *Biological Psychiatry, 27,* 293–304.

Hare, R.D. (1991). *Manual for the Revised Psychopathy Checklist.* Toronto, Canada: Mulithealth Systems.

Hawkins, D., & Catalano, R. (1992). *Communities that care.* San Francisco: Jossey-Bass.

Hayes, S.C., Rincover, A., & Volosin, D. (1980). Variables influencing the acquisition and maintenance of aggressive behavior: Modeling versus sensory reinforcement. *Journal of Abnormal Psychology, 89,* 254–262.

Heilbrun, K. (1997). Prediction vs. management models relevant to risk assessment: The importance of legal decision-making context. *Law and Human Behavior, 21,* 347–359.

Heilbrun, K. (1999, February). *Basic and advanced issues in risk assessment: Approaches, populations, communications, and decision making.* Paper presented at a workshop for the American Academy of Forensic Psychology, Austin, TX.

Henggeler, S.W., Schoenwald, S.K., Borduin, C.M., Rowland, M.D., & Cunningham, P.B. (1998). *Multisystemic treatment of antisocial behavior in youth.* New York: Guilford Press.

Henggeler, S.W., Schoenwald, S.K., Pickel, S.G., Brandino, M.J., Borduin, C.M., & Hall, J.A. (1994). *Treatment manual for family preservation using multisystemic therapy.* Charleston: South Carolina Health and Human Services Finance Commission.

Henry, B., & Moffitt, T.E. (1997). Neuropsychological and neuroimaging studies of juvenile delinquency and adult criminal behavior. In D.M. Stoff, J. Breiling, & J.D. Maser (Eds.), *Handbook of antisocial behavior* (pp. 280–288). New York: Wiley.

Hinshaw, S.P., & Zupan, B.A. (1997). Assessment of antisocial behavior in children and adolescents. In D.M. Stoff, J. Breiling, & J.D. Maser (Eds.), *Handbook of antisocial behavior* (pp. 36–50). New York: Wiley.

Hirschi, T. (1969). *Causes of delinquency.* Berkeley: University of California Press.

Huesmann, L.R., Moise, J.F., & Podolski, C.L. (1997). The effects of media violence on the development of antisocial behavior. In D.M. Stoff, J. Breiling, & J.D. Maser (Eds.), *Handbook of antisocial behavior* (pp. 181–193). New York: Wiley.

Hunt, D.E., & Hardt, R.H. (1965). Developmental stage, delinquency, and differential treatment. *Journal of Research in Crime and Delinquency, 2,* 20–31.

Ilg, F.L., & Ames, L.B. (1955). *Child behavior.* New York: Macmillan.

Katz, L.F., & Gottman, J. (1993). Patterns of marital conflict predict children's internalizing and externalizing behaviors. *Developmental Psychology, 29,* 940–950.

Kaufman, J., & Cicchetti, D. (1989). Effects of maltreatment on children's socioemotional development: Assessments in a day-camp setting. *Developmental Psychology, 25,* 516–524.

Kazdin, A.E. (1995). *Conduct disorders in childhood and adolescence.* Thousand Oaks, CA: Sage.

Kazdin, A.E. (1996). Problem solving and parent management in treating aggressive and antisocial behavior. In E.D. Hibbs & P.S. Jensen (Eds.), *Psychosocial treatments for child and adolescent disorders: Empirically based strategies for clinical practice* (pp. 377–408). Washington, DC: American Psychological Association.

Klein, N.C., Alexander, J.R., & Parsons, B.V. (1977). Impact of family systems intervention on recidivism and sibling delinquency: A model of primary prevention and program evaluation. *Journal of Consulting and Clinical Psychology, 45,* 469–474.

Kolko, D., Moser, J., & Weldy, S. (1990). Medical/health histories and physical evaluation of physically and sexually abused child psychiatric patients: A controlled study. *Journal of Family Violence, 5,* 249–266.

Kramer, R. (1988). *At a tender age: Violent youth and juvenile justice.* New York: Henry Holt.

LaGrange, R.L., & White, H.R. (1983). Age differences in delinquency: A test of theory. *Criminology, 23,* 19–46.

Lahey, B.B., & Loeber, R. (1997). Attention-deficit/hyperactivity disorder, oppositional defiant disorder, conduct disorder, and adult antisocial behavior: A life-span perspective. In D.M. Stoff, J. Breiling, & J.D. Maser (Eds.), *Handbook of antisocial behavior* (pp. 51–59). New York: Wiley.

Lindner, R.M. (1944). *Rebel without a cause.* New York: Grune & Stratton.

Lipsey, M.W. (1992). *The effects of treatment on juvenile delinquents: Results from meta-analysis.* Paper presented at the NIMH meeting for Potential Applicants for Research to Prevent Youth Violence, Bethesda, MD.

Loeber, R. (1988). Natural histories of conduct problems, delinquency, and associated substance use: Evidence for developmental progressions. In B.B. Lahey & A.E. Kazdin (Eds.), *Advances in clinical child psychology* (pp. 73–124). New York: Plenum Press.

Loeber, R., & Stouthamer-Loeber, M. (1998). Development of juvenile aggression and violence. *American Psychologist, 53*(2), 242–259.

Lombroso, C. (1911). *Crime: Its causes and remedies* (H.P. Herton, Trans.). Boston: Little, Brown.

Lowry, L.G. (1944). Delinquent and criminal personalities. In J. McV. Hunt (Ed.), *Personality and the behavior disorders* (Vol. 2). New York: Ronald Press.

Lunden, W.A. (1964). *Statistics on delinquents and delinquency.* Springfield, IL: Thomas.

Mash, E., & Martin, J. (1983). Socialization in the context of the family: Parent-child interaction. In E.M. Hetherington (Ed.), *Handbook of child psychology: Vol. 4. Socialization, personality, and social development* (pp. 1–101). New York: Plenum Press.

McCandless, B.R., & Evans, E.D. (1973). *Children and youth: Psychosocial development.* Hinsdale, IL: Dryden.

McCann, J.T. (1997). The MACI: Composition and clinical applications. In T. Millon (Ed.), *The Millon inventories: Clinical and personality assessment* (pp. 363–388). New York: Guilford Press.

McCord, J., & McCord, W. (1958). Effects of parental role models on criminality. *Journal of Social Issues, 14,* 66–74.

Merton, R.K. (1957). *Social theory and social structure.* Glencoe, IL: Free Press.

Miller, W.B. (1958). Lower class culture as a generation milieu of gang delinquency. *Journal of Social Issues, 14*(3), 5–19.

Millon, T. (1993). *Millon Adolescent Clinical Inventory manual.* Minneapolis, MN: National Computer Systems.

Moffitt, T.E. (1993). Adolescence-limited and life-course persistent antisocial behavior: A developmental taxonomy. *Psychological Review, 100,* 674–701.

Moffitt, T.E. (1993). "Life-course persistent" vs. "adolescence-limited" antisocial behavior: A developmental taxonomy. *Psychological Review, 100,* 674–701.

Monahan, J. (1981). *Predicting violent behavior: An assessment of clinical techniques.* Beverly Hills, CA: Sage.

Mowrer, O.H. (1950). *Learning theory and personality dynamics.* New York: Ronald.

Office of Juvenile Justice and Delinquency Prevention. (1995). *Guide for implementing the comprehensive strategy for serious, violent, and chronic juvenile offenders.* Washington, DC: Author.

Pena, L.M., Megargee, E.I., & Brody, E. (1996). MMPI-A patterns of male juvenile delinquents. *Psychological Assessment, 8*(4), 388–397.

Peterson, D.R., Quay, H.C., & Tiffany, T.L. (1961). Personality factors related to juvenile delinquency. *Child Development, 32,* 613–618.

Phillips, E.L., Phillips, E.A., Fixsen, P.L., & Wolf, M.M. (1973). Behavior-shaping for delinquents. *Psychology Today, 7,* 74–108.

Piliavin, I., & Briar, S. (1964). Police encounters with juveniles. *American Journal of Sociology, 70,* 206–214.

Polk, K. (1967). *Delinquency and community action in nonmetropolitan areas* (In Task Force report: Juvenile delinquency and youth crime, report on juvenile justice and consultant's papers. Task Force on Juvenile Delinquency: The President's Commission on Law Enforcement and Administration of Justice). Washington, DC: U.S. Government Printing Office.

Powers, E., & Witmer, H. (1951). *An experiment in the prevention of delinquency.* New York: Columbia University Press.

President's Commission on Law Enforcement and Administration of Justice. (1967). *Crime in America: The challenge of crime in a free society.* Washington, DC: U.S. Government Printing Office.

Quay, H.C. (1964). Dimensions of personality in delinquent boys as inferred from the factor analysis of case history data. *Child Development, 35,* 479–484.

Quay, H.C. (1966). Personality dimensions in preadolescent delinquent boys. *Educational Psychology and Measurement, 26,* 99–110.

Quay, H.C., & Blumen, L. (1963). Dimensions of delinquent behavior. *Journal of Social Psychology, 61,* 273–277.

Quay, H.C., Peterson, D.R., & Consalvi, C. (1960). The interpretation of three personality factors in juvenile delinquency. *Journal of Consulting Psychology, 24,* 555.

Quay, H.C., & Quay, L.C. (1965). Behavior problems in early adolescence. *Child Development, 36,* 215–220.

Randolph, M.H., Richardson, H., & Johnson, R.C. (1961). A comparison of social and solitary male delinquents. *Journal of Consulting Psychology, 25,* 293–295.

Robins, L.N., & McEvoy, L. (1990). Conduct problems as predictors of substance abuse. In L.N. Robins & M. Rutter (Eds.), *Straight and devious pathways from childhood to adulthood* (pp. 182–204), Cambridge, England: Cambridge University Press.

Robins, L., West, P., & Herjanic, B. (1975). Arrests and delinquency in two generations: A study of Black urban families and their children. *Journal of Child Psychology and Psychiatry, 16,* 125–140.

Rutter, M. (1997). Antisocial behavior: Developmental psychopathology perspectives. In D.M. Stoff, J. Breiling, & J.D. Maser (Eds.), *Handbook of antisocial behavior* (pp. 115–124). New York: Wiley.

Samenow, S.E. (1984). *Inside the criminal mind.* New York: Times Books.

Sameroff, A.J., & Chandler, M.J. (1975). Reproductive risk and the continuum of caretaker casualty. In F.D. Horowitz, E.M. Hetherington, S. Scarr-Salapatek, & G. Siegel (Eds.), *Review of child development research* (pp. 187–244). Chicago: University of Chicago Press.

Schafer, W.E., & Polk, K. (1967). *Delinquency and the schools* (In Task Force report: Juvenile delinquency and youth crime). Washington, DC: U.S. Government Printing Office.

Shaw, C.B. (1938). *Brothers in crime.* Chicago: University of Chicago.

Shaw, D.S., & Winslow E.B. (1997). Precursors and correlates of antisocial behavior from infancy to preschool. In D.M. Stoff, J. Breiling, & J.D. Maser (Eds.), *Handbook of antisocial behavior* (pp. 148–158). New York: Wiley.

Sheldon, W.H. (1949). *Varieties of delinquent youth.* New York: Harper & Row.

Shields, A., & Cicchetti, D. (1998). Reactive aggression among maltreated children: The contributions of attention and emotion dysregulation. *Journal of Clinical Child Psychology, 27,*(4), 381–395.

Short, J.F., Jr. (1960). Differential association as a hypothesis: A panel study of youthful drinking and behavior. *International Journal of the Addictions, 25,* 755–771.

Silverberg, N.E., & Silverberg, M.C. (1971). School achievement and delinquency. *Review of Educational Research, 41,* 17–34.

Sleek, S. (1998). Experts scrambling on school shootings. *American Psychological Association: APA Monitor, 29*(8), 1, 35–36.

Sobel, S. (1979). Psychology and the juvenile justice system. *American Psychologist, 34*(10), 1020–1023.

Supreme Court of the State of New Jersey. (1989). *1989 judicial conference: Juveniles, justice, and the courts: Discussion paper.* Trenton, NJ: Administrative Office of the Courts.

Sutherland, E.H. (1939). *Principles of criminology.* Philadelphia: Lippincott.

Sutherland, E.H., & Cressey, D.R. (1966). *Principles of criminology.* Philadelphia: Lippincott.

Sykes, G.M., & Matza, D. (1957). Techniques of neutralization: A theory of delinquency. *American Sociological Review, 22,* 664–670.

Tannenbaum, F. (1938). *Crime and the community.* New York: Ginn.

Thornberry, T.P., & Krohn, M.D. (1997). Peers, drug use, and delinquency. In D.M. Stoff, J. Breiling, & J.D. Maser (Eds.), *Handbook of antisocial behavior* (pp. 218–233). New York: Wiley.

Toby, J. (1967). *Affluence and adolescent crime* (In Task Force report: Juvenile delinquency and youth crime, report on juvenile justice and consultant's papers.

Task Force on Juvenile Delinquency: The President's Commission on Law Enforcement and Administration of Justice). Washington, DC: U.S. Government Printing Office.

Toman, W. (1969). *Family constellation: Its effects on personality and social behavior.* New York: Springer.

Tracy, P.E., Wolfgang, M.E., & Figlio, R.M. (1985). *Delinquency into birth cohorts: Executive summary: Office of Juvenile Justice and Delinquency Prevention.* Washington, DC: U.S. Government Printing Office.

Trasler, G. (1962). *The explanation of criminality.* London: Routledge & Kegan Paul.

Tredgold, A.F. (1915). *Mental deficiency.* Boston: Wood.

Urist, J. (1977). The Rorschach test and the assessment of object relations. *Journal of Personality Assessment, 41*(1), 3–9.

Vaz, E.W. (1967). Juvenile delinquency in the middle-class youth culture. In E.W. Vaz (Ed.), *Middle-class juvenile delinquency.* New York: Harper & Row.

Webster-Stratton, C. (1996). Early intervention with videotape modeling: Programs for families of children with oppositional defiant disorder or conduct disorder. In E.D. Hibbs & P.S. Jensen (Eds.), *Psychosocial treatments for child and adolescent disorders: Empirically based strategies for clinical practice* (pp. 435–473). Washington, DC: American Psychological Association.

Widom, C.S. (1997). Child abuse, neglect and witnessing violence. In D.M. Stoff, J. Breiling, & J.D. Maser (Eds.), *Handbook of antisocial behavior* (pp. 159–170). New York: Wiley.

Williams, C.L., Butcher, J.N., Ben-Porath, Y.S., & Graham, J.R. (1992). *MMPI-A Content Scales: Assessing psychopathology in adolescents.* Minneapolis: University of Minnesota Press.

Winett, R.A., & Winkler, R.C. (1972). Current behavior modification in the classroom: Be still, be quiet, be docile. *Journal of Applied Behavior Analysis, 5,* 449–504.

Wootton, B. (1959). *Social science and social pathology.* London: George Allen & Unwin.

Yochelson, S., & Samenow, S.E. (1976). *The criminal personality* (Vols. 1 & 2). New York: Aronson.

INTERVENTION STRATEGIES

CHAPTER 40

Parenting: The Child in the Context of the Family

RUSSELL H. JACKSON AND JENNIFER LEONETTI

This chapter presents some factors that professionals should consider when helping parents make responsible decisions about their children, promote more positive functioning within their families, and develop a more realistic context for the family in our society. Our central thesis is that to intervene or advise parents on rearing their children without considering the familial, social, and cultural context and without accepting "normal" parents as capable individuals who are doing the best they can for their children is to invite failure.

This chapter begins by examining development within the family, with a focus on the family unit and the reciprocal, interactive effect parents and children have on each other. The next section emphasizes how society influences changes within the family. We stress the importance of the professional-parent relationship and suggest ways to enhance it while continuing to provide the most therapeutic treatment program in our current world of managed health care. The majority of the chapter focuses on intervention. It is our hope that the brief

The preparation of this chapter was supported in part by the Bureau of Community Health Services, Maternal and Child Health Services Project 920. The authors would like to thank their colleague Gloria Krahn for reading this chapter and sharing her helpful comments.

review of the literature in this area will help professionals determine the most appropriate treatment for the families they encounter.

DEVELOPMENT WITHIN THE FAMILY CONTEXT

THE POTENTIAL FOR PERSONAL GROWTH

There may be no other event that couples look forward to with greater anticipation, or experience with more elation and satisfaction, than the planned birth of a healthy infant. With the arrival of the first infant also comes new responsibilities and multiple opportunities for growth. A key function of the family is the nurturing socialization of the child. Belsky, Lerner, and Spanier (1984) also propose that as the family is a means of socializing children, so it is also a means of socializing adults. The opportunities for personal growth are as great in having children as in being children.

Until relatively recently, parenting research focused on such issues as parental attitudes, mother-infant dyadic interaction, the impact of the child on the caregiver, and, most recently, the role of fathers. Now the scope has broadened and focuses more on the reciprocal and ongoing processes that shape the family as a unit with multiple components. Integral is the social context in which the family operates. Using personal construct theory (Kelly, 1955), Pedersen, Yarrow, Anderson, and Cain (1978) suggest that there are potential benefits from two parents (rather than a single individual) interacting with their infant in the development of complex constructs needed for social exchanges.

PARENTING IN THE CONTEXT OF THE FAMILY

Belsky (1984) conceptualized parenting and child outcomes as significantly influenced by three main factors: parental characteristics (developmental history, personality), child characteristics (temperament, activity level), and social context.

Foss (1996) builds on Belsky's model, which she believes does not adequately address economic issues, family adversity, or stressful life events. Though Belsky's model considers contextual variables, research has largely neglected the cultural context when examining the family. Foss focuses specifically on immigrant populations and outlines the contextual determinants of parenting for these groups. These include premigration, migration, and postmigration experiences, ethnicity, and the social and economic environment.

Accepting these assumptions forces professionals in the field of child development to focus on the family and social environment. Kagan (1976) felt that children who receive food, protection from excessive disease, and physical comfort do not require any specific actions from adults to develop optimally. He based this conclusion, in part, on cross-cultural studies of American, Japanese, and Guatemalan children who were found to be equally adapted to their societies, even though these societies had different conceptions of children. There is always the potential for a debilitating effect when the environment provides social toxins such as poverty, abuse, inappropriate affect, and isolation (Axelrad & Brody, 1978). These reports suggest that children respond to a stable, healthy environment and an emotional bond with adults. They do not identify specific behavior required from parents for children to develop optimally given a stable, healthy environment. See Harris (1998) for the contemporary point of view that parents are not a major determinant in how children develop.

Parents, however, often ask professionals to describe the critical behaviors in successful child rearing. In general, parenting research suggests that parental "responsiveness," "sensitivity," and/or "support" are the important variables in the development of children (Belsky et al., 1984; Rollins & Thomas, 1979; Wahler & Meginnis, 1997). In addition, parents should set some developmentally appropriate limits (Baumrind, 1971, 1975), while encouraging environmental exploration and learning and emphasizing age-appropriate independence (Beckwith, 1990; Kendler, Sham, & MacLean, 1997). Therefore, the responsive, stimulating parent of an infant, the authoritative parent of the preschooler, and the increasingly less restrictive parent of an adolescent share a common skill: the ability to recognize and respond to the developmental capacities of their children and the challenges the children face (Belsky et al., 1984).

A knowledge of child development helps parents make age-appropriate demands and grant children the degree of independence (and support) that they are ready to assume. The professional must be careful not to assume that because parents are effective with a child at one developmental level they will be at others. For example, parents may have difficulty with the clinging dependence of the toddler but thrive on the independence of the adolescent. In addition, parents who feel they are being successful at one developmental level may retain specific strategies that become inappropriate as the child moves on to another developmental level (e.g., spanking the 10-year-old may not be nearly as appropriate or effective as it was for the toddler).

Socialization between children and parents is a two-way process. For example, parents may foster intellectual competence and curiosity in the infant. If the preschooler develops into a child who asks questions of parents and teachers, receives informative answers, and, as a consequence, continues to display intellectual gains, then parents may assume that their behavior directly determined the subsequent intelligence of their child. However, complex reciprocal pathways of influence make connecting parental behavior during infancy to developmental outcome beyond the first years of life extremely difficult.

Finally, the realities of family interaction can help children prepare for the realities of life outside the family. For example, Baumrind (1980) points out that, even within the family, children are faced with (1) scarcity of resources (even the best of parents are not 100% responsive); (2) reciprocity as a pattern of exchange that brings about the mutual dependence of individuals; and (3) imperfect justice, which demands that children develop sufficient resiliency to enable flexible responses to change. A nurturing, supportive parent-child relationship promotes child receptivity to the values of the family and provides experiences that will allow those values to generalize to other social situations (Kagan, 1979).

THE CHANGING FAMILY IN OUR SOCIETY

The changing institution of the family supports both an optimistic and a pessimistic view of social change (Berbardo, 1988). The family is in a perpetual state of evolution as it interfaces with many other social institutions in myriad complex transactions, and it may be an independent variable, a dependent variable, or, most often, an intervening variable: "Its ability to mediate, translate, and incorporate social change in the process of socializing its members is one of its major strengths" (Goode, 1964, p. 2).

Strickland (1997) identified the most important 20th-century changes and considers the impact of these changes in the context of parental role responsibilities and their potential impact on the quality of life for children. Among the most important changes are a shift from a rural farm family environment to an industrialized urban society, the increased impact of the media and outside influences on family values and attitudes, an increase in the number of working mothers (see also Scarr, 1988), a shift to more nontraditional family constellations, and a greater emphasis on personal happiness and self-fulfillment.

The current focus on individualism in our society has affected attitudes toward marriage and family life. Hunt and Hunt (1988) use the term *lifestyle* to refer to the individual focus. They identify some general characteristics of the family that transcend its variations and that differ from the lifestyle approach: (1) families are collective; lifestyles are individuated; (2) families are given; lifestyles are chosen; (3) families are transgenerational; lifestyles

are cohort-specific; (4) families are gendered; lifestyles are genderless; and (5) families are work; lifestyles are play.

Scanzoni (1988) suggests that approximately 20% of U.S. citizens are strongly oriented toward the prevailing paradigm of the conventional family; 20% are strongly oriented toward self-fulfillment; and the rest are somewhere in the middle, where they have the freedom to choose among many lifestyle options. More are choosing not to marry or not to have children if married. There is some evidence that Americans are beginning to take marriage more seriously and to look more carefully at the issues of commitment and responsibility (Kantrowitz et al., 1987). Marriage has not necessarily become more desirable, but the alternatives look even less promising (e.g., lowered standard of living on one income, AIDS). The decision to have children can also create serious conflicts (e.g., the desire to have children is often precluded by the cost). In the United States, for a two-parent family making less than $33,700, the 18-year cost (food, clothing, housing, medical care, education, transportation, recreation, and other expenses) of raising a child is approximately $106,890; $145,320 for a two-parent family making between $33,700 and $56,700; and $211,830 for a two-parent family making more than $56,700 (U.S. Department of Agriculture, 1995).

Some changes in family structure, such as the increase in divorce and subsequent lack of financial support from many noncustodial parents, have caused an increasing number of families to lose their self-sufficiency and has led to the development of legislative efforts to enforce child support. In 1992, children were the most impoverished Americans, with 13.7 million children under 18 years of age living in poverty (U.S. Bureau of the Census, 1995). Glick (1988) reports that for 20 years, the proportion of single-parent families in the United States hovered between 12% (1940) and 14% (1960), then jumped to 28% in 1996. About 32% of children are born to a single mother, and about one quarter of those children are born to teenage mothers. In 1973, divorce became, for the first time, the number one reason for single-parent families rather than death. Forty-three percent of all marriages begun in the late 1980s will end in divorce, and half of the young children alive today will spend at least some time in a single-parent family before the age of 18. Because 75% of those who divorce will eventually remarry, an increasing proportion of children will grow up with stepparents and stepsiblings.

As a result of these changes, there is decreasing contact between parents and children and decreasing parental involvement in child rearing. Bronfenbrenner's 1979 claim that America is an age-segregated society within which children are raised more by peers, television, and day care than by parents is becoming even more true today (Gecas, 1988). Edwards (1988) maintains that the "boundedness" and "unity" of the family are more difficult to maintain on a day-to-day basis. With all of these changes, the family is no longer a private haven, protected from intrusion by political and economic conflicts of society. Welfare and health legislation, along with the subsequent administration of federal programs, has stimulated the development of interest groups and the mobilization of constituencies focusing on the family (Farber, 1988). Regardless of the position these groups take, they may be viewed as breaking down the family as an autonomous domain.

Some researchers take a more optimistic view of the changing pattern. Tallman (1988) points out that families are, in part, problem-solving units and all members of families are, to some degree, problem-solvers. He proposed that each successive generation focuses on solving or altering the problematic conditions of the family life they perceived during their formative years in their families of origin. Tallman predicts a cyclical focus in which the current generation of children will see their children as more important to parents and society.

THE PROFESSIONAL-PARENT RELATIONSHIP

In American society, professionals have looked to the family as an ongoing means of intervention for children. Through adoption, foster care, and small-group living situations, we expect the "family" to remedy problems and enhance a child's quality of life. There is not space to develop this area more than to bring it to the reader's attention.

Society must begin to view parenting as a process in which growth and development continue during adulthood, just as childhood is a period of growth and development preceding adulthood. It is difficult for parents to like their children and enjoy

them when the children's behavior makes a parent feel inadequate. It is when parents feel vulnerable, inadequate, or helpless that they may strike out in anger at their child. Parents need a society that no longer judges, blames, and expects parents to have all the answers simply because they are parents. In the past, the community and the older generation assumed the responsibility of helping younger parents rear children. There is no longer a clear system that provides such long-term transitional support for parents, although many contemporary figures have identified the importance of and need for this support.

At the present time, the professional's interaction with parents is the most difficult and elusive ingredient of a successful therapeutic outcome. Other ingredients for a positive outcome are generally present: (1) parents who are asking for help, (2) appropriate information about child development, (3) behavioral and group techniques for implementing behavior change, and (4) dedicated, trained professionals to work with parents.

Traditionally, the professional has been free from client control of services (Powell, 1987) and free to diagnose and prescribe. However, if the professional takes sole responsibility for the development of treatment plans, then parents are more likely to refuse the treatment program offered, to accept the program initially but drop out before it is completed, and/or to have more difficulty developing an effective generalizable strategy (Miller, 1994; Yoos, Kitzman, Olds, & Overacker, 1995). When professionals do not discuss the parents' needs and feelings with them, the message may become "What you see and feel doesn't matter." Some empirical evidence exists to suggest that direct observation of behavior is more effective when the professional acknowledges the parents' perception (Jackson & Seitz, 1977) and attitude (Parke & Sawin, 1977) about what is occurring in the situation, rather than simply relying on professional interpretation.

If we can facilitate parental requests for help by providing support and appropriate structure, parents not only can tell us much about themselves, but also can become active colleagues who are the "best experts on themselves and are eminently qualified to participate in the development of descriptions and predictions about themselves, not to mention decisions about themselves" (Mischel, 1977, p. 249). Bailey (1987) proposes that for collaborative goal setting to occur between the parent and the professional, at least five skills are necessary: (1) view the family from a systems perspective, (2) systematically assess all relevant family needs, (3) use effective listening and interviewing techniques, (4) negotiate values and priorities to reach a joint solution, and (5) act as case managers.

In keeping with this perspective, family-centered care, a systemwide approach to pediatric care, is based on the assumption that the family is the child's primary source of strength and support. As such, the goal of family-centered care is to include families as full partners in children's health care, and it is marked by five principles: respect, information sharing, collaboration, family-to-family support, and confidence building (Institute for Family-Centered Care, 1998). Similarly, the goal of the early intervention model of working with parents has become to "empower" parents to advocate effectively, make decisions, and solve problems for themselves. Within the early intervention system, Public Law 99-457, Part H, requires the development of an individualized family service plan (IFSP) to empower the family unit and enable it to be responsible for meeting its own needs. Such a change emphasizes the growing awareness of the need to involve families in all aspects of treatment.

In summary, when families are candidates for intervention, the parents' values, priorities, and the context in which they live are receiving more and more emphasis. With all the preceding issues in mind, we now turn to interventions with parents.

INTERVENTIONS WITH PARENTS

PREPARATION FOR PARENTING IN THE CONTEXT OF THE SCHOOLS

At present, no systematic or comprehensive program is available to U.S. students to help them prepare for parenthood. Individual school districts make the decision about whether there will be preparation for parenthood courses and their content. Even when such courses are available, they may not be highly valued by students, teachers, or the community and often have a small enrollment. Other nations have found it important to move toward a more uniform and systematic preparation for parenting in schools (e.g., Finland, Denmark).

Anastasiow (1987) believes that ample information is available for parenting courses and recommends integrating it into classes covering a variety of subjects (e.g., home economics, social studies, civics) and at all levels (e.g., elementary, junior high, and high school).

PROVIDING EARLY SUPPORT TO PARENTS

Although the preparation for parenthood is often inadequate, expectant parents usually make some anticipatory adjustment prior to childbirth to soften its impact. The duration of the pregnancy allows not only for biological growth but for the associated psychological and social adjustment of the parents (Watson, Watson, Wetzel, Bader, & Talbot, 1995). As professionals become more sensitized to the needs of parents and look for ways to be supportive, there are more opportunities for parents to have positive experiences (Strickland, 1997; Watson et al., 1995).

In taking the family perspective, many procedures and practices have become more supportive of parents. For example, there is increased involvement of fathers throughout pregnancy and birth (Watson et al., 1995). Many types of prenatal courses help parents prepare for parenthood (Ladden & Damato, 1992). What is still unclear is whether attending these classes is associated with any differences in the degree of difficulty encountered during adjustment to parenthood (Parke & O'Leary, 1975; Wente & Crockenberg, 1976). Emotional support of the mother by the hospital staff during labor and delivery, the more homelike atmosphere of the birthing room, and less separation of mothers and babies after delivery contribute to the mother's positive feelings (Snyder, 1980). Early familiarizing sessions demonstrating the baby's competence also increases the parents' feelings of competence. In addition, Watson et al. (1995) identify the need for early support to fathers to increase family cohesion and circumvent adjustment and marital difficulties before and after the birth of the baby.

There is increasing focus on the provision of support and intervention from primary care providers, given their regular contact with families (Melnyk & Alpert-Gillis, 1997; Strickland, 1997; Watson et al., 1995). The American Academy of Pediatrics (1998) reports that 90% of pediatricians include advice about discipline when providing guidance to families. It outlines an effective, developmentally based discipline system that contains three vital elements: (1) a learning environment characterized by positive, supportive parent-child relationships; (2) a strategy for systematic teaching and strengthening of desired behaviors (proactive); and (3) a strategy for decreasing or eliminating undesired or ineffective behaviors (reactive). The Academy highlights the need to take a broader view of discipline to include the entire social structure. Cultures in which children display relatively few behavior problems have been characterized by clear role definitions, clear expectations for the child's active work role in the family, very stable family constellations, and involvement of other community members in child care and supervision.

Over the years, professionals have looked for more effective ways of meeting parents in familiar situations, such as public health clinics ("Parents Help Children," 1979) and in conjunction with a pediatric practice (Jackson & Terdal, 1978). Ford (1979) taught parents better skills to decide how and when to consult an appropriate health provider. C. Schroeder (1979) developed a telephone answering service for parents and Pugh (1984) a 24-hour confidential telephone service for acute problems.

Going on the assumption that adults learn best when they have a specific need for information and when the educational opportunity is presented in a way that is easily accessible, appealing, and understandable, a number of state health agencies have developed age-paced newsletters that are keyed to the infant's birth month so that new mothers receive information each month about development and care of babies exactly as old as theirs. Cudaback et al. (1985) found 10 different first-year-of-life newsletter series being distributed in 19 states.

Some states are now sending information about such series to all new parents registered on hospital birth records. A specific example is *The Growing Child*, a monthly newsletter that seeks to provide parents with a coherent and practical understanding of how children change from birth to 6 years of age (Grimley & Robinson, 1986). A separate monthly publication entitled *Growing Parent* focuses on the parents' personal growth and development. Together, the subscription rate grew from 180,070 in 1975 to 266,970 in 1984. In a survey of readers, 99% reported reading some or all of the material each month, and 95% reported that they discussed articles with their spouse. In general, respondents

checked items relating to their own child's growth, learning, nutrition, and safety as most important but also value information dealing with their own needs (e.g., family communication, managing stress, caring for personal needs). There are limitations in the newsletter approach, however. Reading ability is necessary, and there is little evidence that such newsletters are used by parents in low-income homes. Finally, they are geared toward the typical child in each specific age level without specifically relating to deviations in normal growth and development.

Today, there is more and more interest in finding ways to reach parents and help them prevent child-rearing problems. Even if financial resources are available to provide free, flexible, and community-based group programs, the hope of reaching overstretched, low-income mothers who lack confidence has not been achieved (Rosenberg, Reppucci, & Linney, 1983). Some parents decline participation for reasons such as these: (1) the thought of joining a small intensive group of peers is uncomfortable or intimidating; (2) the time demands are too great to be accommodated; and (3) parents are having too much difficulty managing their daily life to attend scheduled meetings twice weekly (Powell, 1987). Musick and Stott (1990) note that past efforts to change the caregiving environment via community-based early interventions have met with mixed results. Specifically, the conclusion drawn was that programs successfully reach parents as people, but not as parents. There is currently little evidence in the family support or parent education literature of moderate or long-term maintenance changes in either parental behavior or infant development. If changing the early caregiving environment involves changing the parent, this must be accomplished in the context of a relationship with the parent. Paraprofessionals are often used in early intervention programs to develop an ongoing relationship with parents.

PARENTHOOD IN THE POPULAR MEDIA

The most widespread means of disseminating advice about child rearing is through popular literature. The 1990 *Books in Print* lists more than 400 books on popular child care. Some magazines are devoted in their entirety to parents (e.g., *Parents Magazine*). Bookstores may carry anywhere from 50 to 175 titles on parenting in regular stock. Levant

(1987) conducted a survey and found that 60% of the respondents had read literature on parenting. However, the respondents also felt there were too many, rather than too few, resources available to them.

The authors of popular child care books address all parents, but the underlying assumption on which they are based is that the readers are young, highly educated, and middle class. Galinsky (1990) pointed out that books for parents are shifting away from telling parents what to do and are emphasizing the parents' own ability to solve problems. From the professional's point of view, many of the popular child-rearing books lack an empirical basis for some of their recommendations and generally disregard individual differences in both children's development and family circumstances.

The Internet is also an increasingly used medium for parenting resources. It is a novel and rapidly growing means of worldwide public communication where families turn for specific medical and mental health information (Widman & Tong, 1997). It is also a place to which more parents are turning for resource libraries and books in print (e.g., Chadwick School Parent Resource Library, http://chadwick-k12.com/library/bibprl.htm; American Academy of Pediatrics, http://www.aap.org.pubserv/adoltoc.htm.

PROBLEM INTERVENTION

Self-Help Books

There are few data regarding the general knowledge of behavioral skills that parents of normal children might have (O'Dell, Tarler-Benlolo, & Flynn, 1979) and fewer that demonstrate a relationship between parents' level of knowledge and their skill in managing child behavior (Eastman & Eyberg, 1981). Self-help books for parents are usually written with the idea of parents changing the child's behavior by using methods that have been tested and are effective under therapist-directed conditions, or by using straightforward behavior principles that do not take the context of the behavior into account. The more circumscribed the child's behavior problem, the more useful the manual for the parent. Ideally, the problem should be specific and confined to a given time and place. For example, see Greene, Clark, and Risley (1977) for specific advice to parents regarding shopping with children. At this level of specificity, parents may experience success reading the manual on their own.

Sweeny (1998) provides an annotated guide to the best publications for parents and professionals regarding children with special needs. Taylor and Biglan (1998) recommend specific books for parents of young children (2+ years) and for adolescents. However, they caution users of self-help books, as these books do not always promote use of empirically validated approaches.

Parent Education

Prior to 1960, parent education was thought to be a panacea for most of the problems related to parenting (Abidin & Carter, 1980). The transition from the lecture-discussion model to a more skill-oriented approach began with Auerbach (1968) and evolved into parent education programs today that target specific populations such as parents of hyperactive children, learning disabled children, aggressive children, and children with disabilities (Abidin & Carter, 1980; Volenski, 1995). See Bodley (1987) for a rather comprehensive list of current parent education programs available, De'Ath (1983) for basic principles that should be included in good programs, and Abidin and Carter for guidelines for conducting parent groups and the basic requirements for the group leader. The fastest growing area of parent education emphasizes primary prevention programs for at-risk families (e.g., teenage mothers, single parents, substance-abusing parents). The relative recency of such programs precludes a thorough evaluation of effectiveness, although preliminary data suggest positive outcomes in a number of areas.

In addition, many popular parent education groups follow a specific theory or point of view, such as Parent Effectiveness Training, behavior management groups, Adlerian groups, and groups based on reality therapy. The focus of most parent groups is on education rather than therapy, and the groups share these characteristics: (1) they provide general information for families rather than treatment for specific child problems; (2) information is presented in a group format rather than individualized; and (3) the focus primarily has been on making good parents better, rather than helping parents who are experiencing difficulty with child rearing. Although thousands of parents have participated in such programs, there is little in the research literature to guide those who would like to know more about the long-term effects of these programs on parents and children (Rogers Wiese &

Kramer, 1988). In a review of 48 articles comparing different parent education programs, Dembo, Switzer, and Lauritzen (1985) concluded that the high number of poorly designed studies in this area precluded "any definitive conclusions or implications regarding the general effectiveness of parent education programs or whether one type of program is more beneficial for a certain type of family or person" (p. 198).

Abidin and Carter (1980) caution that parents may come away from a parent group feeling more depressed and inadequate than before entering, not because of ineffective concepts and methods, but because of the group leader's failure to recognize the general goal of enhancing parental confidence. The group must not increase the disparity between what the parent feels needs to be done and his or her adequacy to cope with it; rather, it must increase the parent's sense of self-respect and confidence in the child-rearing role. The motivation for seeking help in the first place is not just a specific problem confronting a parent in rearing a child but rather the parent's feelings of inadequacy in handling the problem.

Individualized Parent Training
Parent training grew out of both the successes and the failures of parent education programs, and was established to provide individualized, goal-oriented treatment for families experiencing a wide range of problematic behavior. Beginning with Hanf (Hanf & Kling, 1973) and her students at the Oregon Health Sciences University in the 1960s, more focused (and efficient) parent training sessions were developed. Today, Forehand and his colleagues have developed the most widely researched parent training program for the "acting-out" child (Forehand & Long, 1988, 1996). This program is based on the theory that good parenting skills result in good child behavior, and good parenting includes positiveness, consistent but "nonharsh" discipline, and monitoring of the child's behavior and whereabouts. Based on the idea that parents display poor parenting skills because of a lack of knowledge, the program attempts to teach parenting skills in the context of two phases: *Child's Game*, in which the parent learns to increase the range and frequency of rewards while decreasing verbalizations that may be associated with deviant behavior; and *Parent's Game*, in which the parent learns to give appropriate commands and use time-out for

noncompliance. Similar programs have been developed and are currently being implemented at various sites across the nation (e.g., Dumas & Albin, 1986; Eyberg, 1988; Hembree-Kigin & McNeil, 1995; Wahler, 1980; Webster-Stratton, 1985). Generally, all programs focus on improving the interactions between parents and children (Hanf & Kling, 1973) while providing a specific set of behavioral techniques for managing child behavior. This type of program generally has been effective because parents learn new skills and thus serve as their child's therapist, and parents must display a minimum level of competence with each new skill while actually interacting with their child.

Behavioral parent training has been effective in a number of areas, including psychological problems related to somatic complaints, delinquent behavior, ADHD, child abuse, developmental concerns, and speech and language training (Kazdin, 1997b; Miller, 1994; Williams, Williams, & McLaughlin, 1991). Similarly, in a review of research involving parents of children with disabilities, Helm and Kozloff (1986) reported that most studies produced change in both parent and child behavior through a variety of training procedures (see also Gammon & Rose, 1991; Volenski, 1995). By far the most common presenting problem for nearly all programs has been opposition and noncompliance in preschool (Campbell, 1995) and school-age children. Danforth (1998) addresses only noncompliance as the principal target of the Behavior Management Flow Chart.

Although the first parent training programs focused on teaching parents the principles of behavior modification (e.g., Franks & Susskind, 1968; Pumroy & Pumroy, 1965), current programs focus not only on teaching specific skills but also on providing emotional support (Lutzker, McGimsey, McRae, & Campbell, 1983), offering brief marital therapy (Brody & Forehand, 1985), and integrating more traditional theories of treatment (Eyberg, 1988). Taylor and Biglan (1998) provide an excellent review of behavioral family interventions for improving child rearing that have been empirically validated. In addition, Dangel and Polster (1984) provide a comprehensive description and discussion of various parent training programs, and a book edited by Schaefer and Briesmeister (1989) discusses the use of parents as cotherapists for a number of children's behavior problems.

Parent Management Training (PMT) is one of the more well-investigated treatment techniques for children and adolescents (Kazdin, 1997a). Kazdin discusses outcome studies that support several conclusions: PMT has led to marked improvements in child behavior on parent and teacher reports of deviant behavior, direct observation of behavior at home and at school, and institutional records (e.g., school truancy, police contacts, institutionalization). In fact, the magnitude of change has placed conduct problem behavior to within nonclinical levels of functioning at home and at school based on normative data from nonreferred peers. Finally, improvements also have been noted in sibling behavior at home, maternal psychopathology (particularly depression), marital satisfaction, and family cohesion. Providing parents with in-depth knowledge of social learning principles, rather than just teaching them techniques, and supplementing PMT with time during treatment to discuss parental stressors improved outcomes and decreased dropout rates. This may account for the higher levels of treatment persistence with staff therapists than with doctoral-level students. Although PMT principles are quite straightforward, the range of applications that follow from them and the requisite therapist skills in shaping parent behavior require more than just passing familiarity.

Despite the efficacy of such parent training programs, it is estimated that only approximately one third of all participants improve dramatically, whereas one third evidence some improvement, and one third show no improvement at all (e.g., Helm & Kozloff, 1986). In addition, Kazdin (1997a) reports that 40% to 60% of families that begin treatment terminate prematurely. Miller (1994) points out that although parent training documents success, it is also associated with decreased parental involvement, early termination, and decreased long-term success. She attributes the attrition in parent training to a mismatch among expected roles, activities, and goals of treatment. Frankel and Simmons (1992) examined variables related to persistence in treatment with parents applying for an outpatient parent-training intervention at a large university hospital. Multiple variables were examined separately for intake and treatment phases. They found only one parent personality variable associated with persistence during the intake phase: Parents dropping out tended to endorse items reflecting helplessness and negativity. They concluded that the major variable operating against dropout may be a higher degree of positive expectancy of change.

Persistence through treatment was associated only with therapist type: a higher proportion of persisting parents were assigned to staff therapists as opposed to trainees. In their review, Taylor and Biglan (1998) suggest that actively collaborating with parents and understanding their perspective decreases rates of dropout and increases the likelihood of treatment success. One study (Prinz & Miller, 1994) found fewer families dropped out when the therapist regularly scheduled time to discuss parental concerns not related to the child.

Forehand and Long (1988) hypothesized that whereas some parents display poor parenting because they lack appropriate skills, others contend with contextual factors that cause them to display poor parenting. Much of the parent training research in the past decade has focused on factors outside the parent-child relationship that influence treatment outcome; this approach becomes increasingly more important given the contextual approach to child behavior and the multiple roles that parents play in today's society (e.g., individual, spouse, parent, breadwinner). Williams et al. (1991) found that parent training appears to be most effective when provided early in the child's life, when follow-up assistance is provided and gradually reduced, and when parents use self-management strategies to plan, rearrange, and monitor their parenting environment.

Factors that have been found to affect *treatment outcome* include parental psychopathology, such as depression and anxiety (Forehand, Middlebrook, Rogers, & Steffe, 1983; Webster-Stratton & Hammond, 1990); socioeconomic disadvantage (Dadds, Schwartz, & Sanders, 1987; Dumas & Albin, 1986, Webster-Stratton & Hammond, 1990); father's presence and mother's education (Dumas & Albin, 1986); marital status and adjustment (Webster-Stratton & Hammond, 1990); and lack of social support (Dadds et al., 1987). Further research suggests that it may not simply be one of the preceding factors that negatively influences treatment outcome, but rather interactions among factors. Therefore, Wahler and Hann (1984) suggested that multistressed families (with two or more of the listed factors) had poorer treatment outcomes. Further, Wahler and colleagues (Dumas & Wahler, 1983; Wahler & Graves, 1983) suggested that it was socioeconomic disadvantage plus coercive exchanges with kinfolk and outside agencies that predicted poorer outcome. They hypothesized that these coercive exchanges acted as setting events for negative interactions in the parent-child relationship. Dumas (1984) found that mothers who failed in parent training were more aversive in all situations than were their successful counterparts. In addition, these mothers responded aversively to both aversive and nonaversive initiations from their children. Dumas suggested that these women's responses to their children reflected not only the valence of the child behavior but also the nature of the contextual stimuli.

Other studies have suggested that parental perceptions and expectations are often a better predictor of treatment success than actual child behavior. For example, Clark and Baker (1983) discovered that families of children with disabilities demonstrated success rates following parent training similar to families of acting-out children. In addition, they found that "low-proficiency" families (those unable to learn and/or implement techniques) not only had lower socioeconomic status (SES) but also anticipated greater problems in learning the techniques than did "high-proficiency" families. Similarly, Forehand, Furey, and McMahon (1984) reported that parental perception of child adjustment determines whether a particular child will be referred for treatment. They also found that parental perception was affected more by parental distress than by observed child behavior. Forehand et al. concluded that distress contributed not only to completion of the parent training program but also to global satisfaction with child behavior. To test this hypothesis, Middlebrook and Forehand (1985) varied the level of stress for both clinic-referred and non-clinic-referred subjects in an analog situation. They found that, overall, when child behavior was neutral, higher levels of stress produced more perceived deviance. In addition, clinic-referred mothers perceived neutral behavior as inappropriate. It appears as if stress, in a variety of forms, greatly influences parental perception of deviant child behavior.

Therefore, it appears imperative that any parent training program begin with a thorough assessment of both the family and the social system. This would include assessment of parental psychopathology, marital relations, cultural background, SES, relations with other kinfolk, and perceptions of child adjustment.

Research in the area of *satisfaction with parenting programs* has focused on two general areas: Satisfaction with specific behavior modification techniques and satisfaction with the way techniques were taught. Although the number of studies examining satisfaction is far less than those examining treatment outcome, the majority of them suggest that techniques presented as part of a program are more acceptable than techniques presented separately (Calvert & McMahon, 1987). McMahon, Tiedemann, Forehand, and Griest (1984) reported that practice with the child in the clinic was rated as the most useful teaching method. In addition, parents thought that therapist modeling was better than written material for more difficult techniques.

Several studies have found that techniques designed to increase behavior (e.g., rewards, praise, commands) were more acceptable, easier to implement, and more useful than techniques designed to decrease behavior (e.g., Calvert & McMahon, 1987; McMahon et al., 1984). Studies examining only punishment procedures have consistently found that response cost is perceived as more acceptable than time-out, spanking, differential attention, and medication (e.g., Frentz & Kelley, 1986; Heffer & Kelley, 1987). Heffer and Kelley found that less labor-intensive techniques (e.g., spanking, medication) were favored by a majority of their low-income subjects, despite possible side effects. This finding further supports the hypothesis that disadvantaged families may approach child behavior problems differently from middle-income families. Further, Furey and Basili (1988) found that consumer satisfaction in general was based less on decreases in child noncompliance than on the factors discussed previously, including low SES, poor parenting skills, and depression. In fact, Rickert et al. (1988) found that parents reported satisfaction with their program even if their observed behavior did not improve. Overall, the findings support the conclusion that therapists working with families need to consider multiple environmental factors throughout the various phases of treatment.

Maintenance of gains following parent training has received the least attention by researchers. Kazdin (1985) noted that although the primary issue in parent training at the current time should be long-term effectiveness, the majority of studies include follow-up assessment of one year or less. Most short-term follow-up studies have found a low maintenance of treatment gains and no significant differences among treated children and classroom peers (e.g., Strain, Steele, Ellis, & Timm, 1982). The few studies assessing long-term follow-up have produced mixed results (e.g., Daly, Holland, Forrest, & Fellbaum, 1985; Webster-Stratton, 1982). McMahon (1994) reported long-term benefits of PMT 14 years out, and Kazdin (1997a) identified several studies in which treatment gains were maintained one to three years after treatment. Forehand and Long (1988) recently examined their sample of children when they reached early adolescence, 4 to 10 years after treatment. They found that relative to a nonclinic sample, their families were doing well and that few differences emerged on a variety of measures. An interesting finding was that parents who participated in the program continued to view their children more negatively than nonclinic parents, despite no differences in behavior. This finding is particularly disturbing in light of the report from Furey and Basili (1988), who found that, despite continued use of learned parenting skills and improved child behavior, mothers in their sample did not continue to perceive positive gains in their child's adjustment. Therefore, parental perception appears as important for long-term compliance with treatment as it does for predicting short-term treatment outcome.

Many current programs include treatment strategies intended to assist with long-term compliance and maintenance of treatment gains. For example, Dadds et al. (1987) included brief marital therapy for maritally distressed parents. Wahler and Graves (1983) included self-evaluation strategies intended to change the summary reports of disadvantaged insular mothers. Similarly, Graves, Meyers, and Clark (1988) included problem-solving training in their treatment of children's obesity, and Forehand et al. (1984) taught parents generalized social learning principles. Each of these investigators reported fewer dropouts as well as increased satisfaction and maintenance with the implementation of these additional programs.

Another shortcoming of the literature on parent training is the limited discussion of *developmental and cultural differences* and how those differences affect any parent training program (American Academy of Pediatrics, 1998; Robertson, 1984; Yoos et al., 1995). Anderson and Nuttall (1987) emphasized the need for evaluation of parent education programs at different development levels, and Strom (1985) provided developmental differences in an appropriate curriculum for parent education programs. Interestingly, age-appropriate curriculum appears vital if, as Hills and Knowles (1987) suggest, parents are

to establish personal relevance for the information presented. However, few parent training programs differ across developmental levels. The most obvious exceptions to these generalizations are the many programs intended for parents of children with disabilities, which emphasize teaching skills at the appropriate developmental level (Helm & Kozloff, 1986; see also Dangel & Polster, 1984, for examples of such programs). In addition, Serna, Schumaker, Hazel, and Sheldon (1986) asserted that with adolescents, unlike with younger children, communication and reciprocal social training may be the most important component of a parent training package.

Consideration of a family's cultural background and immigration experiences are particularly important in the face of substantial increases in ethnically diverse families in the United States. There is tremendous diversity within and across cultural groups. What constitutes a family, child-rearing practices, and the nature and quality of family relationships may be significantly different from the mainstream culture. Yoos et al. (1995) pointed out that culture plays a critical role in an individual's views of parenting and child development. Each culture has its views on the socialization agenda for children, the role of parents, and the accepted norms of behavior that influence the simplest activities of child care, such as feeding, toileting, discipline, and seeking health care (see also Kagitcibasi, 1992). Sprott (1994) emphasized that clinical professionals must not merely compare mainstream culture's child-rearing practices with those of other cultures and designate differences as deficits. When interacting with culturally diverse families, the challenge for those providing care is to distinguish what merely reflects different styles and perspectives and what reflects dysfunction: "Health care providers can learn about the cultural basis for parenting practices through open discussion with families of how they handle problem situations and why they chose their current childrearing practice" (Yoos et al., 1995, p. 350). Within the framework outlined by Yoos et al., an intervention may then (1) preserve or maintain the client's original cultural perspective and explanatory model; (2) accommodate or negotiate some change while preserving other parts of the original view; or (3) result in restructuring or repatterning of beliefs or behaviors (see Arendell, 1997, for specific parenting styles of African, Asian, Hispanic, and Native Americans; see

Yoos et al., 1995, for review of African American child-rearing beliefs; see Choi, 1995, for review of Korean mothering behaviors). The needs of children and families can be better understood if their socio-cultural context is considered.

In addition to race and ethnicity, SES is a particularly salient factor in determining parenting style and characteristics. Research indicates that SES accounts for a large measure of differences in parenting styles (Arendell, 1997). Cross-cultural research suggests that differences in parenting styles can be more the result of SES differences than cultural differences, and that parenting styles for particular SES groups in other cultures are similar to those in the United States (Fox & Solis-Camara, 1997; Solis-Camara & Fox, 1996). "Race and ethnicity, together with class and gender, constitute interacting hierarchies of resources and rewards that condition the material realities, parenting activities, and subjective experiences of family life" (Arendell, 1997, pp. 14–15). Because racial and ethnic minorities are positioned disproportionately in the lower socio-economic strata, the intersections of class and ethnicity are complex, and their influences on parenting are multifaceted.

Finally, in their reviews of the literature on parent training, Helm and Kozloff (1986) and Kazdin (1985) discuss the relevant *questions for the near future.* These investigators stress increased emphasis on the context of both appropriate and inappropriate behavior, including its functionality and factors outside of the parent child interaction that may influence it. In addition, fundamental research on families and children, including how nonclinic families differ from clinic families, is vital. More specifically, Forehand and Long (1988) suggest continued examination of parental perceptions and their relationship to mental health referrals. Future research endeavors may also increase their emphasis on qualitative as well as quantitative changes, with concomitant changes in assessment instruments and techniques. Finally, the addition of components that account for developmental and cultural differences appears to be the next logical step for many established parent training programs.

SUMMARY

It is hoped that the information in this chapter will be useful to professionals working with families.

There are challenges enough for everyone. As we move into the 21st century, parents must maintain family togetherness despite busy lives and mounting pressures from within and without, allow and support diversity among families, and enjoy children while nurturing and guiding them (Galinsky, 1990). P. Schroeder (1989) suggests a national policy for families with three basic goals: (1) acknowledge the rich diversity of American families; (2) protect families' economic well-being; and (3) provide families with flexible ways to meet their economic and social needs. Given these challenging goals, professionals must make equally challenging decisions in the face of uncertainty and changes in the family and our society. Specifically, given the vast array of research on parenting interventions and emphasis on empirically validated approaches, it will be important to maintain a balance between precise behavioral interventions and supportive approaches to keep families in treatment long enough to make a difference. This will require good clinical judgment to maintain a delicate balance between empowering families to raise and nurture their children, problem-solve, and intervene as independently as possible, and recommending more intensive family involvement in education, therapy, or parent training.

Each therapist must be "professionally and personally equipped to deal with individuals whose personal preferences or experience with life may not be part of his or her own repertoire" (Sporakowski, 1988, p. 374). This suggests that as professionals, we must examine our values and remain open-minded to the increasingly frequent "nontraditional" families who seek our services (Yoos et al., 1995). We know little about how to train "normal" parents to be more effective and whether these parents would really benefit from traditional parent training (Rogers Wiese & Kramer, 1988). Therefore, a thorough assessment is essential to determine what type of intervention best fits the family's needs. For example, many first-time parents simply need assurance and education during developmental transition periods. For these families, parent training may be contraindicated because it could make otherwise competent parents question their abilities.

Because not only families, but the context in which they live, continue to change, professionals will need to help families discover their options and anticipate the consequences of their decisions.

The need for family support is rapidly becoming an obligation that professionals can no longer afford to avoid. Only the form of intervention (e.g., education, therapy) is open to choice (Mancini & Orthner, 1988).

Table 40.1 presents a summary of the family factors, assessment procedures, and intervention strategies that should be considered when developing a treatment plan for parents. Certainly, many families fit the traditional parent training model, and for them, alternative or adjunctive treatment would be a waste of time and resources. As mentioned previously, however, many families do not benefit from traditional parent training, and there are some situations in which such treatment may be harmful. As a general guideline, if a family is experiencing difficulties in more than one area listed under family factors, or if family members are so distressed with the basics of living that they cannot maintain regular appointments or put energy into homework assignments, then an alternative to traditional parent training needs to be developed, for

Table 40.1 Areas to consider when developing a treatment plan for parents.

Family Factors	Assessment Procedures	Intervention Strategies
Cultural Background	Background and Referral Information	Parent Training
Socioeconomic Status Income, living conditions, educational level.	Parent Interview Social-family history.	Consultation with Parents Only Half Parent Training/Half Parent Treatment
History of Family Disruption Moves, illness and hospitalization, sibling problems.	Developmental history of the child. Family routine: work schedule, day care, chores, sibling relationships.	Treatment for Parent(s) Individual or marital therapy.
Parental Psychopathology Drug/alcohol abuse, depression, anxiety.	Description of behavioral concerns. Parental attitudes about child rearing.	Treatment for Child Individual or group therapy. Family Therapy
Marital Relationship Separation, divorce, remarriage, problems in relationship.	Parental value system.	Use of Community Resources Parent support group. Group parent education.
Parenting Characteristics Family of origin, knowledge of child development, religious values, family vs. lifestyle orientation.	Collateral Information Child's teacher. Previously seen professionals. Grandparents and extended family.	Class at community college. School program with parent education component: early intervention, Head Start. Church resources.
Child Characteristics Temperament, handicaps, cognitive level.	Community agencies. Consultation with Other Disciplines Regarding parents and/or child.	Other Community Resources Community health nurse. Children's Services Division.
Previous History with Professionals Medical, psychological, school.	Observational Procedures Structured parent–child interaction.	Respite care. Well baby clinics.
Resources for Family Support Relatives, friends, school, community.	Home observation. School visit and observation.	Other Resources Self-help books. Newsletters.
Overall Stress Level Combination of all factors.	Standardized Assessment Procedures Knowledge of child development. Behavioral questionnaires for parent and child. Marital adjustment and satisfaction. Direct assessment. Cognitive. Personality.	Educational TV programs. Internet.

example, home visits by a community health nurse. On the other hand, parents with marital problems or psychopathology (e.g., depression or substance abuse) may need to address these issues as an adjunct to parent training. Forehand et al. (1984) suggests that one of three strategies may be utilized if distress is identified: (1) begin parent training but monitor distress; (2) address distress before beginning parent training; or (3) focus on distress and parent training concurrently. They continue by suggesting that if distress is high and behavior problems low, use option 2; if behavior problems are high and distress low, use option 1; and if both are high, use option 3. Certainly, the more problematic the family situation, the more difficult it will be to empower the family and give the parents the confidence to rear children effectively. The professional's ability to take all of the areas in Table 40.1 into account and to develop a positive relationship with the parents will be the final determinant of the success of any parenting program.

REFERENCES

Abidin, R.R., & Carter, B.D. (1980). Workshops and parent groups. In R.R. Abidin (Ed.), *Parent education and intervention handbook* (pp. 107–129). Springfield, IL: Thomas.

American Academy of Pediatrics. (1998). Guidance for effective discipline. *Pediatrics, 101,* 723–728.

Anastasiow, N.J. (1987). Programs developed in response to teen pregnancies. *Infant Mental Health Journal, 8,* 65–75.

Anderson, S.A., & Nuttall, P.E. (1987). Parent communications training across three stages of child rearing. *Family Relations: Journal of Applied Family and Child Studies, 36,* 40–44.

Arendell, T. (1997). A social constructionist approach to parenting. In T. Arendell (Ed.), *Contemporary parenting: Challenges and issues* (pp. 1–44). Thousand Oaks, CA: Sage.

Auerbach, A.B. (1968). *Parents learn through discussion: Principles and practices of parent group education.* New York: Wiley.

Axelrad, S., & Brody, S. (1978). *Mothers, fathers and children.* New York: International Universities Press.

Bailey, D.B. (1987). Collaborative goal-setting with families: Resolving differences in values and priorities for services. *Topics in Early Childhood Special Education, 7,* 59–71.

Baumrind, D. (1971). Current patterns of parental authority. *Developmental Psychology Monographs, 4,* 1–102.

Baumrind, D. (1975). *Early socialization and the discipline controversy.* Morristown, NJ: General Learning Press.

Baumrind, D. (1980). New directions in socialization research. *American Psychologist, 35,* 639–652.

Beckwith, L. (1990). Adaptive and maladaptive parenting: Implications for intervention. In S.J. Meisels & J.P. Shonkoff (Eds.), *Handbook of early childhood intervention* (pp. 53–77). New York: Cambridge University Press.

Belsky, J. (1984). The determinants of parenting: A process model. *Child Development, 55,* 83–96.

Belsky, J., Lerner, R.M., & Spanier, G.B. (1984). *The child in the family.* Reading, MA: Addison-Wesley.

Berbardo, F.M. (1988). The American family: A commentary. *Journal of Family Issues, 8,* 426–428.

Bodley, M.J. (1987). Family resources database. *Family Relations, 36,* 229–232.

Brody, G.H., & Forehand, R. (1985). The efficacy of parent training with maritally distressed and nondistressed mothers: A multimethod assessment. *Behaviour Research and Therapy, 23,* 191–296.

Bronfenbrenner, U. (1979). Contexts of child rearing. *American Psychologist, 34,* 844–850.

Calvert, S.C., & McMahon, R.J. (1987). The treatment acceptability of a behavioral parent training program and its components. *Behavior Therapy, 18,* 165–179.

Campbell, S. (1995). Behavior problems in preschool children: A review of recent research. *Journal of Child Psychology and Psychiatry, 36,* 113–149.

Choi, E. (1995). A contrast of mothering behaviors in women from Korea and the United States. *Journal of Obstetric, Gynecologic, and Neonatal Nursing, 24,* 363–369.

Clark, D.B., & Baker, B.L. (1983). Predicting outcome in parent training. *Journal of Consulting and Clinical Psychology, 51,* 309–311.

Cudaback, D., Darden, C., Nelson, P., O'Brien, S., Pinsky, D., & Wiggins, E. (1985). Becoming successful parents: Can age-paced newsletter help? *Family Relations, 34,* 271–275.

Dadds, M.R., Schwartz, S., & Sanders, M.R. (1987). Marital discord and treatment outcome in behavioral treatment of child conduct disorders. *Journal of Consulting and Clinical Psychology, 55,* 396–403.

Daly, R.M., Holland, C.J., Forrest, P.A., & Fellbaum, G.A. (1985). Temporal generalization of treatment effects over a three-year period for a parent training program: Directive parent counseling. *Canadian Journal of Behavioral Sciences, 17,* 379–387.

Danforth, J.S. (1998). The behavior management flow chart: A component analysis of behavior management strategies. *Clinical Psychology Review, 18*(2), 229–257.

Dangel, R.F., & Polster, R.A. (1984). *Parent training: Foundations of research and practice.* New York: Guilford Press.

De'Ath, E. (1983). Teaching parenting skills. *Journal of Family Therapy, 5,* 321–335.

Dembo, M.H., Switzer, M., & Lauritzen, P. (1985). An evaluation of group parent education: Behavioral, PET and Adlerian programs. *Review of Educational Research, 55,* 155–200.

Dumas, J.E. (1984). Interactional correlates of treatment outcome in behavioral parent training. *Journal of Consulting and Clinical Psychology, 52,* 946–954.

Dumas, J.E., & Albin, J.B. (1986). Parent training outcome: Does active parental involvement matter? *Behaviour Research and Therapy, 24,* 227–230.

Dumas, J.E., & Wahler, R.G. (1983). Predictors of treatment outcome in parent training: Mother insularity and socioeconomic disadvantage. *Behavioral Assessment, 5,* 301–313.

Eastman, A.M., & Eyberg, S.M. (1981, March). *The relationship between behavior problems and parent knowledge of behavior management skills.* Paper presented at the 13th Banff International Conference on Behavior Modification, Banff, Alberta, Canada.

Edwards, J.N. (1988). Changing family structure and youthful well-being. *Journal of Family Issues, 8,* 355–372.

Eyberg, S. (1988). Parent-child interaction therapy: Integration of traditional and behavioral concerns. *Child and Family Behavior Therapy, 10,* 33–46.

Farber, B. (1988). The future of the American family: A dialectical account. *Journal of Family Issues, 8,* 431–433.

Ford, J.D. (1979). An interpersonal-effectiveness approach to consumer health education. *Medical Care, 17,* 1061–1067.

Forehand, R.L., Furey, W.M., & McMahon, R.J. (1984). The role of maternal distress in a parent training program to modify child non-compliance. *Behavioural Psychotherapy, 12,* 93–108.

Forehand, R.L., & Long, N. (1988). Outpatient treatment of the acting out child: Procedures, long-term follow-up data, and clinical problems. *Advances in Behaviour Research and Therapy, 10,* 129–177.

Forehand, R.L., & Long, N. (1996). *Parenting the strong-willed child: The clinically proven five-week program for parents of two- to six-year-olds.* Chicago: Contemporary Books.

Forehand, R., Middlebrook, J., Rogers, T., & Steffe, M. (1983). Dropping out of parent training. *Behaviour Research and Therapy, 21,* 663–668.

Foss, G. (1996). A conceptual model for studying parenting behaviors in immigrant populations. *Advanced Nursing Science, 19,* 74–87.

Fox, R.A., & Solis-Camara, P. (1997). Parenting of young children by fathers in Mexico and the United States. *Journal of Social Psychology, 137,* 489–495.

Frankel, F., & Simmons, J.Q. (1992). Parent behavioral training: Why and when some parents drop out. *Journal of Clinical Child Psychology, 21,* 322–330.

Franks, C.M., & Susskind, D.J. (1968). Behavior modification with children: Rationale and technique. *Journal of School Psychology, 6,* 75–88.

Frentz, C., & Kelley, M.L. (1986). Parents' acceptance of reductive treatment methods: The influence of problem severity and perception of child behavior. *Behavior Therapy, 17,* 75–81.

Furey, W.M., & Basili, L.A. (1988). Predicting consumer satisfaction in parent training for noncompliant children. *Behavior Therapy, 19,* 555–564.

Galinsky, E. (1990). Raising children in the 1990s: The challenges for parents, educators, and business. *Young Children, 45*(2), 2–3, 67–69.

Gammon, E., & Rose, S. (1991). The coping skills training program for parents of children with developmental disabilities: An experimental evaluation. *Research on Social Work Practice, 1,* 244–256.

Gecas, V. (1988). Born in the USA in the 1980s: Growing up in difficult times. *Journal of Family Issues, 8,* 434–436.

Glick, P.C. (1988). Fifty years of family demography: A record of social change. *Journal of Marriage and the Family, 50,* 861–873.

Goode, W.J. (1964). *The family.* Englewood Cliffs, NJ: Prentice-Hall.

Graves, T., Meyers, A.W., & Clark, L. (1988). An evaluation of parental problem-solving training in the behavioral treatment of childhood obesity. *Journal of Consulting and Clinical Psychology, 56,* 246–250.

Greene, B.F., Clark, H.B., & Risley, T.R. (1977). *Shopping with children: Advice for parents.* San Rafael, CA: Academic Therapy.

Grimley, L.K., & Robinson, R. (1986). Parent education in early childhood: The growing child model. *Techniques: A Journal for Remedial Education and Counseling, 2,* 81–87.

Hanf, C., & Kling, J. (1973). *Facilitating parent-child interactions: A two-stage training model.* Unpublished manuscript, Oregon Health Sciences University, Portland.

Harris, J. (1998). *The nurture assumption: Why children turn out the way they do: Parents matter less than you think and peers matter more.* New York: Simon & Schuster.

Heffer, R.W., & Kelley, M.L. (1987). Mother's acceptance of behavioral interventions for children: The influence of parent race and income. *Behavior Therapy, 2,* 153–163.

Helm, D.T., & Kozloff, M.A. (1986). Research on parent training: Shortcomings and remedies. *Journal of Autism and Developmental Disorders, 16,* 1–22.

Hembree-Kigin, T., & McNeil, C.B. (1995). *Parent-child interaction therapy.* New York: Plenum Press.

Hills, M.D., & Knowles, D.W. (1987). Providing for personal meaning in parent education programs. *Family Relations, 36,* 158–162.

Hunt, J.G., & Hunt, L.L. (1988). Here to play: From families to lifestyles. *Journal of Family Issues, 8,* 440–443.

Institute for Family-Centered Care. (1998). *The new children's hospital: An opportunity to advance the practice of family-centered care.* Portland, OR: Doernbecher Children's Hospital.

Jackson, R.H., & Seitz, S. (1977). *When parents ask for help.* Unpublished manuscript, Oregon Health Sciences University, Portland.

Jackson, R.H., & Terdal, L. (1978). Parent education within a pediatric practice. *Journal of Pediatric Psychology, 3,* 2–5.

Kagan, J. (1976). The role of family during the first half decade. In V.C. Vaughan & T.B. Brazelton (Eds.), *The family: Can it be saved?* (pp. 161–171). Chicago: Year Book Medical.

Kagan, J. (1979). Family experience and the child's development. *American Psychologist, 34,* 886–891.

Kagitcibasi, C. (1992). Research in child development, parenting, and the family in a cross-cultural perspective. In M.R. Rosenzweig (Ed.), *International psychological science: Progress, problems, and prospects* (pp. 137–160). Washington, DC: American Psychological Association.

Kantrowitz, B., Wingert, P., Gordon, J., Witherspoon, R.M., Witherspoon, D., Calonius, E., Gonzales, D.L., & Turque, B. (1987, August). How to stay married. *Newsweek,* 52–57.

Kazdin, A.E. (1985). *Treatment of antisocial behavior in children and adolescents.* Homewood, IL: Dorsey Press.

Kazdin, A.E. (1997a). Parent management training: Evidence, outcomes, and issues. *Journal of the American Academy of Child and Adolescent Psychiatry, 36,* 1349–1356.

Kazdin, A.E. (1997b). Practitioner review: Psychosocial treatments for conduct disorder in children. *Journal of Child Psychology and Psychiatry, 38,* 161–178.

Kelly, G.A. (1955). *The psychology of personal constructs* (Vols. 1 & 2). New York: Norton.

Kendler, K.S., Sham, P.C., & MacLean, C.J. (1997). The determinants of parenting: An epidemiological multi-informant, retrospective study. *Psychological Medicine, 27,* 549–563.

Ladden, M., & Damato, E. (1992). Parenting and supportive programs. *Nurses Association of the American College of Obstetricians and Gynecologists: Clinical Issues in Perinatal and Women's Health Nursing, 3,* 174–187.

Levant, R.F. (1987). The use of marketing techniques to facilitate acceptance of prevention program: Case example. *Professional Psychology: Research and Practice, 18,* 640–642.

Lutzker, J.R., McGimsey, J.F., McRae, S., & Campbell, R.V. (1983). Behavioral parent training: There's so much more to do. *Behavior Therapist, 6,* 110–112.

Mancini, J.A., & Orthner, D.K. (1988). The context and consequences of family change. *Family Relations, 37,* 363–366.

McMahon, R.J. (1994). Diagnosis, assessment, and treatment of externalizing problems in children: The role of longitudinal data. *Journal of Consulting and Clinical Psychology, 62,* 901–917.

McMahon, R.J., Tiedemann, G.L., Forehand, R., & Griest, D.L. (1984). Parental satisfaction with parent training to modify child noncompliance. *Behavior Therapy, 15,* 295–303.

Melnyk, B.M., & Alpert-Gillis, L. (1997). Building healthier families: Helping parents and children cope with divorce. *Advanced Practice Nursing Quarterly, 2,* 35–43.

Middlebrook, J.L., & Forehand, R. (1985). Maternal perceptions of deviance in child behavior as a function of stress and clinic versus nonclinic status of the child: An analogue study. *Behavior Therapy, 16,* 494–502.

Miller, G. (1994). Enhancing family-based interventions for managing childhood anger and aggression. In M.J. Furlong & D.C. Smith (Eds.), *Anger, hostility, and aggression: Assessment, prevention, and intervention strategies for youth* (pp. 83–116). Brandon, VT: Clinical Psychology.

Mischel, W. (1977). On the future of personality measurement. *American Psychologist, 32,* 246–254.

Musick, J.S., & Stott, F.M. (1990). Paraprofessionals, parenting, and child development: Understanding the problems and seeking solutions. In S.J. Meisels & J.P. Shonkoff (Eds.), *Handbook of early childhood intervention* (pp. 651–667). New York: Cambridge University Press.

O'Dell, S.L., Tarler-Benlolo, L., & Flynn, J.M. (1979). An instrument to measure knowledge of behavioral principles as applied to children. *Journal of Behavior Therapy and Experimental Psychiatry, 10,* 29–34.

Parents help children learn and play in public health clinics and hospital-based schools. (1979). *Hospitals, 53,* 14–15.

Parke, R.D., & O'Leary, S. (1975). Father-mother-infant interaction in the newborn period: Some findings, some observations and some unresolved issues. In K.R. Riegal & J. Meacham (Eds.), *The developing individual in a changing world: Social and environmental issues* (Vol. 2, pp. 653–663). The Hague: Mouton.

Parke, R.D., & Sawin, D.B. (1977). Fathering: It's a major role. *Psychology Today, 11,* 109–111.

Pedersen, F.A., Yarrow, L.J., Anderson, B.J., & Cain, R.L. (1978). Conceptualization of father influences in the infancy period. In M. Lewis & L.A. Rosenblum (Eds.), *The child and its family* (pp. 45–66). New York: Plenum Press.

Powell, D.R. (1987). A neighborhood approach to parent support groups. *Journal of Community Psychology, 15,* 51–62.

Prinz, R.J., & Miller, G.E. (1994). Family-based treatment for childhood antisocial behavior: Experimental influences on dropout and engagement. *Journal of Consulting and Clinical Psychology, 62,* 645–650.

Pugh, G. (1984). Parent education in action. *Early Child Development and Care, 13,* 249–276.

Pumroy, P.K., & Pumroy, S.S. (1965). Systematic observation and reinforcement technique in toilet training. *Psychological Reports, 16,* 467–478.

Rickert, V.I., Sottolano, D.C., Parrish, J.M., Riley, A.W., Hunt, F.M., & Pelco, L.E. (1988). Training parents to become better behavior managers: The need for a competency-based approach. *Behavior Modification, 12,* 475–496.

Robertson, S.E. (1984). Parent education: Current status. *Canadian Counselor, 18,* 100–105.

Rogers Wiese, M.R., & Kramer, J.J. (1988). Parent training research: An analysis of the empirical literature 1975–1985. *Psychology in the Schools, 25,* 325–330.

Rollins, B.C., & Thomas, D.L. (1979). Parental support, power and control techniques in the socialization of children. In W.R. Burr, R. Hill, F.I. Nye, & I.L. Reiss (Eds.), *Contemporary theories about the family* (Vol. 1, pp. 317–364). New York: Free Press.

Rosenberg, M.S., Reppucci, N.D., & Linney, J.A. (1983). Issues in the implementation of human service programs: Examples from a parent training project for high-risk families. *Analysis and Intervention in Developmental Disabilities, 3,* 215–225.

Scanzoni, J. (1988). Families in the 1980s: Time to refocus our thinking. *Journal of Family Issues, 8,* 394–421.

Scarr, S. (1988). The changing realities of employed mothers and young children. In S.E. Goldston (Ed.), *Promoting mental health in early child care settings* (pp. 85–115). Los Angeles: University of California, Neuropsychiatric Institute.

Schaefer, C., & Briesmeister, J. (1989). *Handbook of parent training: Parents as cotherapists for children's behavior problems.* New York: Wiley.

Schroeder, C.S. (1979). Psychologists in a private pediatric practice. *Journal of Pediatric Psychology, 4,* 5–18.

Schroeder, P. (1989). Toward a national family policy. *American Psychologist, 44,* 1410–1413.

Serna, L.A., Schumaker, J.B., Hazel, J.S., & Sheldon, J.B. (1986). Teaching reciprocal social skills to parents and their delinquent adolescents. *Journal of Clinical Child Psychology, 15,* 64–77.

Snyder, D.M. (1980). Future directions in the care of the full-term newborn. *Birth and the Family Journal, 7,* 264–267.

Solis-Camara, P., & Fox, R.A. (1996). Parenting practices and expectations among Mexican mothers with young children. *Journal of Genetic Psychology, 157,* 465–476.

Sporakowski, M.J. (1988). A therapist's views on the consequences of change for the contemporary family. *Family Relations, 37,* 373–378.

Sprott, J. (1994). One person's "spoiling" is another's freedom to become: Overcoming ethnocentric views about parental control. *Social Science and Medicine, 38,* 1111–1124.

Strain, P.S., Steele, P., Ellis, T., & Timm, M.A. (1982). Long-term effects of oppositional child treatment with mothers as therapists and therapist trainers. *Journal of Applied Behavior Analysis, 15,* 163–169.

Strickland, O. (1997). Reframing parenting in the 21st century: Does nursing have a role? *Advanced Practice Nursing, 2*(4), 44–50.

Strom, R.D. (1985). Developing a curriculum for parent education. *Family Relations: Journal of Applied Family and Child Studies, 34,* 161–167.

Sweeny, W.K. (1998). *The special needs reading list: An annotated guide to the best publications for parents and professionals.* Bethesda, MD: Woodbine House.

Tallman, I. (1988). Musings on a theory of family change. *Journal of Family Issues, 8,* 460–463.

Taylor, T., & Biglan, A. (1998). Behavioral family interventions for improving child-rearing: A review of the literature for clinicians and policy makers. *Clinical Child and Family Psychology Review, 1*(1), 41–60.

U.S. Bureau of the Census. (1995). *Statistical abstract of the United States.* Washington, DC: U.S. Government Printing Office.

U.S. Department of Agriculture. (1995). *Expenditures on children by families: 1995 annual report* (U.S. Department of Agriculture Center for Nutrition Policy and Promotion, Miscellaneous Publication 1528). Washington, DC: U.S. Government Printing Office.

Volenski, L.T. (1995). Building school support systems for parents of handicapped children: The parent education and guidance program. *Psychology in the Schools, 32,* 124–129.

Wahler, R.G. (1980). The insular mother: Her problems in parent-child treatment. *Journal of Applied Behavior Analysis, 13,* 207–219.

Wahler, R.G., & Graves, M.G. (1983). Setting events in social networks: Ally or enemy in child behavior therapy? *Behavior Therapy, 14,* 19–36.

Wahler, R.G., & Hann, D.M. (1984). The communication patterns of troubled mothers: In search of a keystone in the generalization of parenting skills. *Education and Treatment of Children, 7,* 335–350.

Wahler, R.G., & Meginnis, K.L. (1997). Strengthening child compliance through positive parenting practices: What works? *Journal of Clinical Child Psychology, 26,* 443–440.

Watson, W.J., Watson, L., Wetzel, W., Bader, E., & Talbot, Y. (1995). Transition to parenthood: What about fathers? *Canadian Family Physician, 41,* 807–812.

Webster-Stratton, C. (1982). Teaching mothers through videotape modeling to change their children's behaviors. *Journal of Pediatric Psychology, 7,* 279–294.

Webster-Stratton, C. (1985). Predictors of treatment outcome in parent training for conduct disordered children. *Behavior Therapy, 16,* 223–243.

Webster-Stratton, C., & Hammond, M. (1990). Predictors of treatment outcome in parent training for families with conduct problem children. *Behavior Therapy, 21,* 319–337.

Wente, A.S., & Crockenberg, S.B. (1976). Transition to fatherhood: Lamaze preparation, adjustment difficulty and the husband-wife relationship. *Family Coordinator, 25,* 351–357.

Widman, L.E., & Tong, D.A. (1997). Requests for medical advice from patients and families to health care providers who publish on the World Wide Web. *Archives of Internal Medicine, 157,* 209–212.

Williams, B., Williams, R., & McLaughlin, T.F. (1991). Treatment of behavior disorders by parents and in the home. *Journal of Developmental and Physical Disabilities, 3,* 385–405.

Yoos, H., Kitzman, H., Olds, D.L., & Overacker, I. (1995). Child rearing beliefs in the African-American community: Implications for culturally competent pediatric care. *Journal of Pediatric Nursing, 10,* 343–353.

CHAPTER 41

Behavior Therapy with Children

SCOTT W. POWERS

Children and families benefit from behavior therapy and cognitive-behavioral therapy in the remediation and management of psychological and behavioral problems (Casey & Berman, 1985; Kazdin, Bass, Ayers, & Rodgers, 1990; Lonigan, Elbert, & Johnson, 1998; Spirito, 1999; Weisz, Donenberg, Han, & Weiss, 1995; Weisz, Weiss, Alicke, & Klotz, 1987; Weisz, Weiss, Han, Granger, & Morton, 1995). In the fields of clinical child and pediatric psychology, various behavior therapies have been shown efficacious for a wide variety of presenting problems, including depressive disorders (Kaslow & Thompson, 1998), phobic and anxiety disorders (Ollendick & King, 1998), autism and pervasive developmental disorders (Rogers, 1998), oppositional defiant and conduct disorders (Brestan & Eyberg, 1998), attention-deficit/hyperactivity disorder (Pelham, Wheeler, & Chronis, 1998), recurrent pediatric headache (Holden, Deichmann, & Levy, 1999), recurrent abdominal pain (Janicke & Finney, 1999), medical procedure-related pain (Powers, 1999), disease-related pain (Walco, Sterling, Conte, & Engel, 1999), severe feeding problems (Kerwin, 1999), pediatric obesity (Jelalian & Saelens, 1999), enuresis and encopresis (Houts, Berman, & Abramson, 1994; Luxem & Christophersen, 1994; Stark et al., 1997), and sleep disorders (Mindell & Durand, 1993). Although many challenges remain for clinical child and pediatric psychology researchers and clinicians

(Kazdin & Kendall, 1998; Weisz & Hawley, 1998), it is clear that behavior therapies and cognitive-behavioral therapies should be included in the health care provided to children and families. Therefore, the purpose of this chapter remains the same as in the two prior editions of this text: to highlight a sampling of the many treatment approaches that have been derived from behavior therapy research and practice. The hope is that clinical child and pediatric psychologists of all therapeutic perspectives will find the contents of this chapter useful.

An introduction to behavior therapy with children might be best accomplished by a brief analysis of behavior therapy in general. Behavior therapy may be considered a multifaceted theoretical model, an experimental methodology, and a set of techniques (Goldfried & Davison, 1994; Phillips, 1998). From a theoretical perspective, principles of learning including classical conditioning (Wolpe, 1958), operant conditioning (Skinner, 1953) and social/observational learning (Bandura, 1969) have been central to the development of behavior therapy. More recently, cognitive, social, physiological, family systems, and developmental principles have been incorporated into behavioral theories (Mash, 1989; Mash & Terdal, 1997). Basic to behavior therapy is a supposition that the same learning principles govern the acquisition and extinction of both adaptive and maladaptive behaviors. In general, events of the present as opposed to those of the past are the focus of intervention.

The essence of behavior therapy is a methodology that permits replication of findings. Behavior therapists are empiricists and adapt their treatment to the client's problems rather than offer a uniform therapeutic approach. Ideally, each behavior therapy case yields results beneficial to the client and at the same time provides data that can be used by other behavior therapists. Behavior therapy is expected to include a detailed description of treatment procedures and measures used to reflect that treatment; the design of the study should permit data collection, analysis, and interpretation. Both single-case and group designs are employed (Barlow & Hersen, 1984; Kazdin, 1998).

Although a chapter on behavior therapy with children also could be organized on the basis of theory or methodology, this discussion is ordered by well-established treatment procedures/techniques. The first section describes operant-based approaches with different populations of children in a variety of settings. Modeling procedures, relaxation therapy, and cognitive-behavioral therapy provide a framework for further illustrations of behavior therapy with children.

Behavior therapy is constantly expanding and evolving. A comprehensive discussion of the vast field of child behavior therapy can be found in Watson and Gresham (1998). Although this chapter does not pretend to be exhaustive, or even entirely representative, of this area, it is a presentation of basic treatment approaches that can be incorporated into any child clinician's repertoire of skills, or at least followed up on by referring to the cited literature. However, though techniques are important and provide for a logical representation of behavior therapy with children, it is important to note that "Developing the techniques for application is easy if you know basic operant and respondent conditioning principles; modifying the techniques to fit a specific case is impossible if you do not" (Linscheid, 1999, p. 215).

OPERANT-BASED TREATMENT

The principles of operant conditioning (Skinner, 1938, 1953), which focus on the relationship among observable events, have powerfully influenced the development of behavior therapy. The following hypothetical example illustrates how operant conditioning principles might guide a behaviorally oriented classroom teacher who is attempting to modify a selected behavior pattern. A schoolchild "talks out" in class on 15 occasions at times when the students have been told to study quietly. An operant approach would first operationally define the target behavior and then have independent observers observe and record the events preceding the talking out, the occurrence of the behavior itself, and the consequences following the behavior; this approach would provide a *functional analysis* (Gelfand & Hartmann, 1984).

Operant extinction is said to take place when a reduction in response frequency is observed following removal of reinforcement. Thus, the teacher might ignore the child's behavior, turning his or her back to the class and becoming busy with paperwork. *Punishment* decreases the probability of a response through the presentation of an aversive event or the removal of a positive event contingent on a response. Because, in this example, the child is not engaging in behavior immediately harmful to self or others (e.g., self-injury), it seems unlikely that the teacher would consider the application of strong aversive events to decrease the frequency of the target behavior. However, a response-cost technique might be used in which the child would forfeit points, exchangeable for backup prizes, following talking out (Little & Kelley, 1989).

In the establishment of control over a target behavior, it is frequently desirable to identify and define behavior incompatible with the unwanted response. In this case, a response incompatible with talking out might consist of not talking and raising one's hand in response to a question. The teacher would define, observe, and record this behavior. To increase hand-raising behavior, either *positive reinforcement* or *negative reinforcement* could be applied following the behavior. Positive reinforcement is defined as the presentation of a stimulus contingent on a response to increase the frequency of that response. Points, exchangeable for backup reinforcers (perhaps a trophy or free time to engage in a preferred activity such as computer or videogames) might be applied with the expectation that hand-raising behavior would increase in frequency. The target behavior also might be increased by removing an aversive stimulus, for example, a noxious noise or uncomfortable temperature contingent on the response. In the situation described, it appears that positive reinforcement would be more easily utilized. However, if the teacher were successful in decreasing the child's talking out behavior, an aversive stimulus, the behavior of "attending to hand-raising" would likely be *negatively reinforced* for the teacher (and hence, become a teacher behavior more likely to occur in the future).

It is probable that the child's new response (hand raising) would be weak, incomplete, and in need of *shaping*. Initially, the teacher would award points for slight movements and abortive lifting of the hand; later, a more fully developed response would be required before the administration of positive reinforcement. Because newly acquired responses are weak, the teacher would choose a near continuous *schedule of reinforcement* to build in the desired response rapidly, administering attention and points for each response. Later, intermittent reinforcement would be applied because such a schedule of reinforcement is associated with response maintenance. Should the child fail to respond to instructions, training procedures might be initiated in special sessions outside the classroom. Perhaps, early in the training sequence, it would be necessary for the teacher to stand next to the child, guiding his or her hand to make the behavior more probable. Instruction paired with guiding, followed by touching, then gestures, and later instructions alone illustrates the use of *prompts* and the systematic *fading* of those prompts. As the training progresses, the teacher might move farther and farther from the child until he or she is standing behind a desk, much as in the actual classroom situation. Utilizing a similarity between training and classroom cues should enhance the probability that *stimulus generalization* will occur and that the child will transfer the target behavior from the training room to the classroom setting. In implementing training outside the classroom setting, the stimulus control gained, helpful in the prompting, shaping, and reinforcement of the target behavior, is a trade-off against the problems likely to be encountered in promoting generalization to the classroom. The newly learned behavior emitted in the classroom will be weak and will likely undergo extinction unless the teacher reinforces it. It has been noted repeatedly that generalization of a target behavior must be programmed, not left to chance (Edelstein, 1989; Stokes & Baer, 1977; Stokes & Osnes, 1989).

Adult attention has been identified as an unintended reinforcer for a variety of inappropriate behaviors. In a seminal study, Williams (1959) reported the successful treatment of tantrum behavior in a 21-month-old male child by the removal of reinforcement. After being put to bed, the child would scream and fuss if the parents left the room; one of the parents was spending up to two hours in the bedroom waiting until the child went to sleep. An extinction procedure was initiated in which the child was put to bed and left screaming and yelling. The amount of time spent in tantrum behavior decreased rapidly after the first session, and by the tenth occasion, the child no longer fussed when the parent left the room, smiling instead. An aunt inadvertently reinstated the tantrum behavior by returning to the child's bedroom while the child was tantruming; similar procedures were instituted, and the behavior was extinguished a second time. No undesirable side effects were observed, and on follow-up the child was described as friendly and outgoing.

The principle of positive reinforcement to help a child achieve and maintain play relationships with peers was employed by Allen, Hart, Buell, Harris, and Wolf (1964). A 4-year-old girl was observed to interact freely with adults but seldom with children. The positive reinforcement procedures consisted of teacher attention to the child for all play with other children, no attention when alone, and minimal attention when she contacted adults only. At the end of the treatment period, she was interacting frequently with peers and was described as a confident, happy member of the group.

Magrab and Papadopoulou (1977) reported the effect of a token reinforcement program on the maintenance of dietary control for four children undergoing dialysis treatment. A prize list was constructed based on the children's personal choices. Points were earned for maintaining acceptable levels of weight, protein breakdown, and potassium level—measures important to a child on hemodialysis. The program resulted in significant improvements in the dietary patterns of each of the four children.

Forehand and his associates (Forehand & McMahon, 1981) have conducted a series of investigations to examine the effectiveness of a parent training program designed specifically to modify child noncompliance. The high-quality research design and methodology that provide data to support the program's efficacy make it an excellent model for teaching parents operant procedures in an outpatient clinic setting. A parental interview followed by clinic observations of parent-child interactions provides a baseline for determining treatment efficacy.

Phase 1 of the training program focuses on teaching the parent to increase the frequency and range of social rewards and to eliminate negative verbal behaviors. The goal is to have the parent give contingent positive attention for desirable child behavior. Although training emphasizes the use of verbal praise statements that label the desirable behavior (e.g., "What a good girl you are to put the toys away!"), alternative rewards such as television time, social outings, and tangible treats are also discussed.

Phase 2 involves training the parent to use a brief time-out procedure. Compliance initiated within five seconds of a parental command is rewarded with positive attention. If the child does not comply, the parent gives a verbal warning of the specific time-out consequences for continued noncompliance. If the child does not comply within five seconds after the warning, the parent places the child on a chair in the corner of the room. After the child has sat quietly on the chair for two to three minutes, the initial parental command is then restated, and compliance is rewarded with positive attention. This sequence of command, warning, and time-out is repeated until compliance is exhibited. The training program also requires that parents, with the therapist's assistance, select target behaviors and develop a home program for practice of their newly acquired skills between clinic training sessions.

The highly structured nature of this parent training program has made it particularly amenable to laboratory as well as clinical investigations in establishing empirical support for treatment efficacy. Feedback from continued research has led to some modifications of training parameters and the development of adjuncts to the basic program (Powers & Roberts, 1995; M.W. Roberts & Powers, 1988, 1990). Investigations of generalization (setting, temporal, sibling), social validity, and comparative effectiveness with other forms of intervention have been conducted; they all indicate further empirical support for this treatment program (McMahon & Wells, 1989). Similar behavioral parent training programs that have empirical support have been developed (Barkley, 1997; Briesmeister & Schaefer, 1998;

Hembree-Kigin & McNeil, 1995; Webster-Stratton & Hammond, 1997).

The behavior of some children is so disordered that home care is extremely difficult and, in some cases, impossible. These children exhibit behavior deficits (little or no language development; failure to acquire ordinary self-help skills, including dressing, toileting, and appropriate eating skills; and a lack of social behaviors) as well as behavior excesses (e.g., self-stimulatory behaviors, self-destructive behaviors, aggressive behaviors) that are highly resistant to modification (R.P. Barrett, 1986).

In the treatment of severely disturbed children, the control of destructive behavior, both self-injury and aggression toward others, must receive high priority. Children banging their heads against walls and other objects have sustained serious injuries; irreversible brain damage and even death can result. O'Leary and Wilson (1987) and Matson and DiLorenzo (1983) have summarized variables related to the administration and effectiveness of contingent punishment, a procedure applicable to self-injurious behavior. The punishing stimulus should have a clear onset and offset and be introduced and maintained at a high intensity. Punishment should follow the problem behavior immediately and occur on a continuous schedule. Because punishment suppresses behavior rather than teaching a new response, alternative appropriate behaviors should be programmed. Also, there are possible negative outcomes of punishment that indicate caution in its use (Ammerman & Hersen, 1995). Some behaviors, such as tantrums, may be exacerbated by punishment, and anxiety responses may be conditioned both to the stimuli present during the event and the stimulus characteristics of the person administering the punishment. In the control of severely disordered, self-injurious behavior, however, punishment is effective and may be considered far kinder than less intrusive techniques that prove ineffective or lead only to slow behavior change (Harris & Ersner-Hershrfield, 1978; Matson & DiLorenzo, 1983).

The following case report illustrates the effective use of punishment to control self-injurious behavior. Tate and Baroff (1966) treated a 9-year-old blind, psychotic child who, since the age of 4, had engaged in frequent self-injurious behavior (e.g., head banging, hitting his shoulder with his chin, and slapping his face with his hands). The child was calm when restrained in bed, but "when left alone and free, he would cry, scream, flail his arms about and hit himself, or bang his head" (p. 282). One treatment procedure consisted of response-contingent electric shock. Self-injurious behavior decreased rapidly in frequency and was eliminated by the 147th day. Time in bed and restraints decreased and time engaging in physical therapy and play activities increased. Interestingly, firm commands, paired with the click of the shock apparatus (without shock delivery) was effective in decreasing other inappropriate behavior, such as retaining saliva in his mouth, posturing, and refusal to swallow food and liquids.

MODELING PROCEDURES

Bandura (1969) observed that "virtually all learning phenomena resulting from direct experiences can occur on a vicarious basis through observation of other persons' behavior and its consequences for them" (p. 118). In a discussion of this ubiquitous behavior change procedure, he identifies separate components: (1) attentional processes that are influenced by modeling both stimuli and characteristics of the observer; (2) retention processes such as symbolic coding and motor rehearsal; (3) motor reproduction processes to include feedback as to accuracy and physical capabilities of the observer; and (4) motivational processes that have to do with external, vicarious, and self-reinforcement. The reader who is interested in a thorough overview of the theoretical and research aspects of social learning is referred to Bandura (1977).

Modeling procedures have been used frequently to modify problem behaviors in children, particularly fears and anxieties (Barrios & O'Dell, 1989; Ollendick & King, 1998). In both institutions and outpatient settings, modeling procedures tend to be used as part of a treatment package. As a treatment component, modeling has frequently served to evoke an adaptive response. Once emitted, many of those responses have reinforcing environmental consequences that do not need to be programmed by the therapist. For other behaviors, the therapist must provide the reinforcing consequences for an initially weak response not under control of the natural environment. The following summaries illustrate the use of modeling in acquiring a new response (learning how to imitate), overcoming the

behavioral deficits of low socialization, and making an adaptive response (entering a hospital for treatment) more comfortable through fear reduction. Other examples of modeling as part of a multicomponent treatment package are discussed in the section on cognitive-behavioral therapies.

A first step in the use of modeling procedures is to assure that the child has available the imitative response itself. Baer, Peterson, and Sherman (1967) demonstrated that severely retarded children who apparently have no imitative responses in their repertoire can be taught to acquire new behavior patterns through modeling. Modeling a simple response, prompting the child to respond imitatively when necessary, and following the response with a food reinforcer accomplished this. After a series of training trials, the children imitated new behaviors demonstrated by the experimenter.

A study by O'Connor (1969) illustrates the modification of a problem behavior, social withdrawal, through modeling techniques. Nursery school children exhibiting marked social withdrawal either watched a film depicting social interactions between children that resulted in reinforcing consequences or viewed a film that did not show social interactions. The group receiving modeling showed an increase in social responsiveness, whereas the other group did not.

Modeling procedures may be used to teach a new pattern of behavior consisting of responses already in the individual's repertoire. The behavior pattern, making an appropriate request of a teacher, consists of many component responses: making eye contact, facing the teacher, speaking fluently, and so on. Most children are capable of exhibiting separately each of these responses, but they may not occur in this particular "request" pattern. As Bandura (1969) has pointed out using other examples, it would be highly uneconomical of time and effort to select out and shape through operant procedures each individual behavior in a pattern.

Melamed and Siegel (1975) used filmed modeling to reduce anxiety in children, ages 4 through 12, who were being hospitalized for surgery. The experimental group viewed a film in which a peer model, although initially somewhat anxious, coped with common hospital scenes in a nonanxious manner. Control group subjects saw a film similar in interest value but not related to hospitalization. Self-report, behavioral, and physiological measures all favored the experimental as compared with the control group. Filmed and taped models offer both convenience and experimental control. Examples of clinical problems that have been treated successfully, in part through the use of filmed modeling, include behavioral distress during invasive medical procedures (Powers, 1999), dental fears (Siegel, 1988), and hospitalization fears (Peterson, Schultheis, Ridley-Johnson, Miller, & Tracy, 1984). Dowrick (1979) presented an imaginative use of filmed modeling. A socially withdrawn 5-year-old boy whose behavior included a low frequency of verbal interactions with other children was given a single 5mg dose of diazepam. A short while later, the child was filmed talking fluently with a peer; this film was later replayed to the child in a series of treatment sessions. Immediately after treatment and in later telephone contacts, the parents reported increased talkativeness in the home environment.

Filmed modeling procedures lend themselves particularly well to the treatment of populations of children with problem behaviors that are not extremely pathological in kind or degree, such as moderate behavioral excesses and deficits, fears, and anxieties (Ollendick, 1986). Some children in almost every educational setting exhibit such behaviors. For example, M.C. Roberts, Wurtele, Boone, Ginther, and Elkins (1981) developed a slide-audiotape package featuring two children who shared their experience of being hospitalized for minor surgery. Children in elementary school who viewed the slide show reported a reduction in general medical fears as well as greater medical knowledge when compared with an attention control group.

RELAXATION TRAINING

Powers and Spirito (1998a, 1998b) describe the use of relaxation training and biofeedback with children. Techniques such as diaphragmatic breathing, progressive muscle relaxation, autogenic training, and imagery are presented. Conceptually, relaxation is associated with high levels of parasympathetic activity and should be capable of inhibiting sympathetic activity and arousal, thus reducing states of anxiety and pain. There is empirical evidence for beneficial effects, in terms of both physiological measures and control of client-presented problems (Holden et al., 1999; Powers, 1999; Walco et al., 1999).

Generalization of the relaxation response is promoted through cue-controlled and differential relaxation. In cue-controlled relaxation, the client achieves relaxation in response to self-produced cues. Paul (1966) describes a procedure in which the relaxed client focuses attention on his or her own breathing, subvocalizing a cue word (e.g., "calm") with each exhalation. The client adequately trained in this technique presumably could evoke relaxation responses in the presence of stressful stimuli by cueing with the word "calm." In differential relaxation, the client learns to relax those muscle groups not involved in the performance of an activity.

Although no one procedure can be described as standard and universally accepted, a manual for helping professions written by Bernstein and Borkovec (1973) illustrates an easily learned training procedure that may serve as the basis for relaxation training for children. Powers and Spirito (1998a, 1998b) also provide specific examples of relaxation training for children. In a discussion of relaxation training for the mentally retarded, Harvey (1979) suggests a number of modifications, including (1) rewarding initial compliance with social or consumable incentives; (2) simplifying the training procedure through the use of plain language and appropriate imagery; (3) nonverbal communication, including gestures and demonstrations; (4) rewarding successive approximations to the desired relaxation response; and (5) beginning training with easily controlled and discriminated parts of the body, such as arms and legs. Cautela and Groden (1978) have produced a manual on relaxation in a programmed learning format that includes suggestions for working with children with physical disabilities and severe behavior problems. Readiness exercises are emphasized, including sitting still for five seconds, maintaining eye contact for three seconds, and following simple instructions. The authors suggest the use of touching, the provision of concrete as well as social reinforcers, and the employment of reinforcers tailored to the particular child's needs.

Koeppen (1974) developed a clever relaxation training script for use with elementary school-age children that capitalizes on the child's willingness to engage in imagery and fantasy. In her approach, the child squeezes a lemon rather than merely making a fist. In stretching and pulling the shoulders, the child is instructed to pretend to be a furry, lazy cat. The following excerpt illustrates tension-release cycles for the shoulder and neck:

> Now pretend you are a turtle. You're sitting out on a rock by a nice, peaceful pond, just relaxing in the warm sun. It feels nice and warm and safe here. Oh—oh! You sense danger. Pull your head into your house. Try to pull your shoulders up to your ears and push your head down into your shoulders. Hold it tight. It isn't easy to be a turtle in a shell. The danger is now passed. You can come out into the warm sunshine, and once again, you can relax and feel the warm sunshine. (p. 18)

Two or three sessions per week, about 15 minutes in length, are recommended. Children are described as variable in their responses, thus timing, pacing, and repetition of scenes should be fashioned to their needs.

In a review of the treatment of children's disorders by relaxation training, Walker (1979) reported success with a diversity of stress-related children's disorders, ranging from fears to biobehavioral disorders. Weil and Goldfried (1973) treated insomnia in an 11-year-old child through self-relaxation procedures. Other problem behaviors treated included headache (Holden et al., 1999), acting-out behavior (Elitzer, 1976), asthma (Creer & Reynolds, 1990), psychotic behavior (Graziano & Kean, 1971), and toilet phobia (Walker, 1979). The following illustration provides a general impression of relaxation as a treatment procedure. Shaw and Walker (1979) employed relaxation training in the short-term treatment of fetishistic behavior in an 8-year-old moderately retarded boy. The boy exhibited inappropriate and excessive sexual responses in the presence of barefoot women. This had apparently resulted from sexual stimulation experienced at a younger age when his mother massaged his stomach with her bare feet. Relaxation was proposed as a self-control response that was incompatible with the inappropriate behavior. The boy was taught to use relaxation in specific situations during which he became sexually aroused *without* eliminating the ability to respond sexually in other situations where such behavior is appropriate. Commercial audiotapes (Lupin, 1976) provided basic relaxation techniques that were also modeled by the therapist. Assessment of learning relaxation was determined by the following three criteria: (1) decrease in time spent to reach relaxation; (2) increase in time spent

voluntarily in relaxation after instructions; and (3) self-report of relaxation. Four sessions were devoted to relaxation training, followed by six sessions with a female assistant who remained barefoot while playing games and socially interacting with the boy. She cued the boy to take a deep breath and relax when he attended to her feet and rewarded him with praise and candy for successful attempts. All the sessions were conducted during one week of hospitalization at a clinical research center. At the time of discharge, the boy was able to be continually in the presence of the barefoot female assistant without becoming sexually aroused or engaging in inappropriate behavior. The parents were trained in the relaxation procedures, provided with audiotapes, and instructed to make relaxation a part of the evening routine at home. Follow-up at 6-, 12-, and 18-month intervals indicated no recurrence of the inappropriate sexual behavior. Parents and teachers also reported that the boy functioned much better at school and that his previous hyperactive behavior was greatly reduced.

Relaxation training is frequently used in combination with other treatment procedures. As part of a classroom strategy to control impulsive behavior, relaxation was combined with problem solving; rewards were forthcoming for those who used the techniques or cued their peers to do so (Schneider & Robin, 1976). Anxiety in hospitalized children was controlled by a treatment package that included imaginal distraction, comforting self-talk, and relaxation training (Peterson & Shigetomi, 1982). A combination of relaxation training and contingency management procedures has been used to control hyperactivity in the classroom (McMahon & Sulzbacher, 1980). Systematic desensitization, the best-known treatment package in which relaxation training is a major component, is discussed in the next section.

SYSTEMATIC DESENSITIZATION THERAPY

In a pioneer study, Jones (1924) explored a number of procedures for the elimination of children's fears. One of these, which she referred to as the method of direct conditioning, associated positive stimuli with fear-provoking stimuli. In one instance, a child almost 3 years old exhibited fear of a white rabbit. The child was placed in a high chair and given food in the presence of the rabbit, placed at a distance that did not elicit fear. During successive sessions, the rabbit was moved closer at a rate the child could tolerate without exhibiting overt signs of emotional arousal. After about two months of treatment, the child played with the rabbit and allowed it to nibble at his fingers.

Similar techniques that manipulate the individual's actual environment to reduce fear and anxiety are referred to as in vivo desensitization. Operations differ across studies, but the goal is to control arousal and anxiety in the presence of stimuli that heretofore have interfered with adequate performance and/or subjective comfort. In vivo desensitization has been employed as a component in the treatment of school phobia (Lazarus, Davison, & Polefka, 1965; Tahmisian & McReynolds, 1971), fear of dogs and public buses (Obler & Terwilliger, 1970), fear of water (Lewis, 1974; Ultee, Griffisen, & Schellekens, 1982), fear of darkness (Leitenberg & Callahan, 1973), elective mutism (Rasbury, 1974), and avoidance of reading (Word & Roznko, 1974).

Wolpe (1958, 1973) developed and provided clinical support for the widely adopted desensitization treatment procedure known as systematic desensitization. As opposed to in vivo desensitization, this treatment typically occurs in an office situation rather than in the environment where the client experiences discomfort. While in a state of relaxation, the client is asked to imagine clearly and vividly anxiety-evoking stimuli with the expectation that relaxation will inhibit anxiety. In the Jones (1924) study, the eating response could be said to have inhibited the effects of the feared stimulus, brought closer in small steps. Wolpe advocated the use of a hierarchy of scenes, beginning with those that the client identifies as producing no emotional discomfort and progressing by small steps to those that described scenes evoking strong emotional reactions. In the procedure, which is viewed as counterconditioning, the relaxation response "reciprocally inhibits" the anxiety response as long as each step in the hierarchy engenders little or no increment in arousal. Empirically, the results of systematic desensitization therapy have been good (Kazdin & Wilcoxon, 1976; Wolpe, 1995).

The treatment of test anxiety in children provides an example of the systematic desensitization approach most frequently employed with adults, in which arousal is countered by relaxation. Mann and Rosenthal (1969) found that both individual and group desensitization successfully reduced test anxiety in junior high school students. Their most effective treatment, however, was a vicarious desensitization procedure in which subjects viewed a peer model undergoing desensitization and gaining control over the fear. Barabasz (1973) demonstrated the effectiveness of group desensitization in reducing test anxiety among highly anxious fifth- and sixth-grade children, although a less anxious group of students receiving the same treatment was not significantly different from a control group on measures of test anxiety. Deffenbacher and Kemper (1974) used desensitization as a counseling procedure for a group of test-anxious sixth-graders and found a significant increase in grade point average.

Multiple phobias in a 10-year-old boy were treated by both imaginal and in vivo systematic desensitization (Miller, 1972). The boy's fears concerning separation from his mother, his own death, and the school situation were treated separately using Wolpe's systematic desensitization procedure. As the boy reported gradual decreases in anxiety to the imagined scenes, his pattern of telephoning his mother at work four to five times each week declined; by the ninth week of treatment, the calls had ceased. Imaginal systematic desensitization was not successful for the death phobia, but a procedure in which the therapist induced relaxation by telephone proved effective; by the sixth week of treatment, the child was able to get to sleep without difficulty, and his reported fears of death had been eliminated. The final treatment phase involved establishing a hierarchy associated with the school phobia. After imaginal desensitization, he agreed to reenter gradually by means of an in vivo desensitization procedure. Follow-up at 3 and 18 months revealed maintenance of all treatment gains and reports that the boy's anxiety level was low.

Miklich (1973) treated a 6.5-year-old boy who had a long history of panic during asthma attacks that interfered with medical treatment. Traditional systematic sensitization procedures were ruled out because of hyperactivity and denial of fear and anxiety associated with the attacks. The first task was to teach the boy "relaxed sitting." Treatment sessions were conducted daily after school. The therapist told him that he could begin playing a game to earn points that could be traded for toys when he was able to sit relaxed for five minutes. The game involved biweekly sessions of imaginal systematic desensitization. Each session began with a three-minute period of relaxation followed by the therapist's describing various frightening scenes (e.g., wild animals in the room, the ceiling falling in). The boy could earn points by maintaining relaxation during the descriptions. After the boy became successfully desensitized to other fears, the asthma panic was introduced. Elimination of the asthma panic as well as considerable improvement in general behavior, particularly hyperactivity, was noted at the end of treatment. At an eight-month follow-up, the treatment gains for asthma panic were maintained; however, hyperactivity had returned to pretherapy rates. The success of this treatment is especially noteworthy because it eliminated the need for sedatives or tranquilizers previously ordered by attending physicians to control the child's asthma attack panic.

COGNITIVE-BEHAVIORAL THERAPY

An early cognitive-behavioral approach with children can be found in Luria's (1961) work in the use of verbal mediators to control overt speech. Vygotsky (1962) later proposed that the ability to internalize verbal commands is crucial for the child's progression from external control to voluntary self-control of behavior. Meichenbaum and Goodman (1971) expanded this basic theoretical model in their development of a cognitive self-instructional training procedure for impulsive children. In a series of four training sessions, the therapist modeled appropriate on-task behavior accompanied by overt self-instruction (thinking aloud) for various tasks ranging from simple sensorimotor skills to more complex problem-solving situations. Task variety was programmed to ensure that the child did not develop task-specific response sets. The self-instruction emphasized four basic performance-relevant skills for each task: (1) defining the problem, (2) focusing attention and response guidance, (3) self-reinforcement, and (4) self-evaluative coping skills and error-correcting options (Meichenbaum, 1979). These skills are illustrated by the following training protocol for a task that required copying line patterns (Meichenbaum & Goodman, 1971):

> Okay, what is it I have to do? You want me to copy the picture with the different lines. I have to go slowly and carefully. Okay, draw the line down, down, good;

then to the right, that's it; now down some more and to the left. Good, I m doing fine so far. Remember, go slowly. Now back up again. No, I was supposed to go down. That's okay. Just erase the line carefully . . . Good. Even if I make an error I can go on slowly and carefully. I have to go down. Finished. I did it! (p. 117)

Each session also involved having the child rehearse the modeled behavior according to the following sequence of task performance instructions: (1) external instruction from therapist, (2) overt self-instruction, (3) faded (whispered) overt self-instruction, and (4) covert self-instruction. The results indicated that self-instructional training was effective in modifying impulsive behavior on a variety of psychometric tests (e.g., Wechsler Intelligence Scale for Children Performance IQ, Matching Familiar Figures Test); training effects, however, did not generalize to teacher ratings of classroom behavior. Douglas, Parry, and Garson (1976) also failed to find significant generalization of training effects to classroom behavior in their use of a similar self-instructional procedure with hyperactive boys. They suggested that combining self-instructional training with contingency management techniques might be a possible solution to the generalization dilemma. Kendall and Finch (1979) responded by developing a training program for impulsive children that combined self-instructions with social praise and a response-cost contingency.

Several variations of the basic self-instructional training paradigm (Meichenbaum & Goodman, 1971) have used modeling videotapes to present the cognitive strategies. For example, Gottman, Gonso, and Schuler (1976) developed a treatment program to increase the social interaction of isolated children. The modeling component consisted of four videotaped vignettes featuring children who want to join a group of peers. Each vignette was narrated by a woman who verbalized the children's thoughts and provided coping self-statements to facilitate social interaction. Other treatment components included teaching the children basic social skills (e.g., giving positive reinforcement, effective listening) through role playing, instructions, and classroom practice. Treatment resulted in greater peer acceptance as measured by sociometric ratings, although there was no change in the total frequency of social interaction. Goodwin and Mahoney (1976) used a similar modeling videotape in their cognitive-behavioral treatment of three aggressive boys. The boys were shown a three-minute videotape of a child being taunted by five peers. Covert self-instructions of the child model were dubbed in on the tape (e.g., "I'm not going to let them bug me"). The first viewing of the tape resulted in no observable treatment effects; however, a second viewing followed by therapist coaching and rehearsal of the cognitive strategy for coping with verbal assault resulted in behavioral improvements that were maintained at one-week follow-up.

The examples of cognitive-behavioral strategies described thus far have been applied to rather broad and/or complex classes of behavior (i.e., impulsivity, hyperactivity, social isolation, and aggression). The strategies are also applicable to more specific problem behaviors. For example, Kanfer, Karoly, and Newman (1975) reported the effectiveness of teaching kindergarten children simple self-instructional statements to reduce their fear of the dark. Teaching the children sentences that emphasized their active control or competence in the fearful situation (e.g., "I'm a brave boy [girl]") was more effective than teaching sentences that reduced the aversive quality of the situation (e.g., "The dark is a fun place to be") or neutral sentences (e.g., "Mary had a little lamb"). Graziano and Mooney (1980, 1982) also found self-instructional training to be effective in treating nighttime fears in school-age children.

Kendall and colleagues have demonstrated the efficacy of a cognitive-behavioral treatment package for children with anxiety disorders (Kendall, 1994; Kendall et al., 1997; Kendall & Southam-Gerow, 1996). This treatment addresses four cognitive foci: (1) recognizing anxious feelings and body reactions to anxiety, (2) clarifying cognitions in anxiety-provoking situations, (3) developing a plan to help cope with the situation, and (4) evaluating the success of the coping strategies and self-reinforcement as appropriate (Ollendick & King, 1998). The package also includes other behavioral procedures, such as modeling, in vivo exposure, role play, relaxation training, and reinforced practice (Kendall et al., 1992). P.M. Barrett, Dadds, and Rapee (1996) have also found this treatment procedure to be effective for children with anxiety disorders.

Another basic cognitive-behavioral intervention is problem-solving training. Spivack, Platt, and Shure (1976) found that emotionally disturbed and behaviorally disruptive children tend to show problem-solving deficits relative to matched controls. They developed a training program in social reasoning skills (Spivack & Shure, 1974) that had significant positive effects on the peer relations of preschool children that were maintained at a one-year follow-up. The program consisted of 30 lessons (presented as games) for teaching the children problem-solving skills (e.g., identifying emotions, learning to gather information about other people, finding alternative solutions). More recently, Shure and colleagues have continued to refine the program and conduct additional studies (Shure, 1996). A number of similar training programs have been developed for other populations, including acting-out preadolescents in a residential treatment setting (Russell & Thoreson, 1976) and normal schoolchildren (Poitras-Martin & Stone, 1977; Stone, Hinds, & Schmidt, 1975).

Clearly, cognitive-behavioral strategies represent an important move toward helping children learn skills to use in determining their own behavior. From pain related to acute medical procedures (Powers, 1999) to anxiety disorders coincident with other comorbidities (Kendall, 1994), research over the past 20 years has increasingly demonstrated the efficacy of cognitive-behavioral therapies with children. Notably, however, most treatment programs that are labeled as cognitive-behavioral therapy consist of procedures derived from respondent, operant, and social learning approaches as well. Weist and Danforth (1998) provide a nice summary of cognitive-behavioral therapy for children and adolescents, including a number of case applications that highlight the inclusion of several treatment techniques into the cognitive-behavioral therapy package.

CONCLUSIONS

Behavior therapy is the treatment of choice for a wide range of mental health and biobehavioral issues that children and families confront. Either used in combination with other forms of therapy (e.g., family therapy) and/or medication (e.g., psychostimulants for attention-deficit/hyperactivity disorder) or used independently, behavior and cognitive-behavioral therapies should be available to all children and families who are served by the health care system. The challenges for the future include ensuring that clinicians are trained to use these therapies, that children and families have access to these therapies, that the health care system will acknowledge and reimburse for these therapies, and that further research is conducted to refine and enhance the efficacy and effectiveness of behavior and cognitive-behavioral therapies for children. Although this chapter sought only to provide a sampling of treatment procedures derived from behavior therapy research and practice, it concludes with a call to action for all clinical child and pediatric psychologists. Children and families deserve treatments that are helpful to them regardless of the background theory or approach. Each of us must play a role—as practitioner, scientist, consumer, employer, advocate, and/or voter—in applying the contents of this chapter, and this entire volume, to the lives of children. There is much work to do, and much benefit to be gained.

REFERENCES

Allen, K.E., Hart, B.M., Buell, J.S., Harris, F.R., & Wolf, M.M. (1964). Effects of social reinforcement in isolate behavior of a nursery school child. *Child Development, 35,* 511–518.

Ammerman, R.T., & Hersen, M. (Eds.). (1995). *Handbook of child behavior therapy in the psychiatric setting.* New York: Wiley.

Baer, D.M., Peterson, R.J., & Sherman, J.A. (1967). The development of imitation by reinforcing behavioral similarity to a model. *Journal of the Experimental Analysis of Behavior, 10,* 405–416.

Bandura, A. (1969). *Principles of behavior modification.* New York: Holt, Rinehart, and Winston.

Bandura, A. (1977). *Social learning theory.* Englewood Cliffs, NJ: Prentice-Hall.

Barabasz, A.F. (1973). Group desensitization of test anxiety in elementary school. *Journal of Psychology, 83,* 295–301.

Barkley, R.A. (1997). *Defiant children: A clinician's manual for assessment and parent training* (2nd ed.). New York: Guilford Press.

Barlow, D.H., & Hersen, M. (1984). *Single case experimental designs: Strategies for studying behavior change* (2nd ed.). New York: Pergamon Press.

Barrett, P.M., Dadds, M.R., & Rapee, R.M. (1996). Family treatment of childhood anxiety: A controlled trial. *Journal of Consulting and Clinical Psychology, 64*(2), 333–342.

Barrett, R.P. (1986). *Severe behavior disorders in the mentally retarded: Non-drug approaches to treatment.* New York: Plenum Press.

Barrios, B.A., & O'Dell, S.L. (1989). Fears and anxieties. In E.J. Mash & R.A. Barkley (Eds.), *Treatment of childhood disorders* (pp. 167–221). New York: Guilford Press.

Bernstein, D.A., & Borkovec, T.D. (1973). *Progressive relaxation training: A manual for the helping professions.* Champaign, IL: Research Press.

Brestan, E.V., & Eyberg, S.M. (1998). Effective psychosocial treatments of conduct-disordered children and adolescents: 29 years, 82 studies, and 5,272 kids. *Journal of Clinical Child Psychology, 27*(2), 180–189.

Briesmeister, J.M., & Schaefer, C.E. (Eds.). (1998). *Handbook of parent training: Parents as co-therapists for children's behavior problems* (2nd ed.). New York: Wiley.

Casey, R.J., & Berman, J.S. (1985). The outcome of psychotherapy with children. *Psychological Bulletin, 98*(2), 388–400.

Cautela, J.R., & Groden, J. (1978). *A comprehensive manual for adults, children, and children wtih special needs.* Champaign, IL: Research Press.

Creer, T.L., & Reynolds, R.V.C. (1990). Asthma. In A.M. Goss & R.S. Drabman (Eds.), *Handbook of clinical behavioral pediatrics* (pp. 183–203). New York: Plenum Press.

Deffenbacher, J.L., & Kemper, C.C. (1974). Counseling test-anxious sixth graders. *Elementary School Guidance and Counseling, 9,* 22–29.

Douglas, V.I., Parry, P., & Garson, C. (1976). Assessment of a cognitive training program for hyperactive children. *Journal of Abnormal Child Psychology, 4,* 389–410.

Dowrick, P.W. (1979). Single dose medication to create a self model film. *Child Behavior Therapy, 1*(2), 193–198.

Edelstein, B.A. (1989). Generalization: Terminological, methodological and conceptual issues. *Behavior Therapy, 20,* 311–324.

Elitzer, B. (1976). Self-relaxation programs for acting-out adolescents. *Adolescence, 11,* 570–572.

Forehand, R.L., & McMahon, R.J. (1981). *Helping the noncompliant child: A clinician's guide to parent training.* New York: Guilford Press.

Gelfand, M.R., & Hartmann, D.P. (1984). *Child behavior analysis and therapy* (2nd ed.). New York: Pergamon Press.

Goldfried, M.R., & Davison, G.C. (1994). *Clinical behavior therapy* (Exp. ed.). New York: Wiley.

Goodwin, S.E., & Mahoney, M.J. (1976). Modification of aggression through modeling: An experimental probe. *Journal of Abnormal Child Psychology, 4,* 179–197.

Gottman, J.M., Gonso, J., & Schuler, P. (1976). Teaching social skills to isolated children. *Journal of Abnormal Child Psychology, 4,* 179–197.

Graziano, A.M., & Kean, J.E. (1971). Programmed relaxation and reciprocal inhibition with psychotic children. In A.M. Graziano (Ed.), *Behavior therapy with children.* Chicago: Aldin.

Graziano, A.M., & Mooney, K.C. (1980). Family self-control instruction for children's nighttime fear reduction.

Journal of Consulting and Clinical Psychology, 48(2), 206–213.

Graziano, A.M., & Mooney, K.C. (1982). Behavioral treatment of "nightfears" in children: Maintenance of improvement at 2 1/2- to 3-year follow-up. *Journal of Consulting and Clinical Psychology, 50*(4), 598–599.

Harris, S.L., & Ersner-Hershrfield, R. (1978). Behavioral suppression of seriously disruptive behavior in psychotic and retarded patients: A review of punishment and its alternatives. *Psychological Bulletin, 35,* 1352–1375.

Harvey, J.R. (1979). The potential of relaxation training for the mentally retarded. *Mental Retardation, 17,* 71–76.

Hembree-Kigin, T.L., & McNeil, C.B. (1995). *Parent-child interaction therapy.* New York: Plenum Press.

Holden, E.W., Deichmann, M.M., & Levy, J.D. (1999). Empirically supported treatments in pediatric psychology: Recurrent pediatric headache. *Journal of Pediatric Psychology, 24*(2), 91–109.

Houts, A.C., Berman, J.S., & Abramson, H. (1994). Effectiveness of psychological and pharmacological treatments for nocturnal enuresis. *Journal of Consulting and Clinical Psychology, 62*(4), 737–745.

Janicke, D.M., & Finney, J.W. (1999). Empirically supported treatments in pediatric psychology: Recurrent abdominal pain. *Journal of Pediatric Psychology, 24*(2), 115–127.

Jelalian, E., & Saelens, B.E. (1999). Empirically supported treatments in pediatric psychology: Pediatric obesity. *Journal of Pediatric Psychology, 24*(3), 223–248.

Jones, M.C. (1924). The elimination of children's fears. *Journal of Experimental Psychology, 7,* 382–390.

Kanfer, F.H., Karoly, P., & Newman, A. (1975). Reduction of children's fear of the dark by competence-related and situational threat-related verbal cues. *Journal of Consulting and Clinical Psychology, 43,* 251–258.

Kaslow, N.J., & Thompson, M.P. (1998). Applying the criteria for empirically supported treatments to studies of psychosocial interventions for child and adolescent depression. *Journal of Clinical Child Psychology, 27*(2), 146–155.

Kazdin, A.E. (1998). *Research design in clinical psychology.* Needham Heights, MA: Allyn & Bacon.

Kazdin, A.E., Bass, D., Ayers, W.A., & Rodgers, A. (1990). Empirical and clinical focus of child and adolescent psychotherapy research. *Journal of Consulting and Clinical Psychology, 58*(6), 729–740.

Kazdin, A.E., & Kendall, P.C. (1998). Current progress and future plans for developing effective treatments: Comments and perspectives. *Journal of Clinical Child Psychology, 27*(2), 217–226.

Kazdin, A.E., & Wilcoxon, L.A. (1976). Systematic desensitization and nonspecific treatment effects: A methodological evaluation. *Psychological Bulletin, 83,* 729–758.

Kendall, P.C. (1994). Treating anxiety disorders in children: Results of a randomized clinical trial. *Journal of Consulting and Clinical Psychology, 62*(1), 100–110.

Kendall, P.C., Chansky, T.E., Kane, M.T., Kim, R.S., Kortlander, E., Ronan, K.R., Sessa, F.M., & Siqueland, L. (1992). *Anxiety disorders in youth: Cognitive-behavioral interventions.* Needham Heights, MA: Allyn & Bacon.

Kendall, P.C., & Finch, A.J., Jr. (1979). Developing nonimpulsive behavior in children: Cognitive-behavioral strategies for self-control. In P.C. Kendall & S.D. Hollon (Eds.), *Cognitive-behavioral interventions: Theory, research and procedures.* New York: Academic Press.

Kendall, P.C., Flannery-Schroeder, E., Panichelli-Mindel, S.M., Southam-Gerow, M., Henin, A., & Warman, M. (1997). Therapy for youths with anxiety disorders: A second randomized clinical trial. *Journal of Consulting and Clinical Psychology, 65*(3), 366–380.

Kendall, P.C., & Southam-Gerow, M.A. (1996). Long-term follow-up of a cognitive-behavioral therapy for anxiety-disordered youth. *Journal of Consulting and Clinical Psychology, 64*(4), 724–730.

Kerwin, M.E. (1999). Empirically supported treatments in pediatric psychology: Severe feeding problems. *Journal of Pediatric Psychology, 24*(3), 193–214.

Koeppen, A.S. (1974). Relaxation training for children. *Elementary School Guidance and Counseling, 9,* 14–21.

Lazarus, A.A., Davison, G.C., & Polefka, D.A. (1965). Classical and operant factors in the treatment of school phobia. *Journal of Abnormal Child Psychology, 70,* 225–229.

Leitenberg, H., & Callahan, E.J. (1973). Reinforced practice and reduction of different kinds of fears in adults and children. *Behaviour Research and Therapy, 11,* 19–30.

Lewis, S.A. (1974). A comparison of behavior therapy techniques in the reduction of fearful avoidance behavior. *Behavior Therapy, 5,* 648–655.

Linscheid, T.R. (1999). Commentary: Response to empirically supported treatments for feeding problems. *Journal of Pediatric Psychology, 24*(3), 215–216.

Little, L.M., & Kelley, M.L. (1989). The efficacy of response cost procedures for reducing children's noncompliance to parental instructions. *Behavior Therapy, 206,* 525–534.

Lonigan, C.J., Elbert, J.C., & Johnson, S.B. (1998). Empirically supported psychosocial interventions for children: An overview. *Journal of Clinical Child Psychology, 27*(2), 138–145.

Lupin, M. (1976). *The family relaxation and self-control program: A therapeutic cassette for both adults and children* [Audiotape]. Houston, TX: Biobehavioral Publishers & Distributors.

Luria, A. (1961). *The role of speech in the regulation of normal and abnormal children.* New York: Liveright.

Luxem, M., & Christophersen, E. (1994). Behavioral toilet training in early childhood: Research, practice, and implications. *Journal of Developmental and Behavioral Pediatrics, 15*(5), 370–378.

Magrab, P., & Papadopoulou, Z. (1977). The effect of a token economy on dietary compliance for children on hemodialysis. *Journal of Applied Behavior Analysis, 10,* 5–13.

Mann, J., & Rosenthal, T. (1969). Vicarious and direct counterconditioning of test anxiety through individual and group desensitization. *Behaviour Research and Therapy, 7,* 359–367.

Mash, E.J. (1989). Treatment of child and family disturbance: A behavioral-systems perspective. In E.J. Mash & R.A. Barkley (Eds.), *Treatment of childhood disorders* (pp. 3–36). New York: Guilford Press.

Mash, E.J., & Terdal, L.G. (1997). Assessment of child and family disturbance: A behavioral-systems approach. In E.J. Mash & L.G. Terdal (Eds.), *Assessment of childhood disorders* (pp. 3–68). New York: Guilford Press.

Matson, J.L., & DiLorenzo, T.M. (1983). *Punishment and its alternative: New perspectives for contemporary behavior therapy.* New York: Springer.

McMahon, R.J., & Sulzbacher, S.I. (1980). Relaxation training as an adjunct to treatment in a hyperactive boy. *Clinical Pediatrics, 19,* 496–498.

McMahon, R.J., & Wells, K.C. (1989). Conduct disorders. In E.J. Mash & R.A. Barkley (Eds.), *Treatment of childhood disorders* (pp. 73–132). New York: Guilford Press.

Meichenbaum, D.H. (1979). Teaching children self-control. In B.B. Lahey & A.E. Kazdin (Eds.), *Advances in clinical child psychology* (Vol. 2). New York: Plenum Press.

Meichenbaum, D.H., & Goodman, J. (1971). Training impulsive children to talk to themselves: A means of developing self-control. *Journal of Abnormal Psychology, 77,* 115–126.

Melamed, B.G., & Siegel, L.J. (1975). Reduction of anxiety in children facing hospitalization and surgery by use of filmed modeling. *Journal of Consulting and Clinical Psychology, 43,* 511–521.

Miklich, D.R. (1973). Operant conditioning procedure with systematic desensitization in a hyperkinetic asthmatic boy. *Journal of Behavior Therapy and Experimental Psychiatry, 4,* 177–182.

Miller, P.M. (1972). The use of visual imagery and muscle relaxation in the counterconditioning of a phobic child: A case study. *Journal of Nervous and Mental Disease, 154,* 457–460.

Mindell, J.A., & Durand, V.M. (1993). Treatment of childhood sleep disorders: Generalization across disorders and effects on family members. *Journal of Pediatric Psychology, 18*(6), 731–750.

Obler, M., & Terwilliger, R.F. (1970). Pilot study on the effectiveness of systematic desensitization with neurologically impaired children with phobic disorders. *Journal of Consulting and Clinical Psychology, 34,* 314–318.

O'Connor, R.D. (1969). Modification of social withdrawal through symbolic modeling. *Journal of Applied Behavior Analysis, 2,* 15–22.

O'Leary, K.D., & Wilson, G.T. (1987). *Behavior therapy: Application and outcome* (2nd ed.). Englewood Cliffs, NJ: Prentice-Hall.

Ollendick, T.H. (1986). Behavior therapy with children and adolescents. In S.L. Garfield & A.E. Bergin (Eds.), *Handbook of psychotherapy and behavior change* (3rd ed., pp. 565–624). New York: Wiley.

Ollendick, T.H., & King, N.J. (1998). Empirically supported treatments for children with phobic and anxiety disorders: Current status. *Journal of Clinical Child Psychology, 27*(2), 156–167.

Paul, G.L. (1966). *Insight vs. desensitization in psychotherapy: An experiment in anxiety reduction.* Stanford, CA: Stanford University Press.

Pelham, W.E., Jr., Wheeler, T., & Chronis, A. (1998). Empirically supported psychosocial treatments for attention-deficit/hyperactivity disorder. *Journal of Clinical Child Psychology, 27*(2), 190–205.

Peterson, L., Schultheis, K., Ridley-Johnson, R., Miller, D.J., & Tracy, K. (1984). Comparison of three modeling procedures on the presurgical and postsurgical reactions of children. *Behavior Therapy, 15,* 197–203.

Peterson, L., & Shigetomi, C. (1982). The use of coping techniques to minimize anxiety in hospitalized children. *Behavior Therapy, 12,* 1–14.

Phillips, S. (1998). Behavior therapy with children and adolescents. In H.S. Ghuman, R.M. Sarles, et al. (Eds.), *Handbook of child and adolescent outpatient, day treatment and community psychiatry* (pp. 265–281). Philadelphia: Brunner/Mazel.

Poitras-Martin, D., & Stone, G. (1977). Psychological education: A skills-oriented approach. *Journal of Counseling, 24,* 153–157.

Powers, S.W., & Roberts, M.W. (1995). Simulation training with parents of oppositional children: Preliminary findings. *Journal of Clinical Child Psychology, 24,* 89–97.

Powers, S.W., & Spirito, A. (1998a). Biofeedback. In J. Noshpitz, J. Coyle, S. Harrison, & S. Eth (Eds.), *Handbook of child and adolescent psychiatry* (Vol. 6, pp. 417–422). New York: Wiley.

Powers, S.W., & Spirito, A. (1998b). Relaxation. In J. Noshpitz, J. Coyle, S. Harrison, & S. Eth (Eds.), *Handbook of child and adolescent psychiatry* (Vol. 6, pp. 411–417). New York: Wiley.

Powers, S.W. (1999). Empirically supported treatments in pediatric psychology: Procedure-related pain. *Journal of Pediatric Psychology, 24*(2), 131–145.

Rasbury, W.C. (1974). Behavioral treatment of selective mutism: A case report. *Journal of Behavior Therapy and Experimental Psychiatry, 5,* 103.

Roberts, M.C., Wurtele, S.K., Boone, R.R., Ginther, L.J., & Elkins, P.D. (1981). Reduction of medical fears by use of modeling: A preventive application in a general population of children. *Journal of Pediatric Psychology, 6*(3), 293–300.

Roberts, M.W., & Powers, S.W. (1988). The compliance test. *Behavioral Assessment, 10,* 375–398.

Roberts, M.W., & Powers, S.W. (1990). Adjusting chair timeout enforcement procedures for oppositional children. *Behavior Therapy, 10,* 375–398.

Rogers, S.J. (1998). Empirically supported comprehensive treatments for young children with autism. *Journal of Clinical Child Psychology, 27*(2), 168–179.

Russell, M., & Thoreson, C. (1976). Teaching decision-making skills to children. In J.D. Krumboltz & C.E. Thoreson (Eds.), *Counseling methods.* New York: Holt, Rinehart, and Winston.

Schneider, M., & Robin, A. (1976). The turtle technique: A method for the self-control of impulsive behavior. In J.D. Krumboltz & C.E. Thoreson (Eds.), *Counseling methods.* New York: Holt, Rinehart, and Winston.

Shaw, W.J., & Walker, C.E. (1979). Use of relaxation in the short-term treatment of fetishistic behavior: An exploratory case study. *Journal of Pediatric Psychology, 4,* 403–407.

Shure, M.B. (1996). I can problem solve (ICPS): An interpersonal cognitive problem solving program for children. In M.C. Roberts (Ed.), *Model programs in child and family mental health* (pp. 47–62). Mahwah, NJ: Erlbaum.

Siegel, L.J. (1988). Dental treatment. In D.K. Routh (Ed.), *Handbook of pediatric psychology* (pp. 448–459). New York: Guilford Press.

Skinner, B.F. (1938). *The behavior of organisms: An experimental analysis.* New York: Appleton.

Skinner, B.F. (1953). *Science and human behavior.* New York: Macmillan.

Spirito, A. (1999). Empirically supported treatments in pediatric psychology. *Journal of Pediatric Psychology, 24*(2), 87–90.

Spivack, G., Platt, J., & Shure, M.B. (1976). *The problem solving approach to adjustment.* San Francisco: Jossey-Bass.

Spivack, G., & Shure, M.B. (1974). *Social adjustment of young children: A cognitive approach to solving real life problems.* San Francisco: Jossey-Bass.

Stark, L.J., Opipari, L.C., Donaldson, D.L., Danovsky, M.B., Rasile, D.A., & DelSanto, A.F. (1997). Evaluation of a standard protocol for retentive encopresis: A replication. *Journal of Pediatric Psychology, 22*(5), 619–633.

Stokes, T.F., & Baer, D.M. (1977). An implicit technology of generalization. *Journal of Applied Behavior Analysis, 10,* 349–367.

Stokes, T.F., & Osnes, P.G. (1989). An operant pursuit of generalization. *Behavior Therapy, 20,* 337–355.

Stone, G., Hinds, W., & Schmidt, G. (1975). Teaching mental health behaviors to elementary school children. *Professional Psychology, 6,* 34–40.

Tahmisian, J.A., & McReynolds, W.T. (1971). Use of parents as behavioral engineers in the treatment of a school-phobic girl. *Journal of Counseling Psychology, 18,* 225–228.

Tate, B.G., & Baroff, G.S. (1966). Aversive control of self-injurious behavior in a psychotic boy. *Behaviour Research and Therapy, 4,* 281–287.

Ultee, C.A., Griffisen, D., & Schellekens, J. (1982). The reduction of anxiety in children: A comparison of the effects of "systemic desensitization *in vitro*" and "systematic desensitization *in vivo*." *Behaviour Research and Therapy, 20,* 61–67.

Vygotsky, L. (1962). *Thought and language.* New York: Wiley.

Walco, G.A., Sterling, C.M., Conte, P.M., & Engel, R.G. (1999). Empirically supported treatments in pediatric psychology: Disease-related pain. *Journal of Pediatric Psychology, 24*(2), 155–167.

Walker, C.E. (1979). Treatment of children's disorders by relaxation training: The poor man's biofeedback. *Journal of Clinical Child Psychology, 8,* 22–25.

Watson, S.T., & Gresham, F.M. (Eds.). (1998). *Handbook of child behavior therapy.* New York: Plenum Press.

Webster-Stratton, C., & Hammond, M. (1997). Treating children with early-onset conduct problems: A comparison of child and parent training interventions. *Journal of Consulting and Clinical Psychology, 65*(1), 93–109.

Weil, G., & Goldfried, M.R. (1973). Treatment of insomnia in an eleven-year-old child through self-relaxation. *Behavior Therapy, 4,* 282–284.

Weist, M.D., & Danforth, J.S. (1998). Cognitive-behavioral therapy for children and adolescents. In H.S. Ghuman, R.M. Sarles, et al. (Eds.), *Handbook of child and adolescent outpatient, day treatment and community psychiatry* (pp. 235–244). Philadelphia: Brunner/Mazel.

Weisz, J.R., Donenberg, G.R., Han, S.S., & Weiss, B. (1995). Bridging the gap between laboratory and clinic in child and adolescent psychotherapy. *Journal of Consulting and Clinical Psychology, 63*(5), 688–701.

Weisz, J.R., & Hawley, K.M. (1998). Finding, evaluating, refining, and applying empirically supported treatments for children and adolescents. *Journal of Clinical Child Psychology, 27*(2), 206–216.

Weisz, J.R., Weiss, B., Alicke, M.D., & Klotz, M.L. (1987). Effectiveness of psychotherapy with children and adolescents: A meta-analysis for clinicians. *Journal of Consulting and Clinical Psychology, 55*(4), 542–549.

Weisz, J.R., Weiss, B., Han, S.S., Granger, D.A., & Morton, T. (1995). Effects of psychotherapy with children and adolescents revisited: A meta-analysis of treatment outcome studies. *Psychological Bulletin, 117*(3), 450–468.

Williams, C.D. (1959). The elimination of tantrum behavior by extinction procedures. *Journal of Abnormal and Social Psychology, 59,* 269.

Wolpe, J. (1958). *Psychotherapy by reciprocal inhibition.* Stanford, CA: Stanford University Press.

Wolpe, J. (1973). *The practice of behavior therapy* (2nd ed.). Oxford, England: Pergamon Press.

Wolpe, J. (1995). Reciprocal inhibition: Major agent of behavior change. In W.T. O'Donohue, L. Krasner, et al. (Eds.), *Theories of behavior therapy: Exploring behavior change* (pp. 23–57). Washington, DC: American Psychological Association.

Word, P., & Roznko, V. (1974). Behavior therapy of an eleven-year-old girl with reading problems. *Journal of Learning Disabilities, 7,* 551–554.

CHAPTER 42

Psychotherapy with Children

SANDRA W. RUSS AND DONALD K. FREEDHEIM

DEVELOPMENT OF CHILD PSYCHOTHERAPY

HISTORICAL PERSPECTIVES

The understanding of behavior disorders in children has changed greatly over time, partly as a function of social and humanistic concerns and partly as a function of the frames of reference used in viewing the behavior. The very terms *mental illness* and *behavior disorder* denote different perceptions of the individual so identified. Children were essentially ignored as individuals, with notable exceptions, until this century, making it unnecessary to differentiate treatment of children from that of adults. Because children were seen as "little adults," the perception of individuals who were seen as "different" pertained to all individuals.

The classic first "case" for clinical psychology was a child who came to Lightner Witmer's clinic at the University of Pennsylvania in 1896 (Witmer, 1909). The child was a poor speller, a prototype for learning problems of today. Witmer published his treatment of the child in his journal *The Psychological Clinic* the same year that Sigmund Freud described his treatment of Little Hans (S. Freud, 1909/1955), which also has implications for modern-day treatments. Freud treated Little Hans through his parent (father), which is again a popular treatment of choice with children under 6 years of age, as in parent-child interaction therapy

(Schuhmann, Foote, Eyberg, & Boggs, 1998). In 1908, Clifford Beers founded the mental hygiene movement, which led to the establishment of child guidance clinics throughout the nation (Rie, 1974). However, all was not complete harmony within the burgeoning ranks of psychotherapists. William James discussed the work of Freud in his lectures at Harvard University and was criticized by Witmer, who wrote an article entitled "Is Psychology Taught at Harvard a National Peril?" (Postman, 1962).

During the 1920s and 1930s, the behavioral experiments of psychologists were paralleled by behavioral treatments of problems in children (Wolman, Egan, & Ross, 1978). During this time, behavioral and educational approaches to childhood problems seemed to hold sway, although there was some understanding that parent-child communication problems formed the basis of many difficulties (Chadwick, 1928; Wickes, 1927).

The psychodynamic or psychoanalytic movement's influence on child treatment began to emerge in the early 1930s and came into its own with the first publication of *The Psychoanalytic Study of the Child* in 1945. The work of Klein (1932/1960) with very young children and Aichorn (1935), particularly with adolescent youth, described various psychoanalytic techniques with children. A treatment emphasizing emotional release to undo depression was stressed by Levy (1938). Baker and Traphagen (1935) applied the theories of S. Freud, Adler, and Jung to children.

In the midst of the strong psychodynamic movement of the 1940s, an alternative to treatments that emphasized verbal exchanges with children was offered by Axline (1947), who described the use of play in therapy in a more nondirective approach. A review of child therapies in the 1940s can be found in Haworth (1947). However, the treatment of children was not entirely through communication and in relationship with a therapist. More severely disturbed children were not amenable to such approaches, and, reminiscent of the Middle Ages, professionals attempted electric shock, albeit with questionable results (Bender, 1947).

The field of child psychotherapy expanded rapidly in the late 1960s and 1970s. No one approach dominated the scene, with the exception of work with the severely and moderately retarded, for whom the advancements in behavior modification therapy were most beneficial (Finch & Kendall, 1979). A whole array of specific techniques were derived for children's learning difficulties, anxiety or behavior disturbances, and for those reacting to traumatic experiences.

Another indispensable approach to child therapy is treatment through the parents (Furman, 1957). Examples of specific guides to parents in treating the problems of their children are found in the work of Wright (1978) and Finch and Kendall (1979). And there are brave souls who treat both parents and children together in family treatment, viewing the family as a systemic, organic unit (German & Kniskern, 1981). In dealing with particularly difficult children with autistic behavior (Galatzer-Levy, 1987; Ross, 1981a) or subtle learning problems (Kenny & Burka, 1980), therapists have stressed the need for multiple and flexible interventions that utilize various approaches at different times with the same child.

In the 1980s and 1990s, there was a sea change in the field of child psychotherapy (Ollendick & Russ, 1999). Several factors contributed to this changing state. First, the move to managed care changed the climate within which child and family psychotherapists worked. There is now a focus on short-term approaches and efficient treatment strategies. There is an increasing need for "effectiveness and efficiency," demanded by third-party payers (Koocher & D'Angelo, 1992). Second, the stress on empirically supported treatments—on treatments that are proven to work—has caused every conscientious therapist to reevaluate his or her practice by reviewing the scientific evidence for treatment effectiveness. Third, the growing awareness in the field about cultural and contextual variables, such as socioeconomic factors, ethnic minority background, and stability of family environment has resulted in an increased sophistication in choosing among treatment approaches.

A DEVELOPMENTAL APPROACH

Embedded in most approaches to child psychotherapy is a developmental framework. Anna Freud was one of the first to see that children are not little adults and that the same manifest symptomatology can mean many different things for children of different ages. She theorized a progressive sequence of hierarchical organization. Mayes and Cohen (1996) discuss the similarities between Anna Freud's principles of development and the basic tenets of contemporary developmental psychopathology. There are many similarities between Anna Freud's concept of developmental lines and organizational hierarchy and developmental psychopathology's organizational perspective of child development and focus on the quality of the integration within and among biological and psychological systems of the individual.

In the 1980s, the impact of a developmental psychopathology framework was felt and has become dominant in conceptualizing childhood disorders (Lease & Ollendick, in press; Sroufe & Rutter, 1984). A developmental psychopathology perspective incorporates general systems theory principles and considers multiple contributors and multiple outcomes in interaction with one another. Sroufe and Rutter (1984) have defined developmental psychopathology as the study of "the origins and course of individual patterns of behavioral maladaptation, whatever the age of onset, whatever the causes, whatever the transformations in behavioral manifestation, and however complex the course of the developmental pattern may be" (p. 18). In short, the developmental psychopathology approach is concerned with the origin and time course of a given disorder, its varying manifestations with development, its precursors and sequelae, and its relation to nondisordered patterns of behavior.

Protective processes and variables that place children at risk are viewed in the context of each other rather than in isolation (Cicchetti & Rogosch,

1996), and an organizational perspective is taken on development. Although this conceptualization of disorder is a rich one, the implications for child treatment of a developmental psychopathology perspective are just beginning to be articulated (Toth & Cicchetti, 1999). Much work in this realm remains to be accomplished.

CURRENT PRACTICE OF INDIVIDUAL CHILD PSYCHOTHERAPY

This chapter focuses on nonbehavioral forms of individual psychotherapy with children that utilize talk and play as major modes of treatment. In most forms of individual child psychotherapy, the child and the therapist meet once or twice a week for 45-minute to one-hour sessions. The mutual agreement between child and therapist is that the therapist is there to help the child understand feelings, thoughts, and behaviors. For some children, a specific problem that the child is concerned about, such as failing in school or feeling unhappy, can be identified. For others who feel they have no problems and resent seeing a therapist, no agreed-upon reason for therapy can be reached, at least initially.

The therapeutic relationship is a professional one, with the therapist there to help the child express feelings and thoughts, understand causes of behavior, and form a relationship with the therapist. The therapist does not take over the parental role. Play is a major tool in therapy. The child communicates with the therapist both verbally and through play. Usually, the child structures the therapeutic hour by choosing the topics, forms of play, and so on. In this way, the child determines the pace of the therapy. The therapist tries to be sensitive to the material that is being presented at a number of different levels. Therapists differ in how much they guide the therapy through comments and interpretations.

It is important to point out that, in most cases, individual work with the child is only one part of a larger treatment program. Parent guidance, family therapy, remediation, school consultation, and/or group therapy frequently occur simultaneously with individual child therapy. In fact, as Koocher and Broskowski (1977) point out, a number of different types of intervention are necessary for optimal treatment of multiproblem families. Thus, it is

actually a disservice in many cases to treat only the child. Also, medication is a frequent supplemental intervention.

A host of practical issues come up in working with children, such as setting reasonable limits, maintaining confidentiality, helping the child separate from the mother in the waiting room, choosing appropriate toys, taking the child to the bathroom (or not), and dealing with vacations. This chapter will not go into the "how tos" of child psychotherapy. For suggestions on how to deal with these issues, Axline (1947), Kessler (1966), Chethik (1989), Gil (1993), and D. Singer, (1993) are good sources.

Both clients and beginning therapists often raise the questions How does change occur by two people meeting and spending a limited amount of time together? What are the mechanisms of change within child psychotherapy?

MECHANISMS OF CHANGE IN INDIVIDUAL CHILD PSYCHOTHERAPY

VARIABLES WITHIN THE THERAPY PROCESS THAT EFFECT CHANGE

The basic premise of many forms of individual psychotherapy with children is that if certain events occur between two people and specific techniques are utilized, specific therapeutic processes will unfold. The therapeutic processes result in changes in the child. Identifying techniques and therapeutic processes has been the focus of much clinical writing and many therapy outcome studies. Applebaum (1978) and Garfield (1980) have identified major ways in which change occurs in psychotherapy with adults. Many of these therapeutic variables are also important in child psychotherapy. The following emerge as major hypothesized mechanisms of change within the child as a result of individual psychotherapy.

Catharsis and Labeling of Feelings
The release of emotion and the expression of feelings are thought to be therapeutic by a number of different schools of child therapy (Axline, 1947; A. Freud, 1965; Moustakas, 1953). Expression of negative feelings, in particular, is important for many children (Moustakas, 1953). Helping children to feel that they can safely express feelings is a

major task of the therapist. The therapist also labels and reflects the feelings that are being expressed. Dorfman (1951) and Ginott (1965) both stressed the importance of reflecting the feeling tone rather than the content of the material. By saying to the child that he or she (or the puppet, doll, etc.) seems to be feeling angry, the clinician connects a label to a feeling state. Words help to put feelings into a context for the child, thus making the feelings less overwhelming.

Corrective Emotional Experience

In this approach, the child's learned expectations are not met. The relationship between therapist and child is especially important for a corrective emotional experience to occur. For example, a child expresses angry thoughts and feelings about mother. The therapist, contrary to the child's expectations, is not angry or punishing. Rather, the therapist is accepting of the feelings and works with the child to help understand the reasons for the anger. After a number of these therapeutic events, a corrective emotional experience occurs. The automatic connection between angry thoughts and guilt or anxiety gradually decreases (or extinguishes). The child no longer reacts so immediately to angry thoughts with guilt or anxiety and a variety of defensive maneuvers and symptoms. A different attitude is developing. Instead of asking the question, "How can I be so angry—what's wrong with me?", the child is now asking, "Why am I so angry?" The child is then more comfortable with feelings and impulses (see Brandell, 1986; Clarizio, 1986).

Insight and Working Through

The child develops cognitive insight into problems. Verbal labeling and cognitive mediation permit understanding of behavior and symptoms. Higher-order reasoning processes can be applied to problem solving (Dollard & Miller, 1950). To develop insight, the therapist links behavior to feelings and thoughts by interpretations. The behavior then becomes understandable to the child. For example, the interpretive statement by the therapist, "You seem to take things from your mother's purse when you are feeling uncared for and alone," puts the behavior into a framework. If this interpretation is well timed (i.e., the child is ready to hear it) and accurate, it also helps the child feel understood. Lowenstein (1956) has a good discussion of the role of speech in psychotherapy.

Equally important to the development of cognitive insight through therapy is the emotional resolution of conflict or the working-through process. That is, the emotional reexperiencing of major developmental conflicts is an important aspect of therapy because it allows the child to express, think about, talk about, play out, and consequently work through ambivalent emotions and conflictual material. Play is particularly important in providing a vehicle to express and resolve conflicts. In many cases, especially with young children, cognitive insight does not occur. Rather, emotional reexperiencing, emotional working through, and mastery do occur and result in symptom reduction and healthy adjustment. This is an important point and is an often overlooked mechanism of change in child treatment. Messer and Warren (1995) also state that the goal of making the unconscious conscious needs to be modified in child play therapy with many children. They suggest that direct verbalization by the child of the meaning of the play may not be as important as the therapist, perhaps in an indirect fashion, conveying understanding of the child's inner world and helping to contain the affect.

Learning Alternative Problem-Solving Techniques and Coping Strategies

Many forms of individual therapy directly help the child to think about alternative ways of handling a problem. The therapist may, in a more directive approach, help the child think of different solutions or may directly suggest another solution to a problem. The therapist might also suggest a different way of viewing a situation. Role playing and modeling of coping strategies are used. D. Singer (1993) gives numerous examples of modeling techniques during therapy.

Development of Internal Structure

Children with structural deficits need to develop structure and processes that permit self-object differentiation, self-esteem regulation, impulse control, object constancy, reality testing, and so on (Kohut, 1977; Mahler, 1968). These children are suffering from early developmental problems. They have not developed the necessary cognitive, affective, and interpersonal processes to help them differentiate fantasy from reality, inside from outside, self from other. The therapist serves as a stable figure who helps the child develop these ego functions as much as possible (Gilpin, 1976). The relationship between therapist and child is probably the most important aspect of therapy that helps the development of these processes. Empathy with the child is a major technique of the therapy.

A Variety of Nonspecific Variables

Nonspecific variables are being increasingly recognized as important in their own right. Possible nonspecific variables in child therapy are that the child no longer feels alone, sees that the problem is being attended to, has expectations of change, or is aware of family involvement (see Gaffney, 1986; Miller, 1988).

SIMILARITIES AND DIFFERENCES IN TYPES OF INDIVIDUAL CHILD PSYCHOTHERAPY WITH SPECIFIC POPULATIONS

Different types of individual psychotherapy emphasize different mechanisms of change within the child. Thus, different mechanisms of change and different techniques are emphasized in different forms of individual psychotherapy. All forms of individual therapy with children have, as a broad goal, to help the child progress along developmental paths. The growth process has been disrupted, and the goal of therapy is to get the child moving again (A. Freud, 1965; Palmer, 1970). Individual therapy is recommended when there are disturbances in emotional and personality development. Psychological assessment is especially important in determining the specific areas of disrupted development as well as the severity and pervasiveness of the problems. Based on this assessment, the therapist decides how to focus the therapy. Increasingly, when individual therapy is recommended, it is in conjunction with a number of other interventions with the family, school, and community.

Kessler (1966) identifies the attributes that many forms of therapy with children have in common. They all involve the release of emotion, the use of play, and the attempt "to re-educate the child through corrective experiences and verbal explanations" (p. 372). Therapists have repeatedly stressed the importance of a warm, accepting, and trusting relationship between the child and the therapist (Axline, 1947; Moustakas, 1953). It is through this relationship that corrective emotional experiences can occur, that emotions and fantasies

can be explored, that risks can be taken, and that the child can internalize the acceptance and understanding offered by the therapist. A good relationship is a basic requirement of all forms of individual therapy with children.

Also of major importance in many forms of individual therapy is the use of play. Play is a major vehicle for change in psychotherapy. Over the years, play has been discussed from a variety of theoretical approaches as being an important function in child development (Axline, 1947; Erikson, 1950; A. Freud, 1946; Piaget, 1951; Schaefer, 1979; D. Singer, & Singer, 1973). Schaefer points out that both Freud and Piaget thought of play as an adaptive function "to help a young child gradually assimilate and gain mastery over unpleasant experiences" (p. 15). Through play, the child expresses affect, calls forth "forbidden" fantasies and feelings, works through and masters developmental problems, and resolves conflicts. Individual therapy provides a safe atmosphere in which the child can use play experiences to resolve conflicts.

The therapy experience adds several elements to the normal play situation. In therapy, an adult is present to provide a permissive and accepting environment for the child. This permissive environment is particularly emphasized by nondirective play therapists (Axline, 1947) and more relationship-oriented therapists (Moustakas, 1959). Also, the therapist labels and interprets the play content. Interpretation is utilized more frequently in psychodynamic approaches (Chethik, 1989; Klein, 1932/1960) in varying degrees by different therapists. Labeling and interpretation by the therapist facilitate the child's own work. Chethik describes the use of play in the working-through process. One of the roles of the therapist is to help the child work toward meaningful play.

Classifying different types of individual psychotherapy with children is a difficult task. Mendelsohn (1975) offers a sophisticated synthesis of major types of individual psychodynamic therapy with children that is consistent with Dewald's (1964) and Weiner's (1975) classification systems with adults. Individual psychotherapy with children includes three broad classifications of treatment. Each type has different treatment goals and emphasizes different techniques and mechanisms of change within the child. These are not "pure" categories in that a mix of techniques is used with each child. Although these broad types of therapy apply mainly to psychodynamic approaches, nondirective play and relationship approaches may also emphasize different techniques and mechanisms of change, depending on the needs of the child.

Insight-Oriented Therapy
The first major type of individual therapy for children is insight-oriented therapy. The goals of this type of therapy are conflict resolution and mastering developmental crises and situational traumas. Interpretation is an important therapeutic technique, as is helping the child deal with forbidden material in fantasy and play so that the material can be thought about, worked through, and mastered. Verbal labeling of unconscious impulses, conflicts, and causes of behavior helps lend higher-order reasoning skills to understanding problems. Forbidden material, as it is expressed and released, is then available for the child to work through in play and fantasy and integrate into the personality. Important mechanisms of change for this type of therapy are insight and working through, catharsis, and corrective emotional experiences.

As Tuma and Russ (1993) pointed out, the form of therapy most associated with the psychodynamic approach is insight-oriented therapy, and it is most appropriate for the child with anxiety and internalized conflict and intense reactions to traumas. This approach is appropriate for children who have age-appropriate ego development, show evidence of internal conflicts, have the ability to trust adults, are able to think about their behavior and what it means, and can use play effectively. Insight-oriented therapy is most often recommended for internalizing disorders such as anxiety and depressive disorder. Children with internalizing disorders often experience internal conflicts and have good ego development and good object relations.

Insight and working through can also be helpful for a child with good inner resources who has experienced a specific trauma (such as the loss of a parent). Altschul (1988) described the use of psychoanalytic approaches in helping children to mourn the loss of a parent. In this application, Webber (1988) stressed that the therapist must first address the question of whether the child can do his or her own psychological work. If not, therapy can be a major aid in the mourning process.

One example of an internalizing disorder was 9-year-old Mark, who said in the intake interview that his main problem was "I have trouble with my vocabulary words because when I get nervous I can't concentrate." Mark was demonstrating a good ability to think about himself and the causes of his behavior, that is, a good "observing ego." He was a good candidate for insight-oriented therapy. Therapy with this boy focused on the expression and understanding of unconscious underlying conflicts that were causing the anxiety and, in turn, school achievement problems. A central conflict concerned his aggressive impulses and associated guilt. Mark was unaware of these feelings and thoughts. The therapist helped Mark to permit this material to surface and to express, verbally and in play therapy, angry feelings toward his father as well as guilt about these feelings. Mark was also afraid of punishment by his father for his aggressive impulses. His conflict regarding aggression resulted in inhibitions in learning situations—a kind of fear of success. The therapist helped Mark to accept these feelings and have access to this material so that it could be worked through. Mark used the therapy well, expressed angry feelings, did a lot of verbalizing, and worked through the conflict to a large degree. There was no longer a need for the inhibition. He was a bright child (IQ 135) and began doing well in school once his anxiety decreased. At the end of that school year, the school felt that Mark was ready for a class for gifted children in a different school. Mark again dealt with a conflict about that issue. He wanted to go but felt bad about leaving his siblings and his friends. He also felt some guilt. Mark, whose father was unemployed, was the youngest of seven children and lived in an inner-city neighborhood. Success for him raised a number of real-life issues. However, he now was able to talk about his feelings and explore all sides of the issue. Because the material was mainly conscious, he was able to talk about it and make his decision during one therapy session. He decided to go to the gifted program, and, at a six-month follow-up, was doing well.

Supportive Therapy
A second major type of individual therapy with children is supportive psychotherapy. It is most appropriate for children with externalizing disorders (Tuma & Russ, 1993). These children frequently act out, have antisocial tendencies, and are impulse-ridden. As Baum (1989) stated, a number of different labels have been used for these children. The broad syndrome of externalizing disorders includes the labels acting-out, antisocial, character

disorders, attention-deficit disorders, and conduct disorders. Theoretically, psychodynamic theory views these children as having major developmental problems. These children have not yet adequately developed the processes necessary for delay of gratification. In addition, they are frequently egocentric, demonstrate an absence of shame and guilt, and their ability to empathize with others is impaired. Kessler (1988) has recommended that structured, supportive therapy is more helpful to these children than any other kind of psychodynamic therapy. Therapy focuses on the here and now and on the development of problem-solving skills and coping resources. For example, the therapist might role-play with the child about how to handle teasing at school or how to be assertive with parents.

At this point, given the effectiveness of behavioral and cognitive-behavioral approaches in working with externalizing disorders, our own view is that supportive psychodynamic psychotherapy is not the treatment of choice. It should be used only as a supplement to other treatment approaches to work on a specific issue. When it is used, supportive psychotherapy focuses on helping the child develop problem-solving techniques and coping strategies. Dewald (1964) and Weiner (1975) both have excellent descriptions of the differences between insight-oriented and supportive therapy. The focus in supportive therapy is on everyday problems and here-and-now conflicts. There is less uncovering of anxiety-producing material. The therapist may help the child think of steps in planning a project rather than focusing on what underlying conflicts were making it difficult to plan in the first place. A major goal in supportive therapy is to improve the child's day-to-day functioning and general adjustment in an immediate fashion. Mechanisms of change that therapists emphasize are catharsis, corrective emotional experience, alternative problem-solving strategies, alternative ways of viewing a situation or oneself, and awareness that someone is there to help and attend.

For example, James, a 16-year-old boy, got into frequent fights in school that were triggered by other boys staring at him. At these times, he would become frightened. He interpreted their staring as meaning that they were going to pick on him and start a fight (he was "beating them to the punch"). At a deeper level, James had fears of homosexual assault and was utilizing the defense of projection of his own aggressive and sexual impulses onto others

a great deal. Much of this material was untouchable in therapy. In a supportive approach, the therapist suggested another way of viewing the situation. The therapist said that many times, when other boys stared at James, it might be for reasons different from wanting to start a fight. It might simply be that they were feeling friendly toward or curious about him. Or it might not mean anything at all. This statement made by the therapist was one of the most therapeutic events of the therapy. It helped James to view the situation differently and to lessen the intensity of his own projection. Fighting decreased considerably and, in time, he began to feel safer with others. It was only within the context of a trusting relationship with the therapist that James was able to hear alternative ways of viewing the situations and truly to consider other possibilities. If this statement had been made early in therapy, it would have been ineffective because it would not have been taken in. The other major mechanism of change for James was his development of trust in the therapist. Trust in the therapist generalized to trust in other people.

Structural Development Approaches

A third major form of child therapy focuses on developing structure in children who have structural deficits that impair a variety of functions. Deficits in structure refer to deficits in cognitive, affective, and interpersonal processes. These children have impaired object relations, self-other boundary disturbances, difficulty distinguishing fantasy from reality, and problems with affect regulation and self-esteem regulation. This impairment is evident in children with psychotic and characterological disorders. These children have early developmental problems with a mix of severe dysfunction in the family and, in the case of borderline children, perhaps a genetic predisposition. Borderline psychotic children and children with narcissistic personality disorders are thought to suffer from internal structural deficits that result in self-other boundary disturbances and the impairment of object relations (Blatt & Wild, 1976; Chethik, 1989; Eckstein, 1966; Galatzer-Levy, 1987; Kohut, 1977; Leichtman & Shapiro, 1980; Mahler, 1968; Masterson, 1972; Pine, 1974). Borderline psychotic children have difficulty distinguishing fantasy from reality, especially in unstructured situations and during times of stress. They also have difficulty integrating positive and negative feelings about an individual. This is a difficult combination of problems. For example, one 10-year-old girl, Donna, became furious with the therapist and threatened to kill her. Because the wish is often equal to the act for these children, Donna needed to hear that wishing someone were dead was not the same as killing and that wishing would not cause the therapist to die. In this way, the therapist was helping Donna distinguish inside from outside, fantasy from reality. She also needed reassurance that the therapist would not let Donna hurt her, nor would the therapist hurt Donna. Donna also needed to hear that she could be angry with the therapist sometimes and feel affection at other times, that it was possible to feel conflicting feelings toward a person. And it was important that the therapist empathize with the anger and attempt to understand and help Donna verbalize the reasons for the anger.

Borderline psychotic children also demonstrate the need-fear dilemma (Blatt & Wild, 1976; Cass & Thomas, 1979). Because they have difficulty differentiating themselves from others, getting close to the therapist or becoming too attached results in a fear of merging or engulfment. If they are too distant from others, there is a fear of annihilation, loss of identity, and personality disorganization. For example, one 12-year-old boy attempted to describe this state as he neared the end of three years of therapy. He drew a picture of a boy on the blackboard. He then said, "I used to be afraid that this would happen to me," and then erased the picture. He was attempting to describe the state of loss of self, of complete annihilation. He also said that he still got those feelings sometimes but now knew that he would be all right.

The primary role of the therapist with these children is to be a stable object that the child can slowly take in (Gilpin, 1976). The therapist's consistency, predictability, empathy, help with self-other differentiation, and help with separating fantasy from reality all develop internal structure in the child. Therapy with children with structural deficits is a slow process, usually taking at least two years of therapy. The major mechanism of change in these children is the development of psychological structure, that is, cognitive, affective, and interpersonal functions necessary for adaptive interaction in the world. Empathy is especially important in helping the borderline child develop more stable object relations. Kohut and Wolfe (1978) describe the role of empathy in facilitating

the development of the self. Russ (1988) discusses the importance of helping the child better integrate raw, drive-laden primary process thinking. As the child develops a better repressive barrier, as self-other differentiation and object relations become more developed, then better integration of primary process thinking becomes possible.

Short-Term Psychotherapy

Russ (1998b) reviewed the area of short-term psychodynamic child psychotherapy. Conceptual frameworks exist for adult forms of brief psychodynamic intervention (Budman & Gurman, 1988; Mann & Goldman, 1982), but not for child forms of brief intervention. However, as Messer and Warren (1995) point out, short-term therapy (6–12 sessions) is a frequent form of psychodynamic intervention. The practical realities of HMOs and of clinical practice in general have led to briefer forms of treatment. Often, the time-limited nature of the therapy is by default, not by plan (Messer & Warren, 1995). The average number of sessions for children in outpatient therapy is six or fewer in private and clinic settings (Dulcan & Piercy, 1985).

There is little research or clinical theory about short-term psychotherapy with children (Clark, 1993; Messer & Warren, 1995). A few research studies have shown that explicit time limits reduced the likelihood of premature termination (Parad & Parad, 1968) and that children in time-limited psychotherapy showed as much improvement as those in long-term psychotherapy (Smyrnios & Kirby, 1993). The time is right for development of theoretically based short-term psychodynamic interventions for children with systematic research studies. Messer and Warren (1995) suggest that the developmental approach utilized by psychodynamic theory provides a useful framework for short-term therapy. One can identify the developmental problems and obstacles involved in a particular case. They also stress the use of play as a vehicle of change and, as Winnicott (1971) has said, of development. They suggest that active interpretation of the meaning of the play can help the child feel understood, which in turn can result in lifelong changes in self-perception and experience. In other words, the understanding of the metaphors in the child's play can give the child insight, or an experience of empathy, or both.

Chethik (1989) discusses focal therapy as therapy that deals with "focal stress events" (p. 194) in the child's life. Chethik listed events such as death in the family, divorce, hospitalization, and illness in the family or of the child as examples of specific stresses. Focal therapy focuses on the problem and is usually of short duration. The basic principles of psychodynamic therapy and play therapy are applied. The basic mechanism of change is insight and working through. Chethik views this approach as working best with children who have accomplished normal developmental tasks before the stressful event occurs.

In general, brief forms of psychodynamic intervention are seen as more appropriate for the child who has accomplished the major developmental milestones. Lester (1968) views problems such as transient regressions, mild exaggerations of age-appropriate behaviors, and acute phobias as most appropriate for brief intervention. Proskauer (1969, 1971) stressed the child's ability to quickly develop a relationship with the therapist, good trusting ability, the existence of a focal dynamic issue, and flexible and adaptive defenses as criteria for short-term intervention. Messer and Warren (1995) conclude that children with less severe psychopathology are more responsive to brief intervention than children with chronic developmental problems. Our own view is that the internalizing disorders are most appropriate for brief psychodynamic intervention. The therapist is active, at times directive, and uses all mechanisms of change in the therapy. Insight and working through are essential, but modeling, rehearsal, and discussing coping strategies are also part of the therapy. Children with major deficits in object relations and with early developmental problems need longer-term structure-building approaches.

Alternatives to Individual Therapy

A few words are called for about contraindications for individual psychotherapy with children. Individual therapy on an outpatient basis should not be recommended if the parents will not support the treatment. If the parents will not be able to bring the child for the therapy sessions or will probably drop out quickly, individual therapy should not be started. Other, more short-term treatment approaches would be more appropriate. If altering situational factors will eliminate the problem, there is no need to work individually with the child. Working with the parents, school, and community would be the appropriate treatment strategies. This often is the case with children under 6 years of age who

have not yet internalized conflicts and who are very responsive to environmental changes. It is true for many other children as well. Often, personality and emotional problems are secondary to problems in other areas of development, such as neurologically based learning disabilities, and chronic illness. Although individual psychotherapy might prove helpful, it should be a supplement to the major intervention in the primary problem area. Finally, when individual psychotherapy might be helpful but is not the optimal intervention, it should not be recommended. This last point is where the field of child psychotherapy runs into trouble. The ultimate purpose of the assessment process is to make optimal treatment decisions (Cole & Magnussen, 1966). When evaluating a child and family, the clinician must ask, What is the probability that individual therapy will make a difference in this child's development? Is individual psychotherapy the most optimal treatment approach? If so, what therapeutic techniques and mechanisms of change should be emphasized in the therapy? What other interventions should be carried out in conjunction with individual therapy? There are few empirically based guidelines for answers to any of these questions.

RESEARCH IN CHILD PSYCHOTHERAPY

In general, the early reviews of child therapy outcome studies concluded that there was little or no support for child therapy. More recent work has concluded that there is support for the effectiveness of child psychotherapy if the research is well-designed.

One of the early classic reviews of child therapy outcome research is that of Levitt (1957). After reviewing 18 child psychotherapy studies, he found that the mean improvement rate for children in treatment was not significantly better than the baseline improvement rate of 72.5%. The 72.5% improvement rate for untreated controls was obtained from studies by Witmer and Keller (1942) and Lehrman, Sirluck, Black, and Glick (1949). In his later work, based on 47 reports of child therapy outcome, Levitt (1963, 1971) concluded that approximately 66% of treated children were improved at the close of treatment. About 80% of that number remained improved at follow-up. The crucial point is that untreated controls, "defectors," showed as much improvement as children who received treatment. Levitt's analysis raised a challenge to the field of child psychotherapy.

A number of authors wrestled with Levitt's conclusions (Halpern, 1968; Heinicke & Goldman, 1960; Hood-Williams, 1960). One of the major issues in this controversy was the adequacy of the use of defectors as the untreated control group. Defectors are children who were evaluated and recommended for treatment but who did not enter into treatment. A number of confounding variables may be operating here that make the defector groups not comparable with the treated groups. Finding adequate control groups has been a difficult task in child therapy research (Hartmann, Roper, & Gelfant, 1977; Strupp & Bergin, 1969).

In general, child psychotherapy outcome research has become more focused and methodologically sophisticated. In addition, the technique of meta-analyses has enabled the field to arrive at a more systematic evaluation of outcome studies. As Weisz and Weiss (1993) noted, meta-analysis is a technique that enables the pooling and statistical summarizing of the results of multiple outcome studies in one analysis.

Weisz and Weiss (1993) reviewed the major meta-analytic studies in the field of child psychotherapy. Casey and Berman (1985) calculated effects of psychotherapy across 64 studies and found a mean effect size (ES) of 0.71, which demonstrated success with children equal to that of adults. A slightly higher ES of 0.79 was found by Weisz, Weiss, Alicke, and Klotz (1987) in a review of 163 treatment-control comparisons. Both studies concluded that the average treated child functioned better after treatment than three-fourths of the untreated groups. Weisz and Weiss concluded that results point to positive effects of therapy.

In general, current reviews of child psychotherapy conclude that psychotherapy of all orientations is more effective than no treatment and that the size of the effect is similar to that found with adults (Casey & Berman, 1985; Kazdin, 1990; Tuma, 1989). Tuma (1986, 1989) reviewed 31 studies of traditional individual psychotherapies with children. In two-thirds of the studies, treated children showed greater improvement than untreated children. Tuma (1989) agreed with Casey and Berman's (1985) conclusion that no treatment modality has been shown to be more effective than any other. However, Weisz and Weiss (1993), in their recent review of major meta-analytic studies, concluded that, in some meta-analyses, behavioral approaches were superior

to nonbehavioral approaches, including psychodynamic. Behavior therapies yielded stronger effects than nonbehavioral approaches, but this finding was not consistent across meta-analyses. Weisz and Weiss also refer to the low number of psychodynamic therapy outcome studies in the literature.

The major reason for the more positive results of the recent child psychotherapy studies is that the studies have been well-designed and focused on specific interventions and variables. Weisz and Weiss (1989, 1993) pointed out that most of the research studies in the meta-analyses involved controlled laboratory interventions. In many of these studies, children were recruited for treatment and were not clinic-referred; samples were homogeneous; there was a focal problem; therapy focused on the target problem; therapists were trained in the specific treatment approaches to be used; and the therapy relied primarily on those techniques. In essence, this was good research that followed many of the methodological guidelines for adequate research design. On the other hand, Weisz and Weiss (1993) cautioned that the evidence for the effectiveness of psychotherapy is based on studies that are not typical of conventional clinical practice. Thus, the findings may not be generalizable to real clinical work. This lack of generalizability may partially explain the discrepancy in the findings between the earlier reviews in the field and these recent meta-analyses. Weisz and Weiss (1989) also make the important point that the control and precision of therapy for research purposes may be needed in clinical practice. Actually, this is the direction that should be followed in the future. Building bridges between research efforts and everyday treatment is essential.

DIRECTION FOR FUTURE RESEARCH

The Need for Specificity

A review of the literature on psychotherapy outcome research indicates several methodological directions for future research. First of all, there is increasing stress on the need for research to become specific. Bergin and Strupp (1972) convincingly argue that research should focus on specific mechanisms in psychotherapy that affect specific variables in the individual. They called for an end to global outcome studies with adults. They point out that outcome studies of behavioral approaches have usually investigated specific processes. Research with other forms of psychotherapy must move in this direction even though the concepts involved may be more difficult to operationalize. Frank (1979) also emphasized the importance of focusing on specific forms of therapy and specific therapist-patient interactions. Kiesler (1966) states that discrete bits of knowledge must be worked on separately in psychotherapy research. Bergin and Lambert (1978) also stressed the importance of investigating specific kinds of change.

In the child area, Barrett, Hampe, and Miller (1978) and Heinicke and Strassman (1975) make the same calls for specificity. Barrett et al. take a close look at Levitt's (1957, 1963) work and the research literature in general, and conclude that one of the major problems in these studies is their global nature. Barrett et al. conclude:

> If we resort to macrovariable research (e.g., combining all kinds of diagnostic categories, patients being seen by therapists with a wide variety of personal styles, each making all kinds of interventions, and then assessing outcome in some gross fashion like improved, partially improved, unimproved) we will continue to demonstrate that 70 percent of disturbed children improve with psychotherapy or with time alone. (p. 430)

They go on to say that the question in psychotherapy research should not be "Does psychotherapy work?" but rather "Which set of procedure is effective when applied to what kinds of patients with which sets of problems and practiced by which sorts of therapists?" (p. 428).

We would suggest becoming even more specific and asking, Which specific interventions affect which specific cognitive, personality, and affective processes? How are these processes related to behavior and practical clinical criteria? Asking these kinds of questions would enable us to identify the developing processes in children that are involved in particular clinical problems. They would also enable us to investigate which interventions facilitate the development of these processes and which do not. Many of the past outcome studies in the child area have either ignored these underlying processes, used inadequate measures, or not made distinctions among them.

Shirk and Russell (1996) have developed a framework for conceptualizing intervention research that ties specific treatment processes to underlying cognitive, affective, and interpersonal processes within a developmental framework. They stress the importance of specific investigation of specific processes and change mechanisms in child psychotherapy.

An important question is: How do we develop the kind of specificity that is called for in child psychotherapy research? The problem is well phrased by Doleys (1989) in a review of enuresis and encopresis. When verbal psychotherapy was found to be effective with these children (in many cases, it was not), it was unclear which specific features of the therapy were effective. He concluded, "Experimental approaches focusing on a component analysis are badly needed to determine which of the factors is most closely associated with success" (p. 304). Russ (1991) concluded that if psychodynamic approaches are to continue to be used, clinical researchers in this area will need to become as specific as researchers of behavioral approaches have been. This need gains increasing impetus given the increasing need for "effectiveness and efficiency" demanded by third-party payers (Koocher & D'Angelo, 1992).

One of the problems in carrying out research in the area of children's play has been the lack of valid objective measures of affective expression in play. One attempt to develop a scale that taps a wide range of affect in fantasy play is the Affect in Play Scale (Russ, 1987, 1993; Russ, Niec, & Seja, in press), which consists of a play task and criteria for rating a variety of affect categories and fantasy. To date, affective expression as measured by the Affect in Play Scale in 6- to 9-year-olds has been significantly related to creativity (Russ & Grossman-McKee, 1990; Russ & Peterson, 1990; Russ, Robins, & Christiano, 1999), coping ability (Christiano & Russ, 1996; Russ & Peterson, 1990; Russ et al., 1999), pain complaints (better affective expression related to fewer pain complaints; Grossman-McKee, 1990), and emotional understanding (Seja & Russ, 1999). The scale could be used to measure changes in play as a result of psychotherapy or the effect of very specific interventions on affective expression. The Affect in Play Scale is an example of a tool that should enable researchers to investigate specific processes in psychotherapy.

Multiple Outcome Criteria

A second guideline that emerges from the literature is the need to use multiple outcome criteria (Barrett et al., 1978; Heinicke & Strassman, 1975; O'Leary & Turkewitz, 1978; Waskow & Parloff, 1975). As Bergin and Lambert (1978) put it, "Divergent methods of criterion measurement must be used to match the divergency of human beings" (p. 171). Hogan, DeSoto, and Solano (1977) point out that many theoretical conceptualizations of the personality are multidimensional in nature; that is, the personality consists of a number of complex dimensions rather than one unitary dimension. The complexity of the person cannot be handled by a few concepts nor, we might extrapolate, by a few measures. In the same vein, Kiesler (1966) speaks of the myth of the one-process dimension in psychotherapy. He speculates that patient change occurs along a number of different dimensions. These dimensions may respond in different ways to different aspects of the therapy process. Stollack, Gershowitz, and Rief (1978) suggest using measures of inner experience as well as behavioral measures.

Strupp and Hadley (1977) have stressed the need for multiple perspectives in evaluation of therapy. In their tripartite model, they suggest using three vantage points in evaluation: the society, the individual, and the mental health professional. The vantage point of society would be reflected in measures of adaptive behavior. For children, adaptive behavior includes measures of school achievement, behavioral adjustment, peer relations, coping strategies, and so on. The point of view of the individual would be reflected in the child's sense of wellbeing. The vantage point of the mental health professional would be reflected in measures of cognitive and personality structure. Strupp and Hadley call for comprehensive evaluations that would use a variety of measures reflecting multiple values in judging therapy outcomes.

Measures of general behavior, such as behavior rating scales, have frequently been used in outcome research, but there are a number of problems involved in using only these measure with children. Similar behaviors may reflect different underlying problems in different children. Similar behaviors have different meanings at different ages. Bedwetting at 6 years may have a different meaning from bedwetting at 14. Behavioral measures are rarely tightly linked to underlying cognitive and personality processes; therefore, changes in these behaviors as a result of intervention tell us little about what specific variables are being influenced, and how. For example, improvements in school achievement as a result of psychotherapy might be due to improved self-esteem, increased motivation, improved impulse control, greater flexibility in problem

solving, or any combination of these factors (as well as a host of others). Different interventions may be optimal for dealing with problems in each of these areas. To tease out the types of therapeutic interactions that are most helpful to problems in emotional integration and to discover how these, in turn, are related to school achievement, we have to formulate very specific empirical questions and use multiple measures that tap different levels of functioning.

Theoretical Validity

This brings us to the third methodological guideline, the need for theoretical validity (Mahoney, 1978). Theoretical validity is the logical bearing an experiment has on a hypothesis. The experimental procedure is relevant to the theoretical model; thus, the measures that are used in outcome studies should be theoretically relevant to the intervention. The measures should "make sense" theoretically and be conceptually linked to the intervention. Heinicke and Strassman (1975) and Bergin and Lambert (1978) stress that the measures should also be theoretically linked to the clinical problem and to the group being investigated. Thus, if we want to improve reading achievement in a group of children with emotionally based learning disorders, we must measure underlying cognitive and personality processes that are components of reading achievement. In this way, we begin to develop a conceptual framework that links the type of intervention to specific cognitive and personality processes, which, in turn, are related to practical clinical criteria. Heinicke's (1969) study of children with reading disorders in psychodynamic psychotherapy is a good example of a study that chose measures of variables, such as ego flexibility and ego integration, that would be expected to be altered by psychodynamic therapy and would in turn affect the reading process. This study made theoretical sense.

Our knowledge of child development and our knowledge of how therapy works should guide us in designing theoretically valid studies. There needs to be a greater synthesis of the research and ideas in child development and those in clinical child psychology. Frequently, the left hand does not know what the right hand is doing and is not particularly interested.

New forms for outcome studies must also be developed (Russ, 1998a). Persons (1991) recently concluded, "Contemporary outcome studies are incompatible with psychotherapy models because the outcome studies treat patients with standardized treatments that are assigned on the basis of psychiatric diagnosis rather than with individualized treatments based on theory-driven psychological assessment of the individual's difficulties" (p. 99). Individualized treatment based on theory-driven assessment is especially true of psychodynamic psychotherapy. Persons suggested ideographic outcome studies using a case formulation approach.

Kazdin (1993) discusses numerous research issues in carrying out systematic assessment and evaluation in clinical practice. He concluded that we need to integrate systematic assessment and evaluation and single-case design wherever possible in clinical practice. Even though single-case designs have been used most frequently to evaluate behavioral interventions, Kazdin suggests that this approach is appropriate for other intervention approaches.

Heinicke and Strassman (1975) cover a number of other methodological issues important for research in the child area, such as the importance of classification according to developmental level. Controlling for maturational effects is a problem unique to the child therapy area (Koocher & Broskowski, 1977). The need for homogeneous treatment groups has been stressed by many (Achenbach, 1978; Hartmann et al., 1977; Kiesler, 1966). The Hartmann et al. review covers a multitude of methodological issues in child psychotherapy research, as does Kazdin's review (1990). Time-limited therapy is an issue of growing import (Sloves & Peterlin, 1986; Uribe, 1988).

The focus in this discussion of child psychotherapy research has been on therapy outcome research that permits inferences about cause and effect. Program evaluation research for children's programs is a broad area with somewhat different goals. Koocher and Broskowski (1977) point out that the primary goal in program evaluation research is to assess program effectiveness and improve service delivery. The primary question in program evaluation research should be Is the program effective? Specific questions about why and how the program is effective are secondary. The Leventhal and Weinberger (1975) study is a good example of a comprehensive program evaluation study that demonstrates the effectiveness of a multimodal program of brief psychotherapy for children. In designing research studies, the authors must be clear about the type of research being done and the primary purpose of the research: to determine if the program is effective, to investigate specific mechanisms of change, or both.

SUMMARY OF RESEARCH GUIDELINES

In summary, a number of psychotherapy researchers in both the adult and child areas are calling for (1) specific processes to be investigated and specific questions to be asked, (2) the use of multiple outcome criteria, and (3) the need for theoretical validity. Many of the past studies in child psychotherapy have not followed these guidelines. A large number of studies have been global in nature, using only a few crude outcome measures. This type of approach has not given much empirical support for the success of child psychotherapy when compared with base rate (Levitt, 1971), nor has it contributed to the knowledge of how psychotherapy effects change.

Fonagy and Moran (1990) have applied many of the current guidelines for psychotherapy outcome research to evaluating the effectiveness of child psychoanalysis. Their studies are models for how to go about investigating the efficacy of psychodynamic approaches. They have carried out different types of studies that are well-suited to the psychoanalytic or psychodynamic approach. In one study (Moran & Fonagy, 1987), they used a time series analysis to study the 184 weeks of treatment of a diabetic teenager. Time series analysis investigates whether or not there is a time-bound relationship between events. The psychodynamic view of brittle diabetes is that, in some cases, intrapsychic conflicts can underlie the mismanagement of diabetes. The mismanagement is an adaption to the anxiety and guilt aroused by unconscious conflict. In this case study, they found a relationship between major themes in analysis and diabetic control. They concluded that the interpretation of conflicts in the treatment brought about an improvement in diabetic control. At times, the improved control led to temporary increases in anxiety and guilt, appearing to increase the likelihood of manifest psychological symptomatology. This pattern fit the psychodynamic understanding of this form of brittle diabetes.

In a second study, an inpatient program for diabetes was evaluated (Fonagy & Moran, 1990).

Eleven patients received psychotherapy and medical supervision, and the comparison group received medical treatment with no psychotherapy. The analytic treatment was well-defined and based on the psychoanalytic understanding of brittle diabetes as being caused by the investment with unconscious emotional significance of the disease or its treatment regimen. This leads to a disregard for normal diabetic care. The goal of therapy was to make conscious the conflicts and anxieties that were interwoven with the regimen and to free the management of diabetes from the maladaptive effects of the symptom. The treated group showed significant improvement in diabetic control; none of the untreated group showed such an improvement. The improvement was maintained at one-year follow-up. Fonagy and Moran stress the importance and feasibility of systematic and specific intervention research that investigates changes in psychic structure such as affect regulation and empathy as a result of psychoanalysis. They report that Wallerstein and his colleagues (Wallerstein, 1988) have developed rating scales for these dimensions. In addition, Kernberg (1995) has also developed a coding system for dimensions relevant to psychodynamic treatment. Shirk and Russell (1996) also review a number of research programs and measures relevant to assessing change in psychodynamic psychotherapy.

Another area where progress is being made in evaluating psychodynamic concepts is play intervention research (Russ, 1995, 1998b). Some studies have investigated the effect of play on specific types of problems or in specific populations. These studies are a good bridge between empirical laboratory studies of play and specific processes, such as creativity, and more global clinical practice outcome studies. Russ (1995) labeled these play intervention studies rather than play therapy because the focus is highly specific. Usually, they involve only a few sessions with no emphasis on forming a relationship with a therapist. On the other hand, these studies differ from specific process research in child development in that they are problem-focused and are not as fine-tuned as they would be in laboratory research. These play intervention studies seem to fit some of Weisz and Weiss's (1993) criteria by including children who were not clinic-referred, by having homogeneous samples, and by having a focal problem that the therapy focused on. Phillips

(1985) reviewed two studies that fall into this play intervention research category. Johnson and Stockdale (1975) and Cassell (1965) found that puppet play reduced anxiety in children undergoing surgery. In an excellent example of a well-designed play intervention study, Milos and Reiss (1982) used play for preschoolers who were dealing with separation anxiety. They identified 64 children who were rated as high-separation-anxiety children by their teachers. The children were randomly assigned to one of four groups. Three play groups were theme related: The free-play group had appropriate toys; the directed-play group had the scene set with a mother doll bringing the child to school; the modeling group had the experimenter playing out a separation scene. A control group also used play with toys irrelevant to separation themes (blocks, puzzles, crayons). All children received three individual 10-minute play sessions on different days. Quality of play was rated. The results showed that all three thematic play conditions were effective in reducing anxiety around separation themes when compared to the control group. An interesting finding was that, when the free-play and directed-play groups were combined, the quality of play ratings were significantly negatively related ($r = -.37$) to a posttest anxiety measure. High-quality play was defined as play that showed more separation themes and attempts to resolve conflicts. One might speculate that the children who were already good players used the intervention to master their separation anxiety. Milos and Reiss concluded that their results support the underlying assumption of play therapy, that play can reduce anxiety associated with psychological problems.

For the field of child psychotherapy to progress, researchers must identify specific interventions that effect specific changes in cognitive and personality functioning and development. Basic questions that relate developmental processes to clinical problems need to be tested before or simultaneously with intervention manipulations. Doing systematic, specific studies is a time-consuming endeavor, but it is necessary to discover which of myriad interventions that occur in the therapy process affect which specific cognitive and personality variables. We need to refine our interventions and our measures. Ultimately, child psychotherapy research cannot be separated from basic research in child personality and cognitive development.

IMPLICATIONS FOR THE FUTURE OF INDIVIDUAL CHILD PSYCHOTHERAPY

We can only speculate about the future of the field of individual therapy for children. Based on the history of the field, the current trends in outcome research, and new developments in the child area in general, what can we predict about the next 50 years? Many of the speculations made in our chapter in the first edition of this book are being realized, and therefore we shall stay with these earlier predictions (Freedheim & Russ, 1983).

The field is realizing and will continue to realize the necessity for obtaining empirical support for therapy practices. A dedication to systematic research programs is beginning to develop, and this is encouraging. It is crucial that we focus on why and how specific interventions effect change. This type of step-by-step research is very time-consuming. It often means validating measures and answering some basic questions empirically before investigating interventions. Ross (1981b), in an appropriately titled paper, "On Rigor and Relevance," has stressed the importance of developing a programmatic series of "interrelated consecutive and simultaneous" studies that are both methodologically rigorous and clinically relevant. He states that it is especially important to have a closer relationship between the clinic and the laboratory. To achieve a systematic accumulation of knowledge, there should be a reciprocal relationship between the clinical case study and the experiment.

As child psychotherapy research becomes more specific, so will child psychotherapy practice. As professionals gain knowledge about how particular interventions affect specific variables with specific groups of children, psychotherapy practice should become more focused. Thus, there may be more specific goals and more deliberate use of specific techniques in therapy. The move in many clinical settings to have specific clinics for different diagnostic groups, such as childhood depression and anxiety disorders, reflects this change. Schaefer and Millman (1977) also see child therapists moving away from one "all-purpose" therapeutic mold to more specific approaches. Kazdin (1990) points out that many current reviews focus on specific areas of child dysfunction and treatment options for specific problems; for example, Gil's (1993) work

with abused children adapts play therapy techniques to a specific population.

The danger involved in becoming more focused is that of losing sight of the whole child. Working with the whole child, focusing on different conflicts as they come up and different developmental levels as the child is ready, has always been a strong advantage of individual therapy. It will be a challenge to the therapist to be optimally focused, emphasizing specific goals and techniques, and yet to remain sensitive to all dimensions of the child.

Developing knowledge about the interaction between cognitive and affective processes will guide what therapists do (Brooks, 1979; Russ, 1987; Russ & Grossman-McKee, 1990; Santosefano, 1980). Research investigating the effect of play on cognitive functioning (Dansky, 1980; Dansky & Silverman, 1973) and the manner in which play in psychotherapy affects children (Russ, 1995; D. Singer & Singer, 1973; J.L. Singer, 1990; J.L. Singer & Singer, 1976; Stollack et al., 1978) should have direct implications for child therapy. Incorporating evolving research-based techniques into clinical practice is important. On the other hand, child therapists have a great deal of knowledge about the interaction of cognitive-affective processes that needs to be shared with and listened to by child development researchers. There needs to be a closer, more reciprocal relationship between the child therapist and the child researcher, for the benefit of both. Harter's (1977) work on a cognitive-developmental approach to children's expression of conflicting feelings is a good example of the integration of child development theory and child psychotherapy practice.

Individual psychotherapy increasingly will be carried out in a situational context. From the beginning of the child guidance movement, there has been an emphasis on working with the child's environment in conjunction with individual therapy. Working with parents and the school has always been a part of treatment plans. Conceptualizations of the reciprocal relationships among systems have been discussed by Bronfenbrenner (1979). The transactional perspective stresses the interactional nature of different systems: each affects the other. The field is becoming increasingly aware of the importance of situational and contextual factors in child development and in intervention (Ollendick & Russ, 1999). The complex interaction of these variables has been emphasized in the developmental psychopathology framework (Cicchetti & Rogosch, 1996). Campbell (1998) emphasized the importance of family and social environmental factors in understanding developmental processes. The importance of understanding cultural factors in working with ethnic minority groups is an important principle. The knowledge base about intervention with minority children is fragmented and studies regarding service delivery, social contexts, and specific problems are separate and distinct (Vraniak & Picketts, 1993). A comprehensive framework needs to be developed. There are some efforts in this area (Vraniak & Picketts, 1993), but there need to be more empirically based guidelines about how to best intervene in different cultures and contexts. These new conceptualizations will affect how the therapist thinks about the child in relation to situational factors. The child therapist will be increasingly involved as a consultant to the school and the community and will need to be knowledgeable in consultation theory and practice.

There will be increasing pressure for short-term interventions, pushing therapists to search for optimal interventions. What will work most quickly and efficiently with a particular child? Conceptualizing in this way often leads to an integration of treatment approaches and techniques. The therapist decides to use both insight and problem-solving approaches. Kazdin (1990) has pointed out that the field of child psychotherapy needs to combine treatment approaches for optimal results. Many children have multiple disorders, with a host of etiological factors involved, which require a combination of intervention techniques. Wachtel's (1977) sophisticated approach to integrating psychodynamic and behavioral techniques in a complementary way should apply to the child area as well as the adult. For example, Knell's (1993) cognitive-behavioral play therapy utilized behavioral interventions within a psychodynamic understanding of the meanings of play. Shirk (1998) describes a cognitive-interpersonal framework in targeting changes in interpersonal schema. Actually, this integration has always been true in child psychotherapy because working with children and families forces one to be pragmatic and to do what works (Russ, 1998a).

In general, the next decades should bring a refinement of interventions, greater use of specific therapy techniques for specific problems and child

populations, and more empirical support for therapy practice. Individual child psychotherapy has always been both an art and a science. It is our hope that the next 50 years will strengthen child psychotherapy as a science while maintaining the art.

REFERENCES

Achenbach, T. (1978). *Research in developmental psychology.* New York: Free Press.

Aichorn, A. (1935). *Wayward youth.* New York: Viking.

Altschul, S. (1988). *Childhood bereavement and its aftermath.* Madison, WI: International University Press.

Applebaum, S. (1978). Pathways to change in psychoanalytic therapy. *Bulletin of the Menninger Clinic, 42,* 239–251.

Axline, V.M. (1947). *Play therapy.* Boston: Houghton-Mifflin.

Baker, H.J., & Traphagen, V. (1935). *The diagnosis and treatment of behavior problem children.* New York: Macmillan.

Barrett, C., Hampe, T.E., & Miller, L. (1978). Research on child psychotherapy. In S. Garfield & A. Bergin (Eds.), *Handbook of psychotherapy and behavior change* (pp. 411–435). New York: Wiley.

Baum, C. (1989). Conduct disorders. In T. Ollendick & M. Hersen (Eds.), *Handbook of child psychopathology* (2nd ed., pp. 171–196). New York: Plenum Press.

Bender, L. (1947). One hundred cases of childhood schizophrenia tested with electric shock. *Transcriptions of the American Neurological Association,* 165–169.

Bergin, A., & Lambert, M. (1978). The evaluation of therapeutic outcome. In S. Garfield & A. Bergin (Eds.), *Handbook of psychotherapy and behavior change* (pp. 139–189). New York: Wiley.

Bergin, A., & Strupp, H. (1972). *Changing frontiers in the science of psychotherapy.* Chicago: Aldine-Atherton.

Blatt, S., & Wild, C. (1976). *Schizophrenia: A developmental analysis.* New York: Academic Press.

Brandell, J.R. (1986). Using children's autogenic stories to assess therapeutic progress. *Journal of Child and Adolescent Psychotherapy, 2,* 285–292.

Bronfenbrenner, U. (1979). *The ecology of human development.* Cambridge, MA: Harvard University Press.

Brooks, R. (1979). Psychoeducational assessment: A broader perspective. *Professional Psychology, 10,* 708–722.

Budman, S.N., & Gurman, A.S. (1988). *Theory and practice of brief therapy.* New York: Guilford Press.

Campbell, S. (1998). Developmental perspectives. In T. Ollendick & M. Hersen (Eds.), *Handbook of child psychopathology* (3rd ed., pp. 3–35). New York: Plenum Press.

Casey, R.J., & Berman, J.S. (1985). The outcome of psychotherapy with children. *Psychological Bulletin, 98,* 388–400.

Cass, L., & Thomas, C. (1979). *Childhood pathology and later adjustment.* New York: Wiley.

Cassell, S. (1965). Effect of brief puppet therapy upon the emotional responses of children undergoing cardiac catheterization. *Journal of Consulting Psychology, 29,* 1–8.

Chadwick, M. (1928). *Difficulties in child development.* New York: John Day.

Chethik, M. (1989). *Techniques of child therapy: Psychodynamic strategies.* New York: Guilford Press.

Christiano, B., & Russ, S. (1996). Play as a predictor of coping and distress in children during an invasive dental procedure. *Journal of Clinical Child Psychology, 25,* 130–138.

Cicchetti, D., & Rogosch, F.A. (1996). Equifinality and multifinality in developmental psychopathology [Special issue]. *Development and Psychopathology, 8*(4), 597–600.

Clarizio, H.F. (1986). Treatment of childhood depression: The state of the art. *Techniques, 2,* 322–332.

Clark, B.E. (1993). Towards an integrated model of time-limited psychodynamic therapy with children. *Dissertation Abstracts International, 54,* 1659B.

Cole, J., & Magnussen, M. (1966). Where the action is. *Journal of Consulting Psychology, 30,* 539–543.

Dansky, J. (1980). Make-believe: A mediator of the relationship between play and associative fluency. *Child Development, 51,* 576–579.

Dansky, J., & Silverman, F. (1973). Effects of play on associative fluency in preschool-aged children. *Developmental Psychology, 9,* 38–43.

Dewald, P. (1964). *Psychotherapy: A dynamic approach.* New York: Basic Books.

Doleys, D. (1989). Enuresis and encopresis. In T. Ollendick & M. Hersen (Eds.), *Handbook of child psychopathology* (2nd ed., pp. 291–314). New York: Plenum Press.

Dollard, J., & Miller, W.E. (1950). *Personality and psychotherapy.* New York: McGraw-Hill.

Dorfman, E. (1951). Play therapy. In C. Rogers (Ed.), *Client-centered therapy* (pp. 235–277). Boston: Houghton Mifflin.

Dulcan, M., & Piercy, P. (1985). A model for teaching and evaluating brief psychotherapy with children and their families. *Professional Psychology: Research and Practice, 16,* 689–700.

Eckstein, R. (1966). *Children of time and space, of action and impulse.* New York: Appleton-Century-Crofts.

Erikson, E.N. (1950). *Childhood and society.* New York: Norton.

Finch, A.J., & Kendall, P.C. (Eds.). (1979). *Clinical treatment and research in child psychopathology.* New York: Spectrum.

Fonagy, P., & Moran, G.S. (1990). Studies on the efficacy of child psychoanalysis. *Journal of Consulting and Clinical Psychology, 58,* 684–695.

Frank, J. (1979). The present status of outcome studies. *Journal of Consulting and Clinical Psychology, 47,* 310–316.

Freedheim, D.K., & Russ, S.W. (1983). Psychotherapy with children. In C.E. Walker & M.E. Roberts (Eds.), *Handbook of clinical child psychology* (pp. 978–994). New York: Wiley.

Freud, A. (1946). *The psychoanalytic treatment of children.* London: Imago.

Freud, A. (1965). Normality and pathology in childhood: Assessments of development. In *The Writings of Anna Freud* (Vol. 6). New York: International Universities Press.

Freud, S. (1955). Analysis of phobia in a five-year-old boy. In *Collected papers* (Vol. 10). London: Hogarth Press. (Original work published 1909)

Furman, E. (1957). Treatment of under-5's by way of parents. In the *Psychoanalytic study of the child* (Vol. 12). New York: International Universities Press.

Gaffney, B. (1986). Toward integration and independence: A four-year-old boy's use of thirteen months of psychotherapy. *Journal of Child Psychotherapy, 12,* 79–97.

Galatzer-Levy, R. (1987). Issues in psychoanalytic treatment of a borderline/severely neurotic child. *Journal of the American Psychoanalytic Association, 35,* 727–737.

Garfield, W. (1980). *Psychotherapy: An eclectic approach.* New York: Wiley.

German, A.S., & Kniskern, D.P. (Eds.). (1981). *Handbook of family therapy.* New York: Brunner/Mazel.

Gil, E. (1993). *The healing power of play.* New York: Guilford Press.

Gilpin, D. (1976). Psychotherapy of borderline psychotic children. *American Journal of Psychotherapy, 30,* 483–496.

Ginott, H.G. (1965). *Between parent and child.* New York: Macmillan.

Grossman-McKee, A. (1990). The relationship between affective expression in fantasy play and pain complaints in first and second grade children. *Dissertation Abstracts International, 50–09B,* 4219.

Halpern, W.I. (1968). Do children benefit from psychotherapy? A review of the literature of follow-up studies. *Bulletin of the Rochester Mental Health Center, 1,* 4–12.

Harter, S. (1977). A cognitive-developmental approach to children's expression of conflicting feelings and a technique to facilitate such expression in play therapy. *Journal of Consulting and Clinical Psychology, 45,* 417–432.

Hartmann, D.P., Roper, B.L., & Gelfant, D.M. (1977). An evaluation of alternative modes of child psychotherapy. In B. Lahey & A.E. Kazdin (Eds.), *Advances in clinical psychology* (Vol. 1, pp. 1–37). New York: Plenum Press.

Haworth, M.R. (Ed.). (1947). *Child psychotherapy* (2nd ed.). New York: Basic Books.

Heinicke, C. (1969). Frequency of psychotherapeutic session as a factor affecting outcome, analysis of clinical ratings and test results. *Journal of Abnormal Psychology, 74,* 553–560.

Heinicke, C., & Goldman, A. (1960). Research on psychotherapy with children: A review and suggestions for further study. *American Journal of Orthopsychiatry, 30,* 483–494.

Heinicke, C., & Strassman, L. (1975). Toward more effective research on child psychotherapy. *Journal of Child Psychiatry, 14,* 561–588.

Hogan, R., DeSoto, C., & Solano, C. (1977). Traits, tests and personality research. *American Psychologist, 32,* 255–264.

Hood-Williams, J. (1960). The results of psychotherapy with children. *Journal of Consulting Psychology, 24,* 84–88.

Johnson, P.A., & Stockdale, D.E. (1975). Effects of puppet therapy on palmar sweating of hospitalized children. *Johns Hopkins Medical Journal, 137,* 1–5.

Kazdin, A.E. (1990). Psychotherapy for children and adolescents. In M.R. Rosenweig & L.W. Porter (Eds.), *Annual review of psychology* (pp. 21–54). Palo Alto, CA: Annual Review.

Kazdin, A.E. (1993). Evaluation in clinical practice: Clinically sensitive and systematic methods of treatment delivery. *Behavior Therapy, 24,* 11–45.

Kenny, T.J., & Burka, A. (1980). Coordinating multiple interventions. In H.E. Rie & E.D. Rie (Eds.), *Handbook of minimal brain dysfunction: A critical review* (pp. 645–665). New York: Wiley.

Kernberg, P. (1995, October). *Child psychodynamic psychotherapy: Assessing the process.* Paper presented at the meeting of the American Academy of Child and Adolescent Psychiatry, New Orleans, LA.

Kessler, J. (1966). *Psychopathology of childhood.* Englewood Cliffs, NJ: Prentice-Hall.

Kessler, J. (1988). *Psychopathology of childhood* (2nd ed.). Englewood Cliffs, NJ: Prentice-Hall.

Kiesler, D. (1966). Some myths of psychotherapy research and the search for a paradigm. *Psychological Bulletin, 65,* 110–136.

Klein, M. (1960). *The psychoanalysis of children.* New York: Grove. (Original work published 1932)

Knell, S. (1993). *Cognitive-behavioral play therapy.* Northvale, NJ: Aronson.

Kohut, H. (1977). *The restoration of the self.* New York: International Universities Press.

Kohut, H., & Wolfe, E.R. (1978). The disorders of the self and their treatment: An outline. *International Journal of Psychoanalysis, 59,* 413–424.

Koocher, G., & Broskowski, A. (1977). Current practices in child psychotherapy. *Professional Psychology, 8,* 583–592.

Koocher, G., & D'Angelo, E.J. (1992). Evolution of practice in child psychotherapy. In D.K. Freedheim (Ed.), *History of psychotherapy* (pp. 457–492). Washington, DC: American Psychological Association.

Lease, C.A., & Ollendick, T.H. (in press). Development and psychopathology. In A.S. Bellack & M. Hersen (Eds.), *Psychopathology in adulthood: An advanced textbook.* New York: Pergamon Press.

Lehrman, L.J., Sirluck, H., Black, B.J., & Glick, S.J. (1949). *Success and failure of treatment of children in the Child Guidance Clinics of the Jewish Board of Guardians* (Research Monograph, No. 1).

Leichtman, M., & Shapiro, S. (1980). An introduction to the psychological assessment of borderline conditions in children: Borderline children and the test process. In J. Kwawer, H. Lerner, P. Lerner, & A. Sugarman (Eds.), *Borderline phenomena and the Rorschach Test* (pp. 343–366). New York: International Universities Press.

Lester, E. (1968). Brief psychotherapy in child psychiatry. *Canadian Psychiatric Association Journal, 13,* 301–309.

Levanthal, T., & Weinberger, G. (1975). Evaluation of a large-scale brief therapy program for children. *American Journal of Orthopsychiatry, 45,* 119–130.

Levitt, E.E. (1957). The results of psychotherapy with children: An evaluation. *Journal of Consulting Psychology, 21,* 189–196.

Levitt, E.E. (1963). Psychotherapy with children: A further evaluation. *Behavior Research and Therapy, 1,* 45–51.

Levitt, E.E. (1971). Research in psychotherapy with children. In A.E. Bergin & S.L. Garfield (Eds.), *Handbook of psychotherapy and behavior change: An empirical analysis* (pp. 474–494). New York: Wiley.

Levy, D. (1938). Release therapy in young children. *Psychiatry, 1,* 387–390.

Lowenstein, R.M. (1956). Some remarks on the role of speech in psychoanalytic techniques. *International Journal of Psychoanalysis, 37,* 460–468.

Mahler, M.S. (1968). *On human symbiosis and the vicissitudes of individuation.* New York: International Universities Press.

Mahoney, M. (1978). Experimental methods and outcome evaluation. *Journal of Consulting and Clinical Psychology, 46,* 660–672.

Mann, J., & Goldman, R. (1982). *A casebook in time-limited therapy.* New York: McGraw-Hill.

Masterson, J. (1972). *Treatment of the borderline adolescent.* New York: Wiley.

Mayes, L., & Cohen, D. (1996). Anna Freud and developmental psychoanalytic psychology. In A. Solnit, P. Newbauer, S. Abrams, & A.S. Dowling (Eds.), *The psychoanalytic study of the child* (Vol. 51, pp. 117–141). New Haven, CT: Yale University Press.

Mendelsohn, R. (1975). A manual for the seminar on psychotherapeutic process. *Collected seminar notes at Washington University Child Guidance Center.* St. Louis, MO.

Messer, S.B., & Warren, C.S. (1995). *Models of brief psychodynamic therapy.* New York: Guilford Press.

Miller, J. (1988). A child losing and finding her objects: An unusual therapeutic intervention in the nursery school. *Bulletin of the Anna Freud Centre, 11,* 75–89.

Milos, M., & Reiss, S. (1982). Effects of three play conditions on separation anxiety in young children. *Journal of Consulting and Clinical Psychology, 50,* 389–395.

Moran, G.S., & Fonagy, P. (1987). Psychoanalysis and diabetic control: A single case study. *British Journal of Medical Psychology, 60,* 357–372.

Moustakas, C. (1953). *Children in play therapy.* New York: McGraw-Hill.

Moustakas, C. (1959). *Psychotherapy with children: The living relationship.* New York: Ballantine.

O'Leary, D., & Turkewitz, N. (1978). Methodological errors in marital and child treatment research. *Journal of Consulting and Clinical Psychology, 46,* 747–758.

Ollendick, T., & Russ, S. (1999). Psychotherapy with children and families: Historical traditions and current trends. In S. Russ & T. Ollendick (Eds.), *Handbook of psychotherapies with children and families* (pp. 3–13). New York: Plenum Press.

Palmer, J. (1970). *The psychological assessment of children.* New York: Wiley.

Parad, L., & Parad, N. (1968). A study of crisis-oriented planned short-term treatment: Part 1. *Social Casework, 49,* 346–355.

Persons, J. (1991). Psychotherapy outcome studies do not accurately represent current models of psychotherapy: A proposed remedy. *American Psychologist, 46,* 99–106.

Phillips, R. (1985). Whistling in the dark? A review of play therapy research. *Psychotherapy, 22,* 752–760.

Piaget, J. (1951). *Play, dreams, and imitation in childhood.* New York: Norton.

Pine, F. (1974). On the concept of "borderline" in children. *Psychoanalytic Study of the Child, 29,* 341–368.

Postman, L. (Ed.). (1962). *Psychology in the making.* New York: Knopf.

Proskauer, S. (1969). Some technical issues in time-limited psychotherapy with children. *Journal of the American Academy of Child and Adolescent Psychiatry, 8,* 154–169.

Proskauer, S. (1971). Focused time-limited psychotherapy with children. *Journal of the American Academy of Child and Adolescent Psychiatry, 10,* 619–639.

Rie, H. (Ed.). (1974). *Perspectives in child psychopathology* (Vol. 3). Minneapolis, MN: University of Minneapolis Press.

Ross, A.O. (1981a). Child psychopathology. *Annual Review of Psychology, 32,* 243–278.

Ross, A.O. (1981b). On rigor and relevance. *Professional Psychology, 12,* 318–327.

Russ, S.W. (1987). Assessment of cognitive affective interaction in children: Creativity, fantasy and play research. In J.E. Butcher & C. Spielberger (Eds.), *Advances in personality assessment* (Vol. 6, pp. 141–155). Hillsdale, NJ: Erlbaum.

Russ, S.W. (1988). Primary process thinking in child development. In H. Lerner & P. Lerner (Eds.), *Primitive mental states and the Rorschach* (pp. 601–618). New York: International Universities Press.

Russ, S.W. (1991). Child psychopathology: State of the art [Review of the book *Handbook of child psychopathology*]. *Contemporary Psychology, 36,* 596–598.

Russ, S.W. (1993). Affect and creativity: The role of affect and play in the creative process. In *The personality assessment series.* Hillsdale, NJ: Erlbaum.

Russ, S.W. (1995). Play psychotherapy research: State of the science. In T. Ollendick & R. Prinz (Eds.), *Advances in clinical child psychology* (pp. 365–391). New York: Plenum Press.

Russ, S.W. (1998a). Introductory comments to special section on developmentally based integrated psychotherapy with children: Emerging models. *Journal of Clinical Child Psychology, 27,* 2–3.

Russ, S.W. (1998b). Psychodynamically based therapies. In T. Ollendick & M. Herson (Eds.), *Handbook of child psychopathology* (3rd ed., pp. 537–556). New York: Plenum Press.

Russ, S.W., & Grossman-McKee, A. (1990). Affective expression in children's fantasy play, primary process thinking on the Rorschach, and divergent thinking. *Journal of Personality Assessment, 54,* 756–771.

Russ, S.W., Niec, L., & Seja, A. (in press). Play assessment of affect: The Affect in Play Scale. In K. Gitlin-Weiner, A. Sangrund, & C. Schaefer (Eds.), *Play diagnoses and assessment.* New York: Wiley.

Russ, S.W., & Peterson, N. (1990). *The Affect in Play Scale: Predicting creativity and coping in children.* Unpublished manuscript.

Russ, S.W., Robins, A., & Christiano, B. (1999). Pretend play: Longitudinal prediction of creativity and affect in fantasy in children. *Creativity Research Journal, 12,* 129–139.

Santosefano, S. (1980). Cognition in personality and the treatment process. A psychoanalytic view. *Psychoanalytic Study of the Child, 35,* 41–66.

Schaefer, C. (Ed.). (1979). *Therapeutic use of child's play.* New York: Aronson.

Schaefer, C., & Millman, H. (1977). *Therapies for children.* San Francisco: Jossey-Bass.

Schuhmann, E.M., Foote, R.C., Eyberg, S.M., & Boggs, S. (1998). Efficacy of parent-child interaction therapy:

Interim report of a randomized trial with short-term maintenance. *Journal of Clinical Child Psychology, 27,* 34–45.

Seja, A., & Russ, S. (1999). Children's fantasy play and emotional understanding. *Journal of Clinical Child Psychology, 28,* 269–277.

Shirk, S.R. (1998). Interpersonal schemata in child psychotherapy: A cognitive-interpersonal perspective. *Journal of Clinical Child Psychology, 27,* 4–16.

Shirk, S.R., & Russell, R. (1996). *Change processes in child psychotherapy: Revitalizing treatment and research.* New York: Guilford Press.

Singer, D. (1993). *Playing for their lives.* New York: Free Press.

Singer, D., & Singer, J.L. (1973). *The child's world of make-believe.* New York: Academic Press.

Singer, J.L. (1990). *The house of make-believe.* Cambridge, MA: Harvard University Press.

Singer, J.L., & Singer, D. (1976). Imaginative play and pretending in early childhood: Some experimental approaches. In A. Davids (Ed.), *Child personality and psychopathology* (Vol. 3, pp. 69, 112). New York: Wiley.

Sloves, R., & Peterlin, K.B. (1986). The process of time-limited psychotherapy with latency-aged children. *Journal of the American Academy of Child Psychiatry, 25,* 847–851.

Smyrnios, K., & Kirby, R.J. (1993). Long-term comparison of brief versus unlimited psychodynamic treatments with children and their families. *Journal of Counseling and Clinical Psychology, 61,* 1020–1027.

Sroufe, L.A., & Rutter, M. (1984). The domain of developmental psychopathology. *Child Development, 55,* 17–29.

Stollack, G., Gershowitz, M., & Rief, T. (1978). *Fantasy play in child psychotherapy.* Paper presented at the meeting of the American Psychological Association, Toronto, Canada.

Strupp, H.H., & Bergin, E. (1969). Some empirical and conceptual bases for coordinated research in psychotherapy: A critical review of issues, trends, and evidence. *International Journal of Psychiatry, 7,* 18–90.

Strupp, H.H., & Hadley, S. (1977). A tripartite model of mental health and therapeutic outcome: With special reference to negative effects in psychotherapy. *American Psychologist, 32,* 187–196.

Toth, S., & Cicchetti, D. (1999). Developmental psychopathology and child psychotherapy. In S. Russ & T. Ollendick (Eds.), *Handbook of psychotherapies with children* (pp. 15–44). New York: Plenum Press.

Tuma, J.M. (1986, August). Current status of traditional therapies with children. In B. Bonner & C.E. Walker (Chairs), *Current status of psychotherapy with children.* Symposium presented at the annual meeting of the American Psychological Association, Washington, DC.

Tuma, J.M. (1989). Traditional therapies with children. In T. Ollendick & M. Hersen (Eds.), *Handbook of child psychopathology* (2nd ed., pp. 419–437). New York: Plenum Press.

Tuma, J.M., & Russ, S.W. (1993). Psychoanalytic psychotherapy with children. In T. Kratochwill & R. Morris (Eds.), *Handbook of psychotherapy with children and adolescents* (pp. 131–161). Boston: Allyn & Bacon.

Uribe, V.M. (1988). Short-term psychotherapy for adolescents: Management of initial resistance. *Journal of the American Academy of Psychoanalysis, 16,* 107–116.

Vraniak, D., & Picketts, S. (1993). Improving interventions with American ethnic minority children: Recurrent and recalcitrant challenges. In T. Kratochwill & R. Morris (Eds.), *Handbook of psychotherapy with children and adolescents* (pp. 502–540). Boston: Allyn & Bacon.

Wachtel, P. (1977). *Psychoanalysis and behavior therapy: Toward an integration.* New York: Basic Books.

Wallerstein, R.S. (1988). Assessment of structural change in psychoanalytic therapy and research. *Journal of the American Psychoanalytic Association, 36*(Suppl.), 241–261.

Waskow, I.E., & Parloff, M.B. (Eds.). (1975). *Psychotherapy change measures.* (DHEW Publication No. ADM 74–120, Supt. Doc. Stock No. 1724–00397). Rockville, MD: NIMH.

Webber, C. (1988). Diagnostic intervention with children at risk. In S. Altschul (Ed.), *Childhood bereavement and its aftermath* (pp. 77–105). Madison, WI: International Universities Press.

Weiner, I.B. (1975). *Principles of psychotherapy.* New York: Wiley.

Weisz, J., & Weiss, B. (1993). *Effects of psychotherapy with children and adolescents.* Newbury Park, CA: Sage.

Weisz, J.R., & Weiss, B. (1989). Assessing the effects of clinic-based psychotherapy with children and adolescents. *Journal of Consulting and Clinical Psychology, 57,* 741–746.

Weisz, J.R., & Weiss, B., Alicke, M.D., & Klotz, M.L. (1987). Effectiveness of psychotherapy with children and adolescents: A meta-analysis for clinicians. *Journal of Consulting and Clinical Psychology, 55,* 542–549.

Wickes, F.G. (1927). *The inner world of childhood.* New York: Wiley.

Winnicott, D.W. (1971). *Playing and reality.* London: Tavistok.

Witmer, H.L. (1909). Clinical psychology. *Psychological Clinic, 1,* 1–9.

Witmer, H.L., & Keller, J. (1942). Outgrowing childhood problems: A study of the value of child guidance treatment. *Smith College Studies in Social Work, 13,* 74–90.

Wolman, B.B., Egan, T., & Ross, A. (Eds.). (1978). *Handbook of treatment of mental disorders in childhood and adolescence.* Englewood Cliffs, NJ: Prentice-Hall.

Wright, L. (1978). *Parent power: A guide to responsible child-rearing.* New York: Psychological Dimensions.

CHAPTER 43

Family Psychology and Therapy

THOMAS V. SAYGER

A child's psychological development is determined by several factors, including genetic predisposition, temperament, and environmental influences. Perhaps the factor most amenable to intervention by a mental health professional is that environmental entity we call "family." As clinicians begin to view the family as an interactive system, it is evident that children's problems are often indicative of family difficulties (Combrinck-Graham, 1989) and are the result of "a sequence of acts between several people" (Haley, 1976, p. 2). Consequently, family therapy has become an increasingly popular therapeutic strategy and philosophy for addressing the psychological disorders of children.

The definition of what family therapy really is remains somewhat elusive because the term can refer to a variety of different methods, procedures, and techniques. The family therapist must formulate new theoretical concepts and therapeutic techniques when confronted with phenomena not explained by individual theory; thus, the family therapy movement continues to experience healthy, developmental growth. This developing perspective has come to be labeled family psychology and represents "the scientific study of the family from a multifaceted perspective—its historical forms and variation, its structure and functioning across time, space, cultures, and generations, and its idiosyncratic and systems attributes" (F.W. Kaslow, 1987, p. 88).

A family therapist emphasizes the family system and the interactive processes that operate within that system to maintain the current patterns of behavior and communication. This chapter focuses on the impact of the family system on the child and the proposed therapeutic strategies for addressing this phenomenon. The goal of this chapter is to provide a brief history of family therapy, an overview of systems philosophy, synopses of selected family therapy theories and their application with children, and a review of recent research issues and concerns. I also describe contraindications for the use of family therapy as an intervention strategy and, where feasible, suggest the treatment of choice for particular childhood disorders. Because this is a brief overview, readers are encouraged to read additional materials in their quest for knowledge regarding family therapy and psychology.

HISTORICAL DEVELOPMENT OF FAMILY THERAPY

The practice of family therapy has expanded tremendously in the past 50 years and much has been written on the topic (Sayger, Homrich, & Horne, 2000). Family therapy seems to have had its beginnings serendipitously in many locations and under the direction of several individuals but is usually noted to have gained recognition as a profession in the 1950s. Some family therapy historians credit Freud with utilizing a family therapy approach and point out that in many cases, when the child was the identified patient, Freud chose to work with the child's parent (e.g., Little Hans). Others point to a manuscript published by John Bowlby in 1949, "The Study and Reduction of Group Tension in the Family," in which he discussed the use of conjoint interviews as an auxiliary to individual sessions at the Tavistock Child Guidance Clinic in London. John Bell, who became aware of Bowlby's work with families, incorporated this approach into his clinical practice and has been labeled by some historians the "father of family therapy."

In the 1950s, Nathan Ackerman asserted that emotional problems could be generated by the immediate environment and by the dynamics of the psyche; thus, interviewing the entire family could be useful in circumventing an impasse with a difficult child. In 1958, Ackerman published *The Psychodynamics of Family Life,* which provided the first book on diagnosis and treatment of family relationships. For Ackerman, the parenting that a child received was closely related to the child's illness.

The clinical research of both Murray Bowen and Lyman Wynne followed on Theodore Lidz's research on the role of the family in the etiology and treatment of schizophrenic disorders. Bowen specialized in treating psychotic children and developed a family systems theory to explain his therapeutic approach. "Wynne was particularly intrigued by the parallel (and sometimes conflicting) needs of a child to develop a sense of personal identity and at the same time develop intimate relationships with others within the family" (I. Goldenberg & H. Goldenberg, 1983, p. 82).

Others credited with the early development of family therapy include Carl Whitaker, the Palo Alto Group, and the Philadelphia Group. Whitaker was characterized by Broderick and Schrader (1981) as "the most irreverent and whimsical of the founding fathers . . . [with his] finely honed therapy of the absurd—a therapy in which he often seems to drive a family sane by appearing more mad than they" (p. 23). Although Whitaker's approaches may have been nontraditional, his emphasis on the family's experience in therapy has provided insight into the therapeutic process.

The Palo Alto Group (Gregory Bateson, Jay Haley, John Weakland, Don D. Jackson, and Virginia Satir) studied the premise that schizophrenia was the product of children's being caught in paradoxical

binds by a parent who "is driven not only to punish the children's demand for love, but also to punish any indication which the child may give that he knows that he is not loved" (Haley, 1976, p. 67). Haley noted that adopting the family therapy perspective meant no longer seeing symptoms or problematic behavior emanating from a single "sick" individual. Instead, dysfunctional behavior was to be viewed as the product of a dysfunctional relationship. The symptom bearer—the "identified patient"—was merely expressing the family's disequilibrium. In 1959, Jackson published a paper on conjoint family therapy, arguing it was more effective than seeing family members individually. At this point, he established the Mental Research Institute (MRI), which was much more focused on family therapy per se, and brought Virginia Satir from Chicago to join the staff. During the mid-1960s, Satir gradually became more involved with a human growth model of family therapy; however, her work was strongly influenced by that of Gregory Bateson and others associated with the Palo Alto Group.

The Philadelphia Group (Boszormenyi-Nagy and associates) has also been an influential cohort in the development of contextual family therapy. Boszormenyi-Nagy was devoted to the therapy of psychotics and the integration of family therapy with psychotherapy as a whole. In the more recent history of family psychology, the work of such behavioral and social learning researchers as Richard Stuart, Gerald Patterson, and Robert Weiss has had a major impact on the development of behavioral family therapy interventions with couples, children, and families. The previously mentioned clinicians and researchers can be credited with adding to our knowledge about families and the development of family therapy and psychology. These individuals and groups were innovators in the system of family psychology, and to identify one as the sole founder of the approach would be inconsistent with the systems perspective of family psychology.

THE SYSTEMS PERSPECTIVE

The goal of all therapy is to assist clients in achieving change, whether this is accomplished by gaining greater insight, restructuring cognitions, improving communication, or developing effective reinforcement contingencies. For the family therapist, it is essential that the family, as an interacting system, be involved in the therapeutic process to ensure the appropriateness and maintenance of these changes. The basic premises of the systems perspective are straightforward and scientifically sound. In essence, a system (family) is an entity comprising elements that are necessarily interdependent. These family systems have subsystems that are separated by boundaries, and interaction across boundaries is governed by implicit rules and patterns. Finally, interactional patterns within a system are circular, and although change is inherent in open systems, families have homeostatic features that maintain the stability of their interactional patterns. The work of the clinician, therefore, is multiplied exponentially when providing therapy for families because facilitating change on the part of the identified child is inadequate unless the professional can also address the potential impact of this change on the client's interactive system.

The systems orientation occupies a preeminent position in the field of family therapy, although the task of integrating systems and other orientations into a workable blend is a difficult issue facing family therapists. The linear/cause-and-effect thinking of the scientific approach attempts to reduce reality into molecular units to determine the causes of individual events or behaviors. This reductionistic perspective deals with parts in isolation, whereas systems approaches focus on the whole and on the relationships that result from the dynamic interaction of its parts. Thus, the context within which interactions occur becomes a primary basis for understanding the functioning or dysfunctioning of the family. H. Goldenberg and Goldenberg (1994) stated that a systems perspective is holistic and attuned to interpersonal relationships and stresses the reciprocity of interactions among people. From a general systems perspective, the family as a whole is different from the sum of its parts, and the clinician must attend to the pattern, not merely to the parts.

In a process that is continuous and ongoing, families have both a history of interaction and an expectation of future interaction and interdependence. The structure or organization of the family indicates how members and subsystems (e.g., spousal, parent-child, sibling) are arranged within the interactive system. Subsystems have their own organization, boundaries, and interactive patterns. Boundaries determine who is to be included within

a certain system and the quality of the interactive process with other related systems. A system seeks to maintain a homeostatic balance, and family members develop systems that cannot be viewed apart from this interpersonal context; therefore, improvement in a child can ultimately threaten the balance of the system itself. Haley (1976) suggested that clues about what function the child's symptom plays can be observed in the initial interview. These clues can become apparent through parent and child interactions, the presentation of the problem, the family seating arrangement, who interrupts whom, reactions of family members to what is being said, and who does the talking.

In relation to circular causality, a basic premise of systems theory, the concept of equifinality suggests that the same results can be obtained by different means and by starting from different points. For example, there is not a single kind of "good parent" subsystem that will produce healthy children (W.C. Nichols & Everett, 1986). Equifinality has practical value for clinicians in that they may start from any one of several different points in the interactional context of the family system or use any one of a variety of different methods, techniques, and approaches to obtain the desired result. Other concepts of systems theory inherently relevant to family psychology include: (1) the family system cannot be understood merely by summing up the attributes or characteristics of the individual members (nonsummativity), although characteristics partially determine the nature of the family; (2) all behavior is considered communication, and communication defines relationships and establishes roles in the family system through the setting of rules; and (3) for the system to maintain itself, a change in one component must correspond to changes in other components of the system (Whitchurch & Constantine, 1993).

APPLICATIONS OF FAMILY THERAPY

The study of the family provides a new, and perhaps more complex, order of theoretical models for thinking about humans and their relationship to nature and the universe. A central theme for all family therapy seems to be the conflict between gaining an individual identity and yet remaining a member of an interactive group (i.e., the family).

Spiegel (1982) noted that all family therapies have three commonalities: (1) they focus on interactive processes and assume that these must change to resolve the problems; (2) observed family behavior is thought to be a surface phenomenon, and therapists look for hidden patterns, distorted or disguised interactions, cultural value systems, metamessages, undiscovered coalitions, and so forth; and (3) therapists bring their unique professional or disciplinary training into their understanding of the family processes.

In this chapter, family theories from the following categories will be discussed: intergenerational (Bowen systems, object relations); communications and strategic (strategic/brief, solution-focused family therapy, Satir's human process model); structural (Minuchin's structural family therapy); and behavioral (social learning/behavioral). The selection of these theories for discussion does not imply that these are the only examples of current family therapy theory, but they do provide a broad spectrum of viewpoints within the field of family psychology.

INTERGENERATIONAL MODELS

Intergenerational family therapies emphasize the family's historical, multigenerational influences and individual family members' intrapsychic functioning as they relate to current dysfunction. These models concurrently focus on what is transpiring inside the individual as well as among members of the family unit and try to facilitate change in both the personal and interpersonal dynamic. As Framo (1992) stated, "The kinds of problems people had with themselves or in their intimate relationships had a lot to do with what they were still working out from their original family" (p. xi).

Bowen Family Systems Therapy

Bowen's approach to family therapy has occupied a central, historical role in the evolution of family therapy. His theory emphasizes emotional functioning as it develops through the processes of differentiation of self, triangulation, the nuclear family emotional system, family projection process, emotional cutoff, multigenerational transmission, sibling position, and process in society. Bowen (1985) believed that children grow up to achieve varying levels of differentiation of self from the nuclear

family and all members of the extended families who still have unresolved emotional dependencies on each other. Differentiation is achieved when the individual can think objectively about emotionally sensitive issues within the family and, thus, can be emotionally close to members of the family or to any other person without fusing into new emotional "onenesses." Some individuals achieve almost complete differentiation of self and become clearly defined individuals with well-defined ego boundaries (i.e., a mature person), whereas the emotionally undifferentiated person experiences psychological difficulties.

For Bowen (1985, p. 174), a triangle represented the "basic building block" of any emotional system. He asserted that, in times of emotional tensions, a two-person system (e.g., mother-father, parent-child) would solicit the participation of a third person, thus permitting the tension to emanate around the triangle and alleviate the intense anxiety. For example, when a parental dyad is in a state of conflict or stress, a child may be brought into the relationship as a comfortable cohort for the most stressed partner in the dyad. Unfortunately, this "triangulation" of the child results in his or her distancing from one parent and becoming overinvolved with the parent who solicited the participation. These triangles have definite relationship patterns that are predictably repeated during periods of stress and calm, resulting in relationships in which two people are generally comfortable and the third person is less comfortable.

The child-focused family is one in which sufficient family anxiety is focused on one or more children (child triangulation) and thus results in serious impairment of a child. The usual approach in family therapy is to defocus the intensity of the emotional involvement with the child and gradually shift the emotional focus to the parents or between parents and families of origin. The strategy is to remove the focus from the child as quickly as possible, remove the children from the therapy sessions as early as possible, and give technical priority to getting the focus on the relationship between the parents at the risk of a temporary increase in the child's symptoms. When the patient is a child, the goal of therapy is to reach a stage when the two parents can work together on their part of the family problem without involving the child. When this stage is reached, the child will automatically improve, according to Bowen, without participation in the family therapy. This process is closely tied to Bowen's philosophy that the original two-person system in tension will automatically resolve its tension within a triangled system if the third person remains emotionally detached; thus, in the case of the triangled child, the therapist removes the third person (i.e., the child) so that the two-person system can resolve its issues.

Family psychotherapy, according to Bowen, involves the two most important people in the family (i.e., parents) and the therapist as a potential triangle. Using this approach, the therapist maintains the role of an interested clinical investigator with many questions to ask about the details of the problem in the family. It is presumed that the emotional problem between two people will resolve automatically, as stated earlier, if they remain in contact (i.e., avoid emotional cutoff) with a third person who can remain free of the emotional field between the two while actively relating to each of them. The therapist is extremely vulnerable to becoming a part of the triangle when listening to the content of the clients' story, because the most uncomfortable client will attempt to bring the therapist into the triangle. Focusing on the therapeutic process rather than on content can help therapists keep their perspective and, thus, their emotional detachment from the triangle. Theoretically, a family system can be changed if any triangle in the family is changed and if that triangle can stay in meaningful emotional contact with the other interlocking triangles. A triangled relationship can also be modified through changes in one family member because creating change in one member of a triangle will predictably change that triangle and the interlocking triangles with which that relationship is associated. The entire family can be changed through one family member if this motivated individual has sufficient dedication and energy to work toward his or her goal in spite of all obstacles.

The nuclear family emotional system describes the patterns of emotional functioning of a family in a single generation. In assessing family functioning, the therapist notes the functioning of the nuclear family and how the functioning of the extended family interrelates with the nuclear family; investigates the functioning of the parental ego mass since marriage; and investigates the two extended families of origin. When any family member makes a move toward differentiation of self, the family emotional system communicates a three-stage verbal and

nonverbal message: (1) You are wrong; (2) Change back; (3) If you do not, these are the consequences (Bowen, 1985). If it is possible to increase differentiation in one family member, this can loosen up the entire family system.

Family projection is the basic process by which parental problems are projected to children. The basic pattern involves a mother whose emotional system is more focused on the children than on her husband and a father who is sensitive to his wife's anxiety and who supports her emotional involvement with the children (Bowen, 1985). The family projection process is selective in that it typically focuses on the child first. Among the most vulnerable for the projection process are oldest children, an only child, and a child born with a defect. Thus, exploring sibling position becomes important, with the goal of helping one parent to "differentiate a self" in the relationship with the child.

The overall goal of Bowen's approach is to help family members become "system experts" who know the family system so well that the family can readjust itself without the help of an outside expert if and when the family system is again stressed. Bowen (1985) noted that families under conditions of chronic stress experience the same process of dysfunction seen in society (i.e., process in society). In this process, families tend to lose contact with their intellectually based principles and revert to emotionally determined decisions for short-term relief, thus laying the foundation for even greater problems in the future. From his research with schizophrenic patients, he speculated that it takes three generations for schizophrenia to develop and that this disorder is characterized by high levels of immaturity (i.e., low differentiation of self) and intense early attachments to the mother. A case presented by Bowen was characterized by a mother who assumed an "overadequate and overinvolved" relationship with her daughter that resulted in the daughter's assuming the role of "helpless and inadequate little child." The father assumed an inadequate role and the relationship between father and mother was one of emotional distance or "emotional divorce." Once the father took a stand against the mother's overinvolvement with the daughter, conflicts arose between the spouses, yet the father continued to participate actively in treatment and the mother became anxious and aggressive toward him. Bowen asserted that this confrontation was the crux of treatment in that the father and mother had established emotional closeness through the father's assuming the "head of the family" role and the mother's becoming more objective about her symbiotic relationship with her daughter. Bowen noted that the daughter's schizophrenic and helpless behaviors decreased markedly when the parents were able to maintain their emotional investment in each other; however, the daughter would regress to her dysfunctional actions when the parents were more invested in their relationship with her.

Family systems theory requires higher motivation and compliance than many other family therapy approaches because of its interests in three-generational patterns and the family of origin (i.e., multigenerational transmission process). Few studies exist that have tested any of its central constructs and none has involved the evaluation of its outcomes. The major pitfall in empirical study is that there are no specific steps to follow other than the general one of being in better contact with parents, siblings, and the larger extended system. M.P. Nichols and Schwartz (1998) reported that Bowenian therapists do at least as well as the standard figures (i.e., one-third of their patients get worse or no better; one-third get somewhat better; and one-third get significantly better); however, evidence for this effectiveness lies primarily in personal experience and clinical reports. Readers are referred to the following publications for information regarding Bowen systems family therapy (Bowen 1976, 1985; Guerin, Fogarty, Fay, & Kautto, 1996; McGoldrick & Gerson, 1985; Papero, 1991).

Object-Relations Family Therapy
"Object-relations theory may be defined as the psychoanalytic study of the origin and nature of interpersonal relationship, and the intrapsychic processes which grow out of infant-adult relationships and remain to influence present interpersonal relationships" (Aradi & Kaslow, 1987, p. 597). The fundamental human drive is the need to be in a relationship. The characteristics of object-relations family therapy include assessment of developmental level, defense and anxiety, group psychoanalytic technique, transference and countertransference, sequencing of individual and couple therapies with family therapy, and the role of play and other techniques with child-rearing families. Object-relations family therapy is influenced by the ethological research of Bowlby, who described the fundamental human need for attachment and the destructive

effects of early separation from caregivers. The infant at birth seeks attachment to his or her mother and is vulnerable to her responses in meeting needs for closeness, comfort, and food. The gratification or frustrating of these needs determines to a large extent the child's attitudes toward family members and eventually his or her relations to others. Object-relations family therapy emphasizes etiology, including unconscious determinism, exploration of the intrapsychic inner world, and the elucidation of psychosexual stages of development. Unhappiness and dysfunction are seen as rooted primarily in the past, existing intrapsychically, and manifested within both the individual's personal world and interpersonal context. This dysfunction is transgenerational and creates a psychological deficit with potentially negative individual and interpersonal consequences.

For Luepnitz (1988), a proponent of feminist object-relations family therapy, treatment:

> begins with the provision of a holding or caring environment so that the family members feel safe enough to make themselves known to the therapist. The aims are to help relieve the symptom in ways that leave the family members better able to understand one another, and to provide a holding environment for one another. The therapist opens up choices to the family that allow them to be less patriarchal, less father-absent, and less isolated from their context [than they have been historically]. (p. 195)

This process is termed *re-membering* the family. The aim of treatment is to enable the patients to review and reexperience what is troublesome, bring about the return of repressed material to consciousness, explore feelings and attitudes, and break up pathological patterns of intrapsychic reacting and interpersonal interacting (Scharff & Scharff, 1987). Consequently, change is achieved by a process of confrontation, clarification, interpretation, and working through.

Skynner (1976) suggested that people with relationship difficulties are "stuck" with expectations that are appropriate only in childhood. What characterizes the analytically oriented approaches seems to be the use of insight to achieve growth of the family members. Object-relations family therapists tend to emphasize the intrapsychic or internal makeup of the child and hold that insight is required for change and developmental progression to occur, and that working through is needed to consolidate gains. Insight occurs when the way the family relates to the therapist reflects the transference of repressed feelings and behavior rooted in earlier experiences with the families of origin. Repetition of these phenomena in the therapeutic setting allows these feelings and the defenses against them to become conscious. Therapist activities primarily consist of listening (for both manifest and latent content), intermittent questioning (to amplify or clarify), interpreting (to make connections and foster insight), and encouraging family members to consider how they wish to be different and how they can help such modifications to occur in light of their idiosyncratic history and talents.

The goals of analytic family therapy are as open-ended as the treatment itself, because goals change as growth occurs. Symptoms are seen as misguided attempts at changing family difficulties. The family is viewed as an interpersonal, cybernetic system that has not been able to adjust to a transition. For the individual family member, the goal of treatment is greater individuation and ego integration. On an interpersonal level, the aim is to enable family members to interact with one another as whole persons, on the basis of current realities rather than unconscious images of the past, and to enable them to individuate as well as to coevolve into a healthier family unit. Implicit in object-relations family therapy is the belief that without treatment, the patient's (family's) prognosis is poor. Successful treatment implies that personality restructuring and increased ego integration will enable each individual family member to handle current and future intra- and interpersonal conflicts more effectively. As a result of the heightened level of individuation, patients will become better equipped to make choices regarding such important matters as mate selection and vocation predicated on conscious, reality-based needs, as opposed to unconscious fantasies and unmet childhood deficiency needs.

Infants, toddlers, and play-age children are included in treatment so that their contribution to the family system can be observed; exclusion of children from the therapeutic process can lead to a fundamentally different perception of family dynamics. Children in the family other than the identified patient may have subtle difficulties that can be detected early if all members are seen, and children may act as allies and cotherapists as they speak and play to express emotion and clarify the unconscious themes. In general, they complete the

picture of the family that is essential to "whole family understanding" (Scharff & Scharff, 1987). Children between the ages of 3 and 10 do not seem to know enough of the family's defenses to know when to keep quiet and what not to say, so they frequently blurt out family "secrets." The impact of parental statements or arguments on the child is explicitly observable by watching the child's response and is frequently more therapeutic than a verbal interpretation by the clinician.

For the object-relations family therapist, play communication is an important source of information. Play is seen as a medium for the expression of the child's internal world and a normal, age-appropriate way of dealing with anxiety for children 6 to 10 years of age. In clinical situations, children also feel substantially more comfortable while engaged in some action. The information from the child about the family is largely nonverbal or "metaverbal" (i.e., beyond the literal meaning of the words) during play; thus, the analytic family therapist emphasizes the affective interactions of play as well as its content.

Given that the constructs studied are not observable (e.g., unconscious conflict, intrapsychic processes) or reliably quantifiable (e.g., differentiation), object-relations family therapy does not readily lend itself to traditional empirical analyses. Rather, evaluation of theory and treatment is phenomenological and constructivistic. Much outcome and process research in object-relations family therapy consists of detailed single-case studies or comparisons of several cases. The methodology used to gather such data tends to be informal and continuous, and consists of the therapist's observing behavior and listening for themes and patterns in patients' spontaneous flow of thoughts and feelings and their interchanges with each other (Scharff, 1992).

COMMUNICATIONS AND STRATEGIC/BRIEF MODELS

The communications schools of family therapy seem ideally suited to families who request only symptomatic relief; however, the intent of therapy is more than elimination of the symptom. These approaches offer a model that is appealing to the resistant family (e.g., those characterized by previous treatment failure or by an unwillingness to follow therapeutic directives) because interaction and communication strategies become the immediate focus. Therapeutic models in this category are generally brief (i.e., less than 20 sessions), emphasize family communications, and tend to be symptom-focused (at least initially).

Strategic/Brief Family Therapy to Solution-Focused Therapy

Although there are two distinct therapeutic approaches under this rubric, strategic (Palo Alto Group) and brief (MRI) family therapy are discussed here as compatible and theoretically consistent therapeutic models. Haley (1976) stated that shifting the therapeutic focus from the individual unit to a social unit of two or more people has certain consequences for a therapist. Not only must therapists think in different ways about human dilemmas, but they must consider themselves as members of the social unit that contains the problem.

Family problems or symptoms are seen as occurring from wrong attempts at changing ordinary difficulties. Segal (1982) noted that these "wrong" actions tend to fall into one of four patterns. First, individuals attempt to solve problems by being "spontaneous deliberately." Usually associated with cases of sleep disorders, sexual dysfunction, and substance abuse, these individuals deliberately attempt to correct the symptom and get trapped in a paradoxical predicament of attempting to force a particular behavior (e.g., forcing themselves to sleep, to not drink). Second, individuals seek a "no-risk" solution where some risk is inevitable. In this instance, the individual is responding to a fear of failure or rejection and either tries too hard or becomes "frozen" when attempting to resolve the problem. Third, a person attempts to reach an interpersonal accord through argument. When attempting to solve problems through discussion and sharing of feelings, individuals become hypersensitive to normal shifts in emotion and create problems where none really exist. Fourth, an individual attracts attention by attempting to be left alone. Consistent with a paranoid reaction, a person utilizing this solution emotionally and/or physically withdraws when sensing a lack of respect or personal attack.

Strategic therapists tend not to use conventional diagnostic systems because they believe that diagnostic labels or labels that present the problem in individualistic terms do nothing more than hamper therapy and present the problem in terms that make treatment more difficult. The goal of strategic family therapy is always clearly set and is to solve the presenting problem. By changing transactional patterns, the family will reorganize in a different manner and thus be able to go on with the process of living their lives.

When working with families in which the child is the identified patient, the strategic therapist first decides who is the focus of the child's concern (i.e., who is being protected by the child and in what way). Madanes (1984) believed that the symptom becomes a protective function for the marital relationship in that it attracts attention to the child and thus distracts the family from the marital problem. The therapy is planned in stages, as it is assumed that the presenting problem usually cannot be solved in one step and that relationships in each family are unique and may require different therapeutic plans even when the presenting problems are similar. Next, the therapist decides on an intervention that will change the family organization to one in which there is a single hierarchy, with the parents in the superior position. The therapist's intervention usually takes the form of a directive about something that the family is to do, both in and out of the interview. These directives may be straightforward or paradoxical, may involve one or two people or the whole family, and have the purpose of changing the interaction patterns of family members. The therapist is not concerned with making family members aware of how communication takes place; if a problem can be solved without the family's knowing how or why, that is satisfactory.

The following strategic family therapy directives, all paradoxical in intent, represent those that seem most amenable to working with children (Madanes, 1984). A paradoxical intervention (e.g., prescribing the symptom) encourages a person to perform the symptom, thus emphasizing that the symptomatic behavior is under the person's control:

1. *Asking parents to prescribe the presenting problem or the symbolic representation of the presenting problem.* The parents are asked to request that the child purposefully have the presenting problem. The parents are to supervise the child in performing the problem behavior and see that he or she does it correctly. Subsequently, this behavior is replaced by more constructive activities by parents and child. The hypothesis behind this paradoxical intervention is that the

symptomatic behavior has a function in relation to the parents; it is part of an interaction in which the child helplessly persists in the disturbing behavior while the parents helplessly insist that it should end but are unable to stop it.

2. *Prescribing the pretending of the symptom.* The parents request the child to pretend to have the presenting problem. The parents are to criticize the performance and make sure that the pretending is accurate, and then they are to behave as they usually do when the child presents the real problem behavior. Parents must be careful to evaluate in a caring and affectionate manner and avoid hostility. In most cases, the therapist does not expect the performance to occur, and the family or child will realize that they do have control over the symptom.

3. *Prescribing a reversal in the family hierarchy.* This directive consists of putting the children in charge of the parents. This approach is appropriate when the parents present themselves as incompetent, helpless, and unable to take charge of their children while complaining that the children are out of control. This approach can also be useful for children who are shy or withdrawn and/or rebellious. This technique is meant to tap into the child's sense of humor and the natural caring that exists between children and parents.

4. *Prescribing who will have the presenting problem.* This directive consists of prescribing the symptom but changing who will have it. This type of therapy prescription is appropriate in cases of severe problems, such as antisocial behavior, drug use, delinquency, bizarre communication, and depression. The hypothesis is that the person with the presenting problem is distracting the family from conflict with a particular family member in a way that is benevolent and prevents the resolution of the original conflict. Thus, by asking another family member to be the "family problem," the therapist expects family members to rebel against this notion and progress to a discussion of the "real" family problems.

Other techniques of the strategic/brief family therapy approaches include *reframing* and *restraining change.* Reframing involves changing the conceptual and/or emotional setting of the situation and placing it in a different frame of reference. Restraining change or benevolent sabotage occurs when the therapist tells the patient to go slow or even emphasizes the dangers of improvement and places an emphasis on consequence. This prescription may continue to be used throughout treatment (Duncan & Solevey, 1989). Theoretically, achieving change will have a snowball effect in that the family or patient will return to his or her normal life situation, do things differently, and continue to grow through natural processes.

In a case of a child experiencing night terrors, the initial therapy interview might attempt to obtain specific information about the night terrors (i.e., sleeping arrangements, family history of night terrors, preceding and antecedent events). The child might be instructed to demonstrate the night terror in session, and the mother asked to discuss her theory of the causes of this problem behavior. Having this information, the therapist might instruct the family members to pretend the symptom every evening. The mother (hearing her child's cries) would wake him and all other family members so they could practice the symptom. An individual session might be held with the child to focus on the night fantasy and change the frightening aspects of his night terrors into more positive images. Treatment would conclude when the child begins to participate in activities with other children and the night terrors disappear.

Perhaps the predominant form of strategic/brief therapy in practice today is solution-focused brief therapy, which directly descends from the MRI model of strategic therapy (M.P. Nichols & Schwartz, 1998). Solution-focused family therapy uses client-generated information through the clinical interviewing process to identify potential solutions for the client's presenting problems. Thus, the clinical emphasis is on the development of positive, effective solutions rather than on the problem per se. Through the identification of periods in which the client is already successfully addressing the problem (e.g., identifying times when a misbehaving child is not misbehaving), the therapist assists the client in expanding on these positive moments and discusses the use of the more effective solutions as a potential course of action for the client.

Solution-focused therapists identify five useful questions (de Shazer & Berg, 1993). First, the presession change question is designed to gather information regarding what the family has done between the time of the initial telephone call with the therapist and the first session. It is assumed that during this time, the family is focused on their concerns and are in a solution-finding mode, so that the problem may be resolved prior to treatment. In such a case, the therapist might ask the family "What do you have to do to keep this [solution-oriented behavior] going?" Second, the miracle question is posed to engage the family in thinking about the possibility that their problem can actually be solved. A miracle question might be presented such as "Suppose a miracle happened, as soon as tonight, while you were sleeping, and the problem that brought you here today is solved. When you wake up, how will you know that a miracle has happened and the problem is solved?" This question would be followed up with "What do you suppose you need to do to make this happen? What is the first step?" Third, exception-finding questions are designed to identify times when the problem does not occur. For example, "Are there times, even now, when parts of the solutions are already happening?" The therapeutic assumption is that every problem has an exception and that there is always a time when the problem does not occur (e.g., a child does not misbehave all the time, a parent does not yell or lose his or her temper all the time). Fourth, scaling questions are designed to assess the client's perceptions with regard to a particular issue. For example, "On a scale of 1 to 10, with 1 being totally disinterested in a solution and 10 very committed to finding a solution, how committed are you to solving this problem?" This questioning can be expanded to determine how each family member feels about how the other family members might rate their commitment and ultimately to ask each family member what he or she needs to do to convince their family he or she is committed to solving the problem. Fifth, coping questions are especially pertinent for clients with chronic or terminal illnesses. A coping question might be "How do you cope each day when you are in so much pain?" or "How did you manage to get out of bed today?" The purpose of the coping question is clear. Given the extreme pain, depression, or difficulty of living with a chronic problem, the client is still able to continue with daily living tasks when others might have succumbed. Solution-focused therapists believe that change is inevitable and occurring constantly; thus, small solutions lead to big solutions, and it is more effective to pay attention to the solutions of problems than to the problems themselves.

Gurman (1988) noted the impressive impact of strategic approaches on family therapy from a clinical perspective, but asserted that there have been no well-designed comparative or control-group studies of any of the strategic variations. Strategic therapy has come under much scrutiny and criticism for its seemingly manipulative techniques (M.P. Nichols & Schwartz, 1998). Haley and Madanes, as the leading proponents of the strategic family approach, have looked to structural family therapy for a more collaborative approach to therapy. Readers are referred to the following books for more information on varying strategic/brief therapy approaches: Fisch, Weakland, and Segal (1982) and M.P. Nichols and Schwartz (1998).

Satir's Human Validation Process Model

Satir's (1983) model holds a very positive belief in human potential and assumes that people are geared toward growth and change and are capable of all kinds of transformation. Furthermore, all humans carry within them all the resources they need to flourish, and the family is a system wherein everyone and everything is impacted by and impacts everyone and everything else. Satir believed that human development is influenced by unchangeable genetic endowments, longitudinal biases that are the result of all the learning an individual acquires, and constant interactions of body and mind. A family system is considered balanced, but the question remains as to what price each part pays to keep it so. Satir's primary goal in therapy is to enhance the individual's potential for becoming more fully evolved as a human being. In family therapy, the goals are to integrate the needs of each family member for independent growth with the integrity of the family system, strengthen and enhance the coping skills of individual family members by teaching them new ways of viewing and handling situations, and make people aware that they have the ability to make choices. These goals focus on the development of health rather than the eradication of symptoms. Satir's goal in life was for people to develop those qualities that help them to become more fully human and to make in themselves the changes necessary for this to occur.

Satir (1983) noted that one of the family's responsibilities is the transmission of culture to the children by parental teaching. This instruction includes roles and/or socially accepted ways to act with others in different social situations, methods of coping with the environment, communication, expression of emotions, recognition of when its members are capable of performing adult roles and functions, and provision for the eventual care of parents by their children. Satir felt that an important aspect of healthy child development was the development of appropriate self-esteem. Self-esteem, Satir believed, was developed by fulfilling the child's needs for physical comfort and continuity of relationships, while learning to influence and predict the responses of others, structure the world, and esteem (or value) the self. Satir hypothesized that the close relationship among parental validation, self-esteem, independence, and uniqueness is demonstrated by observing how a dysfunctional person still clings to his or her parental figures or relates to his or her sexual partner as if that partner were, in fact, a parent.

An important concept in Satir's process model of therapy is that of maturation. The patterns of behaving that characterize a mature person are considered functional because they enable him or her to deal in a relatively competent and precise way with the world in which he or she lives. However, a dysfunctional individual will deliver conflicting messages and will not be able to perform the most important function of good communication (i.e., checking out his or her perceptions to see whether they are congruent with the situation as it really is or with the intended meaning of another). Difficulty in communicating is closely linked to an individual's self-concept (i.e., self-image and self-esteem), with low self-esteem leading to dysfunctional communication. Dysfunction in communication will also follow when the individual is unable to handle "differentness" (i.e., that which makes the individual unique). Therefore, from Satir's perspective, therapy is an attempt to improve inadequate methods of communication.

Satir (1983) advocated the use of a family life chronology or "history-taking process" in therapy; however, the focus of treatment is on "process" issues that occur during the session and a feeling-level focus for the family. Satir and Bitter (2000) stated that it is important to determine under what conditions growth occurs in a positive direction and to provide those conditions. The therapist must be a model of communication and a resource person for the client.

Sculpting (Satir, 1982), which entails having family members take physical postures representing the family's lines of communication, is one technique associated with this model. Family sculptures are incorporated into treatment to demonstrate physically the communication patterns within the family system and to tap into several dimensions of human potential that Satir feels are essential to growth. In general, Satir attempted to access the person's intellectual, emotional, sensual, interactional, contextual, nutritional, physical, and spiritual self.

In working with a misbehaving child, Satir (1982) conceptualized the child's behavior as a signal about family pain and as such, included the child in treatment as a preventive measure. The initial interview began with the Family Life Fact Chronology, which provides information regarding what events had happened, when, who was involved, changes in family membership (e.g., through divorce, death, remarriage), and other specific details. In this approach, Satir supported parental authority while recognizing a child's increasing capacity to make good judgments and decisions. To help family members first identify and then remove blocks to effective communication, Satir had the family form a sculpture of their interactions by placing family members in physical postures that represented their communication style. For example, a blaming parent may stand over the child and point a finger of blame at the child. Family treatment is complete when the blocks to communication have been removed. Satir (1982) wrote, "Working with a family is like weaving a new tapestry, taking the threads from the used one, adding new ones, letting go of out-of-date ones and together creating a new design" (p. 24).

To date, no empirical studies have been conducted to assess the efficacy of the human growth model of family therapy. Satir (1982) stated that she had been clinically successful in most of the more than 5,000 cases she had treated, and this model continues to be widely accepted by practitioners utilizing a family therapy approach to treatment. See Satir and Bitter (2000) for further discussion of the development and current status of Satir's model.

STRUCTURAL MODEL

Structural family therapy seems most suited to families who are disorganized, unmotivated, and authoritarian. Structural family therapy has its therapeutic roots in crisis intervention and treatment of chronically dysfunctional, inner-city, delinquent, and psychotic families. Aradi and Kaslow (1987) noted that structural family therapy is based on changing the organization of the family. When the structure of the family is transformed, the positions of the family members in the group are changed accordingly. Theoretical assumptions include the concepts that all families reflect a structure as defined by hierarchy, boundaries, subsystems, rules, and roles; families are open sociocultural systems in transition; families move through a number of stages that require restructuring as they develop; and, to maintain continuity and enhance the growth of its members, a family must adapt to changing circumstances. Family structures that consistently underfunction and fail to realize the extent of their alternatives can, theoretically, function effectively once system boundaries have been clearly identified and are appropriately flexible.

Minuchin's Structural Family Therapy

Minuchin and Fishman (1981) stated that the family is the natural context for both growth and healing and over time has evolved patterns of interacting that make up the family structure and govern the functioning of family members. A viable form of family structure is needed to perform the family's essential tasks of supporting individuation while providing a sense of belonging. The unit of intervention for structural family therapists is always a holon (family subsystem). Each holon (e.g., the individual, the nuclear family, the extended family, the community) is both a whole system and a part of a larger system. For example, the nuclear family is a holon of the extended family, the extended family of the community, and so on.

. The family is not a static entity, but is in a continuous process of change, as are its social contexts. Therapists, in effect, stop time when they look at families, just as if they were stopping a motion picture to focus on one frame (Minuchin & Fishman, 1981). At the birth of the first child, when new holons are instantly established, the spouse holon must reorganize to deal with new tasks, and new rules must be developed. When children go off to school, the family must relate to a new, well-organized, highly significant system. The entire family must develop new patterns, and as children grow, they also bring new elements into the family system. Healthy family functioning is viewed as a family's ability to respond and adapt to these internal and external family stressors. Continuous

transformation of the positions of family members in relation to one another, for the purpose of individual growth and family continuity, is the hallmark of family health. Dysfunction, or underfunctioning, is caused by a family's inability or refusal to adapt (i.e., change its structure) and accommodate family stressors. Transactional patterns among family members are, therefore, conceptualized as either too inflexible, rigid, and enmeshed, or too chaotic, ambiguous, and disengaged to permit the family to be flexible in response to changing life circumstances. Periodic family stress is considered normal, and family dysfunction during periods of stress is viewed as not uncommon. However, with appropriate family restructuring, the dysfunction can be ameliorated and the family can resume a healthier developmental course.

Therapy consists of the therapist's constructing a map, or organizational schema, of the family. This map describes the structure of the family in terms of its components (subsystems), organization (hierarchy), relationships (boundaries), and processes (coalitions, detouring, etc.). In assessing the family, the clinician focuses on structure, flexibility, and capacity for restructuring; sensitivity to individual members; and family context in terms of support and stress. The family's developmental stage, the tasks required to move through the stage, and the ways in which symptoms are used to maintain the family's transactional patterns are also identified. Minuchin (1984) suggested that the therapist looks for ineffective interactions and relationship but also looks for how boundaries are maintained. Boundaries (generational, sexual, individual), alignments (positive, negative, and neutral connections with people in the family), and balance of forces (whom the individual is connected to in the family has to do with that person's relative importance) provide information about the family structure.

Because dysfunction is viewed as a family's inability to adapt to changing circumstances, change is conceptualized as increasing the family's range of alternatives so that it can become more adaptive. The goal of therapy is to skew the balance (unbalancing) of family members so that a new, more adaptive level of organization can be achieved. The therapist accomplishes this goal through (1) joining the family and establishing a therapeutic system and (2) restructuring the family. To join the family system, the therapist must accept the family's organization and style and blend with them.

Restructuring operations represent specific interventions that create movement toward therapeutic goals. Improvement consists of an infusion of alternatives into the family's repertoire of behaviors.

Minuchin (1984) related the story of an anorectic teenage girl with multiple extreme weight loss, hospitalizations, and refusals of psychological treatment. The family was characterized by high levels of enmeshment and dependency on each other. During initial treatment sessions, the parents (primarily the mother) insisted on responding to questions posed to the daughter. The father seemed reluctant to challenge the mother's power within the family and, consequently, contributed to the continued enmeshment of the family system. The structural therapist attempted to repattern the family in such a way that each member could be a full participant in the functioning of the family. Minuchin (1984, p. 96) posed the therapeutic challenge as one of replacing the family belief of "we are a normal family with an anorectic child and helpful parents" with one of "you are a family that got stuck in your development and must grow up to adjust to the growth of your adolescent children." Therapeutically, Minuchin noted that the suggested solution to the anorectic behavior was that "Loretta [the daughter] is childish; therefore, Margherita [her mother] must grow up" (p. 108). The not-eating behavior was thus reframed as an issue of autonomy, and the client and therapist negotiated a contract in which the client would eat alone, away from the family table, but would agree to be weighed by the therapist prior to each session. Subsequent sessions remained focused on issues of individuation and independence. A follow-up noted that the family had successfully resolved these issues and the identified patient was maintaining appropriate eating behaviors.

Strengths of this model's therapeutic power lie in its clarity, specificity, and teachability; limitations relate to its adaptability. The theoretical assumption that high levels of enmeshment or disengagement among family members are precursors to dysfunction appears too absolute and ethnocentric. It does not acknowledge the adaptive function of these dynamics under certain environmental conditions and for certain ethnic groups. Other criticisms of the structural model are its overemphasis on homeostatic stuckness and resistance while underestimating the system's tendency toward change; overuse of techniques to push a family toward goals set by the therapist rather than letting new patterns of family interaction evolve naturally with less intervention, and an overemphasis on the nuclear family and underemphasis on other system levels including the extended family and larger peer and community networks (Aradi & Kaslow, 1987).

Structural family therapists are one of the few groups that have attempted to attach outcome research to their work. Gurman and Kniskern (1978) believed that structural family therapy is highly amenable to empirical study because it has been successfully taught for years, its technical operations are clear and specific, and positive outcomes have been demonstrated with difficult-to-treat populations. Their research involved problems of delinquency, drug and alcohol addiction, and psychosomaticism. Minuchin (1984) reported great success in treating childhood and adolescent psychosomatic problems with structural family therapy. Treating anorexia, asthma, diabetes, and other psychosomatic symptoms by intervening in the family at a systems level is gaining in popularity and rapidly becoming the treatment of choice for many of these presenting problems (Gurman & Kniskern, 1981).

M.P. Nichols and Schwartz (1998) noted that studies demonstrating the effectiveness of structural family therapy with severely ill psychosomatic children are particularly convincing because the research designs include the use of physiological measures, and are extremely important because of the life-threatening nature of the illnesses. Structural therapy seems to be most effective with disorganized or pathologically organized families. In general, families presenting a symptomatic child in the context of disordered generational boundaries can expect relief of symptoms and overall improvement of family functioning within 8 to 12 sessions of work on their structural imbalances (Minuchin, 1984). For more information on structural family therapy, the reader is referred to Minuchin, Lee, and Simon (1996) and Minuchin (1984).

BEHAVIORAL MODELS

Behavioral models of family therapy attempt to apply principles of human learning in an effort to change the maladaptive behavior in which family members are engaging. Much of the work in this area has actually been parent training, in which the parents are used as agents of change; however, social learning family therapy has a more systemic approach that focuses on the reciprocal interactions of family members in their environment and the role of thoughts, feelings, and complex cognitive events in controlling human behavior. Behavioral family therapists assume that family dysfunction develops through the erosion of positive reinforcement control and is maintained by reciprocal aversive control. Families are systems of "interbehaving" people, and a child's behavior is reinforced and maintained by environmental factors.

Social Learning/Behavioral Family Therapy

"Social learning family therapy is a systematic method of understanding, working with, and evaluating change associated with families" (Horne & Sayger, 2000, p. 455). The common denominator of all behaviorally oriented family therapy approaches is a functional analysis of behavior. The process includes the observation of behavior, baseline assessment of frequency and rate of behaviors, identification of the consequences of behavior, and altering consequences to change behavior. People are seen as attempting to maximize rewards (pleasurable consequences) while minimizing costs (aversive consequences) (Horne & Sayger, 2000). The greater the ratio of costs relative to benefits exchanged in a relationship, the greater the dysfunction.

Family dysfunction is perceived as an interpersonal phenomenon existing in the present through coercive or reciprocal relationships. Coercion refers to a relationship in which family members provide aversive, negatively reinforcing reactions to control the behavior of others. Conversely, reciprocity defines social exchanges in which two people positively reinforce each other at an equitable rate to maintain their relationship (Patterson, 1982). Therefore, deviant behavior is not seen as dysfunctional but as an understandable response to the contingencies of the system. Conceptualizations and treatment are here-and-now focused. As the problem is presented, the therapist redefines it in interactional-systemic terms, which requires understanding the antecedents and consequences of behavior as well as the circularity of the antecedents and consequences for maintaining the dysfunctional system (Horne & Sayger, 1990). Assessment is an integral component of behavioral family therapy and is systematic and precise. The assessment

process is extensive (beginning with the initial interview and continuing through termination and follow-up) and intensive (assessing specific, discrete behaviors). The framework for treatment is likewise clear and specific and includes an initial assessment, development of a treatment plan, increasing positive behaviors, skill acquisition, and generalization and maintenance.

The behavioral family therapist is responsible for having the basic interpersonal skills to establish a therapeutic environment in which family members feel safe and comfortable in discussing their issues (cf. Fleischman, Horne, & Arthur, 1983, pp. 48–49). These therapists hold the basic belief that each person is doing the best he or she can given the circumstances and previous learning experiences. Based on this tenet that interpersonal problems often arise from faulty or inadequate learning, the behavioral approach asserts that appropriate skills training is effective in preventing, as well as solving, family problems. The dysfunctional family pattern is conceptualized as a self-perpetuating, reciprocally reinforcing complex of behaviors that become habitual over time. Social learning family therapy represents the infusion of new behavioral contingencies designed to increase and maintain the rates of positive reinforcement among family members; thus, therapy consists of teaching people more effective and satisfying ways of interacting with others. Through the application of behavioral technology, the behavior therapist teaches family members basic life skills that help equip clients with the ability to deal with problems as they arise and before they become crisis-inducing situations. Skills taught in therapy may include communication, problem solving, negotiation, parenting and child management, self-control, and/or relationship enrichment.

Olson, Russell, and Sprenkle (1980) noted that a behavioral family therapy approach may be considered the treatment of choice for child conduct problems. Sayger, Horne, Walker, and Passmore (1988) and Sayger, Horne, and Glaser (1993) have reported the effectiveness of a social learning family therapy approach for treating families with disruptive and aggressive children. These studies reported significant reductions in aggressive child and family behaviors, increases in positive child and family behaviors, and significant improvements in family cohesion, conflict reduction, and total family relationship. Additionally, Horne and Sayger (1990) outlined a systematic social learning family therapy approach for treating conduct and oppositional defiant disorders in children. This model identifies effective self-control and communication skills, appropriate reinforcement and disciplinary techniques, multiple systems consultation procedures, and factors for ensuring treatment success, generalization, and maintenance.

Horne and Sayger (1990) presented the case of an 11-year-old boy referred for treatment by Child Protective Services. The boy allegedly had been abused physically by his sister's boyfriend and had demonstrated many conduct behavior problems, including fighting, running away, truancy, and arguing. The initial treatment phase was to assess the nature and extent of the family and child problems. This comprehensive overview included members of the family and current living arrangements, problem behaviors (including their antecedents, consequences, family members' feelings and thoughts about these behaviors), discipline strategies utilized, and other agency and school involvement. In such cases, the therapist defines all family members as victims of the system and notes that all family members must change their behavior if they wish to have a happier and more effective family system. The family members then set concrete and specific goals for behavior change, emphasizing the positive counterparts of the ineffective behaviors (e.g., the problem of noncompliance is reframed as acceptable levels of compliance; fighting is reframed to emphasize getting along with friends and family members). Subsequent sessions focus on helping family members maintain control over their anger through relaxation training, positive imagery, and/or cognitive self-instruction. Family members are encouraged to treat each other with respect, dignity, and fairness. Consistency in discipline and family structure is developed. Parents, or in this case, parent and grandparent, negotiated who would be in charge of the children and when, what discipline procedures would be utilized and in what instances. The therapist predicted problems that might arise as the family changed their behaviors (e.g., the parent can expect children to increase negative behaviors when the discipline strategies are implemented as they test the parent's commitment to the new behavior). Weekly telephone calls are utilized to maintain contact with families to ensure implementation of procedures, and in-session rehearsals are conducted when each new technique

is introduced. Open communications were maintained with school personnel and agency staff as the family progressed through treatment, and their assistance was solicited in dealing with school behavior problems and family necessities. An allowance system was developed to reward positive behaviors, and adult family members were assisted in establishing a positive support network. Progress toward treatment goals is reviewed frequently and consistently throughout the treatment program.

Henggeler and Borduin (1990) proposed a multisystemic family therapy model that acknowledged the multiple interrelated systems within which humans develop. These interrelated systems (e.g., family, school, peer group, community) impact, and are impacted by, each other. Effective family therapy models must address these multiple systems if behavior change is to occur and be maintained. For example, children who are experiencing behavior problems at school may precipitate or exacerbate problems between parents and school staff. Multisystemic interventions must include "nonsystemic" interventions (e.g., cognitive behavior therapy) as well as an understanding of the interdependent, systemic nature of individual family members, family units, and their environmental contexts.

Behavioral family therapy approaches have been criticized for being too mechanical and inflexible. Gurman and Kniskern (1978) pointed out that behavioral family therapy is short term and educationally oriented and shows marginal positive generalization to nontargeted behaviors. In addition, approaches indicating success are not clearly defined as "behavioral" because they incorporate strategies that are common to "nonbehavioral" approaches. Questions do exist, however, as to the possibility that some strategies are transtheoretical (Prochaska & DiClemente, 1984); thus, classifying them as behavioral or nonbehavioral may be an error of semantics. In essence, therapy itself is a behavioral enterprise that incorporates a calculated "dance" between therapist interventions and client reactions. Gurman (1988) noted that behavioral therapy is highly teachable and replicable, and many well-designed outcome studies already exist in the areas of behavioral marital therapy and parent-management training for conduct disorders.

Behavioral approaches have been demonstrated to be effective in the treatment of a broad range of problems, including sexual dysfunction, somaticism, phobias, depression, marital conflict, and child conduct. This model's strong adherence to the scientific method results in an evaluative power unsurpassed by any other family therapy approach because its emphasis on a systematic, structured, assessment-based approach to treatment lends itself to both outcome and process empirical research. For more information on behaviorally oriented models of family therapy, the reader is directed to Fleischman et al. (1983) and Horne and Sayger (1990, 2000).

FAMILY THERAPY RESEARCH

Grotevant (1989) stated that researchers' interests in the family can range broadly, from investigating in microanalytic fashion the moment-to-moment processes of family interaction to studying the overall "climate" of the family environment. Psychological approaches to the study of the family have largely been concerned with understanding the socialization of children in a unidirectional parent-to-child approach, with few investigations of the reciprocal effects of children on their parents. Stanton (1988) stated that family therapy's conceptual and data bases differ from most other therapies in that the interpersonal context of a problem and the interplay between this context and symptoms are of primary interest.

Research in family psychology and therapy has typically taken one of two tracks: outcome or process. The most commonly noted problems in this research include the absence or inadequacy of control groups, inconsistent measures of outcome, a lack of or insufficient delay before follow-up assessment, and unclear and inconsistent theoretical basis for treatment. Some theorists have charged, among other things, that traditional research methods are derived from linear and reductionistic paradigms and, therefore, are inappropriate and inadequate to contribute to our knowledge of how systems operate and change. Practitioners have argued that the research conducted in family therapy has little relevance to the clinical practice of therapy, and within the field of family psychology, communication between practitioners and researchers continues to be a problem. This dilemma remains perplexing because the historical beginnings of family therapy were very closely tied to research (Gurman, Kniskern, & Pinsof, 1986).

OUTCOME RESEARCH

In the present state of mental health services, the primary emphasis is on client satisfaction and cost-effectiveness. For these reasons, M.P. Nichols and Schwartz (1998) noted that the majority of current research in the area of family therapy reflects the medical model and is primarily interested in determining the effectiveness of family therapy in general and, more specifically, the effectiveness of family therapy for various disorders. The following comments on outcome research in family therapy are applicable only to those theoretical approaches that have actively conducted studies of their effectiveness and should not be utilized to judge those approaches that have little or no outcome validation. Gurman et al. (1986) wrote that "the practice of family and marital therapy leads to positive outcomes and family therapy no longer needs to justify its existence on empirical grounds" (p. 150). Outcome researchers must deal with a gamut of variables, such as the experience level of the therapist, type of symptoms or referral concerns, severity of family disturbance, length of treatment, what improvement criteria to use for each unit of assessment, and in which unit to assess change.

There is general agreement that family therapy outcome research should give high priority to change in the presenting problem and change in the nuclear family, but less attention has been given to changes in the extended family system or the community. Studies have demonstrated that parents or siblings of the identified patient may, in fact, be "worse" at the end of treatment (Arnold, Levine, & Patterson, 1975). Outcome measures that represent multiple vantage points and assess family interactions, preferably using self-report, other-report, and observational methods, should be employed.

Hazelrigg, Cooper, and Borduin (1987) noted that family therapy outcome research should concentrate on comparative outcome studies with specific populations and with both legitimate alternative treatments and placebo controls. Sayger and Szykula (in press) and Smith, Sayger, and Szykula (1999), in comparisons of strategic and behavior family therapy approaches for treatment of childhood disorders, noted that the two approaches appear to be nearly equal in efficacy with a heterogeneous sample of child referrals to an outpatient psychiatric clinic, though participants in behavior therapy did experience more improvement on the major referral concerns. Measures of outcome included client satisfaction, client perceptions of therapist characteristics, positive and negative side effects, and improvement of the major referral complaint.

Structural and strategic family therapies seem very appropriate for families of delinquents and adolescent drug abusers because ineffective parental authority and control as well as overinvolved or distancing parenting styles are reported, and these approaches emphasize a strong parental hierarchy. Additionally, strategic approaches seem well suited for reducing the resistance that often accompanies court-ordered therapy for substance abusers. Family therapy researchers have not devoted much attention to the applications of family therapy with affective or anxiety disorders, but outcome success has been demonstrated with psychosomatic disorders (e.g., anorexia, bulimia, chronic asthma, diabetes mellitus) using structural family therapy, with substance abusers using an integrated structural-strategic approach, and with conduct disorders (child- and adolescent-onset) utilizing a social learning/behavioral family therapy intervention. The strategic and Bowen systems family therapies have reported success with schizophrenia, Bowen systems with marital conflict, and brief therapy with mixed clinical disorders (Gurman et al., 1986). Gurman et al. stated that "to date [these therapies] have reported meager evidence of the efficacy of their methods" (p. 578); however, they further noted that "absence of evidence of efficacy obviously does not confirm inefficacy" (p. 593).

A recent trend in family therapy has been the integration of strategies from compatible theoretical approaches. Piercy and Frankel (1989) noted that structural, strategic, and behavioral family therapies are compatible for integration because all of these approaches monitor behavior and interpersonal interactions, conceptualize problems interactionally rather than in terms of individual pathology, and appreciate the function of problem behaviors in families. These approaches also conceptualize family process as maintaining problems, emphasize the present over the past, attempt to change behaviors and/or behavioral sequences, and employ instruction and coaching in therapy. Ultimately, these family therapies see their goal as restructuring interactions by way of behavioral and/or cognitive change to alter the presenting problem and utilize homework assignments to produce, generalize, and maintain these changes.

Gurman et al. (1986) stated that the ultimate purpose of family therapy outcome research is to identify "the specific effects of specific interventions by specified therapists at specific points in time with particular types of patients with particular presenting problems" (p. 601). As a whole, outcome research in family therapy has failed to meet these specificity guidelines, yet current research is attempting to overcome these deficits.

PROCESS RESEARCH

Gurman et al. (1986) provide excellent reviews of family therapy process research. The primary task of process research is the identification of the significant relationship between process and outcome variables. Most clinicians feel that what they do in session makes a difference in the outcome of treatment, yet few studies explore this phenomenon. Process research is time-consuming and requires the use of reliable and valid assessment instruments that are sensitive to the salient variables of the therapeutic venture. However, researchers still have not identified or reached a consensus as to which variables need to be measured. Ideally, process research should focus on the critical incidences of therapy and moments when theoretically significant change occurs. To date, a paucity of family therapy process research exists.

Instruments utilized to assess therapy processes must emphasize sequences of behavior and not global evaluations of treatment. Two groups of researchers involved in family process research are located at the Oregon Social Learning Center (OSLC) and the Family Institute of Chicago. The OSLC staff has been investigating the impact of client resistance and cooperation during sessions on the process of therapy (Chamberlain, Patterson, Reid, Kavanaugh, & Forgatch, 1984). The staff of the Family Institute of Chicago has developed instruments that are designed to assess the client's perception of the therapeutic alliance, verbal behaviors of therapists from various theoretical orientations, and client evaluations of whether his or her life has improved, stayed the same, or deteriorated since the last session. Research is underway using, a post hoc extreme-groups design to determine comparative therapy process differences between the most successful and least successful client groups utilizing these instruments (Gurman et al., 1986).

In a project in process, Sayger and Szykula (1998) are developing the Thematic Therapy Interaction Coding System to assess specific critical themes which occur throughout the therapy session. This assessment is designed to identify both the therapist's comments and interventions and client actions and reactions to determine the optimal points of therapeutic interchange.

Kazak, McCannell, Adkins, Himmelberg, and Grace (1989) reported that the unevenness with which established family assessment instruments corresponded with perceptions of normality appears to be reason for concern in research. Their data suggest that standardized family assessment instruments may not be reflecting the standards that different groups of people utilize in thinking about normal families. Their data also suggest that substantial differences in perceptions of normality by developmental variables, ethnic background, and gender exist. These concerns regarding assessment instruments provide even greater challenges for the family therapy process researcher. Process research obviously is in its infancy, but it remains an important part of our understanding of the impact of therapy on the family system.

CONCERNS AND RECOMMENDATIONS

Assessment conducted within a family psychology framework needs to facilitate the simultaneous, integrated consideration of the individual, the family, and the larger context. Although research that links functioning across social systems is beginning to emerge (McDonald & Sayger, 1998), this endeavor is clearly in its formative stages. Major deficiencies still exist in the field of family therapy research and include the need for a broader set of theoretical conceptions (What distinguishes functional from dysfunctional families? What factors outside the family influence interaction within the family? How does the "identified patient" get chosen? Can dysfunction be prevented?) and more attention to cultural influences on family functioning (What is the effect of ethnicity, race, subcultural identity, bilingualism, and worldview on personal and family development?). Family therapy programs need to be extended to new settings (outreach programs into the community, general hospitals, rehabilitation programs, and all of the community's comprehensive

mental health agencies), and more systematic evaluation of family therapy theories and techniques is necessary (What kind of family therapy technique, by what kind of therapist, is most likely to lead to what specific results in which types of families?) (I. Goldenberg & Goldenberg, 1983).

Auerswald (1988) summarized the following recommendations for future family therapy research. First, assess all of the appropriate system levels (individual, marital, parent-child, family, and community). Second, assess presenting symptoms, mediating factors, and ultimate goals. Third, use self-report and behavioral assessment for the most important outcome variables to capture both member and observer perspectives. Fourth, include as many family members as possible in assessment procedures. Fifth, use couple and family scores that best match the methodological assessment with the theoretical constructs. And sixth, use more sophisticated and powerful statistical models and methods for assessing efficacy. For an excellent review of issues regarding family therapy research, the reader is referred to M.P. Nichols and Schwartz (1998).

A FINAL COMMENTARY

Epstein and Loos (1989) point out that the family therapy movement arose in the 1950s and early 1960s in response to the failure of prevalent treatment technologies to work effectively with a number of difficult client populations, including schizophrenics, delinquents, and individuals from poor, multiproblem families. The movement has been widely criticized by professionals from various perspectives. Feminist therapists have been critical of prominent notions of "normal" family functioning that do not take into account power issues and often impute blame (Walter, Carter, Papp, & Silverstein, 1988). Psychoeducational therapists have argued that family therapy has often failed with families of schizophrenics because of notions embedded in family therapy theories that families are responsible for creating the symptoms of schizophrenia. Others have felt that the field, by emphasizing the family-as-a-system, has overlooked the importance of the intrapsychic struggle of the individual. Nevertheless, M.P. Nichols and Schwartz (1998) believe that family therapy has demonstrated its success with a variety of client populations.

Family therapists must become more culturally sensitive if treatment efficacy is to extend to all ethnic groups. DeGenova (1997) stated that family therapy with ethnic minorities requires an organized, culturally sensitive theoretical framework. McGoldrick (1996) stated that ethnicity remains a vital force in this country, a major form of group identification, and a major determinant of family patterns and belief systems. For family therapists, this means increasing their consideration of the cultural system of families who share common history and traditions. Ethnicity is more than race, religion, or national and geographic origin. It describes a sense of commonality transmitted over generations by the family and reinforced by the surrounding community (Boyd-Franklin, 1989; Ingoldsby & Smith, 1995). It involves conscious and unconscious processes that fulfill a deep psychological need for identity and historical continuity. Restoring a stronger sense of identity may require resolving cultural conflicts within the family, between the family and the community, or in the wider context in which the family is embedded.

Two shortcomings of family therapy for dealing with young children who have problems or are "at risk" are that the intrapsychic problems of young children are not often included as part of the family treatment process and are not permitted a genuine "voice," let alone an equal voice with their parents and/or other family members. Guerney and Guerney (1987) noted that to effectively integrate child and family therapy, the child must be empowered as a full participant; the methods used must give the child opportunities to resolve intrapsychic conflicts and/or develop self- and social controls; and parents must be allowed to express and resolve their own conflicts, attitudes, and inhibitions in relation to the child and the system changes. Therapy promotes change in the family system, and intrapsychic and systemic change are sought in an integrative, synergistic fashion. Any attempt to change the child directly without fully integrating other significant family members into the process becomes prey to many disadvantages and dangers. "Efficient, enduring improvement for the child calls not only for parental changes but also for changes that are being fully coordinated in time and nature with the therapeutic changes going on in the child" (Guerney & Guerney, 1987, p. 609).

N.J. Kaslow and Racusin (1990) suggested that family therapy may be contraindicated for children with severe psychopathology because family therapy tends not to fully address the psychological deficits of parents, and the multiple levels of intervention may be overwhelming for the child. Additionally, family therapy may be contraindicated if prior family therapy was unsuccessful, the family sabotages treatment alliances, or the family does not believe in therapeutic efficacy.

The main limitations of most family therapy models concern their failure to appreciate the importance of key variables that pertain to the individual family member and extrafamilial systems. For example, the models often do not take into consideration important individual developmental issues that should influence the therapist's understanding of problems and choice of intervention strategies. Many family therapy models also rarely utilize proven intervention strategies that are derived from other treatment paradigms. Henggeler and Borduin (1990) stated that although the family is certainly the most influential system for the child, he or she directly interacts with, affects, and is affected by several other systems. The primary implication is that the therapist should not assume that any one system is the most appropriate target for intervention.

In summary, family problems are associated with many individual characteristics and extrafamilial variables, as well as with family transactions. The therapist must weigh these issues when choosing to employ family therapy and devise an integrative approach that effectively addresses these concerns.

REFERENCES

Ackerman, N.W. (1958). *The psychodynamics of family life: Diagnosis and treatment of family relationships.* New York: Basic Books.

Aradi, N.S., & Kaslow, F.W. (1987). Theory integration in family therapy: Definition, rationale, content, and process. *Psychotherapy, 24*(S), 595–609.

Arnold, J.E., Levine, A.G., & Patterson, G.R. (1975). Changes in sibling behavior following family interventions. *Journal of Consulting and Clinical Psychology, 43,* 683–688.

Auerswald, E.H. (1988). Epistemological confusion and outcome research. In L.C. Wynne (Ed.), *The state of the art in family therapy research: Controversies and recommendations* (pp. 55–72). New York: Family Process Press.

Bowen, M. (1976). Theory in the practice of psychotherapy. In P.J. Guerin (Ed.), *Family therapy: Theory and practice* (pp. 145–179). New York: Garner Press.

Bowen, M. (1985). *Family therapy in clinical practice.* Northvale, NJ: Aronson.

Bowlby, J. (1949). *The study and reduction of group tension in the family.* London: Tavistock.

Boyd-Franklin, N. (1989). *Black families in therapy: A multisystems approach.* New York: Guilford Press.

Broderick, C.B., & Schrader, S.S. (1981). The history of professional marriage and family therapy. In A.S. Gurman & D.P. Kniskern (Eds.), *Handbook of family therapy* (pp. 5–35). New York: Brunner/Mazel.

Chamberlain, P., Patterson, G., Reid, J., Kavanaugh, K., & Forgatch, M. (1984). Observation of client resistance. *Behavior Therapy, 15,* 144–155.

Combrinck-Graham, L. (Ed.). (1989). *Children in family contexts: Perspectives on treatment.* New York: Guilford Press.

DeGenova, M.K. (1997). *Families in cultural context: Strengths and challenges in diversity.* Mountain View, CA: Mayfield.

de Shazer, S., & Berg, I.K. (1993). Constructing solutions. *Family Therapy Networker, 12,* 42–43.

Duncan, B.L., & Solevey, D. (1989). Strategic brief therapy: An insight-oriented approach. *Journal of Marital and Family Therapy, 15,* 1–10.

Epstein, E.S., & Loos, V.E. (1989). Some irreverent thoughts on the limits of family therapy: Toward a language-based explanation of human systems. *Journal of Family Psychology, 2,* 405–421.

Fisch, R., Weakland, J.H., & Segal, L. (1982). *The tactics of change: Doing therapy briefly.* San Francisco: Jossey-Bass.

Fleischman, M.J., Horne, A.M., & Arthur, J. (1983). *Troubled families: A treatment program.* Champaign, IL: Research Press.

Framo, J.L. (1992). *Family-of-origin therapy: An intergenerational approach.* New York: Brunner/Mazel.

Goldenberg, H., & Goldenberg, I. (1994). *Counseling today's families.* Pacific Grove, CA: Brooks/Cole.

Goldenberg, I., & Goldenberg, H. (1983). Historical roots of contemporary family therapy. In B.B. Wolman & G. Stricker (Eds.), *Handbook of family and marital therapy* (pp. 77–89). New York: Plenum Press.

Grotevant, H.D. (1989). Theory in guiding family assessment. *Journal of Family Psychology, 3,* 104–117.

Guerin, P.J., Fogarty, T.F., Fay, L.F., & Kautto, J.G. (1996). *Working with relationship triangles: The one-two-three of psychotherapy.* New York: Guilford Press.

Guerney, L., & Guerney, B., Jr. (1987). Integrating child and family therapy. *Psychotherapy, 24(S),* 609–614.

Gurman, A.S. (1988). Issues in the specification of family therapy interventions. In L.C. Wynne (Ed.), *The state of the art in family therapy research: Controversies and recommendations* (pp. 125–138). New York: Family Process Press.

Gurman, A.S., & Kniskern, D.P. (1978). Research on marital and family therapy: Progress, perspective, and prospect. In S. Garfield & A. Bergin (Eds.), *Handbook of psychotherapy and behavior change: An empirical analysis* (2nd ed., pp. 546–593). New York: Wiley.

Gurman, A.S., & Kniskern, D.P. (1981). Family therapy outcome research: Knowns and unknowns. In A.S. Gurman & D.P. Kniskern (Eds.), *Handbook of family therapy* (pp. 742–775). New York: Brunner/Mazel.

Gurman, A.S., Kniskern, D.P., & Pinsof, W.M. (1986). Research on marital and family therapy: Progress, perspective, and prospect. In S. Garfield & A. Bergin (Eds.), *Handbook of psychotherapy and behavior change: An empirical analysis* (3rd ed., pp. 565–624). New York: Wiley.

Haley, J. (1976). *Problem solving therapy.* San Francisco: Jossey-Bass.

Hazelrigg, M.D., Cooper, H.M., & Borduin, C.M. (1987). Evaluating the effectiveness of family therapies: An integrative review and analysis. *Psychological Bulletin, 101,* 428–442.

Henggeler, S.W., & Borduin, C.M. (1990). *Family therapy and beyond: A multisystemic approach to treating the behavior problems of children and adolescents.* Pacific Grove, CA: Brooks/Cole.

Horne, A.M., & Sayger, T.V. (1990). *Treating conduct and oppositional defiant disorders in children.* Boston: Allyn & Bacon.

Horne, A.M., & Sayger, T.V. (2000). Behavioral approaches to couple and family therapy. In A.M. Horne (Ed.), *Family counseling and therapy* (3rd ed., pp. 454–486). Itasca, IL: Peacock.

Ingoldsby, B.B., & Smith, S. (1995). *Families in multicultural perspective.* New York: Guilford Press.

Jackson, D.D. (1959). Family interaction, family homeostasis, and some implications for conjoint family therapy. In J. Masserman (Ed.), *Individual and family dynamics* (pp. 165–192). New York: Grune & Stratton.

Kaslow, F.W. (1987). Trends in family psychology. *Journal of Family Psychology, 1,* 77–90.

Kaslow, N.J., & Racusin, G.R. (1990). Family therapy or child therapy: An open or shut case. *Journal of Family Psychology, 3,* 273–289.

Kazak, A.E., McCannell, K., Adkins, E., Himmelberg, P., & Grace, J. (1989). Perception of normality in families: Four samples. *Journal of Family Psychology, 2,* 277–291.

Luepnitz, D.A. (1988). *The family interpreted: Feminist theory in clinical practice.* New York: Basic Books.

Madanes, C. (1984). *Behind the one-way mirror: Advances in the practice of strategic therapy.* San Francisco: Jossey-Bass.

McDonald, L., & Sayger, T.V. (1998). Impact of a family and school based prevention program on protective factors for high risk youth. In J. Valentine, J.A. De-Jong, & N.M. Kennedy (Eds.), *Substance abuse prevention in multicultural communities* (pp. 61–85). New York: Haworth Press.

McGoldrick, M. (1996). Ethnicity and family therapy: An overview. In M. McGoldrick, J.K. Pearce, & J. Giordano (Eds.), *Ethnicity and family therapy* (pp. 1–27). New York: Guilford Press.

Minuchin, S. (1984). *Family kaleidoscope.* Cambridge, MA: Harvard University Press.

Minuchin, S., & Fishman, H.D. (1981). *Family therapy techniques.* Cambridge, MA: Harvard University Press.

Minuchin, S., Lee, W-Y., & Simon, G.M. (1996). *Mastering family therapy: Journeys of growth and transformation.* New York: Wiley.

Nichols, M.P., & Schwartz, R.C. (1998). *Family therapy: Concepts and methods* (4th ed.). Boston: Allyn & Bacon.

Nichols, W.C., & Everett, C.A. (1986). *Systemic family therapy: An integrative approach.* New York: Guilford Press.

Olson, D.H., Russell, C.S., & Sprenkle, D.H. (1980). Marital and family therapy: A decade review. *Journal of Marriage and the Family, 42,* 973–993.

Patterson, G.R. (1982). *Coercive family process.* Eugene, OR: Castalia.

Piercy, F.P., & Frankel, B.R. (1989). The evolution of an integrative family therapy for substance-abusing adolescents: Toward the mutual enhancement of research and practice. *Journal of Family Psychology, 3,* 5–25.

Prochaska, J.O., & DiClemente, C.C. (1984). *The transtheoretical approach: Crossing traditional boundaries of therapy.* Homewood, IL: Dow Jones-Irwin.

Satir, V. (1982). The therapist and family therapy: Process model. In A.M. Horne & M.M. Ohlsen (Eds.), *Family counseling and therapy* (pp. 12–42). Itasca, IL: Peacock.

Satir, V. (1983). *Conjoint family therapy.* Palo Alto, CA: Science and Behavior Books.

Satir, V., & Bitter, J. (2000). The therapist and family therapy: Satir's human validation process model. In A.M. Horne (Ed.), *Family counseling and therapy* (3rd ed., pp. 62–101). Itasca, IL: Peacock.

Sayger, T.V., Homrich, A.M., & Horne, A.M. (2000). Working from a family focus: The historical context of family development and family systems. In A.M. Horne (Ed.), *Family counseling and therapy* (3rd ed., pp. 12–39). Itasca, IL: Peacock.

Sayger, T.V., Horne, A.M., & Glaser, B.A. (1993). Marital satisfaction and social learning family therapy for child conduct problems: Generalization of treatment effects. *Journal of Marital and Family Therapy, 19,* 393–402.

Sayger, T.V., Horne, A.M., Walker, J.M., & Passmore, J.L. (1988). Social learning family therapy with aggressive children: Treatment outcome and maintenance. *Journal of Family Psychology, 1,* 261–285.

Sayger, T.V., & Szykula, S.A. (1998). *Thematic Therapy Interaction Coding System (TTICS).* Unpublished manuscript, University of Memphis at Memphis, TN.

Sayger, T.V., & Szykula, S.A. (in press). Social learning and solution-focused brief family therapy for childhood psychiatric disorders: Assessing clinically reliable behavior change. *Contemporary Family Therapy.*

Scharff, D.E. (1992). *Refining the object and reclaiming the self.* New York: Aronson.

Scharff, D.E., & Scharff, J.S. (1987). *Object relations family therapy.* Northvale, NJ: Aronson.

Segal, L. (1982). Brief family therapy. In A.M. Horne & M.M. Ohlsen (Eds.), *Family counseling and therapy* (pp. 276–301). Itasca, IL: Peacock.

Skynner, A.C.R. (1976). *Systems of family and marital psychotherapy.* New York: Brunner/Mazel.

Smith, W.J., Sayger, T.V., & Szykula, S.A. (1999). Child-focused family therapy: Behavioural family therapy versus brief family therapy. *Australian and New Zealand Journal of Family Therapy, 20,* 83–87.

Spiegel, J. (1982). An ecological model of ethnic families. In M. McGoldrick, J.K. Pearce, & J. Giordano (Eds.), *Ethnicity and family therapy* (pp. 31–51). New York: Guilford Press.

Stanton, M.D. (1988). The lobster quadrille: Issues and dilemmas for family therapy research. In L.C. Wynne (Ed.), *The state of the art in family therapy research: Controversies and recommendations* (pp. 7–31). New York: Family Process Press.

Walters, M., Carter, B., Papp, P., & Silverstein, O. (1988). *The invisible web: Gender patterns in family relationships.* New York: Guilford Press.

Whitchurch, G.G., & Constantine, L.L. (1993). Systems theory. In P.G. Boss, W.J. Doherty, R. LaRossa, W.R. Schumm, & S.K. Steinmetz (Eds.), *Sourcebook of family theories and methods: A contextual approach* (pp. 325–352). New York: Plenum Press.

CHAPTER 44

Residential and Inpatient Treatment of Emotionally Disturbed Children and Adolescents

ROBERT D. LYMAN AND DAVID R. WILSON

Generating an accurate estimate of the number of emotionally disturbed children receiving residential treatment services is difficult because of the diversity of programs and the lack of a central reporting agency. In 1994, there were estimated to be more than 32,000 children in treatment in psychiatric hospitals and residential treatment centers in the United States (Witkin et al., 1998). In addition, more than 120,000 children per year receive short-term treatment for psychiatric disorders in general hospitals (Kiesler, Simpkins, & Morton, 1989). The problems of these children cover the entire range of childhood emotional disturbances, from schizophrenia to conduct disorder, and the duration of their treatment may be as brief as one night or as long as a lifetime. The settings in which these children are treated also vary considerably, from group homes for six or eight children located in suburban neighborhoods to institutional programs for 100 or more, isolated from the community. Almost the only characteristic shared by these children is that their treatment requires them to reside away from their natural homes. This tremendous diversity makes it difficult to adequately review the field of residential and inpatient treatment for disturbed children, but such treatment is important,

both in terms of the number of children served and as one component of a comprehensive service delivery system. This chapter discusses the historical development of residential and inpatient treatment and the position these treatment services occupy in a continuum of mental health services for emotionally disturbed children. The major approaches to residential and inpatient treatment are reviewed and critical dimensions delineated.

HISTORICAL DEVELOPMENT

Residential programs for disturbed children are a relatively recent development. Prior to the seventeenth century, virtually all care of children with emotional or behavioral problems was provided by their immediate families or, in the case of parental absence or abandonment, by relatives, neighbors, or friends. The church provided the only alternative to this informal system of child care by offering limited housing, education, and spiritual training to a few abandoned children without other resources.

The first public, non-church-related system of residential care for children began in England with the establishment of almshouses for destitute children in the 1600s (Mayer, Richman, & Balcerzak, 1977). From that time until today, two parallel systems of residential care for children have existed in Western Europe and the United States. One system is predominantly church related and privately funded and serves mostly dependent children. The other system is largely publicly funded and serves disturbed, handicapped, and delinquent as well as dependent children. During the same period that public almshouses were established in England, the practice of indenturing children to private individuals provided formal legal recognition to the informal process of foster home placement that had existed for centuries (Mayer et al., 1977). The incentive for foster parents (free labor) remained the same, but the process now became part of the public child care network.

For the next several hundred years, this system of institutional child care flourished in Europe and America. Social and political upheaval increased the number of dislocated and homeless children even as it destroyed many of the informal family and community care networks that had existed for centuries. Private and public institutions grew to accommodate this need, and abuses became widespread.

Public awareness of poor conditions in children's institutions, as well as a growing recognition of children's rights in general, led in the late 1800s and early 1900s to a sentiment against large institutional programs for children and in favor of foster care placement or more homelike residential care (Hopkirk, 1944). In response to this sentiment, many institutions adopted a decentralized or "cottage" model, whereas others endeavored to reduce their overall size. Many children were discharged to foster care, often inappropriately. A further result of this focus on deinstitutionalization was the emergence of interest in reuniting children with their natural parents. Historically, child care institutions had viewed their purpose as raising children to adulthood. Now, efforts were made to identify changes in the status of children's natural families that might allow successful return to that environment.

At the same time that these tremendous changes were affecting institutional child care, Freud's psychoanalytic theories were sweeping the mental health world. These theories provided the first systematic rationale for mental health treatment, and their influence was soon felt in the area of child care. Psychoanalytic practitioners postulated a model of residential treatment specifically for children with emotional disturbances. This "milieu therapy" model caused further differentiation in residential child care as emotionally disturbed children were separated from dependent children for the purpose of providing more appropriate treatment, even though, in many cases, the differentiation of the two groups was rather arbitrary. Thus, for the first time, specific residential treatment centers for emotionally disturbed children were identified. Since then there has been a further refinement of the residential treatment model and incorporation of such divergent treatment philosophies as behavior therapy, positive peer culture, and the psychoeducational model. Residential treatment has developed into a unique component in the continuum of treatment alternatives, but to understand it, it must be viewed in perspective with other kinds of mental health intervention.

Residential and inpatient treatment are extremely invasive interventions. They result in changes in virtually every aspect of not only the child's life but the entire family's life as well. Because of the disruptive effects of removing children from their homes for treatment and the dangers of institutionalization and stigmatization that follow, it is important that mental health practitioners consider all aspects of a given clinical situation before making such a treatment decision.

There are four guiding principles that should govern the decision-making process in residential and inpatient care.

THE LEAST DISRUPTIVE SETTING

The first of these principles is that treatment should be provided in the setting that is least disruptive to the child's natural environment. This requires consideration of the full range of treatment alternatives available for emotionally disturbed children and an analysis of each alternative's potential treatment effectiveness in a given case versus the potential for disruption of the child's life. Such analysis is not always simple. Is a month in the sterile, artificial environment of an inpatient psychiatric ward more disruptive to a child's development and role in his or her family than a year in the more natural environment of a group home?

Which of these placements offers the best chance for permanent remediation of the child's (and family's) problems? The following sections describe the major categories of mental health intervention available to the child mental health practitioner in general order of increasing disruption to the child's natural environment.

OUTPATIENT TREATMENT

Outpatient mental health treatment with emotionally disturbed children may range from verbal psychotherapy (Freedheim & Russ, this volume) and play therapy (O'Connor, 1991) to family therapy (Sayger, this volume) and behavior therapy (Marx & Gross, 1998; Powers, this volume). It may continue for years or take place in as few as one or two sessions. Generally, there is little disruption to the child's life. Treatment usually requires a time commitment of no more than one or two hours per week, and a child's school and community activities are generally minimally affected. Treatment may involve only the child or the entire family, and may include somatic treatments such as medication, behavior modification techniques such as a urine alarm for enuresis, or environmental changes instituted by the parents. At times, mental health practitioners may spend extended amounts of time in the child's home environment. Examples of such in-home behavioral interventions include Dry Bed Training for enuresis (Azrin, Sneed, & Foxx, 1974; Scott, Barclay, & Houts, 1992), the Homebuilders model for child behavior problems (Bath, Richey, & Haapala, 1992; Haapala, 1996), and Multisystemic therapy (Henggeler, Schoenwald, Borduin, Rowland, & Cunningham, 1998; Schoenwald, Henggeler, Pickrel, & Cunningham, 1996).

DAY TREATMENT OR SPECIAL EDUCATION PROGRAMS

The provision of mental health services for some, most, or all of the day offers the potential for considerably more therapeutic contact than outpatient treatment, without greatly affecting the child's residential environment or relationships with parents and other family members (Gable, 1989). These mental health services can be provided in regular schools through resource (part-day) or full-time special class placements, combined with individual and group counseling. In other cases, removal to special schools or day treatment centers may be required, although this removal is clearly more invasive than the provision of services in regular schools.

SHELTER OR RESPITE CARE

Residential care provided for short periods of time (12 hours to 3 weeks) is usually termed respite care if the purpose of care is to aid and support parents or other caretakers, and shelter care if the purpose is to protect and help the child or children in a family (Marc & MacDonald, 1988). These two purposes often overlap. Such care is typically provided in response to emergencies such as abuse, abandonment, or parental substance abuse or in response to parental requests for relief from the strain of taking care of a disturbed child. Shelter and respite care programs may offer formal therapeutic interventions including educational programs, or they may provide only temporary housing for the child (Seng, 1989; Weinman, 1984). Contact with parents and other family members is usually limited during a child's stay in shelter or respite care.

FOSTER CARE

Removal of a child from home and placement for an extended period of time in a foster home with adults who may or may not have received special training in working with emotionally disturbed children constitutes a major disruption of the child's natural environment (Steinhauer, 1988). Some aspects of the child's life may be minimally affected, however. In most cases, the child will continue to attend public school (perhaps even the same school). The residential environment also continues to be homelike with surrogate "parents" and usually no more than four or five natural or foster children. There is seldom an intensive treatment focus in foster homes, with the underlying philosophy instead being that exposure to a "good" natural home environment (and removal from a "bad" environment) will ameliorate the child's problems. In some cases, more severely disturbed children have been effectively placed in foster homes where they are the only child and the foster parents have received intensive specialized training. The duration of foster care may range from one month or less to 15 years or more.

GROUP HOME CARE

Group home care is differentiated from foster home care by the number of children placed in one home (up to 10 or 12 at once) and by the more institutional characteristics of the residential environment (Gordon, 1978). In many cases, foster parents act as individual agents, whereas group homes are agencies that employ houseparents, child care workers, social workers, or other staff. A number of group homes may operate under the umbrella of a single agency. Thus, group homes tend to be less homelike and more regimented. Although the group home will frequently have the superficial appearance of a family house, other aspects of its operation reveal its agency characteristics. A formal treatment program or philosophy is usually evident, in contrast with the informal provision of treatment by foster parents. Case records are maintained, and agency personnel think of themselves as treatment staff. In most cases, children in group homes attend an external school; however, some in-house educational programs have been developed. As in foster care, duration of treatment may range from a single month to a number of years.

RESIDENTIAL TREATMENT CENTERS

Programs at residential treatment centers are characterized by stronger agency identification than in group homes and less similarity to children's natural environment (Lyman & Campbell, 1996). The programs are usually more isolated from the community than those of group homes and often provide activities within the facility rather than through community resources. Schooling for at least some children is often provided at the center. There is usually a well-defined treatment program or philosophy and staff other than houseparents to implement it. Some programs utilize child care workers or nursing staff in addition to, or instead of, houseparents. Caseworkers or other professional staff are usually given treatment responsibility. Although such programs may serve 100 or more children, usually functional units of no more than 15 children are identified and housed separately.

Duration of treatment may range from three months to a number of years.

INPATIENT HOSPITALIZATION

The duration of treatment in clearly identified hospital or medically oriented settings is usually shorter (one week to one year) than in residential treatment centers, but the extreme dissimilarity between the hospital environment and the child's natural environment can cause such placements to be more disruptive to a child's life than residential treatment (Dalton, Bolding, Woods, & Daruna, 1987). Typically, nursing staff are utilized rather than child care workers or houseparents, and there is much more regimentation and formality in daily routine. There is often little opportunity for children to engage in such normal activities as room cleaning, snacking, or playing outside. Frequently, schooling is temporarily suspended or offered only on the ward. Parent contacts are often minimal and highly structured. Typically, pharmacotherapy and group, family, or individual psychotherapy are considered to be the primary treatment interventions, with the impact of the hospital milieu accorded less significance. Treatment is usually under the direction of a physician.

INSTITUTIONAL TREATMENT

The primary definitional characteristics of institutional programs are the absence of normalizing or natural environmental experiences and the deemphasis on reentry into the natural environment (Lyman & Campbell, 1996). Institutional programs are frequently physically and attitudinally isolated from the community and regimented and impersonal in daily routine. Few opportunities are available for residents to leave the facility. Generally, the duration of treatment is measured in years, with a common expectation being that the resident will be at the facility for life. Residents frequently have little personal freedom in such areas as dress and room decor, and personal possessions are minimal or discouraged. Parental contact is also often minimal. Schooling is almost always provided in the institution. Although historically, many state psychiatric hospitals have fallen into this category, many have shed, or are currently shedding, their institutional characteristics and are becoming more like residential treatment or inpatient hospital programs. A program of any size, under private or public jurisdiction, may be described as institutional if it fails to provide normalizing life experiences for children and does not actively pursue the goal of reentry into the community for its residents.

As stated earlier, a guiding principle in making treatment placement decisions should be the provision of treatment in the least disruptive environment. Thus, outpatient interventions should generally be considered and tried prior to day treatment, and day treatment should be tried prior to consideration of residential treatment. The appropriate exceptions to this principle are cases requiring immediate placement in shelter or respite care because of danger to the child or parental dysfunction and immediate placement in inpatient care because of a clear need for intensive medical treatment or diagnosis. It is also possible that individual clinical characteristics, such as a severe thought disorder or self-destructive behavior, may suggest consideration of more invasive treatment alternatives without prior implementation of less disruptive options. However, research suggesting that outpatient management of even severe child psychiatric disorders can be highly effective (e.g., McEachin, Smith, & Lovaas, 1993) indicates that caution in considering residential options is advisable.

TREATMENT EFFECTIVENESS

The second guiding principle is that treatment should be provided in the setting that allows for maximum therapeutic effectiveness. For example, it is extremely difficult to treat school behavior problems on an inpatient ward that does not have an educational program. Similarly, communication problems between parents and child cannot be effectively treated if residential placement minimizes or eliminates contact between the parties. Of central importance is the need to maximize generalization of treatment effects from the therapeutic environment back to the child's natural environment. It does little good to achieve significant progress in residential or inpatient treatment only to see the referral problems reappear upon discharge.

One approach to ensuring that treatment effects generalize as much as possible is to minimize dissimilarities between the therapeutic environment and the environment to which the child will return

(Conway & Bucher, 1976). Obviously, more homelike and schoollike treatment programs offer considerable advantages in this regard and should be considered preferred treatment options because of the greater likelihood of effective generalization of treatment effects.

COST-EFFECTIVENESS

The third principle in the consideration of residential treatment is that care should be implemented in as cost-effective a way as possible. Clearly, one component in a comprehensive analysis of cost-effectiveness is treatment effectiveness. A treatment cannot be viewed as cost-effective (even if it is very inexpensive) if it does not produce the desired result. Most evaluations of residential and inpatient treatment report that most children show some improvement while the child is in treatment, with this assessment typically based on a global rating made at or soon after discharge. Research has generally indicated that behavioral approaches are more effective than approaches that emphasize intrapsychic intervention. Long-term follow-up data are also less positive than short-term results (Lyman & Campbell, 1996).

An adequate appraisal of cost-effectiveness must also include consideration of treatment duration and the social cost of treatment failure. Five years of weekly outpatient therapy at $100 per hour may prove far more costly than six months of residential treatment at $200 per day if the above factors are adequately considered. Cost-effectiveness also needs to be considered in comparing different types of residential and inpatient care. For example, if a wilderness therapy program can effectively treat a child for $80 per day, is there any justification for employing $300 per day residential care in a more traditional setting (Lyman & Campbell, 1996)? The question of cost-effectiveness is becoming increasingly important in an era of increasing accountability to third-party payers.

CHILD-PROGRAM COMPATIBILITY

The fourth guiding principle is that a child's clinical condition and behavior should be matched to the philosophy, structure, and capabilities of the treatment environment. Some children require placement in programs with more resources, such as nighttime staff or locked wards, whereas other children require only houseparent supervision. Placement of children in a program with inadequate resources to treat their disorder may lead to staff burnout, little or no progress by the child, creation of a nontherapeutic environment for other children, or dangerously uncontrolled circumstances. Conversely, placement of a child in a program with more structure and resources than necessary may result in failure of the child to assume adequate responsibility for his or her own behavior, loss of treatment effectiveness through decreased generalization to the home environment, as well as inappropriate utilization of limited treatment resources.

Another important aspect of matching a child's needs to a treatment program concerns the fundamental treatment philosophy of a program and the primary intervention techniques utilized there. Children with limited verbal abilities and short attention spans are unlikely to get maximum benefit from a program utilizing traditional verbal psychotherapy as its primary intervention. Similarly, children with problems of depression and anxiety may not derive much benefit from a behavioral treatment program primarily focused on reducing acting-out behaviors. The staffs of hospital inpatient programs are often unfamiliar with academic remediation techniques and may deemphasize the role of learning deficits in a child's adjustment problems. Therefore, such a program might be a poor placement choice for a child with a learning disability resulting in school behavior problems.

To delineate the impact of theoretical orientation on treatment characteristics, the following sections present six theoretical models of residential and inpatient treatment and brief descriptions of their basic characteristics.

MODELS OF TREATMENT

THE PSYCHOANALYTIC MODEL

Beginning with Aichorn (1935) in the 1930s and continuing with the work of Bettelheim (1950) and Redl and Wineman (1957) in the 1940s and 1950s, psychoanalytic practitioners developed a specific model of residential treatment for children with emotional disturbances. Basic elements of this psychoanalytic model, as expressed by Bettelheim (1950, 1974), included the isolation of children from

their parents and the primary role of formal psychoanalysis in treatment. Bettelheim also presented numerous examples of ways in which the residential environment could be used to affect children therapeutically and to allow exploration and resolution of their dynamic conflicts. Redl (1966) emphasized the primary treatment of children by child care workers in the residential environment through the "life space interview," a set of verbal interventions initiated in response to events in the child's daily life. These techniques were analytically based but expressed in practical terms and were intended for use by paraprofessionals. Redl's work, however, conflicted with the child guidance model that represented the mainstream of analytically based residential treatment (Whittaker, 1979). This model emphasizes the therapeutic importance of a treatment team consisting of psychiatrist, psychologist, and social worker, while de-emphasizing the importance of the efforts of on-line child care workers and nursing staff. Individual and group psychotherapy is considered the primary focus of treatment. This model remained the standard for residential treatment programs until the advent of behaviorally oriented programs in the 1960s.

Psychoanalytically based treatment programs have generally not presented much data in support of their effectiveness. Anecdotally, they appear to be more appropriate for highly verbal children from middle-class backgrounds with disorders of emotion rather than conduct. They have not proven effective for children with limited intellectual or verbal abilities, for those with non-middle-class backgrounds, or for children who exhibit behavioral disorders that appear to result primarily from maladaptive social learning. Psychoanalytic concepts, however, continue to be influential in the operation of a number of residential and inpatient facilities for children and adolescents (Stamm, 1989).

THE BEHAVIORAL MODEL

Residential treatment programs based on the principles of learning theory arose as part of a more general questioning of psychoanalytic concepts in mental health. The psychoanalytic model was dominant throughout the first half of the twentieth century, but its limited applicability to some client populations (e.g., retarded, psychotic, economically deprived) and the lack of empirical demonstrations of treatment effectiveness encouraged a search for alternative approaches.

This search led to the application of laboratory-derived learning principles to the treatment of human psychological problems. Wolpe (1958) produced the first widely distributed and accepted work in support of behavior therapy, and Lazarus (1960), Ferster (1961), Ross (1964), and Lovaas, Freitag, Nelson, and Whalen (1967), among others, extended the use of these techniques into the area of child therapy. The next three decades were marked by increasing acceptance of behaviorally based residential treatment. Behaviorally oriented residential treatment programs share a focus on the child's overt behavior rather than on such elements as inner personality states or dynamic conflicts. Maladaptive behaviors are viewed as largely resulting from past learning experiences. Remediation of these behaviors consists of systematic management of positive and negative consequences or control of stimulus-response pairings in accordance with established learning principles. On-line child care workers are usually viewed as the primary treatment agents, as opposed to the child guidance model's view of the psychiatric team as central in importance.

Behavioral treatment programs have generated tremendous quantities of data in support of their treatment effectiveness during the past 30 years. Such programs appear to be effective with a broad range of problem behaviors, including such clinical conditions as anorexia, autism, conduct disorder, phobias, enuresis, and encopresis. Behavioral programs also appear to be more applicable than psychoanalytic programs to children with poor verbal and intellectual abilities. A number of comprehensive models for behaviorally based residential treatment exist, including the Teaching Family Model developed at Achievement Place (Blase, Fixsen, Freeborn, & Jaeger, 1989; Kirigan, 1996).

THE MEDICAL INPATIENT MODEL

Since the formation of the first children's psychiatric units, such as the one begun in the pediatric department of Johns Hopkins Hospital in 1930 (Freedman, Kaplan, & Sadock, 1972), there has been a tremendous increase in the number of such units. Although initially they had a strong psychoanalytic orientation, in recent years many of these units have become more eclectic, with a strong emphasis

on medical diagnosis and interventions (Perry, 1989). The types of problems that appear to be most effectively treated in psychiatric inpatient units are those with organic components and those that are more acute in nature. Given the limited duration of most admissions to inpatient units, long-term interventions are not feasible. As pointed out earlier, inpatient units frequently do not offer good environments for dealing with school or family problems because of the lack of emphasis on educational programming and the limited contact between the child patient and the family. The inpatient staff is also usually more familiar with the process of medical diagnosis and treatment and emphasizes organic etiological factors over family and educational ones. A growing role for medical inpatient units is periodic hospitalization of chronically mentally ill children and adolescents, including those with mental retardation, autism, and thought or conduct disorders, for the purpose of providing respite and crisis stabilization.

THE PSYCHOEDUCATIONAL MODEL

The psychoeducational model is a variant of the behavioral model and is best represented by Project Re-Ed in Tennessee (Hobbs, 1966; Lewis & Lewis, 1989). Like the behavioral model, it stresses the teaching of more appropriate behaviors and coping skills to children and adolescents. A fundamental part of the psychoeducational model is an emphasis on community involvement and continued contact between child and family, if at all possible. As a result, psychoeducational programs appear to be particularly effective in promoting generalization of treatment effects to the home environment. Like behavioral programs, psychoeducational programs appear to have applicability to a broad range of client types and clinical conditions. They are also similar to other behavioral programs in emphasizing the importance of on-line staff, the structuring of daily activities, and the management of positive and negative consequences rather than verbal psychotherapy.

THE PEER CULTURE MODEL

The peer culture model stresses the importance of interpersonal factors in therapeutic programming. Raush, Dittman, and Taylor (1959) and Polsky

(1961) were among the first to formally recognize what had long been informally known: Peer influences are often of far greater significance to a child in residential treatment than the treatment efforts of staff. Following this recognition, a number of authors, including Flackett and Flackett (1970) and Vorrath and Brendtro (1974), offered treatment approaches intended to enlist peer support for positive rather than negative behaviors in residential treatment. Most peer culture programs rely on formal or informal group discussions as well as group control of privileges or rewards. The effectiveness of the treatment derives from both the confrontation and feedback of the group discussions and the reinforcement of appropriate behavior with positive consequences. Staff are significantly involved as participants in the group process, but much of the effectiveness of these programs can be attributed to interactions among residents (Brendtro & Wasmund, 1989).

The peer culture model has become the model of choice for inpatient adolescent substance abuse programs. This is understandable because many substance abuse problems seem to be related to peer pressure. Other conduct disorders also appear to be amenable to treatment through the peer culture model, whereas more internalized disorders appear less appropriate for such an intervention. The peer culture model requires a fairly high level of intellectual and verbal ability for maximum participation and, therefore, is not suited for youngsters with psychotic disorders or mental retardation.

THE WILDERNESS THERAPY MODEL

Camping and contact with nature were assumed to be therapeutic activities long before they became associated with the mental health establishment. The first camps with a consciously therapeutic focus were those developed in the 1920s and 1930s to benefit underprivileged urban youngsters (McNeil, 1962). By the mid-1930s, camps were being developed with a specific focus on mental health benefits rather than on the more general benefits of recreational camping (Young, 1939). In subsequent years, there have been two thrusts to the development of outdoor therapeutic programs. On the one hand, a wide range of camping programs have emerged that use more traditional group and individual therapy techniques to treat children in a camp setting. Many

of these programs are time-limited (usually summer) extensions of year-round treatment programs; others are freestanding and operate year-round. Therefore, the duration of the camp experience for an individual child may vary from a week to a year or more, and activities usually include traditional camp recreation along with more specifically therapeutic experiences. Therapeutic camping programs may range in theoretical orientation from behavioral to psychodynamic. There are a number of published studies suggesting that they offer a cost- and treatment-effective approach to childhood emotional disturbance (e.g., Plouffe, 1981; Rickard & Dinoff, 1974).

Wilderness therapy programs, the second thrust in outdoor therapeutic programming, are primarily derived from the Outward Bound model originated by Kurt Hahn (Richards, 1981). These programs attempt to offer transcendent, real-life experiences in the wilderness that will call forth prosocial values in children and adolescents. Wilderness therapy programs are primarily group-centered and offer challenges to comfort and safety that, when successfully dealt with, provide a new repertoire of coping skills and enhanced self-esteem for the participants. In addition, new modes of relating to others are explored. The challenges offered can range from hiking and mountain climbing to sailing open waters in a small boat or living off the land for extended periods. A number of research studies have demonstrated the effectiveness of these interventions (Burton, 1981; Gibson, 1981).

PROGRAM ELEMENTS

Although there are major theoretical and philosophical differences among all of these program models, a number of practical decisions that are only partly guided by theory also must be made in any program. These decisions can greatly determine the nature and therapeutic effectiveness of any residential or inpatient program, regardless of theoretical orientation.

PHYSICAL FACILITIES

A program's physical characteristics are determined to some degree by theoretical considerations but even more by such practical considerations as available funds, community acceptance, and zoning laws. Attention to physical detail in the residential treatment literature varies; Bettelheim, for example, discusses at length the importance of the appearance of bathrooms in helping children to work through problems in the anal state of psychosexual development (Bettelheim & Sanders, 1979). Most other authorities, however, spend little time addressing the issue of physical facilities. Many treatment programs use converted homes with few modifications; others use specially constructed buildings with such features as childproof windows and secure time-out rooms. There are also major differences among treatment programs in the amount of personal space and privacy allowed children, as well as in the amount of access they have to the community. Although these appear to be critical issues in determining the child's milieu, there are no empirical studies in the research literature to guide the development of physical facilities. A critical concern already mentioned is enhancement of treatment generalization and ease of reintegration into the community. That would suggest that more homelike, community-based facilities would be preferable; however, little research has been done to support this logical conclusion.

STAFFING

The staff is considered critical in every treatment program, but there are significant differences of opinion as to which staff members are primary contributors to treatment. The traditional idea of the psychotherapist as the central figure, with other staff considered secondary and part of the "other 23 hours" (Trieschman, Whittaker, & Brendtro, 1969), to a large extent has given way to the recognition that each member of the milieu is important. This may be due, in part, to the practical reality that few programs can afford to have highly trained treatment staff spend more than a brief time with each child each day. Programs vary widely in how much attention is given to the selection, training, and supervision of paraprofessional staff and how involved such individuals are in treatment planning and implementation. As mentioned earlier, programs also vary in whether line staff are nurses, child care workers, or houseparents. Economic and treatment advantages and disadvantages can be cited for each model, but again, there is little

empirical evidence for the advantages of one staffing philosophy over the others.

CHARACTERISTICS OF CHILDREN SERVED

Most residential and inpatient programs have stated eligibility criteria, with particular behavioral or emotional problems targeted that are assumed to be most responsive to the treatment offered by the program. These tend to be rather vague (e.g., "school behavior problems" or "peer relationship difficulties") and are not based on a careful examination of the program's outcome data. Programs are usually much more specific regarding exclusion criteria (i.e., children with problems that are considered inappropriate, such as fire-setting or suicidal tendencies). Unfortunately, these criteria are often based more on liability concerns or staff uneasiness than on an objective appraisal of the program's capabilities.

It is misleading to focus entirely on the behavior of the child as the only or even the major criterion for admission to residential or inpatient treatment. As mentioned in the first part of this chapter, it is important to examine other factors such as the community's tolerance for particular behaviors, the range of alternative services available, and the willingness and ability of parents and school personnel to work with and manage the child. Residential treatment is necessitated because of an inadequate fit between the particular needs of the child and the resources available in the child's normal environment. Although necessarily focusing on the child, residential programs should also explicitly attend to these other factors, for example, by conducting parent training and various forms of community education.

INVOLVEMENT OF THE CHILD IN TREATMENT

There is wide variation in how much or in what way children are involved in their own treatment. Some programs exclude not only the child but also the entire family from active involvement in treatment planning and implementation. Others specifically provide for such involvement in their treatment procedures. For instance, peer culture programs require that children be major participants in determining their own goals and in evaluating progress (Vorrath

& Brendtro, 1974). Behaviorally oriented programs have also provided for child involvement, with techniques including self-monitoring procedures, contracting, and goal-setting and self-control training (e.g., Lyman, 1984; Stuart, 1971). Points and levels systems may also be used in ways that can either encourage or undermine personal involvement and responsibility (Kazdin, 1977). Some programs have even allowed children to participate in writing their own treatment plans (Dinoff, Rickard, Love, & Elder, 1978).

THE ROLE OF PSYCHOTHERAPY

In the past, psychotherapy was often seen as the main instrument of therapeutic change, with the rest of the residential or inpatient program serving only to house the children and insulate them from countertherapeutic influences. Today, however, programs in which formal psychotherapy is considered the primary agent of treatment are in the minority. "A truly therapeutic milieu cannot be organized around the concept of individual psychotherapy as the central mode of treatment" (Whittaker, 1979, p. 56).

What exactly should the role of psychotherapy be? Results of research in child psychotherapy are mixed (Kazdin, Bass, Ayers, & Rodgers 1990; Weisz & Weiss, 1993) and suggest that verbal psychotherapy is not the treatment of choice for many children. In addition, psychotherapy within the context of residential or inpatient treatment is subject to influences and expectations that differ greatly from those associated with outpatient psychotherapy. Psychotherapy may be requested chiefly when a child is behaving badly and may be viewed by both children and staff merely as an extension of the program's behavior management system. In addition, there are a number of questions concerning confidentiality and client advocacy that must be addressed when a child is seen in psychotherapy in the context of residential or inpatient treatment (Monahan, 1989).

THE ROLE OF THE GROUP

Regardless of the stated theory or model on which a residential or inpatient program is based, much of what happens to a child in treatment will be determined by group factors and influences. Much

power resides in the peer subculture that develops in residential treatment (Polsky, 1961; Polsky & Claster, 1968), and peers frequently reinforce undesirable behaviors (Buehler, Patterson, & Furniss, 1966). The Peer Culture Model attempts to specifically utilize peer influences as a positive force (Brendtro & Wasmund, 1989; Vorrath & Brendtro, 1974), whereas some behavioral programs such as those utilizing the Teaching Family Model have attended to these influences through techniques that include the use of peer managers and peer monitoring (Blase et al., 1989; Phillips, Phillips, Fixsen, & Wolf, 1972).

Other ways to make the group a therapeutic agent include the use of group problem-solving methods (Loughmiller, 1965; Rickard & Lattal, 1974), the use of group contingencies and reinforcement (Swain, Allard, & Holborn, 1982), and reliance on formal group meetings and group therapy. Also of importance is the composition of the group of children in residential treatment at any one time (Lyman, Prentice-Dunn, Wilson, & Taylor, 1989; Redl, 1966).

SPECIFIC SKILLS TRAINING

The learning of adaptive behaviors, such as self-help, prosocial, and academic skills, is an important component of many residential and inpatient treatment programs. Project Re-Ed (Hobbs, 1966; Lewis & Lewis, 1989), for example, "stresses the teaching of competence across the total spectrum of the child's development as the fundamental purpose of the helping environment" (Whittaker, 1979, p. 71). Behavioral programs, such as those utilizing the Teaching Family Model (Blase et al., 1989), have also taken note of the importance of specific skills training, with the learning of adaptive behavior often a targeted goal for children in treatment. Specific intervention techniques that have been used to teach adaptive skills include social skills training (Clark, Caldwell, & Christian, 1979; Shure, 1992), modeling interventions (Marion, 1994), and contingency management procedures applied to academic performance (DuPaul & Eckert, 1997).

BEHAVIOR MANAGEMENT AND CONTROL

Even residential and inpatient programs that consider psychotherapy the primary therapeutic agent must attend to issues of behavioral control and management. Approaches to this issue may vary, from the permissive tolerance of inappropriate behavior seen at the Orthogenic School (Bettelheim, 1974) to the structured interventions implemented at many behavioral programs (Blase et al., 1989). The writings of Redl (1966) may be considered a blending of analytical thought and behavioral practicalities in dealing with issues of control and management. *The Other 23 Hours* (Trieschman et al., 1969) also contains a number of chapters on managing problem behaviors.

Behaviorally oriented programs have attended most explicitly to issues of and techniques for behavior management and control (see Powers, this volume). A number of techniques with documented effectiveness are directly applicable in residential treatment. These include such interventions as points and levels systems (Johnson, 1995), overcorrection techniques (Matson, Manikam, & Ladatto, 1990), behavioral contracting, (Allen, Howard, Sweeney, & McLaughlin, 1993), self-instructional training (Ollendick, Hagopian, & Huntzinger, 1991), and time-out procedures (Roberts & Powers, 1990).

The limitations of behavior management and control techniques should also be recognized. The ultimate purpose of residential and inpatient treatment is to improve functioning in the home environment, not merely to control behavior in the residential setting. These techniques are only truly effective when they are part of a total program for teaching children adaptive skills that will enable them to live better in the less restrictive environment of their homes and communities.

PARENTAL INVOLVEMENT IN TREATMENT

Involving parents closely in residential treatment is often problematic because the child is away from home, with the treatment staff assuming many of what are usually considered to be parental functions. Separation from parents is also a common purpose for residential and inpatient treatment, and parents are, at times, viewed as at least partially responsible for their child's emotional and behavioral problems. Despite these difficulties, most providers of residential or inpatient treatment agree that treatment success is largely dependent on meaningful and sustained involvement of parents in the treatment process and that the child and the family should be jointly regarded as clients

(Jensen & Whittaker, 1989). Geographic factors, parents' personal problems, their feelings of guilt and failure because of their child's placement, or lack of encouragement on the part of the residential facility staff may inhibit parental involvement. In addition, increasing numbers of children in residential and inpatient care lack identifiable parents or are in agency custody, making family involvement unlikely.

Techniques to increase parental involvement include offering parent support groups, providing parent education classes and specific skills training for parents, and actively conducting family therapy sessions. At times, involvement of the parents in nontherapeutic recreational activities at the residential facility can open the door to enhanced therapeutic involvement. Whatever philosophy the intervention is based on, research indicates that for treatment to be successful, change must occur in the child's home environment as well as in the child (Taylor & Alpert, 1973). Treatment of the child without involvement of the parents and family is unlikely to produce meaningful and long-lasting remediation of problem behaviors and emotions.

COMMUNITY LINKAGES

Although residential care, by definition, involves some disruption of a child's life, it is imperative that continuity and communication be maintained between the residential treatment environment and the child's home environment. Preparing for discharge and seeking to enhance treatment generalization should be a continuing concern throughout treatment (Conway & Bucher, 1976). There should be provisions for regular interactions of a child with the home environment while in residential care through home visits, placement in community schools if possible, and parent involvement in family therapy. Only rarely is a residential treatment program justified in severing all contacts between a child and the home environment. On some occasions, it may be necessary for the residential program to create "artificial" community linkages for a particular child who otherwise would not have them. The use of "visiting resources" such as short-term foster homes can create a degree of community involvement for such a child. Residential staff may also be willing to provide community experiences in their own homes for children without other resources.

There should also be linkages between the residential treatment facility and the child's home environment after discharge. The continued support and guidance of treatment staff can be critical in determining the success of posttreatment placement. Community linkages are also critical at the organizational level. To ensure community receptivity to the residential program's mission and to guarantee access to community resources, a high level of communication must be maintained. Coates and Miller (1972) describe some of the community liaison problems that confront residential treatment programs. These range from fear of residents' behavior to concern that property values near the facility will suffer. The most effective way to combat such attitudes is by open communication between residential program staff and community residents.

The issues that have been discussed here must be addressed in any residential or inpatient program. Often, the approaches taken in dealing with these issues will determine the nature and effectiveness of the program far more than its treatment philosophy.

SUMMARY

The provision of residential and inpatient treatment services for children and adolescents is a highly complex field. Different theoretical models and treatment techniques allow for tremendous diversity among programs. Questions of treatment effectiveness and generalization at times appear to threaten the validity of all residential approaches. However, few other interventions offer as much potential for maximum treatment impact. Residential interventions appear likely to continue to be utilized as part of the continuum of services for disturbed children and adolescents in the future. The increasing governmental focus on services for "seriously emotionally disturbed" children (Stroul, 1996) makes it apparent that professionals need to focus even more attention on this unique set of interventions because they are particularly applicable to such children.

REFERENCES

Aichorn, A. (1935). *Wayward youth.* New York: Viking.

Allen, L.J., Howard, V.F., Sweeney, W.J., & McLaughlin, T.F. (1993). Use of contingency contracting to increase on-task behavior with primary students. *Psychological Reports, 72,* 905–906.

Azrin, N.H., Sneed, T.J., & Foxx, R.M. (1974). Drybed training: Rapid elimination of childhood enuresis. *Behavior Research and Therapy, 12,* 147–156.

Bath, H.I., Richey, C.A., & Haapala, D.A. (1992). Child age and outcome correlates in intensive family preservation services. *Children and Youth Services Review, 14,* 389–406.

Bettelheim, B. (1950). *Love is not enough.* New York: Free Press.

Bettelheim, B. (1974). *A home for the heart.* New York: Knopf.

Bettelheim, B., & Sanders, J. (1979). Milieu therapy: The Orthogenic School model. In J.D. Noshpitz (Ed.), *Basic handbook of child psychiatry* (Vol. 3, pp. 216–230). New York: Basic Books.

Blase, K.A., Fixsen, D.L., Freeborn, K., & Jaeger, D. (1989). The behavioral model. In R.D. Lyman, S. Prentice-Dunn, & S. Gabel (Eds.), *Residential and inpatient treatment of children and adolescents* (pp. 43–59). New York: Plenum Press.

Brendtro, L.K., & Wasmund, W. (1989). The peer culture model. In R.D. Lyman, S. Prentice-Dunn, & S. Gabel (Eds.), *Residential and inpatient treatment of children and adolescents* (pp. 81–96). New York: Plenum Press.

Buehler, R.E., Patterson, G.R., & Furniss, J.M. (1966). The reinforcement of behavior in institutional settings. *Behavior Research and Therapy, 4,* 157–167.

Burton, L.M. (1981). A critical analysis and review of the research on Outward Bound and related programs (Doctoral dissertation, Rutgers University, 1981). *Dissertation Abstracts International, 42,* 1581B.

Clark, H.B., Caldwell, C.P., & Christian, W.P. (1979). Classroom training of conversational skills and remote programming for practice of these skills in another setting. *Child Behavior Therapy, 1,* 139–160.

Coates, R.B., & Miller, A.D. (1972). Neutralization of community resistance to group homes. In Y. Bakel (Ed.), *Closing correctional institutions* (pp. 67–84). Lexington, MA: Heath.

Conway, J.B., & Bucher, B.D. (1976). Transfer and maintenance of behavior change in children: A review and suggestions. In J. Mash, L.A. Hamenlynck, & L.C. Handy (Eds.), *Behavior modification and families* (pp. 119–159). New York: Brunner/Mazel.

Dalton, R., Bolding, D.D., Woods, J., & Daruna, J.H. (1987). Short-term psychiatric hospitalization of children. *Hospital and Community Psychiatry, 38,* 973–976.

Dinoff, M., Rickard, H.C., Love, W., & Elder, I. (1978). A patient writes his own report. *Adolescence, 13,* 135–141.

DuPaul, G.J., & Eckert, T.L. (1997). The effects of school-based interventions for attention-deficit/hyperactivity disorder: A meta-analysis. *School Psychology Review, 26,* 5–27.

Ferster, C.B. (1961). Positive reinforcement and behavioral deficits of autistic children. *Child Development, 32,* 437–456.

Flackett, J.M., & Flackett, G. (1970). Criswell House: An alternative to institutional treatment for juvenile offenders. *Federal Probation, 34,* 30–37.

Freedman, A.M., Kaplan, H.I., & Sadock, B.J. (1972). Child psychiatry: Introduction. In A.M. Freedman, H.I. Kaplan, & B.J. Sadock (Eds.), *Modern synopsis of comprehensive textbook of psychiatry* (pp. 574–583). Baltimore: Williams & Wilkins.

Gabel, S. (1989). Outpatient treatment as an alternative to residential treatment or inpatient hospitalization. In R.D. Lyman, S. Prentice-Dunn, & S. Gabel (Eds.), *Residential and inpatient treatment of children and adolescents* (pp. 147–161). New York: Plenum Press.

Gibson, P. (1981). The effects of and the correlates of success in a wilderness therapy program for problem youths (Doctoral dissertation, Columbia University, 1981). *Dissertation Abstracts International, 42,* 140A.

Gordon, J.S. (1978). Group home: Alternative to institutions. *Social Work, 23*(4), 300–305.

Haapala, D.A. (1996). The Homebuilders model: An evolving service approach for families. In M.C. Roberts (Ed.), *Model programs in child and family mental health* (pp. 295–315). Mahwah, NJ: Erlbaum.

Henggeler, S.W., Schoenwald, S.K., Borduin, C.M., Rowland, C.M., & Cunningham, P.B. (1998). *Multisystemic treatment of antisocial behavior in children and adolescents.* New York: Guilford Press.

Hobbs, N. (1966). Helping disturbed children: Psychological and ecological strategies. *American Psychologist, 21,* 1105–1151.

Hopkirk, H.W. (1944). *Institutions serving children.* New York: Sage.

Jensen, J.M., & Whittaker, J.K. (1989). Partners in care: Involving parents in children's residential treatment. In R.D. Lyman, S. Prentice-Dunn, & S. Gabel (Eds.), *Residential and inpatient treatment of children and adolescents* (pp. 207–227). New York: Plenum Press.

Johnson, C.R. (1995). Unit structure and behavioral programming. In R.T. Ammerman & M. Hersen (Eds.), *Handbook of child behavior therapy in the psychiatric setting* (pp. 133–149). New York: Wiley.

Kazdin, A.E. (1977). *The token economy.* New York: Plenum Press.

Kazdin, A.E., Bass, D., Ayers, W.A., & Rodgers, A. (1990). Empirical and clinical focus of child and adolescent psychotherapy research. *Journal of Consulting and Clinical Psychology, 58,* 729–740.

Kiesler, C.A., Simpkins, C., & Morton, T. (1989). The psychiatric inpatient treatment of children and youth in general hospitals. *American Journal of Community Psychology, 17,* 821–830.

Kirigan, K.A. (1996). Teaching-Family Model of group home treatment for children with severe behavior problems. In M.C. Roberts (Ed.), *Model programs in child and family mental health* (pp. 231–247). Mahwah, NJ: Erlbaum.

Lazarus, A. (1960). The elimination of children's phobias by deconditioning. In H.J. Eysenck (Ed.), *Behavior therapy and the neuroses* (pp. 114–122). New York: Pergamon Press.

Lewis, W.W., & Lewis, B.L. (1989). The psychoeducational model: Cumberland House after 25 years. In R.D. Lyman, S. Prentice-Dunn, & S. Gabel (Eds.), *Residential and inpatient treatment of children and adolescents* (pp. 97–113). New York: Plenum Press.

Loughmiller, C. (1965). *Wilderness road.* Austin: University of Texas.

Lovaas, O.I., Freitag, L., Nelson, K., & Whalen, C. (1967). The establishment of imitation and its use for the development of complex behavior in schizophrenic children. *Behavior Research and Therapy, 5,* 171–181.

Lyman, R.D. (1984). The effects of private and public goal setting on classroom on-task behavior of emotionally disturbed children. *Behavior Therapy, 15,* 395–402.

Lyman, R.D., & Campbell, N.R. (1996). *Treating children and adolescents in residential and inpatient settings.* Thousand Oaks, CA: Sage.

Lyman, R.D., Prentice-Dunn, S., Wilson, D.R., & Taylor, G.E., Jr. (1989). Issues in residential and inpatient treatment. In R.D. Lyman, S. Prentice-Dunn, & S. Gabel (Eds.), *Residential and inpatient treatment of children and adolescents* (pp. 3–22). New York: Plenum Press.

Marc, D.L., & MacDonald, L. (1988). Respite care: Who uses it? *Mental Retardation, 26*(2), 93–96.

Marion, M. (1994). Encouraging the development of responsible anger management in young children. *Early Child Development and Care, 97,* 155–163.

Marx, B.P., & Gross, A.M. (1998). Behavioral treatment. In T. Ollendick & M. Hersen (Eds.), *Handbook of child psychopathology* (3rd ed., pp. 581–602). New York: Plenum Press.

Matson, J.L., Manikam, R., & Ladatto, J. (1990). A long-term follow-up of a recreate the scene, DRO, overcorrection, and lemon juice therapy program for severe aggressive biting. *Scandinavian Journal of Behavior Therapy, 19,* 33–38.

Mayer, M.F., Richman, L.H., & Balcerzak, E.A. (1977). *Group care of children: Crossroads and transitions.* New York: Child Welfare League.

McEachin, J., Smith, T., & Lovaas, O.I. (1993). Long-term outcome for children with autism who received early behavioral treatment. *American Journal on Mental Retardation, 97*(4), 359–372.

McNeil, E. (1962). Forty years of childhood: The University of Michigan Fresh Air Camp, 1921–1961. *Michigan Quarterly Review, 1,* 112–118.

Monahan, R.T. (1989). Individual and group psychotherapy. In R.D. Lyman, S. Prentice-Dunn, & S. Gabel (Eds.), *Residential and inpatient treatment of children and adolescents* (pp. 191–205). New York: Plenum Press.

O'Connor, K.J. (1991). *The play therapy primer: An integration of theories and techniques.* New York: Wiley.

Ollendick, T.H., Hagopian, L.P., & Huntzinger, R.M. (1991). Cognitive-behavior therapy with nighttime fearful children. *Journal of Behavior Therapy and Experimental Psychiatry, 22,* 113–121.

Perry, R. (1989). The medical inpatient model. In R.D. Lyman, S. Prentice-Dunn, & S. Gabel (Eds.), *Residential and inpatient treatment of children and adolescents* (pp. 61–79). New York: Plenum Press.

Phillips, E.L., Phillips, E.A., Fixsen, D.L., & Wolf, M.M. (1972). *The teaching family handbook.* Lawrence: University of Kansas Printing Service.

Plouffe, M.M. (1981). A longitudinal analysis of the personality and behavioral effects of participation in the Connecticut Wilderness School: A program for delinquent and pre-delinquent youth (Doctoral dissertation, University of Connecticut, 1981). *Dissertation Abstracts International, 41,* (12-B) 4683.

Polsky, H.W. (1961). *Cottage six: The social system of delinquent boys in residential treatment.* New York: Sage.

Polsky, H.W., & Claster, D.S. (1968). *The dynamics of residential treatment: A social system analysis.* Chapel Hill: University of North Carolina Press.

Raush, H.L., Dittman, A.T., & Taylor, J.J. (1959). The interpersonal behavior of children in residential treatment. *Journal of Abnormal and Social Psychology, 58,* 9–26.

Redl, F. (1966). *When we deal with children.* New York: Free Press.

Redl, F., & Wineman, D. (1957). *The aggressive child.* New York: Free Press.

Richards, A. (1981). *Kurt Hahn: The midwife of educational ideas.* Unpublished doctoral dissertation, University of Colorado, Boulder.

Rickard, H.C., & Dinoff, M. (Eds.). (1974). *Behavior modification in children: Case studies and illustrations from a summer camp.* Tuscaloosa: University of Alabama Press.

Rickard, H.C., & Lattal, K.A. (1974). Group problem-solving in a therapeutic summer camp: An illustration. In H.C. Rickard & M. Dinoff (Eds.), *Behavior modification in children: Case studies and illustrations from a summer camp.* Tuscaloosa: University of Alabama Press.

Roberts, M.W., & Powers, S.W. (1990). Adjusting chair timeout enforcement procedures for oppositional children. *Behavior Therapy, 21,* 257–271.

Ross, A.O. (1964). Learning theory and therapy with children. *Psychotherapy: Theory, Research and Practice, 1,* 102–108.

Schoenwald, S.K., Henggeler, S.W., Pickrel, S.G., & Cunningham, P.B. (1996). Treating seriously troubled youths and families in their contexts: Multisystemic therapy. In M.C. Roberts (Ed.), *Model programs in child and family mental health* (pp. 317–332). Mahwah, NJ: Erlbaum.

Scott, M.A., Barclay, D.R., & Houts, A.C. (1992). Childhood enuresis: Etiology, assessment and current behavioral treatment. In M. Hersen, R.M. Eisler, & P.M. Miller (Eds.), *Progress in behavior modification* (Vol. 28, pp. 83–117). Sycamore, IL: Sycamore.

Seng, M.J. (1989). Child sexual abuse and adolescent prostitution: A comparative analysis. *Adolescence, 24*(95), 665–675.

Shure, M.B. (1992). *I can problem solve (ICPS): An interpersonal cognitive problem solving program.* Champaign, IL: Research Press.

Stamm, I. (1989). A psychoanalytic model. In R.D. Lyman, S. Prentice-Dunn, & S. Gabel (Eds.), *Residential and inpatient treatment of children and adolescents* (pp. 25–42). New York: Plenum Press.

Steinhauer, P.D. (1988). The preventive utilization of foster care. *Canadian Journal of Psychiatry, 33,* 459–467.

Stroul, B.A. (Ed.). (1996). *Children's mental health: Creating systems of care in a changing society.* Baltimore: Brookes.

Stuart, R.B. (1971). Behavioral contracting within the families of delinquents. *Journal of Behavior Therapy and Experimental Psychiatry, 2,* 1–11.

Swain, J.J., Allard, G.B., & Holborn, S.W. (1982). The good toothbrushing game: A school-based dental hygiene program for increasing the toothbrushing effectiveness of children. *Journal of Applied Behavior Analysis, 15,* 171–176.

Taylor, D.A., & Alpert, S.W. (1973). *Continuity and support following residential treatment.* New York: Child Welfare League.

Trieschman, A.E., Whittaker, J.K., & Brendtro, L.K. (1969). *The other 23 hours.* Chicago: Aldine.

Vorrath, H.H., & Brendtro, L.K. (1974). *Positive peer culture.* Chicago: Aldine.

Weinman, K. (1984). Encouraging youth in shelter care. *Individual Psychology: Journal of Adlerian Theory, Research and Practice, 40,* 212–216.

Weisz, J.R., & Weiss, B. (1993). *Effects of psychotherapy with children and adolescents.* Thousand Oaks, CA: Sage.

Whittaker, J.K. (1979). *Caring for troubled children.* San Francisco: Jossey-Bass.

Witkin, M.J., Atay, J.E., Manderscheid, R.W., DeLozier, J., Male, A., & Gillespe, R. (1998). Highlights of organized mental health services in 1994 and major national and state trends. In R.W. Manderscheid & M.J. Henderson (Eds.), *Mental health, United States, 1998* (DHHS Publication No. SMA 99–3285, pp. 143–169). Washington, DC: U.S. Government Printing Office.

Wolpe, J. (1958). *Psychotherapy by reciprocal inhibition.* Stanford, CA: Stanford University Press.

Young, R.A. (1939, April). A summer camp as an integral part of a psychiatric clinic. *Mental Hygiene, 23,* 141–256.

CHAPTER 45

Hospitalization and Medical Care of Children

Lawrence J. Siegel and Paola Conte

Approximately 5.5 million children are hospitalized during a given year, representing 7% of all children under the age of 18 years. The average number of days that a child remains in the hospital for a given period of hospitalization is five (McCerthy & Kozak, 1995). About one-third of all children are hospitalized at least once before they reach adulthood (Prugh, 1983). Although many children remain in the hospital for a brief period of time, often for only one day, they are likely to encounter numerous aversive experiences and invasive medical procedures.

The nature of the child's hospitalization may be elective, episodic, or chronic (Barowsky, 1978). Most admissions to the hospital are planned, and there is an opportunity to prepare the child in advance for events that he or she will experience. Episodic hospitalizations represent emergency admissions and because they are usually unpredictable, they do not typically permit the child to be prepared in advance for the experience. Finally, some children enter the hospital on a chronic, repeated basis, often for prolonged periods of time. This latter group of children most often are diagnosed as having a chronic illness or medical condition such as kidney disease, asthma, or leukemia. In addition, some chronic diseases in children are highly life-threatening, and as a result, admission to the hospital may have a considerably different meaning for these children and their families compared with children who are

hospitalized for elective surgery. Therefore, although all hospitalized children may encounter many similar experiences while in the hospital, the nature of their medical problems and the purpose of the admission can present different challenges to the child's adaptation to the experience (Siegel, 1988, 1998).

This chapter addresses the psychosocial aspects of the medical care of children in the hospital, including the effects of hospitalization on children and approaches for facilitating the child's and family's adjustment to the hospital experience. Although it is recognized that the child's illness certainly will have an impact on his or her adjustment, this chapter considers issues of adjustment primarily as it pertains to the child's response to medical procedures and the hospital experience regardless of the medical or health-related condition of the child.

HISTORICAL DEVELOPMENTS IN THE CARE OF HOSPITALIZED CHILDREN

Advances in the medical treatment of children have, until recently, far surpassed the changes that have occurred in hospital procedures to promote the emotional well-being of the child and his or her family (Siegel, 1998). Despite the large body of research demonstrating children's distress both during and after hospitalization, in the absence of psychological interventions (Vernon & Thompson, 1993), systematic concern with the psychosocial needs of physically ill and hospitalized children is not a universal phenomenon.

James Robertson at the Tavistock Clinic in London was instrumental in changing the practices in hospitals toward the treatment and medical care of children. Robertson made two films in the 1950s, one portraying the intense emotional distress of a young child who was separated from his parents for a week while undergoing minor surgery in the hospital. The other film demonstrated the positive adjustment of a young child whose mother was permitted to remain with him while he was hospitalized for surgery. These films provided the impetus for changing the policies of many hospitals that denied parents the opportunity to remain with their children during their hospitalization.

Another event that called attention to the importance of providing a hospital environment that is responsive to the emotional needs of children was the publication by the National Institute of Mental Health in 1965 of a collection of papers entitled *Red Is the Color of Hurting: Planning for Children in the Hospital* (U.S. Department of Health, Education, and Welfare, 1965). This document resulted in specific recommendations for reducing the unnecessary stress typically encountered by hospitalized children.

Currently, the primary advocacy group for the comprehensive care of hospitalized children is the Association for the Care of Children's Health (ACCH). This multidisciplinary organization has established guidelines for developing hospital programs that are consistent with children's emotional and developmental needs, including advocating parental participation in their children's health care and unlimited visiting rights of parents of hospitalized children, establishing alternative medical care to avoid hospitalization whenever possible, and encouraging the availability of facilities for parents who desire to remain with their child in the hospital overnight (B.H. Johnson, Jeppson, & Redburn, 1992). Guidelines for developing Child Life Programs in hospitals have also been established by providing activities that attempt to facilitate coping with stressful events and normalizing the child's daily experiences while in the hospital (American Academy of Pediatrics, 1993).

Considerable progress has been made during the second half of this century in the overall care that children receive in hospitals. However, the United States continues to lag behind many European countries (Siegel, 1998). In some countries, for example, parents can take paid official leave from work to remain with their child during the duration of the child's hospitalization. Furthermore, special facilities are provided to permit the parents to stay overnight in the hospital.

In 1993, the U.S. Congress passed the Family and Medical Leave Act, which permits primary caregivers to take up to 12 weeks of unpaid leave from their employment. This law pertains only to settings with 25 or more employees. At this time, it is not clear how effective this law has been in enabling parents to remain with their hospitalized child.

PSYCHOLOGICAL EFFECTS OF HOSPITALIZATION AND MEDICAL PROCEDURES

A substantial literature documents the stressful effects of hospitalization and surgery in normal children (Ogilvie, 1990; R.H. Thompson, 1985; Vernon, Foley, Sipowicz, & Schulman, 1965; Vernon & Thompson, 1993). Short-term and long-term emotional and behavioral problems have been reported in as many as 30% of children both during and following the period of hospitalization (Siegel, 1998). Many potential sources of stress for the hospitalized child undergoing medical procedures have been identified, including separation from family members; pain and discomfort from illness, injury, or medical treatment; unfamiliarity with the hospital environment and its personnel; immobility; disruption of typical routines and loss of control over daily events; greater dependency on others; concerns about bodily harm and embarrassment; and distortions and misconceptions about the purpose of the hospitalization and medical procedures (Goslin, 1978; Rae, 1981; Siegel, 1976).

A number of variables potentially influence whether a child perceives the preceding factors as stressful. These moderator variables include the age, sex, and cognitive-developmental level of the child, medical diagnosis, length of hospitalization, previous experience with medical procedures and the hospital, nature and timing of preparation for the hospital experience, prehospital psychological adjustment, and parental ability to function as a supportive resource for the child (Farenfort, Jacobs, Miedema, & Schweizer, 1996; Melamed & Siegel, 1980; Siegel, 1983).

Hospitalization does not uniformly produce psychological distress in children and, in fact, there is some evidence that it can be a positive experience resulting in psychological and emotional benefits for some children (Davenport & Werry, 1970; Mabe, Treiber, & Riley, 1991; Shore, Geiser, & Wolman, 1965; Vernon, Schulman, & Foley, 1966). For example, the hospital experience can provide an opportunity for children to learn to master internal states such as anxiety and environmental stresses such as separation and pain, thereby increasing their self-confidence and coping efficacy (Menke, 1981; Rae, 1981). Furthermore, for children from home environments that are particularly stressful or who have been deprived of normal developmental opportunities, hospitalization can provide physical, social, and emotional experiences that are therapeutically beneficial (Oremland & Oremland, 1973; Rae, 1981; Solnit, 1960).

DEVELOPMENTAL CONSIDERATIONS

A child's response to the hospital experience is influenced by a number of factors. One of the most important to consider is the child's cognitive-developmental level (Siegel, 1988; Siegel & Smith, 1991). In general, the literature consistently supports the finding that younger children tend to be at greater risk for developing emotional and behavioral problems both during and following hospitalization (Melamed & Siegel, 1980). These findings are consistent with the developmental literature that indicates that younger children have a lower level of conceptual understanding of illness and medical procedures, which in turn contributes to their higher level of anxiety and fearful behavior (Siegel et al., 1991).

A number of investigations have documented the relationship between cognitive-developmental level and children's conception of illness in children both with and without a significant medical condition (Bibace & Walsh, 1979; Brewster, 1982; Hergenrather & Rabinowitz, 1991; Sayer, Willet, & Perrin, 1993; Shagena, Sandler, & Perrin, 1988; Susman, Dorn, & Fletcher, 1987). In general, these studies indicate that children's conception of illness becomes more sophisticated as their cognitive abilities mature through the preoperational, concrete operational, and formal operational levels of development (Piaget, 1929).

These research findings have clinical implications when trying to teach children about their own medical condition and management. Educational programs need to be developmentally based, incorporating instructions geared to the child's developmental level. Understanding the child's level of cognitive reasoning also will allow health care providers to respond more effectively to children's fears and concerns related to the medical condition and treatment.

Coping Styles

Children's typical mode of responding to stressful medical procedures influences their reactions to such events and likely affects their ability to benefit from various intervention programs. One approach to assessing children's style of coping has been to identify specific behavioral strategies that children use when confronting medical procedures or other stressful events (Siegel, 1983; Spirito, Starck, & Tyc, 1994). A second approach has been to investigate children's preferences for obtaining or avoiding information related to medical procedures or illness (Field, Alpert, Vega-Lahr, Goldstein, & Perry, 1988; Levenson, Pfefferbaum, Copeland, & Silberberg, 1982; Peterson & Toler, 1986; Smith, Ackerson, & Blotcky, 1989).

There is some evidence that children, like adults, differ in how much information they prefer to have regarding impending stressful events (Peterson & Mori, 1988). Furthermore, several studies suggest that preferred coping style regarding information appears to be related to the duration of the child's illness (Levenson et al., 1982; Smith et al., 1989; Spirito et al., 1994). Children who have had their illness a short period of time are less likely to want information regarding their disease or detailed information during invasive medical procedures necessary for treatment.

If children have preferred coping styles regarding the level of information that they receive about their medical condition or treatment procedures, the question remains whether health care providers should give detailed information to children who would prefer not to have that level of information. For medical conditions that require lifestyle changes and active participation by the child in medical management, it would be difficult not to provide the child with detailed information. Where these factors are not an issue, further research is needed to determine whether providing information to a child who prefers an avoidant coping style may result in even greater emotional distress. Several studies that investigated this issue found, in fact, that providing an intervention that might be inconsistent with the child's preferred coping style does not consistently lead to an adverse response by the child and can in some instances be an effective method for facilitating adaptive functioning (Christiano & Russ, 1998; Smith et al., 1989). Clearly, further research is needed in this area.

PREPARATION FOR HOSPITALIZATION AND MEDICAL PROCEDURES

Although there is no consensus regarding the ideal timing for preparation of children for the hospital experience there is almost universal agreement in the literature on the necessity for some form of preparation to reduce the stress associated with hospitalization (Peterson & Brownlee-Duffeck, 1984; Siegel, 1976, 1983). Most of the work in this area has been in the preparation of children for surgery or invasive diagnostic medical procedures. There is considerable evidence for the effectiveness of various preparation programs in reducing distress before, during, and after hospitalization, and in facilitating adaptive coping during hospitalization (Harbeck-Weber & McKee, 1995; Siegel, 1998; R.H. Thompson, 1985; Vernon & Thompson, 1993).

Most preparation programs with children focus on five major components: (1) giving information, (2) encouraging emotional expression, (3) establishing a trusting relationship between the child and hospital staff, (4) providing the parents with information, and (5) providing coping strategies to the child and/or parents (Elkins & Roberts, 1983; Vernon et al., 1965). Several interventions, which include one or more of these components, have received empirical support with hospitalized children. One approach has been the use of film models. In this method, the child is exposed to various aspects of the hospital experience through the perspective of another child. During various medical procedures, the model typically responds in a manner that demonstrates relatively nonanxious and cooperative behaviors. Various types of information

are provided in film modeling. In this regard, Cohen and Lazarus (1980) have identified four specific types of information that can be provided in the context of medical treatment: the reasons for medical treatment, the actual medical procedures that will be used, the sensations that will be experienced, and specific coping strategies that the patient might use during the forthcoming procedure. Film modeling has been shown to be effective in reducing anxiety and facilitating cooperative behavior in children undergoing hospitalization for surgery (Ferguson, 1979; Melamed & Siegel, 1975) and anesthesia induction (Vernon & Bailey, 1974).

Another method for preparing children for hospitalization and surgery involves training children in specific coping skills. For example, Peterson and Shigetomi (1981) taught children to use several cognitive-behavioral coping strategies that consist of cue-controlled relaxation, distracting imagery (e.g., imagining a pleasant scene), and calming self-instructional phrases during particularly stressful or painful experiences in the hospital. This intervention was effective in reducing distress and increasing cooperative behaviors in children 2 to 10 years old who were hospitalized for elective surgery.

Some investigators have focused on the parents of hospitalized children as the primary point of intervention in facilitating the child's adjustment to the hospital. The rationale for this approach is based on the assumption that anxious parents might communicate their own anxiety to their child and will be less effective in helping their child to regulate his or her emotions and behavior during the hospitalization (Bearison, 1998; Siegel, 1998). A study by Frank, Blount, Smith, Manimala, and Martin (1995) provides research evidence to support this view. Skipper and his colleagues (Skipper & Leonard, 1968; Skipper, Leonard, & Rhymes, 1968) found a reduction in stress responses by mothers and less emotional distress for their children when a supportive nurse provided mothers with information about hospital routines and medical procedures and informed mothers of their role in caring for their child in the hospital. Similar findings are reported by Melnyk (1995) with mothers of young children experiencing unplanned hospitalizations.

Wolfer and Visintainer (1975) developed a preparation program that focused on both the child and parents in the hospital. The mother and child received preparation and supportive care at six "stress points" throughout the hospitalization. The child's preparation included procedural and sensory information, rehearsal of appropriate behaviors, and emotional support. Mothers were provided with support by a nurse that included individual attention at stress points, an opportunity to clarify their feelings and thoughts, accurate information, and an explanation regarding ways in which they could help care for their child. This program was found to reduce distress-related behaviors and facilitate cooperation in the children, decrease self-reported maternal anxiety, and increase satisfaction with the care their child received in the hospital. Campbell, Kirkpatrick, Berry, and Lamberti (1995) report similar findings in child-caregiver dyads with children who were hospitalized for cardiac surgery.

Hospitalized children often experience painful and highly aversive medical procedures. A number of cognitive-behavioral intervention programs have been developed to help children to cope more effectively with these experiences (Ellis & Spanos, 1994; Powers, 1999; Zeltzer, 1994). Children with cancer must endure frequent diagnostic and treatment procedures such as bone marrow aspirations and lumbar punctures, which may be so distressing that the child must be physically restrained to enable the procedures to be performed (Jay, Ozolins, Elliot, & Caldwell, 1983). Hypnosis-related procedures involving progressive muscle relaxation, focused attention, and imagery have been used to help children to manage the acute distress they often experience during these medical tests (Kellerman, Zeltzer, Ellenberg, & Dash, 1983; Zeltzer & LeBaron, 1982).

Jay, Elliot, Ozolins, Olson, and Pruitt (1985) describe a multicomponent treatment program for reducing behavioral distress in preadolescent cancer patients undergoing bone marrow aspirations and lumbar punctures. The treatment program included film modeling, breathing exercises, emotive imagery (fantasies in which superhero figures are used to help the child cope), behavioral rehearsal, and positive reinforcement for cooperative behavior. After each child practiced these techniques, the therapist accompanied the child into the treatment room and "coached" the child in his or her use of these coping techniques during the medical procedure. Results indicated that this program was effective in reducing behavioral distress and self-reported pain in the children. Similar studies have subsequently

provided empirical support for the efficacy of cognitive-behavioral treatment programs for reducing distress-related behaviors in children undergoing a variety of medical procedures (Blount et al., 1992; Kazak et al., 1996; Manne, Bakeman, Jacobsen, Gorfinkle, & Redd, 1994; Powers, Blount, Bachanas, Cotter, & Swan, 1993).

SPECIALIZED HOSPITAL ENVIRONMENTS

Some medical care is inherently more stressful than that encountered during routine elective admission to the hospital. Investigators have examined the psychological problems encountered by children who are exposed to unusually stressful settings within the hospital, including the emergency room, pediatric intensive care units, and isolated or protected environments (Jones, Fisher, & Livingston, 1992; Phipps, 1994).

A study by Roskies, Bedard, Gauvreau-Guilbault, and Lafortune (1975) compared extensive observations of the behavior of children admitted on an emergency basis with the behavior of children having an elective admission. The results indicated that in all the areas evaluated, the emergency admission was considerably more stressful for parents and children. These investigators concluded that given the preeminent medical concerns with the child, "it is possible that during the period of emergency admission itself, little psychological intervention is possible" (p. 580). However, in most cases, it is still possible to provide the child with information about a medical procedure and to assure the child that every effort will be made to make the procedure as brief as possible (Axelrod, 1976).

A child in a pediatric intensive care unit (PICU) is typically immobilized and confronted with periods of overstimulation alternating with periods of sensory deprivation (Rothstein, 1980). Cataldo, Bessman, Parker, Pearson, and Rogers (1979) describe two simple intervention programs where a child life worker interacts with the child with age-appropriate toys. This brief procedure resulted in an increase in the children's interaction with the environment, attention to activities, and positive affect, and a reduction in inappropriate and nonadaptive behaviors.

Where the risk of exposure to infections is high, some children may be confined, often for extended periods of time, to rooms where the air is continuously filtered. These protected environments are most common in the treatment of pediatric cancer patients undergoing intensive chemotherapy or bone marrow transplantation. Prolonged isolation can have a potentially deleterious effect on a child's adjustment because of sensory deprivation resulting from confinement and exposure to a limited number of persons.

Kellerman and his colleagues (Kellerman et al., 1976; Kellerman, Rigler, & Siegel, 1979) developed a comprehensive program designed to mitigate the effects of prolonged isolation for children in protected environments. Access to window views and clocks, the establishment of daily schedules, regular visits from family members, the services of a play therapist and schoolteacher, and counseling for the family were all provided as part of the intervention. These researchers found that this comprehensive program was effective in preventing significant or prolonged psychosocial adjustment problems.

PAIN AND DISCOMFORT

Pain is a special source of stress for children with diseases such as arthritis, hemophilia, sickle cell disease, kidney disease, and cancer (Walco, Siegel, Dolgin, & Varni, 1992). Chronic pain not only results in discomfort for these children but can also interfere with activities of daily living, result in social isolation, and lead to dependence on analgesic medications and the medical care system (Varni & Gilbert, 1982; Walco & Dampier, 1987).

Although pain typically results from underlying organic pathology, environmental consequences can modify and maintain various aspects of chronic pain behavior (Fordyce, 1976). Consequences such as attention and sympathy from others, rest, and avoidance of unpleasant duties and responsibilities, for example, can eventually maintain the behaviors independent of disease-related factors (Bonica, 1977).

Because pain is a private, subjective experience, it is important to evaluate factors that may affect individual differences in pain perception and pain behavior (Varni, 1983). For children, these factors include cognitive-developmental level, the meaning they ascribe to the pain, previous pain experiences, their perceived ability to handle pain, their repertoire of coping skills, and family influences that may provide reinforcement and models for pain behavior (Gaffney, 1993; Siegel & Smith, 1989; Zeltzer, Bursch,

& Walco, 1997). An adequate assessment of pain problems in children includes an evaluation of self-report, cognitive, behavioral, social-environmental, and medical factors (Lavigne, Schulein, & Hahn, 1986a, 1986b; K.L. Thompson & Varni, 1986; Varni, 1983; Zeltzer, 1994).

A variety of behavioral intervention strategies have been used in the management of chronic pain in children (Masek, Russo, & Varni, 1984; Walco et al., 1992; Walco, Sterling, Conte, & Engel, 1999). These techniques can be classified as methods that regulate either pain perception or pain behavior. Pain perception approaches teach the child to regulate or modify his or her perception of pain through self-regulatory methods such as hypnosis, guided imagery, relaxation, and biofeedback training. Techniques to regulate pain behavior involve the manipulation and modification of environmental events that are seen as maintaining pain behaviors. In this latter approach, for example, family members may be taught to respond to the child in ways that reduce pain-related disability and to maximize age-appropriate, adaptive behaviors.

Zeltzer, Dash, and Holland (1979) describe a treatment program for helping adolescents with sickle cell disease to cope more effectively with painful vaso-occlusive crises. The adolescents were taught a self-hypnosis procedure and were instructed in guided imagery involving a pleasant scene and given suggestions for body warmth and dilation of their blood vessels. After learning these techniques, the adolescents were taught to use these procedures at the onset of the painful crisis. Results of this treatment indicated reductions in the frequency and intensity of pain crises and analgesics used. Reductions in outpatient visits and total number of days of hospitalizations were also noted. Similar findings have been reported using the same treatment approach with children experiencing chronic and recurrent pain from juvenile rheumatoid arthritis (Walco, Varni, & Ilowite, 1992) and hemophilia (Varni, 1983; Varni & Gilbert, 1982).

MEDICATION SIDE EFFECTS

A major source of stress for children with chronic illness such as cancer are the side effects of chemotherapy agents used in the treatment of these diseases. Toxic anticancer medications often result in nausea and vomiting that occur within several hours of drug administration. Some patients also develop nausea and vomiting *prior* to taking these drugs. Research with pediatric populations suggests that this anticipatory nausea and vomiting (ANV) occurs in approximately 20% to 30% of patients, and more than 75% experience postchemotherapy nausea and vomiting (Dolgin, Katz, McGinty, & Siegel, 1985; Dolgin, Katz, Zeltzer, & Landsverk, 1989).

The general consensus is that ANV is a conditioned response whose etiology can be attributed to a classical conditioning paradigm (Carey & Burish, 1988). Anticipatory and posttreatment symptoms have been particularly refractory to antiemetic drugs (Oliver, Simon, & Aisner, 1986). A number of cognitive-behavioral treatment approaches have been investigated as alternative methods to reducing these side effects and have been shown to be effective in decreasing the frequency, duration, or severity of either anticipatory or postchemotherapy nausea and vomiting (McQuaid & Nassau, 1999).

Zeltzer and her colleagues (LeBaron & Zeltzer, 1984; Zeltzer, Dolgin, LeBaron, & LeBaron, 1991) found that hypnosis (imagery with suggestion to induce a relaxed/comfortable state) reduced nausea, vomiting, and associated anxiety in children age 6 to 17 years who were receiving chemotherapy. Another intervention that has been used with children involves attention diversion/cognitive distraction techniques. Kolko and Richard-Figueroa (1985) investigated the use of video games as a means of diverting attention away from the chemotherapy experience and potential conditioned stimuli in the environment. This procedure resulted in a reduction in the number of anticipatory symptoms and a decrease in the aversiveness of the postchemotherapy side effects.

ADHERENCE TO TREATMENT PROGRAMS

An important issue in the health care of children is the extent to which the prescribed therapeutic regimens are followed. Studies of adherence to medical treatment programs suggests that a sizable percentage of patients are nonadherent. Estimates range from 10% to 60% in pediatric practice (Dunbar-Jacob, Dunning, & Dwyer, 1993; La Greca, 1988). Researchers acknowledge that adherence is often difficult to operationalize and assess reliably (Cluss & Epstein, 1985; La Greca, 1988; Rudd, 1979). A number of methods have been used to assess treatment adherence, including child or parent monitoring, interview and 24-hour recall, biochemical markers of medication, pill counts, and clinical outcome or health status (Christophersen, 1993; S. Johnson, Silverstein, Rosenbloom, Carter, & Cunningham, 1986; Meichenbaum & Turk, 1987; Parrish, 1986).

Adherence is a dynamic process that is likely to change over time (Meichenbaum & Turk, 1987). In addition, adherence is not an "all or none" phenomenon such that adherence to one aspect of treatment is not necessarily related to other aspects of treatment (S. Johnson et al., 1986; Schafer, Glasgow, McCaul, & Dreher, 1983). Therefore, adherence should be assessed periodically over time and different components of the treatment regimen should be assessed independently.

Among the numerous factors correlated with adherence are duration and complexity of treatment, health beliefs regarding the medical condition, patient's level of knowledge and skill, presence of symptoms and effects of treatment on the symptoms, and the patient's satisfaction with medical treatment and relationship with health care providers. For a more detailed discussion of this literature, the reader is referred to Haynes (1976), Janis (1984), S. Johnson (1993), La Greca (1988), La Greca and Schuman (1995), Meichenbaum and Turk (1987), and Rapoff, (1999).

A number of techniques have been proposed to increase treatment adherence. One practical guideline is to keep treatment demands on the patient and family as simple as possible. It is also important to specify the particular behaviors that the patient should follow. In addition, adherence can be enhanced by attempting to incorporate the treatment regimen into the patient's lifestyle (Meichenbaum & Turk, 1987). One of the most effective means of promoting adherence is to foster a relationship of collaboration between the health care provider and the patient and his or her family (Korsch, Gozzi, & Francis, 1968; Korsch & Negrete, 1972; Meichenbaum & Turk, 1987). Varni and Babani (1986) provide a review of behavioral methods used to facilitate implementation of treatment regimens with specific attention devoted to the antecedents and consequences that may interfere with adherence.

Symptom reduction has been associated with greater adherence to medical treatment (Arnold et al., 1970; Shope, 1981). However, with some medical conditions, adherence may result in painful or aversive symptoms such as nausea, hair loss, and weight gain (Tamaroff, Festa, Adesman, & Walco, 1992). Dolgin, Katz, Doctors, and Siegel (1986) found greater nonadherence associated with more side effects and visible physical changes in children and adolescents with cancer. Health care providers and parents may believe that maintaining good health or preventing future complications should provide sufficient motivation to ensure treatment adherence in children. However, this perception often does not take into consideration developmental issues and concerns about feeling different. To facilitate treatment adherence over long periods of time, Varni and Babani (1986) note that external positive reinforcers may be necessary to maintain a child's adherence behaviors.

The Health Belief Model (Becker & Rosenstock, 1984; Rosenstock, 1985) has been used to examine factors that may contribute to patient adherence. This theoretical model assesses such factors as a patient's perceived susceptibility to future complications, availability of reminders to engage in adherent behaviors, perceived obstacles and costs to engage in adherent behaviors, and self-efficacy. For example, patients' belief regarding their self-efficacy was the strongest predictor of adherence in a study of adolescents with diabetes (McCaul, Glasgow, & Schafer, 1987). Brownlee-Duffeck et al. (1987) found that perceived costs significantly predicted adherence in another group of adolescents with diabetes.

Finally, it is important to recognize that nonadherence may be the result of a conscious decision of the patient. The adaptability of nonadherence has been studied by Deaton (1985) in pediatric patients with asthma. Other researchers have suggested that deciding to adhere or not adhere to a prescribed treatment plan might represent a means by which otherwise powerless patients may exert some control over their condition (Hayes-Bautista, 1976; Stinson, 1974). In addition, although less adaptive, nonadherence may represent a means of indirect self-destructive behavior (Faberow, 1986).

THE FAMILY OF THE MEDICALLY ILL CHILD

A chronic medical condition not only significantly impacts the affected child but influences the interactions and development of intrafamilial relation-

ships (A.E. Kazak, Segal-Andrews, & Johnson, 1995). There also is considerable research that documents the role of the family in the psychological adjustment of the child to his or her medical condition (Wallander & Thompson, 1995).

Research into the effect of a child's medical condition on the family has yielded mixed results. Lack of consistent findings in this area may be attributed to the significant methodological obstacles in the study of family functioning. To date, most research has involved the study of the adjustment of individual members or dyads within the family, which then is extrapolated in an attempt to identify total family functioning. Zeltzer and her colleagues (Zeltzer, LeBaron, & Zeltzer, 1984) conducted a study that attempted to assess overall familial adjustment to the child's diagnosis with cancer. They found that the challenge of understanding the family unit is considerable and that the available research instruments do not fully illuminate familial adjustment or functioning.

Much of the difficulty encountered by families coping with chronic medical conditions may be related to perceived stress and coping resources. A study of families of children with spina bifida (Nevin & McCubbin, 1979) found that those families perceiving themselves to be under low levels of stress were more cohesive, better organized, and lower in conflict than more highly stressed families. Shulman's (1983) study of children with leukemia suggested that 85% of families coped well; factors associated with good family adjustment included a prior history of good coping, good quality of marital and familial relationships, good support systems, religious or spiritual faith, and a trusting relationship with a physician. Similarly, a study of mothers of children with sickle cell disease found that poor maternal adjustment was associated with the use of palliative coping strategies (i.e., avoidance, wishful thinking, blame) and high levels of stress related to daily hassles (R.J. Thompson, Gil, Burbach, Keith, & Kinney, 1993).

Research into the impact of a child's medical condition on the parents' marital relationship suggests either that the relationship is at greater risk for divorce or that intact relationships are brought closer together by the experience (Sabbath & Leventhal, 1984). The evidence regarding the impact of siblings' adjustment is mixed as well. A number of studies have found more adjustment problems in siblings of a child with a chronic medical condition compared with those of healthy children (Breslau,

Weitzman, & Messenger, 1981; Lavigne & Ryan, 1979; Madan-Swan, Sexon, Brown, & Ragab, 1993; Spinetta & Deasy-Spinetta, 1981; Tew & Lawrence, 1975). Other studies, however, have suggested that having a sibling with a chronic medical condition can have a positive impact on peer relationships, social competence, qualities such as compassion and sensitivity, and appreciation for one's own good health (Ferrari, 1984; Grossman, 1972). Factors that have been found to be associated with positive sibling adjustment include good parental communication patterns, level of understanding of the disease affecting the sibling, and good maternal health and emotional adjustment (Carpenter & LeVant, 1994; Gogan & Slavin, 1981; Simensson & McHale, 1981; Tew & Lawrence, 1975).

Holiday (1984) suggests that any of three major coping strategies are utilized by parents who successfully cope with a child's chronic medical condition: (1) obtaining as much information as possible about the child's medical condition, (2) establishing a social support system to share the burden of the child's illness, and (3) attempting to integrate the child into the mainstream of everyday life.

Informational and educational programs that also include skill enhancement and training may be beneficial to families in their efforts to cope with a child who has a chronic illness. Positive results are reported by Kirkham, Schilling, Norelius, and Schinke (1986), who studied a training program designed to enhance social support, reduce stress, and develop coping skills in mothers of handicapped children. An educational program developed for parents of children with cancer was evaluated by Wallace, Bakke, Hubbard, and Pendergrass (1984). They found that increases in knowledge about a child's disease promoted greater parental understanding regarding the effect of cancer on the family. An additional benefit of educational programs for caregivers of children with medical illness involves decreases in feelings of isolation and enhanced opportunities for interactions with staff. Social support groups also can facilitate a family's coping with a chronically ill child (Toseland & Hacke, 1982). Research with Hispanic families of pediatric cancer patients suggests that support groups are particularly appropriate for culturally different families (Saltoun-Moran & Garcia, 1989). Finally, there is some evidence that sibling groups might be beneficial, particularly for the adolescent who has a sibling with a chronic medical condition (McKeever, 1983).

SUMMARY AND CONCLUSIONS

Considerable progress has been made in the past several decades in understanding the psychosocial needs of medically ill and hospitalized children. However, despite growing awareness of the importance of preparing children for hospitalization and medical procedures and the research evidence for the effectiveness of various preparation programs in facilitating the child's adjustment to these stressful experiences, the actual implementation of such programs on a *systematic* basis has yet to be achieved in most pediatric health care settings. Mechanisms for affecting changes in hospital policies that determine routine medical practices with children need to be investigated. A more consistent use of preparation programs with a greater number of children is likely to occur with the development of intervention programs that can be easily implemented within a typical medical setting and that require a minimal investment of professional time (Powers, 1999; Siegel, 1998).

A number of barriers interfere with the ability of children who require medical care and hospitalization to receive the appropriate psychosocial services; these include financial considerations and/or a lack of available services or trained professionals in the health care settings (Sabbeth & Stein, 1990). Furthermore, more recent changes following from health care reform and the managed care movement, with an emphasis on cost-effective care, is likely to have a significant impact on comprehensive care and access to preventive psychosocial interventions for children undergoing hospitalization and medical treatment (Roberts & Hurley, 1997).

Most intervention programs are presented to all children with a given medical condition in a similar manner, with the assumption that they will benefit equally from a particular treatment approach. Future research needs to move beyond merely demonstrating the efficacy of a given intervention to attempting to identify criteria for matching interventions to specific patient characteristics (e.g., coping dispositions, developmental factors, previous experiences) to determine which children respond most favorably to a particular treatment strategy.

The coping skills that children and family members use in their attempts to manage the potential stresses imposed by illness or medical care have received limited research attention (Rudolph,

Denning, & Weisz, 1995). Coping strategies in children with chronic medical conditions need to be evaluated from two perspectives: first, one must study how children negotiate the normal tasks of childhood and adolescence; second, one must focus on disease-related tasks that are unique to a child's particular illness, such as adherence to a specific medical regimen or to tolerate invasive medical procedures. This would permit the identification of specific behaviors associated with the child's attempts to meet the demands imposed by the various illness-related tasks. By systematically identifying adaptive coping strategies, it will be possible to develop more effective intervention programs for children with health problems who require ongoing medical care.

Finally, the preponderance of research in this area has relied on single assessment, cross-sectional designs. There is a greater need for longitudinal evaluation to examine the course of psychosocial and medical adaptation over time as a function of developmental changes. Many of the issues that affect children with chronic medical conditions are not single-episode events and as such, repeated evaluations of the child and/or family over the course of a given period is needed to significantly advance our understanding in this area. This longitudinal approach takes on even greater importance given the multitude of ongoing developmental influences that must be taken into consideration (Siegel, 1995).

REFERENCES

American Academy of Pediatrics, Committee on Hospital Care. (1993). Child life programs. *Pediatrics, 91*, 671–673.

Arnold, R.G., Adebonojo, F.O., Callas, E.R., Callas, J., Carte, E., & Stein, R.C. (1970). Patients and prescriptions: Comprehension and compliance with medical instructions in a suburban pediatric practice. *Clinical Pediatrics, 9*, 648–651.

Axelrod, B.H. (1976). Mental health considerations in the pediatric emergency room. *Journal of Pediatric Psychology, 1*, 14–17.

Barowsky, E.I. (1978). Young children's perceptions and reactions to hospitalization. In E. Gellert (Ed.), *Psychosocial aspects of pediatric care.* New York: Grune & Stratton.

Bearison, D.J. (1998). Pediatric psychology and children's medical problems. In I.G. Siegel & K.A. Renninger (Eds.), *Handbook of child psychology: Vol. 4 Child psychology in practice* (5th ed.). New York: Wiley.

Becker, M.H., & Rosenstock, I.M. (1984). Compliance with medical advice. In A. Steptoe & A. Mathews (Eds.), *Health care and human behavior* (pp. 175–208). New York: Academic Press.

Bibace, R., & Walsh, M.E. (1979). Developmental stages in children's concepts of illness. In G.C. Stone, F. Cohen, & N. Adler (Eds.), *Health psychology: A handbook.* San Francisco: Jossey-Bass.

Blount, R.L., Bachanas, P.J., Powers, S.W., Cotter, M.C., Franklin, A., Chaplin, W., Mayfield, J., Henderson, M., & Blount, S.D. (1992). Training children to cope and parents to coach them during routine immunizations: Effects on child, parent, and staff behaviors. *Behavior Therapy, 23*, 689–705.

Bonica, J.J. (1977). Neurophysiologic and pathologic aspects of acute and chronic pain. *Archives of Surgery, 112*, 750–761.

Breslau, N., Weitzman, M., & Messenger, K. (1981). Psychologic functioning of siblings of disabled children. *Pediatrics, 67*, 344–353.

Brewster, A.B. (1982). Chronically ill hospitalized children's concepts of their illness. *Pediatrics, 69*, 355–362.

Brownlee-Duffeck, M., Peterson, L., Simonds, J.F., Goldstein, D., Kilo, C., & Hoette, S. (1987). The role of health beliefs in the regimen adherence and metabolic control of adolescents and adults with diabetes mellitus. *Journal of Consulting and Clinical Psychology, 55*, 139–144.

Campbell, L.A., Kirkpatrick, S.E., Berry, C.C., & Lamberti, J.J. (1995). Preparing children with congenital heart disease for cardiac surgery. *Journal of Pediatric Psychology, 20*, 313–328.

Carey, M.P., & Burish, T.G. (1988). Etiology and treatment of the psychological side effects associated with cancer chemotherapy: A critical review and discussion. *Psychological Bulletin, 104*, 307–325.

Carpenter, P.J., & LeVant, C.S. (1994). Sibling adaptation to the family crisis of childhood cancer. In D.J. Bearison & R.K. Mulhern (Eds.), *Pediatric psychooncology: Psychological perspectives on children with cancer* (pp. 122–142). New York: Oxford University Press.

Cataldo, M.F., Bessman, C.A., Parker, L.H., Pearson, J.E., & Rogers, M.C. (1979). Behavioral assessment for pediatric intensive care units. *Journal of Applied Behavior Analysis, 12*, 83–97.

Christiano, B., & Russ, S.W. (1998). Matching preparatory interventions to coping style: The effects on children's distress in the dental setting. *Journal of Pediatric Psychology, 23*, 17–27.

Christophersen, E.R. (1993). *Pediatric compliance: A guide for the primary care physician.* New York: Plenum Press.

Cluss, P.A., & Epstein, L.H. (1985). The measurement of medical compliance in the treatment of disease. In P. Karoly (Ed.), *Measurement strategies in health psychology*. New York: Wiley.

Cohen, F., & Lazarus, R.S. (1980). Coping with the stress of illness. In G.C. Stone, F. Cohen, & N.E. Adler (Eds.), *Health psychology: A handbook* (pp. 217–254). San Francisco: Jossey-Bass.

Davenport, H.T., & Werry, J.S. (1970). The effects of general anesthesia, surgery, and hospitalization upon the behavior of children. *American Journal of Orthopsychiatry, 40,* 806–824.

Deaton, A.V. (1985). Adaptive noncompliance in pediatric asthma: The parent as expert. *Journal of Pediatric Psychology, 10,* 1–14.

Dolgin, M.J., Katz, E.R., Doctors, S.R., & Siegel, S.E. (1986). Caregivers' perceptions of medical compliance in adolescents with cancer. *Journal of Adolescent Health Care, 7,* 22–27.

Dolgin, M.J., Katz, E.R., McGinty, K., & Siegel, S.E. (1985). Anticipatory nausea and vomiting in pediatric cancer patients. *Pediatrics, 75,* 547–552.

Dolgin, M.J., Katz, E.R., Zeltzer, L.K., & Landsverk, J. (1989). Behavioral distress in pediatric patients with cancer receiving chemotherapy. *Pediatrics, 84,* 103–110.

Dunbar-Jacob, J., Dunning, E.J., & Dwyer, K. (1993). Compliance research in pediatric and adolescent populations: Two decades of research. In N.P. Krasnegor, L. Epstein, S.B. Johnson, & S.J. Yaffe (Eds.), *Developmental aspects of health compliance behavior* (pp. 29–51). Hillsdale, NJ: Erlbaum.

Elkins, P.D., & Roberts, M.C. (1983). Psychological preparation for pediatric hospitalization. *Clinical Psychology Review, 3,* 1–21.

Ellis, J.A., & Spanos, N.P. (1994). Cognitive-behavioral interventions for children's distress during bone marrow aspirations and lumbar punctures: A critical review. *Journal of Pain and Symptom Management, 9,* 96–108.

Faberow, N.L. (1986). Noncompliance as indirect self-destructive behavior. In K.E. Gerber & A.A. Nehemkis (Eds.), *Compliance: The dilemma of the chronically ill* (pp. 24–43). New York: Springer.

Family and Medical Leave Act of 1993, 29 U.S.C. § 2601 et seq. (1993).

Farenfort, J.J., Jacobs, E.A.M., Miedema, S., & Schweizer, A.T. (1996). Signs of emotional disturbance three years after surgery. *Journal of Pediatric Psychology, 21,* 353–366.

Ferguson, B.F. (1979). Preparing young children for hospitalization: A comparison of two methods. *Pediatrics, 64,* 656–664.

Ferrari, M. (1984). Chronic illness: Psychosocial effects on siblings I. Chronically ill boys. *Journal of Child Psychology and Psychiatry, 25,* 459–476.

Field, T., Alpert, B., Vega-Lahr, N., Goldstein, S., & Perry, S. (1988). Hospitalization stress in children: Sensitizer and repressor coping styles. *Health Psychology, 1,* 433–445.

Fordyce, W.E. (1976). *Behavioral methods for chronic pain and illness.* St. Louis, MO: Mosby.

Frank, N.C., Blount, R.L., Smith, A.J., Manimala, R., & Martin, J.K. (1995). Parent and staff behavior, previous medical experience, and maternal anxiety as they relate to child procedural distress and coping. *Journal of Pediatric Psychology, 20,* 277–289.

Gaffney, A. (1993). Cognitive developmental aspects of pain in school-age children. In N. Schechter, C. Berde, & M. Yaster (Eds.), *Pain in infants, children, and adolescents* (pp. 75–83). Baltimore: Williams & Wilkins.

Gogan, J.L., & Slavin, L. (1981). Interviews with brothers and sisters. In G.P. Koocher & J.E. O'Malley (Eds.), *The Damocles syndrome: Psychosocial consequences of surviving childhood cancer* (pp. 101–111). New York: McGraw-Hill.

Goslin, E.R. (1978). Hospitalization as a life crisis for the preschool child: A critical review. *Journal of Community Health, 3,* 321–326.

Grossman, F.K. (1972). *Brothers and sisters of retarded children: An exploratory study.* New York: Syracuse University Press.

Harbeck-Weber, C., & McKee, D.H. (1995). Prevention of emotional distress in children experiencing hospitalization and chronic illness. In M.C. Roberts (Ed.), *Handbook of pediatric psychology* (2nd ed., pp. 167–184). New York: Guilford Press.

Hayes-Bautista, D.E. (1976). Modifying the treatment: Patient compliance, patient control, and medical care. *Social Science and Medicine, 10,* 233–238.

Haynes, R.B. (1976). A critical review of the "determinants" of patient compliance with therapeutic regimens. In D.L. Sackett & R.B. Haynes (Eds.), *Compliance with therapeutic regimens* (pp. 26–9). Baltimore: Johns Hopkins University Press.

Hergenrather, J.R., & Rabinowitz, M. (1991). Age-related differences in the organization of children's knowledge of illness. *Developmental Psychology, 27,* 952–959.

Holiday, B. (1984). Challenges of rearing a chronically ill child: Caring and coping. *Nursing Clinics of North America, 19,* 361–368.

Janis, I.L. (1984). Improving adherence to medical recommendations: Prescriptive hypotheses derived from recent research in social psychology. In A. Baum, S.E. Taylor, & J.E. Singer (Eds.), *Handbook of psychology and health: Social psychology of aspects of health* (Vol. 4, pp. 113–148). Hillsdale, NJ: Erlbaum.

Jay, S.M., Elliot, C.H., Ozolins, M., Olson, R.A., & Pruitt, S.D. (1985). Behavioral management of children's distress during painful medical procedures. *Behaviour Research and Therapy, 23,* 513–520.

Jay, S.M., Ozolins, M., Elliot, C.H., & Caldwell, S. (1983). Assessment of children's distress during painful medical procedures. *Health Psychology, 2,* 133–147.

Johnson, B.H., Jeppson, E.S., & Redburn, L. (1992). *Caring for children and families: Guidelines for hospitals.* Bethesda, MD: Association for the Care of Children's Health.

Johnson, S.B. (1993). Chronic disease of childhood: Assessing compliance with complex medical regimens. In N.A. Krasnegor, L.H. Epstein, S.B. Johnson, & S.J. Yaffe (Eds.), *Developmental aspects of health compliance behavior* (pp. 159–184). Hillsdale, NJ: Erlbaum.

Johnson, S.B., Siverstein, J., Rosenbloom, A., Carter, R., & Cunningham, W. (1986). Assessing daily management in childhood diabetes. *Health Psychology, 5,* 545–564.

Jones, S.M., Fisher, D.H., & Livingston, R.L. (1992). Behavioral changes in pediatric intensive care units. *American Journal of Diseases of Children, 146,* 375–379.

Kazak, A.E., Penati, B., Boyer, B.A., Himelstein, B., Brophy, P., Waibel, M.K., Blackall, G.F., Daller, R., & Johnson, K. (1996). A randomized controlled prospective outcome study of a psychological and pharmacological intervention protocol for procedural distress in pediatric leukemia. *Journal of Pediatric Psychology, 21,* 615–631.

Kazak, A.E., Segal-Andrews, A.M., & Johnson, K. (1995). Pediatric psychology research and practice: A family/systems approach. In M.C. Roberts (Ed.), *Handbook of pediatric psychology* (2nd ed., pp. 84–104). New York: Guilford Press.

Kellerman, J., Rigler, D., & Siegel, S.E. (1979). Psychological responses of children to isolation in a protected environment. *Journal of Behavioral Medicine, 2,* 263–274.

Kellerman, J., Rigler, D., Siegel, S.E., McCue, K., Pospisil, J., & Uno, R. (1976). Pediatric cancer patients in reverse isolation utilizing protected environments. *Journal of Pediatric Psychology, 1,* 21–25.

Kellerman, J., Zeltzer, L., Ellenberg, L., & Dash, J. (1983). Adolescents with cancer: Hypnosis for the reduction of the acute pain and anxiety associated with medical procedures. *Journal of Adolescent Health Care, 4,* 85–90.

Kirkham, M.A., Schilling, R.F., Norelius, K., & Schinke, S.P. (1986). Developing coping styles and social networks: An intervention. *Child Care Health and Development, 12,* 313–323.

Kolko, D.J., & Richard-Figueroa, J.L. (1985). Effects of video games on the adverse corollaries of chemotherapy in pediatric oncology patients: A single-case analysis. *Journal of Consulting and Clinical Psychology, 53,* 223–228.

Korsch, B., Gozzi, E., & Francis, V. (1968). Gaps in doctor-patient interaction and patient satisfaction. *Pediatrics, 42,* 855–871.

Korsch, B., & Negrete, V. (1972). Doctor-patient communication. *Scientific American, 227,* 66–74.

La Greca, A. (1988). Adherence to prescribed medical regimens. In D.K. Routh (Ed.), *Handbook of pediatric psychology* (pp. 229–320). New York: Guilford Press.

La Greca, A.M., & Schuman, W.B. (1995). Adherence to prescribed medical regimens. In M.C. Roberts (Ed.), *Handbook of pediatric psychology* (2nd ed., pp. 55–83). New York: Guilford Press.

Lavigne, J.V., & Ryan, M. (1979). Psychologic adjustment of siblings of children with chronic illness. *Pediatrics, 63,* 616–627.

Lavigne, J.V., Schulein, M.J., & Hahn, Y.S. (1986a). Psychological aspects of painful medical conditions in children: I. Developmental aspects and assessment. *Pain, 27,* 133–146.

Lavigne, J.V., Schulein, M.J., & Hahn, Y.S. (1986b). Psychological aspects of painful medical conditions in children: II. Personality factors, family characteristics and treatment. *Pain, 27,* 147–169.

LeBaron, S., & Zeltzer, L. (1984). Behavioral intervention for reducing chemotherapy related nausea and vomiting in adolescents with cancer. *Journal of Adolescent Health Care, 5,* 178–182.

Levenson, P.M., Pfefferbaum, B.J., Copeland, D., & Silberberg, Y. (1982). Information preferences of cancer patients ages 11–20 years. *Journal of Adolescent Health Care, 3,* 9–13.

Mabe, P.A., Treiber, F.A., & Riley, W.T. (1991). Examining emotional distress during pediatric hospitalization for school-aged children. *Children's Health Care, 20,* 162–169.

Madan-Swan, A., Sexson, S.B., Brown, R.T., & Ragab, A. (1993). Family adaptation and coping among siblings of cancer patients, their brothers and sisters, and nonclinical controls. *American Journal of Family Therapy, 21,* 60–70.

Manne, S.L., Bakeman, R., Jacobsen, P.B., Gorfinkle, K., & Redd, W.H. (1994). An analysis of a behavioral intervention for children undergoing venipuncture. *Health Psychology, 13,* 556–566.

Masek, B.J., Russo, D.C., & Varni, J.W. (1984). Behavioral approaches to the management of chronic pain in children. *Pediatric Clinics of North America, 31,* 1113–1131.

McCaul, K.D., Glasgow, R.E., & Schafer, L.C. (1987). Diabetes regimen behaviors: Predicting adherence. *Medical Care, 25,* 868–881.

McCerthy, E., & Kozak, L. (1995). *Hospital use by children: United States, 1993.* Washington, DC: National Center for Health Statistics.

McKeever, P. (1983). Siblings of chronically ill children: A literature review with implications for research and practice. *American Journal of Orthopsychiatry, 53,* 209–218.

McQuaid, E.L., & Nassau, J.H. (1999). Empirically supported treatments of disease-related symptoms in pediatric psychology: Asthma, diabetes and cancer. *Journal of Pediatric Psychology, 24,* 305–328.

Meichenbaum, D., & Turk, D.C. (1987). *Facilitating treatment adherence: A practitioner's guidebook.* New York: Plenum Press.

Melamed, B.G., & Siegel, L.J. (1975). Reduction of anxiety in children facing hospitalization and surgery by use of filmed modeling. *Journal of Consulting and Clinical Psychology, 43,* 411–521.

Melamed, B.G., & Siegel, L.J. (1980). *Behavioral medicine: Practical applications in health care.* New York: Springer.

Melnyk, B.M. (1995). Coping with unplanned childhood hospitalizations: The mediating functions of parental beliefs. *Journal of Pediatric Psychology, 20,* 299–312.

Menke, E.M. (1981). School-aged children's perceptions of stress in the school. *Children's Health Care, 9,* 80–86.

Nevin, R.S., & McCubbin, H. (1979). Parental coping with physical handicaps: Social policy implications. *Spina Bifida Therapy, 2,* 151–164.

Ogilvie, L. (1990). Hospitalization of children for surgery: The parent's view. *Children's Health Care, 19,* 49–56.

Oliver, I.N., Simon, R.M., & Aisner, J. (1986). Antiemetic studies: A methodological discussion. *Cancer Treatment Reports, 20,* 555–563.

Oremland, E.R., & Oremland, J.D. (1973). *The effects of hospitalization on children: Models for their care.* Springfield, IL: Thomas.

Parrish, J.M. (1986). Parent compliance with medical and behavioral recommendations. In N.A. Krasnegor, J.D. Arasteh, & M.F. Cataldo (Eds.), *Child health behavior: A behavioral pediatrics perspective* (pp. 453–501). New York: Wiley.

Peterson, L., & Brownlee-Duffeck, M. (1984). Prevention of anxiety and pain due to medical and dental procedures. In M.C. Roberts & L. Peterson (Eds.), *Prevention of problems in childhood: Psychological research and applications* (pp. 266–308). New York: Wiley.

Peterson, L., & Mori, L. (1988). Preparation for hospitalization. In D.K. Routh (Ed.), *Handbook of pediatric psychology* (pp. 460–491). New York: Guilford Press.

Peterson, L., & Shigetomi, C. (1981). The use of coping techniques to minimize anxiety in hospitalized children. *Behavior Therapy, 12,* 1–14.

Peterson, L., & Toler, S.M. (1986). An information seeking disposition in child surgery patients. *Health Psychology, 4,* 343–358.

Phipps, S. (1994). Bone marrow transplantation. In D.J. Bearison & R.K. Mulhern (Eds.), *Pediatric psychooncology: Psychological perspectives on children with cancer* (pp. 143–170). New York: Oxford University Press.

Piaget, J. (1929). *The child's conception of the world.* New York: Harcourt Brace Jovanovich.

Powers, S.W. (1999). Empirically supported treatments in pediatric psychology: Procedure-related pain. *Journal of Pediatric Psychology, 24,* 131–145.

Powers, S.W., Blount, R.L., Bachanas, P.J., Cotter, M.C., & Swan, S.C. (1993). Helping preschool leukemia patients and their parents cope during injections. *Journal of Pediatric Psychology, 18,* 681–695.

Prugh, D. (1983). *The psychosocial aspects of pediatrics.* Philadelphia: Lea & Febiger.

Rae, W.A. (1981). Hospitalized latency-age children: Implications for psychosocial care. *Children's Health Care, 9,* 59–63.

Rapoff, M.A. (1999). *Adherence to pediatric medical regimens.* Boston: Kluwer Academic.

Roberts, M.C., & Hurley, L.K. (1997). *Managing managed care.* New York: Plenum Press.

Rosenstock, I.M. (1985). Understanding and enhancing patient compliance with diabetic regimens. *Diabetes Care, 8,* 610–616.

Roskies, E., Bedard, P., Gauvreau-Guilbault, H., & Lafortune, D. (1975). Emergency hospitalization of young children: Some neglected psychological considerations. *Medical Care, 13,* 570–581.

Rothstein, R. (1980). Psychological stress in families of children in a pediatric intensive care unit. *Pediatric Clinics of North America, 27,* 613–620.

Rudd, P. (1979). In search of the gold standard for compliance measurement. *Archives of Internal Medicine, 139,* 627–628.

Rudolph, K.D., Denning, M., & Weisz, J.R. (1995). Determinants and consequences of children's coping in the medical setting: Conceptualizations, review and critique. *Psychological Bulletin, 118,* 328–357.

Sabbath, B.F., & Leventhal, J.M. (1984). Marital adjustment to chronic childhood illness: A critique of the literature. *Pediatrics, 73,* 762–768.

Sabbath, B.F., & Stein, R.E.K. (1990). Mental health referral: A weak link in the comprehensive care of children with chronic physical illnness. *Journal of Developmental and Behavioral Pediatrics, 11,* 73–78.

Saltoun-Moran, M., & Garcia, D. (1989). *Developing a Latino support group for parents of pediatric oncology patients.* American Cancer Society: California Division.

Sayer, A.G., Willet, J.B., & Perrin, E.C. (1993). Measuring understanding of illness causality in healthy children and children with chronic illness: A construct validation. *Journal of Applied Developmental Psychology, 14,* 11–36.

Schafer, L.C., Glasgow, R.E., McCaul, K.D., & Dreher, M. (1983). Adherence to IDDM regimens: Relationship to psychosocial variables and metabolic control. *Diabetes Care, 6,* 493–498.

Shagena, M.M., Sandler, H.K., & Perrin, E.C. (1988). Concepts of illness and perception of control in healthy children and in children with chronic illnesses. *Developmental and Behavioral Pediatrics, 9,* 252–256.

Shope, J.T. (1981). Medication compliance. *Pediatric Clinics of North America, 28,* 5–21.

Shore, M.F., Geiser, R.L., & Wolman, H.M. (1965). Constructive uses of a hospital experience. *Children, 12,* 3–8.

Shulman, J.L. (1983). Coping with major disease: Child, family, and pediatrician. *Pediatrics, 102,* 988–991.

Siegel, L.J. (1976). Preparation of children for hospitalization: A selected review of the research literature. *Journal of Pediatric Psychology, 1,* 26–30.

Siegel, L.J. (1983). Hospitalization and medical care of children. In C.E. Walker & M.C. Roberts (Eds.), *Handbook of clinical child psychology* (pp. 1089–1108). New York: Wiley.

Siegel, L.J. (1988). Measuring children's adjustment to hospitalization and to medical procedures. In P. Karoly (Ed.), *Handbook of child health assessment: Biosocial perspectives* (pp. 265–302). New York: Wiley.

Siegel, L.J. (1995). Commentary: Children's reactions to aversive medical procedures. *Journal of Pediatric Psychology, 20,* 429–433.

Siegel, L.J. (1998). Children medically at risk. In T.R. Kratochwill & R.J. Morris (Eds.), *The practice of child therapy* (3rd ed.). Needham Heights, MA: Allyn & Bacon.

Siegel, L.J., & Smith, K.S. (1989). Children's strategies for coping with pain. *Pediatrician: International Journal of Child and Adolescent Health, 16,* 110–118.

Siegel, L.J., & Smith, K.E. (1991). Coping and adaption in children's pain. In J.P. Bush & S.W. Hawking (Eds.), *Children in pain: Clinical and research issues from a developmental perspective* (pp. 149–170). New York: Springer-Verlag.

Simensson, R.J., & McHale, S.M. (1981). Review: Research on handicapped children: Sibling relationships. *Child Care Health and Development, 7,* 153–171.

Skipper, J.K., & Leonard, R.C. (1968). Children, stress, and hospitalization: A field experiment. *Journal of Health and Social Behavior, 9,* 275–287.

Skipper, J.K., Leonard, R.C., & Rhymes, J. (1968). Child hospitalization and social interaction: An experimental study of mothers' feelings of stress, adaptation, and satisfaction. *Medical Care, 6,* 496–506.

Smith, K.E., Ackerson, J.D., & Blotcky, A.D. (1989). Reducing distress during invasive medical procedures: Relating behavioral interventions to preferred coping style in pediatric cancer patients. *Journal of Pediatric Psychology, 14,* 405–419.

Solnit, A.J. (1960). Hospitalization: An aid to physical and psychological health in childhood. *American Journal of Diseases of Children, 99,* 155–163.

Spinetta, J.J., & Deasy-Spinetta, P. (Eds.). (1981). *Living with childhood cancer.* St. Louis, MO: Mosby.

Spirito, A., Starck, L.J., & Tyc, V.L. (1994). Stressors and coping strategies described during hospitalization by chronically ill children. *Journal of Clinical Child Psychology, 23,* 314–322.

Stinson, G.V. (1974). Obeying doctor's orders: A view from the other side. *Social Science and Medicine, 8,* 97–104.

Susman, E.J., Dorn, L.D., & Fletcher, J.C. (1987). Reasoning about illness in ill and healthy children and adolescents: Cognitive and emotional developmental aspects. *Developmental and Behavioral Pediatrics, 8,* 266–273.

Tamaroff, M.H., Festa, R.S., Adesman, A.R., & Walco, G.A. (1992). Therapeutic adherence to oral medication regimens by adolescents with cancer: 2. Clinical and psychological correlates. *Journal of Pediatrics, 120,* 812–817.

Tew, B., & Lawrence, K.M. (1975). Some sources of stress in mothers of spina bifida children. *British Journal of Prevention and Social Medicine, 29,* 27–30.

Thompson, K.L., & Varni, J.W. (1986). A developmental cognitive-biobehavioral approach to pediatric pain assessment. *Pain, 25,* 283–296.

Thompson, R.H. (1985). *Psychosocial research on pediatric hospitalization and health care: A review of the literature.* Springfield, IL: Thomas.

Thompson, R.H., Gil, K.M., Burbach, D.J., Keith, B.R., & Kinney, T.R. (1993). Psychological adjustment of mothers of children and adolescents with sickle cell disease: The role of stress, coping methods, and family functioning. *Journal of Pediatric Psychology, 18,* 549–559.

Toseland, R., & Hacke, L. (1982). Self-help groups and professional development. *Social Work, 27,* 341–347.

United States Department of Health, Education, and Welfare. (1965). *Red is the color of hurting: Planning for children in the hospital.* Washington, DC: National Clearinghouse for Mental Health Information.

Varni, J.W. (1983). *Clinical behavioral pediatrics: An interdisciplinary biobehavioral approach.* New York: Pergamon Press.

Varni, J.W., & Babani, L. (1986). Long-term adherence to health care regimens in pediatric chronic disorders. In N.A. Krasnegor, J.D. Arasteh, & M.F. Cataldo (Eds.), *Child health behavior: A behavioral pediatrics perspective* (pp. 502–520). New York: Wiley.

Varni, J.W., & Gilbert, A. (1982). Self-regulation of chronic arthritic pain and long-term analgesic dependence in a hemophilia. *Rheumatology and Rehabilitaiton, 21,* 171–174.

Vernon, D.T.A., & Bailey, W.C. (1974). The use of motion pictures in the psychological preparation of children for induction of anesthesia. *Anesthesiology, 40,* 68–74.

Vernon, D.T.A., Foley, J.M., Sipowicz, R.R., & Schulman, J.L. (1965). *The psychological responses of children to hospitalization and illness.* Springfield, IL: Thomas.

Vernon, D.T.A., Schulman, J.L., & Foley, J.M. (1966). Changes in children's behavior after hospitalization. *American Journal of Diseases of Children, 111,* 581–593.

Vernon, D.T.A., & Thompson, R.H. (1993). Research on the effect of experimental interventions on children's behavior after hospitalization: A review and synthesis. *Journal of Developmental and Behavioral Pediatrics, 14,* 36–44.

Walco, G.A., & Dampier, C.D. (1987). Chronic pain in adolecent patients. *Journal of Pediatric Psychology, 12,* 215–225.

Walco, G.A., Siegel, L.J., Dolgin, M.J., & Varni, J.W. (1992). Pediatric pain. In V.B. Van Hasselt & D.J. Kolko (Eds.), *Inpatient behavior therapy for children and adolescents* (pp. 183–203). New York: Plenum Press.

Walco, G.A., Sterling, C.M., Conte, P.M., & Engel, R.G. (1999). Empirically supported treatments in pediatric pain. *Journal of Pediatric Psychology, 24,* 155–167.

Walco, G.A., Varni, J.W., & Ilowite, N.T. (1992). Cognitive-behavioral pain management in children with juvenile rheumatoid arthritis. *Pediatrics, 89,* 1075–1079.

Wallace, M.H., Bakke, K., Hubbard, A., & Pendergrass, T.W. (1984). Coping with childhood cancer: An educational program for parents of children with cancer. *Oncology Nursing Forum, 11,* 30–35.

Wallander, J.L., & Thompson, R.J. (1995). Psychological adjustment of children with chronic physical conditions. In M.C. Roberts (Ed.), *Handbook of pediatric psychology* (2nd ed., pp. 124–141). New York: Guilford Press.

Wolfer, J.A., & Visintainer, M.A. (1975). Pediatric surgical patients' and parents' stress responses and adjustment. *Nursing Research, 24,* 244–255.

Zeltzer, L. (1994). Pain and symptom management. In D.J. Bearison & R.K. Mulhern (Eds.), *Pediatric psychooncology: Psychological perspectives in children with cancer* (pp. 61–83). New York: Oxford University Press.

Zeltzer, L., Bursch, B., & Walco, G.A. (1997). Pain responsiveness and chronic pain: A psycho-biological perspective. *Developmental and Behavioral Pediatrics, 18,* 413–422.

Zeltzer, L.K., Dash, J., & Holland, J.P. (1979). Hypnotically induced pain control in sickle cell anemia. *Pediatrics, 64,* 533–536.

Zeltzer, L.K., Dolgin, M.J., LeBaron, S., & LeBaron, C. (1991). A randomized controlled study of behavioral intervention for chemotherapy distress in children with cancer. *Pediatrics, 88,* 34–42.

Zeltzer, L., & LeBaron, S. (1982). Hypnosis and nonhypnotic techniques for reduction of pain and anxiety during painful procedures in children and adolescents with cancer. *Journal of Pediatrics, 101,* 1032–1035.

Zeltzer, L.K., LeBaron, S., & Zeltzer, P.M. (1984). The effectiveness of behavioral intervention for reduction of nausea and vomiting in children and adolescents receiving chemotherapy. *Journal of Clinical Oncology, 2,* 683–690.

CHAPTER 46

Pediatric Psychology: Contemporary Issues

LARRY L. MULLINS AND JOHN M. CHANEY

Pediatric psychology as an interdisciplinary field has witnessed substantial growth and change over the course of the past three decades. Not unlike other subdisciplines within clinical psychology, advancements in scientific research, medical technology, clinical practice, and a changing health care marketplace have culminated in a highly unique and clearly identifiable area of study. It is the purpose of this chapter to delineate the critical features of the evolving field of pediatric psychology, with a focus on contemporary definitions, training issues, research findings, professional issues, and future directions.

DEFINITIONS OF PEDIATRIC PSYCHOLOGY

Although the historic roots of pediatric psychology can be traced to Lightner Witmer in the nineteenth century (Roberts & McNeal, 1995), formal definitions of the field were first offered in the 1960s. Beginning with Kagan's (1965) call for collaboration between pediatrics and psychology, contributions began to emerge in the literature arguing for the genesis of a new area of study. In 1967, Logan Wright published an article in *American Psychologist* outlining what he believed to be the necessary role and training for the pediatric psychologist. By 1968, the Society of Pediatric Psychology was born and

became formally affiliated with the American Psychological Association, Division 12, Section on Clinical Child Psychology (Roberts & McNeal, 1995).

Through the 1970s, clearer and more comprehensive definitions emerged. Walker (1979) defined pediatric psychology as a subspecialty of behavioral medicine that allows for a behavioral-developmental perspective on child problems in the pediatric medical context. Importantly, he noted that pediatric psychology differed from traditional clinical psychology in terms of conceptualization and both points of intervention and manner of intervention. Yet, perhaps the most contemporary and inclusive definition of pediatric psychology is found in the masthead statement of the *Journal of Pediatric Psychology* (Roberts, La Greca, & Harper, 1988). To summarize:

> Pediatric psychology is an interdisciplinary field addressing physical, cognitive, social, and emotional functioning and development as they relate to health and illness issues in children, adolescents, and families . . . it explores the interrelationship between psychological and physical well-being of children, adolescents, and families including: psychosocial and developmental factors contributing to the etiology, course, treatment, and outcome of pediatric conditions; assessment and treatment of behavioral and emotional concomitants of disease, illness, and developmental disorders; the role of psychology in health-care settings; behavioral aspects of pediatric medicine;

the promotion of health and health related behaviors; the prevention of illness and injury among children and youth; and issues related to the training of pediatric psychologists. (p. 2)

Thus, pediatric psychology has evolved beyond early definitions of the field that were narrow in scope and based almost exclusively on the role of pediatric psychologists in the medical setting. Although not embraced by all pediatric psychologists, more contemporary definitions of the field capture more accurately the broad range of responsibilities and health care contexts in which pediatric psychologists function (Roberts & McNeal, 1995).

SCOPE OF STUDY AND ROLE DEFINITIONS

Given this definition of pediatric psychology, what then would be the scope of study for such a diverse field? An examination of representative articles published in the *Journal of Pediatric Psychology* over the past few years offers insight into this question. Publications include examination of social support and adjustment among adolescents with cancer (Manne & Miller, 1998), child-rearing practices of parents of children with sickle cell disease (Noll, McKellop, Vannatta, & Kalinyak, 1998), preparatory interventions for children undergoing dental procedures (Christiano & Russ, 1998), role of the family system in HIV risk reduction (Parsons et al., 1998), effects of television safety models on child risk taking (Potts & Swisher, 1998), illness uncertainty and attributional style in adolescents with asthma (Mullins, Chaney, Pace, & Hartman, 1997), interactions between infants with orofacial clefts and their mothers (Endriga & Speltz, 1997), and mother's causal attributions about infant growth deficiency (Sturm, Drotar, Laing, & Zimet, 1997), to name but a few.

Thus, the scope of study in pediatric psychology is quite varied, which has direct implications for professional role definitions. Numerous articles describe the various and multifaceted roles and activities engaged in by pediatric psychologists (e.g., Drotar, 1995a; Roberts, 1986). Pediatric psychologists serve in the roles of educator, consultant, supervisor, diagnostician, practitioner, facilitator, program designer, and administrator; importantly, many pediatric psychologists serve multiple roles within the same job description. Integration of roles is the norm, and the bifurcation of clinical practice and research, which pervades much of clinical psychology, has largely been avoided in the field (Roberts & McNeal, 1995).

Surveys indicate that the majority of pediatric psychologists work in clinical settings, specifically medical/pediatric systems (Drotar, Sturm, Eckerle, & White, 1993). Thus, although pediatric psychologists are often involved in the traditional roles of teaching, supervision, service delivery, program development, and research (Koocher, Sourkes, & Keane, 1979), they are unique in that they operate in the context of the medical health care delivery system (Peterson & Harbeck, 1988). As care providers, they often work at the behest of or collaboratively with pediatricians or other primary medical professionals. In this regard, they serve as consultants to both the pediatrician and pediatric health care team in general, in addition to their responsibilities as care providers to the ill child and his or her immediate family system (Mullins, Gillman, & Harbeck, 1991). The pediatric psychologist's consultation role may be further extended to include social, educational, and legal systems as deemed relevant to a particular case.

Because of the nature of pediatric psychology practice, some have logically argued that role definitions be expanded to include that of *primary care practitioner*. Such a role definition would make sense, in that pediatric psychologists are already involved in prevention, early identification, and treatment of a wide variety of pediatric problems. Indeed, efforts have been made to more closely align and establish a joint mission with pediatric medicine colleagues through active collaboration with the American Academy of Pediatrics (Armstrong, 1998). It remains to be seen, however, whether formalization of this new role will occur, and opposition to this has already been encountered on a variety of professional fronts, most notably from the field of child psychiatry.

TRAINING ISSUES

The diverse and complex roles of the pediatric psychologist pose particular challenges for training. Coupled with the rapidly advancing knowledge base of health-related conditions and a changing health care marketplace, the need for a comprehensive and evolving training curriculum is critical. A number of training models have been proposed over time (e.g., Davidson, 1988; La Greca, Stone, Drotar, & Maddux, 1988; La Greca, Stone, & Swales, 1989; Peterson & Harbeck, 1988). Although a relative lack of agreement still exists as to the requisite components and sequencing of training experiences (Pruitt & Elliott, 1992; Peterson & Harbeck, 1988), a number of important common perspectives are shared.

First, initial training in pediatric psychology should involve a generic, broad-based training background in psychology, including core courses in biological, social, experimental, and developmental psychology coupled with clinical courses in child assessment, treatment, and practicum. Subsequent experiences should then involve more specialized training in both clinical child psychology and health psychology (Davidson, 1988; Peterson & Harbeck, 1988). Such coursework should also include an emphasis on behavioral approaches, family therapy, and research methods (Peterson & Harbeck, 1988). Specialized graduate practica in pediatric psychology are also suggested, although many graduate programs in psychology lack the necessary resources (i.e., available supervising faculty, pediatric referral sources, or medical center) for such practica to be implemented. In this regard, specialized clinical training is most likely to take place at the predoctoral internship or postdoctoral level, which many pediatric psychologists believe to be the ideal sequence (LaGreca et al., 1988). Fortunately, the number of pre- and postdoctoral training opportunities in this area rose steadily through the 1980s (Tuma, 1987).

Despite these efforts, no current model of training or specification of competency criteria for pediatric psychology has been officially endorsed by an existing governing body, such as APA or the Society of Pediatric Psychology. However, with the formation of the Commission for Recognition of Specialties and Proficiencies in Professional Psychology (CRSPPP) and new APA accreditation guidelines (American Psychological Association, 1996), it is likely that pressure will only increase to adopt a set of "aspirational" guidelines. Recently, a number of new models and competencies have been recommended for clinical child psychology (La Greca & Hughes, 1999; Roberts et al., 1998). In addition to the standard topics of developmental psychology/psychopathology and child assessment and treatment, these models recommend training areas such

as cultural diversity, interdisciplinary collaboration and systems consultation, primary prevention and health promotion, and development of administration/entrepreneurial skills. Given the overlap between the two subspecialties, such models could serve as blueprints for developing similar guidelines in the field of pediatric psychology.

PRIMARY PREVENTION AND PROMOTION OF HEALTHY BEHAVIORS

As noted in the masthead statement of the *Journal of Pediatric Psychology,* a defining feature of the field is the *promotion* of healthy behaviors and the *prevention* of untoward health effects in children. Indeed, Peterson and Harbeck (1988) have noted that, in contrast to other fields of medicine, pediatrics in general has historically attended to the prevention of disease in a proactive manner. Given the emphasis of pediatric psychology on developmental aspects of children's problems, it makes sense that promotion and prevention efforts would be of paramount importance. Yet, it has only been in the past decade or so that behavioral researchers have devoted serious attention to prevention and early intervention efforts. Other chapters in this volume provide comprehensive reviews of these efforts (see Peterson & DiLillo, this volume). In the present chapter, we have tried to briefly summarize the current trends in this area.

Clearly, the most serious health-related concerns facing Americans today are related to problematic or unhealthy lifestyles (Wurtele, 1995). Overeating, lack of exercise, smoking, alcohol and other drug abuse, and risk-taking behaviors contribute to the onset and exacerbation of a host of health-related problems. Undeniably, these behavior patterns have their genesis in childhood. It has been cogently argued that the ideal time to maximize the long-term impact of healthy lifestyles occurs at early developmental periods in a child's life. Wurtele has summarized the primary objectives for these target lifestyle behaviors. As examples, Wurtele offered specific recommendations for enhancing children's lifestyles, such as promoting cardiovascular fitness and reducing obesity by increasing moderate daily activity, reducing the incidence of smoking, decreasing alcohol-related motor vehicle accidents, and providing quality school-based health promotion/education.

Thus, active efforts are being made by pediatric psychologists to address issues of health promotion and primary prevention. This contemporary trend is most evident in the area of injury prevention. Numerous articles, both theoretical and empirical, have documented the need to reduce the number of injuries sustained by children (Dershowitz & Williamson, 1977; Finney, 1995; Peterson & Oliver, 1995; Rodriguez, 1990; Routh, 1997). Researchers are also actively investigating children's perspectives on injuries and near-injuries (Morrongielo, 1997), factors influencing risk taking (Jelalian et al., 1997; Potts, Martinez, & Dedmon, 1995), the effects of televised safety models (Potts & Swisher, 1998), and attributions about naturally occurring minor illnesses (Gable & Peterson, 1998). Collectively, these research efforts reflect the growing concern about the prevention of health-related difficulties in children.

ADAPTATION TO CHRONIC ILLNESS

Perhaps no other area of pediatric psychology has received as much attention in the past decade as the study of emotional and behavioral adaptation to chronic medical conditions (La Greca, 1997). There are several reasons for this. Primarily due to advances in biomedical technology, greater numbers of children are surviving childhood medical conditions that would have resulted in death not so long ago (Thompson & Gustafson, 1996). Estimates suggest that as many as one million children in this country live with chronic medical conditions that significantly influence their daily lives and the lives of those in their immediate environment (Perrin & MacLean, 1988). Also, the changing complexion of childhood medical illnesses has resulted in similar changes in the practice of primary medical care, such that chronically ill children now constitute a substantial portion of pediatric practice. Chronically ill children utilize a vast array of medical services, and greater numbers of children and their families must learn to deal with the challenges of chronic conditions for longer periods of time (Olson, Mullins, Chaney, & Gillman, 1994; Thompson & Gustafson, 1996).

To keep pace with the increasing complexity of demands faced by children, their families, and the health care environment, the past 10 years or so

have witnessed significant advances in the study of pediatric chronic illness. Not only has the quantity of research increased dramatically, but the quality and rigor of these studies has advanced as well. For example, several special issues of the *Journal of Pediatric Psychology* (e.g., August 1995; December 1997), entire texts (e.g., Thompson & Gustafson, 1996), and substantial portions of other volumes (e.g., Olson, Mullins, Gillman, & Chaney, 1994; Roberts, 1995) have been dedicated to this topic. Because the scope of this chapter does not allow for an exhaustive review of the literature, we refer the reader to Thompson and Gustafson (1996), Roberts, and Olson, Mullins, Gillman, et al. (1994) for more thorough reviews of research and treatment issues pertaining to pediatric chronic illness.

In our view, several important conceptual and methodological developments in the study of adaptation to pediatric chronic illness stand out. Glasgow and Anderson (1995) provided a succinct analysis and synthesis of these issues: (1) conceptual issues, (2) sample considerations, (3) self-management (adherence) measurement, (4) research design, (5) behavior-health outcome issues, and (6) data analysis concerns. In this chapter, we have chosen to highlight issues concerning theory-driven research and issues related to research design and analysis.

CONCEPTUAL ISSUES

We agree with Glasgow and Anderson (1995) that studies of pediatric chronic illness need to be theory-driven and based on sound conceptual grounds. Moreover, because management and adaptation to chronic illness requires the involvement of the family and other significant systems in the child's environment, we believe that current models examining adaptation from family contextual/systems perspectives (e.g., Kazak, 1997) constitute a significant advancement in the field (Drotar, 1997b). Moreover, the literature indicates a growing interest in family systems theory and practice among pediatric psychologists (e.g., Kazak, 1989; Mullins, Harbeck-Weber, Olson, & Hartman, 1996). A number of these types of models have been suggested in recent years.

Wallander et al. (1989) emphasize the importance of risk and resistance factors (e.g., perceived role strain and family support) that operate at the family level to determine more or less advantageous coping with chronic conditions. Thompson and colleagues (1992) promote a transactional stress and coping conceptualization of pediatric chronic illness, which takes into account the effects of illness (e.g., severity) on both children and parents. Further, this model highlights the importance of reciprocal behavioral and emotional transactions that occur among family members (e.g., parent-child, parent-parent) to influence coping and adaptation to illness. Similarly, biobehavioral models have been advanced that emphasize the direct influence of emotions on biomedical aspects of disease and family/larger systems influences on chronic illness adjustment, such as school, peers, and the health care context. Biobehavioral models also suggest the need to focus more closely on the physiological vulnerability of some children with chronic illnesses and the potential role of physiological vulnerability in response to specific stressors, such as family conflict (Wood, 1993, 1995; Wood et al., 1989).

In general, these models have generated a wealth of conceptually sound research supporting the notion that adaptation to pediatric illness occurs in the context of a complex set of emotional, physiological, and social transactions. Studies suggest that family risk and resistance factors function to determine parental psychological adjustment, which may have both direct and indirect effects on children's adjustment (e.g., Drotar, Agle, Eckl, & Thompson, 1997; Mullins et al., 1991; Wallander & Venters, 1995). Further, investigations consistently support the role of family functioning and, more specifically, dyadic transactions (e.g., parent-child) in determining the emotional adjustment of both parents and children to chronic medical conditions (e.g., Chaney et al., 1997; Holmbeck et al., 1997; Manne et al., 1995; Mullins et al., 1995; Sheeran, Marvin, & Pianta, 1997; Thompson, Gil, Burbach, Keith, & Kinney, 1993). Finally, a number of interesting articles utilizing biobehavioral models have emerged, indicating that some children with chronic conditions demonstrate both excessive psychological and physiological reactivity in response to distressful environmental conditions (Miller & Wood, 1994, 1997), which may have direct effects on their physical functioning.

RESEARCH DESIGN

Methodological improvements in the study of adaptation to chronic illness have also been observed. Glasgow and Anderson (1995) commented that the field should continue to implement innovative research designs to get away from cross-sectional descriptive studies and to narrow our focus to more specific relationships among variables and specific experimental effects of interventions on adaptation (see also Drotar, 1997a; Roberts, McNeal, Randall, & Roberts, 1996). Several studies of this type can be found in the recent chronic illness literature.

Longitudinal or "growth" studies have advanced cross-sectional findings in the field, primarily because studies of this type are more consistent with the developmental approach inherent in the field of pediatric psychology and because they give us a better idea of the nature of relationships over time (Drotar, 1997a). These investigations have yielded important information regarding stability and change in both parent and child adaptation to illness across a number of chronic conditions, including diabetes, cystic fibrosis, cancer, juvenile rheumatoid arthritis, and sickle cell disease (e.g., Chaney et al., 1997; Dahlquist, Czyzewski, & Jones, 1996; Jacobsen, Hauser, et al., 1994; Kovacs, Iyengar, Goldston, Obrosky, Marsh, et al., 1990; Kovacs, Iyengar, Goldston, Obrosky, Stewart, et al., 1990; Manne et al., 1995; Northam, Anderson, Adler, Werther, & Warne, 1996; Thompson, Gil, et al., 1994; Thompson, Gustafson et al., 1994; Timko, Stovel, & Moos, 1992).

A number of studies have also emerged in recent years that reflect the growing concern for experimental and applied research in this area (e.g., Hains, Davies, Behrens, & Biller, 1997; Ireys, Sills, Kolodner, & Walsh, 1996; Wysocki et al., 1997). Perhaps one of the most influential papers on this topic was provided by Kaslow et al. (1997). We have highlighted this paper because it focuses specifically on a family-based approach to treatment with ill children and delineates a number of important requirements for an intervention to be considered an empirically validated approach. Kaslow and colleagues promote (1) the use of manual-based approaches because they allow clinicians greater access to standardized treatments; (2) subject selection based on inclusion/exclusion criteria and subject randomization to treatment groups; (3) specific definitions of target outcomes; and (4) follow-up data to demonstrate long-term effects of the intervention. Also, Kaslow et al. highlight the need to implement interventions that are sensitive to the specific features of culturally diverse families.

We suggest that in addition to treatment studies, there is tremendous need for more experimental studies in the area of pediatric chronic illness.

Much of the existing literature is based on self-report data and multivariate correlational designs, making firm conclusions difficult regarding the causal nature of variables in the adaptation process. Experimental designs allow for a closer examination of psychosocial variables directly affecting physical functioning (e.g., Miller & Wood, 1994, 1997) and for examining children's appropriate coping responses to specific illness information (e.g., Rietveld, Kolk, & Prins, 1996). These types of studies also allow for more precise testing of theoretical models of adaptation. For example, in a recent study, Chaney and colleagues (1999) provided a demonstration of experimentally induced learned helplessness deficits in a group of older youth with long-standing asthma. Utilizing a laboratory analogue procedure to simulate behavior-outcome non-contingency, these authors found that individuals with asthma (compared to an age-matched healthy cohort) exhibited an increased vulnerability for cognitive, affective, and problem-solving difficulties in response to noncontingent feedback on an experimental learning task. Findings of this nature help to develop a more accurate understanding of disease-specific aspects of childhood chronic illness and have direct implications for disease management and psychosocial adaptation to illness.

STATISTICAL APPROACHES

In addition to longitudinal designs and a greater emphasis on experimental data, the field has begun to implement more sophisticated statistical analyses to address specific questions that are more consistent with theory-driven hypotheses. Because research on pediatric chronic illness is no longer considered in its infancy, studies rarely rely on exploratory data analysis methods, such as bivariate relationships between variables, or on inadequate multivariate designs, such as stepwise regression models. Instead, current approaches to studying adaptation to pediatric chronic illness more often utilize hierarchical regression approaches that allow for the construction of theoretically driven regression equations to examine more precisely the unique contribution of key variables (see Chaney et al., 1997; Kliewer & Lewis, 1995; Thompson, Gustafson, et al., 1994).

Also, as pointed out by Peyrot (1996), the statistical approaches implemented in many studies of pediatric chronic illness leave a number of important relationships unexamined by not including potential mediator or moderator variables (see Baron & Kenny, 1986) in the analyses. Recent studies have begun to utilize these types of analysis to get a more precise picture of relationships among variables and potential routes leading to adaptive outcomes (e.g., Lewis & Kliewer, 1996; Lustig, Ireys, Sills, & Walsh, 1996; Mullins et al., 1997; Overstreet et al., 1995; Silver, Stein, & Dadds, 1996).

DEVELOPMENTAL PROBLEMS

Pediatric psychology by definition emphasizes developmental issues, and problems associated with "faulty developmental processes" have long been the target of assessment and intervention. This area of pediatric psychology is quite broad in scope; thus, primarily for illustrative purposes, we have chosen to describe four representative problems: high-risk infants, failure to thrive, feeding problems, and elimination disorders.

HIGH-RISK INFANTS

The term "high-risk infants" encompasses a broad range of developmental problems associated with the pre-, peri-, and neonatal time periods. Children are placed at risk by a variety of factors, including prematurity, congenital physical anomalies, and prenatal exposure to drugs, alcohol, and HIV, among others (Bendell-Estroff, Field, Shelton, & Saylor, 1996). More specifically, these infants may experience a variety of physical compromises as a result, including acute respiratory insufficiency, brain hemorrhages, fetal infection, convulsions, bradycardia, and acidosis (e.g., Bottos, Barba, D'Este, & Tronick, 1996; Nowicki, 1994). All these problems may represent an immediate life-threatening situation that must be attended to by both the parents and multiple health care professionals.

The potential activities and points of intervention for the pediatric psychologist are numerous. Bendell-Estroff (1994) states that the initial assessment and treatment of the high-risk infant falls into six interrelated areas: (1) the parents; (2) the neonate, focusing on specific medical problems; (3) enhancement of the infant's health status; (4) the environment of the neonatal intensive care unit (NICU); (5) the infant-parent relationship; and

(6) the impact of the NICU environment on medical personnel. Thus, the pediatric psychologist may be working simultaneously with the parents on coping issues, monitoring the child's health status and facilitating the decision-making process, consulting with parents on attachment issues, and helping medical personnel communicate more effectively with distraught parents. Through these efforts, the goal of the pediatric psychologist is to enhance optimal family functioning until hospital discharge can be achieved.

Although medical advancements have greatly reduced mortality and morbidity for high-risk infants, (Bendell-Estroff, 1994), a subset of these children remains at significant risk for many years. Thus, pediatric psychologists are also involved in assessment and treatment of high-risk infants following discharge from the hospital, often for extended periods of time. O'Brien, Soliday, and McCluskey-Fawcett (1995) offer a comprehensive review of the various physical health, cognitive, social-emotional, and behavioral sequelae of the preterm infant that may become the target for later intervention efforts. Specifically, mother-child bonding difficulties, learning disabilities, attentional problems, child abuse and neglect, and externalizing behavior disorders may necessitate treatment on the part of the pediatric psychologist (e.g., K. Katz et al., 1996; Lloyd, Wheldall, & Perks, 1988; O'Brien et al., 1995).

FAILURE TO THRIVE

Failure to thrive (FTT) represents another primary developmental problem addressed by pediatric psychologists. In general, FTT is a nonspecific descriptive term used to diagnose children exhibiting a nonnormative downward deviation in growth pattern (Domek, 1994; Drotar, 1995b). Specific criteria for FTT include (1) weight for age below the fifth percentile (Hammill et al., 1979); (2) a significant deceleration in rate of weight gain, that is, failure to gain weight in an appropriate developmental fashion (Bithoney & Rathbun, 1983); and (3) weight for height below the tenth percentile and downward crossing of the two percentiles on weight charts (Frank & Zeisel, 1988). In essence, FTT represents a heterogeneous category of growth problems involving multiple etiologic factors, including both medical and psychosocial influences. Drotar and Sturm

(1994) note that the current classification of FTT falls into three categories: (1) organic failure to thrive (OFT), wherein a physical cause is responsible for the growth deficiency; (2) nonorganic failure to thrive (NOFT), wherein psychosocial factors appear to be the primary causal factor; and (3) mixed FTT, in which both medical and psychosocial factors contribute.

Numerous medical and psychosocial consequences result from FTT, many of which pediatric psychologists are called on to address. These problems include feeding problems, parent stress, parent-child interaction difficulties, withdrawal, self-stimulatory behavior, and demandingness (Drotar, Malone, & Negray, 1980; Linscheid & Rasnake, 1985). Drotar and Sturm (1994) provide a comprehensive overview of clinical assessment aimed at identifying FTT-related problems and associated intervention strategies. Because growth deficiencies often result in a plethora of interrelated problems, an interdisciplinary team approach is typically in order to successfully treat these difficulties (Drotar, 1995b). Although the pediatric psychologist's role is not always well defined in these teams, they often serve as influential team members or act as consultants in the treatment process, given the nature of their expertise. Drotar (1995a) further notes that it is critical for the pediatric psychologist to operate in a concerted fashion with other team members to maximize the success of the overall care plan.

FEEDING PROBLEMS

Children in the pediatric context often present with various types of feeding problems. Linscheid (1992) has estimated that incidence of feeding problems is as high as 25% to 35%. This figure may be on the rise as medical technology increases the survival rates of high-risk infants, an at-risk population for developing problematic eating patterns. In general, these problems can be classified as organic in nature, as resulting from behavioral mismanagement of eating behavior, or as a combination of both (Linscheid, Budd, & Rasnake, 1995). For example, an eating disorder in a young child may result initially from a needed medical procedure (e.g., a Nissan fundoplication for gastroesophageal reflux), which is then complicated by parents who inadvertently reinforce subsequent food refusal.

To effectively intervene, careful interdisciplinary assessment of the child must take place, preferably in an inpatient setting (Linscheid et al., 1995). Clinical assessment typically involves the implementation of a food diary system charted by caregivers and health care staff (e.g., nurses, occupational therapists) and observations of child-feeder interactions by the pediatric psychologist. In this manner, the pediatric psychologist can rate preferred/non-preferred foods, the child's manner of refusal, associated behavior problems, effective/noneffective feeding strategies on the part of the caregiver, and reinforcement contingencies.

After an analysis of these component processes, treatment is based largely on behavioral principles (Linscheid et al., 1995). Contingent social attention in the form of praise and tactile stimulation is typically utilized for successive approximations to the target goal of food intake, coupled with ignoring of food refusal behavior (Linscheid, 1992; Stark et al., 1993). Other incentives have also been used as rewards for target eating behavior, including play time, gaining access to a preferred food, or tokens (e.g., Luiselli & Gleason, 1987; Stark, Bowen, Tyc, Evans, & Passero, 1990). Shaping and fading procedures that alter the type and texture of food are also typically implemented (e.g., Johnson & Bobbitt, 1993; Linscheid, Tarnowski, Rasnake, & Brams, 1987). Many eating programs are initiated in the context of appetite manipulation, which restricts supplemental food intake (e.g., reducing caloric intake via gastro-tube).

Pediatric psychologists play a primary role in most comprehensive feeding programs. Often, they are called on to perform a thorough assessment of psychosocial/behavioral contributions to the problem, construct the feeding program itself, and coordinate treatment efforts. Not unlike interventions with FTT, feeding cases typically involve an interdisciplinary team approach. In these cases, the pediatric psychologist is often considered the team leader in conjunction with medical staff.

ELIMINATION DISORDERS

Enuresis (the repeated voiding of urine in inappropriate places) and encopresis (the repeated passing of feces in inappropriate places) represent two of the most commonplace problems referred to the pediatric psychologist (Walker, 1995). In contrast to the above-mentioned developmental problems, enuresis and encopresis both represent distinct *DSM-IV* (American Psychiatric Association, 1994) disorders. Enuresis is defined by (1) repeated voiding of urine into the bed or clothes; (2) the child has reached at least 5 years of age; (3) the wetting must be clinically significant, as indicated by a frequency of two times per week for three months or the presence of clinically significant distress/impairment in important areas of functioning; and (4) a functional etiology. In contrast, for encopresis, the *DSM-IV* requires an age of at least 4 years and inappropriate expelling of feces at least once a month for at least three months.

Although a variety of etiological models, including biological, emotional, and learning approaches, have been proposed to explain problems of elimination, the predominant, empirically supported treatment regimens are largely based on behavioral learning principles (see Calkins, Walker, & Howe, 1994, and Walker, 1995, for comprehensive reviews). Urine alarms (bell and pad), multidimensional behavioral programs, urine retention and sphincter control exercises, and combined pharmacological treatments have all been successfully used for treating enuresis (e.g., Azrin, Sneed, & Foxx, 1974; Howe & Walker, 1992; Walker, 1979). For retentive encopresis, the most common form of encopresis, behavioral treatment modalities have again received much support (e.g., Houts & Abramson, 1990; Walker, 1979). Many of the more effective treatments for encopresis involve behavioral programs combined with medical interventions (i.e., use of suppositories and implementing a high-fiber diet). Walker (1995) notes that success rates are nearly as high as 100% for many such programs.

MANAGEMENT OF PAIN AND DISTRESS

One of the most common and yet challenging presenting problems for the pediatric psychologist is managing children's pain and distress. Indeed, pain and distress are almost synonymous with pediatric procedures and hospitalization. Venipunctures, immunizations, spinal taps, bone marrow aspirations, endoscopic evaluations, and presurgical anesthesia represent just a few of the many painful procedures that are routinely experienced by children in the medical care system. Coupled with the number of children who experience minor or major traumatic injuries (e.g., falls, motor vehicle accidents, burns) or who are diagnosed with a painful chronic medical condition (e.g., sickle cell anemia, juvenile rheumatoid arthritis), the sheer number of children experiencing some form of painful event is staggering. It is not surprising, then, that pediatric psychologists are called on with great regularity to assess and treat children's pain and distress.

Notably, the empirical literature on pain and distress has grown dramatically in the past decade (Varni, Blount, Waldron, & Smith, 1995). Numerous comprehensive reviews and textbooks have summarized this large body of information (e.g., Bush & Harkins, 1991; Carter, Bennett, & Urey, 1994; McGrath, 1990; Ross & Ross, 1988; Varni et al., 1995), and any attempt to cover this topic in detail is beyond the scope of this chapter. For illustrative reasons, we briefly review select aspects of the pediatric pain and distress literature, including current typologies, trends in assessment, and treatment procedures.

TYPOLOGIES OF PAIN AND DISTRESS

Pain is inherently a perceptual and psychosocial phenomenon (Karoly, 1991), reflecting a subjective experience. Thus, a given child's pain experience is influenced by a host of factors, including age, sex, development, culture, and previous pain experience (McGrath, 1990). Although different typologies exist, most experts agree that there are at least four categories of pediatric pain (Varni, 1983; McGrath, 1990): (1) pain resulting from or associated with some type of chronic illness, (2) pain resulting from physical injury or trauma, (3) pain associated with less well-defined disease or injury, and (4) acute pain, often associated with medical procedures. Importantly, these distinctions do not represent mutually exclusive categories, and a given child may experience two or more of these types of pain. They do, however, serve as a useful heuristic for clinical and research purposes.

ASSESSMENT OF PAIN AND DISTRESS

Assessment of pain is a complex, multidimensional task and varies as a function of the type of pain, the purpose of the assessment, the context, and the child's developmental level (Karoly, 1991; McGrath, 1990). Whereas 20 years ago, most pediatric pain assessment methods were crude and utilized adult-based measures, today, a large number of assessment tools are available to measure children's pain. Most of these measures can be broken down into parent report, child report, and independent observer report types of formats.

The Pediatric Pain Questionnaire (PPQ; Varni & Thompson, 1985) serves as an excellent example of a multidimensional parent and child report pain measure. The PPQ is a developmentally based instrument designed to assess acute, chronic, and recurrent pain in children (Varni et al., 1995). It includes child, adolescent, and parent response forms. In addition to assessing pain intensity and sensory and affective components of pain, it also assesses social, environmental, and functional status factors. Pertinent medical and pain history is gathered for both the child and other family members. In addition, pain is assessed through use of a visual analogue scale (VAS), body outline figures for location of pain, and use of pain descriptor checklists. The PPQ is best known for its use in research on juvenile rheumatoid arthritis (JRA), although it is an appropriate measure for assessing pain in a variety of chronic conditions.

Whereas the PPQ was developed to assess parent and child report, other measures rely on a direct observation format. Much of the original research on the development of these assessment methods was conducted on pediatric cancer populations, primarily children undergoing lumbar punctures and bone marrow aspiration. Three measures stand out as examples of highly reliable and often used direct observations of distress and pain: (1) the Procedural Behavior Rating Scale–Revised (PBRS-R; E. Katz, Kellerman, & Siegel, 1980), (2) the Observation Scale of Behavioral Distress (OSBD; Jay, Ozolins, Elliott, & Caldwell, 1983), and (3) the Child-Adult Procedure Interaction Scale (CAMPIS; Blount et al., 1998). The CAMPIS is a notable development in the field, in that it offers an intricate analysis of verbal interaction patterns among parent, staff, and child during medical procedures. Such an approach allows for more specific delineation of behaviors that promote adaptation versus those that exacerbate distress.

Overall, these and other measures (see McGrath, 1990, for a detailed review) have proven quite useful in understanding the nature of pediatric pain and in developing treatment strategies. A brief review of treatment issues follows.

TREATMENT OF CHILDREN'S PAIN AND DISTRESS

The area of pediatric pain and distress is notable for empirically driven intervention efforts and ample documentation of their effectiveness. Targets of interventions for specific procedures have included children undergoing venipunctures, immunizations, lumbar punctures, bone marrow aspirations, chemotherapy, cast removal, debridement of burns, and tanking procedures, among others (e.g., Jay, Elliott, Fitzgibbons, Woody, & Siegel, 1995; Manne, Bakeman, Jacobson, Gorfinkle, & Redd, 1994). Other targets of intervention have been children with more enduring episodic pain conditions, such as those diagnosed with sickle cell disease (Kaslow et al., 1997) and JRA (Varni, Rapoff, & Waldron, 1994).

The majority of these interventions have been behaviorally or cognitive-behaviorally based. Types of interventions include positive reinforcement, imagery/distraction strategies, relaxation techniques, modeling, role playing, and coaching by the therapist. Collectively, these studies demonstrate (1) that behavioral and cognitive-behavioral interventions significantly reduce pain and distress across a variety of procedures and conditions, and (2) that children are rated as more cooperative during the distressing procedures, which allows for more effective treatment (e.g., Elliott & Olson, 1983; Jay, Elliott, Katz, & Spiegel, 1987; Turk, Meichenbaum, & Genest, 1983).

Importantly, integrated, multimodal interdisciplinary pain programs may be the most efficacious means of intervention (e.g., McGrath, 1990). Such programs involve both nonpharmacological and pharmacological strategies of intervention and include physicians, psychologists, nurses, and other members of the health care team. Such an approach not only enhances the likelihood of comprehensive care, but also maximizes consistency and quality of care.

Currently, the question is not whether pediatric psychologists can effectively reduce children's pain and distress, but what interventions are most effective (singularly or in combination) for which painful conditions. In addition, questions are raised regarding who will implement treatment and who

will pay for services. Although many interventions can be presented via videotape or by paraprofessionals, the number of children needing these services is daunting. Notably, recent research suggests that although the use of empirically supported pain interventions with pediatric populations is increasing, a significant number of pediatric hospitals have yet to adopt these contemporary techniques (e.g., teaching coping strategies, use of filmed modeling) (O'Byrne, Peterson, & Saldana, 1997). Pediatric psychologists must attend to these issues if the needs of children in pain and distress are to be adequately served.

PROFESSIONAL ISSUES

As pediatric psychology passes the millennium mark, professional issues abound. For brevity's sake, we have chosen to focus on a limited number of topic areas. These areas include ethical and legal issues, development of the *Diagnostic and Statistical Manual for Primary Care (DSM-PC)*, and attempts to gain APA division status.

ETHICAL AND LEGAL ISSUES

As has been aptly pointed out, ethical considerations are particularly problematic in both pediatric psychology and clinical child psychology (Rae, Worchel, & Brunnquell, 1995). Despite increasingly sophisticated and specific guidelines set forth by the American Psychological Association (1992), the complexities of ethical/legal decision making in the general area of child heath psychology present numerous dilemmas for the pediatric psychologist. Ethical decisions must be made in the context of the demands of an intricate health care system, ambiguous constitutional rights of children, idiosyncratic jurisdictional statutes, the family system, and the needs of the larger society (Melton & Ehrenreich, 1992; Schaefer & Call, 1994).

Such complexities are evident as they concern the more general principles of informed consent and confidentiality. A central focus of APA guidelines is protection of the patient's right to be a freely informed participant in psychological care. Yet, almost by definition, children lack the necessary cognitive/developmental capacity to comprehend fully the gravity and nature of their treatment and to make informed decisions (Rae et al., 1995). Because children in the pediatric context often have multiple decisions made for them (e.g., medical regimen course, need for hospitalization), psychologists must necessarily focus on issues of (1) the voluntary nature of the decision, (2) available knowledge, and (3) capacity to make a decision. More specifically, children should be able to participate in treatment without coercion, having information presented to them in an understandable fashion, consistent with their capacity to understand the information (Rae et al., 1995). Although legally, children may not be able to consent to a given treatment(s), they should be given the opportunity to "assent" to treatment (Koocher & Keith-Spiegel, 1990), thereby allowing them a sense of agency and participation in the decision-making process.

Similarly, pediatric psychologists must address issues of confidentiality. Although children are not accorded the same right to confidentiality as adults due to their minor status, establishing a therapeutic atmosphere of trust is essential. Children must be informed of the limits of confidentiality in language they can understand, although a substantial minority of pediatric psychologists do not actually assess a child's ability to cognitively appreciate this tenet (Rae & Worchel, 1991).

More specific to the context of pediatric psychology are changes occurring in the realm of bioethics (Rae et al., 1995). Advancements in medical technology and the attendant complexities of medical decision making have led to the creation of numerous policies, procedures, and institutional structures for ensuring the rights of consumers. Hospital ethics committees are now a standard reinforced by state and federal legislation. A new profession has been created, the biomedical ethicist, whose specialized training places him or her in the role of consultant to medical ethics boards (LaPuma & Scheidermayer, 1991). Rae et al. (1995) point out that the role of the biomedical ethicist is particularly critical in cases of neonatal medicine, including the right to treatment, right to refuse treatment, withholding or withdrawing life-sustaining treatment, establishment of advance directives, and issues of religious faith dictating treatment course.

Because of their unique training and expertise, pediatric psychologists are likely to play a central role in the bioethical decision-making process, and as such must stay abreast of developments in this arena. Schaefer and Call (1994) provide a list of practical suggestions for proactively approaching ethical issues in the pediatric context. Consistent with trends in other areas of medicine, the complexities of ethics in pediatric psychology are likely to increase with technological advancements and changing societal norms.

DIAGNOSTIC AND STATISTICAL MANUAL FOR PRIMARY CARE (DSM-PC)

In what has been referred to as a landmark event (Jellinek, 1997), the *DMS-PC Child and Adolescent Version* was developed as a new classification scheme for coding behavioral and developmental problems seen in primary care (Wolraich, Felice, & Drotar, 1996). The development of *DSM-PC* began in 1989, representing a unique collaboration among the American Academy of Pediatrics, the American Psychiatric Association, the American Psychological Association (particularly the Society of Pediatric Psychology), the Society for Developmental and Behavioral Pediatrics, the American Academy of Child and Adolescent Psychology, the American Academy of Family Physicians, the Canadian Pediatric Society, the Zero to Three National Center for Clinical Infant Programs, the Maternal and Child Health Bureau, and the National Institute of Mental Health (Wolraich, 1997). The primary motivating factor for the *DSM-PC* was the longstanding dissatisfaction with the *DSM* for mental disorders (American Psychiatric Association, 1994), which primary care physicians found inappropriate for many of the child problems encountered in their practices.

Drotar (1997c) notes that the *DSM-PC* was largely predicated on four assumptions: (1) environmental factors impact children's mental health; (2) a functional mental health classification scheme must be clear, concise, and amenable to change based on research findings; (3) children's symptoms are on a continuum from normal variation to mental disorders; and (4) any new system must be compatible with existing coding systems. Accordingly, the manual is organized such that the clinician can describe the impact of negative environmental situations or stressors on the child, noting risk and protective factors. Behavioral clusters, based on presenting complaints, are used to describe various child problem manifestations, with each cluster having three levels or categories: developmental variations, problems, and disorders (Drotar, 1997c). Clinicians are also given developmental guidelines for the coding of a given problem in specific age groups. Finally, the *DSM-PC* allows for differential diagnosis and coding of severity.

The emergence of the *DSM-PC* has significant relevance for the practice of pediatric psychology. At a conceptual level, the manual represents a much clearer taxonomy for describing the types of problems typically encountered in pediatric practice, thereby advancing concepts of behavioral diagnosis (Drotar, 1997c). It is hoped that this will allow clinicians to better communicate with each other, both within the discipline of psychology and across disciplines with primary care physicians. Drotar also notes that the *DSM-PC* may potentiate and enhance collaboration training efforts with pediatricians, promote research on primary care providers, and facilitate reimbursement of psychological services.

What will be the future of *DSM-PC*? Unfortunately, much will probably depend on how well the manual is adopted by existing health care plans, which must be "sold" on the advantages/cost-effectiveness of the new system. It is highly unlikely that clinicians will use a classification scheme that does not lend itself to reimbursement or results in significant complexity in billing for their services. The adoption of this new taxonomy will partially rest on pediatric psychologists determining its reliability and utility in the context of both explicative and intervention research. Empirical demonstrations of the *DSM-PC* as a valid and functional classification scheme will legitimize its acceptance into mainstream pediatric medicine and pediatric psychology.

PEDIATRIC PSYCHOLOGY AS A
NEW DIVISION IN APA

At the time of this writing, the Society of Pediatric Psychology (SPP) had changed in status from a section in Division 12 of APA to a full division (Division 54) in its own right (Black, 1998). Coordinating efforts with Section 1 (Clinical Child Psychology), which also was moving toward division status, the SPP met with various APA officials to lay the groundwork for this advancement. Black has pointed out that attaining division status is a potential milestone in the development of pediatric psychology as a profession, and will help ensure recognition, support, and governance responsibilities within APA. Indeed, with division status granted, the visibility of pediatric psychology as a legitimate subspecialty within psychology will certainly be enhanced.

SUMMARY AND
FUTURE DIRECTIONS

Pediatric psychology has witnessed rapid change as an area of specialization over the past 30 years, and not unlike other specialties within psychology, continual change is inevitable as scientific knowledge is expanded. Because of pediatric psychology's unique relationship with the health care delivery system, however, such changes are likely to be even more dramatic. For example, in the health care context, "corporatization" of the private sector and "privatization" of the public sector led to over 56 million Americans obtaining medical services through health maintenance organizations in 1995 (Belar, 1997). Managed care plans are increasingly dictating who receives mental health services, how much service can be received, who will be the service providers, and how much they will be reimbursed. Pediatric psychology as a practicing profession has certainly felt the negative impact of these changes.

On a positive note, the pediatric psychologist has long been known to offer brief assessment and intervention services, many of which are short term in nature, targeted toward specific, identifiable behaviors, and most often guided by empirical findings. In this regard, pediatric psychologists are in a unique position to market their services to managed care companies and their patient subscribers (Resnick & Kruczek, 1996). Nonetheless, increased efforts are needed in two critical areas: intervention research and cost-benefit analysis (La Greca & Varni, 1993). Not unlike clinical health psychology in general (Belar, 1997), pediatric psychology is sorely lacking in these two areas. A recent review by Kibby, Tyc, and Mulhern (1998) identified only 42 studies of psychological interventions for children and adolescents with chronic medical conditions for the years 1990 to 1995. Notably, only one study was found that examined prevention in this age group. Notwithstanding the recent efforts of the editorial board of the *Journal of Pediatric Psychology* to encourage intervention research (La Greca &

Varni, 1993), considerably more work is needed in this area.

Importantly, medical advancements are likely to also change the practice landscape for pediatric psychology in other ways. New, innovative treatments have already resulted in more complicated and demanding medical regimens for certain chronic illnesses, with increasing task demands for both children and their parents. Conversely, genetic screenings, in utero surgical procedures, and newer medications may well make some conditions curable or more readily managed. In either case, *how* pediatric psychologists will intervene in the lives of their young patients is likely to change as well.

In all likelihood, pediatric psychology will continue to define and develop its interdisciplinary role vis-à-vis other professions in the health care setting. Because collaboration is the cornerstone in the practice of pediatric psychology, this philosophy will most likely prove to be the key to enhancing the future status of the discipline (Drotar, 1993). Unfortunately, previous efforts to establish true collaboration with our pediatric medicine colleagues have been underexplored. More recent attempts by the Society of Pediatric Psychology to combine forces with the American Academy of Pediatrics reflects the potential benefits of a shared vision of serving children and their families (Armstrong, 1998).

REFERENCES

American Psychiatric Association. (1994). *Diagnostic and statistical manual of mental disorders* (4th ed.). Washington, DC: Author.

American Psychological Association. (1992). Ethical principles of psychologists and code of conduct. *American Psychologist, 47,* 1597–1611.

American Psychological Association. (1996). *Guidelines and principles for accreditation of programs in professional psychology and accreditation procedures.* Washington, DC: Author.

Armstrong, D. (1998). SPP Updates: American Academy of Pediatrics presidential address to SPP at APA. *Progress Notes: Newsletter of the Society of Pediatric Psychology, 22,* 13.

Azrin, N., Sneed, T., & Foxx, R. (1974). Dry bed training: Rapid elimination of childhood enuresis. *Behavioral Research and Therapy, 12,* 147–156.

Baron, R., & Kenny, D. (1986). The moderator-mediator variable distinction in social psychological research: Conceptual, strategic, and statistical considerations. *Journal of Personality and Social Psychology, 51,* 1173–1182.

Belar, C. (1997). Clinical health psychology: A specialty for the 21st century. *Health Psychology, 16,* 411–416.

Bendell-Estroff, D. (1994). Neonatal problems: Psychological issues. In R. Olson, L. Mullins, J. Gillman, & J. Chaney (Eds.), *Sourcebook of pediatric psychology* (pp. 17–25). Needham Heights, MA: Allyn & Bacon.

Bendell-Estroff, D., Field, T., Shelton, T., & Saylor, C. (1996). Editorial: High risk infants. *Journal of Pediatric Psychology, 21,* 753–754.

Bithoney, W., & Rathbun, J. (1983). Failure to thrive. In M. Levine, W. Carey, A. Crocker, & R. Gross (Eds.), *Developmental behavioral pediatrics* (pp. 557–562). Philadelphia: Saunders.

Black, M. (1998). The president's message. *Progress Notes: Newsletter of the Society of Pediatric Psychology, 22,* 1.

Blount, R., Corbin, S., Sturges, J., Wolfe, V., Prater, J., & James, C. (1998). The relationship between adult's behavior and child coping and distress during BMA/LP procedures: A sequential analysis. *Behavior Therapy, 20,* 585–601.

Bottos, M., Barba, B., D'Este, A., & Tronick, E. (1996). The Neurobehavioral Assessment Scale as an instrument for early long-term prognosis and intervention in major disability in high-risk infants. *Journal of Pediatric Psychology, 21,* 755–770.

Bush, J.P., & Harkins, S.W. (Eds.). (1991). *Children in pain: Clinical and research issues from a developmental perspective.* New York: Springer-Verlag.

Calkins, D., Walker, C., & Howe, A. (1994). Elimination disorders: Psychological issues. In R. Olson, L. Mullins, J. Gillman, & J. Chaney (Eds.), *Sourcebook of pediatric psychology* (pp. 46–54). Needham Heights, MA: Allyn & Bacon.

Carter, B., Bennett, D., & Urey, J. (1994). Burn injuries: Psychological issues. In R. Olson, L. Mullins, J. Gillman, & J. Chaney (Eds.), *Sourcebook of pediatric psychology* (pp. 244–256). Needham Heights, MA: Allyn & Bacon.

Chaney, J., Mullins, L., Frank, R., Peterson, L., Mace, L., Kashani, J., & Goldstein, D. (1997). Transactional patterns of child, mother, and father adjustment in insulin-dependent diabetes mellitus: A prospective study. *Journal of Pediatric Psychology, 22,* 229–244.

Chaney, J., Mullins, L., Uretsky, D., Pace, T., Werden, D., & Hartman,V. (1999). An experimental examination of learned helplessness in older adolescents and young adults with long-standing asthma. *Journal of Pediatric Psychology, 24,* 259–270.

Christiano, B., & Russ, S. (1998). Matching preparatory intervention with coping style: The effects on children's distress in the dental setting. *Journal of Pediatric Psychology, 23,* 17–28.

Dahlquist, L., Czyzewski, D., & Jones, C. (1996). Parents of children with cancer: A longitudinal study of emotional distress, coping style, and marital adjustment two and twenty months after diagnosis. *Journal of Pediatric Psychology, 21,* 541–554.

Davidson, C. (1988). Training the pediatric psychologist and the developmental behavioral pediatrician. In D. Routh (Ed.), *Handbook of pediatric psychology* (pp. 507–537). New York: Guilford Press.

Dershowitz, R., & Williamson, J. (1977). Prevention of childhood household injuries: A controlled clinical trial. *American Journal of Public Health, 67,* 1148–1153.

Domek, D. (1994). Failure to thrive: Medical issues. In R. Olson, L. Mullins, J. Gillman, & J. Chaney (Eds.), *Sourcebook of pediatric psychology* (pp. 26–28). Needham Heights, MA: Allyn & Bacon.

Drotar, D. (1993). Influences on collaborative activities among psychologists and pediatricians: Implications for practice, training, and research. *Journal of Pediatric Psychology, 18,* 159–172.

Drotar, D. (1995a). *Consulting with pediatricians: Psychological perspectives.* New York: Plenum Press.

Drotar, D. (1995b). Failure to thrive (growth deficiency). In M.C. Roberts (Ed.), *Handbook of pediatric psychology* (2nd ed., pp. 516–536). New York: Guilford Press.

Drotar, D. (1997a). Intervention research: Pushing back the frontiers of pediatric psychology. *Journal of Pediatric Psychology, 22,* 593–606.

Drotar, D. (1997b). Relating parent and family functioning to the psychological adjustment of children with chronic health conditions: What have we learned? What do we need to know? *Journal of Pediatric Psychology, 22,* 149–166.

Drotar, D. (1997c, May). *What's new in behavior diagnosis?* Paper presented at the 15th annual Conference of Developmental Behavioral Disorders and a Spectrum of Pediatric Challenges, Hilton Head, SC.

Drotar, D., Agle, D., Eckl, C., & Thompson, P. (1997). Correlates of psychological distress among mothers of children and adolescents. *Journal of Pediatric Psychology, 22,* 1–14.

Drotar, D., Malone, C.A., & Negray, J. (1980). Environmentally-based failure to thrive and children's intellectual development. *Journal of Clinical Child Psychology, 9,* 236–240.

Drotar, D., & Sturm, L. (1994). Failure to thrive: Psychological issues. In R. Olson, L. Mullins, J. Gillman, & J. Chaney (Eds.), *Sourcebook of pediatric psychology* (pp. 29–41). Needham Heights, MA: Allyn & Bacon.

Drotar, D., Sturm, L., Eckerle, D., & White, S. (1993). Pediatric psychologists' perceptions of their work settings. *Journal of Pediatric Psychology, 18,* 237–248.

Elliott, C., & Olson, R. (1983). The management of children's distress in response to painful medical treatment for burn injuries. *Behavior Research and Therapy, 21,* 675–683.

Endriga, M., & Speltz, M. (1997). Face-to-face interaction between infants with orofacial clefts and their mothers. *Journal of Pediatric Psychology, 22,* 439–454.

Finney, J. (1995). Pediatric injury control: Adding pieces to the puzzle. *Journal of Pediatric Psychology, 20,* 1–3.

Frank, D., & Zeisel, S. (1988). Failure to thrive. *Pediatric Clinics of North America, 34,* 1187–1206.

Gable, S., & Peterson, L. (1998). School-age children's attributions about their own naturally occurring minor injuries: A process analysis. *Journal of Pediatric Psychology, 23,* 323–332.

Glasgow, R., & Anderson, B. (1995). Future directions for research on pediatric chronic disease management: Lessons from diabetes. *Journal of Pediatric Psychology, 20,* 389–402.

Hains, A., Davies, W., Behrens, D., & Biller, J. (1997). Cognitive behavioral interventions for adolescents with cystic fibrosis. *Journal of Pediatric Psychology, 22,* 669–688.

Hammill, P., Drizd, T., Johnson, C., Reed, R., Roche, A., & Moore, W. (1979). Physical growth: National Center for Health Statistics percentages. *American Journal of Clinical Nutrition, 32,* 607–629.

Hoekstra-Weebers, J., Heuval, F., Jaspers, J., Kamps, W., & Klip, E. (1998). An intervention program for parents of pediatric cancer patients: A randomized controlled trial. *Journal of Pediatric Psychology, 23,* 207–214.

Holmbeck, G., Gorey-Ferguson, L., Hudson, T., Seefeldt, T., Shapera, W., Turner, T., & Uhler, J. (1997). Maternal, paternal, and marital functioning in families of preadolescents with spina bifida. *Journal of Pediatric Psychology, 22,* 167–182.

Houts, A., & Abramson, H. (1990). Assessment and treatment of functional childhood enuresis and encopresis: Toward a partnership between health psychologists and physicians. In S. Morgan & T. Okwamabua (Eds.), *Child and adolescent disorders: Developmental and health psychology perspectives* (pp. 47–103). Hillsdale, NJ: Erlbaum.

Howe, A., & Walker, C. (1992). Behavioral management of toilet-training, enuresis, and encopresis. *Pediatric Clinics of North America, 39,* 413–432.

Ireys, H., Sills, E., Kolodner, K., & Walsh, B. (1996). A social support intervention for parents of children with juvenile rheumatoid arthritis: Results of a randomized trial. *Journal of Pediatric Psychology, 21,* 633–642.

Jay, S., Elliott, C., Fitzgibbons, I., Woody, P., & Siegel, S. (1995). A comparative study of cognitive-behavioral therapy versus general anesthesia for painful medical procedures in children. *Pain, 62,* 3–9.

Jay, S., Elliott, C., Katz, E., & Siegel, S. (1987). Cognitive-behavioral and pharmacological interventions for children's distress during painful medical procedures. *Journal of Consulting and Clinical Psychology, 55,* 860–865.

Jay, S., Ozolins, M., Elliott, C., & Caldwell, S. (1983). Assessment of children's distress during painful medical procedures. *Health Psychology, 2,* 133–147.

Jelalian, E., Spirito, A., Rasile, D., Vinnick, L., Rohrback, C., & Arrigan, M. (1997). Risk-taking, reported injury, and perception of future injury among adolescents. *Journal of Pediatric Psychology, 22,* 513–531.

Jellinek, M. (1997). *DSM-PC:* Bridging pediatric primary care and mental health services. *Developmental and Behavioral Pediatrics, 18,* 173–174.

Johnson, C., & Bobbitt, R. (1993). Antecedent manipulation in the case of primary solid food refusal. *Behavior Modification, 17,* 510–521.

Kagan, J. (1965). The new marriage: Pediatrics and psychology. *American Journal of Diseases of Children, 110,* 272–278.

Karoly, P. (1991). Assessment of pediatric pain. In J. Bush & S. Harkins (Eds.), *Children in pain: Clinical and research issues from a developmental perspective* (pp. 59–82). New York: Springer-Verlag.

Kaslow, N., Collins, M., Loundy, M., Brown, F., Hollins, L., & Eckman, J. (1997). Empirically validated family interventions for pediatric psychology: Sickle cell disease as an exemplar. *Journal of Pediatric Psychology, 22,* 213–228.

Katz, E., Kellerman, J., & Siegel, S. (1980). Distress behavior in children with cancer undergoing medical procedures: Developmental considerations. *Journal of Consulting and Clinical Psychology, 48,* 356–365.

Katz, K.S., Dubowitz, L.M.S., Henderson, S., Jongmans, M., Kay, G.G., Nolte, C.A., & de Vries, L.C. (1996). Effects of cerebral lesions on continuous test responses of school age children born prematurely. *Journal of Pediatric Psychology, 21,* 841–856.

Kazak, A. (1989). Families of chronically ill children: A systems and social-ecological model of adaptation and challenge. *Journal of Consulting and Clinical Psychology, 57,* 25–30.

Kazak, A. (1997). A contextual family/systems approach to pediatric psychology: Introduction to the special issue. *Journal of Pediatric Psychology, 22,* 141–148.

Kibby, M., Tyc, V., & Mulhern, R. (1998). Effectiveness of psychological intervention for children and adolescents with chronic medical illness: A meta-analyses. *Clinical Psychology Review, 18,* 103–117.

Kliewer, W., & Lewis, H. (1995). Family influences on coping processes in children and adolescents with sickle cell disease. *Journal of Pediatric Psychology, 20,* 511–526.

Koocher, G., & Keith-Spiegal, P. (1990). *Children, ethics, and the law.* Lincoln: University of Nebraska Press.

Koocher, G., Sourkes, B., & Keane, W. (1979). Pediatric oncology consultation: A generalizable model for medical settings. *Professional Psychology, 10,* 467–474.

Kovacs, M., Iyengar, S., Goldston, D., Obrosky, D., Marsh, J., & Stewart, J. (1990). Psychological functioning of children with insulin-dependent diabetes mellitus: A longitudinal study. *Journal of Pediatric Psychology, 15,* 619–632.

Kovacs, M., Iyengar, S., Goldston, D., Obrosky, D., Stewart, J., & Marsh, J. (1990). Psychological functioning among mothers of children with insulin-dependent diabetes mellitus: A longitudinal study. *Journal of Consulting and Clinical Psychology, 58,* 189–195.

La Greca, A. (1997). Reflections and perspectives on pediatric psychology: Editor's vale dictum. *Journal of Pediatric Psychology, 22,* 759–770.

La Greca, A., & Hughes, J. (1999). United we stand, divided we fall: The education and training of clinical child psychologists. *Journal of Clinical Child Psychology, 28,* 435–447.

La Greca, A., Stone, W., Drotar, D., & Maddux, J. (1988). Training in pediatric psychology: Survey results and recommendations. *Journal of Pediatric Psychology, 13,* 121–139.

La Greca, A., Stone, W., & Swales, T. (1989). Pediatric psychology training: An analysis of graduate, internship, and postdoctoral prognosis. *Journal of Pediatric Psychology, 14,* 103–116.

La Greca, A., & Varni, J. (1993). Editorial: Intervention in pediatric psychology: A look toward the future. *Journal of Pediatric Psychology, 18,* 667–679.

LaPuma, J., & Scheidermayer, D. (1991). Ethics consultation: Skills, roles, and training. *Annals of Internal Medicine, 114,* 156–160.

Lewis, H., & Kliewer, W. (1996). Hope, coping, and adjustment among children with sickle cell disease: Tests of mediator and moderator models. *Journal of Pediatric Psychology, 21,* 25–42.

Linscheid, T. (1992). Eating problems in children. In C.E. Walker & M.C. Roberts (Eds.), *Handbook of clinical child psychology* (2nd ed., pp. 451–473). New York: Wiley.

Linscheid, T., Budd, K., & Rasnake, L. (1995). Pediatric feeding disorders. In M.C. Roberts (Ed.), *Handbook of pediatric psychology* (2nd ed., pp. 501–515). New York: Guilford Press.

Linscheid, T., & Rasnake, L. (1985). Behavioral approaches to the treatment of failure-to-thrive. In D. Drotar (Ed.), *New directions in failure-to-thrive: Implications for research and practice* (pp. 279–294). New York: Plenum Press.

Linscheid, T., Tarnowski, K., Rasnake, L., & Brams, J. (1987). Behavioral treatment of food refusal in a child with short-gut syndrome. *Journal of Pediatric Psychology, 12,* 451–460.

Lloyd, B., Wheldall, K., & Perks, D. (1988). Controlled study of intelligence and school performance of very low birthweight children from a defined geographical area. *Developmental Medicine and Child Neurology, 30,* 36–42.

Luiselli, J., & Gleason, D. (1987). Combining sensory reinforcement and texture fading procedures to overcome chronic food refusal. *Journal of Behavior Therapy and Experimental Psychology, 18,* 149–155.

Lustig, J.L., Iveys, H.T., Sills, E.M., & Walsh, B.B. (1996). Mental health of mothers of children with juvenile rheumatoid arthritis: Appraisal as a mediator. *Journal of Pediatric Psychology, 21*(5), 719–733.

Manne, S., Bakeman, R., Jacobson, P., Gorfinkle, K., & Redd, W. (1994). An analysis of a behavioral intervention for children undergoing venipuncture. *Health Psychology, 13,* 556–566.

Manne, S., Lesanics, D., Meyers, P., Wollner, N., Steinherz, P., & Redd, W. (1995). Predictors of depressive symptomatology among parents of newly diagnosed children with cancer. *Journal of Pediatric Psychology, 20,* 491–510.

Manne, S., & Miller, P. (1998). Social support, social conflict, and adjustment among adolescents with cancer. *Journal of Pediatric Psychology, 23,* 121–130.

McGrath, P.A. (1990). *Pain in children: Nature, assessment, and treatment.* New York: Guilford Press.

Melton, G., & Ehrenreich, N. (1992). Ethical and legal issues in mental health for children. In C.E. Walker & M.C. Roberts (Eds.), *Handbook of clinical child psychology* (pp. 1035–1056). New York: Wiley.

Miller, B.D., & Wood, B.L. (1994). Psychophysiologic reactivity on asthematic children: A cholmergically mediated confluence of pathways. *Journal of the American Academy of Child and Adolescent Psychiatry, 33*(9), 1236–1245.

Miller, B.D., & Wood, B.L. (1997). Influence of specific emotional states on autonomic reactivity and pulmonary function on asthematic children. *Journal of the Academy of Child and Adolescent Psychiatry, 36,* 669–677.

Morrongielo, B. (1997). Children's perspectives on injuries and close call experiences: Sex differences in injury-outcome process. *Journal of Pediatric Psychology, 22,* 499–512.

Mullins, L., Chaney, J., Hartman, V., Olson, R., Youll, L., Reyes, S., & Blackett, P. (1995). Child and maternal adaptation to cystic fibrosis and insulin-dependent diabetes mellitus: Differential patterns across disease states. *Journal of Pediatric Psychology, 20,* 173–186.

Mullins, L., Chaney, J., Pace, T., & Hartman, V. (1997). Illness uncertainty, attributional style, and psychological adjustment in older adolescents and young adults with asthma. *Journal of Pediatric Psychology, 22,* 871–880.

Mullins, L., Gillman, J., & Harbeck, C. (1991). Multiple level interventions in pediatric settings: A behavioral-systems perspective. In A. La Greca, L. Siegel, J. Wallander, & C.E. Walker (Eds.), *Stress and coping in child health* (pp. 377–399). New York: Guilford Press.

Mullins, L., Harbeck-Weber, C., Olson, R., & Hartman, V. (1996). Systems theory orientation and clinical practice: A survey of pediatric psychologists. *Journal of Pediatric Psychology, 21,* 577–582.

Noll, R., McKellop, M., Vannatta, K., & Kalinyak, K. (1998). Child-rearing practices of primary caregivers of children with sickle cell disease: The perspective of professionals and caregivers. *Journal of Pediatric Psychology, 23,* 131–140.

Northam, E., Anderson, P., Adler, R., Werther, G., & Warne, G. (1996). Psychosocial and family functioning in children with insulin-dependent diabetes at diagnosis and one year later. *Journal of Pediatric Psychology, 21,* 699–718.

Nowicki, P. (1994). Neonatal problems: Medical issues. In R. Olson, L. Mullins, J. Gillman, & J. Chaney (Eds.), *Sourcebook of pediatric psychology* (pp. 11–16). Needham Heights, MA: Allyn & Bacon.

O'Brien, M., Soliday, E., & McCluskey-Fawcett, K. (1995). Prematurity and the neonatal intensive care unit. In M.C. Roberts (Ed.), *Handbook of pediatric psychology* (2nd ed., pp. 463–478). New York: Guilford Press.

O'Byrne, K., Peterson, L., & Saldana, L. (1997). Survey of pediatric hospitals' preparation programs: Evidence of the impact of health psychology research. *Health Psychology, 16,* 147–154.

Olson, R., Mullins, L., Chaney, J., & Gillman, J. (1994). The role of the pediatric psychologist in a consultation/liaison service. In R. Olson, L. Mullins, J. Gillman, & J. Chaney (Eds.), *Sourcebook of pediatric psychology* (pp. 1–8). Needham Heights, MA: Allyn & Bacon.

Olson, R., Mullins, L., Gillman, J., & Chaney, J. (Eds.). (1994). *Sourcebook of pediatric psychology.* Needham Heights, MA: Allyn & Bacon.

Overstreet, S., Goins, J., Chen, R., Holmes, C., Breer, T., Dunlap, W., & Frentz, J. (1995). Family environment and the interrelation of family structure, child behavior, and metabolic control for children with diabetes. *Journal of Pediatric Psychology, 20,* 435–448.

Parsons, J., Butler, R., Kocik, S., Norman, L., Nuss, R., and the Adolescent Hemophilia Behavioral Intervention Evaluation Projects (AHIEP) Study Group. (1998). The role of the family system in HIV risk reduction: Youth with hemophilia and HIV infection and their parents. *Journal of Pediatric Psychology, 23,* 57–66.

Perrin, J.M., & MacLean, W.E. (1988). Biomedical and psychosocial dimensions of chronic illness in childhood. In P. Karoly (Ed.), *Handbook of child health assessment: Biopsychosocial perspectives* (pp. 11–29). New York: Wiley.

Peterson, L., & Harbeck, C. (1988). *The pediatric psychologist: Issues in professional development and practice.* Champaign, IL: Research Press.

Peterson, L., & Oliver, K. (1995). Prevention of injuries and disease. In M.C. Roberts (Ed.), *Handbook of pediatric psychology* (2nd ed., pp. 185–199). New York: Guilford Press.

Peyrot, M. (1996). Causal analysis: Theory and application. *Journal of Pediatric Psychology, 21,* 3–24.

Potts, R., Martinez, I., & Dedmon, A. (1995). Childhood risk-taking and injury: Self-report and informant measures. *Journal of Pediatric Psychology, 20,* 5–12.

Potts, R., & Swisher, L. (1998). Effects of televised safety models on children's risk-taking and hazard identification. *Journal of Pediatric Psychology, 23,* 157–164.

Pruitt, S., & Elliot, C. (1992). Pediatric psychology: Current issues and developments. In C.E. Walker & M.C. Roberts (Eds.), *Handbook of clinical child psychology* (pp. 859–872). New York: Wiley.

Rae, W., & Worchel, F. (1991). Ethical beliefs and behaviors of pediatric psychologists: A survey. *Journal of Pediatric Psychology, 16,* 727–745.

Rae, W., Worchel, F., & Brunnquell, D. (1995). Ethical and legal issues in pediatric psychology. In M.C. Roberts (Ed.), *Handbook of pediatric psychology* (2nd ed., pp. 19–36). New York: Guilford Press.

Resnick, R., & Kruczek, T. (1996). Pediatric consultation: New concepts in training. *Professional Psychology: Research and Practice, 27,* 194–197.

Rietveld, S., Kolk, A., & Prins, P. (1996). The influence of lung function information on self-reports of dyspnea by children with asthma. *Journal of Pediatric Psychology, 21,* 367–378.

Roberts, M. (1986). *Pediatric psychology: Psychological interventions and strategies for pediatric problems.* Elmford, NY: Pergamon Press.

Roberts, M., Carlson, C., Erickson, M., Friedman, R., La Greca, A., Lemanek, K., Russ, S., Schroeder, C., Vargas, L., & Wohlford, P. (1998). A model for training psychologists to provide services for children and adolescents. *Professional Psychology: Research and Practice, 29,* 293–299.

Roberts, M., La Greca, A., & Harper, D. (1988). Journal of Pediatric Psychology: Another stage of development. *Journal of Pediatric Psychology, 13,* 1–5.

Roberts, M., & McNeal, R. (1995). Historical and conceptual foundations of pediatric psychology. In M. Roberts (Ed.), *Handbook of pediatric psychology* (2nd ed., pp. 3–18) New York: Guilford Press.

Roberts, M., McNeal, R., Randall, C., & Roberts, J. (1996). A necessary reemphasis on integrating explicative research with the pragmatics of pediatric psychology. *Journal of Pediatric Psychology, 21,* 107–114.

Roberts, M.C. (Ed.). (1995). *Handbook of pediatric psychology* (2nd ed.). New York: Guilford Press.

Rodriguez, J.G. (1990). Childhood injuries in the United States: A priority issue. *American Journal of Diseases of Children, 144,* 625–626.

Ross, D., & Ross, S. (1988). *Childhood pain: Current issues, research and management.* Baltimore: Urban and Schwarzenberg.

Routh, D. (1997). Injury control research in pediatric psychology: A commentary and proposal. *Journal of Pediatric Psychology, 22* 495–498.

Schaefer, A., & Call, J. (1994). Legal and ethical issues. In R. Olson, L. Mullins, J. Gillman, & J. Chaney (Eds.), *Sourcebook of pediatric psychology* (pp. 405–413). Needham Heights, MA: Allyn & Bacon.

Sheeran, T., Marvin, R., & Pianta, R. (1997). Mothers' resolution of their child's diagnosis and self-reported measures of parenting stress, marital relations, and social support. *Journal of Pediatric Psychology, 22,* 197–212.

Silver, E., Stein, R., & Dadds, M. (1996). Moderating effects of family structure on the relationships between physical and mental health in urban children with chronic illness. *Journal of Pediatric Psychology, 21,* 43–56.

Silver, E., Westbrook, L., & Stein, R. (1998). Relationship of psychological distress to consequences of chronic health conditions in children. *Journal of Pediatric Psychology, 23,* 5–16.

Stark, L., Bowen, A., Tyc, V., Evans, S., & Passero, M. (1990). A behavioral approach to increasing calorie consumption in children with cystic fibrosis. *Journal of Pediatric Psychology, 15,* 309–326.

Stark, L.J., Knapp, L.G., Bowen, A.M., Powers, S.W., Jelalian, E., Evans, S., Passero, M.A., Mulvihill, M.M., & Hovell, M. (1993). Increasing calorie consumption in children with cystic fibrosis: Replication with a 2-year follow-up. *Journal of Applied Behavior Analysis, 26,* 435–450.

Sturm, L., Drotar, D., Laing, K., & Zimet, G. (1997). Mothers' beliefs about the causes of infant growth deficiency: Is there attributional bias? *Journal of Pediatric Psychology, 22,* 329–344.

Thompson, R.J., Jr., Gil, K.M., Burbach, D.J., Keith, B., & Kinney, T.R. (1993). The role of child and maternal processes in the psychological adjustment of children with sickle cell disease. *Journal of Consulting and Clinical Psychology, 61,* 468–474.

Thompson, R.J., Jr., Gil, K.M., Keith, B.R., Gustafson, K.E., George, L.K., & Kinney, T.R. (1994). Psychological adjustment of children with sickle cell disease: Stability and change over a ten-month period. *Journal of Consulting and Clinical Psychology, 62,* 856–860.

Thompson, R.J., Jr., & Gustafson, K.E. (1996). *Adaptation to chronic childhood illness.* Washington, DC: American Psychological Association.

Thompson, R.J., Jr., Gustafson, K.E., George, L.K., & Spock, A. (1994). Change over on 12-month period in the psychological adjustment of adolescents with cystic fibrosis. *Journal of Pediatric Psychology, 19,* 189–204.

Thompson, R.J., Jr., Gustafson, K.E., Hamlett, K.W., & Spock, A. (1992). Psycological adjustment of children with cystic fibrosis: The role of child cognitive processes and material adjustment. *Journal of Pediatric Psychology, 17,* 741–755.

Timko, C., Stovel, K., & Moos, R. (1992). Functioning of mothers and fathers of children with juvenile rheumatic disease: A longitudinal study. *Journal of Pediatric Psychology, 17,* 705–724.

Tuma, J. (1987). *Directory of internship programs in clinical child and pediatric psychology.* Baton Rouge, LA: Author.

Turk, D., Meichenbaum, D., & Genest, M. (1983). *Pain and behavioral medicine: A cognitive-behavioral perspective.* New York: Guilford Press.

Varni, J., Blount, R., Waldron, S., & Smith, A. (1995). Management of pain and distress. In M.C. Roberts (Ed.), *Handbook of pediatric psychology* (2nd ed., pp. 105–123). New York: Guilford Press.

Varni, J., Rapoff, M., & Waldron, S. (1994). Juvenile rheumatoid arthritis: Psychological issues. In R. Olson, L. Mullins, J. Gillman, & J. Chaney (Eds.), *Sourcebook of pediatric psychology* (pp. 75–89). Needham Heights, MA: Allyn & Bacon.

Varni, J., & Thompson, K. (1985) *The Varni/Thompson Pediatric Pain Questionnaire.* Unpublished manuscript.

Walker, C.E. (1979). Behavioral intervention in a pediatric setting. In J. McNamara (Ed.), *Behavioral approaches to medicine: Application and analyses* (pp. 227–266). New York: Plenum Press.

Walker, C.E. (1995). Elimination disorders: Enuresis and encopresis. In M.C. Roberts (Ed.), *Handbook of pediatric psychology* (2nd ed., pp. 537–557). New York: Guilford Press.

Wallander, J., & Venters, T. (1995). Perceived role restriction and adjustment of mothers of children with chronic physical disability. *Journal of Pediatric Psychology, 20,* 619–632.

Wallander, J.L., Varni, J.W., Babari, L.V., Baris, H.T., & Wilcox, K.T. (1989). Family resources as resistive factors for psychological maladjustment in chronically ill and handicapped children. *Journal of Pediatric Psychology, 14,* 157–173.

Wolraich, M. (1997). Diagnostic and statistical manual for primary care *(DSM-PC)* child and adolescent version: Design, intent, and hopes for the future. *Developmental and Behavioral Pediatrics, 18,* 171–172.

Wolraich, M., Felice, M., & Drotar, D. (1996). *The classification of child and adolescent mental diagnosis in primary care: Diagnostic and Statistical manual for Primary Care (DSM-PC) child and adolescent version.* Elk Grove Village, IL: American Academy of Pediatrics.

Wood, B.L. (1993). Beyond the "psychosomatic family": A biobehavioral family model of pediatric illness. *Family Process, 32*(3), 261–278.

Wood, B.L. (1995). A developmental biopsychosocial approach to the treatment of chronic illness in children and adolescents. In R.H. Mikesell & D.D. Lusterman (Eds.), *Integrating family therapy: Handbook of family psychology and systems theory* (pp. 437–455). Washington, DC: American Psychological Association.

Wood, B.L., Watkins, J.B., Boyle, J.T., Nogueira, J., Zimand, E., & Carroll, L. (1989). The "psychosomatic family" model: An empirical and theoretical analysis. *Family Process, 28*(4), 399–417.

Wright, L. (1967). The pediatric psychologist: A role model. *American Psychologist, 22,* 323–325.

Wurtele, S.K. (1995). Health promotion. In M.C. Roberts (Ed.), *Handbook of pediatric psychology* (2nd ed., pp. 200–218). New York: Guilford Press.

Wysocki, T., Harris, M., Greco, P., Harvey, L., McDonell, K., Danda, C., Bubb, J., & White, N. (1997). Social validity of support group and behavior therapy interventions for families of adolescents with insulin-dependent diabetes mellitus. *Journal of Pediatric Psychology, 22,* 635–650.

CHAPTER 47

Pharmacotherapy

ALAIN KATIC AND RONALD J. STEINGARD

T he birth of child psychopharmacology is generally considered to have begun with Charles Bradley's report in 1937 on the effects of amphetamine sulfate (Benzedrine) on various behavioral disturbances in 30 children age 5 to 14 years. Although significant progress has transpired from the past 25 years of research, the field of pediatric psychopharmacology continues to lag behind advances in adult psychopharmacology. A number of factors probably account for this lag. In addition to ongoing concerns about the safety and efficacy of psychotropic agents in children, the acceptance of the fact that children can suffer from the same disorders as adults is still an issue debated in the field. Furthermore, until recently, funding for controlled trials of psychotropic medications in children and adolescents has been severely limited. In spite of these limitations, the introduction of more psychiatric medications and research showing their efficacy for a variety of disorders has resulted in psychopharmacology's becoming a more widely accepted component of the treatment of psychiatric conditions in children.

This chapter covers the major classes of medications currently used in child psychopharmacology as well as the diagnostic categories for which there is research and clinical experience indicating pharmacologic efficacy in treating these disorders.

SPECIAL ISSUES IN PEDIATRIC PSYCHOPHARMACOLOGY

Whereas many aspects of the practice of pediatric psychopharmacology mirror the practice with adults, treating children and adolescents requires attention to key differences. The most salient differences relate to the significant developmental variability that exists within this population and the developmental differences that exist between children and adults.

Differences in height, body weight, and pubertal status are the most obvious examples of variability within this population. A more important concern, especially regarding the assessment and treatment of psychiatric illness, is the marked variability in emotional and cognitive development. A typical 6-year-old is not only smaller than most 18-year-olds, but has had less time to develop coping skills that would allow the child to handle adversity, such as psychiatric illness or psychosocial stress. This developmental "immaturity" may adversely affect the child's ability to respond rapidly to treatment interventions, prolonging the duration of his or her illness.

Cognitive differences between adults and children, such as the ability to sequence events temporally, may impede the pediatric clinician's ability to elicit accurate histories from children with regard to the exact nature of their perceived affect, the sequencing of symptom onset, and the duration of symptoms. Thus, the pediatric clinician is much more dependant on the behavioral observations of parents, teachers, and other caretakers in making an initial diagnosis.

Developmental variability will also impact decisions regarding dosing and frequency of dosing. Children metabolize medications more efficiently than adults. Therefore, children are typically given higher mg/kg doses of medication and may require more frequent doses.

Additionally, children and adolescents are more dependent on the systems in which they live. The management of their medications always includes other parties, such as parents, schools, day-care centers, and pediatricians, who will need to be informed about the indications, potential benefits, and potential risks of the proposed trial. Furthermore, children and adolescents cannot provide consent for medication trials. The decision-making process for a psychopharmacological intervention always includes at least one other party, such as a parent or legal guardian.

Finally, most of the current interventions for children have not yet been approved by the Food and Drug Administration (FDA). The FDA allows for "off-label" use: "If the course of the disease and the effects of the drug are sufficiently similar in the pediatric and adult populations, then the adult experience can be used to guide use in the pediatric population" (FDA, 1995). The informed consent process for children and adolescents needs to address the fact that most drugs used in pediatric psychopharmacology are not FDA-approved for use in children.

TREATMENT STRATEGIES IN PEDIATRIC PSYCHOPHARMACOLOGY

Initiating treatment with pediatric patients begins with a comprehensive evaluation of the child's world. A thorough evaluation includes not only an assessment of the child, but a careful review of behavior and interactions with peers, teachers, and other caretakers. Treatment is typically multimodal in nature and attempts to not only ameliorate the primary symptoms of the existing psychiatric

disorder, but also to provide remediation in areas of dysfunction that have accrued as a result of being ill. For example, depressed children develop problems in almost all areas of psychosocial functioning. This dysfunction often persists after the index episode of depression has abated. Therefore, in addition to pharmacotherapy, remedial help may be needed in the development of age-appropriate social skills, family-centered behavioral interventions may be required to reduce difficulties in familial functioning, and educational assistance may be needed to help the child return to grade-level performance.

When pharmacotherapy is recommended, the parent's (or legal guardian's) consent to treatment needs to be obtained. In addition, the purpose of the medication should be carefully explained to the child and the child's assent obtained if at all possible. The informed consent process typically requires extensive education and support and can be the cornerstone to the development of an adequate treatment alliance with the family. This process needs to be an open discussion among patient, parents, and physician. The clinician must be compassionate to the fact that the parents are making a decision to medicate their child, not themselves, and that this can be a difficult process. The educational phase of the intervention also involves communication with pediatricians and schools. Once a treatment is devised, medications are usually initiated at low doses to attempt to mitigate against treatment-emergent side effects. This is critical in maintaining a treatment alliance with parents, and the clinician should allow for frequent phone contact and office visits during this phase of treatment.

ATTENTION-DEFICIT/HYPERACTIVITY DISORDER (ADHD)

The diagnosis of ADHD is a clinical diagnosis that should take several important factors into account, including persistence of symptoms, pervasiveness of symptoms across environments, and functional impairment. Although there is no specific test for ADHD, there are multiple sources of information that can assist in making the diagnosis, including parent and child interviews, school reports, behavioral rating scales, cognitive testing, and physical/neurological evaluation.

ADHD is the most common child psychiatric disorder, with a prevalence in the pediatric population of 3% to 5% and a 4:1 ratio of boys to girls (Popper & Steingard, 1994). Thus, ADHD is one of the more frequent reasons for referral to a child psychiatrist. Studies have shown that ADHD persists even into adulthood (Gittelman, Mannuzza, Shenker, & Bonagura, 1985; Mannuzza, Klein, Bessler, Malloy, & LaPadula, 1993; Mannuzza et al., 1991). Comorbidity is a significant concern in ADHD, as up to two-thirds of children with the disorder carry a comorbid diagnosis. Common comorbid conditions include conduct disorder, oppositional defiant disorder, mood disorders, anxiety disorders, Tourette's syndrome or chronic tics, and learning disorders.

Stimulants

The most commonly prescribed drugs for the treatment of ADHD are the stimulants, with up to 75% to 80% of children responding positively to one of these agents. If a child fails to respond to one agent, a trial of a different stimulant is indicated, as children can respond positively to a second stimulant medication. The same holds true for side effects. Even though stimulants share side effect profiles, children may respond better to one drug than another. Stimulant medications include methylphenidate, dextroamphetamine, and magnesium pemoline as well as adderall, a newer stimulant combination of four amphetamine salts (d-amphetamine saccharate, d-amphetamine sulfate, d,l-amphetamine sulfate, and d,l-amphetamine aspartate).

Stimulants all share a basic mechanism of action: They increase release of dopamine and norepinephrine at presynaptic terminals, and they are metabolized by the liver with subsequent renal excretion. Although pharmacokinetics varies among these agents and among individuals, they are short-acting compounds. Peak plasma levels of methylphenidate and dextroamphetamine occur within one hour of administration, with clinical effect lasting approximately three to five hours depending on individual metabolism. Both agents also come in "slow release" forms, which delay the onset of action to one hour and add possibly one to two hours of clinical effect over the regular forms of these drugs. Thus, multiple daily dosing of these agents is required to maintain peak clinical effect. Because of the short half-life of stimulants, they should be given in divided doses two or three times a day, usually four hours apart. One must attempt to obtain a detailed history of clinical response to these agents to maximize efficacy by appropriately

spacing dosing intervals, rather than by simply increasing individual milligram dosages. The total daily dose is generally 0.3 to 2 mg/kg/day depending on the agent used. In general, starting doses are 2.5 to 5 mg twice a day (morning and noon), with subsequent dose titrations of 2.5 to 5 mg per dose occurring every five to seven days depending on clinical response. Three-times-a-day dosing is sometimes necessary to cover symptoms into the early evening hours. Stimulants should be administered on a seven-days/week basis unless the family feels comfortable handling untreated ADHD symptoms over weekends.

There are over 152 controlled studies of stimulants in children and adolescents reporting positive response rates of up to 70%. With the recent addition of adderall, Swanson et al. (1998) reported the first double-blind crossover study of this agent in 30 children with ADHD evaluating the time course of adderall, methylphenidate, and placebo. Adderall and methylphenidate both resulted in improvement of ADHD symptomatology. No distinction was made between the efficacy of methylphenidate and that of adderall. However, it was noted that adderall produced a dose-related improvement in behavioral measures as well as a dose-dependent duration of action with an average of 6.4 hours for a 20 mg dose. Thus, given the significant number of studies reporting stimulant efficacy, these agents are the first-line treatment for ADHD.

Pemoline has been purported to have a clinical efficacy of up to 24 hours. In more recent studies by Pelham, Swanson, Furman, and Schwindt (1995), however, its kinetics have actually been shown to be approximately 8 to 10 hours with peak onset within two hours. The typical starting dose for pemoline is 18.75 to 37.5 mg per day, with increments of 18.75 mg occurring every few days thereafter, depending on clinical response. It should also be noted that as recently as January 1997, the manufacturer of pemoline released a drug alert reporting 13 cases of drug-induced hepatitis occurring with pemoline administration since its release in 1975. Of these 13 cases, 11 resulted in either death or liver transplantation. Thus, pemoline should not be used as a first-line agent for the treatment of ADHD, and when used, this should be done with caution and active monitoring of liver function tests.

Common side effects associated with stimulant use include appetite suppression, upset stomach, headaches, and possible sleep disturbance. Weight should be closely monitored and, if weight loss is significant, dietary caloric increases should be initiated. If nutritional changes do not promote adequate weight gain, consideration should be given to lowering stimulant dosage or instituting "drug holidays." Finally, although sleep disturbances, consisting of delayed sleep initiation, are reported to occur with these agents, recent studies looking specifically at this issue suggest that this is not a clinically significant side effect (Kent, Blader, Koplewicz, Abikoff, & Foley, 1995; Stein et al., 1996; Tirosh, Sadeh, Munvez, & Lavie, 1993).

Less commonly reported side effects include mood disturbance, psychosis, and onset of motor and/or vocal tics. Mood disturbances can include symptoms such as general irritability, tearfulness, and even full-blown major depressive symptoms (D. Klein, Gittelman, Quitkin, & Rifkin, 1980). A toxic psychosis can occur with administration of stimulants, particularly at higher dosages or when rapid titration is pursued.

The precipitation of motor/vocal tics with stimulants has been reported extensively in the literature. Current research shows that stimulant-induced tics occur with greater frequency in individuals with a family history of tic disorders, and that tics generally, but not always, subside with cessation of stimulant treatment. A recent report by Gadow, Nolan, Sprafkin, and Sverd (1995) examined the use of stimulants in children who had a preexisting history of tics and found that the tics continued but did not increase in frequency or severity either acutely or with continued drug treatment. Castellanos et al. (1997) reported similar results in a double-blind crossover study of 20 subjects with ADHD and comorbid Tourette's. High dosages of methylphenidate and dexedrine resulted in increases in tics, which were sustained with dexedrine but attenuated with methylphenidate. Fourteen of 20 subjects continued on stimulants for one to three years, with improvement in ADHD symptoms and acceptable effects on tics. Consideration of ongoing treatment in the face of tic precipitation should occur in the greater context of assessing clinical improvement and whether drug therapy is deemed necessary to maintain such improvement, as well as reviewing other treatment options.

Alpha-2 Agonists

More recent studies have shown the alpha-2 agonists clonidine and guanfacine to be effective in treating ADHD symptoms. The alpha agonists act on presynaptic alpha-2 adrenoreceptors, resulting in decreased release of noradrenaline into the synaptic cleft. It has been postulated, based on animal models, that the alpha-2-agonists may enhance inhibitory circuits in the prefrontal cortex as well as decrease spontaneous firing in the locus coeruleus (LC), thereby enhancing responses to relevant stimuli (Arnsten, Steere, & Hunt, 1996). This effect is believed to potentially contribute to improved attention and decreased motor hyperactivity.

Clonidine (Catapres). Clonidine is well absorbed from the GI tract and peak plasma levels occur in one to three hours, with a half-life of 6 to 20 hours. The most common side effect is sedation, which tends to diminish with continued use. It is prudent to initiate treatment with as low a dose as possible to minimize this effect. Other common side effects include dry mouth, dizziness, nausea, constipation, and potential hypotension. There are no firm guidelines for dosing of clonidine in children. Typical starting doses are 0.025 mg twice a day or three times a day, with subsequent increases of 0.05 mg/day in divided doses every three to five days. Various studies have used final total dose ranges of 2 to 10 mcg/kg/day. As individual doses increase, it is common to go to a four times a day dosing schedule. Blood pressure and pulse should be monitored regularly, particularly with dosing increases, though hypotension is frequently not clinically significant. Cessation of drug treatment with clonidine should be done in a gradual taper to avoid any potential for rebound hypertension, though this too is uncommon.

Among the studies of clonidine in ADHD treatment, Hunt, Menderaa, and Cohen (1985) conducted a double-blind placebo-controlled crossover study in 12 children with dosages of 4 to 5 mcg/kg/day. Statistically significant improvements were seen for the group as a whole, with the best responders being those children with overactivity and impulsivity.

Guanfacine (Tenex). Guanfacine is readily absorbed from the GI tract, and peak plasma levels occur in one to four hours. Half-life ranges from 10 to 30 hours (average 17 hours); in younger patients, guanfacine tends to have a shorter half-life of 13 to 14 hours. Although guanfacine is felt to have less propensity to cause sedation than clonidine, sedation is a common side effect, as are dry mouth, dizziness, and constipation. Adverse effects tend to diminish with continued usage. Again there are no firm guidelines for dosing of guanfacine. Typical starting doses are 0.25 to 0.5 mg twice a day, with subsequent increases of 0.5 mg/day every three to five days. In studies thus far, final total dosages have ranged from 0.5 to 3.5 mg/day. The manufacturer does not recommend doses above 3 mg/day, as there is no evidence of increased efficacy (in adults treated for hypertension). Blood pressure and pulse should be monitored regularly, particularly with dose increases. Cessation of guanfacine should occur in a gradual taper fashion to avoid the potential risk of rebound hypertension.

Guanfacine has been studied in the treatment of ADHD. Hunt, Arnsten, and Asbell (1995) reported on an open trial of guanfacine in 13 subjects diagnosed with ADHD. Mean optimal dose was 3.5 mg/day in four divided doses. Conner's Parent Rating Scale scores after one month of treatment showed significant improvement in factor scores of hyperactivity, inattention, and immaturity. Side effects included fatigue, headaches, and stomach aches, which resolved in two weeks. Chapell et al. (1995) reported an open study of 10 subjects diagnosed with ADHD and Tourette's syndrome. Three subjects had moderate improvement on the 48-item Conner's Parent Rating Scale and one subject had marked improvement. The analysis of the group as a whole did not show significant improvement in ADHD symptoms. Group results for tics showed decreased severity of tics in ratings by clinicians and patients.

Other Agents
Other pharmacologic agents used in the treatment of ADHD include the tricyclic antidepressants (TCAs), bupropion, and occasionally mood stabilizers. The TCAs are well studied and have been shown to be effective in up to 60% to 70% of children with ADHD (Biederman, Baldessarini, Wright, Knee, & Harmatz, 1989; Garfinkel, Wender, Sloman, & O'Neill, 1983; Rapoport, Quinn, Bradbard, Riddle, & Brooks, 1974; Saul, 1985; Wilens, Biederman, Geist, Steingard, & Spencer, 1993). TCA use is limited by concerns about cardiac side effects, particularly cardiac arrhythmias, and the possibility of sudden death (TCAs are covered in more detail under depression).

Barrickman et al. (1995) reported on the first study to compare bupropion to methylphenidate in the treatment of ADHD. Bupropion was found to be effective in reducing ADHD symptoms using a number of rating scales. There was no significant difference between methylphenidate and bupropion in

overall efficacy, but results of nearly all the rating scales showed trends in favor of methylphenidate. Other studies have reported bupropion's efficacy in comparison to placebo (Casat, Pleasants, & Van Wyck Fleet, 1987; Simeon, Ferguson, & Van Wyck Fleet, 1986).

There have been few studies examining the efficacy of mood stabilizers such as lithium and carbamazepine in treating children with ADHD. Symptoms of ADHD did not improve in a three-month controlled trial of lithium in nine children with ADHD (Greenhill, Rieder, Wender, Bushbaum, & Zahn, 1973). A recent review and meta-analysis by Silva, Munoz, and Alpert (1996) of carbamazepine in treating ADHD symptoms found three double-blind studies where carbamazepine was significantly more effective than placebo in controlling target symptoms (Silva et al., 1996).

There has also been recent research in novel pharmacologic approaches to treatment of pediatric ADHD, including the use of newer antidepressants, such as venlafaxine, and even anxiolytics, such as buspirone. Olvera, Pliszka, Luh, and Tatum (1996) reported a five-week open-label study of venlafaxine in 16 children age 8 to 17 with ADHD diagnosis and comorbid conduct disorder, oppositional defiant disorder, or anxiety disorders. Low dosages (mean daily dose of 60mg/day) resulted in improvement in 7 out of 16 subjects with a decrease of at least one standard deviation from baseline on Conner's Parent Rating Scale, but no improvement of performance on Conner's Continuous Performance Test. Three subjects also had worsening of their hyperactivity and had to discontinue venlafaxine. Malhotra and Santosh (1998) reported a six-week open trial of buspirone in 12 children age 6 to 12 with ADHD. Using the Conner's Parent Abbreviated Index and Children's Global Assessment Scale, all 12 subjects showed significant improvement over baseline scores, with reemergence of symptoms two weeks after discontinuation of buspirone.

MOOD DISORDERS

Major Depression
The present diagnostic criteria for major depression in children are identical to those in adults, with the following adjustments: irritable mood can substitute for the symptom requirement of depressed mood,

and failure to make expected weight gains can be considered a positive symptom of appetite disturbance. Recent epidemiologic studies indicate a prevalence rate of 0.4% to 2.5% in children and 0.4% to 8.3% in adolescents for major depression (Fleming & Offord, 1990). Major depression occurs in children at the same rate in both girls and boys, whereas in adolescents, the female:male ratio begins to approach 2:1, as it does in adults. Symptoms of depression parallel those in adults but also evidence some developmental differences. Younger children more frequently manifest somatic symptoms, withdrawal, irritability, and behavioral disturbances. As symptoms of suicidality, melancholia, and impaired functioning increase with age, by adolescence, symptoms more closely resemble adult depression. Many comorbid conditions occur, such as dysthymia, anxiety disorders, disruptive behavior disorders, and substance abuse. Epidemiologic studies have shown that 40% to 70% of depressed children and adolescents suffer from a comorbid psychiatric diagnosis. Thus, it is important to be as rigorous as possible in the initial diagnosis and assessment of children presenting with symptoms of depression.

Selective Serotonin Reuptake Inhibitors (SSRIs). In current practice, the SSRIs are used more frequently than the TCAs for treating depression in children due to their ease of administration, low side effect profile, and low lethality in overdose. Drugs included in this class are fluoxetine (Prozac), sertraline (Zoloft), paroxetine (Paxil), fluvoxamine (Luvox), and citalopram (Celexa). All the SSRIs share a common mechanism of action, namely, inhibition of the reuptake of serotonin. The various compounds differ in their potency with regard to this action; however, this does not appear to impact on their clinical efficacy. They also share the characteristic of essentially being devoid of receptor antagonism at acetylcholinergic and histaminergic receptors, resulting in more tolerable side effect profiles.

The major differences among the SSRIs lies in their pharmacokinetic characteristics, specifically their half-lives and level of activity at the cytochrome P450 enzyme system. Fluoxetine has the longest half-life (approximately 2 to 3 days) as well as having an active metabolite with an even longer half-life (approximately 5 to 10 days). The other SSRIs generally have half-lives approaching 18 to 24 hours and do not have clinically active metabolites. Although the SSRIs have been shown to inhibit the metabolism of other drugs through their action on the cytochrome P450 liver enzyme system, the intensity and specificity of these effects vary among the agents (e.g., fluoxetine has a potent effect on the IID6 subsystem, while fluvoxamine potently inhibits IA2 and IIIA4) (Nemeroff, DeVane, & Pollock, 1996).

The most common side effects encountered with the SSRIs consist of GI symptoms, including nausea, anorexia, dyspepsia, and diarrhea. Other side effects include headaches, nervousness, particularly with treatment initiation, insomnia and somnolence, and rashes. A frequently overlooked side effect is sexual dysfunction, including anorgasmia, and delayed or retrograde ejaculation.

The SSRIs are most commonly used to treat major depression and anxiety disorders. Open studies have reported 70% to 90% response rates to fluoxetine in adolescents with major depressive disorder (MDD) (Boulos, Kutcher, Gardner, & Young, 1992; Colle, Belair, DiFeo, Weiss, & LaRoache, 1994; Jain, Birmaher, Garcia, Al-Shabbout, & Ryan, 1992). To date, there is one double-blind placebo-controlled study by Emslie et al. (1997) involving 96 children and adolescents with MDD that found a statistically significant improvement in subjects taking fluoxetine versus placebo.

Present clinical practice generally follows a course of treatment initiating drug therapy with an SSRI beginning at half the recommended dose for adults (e.g., 10 mg fluoxetine, 25 mg sertraline), with gradual dose titration over the ensuing three to four weeks depending on response. Final dose ranges used in published or ongoing clinical trials have been comparable to those used in adults (fluoxetine 10 to 80 mg/day; sertraline 25 to 200 mg/day; paroxetine 10 to 60 mg/day; fluvoxamine 50 to 200 mg/day; citalopram 20 to 40 mg/day). As with adults, an adequate medication trial should consist of six to eight weeks at a standard therapeutic dose. Further increases in dosage should be pursued only if some partial response has been obtained and if, on further increases, one continues to capture additional therapeutic symptom resolution. For children who fail one trial of an SSRI, it is common practice to attempt a trial with an alternative SSRI, as the possibility of response to alternative agents is present. However, if a patient has failed two successive trials of SSRIs, then consideration should be given to a trial of a TCA or possibly one of the novel antidepressants now available.

Tricyclic Antidepressants (TCAs). Numerous studies investigating TCAs have shown response rates ranging from 30% to 80% for children and adolescents treated with TCAs. On the other hand, placebo response rates are 50% or more, thereby not supporting a significant difference in response rates for drug and placebo. Since 1982, there have been six double-blind placebo-controlled studies in children (total N for all six studies = 134), and five such studies in adolescents (total $N = 172$) (Birmaher, Ryan, Williamson, Brent, & Kaufman, 1996). Study drugs have included imipramine, amitriptyline, nortriptyline, and desipramine. Only one study, by Preskorn, Weller, Hughes, Weller, & Bolte (1987), found a statistically significant but small antidepressant effect in one outcome measurement. Due to the small N per study, each study had decreased power to detect the efficacy of TCAs. Another possible explanation for the lack of effect is the brief treatment (average four to eight weeks), providing an insufficient opportunity for clinical response.

The TCAs initiate their action by blocking the reuptake of norepinephrine and serotonin, resulting in a functional increase in the amount of these neurochemicals in the synaptic gaps between neurons. The delay in onset of clinical effect, however, is most likely related to the adaptive response of the nervous system and physiologic changes that occur in the postsynaptic neuron (Hyman & Nestler, 1996).

All of these compounds have long half-lives ranging from 10 to 70 hours in adults. Consequently, they are most commonly dosed once a day and reach steady-state plasma levels within five to seven days. In children, who tend to be more efficient metabolizers, these drugs have a half-life of approximately 12 to 24 hours and may require twice-a-day dosing in some patients (P. Klein & Riddle, 1995). These drugs are metabolized by the cytochrome P450 enzymes and can subsequently be affected by other drugs that inhibit or induce this enzyme system.

The TCAs also block muscarinic acetylcholine and histamine receptors, which is felt to result in some of their side effects. Common side effects include sedation, dry mouth, constipation, and orthostatic hypotension. Other possible side effects include blurred vision, urinary retention, possible

anticholinergic-induced delirium, and triggering of mania in bipolar patients. Abrupt cessation of TCAs can result in cholinergic rebound and subsequent flulike symptoms, including vomiting, headaches, and malaise. Therefore, children should be tapered off TCAs gradually.

Another important side effect of this class of drugs is their effect on cardiac electrophysiology, particularly in light of reports in the early 1990s of sudden death occurrences in five children on desipramine. More recently, two more cases of sudden death in children treated with TCAs, one with desipramine and one with imipramine, were reported by Varley and McClellan (1997). It is well-known that TCAs prolong conduction time, cause tachycardia, and can be arrhythmogenic in overdosage. TCAs should be avoided in children with known cardiac histories, particularly conduction defects, or initiated only after consultation with a pediatric cardiologist.

Prior to initiating treatment with a TCA, a baseline EKG should be obtained to rule out any possible conduction defect. Treatment is then generally initiated with a 10 mg or 25 mg dose depending on the size and age of the child (approximately 1 mg/kg/day starting dose). Subsequent dose titrations should occur slowly, about every 10 to 14 days depending on clinical response. Dose increases should consist of 10 to 25 mg increases with endpoints of 3 to 5 mg/kg/day total dose for imipramine/desipramine, and 1 to 3 mg/kg/day total dose for amitriptyline/nortriptyline. With each subsequent dose increase, a repeat EKG should be obtained to monitor drug effect on conduction times. Blood levels can be obtained for amitriptyline/nortriptyline and imipramine/desipramine, particularly to monitor for toxic levels, although the clinical implications of these levels are unclear (Geller, Cooper, Chestnut, Anker, & Schluchter, 1986).

Novel Antidepressants. New antidepressants released in the last five years include agents such as venlafaxine, nefazadone, and mirtazapin. Bupropion is also included in this grouping, even though it has been in clinical use for over 10 years. Each of these agents is chemically and structurally different and will therefore be reviewed independently. It should also be noted that there are no controlled trials of these medications for pediatric depression, though some open trials and case reports exist.

VENLAFAXINE (EFFEXOR). Venlafaxine is structurally unrelated to tricyclic, tetracyclic, or other SSRIs. Venlafaxine and its active metabolite O-desmethylvenlafaxine (ODV) are potent inhibitors of neuronal serotonin and norepinephrine reuptake as well as being weak inhibitors of dopamine reuptake. At the same time, venlafaxine lacks significant affinity for muscarinic, histaminergic, or alpha adrenergic receptors. These properties are postulated to account for the drug's clinical efficacy and lack of side effects, such as sedation and cardiovascular effects seen with other antidepressants. Venlafaxine is rapidly absorbed on administration with typical half-lives of 5 to 7 hours for venlafaxine and 11 to 13 hours for ODV. Thus, steady-state plasma levels are obtained within three days of continuous dosing on a twice or three times a day schedule.

Side effects commonly associated with venlafaxine include anxiety/nervousness, anorexia, somnolence/insomnia, and dizziness; other side effects include abnormal ejaculation/anorgasmia, asthenia, and sweating. Of importance is the clear association of venlafaxine-induced hypertension with sustained elevations in supine diastolic blood pressure noted to occur with increasing dosages and particularly dosages above 300 mg/day. Therefore, it is strongly recommended that patients be regularly monitored for increases in blood pressure, and, if hypertension should occur, dose reduction or discontinuation of venlafaxine should be considered.

In adults, recommended starting dose is 75 mg/day. Dose can be increased every four to seven days to a recommended dose of 225 mg/day. More severely depressed patients may require higher dosing (recommended maximum dose is 375 mg/day). In adults, venlafaxine has been shown to be effective in the treatment of major depression and anxiety disorders (Pollack et al., 1996).

To date, there is limited data on the efficacy of venlafaxine in pediatric major depression. Mandoki, Tapia, Tapia, Sumner, and Parker (1997) reported a six-week double-blind placebo-controlled study in 33 subjects age 8 to 17 diagnosed with major depression, treated either with venlafaxine and therapy or placebo and therapy. Both groups improved, but there was no statistically significant difference between medication and placebo groups.

NEFAZADONE (SERZONE). Nefazadone is structurally unrelated to other tricyclic, tetracyclic, or SSRI antidepressants. Nefazadone is a phenylpiperazine shown to inhibit neuronal reuptake of serotonin and norepinephrine. Nefazadone acts as an antagonist at central 5-HT2 receptors, and it also antagonizes alpha-1-adrenergic receptors, which may be associated with the side effect of postural hypotension.

Nefazadone is rapidly absorbed but undergoes extensive metabolism affecting its bioavailability. Both nefazadone and its metabolite hydroxynefazadone, which is believed to share a similar pharmacological profile to nefazadone, undergo nonlinear kinetics. This results in greater accumulation of nefazadone and its metabolite with increasing milligram dosages and dosage frequency. Peak plasma levels occur within one hour of ingestion, with nefazadone displaying a half-life of approximately 2 to 4 hours, whereas hydroxynefazadone appears to have a half-life of 18 hours. Steady-state plasma concentrations are usually attained by four to five days. Nefazadone is also a known inhibitor of cytochrome P450-3A4, resulting in increased levels of drugs metabolized via this cytochrome, such as triazolam, alprazolam, terfenadine, and astemizole. Thus, it is strongly recommended that nefazadone not be given in combination with drugs such as terfenadine and astemizole, as elevated blood levels can cause cardiovascular effects such as prolonged QT intervals and ventricular arrhythmias.

Side effects commonly associated with nefazadone include sedation, dry mouth, dizziness, lightheadedness, nausea, constipation, and possibly blurred vision. Incidence of side effects increases with higher dosages, particularly at dosages greater than 300 mg/day.

Nefazadone is indicated in the treatment of depression. Typical starting dosages in adults are 200 mg/day given in a twice a day dosing schedule, with greater efficacy for antidepressant activity usually noted at dosages above 300 mg/day. Dose increases usually consist of 100 mg/day increases, again in divided doses, after intervals of one to three weeks at any given dose. There are no dosing guidelines as of yet in pediatric populations, and the only published case report in children used doses between 200 and 600 mg/day (mean daily dose of 357 mg/day) (Wilens, Spencer, Biederman, & Schleifer, 1997).

BUPROPION (WELLBUTRIN). Bupropion hydrochloride is an antidepressant of the aminoketone class and is chemically unrelated to tricyclic, tetracyclic, and other antidepressant classes. The exact therapeutic mechanism of action is unknown. However, bupropion does inhibit the reuptake of serotonin, norepinephrine, and dopamine, though compared to other TCAs and SSRIs, it does so weakly. Bupropion is rapidly absorbed, reaching peak plasma levels within two hours, and its half-life is approximately 14 hours. Several of the known metabolites of bupropion are pharmacologically active and have longer elimination half-lives; however, their effect on bupropion's overall clinical efficacy is unknown.

Side effects commonly seen with bupropion administration include nausea, vomiting, headaches, agitation, and sleep disturbance. Of most concern is the increased risk of seizures reported to occur in approximately 0.4% (4/1,000) of patients. The risk of seizure is related to dosage and predisposing factors such as seizure disorder or history of seizures, head trauma, CNS tumor, or concomitant administration of drugs that lower seizure threshold. Therefore, current recommendations are that the total daily dose of bupropion not exceed 450 mg, that no single dose be larger than 150 mg (thus requiring three times a day dosing), and that dose titration occur gradually. Bupropion has also been released in a sustained release (SR) form that allows for twice a day dosing. With bupropion SR, no single dose may exceed 200 mg and a total maximal dose is 400 mg/day.

Bupropion is approved for the treatment of depression in adults; however, it has also been used in pediatric populations for the treatment of ADHD (Barrickman et al., 1995; Wender, 1988). Typical starting dosages for adults with depression are 200 mg/day given on a twice a day dosing schedule. Subsequent increases should occur no sooner than day four after initiation, with a shift to three times a day dosing and gradual increases as clinically indicated thereafter. In pediatric populations, it is common to start at a lower dosage of 75 mg twice a day or 100 mg SR once a day, and then follow adult guidelines.

MIRTAZAPINE (REMERON). Mirtazapine is a novel antidepressant with a unique pharmacologic profile in comparison with other antidepressants. It is postulated that mirtazapine results in an increased release of both norepinephrine and serotonin and blocks the 5-HT2 and 5-HT3 receptors, resulting in a more favorable side effect profile than the SSRIs, while maintaining comparable efficacy. Mirtazapine is indicated for the treatment of depression in adults. There have been no formal studies done on pediatric populations to date.

BIPOLAR DISORDER

The diagnostic criteria and the typical clinical presentation of bipolar disorder in children are the same as in adults; however, the presence of irritability and emotional lability are often more common in pediatric patients than symptoms of elation, euphoria, and grandiosity. A developmental approach to symptom evaluation is necessary, as grandiosity in a child, for instance, may present as harassment of teachers because the child believes he or she understands the material better than the teacher. The estimated base rate of bipolar disorder is even lower than that of MDD, but the occurrence of bipolar illness in children and adolescents is often associated with a very pernicious course. Furthermore, identification of the disorder at the onset of the illness is complicated by the fact that the episodes may be less discrete in nature, tending to blend with burgeoning behavioral difficulties that often outlast the episodes of mania or depression themselves. Common comorbid conditions include ADHD, conduct disorder, anxiety disorders, and substance abuse.

Data from open studies suggest that lithium therapy is helpful in the acute management and prophylaxis of bipolar illness (Delong & Aldershop, 1987; Strober et al., 1988; Varanka, Weller, Weller, & Fristad, 1988). However, these studies are complicated by the open nature of the treatment, the use of adjunctive pharmacotherapies, and the presence of comorbid psychiatric conditions. Similarly, there is an absence of controlled data on children and adolescents using other mood stabilizers, such as carbamazepine and valproic acid. The available open trial data support the use of valproic acid in the acute management of juvenile bipolar disorder (Papatheodorou, Kutcher, Katic, & Szalai, 1995). To date, there is only one published controlled study of pharmacologic treatment of bipolar disorder in pediatrics (reviewed below).

Mood Stabilizers/Anticonvulsants
Currently, there are several different types of compounds used to treat bipolar illness, including lithium, valproate, and carbamezapine. To date, only lithium has FDA approval for the treatment of

manic phases and maintenance treatment of bipolar disorder in patients 12 years and older.

Lithium Carbonate. Lithium is most commonly administered in the form of a salt, lithium carbonate, which is easily absorbed from the GI tract. Although the exact mechanism of action for lithium is unclear, current research indicates that lithium may affect second messenger systems by inhibiting inositol phosphatases within neurons. Such inhibition results in decreased cellular responses to neurotransmitters that are linked to the phosphatidylinositol second messenger system (Baraban, Worley, & Snyder, 1989). Peak plasma levels occur within 2 to 4 hours, with a half-life of approximately 20 to 24 hours. Steady-state plasma levels are reached in five to seven days. Lithium is almost entirely eliminated via the kidneys; thus, renal function can impact on lithium excretion and blood levels. Lithium acts as an antagonist to antidiuretic hormones, resulting in polyuria due to decreased reabsorption of fluid at the distal tubules. One must take into account decreased renal function, other possible medical conditions, and concomitant drug administration that can affect lithium excretion. Diuretics can increase or decrease lithium levels based on their mechanism of action. Other commonly administered medications in pediatric populations, such as tetracycline, can increase lithium levels, whereas anti-inflammatory medications such as ibuprofen, naproxen, indomethacin, and phenylbutazone can increase plasma levels. Thus, caution is always advised when coadministering lithium with other medications, and a search for possible drug interactions is prudent.

Common side effects associated with lithium administration include tremor, polydipsia and polyuria, nausea, and diarrhea. Other side effects include weight gain, thyroid abnormalities (hypothyroidism, generally), fatigue, dermatologic abnormalities, and leukocytosis. Long-term side effects include possible decreased renal function, with glomerular and interstitial fibrosis having been reported in adults on chronic lithium therapy.

Of particular concern is lithium's narrow therapeutic index with ensuing toxicity. Initially, lithium toxicity is marked by diarrhea, vomiting, ataxia, tremor, sedation, slurred speech, and poor coordination. If no intervention occurs and lithium levels continue to rise, increasingly life-threatening toxic effects are seen, including cardiac arrhythmias, confusion, stupor, and eventually coma and death. Lithium toxicity in its mild to moderate form tends to occur at blood levels between 1.5 and 2 mEq/L, with moderate to severe toxicity occurring above 2 mEq/L. If severe toxicity occurs, hospital admission is indicated, as the patient will most likely require close cardiac monitoring, possible hemodialysis, and other supportive measures.

Current indications for the use of lithium include mania and maintenance treatment of bipolar disorder. Other possible indications include severe aggressive behaviors in conduct disordered children and developmentally disabled children. Typical starting dosages of lithium are 150 to 300 mg twice a day, with serum blood levels obtained at day five and subsequent dose titration based on blood level results and clinical improvement. Weller, Weller, and Fristad (1986) published a guideline for rapid titration of lithium dosage while attempting to avoid undue side effects and toxic blood levels. Most recently, Geller et al. (1998) reported a six-week double-blind placebo-controlled study of lithium in 25 adolescents diagnosed with bipolar disorder and comorbid substance dependency. Significant differences were reported in both psychopathology measures and random urine drug screens between groups. The mean serum lithium level in responders was 0.9 mEq/L.

Valproic Acid (Depakene)/Divalproex Sodium (Depakote). Valproate is a carboxylic acid that has known anticonvulsant effects and has been shown to be effective in the treatment of bipolar I disorder in adults. The mechanism of action of valproate is unknown, but there is speculation that its therapeutic effect may be mediated by the drug's effect on gamma-aminobutyric acid (GABA). Valproate has been shown to both increase and decrease the synthesis of GABA. It is postulated that valproate may increase the effect of GABA postsynaptically, though a causal relation to its therapeutic effect remains unclear.

Valproate is converted to valproic acid in the stomach. Its peak plasma level can be affected by the concomitant ingestion of food, which decreases its absorption, though generally, peak plasma level occurs within 1 to 4 hours. The half-life of valproate is approximately 6 to 18 hours, resulting in the need for two- to three-times-a-day dosing. Steady-state plasma levels are commonly reached by day five to seven of administration, with a therapeutic blood level ranging from 50 to 150 mg/ml.

Side effects encountered with valproate include GI symptoms such as nausea, vomiting, and diarrhea. GI side effects are common during the initiation of treatment and tend to subside with continued use; they can also potentially be minimized by slow drug initiation and titration. Other side effects include sedation, ataxia, tremor, weight gain, and, rarely, hair loss. In some patients, there is persistent elevation of liver transaminases, which is benign and resolves with drug discontinuation. At the same time, there have been reports of drug-induced hepatitis resulting in death, particularly in younger children on multidrug therapy.

The initial starting dosage of valproate can be 250 mg twice a day; if possible, a more gradual titration beginning with 125 to 250 mg once a day may result in less significant GI side effects. Lower initial dosages should be used in younger children, with initiation dosages of 15 mg/kg and a maximum dose of 60 mg/kg. Valproate dosages can safely be increased every five to seven days by adding a second or third dose or increasing individual doses. Plasma levels should be obtained at dose titration points, with blood levels being drawn in the morning prior to the first dose.

There are no current approved indications for the use of valproate in pediatric psychiatry other than for the treatment of seizure disorder. There are reports of its possible efficacy in the treatment of mania and conduct disorder in children (Kastner, Finesmith, & Walsh, 1993; Kastner, Friedman, Plummer, Ruiz, & Henning, 1990; Papatheodorou et al., 1995; West et al., 1994).

Carbamazepine (Tegretol). Carbamazepine is structurally related to imipramine. It is currently indicated for the treatment of seizure disorders, particularly partial complex seizures, as well as trigeminal neuralgia. There is no current approved usage in pediatric psychiatry. In adult psychiatry, there is extensive literature indicating the efficacy of carbamazepine in the treatment of acute mania and maintenance treatment of bipolar disorder.

The mechanism of action of carbamazepine is unknown. Current theory proposes that carbamazepine's therapeutic effect could be related to interactions at GABA receptors centrally and peripherally with subsequent inhibition of calcium channels, as well as possible antikindling properties due to polysynaptic inhibition.

Carbamazepine is variably absorbed from the GI tract, and absorption is enhanced when the drug is taken with meals. Carbamazepine is metabolized by the liver and excreted by the kidneys. Peak plasma levels are reached in 2 to 8 hours. The half-life of carbamazepine varies as the drug induces its own metabolism, but this tends to stabilize after several months administration; thus, after chronic administration, the half-life approaches 12 to 18 hours. During dose titration, plasma levels should be obtained four to six days after steady dosage or at dosage increases. Therapeutic blood levels range from 4 to 12 mg/ml, and blood levels should be drawn in the morning prior to the first dose.

Common side effects include dizziness, drowsiness, ataxia, nausea, and vomiting. Side effects can be minimized by gradual dose titration and tend to be time-limited, with the most acute side effects occurring at drug initiation. Other side effects include blood dyscrasias including aplastic anemia and agranuloctyosis. Patients should be warned that the development of fever, sore throat, bruising, petechiae, and easy bleeding could be indications of a severe blood dyscrasia and that their physician should be contacted immediately. At the same time, carbamazepine can also cause a benign decrease in the white blood cell count, with values remaining above 3,000. Carbamazepine has also been associated with a drug-induced hepatitis, usually within the first few weeks of therapy, necessitating the cessation of drug therapy as the hepatitis can be fatal. Thus, baseline blood chemistries, including a complete blood count and liver function enzymes, should be obtained prior to drug initiation and at regular subsequent intervals.

Initial dosages of carbamazepine in children 6 to 12 years of age are 100 mg twice a day, with increases occurring weekly using 100 mg increases and going to a three or even four times a day schedule until therapeutic blood levels are obtained. In children over 12 years of age, initial doses are typically 200 mg three times a day, with weekly dose increases of 200 mg per day and going to a three or four times a day dosing schedule. It is recommended that dosages not exceed 1,000 mg/day in children 12 to 15 years of age, and 1,200 mg/day in children over 15 years of age.

There are no currently approved usages of carbamazepine in pediatric psychiatry. A meta-analysis by Silva et al. (1996) suggests that carbamazepine may have a role in the treatment of ADHD symptoms. A more recent double-blind placebo-controlled study of carbamazepine in aggressive children with conduct disorder did not demonstrate efficacy of carbamazepine in reducing aggressive behaviors (Cueva et al., 1996).

SCHIZOPHRENIA

Fortunately, schizophrenia is a rare condition in childhood and tends more typically to present in mid- to later adolescence. The current diagnostic criteria for schizophrenia in pediatric populations are the same as those for adults in terms of characteristic symptoms (delusions, hallucinations, disorganized speech, disorganized behavior, and negative symptoms). Two or more symptoms must be present and the disturbance must persist for six months. Consideration is given to developmental aspects with regard to social/occupational dysfunction because failure to achieve expected levels of interpersonal, academic, or occupational achievement can be diagnostic for children.

Epidemiologic data are limited due to the rarity of this condition. The course of illness in childhood-onset schizophrenia appears to be one of chronic illness with a poor prognosis for improvement. Comorbid conditions can include affective disorders, especially bipolar disorder, where children who are manic present with psychotic symptoms and are often misdiagnosed as schizophrenic. Other comorbid conditions can include disruptive behavior disorders (ADHD and conduct disorder) and learning disorders.

Treatment of psychotic symptoms in children is similar to that for adults, with the various antipsychotic medications having comparable efficacy in reducing symptoms. Due to the potential for chronic administration of these agents in children, current practice is to initiate treatment with one of the newer antipsychotics (risperidone, olanzapine), which may have a lower risk for potential tardive dyskinesia and dystonias. The classic antipsychotics have shown efficacy in children, typically at dosages equivalent to those in adults (400 to 600 mg/70 kg chlorpromazine equivalents).

Antipsychotics
As a class of drugs, these compounds were initially used in pediatric psychiatry for a broad variety of nonpsychotic indications, such as agitation, impulsivity, ADHD-type symptoms, and aggressive behavior. Over the past several decades, however, as other phar-macologic options have become available, their use has become more circumscribed and more consistent with adult indications. At the present time, antipsychotics are the drug of choice in childhood schizophrenia and psychotic disorders. They are also effective in treating some symptoms of autism, mental retardation syndromes, and motor/vocal tics in Tourette's syndrome. This class of drugs includes a diverse group of compounds that all share the common action of antagonism at dopamine receptors.

Classic Antipsychotics. The classic antipsychotics all block dopamine at the D2 receptor site with varying degrees of affinity. The low-potency drugs (chlorpromazine, thioridazine) have a lower affinity for the D2 receptor, while high-potency drugs (haloperidol, fluphenazine) have high affinity for this receptor. These in vitro effects coincide with their in vivo clinical potency. In spite of this common primary action, generalizing that this is the reason for their antipsychotic effect oversimplifies matters. Antagonism at the D2 receptor site occurs within several doses of drug initiation, whereas therapeutic effects take several days to weeks to occur. It is known that dopaminergic neurons decrease their firing rates after long-term administration but not after short-term administration of dopamine antagonists. Thus, some as yet unknown change at the synaptic, postsynaptic, intracellular, or even genetic level accounts for antipsychotic effect and takes time to develop, unlike the immediate receptor blockade that occurs with drug initiation.

These compounds display various half-lives ranging from 10 to 36 hours in adults, allowing for once-a-day dosing. Peak plasma levels are attained within 1 to 4 hours after ingestion. It is unknown if the same pharmacokinetic profiles are true for children. Rivera-Calimlim, Griesbach, and Perlmutter (1979) reported the result of plasma chlorpromazine levels in a study of 24 children age 8 to 16 years. A wide range of plasma levels was noted for any given dose, and study subjects had plasma levels that were 2 to 3.5 times lower than those for adults for a given dose per kilogram body weight. Another observation of the study was that plasma levels declined over time in most patients in spite of fixed doses, suggesting possible autoinduction of enzymes that metabolize chlorpromazine.

Most of these compounds also have significant effects at a number of other receptor sites, including adrenergic, histaminergic, and cholinergic receptors. These other sites of action are not felt to contribute to therapeutic action but are frequently associated with some of the common side effects encountered with these drugs. For instance, the low-potency drugs have significant anticholinergic and anti-alpha-1-adrenergic effects that result in side effects such as dry mouth and constipation, and orthostasis, respectively. Other important side effects include lowering of seizure threshold, particularly with low-potency neuroleptics, galactorrhea, amenorrhea, and sexual side effects.

Of most concern is the potential for acute dystonic reactions, akathisia, parkinsonian symptoms, cognitive dulling, tardive dyskinesia, and the possibility of neuroleptic malignant syndrome. Acute dystonic reactions tend to occur with drug initiation, during the first week of drug therapy, and with subsequent dose increases. Such reactions can be very frightening, and patients should be informed of these prior to drug initiation. Fortunately, acute dystonic reactions respond rapidly to anticholinergic and antiparkonsonian drugs such as diphenhydramine (Benadryl) 25 to 50 mg orally or intramuscularly, or benztropine (Cogentin) 1 to 2 mg orally or intramuscularly. Consideration should be given to either using prophylactic doses of diphenhydramine or benztropine during the first four to six weeks, the period of highest risk, or giving the patient instructions on how to use these medications on an as-needed basis if a dystonic reaction occurs.

Akathisia consists of a feeling of inner restlessness, particularly in the lower extremities, and the inability to sit still or an irresistible urge to move about. Again, the period of highest risk for developing akathisia is with drug initiation and during the first several months of drug treatment. Akathisia may or may not respond to antiparkinsonian drugs such as benztropine; other treatment options include the use of propranolol or benzodiazepines. Parkinsonian symptoms include tremor, cogwheeling rigidity, akinesia (slowness in movement), and a decrease in facial expression or masklike face. The period of maximum risk for developing parkinsonian side effects tend to be within the first days to month of drug initiation. These symptoms do respond to antiparkinsonian drugs, such as benztropine 1 to 2 mg given two to three times a day. Efforts should be made to gradually withdraw antiparkinsonian agents after two to three weeks of treatment to determine if their use is still clinically necessary.

Tardive dyskinesia (TD) is a movement disorder precipitated by long-term administration, usually emerging after several months to years use of antipsychotic medication (though there have been reports of TD developing within three days of drug initiation). Common manifestations of TD include choreoathetotic movements of the head, neck, mouth, and tongue, as well as involuntary movement of the trunk and upper and lower extremities. Of particular concern is the potential that TD will become irreversible. Given the age of the patient and the inherent possibility of long-term administration, the clinician should be cautious about the use of these agents. As a precaution against development of TD, all children receiving antipsychotic medication should undergo baseline screening using the abnormal involuntary movement scale (AIMS) and serial AIMS during drug therapy.

Neuroleptic malignant syndrome (NMS) is a potentially life-threatening adverse reaction to antipsychotic medication that requires immediate cessation of drug therapy and institution of medical treatment.

Typical dosages for antipsychotic drugs range from 3 to 6 mg/kg/day for the low-potency drugs and 0.1 to 0.5 mg/kg/day for the high-potency drugs. Initially, it is common to use two or even three times a day dosing of neuroleptics with drug initiation. Due to their relatively long half-life, once clinical response is achieved, changing to once-a-day dosing is possible. Typical therapeutic response to these drugs commonly takes two to four weeks to occur, so it is advisable not to increase dosages too rapidly at drug initiation to avoid excessively high doses.

Atypical Antipsychotics. Currently, clozapine, risperidone, and olanzapine can be classified as atypical antipsychotics due to their simultaneous receptor blockade at both dopamine and serotonin receptors. It is hypothesized that this dual action contributes to the increased efficacy in reducing "negative" symptoms of schizophrenia, while also resulting in a decreased incidence of extrapyramidal side effects in comparison to classic antipsychotics.

CLOZAPINE (CLOZARIL). Clozapine is the original atypical antipsychotic. It has a unique pharmacologic profile in that it is a low-potency D2 receptor antagonist, but has a much higher potency as an antagonist at the D1 and D4 receptors, serotonin type 2

(5-HT2) receptor, and noradrenergic alpha receptors, particularly alpha-1. Of interest is that clozapine is more potent in affecting the mesolimbic dopaminergic neurons than those projecting to the basal ganglia (nigrostriatal neurons). It is hypothesized that this selectivity contributes to clozapine's effectiveness in improving both positive and negative schizophrenic symptoms with rare concomitant extrapyramidal effects. Clozapine was approved by the FDA in 1990 for use in treatment-resistant schizophrenic patients. To date, there is no approved usage of this drug in pediatric psychiatry.

Clozapine is a dibenzodiazepine that is rapidly absorbed from the GI tract, reaching peak plasma levels in 1 to 4 hours. It has a half-life of 10 to 16 hours in adults, resulting in the need for two or three times a day dosing. Clozapine has a number of important side effects, including cardiac side effects, agranulocytosis, and an increased risk of seizures. Cardiac side effects include tachycardia, hypotension with potential syncopal events, and nonspecific EKG changes, including ST-T wave changes, T wave flattening, and T wave inversion. Syncopal episodes can be minimized by starting at very low dosages such as 12.5 to 25 mg/day with gradual dose titration thereafter.

The incidence of agranulocytosis in clozapine-treated patients is 1% to 2%. Agranulocytosis is defined as a decrease in the number of white blood cells. It is potentially fatal if not recognized early and clozapine therapy discontinued. Thus, weekly blood counts are currently required to obtain further clozapine prescriptions. Agranulocytosis typically occurs in the first six months of drug initiation but can occur at later points in drug therapy. Current recommendations are that if a patient experiences agranulocytosis, clozapine is discontinued and future use of clozapine is contraindicated for that patient.

Clozapine can also increase the risk of seizures. Between 1% and 5% of patients taking clozapine experience drug-related seizures. If a seizure occurs, clozapine should be discontinued. Consideration should then be given to beginning an anticonvulsant with gradual reinstitution of clozapine versus complete discontinuation of clozapine.

Other common side effects include sedation, constipation, sialorrhea (excessive salivation), and fever. Sialorrhea can be significant; however, due to clozapine's anticholinergic effects, it is not advisable to use anticholinergic drugs to treat this side effect.

Typical starting doses of clozapine are 12.5 mg twice a day or 25 mg once a day with subsequent daily increases of up to 25 mg to reach a total dose of 300 to 450 mg in two to three weeks. Subsequent increases of 100 mg/day (usually in divided doses) can occur on a weekly basis depending on clinical response. A total dose of 900 mg/day is not to be exceeded.

Clozapine has no current FDA-approved usage in children under the age of 16. However, it should be considered in those patients with severe schizophrenic symptoms who have not responded to two adequate trials of classic antipsychotics or who could not tolerate such medications due to overwhelming adverse effects. Frazier et al. (1994) have reported on the use of clozapine in an open trial, and Kumra, Frazier et al. (1997) reported a six-week double-blind parallel comparison of clozapine and haloperidol. Both studies treated adolescents with schizophrenia and demonstrated positive responses. Side effects in the studies included tachycardia, sedation, sialorrhea, weight gain, constipation, enuresis, orthostasis, nausea, dizziness, neutropenia, akisthisia, and coarse tremors.

RISPERIDONE (RISPERDAL). Risperidone is a benzisoxazole, making it chemically distinct from other antipsychotic drugs. Risperidone is a potent antagonist at the D2 receptor site, like classic neuroleptics, but also has potent antagonism at the serotonin type 2 (5HT2) receptor. This multireceptor affinity is believed to contribute to its therapeutic effect on both positive and negative symptoms of schizophrenia while decreasing its potential for extrapyramidal effects (EPS).

Risperidone is rapidly absorbed in the GI tract, with peak plasma levels occurring within 1 to 2 hours. It is metabolized in the liver by cytochrome P450 IID6 and thus can be affected by other drugs metabolized via this same cytochrome. The typical half-life ranges from 3 to 20 hours, thus requiring two or three times a day dosing.

Common side effects include weight gain, somnolence, constipation, orthostatic hypotension, and dizziness. EPS can occur even at low doses. There have also been reports of TD associated with risperidone, though the incidence of TD appears to be lower with risperidone compared to classic antipsychotics. Of importance in pediatric populations are cardiac side effects, including tachycardia, and EKG changes, including increases in QTc. A recent case study by Kumra, Herion, Jacobsen, Briguglia, and Grothe (1997) reported the occurrence of liver dysfunction and steatohepatitis in 2 children out of 13 treated with risperidone. In each case, liver damage was reversible after drug discontinuation. Recommendations included that pediatric patients treated with risperidone have baseline and periodic liver function tests and careful monitoring of weight gain.

The typical starting dose for risperidone is 0.5 to 1 mg twice a day with gradual dose increases of 1 to 2 mg/day occurring every week if necessary. Again, therapeutic effect can take weeks to begin, so rapid dose titration is contraindicated, as excessive doses may be used when lower doses would have been sufficient. Quintana and Keshavan (1995) reported results of four cases of schizophrenic adolescents age 12 to 17 treated with risperidone. They reported improvement in three of the four cases using low doses of risperidone (4 to 5 mg/day). Armenteros, Whitaker, Welikson, Stedge, and Gorman (1997) reported the short-term efficacy of risperidone in a six-week open-label study of 10 adolescents age 11 to 18 with a diagnosis of schizophrenia. Risperidone resulted in statistically significant improvement on the Positive and Negative Syndrome Scale for Schizophrenia, Brief Psychiatric Rating Scale, and Clinical Global Impression scale at dosages of 4 to 10 mg per day.

OLANZAPINE (ZYPREXA).   Olanzapine is a thienobenzodiazepine with antagonist activity at serotonin type 2 (5HT2) and dopamine receptor sites. These sites of activity are felt to contribute to its clinical efficacy. Olanzapine also has high affinity for muscarinic, histamine, and alpha-1-adrenergic receptors, which are felt to account for some of its side effects.

Olanzapine is rapidly absorbed and reaches peak plasma levels within six hours of ingestion in adults. Its half-life ranges from 21 to 54 hours, allowing for once-a-day dosing. Although olanzapine is partially metabolized via the cytochrome P450 IID6, it is felt to be a minor pathway, as subjects deficient in this enzyme did not display elevated plasma levels of olanzapine.

Common side effects include orthostatic hypotension, constipation, weight gain, dizziness, and akathisia. In preclinical trials, akathisia occurred at a statistically significant higher rate compared to placebo, particularly at doses > 10 mg. Other EPS symptoms such as parkinsonism, dystonias, and dyskinesias also occurred.

Typical starting dosages are 5 to 10 mg/day in adults, with further increases occurring on a weekly basis if indicated. Antipsychotic effect was shown to occur at dosages of 10 to 15 mg/day; however, dosages above 10 mg were not more effective. Current recommendations are to proceed above 10 mg/day only after careful clinical assessment; there is no current indication to proceed above 20 mg/day. There is currently no approved indication for the use of olanzapine in pediatric psychiatry. A recent study by Kumra et al. (1998) reported an eight-week open-label trial of olanzapine in 8 adolescent patients and compared their outcome to 15 adolescents treated openly with clozapine for six weeks. Eight of the 15 patients treated with clozapine versus 0 of 8 olanzapine-treated patients were considered responders at week six, but by week eight, two of the eight olanzapine treated patients were considered responders and one was considered a partial responder.

ANXIETY DISORDERS

With the introduction of the *Diagnostic and Statistical Manual of Mental Disorders Fourth Edition (DSM-IV)*, anxiety disorders in children, like mood disorders, are diagnosed using the same criteria used for adults. The *DSM-III-R* had included separate childhood classifications of anxiety disorders: separation anxiety disorder (SAD), overanxious disorder (OAD), and avoidant disorder (AD). Only the classification of SAD remains in the *DSM-IV*. The other disorders have been fully subsumed under the adult disorders (i.e., OAD subsumed under generalized anxiety disorder and AD subsumed under social phobia). In addition, it is clear that adult-onset anxiety disorders, such as panic disorder (PD) with and without agoraphobia, can occur in childhood with the same symptomatology and morbidity that accompany the disorders in adults.

Anxiety symptoms appear to be highly prevalent in children. Approximately 8% to 9% of children in community samples will report the presence of an anxiety disorder that causes some degree of psychosocial dysfunction (Costello, 1989; Kashani & Sherman, 1988). Prevalence rates for anxiety disorders in children suggest that the scope of the problem is not trivial: 2% to 5% SAD, 1% to 2% AD, 3% to 5% OAD, and 6% PD in a clinically referred sample (Costello et al., 1988). Similar patterns of comorbidity seen in adults (i.e., high rates of co-occurrence of mood disorders) are also seen in children and adolescents. As with other disorders, the number of available studies investigating the use of pharmacotherapy in childhood anxiety disorders is limited. The focus of these studies has been on antidepressant and antianxiety agents, reflecting the already established adult treatment literature.

Clinical trials of both TCAs and SSRIs suggest a role for antidepressants in the management of anxiety disorders (Berney et al., 1981; Birmaher et al., 1994; Gittelman-Klein & Klein, 1971; R. Klein, Koplewicz, & Kannew, 1992). Only imipramine and clomipramine have been studied in placebo-controlled trials (Berney et al., 1981; Gittelman-Klein & Klein, 1971; R. Klein et al., 1992). In the first controlled study of these agents, 45 children (age range 6–14; mean age 10.8 years) with SAD were enrolled in a six-week double-blind placebo-controlled trial of imipramine. At the end of the trial, there was a significant difference between the drug and placebo group, using regular return to school as an outcome measure. The only side effect of significance was dry mouth. In a comparable study of clomipramine, (Berney et al., 1981), 46 children (age range 9–14 years) with school refusal were enrolled in a 12-week double-blind placebo-controlled trial. There were no differences between the groups on any outcome measures at the end of the trial. Likewise, a second study of imipramine failed to demonstrate any clear response. R. Klein et al. (1992) enrolled 21 children (age range 6–15 years; mean age 9.5 years) who met *DSM-II* criteria for SAD and had failed intensive behavioral therapy in a six-week double-blind placebo trial. In this study, there was no significant difference in symptoms between the groups, and the drug group experienced significantly more side effects, including irritability, dry mouth, and sedation. Another recent open-label study has shown preliminary efficacy of fluoxetine in separation anxiety, social phobia, and generalized anxiety (Birmaher et al., 1994). A recent double-blind placebo-controlled trial of fluoxetine demonstrated improvement in selective mutism by parental report.

Antianxiety agents
Current compounds used to treat anxiety disorders in pediatric psychiatry include the benzodiazepines and, less commonly, buspirone. In the following section, we review the benzodiazepines and buspirone separately.

Benzodiazepines. The benzodiazepines are generally considered to be the most effective and rapid-onset compounds to address anxiety symptoms. Although this is a varied group of drugs with various half-lives and metabolites, they all share a common mechanism of action. These compounds all share affinity for the benzodiazepine receptor site on GABAa, where they act as agonists and enhance the activity of the neurochemical GABA at its receptor. This results in sustained activity at the chloride ion channel, allowing the increased passage of chloride into the neuron to hyperpolarize neurons, leading to CNS inhibition.

The pharmacokinetics of the benzodiazepines varies greatly, with factors such as lipophilicity contributing to rapid onset of drug effects and peak plasma levels of one to three hours for compounds such as diazepam (Valium), alprazolam (Xanax), lorazepam (Ativan), and triazolam (Halcion). The half-life of benzodiazepines is dependent on whether they undergo multistep biotransformation, often resulting in active metabolites, or direct metabolism by glucuronidation and have no active metabolites. Whereas compounds that undergo several steps in their metabolism have long half-lives, such as diazepam, chlordiazepoxide (Librium), and clonazepam (Klonopin), other compounds such as alprazolam, lorazepam, and oxazepam (Serax) have short half-lives.

Common side effects include sedation, confusion, dizziness, and ataxia. Benzodiazepines can also result in anterograde amnesia and other possible side effects such as paradoxical aggression and behavioral disinhibition. Symptoms of benzodiazepine intoxication at higher dosages can include slurred speech, ataxia, hyporeflexia, and respiratory depression. Particular caution should be given to not coadminister other sedative medications as compounding of effect can occur.

Typical starting dosages of benzodiazepines in pediatric populations vary depending on the potency of the agent. These compounds are used in the pediatric population for the treatment of anxiety disorders, including panic disorder, obsessive-compulsive disorder, and some sleep disorders (Graee, Milnew, Rizzotto, & Klein, 1994; R. Klein & Last, 1989; Kutcher & MacKenzie, 1988; Pfefferbaum et al., 1987; Ross & Pigott, 1993; Simeon et al., 1992). Although the FDA has approved the use of some of these agents for children as young as 6 years, there remains limited clinical and research guidelines for dosing and ongoing use.

Like the antidepressants, open-label trials and case reports suggest a role for antianxiety agents in childhood-onset anxiety disorders (Grace et al., 1994; R. Klein & Last, 1989; Kutcher & MacKenzie, 1988; Ross & Pigott, 1993; Simeon et al., 1992). However, controlled trials are sparse and not as supportive (Grace et al., 1994; Simeon & Ferguson, 1987). Simeon and Ferguson enrolled 30 children (age range 8–17 years; mean age 12.6 years) with OAD or AD in a six-week double-blind placebo-controlled trial of alprazolam. The medication was well tolerated, but there were no significant differences between the groups at the end of the treatment trial. Grace et al. (1994) enrolled 15 children (age range 7–13 years; mean age 9.8 years) with various anxiety disorders in an eight-week double-blind placebo-controlled crossover study of clonazepam. Although individual patients demonstrated significant clinical improvement on active drug, there was no significant difference between periods on placebo and active drug. Side effects included drowsiness, irritability, and oppositional behavior. Furthermore, two children dropped out of the study secondary to serious disinhibition. Thus, it is recommended that these compounds be limited to short-term usage with frequent reassessment of indications for ongoing medication treatment.

Buspirone (Buspar).   Buspirone is a novel compound with anxiolytic properties, which is not pharmacologically related to the benzodiazepines. Buspirone is unlike the benzodiazepines in that it does not have any direct effects at the GABA neurotransmitter complex. It also does not have sedative, hypnotic, muscle relaxant, or anticonvulsant effects. Buspirone does not have cross-tolerance with benzodiazepines, and it does not produce a withdrawal syndrome or have significant potential for abuse.

Buspirone's primary site of action is as an agonist on serotonin type 1a (5HT1a) receptors. It also has activity at 5HT2 and dopamine type 2 (D2) receptors, but the contribution of these sites to its overall pharmacologic effect is poorly understood. Buspirone has been shown in animal models to reduce the release of serotonin in the hippocampus and reduce the rate of firing of serotonergic neurons in the median raphe nuclei. It is postulated that this effect is related to its clinical effect; the fact that buspirone takes two to three weeks to exert therapeutic effects, however, probably indicates that modulation of several neurotransmitters or intracellular processes is involved.

Buspirone is rapidly absorbed from the GI tract, with peak plasma levels occurring in 60 to 90 minutes. Buspirone has a short half-life of two to three hours, necessitating three-times-a-day dosing. Its first metabolite is active but less potent than the parent compound, and has a twice-as-long half-life. The most common side effects include headache, nausea, dizziness, drowsiness, and insomnia.

Typical starting dosages in adults are 5 mg three times a day with subsequent titrations occurring at three days or longer intervals and consisting of 5 mg increases. Typical dose ranges are 15 to 30 mg/day with a maximum of 60 mg/day. There are no firm guidelines for dosages in children and adolescents. However, if one chooses to use buspirone, a more conservative dosing schedule should be tried.

Buspirone has been approved for the treatment of anxiety disorders in adults, but there is no current approved indication for the use of buspirone in children under 18 years of age. It has been reported to be effective in case reports for the treatment of generalized anxiety (Kranzler, 1988; Simeon et al., 1994) and in social phobia (Zwier & Rao, 1994).

OBSESSIVE-COMPULSIVE DISORDER

The clinical presentation of obsessive-compulsive disorder (OCD) in children and adolescents is similar to the presentation seen in adults, and the same clinical criteria are used for making a diagnosis in juveniles. Prevalence rates in juveniles are estimated at 2% to 4%. Males tend to predominate in childhood OCD. Although the mean age of onset in clinical populations that have been studied is approximately 10 years old, diagnosis is often delayed. Furthermore, there is a high rate of comorbidity in juvenile samples. Mood disorders, anxiety disorders, and tic disorders are most common, but increased rates of disruptive behavior disorders and specific developmental disorders have also been comorbidly reported. Outcome studies suggest chronicity and the risk of development of other psychiatric disorders, particularly mood and anxiety disorders.

The extant literature strongly supports the role of pharmacotherapy in the treatment of OCD in juveniles. Including the initial report by Flament et al. (1985), which demonstrated at least moderate improvement in 75% of juveniles with OCD treated with clomipramine in a double-blind placebo-controlled crossover study, there have been 12 published reports regarding the use of pharma-cotherapy in OCD treatment (Apter et al., 1994; Como & Kurlan, 1991; DeVaugh-Geiss et al., 1992; Flament et al., 1985; Geller, Biederman, Reed, Spencer, & Wilens, 1995; Leonard et al., 1989, 1991; Liebowitz, Hollander, Fairbanks, & Campeas, 1990; Riddle et al., 1990, 1992, 1996; Simeon, Thatte, & Wiggins, 1990). These studies involved close to 400 juvenile OCD patients and included six randomized double-blind trials (five placebo-controlled and one crossover design of desipramine vs. clomipramine), five open-label studies, and one retrospective treatment review. The studies investigated both SSRIs (fluoxetine [$N = 5$] and fluvoxamine [$N = 3$]) and clomipramine ($N = 4$). Response rates ranged from 50% to 75%, and the children experienced a 25% to 60% reduction in symptoms. A recent report using the newly release SSRI, citalopram, by Thomsen (1997) reported a 10-week open trial in 23 children (age 9 to 18) with OCD. Four patients had a greater than 50% reduction in Children's Yale–Brown Obsessive Compulsive Scale (CY-BOCS), 14 patients showed a 20% to 43% reduction in CY-BOCS scores, and no patient worsened during citalopram therapy.

Given the lower side effect profile, particularly with regards to cardiac issues, the SSRIs are currently first-line agents in the treatment of pediatric OCD, with fluvoxamine and sertraline having FDA-approved indications for pediatric OCD. March et al. (1998) reported a 12-week multicenter randomized controlled trial of sertraline in 187 children and adolescents age 6 to 17. Sertraline was titrated to a dosage of 200mg/day by week four and continued at that dose for eight more weeks. Patients treated with sertraline showed significantly greater improvement than the placebo group on CY-BOCS and Clinical Global Improvement scale (CGI). Also, recent investigations by March, Mulle, and Herbel (1994) using a manualized cognitive-behavioral treatment protocol suggested that the use of this intervention results in significant symptom reduction in 60% of patients. It appears that this intervention can augment the effect of medications and, in some cases, allows for the discontinuation of medications with continued improvement. Given this experience, the treatment of juvenile OCD typically involves the combination of cognitive-behavioral therapies and pharmacotherapy.

AUTISM/PERVASIVE DEVELOPMENTAL DISORDER (PDD)

In *DSM-IV*, autism and PDD/NOS are classified under the larger category of pervasive developmental disorders that also include disorders such as Rett's syndrome, Asperger's disorder, and childhood disintegrative disorder. Autism is a developmental disability in which patients display marked impairment in age-appropriate social and language/play development, as well as displaying repetitive and/or stereotypical behaviors.

The prevalence of autism is 4 to 5 per 10,000 children, with a higher prevalence for PDD/NOS that approaches 10 to 15 per 10,000 children. Both disorders occur more commonly in boys than girls, with a ratio of 3:1. Mental retardation is frequently comorbid, and 40% to 60% of children with autism have cognitive deficits. Language disorders also present comorbidly and need to be carefully distinguished from autism. Children with language disorders can present with poor socialization, but as their language improves, they display less autistic traits. Autism is a chronic condition, with up to two-thirds of autistic adults remaining severely handicapped and requiring supervised living arrangements. Prognosis is closely linked to cognitive ability and the level of language development that occurs. Only 1% to 2% of autistic patients achieve independent living status.

A number of pharmacologic agents have been used to address symptoms in autism of hyperactivity, OCD, aggression, self-injury, and depression. Although a number of agents have resulted in clinical improvement for autistic individuals, they tend to provide only symptomatic relief and do not significantly alter the course of the disorder.

The antipsychotics are the best-studied agents, with several studies having shown the efficacy of haloperidol in the treatment of disruptive behaviors and with improvement in learning (Anderson et al., 1989; Campbell et al., 1978). A more recent case study by Hardan, Johnson, Johnson, and Hrecznyj (1996) reported the efficacy of risperidone in an open clinical trial of 20 subjects (age 8 to 17 years) with various developmental disorders, including autism, PDD/NOS, and mental retardation. Target symptoms included hyperactivity, aggression, and self-injury. Clinical efficacy was demonstrated in 13 subjects as measured by the Aberrant Behavior Checklist (ABC) and Conners scales. McDougle et al. (1997) also reported a 12-week open trial of risperidone in 18 subjects (age 5–18 years) with autism, Asperger's disorder, childhood disintegrative disorder, and PDD/NOS. Significant improvement was seen in aggression and impulsivity, interfering repetitive behavior, and some elements of impaired social relatedness.

Naltrexone, an opiate antagonist, has been studied in the treatment of self-injurious behavior with mixed results. In the only double-blind placebo-controlled trial by Campbell et al. (1993), naltrexone was shown to reduce hyperactivity but had no effect on learning and self-injurious behavior. Clomipramine has been studied as a possible agent to address repetitive behaviors in autism. Gordon, State, Nelson, Hamburger, and Rapoport (1993) reported a double-blind study of 24 subjects age 6 to 18 years, comparing clomipramine, desipramine, and placebo in autism. Clomipramine was superior to placebo in reducing stereotypical behavior, compulsive behavior, and anger, with mean dosages of 152 mg having been used. Clomipramine and desipramine were effective in reducing hyperactivity as well.

Other drugs that have shown symptomatic improvement in autism include fluoxetine, stimulants, and clonidine. Cook, Rowlett, Jaselskis, and Leventhal (1992) reported an open trial of fluoxetine in 23 subjects with autism and 16 with mental retardation. They found improvement in Clinical Global Impressions rating of clinical severity in 15 of 23 autistic subjects and 10 of 16 subjects with mental retardation. Birmaher, Quintana, and Greenhill (1988) treated nine hyperactive autistic children (ages 4–16 years) with 10 to 50 mg of methylphenidate per day, with eight of nine children improving on all rating scales. Jaselskis, Cook, Fletcher, and Leventhal (1992) reported treating eight male autistic subjects (age 5–13 years) with clonidine in a double-blind, placebo-controlled, crossover study. On Conners Abbreviated Parent and Teacher questionnaires, both parents and teachers reported significant improvement on clonidine compared to placebo. Clinician ratings, however, showed no significant differences between clonidine and placebo.

CONCLUDING REMARKS

The past twenty years have yielded significant gains in child psychiatry that have been built on (1) the introduction of a structured diagnostic system, (2) the recognition of the onset of psychiatric illness in childhood, (3) the implementation of longitudinal studies of psychopathology beginning in childhood, (4) investigations of temperament and its relationship to subsequent psychopathology, and (5) longitudinal studies of and (6) interventional studies with at-risk children. However, controlled investigations of psychopharmacological interventions in children have been lacking. The practice of pediatric psychopharmacology is based largely on studies conducted in adult patients; however, generalizing research results from adults to children is not adequate. Children are different from adults in many clinically important ways; therefore, clinical investigations of psychopharmacologic interventions in children are needed.

Many of the disorders that occur in childhood are associated with significant morbidity and functional impairment. The evaluation of children should include a careful assessment of coexisting psychosocial stressors that may be contributing to the child's presentation. Proper intervention typically involves the use of multiple modalities. Pharmacotherapy, when used appropriately, may act to diminish symtom severity and assist in the process of recovery in pediatric patients. Successful pharmacotherapy of children begins with the development of an active and reciprocal alliance with patient and family that allows for the sharing of critical information and the provision of support. The alliance should be built on an open discourse regarding the nature of the child's diagnosis. The initiation of treatment should also include a clear definition of target symptoms, the potential risks and benefits of the proposed intervention, and a discussion that includes a review of the current experience in both adult and child psychiatry with this intervention. Finally, the establishment of a method that allows for adequate monitoring of both response and side effects is critical. Although this type of carefully monitored approach to treatment cannot supplant the need for controlled trials, the use of a structured approach to psychopharmacological treatment can further the development of clinically relevant observations and reports and can enhance the practitioner's ability to safely monitor response and side effects. Pediatric pharmacotherapy is a field in its infancy; until the critical need for more controlled studies is sufficiently met, practitioners must be acutely aware of the limitations of the existing knowledge base concerning psychopharmacological interventions in children.

REFERENCES

Anderson, L.T., Campbell, M., Adams, P., Small, A.M., Perry, R., & Shell, J. (1989). The effects of haloperidol on discrimination learning and behavioral symptoms in autistic children. *Journal of Autism and Developmental Disorders, 19,* 227–239.

Apter, A., Ratzoni, G., King, R., Weizman, A., Iancu, I., Binder, M., & Riddle, M.A. (1994). Fluvoxamine open-label treatment of adolescent inpatients with obsessive-compulsive disorder or depression. *Journal of the American Academy of Child and Adolescent Psychiatry, 33,* 342–348.

Armenteros, J.L., Whitaker, A.H., Welikson, M., Stedge, D.J., & Gorman, J. (1997). Risperidone in adolescents with schizophrenia: An open pilot study. *Journal of the American Academy of Child and Adolescent Psychiatry, 36,* 694–700.

Arnsten, A.F., Steere, J.C., & Hunt, R.D. (1996). The contribution of alpha-2 noradrenergic mechanisms to prefrontal cortical cognitive function: Potential significance for attention-deficit hyperactivity disorder. *Archives of General Psychiatry, 53,* 448–455.

Baraban, J.M., Worley, P.F., & Snyder, S.H. (1989). Second messenger systems and psychoactive drug action: Focus on the phosphoinositide system and lithium. *American Journal of Psychiatry, 146,* 1251–1260.

Barrickman, L.L., Perry, P.J., Allen, A.J., Kuperman, S., Arndt, S.V., Herrmann, K.J., & Schumacher, E. (1995). Bupropion vs. methylphenidate in the treatment of ADHD. *Journal of the American Academy of Child and Adolescent Psychiatry, 34,* 649–657.

Berney, T., Kolvin, I., Bhate, S.R., Garside, R.F., Jeans, J., Kay, B., & Scarth, L. (1981). School phobia: A therapeutic trial with clomipramine and short-term outcome. *British Journal of Psychiatry, 138,* 110–118.

Biederman, J., Baldessarini, R., Wright, V., Knee, D., & Harmatz, J. (1989). A double-blind placebo controlled study of desipramine in the treatment of attention-deficit disorder: I. Efficacy. *Journal of the American Academy of Child and Adolescent Psychiatry, 28,* 777–784.

Birmaher, B., Quintana, H., & Greenhill, L.L. (1988). Methylphenidate treatment of hyperactive autistic children. *Journal of the American Academy of Child and Adolescent Psychiatry, 27,* 248–251.

Birmaher, B., Ryan, N.D., Williamson, D.E., Brent, D.A., & Kaufman, J. (1996). Childhood and adolescent depression: A review of the past 10 years: Part II. *Journal of the American Academy of Child and Adolescent Psychiatry, 35,* 1575–1583.

Birmaher, B., Waterman, G.S., Ryan, N., Cully, M., Balach, L., Ingram, J., & Brodsky, M. (1994). Fluoxetine for childhood anxiety disorders. *Journal of the American Academy of Child and Adolescent Psychiatry, 33,* 993–999.

Boulos, C., Kutcher, S., Gardner, D., & Young, E. (1992). An open naturalistic trial of fluoxetine in adolescents and young adults with treatment resistant major depression. *Journal of Child and Adolescent Psychopharmacology, 2,* 103–111.

Bradley, C. (1937). The behavior of children receiving Benzedrine. *American Journal of Psychiatry, 94,* 577–585.

Campbell, M., Anderson, L.T., Meier, M., Cohen, I.L., Small, A.M., Samit, C., & Sachar, E.J. (1978). A comparison of haloperidol and behavior therapy and their interaction in autistic children. *Journal of the American Academy of Child Psychiatry, 17,* 640–655.

Campbell, M., Anderson, L.T., Small, A.M., Adams, P., Gonzalez, N.M., & Ernst, M. (1993). Naltrexone in autistic children: Behavioral symptoms and attentional learning. *Journal of the American Academy of Child and Adolescent Psychiatry, 32,* 1283–1291.

Casat, C.D., Pleasants, D.Z., & Van Wyck Fleet, J. (1987). A double blind trial of bupropion in children with attention deficit disorder. *Psychopharmacology Bulletin, 23,* 120–122.

Castellanos, F.X., Giedd, J.N., Elia, J., Marsh, W.L., Ritchie, G.F., Hamburger, S.D., & Rapoport, J.L. (1997). Controlled stimulant treatment of ADHD and comorbid Tourette's syndrome. Effects of stimulant and dose. *Journal of the American Academy of Child and Adolescent Psychiatry, 36,* 589–596.

Chapell, P.B., Riddle, M.A., Scahill, L., Lynch, K.A., Schultz, R., Arnsten, A.F., Leckman, J.F., & Cohen, D.J. (1995). Guanfacine treatment of comorbid attention-deficit-hyperactivity disorder and Tourette's syndrome: Preliminary clinical experience. *Journal of the American Academy of Child and Adolescent Psychiatry, 34,* 1140–1146.

Colle, L.M., Belair, J.F., DiFeo, M., Weiss, J., & LaRoache, C. (1994). Extended open-label fluoxetine treatment of adolescents with major depression. *Journal of Child and Adolescent Psychopharmacology, 4,* 225–232.

Como, P.G., & Kurlan, R. (1991). An open-label trial of fluoxetine for obsessive-compulsive disorder in Gilles de la Tourette's syndrome. *Neurology, 41,* 872–874.

Cook, E.H., Jr., Rowlett, R., Jaselskis, C., & Leventhal, B.L. (1992). Fluoxetine treatment of children and adults with autistic disorder and mental retardation. *Journal of the Academy of Child and Adolescent Psychiatry, 31,* 739–745.

Costello, E.J. (1989). Child psychiatric disorders and their correlates: A primary care pediatric sample. *Journal of the American Academy of Child and Adolescent Psychiatry, 28,* 851–859.

Costello, E.J., Costello, A.J., Edelbrock, C., Burns, B.J., Dulcan, M.K., Brent, D., & Janiszewski, S. (1988). Psychiatric disorders in pediatric primary care: Prevalence and risk factors. *Archives of General Psychiatry, 45,* 1107–1116.

Cueva, J.E., Overall, J.E., Small, A.M., Armenteros, J.L., Perry, R., & Campbell, M. (1996). Carbamazepine in aggressive children with conduct disorder: A double-blind and placebo-controlled study. *Journal of the American Academy of Child and Adolescent Psychiatry, 35,* 480–490.

DeLong, G.R., & Aldershop, A.L. (1987). Long-term experience with lithium treatment in childhood: Correlation with clincial diagnosis. *Journal of the American Academy of Child and Adolescent Psychiatry, 26,* 389–394.

DeVaugh-Geiss, J., Moroz, G., Biederman, J., Cantwell, D., Fontaine, R., Greist, J., Reichler, R., Katz, R., & Landau, P. (1992). Clomipramine hydrochloride in childhood and adolescent obsessive-compulsive disorder: A multicenter trial. *Journal of the American Academy of Child and Adolescent Psychiatry, 31,* 34–49.

Emslie G., Rush, A.J., Weinberg, W.A., Kowatch, R.A., Hughes, C.W., Carmody, T., & Rintelmann, J. (1997). A double-blind, randomized placebo-controlled trial of fluoxetine in depressed children and adolescents. *Archives of General Psychiatry, 54,* 1031–1037.

Federal Drug Administration. (1995, August). *Federal Drug Administration bulletin* (p. 3). Washington, DC: Author.

Flament, M.F., Rapoport, J.L., Berg, C.J., Sceery, W., Kilts, C., Mellstrom, B., & Linnoila, M. (1985). Clomipramine treatment of childhood obsessive-compulsive disorder: A double-blind controlled study. *Archives General Psychiatry, 42,* 977–983.

Fleming, J.E., & Offord, D.R. (1990). Epidemiology of childhood depressive disorders: A critical review. *Journal of the American Academy of Child and Adolescent Psychiatry, 29,* 571–580.

Frazier, J.A., Gordon, C.T., McKenna, K., Lenane, M.C., Jih, D., & Rapoport, J.L. (1994). An open trial of clozapine in 11 adolescents with child-onset schizophrenia. *Journal of the American Academy of Child and Adolescent Psychiatry, 33,* 658–663.

Gadow, K.D., Nolan, E., Sprafkin, J., & Sverd, J. (1995). School observations of children with attention-deficit-hyperactivity disorder and comorbid tic disorder: Effects of methylphenidate treatment. *Journal of Developmental and Behavioral Pediatrics, 16,* 167–176.

Garfinkel, B.D., Wender, P.H., Sloman, L., & O'Neill, I. (1983). Tricyclic antidepressant and methylphenidate treatment of attention deficit disorder in children. *Journal of the American Academy of Child Psychiatry, 22,* 343–348.

Geller, B., Cooper, T.B., Chestnut, E.C., Anker, J.A., & Schluchter, M.D. (1986). Preliminary data on the relationship between nortriptyline plasma level and responses in depressed children. *American Journal of Psychiatry, 143,* 1283–1286.

Geller, B., Cooper, T.B., Sun, K., Zimerman, B., Frazier, J., Williams, M., & Heath, J. (1998). Double-blind and placebo-controlled study of lithium for adolescent bipolar disorders with secondary substance dependency. *Journal of the American Academy of Child and Adolescent Psychiatry, 37,* 171–178.

Geller, D., Biederman, J., Reed, E., Spencer, T., & Wilens, T. (1995). Similarities in response to fluoxetine in the treatment of children and adolescents with obsessive-compulsive disorder. *Journal of the American Academy of Child and Adolescent Psychiatry, 34,* 36–44.

Gittelman, R., Mannuzza, S., Shenker, R., & Bonagura, N. (1985). Hyperactive boys almost grown up: I. Psychiatric status. *Archives of General Psychiatry, 42,* 937–947.

Gittelman-Klein, R., & Klein, D. (1971). Controlled imipramine treatment of school phobia. *Archives of General Psychiatry, 25,* 204–207.

Gordon, C.T., State, R.C., Nelson, J.E., Hamburger, S.D., & Rapoport, J.L. (1993). A double-blind comparison of clomipramine, desipramine, and placebo in the treatment of autistic disorder. *Archives of General Psychiatry, 50,* 441–447.

Grace, F., Milner, J., Rizzotto, L., & Klein, R.G. (1994). Clonazepam in childhood anxiety disorders. *Journal of the American Academy of Child and Adolescent Psychiatry, 33,* 372–376.

Greenhill, L.L., Rieder, R.O., Wender, P.H., Bushbaum, M., & Zahn, T.P. (1973). Lithium carbonate in the treatment of hyperactive children. *Archives of General Psychiatry, 28,* 636–640.

Hardan, A., Johnson, K., Johnson, C., & Hrecznyj, B. (1996). Case study: Risperidone treatment of children and adolescents with developmental disorders. *Journal of the American Academy of Child and Adolescent Psychiatry, 35,* 1551–1556.

Hunt, R.D., Arnsten, A.F.T., & Asbell, M.D. (1995). An open trial of guanfacine in the treatment of attention-deficit-hyperactivity disorder. *Journal of the American Academy of Child Adolescent Psychiatry, 34,* 50–54.

Hunt, R.D., Menderaa, R.B., & Cohen, D.J. (1985). Clonidine benefits children with attention-deficit disorder and hyperactivity: Report of a double-blind placebo-crossover therapeutic trial. *Journal of the American Academy of Child Psychiatry, 24,* 617–629.

Hyman, S.E., & Nestler, E.J. (1996). Initiation and adaptation: A paradigm for understanding psychotropic drug action. *American Journal of Psychiatry, 153,* 151–162.

Jain, U., Birmaher, B., Garcia, M., Al-Shabbout, M., & Ryan, N. (1992). Fluoxetine in children and adolescents with mood disorders: A chart review of efficacy and adverse effects. *Journal of Child and Adolescent Psychopharmacology, 2,* 259–265.

Jaselskis, C.A., Cook, E.H., Fletcher, K.E., & Leventhal, B.L. (1992). Clonidine treatment of hyperactive and impulsive children with autistic disorder. *Journal of Clinical Psychopharmacology, 12,* 322–327.

Kashani, J.H., & Sherman, D.D. (1988). Childhood depression: Epidemiology, etiological models, and treatment implications. *Integrative Psychiatry, 6,* 1–8.

Kastner, T., Finesmith, R., & Walsh, K. (1993). Long-term adminstration of valproic acid in the treatment of affective symptoms in people with mental retardation. *Journal of Clinical Psychopharmacology, 13,* 448–451.

Kastner, T., Friedman, D.L., Plummer, A.T., Ruiz, M.Q., & Henning, D. (1990). Valproic acid for the treatment of children with mental retardation and mood symptomatology. *Pediatrics, 86,* 467–472.

Kent, J.D., Blader, J.C., Koplewicz, H.S., Abikoff, H., & Foley, C.A. (1995). Effects of late-afternoon methylphenidate administration on behavior and sleep in attention-deficit-hyperactivity disorder. *Pediatrics, 96,* 320–325.

Klein, D.F., Gittelman, R., Quitkin, F., & Rifkin, A. (1980). Diagnosis and treatment of childhood disorders. In *Diagnosis and drug treatment of psychiatric disorders: Adults and children.* Baltimore: Williams & Wilkins.

Klein, P.D., & Riddle, M.A. (1995). Pharmacokinetics in children and adolescents. *Child and Adolescent Psychiatry Clinic of North America, 4,* 59–75.

Klein, R.G., Koplewicz, H.S., & Kannew, A. (1992). Imipramine treatment of children with separation anxiety disorder. *Journal of the American Academy of Child and Adolescent Psychiatry, 31,* 21–28.

Klein, R.G., & Last, C.G. (1989). *Anxiety disorders in children.* Newbury Park, CA: Sage.

Kranzler, H.R. (1988). Use of buspirone in an adolescent with overanxious disorder. *Journal of the American Academy of Child and Adolescent Psychiatry, 27,* 789–790.

Kumra, S., Frazier, J.A., Jacobsen, L.K., McKenna, K., Gordon, C.T., Lenane, M.C., Hamburger, S.D., Smith, A.K., Albus, K.E., Alaghband-Rad, J., & Rapoport, J.L. (1997). Childhood-onset schizophrenia: A double blind clozapine-haloperidol comparison. *Archives of General Psychiatry, 53,* 1090–1097.

Kumra, S., Herion, D., Jacobsen, L.K., Briguglia, C., & Grothe, D. (1997). Case study: Risperidone-induced hepatotoxicity in pediatric patients. *Journal of the American Academy of Child and Adolescent Psychiatry, 36,* 701–705.

Kumra, S., Jacobsen, L.K., Lenane, M., Karp, B.I., Frazier, J.A., Smith, A.K., Bedwell, J., Lee, P., Malanga, C.J., Hamburger, S.D., & Rapoport, J.L. (1998). Childhood-onset Schizophrenia: An open label study of olanzapine

in adolescents. *Journal of the American Academy of Child and Adolescent Psychiatry, 37,* 377–385.

Kutcher, S.P., & MacKenzie, S. (1988). Successful clonazepam treatment of adolescents with panic disorder [Letter]. *Journal of Clinical Psychopharmacology, 8,* 299–301.

Leonard, H.L., Swedo, S.E., Rapoport, J.L., Koby, E., Lenane, M.C., Cheslow, D.L., & Hamburger, S.D. (1989). Treatment of obsessive-compulsive disorder with clomipramine and desipramine in children and adolescents. *Archives of General Psychiatry, 46,* 1088–1092.

Leonard, H.L., Swedo, S.E., Lenane, M.C., Rettew, D.C., Cheslow, D.L., Hamburger, S.D., & Rapoport, J.L. (1991). A double-blind desipramine substitution during long-term clomipramine treatment in children and adolescents with obsessive-compulsive disorder. *Archives of General Psychiatry, 48,* 922–927.

Liebowitz, M.R., Hollander, E., Fairbanks, J., & Campeas, R. (1990). Fluoxetine for adolescents with obsessive-compulsive disorder [Letter; comment]. *American Journal of Psychiatry, 47,* 370–371.

Malhotra, S., & Santosh, P.J. (1998). An open clinical trial of buspirone in children with attention-deficit-hyperactivity disorder. *Journal of the American Academy of Child and Adolescent Psychiatry, 37,* 364–371.

Mandoki, M.W., Tapia, M.R., Tapia, M.A., Sumner, G.S., & Parker, J.L. (1997). Venlafaxine in the treatment of children and adolescents with major depression. *Psychopharmacology Bulletin, 33,* 149–154.

Mannuzza, S., Klein, R.G., Bessler, A., Malloy, P., & LaPadula, M. (1993). Adult outcome of hyperactive boys: Educational achievement, occupational and psychiatric status. *Archives of General Psychiatry, 50,* 565–576.

Mannuzza, S., Klein, R.G., Bonagura, N., Malloy, P., Giampino, T.L., & Addalli, K.A. (1991). Hyperactive boys almost grown up: V. Replication of psychiatric status. *Archives of General Psychiatry, 48,* 77–83.

March, J.S., Biederman, J., Wolkow, R., Safferman, A., Mardekian, J., Cook, E.H., Cutler, N.R., Dominguez, R., Ferguson, J., Muller, B., Riesenberg, R., Rosenthal, M., Sallee, F.R., & Wagner, K.D. (1998). Sertraline in children and adolescents with obsessive-compulsive disorder: A multicenter randomized controlled trial. *Journal of the American Medical Association, 280,* 1752–1756.

March, J.S., Mulle, K., & Herbel, B. (1994). Behavioral psychotherapy for children and adolescents with obsessive-compulsive disorder: An open trial of a new protocol-driven treatment package. *Journal of the American Academy of Child and Adolescent Psychiatry, 33,* 333–341.

McDougle, C.J., Holmes, J.P., Bronson, M.R., Anderson, G.M., Volkmar, F.R., Price, L.H., & Cohen, D.J. (1997).

Risperidone treatment of children and adolescents with pervasive developmental disordes: A prospective open-label study. *Journal of the American Academy of Child and Adolescent Psychiatry, 36,* 685–693.

Nemeroff, C.B., DeVane, C.L., & Pollock, B.G. (1996). Newer antidepressants and the cytochrome P450 system. *American Journal of Psychiatry, 153,* 311–320.

Olvera, R.L., Pliszka, S.R., Luh, J., & Tatum, R. (1996). An open trial of venlafaxine in the treatment of attention-deficit-hyperactivity disorder in children and adolescents. *Journal of Child and Adolescent Psychopharmacology, 6,* 241–250.

Papatheodorow, G., Kutcher, S.P., Katic, M., & Szalai, J.P. (1995). The efficacy and safety of divalproex sodium in the treatment of acute mania in adolescents and young adults: An open clinical trial. *Journal of Clinical Psychopharmacology, 15,* 110–115.

Pelham, W.E., Swanson, J.M., Furman, M.B., & Schwindt, H., (1995). Pemoline effects on children with ADHD: A time-response by dose-response analysis on classroom measures. *Journal of the American Academy of Child Adolescent Psychiatry, 34,* 1504–1513.

Pfefferbaum, G., Overall, J.E., Boren, H.A., Frankel, L.S., Sullivan, M.R., & Johnson, K. (1987). Alprazolam in the treatment of anticipatory and acute situational anxiety in children with cancer. *Journal of the American Academy of Child and Adolescent Psychiatry, 26,* 532–535.

Pollack, M.H., Worthington, J.J., III, Otto, M.W., Maki, K.M., Smoller, J.W., Manfro, G.G., Rudolph, R., & Rosenbaum, J.F. (1996). Venlafaxine for panic disorder: Results from a double-blind placebo-controlled study. *Psychopharmacology Bulletin, 32,* 667–670.

Popper, C.W., & Steingard, R.J. (1994). Disorders usually first diagnosed in infancy, childhood, or adolescence. In R.E., Hales, S.C. Yudofsky, & J.A. Talbott (Eds.), *Textbook of psychiatry* (2nd ed., pp. 729–832). Washington, DC: American Psychiatric Press.

Preskorn, S.H., Weller, E.B., Hughes, C.W., Weller, R.A., & Bolte, K. (1987). Depression in prepubertal children: Dexamethasone nonsuppression predicts differential response to imipramine vs. placebo. *Psychopharmacology Bulletin, 23,* 128–133.

Quintana, H., & Keshavan, M. (1995). Case study: Risperidone in children and adolescents with schizophrenia. *Journal of the American Academy of Child Psychiatry, 34,* 1292–1296.

Rapoport, J.L., Quinn, P.O., Bradbard, G., Riddle, D., & Brooks, E. (1974). Imipramine and methylphenidate treatment of hyperactive boys. *Archives of General Psychiatry, 30,* 789–798.

Riddle, M.A., Claghorn, J., Gaggney, G., Greist, J., Holland, D., Landbloom, R., McConville, B., Piggott, T., Pravetz, M., Walkup, J., Yaryura-Tobias, J., & Houser, V. (1996). *Fluvoxamine for children and adolescents with obsessive compulsive disorder: A controlled multicenter trial.* Abstract from the Scientific Proceedings of the 43rd annual meeting of the American Academy of Child and Adolescent Psychiatry, Philadelphia.

Riddle, M.A., Scahill, L., King, R., Hardin, M., Anderson, G., Ort, S., Smith, J.C., Leckman, J.F., & Cohen, D.J. (1992). Double-blind, crossover trial of fluoxetine and placebo in children and adolescents with obsessive-compulsive disorder. *Journal of the American Academy of Child and Adolescent Psychiatry, 31,* 1062–1069.

Riddle, M.A., Scahill, L., King, R., Hardin, M.T., Towbin, K.E., Ort, S.I., Leckman, J.F., & Cohen, D.J. (1990). Obsessive compulsive disorder in children and adolescents: Phenomenology and family history. *Journal of the American Academy of Child and Adolescent Psychiatry, 29,* 766–767.

Rivera-Calimlim, L., Griesbach, P.H., & Perlmutter, R. (1979). Plasma chlorpromazine concentrations in children with behavioral disorders and mental illness. *Clinical Pharmacol Therapy, 26,* 14–121.

Ross, D.C., & Pigott, L.R. (1993). Clonazepam for OCD [Letter]. *Journal of the American Academy of Child and Adolescent Psychiatry, 32,* 470–471.

Saul, R.C. (1985). Nortriptyline in attention deficit disorder. *Clinical Neuropharmacology, 8,* 382–384.

Silva, R.R., Munoz, D.M., & Alpert, M. (1996). Carbamazepine use in children and adolescents with features of attention-deficit hyperactivity disorder: A meta-analysis. *Journal of the American Academy of Child and Adolescent Psychiatry, 35,* 352–358.

Simeon, J.G., & Ferguson, H.B. (1987). Alprazolam effects in children with anxiety disorders. *Canadian Journal of Psychiatry, 32,* 570–574.

Simeon, J.G., Ferguson, H.B., Knott, V., Roberts, N., Gauthier, B., Dubois, C., & Wiggins, D. (1992). Clinical, cognitive, and neurophysiological effects of alprazolam in children and adolescents with overanxious and avoidant disorders. *Journal of the American Academy of Child and Adolescent Psychiatry, 31,* 29–33.

Simeon, J.G., Ferguson, H.B., & Van Wyck Fleet, J. (1986). Bupropion effects in attention deficit and conduct disorders. *Canadian Journal of Psychiatry, 31,* 581–585.

Simeon, J.G., Knott, V.J., DuBois, C., Wiggins, D., Geraets, I., Thatte, S., & Miller, W. (1994). Buspirone therapy of mixed anxiety disorders in childhood and adolescence: A pilot study. *Journal of Child and Adolescent Psychopharmacology, 4,* 159–170.

Simeon, J.G., Thatte, S., Wiggins, D. (1990). Treatment of adolescent obsessive-compulsive disorder with a clomipramine-fluoxetine combination. *Psychopharmacology Bulletin, 26(3),* 285–290.

Stein, M.A., Blondis, T.A., Schnitzler, E.R., O'Brien, T., Fishkin, J., Blackwell, B., Szumowski, E., & Roizen, N.J. (1996). Methylphenidate dosing: Twice daily versus three times daily. *Pediatrics, 98,* 748–756.

Strober, M., Morrell, W., Burroughs, J., Lampert, C., Danforth, H., & Freeman, R. (1988). A family study of bipolar I disorder in adolescence: Early onset of symptoms linked to increased familial loading and lithium resistance. *Journal of Affective Disorder, 14,* 255–268.

Swanson, J.M., Wigal, S., Greenhill, L.L., Browne, R., Waslik, B., Lerner, M., Williams, L., Flynn, D., Agler, D., Crowley, K., Fineberg, E., Baren, M., & Cantwell, D. (1998). Analog classroom assessment of adderall in children with ADHD. *Journal of the American Academy Child Adolescent Psychiatry, 37,* 519–526.

Thomsen, P.H. (1997). Child and adolescent obsessive-compulsive disorder treated with citalopram: Findings from an open trial of 23 cases. *Journal of Child and Adolescent Psychopharmacology, 7,* 157–166.

Tirosh, E., Sadeh, A., Munvez, R., & Lavie, P. (1993). Effects of methylphenidate on sleep in children with attention-deficient-hyperactivity disorder: An activity monitor study. *American Journal of Diseases in Children, 147,* 1313–1315.

Varanka, T.M., Weller, R.A., Weller, E.B., & Fristad, M.A. (1988). Lithium treatment of manic episodes with psychotic features in prepubertal children. *American Journal of Psychiatry, 145,* 1557–1559.

Varley, C.K., & McClellan, J. (1997). Case study: Two additional sudden deaths with tricyclic antidepressants. *Journal of the American Academy of Child and Adolescent Psychiatry, 36,* 390–394.

Weller, E.B., Weller, R.A., & Fristad, M.A. (1986). Lithium dosage guide for prepubertal children: A preliminary report. *Journal of the American Academy of Child Psychiatry, 25,* 92–95.

Wender, P.H. (1988). Attention-deficit-hyperactivity disorder. In J.G. Howells (Ed.), *Modern perspectives in clinical psychiatry* (pp. 149–169). New York: Brunner/Mazel.

West, S.A., Keck, P.E., McElroy, S.L., Strakowske, S.M., Minnery, K.L., McConville, B.J., & Sorter, M.T. (1994). Open trial of valproate in the treatment of adolescent mania. *Journal of Child and Adolescent Psychopharmacology, 4,* 263–267.

Wilens, T.E., Biederman, J., Geist, D.E., Steingard, R., & Spencer, T. (1993). Nortriptyline in the treatment of ADHD: A chart review of 58 cases. *Journal of the American Academy of Child and Adolescent Psychiatry, 32,* 343–349.

Wilens, T.E., Spencer, T.J., Biederman, J., & Schleifer, D. (1997). Case study: Nefazadone for juvenile mood disorders. *Journal of the American Academy of Child and Adolescent Psychiatry, 36,* 481–485.

Zwier, K.J., & Rao, U. (1994). Buspirone use in an adolescent with social phobia and mixed personality disorder (cluster A type). *Journal of the American Academy of Child and Adolescent Psychiatry, 33,* 1007–1011.

SECTION SEVEN

SPECIAL TOPICS

CHAPTER 48

Cultural and Ethnic Diversity Issues in Clinical Child Psychology

RUSSELL T. JONES, CHRISTINA KEPHART, AUDRA K. LANGLEY,
MARY N. PARKER, UMA SHENOY, AND CHERI WEEKS

Research suggests that within the next several years, this country will realize significant demographic changes in its cultural makeup. Further, estimates predict that by the year 2050, 50% of the American population will be of ethnic minority descent (Victor, et al., 1996), and a majority of these individuals will be children and adolescents. These projections pose significant problems for our society in that the majority of its institutions (e.g., educational, mental health) primarily embrace a Eurocentric cultural framework and do not encompass cultures of many individuals of color. Given that growing numbers of children and adolescents of color are coming to the attention of mental health professionals, it is imperative that efforts be made to identify the specific needs of these populations and then integrate them into the conceptualization, development, and delivery of mental health services (American Psychiatric Association [APA], 1994).

The purpose of this chapter is to explore many of the clinical issues that are specific to African American, Latino/Latina, Native American, and Asian American children. More specifically, this chapter focuses on clinical issues related to the assessment, diagnosis, and treatment of psychological disorders in children of color. The central aim of this chapter is to make recommendations to enhance the effectiveness of mental health professionals who serve people of color. The term "individuals of color" is a generic title typically used to refer to persons who are not of European descent, including individuals of African, Asian, and Latin or Hispanic descent and Native Americans. These nationalities represent distinct groups of individuals who possess their own unique cultural histories, values, and practices. Even the histories of these groups in the United States are very distinct, ranging from forced slavery, indentured servitude, and displacement to voluntary immigration with the goal of obtaining a better life. Research suggests that the history of individuals in this society is an important factor that serves as a major determinant in the expression of psychological phenomena. When possible, we attempt to identify cultural factors that impact clinical issues in each of these diverse groups of individuals.

Recently, psychologists have begun to examine the role that culture and ethnicity play in the development, maintenance, and expression of psychopathology. Culture and ethnicity are terms that are often engaged to refer to the same phenomena within various psychological research efforts; however, these constructs are qualitatively different.

Culture is defined as a set of norms and values that influence the way a person thinks, behaves, and feels. It is influenced by society and affects ways that relationships are formed (Parron, 1994). Therefore, culture appears to be a far-reaching entity that influences all aspects of functioning. In contrast, ethnicity refers to a person's racial heritage. Ethnicity is a dynamic system of genetic, morphological, and anthropological characteristics (Parron, 1994). A common misconception has been that ethnic groups harbor a set of beliefs and behaviors that are static and homogeneous. From the above definitions, ethnicity does not influence behavior and belief; rather, these are influenced by a complex set of commonly held cultural beliefs. In this chapter, we view culture as an overarching construct that impacts the psychological functioning of all children of color. Four major groups of children of color (African American, Asian, Latino, and American Indian) are discussed. Unique issues related to the assessment, diagnosis, and treatment of disorders are discussed, followed by recommendations to inform those who serve these populations.

AFRICAN AMERICAN CHILDREN AND ADOLESCENTS

POPULATION AND CULTURAL CHARACTERISTICS

Thirteen percent of the U.S. population is African American, 30% of whom are children under 18 years of age. The U.S Census Bureau defines African Americans as American-born persons of either African or Hispanic descent (U.S. Bureau of the Census, 1996).

Although African Americans share the same history and similar experiences, it is important to note that they are not a homogeneous group. Within-group differences are often overlooked by researchers and clinicians, which leads to overgeneralizations. Boyd-Franklin (cited in Dillon, 1994) writes: "The great diversity of values, characteristics, and lifestyles that arise from such elements as geographic origin, level of acculturation, socioeconomic status, education, religious background, and age reveals such categorization to be inaccurate and ultimately unproductive as an assessment tool" (p. 131). It is therefore important that researchers and clinicians recognize the need to "match" conceptualizations of psychological

functioning as well as clinical formulations to the unique qualities of diverse African American individuals.

MENTAL HEALTH STATUS

African Americans, and minorities in general, have been reported to exhibit higher rates of psychological problems than the larger population (Gibbs & Huang, 1989). African American children are diagnosed with higher rates of conduct disorder and are hospitalized at two to three times the rate of their White counterparts (Gibbs, 1988). Additionally, African American adults and children are more likely to be diagnosed with psychotic disorders, whereas the diagnosis of affective disorders is often overlooked (Adebimpe, 1981; Baker, 1988; Canino & Spurlock 1994). These reports make a compelling case for further investigation of those issues that impact the psychological functioning of African American children. They also indicate the necessity of addressing issues that may impact the dissemination of services of mental health to individuals in this community.

The majority of the social institutions in the United States have their roots in the majority culture; the incongruence between an African American's cultural values and that of the dominant culture have been shown to result in stress. This type of stress, referred to as African American status stress, is conceptualized as chronic in that it has a persistent impact on every area of an African American's life. It results not only from inconsistencies between a Eurocentric and an Afrocentric framework but also from the perception and treatment of African Americans, historically and presently, in American society. More specifically, these stressors often result from a variety of factors, including discrimination in corporate and educational institutions, overt racism, police brutality, poorer medical health care, conservative backlash, and political inequality. These types of stressors may have a direct effect on the psychological functioning of African American children or an indirect effect by impacting their parents.

Poverty, violence, unemployment, and incarceration affect all Americans in the United States; however, African Americans are highly visible in all of these categories. A majority of African Americans live in urban areas that are characterized by poverty, substandard housing, inadequate

ASSESSMENT

Clinicians working with minority children may be challenged to earn the trust of the child and the family, which is essential for the establishment of a viable therapeutic relationship. For example, traditionally, African Americans have been skeptical of psychological assessment. Early psychological investigations reported that African Americans were both mentally and emotionally inferior to Whites (R.T. Jones, Brown, Davis, Jefferies, & Shenoy, 1998). Such claims, based on faulty data, have done much to discourage confidence in the psychological assessment process.

The traditional mode of assessment for African American populations has been much like that for majority group members. This approach has often succeeded only in revealing differences among racial groups without providing a clear understanding of how such differences may be accounted for and how test scores might be employed to effect desired change. Few of the popular test instruments have been normed on African Americans, and many clinicians erroneously interpret the results. This is a dangerous practice in that it increases the number of Type II errors and, according to Malgady (1996), is most detrimental to ethnic minority clients because of the danger of misdiagnosis. One consequence of this practice has been the overrepresentation of African American children in special education classrooms (R.L. Jones, 1972, 1988). Although the Wechsler Intelligence Scale for Children (WISC) and WISC-R have both shown predictive validity for minority children in studies that show correlations up to .60 between test scores and school performance (Hartlage & Steele, 1977; Sattler, 1974), one criticism of intellectual assessment measures and their utility with African American children is that they lack sufficient items that assess right brain functioning (cited in R.T. Jones & Herndon, 1992). Kaufman (1979) has argued that this may negatively affect the test scores of African American children because these children demonstrate right brain preference through their use of gestural language and emphasis on movement and music (C. Carter, 1977). Intellectual assessment

measures have also been criticized for being biased against African American children because of their content, which emphasizes White, middle-class norms and values. However, Kaufman asserts that the bias does not come from the inclusion of these items, but rather from the lack of items that measure certain aspects of intelligence.

Few instruments have been designed for the assessment of general psychological functioning in African Americans; however, several promising strategies have recently emerged. For example, the potential employment of the Culturally Informed Functional Assessment (CIFA) interview by Tanaka-Matsumi, Seiden, and Lam (1996) is noteworthy. This instrument is comprehensive in that it is designed to assess clients on individual, familial, and group levels for each of these variables.

A child's level of racial identity resolution is also important to his or her psychological functioning (R.T. Carter, 1995; Phinney & Rotheram, 1987). Therefore, it is important to determine level of racial identity and acculturation as a component of the assessment process.

Clinicians should be wary of relying solely on results from a single assessment tool; care should be exercised to use an eclectic mix of assessment instruments that utilize different techniques, such as interviews and projective and objective techniques (Malgady, 1996). The involvement of culturally competent clinicians is also an important predictor of reliable and valid assessments.

DIAGNOSIS

The clinician should be mindful of several factors in diagnosing African American children, including contextual variables that have an effect on the expression of psychopathology and the level of impairment involved. If a child meets diagnostic criteria for a disorder, the clinician should consider the level of impairment in combination with other relevant circumstances. Clinicians should also be cognizant of the limitations of the *Diagnostic and Statistical Manual of Mental Disorders*, 4th edition (*DSM-IV*; APA, 1994) classification system for ethnic minorities.

Special caution must be exercised when a clinician from one ethnic or cultural group uses the *DSM-IV* classification to evaluate an individual from a different ethnic or cultural group. As stated in the *DSM-IV*:

A clinician who is unfamiliar with the nuances of an individual's cultural frame of reference may incorrectly judge as psychopathology those normal variations in behavior, belief, or experience that are particular to the culture as forms of psychopathology. For example, certain religious practices or beliefs (e.g., hearing or seeing a deceased relative during bereavement) may be misdiagnosed as manifestations of a psychotic disorder. (APA, p. xxiv)

Likewise, "speaking in tongues" may be interpreted as disorganized speech (R.T. Jones, 1999). Specific to African Americans, the use of culture-bound syndromes as spelled out in the *DSM-IV* to interpret locality-specific patterns of aberrant or troubling experiences (e.g., spelling) may avoid misdiagnosis. Additionally, applying personality disorder criteria across cultural settings may be especially difficult because of the wide cultural variations in concepts of self, styles of communication, and coping mechanisms. When diagnosing ethnic minorities, it is important to consider Axes IV and V, where the social and environmental contexts of the client are taken into account, perhaps explaining various "deviations" in functioning.

Several disorders require special attention when diagnosing African American children, including childhood depression, schizophrenia, and disruptive behavior disorders. These disorders stand out because of the tendency for these children to be diagnosed with psychotic and conduct disorder, whereas the diagnosis of mood disorders is often overlooked. A diagnosis of depression is seldom made because somatization of depression is often observed in African American groups even though children who present with disruptive behavior disorder often suffer from the effects of depression (Canino & Spurlock, 1994). Additionally, the chronic stress that African American children face can predispose them to depression and other affective disorders. Many African American children reside in the inner city (U.S. Census Bureau, 1996), where they may be exposed to high levels of crime and violence (Cunningham, Jones, & Yang, 1994). When presented to the mental health system, these children often warrant a dual diagnosis of depression and posttraumatic stress disorder (PTSD). Due to high rates of depression, the number of African American children who commit suicide has climbed in recent years (Canino & Spurlock, 1994; Gibbs, 1988). This has been explained by the

limited resources and supports available to many African American children, as well as easy accessibility to guns (Canino & Spurlock, 1994; R.L. Jones, 1972; Myers & King, 1983). Additionally, because African American children face numerous stressors due to racist practices, attending a new school in a predominately White neighborhood, for example, may lead to a variety of psychological problems. Although such changes affect all children, clinicians who are informed about the level of minority status stress faced by African American children may make better diagnostic decisions and provide more informed treatment than those unfamiliar with such stressors.

TREATMENT

Although studies suggest that the key to successful treatment is accurate assessment and diagnosis, the fact that African Americans represent a heterogeneous group presents a challenge to those conceptualizing and implementing treatment programs. Canino and Spurlock (1994) maintain that the following steps are likely to enhance treatment effectiveness of minority children: (1) clients should be involved in the selection of a treatment strategy; (2) clients, as well as their caretaker, should agree on the treatment; (3) if a client or family does not agree on the technique, steps should be taken to devise a plan that is acceptable to the group; and (4) when necessary, the assistance of laypeople within the community (e.g., teacher, minister, mentor) should be enlisted to aid in treatment implementation.

Some researchers have attempted to develop treatment techniques that have specific utility with African American children. For example, N. Banks (1993) describes a treatment termed cognitive ebonization aimed at increasing a child's knowledge about racism and developing a strong sense of self-worth and self-love.

Neal-Barnett and Smith (1996) present an Afrocentric approach to behavior therapy with children. The Afrocentric approach goes beyond traditional aspects of behavior therapy in that it specifies that intervention take place at all levels of the child's functioning. This view encourages the clinician and the child to work on the environment at both the individual and community levels to effect a positive change for the child (Neal-Barnett & Smith,

1996). Clinicians are encouraged to educate themselves about the African American child and the child's community to become more effective change agents.

Jones and Herndon (1992) provide several intervention techniques that are effective treatment tools with African American children in the classroom, including token reinforcement, contingency contracts, and self-management. They feel that the behavioral and cognitive-behavioral approaches to behavioral change are beneficial because they encourage functional analyses of problem behavior followed by systematic implementation of empirically sound treatment strategies.

In conclusion, effective assessment, diagnosis, and treatment of African American children's problem behavior should be carried out by culturally competent change agents. Psychologists must develop and implement culturally sensitive strategies to assess, diagnose, and treat children with various psychological disorders. Although the *DSM-IV* reflects an attempt to address the changing demographics of American society as well as reduce diagnostic and cultural discrimination, it is essential that clinicians incorporate cultural components into their clinical formulations and research efforts. The paucity of research on issues related to assessment, diagnosis, and treatment of African American children has significantly hindered clinical efforts (R.T. Jones et al., 1998). The changing demographics of society call for continued research in these areas for the field of cross-cultural psychology to progress.

LATINO CHILDREN AND ADOLESCENTS

POPULATION AND CULTURAL CHARACTERISTICS

In the year 2000, there are an estimated 31 million Latinos in the United States. Organista and Muñoz (1996) define Latinos as "individuals with personal and family roots in the countries of Latin America. Many Latinos speak Spanish, and most engage in blended cultural traditions of the Spanish colonists and the indigenous peoples of the Americas. Latinos may belong to any racial group, including those with roots in Europe, Africa, Asia, and the Middle East" (p. 256). Mexican Americans make up the majority of Latinos in the United States (62%), followed by Puerto Ricans (12.7%), Cubans (5.3%), Central and South Americans (11.5%), and other Latinos (8.5%) (e.g., not self-identified with the above groups; Marger, 1991).

It is important to be aware of the significant elements Latino cultures have in common and how they may differ from the majority culture, but clinicians must also take intragroup differences into consideration. There is notable diversity among Latino groups in the United States, and thus there are inherent risks in attempts to generalize from one group to another. For example, although Latino cultures have some important elements in common (e.g., emphasis on cooperation, mutual aid, support of family and community, conviviality, recognition of dignity and respect regardless of station in life) that distinguish them from the majority American culture, it is important to assess individual differences along such variables as geographic place of birth, degree of exposure to other members of one's ethnic group, and generational stage (Canino & Spurlock, 1994). Given this fact, the dearth of research on children from any single Latino subgroup requires one to focus on available literature, most of which consists of samples from predominantly Mexican American and Puerto Rican populations of low socioeconomic status (SES; Zayas & Solari, 1994).

Latino parents have goals for their children that are in part culturally determined. Therefore, their behaviors, reactions, and appraisals may differ from those of majority group members (Garcia-Coll, 1990). In most Latino families, parents socialize children to behave in ways important to the family's culture, which is elevated in importance above autonomy whether or not it is in accordance with the norms of the dominant culture. By following culturally influenced values and beliefs, parents try to foster social competencies during childhood and adolescence that are in line with successful functioning in a system of similarly held values and beliefs (Ogbu, 1981).

The definition of family in Latino culture extends well beyond a child's parents and siblings. Canino and Spurlock (1994) point out that the acceptance of extended family as a unit of analysis reveals strengths and resources that may be overlooked with a more narrow American view of the term "family." A Latino child's attachment to several significant adult relatives may be an important source of socialization (Garcia-Coll, 1990). In

Latino families, parents and the extended family serve an important role in transmitting cultural values. Latino families place an emphasis on family solidarity and the individual's sense of obligation to the family, which helps to both protect the family's continuity and preserve its culture (Zayas & Palleja, 1988).

MENTAL HEALTH STATUS

This population presents with unique mental health needs deserving of specialized attention and assessment (Organista & Muñoz, 1996). Working with Latino children requires an assessment of the contextual and cultural variables relevant to the client's socialization and development. Children's behaviors are a result of specific cultural values enveloped in their socialization process. Latino parents use particular beliefs and behaviors, determined largely by their cultural and socioeconomic situation, in the socialization of their children (Zayas & Solari, 1994). Thus, an understanding of these beliefs as they relate to a given child must be an integral part of the assessment, diagnosis, and treatment process.

Information on the prevalence of psychopathology in Latinos in the United States has been acquired over the past 15 years. According to the National Comorbidity Survey (NCS; Kessler et al., 1994), based on a national probability sample ($N = 8,098$) including a representative number of Latinos, Latinos had significantly higher prevalence of currently diagnosable affective disorders and active comorbidity, meeting three or more concurrent mental disorders, as compared to non-Latino Whites and African Americans. Data from the NCS, as well as the Epidemiological Catchment Area study (ECA; Weissman, Bruce, Leaf, & Holzer, 1991) and the Hispanic Health and Nutrition Examination Surveys (H-HANES), suggest that Latinos may be at greater risk than the general population for depression, anxiety, and somatization disorders (Organista & Muñoz, 1996). However, the extent to which differences remain after controlling for SES has yet to be evaluated.

Latinos tend to underutilize mental health services due to issues of cultural acceptability, service availability, and accessibility (Parron, 1982), but they tend to overutilize physicians for emotional and psychological problems (Organista & Muñoz, 1996). For example, Muñoz and Ying (1993) found rates of current major depression in Spanish-speaking primary care patients to be more than double the rate in the general population. According to Miranda (1976), the expectations of traditional Latino patients (e.g., traditional value orientation, low level of acculturation) include immediate symptom relief, guidance and advice, and a problem-centered approach. Additionally, 39% of Puerto Ricans, 30% of Mexican Americans, and 18% of Cuban Americans live below the poverty level, compared with only 10% of non-Latino Whites (Healey, 1995).

Cultural expectations of child development and behavior and cultural attitudes toward psychological services both emerge in the clinical setting. The clinician, then, must consider the influence of culture on child-rearing practices, language, fluency, religion, appearance, and behavior during sessions. An understanding of cultural norms in this area will circumvent inaccurate clinical judgments because observation and evaluation will be set in the context of the individual child's cultural experience.

Another issue to be considered when working with Latino children is the effect of pre- and post-migration experiences. This may be particularly relevant to Central Americans. Latino immigrants from many war-torn Central American countries have been exposed to various factors that may predispose them to psychopathology, especially PTSD (Masser, 1992). In fact, Central American children who have suffered the effects of war are distinct from other war-traumatized children in that guerrilla warfare has been found to be more stressful for children than conventional warfare (Arroyo & Eth, 1985). The poor diet and poverty of medical resources in Central America have also been cited as factors predisposing children to psychopathology, in addition to limiting their growth, development, central nervous system maturation, and attachment behavior. Studies of community samples of Central Americans in the United States report elevated symptom levels of depression, anxiety, somatization, and interpersonal sensitivity as compared to American norms (Plante, Manuel, Menendez, & Marcotte, 1995). Additionally, Central Americans have more symptoms of depression and migration-related stress (Salgado de Snyder, Cervantes, & Padilla, 1990) as well as PTSD (Cervantes, Salgado de Snyder, & Padilla, 1989) than do Mexican immigrants.

It is also important that assessment and treatment be delivered in a language that the Latino child or adolescent and his or her family can both understand and use. Language here refers to words, syntax, and local idiomatic expressions as well as symbols and concepts shared by the cultural group (Canino & Spurlock, 1994). To be most effective, language must be culturally and developmentally appropriate as well as compatible with the local vernacular. Because language often conveys culture, treatment delivered in the language of the target population assumes an integration of culture. This reciprocal interaction between language and culture is exemplified in Mexican Spanish, which contains many diminutives, hand gestures, and required formalities because directness is not viewed as a virtue in Mexican culture.

Other important elements include the concept of time and relationship protocol. In many Latino societies, time is polychronic; that is, many things happen at once, and interruptions and delays are common. This is a process-oriented culture where relationships are more important than schedules. This concept may also impact treatment options. For example, short-term and present-time orientation therapies have been found to be most consonant with the Puerto Rican culture, where long-term commitments to therapy are difficult to achieve (Rossello & Bernal, 1996). Time must be spent in the exchange of pleasantries and personal conversation before "getting down to business."

ASSESSMENT

It is important for the clinician to determine how the child client from a Latino background identifies himself or herself. This may be done by exploring the importance of ethnic values and traditions to the family, as well as the degree to which the individual is influenced by Latino culture. Felix-Ortiz, Newcomb, and Myers (1994) have created a multidimensional measure of cultural identity for Latino/Latina adolescents. The measure includes scales for language, behavior/familiarity, and values/attitudes, and has been found to differentiate highly bicultural, Latino-identified, American-identified, and low-level bicultural individuals. It is also imperative to recognize that the pathways influencing ethnic differences in the outcome of psychological intervention include not only cultural factors, but minority status, SES, level of acculturation, and immigration experiences (Alvidrez, Azocar, & Miranda, 1996). Each of these should be addressed during the assessment process in the most objective manner possible.

Alvidrez et al. (1996) refer to minority status as "the designation of members of particular groups as inappropriate, unwelcome, or inferior, that justifies and perpetuates their systematic exclusion from full participation in society or access to its rewards" (p. 905). The personal or collective experience of discrimination and/or marginalization of ethnic minorities will have an impact on beliefs, attitudes, and behaviors, which may influence psychological assessment. For example, the effects of minority status may impact the Latino client's level of trust toward the clinician, as well as the amount of self-disclosure. Felix-Ortiz et al. (1994) have created a Cultural Identity Scale with a subscale of perceived discrimination, which may be useful in assessing minority status effects.

Acculturation is the process of psychosocial change that occurs when an individual or group comes into contact with another culture and has been measured by assessing the use of language, values, beliefs, attitudes, skills, preference for leisure activities, observance of holidays, and cultural self-identity. An essential part of this measurement process with Latinos is assessing the use of language. Language, in fact, has been found to account for much of the total variance in acculturation (Alvidrez et al., 1996). Measures that capture both adherence to traditional culture as well as exposure to the dominant culture are recommended. Marin and Marin (1991) provide a review of several acculturation scales useful with Latino populations. Additionally, Phinney (1992) has created a brief ethnic identity scale useful with any ethnic group.

Another integral factor to include in the assessment of Latino children is immigration experience. The unique stresses created by the process of immigration into another country and the need for grieving the loss of the home country and loved ones are important psychological processes confronted by all immigrants and refugees (Espin, 1987).

DIAGNOSIS

An understanding of the belief systems integral to Latino culture is also an essential component in making diagnoses. All disorders and treatments are culture-specific in the sense that a diagnosis may have different behavioral manifestations according to the ethnicity of the patient. Recognizing that the *DSM-IV* outlines the importance of integrating an account of the individual's ethnic and cultural context in the evaluation of each of the *DSM-IV* axes may prove to be of extreme value. It calls for the "systematic review of the individual's cultural background, the role of the cultural context in the expression and evaluation of symptoms and dysfunction, and the effect that cultural differences may have on the relationship between the individual and the clinician" (APA, 1994, p. 843). Furthermore, as stated earlier, the *DSM-IV* defines various culture-bound syndromes, several of which may be meaningful in making clinical diagnoses with Latino children. Culture-bound syndromes are "generally limited to specific societies or culture areas and are localized, folk, diagnostic categories that frame coherent meanings for certain repetitive, patterned, and troubling sets of experiences and observations" (p. 844). Those that may be relevant to Latino populations are discussed next.

Nervios refers both to a general state of vulnerability to stressful life experiences and to a syndrome brought on by difficult life circumstances. The term includes a wide range of symptoms of emotional distress, somatic disturbance, and inability to function (e.g., headaches, irritability, sleep difficulties, nervousness, *mareos* or dizzy spells). Nervios tends to be an ongoing problem and is quite variable in the degree of disability manifested. *Ataque de nervios,* principally reported among Latinos from the Caribbean but recognized among many Latin American and Latin Mediterranean groups, features a sense of being out of control. Commonly reported symptoms include uncontrollable shouting, attacks of crying, trembling, and verbal or physical aggression. Dissociative experiences, fainting, or suicidal gestures may also be present. Ataques de nervios frequently occur in response to a stressful event in the family. The association of this precipitating event and the absence of acute fear or apprehension distinguish them from panic disorder. Ataques span the range from normal expressions of distress to symptom presentations associated with the diagnosis of anxiety, mood, dissociative, or somatoform disorders.

Locura is a term used by Latinos in the United States and Latin America to refer to a severe form of chronic psychosis, which is attributed to an inherited vulnerability to the effect of multiple life difficulties. Symptoms include incoherence, agitation, auditory and visual hallucinations, inability to follow rules of social interaction, unpredictability, and possible violence. *Bilis* and *colera* refer to syndromes caused by strong anger or rage. Among many Latino groups, anger is viewed as a powerful emotion that may profoundly affect the body by disturbing the balance between hot and cold (and/or material and spiritual) valences. Symptoms can include acute nervous tension, headache, trembling, screaming, stomach disturbances, and, in more severe cases, loss of consciousness. Chronic fatigue may result from the acute episode. *Mal puesto* or *brujeria* refers to a set of cultural interpretations in Latin American societies that ascribe illness to hexing, witchcraft, sorcery, or the evil influence of another person. Symptoms may include generalized anxiety and gastrointestinal complaints, weakness, dizziness, the fear of being poisoned, and even the fear of death.

Susto (fright or soul loss) is a folk illness prevalent among Latinos in the United States and among people in Mexico, Central America, and South America. It is also referred to as *espanto, pasmo, tripa ida, perdida del alma,* and *chibih* and is attributed to frightening events that cause the soul to leave the body and results in unhappiness and sickness. Symptoms include appetite and sleep disturbances, troubling dreams, feelings of sadness, lack of motivation, and feelings of low self-worth or dirtiness. These symptoms may appear any time from days to years after the frightening event is experienced. Ritual healings focus on calling the soul back to the body and cleansing the person to restore bodily and spiritual balance. Different experiences of susto may be related to major depressive disorder, PTSD, and somatoform disorders.

TREATMENT

Beliefs and values central to Latino culture must be taken into account when conceptualizing an effective treatment plan with Latino children. The objective introduction of the cultural context may enable a greater degree of compatibility when one chooses an established treatment modality that allows for greater influence of the child's culture. A variety of cultural models for individual psychotherapy (e.g., Comas-Diaz & Griffith, 1988) and culturally sensitive frameworks for clinicians conducting psychotherapy (G. Bernal, Bonilla, & Bellido, 1995) have been developed. However, little research on treatment outcomes has been done and much of the treatment outcome research carried out with children is not generalizable to ethnic minority populations. The literature shows very few studies that include Latinos (H. Bernal, 1993). S. Sue, Fujino, Hu, Takeuchi, and Zane (1991) found that the matching of culturally sensitive treatments on the basis of ethnicity and language was related to better treatment outcome and lower dropout rates in Latino patients with low acculturation. There is an evident need to develop, adapt, and test empirically based treatment approaches that show promise with Latino populations.

In accordance with the expectations of low-income groups whose pressing life circumstances frequently demand immediate attention and interfere with long-term treatment (Torres-Matrullo, 1982), short-term, directive, problem-solving therapies seem to be an appropriate treatment choice for this population. Consistent with this notion, studies have found cognitive-behavioral therapy (CBT) to be effective in treating depression in Spanish-speaking Puerto Rican mothers from low SES backgrounds (Comas-Diaz, 1992) and with low-income, Spanish-speaking Latino outpatients (Organista, Muñoz, & Gonzalez, 1994).

An additional advantage of using CBT with Latino clients is that the use of therapy manuals and workbooks, homework assignments, and didactic presentation may lead to the client's perceiving therapy as more of a classroom experience. This may alleviate the cultural stigma attached to psychotherapy. In fact, Organista and Muñoz (1996) point out that many of their Mexican and Central American immigrant clients have stated that the stigma of utilizing mental health services is very strong in their countries of origin, "where scarce mental health services are reserved almost exclusively for psychotic patients in mental hospitals" (p. 259). There are some ways to alter CBT to be more culturally sensitive to Latino clients. An example of this is Organista and Muñoz's recommendation to shift from the more traditional A-B-C-D (Activating events, Beliefs about the event, emotional Consequences of beliefs, and Disputing irrational beliefs; Ellis & Grieger, 1977) model of cognitive restructuring to a more simplistic differentiation between "helpful" and "unhelpful" thoughts.

Religion is another important construct to be understood and integrated in the cognitive domain when treating traditional or religious Latino clients. Within CBT, Organista and Muñoz (1996) advocate the reinforcement of church attendance and prayer as a way of helping the client deal with stress and negative mood states, while challenging forms of prayer that lessen the probability of active problem solving. One way of reframing prayers of this nature is to help the client shift them into a more active direction, with the idea that "God helps those who help themselves" (p. 262). For example, the prayers may shift from asking God to help them with their problems (and thus not completing their homework) to asking God to help them try out new behaviors, attend therapy, and help themselves.

Culturally specific treatment modalities involve actually bringing cultural elements directly into treatment. An example of this is the *cuento*, or folktale, which has the ability to meld traditional Latino culture and Anglo-American culture by integrating new elements while maintaining the original content of the tale. Some hold the view that the acculturation of Latino youths in dominant American society rests on their ability to bridge the gap between their Latino heritage and prevailing American values. Originally developed in the framework of modeling therapy, cuentos convey a message or moral to be emulated by others (Costantino & Malgady, 1996).

When implementing any therapy, it is important to examine whether or not the underlying concepts are congruent with the concepts and belief systems of Latino culture. This conceptual congruence, along with an understanding of familial interdependence, must be incorporated in the therapist's treatment delivery. For example, it is important to know what behaviors are highly desired by the parents and reflected in their own cultural background. In psychotherapy with Latino children, similar considerations must first be given to the influence of parents' stated desires about how they perceive their children's behavior and how they want their children to behave. For example, traditionally oriented Latino parents may find it insulting when therapists encourage children's behavioral and verbal assertiveness toward them. Promoting such expressiveness may be perceived by parents as undermining their authority. It is not unusual for family therapists to encounter Latino children who are unwilling to be negatively demonstrative toward their parents in a public forum. Thus, parental goals should be carefully evaluated and integrated into treatment consideration.

In summary, given the specific mental health needs of this target population, careful consideration should be provided to issues related to assessment, diagnosis, and treatment. The role of extended family, the effects of pre- and postmigration experiences, and the impact of Latino traditions should each be taken into account when addressing problems with children from this cultural background. Of course, cultural context must be a necessary component of any clinical formulation if desired improvement is to be forthcoming.

NATIVE AMERICAN CHILDREN AND ADOLESCENTS

POPULATION AND CULTURAL CHARACTERISTICS

Census data indicate that Native Americans make up approximately 0.9% of the American population (U.S. Census, 1998). Quantification of Native American culture as a single entity is particularly difficult due to the degree of variation found among the cultures and traditions of each of the 517 bands currently recognized by the federal government (Herring, 1991). However, mental health professionals who have worked with Native American youth recognize that they view the world in quantifiably different ways from their White counterparts (Manson, Walker, & Kivlahan, 1987). For the purposes of this discussion, only those cultural features that apply most generally to the Native American population, such as worldview, and that distinguish it from the majority population are considered.

Differences in cultural teachings and expectations between the Native American and the majority cultures point to issues that must be addressed by the clinician in terms of how the Native American child might best be served. Important cultural variables to consider may include, but are not limited to, parent-child interaction style, worldview and relationship to the physical world, and collectivity versus individuality. Each of these variables, the extent to which each differs in the Native American population from the majority population, and potential effects on assessment, diagnosis, and treatment processes are discussed.

In many ways, the learning experience of Native American children is very different from that of children of the majority culture. In mainstream American culture, children are thought to be the responsibility, even the "property," of their parents. The parents are expected to shape the youngster, closely monitoring and guiding his or her development. This perspective is in sharp contrast to the Native American value of noninterference, in which individuals defer to one another while minimizing the power differential between them (Sage, 1991). Consistent with this value, adults view even young children as autonomous individuals, capable of making their own decisions (Yates, 1987). Parents allow their children to develop in their own time and with few rules. To attempt to direct or control behavior of another individual is considered disrespectful (Morrissette, 1991). Such a parenting style may be viewed in the majority culture as lax at best and neglectful at worst. Thus, Native American parents, while demonstrating respect for the child as an individual and concern for the child's development and well-being according to the values of their own culture, may be inaccurately described as uninvolved or even negligent by clinicians from the majority culture (Yates, 1987).

Nonverbal communication is highly valued in Native American culture, in direct contrast to the majority culture, which teaches children to speak up for themselves (Yates, 1987). Native American children are expected to learn through observation, and instruction is given only when specifically elicited. Peers and siblings often teach through nonverbal encouragement and example. Words are to be chosen wisely, and even when an elder is asked for advice, it may not be given if the elder does not feel that he or she has expertise in that area (Morrissette, 1991). In some tribes, such as the Papago and the Yaqui, there is little conversation in the home. When children are learning to speak, "baby talk" is not tolerated, and children are often punished for bad behavior by being ignored (Blanchard, 1983).

Native American culture views all aspects of life as interactive and inseparable. Life has a natural course and should not be consciously altered. Many majority culture interventions are therefore viewed as distorting the natural progression of life (Yates, 1987). Thinking is holistic and intuitive in nature, whereas the majority culture values the scientific method and empirical validation over intuition.

In addition, time is thought to be fluid and unstructured in Native American culture. Events transpire "when the time is right," and emphasis is placed on the present time. Deadlines imposed by the majority culture are meaningless because time, like life itself, cannot be broken down into discrete units (Morrissette, 1991). Deadlines also indicate a concern for time in the future, which cannot be predicted and thus is not as important as what is happening in the present. This perspective contrasts sharply with the treatment of time as a highly valued and structured entity in the majority culture. Because Native American children may be unconcerned with such matters as when class begins or when homework is due, they are often regarded as lazy or irresponsible by the majority culture (Yates, 1987). Such misunderstandings occur when the discrepancy between the two cultures is not recognized.

MENTAL HEALTH STATUS

The following describes the proliferation of data that have been collected documenting the alarming rates of substance use and suicide in the Native American population, especially in adolescents. The roles of specified risk factors and associated variables are also considered.

Empirical studies have repeatedly shown that Native American youth report using alcohol more heavily and at an earlier age than do their non-Native peers, although the numbers vary widely from tribe to tribe (Austin, 1988; Beauvais, Oetting, & Wolfe, 1989; U.S. Congress, 1990; Welte & Barnes, 1987). By age 11, nearly one third of Native American children have tried alcohol (May, 1986). In a study by Beauvais, Oetting, and Wolf (1989), 81% of Native American students in grades 7 to 12 reported having used alcohol at some time, compared to 57% of non-Native students. These high usage rates appear to continue throughout adolescence, putting Native American youth at risk for problem drinking and alcoholism as adults (Moncher, Holden, & Trimble, 1990). Abuse of other drugs has also been shown to be a significant problem among Native American youth (Welte & Barnes, 1987). In the survey of children in grades 7 to 12 cited previously, 61% of Native American children had used marijuana, 24% had used inhalants, and 25% had used stimulants (Beauvais et al., 1989). The National Institute on Drug Abuse found that non-Native youth were much less likely to have used each of these drugs (U.S. Congress, 1990). Again, high levels of use continue throughout adolescence (Beauvais et al., 1989; U.S. Congress, 1990). Mari-

juana use in Native American youth remains double that of non-Native youth and approaches the level of alcohol use (Oetting & Beauvais, 1986). Only inhalant use appears to decline with age as other substances become more readily available.

Many factors may contribute to these high levels of substance use. Sigelman and colleagues (Sigelman, Didjurgis, Marshall, Vargas, & Stewart, 1992) found that when sixth-grade children were presented with a vignette describing excessive alcohol use by a teenage boy, Native American children rated the problem as less serious than their non-Native counterparts. The Native American children did not support aggressive treatment as much as the other children, and they also endorsed a disease model of alcoholism more strongly than did the non-Native children. These attitudes may be the result of Native American children's having seen problem drinking more often than their non-Native peers. Native American children may be more aware of the difficulty of rehabilitation and therefore may not see intervention as very helpful. The fact that these children adhere to a disease model of alcoholism suggests that they may view individuals as having less control over their drinking habits than do non-Native children.

Because of the policy of noninterference, Native American parents are reluctant to intervene or to warn against substance use. This lack of clear sanctions against substance use may convey an attitude of permissiveness to children. Furthermore, drinking within the family seems to influence alcohol use in Native American children; one third report having their first drink with a family member (Weibel-Orlando, 1984). Due to the high rates of alcohol use among Native American adults, children may see drinking as normative and a sign of adulthood to a greater degree than do non-Native children (Edwards & Edwards, 1988).

Peer pressure has also been found to influence substance use. Relationships between peer associations and substance use have been found to be extremely high, especially among younger children (Oetting, Beauvais, & Edwards, 1988; Welte & Barnes, 1987). In peer groups where substance use is sanctioned, it may even be considered disrespectful to refuse someone who offers drugs or alcohol (Herring, 1994; Westermeyer & Neider, 1985).

Other psychosocial factors that have been found to be related to substance abuse are prominent in the Native American community. These include high unemployment rates and poverty. In addition, cultural identity uncertainty, poor school adjustment, high mortality rates, and lack of opportunity are all considered risk factors for substance use to which Native American children are exposed significantly more often than non-Native children (Edwards & Edwards, 1988; Oetting et al., 1988).

Suicide rates among Native American youth range from 3 to 10 times the rates recorded for non-Native youth (May, 1987; Sigurdson, Staley, Matas, Hildahl, & Squair, 1994), and suicide is the second major cause of death among these adolescents. Substance use has been implicated in approximately 60% of these deaths (Sigurdson et al., 1994). In a recent survey of Native American adolescents that included more than 13,000 respondents, 22% of females and 12% of males reported having attempted suicide at some time (Blum, Hamon, Harris, Berguisen, & Resnick, 1992). The suicide rate in the Native American population peaks during adolescent and young adult years, then subsides (McIntosh & Santos, 1981). Speculations concerning etiological factors implicate, as in substance abuse, a relationship between acculturation and suicide (Dinges & Duong-Tran, 1993).

ASSESSMENT

Assessment may be difficult to accomplish with the Native American child, as the goal of the clinician is often to separate, or compartmentalize, different aspects of life, in direct contrast to the Native American view of life as circular in nature and unable to be broken down into pieces (Morrissette, 1991). Because verbal assertion is not valued in Native American culture and may even be deemed disrespectful in some situations, children's behavior in an assessment situation may be misinterpreted as withdrawn or uninterested (Powless & Elliott, 1993). Children may also be viewed as unmotivated or resistant, when they are actually learning and observing (Morrissette, 1991). The importance of the family as a unit may make it difficult for a child to delineate his or her feelings and thoughts from the overriding attitudes and dispositions of the family.

To objectively assess issues of substance abuse and suicide among Native American youth requires the development of culturally sensitive assessment instruments. Current instruments developed to assess potential causal factors contributing to these two phenomena may not be integrating cultural

differences into the conceptualization of causes of treatment of these problem areas. For example, the fact that Native American youth see higher rates of alcohol use in their everyday lives suggests that their view of "normal" drinking behavior may be very different from that of non-Native youth (Sigelman et al., 1992). Thus, accurate assessment of substance use will necessitate very detailed description of use without using such vague terms as "too much" or "too often."

In addition to the cultural variables that may lead to misinterpretation or inaccuracy of conclusions, clinicians must also be aware of the limitations of the instruments they use in assessing Native American children. In the development of many commonly used measures, Native Americans were not included in the normative sample, rendering these instruments insufficient in terms of providing meaningful results when used to evaluate individuals from this group. Applying assessment instruments to any group of people who were not included in the standardization of the instrument can lead to erroneous and inaccurate conclusions.

DIAGNOSIS

There is some evidence that Native American youth do suffer more mental health problems than do children in the general population (Beals et al., 1997; Blum et al., 1992). The stress that Native American children experience when attempting to bridge the gap between the values that have been instilled in them in their native culture and the values to which they are exposed through their experiences in the majority culture is one factor that may contribute to the elevated rates of psychopathology. Other negative aspects of the psychosocial environment, such as high unemployment rates and levels of poverty, are also contributing factors to the differential rates of diagnosis, especially as they relate to substance abuse and suicide rates (Dauphinais & King, 1992). Unemployment rates among the Native American population are more than double the national average, and 31.7% of Native American families live below the poverty level, a number much higher than the national average of 13.1% (U.S. Department of Health and Human Services, 1994).

The *DSM-IV* (APA, 1994) recognizes one pattern of symptoms unique to the Native American population in the section on cultural-bound syndromes.

Ghost sickness is described as absorption in the theme of death. Symptoms may include disturbing dreams, loss of appetite, dizziness, hallucinations, fear, anxiety, loss of consciousness, and feelings of suffocation. This preoccupation with death may be related in some way to the elevated suicide rates among Native American youth.

TREATMENT

The contrasts between Native American culture and the majority culture apply not only to the assessment of Native American children but to the treatment process as well. Generally, treatments prescribed from the majority perspective are not likely to be effective with Native American children due to the differing teachings, values, and worldviews of the two cultures. Native American children are apt to be labeled resistant or unmotivated in a treatment setting due to the differences in communication style between their culture and the majority culture. They are not likely to express their emotions in therapy because they are taught that such expression is disrespectful to elders. Clinicians attempting to treat Native American children from the viewpoint of the majority culture may easily underestimate the importance of involving extended family members in the treatment process. Because of the Native American policy of noninterference, parents may also feel that treatment is the responsibility of the child and that they should not intervene in the child's development. Clinicians in the majority culture are likely to find this unwillingness to participate very frustrating and may have to be creative in attempts to involve the entire family. Due to cultural differences in self-worth and perceived control over certain behaviors, clinicians are likely to find that current treatments for substance abuse or suicidal Native American youth may be largely ineffective.

ASIAN AMERICAN CHILDREN AND ADOLESCENTS

POPULATION AND CULTURAL CHARACTERISTICS

Currently, it is believed that approximately 2% of the U.S. population is Asian American (Ho, 1992; Yeh, Takeuchi, & Sue, 1994). Heterogeneity and homogeneity are both encompassed in the usage of the term Asian American. The diverse countries this term subsumes, for example, China, Japan, India, the Philippines, and Vietnam, give it its heterogeneous quality. In general, the term has been loosely used to denote anyone of Asian origin. Another type of diversity arises from its simultaneous usage for both recent immigrants and individuals of Asian origin born in the United States. Due to its loose application, current published reports on Asian Americans differ widely in the nature of their samples (Feng & Cartledge, 1996; Rosenblatt & Attkisson, 1992; Stone, 1992). There is a lack of consensus regarding inclusion and exclusion criteria for this group, which precludes integrative information that could be useful in designing psychological and educational interventions. However, the unity in this diversity is assumed to be derived from the common collectivistic or communal orientation that is characteristic of Eastern cultures (Triandis, 1995). It is this collective orientation that makes it possible to consider individuals from the diverse Asian countries as one group.

To build a successful conceptual model to guide assessment, diagnostic, and treatment efforts in this population, it is necessary to discuss the concept of collectivism. Collectivism is a syndrome of feelings, thoughts, beliefs, ideas, and behaviors related to interpersonal concern (Hui & Triandis, 1986). Collectivists have been conceptualized as having an interdependent self, a propensity to select goals that are compatible with their in-groups, behaving in accordance with norms, and giving priority to relationships even if they are not cost-effective (Triandis, 1995). Due to this value orientation, individuality is conceptualized as being subordinate to collective solidarity, and one's ego as being suppressed into the collective ego of the family (Laungani, 1995). Consequently, personal choice is thought to be virtually nonexistent in such individuals (Laungani, 1995). Collectivists have a willingness to confirm and accept opinions of other in-group members because they are socialized for duty and obedience. Relationships are vertical in nature; for example, parent-child relationships are stronger than bonds between spouses (Hart & Poole, 1995).

Collectivistic attributes could potentially lead to or exacerbate problems of Asian American children in an individualistic culture such as the United States. The child's knowledge of and fluency with the English language should be determined, as deficiencies in either could serve as a contributing factor to the child's psychological functioning. Thus, different assessment, diagnostic, and treatment methods may need to be considered if the child is not conversant with the English language. In some cases, matching the child to an ethnically similar therapist may be necessary. Because collectivistic traditions emphasize subordination of the child to authority figures and require obedience and acceptance of others' opinions, this too may lead to problems in the individualistic culture of the United States. The clinician should be keenly aware of the potential impact of this tradition on the child's functioning and prevent the designation of inappropriate labels (e.g., low self-esteem). In addition, collective cultures emphasize restriction of expression of negative feelings in public, which may also have implications for assessment and treatment.

Asian American families may have experienced stressors related to difficulties in immigration, especially for illegal immigrants, which may need to be addressed. Due to the collective orientation of Asian Americans, it is more likely that children will be living in joint families. If potentially influential members other than parents are present (e.g., grandparents), they should play a role in intervention efforts.

MENTAL HEALTH STATUS

Investigations regarding educational and psychological difficulties, although uncommon (Ho, 1992; S. Sue & Chin, 1996), have begun to reveal increasing problems in this group. Koh and Koh (1982) reported that of 3,500 Korean children enrolled during a two-year school period in the Greater Chicago area, 0.01% were referred for psychological evaluation. Learning problems, poor peer relations, educational guidance, and behavioral and emotional disturbances were the reasons for these referrals. Millard (1987) stated that Chinese American youth constituted 5% of 8,000 juvenile offenders in San Francisco in 1986, although only 12% of the population were Chinese American.

Although such reports are not extensive, they suggest a growing need to address problems exhibited by Asian American children. However, little attention has been diverted to this issue, and consequently, psychological efforts in this population in

the areas of diagnosis, assessment, and treatment continue to be based on Western ethnocultural values and beliefs. Furthermore, Asian Americans continue to be underrepresented in the American mental health system (Bui & Takeuchi, 1992; Rosenblatt & Attkisson, 1992; S. Sue, 1977).

ASSESSMENT

In the past, instruments standardized on Western populations, such as commonly used intelligence tests, have been employed to assess Asian Americans. Recent studies have pointed out potential problems with such practices. For example, Stone (1992) reported that intelligence tests that are verbally laden may be biased against Asian Americans and may underpredict achievement. Regarding symptom expression, several authors have reported a predominant somatic tendency (Atkinson, Morton, & Sue, 1979; Canino & Spurlock, 1994; S. Sue, 1982) in this group. Because most psychological instruments tap into psychological idioms of distress, these may be inappropriate for use with Asian Americans and lead to underreporting of symptoms (S. Sue, 1982). Because of these problems, culturally relevant assessment processes should include the following considerations.

Instruments that are sensitive to culture-specific ways of symptom expression need to be developed. Vijver and Leung (1997) have pointed out the important distinction between applicability and adaptability of instruments in this regard. The former is conceptualized as issues related to direct use in one culture of an instrument normed on another culture; the latter is related to whether an instrument needs to be modified for use in another culture. Specifically, on consultation with appropriate professionals from that culture or from a cultural analysis, the therapist may better determine applicability of an assessment instrument. For example, Western-based psychological instruments may be appropriate for a highly acculturated Asian American family who has been in the United States for several years. However, for a recent immigrant family, it may be necessary to adapt instruments or actually replace them. Adaptability can take two forms. If it is determined that current instruments are appropriate with modifications, then such modifications should be made. On the other hand, if it is determined that a specific disorder (as defined in the *DSM-IV*) has little cultural significance for a particular individual or group, attempts to use a more appropriate culture-specific disorder should be made. For example, Kleinman (1988) pointed out that Western notions of depression and anxiety collectively represent a Chinese disorder translated as "neurasthenia." In this case, it may be more relevant to examine and treat neurasthenia than symptoms of depression and anxiety. Instrument usage should also be compatible to language ability. If it is deemed that the client is not familiar with the English language, then appropriate translation procedures should be employed (Vijver & Leung, 1997).

DIAGNOSIS

Underreporting of psychiatric problems in this group has been commonly reported in the literature (S. Sue, 1982; Touliatos & Lindholm, 1980). Such underreporting of problems enhances the possibility of negative error rate (Type II error). Like the problems regarding assessment instruments outlined earlier, this issue requires careful consideration of culture-related ways of interactions, self-concept, and symptom expression. For example, the lack of emphasis on self is appropriate in most Asian cultures, and therefore should not be interpreted as an indicator of internalizing disorders or low self-esteem. To ensure appropriate diagnoses of Asian American children, it is essential that parental input is obtained, as parents play an influential and dominant role in the lives of their children. Their perceptions of problem behaviors are essential. For instance, in some cases, parents may not view an inattentive child as suffering from attention-deficit disorder because certain practices or cultural beliefs may allow or encourage such behavior.

TREATMENT

Several studies have pointed out the low rates of help-seeking behavior and high dropout rates of Asian Americans from mental health centers (Rosenblatt & Attkisson, 1992; Yeh, Takeuchi, et al., 1994). These are indicative of a need to revise current treatment approaches and develop new strategies for this population. Unfortunately, standard treatment approaches continue to be used for ethnically

different populations, which may discourage clients from seeking or continuing therapy. Specific guidelines to enhance therapy effectiveness for Asian American children and adolescents follow.

Based on an assessment of a child's ease of communication in the English language and his or her level of acculturation, the clinician should select culture-specific therapies such as cuento therapy and hero/heroine modeling therapy (Costantino & Malgady, 1996). Also, the use of nonverbal therapy modes including play therapy and art therapy should be considered. In some cases of low acculturation in Western culture, the possibility of having treatments administered by ethnically matching clinicians needs to be considered. Some investigations have demonstrated that ethnic matching is a significant predictor of dropout rate for Asian American children (Yeh, Eastman, & Cheung, 1994).

SUMMARY

In light of the predicted demographic changes in the cultural makeup of the United States, the need for the mental health professions, especially psychologists, to keep pace with these changes is essential if the needs of these groups are to be met. Given the growing demands and stressors likely to confront children and adolescents, particularly those of color, in the coming millennium, psychological assessment, diagnosis, and treatment must rise to the occasion if appropriate functioning across a variety of settings, including home, school, and social environment, is to be ensured. To do so, cultural, ethnic, and contextual variables must be considered. Heritage, traditions, expectations, family values, and worldviews relevant to the client's socialization and development must be embraced and integrated into the efforts of psychologists and other change agents.

Culture-specific frameworks (e.g., Afrocentrism, collectivism, collectivity), a reemphasis on nonverbal communication, and the importance of intuition over the scientific method must be embraced and integrated into novel ways of thinking and conceptualizing efforts related to the change process. When formulating such efforts, we must be willing to "rotate our conceptual axes" to broaden our thinking and to gain a greater appreciation of other worldviews. The need to embrace non-Westernized

European constructs that may potentially mediate or moderate various patterns of behavior (e.g., minority status stress, acculturation) is essential if meaningful, long-lasting change is to be forthcoming.

Although several existing modes of assessment have proven to be appropriate and sensitive to non-White populations, the continued development of more culturally sensitive instruments should become a high priority for those dedicated to precise and sensitive assessment of problem behavior. Assessment of the following levels should be carefully considered and incorporated into one's functional analyses: child, parent, family, school and community, and politicocultural context. Regarding diagnoses, advances in the field to target concerns of non-Caucasian clients, including the development of culture-bound syndromes, should continue to prove useful in the categorization of diagnostic levels of functioning. The need for change agents to be aware of and appreciate syndromes within a cultural context is essential to inform effective intervention efforts.

REFERENCES

Adebimpe, V.R. (1981). Overview: White norms and psychiatric diagnosis of Black patients. *American Journal of Psychiatry, 138,* 279–285.

Alvidrez, J., Azocar, F., & Miranda, J. (1996). Demystifying the concept of ethnicity for psychotherapy researchers. *Journal of Consulting and Clinical Psychology, 64,* 903–908.

American Psychiatric Association. (1994). *Diagnostic and statistical manual of mental disorders* (4th ed.). Washington, DC: Author.

Arroyo, W., & Eth, S. (1985). Children traumatized by Central American warfare. In S. Eth & R.S. Pynoos (Eds.), *Post-traumatic stress disorder in children* (pp. 101–117). Washington, DC: American Psychiatric Press.

Atkinson, D.R., Morton, G., & Sue, D.W. (1979). *Counseling American minorities: A cross-cultural perspective.* Dubuque, IA: Brown.

Austin, G.A. (1988). *Substance abuse among minority youth: Native Americans* (Prevention Research Update No. 2). Portland, OR: Western Center for Drug-Free Schools and Communities.

Baker, F.M. (1988). Afro-Americans. In L. Comas-Diaz & E.H. Griffith (Eds.), *Clinical guidelines in cross-cultural mental health* (pp. 151–181). New York: Wiley.

Banks, N. (1993). Identity work with Black children. *Educational and Child Psychology, 10*(3), 43–46.

Beals, J., Piasecki, J., Nelson, S., Jones, M., Keane, E., Dauphinais, P., Red Shirt, R., Sack, W.H., & Spero, M.M. (1997). Psychiatric disorder among American Indian adolescents: Prevalence in Northern Plains youth. *Journal of the American Academy of Child and Adolescent Psychiatry, 36,* 1252–1259.

Beauvais, F., Oetting, E.R., & Wolf, W. (1989). American Indian youth and drugs, 1976–1987: A continuing problem. *American Journal of Public Health, 79,* 634–636.

Bernal, G., Bonilla, J., & Bellido, C. (1995). Ecological validity and cultural sensitivity for outcome research: Issues for the cultural adaptation and development of psychosocial treatment with Hispanics. *Journal of Abnormal Child Psychology, 23,* 67–82.

Bernal, H. (1993). A model for delivering culture-relevant care in the community. *Public Health Nursing, 10*(4), 228–232.

Blanchard, E.L. (1983). The growth and development of American Indian and Alaskan Native children. In G.J. Powell (Ed.), *The psychosocial development of minority group children* (pp. 59–71). New York: Brunner/Mazel.

Blum, R.W., Hamon, B., Harris, L., Berguisen, L., & Resnick, M.D. (1992). American Indian–Alaska Native youth health. *Journal of the American Medical Association, 267,* 1637–1644.

Bui, K.T., & Takeuchi, D. (1992). Community mental heath services for ethnic minority children. *American Journal of Community Psychology, 20,* 403–415.

Canino, I.A., & Spurlock, J. (1994). *Culturally diverse children and adolescents: Assessment, diagnosis, and treatment.* New York: Guilford Press.

Carter, C. (1977). Prospectus on Black communications. *School Psychology Digest, 6,* 23–30.

Carter, R.T. (1995). *The influence of race and racial identity in psychotherapy: Toward a racially inclusive model.* New York: Wiley.

Cervantes, R.C., Salgado de Snyder, V.N., & Padilla, A.M. (1989). Posttraumatic stress disorder among immigrants from Central America and Mexico. *Hospital and Community Psychology, 40,* 615–619.

Comas-Diaz, L. (1992). The future of psychotherapy with ethnic minorities. *Psychotherapy, 29*(4), 89–94.

Comas-Diaz, L., & Griffith, E.E.H. (Eds.). (1988). *Clinical guidelines in cross-cultural mental health.* New York: Wiley.

Costantino, G., & Malgady, R.G. (1996). Culturally sensitive treatment: Cuento and hero/heroine modeling therapies for Hispanic children and adolescents. In E.D. Hibbs & P.S. Jensen (Eds.), *Psychosocial treatments for child and adolescent disorders: Empirically based strategies for clinical practice* (pp. 639–669). Washington, DC: American Psychological Association.

Cunningham, P.B., Jones, R.T., & Yang, B. (1994). *Impact of community violence on African-American children and preliminary findings.* Poster presented at the seventh annual Research Conference: A system of care for children's mental health: Expanding the research base, Tampa, FL.

Dauphinais, P.L., & King, J. (1992). Psychological assessment with American Indian children. *Applied and Preventive Psychology, 1,* 97–110.

Dillon, D. (1994). Understanding and assessment of intragroup dynamics in family foster care: African American families. *Child Welfare, 73*(2), 129–139.

Dinges, N.G., & Duong-Tran, Q. (1993). Stressful life events and co-occurring depression, substance abuse and suicidality among American Indian and Alaska Native adolescents. *Culture, Medicine, and Psychiatry, 16,* 487–502.

Edwards, E.D., & Edwards, M.E. (1988). Alcoholism prevention/treatment and Native American youth: A community approach. *Journal of Drug Issues, 18,* 103–115.

Ellis, A., & Grieger, R. (1977). *Handbook of rational emotive therapy.* New York: Holt, Rinehart, and Winston.

Espin, O.M. (1987). Psychological impact of migration on Latinas. *Psychology of Women Quarterly, 11,* 489–503.

Felix-Ortiz, M., Newcomb, M.D., & Myers, H. (1994). A multidimensional measure of cultural identity for Latino and Latina adolescents. *Hispanic Journal of Behavioral Sciences, 16,* 99–115.

Feng, H., & Cartledge, G. (1996). Social skills assessment of inner city Asian, African, and European American students. *School Psychology Review, 25*(2), 228–239.

Garcia-Coll, C.T. (1990). Developmental outcome of minority infants: A process-oriented look into our beginnings. *Child Development, 61,* 270–289.

Gibbs, J.T. (1988). Mental health issues of Black adolescents: Implications for policy and practice. In A.R. Stiffman & L.E. Davis (Eds.), *Ethnic issues in adolescent mental health* (pp. 21–52). Newbury Park, CA: Sage.

Gibbs, J.T., & Huang, L.N. (1989). A conceptual framework for assessing and treating minority youth. In J.T. Gibbs & L.N. Huang (Eds.), *Children of color: Psychological interventions with minority youth* (pp. 375–403). San Francisco: Jossey-Bass.

Hart, I., & Poole, G.D. (1995). Individualism and collectivism as considerations in cross-cultural health research. *Journal of Social Psychology, 135*(1), 97–99.

Hartlage, L.C., & Steele, C.T. (1977). WISC and WISC-R correlates of academic achievement. *Psychology in the Schools, 14*(1), 15–18.

Healey, J.F. (1995). Hispanic Americans: Colonization, immigration, and ethnic enclaves. In J.F. Healey (Ed.), *Race, ethnicity, gender, and class: The sociology of group conflict and change* (pp. 341–401). Thousand Oaks, CA: Pine Forge Press.

Herring, R.D. (1991). Counseling Native American youth. In C.C. Lee & B.L. Richardson (Eds.), *Multicultural issues in counseling: New approaches to diversity*

(pp. 37–50). Alexandria, VA: American Association for Counseling and Development.

Herring, R.D. (1994). Substance use among Native American Indian youth: A selected review of causality. *Journal of Counseling and Development, 7,* 578–583.

Ho, M.K. (1992). *Minority children and adolescents in therapy.* Newbury Park, CA: Sage.

Hui, C.H., & Triandis, H.C. (1986). Individualism-collectivism: A study of cross-cultural researchers. *Journal of Cross-Cultural Psychology, 17*(2), 225–248.

Jones, R.L. (1972). Introduction. In R.L. Jones (Ed.), *Black psychology* (pp. 285–294). New York: Harper & Row.

Jones, R.L. (1988). *Psychoeducational assessment of minority group children: A casebook.* Berkeley, CA: Cobb & Henry.

Jones, R.T., Brown, V.R. Davis, M., Jefferies, R., & Shenoy, U. (1998). African Americans in behavioral therapy and research. In R.L. Jones (Ed.), *African American mental health.* Hampton, VA: Cobb & Henry.

Jones, R.T., & Herndon, C. (1992). The status of Black children and adolescents in the academic setting: Assessment and treatment issues. In C.E. Walker & M.C. Roberts (Eds.), *Handbook of clinical child psychology* (2nd ed., pp. 901–917). New York: Wiley.

Kaufman, A.S. (1979). *Intelligence testing with the WISC-R.* New York: Wiley.

Kessler, R.C., McGonagle, K.A., Zhao, S., Nelson, C.B., Hughes, M., Eshleman, S., Wittchen, H., & Kendler, K.S. (1994). Lifetime and 12-month prevalence of *DSM-III-R* psychiatric disorders in the United States. *Archives of General Psychiatry, 51,* 8–19.

Kleinman, A. (1988). *Rethinking psychiatry: From cultural category to personal experience.* New York: Free Press.

Koh, T., & Koh, S. (1982). A note on the psychological evaluation of Korean school children. *Pacific/Asian American Mental Health Review, 1,* 1–2.

Laungani, P. (1995). Series in stress and emotion: Anxiety, anger, and curiosity. In C.D. Spielberger, I.G. Sarason, J.M.T. Brebner, E. Greenglass, P. Laungani, & A.M. O'Roark (Eds.), *Stress and emotion: Anxiety, anger, and curiosity* (Vol. 15, pp. 265–280). Washington, DC: Taylor & Francis.

Malgady, R.G. (1996). The question of cultural bias in assessment and diagnosis of ethnic minority clients: Let's reject the null hypothesis. *Professional Psychology: Research and Practice, 27*(1), 73–77.

Manson, S.M., Walker, R.D., & Kivlahan, D.R. (1987). Psychiatric assessment and treatment of American Indians and Alaska Natives. *Hospital and Community Psychiatry, 38,* 165–173.

Marger, M.N. (1991). Hispanic Americans. In M.N. Marger (Ed.), *Race and ethnic relations: American and global perspectives* (2nd ed., pp. 279–320). Belmont, CA: Wadsworth.

Marin, G., & Marin, B. (1991). *Research with Hispanic populations.* Newbury Park, CA: Sage.

Masser, D.S. (1992). Psychosocial functioning of Central American refugee children. *Child Welfare, 71,* 439–456.

May, P.A. (1986). Alcohol and drug misuse prevention programs for Native Americans: Needs and opportunities. *International Journal of the Addictions, 17,* 1185–1209.

May, P.A. (1987). Suicide and self-destruction among American Indian youths. *American Indian and Alaska Native Mental Health, 1,* 52–69.

McAdoo, H.P., & McAdoo, J.L. (Eds.). (1985). *Black children: Social, educational and parental environment.* New York: Sage.

McIntosh, J.L., & Santos, J.F. (1981). Suicide among Native Americans: A compilation of findings. *Omega, 11,* 303–316.

Millard, M. (1987, November 6). Problems of Asian juvenile offenders brings outcry for better system in San Francisco. *East-West News,* pp. 1, 8–9.

Miranda, M.R. (Ed.). (1976). *Psychotherapy with the Spanish-speaking: Issues in research and service delivery* (Monograph No. 3). Los Angeles: University of California, Spanish-Speaking Mental Health Research Center.

Moncher, M.S., Holden, G.W., & Trimble, J.E. (1990). Substance use among Native American youth. *Journal of Consulting and Clinical Psychology, 58,* 408–415.

Morrissette, P.J. (1991). The therapeutic dilemma with Canadian Native youth in residential care. *Child and Adolescent Social Work, 8,* 89–99.

Muñoz, R.F., & Ying, Y.W. (1993). *The prevention of depression: Research and practice.* Baltimore: Johns Hopkins University Press.

Myers, H.F., & King, L.M. (1983). Mental health issues in the development of the Black American child. In G.J. Powell (Ed.), *The psychosocial development of minority group children* (pp. 275–306). New York: Brunner/Mazel.

Neal-Barnett, A.M., & Smith, J.M., Sr. (1996). African American children and behavior therapy: Considering the Afrocentric approach. *Cognitive and Behavioral Practice, 3*(2), 351–370.

Oetting, E.R., & Beauvais, F. (1986). Peer cluster theory, socialization characteristics and adolescent drug use: A path analysis. *Journal of Counseling Psychology, 34,* 205–213.

Oetting, E.R, Beauvais, F., & Edwards, R. (1988). Alcohol and Indian youth: Social and psychological correlates and prevention. *Journal of Drug Issues, 18,* 87–101.

Ogbu, J.U. (1981). Origins of human competence: A cultural ecological perspective. *Child Development, 52,* 13–429.

Organista, K.C., & Muñoz, R.F. (1996). Cognitive behavioral therapy with Latinos. *Cognitive and Behavioral Practice, 3,* 255–270.

Organista, K.C., Muñoz, R.F., & Gonzalez, G. (1994). Cognitive behavioral therapy for depression in low-income and minority medical outpatients: Description of a program and exploratory analyses. *Cognitive Therapy and Research, 18,* 241–259.

Parron, D.L. (1982). An overview of minority group mental health needs and issues as presented to the President's Commission on Mental Health. In F.V. Muñoz & R. Endo (Eds.), *Perspectives on minority group mental health* (pp. 3–22). Washington, DC: University Press of America.

Parron, D.L. (1994). *DSM-IV:* Making it culturally relevant. In S. Friedman (Ed.), *Anxiety disorders in African Americans* (pp. 149–165). New York: Springer.

Phinney, J.S. (1992). The multigroup ethnic identity measure: A new scale for use with diverse groups. *Journal of Adolescent Research, 7,* 156–176.

Phinney, J.S., & Rotheram, M.J. (Eds.). (1987). *Children's ethnic socialization: Pluralism and development.* Newbury Park, CA: Sage.

Plante, T.G., Manuel, G.M., Menendez, A.V., & Marcotte, D. (1995). Coping with stress among Salvadoran immigrants. *Hispanic Journal of Behavioral Sciences. 17*(4), 471–479.

Powless, D.L., & Elliott, S.N. (1993). Assessment of social skills of Native American preschoolers: Teachers' and parents' ratings. *Journal of School Psychology, 31,* 293, 307.

Rosenblatt, A., & Attkisson, C.C. (1992). Integrating systems of care in California for youth with severe emotional disturbance: I. A descriptive overview of the California AB377 Evaluation Project. *Journal of Child and Family Studies, 1*(1), 93–113.

Rossello, J., & Bernal,G. (1996). Adapting cognitive-behavioral and interpersonal treatments for depressed Puerto Rican adolescents. In E.D. Hibbs, & P.S. Jensen (Eds.), *Psychosocial treatments for child and adolescent disorders: Empirically based strategies for clinical practice* (pp. 157–185). Washington, DC: American Psychological Association.

Sage, G.P. (1991). Counseling American Indian adults. In C.C. Lee & B.L. Richardson (Eds.), *Multicultural issues in counseling: New approaches to diversity* (pp. 23–35). Alexandria, VA: American Association for Counseling and Development.

Salgado de Snyder, V.N., Cervantes, R.C., & Padilla, A.M. (1990). Gender and ethnic differences in psychosocial stress and generalized distress among Hispanics. *Sex Roles, 22,* 441–453.

Sattler, J.M. (1974). *Assessment of children's intelligence.* Philadelphia: Saunders.

Sigelman, C., Didjurgis, T., Marshall, B., Vargas, F., & Stewart, A. (1992). Views of problem drinking among Native American, Hispanic, and Anglo children. *Child Psychiatry and Human Development, 22,* 265–276.

Sigurdson, E., Staley, D., Matas, M., Hildahl, K., & Squair, K. (1994). A five year review of youth suicide in Manitoba. *Canadian Journal of Psychiatry, 39*, 397–403.

Stiffman, A.R., & Davis, L.E. (Eds.). (1990). *Ethnic issues in adolescent mental health.* Newbury Park, CA: Sage.

Stone, B.J. (1992). Prediction of achievement by Asian American and White children. *Journal of School Psychology, 30*(1), 91–99.

Sue, D.W., & Sue, S. (1979). Counseling Chinese-Americans. In D.R. Atkinson, G. Morton, & D.W. Sue (Eds.), *Counseling American minorities: A cross-cultural perspective* (pp. 95–104). Dubuque, IA: Brown.

Sue, S. (1977). Community mental health services to minority groups: Some optimism, some pessimism. *American Psychologist, 32*, 616–624.

Sue, S. (1982). *The mental health of Asian-Americans.* San Francisco: Jossey-Bass.

Sue, S., & Chin, R. (1996). Mental health of Chinese-American children. In, G.J. Powell (Ed.), *The psychosocial development of minority group children* (pp. 362–372).

Sue, S., Fujino, D.C, Hu, L., Takeuchi, D.T., & Zane, N. (1991). Community mental health services for ethnic minority groups: A test of the cultural responsiveness hypothesis. *Journal of Consulting and Clinical Psychology, 59*, 533–540.

Tanaka-Matsumi, J., Seiden, D.Y., & Lam, K.N. (1996). The Culturally Informed Functional Assessment (CIFA) interview: A strategy for cross-cultural behavioral practice. *Cognitive and Behavioral Practice, 3*(2), 215–235.

Torres-Matrullo, C. (1982). Cognitive therapy of depressive disorders in the Puerto Rican female. In R.M. Becerra, M. Karno, & J.I. Escobar (Eds.), *Mental health and Hispanic Americans* (pp. 101–113). New York: Grune & Stratton.

Touliatos, J., & Lindholm, B. (1980). Behavior disturbances of children of native-born and immigrant parents. *Journal of Community Psychology, 8*(1), 334–348.

Triandis, H.C. (1995). The self and social behavior in differing cultural contexts. In N.R. Goldberger & J.B. Veroff (Eds.), *The culture and psychology reader* (pp. 326–365). New York: New York University Press.

U.S. Bureau of the Census. (1996). *Statistical abstract of the United States 1996* (113th ed.). Washington, DC: Author.

U.S. Census Bureau. (1998). *1998 statistical abstract* [Online]. Available: http://www.census.gov/

U.S. Congress, Office of Technology Assessment. (1990, January). *Indian adolescent mental health* (OTA-H-446). Washington, DC: U.S. Government Printing Office.

U.S. Department of Health and Human Services. (1994). *Trends in Indian health.* Public Health Service, Indian Health Service. Washington DC: U.S. Government Printing Office.

Victor, J.B., Dent, H., Lane, K., Chambers, A., Franklin, D., & Turner, K. (1996). *Dimensions of personality in African-American children.* Paper presented at the sixth annual Virginia Beach Conference: Children and Adolescents with Emotional and Behavioral Disorders, Virginia Beach, VA.

Vijver, F. van de, & Leung, K. (1997). Methods and data analysis of comparative research. In J.W. Berry, Y. Poortinga, & J. Pandey (Eds.), *Handbook of cross-cultural psychology* (Vol. 1, pp. 257–300). Boston: Allyn & Bacon.

Weibel-Orlando, J. (1984). Culture-specific treatment modalities: Assessing client-to-treatment fit in Indian alcoholism programs. In W.M. Cox (Ed.), *Treatment and prevention of alcohol problems: A resource manual* (pp. 261–283). Orlando, FL: Academic Press.

Weissman, M.M., Bruce, M.L., Leaf, P.J., & Holzer, C., III. (1991). Affective disorders. In L.N. Robins & D.A. Regier (Eds.), *Psychiatric disorders in America: The Epidemiologic Catchment Area Study* (pp. 53–80). New York: Free Press.

Welte, J.W., & Barnes, G.M. (1987). Alcohol use among adolescent minority groups. *Journal of Studies on Alcohol, 48*, 329–336.

Westermeyer, J., & Neider, J. (1985). Cultural affiliation among American Indian alcoholics: Correlations and change over a ten year period. *Journal of Operational Psychiatry, 16*, 17–23.

Yates, A. (1987). Current status and future directions of research on the American Indian child. *American Journal of Psychiatry, 144*, 1135–1142.

Yeh, M., Eastman, K., & Cheung, M. (1994). Children and adolescents in community health centers: Does the ethnicity or the language of the therapist matter? [Special issue: Asian-American Mental Health]. *Journal of Community Psychology, 22*(2), 153–163.

Yeh, M., Takeuchi, D., & Sue, S. (1994). Asian-American children treated in the mental health system: A comparison of parallel and mainstream outpatient service centers. *Journal of Clinical Child Psychology, 23*(1), 5–12.

Zayas, L.H., & Palleja, J. (1988). Puerto Rican familism: Implications for family therapy. *Family Relations, 37*, 260–264.

Zayas, L.H., & Solari, F. (1994). Early childhood socialization in Hispanic families: Context, culture, and practice implications. *Professional Psychology: Research and Practice, 25*, 200–206.

CHAPTER 49

Prevention of Childhood Disorders

DAVID DiLILLO AND LIZETTE PETERSON

Psychologists have traditionally directed the majority of their efforts toward the development and evaluation of interventions to ameliorate mental disorders once they have been fully manifested. These efforts have yielded a number of innovative and successful psychotherapeutic interventions, which can greatly reduce the suffering associated with a variety of psychological problems. Many patients who previously were forced simply to endure the pain of depression, anxiety, attention-deficit/hyperactivity disorder (ADHD), and other disorders can now enjoy a substantial degree of relief from their symptoms.

Despite the many unequivocal successes achieved by the field, traditional victim-oriented approaches to mental health treatment have at least one obvious limitation. Even the most sophisticated after-the-fact treatment approaches are incapable of reducing the initial incidence rates of a disorder (Bloom, 1979). As Albee (1982) notes, regardless of our best efforts, no disease or mental disorder can be conquered in a solely reactive fashion by treating only those already affected. In fact, some have argued that by focusing on treatment to the exclusion of prevention, mental health professionals have sometimes labored under an illusion that social problems are being solved, when they actually are not (Heller, Jenkins, Steffen, & Swindle, 2000).

Prevention of disorders before they occur is an appealing proposition, especially when applied to children. Who would dispute the value in teaching children skills and bolstering their competencies to spare them later physical and psychological distress? Periodically over the years, the virtues of prevention have been espoused by various mental health advocates, but these sentiments have typically been overlooked by the broader treatment community (Heller, 1996).

Why has the mental health community been reluctant to embrace such an inherently attractive concept as prevention? Several factors may have contributed to prevention's apparent lack of staying power. First, as noted, the established mental health treatment community historically has concerned itself with the remediation of existing deficits in individual patients. The sheer inertia of this orientation, along with early advocates' sometimes poor articulation of the prevention concept, has made it difficult for preventionist movements to gain a strong constituency. Second, it has been suggested by Felner, Felner, and Silverman (2000) that our society seems to believe that a certain level of human suffering and loss is acceptable or even necessary. Felner et al. maintain that the adoption of a goal of zero tolerance toward human casualties is necessary for prevention as a concept to be effective and widely accepted. Finally, the movement toward prevention has periodically been slowed by critics arguing that prevention had yet to prove its worth (e.g., Lamb & Zusman, 1979; Moscowitz, 1989).

Over the past several years, however, a clear groundswell of support for the prevention of mental disorders has once again emerged. Managed care organizations have begun to tout early detection and prevention in an effort to curb rising health care costs. These organizations hope to reduce the traditional reliance on more expensive acute care delivery systems. The Institute of Medicine (IOM) and the National Institute of Mental Health (NIMH) have each released reports, authored by prominent and influential preventionists, reviewing the current state of mental health prevention and calling for a strong national prevention research agenda (Mrazek & Haggerty, 1994; NIMH, 1994). These reports provide increased acknowledgment of the merits of prevention research on the federal level. Influential psychologist and past president of the American Psychological Association Martin Seligman has also spoken widely of the need to refocus psychology on prevention and promotion of more positive human attributes (Clay, 1997). Together, these events signal that, once again, the time is ripe for prevention. No groups stand to gain more from this renewed emphasis on prevention than children and adolescents.

DIFFERING DEFINITIONS

Most public health and psychological interventions in the past have delineated three types of prevention: primary, secondary, and tertiary. Primary prevention, the most commonly investigated of the forms of preventive interventions, designates those interventions that occur prior to the beginning of any sign of difficulty. Education programs designed to prevent children from ever using drugs are representative of primary prevention efforts. Secondary prevention refers to prevention that is cued by signs that, in the absence of an intervention, problems may develop. Interventions that target very active and socially unskilled preschool children who might potentially become aggressive would be regarded as secondary prevention. Tertiary prevention designates prevention of further damage to individuals who are already experiencing signs of a disorder or illness. Preventing adolescents who are abusing alcohol from continuing on to a pattern of more serious addiction is one example of tertiary prevention.

The IOM report (Mrazek & Haggerty, 1994) noted that confusion has surrounded the usage of the traditional public health classification system of primary, secondary, and tertiary prevention. For example, the use of the term "prevention," which implies the avoidance of a disorder altogether, has frequently been applied to interventions targeting individuals who have already met or nearly met the diagnostic criteria for a disorder. Thus, the Committee on Prevention of Mental Disorders has recommended that the label "prevention" be used on a continuum, with primary prevention indicating only those interventions that occur prior to the initial onset of a clinically diagnosable disorder. In delineating the full spectrum of mental health interventions, the IOM committee recommended that interventions occurring after a disorder meets formal diagnostic criteria be termed "treatment interventions," and that those interventions taking place after an initial acute episode of a disorder has subsided be classified as "maintenance interventions."

The IOM also proposed a breakdown of preventive interventions into three subcategories that are similar to types of primary prevention described earlier. These are universal, selective, and indicated preventive interventions. Universal interventions are those targeting an entire population; they are not applied differentially to high-risk groups. Selective interventions are aimed at a subgroup of the population who, because of biological, psychological, or social risk factors, are at risk of developing a particular mental disorder but have not yet become dysfunctional. Indicated interventions are intended for those members of high-risk groups who have already been identified as having experienced the precursors to or some minimal symptomology associated with a mental disorder.

Discussed here are some of the significant intervention efforts developed to prevent childhood disorders. The chapter is organized in a developmental sequence, from infancy through adolescence. During each phase of development, children are faced with new tasks—motor, cognitive, and social—which they must attempt and, ideally, master. At times, however, the acquisition of these new skills and competencies is hampered by physical or psychological difficulties, each of which is associated with a unique set of risk factors. Most intervention efforts with children seek to reduce these risk factors and to enhance the protective conditions known to shield children from a particular disorder. Here, interventions targeting several of the most prevalent childhood problems are sampled. For each, we briefly note the nature and scope of the problem, then provide an illustrative sample of the major efforts undertaken to prevent that disorder.

PRENATAL CARE

Proper care and protection of the developing fetus is commonly known to prevent prematurity, low birthweight, and specific disabilities and disorders in newborns. Conversely, lack of quality prenatal care has been related to a variety of preventable disorders that appear in low birthweight babies. Low birthweight babies constitute approximately 60% of infant deaths in the United States, and those underweight babies who do survive often experience significant disorders throughout their lives, including mental retardation, cerebral palsy, and other psychosocial problems (IOM, 1985). In a review of prenatal care intervention programs, the IOM (1988) noted that the small number of interventions with premature infants that have been conducted have been plagued by biases in the selection of participants and a failure to utilize random assignment of participants to treatment conditions. They further commented that the determination of the impact of individual program elements in prenatal programs is made difficult if not impossible due to the complexity of the programs.

As part of its Healthy People 2000 campaign, the U.S. Public Health Service expressed a commitment to providing all infants with a healthy start in life by ensuring that quality prenatal health care be universally available (Department of Health and Human Services, 1991). Early drafts of the *Healthy People 2010* report (Department of Health and Human Services, 1999) document increases in prenatal care received by African American and Hispanic mothers. Nevertheless, there continue to be large numbers of women, particularly young mothers and those from economically and socially disadvantaged groups, who receive substandard prenatal care in the United States (IOM, 1988).

As an example of one of the few well-evaluated prenatal intervention programs to avoid these pitfalls, Olds, Henderson, Chamberlin, and Tatelbaum (1986) examined the effects of prenatal home visitations conducted with 400 primiparous women in upstate New York. This selective intervention focused on women who were teenagers, unmarried,

or of low socioeconomic status (SES). The program coordinated nutritional assessment, health education, and prenatal medical care through the use of home nurses. Findings revealed that home visitations appeared to improve women's prenatal health-related behaviors, social support, and use of services, and the infant's birthweight and length of gestation. The intervention also was associated with long-term benefits (detailed later in this chapter). Further investigation is needed if the potential impact of prenatal intervention programs is to be learned.

INTERVENTIONS FOR INFANTS AND YOUNG CHILDREN

The first five years of life are crucial for the development of verbal, motor, and intellectual skills, as well as for the formation of healthy parent-child attachment. There are many prevention programs that target multiple aspects of the child's emerging abilities, such as Parents as Teachers and Head Start. As an example of important prevention efforts, this chapter focuses on one vitally important class of behaviors: those adult or child behaviors that eventually result in the child's being harmed, either unintentionally because of florid neglect or through deliberate acts of maltreatment. Unintentional injuries, physical abuse, and neglect pose significant threats to youth development, for children who experience these events often suffer serious impairment in their long-term physical and psychological adjustment (Cicchetti, 1989).

Interventions during the early years seek to reduce risk factors that interfere with the achievement of important developmental milestones. Increasingly, economic deprivation has been recognized as a risk factor associated with a variety of mental and physical health problems experienced by young children (Farrington et al., 1990). In response to this, many early child interventions are selectively aimed at individuals from lower socioeconomic groups. Also, because preschool children's cognitive and verbal abilities have not fully emerged, most preventive interventions at this age target children indirectly, through intervention efforts focusing on parents' and caregivers' behaviors.

Prevention of Physical Abuse and Neglect

The incidence of reported physical abuse and neglect cases in the United States is shockingly high. In 1993 alone, there were 3 million child maltreatment reports (Department of Health and Human Services, 1995). With over half of the children abused or neglected in 1993 being under the age of 8, and a full one-third between the ages of 3 and 7 (Department of Health and Human Services, 1995), young children are among the most likely to be abused or maltreated.

Multiple aspects of children's long-term functioning may be disrupted by repeated physical abuse and neglect. Maltreated children show more difficulties in social functioning than do their non-mistreated peers (Cicchetti & Carlson, 1989), suggesting that abuse interferes with their ability to establish competent social relations with peers. Externalizing behaviors such as aggression, noncompliance, and impulsivity (Alessandri, 1991; Bousha & Twentyman, 1984; Hoffman-Plotkin & Twentyman, 1984), as well as internalizing disorders of depression, avoidance, and anxiety, are associated with having been abused (Jaffe, Wolfe, Wilson, & Zak, 1986; Klimes-Dougan & Kistner, 1990).

In an effort to spare young children from these and other undesirable outcomes, researchers have attempted to identify those at risk for abuse and devise interventions to prevent the initial onset and repeated occurrence of maltreatment. These interventions have taken several forms, targeting parenting skills, parent-child interactions, the nature of the home environment, abuse potential, and other factors associated with abuse. Only a handful of studies have utilized actual reported abuse as an outcome measure. The majority of these studies have employed didactic approaches as a means to modify parenting behaviors. Such methods have proven to be relatively ineffective in preventing abuse (Daro, 1988). More promising appear to be interventions offering multiple social support mechanisms to caregivers, thereby potentially impacting a number of risk factors for abuse.

One such intervention, developed by Olds et al. (1986), targeted 400 low-income teenage mothers beginning during the prenatal period and extending through their children's second birthdays. Home visiting by nurses consisted of teaching parenting skills, providing education about child health and development, strengthening social support, and linking the family to community services. Data obtained two years following the intervention showed gains such as reduced rates of subsequent pregnancy, increased employment, and reduced dependence on government aid were maintained two years following termination of the intervention. These improvements were still evident even 15 years following treatment, as were additional benefits, such as a lower incidence of criminal behavior, child abuse, and neglect (Olds et al., 1997). What appears to be a very costly intervention, with a caseworker assigned weekly for many months, may in the end be cost-effective. To convince legislators who control the aid for high-risk women, these studies may have to include clear cost-benefit ratios in their outcome data. One difficulty of our present legislative process is that a legislator must convince his or her constituency of the value of spending money now, when the real value of the program may not be seen during that legislator's term.

A small number of behavioral interventions employing time-limited treatments have been shown to be effective with adjudicated abusing parents (e.g., Lutzker & Rice, 1984; Wolfe, 1994), as well as promising interventions with high-risk but non-adjudicated parents (e.g., Peterson, Gable, Doyle, & Ewigman, 1997). Still, there remains the need for demonstration of a practical and effective multicomponent behavioral treatment program for parents who are at high risk, yet not actively maltreating their children. Multisystemic therapy (Henggeler, Schoenwald, Borduin, Rowland, & Cunningham, 1998), which has been successfully implemented in families with older juvenile offenders, represents one broad-based approach that could be employed earlier in a child's life to reduce overall conflict abuse potential in at-risk homes.

Prevention of Unintentional Injuries

Unintentional injuries are responsible for more childhood deaths in the United States than the next nine leading causes of death combined (Dershewitz & Williamson, 1977). Injuries result in 600,000 child hospitalizations and 16 million emergency room visits annually (Rodriguez, 1990). Children under the age of 5 experience a disproportionate number of these injuries (Baker, O'Neill, Ginsburg, & Li,

1992). Perhaps most disturbing is that, in hindsight, it is clear that a large proportion of unintentional injuries could have been prevented altogether.

Environmental Change
Early efforts to reduce injuries to young children emphasized the physical separation of children from environmental hazards (Grantz, 1979; Rivara & Mueller, 1987). Such efforts are aimed at restructuring children's surroundings to minimize the likelihood of injury. In many instances, these interventions have succeeded. Children's poisonings plummeted when medicines and other toxic substances were placed in child-resistant containers (Walton, 1982). Child safety gates and bars on windows have drastically reduced the number of injuries sustained from falls (Wilson, Baker, Teret, Shock, & Garbarino, 1991). Bicycle helmets can reduce the risk for head injury in children by as much as 85% (Rivara, 1982). Where relevant, environmental modifications are the preferred means of reducing injuries.

Targeting Caregivers
Unfortunately, approaches to injury control that emphasize solely environmental modifications have some serious limitations. For the most part, children live in a world designed for and by adults. Thus, it is not always possible to alter the adult-oriented environment to effectively isolate children from potential agents of injury. For instance, there is no feasible way to guarantee that young children will not place dangerous objects in their mouths (e.g., pennies, thumbtacks, paperclips).

In situations where environmental and product modification approaches fall short or are not applicable, some voluntary, self-regulatory behavior on the part of either caregiver or child is necessary if an injury is to be averted. Many of the most common injuries sustained by toddlers fall into this category (e.g., bathtub drownings, burns, suffocation). Toddlers and younger children must depend on effective caregiving if they are to avoid these injuries. Educational interventions directed at caregivers have been the most common ways of promoting safe parenting practices. Such interventions presume that parents who are well-informed about the causes of childhood injury will independently take steps to keep their children safe. Though many of these interventions are well-planned and have good face validity, this type of populationwide educational

intervention has proven relatively ineffective. In a classic example of a community education program, a home safety campaign was directed at parents of young children living in Rockland County, New York (Schlesinger et al., 1966). The intervention group in this study was exposed to extensive didactic sessions, neighborhood discussion groups, and a periodic newsletter. However, in comparison to controls, these parents showed no significant gains in terms of reduced injury rates. Although the project utilized "state of the art" techniques and reached a majority of its target population, its overly broad objectives (Pless & Arsenault, 1987) and lack of consequences for responding or failing to respond (Peterson & Cook, 1994) appeared to have been the fatal flaws.

Behavior Change and the Use of Consequences
Most teaching-type interventions that have demonstrated effectiveness target a limited number of well-defined goals and typically offer explicit consequences. They also provide feedback to parents, as well as incentives to reinforce desired safety behaviors. For example, Roberts, Fanurik, and Wilson (1988) used behavioral procedures involving rewards, prompting, and feedback to successfully increase children's safety belt use. In their assessment of the study, Roberts et al. concluded that merely providing safety information to individuals is insufficient to motivate behavior change. It is with rewards and behavioral rehearsal that safety behaviors are most likely to be adopted and maintained.

Future injury research with young children will need to uncover the means and behavioral mechanisms by which parents socialize their children about injury. With this knowledge, selective interventions can be devised to help teach parents the most appropriate and safe ways to supervise young children.

INTERVENTIONS FOR SCHOOL-AGE CHILDREN

Pervasive social and cognitive changes characterize the ages between 5 and 12. Children's information-processing abilities increase greatly during this time, resulting in the improved memory and learning capacities necessary for successful scholastic achievement. Poor academic performance places children at an increased risk for various mental and behavioral disorders, prompting researchers to devise programs to address risk factors associated with poor academic performance. Middle childhood is also a time when conduct problems, which themselves place children at risk for more serious adult adjustment difficulties, begin to emerge in full force. Finally, during the elementary school years, unsuspecting children become particularly vulnerable to sexual abuse committed by both intra- and extrafamilial perpetrators. To protect children from these threats, researchers have devised programs to assist youth in recognizing and avoiding sexually abusive situations. In general, interventions during this stage are aimed at both adult caregivers and children themselves, who now possess increased verbal abilities and improved behavioral self-control.

ENHANCEMENT OF ACADEMIC PERFORMANCE

Studies have related poor academic achievement to various undesirable outcomes, such as school dropout, misbehavior (Gold & Mann, 1984), delinquency, and substance abuse (Blumstein, Cohen, Roth, & Visher, 1986; Gottfredson, 1981). These findings have led to the investigation of enhancement of school performance as a significant component of prevention interventions. In one such investigation, O'Donnell, Hawkins, Catalano, Abbott, and Day (1995) reported results based on the 177 low-income elementary school children participating in the Seattle Social Development Project. This multicomponent selective intervention took place over four years, beginning when children entered the first grade, with the goal of reducing school failure, substance abuse, and delinquency. To improve children's classroom performance, teachers in the intervention condition were trained to implement proactive classroom management (to promote learning and minimize disruptive behavior), interactive teaching (which involves frequent assessment of children's comprehension of subject matter), and cooperative learning (utilization of small groups to foster teamwork). Outcome data collected when children entered the fifth grade showed some improvements in important areas of academic functioning. Compared to controls, boys receiving the intervention showed significant improvement in study skills and persistence in completing schoolwork. Boys in the treatment condition

also obtained better grades and performed better in math, reading, and language arts on a standardized achievement test. Though the authors provide no definite explanation to account for the study's differential impact on boys and girls, the project demonstrates at least some effectiveness in enhancing school performance with one segment of a high-risk sample.

PREVENTION OF CONDUCT DISORDERS

The prevalence of conduct and behavioral disorders among elementary-age children in the United States has been estimated at 3% to 6% of the general population (Kazdin, Mazurick, & Bass, 1993). A significant proportion of these children will go on to face later problems, including school dropout, teen pregnancy, and interpersonal difficulties (Kazdin et al., 1993; Walker, Colvin, & Ramsey, 1995). Thus, with successful implementation of prevention programs, many children can be spared a variety of increasingly serious long-term difficulties.

Patterson and colleagues (Patterson, 1982) have devised a model of social interaction that provides insight into the family processes that contribute to the development of antisocial behavior and conduct disorders in young children. Specifically, harsh, coercive, and inconsistent parenting practices have been found to predict the onset and maintenance of oppositional behaviors and conduct disorders. These disruptive behaviors in turn prompt additional and more intense harsh parental reactions, forming a positive feedback loop (more child opposition yields harsher discipline, which in turn yields more opposition). This mutually coercive cycle of escalating, intensified behaviors can contribute to the development of conduct disorders (Patterson, 1982; Webster-Stratton, 1993).

Interventions that interrupt this coercive cycle in its early stages hold promise for the reduction of subsequent conduct disorders. The Montreal Longitudinal Study (Tremblay et al., 1991) utilized three groups—an experimental, an observational placebo, and a control group—to evaluate the efficacy of a treatment program for disruptive boys between the age of 7 and 9. The two-pronged intervention included a parent training component based on Patterson's (1982) model and a variety of school-based social skills training for target boys in small groups with prosocial peers. Initial follow-ups following this 17 to 19-session intervention showed few treatment gains, which the authors attributed to treatment practices that may have oversensitized mothers to disruptive and inattentive behaviors in their sons. Two years after the intervention, however, the treated boys reported less fighting and theft as well as better classroom behavior than untreated subjects, suggesting that some positive effect of the treatment was realized.

Bry's (1982) indicated intervention program lasted three years and targeted samples of seventh-grade children who were at risk for delinquency due to low academic motivation, alienation from family, and previous school conduct problems. Children were placed in pairs matched for previous academic performance and randomly assigned to either an intervention or a control group. The intervention included weekly report cards sent home to parents to monitor classroom behavior, and rewards (e.g., praise and approval from staff) for desirable school conduct. Close contact was maintained between school officials and parents regarding children's progress during the intervention. Biweekly booster sessions were conducted for two years following the initial intervention phase. Data from school records, arrest reports, and interviews showed that rates of delinquent and criminal behavior among the treatment group members were significantly lower than those of the control group at both one- and five-year follow-ups.

Together, these studies suggest that multicomponent interventions show promise for reducing disruptive behaviors among elementary school children. In a recent review of empirically supported treatments for conduct-disordered children, Brestan and Eyberg (1998) highlighted several key issues to consider in the development of future interventions with this population; these issues are also relevant to the development of efficacious preventive interventions. For instance, past studies often included only boys, and as such, are not necessarily applicable to girls, who represent a substantial minority of those diagnosed with conduct problems. Investigations should also take into account potentially related variables such as the SES and ethnic makeup of study participants, as families from minority backgrounds constitute a growing proportion of the general population. Finally, with few exceptions (e.g., Tremblay, Pagani-Kurtz, Masse, Vitaro, & Pihl, 1995), most true preventive interventions in this area target older preadolescent

or adolescent children. Evidence that the origins of disruptive behavior patterns may lie in early parent-child interactions (Patterson, 1982) suggests a greater need for true selective prevention efforts to begin at an early age, before disruptive behavior patterns have been fully manifested.

PREVENTION OF SEXUAL ABUSE

Estimating the prevalence of child sexual abuse (CSA) is difficult because only a small number of the sex crimes committed are ever reported (Kilpatrick, Edmunds, & Seymour, 1992). National surveys, which are not dependent on official reports, may be the best indicators of sexual abuse rates. A recent nationwide telephone survey of 10 to 16-year-old boys and girls found that 15.3% of girls and 5.9% of boys had experienced attempted or completed sexual abuse of another (Finkelhor & Dziuba-Leatherman, 1994). Although responses of survivors to their abuse vary greatly (Kendall-Tackett, Williams, & Finkelhor, 1993), CSA is clearly predictive of a variety of long-term emotional, social, and sexual difficulties (Polusny & Follette, 1995).

Several programs have been developed to help children avoid sexual molestation. Among the most prevalent are school-based interventions, which are mandated in over one third of the states in this country (Kohl, 1993). The primary goals of these intervention programs are to help children detect and then effectively resist sexual assault. These interventions typically teach children to identify inappropriate sexual advances by using their feelings to differentiate among "good, bad, and confusing" touches from adults (Tharinger et al., 1988). Following recognition of an abusive situation, children must then utilize some resistive response, either verbal or behavioral, if they are to avoid an assault. In training situations, both preschool- and elementary-age children have demonstrated the ability to learn appropriate responses to sexual abuse encounters (Harvey, Forehand, Brown, & Holmes, 1988; Kolko, Moser, & Hughes, 1989; Miltenberger & Thiesse-Duffy, 1988; Sarno & Wurtele, 1997). It is currently unclear, however, whether these programs, which depend upon children's assertiveness, work in the face of an actual abusive interaction. Empirical investigation of this question is hampered by the relatively low base rate of reported sexual abuse as well as ethical concerns involved in subjecting children to situations that simulate abusive encounters.

INTERVENTIONS FOR ADOLESCENTS

Adolescence is characterized by a multitude of developmental changes, many of which may be accompanied by serious psychosocial difficulties. Prevention efforts are typically designed to help adolescents deal with and avoid the problems that can arise during the difficult transition to adulthood. The physical changes that occur during puberty result in sexual maturity, which increases the likelihood of unplanned pregnancies, sexually transmitted diseases (STDs), and AIDS. Adolescents' search for a sense of identity and their attempts to manage difficult life stresses can lead to experimentation with alcohol and drugs, possibly evolving into more serious substance abuse and dependency problems. Finally, overwhelmed by the inability to cope, some teens come to view suicide as the only solution to their suffering. Preventive programs targeting teens have been devised to address these and other problems they commonly encounter. The developmental processes occurring at this stage may sometimes facilitate preventive efforts. No longer restrained by the cognitive limitations present at earlier developmental levels, adolescents become more capable of the self-reflection and self-directed behavior changes necessary to avoid problems. Thus, preventive efforts at this point can successfully target adolescents directly, rather than relying primarily on caregiver interventions.

PREVENTION OF AIDS, STDs, AND UNWANTED PREGNANCY

Sexual experimentation is one of the most common risk behaviors in which adolescents engage. The physical changes that accompany puberty equip adolescents with the ability and desire to engage in sexual activity at a time when many have not acquired the social and psychological skills to practice it safely. Unsafe sex practices have led to unacceptably high rates of STDs, HIV infection, and unwanted pregnancies. Figures indicate that nationally, teenagers make up one in four cases of

HIV infection (Hingson, Strunin, Berlin, & Heeren, 1990). When unplanned pregnancies result in childbirth, the long-term consequences are shared by society as well as the individuals involved, with total societal costs associated with teen parenting estimated at between $9 billion and $29 billion annually (Furstenberg, 1991; Maynard, 1996). The fact that nearly all STDs and unplanned pregnancies are readily and simply preventable makes these figures even more disturbing.

It has been noted that sexual activity—the means by which AIDS, STDs, and unwanted pregnancies occur—is a biologically driven behavior that is unlikely to be altered simply because teens acquire knowledge of the associated risks (Botvin, Schinke, & Orlandi, 1995). To be effective, intervention strategies must also contend with adolescents' general feelings of invulnerability to harm, their perceptions that birth control (e.g., condom use) reduces sexual pleasure, and the added resistance to behavior change proffered by teens who are already sexually active. It should come as little surprise then, that early interventions that relied exclusively on dissemination of information emphasizing the consequences of risky sexual behaviors were largely unsuccessful (Kirby, 1992).

The steady increase in the incidence of HIV infection among adolescents at a time when fundamental knowledge about the syndrome and major prevention methods has been on the rise suggests that the provision of information alone is an insufficient means of promoting sexual behavior change among adolescents (Anderson & Christenson, 1991; Hingson et al., 1990; Sonenstein, Pleck, & Ku, 1989). Botvin et al. (1995) delineate factors they consider to be key elements of successful risk-reduction interventions: open communication with sexual partners, the ability to defy peer norms regarding sexual behaviors, support for condom use among sex partners, and frequent parent-adolescent communication.

Schools provide the most convenient and cost-effective access to large numbers of children and therefore are a logical place to implement AIDS, STD, and pregnancy prevention programs. However, because of the heightened political sensitivity to programs dealing with sexual issues, school-based AIDS, STD, and pregnancy reduction efforts may face more than the usual obstacles to implementation. Further, school-based interventions may not reach many adolescents who are at the highest risk for AIDS, STDs, and unwanted pregnancies. For instance, there is evidence that teens whose school attendance may be more sporadic (e.g., incarcerated or homeless youth) face a greater risk of HIV infection yet are less knowledgeable about the basic facts of AIDS than the average teen (DiClemente, Lanier, Horan, & Lodico, 1991; Sondheimer, 1992).

The bottom-line conclusion reached by Botvin and colleagues (1995), one worth repeating here, is that the next generation of interventions in this area will have to go beyond providing information about the causes of STDs and unwanted pregnancies, and place a greater emphasis on helping adolescents learn effective strategies for modifying their sexual behaviors. An example of one such program was developed by Jemmott, Jemmott, and Fong (1992), who randomly assigned 157 African-American male adolescents to one of two groups. In the treatment condition, participants took part in a day-long intervention comprised of HIV/AIDS education, practicing social skills, and role playing, all conducted by a trained facilitator. Participants in the control condition received similarly presented information about career opportunities. At a three-month follow-up, treatment participants reported having fewer incidents of sexual intercourse, fewer sexual partners, and greater rates of condom use.

PREVENTION OF SUBSTANCE ABUSE

Risk taking among adolescents is not limited to sexual behaviors. A recent national sample of high school seniors found that 77% had used alcohol within the past year and 27% had used at least one illicit drug (Johnston, O'Malley, & Bachman, 1993). Early experimentation with drugs is predictive not only of later-life substance use disorders (Kandel, Yamaguchi, & Chen, 1992; Robins & Przybeck, 1985), but also of a host of other unfavorable outcomes such as diminished educational achievement, poor job stability, and increased likelihood of criminal behavior (Newcomb & Bentler, 1988).

These findings underscore the importance of intervening with children to prevent, or postpone, first use of tobacco, alcohol, and illicit drugs. For the past 20 or so years, drug prevention programs have been widely implemented in public schools. The most popular of these programs is Drug Abuse Resistance Education (DARE), a school-based intervention to reduce future use of tobacco, alcohol, and marijuana. With approximately half of local school districts using the program, DARE generally enjoys considerable community support. The program curriculum, which primarily utilizes a social influence approach to drug resistance (Ringwalt, Ennett, & Holt, 1991), includes 17 classroom lessons conducted by a law enforcement officer. One of the three DARE curricula targets children in the last year of elementary school, prior to the time when drug experimentation typically begins.

DARE's rapid proliferation appears to have outstripped the evidence for its efficacy from controlled research studies. Data from investigations incorporating pre- and posttest evaluations and adequate control conditions suggest that DARE does engender less favorable views toward drug use among students (Clayton, Cattarello, Day, & Walden, 1991; Harmon, 1993; Ringwalt et al., 1991) and possibly increases assertiveness (Harmon, 1993; Ringwalt et al., 1991). However, the impact of DARE on actual drug use behaviors has been less favorable. Major evaluation studies have found that DARE has very little if any influence on adolescent drug use, either immediately after the intervention (Harmon, 1993; Ringwalt et al., 1991) or at 1-, 2-, 3-, or 10-year follow-ups (Clayton, Cattarello, & Walden, 1991; Ennett, Rosenbaum et al., 1994; Lynam et al., 1999).

Some have suggested that the young age of students participating in DARE, relative to the age when drug use typically starts, may be responsible for the program's poor performance (Clayton, Cattarello, Day, & Walden, 1991). Other school-based social-influence-oriented prevention programs (e.g., Ellikson & Bell, 1990; Murray, Pirie, Luepker, & Pallonen, 1989; Pentz et al., 1989), targeting slightly older, middle-school-age children, have met with greater success than DARE. For example, Pentz and colleagues implemented the Midwestern Prevention Project, a six-year community-based multicomponent intervention program. The program included a 10-week classroom curriculum, parent-child homework, one-year booster sessions, education and training of parents and community leaders regarding positive communication with children and drug prevention strategies, and an antidrug media campaign. This universal intervention resulted in lower rates of cigarette smoking and marijuana at a three-year follow-up (Johnson et al., 1990). A significant effect on alcohol use found one year after the intervention was not present at the three-year follow-up (Pentz et al., 1989). Nevertheless, these results suggest that multicomponent, community-based programs may have the potential to positively impact substance use.

SUICIDE PREVENTION

For some youths, adolescence is characterized by conflict with parents, school difficulties, and social isolation. These difficulties sometimes escalate to seemingly unmanageable levels, leading many adolescents to contemplate suicide as a means of escape from their difficulties. In recent years, there has been a startling upsurge in the rate of adolescent suicide. Suicide is now the leading cause of death among 15 to 19-year-olds in the United States (National Institute of Mental Health, 1992).

The problem of child and adolescent suicide has received attention from parents, schools, and the helping community. In schools alone, over 1,700 suicide prevention programs were established in the late 1970s and 1980s (Garland, Shaffer, & Whittle, 1989). The low base rate of suicide, combined with the large number of unreported suicide attempts, make evaluation of these programs difficult. One recent national survey found that only 2% of adolescent suicide attempts are reported as such to medical authorities (Kann, Warren, & Harris, 1996).

Suicide prevention efforts have taken many different forms. Crisis centers and hotlines are available to the public in virtually every major city in the United States. These services are based on the belief that suicidal behavior is precipitated by some critical incident that pushes an individual "over the edge." Crisis workers provide support to callers and attempt to dissuade them from self-harm. If crisis centers and hotlines are effective, then cities in which they are located should have reduced rates of suicide. Although no data exist on the impact of crisis services on teen suicide specifically, there are some very limited data from an adult study conducted in the United States. Miller, Coombs, Leeper, and Barton (1984) utilized time-series analysis to compare suicide rates over a six-year period in 50 U.S. counties with suicide prevention services and 25 counties without such services. A significant reduction in suicide rate among young White females was found in counties with crisis centers. However, it is impossible to draw conclusions about the efficacy of community crisis intervention services based on this study alone. The lack of adequate data evaluating crisis intervention services is of particular concern considering their wide proliferation and the vast amount of resources utilized by them.

As noted, increases in the number of school-based suicide intervention programs accompanied the recent increase in adolescent suicide rates. In fact, the number of school-based intervention programs doubled during the mid-1980s (Garland et al., 1989). Garland et al. found that most school-based programs focus on a similar set of goals: (1) to heighten awareness of suicide among students; (2) to assist with identification of those students at risk; and (3) to provide students and school personnel with information about resources available to them. In a recent review, Mazza (1997) seriously questions the efficacy of most school-based suicide prevention programs, citing major concerns that merit reiteration here. First, the vast majority of school prevention programs are based on the notion that suicide attempts result from an accumulation of unmanageable life stress (Garland et al., 1989). This approach ignores a significant amount of literature (e.g., Brent et al., 1986, 1993; Shafii, Carrigan, Whittinghill, & Derrick, 1985) relating suicidal behavior to mental illness and psychopathology. By missing this association, prevention approaches may be limiting their ability to identify and assist many troubled students. A second concern is that most school-based approaches are universal in nature, targeting entire student bodies rather than focusing on those who are most at risk. Mazza contends that the latter approach would be more efficient and effective in preventing a low base rate behavior such as suicide.

CONCLUSIONS

This chapter has delineated a few examples from the many areas in which preventive interventions have been attempted with children and adolescents. In reviewing this area of research, a theme worth noting is that many intervention approaches have adopted a similar initial strategy for promoting change, one that focuses primarily on public education. That is, recognition of a problem area is typically followed by relatively weak but low-cost intervention attempts that are exclusively educational in nature. This strategy is based on the assumption that increased awareness and factual knowledge about a problem will automatically result in corrective behavior changes. The unfortunate conclusion, however, seems to be that these initial educational endeavors rarely succeed. The behaviors addressed by these interventions (e.g., drug abuse, teen pregnancy, inadequate parenting practices including abuse and neglect) are maintained by social and biological processes that are largely resilient to purely didactic interventions. Educational approaches may well improve knowledge levels or attitudes about a particular problem area, but more promising are interventions that combine dissemination of information with helping individuals learn and rehearse the skills and strategies needed to avoid specific problem areas. Effective acquisition of these skills, in fact, should involve a large component of behavioral rehearsal, combined with feedback and performance-contingent reinforcement. Only then is it realistic to expect that individuals will manage their behaviors effectively in real-life situations.

As noted at the outset of this chapter, the field of prevention periodically has had detractors who have expressed (sometimes legitimate) skepticism about the viability of its interventions on the basis of perceived weak conceptual and empirical foundations (e.g., Lamb & Zusman, 1979, 1981). In the past decade, however, a significant number of methodologically rigorous and theoretically sound prevention investigations have been conducted. A recent meta-analysis of the field conducted by Durlak and Wells (1997) reviewed 177 interventions designed to prevent a variety of behavioral and social problems during childhood. Cowen (1997), in commenting on this meta-analysis, summarized what he considers to be the current state of the field: "Based on many studies, each meeting at least minimal scientific standards, involving many different genera of primary prevention programs for children, conducted with many different groups, there is consistent evidence of the efficacy of the overall approach and its principal variants" (p. 155). Thus, with basic questions of its own worthiness answered, perhaps the field itself is transitioning from adolescence to the early stages of maturity.

Nevertheless, formidable tasks lie ahead for prevention intervention research. Several authors (e.g., Durlak & Wells, 1997; Kessler & Goldston, 1986;

McGuire & Earls, 1991) have discussed some of the challenges faced by preventionists. Durlak and Wells highlight a few of these hurdles, including the fact that prevention efforts must always contend with the difficulties inherent in demonstrating the absence of a phenomenon—that is, that a clinical disorder has *not* occurred. Second, for many of the disorders we wish to prevent, the exact etiology and developmental course of the problem remains unclear. Consequently, it is difficult to identify the risk and protective factors that should be targeted for modification or the optimal time or times at which to attempt interventions. Third, prevention efforts are often aimed at distal outcomes, which require expensive and time-consuming long-term follow-ups to be evaluated. It is of concern, then, that only 25% of the studies reviewed by Durlak and Wells included follow-ups of one year or more. Finally, because many of the problems targeted for elimination are low base rate events, it is frequently a challenge to obtain large enough samples to effectively evaluate intervention outcomes.

The IOM report (Mrazek & Haggerty, 1994) recognized psychology as the discipline that has made the most significant contribution to mental health prevention research. Thus, unless psychologists persist in this work, progress in prevention research stands to suffer greatly (Muñoz, Mrazek, & Haggerty, 1996). There are new challenges to meet in the near future of prevention research. In the current health care climate, preventionists must be prepared for increasingly rigorous evaluation of their interventions, as the push to become time-limited and cost-effective becomes increasingly urgent. These evaluations may include direct comparisons of the cost-effectiveness of prevention strategies with traditional treatment approaches (Muñoz et al., 1996). Finally, a particular challenge will be to devise ways to move successful intervention programs into the public arena for wider dissemination in a cost-effective manner; interventions with demonstrated positive outcomes are of minimal value until they reach the wider public. Finding cost-effective methods of accomplishing these objectives and then representing them cogently to educational and hospital administrators, legislators, and anyone else who assists in decision making in state and community organizations may be the best way that psychologists can help move the field of prevention forward in the future.

REFERENCES

Albee, G.W. (1982). Preventing psychopathology and promoting human potential. *American Psychologist, 32,* 150–161.

Alessandri, S.M. (1991). Play and social behavior in maltreated preschoolers. *Development and Psychopathology, 3,* 191–205.

Anderson, M.D., & Christenson, G.M. (1991). Ethnic breakdown of AIDS related knowledge and attitudes from the National Adolescent Student Health Survey. *Journal of Health Education, 22,* 30–34.

Baker, S.P., O'Neill, B., Ginsburg, M.J., & Li, G. (1992). *The injury fact book* (2nd ed.). Lexington, MA: Lexington Books.

Bloom, B.L. (1979). Prevention of mental disorders: Recent advances in theory and practice. *Community Mental Health Journal, 15,* 179–191.

Blumberg, E.J., Chadwick, M.W., Fogarty, L.A., Speth, T.W., & Chadwick, D.L. (1991). The touch discrimination component of sexual abuse prevention training unanticipated positive consequences. *Journal of Interpersonal Violence, 6,* 12–28.

Blumstein, A., Cohen, F., Roth, J.A., & Visher, C.A. (1986). *Criminal careers and "career criminals"* (Vol. 1). Washington DC: National Academy Press.

Botvin, G.L., Schinke, S., & Orlandi, M.A. (1995). School-based health promotion: Substance abuse and sexual behavior. *Applied and Preventive Psychology, 4,* 167–184.

Bousha, D.M., & Twentyman, C.T. (1984). Mother-child interactional style in abuse, neglect, and control groups: Naturalistic observations in the home. *Journal of Abnormal Psychology, 93,* 106–114.

Brent, D.A., Kalas, R., Edelbrock, C., Costello, A.J., Dulcan, M.K., & Conover, N. (1986). Psychopathology and its relationship to suicidal ideation in childhood and adolescents. *Journal of the American Academy of Child and Adolescent Psychiatry, 25,* 666–673.

Brent, D.A., Perper, J.A., Moritz, G., Allman, C.J., Friend, A., Roth, C., Schweers, J., Balach, L., & Baugher, M. (1993). Psychiatric risk factor for adolescent suicide: A case control study. *Journal of the American Academy of Child and Adolescent Psychiatry, 32,* 521–529.

Brestan, E.V., & Eyberg, S.M. (1998). Effective psychosocial treatments of conduct-disordered children and adolescents: 29 years, 82 studies, and 5,272 kids. *Journal of Clinical Child Psychology, 27*(2), 180–189.

Bry, B.H. (1982). Reducing the incidence of adolescent problems through preventive intervention: One- and five-year follow-up. *American Journal of Community Psychology, 10,* 265–276.

Cicchetti, D. (1989). How research on child maltreatment has informed the study of child development: Perspectives from developmental psychopathology. In D. Cicchetti & V. Carlson (Eds.), *Child maltreatment: Theory and research on the causes and consequences of child abuse and neglect* (pp. 377–431). New York: Cambridge University Press.

Cicchetti, D., & Carlson, V. (Eds.). (1989). *Child maltreatment: Theory and research on the causes and consequences of child abuse and neglect.* New York: Cambridge University Press.

Clay, R.A. (1997, September). Prevention is the theme of the '98 presidential year. *APA Monitor,* 35.

Clayton, R.R., Cattarello, A., Day, L.E., & Walden, K.P. (1991). Persuasive communications and drug abuse preventions: An evaluation of the DARE program. In H. Sypher, L. Donohew, & W. Bukoski (Eds.), *Persuasive communications and drug abuse preventions* (pp. 51–84). Hillsdale, NJ: Erlbaum.

Clayton, R.R., Cattarello, A., & Walden, K.P. (1991). Sensation seeking as a potential mediating variable for school-based prevention: A two-year follow-up of DARE. *Health Communication, 3,* 229–239.

Cowen, E.L. (1997). The coming of age of primary prevention: Comments on Durlak and Wells' meta-analysis. *American Journal of Community Psychology, 25,* 153–164.

Daro, D. (1988). *Confronting child abuse for effective program design.* New York: Free Press.

Department of Health and Human Services. (1991). *Healthy People 2000: National health promotion and disease prevention objectives* (DHHS Publication No. PHS 91–50212). Washington, DC: U.S. Government Printing Office.

Department of Heath and Human Services. (1995). *Child maltreatment 1993: Reports from the states to the National Center on Child Abuse and Neglect.* Washington DC: Author.

Department of Health and Human Services. (1999). *Healthy People 2010: Draft for public comment* [On-line]. Available: http://web.health.gov/healthypeople/default.htm

Dershewitz, R.A., & Williamson, J.W. (1977). Prevention of childhood household injuries: A controlled clinical trial. *American Journal of Public Health, 67,* 1148–1153.

DiClemente, R.J., Lanier, M.M., Horan, P.F., & Lodico, M. (1991). Comparison of AIDS knowledge, attitudes, and behaviors among incarcerated adolescents and a public school sample in San Francisco. *American Journal of Public Health, 81,* 628–630.

Durlak, J.A., & Wells, A.M. (1997). Primary prevention mental health programs for children and adolescents: A meta-analytic review. *American Journal of Community Psychology, 25,* 115–142.

Ellikson, P.L., & Bell, R.M. (1990). Drug prevention in junior high: A multi-site longitudinal test. *Science, 247,* 1299–1305.

Ennett, S.T., Rosenbaum, D.P., Flewelling, R.L., Bieler, G.S., Ringwalt, C.L., & Bailey, S.L. (1994). Long-term evaluation of drug abuse resistance education. *Addictive Behaviors, 19,* 113–125.

Farrington, D.P., Loeber, R., Elliot, D.S., Hawkins, J.D., Kandel, D.B., Klein, M.W., McCord, J., Rowe, D.C., & Tremblay, R.E. (1990). Advancing knowledge about the onset of delinquency and crime. In B.B. Lahey & A.E. Kazdin (Eds.), *Advances in clinical child psychology* (Vol. 13, pp. 283–342). New York: Plenum Press.

Felner, R.D., Felner, T.Y., & Silverman, M.M. (2000). Prevention in mental health and social intervention: Conceptual and methodological issues in the evolution of the science and practice of prevention. In J. Rappaport & E. Seidman (Eds.), *Handbook of community psychology* (pp. 9–42). New York: Plenum Press.

Finkelhor, D., & Dziuba-Leatherman, J. (1994). Children as victims of violence: A national survey. *Pediatrics, 94,* 413–420.

Furstenberg, F.F., Jr. (1991). As the pendulum swings: Teenage childbearing and social concern. *Family Relations, 40,* 127–138.

Garland, A.F., Shaffer, D., & Whittle, B.A. (1989). A national survey of school-based, adolescent suicide prevention programs. *Journal of the American Academy of Child and Adolescent Psychiatry, 48,* 169–182.

Gold, M., & Mann, D.W. (1984). *Expelled to a friendlier place: A study of effective alternative schools.* Ann Arbor: University of Michigan Press.

Gottfredson, G.D. (1981). Schooling and delinquency. In S.W. Martin, L.B. Sechrest, & R. Redner (Eds.), *New directions in the rehabilitation of criminal offenders* (pp. 424–469). Washington DC: National Academy Press.

Grantz, R.R. (1979). Accidental injury in childhood: A literature review on pediatric trauma. *Journal of Trauma, 19,* 551–555.

Harbeck, C., Peterson, L., & Starr, L. (1992). Previously abused child victims' response to a sexual abuse prevention program: A matter of measures. *Behavior Therapy, 23,* 375–387.

Harmon, M.A. (1993). Reducing the risk of drug involvement among early adolescents. *Evaluation Review, 17,* 221–239.

Harvey, P., Forehand, R., Brown, C., & Holmes, T. (1988). The prevention of sexual abuse: Examination of the effectiveness of a program with kindergarten-age children. *Behavior Therapy, 19,* 429–435.

Heller, K. (1996). Coming of age of prevention science: Comments on the 1994 National Institute of Mental Health–Institute of Medicine prevention reports. *American Psychologist, 51,* 1123–1127.

Heller, K., Jenkins, R.A., Steffen, A.M., & Swindle, R.W., Jr. (2000). Prospects for a viable community mental health system: Recording ideology, professional traditions, and political reality. In J. Rappaport & E. Seidman (Eds.), *Handbook of community psychology* (pp. 445–470). New York: Plenum Press.

Henggeler, S.W., Schoenwald, S.K., Borduin, C.M., Rowland, M.D., & Cunningham, P.B. (1998). *Multisystemic treatment of antisocial behavior in children and adolescents.* New York: Guilford Press.

Hingson, R.W., Strunin, L., Berlin, B., & Heeren, T. (1990). Beliefs about AIDS, use of alcohol and drugs, and unprotected sex among Massachusetts adolescents. *American Journal of Public Health, 80,* 295–299.

Hoffman-Plotkin, D., & Twentyman, C.T. (1984). A multimodal assessment of behavioral and cognitive deficits in abused and neglected preschoolers. *Child Development, 55,* 794–802.

Institute of Medicine. (1985). *Preventing low birthweight.* Washington, DC: National Academy Press.

Institute of Medicine. (1988). *Prenatal care: Reaching mothers, reaching infants.* Washington, DC: National Academy Press.

Jaffe, P., Wolfe, D., Wilson, S., & Zak, L. (1986). Similarities in behavioral and social maladjustment among child victims and witnesses to family violence. *American Journal of Orthopsychiatry, 56,* 142–146.

Jemmott, J.B., III, Jemmott, L.S., & Fong, G.T. (1992). Reduction in HIV risk-associated sexual behaviors among Black male adolescents: Effects of an AIDS prevention intervention. *American Journal of Public Health, 82,* 372–377.

Johnson, C.A., Pentz, M.A., Weber, M.D., Dwyer, J.H., Baer, N., MacKinnon, D.P., Hanson, W.B., & Flay, B.R. (1990). Relative effectiveness of comprehensive community programming for drug abuse prevention with high-risk and low-risk adolescents. *Journal of Consulting and Clinical Psychology, 58,* 447–456.

Johnston, L., O'Malley, P.M., & Bachman, J.G. (1993). *National survey results on drug use from the Monitoring the Future Study, 1975–1992 (Vol. I: Secondary School Students).* Rockville, MD: National Institute of Drug Abuse.

Kandel, D.B., Yamaguchi, K., & Chen, K. (1992). Stages of progression in drug involvement from adolescence to adulthood: Further evidence for the gateway theory. *Journal of Studies on Alcohol, 53,* 447–457.

Kann, L., Warren, C.W., & Harris, W.A. (1996). Youth risk behavior surveillance: U.S., 1993. *Journal of School Health, 66,* 365–377.

Kazdin, A.E., & Kendall, P.C. (1998). Current progress and future plans for developing effective treatments: Comments and perspectives. *Journal of Clinical Child Psychology, 27,* 217–226.

Kazdin, A.E., Mazurick, J.L., & Bass, D. (1993). Risk for attrition in treatment of antisocial children and families. *Journal of Clinical Child Psychology, 22,* 2–16.

Kendall-Tackett, K., Williams, L., & Finkelhor, D. (1993). Impact of sexual abuse on children: A review and synthesis of recent empirical studies. *Psychological Bulletin, 113,* 164–180.

Kessler, M., & Goldston, S.E. (Eds.). (1986). *A decade of progress in primary prevention.* Hanover, NH: University Press of New England.

Kilpatrick, D.G., Edmunds, C.N., & Seymour, A.K. (1992). Rape in America: A report to the nation. *National Victim Center.*

Kirby, D. (1992). School-based prevention programs: Design, evaluation, and effectiveness. In R. DiClemente (Ed.), *Adolescents and AIDS: A generation in jeopardy* (pp. 159–180). Thousand Oaks, CA: Sage.

Klimes-Dougan, B., & Kistner, J. (1990). Physically abused preschoolers' responses to peers' distress. *Developmental Psychology, 26,* 599–602.

Kohl, J. (1993). School-based child sexual abuse prevention programs. *Journal of Family Violence, 2,* 137–150.

Kolko, D.J., Moser, J.T., & Hughes, J. (1989). Classroom training in sexual victimization awareness and prevention skills: An extension of the Red Flag/Green Flag People Program. *Journal of Family Violence, 4,* 25–45.

Lamb, H.R., & Zusman, J. (1979). Primary prevention in perspective. *Psychiatry, 136,* 12–17.

Lamb, H.R., & Zusman, J. (1981). A new look at primary prevention. *Hospital and Community Psychiatry, 32,* 843–848.

Lutzker, J.R., & Rice, J.M. (1984). Project 12-Ways: Treating child abuse and neglect from an ecobehavioral perspective. In R.F. Dangel & R.A. Polster (Eds.), *Parent training: Foundations of research and practice* (pp. 260–293). New York: Guilford Press.

Lynam, D.R., Milich, R., Zimmerman, R., Novak, S.P., Logan, T.K., Martin, C., Leukefeld, C., & Clayton, R. (1999). Project DARE: No effects at 10-year follow-up. *Journal of Consulting and Clinical Psychology, 67,* 590–593.

Maynard, R.A. (1996). *Kids having kids: A Robin Hood Foundation special report on the costs of adolescent childbearing.* Washington, DC: Urban Institute.

Mazza, J.J. (1997). School-based suicide prevention programs: Are they effective? *School Psychology Review, 26,* 382–396.

McGuire, J., & Earls, F. (1991). Prevention of psychiatric disorders in early childhood. *Journal of Child Psychology and Psychiatry, 32,* 129–153.

Miller, H.L., Coombs, D.W., Leeper, J.D., & Barton, S.N. (1984). An analysis of the effects of suicide prevention facilities on suicide rates in the United States. *American Journal of Public Health, 74,* 340–343.

Miltenberger, R.G., & Thiesse-Duffy, E. (1988). Evaluation of home-based programs for teaching personal safety skills to children. *Journal of Applied Behavior Analysis, 21,* 81–87.

Moscowitz, J.M. (1989). The primary prevention of alcohol problems: A critical review of the research literature. *Alcohol Study, 50,* 54–88.

Mrazek, P.J., & Haggerty, R.J. (1994). *Reducing risks for mental disorders: Frontiers for preventive intervention research.* Washington, DC: National Academy Press.

Muñoz, R.F., Mrazek, P.J., & Haggerty, R.J. (1996). Institute of Medicine report on prevention of mental disorders. *American Psychologist, 51,* 1116–1122.

Murray, D.M., Pirie, P., Luepker, R.V., & Pallonen, U. (1989). Five- and six-year follow-up results from four seventh-grade smoking prevention studies strategies. *Journal of Behavioral Medicine, 12,* 207–218.

National Institute of Mental Health. (1992, March). *Suicide facts.* Bethesda, MD: Author.

National Institute of Mental Health Prevention Research Steering Committee. (1994). *The prevention of mental disorders: A national research agenda.* Washington, DC: Author.

Newcomb, M.D., & Bentler, P.M. (1988). *Consequences of adolescent drug use: Impact on the lives of young adults.* New York: Sage.

O'Donnell, J., Hawkins, J.D., Catalano, R.F., Abbott, R.D., & Day, L.D. (1995). Preventing school failure, drug use, and delinquency among low-income children: Long-term intervention in elementary schools. *American Journal of Orthopsychiatry, 65,* 87–100.

Olds, D.L., Eckenrode, J., Henderson, C.R., Jr., Kitzman, H., Powers, J., Cole, R., Sidora, K., Morris, P., Pettitt, L.M., & Luckey, D. (1997). Long-term effects of home visitation on maternal life course and child abuse and neglect: Fifteen-year follow-up of a randomized trial. *Journal of the American Medical Association, 278,* 637–643.

Olds, D.L., Henderson, C.R., Jr., Chamberlin, R., & Tatelbaum, R. (1986). Preventing child abuse and neglect: A randomized trial of nurse home visitation. *Pediatrics, 78,* 65–78.

Patterson, G.R. (1982). *A social learning approach: Coercive family process.* Eugene, OR: Castilia.

Pentz, M.A., Dwyer, J.H., MacKinnon, D.P., Flay, B.R., Hansenm, W.B., Wang, E.Y.I., & Johnson, C.A. (1989). A multicommunity trial for primary prevention of adolescent drug abuse. *Journal of the American Medical Association, 261,* 3259–3266.

Peterson, L., & Cook, S.C. (1994). Preventing injuries: Psychological issues. In R.A. Olson, L.L. Mullins, J.B. Gillman, & J.M. Chaney (Eds.), *The sourcebook of pediatric psychology* (pp. 304–313). Boston: Allyn & Bacon.

Peterson, L., Gable, S., Doyle, C., & Ewigman, B. (1997). Beyond parenting skills: Battling barriers and building bonds to prevent child abuse and neglect. *Cognitive and Behavioral Practice, 4,* 53–74.

Pless, I.B., & Arsenault, L. (1987). The role of health education in the prevention of injuries to children. *Journal of Social Issues, 43,* 87–104.

Polusny, M.A., & Follette, V.M. (1995). Long-term correlates of child sexual abuse: Theory and review of the empirical literature. *Applied and Preventive Psychology, 4*, 143–166.

Ringwalt, C.R., Ennett, S.T., & Holt, K.D. (1991). An outcome valuation of Project DARE (Drug Abuse Resistant Education). *Health Education Research, 6*, 327–337.

Rivara, F.P. (1982). Epidemiology of childhood injuries. *American Journal of Diseases of Children, 136*, 399–405.

Rivara, F.P., & Mueller, B. (1987). The epidemiology and causes of childhood injuries. *Journal of Social Issues, 43*, 13–31.

Roberts, M.C., Fanurik, D., & Wilson, D.R. (1988). A community program to reward children's use of seat belts. *American Journal of Community Psychology, 16*, 395–407.

Robins, L.N., & Przybeck, T.R. (1985). Age of onset of drug use as a factor in drug and other disorders. *National Institute on Drug Abuse: Research Monograph Series, 56*, 178–192.

Rodriguez, J.G. (1990). Childhood injuries in the United States: A priority issue. *American Journal of Diseases of Children, 144*, 625–626.

Sarno, J.A., & Wurtele, S.K. (1997). Effects of a personal safety program on preschoolers' knowledge, skills, and perceptions of child sexual abuse. *Child Maltreatment, 2*, 35–45.

Schlesinger, E.R., Dickson, D.G., Westaby, J., Lowen, L., Logrillo, V.M., & Maiwald, A.A. (1966). A controlled study of health education in accident prevention: The Rockland County Child Injury Project. *American Journal of Diseases of Children, 3*, 490–496.

Shafii, M., Carrigan, S., Whittinghill, J.R., & Derrick, A. (1985). Psychological autopsy of completed suicides in children and adolescents. *American Journal of Psychiatry, 142*, 1061–1064.

Sondheimer, D.L. (1992). HIV infection and disease among homeless adolescents. In R. DiClemente (Ed.), *Adolescents and AIDS: A generation in jeopardy* (pp. 71–85). Thousand Oaks, CA: Sage.

Sonenstein, F., Pleck, J., & Ku, L. (1989). Sexual activity, condom use, and AIDS awareness among adolescent males. *Family Planning Perspectives, 21*, 152–158.

Tharinger, D.J., Krivacaska, J.J., Laye-McDonough, M., Jamison, L., Vincent, G.G., & Hedlund, A.D. (1988). Prevention of child sexual abuse: An analysis of issues in educational programs, and research finding. *School Psychology Review, 17*, 614–634.

Tremblay, R. E., McCord, J., Boileau, H., Charlebois, P., Gagnon, C., Le Blanc, M., & Larivee, S. (1991). Can disruptive boys be helped to become competent? *Psychiatry, 54*, 148–161.

Tremblay, R.E., Pagani-Kurtz, L., Masse, L.C., Vitaro, F., & Pihl, R.O. (1995). A bimodal preventive intervention for disruptive kindergarten boys: Its impact through mid-adolescence. Special Section: Prediction and prevention of child and adolescent antisocial behavior. *Journal of Consulting and Clinical Psychology, 63*, 560–568.

Walker, H.M., Colvin, G., & Ramsey, E. (1995). *Antisocial behavior in school: Strategies and best practices*. Pacific Grove, CA: Brooks/Cole.

Walton, W.W. (1982). An evaluation of the Poison Prevention Packaging Act. *Pediatrics, 69*, 363–370.

Webster-Stratton, C. (1993). Randomized trial of two parent-training programs for families with conduct disordered children. *Journal of Consulting and Clinical Psychology, 57*, 666–678.

Wilson, M.H., Baker, S.P., Teret, S.P., Shock, S., & Garbarino, J. (1991). *Saving children: A guide to injury prevention*. New York: Oxford University Press.

Wolfe, D.A. (1994). The role of intervention and treatment services in the prevention of child abuse and neglect. In G.B. Melton & F.D. Barry (Eds.), *Protecting children from abuse and neglect* (pp. 182–223). New York: Guilford Press.

CHAPTER 50

Child Maltreatment

BARBARA L. BONNER, MARY BETH LOGUE, KEITH L. KAUFMAN, AND LARISSA N. NIEC

Child maltreatment is now recognized as a major social and mental health problem in the United States and increasingly throughout the world. Since the publication of the seminal article describing the "battered child syndrome" in 1962 by Kempe and his colleagues, (Kempe, Silverman, Steele, Droegemuller, & Silver, 1962), the fields of medicine, social work, law, psychology, law enforcement, and, more recently, dentistry and public health have increased their focus on the diagnosis, treatment, prosecution, and prevention of child abuse and neglect. Various progressive measures have been taken to protect children at the state and federal levels, such as the enactment of laws mandating the reporting of suspected abuse or neglect, the establishment of a nationwide system to protect children (Child Protective Services, CPS), and the creation in 1974 of the National Center on Child Abuse and Neglect (now the Office of Child Abuse and Neglect, OCAN). In spite of these efforts, the U.S. Advisory Board on Child Abuse and Neglect (1990) concluded "that child abuse and neglect in the United States now represents a national emergency" (p. 2), and a recent report by the U.S. Department of Health and Human Services (1998) stated, "One of our nation's most compelling problems is the maltreatment of our children" (p. ix).

Efforts at the federal level to obtain accurate figures on the incidence and prevalence of child abuse and neglect in the United States continue to encounter serious methodological problems. In the most recent national data from 1997, information was gathered from state and national findings on the sources and number of child abuse and neglect reports, the types of maltreatment, the dispositions of the investigations, the child protective investigations and services, the characteristics of the child victims, and the children's relationship to the perpetrators (U.S. Department of Health and Human Services, 1999). However, due to the variations across the entities in definition, investigatory factors, and substantiation criteria, the information gathered is not consistent across the states.

Based on the 1997 figures, CPS determined that just under one million children had cases of indicated or substantiated abuse or neglect, a decrease from more than one million victims in 1996 (U.S. Department of Health and Human Services, 1999). In 1997, CPS agencies investigated more than two million reports involving more than three million children and substantiated 967 deaths due to maltreatment. The national rate of victimization was 13.9 victims per 1,000 children under age 18 in the U.S. population, which is slightly higher than 13.4 victims per 1,000 children in 1990. The rate of child victims peaked in 1993 at 15.3 victims per 1,000 and has continued to drop since that time. However, the National Research Council (1993) reviewed the extant data and recommended numerous changes in the data gathering methods in order to reduce the disparity in epidemiological reports.

Establishing the prevalence of child maltreatment in the United States is hampered by problems of definition, differences in criteria for substantiation across agencies, and methodological problems, such as basing figures on retrospective studies of adults. In the 1970s, it was estimated that 14% of U.S. children had been involved in abusive violence (Straus, 1979), whereas reports in the 1980s used figures of 2% to 3% nationally (National Center on Child Abuse and Neglect, 1988). This difference in reported prevalence rate resulted in criticism of underreporting (Russell & Trainor, 1984). Prevalence figures are best established in the area of sexual abuse, with figures of approximately 20% of all women and 5% to 10% of all men being victimized as children (Finkelhor, 1994).

During the past decade, several events and issues have had a positive effect on the field of child maltreatment. These are described below:

- The American Professional Society on the Abuse of Children (APSAC), an interdisciplinary organization, was established and began conducting an annual national colloquium on child maltreatment. In addition, APSAC publishes a journal, *Child Maltreatment*, and has published six guidelines for practice in the fields of medicine, mental health, and ethics.
- The Section on Child Maltreatment was established by Division 37 of the American Psychological Association.
- Multidisciplinary teams have been established in many communities to assist in the investigation, prosecution, and case management of child maltreatment cases. A national organization, the National Alliance for Children, has been organized to set criteria for team structure and provide ongoing training and technical support.
- Increased focus has been placed on improving techniques to interview children in cases of child sexual abuse due to criticism of inappropriate or leading questioning of young children.
- Interdisciplinary Child Death Review Boards have been established at both local and state levels to review deaths of children from child abuse and neglect, and in many cases, all child deaths. The boards are designed to review cases and make recommendations for changes in systems dealing with the investigation of child deaths or in state legislation to assist in reducing child deaths.
- Research by psychologists, sociologists, physicians, dentists, social workers, and other social scientists has grown dramatically, with over 500 articles on child maltreatment being published annually since 1990.
- The prevention of child maltreatment has taken a major role, with development and implementation of various local, state, and national programs, the most visible of which have been home visitation programs.

Over the past 20 years, mental health professionals have assessed and treated increasing numbers of child, adolescent, and adult victims of child maltreatment, abusing and nonabusing parents, and adolescents and adults who sexually abuse children. During the late 1980s and throughout the 1990s, increasing numbers of preschool and school-age children with inappropriate and aggressive sexual behavior have been referred for psychological intervention (Bonner, Walker, & Berliner, 1999). Specialized treatment programs for victims and offenders have been established in outpatient and inpatient facilities by both public and private agencies.

Although the treatment of an abused child's caregivers, particularly the nonabusing parent(s), is a critical component of a comprehensive treatment program, this chapter focuses primarily on the psychological assessment and treatment of abused children. General information and additional references are provided for the treatment of parents and other family members.

The first section uses the physically abused child as a model and discusses the assessment and treatment of psychological symptoms from a developmental perspective. Although developmental psychologists and others have long emphasized the importance of taking children's development into consideration when explaining the effects of various events, such as natural disasters and victimization, it is heartening to note that the field of child maltreatment has become more sensitive to these issues over the past decade (e.g., Cicchetti & Toth, 1995; Finkelhor, 1995).

PHYSICAL ABUSE

Physical child abuse represents an act of commission on the part of a parent or caregiver involving excessive discipline, beatings, or some other form of overt physical violence that results in injuries to a child that may include fractures, bruises, lacerations, burns, or internal injuries (National Center on Child Abuse and Neglect, 1981). The victims of physical abuse span the age continuum, with children under 5 years at the greatest risk of serious injury. Reports indicate that boys are more likely to be victims of abusive violence than girls, particularly in the category of very severe abuse. Children are most often abused by a parent (75%), in most cases, a natural parent (U.S. Department of Health and Human Services, 1999). The figures on the incidence of physical abuse are based on estimates and do not reflect the true incidence of abuse, but figures show an estimated 35% increase in cases of physical abuse from 1980 to 1986, from 199,100 to 269,700 cases (Sedlak, 1990). Recent figures report over 278,000 cases of physical abuse across the United States in 1997, constituting approximately 25% of all substantiated or indicated cases in that year (U.S. Department of Health and Human Services, 1999).

Initial clinical and research efforts in this area focused almost exclusively on the abusive parent. As a result, an extensive literature exists regarding (1) the offender's personal characteristics, such as deficits in child management skills, inappropriate developmental expectations, and anger and impulse control difficulties (see Kolko, 1996); and (2) the offender's social and situational circumstances, such as social isolation (J.S. Milner, 1998), poverty and unemployment (Gelles, 1973), and single-parent household (D. Gil, 1970).

A model for a comprehensive approach to the assessment and treatment of abused children and their families has been developed by Walker, Bonner, and Kaufman (1988). The model assesses five factors: the abuser, the nonabusing family members, the child victim, the social context, and the situational context (see Figure 50.1). These five factors were identified from a logical analysis of the

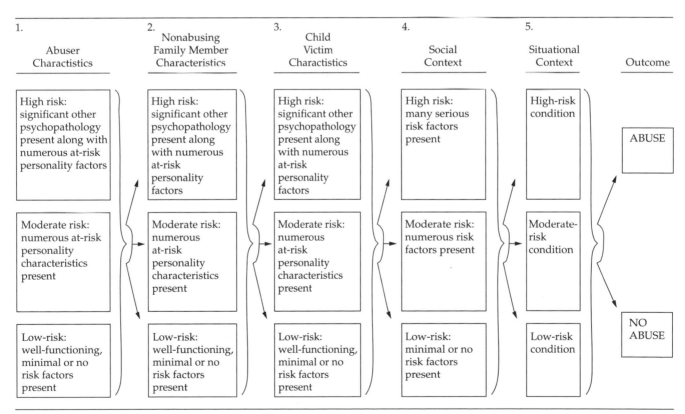

Figure 50.1 Assessment of abuse model. From *The Physically and Sexually Abused Child: Evaluation and Treatment* (p. 110), by C.E. Walker, B.L. Bonner, and K.L. Kaufman, 1988. New York: Pergamon Press. Copyright 1988 by Pergamon Press. Reprinted by permission.

extant literature as being implicated in the process that results in abuse. Three levels are indicated for each of the five factors, from low risk to high risk. However, clinicians should note that these levels are viewed as representing a continuum. The two possible outcomes are *abuse* or *no abuse.* The model is intended to be descriptive and to facilitate assessment and effective treatment planning.

This five-factor model can be used to assess a family at a given time and to determine the likelihood that abuse will occur in the near future in the family. If a family has several factors in the high-risk category, such as an alcoholic mother who has previously been reported for abuse, an unemployed father, and an overactive young child, this would place the family in a highly at-risk category. Similarly, if only one factor were at high risk and several factors showed low risk, the family would be seen as less likely for abuse to occur. A complete description of the model can be found in Walker et al. (1988). The following sources are suggested for further reading on the treatment of abusive families: Azar (1997); Donohue, Miller, Van Hasselt, and Hersen (1998); K. Kaufman and Rudy (1991); and Kolko (1996).

Until recently, studies targeting abused children have focused primarily on documenting particular deficit areas assumed to result from their victimization, such as low self-esteem, poor peer relations, and behavioral difficulties. Literature offering an integration of these research findings into a comprehensive approach to the assessment and treatment of child victims has been lacking, with a few exceptions (e.g., Azar & Wolfe, 1989; Wolfe, 1987). The following discussion focuses on a comprehensive approach to the assessment and treatment of child physical abuse victims. It is oriented toward issues relevant to practicing clinicians while also providing a literature-based approach for the selection of particular assessment and treatment target areas. (For additional information on assessment and treatment, see Kolko, 1996, and Friedrich, 1996.)

ASSESSMENT TECHNIQUES

The assessment of child abuse victims should be considered an ongoing process that begins with the initial discovery of abuse. It should be developmentally based, ensuring the use of appropriate language, questions, and assessment measures. Evaluation devices should have adequate reliability and validity and incorporate input from multiple respondents. When possible, information should be obtained from objective, nonfamilial sources such as babysitters, teachers, or day-care personnel. The assessment proceeds from a general screening to a more specific and extensive examination of particular deficit areas.

At each developmental level, consideration should be given to the child's relative strengths as well as the deficits mentioned earlier. In many cases, relative strengths can become targets for intervention and amplified to enhance a child's or adolescent's functioning. The presence of these skills, attitudes, and competencies may explain why some children and adolescents seem less seriously affected by an abusive experience. Mrazek and Mrazek (1987) suggest that certain protective factors, such as disassociation of affect or decisive risk taking, may mediate against maladaptive outcomes. They go on to argue that supportiveness of more general life circumstances, for example, access to health services, may act to further ameliorate the impact of abuse on a child.

The assessment should begin with a review of information obtained as part of the local CPS investigation. Typically, transcripts or notes resulting from the investigation are available from the CPS worker involved with the case. A clinical interview of the child and an adult who is familiar with the child's behavior (e.g., nonabusing parent, other relative, foster parent) is the next step in the process. In general, information should be obtained in the following areas: the severity, type, and duration of the abuse; the child's understanding of the parent's abusive behavior; a description of previous and current living situations; past and current behavioral problems and emotional difficulties, such as aggression, depression, or anxiety; cognitive and developmental delays; social and interpersonal relationships; and academic performance.

The interview and subsequent psychometric evaluation should be tailored to the individual child, based on his or her developmental level, and consider the associated context. To that end, the following discussion will be divided by age range: infants (birth–18 months); toddlers and preschool children (19 months to 4 years); school-age children (5–12 years); and adolescents (13–17 years). Table 50.1 reflects key assessment techniques and approaches for

Table 50.1 Assessment instruments by age range and focus area.

Focus Area	Age Range			
	Infancy	*Toddler/Preschool*	*School-Age*	*Adolescence*
Attachment/bonding	Behavioral observations Parent interview			
Development/ adaptive skills	1. Denver-II (14 days–6.4 yrs). 2. BSID-II (1 mo.–3.5 yrs.) 3. VABS (birth–18 yrs.)			
Cognitive development		4. SBIS-R (2+ yrs.) 5. WPPSI-R (4.5–6.5 yrs.) 6. K-ABC (2.5–12.5 yrs.)	12. WISC-III (6.5–16.5 yrs.)	25. WAIS-III (> 16.5 yrs.) 26. ASPP (13–18 yrs.)
School achievement			13. WJ-R (6 yrs.–adult) 14. WRAT-III (5 + yrs.)	
Behavior		7. CRS-R-Parent Form (3–17 yrs.) 8. PIC (3–16 yrs.) 9. CBCL-Parent Form (2–18 yrs.) 10. BASC-Teacher Form (2.5–18 yrs.) BASC-Parent Form (2.5–18 yrs.)	CRS-R-Teacher Form (5–17 yrs.) CBCL-Teacher Form (6–18 yrs.) CBCL-Youth Self Report (11–18 yrs.) BASC-Self Report Form (8–18 yrs.)	
Affect		11. CAT (3–10 yrs.)	15. PHSCS (8–17 yrs.) 16. SPPC (8–12 yrs.) 17. CDI (8–17 yrs.) 18. CSADS (6–18 yrs.) 19. RCMAS (6–18 yrs.) 20. STAIC (8–17 yrs.) 21. FSSC-R (6+ yrs.) 22. TAT (6+ yrs.) 23. RIT (6+ yrs.) 24. RAT (6–15 yrs.)	27. MMPI-A (14–18 yrs.) 28. MAPI (13–18 yrs.)

Assessment Instrument Abbreviations: 1. DDST-II: Denver Developmental Screening Test II; 2. BSID-II: Bayley Scales of Infant Development II; 3. VABS: Vineland Adaptive Behavior Scales; 4. SBIS-R: Stanford–Binet Intelligence Scale–Revised; 5. WPPSI-R: Wechsler Preschool and Primary Scales of Intelligence–Revised; 6. K-ABC: Kaufman Assessment Battery for Children; 7. CSC-R: Conners Symptom Checklist–Revised; 8. PIC: Personality Inventory for Children; 9. CBCL: Child Behavior Checklist; 10. BASC: Behavior Assessment System for Children; 11. CAT: Children's Apperception Test; 12. WISC-III: Wechsler Intelligence Scale for Children III; 13. WJ-R: Woodcock–Johnson Psychoeducational Battery–Revised; 14. WRAT-III: Wide Range Achievement Test III; 15. PHSCS: Piers–Harris Self-Concept Scale; 16. SPPC: Self-Perception Profile for Children; 17. CDI: Children's Depression Inventory; 18. CSADS: Children's Schedule for Affective Disorders; 19. RCMAS: Revised Children's Manifest Anxiety Scale; 20. STAIC: State-Trait Anxiety Inventory for Children; 21. FSSC-R: Fear Survey Schedule for Children–Revised; 22. TAT: Thematic Apperception Test; 23. RIT: Rorschach Inkblot Test; 24. RAT: Roberts Apperception Test; 25. WAIS-III: Wechsler Adult Intelligence Scale III; 26. ASPP: Adolescent Self-Perception Profile; 27. MMPI-A: Minnesota Multiphasic Personality Inventory–Adolescent; 28. MAPI: Million Adolescent Personality Inventory.
Age ranges for assessment devices are in parentheses and are based on norms, test critique information, or the testing manual.
References for all assessment instruments are contained in the body of the chapter.

specific difficulties encountered in these particular age ranges.

Assessment of Infants
Infancy represents a critical time for the development of attachment with the child's primary caretaker. Evidence suggests that abuse is often associated with insecure attachment relationships during this critical phase (Crittenden & Ainsworth, 1989). Declining developmental skills (Egeland, 1991b) and a lack of social sensitivity and empathy have also been linked to the disruption of the attachment process (Frodi & Smetana, 1984). A lack of secure attachments may also predispose some children to later adjustment difficulties (e.g., Lewis, Feiring, McGuffog, & Jaskir, 1984).

The assessment of developmental progress is especially important given the foundation that early skills represent for later development and the empirical evidence that children with such delays may be at risk for further abuse (Starr, 1982). The assessment of an infant's developmental progress can be accomplished through a screening device such as the Denver II (Frankenburg, Dodds, Archer, Shapiro, & Bresnick, 1990) or through a more comprehensive instrument such as the Bayley Scales of Infant Development (BSID-II; Bayley, 1993). These measures are behaviorally oriented and can be repeated to assess progress over the course of treatment. The Vineland Adaptive Behavior Scales (VABS; Sparrow, Balla, & Cicchetti, 1984) measure developmental and adaptive skills in children approximately 1 to 18 years and identify areas in which a child may be behind his or her chronological peers.

Consideration should also be given to a child's physical health and nutritional status as part of the assessment process. A poor diet, illnesses or accidental injuries that do not receive proper medical care, the ingestion of toxic substances such as paint containing lead, a lack of proper timely immunizations, and/or nonorganic failure to thrive may also be present in families identified because of physical abuse. A thorough physical evaluation by a medical professional should be completed as part of the assessment process. Ongoing communication with the child's physician is critical to prevent further medically related problems.

Assessment of Toddlers and Preschool Children
Normal developmental changes during the toddler and preschool period are marked by the emergence of more sophisticated language and motoric capabilities as well as increased adaptive skills (e.g., self-care). The Denver II and the VABS continue to be useful in assessing children's abilities relative to their peers in these areas. Referrals for more in-depth speech and hearing evaluations or medical consultations may be necessary to clarify language or motor deficits identified on screening devices.

The recognition of cognitive delays prior to a child's school enrollment has important preventive implications (Wolfe, 1988). Such difficulties may stem from lack of a stimulating environment or more directly from ongoing parent-child conflict, yet they may be confused with motivational or learning difficulties when the child begins school. The need to identify cognitive deficits at an early age is underscored by findings that document significant differences in intelligence scores between abused and nonabused preschoolers (e.g., Hoffman-Plotkin & Twentyman, 1984). A variety of measures are appropriate for assessing children's cognitive abilities in the toddler-preschool age range, including the Stanford-Binet Intelligence Scale, 4th edition (SBIS-4; Thorndike, Hager, & Sattler, 1986), Wechsler Preschool and Primary Scale of Intelligence–Revised (WPPSI-R; Wechsler, 1989), and the Kaufman Assessment Battery for Children (K-ABC; A. Kaufman & Kaufman, 1983).

As toddlers develop the capacity for purposeful communication and independent ambulation, their social sphere begins to include other children. Physically abused preschoolers have been identified as having difficulties maintaining self-control (Gaensbauer & Sands, 1979) and moderating their aggressive behavior toward peers (George & Main, 1979; Hoffman-Plotkin & Twentyman, 1984). The parents or caregivers can be asked to complete measures such as the Conners' Rating Scale–Revised (CRS-R; Conners, 1997), the Behavior Assessment System for Children (BASC; Reynolds & Kamphaus, 1992), or the Child Behavior Checklist (CBCL; Achenbach, 1991). Parallel forms of the CRS-R, the BASC, and the CBCL can be completed by parents and teachers or day-care staff to provide collateral perspectives. Behavioral observations of a child interacting with parents, siblings, and peers may also prove useful in clarifying the child's social or behavioral difficulties.

Affective difficulties related to abuse are more easily recognized as the child enters the toddler-preschool stage. Projective techniques such as the

Children's Apperception Test (CAT; Bellak, 1993) can be useful with young children. Depression and social withdrawal may be assessed by the parents' report on the CBCL or the BASC. Evidence of anxiety-related difficulties may be gleaned from the CBCL or the BASC and from observations of the child at play, in school, or while interacting with the parents. Reports from other caretakers may also be useful in identifying the anxious child.

Assessment of School-Age Children

A child's entrance into the academic arena can be a source of great success, moderate accomplishment, or profound failure. Evidence suggests that school-related difficulties are commonplace for victims of physical abuse (Salinger, Kaplan, Pelcovitz, Samit, & Kreiger, 1984). Salinger et al. found that abused children were significantly more likely to be two grade levels behind in math and verbal skills and at risk for failed classes and/or placement in special classes when compared with nonabused controls. The potential for hyperactivity, attentional problems, learning disabilities, and neurological impairments is present in all abuse cases and is of particular concern in situations where the abuse may have involved trauma to the head.

A general evaluation of school-age children's intellectual potential may be accomplished by administering a standard intelligence measure such as the Wechsler Intelligence Scale for Children III (WISC-III; Wechsler, 1991). An assessment of the child's current academic performance could include the Woodcock–Johnson Psychoeducational Battery–Revised (WJ-R; Woodcock & Johnson, 1990), which measures reading, mathematics, written language, science, social studies, and the humanities, or the Wide Range Achievement Test III (WRAT-III; Wilkinson, 1993), a briefer measure of reading, word recognition, and pronunciation, written spelling, and arithmetic computation. If significant academic problems or possible learning disabilities are present, more extensive testing would be necessary.

Behavior disorders can be particularly problematic to the school-age abuse victim, both at home and in the classroom (Wolfe, 1988). High levels of externalizing behaviors continue to be cited in the literature as effects of physical abuse. These include conduct disorders, serious aggressiveness, hyperactivity, and delinquency (e.g., Kolko, 1996; J.S. Milner & Crouch, 1993; Williamson, Borduin, & Howe, 1991). Academic frustrations may be acted out in displays of inappropriate behavior in the classroom, or the violent nature of parent-child interactions may be replayed as aggression directed at classmates. Parent and teacher versions of the CBCL, the CRS-R, and the BASC are excellent sources of information regarding a child's behavioral problems and socialization. A school observation of the child's behavior and social interactions is often a necessary part of the assessment process. Behaviors should be sampled at different times of the day and when the child is engaged in tasks demanding various amounts of structure, independence, responsibility, and social interaction.

The affective impact of physical abuse on the school-age child may take on a variety of forms. Studies have documented abuse victims' decreased self-esteem and social withdrawal (Oates, Forrest, & Peacock, 1985), depression (Blumberg, 1981), and anxiety (Wolfe & Mosk, 1983). Several instruments can be used to assess affective factors in children. The Piers–Harris Self-Concept Scale (PHSCS; Piers & Harris, 1996) has norms available for fourth- to twelfth-grade children and taps personal satisfaction as well as specific self-evaluation in the areas of behavior, school and intellectual status, physical appearance, anxiety, and popularity. The Self-Perception Profile for Children (SPPC; Harter, 1985) can be used with children age 8 to 12 to assess somewhat similar dimensions of self-concept. The Children's Depression Inventory (CDI; Kovacs, 1992) is a relatively brief self-report measure of depression in children 8 to 17 years of age.

Other tests that can be useful include the Personality Inventory for Children (PIC; Wirt, Lachar, Klinedinst, & Seat, 1990); the State-Trait Anxiety Inventory for Children (STAIC; Speilberger, 1973), a measure that assesses both immediate (state) and stylistic (trait) anxiety dimensions in a brief self-report form; and the Revised Children's Manifest Anxiety Scale (RCMAS; Reynolds & Richmond, 1985), a 37-item self-report inventory that measures the level and nature of anxiety in 6- to 19-year-olds. Childhood fears can be assessed with the Fear Survey Schedule for Children–Revised (FSSC-R; Ollendick, 1983). Additionally, projective techniques may be useful in obtaining a child's affective information as well as evaluating a child's contact with reality. The Children's Apperception Test (CAT; Bellak, 1993), the Thematic Apperception Test (TAT; Bellak, 1993), the Rorschach Inkblot Test (RIT; Exner, 1978, 1986), and the Roberts Apperception Test for

Children (RATC; McArthur & Roberts, 1990) can be used with this age child. Considerable information regarding a child's affective state can also be obtained through clinical interviews and behavioral observations in the clinic, the school setting, and if possible, in the home.

Assessment of Adolescents

Studies investigating the maltreatment of adolescents were visibly absent in the abuse literature until the 1970s and 1980s (Doueck, Ishisaka, Sweany, & Gilchrist, 1987; Farber & Joseph, 1985; Mogan, 1977). A number of factors may explain the lack of attention to the abuse of adolescents: (1) adolescents have been perceived as able to defend themselves against physical attacks by parents; (2) developmentally appropriate behavior exhibited during adolescence, such as proactive and boundary-testing behaviors, may be construed as justification for physically punitive discipline on the part of the parent; and (3) adolescents who are in trouble at home are more likely to come to the attention of the mental health system or the juvenile justice system than the child protective or social service system (Fisher & Berdie, 1978; Garbarino, 1989). This can result in the adolescent's being viewed as psychologically disturbed or delinquent rather than in need of services from a child protection agency.

Adolescent maltreatment may reflect a continuing pattern of abuse that began when the child was young, a progression to more physically violent forms of punishment and discipline as the child grew older, or abuse that was precipitated by factors related to the onset of adolescence. In one study of adolescent maltreatment, 75% of the victims were described as having been abused or neglected when they were younger (Berdie, Berdie, Wexler, & Fisher, 1983). However, a number of authors have suggested that adolescent maltreatment more closely resembles spouse abuse than the maltreatment of younger children (Garbarino & Gilliam, 1980). In both adolescent and spouse abuse, the central themes involve power and autonomy. Moreover, the victims in both cases are perceived as being able to express dissatisfaction with their treatment and seek outside help if necessary.

Findings from studies of the relationships between physical abuse and maladaptive behavior in adolescents link histories of physical abuse with (1) court involvement, ungovernable behaviors, and juvenile delinquency during adolescence (Alfaro,

1981); (2) greater use of violence in the commission of delinquent acts (Tarter, Hegedus, Winsten, & Alternman, 1984); and (3) difficulties with alcoholism, mental illness, and premature death (McCord, 1979). The saliency of these relationships may be due in part to the inherently violent nature of the adolescent's family environments (Wolfe, 1988). Despite the emphasis on extremely negative consequences of maltreatment, it is likely that many adolescents experience a variety of less severe sequelae. Such difficulties may include disruptions in social relationships, affective disorders, substance abuse, and acting-out behaviors.

Instruments used to assess self-esteem and affective, behavioral, and cognitive functioning in children are also applicable to adolescents. Several additional instruments, specific to the adolescent age, include the Wechsler Adult Intelligence Scales III (WAIS III; Wechsler, 1997), the Millon Adolescent Personality Inventory (MAPI; Millon, Green, & Meagher, 1982), the Adolescent Self-Perception Profile (Harter, 1988), and the Minnesota Multiphasic Personality Inventory–Adolescent (MMPI-A; Butcher et al., 1992).

TREATMENT APPROACHES

In families where physical abuse has occurred, treatment has typically focused on the abusive parents and, until recently, failed to assess and provide treatment for the needs of the children. Two comprehensive literature reviews on treatment with abusive parents and their children reported that (1) the most frequently used treatment for children is therapeutic day care, and (2) more methodologically sound research designs and longer-term follow-up of families are necessary (Oates & Bross, 1995; Wolfe & Wekerle, 1993). These reviews highlight the lack of research treatment interventions with physically abused school-age children and adolescents.

As a relatively new area of clinical intervention, the treatment of child physical abuse victims must rely on techniques and approaches from other child treatment areas. At present, clinicians are encouraged to (1) draw from as varied a repertoire of approaches as necessary to meet the child's particular treatment needs; (2) use treatment approaches that are consistent with the child's developmental and cognitive level of functioning; and (3) select techniques that have demonstrated effectiveness in ameliorating the target symptoms. In some cases, this may mean modifying an existing intervention strategy or combining components of a number of approaches.

The clinician should strive to create a treatment plan that follows directly from a comprehensive assessment and emphasizes the unique strengths of the child. The needs and weaknesses of the child that were identified during the assessment phase should be prioritized based on the degree to which the deficits and problems interfere with the child's day-to-day functioning. Often, more than one target area can be addressed simultaneously. It is important to begin the treatment process with an emphasis on gaining the child's trust, reducing his or her fears, and fostering the child's mastery and sense of control over his or her environment. As such, goals for the initial session should be minimal and requests of the child should be limited to things that are likely to be completed successfully. Tasks should be chosen during these sessions with input from the child.

Consideration should also be given to the structure, frequency, and duration of the therapy sessions and, perhaps, the gender of the therapist. For example, younger children are likely to benefit from the incorporation of more structure into therapy. At the same time, their attention span may dictate shorter, more frequent sessions. Although children who have been severely abused by a male figure will unquestionably need to resolve issues with adult males, fearfulness and anxiety in response to a male therapist may limit their participation in the therapy process. Initially, these children may work more effectively with a female therapist who does not elicit fear or withdrawal. This would not, however, preclude dealing with the child's feelings about adult males at a later time in therapy.

The treatment of abused children is discussed in the same context of developmental stages used to discuss assessment techniques. Table 50.2 offers a graphic representation of treatment strategies that can be utilized in responding to the problem areas previously identified. These approaches are suggested as general guidelines for intervention and can be modified to meet the child's particular needs.

Interventions with Infants
The focus of treatment with abused infants is on increasing the parents' or caretakers' knowledge about appropriate development, improving the caretaker-child relationship, and promoting the child's progress in overall development. Remediating existing developmental delays and preventing additional deficits requires a stimulating environment that offers the child an adequate range of behavior to model as well as sufficient opportunities to practice and develop new skills. Frequently, abusive parents find it difficult to meet even one of the conditions. However, Lutzker and colleagues demonstrated the effectiveness of visual prompts for increasing mother-baby stimulation in at-risk and abusive single mothers (S. Lutzker, Lutzker, Braunling-McMorrow, & Eddleman, 1987). For each target behavior, a prompting guide was developed to help parents remember the elements involved in a particular type of parent-infant interaction (e.g., use of affectionate words). Often, infant stimulation programs are available through occupational and physical therapy departments of local hospitals. A study by Field (1988) found that a physical stimulation program offered to premature infants facilitated significant developmental gains.

Problems of attachment may be addressed by changing the parents' perceptions of what constitutes a caring and attentive relationship and helping parents develop more positive models of the parent-child relationship. This involves addressing the relationship that they had with their parents and the ways in which they were reared and disciplined (Guidano & Liotti, 1983).

Considerable gains can be made by improving parents' knowledge of age-appropriate developmental behaviors and offering suggestions for the parents to practice delayed adaptive skills with their child on a regular basis. The VABS can be a useful intervention as well as assessment device. It can provide information about expected development and target behaviors as well as giving parents information about their infant's particular development.

Ensuring that the family has a primary care physician and attends scheduled well-care visits will also bolster the parents' ability to view their child in a developmentally appropriate manner. The development of an ongoing relationship with a community pediatrician may improve the parents' trust of professionals and increase future utilization of such services.

Intervention with Toddlers and Preschool Children
As with infants, toddlers and preschool children who have experienced abuse may show developmental delays and a disturbed parent-child relationship. Additionally, these children may have

Table 50.2 Treatment approaches by age range and focus area.

Focus Area	Age Range			
	Infancy	*Toddler/Preschool*	*School-Age*	*Adolescence*
Attachment/bonding	Parent education			
Developmental deficits	Infant stimulation Prompted mother-baby stimulation	Developmental preschool		
Adaptive difficulties	Guided practice "Well-child" visits	Developmental preschool Modeling/role plays		
Cognitive-academic deficits		Developmental preschool	School consultation	
Behavioral difficulties		Social learning approaches Parent-child interaction therapy	Special school placement Simulated behavioral home environment Cognitive-behavioral (CBT) approach for self-control, problem solving, and self-monitoring	Behavioral contracting Crisis intervention Placement outside home Problem-solving communication training
Affective difficulties		Play therapy	CBT for depression Relaxation training Systematic desensitization and hypnosis for anxiety Structured practice for anger management	Anger diary
Disruption of peer relations		Peer/teacher-prompted interactions	Social skills training Teacher reinforced prosocial behavior Peer modeled social interactions Filmed modeling Cognitive control therapy	Social exposure Social problem solving Practice dating

developed behavior problems and affective difficulties as a result of the abuse. Treatment with these young children focuses on interventions with the child directly and on the parent-child relationship. In some instances, the day-care program is part of a family preservation program that provides comprehensive services to a family to prevent out-of-home placement of the child or to facilitate the child's reentry to the home (Ayoub, 1991).

Behaviorally based programs designed to increase the stimulation provided to abused children, enhance their language skills, and improve their overall functioning have resulted in positive outcomes (Wolfe, Edwards, Manion, & Koverola, 1988; Wolfe & Wekerle, 1993). Developmentally oriented preschool programs offer an additional resource for remediating developmental deficits in delayed, abused children (Parish, Myers, Brander, & Templin, 1985). A connection between the security of a child's attachment and his or her syntactic and linguistic performance has been described in the literature (Gersten, Coster, Schneider-Rosen, Carlson, & Cicchetti, 1986). This finding suggests that improvements in a child's attachment to significant others may have implications for the quality of language skills.

One program designed to modify dysfunctional parent-child interactions, Parent-Child Interaction Therapy (PCIT), is based on the work of Eyberg (1979; Eyberg & Boggs, 1989). The training involves a focus on both child-directed and parent-directed interactions. PCIT relies heavily on social learning principles, including therapist modeling of treatment skills, role playing, daily home practice, and direct coaching of parents with a bug-in-the-ear device. (For a full description of the program, see Hembree-Kigin & McNeil, 1995.) J. Lutzker, Megson, Dachman, and Webb (1985) described a similar but more general version of adult-child interaction training that was designed for use with abusive and neglectful parents. Findings from a clinical trial seem promising despite the limited sample size in the study.

Behavior problems of the abused child may parallel any of the forms typical for children in this age group (e.g., bed wetting, nightmares, noncompliance). Behaviorally oriented approaches to common behavioral problems, as described by Ross (1981) and L. Schaefer and Millman (1981), offer effective strategies for intervention with such difficulties.

In addition to these more typical childhood problems, physically abused children tend to exhibit particular difficulties with aggressive behavior and social withdrawal (Azar & Wolfe, 1989). A combination of reward-oriented techniques for appropriate behaviors, such as verbal praise or a star chart, and the use of time-out for aggressive behaviors is likely to reduce the frequency and intensity of target behaviors. Any intervention will be more effective if similar approaches are used consistently by all caregivers and across settings (i.e., foster home, parental visits, day care). Other strategies for intervening with aggressive children are described in detail by Patterson (1982), and Forehand and McMahon (1981) offer excellent suggestions for treating the noncompliant child.

Children's social withdrawal has also been significantly impacted through the use of behavioral techniques that include peer and teacher-prompted interactions (see the next section for details). Often, simply arranging for a child to be involved in structured group activities such as community or recreation center programs will offer the opportunity for exposure to peers that has previously been absent. The therapist should anticipate, however, that the parents or caregivers will require assistance in responding to the child's initial reactions to peer interactions (e.g., fears, clinging behavior). Suggestions for patience, minimal expectations for the first few attempts, and guidance in helping the child slowly integrate into the group situation will greatly facilitate the process.

Treatment approaches should strive to bolster the child's self-esteem and sense of self-control over his or her environment. The therapist can work with caregivers to arrange mastery experiences that allow the child to build on relative strengths or develop new areas of competency (Walker et al., 1988). Efforts to alleviate fears and anxieties may also enhance the child's self-concept. Caregivers should be instructed to offer the child as many appropriate choices as possible to highlight the control that they do have over their environment. For children who have not previously had the opportunity to participate in decisions or making choices, some encouragement will be necessary.

Finally, consideration should be given to involving some victims of physical abuse in play therapy (E. Gil, 1991). Children who are withdrawn or depressed or who have had a history of inconsistent adult relationships may find this intervention modality particularly helpful. This approach to treatment offers an opportunity to establish an ongoing relationship with a caring adult professional as well as a chance to work through affective issues such as anger, sadness, or fear in a familiar yet nonthreatening setting.

Intervention with School-Age Children

In addition to behavioral and affective problems experienced by younger children who have been abused, school-age children may present with problems in their cognitive or academic functioning and in developing social relationships. A prompt assessment of cognitive skills and school achievement capabilities can offer guidance with regard to abuse victims' intervention needs. Often, the therapist can serve as an advocate for this child in assuring proper placement and services. In cases where a child is failing in school but does not meet the school system's criteria for special education classes, arrangements for a home tutor may be indicated. The therapist may also be of assistance in helping the family develop a structured system for regular study times and the completion of homework assignments. Simple behavioral programs, such as the use of contingent reinforcement or sticker charts, are often quite effective for this type of target behavior.

Effective behavioral approaches to classroom difficulties have emphasized the modification of teacher attention, differential reinforcement of appropriate behaviors, positive practice procedures, use of tokens, teaching self-management strategies, and consequences for inappropriate behaviors (see reviews by Ross, 1981; Ruggles & LeBlanc, 1982). When treatment for the child is provided as a component of a group format parent training program (e.g., Wolfe, Kaufman, Aragona, & Sandler, 1981), consideration should be given to involving abused children in a behaviorally oriented, simulated home environment. The intent is to teach children the responses that complement the techniques their parents have been instructed to use at home. The simulated environment approximates the rules, contingencies, and rewards that the parents are expected to utilize at home while allowing other problem areas to be addressed (e.g., social skills training) within this context. This approach proved to be quite successful in the treatment program implemented by Wolfe and his colleagues.

Although minimal empirical research on treatment outcome of physically abused children is available, a variety of cognitive-behavioral treatment (CBT) approaches have been utilized to remediate children's behavioral and social problems. Cognitive control therapy as described by Santostefano (1985) has been used with maltreated children displaying social deficits (Cicchetti, Toth, & Bush, 1988). Other CBT interventions include modeling (Howes & Espinosa, 1985), social skills training (R. Kelly & Hansen, 1987), and interventions for depression (Leahy, 1988). Difficulties related to anxiety and anger may be addressed with a combination of relaxation training, deep breathing, guided imagery, systematic desensitization, and structured practice in dealing with anger-eliciting prompts (see Walker et al., 1988, pp. 74–76, 84, for additional details).

Kolko (1996) published one of the few empirical studies in recent years on physically abusive parents and their children. The families were randomly assigned to either CBT or family therapy (FT) and were assessed weekly over 12 sessions. Although the results indicated continuing high levels of physical discipline, parental anger, and family problems, the CBT children and parents reported lower levels of physical discipline and parental anger than FT parents. Kolko suggested that the results might be improved through increasing the length of treatment and the comprehensiveness of the treatment interventions.

As with younger children, play therapy approaches may benefit school-age children who

require an opportunity to express the emotional impact of their abuse in an indirect, less threatening fashion (E. Gil, 1991). Individual therapy may provide a vehicle for addressing a number of other affective disorders related to physical abuse. In cases of severe psychopathology resulting from abuse, such as dissociative disorders or severe depression, the use of psychotropic medications and inpatient psychiatric hospitalization may be warranted.

Interventions with Adolescents
As described in the assessment section, adolescents who have been abused may exhibit a wide range of behavioral and emotional difficulties related to their abuse. Treatment interventions may need to focus on the parent-child relationship, academic or cognitive deficits, peer relationships, acting-out behavior, or affective problems. In many instances, opportunities to address academic and/or cognitive deficits are hampered by more acute behavioral or familial difficulties. However, unidentified or unaddressed learning disabilities and placement beyond an adolescent's academic capabilities create a fertile environment for the development of behavioral, attendance, and self-esteem difficulties. In many respects, a thorough cognitive and educational assessment represents the most effective initial intervention. A tailored educational plan for responding to academic deficits should follow this evaluation. A detailed discussion of specific educational interventions is beyond the scope of this chapter, but Schloss and his associates offer a comprehensive discussion of such techniques (Schloss, Smith, & Schloss, 1990).

Adolescents engage in many of the same behaviors that younger children get into trouble for exhibiting. For example, they may be noncompliant with their parents' or teachers' requests, they may lie, and they may get into verbal and physical fights with peers. In contrast, some inappropriate behaviors are seen more frequently in adolescents (e.g., substance abuse, delinquency, indiscriminate sexual behavior). Consequently, the problem behaviors presented by adolescents may necessitate a qualitatively different approach to intervention. As some adolescents remove themselves from the source of the abuse in ways that young children cannot, by running away or obtaining financial resources from sources other than their parents, consideration must be given to interventions that anticipate and correct such possibilities. This is not to say that the behavioral interventions utilized with younger children will prove ineffective with all adolescents, but rather, that the treatment of adolescents is enhanced by using fewer power-based techniques and more negotiation. One well-researched intervention, multisystemic therapy, has had excellent results with delinquent behavior problems (Henggeler & Borduin, 1990).

The need for crisis intervention services and/or resources for the temporary placement of adolescents whose behavior has exceeded their parents' tolerance should be viewed in the context of proactive strategies rather than as a last resort. Because evidence suggests that many physically abused adolescents are treated as status offenders (i.e., ungovernable) or attain this status by virtue of attempting to escape the abuse by running away, a therapist's efforts to arrange temporary or respite placement of an adolescent may defuse a difficult situation and at the same time maintain the greatest number of future options (Doueck et al., 1987; Fisher, Berdie, Cook, & Day, 1980). Opportunities for informal placement with other family members or friends may offer the respite that both the parents and the adolescent need to reapproach the situation in a more productive fashion. Therapists should also investigate the crisis intervention and ongoing service resources that their particular community offers. When adolescents exhibit socialization difficulties, three major areas are typically targeted for intervention: social skills, social exposure, and social problem solving (R. Kelly & Hansen, 1987). The goals of social skills training are to teach adolescents to deal effectively with actual social interactions through social situation simulations and role plays. Training programs include didactic instruction, modeling, behavioral rehearsal, and feedback (J. Kelly, 1982).

For many adolescents, opportunities to practice acquired skills are insufficient. Arrangements by the therapist to increase the adolescent's peer and dating interactions can offer the chance to apply competencies learned during social skills training. This may involve encouraging the adolescent to partake in organized social events such as school or church dances, sports programs, or afterschool activities. In some cases, it may be necessary to more formally organize or refer an adolescent to group treatment for date-related anxiety.

Most adolescents would also benefit from social problem-solving training that facilitates the development of cognitive problem-solving skills to deal with socially difficult situations. Training of this nature incorporates the use of a problem-solving methodology with representative practice scenarios reflecting a social conflict or dilemma (D'Zurilla & Goldfried, 1971).

As with younger children, disturbances of affect in the maltreated adolescent may assume many forms. Cognitive-behavioral strategies are indicated when depression is a significant concern (Leahy, 1988). Difficulties related to anxiety may be treated with relaxation training, systematic desensitization, and/or hypnosis/self-hypnosis (E. Barnett, 1984; Turner, Calhoun, & Adams, 1981). Adolescents may be taught to moderate their feelings of anger and frustration through the use of an anger diary and structured practice coping with anger-eliciting stimuli (Walker et al., 1988, pp. 74–76, 84). Poor self-esteem may also be addressed through cognitive-behavioral strategies or more process-oriented individual psychotherapy. Conflicts between adolescents and their parents constitute a predictable part of normal development. However, such conflict may be likely to escalate into episodes of adolescent maltreatment in families characterized by parents who are (1) having difficulty resolving their own midlife issues, (2) rigid or overindulgent, or (3) physically punitive or have previously abused a child (Fisher et al., 1980; Pelcovitz, Kaplan, Samit, Krieger, & Cornelius, 1984).

Consideration should also be given to the use of family therapy in resolving parent-adolescent conflicts. Family therapy is indicated in cases where family members are either uncooperative in learning components of a skills-based approach or in situations where family members have such skills in their repertoire but are unwilling to utilize them. Resolution of family issues through structural (Minuchin & Fishman, 1981), strategic (Madanes, 1984), systemic (Tomm, 1984), or multisystemic (Henggeler & Borduin, 1990) family therapy approaches may foster later involvement in skills-based training. (For additional reading on treatment of abused adolescents, see Chaffin, Bonner, Worley, & Lawson, 1996.)

Treatment Compliance and Follow-up

The majority of maltreated children will be dependent on their parents for transportation to assessment and treatment sessions. Given that high attrition rates have been associated with treatment approaches directed at abusive parents, consideration should be given to methods of assuring the child victim's involvement (Irueste-Montes & Montes, 1988; Nicol et al., 1988). The use of client "salaries" and small gifts for completing assigned tasks and attending sessions has proven somewhat successful with this population (Fleischman, 1979; Wolfe & Manion, 1984). Evidence also supports the utility of a specific court order for treatment in maintaining abusive parents in treatment (Irueste-Montes & Montes, 1988; Wolfe, Aragona, Kaufman, & Sandler, 1980). Compliance may also be increased by scheduling parent treatment sessions to coincide with child victim sessions, offering services at convenient times, utilizing parent input in prioritizing target areas to address, defining the therapist's role as separate from the child protective service system, and setting goals with the parents that will facilitate their family's independence from social service involvement.

The criterion-based approach to treatment described by Wolfe and his colleagues should be used as a model for intervention and follow-up (Wolfe et al., 1981). Clinical and psychometric indicators should be utilized to determine when a child has met the treatment goals. Follow-up sessions should be planned as part of the termination process and reassessment of treated target areas at follow-up should be used as the basis for "booster sessions" if necessary. Parents and collaterals (e.g., teacher, caseworker) should be informed of the need to recontact the therapist if the child begins to display behaviors that suggest additional difficulties. Specific examples of early indicators of problems should be offered to facilitate accurate identification.

SEXUAL ABUSE

Similar to other types of abuse, child sexual abuse is a term that is defined differently depending on the purpose of the definition (e.g., investigation vs. treatment vs. research). Professionals from mental health, law, medicine, and social services often have different interpretations of the events that constitute abuse because of differences in their professional roles. This lack of an accepted standard definition has hampered investigation, substantiation, treatment, and research in the area of child

sexual abuse. However, addressing sexual abuse through multidisciplinary teams may foster better understanding of terminology and definitions among professionals.

Despite the lack of a universally accepted definition, child sexual abuse can be broadly defined as the involvement of dependent, developmentally immature children and adolescents in sexual activities they do not fully comprehend and to which they are unable to give informed consent. These activities also violate the social taboos of society (Krugman & Jones, 1987). The definition of child sexual abuse is frequently based on several dimensions: (1) the age of the child (17 to 18 or younger); (2) the relationship of the child to the perpetrator (i.e., intrafamilial or extrafamilial); (3) the difference in age, developmental level, or power status between the victim and the offender; and (4) the type of abuse, that is, touching the victim's body versus nonbody contact (Wyatt & Peters, 1986).

Children of all ages, including very young infants, are sexually abused. Evidence suggests, however, that some children are more vulnerable to sexual abuse than others. For example, in substantiated reports of sexual abuse, girls are approximately three times more likely to be sexually abused than boys, and there are disproportionate numbers of abused children from families with low socioeconomic status (Sedlak & Broadhurst, 1996). A retrospective study of 710 women found that having a mother who is mentally ill, experiencing physical abuse, and being isolated from social support were factors associated with a higher incidence of child sexual abuse (Fleming, Mullen, & Bammer, 1997).

In the United States, cases of child sexual abuse typically represent about 13% to 15% of all substantiated child abuse cases in a given period. Based on a review of studies with differing methodologies and definitions, Cosentino and Collins (1996) estimated that approximately 1 in 4 girls and 1 in 10 boys are sexually victimized before the age of 18. The most recent national study of child abuse and neglect (U.S. Department of Health and Human Services, 1999) found that 12.5% or 123,000 children and adolescents were substantiated for sexual abuse in 1997.

As child sexual abuse continues to occur at high rates, theoretically sound and empirically validated treatments for sexually abused children become increasingly important. Unfortunately, the empirical research on child sexual abuse has historically contained numerous methodological problems, including inconsistent definitions of sexual abuse across studies, small sample sizes, lack of control for preabuse psychopathology, heterogeneous samples with multiple types of abuse experiences, and use of unstandardized assessment instruments (Slusser, 1995). Although multiple problems remain in the child sexual abuse literature, there have been marked improvements over the past 10 years.

A wide range of symptoms have been observed in sexually abused children. In a 1988 study, the following symptoms were documented: fearfulness of abuse stimuli (30%), nightmares and sleep disorders (20%), depression (19%), repressed anger or hostility (19%), behavior problems (14%), and somatic complaints (10%) (Conte & Schuerman, 1988). In one of the few investigations of young male victims, the parent-reported behaviors of sexually abused, nonabused, and allegedly abused boys 3 to 15 years old were compared (Wells, McCann, Adams, Voris, & Dahl, 1997). The symptoms most common in the sexually abused sample were sudden emotional/behavioral changes (72%), fearfulness of being left alone (68%), difficulty getting to sleep (65%), crying easily (62%), and knowing more about sex (58%). Overall, the sexually abused boys had more behavior problems reported than the allegedly abused or the nonabused boys. Studies to date have found child sexual abuse to have an impact on boys similar to that for girls (Cosentino & Collins, 1996; Wells et al., 1997). There is some evidence, however, that boys are more likely than girls to demonstrate externalizing behavior problems such as general aggressive behaviors and sexual aggression.

Recently, abuse-related changes at the biological level have been discovered in sexually abused girls. A longitudinal study of sexually abused girls 6 to 15 years of age found several major physiological stress response systems to be impacted by sexual abuse (Putnam & Trickett, 1997). These physiological dysregulations can subsequently impact socioemotional and behavioral functioning. Preliminary evidence has suggested, for example, that sexual abuse increases catecholamine levels, which may be exhibited behaviorally as restlessness and hyperactivity. There may also be detrimental effects to immune function and physiological development. As more definitive information is gathered regarding the psychobiological effects of sexual abuse, it will be increasingly important to consider these changes in assessment and treatment planning.

Based on investigations of the initial effects of sexual abuse, it appears that sexually abused children present with a wide variety of symptoms and with a range of symptom severity. Symptoms experienced by child victims of sexual abuse have generally been found to be more severe than the symptoms of nonabused children but less severe than the symptoms of other child outpatient populations (Berliner, 1991; Cosentino & Collins, 1996). The symptoms that have most often been found to discriminate sexually abused children from children experiencing other types of abuse and from nonabused clinical populations are inappropriate sexual behaviors (Cosentino & Collins, 1996; Friedrich, 1997; Friedrich et al., 1992; Mian, Marton, & LeBaron, 1996; Slusser, 1995). These behaviors may range in severity from repeatedly exposing the genitals and compulsive masturbation to forced sexual interactions with others (Friedrich, 1997).

Studies on the long-term effects of sexual abuse also reveal a wide range of symptoms. The effects that have clearest documentation are dissociation, anxiety, drug and alcohol abuse, depression, and sexual problems (Bagley & Ramsay, 1985; Briere & Runtz, 1988; Finkelhor, 1988; Peters, 1988; Sedney & Brooks, 1984). A meta-analysis by Jumper (1995) of the relationship between child sexual abuse and adult functioning reviewed 26 published studies to evaluate the effect size of depression, self-esteem deficits, and other psychological symptomatology (e.g., anxiety disorders, personality disorders, suicide attempts). The results found that child sexual abuse accounted for a small but significant amount of the variance across multiple sampling methods, definitions of sexual abuse, and gender of subjects, thus supporting the hypothesis that sexual abuse can have long-term impact on individuals' psychological functioning.

Although it is generally agreed that child sexual abuse can have a devastating impact on a child's ability to successfully navigate important developmental tasks, clinical experience and empirical findings suggest that not all sexually abused children exhibit clinical levels of symptoms. In several studies, up to 40% of the sexually abused children appeared to have none of the expected abuse-related problems (Kendall-Tackett, Williams, & Finkelhor, 1993). These children have been described as resilient, and some studies have attempted to identify factors that promote children's resiliency in cases of abuse (Farber & Egeland, 1987; J. Kaufman, Cook, Arney, Jones, & Pittinsky, 1994). Factors that have been associated with resilience to the impact of child sexual abuse include support of a nonoffending parent and the level of abuse stressors experienced (Spaccarelli & Kim, 1995). Caution must be used, however, to ensure that more subtle signs of distress, such as the subjective experiences of depression and anxiety, are not overlooked in children who are functioning successfully in other areas. Further research on resiliency will provide useful information about the child and family variables that should be targeted for change in prevention and intervention efforts.

Theoretical Models

In an effort to conceptualize the effects of sexual abuse, several models have been proposed. These models can assist clinicians in assessing the effects of sexual abuse, planning treatment interventions, and anticipating future problems to which children may be vulnerable. Finkelhor and Browne (1985) developed a model called the Traumagenic Dynamics Model of Child Sexual Abuse. A traumagenic dynamic is defined as "an experience that alters a child's cognitive or emotional orientation to the world and causes trauma by distorting the child's self-concept, world view or affective capacities" (Finkelhor, 1988, p. 68). The model proposes that four key experiences in child sexual abuse impact the manifestation of psychopathology: traumatic sexualization, stigmatization, betrayal, and powerlessness.

Traumatic sexualization is the process by which a child's sexuality becomes developmentally inappropriate and interpersonally dysfunctional. Sexually abused children may have distorted views of sexual norms, become confused about their sexual orientation, or become sexually aggressive. Abuse-related behaviors such as sexual precocity, compulsive sexuality, and sexual aversion may be understood through traumatic sexualization. The second traumagenic factor, stigmatization, appears to result from the nonsupportive reaction of others to the child's disclosure of the abuse and/or from the offender's blaming and denigrating the victim. The behavioral and emotional impact on the child may be feelings of guilt and shame, lowered self-esteem, and a sense of being different from others.

Betrayal, the third traumagenic factor, frequently occurs because the child's sense of trust and vulnerability are manipulated by the offender. The effects of this manipulation can be compounded by a lack of support from other adults, resulting in significant damage to the child's normal expectation that others will provide care and protection. In response, the child may experience grief, depression, or an impaired ability to judge the trustworthiness of others. Behaviorally, the child may become hostile, angry, or aggressive. The fourth traumagenic factor, powerlessness, often results from the unwanted invasion of a child's body or an inability to convince trusted adults that the abuse occurred. These events may result in feelings of vulnerability and a lack of self-efficacy. The behavioral and emotional impact may include anxiety, phobias, eating and sleeping disorders, depression, running away, and truancy.

A second model that can be employed in assessing and treating children who have been sexually abused is the transactional model proposed by Spaccarelli (1994). Based on the theory that a healthy or pathological developmental outcome depends on a series of individual-environment transactions (Sameroff & Fiese, 1990), Spaccarelli's model proposes multiple factors that may buffer or exacerbate children's responses to the experience of sexual abuse.

The model's first tenet is that victims of sexual abuse experience a series of stressors including and beyond the stress of the abuse itself. These include the abuse experience (e.g., perpetrator-child interactions), events related to the abuse (e.g., family conflict), and events related to the public disclosure of the abuse (e.g., interviews, physical exams, adjudication). The second tenet is that the effects of these abuse stressors are mediated by the child's cognitive appraisals of the events and the type of coping strategies employed. For example, a child using an avoidant coping response may not tell anyone, thereby increasing the social isolation experienced and exacerbating feelings of depression, whereas a child using a support-seeking response may elicit help. The third tenet is that influences among the abuse stressors, children's responses (appraisals, coping), and the impact of the abuse are bidirectional. For example, negative appraisals of the abuse may be exhibited as depression, which in turn may reduce effective use of coping strategies. This model emphasizes that a thorough assessment of a child who has been sexually abused should include not only the child's behavioral and emotional responses to the abuse, but also the types of abuse stress experienced before and after the disclosure, as well as the ability of the family and community environment to provide appropriate support for the child.

ASSESSMENT TECHNIQUES

The assessment and treatment of child sexual abuse victims is currently a developing area of clinical practice. The preceding models, based on clinical experience and recent research, can assist clinicians in understanding child victims and planning a more effective treatment program. Although this section focuses primarily on the assessment and treatment of children and adolescents, because of the particular importance of parental response in the outcome of sexually abused children, this section also briefly mentions some types of interventions involving the caregiver.

In cases of child sexual abuse, assessments may be conducted for the purpose of forensic investigation or for the purpose of clinical evaluation. Clinicians should be aware that there are distinct differences in method and approach between these types of assessments (American Academy of Child and Adolescent Psychiatry [AACAP], 1997). For more information on conducting forensic assessments, see AACAP, American Professional Society on the Abuse of Children (APSAC 1995a, 1997), and T. Ney (1995). This section focuses on the clinical evaluation of children and adolescents for the purpose of planning treatment. The assessment section on physical abuse can be reviewed for additional information.

The purpose of the assessment phase is to understand what happened to the child, how the child copes with the conflicts that arise from the abuse, the extent of the child's current symptoms or discomfort, and what problems lie ahead. During this phase, the clinician should formulate a diagnostic impression, initial goals for therapy, and prognosis for the child's mental health at subsequent developmental stages. The range of responses to the experience of sexual abuse is wide. Most children who have been sexually abused exhibit a mild to moderate response that may require brief to intensive outpatient therapy. Some children present with severe psychopathology that may need to be treated in an inpatient psychiatric facility. Others show no

significant distress, but may benefit from brief preventive work with the child and caregivers.

A variety of assessment techniques may be used to help understand the child victim (see Table 50.1). When working with children who have been sexually abused, it is important to use both broad-scale assessment measures and instruments specific to sexual abuse. The assessment techniques and instruments described in the previous section on physical abuse can be used with children of different ages to provide information on their current level of academic, behavioral, and affective functioning. Clinicians should remember, however, that the child's display of symptomatic behavior may vary with the phase of disclosure and involvement with the legal system (Wolfe & Wolfe, 1988). For example, the process of disclosure may lead to stress-related symptoms that may decline once the child's situation has stabilized, but that may reappear if the child is required to testify in court.

As with all child clients, a thorough understanding of the child's home environment is important. Structured behavioral observations of the child with the parents are useful to uncover information about (1) the parent-child relationship; (2) the parents' ability to give appropriate directions, praise, and punishment; and (3) the child's level of compliance (Hembree-Kigin & McNeil, 1995). A thorough clinical interview and history with the child and family members will elicit information about the child's characteristics and preabuse functioning and the adults' ability to support and protect the child.

For preschool children, a diagnostic play interview can be useful to assess the child's ability to separate from the parents, explore an unfamiliar environment, and establish a relationship with an unfamiliar adult. In addition, the clinician can informally assess the child's developmental level. As rapport is established, the clinician may become more direct and ask specific questions about the child's family, day-care situation, wishes, and fears. Specific tests to evaluate the child's developmental level, behavior, and affect are described in the earlier section.

Measures appropriate for preschoolers have been developed to evaluate behaviors specific to sexual abuse. The Weekly Behavior Report (WBR; Cohen & Mannarino, 1996), developed from the current empirical data regarding sexual-abuse-specific symptoms, has helped to fill a gap in the available measures, as other similar measures were created for school-age and older children. The WBR is a 26-item checklist, completed by the caregiver, that assesses anxiety, inappropriate sexual behaviors, and regressive, aggressive, and oppositional behaviors. Preliminary data demonstrate adequate test-retest reliability and internal consistency. The WBR has been shown to be sensitive to change following treatment, which makes it a potential tool to assess treatment progress.

With school-age children and adolescents, self-report instruments are useful for assessing the child's reaction to the abuse and the disclosure. Self-report methods that require the child to make a yes-no or scaled response may be more effective in eliciting disclosure of negative affect than open-ended questions (Wolfe & Wolfe, 1988). In comprehensive assessments of sexually abused children, self-report instruments that assess physiological, cognitive, and behavioral components of anxiety and depression should especially be included, because caregivers have been found to underreport internalizing problems in their children.

There are several recently developed measures that assess sexual-abuse-specific symptoms in school-age children. Many of these new measures focus on assessing the children's perceptions and attributions of the abuse experience. The Negative Appraisals of Sexual Abuse Scale (NASAS; Spaccarelli, 1994) is a self-report measure based on the conceptualization that an individual's perception of personal harm or loss during a stressful event may impact his or her psychological adjustment. The NASAS is a 56-item measure assessing eight types of negative appraisals (e.g., self and sexuality, physical damage, negative evaluation by others). The measure has shown good internal consistency and relationships with theoretically relevant variables (e.g., PTSD symptoms, parent- and self-reported depression and anxiety).

The Trauma Symptom Checklist for Children (TSC-C; Briere, 1996) was developed as a self-report measure to assess various aspects of distress in children who have experienced sexual abuse or other traumatic events. The 54-item inventory provides information on children's and adolescents' level of symptomatology in six areas: anxiety, depression, anger, posttraumatic stress, dissociation, and sexual concerns.

Other sexual-abuse-specific measures are in the format of child or caregiver interviews. The Children's Impact of Traumatic Events Scale–Revised (CITES-R), a 78-item standardized interview with objective response options, was developed to assess the child's perspective on the impact of the abuse (Wolfe, Gentile, Michienzi, Sas, & Wolfe, 1991). Children are asked to recall the victimization experience and then respond to questions about intrusive thoughts and perceptions of blame, guilt, betrayal, stigmatization, and helplessness. The measure has shown preliminary evidence for convergent validity and good internal consistency.

The Children's Attributions and Perceptions Scale (CAPS) is another measure that attempts to assess children's perceptions of why the abuse occurred and how it has affected them (Mannarino & Cohen, 1996; Mannarino, Cohen, & Berman, 1994). Four types of attributions are assessed with 18 items: (1) feeling different from peers; (2) personal attributions for negative events; (3) perceived credibility; and (4) interpersonal trust. The CAPS has also shown preliminary indications of validity and reliability, in that the CAPS total score was significantly higher for sexually abused than nonabused children and it correlated with self-reported symptoms of anxiety, depression, and self-esteem in the abused group. Initial test-retest and internal consistency findings have been adequate to good for the four scales.

As the stressful events of the sexual abuse experience have been conceptualized as an important factor impacting children's subsequent functioning, it is helpful to evaluate the number and severity of stressors experienced by the sexually abused child. The Checklist of Sexual Abuse and Related Stressors (C-SARS; Spaccarelli, 1994) is a 70-item child-report measure designed to assess not only the events associated with the abuse contact itself, but also events that may have occurred before (e.g., grooming by the perpetrator) and after the abuse (e.g., family reaction, legal and social responses). The C-SARS has shown high internal consistency and has been positively related to parent-reported behavior problems, therapists' ratings of abuse stress, and number of types of sexual abuse. Another measure assessing children's perceived abuse-related stress is the Intervention Stressors Inventory (ISI; Runyan, Hunter, Everson, Whitcomb, & DeVos, 1994). The ISI focuses exclusively on the events occurring as a result of societal interventions subsequent to disclosure of the abuse. At this time, the scale has been suggested as being most appropriate as a research tool.

Different from the above measures, the Structured Interview for Symptoms Associated with Sexual Abuse (SASA) was developed to provide caregivers, rather than children or adolescents, the opportunity to report on physical, emotional, and behavioral symptoms specific to sexual abuse (Wells et al., 1997; Wells, McCann, Adams, Voris, & Ensign, 1995). The scale assesses the existence, duration, and onset of 30 symptoms and has shown preliminary validity on both male and female populations of children, in that overall scores differentiated groups of abused and nonabused children.

Sexually abused children may present with inappropriate sexual behaviors as a reported problem, and an assessment of these behaviors may be necessary. The Child Sexual Behavior Inventory (CSBI; Friedrich, 1997), a 38-item caregiver-report measure, was developed for use with children 2 to 12 years of age. The CSBI assesses the number and frequency of sexual behaviors a child may exhibit. Two clinical scales are available that aid in interpretation of the child's sexual behaviors: the Developmentally Related Sexual Behavior Scale and the Sexual Abuse Specific Items. Items on the Sexual Abuse Specific Scale are those that statistically differentiated an abused from a nonabused normative sample. These items differ depending on the gender and age of the child.

As is apparent from the above descriptions, investigations of the impact of sexual abuse have led to an increased number of measures to assess abuse-related symptoms. It should be noted, however, that the adequacy of the psychometric characteristics of most measures is still being evaluated. Although many of these measures have potential for clinical use, the clinician should understand the stability, validity, and available norms for the individual scales before the measure is used to draw conclusions about a child's functioning.

TREATMENT TECHNIQUES

By the end of the assessment phase, the clinician should be ready to formulate a specific treatment plan. Components of the plan may be individual psychotherapy, group therapy, parent-child dyad, or family therapy. This section discusses treatment techniques that can be used with children from approximately age 3 years through adolescence. Although infants and very young children are sexually

abused, it occurs less frequently than physical abuse, and the treatment is usually focused on the adult family members. Techniques to improve the parent-child relationship described in the previous section can be implemented with these children. (For additional reading on family treatment programs that involve children, see Ayoub, 1991; Friedrich, 1990; Hembree-Kigin & McNeil, 1995.)

Interventions with Preschool Children

Young children present several difficulties in treatment and prevention of reabuse: (1) they are not sufficiently cognitively advanced to thoroughly understand what has happened to them or the motives of adults who are trying to help them; (2) they have limited verbal abilities; and (3) they have limited understanding of emotions. Based on these limitations, treatment for the child involving close work with the caregivers is often useful. Conjoint parent work can, for example, be used to teach parents how to increase their child's adaptive and appropriate behaviors outside of the clinic setting. In addition, in the case of child sexual abuse, parents' reactions to the abuse and support of the child have been found to be strongly associated with children's behavioral and emotional treatment outcome (Cohen & Mannarino, 1996, 1998). Thus, teaching parents how to respond to their children in a developmentally appropriate, nurturing manner about abuse issues is a valuable goal of treatment. Although there are many different orientations and techniques for the treatment of sexually abused children, work with caregivers is a component that can be readily integrated with all approaches.

Play therapy is one approach frequently used with young sexually abused children. "In practice, therapists assume that a child's play is a reflection of feelings, conflicts, thoughts, and perceptions of reality. These are expressed through play because the child is not yet able to express them verbally" (Knell, 1993, p. 8). Techniques used in play therapy range widely and may include nondirective, child-centered approaches (Axline, 1964); interpretive, psychoanalytic approaches (Klein, 1932); and directive, cognitive-behavioral approaches (Knell, 1993). (For additional information on play therapy with sexually abused children, see E. Gil, 1991; Webb, 1991.)

There have not yet been sufficient large-scale, well-controlled studies to draw conclusions regarding the relative effectiveness of various treatment approaches for sexually abused children (Finkelhor & Berliner, 1995). However, several studies suggest that structured behavioral and cognitive-behavioral interventions may be more effective than less directive approaches (O'Donohue & Elliot, 1992). In an effectiveness comparison study with random subject assignment to cognitive-behavioral group treatment or nondirective supportive group therapy, Cohen and Mannarino (1998) found that assignment to the cognitive-behavioral group was the strongest predictor of preschoolers' positive behavioral and emotional outcome at posttreatment and at 12-month follow-up. Celano, Hazzard, Webb, and McCall (1996) randomly assigned sexually abused children and their nonoffending mothers to a structured or unstructured treatment program and found both treatments effective in reducing children's distress, but found the structured intervention more effective in increasing caregiver support of the child and decreasing negative attributions by the caregiver (e.g., self-blame).

Behavioral techniques are useful to reduce both a child's internalizing symptoms (e.g., depression, anxiety) and their externalizing symptoms (e.g., noncompliance, inappropriate sexual behaviors). Ruma (1993) described the effective use of behavioral techniques in the treatment of a 3½-year-old who was sexually abused by her preschool teacher. The child exhibited nightmares, refusal to sleep in her own bed, and sexualized touching of her mother and dolls. Redirection, contingency management, and differential reinforcement were taught to the child's mother to help the child increase her adaptive behaviors. The child earned stars for each night she slept in her own bed and was allowed to choose one night a week to sleep in the mother's bed. Appropriate affection-seeking behaviors were praised, and inappropriate sexualized behaviors were redirected. It was reported that inappropriate sexual behaviors and sleep problems subsided within a three-month period.

Children presenting with externalizing behavior disorders may also benefit from behavioral techniques to reduce their inappropriate behavior. For example, excessive noncompliance may respond to techniques such as shaping and modeling acceptable behavior. For children with internalizing behavior disorders, other useful techniques include developing relaxation skills, creating relaxation tapes for use at bedtime, and creating booklets with pictures and names of supportive people in their

lives. Clinicians can refer to Hembree-Kigin and McNeil (1995) and C. Schaefer and Briesmeister (1989) for other examples of behavioral programs designed for parents and children.

Bibliotherapy can be useful even with young children. The therapist can use the reading materials as a stimulus to promote discussion of abuse-related issues. Books that are helpful for young children to deal with stigmatization include *Alice Doesn't Babysit Anymore* (McGovern, 1985) and *No More Secrets for Me* (Wachter, 1983). Books that may help teach prevention skills and reduce a sense of powerlessness include *Talking about Touching for Parents and Kids* (Beland, 1985) and *My Body Is Private* (Girard, 1984). In addition to reading books that describe prevention skills, it is important with preschoolers to practice role-playing prevention behavior such as saying "No!" in a loud voice, running away, and telling an adult what happened to them.

Although group treatment has historically targeted school-age children and adolescents, recent studies have demonstrated the usefulness of group treatment with preschool-age children (Cohen & Mannarino, 1996, 1998; Stauffer & Deblinger, 1996). The group format can be used to help children learn age-appropriate social skills, reduce aggressive and inappropriate sexual behaviors, gain a better understanding of the abuse, and practice prevention skills. Children learn in vivo through their rehearsal of skills with others in the group.

Another useful component of group treatment is a child-focused parallel group for caregivers. Such groups can teach caregivers ways to respond supportively to the child, to manage problematic abuse-related behaviors, and to help the children generalize their new skills. Because of the difficulty in substantiating sexual abuse in young children, clinicians are sometimes faced with the treatment of children who are only suspected of being sexually abused. In response to this circumstance, treatment groups have recently been developed that focus on decreasing children's sexualized behaviors, increasing their adaptive problem solving, and increasing appropriate expression of feelings, without discussing abuse-specific topics (Silovsky & Niec, 1998).

Interventions with School-Age Children
Because school-age children are able to think logically and have increased verbal skills, they are

more likely than preschool children to benefit from a cognitive approach. Cognitive-behavioral techniques may be useful to increase a child's impulse control and to gain control over unacceptable behavior. Three commonly used problem-solving strategies with children are interpersonal cognitive problem solving (Shure & Spivack, 1978; Spivack, Platt, & Shure, 1976), self-instructional training (Kendall & Finch, 1979; Meichenbaum, 1977), and the turtle technique (Robin, Schneider, & Dolnick, 1976). Cognitive-behavioral therapy may also be useful in decreasing a child's abuse-related depression and anxiety. For example, specific interventions can teach the child to change distorted attributions and perceptions about the abuse (e.g., self-blame) and develop thought-stopping and positive imagery skills to reduce intrusive thoughts.

Other cognitive-behavioral techniques address somatic components of anxiety and depression (e.g., hyperarousal). These skills can be taught using creative games that decrease the threat of the material and encourage children's participation. For example, teaching children to challenge their distorted self-statements can be presented in the metaphor of a detective looking for clues before drawing conclusions. The child can then be reinforced for being a "good detective." As with preschool children, it is valuable to include caregivers in the treatment of school-age children, as the adult's participation demonstrates support and can encourage the child to use newly learned adaptive strategies outside the therapy setting (Deblinger, Lippmann, & Steer, 1996). For more details regarding cognitive-behavioral techniques, see Kendall (1991).

Bibliotherapy can be used with school-age children for sex education and to address issues of age-appropriate sexuality. Books that may be useful include *How You Were Born* (Cole, 1993), *So That's How I Was Born!* (Brooks, 1983), *The Playbook for Kids about Sex* (Blank, 1980), or *Let's Talk about . . . S-E-X* (Gitchel & Foster, 1982). These books can be read together during a therapy session or read at home and discussed with the therapist later. The books mentioned earlier can also be useful to elicit a discussion of the abuse with the school-age child.

Writing activities may also be employed with this age group. Letters to judges, lawyers, perpetrators, and other family members may be productive to increase a child's sense of mastery and decrease feelings of powerlessness, whether the letters are kept or sent. For children who respond to less direct therapeutic interventions, clinicians advocate the use of art therapy (Sgroi, 1982) and poetry therapy (Mazza, Magaz, & Scaturro, 1987).

Group therapy, which is frequently utilized with school-age children, has been found to be effective in the treatment of child sexual abuse (Reeker, Ensing, & Elliott, 1997). Although groups may vary in treatment focus, common goals that have been described include validating conflicting emotional and physical feelings associated with the abuse, providing adaptive ways to express and organize abuse-related thoughts and feelings, teaching age-appropriate means of expressing and eliciting physical affection, learning to identify and maintain physical and sexual boundaries, developing a prevention plan, and preparing children for other forms of treatment (e.g., family, mother-daughter dyad) (Sturkie, 1994).

For 6- to 12-year-old children, it is important to address peer issues in a treatment program. Children who have been involved in abusive situations sometimes have poor social skills and only limited interactions with their peers outside school. Important social skills can be learned through the utilization of behavioral techniques such as modeling, shaping, and reinforcement in individual or group therapy. The therapist can help children learn basic skills that will assist them in making friends, such as how to approach another child, what to talk about, and how to invite a friend to a movie. In addition, the techniques mentioned above (e.g., relaxation strategies, turtle technique, differential reinforcement) may be used to reduce inappropriate sexual behaviors that would interfere with normal peer relationships. Children's aggressive feelings can be channeled into acceptable physical activities such as karate, swimming, running, or skating that may not only decrease aggression with peers but can also provide increased opportunities for positive social contact.

Interventions with Adolescents

Many of the cognitive-behavioral, reading, and writing techniques described for school-age children are also useful with adolescents. However, because of the multiple developmental changes occurring during these years, sexually abused adolescents present unique characteristics that should be considered in developing a treatment plan. For example, whereas young children are likely to present with sexual behavior problems, adolescents appear more likely to present with symptoms of low self-esteem, depression, and suicidal ideation or behavior; therefore, suicidal risk should be sensitively assessed and treated (Beitchman, Zucker, Hood, DaCosta, & Akman, 1991). As is developmentally appropriate, teenagers are beginning to develop autonomy from their families and view peer relationships as highly important. As a result, concerns about how peers will view their sexual abuse may promote avoidance of peer relations. Treatment in such cases should facilitate the development of positive, close peer relationships.

Another developmental aspect that separates adolescents from 6- to 12-year-olds is their advanced cognitive development. If not cognitively delayed, many adolescents are capable of abstract and introspective thinking, which facilitates their articulation of abuse-related attributions (Celano, 1992). Articulation of these thoughts makes it possible to directly address maladaptive attributions. Adolescents' cognitive development also allows them to benefit from didactic information. For example, educational readings about abuse effects can validate and normalize a victim's feelings and experiences (Chaffin et al., 1996).

Education about sex and sexuality is also recommended for sexually abused adolescents. Chaffin et al. (1996) discuss six reasons for the importance of sex education: (1) to provide a common language for discussing sexuality; (2) to correct misconceptions; (3) to promote a healthy body image; (4) to differentiate abusive from healthy sexual relationships; (5) to decrease the risk of revictimization; and (6) to prevent pregnancy and sexually transmitted diseases. Books written for teenagers, such as *The New Our Bodies, Our Selves* (Boston Women's Health Book Collective, 1999), may be helpful in providing accurate health information. Emphasis has been placed on group treatment of sexually abused adolescents because of the advantages to teenagers of addressing abuse issues through peer interactions (Chaffin et al., 1996).

Group treatment with adolescents typically focuses on two broad goals: coping with the aftereffects of the abuse and successfully negotiating the normal developmental tasks of adolescence. Group treatment is seen as especially beneficial for sexually abused adolescents to decrease their feelings of alienation, isolation, and blame by discussing their abuse with others who have had similar experiences. It can also be a less threatening format for providing sex education. Because many of the adolescents have experienced inadequate family boundaries, a group can be an excellent environment for learning to set personal boundaries and to respect other people's boundaries. Other group methods used to reduce anxiety include the use of relaxation and imagery techniques. Additional useful activities with this age group include charting genograms, utilizing family sculptures, and producing a videotape (Sirles, Walsma, Lytle-Barnaby, & Lander, 1988).

Normal developmental tasks that can be worked on in a group format include (1) individuation from family, (2) identity formation, (3) learning to have successful peer relationships, and (4) clarifying life goals. Although substance abuse and eating disorders are sometimes discussed in a group setting, individuals with these problems should be referred for specialized treatment.

PREVENTION OF SEXUAL ABUSE

As public awareness of sexual abuse has increased, efforts to prevent the sexual abuse of children have also increased dramatically over the past decade. For clinicians treating child abuse victims and focusing on the prevention of revictimization, knowledge of the prevention literature is helpful. For example, it has been shown that programs that include development of self-protection skills through explicit training are more effective than programs teaching concepts of sexual abuse (Rispens, Aleman, & Goudena, 1997). It has also been shown that young children appear to lose their skills more quickly and thus may benefit from repeated practice over time. Prevention programs may be more effective overall if they consider the developmental level of the participants. The reader interested in learning more about sexual abuse prevention is encouraged to read Finkelhor and Dziuba-Leatherman (1995); Reppucci, Land, and Haugaard (1998); and Rispens et al, (1997) for more information.

PSYCHOLOGICAL MALTREATMENT

Psychological maltreatment has gained increasing attention from mental health professionals, researchers, CPS personnel, and policymakers in the past decade (APSAC, 1995b; Browne & Lynch, 1997; McGee, Wolfe, Yuen, Wilson, & Carnochan, 1995;

National Research Council, 1993). Recent research has heightened the focus on psychological maltreatment as the most frequent form of child maltreatment and the form that occurs in most cases of child abuse and neglect (Brassard & Hardy, 1997; Hart, Binggeli, & Brassard, 1998). A major indication of the increased focus on psychological maltreatment is the publication of a new journal, *Journal of Emotional Abuse,* with its first issue in 1998.

The problem of definition has been more pronounced in psychological maltreatment than in all other forms of abuse (D. Barnett, Manly, Cicchetti, 1991; Egeland, 1991a; McGee & Wolfe, 1991; O'Hagan, 1995; Thompson & Kaplan, 1996). The initial federal definition of child abuse and neglect was "the physical and mental injury, sexual abuse, negligent treatment, or maltreatment of a child under the age of eighteen by a person who is responsible for the child's welfare under circumstances which indicate that the child's health or welfare is harmed or threatened" (Child Abuse Prevention and Treatment Act, 1983). Although revisions of the act have more clearly defined physical and sexual abuse, and in some respects neglect, little has been done to clarify "mental injury." This has resulted in a "child welfare system that is committed to the protection of children's physical well-being but slow to recognize and deal systemically with the mandate to protect their psychological well-being" (Brassard & Hardy, 1997, p. 393).

A generally accepted definition of psychological maltreatment is a repeated pattern or extreme instances on the part of the caregiver that express to a child that he or she is worthless, unloved, unwanted, endangered, or of value only in meeting someone else's needs (APSAC, 1995b; Brassard, Hart, & Hardy, 1991). Psychological maltreatment is currently described as falling into one of the six categories described below (for a full discussion, see Brassard & Hardy, 1997):

1. *Spurning:* A type of verbal battering that is a combination of rejection and hostile degradation. The parent may actively refuse to help a child or even to acknowledge the child's request for help. Spurning also includes calling a child debasing names, labeling the child as inferior, and publicly humiliating the child.
2. *Terrorizing:* Threatening to physically hurt, kill, or abandon the child if he or she does not behave. It also includes exposing a child to violence (see Rossman & Rosenberg, 1997) or

threats directed toward loved ones and leaving a young child unattended.
3. *Isolating:* Entails the active isolation of a child by an adult. The child may be locked in a closet or room for an extended length of time, or the adult may limit or refuse to allow any interaction with peers or adults outside the family.
4. *Exploiting/Corrupting:* Involves modeling antisocial acts and unrealistic roles or encouraging and condoning deviant standards or beliefs. This includes teaching the child criminal behavior, keeping a child home in the role of a servant or surrogate parent in lieu of school attendance, or encouraging a child to participate in the production of pornography.
5. *Denying Emotional Responsiveness:* Includes acts by the caregiver that ignore a child's needs and attempts to interact. The caregiver shows no emotion when interacting with the child and fails to express caring, affection, and love to the child. Parents who behave this way communicate through acts of omission that they are not interested in the child and are emotionally unavailable.
6. *Unwarranted Withholding of Medical Care, Mental Health Services, or Education:* Includes caregiver acts that ignore, refuse to allow, or fail to provide necessary treatment for serious emotional, behavioral, physical health, or educational needs of the child.

Although these categories and definitions are generally accepted in the field, they have not been universally adopted, and suggestions continue to be made to improve them (e.g., D. Barnett et al., 1991; Burnett, 1993; Hart et al., 1998; C. Schaefer, 1997; Thompson & Kaplan, 1996). It is interesting to note that although psychological maltreatment typically occurs in a caregiver-child relationship, other recent literature has described the behavior in other relationships, such as by siblings (Whipple & Finton, 1995), in the context of separation and divorce (Klosinski, 1993), in adolescent dating relationships (Jezl, Molidor, & Wright, 1996; Kasian & Painter, 1992), and in schools (Elbedour, Center, Maruyama, & Assor, 1997).

The current definitions continue to present insufficient direction for consistent application by the various professionals involved in investigation, prosecution, and treatment of these cases. CPS personnel, attorneys, judges, mental health professionals, and researchers, operating from different perspectives, use different definitions for different purposes. A number of issues persist in confounding the issue: (1) psychological maltreatment is manifested in both acts of commission and acts of omission; (2) there is an absence of physical evidence; (3) it can exist alone or with other forms of maltreatment; (4) it can be defined only within an interpersonal context; and (5) the definition is often dependent on the developmental stage of the victim. Without a generally agreed upon and operationalized definition, it will continue to be problematic to identify and provide appropriate protective and clinical services to psychologically maltreated children.

It is clear that accurate data on the incidence and prevalence of psychological maltreatment are virtually impossible to obtain. The 1997 national data indicate that 6% of the 984,000 child victims suffered emotional abuse (U.S. Department of Health and Human Services, 1999). Estimates of the incidence of psychological maltreatment vary widely in the literature, which is a clear indication of the definitional confusion that continues to plague the field. It is generally accepted that only a small percentage of cases of psychological maltreatment are reported, investigated, substantiated, or successfully prosecuted. When a case is reported, it is less likely than other forms of maltreatment to become an active child welfare case, to result in court action, or to receive mental health services. This lack of CPS, legal, and mental health involvement in cases of psychological maltreatment is related to the problem of definition and establishing a chain of cause and effect. For a child to be identified as psychologically maltreated, the professionals must establish three components to the case: (1) there must be identifiable parental behavior that could cause harm; (2) harm to the child must be demonstrated; and (3) a causal link between the parental behavior and the harm to the child must be established (Duquette & Faller, 1988).

THEORETICAL ASSUMPTIONS

Due to the lack of a consistent definition and its frequent occurrence with other forms of maltreatment, minimal information is available on families that psychologically maltreat their children, either as the sole form of abuse or in conjunction with other forms of abuse or neglect. Child development research indicates that infants and children do not initially elicit psychological abuse, but are its victims. It is still postulated that the maltreatment is a result of the problems and conflicts between adults (Herrenkohl, Herrenkohl, & Egolf, 1983), and that children can learn maladaptive social behavior from a rejecting parent as early as 1 to 3 years of age (Main & Goldwyn, 1984).

As psychological maltreatment is usually seen as a symptom of parental dysfunction, most interventions have focused on changing parents or the home environment rather than on direct treatment of children, except in cases where a child is removed from the home and provided with treatment. This approach rarely relieves the child's emotional response to the maltreatment and leaves the child vulnerable to repeating problematic patterns of relating in all other relationships, most notably in future relationships with his or her own children (Kagan & Schlosberg, 1989).

Although still sparse, there is empirical cause-and-effect evidence for samples of children and adolescents (for a recent review, see Hart et al., 1998). Clausen and Crittenden (1991) compared a sample of 175 physically abused children, 39 receiving mental health services, and 176 normative controls. They found that (1) psychological maltreatment can occur alone; (2) psychological maltreatment was present in all cases of physical abuse; (3) psychological maltreatment was related more to negative outcome for children than was the severity of the physical injury; and (4) psychological maltreating behavior and negative child outcomes were highly related. In this community sample, it was found that psychological maltreatment occurred at a rate five times higher than physical abuse, which suggests that it may occur more frequently than other forms of abuse and neglect in the general population.

A major empirical longitudinal study on children is the Minnesota Mother-Child Interaction Project, a study initiated in 1975 of primiparous women at risk for abusive caretaking. Children who were subsequently abused were classified into four groups, and those children whose mothers were psychologically unavailable showed particular problems, including evidence of an anxious/avoidant attachment, a severe decline in functioning in the early years, and later lack of social-emotional competence (Egeland, 1991b; Erickson, Egeland, & Pianta,

1989). The project was designed to differentiate the impact of various forms of child maltreatment at different developmental stages. It found that even when the effects of poverty and other aversive environmental conditions were controlled for, the maltreated children showed maladaption at each time of assessment (Egeland, 1991b).

A recent study of 60 adolescents' perceptions of their abuse experiences found that psychological maltreatment was the most potent predictive type of maltreatment (McGee, Wolfe, & Wilson, 1997). Youth who had a documented history of severe psychological maltreatment (i.e., according to CPS standards) had the highest level of internalizing problems, and the authors speculated that the maltreatment interrupts the development of the self-system. This study is important in that it furthers our understanding of the impact of maltreatment and empirically documents the predictive value of the perceptions of adolescents about their maltreatment experiences. This research is unique in targeting an adolescent population, and yet the results converge with previous studies of younger children in showing the "ubiquitous nature of psychological maltreatment" (p. 146).

ASSESSMENT

Mental health professionals will increasingly be called on to conduct evaluations of families in which allegations of psychological maltreatment have been made. This is obviously a difficult task with significant psychological and possible legal consequences for the child and caregivers. In addition to the standardized instruments listed in Table 50.1, a set of professional guidelines and several instruments are now available to assist in assessing psychologically maltreating behavior in parents and the effects of such behavior on children. However, due to the lack of a clear definition and the problems discussed previously, professionals should approach such an evaluation with caution and collaboration with other professionals.

APSAC developed a set of practice guidelines, *Psychosocial Evaluation of Suspected Psychological Maltreatment in Children and Adolescents* (1995b), to provide a structure for assessing whether or not children have been psychologically maltreated. The guidelines are designed to assist in the assessment, treatment, legal decisions, and case management of

cases in which psychological maltreatment occurs. Several important points are made in the APSAC guidelines for evaluating families for possible psychological maltreatment: (1) confidentiality and informal consent are explained; (2) the differences between a forensic evaluation and solicited therapy are pointed out; (3) recommendations for the level of training and experience of the assessor are included; (4) the importance of the child's developmental level is pointed out; (5) suggestions are made for determining the level of severity; (6) four areas of assessment are described; and (7) suggestions are listed for report writing and testifying in court.

Observation of the parent-child interaction is a major source of information in identifying psychological maltreatment by relatives, school personnel, or neighbors, who report most of the abuse. Professionals also rely on observation in a clinic or home setting, along with other, more structured forms of observation. One widely used instrument to make standardized home observations is the Childhood Level of Living Scale (CLL; Polansky, Chalmers, Buttenwieser, & Williams, 1978, 1981). Originally developed to assess neglect, the instrument evaluates the degree to which the environment of families with young children offers minimally safe, hygienic levels of comfort. By assessing the degree to which mothers provide minimal levels of stimulation, cultural enrichment, and emotional support for development, the scale also measures emotional neglect.

In the past decade, several instruments have been developed that have the potential to be used as part of a battery to assess psychological maltreatment. The Psychological Maltreatment Rating Scale (PMRS; Brassard, Hart, & Hardy, 1993) uses four scales to assess spurning, terrorizing, corrupting/ exploiting, and denying emotional responsiveness, and nine scales to assess prosocial parenting, the absence of which indicates psychological neglect. A validation study showed that the PMRS is a moderately reliable and valid measure of psychological maltreatment that can discriminate between maltreating and comparison mothers.

The Child-Adult Relationship Experimental Index (CARE Index) utilizes a three-minute videotaped play episode to rate 52 items on a behavioral rating system (Crittenden, 1988a). The CARE Index has been used to discriminate among adequate, abusive, neglectful, abusive-neglectful, and marginally maltreating families. Observations are coded on three types of adult behaviors (sensitive, controlling, responsive) and four types of infant behavior (cooperative, difficult, passive, compulsive/compliant). Although the CARE Index was developed to examine mother-infant interactions, the author notes that the behaviors coded are relevant across the life span. Crittenden reports 81% to 89% agreement among highly trained raters on this instrument.

Another instrument has been designed as a comprehensive documentation of a child's or adolescent's victimization history. The Record of Maltreatment Experiences (ROME) is an 87-item instrument with five subscales that measure psychological maltreatment, constructive parenting behavior, sexual abuse, physical abuse, and exposure to family violence (McGee, Wolfe, & Wilson, 1990; Wolfe & McGee, 1994).

As the assessment of psychological maltreatment typically uses information from a variety of sources, Kaufman and her colleagues developed the Emotional Maltreatment Scale, a system for integrating information from CPS workers, medical records, parent interviews, and clinical observations (J. Kaufman, Jones, Stieglitz, Vitulano, & Mannarino, 1994). The scale is scored from 0 (no evidence of emotional maltreatment or rejection) to 4 (extreme parental rejection in addition to exposure to drug/alcohol abuse and/or marital violence). Parents were found to be a particularly useful source, as they provided the majority of information on new instances of maltreatment. However, the authors noted that parental reports and CPS reports were both needed to obtain a comprehensive picture.

There is only one measure of psychological abuse with national norms, the Verbal/Symbolic Aggression Index of the Conflict Tactics Scales (CTS; Straus, 1996). The CTS is a short, self-report instrument that assesses nonviolent discipline, psychological aggression, and physical assault in parent-child and other family relationships. The Psychological Aggression and Physical Assault Scales provide information for diagnosing psychological maltreatment and physical abuse (for a full discussion, see Straus & Hamby, 1997). The strengths of the instrument are that it does not appear to be affected by social desirability; the questions are posed as conflict resolution rather than child abuse and so are more readily answered by caregivers; it has concurrent validity for spouse abuse; and its history indicates

that parents will report abusive behavior to other individuals (Brassard & Hardy, 1997; Sounders, 1986). The shortcomings of the instrument in the area of psychological maltreatment are the level of internal consistency (.62–.77), the small number of items included, the lack of items to assess infants and toddlers, and the lack of concurrent validity studies (Brassard & Hardy, 1997).

There is a new version, the CTS 2, that can be obtained from the author (Straus, 1995). This self-report scale asks the parent to describe his or her own behavior as well as the other parent's behavior, giving a broader picture of family interactions. It also has supplemental scales that assess weekly discipline, neglect, and sexual abuse.

A comprehensive evaluation includes an assessment of the family, parental factors, parent-child interactions, and the child's behavior and personality. The following instruments may be useful in assessing these factors:

- *Family Factors:* Family Adaptability and Cohesion Evaluation Scale (FACES II; Olson, Portner, & Bell, 1982); Family Environment Scale (FES; Moos & Moos, 1981); Interparental Conflict and Influence Scales (IPC; Schwartz & Zuroff, 1979).
- *Parental Factors and Parent-Child Interactions:* Parental Acceptance-Rejection Questionnaire (Rohner & Rohner, 1980); Children's Reports of Parental Behavior Inventory (E. Schaefer, 1965); Michigan Screening Profile of Parenting (MSPP; Helfer, Schneider, & Hoffmeister, 1978); Child Abuse Potential Inventory (CAP; J.S. Milner, 1986); and Parenting Stress Index (PSI; Abidin, 1983).
- *Child's Behavior and Personality:* See Table 50.1 and the previous section on the assessment of the physically abused child. (For additional information on assessment in psychological maltreatment cases, see Brassard & Hardy, 1997; Hart, Brassard, & Karlson, 1996).

Researchers have used structured tasks in the home or laboratory to identify parent-child or familial interactions that discriminate between maltreating and controlling families. Parental behaviors of interest include the six subtypes of psychological maltreatment mentioned earlier, as well as positive parental attention. Child behaviors that are examined tend to be the degree to which a child is actively hostile toward the parent, or displays avoidance, out-of-control behavior, or hypervigilance. Recently, compulsive compliance has been identified as a pattern typical of severely maltreated children (Crittenden, 1988b).

TREATMENT

Clinical experience and treatment research with abusive families document that they are frequently difficult to work with (Cohn & Daro, 1987) and, in cases of psychological maltreatment, are often not referred to CPS (e.g., Claussen & Crittenden, 1991). Hart and his colleagues (1996) recommend an approach that (1) is empirically based; (2) combines treatment with prevention; (3) is available to all families, thus reducing the stigma; and (4) is longer term, to continue throughout the child's developmental periods. They recommend home visitors, school-based health and mental health services for children and their families, and a CPS system that is client-data-driven, using J. Lutzker's (1984) ecobehavioral model. A recent review of the evaluation of home visiting programs indicated that results varied widely across program models, program sites using the same model, and families at a single program site (David and Lucile Packard Foundation, 1999). The report's executive summary concluded that (1) the benefits cannot be generalized from one program model to another; (2) although human behavior is difficult to change, programs should continue to provide support for families with young children; and (3) changes are necessary in the current home visiting models before widespread and consistent benefits will be achieved.

Treatment interventions for psychologically maltreated children and adolescents remain in their infancy. Few research studies exist to document treatment effectiveness at any age. The treatment approaches described in earlier sections of this chapter may be utilized to address various affective and behavioral problems seen in psychologically abused children.

Brassard and her colleagues (Brassard, Germain, & Hart, 1987; Brassard et al., 1991) developed a comprehensive treatment model derived from a combination of ecological-systemic theory, psychoanalytically influenced organizational theory, and social learning theory. Because multiproblem families are often

less resistant to outside intervention during crisis periods, the treatment model uses each crisis as an opportunity to build a supportive, consistent relationship with the family. As they work with the family to deal with the crisis on a concrete level, clinicians not only demonstrate and teach appropriate problem-solving skills but present more rewarding models of interpersonal relationships and provide opportunities for family members to come to terms with past traumas.

Critical to engaging these families in treatment is establishing a working relationship. Unresolved issues from a parent's own childhood can have an enormous impact on his or her parenting behavior. In maltreating families, the unmet psychological needs of the adults can prohibit their empathizing with and protecting their children (Fraiberg, 1983). Parents who were abused as children need assistance in learning new models of relating to and communicating with others. They must have an opportunity to work through, cognitively and affectively, the painful experiences of childhood trauma that prevent them from forming nurturing relationships with their children. Whether conceptualized as transference issues (Fraiberg, 1983), dysfunctional representational working models of relationships (Bretherton, 1985; Sroufe & Fleeson, 1986), unresolved issues in the parents' family of origin (Bowen, 1978), or a cognitive developmental immaturity (Ivey, 1987; Newberger, 1980), maltreating parents are often found to be psychologically unable to assume the role of adult and parent because of unmet needs and concomitant delays in their cognitive and emotional development.

In many maltreating families, the parents need extensive individual attention and nurturance before effective interventions with other family members can occur. As the therapeutic relationship with a mother is developed and stabilized, this individual attention can be balanced by attempts to engage her partner in the treatment process. Marital issues are an important part of the treatment of maltreating families, but the existence of drug or alcohol problems greatly impedes all interventions to improve family functioning and eliminate abuse (Daro, 1988).

A lack of skills for solving both interpersonal and concrete problems exacerbates the psychological neediness and social isolation that these families experience. The treatment provider needs to offer the parents assistance in acquiring specific skills, such as (1) parenting-child management, knowledge of and how to facilitate child development; (2) forming and maintaining relationships: communication, social skills, problem solving, perspective taking; (3) anger management; and (4) basic life skills: money management, assertiveness with institutions such as welfare, hospitals, schools. Behavior therapists have demonstrated the effectiveness of behavioral interventions with maltreating parents in these areas (Goldstein, Keller, & Erné, 1985; J. Lutzker, 1984; Wolfe, 1987).

For work with infants, Fraiberg's (1983) clinical infant mental health program and the University of Minnesota's Steps Toward Effective and Enjoyable Parenting (STEEP) Project (Erickson, 1988) are two examples of intervention projects that appear to be successful in treating maltreating families with infants. For preschool children, play therapy has had some success (Mann & McDermott, 1983). For school-age children, group therapy (Steward, Farquhar, Dicharry, Glick, & Martin, 1986) and behavioral programs to address relationship problems and promote social competence, such as the Prepare Curriculum (Goldstein, 1990), merit further evaluation. The latter has been demonstrated to be effective with adolescent delinquents, a group known for its relationship disorders (Goldstein, Glick, Irwin, Pask-McCartney, & Rubama, 1989).

In a recent work, Hart and his colleagues have strongly recommended that schools should play a major role in intervening and preventing psychological maltreatment through school-based services for children (Hart et al., 1996). The reasons are: (1) many schools already have trained staff such as school psychologists, nurses, guidance counselors, and social workers available; (2) children are observed on a daily basis and problems can be addressed early in their development; (3) services delivered in the school are more accessible to children and families than clinic-based interventions; (4) schools are settings that promote achievement and social development in children; and (5) school personnel are excellent sources for role models and compensatory relationships for maltreated children.

Psychologically maltreated children and adolescents need many of the same types of interventions that their parents and other abused children need. Results of clinical experience and a number of studies suggest that therapeutic intervention can make a real and lasting difference in some children's lives if clinicians offer them an alternative model of relationships and provide a safe environment. Children and adolescents need supportive relationships to resolve the effects of their trauma, address areas of developmental delay, promote competence in areas of strength, and develop their significant relationships (Egeland, Jacobvitz, & Sroufe, 1988; Fraiberg, 1983; Main & Goldwyn, 1984; Werner, 1988). Group therapy, socially based interventions, and cognitive techniques may be useful in addressing faulty cognitions and self-definitions found in maltreated adolescents who have low self-esteem or are depressed (DuRubeis & Beck, 1988).

The problems of these families and the children in them are often so numerous and severe that it is quite easy for professionals dealing with the family to become as overwhelmed and hopeless as the family members themselves. It is a vital aspect of the treatment process to emphasize the family's resources and the personal strengths of its members (Karpel, 1986). These strengths are not always readily apparent, yet they must be identified, actively validated, and built upon.

NEGLECT

Child neglect is perhaps the most forgotten type of child maltreatment (Cantwell, 1997). Contrasted with other forms of maltreatment that generally arise from acts of commission, neglect arises from acts of omission on the part of the caretaker. It is defined as the chronic failure of a parent or caretaker to provide children under 18 with basic needs such as food, clothing, shelter, medical care, educational opportunity, protection, and supervision. According to Daro (1988), several types of neglect exist: physical neglect, deprivation of necessities, educational neglect or deprivation, medical care neglect, intentional drugging, abandonment or lack of supervision, failure to provide, and fostering delinquency. Erickson and Egeland (1996) add emotional neglect, defined as parental emotional unavailability to the child, and mental health neglect to this list. The apparent simplicity of this list of types of neglect belies the difficulty of defining and determining the presence of neglect, its impact on children of different ages (Cicchetti & Toth, 1995), and the myriad contexts within which it occurs (Belsky, 1993). Definitions of neglect evolve and change over time and are heavily influenced by culture (e.g.,

Rose & Meezan, 1996). In defining neglect, clinicians must pay careful attention to the idea of community standards of care.

Other considerations in defining child neglect are related to the chronicity and acuteness of the neglect and the impact on the child. Certainly, some of the most devastating and long-lasting effects of neglect arise from the chronic failure of parents to provide for the needs of the child (e.g., nonorganic failure to thrive; Oates & Kempe, 1997). However, even brief episodes of neglect—most often, lack of adequate supervision—can have devastating effects. For example, child deaths due to drowning are almost always caused, in part, by the failure of the caretaker to provide adequate supervision to ensure the safety of the child. So, too, are the deaths of children from fires. Children are most likely to die in child-set fires that occur in the absence of appropriate adult supervision (Bonner, Crow, & Logue, 1999). These deaths may be the result of momentary instances of neglect or part of more long-standing patterns of neglect. Other forms of fatal neglect occur as a result of chronic failure to provide care, as in cases of medical neglect (e.g., Geffken, Johnson, Silverstein, & Rosenbloom, 1992).

Incidence rates show that more children suffer from neglect than from any form of abuse. The most recent statistics indicate that 56% of all substantiated cases of child maltreatment were cases of neglect (U.S. Department of Health and Human Services, 1999). This means that over 551,000 children were neglected in 1997, a proportional increase of 7.5% since 1990. In spite of neglect's having the highest rate of occurrence, it is the area of abuse that has received the least attention, both in service provision and research. In medical settings, when the presence of symptoms of trauma receive high rates of attention, neglect may be overlooked (McHugh, 1992). Even in social services agencies, neglectful families may receive fewer services than abusing families (Wilding & Thoburn, 1997).

Research in child neglect still lags behind studies on other forms of child maltreatment, although recently there has been an increase in research that focuses on neglect. A review of Medline and PsychInfo databases revealed over 1,500 articles pertaining to child neglect or abuse. Fewer than 5% of these articles separated neglect from abuse or were about neglect alone, yet the articles reflect an increase in empirical interest in neglect as a separate form of child maltreatment as compared to the

earlier part of this decade. Studying neglect as an individual phenomenon is difficult, as many instances of child maltreatment involve more than one type of maltreatment, and neglect, especially psychological neglect, is often thought to be a part of all other forms of maltreatment. Further, the effects of other problems that impact children are confounded with neglect. Poverty, general family dysfunction, and environmental chaos are difficult to separate from neglect and have profound effects on the lives of children (Daro, 1988; Erickson & Egeland, 1996; Gaudin, Polansky, Kilpatrick, & Shilton, 1996).

THEORETICAL ASSUMPTIONS

As stated above, neglect does not occur in a vacuum. It may arise as the result of other influences on the family, such as poverty, family dysfunction, parental mental illness, and child factors. In some families in poverty, but certainly not all, basic survival needs consume the family's energy and little energy may be left to care for the children. Children reported for child neglect often live with one parent, and these caregivers are unemployed (American Association for Protecting Children, 1986). Even in two-parent families, parental resources are seen as inadequate: mothers in two-parent neglectful families rated their partners as less supportive and more violent than the mothers of male partners in abusive families (Lacharite, Ethier, & Couture, 1996). According to Daro (1988), the National Clinical Evaluation Study found that 96% of neglecting families reported financial difficulties compared with approximately 75% of other maltreating families.

Poverty, although closely associated with neglect (Drake & Pandey, 1996), is not solely predictive of child neglect (Nelson, Cross, Landsman, & Tyler, 1996; Nelson, Saunders, & Landsman; 1993), but is the best predictor of physical neglect (Jones & McCurdy, 1992). In addition, more than 75% of neglecting families lacked knowledge about child development, exhibited an "inaccurate sense" of the child's needs, showed low self-esteem, and were unable to manage their households (Daro, 1988).

A population-based study of parents who reported neglecting or abusing their children indicated that a lifetime history of mental illness (especially alcohol abuse and anxiety disorders), low SES, and greater numbers of children in the household were associated with increased rates of neglect (Egami, Ford, Greenfield, & Crum, 1996). Mothers who were found to be neglectful of adequately supervising their children also showed poorer problem-solving skills, had less education, and were more likely to be in multiproblem families than were nonneglecting mothers (Coohey, 1998).

It is not only parent factors that are found to be related to child neglect. Dubowitz and colleagues (Harrington, Black, Starr, & Dubowitz, 1998) found that children whose temperaments were rated by their mothers as "difficult" were more likely to be emotionally neglected. This effect was buffered, however, by family support. Thus, the context within which neglect occurs is complex and requires that any effective assessment or treatment attend to multiple facets of the problem, not just the effects on the child.

A careful evaluation of demonstration projects designed to address the problem of neglect indicates only minimal success in preventing continued neglect and reducing the probability of future maltreatment. Daro (1988) evaluated 19 clinical intervention projects with abusive and neglectful families and found a success rate of only 30% in neglect cases. During the course of intervention, abuse or neglect recurred in 66% of the cases. A review of 89 federally funded child abuse and neglect projects from 1974 to 1982 indicated that the most effective intervention strategies included (1) group approaches, (2) the use of nonprofessional laypeople, (3) skills training to supplement professional help, and (4) parent education and support groups (Gaudin, Wodarski, Arkinson, & Avery, 1991). The least successful projects were those that lasted less than six months, relied solely on casework, or focused on traditional parent counseling techniques. Cohn and Daro (1987) concluded that successful interventions with neglectful and abusing families must have multicomponent programs that include group approaches.

The effects of neglect on children are documented in studies conducted over the past 20 years. Compared with nonabused children, physically neglected children appear to display more behavior problems (Aragona & Eyberg, 1981); apathy and passivity, as well as less flexibility, persistence and enthusiasm (Crittenden, 1981); and academic problems (Hoffman-Plotkin & Twentyman, 1984; Kendall-Tackett & Eckenrode, 1996; Kent, 1976; Reidy, 1977). When compared with physically abused children, neglected children show poorer academic performance and have greater developmental delays and cognitive difficulties (Kent, 1976) and poorer or more delayed language development (Fox, Long, & Langlois, 1988). In addition, they seem to display more social and emotional withdrawal (Hoffman-Plotkin & Twentyman, 1984), lower self-esteem, and less confidence and assertiveness when given learning tasks (Egeland, Sroufer, & Erickson, 1983). In fact, Egeland and his colleagues wrote that physically neglected children present "the least positive and most negative affect" of all types of maltreated children (p. 469).

Extreme forms of psychological neglect can lead to nonorganic failure to thrive, a condition that can have devastating life-long consequences for the child (Erikson & Egeland, 1996; Mackner, Starr, & Black, 1997). Other long-term effects include disturbances in attachment and other psychological functioning in early adulthood (Gauthier, Stollak, Messé, & Aronoff, 1996). Finally, neglect has been determined to be a precursor to some forms of abuse of the neglected children (P. Ney, Fung, & Wickett, 1993, 1994).

Obviously, neglected children are at great risk for physical, academic, and psychological problems unless they and their families receive sustained intervention services. Although this need is clear, few studies exist that document successful assessment strategies and treatment programs for neglectful parents and their children.

ASSESSMENT

Many of the general assessment techniques utilized with physically, sexually, and psychologically maltreated children and families are also appropriate with neglectful families. Specific measures to assess children's cognitive, behavioral, and affective functioning and the family's functioning can be reviewed in the physical abuse section of this chapter. A series of instruments were developed and used during the 1980s to assess cases of neglect. One of the early measures was the CLL, an 80-item instrument developed by Polansky et al. (1978, 1981). The CLL measures physical care and emotional cognitive care. Items are scored as yes or no by a professional familiar with the family. Another instrument is the Home Observation for Measurement of the Environment (HOME; Bradley & Caldwell, 1979), a

45-item checklist that measures the quality and quantity of social, emotional, and cognitive support available to children. Items are scored by direct observation or parental report and result in six subscales. A separate form is available for infants to 3-year-olds and 3- to 5-year-old children. Several other measures can be used in the assessment process: the Home Accident Prevention Inventory (J. Lutzker, 1984); the Checklist for Living Environments to Assess Neglect (CLEAN), which measures home cleanliness (Watson-Perczel, Lutzker, Greene, & McGimpsey, 1988); the Child Neglect Severity Scale (Edgington, Hall, & Rosser, 1980); and the Indicators of the Caretaking Environment for Children Scale (Halper & Jones, 1981).

There has been an increase in interest in developing measures specific to neglect. New measures are being developed with special attention to psychometric properties, such as reliability and validity, which allow meaningful conclusions to be drawn from their use.

The Child Well-Being Scales (Gaudin, Polansky, & Kilpatrick, 1992) is a measure of physical and psychological care of children that has been shown to adequately differentiate neglecting and nonneglecting parents. The Ontario Child Neglect Index (Trocme, 1996) is a promising new instrument that rates the type and severity of neglect as observed by CPS workers. Initial investigations show that the instrument has adequate validity and reliability and is easy to use. The Scale of Parental Caregiving is a recently developed and yet-to-be validated brief checklist designed to be used by CPS workers in evaluating child neglect in individual families (Mindy & Pattinson, 1994).

In addition to the preceding checklists, Wolfe and his colleagues recommend that clinicians assess parent characteristics such as family background, marital relationship, parent psychopathology, health concerns, and parental stress, as well as child characteristics such as behavior problems, emotional problems, adaptive abilities, fears, and anxieties (Wolfe, 1988; Wolfe & Bourdeau, 1987). Writing about abuse and neglect, Belsky (1993) asserted that assessment should include parent factors (e.g., developmental history, history of abuse or neglect, personality, psychological resources); child factors (e.g., age, physical health, behavior); the parent-child interaction; and broader societal factors (e.g., availability and utilization of community and social support, and cultural resources). Clinicians should utilize self-report measures, reports of those familiar with the family, and direct observation to obtain a comprehensive view of the family.

As part of the assessment process, all children from neglectful families should be referred to a physician for a complete medical evaluation, if one has not been recently performed. Clinicians can assist parents in finding medical resources that are accessible to the family and monitor the family's medical appointments and proper use of any medication prescribed during the course of treatment.

TREATMENT

Outcome research in the treatment of neglect is sparse, owing to the tendency to combine abused and neglected children in treatment programs and to the poor methodology utilized in outcome studies (Heneghan, Horwitz, & Leventhal, 1996). Few treatment reports of neglectful families are available. One exception is the study of three neglectful parents by Dawson, deArmas, McGrath, and Kelly (1986). This study used behavioral techniques including modeling, shaping, practice, and feedback to improve parents' child care and problem-solving skills. The authors reported that the parents' skills improved and also generalized to untrained problem situations.

Perhaps one of the best-documented treatment programs for abusive and neglectful families is Project 12-Ways (J. Lutzker & Newman, 1986). The project provides in vivo treatment (e.g., in homes and schools) in an effort to improve generalization and reduce the stigma that may be attached to clinic-based programs. The services provided include training in parenting, stress reduction, assertiveness, self-control, leisure-time activities, job location, money management, health maintenance and nutrition, home safety, and behavior management in multiple settings. Other program components include basic skills training for children, marital counseling, social support groups, alcohol treatment and referral, and unwed mother services.

Based on recidivism data from 352 families receiving services from Project 12-Ways and 358 comparison families, Project 12-Ways appears to be successful in reducing future child abuse and neglect (J. Lutzker & Rice, 1987). However, abuse and neglect were not separated in this study, and it is unclear what percentage of the treatment families or families with repeated offences were neglectful families.

A home visitation program developed by Olds and colleagues (Olds, Henderson, & Kitzman, 1994; Olds, Henderson, Kitzman, & Cole, 1995; Olds et al., 1997) used nurses to visit first-time mothers and showed lower rates of child abuse and neglect, dependence on welfare, criminal behavior, and child behavior problems in a 15-year follow-up. As in other studies, abuse and neglect were not separated in this study.

A unique study, in that it focused specifically on neglectful families, was designed to reduce neglectful parenting through strengthening the informal support networks of the parents (Gaudin et al., 1991). The authors reported that two factors were significant obstacles in working with this sample of neglectful families: their lack of motivation and their extreme mobility. The project demonstrated that a social network intervention model that utilizes intensive casework, case management, advocacy, and interventions to strengthen the parents' informal network can improve the adequacy of both rural and urban low SES parents. There were significant improvements in parents' practices and attitudes over a 6- to 12-month intervention period when compared with matched control families who received only casework and case management services during the same period. However, the authors caution that, based on caseworker assessments, almost two-thirds of the parents in the project were seen as likely to maltreat again under stressful conditions.

CONCLUSIONS

Professionals and the general public now recognize child abuse and neglect as a major health and social problem with significant short- and long-term effects for children and their families. During the past decade, empirical research has focused primarily on the area of sexual abuse with only minimal research being conducted in other areas of maltreatment. However, overall progress has been made in the field through the development of professional organizations such as APSAC, the implementation of home visitation programs, and the formation of multidisciplinary teams to improve detection, diagnosis, and treatment of abused children.

During the 1990s, the American Psychological Association (APA) appointed an Oversight Committee and three Working Groups on child abuse issues. In addition, the Section on Child Maltreatment was established by Division 37 to increase psychologists' communication and research on maltreatment. These efforts have resulted in increased focus and publications, both empirical studies and information for the general public, by the APA.

Although progress has been made over the past 10 years, this chapter clearly reflects the major work to be done in effectively treating and preventing child maltreatment. Developing and empirically validating effective treatment and prevention programs for abused children and their families continues to be a major challenge for psychologists and other professionals during the next decade. In a field where the need for clinical expertise has not yet been matched by the availability of quality data to guide treatment decisions, implementation of the scientist-practitioner model by both researchers and clinicians is needed to improve the treatment of this increasingly referred population of children.

Clearly, the rates of neglect and the far-reaching consequences of neglect beg for more attention to effective assessment and intervention. The trend has begun, and future research should continue to use standardized measures, separate neglect from other types of abuse, and measure outcome through recidivism data as well as the children's long-term health, academic performance, and psychological adjustment. Innovative programs that address the most difficult aspects and concomitants of neglect (e.g., parental apathy, poverty, chaotic context in which neglect occurs) are necessary and should receive increased attention from researchers, treatment providers, and policymakers.

REFERENCES

Abidin, R. (1983). *Parenting Stress Index manual.* Charlottesville, VA: Pediatric Psychology Press.

Achenbach, T.M. (1991). *Manual for the Child Behavior Checklist 4–18 and 1991 profile.* Burlington: University of Vermont, Department of Psychiatry.

Alfaro, J.D. (1981). Report on the relationship between child abuse and neglect and later socially deviant behavior. In R.J. Hunner & Y.E. Walker (Eds.), *Exploring the relationship between child abuse and delinquency* (pp. 175–219). Montclair, NJ: Allanheld, Osmun.

American Academy of Child and Adolescent Psychiatry (AACAP). (1997). Practice parameters for the forensic evaluation of children and adolescents who may have been physically or sexually abused. *Journal of the American Academy of Child and Adolescent Psychiatry, 36*, 423–442.

American Association for Protecting Children. (1986). *Highlights of official child neglect and abuse reporting 1985*. Denver, CO: American Humane Association.

American Professional Society on the Abuse of Children (APSAC). (1995a). *Practice guidelines: Use of anatomical dolls in child sexual abuse assessments*. Chicago: Author.

American Professional Society on the Abuse of Children (APSAC). (1995b). *Psychosocial evaluation of suspected psychological maltreatment in children and adolescents*. Chicago: Author.

American Professional Society on the Abuse of Children (APSAC). (1997). *Guidelines for psychosocial evaluation of suspected sexual abuse in young children*. Chicago: Author.

Aragona, J.A., & Eyberg, S.M. (1981). Neglected children: Mothers' report of child behavior problems and observed verbal behavior. *Child Development, 52*, 596–602.

Axline, V. (1964). *Dibs in search of self*. New York: Ballantine.

Ayoub, C. (1991). Physical violence and preschoolers: The use of therapeutic day care in the treatment of physically abused children and children from violent families. *APSAC Advisor, 4*, 1–16.

Azar, S.T. (1997). A cognitive behavioral approach to understanding and treating parents who physically abuse their children. In D.A. Wolfe, R.J. McMahon, & R.D. Peters (Eds.), *Banff International Behavioral Science Series: Vol. 4. Child abuse: New directions in prevention and treatment across the lifespan* (pp. 79–101). Thousand Oaks, CA: Sage.

Azar, S.T., & Wolfe, D.A. (1989). Child abuse and neglect. In E.J. Mash & R.A. Barkley (Eds.), *Treatment of childhood disorders* (pp. 451–493). New York: Guilford Press.

Bagley, C., & Ramsay, R. (1985). Disrupted childhood and vulnerability to sexual assault: Long-term sequels with implications for counseling. *Social Work and Human Sexuality, 4*, 33–48.

Barnett, D., Manly, J.T., & Cicchetti, D. (1991). Continuing toward an operational definition of psychological maltreatment. *Development and Psychopathology, 3*, 19–29.

Barnett, E.A. (1984). Hypnosis in the treatment of anxiety and chronic stress. In W.C. Wester, II, & A.H. Smith, Jr. (Eds.), *Clinical hypnosis: A multidisciplinary approach* (pp. 458–475). Philadelphia: Lippincott.

Bayley, N. (1993). *Bayley Scales of Infant Development II (BSID-II)*. New York: Psychological Corporation.

Beitchman, J., Zucker, K., Hood, J., DaCosta, G., & Akman, D. (1991). Short-term effects of child sexual abuse. *Child Abuse and Neglect, 15*, 537–556.

Beland, K. (1985). *Talking about touching for parents and kids*. Seattle, WA: Committee for Children.

Bellak, L. (1993). *The Thematic Apperception Test, the Children's Apperception Test, and the Senior Apperception Technique in Clinical Use* (5th ed.). Boston: Allyn & Bacon.

Belsky, J. (1993). Etiology of child maltreatment: A developmental-ecological analysis. *Psychological Bulletin, 114*, 413–434.

Berdie, J., Berdie, M., Wexler, S., & Fisher, B. (1983). *An empirical study of families involved in adolescent maltreatment*. San Francisco: URSA Institute.

Berliner, L. (1991). Clinical work with sexually abused children. In C. Hollin & K. Howells (Eds.), *Clinical approaches: Sex offenders and their victims* (pp. 209–228). New York: Wiley.

Blank, J. (1980). *The playbook for kids about sex*. Burlingame, CA: Yes Press.

Blumberg, M. (1981). Depression in abused and neglected children. *American Journal of Psychotherapy, 35*, 342–355.

Bonner, B.L., Crow, S.M., & Logue, M.B. (1999). Fatal child neglect. In H. Dubowitz (Ed.), *Neglected children* (pp. 156–173). Thousand Oaks, CA: Sage.

Bonner, B.L., Walker, C.E., & Berliner, L. (1999). *Children with sexual behavior problems: Assessment and treatment: Final report*. Washington, DC: Office of Child Abuse and Neglect.

Boston Women's Health Book Collective. (1999). *The new our bodies, ourselves*. New York: Simon & Schuster.

Bowen, M. (1978). *Family therapy in clinical practice*. New York: Aronson.

Bradley, R.H., & Caldwell, B.M. (1979). Home Observation for Measurement of the Environment: A revision of the preschool scale. *American Journal of Mental Deficiency, 84*, 235–244.

Brassard, M.R., Germain, R., & Hart, S.N. (1987). *Psychological maltreatment of children and youth*. New York: Pergamon Press.

Brassard, M.R., & Hardy, D.B. (1997). Psychological maltreatment. In M.E. Helfer, R.S. Kempe, & R.D. Krugman (Eds.), *The battered child* (5th ed., pp. 392–412). Chicago: University of Chicago Press.

Brassard, M.R., Hart, S.N., & Hardy, D.B. (1991). Psychological and emotional abuse of children. In T. Ammerman & M. Hersen (Eds.), *Case studies in treating family violence* (pp. 255–270). Boston: Allyn & Bacon.

Brassard, M.R., Hart, S.N., & Hardy, D.B. (1993). The Psychological Maltreatment Rating Scale. *Child Abuse and Neglect, 17*, 715–729.

Bretherton, I. (1985). Attachment theory: Retrospect and prospect. In I. Bretherton & E. Waters (Eds.), *Growing points in attachment theory and research: Monographs of the Society for Research in Child Development, 50*(1–2, Serial No. 209). Chicago: University of Chicago Press.

Briere, J. (1996). *Trauma Symptom Checklist for Children (TSCC): Professional manual*. Odessa, FL: Psychological Assessment Resources.

Briere, J., & Runtz, M. (1988). Post sexual abuse trauma. In G.E. Wyatt & G.J. Powell (Eds.), *Lasting effects of child sexual abuse* (pp. 85–99). Newbury Park, CA: Sage.

Brooks, R. (1983). *So that's how I was born*. New York: Simon & Schuster.

Browne, K.D., & Lynch, M.A. (Eds.). (1997). Special issue on emotional maltreatment of children. *Child Abuse Review, 6*, 313–390.

Burnett, B.B. (1993). The psychological abuse of latency age children: A survey. *Child Abuse and Neglect, 17*, 441–454.

Butcher, J.N., Williams, C.L., Graham, J.R., Archer, R.P., Tellegen, A., Ben-Porath, Y.S., & Kaemmer, B. (1992). *Minnesota Multiphasic Personality Inventory–Adolescent*. Minneapolis: University of Minnesota Press.

Cantwell, H.B. (1997). The neglect of child neglect. In M.E. Helfer, R.S. Kemp, & R.D. Krugman (Eds.), *The battered child* (5th ed., pp. 347–373). Chicago: University of Chicago Press.

Celano, M. (1992). A developmental model of victims' internal attributions of responsibility for sexual abuse. *Journal of Interpersonal Violence, 7*, 57–69.

Celano, M., Hazzard, A., Webb, C., & McCall, C. (1996). Treatment of traumagenic beliefs among sexually abused girls and their mothers: An evaluation study. *Journal of Abnormal Child Psychology, 24*, 1–17.

Chaffin, M., Bonner, B., Worley, K., & Lawson, L. (1996). Treating abused adolescents. In J. Briere, L. Berliner, J. Bulkley, C. Jenny, & T. Reid (Eds.), *The APSAC handbook of child maltreatment* (pp. 119–139). Thousand Oaks, CA: Sage.

Child Abuse Prevention and Treatment Act, 42 U.S.C. § 107, 5102 (1983).

Cicchetti, D., & Toth, S.L. (1995). A developmental psychopathology perspective on child abuse and neglect. *Journal of the American Academy of Child and Adolescent Psychiatry, 34*, 541–565.

Cicchetti, D., Toth, S., & Bush, M. (1988). Developmental psychopathology and incompetence in childhood: Suggestions for intervention. In B.B. Lahey & A.E. Kazdin (Eds.), *Advances in clinical child psychology* (pp. 1–71). New York: Plenum Press.

Claussen, A.H., & Crittenden, P.M. (1991). Physical and psychological maltreatment: Relations among the types of maltreatment. *Child Abuse and Neglect, 15*, 5–18.

Cohen, J., & Mannarino, A. (1996). Factors that mediate treatment outcome of sexually abused preschool children. *Journal of the American Academy of Child and Adolescent Psychiatry, 34*, 1402–1410.

Cohen, J., & Mannarino, A. (1998). Factors that mediate treatment outcome of sexually abused preschool children: Six and 12-month follow-up. *Journal of the American Academy of Child and Adolescent Psychiatry, 37*, 44–51.

Cohn, A.H., & Daro, D. (1987). Is treatment too late? What ten years of evaluative research tell us. *Child Abuse and Neglect, 11*, 433–442.

Cole, J. (1993). *How you were born*. New York: Morrow Junior Books.

Conners, K. (1997). *Conners' Rating Scale–Revised (CRS-R): Parent and teacher form*. Tonawanda, NY: Multi Health Systems.

Conte, J.R., & Schuerman, J.R. (1988). The effects of sexual abuse on children: A multidimensional view. In G.E. Wyatt & G.J. Powell (Eds.), *Lasting effects of child sexual abuse* (pp. 157–170). Newbury Park, CA: Sage.

Coohey, C. (1998). Home alone and other inadequately supervised children. *Child Welfare, 77*, 291–310.

Cosentino, C., & Collins, M. (1996). Sexual abuse of children: Prevalence, effects, and treatment. *Annals of the New York Academy of Sciences, 789*, 45–65.

Crittenden, P.M. (1981). Abusing, neglecting, problematic, and adequate dyads: Differentiating by patterns of interaction. *Merrill-Palmer Quarterly, 27*, 201–218.

Crittenden, P.M. (1988a). Family and dyadic patterns of functioning in maltreating families. In K. Brown, C. Davies, & P. Stratton (Eds.), *Early prediction and prevention of child abuse* (pp. 161–189). New York: Wiley.

Crittenden, P.M. (1988b). Relationships at risk. In J. Belsky & T. Nezworski (Eds.), *Clinical implications of attachment* (pp. 137–174). Hillsdale, NJ: Erlbaum.

Crittenden, P.M., & Ainsworth, M.D.S. (1989). Child maltreatment and attachment theory. In D. Cicchetti & V. Carlson (Eds.), *Child maltreatment* (pp. 432–463). New York: Cambridge University Press.

Daro, D. (1988). *Confronting child abuse: Research for effective program design*. New York: Free Press.

David and Lucile Packard Foundation. (1999). Home visiting: Recent program evaluations. *Future of Children, 9*, 2–7.

Dawson, B., deArmas, A., McGrath, M.L., & Kelly, J.A. (1986). Cognitive problem-solving training to improve the child-care judgment of child neglectful parents. *Journal of Family Violence, 1*, 209–221.

Deblinger, E., Lippman, N.J., & Steer, R. (1996). Sexually abused children suffering post traumatic stress symptoms: Initial treatment outcome findings. *Child Maltreatment, 1*, 310–321.

Donohue, B., Miller, E.R., Van Hasselt, V.B., & Hersen, M. (1998). An ecobehavioral approach to child maltreatment. In V.B. Van Hasselt & M. Hersen (Eds.), *The LEA series in personality and clinical psychology: Handbook of psychological treatment protocols for children and adolescents* (pp. 279–356). Mahwah, NJ: Erlbaum.

Doueck, H.J., Ishisaka, A.H., Sweany, S.L., & Gilchrist, L.D. (1987). Adolescent maltreatment: Themes from the empirical literature. *Journal of Interpersonal Violence, 2,* 139–153.

Drake, B., & Pandey, S. (1996). Understanding the relationship between neighborhood poverty and specific types of child maltreatment. *Child Abuse and Neglect, 20,* 1003–1018.

Duquette, D.N., & Faller, K.C. (1988). Interdisciplinary teams in professional schools: A case study. In D.C. Bross, R.D. Krugman, M.R. Lenherr, D.A. Rosenberg, & B.D. Schmitt (Eds.), *The new child protection team handbook* (pp. 536–547). New York: Garland.

DuRubeis, R., & Beck, A. (1988). Cognitive therapy. In K. Dobson (Ed.), *Handbook of cognitive-behavioral therapists* (pp. 273–307). New York: Guilford Press.

D'Zurilla, T.J., & Goldfried, M.R. (1971). Problem solving and behavior modification. *Journal of Abnormal Psychology, 78,* 107–126.

Edington, A., Hall, M., & Rosser, R.S. (1980, June). *Neglectful families: Measurement of treatment outcome.* Paper presented at the Tri-regional Workshop for Social Workers in Maternal and Child Health, Raleigh, NC.

Egami, Y., Ford, D.E., Greenfield, S.F., & Crum, R.M. (1996). Psychiatric profile and sociodemographic characteristics of adults who report physically abusing or neglecting children. *American Journal of Psychiatry, 153,* 921–928.

Egeland, B. (1991a). From data to definition. *Development and Psychopathology, 3,* 37–43.

Egeland, B. (1991b). A longitudinal study of high-risk families: Issues and findings. In R.H. Starr & D.A. Wolfe (Eds.), *The effects of child abuse and neglect* (pp. 33–56). New York: Guilford Press.

Egeland, B., Jacobvitz, D., & Sroufe, L.A. (1988). Breaking the cycle of abuse. *Child Development, 59,* 1080–1088.

Egeland, B.A., Sroufe, L.A., & Erickson, M.F. (1983). The development of consequences of different patterns of maltreatment. *Child Abuse and Neglect, 7,* 459–469.

Elbedour, S., Center, B.A., Maruyama, G.M., & Assor, A. (1997). Physical and psychological maltreatment in schools. *School Psychology International, 18,* 201–215.

Erickson, M.F. (1988, March). *School psychology in preschool settings.* Paper presented at the annual meeting of the National Association of School Psychologists, Chicago.

Erickson, M.F., & Egeland, B. (1996). Child neglect. In J. Briere, J. Berliner, J. Bulkley, C. Jenney, & T. Reid (Eds.), *The APSAC handook on child maltreatment* (pp. 4–20). Thousand Oaks, CA: Sage.

Erickson, M.F., Egeland, B., & Pianta, R. (1989). The effects of maltreatment on the development of young children. In D. Cicchetti & V. Carlson (Eds.), *Child maltreatment: Theory and research on the causes and consequences of child abuse and neglect* (pp. 647–684). New York: Cambridge University Press.

Exner, J.E. (1978). *The Rorschach: A comprehensive system. Volume 1: Basic foundations.* New York: Wiley.

Exner, J.E. (1986). *The Rorschach: A comprehensive system. Volume 2: Basic foundations.* New York: Wiley.

Eyberg, S.M. (1979, April). *A parent-child interaction model for the treatment of psychological disorders in early childhood.* Paper presented at the annual meeting of the Western Psychological Association, San Diego, CA.

Eyberg, S.M., & Boggs, S.R. (1989). Parent training for oppositional-defiant preschoolers. In C.E. Schafer & J.M. Briesmeister (Eds.), *Handbook of parent training: Parents as co-therapists for children's behavior problems* (pp. 105–132). New York: Wiley.

Farber, E.A., & Egeland, B. (1987). Invulnerability among abused and neglected children. In E.J. Anthony & B.J. Cohler (Eds.), *The invulnerable child* (pp. 253–288). New York: Guilford Press.

Farber, E.A., & Joseph, J. (1985). The maltreated adolescent: Patterns of physical abuse. *Child Abuse and Neglect, 9,* 201–206.

Field, T. (1988). Stimulation of preterm infants. *Pediatric Review, 10,* 149–153.

Finkelhor, D. (1988). The trauma of child sexual abuse: Two models. In G.E. Wyatt & G.J. Powell (Eds.), *Lasting effects of child sexual abuse* (pp. 63–82). Newbury Park, CA: Sage.

Finkelhor, D. (1994). Current information on the scope and nature of child sexual abuse. *Future of Children, 4,* 31–53.

Finkelhor, D. (1995). The victimization of children: A developmental perspective. *American Journal of Orthopsychiatry, 65,* 177–193.

Finkelhor, D., & Berliner, L. (1995). Research on the treatment of sexually abused children: A review and recommendations. *Journal of the American Academy of Child and Adolescent Psychiatry, 34,* 1408–1423.

Finkelhor, D., & Browne, A. (1985). The traumatic impact of child sexual abuse: A conceptualization. *American Journal of Orthopsychiatry, 55,* 530–541.

Finkelhor, D., & Dziuba-Leatherman, J. (1995). Victimization prevention programs: A national survey of children's exposure and reactions. *Child Abuse and Neglect, 19,* 129–139.

Fisher, B., & Berdie, J. (1978). Adolescent abuse and neglect: Issues of incidence, intervention, and service delivery. *Child Abuse and Neglect, 2,* 178–192.

Fisher, B., Berdie, J., Cook, J., & Day, N. (1980). *Adolescent abuse and neglect: Intervention strategies.* Washington, DC: U.S. Government Printing Office.

Fleischman, M.J. (1979). Using parent salaries to control attrition and cooperation in therapy. *Behavior Therapy, 10*, 111–116.

Fleming, J., Mullen, P., & Bammer, G. (1997). A study of potential risk factors for sexual abuse in childhood. *Child Abuse and Neglect, 21*, 49–58.

Forehand, R.L., & McMahon, R.J. (1981). *Helping the noncompliant child: A clinician's guide to parent training.* New York: Guilford Press.

Fox, L., Long, S.H., & Langlois, A. (1988). Patterns of language comprehension deficit in abused and neglected children. *Journal of Speech and Hearing Disorders, 53*, 239–244.

Fraiberg, S. (Ed.). (1983). *Clinical studies in infant mental health: The first year of life.* New York: Basic Books.

Frankenburg, W.K., Dodds, J.B., Archer, P., Shapiro, H., & Bresnick, B. (1990). *Denver-II screening manual.* Denver, CO: Denver Developmental Materials.

Friedrich, W.N. (1990). *Psychotherapy of sexually abused children and their families.* New York: Norton.

Friedrich, W.N. (1996). An integrated model of psychotherapy for abused children. In J. Briere, L. Berliner, J. Bulkley, C. Jenny, & T. Reid (Eds.), *The APSAC handbook on child maltreatment* (pp. 104–118). Thousand Oaks, CA: Sage.

Friedrich, W.N. (1997). *Child Sexual Behavior Inventory: Professional manual.* Odessa, FL: Psychological Assessment Resources.

Friedrich, W., Grambsch, P., Damon, L., Hewitt, S., Koverola, C., Lang, R., Wolfe, V., & Broughton, D. (1992). Child Sexual Behavior Inventory: Normative and clinical comparisons. *Psychological Assessment, 4*, 303–311.

Frodi, A., & Smetana, J. (1984). Abused, neglected and nonmaltreated preschoolers' ability to discriminate emotions in others: The effects of IQ. *Child Abuse and Neglect, 8*, 459–465.

Gaensbauer, T.J., & Sands, K. (1979). Distorted affective communication in abused/neglected infants and their potential impact on caregivers. *Journal of the American Academy of Child Psychiatry, 18*, 236–250.

Garbarino, J. (1989). Troubled youth, troubled families: The dynamics of adolescent maltreatment. In D. Cicchetti & V. Carlson (Eds.), *Child maltreatment: Theory and research on the causes and consequences of child abuse and neglect* (pp. 685–706). New York: Cambridge University Press.

Garbarino, J., & Gilliam, G. (1980). *Understanding abusive families.* Lexington, MA: Lexington Books.

Gaudin, J.M., Polansky, N.A., & Kilpatrick, A.C. (1992). The child well-being scales: A field trial. *Child Welfare, 4*, 319–328.

Gaudin, J.M., Jr., Polansky, N.A., Kilpatrick, A.C., & Shilton, P. (1996). Family functioning in neglectful families. *Child Abuse and Neglect, 20*, 363–377.

Gaudin, J.M., Jr., Wodarski, J.S., Arkinson, M.K., & Avery, L.S. (1991). Remedying child neglect: Effectiveness of social network interventions. *Journal of Applied Social Sciences, 15*, 97–123.

Gauthier, L., Stollak, G., Messé, L., & Aronoff, J. (1996). Recall of childhood neglect and physical abuse as differential predictors of current psychological functioning. *Child Abuse and Neglect, 20*, 549–559.

Geffken, G., Johnson, S.B., Silverstein, J., & Rosenbloom, A. (1992). The death of a child with diabetes from neglect: A case study. *Clinical Pediatrics, 31*, 325–330.

Gelles, R.J. (1973). Child abuse as psychopathology: A sociological critique and reformulation. *American Journal of Orthopsychiatry, 43*, 611–621.

George, C., & Main, M. (1979). Social interactions of young abused children: Approach, avoidance, and aggression. *Child Development, 50*, 306–318.

Gersten, M., Coster, W., Schneider-Rosen, K., Carlson, V., & Cicchetti, D. (1986). The socio-emotional bases of communicative functioning: Quality of attachment, language development, and early maltreatment. In M.E. Lamb, A.L. Brown, & B. Rogoff (Eds.), *Advances in developmental psychology* (Vol. 4, pp. 105–151). Hillsdale, NJ: Erlbaum.

Gil, D.G. (1970). *Violence against children: Physical child abuse in the United States.* Cambridge, MA: Harvard University Press.

Gil, E. (1991). *The healing power of play: Working with abused children.* New York: Guilford Press.

Girard, L. (1984). *My body is private.* Morton Grove, IL: Albert Whitman.

Gitchel, S., & Foster, L. (1982). *Let's talk about . . . S-E-X.* Fresno, CA: Planned Parenthood.

Goldstein, A.P. (1990). *The prepare curriculum.* Champaign, IL: Research Press.

Goldstein, A.P., Glick, B., Irwin, M.J., Pask-McCartney, C., & Rubama, L. (1989). *Reducing delinquency: Intervention in the community.* New York: Pergamon Press.

Goldstein, A.P., Keller, H., & Erné, D. (1985). *Changing the abusive parent.* Champaign, IL: Research Press.

Guidano, V.F., & Liotti, G. (1983). *Cognitive processes and emotional disorders: A structural approach to psychotherapy.* New York: Guilford Press.

Halper, G., & Jones, M.A. (1981). *Serving families at risk of dissolution: Public preventative services in New York City.* New York: City of New York Human Resources Administration.

Harrington, D., Black, M.M., Starr, R.H., Jr., & Dubowitz, H. (1998). Child neglect: Relationship to child temperament and family context. *American Journal of Orthopsychiatry, 68*, 108–116.

Hart, S.N., Binggeli, N.J., & Brassard, M.R. (1998). Evidence for the effects of psychological maltreatment. *Journal of Emotional Abuse, 1*, 27–58.

Hart, S.N., Brassard, M.R., & Karlson, H.C. (1996). Psychological maltreatment. In J. Briere, L. Berliner, J. Bulkley, C. Jenny, & T. Reid (Eds.), *The APSAC handbook on child maltreatment* (pp. 72–89). Thousand Oaks, CA: Sage.

Harter, S. (1985). *Manual for the Self-Perception Profile for Children.* Denver, CO: University of Denver.

Harter, S. (1988). *Manual for the Adolescent Self-Perception Profile.* Denver, CO: University of Denver.

Helfer, R.E., Schneider, C.J., & Hoffmeister, J.K. (1978). *Report on research using the Michigan Screening Profile of Parenting (MSPP): A 12-year study to develop and test a predictive questionnaire.* Washington, DC: Department of Education, Office of Child Development.

Hembree-Kigin, T., & McNeil, C. (1995). *Parent-child interaction therapy.* New York: Plenum Press.

Heneghan, A.M., Horwitz, S.M., & Leventhal, J.M. (1996). Evaluating intensive family preservation programs: A methodological review. *Pediatrics, 97,* 535–542.

Henggeler, S.W., & Borduin, C.M. (1990). *Family therapy and beyond: A multisystemic approach to treating the behavior problems of children and adolescents.* Pacific Grove, CA: Brooks/Cole.

Herrenkohl, R.C., Herrenkohl, E.C., & Egolf, B.P. (1983). Circumstances surrounding the occurrence of child maltreatment. *Journal of Consulting and Clinical Psychology, 51,* 424–431.

Hoffman-Plotkin, D., & Twentyman, C.T. (1984). A multimodal assessment of behavioral and cognitive deficits in abused and neglected preschoolers. *Child Development, 55,* 794–802.

Howes, C., & Espinosa, M. (1985). The consequences of child abuse for the formation of relationships with peers. *Child Abuse and Neglect, 9,* 397–404.

Irueste-Montes, A.M., & Montes, F. (1988). Court-ordered vs. voluntary treatment of abusive and neglectful parents. *Child Abuse and Neglect, 12,* 33–39.

Ivey, A. (1987). *Developmental therapy.* San Francisco, Jossey-Bass.

Jezl, D.R., Molidor, C.E., & Wright, T.L. (1996). Physical, sexual and psychological abuse in high school dating relationships: Prevalence rates and self-esteem issues. *Child Abuse and Neglect, 13,* 69–87.

Jones, E.D., & McCurdy, K. (1992). The links between types of child maltreatment and demographic characteristics of children. *Child Abuse and Neglect, 16,* 201–215.

Jumper, S. (1995). A meta-analysis of the relationship of child sexual abuse to adult psychological adjustment. *Child Abuse and Neglect, 19,* 715–728.

Kagan, R., & Schlosberg, S. (1989). *Families in perpetual crisis.* New York: Norton.

Karpel, M. (Ed.). (1986). *Family resources: The hidden partner in family therapy.* New York: Guilford Press.

Kasian, M., & Painter, S.L. (1992). Frequency and severity of psychological abuse in a dating population. *Journal of Interpersonal Violence, 7,* 350–364.

Kaufman, A.S., & Kaufman, N.L. (1983). *K-ABC: Kaufman Assessment Battery for Children.* Circle Pines, MN: American Guidance Services.

Kaufman, J., Cook, A., Arney, L., Jones, B., & Pittinsky, T. (1994). Problems defining resiliency: Illustrations from the study of maltreated children. *Development and Psychopathology, 6,* 215–229.

Kaufman, J., Jones, B., Stieglitz, E., Vitulano, L., & Mannarino, A.P. (1994). The use of multiple informants to assess children's maltreatment experiences. *Journal of Family Violence, 9,* 227–248.

Kaufman, K., & Rudy, L. (1991). Future directions in the treatment of physical child abuse. *Criminal Justice and Behavior, 18,* 82–97.

Kelly, J.A. (1982). *Social-skills training: A practical guide for interventions.* New York: Springer.

Kelly, R.J., & Hansen, D.J. (1987). Social interactions and adjustments. In V.B. Van Hasselt & M. Hersen (Eds.), *Handbook of adolescent psychology* (pp. 131–146). New York: Pergamon Press.

Kempe, C.H., Silverman, F.N., Steele, B.F., Droegemuller, W., & Silver, H.K. (1962). The battered child syndrome. *Journal of the American Medical Association, 181,* 17–24.

Kendall, P. (1991). *Child and adolescent therapy: Cognitive-behavioral procedures.* New York: Guilford Press.

Kendall, P., & Finch, A. (1979). Changes in verbal behavior following a cognitive-behavioral treatment for impulsivity. *Journal of Abnormal Child Psychology, 7,* 455–463.

Kendall-Tackett, K.A., & Eckenrode, J. (1996). The effects of neglect on academic achievement and disciplinary problems: A developmental perspective. *Child Abuse and Neglect, 20,* 161–169.

Kendall-Tackett, K.A., Williams, L.M., & Finkelhor, D. (1993). Impact of sexual abuse on children: A review and synthesis of recent empirical studies. *Psychological Bulletin, 113,* 164–180.

Kent, J. (1976). A follow-up study of abused children. *Journal of Pediatric Psychology, 1,* 24–31.

Klein, M. (1932). *The psycho-analysis of children.* London: Hogarth Press.

Klosinski, G. (1993). Psychological maltreatment in the context of separation and divorce. *Child Abuse and Neglect, 17,* 557–563.

Knell, S. (1993). *Cognitive-behavioral play therapy.* Northvale, NJ: Aronson.

Kolko, D.J. (1996). Child physical abuse. In J. Briere, L. Berliner, J. Bulkley, C. Jenny, & T. Reid (Eds.), *The APSAC handbook on child maltreatment* (pp. 21–50). Thousand Oaks, CA: Sage.

Kovacs, M. (1992). *Children's Depression Inventory manual.* Los Angeles: Western Psychological Services.

Krugman, R., & Jones, D.P.H. (1987). Incest and other forms of sexual abuse. In R.E. Helfer & R.S. Kempe (Eds.), *The battered child* (4th ed., pp. 286–300). Chicago: University of Chicago Press.

Lacharite, C., Ethier, L., & Couture, G. (1996). The influence of partners on parental stress of neglectful mothers. *Child Abuse Review, 5,* 18–33.

Leahy, R.L. (1988). Cognitive therapy of childhood depression: Developmental considerations. In S.R. Shirk (Ed.), *Cognitive development and child psychotherapy* (pp. 187–206). New York: Plenum Press.

Lewis, D.O., Feiring, C., McGuffog, C., & Jaskir, J. (1984). Predicting psychopathology in six-year-olds from early social relations. *Child Development, 55,* 123–136.

Lutzker, J.R. (1984). Project 12-Ways: Treating child abuse and neglect from an ecobehavioral perspective. In R.F. Dangel & R.A. Polster (Eds.), *Parent training: Foundations of research and practice* (pp. 260–297). New York: Guilford Press.

Lutzker, J.R., Megson, D.A., Dachman, R., & Webb, M.E. (1985). Validating and training adult-child interaction skills to professionals and to parents indicated for child abuse and neglect. *Journal of Child and Adolescent Psychotherapy, 2,* 91–104.

Lutzker, J.R., & Newman, M.R. (1986). Child abuse and neglect: Community problem, community solutions [Special issue: Health promotion in children: A behavior analysis and public health perspective]. *Education and Treatment of Children, 9,* 344–354.

Lutzker, J.R., & Rice, J.M. (1987). Using recidivism data to evaluate Project 12-Ways: An ecobehavioral approach to the treatment and prevention of child abuse and neglect. *Journal of Family Violence, 2,* 283–290.

Lutzker, S.Z., Lutzker, J.R., Braunling-McMorrow, D., & Eddleman, J. (1987). Prompting to increase mother-baby stimulation with single mothers. *Journal of Child and Adolescent Psychotherapy, 4,* 2–12.

Mackner, L.M., Starr, R.H., Jr., & Black, M.M. (1997). The cumulative effect of neglect and failure-to-thrive on cognitive functioning. *Child Abuse and Neglect, 21,* 691–700.

Madanes, C. (1984). *Behind the one-way mirror: Advances in the practice of strategic therapy.* San Francisco: Jossey-Bass.

Main, M., & Goldwyn, R. (1984). Predicting rejection of her infant from mother's representation of her own experience: Implications for the abused-abusing intergenerational cycle. *Child Abuse and Neglect, 8,* 203–271.

Mann, E., & McDermott, J.F., Jr. (1983). Play therapy for victims of child abuse and neglect. In C. Schaefer & K. O'Connor (Eds.), *Handbook of play therapy* (pp. 283–307). New York: Wiley.

Mannarino, A., & Cohen, J. (1996). Abuse-related attributions and perceptions, general attributions, and locus of control in sexually abused girls. *Journal of Interpersonal Violence, 11,* 162–180.

Mannarino, A., Cohen, J., & Berman, S. (1994). The children's attributions and perceptions scale: A new measure of sexual abuse-related factors. *Journal of Clinical Child Psychology, 23,* 204–211.

Mazza, N., Magaz, C., & Scaturro, J. (1987). Poetry therapy and abused children. *Arts in Psychotherapy, 14,* 85–92.

McArthur, D.S., & Roberts, G.E. (1990). *Roberts Apperception Test for Children manual.* Los Angeles: Western Psychological Services.

McCord, J. (1979). A forty year perspective on effects of child abuse and neglect. *Child Abuse and Neglect, 7,* 265–270.

McGee, R.A., & Wolfe, D.A. (1991). Psychological maltreatment: Toward an operational definition. *Development and Psychopathology, 3,* 3–18.

McGee, R.A., Wolfe, D.A., & Wilson, S.K. (1990). *A record of maltreatment experiences.* Toronto: Institute for the Prevention of Child Abuse. (Available from D.A. Wolfe, Institute for the Prevention of Child Abuse, 25 Spadina Road, Toronto, Ontario, Canada, M5 R259)

McGee, R.A., Wolfe, D.A., & Wilson, S.K. (1997). Multiple maltreatment experiences and adolescent behavior problems: Adolescents' perspectives. *Development and Psychopathology, 9,* 131–149.

McGee, R.A., Wolfe, D.A., Yuen, S.A., Wilson, S.K., & Carnochan, J. (1995). The measurement of maltreatment: A comparison of approaches. *Child Abuse and Neglect, 12,* 233–249.

McGovern, K.B. (1985). *Alice doesn't babysit anymore.* Portland, OR: McGovern & Mulbacker Books.

McHugh, M. (1992). Child abuse in a sea of neglect: The inner-city child. *Pediatric Annals, 21,* 504–507.

Meichenbaum, D. (1977). *Cognitive-behavioral modification: An integrative approach.* New York: Plenum Press.

Mian, M., Marton, P., & LeBaron, D. (1996). The effects of sexual abuse on 3- to 5-year-old girls. *Child Abuse and Neglect, 20,* 731–745.

Millon, T., Green, C.J., & Meagher, R.B. (1982). *Millon Adolescent Personality Inventory manual (MAPI).* Minneapolis, MN: Interpretive Scoring Systems.

Milner, J.S. (1986). *The child abuse potential inventory: Manual* (Rev. ed.). Webster, NC: Psytec.

Milner, J.S. (1998). Individual and family characteristics associated with intrafamilial child physical and sexual abuse. In P.K. Trickett & C.J. Schellenbach (Eds.), *Violence against children in the family and the community* (pp. 141–170). Washington, DC: American Psychological Association.

Milner, J.S., & Crouch, J.L. (1993). Physical child abuse. In R.L. Hampton, T.P. Gullottoa, G.R. Adams, E.H. Potter,

& R.P. Weissberg (Eds.), *Family violence: Prevention and treatment* (pp. 25–55). Newbury Park, CA: Sage.

Mindy, B., & Pattinson, G. (1994). The nature of child neglect. *British Journal of Social Work, 24,* 733–747.

Minuchin, S., & Fishman, H.C. (1981). *Family therapy techniques.* Cambridge, MA: Harvard University Press.

Moos, R.H., & Moos, B.S. (1981). *Manual for the Family Environment Scale.* Palo Alto, CA: Consulting Psychologists Press.

Morgan, R. (1977). The battered adolescent: A developmental approach to identification and intervention. *Child Abuse and Neglect, 1,* 343–348.

Mrazek, P.J., & Mrazek, D.A. (1987). Resilience in child maltreatment victims: A conceptual exploration. *Child Abuse and Neglect, 11,* 357–366.

National Center on Child Abuse and Neglect. (1981). *Study findings: National study of the incidence and severity of child abuse and neglect* (Publication No. OHDS 81–30325). Washington, DC: U.S. Department of Health and Human Services.

National Center on Child Abuse and Neglect. (1988). *Study findings: Study of the national incidence and prevalence of child abuse and neglect.* Washington, DC: U.S. Department of Health and Human Services.

National Research Council. (1993). *Understanding child abuse and neglect.* Washington, DC: National Academy Press.

Nelson, K.E., Cross, T., Landsman, M.J., & Tyler, M. (1996). Native American families and child neglect. *Children and Youth Services Review, 18,* 505–522.

Nelson, K.E., Saunders, E.J., & Landsman, M.J. (1993). Chronic child neglect in perspective. *Social Work, 38,* 661–671.

Newberger, C.M. (1980). The cognitive structure of parenthood: The development of a descriptive measure. In R. Selman & R. Yando (Eds.), *New directions of child development: Clinical developmental research* (Vol. 7, pp. 45–67). San Francisco: Jossey-Bass.

Ney, P.G., Fung, T., & Wickett, A.R. (1993). Child neglect: The precursor to child abuse. *Pre- and Perinatal Psychology Journal, 8,* 95–112.

Ney, P.G., Fung, T., & Wickett, A.R. (1994). The worst combinations of child abuse and neglect. *Child Abuse and Neglect, 18,* 705–714.

Ney, T. (Ed.). (1995). *True and false allegations of child sexual abuse: Assessment and case management.* New York: Brunner/Mazel.

Nicol, A.R., Smith J., Kay, B., Hall, D., Barlow, J., & Williams, B. (1988). A focused casework approach to the treatment of child abuse: A controlled comparison. *Journal of Child Psychology and Psychiatry, 29,* 703–711.

Oates, R.K., & Bross, D.C. (1995). What have we learned about treating physical abuse? A literature review of the last decade. *Child Abuse and Neglect, 19,* 463–473.

Oates, R.K., Forrest, D., & Peacock, A. (1985). Self-esteem of abused children. *Child Abuse and Neglect, 9,* 159–163.

Oates, R.K., & Kempe, R.S. (1997). Growth failure in infants. In M.E. Helfer, R.S. Kempe, & R.D. Krugman (Eds.), *The battered child* (5th ed., pp. 374–391). Chicago: University of Chicago Press.

O'Donohue, W., & Elliott, A. (1992). Treatment of the sexually abused child: A review. *Journal of Clinical Child Psychology, 21,* 218–228.

O'Hagan, K. (1995). Emotional and psychological abuse: Problems of definition. *Child Abuse and Neglect, 19,* 449–461.

Olds, D.L., Eckenrode, J., Henderson, C.R., Jr., Kitzman, H., Powers, J., Cole, R., Sidora, K., Morris, P., Pettitt, L.M., & Luckey, D. (1997). Long-term effects of home visitation on maternal life course and child abuse and neglect: Fifteen-year follow-up of a randomized trial. *Journal of the American Medical Association, 278,* 637–643.

Olds, D.L., Henderson, C.R., & Kitzman, H. (1994). Does prenatal and infancy nurse home visitation have enduring effects on qualities of parental caregiving and child health at 25 and 50 months of life? *Pediatrics, 93,* 89–98.

Olds, D.L., Henderson, C.R., Kitzman, H., & Cole, R. (1995). Effects of prenatal and infancy nurse home visitation on surveillance of child maltreatment. *Pediatrics, 95,* 365–372.

Ollendick, T.H. (1983). Realiability and validity of the Revised Fear Survey Schedule for Children (FSSC-R). *Behaviour Research and Therapy, 21,* 685–692.

Olson, D.H., Portner, J., & Bell, R. (1982). *Family Adaptability and Cohesion Scales (FACES II).* St. Paul: University of Minnesota.

Parish, R., Myers, P., Brander, A., & Templin, K. (1985). Developmental milestones in abused children and their improvement with a family oriented approach to the treatment of child abuse. *Child Abuse and Neglect, 9,* 245–250.

Patterson, G.R. (1982). *Coercive family process.* Eugene, OR: Castalia.

Pelcovitz, D., Kaplan, S., Samit, C., Krieger, R., & Cornelius, P. (1984). Adolescent abuse: Family structure and implications for treatment. *Journal of the American Academy of Child Psychiatry, 23,* 85–90.

Peters, S.D. (1988). Child sexual abuse and later psychological problems. In G.E. Wyatt & G.J. Powell (Eds.), *Lasting effects of child sexual abuse* (pp. 101–117). Newbury Park, CA: Sage.

Piers, E.V., & Harris, D.B. (1996). *Piers–Harris Self-Concept Scale (PHSCS).* Los Angeles: Western Psychological Services.

Polansky, N.A., Chalmers, M.A., Buttenwieser, E.N., & Williams, D.D. (1978). Assessing adequacy of child caring: An urban scale. *Child Welfare, 576,* 441–449.

Polansky, N.A., Chalmers, M.A., Buttenwieser, E.N., & Williams, D.D. (1981). *Damaged parents: An anatomy of child neglect.* Chicago: University of Chicago Press.

Putnam, F., & Trickett, P. (1997). Psychobiological effects of sexual abuse. *Annals of the New York Academy of Sciences, 821,* 150–159.

Reeker, J., Ensing, D., & Elliott, R. (1997). A meta-analytic investigation of group treatment outcomes for sexually abused children. *Child Abuse and Neglect, 21,* 669–680.

Reidy, T.J. (1977). The aggressive characteristics of abused and neglected children. *Journal of Clinical Psychology, 33,* 1140–1145.

Reppucci, N.D., Land, D., & Haugaard, J.J. (1998). Child sexual abuse prevention programs that target young children. In P.K. Trickett & C.S. Schellenbach (Eds.), *Violence against children in the family and in the community* (pp. 317–338). Washington, DC: American Psychological Association.

Reynolds, C.R., & Kamphaus, R.W. (1992). *The Behavior Assessment System for Children (BASC).* Circle Pines, MN: American Guidance Service.

Reynolds, C.R., & Richmond, B.O. (1985). *Revised Children's Manifest Anxiety Scale.* Los Angeles: Western Psychological Services.

Rispens, J., Aleman, A., & Goudena, P. (1997). Prevention of child sexual abuse victimization: A meta-analysis of school programs. *Child Abuse and Neglect, 21,* 975–987.

Robin, A., Schneider, M., & Dolnick, M. (1976). The turtle technique: An extended case study of self-control in the classroom. *Psychology in the Schools, 13,* 449–453.

Rohner, R.P., & Rohner, E.C. (1980). Antecedents and consequences of parental rejection: A theory of emotional abuse. *Child Abuse and Neglect, 4,* 189–198.

Rose, S.J., & Meezan, W. (1996). Variations in perceptions of child neglect. *Child Welfare, 75,* 139–160.

Ross, A. (1981). *Child behavior therapy.* New York: Wiley.

Rossman, B.B.R., & Rosenberg, M.S. (1997). Psychological maltreatment: A needs analysis and application for children in violent families. *Journal of Aggression, Maltreatment, and Trauma, 1,* 245–262.

Ruggles, T.R., & LeBlanc, J.M. (1982). Behavior analysis procedures in classroom teaching. In A.S. Bellack, M. Hersen, & A.E. Kazdin (Eds.), *International handbook of behavior modification and therapy* (pp. 959–996). New York: Plenum Press.

Ruma, C. (1993). CBPT with sexually abused children. In S. Knell (Ed.), *Cognitive-behavioral play therapy* (pp. 197–230). Northvale, NJ: Aronson.

Runyan, D., Hunter, W., Everson, M., Whitcomb, D., & DeVos, E. (1994). The Intervention Stressors Inventory: A measure of the stress of intervention for sexually abused children. *Child Abuse and Neglect, 18,* 319–329.

Russell, A.B., & Trainor, C.M. (1984). *Trends in child abuse and neglect: A national perspective.* Denver, CO: American Humane Association.

Salinger, S., Kaplan, S., Pelcovitz, D., Samit, C., & Kreiger, R. (1984). Parent and teacher assessment of children's behavior in child maltreating families. *Journal of the American Academy of Child Psychiatry, 23,* 458–464.

Sameroff, A., & Fiese, B. (1990). Transactional regulations and early intervention. In S.J. Meisels & J.P. Shonkoff (Eds.), *Handbook of early childhood intervention* (pp. 119–149). Cambridge, England: Cambridge University Press.

Santostefano, S. (1985). *Cognitive control therapy with children and adolescents.* New York: Pergamon Press.

Schaefer, C. (1997). Defining verbal abuse of children: A survey. *Psychological Reports, 18,* 626.

Schaefer, C., & Briesmeister, J. (1989). *Handbook of parent training: Parents as co-therapists for children's behavior problems.* New York: Wiley.

Schaefer, E.S. (1965). Children's reports of parental behavior: An inventory. *Child Development, 36,* 413–424.

Schaefer, L.E., & Millman, H.L. (1981). *How to help children with common problems.* New York: Van Nostrand-Reinhold.

Schloss, P.J., Smith, M.A., & Schloss, C.N. (1990). *Instructional methods for adolescents with learning and behavior problems.* Boston: Allyn & Bacon.

Schwartz, J.C., & Zuroff, D.C. (1979). Family structure and depression in female college students: Effects of parental conflict, decision making power, and inconsistency of love. *Journal of Abnormal Psychology, 88,* 398–406.

Sedlak, A.J. (1990). *Technical amendment to the study findings: National incidence and prevalence of child abuse and neglect: 1988.* Rockville, MD: Westat.

Sedlak, A., & Broadhurst, D. (1996). *Executive summary of the third national incidence study of child abuse and neglect.* Washington, DC: U.S. Department of Health and Human Services.

Sedney, M.S., & Brooks, B. (1984). Factors associated with a history of childhood sexual experience in a nonclinical female population. *Journal of the American Academy of Child Psychiatry, 23,* 215–218.

Sgroi, S.M. (1982). *Handbook of clinical intervention in child sexual abuse.* Lexington, MA: Lexington Books.

Shure, M., & Spivack, G. (1978). *Problem-solving techniques in childrearing.* San Francisco: Jossey-Bass.

Silovsky, J.F., & Niec, L.N. (1998). *Group treatment for preschool children with problematic sexualized behavior: Program manual.* Unpublished treatment manual, University of Oklahoma Health Sciences Center, Oklahoma City.

Sirles, E.A., Walsma, J., Lytle-Barnaby, R., & Lander, L.C. (1988). Group therapy techniques for work with child sexual victims. *Social Work with Groups, 11,* 67–78.

Slusser, M. (1995). Manifestations of sexual abuse in preschool-aged children. *Issues in Mental Health Nursing, 16,* 481–491.

Sounders, P.G. (1986). When battered women use violence: Husband abuse or self-defense? *Violence and Victims, 1,* 49–60.

Spaccarelli, S. (1994). Stress, appraisal, and coping in child sexual abuse: A theoretical and empirical review. *Psychological Bulletin, 116,* 340–362.

Spaccarelli, S., & Kim, S. (1995). Resilience criteria and factors associated with resilience in sexually abused girls. *Child Abuse and Neglect, 19,* 1171–1182.

Sparrow, S.S., Balla, D.A., & Cicchetti, D.V. (1984). *Vineland Adaptive Behavior Scales: Expanded form manual* (Linterview ed.). Circle Pines, MN: American Guidance Service.

Spielberger, C.D. (1973). *Preliminary manual for the State-Trait Anxiety Inventory for Children.* Palo Alto, CA: Consulting Psychologists Press.

Spielberger, C.D., Gorsuch, R.L., & Lushene, R.E. (1970). *Manual for the State-Trait Anxiety Inventory.* Palo Alto, CA: Consulting Psychologists Press.

Spivack, G., Platt, J., & Shure, M. (1976). *Social adjustment of young children: A cognitive approach to solving real-life problems.* San Francisco: Jossey-Bass.

Sroufe, L.A., & Fleeson, J. (1986). Attachment and the construction of relationships. In W.W. Hartup & Z. Rubin (Eds.), *Relationships and development* (pp. 51–72). Hillsdale, NJ: Erlbaum.

Starr, R.H., Jr. (1982). A research based approach to the prediction of child abuse. In R.H. Starr, Jr. (Ed.), *Child abuse prediction: Policy implications* (pp. 105–134). Cambridge, MA: Ballinger.

Stauffer, L., & Deblinger, E. (1996). Cognitive behavioral groups for nonoffending mothers and their young sexually abused children: A preliminary treatment outcome study. *Child Maltreatment, 1,* 65–76.

Steward, M.S., Farquhar, L.C., Dicharry, D.C., Glick, D.R., & Martin, P.W. (1986). Group therapy: A treatment of choice for young victims of child abuse. *International Journal of Group Psychotherapy, 36,* 261–277.

Straus, M.A. (1979). Family patterns and child abuse in a nationally representative American sample. *Child Abuse and Neglect, 3,* 213–225.

Straus, M.A. (1995). *Manual for the Conflict Tactics Scale (CTS) and test forms for the revised Conflict Tactics Scale.* Durham: University of New Hampshire, Family Research Laboratory.

Straus, M.A. (1996). *Manual for the Conflict Tactics Scales.* Durham: University of New Hampshire, Family Research Laboratory.

Straus, M.A., & Hamby, S.L. (1997). Measuring physical and psychological maltreatment of children with the Conflict Tactics Scales. In G. Kaufman Kantar & M. Hersen (Eds.), *Out of the darkness: Contemporary perspectives on family violence* (pp. 119–135). Thousand Oaks, CA: Sage.

Sturkie, K. (1994). Group treatment for sexually abused children. *Child and Adolescent Psychiatric Clinics of North America, 3,* 813–829.

Tarter, R.E., Hegedus, A.E., Winsten, N.E., & Alternman, A.I. (1984). Neuropsychological, personality, and familiar characteristics of physically abused delinquents. *Journal of the American Academy of Child Psychiatry, 23,* 668–674.

Thompson, A.E., & Kaplan, C.A. (1996). Childhood emotional abuse. *British Journal of Psychiatry, 168,* 143–148.

Thorndike, R.L., Hager, E.P., & Sattler, J.M. (1986). *Guide for administering and scoring the Stanford–Binet Intelligence Scale* (4th ed.). Chicago: Riverside.

Tomm, K. (1984). One perspective on the Milan systemic approach: Part II. Description of session format, interviewing style, and interventions. *Journal of Marital and Family Therapy, 10,* 253–271.

Trocme, N. (1996). Development and preliminary evaluation of the Ontario Neglect Index. *Child Maltreatment, 1,* 145–155.

Turner, S.M., Calhoun, K.S., & Adams, H.E. (1981). *Handbook of clinical behavior therapy.* New York: Wiley.

U.S. Advisory Board on Child Abuse and Neglect. (1990). *Child abuse and neglect: Critical first steps in response to a national emergency* (Stock No. 014–092–00104–5). Washington, DC: U.S. Government Printing Office.

U.S. Department of Health and Human Services, Children's Bureau. (1998). *Child maltreatment 1996: Reports from the states to the national child abuse and neglect data system.* Washington, DC: U.S. Government Printing Office.

U.S. Department of Health and Human Services, Children's Bureau. (1999). *Child maltreatment 1997: Reports from the states to the national child abuse and neglect data system.* Washington, DC: U.S. Government Printing Office.

Wachter, O. (1983). *No more secrets for me.* Boston: Little, Brown.

Walker, C.E., Bonner, B.L., & Kaufman, K.L. (1988). *The physically and sexually abused child: Evaluation and treatment.* New York: Pergamon Press.

Watson-Perczel, M., Lutzker, J.R., Greene, B.F., & McGimpsey, B.J. (1988). Assessment and modification of home cleanliness among families adjudicated for child neglect. *Behavior Modification, 12,* 57–81.

Webb, N. (Ed.). (1991). *Play therapy with children in crises.* New York: Guilford Press.

Wechsler, D. (1989). *Manual for the Wechsler Preschool and Primary Scale of Intelligence–Revised.* New York: Psychological Corporation.

Wechsler, D. (1991). *Manual for the Wechsler Intelligence Scale for Children III.* New York: Psychological Corporation.

Wechsler, D. (1997). *Manual for the Wechsler Adult Intelligence Scale III (WAIS-III)*. San Antonio, TX: Psychological Corporation.

Wells, R., McCann, J., Adams, J., Voris, J., & Dahl, B. (1997). A validational study of the structured interview of Symptoms Associated with Sexual Abuse (SASA) using three samples of sexually abused, allegedly abused, and nonabused boys. *Child Abuse and Neglect, 21,* 1159–1167.

Wells, R., McCann, J., Adams, J., Voris, J., & Ensign, J. (1995). Emotional, behavioral, and physical symptoms reported by parents of sexually abused, nonabused, and allegedly abused prepubescent females. *Child Abuse and Neglect, 19,* 155–163.

Werner, E. (1988). Individual differences, universal needs: A 30 year study of resilient high risk infants. *Bulletin of the National Center for Clinical Infant Programs, 8,* 1–5.

Whipple, E.E., & Finton, S.E. (1995). Psychological maltreatment by siblings: An unrecognized form of abuse. *Child and Adolescent Social Work Journal, 12,* 135–146.

Wilding, J., & Thoburn, J. (1997). Family support plans for neglected and emotionally maltreated children. *Child Abuse Review, 6,* 343–356.

Wilkinson, G.S. (1993). *Wide Range Achievement Test III (WRAT-III)*. Wilmington, DE: Jastak Associates.

Williamson, J.M., Borduin, C.M., & Howe, B.A. (1991). The ecology of adolescent maltreatment: A multilevel examination of adolescent physical abuse, sexual abuse, and neglect. *Journal of Consulting and Clinical Psychology, 59,* 449–457.

Wirt, R.D., Lachar, D., Klinedinst, J.K., & Seat, P.D. (1990). *Multidimensional description of child personality: A manual for the Personality Inventory for Children*. Los Angeles: Western Psychological Services.

Wolfe, D.A. (1987). *Child abuse: Implications for child development and psychopathology*. Newbury Park, CA: Sage.

Wolfe, D.A. (1988). Child abuse and neglect. In E.J. Mash & L.G. Terdal (Eds.), *Behavior assessment of childhood disorders* (2nd ed., pp. 627–669). New York: Guilford Press.

Wolfe, D.A., Aragona, J., Kaufman, K., & Sandler, J. (1980). The importance of adjudication in the treatment of child abuse: Some preliminary findings. *Child Abuse and Neglect, 4,* 127–135.

Wolfe, D.A., & Bourdeau, P.A. (1987). Current issues in the assessment of abusive and neglectful parent-child relationships. *Behavioral Assessment, 9,* 271–290.

Wolfe, D.A., Edwards, B., Manion, I., & Koverola, C. (1988). Early intervention for child abuse and neglect: A preliminary investigation. *Journal of Consulting and Clinical Psychology, 56,* 40–47.

Wolfe, D.A., Kaufman, K., Aragona, J., & Sandler, J. (1981). *A child management program for abusive parents: Procedures for developing a child abuse intervention program*. Orlando, FL: Anna.

Wolfe, D.A., & Manion, I.G. (1984). Impediments to child abuse prevention: Issues and directions. *Advances in Behavior Research and Therapy, 6,* 47–62.

Wolfe, D.A., & McGee, R.A. (1994). Dimensions of child maltreatment and their relationship to adolescent adjustment. *Development and Psychopathology, 6,* 165–182.

Wolfe, D.A., & Mosk, M.D. (1983). Behavioral comparisons of children from abusive and distressed families. *Journal of Consulting and Clinical Psychology, 51,* 702–708.

Wolfe, D.A., & Wekerle, C. (1993). Treatment strategies for child physical abuse and neglect: A critical progress report. *Clinical Psychology Review, 13,* 473–500.

Wolfe, V., Gentile, C., Michienzi, T., Sas, L., & Wolfe, D. (1991). The Children's Impact of Traumatic Events Scale: A measure of post-sexual-abuse PTSD symptoms. *Behavioral Assessment, 13,* 359–383.

Wolfe, V.V., & Wolfe, D.A. (1988). The sexually abused child. In E.J. Mash & L.G. Terdal (Eds.), *Behavioral assessment of childhood disorders* (2nd ed., pp. 670–714). New York: Guilford Press.

Woodcock, R.W., & Johnson, M.B. (1990). *Woodcock–Johnson Psycho-Educational Battery–Revised (WJ-R)*. Allen, TX: DLM Teaching Resources.

Wyatt, G.E., & Peters, S.D. (1986). Issues in the definition of child sexual abuse in prevalence research. *Child Abuse and Neglect, 10,* 231–240.

CHAPTER 51

Children and Divorce

H. ELIZABETH KING

Nearly one million children a year in the United States will experience their parents' divorce (U.S. Bureau of Census, 1992). It appears that 50% to 60% of American children will live in a single-parent household, typically headed by mothers, for some period of their life. Almost three-quarters of the fathers and two-thirds of the mothers will remarry (Booth & Edwards, 1992; Cherlin & Furstenberg, 1994). Because the rate of divorce is 10% higher for second marriages than for first marriages, many of these remarriages will also fail (Cherlin & Furstenberg, 1994), particularly those involving once-divorced women. Almost half of all the children whose parents divorce will be in a stepfamily within four years, and the rate of divorce for remarried families in which children are present is 50% higher. Statistics vary from country to country, but divorce has become commonplace.

THE PROCESS OF DIVORCE

There are significant difficulties in most families prior to divorce. The decision to dissolve a marriage, particularly one involving children, is typically reached only after years of unhappiness and conflict. Separating or divorcing adults are significantly distressed. Children are exposed to unhappy, if not depressed, parents with an impaired ability to provide a happy, supportive home environment.

In some cases, helpless and frightened children have viewed unhappy scenes, rage attacks, or losses of control by one or both parents. Parents often model behaviors that, when exhibited by the child, are of great concern to parents, schoolteachers, and mental health professionals alike. The extent to which the divorced parents can achieve a harmonious coparenting relationship is a crucial factor in children's postdivorce adjustment.

The postdivorce adjustment period for parents can be lengthy. Hetherington, Cox, and Cox (1977) noted a two-year course of emotional adjustment postdivorce for both mothers and fathers. Wallerstein and Corbin (1989) reported that many parents had not yet adjusted to the divorce two or three years later. The length of time parents are consumed with their own emotional reactions is significant, causing them to have reduced parenting capacities.

The divorce process also entails many changes in family roles and relationships. Changes in the family structure and the child's loss of time with both parents are inevitable. Each parent is coping with new responsibilities and an altered lifestyle. In most families (70% to 90%), the children will reside primarily with the mother. Most women who must cope with new financial demands and less free time find the challenges of being a custodial parent exhausting. Children are faced with two losses: (1) the father no longer resides with the child; and (2) the mother is not as available physically or emotionally. Fathers find themselves living apart from their children and must create a new relationship in circumstances that may feel artificial and constrained. Not only are parental roles changing, but parents are also adapting to a new relationship with each other.

CHILDREN'S EMOTIONAL REACTIONS TO DIVORCE AND LONG-TERM IMPACT

WALLERSTEIN'S LONGITUDINAL STUDIES

Wallerstein and Kelly (1980) conducted the first major large-scale longitudinal study of children and their parents after divorce. Their findings indicate that the initial reactions of children of all ages include distress, sadness, and anger. This reaction is expressed in behaviors typical for the developmental stage of the child, but regression is frequent. After the initial disequilibrium, a period of adjustment occurs during the next two to three years. Their work indicated that child factors most related to short-term and intermediate adjustment included sex, age, developmental level of the child, and child temperament. Quality of life in the single-parent home, quality of parenting, interparental cooperation, and the social support system of the child were the external factors noted to significantly impact the child's adjustment to divorce.

Wallerstein (1984, 1985, 1986, 1987) conducted a 10-year follow-up of the children in her original study. Children who were preschoolers at the time of divorce had no memory of their intact family, but they felt that divorce was an important aspect of their lives. These children had an intense awareness of their father, regardless of the amount of contact with them. One-third of the children had irregular visits (extended vacations or five times a year) with their father, and one-fourth had one contact a year at most. During adolescence, many of these children attempted to reach out and reestablish a relationship with their father.

School-age children at the time of the divorce were concerned with issues of loss, particularly loss of their father and the protective family unit. Forty percent of the children had tried living with their father, and 25% moved into the father's home permanently. For those who still resided with their mother, fewer than 10% had no contact with the father. The frequency of visits was not important to

the long-term outcome for boys or girls; however, the quality of the father-son relationship was significantly related to the psychological outcome for boys. One-third of the teenagers were viewed as doing well at the 10-year follow-up; however, half of the boys and one-fourth of the girls had moderate to clinical levels of depression and had difficulties in relationships.

Adolescents at the time of the divorce, who were young adults 19 to 28 years of age at the time of the follow-up, were generally undereducated. Only 50% were in school at follow-up. Of the 50% out of school, 30% were unemployed. Only 66% were attending or had graduated from college or graduate school, in contrast to the 85% rate of the graduates from their high school. Lack of finances was the major factor in failure to attend college. Two-thirds of the fathers failed to assist with college tuition regardless of financial circumstances. Two-thirds of this group felt that their childhood or adolescence had been burdened by the divorce, and fully one-third of the women were having problems in heterosexual relationships as adults.

Wallerstein and Lewis (1998) provided 25-year follow-up data on the children who were between 2.5 and 6 years of age at the time of the divorce. This group was viewed as the most vulnerable because of their needs for physical care and emotional nurturance. A great part of their childhood was spent in a single-parent or stepfamily. The 26 preschoolers who were in the initial study were 27 to 32 years of age at follow-up. Half of the sample were involved with serious drug and alcohol abuse. Although 25% of the fathers refused any further support when the children were 18 years of age, and only 6 of the 26 received full financial support for their higher education from parents or stepfathers, over 40% received a college degree.

Relationships with fathers were less stable than expected in spite of little interparental conflict. The fathers' interest in their children had fluctuated widely as a function of vocational issues or romantic relationships. Remarriage was prevalent. The stepmothers' attitude and the presence of children within the new family were powerful influences on the fathers' contact with and financial generosity to their children. When fathers were unable to adapt to or understand the child's changing needs, visits deteriorated. Young adolescent girls appeared especially problematic for their fathers.

Intense anger at their father was expressed by a subgroup of children who were forced to maintain a strict schedule of visits in spite of the child's changing developmental and social needs. None of the children who had a rigidly enforced court-ordered visitation schedule or unmodified arrangement had a good relationship with their father in adulthood. These children objected to their lack of input about their lives. They felt they had less freedom or control over their lives than did their peers. This failure of parents (and the legal system) to acknowledge these children's changing developmental requirements was a major problem.

Although largely clinical in nature, Wallerstein's work and subsequent articles have humanized the children of divorce, and she has provided a better understanding of the additional coping tasks faced by these families. The lack of control groups limits the conclusions that can be drawn, and these findings may overpathologize the children of divorce. Societal changes have reduced the stigma of divorce, increased awareness of the importance of addressing higher education in divorce decrees, and focused attention on the important role of fathers in their children's development. Although many past problems might be mitigated and current divorces may be less destructive, the child's interpretation of divorce and the negative psychological consequences remain.

KALTER'S THEORETICAL MODEL OF DIVORCE IMPACT

Kalter (1987) has offered a helpful theoretical model of divorce as a process with two developmental components, one within the child and one within the unfolding developmental process of the divorce. Kalter contends that divorce can potentially interfere with three key developmental achievements in children. The first is the capacity to modulate aggression. The child's feelings of hurt, created by one parent's departure, are defended against by anger or aggression. Maladaptive models of conflict resolution are presented to the child by the parents, and parental attempts to model self-control frequently fail. Children may undercontrol or overcontrol angry feelings. Some children may act out with noncompliance and aggression. Excessive inhibition of aggression may occur in other children who feel inadequate or unaccepted.

The child's ability to emotionally separate from his or her parents is a second key developmental task. The feeling of firm psychological and emo-

tional acceptance at home is necessary to become independent and feel secure in leaving home. Fathers often serve as a bridge for independence and autonomy. In single-parent homes, the children often feel less secure and confident about separating.

The third task Kalter (1987) notes is that of development of gender identity. Divorce with frequent father absence often means the lack of a positive masculine role model for boys' gender identification. Girls may feel abandoned and rejected and view their feminine role model, the mother, as rejected as well. The distant or absent father cannot assist the girl in valuing her femininity, nor is he available to assist her in learning feminine behaviors.

Kalter's assertion that divorce complicates children's positive gender identification has been supported empirically. Many of the girls in Wallerstein's (1985) group were having significant difficulties with heterosexual relationships in young adulthood. Hetherington (1972) reported that adolescent girls from divorced homes had more negative attitudes and more conflicts with their fathers and also had more heterosexual activity than did girls from intact families or girls whose fathers had died. Kalter, Riemer, Brickman, and Chen (1985) suggested that the sexually precocious behavior of girls from divorced families might be in part the result of a devalued sense of femininity. Low feminine self-esteem may be caused by the father's absence and the resulting failure to confirm the girl's femininity and make her feel valued. In their follow-up study of the same girls, Hetherington et al., (1977) found that daughters from divorced families married younger, had a higher incidence of pregnancy at the time of marriage, and had a higher divorce rate than daughters of widows or daughters from intact families. Girls from divorced homes also had the most negative perception of their father, husband, and men in general. In a large study of Finnish children age 16 to 22, Palosaari, Aro, and Laippala (1996) found depression more common among the offspring of divorced families. Moreover, the long-term impact of divorce among girls was mediated via low self-esteem and lack of closeness to the father. When the girls had a close relationship with their father, no excess risk of depression was noted. This study also supported Kalter's hypothesis that fathers assist girls in separating from their mothers.

It does appear that the loss of the father as a role model for boys and as a facilitator of developing self-esteem and comfort with sexual identity for girls can be very problematic. It is less clear how much contact is needed to ameliorate these problems. At the present time, it appears that the loss of sufficient contact with the father postdivorce is likely to impact boys most significantly during the latency years, and that their problems will largely be academic or behavioral. The difficulties for girls appear to be related to self-esteem, depression, and heterosexual relationships and are most likely to emerge during adolescence.

FACTORS AFFECTING CHILDREN'S ADJUSTMENT TO DIVORCE

AGE

Wallerstein and Corbin (1989) contend that preschoolers are at greatest risk for problems postdivorce. They spend the least amount of time in the nuclear family, are often confused about family events, and may blame themselves for the divorce. In addition, preschoolers do not understand the abrupt and multiple changes or losses and are likely to experience much loss or abandonment because they are also least able to reach out and obtain support from others. Allison and Furstenberg (1989) and Zill, Morrison, and Coiro (1993) found preschoolers more likely to develop long-term problems in social and emotional development. Confounding variables such as length of time since divorce and remarriage, as well as factors such as father access and conflict, make conclusions about age effects impossible. Findings supportive of a "vulnerable period" in childhood for the parental divorce were reported by Pagani, Boulerice, Tremblay, and Vitaro (1997). They followed 1,316 children from divorced, never remarried families from the end of kindergarten until the beginning of adolescence. They used parent and teacher ratings and controlled for preceding behavioral predispositions while in the intact family. Children who experienced their parents' divorce before the age of 6 exhibited comparatively more behavioral problems than children whose parents divorced later. Early childhood divorce was linked to increases in anxiety, hyperactivity, and oppositional behavior during later childhood.

Adolescence is another vulnerable period. Adolescents in divorced families are likely to become involved in alcohol abuse and sexual acting-out and show symptoms of depression (Wallerstein &

Corbin, 1989). Hetherington (1993; Hetherington & Jodl, 1994) notes that in contrast to the 10% of adolescents in intact families, 25% to 33% of adolescents in divorced and remarried families become disengaged from their families. Hetherington and Jodl noted that adolescents spend little time at home and avoid communication, interaction, and activities with family members. Disengagement may be a positive solution to a disruptive or conflicted family situation, or it may result in antisocial behavior and academic problems in adolescents (Hetherington, 1993).

GENDER

Earlier reports suggested that divorce was more harmful for boys, but recent data suggest inconsistencies. Some researchers suggested that boys respond to divorce with externalizing behaviors such as conduct disorder, and girls internalize distress, which results in depressive symptomology (Emery, 1982); however, both male and female adolescents from divorced families show higher rates of depression and conduct disorder than do those from intact families (Amato & Keith, 1991a; Hetherington, 1993; Hetherington & Clingempeel, 1992; Hetherington & Jodl, 1994). Although both males and females are likely to become teenage parents, girls are more likely to drop out of school, and pregnancy has more adverse consequences for them (McLanahan & Sandefur, 1994).

PARENTAL FUNCTIONING AND PARENT-CHILD RELATIONSHIP

As is true for intact families, the mental health and parenting skills of the parents and the quality of the parent-child relationship are strongly related to the child's well-being in divorced families. Parents who divorce may have problems in relation to their children as much as 8 to 12 years prior to divorce. Parenting difficulties include irritable, erratic, and nonauthoritative behaviors (Amato & Booth, 1996; Block, Block & Gjerde, 1986). Some of the behavior problems noted in children of divorce may be a function of genetics or child-rearing practices rather than the divorce itself. Additionally, children have been found to have poor adjustment prior to divorce (Amato & Keith, 1991b; Block et al., 1986; Cherlin et al., 1991). When research has controlled for child problems occurring before the divorce, the differences between divorced and intact families were significantly reduced (Cherlin et al., 1991).

Wallerstein (1986) found that chronic anger or psychopathology in the custodial parent was related to poor outcome for the child. In her study, the quality of the relationship of the child with both parents was important. The child's relationship with the mother was related to short- and long-term outcomes. The relationship with the father was related to long-term outcome.

Child temperament, including irritability, reactivity, and adaptability, are important to consider. Difficult children create more problems in families and may elicit more rejection or negative behaviors from parents or other adults. Adaptable, easygoing children who have a sense of humor are temperamentally better prepared to weather any family crisis and are better able to elicit support from others (Hetherington, Bridges, & Insabella, 1998).

ECONOMIC DISADVANTAGES

Divorce is associated with a marked decline in income for households in which mothers retain custody. Forty-three percent of divorced custodial mothers have an annual income of less than $10,000 (Hernandez, 1988). Most divorced women lack the education, skills, and job experience to successfully compete in the economic marketplace and they cannot support their children comfortably. Kalter (1987) reported that 33% of the children of divorced parents live at or below the poverty level. Of the remaining 67%, many experience wrenching economic changes. This financial disruption may in part be a result of the fact that large proportions of fathers fail to pay child support (Haskins, Schwartz, Akin, & Dobelstein, 1985).

Economic changes postdivorce result in changes in residence, school, and neighborhood. New neighborhoods are seldom of the same socioeconomic status as the previous one, and the schools may be poorly financed with inadequate resources (e.g., books, magazines, computers). Most children are conscious of the decreased socioeconomic level and may feel stigmatized by their reduced economic circumstance.

Studies have noted that such sudden downward shifts in socioeconomic status are frequently correlated with child adjustment difficulties (Hetherington, 1979a, 1979b; Hodges, Wechsler, &

Ballantine, 1979). Other studies have shown that when family income is statistically equated, differences between rates of behavior problems in children from divorced and from intact families are eliminated (Colletta, 1979; MacKinnon, Brody, & Stoneman, 1982). Desimone-Luis, O'Mahoney, and Hunt (1978) found that those children with the most pronounced behavior difficulties following divorce were from homes with severe economic loss immediately following the divorce.

Guidubaldi, Cleminshaw, Perry, and McLoughlin (1983) reported that without controls for income, children in divorced families scored significantly lower than children in intact families on 27 of 34 outcome measures. When income levels were controlled, the differences shrunk to only 14 of the 34 outcome variables. The authors concluded that children from divorced homes do more poorly, particularly with regard to academic issues, in large part because they are economically disadvantaged.

Social and legal changes in child support guidelines and women's increased advancement in the workplace have made an impact on the economic situation. Although the economic picture may be improving for mother-only families, the changes are not sufficient. Most recent data indicate that poverty rates for mother-only families in 1989 were 43%. The contrast to father-only families is stark: Those families had poverty rates of only 18%. Fathers heading families have mean personal incomes almost twice that of mothers heading families: $24,000 to $13,000 in 1989 (Meyer & Garasky, 1993). In a recent review, Bianchi, Subaiya, and Kahn (1997) found that custodial mothers experience the loss of 25% to 50% of their predivorce income in comparison to only 10% for custodial fathers.

PARENTAL CONFLICT

Many children of divorce witness a continued conflictual relationship between their parents. Several investigators have proposed that the most important mediating variable associated with divorce and child adjustment is this conflict. There is evidence to suggest that parental conflict, not parental separation, is the major factor responsible for postdivorce child maladjustment.

Whitehead (1979) studied children's responses to family discord and separation. The results suggested that discord is more detrimental than separation and that antisocial behavior associated with marital tension is more likely to be exhibited at school by boys. Hess and Camara (1979) found that the level of parental harmony, mother-child relations, and father-child relations were better predictors of aggressive behavior than divorce. Wallerstein and Kelly (1980) and Hetherington (1989) noted that parental conflict was a critical mediating variable for child problems postdivorce. The finding that parental conflict, not divorce, is the underlying factor causing most long-term behavior problems in the children of divorce is prevalent in the literature (Hess & Camara, 1979; Jacobson, 1978; Johnston, Kline, & Tschann, 1989; Kurdek & Fine, 1993; Leupnitz, 1982).

When conditions of high conflict continue with divorced parents, frequent contact with noncustodial parents may exacerbate children's problems. Johnston, Gonzales and Campbell (1987) and Johnston et al. (1989) found that children in high-conflict, frequent contact situations were depressed, withdrawn, and uncommunicative. This situation was particularly adverse for girls' adjustment.

Longitudinal studies suggest that divorce improves the adjustment of children removed from conflictual marriages, but harms children removed from nonconflictual marriages (Amato, Loomis, & Booth, 1995). Maccoby and colleagues contend that the type of conflict is also important. Their studies (Buchanan, Maccoby, & Dornbusch, 1991; Maccoby, Buchanan, Mnookin, & Dornbusch, 1993; Maccoby & Mnookin, 1992) demonstrate that conflicts involving the children are the most detrimental to the children's well-being.

COMPARATIVE ANALYSIS OF THREE FACTORS RELATED TO CHILD OUTCOME

Amato and Keith (1991a) conducted a meta-analysis of 92 studies involving over 13,000 children to evaluate three central notions frequently used to explain the negative impact of divorce on children: parental absence, economic disadvantage, and family conflict. Their analysis states that contact appears to operate in a complex fashion, with factors such as sex of child and parent, relationship of child and parent, and relationship between parents playing significant roles. The impact of economic disadvantage was an important factor causing the children of divorce to fare poorly. Economic decline

accounted for some, but certainly not all, of the negative consequences of divorce. The family conflict perspective was most strongly supported. The majority of studies relating postdivorce conflict with children's well-being found a significant association between conflict and a child's problems. The data support the notion that conflict between parents is a critically important variable underlying children's problems postdivorce.

SUMMARY

In Amato and Keith's (1991b) review, more than two-thirds of the studies found that children with divorced parents had lower levels of well-being than did children from intact homes. They note, however, that the effect sizes in the literature are weak rather than strong. Further, they contend that the negative implications of parental divorce for children's well-being have become less pronounced since the 1950s and 1960s. They argue that the adjustment of children from divorced or remarried families is similar to that of children from intact families (Amato & Keith, 1991b; Cherlin & Furstenberg, 1994; Hetherington, 1989). Most of these children do not have problems and will become normal, competent individuals (Emery & Forehand, 1994).

Other authors assert that children of divorce are more vulnerable to problems in adjustment and more likely to have problems with academics, self-esteem, social skills, and behavior. As adolescents, the children of divorce are more likely to exhibit behavior problems, drop out of school, become sexually active, and have social problems (Amato & Keith, 1991a; Hetherington et al., 1998; Hetherington & Clingempeel, 1992). There is disagreement as to the size of divorce-related effects on children's adjustment. Some researchers view these effects as modest (Amato & Keith, 1991a). Others note that the children of divorce are twice as likely to have problems as children from intact families (Hetherington, 1989, 1991a; Hetherington & Clingempeel, 1992; Hetherington & Jodl, 1994; Zill et al., 1993).

The complexity of the many factors contributing to children's difficulties postdivorce is discussed in detail by Hetherington et al. (1998). They conclude that conflictual family relationships between parents, parents and children, and siblings are a significant factor. Other factors—the individual vulnerability of parents and/or children; family composition, parental absence; stress, including socioeconomic factors; and parental distress leading to problematic parenting—also play a role. Some may have a direct effect, others, such as parenting abilities, are mediated through the impact on the family process, but all appear relevant to children's adjustment postdivorce.

TYPES OF CUSTODIAL ARRANGEMENTS

MOTHER CUSTODY

Approximately 84% of children reside with their mothers following divorce (Seltzer, 1994). The mother's relationship with her children changes dramatically. The vast majority of divorced women work full time, and preschool children often feel abandoned postdivorce. Placement in a day-care facility often results in multiple illnesses for at least the first year. Also, many mothers resent or feel unhappy working even if highly trained. Additionally, studies suggest that divorce and maternal employment have a negative impact on the environments of preschool children. MacKinnon et al. (1982) reported that preschool children in mother-headed divorced households experienced less stimulation than children from intact households even when family income was controlled. Eighteen months later, children from mother-headed households were receiving more stimulation at follow-up than at the initial assessment, but they continued to receive less cognitive and social stimulation than children in married households.

Hetherington, Cox, and Cox (1977, 1979) found that although the divorce group improved over two years postdivorce, differences still existed in the social behavior of children from divorced and married households. Immediately after divorce, there is often a period of disruptive or maladaptive parenting characterized by irritability, coercion, diminished communication, less affection, and inconsistency in control and monitoring (Hetherington, 1991a, 1991b, 1993; Simons & Johnson, 1996). Hetherington (1991a) noted that the parenting of divorced mothers improves over the course of two years, but remains less authoritative than that of nondivorced mothers. Problems in control and

coercive exchanges between divorced mothers and sons may remain high.

Santrock and Warshak (1979; Santrock, Warshak, & Elliott, 1982) compared the social development of children from father custody, mother custody, and intact homes. Observation of parent-child interactions nearly three years postdivorce found mother-custody homes were associated with girls being less demanding and more mature, sociable, and independent than boys. Father-custody boys were mature, warm, and independent; however, girls in father custody were less warm, mature, sociable, and independent. The authors conclude that custody by the same-sex parent is related to more positive social behaviors for children. Support for the same-sex hypothesis was also noted by Camara and Resnick (1989). Other studies indicate that the same-sex custodial parent has greater influence on the adjustment of adolescents in divorced homes (Furman & Buhrmester, 1992; Kurdek & Fine 1993).

Positive adjustment in children and adolescents is typically found with custodial mothers who have close relationships with their children. Supportive, authoritative mothers who exert firm, consistent control and supervision and who are warm are generally associated with children's positive adjustment (Bray & Berger, 1993; Forehand, Thomas, Wierson, Brody, & Fauber, 1990; Hetherington, 1989, 1993; Hetherington & Clingempeel, 1992; Maccoby et al., 1993; Simons & Johnson, 1996). During adolescence, there is a notable increase in conflict between mothers and their daughters (Hetherington, 1991a; Hetherington & Clingempeel, 1992). Low levels of parental supervision were noted by Demo and Acock (1996).

FATHER CUSTODY

Father-headed families are the fastest growing family type in the United States (Meyer & Garasky, 1993). Fathers who seek custody of their children are often more involved and capable; therefore, custodial fathers are a very select group of fathers who are more likely to be child-oriented than most fathers. Custodial fathers report less child-rearing stress, better parent-child relations, and fewer behavior problems in their children than do custodial mothers (Amato & Keith, 1991a; Clarke-Stewart & Hayward, 1996; Furstenberg, 1988). Fathers, however, appear to have more problems with communication, self-disclosure, and monitoring of their children's activities (Chase-Lansdale & Hetherington, 1990; Furstenberg, 1988; Warshak, 1986), in particular, with monitoring adolescent behaviors, especially those of daughters (Maccoby et al., 1993).

Clarke-Stewart and Hayward (1996) reported on a recent study of 187 school-age children. Children in father-custody were doing better than children in mother-custody in terms of psychological well-being, self-esteem, depression, anxiety, and exhibition of "deficient problem behaviors." This advantage was most clear for boys, but true for both sexes. The authors note the advantages of the custodial fathers: higher income, fewer children, and a better emotional support system. Additionally, the authors note that the noncustodial parent, the mother, continued to be involved with the children. Further, although children in the father-custody group were doing better than the children in mother custody, children in mother custody who had high levels of contact with their father were functioning equally as well. This study provides support for the notion that fathers can be excellent custodial parents. Equally important are the findings that involvement with both parents was a critical factor in good adjustment for boys and girls regardless of custody arrangement.

NONCUSTODIAL MOTHERS AND THEIR CHILDREN

Although noncustodial mothers are less competent than custodial mothers in monitoring and controlling their children's behavior, they are more effective in this than are noncustodial fathers (Furstenberg & Nord, 1987; Lindner-Gunnoe, 1993). Overall, noncustodial mothers are more active and supportive in response to the needs of their children than are noncustodial fathers (Furstenberg & Nord, 1987; Lindner-Gunnoe, 1993; Santrock & Sitterle, 1987). Children report talking more with their noncustodial mothers than to noncustodial fathers.

In a study by Clarke-Stewart and Hayward (1996) comparing mother-custody and father-custody homes, the role of the noncustodial mother in children's adjustment was critical. Noncustodial mothers remained more involved with their children than did noncustodial fathers. This finding of continued emotional closeness occurred despite the fact that there was no difference between the noncustodial parents in the amount or kind of contact.

Further, children in father custody who had a negative relationship with their noncustodial mother had poorer psychological well-being than children whose relationship was good. No similar findings occurred with regard to noncustodial fathers.

NONCUSTODIAL FATHERS AND CHILDREN

For most children of divorce, their relationship with their father alters significantly. For many children, the relationship is lost. In Hetherington et al.'s (1977) two-year longitudinal study of divorced fathers, almost 20% of the fathers decreased their visits over time, and complete loss of contact did occur in some cases. In a national survey of children between 11 and 16 years of age, Furstenberg and Saltzer (1983) indicated that almost half of the children of divorce had not had any contact with the visiting parent during the preceding five years. Furstenberg, Nord, Peterson, and Zill (1983) found that the loss of the relationship with the father occurs at separation and escalates over the period of separation. For children whose parents had divorced seven years previously, 33% of the children saw their fathers two to three times a year or less and 37% did not see their fathers at all. There appeared to be a high correlation of lack of father contact with remarriage of either parent. These data indicate less frequent father-child contact than reported by Wallerstein (1986; Wallerstein & Blakeslee, 1989), but may be more representative.

The postdivorce parenting behavior of fathers is less predictable from their predivorce behavior than is the case with mothers (Hetherington, Cox, & Cox, 1985). Noncustodial fathers appear less likely than nondivorced fathers to monitor or control their children's behavior or to participate in tasks such as homework (Bray & Berger, 1993; Furstenberg & Nord, 1987; Hetherington, 1991b). Perhaps because of the limited access to their children and the desire for contacts to be positive, most noncustodial fathers have more of a companion relationship than a traditional parenting relationship with their children (Furstenberg & Nord, 1987; Hetherington et al., 1979).

Frequency of contact of noncustodial fathers is usually unrelated to adjustment in children (Amato & Keith, 1991b). Quality of the parental relationship with the child appears most important (Amato, 1993; Emery, 1988). Factors that impact the father's ability to maintain a good relationship include the father's interest in the child, his ability to focus on the child's needs and to appropriately alter activities, the ability of the mother to support the child's relationship with the father, and the lack of parental conflict.

PARENTS WITH JOINT CUSTODY

Joint custody has become a frequently used post-divorce arrangement in the past 20 years. It is believed to be an advantageous arrangement because it (1) continues the active involvement of both parents, (2) encourages child support payments because of this involvement, and (3) provides relief from child care for both parents, thus improving their quality of life. The lack of consistent operational definitions regarding joint custody complicates any discussion or assessment of this arrangement. Further, the profound differences between families who voluntarily enter this arrangement and those who enter it reluctantly (via mediation or custody evaluations) and those on whom it is enforced (litigation) make assessment problematic. The literature is far from conclusive.

Initial studies of joint custody involved highly educated, upper-middle-class families with fewer than three children who voluntarily chose the custodial arrangement. These studies focused on parental adjustment and parental satisfaction with different forms of custody, and found that both parents maintained active roles in the lives of their children and were satisfied with the arrangement (Ahrons, 1980; Arbabanel, 1979; Grief, 1979; Rothberg, 1983; Steinman, 1981). In a critical review of the research literature, Benjamin and Irving (1989) found that only 5 of 21 studies provided any data about the children.

Leupnitz (1982) compared children from maternal custody, paternal custody, and joint custody families on a variety of psychological measures and found no differences based on type of custody. Similar findings were reported by Leupnitz (1986), Wolchik, Braver, and Sandler (1985), and Kline, Tschann, Johnston, and Wallerstein (1989). Although Shiller (1986a, 1986b) reported that boys in joint custody had fewer behavioral difficulties and were less distressed than boys in sole maternal custody, the joint custody parents had less current parental conflict than the parents in the sole custody group; therefore, the reason for differences in child outcome was unclear.

Johnston (1995) reviewed five major custody studies: Kline et al. (1989), Maccoby and Mnookin (1992), Pearson and Thoennes (1990), Johnston et al. (1989), and Johnston (1992). Johnston found few, if any, differences in child adjustment as a function of custody type. She noted that one-third of the joint custody children drifted into the primary care of the mother. Those families remaining in a joint custody arrangement typically had parents who were more educated and financially stable.

A small minority of divorcing parents remain in ongoing conflict for two or more years (Johnston et al., 1989; Maccoby & Mnookin, 1992), and this conflict has a detrimental impact on children, particularly in situations where children experience frequent access (as in joint custody). Those arrangements are associated with more emotional and behavioral disturbances among children, especially girls (e.g. depressed, withdrawn, aggressive, somatic complaints, and peer problems). Johnston et al. (1989) noted that the most problematic arrangements appear to be court-ordered joint custody arrangements.

CONCLUSIONS REGARDING CUSTODY/PARENTAL ACCESS

Few, if any, consistent differences in the adjustment of children in different custody arrangements were noted. The actual physical custody and visitation arrangements were less important than the quality of the ensuing family relationships. Good adjustment for children was highly related to the parents' psychological functioning and the quality of the parent-child relationships. A warm, supportive relationship with a custodial parent who is able to maintain consistent expectations and appropriate monitoring of the child protects the child's development (Buchanan, Maccoby, & Dornbusch, 1992; Kline, Johnston, & Tschann, 1991; Pearson & Thoennes, 1990).

Children benefit from regular predictable access to both parents, but access patterns should be influenced by the child's developmental needs and must be responsive to development and social needs. Child adjustment is enhanced by a stable support system, including school, social activities, and peers. Frequent transitions between homes and/or high degrees of access to both parents in situations of high conflict is detrimental and likely to result in emotional and behavioral problems in boys and girls.

Successful joint physical custody arrangements typically involve parents who are better educated and have higher incomes (Maccoby & Mnookin, 1992; Pearson & Thoennes, 1990). The logistical difficulties and level of parental involvement and commitment require flexibility, accommodation, and determination on the part of both parents. The child's characteristics are important. The child must have sufficient adaptability so that transitions between homes are not confusing or distressing. There is a tendency over time for self-selection in the custody arrangement best suited for the individual family. Children in joint residential arrangements often drifted back into the primary care of the mothers. Children who remain in the joint care of their parents do so because the arrangement suits them and their parents.

PSYCHOLOGICAL INTERVENTION

Many types of interventions are available and have been utilized with children and parents who are divorcing (Benedek & Benedek, 1979) or who have divorced. Advice to the separating parent, individual psychotherapy with the child (Gardner, 1976; Tessman, 1978), and children's groups (Kalter & Rubin, 1989; Stolberg & Walsh, 1988; Wilkinson & Black, 1977) are among the most popular interventions. Some therapists advocate a strategy of family therapy with the single-parent unit. Kalter (1984) describes conjoint mother-daughter treatment. The choice of intervention strategy for clinicians will be a function of the particular family situation, the needs of the child, the child's age and developmental level, the parents' concerns about the children, their openness to therapy, and their ability to resolve continuing conflict with each other. Indirect intervention in the form of bibliotherapy can be useful as well.

INTERVENTION WITH PARENTS

Predivorce Counseling with One or Both Parents
The decision to separate is difficult, and many parents request assistance in making decisions regarding custody, patterns of visitation, and communication of the news of the separation to the child. Custodial recommendations are to be avoided

unless the professional has conducted a custody evaluation. Discussions about custody or visitation arrangements should focus on the child's stage of development as well as personality, temperament, and current relationships. It is often helpful to review for parents that infants or preschoolers have difficulties with separation and lack a concept of time. Parents should be encouraged to make arrangements that facilitate the child's relationship with both parents but do not tax the child's coping abilities. It is useful to suggest that different schedules or patterns of access will be needed during the child's changing stages of development. Issues that are typical for children when their parents separate, such as regressive behaviors, should be addressed and normalized. Difficulties and transitions should also be anticipated and coping techniques discussed with both parents. Collaboration between parents should be encouraged.

Parents often need assistance with when and how to inform a child of the impending separation. Lengthy, confusing, adult-oriented discussions or "blaming" talks should be avoided. Parents should be helped to monitor their distress and to explain the separation without intense expressions of anger toward each other. Parents should be encouraged to inform others such as pediatricians, school, and neighbors of the separation. Children benefit from having support from neutral adults during this period of crisis.

Recommendations should include the avoidance of additional stress. Changes such as moving into a new home, going to a different school, obtaining a new housekeeper, or placing children in day care should be avoided or postponed if possible. Divorce, like any other crisis, is best dealt with in a manner that maximizes the child's coping skills. This most frequently occurs when children are in familiar surroundings and can utilize their already established social support systems.

Postdivorce Counseling
The focus of intervention with recently separated parents is typically twofold: the clinician must be supportive and helpful to the parents regarding their personal difficulties and problems in adjustment and, equally important, must provide constructive and helpful guidance regarding the child. Education about divorce from the child's perspective and typical reactions of children to stress is a major component of such counseling. Parent coordinators are

being used more frequently in difficult or high-conflict situations. The professional is asked to assist the parents in determining appropriate decisions for their child in varying custody and visitation arrangements. These decisions include length of vacations, transition arrangements, school choices, and discussions about relocation. Obviously, the professional must be sensitive to issues of child development, as well as able to use strategies for couples in counseling and mediation. Therapists often find articles or books regarding divorce useful in terms of educating parents about the divorce process. *Surviving the Breakup* (Wallerstein & Kelly, 1980), *The Parent's Book about Divorce* (Gardner, 1979), *Divorced Dads* (Shepard & Goldman, 1980), and *Second Chances* (Wallerstein & Blakeslee, 1989) are four that are helpful.

INTERVENTION WITH CHILDREN

Children are seen in brief psychotherapy to assist their recognizing the reality of the separation and divorce, dealing with the loss of the intact family unit, resolving their fears that the divorce is their fault, and detriangulating from the parental discord that so frequently accompanies separation and divorce. In addition to providing a safe and supportive atmosphere for grieving, the child often needs permission to express the anger and rage experienced as a result of the divorce or separation. Children may fear abandonment and will be relieved to learn that the noncustodial parent does not plan to leave them.

Some children experience overwhelming and immobilizing feelings that can damage their self-esteem and self-concept. The therapist should be reassuring and focus on repairing the damaged self-esteem. Additionally, the therapist can often assist the child in recognizing that these negative feelings of sadness and powerlessness are appropriate in such a situation.

Books such as *The Boys' and Girls' Book of Divorce* (Gardner, 1970), *What Every Child Wants His Parents to Know* (Salk, 1973), and *The Dinosaur's Divorce* (Brown & Brown, 1986) have proved to be very successful with school-age children and adolescents. Johnston and Roseby's (1997a) *High-Conflict, Violent and Separating Families: A Group Treatment Manual for School-Age Children* is an excellent resource for clinicians dealing with this population.

School-Based Child-Directed Groups

Child groups conducted in schools are a relatively new area of intervention that appears to be a very useful modality for assisting children of divorce in understanding their situation and preventing or reducing psychopathology. The Divorce Adjustment Project: Children's Support Group (CSG) (Stolberg & Garrison, 1985), the subsequent spinoff, Children of Divorce Intervention Project (CODIP) (Pedro-Corrall & Cowen, 1985), and Kalter and Rubin's (1989) school-based support groups are similar. The focus of these groups is (1) to help children understand divorce-related events, thereby reducing their anger, frustration, and self-blame; (2) to help children adapt to the changes in their lives; and (3) to help build internal controls in the children by teaching them problem-solving skills and cognitive-behavioral strategies. Groups provide peer and adult support to the children and help normalize the divorce process.

SUMMARY

Successful interventions range from traditional play therapy to nontraditional family therapy and innovative children's groups in schools. Therapists' knowledge of the short- and long-term effects of divorce on parents and children, as well as the salient age and gender variables, is critical. Finally, anyone conducting therapy with divorced parents or children from divorced homes needs to recognize the most predictable problematic factors: (1) reaction of the child to the loss of the intact family, (2) ongoing parental discord, and (3) reaction of the child to deprivation of a relationship with the noncustodial parent. The particular strategy of intervention is less important than the therapist's ability to provide emotional support to the parent and/or the child while dealing with the preceding factors. Clinicians will find excellent resources in *Children of Parting Parents* (Tessman, 1978), *Psychotherapy with Children of Divorce* (Gardner, 1976), *Children of Divorce* (Wolchik & Karoly, 1988), and Wallerstein and Blakeslee's (1989) *Second Chances*. Kalter's articles "Conjoint Mother-Daughter Therapy" (1984) and "Long-Term Effects of Divorce on Children" (1987) are also valuable resources. Therapists who elect to work with parents who are conflicted postdivorce will find *Impasses of Divorce* (Johnston & Campbell, 1988), *Caught in the Middle,* (Garrity & Baris, 1994), and *In the Name of the Child* (Johnston & Roseby, 1997b) useful resources.

REFERENCES

Ahrons, C. (1980). Joint custody arrangements in the post-divorce family. *Journal of Divorce, 3,* 189–205.

Allison, P.D., & Furstenberg, F.F., Jr. (1989). How marital dissolution affects children: Variations by age and sex. *Developmental Psychology, 25,* 540–549.

Amato, P.R. (1993). Children's adjustment to divorce: Theories, hypotheses, and empirical support. *Journal of Marriage and the Family, 55,* 23–38.

Amato, P.R., & Booth, A. (1996). A perspective study of divorce and parent-child relationships. *Journal of Marriage and the Family, 58,* 356–365.

Amato, P.R., & Keith, B. (1991a). Parental divorce and adult well being: A meta-analysis. *Journal of Marriage and the Family, 53,* 43–58.

Amato, P.R., & Keith, B. (1991b). Parental divorce and the well being of children: A meta-analysis. *Psychological Bulletin, 110,* 26–46.

Amato, P.R., Loomis, L.S., & Booth, A. (1995). Parental divorce, marital conflict, and offspring well-being during adulthood. *Social Forces, 73,* 895–915.

Arbabanel, A. (1979). Shared parenting after separation and divorce: A study of joint custody. *American Journal of Orthopsychiatry, 49,* 320–329.

Benedek, R., & Benedek, E. (1979). Children of divorce: Can we meet their needs? *Journal of Social Issues, 35,* 155–169.

Benjamin, M., & Irving, H.H. (1989). Shared parenting: Critical review of the research literature. *Family and Conciliation Courts Review, 27,* 21–35.

Bianchi, S.M., Subaiya, L., & Kahn, J. (1997, March). Economic well-being of husbands and wives after marital disruption. Paper presented at the annual meeting of the Population Association of America, Washington, DC.

Block, J.H., Block, J., & Gjerde, P.F. (1986). The personality of children prior to divorce: A prospective study. *Child Development, 57,* 827–840.

Booth, A., & Edwards, J.N. (1992). Starting over: Why remarriages are more unstable. *Journal of Family Issues, 13,* 179–194.

Bray, J.H., & Berger, S.H. (1993). Developmental issues in Stepfamilies Research Project: Family relationships and parent-child interactions. *Journal of Family Psychology, 7,* 76–90.

Brown, L.K., & Brown, M. (1986). *The dinosaur's divorce.* Boston: Little, Brown.

Buchanan, C.M., Maccoby, E.E., & Dornbusch, S.M. (1991). Caught between parents: Adolescents' experience in divorced homes. *Child Development, 62,* 1008–1029.

Buchanan, C.M., Maccoby, E.E., & Dornbusch, S.M. (1992). Adolescents and their families after divorce: Three residential arrangements compared. *Journal of Research on Adolescence, 2,* 261–291.

Camara, K.A., & Resnick, G. (1989). Styles of conflict resolution and cooperation between divorced parents: Effects on child behavior and adjustment. *Journal of Orthopsychiatry, 59,* 560–575.

Chase-Lansdale, P.L., & Hetherington, E.M. (1990). The impact of divorce on life-span development: Short and long term effects. In P.D. Baltes, D.L. Featherman, & R.M. Lerner (Eds.), *Life-span development and behavior* (Vol. 10, pp. 105–150). Hillsdale, NJ: Erlbaum.

Cherlin, A.J., & Furstenberg, F.F. (1994). Stepfamilies in the United States: A reconsideration. In J. Blake & J. Hagen (Eds.), *Annual review of sociology* (pp. 359–381). Palo Alto, CA: Annual Reviews.

Cherlin, A.J., Furstenberg, F.F., Chase-Lansdale, P.L., Kiernan, K.E., Robins, P.K., Morrison, D.R., & Teitler, J.O. (1991). Longitudinal studies of effects of divorce in children in Great Britain and the United States. *Science, 252,* 1386–1389.

Clarke-Stewart, K.A., & Hayward, C. (1996). Advantages of father custody and contact for the psychological well-being of school-age children. *Journal of Applied Developmental Psychology, 17,* 239–270.

Colletta, N. (1979). The impact of divorce: Father absence or poverty? *Journal of Divorce, 3,* 27–35.

Demo, D.H., & Acock, A.C. (1996). Family structure, family process, and adolescent well-being. *Journal of Research on Adolescence, 6,* 457–488.

Desimone-Luis, J., O'Mahoney, K., & Hunt, D. (1978). Children of separation and divorce: Factors influencing adjustment. *Journal of Divorce, 3,* 37–42.

Emery, R.E. (1982). Interpersonal conflict and the children of discord and divorce. *Psychological Bulletin, 92,* 310–330.

Emery, R.E. (1988). *Marriage divorce and children's adjustment.* Newbury Park, CA: Sage.

Emery, R.E., & Forehand, R. (1994). Parental divorce and children's well-being: A focus on resilience. In R.J. Haggerty, L.R. Sherrod, N. Garmezy, & M. Rutter (Eds.), *Stress, risk and resilience in children and adolescents* (pp. 64–99). Cambridge, England: Cambridge University Press.

Forehand, R., Thomas, A.M., Wierson, M., Brody, G., & Fauber, R. (1990). Role of maternal functioning and parenting skills in adolescent functioning following divorce. *Journal of Abnormal Psychology, 99,* 278–283.

Furman, W., & Buhrmester, D. (1992). Age and sex differences in perceptions of networks of personal relationships. *Child Development, 63,* 103–115.

Furstenberg, F.F., Jr. (1988). Child care after divorce and remarriage. In E.M. Hetherington & J.D. Arasteh

(Eds.), *Impact of divorce, single parenting, and stepparenting on children* (pp. 245–261). Hillsdale, NJ: Erlbaum.

Furstenberg, F.F., Jr., & Nord, C.W. (1987). Parenting apart: Patterns of childbearing after marital disruption. *Journal of Marriage and the Family, 47,* 893–904.

Furstenberg, F.F., Jr., Nord, C.W., Peterson, J.L., & Zill, N. (1983). The life course of children of divorce: Marital disruption and parental contact. *American Sociological Review, 48,* 656–668.

Furstenberg, F.F., & Saltzer, J.A. (1983). *Divorce and child development.* Paper presented at a meeting of the American Orthopsychiatric Association, Boston.

Gardner, R. (1970). *The boys' and girls' book about divorce.* New York: Aronson.

Gardner, R. (1976). *Psychotherapy with children of divorce.* New York: Aronson.

Gardner, R. (1979). *The parents' book about divorce.* NewYork: Bantam Books.

Garrity, C.B., & Baris, M.A. (1994). *Caught in the middle: Protecting the children of high-conflict divorce.* New York: Lexington Books.

Grief, J.B. (1979). Fathers, children and joint custody. *American Journal of Orthopsychiatry, 49,* 311–319.

Guidubaldi, J., Cleminshaw, H.K., Perry, J.D., & McLoughlin, C.S. (1983). The impact of parental divorce on children: Report of the nationwide NASP study. *School Psychology Review, 12,* 300–323.

Haskins, R., Schwartz, J.B., Akin, J.S., & Dobelstein, A.W. (1985). How much support can absent fathers pay? *Policy Studies Journal, 14,* 201–222.

Hernandez, D.J. (1988). Demographic trends and the living arrangements of children. In E.M. Hetherington & J.D. Arasteh (Eds.), *Impact of divorce, single-parenting and step-parenting on children* (pp. 3–22). Hillsdale, NJ: Erlbaum.

Hess, R., & Camara, K.A. (1979). Postdivorce family relationships as mediating factors in the consequences of divorce for children. *Journal of Social Issues, 35,* 79–97.

Hetherington, E.M. (1972). Effects of father absence on personality development in adolescent daughters. *Developmental Psychology, 7,* 313–326.

Hetherington, E.M. (1979a, August). *Children and divorce.* Presidential address: Division 7, American Psychological Associates Convention, New York.

Hetherington, E.M. (1979b). A child's perspective. *American Psychologist, 34,* 851–858.

Hetherington, E.M. (1989). Coping with family transitions: Winners, losers, and survivors. *Child Development, 60,* 1–14.

Hetherington, E.M. (1991a). Families, lies, and videotapes. *Journal of Research on Adolescence, 1,* 323–348.

Hetherington, E.M. (1991b). The role of individual differences in family relations in coping with divorce and remarriage. In P. Cowan & E.M. Hetherington (Eds.), *Advances in family research: Family transitions* (Vol. 2, pp. 165–194). Hillsdale, NJ: Erlbaum.

Hetherington, E.M. (1993). An overview of the Virginia Longitudinal Study of Divorce and Remarriage with a focus on early adolescence. *Journal of Family Psychology, 7,* 39–56.

Hetherington, E.M., Bridges, M., & Insabella, G.M. (1998). What matters? What does not? Five perspectives on the association between marital transitions and children's adjustment. *American Psychologist, 53,* 167–184.

Hetherington, E.M., & Clingempeel, W.G. (1992). Coping with marital transitions: A family systems perspective. *Monographs of the Society for Research in Child Development, 57*(2–3, Serial No. 227).

Hetherington, E.M., Cox, M., & Cox, R. (1977). The aftermath of divorce. In J.H. Stevens, Jr. & M. Matthews (Eds.), *Mother-child, father-child relations* (pp. 110–155). Washington, DC: National Association for the Education of Young Children.

Hetherington, E.M., Cox, M., & Cox, R. (1979). Family interaction and the social, emotional, and cognitive development of children following divorce. In V. Vaughn & T. Brazelton (Eds.), *The family: Setting priorities* (pp. 89–128). New York: Science and Medicine.

Hetherington, E.M., Cox, M., & Cox, R. (1985). Long-term effects of divorce and remarriage on the adjustment of children. *Journal of the American Academy of Child Psychiatry, 24,* 518–539.

Hetherington, E.M., & Jodl, K.M. (1994). Stepfamilies as settings for child development. In A. Booth & J. Dunn (Eds.), *Stepfamilies: Who benefits? Who does not?* (pp. 55–79). Hillsdale, NJ: Erlbaum.

Hodges, W., Wechsler, R., & Ballantine, C. (1979). Divorce and the preschool child: Cumulative stress. *Journal of Divorce, 3,* 55–67.

Jacobson, D.S. (1978). The impact of marital separation/divorce on children II. Interparental hostility and child adjustment. *Journal of Divorce, 2,* 3–19.

Johnston, J.R. (1992). *Guidelines for the resolution of disputed custody and visitation for children of domestic violence* (Final report to the Judicial Council of California, Administrative Office of the Courts). San Francisco: Judicial Council of California.

Johnston, J.R. (1995). Research update: Children's adjustment in sole custody compared to joint custody families and principles for custody decision making. *Family and Conciliation Courts Review, 33,* 415–425.

Johnston, J.R., & Campbell, L.E. (1988). *Impasses of divorce: The dynamics and resolution of family conflict.* New York: Free Press.

Johnston, J.R., Gonzales, R., & Campbell, L.E.G. (1987). Ongoing postdivorce conflict and child disturbance. *Journal of Abnormal Child Psychology, 15,* 493–509.

Johnston, J.R., Kline, M., & Tschann, J.M. (1989). Ongoing postdivorce conflict: Effects on children of joint custody and frequent access. *American Journal of Orthopsychiatry, 59,* 576–592.

Johnston, J.R., & Roseby, V. (1997a). *High-conflict, violent and separating families: A group treatment manual for school-age children.* New York: Free Press.

Johnston, J.R., & Roseby, V. (1997b). *In the name of the child: A developmental approach to understanding and helping children of conflicted and violent divorce.* New York: Free Press.

Kalter, N. (1984). Conjoint mother-daughter treatment: A beginning phase of psychotherapy with adolescent daughters of divorce. *American Journal of Orthopsychiatry, 54,* 490–497.

Kalter, N. (1987). Long-term effects of divorce on children: A developmental vulnerability model. *American Journal of Orthopsychiatry, 57,* 587–600.

Kalter, N., Riemer, B., Brickman, A., & Chen, J.W. (1985). Implications of parental divorce for female development. *Journal of the American Academy of Child Psychiatry, 24,* 538–544.

Kalter, N., & Rubin, S. (1989). *School-based therapy groups for children of divorce.* Paper presented at the annual meeting of the American Psychological Association, New Orleans, LA.

Kline, M., Johnston, J.R., & Tschann, J.M. (1991). The long shadow of marital conflict: A model of children's post-divorce adjustment. *Journal of Marriage and the Family, 53,* 297–309.

Kline, M., Tschann, J.M., Johnston, J.R., & Wallerstein, J.S. (1989). Children's adjustment in joint and sole physical custody families. *Developmental Psychology, 25,* 430–438.

Kurdek, L.A., & Fine, M.A. (1993). Parent and nonparent residential family members as providers of warmth, support, and supervision to young adolescents. *Journal of Family Psychology, 7,* 245–249.

Leupnitz, D.A. (1982). *Child custody: A study of families after divorce.* Lexington, MA: Lexington Books.

Leupnitz, D.A. (1986). A comparison of maternal, paternal, and joint custody: Understanding the varieties of post-divorce family life. *Journal of Divorce, 9,* 1–12.

Lindner-Gunnoe, M. (1993). *Noncustodial mothers' and fathers' contributions to the adjustment of adolescent stepchildren.* Unpublished doctoral dissertation, University of Virginia, Charlottesville.

Maccoby, E.E., Buchanan, C.M., Mnookin, R.H., & Dornbusch, S.M. (1993). Postdivorce roles of mothers and fathers in the lives of their children. *Journal of Family Psychology, 7,* 24–38.

Maccoby, E.E., & Mnookin, R.H. (1992). *Dividing the child: Social and legal dilemmas of custody.* Cambridge, MA: Harvard University Press.

MacKinnon, C.E., Brody, G.H., & Stoneman, Z. (1982). The effects of divorce and maternal employment on the home environments of preschool children. *Child Development, 53,* 1392–1399.

McLanahan, S., & Sandefur, G. (1994). *Growing up with a single parent: What hurts, what helps?* Cambridge, MA: Harvard University Press.

Meyer, D.R., & Garasky, S. (1993). Custodial fathers: Myths, realities and child support policy. *Journal of Marriage and the Family, 55,* 73–89.

Pagani, L., Boulerice, B., Tremblay, R.E., & Vitaro, F. (1997). Behavioural development in children of divorce and remarriage. *Journal of Child Psychology and Psychiatry, 38,* 769–781.

Palosaari, U., Aro, H., & Laippala, P. (1996). Parental divorce and depression in young adulthood: Adolescents' closeness to parents and self-esteem as mediating factors. *Acta Psychiatrica Scandinavica, 93,* 20–26.

Pearson, J., & Thoennes, N. (1990). Custody after divorce: Demographic attitudinal patterns. *American Journal of Orthopsychiatry, 60,* 233–249.

Pedro-Corrall, J.L., & Cowen, E.L. (1985). The Children of Divorce Intervention Program: An investigation of the efficacy of a school-based prevention program. *Journal of Consulting Clinical Psychology, 53,* 603–611.

Rothberg, B. (1983). Joint custody: Parental problems and satisfaction. *Family Process, 22,* 43–52.

Salk, L. (1973). *What every child wants his parents to know.* New York: Warner.

Santrock, J.W., & Sitterle, K.A. (1987). Parent-child relationships in stepmother families. In K. Palsey & M. Ihinger-Tallman (Eds.), *Remarriage and stepparenting: Current research and theory* (pp. 273–299). New York: Guilford Press.

Santrock, J.W., & Warshak, R.A. (1979). Father custody and social development in boys and girls. *Journal of Social Issues, 35,* 112–125.

Santrock, J.W., Warshak, R.A., & Elliott, G.L. (1982). Social development and parent-child interaction in father-custody and stepmother families. In M. Lamb (Ed.), *Nontraditional families: Parenting and child development* (pp. 289–314). Hillsdale, NJ: Erlbaum.

Seltzer, J.A. (1994). Consequences of marital dissolution for children. *Annual Review of Sociology, 20,* 235–266.

Shepard, M., & Goldman, G. (1980). *Divorced dads.* New York: Berkley Books.

Shiller, V.M. (1986a). Joint versus maternal custody for families with latency age boys: Parent characteristics and child adjustment. *American Journal of Orthopsychiatry, 56,* 486–489.

Shiller, V.M. (1986b). Loyalty conflicts and family relationships in latency age boys: A comparison of joint and maternal custody. *Journal of Divorce, 9,* 17–38.

Simons, R.L., & Johnson, C. (1996). Mother's parenting. In R.L. Simons & Associates (Eds.), *Understanding differences between divorced and intact families: Stress, interaction, and child outcome* (pp. 81–93). Thousand Oaks, CA: Sage.

Steinman, S. (1981). The experience of children in a joint custody arrangement: A report of a study. *American Journal of Orthopsychiatry, 51*, 403–414.

Stolberg, A.L., & Garrison, K.M. (1985). Evaluating a primary prevention program for children of divorce. *American Journal of Community Psychology, 13*, 111–124.

Stolberg, A.L., & Walsh, P. (1988). A review of treatment methods for children of divorce. In S.A. Wolchik & P. Karoly (Eds.), *Children of divorce* (pp. 299–321). New York: Gardner Press.

Tessman, L.H. (1978). *Children of parting parents.* New York: Aronson.

U.S. Bureau of the Census. (1992). *Marital status and living arrangements: March 1992* (No. 468, Tables G & 5, Current Population Reports, Series P–20). Washington, DC: U.S. Government Printing Office.

Wallerstein, J.S. (1984). Children of divorce: Preliminary report of a ten-year follow-up of young children. *American Journal of Orthopsychiatry, 54*, 444–458.

Wallerstein, J.S. (1985). Children of divorce: Preliminary report of a ten-year follow-up of older children and adolescents. *Journal of the American Academy of Child Psychiatry, 24*, 545–553.

Wallerstein, J.S. (1986). *Children of divorce workshop.* Presented at the Cape Cod Institute, Massachusetts.

Wallerstein, J.S. (1987). Children of divorce: Report of a ten-year follow-up of early latency-age children. *American Journal of Orthopsychiatry, 57*, 199–211.

Wallerstein, J.S., & Blakeslee, S. (1989). *Second chances: Men, women and children.* New York: Ticknor and Fields.

Wallerstein, J.S., & Corbin, S.B. (1989). Daughters of divorce: Report from a ten-year follow-up. *American Journal of Orthopsychiatry, 59*, 593–604.

Wallerstein, J.S., & Kelly, J.B. (1980). *Surviving the breakup: How children and parents cope with divorce.* New York: Basic Books.

Wallerstein, J.S., & Lewis, J. (1998). The long-term impact of divorce on children: A first report from a 25-year study. *Family and Conciliation Courts Review, 36*, 368–383.

Warshak, R.A. (1986). Father custody and child development: A review and analysis of psychological research. *Behavioral Sciences and the Law, 4*, 185–202.

Whitehead, L. (1979). Sex differences in children's responses to family stress: A reevaluation. *Journal of Child Psychology and Psychiatry, 20*, 247–254.

Wilkinson, G.S., & Black, R.T. (1977). Children's divorce groups. *Elementary School Guidance and Counseling, 11*, 205–213.

Wolchik, S.A., Braver, S.L., & Sandler, I.N. (1985). Maternal versus joint custody: Children's post-separation experiences and adjustment. *Journal of Clinical Child Psychology, 14*, 5–10.

Wolchik, S.A., & Karoly, P. (1988). *Children of divorce: Empirical perspectives on adjustment.* New York: Gardner Press.

Zill, N., Morrison, D.R., & Coiro, M.J. (1993). Long-term effects of parental divorce on parent-child relationships, adjustment, and achievement in young adulthood. *Journal of Family Psychology, 7*, 91–103.

CHAPTER 52

Children with Grief

LINDA SAYLER GUDAS AND GERALD P. KOOCHER

A range of complex emotions confront children experiencing a death or loss. Sadness, anger, numbness, confusion, and fear can be felt by children facing events that are both difficult for them to comprehend and unfamiliar within their scope of experience. Nothing is easy about grief, for children or for adults. Clinicians assisting children and families coping with grief must develop a high degree of comfort with death and educate themselves about the uniqueness of children's grief. Not doing so may result in potential transference issues, "professional exhaustion" (Marquis, 1993), and vicarious traumatization.

This discussion of clinical issues and intervention strategies focuses on three subgroups of children, each with a different context for confronting death. First are children who encounter death in the course of "normal" life events, but who are not directly confronting a significant personal loss. Second, the circumstances of children with their own life-threatening illness are addressed. In such instances, a variety of special factors demand attention, including the child's awareness of his or her own condition. The third subgroup is those children who are bereaved by the loss of a parent, sibling, or other significant person. Although the thrust of clinical work and the nature of the interventions proposed necessarily differ for each of these subgroups, common developmental responses to death, loss, and grief can be identified.

CHILDREN'S AWARENESS OF DEATH AND LOSS

Early classics in what has become a substantial body of literature regarding children's conceptions of death and loss are studies by Anthony (1940) and Nagy (1948). Both represented initial attempts to address children's awareness of death from a systematic, age-related, developmental perspective and provided support for the theory that such conceptions follow a stepwise progression. Although each study had major sampling problems, together they represented nearly the whole body of material on the topic for two decades. As a result, many writers simply accepted and repeated these early findings without question or additional investigation (e.g., Kübler-Ross, 1969, pp. 178–179). Affective, social, environmental, and cognitive variables in shaping children's unique reactions were not identified.

Subsequent research has provided firm empirical documentation that children's response to death is strongly determined by the manner in which the death concept develops. The specific concerns and fantasies expressed by children of different ages with respect to death are reflective of their cognitive understanding about it. A Piagetian framework has been applied to demonstrate how children's responses to questions about death reflect their level of cognitive development (Koocher, 1981,

1985). Other developmental studies have documented acquisition of the universality and irrevocability of death concepts (Jenkins & Cavanaugh, 1985/1986; Orbach, Talmon, Kedem, & Har-even, 1987; Worden, 1996), as well as highlighting children's own awareness of their potential death (Sourkes, 1982, 1995; Spinetta, 1974). These studies suggest that the egocentrism and magical thinking characteristic of preoperational thought dominate concerns about death in young children. Young children's conceptualizations are limited by their own reality. Death is therefore considered solely in terms of the child's experiences by analogy with sleep, separation, and injury. At this stage, children are not yet able to regard death as an irreversible process, and they are most worried about the duration of separation from loved ones that death implies.

With the arrival of concrete operations at about age 6 or 7, children can distinguish self from others, become capable of comprehending the experiences of other people, and thereby recognize the permanence of death. However, the child may still think of death as something that occurs as a specific consequence of illness or injury rather than as the outcome of a biological process. When children become capable of concrete operations, they are able to use information gleaned from the media, from peers, and from parents in forming their impressions. The child's predictions gradually become more accurate over time. At this stage, youngsters are most concerned with issues of pain and inflicted injury, although separation concerns remain an issue as well.

The onset of adolescence brings formal operational reasoning and the ability to make use of abstract reasoning. For the first time, the child is able to truly realize that *what is* may differ from *what might be*. Conceptions of death begin to involve more issues of uncertainty as well as theological and philosophical elements. With the onset of formal operational thought comes a more encompassing comprehension of death as a concept. An accompanying fascination with dramatic or romanticized death and suicide may also occur.

The need to differentiate between the recently deceased and the living is a common cognitive adaptation mechanism that crosses developmental ages and stages. Adults are not immune to magical thinking, but children have a particular need to distinguish between real and imaginary causes of death. Death is an abstract experience, and children have difficulty coping with abstractions. However, Lonetto (1980) notes that the same phenomena that make abstractions difficult for young children to grasp also make them more tolerant of ambiguities in learning about death.

Some authorities (Kohlberg, 1968) argue that the understanding of concepts such as life and death evolve by a natural process through developmental stages and interpret Piaget's work as implying that the child's normal maturational sequence cannot be accelerated by direct intervention. At least one experimental design, however, yielded convincing evidence that 4 to 8-year-old children provided with educational presentations about death make significantly greater gains in understanding the concept than did a control group of children who did not participate in the program (Schonfeld & Kappelman, 1990).

Emotional as well as cognitive responses to loss are related to children's developmental efforts to make sense of and master the concepts of death and the experience of grief. Loss and separation issues in childhood have been well represented in the literature of child development, psychology, and psychiatry. Anna Freud and colleagues (Freud & Burlingham, 1944; Freud & Dann, 1951) were the first authors to refer to children's grief reactions as qualitatively different from adults' and to refer to such behaviors as "grief." In 1944, Lindemann described the symptomatology and management of acute grief in adults. Two outcomes of his work are relevant to children. First, Lindemann acknowledged the long-term impact of bereavement on children; second, he connected the experience of separation and loss with grief. The work of Bowlby (1960, 1973) in describing protest, despair, and detachment in the mourning of very young children remains a standard. Rochlin's (1953) study of children's play representations of fears associated with death is another important work. Kübler-Ross's (1969) seminal work on adult adjustment to terminal illness provided five stages of grief (denial, anger, bargaining, depression, and acceptance). Although Kübler-Ross's work does not consider child developmental issues, and the empirical validity of her stage theory has been questioned, her stages should be considered a roster of flexible reactions in all persons that may occur in any sequence, remit and reappear, or never occur at all. In children, such reactions will often be acted out or expressed in play.

What clinicians and researchers have now begun to document observing in situations of loss and terminal illness are phases or "schemas" (Rando, 1993) of a process of grief, many of which encompass the responses described by Kübler-Ross. References to psychological tasks rather than stages that children should master to cope effectively are also appearing (Worden, 1996).

In summary, distinct developmental trends occur in the normal process of acquiring a concept of death that influence the style and substance of adaptive reactions in the face of a loss and the grief reaction that follows. It is important for the reader to become familiar with accounts of these trends (Gudas, 1993; Koocher, 1981; Lonetto, 1980; Orbach et al., 1987) prior to beginning therapeutic work on this topic with children.

CHILDREN WHO ENCOUNTER DEATH THROUGH LIFE EVENTS

NORMAL EXPERIENCES

During the course of life events, children encounter death. A dying pet, a movie such as *Bambi* or *The Lion King,* and a racing ambulance are everyday occurrences from which to begin a discussion with an inquiring child. Family discussions of such matters at naturally occurring teaching moments as well as death education curricula in schools (see Brown & Brown, 1996; Duncan, 1979; Schonfield & Kappelman, 1990) are both important. A preventative approach is the best strategy for helping all children cope with death and grief issues. One should not wait until the death of an important person in the child's life to begin thinking about how to communicate on these issues.

When discussing death with children, avoidance of adult metaphors and euphemisms is important. One adult may talk to another about a friend who "lost a father last week," but a 3-year-old might worry, "Why couldn't they find him?" One must also be cautious with spiritual and philosophical statements or concepts explaining death, especially in the absence of close family supports (Furman, 1974). "She was so special, she went to a better place" may cause a 6-year-old to be fearful of being "special" to anyone. Attention to the questions the child asks and the comments he or she makes help

gain perspective about what the child understands about death. Gently posing questions to the child such as "What makes you think that?" or "What do you know about that?" may give insight into the child's fear or confusion and provide a baseline for teaching. Vocabulary to discuss death should be developmentally understandable and accurate (e.g., the family pet is not "sleeping," she is dead). Descriptions should be concise, direct, and clear (e.g., "Johnny's grandmother had a heart attack. Her heart stopped beating forever. She died and will never be alive again. Maybe we can write Johnny a note to say we are sorry.").

Unarticulated concerns about death often include questions such as "Could this happen to me (or my parents)?" and "Who would take care of me?" As such questions are addressed, the child can be thoughtfully reassured that all people worry about such concerns. Discussions of how people cope with sadness, cultural differences among groups, and the purpose of memorial services, cemeteries, and funeral homes can all be a part of answering children's questions. This can also be a time for explaining etiquette when someone dies; examples include what to say to someone who is mourning and participating in selecting a condolence card.

Rituals and religious services can be important to children of all ages but only if they are well integrated with family values. A religious funeral, for example, may actually be more frightening than reassuring to a child whose family never participates in such events. Fables or similar religious stories raise potential problems for children whose developmental level makes them prone to concrete, literal interpretation. On the other hand, a child may gain considerable comfort and support from participating in rituals or services involving well-known contexts and familiar people. One must carefully assess whether the child's participation in such events meets the child's needs or is being dictated for the vicarious benefit of adults (Rando, 1993). Clinicians can work with parents to help them objectively describe anticipated memorializing events to the child and encourage him or her to express choices that are free of guilt. For example, in discussing an upcoming funeral, one might tell a child, "There will be people talking about the person who died and some may cry because they are sad. The body will be in a box called a casket. Some people like to go to funerals so they can be with other people when they feel sad or so they can tell the person's family they are thinking of them. Others would rather not go and remember the person in other ways. What would you like to do?"

A "debriefing" with the child may also be helpful following discussions about death (see Brooks & Siegel, 1996, for a detailed explanation of debriefing). The child can be encouraged to restate key elements of the explanation or talk about feelings relative to the discussion or events just passed. For example, "Tell me what you think you might see at the funeral home" or "How do you think Anne will feel when she goes back to school after her dad's funeral?" Misconceptions, potentially anxiety-arousing communication errors, and ways of responding to the bereft can all be clarified at such a time.

DEATH, LOSS, AND DISASTER

Virtually every child in America will witness at least one disaster that involves death. Exposure to such catastrophes occurs either directly or through what Brooks and Siegel (1996) refer to as "trauma by proxy," where the event is experienced through the media. The loss and devastation for a child who directly lives through a disaster is significant and has long-term psychological implications. However, the effects on any child of repetitive news coverage of horrific scenes of near or distant events must also be addressed, especially if those scenes involve danger and death to peers. Children of the new millennium have been exposed to disastrous events in ways that previous generations never or rarely experienced (American Academy of Pediatrics, 1999), resulting in the lack of a "geographical safety zone" (Brooks & Siegel, 1996); that is, children cannot retreat from such events (Monahon, 1993). Despite the onslaught of public interest, research on children experiencing such disasters has been scant (Rozensky, Sloan, Schwarz, & Kowalski, 1993).

The effect of the simultaneous occurrence of disaster and death for children complicates the bereavement process (Gudas, 1993). Rando (1993), for example, describes how disaster-related bereavement reawakens the most basic death anxiety and fear of annihilation. In such situations, one is forced to confront the general destructiveness of humankind or nature. Life assumptions are shattered, and a sense of personal vulnerability and helplessness emerges (Gillis, 1993).

"Children have a specific postdisaster clinical presentation, along with some varying symptoms" (Sugar, 1999, p. 192). This presentation is similar to acute and posttraumatic stress disorder. Factors related to the degree of reported grief include the degree of exposure to this and previous disasters, acquaintance with the deceased, degree of secondary losses, duration and disruption of normal routines, presence of violence, personal injury, parental reaction, and poor and disorganized living conditions (American Academy of Pediatrics, 1999; Rozensky et al., 1993; Sugar, 1999). Cultural reactions to disaster have also been found among Whites, Asians, African Americans, Hispanics, Native Americans, and immigrants (Sugar, 1999). Individual children of all races and cultures have variable abilities to cope; some are often quite resilient, with little evidence of the emotional residual of a disaster (Monahon, 1993; Sugar, 1999). However, asymptomatic children should be monitored for delayed effects, especially when a death is involved.

Terr et al. (1997) undertook an important study following the *Challenger* spacecraft explosion that instantly killed all six astronauts and a high school teacher on board. The disaster provided an opportunity to study normal children after a sudden and distant disaster. The selected population ($n = 153$) included children from the teacher's hometown of Concord, New Hampshire, all of whom were watching the spacecraft on TV when it exploded, and children from a well-matched West Coast town, all of whom learned of the event after it happened. A group of children sent to Cape Canaveral from Concord to watch the takeoff served as a comparison. Among the findings were six patterns of thinking similar to psychic trauma: denial, avoidance of thought, fantasies, omens, paranormal phenomena, and negative attitudes about the world's future. Such thinking is also often found in grief reactions. Similar studies of "more involved" versus "less involved" children who experience disasters and death would provide further valuable data, especially in light of the amount of children who have been affected by the recent series of school shootings.

Children reacting to disasters are simultaneously faced with both trauma and loss issues. Researchers unanimously agree that trauma effects of the disaster must be dealt with first before grief work can be comprehensively addressed (Gillis,

1993; Monahon, 1993; Raphael & Martinek, 1997). Early intervention is critical. Opportunities to discuss facts around the event should be provided. Such discussions clarify misconceptions, clear up cognitive distortions (Gillis, 1993; Monahon, 1993), and normalize the information (Rando, 1993). Parents should be actively present with their child and supervise media coverage of frightening events as best as possible. Parents may be told to expect repetitious telling and retelling or playing and replaying of the event, as the child tries to cognitively master the experience (Gillis, 1993; Monahon, 1993). To establish predictability of and control in the environment, maintaining routines is also valuable (American Academy of Pediatrics, 1999; Monahon, 1993). The protective influence of the family and the community must be stressed, as children need to feel both physically safe and emotionally secure in a world that just demonstrated that it is not always so.

THE CHILD WITH LIFE-THREATENING ILLNESS

The dying child's awareness of death has long been a topic of concern to health care providers (Spinetta, 1974). It has become increasingly clear that even young children are aware of the seriousness of their illness and are eager to have someone to talk with about it. A number of empirical studies have yielded confirming results (Koocher & O'Malley, 1981; Spinetta & Maloney, 1975; Spinetta, Rigler, & Karon, 1973, 1974). Just as Kübler-Ross's (1969) work emphasized the importance of systematic psychological intervention for the adult with terminal illness, the parallel needs of children have also been recognized as routine in publications as diverse as an Institute of Medicine study (Osterweis, Solomon, & Green, 1984) and a special issue of the *APA Monitor* (June 1999).

Reviews of professional opinion and research data have consistently stressed that children as young as 5 or 6 have a very real understanding of the seriousness of their illness, and still younger children show definite reactions to increased parental stress and other concomitants of a terminal diagnosis on the family (Slavin, 1981; Spinetta, 1974). Despite this recognition by children of their serious illness, conceptualizations of death and loss issues do not differ from the general developmental trends

noted above. The predominant modes of response tend to reflect age-related concerns about separation, pain, and disruption of usual life activities.

Recent advances in modern medical diagnoses and therapeutics have altered the natural histories of many chronic, life-threatening diseases. Illnesses that were acutely fatal just two or three decades ago have been converted into conditions that still threaten death but are much more chronic than acute in their course; childhood cancer and cystic fibrosis are good examples. New survival statistics of such illnesses have generated a whole host of psychological stress issues, including the matter of long-term uncertainty and the helplessness this induces for many patients. And what of the families of such patients? Should they attempt to anticipate the child's death and accommodate to the loss, or should they stifle their anxieties about a potential loss while hoping for the best? Either course may lead to psychological distress over the long term. The uncertainty component cannot be overlooked when considering the psychological adaptation of the child patient and his or her family members.

PSYCHOLOGICAL REACTIONS OF THE CHILD WITH TERMINAL ILLNESS

Children who are terminally ill or who face an uncertain but potentially fatal outcome from chronic illness are at substantial risk for emotional disturbance as a function of stress. A multitude of publications (Gogan, O'Malley, & Foster, 1977; Slavin, 1981; Sourkes, 1982, 1995; Spinetta, 1974) have documented and detailed the core stresses and common symptoms. Depending on the course and trajectory of the disease process, even children who were quite "normal" prior to becoming ill may develop increased anxiety, loss of appetite, insomnia, social isolation, emotional withdrawal, depression and apathy, and marked ambivalence toward those adults who are providing care.

The nature of these signs and symptoms are generally regarded as responses to acute or chronic stress rather than as functional psychopathology. It is predictable, however, that children or families with preexisting emotional pathology will experience an exacerbation. The concept of learned helplessness (Seligman, 1975) helps explain this phenomenon. When one believes that the outcome one confronts (i.e., death) is independent of one's own behavior, the hopelessness and accompanying emotional stress is dramatic (Seligman, 1975).

Empirical studies have demonstrated that anxiety levels of childhood leukemia patients increase parallel to increases in the frequency of outpatient clinic visits (Spinetta & Maloney, 1975). This finding is the opposite of what one would expect to find in youngsters with chronic non-life-threatening illnesses, where habituation and familiarity would tend to reduce stress over time. Other reports (Sourkes, 1982, 1995; Spinetta et al., 1974) demonstrate the increasing sense of isolation that dying children often experience.

Even children who otherwise seem to be coping quite well through a prolonged illness course may develop specific problems, such as conditioned-reflex vomiting, anxiety linked to specific medical procedures, depressive reactions to progressive loss of physical capacity, or family communication inhibitions. Sometimes, children and their families cope quite well during periods of active treatment, only to become overwhelmed when the need for continued treatment is over. Although this type of reaction may seem paradoxical, hospitalizations and even harsh treatment regimens may come to be imbued with some protective value that takes on functional autonomy.

Psychotherapeutic Interventions for the Child at Risk for Death

For those children with fatal or life-threatening illnesses who require mental health services, there are two basic paradigms. First, by virtue of preexisting difficulties, is the child or family for whom psychological intervention would have been needed even without the illness. Second is the child and family struggling with acute stress as a function of the illness, affecting a heretofore well-adapted psychosocial system. Both groups will be in need of supportive treatment and crisis intervention at various points in the treatment of the child's illness.

Most children with chronic life-threatening illnesses will require relatively sophisticated medical care and will probably be treated at or in consultation with major medical centers. In the ideal circumstance, mental health services will be available at these centers through the primary care team. Even in the best of circumstances, however, powerful stresses will exist among children, parents, and the

treatment staff (Koocher, 1980). Mental health personnel must become familiar with the history of and treatments for the illnesses of their patients, and medical staff must be able to incorporate the psychological components of their patients into the treatment plan. A variety of models for providing such care has been well described in the literature (Adams, 1979; Kellerman, 1980; Koocher & O'Malley, 1981; Koocher, Sourkes, & Keane, 1979; Rando, 1993).

The precise nature of intervention strategies and techniques varies as a function of the individual patient's needs. The basic intervention should include consideration of the following clinical questions: What has the child been told about the illness? Are there any discrepant opinions regarding what/what not and how much to tell the child? What surface concerns does the child have? What sources of support are available? What sources of stress are anticipated?

Knowing exactly what information has been communicated to the child and family is important, but it is also critical to recognize that what has been understood may differ from what information was offered (or overheard). The nature of the anxieties a child may face is quite complex, and some facets are more easily verbalized than others; these surface concerns should be addressed first. This strategy establishes a climate within which the child will later be able to verbalize more complex worries. Sources of support include the child's own coping abilities as well as the emotional support available from family, friends, and the medical team. Although predicting the precise timing of stress events associated with the treatment of life-threatening illnesses is not always possible, the events themselves are well-known to those who treat such children (e.g., alopecia among cancer patients). Lessening the psychological stress of such events by preparing the child in advance is often possible. The clinician who explores these issues with the child will have begun the most important parts of a constructive intervention program.

Answering the question "Am I going to die?" and preparing the child for dying is one of the most burdensome tasks an adult can undertake. However, if one waits until it is evident that death is near to initiate such discussions, a tragic error has been made. Even young children can be told at diagnosis if their illness is "a very serious disease: People can die from it." Such statements can be followed by other information about promising treatments and how the medical staff plans to "fight the disease," soliciting the child in the battle. From the very beginning, the child should be engaged in an emotional climate that encourages supportive discussion of even the most stressful events.

During the course of treatment for the illness, the clinician might routinely explore the child's concerns, even asking specifically, "Do you ever worry about dying?" If the child answers affirmatively, a discussion should proceed. If such fears are denied, one can state, "Well, I'm glad you don't, but if you do get worried, I hope you'll let me (or your parents) know so we can talk about it."

When a child is clearly entering a terminal trajectory, a meeting with the parents and medical team to explore ways to handle communication is helpful. Some children will be open, direct, and straightforward about their dying. In such cases, part of the clinician's work may focus on helping family and staff deal with their own feelings about discussing death. When the child denies concern but shows obvious symptoms of distress (such as separation anxiety), help the child to see that he or she is not alone or provide interventions without directly confronting the issue of death. Statements such as "Today seems to be a tough day for you" may provide support and open further discussion.

THE BEREAVED CHILD

A number of studies have focused specifically on patterns of mourning and bereavement in children. Some have reported descriptions of bereavement in children as young as 3 years, although most tend to make rather gross age distinctions and focus on middle childhood and adolescence. Regression, denial, hopelessness, and animistic fantasies are described as a child struggles to cope with the loss of a loved one. Retrospective studies have attempted to link losses in childhood to adult depression and physical illness. Summaries of these studies (Fleming, 1980; Osterweis et al., 1984) conclude that the course and outcome of childhood bereavement experiences may influence adult affective disturbance years later, but the nature of the relationship is not clear.

Worden (1996) describes four tasks involved in the mourning process for children. The first task, accepting the reality of the loss, requires some concept of death's permanency. Also, young children can confront loss only in small amounts and for brief periods. The second task, experiencing the pain or emotional aspects of the loss, is accomplished gradually, and the child must feel safe to do so. Adjusting to the new environment from which the deceased person is missing is the third task. This adjustment requires accepting new roles and investing in new relationships and activities. The fourth task, relocating the deceased person in one's own life, does not require a "letting go" or resolution of the relationship, as has traditionally been encouraged. Rather, the "relocating" involves a cognitive and emotional accommodation process (in the true Piagetian sense) that takes place in a social context of which the deceased is a part. This continuing bond (Klass, Silverman, & Nickman, 1996) provides an ongoing representation of the deceased as a way of active remembering and finding ways to memorialize the person. An additional task that should be considered is the return of the child to age-appropriate tasks.

Factors that may help or hinder the child's adjustment and sense of loss include the circumstances of the death and the attendant rituals, preloss psychological adjustment of the child, functioning of the surviving parent or caretakers, qualitative aspects of the child's relationship with the deceased person, social support, family stresses, and individual characteristics (e.g., age, gender, and social skills). An adult who is consistently able to both meet the child's needs and enable discussions about the loss is invaluable (Worden & Silverman, 1993). The presence of such an adult is repeatedly mentioned in the literature as the most important factor in helping the child with grief.

The death of a family member is, inevitably, the most difficult of losses for a child. Klass et al. (1996) write of a child's continuing need to have an ongoing, inner representation of a deceased parent as well as an active way to keep the parent in his or her life. The death of a sibling places intense stress on the family and surviving children. Parents may be less emotionally available and marital tensions are likely to increase (Worden & Monahon, 1993). Parents may make conscious or unconscious efforts to replace the lost child, overprotect surviving children, or be so grief-stricken that they are emotionally unavailable. Idealization of the deceased child often occurs. Hindmarch (1995) refers to the many secondary losses a child sustains when a sibling dies. Unfortunately, one of these losses is often a secure and stable family environment. In addition, internally generated survivor guilt among siblings is not uncommon (McCown & Pratt, 1985).

Children can manifest both cognitive and emotional disruption in the aftermath of a family member's death almost without regard to the specific circumstances of the loss. In some instances (i.e., parent suicide), the reactions may be unusually intense and prolonged (Rando, 1993). Even the death of a public figure with parent surrogate qualities can evoke a significant mourning response in both children and adults, as was well illustrated by children's reactions to John Kennedy's assassination (Wolfenstein & Kliman, 1965) and Christa MacAuliffe's death in the *Challenger* explosion (Terr et al., 1997).

Bryer's (1979) paper on the Amish way of preparing for death throughout life underscores the importance of the family as a support system in the face of death. Bryer demonstrates how community orientation, family structure, and cultural attitudes toward life and death can facilitate bereavement in a supportive atmosphere that tends to minimize emotional trauma associated with the loss. The importance of family rituals, such as a funeral, has been well documented in a variety of cultures, and the welfare of survivors is regarded as of paramount importance to most ethnic groups.

PSYCHOTHERAPEUTIC CARE OF THE BEREAVED CHILD

A major goal in working with grieving children is to prevent the development of psychopathology and maladaptation in the aftermath of loss (Koocher, 1994). The clinician will be challenged to use a variety of therapeutic methods, including psychoeducational, developmental, psychodynamic, and behavioral interventions (Gudas, 1999). The questions a child may be presumed to worry about in the aftermath of a salient death include: Why did that person die? Will that happen to me (or someone I care about)? Did I have anything to do with it? Who will take care of me now? Why did this happen to me? These questions may not be specifically articulated by the child, but they are almost always a part of the underlying concerns that accompany grief. Obsessive ruminating or pessimistic, hopeless thinking can also be found, especially if there is self-blame or guilt over the death.

Lonetto (1980) describes cognitive developmental approaches to illustrate the use of play and drawings as a meaningful way of reducing the abstraction and ambiguity of death and dying for children in various age groups. Writing from a different frame of reference, Rochlin (1953) uses the psychoanalytic model to arrive at similar conclusions. He notes that the child's play is organized to protect the self against fears associated with an understanding of death.

Hindmarch (1995) refers to several needs of children who have lost a sibling, but these needs apply to all children coping with grief. First is a need for information, which should be developmentally appropriate and accurate. Terr et al. (1997) also noted that 95% of the children in the *Challenger* study attempted to cope with the disaster by seeking and acquiring information. Remaining needs are a sense of reassurance and understanding, attention, and security.

The question of pharmacological treatment may arise when bereft children present with difficult behaviors or symptoms. The behaviors or symptoms of concern must be considered in relation to past and present mental status, ability to perform routine activities, available supports, and success of other therapeutic interventions. In certain situations, the use of medication is prudent for symptom relief (e.g., incapacitating anxiety). However, parents and children must be educated that the psychological work of grieving still needs to be done.

ASSESSMENT OF CHILDREN AT RISK

Assessment of potential risk factors in the child with grief involves gauging the intensity, duration, and severity of the grief reaction and the degree to which psychological defense mechanisms are successful in protecting the child from anxiety (Fleming, 1980; Lindemann, 1944; Rochlin, 1953).

The natural dependency of childhood, along with the potential for animistic and magical thinking, make children vulnerable to psychological sequelae following an important loss. At the same time, the absence of any symptoms of acute grief or a sharply truncated reaction may herald premature application of denial or avoidance defenses, with the potential for emergence of symptoms at a later time. Dramatic shifts in affect that would seem pathological in an adult are more the norm in children.

A child or adolescent in the process of adapting to a loss should be able to verbalize sadness and related feelings in the course of a psychodiagnostic evaluation. Inability to discuss the loss, denial of affect, or anxiety and guilt themes in relation to the deceased or family members are all indicators that some additional evaluation or psychotherapeutic intervention may be warranted.

Time can also be a factor in assessing adaptation to loss. Although the intensity of the depressive symptoms will often abate over a period of weeks, "anniversary phenomena" (holidays, family events) or reminders of the deceased (a song, a toy) may trigger renewed symptoms along with thoughts of the deceased person. Usually, these recurrences are much less intense than in the acute mourning period. Such "connections" to the deceased (Klass et al., 1996) are expectable and normal, but often painfully bittersweet. If recurrences persist more than several days following the stimulus event or evoke a heretofore unseen intensity, a diagnostic evaluation is suggested.

The clinician must also be sensitive to the principle that the bereaved child cannot accurately be evaluated outside of the family context. Grief reactions in children are subject to both amelioration and exacerbation based on the presence or absence of emotional supports within the surviving family (Rando, 1993). Behavioral contagion and social learning also play roles in determining a child's response. Religious and cultural rituals and family behavior patterns provide opportunities for observational learning and imitation that may be either facilitative or inhibitory with respect to the child's adaptation. Children may also react to mourning, depression, or anxiety in their parents or caretakers even though they have had no personal contact with the deceased individual. Such reactions may occur in national tragedies or distant disasters.

Factors that could place a child at risk for complicated bereavement include a history of past or current losses; many disruptions or traumas in the child's life; poor functioning or unavailable parents; if the loss makes no sense (i.e. a drowning, a shooting); and when the death is sudden, violent, or traumatic. Additionally, the child who presents with risk-taking behaviors, persistent blame, guilt, or sense of responsibility; trauma symptoms (flashbacks, hyperarousal); complaints of ongoing somatic or psychosomatic ailments; or a desire to die or talk of suicide should be assessed. Although no one symptom or symptom cluster is "diagnostic" of grief, the following may be found in children's grief reactions: separation anxiety, increase in unfocused activity, appetite and sleep changes, decreased attention span, loss of interest in favorite pastimes, tearfulness, numbness, preoccupation with the deceased, decreased effectiveness in school, regression, and a pessimistic or hopeless view of the future. Such symptoms need to be evaluated in terms of severity and intensity.

CONCLUSION

All children think about death, encounter death in everyday events, and experience separations from loved ones. Spontaneous questions and concerns about death and loss are a normal part of growing up and should be treated as such by adults. The thoughts and fantasies of children dealing with death and loss are acted out in play and translated into many questions and ideas that can create myriad emotions in adults, including sadness and anxiety.

Whether one is considering the needs of the general population of children, the child with a life-threatening illness, or the child who has lost a loved one, emotional climate is the paramount guarantor of security and adaptation. The need for ongoing support from others is crucial for the grieving child, especially as such support has been found to decrease dramatically within weeks of the death and, in fact, even fall below the original baseline (Koocher, 1994). When the social and emotional context provides a sense of trust and empathic understanding, coping is greatly facilitated. Establishing such a context within the family and in psychotherapy, along with a recognition of salient issues from the child's standpoint, is the most effective base on which to begin dealing with grief and loss in childhood.

REFERENCES

Adams, D.W. (1979). *Childhood malignancy: The psychosocial care of the child and his family.* Springfield, IL: Thomas.

American Academy of Pediatrics, Committee on Psychosocial Aspects of Child and Family Health. (1999).

How pediatricians can respond to the psychosocial implications of disasters. *Pediatrics, 103,* 521–523.

Anthony, S. (1940). *The child's discovery of death.* New York: Harcourt Brace.

APA Monitor. (1999, June). (Vol. 30).

Bowlby, J. (1960). Grief and mourning in infancy and early childhood. *Psychoanalytic Study of the Child* (Vol. 15, pp. 9–15). New York: International Universities Press.

Bowlby, J. (1973). *Separation: Anxiety and anger.* New York: Basic Books.

Brooks, B., & Siegel, P.M. (1996). *The scared child.* New York: Wiley.

Brown, L.K., & Brown, M.T. (1996). *When dinosaurs die: A guide to understanding death.* Boston: Little, Brown.

Bryer, K. (1979). The Amish way of death: A study of family support systems. *American Psychologist, 34,* 255–261.

Duncan, C. (1979). *Teaching children about death: A rationale and model for curriculum.* Doctoral dissertation, Boston College, Chestnut Hill, MA.

Fleming, S. (1980). Childhood bereavement. In R. Lonetto (Ed.), *Children's conceptions of death* (pp. 178–187). New York: Springer.

Freud, A., & Burlingham, D. (1944). *Infants without families.* New York: International Universities Press.

Freud, A., & Dann, S. (1951). An experiment in group upbringing. *Psychoanalytic Study of the Child* (Vol. 6, pp. 127–168). New York: International Universities Press.

Furman, E. (1974). *A child's parent dies.* New Haven, CT: Yale University Press.

Gillis, H.M. (1993). Individual and small-group psychotherapy for children involved in trauma and disaster. In C.F. Saylor (Ed.), *Children and disasters* (pp. 165–186). New York: Plenum Press.

Gogan, J.L., O'Malley, J.E., & Foster, D.J. (1977). Treating the pediatric cancer patient: A review. *Journal of Pediatric Psychology, 2,* 42–48.

Gudas, L. (1993). Concepts of death and loss in childhood and adolescence: A developmental perspective. In C.F. Saylor (Ed.), *Children and disasters* (pp. 67–84). New York: Plenum Press.

Gudas, L. (1999). Bereavement interventions when a child dies. *Progress Notes: Newsletter of the Society of Pediatric Psychology, 23,* 4–5, 16.

Hindmarch, C. (1995). Secondary losses for siblings. *Child: Health and Development, 21,* 425–431.

Jenkins, R.A., & Cavanaugh, J.C. (1985/1986). Examining the relationship between the development of death and overall cognitive development. *Omega, 16,* 193–199.

Kellerman, J. (Ed.). (1980). *Psychological aspects of childhood cancer.* Springfield, IL: Thomas.

Klass, D., Silverman, P.R., & Nickman, S.L. (Eds.). (1996). *Continuing bonds.* Washington, DC: Taylor & Francis.

Kohlberg, L. (1968). Early education: A cognitive-developmental view. *Child Development, 39,* 1013–1062.

Koocher, G.P. (1980). Pediatric cancer: Psychosocial problems and the high costs of helping. *Journal of Clinical Child Psychology, 9,* 2–5.

Koocher, G.P. (1981). Development of the death concept in childhood. In R. Bibace & M.E. Walsh (Eds.), *The development of concepts related to health: Future directions in developmental psychology* (pp. 85–99). San Francisco: Jossey-Bass.

Koocher, G.P. (1985). Promoting coping with illness in childhood. In J.C. Rosen & L.J. Solomon (Eds.), *Prevention in health psychology* (pp. 311–327). Hanover, NH: University Press of New England.

Koocher, G.P. (1994). Preventive intervention following a child's death. *Psychotherapy, 31,* 377–382.

Koocher, G.P., & O'Malley, J.E. (1981). *The Damocles syndrome: Psychosocial consequences of surviving childhood cancer.* New York: McGraw-Hill.

Koocher, G.P., Sourkes, B.M., & Keane, M.W. (1979). Pediatric oncology consultations: A generalizable model for medical settings. *Professional Psychology, 10,* 467–474.

Kübler-Ross, E. (1969). *On death and dying.* New York: Macmillan.

Lindemann, E. (1944). Symptomatology and management of acute grief. *American Journal of Psychiatry, 101,* 141–148.

Lonetto, R. (1980). *Children's conceptions of death.* New York: Springer.

Marquis, S. (1993). Death of the nursed: Burnout of the provider. *Omega, 27,* 17–33.

McCown, D.E., & Pratt, C. (1985). The impact of sibling death on children's behavior. *Death Studies, 9,* 323–335.

Monahon, C. (1993). *Children and trauma.* San Francisco: Jossey-Bass.

Nagy, M. (1948). The child's theories concerning death. *Journal of Genetic Psychology, 73,* 3–27.

Orbach, I., Talmon, O., Kedem, P., & Har-even, D. (1987). Sequential patterns of five subconcepts of human and animal death in children. *Journal of the American Academy of Child and Adolescent Psychiatry, 26,* 578–582.

Osterweis, M., Solomon, F., & Green, M. (Eds.). (1984). *Bereavement: Reactions, consequences, and care.* Washington, DC: National Academy Press.

Rando, T. (1993). *The treatment of complicated mourning.* Champaign, IL: Research Press.

Raphael, B., & Martinek, N. (1997). Assessing traumatic bereavement and posttraumatic stress disorder. In J.P. Wilson & T.M. Keane (Eds.), *Assessing psychological trauma and PTSD.* New York: Guilford Press.

Rochlin, G. (1953). Loss and restitution. *Psychoanalytic Study of the Child, 8,* 288–309.

Rozensky, R.H., Sloan, I.H., Schwarz, E.D., & Kowalski, J.M. (1993). Psychological response of children to shootings and hostage situations. In C.F. Saylor (Ed.),

Children and disasters (pp. 123–136). New York: Plenum Press.

Schonfeld, D.J., & Kappelman, M. (1990). The impact of school-based education on the young child's understanding of death. *Developmental and Behavioral Pediatrics, 11*, 247–252.

Seligman, M.E.P. (1975). *Helplessness.* San Francisco: Freeman.

Slavin, L.A. (1981). Evolving psychosocial issues in the treatment of childhood cancer: A review. In G.P. Koocher & J.E. O'Malley (Eds.), *The Damocles syndrome: Psychosocial consequences of surviving childhood cancer* (pp. 1–30). New York: McGraw-Hill.

Sourkes, B.M. (1982). *The deepening shade: Psychological aspects of life-threatening illness.* Pittsburgh, PA: University of Pittsburgh Press.

Sourkes, B.M. (1995). *Armfuls of time: The psychological experience of the child with a life-threatening illness.* Pittsburgh, PA: University of Pittsburgh Press.

Spinetta, J.J. (1974). The dying child's awareness of death: A review. *Psychological Bulletin, 81*, 256–260.

Spinetta, J.J., & Maloney, L.J. (1975). Death anxiety in the outpatient leukemic child. *Pediatrics, 65*, 1034–1037.

Spinetta, J.J., Rigler, D., & Karon, M. (1973). Anxiety in the dying child. *Pediatrics, 52*, 841–845.

Spinetta, J.J., Rigler, D., & Karon, M. (1974). Personal space as a measure of a dying child's sense of isolation. *Journal of Consulting and Clinical Psychology, 42*, 751–756.

Sugar, M. (1999). Disasters. In M.D. Levine, W.B. Carey, & A.C. Crocker (Eds.), *Developmental-behavioral pediatrics* (3rd ed., pp. 192–195). Philadelphia: Saunders.

Terr, L.C., Bloch, D.A., Michel, B.A., Hong Shi, M.S., Reinhardt, J.A., & Metayer, S. (1997). Children's thinking in the wake of *Challenger. American Journal of Psychiatry, 154*, 744–751.

Wolfenstein, M., & Kliman, G. (Eds.). (1965). *Children and the death of a president.* Garden City, NY: Doubleday.

Worden, J.W. (1996). *Children and grief: When a parent dies.* New York: Guilford Press.

Worden, J.W., & Monahan, J. (1993). Bereaved parents. In A. Armstrong-Dailey & S. Goltzer (Eds.), *Hospice care for children* (pp. 122–139). Oxford, England: Oxford University Press.

Worden, J.W., & Silverman, P.R. (1993). Grief and depression in newly widowed parents with school-age children. *Omega, 27*, 251–260.

CHAPTER 53

The Psychological Impact of a Parent's Chronic Illness on the Child

KELLY M. CHAMPION AND MICHAEL C. ROBERTS

INTRODUCTION

Pediatric psychologists and child health psychologists have extensively researched psychosocial factors surrounding children's chronic illness in terms of impact on the child and the parents. Similarly, health psychologists have extensively researched the impact on adults who have a chronic illness. Much less attention has been given to the psychosocial adjustment of children and families who have a parent with a chronic illness, including both physical and mental illnesses. Children are seemingly ignored by health psychologists studying adults with chronic illness, and pediatric psychologists are interested in children and do not study adult chronic illness.

ADULT CHRONIC ILLNESS

The prevalence of chronic illness in adults is substantial and the impact is potentially immense on the psychosocial aspects of their lives. Verbrugge and Patrick (1995) provide this definition:

Chronic conditions are long-term diseases, injuries with long sequelae, and enduring structural, sensory, and communication abnormalities. They are physical or mental (cognitive and emotional) in nature, and their onset time ranges from before birth to late in life. Their defining aspect is duration. Once they are past certain symptomatic or diagnostic thresholds, chronic conditions are essentially permanent features for the rest of life. Medical and personal regimens can sometimes control but can rarely cure them. (p. 173)

Types of chronic conditions in adults include diseases such as asthma, diabetes, hemophilia, cancer/leukemia, and chronic pain, which can be present across the life span, and conditions such as multiple sclerosis and dystrophies, end stage renal disease, fibrocystic breast disease, endometriosis, arthritic illnesses, systemic lupus erythematosus, emphysema, heart and coronary disease, and stroke, which appear or are more prevalent in adulthood. These chronic conditions frequently are associated with substantial challenges to vocational aspirations and fulfillment, recreational and educational activities, and interpersonal and family relationships.

A considerable amount of research has investigated psychological effects such as adjustment of the adult patient, adjustment of the adult patient's spouse, sexual functioning, work-related outcomes, financial resources, and role restructuring (e.g.,

Preparation of this chapter was facilitated by a Research, Creativity, and Scholarship Grant from Gustavus Adolphus College to the first author.

Coyne & Fiske, 1992). In addition, a few researchers have examined the effects of family support and conflict among family members (e.g., Jacobs, 1992). To gauge the potential size of this phenomenon, Benson and Marano (1994) estimated that over 10 million adults in the parenting ages 18 to 44 had a chronic health condition. Nonetheless, when studying the effects of adult chronic illness, only a small percentage of the adult chronic illness research has investigated the psychological and behavioral functioning of children whose parent has a chronic illness.

Most discussions on the impact of chronic illness rely on some aspects of the stress and coping models in the pediatric and health psychology literature that attend to physical conditions and psychosocial adjustment. In the pediatric psychology arena, theoretical models have emphasized the ill or disabled child and examined the concomitant effects on self, parents, and family, and the patient's environment (e.g., Wallander & Thompson, 1995). In the adult health arena, attention has been narrowly focused on the psychological functioning of the ill adult and perhaps that of a partner (e.g., Coyne & Fiske, 1992). For the present topic, the attention is on the psychosocial functioning of the child growing up in the context of a parent's health condition and the concomitant effects on development and adjustment. This focus widens the parameters of typical adult health psychology models to include the adjustment and coping of offspring of chronically ill adults and reverses the direction of influence from previous pediatric psychology models of effects of chronic illness.

Although few researchers in the past examined the impact of parental health problems on children and adolescents (Drotar, 1994), there have been more recent publications reporting research on the impact of parents' cancer on children (Compas et al., 1994; Grant & Compas, 1995) or HIV/AIDS in parents and the effects on their children (Armistead, Klein, & Forehand, 1995; Forehand et al., 1998). In general, these studies have found that some differences do emerge in child functioning when a parent has a chronic illness. Nonetheless, many aspects of adult chronic illness and concomitant effects on child outcomes remain unexamined. For example, many chronic illnesses and a variety of psychosocial variables have not been examined at all. As Pless and Perrin (1985) stated, a disease needs to be examined in terms of severity, prognosis, functional

status, type of disability, and visibility. Additionally, attention needs to be given to phenomenological variables for the adult as the person with the disease and for his or her multiple roles in life (including parenting). Phenomenological or perception variables also need to be investigated for the child as a member of a family in which a parent has a chronic illness. For example, some of the studies have found that the subjective experience (e.g., the cognitive appraisal of seriousness or stress) of those involved in the situation is as important as the objective characteristics (e.g., diagnosis severity).

ADULT DISABILITY

Thus far, the focus has been on chronic illness. However, parental disability also has a potential impact on children's development and functioning. Disabled parents are a markedly heterogeneous group that includes parents with sensory disabilities (e.g., blind, deaf), physical disability (e.g., paraplegic, spastic gait, chronic pain), cognitive disabilities (e.g., mental retardation, dementia, learning disabilities), and psychiatric disabilities (e.g., major depression, schizophrenia). A chronic illness can cause a physical disability, as in the case of multiple sclerosis and polio. Treatment of an illness also can cause disability (e.g., bone cancer, amputation). Cognitive and psychiatric disabilities are also associated with some chronic illness, such as the effects of stroke due to arteriolosclerosis and multiple sclerosis. In other cases, cognitive impairments may fluctuate with control of the disease, as is the case with some individuals with diabetes and changes in blood glucose levels. Thus, potentially large individual differences exist in the status of disability and related psychosocial functioning. For example, in a large survey of disabled adults conducted by the Berkeley Planning Associates (Barker & Maralani, 1997), disabled parents ranged from fully employed to living on public assistance or disability insurance and from a graduate school education to less than a high school diploma.

This survey of disabled parents examined the needs and resources of a large sample (Barker & Maralani, 1997). The results suggested a vast range in the needs of disabled parents, despite limitations in participant recruitment. About 75% of those surveyed experienced difficulties obtaining employment or engaging in recreation with their families;

80% had difficulty obtaining reliable transportation that allowed them to escort their child in a vehicle. When handicapped transportation services were available, typically there were no child safety seats or safe accommodations or children were forbidden to ride in the transportation. Other barriers to parenting identified by the survey included lack of medical expertise in the challenges faced by a disabled parent, lower income than nondisabled parents, more expenses for services and adaptive equipment, lack of appropriate adaptive equipment specific to child care, and lack of access to appropriate assistance. Although some of the barriers affecting parents with a disability might be related to low-income status in areas such as transportation and recreation, the overwhelming prevalence of these problems suggests that it is related to disability. Overall, the findings from the Berkeley Planning Associates identify some of the challenges that disabled parents confront beyond the challenges confronted by nondisabled parents. The effect of parental disability on child outcome remains to be studied.

Given the complex relationship between chronic illness and disability, many of the challenges identified by disabled parents are likely to be experienced also by parents with chronic illness. In a review of the literature of an earlier generation of research, however, Buck and Hohmann (1983) argued that researchers needed to conceptualize and measure impact of parental illness and parental disability status separately. Other authors have not found the need to separate these groups compelling (e.g., Peters & Esses, 1985). Moreover, separating these groups definitively may be impossible. The most promising approach may be that proposed by Kahle and Jones (1998), which holds that the focus should be "on the dimensions of either condition that might interfere with parenting and access[ing] those dimensions as directly as possible" (p. 396).

IMPORTANCE FOR CLINICAL CHILD PSYCHOLOGY

The fact that an adult is the one with the chronic condition should not lessen the interest of practitioners and researchers in clinical child psychology. Parental chronic illness may intrude into the normal developmental pathways and effect a child in the same way as do other potentially adverse phenomena in a child's life, such as parental

divorce, absence, alcoholism, or death. A child may have to cope with restrictions in the parent's ability to visit school or to participate in family activities, with real or perceived threats of death, with financial costs and limitations, with frequent disruptions of schedule due to doctors' visits or hospitalization, for example. The adverse impact of illness-related demands on the psychological well-being of the child is of greatest concern; however, any potential positive aspects are also of interest. In this chapter, we examine the scientific and professional literature for the existing conceptualizations of parenting with a chronic illness in the context of previous research, and present relevant findings regarding the impact of a parental chronic illness on child functioning, family functioning, and coping behaviors. We then present an expanded conceptualization for guiding research and interventions, describe the research needs, and outline some considerations for clinical interventions.

THEORETICAL CONCEPTUALIZATIONS

No single conceptual model or theory has been formulated with a focus on delineating the many variables, which have been discussed in relation to the impact of parental chronic illness on a child, in a comprehensive way that explicates the relationships among all the variables. The investigators researching this topic typically have not relied on a theoretical model; they have studied important variables, but these have rarely been interlinked theoretically to form a comprehensive perspective. The lack of a conceptualization has limited empirical investigation and hindered development of services that may improve children's functioning when a parent is diagnosed with a disease. As will be noted later in this chapter, recently emerging conceptualizations have guided program development such as the Family Health Project for HIV-seropositive parents (Family Health Project Research Group, 1998; Forehand et al., 1998).

COMBINED THEORETICAL PERSPECTIVES

Most authors writing about this topic have described the application of various theoretical perspectives that might be useful in organizing work in this area. For example, Kahle and Jones (1998) suggested that outcomes for children might be conceptualized through four traditional and theoretical perspectives: developmental, family systems, psychodynamic, and social learning. The developmental perspective predicts that parental chronic illness interferes with the child's normal developmental transitions and that a child's response to the illness might change depending on his or her developmental status. The family systems perspective views the reciprocally interacting aspects of the family as important in that changes to one part of the family (namely, the health of the parent) change the roles and functions of other parts of the unit (e.g., the child). The family system adapts to the parental illness in various ways that might be effective or ineffective. The psychodynamic perspective, as outlined by Kahle and Jones, holds that personality characteristics of the parent are affected by the chronic illness, which, in term, affects the child. Through this perspective, for example, the child may become poorly attached due to identification with the parent who is chronically ill. The social learning perspective also involves identification with and modeling by the ill parent, by which the child learns illness behavior and coping responses to illness. Finney and Miller (1998) endorsed a social learning model as a pathway of influence based on imitation or modeling of behaviors. This approach predicts somatic complaints in the children when a parent is physically ill or the child is modeling other illness-related behaviors. Additionally, Finney and Miller included the impact of parental chronic illness on the family system with concomitant effects on a child's functioning. These authors further incorporated a developmental perspective in understanding children's responses and coping with parental chronic illness. However, the mechanism by which developmental status influences the relationship was not proposed. A social learning perspective has also been taken by researchers and other authors in this area. Some research has supported the social learning approach while revealing that there are multiple impacts likely resulting from different mechanisms (Stein & Newcomb, 1994).

DISRUPTED PARENTING

Armistead et al. (1995) took the position that understanding the relationship between parental illness and child adjustment requires an examination of

the mechanisms by which a relationship might occur. They proposed a tentative model wherein disrupted parenting, broadly defined, can account for some child maladjustment due to parental chronic illness. Disruption of parenting may include such mechanisms as "reduced parental support for the child; fewer efforts at discipline; neglect of child due to reorganization of family around illness; changes in family routines; parental absence" (p. 418). Additionally, they postulated that the mechanisms influencing child functioning may include parental depression, interfamilial conflict, and parental divorce, as related to the illness.

Armistead and Forehand (1995) offered a more specific conceptual model focused on mothers who are HIV infected. In this context, they outlined elements of the broader environmental context of life (in which stigma and associated stressors of the parent living with HIV are experienced) and daily challenges (e.g., day-to-day parenting requirements and other caregiving burdens). In this model, the woman with HIV must also make major decisions about conceiving and giving birth, disclosing to others that she is seropositive, and making future living arrangements for her child after death. All of these components and relational mechanisms are presumed to influence the child's functioning. This model posits that a mother who is HIV infected faces a range of difficulties, including stigmatization by society, rejection by potential social supports and related disclosure issues, compromised parenting, hospitalization and separation of mother and child, maternal depression, and worries related to her child (Armistead & Forehand, 1995; Family Health Project Research Group, 1998; Forehand et al., 1998). The delineation of this model allowed this research group to empirically test the relationships. Confirmation of the model would seem to lead directly to interventions.

INCREASED STRESS

Compas and his colleagues identified stress as a marker of increased risk for children of chronically ill parents and sought to determine a mechanism or process by which stress influences children's psychological health (Compas et al., 1994). They found that girls whose mothers were diagnosed with cancer had more anxious-distressed symptoms than boys (and than girls whose fathers were ill). They postulated and generally confirmed that the girls with ill mothers experienced more stressful events related to increased family responsibilities (Grant & Compas, 1995). These authors also suggested that the assumption of caretaking roles may contribute to the adolescent girls' maladjustment because "they may not have developed adaptive capacities to cope with the role of caring for others" or because these new responsibilities come "into conflict with other developmentally appropriate goals (e.g., school achievement, relationships with friends, increased autonomy outside the family)" (p. 1019). Thus, this line of research takes a family systems perspective coupled with a developmental perspective in examining coping mechanisms.

REVIEW OF THE EXISTING LITERATURE: CHILD FUNCTIONING, FAMILY FUNCTIONING, AND COPING

Parental chronic illness is a potentially persistent source of stress that can affect children and families (Drotar, 1994). The earliest research (Buck & Hohmann, 1983) suggested that parental chronic illness is positively associated with poor child adjustment, behavior problems, and anxieties. The conclusions of these few early studies, however, are limited by weak underlying theories and methodological problems, which include small sample size, subjective measures of children's behavior and symptomology, an absence of comparison populations, and a failure to distinguish among parental physical illness, stable parental disability, and parental psychiatric illness (Buck & Hohmann, 1983). Research completed since Buck and Hohmann's review remains sparse. Some research employs improved methodology, but many of the same criticisms can be made of current research.

Child Functioning

Studies completed after the review by Buck and Hohmann (1983) also demonstrated that children of physically ill parents are at greater risk for social, emotional, and behavioral problems when compared to children of physically healthy parents on a broad range of child adjustment variables. In a study of families with a terminally ill parent, ill parents reported more internalizing problems

(anxiety, fear, and depression), externalizing problems (aggressive, inattentive, and impulsive behavior), and poorer school performance in their children than parents drawn from a community sample (Siegel et al., 1992). Children of terminally ill parents also self-reported more anxiety and depression than comparison children (Siegel et al., 1992). In a second paper completed by this group, the most adversely affected children had either a history of psychological problems or family disruption prior to the parental illness (Christ et al.,1993). These results support a move beyond a simple deficit model, because differences also exist among children of chronically ill parents. Both of these projects are limited by a small and homogeneous sample. The results may not apply to children who are coping with a parent's non-life-threatening disease, because the sample was restricted to families in which the parent died within six months of the initial interview.

In a series of studies of parental HIV infection, Forehand and colleagues found an association between maternal HIV infection and difficulties across multiple domains of child functioning (Forehand et al., 1998). Results supported the authors' hypotheses that children show disruptions in different domains and that reports of disruptions in functioning vary by informant. For example, HIV-infected mothers reported more difficulties with their child's cognitive and social competence than did noninfected mothers. Children of HIV-infected mothers self-reported more internalizing and externalizing symptoms than children of noninfected mothers, although mothers' reports of psychopathology in their children did not differ according to health status. Children's self-reports of social and cognitive competence were judged unreliable and could not be analyzed. Findings by Forehand's team suggest that a failure to consider multiple domains from more than one perspective may mask disruptions related to parental illness (Forehand et al., 1998). Conclusive generalizations, however, are limited by the fact that all participating children were African American and from inner-city, economically impoverished homes. The same mechanisms may not apply to majority culture adolescents or wealthier adolescents.

The literature on parents with mood disorders, when physically ill parents are used as a comparison group, provides additional support for an association between chronic illness and poorer child functioning. Anderson and Hammen (1993) compared children of mothers with an affective illness to children of parents without any diagnoses (normative group) and children of mothers diagnosed with a chronic illness (insulin-dependent diabetes or severe arthritis). Physically ill mothers reported rates of significant and chronic psychiatric symptoms in their children similar to rates reported by psychiatrically ill mothers. Both groups of children thus appear to be at equal risk for chronic adjustment problems. Significance testing also indicated that physically ill mothers reported fewer symptoms of psychiatric conditions on average than psychiatrically ill mothers but more than mothers in the normative group. Unfortunately, differences between children of normal parents and children of chronically ill parents were not tested for significance (Anderson & Hammen, 1993).

ILLNESS SEVERITY

Recent research has attempted to identify the illness characteristics mechanisms that interfere with child functioning. For example, Kotchick et al. (1997) examined the effects of parental illness severity on the psychosocial adjustment of children age 6 to 11 from urban, poor, African-American families confronting maternal HIV infections. Participating families were classified into two groups representing the severity of their disease: symptomatic and asymptomatic AIDS. A comparison sample was drawn from the local schools. No significant effects were found for illness severity on child functioning. In a follow-up study of the same sample, Dorsey, Chance, Forehand, Morse, and Morse (1999) hypothesized a link between disease severity and the effects of other adults in the home on child adjustment in families experiencing HIV infections. Results indicated no direct relationship between disease severity and the number of adults in the home. Women with symptoms of AIDS, however, were more likely than asymptomatic women to have fewer children living with them and to be living with another adult female, although the presence of additional adults was not protective for children as hypothesized. In fact, although asymptomatic HIV-infected mothers did not report more internalizing or externalizing problems in their children when more adults resided in the home, children of AIDS-symptomatic mothers did report experiencing more symptoms when more adults were present in the home. The authors suggested

that they may have placed too much importance on coresidence and suggested future studies attend to *important* adults in and out of the home (Dorsey et al., 1999). Given the specific sample and the main effects for symptomatic versus asymptomatic HIV status, generalizations from these results may be limited to African-American families living in poverty. Nonetheless, this limitation is also a strength because of a differential risk for HIV-infection in minority populations and the fact that minority groups are typically understudied. For a more complete discussion of the research with this population, see a review of the work by the Family Health Project Research Group (1998).

CHILD AND FAMILY PERCEPTIONS

Researchers also have examined the effects of illness-related cognitions on child and family outcomes. Steele, Tripp, Kotchick, Summers, and Forehand (1997) assessed the effects of perceptions of uncertainty (evidenced by a lack of clarity regarding knowledge and expectations of the possible outcome of the disease) on psychosocial adjustment in families coping with paternal hemophilia and HIV infection. Children's internalizing symptoms were positively correlated with their own uncertainty about their father's disease. Child internalizing symptoms were indirectly related to the father's uncertainty, so that fathers' feelings of uncertainty correlated with children's uncertainty. Maternal uncertainty, in contrast, was directly associated with children's self-reports of anxiety and unrelated to child uncertainty. Consistent with cognitive approaches to stress and coping, no significant relationships were found between objective measures of parental disease severity and children's internalizing symptoms (Steele, Tripp, et al., 1997). Results suggest that the influence of parents' knowledge and expectations about parental disease on children varies depending on the gender of the parent and/or on whether the ill parent's assessment or nonill parent's assessment is being considered. This study did not address that question.

Similarly, Compas and his colleagues have conducted a set of studies exploring the effects of perceived and objective disease severity on family members' coping and adjustment shortly after a parent was diagnosed with cancer (Compas et al., 1994; Compas, Worsham, Ey, & Howell, 1996). In one of these studies, children, youth, and young adults whose parent had an objectively poorer prognosis or was in a more advanced stage of cancer were more likely to report avoidance coping but were no more likely to report anxiety or depression (Compas et al., 1996). Again, perceptions of stress related to parental illness—not prognosis or illness severity—were positively associated with depression and anxiety (Compas et al., 1994, 1996). Further, Compas et al. (1994) found that children of parents with cancer who perceived the illness to be more severe were more likely to experience stress-related symptoms, such as intrusive thoughts. Symptoms of emotional distress, however, also varied by age (Compas et al., 1994, 1996) and gender (Compas et al., 1994) of the parent and the offspring. Adolescent daughters of mothers with cancer reported the highest levels of distress.

In a follow-up study, Grant and Compas (1995) examined potential processes to explain adolescent girls' increased risk. Although adolescent daughters, in this study, relied more on ruminative coping, coping style did not account entirely for higher levels of anxiety and depression. Greater perceived demands and more stress related to family responsibilities, such as caring for younger children and household chores, however, did account for high levels of symptomology. The authors conclude that, consistent with the literature on stress, illness-related minor and daily hassles may mediate adjustment to parental illness. Moreover, these studies highlight the reciprocal and interactive influences on outcomes for family members, as we discuss further in the section on coping.

FAMILY FUNCTIONING

In contrast to the effects of parental illness on individual family members, some studies have considered the effects on family functioning as a unit. Dura and Beck (1988) found that families in which the mother was chronically ill (insulin-dependent diabetes or chronic back or neck pain) perceived less cohesion and more control when compared to families with physically healthy mothers. Children of women with multiple sclerosis (MS) also reported lower levels of cohesion and higher levels of conflict along with lower levels of intellectual-cultural activities (Peters & Esses, 1985). These studies suggest the profound effect that parental illness can have on children's perceptions of the family environment, although larger replications

are needed. Potentially, higher levels of conflict and lower levels of cohesion reflect the challenges and disruptions that families most often confront with parental illness so that differences between families with physically healthy parents and chronically ill parents may be mediated by the degree of physical disability or illness severity (Peters & Esses, 1985). This proposal, however, remains an empirical question; measures of this variable were not taken in either study.

Crist (1993) conducted a unique observational study of the interactions between mothers with MS and their preadolescent daughters. She predicted that mothers with MS would have more negative interactions with their daughters than physically healthy mothers and that mothers with MS who were also disabled would have more negative interactions with their daughters (age 8–22) than mothers with MS and no disability. She found no differences in the behaviors of mothers or daughters on an observational measure of the characteristics of interactive exchanges between mothers with and without MS and their daughters. Additional research, however, is still needed to explore discrepancies between self-reported adjustment problems and observed parent-child interactions.

In a study of HIV-infected inner-city minority mothers living in poverty, ill mothers reported less monitoring of their children outside the home (age 6–11 years) and poorer quality in the mother-child relationship when compared to physically healthy mothers (Kotchick et al., 1997). The objective severity of the disease was unrelated to parenting behavior, which is consistent with some of the findings discussed previously. Nonetheless, parenting behaviors and parent-child relationship quality predicted child adjustment in families with maternal HIV and without maternal HIV. The authors concluded that HIV infection may have a direct effect on maternal parenting, which can explain poorer child psychosocial adjustment in families experiencing maternal HIV infections. The authors recognized, however, that HIV infection may have a number of indirect effects such as maternal depression and loss of social support that contribute to parenting and to children's psychosocial adjustment beyond the normative processes (Kotchick et al., 1997). This is an important question, given the literature demonstrating increased risk for psychosocial problems among children of depressed mothers (Downey & Coyne, 1990). The degree to which these findings are mediated by marital status and other transitions was not considered in this study. Clarifying the additional sources of stress can contribute to intervention efforts by identifying both outside resources as well as sources of distress.

The effects of parental illness on child outcomes also may be related to effects on the interactions among other family members. In a study of mothers with cancer, Lewis and her colleagues found that school-age children (6–12 years) had better relationships with peers when families engaged in more reflection and introspection about a parental diagnosis (Lewis, Hammond, & Woods, 1993). Nonill partners tended to have more frequent interactions with the child and a more positive marital adjustment when the family engaged in reflection about the cancer and related problems. The greater the illness demands on the family, the more likely parents were to report feeling depressed and the less likely the family was to engage in introspection and reflection. These findings emphasize the potentially indirect effects of illness severity on child functioning effecting processes within the family such as coping and adult adjustment.

Studies that have taken a conceptual approach to understanding the adjustment and functioning of families in the context of parental chronic illness have highlighted the complex and interactive processes that influence child outcomes. At this point, there seems to be sufficient evidence to avoid any additional studies based on simple deficit models. Disruptions in functioning likely are related to disruptions in normative parenting processes and adjustment-related processes. Below, we specifically review the findings on coping to highlight the importance of conceptualizing individual differences in outcomes for children in families with parental illness according to complex interactions among family members and with people outside the family.

COPING AS AN INTERACTIVE PROCESS

In studies of families experiencing maternal cancer, Compas et al. (1996) found that most children, including adult children of ill mothers, perceived little personal control over their parents' illness. Consistent with the literature on coping with uncontrollable events, these children tended to use emotion-focused coping. Children of parents with a more serious stage of cancer and a less optimistic prognosis tended to perceive the cancer as more serious and to use more emotion-focused coping than children of parents with a more optimistic prognosis. Most emotion-focused coping efforts were attempts at avoiding the stress or feelings related to the cancer. Emotion-focused coping efforts, however, predicted more symptoms of stress, depression, and anxiety (Compas et al., 1996). Of note, adolescents and young adults in this sample were more likely to engage in emotion-focused coping, which was less effective and positively associated with symptoms of distress. According to the authors, a diagnosis of parental cancer may leave children of all ages with few opportunities to experience a sense of personal control and develop effective coping solutions.

Coping is a process, however, that may be influenced by more than individual perceptions and efforts. Family members can facilitate or hinder each other's adjustment. Kotchick et al. (1997) found that avoidant coping by one spouse increased the psychological distress of the other spouse. The coping behaviors of one spouse, however, did not directly predict the coping behavior of the other spouse. Frequent use of avoidant coping by either parent also increased the likelihood that children would experience behavior problems and/or more depression and anxiety. The relationship between mothers' coping and family members' adjustment was stronger than the relationship between fathers' coping and family members' adjustment (Kotchick et al., 1997).

Steele, Forehand, and Armistead (1997) tested a more complex model of the processes related to child outcomes in families experiencing paternal hemophilia with or without HIV infection. They found that the severity of the disease increased parental depression, which directly predicted parent-child relationship problems. These parent-child relationship problems predicted higher levels of self-reported anxiety and depression in children of ill fathers and more avoidant coping in children. Also, when parents used avoidant coping, children were more likely to use avoidant coping and to experience poorer adjustment. Again, the mother's coping affected her child's adjustment more strongly than the father's. These findings highlight the importance of considering the interactive influence of family members on processes such as coping and adjustment.

PARENTING WITH DISABILITY

Very few studies have examined the effects of physical disability on parents and their children. The degree to which disability influences parenting remains largely ignored (see Crist, 1993, for an exception). One difficulty is the complicated and entangled relationship between disability and chronic illness, discussed earlier. A second major limitation to research on parenting with a disability is the use of samples that include a number of different types of disability in a single sample. Although it can be quite difficult to entirely separate different types of disability, particularly among chronically ill populations, research must first demonstrate that these conditions each have a similar effect on child development and adjustment.

EXPANDED CONCEPTUALIZATION OF THE EFFECTS OF PARENTAL CHRONIC ILLNESS

Family members affect each other's behavior in diverse and complex ways. Few strong conclusions can be made regarding the processes that create, control, or exacerbate adjustment problems for all family members. Early evidence indicated a modest relationship between parental illness and negative outcomes for children and families (Buck & Hohmann, 1983). Simple comparisons, however, between children of ill parents and children with physically healthy parents on measures of psychopathology and distress fail to provide much information beyond justifying further research.

A number of variables potentially related to child development and adjustment in the context of parental chronic illness can be identified in the literature on parenting with chronic illness and the normative developmental literature. We propose that a broad perspective on this topic can be informed by variables from each domain discussed below and the potential interactions among them. However, no single study can be expected to capture all the domains identified and additional domains will likely emerge as more research is completed. As knowledge of particular processes or variables advances, we suggest that findings be interpreted as one part of a larger picture encompassing all of these domains. In addition, theoretical work is needed to develop specific models demonstrating how these pieces fit together.

INDIVIDUAL CHARACTERISTICS OF CHILD AND ADULT

Some of the individual differences that may be important to adjustment to parental illness include age, gender, cultural and ethnic background, and preexisting conditions. The few studies that have examined these individual characteristics and children's responses to parental illness found that the effects of individual differences are not simple. The gender of both the child and the parent is related to the child's adjustment to chronic illness (Compas et al., 1994; Grant & Compas, 1995; Steele, Tripp, et al., 1997). The processes that increase risk remain to be studied. Compas's team has postulated that the relation between gender and social role is one mechanism by which this may occur (Grant & Compas, 1995).

Ethnic and cultural identification provide an additional source of individual differences because these are the social lenses through which people perceive and interpret events. Thus, these variables should be considered in both research and applied work. The functioning of individual family members and the family system as a unit, for example, may differ according to distinct cultural and social values. In addition, specific detailed knowledge of marginalized and understudied groups coping with health issues decreases false generalizations about group differences. A careful study of marginalized groups can facilitate the identification of protective factors for specific groups and clarify the effects of interventions (Mann & Kato, 1996). The efforts by Forehand and colleagues to develop a body of knowledge about urban, African-American mothers infected with HIV and living in poverty is a good example of such work (Family Health Project Research Group, 1998; Forehand et al., 1998; Kotchick et al., 1997).

Much more work, however, is needed regarding the influence of developmental stages on functioning in families with chronically ill parents because parents and children all have a past and future beyond the snapshots taken by research studies. For example, how do the cognitive representations of parental illness change as children age? In what ways do the cognitive limitations of young children act as a protective factor or a risk factor? Answers to these questions may inform intervention efforts in important ways.

In addition, a number of preexisting characteristics of the child and the adult exist, which may have important effects on the relationship among parental health problems, the child, and the child's family. Such conditions can color the entire process of the child's and family's reaction to the onset and continuing existence of a disease (e.g., prior coping strategies, adjustment patterns, and behavioral and personality functioning with which the individual enters the process). It appears that no one has examined relationships between parental and child premorbid personality characteristics and the effects of parental chronic illness. Research is needed to identify individual differences that affect the degree of risk parental illness poses for children and families. The quality of the relationship between parent and child is another preexisting characteristic that may have a major effect on child development. Preexisting individual characteristics also may have a direct relation to the parent's risk for illness. Intravenous drug abuse, for example, is one risk factor for infection and for disruptions in adult functioning independent of the infection, which include disruptions in education, occupation, social functioning, and parenting. In light of these possibilities, researchers should take care to avoid generalizations regarding the effects of parental HIV infection that fail to account for the effects of the risks co-occurring, but not necessarily present, for all HIV-infected persons.

The effects of premorbid characteristics are absent in the current emphasis on cross-sectional studies. Opportunities for gathering information on a population before the symptoms of illness develop, however, are quite limited. Other means of capturing some of this information may be to conduct archival assessments such as children's school records and medical records.

CHARACTERISTICS OF THE STRESSOR

The designation "chronically ill" or "disabled" captures a large group within which persons may have vastly different experiences. These differences pose challenges to generalizing findings from one population to another. Although our review has attempted to summarize some of the findings across different diseases and conditions, we know of no studies demonstrating that findings with families experiencing one condition can be applied to families experiencing a different illness or disability. Even within a diagnostic category, the effects of an illness can vary widely. The physical effects of MS, for example, range from a series of hassles to parental morbidity from complications, which creates significant variability among families (Rosner & Ross, 1987). Thus, researchers should attend to the sources of individual differences within specific diagnoses or conditions. Whether one model can fit a single diagnostic group or capture the effects across a range of conditions remains to be seen.

Potentially, studies of the dimensions of physical conditions in conjunction with diagnostic category will provide findings that can be generalized across conditions. Dimensions of health status that are definable and that potentially influence the impact of illness or disability on adults and children include the physical effects of the condition (e.g., hair loss, amputation, fatigue), predictability of symptoms and course of the condition, functional status and any type of disability associated with the chronic illness, and visibility of the symptoms of the illness. The course or perceived course of a particular illness, rather than the presence of that illness, has a more important role in adjustment of both children and families.

The exact nature of the challenges confronting parents in families experiencing a parental illness also can vary widely. Sources of stress are likely to vary from one family to another independent of parental diagnosis. Rather than attributing all group differences to the presence of a parental illness, research must evaluate the extent to which parental illness is exacerbating normative sources of stress (e.g., typical parenting demands to nurture and discipline, or life events affecting families such as school entry, marital separation, or geographic relocation) and/or creating illness-related stress, such as emotional, financial, and personal demands of treatment, or debilitating symptoms and treatment regimens that interfere with providing physical care and emotional nurturing. Information about the specific demands that chronic illness places on parents, beyond the typical demands of parenting, contributes to developing an understanding of the relationships between parental illness and disturbances in child and family functioning by moving away from a simple deficit model. Finally, professionals should assess some of the challenging experiences that parents with chronic illness face for the potential to facilitate child development. For example, the experience of parental disability may actually improve communication in the family (Alessandri, 1992; Johnston, Martin, Martin, & Gumaer, 1992).

Qualitative studies of parents disabled by either chronic illness or injury further highlight the need for more attention to specific challenges confronted by parents. Thorne (1990) and Crook (1982) found that mothers experienced the demands of treatment and medical prescriptions to be incompatible with the demands of child care. Thus, attention to specific demands of parenting in the context of chronic illness may facilitate better medical and psychological interventions.

In addition, studies should specify the duration of the parent's illness for the sample. In cases where the parent was diagnosed prior to the child's birth, children are not adjusting to parental illness, but are developing in the context of parental chronic illness. Conversely, a child whose mother is diagnosed with cancer when the child is 10 years old is adjusting to parental illness and developing in the context of parental chronic illness. The effects of the disease characteristics are not likely to be the same across developmental stages. Individual differences can be expected to interact with the duration of the illness and its location in time.

We limited our literature review to studies of populations in which a parent is experiencing and receiving treatment for a diagnosed chronic disorder or disability. Another approach to parental health and child development is to consider parental health status and risks in general (e.g., smoking, diet, substance abuse, health care utilization). Such an approach provides the opportunity to broaden the topic of parental illness further but also poses challenges in formulating operational definitions of parental health problems (Drotar, 1994). The effects of parents' health risks on their children is clearly important from a preventive health perspective. Whether parental smoking falls within the domain of parental health problems to an extent equal to parental diabetes, for example, is a question. Nonetheless, prospective studies of adults with certain health risk factors will identify specific at-risk populations with a greater likelihood of developing a chronic illness of potential impact on children.

ADJUSTMENT PROCESSES

Individuals do not confront stress passively. Appraisals of events and coping responses are important factors mediating individual differences in response to stress (Lazarus & Folkman, 1984). Therefore, in addition to carefully defining the stress, researchers should consider processes that mediate outcomes for family members. For example, within the family, the flexibility of perceptions of gender roles may be related to a family's ability to adapt. In general, society holds women to be more responsible than men for the emotional and behavioral outcomes of their children. These perceptions are reflected as well in the research on parenting by the overwhelming number of articles examining mothers and excluding fathers (Phares & Compas, 1992). The rigidity of such perceptions may affect adjustment by placing a parent in a new role with more or less child-related responsibilities. For the chronically ill mother, disease-related interference with her role as primary caregiver may lead to adjustment difficulties, whereas chronically ill fathers, if unable to maintain employment outside the home, may have difficulty adjusting to more caregiving responsibilities. Little research has examined the effects of illness on perceived social roles and illness-related challenges to those roles.

In addition to individual differences in coping, adjustment processes can capture the effects of family members on each other and the effects of individuals outside the family. Parental loss of social support, for example, may disrupt parenting more than the presence of the illness itself (Dorsey et al., 1999). Much more attention is needed to the effects of resources outside the immediate family to facilitate or prevent adequate adjustment. Research on coping by parents, moreover, has demonstrated significant relationships among children's coping, parents' coping, and adjustment. Although research to date has not explored the influence of child coping and adjustment on parental outcomes, parents and children potentially influence adaptation both positively and negatively.

OUTCOMES

The attempt to establish definitive outcomes in any study of illness and adaptation is inherently complex because of the interaction between psychosocial and biomedical variables. Researchers are advised to draw from existing models when selecting specific child outcome variables to ensure that adequate attention is given to constellations of behavioral and emotional outcomes. Nonetheless, it is not always clear which variable is driving the relationship. For example, illness-related demands modestly predict stress-related outcomes (Compas et al., 1994). Conversely, denial of one's disease can interfere with treatment demands and exacerbate the illness, and cognitive aspects of depression such as lack of optimism have been found to be predictive of an increased risk for chronic and life-threatening physical conditions (Peterson & Bossio, 1991). Thus, psychosocial variables such as depression can be direct outcomes of the disease, a preexisting condition, or difficulties coping with an illness, or a variable that interacts with the disease and both exacerbates the disease process and undermines effective coping.

We propose that examination of the effects of chronic illness on the adjustment of ill parents includes careful attention to the relationships between biological effects and psychosocial effects related to the physical condition and the patient's adjustment. Although in one study, depression or stress-response symptoms may represent a patient's adjustment to a chronic physical condition, in another, depression may represent a preexisting condition or a process that exacerbates the symptoms and hastens the progress of the disease. We do not propose that research emphasize psychological characteristics as important causal factors for the disease. A fine balance exists between an appropriate biopsychosocial perspective and a "victim-blaming" approach, which suggests that if the individual were coping better, he or she would not be experiencing illness. Rather, we propose that studies of psychological adjustment to chronic parental illness avoid too much emphasis on psychological outcomes independent of the interaction between physical and psychological variables. The best studies will likely be the product of interdisciplinary perspectives that include expertise in the biomedical effects of the illness and the psychological variables related to adjustment and coping. In this way, respectful and informative research and applications will emerge.

Similarly, parental illness is presumed to disrupt child development via the same processes in any source of chronic stress. Anecdotally, however, children of ill or disabled parents often assist the ill parent to meet illness-related demands. Such early demands of the environment potentially facilitate earlier development of perspective-taking skills or a greater tolerance of physical differences.

A broad perspective that interprets findings in the context of pathways and processes related to differences in outcomes further helps to ensure that resiliency as well as risk factors are considered (Drotar, 1994). The experiences and processes in families that provide protection from stress or exacerbate stress likely will be similar for individuals experiencing any chronic stress. Moreover, efforts to explore the rich and complex variables that relate to child development in families experiencing chronic illness have raised important questions that extend beyond this specific population. For example, how does coping change with maturation? Do individual differences in coping change in the context of chronic parental illness (Compas et al., 1996). Such questions suggest that exploring development in the context of parental illness can contribute to a better understanding of basic developmental processes in typical populations.

Finally, researchers should give careful attention to specific measures of adjustment as knowledge advances. For example, Compas found that stress-response symptoms were more consistently related to perceptions of illness-related stress than depression or anxiety. At this time, we endorse the approaches of both the Forehand and Compas research teams, which is to include multiple outcome measures from multiple perspectives (e.g., Compas et al., 1994, 1996; Forehand et al., 1998).

RESEARCH NEEDS

Despite the improvements in empirical research conducted since the review by Buck and Hohmann (1983), many issues remain inadequately explored and many of the same criticisms of earlier reviews, including use of small, homogeneous samples, still apply (Drotar, 1994). For future research, we recommend the following methodological improvements to facilitate the development of more specific research models of child and family outcomes and improve generalizations across samples: (1) larger samples, which include adequate representation of different age groups; (2) standardized measures applicable across research studies; (3) multidimensional and multimethod assessments; (4) attention to marginalized populations; and (5) longitudinal follow-up to explore preexisting and developmental factors. Further, considerably more work is needed regarding the processes by which a parental illness might disrupt family environments and functioning. Multiple sources of confounding variables affect these families, including poverty, overlapping illnesses, cognitive and psychiatric disabilities, and socioeconomic disruptions such as job loss. Studies that draw conclusions from heterogeneous samples perpetuate the assumption that physical, cognitive, and psychiatric disabilities inherently co-occur. Such biased assumptions have contributed to previous research designed to demonstrate disruptions in emotional functioning and psychiatric problems of children of disabled parents and have interfered with appropriate attention to the interpersonal processes that are associated with adjustment of children in families with a physically disabled or sensory-impaired parent. Research that examines and replicates specific explanatory models of the ways in which parental illness can influence parenting are needed (1) to avoid a solely deficit/disruption model and examine a range of responses and identify what might protect the child in this situation, including prosocial outcomes; (2) to hypothesize and empirically evaluate the mechanisms or processes by which important variables are related to each other, which requires multivariate and longitudinal research (Armistead et al., 1995; Grant & Compas, 1995); (3) to specify the nature of stress and specific illness-related and normative demands confronted by families; (4) to attend to the functional disruptions related to the parent's illness; and (5) to give more sophisticated attention to parental health and illness to account for the fact that many adults experience overlapping chronic illnesses and/or disabling conditions (Drotar, 1994). In addition, attention should be given to fathers and to influences outside of the immediate family. Only a few studies have included fathers; only one of the studies reviewed here (Dorsey et al., 1999) considered the effects of extended family members. It also may be important to consider the resources that families have beyond the nuclear system. Furthermore, case studies have suggested that the impact of parental illness disrupts the entire family, which may have ramifications on child adjustment (Armistead et al., 1995). A few of the research needs suggested by these weaknesses

include: (1) assessments by family members other than mothers, specifically fathers, as well as teachers, peers, and health care providers; (2) assessments of the influences of social and cultural values; and (3) assessments of disruptions in the surrounding ecosystems. Finally, the relative recency of empirical studies on the effects of parental chronic illness on children has left most practitioners with few to no guidelines for treatment. There is a significant need to examine and determine what variables are amenable to intervention and how to successfully intervene. For example, changing a child's gender or age is not possible; however, targeting the issues associated with gender or age is not only possible but recommended. Moreover, empirical studies of the effectiveness of interventions are also needed.

CLINICAL INTERVENTIONS

Mental health professionals are often consulted to provide services or design intervention programs responding to the potential problems facing children who have parents with a chronic illness or disability. Theoretically driven empirical research, as opposed to case descriptions of clinical experience or postulated relationships of different variables, is needed to guide prevention and therapeutic interventions. The value of developing theoretical frameworks for conceptualizing relationships between characteristics of the situation for children and their families when a parent is ill and empirical confirmation of these relationships is that the improved understanding can lead directly to intervention. For example, if parental depression resulting from the diagnosis and treatment of the chronic illness increases problems in family systems and disrupts coping mechanisms (Steele, Forehand, et al., 1997), then professionals can target that parental depression to help the children in the family. If the parental illness has disrupted the parent-child relationship, then interventions can bolster the child's relationship with the nonill parent (Steele, Forehand, et al., 1997). Similarly, research confirming that adolescent daughters in particular have increased family caretaking responsibilities, which lead to stress and poor coping (Grant & Compas, 1995), suggests that a logical intervention would be to work on alleviating those responsibilities and providing support for the daughters. Also, studies indicating that nonadaptive coping styles by adolescents are related to parental chronic illness support interventions that reduce the use of denial and avoidant or ruminative coping strategies (Grant & Compas, 1995; Steele, Forehand, et al., 1997; Wills, Schreibman, Benson, & Vaccaro, 1994). Professionals may also determine to intervene to change noneffective parenting practices such as low monitoring of child activities that may be associated with parental illness and are disruptive to child psychosocial adjustment (Kotchick et al., 1997).

When research has identified the critical linkages of psychological and physical support for parenting, then interventions should be organized to provide that support through home visitation programs, for example, for those with economic disadvantage (Black, Nair, & Harrington, 1994). When studies have shown that some positive outcomes are possible, then interventions should not just assume that negative outcomes are the norm (Armistead et al., 1995; Kahle & Jones, 1998) or focus only on preventing negative outcomes; professionals should work to facilitate positive developmental results. Thus, as illustrated in these examples, basic research investigating the relationships of various aspects of the parental chronic illness can assist clinical professionals in determining where and how to make the most effective interventions.

Other aspects of interventions can come through theoretical and professional perspectives identifying that certain key psychological components need to be present in children's lives. For example, providing support and access to psychotherapy and medical health services seems essential (Drotar, 1994). Organizing groups or dyads of parents to provide parent-to-parent support for both the ill and the nonill parent also flows from other mental health interventions. Several professionals have relied on the family perspective of focus on ongoing family care and support (e.g., Black et al., 1994; Siegel et al., 1992).

As should be emphasized with all psychotherapeutic interventions in clinical child psychology, cultural- and gender-sensitive programs are required for maximal effectiveness (e.g., Black et al., 1994; Drotar, 1994; Rotheram-Borus, Murphy, Miller, & Draimin, 1997; chapter by Jones et al. in this volume). A developmental perspective also is essential for individualizing prevention and intervention efforts for children and adolescents. The phenomenology of the child's experience, the subjective aspects,

and his or her appraisals of the meaning of the disease and its treatment are important considerations. A simple formulation of the more objective characteristics (e.g., type and severity of disease, gender, socioeconomic status) will ignore significant changes in the perceptions of the child such as the child's individualized manifestations of stress or perceptions of uncertainty (Steele, Tripp, et al., 1997).

Professionals working with children whose parents have a chronic illness need to gain an understanding of what the child knows about the disease and, importantly, what inaccurate beliefs he or she may hold about the cause, the course, and the outcome of the disease process. The professional can provide educative and accurate information in a sensitive, developmentally appropriate manner as a basic step, but without the assumption that information alone will prevent or remediate all potential misconceptions, maladaptive coping, or poor adjustment. There are numerous information resources available and organizations exist for almost all major diseases to advocate, provide accurate information, conduct research, and fund treatment. Some of the resources provided by these national organizations (often with state or local chapters) are specifically targeted to the children of the adults who have the disease. However, in most cases, these materials do not appear to have been empirically tested for educational or therapeutic effects. With the development of the World Wide Web, both accurate and inaccurate information have become easily accessible; the clinical child psychology professional will want to evaluate these before recommending them to patients. Some major Web sites include American Cancer Society (www.cancer.edu), National Multiple Sclerosis Society (www.nmss.org/index.html), American Diabetes Association (www.diabetes.org), American Heart Association (www.amhrt.org), Arthritis Foundation (www.arthritis.org), National Kidney Foundation (www.kidney.org), CFIDS Association of America for chronic fatigue and immune dysfunction syndrome (www.cfids.org), and the National Alliance for the Mentally Ill (www.nami.org).

We describe a few interventions here with the important caveat that most interventions conducted in practice and some described in the various professional literatures have not been subjected to systematic program evaluation. Some interventions are undergoing research validation.

In an unevaluated bibliotherapeutic intervention, Kathleen McCue (1994) authored a self-help book entitled *How to Help Children Through a Parent's Serious Illness*. Although not tested empirically, the advice and information contained in this book based on the author's work as a child life specialist seem quite consistent with the developing literature in this area. The book is directed at parents, both ill and nonill, on how to recognize the needs of children, how to explain illness, what to look for in children's responses, and how to help adjustment. Similarly, a variety of intervention strategies were outlined by Blackford (1992) for nurses to use when they identify parents with MS. In addition to providing information about the disease in understandable form for children, she suggested that the whole family should meet to share emotional responses and to engage in problem solving together while the parent is hospitalized, mainly at the initial diagnosis phase. She also recommended that visiting nurses can facilitate information provision and problem-solving discussions at home, specifically on issues of heredity of MS, aspects of deterioration and disability, and death. Peer groups may also be used to share experiences and perspectives. Blackford suggests that group affiliation will produce "a feeling of acceptance and a more positive self-identity" (p. 53). In a comprehensive intervention program, Rotheram-Borus et al. (1997) described an intervention for adolescents whose parents are living with AIDS. They adapted cognitive-behavioral principles in attempting to increase the coping skills of the adolescents and parents. The intervention program used three organizational modules focusing on (1) the ill parent's coping with the illness, fear, and anger; (2) the illness, its meanings and implications for the mother in dealing with her children's issues, and the adolescent's knowledge, coping, and anger management; and (3) the grieving process for the adolescent. In multiple sessions, professionals teach coping strategies, relaxation, and problem-solving skills. This clinical research team is currently evaluating this well-designed intervention program.

Another brief preventive intervention program was described by Christ, Siegel, Mesagno, and Langosch (1991) for children who are bereaved due to parental death after a protracted illness (in this case, terminal cancer). These professionals hold that, by intervening before the parent's death, the child can become prepared for the loss and change in the family. The program is implemented in the terminal phase (approximately six months prior to anticipated death) and extends through six months afterwards and uses a standardized format. The program seeks to build on the relationship of the child with the surviving parent through a parent-guidance approach. The program attempts to enhance "the ability of these parents to meet their children's heightened needs for emotional support and physical care, on encouraging open communication with the children about the illness and its prognosis, and on maintaining as much stability and predictability in the children's environment as possible" (p. 169). Preliminary evaluation suggested that this program is successful in involving parents in prevention efforts for children anticipating the grieving process.

Although most of the interventions have not received comprehensive validation, the field of clinical child psychology and its related mental health disciplines is becoming more oriented to empirically supporting its psychotherapeutic interventions (Lonigan, Elbert, & Johnson, 1998; Spirito, 1999). Interventions for children and families where a parent has a chronic illness or disability also require much more validation than has been provided to this point, although this is increasing in some areas (e.g., Family Health Project Research Group, 1998).

CONCLUSIONS

Is the impact of a parental health problem on a child a major life event? Is it as major as having a disease oneself? In the context of all the potential developmental influences, where does the impact of a parental illness rate in significance? Like most of the biopsychosocial influences on development, the impact of this one probably "depends" on the range of factors outlined in our model. And like most biopsychosocial phenomena, more research needs to be done to answer the question Does a parental health problem impact significantly on children? Parents assume a major role in their children's lives. The theorizing and research on the impact on children of parental chronic illness parallel conceptualization and empirical research regarding the impact on and psychological adjustment of (1) children of parental divorce (see King, in this volume), (2) children with a parent who is alcoholic or drug abusing (e.g., Rotunda, Scherer, & Imm, 1995), and (3) children with a parent who has a significant emotional/mental disorder (Downey & Coyne, 1990; Scherer, Melloh, Buyck, Anderson, & Foster, 1996). This area is one where more empirical research work and intervention evaluation by clinical child and health psychologists can demonstrate how the phenomenon of a parent's chronic illness or disability influences child development and where preventive and therapeutic interventions can be made to ameliorate those problems so identified.

REFERENCES

Alessandri, S.M. (1992). Effects of maternal work status in single-parent families on children's perception of self and family and school achievement. *Journal of Experimental Psychology, 54*, 417–423.

Anderson, C.A., & Hammen, C.L. (1993). Psychosocial outcomes of children of unipolar depressed, bipolar, medically ill, and normal women: A longitudinal study. *Journal of Experimental Psychology, 54*, 417–423.

Armistead, L., & Forehand, R. (1995). For whom the bell tolls: Parenting decisions and challenges faced by mothers who are HIV seropositive. *Clinical Psychology: Research and Practice, 2*, 239–250.

Armistead, L., Klein, K., & Forehand, R. (1995). Parental physical illness and child functioning. *Clinical Psychology Review, 15*, 409–422.

Barker, L.T., & Maralani, V. (1997). *Challenges and strategies of disabled parents: Findings from a national survey of parents with disabilities.* Berkeley, CA: Berkeley Planning Associates.

Benson, V., & Marano, M. (1994). *Current estimates from the National Health Interview Survey.* National Center for Health Statistics, Vital and Health Statistics (Series 10, No. 189). Washington, DC: U.S. Government Printing Office.

Black, M.M., Nair, P., & Harrington, D. (1994). Maternal HIV infection: Parenting and early child development. *Journal of Pediatric Psychology, 19*, 595–616.

Blackford, K.A. (1992, December). Strategies for intervention and research with children or adolescents who have a parent with multiple sclerosis. *Axon,* 50–54.

Buck, F.M., & Hohmann, G.W. (1983). Parental disability and children's adjustment. *Annual Review of Rehabilitation, 3*, 203–241.

Christ, G.H., Siegel, K., Freund, B., Langosch, D., Hendersen, S., Sperber, D., & Weinstein, L. (1993). Impact of parental terminal cancer on latency-age children. *American Journal of Orthopsychiatry, 63*, 417–425.

Christ, G.H., Siegel, K., Mesagno, F.P., & Langosch, D. (1991). A preventive intervention program for bereaved children: Problems of intervention. *American Journal of Orthopsychiatry, 61*, 168–178.

Compas, B., Worsham, N., Epping-Jordan, J., Grant, K., Mireault, G., Howell, D., & Malcarne, V. (1994). When Mom or Dad has cancer: Markers of psychological distress in cancer patients, spouses, and children. *Health Psychology, 13*, 507–515.

Compas, B.E., Worsham, N.L., Ey, S., & Howell, D.C. (1996). When Mom or Dad has cancer II. Coping, cognitive appraisals, and psychological distress in children of cancer patients. *Health Psychology, 15*, 167–175.

Coyne, J.C., & Fiske, V. (1992). Couples coping with chronic and catastrophic illness. In T.J. Akamatsu, M.A.P. Stephens, S.E. Hobfall, & J.H. Crowther (Eds.), *Family health psychology* (pp. 129–149). Washington, DC: Hemisphere.

Crist, P. (1993). Contingent interaction during work and play tasks for mothers with multiple sclerosis and their daughters. *American Journal of Occupational Therapy, 47*, 121–131.

Crook, J. (1982). Women with chronic pain. In R. Roy & E. Tunks (Eds.), *Chronic pain: Psychosocial factors in rehabilitation* (pp. 69–78). Baltimore: Williams & Wilkins.

Dorsey, S., Chance, M.W., Forehand, R., Morse, E., & Morse, P. (1999). Children whose mothers are HIV infected: Who resides in the home and is there a relationship to child psychosocial adjustment? *Journal of Family Psychology, 13*, 103–117.

Downey, G., & Coyne, J.C. (1990). Children of depressed parents: An integrative review. *Psychological Bulletin, 108*, 50–76.

Drotar, D. (1994). Impact of parental health problems on children: Concepts, methods, and unanswered questions. *Journal of Pediatric Psychology, 19*, 525–536.

Dura, J.R., & Beck, S.J. (1988). A comparison of family functioning when mothers have chronic pain. *Pain, 35*, 79–89.

Family Health Project Research Group. (1998). The Family Health Project: A multidisciplinary longitudinal investigation of children whose mothers are HIV infected. *Clinical Psychology Review, 18*, 839–856.

Finney, J.W., & Miller, K.M. (1998). Children of parents with medical illness. In W.K. Silverman & T.H. Ollendick (Eds.), *Developmental issues in the clinical treatment of children* (pp. 433–442). Needham Heights, MA: Allyn & Bacon.

Forehand, R., Steele, R., Armistead, L., Morse, E., Simon, P., & Clark, L. (1998). The Family Health Project: Psychosocial adjustment of children whose mothers are HIV infected. *Journal of Consulting and Clinical Psychology, 66*, 513–520.

Grant, K.E., & Compas, B.E. (1995). Stress and anxious-depressed symptoms among adolescents: Searching for mechanisms of risk. *Journal of Consulting and Clinical Psychology, 63*, 1015–1021.

Jacobs, J. (1992). Understanding family factors that shape the impact of chronic illness. In T.J. Akamatsu, M.A.P. Stephens, S.E. Hobfall, & J.H. Crowther (Eds.), *Family health psychology* (pp. 111–127). Washington, DC: Hemisphere.

Johnston, M., Martin, D., Martin, M., & Gumaer, J. (1992). Long-term parental illness and children: Perils and promises. *School Counselor, 39,* 225–231.

Kahle, A., & Jones, G.N. (1998). Adaptation to parental chronic illness. In A.J. Goreczny & M. Hersen (Eds.), *Handbook of pediatric and adolescent health psychology* (pp. 387–399). Needham Heights, MA: Allyn & Bacon.

Kotchick, B., Forehand, R., Brody, G., Armistead, L., Morse, E., Simon, P., & Clark, L. (1997). The impact of maternal HIV infection on parenting in the inner-city. *Journal of Family Psychology, 11,* 447–461.

Lazarus, R.S., & Folkman, S. (1984). *Stress, appraisal, and coping.* New York: Springer.

Lewis, F.M., Hammond, M.R., & Woods, N.F. (1993). The family's functioning with newly diagnosed breast cancer in the mother: The development of an explanatory model. *Journal of Behavioral Medicine, 16,* 351–370.

Lonigan, C.J., Elbert, J.C., & Johnson, S.B. (1998). Empirically supported psychosocial interventions for children: An overview. *Journal of Clinical Child Psychology, 27,* 138–145.

Mann, T., & Kato, P. (1996). Diversity issues in health psychology. In P.M. Kato & T. Mann (Eds.), *Handbook of diversity issues in health psychology* (pp. 3–18). New York: Plenum Press.

McCue, K. (1994). *How to help children through a parent's serious illness.* New York: St. Martin's Press.

Peters, L.C., & Esses, L.M. (1985). Family environment as perceived by children with a chronically ill parent. *Journal of Chronic Diseases, 38,* 301–308.

Peterson, C., & Bossio, L.M. (1991). *Health and optimism.* New York: Free Press.

Phares, V., & Compas, B.E. (1992). The role of fathers in child and adolescent psychopathology: Make room for Daddy. *Psychological Bulletin, 111,* 387–412.

Pless, I.B., & Perrin, J.M. (1985). Issues common to a variety of illnesses. In N. Hobbs & J.M. Perrin (Eds.), *Issues in the care of children with chronic illness: A source book on problems, services, and policies* (pp. 41–60). San Francisco: Jossey-Bass.

Rosner, L.J., & Ross, S. (1987). *Multiple sclerosis.* New York: Prentice-Hall.

Rotheram-Borus, M.J., Murphy, D.A., Miller, S., & Draimin, B.H. (1997). An intervention for adolescents whose parents are living with AIDS. *Clinical Child Psychology and Psychiatry, 2,* 201–219.

Rotunda, R.J., Scherer, D.G., & Imm, P.S. (1995). Family systems and alcohol misuse: Research on the effects of alcoholism on family functioning and effective family interventions. *Professional Psychology: Research and Practice, 26,* 95–104.

Scherer, D.G., Melloh, T., Buyck, D., Anderson, C., & Foster, A. (1996). Relation between children's perceptions of maternal mental illness and children's psychological adjustment. *Journal of Clinical Child Psychology, 25,* 156–159.

Siegel, K., Mesagno, F.P., Karus, D., Christ, G., Banks, K., & Moynihan, R. (1992). Psychosocial adjustment of children with a terminally ill parent. *Journal of the American Academy of Child and Adolescent Psychiatry, 31,* 327–333.

Spirito, A. (1999). Empirically supported treatments in pediatric psychology: Introduction. *Journal of Pediatric Psychology, 24,* 87–90.

Steele, R.G., Forehand, R., & Armistead, L. (1997). The role of family processes and coping strategies in the relationship between parental chronic illness and childhood internalizing problems. *Journal of Abnormal Child Psychology, 25,* 83–94.

Steele, R.G., Tripp, G., Kotchick, B.A., Summers, P., & Forehand, R. (1997). Family members' uncertainty about parental chronic illness: The relationship of hemophilia and HIV infection to child functioning. *Journal of Pediatric Psychology, 22,* 577–591.

Stein, J.A., & Newcomb, M.D. (1994). Children's internalizing and externalizing behaviors and maternal health problems. *Journal of Pediatric Psychology, 19,* 571–594.

Thorne, S.E. (1990). Mothers with chronic illness: A predicament of social construction. *Health Care for Women International, 11,* 209–221.

Verbrugge, L.M., & Patrick, D.L. (1995). Seven chronic conditions: Their impact on U.S. adults' activity levels and use of medical services. *American Journal of Public Health, 85,* 173–182.

Wallander, J.L., & Thompson, R.J. (1995). Psychosocial adjustment of children with chronic physical conditions. In M.C. Roberts (Ed.), *Handbook of pediatric psychology* (2nd ed., pp. 124–141). New York: Guilford Press.

Wills, T.A., Schreibman, D., Benson, G., & Vaccaro, D. (1994). Impact of parental substance use on adolescents: A test of a mediational model. *Journal of Pediatric Psychology, 19,* 537–556.

CHAPTER 54

Ethical and Legal Issues in
Mental Health Services for Children

GARY B. MELTON, NANCY S. EHRENREICH, AND PHILLIP M. LYONS, JR.

Whether treating adolescents in a state hospital, counseling runaways at a storefront clinic, or leading therapy groups for abused children, child clinicians confront special legal and ethical issues. Clinicians are treating clients who are doubly disadvantaged (i.e., by both age and disability) and arguably in need of special protection. Furthermore, both ethically and legally, clinicians are required to consider the impact of their actions not only on child clients, but also on the rights, responsibilities, and relationships that tie children to their parents. The purpose of this chapter is to explore these special issues of clinical child practice and the related policy concerns.

TRENDS IN LAW ON
CHILDREN'S RIGHTS

The law concerning the relationship between children and their parents has become significantly more complex during the past 25 years, primarily because the general legal status of children has been in flux. Prior to *In re Gault* (1967) and *Tinker v. Des Moines Independent School District* (1969), it was not clear that minors were to be considered "persons" under the Fourteenth Amendment, which applies the Bill of Rights to the states. In *Gault*, how-

ever, the Supreme Court held that basic procedural protections under the Fifth and Sixth Amendments belonged to juvenile respondents in delinquency proceedings and, in *Tinker*, that minors had First Amendment rights to freedom of expression.

This trend toward recognition of minors' constitutional rights and concomitant increased self-determination for children has been further supported by a line of Supreme Court cases recognizing that minors have a constitutional right to privacy (e.g., *Carey v. Population Services International*, 1977). Initially articulated in cases dealing with adults' rights to purchase contraceptives (*Eisenstadt v. Baird*, 1972; *Griswold v. Connecticut*, 1965), the right to privacy now often is thought to encompass a broader right to be free from unwanted violations of bodily integrity. The right to privacy has been cited by the Supreme Court as the basis for granting both minors (*Planned Parenthood of Central Missouri v. Danforth*, 1976; *Planned Parenthood of Southeastern Pennsylvania v. Casey*, 1992) and adults (*Planned Parenthood of Southeastern Pennsylvania v. Casey*, 1992; *Roe v. Wade*, 1973) a limited right to obtain abortions (see generally, e.g., Schmidt, 1993).

Despite these developments, the limits of autonomy for minors remain so unclear that the post-*Gault* era has featured a remarkably broad array of Supreme Court cases on the application of constitutional rights to minors. One of the sources of ambiguity is the constraints placed on autonomy by the child's level of competence to make a particular decision. The abortion decisions, for example, have been predicated on a right to privacy for mature minors (e.g., *Bellotti v. Baird*, 1979). Furthermore, in denying minors due process rights when they are being "voluntarily" admitted to mental hospitals by their parents, the Court has assumed that "most children, even in adolescence, simply are not able to make sound judgments concerning many decisions, including their need for medical care or treatment. Parents can and must make those judgments" *(Parham v. J.R.*, 1979, p. 603).

The emphasis on competence has been variously based on two legal theories. First, if minors are so incompetent as decision makers that they cannot reasonably be assumed to be full members of the moral community (see Moore, 1984), then they may not have the rights accorded people who have moral and legal status as persons. Such an argument would seem to have been foreclosed by *Gault* and *Tinker*, but it persists in the form of lower standards for infringement of rights of minors than of adults—in effect, making minors half-persons—and in the tendency to regard rights as relatively unmeaningful for children and adolescents.

Second, even if minors are believed, in the abstract, to have the full panoply of rights due adults, those rights may be limited when the state has a compelling interest in doing so. Thus, for example, the state may infringe on minors' freedom of association, expression, and movement to such a degree that it can require their attendance in school for a number of hours a day and regulate their behavior there in ways that would be plainly unconstitutional if applied to adults. Such gross restrictions on autonomy are justified by the state's interest in the education of future workers and voters. In the same vein, competence enters the picture in most debates about minors' autonomy because of the interest of the state as parens patriae (the sovereign as parent) in protecting minors from the consequences of ill-conceived decisions.

Determination that a minor is competent as a decision maker does not end the ambiguity about whether he or she is entitled to exercise a right. The autonomy of even mature minors may be limited by the state's deference to parental decisions about what is best for them. Historically, children were viewed essentially as the property of their biological parents, who had the right (and responsibility) to control and provide for them. To a large extent, this view has persisted in notions about parents' liberty to rear children as they see fit without interference, so long as the parents do not constitute threats to the children's health and safety (see, e.g., *Ginsberg v. New York*, 1968; *Meyer v. Nebraska*, 1923; Pagliocca, Melton, Weisz, & Lyons, 1995; *Wisconsin v. Yoder*, 1972). Although such respect for parental autonomy sometimes emanates from a belief that it is necessary to protect child welfare (see, e.g., Goldstein, Freud, & Solnit, 1973, 1979; Solnit, Nordhaus, & Lord, 1992), it also is based on respect for the family as an institution, regardless of whether such deference is necessary to child welfare.

Still, the courts have never viewed parental control over offspring as unlimited. Rather, they have held that the state has the authority (and the duty) to protect children from serious harm when their parents cannot or will not do so. The state's parens patriae power derives at least in part from its interest in protecting members of society who cannot protect themselves (so that, e.g., their estates—and the taxes that would be derived from them—are not squandered) and in assuring that children grow up to be productive, responsible citizens. It has been used, for example, to uphold compulsory education (e.g., *Pierce v. Society of Sisters*, 1925; see Moshman, 1989) and child labor laws (e.g., *United States v. Darby*, 1940), to support the termination of parental rights based on abuse or neglect (cf. *Santosky v. Kramer*, 1982), and to override parental refusals to consent to lifesaving medical treatment, even when those refusals were based on religious grounds (e.g., *In re Hudson*, 1942; *In re Sampson*, 1970; *In re Seiferth*, 1955; *State v. Perricone*, 1962).

Finally, the "true" allocation of decision-making power is further obfuscated by controversies concerning the proper limits of state authority in shaping the lives of children. The child advocacy movement itself has long been split on this point (Mnookin, 1978; Rogers & Wrightsman, 1978). Although some commentators argue for further extension of self-determination rights to minors, others believe strongly in the appropriateness and effectiveness of state intervention in the lives of children and families even where neither the child nor the parents desire much "help." The child helping professions have grown up with such an ideology (for historical reviews, see Bakan, 1971; Levine, Ewing, & Hager, 1987; Levine & Levine, 1992). For example, early child guidance clinics developed around the juvenile court system, in which due process and concern for the respondents' personal liberty were sacrificed in the name of "treatment," often for noncriminal behavior that was, although perhaps bothersome, arguably a product of "normal" adolescent group norms.

Indeed, as a practical matter, the central purpose of the child mental health professions may be social control (Melton, 1990a), a theory that is given credence by the fact that the primary problem for which children are referred for treatment (whether administered in the mental health, juvenile justice, child welfare, or special educational system) is simply misbehavior (Melton, Lyons, & Spaulding, 1998; Silver et al., 1992). Perhaps contrary to popular belief, the deeper children are in the service system (i.e., the more restrictive the setting in which they are served), the less likely they are to have classical mental health symptoms and the more likely that they are to demonstrate conduct disorders.

Conflicts among child, family, and state thus are ubiquitous in the practice of clinical child psychology (see Szasz, 1979, for one analysis of these conflicts; for further examples, see Mnookin & Weisberg, 1989). Children rarely come to a therapist on a purely voluntary basis, and if they do, it may well be without parental knowledge or consent. Is the therapist's primary allegiance to the child, the parent, or the state as parens patriae? Under what conditions does the allegiance shift? Because the law is not clear, standards for clinicians' decision making on this point also may be unclear. Furthermore, child clinicians can find little guidance in professional ethical standards (but see Koocher, 1983, and Koocher & Keith-Spiegel, 1990, for sensitive discussions of the issues). The American Psychological Association's (APA, 1992) Ethical Principles of Psychologists and Code of Conduct, for example, states:

> When a psychologist agrees to provide services to several persons who have a relationship (such as husband and wife or parents and children), the psychologist attempts to clarify at the outset (1) which of the individuals are patients or clients and (2) the relationship the psychologist will have with each person. (Standard. 4.03; see also Standard. 4.02, Informed Consent to Therapy)

Thus, although the Ethical Principles prescribe the need to clarify, little is offered by way of concrete rules as to how such clarification is to occur. Clinicians trying to make practical case decisions in a manner consonant with societal values face a complex and contradictory sociolegal context characterized by unprecedented levels of respect for child liberty, deference to family privacy, intrusive state authority in response to irresponsible behavior by parents and/or children, and intrusive exercise of state authority in the name of public health (Melton, 1987b). The dilemma for the clinician is exacerbated because parents, teachers (commonly, representatives of the state), and children rarely have the same view of the problem in a particular case. In Rutter's classic epidemiological studies (reviewed in Gould, Wunsch-Hitzig, & Dohrenwend, 1980), parents and teachers agreed on clinically significant behavior ratings in only 7% of cases. Children themselves generally deny that their mental health problems are serious, and they tend to ascribe the problems they do have to the family as a whole (see, e.g., Achenbach, 1980). The disparity between parents' accounts of their children's problems and self-reports by children themselves is well documented and has persisted over time (e.g., Duchnowski, Johnson, Hall, Kutash, & Friedman, 1993).

Child mental health professionals thus frequently find themselves in complex ethical and legal situations in which there are not only symbolic conflicts among child, family, and state but also real disputes over the facts. Fortunately, though, at least when parents and children are given real alternatives, their interests converge in the end. The child's interest in preservation of liberty and privacy, the parents' interest in protection of family integrity, and the state's interest in cost-effective treatment all typically can be accommodated by intensive family and community-based treatment models (Melton et al., 1998).

The qualifier, *at least when parents and children are given real alternatives,* is an important one. In most communities, when a child with serious emotional disturbance (typically, conduct disorder) enters one of the child and family service systems, the clinician, the child, and the parents face terrible choices. The services that are available often are so limited that they cannot reasonably be expected to make a significant impact on the array of social, emotional, family, and educational problems commonly present (e.g., one hour per week of psychotherapy). They often, in the alternative, involve removal of the child from the family, with unnecessary intrusions on family privacy and child liberty and little hope of significant change that will be sustained if and when the child returns to the home and community. As two of us observed elsewhere, "Parents of children with serious emotional disturbance are confronted with only two alternatives: cope with their problems as well as they can largely by themselves, or turn the child over completely to someone else" (Melton et al., 1998, p. 2; see also Knitzer, 1982). Moreover, if juvenile justice, child welfare, or school authorities find the child's behavior sufficiently irritating, parents may find themselves with little choice other than to "volunteer" the child for some form of residential treatment.

Thus, the most fundamental ethical problem for child clinicians frequently is not the oft-discussed question of who will decide, but instead the question of whether any services should be provided at all when research suggests that those available are likely to be intrusive (for both parents and children), expensive, and largely ineffective. At what point does "doing something" become indefensible, even though the child being assessed presents persistent and pervasive mental health problems? How do clinicians maintain the integrity of their helping role when they are pushed by fiscal, political, and professional considerations toward service plans that seem ultimately to serve no one's interests? Does the child clinician have a duty to become an effective politician to increase the alternatives available to troubled children and their families (see Melton, 1983a, 1987a)?

Such questions are complicated by the fact that the legal-political context, not simply the substantive questions of law, is complex in child and family services. As a result of blurred agency boundaries and privatization, a single facility may be at once a residential treatment center in the mental health system, a group care facility in the social service system, a residential placement in the juvenile justice system, and a residential school in the special education system (e.g., Melton et al., 1998). Because each of these systems has a mission of treatment and each serves essentially the same clientele, especially in more restrictive forms of treatment, reforms to tighten procedures in one system may simply "transinstitutionalize" youth to another (Warren, 1981). Indeed, those differences that do exist in the population served generally reflect financial and social factors (e.g., race) that should be irrelevant to a child's placement. In this complex

political-legal context, clinicians and mental health policymakers must be especially careful, because multiple and sometimes conflicting bodies of law (e.g., mental health law and education law) may apply in a given case and because unintended side effects are an omnipresent reality in child and family policy.

Recognizing that the conflicting interests and ambiguous case law in child mental health preclude simple answers, we nevertheless attempt in this chapter to clarify the ethical issues and identify the prevailing legal trends affecting clinical child practice, particularly with regard to consent, refusal of consent, treatment in institutions, and confidentiality.

MINORS AND INFORMED CONSENT

THE DOCTRINE OF INFORMED CONSENT

The legal principles relating to juveniles' access to treatment stem primarily from the common law, a set of general rules developed by courts through case-by-case decision making. However, many of these principles have also been enacted into statutory law by state legislatures. Although we focus on the general trends in minors' consent to treatment, states vary widely in the extent to which they follow the dominant trends in the common law, and, for the most part, questions in children's law are matters of state rather than federal law. Thus, it is important for individual clinicians to consult the applicable statutes and relevant case law in their own states to determine the specific rules governing mental health practice there.

The most important principle applying to the treatment of adult patients is the doctrine of *informed consent*. That doctrine provides that a health professional can be held liable for battery or negligence if treatment is provided to an individual without appropriately informing that person of the risks and benefits attendant to that treatment and its alternatives and obtaining the client's voluntary consent to receive it. Whether a particular disclosure is legally sufficient likely will depend on the application of one of three standards used in jurisdictions in the United States. Those standards involve the evaluation of the disclosure vis-à-vis (1) that which clinicians generally provide (e.g.,

Natanson v. Kline, 1960), (2) that which would be material to the decision of a reasonable person (e.g., *Canterbury v. Spence,* 1972), or, rarely, (3) that which would be material to the decision of the particular client (e.g., *Scott v. Bradford,* 1979). As a matter of ethics, though, the three standards are listed in increasing level of propriety, because they reflect a hierarchy of concern for the client's own wishes (see Katz, 1984; Lidz et al., 1984).

Being *informed* is not enough for legally valid consent. In legal jargon, the standard for informed consent typically is that it be knowing (informed), intelligent (competent), and voluntary. As for the second criterion, the standard for competence to consent rarely is well articulated in law. The clearest explication of possible standards has been offered by Roth, Meisel, and Lidz (1977; see also Weithorn, 1982). The standard most deferential to individual autonomy is *expression of preference:* as long as the client makes a choice, he or she is presumed competent. At a somewhat higher level, the state might require clients to demonstrate an *understanding* of the nature of the proposed treatment, its alternatives, and their risks and benefits. A variant of the standard of understanding is a requirement that the client *appreciate* the personal significance of the information that has been disclosed. At a still higher level, clients might have to show not only that they comprehended the information disclosed to them but also that they weighed it rationally— that they exhibited a *reasonable process* of decision making. Finally, the state might define competence in terms of a *reasonable outcome* of decision making; in other words, the state might pay no attention to understanding of relevant information or rational analysis of that information but instead rest the determination of competence on the actual decision made. No matter how rational the process by which the decision was made, the client would be regarded as competent if the choice was one that a reasonable person would make. Obviously, such a standard, which is rarely the *articulated* standard for competence, negates the purpose of informed consent by failing to recognize unconventional but rational decisions as competent.

The approach to categorizing definitions of informed consent described above relies heavily— indeed, almost exclusively—on studies and conceptualizations of adult decisional processes. Recent work with adults has clarified the decisional capacities involved (e.g., Grisso & Appelbaum, 1995) and

provided useful instruments for assessing those capacities (Grisso, Appelbaum, Mulvey, & Fletcher, 1995). To evaluate the propriety of treating children's capacities to consent differently from those of adults, research on adult capacities must be extended to children. A recent undertaking in this regard (Mulvey & Peeples, 1996) showed differences between the treatment decisions of children with mental disorders and of children without disorders that paralleled differences between treatment decisions by adults with and without mental disorders. Whatever the advisability of treating children's consent to treatment differently from adults' consent to treatment, the fact is that the law does draw such distinctions. Concerns about consent, though, go beyond the various underlying rational capacities.

The final element of informed consent is that it is voluntary. To a hard determinist, this standard is essentially nonsensical. Beyond the ancient philosophical debate about voluntariness, clinicians often face a difficult question: whether the pressure placed on a client is so intense that his or her decision is the product of duress. Such a question is especially acute in the case of minors (who generally have been "volunteered" for treatment by someone else; see, e.g., Hoge, Davidson, Hill, Turner, & Ameli, 1992; Melton et al., 1998) and institutionalized persons (who literally are a captive audience, typically with limited authority to make even the most mundane decisions) (e.g., Grisso, 1996).

The concept of informed consent is sufficiently ingrained in the law and ethics of the health professional that it is nearly inviolate in theory if not in practice (see Lidz et al., 1984). Just two exceptions to the informed consent requirements commonly are available in law, and neither has much relevance in the ordinary practice of clinical child psychology. First, the treatment provider need not obtain consent if faced with an *emergency* situation where the time necessary to obtain such consent could result in loss of life or serious bodily injury. Second, clinicians in some jurisdictions may exercise a *therapeutic privilege* not to disclose very severe and perhaps unlikely consequences of the treatment when such a disclosure would worsen the patient's condition and prevent him or her from reaching a rational decision about the treatment. This privilege is eroding, however, largely because it might have the effect of negating the very purpose of the informed consent doctrine, which is to "humanize" the clinician-patient relationship by discouraging unilateral decisions by the clinician and supporting individual liberty and privacy.

Beyond these general exceptions, several special issues affect the application of the informed consent doctrine to minors' access to treatment. In most jurisdictions, minors are considered to be per se incompetent (see, e.g., Pagliocca et al., 1995; Rodham, 1973). That is, they are presumed, by virtue of their age alone, to lack the ability to make treatment decisions. Traditionally, parents have been authorized to make such decisions, not only because of the original concept in natural philosophy of the parents' right to control their children's lives but also because of the more recent belief that parents should protect their children from unnecessary or harmful treatment. When a parent is not available, a guardian or other person or agency acting in loco parentis (in place of the parent) is authorized to provide consent.

Thus, when applied to the treatment of children, the informed consent doctrine has been held to give parents, not the child, the right to be informed and consulted. As a matter of law, consent or refusal by the child is considered to be not only insufficient but also irrelevant, for once the parent has consented, treatment can be provided even over the child's objection.

However, as will be described in more detail later, there are several situations in which the per se incompetence rule does not apply and children are authorized to consent to or refuse treatment on their own. Under such circumstances, however, clinicians should not assume that they are now free to treat a consenting child. Rather, clinicians should refer to and follow the general requirements for adult consent, because a clinician still may be liable for treatment without informed consent if the child client is de facto incompetent to give consent or does not consent voluntarily. Nonetheless, the exceptions to the per se rule at least raise the possibility of minors' consenting to treatment independently of their parents. Those exceptions are thus worthy of some discussion.

EXCEPTIONS TO THE REQUIREMENT FOR PARENTAL PERMISSION

Emancipation

Under certain circumstances, courts will hold that a minor is sufficiently independent of and separate from his or her parents to justify treating the child as an adult for certain purposes. For example, an *emancipated minor*, as such a child is called, might be able to enter into valid contracts, make a will, or consent to a blood test. The evidence that establishes emancipation varies from state to state, and although some states statutorily define this term, most leave its application to case-by-case judicial determinations. Factors commonly cited as indicative of emancipation include financial independence, living separate from the parents, enlistment in the Armed Forces, marriage, and parental acquiescence in such assertions of independence. If minors are found to be emancipated, courts generally will hold that they are legally presumed competent to consent to psychological treatment, and the children (actually, adolescents) probably will be sufficiently competent in fact to make such decision.

Mature Minors

Apparently responding either to social welfare concerns that a parental consent requirement might prevent minors from obtaining treatment or to libertarian concerns that minors' privacy in health-related matters should be respected, courts have created a specific exception to the parental consent rule, known as the *mature minor* exception (e.g., *Belcher v. Charleston Area Medical Center*, 1992; Bossing, 1998; *Lacey v. Laird*, 1956; *Younts v. Saint Francis Hospital and School of Nursing Inc.*, 1970). Wadlington (1973; Davis, Scott, Wadlington, & Whitebread, 1997) has summarized the common elements of cases in which that exception is applied: (1) the child is of a relatively mature age; (2) the treatment is beneficial to the child himself or herself (as opposed to being for the benefit of another person); (3) the child has the capacity to understand the nature of the procedure to which he or she consented; and (4) the treatment is not considered to be major.

Mature Minor Statutes   Although a few states have adopted statutory versions of the mature minor rule (e.g., Illinois, 1997; Mississippi, 1990), in most, it is purely a judicially created doctrine. In federal case law, it has been adopted most clearly in cases involving minors' access to abortions (see, e.g., *Bellotti v. Baird*, 1979; *Hodgson v. Minnesota*, 1990; *Planned Parenthood of Central Missouri v. Danforth*, 1976). Unfortunately, the courts rarely provide a definitive articulation of the factors relevant to a finding of "maturity" to which a psychologist can refer in deciding whether to provide treatment to a given minor (see, e.g., *H.L. v. Matheson*, 1981; see also *Hodgson v. Minnesota*, 1990, dissenting opinion of Justice Marshall). Thus, although judicial decisions in which a physician is held liable for nonnegligent treatment of a child older than 15 years are extremely unlikely (see Pilpel, 1972), the variable definition and retrospective application of this rule will no doubt still deter some mental health professionals (as well as physicians in general) from providing treatment to minors whom they are not certain the law will view as mature.

Minor Consent Statutes In recent years, most states have enacted one or more statutes specifically authorizing children to consent to certain types of treatment. Concluding that the societal interest in assuring that such treatment will be received outweighs both the parents' interest in controlling their children's conduct and any danger that children will receive unneeded services, many states have statutorily authorized minors to consent to the provision of pregnancy-related services, treatment for venereal disease, and drug and alcohol abuse treatment. A smaller number have also passed such a law allowing minors' consent to mental health services (e.g., Virginia, 1998). In addition, some have adopted a more general approach, authorizing children to consent to all medical treatment (e.g., Arkansas, 1997). Some minor consent statutes include a minimum age at which children can consent—and the age may vary with the treatment—whereas others provide no floor (cf. Arkansas, 1997; Delaware, 1998).

Although these laws provide helpful guidance to many professionals who deal with children, they often tend to raise as many questions as they answer. For example, they frequently fail to address the role, if any, that the parent should play in the treatment process. Can treatment under such a law be based on parental consent alone, or does the child have the right to refuse treatment as well as consent to it? Can the provider inform parents that their child is in treatment? Can the provider inform parents of the details of such treatment? Is the parent liable for necessary medical treatment provided under such statutes? In addition, such laws may authorize consent to pregnancy-related services without specifying which specific professionals and which treatments are included. Finally, these statutes do not alter the fact that the psychologist

probably has an ethical obligation to determine whether a given client does in fact have the capacity to consent to the treatment being rendered (APA, 1992, Standard 4.02).

Another impediment to the effectiveness of minor consent statutes is that they are not always effectively disseminated to the people they will affect. Thus, more than one year after the passage by one state legislature of a broad statute authorizing juveniles to consent to psychotherapy (Virginia, 1998), 39% of the community mental health clinics in the state were unaware of the existence of the law (Melton, 1981). Furthermore, virtually none of the clinics that did know the law disseminated information concerning it to minors themselves. Not surprisingly, no substantial change in the number of children seeking treatment was reported by the clinics, although the one agency that had established an outreach program to inform minors of their right to consent to mental health treatment experienced a significant increase in its total case load.

State Authority to Order Treatment over Parental Objections

The parens patriae power of the state authorizes a court to override parental preferences where the matter at issue is sufficiently important to the state's interest in the welfare of the child. In the area of consent to medical or mental health treatment, the state intervention usually takes place under the rubric of the neglect laws. Because parents have a legal obligation to provide necessary medical treatment to their children, a parent's refusal to consent to such treatment can result in a finding that the child is neglected and a court order that mandates treatment. In such a situation, the child's preferences may be considered by the court, but the child has no independent right to consent to or refuse the treatment.

"Necessary" medical treatment has traditionally been interpreted to mean only treatment necessary to save the life of the child (e.g., *In re Hudson*, 1942; *In re Seiferth*, 1955). However, in recent years, the courts have become more willing to order desirable, but not life-preserving, medical procedures over parental objection (e.g., *In re Karwath*, 1972; *In re Sampson*, 1970). Nevertheless, cases holding that mental health services constitute necessary medical treatment are very rare (but see *In re Carstairs*, 1952).

FINANCIAL LIABILITY FOR TREATMENT

Even if a given child is able to give valid consent and has done so, the would-be client may be precluded from obtaining treatment because of an absence of funds to pay for it. Although parents generally are liable for their children's necessary medical expenses, they probably would not be required to pay for nonemergency treatment to which they had refused consent or about which they had not been consulted. Thus, it is unlikely that parents would be required to pay for routine psychological services provided to their child without their consent unless the services were considered to be *necessaries*. Similarly, courts usually refuse to require the parents of an emancipated child to pay his or her medical bills.

Statutes have been proposed to make insurance companies liable, under certain circumstances, for treatment of children to which the parents (the policyholders) did not consent (Institute of Judicial Administration/American Bar Association [IJA/ABA], 1980b). Nevertheless, such statutes might not fully solve the problem. Ubiquitous requirements for deductibles and copayments would make it difficult for a child to contact an insurance company and obtain coverage for a claim without the parents' discovering that treatment was being obtained. In such a circumstance, a legal authorization for independent consent and confidential treatment of a minor would be meaningless in practice, unless the clinician waived his or her fee.

When parents are not financially liable as a result of their child's emancipation, minors seeking treatment independently will clearly be legally responsible for the cost of treatment, although they still may simply not have the funds to pay. When a minor is not emancipated, however, his or her liability depends on whether the minor was competent to enter into a binding contract for services (i.e., treatment). Minors are generally considered competent to enter into (and are bound by) contracts only if the contracts are for the purchase of necessaries. In other words, children cannot use their minor status as a basis for disaffirming (backing out of) such a contract. Once an agreement has been made to purchase necessaries, the minor is legally obligated to pay for them. (Note, however, that the problem of penniless purchasers can occur here also.) Both medical and dental care are generally considered to be necessaries. Therefore, psychiatric treatment,

especially for a severe emotional disturbance, would probably be included as well. Mental health services provided by psychologists and nonmedical professionals, however, are less likely to be viewed by the courts as necessaries. Therefore, it is conceivable that in some circumstances, neither the child nor the parent would be liable for treatment to which the parent did not consent.

SCHOOL-BASED PROGRAMS

The substantial legal impediments to the provision of mental health services to minors may not be quite so formidable in school settings. Consistent with the country's educational goals for the year 2000 (National Educational Goals Panel, 1996), school-based programs have become an increasingly important part of school reform efforts. With service integration as an overarching goal (e.g., Melaville, Blank, & Asayesh, 1993), school-based initiatives have involved clinics addressing not only primary health care (e.g., "Making the Grade," 1996) but also mental health needs (e.g., McKinney & Peak, 1994). The need for the latter stems, at least in part, from the fact that, of the clinicians traditionally hired by schools, "few were trained to deal with either the psychosocial problems of today's teens or the therapeutic and social welfare needs of their parents" (Dryfoos, 1997, p. 27). The location of school-based treatment programs, of course, provides access to children in a context where parental consent is largely irrelevant (but see, e.g., Pagliocca et al., 1995).

REFUSAL OF TREATMENT

THEORETICAL FOUNDATION

As the discussion thus far has revealed, the children's rights movement in general and the right to consent to treatment in particular have been supported by two very different lines of reasoning, one advocating child protection, the other child autonomy. It is important to note, however, that these two strains of analysis necessarily lead to diametrically opposed positions on the question of whether a de facto competent child who has been given the right to consent to treatment is also entitled to refuse it.

Briefly, the parens patriae approach, sometimes referred to as *child saving*, approves of minor consent to encourage beneficial treatment and thereby protect the child from harm. Thus, this view is not only inconsistent with but arguably even prohibits the granting of a right to refuse treatment to children, because such a right could prevent minors from receiving needed help.

The child autonomy, or *kiddie lib* position, on the other hand, supports a right to consent to treatment, because (1) basic respect for children as human beings requires that they be allowed to participate in decisions regarding their lives to the maximum extent that they are capable, and (2) neither parents nor state can be relied on to act in the child's best interests anyway. This approach, of course, logically implies that a child who is legally and mentally competent to consent to a given treatment should also be allowed to refuse that treatment if he or she wishes to do so. Such deference to child autonomy and privacy, absent a compelling state interest to the contrary, is an increasingly accepted norm. Notably, the United Nations Convention on the Rights of the Child (1989), adopted unanimously by the General Assembly and ratified by every nation except Somalia and the United States, places an obligation on anyone acting under color of law to solicit the views of children able to express a preference in any matters pertaining to them. Although the UN Convention has not been ratified and, thus, does not directly carry the weight of law in the United States, it can be said to be customary international law and thus nonetheless legally binding (see D'Amato, 1971; Paust, 1988). Moreover, because the president signed the Convention, at a minimum, the United States is compelled by the Vienna Convention on the Law of Treaties (1969) to refrain from adopting policies inconsistent with the former. Regardless of its legal force, the Convention is a valuable guidepost to children's policy and professional practice.

MINOR CONSENT STATUTES

In interpreting minor consent statutes, courts generally have assumed that they were intended to support child autonomy. Thus, for example, in *In re Smith* (1973), the Maryland Supreme Court was asked to construe a state law that provided that, for pregnancy-related treatment, "a minor shall have the same capacity to consent as an adult." The case involved a pregnant 16-year-old girl who had been ordered by a juvenile court to obey her mother's direction to get an abortion. The girl preferred to marry her boyfriend and have her child, and the physician to whom her mother brought her refused to perform the operation without the girl's consent. The Maryland high court had no trouble interpreting the statute as implying a right to refuse abortion, possibly because of the law's explicit presumption of competency. In a similar case (*Melville v. Sabatino*, 1972), the Connecticut Supreme Court held that a statute authorizing children aged 16 or older to admit themselves to mental hospitals necessarily implied that a 17-year-old boy who had been "voluntarily" admitted to a hospital by his parents two years earlier could sign himself out against their wishes.

LIMITED RIGHT TO RESIST CERTAIN TREATMENTS

Even where a right to consent to treatment has not been provided, however, there may be reason to grant the child a limited right to refuse. Particularly where a significant deprivation of rights could result, such as when hospitalization or an intrusive or aversive therapy is proposed, reliance on the parent's judgment alone might not be warranted. In such situations, it has been argued, the child's objection to the parent's decision should trigger an external review of the need for treatment.

Hospitalization of Adults

Adults enter mental hospitals in two ways. First, individuals may be subject to petitions for involuntary commitment. In such situations, the due process clause of the Constitution mandates that respondents be given a hearing at which they are represented by counsel and have a right to offer evidence (see, e.g., *Hawks v. Lazaro*, 1974; *Heryford v. Parker*, 1967; *Lessard v. Schmidt*, 1972). In most jurisdictions, judges hearing such petitions can order hospitalization only if they find the respondent to be both mentally ill and either (1) dangerous to himself or herself, (2) dangerous to others, or (3) unable to care for himself or herself. Furthermore, institutionalization can be used only if no less restrictive alternative forms of treatment are available, and its appropriateness must be periodically reviewed (see, generally, Hoffman & Foust, 1977).

Second, individuals can enter the hospital voluntarily. If mentally competent to make such a decision, they can simply request admission to the facility, which can admit them even if they do not meet the preceding criteria for civil commitment. Whenever voluntary patients decide to leave, the hospital must discharge them, although it typically can require that notice of an intention to leave be given one or two days beforehand so that the hospital will have the opportunity to file a petition for involuntary commitment of the patient. In addition, in some states, voluntary patients have the right to refuse medication or other treatments to which they object (*Rogers v. Commissioner*, 1983; *Washington v. Harper*, 1990).

Hospitalization of Minors

Like adults, children can enter psychiatric hospitals as either voluntary or involuntary patients. In most states, however, it is the parent rather than the child who is authorized to request the latter's "voluntary" admission, which will be granted as long as the hospital staff agrees that the child needs treatment. The parent is also authorized to exercise the other rights that accrue to a voluntary patient: the right to petition for (and receive) discharge and to consent to, or refuse, medication.

The Supreme Court upheld the "voluntary" admission of children by their parents in *Parham v. J.R.* (1979). That case was an appeal from a three-judge federal court's decision declaring unconstitutional a Georgia statute that allowed parents to admit their children to mental hospitals "voluntarily" and provided no judicial review of the need for inpatient treatment. Rejecting the lower court's conclusion that parents should not be assumed to act in their children's best interests, the Court held that a minor can be constitutionally confined in a mental hospital without a hearing of any kind.

In reaching this result, Chief Justice Burger, writing for the majority, emphasized that a formal hearing could disrupt the parent-child relationship and further upset an already emotionally unstable child. He also concluded that such a hearing could deter parents from seeking needed treatment for their offspring and that the admitting mental health professional's judgment was a sufficient safeguard against a misguided placement. Even when the minor was in the custody of a state agency, the Court held, the agency could act in the same way that a parent could and no further safeguards were warranted.

This faith in parental and professional decision making was reiterated in *Secretary of Public Welfare v. Institutionalized Juveniles* (1979), a companion case to *Parham* decided the same day. In that case, the Supreme Court overturned a federal court in Pennsylvania, which had ruled that children in that state were constitutionally entitled to a full adversary hearing prior to hospitalization. Quoting language in *Parham* requiring a "neutral factfinder" who interviews the prospective patient, the Court held that a psychiatric examination conducted on admission by the hospital treatment team satisfied this requirement. The Court also emphasized that periodic reassessment of a child's condition is necessary to ensure that the initial admission decision is made correctly and ruled that state regulations requiring review of a patient's condition every 30 days constituted sufficient periodic review.

The Supreme Court's decisions in *Parham* and *Institutional Juveniles* do not prohibit a state from providing additional procedural protections for minors who may be hospitalized. These decisions merely state that such protections are not constitutionally required. Mandating more adversarial procedures than the Constitution requires for the hospitalization of certain juveniles, several states have at least partially adopted the approach taken by the lower federal courts in *Parham* and *Institutionalized Juveniles*.

Moreover, *Parham* should not be read as carte blanche to states to exercise unfettered control over the lives of children whose parents have "volunteered" them for mental health treatment. The Court left open the nature of the postadmission review that is necessary when children are hospitalized voluntarily by their parents. The Court also gave extensive attention to the nature of the community mental health system in Georgia at the time. Although the Court was not altogether honest in examining the histories even of the representatives (J.L. and J.R.) of the class before them (Melton, 1984; Perry & Melton, 1984), the Court did note that Georgia had established a sufficiently strong community mental health system that some level of evaluation and treatment typically would precede institutionalization of children. Accordingly, the

Court was not entirely clear whether its deference in *Parham* to informal decision making by parents and clinicians would apply in a jurisdiction with minimally developed community-based alternatives.

A narrow reading of *Parham* is supported by two other facts. First, the Court did make clear that the child's interests at stake in commitment are of constitutional proportion. Second, despite expansive verbiage about child-parent relations and the nature of the mental health system, *Parham* has been cited primarily as a procedure case (Perry & Melton, 1984). No matter what the legal context, judges cite *Parham* whenever they do not want to make decisions themselves.

Whatever the state of the law, mental health professionals should recognize that civil commitment, even when nominally voluntary, entails a "massive curtailment of liberty" (*Humphrey v. Cady*, 1972, p. 509) that is experienced as such by most child patients and that is of dubious efficacy (Melton et al., 1998). Under such circumstances, it is especially important, at least as a matter of ethics if not always of law, that clinicians involve children themselves in decision making and search diligently for alternatives less restrictive of children's liberty (see, e.g., Earle & Forquer, 1995; Melton et al., 1998), less intrusive on their privacy (see, e.g., Melton, 1983b), and more protective of family integrity (e.g., *Prince v. Mass.*, 1944, p. 166; see also Melton, 1999).

CONFIDENTIALITY

ADULTS

Although usually considered separately from informed consent, confidentiality is closely related to it, because it concerns the limits of personal control over decision making about release of information. Confidentiality involves an individual's right to prohibit his or her therapist from disclosing to others information that the individual communicates during the course of treatment. It is related to, but different from, testimonial *privileges*, which we discuss later. Mental health professionals have both ethical (e.g., APA, 1992, Standards 5.01–5.09) and, in many states, legal duties to preserve the confidences of their clients. This duty has been imposed not only out of concern for the client's personal feelings and rights but also for two more practical, policy-oriented reasons. First, the knowledge that

their communications will be confidential encourages people to seek needed treatment in the first place. Second, that knowledge facilitates the development of a trusting relationship and a willingness to be completely honest with the therapist, thereby increasing the chances that the treatment will be successful.

Also for reasons of social policy, the confidentiality of therapist-client communications is not absolute. Thus, for instance, to protect the general welfare, a professional whose patient has a contagious disease is often legally required to inform anyone who might come in contact with that person, and all states either authorize or require a professional who suspects that a child has been abused to report that suspicion to a social services agency. Some courts have even required mental health professionals with dangerous clients either to warn the known potential victims of such violence or to take other actions to prevent it (see Fulero, 1988, for an annotated list of cases).

CHILDREN

Although the legal rules regarding confidentiality of adults' records and communications are currently in a state of flux, those regarding children are even less clear. It should be noted, however, that the legal rules concerning confidentiality in some contexts are spelled out in meticulous detail. The most important example of such a detailed articulation of confidentiality rules is the federal regulations on substance abuse treatment that govern any state agency that receives federal funds ("Confidentiality," 1990). Those regulations have produced their own set of problems, which there is insufficient space to discuss here, but the regulations should certainly be read closely by any clinician who deals with substance-abusing children.

WHERE PARENTS HAVE CONSENTED TO TREATMENT

In general, parents are authorized to have access to their children's records, whether they are in the custody of a mental health professional, a school, or a juvenile court. However, parents do not necessarily have the right to control the disclosure of such records. For instance, many states allow attorneys, welfare departments, and insurance companies to obtain a child's mental hospital records, and some even have a catchall provision authorizing disclosure whenever it is in the minor's best interest (see Wilson, 1978, p. 261). Similarly, although juvenile court records, often containing reports of psychological evaluations and social history materials, are generally confidential, special exceptions for school officials and others are frequently found (Wilson, 1978; see also Youth Law Center, 1993).

It could be argued, of course, that even children who have not consented to their treatment independently might still be capable of appreciating the importance and meaning of confidentiality and resent disclosure to parents or others of information that they have conveyed to therapists. Nevertheless, parental access is probably appropriate in such situations, if for no other reason than that parents are responsible for consenting to third-party access and they need to be familiar with the records to make such decisions. At a minimum, however, children should be informed by a mental health professional of the limited confidentiality that will be accorded to their communications (APA, 1992, Standard 5.01). In addition, the clinician can attempt to obtain the parents' permission to delete extremely sensitive material before giving the records to them.

Where the Child Has Consented to Treatment

The confidentiality rights of children who have consented to treatment independently are far less clear than those of adults who have so consented. Statutes in this area frequently fail to address the issue of confidentiality at all and, when they do address it, often do so inadequately or inconsistently. Some minor consent statutes, for example, are silent on the question of whether a minor not only has the right to consent to treatment but also has a concomitant right to control access to the records of that treatment. Others specifically authorize the service provider to inform the parents that their child is receiving treatment but may still be unclear as to whether the clinician can also disclose the details of such treatment to them. In the absence of a minor consent statute, the situation is murkier still. Only in the abortion context is there case law on the privacy rights possessed by mature minors during the course of treatment to which they have provided valid consent.

In support of full disclosure to the parent whose child has independently consented to treatment, it can be argued that mental health treatment is rarely effective if the family is not included and that the parents cannot effectively fulfill their duty to care for and protect their offspring unless they are aware of all significant factors in the child's life. On the other hand, mandatory disclosure arguably vitiates a primary purpose of the mature minor rule: the encouragement of treatment that the minor would be unlikely to seek if parental consent were required. In other words, merely the knowledge that parents will be informed of the treatment, even where parents cannot prohibit it, might be sufficient to dissuade some children from seeking such treatment. In addition, respect for mature minors' autonomy, privacy, and judgment dictates that their confidentiality rights should be recognized.

Few would argue, though, that clinicians' duty to preserve confidences is or should be exactly the same for juvenile clients as for adult clients. For example, as mentioned earlier, it has been held that clinicians have a duty to protect the potential victim of an adult client when specific threats have been made (e.g., *Tarasoff v. Board of Regents*, 1976), and that duty can logically be extended to clinicians who treat juveniles (*McIntosh v. Milano*, 1979). Although there is no corresponding duty to warn the family of an adult client's suicidal tendencies (*Bellah v. Greenson*, 1978), the fact that both the parents and the state are legally obligated to protect dependent minors from harm might constitute sufficient reason to impose such a duty when the therapist is treating a minor. In fact, it could even be argued that the parents' duty to care for and control their children entitles them to be informed of self-destructive or violent behavior that does not reach suicidal or homicidal proportions. There is, however, little case law on this question. Therefore, the clinician is well advised to establish a policy regarding disclosures to parents, to discuss that policy with clients when beginning treatment, and to document carefully both the policy itself and the reasons for any exceptions made to it.

One interesting approach to reconciling the competing concerns in this area was suggested by the Institute of Judicial Administration/American Bar Association (1980b) Juvenile Justice Standards Project (Standards Relating to Rights of Minors,

Standard 4.2 and accompanying Commentary). In its proposal, the Project distinguished between drug treatment and pregnancy-related treatment (including abortions and treatment for venereal disease) on the one hand, and treatment for emotional or mental disorders on the other. The Standards would allow a child of any age to consent to drug- or pregnancy-related treatment (if competent to do so), and they would prohibit disclosure of such treatment to parents without the child's consent unless failure to notify them could seriously jeopardize the child's health. However, the Standards would require notification of parents whose child is receiving mental health treatment (which can be consented to only by children over 14) after three therapy sessions and prohibit further treatment without parental consent. The Project justified these restrictions on the grounds that such treatment has a potential impact on familial relationships, requires family involvement to be effective, and could continue for a prolonged period of time.

WHERE A COURT HAS ORDERED TREATMENT

Confidentiality questions also arise when the child is receiving treatment under a court order. Such treatment is often imposed as a condition of probation, in which case, the child's failure to comply with the court's order could result in a revocation of the probation and confinement in a juvenile institution. Thus, a mental health professional treating a minor pursuant to a court order may be asked to inform the probation officer or the judge if the client stops treatment or misses an appointment. In states where the juvenile court is authorized to order state agencies to provide services to a child, the therapist may even be ordered to report any absence to the court. If no such order exists, clinicians are left to their own judgment of the appropriate action to take. If clinicians decide to notify the court in such situations, they should at least inform all child clients beforehand that they will report any willful failure to comply with a court order mandating treatment (see IJA/ABA, 1980a, Standards Relating to Dispositions, Standard 5.4). Even when operating under a court order mandating notification of the judge, however, the clinician should first attempt to determine whether the client had a legitimate reason for missing an appointment to ensure that the

judge's subsequent action is based on a full understanding of the situation.

In general, many of the problems regarding court-ordered treatment can be avoided by clearly working out with the judge ahead of time the terms of disclosure of confidential information. Such discussions with court personnel will not only prevent conflict or confusion on individual cases but might also lead to increased understanding on the part of the judge of the importance of confidentiality in treatment and encourage the court to agree to more limited disclosure in such situations.

TESTIMONIAL PRIVILEGE

Adults

The physician-patient privilege provides that a doctor can be prohibited from testifying in court regarding a confidential communication that related to the treatment sought and that was made by his or her patient in the course of receiving treatment. All but nine states have adopted the privilege either by statute or through case law (Alexander, 1993). Unfortunately, however, the privilege is sometimes interpreted as covering only treatment for physical illness, so that not only psychologists (who are excluded because they are not medically trained) but also psychiatrists may have to testify in court.

The purpose of the privilege is to assure the confidentiality necessary to encourage people to seek and to facilitate the successfulness of necessary medical treatment. For similar reasons, most states protect other relationships such as the attorney-client and the priest-penitent relationship through privileges as well. The doctor-patient privilege can be asserted only by the patient; in other words, the physician cannot refuse to testify if the patient has no objection. Also, it may be eliminated for compelling policy reasons, such as preventing epidemics or protecting criminal defendants' due process rights, that the judge decides are sufficiently crucial to override the patient's confidentiality rights. Finally, the privilege cannot be asserted where the very condition for which the patient sought treatment has been put at issue by the patient.

In addition to physician-patient privilege statutes, many jurisdictions have passed specific psychotherapist-patient privilege statutes as well. These laws, however, usually list the particular professions included and whether certification is required, and courts often refuse to extend coverage to types of clinicians not specifically mentioned. Thus, not only are psychiatric social workers often excluded, but psychologists and even psychiatrists may also find themselves covered by neither the physician-patient nor the psychotherapist-patient statute in their state (Wilson, 1978).

Children

It is possible that, where parents have consented to the treatment of their child, the assertion or waiver of the therapist-patient privilege will be held to be up to them. Privilege laws rarely address this question directly, but conclusions can sometimes be drawn from the statutory language. For example, if the term *patient* is defined to include minors and the patient is specifically given the power to assert the privilege, then parents are less likely to be able to do so on behalf of their children (cf. Conn. Gen. Stat. Ann., 1991). However, statutes usually provide little guidance, and the courts have rarely addressed the issue. Therefore, in the absence of a statutory provision to the contrary, a clinician should probably inform minor clients, where such a possibility is likely, that the clinician could be required to testify in court as to their confidential communications if their parents consent to such disclosures.

Where children themselves have consented to treatment, the arguments in favor of allowing them to assert the testimonial privilege are the same as those concerning the confidentiality of records: personal dignity, autonomy, privacy, promotion of full disclosure during therapy, and the potential for parents to fail to act in their children's best interests. Here, as in the broader confidentiality area, there is little case law concerning how these considerations should be balanced against parental rights and obligations. Thus, until this issue is resolved by the courts, the best that clinicians can do is to inform their child clients that waiver of the privilege by their parents might be allowed by a court.

CONDITIONS OF TREATMENT

Institutional settings present special issues in terms of the rights of minors to access to treatment. There is a substantial body of case law holding that minors residing involuntarily in state institutions have a right to receive treatment while confined (e.g., *Inmates of Boys' Training School v. Affleck*, 1972; *Martarella v. Kelley*, 1972; *Morales v. Turman*, 1974; *Nelson v. Heyne*, 1974). Federal courts have recognized such a right for children who are temporarily detained (*Martarella*), who are adjudicated delinquents (*Morales*), who are status offenders (e.g., children found to be "in need of services"; *Nelson* and *Morales*), who are neglected (*Boys' Training School*), and who have been "voluntarily" admitted into facilities by their parents (*Boys' Training School*). Rights to mental health treatment also can be conferred by the U.S. Congress through federal legislation (cf. Americans with Disabilities Act of 1990; *Olmstead v. L.C. ex rel. Zimring*, 1999). The application and breadth of such a right remains questionable, though, because of a series of Supreme Court cases. When presented with the question of the existence of a constitutional right to treatment, the Court has issued narrow rulings in which it has expressly declined to reach a decision about the existence of a broad constitutional right (see, e.g., *O'Connor v. Donaldson*, 1975).

The holding most on point came in *Youngberg v. Romeo* (1982). In that case, the Court held that institutionalized persons with mental retardation are owed, at a minimum, safety, freedom from undue restraint, and "minimally adequate or reasonable training" necessary to ensure those liberty interests. Specifically, the Court held that Romeo, an institutionalized person with profound mental retardation, was owed minimally adequate or reasonable training to reduce his self-injurious behavior so that he could live safely without being confined in physical restraints. The Court limited the means of vindicating even this narrow right by holding that state officials were immune from liability for violating such a right if they acted on the basis of a reasonable professional judgment. Accordingly, the Court effectively reduced the standard for violation of the right to treatment or habilitation (however it ultimately is defined) to that of professional malpractice—a tort for which remedies are already available.

Moreover, the Court has made clear its general reluctance to recognize entitlements for services. In *Pennhurst State School and Hospital v. Halderman* (1981), the Court declined to enforce the Bill of Rights in the Developmental Disabilities Assistance and Bill of Rights Act of 1975 because the majority viewed Congress's intent to make the bill binding to be insufficiently explicit. The Court also has refused to recognize a constitutional right to education (*San Antonio Independent School District v. Rodriguez*, 1973) or to protection when a social service worker is aware of a case of child maltreatment (*DeShaney v. Winnebago County Department of Social Services*, 1989). Suggestive language in *Youngberg* also indicated that even the minimal right to habilitation that the Court recognized in that case applied only because the state had agreed to take Romeo into its care; it had no constitutional obligation to offer services initially.

In any event, right to treatment cases rarely have focused primarily on access to services (but see, e.g., *Nelson v. Heyne*, 1974). Rather, such cases typically have been brought against state facilities that lacked even the rudiments of decent care. Consequently, even expansive orders emanating from such cases typically have been most detailed in their guarantee of humane care as an element of "treatment." In that regard, the best-established principle in case law on conditions of confinement of people with mental disabilities is that they cannot be held under conditions that, if applied to prisoners, would violate the Eighth Amendment's prohibition of cruel and unusual punishment (see, e.g., Melton & Garrison, 1987).

There are several reasons, though, to conclude that the courts still may be an effective avenue for redress of children's rights while in the care of the state. First, the Individuals with Disabilities Education Act provides a clear statutory basis for a therapeutic education program in the least restrictive alternative for most children in residential treatment. Statements of legislative intent in state statutes authorizing the establishment of public agencies for child and family services (e.g., juvenile courts) often offer another ground for asserting a right to rehabilitative services for troubled children. The U.S. Supreme Court recently found a statutory basis for community-based treatment in the Americans with Disabilities Act (1990). The Court handed down its ruling in a case filed by patients of a state psychiatric hospital who challenged their confinement in the institution (*Olmstead v. L.C. ex rel. Zimring*, 1999).

Second, the right to personal security can be said to encompass a general right to protection from harm. In that regard, Justices Brennan and O'Connor joined Justice Blackmun in declaring in a concurring opinion in *Youngberg* that such a right implies a right to treatment or habilitation to avoid regression. Analogous cases involving persons with mental retardation suggest that a right to avoid regression and unnecessary restrictions on liberty implies a broad right to habilitation for developmentally immature individuals in the state's care (see Rothman & Rothman, 1984, for a detailed account of the development of this idea in litigation concerning Willowbrook State School).

Third, subsequent cases have suggested that the *DeShaney* holding may be quite limited. Not only does *DeShaney* not apply to children for whom the state has assumed custody (rather than simply agreed to supervise for protective purposes), but theories other than the one posited in *DeShaney* of a substantive due process right to freedom from intrusions on personal security may justify an entitlement to diligent action by child protective authorities. Notably, the Fifth Circuit Court of Appeals (*Chrissy F. v. Mississippi Department of Public Welfare*, 1991) held (1) that a social service agency's failure to investigate and a prosecutor's concomitant refusal to file a civil child protection petition in a case of alleged sexual abuse may have violated the child's constitutional right of meaningful access to the courts (under the First, Fifth, and Fourteenth Amendments), and (2) that neither sovereign immunity nor prosecutorial (quasi-judicial) immunity applied to protect the public officials from liability. The circuit court also found a "clearly established" Fourteenth Amendment liberty interest in not being abused that is implicated whenever state action begins.

Fourth, some courts have read *Youngberg* to provide a right to treatment, including treatment in the community, when such a service is recommended by a mental health professional exercising a reasonable professional judgment for a client who is subject to state control (see Small & Otto, 1991, and cases cited therein for expositions of this theory). Under the guise of deference to state experts, this line of cases and parallel cases in which courts have showed deference to professional standards for administration of state institutions (see, e.g., *Woe v. Cuomo*, 1986) have left the door open to legal enforcement of such standards for humane care and reasonable treatment. In that regard, the most expansive orders in institutional litigation typically have arisen in "friendly" litigation in which state administrators have consented to decrees fashioned in concert with national experts on the state of the art in habilitation and treatment services (see, e.g., Johnson, 1976; Rothman & Rothman, 1984).

CONCLUSIONS: THE LAW AS GUIDEPOST AND FRAMEWORK

Use of professional standards to guide constitutional litigation involving institutions is illustrative of a general phenomenon of reciprocal influences between the law and the mental health professions. Not only do professional standards guide legal decision making, but legal decisions do change professionals' judgments about the bounds of humane care, even when decrees are the products of friendly negotiation between the plaintiffs and the defendants for conditions of service that go beyond those the court would have enforced without the consent of the parties. Such a process of interplay between law and professional ethics is explicit for psychologists, who must "accord appropriate respect to the fundamental rights, dignity, and worth of all people" (APA, 1992, Principle D).

Even if the law offers few avenues for vindication of clients' rights in any given case, it can serve as an educator of those who seek the moral guidance of the community (see Melton, 1986; Melton & Saks, 1985). Thus, mental health law probably has had a salutary effect on mental health practice. It is important to remember in this regard that many of the most egregious intrusions on the rights of children have been in the name of treatment. Even the most minimal respect for clients and a spirit of beneficence should translate at least into a duty to avoid harm to clients (e.g., APA, 1992, Standard 1.14; *Halderman v. Pennhurst State School & Hospital*, 1985; *New York State Association for Retarded Children, Inc. v. Rockefeller*, 1973; *Youngberg v. Romeo*, 1982). Not only has "grotesque" discrimination against people with mental disabilities (*City of Cleburne v. Cleburne Living Center, Inc.*, 1985) been sanctioned historically by the mental health professions, but the institutions that have been found to be so inhumane that they would constitute cruel and unusual punishment for convicted felons have been supervised by mental health professionals. Too often, even expensive, highly professionalized treatment programs for children remain so cavalier about their child clients' rights that they could be fairly described as psychologically abusive (Melton & Davidson, 1987; see, e.g., *Milonas v. Williams*, 1982).

Although this chapter has focused primarily on the law affecting child mental health services, the law should be viewed as a guidepost, not an end in itself. Conformity to the law does not make an individual's judgments ethical. At its best, though, the law provides a framework for decision making consistent with respect for clients' dignity.

In children's law, we know of no instrument that better meets this standard than the United Nations Convention on the Rights of the Child (1989). Unfortunately, the United States has failed to join most of the rest of the world in ratifying the Convention, although our government did participate in drafting it and did vote for its adoption by the General Assembly. The Convention gained acceptance in the global community with unprecedented speed. Within seven years of its adoption by the General Assembly, the Convention had been ratified by all but six countries in the world. Within a year after that, only the United States and Somalia had failed to ratify it (Cohen, 1998).

Even if the Convention is not directly legally enforceable in the United States (as discussed elsewhere in this chapter), its comprehensiveness and conceptual coherence make it an excellent tool for policymakers, program administrators, and clinicians puzzled by ethical issues involving child clients. When read "constitutionally," the Convention provides a blueprint for child mental health policy and practice. From the Convention, one of us (Melton, 1990b, 1991b; see also Melton, 1991a, on child protection policy) has derived the following principles to guide mental health work:

1. The provision of high-quality services for children should be a matter of the highest priority for public mental health services.
2. Children should be viewed as active partners in child mental health services, with heavy weight placed on protection of their liberty and privacy.
3. Mental health services for children should be respectful of parents and supportive of family integrity.
4. States should apply a strong presumption against residential placement of children for the purpose of treatment, with due procedural care in decision making about treatment and with provision of community-based alternatives.

When out-of-home placement is necessary for the protection or treatment of the child, it should be in the most familylike setting consistent with those objectives.

5. When the state does undertake the care and custody of emotionally disturbed children, it also assumes an especially weighty obligation to protect them from harm.

6. Prevention should be the cornerstone of child mental health policy.

Although the wisdom and morality of these principles may evoke little argument, the mental health professions have far to go before such principles are routinely followed in child mental health policy and practice. There is no magic in the process of their application. Rather, there must be a moral commitment to take children seriously as persons and a commensurate diligence in understanding children's experience and concerns and fashioning policy and practice accordingly (see Melton, 1987a). To a large extent, the children's field has lacked the moral fervor, political acumen, economic resources, and intellectual discipline necessary to develop and fulfill such a vision. With the fashioning of a new international consensus that children are indeed people and that adults' behavior should change accordingly, the time is ripe for a new, more respectful, and more thoughtful approach to child mental health.

REFERENCES

Achenbach, T. (1980). *DSM-III* in light of empirical research on the classification of child psychopathology. *Journal of the American Academy of Child Psychiatry, 19,* 395–412.

Alexander, L.C. (1993). Should Alabama adopt a physician-patient evidence privilege? *Alabama Law Review, 45,* 261–274.

American Psychological Association. (1992). Ethical principles of psychologists and code of conduct. *American Psychologist, 47,* 1597–1611.

Americans with Disabilities Act of 1990, 42 U.S.C. §§ 12101–12213 (Supp. III, 1991).

Ark. Stat. Ann. § 20-9-602 (1997).

Bakan, D. (1971). Adolescence in America: From idea to social fact. In J. Kagan & R. Coles (Eds.), *Twelve to sixteen: Early adolescence* (pp. 73–89). New York: Norton.

Belcher v. Charleston Area Medical Center, 422 S.E.2d 827 (W.Va. 1992).

Bellah v. Greenson, 81 Cal. App. 3d 614 (1978).

Bellotti v. Baird, 443 U.S. 622 (1979).

Bossing, L. (1998). Now sixteen could get you life: Statutory rape, meaningful consent, and the implications for federal sentencing enhancement. *New York University Law Review, 73,* 1205–1250.

Canterbury v. Spence, 464 F.2d 772 (D.C. Cir. 1972).

Carey v. Population Services International, 431 U.S. 678 (1977).

Chrissy F. v. Mississippi Department of Public Welfare, 925 E.2d 844 (5th Cir. 1991).

City of Cleburne v. Cleburne Living Center Inc., 473 U.S. 432 (1985).

Cohen, C.P. (1998). United Nations Convention on the Rights of the Child: Prospects for the year 2000. *Loyola Poverty Law Journal, 4,* 3–8.

Confidentiality of Alcohol and Drug Abuse Patient Records, 42 C.F.R. 2 (1990).

Conn. Gen. Stat. Ann., § 52-146d(6) (1991).

D'Amato, A. (1971). *The concept of custom in international law.* Ithaca, NY: Cornell University Press.

Davis, S.M., Scott, E.S., Wadlington, W.L., & Whitebread, C.H. (1997). *Children in the legal system: Cases and materials* (2nd ed.). Westbury, NY: Foundation Press.

Del. Code Ann. tit. 13, § 708 (Cum. Supp. 1998).

DeShaney v. Winnebago County Department of Social Services, 489 U.S. 189 (1989).

Developmental Disabilities Assistance and Bill of Rights Act of 1975, 42 §§ 6000–6009.

Dryfoos, J.G. (1997). School-based youth programs: Exemplary models and emerging opportunities. In R.J. Illback, C.T. Cobb, & H.J. Joseph Jr. (Eds.), *Integrated services for children and families: Opportunities for psychological practice* (pp. 23–52). Washington, DC: American Psychological Association.

Duchnowski, A.J., & Friedman, R.M. (1990). Children's mental health: Challenges for the nineties. *Journal of Mental Health Administration, 17,* 3–12.

Duchnowski, A.J., Johnson, M.K., Hall, K.S., Kutash, K., & Friedman, R.M. (1993). The alternatives to residential treatment study: Initial findings. *Journal of Emotional and Behavioral Disorders, 1,* 17–26.

Earle, K.A., & Forquer, S.L. (1995). Use of seclusion with children and adolescents in public psychiatric hospitals. *Social Work, 39,* 588–594.

Education for all Handicapped Children Act of 1974, 20 U.S.C. §§ 1400–1445 (1982). [Originally enacted as the Education of the Handicapped Act and subsequently known as the Individuals with Disabilities Education Act, Pub. L. No. 101-476 (1990), 20 U.S.C.A. §§ 1400–1485 (West Supp. 1991). Name change to IDEA was enacted by Pub. L. No. 101-476 and required no change in text.]

Eisenstadt v. Baird, 405 U.S. 438 (1972).

Ellis, J.W. (1974). Volunteering children: Commitment of minors to mental institutions. *California Law Review, 62,* 840–916.

Fulero, S.M. (1988). *Tarasoff:* 10 years later. *Professional Psychology: Research and Practice, 19,* 184–190.

Ginsberg v. New York, 390 U.S. 629 (1968).

Goldstein, J., Freud, A., & Solnit, A.J. (1973). *Beyond the best interests of the child.* New York: Free Press.

Goldstein, J., Freud, A., & Solnit, A.J. (1979). *Before the best interests of the child.* New York: Free Press.

Gould, M.S., Wunsch-Hitzig, R., & Dohrenwend, B.P. (1980). Formulation of hypotheses about the prevalence, treatment, and prognostic significance of psychiatric disorders in children in the United States. In B.P. Dohrenwend, B.S. Dohrenwend, M.S. Gould, B. Link, R. Neugebauer, & R. Wunsch-Hitzig (Eds.), *Mental illness in the United States: Epidemiological estimates* (pp. 9–44). New York: Praeger.

Grisso, T. (1996). Voluntary consent to research participation in the institutional context. In B.H. Stanley, J.E. Sieber, & G.B. Melton (Eds.), *Research ethics: A psychological approach* (pp. 207–224). Lincoln: University of Nebraska Press.

Grisso, T., & Appelbaum, P.S. (1995). The MacArthur Treatment Competence Study III: Abilities of patients to consent to psychiatric and medical treatments. *Law and Human Behavior, 19,* 149–174.

Grisso, T., Appelbaum, P.S., Mulvey, E.P., & Fletcher, K. (1995). The MacArthur Treatment Competence Study II: Measures of abilities related to competence to consent to treatment. *Law and Human Behavior, 19,* 127–148.

Griswold v. Connecticut, 381 U.S. 479 (1965).

H.L. v. Matheson, 450 U.S. 398 (1981).

Halderman v. Pennhurst State Sch. & Hosp., 610 F. Supp. 1221 (E.D. Pa. 1985).

Hawks v. Lazaro, 157 W. Va. 417 (1974).

Heryford v. Parker, 396 F.2d 393 (10th Cir. 1967).

Hodgson v. Minnesota, 1497 U.S. 417 (1990).

Hoffman, P.B., & Foust, L. (1977). Least restrictive treatment of the mentally ill: A doctrine in search of its senses. *San Diego Law Review, 14,* 1100–1154.

Hoge, M.A., Davidson, L., Hill, W.L., Turner, V.E., & Ameli, R. (1992). The promise of partial hospitalization: A reassessment. *Hospital and Community Psychiatry, 43,* 345–354.

Humphrey v. Cady, 405 U.S. 504 (1972).

Ill. Comp. Stat. Ann. Chapt. 410 § 210/4 (West 1997).

Individuals with Disabilities Education Act, Pub. L. No. 101-476 (1990), 20 U.S.C.A. §§ 1400–1485 (West Supp. 1991). [Originally enacted as the Education of the Handicapped Act and subsequently known as the Education for All Handicapped Children Act, first enacted in 1975. Name change to IDEA was enacted by Pub. L. No. 101-476 and required no change in text.]

In re Carstairs, 115 N.Y.S.2d 314 (1952).

In re Gault, 387 U.S. 1 (1967).

In re Hudson, 13 Wash. 2d 673 (1942).

In re Karwath, 199 N.W.2d 147 (Iowa 1972).

In re Sampson, 65 Misc.2d 658 (N.Y. 1970).

In re Seiferth, 309 N.Y. 80 (1955).

In re Smith, 16 Md. App. 209 (1973).

Inmates of Boys' Training School v. Affleck, 346 F. Supp. 3154 (D.R.I. 1972).

Institute of Judicial Administration/American Bar Association Juvenile Justice Standards Project. (1980a). *Standards relating to dispositions.* Cambridge, MA: Ballinger.

Institute of Judicial Administration/American Bar Association Juvenile Justice Standards Project. (1980b). *Standards relating to juvenile records and information.* Cambridge, MA: Ballinger.

Johnson, F.M. (1976). The Constitution and the federal district judge. *Texas Law Review, 54,* 903–916.

Katz, J. (1984). *The silent world of doctor and patient.* New York: Free Press.

Knitzer, J. (1982). *Unclaimed children: The failure of public responsibility to children and adolescents in need of mental health services.* Washington, DC: Children's Defense Fund.

Koocher, G.P. (1983). Competence to consent: Psychotherapy. In G.B. Melton, G.P. Koocher, & M.J. Saks (Eds.), *Children's competence to consent* (pp. 111–128). New York: Plenum Press.

Koocher, G.P., & Keith-Spiegel, P.C. (1990). *Children, ethics and the law: Professional issues and cases.* Lincoln: University of Nebraska Press.

Lacey v. Laird, 166 Ohio St. 12 (1956).

Lessard v. Schmidt, 349 F. Supp. 1078 (E.D. Wis. 1972), *vacated on other grounds,* 414 U.S. 473 (1974), *reheard,* 379 F. Supp. 1376 (E.D. Wis. 1974), *vacated,* 421 U.S. 957 (1975), *prior judgment reinstated,* 413 F. Supp. 1318 (E.D. Wis. 1976).

Levine, M., Ewing, C.P., & Hager, R. (1987). Juvenile and family law in sociohistorical context. *International Journal of Law and Psychiatry, 10,* 91–109.

Levine, M., & Levine, A. (1992). *Helping children: A social history.* New York: Oxford University Press.

Lidz, C., Meisel, A., Zerubavel, E., Carter, M., Sestak, R.M., & Roth, L.H. (1984). *Informed consent: A study of decisionmaking in psychiatry.* New York: Guilford Press.

Making the grade. (1996). *Access.* Washington, DC: George Washington University.

Martarella v. Kelley, 349 F. Supp. 575 (S.D.N.Y. 1972).

McIntosh v. Milano, 168 N.J. Super. 466 (1979).

McKinney, D., & Peak, G. (1994). *School-based and school-linked health centers: Update 1993.* Washtington, DC: Center for Population Options.

Melaville, A., Blank, M., & Asayesh, G. (1993). *Together we can: A guide for crafting a profamily system of education and human services.* Washington, DC: U.S. Government Printing Office.

Melton, G.B. (1981). Effects of a state law permitting minors to consent to psychotherapy. *Professional Psychology: Research and Practice, 12,* 246–252.

Melton, G.B. (1983a). *Child advocacy: Psychological and legal issues.* New York: Plenum Press.

Melton, G.B. (1983b). Minors and privacy: Are legal and psychological concepts compatible? *Nebraska Law Review, 62*, 455–493.

Melton, G.B. (1984). Family and mental hospitals as myths. In N.D. Reppucci, L.A. Weithorn, E.P. Mulvey, & J. Monahan (Eds.), *Children, mental health, and the law* (pp. 151–167). Beverly Hills, CA: Sage.

Melton, G.B. (1986). Litigation in the interests of children: Does anybody win? *Law and Human Behavior, 10*, 337–354.

Melton, G.B. (1987a). Children, politics, and morality: The ethics of child advocacy. *Journal of Clinical Child Psychology, 16*, 357–367.

Melton, G.B. (1987b). Law and random events: The state of child mental health policy. *International Journal of Law and Psychiatry, 10*, 81–90.

Melton, G.B. (1990a). Children as objects of social control: Implications for training in children's services. In P.R. Magrab & P. Wohlford (Eds.), *Clinical training in psychology: Improving psychological services for children and adolescents with severe mental disorders* (pp. 151–156). Washington, DC: American Psychological Association.

Melton, G.B. (1990b). Promoting children's dignity through mental health services. In C.P. Cohen & H.A. Davidson (Eds.), *Children's rights in America: The U.N. Convention on the Rights of the Child compared with United States law* (pp. 239–258). Washington, DC: American Bar Association, Center on Children and the Law, and Defense for Children International–USA.

Melton, G.B. (1991a). Preserving the dignity of children around the world. *Child Abuse and Neglect, 15*, 343–350.

Melton, G.B. (1991b). Socialization in the global community: Respect for the dignity of children. *American Psychologist, 46*, 66–71.

Melton, G.B. (1999). Privacy issues in child mental health services. In B.S. Arons & J.J. Gates (Eds.), *Privacy and confidentiality in mental health care* (pp. 47–70). Baltimore: Brookes.

Melton, G.B., & Davidson, H.A. (1987). Child protection and society: When should the state intervene? *American Psychologist, 42*, 172–175.

Melton, G.B., & Garrison, E.G. (1987). Fear, prejudice, and neglect: Discrimination against mentally disabled persons. *American Psychologist, 42*, 1007–1026.

Melton, G.B., Lyons, P.M., Jr., & Spaulding, W.J. (1998). *No place to go: The civil commitment of minors.* Lincoln: University of Nebraska Press.

Melton, G.B., & Saks, M.J. (1985). The law as an instrument of socialization and social structure. In G.B. Melton (Ed.), *Nebraska Symposium on Motivation: Vol. 33. The law as a behavioral instrument* (pp. 235–277). Lincoln: University of Nebraska Press.

Melville v. Sabatino, 30 Conn. 320 (1972).

Meyer v. Nebraska, 262 U.S. 390 (1923).

Milonas v. Williams, 691 F. 2d 931 (10th Cir. 1982).

Miss. Code Ann. § 41-41-3(h) (1990).

Mnookin, R.H. (1978). Children's rights: Beyond kiddie libbers and child savers. *Journal of Clinical Child Psychology, 7*, 163–167.

Mnookin, R.H., & Weisberg, K. (1989). *Child, family, and state: Problems and materials on children and the law* (2nd ed.). Boston: Little, Brown.

Moore, M.S. (1984). *Law and psychiatry: Rethinking the relationship.* Cambridge, England: Cambridge University Press.

Morales v. Turman, 383 F. Supp. 52 (E.D. Tex. 1974), *rev'd on other grounds*, 535 F.2d 864 (5th Cir. 1976), *rev'd per curiam*, 430 U.S. (1977).

Moshman, D.N. (1989). *Children, education, and the first amendment: A psycholegal analysis.* Lincoln: University of Nebraska Press.

Mulvey, E.P., & Peeples, F.L. (1996). Are disturbed and normal adolescents equally competent to make decisions about mental health treatment? *Law and Human Behavior, 20*, 273–287.

Natanson v. Kline, 350 P.2d 1093 (Kan. 1960).

National Educational Goals Panel. (1996). *The national education goals report 1995.* Washington, DC: U.S. Government Printing Office.

Nelson v. Heyne, 491 F.2d 352 (7th Cir. 1974), *cert. den.*, 417 U.S. 976 (1974).

New York State Ass'n for Retarded Children, Inc. v. Rockefeller, 357 F. Supp. 752 (E.D.N.Y. 1973).

O'Connor v. Donaldson, 422 U.S. 563 (1975).

Olmstead v. L.C. *ex rel.* Zimring, 67 U.S.L.W. 3683 (1999).

Pagliocca, P.M., Melton, G.B., Weisz, V., & Lyons, P.M., Jr. (1995). Parenting and the law. In M.H. Bornstein (Ed.), *Handbook of parenting* (pp. 437–457). Hillsdale, NJ: Erlbaum.

Parham v. J.R., 422 U.S. 584 (1979).

Paust, J.J. (1988). Rediscovering the relationship between congressional power and international law: Exceptions to the last in time rule and the primacy of custom. *Virginia Journal of International Law, 28*, 393–449.

Pennhurst State School & Hospital v. Halderman, 451 U.S. 1 (1981).

Perry, G.S., & Melton, G.B. (1984). Precedential value of judicial notice of social facts: *Parham* as an example. *Journal of Family Law, 22*, 633–676.

Pierce v. Society of Sisters, 268 U.S. 510 (1925).

Pilpel, H.F. (1972). Minors' rights to medical care. *Albany Law Review, 36*, 462–487.

Planned Parenthood of Central Missouri v. Danforth, 428 U.S. 52 (1976).

Planned Parenthood of Southeastern Pennsylvania v. Casey, 505 U.S. 833 (1992).

Prince v. Massachusetts, 321 U.S. 158 (1944).

Rodham, H. (1973). Children under the law. *Harvard Education Review, 43,* 487–514.

Roe v. Wade, 410 U.S. 113 (1973).

Rogers v. Commissioner, 458 N.E.2d 308 (Mass. 1983).

Rogers, C.M., & Wrightsman, L.S. (1978). Attitudes toward children's rights: Nurturance or self-determination. *Journal of Social Issues, 34*(2), 59–68.

Roth, L.H., Meisel, A., & Lidz, C.W. (1977). Tests of competency to consent to treatment. *American Journal of Psychiatry, 134,* 279–284.

Rothman, D.J., & Rothman, S. (1984). *The Willowbrook wars.* New York: Harper & Row.

San Antonio Independent School District v. Rodriguez, 411 U.S. 1 (1973).

Santosky v. Kramer, 455 U.S. 745 (1982).

Schmidt, C.G. (1993). Where privacy fails: Equal protection and the abortion rights of minors. *New York University Law Review, 68,* 597–638.

Scott v. Bradford, 606 P.2d 554 (Okla. 1979).

Secretary of Public Welfare v. Institutional Juveniles, 442 U.S. 640 (1979).

Silver, S.E., Duchnowski, A.J., Kutash, K., Friedman, R.M., Eisen, M., Prange, M.E., Brandenburg, N.A., & Greenbaum, P.E. (1992). A comparison of children with serious emotional disturbance served in residential and school settings. *Journal of Child and Family Studies, 1,* 43–59.

Small, M.A., & Otto, R.K. (1991). Utilizing the "professional judgment standard" in child advocacy. *Journal of Clinical Child Psychology, 20,* 71–77.

Solnit, A.J., Nordhaus, B.F., & Lord, R. (1992). *When home is no heaven: Child placement issues.* New Haven, CT: Yale University Press.

State v. Perricone, 37 N.J. 463 (1962).

Szasz, T.S. (1979). Critical reflections on child psychiatry. *Children and Youth Services Review, 1,* 7–29.

Tarasoff v. Board of Regents, 17 Cal.3d 425 (1976).

Tinker v. Des Moines Independent School District, 393 U.S. 503 (1969).

United Nations Convention on the Rights of the Child, U.N. Doc. A/Res/44/25 (1989).

United States v. Darby, 312 U.S. 100 (1940).

Va. Code Ann. § 54.1-2969(D)(4) (1998).

Vienna Convention on the Law of Treaties, U.N. Doc. A/Conf./39/27 (1969, May 23).

Wadlington, W.L. (1973). Minors and health care: The age of consent. *Osgoode Hall Law Journal, 11,* 115–125.

Warren, C.A.B. (1981). New forms of social control: The myth of deinstitutionalization. *American Behavioral Scientist, 24,* 724–740.

Washington v. Harper, 494 U.S. 210 (1990).

Weithorn, L.A. (1982). Developmental factors and competence to make informed treatment decisions. In G.B. Melton (Ed.), *Legal reforms affecting child and youth services* (pp. 85–100). New York: Haworth Press.

Wilson, J.P. (1978). *The rights of adolescents in the mental health system.* Lexington, MA: Lexington Books.

Wisconsin v. Yoder, 406 U.S. 205 (1972).

Woe v. Cuomo, 801 F.2d 627 (2d Cir. 1986).

Youngberg v. Romeo, 457 U.S. 307 (1982), *vacating and remanding* 644 F.2d. 147 (3d Cir. 1980).

Younts v. Saint Francis Hospital and School of Nursing, Inc., 205 Kan. 292 (1970).

Youth Law Center. (1993, March). *Glass walls: Confidentiality provisions and interagency collaborations.* San Francisco: Author.

CHAPTER 55

Forensic Evaluations of Children and Expert Witness Testimony

ARLENE B. SCHAEFER

Although scholarly and procedural attention has been paid to the interface of psychology and the law for many decades, it was not until 1984 that texts focusing specifically on forensic assessment and the expert witness testimony based on it emerged (Grisso, 1987). There has been a proliferation of information since that time, emanating from academicians and practitioners in both the legal and the mental health communities, as well as from those professionals who are dual citizens of what, at times, appear to be two very different worlds.

One important area that has been addressed is the need to get into the legal system the psychological knowledge base pertinent to the types of cases being heard. It has been noted that the expert witness testimony of mental health professionals "may represent psychology's greatest influence on the legal process" (Grisso, 1987, p. 832). Most of the extant research knowledge is found in journals, and a survey of judges and other court personnel revealed that few of them read psychology or psychology-law journals (Grisso & Melton, 1987). Mental health professionals must, therefore, assume the responsibility for presenting germane research findings in court.

The responsibility is a significant one. It requires that mental health professionals stay current with pertinent psychological research (Sales, 1982). In addition, it creates an ethical obligation to be complete and accurate, that is, to present all information, including that which may contradict the position of the party who solicited the testimony of the expert (Weithorn, 1987a). The latter responsibility also applies to clinical data gathered in a case and presented as evidence.

The duty of the mental health professional to refrain from a selective presentation of data often conflicts with the basic nature of the adversarial system in which each side in a dispute presents evidence favorable to its position and unfavorable to the position of the other party. By following rules of law and procedures based on case precedent, including direct and cross-examination of witnesses and the introduction of rebuttal evidence, it is believed that a true picture will be created on which a decision is made by the trier of fact (i.e., the judge or jury). Justice refers not to the decision that is rendered, but to the opportunity for individuals to have their fair say in court (Melton & Limber, 1989; Weithorn, 1987a).

The pursuit of justice via the adversarial system and the pursuit of the "helping ethic" by mental health practitioners rest on different conceptualizations, procedures, and values (Melton, Petrila, Poythress, & Slobogin, 1997). These differences create the need for mental health practitioners who do evaluations for forensic purposes and who testify as expert witnesses to have specialized training, experience, and knowledge (Anderten, Staulcup, & Grisso, 1980; Blau, 1998; Grisso, 1987; Melton et al., 1997; Poythress, 1979; Shapiro, 1984). Although mental health practitioners may perform with excellence in the clinical arena, the typical training they receive does not suffice for them to function competently and ethically in the forensic arena (Butcher & Pope, 1993; Melton et al., 1997).

Lack of specialized competence and/or naïveté can be dangerous to the individual practitioner, the clients served (e.g., examinees, agencies, courts), the public interest, and the mental health professions. With respect to the individual practitioner, there is increased exposure to ethical complaints against psychologists who provide services in forensic cases involving disputes over child custody (Weithorn, 1987b). Many authors (e.g., Grisso, 1987; Haas, 1993; Melton et al., 1997; Poythress, 1979; Wells, 1986) have addressed the importance of the relationship between the quality of forensic work done by mental health professionals and the public image of psychology as a profession. The public image of the mental health professions created through expert testimony can, in turn, affect the public's use of mental health services and the allocation of funds for research and service delivery (Sales & Shuman, 1993). Finally, the forensic activities of mental health professionals can affect the welfare of clients in profound ways because fundamental legal and civil rights and important personal and social interests are at stake in the context of courtroom litigation (Grisso, 1987; Haas, 1993; Melton et al., 1997; Poythress, 1979; Wells, 1986).

According to Grisso and Melton (1987), the categories of interests that the contemporary system of juvenile justice attempts to protect include the constitutional rights of children and families, the best interests of the child, and community interests that may be compromised by the delinquent behavior of juveniles. The specific kinds of cases in which legal determinations involving children are made include abuse and neglect, guardianship, divorce custody, and delinquency. Depending on the nature of the legal issue and the structure of the court system in a jurisdiction, these cases may be heard in juvenile court, domestic relations or family court, and/or other civil or criminal courts. Mental health professionals may be involved in different phases of the

legal actions in any of these courts. Melton and his colleagues (1997) present a thorough description of the structure of court systems, the legal processes in which mental health professionals may participate, and the different role functions they may perform. This chapter is limited to a consideration of forensic psychological evaluations done in the context of divorce custody determinations. The topic was chosen for review as an example of forensic cases involving children because of the relative frequency with which mental health professionals are incorporating these evaluations into their practices (Grisso, 1990), the complexity of the issues involved, the elevated risk of an ethics complaints or civil suit against psychologists who perform these evaluations, and the implications for children's welfare and development.

Before addressing divorce custody evaluations, however, important issues related to forensic evaluations in general and expert witness testimony are presented as an orienting framework. It should be noted that all of the complex issues and even the fundamental knowledge base cannot be considered in a single chapter. Although reading alone is not a substitute for specialized educational programs and practical training, there are several texts that provide the kind of coverage not feasible here. These include books authored by Blau (1998), Grisso (1986), Melton and colleagues (1997), and Shapiro (1984).

OVERVIEW

FORENSIC EVALUATIONS

Professional Expertise

In view of the significant potential implications discussed previously, mental health practitioners who undertake the conduct of forensic evaluations must ensure that they have the necessary expertise. Two decades ago, it was noted that forensic clinicians gained the requisite knowledge principally through their efforts to read the relevant literature and attend seminars and workshops (Anderten et al., 1980). At that time (Poythress, 1979), the need for specialized training that is interdisciplinary in nature was emphasized. Such training might be obtained through the completion of a joint degree program in one of the mental health professions and the law, by taking law-related or interdisciplinary courses at the graduate level, or through postdoctoral or other postgraduate training (Otto, Heilbrun, & Grisso, 1990). Butcher and Pope (1993) are emphatic about the need for specialized graduate courses and internships as the foundation for competent, and therefore ethical, forensic practice.

In reality, there are many clinicians who perform forensic evaluations without benefit of formal education and training in the area. As noted earlier, typical clinical training is not considered sufficient, and mental health practitioners who seldom do forensic assessments may not be knowledgeable about the special issues involved (Grisso, 1987; Melton et al., 1997). In a departure from the traditional specialized training model, Melton and his colleagues suggest that the best way to facilitate functioning in the forensic arena is for mental health professionals to establish a practice that focuses only, or at least principally, on the delivery of forensic services. Those authors maintain that the requirements of developing and maintaining a forensic mental health practice will naturally create the specialized knowledge base and expertise of the true "forensic specialist" (Melton et al., 1997).

A critical facet of forensic expertise is the possession of knowledge and professional experience *in areas relevant to the particular case at hand* (Blau, 1998; Clark, 1990; Melton et al., 1997; Shapiro, 1984; Smith, 1989). In addition to knowledge of the literature, assessment procedures, and statutes and case law specific to the psycholegal issue being addressed, expertise also requires familiarity with the special legal and ethical issues that attach to forensic evaluations and the role of the expert witness, consultation skills, knowledge of how to write a forensic report, and sensitivity to issues concerning the need for careful preparation to testify, appropriate courtroom demeanor, and the effective presentation of oral testimony.

Procedural Issues
According to Melton et al. (1997), the initial contact with the referral source (i.e., the legal representative of the potential client) is extremely important; the parameters of the evaluation must be established when the referral is made. It is incumbent upon the mental health professional to find out from the attorney what legal issues are to be addressed in the case and the attorney's expectations of the mental health professional. Melton and his colleagues (1997) suggest that it is the responsibility of the

mental health practitioner to convey to the referral source (1) the limits of knowledge in the area; (2) limitations on assessing the issue in question and making predictions about it; (3) the potential outcomes; and (4) what position is taken regarding ultimate issue testimony.

The costs for the services and who will be responsible for payment should be clarified with the referral source. It behooves practitioners to require payment in advance of testifying in court, both to enhance the likelihood that they will be paid and to make it clear that any findings or opinions offered are not being influenced by the potentiality of payment (Blau, 1998; Shapiro, 1984). Also, it is necessary to disclose relationships or activities that could create a conflict of interest (Committee on Ethical Guidelines for Forensic Psychologists, 1991).

The prudent practitioner will not embark on a forensic evaluation without first having thoroughly explored the pertinent issues with the client's legal representative. In addition, clarification of these issues is necessary to enable the referral source to make an informed decision about whether or not to retain a particular mental health professional (Committee on Ethical Guidelines for Forensic Psychologists, 1991).

If mutual agreement is reached between the referral source and the practitioner, the next step is usually an interview with the client (although the practitioner might want first to review pertinent documents). It is important for mental health practitioners to be aware that individuals assessed for legal purposes differ from other patients in that they may be reluctant to participate in the evaluation process, they may be motivated by real or perceived coercion, and they are subject to other influences that inhere in the adversarial context (Rogers, 1987). Individuals in these circumstances typically have more investment in the outcome of their legal case (which often has profound personal implications) than in honest self-disclosure (Lanyon, 1986). These factors must be taken into account in the conduct of the evaluation and in the interpretation of the results of it.

At the time of the initial contact with the client, it is the ethical responsibility of a psychologist to discuss the following issues:

1. The examinee's understanding of and expectations about the evaluation process.
2. The examinee's right to refuse to participate in the evaluation (unless that right has been restricted by court order).

3. The questions that will be addressed in the evaluation and what procedures will be used.
4. Limits on confidentiality and privilege, that is, who will or may have access to the information gathered.
5. Possible implications of the results. (Melton et al., 1997)

In addition, if the client will be responsible for payment, fees and payment policies should be discussed (Blau, 1998; Shapiro, 1984). If there is mutual agreement for the evaluation to be conducted, it will most likely consist of multiple interviews, the administration of psychological tests, gathering corroborative information (pertinent documents and interviews with relevant parties), integration of results, and preparation of a report. Oral testimony may or may not be necessary.

A crucial procedural guideline is to design assessments to be specific to the legal issue at hand (Grisso, 1986; Melton et al., 1997), as well as to be sufficiently comprehensive (by using multiple assessment tools and corroborative sources of information) that the reliability and validity of the findings are enhanced (Lanyon, 1986). Grisso (1986) has developed an excellent model for conducting forensic assessments that construes the legal issues typically addressed as "competencies" (e.g., parenting competency), which have six characteristics: functional, contextual, causal, interactive, judgmental, dispositional. These characteristics are operationally defined by Grisso to provide for the legal relevance of psychological evaluations.

Psychological Testing
In 1979, Poythress noted that clinical psychologists commonly err in using standard test batteries that were neither intended nor validated for forensic issues. More recently, Butcher and Pope (1993, p. 271) described the use of a standard battery of tests with which forensic practitioners feel "comfortable" as "a special occupational hazard." According to Grisso (1986), the unvalidated use of traditional tests to answer legal questions is a major problem in forensic assessments.

In a special issue of *Law and Human Behavior*, Elwork (1984) addressed the need for assessment techniques specific to legal questions. In an elaboration of that need, Grisso (1986) cogently argued for the development and use of "forensic assessment instruments," defined as psychological tests or techniques that assess competencies of psycholegal interest. Instruments extant at the time that were designed for forensic application or that might be used for that purpose are extensively reviewed. Although somewhat dated by the subsequent emergence of many forensic assessment instruments, Grisso's 1986 volume remains an indispensible resource for clinicians who use psychological tests in forensic assessments; the conceptual model is unsurpassed.

The development of forensic assessment devices has made a major contribution to the field. Examples include instruments to address competency to stand trial, criminal responsibility, parenting in the context of child custody disputes, guardianship, and risk of violence (Borum, 1998). Despite meeting the criterion of psycholegal relevance, these instruments still necessitate circumspection. Users must be familiar with the methodology of administration and interpretation, the normative data, and their known reliability and validity (Ewing, 1996).

Report Preparation
Because psychological reports in legal cases may be read by many individuals, submitted into evidence in court and thereby become part of the public record, and otherwise get into the public arena, it is recommended and ethically imperative that they be conservative and objective in nature (Blau, 1998; Melton et al., 1997). The following guidelines are a distillation of information contained in Melton et al., a source that should be consulted for further elaboration of appropriate and ethical report writing and for examples of reports of assessments done in response to a variety of psycholegal questions:

1. Present the facts/observations gathered and any inferences/opinions/conclusions reached, with a clear separation between the former and the latter. Subject matter to be included is the circumstances surrounding the referral; relevant background information; types of services and the dates rendered; sources of information relied on; the clinical findings (if psychological testing contributed to the conclusions and/or opinions offered, the reported findings should include test results and interpretations); and a psycholegal formulation (i.e., the relationship between clinical findings and the legal issue). Ethical principles also require that the limitations inherent in the

assessment and contradictory, alternative, and/or disconfirmatory information be disclosed. Recommendations for ameliorative interventions (e.g., psychotherapy) may be made, but recommendations concerning the legal disposition of the case are generally not considered to be within the purview of mental health practitioners. Melton and his colleagues (1997, p. 17) have noted the "near-unanimity among scholarly commentators" that it is unacceptable for mental health professionals to render opinions about the ultimate legal issue (e.g., which parent should have custody; whether a child's report of sexual abuse is sufficiently credible that the noncustodial father can be declared the perpetrator and visitation with him restricted).

2. Limit the report contents to the parameters defined by the referral question.

3. Further limit the report to information likely to be perceived as relevant by the trier of fact. Judges and juries may feel "overloaded" by too much information, and neither they nor attorneys may read extensive reports.

4. Try to avoid the use of jargon. If a technical term must be used, it should be clearly defined.

Ethical Issues

The conduct of forensic evaluations opens up a veritable Pandora's box of ethical issues. Although naïveté or ignorance may lead to unethical practices, many commentators (e.g., McCloskey, Egeth, & McKenna, 1986; Melton et al., 1997; Rogers, 1987; Weithorn, 1987a) have suggested that antagonistic legal and ethical demands, the complexity of the issues, and problems in defining who the clients are and conflicts of interest among them may make the capacity to operate totally under an ethical rubric more illusory than real.

The American Psychological Association (APA, 1992) makes it obligatory for member psychologists to abide by the *Ethical Principles of Psychologists and Code of Conduct* (hereafter referred to as the Ethics Code). The most recent revision of the Ethics Code (APA, 1992) provides greater guidance than previous versions by elucidating ethical standards specific to forensic activities, with reference made to relevant standards elsewhere in the Ethics Code. In addition, building on the previously published *Ethical Principles of Psychologists* (APA, 1990), *Specialty Guidelines for Forensic Psychologists* (Committee on Ethical Guidelines for Forensic Psychologists, 1991) have been developed to enhance the professional conduct of psychologists who function within the forensic arena.

A fundamental ethical obligation of psychologists working in the forensic arena is to be competent in the relevant area. The criteria for the establishment of expertise mentioned previously are components of the ethical obligation of psychologists who perform forensic assessments both to have the competence to do so *and* to stay within the boundaries of their competence. With respect to the former, the practitioner must have not only the clinical skills relevant to the psycholegal issue at hand, but also knowledge of the psychological literature in the area (Clark, 1990; Sales, 1982) and of the germane legal and ethical standards (Clark, 1990; Grisso, 1986; Melton et al., 1997). With respect to the latter, it has been noted frequently that psychologists do not have the training nor the expertise to make legal decisions; to render conclusions on legal issues is therefore outside the ethical boundaries of competent practice (e.g., Clark, 1990; Grisso, 1986; Melton et al., 1997; Morse, 1978).

Even if they do not overstep their boundaries of competence by making legal determinations, psychologists can ethically exceed their competence by making overgeneralizations clinically that cannot be supported by the specific findings nor by the techniques used (Shapiro, 1988). If psychological tests were used and therefore may have an impact on the legal decision, practitioners have the ethical duty to be competent in their use (Blau, 1984; Butcher & Pope, 1993). Special considerations apply to the ethical use of tests that are scored and interpreted by computer (APA, 1986; Butcher & Pope, 1993; Shapiro, 1988).

In addition to the obvious threats to competence inherent in inadequate knowledge of the legal system and of the data relevant to the case at hand, Haas (1993) describes several factors that can impede competent functioning by forensic psychologists (and, by extension, other forensic mental health practitioners). Personal variables that can lead to incompetent performance, rarely addressed in the literature, include arrogance, cynicism, psychological impairment, and greed (Haas, 1993).

Several of the standards in the Ethics Code specific to forensic activities pertain to assessments, together emphasizing the obligation to be able to substantiate findings with data appropriate to the scope of conclusions reached or recommendations made. Of particular note is that psychologists are discouraged from offering opinions about individuals they have not directly assessed. If they do so, psychologists are obligated to be circumspect and to disclose the limitations inherent in these opinions. Practitioners are sometimes asked, for example, to offer opinions about individuals not formally assessed based on their presentation while testifying. As Brodsky (1998, p. 484) aptly notes, "One should not consider observation of other witnesses' behavior on the stand to be remotely equivalent to findings from conventional psychological assessments."

Of related interest is the absolute proscription against the offering of professional opinions about individuals not actually seen or formally evaluated in the *Code of Conduct* developed by the Association of State and Provincial Psychology Boards (ASPPB, 1991) for use by agencies that are legally empowered to regulate psychologists. The *Code of Conduct* has been adopted by the regulatory board in at least one jurisdiction as part of its enforceable Code of Ethics (Oklahoma State Board of Examiners of Psychologists, 1999).

Other ethical standards are relevant to objectivity and full disclosure in the forensic area, enjoining psychologists to be truthful and circumspect in their presentations, to avoid role confusion and conflicts, and to disclose potential conflicts of interest to appropriate parties. Finally, psychologists are to be aware of the competing requirements of their ethics and of the legal system that sometimes occur; they are to make evident their adherence to the Ethics Code and attempt to resolve such conflicts responsibly. Naturally, APA member psychologists who function in the forensic arena, like all other member psychologists, are bound by the entire Ethics Code.

The ethical standards regarding confidentiality have a complex relationship to forensic assessments and the presentation of the results of them. According to Melton et al. (1997), practitioners have an ethical obligation to determine for themselves, and then to explain to the examinee, the limits of confidentiality. A particularly sensitive ethical issue is that the information provided by the examinee could influence the outcome in such a way that his or her legal cause is not promoted, a conflict that also bears on the practitioner's duty to avoid the compromise of clients' legal rights (Melton et al., 1997). Even though a client may have waived the statutory privilege that normally protects psychotherapist-patient communications by participating in a forensic evaluation (Shapiro, 1988, 1990), sound ethical practice suggests the need for written, informed consent to release the information gathered to specific parties (e.g., attorneys, the court). Clients often do not understand that they are abdicating their right to privileged communications by their participation in an evaluation, or they may have signed a consent form in their attorney's office to release information without fully appreciating to what they are agreeing. Rogers (1987) suggests that practitioners also obtain written consent for confidential information to be released to them from other sources (e.g., physicians, treating psychologists), regardless of the legal waiver of privilege.

Principles regarding confidentiality and public statements make it unethical for psychologists to reveal information about clients in written reports and oral testimony that is not relevant to the reason for the evaluation (Melton et al., 1997). For example, although the inquiry in child custody litigation is broad, discussion of a parent's sexual dysfunction during a prior marriage is inappropriate unless it bears on the individual's functioning as a parent in the extant custody litigation.

There are several general principles in the Ethics Code that are aspirational in nature and that subsume the specific standards cited above. An overarching tenet, sweeping in its scope, is respect for and protection of the welfare of consumers. Among its ramifications are the duties to clarify the nature of relationships with and to all parties (Melton et al., 1997; Rogers, 1987), to obtain informed consent from clients (Melton et al., 1997), to clarify fees and payment policies in advance (Blau, 1998; Shapiro, 1984), and to provide some services pro bono (i.e., free) (Blau, 1998; Committee on Ethical Guidelines for Forensic Psychologists, 1991; Smith, 1989). Inadequate preparation to testify in court may compromise the welfare of consumers (Anderten et al., 1980). The ethical proscription against multiple relationships that impair objectivity means that psychologists cannot serve as both therapist and forensic evaluator with the same client (Clark, 1990; Shapiro, 1988).

The type of role the psychologist assumes in a forensic case has ethical implications governed by the principle of responsible behavior. Although concerned with expert testimony based on experimental psychology rather than clinical practice, most of the participants in a conference to address the ethical issues surrounding advocacy versus impartiality of psychologists as expert witnesses concluded that being an "impartial educator" is the "only ethically defensible position" (McCloskey et al., 1986, p. 5). Assuming the role of advocate, a position favored by the adversarial system, promotes the suppression of unfavorable findings. As noted earlier, ethically responsible practice mandates the communication of the limitations of procedures used and of the findings, knowledge, opinions, and recommendations offered, as well as full disclosure of unfavorable or contradictory findings and alternative explanations for the results of the evaluation (Anderten et al., 1980; Blau, 1998; Elwork, 1984; Melton et al., 1997; Rogers, 1987; Weithorn, 1987a). A specific mandate subsumed by the ethical standard regarding truthfulness, one not often mentioned in the psychology literature, is the obligation of all witnesses, including experts, to adhere to the courtroom oath "to tell the truth" (Saks, 1990; Smith, 1989).

Standards for Competent Practice

In 1984, Shapiro commented on the absence of specific policies and procedures for private practitioners functioning in the legal arena. He suggested using the standard for deciding professional malpractice cases, that is, doing what "the reasonably prudent practitioner" would do. Reasonably prudent practice means, in part, adhering to the *Ethical Principles of Psychologists and Code of Conduct* (APA, 1992) and applying the entire Ethics Code to forensic issues. According to Shapiro (1984, 1990), reasonably prudent practice also can be defined by the various applicable practice guidelines. Practice guidelines are aspirational and not mandated for psychologists by the adopting group within APA. They can be and have been employed by the legal system, however, not only as representative of the standard of psychological practice in malpractice suits but also for judging the admissibility of expert testimony (Schaefer, 1998). In the forensic area, important examples are the *Specialty Guidelines for Forensic Psychologists* (Committee on Ethical Guidelines for Forensic Psychologists, 1991), *General Guidelines for Providers of Psychological Services* (APA, 1987), *Specialty Guidelines for the Delivery of Services* (e.g., by Clinical Psychologists) (APA, 1981), *Standards for Educational and Psychological Testing* (American Educational Research Association, American Psychological Association, &

National Council on Measurement in Education, 1999), and *Guidelines for Computer-Based Tests and Interpretations* (APA, 1986).

EXPERT WITNESS TESTIMONY

Qualifications of Expert Witnesses

The legal status as expert witness is conferred by each state's rules of evidence that are generally based on the Federal Rules of Evidence. The rules essentially define an expert as an individual who, by virtue of specialized knowledge, education, and/or experience, can provide testimony in court that is likely to assist the trier of fact in understanding the evidence and/or in making a legal decision (Blau, 1998; Melton et al., 1997).

As noted previously, scholarly commentators in the mental health professions advance the view that it is particularly important to have qualifications relevant to the distinctive psycholegal case at hand. When the professional is being qualified as an expert in court, it is those case-specific qualifications that should be emphasized (Green & Schaefer, 1984; Shapiro, 1984; Smith, 1989). Ziskin (1981) has severely criticized the manner of qualification of mental health professionals as expert witnesses, particularly on such flimsy credentials as membership in professional organizations. According to Ziskin, teaching experience and publications relevant to a particular legal case may constitute meaningful qualifications.

Admissibility of Expert Witness Testimony

The rules of evidence provide for the admission of expert witness testimony if it is sufficiently specialized to exceed what the average person is likely to know, if it is relevant and reliable, if it will be of assistance to the trier of fact while not being unduly influential, and if its helpfulness is likely to be greater than its potential to be prejudicial (Melton et al., 1997). Melton and his colleagues support liberal standards for the admission of testimony by mental health practitioners, noting that it is no more speculative than testimony offered by experts in other fields that is routinely admitted, and that it is specialized knowledge of a type that can help inform legal decisions.

Faust and Ziskin (1988a, 1988b) clearly disagree with that position. They contend that the legal standards for the admissibility of mental health professionals' expert witness testimony lend themselves to empirical articulation; that is, "Can expert witnesses in psychology and psychiatry answer forensic questions with reasonable accuracy?" and "Can experts help the judge and jury reach more accurate conclusions than would otherwise be possible?" (Faust & Ziskin, 1988a, p. 31). Based on a selective consideration of empirical data, the authors suggest that neither criterion is met. The president and president-elect of the American Psychological Association at the time (Fowler & Matarazzo, 1988), on behalf of the membership, contradicted the approach taken and the conclusions reached by Faust and Ziskin.

Faust and Ziskin (1988a) further conclude that because mental health professionals have little of value to offer the courts, their testimony should not be admitted because to do so is too costly both in terms of the court's time and the public's money. Even those who disagree with the extreme position taken by Faust and Ziskin, believing that mental health professionals can have an enhancing role in the legal system, are critical of the quality of expert testimony that is admitted (Elwork, 1984; Grisso, 1986, 1987; Melton et al., 1997; Morse, 1978; Smith, 1989). A summary of the complaints that, unfortunately, are often valid is that testimony by mental health professionals tends to be irrelevant to the psycholegal issue being addressed, intrudes on the domain of the fact-finder by reaching a legal conclusion, is not credible because it fails to meet scientific standards (Grisso, 1986), and is presented in a manner that is not clear and understandable to the trier of fact (Elwork, 1984).

A legal case dating back to 1923, *Frye v. United States*, has been used as precedent in the admission of expert testimony. Commonly referred to as the *Frye* test, it holds that in order for scientific evidence to be admitted, it must generally be accepted by the scientific community from which it emanates (Blau, 1984). The *Frye* test has been applied to psychological procedures and tests as well as to certain kinds of data, such as clinical syndromes offered to characterize various types of individuals.

There have been criticisms of the *Frye* test by experts in the mental health professions. One criticism, offered by Blau (1984), is that the *Frye* test does not address the true scientific merits of psychological evidence, such as reliability and validity. According to Smith (1989), it should be mandatory

that evidence of a psychological nature meet those kinds of scientific standards to be admissible. Another criticism that can be applied to the *Frye* test is that tests, techniques, and procedures must have been available for a fairly long period of time to have general acceptance (Suggs, 1979). Case precedents, including *Frye v. United States*, are important to the way the legal system functions and tend to mitigate against higher-quality testimony because better methodologies and newer research findings may not be admitted (Grisso, 1987). A succinct criticism of the *Frye* test by Melton and his colleagues (1997) is its allowance for the introduction of "scientific" evidence that is accepted by psychologists but is not statistically reliable or valid, and the failure to admit testimony based on evidence that is novel but scientifically reliable.

By and large, legal analysts deem the *Frye* standard too conservative, that is, unnecessarily restrictive (Melton et al., 1997). Partially in an effort to liberalize the standards for the admissibility of scientific evidence, the Supreme Court of the United States established new guidelines for the Federal Courts in 1993 in what has become a landmark case, *Daubert v. Merrell Dow Pharmaceuticals, Inc.* In essence, the Supreme Court decided that the Federal Rules of Evidence supersede the *Frye* test and made the judge the "gatekeeper" for scientific testimony on a case-by-case basis. By way of explication of the Federal Rule that the evidence proffered be helpful to the trier of fact in understanding the matter being heard, the Court enumerated factors to be considered in evaluating the admissibility of scientific evidence. Those factors include (1) whether the theory or technique relied on is based on methods that have been or can be tested; (2) whether the theory or technique has been subjected to peer review and published; (3) whether there is a known rate of error in the application of the theory or technique; and (4) whether the theory or technique has gained general acceptance in the relevant scientific community. The fourth factor is, of course, the *Frye* test.

Although the application of *Daubert* was thought by the Supreme Court to make decisions about the admissibility of expert testimony less restrictive, Tomkins (1995) has noted with respect to forensic psychology that "expert testimony will be subject to the broader trend of heightened judicial scrutiny and management" (p. 129). The potential impact is great if one considers how much testimony by psychologists is clinical in nature, rather than scientific, and could be referred to as "speculation," "art," or "naïve empiricism" as opposed to science (Rotgers & Barrett, 1996).

Scope of Expert Witness Testimony
The scope of expert testimony that various commentators believe to be legally, professionally, and ethically acceptable occupies a broad continuum. At the conservative end are Faust and Ziskin (1988a), who conditionally support testimony based on valid and reliable actuarial data. Although still at the conservative end of the spectrum, in addition to actuarial data, Morse (1978) would have psychologists testify to behavioral observations of the kind unlikely to be made by laypersons (e.g., clients' answers to questions that have diagnostic significance). The modal area of the continuum is occupied by those who endorse testimony that might include facts, observations, actuarial and clinical findings, inferences, and restricted kinds of clinical opinions and recommendations, but that precludes opinions that embrace the elements of or directly address the ultimate legal issue (Bazelon, 1982; Bersoff, 1986; Blau, 1998; Clark, 1990; Grisso, 1986; Melton et al., 1997; Monahan, 1980; Morse, 1982; Poythress, 1982; Wagenaar, 1988; Weithorn, 1987b). At the extreme end of the continuum of scholarly commentators, an apparently desolate place, are those who support the rendering of ultimate issue opinions by mental health professionals (Rogers & Ewing, 1989; Smith, 1989).

Rogers and Ewing (1989) offer several cogent arguments for ultimate issue testimony, and the observation has been made that many legal professionals want and request opinion testimony on the legal decision in question, and that many mental health expert witnesses (all too frequently) give it (Bazelon, 1982; Blau, 1998; Grisso, 1986, 1987; Melton et al., 1997; Morse, 1982; Poythress, 1982; Slobogin, 1989; Wagenaar, 1988). The Federal Rules of Evidence permit expert witnesses to offer opinions that concern the ultimate legal decision to be made by the trier of fact, and some states require it on certain legal issues (Bisbing & Faust, 1990; Poythress, 1982). As Melton and his colleagues (1997) have aptly noted, however, the Federal Rules of Evidence limit testimony to opinions based on specialized knowledge. It is widely believed that mental health professionals do not have special expertise in making findings of fact, reaching legal conclusions, or making the moral, value, and social policy judgments that are typically the basis for legal decisions (Bazelon, 1982; Bersoff, 1986; Blau, 1998; Grisso, 1986; Melton et al., 1997; Morse, 1978; Slobogin, 1989; Weithorn, 1987b). In an interesting treatment of the topic, Bersoff suggests that mental health experts should be permitted to give ultimate opinion testimony if they can empirically demonstrate expertise not only in their profession but also as social policymakers. Rogers and Ewing (1989) disagree with the premise so often advanced that ultimate issue testimony requires or implies moral and legal expertise. Rather, they state, ultimate issue testimony represents "an attempt to generalize from empirical studies to clinical situations involving legal standards" (p. 364). Smith (1989) would permit such testimony if the mental health expert can demonstrate knowledge of the relevant legal test and concepts and how they are pertinent to the current findings. The proponents appear to overlook the observation made by the opponents that legal decisions usually imply the prediction of outcomes for which there is no adequate scientific basis (e.g., Grisso, 1986; Melton et al., 1997; Morse, 1978). Ultimate issue testimony therefore often reflects the personal values and preferences of the mental health professional.

The question of the appropriate scope of expert testimony remains controversial. If a mental health practitioner accepts the majority opinion that offering opinions or conclusions about legal issues goes beyond the domain of professional competence, there are obvious ethical implications of doing so.

Ethical, Competent, and Effective Testimony
Most of the specific issues concerning ethical and competent expert witness testimony have been addressed previously under the relevant headings in the section on forensic evaluations. One of those issues, however, is so important to the role of the mental health professional in the public arena of the courtroom that it merits additional elaboration.

The issue in question concerns whether a mental health professional should be an advocate or an impartial educator. Although the dichotomy between advocacy and impartiality is most often addressed in the literature, Saks (1990) compellingly recasts the dichotomy as one between the role of advocate and the role of witness. According to Saks, an expert witness has a prescribed role just as other witnesses do, which is to provide evidence that is sworn under oath to be truthful. Advocacy for a party of a particular outcome, for example, by omitting unfavorable findings, is incompatible with an expert witness's obligation to tell the truth. It is the attorney whose role is defined as advocate. In court, attorneys are not required to take the oath. Although attorneys are not permitted to knowingly present false evidence, they are not obliged to present all evidence known to them. Indeed, attorneys operate under the ethical imperative to be vigorous advocates, a role that obligates them to present evidence that supports their client's legal cause.

Although the law expects mental health experts to be witnesses and not advocates, it does not formally sanction those who assume the role of "assistant advocate" (Saks, 1990). Sanctions come obliquely in the form of suspicions about mental health expert witnesses (Saks, 1990) and in the nullification of the value of their testimony in the court's eyes (Wagenaar, 1988).

Most people are familiar with the disreputable "hired gun," the expert who testifies to advance the cause of the paying party (Saks, 1990). The role of hired gun is patently unethical, and advocacy by the expert also has ethical implications because there is never perfect congruence between the expert's data and a particular position (Saks, 1990). To be an advocate, therefore, the expert witness would have to distort the data presented. As noted earlier, mental health experts have an ethical duty to be impartial educators rather than advocates (McCloskey et al., 1986; Melton et al., 1997). Others (e.g., Blau, 1998; Clark, 1990; Goldman, 1986; Haas, 1993) have enjoined mental health professionals to avoid the role of advocate, with the possible exception of advocating one's opinion (Shapiro, 1984).

Even those experts who intend to be impartial may find themselves losing their neutral position under the pressures of the adversarial system (Brodsky, 1991; Goldman, 1986; Haas, 1993; Loftus, 1986; Saks, 1990). Because attorneys seem to prefer advocacy as opposed to impartiality in their expert witnesses, impartial experts may find themselves at best in conflicted, tense relationships with attorneys (Saks, 1990). Several commentators have observed that experts who are unwilling to advocate for an attorney's case are unlikely to get forensic referrals (Loftus, 1986; McCloskey et al., 1986; Saks, 1990).

An expert witness who is appointed by the court is less vulnerable to adversarial pressures. The courts have the power to appoint expert witnesses under the Federal Rules of Evidence, but generally underuse it (Smith, 1989). Smith encourages the legal system to appoint mental health professionals as the court's witnesses, and Schofield (1956) strongly urges professionals to seek court-appointed status to formalize their role as impartial experts. Both Schofield and Wells (1986) point to the enhanced status of the court-appointed expert, and Weithorn (1987a) mentions the greatly augmented control the expert has over the information that is presented. Greater control over the nature and extent of the data offered in turn increases the likelihood of ethical and competent testimony. In lieu of being the court's expert, Wells suggests that a guiding principle for mental health professionals is to give testimony that would be identical whether one is called by the prosecution or the defense (or, alternatively, the plaintiff or the defendant, the petitioner or the respondent).

In summary, the majority opinion suggests that ethical and competent performance of the role of expert witness rests on undertaking evaluations only in areas for which the mental health professional has demonstrable expertise, conducting the evaluation under the rubric of relevant legal and ethical standards and within appropriate practice guidelines, assuming the posture of impartiality rather than advocacy, and not making dispositional decisions but rather offering evidence of the highest caliber in an effort to enhance the legal decision-making process. Related goals include protecting the image of the profession as a whole and maintaining one's own professional dignity and reputation.

To be dignified and effective in the courtroom, careful pretrial preparation and knowledge of courtroom protocol are essential. Excellent coverage of these issues can be found in Blau (1998), Brodsky (1991), Melton et al. (1997), and Shapiro (1984). Only a brief summary is offered here.

Adequate preparation entails a review of the entire case file and related materials (e.g., reliability and validity data of the tests used, pertinent research, corroborative documents) that will form the content of the testimony. Consultation with experienced legal and mental health professionals who are not involved in the case is useful and often essential. A pretrial meeting with the attorney who will be conducting the direct examination is mandatory to the development of questions that will enable the expert to bring the necessary information before the court and to help the expert anticipate the nature of the cross-examination. Mental health professionals should be aware of the different styles of direct and cross-examination (Call, 1995) and be prepared for aggressive cross-examination.

Courtroom demeanor is important. The witness should address himself or herself to the trier of fact, either the judge or jury, in a clear and comprehensible manner. Answers should be responsive to the questions. It is permissible and recommended that if the expert is unable to answer a question, he or she state, "I do not know the answer." If the expert does not understand a question, a request for clarification or rephrasing is advised. Melton and his colleagues (1997, pp. 543–546) offer excellent guidance on avoiding pressures to give ultimate legal issue opinions if the expert opposes doing so.

DIVORCE CUSTODY EVALUATIONS

PSYCHOLEGAL ISSUES

Custodial Arrangements

The legal dissolution of a marriage in which there are minor children necessitates that the parents' rights and responsibilities relative to the children be restructured (Wyer, Gaylord, & Grove, 1987). If the divorcing parents are among the minority who are unable to agree on the form the restructuring will take (Melton et al., 1997), then the court will determine how the parents' legal rights and responsibilities and the amount of physical contact each will have with the children will be distributed (Wyer et al., 1987).

There are a variety of possible permutations, assuming that both parents are fit. The most typical arrangement is that one parent has sole legal custody and the noncustodial parent has only the legal right to physical possession of the children on occasion (i.e., visitation). The second most frequent arrangement, joint custody, has two components. Joint legal custody refers to each parent's having equal rights to make major decisions concerning the children, whereas joint physical custody has reference to a distribution of the time that the children reside with each parent that approaches equivalence (Atkinson, 1984; Felner & Terre, 1987). Physical custody actually can be allocated in an infinite variety of ways under the rubric of joint legal custody, and may be by the

parents themselves despite the provisions of the court's order (McKinnon & Wallerstein, 1986). Only rarely do courts provide for split custody, an arrangement by which each parent has sole legal custody of one or more of the children (Atkinson, 1984). Judges (Pearson & Ring, 1982–1983) and experienced child custody evaluators (Keilin & Bloom, 1986) generally oppose splitting sibships, but there is virtually no empirical evidence to support the opposition. In a small sample of chronically contesting families, however, Hauser (1985) did find that the few (six) children who were parties to split custody arrangements tended to be the more poorly adjusted.

Prior to the twentieth century, fathers had legal entitlement to the custody of their children. In the 1900s, account began to be taken of the best interests of the child. Until the latter part of the twentieth century, those interests were defined by the tender years doctrine, which holds that the best interests of young children are served by being in the custody and care of their mother. Because the maternal presumption inherent in the tender years doctrine violates the due process and equal protection clauses of the Constitution, it has been replaced by a generic "best interest of the child" standard (Atkinson, 1984).

Definition of the Legal Standard

Simply stated, the court is to make the decision concerning custody at the time of a divorce based on what is deemed to be in the best interests of the child. By either state statute or case law, the standard has been adopted by all 50 states (Atkinson, 1984; Grisso, 1986; Melton et al., 1997; Shuman, 1986). No criteria for defining the best interests of the child are specified in most states (Wyer et al., 1987), but some states have adopted the model contained in the Uniform Marriage and Divorce Act, or UMDA (Atkinson, 1984; Melton et al., 1997; Rohman, Sales, & Lou, 1987). The UMDA model states that the court shall take into account "all relevant factors" in making a custody determination. Among the factors to be considered are (1) the preferences of the parents and child regarding the custodial arrangement; (2) the nature of the child's relationships with each of his or her parents, siblings, and other important persons in the child's life; (3) the child's adaptation to the home, school, and community environments; and (4) the physical and mental well-being of all of the parties. The UMDA enjoins the court to disregard parental behavior that does not impinge on the relationship with the child (see Melton et al., 1997, p. 488, for the pertinent portion of the UMDA).

The best interests standard may be variously defined by legal presumptions created by some states' statutes and case law. Legal presumptions are believed to be an inadequate foundation for custody decisions (Black & Cantor, 1989), are generally not supported by social science data (Browne & Giampetro, 1985; Felner & Terre, 1987; Wallerstein, 1986; Warshak, 1986), and probably violate due process (Atkinson, 1984). Depending on the jurisdiction, presumptive status may be accorded to biological over nonbiological parent-child relationships (Musetto, 1981), maternal custody (Atkinson, 1984; Davis & Dudley, 1985; Musetto, 1981; Wyer et al., 1987), joint custody (Atkinson, 1984; Melton et al., 1997; Wallerstein, 1986), the parent who has been the primary caregiver (Atkinson, 1984; Black & Cantor, 1989; Davis & Dudley, 1985; Melton et al., 1997; Musetto, 1981), the child's preference (Black & Cantor, 1989), or to the parent with whom the child has been residing since the parents' separation (Black & Cantor, 1989). It has been noted that psychological theories may be used as informal presumptions (Elster, 1987).

Application of the Legal Standard
Divorce custody cases have been described as "agonizing" for all parties involved (Elster, 1987). In the majority of cases, the disparities between the parents are small. The decision as to which of two seemingly competent (Davis & Dudley, 1985; Simons & Meyer, 1986) or equally incompetent (Weiner, Simons, & Cavanaugh, 1985) parents will have custody is considered the most difficult for judges to make. Although judges dislike child custody cases (Settle & Lowery, 1982), they apparently value the best interests standard because it is simple and flexible (Shuman, 1986) and therefore allows them to make individualized decisions in these complex cases (Pearson & Ring, 1982–1983). Interestingly, however, a survey of judges revealed that only half of them considered the best interests of the child one of the five most important factors they used in determining custody (Felner et al., 1985).

Rather than describing it as flexible, most commentators have referred to the standard as "abstract and imprecise" (Musetto, 1981), "largely undefined" (Rohman et al., 1987), "indeterminate" (Browne & Giampetro, 1985; Davis & Dudley, 1985; Elster, 1987; Melton et al., 1997; Wyer et al., 1987), "speculative" (Hauser, 1985), "nebulous" (Jones, 1984), and not allowing for generalizations about its content or meaning (Shuman, 1986). The indeterminacy of the standard gives judges enormous discretion in custody cases (Browne & Giampetro, 1985; Wyer et al., 1987). There is a lack of uniformity in their decisions because judges often base them on personal biases, values, or whims (Rohman et al., 1987; Scott & Emery, 1987; Wyer et al., 1987) rather than on the law or expert opinions (Atkinson, 1984). Judges themselves stated in a survey that they usually make decisions ultimately on their "gut reactions" (Settle & Lowery, 1982). The personal biases underlying their opinions may not be made known by judges, and their decisions are unlikely to be reversed if appealed (Atkinson, 1984; Jones, 1984; Wyer et al., 1987).

That judges as well as other individuals continue to have a strong bias favoring mothers over fathers (Black & Cantor, 1989; Bolocofsky, 1989; Wyer et al., 1987) is attested to in several ways. Among the older judges in one survey (Pearson & Ring, 1982–1983), the tender years presumption was found to be an important criterion for making custody decisions. Both judges and attorneys have reported suspicions about fathers' motivations for seeking custody (Felner & Terre, 1987; Pearson & Ring, 1982–1983) and are likely to dissuade them from doing so despite the probable violation of fathers' due process and equal protection rights (Rohman et al., 1987). Most compelling of all are the reports in the literature that mothers are still overwhelmingly chosen to be the sole custodial parent in both uncontested and contested custody cases (Lowery, 1986; Santilli & Roberts, 1990).

Contributions by Mental Health Professionals
Judges obviously have extraordinary power to personally determine the restructuring of relationships and the future well-being of children and their parents. Whether they have the mental health training or expertise to make informed decisions that are in the child's interests is questionable (Bolocofsky, 1989; Wallerstein, 1986). According to Blau (1998), judges' knowledge of child development, marital relationships, and parenting is quite variable. An important contribution that mental health professionals can make is the elucidation of

pertinent clinical and research knowledge and theory for the trier of fact (Blau, 1998; Browne & Giampetro, 1985; Grisso, 1986; Melton et al., 1997; Rohman et al., 1987; Warshak, 1986; Weithorn & Grisso, 1987), as well as what is *not* known in the behavioral sciences (Melton et al., 1997).

Although the legal system may have the capacity to promote satisfactory and amicable resolutions of child custody disputes (Hauser, 1985), the bulk of scholarly opinion is that the adversarial context is unsuitable for arriving at custody determinations (Elster, 1987; Gardner, 1989; Musetto, 1981; Scott & Emery, 1987). A particularly compelling criticism is that although the legal standard for deciding the outcome is the child's best interests, the child is not a disputant in the litigation; however, the parents as the litigants are represented by legal counsel ethically obliged to promote their client's interests (Scott & Emery, 1987). Furthermore, the adversarial system fosters polarization of the parties and thus may create or exacerbate hostility (Scott & Emery, 1987) or psychological dysfunction in the parents (Gardner, 1989). The more heated the conflict, the more parental interests are likely to dominate the interests of the child (Musetto, 1981). Not only may the parents and their attorneys lose sight of the child's interests, but the judge also may be too concerned about parents' interests at the expense of the interests of the child (Elster, 1987). It has been said, therefore, that it is in the best interests of children that custody not be litigated (Musetto, 1981). Mental health professionals can help promote the true interests of children in being protected from parental warfare and deterioration by mediating child custody disputes as an alternative to litigation (Gardner, 1989; Ochroch, 1982; Scott & Emery, 1987).

In the present context of the adversarial system, several reforms designed to protect the child's interests have been suggested. These reforms include the appointment of an attorney or guardian ad litem to represent the child; more importance attached to the child's preference for custodial arrangements; and the court's appointment of a mental health professional as an impartial expert (Melton et al., 1997; Scott & Emery, 1987).

Both the need for the child to have legal representation and the rarity of that occurrence have been noted (Melton et al., 1997; Rohman et al., 1987; Scott & Emery, 1987). A majority of family law attorneys and judges in one survey reported being opposed to

legal representation for children in custody cases and only rarely or occasionally requesting it (Felner et al., 1985). Mental health professionals, as advocates for children's welfare, could promote the need for this reform.

The issue concerning the child's preference is complex. As noted previously, the child's preference for custody is included as a relevant factor in the UMDA model. Consideration of the child's preference is allowed or mandated in each state by statute or case law (Atkinson, 1984; Jones, 1984; Scott & Emery, 1987), but the child is not legally obligated to state a preference (Scott & Emery, 1987). The manner in which the preference is elicited (Jones, 1984; Scott & Emery, 1987) and how much weight to accord it (Wyer et al., 1987) may be legally indeterminate and therefore a matter of judicial discretion. Whether or not to elicit a preference and how much weight to give one that is stated are generally based on such factors as the child's age, intelligence, and maturity (Atkinson, 1984; Felner et al., 1985; Scott & Emery, 1987), and it has been noted that there tends to be congruence between social science data and children's ages (i.e., beginning in early adolescence) at which judges appear to give more weight to preferences (Rohman et al., 1987). Judges consider the child's preference to be of relatively little importance, however, compared to other criteria in making custody determinations (Felner et al., 1985; Lowery, 1981). In addition to problems they report in knowing how to properly elicit and weigh a preference, judges are concerned that asking for a statement of preference may have negative effects on the child (Felner et al., 1985). In fact, there appears to be widespread concern of this nature among professionals, including mental health practitioners, although there are no empirical data to support it (Melton et al., 1997; Scott & Emery, 1987).

Gardner (1989) has expressed opposition to eliciting a child's preference because the preference may be specious, transitory, or colored by the child's feelings in reaction to the context of the divorce. Elster (1987) has also noted that the preference may be transitory and that a child may not have the knowledge necessary to place differential values on the possible outcomes. Based on developmental cognitive research, however, Weithorn (1984) concluded that between the ages of 12 and 14, children are likely to be competent to state a custodial preference. The child's level of cognitive development is the critical variable, and some younger children may be able to contribute meaningful preferential input. Competency to state a preference is defined psychologically by the child's cognitive ability to understand the alternatives and the possible consequences of his or her choice (Weithorn, 1984). The legal definition, if competency is not statutorily determined by age, appears to be the opinion of the judge that the preference is reasonable or based on rational thinking processes (Garrison, 1991). In an empirical test that combines the elements of the cognitive and legal standards of competency, Garrison confirmed that 14-year-olds were as competent as adults (18-year-old subjects) to state a custodial preference based on hypothetical divorce custody situations. Garrison also found that the 9- and 10-year-old children could meet at least one criterion of competency, according to the ratings of domestic relations judges.

Commentators have supported the importance of the child's preference in custody determinations as a means of fostering the child's adaptation to the trauma of family disruption by having some actual control over his or her situation (Black & Cantor, 1989), at least for minors who are willing and competent to state a preference (Garrison, 1991). In an initial presentation of the findings of a 25-year follow-up of children of divorce in their youngest cohort, Wallerstein and Lewis (1998) confirmed the importance of preferences of children whose parents divorce. A frequent complaint concerning the impact of divorce on them by the young adults interviewed was the lack of regard for their wishes in the subsequent years. Despite the developmental changes in their needs, these children were forced to adhere to plans others had made for them (Wallerstein & Lewis, 1998).

Mental health professionals can be helpful in a variety of ways where the role of the child's preference is concerned. They can educate legal professionals about the potential benefits to the child of stating a preference. They can provide the judge with information about the child's developmental cognitive functioning to enable the trier of fact to determine how much weight to accord the child's preference. Skillful ways of eliciting a preference from the child can be taught to judges. Mental health professionals themselves may ascertain the child's preference (Black & Cantor, 1989). If they do so, the court should be informed as to how an opinion regarding the preference was reached (Davis & Dudley, 1985).

The best interests standard allows for but does not mandate expert testimony by mental health professionals in custody cases (Shuman, 1986), and only a small percentage of contested cases include such testimony (Melton et al., 1997). In contrast to the apparent belief among professionals that custody litigation is the type of case in which they can be the most helpful (Melton et al., 1997), judges do not appear to give much weight to the testimony of mental health experts in divorce custody cases (Grisso, 1986; Pearson & Ring, 1982–1983; Settle & Lowery, 1982). It is perhaps for this reason that judges infrequently appoint even experienced custody evaluators to serve as the court's expert (Keilin & Bloom, 1986).

It is recommended that mental health professionals actively seek appointment by the court in child custody cases. Adversarial pressures in these cases are great, and serving as the court-appointed expert may be the best way for mental health professionals to protect their impartial status rather than being drawn into the improper role of advocate for a parent (Blau, 1998; Scott & Emery, 1987; Simons & Meyer, 1986; Weiner et al., 1985; Weithorn, 1987b). Impartiality enhances the likelihood that the parents will perceive the overall proceedings as fair (Black & Cantor, 1989; Keilin & Bloom, 1986) and that the judge will give more weight to the testimony (Bolocofsky, 1989). Of great import in serving as the court-appointed expert is that the mental health professional does not become enmeshed in the adversarial polarization of the dissolving family and function as another catalyst for the potentially destructive effects of the system on the child and his or her parents. Finally, court appointment confers upon the mental health practitioner immunity from civil suits (but not from disciplinary actions by professional regulatory boards) arising out of the performance of his or her role as expert witness.

Procedural Issues

Scope of the Evaluation

The fundamental legal question in divorce custody cases is which custodial arrangement will serve the best interests of the child. The failure of social science data to demonstrate differential outcomes for children as a primary function of particular custody dispositions (Beaber, 1982; Black & Cantor, 1989; Felner & Terre, 1987: Grisso, 1986, 1990; Lowery, 1986;

Melton et al., 1997; Schutz, Dixon, Lindenberger, & Ruther, 1989; Warshak, 1986) mitigates against the design of evaluations to answer that question. The clinical methodologies and knowledge base of the behavioral sciences, however, lend themselves well to the investigation and assessment of the specific factors defined by statutes and case law as relevant considerations in the legal determination of a child's best interests on an individualized basis (Grisso, 1986; Lowery, 1981; Rohman et al., 1987; Schutz et al., 1989; Weithorn & Grisso, 1987). These factors include (1) child variables (e.g., age, sex, physical and psychological status, psychological needs, and the child's preference); (2) parent variables (e.g., physical and psychological functioning, historical and present ability to meet the child's medical, educational, emotional, and other needs); (3) environmental variables (e.g., the degree to which each prospective environment offers continuity and stability to the child); and (4) interactive variables (e.g., the quality of the child's relationship to each parent and other significant persons in these environments) (Weithorn & Grisso, 1987).

Grisso's (1986) model, in which parenting competency is defined as the core issue in child custody cases, provides an excellent framework for defining the scope of an evaluation that incorporates the legal variables of interest. An evaluation conducted according to Grisso's model would include a thorough assessment of the adult parties' functional abilities as parents and of the developmental history, status, and needs of the child and, most important of all, an assessment of the congruence or goodness of fit between each parent's abilities and the particular needs of the child as the three principal elements (Weithorn & Grisso, 1987).

Included in the assessment of the parents is the need to address the possible reasons for any functional deficits observed and the potential for remediation. A particularly important issue in this regard is the possibility that the functional deficit is the temporary product of stress induced by the divorce context, for it is known that marked deterioration in parenting ability is a frequent by-product of marital dissolution (Wallerstein & Kelly, 1980). A related area of inquiry is the consideration or actual assessment of ancillary caretakers who reside in the household (relatives or nonrelatives) and who may compensate for the parent's deficiencies. In addition, the quality of the relationships between those parties and the child is important information in its own right.

A complete assessment of the child necessitates knowledge of the child's functioning in contexts outside of the home (e.g., in school), the quality of the child's relationships with others (e.g., teachers, peers), and information that others (e.g., teachers, physicians) have about the child's developmental status, in addition to those data about the child that are obtained through direct evaluation. Clinical findings on the child are also likely to be affected by the family's disruption (Rohman et al., 1987), a situational stress that should be taken into account in interpreting the findings (Melton et al., 1997).

Finally, the assessment should include an inquiry into the total environment that each parent offers the child. Important considerations are not only the qualitative aspects of the environment (e.g., opportunities for enrichment, access to a good education and medical care), but also the degree of continuity and stability that each environment can provide for the child.

Schutz and his colleagues (1989) provide a helpful summary of variables to be considered in divorce custody evaluations that is consistent with the model advanced by Grisso (1986). Based on a brief, representative review of the literature, the authors conclude that there is sufficient knowledge available to articulate the most important components of good parenting. Some of those components are the quality of the parent's attachment to the child, a realistic perception of the child, recognition of the child as a separate individual, and consistency in expectations and limit-setting. In addition, Schutz and his colleagues describe child variables of interest and the variables that address the congruence between the parents' functional abilities and the specific needs of the child. Finally, the authors emphasize the need to address other variables that bear on the quality of the parent-child relationship. In the latter category, Schutz and his colleagues include (1) the ability of the parents to cooperate with each other and their willingness to foster a relationship between the child and the other parent, factors known from the research of Wallerstein and Kelly (1980) to be especially important to children's postdivorce adjustment; (2) the child's preference as a reflection of the congruence of the relationship with each parent; (3) the identification of the parent who historically has been the primary caregiver, an especially important variable if the child is very young (Rohman et al., 1987); and (4) a history of abuse or neglect.

The reader is cautioned that the above information represents merely the skeleton of variables that may be addressed in divorce custody evaluations, and that the scope of the evaluation is determined by the specific psycholegal question(s) raised in the individual case. The suggestions, however, are intended to be compatible with the recommendations advanced by Weithorn and Grisso (1987) as part of the effort of the Committee on Child Custody of Division 37 of the American Psychological Association, with the collaboration of Division 41 (Weithorn, 1987c), and with the forensic assessment model and the "evolving guidelines" in custody cases flowing from it advanced by Grisso (1986, 1990).

The efforts referred to above can be readily identified as substantial components of the foundation for the *Guidelines for Child Custody Evaluations in Divorce Proceedings,* developed by the Committee on Professional Practice and Standards of the American Psychological Association (APA, 1994). Though aspirational in nature, they provide the kind of guidance that defines "reasonably prudent practice" (Shapiro, 1984) in this particularly thorny area of forensic specialization. Although noting that the scope of the assessment is to be determined by the practitioner as a function of the nature of the referral or of case-specific issues, the Custody Guidelines advise evaluators to maintain a focus on the interests of the child and to follow the tripartite model that considers the parenting capacities of the potential custodians, the developmental functioning and needs of the child, and the goodness of fit between the former and the latter. The Custody Guidelines include consideration of the child's preference if appropriate and accord secondary importance to adult psychopathology.

The interested reader may also want to refer to the *Association of Family and Conciliation Courts Model Standards of Practice for Child Custody Evaluation,* which were developed by the multidisciplinary Association of Family and Conciliation Courts (AFCC, 1994) to provide standards of practice for its members who conduct child custody evaluations. The AFCC Standards (AFCC, 1994) are similar in intent, guiding principles, and comprehensiveness to the Custody Guidelines (APA, 1994).

Methodology
Prior to the appearance of the aspirational Custody Guidelines (APA, 1994) for conducting divorce custody evaluations, there was agreement on the need

for multiple assessment methods and samples of behavior to produce convergent validity (Black & Cantor, 1989; Schutz et al., 1989; Weithorn & Grisso, 1987). In this regard, Weithorn and Grisso suggested that all opinions and inferences be supported by at least two sources of data. Multiple procedures and samples are also necessitated by the breadth of the court's inquiry (Grisso, 1986; Melton et al., 1997; Weithorn & Grisso, 1987). The methods typically used are interviews, observations, psychological tests, and the gathering of information from collateral sources (Weithorn & Grisso, 1987). The recommendations for a multimethod, multisource inquiry, convergent validity, and sufficient support for opinions and conclusions are incorporated into the Custody Guidelines.

Individual clinical interviews with each parent and the child have been reported by experienced child custody evaluators to be the foundation of their assessments (Keilin & Bloom, 1986). A recent replication and expansion of Keilin and Bloom's 1986 survey by Ackerman and Ackerman (1997) revealed no change in the reliance on interviews by experienced evaluators. Most commentators recommend a series of interviews that includes not only multiple sessions with each individual, but also sessions with the parents together, the child or children with each parent, and perhaps the entire family (Black & Cantor, 1989; Davis & Dudley, 1985; Gardner, 1989; Grisso, 1986; Schutz et al., 1989; Shapiro, 1984; Simons & Meyer, 1986; Weiner et al., 1985).

Actual parenting behaviors in relationship to the child are most powerfully assessed by the direct observation of their interactions in conjoint sessions (Beaber, 1982). If the child is too young to participate in a conjoint interview, then an observation of the parent and child in a free play situation may be substituted (Shapiro, 1984). Structured observation sessions of parent-child interactions may be scheduled in addition to or in lieu of conjoint interviews in cases involving older as well as younger children (Schutz et al., 1989).

The practice of directly observing and evaluating parent-child interactions is strongly endorsed in the Custody Guidelines (APA, 1994). The practices of experienced evaluators are apparently consistent with that endorsement; the survey by Ackerman and Ackerman (1997) revealed that the vast majority of evaluators (91%) employ conjoint sessions for observing interactions between each parent and the child or children.

Specific inquiry into evaluators' use of conjoint interviews with the contesting parents is not reported by Ackerman and Ackerman (1997). Such interviews might enable the evaluator to assess the quality of the relationship between the parents as well as each parent's support of the other's relationship with the child, variables noted earlier to be influential in the child's ongoing adjustment (Lanyon, 1986; Schutz et al., 1989).

The majority of experienced custody evaluators endorse the use of and routinely administer psychological tests and instruments to both parents and children (Ackerman & Ackerman, 1997; Keilin & Bloom, 1986). The instruments most commonly used, according to the earlier survey (Keilin & Bloom, 1986), are those that constitute the typical batteries administered in general clinical practice, for example, the Minnesota Multiphasic Personality Inventory (MMPI), Rorschach, Thematic or Children's Apperception Test, one of the Wechsler scales, and projective drawings. Several changes have occurred over the past decade, some of which give cause for concern (Ackerman & Ackerman, 1997). The MMPI, reported to be the most frequently used instrument in custody evaluations in 1986 despite the lack of any demonstrable validity as a measure of parenting, is now being used even more frequently. Absent any supportable reason in custody cases for routinely using a test whose normative data are derived from a clinical population, there is currently fairly widespread and frequent use of the Millon Clinical Multiaxial Inventories (Ackerman & Ackerman, 1997). Finally, Ackerman and Ackerman report an increased use of projective drawings.

Melton and his colleagues (1997) severely criticize the routine use of psychological tests in custody evaluations and join Brodzinsky (1993) in recommending their limited, selective employment only when needed to address an issue they were developed to address. Such usage is consistent with Grisso's (1986) support of these tests in understanding any functional deficits the parents might possess. Grisso and Blau (1984), however, endorse the somewhat more liberal position that well-established, traditional psychological tests are also appropriate and valuable in divorce custody evaluations to assess the developmental status and needs of the child. The use of such instruments to assess parenting per se is a highly questionable practice at best, however (Bolocofsky,

1989; Grisso, 1986; Lanyon, 1986). In lieu of that practice, Grisso promotes the need for legally relevant assessment devices that specifically address parenting ability and those that have "parallel dimensions," that is, instruments that assess similar variables in the parent and the child (e.g., the parent's capacity to set and enforce limits and the child's need for structure and firm guidance).

In his 1986 publication, Grisso thoroughly reviewed assessment devices (i.e., questionnaires) available at the time that were designed to address parenting ability. He cautioned that the instruments were not specifically developed for use in custody cases. Even more important is the caveat that these devices address knowledge, self-reported behavior, and/or attitudes that may not correspond accurately to actual parenting practices (Bolocofsky, 1989; Grisso, 1986; Lanyon, 1986).

Since the time of Grisso's important work (1986) and the survey of Keilin and Bloom (1986), there has been a response to the call for forensic assessment instruments specifically designed to answer the psycholegal questions raised in custody cases. Notable among them are the family of instruments developed by Bricklin (1995), the initial one of which was published in 1984 (Bricklin, 1984), the Custody Quotient (Gordon & Peek, 1989), and the Ackerman–Schoendorf Scales for Parent Evaluation of Custody, or ASPECT (Ackerman & Schoendorf, 1992). Surveys of psychologist custody evaluators with experience (Ackerman & Ackerman, 1997) and those who are diplomates of the American Board of Forensic Psychology (Heinze & Grisso, 1996) indicated that these instruments are being employed. In addition, some of those professionals have incorporated parenting instruments not specifically designed for psycholegal cases into their custody evaluations (Ackerman & Ackerman, 1997; Heinze & Grisso, 1996). Heinze and Grisso critically reviewed three of the latter instruments: the Child Abuse Potential Inventory (CAP; Milner, 1986), the Parent-Child Relationship Inventory (PCRI; Gerard, 1994), and the Parenting Stress Index (PSI; Abidin, 1990). Circumspect use of these instruments is endorsed in custody cases to assess the specific variables for which they were designed (Heinze & Grisso, 1996).

Instruments designed to assess parenting in custody cases are reviewed by Heinze and Grisso (1996) and by Melton and his colleagues (1997). The critiques by these distinguished authorities are decidedly negative regarding their use. Formal scoring of the results and reporting of the values so derived are discouraged due to the absence of demonstrable reliability and validity (Melton et al., 1997) and because of the danger of misleading the court by the appearance of a *scientific* determination of the parents' abilities and meaningful differences between them (Heinze & Grisso, 1996). Despite the negative appraisal, a possible circumscribed utilization of some of the instruments is cautiously accepted to "facilitate gathering useful responses regarding parents' attitudes, knowledge, or values with respect to raising their children" (Melton et al., 1997, p. 504).

One instrument that appears to warrant its use for the above purpose (i.e., investigative or focused data gathering) is the Custody Quotient (Gordon & Peek, 1989), an instrument that was endorsed earlier (Call, 1989). The Custody Quotient was specifically designed to address those aspects of parenting that are deemed important in child custody evaluations because they are consistent with the UMDA, statutes and case law, the opinions of family law judges and attorneys and of mental health practitioners, and with social science data. Another advantage of the Custody Quotient is that it takes into account the multiple sources of data that are incorporated into comprehensive custody evaluations. Also, various forms of validity for the instrument have been demonstrated. Finally, the Custody Quotient yields information on the feasibility of joint custody and the willingness of parents to admit to common shortcomings ("frankness") as opposed to attempting to create a positive impression.

The major disadvantage of the Custody Quotient is that the authors have not collected normative data as originally intended; at the present time, the overall results for each of the parents (their Custody Quotient or CQ) are compared to a theoretical normal curve of parenting ability. Absent normative data and stronger evidence for its validity and reliability, the presentation of numerical results would create an impression of psychometric soundness and scientific accuracy that is probably not justified. Furthermore, the use of the Custody Quotient as a psychometric instrument, rather than as a structured interview, might render it inadmissible under *Daubert*.

Another instrument designed specifically to be consistent with the legal definition of the best interests standard and to be used in child custody evaluations is the Bricklin Perceptual Scales: Child Perception of Parent Series (Bricklin, 1990). Through the use of verbal and nonverbal responses, the Bricklin intends to assess the child's overt (and perhaps coached) and less conscious (and therefore theoretically more genuine) preference for custodial parent by asking the child to indicate how well he or she perceives each parent as functioning on 32 items.

In 1986, Lanyon opined that the Bricklin was a promising instrument that needed more psychometric refinement, and others (Call, 1989; Schutz et al., 1989) subsequently recommended its use in custody evaluations. A more recent, thorough review of the psychometric data (Heinze & Grisso, 1996), however, suggests caution at the very least in the interpretation and presentation of the results. Numerically based comparisons between the parents do not appear warranted.

A more clinical, descriptive approach to the Bricklin is perhaps to use it as a source of hypotheses regarding the child's view of his or her parents and custodial preference. Another possible use of the instrument, if the clinical/descriptive approach is taken, is the comparison of the areas addressed by the Bricklin (the child's perception of each parent's supportiveness, competency, consistency, and possession of admirable characteristics) with specific domains of parental functioning defined by the Custody Quotient (e.g., emotional needs, good parenting, values). This type of comparison may shed light on the congruence between some aspects of parenting and the child's report of how well the parents are performing in those areas.

As noted previously, there is no standard protocol for child custody assessments, nor is any recommended in the Custody Guidelines (APA, 1994). The main considerations in the selection and use of instruments are that they are relevant to the psycholegal question, that the user is familiar with the standards for administration and with their psychometric properties, and that disclosure is made concerning their limitations (Blau, 1984, 1998; Grisso, 1986; Lanyon, 1986; Melton et al., 1997; Weithorn & Grisso, 1987).

Another type of data considered important in divorce custody evaluations is information obtained from collateral sources (APA, 1994). Such information may include the verbal reports of individuals who know family members (e.g., teachers, physicians, mental health professionals) and pertinent documents (e.g., medical records, school report cards, reports of prior psychological evaluations and/or treatment) (Black & Cantor, 1989; Gardner, 1989; Grisso, 1986; Melton et al., 1997; Schutz et al., 1989; Simons & Meyer, 1986; Weiner et al., 1985; Weithorn & Grisso, 1987). These data are useful in the comprehensive evaluation of the functioning of parents and children. In addition, and perhaps most important, they provide potentially corroborative information that can be used as a check against the distortions likely in self-reports and on psychological tests in custody cases (Beaber, 1982; Bricklin, 1990; Gardner, 1989; Gordon & Peek, 1989; Grisso, 1986; Lanyon, 1986; Simons & Meyer, 1986). Although most evaluators are said to fail to take into account the possibility that the child is dissimulating (Beaber, 1982), Gardner reports from his clinical experience that children are frequently influenced by their parents or by their own needs to distort their relationships with their parents.

Communication of Findings

Procedural issues considered earlier concerning forensic report writing and oral testimony are applicable to divorce custody cases. Some of those issues deserve elaboration here because they are particularly problematic or especially meaningful in the context of custody evaluations.

It is apparently common practice for child custody evaluators to make dispositional recommendations to the court, that is, to offer an opinion or conclusion as to which custodial arrangement will be in the child's best interests (Bolocofsky, 1989; Karras & Berry, 1985; Keilin & Bloom, 1986). In the recent survey by Ackerman and Ackerman (1997), 65% of participating psychologists endorsed ultimate issue testimony (a surprising 6% indicated not knowing what "ultimate issue" means). According to Melton and his colleagues (1997, p. 484), "There is probably no forensic question on which overreaching by mental health professionals has been so common and so egregious." Although some judges believe that mental health professionals might better make these difficult decisions (Settle & Lowery, 1982), other judges are critical of mental health experts who offer evaluative opinions rather than factual findings, and those judges report that they disregard the recommendations made (Pearson & Ring, 1982–1983). Regardless of the practices of professionals and the opinions of judges, the weight of supportable scholarly opinion is that mental health

practitioners should not make recommendations concerning custodial arrangements (Beaber, 1982; Black & Cantor, 1989; Blau, 1998; Bolocofsky, 1989; Faust & Ziskin, 1988a; Grisso, 1986; Weithorn, 1987b; Weithorn & Grisso, 1987).

Grisso (1986) would also preclude global comparative statements that one parent is better overall than the other because the law does not specify degrees of congruency in parent-child relationships that would lend themselves to such comparisons and because such comparisons are based on value judgments rather than empiricism. For example, there are no empirical data that would allow for the conclusion that one parent is better than the other in a family in which the mother more openly expresses affection but is less consistent in enforcing rules in comparison to the father. Schutz and his colleagues (1989) would allow comparative statements if either of the following stringent criteria is met: (1) each parent has "reportable" findings on all variables relating to parenting characteristics and all of the findings favor one parent; (2) one parent presents a clear danger to the child (e.g., there is substantiation of recent or ongoing abuse).

How far the expert should go in reporting findings, inferences, and opinions remains controversial (APA, 1994). There is, however, no dispute over the need minimally to report (1) the nature and scope of the referral question; (2) the facts and observations gathered; (3) the methodologies and sources relied on; (4) inferences and opinions formulated and the underlying data supporting them; (5) relevant social science data; (6) discrepancies and limitations pertinent to procedures and findings; and (7) recommendations for treatment interventions. To briefly review the scope of clinical findings in an individual case, it might include facts and observations concerning, at a minimum, each prospective custodian's past and current parenting behavior, attitudes, and knowledge; the overall adjustment of each parent, particularly as it pertains to any functional deficits in parenting and their potential for remediation; the child's past and present developmental functioning and needs and adjustment to various environmental contexts; the congruence between each prospective custodian's parenting capacities and the specific needs of the child; the nature of the relationships between the child and each parent, the child and significant others, and between the parents themselves; the nature of the environment provided by each parent; and the child's preference in appropriate cases. Further specification might include each parent's support of the relationship between the child and the other parent; which parent has been the primary caregiver of a very young child; the proximity of the prospective custodial homes; a parental history of alcoholism and convictions of driving while intoxicated; parental consistency in limit-setting; and the child's need for special educational interventions.

The reader is again referred to such sources as Black and Cantor (1989), Grisso (1986), Melton et al. (1997), Rohman et al. (1987), and Schutz et al. (1989) for descriptions of specific variables to be addressed in custody cases that are legally relevant and have an empirical foundation. Melton and his colleagues and Schutz and his colleagues are excellent resources for specific procedural guidelines and for principles of report writing and testifying in child custody cases. Finally, there is a promising new model constructed according to family systems theory that provides an organizational approach to child custody evaluations (Jameson, Ehrenberg, & Hunter, 1997). In the model, individual items rated by experienced psychologists according to their importance in custody assessments are grouped into the domains of relational assessment, needs-of-the-child assessment, and abilities-of-the-parents assessment, which are subsumed under the defining criterion of the best interests of the child. The items were preselected from legal definitions of the best interests of the child standard, as well as from a review of the empirical literature on the effects of divorce and custody arrangements on children (Jameson et al., 1997).

ETHICAL ISSUES

Psychologists who conduct evaluations and offer expert testimony in divorce custody cases are quite vulnerable to committing ethical violations and to having a complaint filed against them (APA Ethics Committee, 1990; Hall & Hare-Mustin, 1983; Weithorn, 1987b). According to Weithorn (p. 183), divorce custody cases might be characterized "as a potential minefield for psychologists from the standpoint of ethics." A thoughtful analysis of the relationship between custody litigation and clinical practice led Weithorn to the following summary of factors that may account for the relatively high level of vulnerability to unethical

professional behavior: (1) the indeterminacy of the legal standard and adversarial pressures; (2) the difficult nature and complexity of custody cases; (3) the magnitude of the consequences to the parties of the decision that is made; (4) the lack of clarity concerning the nature of relationships and invitations or pressures to become involved in dual relationships; (5) the complexities surrounding confidentiality issues; and (6) the lack of formalized standards of practice in divorce custody cases. Some salient examples of unethical practices in divorce custody cases are making inferences or drawing conclusions about a parent who was not directly evaluated, which would include making comparative statements about parents or a recommendation for custodial placement when only one parent was seen (APA Ethics Committee, 1987); performance of a custody evaluation of a child while on visitation with the noncustodial parent without the knowledge or consent of the custodial parent (APA, 1988); reaching conclusions that go beyond the limitations of the clinical data (APA, 1988); reaching conclusions that are matters of law (Ochroch, 1982; Weithorn, 1987b); serving as mediator for a family or psychotherapist for one of the parties and subsequently conducting a custody evaluation (Weithorn, 1987b); and failure to obtain a written statement of the referral request that would clarify the nature and scope of the issues to be addressed in the evaluation (APA, 1988).

The above examples are merely representative and do not exhaust the potential for ethical violations in child custody cases. With the exception of the principles governing human and animal research, all sections of the *Ethical Principles of Psychologists and Code of Conduct* (APA, 1992) are pertinent to forensic cases in general (Blau, 1998) and to divorce custody cases (Ochroch, 1982) as a particular example of forensic evaluations and expert witness testimony. The potential for ethical violations is apparently unlimited in custody cases. The following suggestions, based principally on Weithorn's (1987b) detailed consideration of the interaction of legal, clinical, and ethical variables, should not be assumed to include all means of avoiding unethical practices. These suggestions also find a basis in the Custody Guidelines (APA, 1994).

Prior to undertaking a divorce custody evaluation, the clinician should ascertain whether he or she has the competence necessary to do so. The functional criteria for determining expertise on an individual case basis as suggested by Melton and his colleagues (1997) and others were discussed earlier, and can certainly be applied to professional competence in custody matters. Weithorn (1987b) suggests that competence to perform divorce custody evaluations could be achieved through formal graduate training in the assessment and treatment of children and adults and postgraduate education in the forensic area. In addition, the psychologist needs to acquire knowledge of the relevant literature, observe the performance of custody evaluations by more experienced clinicians or participate in them as a secondary evaluator, and independently conduct initial evaluations under the supervision of a practitioner with experience in these cases. Bolocofsky (1989) reports findings related to competence of an Interdisciplinary Committee on Child Custody, composed of experienced family law judges and attorneys and mental health professionals involved in child custody cases. That group recommends that custody evaluators be knowledgeable about (1) the development of children; (2) the dynamics of functional and dysfunctional families; (3) psychopathology in children; (4) psychopathology in adults and its potential effects on parenting; (5) the parameters of parenting effectiveness; (6) how changing family structures affect family members; (7) appropriate assessment techniques; (8) relevant legal and ethical standards and the proper role of the mental health expert; and (9) the range of custody and visitation alternatives.

If the psychologist confirms that he or she has the competence to undertake a custody evaluation, the next ethical duty involves clarification with the referral source of the nature and scope of the referral question, the role to be assumed by the evaluator and the nature of the relationships to the parties, the procedures to be used and the potential outcomes (including whatever limitations are involved), the estimated cost of the evaluation and policies regarding payment, and expectations regarding the presentation of the findings. Schutz and his colleagues (1989) provide examples of letters of agreement that may be helpful in establishing documentation of these issues.

As noted previously, the preferred role for the mental health expert is to be appointed by the court and thereby be provided with access to all relevant parties and formalize one's status as impartial. The second best alternative is to have the

referral originate by agreement of the parties. A less preferable means of entering a case is to be hired by one attorney and have access to the other parent through court order or other forms of coercion. The least desirable situation is to be retained by one party and have no opportunity to evaluate the other parent. Although performing an evaluation in the last circumstance is not unethical, making evaluative statements about a parent who was not seen or offering comparisons between the parents or recommendations for custody are not desirable (APA, 1994) or ethically acceptable practices (APA Ethics Committee, 1987). If the psychologist has a prior relationship with any of the parties that creates or gives the appearance of a conflict of interest or compromised objectivity, he or she is ethically bound to decline to conduct an evaluation. The ethical duties to be impartial and objective and to protect consumers and the public image of psychology are abundantly clear.

To fulfill the ethical obligations concerning informed consent, the psychologist must clarify with the parents the same issues that were addressed with the referral source. Such clarification should be done in even more detail to ensure that the consent of the parties is truly informed. The psychologist's role, the procedures to be used and for what purpose, the time and money involved, who will be responsible for payment and how payment is expected to be made, what kinds of data will be reported and to whom and in what form, the limits on confidentiality, and the right of the individuals to decline to participate (which may not exist in some cases and is more illusory than real in others) must be clearly understood by the parties (and the child if he or she is mature enough to understand these issues).

Although certainly not exhaustive of all of the concrete, practical matters involved in obtaining informed consent, there are some specific items especially worthy of note. First, all parties should be informed at the outset that the needs of the child will be the main focus of the evaluation (APA, 1994; Simons & Meyer, 1986). Second, *all* procedures to be used in generating findings (and, of course, their limitations) must be disclosed to the parties. According to Karras and Berry (1985), making surreptitious observations in the waiting room or unannounced home visits constitutes both a failure to obtain informed consent and an undue invasion of privacy. Third, it is recommended that there be written documentation of the parameters of the evaluation and the signed consent of the parties to the stipulated agreements. Fourth, it is suggested that the parties be informed that payment is expected contemporaneously with or in advance of the delivery of services and, most important, before a report is rendered or testimony is offered (Keilin & Bloom, 1986; Simons & Meyer, 1986; Weiner et al., 1985). Disclosure must be made to the parties if the psychologist has a policy of declining further participation in the evaluation if payments are not made according to the established agreement, and an explanation given as to how any monies already collected will be handled (Schutz et al., 1989). Psychologists must be aware that once the evaluation is completed, it is probably impossible and at least questionable ethically to withhold the results obtained due to the parties' failure to pay. A final issue concerning financial disclosure is the ethical obligation to inform the parties that most insurance companies will not make reimbursement for custody evaluations (Karras & Berry, 1985). For the psychologist to misrepresent the services provided on an insurance claim to obtain reimbursement is patently unethical and fraudulent as well. Fifth, if the psychologist assumes the position of not offering ultimate issue testimony, the parents and the referral source must be informed that recommendations regarding custody will not be made, as most laypersons and legal professionals will probably anticipate them. Sixth, any child from whom a custodial preference has been elicited has the right to know how that information will be used. The child must be protected from any potential emotional harm contingent upon stating a preference (e.g., by believing that he or she will be solely responsible for the decision that is made).

The ethical parameters governing confidentiality are complex. It is incumbent on the psychologist to understand the statutes governing privileged communications and the ethical constraints on confidentiality in custody cases and to communicate this understanding to the parties so they have informed choices regarding disclosure of information. Collateral sources and the clients themselves must be made aware that the information disclosed by third parties will not be held in confidence. It is suggested that written consent be obtained from the parents to obtain information from other parties and to release the results of the evaluation to the intended recipients (e.g., the court, the attorneys, the other parent).

Demonstrable support for any inferences or opinions is both an ethical and a legal requirement. Not only must the psychologist have rational clinical and scientific bases for inferences and opinions, he or she must also adequately document the clinical data. Detailed, contemporaneous written notes are a minimum requirement, the quality of which is expected to be above general clinical practice standards (Committee on Ethical Guidelines for Forensic Psychologists, 1991).

Ethically, psychologists cannot release test data to individuals who are not qualified to interpret them. If one's records are subpoenaed, this ethical principle presents a thorny problem. The psychologist may need to retain an attorney to protect his or her ethical obligations regarding test data. Despite the position taken by the psychologist, the court may order that the records be turned over to the requesting party. At this juncture, the psychologist faces a dilemma between violating ethical principles and being held in contempt of court. A reasonable solution is to explain to the court the basis for resistance to turning over the raw data. The court may issue an order to protect the data or may heed the psychologist's recommendation that the data be turned over for review to a qualified professional retained by the attorney seeking the disclosure. The Committee on Psychological Tests and Assessment of APA (1996) prepared a *Statement on the Disclosure of Test Data* that is not meant to establish guidelines or professional standards in the area but to inform psychologists in their ethical decision making. Psychologists should be aware that records taken to a deposition or into the courtroom when they are testifying are subject to disclosure and admittance into evidence.

Psychologists are ethically obligated in custody cases to be knowledgeable about the relevant legal standards in their jurisdiction and to design their evaluations to adequately assess the variables of import. The procedures used must be ones for which the psychologist has adequate competence and that are valid for the specific purpose. The psychologist must be familiar with the literature that can serve to guide the selection of procedures and the interpretation of findings. Psychologists also have an ethical obligation to prevent misuse of their data.

In reporting the results of the custody evaluation, psychologists have an ethical duty to indicate the limitations of their methods, the data gathered, and the available research knowledge. They must also disclose contradictory findings and alternative explanations for them. Full disclosure is an ethical imperative as well as a component of the sworn oath the expert witness takes. There is also the ethical obligation to refrain from an unnecessary invasion of privacy.

As noted earlier, this section was not intended to cover all of the ethical parameters of divorce custody evaluations. The reader is advised to consult Weithorn (1987b), Melton et al. (1997), and the Custody Guidelines (APA, 1994) for a more detailed development of the issues presented here and to become familiar with other issues that were not addressed. The importance of ethics in custody evaluations cannot be emphasized too much, as divorce and the child custody litigation accompanying it involve important civil and legal rights, the immediate welfare of children and families, and an outcome that may affect the lives of family members in as profound a way as any other event in their history.

REFERENCES

Abidin, R.R. (1990). *Parenting Stress Index* (3rd ed.). Odessa, FL: Psychological Assessment Resources.

Ackerman, M.J., & Ackerman, M.C. (1997). Custody evaluation practices: A survey of experienced professionals (revisited). *Professional Psychology: Research and Practice, 28,* 137–145.

Ackerman, M.J., & Schoendorf, K. (1992). *Ackerman–Schoendorf Scales for Parent Evaluation of Custody (ASPECT).* Los Angeles: Western Psychological Services.

American Educational Research Association, American Psychological Association, & National Council on Measurement in Education. (1999). *Standards for educational and psychological testing.* Washington, DC: Author.

American Psychological Association. (1981). Specialty guidelines for the delivery of services by clinical psychologists. *American Psychologist, 36,* 640–651.

American Psychological Association. (1986). *Guidelines for computer-based tests and interpretations.* Washington, DC: Author.

American Psychological Association. (1987). *General guidelines for providers of psychological services.* Washington, DC: Author.

American Psychological Association. (1990). Ethical principles of psychologists (amended June 2, 1989). *American Psychologist, 45,* 390–395.

American Psychological Association. (1992). Ethical principles of psychologists and code of conduct. *American Psychologist, 47,* 1597–1611.

American Psychological Association Committee on Professional Practice and Standards. (1994). Guidelines for child custody evaluations in divorce proceedings. *American Psychologist, 49,* 677–680.

American Psychological Association Committee on Professional Standards. (1988). Casebook for providers of psychological services. *American Psychologist, 43,* 557–563.

American Psychological Association Committee on Psychological Tests and Assessment. (1996). Statement on the disclosure of test data. *American Psychologist, 51,* 644–648.

American Psychological Association Ethics Committee. (1987). *Casebook on ethical principles of psychologists.* Washington, DC: American Psychological Association.

American Psychological Association Ethics Committee. (1990). Report of the ethics committee: 1988. *American Psychologist, 45,* 873–874.

Anderten, P., Staulcup, V., & Grisso, T. (1980). On being ethical in legal places. *Professional Psychology: Research and Practice, 11,* 764–773.

Association of Family and Conciliation Courts. (1994). Association of Family and Conciliation Courts model standards of practice for child custody evaluation. *Family and Conciliation Courts Review, 32,* 504–513.

Association of State and Provincial Psychology Boards. (1991). *ASPPB code of conduct.* Montgomery, AL: Author.

Atkinson, J. (1984). Criteria for deciding child custody in the trial and appellate courts. *Family Law Quarterly, 18,* 1–42.

Bazelon, D.L. (1982). Veils, values, and social responsibility. *American Psychologist, 37,* 115–121.

Beaber, R.J. (1982). Custody quagmire: Some psycholegal dilemmas. *Journal of Psychiatry and Law, 10,* 309–326.

Bersoff, D.N. (1986). Psychologists and the judicial system: Broader perspectives. *Law and Human Behavior, 10,* 151–165.

Bisbing, S.B., & Faust, D. (1990). *Psychological expert testimony: Avoiding common errors in evaluating and testifying.* Paper presented at the 98th annual convention of the American Psychological Association, Boston.

Black, J.C., & Cantor, D.J. (1989). *Child custody.* New York: Columbia University Press.

Blau, T.H. (1984). Psychological tests in the courtroom. *Professional Psychology: Research and Practice, 15,* 176–186.

Blau, T.H. (1998). *The psychologist as expert witness* (2nd ed.). New York: Wiley.

Bolocofsky, D.N. (1989). Use and abuse of mental health experts in child custody determinations. *Behavioral Sciences and the Law, 7,* 197–213.

Borum, R. (1998). Forensic assessment instruments. In G.P. Koocher, J.C. Norcross, & S.S. Hill (Eds.), *Psychologists' desk reference* (pp. 487–491). New York: Oxford University Press.

Bricklin, B. (1984). *Bricklin Perceptual Scales: Child Perception of Parent Series.* Doylestown, PA: Village.

Bricklin, B. (1990). *Bricklin Perceptual Scales: Child Perception of Parent Series* (Rev. ed.). Doylestown, PA: Village.

Bricklin, B. (1995). *The custody evaluation handbook: Research-based solutions and applications.* New York: Brunner/Mazel.

Brodsky, S.L. (1991). *Testifying in court: Guidelines and maxims for the expert witness.* Washington, DC: American Psychological Association.

Brodsky, S.L. (1998). Forensic evaluations and testimony. In G.P. Koocher, J.C. Norcross, & S.S. Hill (Eds.), *Psychologists' desk reference* (pp. 483–485). New York: Oxford University Press.

Brodzinsky, D.M. (1993). On the use and misuse of psychological testing in child custody evaluations. *Professional Psychology: Research and Practice, 24,* 213–219.

Browne, M.N., & Giampetro, A. (1985). The contribution of social science data to the adjudication of child custody disputes? *Capital University Law Review, 15,* 43–58.

Butcher, J.N., & Pope, K.S. (1993). Seven issues in conducting forensic assessments: Ethical responsibilities in light of new standards and new tests. *Ethics and Behavior, 3*(3–4), 267–288.

Call, J.A. (1989). Evaluating parenting: The real task of child custody evaluations. *Oklahoma Bar Association Family Law Update, 4,* 1–7.

Call, J.A. (1995). Examining the psychological expert in a custody case. *American Journal of Family Law, 9,* 175–186.

Clark, C.R. (1990). Agreeing to be an expert witness: Considerations of competence and role integrity. *Register Report, 16,* 4.

Committee on Ethical Guidelines for Forensic Psychologists. (1991). Specialty guidelines for forensic psychologists. *Law and Human Behavior, 15,* 655–665.

Daubert v. Merrell Dow Pharmaceuticals, Inc., 113 S.Ct. 2786 (1993).

Davis, P.C., & Dudley, R.G. (1985). Family evaluation and the development of standards for child custody determination. *Columbia Journal of Law and Social Problems, 19,* 505–515.

Elster, J. (1987). Solomonic judgments: Against the best interest of the child. *University of Chicago Law Review, 54,* 1–45.

Elwork, A. (1984). Psycholegal assessment, diagnosis, and testimony: A new beginning. *Law and Human Behavior, 8,* 197–203.

Ewing, C.P. (1996). Introduction to psychological testing and the law. *Behavioral Sciences and the Law, 14,* 269–270.

Faust, D., & Ziskin, J. (1988a). The expert witness in psychology and psychiatry. *Science, 241,* 31–35.

Faust, D., & Ziskin, J. (1988b). Response to Fowler and Matarazzo. *Science, 241,* 1143–1144.

Felner, R.D., & Terre, L. (1987). Child custody dispositions and children's adaptation following divorce. In L.A. Weithorn (Ed.), *Psychology and child custody determinations: Knowledge, roles, and expertise* (pp. 106–153). Lincoln: University of Nebraska Press.

Felner, R.D., Terre, L., Goldfarb, A., Farber, S.S., Primavera, J., Bishop, T.A., & Aber, M.S. (1985). Party status of children during marital dissolution: Child preference and legal representation in custody decisions. *Journal of Clinical Child Psychology, 14,* 42–48.

Fowler, R.D., & Matarazzo, J.D. (1988). Psychologists and psychiatrists as expert witnesses. *Science, 241,* 1143.

Frye v. United States, 293 F. 1013 (D.C. Cir. 1923).

Gardner, R.A. (1989). *Family evaluation in child custody mediation, arbitration, and litigation.* Cresskill, NJ: Creative Therapeutics.

Garrison, E.G. (1991). Children's competence to participate in divorce custody decisionmaking. *Journal of Clinical Child Psychology, 20,* 78–87.

Gerard, A.B. (1994). *Parent-Child Relationship Inventory (PCRI): Manual.* Los Angeles: Western Psychological Services.

Goldman, A.H. (1986). Cognitive psychologists as expert witnesses: A problem in professional ethics. *Law and Human Behavior, 10,* 29–45.

Gordon, R., & Peek, L.A. (1989). *The Custody Quotient: Research manual* (Rev. ed.). Dallas, TX: Wilmington Institute.

Green, R.K., & Schaefer, A.B. (1984). *Forensic psychology: A primer for legal and mental health professionals.* Springfield, IL: Thomas.

Grisso, T. (1986). *Evaluating competencies: Forensic assessments and instruments.* New York: Plenum Press.

Grisso, T. (1987). The economic and scientific future of forensic psychological assessment. *American Psychologist, 42,* 831–839.

Grisso, T. (1990). Evolving guidelines for divorce/custody evaluations. *Family and Conciliation Courts Review, 28,* 35–41.

Grisso, T., & Melton, G.B. (1987). Getting child development research to legal practitioners: Which way to the trenches? In G.B. Melton (Ed.), *Reforming the law: Impact of child development research* (pp. 146–176). New York: Guilford Press.

Haas, L.J. (1993). Competence and quality in the performance of forensic psychologists. *Ethics and Behavior, 3*(3–4), 251–266.

Hall, J.E., & Hare-Mustin, R.T. (1983). Sanctions and the diversity of ethical complaints against psychologists. *American Psychologist, 38,* 714–729.

Hauser, B.B. (1985). Custody in dispute: Legal and psychological profiles of contesting families. *Journal of the American Academy of Child Psychiatry, 24,* 575–582.

Heinze, M.C., & Grisso, T. (1996). Review of instruments assessing parenting competencies used in child custody evaluations. *Behavioral Sciences and the Law, 14,* 293–313.

Jameson, B.J., Ehrenberg, M.F., & Hunter, M.A. (1997). Psychologists' ratings of the best-interests-of-the-child custody and access criterion: A family systems assessment model. *Professional Psychology: Research and Practice, 28,* 253–262.

Jones, C.J. (1984). Judicial questioning of children in custody and visitation proceedings. *Family Law Quarterly, 18,* 43–91.

Karras, D., & Berry, K.K. (1985). Custody evaluations: A critical review. *Professional Psychology: Research and Practice, 16,* 76–85.

Keilin, W.G., & Bloom, L.J. (1986). Child custody evaluation practices: A survey of experienced professionals. *Professional Psychology: Research and Practice, 17,* 338–346.

Lanyon, R.I. (1986). Psychological assessment procedures in court-related settings. *Professional Psychology: Research and Practice, 17,* 260–268.

Loftus, E.F. (1986). Experimental psychologist as advocate or impartial educator. *Law and Human Behavior, 10,* 63–78.

Lowery, C.R. (1981). Child custody decisions in divorce proceedings: A survey of judges. *Professional Psychology: Research and Practice, 12,* 492–498.

Lowery, C.R. (1986). Maternal and joint custody: Differences in the decision process. *Law and Human Behavior, 10,* 303–315.

McCloskey, M., Egeth, H., & McKenna, J. (1986). The experimental psychologist in court: The ethics of expert testimony. *Law and Human Behavior, 10,* 1–13.

McKinnon, R., & Wallerstein, J.S. (1986). Joint custody and the preschool child. *Behavioral Sciences and the Law, 4,* 169–183.

Melton, G.B., & Limber, S. (1989). Psychologists' involvement in cases of child maltreatment: Limits of role and expertise. *American Psychologist, 44,* 1225–1233.

Melton, G.B., Petrila, J., Poythress, N.G., & Slobogin, C. (1997). *Psychological evaluations for the courts: A handbook for mental health professionals and lawyers* (2nd ed.). New York: Guilford Press.

Milner, J.S. (1986). *The Child Abuse Potential Inventory: Manual* (2nd ed.). Webster, NC: Psytec.

Monahan, J. (Ed.). (1980). *Who is the client? The ethics of psychological intervention in the criminal justice system.* Washington, DC: American Psychological Association.

Morse, S.J. (1978). Law and mental health professionals: The limits of expertise. *Professional Psychology: Research and Practice, 9,* 389–399.

Morse, S.J. (1982). Reforming expert testimony: An open response from the tower (and the trenches). *Law and Human Behavior, 6,* 45–47.

Musetto, A.P. (1981). Standards for deciding contested child custody. *Journal of Clinical Child Psychology, 10,* 51–55.

Ochroch, R. (1982). *Ethical pitfalls in child custody cases.* Paper presented at the 90th annual convention of the American Psychological Association, Washington, DC.

Oklahoma State Board of Examiners of Psychologists. (1999). *Psychologists licensing act and rules of the board.* Oklahoma City: Central Printing.

Otto, R.K., Heilbrun, K., & Grisso, T. (1990). Training and credentialing in forensic psychology. *Behavioral Sciences and the Law, 8,* 217–231.

Pearson, J., & Ring, M.A.L. (1982–1983). Judicial decision-making in contested custody cases. *Journal of Family Law, 21,* 703–724.

Poythress, N.G., Jr. (1979). A proposal for training in forensic psychology. *American Psychologist, 34,* 612–621.

Poythress, N.G., Jr. (1982). Concerning reform in expert testimony: An open letter from a practicing psychologist. *Law and Human Behavior, 6,* 39–43.

Rogers, R. (1987). Ethical dilemmas in forensic evaluations. *Behavioral Sciences and the Law, 5,* 149–160.

Rogers, R., & Ewing, C.P. (1989). Ultimate issue proscriptions: A cosmetic fix and a plea for empiricism. *Law and Human Behavior, 13,* 357–374.

Rohman, L.W., Sales, B.D., & Lou, M. (1987). The best interests of the child in custody disputes. In L.A. Weithorn (Ed.), *Psychology and child custody determinations: Knowledge, roles, and expertise* (pp. 59–105). Lincoln: University of Nebraska Press.

Rotgers, F., & Barrett, D. (1996). *Daubert v. Merrell Dow* and expert testimony by clinical psychologists: Implications and recommendations for practice. *Professional Psychology: Research and Practice, 27,* 467–474.

Saks, M.J. (1990). Expert witnesses, nonexpert witnesses, and nonwitness experts. *Law and Human Behavior, 14,* 291–313.

Sales, B.D. (1982). The legal regulation of psychology: Scientific and professional interactions. In C.J. Scheirer & B.L. Hammonds (Eds.), *Psychology and the law: The Master Lecture Series* (Vol. 2, pp. 9–35). Washington, DC: American Psychological Association.

Sales, B.D., & Shuman, D.W. (1993). Reclaiming the integrity of science in expert witnessing [Guest editorial]. *Ethics and Behavior, 3*(3–4), 223–229.

Santilli, L.E., & Roberts, M.C. (1990). Custody decisions in Alabama before and after the abolition of the tender years doctrine. *Law and Human Behavior, 14,* 123–137.

Schaefer, A.B. (1998, Spring). Admissibility of expert witness testimony by psychologists: Recent developments. *Oklahoma Psychologist, 1.*

Schofield, W. (1956). Psychology, law, and the expert witness. *American Psychologist, 11,* 1–7.

Schutz, B.M., Dixon, E.B., Lindenberger, J.C., & Ruther, N.J. (1989). *Solomon's sword: A practical guide to conducting child custody evaluations.* San Francisco: Jossey-Bass.

Scott, E.S., & Emery, R. (1987). Child custody dispute resolution: The adversarial system and divorce mediation. In L.A. Weithorn (Ed.), *Psychology and child custody determinations: Knowledge, roles, and expertise* (pp. 25–36). Lincoln: University of Nebraska Press.

Settle, S.A., & Lowery, C.R. (1982). Child custody decisions: Content analysis of a judicial survey. *Journal of Divorce, 6,* 125–138.

Shapiro, D.L. (1984). *Psychological evaluation and expert testimony: A practical guide to forensic work.* New York: Van Nostrand-Reinhold.

Shapiro, D.L. (1988). Ethical constraints in forensic settings: Understanding the limits of our expertise. *Psychotherapy in Private Practice, 6,* 71–86.

Shapiro, D.L. (1990). *Dilemmas for the psychotherapist in an age of litigation: Ethics, confidentiality, and legal liability.* Paper presented at the 98th annual convention of the American Psychological Association, Boston.

Shuman, D.W. (1986). *Psychiatric and psychological evidence.* Colorado Springs, CO: Shepard's.

Simons, V., & Meyer, K.G. (1986). The child custody evaluation: Issues and trends. *Behavioral Sciences and the Law, 4,* 137–156.

Slobogin, C. (1989). The "ultimate issue" issue. *Behavioral Sciences and the Law, 7,* 259–266.

Smith, S.R. (1989). Mental health expert witnesses: Of science and crystal balls. *Behavioral Sciences and the Law, 7,* 145–180.

Suggs, D.L. (1979). The use of psychological research by the judiciary. *Law and Human Behavior, 3,* 135–148.

Tomkins, A.J. (1995). Introduction to behavioral science evidence in the wake of *Daubert. Behavioral Sciences and the Law, 13,* 127–130.

Wagenaar, W.A. (1988). The proper seat: A Bayesian discussion of the position of expert witnesses. *Law and Human Behavior, 12,* 499–510.

Wallerstein, J.S. (1986). Child of divorce: An overview. *Behavioral Sciences and the Law, 4,* 105–118.

Wallerstein, J.S., & Kelly, J.B. (1980). *Surviving the breakup: How children and parents cope with divorce.* New York: Basic Books.

Wallerstein, J.S., & Lewis, J. (1998). The long-term impact of divorce on children: A first report from a 25-year study. *Family and Conciliation Courts Review, 36,* 368–383.

Warshak, R.A. (1986). Father-custody and child development: A review and analysis of psychological research. *Behavioral Sciences and the Law, 4,* 185–202.

Weiner, B.A., Simons, V.A., & Cavanaugh, J.L., Jr. (1985). The child custody dispute. In D.H. Schetky & E.P. Benedek (Eds.), *Emerging issues in child psychiatry and the law* (pp. 59–75). New York: Brunner/Mazel.

Weithorn, L.A. (1984). Children's capacities in legal contexts. In N.D. Reppucci, L.A. Weithorn, E.P. Mulvey, & J. Monahan (Eds.), *Children, mental health, and the law* (pp. 25–55). Beverly Hills, CA: Sage.

Weithorn, L.A. (1987a). Professional responsibility in the dissemination of psychological research in legal contexts. In G.B. Melton (Ed.), *Reforming the law: Impact of child development research* (pp. 253–279). New York: Guilford Press.

Weithorn, L.A. (1987b). Psychological consultation in divorce custody litigation: Ethical considerations. In L.A. Weithorn (Ed.), *Psychology and child custody determinations: Knowledge, roles, and expertise* (pp. 182–209). Lincoln: University of Nebraska Press.

Weithorn, L.A. (Ed.). (1987c). *Psychology and child custody determinations: Knowledge, roles, and expertise.* Lincoln: University of Nebraska Press.

Weithorn, L.A., & Grisso, T. (1987). Psychological evaluations in divorce custody: Problems, principles, and procedures. In L.A. Weithorn (Ed.), *Psychology and child custody determinations: Knowledge, roles, and expertise* (pp. 157–181). Lincoln: University of Nebraska Press.

Wells, G.L. (1986). Expert psychological testimony: Empirical and conceptual analyses of effects. *Law and Human Behavior, 10,* 83–95.

Wyer, M.M., Gaylord, S.J., & Grove, E.T. (1987). The legal context of child custody evaluations. In L.A. Weithorn (Ed.), *Psychology and child custody determinations: Knowledge, roles, and expertise* (pp. 3–22). Lincoln: University of Nebraska Press.

Ziskin, J. (1981). *Coping with psychiatric and psychological testimony* (Vol. 1, 3rd ed.). Venice, CA: Law and Psychology Press.

Author Index

Boe, E.E., 572
Boer, H., 217
Bogart, L.C., 536
Boggs, S., 27, 76, 85, 279, 840, 998
Bohlin, G., 523
Bohlmeyer, E.M., 719
Bohman, M., 758–759
Boivin, M., 271
Bolding, D.D., 884
Bolger, K.E., 57–58
Boll, T.J., 151–154, 156–157, 160–166
Bollard, R.J., 464–465
Bolles, R.N., 750
Bolocofsky, D.N., 1105, 1107, 1110, 1112, 1114
Bolstad, O.D., 104
Bolte, K., 934
Boltke, K., 385
Bolton, P., 211–212, 231, 440, 442
Bolton, V., 216, 231
Bonagura, N., 477, 930
Bond, T., 325
Bondy, A.S., 306
Bonica, J.J., 900
Bonilla, J., 963
Bonner, B.L., 465, 990, 991, 1001, 1017
Boocock, S.S., 564
Booksetin, F.L., 474
Boone, R.R., 830
Booth, A., 1031, 1034, 1036
Bootzin, R.R., 306
Borchardt, C.M., 233
Bordin, E.S., 746
Borduin, C.M., 408, 794, 874–875, 878, 883, 977, 995, 1001
Bordwell, R., 405
Borgen, F.H., 743
Borghgraef, M., 551
Boris, N., 53
Borjas, G.J., 14
Borkovec, T.D., 362
Borkowski, J.G., 112
Borneman, E., 495
Bornstein, M.T., 105
Bornstein, P.H., 105
Borquez, J., 60
Borum, R., 1097
Bose, S., 181
Boshes, L.D., 344
Bossing, L., 1079
Bossio, L.M., 1068
Botash, A.S., 328
Bottomley, V., 511
Bottos, M., 915
Botvin, G.L., 981–982
Bouchard, T.J., Jr., 209–210, 233
Boulerice, B., 1034
Boulos, C., 933
Bourdeau, P.A., 1019

Bousha, D.M., 971
Boutin, P., 227
Bowen, A., 531, 917
Bowen, M., 863–865, 1015
Bowerman, N., 547
Bowery, N.G., 224
Bowlby, J., 380, 396, 548, 777, 1047
Bowman, E.S., 420
Bowman, S.L., 739
Boyar, R., 299
Boyce, T.W., 367
Boyce, W.T., 38, 395
Boyd-Franklin, N., 878
Boyer, D., 680
Boyle, M., 234
Boyle, M.H., 37, 93–94, 97, 645–646
Boyle, M.P., 327
Bradbard, G., 932
Bradburn, N.M., 35
Bradfer-Blomart, J., 181
Bradford, J.M.W., 680
Bradley, C., 928
Bradley, L.A., 331
Bradley, R.H., 54, 66, 1018
Bradley, S.J., 508–509, 511, 676, 681–682, 685
Bradley S.J., 299, 308
Brady, E.U., 378
Brady, J., 328
Brady, K.T., 760
Brainerd, C.J., 546
Brakarsh, D., 758
Brambilla, P., 217
Brams, J., 367, 525, 917
Brand, M., 639–640
Brandell, J.R., 843
Brandenburg, N.A., 643–644, 650
Brander, A., 998
Brandys, C.F., 577
Brassard, M.R., 118, 1011, 1013–1015
Braswell, L., 474
Braucht, G.N., 758
Braukmann, C.J., 407
Braunling-McMorrow, D., 997
Braver, S.L., 1039
Bravo, M., 37
Bray, J.H., 1037–1038
Bray, N.W., 546
Brazeal, T.J., 304
Brazelton, T., 12, 453–455, 457
Breakfield, X.O., 232
Bream, L.A., 395
Breaux, A.M., 264
Bremer, F.J., 6
Brendtro, L.K., 888–890
Brennan, D., 610
Brennan, P.A., 781
Brent, D., 40, 667, 934, 983
Breslau, N., 54, 902
Bresnick, B., 994

Bressman, S., 341
Brestan, E.V., 398, 825, 980
Breston, E., 279
Bretherton, I., 1015
Breton, J.J., 37
Brett, E.A., 422
Brett, P.M., 343
Brewer, E.J., 362
Brewin, C.R., 423
Brewster, A.B., 361, 897
Briar, S., 785
Bricker, D., 253
Bricker, W., 397
Bricklin, B., 186, 1110–1112
Brickman, A., 1033
Bridges, M., 1035
Briere, J., 35, 420, 1003, 1006
Briesmeister, J., 814, 828, 1008
Brigham, T.A., 407
Briguglia, C., 942
Brink, J.D., 163–164
Brinkman, D.C., 624
Britner, P.A., 274
Britten, C., 695
Broadhurst, D., 1002
Broder, H.L., 611
Broderick, C.B., 861
Brodsky, M., 39
Brodsky, S.L., 1099, 1103
Brody, G., 60–61, 67, 280, 814, 1035, 1037
Brody, S., 272, 345, 808
Brodzinsky, D.M., 87, 1110
Brodzinsky, D.M., 87, 1110
Brondino, M.J., 408
Bronfenbrenner, U., 52, 56, 408, 716, 731, 810, 854
Brook, J.S., 298, 394, 759
Brooks, B., 1003, 1049
Brooks, E., 932
Brooks, L., 730
Brooks, R., 854, 1009
Brooksbank, D.J., 419
Brooks-Gunn, J., 49, 50, 53–54, 62, 67, 252, 507, 549, 675–676, 678, 693, 723, 768
Brophy, C., 292
Brophy, J.E., 564
Broskowski, A., 842, 852
Bross, D.C., 996
Broughton, D., 496
Broughton, R., 322, 324
Brouilette, C., 697
Broussard, B.A., 696
Brower, A.M., 222
Brown, A.L., 112
Brown, B.F., 725
Brown, C., 980
Brown, E., 515
Brown, F., 90, 483
Brown, J.L., 55

Subject Index